Baseball America

2025 ALMANAC

BASEBALL AMERICA INC. · DURHAM, N.C.

Baseball America

ESTABLISHED 1981

P.O. BOX 12877, DURHAM, NC 27709 • PHONE (800) 845-2726

BASEBALL AMERICA is published monthly, 12 issues per year, by Baseball America Enterprises, LLC, 650 Fifth Avenue, Suite 2400, New York, NY 10019. Subscription rate is $109.99 for one year; Canada $112.99 (U.S. funds); all other foreign $125.99 per year (U.S. funds). Periodicals postage paid at New York NY, & additional mailing offices. Occasionally our subscriber list is made available to reputable firms offering goods and services we believe would be of interest to our readers. If you prefer to be excluded, please send your current address label and a note requesting to be excluded from these promotions to Baseball America Enterprises, LLC, PO Box 12877, Durhan, NC 27709, Attn: Privacy Coordinator. POSTMASTER: Send all UAA to CFS (See DMM 707.4.12.5); NONPOSTAL & MILITARY FACILITIES: send address corrections to Baseball America, P.O. Box 420235, Palm Coast, FL 32142-0235. CANADA POST: Return undeliverable Canadian addresses to IMEX Global Solutions, P.O. Box 25542, London, ON N6C 6B2. Please contact 1-800-381-1288 to start carrying Baseball America in your store.

Baseball America
2025 ALMANAC

Editor
J.J. Cooper

Associate Editors
King Kaufman, Josh Norris, Matt Eddy

Contributing Editors
Carlos Collazo, Peter Flaherty

Design & Production
Seth Mates

Cover Photo
MAIN PHOTO: Bobby Witt Jr.
PHOTO BY: Ed Zurga/Getty Images

For additional copies, visit our Website at
BaseballAmerica.com or call 1-800-845-2726 to order.
US $36.95 / CAN $49.95, plus shipping and handling per order. Expedited shipping available.
Distributed by Simon & Schuster.
ISBN-13: 979-8-9869573-7-1
Statistics provided by Major League Baseball Advanced Media and Compiled by Baseball America.

EDITOR'S NOTE: Major league statistics are based on final, unofficial 2024 averages.

» The organization statistics, which begin on Page 45, include all players who participated in at least one game during the 2024 season.

» Pitchers' batting statistics are not included, nor are the pitching statistics of position players who pitched in fewer than five games.

TABLE OF CONTENTS

Paul Skenes

DUSTIN SATLOFF/GETTY IMAGES

MAJOR LEAGUES 6

2024 IN REVIEW

AMERICAN LEAGUE

NATIONAL LEAGUE

POSTSEASON

MAJOR LEAGUES

Dodgers go all the way

Baseball isn't fair. Random acts—or, if you prefer, low-probability outcomes—can happen.

A line drive with a 110 mph exit velocity can be an out, and a dribbler hit 46 mph can be a hit. Pitchers can hit their spots with nasty stuff and get a swing and miss, only to then forget to cover first base, or have the first baseman get beat to the bag by a hard-charging runner. Or the pitcher can get into a jam, roll that ground ball he was looking for . . . and watch it duck under a fielder's glove for an error.

Teams can spend hundreds of millions of dollars in payroll and run up 100-win seasons, only to get tripped up by the randomness of the postseason. In the absence of a salary cap (or floor) and other mechanisms present in other U.S. professional sports that encourage parity, Major League Baseball has instead utilized the randomness of the game as the method to give smaller- and middle-revenue clubs a chance to win championships. In many ways, this has worked. The league hasn't had a repeat champion in the 21st century, and every club has made the playoffs at least once since 2014. The 2023 postseason was the most recent example, with Texas and Arizona—each a wild-card entrant—meeting in a World Series which provided some drama but generated little buzz and minor television ratings.

In 2024, randomness lost. For once, the team that won the offseason actually had the best regular season, and then won the World Series championship as well. The Los Angeles Dodgers won 98 games—the best record in MLB but their worst regular-season record since 2018—then advanced to their first World Series since their last title in 2020. Once there, the Dodgers dispatched the Yankees—winners of their first pennant in 15 seasons—in five games. It's the eighth championship for the franchise and its seventh since moving to Los Angeles in 1958.

For the Dodgers, 2024 proved a validation of their approach to recent seasons, assembling a major league juggernaut with help of the Guggenheim ownership group, which purchased the team in 2012. First, ownership brought in club president Andrew Friedman from the Tampa Bay Rays. Friedman then built one of the best scouting and player development machines of the 21st century. That foundation, and the financial flexibility that allowed them to poach superstar Mookie Betts from the Red Sox in February 2020, helped bring the Dodgers a World Series title at the end of the Covid-shortened season, which also included an expanded and more grueling playoff setup.

ELSA/GETTY IMAGES

Shohei Ohtani hit .310 with 54 homers and 59 stolen bases and won the World Series

The Dodgers didn't get to have a parade after their 2020 title and craved another, spending handsomely to pursue it. In this second phase, the Dodgers have been baseball's biggest, baddest power, robustly pursuing and signing free agents such as first baseman Freddie Freeman and twice breaking records for pitcher contracts, first on the ill-fated Trevor Bauer deal (remember him? Don't . . .) and last offseason for Japanese ace Yoshinobu Yamamoto.

The biggest deal of them all was signing Shohei Ohtani, fresh off his second MVP season with the Los Angeles Angels, as a free agent in the offseason. The Dodgers landed the reigning American League MVP for a record 10-year, $700 million contract, with $680 million of it deferred as Ohtani sought to give the Dodgers the payroll flexibility to acquire supporting pieces and help him win a World Series to go with his 2023 World Baseball Classic crown and an NPB championship.

Yamamoto received a 12-year, $325 million guarantee, the largest ever given to a pitcher.

The Dodgers kept splurging, trading for righthander Tyler Glasnow, then signing the nearby Newhall, Calif., native to a five-year extension worth more than $136 million. They polished off their purchases with a one-year, $23 million deal for a needed righthanded power bat in outfielder Teoscar Hernandez.

Despite a slew of pitching injuries that sapped their depth to the point that they used bullpen games in each playoff series, the Dodgers finished the regular year with 98 wins and entered October as the top seed. Led by Ohtani and Betts, they finished second in the majors in runs (842) and third in home runs (233). The pitching was good enough to toss 24 consecutive scoreless innings to finish off a five-game Division Series win against San Diego, the first time LA had advanced beyond the first round of the postseason since 2020.

Manager Dave Roberts went on Betts' podcast after the Series and said the Dodgers, who lost eight of 13 to San Diego in the regular season, considered the Padres their biggest obstacle to overcome, saying, "I felt, from my perspective, that was the World Series . . . I felt that in that moment in time, when we started the postseason, they were 1-to-26 the best team," to which Betts chimed in, "One hundred percent."

Then LA's offense proved too much for the Mets in the National League Championship Series and the Yankees in the World Series.

"We did go through a lot, but I'll say we still had the best record in all of baseball this year," Roberts said when the World Series was over. "It wasn't easy, but our guys fought and played every day the right way, played to win.

"There was a lot of backfilling on talent because of injury, a lot of young players cut their teeth, which is good. But one thing is that we just kept going. Even in the postseason, I don't think anyone had us picked. I don't think they had us picked to get out of the first series. For us to go out there and fight and scratch and claw and win 11 games in October, that's a credit to our guys."

Ohtani's Wild Ride

Ohtani's move to the Dodgers seemed preordained in some ways, but his season got off to an unexpectedly rocky start owing in part to the new era of legalized sports gambling. His interpreter and friend, Ippei Mizuhara, was ensnared in a gambling debt scandal that exploded into the news as the Dodgers opened the regular season in Seoul, South Korea, for a two-game series against the Padres.

Mizuhara had served as Ohtani's interpreter and personal assistant since he arrived from Japan to play for the Angels in 2018. He made the move with Ohtani to the Dodgers and was in Dodgers camp with Ohtani all spring. On March 18, news began to surface of Ohtani's name appearing on records of financial wire transfers to Mathew Bowyer, a Southern California bookmaker whom Mizuhara had met in 2021.

That led to a 48-hour news frenzy in which Ohtani admitted he had helped Mizuhara pay off debts of $4.5 million to Bowyer. Meanwhile, Mizuhara made the trip to Korea and was in the dugout with Ohtani during the season-opening 5-2 victory. But while in Korea, Ohtani's story changed from bailing out his friend to asserting that Mizuhara, who had access to Ohtani's bank accounts, had committed theft to feed his gambling habit.

The Dodgers fired Mizuhara March 20 after Ohtani's attorneys, Berk Brettler LLP, issued a statement to ESPN that read: "In the course of responding to recent media inquiries, we discovered that Shohei has been the victim of a massive theft, and we are turning the matter over to the authorities."

Ohtani's two-way talents have earned him comparisons to Babe Ruth, who helped save MLB from the Black Sox scandal that followed the 1919 World Series. Now, Ohtani was potentially being ensnared by a gambling scandal of his own due to Mizuhara, who appeared to be crucial not only to Ohtani the player but to his agent, Nez Balelo of CAA, who had negotiated Ohtani's $700 million contract but who also relied on Mizuhara as a conduit to Ohtani. Even the Dodgers and investigators who had been dealing with Ohtani had been doing so through Mizuhara.

On March 21, the Dodgers assigned longtime club employee Will Ireton as Ohtani's new interpreter, and Mizuhara's story began to unravel. His resume apparently included claims he'd graduated from UC Riverside (which the school denied) and worked as a translator for the Red Sox with Japanese lefthander Hideki Okajima 17 years prior (which the Red Sox denied). Four days later, Ohtani addressed the media in Japanese with Ireton translating.

"I'm very saddened and shocked that someone I trusted has done this," he said, and later continued, "I never bet on baseball or any other sports. I have never asked anybody to do that on my behalf. I have never gone through a bookmaker to bet on sports.

"Up until a couple of days ago, I didn't know this was happening. Just to go over the result,

JIM MCISAAC/GETTY IMAGES

Offseason trade acquisition Juan Soto was exceptional in his first season in New York.

Ippei has been stealing money from my account, and has told lies."

On April 11, Mizuhara was formally charged with bank fraud for stealing more than $16 million from Ohtani, with federal prosecutors corroborating Ohtani's side of the story that he was a victim and had no prior knowledge that Mizuhara was stealing from him to feed his gambling problem.

Mizuhara surrendered to authorities the next day and pleaded guilty on June 4 to bank fraud and tax fraud. That day, MLB closed its own investigation into the Mizuhara/Ohtani affair. If Ohtani was bothered by the scandal, his play didn't indicate it.

Ohtani had a season for the ages while playing DH the entire season and not pitching as he rehabbed his right arm from significant elbow surgery. He posted the first 50-50 season in MLB history, with an NL-leading 54 homers to go with 59 stolen bases (in just 63 attempts). He hit .310/.390/.646 with a major league-leading 411 total bases and 134 runs scored, and finally got to play in a postseason after six mostly spectacular and yet fruitless seasons toiling east on the freeway in Anaheim.

"We were able to get through the regular season, I think, because of the strength of this team, this organization," Ohtani said after the World Series. "And the success of the postseason is very similar to how we were able to pull it off during the regular season . . . Extremely honored to be a part of this."

Japanese fans paid attention, as an average of 12.1 million fans watched the five games of the World Series in Japan, even though the games started at 9 a.m. local time. That's the highest rated MLB World Series ever in Japan, and Games One (14.4 million) and Two (15.9 million) were the most-watched postseason games ever in Japan.

Ohtani's star power, plus that of the Yankees and Dodgers franchises, helped make this MLB's highest-rated World Series since 2017 (Astros-Dodgers), with an average of 15.8 million fans viewing over Fox TV's various platforms, an increase of 67% from the 2023 Series.

Yankees Are Fairly Dandy

The Dodgers and Yankees have faced off in the World Series 12 times now, with the Dodgers winning in 2024, 1981, 1963 and 1955.

Despite never being satisified with second place, the Yankees should feel no shame in losing to their longtime rivals. They won their first pennant since 2009 and finished with the best record in the American League.

The Bronx Bombers powered their way to October with 237 home runs to lead MLB, helping them top the AL in runs (815). No team had a duo as productive as the Yanks with team captain Aaron Judge and his 2024 running-mate, Juan Soto. A free agent after the season, Soto had won a World Series with his original organization, the Washington Nationals, in 2019, then was traded to San Diego in 2022 and spent parts of two seasons there, including a shockingly disappointing 82-win campaign in 2023.

With the Padres needing to trim payroll, they dealt Soto to the Yankees for a robust trade package that included righthander Michael King, who emerged as a frontline starter in his first full year in a rotation.

While King helped the Padres reach the playoffs and throw a scare into the Dodgers, Soto joined Judge to form one of baseball's most lethal 1-2 punches since Ruth and Gehrig. Judge hit 58 home runs–his third season with 50-plus–and hit .322/.458/.701 while leading the AL in homers, RBIs (144), OBP, slugging and total bases (392).

Soto, meanwhile, finished second to Judge in OBP and walks (after leading the majors in walks for three straight years) during his own .288/.419/.569 season, with a career-best 41 home runs and league-high 128 runs scored.

Soto, a Scott Boras Corporation client, became

PLAYER OF THE YEAR

Judge makes history—again

BY MATT EDDY

The Yankees take the title of captain seriously.

Aaron Judge is the 16th captain in Yankees franchise history, following the likes of Derek Jeter, Don Mattingly, Thurman Munson, Lou Gehrig, Babe Ruth and others.

This season, Judge truly earned the "C" designation.

He led all major league hitters with a .458 on-base percentage, a .701 slugging percentage, 58 home runs, 144 RBIs, 133 walks, a 218 wRC+ and 11.2 fWAR.

He hit a career-high .322 to trail only Bobby Witt Jr. and Vladimir Guerrero Jr. in the batting race.

On top of his offensive exploits, Judge took on his largest share of center field. He made 105 starts in center and helped optimize the Yankees' lineup as they won 94 games and later the American League pennant.

Here, we recount our three favorite facts about Judge's historic 2024 season.

218 wRC+

Weighted runs created plus is an index metric which places a hitter's offensive contributions in the context of league run environment and home ballpark. Judge this season had a 218 wRC+, which means that he produced offense at a rate 118% higher than the average American League hitter.

Any hitter who reaches 200 by this metric is having an all-time season. Ten different hitters have reached the 200 wRC+ benchmark in a season of at least 500 plate appearances since 1901.

DUSTIN SATLOFF/MLB PHOTOS VIA GETTY IMAGES

Aaron Judge led MLB in multiple key hitting categories, just as he did in 2022.

Since baseball embarked on its expansion era in 1961—a total of 63 seasons—Judge is one of just four hitters to better a 200 wRC+ in a season of 500 PAs, joining Barry Bonds, Mark McGwire and Frank Thomas. In fact, Judge has now done it twice.

Three 50-Homer Seasons

Both Judge and Shohei Ohtani reached 50 home runs this season, but don't be fooled. Hitting the half-century mark for home runs is a rare feat.

It has happened just 50 times in baseball history. Judge has three of those seasons, making him one of just 10 hitters to hit 50 home runs multiple times.

Fastest To 300 Home Runs

Judge's signature skill is his power, so it's only fitting that he reached the 300-home run milestone faster than any hitter in history.

With his home run on Aug. 14, Judge reached 300 for his career. The blast was hit in his 955th career game, shattering the previous record of 1,087 held by Ralph Kiner.

Judge hit his 300th home run in his 3,431st at-bat, which was 400 at-bats faster than Babe Ruth (3,831) and a few ticks faster than Mark McGwire (3,837) or Kiner (3,883), according to the Elias Sports Bureau. ■

LAST 10 WINNERS

2014: Clayton Kershaw, LHP, Dodgers
2015: Bryce Harper, OF, Nationals
2016: Mike Trout, OF, Angels
2017: Jose Altuve, 2B, Astros
2018: Mike Trout, OF, Angels
2019: Justin Verlander, RHP, Astros
2020: Freddie Freeman, 1B, Braves
2021: Shohei Ohtani, DH/RHP, Angels
2022: Aaron Judge, OF, Yankees
2023: Shohei Ohtani, DH/RHP, Angels

Full list: search "Baseball America awards"

a free agent at season's end. He was just part of the tweaks that longtime general manager Brian Cashman made to the roster as the Yankees bounced back from an 82-win, fourth-place finish in 2023. The biggest was the trade deadline acquisition of versatile Marlins star Jazz Chisholm Jr., who shifted from center field to third base for the Yankees and provided a needed lefthanded-hitting jolt of energy to the offense (.825 OPS, 11 HR, 18 SB in 46 games).

Rookie Luis Gil was a first-half stalwart, helping ease the pain of ace Gerrit Cole's injury-plagued first half en route to a 15-win season. Free agent signee Marcus Stroman provided 154 innings but didn't earn a spot in the postseason rotation, while 2023 signee Luke Weaver evolved from an interesting relief piece to the closer by season's end, supplanting Clay Holmes, who saved 30 games but led the majors in blown saves (13).

The Yankees had flaws but finished with 94 wins, most in the AL and three games better than the Orioles, who won the division in 2023 with 101 victories but faded in the second half in 2024 and were swept at home in the Wild Card Series by Kansas City. The Yankees defeated the Royals in four games in the Division Series, then prevailed against Cleveland in a relatively dramatic but short five-game ALCS.

AL Goes To Extremes

Cleveland had ranked second in the AL with 92 victories to win the AL Central for the second time in three seasons and for the first time under new manager Stephen Vogt, who replaced Terry Francona after the two-time World Series champion had stepped aside for health reasons. Vogt, whose playing career ended with the Athletics in 2022, breathed new life into the Guardians and managed one of the best, most valuable bullpens of all time. Cleveland got 7.5 bWAR from its bullpen; the Braves ranked second in MLB with 3.9 WAR.

The Guardians needed that pen due to a shaky rotation, which lost former Cy Young Award winner Shane Bieber to injury after just two starts. They also needed everything they could get with the newfound strength of the Central Division, which produced four teams with winning records and three playoff teams. The Royals and Tigers both finished strong, streaked past the 82-win Twins (who won just 12 of their final 39 games) and joined the Guardians in the postseason, earning wild card berths with 86 victories.

The Royals featured a massive step forward for 2019 No. 2 overall pick Bobby Witt Jr., who posted an MVP-caliber season. He hit .332/.389/.588 to win the batting title, led the league with 211 hits (88 for extra bases) and went 30-30 with 32 home runs and 31 stolen bases. It was Kansas City's first playoff spot since it won the 2015 World Series.

Detroit sold at the deadline, trading righty Jack Flaherty to the Dodgers, where he wound up starting Game One of the World Series. But they kept ace lefty Tarik Skubal (18-4, 2.39), had young players such as Spencer Torkelson and Parker Meadows improve after returning from the minor leagues, and used a deep, young pitching staff to unleash "pitching chaos" with multiple bullpen games per week in August and September.

AMERICAN LEAGUE STANDINGS

East	W	L	PCT	GB	Manager	General Manager	Attendance	Average	Last Penn.
New York Yankees	94	68	.580	—	Aaron Boone	Brian Cashman	3,309,838	41,897	2024
Baltimore Orioles	91	71	.562	3	Brandon Hyde	Mike Elias	2,281,129	28,162	1983
Boston Red Sox	81	81	.500	13	Alex Cora	Craig Breslow	2,659,949	32,839	2018
Tampa Bay Rays	80	82	.494	14	Kevin Cash	Erik Neander	1,337,739	16,515	2020
Toronto Blue Jays	74	88	.457	20	John Schneider	Ross Atkins	2,681,236	33,102	1993
Central	**W**	**L**	**PCT**	**GB**	**Manager**	**General Manager**	**Attendance**	**Average**	**Last Penn.**
Cleveland Guardians	92	69	.571	—	Stephen Vogt	Chris Antonetti	2,056,264	25,703	2016
Kansas City Royals	86	76	.531	6.5	Matt Quatraro	J.J. Picollo	1,658,347	20,473	2015
Detroit Tigers	86	76	.531	6.5	A.J. Hinch	Scott Harris	1,858,295	23,824	2012
Minnesota Twins	82	80	.506	10.5	Rocco Baldelli	Derek Falvey	1,951,616	24,094	1991
Chicago White Sox	41	121	.253	51.5	Pedro Grifol/Grady Sizemore	Chris Getz	1,380,733	17,932	2005
West	**W**	**L**	**PCT**	**GB**	**Manager**	**General Manager**	**Attendance**	**Average**	**Last Penn.**
Houston Astros	88	73	.547	—	Joe Espada	Dana Brown	2,835,234	35,003	2022
Seattle Mariners	85	77	.525	3.5	Scott Servais/Dan Wilson	Jerry Dipoto	2,555,813	31,553	Never
Texas Rangers	78	84	.481	10.5	Bruce Bochy	Chris Young	2,651,553	32,735	2023
Oakland Athletics	69	93	.426	19.5	Mark Kotsay	David Forst	922,286	11,529	1990
Los Angeles Angels	63	99	.389	25.5	Ron Washington	Perry Minasian	2,577,597	31,822	2002

Wild Card Series: Tigers defeated Astros 2-0 and Royals defeated Orioles 2-0 in best-of-three. **Division Series:** Guardians defeated Tigers 3-2 and Yankees defeated Royals 3-1 in best-of-five. **Championship Series:** Yankees defeated Guardians 4-1 in best-of-seven.

ROOKIE OF THE YEAR

Skenes comes up aces for Pirates

BY MATT EDDY

From No. 1 pick to No. 1 starter in less than a year.

That summarizes the rise of Pirates righthander Paul Skenes, who won a national championship with LSU in 2023, went first overall in the draft that year and then made his MLB debut on May 11, 2024.

While the Pirates did not contend for a national championship in 2024, it wasn't for lack of a frontline ace. Skenes pitched as advertised as a rookie, going 11-3 with a 1.96 ERA and 170 strikeouts and 32 walks in 133 innings. He allowed 10 home runs in 23 starts.

Even in a crowded rookie field that also included the Padres' Jackson Merrill and the Brewers' Jackson Chourio, Skenes stood out. He turned in one of the strongest seasons by a rookie pitcher in the Wild Card Era.

The various statistics outlined here illustrate how Skenes came up aces.

1.96 ERA

Some baseball numbers require no context. An ERA hovering near 2.00 over a sizable sample is one such example.

Skenes fell about 30 innings short of qualifying for the ERA title, but his 1.96 ERA was the lowest of any pitcher with at least 120 innings this season. In fact, it is one of the lowest ERAs for any pitcher with as many innings during the Wild Card Era.

In the past 30 seasons, 10 different pitchers have posted a sub-2.00 ERA in a season of 120 innings or more. The list includes Clayton Kershaw (three times) and Pedro Martinez (two), with single appearances from Jake Arrieta, Kevin Brown, Roger Clemens, Jacob deGrom, Zack Greinke, Greg Maddux, Blake Snell and Justin Verlander.

While those pitchers threw a lot more innings than Skenes did this year, they also were not rookies and were not pitching for a last-place team like the 2024 Pirates.

26.8 K-BB%

Analysts say strikeout percentage minus walk percentage is the best predictor of ERA.

If that's the case, then Skenes is in great shape for 2025.

JIM MCISAAC/GETTY IMAGES

The Pirates' Paul Skenes pitched like an ace as a 22-year-old rookie.

His 33.1% strikeout rate and 6.2% walk rate yield a 26.8 K-BB% that stands as the second-best ever for a rookie pitcher with at least 120 innings. Braves righthander Spencer Strider holds the rookie record with a 29.7 K-BB% mark in 2022.

100 Pitches At 100 mph

Power is key to Skenes' success. No starting pitcher threw more pitches at 100 mph or faster than he did in 2024.

Skenes threw exactly 100 pitches at the century mark in 2024—no rounding up—more than twice as many as the Angels' Jose Soriano, who threw 46 fastballs at 100 mph.

In the Statcast era, Skenes already has thrown the sixth-most pitches at 100 mph among starters. Everybody ahead of him—Hunter Greene, Jacob deGrom, Noah Syndergaard, Nathan Eovaldi and Gerrit Cole—has at least three MLB seasons. ■

LAST 10 WINNERS

2014: Jose Abreu, 1B, White Sox
2015: Kris Bryant, 3B, Cubs
2016: Corey Seager, SS, Dodgers
2017: Aaron Judge, OF, Yankees
2018: Shohei Ohtani, RHP/DH, Angels
2019: Pete Alonso, 1B, Mets
2020: Tony Gonsolin, RHP, Dodgers
2021: Jonathan India, 2B, Reds
2022: Julio Rodriguez, OF, Mariners
2023: Corbin Carroll, OF, Diamondbacks

Full list: search "Baseball America awards"

The Tigers went 34-19 in those months to pass Boston, Seattle and Minnesota for a postseason berth, Detroit's first since 2014, leaving the Angels (also 2014) with the longest active playoff drought in MLB.

The Angels, having lost Ohtani to the Dodgers and losing Mike Trout once again to an early-season injury, lost a franchise-record 99 games. They still would have had a 22-game lead on the White Sox, however. The last place team in the Central also set an MLB record for losses in a season with 121 in a truly embarrassing season.

The White Sox surpassed the 1962 Mets' loss total but won five of their final six games to avoid the worst winning percentage of all time, with their .252 mark ranking fourth-worst in history. They struggled despite having fairly strong starting pitching, even after trading away ace Dylan Cease in spring training to the Padres for a package of prospects. But they transitioned lefty Garrett Crochet, their 2020 first-round pick, to the rotation successfully and made a shrewd signing of free-agent righthander Erick Fedde, a 2014 Nationals first-round pick who had failed in the big leagues but thrived in Korea's KBO in 2023.

The rest of the team was ... historically bad. Despite Crochet earning a deserved all-star nod and Fedde providing above-average run prevention in bulk, the Sox still finished third from the bottom in runs allowed. Offensively, the Sox ranked last in the majors with 507 runs scored, nearly 100 fewer runs than the next-worst club, Tampa Bay, and the 507 runs were the fewest scored by a team since the DH first arrived in MLB in 1973. They ranked last in the league in the triple-slash categories as well at .221/.278/.340.

That level of ineptitude led to three double-digit losing streaks, starting with a franchise-record 14-game streak in May and June. Then they tied an American League record with a 21-game streak July 10-Aug. 6, with manager Pedro Grifol losing his job two days later. Former all-star outfielder Grady Sizemore took over as interim manager and had his own 12-game losing streak which lasted into September.

Through it all the White Sox wound down Crochet's workload to keep him healthy, traded Fedde to the Cardinals at the trade deadline and unloaded two key pieces of their last rebuild, righty Michael Kopech (to the Dodgers in the three-team Fedde trade) and DH Eloy Jimenez (to Baltimore), in deals that were panned in the industry for not bringing back enough prospects.

Club owner Jerry Reinsdorf had fired longtime club president Kenny Williams and GM Rick Hahn in August 2023 but stayed inside the organization, promoting farm director Chris Getz to the GM spot. Reinsdorf penned a letter to fans in September, calling the season "a failure" and "embarrassing" while expressing confidence in Getz to rebuild "the foundation of our baseball operations department." But Getz went into the offseason talking about drawing down payroll on the South Side, where a turnaround appears to be a long way off.

End Of An Era

No major league franchise has been as nomadic as the Athletics, who launched in Philadelphia in 1901, managed and later owned by Connie Mack

NATIONAL LEAGUE STANDINGS

East	W	L	PCT	GB	Manager	General Manager	Attendance	Average	Last Penn.
Philadelphia Phillies	95	67	.586	—	Rob Thomson	Dave Dombrowski	3,363,712	41,527	2022
Atlanta Braves	89	73	.549	6	Brian Snitker	Alex Anthopoulos	3,011,755	37,647	2021
New York Mets	89	73	.549	6	Carlos Mendoza	David Stearns	2,329,299	29,485	2015
Washington Nationals	71	91	.438	24	Dave Martinez	Mike Rizzo	1,967,302	24,288	2019
Miami Marlins	62	100	.383	33	Skip Schumaker	Peter Bendix	1,087,455	13,425	2003
Central	**W**	**L**	**PCT**	**GB**	**Manager**	**General Manager**	**Attendance**	**Average**	**Last Penn.**
Milwaukee Brewers	93	69	.574	—	Pat Murphy	Matt Arnold	2,537,202	31,323	1982 (AL)
Chicago Cubs	83	79	.512	10	Craig Counsell	Jed Hoyer	2,909,794	35,923	2016
St. Louis Cardinals	83	79	.512	10	Oliver Marmol	John Mozeliak	2,878,115	35,532	2013
Cincinnati Reds	77	85	.475	16	David Bell/Freddie Benavides	Nick Krall	2,024,186	24,990	1990
Pittsburgh Pirates	76	86	.469	17	Derek Shelton	Ben Cherington	1,720,361	21,239	1979
West	**W**	**L**	**PCT**	**GB**	**Manager**	**General Manager**	**Attendance**	**Average**	**Last Penn.**
Los Angeles Dodgers	98	64	.605	—	Dave Roberts	Andrew Friedman	3,941,251	48,657	2024
San Diego Padres	93	69	.574	5	Mike Shildt	A.J. Preller	3,330,545	41,118	1998
Arizona Diamondbacks	89	73	.549	9	Torey Lovullo	Mike Hazen	2,341,876	28,912	2023
San Francisco Giants	80	82	.494	18	Bob Melvin	Farhan Zaidi	2,647,736	33,097	2014
Colorado Rockies	61	101	.377	37	Bud Black	Bill Schmidt	2,540,195	31,360	2007

Wild Card Series: Mets defeated Brewers 2-1 and Padres defeated Braves 2-0 in best-of-three. **Division Series:** Mets defeated Phillies 3-1 and Dodgers defeated Padres 3-2 in best-of-five. **Championship Series:** Dodgers defeated Mets 4-2 in best-of-seven.

EZRA SHAW/GETTY IMAGES

The Athletics bid farewell to Oakland, their home for 57 seasons. The franchise moves to Sacramento for at least the 2025 through 2027 seasons as a step toward their planned move to Las Vegas.

through 1950. They moved to Kansas City for the 1955 season, but that proved just a pit stop on the way to Oakland, the East Bay city they called home starting in 1968.

The A's were one of baseball's great dynasties from 1972-74 and nearly were again with three straight AL pennants 1988-90 and a Series title in '89. They won new followers under then-GM (now club president) Billy Beane as the 2002 "Moneyball" club, now immortalized in a movie, won 20 games in a row.

But the Oakland Coliseum, which has known many corporate sponsor names over the years, had fallen behind other facilities, first thanks to time, then due to a football-driven renovation which ruined its sightlines, then due to lack of investment as the club's owners wrangled with local officials over the site and costs of a new and/or renovated ballpark. Ultimately, current owner John Fisher seemed determined to get the best deal he could get for himself, whether or not it was best for MLB or even for the franchise.

The A's announced the move to Las Vegas in April 2023, but their immediate future took shape in 2024, when they announced plans to play the 2025-27 seasons in Sacramento, sharing Sutter Health Park with the Giants' Triple-A franchise. The move gives Las Vegas time to build its ballpark, set to open in 2028, while the A's get out of the Coliseum while still fulfilling their local TV contract by staying close to the Bay Area.

The A's ended their 57-year stay in Oakland by going 63-99, including 32-32 after the All-Star Game, after being predicted to be baseball's worst team in the preseason. Manager Mark Kotsay shepherded a young lineup that developed multiple power threats while dealing with the fan boycotts, franchise chaos and the impending move. Oakland fans came out in droves for the final game, as a crowd of 46,889 came to say goodbye on Sept. 26.

"That was by far the coolest game I've ever played in," second-year outfielder Lawrence Butler said. "The coolest crowd I've ever played in front of. Greatest atmosphere I've ever played in front of. This last game will stick with me forever."

Kotsay added, "I've never been to a World Series before, but I feel like today is one of those days that you can kind of experience the emotion of that. The magnitude of it, driving in today and seeing the fullness of a parking lot and feeling the energy and emotion, that's something I'll treasure for the rest of my life."

Skenes On An Elite Plane

The hotshot pitching phenom has been a staple of modern baseball, from Mark "The Bird" Fidrych electrifying fans in 1976 to Dwight Gooden's mid-1980s exploits, down to Kerry Wood's 20-strikeout gem in his 1998 rookie season and the sheer dominance of Stephen Strasburg during his 14-strikeout debut in 2010, only one year after he was the No. 1 overall pick in the draft.

In an age when starting pitchers have been diminished by bullpen games, injuries and a blurred line between starter and reliever, Paul

ALL-ROOKIE TEAM 2024

Pos	Player, Team	Age	PA	HR	RBI	SB	AVG	OBP	SLG	Summary
C	Austin Wells, Yankees	24	414	13	55	1	.229	.322	.395	LH hitter with power and patience; strong pitch framer
1B	Michael Busch, Cubs	26	567	21	65	2	.248	.335	.440	Thrived in everyday role after breaking free from Dodgers
2B	Tyler Fitzgerald, Giants	26	341	15	34	17	.280	.334	.497	Late-bloomer who runs and defends; showed life in bat
3B	Joey Ortiz, Brewers	25	511	11	60	11	.239	.329	.398	Lockdown glove held down weak position for Brewers
SS	Masyn Winn, Cardinals	22	637	15	57	11	.267	.314	.416	Youngster morphed into leadoff hitter, Gold Glove finalist
OF	Jackson Chourio, Brewers	20	573	21	79	22	.275	.327	.464	Youngest 20-20 hitter in MLB history and a future star
OF	Colton Cowser, Orioles	24	561	24	69	9	.242	.321	.447	Powerful bat and strong glove in spacious Baltimore LF
OF	Jackson Merrill, Padres	21	593	24	90	16	.292	.326	.500	Does-it-all center fielder who had a knack for the big hit
DH	Wyatt Langford, Rangers	22	557	16	74	19	.253	.325	.415	Started slowly but improved dramatically in second half

Pos	Pitcher, Team	Age	IP	W	L	BB	SO	HR	ERA	Summary
SP	Paul Skenes, Pirates	22	133	11	3	32	170	10	1.96	One of the most dominant rookie pitcher seasons ever
SP	Shota Imanaga, Cubs	30	173	15	3	28	174	27	2.91	NPB vet and flyball pitcher succeeded with elite K-BB%
SP	Luis Gil, Yankees	26	152	15	7	77	171	18	3.50	Older rookie made triumphant return from Tommy John
SP	Spencer Schwellenbach, Braves	24	117	8	7	23	122	14	3.47	Athletic starter helped keep Braves alive amid injuries
RP	Cade Smith, Guardians	25	75	6	1	17	103	1	1.91	Workhorse rookie led all relievers in FIP and fWAR
RP	Mason Miller, Athletics	25	65	2	2	21	104	6	2.49	100 mph closer saved 28 games, made all-star team

Skenes did everything he could to join the list of phenoms. The California prep product built the hype by helping Louisiana State win the 2023 College World Series, then was the No. 1 pick by the Pirates in the '23 draft.

He made five brief starts in the minors after signing and needed just seven more in 2024 before debuting May 11 against the Cubs, with a crowd of 34,924 coming to PNC Park in Pittsburgh to see it. He pitched into the fifth inning, yielding two hits to open the frame; the Pirates' bullpen gave up seven runs in the fifth after he left. But in his return engagement six days later in Chicago against the same Cubs, Skenes dazzled, striking out 11 over six no-hit innings while featuring a 100-mph fastball and a new pitch for him, the hybrid split-finger/two-seam "splinker". He struck out 11 again nearly two months later, July 11 at Milwaukee, in seven no-hit innings, and was named the NL's All-Star Game starter the next day. He learned the news live on the Dan Patrick Show when Diamondbacks manager Torey Lovullo called in while Patrick interviewed Skenes and broke the news.

"That's normally not what the protocol is," Skenes said on the show. "You don't do an interview and find out while you're on an interview from the actual National League manager. I wasn't expecting that."

The first Pirate to be the starting pitcher in an All-Star Game since Jerry Reuss in 1975, Skenes tossed a scoreless inning and became just the second drafted rookie to start an All-Star Game, joining Fidrych, a 1974 draftee who started the game in '76. Skenes was the first rookie to start the Game since Japan's Hideo Nomo of the Dodgers in 1995.

Skenes wound up averaging 98.8 mph on his four-seam fastball, firmest of any starter in the game and eighth-best overall among pitchers who threw at least 500 pitches. Fellow Pirates rookie Jared Jones (97.3 mph) joined him among the top five starters in fastball velocity, giving Pittsburgh fans some hope amidst another dreary 76-86 season.

Odds & Ends

■ Commissioner Rob Manfred has instituted plenty of changes across the sport since replacing Bud Selig in 2015, including expanded playoffs and the pitch clock. He signed a third five-year contract in July 2024 as commissioner but also announced that he would retire at the end of the 2029 season, making this his final term. He has worked for MLB since 1987.

"You can only have so much fun in one lifetime," Manfred told reporters at the time. "I have been open with (owners) about the fact that this was going to be my final term."

Manfred's next major move appears to be tackling the strike zone and using technology to either call balls and strikes or aid it. Triple-A leagues used a mix of a full ABS (automated ball-strike system) and a challenge system, in which hitters or pitchers could challenge individual calls, during the first half of the season. In the second half, they used strictly the challenge system, and Manfred said in various media interviews the week of the World Series that MLB would use the challenge system in spring training in 2025.

■ Another Manfred initiative has been the implementation of jewel event games in the regular season, such as games in London (this year between the Mets and Phillies), the Field of Dreams games in past years and the now-annual Little League classic played in Williamsport, Pa.

MARY DECICCO/MLB PHOTOS VIA GETTY

The Giants and Cardinals played a game at Rickwood Field in Birmingham, Ala., on June 20. The game became especially poignant when Willie Mays died just two days before the event.

For 2024, the event was a Cardinals-Giants game at Rickwood Field in Birmingham, Ala.

Rickwood Field is the oldest ballpark in the U.S., as it began hosting games in August 1910, and served as a home for independent minor league teams, affiliated minor league clubs (the Double-A Birmingham Barons have played annual "Turn Back the Clock" games there since 1996) and segregated Negro League clubs. Willie Mays got his professional start at Rickwood Field in 1947 and led the Birmingham Black Barons to a Negro League World Series victory the next year before later embarking on his Hall of Fame career with the Giants.

The 2024 Rickwood Classic was intended to honor Mays, but the greatest living player died June 18, two days before the game. The game was still played and became a poignant sendoff for Mays, 93, who finished his career with three MVP awards, 24 All-Star Game appearances and 660 home runs as one of the most dazzling center fielders who ever played.

"All of Major League Baseball is in mourning today as we are gathered at the very ballpark where a career and a legacy like no other began," commissioner Manfred said from Birmingham. "Willie Mays took his all-around brilliance from the Birmingham Black Barons of the Negro American League to the historic Giants franchise. From coast to coast . . . Willie inspired generations of players and fans as the game grew and truly earned its place as our National Pastime."

■ All-time MLB hits leader Pete Rose died at age 83 on Sept. 30, leaving a tangled legacy as the Hit King who rackeed up 4,256 hits and played in more games (and more wins) than anyone in MLB history. He also was banned from baseball in 1989 for his involvement in gambling on baseball games as manager of the Reds. He denied the gambling scandal for nearly 15 years before admitting his culpability in his 2004 autobiography.

■ Longtime Orioles owner Peter Angelos died March 23 at age 94, just days before his family was expected to complete the sale of the Orioles, a franchise it had owned since 1992. The sale did go through to billionaire businessman David Rubenstein, the only ownership change in MLB in 2024.

Despite the change in ownership and apparent change in vibes, the Orioles could not follow up on their 101-win 2023 breakthrough, dropping to 91 wins, including a 33-33 second half. Baltimore hosted a wild-card series against Kansas City but scored only one run in two games while being swept.

In other franchise sale news, the Twins went on the block in October. Carl Pohlad bought the club in 1984, and his grandson Joe Pohlad, in his second year as the club's control person, said the family was seeking a buyer. Only Reinsdorf (1981) and the Steinbrenner family, owners of the Yankees (1973), have owned their current franchises longer than the Pohlads have owned the Twins.

An official statement from Twins executive chair Joe Pohlad, issued Oct. 10, stated, We've never taken lightly the privilege of being stewards of this franchise. However, after months of thoughtful consideration, our family reached a decision this summer to explore selling the Twins. As we enter the next phase of this process, the time is right to make this decision public . . . It's our objective to find an ownership group who all of us can be proud of and who will take care of the Minnesota Twins."

■ The White Sox's Grifol was the first manager fired during the season, while Cincinnati fired David Bell in the season's final week. While Bell was a third-generation big leaguer, he was replaced in the offseason with a second-generation player and longtime veteran manager in Terry Francona, who will return to the dugout in 2025 after a year off after stepping down as Cleveland's manager after the 2023 season.

The other in-season managerial change came in Seattle after the Mariners led the AL West for much of the season. They led by 10 games on June 18 but less than two months later had fallen behind the Astros and fired manager Scott Servais when they were 64-64, replacing him with former Mariners catcher and longtime organization coach Dan Wilson. Seattle pitchers led MLB in ERA (3.49) and WHIP (1.077) but the offense ranked 21st in runs and the club missed the playoffs. The Mariners still have only one postseason berth (2022) since its 116-win season in 2001, Ichiro Suzuki's rookie year.

■ The Giants missed the playoffs for the seventh time in eight seasons, and it cost president of baseball operations Farhan Zaidi his post. Zaidi had replaced Bobby Evans in November 2018 and had produced one season above .500. Of course, that was 2021, when the Giants won 107 games, breaking a franchise record that had stood since manager John McGraw led the New York Giants to 106 wins in 1904 (and then refused to play in the World Series).

The magic of '21 never returned, though, and the Giants and their fans grew impatient of losing their luster while the Dodgers' star soared. The shock wasn't that Zaidi lost his job in October; it was that former all-star catcher Buster Posey, who retired after the 2021 season, was named as his successor. Posey already had a seat on the club's ownership group since 2022 and promoted pro scouting director Zack Minasian to replace Pete Putila as general manager. Minasian's brother Perry already is GM of the Angels.

■ In 2023, the top three payrolls failed to make the playoffs in the Mets, Padres and Yankees. In 2024, the Mets again had the largest payroll due in part to paying players who no longer played

AMERICAN LEAGUE BEST TOOLS

A Baseball America survey of American League managers, conducted in August 2024, ranked players with the best tools.

Best Hitter
1. Aaron Judge, Yankees
2. Juan Soto, Yankees
3. Steven Kwan, Guardians

Best Power
1. Aaron Judge, Yankees
2. Gunnar Henderson, Orioles
3. Yordan Alvarez, Astros

Best Bunter
1. Cedric Mullins, Orioles
2. Jose Altuve, Astros
3. Daulton Varsho, Blue Jays

Best Strike-Zone Judgment
1. Juan Soto, Yankees
2. Kyle Tucker, Astros
3. Steven Kwan, Guardians

Best Hit-And-Run Artist
1. Steven Kwan, Guardians
2. Jose Altuve, Astros
3. Salvador Perez, Royals

Best Baserunner
1. Bobby Witt Jr., Royals
2. Jose Ramirez, Guardians
3. Jarren Duran, Red Sox

Fastest Baserunner
1. Bobby Witt Jr., Royals
2. Byron Buxton, Twins
3. Dairon Blanco, Royals

Most Exciting Player
1. Gunnar Henderson, Orioles
2. Bobby Witt Jr., Royals
3. Aaron Judge, Yankees

Best Pitcher
1. Corbin Burnes, Orioles
2. Tarik Skubal, Tigers
3. George Kirby, Mariners

Best Fastball
1. Mason Miller, Athletics
2. Cole Ragans, Royals
3. Emmanuel Clase, Guardians

Best Curveball
1. Seth Lugo, Royals
2. Corbin Burnes, Orioles
3. Justin Verlander, Astros

Best Slider
1. Tanner Houck, Red Sox
2. Griffin Jax, Twins
3. Hunter Gaddis, Guardians

Best Changeup
1. Michael Wacha, Royals
2. Tyler Anderson, Angels
3. Tanner Houck, Red Sox

Best Control
1. George Kirby, Mariners
2. Zach Eflin, Rays
3. Joe Ryan, Twins

Best Pickoff Move
1. Jon Gray, Rangers
2. Tanner Bibee, Guardians
3. Nestor Cortes, Yankees

Best Reliever
1. Emmanuel Clase, Guardians
2. Mason Miller, Athletics
3. Andres Muñoz, Mariners

Best Defensive C
1. Cal Raleigh, Mariners
2. Jonah Heim, Rangers
3. Jose Trevino, Yankees

Best Defensive 1B
1. Nathaniel Lowe, Rangers
2. Carlos Santana, Twins
3. Vladimir Guerrero Jr., Blue Jays

Best Defensive 2B
1. Marcus Semien, Rangers
2. Andres Gimenez, Guardians
3. Nicky Lopez, White Sox

Best Defensive 3B
1. Josh Rojas, Mariners
2. Alex Bregman, Astros
3. Jose Ramirez, Guardians

Best Defensive SS
1. Bobby Witt Jr., Royals
2. Gunnar Henderson, Orioles
3. JP Crawford, Mariners

Best Infield Arm
1. Carlos Correa, Twins
2. Bobby Witt Jr., Royals
3. Gunnar Henderson, Orioles

Best Defensive OF
1. Daulton Varsho, Blue Jays
2. Byron Buxton, Twins
3. Leody Taveras, Rangers

Best Outfield Arm
1. Adolis Garcia, Rangers
2. Kevin Kiermaier, Blue Jays
3. Colton Cowser, Orioles

Best Manager
1. Bruce Bochy, Rangers
2. Kevin Cash, Rays
3. Brandon Hyde, Orioles

ORGANIZATION OF THE YEAR

Setting a new standard in San Diego

BY JEFF SANDERS

Xander Bogaerts spoke quietly as reporters gathered around him in the tiny visiting clubhouse at Dodger Stadium. The finality of the Padres' Game 5 loss in the National League Division Series had only begun to wash over the 32-year-old shortstop as he and his teammates dressed for a bus ride back to Petco Park and into the offseason.

They had planned to go so much further.

"Roster wise, we had it all, to be honest," Bogaerts said.

The injury-ravaged Dodgers, buoyed by National League MVP Shohei Ohtani and an MLB-high $328.5 million payroll, went on to win the World Series, stiff-arming both expensive New York clubs on the way to their first full-season title since 1988.

Los Angeles' biggest test in 2024 resided some two hours down Interstate 5 in the form of a Padres team that rose from the ashes of the most disappointing season in franchise history, the death of a beloved owner and a sobering new financial reality to push baseball's No. 1 seed to the brink of elimination.

To orchestrate a rebound with a heavy heart following chairman Peter Seidler's death from an infection related to a compromised immune system, the Padres traded away Juan Soto to begin to rebuild a competitive roster minus some $90 million from the 2023 Opening Day payroll.

They paired some of the fruit of that Soto trade with several Day One draft picks, including their last two first-rounders, to add stars to the mix. They called up Jackson Merrill—one of the top prospects in baseball—changed

SEAN M. HAFFEY/GETTY IMAGES

A.J. Preller's creativity and quick-strike mentality pushed the Padres to 93 wins.

his position and watched him blossom into an all-star. Jurickson Profar started the All-Star Game as a $1 million lottery ticket signed on the eve of spring training.

The Padres' pro scouting department recommended important role players for both the lineup and the bullpen. And they reloaded the farm system via another top international signee and several early 2024 draft picks with promising upside.

The Padres' creativity, resilience and overall excellence make them the Baseball America Organization of the Year for 2024.

"I don't think I'll ever be in a situation like that again (with the death of) somebody who I obviously worked closely with and love and respect," Padres president of baseball operations A.J. Preller said.

"That kind of had a huge effect on the whole organization. I think we rallied around that, rallied around everything as a group. Each offseason brings up a lot of questions, always . . . and brings up its own set of challenges.

"It's kind of one of the fun parts of the job." ■

LAST 10 WINNERS

2014: Kansas City Royals
2015: Pittsburgh Pirates
2016: Chicago Cubs
2017: Los Angeles Dodgers
2018: Milwaukee Brewers
2019: Tampa Bay Rays
2020: Los Angeles Dodgers
2021: Tampa Bay Rays
2022: Seattle Mariners
2023: Texas Rangers

Full list: search "Baseball America awards"

ACTIVE LEADERS

Career leaders among players who played in a game in 2024. Batters require 3,000 plate appearances and pitchers 1,000 innings to qualify for percentage titles.

BATTERS			PITCHERS		
AVG	Jose Altuve	.306	**ERA**	Clayton Kershaw	2.50
OBP	Juan Soto	.421	**SO/9**	Blake Snell	11.23
SLG	Aaron Judge	.604	**BB/9**	Miles Mikolas	1.72
OPS	Aaron Judge	1.010	**HR/9**	Clayton Kershaw	0.74
R	Freddie Freeman	1,298	**W**	Justin Verlander	262
H	Freddie Freeman	2,267	**L**	Justin Verlander	147
2B	Freddie Freeman	508	**SV**	Kenley Jansen	447
3B	Charlie Blackmon	68	**IP**	Justin Verlander	3,415.2
HR	Giancarlo Stanton	429	**SO**	Justin Verlander	3,416
RBI	Freddie Freeman	1,232	**BB**	Justin Verlander	952
BB	Carlos Santana	1,278	**AVG**	Clayton Kershaw	.210
SO	Giancarlo Stanton	1,963	**G**	Kenley Jansen	871
XBH	Freddie Freeman	882	**GS**	Justin Verlander	526
SB	Starling Marte	354	**HR**	Justin Verlander	355

for them (such as Max Scherzer, Justin Verlander and James McCann, among others). But these Mets rallied from a 22-33 start to zoom into a wild card spot, riding a breakout season from second-year third baseman Mark Vientos (team-best .516 slugging), strong seasons from veterans such as lefthander Sean Manaea (12-6, 3.47) and infielder Jose Iglesias (.337/.381/.448), and the sustained excellence of shortstop Francisco Lindor (.273/.344/.500, 33 HR).

The Mets' playoff run also ended the year of one of the league's surprise teams in Milwaukee, as New York beat the Brewers in a three-game wild-card tilt when Pete Alonso hit a three-run, ninth-inning homer off Brewers closer Devin Williams, the first home run hit off Williams' changeup in 2024. Milwaukee ran away with the NL Central crown, its 10-game margin over both St. Louis and Chicago being the largest division lead in the majors. That's despite losing manager Craig Counsell to the Cubs in the offseason; Pat Murphy, who coached Counsell at Notre Dame in the early 1990s and was his bench coach in Milwaukee, succeeded him and piloted one of baseball's most athletic and aggressive rosters.

The Brew Crew ranked second in the majors with 217 stolen bases and third in walks (597), so even though their 177 homers were slightly below the league average, they still finished sixth in runs scored. GM Matt Arnold refashioned the rotation in the offseason, trading impending free agent Corbin Burnes to Baltimore (netting rookie third baseman Joey Ortiz for starters) and losing Brandon Woodruff to a season-long shoulder injury. But Milwaukee persevered with holdover Freddy Peralta, well-traveled rookie Tobias Myers

NATIONAL LEAGUE BEST TOOLS

A Baseball America survey of National League managers, conducted in August 2024, ranked players with the best tools.

Best Hitter
1. Shohei Ohtani, Dodgers
2. Bryce Harper, Phillies
3. Mookie Betts, Dodgers

Best Power
1. Shohei Ohtani, Dodgers
2. Bryce Harper, Phillies
3. Oneil Cruz, Pirates

Best Bunter
1. Jacob Young, Nationals
2. TJ Friedl, Reds
3. Jake McCarthy, D-backs

Best Strike-Zone Judgment
1. Freddie Freeman, Dodgers
2. Mookie Betts, Dodgers
3. Andrew McCutchen, Pirates

Best Hit-And-Run Artist
1. Luis Arraez, Padres
2. William Contreras, Brewers
3. Nico Hoerner, Cubs

Best Baserunner
1. Elly De La Cruz, Reds
2. Corbin Carroll, D-backs
3. Trea Turner, Phillies

Fastest Baserunner
1. Elly De La Cruz, Reds
2. Trea Turner, Phillies
3. Victor Scott II, Cardinals

Most Exciting Player
1. Shohei Ohtani, Dodgers
2. Elly De La Cruz, Reds
3. Paul Skenes, Pirates

Best Pitcher
1. Zack Wheeler, Phillies
2. Chris Sale, Braves
3. Paul Skenes, Pirates

Best Fastball
1. Paul Skenes, Pirates
2. Hunter Greene, Reds
3. Reynaldo Lopez, Braves

Best Curveball
1. Aaron Nola, Phillies
2. Tyler Glasnow, Dodgers
3. Max Fried, Braves

Best Slider
1. Chris Sale, Braves
2. Ryan Helsley, Cardinals
3. Dylan Cease, Padres

Best Changeup
1. Cristopher Sanchez, Phillies
2. Logan Webb, Giants
3. Freddy Peralta, Brewers

Best Control
1. Aaron Nola, Phillies
2. Logan Webb, Giants
3. Shota Imanaga, Cubs

Best Pickoff Move
1. Charlie Morton, Braves
2. Patrick Corbin, Nationals
3. Max Fried, Braves

Best Reliever
1. Ryan Helsley, Cardinals
2. Tanner Scott, Marlins
3. Robert Suarez, Padres

Best Defensive C
1. Patrick Bailey, Giants
2. JT Realmuto, Phillies
3. Gabriel Moreno, Dbacks

Best Defensive 1B
1. Christian Walker, D-backs
2. Freddie Freeman, Dodgers
3. Matt Olson, Braves

Best Defensive 2B
1. Brice Turang, Brewers
2. Ketel Marte, D-backs
3. Nico Hoerner, Cubs

Best Defensive 3B
1. Matt Chapman, Giants
2. Ke'Bryan Hayes, Pirates
3. Ryan McMahon, Rockies

Best Defensive SS
1. Ezequiel Tovar, Rockies
2. Dansby Swanson, Cubs
3. Elly De La Cruz, Reds

Best Infield Arm
1. Masyn Winn, Cardinals
2. Oneil Cruz, Pirates
3. Elly De La Cruz, Reds

Best Defensive OF
1. Brenton Doyle, Rockies
2. Jacob Young, Nationals
3. Michael Siani, Cardinals

Best Outfield Arm
1. Nolan Jones, Rockies
2. Fernando Tatis Jr., Padres
3. Brenton Doyle, Rockies

Best Manager
1. Rob Thomson, Phillies
2. Pat Murphy, Brewers
3. Dave Roberts, Dodgers

(9-6, 3.00) and one of the majors' best bullpens to post a 3.65 team ERA, fifth-best in baseball.

■ Hurricane Helene delayed games the final week of MLB's season, affecting the National League wild-card chase involving the Mets, Braves

MAJOR LEAGUE ALL-STARS

SELECTED BY BASEBALL AMERICA

FRANK JANSKY/ICON SPORTSWIRE VIA GETTY IMAGES

Emmanuel Clase allowed a microscopic 0.61 ERA as the Guardians' closer

ORLANDO RAMIREZ/GETTY IMAGES

As a rookie, Jackson Merrill made an immediate impact in center field

FIRST TEAM

Pos	Player, Team	Age	AVG	OBP	SLG	PA	R	H	2B	3B	HR	RBI	BB	SO	SB	bWAR
C	William Contreras, Brewers	26	.281	.365	.466	679	99	167	37	2	23	92	78	139	9	4.9
1B	Vladimir Guerrero Jr., Blue Jays	25	.323	.396	.544	697	98	199	44	1	30	103	72	96	2	6.2
2B	Ketel Marte, D-backs	30	.292	.372	.560	583	93	147	23	2	36	95	65	106	7	6.9
3B	Jose Ramirez, Guardians	31	.279	.335	.537	682	114	173	39	2	39	118	54	82	41	6.8
SS	Bobby Witt Jr., Royals	24	.332	.389	.588	709	125	211	45	11	32	109	57	106	31	9.4
OF	Yordan Alvarez, Astros	27	.308	.392	.567	635	88	170	34	2	35	86	69	95	6	5.4
OF	Aaron Judge, Yankees	32	.322	.458	.701	704	122	180	36	1	58	144	133	171	10	10.8
OF	Juan Soto, Yankees	25	.288	.419	.569	713	128	166	31	4	41	109	129	119	7	7.9
DH	Shohei Ohtani, Dodgers	29	.310	.390	.646	731	134	197	38	7	54	130	81	162	59	9.2

Pos	Pitcher, Team	Age	W	L	ERA	G	SV	IP	H	R	ER	HR	BB	SO	WHIP	bWAR
SP	Seth Lugo, Royals	34	16	9	3.00	33	33	207	177	75	69	16	48	181	1.09	5.3
SP	Cole Ragans, Royals	26	11	9	3.14	32	0	186	146	71	65	15	67	223	1.14	5.0
SP	Chris Sale, Braves	35	18	3	2.38	29	0	178	141	48	47	9	39	225	1.01	6.2
SP	Tarik Skubal, Tigers	27	18	4	2.39	31	0	192	142	54	51	15	35	228	0.92	6.3
SP	Zack Wheeler, Phillies	34	16	7	2.57	32	0	200	139	62	57	20	52	224	0.96	6.0
RP	Emmanuel Clase, Guardians	26	4	2	0.61	74	47	74	39	10	5	2	10	66	0.66	4.5

SECOND TEAM

Pos	Player, Team	Age	AVG	OBP	SLG	PA	R	H	2B	3B	HR	RBI	BB	SO	SB	bWAR
C	Cal Raleigh, Mariners	27	.220	.312	.436	628	73	120	16	0	34	100	70	176	6	4.7
1B	Bryce Harper, Phillies	31	.285	.373	.525	631	85	157	42	0	30	87	76	138	7	4.8
2B	Jose Altuve, Astros	34	.295	.350	.439	682	94	185	31	0	20	65	47	119	22	3.4
3B	Rafael Devers, Red Sox	27	.272	.354	.516	601	87	143	34	5	28	83	67	147	3	3.7
SS	Gunnar Henderson, Orioles	23	.281	.364	.529	719	118	177	31	7	37	92	78	159	21	8.9
OF	Jarren Duran, Red Sox	27	.285	.342	.492	735	111	191	48	14	21	75	54	160	34	8.7
OF	Riley Greene, Tigers	23	.262	.348	.479	584	82	134	27	6	24	74	64	156	4	5.4
OF	Jackson Merrill, Padres	21	.292	.326	.500	593	77	162	31	6	24	90	29	101	16	4.4
DH	Brent Rooker, Athletics	29	.293	.365	.562	614	82	160	26	2	39	112	59	177	11	5.6

Pos	Pitcher, Team	Age	W	L	ERA	G	SV	IP	H	R	ER	HR	BB	SO	WHIP	bWAR
SP	Dylan Cease, Padres	28	14	11	3.47	33	33	189	137	80	73	18	65	224	1.07	4.1
SP	Logan Gilbert, Mariners	27	9	12	3.23	33	0	209	148	83	75	26	37	220	0.89	2.8
SP	Reynaldo Lopez, Braves	30	8	5	1.99	25	0	136	108	32	30	10	42	148	1.11	5.0
SP	Paul Skenes, Pirates	22	11	3	1.96	23	0	133	94	31	29	10	32	170	0.95	6.0
SP	Logan Webb, Giants	27	13	10	3.47	33	0	205	202	83	79	11	50	172	1.23	3.8
RP	Ryan Helsley, Cardinals	29	7	4	2.04	65	49	66	50	19	15	3	23	79	1.10	3.0

MAJOR LEAGUES

EXECUTIVE OF THE YEAR

AARON GASH/MLB PHOTOS VIA GETTY IMAGES

Matt Arnold

The Brewers had every excuse to take a significant step back in 2024.

They lost their manager. They traded their ace. They suffered through myriad injuries to key players. Their payroll once again matched their status as baseball's smallest-market team.

In the end, none of that mattered.

Thanks in large part to the deft decision-making of general manager Matt Arnold, the Brewers went on to win the National League Central division and make their sixth postseason appearance in the last seven years.

"Matt has been the glue in our baseball ops group," Brewers principal owner Mark Attanasio said.

Arnold, 45, has been with the Brewers since October 2015, when he joined as right-hand man to then-GM David Stearns. Arnold ascended to the top spot in baseball operations in October 2022 after Stearns stepped into an advisory role for what would be his final year with the Brewers.

LAST 10 WINNERS

2014: Dan Duquette, Orioles
2015: Sandy Alderson, Mets
2016: Chris Antonetti, Indians
2017: Brian Cashman, Yankees
2018: Dave Dombrowski, Red Sox
2019: Mike Rizzo, Nationals
2020: Andrew Friedman, Dodgers
2021: Farhan Zaidi, Giants
2022: Alex Anthopoulous, Braves
2023: Mike Elias, Orioles

Full list: search "Baseball America awards"

MANAGER OF THE YEAR

AL BELLO/GETTY IMAGES

Dave Roberts

Over his nine years as manager of the Dodgers, Dave Roberts has learned something about his position.

When the Dodgers win—and they have won more than any other team since 2016—it is never because of Roberts. It is rationalized as their resources and payroll and their sophisticated front office that brings together the star power that makes winning inevitable.

But when the Dodgers lose, the blame falls on Roberts more than anyone else. He took the pitcher out too soon, brought in the wrong reliever, was too wedded to analytics or was not guided enough by analytics.

"I've learned to have thicker skin and try to appreciate the fact that there's always going to be criticism—maybe more jaded at times," Roberts said this fall. "But it is a results business, and I get that."

It is absolutely a results business. And Roberts got the results in 2024, when the Dodgers won the World Series in five games.

LAST 10 WINNERS

2014: Buck Showalter, Orioles
2015: Joe Maddon, Cubs
2016: Terry Francona, Indians
2017: A.J. Hinch, Astros
2018: Bob Melvin, Athletics
2019: Craig Counsell, Brewers
2020: Brian Snitker, Braves
2021: Dusty Baker, Astros
2022: Brandon Hyde, Orioles
2023: Torey Lovullo, Dbacks

Full list: search "Baseball America awards"

and Diamondbacks and forcing the Mets and Braves to play a doubleheader the day after the rest of MLB's season was over to determine the final spots. The teams split, leaving Arizona the odd team out.

Two weeks later, Hurricane Milton roared across the Gulf of Mexico and slammed into the Tampa Bay region, causing hundreds of millions of dollars in damage and killing at least 35. The symbol of the storm's destruction became Tropicana Field, the Rays' home ballpark. As the storm passed, TV cameras focused on the Trop, revealing the structure's teflon-coated roof had been ripped to shreds by the storm's 100 mph winds.

The Trop originally opened in 1990 and has been the Rays' much-maligned home ballpark since the club's inception in 1998. The Rays in late May had unveiled detailed plans for their new ballpark, which is planned to open in 2028 in what currently is Tropicana Field's parking lot.

The storm's damage rendered The Trop unplayable for at least the 2025 season, which the Rays will spend at Steinbrenner Field, which houses the Yankees during spring training and their Low-A affiliate in the regular season. The move rankled local officials in Pinellas County to the point that the bonds needed for the Rays' new home are now in question. The move also means that two of MLB's 30 clubs, the A's and Rays, will play home games in minor league ballparks in 2025. ■

Duran HR continues AL dominance

BY J.J. COOPER

After a brief siesta in 2023, the American League's dominance of the All-Star Game continued in Dallas.

A night after Teoscar Hernandez hung on to beat Bobby Witt Jr. in the Home Run Derby, the sellout crowd got to see plenty of stars rise to the occasion in the All-Star Game.

National League DH Shohei Ohtani hit a three-run home run off of Tanner Houck to give the National League a lead in the third inning.

A Juan Soto two-run double and a David Fry RBI single off Logan Webb evened the score in the bottom of the third.

All-Star MVP Jarren Duran hit a two-run home run off Hunter Greene in the fifth inning, breaking the tie and giving the American League a 5-3 lead.

Cole Ragans, Seth Lugo, Kirby Yates and Emmanuel Clase made that lead stick, making a winner out of A's reliever Mason Miller, who was had reached back for 103.6 mph in a perfect, two-strikeout, 12-pitch fifth inning.

Miller's peak velocity set an All-Star Game record in the Statcast era, topping Aroldis Chapman's 103.4 mph pitch in the 2015 All-Star Game. Miller threw eight fastballs. All topped 100 mph, and four were 102+ mph.

Pirates rookie Paul Skenes was named the NL starter, becoming only the fifth rookie pitcher to start the All-Star Game. He was the first to do so since Hideo Nomo started the 1995 All-Star Game. He handled the honor with aplomb, recording a clean inning as he allowed one walk.

This was the American League's tenth win in the past 11 All-Star games. The National League dominated the midseason classic for decades, and won 19 of 20 All-Star Games from 1963 to 1982.

But that balance of power has clearly shifted. The American League has won 27 of the past 35 games with the National League winning seven and one very famous tie.

The American League now leads the All-Star Game with 48 wins to the National League's 44, with two ties. ■

ALL-STAR GAME

All-Star Game MVP Jarren Duran

STACY REVERE/GETTY IMAGES

2024 ALL-STAR GAME

JULY 15, 2024
AL 5, NL 3

National	AB	R	H	RBI	American	AB	R	H	RBI
Marte, K, 2B	3	1	1	0	Kwan, LF	1	1	0	0
McMahon, 2B	1	0	0	0	Greene, R, LF	2	0	0	0
Ohtani, DH	2	1	1	3	Henderson, SS	2	0	0	0
Ozuna, PH-DH	1	0	0	0	Seager, SS	1	0	0	0
Turner, SS	3	0	1	0	Witt Jr., SS	1	0	0	0
Abrams, SS	1	0	0	0	Soto, J, RF	1	1	1	2
Harper, 1B	3	0	1	0	Santander, RF	2	1	1	0
Ramos, RF	1	0	0	0	Judge, CF	2	0	0	0
Contreras, Wm, C	2	0	0	0	Duran, Ja, CF	2	1	1	2
Smith, W.D., C	2	0	1	0	Alvarez, Y, DH	0	0	0	0
Yelich, RF	2	0	0	0	Fry, PH-DH	2	0	1	1
Freeman, F, PH-1B	1	0	0	0	Castro, W, PH-DH	1	0	0	0
Alonso, 1B	1	0	0	0	Ramirez, Jo, 3B	2	0	0	0
Bohm, 3B	2	0	1	0	Paredes, 3B	1	0	0	0
De La Cruz, E, 3B	2	0	1	0	Guerrero Jr., 1B	2	0	0	0
Hernandez, T, CF	2	0	0	0	Naylor, J, 1B	1	0	0	0
Merrill, CF	2	0	1	0	Rutschman, C	2	0	0	0
Profar, J, LF	2	1	1	0	Perez, S, C	1	0	0	0
Reynolds, B, LF	2	0	1	0	Semien, 2B	2	1	1	0
					Westburg, 2B	1	0	0	0
Totals	**35**	**3**	**10**	**3**	**Totals**	**29**	**5**	**5**	**5**

2B: Harper (1, Burnes); Soto, J (1, Webb). **HR:** Ohtani (1, 3rd inning off Houck, 2 on, 0 out); Duran, Ja (1, 5th inning off Greene, H, 1 on, 2 out). **TB:** Bohm; De La Cruz, E; Harper 2; Marte, K; Merrill; Ohtani 4; Profar, J; Reynolds, B; Smith, W.D.; Turner; Duran, Ja 4; Fry; Santander; Semien; Soto, J 2. **RBI:** Ohtani 3 (3); Duran, Ja 2 (2); Fry (1); Soto, J 2 (2). **GIDP:** Freeman, F; Harper. **DP:** 2 (Semien-Henderson-Guerrero Jr.; Naylor, J-Witt Jr.-Naylor, J).

Time of Game: 2:28. **Attendance:** 39,343.

National	IP	H	R	SO	American	IP	H	R	SO
Skenes	1.0	0	0	0	Burnes	1.0	1	0	0
Fried	1.0	0	0	0	Skubal	1.0	0	0	0
Webb (BS)	1.0	3	3	1	Houck	1.0	4	3	1
Imanaga	1.0	0	0	1	Crochet	1.0	1	0	1
Greene, H (L)	1.0	2	2	0	Miller, M (W)	1.0	0	0	2
Sanchez, C	0.2	0	0	0	Ragans (H)	1.0	1	0	0
Lopez, R	0.1	0	0	1	Lugo, S (H)	1.0	2	0	1
Suarez, Ro	0.2	0	0	2	Yates (H)	1.0	0	0	2
Strahm	0.1	0	0	1	Clase, E (Sv)	1.0	1	0	2
Scott, Tan	0.2	0	0	0					
Hoffman	0.1	0	0	0					
Totals	**8**	**5**	**5**	**6**	**Totals**	**9**	**10**	**3**	**9**

MAJOR LEAGUE DEBUTS

ARIZONA DIAMONDBACKS
Blaze Alexander....Mar 28
Jorge Barrosa.......... Apr 1
Blake Walston........ May 1
Cristian Mena ....Jul 3
Yilber Diaz ....Jul 8
Adrian Del Castillo ..Aug 7

ATLANTA BRAVES
Spencer Schwellenbach..May 29
Hurston Waldrep .... Jun 9
Grant Holmes ....Jun 16
Nacho Alvarez Jr. ....Jul 22
Parker Dunshee ..Aug 826

BALTIMORE ORIOLES
Jackson Holliday... Apr 10
David Bañuelos..... Apr 16
Connor Norby .... Jun 3
Cade Povich .... Jun 6
Chayce McDermott .Jul 24
Coby Mayo.............Aug 2

BOSTON RED SOX
Justin Slaten.........Mar 30
Cam Booser .... Apr 19
Naoyuki Uwasawa . May 2
Jamie Westbrook..... Jun 2
Bailey Horn............Jun 29
Nick Sogard ....Aug 2
Mickey Gasper ......Aug 12
Chase Shugart ......Aug 15
Richard Fitts .... Sep 8
Luis Guerrero .... Sep 8
Zach Penrod.......... Sep 14

CHICAGO CUBS
Ben Brown............Mar 30
Shota Imanaga....... Apr 1
Porter Hodge....... May 22
Luis Vazquez........ May 22
Hunter Bigge ....Jul 9
Jack Neely.............Aug 21
Kevin Alcantara .... Sep 25

CHICAGO WHITE SOX
Jordan Leasure .....Mar 30
Nick Nastrini......... Apr 15
Jonathan Cannon . Apr 17
Bryan Ramos......... May 4
Zach DeLoach ...... May 22
Duke Ellis................ Jun 4
Drew Thorpe..........Jun 11
Brooks Baldwin ......Jul 19
Fraser Ellard...........Jul 30
Ky Bush...................Aug 5
Jairo Iriarte............ Sep 3
Sean Burke .... Sep 10
Jake Eder .... Sep 17

CINCINNATI REDS
Jacob Hurtubise... May 13
Blake Dunn............. Jun 4
Levi Jordan ....Jun 24
Yosver Zulueta ....Jun 25
Rece Hinds................Jul 8
Eric Yang ....Jul 31
Julian Aguiar ....Aug 19
Evan Kravetz ....Aug 28
Rhett Lowder........Aug 30

CLEVELAND INDIANS
Cade Smith ....Mar 30
Kyle Manzardo....... May 6
Johnathan Rodriguez ..May 21
Daniel Schneemann Jun 2
Angel Martinez.....Jun 22
Jhonkensy Noel ....Jun 26
Joey Cantillo ....Jul 28
Connor Gillispie ......Aug 4
Erik Sabrowski .... Sep 4
Andrew Walters.... Sep 12

COLORADO ROCKIES
Anthony Molina....Mar 28
Jordan Beck.......... Apr 30
Angel Chivilli .... Jun 3
Greg Jones.............. Jun 6
Adael Amador .... Jun 9
Aaron Schunk ....Jun 29
Tanner Gordon..........Jul 7
Drew Romo ....Aug 17
Jeff Criswell ....Aug 21
Luis Peralta...........Aug 24
Seth Halvorsen .....Aug 30
Jaden Hill .... Sep 7

DETROIT TIGERS
Colt Keith..............Mar 28
Wenceel Perez .... Apr 8
Keider Montero.... May 29
Justyn-Henry Malloy ... Jun 3
Dillon Dingler ....Jul 29
Bryan Sammons .....Jul 29
Brant Hurter ....Aug 4
Jace Jung..............Aug 16
Trey Sweeney ....Aug 16
Ty Madden............Aug 26
Jackson Jobe......... Sep 25

HOUSTON ASTROS
Blair Henley............ Apr 8
Spencer Arrighetti Apr 10
Forrest Whitley..... Apr 16
Joey Loperfido...... Apr 30
Jake Bloss ....Jun 21
Luis Contreras........Jun 23
Bryan King.............Jun 23
Pedro Leon ....Aug 3
Zach Dezenzo ....Aug 6
Shay Whitcomb ....Aug 17

KANSAS CITY ROYALS
Matt Sauer..............Mar 31
Will Klein ....Apr 28
CJ Alexander............Jun 24
Walter Pennington......Jul 5
Tyler Gentry.............Aug 25

LOS ANGELES ANGELS
Zac Kristofak......... Apr 28
Jack Kochanowicz...Jul 11
Niko Kavadas........Aug 16
Ryan Zeferjahn .....Aug 25
Ryan Miller...........Aug 27
Sam Aldegheri......Aug 30
Caden Dana .... Sep 1
Bryce Teodosio........ Sep 7
Eric Wagaman ...... Sep 10
Gustavo Campero . Sep 15

LOS ANGELES DODGERS
Yoshinobu Yamamoto.. Mar 21
Ricky Vanasco .... Apr 15
Andy Pages........... Apr 16
Landon Knack....... Apr 17
Michael Petersen...Jun 18
Justin Wrobleski ....Jul 7
River Ryan ....Jul 22
Hunter Feduccia......Jul 31
Ben Casparius ....Aug 31
Edgardo Henriquez....Sep 24

MIAMI MARLINS
Jhonny Pereda...... Apr 17
Roddery Muñoz.... Apr 20
Anthony Maldonado . Apr 26
Emmanuel Ramirez ... Apr 28
Eli Villalobos .... May 5
Valente Bellozo......Jun 26
Austin Kitchen ....Jul 30
Griffin Conine ....Aug 26
Jonathan Bermudez .... Aug 27
Javier Sanoja .... Sep 7
Lake Bachar........... Sep 8

MILWAUKEE BREWERS
Jackson Chourio....Mar 29
Oliver Dunn ....Mar 30
Tobias Myers......... Apr 23
Tyler Black .... Apr 30
Robert Gasser...... May 10
Chris Roller.......... May 15
James Meeker......... Jun 7
Carlos Rodriguez....Jun 11
Bradley Blalock.......Jun 20
Isaac Collins........... Sep 8

MINNESOTA TWINS
Ryne Harper.......March 31
Austin Martin ....Mar 30
Jair Camargo......... Apr 16
David Festa ....Jun 27
Brooks Lee ....Jul 3
Zebby Matthews....Aug 13
Michael Helman ..... Sep 3
DaShawn Keirsey.... Sep 5

NEW YORK METS
Dedniel Nuñez........ Apr 9
Tyler Jay................ Apr 11
Christian Scott....... May 4
Eric Orze ....Jul 8
Luisangel Acuña ... Sep 14

NEW YORK YANKEES
Clayton Beeter......Mar 29
Josh Maciejewski.... Apr 8
Ben Rice ....Jun 18
Carlos Narvaez........Jul 20
Will Warren.............Jul 30

OAKLAND ATHLETICS
Darell Hernaiz.......Mar 28
Mitch Spence........Mar 29
Kyle McCann.........Mar 30
Max Schuemann... Apr 12
Brett Harris........... May 3
Tyler Ferguson .... May 7
Jack O'Loughlin ... May 26
Brady Basso .... May 31
Michel Otañez ....Jun 10
Armando Alvarez...Jun 22
Jacob Wilson...........Jul 19
Grant Holman.......Aug 17
J.T. Ginn ....Aug 21

PHILADELPHIA PHILLIES
Michael Mercado...Jun 24
Tyler Phillips ....Jul 7
Max Lazar.............Aug 10
Seth Johnson.......... Sep 8

PITTSBURGH PIRATES
Jared Jones...........Mar 30
Paul Skenes .... May 11
Grant Koch........... May 29
Brady Feigl ....Aug 26
Billy Cook................ Sep 8
Nick Yorke............. Sep 16
Mike Burrows .... Sep 28

ST. LOUIS CARDINALS
Victor Scott II........Mar 28
Ryan Fernandez...... Apr 3
Pedro Pages............ Apr 7
Chris Roycroft .... May 7
Ryan Loutos............. Jun 1
Adam Kloffenstein.Jun 20
Gordon Graceffo ....Jun 29
Michael McGreevy ..Jul 31
Thomas Saggese... Sep 10

SAN DIEGO PADRES
Yuki Matsui...........Mar 20
Jackson Merrill .....Mar 20
Graham Pauley.....Mar 20
Stephen Kolek ......Mar 21
Adam Mazur........... Jun 4
Sean Reynolds........Jul 14
Brandon Lockridge ....Sep 13

SAN FRANCISCO GIANTS
Jung Hoo Lee........Mar 28
Erik Miller ....Mar 28
Landen Roupp ......Mar 29
Kai-Wei Teng ....Mar 31
Nick Avila................ Apr 1
Randy Rodriguez ... May 4
Mason Black.......... May 6
Trenton Brooks .... May 28
Spencer Bivens ......Jun 16
Raymond Burgos...Jun 24
Hayden Birdsong ..Jun 26
Grant McCray........Aug 14
Trevor McDonald .. Sep 29

SEATTLE MARINERS
Jonatan Clase .... Apr 15
Leo Rivas .... Apr 28
Ryan Bliss............ May 27
Tyler Locklear.......... Jun 9
Troy Taylor ....Aug 11

TAMPA BAY RAYS
Austin Shenton.....Mar 31
Justin Sterner ...... May 31
Kameron Misner.....Aug 2
Logan Driscoll......... Sep 3
Mason Montgomery....Sep 5

TEXAS RANGERS
Wyatt Langford ....Mar 28
Justin Foscue .... Apr 5
Davis Wendzel .... Apr 9
Cole Winn .... Apr 14
Jack Leiter .... Apr 18
Gerson Garabito... May 26
Daniel Robert ....Jul 10
Sandro Fabian .... Sep 6
Kumar Rocker .... Sep 12
Marc Church .... Sep 28
Dustin Harris......... Sep 28

TORONTO BLUE JAYS
Yariel Rodriguez ... Apr 13
Addison Barger..... Apr 24
Brandon Eisert.......Jun 17
Orelvis Martinez ....Jun 21
Steward Berroa......Jun 23
Leo Jimenez..............Jul 4
Luis De Los Santos ..Jul 31
Will Wagner..........Aug 12

WASHINGTON NATIONALS
Trey Lipscomb.......Mar 30
Nasim Nuñez ....Mar 30
Mitchell Parker..... Apr 15
DJ Herz .... Jun 4
James Wood ....Jul 1
Andres Chaparro...Aug 13
Orlando Ribalta ....Aug 13
Dylan Crews...........Aug 26
Darren Baker .... Sep 1
Zach Brzykcy........... Sep 1

AMERICAN LEAGUE 2024 STATISTICS

CLUB BATTING

	AVG	G	AB	R	H	2B	3B	HR	RBI	BB	SO	SB	OBP	SLG
Houston	.262	161	5530	740	1448	264	16	190	701	448	1176	93	.322	.418
Boston	.252	162	5577	751	1404	311	30	194	724	493	1570	144	.319	.423
Baltimore	.250	162	5567	786	1391	262	33	235	759	489	1359	98	.315	.435
New York	.248	162	5450	815	1352	243	15	237	782	672	1326	88	.333	.429
Kansas City	.248	162	5421	735	1343	264	35	170	711	429	1161	134	.306	.403
Minnesota	.246	162	5490	742	1352	309	23	183	702	473	1306	65	.315	.411
Toronto	.241	162	5410	671	1306	280	26	156	640	510	1233	72	.313	.389
Texas	.238	162	5472	683	1302	220	15	176	652	490	1284	97	.305	.380
Cleveland	.238	161	5310	708	1263	245	18	185	670	466	1196	148	.307	.395
Detroit	.234	162	5442	682	1273	244	47	162	656	476	1461	76	.300	.385
Oakland	.233	162	5432	643	1267	240	19	196	619	493	1502	98	.301	.393
Tampa Bay	.230	162	5389	604	1241	245	23	147	564	493	1485	178	.302	.366
Los Angeles	.229	162	5357	635	1227	227	15	165	596	482	1416	133	.301	.369
Seattle	.224	162	5330	676	1195	228	13	185	642	571	1625	140	.311	.376
Chicago	.221	162	5383	507	1187	226	9	133	485	395	1403	90	.278	.340

CLUB PITCHING

	ERA	G	CG	SHO	SV	IP	H	R	ER	HR	BB	SO	AVG
Seattle	3.49	162	1	15	34	1433	1174	607	556	183	369	1416	.220
Cleveland	3.61	161	0	12	53	1428	1224	621	572	179	492	1410	.230
Detroit	3.61	162	1	10	45	1447	1265	642	581	159	416	1354	.233
Houston	3.74	161	2	11	43	1432	1238	649	595	183	544	1479	.231
New York	3.74	162	0	14	45	1453	1272	668	604	181	533	1457	.233
Kansas City	3.76	162	2	11	41	1428	1303	644	596	146	472	1339	.241
Tampa Bay	3.77	162	0	12	51	1441	1286	663	604	196	445	1406	.236
Baltimore	3.94	162	0	9	46	1442	1303	699	632	175	481	1380	.238
Boston	4.04	162	1	13	40	1453	1363	747	652	189	461	1353	.246
Minnesota	4.26	162	1	8	43	1440	1333	735	682	190	433	1500	.242
Toronto	4.29	162	3	9	36	1427	1316	743	681	208	503	1314	.243
Texas	4.35	162	0	12	38	1428	1323	738	690	198	530	1371	.243
Oakland	4.37	162	1	12	35	1437	1385	764	698	169	530	1263	.253
Los Angeles	4.56	162	0	7	35	1431	1328	797	725	202	601	1252	.246
Chicago	4.67	162	0	7	21	1420	1397	813	737	201	643	1366	.255

CLUB FIELDING

	PCT	PO	A	E	DP
Minnesota	.988	4321	1230	70	75
Texas	.987	4283	1366	73	106
Detroit	.986	4341	1409	80	129
Seattle	.986	4299	1293	79	95
Baltimore	.986	4326	1336	81	100
Oakland	.985	4310	1360	84	142
Kansas City	.985	4284	1423	85	125
Houston	.985	4296	1312	84	130

	PCT	PO	A	E	DP
Cleveland	.985	4284	1377	87	130
Tampa Bay	.984	4322	1265	90	108
Chicago	.984	4260	1276	90	115
Toronto	.984	4282	1355	92	125
New York	.984	4358	1320	93	112
Los Angeles	.983	4293	1439	97	152
Boston	.981	4358	1449	115	117

INDIVIDUAL BATTING LEADERS

	AVG	G	AB	R	H	2B	3B	HR	RBI	BB	SO	SB
Bobby Witt Jr., Kansas City	.332	161	636	125	211	45	11	32	109	57	106	31
Vladimir Guerrero Jr., Toronto	.323	159	616	98	199	44	1	30	103	72	96	2
Aaron Judge, New York	.322	158	559	122	180	36	1	58	144	133	171	10
Yordan Alvarez, Houston	.308	147	552	88	170	34	2	35	86	69	95	6
Yandy Diaz, Houston	.299	148	585	70	175	29	3	16	84	24	107	2
Jose Altuve, Houston	.295	153	628	94	185	31	0	20	65	47	119	22
Brent Rooker, Oakland	.293	145	546	82	160	26	2	39	112	59	177	11
Steven Kwan, Cleveland	.292	122	480	83	140	16	3	14	44	53	51	12
Juan Soto, New York	.288	157	576	128	166	31	4	41	109	129	119	7
Jarren Duran, Boston	.285	160	671	111	191	48	14	21	75	54	160	34

INDIVIDUAL PITCHING LEADERS

	W	L	ERA	G	GS	CG	SV	IP	H	R	ER	BB	SO
Tarik Skubal, Detroit	18	4	2.39	31	31	0	0	192	142	54	51	35	228
Ronel Blanco, Houston	13	6	2.80	30	29	1	0	167	114	56	52	68	166
Framber Valdez, Houston	15	7	2.91	28	28	1	0	176	140	60	57	55	169
Corbin Burnes, Baltimore	15	9	2.92	32	32	0	0	194	165	76	63	48	181
Bryce Miller, Seattle	12	8	2.94	31	31	0	0	180	131	62	59	45	171
Seth Lugo, Kansas City	16	9	3.00	33	33	1	0	207	177	75	69	48	181
Tanner Houck, Boston	9	10	3.12	30	30	1	0	179	156	75	62	48	154
Cole Ragans, Kansas City	11	9	3.14	32	32	1	0	186	146	71	65	67	223
Logan Gilbert, Seattle	9	12	3.23	33	33	1	0	209	148	83	75	37	220
Michael Wacha, Kansas City	13	8	3.35	29	29	0	0	167	154	65	62	45	145

AWARD WINNERS

Selected by Baseball Writers Association of America

MOST VALUABLE PLAYER

Player	1st	2nd	3rd	Total
Aaron Judge, Yankees	30	—	—	420
Bobby Witt Jr., Royals	—	30	—	270
Juan Soto, Yankees	—	—	21	229
Gunnar Henderson, Orioles	—	—	6	208
Jose Ramirez, Guardians	—	—	3	184
Vladimir Guerrero Jr., Blue Jays	—	—	—	99
Tarik Skubal, Tigers	—	—	—	93
Jarren Duran, Red Sox	—	—	—	90
Yordan Alvarez, Astros	—	—	—	75
Brent Rooker, Athletics	—	—	—	40
Emmanuel Clase, Guardians	—	—	—	36
Cal Raleigh, Mariners	—	—	—	12
Rafael Devers, Red Sox	—	—	—	5
Anthony Santander, Orioles	—	—	—	4
Jose Altuve, Astros	—	—	—	1
Tyler Holton, Tigers	—	—	—	1
Seth Lugo, Royals	—	—	—	1
Corey Seager, Rangers	—	—	—	1
Framber Valdez, Astros	—	—	—	1

CY YOUNG AWARD

Player	1st	2nd	3rd	Total
Tarik Skubal, Tigers	30	—	—	210
Seth Lugo, Royals	—	14	9	93
Emmanuel Clase, Guardians	—	9	7	66
Cole Ragans, Royals	—	3	6	48
Corbin Burnes, Orioles	—	3	4	47
Logan Gilbert, Mariners	—	1	2	25
Framber Valdez, Astros	—	—	2	17
Kirby Yates, Rangers	—	—	—	2
Yusei Kikuchi, Astros	—	—	—	1
Cade Smith, Guardians	—	—	—	1

ROOKIE OF THE YEAR

Player	1st	2nd	3rd	Total
Luis Gil, Yankees	15	10	1	106
Colton Cowser, Orioles	13	11	3	101
Austin Wells, Yankees	—	3	8	17
Mason Miller, Athletics	1	2	5	16
Cade Smith, Guardians	1	1	4	12
Wilyer Abreu, Red Sox	—	2	5	11
Wyatt Langford, Rangers	—	1	4	7

MANAGER OF THE YEAR

Player	1st	2nd	3rd	Total
Stephen Vogt, Guardians	27	2	1	142
Matt Quatraro, Royals	2	19	6	73
A.J. Hinch, Tigers	1	6	18	41
Joe Espada, Astros	—	1	3	6
Aaron Boone, Yankees	—	1	—	3
Mark Kotsay, Athletics	—	1	—	3
Rocco Baldelli, Twins	—	—	1	1
Alex Cora, Red Sox	—	—	1	1

GOLD GLOVE WINNERS

P—Seth Lugo, Royals. **C**—Cal Raleigh, Mariners. **1B**—Carlos Santana, Twins. **2B**—Andres Gimenez, Guardians. **3B**—Alex Bregman, Astros. **SS**—Bobby Witt Jr., Royals. **LF**—Steven Kwan, Guardians. **CF**—Daulton Varsho, Blue Jays. **RF**—Wilyer Abreu, Red Sox. **UT**—Dylan Moore, Mariners.

AMERICAN LEAGUE DEPARTMENT LEADERS

BATTING

GAMES
Bobby Witt Jr., Kansas City 161
Anthony Volpe, New York 160
Jarren Duran, Boston 160
Vladimir Guerrero Jr., Toronto 159
Gunnar Henderson, Baltimore 159
Marcus Semien, Texas 159
JJ Bleday, Oakland 159

AT-BATS
Jarren Duran, Boston 671
Marcus Semien, Texas 650
Anthony Volpe, New York 637
Bobby Witt Jr., Kansas City 636
Gunnar Henderson, Baltimore 630

PLATE APPEARANCES
Jarren Duran, Boston 735
Gunnar Henderson, Baltimore 719
Marcus Semien, Texas 718
Juan Soto, New York 713
Bobby Witt Jr., Kansas City 709

RUNS
Juan Soto, New York 128
Bobby Witt Jr., Kansas City 125
Aaron Judge, New York 122
Gunnar Henderson, Baltimore 118
Jose Ramirez, Cleveland 114

HITS
Bobby Witt Jr., Kansas City 211
Vladimir Guerrero Jr., Toronto 199
Jarren Duran, Boston 191
Jose Altuve, Houston 185
Aaron Judge, New York 180

TOTAL BASES
Aaron Judge, New York 392
Bobby Witt Jr., Kansas City 374
Vladimir Guerrero Jr., Toronto 335
Gunnar Henderson, Baltimore 333
Jose Ramirez, Cleveland 333

DOUBLES
Jarren Duran, Boston 48
Bobby Witt Jr., Kansas City 45
Vladimir Guerrero Jr., Toronto 44
JJ Bleday, Oakland 43
Jose Ramirez, Cleveland 39

TRIPLES
Jarren Duran, Boston 14
Bobby Witt Jr., Kansas City 11
Kyle Isbel, Kansas City 8
Gunnar Henderson, Baltimore 7
Daulton Varsho, Toronto 7
Anthony Volpe, New York 7

EXTRA-BASE HITS
Aaron Judge, New York 95
Bobby Witt Jr., Kansas City 88
Jarren Duran, Boston 83
Jose Ramirez, Cleveland 80
Juan Soto, New York 76

HOME RUNS
Aaron Judge, New York 58
Anthony Santander, Baltimore 44
Juan Soto, New York 41
Jose Ramirez, Cleveland 39
Brent Rooker, Oakland 39

RUNS BATTED IN
Aaron Judge, New York 144
Jose Ramirez, Cleveland 118
Brent Rooker, Oakland 112
Juan Soto, New York 109
Bobby Witt Jr., Kansas City 109

Bobby Witt Jr.

SACRIFICES
Kyle Isbel, Kansas City 8
Nicky Lopez, Chicago 6
Victor Robles, Seattle 5
Christian Vazquez, Minnesota 5
Kevin Kiermaier, Toronto 5
Max Schuemann, Oakland 5

SACRIFICE FLIES
Vinnie Pasquantino, Kansas City 13
Alex Verdugo, New York 10
Alejandro Kirk, Toronto 9
4 tied with 8

HIT BY PITCHES
Randy Arozarena, Seattle/TB 22
Willi Castro, Minnesota 21
Luke Raley, Seattle 20
Tyler Freeman, Cleveland 19
Josh H. Smith, Texas 18

WALKS
Aaron Judge, New York 133
Juan Soto, New York 129
Gunnar Henderson, Baltimore 78
Randy Arozarena, Seattle/TB 73
Vladimir Guerrero Jr., Toronto 72

STOLEN BASES
Jose Caballero, Tampa Bay 44
Jose Ramirez, Cleveland 41
Maikel Garcia, Kansas City 37
Jarren Duran, Boston 34
David Hamilton, Boston 33

STOLEN BASE PERCENTAGE
Aaron Judge, New York 1.000
Maikel Garcia, Kansas City .949
George Springer, Toronto .941
Nolan Schanuel, Los Angeles .909
Zack Gelof, Oakland .893

STRIKEOUTS
Zack Gelof, Oakland 188
Adolis Garcia, Texas 177
Brent Rooker, Oakland 177
Cal Raleigh, Seattle 176
Colton Cowser, Baltimore 172

STRIKEOUT PERCENTAGE
Zack Gelof, Oakland 34.4
Colton Cowser, Baltimore 30.7
Logan O'Hoppe, Los Angeles 29.7
Brent Rooker, Oakland 28.8
Cal Raleigh, Seattle 28.0

MULTI-HIT GAMES
Bobby Witt Jr., Kansas City 61
Aaron Judge, New York 55
Vladimir Guerrero Jr., Toronto 54
Yordan Alvarez, Houston 53
Jose Altuve, Houston 53

ON-BASE PERCENTAGE
Aaron Judge, New York .458
Juan Soto, New York .419
Vladimir Guerrero Jr., Toronto .396
Yordan Alvarez, Houston .392
Bobby Witt Jr., Kansas City .389

ON-BASE PLUS SLUGGING
Aaron Judge, New York 1.159
Juan Soto, New York .988
Bobby Witt Jr., Kansas City .977
Yordan Alvarez, Houston .959
Vladimir Guerrero Jr., Toronto .940

Tarik Skubal

PITCHING

WINS
Tarik Skubal, Detroit 18
Jose Berrios, Toronto 16
Seth Lugo, Kansas City 16
Carlos Rodon, New York 16
4 tied with 15

LOSSES
Kutter Crawford, Boston 16
Chris Flexen, Chicago 15
Tyler Anderson, Los Angeles 15
Chris Bassitt, Toronto 14
Andrew Heaney, Texas 14

GAMES
T.J. McFarland, Oakland 79
Bryan Abreu, Houston 78
Hunter Gaddis, Cleveland 78
Tim Herrin, Cleveland 75
Emmanuel Clase, Cleveland 74
Cade Smith, Cleveland 74

GAMES STARTED
Kutter Crawford, Boston 33
Logan Gilbert, Seattle 33
George Kirby, Seattle 33
Seth Lugo, Kansas City 33
9 tied with 32

GAMES FINISHED
Emmanuel Clase, Cleveland 66
Josh Hader, Houston 62
Clay Holmes, New York 50
Kirby Yates, Texas 50
Mason Miller, Oakland 44

COMPLETE GAMES
Kevin Gausman, Toronto 2
10 tied with 1

SHUTOUTS
Tanner Houck, Boston 1
Ronel Blanco, Houston 1
Kevin Gausman, Toronto 1
Joey Estes, Oakland 1
Keider Montero, Detroit 1

INNINGS PITCHED
Logan Gilbert, Seattle 209
Seth Lugo, Kansas City 207

ED ZURGA/GETTY IMAGES (WITT JR.), ALEX SLITZ/GETTY IMAGES (SKUBAL)

AMERICAN LEAGUE DEPARTMENT LEADERS

Corbin Burnes, Baltimore	194
Jose Berrios, Toronto	192
Tarik Skubal, Detroit	192

HITS ALLOWED

George Kirby, Seattle	181
Pablo Lopez, Minnesota	180
Chris Bassitt, Toronto	180
Chris Flexen, Chicago	180
Seth Lugo, Kansas City	177

RUNS ALLOWED

Griffin Canning, Los Angeles	105
Kutter Crawford, Boston	97
Chris Flexen, Chicago	95
JP Sears, Oakland	93
Chris Bassitt, Toronto	91

HOME RUNS ALLOWED

Kutter Crawford, Boston	34
Jose Berrios, Toronto	31
Griffin Canning, Los Angeles	31
Carlos Rodon, New York	31
Nick Pivetta, Boston	28
JP Sears, Oakland	28

WALKS ALLOWED

Luis Gil, New York	77
Tyler Anderson, Los Angeles	73
Chris Bassitt, Toronto	70
Ronel Blanco, Houston	68
Cole Ragans, Kansas City	67

LOWEST WALKS PER NINE

George Kirby, Seattle	1.08
Logan Gilbert, Seattle	1.60
Tarik Skubal, Detroit	1.64
Pablo Lopez, Minnesota	1.99
Nestor Cortes, New York	2.01

HIT BATTERS

Chris Bassitt, Toronto	16
Tanner Houck, Boston	16
JP Sears, Oakland	14
Austin Adams, Oakland	13
Jose Berrios, Toronto	13

STRIKEOUTS

Tarik Skubal, Detroit	228
Cole Ragans, Kansas City	223
Logan Gilbert, Seattle	220
Garrett Crochet, Chicago	209
Yusei Kikuchi, Houston, Toronto	206

Mason Miller

STRIKEOUTS PER NINE

Cole Ragans, Kansas City	10.77
Tarik Skubal, Detroit	10.69
Carlos Rodon, New York	10.03
Tanner Bibee, Cleveland	9.69
Bailey Ober, Minnesota	9.62
Pablo Lopez, Minnesota	9.62

STRIKEOUTS PER NINE
(Relievers)

Mason Miller, Oakland	14.40
Josh Hader, Houston	13.31
Garrett Crochet, Chicago	12.88
Craig Kimbrel, Baltimore	12.55
Kirby Yates, Texas	12.41

DOUBLE PLAYS

Framber Valdez, Houston	32
Jose Berrios, Toronto	21
Seth Lugo, Kansas City	18
Griffin Canning, Los Angeles	17
Michael Wacha, Kansas City	17

PICKOFFS

Nestor Cortes, New York	4
Tanner Bibee, Cleveland	4
Alec Marsh, Kansas City	3
Ben Lively, Cleveland	3
Griffin Canning, Los Angeles	3
Tyler Alexander, Tampa Bay	3

WILD PITCHES

Trevor Richards, Toronto, Minnesota	13
Cole Ragans, Kansas City	11
Logan Gilbert, Seattle	11
David Robertson, Texas	8
Framber Valdez, Houston	8
Mitch Spence, Oakland	8

WHIP

Logan Gilbert, Seattle	0.89
Tarik Skubal, Detroit	0.92
Bryce Miller, Seattle	0.98
Bailey Ober, Minnesota	1.00
George Kirby, Seattle	1.07

OPPONENT AVERAGE

Ronel Blanco, Houston	.190
Logan Gilbert, Seattle	.196
Bryce Miller, Seattle	.200
Tarik Skubal, Detroit	.201
Bailey Ober, Minnesota	.208

WORST ERA

Griffin Canning, Los Angeles	5.19
Brayan Bello, Boston	4.49
JP Sears, Oakland	4.38
Kutter Crawford, Boston	4.36
Chris Bassitt, Toronto	4.16

FIELDING

PITCHER

PCT	Bryan Abreu, Houston	1.000
PO	Tanner Houck, Boston	32
A	Seth Lugo, Kansas City	29
DP	Casey Mize, Detroit	4
	Michael Lorenzen, Texas/KC	4
E	Corbin Burnes, Baltimore	4
	Alec Marsh, Kansas City	4

CATCHER

PCT	Jake Rogers, Detroit	.996
PO	Cal Raleigh, Seattle	1138
A	Cal Raleigh, Seattle	51
	Shea Langeliers, Oakland	51
E	Austin Wells, New York	11
CS	Cal Raleigh, Seattle	32
PB	Korey Lee, Chicago	9

FIRST BASE

PCT	Ryan Mountcastle, Baltimore	.997
PO	Nolan Schanuel, Los Angeles	1018
A	Nathaniel Lowe, Texas	92
	Carlos Santana, Minnesota	92
DP	Nolan Schanuel, Los Angeles	127
E	Vladimir Guerrero Jr., Toronto	10

SECOND BASE

PCT	Jose Altuve, Houston	.989
PO	Zack Gelof, Oakland	264
A	Andres Gimenez, Cleveland	396
DP	Andres Gimenez, Cleveland	93
E	Gleyber Torres, New York	18

THIRD BASE

PCT	Alex Bregman, Houston	.972
PO	Alex Bregman, Houston	103
A	Alex Bregman, Houston	242
DP	Rafael Devers, Boston	12
E	Alex Bregman, Houston	23
	Jose Ramirez, Cleveland	23

SHORTSTOP

PCT	Corey Seager, Texas	.983
PO	Gunnar Henderson, Baltimore	232
A	Zach Neto, Los Angeles	405
DP	Zach Neto, Los Angeles	103
E	Gunnar Henderson, Baltimore	25

OUTFIELD

PCT	Jake Meyers, Houston	.997
PO	JJ Bleday, Oakland	392
A	Jarren Duran, Boston	12
DP	3 tied with	7
E	Steven Kwan, Cleveland	3
	Adolis Garcia, Texas	3

RICH SCHULTZ/GETTY IMAGES

NATIONAL LEAGUE 2024 STATISTICS

CLUB BATTING

	AVG	G	AB	R	H	2B	3B	HR	RBI	BB	SO	SB	OBP	SLG
San Diego	.263	162	5526	760	1456	259	18	190	726	458	1077	120	.324	.420
Arizona	.263	162	5522	886	1452	271	37	211	845	569	1265	119	.337	.440
Los Angeles	.258	162	5522	842	1423	291	26	233	815	602	1336	136	.335	.446
Philadelphia	.257	162	5534	784	1423	285	24	198	750	515	1370	148	.325	.425
Milwaukee	.248	162	5472	777	1359	249	33	177	742	597	1459	217	.326	.403
St. Louis	.248	162	5507	672	1363	257	21	165	639	478	1318	91	.312	.392
New York	.246	162	5510	768	1357	279	15	207	735	514	1382	106	.319	.415
Miami	.244	162	5522	637	1347	243	23	150	611	403	1410	125	.300	.378
Atlanta	.243	162	5481	704	1333	273	15	213	674	485	1461	69	.309	.415
Washington	.243	162	5374	660	1306	267	18	135	621	456	1220	223	.309	.375
Chicago	.242	162	5441	736	1318	253	29	170	696	546	1362	143	.317	.393
Colorado	.242	162	5454	682	1319	277	25	179	655	453	1617	85	.304	.400
San Francisco	.239	162	5460	693	1303	266	30	177	661	492	1452	68	.305	.396
Pittsburgh	.234	162	5477	665	1283	236	17	160	643	485	1506	106	.301	.371
Cincinnati	.231	162	5325	699	1230	257	29	174	663	496	1459	207	.305	.388

CLUB PITCHING

	ERA	G	CG	SHO	SV	IP	H	R	ER	HR	BB	SO	AVG
Atlanta	3.49	162	2	17	40	1443	1277	607	559	150	449	1553	.236
Milwaukee	3.65	162	0	14	53	1446	1289	641	586	196	494	1373	.237
Chicago	3.78	162	1	11	38	1432	1302	669	602	181	485	1348	.239
Philadelphia	3.85	162	5	14	37	1443	1339	671	617	181	444	1433	.243
San Diego	3.86	162	1	16	44	1439	1296	669	617	169	462	1453	.238
Los Angeles	3.90	162	1	13	50	1446	1273	686	626	198	501	1390	.235
New York	3.96	162	1	9	39	1442	1232	697	634	165	586	1455	.230
St. Louis	4.04	162	0	9	55	1444	1363	719	648	174	454	1308	.249
Cincinnati	4.09	162	1	8	36	1428	1302	694	649	196	487	1370	.239
San Francisco	4.10	162	2	12	36	1434	1339	699	653	153	526	1436	.246
Pittsburgh	4.15	162	1	12	43	1439	1369	739	664	166	515	1356	.250
Washington	4.30	162	0	6	40	1434	1429	764	685	168	473	1314	.258
Arizona	4.62	162	0	10	38	1443	1468	788	741	181	481	1313	.262
Miami	4.73	162	1	7	33	1437	1431	841	755	195	556	1317	.257
Colorado	5.47	162	0	1	37	1427	1604	929	867	221	563	1118	.285

CLUB FIELDING

	PCT	PO	A	E	DP
Arizona	.989	4330	1456	62	138
Atlanta	.988	4330	1436	68	131
St. Louis	.987	4332	1525	75	155
San Diego	.987	4318	1297	75	116
Chicago	.987	4297	1349	76	91
Colorado	.986	4280	1564	82	164
Philadelphia	.986	4328	1467	85	120
San Francisco	.985	4301	1558	87	135
Los Angeles	.985	4337	1366	88	119
Milwaukee	.985	4338	1348	89	113
Pittsburgh	.984	4316	1370	91	139
New York	.984	4327	1408	94	127
Cincinnati	.983	4284	1213	96	100
Washington	.981	4302	1438	109	155
Miami	.980	4312	1432	117	123

INDIVIDUAL BATTING LEADERS

	AVG	G	AB	R	H	2B	3B	HR	RBI	BB	SO	SB
Luis Arraez, Miami/San Diego	.314	150	637	83	200	32	3	4	46	24	29	9
Shohei Ohtani, Los Angeles	.310	159	636	134	197	38	7	54	130	81	162	59
Marcell Ozuna, Atlanta	.302	162	606	96	183	31	0	39	104	74	170	1
Trea Turner, Philadelphia	.295	121	505	88	149	25	0	21	62	27	98	19
Jackson Merrill, San Diego	.292	156	554	77	162	31	6	24	90	29	101	16
Ketel Marte, Arizona	.292	136	504	93	147	23	2	36	95	65	106	7
Mookie Betts, Los Angeles	.289	116	450	75	130	24	5	19	75	61	57	16
Bryce Harper, Philadelphia	.285	145	550	85	157	42	0	30	87	76	138	7
Seiya Suzuki, Chicago	.283	132	512	74	145	27	6	21	73	63	160	16
Freddie Freeman, Los Angeles	.282	147	542	81	153	35	2	22	89	78	100	9

INDIVIDUAL PITCHING LEADERS

	W	L	ERA	G	GS	CG	SV	IP	H	R	ER	BB	SO
Chris Sale, Atlanta	18	3	2.38	29	29	0	0	178	141	48	47	39	225
Zack Wheeler, Philadelphia	16	7	2.57	32	32	0	0	200	139	62	57	52	224
Shota Imanaga, Chicago	15	3	2.91	29	29	0	0	173	149	66	56	28	174
Michael King, San Diego	13	9	2.95	31	30	0	0	174	144	71	57	63	201
Max Fried, Atlanta	11	10	3.25	29	29	2	0	174	146	71	63	57	166
Jameson Taillon, Chicago	12	8	3.27	28	28	0	0	165	154	67	60	33	125
Cristopher Sanchez, Philadelphia	11	9	3.32	31	31	2	0	182	182	76	67	44	153
Sean Manaea, New York	12	6	3.47	32	32	0	0	182	134	75	70	63	184
Dylan Cease, San Diego	14	11	3.47	33	33	1	0	189	137	80	73	65	224
Logan Webb, San Francisco	13	10	3.47	33	33	1	0	205	202	83	79	50	172

AWARD WINNERS

Selected by Baseball Writers Association of America

MOST VALUABLE PLAYER

Player	1st	2nd	3rd	Total
Shohei Ohtani, Dodgers	30	—	—	420
Francisco Lindor, Mets	—	23	7	263
Ketel Marte, Diamondbacks	—	5	13	229
Marcell Ozuna, Braves	—	1	6	134
William Contreras, Brewers	—	—	3	132
Bryce Harper, Phillies	—	—	—	130
Chris Sale, Braves	—	1	—	99
Elly De La Cruz, Reds	—	—	—	89
Jackson Merrill, Padres	—	—	—	57
Willy Adames, Brewers	—	—	—	54
Matt Chapman, Giants	—	—	1	37
Zack Wheeler, Phillies	—	—	—	31
Mookie Betts, Dodges	—	—	—	24
Jurickson Profar, Padres	—	—	—	23
Kyle Schwarber, Phillies	—	—	—	15
Manny Machado, Padres	—	—	—	12
Freddie Freeman, Dodgers	—	—	—	6
Luis Arraez, Padres	—	—	—	4
Paul Skenes, Pirates	—	—	—	3
Teoscar Hernandez, Dodgers	—	—	—	3
Ezequiel Tovar, Rockies	—	—	—	3
Jackson Chourio, Brewers	—	—	—	1
Dylan Cease, Padres	—	—	—	1

CY YOUNG AWARD

Player	1st	2nd	3rd	Total
Chris Sale, Braves	26	4	—	198
Zack Wheeler, Phillies	4	25	—	130
Paul Skenes, Pirates	—	1	13	53
Dylan Cease, Padres	—	—	6	45
Shota Imanaga, Cubs	—	—	7	38
Logan Webb, Giants	—	—	2	18
Michael King, Padres	—	—	1	14
Hunter Greene, Reds	—	—	1	5
Ryan Helsley, Cardinals	—	—	—	4
Cristopher Sanchez, Phillies	—	—	—	2
Reynaldo Lopez, Braves	—	—	—	1
Sean Manaea, Mets	—	—	—	1
Aaron Nola, Phillies	—	—	—	1

ROOKIE OF THE YEAR

Player	1st	2nd	3rd	Total
Paul Skenes, Pirates	23	7	—	136
Jackson Merrill, Padres	7	23	—	104
Jackson Chourio, Brewers	—	—	26	26
Shota Imanaga, Cubs	—	—	4	4

MANAGER OF THE YEAR

Player	1st	2nd	3rd	Total
Pat Murphy, Brewers	27	3	—	144
Mike Shildt, Padres	1	19	8	70
Carlos Mendoza, Mets	1	6	12	35
Torey Lovullo, Diamondbacks	—	2	2	8
Rob Thomson, Phillies	1	—	—	5
Brian Snitker, Braves	—	—	4	4
Dave Roberts, Dodgers	—	—	3	3
Oliver Marmol, Cardinals	—	—	1	1

GOLD GLOVE WINNERS

P—Chris Sale, Braves. **C**—Patrick Bailey, Giants. **1B**—Christian Walker, D-backs. **2B**—Brice Turang, Brewers. **3B**—Matt Chapman, Giants. **SS**—Ezequiel Tovar, Rockies. **LF**—Ian Happ, Cubs. **CF**—Brenton Doyle, Rockies. **RF**—Sal Frelick, Brewers. **UT**—Jared Triolo, Pirates.

NATIONAL LEAGUE DEPARTMENT LEADERS

BATTING

GAMES
Pete Alonso, New York 162
Nick Castellanos, Philadelphia 162
Matt Olson, Atlanta 162
Marcell Ozuna, Atlanta 162
Willy Adames, Milwaukee 161

AT-BATS
Ezequiel Tovar, Colorado 655
Luis Arraez, SD/Miami 637
Shohei Ohtani, Los Angeles 636
Bryan Reynolds, Pittsburgh 622
Francisco Lindor, New York 618
Elly De La Cruz, Cincinnati 618

PLATE APPEARANCES
Shohei Ohtani, Los Angeles 731
Elly De La Cruz, Cincinnati 696
Ezequiel Tovar, Colorado 695
Pete Alonso, New York 695
Bryan Reynolds, Pittsburgh 692
Kyle Schwarber, Philadelphia 692

RUNS
Shohei Ohtani, Los Angeles 134
Corbin Carroll, Arizona 121
Kyle Schwarber, Philadelphia 110
Francisco Lindor, New York 107
Elly De La Cruz, Cincinnati 105

HITS
Luis Arraez, SD/Miami 200
Shohei Ohtani, Los Angeles 197
Marcell Ozuna, Atlanta 183
Ezequiel Tovar, Colorado 176
Bryan Reynolds, Pittsburgh 171

TOTAL BASES
Shohei Ohtani, Los Angeles 411
Marcell Ozuna, Atlanta 331
Francisco Lindor, New York 309
Ezequiel Tovar, Colorado 307
Teoscar Hernandez, Los Angeles 295

DOUBLES
Ezequiel Tovar, Colorado 45
Alec Bohm, Philadelphia 44
Bryce Harper, Philadelphia 42
Matt Chapman, San Francisco 39
Francisco Lindor, New York 39

TRIPLES
Corbin Carroll, Arizona 14
Elly De La Cruz, Cincinnati 10
Mike Yastrzemski, San Francisco 9
Jake McCarthy, Arizona 7
Shohei Ohtani, Los Angeles 7

EXTRA-BASE HITS
Shohei Ohtani, Los Angeles 99
Ezequiel Tovar, Colorado 75
Francisco Lindor, New York 73
Bryce Harper, Philadelphia 72
Elly De La Cruz, Cincinnati 71

HOME RUNS
Shohei Ohtani, Los Angeles 54
Marcell Ozuna, Atlanta 39
Kyle Schwarber, Philadelphia 38
Ketel Marte, Arizona 36
Pete Alonso, New York 34

RUNS BATTED IN
Shohei Ohtani, Los Angeles 130
Willy Adames, Milwaukee 112
Manny Machado, San Diego 105

Elly De La Cruz

Marcell Ozuna, Atlanta 104
Kyle Schwarber, Philadelphia 104

SACRIFICES
Michael Siani, St. Louis 11
Jacob Young, Washington 9
Pete Crow-Armstrong, Chicago 8
Johan Rojas, Philadelphia 8
Geraldo Perdomo, Arizona 7
Nick Fortes, Miami 7
Jose Herrera, Arizona 7

SACRIFICE FLIES
Eugenio Suarez, Arizona 11
Ketel Marte, Arizona 9
Corbin Carroll, Arizona 9
Bryson Stott, Philadelphia 9
5 tied with 8

HIT BY PITCHES
Joc Pederson, Arizona 18
Jurickson Profar, San Diego 18
CJ Abrams, Washington 16

Jonathan India, Cincinnati 15
Jake McCarthy, Arizona 14

WALKS
Kyle Schwarber, Philadelphia 106
Shohei Ohtani, Los Angeles 81
Jonathan India, Cincinnati 80
Ian Happ, Chicago 80
William Contreras, Milwaukee 78
Freddie Freeman, Los Angeles 78

STOLEN BASES
Elly De La Cruz, Cincinnati 67
Shohei Ohtani, Los Angeles 59
Brice Turang, Milwaukee 50
Corbin Carroll, Arizona 35
Jacob Young, Washington 33

STOLEN BASE PERCENTAGE
Brandon Nimmo, New York 1.000
Paul Goldschmidt, Arizona 1.000
Oneil Cruz, Pittsburgh .957
Shohei Ohtani, Los Angeles .937

Francisco Lindor

Bryson Stott, Philadelphia .914

STRIKEOUTS
Elly De La Cruz, Cincinnati 218
Ezequiel Tovar, Colorado 200
Kyle Schwarber, Philadelphia 197
Teoscar Hernandez, Los Angeles 188
Ryan McMahon, Colorado 185

STRIKEOUT PERCENTAGE
Elly De La Cruz, Cincinnati 31.3
Oneil Cruz, Pittsburgh 30.2
Teoscar Hernandez, Los Angeles 28.8
Ezequiel Tovar, Colorado 28.8
Rhys Hoskins, Milwaukee 28.8

MULTI-HIT GAMES
Luis Arraez, Miami/SD 62
Shohei Ohtani, Los Angeles 61
Francisco Lindor, New York 53
Marcell Ozuna, Atlanta 51
Ezequiel Tovar, Colorado 50

ON-BASE PERCENTAGE
Shohei Ohtani, Los Angeles .390
Jurickson Profar, San Diego .380
Marcell Ozuna, Atlanta .378
Freddie Freeman, Los Angeles .378
Bryce Harper, Philadelphia .373

ON-BASE PLUS SLUGGING
Shohei Ohtani, Los Angeles 1.036
Ketel Marte, Arizona .932
Marcell Ozuna, Atlanta .924
Bryce Harper, Philadelphia .898
Mookie Betts, Los Angeles .863

PITCHING

WINS
Chris Sale, Atlanta 18
Zack Wheeler, Philadelphia 16
Shota Imanaga, Chicago 15
Aaron Nola, Philadelphia 14
Dylan Cease, San Diego 14
Zac Gallen, Arizona 14

LOSSES
Jake Irvin, Washington 14
Patrick Corbin, Washington 13
5 tied with 12

GAMES
Tyler Rogers, San Francisco 77
Ryan Walker, San Francisco 76

JEFF DEAN/GETTY IMAGES (DE LA CRUZ), AL BELLO/GETTY IMAGES (LINDOR)

NATIONAL LEAGUE

DEPARTMENT LEADERS

Derek Law, Washington	75
Joe Mantiply, Arizona	75
Andrew Kittredge, St. Louis	74

GAMES STARTED

Dylan Cease, San Diego	33
Aaron Nola, Philadelphia	33
Logan Webb, San Francisco	33
Jake Irvin, Washington	33
7 tied with	32

GAMES FINISHED

Ryan Helsley, St. Louis	62
Kyle Finnegan, Washington	58
Robert Suarez, San Diego	55
Raisel Iglesias, Atlanta	52
Alexis Diaz, Cincinnati	50

COMPLETE GAMES

Cristopher Sanchez, Philadelphia	2
Max Fried, Atlanta	2
12 tied with	1

SHUTOUTS

11 tied with	1

Chris Sale

INNINGS PITCHED

Logan Webb, San Francisco	205
Zack Wheeler, Philadelphia	200
Aaron Nola, Philadelphia	199
Dylan Cease, San Diego	189
Jake Irvin, Washington	188

HITS ALLOWED

Patrick Corbin, Washington	208
Logan Webb, San Francisco	202
Miles Mikolas, St. Louis	194
Aaron Nola, Philadelphia	189
Brandon Pfaadt, Arizona	183

RUNS ALLOWED

Patrick Corbin, Washington	114
Miles Mikolas, St. Louis	106
Brandon Pfaadt, Arizona	103
Jake Irvin, Washington	97
Ryan Feltner, Colorado	94

HOME RUNS ALLOWED

Austin Gomber, Colorado	30
Aaron Nola, Philadelphia	30
Colin Rea, Milwaukee	29
Jake Irvin, Washington	29
Shota Imanaga, Chicago	27

WALKS ALLOWED

Cal Quantrill, Colorado	69
Freddy Peralta, Milwaukee	68
Kyle Gibson, St. Louis	68
Frankie Montas, Cin/Mil	66
Charlie Morton, Atlanta	65
MacKenzie Gore, Washington	65
Dylan Cease, San Diego	65

LOWEST WALKS PER NINE

Miles Mikolas, St. Louis	1.31
Shota Imanaga, Chicago	1.45
Jameson Taillon, Chicago	1.80
Chris Sale, Atlanta	1.98
Austin Gomber, Colorado	2.07

HIT BATTERS

Hunter Greene, Cincinnati	19
Nick Lodolo, Cincinnati	18
Charlie Morton, Atlanta	18
Mitch Keller, Pittsburgh	15
5 tied	11

STRIKEOUTS

Chris Sale, Atlanta	225
Zack Wheeler, Philadelphia	224
Dylan Cease, San Diego	224
Sonny Gray, St. Louis	203
Michael King, San Diego	201

STRIKEOUTS PER NINE

Chris Sale, Atlanta	11.40
Sonny Gray, St. Louis	10.98
Dylan Cease, San Diego	10.65
Michael King, San Diego	10.42
Freddy Peralta, Milwaukee	10.36

STRIKEOUTS PER NINE
(Relievers)

Fernando Cruz, Cincinnati	14.72
Aroldis Chapman, Pittsburgh	14.40
Edwin Diaz, New York	14.09
Jeremiah Estrada, San Diego	13.87
Reed Garrett, New York	13.03

DOUBLE PLAYS

Logan Webb, San Francisco	25
Kyle Gibson, St. Louis	21
MacKenzie Gore, Washington	21
Max Fried, Atlanta	20
Charlie Morton, Atlanta	20
Jake Irvin, Washington	20

PICKOFFS

Charlie Morton, Atlanta	6
Aroldis Chapman, Pittsburgh	5
14 tied with	3

WILD PITCHES

MacKenzie Gore, Washington	14
Dylan Cease, San Diego	12
Andre Pallante, St. Louis	12
Tyler Glasnow, Los Angeles	12
Gavin Stone, Los Angeles	9

WALKS PLUS HITS PER INNING

Zack Wheeler, Philadelphia	0.96
Chris Sale, Atlanta	1.01
Shota Imanaga, Chicago	1.02
Dylan Cease, San Diego	1.07
Sean Manaea, New York	1.08

OPPONENT AVERAGE

Zack Wheeler, Philadelphia	.192
Dylan Cease, San Diego	.200
Sean Manaea, New York	.202
Chris Sale, Atlanta	.216
Michael King, San Diego	.221

WORST ERA

Patrick Corbin, Washington	5.62
Miles Mikolas, St. Louis	5.35
Austin Gomber, Colorado	4.75
Brandon Pfaadt, Arizona	4.71
Ryan Feltner, Colorado	4.49

FIELDING

PITCHER

PCT	Andrew Abbott, Cincinnati	1.000
PO	Zack Wheeler, Philadelphia	21
A	Logan Webb, San Francisco	33
DP	Logan Webb, San Francisco	5
E	5 tied with	5

CATCHER

PCT	Keibert Ruiz, Washington	.998
PO	William Contreras, Milwaukee	1054
A	Will Smith, Los Angeles	58
E	Nick Fortes, Miami	9
	Kyle Higashioka, San Diego	9
CS	Will Smith, Los Angeles	32
PB	Francisco Alvarez, New York	11

FIRST BASE

PCT	Christian Walker, Arizona	.998
PO	Matt Olson, Atlanta	1259
A	Freddie Freeman, Los Angeles	115
DP	Paul Goldschmidt, Arizona	137
E	Michael Toglia, Colorado	8

SECOND BASE

PCT	Bryson Stott, Philadelphia	.993
PO	Brice Turang, Milwaukee	240
A	Brice Turang, Milwaukee	379
DP	Brendan Rodgers, Colorado	89
E	Luis Garcia, Washington	10
	Nolan Gorman, St. Louis	10

THIRD BASE

PCT	Mark Vientos, New York	.980
PO	Nolan Arenado, St. Louis	103
A	Ryan McMahon, Colorado	323
DP	Matt Chapman, San Francisco	34
E	Ryan McMahon, Colorado	15
	Matt Chapman, San Francisco	15

SHORTSTOP

PCT	Dansby Swanson, Chicago	.990
PO	Elly De La Cruz, Cincinnati	247
A	Ezequiel Tovar, Colorado	435
DP	Ezequiel Tovar, Colorado	113
E	Elly De La Cruz, Cincinnati	29

OUTFIELD

PCT	Jackson Chourio, Milwaukee	1.000
PO	Brenton Doyle, Colorado	426
A	Ian Happ, Chicago	11
	Bryan Reynolds, Pittsburgh	11
DP	Jackson Merrill, San Diego	4
E	Jacob Young, Washington	8

TODD KIRKLAND/GETTY IMAGES

MARY DECICCO/MLB PHOTOS VIA GETTY IMAGES

Giancarlo Stanton hit seven postseason home runs to help lead the Yankees to the World Series

Dodgers Overcome Injuries; Yankees Return To Series

BY J.J. COOPER

In 2023, the Los Angeles Dodgers ran out of pitching, which is why they were run out of the playoffs.

In response, they went overboard to fix the problem all offseason. Yoshinobu Yamamoto and James Paxton were signed as free agents, Tyler Glasnow was acquired through trade and Clayton Kershaw was re-signed.

Yet here they were in the World Series, once again effectively out of pitching. With Game Five on the line, in jogged Walker Buehler to pitch the ninth. Buehler was scheduled to be the Dodgers' Game Seven starter, but a win here would ensure the series didn't get to that point.

"Obviously if I have to use the potential Game Seven starter in the ninth inning, that just speaks to we didn't have enough pitching," Dodgers manager Dave Roberts said.

Buehler retired all three batters he faced. Game Six and Game Seven became unnecessary. And the Dodgers had their second World Series title in five years. When Los Angeles halted its 32-year World Series title drought in 2020, there wasn't any parade because of the coronavirus pandemic. Some grumbled that a World Series title after a shortened 60-game season deserved an asterisk. There can be no caveats or qualifiers attached to this one. The Dodgers, a perennial power, are now the dynasty of the 2020s.

The Dodgers seemed likely to have to worry about Game Six early in Game Five. Yankees' ace Gerrit Cole was staked to a five-run early lead as Jack Flaherty was knocked out in the second inning. Cole rolled through the first four innings, but Kiké Hernandez led off with a single in the fifth inning.

Tommy Edman then hit a line drive straight to Yankees center fielder Aaron Judge, but Judge dropped it for a costly error. Will Smith then hit a grounder to shortstop Anthony Volpe. Volpe tried to throw to third to nab Hernandez but he bounced the throw. A second costly error and the bases were loaded.

Even after two errors, no runs had scored. Cole struck out Gavin Lux and Shohei Ohtani, and then he induced a grounder from Mookie Betts to first baseman Anthony Rizzo.

It had been a scare, but here was a fifth potential out to get the Yankees out of the inning with no harm done.

But when Rizzo fielded the ball, he looked to toss the ball to Cole covering first base, Cole had taken an angle to try to field the ball. When the ball got through, he didn't immediately head to first base. So there was no one covering first as Betts flew down the line. It was scored as an RBI single, but everyone watching knew it should have ended the inning.

The dam broke. Freddie Freeman fouled off a quality changeup with two strikes and then hit a two-run single to center field. Teoscar Hernandez drove in two more with a double. A five-run deficit quickly turned into a 5-5 tie game.

"Yeah, just we didn't take care of the ball well enough in that inning. Against a great team like that, they took advantage. It looked like just kind of that sinking liner that just Judgey missed," Yankees manager Aaron Boone said. "The play to Volpe, the right move obviously going to third, a little bit of a short hop over there at third, didn't complete the play. And then Mookie hits a squibber so Rizz couldn't really run through it. He kind of had to stay there and make sure he secured the catch because of the spin on the ball. And I think Gerrit just—all that he went through in that inning, kind of spent and kind of almost working his way out of it, just didn't react quick enough to get over."

A Giancarlo Stanton sacrifice fly gave the Yankees the lead back in the sixth inning, but reliever Tommy Kahnle gave up a pair of singles and a walk to the three batters he faced. Lux and Betts drove in a pair of runs with sacrifice flies to give the Dodgers a 7-6 lead.

The Yankees got a double from Aaron Judge and a walk from Jazz Chisholm in the eighth, but Stanton flew out and Rizzo struck out to leave those runners stranded. Buehler then got a ground out from Volpe and struck out Austin Wells and Alex Verdugo to finish off the Dodgers' eighth World Series title.

LUKE HALES/GETTY IMAGES

Dodgers first baseman Freddie Freeman won his second World Series title in four years.

Freeman Wins World Series MVP

Freddie Freeman was named World Series MVP in one of the easiest decisions in Fall Classic history. Freeman had been battling an ankle injury for much of the postseason, but he was the star of the World Series.

In Game One, Freeman hit a dramatic walk-off grand slam in the 10th inning, evoking comparisons to Kirk Gibson's dramatic Game One home run in the 1988 World Series. Both were hit to right field in Dodgers stadium at 8:37 p.m. PT.

Freeman homered again in Game Two off Carlos Rodon, providing the final run in Los Angeles' 4-2 Game 2 win. His two-run first-inning home run off Clarke Schmidt got the scoring started in the Dodgers' 4-2 Game Three win. Freeman's two-run home run off Luis Gil in the first inning gave the Dodgers a lead again in Game Four, but the Dodgers did rally for six runs in the final four innings to win 11-4, avoiding elimination.

With his two-RBI single in Game Five, Freeman finished with a .300/.364/1.000 stat line for the World Series. He had four home runs, 12 RBIs and five runs scored.

"You don't really think about it when you're up there. Things seem to be slowing down. That's kind of what you're just trying to do. And I think obviously experience definitely helps in this situation," Freeman said. "I did a lot of work in between the NLCS and the World Series. Thankfully, my ankle got into a good spot where I could work on my swing, and I found a cue that really worked for me. I was able to slow things down. All you're trying to do is swing at strikes, take balls, and hit the mistakes. Thankfully, I was able to do that for five games."

Just Enough Pitching

The Dodgers managed to win the World Series with reliever Ben Casparius making a start. The Dodgers had to resort to a bullpen game in each of their three playoff series. Los Angeles had more than a full rotation on the injured list. Glasnow was shut down with elbow inflammation. A toe injury ended Kershaw's season. Paxton tore a calf muscle. Dustin May, already on the IL because of a flexor tendon injury, saw his season ended by an esophageal injury. Gavin Stone went down with a shoulder injury. Bobby Miller went on the IL with a shoulder injury. River Ryan and Emmet Sheehan each had Tommy John surgery. There was hope that Tony Gonsolin would make it back from Tommy John surgery in time for the postseason, but his return was pushed to 2025. Shohei Ohtani also was limited to DH because of his 2023 Tommy John surgery.

That's 10 injured starting pitchers. Somehow, the Dodgers managed to survive thanks to the trade deadline acquisition of Flaherty, the return to form of Buehler and the strong pitching of Yamamoto.

"I don't let my mind go there too far because, yeah, to have Clayton, Glasnow, May, Emmet Sheehan, all those guys, it would be fun. It would be great," Roberts said. "To be quite honest, I didn't know who Ben Casparius was at the start of the season. So to that point—and Edgardo Henriquez, who pitched big innings for us in the DS and CS. I didn't know those guys.

"We did go through a lot, but I'll say we still had the best record in all of baseball this year. It wasn't easy, but our guys fought and played every day the right way, played to win," Roberts continued. "There was a lot of backfilling on talent because of injury, a lot of young players cut their teeth, which is good. But one thing is that we just kept going. Even in the postseason, I don't think anyone had us picked. I don't think they had us picked to get out of the first series. For us to go out there and fight and scratch and claw and win 11 games in October, that's a credit to our guys."

"It's the war of attrition sometimes. That's how they've had to do it. They've had obviously a number of guys get hurt, which, credit to them, they've gotten creative and worked some things out, figured some things out to the point they're playing for a world championship," Aaron Boone said. "There's a lot of ways to skin a cat. It doesn't always have to be conventional, and they've had to get creative with some of the injuries they've had."

AMERICAN LEAGUE CHAMPIONS, 1999-2024

American League postseason results from 1998 to present, where (*) denotes wild card playoff entrant.

YEAR	CHAMPIONSHIP SERIES	ALCS MVP	DIVISION SERIES	DIVISION SERIES
2024	New York 4, Cleveland 1	Giancarlo Stanton, DH, New York	Cleveland 3, Detroit* 2	New York 3, Kansas City* 1
2023	Texas 4, Houston 3	Adolis Garcia, OF, Texas	Houston 3, Minnesota 1	Texas* 3, Baltimore 0
2022	Houston 4, New York 0	Jeremy Peña, SS, Houston	Houston 3, Seattle* 0	New York 3, Cleveland 2
2021	Houston 4, Boston 2	Yordan Alvarez, OF, Houston	Houston 3, Chicago 1	Boston* 3, Tampa Bay 1
2020	Tampa Bay 4, Houston 3	Randy Arozarena, OF, Tampa Bay	Tampa Bay 3, New York* 2	Houston* 3, Oakland 1
2019	Houston 4, New York 2	Jose Altuve, 2B, Houston	Houston 3, Tampa Bay* 2	New York 3, Minnesota 0
2018	Boston 4, Houston 1	Jackie Bradley Jr., OF, Boston	Boston 3, New York* 1	Houston 3, Cleveland 0
2017	Houston 4, New York 3	Justin Verlander, RHP, Houston	New York* 3, Cleveland 2	Houston 3, Boston 1
2016	Cleveland 4, Toronto 1	Andrew Miller, LHP, Cleveland	Toronto* 3, Texas 0	Cleveland 3, Boston 0
2015	Kansas City 4, Toronto 2	Alcides Escobar, SS, Kansas City	Kansas City 3, Houston* 2	Baltimore 3, Texas 2
2014	Kansas City 4, Baltimore 0	Lorenzo Cain, OF, Kansas City	Kansas City 3, Los Angeles 0	Baltimore 3, Detroit 0
2013	Boston 4, Detroit 2	Koji Uehara, RHP, Boston	Boston 3, Tampa Bay* 1	Detroit, 3, Oakland 2
2012	Detroit 4, New York 0	Delmon Young, OF, Detroit	New York 3, Baltimore* 2	Detroit 3, Oakland 2
2011	Texas 4, Detroit 2	Nelson Cruz, OF, Texas	Detroit 3, New York 2	Texas 3, Tampa Bay* 1
2010	Texas 4, New York 2	Josh Hamilton, OF, Texas	Texas 3, Tampa Bay 2	New York* 3, Minnesota 0
2009	New York 4, Los Angeles 2	C.C. Sabathia, LHP, New York	New York 3, Minnesota 0	Los Angeles 3, Boston* 0
2008	Tampa Bay 4, Boston 3	Matt Garza, RHP, Tampa Bay	Boston* 3, Los Angeles 1	Tampa Bay 3, Chicago 1
2007	Boston 4, Cleveland 3	Josh Beckett, RHP, Boston	Boston 3, Los Angeles 0	Cleveland 3, New York* 1
2006	Detroit 4, Oakland 0	Placido Polanco, 2B, Detroit	Detroit* 3, New York 1	Oakland 3, Minnesota 0
2005	Chicago 4, Los Angeles 1	Paul Konerko, 1B, Chicago	Chicago 3, Boston* 0	Los Angeles 3, New York 2
2004	Boston 4, New York 3	David Ortiz, DH, Boston	Boston* 3, Anaheim 0	New York 3, Minnesota 1
2003	New York 4, Boston 3	Mariano Rivera, RHP, New York	New York 3, Minnesota 1	Boston* 3, Oakland 2
2002	Anaheim 4, Minnesota 1	Adam Kennedy, 2B, Anaheim	Anaheim* 3, New York 1	Minnesota 3, Oakland 2
2001	New York 4, Seattle 1	Andy Pettitte, LHP, New York	Seattle 3, Cleveland 2	New York 3, Oakland* 2
2000	New York 4, Seattle 2	David Justice, OF, New York	New York 3, Oakland 2	Seattle* 3, Chicago 0
1999	New York 4, Boston 1	Orlando Hernandez, RHP, New York	Boston* 3, Cleveland 2	New York 3, Texas 0

Ohtani Gets His Title

The World Series also provided the much-awaited first World Series title for Ohtani, who injured his left shoulder in Game 2. After the World Series ended, he had surgery to repair a labrum tear, but he didn't miss a game, even if his swing seemed to be affected.

Ohtani hit .230/.373/.393 overall in the postseason, driving in 10 runs thanks to him hitting .409 with runners in scoring position. His 14 runs scored were tied with Betts for most in the 2024 postseason.

"I'm thrilled. Six years in the States, arguably the best player in the big leagues. So he committed to us, and he wanted to play for a championship. For it to kind of come to fruition in his first year is pretty remarkable," Roberts said. "What Shohei's done to our ballclub, the Dodger fan base domestically, globally, I just don't think you can quantify. And he's just such a good guy. He was playing with one arm in the postseason. So most guys would probably tap out, but he was going to not be denied at playing and posting and being in the lineup. So for him to hoist that World Series trophy, that's something he dreamed of, I'm sure, for quite some time."

A Bitter End, But A Strong Season

The Yankees avoided being swept in the World Series, but losing four games to one leaves little room to wonder how one or two different decisions could have changed the World Series.

New York's return to the World Series was a step forward for a team that had gone 14 years without an appearance in the Fall Classic. For most teams, a 15-year World Series drought is expected. For the Yankees, it's a cause for much concern.

New York had added Juan Soto from the Padres in an offseason trade. He proved the perfect addition. He hit .327/.469/.633 in the postseason with 12 runs scored, three doubles and four home runs. He walked 14 times in 14 postseason games.

Stanton was also excellent. He carried the Yankees in the ALCS, hitting home runs in four consecutive games. He hit seven homers in the postseason as a whole, two more than anyone else. He also led all hitters with 39 total bases in the 2024 postseason.

The postseason was much tougher for Judge, who was once again the best hitter and slugger in the American League during the regular season. He had struggled in April, but from May through September, he averaged over 10 home runs a month.

But as the temperatures dipped in October, he looked as cold as he had in April. He hit .184/.344/.408 in the postseason with 20 strikeouts in 64 plate appearances. He was intentionally walked a league-leading 20 times in the regular season. He was intentionally walked only once in postseason, and his error in center field in the final game opened the floodgates for the Dodgers.

NATIONAL LEAGUE CHAMPIONS, 1999-2024

National League postseason results from 1998 to present, where (*) denotes wild card playoff entrant.

YEAR	CHAMPIONSHIP SERIES	NLCS MVP	DIVISION SERIES	DIVISION SERIES
2024	Los Angeles 4, New York* 2	Tommy Edman, SS/OF, Los Angeles	New York* 3, Philadelphia 1	Los Angeles 3, San Diego* 2
2023	Arizona 4, Philadelphia 3	Ketel Marte, 2B, Arizona	Philadelphia* 3, Atlanta 1	Arizona* 3, Los Angeles 0
2022	Philadelphia 4, San Diego 1	Bryce Harper, OF, Philadelphia	Philadelphia* 3, Atlanta 1	San Diego* 3, Los Angeles 1
2021	Atlanta 4, Los Angeles 2	Eddie Rosario, OF, Atlanta	Atlanta 3, Milwaukee 1	Los Angeles* 3, San Francisco 2
2020	Los Angeles 4, Atlanta 3	Corey Seager, SS, Los Angeles	Los Angeles 3, San Diego* 0	Atlanta 3, Miami* 0
2019	Washington 4, St. Louis 0	Howie Kendrick, 2B, Washington	Washington* 3, Los Angeles 2	St. Louis 3, Atlanta 2
2018	Los Angeles 4, Milwaukee 3	Cody Bellinger, 1B/OF, Los Angeles	Los Angeles 3, Atlanta 1	Milwaukee 3, Colorado 0*
2017	Los Angeles 4, Chicago 1	Justin Turner, 3B/Chris Taylor, CF, L.A.	Los Angeles 3, Arizona* 0	Chicago 3, Washington 2
2016	Chicago 4, Los Angeles 2	Javier Baez, 2B/Jon Lester, LHP, Chicago	Chicago 3, San Francisco* 1	Los Angeles 3, Washington 2
2015	New York 4, Chicago 0	Daniel Murphy, 2B, New York	New York 3, Los Angeles 2	Chicago* 3, St. Louis 1
2014	San Francisco 4, St. Louis 1	Madison Bumgarner, LHP, San Francisco	San Francisco 3, Washington 1	St. Louis 3, Los Angeles 1
2013	St. Louis 4, Los Angeles 2	Michael Wacha, RHP, St. Louis	St. Louis 3, Pittsburgh* 2	Los Angeles 3, Atlanta 1
2012	San Francisco 4, St. Louis 3	Marco Scutaro, 2B, San Francisco	St. Louis* 3, Washington 2	San Francisco 3, Cincinnati 2
2011	St. Louis 4, Milwaukee 2	David Freese, 3B, St. Louis	St. Louis* 3, Philadelphia 2	Milwaukee 3, Arizona 2
2010	San Francisco 4, Philadelphia 2	Cody Ross, OF, San Francisco	Philadelphia 3, Cincinnati 0	San Francisco 3, Atlanta* 1
2009	Philadelphia 4, Los Angeles 1	Ryan Howard, 1B, Philadelphia	Los Angeles 3, St. Louis 0	Philadelphia 3, Colorado* 1
2008	Philadelphia 4, Los Angeles 1	Cole Hamels, LHP, Philadelphia	Los Angeles 3, Chicago 0	Philadelphia 3, Milwaukee* 1
2007	Colorado 4, Arizona 0	Matt Holliday, OF, Colorado	Arizona 3, Chicago 0	Colorado* 3, Philadelphia 0
2006	St. Louis 4, New York 3	Jeff Suppan, RHP, St. Louis	New York 3, Los Angeles* 0	St. Louis 3, San Diego 1
2005	Houston 4, St. Louis 2	Roy Oswalt, RHP, Houston	St. Louis 3, San Diego 0	Houston* 3, Atlanta 1
2004	St. Louis 4, Houston 3	Albert Pujols, 1B, St. Louis	St. Louis 3, Los Angeles 1	Houston* 3, Atlanta 2
2003	Florida 4, Chicago 3	Ivan Rodriguez, C, Florida	Florida* 3, San Francisco 1	Chicago 3, Atlanta 2
2002	San Francisco 4, St. Louis 1	Benito Santiago, C, San Francisco	San Francisco* 3, Atlanta 2	St. Louis 3, Arizona 0
2001	Arizona 4, Atlanta 1	Craig Counsell, SS, Arizona	Atlanta 3, Houston 0	Arizona 3, St. Louis* 2
2000	New York 4, St. Louis 1	Mike Hampton, LHP, New York	St. Louis 3, Atlanta 0	New York* 3, San Francisco 1
1999	Atlanta 4, New York 2	Eddie Perez, C, Atlanta	Atlanta 3, Houston 1	New York* 3, Arizona 1

THE WORLD SERIES YEAR-BY-YEAR

Year	Winner	Loser	Result
1903	Boston (AL)	Pittsburgh (NL)	5-3
1904	NO SERIES		
1905	New York (NL)	Philadelphia (AL)	4-1
1906	Chicago (AL)	Chicago (NL)	4-2
1907	Chicago (NL)	Detroit (AL)	4-0
1908	Chicago (NL)	Detroit (AL)	4-1
1909	Pittsburgh (NL)	Detroit (AL)	4-3
1910	Philadelphia (AL)	Chicago (NL)	4-1
1911	Philadelphia (AL)	New York (NL)	4-2
1912	Boston (AL)	New York (NL)	4-3-1
1913	Philadelphia (AL)	New York (NL)	4-1
1914	Boston (NL)	Philadelphia (AL)	4-0
1915	Boston (AL)	Philadelphia (NL)	4-1
1916	Boston (AL)	Brooklyn (NL)	4-1
1917	Chicago (AL)	New York (NL)	4-2
1918	Boston (AL)	Chicago (NL)	4-2
1919	Cincinnati (NL)	Chicago (AL)	5-3
1920	Cleveland (AL)	Brooklyn (NL)	5-2
1921	New York (NL)	New York (AL)	5-3
1922	New York (NL)	New York (AL)	4-0
1923	New York (AL)	New York (NL)	4-2
1924	Washington (AL)	New York (NL)	4-3
1925	Pittsburgh (NL)	Washington (AL)	4-3
1926	St. Louis (NL)	New York (AL)	4-3
1927	New York (AL)	Pittsburgh (NL)	4-0
1928	New York (AL)	St. Louis (NL)	4-0
1929	Philadelphia (AL)	Chicago (NL)	4-1
1930	Philadelphia (AL)	St. Louis (NL)	4-2
1931	St. Louis (NL)	Philadelphia (AL)	4-3
1932	New York (AL)	Chicago (NL)	4-0
1933	New York (NL)	Washington (AL)	4-1
1934	St. Louis (NL)	Detroit (AL)	4-3
1935	Detroit (AL)	Chicago (NL)	4-2
1936	New York (AL)	New York (NL)	4-2
1937	New York (AL)	New York (NL)	4-1
1938	New York (AL)	Chicago (NL)	4-0
1939	New York (AL)	Cincinnati (NL)	4-0
1940	Cincinnati (NL)	Detroit (AL)	4-3
1941	New York (AL)	Brooklyn (NL)	4-1
1942	St. Louis (NL)	New York (AL)	4-1
1943	New York (AL)	St. Louis (NL)	4-1
1944	St. Louis (NL)	St. Louis (AL)	4-2
1945	Detroit (AL)	Chicago (NL)	4-3
1946	St. Louis (NL)	Boston (AL)	4-3
1947	New York (AL)	Brooklyn (NL)	4-3
1948	Cleveland (AL)	Boston (NL)	4-2
1949	New York (AL)	Brooklyn (NL)	4-1
1950	New York (AL)	Philadelphia (NL)	4-0
1951	New York (AL)	New York (NL)	4-2
1952	New York (AL)	Brooklyn (NL)	4-3
1953	New York (AL)	Brooklyn (NL)	4-2
1954	New York (NL)	Cleveland (AL)	4-0
1955	Brooklyn (NL)	New York (AL)	4-3
1956	New York (AL)	Brooklyn (NL)	4-3
1957	Milwaukee (NL)	New York (AL)	4-3
1958	New York (AL)	Milwaukee (NL)	4-3
1959	Los Angeles (NL)	Chicago (AL)	4-2
1960	Pittsburgh (NL)	New York (AL)	4-3
1961	New York (AL)	Cincinnati (NL)	4-1
1962	New York (AL)	San Francisco (NL)	4-3
1963	Los Angeles (NL)	New York (AL)	4-0
1964	St. Louis (NL)	New York (AL)	4-3
1965	Los Angeles (NL)	Minnesota (AL)	4-3
1966	Baltimore (AL)	Los Angeles (NL)	4-0
1967	St. Louis (NL)	Boston (AL)	4-3
1968	Detroit (AL)	St. Louis (NL)	4-3
1969	New York (NL)	Baltimore (AL)	4-1
1970	Baltimore (AL)	Cincinnati (NL)	4-1

Commissioner's Trophy

CATO CATALDO

Year	Winner	Loser	Result
1971	Pittsburgh (NL)	Baltimore (AL)	4-3
1972	Oakland (AL)	Cincinnati (NL)	4-3
1973	Oakland (AL)	New York (NL)	4-3
1974	Oakland (AL)	Los Angeles (NL)	4-1
1975	Cincinnati (NL)	Boston (AL)	4-3
1976	Cincinnati (NL)	New York (AL)	4-0
1977	New York (AL)	Los Angeles (NL)	4-2
1978	New York (AL)	Los Angeles (NL)	4-2
1979	Pittsburgh (NL)	Baltimore (AL)	4-3
1980	Philadelphia (NL)	Kansas City (AL)	4-2
1981	Los Angeles (NL)	New York (AL)	4-2
1982	St. Louis (NL)	Milwaukee (AL)	4-3
1983	Baltimore (AL)	Philadelphia (NL)	4-1
1984	Detroit (AL)	San Diego (NL)	4-1
1985	Kansas City (AL)	St. Louis (NL)	4-3
1986	New York (NL)	Boston (AL)	4-3
1987	Minnesota (AL)	St. Louis (NL)	4-3
1988	Los Angeles (NL)	Oakland (AL)	4-1
1989	Oakland (AL)	San Francisco (NL)	4-0
1990	Cincinnati (NL)	Oakland (AL)	4-0
1991	Minnesota (AL)	Atlanta (NL)	4-3
1992	Toronto (AL)	Atlanta (NL)	4-2
1993	Toronto (AL)	Philadelphia (NL)	4-2
1994	NO SERIES		
1995	Atlanta (NL)	Cleveland (AL)	4-2
1996	New York (AL)	Atlanta (NL)	4-2
1997	Florida (NL)	Cleveland (AL)	4-3
1998	New York (AL)	San Diego (NL)	4-0
1999	New York (AL)	Atlanta (NL)	4-0
2000	New York (AL)	New York (NL)	4-1
2001	Arizona (NL)	New York (AL)	4-3
2002	Anaheim (AL)	San Francisco (NL)	4-3
2003	Florida (NL)	New York (AL)	4-2
2004	Boston (AL)	St. Louis (NL)	4-0
2005	Chicago (AL)	Houston (NL)	4-0
2006	St. Louis (NL)	Detroit (AL)	4-1
2007	Boston (AL)	Colorado (NL)	4-0
2008	Philadelphia (NL)	Tampa Bay (AL)	4-1
2009	New York (AL)	Philadelphia (NL)	4-2
2010	San Francisco (NL)	Texas (AL)	4-1
2011	St. Louis (NL)	Texas (AL)	4-3
2012	San Francisco (NL)	Detroit (AL)	4-0
2013	Boston (AL)	St. Louis (NL)	4-2
2014	San Francisco (NL)	Kansas City (AL)	4-3
2015	Kansas City (AL)	New York (NL)	4-1
2016	Chicago (NL)	Cleveland (AL)	4-3
2017	Houston (AL)	Los Angeles (NL)	4-3
2018	Boston (AL)	Los Angeles (NL)	4-1
2019	Washington (NL)	Houston (AL)	4-3
2020	Los Angeles (NL)	Tampa Bay (AL)	4-2
2021	Atlanta (NL)	Houston (AL)	4-2
2022	Houston (AL)	Philadelphia (NL)	4-2
2023	Texas (AL)	Arizona (NL)	4-1
2024	Los Angeles (NL)	New York (AL)	4-1

WORLD SERIES BOX SCORES

GAME ONE *October 25, 2024*

L.A. DODGERS 6, NEW YORK YANKEES 3 (10)

	1	2	3	4	5	6	7	8	9	10	R	H	E
NY YANKEES	0	0	0	0	0	2	0	0	0	1	3	10	1
LA DODGERS	0	0	0	0	1	0	0	1	0	4	6	7	1

NY YANKEES	AB	R	H	RBI	BB	SO	LOB	AVG
Torres, 2B	5	0	2	0	0	0	1	.310
1-Domínguez, PR	0	0	0	0	0	0	0	.000
Cabrera, O, 2B	0	0	0	0	0	0	0	.167
Soto, J, RF	3	1	1	0	2	0	1	.333
Judge, CF	5	0	1	0	0	3	4	.167
Stanton, DH	5	1	1	2	0	2	2	.282
Chisholm Jr., 3B	5	1	2	0	0	1	2	.179
Rizzo, 1B	4	0	1	0	1	2	1	.389
Volpe, SS	4	0	0	1	1	2	2	.273
Wells, A, C	5	0	1	0	0	2	2	.105
Verdugo, LF	4	0	1	0	0	1	4	.200
Cole, P	0	0	0	0	0	0	0	.000
Holmes, C, P	0	0	0	0	0	0	0	.000
Kahnle, P	0	0	0	0	0	0	0	.000
Weaver, P	0	0	0	0	0	0	0	.000
Cousins, P	0	0	0	0	0	0	0	.000
Cortes, P	0	0	0	0	0	0	0	.000
TOTALS	**40**	**3**	**10**	**3**	**4**	**13**	**19**	**.250**

1-Ran for Torres in the 9th. 2B: Torres (3, Kopech). HR: Stanton (6, 6th inning off Flaherty, 1 on, 1 out). TB: Chisholm Jr. 2; Judge; Rizzo; Soto, J; Stanton 4; Torres 3; Verdugo; Wells, A. RBI: Stanton 2 (13); Volpe (2). Runners left in scoring position, 2 out: Wells, A; Judge; Chisholm Jr.; Verdugo 3. GIDP: Soto, J. Team RISP: 1-for-8. Team LOB: 11. SB: Chisholm Jr. 3 (5, 2nd base off Banda/Smith, W.D., 2nd base off Treinen/Smith, W.D., 3rd base off Treinen/Smith, W.D.); Volpe (3, 2nd base off Treinen/Smith, W.D.). E: Soto, J (1, throw)..

LA DODGERS	AB	R	H	RBI	BB	SO	LOB	AVG
Ohtani, DH	5	1	1	0	0	1	3	.277
Betts, RF	3	1	0	1	1	0	1	.277
Freeman, F, 1B	5	1	2	4	0	0	1	.243
Hernández, T, LF	4	0	1	0	0	0	1	.205
Muncy, 3B	3	0	0	0	0	1	0	.222
Hernández, K, CF	3	1	1	0	0	1	0	.306
Smith, W.D., C	3	0	0	1	0	1	2	.146
Lux, 2B	3	0	0	0	1	0	2	.185
1-Taylor, Ch, PR	0	1	0	0	0	0	0	.250
Edman, SS	4	1	2	0	0	0	0	.354
Flaherty, P	0	0	0	0	0	0	0	.000
Banda, P	0	0	0	0	0	0	0	.000
Graterol, P	0	0	0	0	0	0	0	.000
Vesia, P	0	0	0	0	0	0	0	.000
Kopech, P	0	0	0	0	0	0	0	.000
Treinen, P	0	0	0	0	0	0	0	.000
TOTALS	**33**	**6**	**7**	**6**	**2**	**4**	**10**	**.212**

1-Ran for Lux in the 10th. 2B: Edman (4, Cole); Ohtani (1, Kahnle). 3B: Freeman, F (1, Cole); Hernández, K (1, Cole). HR: Freeman, F (1, 10th inning off Cortes, 3 on, 2 out). TB: Edman 3; Freeman, F 7; Hernández, K 3; Hernández, T; Ohtani 2. RBI: Betts (13); Freeman, F 4 (5); Smith, W.D. (7). 2-out RBI: Freeman, F 4. Runners left in scoring position, 2 out: Freeman, F; Lux 2; Hernández, T. SAC: Hernández, K. SF: Betts; Smith, W.D. Team RISP: 1-for-8. Team LOB: 4. E: Edman (1, fielding). DP: (Edman-Freeman, F).

NY YANKEES	IP	H	R	ER	BB	SO	HR	ERA
Cole	6	4	1	1	0	4	0	2.82
Holmes, C (H, 4)	0.2	0	0	0	0	0	0	3.24
Kahnle (H, 3)	0.2	1	1	0	0	0	0	0.00
Weaver (BS, 2)	1.2	0	0	0	0	0	0	2.25
Cousins (L, 0-1)(H, 1)	0.1	1	2	2	1	0	0	12.00
Cortes (BS, 1)	0.1	1	2	2	1	0	1	54.00
TOTALS	**9.2**	**7**	**6**	**5**	**2**	**4**	**1**	**4.66**

LA DODGERS	IP	H	R	ER	BB	SO	HR	ERA
Flaherty	5.1	5	2	2	1	6	1	6.10
Banda	0.2	2	0	0	1	2	0	1.42
Graterol	1	1	0	0	0	1	0	0.00
Vesia	1	0	0	0	0	2	0	0.00
Kopech	0.2	1	0	0	1	0	0	1.50
Treinen (W, 1-0)	1.1	1	1	1	1	2	0	1.93
TOTALS	**10**	**10**	**3**	**3**	**4**	**13**	**1**	**2.70**

Cole pitched to 1 batter in the 7th. IBB: Volpe (by Banda); Soto, J (by Kopech); Rizzo (by Treinen); Betts (by Cortes). HBP: Muncy (by Holmes, C). Pitches-strikes: Cole 88-61; Holmes, C 5-2; Kahnle 8-7; Weaver 19-12; Cousins 14-7; Cortes 2-2; Flaherty 90-55; Banda 15-11; Graterol 18-12; Vesia 16-9; Kopech 10-5; Treinen 22-14. Groundouts-flyouts: Cole 3-6; Holmes, C 1-0; Kahnle 2-0; Weaver 0-2; Cousins 0-1; Cortes 0-1; Flaherty 7-1; Banda 0-0; Graterol 1-0; Vesia 0-0; Kopech 2-0; Treinen 1-0. Batters faced: Cole 22; Holmes, C 3; Kahnle 3; Weaver 5; Cousins 3; Cortes 3; Flaherty 22; Banda 5; Graterol 4; Vesia 3; Kopech 4; Treinen 6. Inherited runners-scored: Holmes, C 1-0; Kahnle 2-0; Weaver 1-1; Cortes 2-2; Treinen 2-0. Umpires: HP: Carlos Torres. 1B: Mark Carlson. 2B: Doug Eddings. 3B: Mark Ripperger. LF: Chad Fairchild. RF: Todd Tichenor. Official Scorer: Ed Munson Weather: 76 degrees, Clear. Wind: 5 mph, R To L. First pitch: 5:11 PM. T: 3:27. Att: 52,394. Venue: Dodger Stadium

GAME TWO *October 26, 2024*

LOS ANGELES DODGERS 4, NEW YORK YANKEES 2

	1	2	3	4	5	6	7	8	9	R	H	E
NY YANKEES	0	0	1	0	0	0	0	0	1	2	4	0
LA DODGERS	0	1	3	0	0	0	0	0	X	4	8	0

NY YANKEES	AB	R	H	RBI	BB	SO	LOB	AVG
Torres, 2B	3	0	0	0	1	0	0	.289
Soto, J, RF	4	2	2	1	0	0	1	.350
Judge, CF	4	0	0	0	0	3	2	.150
Stanton, DH	4	0	1	1	0	0	1	.279
Chisholm Jr., 3B	4	0	1	0	0	0	0	.186
Rizzo, 1B	1	0	0	0	1	1	0	.368
1-Cabrera, O, PR	0	0	0	0	0	0	0	.167
Volpe, SS	4	0	0	0	0	2	5	.243
Wells, A, C	3	0	0	0	0	1	1	.098
a-Trevino, PH	1	0	0	0	0	0	3	.333
Verdugo, LF	3	0	0	0	0	0	0	.184
Rodón, P	0	0	0	0	0	0	0	.000
Cousins, P	0	0	0	0	0	0	0	.000
Hill, T, P	0	0	0	0	0	0	0	.000
Holmes, C, P	0	0	0	0	0	0	0	.000
Leiter Jr., P	0	0	0	0	0	0	0	.000
TOTALS	**31**	**2**	**4**	**2**	**2**	**7**	**13**	**.197**

1 Ran for Torres in the 9th. 2B: Torres (3, Kopech). HR: Stanton (6, 6th inning off Flaherty, 1 on, 1 out). TB: Chisholm Jr. 2; Judge; Rizzo; Soto, J; Stanton 4; Torres 3; Verdugo; Wells, A. RBI: Stanton 2 (13); Volpe (2). Runners left in scoring position, 2 out: Wells, A; Judge; Chisholm Jr.; Verdugo 3. GIDP: Soto, J. Team RISP: 1-for-8. Team LOB: 11. SB: Chisholm Jr. 3 (5, 2nd base off Banda/Smith, W.D., 2nd base off Treinen/Smith, W.D., 3rd base off Treinen/Smith, W.D.); Volpe (3, 2nd base off Treinen/Smith, W.D.). E: Soto, J (1, throw).

LA DODGERS	AB	R	H	RBI	BB	SO	LOB	AVG
Ohtani, DH	3	0	0	0	1	1	1	.260
Betts, RF	4	1	2	0	0	1	1	.294
Hernández, T, LF	4	1	2	2	0	0	1	.229
Taylor, Ch, LF	0	0	0	0	0	0	0	.250
Freeman, F, 1B	4	1	1	1	0	0	2	.244
Edman, CF	4	1	2	1	0	1	1	.365
Hernández, K, 2B	3	0	0	0	0	0	1	.282
Muncy, 3B	3	0	0	0	0	2	0	.205
Smith, W.D., C	3	0	1	0	0	0	0	.159
Rojas, M, SS	3	0	0	0	0	1	1	.182
Yamamoto, P	0	0	0	0	0	0	0	.000
Banda, P	0	0	0	0	0	0	0	.000
Kopech, P	0	0	0	0	0	0	0	.000
Treinen, P	0	0	0	0	0	0	0	.000
Vesia, P	0	0	0	0	0	0	0	.000
TOTALS	**31**	**4**	**8**	**4**	**1**	**6**	**8**	**.234**

2B: Edman (5, Rodón); Smith, W.D. (1, Cousins). HR: Edman (2, 2nd inning off Rodón, 0 on, 0 out); Hernández, T (3, 3rd inning off Rodón, 1 on, 2 out); Freeman, F (2, 3rd inning off Rodón, 0 on, 2 out). TB: Betts 2; Edman 6; Freeman, F 4; Hernández, T 5; Smith, W.D. 2. RBI: Edman (13); Freeman, F (6); Hernández, T 2 (10). 2-out RBI: Freeman, F; Hernández, T 2. Runners left in scoring position, 2 out: Hernández, K; Ohtani. Team RISP: 0-for-3. Team LOB: 4. SB: Edman (4, 3rd base off Rodón/Wells, A). CS: Ohtani (2, 2nd base by Holmes, C/Wells, A).

NY YANKEES	IP	H	R	ER	BB	SO	HR	ERA
Rodón (L, 1-2)	3.1	6	4	4	0	3	3	5.60
Cousins	1	2	0	0	0	0	0	9.00
Hill, T	1.1	0	0	0	0	1	0	1.29
Holmes, C	1.1	0	0	0	1	2	0	2.79
Leiter Jr.	1	0	0	0	0	0	0	2.70
TOTALS	**8**	**8**	**4**	**4**	**1**	**6**	**3**	**4.58**

LA DODGERS	IP	H	R	ER	BB	SO	HR	ERA
Yamamoto (W, 2-0)	6.1	1	1	1	2	4	1	3.86
Banda (H, 2)	0.2	0	0	0	0	0	0	1.29
Kopech (H, 3)	1	0	0	0	0	1	0	1.29
Treinen (H, 2)	0.2	3	1	1	0	2	0	2.70
Vesia (S, 1)	0.1	0	0	0	0	0	0	0.00
TOTALS	**9**	**4**	**2**	**2**	**2**	**7**	**1**	**2.37**

WP: Treinen. HBP: Rizzo 2 (by Banda, by Treinen). Pitches-strikes: Rodón 63-40; Cousins 21-12; Hill, T 14-10; Holmes, C 23-13; Leiter Jr. 9-8; Yamamoto 86-54; Banda 16-9; Kopech 14-9; Treinen 33-19; Vesia 1-1. Groundouts-flyouts: Rodón 1-3; Cousins 2-1; Hill, T 0-0; Holmes, C 1-0; Leiter Jr. 2-0; Yamamoto 9-3; Banda 0-2; Kopech 1-0; Treinen 0-0; Vesia 0-1. Batters faced: Rodón 16; Cousins 5; Hill, T 4; Holmes, C 4; Leiter Jr. 3; Yamamoto 22; Banda 3; Kopech 3; Treinen 6; Vesia 1. Inherited runners-scored: Hill, T 1-0; Vesia 3-0. Umpires: HP: Andy Fletcher. 1B: Doug Eddings. 2B: Mark Ripperger. 3B: Chad Fairchild. LF: Todd Tichenor. RF: Carlos Torres. Official Scorer: Ed Munson Weather: 77 degrees, Partly Cloudy Wind: 5 mph, L To R First pitch: 5:15 PM T: 2:53 Att: 52,725

GAME 3 *October 28, 2024*

LOS ANGELES DODGERS 4, NEW YORK YANKEES 2

	1	2	3	4	5	6	7	8	9	R	H	E
LA DODGERS	2	0	1	0	0	1	0	0	0	4	5	0
NY YANKEES	0	0	0	0	0	0	0	0	2	2	5	1

LA DODGERS	AB	R	H	RBI	BB	SO	LOB	AVG
Ohtani, DH	3	1	0	0	1	1	3	.245
Betts, RF	4	0	1	1	1	0	4	.291
Freeman, F, 1B	3	1	1	2	1	0	1	.250
Hernández, T, LF	4	0	1	0	0	0	3	.231
Taylor, Ch, LF	0	0	0	0	0	0	0	.250
Muncy, 3B	3	0	0	0	1	2	3	.190
Smith, W.D., C	4	0	0	0	0	0	3	.146
Lux, 2B	2	1	0	0	1	2	0	.172
Hernández, K, CF	4	0	2	1	0	1	0	.302
Edman, SS	3	1	0	0	1	1	3	.345
Buehler, P	0	0	0	0	0	0	0	.000
Graterol, P	0	0	0	0	0	0	0	.000
Vesia, P	0	0	0	0	0	0	0	.000
Hudson, Dan, P	0	0	0	0	0	0	0	.000
Banda, P	0	0	0	0	0	0	0	.000
Brasier, P	0	0	0	0	0	0	0	.000
Kopech, P	0	0	0	0	0	0	0	.000
TOTALS	**30**	**4**	**5**	**4**	**6**	**7**	**20**	**.213**

HR: Freeman, F (3, 1st inning off Schmidt, 1 on, 1 out). TB: Betts; Freeman, F 4; Hernández, K 2; Hernández, T. RBI: Betts (14); Freeman, F 2 (8); Hernández, K (6). Runners left in scoring position, 2 out: Smith, W.D. 2; Muncy; Betts. GIDP: Betts; Muncy. Team RISP: 2-for-8. Team LOB: 7. SB: Lux (1, 2nd base off Cousins/Trevino). CS: Hernández, K (1, 2nd base by Cousins/Trevino). Outfield assists: Hernández, T (Stanton at home).

NY YANKEES	AB	R	H	RBI	BB	SO	LOB	AVG
Torres, 2B	3	0	0	0	2	1	2	.271
Soto, J, RF	3	0	0	0	1	0	2	.326
Judge, CF	3	0	0	0	1	1	2	.140
Stanton, DH	4	0	2	0	0	1	2	.298
Chisholm Jr., 3B	4	0	0	0	0	1	4	.170
Volpe, SS	4	0	1	0	0	3	0	.244
Rizzo, 1B	3	1	1	0	1	1	0	.364
Trevino, C	2	0	0	0	0	1	0	.200
a-Wells, A, PH-C	2	0	0	0	0	1	2	.093
Verdugo, LF	3	1	1	2	1	1	0	.195
Schmidt, P	0	0	0	0	0	0	0	.000
Leiter Jr., P	0	0	0	0	0	0	0	.000
Cortes, P	0	0	0	0	0	0	0	.000
Cousins, P	0	0	0	0	0	0	0	.000
Hill, T, P	0	0	0	0	0	0	0	.000
Holmes, C, P	0	0	0	0	0	0	0	.000
Kahnle, P	0	0	0	0	0	0	0	.000
Weaver, P	0	0	0	0	0	0	0	.000
TOTALS	**31**	**2**	**5**	**2**	**6**	**11**	**14**	**.186**

a-Struck out for Trevino in the 7th. 2B: Stanton (3, Buehler). HR: Verdugo (1, 9th inning off Kopech, 1 on, 2 out). TB: Rizzo; Stanton 3; Verdugo 4; Volpe. RBI: Verdugo 2 (5). 2-out RBI: Verdugo 2. Runners left in scoring position, 2 out: Torres; Chisholm Jr. Team RISP: 2-for-6. Team LOB: 8. E: Chisholm Jr. (2, fielding). DP: 3 (Torres-Rizzo; Trevino-Volpe; Volpe-Torres-Rizzo).

LA DODGERS	IP	H	R	ER	BB	SO	HR	ERA
Buehler (W, 1-1)	5	2	0	0	2	5	0	3.86
Graterol	0.2	1	0	0	1	0	0	0.00
Vesia (H, 3)	0.1	0	0	0	0	0	0	0.00
Hudson, Dan	0.2	1	0	0	0	2	0	1.80
Banda	0.1	0	0	0	1	1	0	1.23
Brasier	1	0	0	0	1	2	0	4.50
Kopech	1	1	2	2	1	1	1	3.38
TOTALS	**9**	**5**	**2**	**2**	**6**	**11**	**1**	**2.25**

NY YANKEES	IP	H	R	ER	BB	SO	HR	ERA
Schmidt (L, 0-1)	2.2	2	3	3	4	3	1	5.25
Leiter Jr.	0.2	1	0	0	1	0	0	2.25
Cortes	1.2	0	0	0	0	1	0	9.00
Cousins	1	1	1	1	0	1	0	9.00
Hill, T	0.2	0	0	0	1	0	0	1.17
Holmes, C	0.2	1	0	0	0	1	0	2.61
Kahnle	1	0	0	0	0	1	0	0.00
Weaver	0.2	0	0	0	0	0	0	2.13
TOTALS	**9**	**5**	**4**	**4**	**6**	**7**	**1**	**4.39**

WP: Kopech. HBP: Lux (by Cousins); Ohtani (by Weaver). Pitches-strikes: Buehler 76-45; Graterol 18-8; Vesia 4-2; Hudson, Dan 22-13; Banda 10-4; Brasier 22-13; Kopech 24-15; Schmidt 68-37; Leiter Jr. 17-8; Cortes 15-10; Cousins 17-10; Hill, T 17-10; Holmes, C 12-7; Kahnle 11-8; Weaver 6-2. Groundouts-flyouts: Buehler 3-3; Graterol 2-0; Vesia 1-0; Hudson, Dan 0-0; Banda 0-0; Brasier 0-0; Kopech 1-0; Schmidt 2-2; Leiter Jr. 2-0; Cortes 2-0; Cousins 0-0; Hill, T 1-0; Holmes, C 0-0; Kahnle 1-0; Weaver 1-0. Batters faced: Buehler 18; Graterol 4; Vesia 1; Hudson, Dan 3; Banda 2; Brasier 4; Kopech 5; Schmidt 14; Leiter Jr. 4; Cortes 5; Cousins 4; Hill, T 3; Holmes, C 3; Kahnle 3; Weaver 2. Inherited runners-scored: Vesia 2-0; Banda 1-0; Leiter Jr. 3-0; Cortes 2-0; Holmes, C 1-0. Umpires: HP: Mark Carlson. 1B: Mark Ripperger. 2B: Chad Fairchild. 3B: Todd Tichenor. LF: Carlos Torres. RF: Andy Fletcher. Official Scorer: Billy Altman. Weather: 52 degrees, Clear Wind: 5 mph, In From LF First pitch: 8:17 PM T: 3:25 Att: 49,368

GAME 4 *October 29, 2024*

NEW YORK YANKEES 11, LOS ANGELES DODGERS 4

	1	2	3	4	5	6	7	8	9	R	H	E
LA DODGERS	2	0	0	0	2	0	0	0	0	4	6	1
NY YANKEES	0	1	4	0	0	1	0	5	X	11	9	0

LA DODGERS	AB	R	H	RBI	BB	SO	LOB	AVG
Ohtani, DH	4	0	1	0	0	1	1	.246
Betts, RF	4	1	1	0	0	1	3	.288
Freeman, F, 1B	4	1	1	3	0	0	1	.250
Hernández, T, LF	4	0	1	0	0	1	1	.232
Muncy, 3B	3	0	0	0	1	3	1	.178
Hernández, K, CF	4	0	0	0	0	1	2	.277
Lux, 2B	3	0	1	0	0	0	1	.188
a-Taylor, Ch, PH	1	0	0	0	0	0	0	.231
Smith, W.D., C	4	1	1	1	0	1	1	.154
Edman, SS	1	1	0	0	2	0	1	.339
Casparius, P	0	0	0	0	0	0	0	.000
Hudson, Dan, P	0	0	0	0	0	0	0	.000
Knack, P	0	0	0	0	0	0	0	.000
Honeywell, P	0	0	0	0	0	0	0	.000
TOTALS	**32**	**4**	**6**	**4**	**3**	**8**	**12**	**.206**

a-Grounded out for Lux in the 9th. 2B: Betts (5, Gil); Lux (1, Gil). HR: Freeman, F (4, 1st inning off Gil, 1 on, 1 out); Smith, W.D. (3, 5th inning off Gil, 0 on, 0 out). TB: Betts 2; Freeman, F 4; Hernández, T; Lux 2; Ohtani; Smith, W.D. 4. RBI: Freeman, F 3 (11); Smith, W.D. (8). Runners left in scoring position, 2 out: Betts. Team RISP: 1-for-7. Team LOB: 4. SB: Edman (5, 2nd base off Leiter Jr./Wells, A). E: Edman (2, fielding). DP: (Lux-Edman-Freeman, F).

NY YANKEES	AB	R	H	RBI	BB	SO	LOB	AVG
Torres, 2B	5	1	1	3	0	0	2	0.264
Soto, J, RF	4	1	1	0	1	2	0	.319
Judge, CF	3	1	1	1	1	0	0	.152
Chisholm Jr., 3B	4	1	1	0	1	0	3	.176
Stanton, DH	4	1	0	0	1	1	5	.275
Rizzo, 1B	4	0	0	0	0	1	5	.308
Volpe, SS	3	3	2	4	1	0	2	.273
Wells, A, C	3	2	2	1	1	0	0	.130
Verdugo, LF	4	1	1	2	0	0	2	.200
Gil, P	0	0	0	0	0	0	0	.000
Hill, T, P	0	0	0	0	0	0	0	.000
Holmes, C, P	0	0	0	0	0	0	0	.000
Leiter Jr., P	0	0	0	0	0	0	0	.000
Weaver, P	0	0	0	0	0	0	0	.000
Mayza, P	0	0	0	0	0	0	0	.000
TOTALS	**34**	**11**	**9**	**11**	**6**	**4**	**19**	**.206**

2B: Wells, A (1, Casparius); Volpe (2, Honeywell); Soto, J (3, Honeywell). HR: Volpe (1, 3rd inning off Hudson, Dan, 3 on, 2 out); Wells, A (2, 6th inning off Knack, 0 on, 0 out); Torres (2, 8th inning off Honeywell, 2 on, 1 out). TB: Chisholm Jr.; Judge; Soto, J 2; Torres 4; Verdugo; Volpe 6; Wells, A 6. RBI: Judge (7); Torres 3 (8); Verdugo 2 (7); Volpe 4 (6); Wells, A (4). 2-out RBI: Volpe 4. Runners left in scoring position, 2 out: Stanton 3; Volpe; Torres. GIDP: Torres. Team RISP: 4-for-15. Team LOB: 6. SB: Volpe 2 (5, 2nd base off Casparius/Smith, W.D., 3rd base off Honeywell/Smith, W.D.); Chisholm Jr. (6, 2nd base off Hudson, Dan/Smith, W.D.); Wells, A (1, 2nd base off Honeywell/Smith, W.D.); Judge (2, 2nd base off Honeywell/Smith, W.D.). DP: (Rizzo-Volpe).

LA DODGERS	IP	H	R	ER	BB	SO	HR	ERA
Casparius	2	1	1	1	3	1	0	1.42
Hudson, Dan (L, 0-1)	1	2	4	4	1	1	1	7.5
Knack	4	2	1	1	1	2	1	7.71
Honeywell	1	4	5	5	1	0	1	9.35
TOTALS	**8**	**9**	**11**	**11**	**6**	**4**	**3**	**4.50**

NY YANKEES	IP	H	R	ER	BB	SO	HR	ERA
Gil	4	5	4	4	2	1	2	6.75
Hill, T	0.2	1	0	0	0	0	0	1.08
Holmes, C (W, 3-1)	1.1	0	0	0	0	2	0	2.31
Leiter Jr. (H, 1)	0.2	0	0	0	1	2	0	1.93
Weaver (H, 1)	1.1	0	0	0	0	3	0	1.93
Mayza	1	0	0	0	0	0	0	0.00
TOTALS	**9**	**6**	**4**	**4**	**3**	**8**	**2**	**4.29**

Gil pitched to 2 batters in the 5th. HBP: Judge (by Hudson, Dan). Pitches-strikes: Casparius 43-23; Hudson, Dan 20-11; Knack 56-33; Honeywell 50-32; Gil 67-40; Hill, T 5-3; Holmes, C 13-9; Leiter Jr. 18-8; Weaver 21-14; Mayza 15-9. Groundouts-flyouts: Casparius 3-2; Hudson, Dan 0-1; Knack 3-6; Honeywell 2-1; Gil 3-2; Hill, T 2-0; Holmes, C 1-1; Leiter Jr. 0-0; Weaver 0-1; Mayza 2-0. Batters faced: Casparius 10; Hudson, Dan 7; Knack 15; Honeywell 9; Gil 18; Hill, T 3; Holmes, C 4; Leiter Jr. 3; Weaver 4; Mayza 3. Inherited runners-scored: Hill, T 1-1; Holmes, C 1-0; Weaver 1-0. Umpires: HP: Doug Eddings. 1B: Chad Fairchild. 2B: Todd Tichenor. 3B: Carlos Torres. LF: Andy Fletcher. RF: Mark Carlson. Official Scorer: Howie Karpin. Weather: 61 degrees, Cloudy Wind: 10 mph, R To L First pitch: 8:08 PM T: 3:16 Att: 49,354

GAME 5 *October 30, 2024*

LOS ANGELES DODGERS 7, NEW YORK YANKEES 6

	1	2	3	4	5	6	7	8	9	R	H	E
LA DODGERS	0	0	0	0	5	0	0	2	0	7	7	0
NY YANKEES	3	1	1	0	0	1	0	0	0	6	8	3

LA DODGERS	AB	R	H	RBI	BB	SO	LOB	AVG
Ohtani, DH	4	0	0	0	0	1	4	.230
Betts, RF	3	1	1	2	1	0	0	.290
Freeman, F, 1B	4	1	1	2	1	1	3	.250
Hernández, T, LF	4	0	2	2	1	1	1	.250
1-Taylor, Ch, PR-LF	0	0	0	0	0	0	0	.231
Muncy, 3B	4	0	0	0	1	2	4	.163
Hernández, K, CF	4	2	2	0	1	0	2	.294
Edman, SS	5	2	1	0	0	2	3	.328
Smith, W.D., C	4	1	0	0	1	1	4	.143
Lux, 2B	2	0	0	1	1	1	3	.176
Flaherty, P	0	0	0	0	0	0	0	.000
Banda, P	0	0	0	0	0	0	0	.000
Brasier, P	0	0	0	0	0	0	0	.000
Kopech, P	0	0	0	0	0	0	0	.000
Vesia, P	0	0	0	0	0	0	0	.000
Graterol, P	0	0	0	0	0	0	0	.000
Treinen, P	0	0	0	0	0	0	0	.000
Buehler, P	0	0	0	0	0	0	0	.000
TOTALS	**34**	**7**	**7**	**7**	**7**	**9**	**24**	**.206**

1-Ran for Hernández, T in the 9th. 2B: Hernández, T (1, Cole). TB: Betts; Edman; Freeman, F; Hernández, K 2; Hernández, T 3. RBI: Betts 2 (16); Freeman, F 2 (13); Hernández, T 2 (12); Lux (4). 2-out RBI: Freeman, F 2; Hernández, T 2; Betts. Runners left in scoring position, 2 out: Hernández, K; Freeman, F; Smith, W.D.; Muncy 2. SF: Betts; Lux. Team RISP: 3-for-12. Team LOB: 10.

NY YANKEES	AB	R	H	RBI	BB	SO	LOB	AVG
Torres, 2B	5	0	0	0	0	1	5	0.241
Soto, J, RF	2	2	1	0	3	0	0	.327
Judge, CF	3	1	2	2	2	0	2	.184
Chisholm Jr., 3B	4	1	1	1	1	1	7	.182
Stanton, DH	4	1	1	2	0	0	2	.273
Rizzo, 1B	4	0	0	0	1	2	2	.267
Volpe, SS	5	1	2	0	0	0	2	.286
Wells, A, C	4	0	0	0	0	3	1	.120
Verdugo, LF	3	0	1	1	2	2	0	.208
Cole, P	0	0	0	0	0	0	0	.000
Holmes, C, P	0	0	0	0	0	0	0	.000
Kahnle, P	0	0	0	0	0	0	0	.000
Weaver, P	0	0	0	0	0	0	0	.000
Leiter Jr., P	0	0	0	0	0	0	0	.000
TOTALS	**34**	**6**	**8**	**6**	**9**	**9**	**21**	**.212**

2B: Volpe (3, Flaherty); Judge (2, Treinen). HR: Judge (3, 1st inning off Flaherty, 1 on, 1 out); Chisholm Jr. (2, 1st inning off Flaherty, 0 on, 1 out); Stanton (7, 3rd inning off Brasier, 0 on, 0 out). TB: Chisholm Jr. 4; Judge 6; Soto, J; Stanton 4; Verdugo; Volpe 3. RBI: Chisholm Jr. (2); Judge 2 (9); Stanton 2 (16); Verdugo (8). Runners left in scoring position, 2 out: Rizzo; Volpe; Torres 2; Chisholm Jr. 3. SF: Stanton. Team RISP: 1-for-10. Team LOB: 12. E: Judge (1, fielding); Volpe (2, throw), Wells, A (1, catcher interference).

LA DODGERS	IP	H	R	ER	BB	SO	HR	ERA
Flaherty	1.1	4	4	4	1	1	2	7.36
Banda	0.2	0	0	0	2	1	0	1.13
Brasier	1	1	1	1	0	1	1	5.00
Kopech	1	1	0	0	1	1	0	3.00
Vesia	1	1	0	0	1	0	0	0.00
Graterol	0.2	0	1	1	3	0	0	3.86
Treinen (W, 2-0)	2.1	1	0	0	1	3	0	2.19
Buehler (S, 1)	1	0	0	0	0	2	0	3.60
TOTALS	**9**	**8**	**6**	**6**	**9**	**9**	**3**	**4.80**

NY YANKEES	IP	H	R	ER	BB	SO	HR	ERA
Cole	6.2	4	5	0	4	6	0	2.17
Holmes, C (H, 5)	0.1	0	0	0	1	1	0	2.25
Kahnle (L, 1-1)	0	2	2	2	1	0	0	2.08
Weaver (BS, 3)	1.1	1	0	0	1	1	0	1.76
Leiter Jr.	0.2	0	0	0	0	1	0	1.69
TOTALS	**9**	**7**	**7**	**2**	**7**	**9**	**0**	**3.83**

Kahnle pitched to 3 batters in the 8th. WP: Banda. Balk: Weaver. Disengagement violations: Weaver. HBP: Wells, A (by Vesia). Pitches-strikes: Flaherty 35-18; Banda 16-8; Brasier 12-8; Kopech 18-11; Vesia 23-12; Graterol 24-12; Treinen 42-25; Buehler 16-10; Cole 108-76; Holmes, C 11-4; Kahnle 8-3; Weaver 22-13; Leiter Jr. 7-4. Groundouts-flyouts: Flaherty 2-0; Banda 1-0; Brasier 0-1; Kopech 0-1; Vesia 1-1; Graterol 1-1; Treinen 3-1; Buehler 1-0; Cole 6-6; Holmes, C 0-0; Kahnle 0-0; Weaver 0-3; Leiter Jr. 1-0. Batters faced: Flaherty 9; Banda 4; Brasier 4; Kopech 5; Vesia 6; Graterol 5; Treinen 9; Buehler 3; Cole 30; Holmes, C 2; Kahnle 3; Weaver 7; Leiter Jr. 2. Inherited runners-scored: Banda 1-0; Treinen 2-0; Holmes, C 1-0; Weaver 3-2, Leiter Jr. 2-0. Umpires: HP: Mark Ripperger 1B: Todd Tichenor. 2B: Carlos Torres. 3B: Andy Fletcher. LF: Mark Carlson. RF: Doug Eddings. Official Scorer: Jordan Sprechman. Weather: 67 degrees, Partly Cloudy Wind: 5 mph, Out To LF First pitch: 8:09 PM T: 3:42 Att: 49,263

AMERICAN LEAGUE WILD CARD SERIES

KANSAS CITY ROYALS VS. BALTIMORE ORIOLES

KANSAS CITY	AVG	G	AB	R	H	2B	3B	HR	RBI	BB	SO	SB
Michael Massey	.375	2	8	1	3	1	0	0	0	0	1	0
Bobby Witt Jr.	.333	2	9	0	3	0	0	0	2	0	1	0
Vinnie Pasquantino	.286	2	7	0	2	0	0	0	1	2	2	0
Salvador Perez	.250	2	8	0	2	0	0	0	0	0	3	0
Kyle Isbel	.200	2	5	1	1	0	0	0	0	1	0	0
Maikel Garcia	.167	2	6	1	1	0	0	0	0	1	2	2
Yuli Gurriel	.143	2	7	0	1	0	0	0	0	1	1	0
MJ Melendez	.143	2	7	0	1	0	0	0	0	0	2	0
Tommy Pham	.000	2	4	0	0	0	0	0	0	0	1	0
Hunter Renfroe	.000	1	3	0	0	0	0	0	0	1	1	0
Totals	**.219**	**32**	**64**	**3**	**14**	**1**	**0**	**0**	**3**	**6**	**14**	**3**

KANSAS CITY	W	L	ERA	G	GS	SV	IP	H	R	ER	BB	SO
Kris Bubic	0	0	0.00	2	0	0	1.2	2	0	0	1	0
Lucas Erceg	0	0	0.00	2	0	2	2.1	0	0	0	1	3
Sam Long	0	0	0.00	2	0	0	1.2	0	0	0	1	1
Cole Ragans	1	0	0.00	1	1	0	6	4	0	0	0	8
John Schreiber	0	0	0.00	1	0	0	1	0	0	0	0	2
Angel Zerpa	1	0	0.00	1	0	0	1	0	0	0	0	2
Seth Lugo	0	0	2.08	1	1	0	4.1	5	1	1	1	6
Totals	**2**	**0**	**0.50**	**10**	**2**	**2**	**18**	**11**	**1**	**1**	**4**	**22**

BALTIMORE	AVG	G	AB	R	H	2B	3B	HR	RBI	BB	SO	SB
Ryan O'Hearn	.500	2	2	0	1	0	0	0	0	1	0	0
Austin Slater	.500	1	2	0	1	0	0	0	0	0	1	0
Cedric Mullins	.429	2	7	1	3	1	0	1	1	0	1	0
Ramón Urías	.286	2	7	0	2	1	0	0	0	0	1	0
Jordan Westburg	.167	2	6	0	1	0	0	0	0	1	1	0
Colton Cowser	.143	2	7	0	1	0	0	0	0	0	3	0
Adley Rutschman	.125	2	8	0	1	0	0	0	0	0	2	0
Anthony Santander	.125	2	8	0	1	0	0	0	0	0	2	0
Gunnar Henderson	.000	2	7	0	0	0	0	0	0	2	4	0
Heston Kjerstad	.000	2	2	0	0	0	0	0	0	0	1	0
James McCann	.000	1	2	0	0	0	0	0	0	0	2	0
Ryan Mountcastle	.000	2	7	0	0	0	0	0	0	0	4	0
Emmanuel Rivera	.000	1	1	0	0	0	0	0	0	0	0	0
Totals	**.167**	**33**	**66**	**1**	**11**	**2**	**0**	**1**	**1**	**4**	**22**	**0**

BALTIMORE	W	L	ERA	G	GS	SV	IP	H	R	ER	BB	SO
Keegan Akin	0	0	0.00	1	0	0	0.2	0	0	0	1	0
Yennier Cano	0	0	0.00	1	0	0	1.1	2	0	0	1	1
Danny Coulombe	0	0	0.00	1	0	0	0.2	1	0	0	0	1
Seranthony Domínguez	0	0	0.00	2	0	0	1.2	0	0	0	0	2
Gregory Soto	0	0	0.00	1	0	0	0.2	0	0	0	1	1
Jacob Webb	0	0	0.00	1	0	0	0.2	0	0	0	1	2
Corbin Burnes	0	1	1.13	1	1	0	8	5	1	1	1	3
Zach Eflin	0	0	2.25	1	1	0	4	4	1	1	1	3
Cionel Pérez	0	1	27.00	1	0	0	0.1	2	1	1	0	1
Totals	**0**	**2**	**1.50**	**10**	**2**	**0**	**18**	**14**	**3**	**3**	**6**	**14**

SCORE BY INNINGS

KANSAS CITY	1	0	0	0	0	2	0	0	0	3
BALTIMORE	0	0	0	0	1	0	0	0	0	1

DETROIT TIGERS VS. HOUSTON ASTROS

DETROIT	AVG	G	AB	R	H	2B	3B	HR	RBI	BB	SO	SB
Andy Ibáñez	.667	2	3	0	2	2	0	0	3	0	0	0
Justyn-Henry Malloy	.667	2	3	0	2	0	0	0	0	1	1	0
Wenceel Pérez	.400	1	5	1	2	0	0	0	0	0	1	0
Jake Rogers	.375	2	8	1	3	0	0	0	1	0	3	0
Zach McKinstry	.333	2	3	0	1	1	0	0	0	0	0	0
Matt Vierling	.250	2	8	1	2	0	0	0	1	2	4	0
Parker Meadows	.222	2	9	2	2	0	0	1	1	0	3	1
Kerry Carpenter	.167	2	6	1	1	0	0	0	0	0	1	0
Trey Sweeney	.143	2	7	0	1	0	0	0	1	1	3	1
Riley Greene	.111	2	9	0	1	1	0	0	0	1	3	0
Colt Keith	.000	2	3	1	0	0	0	0	0	4	1	0
Spencer Torkelson	.000	2	5	1	0	0	0	0	0	3	3	0
Totals	**.246**	**35**	**69**	**8**	**17**	**4**	**0**	**1**	**7**	**12**	**23**	**2**

DETROIT	W	L	ERA	G	GS	SV	IP	H	R	ER	BB	SO
Anthony Banda	0	0	0.00	3	0	0	3	2	0	0	1	4
Beau Brieske	0	0	0.00	2	0	1	2.1	0	0	0	2	1
Sean Guenther	1	0	0.00	1	0	0	1.2	0	0	0	0	0
Brenan Hanifee	0	0	0.00	1	0	0	1.2	1	0	0	1	2
Tyler Holton	0	0	0.00	2	1	0	1.1	0	0	0	0	1
Brant Hurter	0	0	0.00	1	0	0	1.2	2	0	0	1	0
Tarik Skubal	1	0	0.00	1	1	0	6	4	0	0	1	6
Will Vest	0	0	0.00	2	0	1	2.2	0	0	0	0	5
Jason Foley	0	0	27.00	1	0	0	0.1	3	1	1	0	0
Jackson Jobe	0	0	54.00	1	0	0	0.1	2	2	2	0	0
Totals	**2**	**0**	**1.50**	**12**	**2**	**2**	**18**	**12**	**3**	**3**	**5**	**15**

HOUSTON	AVG	G	AB	R	H	2B	3B	HR	RBI	BB	SO	SB
Mauricio Dubón	.400	2	5	0	2	0	0	0	0	0	0	0
Alex Bregman	.375	2	8	0	3	0	0	0	0	0	0	0
Yordan Alvarez	.286	2	7	0	2	1	0	0	0	1	1	0
Yainer Diaz	.286	2	7	0	2	0	0	0	1	1	1	0
Victor Caratini	.167	2	6	1	1	0	0	0	0	0	3	0
Jeremy Peña	.167	2	6	1	1	0	0	0	0	1	3	0
Jose Altuve	.143	2	7	0	1	0	0	0	1	0	2	0
Jason Heyward	.000	2	3	0	0	0	0	0	0	0	2	0
Chas McCormick	.000	2	2	0	0	0	0	0	0	1	0	1
Jake Meyers	.000	2	2	0	0	0	0	0	0	0	1	0
Jon Singleton	.000	2	2	0	0	0	0	0	1	0	0	0
Kyle Tucker	.000	2	7	0	0	0	0	0	0	1	2	0
Totals	**.194**	**35**	**62**	**3**	**12**	**1**	**0**	**0**	**3**	**5**	**15**	**1**

HOUSTON	W	L	ERA	G	GS	SV	IP	H	R	ER	BB	SO
Bryan Abreu	0	0	0.00	1	0	0	1.1	0	0	0	1	2
Ronel Blanco	0	0	0.00	1	0	0	2	1	0	0	3	4
Caleb Ferguson	0	0	0.00	1	0	0	0.1	0	0	0	0	0
Bryan King	0	0	0.00	1	0	0	0.2	1	0	0	0	1
Héctor Neris	0	0	0.00	1	0	0	0.2	0	0	0	1	2
Hunter Brown	0	0	1.59	1	1	0	5.2	2	1	1	2	9
Josh Hader	0	0	3.86	2	0	0	2.1	4	1	1	2	0
Framber Valdez	0	1	6.23	1	1	0	4.1	7	3	3	2	3
Ryan Pressly	0	1	40.50	1	0	0	0.2	2	3	3	1	2
Totals	**0**	**2**	**4.00**	**10**	**2**	**0**	**18**	**17**	**8**	**8**	**12**	**23**

SCORE BY INNINGS

DETROIT	0	3	0	0	0	1	0	4	0	8
HOUSTON	0	0	0	0	0	0	2	0	1	3

AMERICAN LEAGUE DIVISION SERIES

NEW YORK YANKEES VS. KANSAS CITY ROYALS

NY YANKEES	AVG	G	AB	R	H	2B	3B	HR	RBI	BB	SO	SB
Giancarlo Stanton	.375	4	16	1	6	2	0	1	4	2	2	1
Jon Berti	.286	2	7	0	2	0	0	0	0	1	1	0
Juan Soto	.286	4	14	1	4	1	0	0	2	3	4	0
Anthony Volpe	.250	4	12	1	3	0	0	0	1	4	1	1
Alex Verdugo	.214	4	14	3	3	0	0	0	1	1	0	0
Oswaldo Cabrera	.200	2	5	0	1	1	0	0	0	3	3	0
Gleyber Torres	.200	4	15	4	3	1	0	1	3	5	3	0
Aaron Judge	.154	4	13	2	2	1	0	0	0	5	5	1
Jazz Chisholm Jr.	.133	4	15	2	2	0	0	1	1	1	3	1
Austin Wells	.125	4	16	0	2	0	0	0	2	2	6	0
Totals	**.220**	**57**	**127**	**14**	**28**	**6**	**0**	**3**	**14**	**27**	**28**	**4**

NY YANKEES	W	L	ERA	G	GS	SV	IP	H	R	ER	BB	SO
Jake Cousins	0	0	0.00	1	0	0	0.1	0	0	0	1	0
Ian Hamilton	0	0	0.00	1	0	0	1.1	1	0	0	0	3
Tim Hill	0	0	0.00	2	0	0	1	1	1	0	0	0
Clay Holmes	1	0	0.00	4	0	0	5	3	0	0	1	3
Tommy Kahnle	1	0	0.00	3	0	0	3	0	0	0	2	3
Tim Mayza	0	0	0.00	1	0	0	0.2	1	0	0	0	1
Luke Weaver	0	0	0.00	4	0	3	4.1	2	0	0	0	5
Gerrit Cole	1	0	3.00	2	2	0	12	13	5	4	2	8
Clarke Schmidt	0	0	3.86	1	1	0	4.2	4	2	2	1	4
Carlos Rodón	0	1	9.82	1	1	0	3.2	7	4	4	0	7
Totals	**3**	**1**	**2.50**	**20**	**4**	**3**	**36**	**32**	**12**	**10**	**7**	**34**

KANSAS CITY	AVG	G	AB	R	H	2B	3B	HR	RBI	BB	SO	SB
Garrett Hampson	1.000	2	3	1	3	0	0	0	3	1	0	0
Tommy Pham	.455	4	11	2	5	0	0	0	2	0	2	1
Maikel Garcia	.375	4	16	0	6	0	0	0	1	0	3	1
Adam Frazier	.333	1	3	1	1	0	0	0	0	0	1	0
Michael Massey	.267	4	15	0	4	0	1	0	1	2	5	0
Kyle Isbel	.222	4	9	1	2	1	0	0	1	0	4	0
Yuli Gurriel	.214	4	14	4	3	1	0	0	0	2	0	0
Salvador Perez	.188	4	16	1	3	0	0	1	1	0	4	0
MJ Melendez	.154	4	13	1	2	0	0	1	2	0	1	0
Bobby Witt Jr.	.118	4	17	1	2	0	0	0	0	1	5	0
Vinnie Pasquantino	.063	4	16	0	1	1	0	0	1	1	7	0
Hunter Renfroe	.000	1	2	0	0	0	0	0	0	0	2	0
Totals	**.237**	**63**	**135**	**12**	**32**	**3**	**1**	**2**	**12**	**7**	**34**	**2**

KANSAS CITY	W	L	ERA	G	GS	SV	IP	H	R	ER	BB	SO
John Schreiber	0	0	0.00	4	0	0	2.2	0	0	0	4	2
Brady Singer	0	0	0.00	1	0	0	0.1	0	0	0	0	1
Cole Ragans	0	0	2.25	1	1	0	4	3	1	1	4	5
Kris Bubic	0	1	3.00	2	0	0	3	3	1	1	2	3
Angel Zerpa	1	0	3.00	4	0	0	3	2	1	1	3	3
Seth Lugo	0	0	3.60	1	1	0	5	2	2	2	4	2
Sam Long	0	0	3.86	3	0	0	2.1	1	1	1	3	1
Michael Lorenzen	0	1	3.86	2	0	0	2.1	3	1	1	1	3
Lucas Erceg	0	0	4.91	3	0	1	3.2	4	2	2	2	3
Michael Wacha	0	1	5.19	2	2	0	8.2	10	5	5	4	5
Totals	**1**	**3**	**3.60**	**23**	**4**	**1**	**35**	**28**	**14**	**14**	**27**	**28**

SCORE BY INNING

	1	2	3	4	5	6	7	8	9	R
NY YANKEES	1	0	4	0	3	2	1	0	2	13
KANSAS CITY	0	1	0	10	0	3	0	0	0	14

DETROIT TIGERS VS. CLEVELAND GUARDIANS

CLEVELAND	AVG	G	AB	R	H	2B	3B	HR	RBI	BB	SO	SB
Steven Kwan	.524	5	21	6	11	1	0	0	0	2	3	1
Brayan Rocchio	.375	5	16	1	6	2	0	0	1	2	3	0
Lane Thomas	.316	5	19	2	6	0	0	2	9	0	3	0
David Fry	.250	5	16	3	4	1	0	1	5	1	6	1
Will Brennan	.200	3	5	0	1	1	0	0	0	0	1	0
Josh Naylor	.200	5	20	1	4	1	0	0	1	0	3	0
José Ramírez	.188	5	16	3	3	1	0	1	3	3	3	0
Andrés Giménez	.167	5	18	2	3	1	0	0	0	0	7	1
Kyle Manzardo	.167	4	6	0	1	0	0	0	0	0	1	0
Austin Hedges	.000	4	5	0	0	0	0	0	0	0	3	0
Angel Martínez	.000	1	1	0	0	0	0	0	0	0	0	0
Bo Naylor	.000	5	11	0	0	0	0	0	0	0	3	0
Jhonkensy Noel	.000	5	13	1	0	0	0	0	0	1	5	0
Totals	**.234**	**88**	**167**	**19**	**39**	**8**	**0**	**4**	**19**	**9**	**41**	**31**

CLEVELAND	W	L	ERA	G	GS	SV	IP	H	R	ER	BB	SO
Matthew Boyd	0	0	0.00	2	2	0	6.2	5	0	0	3	10
Joey Cantillo	0	0	0.00	1	0	0	1	0	0	0	0	1
Erik Sabrowski	0	0	0.00	2	0	0	1.2	0	0	0	2	2
Cade Smith	1	0	1.42	5	0	0	6.1	2	1	1	1	12
Tanner Bibee	0	0	2.08	2	2	0	8.2	8	2	2	3	9
Hunter Gaddis	1	0	2.25	4	0	0	4	5	1	1	3	6
Tim Herrin	1	0	2.25	5	0	0	4	3	1	1	4	4
Eli Morgan	0	0	5.40	3	0	0	1.2	2	1	1	1	4
Alex Cobb	0	1	6.00	1	1	0	3	3	2	2	1	2
Emmanuel Clase	0	1	6.35	4	0	2	5.2	5	4	4	0	6
Andrew Walters	0	0	6.75	2	0	0	1.1	1	1	1	1	2
Totals	**3**	**2**	**2.66**	**31**	**5**	**2**	**44**	**34**	**13**	**13**	**19**	**58**

DETROIT	AVG	G	AB	R	H	2B	3B	HR	RBI	BB	SO	SB
Justyn-Henry Malloy	.600	5	5	1	3	1	0	0	0	1	0	0
Zach McKinstry	.500	3	4	1	2	1	0	1	1	1	0	0
Kerry Carpenter	.308	5	13	2	4	0	0	1	4	1	6	0
Riley Greene	.294	5	17	1	5	0	0	0	1	3	2	0
Parker Meadows	.294	5	17	1	5	2	0	0	0	3	3	2
Spencer Torkelson	.250	5	16	1	4	3	0	0	1	0	8	0
Jake Rogers	.214	5	14	2	3	1	0	0	1	3	5	0
Wenceel Pérez	.200	5	15	0	3	1	0	0	1	0	6	0
Colt Keith	.133	5	15	2	2	1	0	0	1	2	7	0
Matt Vierling	.100	5	20	0	2	1	0	0	1	2	10	0
Trey Sweeney	.067	5	15	2	1	0	0	0	1	2	9	0
Andy Ibáñez	.000	5	6	0	0	0	0	0	0	0	2	0
Jace Jung	.000	2	2	0	0	0	0	0	1	1	0	0
Totals	**.214**	**84**	**159**	**13**	**34**	**11**	**0**	**2**	**13**	**19**	**58**	**2**

DETROIT	W	L	ERA	G	GS	SV	IP	H	R	ER	BB	SO
Brant Hurter	1	0	0.00	1	0	0	3.1	5	0	0	1	1
Keider Montero	0	0	0.00	2	1	0	3	1	0	0	0	3
Reese Olson	0	0	2.00	2	1	0	9	8	2	2	2	8
Beau Brieske	0	1	2.45	4	0	1	3.2	1	1	1	0	5
Will Vest	1	0	2.70	4	0	0	3.1	3	1	1	0	4
Tarik Skubal	0	1	3.46	2	2	0	13	9	5	5	1	14
Sean Guenther	0	0	6.75	3	0	0	1.1	2	1	1	1	0
Jackson Jobe	0	0	6.75	1	0	0	1.1	3	1	1	0	0
Tyler Holton	0	1	12.46	4	1	1	4.1	6	6	6	1	5
Ty Madden	0	0	27.00	1	0	0	0.2	1	2	2	3	1
Totals	**2**	**3**	**3.98**	**24**	**5**	**2**	**43**	**39**	**19**	**19**	**9**	**41**

SCORE BY INNINGS

	1	2	3	4	5	6	7	8	9	R
DETROIT	1	1	1	0	2	3	1	0	4	13
CLEVELAND	6	0	0	0	6	2	3	1	1	19

AMERICAN LEAGUE CHAMPIONSHIP SERIES

NEW YORK YANKEES VS. CLEVELAND GUARDIANS

NEW YORK	AVG	G	AB	R	H	2B	3B	HR	RBI	BB	SO	SB
Jose Trevino	.500	2	2	0	1	0	0	0	1	0	0	0
Anthony Rizzo	.429	5	14	1	6	1	0	0	0	2	3	0
Juan Soto	.368	5	19	5	7	1	0	3	6	4	3	0
Gleyber Torres	.364	5	22	5	8	1	0	0	2	2	2	0
Anthony Volpe	.353	5	17	5	6	1	0	0	0	4	5	1
Giancarlo Stanton	.222	5	18	5	4	0	0	4	7	3	5	0
Alex Verdugo	.176	5	17	1	3	2	0	0	2	3	4	0
Aaron Judge	.167	5	18	4	3	0	0	2	6	2	8	0
Jazz Chisholm Jr.	.158	5	19	0	3	1	0	0	0	1	8	1
Austin Wells	.059	5	17	1	1	0	0	1	1	1	9	0
Jon Berti	.000	2	4	1	0	0	0	0	0	0	2	0
Oswaldo Cabrera	.000	3	1	0	0	0	0	0	0	0	0	0
Totals	**.250**	**81**	**168**	**29**	**42**	**7**	**0**	**10**	**25**	**22**	**49**	**2**

NEW YORK	W	L	ERA	G	GS	SV	IP	H	R	ER	BB	SO
Tommy Kahnle	0	0	0.00	3	0	1	4	3	0	0	4	3
Tim Mayza	0	0	0.00	1	0	0	0.2	1	0	0	2	0
Tim Hill	0	0	1.93	5	0	0	4.2	5	1	1	1	2
Carlos Rodón	1	0	2.53	2	2	0	10.2	8	3	3	1	15
Mark Leiter Jr.	1	0	3.86	2	0	0	2.1	2	1	1	3	2
Clarke Schmidt	0	0	3.86	1	1	0	4.2	5	2	2	2	2
Gerrit Cole	0	0	4.15	1	1	0	4.1	6	2	2	4	4
Luis Gil	0	0	4.50	1	1	0	4	3	2	2	3	3
Luke Weaver	1	0	4.50	4	0	1	6	5	3	3	1	7
Jake Cousins	0	0	7.71	2	0	0	2.1	2	2	2	2	6
Clay Holmes	1	1	10.13	4	0	0	2.2	4	3	3	2	3
Ian Hamilton	0	0	27.00	1	0	0	0.1	0	1	1	1	0
Totals	**4**	**1**	**3.86**	**27**	**5**	**2**	**46.2**	**44**	**20**	**20**	**26**	**47**

CLEVELAND	AVG	G	AB	R	H	2B	3B	HR	RBI	BB	SO	SB
Kyle Manzardo	.385	5	13	2	5	1	0	1	2	0	3	0
Bo Naylor	.364	5	11	2	4	2	0	0	1	0	3	0
David Fry	.333	5	12	1	4	0	0	1	3	1	5	0
Brayan Rocchio	.294	5	17	3	5	0	0	1	1	3	4	0
Andrés Giménez	.263	5	19	2	5	1	0	0	1	2	6	1
José Ramírez	.263	5	19	2	5	2	0	1	3	4	2	2
Josh Naylor	.250	5	20	1	5	1	0	0	4	2	7	0
Jhonkensy Noel	.250	4	8	1	2	0	0	1	2	1	3	0
Steven Kwan	.238	5	21	4	5	0	0	0	2	4	1	1
Will Brennan	.143	4	7	0	1	1	0	0	1	0	3	0
Austin Hedges	.143	4	7	0	1	1	0	0	0	2	2	0
Lane Thomas	.118	5	17	2	2	1	0	0	0	7	6	1
Daniel Schneemann	.000	3	7	0	0	0	0	0	0	0	2	0
Totals	**.247**	**94**	**178**	**20**	**44**	**10**	**0**	**5**	**20**	**26**	**47**	**5**

CLEVELAND	W	L	ERA	G	GS	SV	IP	H	R	ER	BB	SO
Pedro Avila	1	0	0.00	3	0	0	4	0	0	0	2	3
Tim Herrin	0	0	0.00	4	0	0	4.1	3	0	0	1	2
Ben Lively	0	0	0.00	1	0	0	1.1	1	0	0	1	2
Eli Morgan	0	0	0.00	3	0	0	2.1	0	1	0	1	2
Andrew Walters	0	0	0.00	2	0	0	1.2	0	0	0	1	2
Matthew Boyd	0	0	1.80	1	1	0	5	2	1	1	3	4
Erik Sabrowski	0	0	2.45	3	0	0	3.2	4	2	1	1	6
Tanner Bibee	0	1	5.14	2	2	0	7	11	5	4	1	7
Joey Cantillo	0	0	6.75	2	0	0	1.1	0	1	1	4	2
Cade Smith	0	0	7.36	4	0	0	3.2	3	3	3	1	4
Hunter Gaddis	0	1	8.10	4	0	0	3.1	3	6	3	2	6
Alex Cobb	0	1	10.13	1	1	0	2.2	5	3	3	3	3
Gavin Williams	0	0	11.57	1	1	0	2.1	3	3	3	0	4
Emmanuel Clase	0	1	15.43	3	0	0	2.1	7	4	4	1	2
Totals	**1**	**4**	**4.60**	**34**	**5**	**0**	**45**	**42**	**29**	**23**	**22**	**49**

SCORE BY INNINGS

	1	2	3	4	5	6	7	8	9	10	R
CLEVELAND	1	1	3	0	3	2	3	2	3	2	20
NY YANKEES	3	4	3	1	0	6	3	3	3	3	29

NATIONAL LEAGUE WILD CARD SERIES

SAN DIEGO PADRES VS. ATLANTA BRAVES

SAN DIEGO	AVG	G	AB	R	H	2B	3B	HR	RBI	BB	SO	SB
Fernando Tatis Jr.	.667	2	6	2	4	0	0	1	2	2	0	0
Jackson Merrill	.429	2	7	0	3	1	1	0	2	0	1	0
Kyle Higashioka	.400	2	5	2	2	0	0	2	3	1	0	0
Luis Arráez	.333	2	9	2	3	0	0	0	0	0	0	0
Manny Machado	.143	2	7	1	1	1	0	0	2	0	3	0
Jurickson Profar	.143	2	7	1	1	0	0	0	0	0	1	0
Donovan Solano	.143	2	7	0	1	0	0	0	0	0	2	0
Xander Bogaerts	.000	2	7	0	0	0	0	0	0	0	0	0
Jake Cronenworth	.000	2	6	1	0	0	0	0	0	0	4	0
Totals	**.246**	**27**	**61**	**9**	**15**	**2**	**1**	**3**	**9**	**3**	**11**	**0**

WASHINGTON	W	L	ERA	G	GS	SV	IP	H	R	ER	BB	SO
Jeremiah Estrada	0	0	0.00	1	0	0	0.2	2	0	0	0	0
Michael King	1	0	0.00	1	1	0	7	5	0	0	0	12
Tanner Scott	0	0	0.00	1	0	0	1.1	0	0	0	1	2
Robert Suarez	0	0	0.00	2	0	1	2	1	0	0	0	0
Joe Musgrove	0	0	2.45	1	1	0	3.2	1	1	1	0	4
Bryan Hoeing	1	0	6.75	1	0	0	1.1	1	1	1	0	1
Jason Adam	0	0	9.00	2	0	0	2	3	2	2	0	4
Totals	**2**	**0**	**2.00**	**9**	**2**	**1**	**18**	**13**	**4**	**4**	**1**	**23**

ATLANTA	AVG	G	AB	R	H	2B	3B	HR	RBI	BB	SO	SB
Michael Harris II	.625	2	8	2	5	1	0	1	2	0	1	0
Marcell Ozuna	.286	2	7	0	2	0	0	0	1	0	4	0
Jorge Soler	.286	2	7	1	2	0	0	1	1	1	2	0
Travis d'Arnaud	.200	2	5	0	1	1	0	0	0	0	1	0
Orlando Arcia	.167	2	6	1	1	0	0	0	0	0	2	0
Ozzie Albies	.125	2	8	0	1	0	0	0	0	0	4	1
Matt Olson	.125	2	8	0	1	0	0	0	0	0	1	0
Ramón Laureano	.000	2	8	0	0	0	0	0	0	0	4	0
Sean Murphy	.000	1	3	0	0	0	0	0	0	0	2	0
Gio Urshela	.000	2	6	0	0	0	0	0	0	0	2	0
Totals	**.197**	**29**	**66**	**4**	**13**	**2**	**0**	**2**	**4**	**1**	**23**	**1**

ATLANTA	W	L	ERA	G	GS	SV	IP	H	R	ER	BB	SO
Aaron Bummer	0	0	0.00	1	0	0	2.2	0	0	0	1	1
Jesse Chavez	0	0	0.00	1	0	0	2	0	0	0	0	1
Daysbel Hernández	0	0	0.00	1	0	0	2.1	1	0	0	1	3
Joe Jiménez	0	0	0.00	1	0	0	1	0	0	0	1	1
Pierce Johnson	0	0	0.00	1	0	0	1	0	0	0	0	0
Dylan Lee	0	0	0.00	1	0	0	1.2	1	0	0	0	0
Luke Jackson	0	0	4.50	1	0	0	2	1	1	1	0	2
AJ Smith-Shawver	0	1	20.25	1	1	0	1.1	4	3	3	0	1
Max Fried	0	1	22.50	1	1	0	2	8	5	5	0	2
Totals	**0**	**2**	**5.06**	**9**	**2**	**0**	**16**	**15**	**9**	**9**	**3**	**11**

SCORE BY INNINGS

ATLANTA	1	0	0	0	1	0	0	2	0	4
SAN DIEGO	2	6	0	0	0	0	0	1	0	9

NEW YORK METS VS. MILWAUKEE BREWERS

NY METS	AVG	G	AB	R	H	2B	3B	HR	RBI	BB	SO	SB
Starling Marte	.333	3	9	1	3	0	0	0	2	2	1	1
Brandon Nimmo	.250	3	12	2	3	0	0	0	1	0	2	0
Mark Vientos	.250	3	12	2	3	0	0	0	2	0	5	0
Pete Alonso	.222	3	9	2	2	0	0	1	3	3	2	0
Francisco Lindor	.222	3	9	2	2	1	0	0	1	4	1	0
J.D. Martinez	.200	2	5	0	1	0	0	0	2	1	2	0
Jesse Winker	.200	3	5	2	1	0	1	0	2	0	1	1
Tyrone Taylor	.167	3	12	2	2	1	0	0	0	0	4	0
Jose Iglesias	.143	3	14	2	2	0	0	0	1	0	3	0
Francisco Alvarez	.091	3	11	0	1	0	0	0	1	0	3	0
Totals	**.204**	**46**	**98**	**15**	**20**	**2**	**1**	**1**	**15**	**10**	**24**	**2**

NY METS	W	L	ERA	G	GS	SV	IP	H	R	ER	BB	SO
Edwin Díaz	1	0	0.00	1	0	0	1.2	0	0	0	2	3
Reed Garrett	1	0	0.00	0	0	0	1	1	0	0	0	1
David Peterson	1	0	0.00	0	0	1	1	1	0	0	0	1
Jose Quintana	1	1	0.00	0	0	0	6	4	0	0	1	5
Ryne Stanek	2	0	0.00	0	0	0	2	0	0	0	0	1
Sean Manaea	1	1	3.60	0	0	0	5	6	2	2	0	4
Luis Severino	1	1	4.50	1	0	0	6	8	4	3	2	3
José Buttó	2	0	7.71	0	0	0	2.1	2	2	2	0	3
Phil Maton	1	0	27.00	0	1	0	1	4	3	3	0	0
Totals	**11**	**3**	**3.46**	**2**	**1**	**1**	**26**	**26**	**11**	**10**	**5**	**21**

MILWAUKEE	AVG	G	AB	R	H	2B	3B	HR	RBI	BB	SO	SB
Blake Perkins	.500	2	6	0	3	0	0	0	1	1	1	1
Jackson Chourio	.455	3	11	3	5	0	0	2	3	1	1	1
Brice Turang	.455	3	11	3	5	3	0	0	0	1	1	2
Sal Frelick	.364	3	11	2	4	1	0	1	1	0	1	0
Jake Bauers	.333	2	6	1	2	0	0	1	1	0	3	0
Gary Sánchez	.286	2	7	0	2	1	0	0	0	0	2	0
Garrett Mitchell	.250	2	4	1	1	0	0	1	2	1	1	0
Willy Adames	.182	3	11	1	2	0	0	0	0	1	3	1
William Contreras	.167	3	12	0	2	0	0	0	2	0	3	0
Rhys Hoskins	.000	3	9	0	0	0	0	0	1	0	3	0
Joey Ortiz	.000	3	11	0	0	0	0	0	0	0	2	0
Totals	**.263**	**46**	**99**	**11**	**26**	**5**	**0**	**5**	**11**	**5**	**21**	**5**

MILWAUKEE	W	L	ERA	G	GS	SV	IP	H	R	ER	BB	SO
Aaron Civale	1	0	0.00	0	0	0	3	0	0	0	1	2
Jared Koenig	1	0	0.00	0	0	0	0.2	1	0	0	0	0
Nick Mears	2	0	0.00	0	0	0	2.1	0	0	0	0	3
Trevor Megill	2	0	0.00	0	0	0	2.1	0	0	0	0	4
Tobias Myers	1	1	0.00	0	0	0	5	2	0	0	0	5
Joe Ross	2	0	0.00	1	0	0	1.2	0	0	0	1	0
Frankie Montas	1	1	2.45	0	0	0	3.2	6	3	1	1	3
Freddy Peralta	2	1	5.40	0	0	0	5	2	3	3	1	5
Joel Payamps	2	0	16.20	0	1	0	1.2	3	3	3	3	1
Devin Williams	2	0	21.60	0	1	1	1.2	3	4	4	1	1
Aaron Ashby	1	0	inf	0	0	0	0	3	2	2	2	0
Totals	**17**	**3**	**4.33**	**1**	**2**	**1**	**27**	**20**	**15**	**13**	**10**	**24**

SCORE BY INNINGS

NY METS	1	5	0	0	5	0	0	0	4	15
MILWAUKEE	3	0	0	2	1	0	2	3	0	11

NATIONAL LEAGUE DIVISION SERIES

SAN DIEGO PADRES VS. LOS ANGELES DODGERS

LA DODGERS	AVG	G	AB	R	H	2B	3B	HR	RBI	BB	SO	SB
Enrique Hernández	.333	3	9	2	3	0	0	1	1	0	2	0
Teoscar Hernández	.333	5	18	3	6	0	0	2	7	2	4	1
Freddie Freeman	.286	4	14	0	4	0	0	0	0	0	2	1
Gavin Lux	.278	5	18	3	5	0	0	1	3	1	2	0
Miguel Rojas	.250	3	8	0	2	0	0	0	0	0	0	0
Tommy Edman	.235	5	17	1	4	0	0	0	1	0	2	2
Mookie Betts	.222	5	18	4	4	0	0	2	3	3	3	0
Shohei Ohtani	.200	5	20	3	4	0	0	1	4	2	10	0
Max Muncy	.167	5	18	3	3	1	0	1	1	1	6	0
Will Smith	.125	5	16	4	2	0	0	1	2	4	2	1
Andy Pages	.000	3	2	1	0	0	0	0	0	0	1	0
Chris Taylor	.000	4	4	0	0	0	0	0	0	0	4	0
Totals	**.228**	**81**	**162**	**24**	**37**	**1**	**0**	**9**	**22**	**13**	**38**	**5**

WASHINGTON	W	L	ERA	G	GS	SV	IP	H	R	ER	BB	SO
Anthony Banda	0	0	0.00	3	0	0	3	2	0	0	1	4
Daniel Hudson	0	0	0.00	3	0	0	2.1	1	0	0	0	1
Landon Knack	0	0	0.00	1	0	0	1	1	0	0	0	1
Michael Kopech	0	0	0.00	4	0	0	3.1	1	0	0	2	5
Evan Phillips	1	0	0.00	3	0	0	4.1	0	0	0	0	4
Blake Treinen	0	0	0.00	3	0	2	3.2	3	0	0	2	4
Alex Vesia	0	0	0.00	3	0	0	3	1	0	0	1	4
Ryan Brasier	1	0	4.91	3	1	0	3.2	3	2	2	0	2
Yoshinobu Yamamoto	1	0	5.63	2	2	0	8	7	5	5	3	3
Jack Flaherty	0	1	6.75	1	1	0	5.1	5	4	4	1	2
Walker Buehler	0	1	10.80	1	1	0	5	7	6	6	1	0
Michael Grove	0	0	27.00	1	0	0	0.1	1	1	1	0	1
Edgardo Henriquez	0	0	27.00	1	0	0	1	4	3	3	0	1
Totals	**3**	**2**	**4.30**	**29**	**5**	**2**	**44**	**36**	**21**	**21**	**11**	**32**

SAN DIEGO	AVG	G	AB	R	H	2B	3B	HR	RBI	BB	SO	SB
Fernando Tatis Jr.	.350	5	20	6	7	3	0	3	5	1	2	0
David Peralta	.308	5	13	2	4	1	0	1	4	0	1	0
Xander Bogaerts	.235	5	17	2	4	1	0	1	4	2	3	0
Jurickson Profar	.222	5	18	0	4	0	0	0	1	3	3	0
Kyle Higashioka	.214	5	14	1	3	1	0	1	2	0	3	0
Manny Machado	.190	5	21	3	4	0	0	1	2	0	6	0
Jake Cronenworth	.188	5	16	1	3	0	1	0	0	2	5	0
Luis Arráez	.182	5	22	2	4	0	0	0	0	0	1	0
Jackson Merrill	.176	5	17	4	3	0	0	1	3	3	5	0
Elias Díaz	.000	1	1	0	0	0	0	0	0	0	1	0
Donovan Solano	.000	3	7	0	0	0	0	0	0	0	2	0
Totals	**.217**	**76**	**166**	**21**	**36**	**6**	**1**	**8**	**21**	**11**	**32**	**0**

SAN DIEGO	W	L	ERA	G	GS	SV	IP	H	R	ER	BB	SO
Jason Adam	0	0	0.00	3	0	0	3.1	1	0	0	0	2

	W	L	ERA	G	GS	SV	IP	H	R	ER	BB	SO
Jeremiah Estrada	0	0	0.00	3	0	0	3.2	3	1	0	1	5
Yuki Matsui	0	0	0.00	1	0	0	1	1	0	0	0	1
Tanner Scott	0	0	0.00	4	0	0	3	2	0	0	1	5
Robert Suarez	0	0	0.00	1	0	1	1.1	0	0	0	0	2
Yu Darvish	1	1	1.98	2	2	0	13.2	6	3	3	3	7
Adrián Morejón	0	1	3.86	2	0	0	2.1	2	1	1	2	1
Alek Jacob	0	0	4.50	2	0	0	2	1	3	1	1	2
Wandy Peralta	0	0	6.75	1	0	0	1.1	2	1	1	0	3
Michael King	1	0	9.00	1	1	0	5	5	5	5	1	3
Bryan Hoeing	0	0	13.50	2	0	0	1.1	4	2	2	1	1
Dylan Cease	0	1	14.40	2	2	0	5	10	8	8	3	6
Totals	**2**	**3**	**4.40**	**24**	**5**	**1**	**43**	**37**	**24**	**21**	**13**	**38**

SCORE BY INNINGS

SAN DIEGO	**4**	**8**	**2**	**0**	**0**	**1**	**0**	**3**	**3**	**21**
LA DODGERS	**2**	**7**	**6**	**3**	**1**	**0**	**4**	**0**	**1**	**24**

NEW YORK METS VS. PHILADELPHIA PHILLIES

NY METS	AVG	G	AB	R	H	2B	3B	HR	RBI	BB	SO	SB
Mark Vientos	.563	4	16	3	9	2	0	2	5	2	5	0
J.D. Martinez	.333	4	9	1	3	0	0	0	1	1	2	0
Pete Alonso	.308	4	13	3	4	1	0	2	3	4	6	1
Brandon Nimmo	.286	4	14	4	4	0	0	1	3	4	3	0
Francisco Lindor	.278	4	18	4	5	2	0	1	5	2	6	0
Jose Iglesias	.267	4	15	1	4	0	0	0	2	1	4	0
Jesse Winker	.250	2	4	1	1	0	0	1	1	2	0	0
Francisco Alvarez	.200	4	15	1	3	0	0	0	0	0	6	0
Harrison Bader	.167	4	6	3	1	0	0	0	0	0	1	2
Starling Marte	.091	4	11	1	1	0	0	0	3	1	5	0
Tyrone Taylor	.091	4	11	1	1	0	0	0	0	1	4	0
Luisangel Acuña	.000	3	2	0	0	0	0	0	0	0	2	0
Totals	**.269**	**62**	**134**	**23**	**36**	**5**	**0**	**7**	**23**	**18**	**44**	**3**

NY METS	W	L	ERA	G	GS	SV	IP	H	R	ER	BB	SO
José Buttó	0	0	0.00	1	0	0	0.2	1	0	0	0	0
Reed Garrett	1	0	0.00	2	0	0	2.2	0	0	0	1	3
David Peterson	1	0	0.00	2	0	0	5.1	3	0	0	3	2
Jose Quintana	0	0	0.00	1	1	0	5	2	1	0	2	6
Sean Manaea	1	0	1.29	1	1	0	7	3	1	1	2	6
Ryne Stanek	0	0	3.86	2	0	0	2.1	2	1	1	1	2
Kodai Senga	0	0	4.50	1	1	0	2	1	1	1	1	3
Luis Severino	0	0	4.50	1	1	0	6	6	3	3	0	7
Phil Maton	0	0	5.40	2	0	0	1.2	3	1	1	1	3
Tylor Megill	0	1	6.75	1	0	0	1.1	1	1	1	2	2
Edwin Díaz	0	0	16.20	2	0	1	1.2	2	3	3	3	4
Totals	**3**	**1**	**2.78**	**16**	**4**	**1**	**35.2**	**24**	**12**	**11**	**16**	**38**

PHILADELPHIA	AVG	G	AB	R	H	2B	3B	HR	RBI	BB	SO	SB
Nick Castellanos	.412	4	17	2	7	1	0	1	3	0	3	0
Kody Clemens	.400	4	5	0	2	1	0	0	1	0	2	0
Bryce Harper	.333	4	12	3	4	2	0	1	3	5	5	0
Edmundo Sosa	.250	2	4	1	1	0	0	0	0	0	2	0
Johan Rojas	.200	3	5	0	1	0	0	0	0	1	1	1
Trea Turner	.200	4	15	2	3	0	0	0	0	2	5	2
Bryson Stott	.182	4	11	1	2	0	1	0	2	2	4	0
Kyle Schwarber	.125	4	16	2	2	0	0	1	1	2	6	0
Alec Bohm	.077	4	13	0	1	0	0	0	0	1	0	0
Brandon Marsh	.077	4	13	0	1	0	0	0	0	0	3	0
Austin Hays	.000	2	4	0	0	0	0	0	0	0	3	0
J.T. Realmuto	.000	4	11	1	0	0	0	0	1	3	4	0
Weston Wilson	.000	2	3	0	0	0	0	0	0	0	0	0
Totals	**.186**	**66**	**129**	**12**	**24**	**4**	**1**	**3**	**11**	**16**	**38**	**3**

PHILADELPHIA	W	L	ERA	G	GS	SV	IP	H	R	ER	BB	SO
Ranger Suárez	0	0	0.00	1	1	0	4.1	5	0	0	4	8
Zack Wheeler	0	0	0.00	1	1	0	7	1	0	0	4	9
Orion Kerkering	0	0	2.45	4	0	0	3.2	4	1	1	2	5
Carlos Estévez	0	0	3.38	3	0	0	2.2	2	2	1	1	4
Cristopher Sánchez	0	0	3.60	1	1	0	5	5	2	2	1	5
José Ruiz	0	0	6.75	2	0	0	1.1	4	1	1	0	0
Aaron Nola	0	1	7.20	1	1	0	5	5	4	4	2	8
Tanner Banks	0	0	9.00	1	0	0	1	2	1	1	0	2
Matt Strahm	0	0	18.00	3	0	0	2	4	4	4	0	1
José Alvarado	0	0	27.00	1	0	0	0.2	1	2	2	2	1
Jeff Hoffman	1	2	40.50	3	0	0	1.1	3	6	6	2	1
Totals	**1**	**3**	**5.82**	**21**	**4**	**0**	**34**	**36**	**23**	**22**	**18**	**44**

SCORE BY INNINGS

PHILADELPHIA	**1**	**0**	**0**	**1**	**0**	**3**	**0**	**5**	**2**	**12**
NY METS	**0**	**1**	**2**	**1**	**0**	**7**	**3**	**6**	**3**	**23**

NATIONAL LEAGUE CHAMPIONSHIP SERIES

LOS ANGELES DODGERS VS. NEW YORK METS

LA DODGERS	AVG	G	AB	R	H	2B	3B	HR	RBI	BB	SO	SB
Tommy Edman	.407	6	27	5	11	3	0	1	11	0	4	1
Chris Taylor	.375	4	8	2	3	0	0	0	0	2	1	1
Shohei Ohtani	.364	6	22	9	8	0	0	2	6	9	7	0
Mookie Betts	.346	6	26	6	9	4	0	2	9	5	5	2
Max Muncy	.333	6	15	5	5	0	0	2	4	11	4	2
Enrique Hernández	.292	6	24	6	7	0	0	1	4	3	6	0
Andy Pages	.235	5	17	2	4	0	0	2	4	0	5	0
Will Smith	.182	6	22	3	4	0	0	1	4	3	4	0
Freddie Freeman	.167	4	18	1	3	0	0	0	1	1	4	0
Teoscar Hernández	.091	6	22	4	2	0	0	0	1	7	9	0
Kevin Kiermaier	.000	4	2	2	0	0	0	0	0	0	1	0
Gavin Lux	.000	3	6	1	0	0	0	0	0	1	1	0
Totals	**.268**	**90**	**209**	**46**	**56**	**7**	**0**	**11**	**44**	**42**	**51**	**6**

LA DODGERS	W	L	ERA	G	GS	SV	IP	H	R	ER	BB	SO
Walker Buehler	0	0	0.00	1	1	0	4	3	0	0	2	6
Ben Casparius	1	0	0.00	3	0	0	4.1	2	0	0	2	4
Evan Phillips	1	0	0.00	2	0	0	2.1	3	0	0	3	2
Blake Treinen	0	0	2.08	3	0	1	4.1	4	1	1	0	7
Edgardo Henriquez	0	0	2.25	2	0	0	4	4	1	1	3	2
Anthony Banda	0	0	3.38	3	0	0	2.2	2	1	1	1	3
Yoshinobu Yamamoto	0	0	4.15	1	1	0	4.1	4	2	2	1	8
Daniel Hudson	0	0	4.50	2	0	0	2	3	1	1	1	2
Michael Kopech	1	0	4.50	2	1	0	2	1	1	1	2	2
Brent Honeywell Jr.	0	0	4.70	2	0	0	7.2	8	4	4	2	2
Ryan Brasier	0	1	5.40	3	1	0	3.1	4	2	2	2	2
Jack Flaherty	1	1	7.20	2	2	0	10	10	8	8	6	6
Landon Knack	0	0	22.50	1	0	0	2	5	5	5	3	2
Totals	**4**	**2**	**4.42**	**27**	**6**	**1**	**53**	**53**	**26**	**26**	**28**	**48**

NY METS	AVG	G	AB	R	H	2B	3B	HR	RBI	BB	SO	SB
Francisco Alvarez	.412	6	17	3	7	1	0	0	2	2	4	0
Jesse Winker	.385	5	13	4	5	0	1	0	1	5	3	0
Starling Marte	.333	6	27	2	9	4	0	0	4	0	5	0
Francisco Lindor	.292	6	24	5	7	0	1	1	2	4	6	0
Pete Alonso	.273	6	22	5	6	0	0	1	4	5	7	1
Jose Iglesias	.267	5	15	0	4	0	0	0	0	1	2	0
Mark Vientos	.222	6	27	3	6	0	0	3	7	1	9	0
Tyrone Taylor	.214	6	14	3	3	1	0	0	1	3	0	0
Jeff McNeil	.182	5	11	0	2	0	0	0	3	0	1	0
Brandon Nimmo	.167	6	24	1	4	0	0	0	2	3	6	0
Luisangel Acuña	.000	3	1	0	0	0	0	0	0	0	0	0
Harrison Bader	.000	5	3	0	0	0	0	0	0	0	2	0
J.D. Martinez	.000	2	4	0	0	0	0	0	0	4	3	0
Luis Torrens	.000	1	1	0	0	0	0	0	0	0	0	0
Totals	**.261**	**95**	**203**	**26**	**53**	**6**	**2**	**5**	**26**	**28**	**48**	**1**

LOS ANGELES	W	L	ERA	G	GS	SV	IP	H	R	ER	BB	SO
Edwin Díaz	0	0	0.00	3	0	1	5.1	2	0	0	2	6
Luis Severino	0	1	0.00	1	1	0	4.2	3	0	2	4	3
Phil Maton	0	0	4.91	3	0	0	3.2	4	2	2	3	3
Ryne Stanek	1	0	4.91	3	0	0	3.2	3	2	2	2	5
David Peterson	0	0	6.00	2	1	0	6	10	4	5	5	5
José Buttó	0	0	6.75	3	0	0	4	3	3	4	3	5
Danny Young	0	0	7.36	2	0	0	3.2	4	3	3	3	3
Sean Manaea	1	1	9.00	2	2	0	7	8	7	8	6	9
Reed Garrett	0	0	9.64	4	0	0	4.2	4	5	5	1	6
Tylor Megill	0	0	12.00	1	0	0	3	5	4	4	3	3
Jose Quintana	0	1	13.50	1	1	0	3.1	5	5	5	4	2
Kodai Senga	0	1	18.00	2	1	0	3	5	6	6	6	1
Totals	**2**	**4**	**7.10**	**27**	**6**	**1**	**52**	**56**	**41**	**46**	**42**	**51**

SCORE BY INNINGS

LA DODGERS	**5**	**4**	**6**	**6**	**4**	**8**	**0**	**12**	**1**	**46**
NY METS	**6**	**5**	**6**	**4**	**0**	**1**	**1**	**1**	**2**	**26**

ORGANIZATION STATISTICS

Arizona Diamondbacks

SEASON SYNOPSIS: A Cinderella run to the 2023 National League pennant raised expectations for 2024, and the D-backs scored 44 more runs than any team in baseball. But a slow 25-32 start set them back, as did inconsistent starting pitching and a late-season bullpen slide. Arizona lost five of its last seven to finish at 89-73 and out of a wild card by virtue of losing head-to-head tiebreakers to the Braves and Mets.

HIGH POINT: Arizona broke out in the first half of August, winning 11 of its first 13 games, including series wins against eventual division winners Cleveland and Philadelphia. Rookie Adrian Del Castillo walked off the Phillies in a 3-2 win on Aug. 9, and Arizona won blowouts the next two games, homering four times on the 10th in an 11-1 win, then pounding 18 hits in a 12-5 series finale. Outfielder Corbin Carroll, who had a disastrous start to the season, continued to warm up with homers in each of the blowouts.

LOW POINT: The D-backs lost five of their last seven to squander a three-game wild card advantage over the Braves, a streak that started when they blew an 8-0 lead on Sept. 22 in Milwaukee. Jordan Montgomery couldn't make it through the fifth inning, and the Brewers scored seven runs in the last three frames to pull out a 10-9 victory. Then the Arizona offense fell silent, with two shutouts in the final six games.

NOTABLE ROOKIES: Dominican righthander Justin Martinez emerged as the club's top reliever and hardest thrower, using a 100 mph sinker to power a 5-6, 2.48 season with eight saves. Righty Slade Cecconi was part of a rotating crew at the back of the rotation, going 2-7, 6.66. Righty Bryce Jarvis, the club's 2020 first-round pick, posted a 3.19 ERA in 59 innings. Blaze Alexander was a credible fill-in at second base, third and shortstop and posted a .664 OPS.

KEY TRANSACTIONS: After using bullpen games liberally in the 2023 postseason, Arizona thought it boosted its rotation by signing free agent lefties Eduardo Rodriguez (four years/$80 million) and Montgomery (one year/$25 million). A shoulder strain sidelined Rodriguez until August and limited him to 10 starts. Montgomery signed in late March, never got into a groove and wound up 8-7, 6.23. Club owner Ken Kendrick took the blame for the Montgomery deal in a postseason radio interview, saying it was his call and labeling it a "horrible decision" on "The Burns & Gumbo Show."

OPENING DAY PAYROLL: $140,825,700 (17th)

PLAYERS OF THE YEAR

MAJOR LEAGUE

Ketel Marte
2B
.292/.372/.560
36 HR
93 R, 95 RBIs

MINOR LEAGUE

Adrian Del Castillo
C
(AAA)
.312/.399/.603
26 HR, 36 2B, 75 RBIs

ORGANIZATION LEADERS

Batting		*Qualifiers
MAJORS		
* AVG	Ketel Marte	.292
* OPS	Ketel Marte	.932
HR	Ketel Marte	36
RBI	Eugenio Suarez	101
MINORS		
* AVG	Demetrio Crisantes, Visalia/ACL D-backs	.341
* OBP	Demetrio Crisantes, Visalia/ACL D-backs	.429
* SLG	Adrian Del Castillo, Reno	.603
* OPS	Adrian Del Castillo, Reno	1.002
R	Adrian Del Castillo, Reno	90
H	Tim Tawa, Reno/Amarillo	153
TB	Tim Tawa, Reno/Amarillo	285
2B	Albert Almora, Reno	45
3B	Jansel Luis, Visalia	10
HR	Tim Tawa, Reno/Amarillo	31
RBI	Kyle Garlick, Reno	105
BB	Druw Jones, Visalia	85
SO	Kyle Garlick, Reno	171
SB	Anderdson Rojas, Visalia	34

Pitching		#Qualifiers
MAJORS		
W	Zac Gallen	14
# ERA	Zac Gallen	3.65
SO	Brandon Pfaadt	185
SV	Paul Sewald	16
MINORS		
W	Tommy Henry, Reno	10
L	Dylan File, Reno/Amarillo	10
L	Spencer Giesting, Hillsboro/Amarillo	10
# ERA	Spencer Giesting, Hillsboro/Amarillo	3.31
G	Austin Pope, Reno	55
GS	Billy Corcoran, Hillsboro/Amarillo	25
GS	Spencer Giesting, Hillsboro/Amarillo	25
SV	Alfred Morillo, Hillsboro	13
IP	Spencer Giesting, Hillsboro/Amarillo	141
BB	Denny Larrondo, Visalia	68
SO	Spencer Giesting, Hillsboro/Amarillo	154
# AVG	Roman Angelo, Visalia/Hillsboro	.219

2024 PERFORMANCE

General Manager: Mike Hazen. **Farm Director:** Shaun Larkin. **Scouting Director:** Ian Rebhan.

Class	Team	League	W	L	PCT	Finish	Manager
Majors	Arizona Diamondbacks	National	89	73	.549	5 (15)	Torey Lovullo
Triple-A	Reno Aces	Pacific Coast	79	70	.530	4 (10)	Blake Lalli
Double-A	Amarillo Sod Poodles	Texas	58	79	.423	8 (10)	Tim Bogar
High-A	Hillsboro Hops	Northwest	69	62	.527	3 (6)	Javier Colina
Low-A	Visalia Rawhide	California	67	64	.511	5 (8)	Dee Garner
Rookie	ACL D-backs	Arizona Complex	39	21	.650	2 (15)	Gift Ngoepe
Rookie	DSL Arizona Black	Dominican	12	43	.218	51 (51)	Luis Alen
Rookie	DSL Arizona Red	Dominican	36	20	.643	10 (51)	Izzy Alcantara
Overall 2024 Minor League Record			**360**	**359**	**.501**	**15th (30)**	

ORGANIZATION STATISTICS

ARIZONA DIAMONDBACKS

NATIONAL LEAGUE

Batting	B-T	Ht.	Wt.	DOB	AVG	OBP	SLG	G	PA	AB	R	H	2B	3B	HR	RBI	BB	HBP	SH	SF	SO	SB	CS	BB%	SO%
Alexander, Blaze	R-R	5-11	160	6-11-99	.247	.321	.343	61	185	166	19	41	7	0	3	21	15	3	1	0	49	3	1	8.11	26.49
Barnhart, Tucker	L-R	5-11	192	1-7-91	.173	.287	.210	31	96	81	13	14	3	0	0	6	13	0	2	0	31	1	0	13.54	32.29
Barrosa, Jorge	B-L	5-5	165	2-17-01	.176	.176	.294	8	18	17	3	3	2	0	0	1	0	0	1	0	2	1	0	0.00	11.11
Bell, Josh	B-R	6-4	261	8-14-92	.279	.361	.436	41	162	140	24	39	5	1	5	22	17	1	0	0	32	0	1	10.49	19.75
Carroll, Corbin	L-L	5-10	165	8-21-00	.231	.322	.428	158	684	589	121	136	22	14	22	74	73	10	3	9	130	35	8	10.67	19.01
Del Castillo, Adrian	L-R	5-9	208	9-27-99	.313	.368	.525	25	87	80	12	25	5	0	4	19	7	0	0	0	28	1	1	8.05	32.18
Grichuk, Randal	R-R	6-2	216	8-13-91	.291	.348	.528	106	279	254	40	74	20	2	12	46	20	3	0	2	46	0	0	7.17	16.49
Guillorme, Luis	L-R	5-10	190	9-27-94	.162	.347	.216	18	49	37	6	6	2	0	0	4	11	0	0	1	8	3	0	22.45	16.33
Gurriel, Lourdes	R-R	6-4	215	10-10-93	.279	.322	.435	133	553	513	72	143	22	2	18	75	29	6	0	5	101	7	1	5.24	18.26
Herrera, Jose	B-R	5-10	217	2-24-97	.227	.290	.320	42	114	97	11	22	4	1	1	13	9	0	7	1	27	0	0	7.89	23.68
Marte, Ketel	B-R	6-1	210	10-12-93	.292	.372	.560	136	583	504	93	147	23	2	36	95	65	5	0	9	106	7	1	11.15	18.18
McCarthy, Jake	L-L	6-2	215	7-30-97	.285	.349	.400	142	495	442	66	126	13	7	8	56	31	14	5	3	78	25	6	6.26	15.76
McGough, Scott	R-R	5-11	190	10-31-89	.000	.000	.000	26	1	1	0	0	0	0	0	0	0	0	0	0	1	0	0	0.00	100.00
Moreno, Gabriel	R-R	5-11	195	2-14-00	.266	.353	.380	97	351	305	39	81	18	1	5	45	41	2	0	3	52	3	1	11.68	14.81
Newman, Kevin	R-R	6-1	195	8-4-93	.278	.311	.375	111	311	288	41	80	17	1	3	28	15	0	6	2	48	8	1	4.82	15.43
Pederson, Joc	L-L	6-1	220	4-21-92	.275	.393	.515	132	449	367	62	101	17	1	23	64	55	18	1	3	105	7	4	12.25	23.39
Perdomo, Geraldo	B-R	6-2	203	10-22-99	.273	.344	.374	98	388	337	61	92	21	2	3	37	36	3	7	5	58	9	1	9.28	14.95
Peterson, Jace	L-R	6-0	215	5-9-90	.045	.154	.045	14	26	22	2	1	0	0	0	1	3	0	0	1	6	0	0	11.54	23.08
Smith, Pavin	L-L	6-2	208	2-6-96	.270	.348	.547	60	158	137	26	37	11	0	9	36	18	0	0	3	31	1	0	11.39	19.62
Suarez, Eugenio	R-R	5-11	213	7-18-91	.256	.319	.469	158	640	571	90	146	28	2	30	101	49	9	0	11	176	2	1	7.66	27.50
Thomas, Alek	L-L	5-11	175	4-28-00	.189	.245	.358	39	103	95	13	18	5	1	3	17	7	0	1	0	17	4	1	6.80	16.50
Walker, Christian	R-R	6-0	208	3-28-91	.251	.335	.468	130	552	479	72	120	26	0	26	84	55	10	0	8	133	2	2	9.96	24.09

Pitching	B-T	Ht.	Wt.	DOB	W	L	ERA	G	GS	SV	IP	Hits	Runs	ER	HR	BB	SO	AVG	OBP	SLG	SO%	BB%	BF
Allen, Logan	R-L	6-3	200	5-23-97	0	1	5.46	12	0	1	28	32	17	17	3	10	21	.281	.344	.412	16.41	7.81	128
Barnhart, Tucker	L-R	5-11	192	1-7-91	0	0	18.00	1	0	0	1	4	2	2	1	0	0	.571	.571	1.000	0.00	0.00	7
Bowman, Matt	R-R	6-0	185	5-31-91	0	0	8.10	4	0	0	7	8	6	6	1	2	4	.276	.323	.552	12.90	6.45	31
Castellanos, Humberto	R-R	5-11	222	4-3-98	0	0	5.23	7	0	1	10	11	6	6	0	4	7	.268	.354	.341	14.58	8.33	48
Castro, Miguel	R-R	6-7	201	12-24-94	0	0	5.93	11	0	0	14	20	9	9	3	3	8	.339	.381	.610	12.50	4.69	64
Cecconi, Slade	R-R	6-4	219	6-24-99	2	7	6.66	20	13	0	77	92	57	57	16	17	64	.294	.335	.527	18.93	5.03	338
Diaz, Yilber	R-R	6-0	190	8-19-00	1	1	3.81	7	4	0	28	27	13	12	3	12	19	.257	.328	.429	15.97	10.08	119
Floro, Dylan	L-R	6-2	203	12-27-90	3	1	9.37	15	0	0	16	23	17	17	4	4	8	.333	.373	.580	10.67	5.33	75
Frias, Luis	R-R	6-3	245	5-23-98	0	1	9.95	7	0	0	6	11	8	7	1	4	7	.423	.484	.654	22.58	12.90	31
Gallen, Zac	R-R	6-2	189	8-3-95	14	6	3.65	28	28	0	148	133	62	60	13	54	156	.237	.308	.376	25.12	8.70	621
Ginkel, Kevin	L-R	6-4	235	3-24-94	8	3	3.21	72	0	5	70	69	31	25	6	15	77	.256	.300	.389	26.46	5.15	291
Henry, Tommy	L-L	6-3	205	7-29-97	2	3	7.04	9	7	0	38	49	31	30	9	18	30	.312	.392	.586	16.48	9.89	182
Hughes, Brandon	S-L	6-2	215	12-1-95	0	0	8.15	15	2	0	18	24	16	16	8	10	21	.316	.404	.697	23.60	11.24	89
Jacques, Joe	L-L	6-4	210	3-11-95	0	0	13.50	1	0	0	1	3	2	2	1	1	0	.500	.571	1.000	0.00	14.29	7
Jarvis, Bryce	L-R	6-2	195	12-26-97	1	2	3.19	44	0	0	59	52	25	21	6	33	38	.239	.349	.362	14.73	12.79	258
Kelly, Merrill	R-R	6-2	202	10-14-88	5	1	4.03	13	13	0	74	67	35	33	11	19	63	.242	.294	.426	21.00	6.33	300
Mantiply, Joe	R-L	6-4	219	3-1-91	6	2	3.92	75	2	1	60	52	27	26	1	18	53	.231	.288	.342	21.81	7.41	243
Martinez, Justin	R-R	6-3	180	7-30-01	5	6	2.48	64	0	8	73	59	26	20	2	36	91	.221	.316	.288	29.55	11.69	308
McGough, Scott	R-R	5-11	190	10-31-89	1	3	7.44	26	2	0	33	34	30	27	6	21	25	.274	.373	.532	16.67	14.00	150
Mena, Cristian	R-R	6-2	170	12-21-02	0	0	12.00	1	1	0	3	4	4	4	2	3	2	.333	.467	.833	13.33	20.00	15
Montgomery, Jordan	L-L	6-6	228	12-27-92	8	7	6.23	25	21	1	117	149	83	81	14	44	83	.312	.369	.496	15.60	8.27	532
Nelson, Kyle	L-L	6-1	175	7-8-96	0	0	4.22	11	0	0	11	8	5	5	2	4	8	.216	.286	.405	19.05	9.52	42
Nelson, Ryne	R-R	6-3	184	2-1-98	10	6	4.24	28	25	1	151	155	73	71	17	34	126	.266	.308	.446	20.00	5.40	630
Pfaadt, Brandon	R-R	6-4	220	10-15-98	11	10	4.71	32	32	0	182	183	103	95	24	42	185	.259	.302	.421	24.34	5.53	760
Puk, A.J.	L-L	6-7	248	4-25-95	0	1	1.32	30	0	2	27	15	4	4	2	5	43	.155	.204	.278	41.75	4.85	103
Rodriguez, Eduardo	L-L	6-2	231	4-7-93	3	4	5.04	10	10	0	50	56	29	28	8	19	47	.277	.341	.475	20.98	8.48	224
Saalfrank, Andrew	L-L	6-3	205	8-18-97	0	0	36.00	2	0	0	1	2	4	4	0	4	0	.500	.750	1.000	0.00	50.00	8
Seward, Paul	R-R	6-3	219	5-26-90	1	2	4.31	42	0	16	40	35	19	19	6	10	43	.232	.291	.437	26.06	6.06	165

Smith, Pavin	L-L	6-2	208	2-6-96	0	0	0.00	1	0	0	1	0	0	0	0	1	0	.000	.400	.000	0.00	20.00	5
Thompson, Ryan	R-R	6-5	210	6-26-92	7	5	3.26	67	0	2	66	64	26	24	5	15	52	.254	.296	.377	19.12	5.51	272
Vieira, Thyago	R-R	6-3	265	7-1-93	0	1	2.87	11	0	0	16	11	6	5	2	9	14	.196	.303	.375	21.21	13.64	66
Walston, Blake	L-L	6-5	175	6-28-01	1	0	4.42	7	2	0	18	16	12	9	4	10	18	.229	.349	.429	21.69	12.05	83

Fielding

Catcher	PCT	G	PO	A	E	DP	PB
Barnhart	.991	31	214	9	2	1	1
Del Castillo	.983	24	171	7	3	1	0
Herrera	.997	40	314	7	1	1	3
Moreno	.997	93	636	31	2	4	3

First Base	PCT	G	PO	A	E	DP
Bell	1.000	31	213	15	0	19
Gurriel	.000	1	0	0	0	0
Newman	1.000	10	22	1	0	1
Smith	1.000	17	57	5	0	5
Walker	.998	129	977	76	2	104

Second Base	PCT	G	PO	A	E	DP
Alexander	.985	17	22	43	1	8
Guillorme	1.000	16	15	27	0	7
Marte	.990	113	216	289	5	73
Newman	.992	44	43	83	1	21
Peterson	1.000	4	4	4	0	2

Third Base	PCT	G	PO	A	E	DP
Alexander	.933	8	2	12	1	1
Guillorme	1.000	1	0	1	0	0
Herrera	1.000	1	0	1	0	0
Newman	.800	6	2	2	1	0
Peterson	1.000	1	0	1	0	0
Suarez	.974	155	88	292	10	33

Shortstop	PCT	G	PO	A	E	DP
Alexander	.915	20	21	22	4	7
Marte	.000	1	0	0	0	0
Newman	.983	55	46	127	3	30
Perdomo	.987	97	112	261	5	55
Peterson	1.000	5	3	8	0	1

Outfield	PCT	G	PO	A	E	DP
Barrosa	.909	6	10	0	1	0
Carroll	.995	159	358	6	2	2
Grichuk	1.000	57	97	1	0	0
Gurriel	.980	127	239	4	5	0
McCarthy	.993	161	270	2	2	1
Newman	1.000	1	1	0	0	0
Smith	1.000	33	41	2	0	0
Thomas	1.000	35	57	0	0	0

RENO ACES — TRIPLE-A

PACIFIC COAST LEAGUE

Batting	B-T	Ht.	Wt.	DOB	AVG	OBP	SLG	G	PA	AB	R	H	2B	3B	HR	RBI	BB	HBP	SH	SF	SO	SB	CS	BB%	SO%
Alcantara, Sergio	B-R	6-4	151	7-10-96	.279	.391	.434	112	450	376	70	105	20	7	8	57	69	2	0	3	82	8	0	15.33	18.22
Alexander, Blaze	R-R	5-11	160	6-11-99	.276	.353	.444	51	225	196	27	54	12	3	5	20	19	6	0	3	69	4	1	8.44	30.67
Almora, Albert	R-R	6-2	190	4-16-94	.292	.349	.438	127	576	520	79	152	45	2	9	69	42	5	5	4	81	20	7	7.29	14.06
Barrosa, Jorge	B-L	5-5	165	2-17-01	.270	.360	.421	75	329	285	46	77	17	1	8	43	38	3	1	2	59	12	4	11.55	17.93
Beaty, Matt	L-R	6-0	215	4-28-93	.148	.303	.185	8	33	27	3	4	1	0	0	3	4	2	0	0	6	0	1	12.12	18.18
Brigman, Bryson	R-R	5-11	180	6-19-95	.334	.383	.474	113	404	365	63	122	18	3	9	61	26	5	3	4	62	10	4	6.44	15.35
Castillo, Neyfy	R-R	6-1	175	3-2-01	.286	.375	.429	2	8	7	1	2	1	0	0	0	1	0	0	0	4	0	0	12.50	50.00
Chaparro, Andres	R-R	6-0	200	5-4-99	.332	.403	.564	95	414	367	69	122	26	1	19	75	41	4	0	2	73	3	0	9.90	17.63
Cintron, Jancarlos	R-R	5-8	170	12-1-94	.230	.317	.279	39	139	122	21	28	4	1	0	12	12	4	0	1	14	5	1	8.63	10.07
Corniel, Juan	B-R	5-11	150	10-2-02	.316	.350	.368	4	20	19	4	6	1	0	0	1	0	1	0	0	1	0	0	0.00	5.00
De Los Santos, Deyvison	R-R	5-11	185	6-21-03	.289	.338	.588	49	210	194	33	56	14	1	14	47	11	4	0	1	48	0	0	5.24	22.86
Del Castillo, Adrian	L-R	5-9	208	9-27-99	.312	.399	.603	105	474	413	90	129	36	3	26	75	55	5	0	1	80	0	0	11.60	16.88
English, Tristin	R-R	6-0	208	5-14-97	.263	.326	.424	111	479	434	73	114	18	2	16	63	32	10	0	3	95	3	4	6.68	19.83
Garlick, Kyle	R-R	6-1	210	1-26-92	.237	.329	.444	136	623	540	87	128	22	3	28	105	71	6	0	6	171	1	1	11.40	27.45
Grichuk, Randal	R-R	6-2	216	8-13-91	.286	.375	.500	4	16	14	5	4	0	0	1	2	1	1	0	0	3	0	0	6.25	18.75
Hernandez, Ronaldo	R-R	6-1	230	11-11-97	.311	.357	.507	63	237	219	29	68	10	0	11	36	11	5	0	0	36	0	0	4.64	15.19
Herrera, Jose	B-R	5-10	217	2-24-97	.260	.351	.362	37	149	127	23	33	5	1	2	19	19	0	1	2	23	0	1	12.75	15.44
Johnson, Brett	L-R	5-11	195	1-6-00	.211	.348	.434	28	92	76	15	16	5	3	2	16	16	0	0	0	27	1	1	17.39	29.35
Knizner, Andrew	R-R	6-1	225	2-3-95	.263	.355	.388	22	93	80	16	21	4	0	2	12	10	2	0	1	20	1	0	10.75	21.51
Lawlar, Jordan	R-R	6-1	190	7-17-02	.367	.439	.592	12	58	49	6	18	3	1	2	12	7	0	1	1	17	1	2	12.07	29.31
Newman, Kevin	R-R	6-1	195	8-4-93	.364	.407	.636	6	27	22	6	8	1	1	1	7	3	0	0	2	8	1	0	11.11	29.63
Patino, Wilderd	R-R	6-1	175	7-18-01	.091	.333	.091	6	15	11	5	1	0	0	0	2	3	1	0	0	4	0	1	20.00	26.67
Perdomo, Geraldo	B-R	6-2	203	10-22-99	.143	.250	.143	4	16	14	1	2	0	0	0	2	2	0	0	0	0	0	1	12.50	0.00
Perez, Michael	L-R	5-10	195	8-7-92	.354	.444	.622	24	99	82	17	29	10	0	4	13	13	2	0	2	16	0	0	13.13	16.16
Smith, Pavin	L-L	6-2	208	2-6-96	.318	.433	.564	62	289	236	51	75	15	2	13	51	49	1	0	3	49	1	1	16.96	16.96
Stumpo, Mitchell	R-R	6-2	205	6-17-96	.000	.000	.000	9	0	0	1	0	0	0	0	0	0	0	0	0	0	0	0	—	—
Tawa, Tim	R-R	5-10	196	4-7-99	.304	.376	.616	37	157	138	25	42	11	1	10	26	13	4	0	2	32	3	0	8.28	20.38
Thomas, Alek	L-L	5-11	175	4-28-00	.286	.333	.444	16	69	63	14	18	4	0	2	12	5	0	0	1	11	1	0	7.25	15.94
Valdez, Jesus	R-R	5-9	175	12-29-97	.414	.433	.621	9	30	29	4	12	0	0	2	5	1	0	0	0	6	0	1	3.33	20.00
Vukovich, A.J.	R-R	6-2	210	7-20-01	.273	.273	.273	4	11	11	1	3	0	0	0	0	0	0	0	0	4	0	0	0.00	36.36
Warmoth, Logan	R-R	5-10	195	9-6-95	.100	.296	.100	10	27	20	4	2	0	0	0	1	4	2	0	1	3	2	0	14.81	11.11
Weber, Andy	L-R	5-11	190	7-24-97	.263	.275	.500	11	41	38	6	10	1	1	2	8	1	0	1	1	11	1	0	2.44	26.83
Wong, Kolten	L-R	5-7	185	10-10-90	.271	.339	.383	31	121	107	15	29	6	0	2	16	10	2	0	2	22	2	0	8.26	18.18

Pitching	B-T	Ht.	Wt.	DOB	W	L	ERA	G	GS	SV	IP	Hits	Runs	ER	HR	BB	SO	AVG	OBP	SLG	SO%	BB%	BF
Allen, Logan	R-L	6-3	200	5-23-97	6	3	5.23	20	19	0	96	118	59	56	13	39	83	.306	.364	.499	18.95	8.90	438
Amendt, Kyle	R-R	6-5	237	4-5-00	3	2	5.25	13	0	0	12	12	7	7	1	14	18	.245	.413	.347	28.57	22.22	63
Backhus, Kyle	L-L	6-4	185	1-31-98	2	3	3.94	35	0	1	32	25	17	14	4	18	38	.205	.329	.320	26.03	12.33	146
Barnes, Zach	R-R	6-0	180	4-10-99	0	1	13.50	10	0	0	17	28	27	25	3	12	11	.368	.467	.566	11.96	13.04	92
Brigman, Bryson	R-R	5-11	180	6-19-95	0	0	27.00	1	0	0	1	3	3	3	1	0	0	.500	.500	1.333	0.00	0.00	6
Castellanos, Humberto	R-R	5-11	222	4-3-98	9	1	3.81	21	20	0	104	84	44	44	21	39	102	.220	.293	.455	23.83	9.11	428
Castillo, Jose	L-L	6-6	252	1-10-96	1	0	4.35	21	0	0	21	18	10	10	1	7	21	.234	.306	.338	24.42	8.14	86
Castro, Miguel	R-R	6-7	201	12-24-94	0	0	0.00	2	0	0	3	1	0	0	0	2	2	.111	.273	.111	18.18	18.18	11
Cecconi, Slade	R-R	6-4	219	6-24-99	4	2	3.06	18	5	3	47	34	17	16	5	14	54	.202	.264	.357	29.51	7.65	183
Chalmers, Dakota	R-R	6-3	175	10-8-96	0	5	9.57	25	0	1	26	22	30	28	2	34	44	.227	.453	.371	31.88	24.64	138
Chatwood, Tyler	R-R	5-11	200	12-16-89	0	0	45.00	2	0	0	1	3	5	5	0	3	0	.600	.700	.800	0.00	30.00	10
Clarkin, Ian	L-L	6-2	215	2-14-95	1	0	10.00	6	0	0	9	16	12	10	2	5	12	.381	.458	.667	25.00	10.42	48
Diaz, Yilber	R-R	6-0	190	8-19-00	3	4	3.22	10	8	0	50	47	23	18	4	18	63	.246	.313	.372	29.86	8.53	211
Ellis, Chris	L-R	6-5	205	9-22-92	2	7	9.09	15	15	0	64	77	66	65	14	45	44	.297	.403	.537	14.19	14.52	310
English, Tristin	R-R	6-0	208	5-14-97	1	0	0.00	1	0	0	2	0	2	0	0	0	0	.000	.000	.000	0.00	0.00	6

File, Dylan	R-R	6-1	205	6-4-96	0	3	10.24	3	2	0	10	16	13	11	2	3	4	.372	.420	.558	8.00	6.00	50
Frias, Luis	R-R	6-3	245	5-23-98	1	3	4.88	21	0	4	24	24	17	13	5	11	24	.261	.352	.478	22.02	10.09	109
Green, Josh	R-R	6-3	211	8-31-95	1	0	6.35	13	1	0	17	22	13	12	1	12	8	.338	.449	.446	10.26	15.38	78
Henry, Tommy	L-L	6-3	205	7-29-97	10	1	4.25	20	20	0	108	109	54	51	10	54	114	.266	.351	.420	24.20	11.46	471
Hill, Jamison	R-R	6-1	180	3-28-99	0	1	10.38	1	1	0	4	5	6	5	2	4	2	.294	.409	.647	9.09	18.18	22
Hollowell, Gavin	R-R	6-7	215	11-4-97	1	1	3.63	18	0	0	17	15	8	7	1	13	24	.234	.367	.328	30.38	16.46	79
Hughes, Brandon	S-L	6-2	215	12-1-95	1	4	2.03	40	0	1	49	41	15	11	3	18	50	.229	.310	.341	24.88	8.96	201
Jacques, Joe	L-L	6-4	210	3-11-95	3	0	4.30	35	0	0	38	37	20	18	0	15	33	.252	.339	.313	19.64	8.93	168
Karcher, Ricky	R-R	6-4	230	9-18-97	0	0	8.46	21	0	0	22	13	22	21	1	31	31	.171	.413	.289	28.44	28.44	109
Lin, Yu-Min	L-L	5-11	160	7-12-03	0	0	1.93	1	1	0	5	4	1	1	0	3	2	.222	.333	.222	9.52	14.29	21
Martin, Corbin	R-R	6-2	225	12-28-95	0	0	9.00	2	0	0	3	3	3	3	1	3	3	.273	.429	.545	21.43	21.43	14
Martinez, Justin	R-R	6-3	180	7-30-01	0	0	2.70	6	0	3	7	4	5	2	1	3	14	.167	.286	.375	50.00	10.71	28
McGough, Scott	R-R	5-11	190	10-31-89	1	2	3.22	33	0	8	36	31	19	13	2	18	37	.226	.314	.343	23.72	11.54	156
Mena, Cristian	R-R	6-2	170	12-21-02	4	2	4.61	19	19	0	96	101	54	49	15	46	102	.272	.357	.452	24.06	10.85	424
Montes De Oca, Christian	R-R	6-4	230	8-30-99	4	5	5.24	47	0	8	57	62	39	33	7	21	47	.274	.345	.447	18.29	8.17	257
Montgomery, Jordan	L-L	6-6	228	12-27-92	0	0	10.57	2	2	0	8	12	9	9	2	5	9	.364	.436	.667	23.08	12.82	39
Montilla, Emailin	L-L	4-4	255	10-2-95	0	0	18.00	2	0	0	2	2	4	4	0	2	1	.286	.500	.571	9.09	18.18	11
Morales, Francisco	R-R	6-4	185	10-27-99	1	4	9.15	19	0	0	21	20	23	21	3	21	31	.274	.461	.493	30.39	20.59	102
Pilkington, Konnor	L-L	6-3	240	9-12-97	3	5	5.91	33	21	0	78	88	52	51	7	49	79	.289	.390	.426	22.01	13.65	359
Pope, Austin	R-R	6-3	210	10-26-98	6	5	5.72	55	0	1	57	67	40	36	4	33	70	.289	.379	.405	26.02	12.27	269
Rashi, Taylor	R-R	6-4	220	1-15-96	0	0	6.75	3	0	0	4	4	3	3	0	4	3	.267	.400	.333	15.00	20.00	20
Rice, Jake	L-L	6-1	220	7-19-97	1	0	1.35	5	0	0	7	8	1	1	0	6	8	.308	.455	.385	24.24	18.18	33
Rodriguez, Chris	R-R	6-2	185	7-20-98	2	2	5.80	25	1	0	36	39	25	23	6	30	28	.287	.417	.500	16.67	17.86	168
Saalfrank, Andrew	L-L	6-3	205	8-18-97	4	1	2.63	18	0	3	24	17	7	7	2	10	28	.205	.287	.313	29.47	10.53	95
Sewald, Paul	R-R	6-3	219	5-26-90	0	0	0.00	1	0	0	1	2	1	0	0	1	2	.500	.600	.500	40.00	20.00	5
Stumpo, Mitchell	R-R	6-2	205	6-17-96	0	1	14.04	8	0	0	8	13	13	13	1	7	8	.382	.455	.647	18.18	15.91	44
Uelmen, Erich	R-R	6-3	195	5-19-96	1	0	6.18	23	1	0	28	36	22	19	4	16	25	.310	.416	.466	18.25	11.68	137
Walston, Blake	L-L	6-5	175	6-28-01	3	2	4.85	14	13	0	65	69	36	35	8	31	68	.275	.368	.438	23.21	10.58	293

Fielding

Catcher	PCT	G	PO	A	E	DP	PB
Del Castillo	.991	61	522	24	5	2	6
Hernandez	.967	15	113	6	4	0	2
Herrera	.982	35	355	28	7	4	2
Knizner	.985	20	181	11	3	1	1
Perez	1.000	21	199	9	0	2	0

First Base	PCT	G	PO	A	E	DP
Beaty	1.000	3	19	1	0	3
Chaparro	.992	16	106	16	1	16
De Los Santos	.986	36	253	21	4	38
English	.997	42	283	26	1	27
Garlick	1.000	1	9	0	0	0
Hernandez	1.000	10	65	4	0	4
Smith	.978	31	195	24	5	23
Tawa	1.000	16	113	8	0	23
Wong	1.000	1	12	0	0	2

Second Base	PCT	G	PO	A	E	DP
Alcantara	.986	17	35	34	1	13
Alexander	1.000	5	9	11	0	5
Brigman	.975	78	145	161	8	50
Cintron	1.000	21	32	47	0	16
Tawa	.955	5	8	13	1	4
Valdez	1.000	4	5	6	0	4
Warmoth	.889	7	3	13	2	1
Weber	.972	10	12	23	1	5
Wong	1.000	22	40	38	0	12

Third Base	PCT	G	PO	A	E	DP
Alcantara	1.000	8	4	9	0	0
Alexander	1.000	22	12	54	0	9
Chaparro	.961	72	57	139	8	13
Cintron	.933	6	7	7	1	0
De Los Santos	.969	10	9	22	1	2
English	.953	17	13	28	2	7
Lawlar	1.000	4	4	7	0	0
Tawa	.875	4	4	10	2	2
Valdez	.900	5	2	7	1	0
Wong	.923	6	4	8	1	0

Shortstop	PCT	G	PO	A	E	DP
Alcantara	.963	90	116	218	13	48
Alexander	.964	24	40	67	4	22
Brigman	1.000	3	2	2	0	0
Cintron	.927	14	14	24	3	8
Corniel	1.000	4	2	11	0	1
Lawlar	.914	8	15	17	3	3
Newman	1.000	5	6	14	0	6
Perdomo	.889	3	4	4	1	1
Warmoth	.900	3	2	7	1	4
Weber	1.000	1	0	1	0	0
Wong	.750	1	2	1	1	0

Outfield	PCT	G	PO	A	E	DP
Weber	.000	1	0	0	0	0
Castillo	.667	2	1	1	1	0
Vukovich	.889	3	8	0	1	0
Thomas	.923	12	24	0	2	0
Johnson	.925	26	35	2	3	2
Smith	.940	29	46	1	3	0
Tawa	.957	16	22	0	1	0
Garlick	.977	105	167	2	4	0
Brigman	.979	32	46	1	1	0
Almora	.992	128	243	2	2	0
Barrosa	.993	76	150	2	1	1
English	1.000	44	84	4	0	3
Grichuk	1.000	3	5	0	0	0
Patino	1.000	4	7	0	0	0
Wong	1.000	2	1	0	0	0

AMARILLO SOD POODLES — *DOUBLE-A*

TEXAS LEAGUE

Batting	B-T	Ht.	Wt.	DOB	AVG	OBP	SLG	G	PA	AB	R	H	2B	3B	HR	RBI	BB	HBP	SH	SF	SO	SB	CS	BB%	SO%
Beaty, Matt	L-R	6-0	215	4-28-93	.297	.380	.424	45	179	158	21	47	5	0	5	20	14	7	0	0	18	0	0	7.82	10.06
Brigman, Bryson	R-R	5-11	180	6-19-95	.500	.667	.500	1	3	2	2	1	0	0	0	0	1	0	0	0	1	0	0	33.33	33.33
Castillo, Neyfy	R-R	6-1	175	3-2-01	.206	.272	.345	49	213	194	22	40	10	1	5	23	17	1	0	1	77	5	1	7.98	36.15
Cerda, Christian	R-R	6-0	190	12-27-02	.200	.394	.260	17	66	50	7	10	3	0	0	7	16	0	0	0	22	1	0	24.24	33.33
Chen, Sheng-Ping	L-R	5-9	165	10-27-00	.183	.236	.244	25	90	82	3	15	2	0	1	8	5	1	1	1	22	2	0	5.56	24.44
Cintron, Jancarlos	R-R	5-8	170	12-1-94	.241	.290	.321	80	344	315	45	76	14	1	3	35	19	4	3	3	50	4	3	5.52	14.53
Conticello, Gavin	L-R	6-4	195	6-11-03	.227	.292	.455	6	24	22	4	5	0	1	1	3	2	0	0	0	7	0	0	8.33	29.17
D'Orazio, J.J.	R-R	6-1	170	12 28-01	.223	.290	.328	73	284	256	33	57	12	0	5	25	23	2	1	2	61	0	1	8.10	21.48
De Los Santos, Deyvison	R-R	5-11	185	6-21-03	.372	.426	.696	38	162	148	28	55	4	1	14	37	12	2	0	0	36	1	1	7.41	22.22
Fernandez, Jose	R-R	6-3	165	9-22-03	.000	.000	.000	2	5	4	0	0	0	0	0	0	0	0	1	0	0	0	0	0.00	0.00

Graham, Kevin	L-R	6-1	195	8-12-99	.213	.292	.326	94	347	310	44	66	16	2	5	31	32	3	1	1	106	6	0	9.22	30.55
Groover, Gino	R-R	6-2	212	4-16-02	.340	.400	.600	13	55	50	8	17	4	0	3	6	5	0	0	0	9	1	0	9.09	16.36
Lawlar, Jordan	R-R	6-1	190	7-17-02	.143	.333	.143	2	9	7	0	1	0	0	0	0	2	0	0	0	2	0	0	22.22	22.22
Lin, Lyle	R-R	6-1	200	6-26-97	.409	.480	.568	14	50	44	3	18	4	0	1	7	3	3	0	0	6	0	0	6.00	12.00
Melendez, Ivan	R-R	6-3	225	1-24-00	.238	.312	.434	107	442	399	58	95	10	1	22	47	34	9	0	0	133	3	1	7.69	30.09
Partino, Wilderd	R-R	6-1	175	7-18-01	.221	.279	.307	65	268	244	28	54	9	0	4	14	17	3	94	3	1	17	3	6.34	35.07
Pintar, Andrew	R-R	6-2	190	3-23-01	.184	.289	.237	10	46	38	4	7	2	0	0	6	6	0	1	1	12	1	0	13.04	26.09
Roberts, Caleb	L-R	5-11	195	2-9-00	.243	.339	.454	113	485	416	68	101	20	4	20	65	55	8	1	5	120	11	2	11.34	24.74
Robinson, Kristian	R-R	6-3	190	12-11-00	.214	.337	.350	110	419	351	48	75	13	1	11	42	63	3	0	2	150	10	4	15.04	35.80
Tawa, Tim	R-R	5-10	196	4-7-99	.270	.340	.487	105	456	411	62	111	22	2	21	64	40	4	0	1	96	11	6	8.77	21.05
Valdez, Jesus	R-R	5-9	175	12-29-97	.237	.312	.374	67	222	198	26	47	10	1	5	15	22	0	1	1	64	2	1	9.91	28.83
Vukovich, A.J.	R-R	6-2	210	7-20-01	.270	.342	.458	121	512	456	59	123	29	3	17	80	48	4	0	4	153	6	3	9.38	29.88
Walters, Jean	B-R	5-11	155	8-13-01	.214	.254	.286	33	130	112	10	24	3	1	1	13	6	1	8	3	22	2	2	4.62	16.92
Warmoth, Logan	R-R	5-10	195	9-6-95	.193	.320	.247	45	181	150	15	29	5	0	1	21	28	1	0	2	44	5	1	15.47	24.31
Weber, Andy	L-R	5-11	190	7-24-97	.328	.388	.522	34	149	134	21	44	14	0	4	15	12	1	2	0	29	2	1	8.05	19.46

Pitching	B-T	Ht.	Wt.	DOB	W	L	ERA	G	GS	SV	IP	Hits	Runs	ER	HR	BB	SO	AVG	OBP	SLG	SO%	BB%	BF
Albright, Luke	R-R	6-4	215	12-13-99	0	2	9.79	18	3	0	34	40	39	37	10	30	37	.288	.425	.561	21.26	17.24	174
Alvarez, Jhosmer	R-R	6-1	155	6-29-01	0	4	3.24	24	0	2	25	25	11	9	2	10	16	.269	.349	.366	14.81	9.26	108
Amendt, Kyle	R-R	6-5	237	4-5-00	1	1	2.89	19	0	3	19	8	6	6	1	8	30	.127	.222	.222	41.67	11.11	72
Baker, Alec	R-R	6-3	202	12-4-99	0	0	12.46	3	0	0	4	6	6	6	1	5	7	.316	.458	.684	29.17	20.83	24
Barnes, Zach	R-R	6-0	180	4-10-99	2	3	4.99	24	0	0	31	35	18	17	5	12	32	.278	.345	.524	22.86	8.57	140
Clayton, Logan	R-R	6-5	188	5-2-00	0	2	5.96	9	3	0	23	27	17	15	7	4	16	.281	.320	.521	15.38	3.85	104
Corcoran, Billy	R-R	6-8	220	8-21-99	6	8	4.92	20	20	0	106	106	66	58	15	30	78	.262	.316	.455	17.49	6.73	446
Diaz, Yilber	R-R	6-0	190	8-19-00	3	5	4.33	11	11	0	54	38	26	26	5	29	77	.196	.302	.314	34.22	12.89	225
Elbis, Joe	R-R	6-1	150	9-24-02	0	3	4.60	8	8	0	45	40	25	23	4	18	37	.241	.317	.398	19.58	9.52	189
File, Dylan	R-R	6-1	205	6-4-96	5	7	4.78	18	18	0	98	111	53	52	12	15	70	.291	.329	.445	17.11	3.67	409
Giesting, Spencer	L-L	6-4	200	7-2-01	4	7	4.65	15	15	0	81	84	45	42	10	31	87	.267	.344	.435	24.51	8.73	355
Graham, Kevin	L-R	6-1	195	8-12-99	0	0	9.00	1	0	0	1	1	1	1	1	0	0	.250	.400	1.000	0.00	0.00	5
Grammes, Conor	R-R	6-1	200	7-13-97	2	2	5.13	40	1	1	47	43	32	27	3	36	50	.242	.385	.343	22.62	16.29	221
Green, Josh	R-R	6-3	211	8-31-95	0	0	4.50	2	0	0	2	3	1	1	0	1	2	.375	.444	.375	22.22	11.11	9
Gutierrez, Gerardo	R-R	6-0	177	9-15-98	1	1	5.48	38	0	3	43	45	32	26	7	26	36	.274	.381	.433	18.46	13.33	195
Hill, Jamison	R-R	6-1	180	3-28-99	3	5	7.26	27	12	0	84	102	72	68	18	34	77	.296	.362	.516	19.79	8.74	389
Larsen, Dillon	R-L	6-5	230	7-9-98	1	1	5.66	13	1	0	21	25	14	13	0	16	19	.313	.424	.413	19.19	16.16	99
Lin, Yu-Min	L-L	5-11	160	7-12-03	3	6	4.28	19	19	0	95	104	59	45	14	33	90	.282	.353	.477	21.74	7.97	414
Mabrey, Will	L-L	6-0	185	9-23-00	3	2	3.52	43	0	2	46	45	22	18	5	24	49	.249	.338	.387	23.67	11.59	207
Matthews, John	R-R	6-1	190	1-21-98	3	0	8.06	28	0	0	26	33	25	23	3	15	19	.311	.434	.509	14.73	11.63	129
Meza, Carlos	L-L	6-1	155	2-10-01	0	1	12.00	5	0	0	6	4	9	8	1	10	7	.190	.455	.476	21.21	30.30	33
Montes De Oca, Christian	R-R	6-4	230	8-30-99	0	0	0.00	3	0	2	4	1	1	0	0	0	6	.067	.125	.067	37.50	0.00	16
Montilla, Emailin	L-L	4-4	255	10-2-95	1	0	8.15	16	0	0	18	28	19	16	3	12	15	.354	.426	.557	15.96	12.77	94
Morales, Francisco	R-R	6-4	185	10-27-99	1	1	14.29	4	0	0	6	9	11	9	1	5	8	.333	.472	.519	22.22	13.89	36
Percival, Cole	R-R	6-5	220	2-26-99	3	6	4.99	14	9	0	49	47	27	27	9	20	47	.250	.321	.452	22.49	9.57	209
Rashi, Taylor	R-R	6-4	220	1-15-96	7	3	4.53	38	0	3	48	46	35	24	7	26	59	.246	.338	.412	26.82	11.82	220
Ray, Dylan	R-R	6-3	230	5-9-01	2	5	5.22	16	16	0	71	77	48	41	16	32	68	.280	361	.491	21.94	10.32	310
Rice, Jake	L-L	6-1	220	7-19-97	2	1	3.47	41	0	0	49	38	26	19	3	27	58	.210	.313	.293	26.85	12.50	216
Rodriguez, Chris	R-R	6-2	185	7-20-98	0	0	2.79	9	0	0	10	7	3	3	0	4	9	.226	.342	.323	23.08	10.26	39
Sosa, Listher	R-R	6-4	208	9-6-01	0	1	3.46	8	1	1	13	11	5	5	1	4	12	.250	.346	.341	23.08	7.69	52
Stumpo, Mitchell	R-R	6-2	205	6-17-96	5	2	4.01	33	0	10	34	34	18	15	7	10	39	.264	.321	.465	27.86	7.14	140
Valdez, Jesus	R-R	5-9	175	12-29-97	0	0	27.00	2	0	0	2	6	6	6	1	0	1	.545	.583	.818	8.33	0.00	12

Fielding

Catcher	PCT	G	PO	A	E	DP	PB
Cerda	.981	11	90	12	2	0	2
D'Orazio	.989	59	510	33	6	3	8
Lin	1.000	8	68	7	0	0	0
Roberts	.986	62	499	54	8	4	21

First Base	PCT	G	PO	A	E	DP
Beaty	1.000	34	227	19	0	22
Castillo	1.000	18	123	11	0	13
De Los Santos	.986	34	269	23	4	21
Graham	1.000	2	12	1	0	0
Melendez	.992	37	251	12	2	31
Tawa	1.000	20	111	8	0	9

Second Base	PCT	G	PO	A	E	DP
Chen	.967	14	24	35	2	5
Cintron	.957	10	21	24	2	6
Fernandez	1.000	1	1	1	0	1
Groover	.977	7	20	23	1	10
Tawa	.970	53	104	121	7	28
Valdez	.984	18	29	31	1	9
Walters	.984	27	55	69	2	18
Warmoth	1.000	10	16	25	0	6
Weber	.923	2	5	7	1	3

Third Base	PCT	G	PO	A	E	DP
Melendez	.923	68	46	98	12	12
Valdez	.938	44	28	77	7	6
Chen	1.000	2	0	1	0	0
Cintron	1.000	10	8	16	0	2
Fernandez	1.000	1	0	1	0	1
Groover	1.000	6	0	13	0	3
Tawa	1.000	9	11	18	0	1
Walters	1.000	2	0	3	0	1

Shortstop	PCT	G	PO	A	E	DP
Chen	.865	10	11	21	5	5
Weber	.943	32	34	82	7	13
Cintron	.961	55	86	136	9	29
Warmoth	.978	33	43	90	3	15
Brigman	1.000	1	2	3	0	1
Lawlar	1.000	2	3	1	0	1
Tawa	1.000	2	1	7	0	1
Walters	1.000	3	1	7	0	2

Outfield	PCT	G	PO	A	E	DP
Roberts	.000	1	0	0	0	0
Robinson	.960	106	210	6	9	1
Tawa	.978	17	43	1	1	0
Graham	.983	69	118	1	2	0
Vukovich	.995	118	199	7	1	1
Castillo	1.000	30	38	3	0	0
Cintron	1.000	4	4	1	0	0
Conticello	1.000	6	10	0	0	0
Pintar	1.000	8	16	0	0	0
Warmoth	1.000	2	2	0	0	0

HILLSBORO HOPS — HIGH-A

NORTHWEST LEAGUE

Batting	B-T	Ht.	Wt.	DOB	AVG	OBP	SLG	G	PA	AB	R	H	2B	3B	HR	RBI	BB	HBP	SH	SF	SO	SB	CS	BB%	SO%
Boyd, Jermiah	R-R	5-10	225	7-1-00	.000	.182	.000	4	11	9	0	0	0	0	0	1	1	1	0	0	4	0	0	9.09	36.36
Castillo, Neyfy	R-R	6-1	175	3-2-01	.225	.313	.359	61	265	231	28	52	7	3	6	36	24	7	0	3	84	8	5	9.06	31.70
Cerda, Christian	R-R	6-0	190	12-27-02	.243	.364	.332	88	354	292	46	71	11	0	5	36	55	3	0	4	62	4	3	15.54	17.51
Conticello, Gavin	L-R	6-4	195	6-11-03	.282	.346	.429	126	542	489	64	138	31	7	9	65	46	3	0	3	115	20	4	8.49	21.22
Corniel, Juan	B-R	5-11	150	10-2-02	.193	.252	.217	77	275	254	22	49	6	0	0	18	17	3	1	0	62	6	6	6.18	22.55
Crenshaw, Wyatt	L-R	6-0	180	4-21-00	.143	.270	.143	28	75	63	12	9	0	0	0	1	8	3	1	0	27	1	0	10.67	36.00
Feltner, Jackson	R-R	6-2	225	9-19-01	.162	.219	.294	20	73	68	4	11	3	0	2	7	4	1	0	0	29	0	0	5.48	39.73
Fernandez, Jose	R-R	6-3	165	9-22-03	.256	.292	.344	101	387	363	40	93	7	2	7	43	17	2	3	2	85	10	5	4.39	21.96
Franco, Junior	L-L	5-9	165	9-13-02	.241	.302	.333	55	215	195	24	47	5	2	3	21	18	0	0	2	42	21	3	8.37	19.53
Groover, Gino	R-R	6-2	212	4-16-02	.272	.360	.457	40	175	151	21	41	7	0	7	25	20	2	0	2	24	3	0	11.43	13.71
Hurley, Jack	L-R	6-0	185	3-13-02	.245	.305	.404	117	505	458	67	112	29	4	12	61	36	6	0	5	136	14	6	7.13	26.93
Johnson, Brett	L-R	5-11	195	1-6-00	.136	.304	.227	16	56	44	6	6	2	1	0	5	10	1	0	1	15	2	1	17.86	26.79
Lin, Lyle	R-R	6-1	200	6-26-97	.231	.286	.231	6	14	13	1	3	0	0	0	1	1	0	0	0	2	0	0	7.14	14.29
Logan, Gavin	L-R	5-9	212	1-14-00	.182	.324	.336	52	176	143	15	26	9	2	3	15	25	6	0	2	56	4	2	14.20	31.82
Martin, David	L-R	6-1	185	10-28-00	.188	.296	.224	25	98	85	6	16	3	0	0	4	7	6	0	0	17	0	0	7.14	17.35
Patino, Wilderd	R-R	6-1	175	7-18-01	.258	.395	.452	13	38	31	6	8	1	1	1	4	4	3	0	0	14	5	0	10.53	36.84
Pena, Manuel	L-R	6-1	170	12-5-03	.275	.327	.370	116	491	451	45	124	27	2	4	51	33	3	2	2	106	10	10	6.72	21.59
Pintar, Andrew	R-R	6-2	190	3-23-01	.304	.403	.516	57	254	217	40	66	13	3	9	32	35	1	0	0	43	17	1	13.78	16.93
Rios, Alejandro	R-R	5-11	150	3-30-05	.000	.143	.000	2	7	6	0	0	0	0	0	0	1	0	0	0	4	0	0	14.29	57.14
Roberts, Cole	R-R	5-9	165	10-9-00	.192	.353	.192	10	34	26	5	5	0	0	0	5	7	0	0	1	7	1	0	20.59	20.59
Sim, Kevin	R-R	6-2	210	2-7-02	.199	.269	.317	107	391	356	43	71	16	1	8	31	28	6	0	1	104	5	3	7.16	26.60
Troy, Tommy	R-R	5-10	197	1-17-02	.227	.319	.347	65	288	251	39	57	13	1	5	20	30	5	0	2	64	16	5	10.42	22.22
Walters, Jean	B-R	5-11	155	8-13-01	.293	.335	.376	55	198	181	23	53	6	3	1	15	13	0	1	3	36	3	4	6.57	18.18

Pitching	B-T	Ht.	Wt.	DOB	W	L	ERA	G	GS	SV	IP	Hits	Runs	ER	HR	BB	SO	AVG	OBP	SLG	SO%	BB%	BF
Abner, Philip	L-L	6-1	220	5-5-02	3	0	3.14	14	0	0	14	14	7	5	0	6	10	.255	.339	.327	16.13	9.68	62
Alvarez, Jhosmer	R-R	6-1	155	6-29-01	1	1	4.15	10	0	2	13	12	8	6	0	5	12	.250	.315	.271	22.22	9.26	54
Amendt, Kyle	R-R	6-5	237	4-5-00	1	1	0.68	11	0	5	13	8	2	1	0	2	27	.167	.196	.167	52.94	3.92	51
Angelo, Roman	R-R	6-5	220	5-17-00	5	5	3.46	17	17	0	96	75	41	37	8	33	111	.216	.293	.349	27.82	8.27	399
Baker, Alec	R-R	6-3	202	12-4-99	3	2	2.37	28	3	1	65	57	24	17	4	16	63	.232	.294	.350	23.25	5.90	271
Cabrera, Jose	R-R	6-3	190	5-30-02	4	2	2.32	11	11	0	66	44	21	17	5	18	62	.187	.250	.289	23.85	6.92	260
Cerda, Junior	R-R	5-11	170	6-15-00	2	1	4.30	18	0	0	23	17	15	11	2	22	33	.195	.386	.322	28.95	19.30	114
Chalas, Yordin	R-R	6-3	175	2-22-04	0	2	4.82	23	0	3	28	28	17	15	3	15	39	.257	.346	.376	30.71	11.81	127
Clayton, Logan	R-R	6-5	188	5-2-00	4	6	4.50	17	17	0	86	84	47	43	7	32	72	.257	.324	.401	19.46	8.65	370
Corcoran, Billy	R-R	6-8	220	8-21-99	2	0	2.22	5	5	0	28	24	8	7	2	7	36	.231	.289	.317	31.30	6.09	115
Durke, Hayden	R-R	6-1	206	5-1-02	2	1	11.57	5	0	0	5	4	6	6	1	9	3	.267	.519	.533	10.71	32.14	28
Elbis, Joe	R-R	6-1	150	9-24-02	7	3	2.79	16	16	0	90	74	32	28	5	29	75	.218	.286	.304	20.05	7.75	374
Giesting, Spencer	L-L	6-4	200	7-2-01	5	3	1.50	10	10	0	60	39	13	10	2	13	67	.180	.236	.253	28.76	5.58	233
Gutierrez, Gerardo	R-R	6-0	177	9-15-98	0	0	0.00	4	0	1	6	4	1	0	0	2	5	.200	.273	.250	21.74	8.70	23
Kelly, Merrill	R-R	6-2	202	10-14-88	0	0	6.75	1	1	0	4	6	3	3	1	0	2	.333	.333	.611	11.11	0.00	18
Larsen, Dillon	R-L	6-5	230	7-9-98	0	1	8.10	2	0	0	3	2	3	3	0	3	5	.182	.357	.273	35.71	21.43	14
Linskey, Matthew	R-R	6-7	245	4-19-02	0	1	8.53	6	0	0	6	6	7	6	1	6	7	.273	.452	.500	22.58	19.35	31
Mendez, Teofilo	R-R	5-11	170	10-8-01	1	0	9.45	5	0	0	7	10	7	7	2	4	6	.345	.424	.621	18.18	12.12	33
Meza, Carlos	L-L	6-1	155	2-10-01	1	1	4.24	24	0	0	23	23	12	11	1	19	30	.261	.402	.341	26.79	16.96	112
Minyety, Jorge	R-R	6-1	170	1-4-03	0	0	13.50	2	0	0	2	2	3	3	1	3	2	.250	.455	.625	18.18	27.27	11
Morillo, Alfred	R-R	6-3	190	11-14-01	3	1	2.41	34	0	13	37	19	11	10	3	21	45	.148	.281	.266	29.22	13.64	154
Norris, Liam	L-L	6-4	215	8-13-01	0	0	0.00	4	0	0	3	2	0	0	0	4	6	.167	.375	.167	37.50	25.00	16
Otano, Peniel	R-R	6-4	190	10-7-00	1	1	7.64	19	0	0	18	17	19	15	0	18	13	.250	.429	.338	14.13	19.57	92
Percival, Cole	R-R	6-5	220	2-26-99	1	0	3.86	3	3	0	14	15	6	6	0	3	12	.263	.311	.351	19.67	4.92	61
Rey, Carlos	L-L	6-2	180	5-19-02	0	0	3.86	4	0	0	2	2	4	1	0	5	4	.200	.500	.500	25.00	31.25	16
Russell, Zane	R-R	6-2	196	6-12-02	4	5	5.54	41	0	2	37	30	28	23	3	27	48	.222	.350	.341	29.45	16.56	163
Saul, Eli	L-R	6-5	215	8-16-01	1	3	5.40	36	0	3	35	47	34	21	4	15	26	.333	.411	.489	15.76	9.09	165
Short, Avery	R-L	6-1	205	3-14-01	7	9	3.51	24	23	0	128	113	58	50	10	36	112	.238	.298	.364	21.21	6.82	528
Sims, Landon	R-R	6-2	227	1-3-01	2	0	2.12	25	0	1	34	33	13	8	1	14	45	.254	.336	.331	30.00	9.33	150
Sosa, Listher	R-R	6-4	208	9-6-01	4	2	3.07	31	0	4	44	35	20	15	2	14	45	.222	.295	.310	25.00	7.78	180
Steinmetz, Jacob	R-R	6-5	220	7-19-03	1	5	4.37	13	13	0	58	63	31	28	4	25	54	.283	.370	.390	20.69	9.58	261
Telfer, Shane	L-L	6-1	185	7-17-01	1	0	3.29	6	0	0	14	9	5	5	0	7	9	.188	.310	.271	15.52	12.07	58
Vasquez, Armando	L-L	5-11	160	5-4-01	1	1	6.44	34	0	0	36	27	29	26	5	25	43	.211	.348	.391	27.04	15.72	159
Walters, Jean	S-R	5-11	155	8-13-01	0	0	0.00	2	0	1	1	0	0	0	0	0	0	.000	.200	.000	0.00	0.00	5
Wendell, Wyatt	R-R	6-5	215	2-11-00	0	2	4.20	6	3	0	15	17	13	7	1	8	6	.298	.420	.404	8.57	11.43	70
Yan, Ricardo	R-R	6-4	180	11-14-02	2	3	3.68	9	9	0	37	24	25	15	2	31	36	.185	.355	.308	21.69	18.67	166

Fielding

Catcher	PCT	G	PO	A	E	DP	PB
Boyd	1.000	1	1	0	0	0	0
Cerda	.991	78	703	42	7	3	16
Lin	.929	4	24	2	2	0	1
Logan	.988	51	399	21	5	4	6
Martin	.958	6	44	2	2	0	0
Rios	.909	2	9	1	1	0	0

First Base	PCT	G	PO	A	E	DP
Castillo	.987	17	139	10	2	14
Conticello	1.000	16	124	8	0	14
Feltner	1.000	11	79	5	0	6
Fernandez	1.000	8	59	5	0	3
Groover	1.000	1	4	1	0	1
Lin	1.000	2	7	0	0	0
Martin	.905	3	19	0	2	2
Sim	.992	84	563	33	5	50

Second Base	PCT	G	PO	A	E	DP
Corniel	.889	3	2	6	1	2
Fernandez	1.000	1	4	4	0	1
Groover	.968	7	11	19	1	3
Pena	.965	88	162	221	14	56
Roberts	1.000	1	0	3	0	0

	PCT	G	PO	A	E	DP
Troy	.980	12	21	28	1	3
Walters	1.000	20	36	53	0	12

Third Base	PCT	G	PO	A	E	DP
Corniel	1.000	7	2	10	0	1
Crenshaw	1.000	1	1	0	0	0
Fernandez	.924	69	37	122	13	13
Groover	.872	23	10	31	6	2
Pena	1.000	1	0	1	0	0
Sim	.930	21	18	35	4	1
Walters	1.000	18	11	29	0	4

Shortstop	PCT	G	PO	A	E	DP
Corniel	.968	66	79	162	8	29
Fernandez	.956	16	28	37	3	8
Troy	.909	44	45	114	16	19
Walters	.973	9	20	16	1	7

Outfield	PCT	G	PO	A	E	DP
Castillo	1.000	26	39	1	0	0
Conticello	.980	103	184	14	4	0
Crenshaw	.929	18	39	0	3	0
Feltner	1.000	3	2	0	0	0
Franco	.959	43	70	1	3	1
Hurley	.980	118	234	7	5	0
Johnson	.909	17	20	0	2	0
Patino	.971	14	32	1	1	0
Pena	1.000	8	13	0	0	0
Pintar	.991	54	112	3	1	0
Roberts	.833	8	4	1	1	0
Walters	.500	2	1	0	1	0

VISALIA RAWHIDE — *LOW-A*

CALIFORNIA LEAGUE

Batting	B-T	Ht.	Wt.	DOB	AVG	OBP	SLG	G	PA	AB	R	H	2B	3B	HR	RBI	BB	HBP	SH	SF	SO	SB	CS	BB%	SO%
Barriga, Alberto	R-R	5-9	155	11-15-04	.105	.150	.211	6	20	19	3	2	2	0	0	0	1	0	0	0	10	0	0	5.00	50.00
Boyd, Jermiah	R-R	5-10	225	7-1-00	.000	.125	.000	2	8	7	0	0	0	0	0	0	1	0	0	0	3	0	0	12.50	37.50
Castillo, Kenny	R-R	6-2	170	5-13-04	.280	.325	.376	88	382	346	36	97	21	0	4	55	21	6	1	8	93	2	0	5.50	24.35
Castillo, Neyfy	R-R	6-1	175	3-2-01	.304	.385	.609	5	26	23	7	7	1	0	2	9	2	1	0	0	5	1	0	7.69	19.23
Crenshaw, Wyatt	L-R	6-0	180	4-21-00	.250	.286	.313	11	35	32	7	8	0	1	0	3	2	0	0	1	8	1	1	5.71	22.86
Crisantes, Demetrio	R-R	6-0	178	9-5-04	.333	.429	.478	63	295	249	58	83	16	1	6	40	38	5	0	2	47	20	2	12.88	15.93
De Leon, Adrian	R-R	5-7	180	2-9-04	.208	.380	.320	74	298	231	43	48	11	0	5	32	50	15	1	1	79	5	0	16.78	26.51
Feltner, Jackson	R-R	6-2	225	9-19-01	.260	.391	.413	63	256	208	30	54	9	1	7	36	42	4	0	2	75	2	1	16.41	29.30
Franco, Junior	L-L	5-9	165	9-13-02	.286	.373	.416	43	185	161	20	46	5	2	4	22	20	3	0	1	31	11	5	10.81	16.76
Jones, Druw	R-R	6-4	180	11-28-03	.275	.409	.405	109	471	378	74	104	15	8	6	65	85	3	1	4	132	21	6	18.05	28.03
Josepha, Jakey	L-R	6-2	135	5-15-04	.114	.215	.129	21	81	70	10	8	1	0	0	3	8	1	2	0	34	1	0	9.88	41.98
Luis, Jansel	B-R	6-0	170	3-6-05	.265	.337	.414	109	523	471	73	125	29	10	7	50	40	11	1	0	109	20	10	7.65	20.84
Marte, Modeifi	R-R	6-1	200	7-31-02	.218	.309	.296	62	249	216	28	47	8	0	3	35	26	4	0	3	55	8	1	10.44	22.09
McLaughlin, Ben	L-R	6-3	200	5-30-02	.233	.406	.356	24	102	73	10	17	3	0	2	17	23	1	1	4	25	1	1	22.55	24.51
Ortiz, Angel	L-L	6-0	180	10-3-02	.300	.381	.471	88	376	327	60	98	22	5	8	53	37	8	1	3	70	4	6	9.84	18.62
Pena, Jefferson	R-R	5-8	160	1-13-04	.200	.294	.250	90	323	280	37	56	8	0	2	29	31	7	3	2	85	16	5	9.60	26.32
Roberts, Cole	R-R	5-9	165	10-9-00	.198	.274	.279	30	96	86	13	17	3	2	0	7	9	0	1	0	22	8	2	9.38	22.92
Rojas, Anderdson	L-R	5-10	150	3-8-04	.246	.315	.354	106	446	395	67	97	16	6	5	46	37	6	2	6	74	34	9	8.30	16.59
Santana, Ruben	R-R	6-0	190	2-16-05	.219	.328	.305	106	454	384	48	84	11	5	4	51	59	6	0	5	121	11	0	13.00	26.65
Soler, Yassel	R-R	5-11	185	1-26-06	.125	.222	.125	2	9	8	0	1	0	0	0	1	1	0	0	0	2	0	0	11.11	22.22
Torin, Cristofer	R-R	5-10	155	5-26-05	.255	.381	.344	108	512	419	78	107	19	3	4	50	81	6	3	3	84	15	5	15.82	16.41
Waldschmidt, Ryan	R-R	6-1	205	10-7-02	.273	.485	.318	14	66	44	11	12	2	0	0	7	15	5	0	2	9	4	2	22.73	13.64

Pitching	B-T	Ht.	Wt.	DOB	W	L	ERA	G	GS	SV	IP	Hits	Runs	ER	HR	BB	SO	AVG	OBP	SLG	SO%	BB%	BF
Abner, Philip	L-L	6-1	220	5-5-02	0	0	0.53	9	0	0	17	6	1	1	0	3	25	.105	.190	.175	39.68	4.76	63
Alvarez, Jhosmer	R-R	6-1	155	6-29-01	1	0	1.80	7	0	0	10	6	2	2	0	4	15	.150	.244	.175	33.33	8.89	45
Anderson, Casey	R-R	6-4	185	8-31-00	6	8	6.37	21	21	0	89	87	66	63	12	47	93	.254	.363	.418	22.57	11.41	412
Angelo, Roman	R-R	6-5	220	5-17-00	2	1	3.60	6	5	1	25	21	11	10	1	17	40	.231	.364	.308	36.36	15.45	110
Britton, Rio	S-L	6-2	189	12-23-02	1	4	3.97	35	1	1	68	69	36	30	5	34	77	.270	.365	.375	25.93	11.45	297
Cerda, Junior	R-R	5-11	170	6-15-00	0	1	13.50	2	0	0	2	5	5	3	0	0	6	.417	.462	.500	46.15	0.00	13
Chalas, Yordin	R-R	6-3	175	2-22-04	1	3	3.18	18	0	4	23	18	13	8	2	11	33	.217	.305	.349	34.02	11.34	97
Craig, Luke	L-L	6-2	205	8-6-01	0	0	1.13	7	0	1	8	6	1	1	0	2	11	.207	.281	.207	34.38	6.25	32
Dominguez, Eric	L-L	6-3	180	1-12-03	3	1	3.09	9	0	1	32	22	11	11	3	10	35	.193	.260	.316	27.34	7.81	128
Durke, Hayden	R-R	6-1	206	5-1-02	2	0	2.33	34	0	2	46	22	13	12	3	36	69	.142	.314	.226	35.20	18.37	196
Fitzgibbons, Jake	L-L	5-11	175	3-21-02	0	0	5.93	10	0	1	14	8	9	9	2	17	19	.174	.415	.370	29.23	26.15	65
Garnett, Travis	R-L	6-6	225	1-19-03	0	1	9.00	3	0	0	2	0	2	2	0	9	2	.000	.600	.000	13.33	60.00	15
Grice, Caden	L-L	6-6	240	6-15-02	3	3	3.75	12	11	0	50	37	24	21	4	29	68	.207	.339	.324	31.19	13.30	218
Isea, Edgar	R-R	6-3	185	8-20-02	3	4	4.46	32	0	2	34	18	18	17	1	30	48	.161	.362	.188	31.58	19.74	152
Knowlton, Sam	R-R	6-7	255	6-15-00	4	4	5.66	31	0	3	35	37	28	22	1	33	43	.276	.428	.366	24.57	18.86	175
Larrondo, Denny	R-R	6-2	180	5-31-02	6	5	3.56	23	23	0	94	76	52	37	7	68	107	.226	.371	.368	25.36	16.11	422
Liebano, Alexis	R-R	6-1	175	3-8-03	4	6	5.60	34	0	9	35	35	27	22	6	17	48	.252	.342	.439	30.19	10.69	159
Linskey, Matthew	R-R	6-7	245	4-19-02	1	0	1.59	13	0	0	23	13	7	4	0	9	37	.167	.267	.244	41.11	10.00	90
Marriott, Mason	L-R	6-2	188	8-14-02	0	0	2.57	3	0	0	7	6	2	2	0	1	6	.231	.259	.269	22.22	3.70	27
Marte, Modeifi	R-R	6-1	200	7-31-02	0	0	0.00	1	0	0	1	0	0	0	0	1	0	.000	.250	.000	0.00	25.00	4
Mendez, Teofilo	R-R	5-11	170	10-8-01	0	0	1.41	23	0	0	45	38	15	7	1	17	51	.228	.303	.299	27.13	9.04	188
Minyety, Jorge	R-R	6-1	170	1-4-03	3	0	2.38	11	0	0	23	13	9	6	1	9	18	.165	.287	.278	19.15	9.57	94
Nunez, Daniel	R-R	6-0	196	4-3-03	3	1	3.21	20	11	0	67	65	26	24	3	12	72	.248	.290	.359	25.71	4.29	280
Otano, Peniel	R-R	6-4	190	10-7-00	4	0	1.42	13	0	0	19	14	5	3	0	12	21	.194	.314	.236	24.42	13.95	86
Paredes, Wilkin	L-L	6-2	180	9-19-03	6	5	5.49	16	16	0	82	96	56	50	13	17	69	.284	.321	.467	19.11	4.71	361
Perez, Adonys	L-L	6-3	185	10-10-03	5	8	6.63	22	21	0	96	110	76	71	13	44	95	.293	.378	.473	21.74	10.07	437
Pinales, Darlin	R-R	6-4	240	8-28-02	0	1	8.24	16	0	0	20	17	22	18	1	24	30	.227	.426	.347	29.70	23.76	101
Quinn, Braden	L-L	6-3	210	6-24-03	1	0	0.00	3	0	1	7	2	1	0	0	2	9	.087	.192	.087	34.62	7.69	26
Reid, Rocco	R-L	5-11	190	10-16-02	0	1	11.25	4	0	0	4	4	5	5	0	3	5	.286	.368	.429	25.00	15.00	20
Rey, Carlos	L-L	6-2	180	5-19-02	0	0	3.86	4	0	0	2	2	4	1	0	5	4	.200	.500	.500	25.00	31.25	16
Roberts, Cole	R-R	5-9	165	10-9-00	1	0	4.50	1	0	0	2	2	2	1	1	0	1	.286	.286	.714	14.29	0.00	7
Savino, Nate	L-L	6-3	210	1-24-02	0	4	9.66	11	11	0	32	31	42	34	6	22	31	.246	.378	.444	19.87	14.10	156
Sierra, Diomede	L-L	6-2	170	9-11-01	0	0	18.00	5	0	0	4	8	8	8	0	11	3	.421	.645	.474	9.68	35.48	31
Sims, Landon	R-R	6-2	227	1-3-01	2	0	4.38	16	1	1	25	20	12	12	2	14	40	.220	.336	.352	37.38	13.08	107
Sosa, Listher	R-R	6-4	208	9-6-01	0	0	6.75	2	0	1	4	2	3	3	2	2	5	.154	.267	.615	33.33	13.33	15

Pitching	B-T	Ht.	Wt.	DOB	W	L	ERA	G	GS	SV	IP	Hits	Runs	ER	HR	BB	SO	AVG	OBP	SLG	SO%	BB%	BF
Steinmetz, Jacob	R-R	6-5	220	7-19-03	2	2	3.60	10	10	0	50	53	21	20	2	17	59	.277	.335	.393	27.70	7.98	213
Telfer, Shane	L-L	6-1	185	7-17-01	0	0	3.60	6	0	0	10	10	6	4	0	9	9	.278	.404	.389	19.15	19.15	47

Fielding

Catcher	PCT	G	PO	A	E	DP	PB
Barriga	1.000	2	20	3	0	1	0
Boyd	1.000	2	24	4	0	1	1
Castillo	.991	71	724	42	7	4	15
De Leon	.985	61	615	38	10	2	16

First Base	PCT	G	PO	A	E	DP
Crisantes	1.000	9	67	6	0	9
Feltner	.993	39	275	16	2	38
Marte	.981	43	294	21	6	31
McLaughlin	1.000	20	152	10	0	14
Santana	.983	25	165	9	3	17

Second Base	PCT	G	PO	A	E	DP
Crenshaw	1.000	1	0	1	0	0
Crisantes	.980	36	60	87	3	24
Luis	.966	25	32	53	3	11
Roberts	.981	17	16	35	1	8
Rojas	.991	26	40	67	1	24
Torin	.984	32	41	86	2	21

Third Base	PCT	G	PO	A	E	DP
Crisantes	1.000	12	7	21	0	0
Luis	.965	25	10	45	2	4
Rojas	.882	19	7	23	4	5
Santana	.937	80	39	124	11	12
Soler	1.000	2	0	3	0	0

Shortstop	PCT	G	PO	A	E	DP
Luis	.965	49	50	114	6	31
Rojas	.958	14	14	32	2	7
Torin	.943	71	98	182	17	45

Outfield	PCT	G	PO	A	E	DP
Castillo	1.000	5	4	0	0	0
Crenshaw	1.000	9	13	0	0	0
Feltner	1.000	2	1	0	0	0
Franco	.980	35	47	2	1	1
Jones	.978	105	215	7	5	2
Josepha	.938	19	27	3	2	1
Marte	1.000	2	4	0	0	0
Ortiz	.973	83	138	5	4	2
Pena	.952	89	128	12	7	4
Roberts	1.000	6	6	2	0	0
Rojas	.971	39	64	2	2	0
Waldschmidt	.926	13	23	2	2	1

ACL D-BACKS

ROOKIE

ARIZONA COMPLEX LEAGUE

Batting	B-T	Ht.	Wt.	DOB	AVG	OBP	SLG	G	PA	AB	R	H	2B	3B	HR	RBI	BB	HBP	SH	SF	SO	SB	CS	BB%	SO%
Alcala, Moises	B-R	5-9	155	2-10-03	.286	.500	.429	4	10	7	0	2	1	0	0	0	3	0	0	0	1	0	0	30.00	10.00
Alpuria, Jose	B-R	6-2	160	2-12-05	.287	.430	.357	42	165	129	21	37	2	2	1	17	19	15	0	2	42	16	2	11.52	25.45
Aparicio, Juan	R-R	6-0	165	9-25-02	.189	.317	.208	24	63	53	11	10	1	0	0	2	8	2	0	0	14	0	0	12.70	22.22
Barriga, Alberto	R-R	5-9	155	11-15-04	.276	.362	.432	46	213	185	40	51	13	2	4	26	23	3	0	2	42	12	5	10.80	19.72
Barrosa, Jorge	B-L	5-5	165	2-17-01	.235	.289	.412	9	38	34	4	8	1	1	1	7	2	1	0	1	7	1	1	5.26	18.42
Benitez, Johan	B-R	6-3	170	8-7-03	.136	.282	.153	21	71	59	10	8	1	0	0	3	12	0	0	0	24	0	1	16.90	33.80
Benua, Alexander	R-R	6-2	185	10-19-03	.301	.385	.478	44	161	136	31	41	8	2	4	31	18	3	0	4	38	11	1	11.18	23.60
Cabeza, Diosfran	B-R	5-10	155	5-13-03	.273	.321	.325	24	84	77	12	21	4	0	0	14	5	1	0	1	13	1	0	5.95	15.48
Cabral, Riquelmin	B-R	5-10	165	5-12-03	.210	.275	.290	22	70	62	8	13	1	2	0	8	6	0	1	1	20	1	0	8.57	28.57
Crisantes, Demetrio	R-R	6-0	178	9-5-04	.355	.431	.521	29	144	121	31	43	7	5	1	20	17	2	0	4	22	10	1	11.81	15.28
De La Cruz, Abdias	R-R	6-3	175	11-3-04	.301	.399	.435	52	224	186	39	56	15	5	0	32	32	1	1	4	46	11	3	14.29	20.54
Groover, Gino	R-R	6-2	212	4-16-02	.222	.353	.333	8	34	27	5	6	1	1	0	4	5	1	0	1	3	0	1	14.71	8.82
Josepha, Jakey	L-R	6-2	135	5-15-04	.262	.340	.410	48	213	183	38	48	13	1	4	38	20	4	1	5	70	9	2	9.39	32.86
Lawlar, Jordan	R-R	6-1	190	7-17-02	.276	.405	.379	9	37	29	7	8	3	0	0	8	5	2	0	1	4	5	0	13.51	10.81
Moreno, Gabriel	R-R	5-11	195	2-14-00	.500	.667	1.000	1	3	2	1	1	1	0	0	0	1	0	0	0	0	0	0	33.33	0.00
Nin, Yerald	L-R	6-0	170	8-18-05	.269	.384	.326	51	211	175	33	47	6	2	0	23	32	2	0	2	53	23	4	15.17	25.12
Ortiz, Angel	L-L	6-0	180	10-3-02	.000	.375	.000	2	8	4	0	0	0	0	0	1	3	0	0	1	1	0	0	37.50	12.50
Perdomo, Geraldo	B-R	6-2	203	10-22-99	.125	.273	.125	3	11	8	1	1	0	0	0	2	2	0	0	1	3	0	0	18.18	27.27
Pintar, Andrew	R-R	6-2	190	3-23-01	.250	.333	.250	2	9	8	1	2	0	0	0	0	1	0	0	0	3	1	0	11.11	33.33
Polanco, Ronny	R-R	5-11	180	8-23-03	.211	.320	.266	32	128	109	19	23	3	0	1	9	13	5	0	1	32	3	1	10.16	25.00
Rios, Alejandro	R-R	5-11	150	3-30-05	.000	.167	.000	2	6	5	1	0	0	0	0	2	1	0	0	0	2	0	0	16.67	33.33
Rodriguez, Adrian	R-R	6-0	170	10-21-03	.290	.391	.383	35	128	107	24	31	1	3	1	18	15	4	0	2	28	3	2	11.72	21.88
Soler, Yassel	R-R	5-11	185	1-26-06	.303	.351	.472	53	239	218	36	66	15	2	6	35	16	2	0	3	41	6	0	6.69	17.15
Thomas, Alek	L-L	5-11	175	4-28-00	.538	.563	.846	5	16	13	3	7	1	0	1	3	2	0	0	1	1	0	0	12.50	6.25
Troy, Tommy	R-R	5-10	197	1-17-02	.318	.308	.545	7	26	22	3	7	3	1	0	5	1	0	0	3	7	0	0	3.85	26.92
Weber, Andy	L-R	5-11	190	7-24-97	.258	.314	.419	8	35	31	6	8	2	0	1	6	3	0	0	1	3	0	0	8.57	8.57
Zapata, Gian	L-L	6-4	195	9-13-05	.100	.262	.180	15	61	50	8	5	1	0	1	7	9	2	0	0	27	2	3	14.75	44.26

Pitching	B-T	Ht.	Wt.	DOB	W	L	ERA	G	GS	SV	IP	Hits	Runs	ER	HR	BB	SO	AVG	OBP	SLG	SO%	BB%	BF
Abner, Philip	L-L	6-1	220	5-5-02	0	0	3.38	3	2	0	3	2	1	1	0	1	3	.200	.273	.200	27.27	9.09	11
Amparo, Jeffrey	R-R	6-3	175	9-24-04	1	1	3.95	5	1	0	14	12	7	6	0	16	17	.235	.426	.294	25.00	23.53	68
Aparicio, Juan	R-R	6-0	165	9-25-02	0	0	0.00	1	0	0	1	0	0	0	0	0	1	.000	.000	.000	50.00	0.00	2
Backhus, Kyle	L-L	6-4	185	1-31-98	0	0	2.45	3	1	0	4	1	2	1	0	0	6	.083	.154	.083	46.15	0.00	13
Barnes, Zach	R-R	6-0	180	4-10-99	0	0	0.00	2	0	0	2	0	0	0	0	0	3	.000	.000	.000	50.00	0.00	6
Benitez, Johan	S-R	6-3	170	8-7-03	1	0	7.71	2	0	1	2	3	3	2	0	1	2	.375	.500	.500	20.00	10.00	10
Cardenas, Anderson	R-R	6-2	160	6-21-06	4	1	3.38	12	3	0	35	22	13	13	3	13	39	.185	.287	.294	28.68	9.56	136
Castillo, Jose	L-L	6-6	252	1-10-96	0	0	0.00	3	2	0	3	1	0	0	0	2	8	.083	.214	.083	57.14	14.29	14
Castro, Miguel	R-R	6-7	201	12-24-94	0	0	0.00	2	2	0	3	2	0	0	0	0	5	.200	.200	.200	50.00	0.00	10
Chatwood, Tyler	R-R	5-11	200	12-16-89	0	0	0.00	1	1	0	1	1	0	0	0	1	1	.250	.400	.250	20.00	20.00	5
Digon, Jairon	R-R	6-0	165	11-7-05	1	0	4.86	6	0	0	17	18	9	9	1	13	17	.281	.410	.391	21.79	16.67	78
Dominguez, Eric	L-L	6-3	180	1-12-03	1	1	2.20	9	5	0	41	27	16	10	1	19	53	.188	.293	.236	31.55	11.31	168
Escobar, Jesus	R-R	6-0	150	2-28-06	0	0	16.20	3	0	0	3	4	6	6	0	7	2	.286	.545	.429	9.09	31.82	22
Fitzgibbons, Jake	L-L	5-11	175	3-21-02	1	0	0.00	4	0	0	4	2	0	0	0	0	9	.143	.143	.214	64.29	0.00	14
Frias, Luis	R-R	6-3	245	5-23-98	0	0	0.00	1	1	0	1	1	0	0	0	1	1	.333	.500	.667	25.00	25.00	4
Fuerte, Abel	R-R	6-2	175	1-1-05	2	3	8.10	12	0	0	17	26	19	15	1	17	15	.371	.505	.500	16.30	18.48	92
Gonzalez, Joangel	R-R	6-4	210	7-1-04	5	0	4.98	15	1	1	34	31	20	19	2	14	40	.237	.329	.336	26.85	9.40	149
Green, Josh	R-R	6-3	211	8-31-95	1	0	0.00	2	0	0	3	0	0	0	0	1	6	.000	.091	.000	54.55	9.09	11

Guzman, Alvin	R-R	6-1	166	10-20-01	0	0	4.91	4	0	0	4	5	2	2	0	3	5	.333	.444	.400	27.78	16.67	18
Hitt, Grayson	R-L	6-3	195	12-11-01	0	0	15.00	6	5	0	6	5	11	10	1	11	9	.217	.471	.391	26.47	32.35	34
Isea, Edgar	R-R	6-3	185	8-20-02	0	0	0.00	1	0	0	1	0	0	0	0	3	1	.000	.600	.000	20.00	60.00	5
Jacques, Joe	L-L	6-4	210	3-11-95	0	0	9.00	1	1	0	1	2	1	1	0	0	1	.400	.400	.400	20.00	0.00	5
Larsen, Dillon	R-L	6-5	230	7-9-98	1	0	1.04	6	0	2	9	8	1	1	0	7	6	.308	.455	.308	18.18	21.21	33
Lin, Yu-Min	L-L	5-11	160	7-12-03	0	0	1.80	1	1	0	5	1	1	1	0	2	9	.067	.176	.067	52.94	11.76	17
Linskey, Matthew	R-R	6-7	245	4-19-02	0	0	0.00	3	0	0	3	1	0	0	0	1	7	.091	.167	.091	58.33	8.33	12
Minyety, Jorge	R-R	6-1	170	1-4-03	2	1	1.53	12	0	3	18	20	11	3	0	7	31	.270	.345	.324	36.90	8.33	84
Morales, Francisco	R-R	6-4	185	10-27-99	0	0	2.25	4	0	0	4	1	1	1	0	3	6	.077	.294	.231	35.29	17.65	17
Norris, Liam	L-L	6-4	215	8-13-01	1	0	10.38	4	1	0	4	5	5	5	0	5	2	.333	.476	.467	9.09	22.73	22
Nunez, Daniel	R-R	6-0	196	4-3-03	0	0	7.20	3	0	1	5	10	4	4	1	2	11	.400	.444	.560	40.74	7.41	27
Paredes, Wilkin	L-L	6-2	180	9-19-03	2	0	1.13	2	0	0	8	6	1	1	0	1	8	.207	.233	.207	26.67	3.33	30
Pinales, Darlin	R-R	6-4	240	8-28-02	0	0	2.37	16	0	7	19	10	5	5	0	18	30	.161	.381	.226	35.29	21.18	85
Ramirez, Santiago	R-R	6-2	190	8-30-04	1	3	6.53	13	0	0	21	24	19	15	1	8	27	.279	.364	.407	27.27	8.08	99
Ray, Dylan	R-R	6-3	230	5-9-01	0	0	0.00	1	1	0	3	2	0	0	0	1	6	.222	.300	.333	60.00	10.00	10
Reynoso, Erick	R-R	6-4	185	11-21-02	2	0	5.03	11	7	0	39	29	23	22	5	32	34	.212	.373	.380	19.21	18.08	177
Rodriguez, Chris	R-R	6-2	185	7-20-98	1	0	0.00	2	0	0	3	0	0	0	0	0	5	.000	.000	.000	55.56	0.00	9
Sanchez, Junior	R-R	5-10	175	9-16-05	3	2	3.78	13	0	1	33	34	18	14	2	18	37	.266	.354	.398	25.17	12.24	147
Santana, Sandro	L-L	5-10	150	3-7-05	2	0	7.11	8	1	1	19	18	16	15	3	13	19	.265	.386	.441	22.62	15.48	84
Savino, Nate	L-L	6-3	210	1-24-02	0	1	1.32	9	7	0	14	6	6	2	0	12	20	.130	.339	.130	32.26	19.35	62
Serda, Dawel	R-R	6-3	165	10-13-04	2	1	5.82	11	8	0	34	31	26	22	5	19	28	.242	.342	.406	18.79	12.75	149
Sewald, Paul	R-R	6-3	219	5-26-90	0	0	0.00	1	0	0	1	0	0	0	0	0	2	.000	.000	.000	50.00	0.00	4
Sierra, Diomede	L-L	6-2	170	9-11-01	2	0	6.48	8	0	1	8	11	7	6	0	11	6	.333	.500	.394	13.64	25.00	44
Uelmen, Erich	R-R	6-3	195	5-19-96	0	0	0.00	2	2	0	3	1	0	0	0	1	3	.111	.200	.111	30.00	10.00	10
Valdez, Vitico	R-R	6-4	175	11-6-03	2	3	4.81	12	7	0	43	48	31	23	0	28	44	.284	.401	.367	21.67	13.79	203
Zapata, Deyer	L-L	6-0	150	12-4-03	1	4	3.89	15	0	0	35	33	17	15	4	19	41	.248	.342	.451	26.45	12.26	155

Fielding

C: Barriga 38, Cabeza 22, Alcala 3, Rios 2, Moreno 1. 1B: Polanco 24, Benitez 17, Cabral 13, Aparicio 6, Groover 3, Crisantes 2. 2B: Crisantes 18, Nin 17, Rodriguez 17, Aparicio 14, Weber 1, Groover 1. 3B: Soler 45, Crisantes 7, Cabral 6, Groover 3, Aparicio 3, Lawlar 2, Rodriguez 1. SS: Nin 38, Rodriguez 17, Weber 6, Lawlar 6, Troy 5, Perdomo 2. LF: De La Cruz 26, Benua 15, Josepha 11, Alpuria 8, Ortiz 2, Barrosa 1, Benitez 1. CF: Josepha 18, Alpuria 13, De La Cruz 11, Zapata 7, Barrosa 7, Benua 7, Thomas 4, Pintar 2. RF: Alpuria 21, Benua 15, Josepha 14, Zapata 7, De La Cruz 3.

DSL ARIZONA RED — *ROOKIE*

DOMINICAN SUMMER LEAGUE

Batting	B-T	Ht.	Wt.	DOB	AVG	OBP	SLG	G	PA	AB	R	H	2B	3B	HR	RBI	BB	HBP	SH	SF	SO	SB	CS	BB%	SO%
Alejos, Eliesbert	R-R	6-0	175	6-9-06	.309	.377	.387	53	224	194	30	60	10	1	1	29	16	7	4	3	20	8	4	7.14	8.93
Alvarez, Juan	B-R	6-1	190	3-3-06	.194	.325	.274	24	77	62	9	12	2	0	1	12	12	1	0	2	20	1	1	15.58	25.97
Araujo, Gabriel	R-R	6-0	175	9-7-04	.266	.420	.313	25	81	64	9	17	3	0	0	8	15	2	0	0	15	7	2	18.52	18.52
Benzan, Alfredo	B-R	6-2	165	4-21-07	.248	.300	.297	28	112	101	17	25	5	0	0	10	7	1	2	1	28	6	1	6.25	25.00
Blanco, Pedro	L-R	6-1	205	4-22-07	.218	.271	.382	14	59	55	10	12	3	0	2	8	4	0	0	0	19	1	0	6.78	32.20
Carpio, Albert	R-R	5-9	150	8-12-05	.254	.357	.310	27	85	71	11	18	2	1	0	9	6	6	1	1	7	2	4	7.06	8.24
Encarnacion, Andy	R-R	6-1	160	1-18-05	.250	.358	.375	44	151	128	24	32	6	2	2	18	20	2	0	1	33	13	6	13.25	21.85
Fernandez, Johan	R-R	6-0	180	3-10-07	.130	.355	.130	13	32	23	4	3	0	0	0	1	6	2	1	0	7	0	0	18.75	21.88
Gallardo, Leo	L-R	6-0	185	11-2-05	.000	.000	.000	2	3	3	0	0	0	0	0	0	0	0	0	0	1	0	0	0.00	33.33
Gallegos, Alonso	R-R	5-9	150	2-23-07	.306	.433	.341	35	104	85	10	26	3	0	0	12	18	1	0	0	20	4	4	17.31	19.23
Gonzalez, Dauwin	R-R	6-1	170	2-19-06	.229	.304	.375	15	56	48	10	11	1	0	2	10	5	1	0	2	12	3	1	8.93	21.43
Guanchez, Alfredo	B-R	6-0	150	10-17-05	.275	.410	.376	49	188	149	31	41	5	2	2	21	34	2	0	3	37	23	5	18.09	19.68
Lara, Jorge	B-R	5-6	145	10-24-05	.234	.403	.319	15	62	47	9	11	1	0	1	3	8	6	0	1	14	4	3	12.90	22.58
Liriano, Raily	R-R	6-2	160	1-9-07	.227	.346	.288	19	81	66	12	15	4	0	0	8	12	1	0	2	32	5	3	14.81	39.51
Molina, Carlos	R-R	6-0	170	4-25-07	.136	.240	.136	13	26	22	3	3	0	0	0	2	2	1	1	0	6	2	0	7.69	23.08
Perez, Enyervert	R-R	5-11	180	10-20-05	.293	.399	.489	54	223	188	30	55	17	1	6	26	23	11	0	1	53	4	3	10.31	23.77
Perez, Miguel	R-R	6-0	155	6-1-06	.111	.200	.111	5	10	9	1	1	0	0	0	0	0	1	0	0	1	2	0	0.00	10.00
Radney, Adriel	R-R	6-3	180	6-23-07	.209	.303	.299	20	76	67	10	14	2	2	0	6	7	2	0	0	15	1	0	9.21	19.74
Ramos, Santiago	L-R	5-10	170	1-3-07	.357	.438	.357	7	16	14	0	5	0	0	0	1	1	1	0	0	3	0	0	6.25	18.75
Rivera, Belfi	L-R	6-0	165	12-16-06	.059	.292	.059	5	25	17	3	1	0	0	0	3	6	0	1	1	6	0	0	24.00	24.00
Sinzza, Kyle	R-R	5-9	160	4-11-07	.356	.455	.533	14	55	45	14	16	2	0	2	8	6	3	0	1	7	3	0	10.91	12.73
Urbina, Jose	R-R	5-11	195	5-14-06	.300	.400	.367	12	35	30	5	9	2	0	0	3	3	2	0	0	4	1	0	8.57	11.43
Virahonda, Carlos	R-R	5-11	180	12-12-05	.156	.279	.231	49	190	160	20	25	9	0	1	17	15	13	0	2	30	2	1	7.89	15.79
Zapata, Gian	L-L	6-4	195	9-13-05	.299	.457	.433	21	92	67	17	20	7	1	0	13	17	5	0	3	19	5	3	18.48	20.65

Pitching	B-T	Ht.	Wt.	DOB	W	L	ERA	G	GS	SV	IP	Hits	Runs	ER	HR	BB	SO	AVG	OBP	SLG	SO%	BB%	BF
Andujar, Luis	R-R	6-2	160	8-16-05	3	2	3.42	12	0	0	24	17	10	9	0	19	25	.200	.367	.235	22.94	17.43	109
Bello, Samuel	R-R	6-3	195	10-18-04	0	0	1.42	5	0	0	6	5	1	1	0	4	7	.217	.357	.261	25.00	14.29	28
Beltran, Angel	R-R	6-4	230	7-13-07	0	0	6.75	2	0	0	4	1	3	3	0	4	2	.083	.421	.083	10.53	21.05	19
Brea, Victor	L-L	6-4	170	10-8-02	2	0	3.86	13	0	2	14	5	7	6	0	10	18	.106	.283	.106	30.00	16.67	60
Calvo, Jeison	R-R	6-2	200	10-31-05	1	3	3.46	11	9	0	39	31	19	15	0	16	43	.218	.302	.324	26.54	9.88	162
Carrasco, Luis	L-L	6-1	175	1-22-05	0	0	0.00	2	0	0	5	5	0	0	0	3	4	.263	.364	.263	18.18	13.64	22
Ciprian, Junior	R-R	6-3	180	6-2-05	1	1	3.60	11	3	1	25	22	12	10	0	14	32	.232	.336	.263	29.09	12.73	110
De Aza, Luis	R-R	6-4	190	10-21-04	1	1	3.18	11	0	1	17	20	8	6	0	7	18	.299	.382	.388	23.68	9.21	76
Digon, Jairon	R-R	6-0	165	11-7-05	2	0	0.90	2	2	0	10	1	1	1	0	3	17	.032	.118	.032	50.00	8.82	34
Echegarreta,, Oscar	R-R	6-1	170	10-7-03	2	0	3.38	4	0	0	5	5	3	2	0	5	3	.263	.417	.368	12.00	20.00	25
Espinal, Jeury	R-R	5-11	165	1-5-07	2	1	3.12	11	4	1	40	31	15	14	4	8	58	.208	.259	.342	35.80	4.94	162
Fell, Mervin	R-R	6-1	215	2-22-03	5	2	3.27	12	5	0	33	23	13	12	0	17	40	.202	.308	.237	29.85	12.69	134

Frias, Frederic	R-R	6-3	180	6-24-04	0	1	40.50	1	0	0	1	0	3	3	0	2	0	.000	.600	.000	0.00	40.00	5
Gonzalez, Samuel	R-R	6-3	185	1-18-05	0	0	3.86	2	1	0	2	2	2	1	0	2	2	.200	.333	.300	16.67	16.67	12
Jimenez, Onias	R-R	6-1	170	5-23-04	0	0	1.80	14	0	5	15	13	3	3	0	10	19	.241	.354	.259	29.23	15.38	65
Marin, Alexis	R-R	6-6	205	9-18-04	0	0	0.00	1	0	0	1	0	0	0	0	1	2	.000	.200	.000	40.00	20.00	5
Martinez, Argenis	L-L	6-0	180	4-26-04	1	0	9.82	5	0	0	7	14	9	8	1	5	10	.412	.475	.588	25.00	12.50	40
Mena, Walvin	R-R	6-1	195	9-30-05	1	1	3.60	9	8	0	30	18	15	12	4	13	30	.173	.273	.337	24.59	10.66	122
Morales, Victor	R-R	5-10	165	10-10-01	0	0	9.00	4	0	0	4	3	4	4	0	3	8	.188	.350	.188	40.00	15.00	20
Parra, Nixon	R-R	6-2	170	1-7-04	2	2	2.08	12	0	2	17	9	6	4	0	9	13	.161	.294	.196	19.12	13.24	68
Pena, Geremias	R-R	6-2	165	10-12-06	0	0	0.00	1	1	0	2	1	0	0	0	1	1	.200	.429	.400	14.29	14.29	7
Rosario, Kelvin	L-L	6-2	140	8-28-06	4	2	2.97	10	5	0	39	34	14	13	4	15	41	.233	.323	.370	24.55	8.98	167
Rosario, Naimer	L-L	6-0	160	7-18-06	3	2	4.18	9	2	2	24	13	12	11	0	17	25	.155	.330	.238	23.58	16.04	106
Rubio, Alexis	R-R	5-9	190	8-9-02	0	0	1.50	4	0	0	6	3	1	1	0	5	5	.143	.308	.190	19.23	19.23	26
Sanchez, David	R-R	6-1	165	2-14-07	1	0	8.22	7	0	0	8	7	7	7	1	6	7	.226	.351	.323	18.92	16.22	37
Suarez, Josdanner	R-R	6-3	170	10-4-04	2	1	2.76	12	6	0	33	30	11	10	1	12	33	.248	.321	.331	24.63	8.96	134
Terrero, Robert	R-R	6-4	160	1-8-07	2	0	2.33	9	5	0	19	15	8	5	0	20	19	.224	.418	.299	20.88	21.98	91
Vasquez, Daury	R-R	6-2	170	4-17-06	1	1	4.45	9	5	0	32	23	17	16	0	17	38	.200	.321	.270	27.74	12.41	137

Fielding

C: Virahonda 37, Fernandez 13, Urbina 11, Ramos 7, Molina 4. 1B: Guanchez 31, Perez 23, Alvarez 11, Molina 1, Ramos 1. 2B: Perez 29, Gallegos 18, Lara 14, Sinzza 1. 3B: Alejos 17, Carpio 17, Guanchez 15, Gallegos 12, Perez 2, Encarnacion 1, Blanco 1. SS: Alejos 36, Carpio 13, Sinzza 13, Gallegos 1. LF: Araujo 20, Encarnacion 15, Gonzalez 10, Blanco 7, Guanchez 3, Perez 3, Zapata 2, Alvarez 2, Benzan 2, Radney 1. CF: Benzan 22, Encarnacion 14, Zapata 11, Liriano 7, Rivera 5, Gonzalez 2, Guanchez 1. RF: Encarnacion 18, Radney 12, Liriano 11, Zapata 8, Guanchez 5, Benzan 4, Gonzalez 4, Alejos 1, Araujo 1, Perez 1.

DSL ARIZONA BLACK — ROOKIE

DOMINICAN SUMMER LEAGUE

Batting	B-T	Ht.	Wt.	DOB	AVG	OBP	SLG	G	PA	AB	R	H	2B	3B	HR	RBI	BB	HBP	SH	SF	SO	SB	CS	BB%	SO%
Alvarez, Juan	B-R	6-1	190	3-3-06	.167	.286	.167	9	28	24	4	4	0	0	0	1	3	1	0	0	10	0	1	10.71	35.71
Aponte, Oscar	R-R	5-11	160	10-16-06	.227	.298	.309	36	124	110	10	25	4	1	1	12	5	6	2	0	22	8	7	4.03	17.74
Araujo, Gabriel	R-R	6-0	175	9-7-04	.316	.395	.447	13	43	38	6	12	3	1	0	4	3	2	0	0	8	3	0	6.98	18.60
Benzan, Alfredo	B-R	6-2	165	4-21-07	.268	.353	.338	20	85	71	16	19	5	0	0	10	11	0	0	3	13	8	4	12.94	15.29
Blanco, Pedro	L-R	6-1	205	4-22-07	.275	.375	.480	31	120	102	21	28	6	0	5	18	14	3	0	1	27	6	1	11.67	22.50
De La Cruz, Erick	R-R	6-0	160	11-15-06	.244	.364	.489	13	55	45	13	11	2	0	3	12	7	2	0	1	16	4	2	12.73	29.09
Fernandez, Johan	R-R	6-0	180	3-10-07	.250	.318	.450	7	22	20	1	5	4	0	0	3	1	1	0	0	4	0	1	4.55	18.18
Gonzalez, Dauwin	R-R	6-1	170	2-19-06	.224	.375	.289	27	96	76	11	17	0	1	1	6	18	1	0	1	17	2	1	18.75	17.71
Lantigua, Robert	L-R	5-9	175	5-24-07	.205	.250	.295	18	48	44	2	9	0	2	0	6	2	1	0	1	16	1	1	4.17	33.33
Liriano, Raily	R-R	6-2	160	1-9-07	.146	.271	.236	26	107	89	12	13	5	0	1	8	13	3	0	2	47	5	1	12.15	43.93
Martinez, Luis	L-R	6-1	190	9-19-05	.283	.417	.386	42	163	127	20	36	7	0	2	21	30	2	0	4	36	2	2	18.40	22.09
Medina, Steven	B-R	6-0	175	3-4-03	.214	.267	.250	9	30	28	3	6	1	0	0	4	1	1	0	0	7	0	0	3.33	23.33
Molina, Carlos	R-R	6-0	170	4-25-07	.182	.357	.455	4	14	11	1	2	0	0	1	2	2	1	0	0	5	0	1	14.29	35.71
Penuela, Wilmeyber	B-R	5-10	165	10-18-06	.222	.361	.313	35	123	99	21	22	2	2	1	15	22	0	1	1	38	5	2	17.89	30.89
Perez, Eddy	B-R	5-10	150	9-3-05	.221	.314	.327	40	119	104	19	23	1	5	0	9	12	2	1	0	53	8	3	10.08	44.54
Perez, Miguel	R-R	6-0	155	6-1-06	.274	.489	.403	28	90	62	22	17	5	0	1	7	23	4	0	1	23	6	0	25.56	25.56
Radney, Adriel	R-R	6-3	180	6-23-07	.250	.370	.273	14	54	44	6	11	1	0	0	5	7	2	0	1	10	0	1	12.96	18.52
Ramos, Santiago	L-R	5-10	170	1-3-07	.235	.297	.324	12	37	34	6	8	0	0	1	3	3	0	0	0	9	1	0	8.11	24.32
Rivera, Belfi	L-R	6-0	165	12-16-06	.198	.298	.265	44	188	162	26	32	6	1	1	7	22	2	0	2	58	7	2	11.70	30.85
Rodriguez, Jose	R-R	5-8	175	4-11-07	.238	.484	.238	8	31	21	2	5	0	0	0	0	4	6	0	0	6	0	0	12.90	19.35
Sinzza, Kyle	R-R	5-9	160	4-11-07	.252	.379	.270	35	141	115	16	29	2	0	0	8	22	2	1	1	21	11	1	15.60	14.89
Surun, Ezequiel	R-R	6-0	150	7-7-04	.297	.378	.405	45	172	148	21	44	6	2	2	17	15	6	0	3	45	9	1	8.72	26.16
Urbina, Jose	R-R	5-11	195	5-14-06	.263	.357	.400	26	112	95	13	25	4	0	3	25	9	6	0	2	24	0	1	8.04	21.43

Pitching	B-T	Ht.	Wt.	DOB	W	L	ERA	G	GS	SV	IP	Hits	Runs	ER	HR	BB	SO	AVG	OBP	SLG	SO%	BB%	BF
Almonte, Raminel	R-R	6-0	150	4-17-07	0	2	12.71	3	1	0	6	7	8	8	0	6	4	.333	.483	.381	13.33	20.00	30
Beltran, Angel	R-R	6-4	230	7-13-07	0	2	3.78	9	9	0	33	31	23	14	2	22	29	.244	.366	.339	18.71	14.19	155
Caicedo, Reinel	R-R	6-2	190	3-22-07	0	0	20.25	1	0	0	1	0	4	3	0	4	1	.000	.625	.000	12.50	50.00	8
Carrasco, Luis	L-L	6-1	175	1-22-05	1	0	2.95	6	1	0	18	12	7	6	0	5	12	.190	.271	.302	16.90	7.04	71
De Los Santos, Greudis	R-R	6-4	175	11-22-05	0	4	8.89	8	6	0	27	30	36	27	2	22	32	.280	.448	.421	22.38	15.38	143
Echegarreta,, Oscar	R-R	6-1	170	10-7-03	1	1	2.20	7	1	0	16	12	5	4	0	13	11	.211	.366	.228	15.49	18.31	71
Frias, Frederic	R-R	6-3	180	6-24-04	0	2	9.22	14	0	1	14	15	16	14	0	19	16	.273	.474	.291	21.05	25.00	76
Gonzalez, Samuel	R-R	6-3	185	1-18-05	0	2	27.00	4	1	0	4	3	11	11	0	8	7	.214	.593	.286	25.93	29.63	27
Kelly, Jaitoine	R-R	6-3	257	6-29-07	0	4	6.08	11	10	0	37	36	30	25	3	33	35	.261	.415	.384	19.89	18.75	176
Lugo, Alexander	L-L	6-1	160	8-29-06	0	0	6.75	17	0	0	20	20	17	15	1	17	10	.274	.423	.479	10.20	17.35	98
Marcano, Alan	R-R	6-4	175	4-24-07	1	3	10.80	11	1	0	20	21	25	24	2	23	23	.266	.473	.443	20.54	20.54	112
Marin, Alexis	R-R	6-6	205	9-18-04	1	2	7.71	9	5	0	28	29	29	24	3	25	30	.261	.401	.387	21.90	18.25	137
Martinez, Argenis	L-L	6-0	180	4-26-04	1	1	2.70	10	0	0	13	11	6	4	1	5	16	.224	.296	.306	29.63	9.26	54
Monegro, Cristian	R-R	6-3	170	4-11-05	1	0	10.50	5	0	0	6	3	8	7	0	11	10	.150	.455	.200	30.30	33.33	33
Nolasco, Daniel	R-R	6-3	190	11-17-05	0	1	7.56	15	0	1	17	15	15	14	1	19	13	.250	.458	.400	15.66	22.89	83
Nunez, Ariel	R-R	6-5	190	10-5-04	0	1	13.50	3	0	0	4	6	6	6	0	5	3	.400	.545	.667	13.64	22.73	22
Otero, Amauri	L-L	6-1	175	2-19-05	0	2	5.03	10	3	0	20	20	15	11	1	13	14	.267	.378	.413	14.44	15.55	90
Pena, Geremias	R-R	6-2	165	10-12-06	0	0	7.94	2	2	0	6	6	5	5	0	3	5	.286	.400	.429	19.23	11.54	26
Perez, Elquis	R-R	6-1	170	7-11-06	0	1	11.37	14	0	0	13	17	18	16	0	22	9	.321	.538	.377	11.53	28.20	78
Perez, Fabian	R-R	5-11	180	7-20-04	0	2	8.40	14	0	0	15	9	19	14	2	25	15	.173	.458	.346	18.07	30.12	83
Ramirez, Oscar	R-R	6-2	185	9-18-03	0	2	5.68	7	4	0	13	9	8	8	0	13	15	.200	.393	.267	24.59	21.31	61
Reina, Abraham	R-R	6-1	185	9-5-06	1	4	14.46	10	2	0	19	22	34	30	4	31	21	.306	.528	.556	19.27	28.44	109
Rogers, Stiven	R-R	6-2	170	1-20-07	4	2	7.52	11	3	0	32	42	32	27	3	16	31	.313	.420	.463	19.02	9.82	163
Rosario, Naimer	L-L	6-0	160	7-18-06	0	1	3.75	3	3	0	12	10	5	5	0	5	14	.250	.367	.325	28.57	10.20	49

Rubio, Alexis	R-R	5-9	190	8-9-02	0	1	31.50	3	0	0	2	7	9	7	0	4	2	.538	.667	.692	11.11	22.22	18
Sanchez, David	R-R	6-1	165	2-14-07	1	0	5.40	9	0	1	12	12	9	7	0	10	10	.279	.411	.302	17.54	17.54	57
Terrero, Robert	R-R	6-4	160	1-8-07	0	0	7.20	3	2	0	5	3	4	4	0	6	1	.176	.417	.176	4.17	25.00	24
Vargas, Modesto	R-R	6-2	195	12-14-04	0	2	10.93	14	0	0	14	14	23	17	0	26	14	.246	.482	.263	16.28	30.23	86
Vasquez, Daury	R-R	6-2	170	4-17-06	0	1	2.35	2	1	0	8	4	4	2	0	4	7	.138	.265	.241	20.59	11.76	34

Fielding

C: Urbina 21, Lantigua 17, Ramos 9, Rodriguez 7, Fernandez 7, Martinez 2, Molina 1. 1B: Martinez 32, Alvarez 8, Aponte 7, Blanco 7, Surun 7. 2B: Penuela 25, Surun 17, De La Cruz 9, Benzan 6, Sinzza 5. 3B: Perez 35, Penuela 12, Surun 7, Sinzza 5, Benzan 5. SS: Sinzza 27, Surun 20, Benzan 8, De La Cruz 4, Penuela 1. LF: Perez 15, Aponte 14, Blanco 13, Gonzalez 9, Medina 6, Perez 3, Araujo 2. CF: Rivera 35, Liriano 12, Perez 5, Aponte 5, Gonzalez 1. RF: Gonzalez 16, Radney 11, Aponte 10, Araujo 8, Liriano 6, Perez 6, Medina 1, Rivera 1.

Atlanta Braves

SEASON SYNOPSIS: Other teams may have had more injuries, but few had more impactful injuries than Atlanta, which played without ace Spencer Strider (two starts) and 2023 MVP Ronald Acuña Jr. (49 games) for most of the season while also missing third baseman Austin Riley and second baseman Ozzie Albies for swaths of the second half. They fell short of winning the National League East for the first time since 2017 and were swept out of the wild-card series by the Padres.

HIGH POINT: Lefty Chris Sale tossed seven shutout innings May 14 to beat the Cubs 7-0 to improve to 26-13, tied with the Phillies in the loss column. Sale, acquired from the Red Sox in the offseason for Vaughn Grissom and salary relief for Boston, Sale won the NL pitching triple crown, going 18-3, 2.38 with 225 strikeouts in 177.2 innings.

LOW POINT: The Braves were in a tight wild card race when Hurricane Helene's arrival rained out two games of a series against the Mets in the season's final week, leading to a doubleheader on what was supposed to be an off day. Sale was supposed to start one of the games but physically wasn't able to go. Even though Atlanta won to earn a wild-card spot, Sale still couldn't pitch in the wild-card series in San Diego. The Padres jumped A.J. Smith-Shawver in the 4-0 opening victory before sending Atlanta home without a playoff series victory since the 2021 World Series.

NOTABLE ROOKIES: Former Nebraska shortstop/closer Spencer Schwellenbach was the Braves' best rookie and best player development story, going 8-7, 3.35 with 127 strikeouts and just 23 walks in 123.2 innings to help save the rotation. Righty Grant Holmes, a 2014 first-round pick who had turned into a minor league journeyman, finally got his shot with the Braves, tossed four scoreless innings in the season finale and went 2-1, 3.56 overall in 68 innings.

KEY TRANSACTIONS: The Sale trade helped make the Braves' season, and free-agent signee Reynaldo Lopez (8-5, 1.99 in 135 IP) was a big win after returning to a starter's role. Atlanta absorbed Evan White's contract in a deal with Seattle that netted left fielder Jarred Kelenic, who struggled (.231/.286/.393, career-high 15 HR). Needing a trade deadline boost, the Braves reunited with DH/OF Jorge Soler and righty reliever Luke Jackson, 2021 Series winners who were acquired from the Giants.

OPENING DAY PAYROLL: $217,290,000 (8th)

PLAYERS OF THE YEAR

MAJOR LEAGUE

Chris Sale
LHP
18-3, 2.38
225 SO in 178 IP
Pitching triple crown

MINOR LEAGUE

Drake Baldwin
C
(AA/AAA)
.276/.370/.423
16 HR, 72 BB, 88 RBIs

ORGANIZATION LEADERS

Batting		*Qualifiers
MAJORS		
*AVG	Marcell Ozuna	.302
*OPS	Marcell Ozuna	.925
HR	Marcell Ozuna	39
RBI	Marcell Ozuna	104
MINORS		
*AVG	Alejo Lopez, Gwinnett	.307
*OBP	Drew Compton, Augusta/Rome	.394
*SLG	Drake Baldwin, Mississippi/Gwinnett	.423
*OPS	Drew Compton, Augusta/Rome	.808
R	Kevin Kilpatrick, Rome	78
H	Drake Baldwin, Mississippi/Gwinnett	129
TB	Drake Baldwin, Mississippi/Gwinnett	198
2B	E.J. Exposito, Rome	29
3B	Cody Milligan, Mississippi	8
HR	Drake Baldwin, Mississippi/Gwinnett	16
HR	Andrew Velazquez, Gwinnett	16
RBI	Drake Baldwin, Mississippi/Gwinnett	88
BB	Drake Baldwin, Mississippi/Gwinnett	72
SO	Andrew Velazquez, Gwinnett	157
SB	Justin Dean, Mississippi/Gwinnett	61

Pitching		#Qualifiers
MAJORS		
W	Chris Sale	18
# ERA	Reynaldo Lopez	1.99
SO	Chris Sale	225
SV	Raisel Iglesias	34
MINORS		
W	Bryce Elder, Gwinnett	10
L	Luis De Avila, Mississippi	10
# ERA	Allan Winans, Gwinnett	2.85
G	Domingo Gonzalez, Mississippi/Gwinnett	45
GS	Drue Hackenberg, Mississippi/Gwinnett/Rome	25
SV	Domingo Gonzalez, Mississippi/Gwinnett	9
IP	Lucas Braun, Rome/Mississippi	144
BB	Drue Hackenberg, Mississippi/Gwinnett/Rome	62
SO	Lucas Braun, Rome/Mississippi	162
# AVG	Drue Hackenberg, Mississippi/Gwinnett/Rome	.212

2024 PERFORMANCE

General Manager: Alex Anthopoulos. **Farm Director:** Ben Sestanovich. **Scouting Director:** Ronit Shah.

Class	Team	League	W	L	PCT	Finish	Manager
Majors	Atlanta Braves	National	89	73	.549	6 (15)	Brian Snitker
Triple-A	Gwinnett Stripers	International	72	78	.480	12 (20)	Kanekoa Texeira
Double-A	Mississippi Braves	Southern	63	73	.463	6 (8)	Angel Flores
High-A	Rome Braves	South Atlantic	64	64	.500	6 (12)	Cody Gabella
Low-A	Augusta GreenJackets	Carolina	49	80	.380	12 (12)	Wynston Sawyer
Rookie	FCL Braves	Florida Complex	20	39	.339	14 (15)	Nestor Perez
Rookie	DSL Braves	Dominican	15	37	.288	49 (51)	Maikol Gonzalez
Overall 2024 Minor League Record			**283**	**371**	**.433**	**30th (30)**	

ATLANTA BRAVES

ORGANIZATION STATISTICS

ATLANTA BRAVES

NATIONAL LEAGUE

Batting	B-T	Ht.	Wt.	DOB	AVG	OBP	SLG	G	PA	AB	R	H	2B	3B	HR	RBI	BB	HBP	SH	SF	SO	SB	CS	BB%	SO%
Acuna, Ronald	R-R	6-0	205	12-18-97	.250	.351	.365	49	222	192	38	48	8	1	4	15	27	3	0	0	53	16	3	12.16	23.87
Albies, Ozzie	B-R	5-8	165	1-7-97	.251	.303	.404	99	435	399	52	100	29	1	10	53	27	5	0	4	65	8	1	6.21	14.94
Alvarez, Ignacio	R-R	5-11	190	4-11-03	.100	.156	.100	8	32	30	1	3	0	0	0	0	0	2	0	0	10	0	0	0.00	31.25
Anderson, Brian	R-R	6-2	215	5-19-93	.000	.000	.000	3	5	5	0	0	0	0	0	0	0	0	0	0	2	0	0	0.00	40.00
Arcia, Orlando	R-R	6-0	187	8-4-94	.218	.271	.354	157	602	551	50	120	24	0	17	46	41	2	1	7	128	2	0	6.81	21.26
Biggio, Cavan	L-R	6-2	200	4-11-95	.200	.200	.200	4	5	5	1	1	0	0	0	0	0	0	0	0	2	0	0	0.00	40.00
d'Arnaud, Travis	R-R	6-2	210	2-10-89	.238	.302	.436	99	341	307	40	73	16	0	15	48	24	6	0	4	89	1	0	7.04	26.10
Duvall, Adam	R-R	6-1	215	9-4-88	.182	.245	.323	104	330	303	29	55	10	0	11	30	21	5	0	1	99	0	0	6.36	30.00
Fletcher, David	R-R	5-9	185	5-31-94	.250	.222	.250	5	9	8	0	2	0	0	0	2	0	0	0	1	1	0	0	0.00	11.11
Guillorme, Luis	L-R	5-10	190	9-27-94	.150	.190	.250	10	21	20	2	3	2	0	0	3	1	0	0	0	5	0	0	4.76	23.81
Harris, Michael	L-L	6-0	195	3-7-01	.264	.304	.418	110	470	440	58	116	14	3	16	48	23	4	0	3	94	10	6	4.89	20.00
Kelenic, Jarred	L-L	6-1	206	7-16-99	.231	.286	.393	131	449	412	49	95	18	2	15	45	32	1	1	3	133	7	2	7.13	29.62
Laureano, Ramon	R-R	5-11	203	7-15-94	.296	.327	.505	67	226	216	28	64	13	1	10	29	8	2	0	0	64	5	2	3.54	28.32
Martinez, J.P.	L-L	5-8	174	3-21-96	.200	.200	.300	7	10	10	2	2	1	0	0	0	0	0	0	0	4	1	0	0.00	40.00
Merrifield, Whit	R-R	6-1	195	1-24-89	.248	.348	.336	42	161	137	23	34	5	2	1	4	20	1	3	0	33	6	2	12.42	20.50
Murphy, Sean	R-R	6-3	228	10-4-94	.193	.284	.352	72	264	233	19	45	5	1	10	25	27	3	0	1	67	0	0	10.23	25.38
Olson, Matt	L-R	6-5	225	3-29-94	.247	.333	.457	162	685	600	78	148	37	1	29	98	71	9	0	5	170	0	0	10.36	24.82
Ozuna, Marcell	R-R	6-1	225	11-12-90	.302	.378	.546	162	688	606	96	183	31	0	39	104	74	3	0	4	170	1	0	10.76	24.71
Riley, Austin	R-R	6-3	240	4-2-97	.256	.322	.461	110	469	425	63	109	26	2	19	56	37	5	0	2	118	0	0	7.89	25.16
Rosario, Eddie	L-R	6-1	180	9-28-91	.154	.181	.282	24	84	78	7	12	1	0	3	9	3	0	1	2	23	1	0	3.57	27.38
Short, Zack	R-R	5-10	180	5-29-95	.148	.313	.204	30	69	54	9	8	3	0	0	5	12	1	2	0	16	2	0	17.39	23.19
Soler, Jorge	R-R	6-4	235	2-25-92	.243	.356	.493	49	182	152	27	37	11	0	9	24	24	3	0	1	44	0	0	13.19	24.18
Tromp, Chadwick	R-R	5-8	221	3-21-95	.250	.259	.365	19	54	52	3	13	6	0	0	6	1	0	0	1	17	0	0	1.85	31.48
Urshela, Gio	R-R	6-0	215	10-11-91	.265	.287	.424	36	136	132	9	35	9	0	4	15	4	0	0	0	23	0	0	2.94	16.91
Wall, Forrest	L-R	6-0	195	11-20-95	.241	.313	.241	13	32	29	3	7	0	0	0	1	3	0	0	0	6	3	3	9.38	18.75
White, Eli	R-R	6-2	195	6-26-94	.282	.333	.436	35	42	39	9	11	1	1	1	4	1	2	0	0	12	3	1	2.38	28.57
Williams, Luke	R-R	6-0	186	8-9-96	.196	.275	.261	37	52	46	8	9	3	0	0	4	4	1	1	0	13	3	0	7.69	25.00

Pitching	B-T	Ht.	Wt.	DOB	W	L	ERA	G	GS	SV	IP	Hits	Runs	ER	HR	BB	SO	AVG	OBP	SLG	SO%	BB%	BF
Brebbia, John	L-R	6-1	200	5-30-90	0	0	2.70	5	0	0	7	4	2	2	2	2	9	.167	.231	.417	34.62	7.69	26
Bummer, Aaron	L-L	6-3	215	9-21-93	4	3	3.58	56	0	0	55	61	24	22	2	18	69	.277	.333	.364	28.28	7.38	244
Chavez, Jesse	R-R	6-1	175	8-21-83	2	2	3.13	46	0	0	63	60	27	22	10	19	55	.249	.304	.427	20.83	7.20	264
Dodd, Dylan	L-L	6-2	210	6-6-98	0	0	9.00	1	0	0	2	4	2	2	0	1	2	.500	.556	.625	22.22	11.11	9
Dunshee, Parker	R-R	6-0	215	2-12-95	0	0	19.29	1	0	0	2	4	5	5	2	2	3	.364	.500	1.000	21.43	14.29	14
Elder, Bryce	R-R	6-2	220	5-19-99	2	5	6.52	10	10	0	50	64	37	36	8	17	46	.311	.367	.490	20.35	7.52	226
Fried, Max	L-L	6-4	190	1-18-94	11	10	3.25	29	29	0	174	146	71	63	13	57	166	.226	.295	.315	23.25	7.98	714
Guillorme, Luis	L-R	5-10	190	9-27-94	0	0	36.00	1	0	0	1	3	4	4	1	1	0	.500	.571	1.000	0.00	14.29	7
Herget, Jimmy	R-R	6-3	170	9-9-93	0	1	4.38	8	0	0	12	13	6	6	2	3	15	.265	.308	.449	28.85	5.77	52
Hernandez, Daysbel	R-R	5-10	220	9-15-96	3	0	2.50	16	0	0	18	10	6	5	0	10	26	.159	.284	.175	35.14	13.51	74
Holmes, Grant	L-R	6-0	226	3-22-96	2	1	3.56	26	7	0	68	66	27	27	7	15	70	.252	.294	.370	24.82	5.32	282
Iglesias, Raisel	R-R	6-2	190	1-4-90	6	2	1.95	66	0	34	69	38	19	15	4	13	68	.160	.211	.248	26.25	5.02	259
Jackson, Luke	R-R	6-2	210	8-24-91	0	1	4.50	16	0	0	18	17	11	9	2	11	26	.239	.345	.366	30.95	13.10	84
Jimenez, Joe	R-R	6-3	277	1-17-95	1	5	2.62	69	0	3	69	45	22	20	2	23	82	.181	.260	.242	29.60	8.30	277
Johnson, Pierce	R-R	6-2	202	5-10-91	6	6	3.67	58	0	2	56	48	25	23	6	25	67	.230	.318	.364	28.39	10.59	236
Kerr, Ray	L-L	6-3	185	9-10-94	1	2	5.64	10	2	0	22	29	14	14	4	7	27	.315	.379	.533	26.21	6.80	103
Lee, Dylan	L-L	6-3	214	8-1-94	4	2	2.11	52	0	0	60	49	19	14	7	17	76	.222	.276	.376	31.67	7.08	240
Lopez, Reynaldo	R-R	6-1	225	1-4-94	8	5	1.99	26	25	0	136	108	32	30	10	42	148	.220	.280	.333	27.26	7.73	543
Matzek, Tyler	L-L	6-3	230	10-19-90	0	0	9.90	11	0	0	10	16	11	11	3	3	10	.356	.396	.622	20.83	6.25	48
Minter, A.J.	L-L	6-0	215	9-2-93	5	4	2.62	39	0	1	34	24	10	10	6	11	35	.198	.271	.364	26.12	8.21	134
Morton, Charlie	R-R	6-5	215	11-12-83	8	10	4.19	30	30	0	165	154	85	77	23	65	167	.251	.339	.427	23.82	9.27	701
Sale, Chris	L-L	6-6	183	3-30-89	18	3	2.38	29	29	0	178	141	48	47	9	39	225	.216	.269	.319	32.05	5.56	702
Schwellenbach, Spencer	R-R	6-1	200	5-31-00	8	7	3.35	21	21	0	124	106	49	46	14	23	127	.226	.271	.391	25.40	4.60	500
Smith-Shawver, AJ	R-R	6-3	205	11-20-02	0	0	0.00	1	1	0	4	3	0	0	0	2	4	.188	.278	.188	22.22	11.11	18
Stephens, Jackson	R-R	6-2	220	5-11-94	0	0	2.70	3	0	0	3	5	1	1	1	1	2	.333	.412	.533	11.76	5.88	17

Pitching	B-T	Ht.	Wt.	DOB	W	L	ERA	G	GS	SV	IP	Hits	Runs	ER	HR	BB	SO	AVG	OBP	SLG	SO%	BB%	BF
Strider, Spencer	R-R	6-0	195	10-28-98	0	0	7.00	2	2	0	9	10	7	7	2	5	12	.270	.357	.486	28.57	11.90	42
Vines, Darius	R-R	6-1	190	4-30-98	0	1	8.56	4	2	0	14	21	14	13	4	4	9	.356	.394	.627	13.64	6.06	66
Waldrep, Hurston	R-R	6-2	205	3-1-02	0	1	16.71	2	2	0	7	9	13	13	3	8	3	.333	.500	.704	8.33	22.22	36
Williams, Luke	R-R	6-0	186	8-9-96	0	0	4.50	3	0	0	4	5	2	2	0	1	0	.294	.368	.294	0.00	5.26	19
Winans, Allan	R-R	6-2	165	8-10-95	0	2	15.26	2	2	0	8	14	14	13	3	4	4	.378	.439	.811	9.76	9.76	41

Fielding

Catcher	PCT	G	PO	A	E	DP	PB
d'Arnaud	.996	89	716	25	3	3	2
Murphy	.993	69	709	27	5	3	2
Tromp	1.000	19	131	7	0	0	0

First Base	PCT	G	PO	A	E	DP
Olson	.996	162	1259	105	6	125

Second Base	PCT	G	PO	A	E	DP
Albies	.992	99	153	239	3	57
Alvarez	1.000	7	8	12	0	3
Biggio	1.000	4	3	4	0	2
Fletcher	1.000	5	6	14	0	4
Guillorme	1.000	7	5	15	0	2
Merrifield	.986	40	46	96	2	19
Short	.667	2	0	2	1	0
White	1.000	1	2	0	0	0
Williams	.913	8	8	13	2	3

Third Base	PCT	G	PO	A	E	DP
Alvarez	1.000	1	0	1	0	0
Anderson	.000	1	0	0	0	0
Merrifield	1.000	1	1	0	0	0
Riley	.960	109	60	178	10	17
Short	.929	15	4	22	2	1
Urshela	.980	36	22	77	2	15
Williams	1.000	6	2	11	0	1

Shortstop	PCT	G	PO	A	E	DP
Arcia	.981	157	168	393	11	87
Guillorme	1.000	1	2	2	0	1
Short	.917	10	3	8	1	1
Urshela	.000	1	0	0	0	0
Williams	1.000	1	1	6	0	0

Outfield	PCT	G	PO	A	E	DP
Acuna	.980	48	98	2	2	0
Anderson	1.000	2	3	0	0	0
Duvall	.987	95	151	4	2	0
Harris	.991	110	232	1	2	0
Kelenic	.987	126	231	4	3	0
Laureano	.989	72	86	2	1	0
Martinez	1.000	5	4	0	0	0
Rosario	1.000	24	35	2	0	1
Soler	.984	46	60	2	1	0
Wall	1.000	12	18	0	0	0
White	1.000	31	26	0	0	0
Williams	1.000	4	4	0	0	0

GWINNETT STRIPERS — *TRIPLE-A*

INTERNATIONAL LEAGUE

Batting	B-T	Ht.	Wt.	DOB	AVG	OBP	SLG	G	PA	AB	R	H	2B	3B	HR	RBI	BB	HBP	SH	SF	SO	SB	CS	BB%	SO%
Albies, Ozzie	B-R	5-8	165	1-7-97	.500	.556	.875	2	9	8	1	4	0	0	1	3	1	0	0	0	0	0	0	11.11	0.00
Alvarez, Ignacio	R-R	5-11	190	4-11-03	.297	.398	.463	64	289	246	47	73	9	1	10	42	37	5	0	1	45	10	2	12.80	15.57
Anderson, Brian	R-R	6-2	215	5-19-93	.205	.292	.291	42	171	151	21	31	4	0	3	21	18	1	0	1	54	0	0	10.53	31.58
Baldwin, Drake	L-R	6-0	210	3-28-01	.298	.407	.484	72	334	275	40	82	13	1	12	55	52	2	0	5	54	1	0	15.57	16.17
Biggio, Cavan	L-R	6-2	200	4-11-95	.200	.200	.200	1	5	5	1	1	0	0	0	1	0	0	0	0	1	0	0	0.00	20.00
Bolt, Skye	B-R	6-2	194	1-15-94	.236	.339	.349	39	127	106	20	25	4	1	2	18	18	0	0	3	33	1	0	14.17	25.98
Casteel, Ryan	R-R	5-11	205	6-6-91	.213	.245	.362	14	49	47	4	10	1	0	2	6	2	0	0	0	20	0	0	4.08	40.82
Dean, Justin	R-R	5-8	185	12-6-96	.257	.367	.324	25	90	74	13	19	3	1	0	7	12	2	0	2	30	14	1	13.33	33.33
Evans, Phillip	R-R	5-10	210	9-10-92	.222	.305	.324	51	200	176	17	39	3	0	5	18	20	2	0	2	36	1	0	10.00	18.00
Fletcher, David	R-R	5-9	185	5-31-94	.246	.319	.275	39	160	142	16	35	4	0	0	18	16	0	0	2	17	5	0	10.00	10.63
Garcia, Leury	B-R	5-8	190	3-18-91	.320	.374	.450	27	116	100	18	32	6	2	1	14	9	2	1	4	21	4	0	7.76	18.10
Gurriel, Yuli	R-R	6-0	215	6-9-84	.292	.378	.485	75	333	291	38	85	18	1	12	48	39	2	0	1	49	11	1	11.71	14.71
Harris, Michael	L-L	6-0	195	3-7-01	.435	.500	.565	6	26	23	2	10	0	0	1	2	3	0	0	0	3	0	0	11.54	11.54
Laureano, Ramon	R-R	5-11	203	7-15-94	.362	.424	.603	14	66	58	13	21	3	1	3	12	6	1	0	1	17	0	0	9.09	25.76
Leon, Sandy	B-R	5-10	235	3-13-89	.181	.328	.262	79	297	237	20	43	4	0	5	26	51	2	4	3	85	0	0	17.17	28.62
Liberato, Luis	L-L	5-11	175	12-18-95	.265	.321	.385	72	280	257	29	68	17	1	4	39	21	1	0	1	71	7	0	7.50	25.36
Lopez, Alejo	B-R	5-8	170	5-5-96	.307	.392	.397	112	473	411	63	126	21	2	4	55	47	12	1	2	64	21	7	9.94	13.53
Martinez, J.P.	L-L	5-8	174	3-21-96	.233	.334	.350	107	438	377	62	88	22	2	6	30	53	5	1	2	118	37	8	12.10	26.94
Murphy, Sean	R-R	6-3	228	10-4-94	.278	.316	.667	4	19	18	4	5	1	0	2	4	1	0	0	0	4	0	0	5.26	21.05
Ramirez, Harold	R-R	5-10	232	9-6-94	.231	.278	.275	22	97	91	8	21	4	0	0	9	6	0	0	0	20	2	0	6.19	20.62
Rivero, Sebastian	R-R	6-1	210	11-16-98	.213	.271	.258	29	97	89	8	19	4	0	0	7	7	0	1	0	20	1	0	7.22	20.62
Rosario, Eddie	L-R	6-1	180	9-28-91	.273	.333	.727	3	12	11	3	3	0	1	1	1	1	0	0	0	1	0	1	8.33	8.33
Sanchez, Yolbert	R-R	5-9	176	3-3-97	.250	.238	.250	8	22	20	1	5	0	0	0	2	0	0	0	1	1	0	0	0.00	4.55
Short, Zack	R-R	5-10	180	5-29-95	.216	.361	.273	29	109	88	18	19	3	1	0	7	19	1	1	0	27	3	0	17.43	24.77
Tromp, Chadwick	R-R	5-8	221	3-21-95	.303	.378	.457	60	267	234	32	71	15	0	7	48	29	1	0	3	48	0	0	10.86	17.98
Velazquez, Andrew	R-R	5-9	170	7-14-94	.242	.298	.394	118	473	429	62	104	17	0	16	48	34	1	6	3	157	33	1	7.19	33.19
Waddell, Luke	L-R	5-7	180	7-13-98	.235	.317	.322	111	464	404	57	95	21	4	2	55	41	10	2	6	64	12	3	8.84	13.79
Wall, Forrest	L-R	6-0	195	11-20-95	.279	.380	.411	51	231	197	34	55	7	2	5	18	28	4	2	0	58	12	5	12.12	25.11
White, Eli	R-R	6-2	195	6-26-94	.294	.388	.447	78	340	293	56	86	17	2	8	40	38	8	0	1	76	24	2	11.18	22.35
Williams, Luke	R-R	6-0	186	8-9-96	.282	.344	.495	55	241	216	30	61	19	0	9	40	21	1	0	3	62	18	4	8.71	25.73
Worrell, Bryson	B-R	6-2	226	11-7-98	.182	.182	.545	3	11	11	2	2	1	0	1	2	0	0	0	0	7	0	0	0.00	63.64

Pitching	B-T	Ht.	Wt.	DOB	W	L	ERA	G	GS	SV	IP	Hits	Runs	ER	HR	BB	SO	AVG	OBP	SLG	SO%	BB%	BF
Anderson, Ian	R-R	6-3	170	5-2-98	3	2	3.96	10	10	0	52	48	25	23	7	27	53	.241	.333	.412	23.25	11.84	228
Bowden, Ben	L-L	6-4	249	10-21-94	2	1	4.03	27	0	0	29	26	13	13	4	17	35	.243	.349	.421	27.13	13.18	129
Carasiti, Matt	R-R	6-2	205	7-23-91	1	0	3.46	11	0	0	13	8	5	5	1	15	19	.178	.383	.356	31.15	24.59	61
Casteel, Ryan	R-R	5-11	205	6-6-91	0	0	45.00	1	0	0	1	5	5	5	0	2	0	.625	.700	1.000	0.00	20.00	10
Dodd, Dylan	L-L	6-2	210	6-6-98	2	7	5.35	25	20	1	108	131	75	64	18	32	98	.297	.346	.512	20.33	6.64	482
Doyle, Tommy	R-R	6-6	244	5-1-96	3	2	3.57	32	0	3	40	35	19	16	5	17	43	.227	.306	.396	24.86	9.83	173
Dunshee, Parker	R-R	6-0	215	2-12-95	1	1	3.83	26	0	3	45	38	23	19	1	23	55	.228	.325	.299	27.78	11.62	198
Elder, Bryce	R-R	6-2	220	5-19-99	10	6	3.73	17	17	0	101	92	45	42	6	40	102	.239	.310	.332	23.78	9.32	429
Evans, Phillip	R-R	5-10	210	9-10-92	0	0	18.00	1	0	0	1	3	2	2	1	0	1	.500	.500	1.000	16.67	0.00	6
Fletcher, David	R-R	5-9	185	5-31-94	0	1	6.55	5	1	0	11	10	8	8	0	7	10	.244	.385	.293	19.23	13.46	52
Giles, Ken	R-R	6-3	197	9-20-90	4	2	6.28	42	0	4	39	31	28	27	8	22	58	.215	.329	.451	33.92	12.87	171
Gonzalez, Domingo	R-R	6-0	185	9-27-99	3	2	3.41	24	1	2	29	18	11	11	2	13	45	.175	.301	.282	36.29	10.48	124
Hackenberg, Drue	R-R	6-2	220	4-1-02	1	0	1.52	4	4	0	24	14	5	4	0	15	18	.175	.305	.175	18.95	15.79	95
Halligan, Patrick	R-R	6-6	230	10-4-99	0	0	6.75	4	1	0	5	5	4	4	0	8	5	.250	.448	.250	17.24	27.59	29
Harris, Hayden	L-L	6-0	186	3-2-99	1	3	7.36	22	0	2	22	25	18	18	5	16	35	.294	.408	.506	33.33	15.24	105

Herget, Jimmy	R-R	6-3	170	9-9-93	0	1	3.06	15	0	3	18	20	6	6	1	6	21	.286	.342	.414	27.27	7.79	77
Hernandez, Daysbel	R-R	5-10	220	9-15-96	4	2	2.59	33	0	3	42	35	16	12	2	25	52	.230	.354	.309	28.42	13.66	183
Holmes, Grant	L-R	6-0	226	3-22-96	3	2	2.63	18	3	4	41	34	14	12	4	14	51	.225	.293	.338	30.36	8.33	168
Kerr, Ray	L-L	6-3	185	9-10-94	0	1	4.50	9	1	3	14	13	9	7	5	5	22	.245	.322	.623	37.29	8.47	59
Lee, Dylan	L-L	6-3	214	8-1-94	0	0	0.00	2	0	0	3	1	0	0	0	0	4	.100	.100	.100	40.00	0.00	10
Leon, Sandy	S-R	5-10	235	3-13-89	0	0	2.45	3	0	0	4	2	2	1	1	0	0	.154	.154	.385	0.00	0.00	13
Logue, Zach	L-L	6-0	165	4-23-96	5	6	2.68	23	12	1	91	70	29	27	8	27	86	.217	.291	.347	23.50	7.38	366
Lopez, Reynaldo	R-R	6-1	225	1-4-94	0	0	6.75	1	1	0	4	6	3	3	0	1	4	.353	.421	.529	21.05	5.26	19
Martinez, Daniel	L-R	5-11	190	7-28-98	0	1	18.90	1	0	0	3	3	8	7	2	4	3	.231	.444	.769	15.79	21.05	19
Matzek, Tyler	L-L	6-3	230	10-19-90	0	1	4.76	4	0	0	6	5	3	3	1	2	5	.238	.304	.381	21.74	8.70	23
Mejia, Ian	R-R	6-3	205	1-31-00	0	1	33.75	1	1	0	1	5	5	5	2	3	1	.556	.667	1.222	8.33	25.00	12
Minter, A.J.	L-L	6-0	215	9-2-93	0	0	4.50	2	0	0	2	0	1	1	0	2	0	.000	.286	.000	0.00	28.57	7
Moran, Brian	L-L	6-4	225	9-30-88	2	1	5.91	27	2	0	46	56	33	30	6	16	48	.301	.371	.473	22.86	7.62	210
Parrish, Drew	L-L	5-11	200	12-8-97	0	0	2.45	2	1	0	7	3	2	2	0	4	4	.130	.286	.217	14.29	14.29	28
Smith-Shawver, AJ	R-R	6-3	205	11-20-02	3	7	4.86	20	20	0	87	69	47	47	20	40	104	.215	.304	.442	28.49	10.96	365
Stephens, Jackson	R-R	6-2	220	5-11-94	2	7	3.86	29	1	1	47	46	27	20	3	17	49	.260	.332	.379	24.38	8.46	201
Vines, Darius	R-R	6-1	190	4-30-98	3	3	5.14	14	14	0	77	82	45	44	14	22	54	.276	.329	.502	16.56	6.75	326
Vizcaya, Anthony	R-R	6-0	220	10-24-93	0	0	9.00	1	0	0	1	2	1	1	0	2	0	.400	.571	.600	0.00	28.57	7
Waldrep, Hurston	R-R	6-2	205	3-1-02	2	2	3.38	8	8	0	40	34	15	15	3	24	43	.234	.339	.338	25.00	13.95	172
Walsh, Jake	R-R	6-1	192	7-20-95	2	1	2.31	11	0	0	12	10	5	3	0	8	8	.222	.340	.244	15.09	15.09	53
Widener, Taylor	L-R	6-0	203	10-24-94	3	5	6.51	22	11	0	57	64	44	41	11	30	59	.279	.374	.520	22.18	11.28	266
Wilson, Brooks	L-R	6-2	205	3-15-96	4	2	4.12	26	0	0	44	32	21	20	6	29	57	.201	.328	.327	29.69	15.10	192
Winans, Allan	R-R	6-2	165	8-10-95	7	5	3.30	24	16	0	115	103	44	42	15	31	100	.235	.294	.404	20.83	6.46	480
Ynoa, Huascar	R-R	6-2	220	5-28-98	1	3	6.15	12	5	0	26	27	19	18	3	13	22	.273	.365	.465	19.13	11.30	115

Fielding

Catcher	PCT	G	PO	A	E	DP	PB
Baldwin	.985	43	384	19	6	3	6
Casteel	1.000	5	32	2	0	0	0
Leon	.996	53	479	30	2	2	1
Murphy	1.000	2	8	2	0	0	0
Rivero	.984	27	240	11	4	1	2
Tromp	1.000	28	246	11	0	1	1

First Base	PCT	G	PO	A	E	DP
Anderson	.989	24	167	7	2	17
Casteel	1.000	4	21	1	0	0
Evans	.995	28	176	22	1	12
Gurriel	.996	58	442	42	2	39
Liberato	.990	13	94	5	1	7
Rivero	1.000	1	6	1	0	0
Tromp	1.000	6	46	4	0	5
Williams	.987	19	140	10	2	14

Second Base	PCT	G	PO	A	E	DP
Albies	.857	2	4	2	1	1
Alvarez	1.000	1	4	4	0	0
Biggio	1.000	1	2	3	0	1
Fletcher	.991	32	44	71	1	16
Garcia	1.000	4	9	6	0	1
Gurriel	1.000	4	5	12	0	3
Lopez	.989	25	34	56	1	17
Sanchez	1.000	8	6	15	0	1
Short	.969	10	9	22	1	5
Velazquez	.985	48	73	125	3	21
Waddell	.986	19	20	49	1	7
Williams	1.000	7	15	23	0	4

Third Base	PCT	G	PO	A	E	DP
Alvarez	.974	33	21	53	2	6
Anderson	1.000	3	0	2	0	0
Evans	.917	14	3	19	2	3
Garcia	.667	3	0	2	1	0
Gurriel	1.000	3	1	9	0	1
Lopez	.962	68	58	94	6	8
Short	1.000	2	2	2	0	0
Waddell	.968	11	9	21	1	3
Williams	.955	22	11	31	2	3

Shortstop	PCT	G	PO	A	E	DP
Alvarez	.943	31	42	58	6	13
Fletcher	1.000	1	1	2	0	1
Short	.984	18	24	36	1	11
Velazquez	.924	20	27	46	6	7
Waddell	.976	84	91	190	7	37
Williams	.667	1	1	1	1	0

Outfield	PCT	G	PO	A	E	DP
Anderson	1.000	14	29	1	0	0
Bolt	1.000	31	35	0	0	0
Dean	1.000	26	45	3	0	1
Garcia	.935	14	29	0	2	0
Harris	1.000	2	6	0	0	0
Laureano	.962	14	25	0	1	0
Liberato	1.000	59	116	4	0	1
Lopez	1.000	17	27	0	0	0
Martinez	.974	104	183	2	5	2
Ramirez	1.000	19	23	0	0	0
Rosario	1.000	2	1	0	0	0
Velazquez	.975	43	77	0	2	0
Wall	.978	45	86	2	2	1
White	.993	73	136	4	1	0
Williams	1.000	7	10	0	0	0
Worrell	1.000	3	9	0	0	0

MISSISSIPPI BRAVES

DOUBLE-A

SOUTHERN LEAGUE

Batting	B-T	Ht.	Wt.	DOB	AVG	OBP	SLG	G	PA	AB	R	H	2B	3B	HR	RBI	BB	HBP	SH	SF	SO	SB	CS	BB%	SO%
Alvarez, Ignacio	R-R	5-11	190	4-11-03	.265	.381	.312	48	202	170	18	45	6	1	0	15	29	3	0	0	38	16	1	14.36	18.81
Baldwin, Drake	L-R	6-0	210	3-28-01	.244	.313	.337	52	217	193	18	47	6	0	4	33	20	1	0	3	41	1	1	9.22	18.89
Bunnell, Cade	L-R	5-11	190	5-14-97	.155	.312	.230	73	247	200	17	31	12	0	1	10	46	0	0	1	97	1	2	18.62	39.27
Conley, Cal	B-R	5-8	185	7-17-99	.242	.305	.312	126	515	462	54	112	21	1	3	35	43	1	4	5	91	42	10	8.35	17.67
Dean, Justin	R-R	5-8	185	12-6-96	.244	.331	.321	92	362	315	44	77	11	2	3	31	39	4	0	4	92	47	7	10.77	25.41
Fletcher, David	R-R	5-9	185	5-31-94	.218	.276	.246	54	156	142	15	31	2	1	0	7	11	1	0	2	23	10	1	7.05	14.74
Horne, Bryson	L-R	5-10	220	3-6-99	.238	.290	.355	107	396	366	34	87	15	2	8	48	27	1	0	2	115	6	2	6.82	29.04
Jones, Colby	R-R	5-11	180	9-30-03	.250	.250	.250	1	4	4	0	1	0	0	0	0	0	0	0	0	0	1	0	0.00	0.00
Magee, Cam	L-R	6-1	190	6-1-02	.500	.500	.750	1	4	4	0	2	1	0	0	0	0	0	0	0	2	1	0	0.00	50.00
McCabe, David	B-R	6-3	230	3-25-00	.137	.284	.214	35	141	117	12	16	3	0	2	9	24	0	0	0	42	2	0	17.02	29.79
Milligan, Cody	L-R	5-9	170	12-23-98	.242	.306	.358	105	426	388	45	94	18	6	5	38	33	3	1	1	104	38	8	7.75	24.41
Ogans, Keshawn	R-R	5-8	180	8-26-01	.218	.286	.275	100	393	357	40	78	13	2	1	26	27	7	1	1	75	16	8	6.87	19.08
Parker, Brandon	R-R	6-0	205	5-27-99	.198	.268	.362	74	257	232	27	46	11	0	9	29	17	6	0	2	95	7	1	6.61	36.96
Quintero, Geraldo	B-R	5-5	155	10-10-01	.240	.334	.319	94	338	288	47	69	8	3	3	29	33	10	0	4	66	32	16	9.76	19.53
Rivero, Sebastian	R-R	6-1	210	11-16-98	.169	.220	.243	46	162	148	7	25	8	0	1	19	7	3	3	1	38	0	0	4.32	23.46
Sanchez, Yolbert	R-R	5-9	176	3-3-97	.299	.325	.367	84	331	308	40	92	13	1	2	32	13	2	1	6	53	4	4	3.93	16.01
Tolve, Tyler	L-R	6-0	200	7-16-00	.213	.270	.397	84	326	300	35	64	20	1	11	43	16	8	0	2	112	0	0	4.91	34.36
Valdes, Javier	R-R	5-10	205	11-19-98	.190	.253	.321	25	91	84	8	16	2	0	3	11	5	2	0	0	14	0	0	5.49	15.38
Workinger, Ethan	R-R	6-0	185	10-19-01	.207	.273	.288	30	121	111	15	23	4	1	1	11	10	0	0	0	19	1	1	8.26	15.70
Worrell, Bryson	B-R	6-2	226	11-7-98	.119	.178	.209	22	73	67	6	8	0	0	2	7	4	1	0	1	32	1	0	5.48	43.84
Zebrowski, Adam	R-R	6-0	230	9-28-00	.216	.286	.235	15	56	51	2	11	1	0	0	4	5	0	0	0	5	0	0	8.93	8.93

Pitching	B-T	Ht.	Wt.	DOB	W	L	ERA	G	GS	SV	IP	Hits	Runs	ER	HR	BB	SO	AVG	OBP	SLG	SO%	BB%	BF
Bourassa, Ryan	R-R	6-0	230	12-18-99	0	1	9.00	5	0	0	5	6	5	5	2	6	5	.286	.444	.714	18.52	22.22	27
Braun, Lucas	R-R	6-0	185	8-26-01	5	2	2.38	13	13	0	79	59	22	21	5	26	87	.207	.272	.302	27.71	8.28	314
De Avila, Luis	L-L	5-9	215	5-29-01	4	10	3.74	19	19	0	101	95	49	42	2	46	79	.247	.330	.325	18.04	10.50	438
Dunshee, Parker	R-R	6-0	215	2-12-95	1	1	1.84	11	0	1	15	9	4	3	0	5	28	.164	.246	.218	45.16	8.06	62
Farris, Mitch	L-L	6-2	187	2-14-01	0	1	12.00	1	1	0	3	5	4	4	2	4	1	.357	.500	.857	5.56	22.22	18
Fletcher, David	R-R	5-9	185	5-31-94	3	7	6.37	17	17	0	89	108	67	63	12	37	32	.308	.394	.467	7.88	9.11	406
Gonzalez, Domingo	R-R	6-0	185	9-27-99	1	1	2.28	21	0	7	24	10	8	6	1	9	38	.128	.236	.231	42.22	10.00	90
Hackenberg, Drue	R-R	6-2	220	4-1-02	3	2	3.13	9	9	0	46	39	17	16	0	19	64	.232	.320	.292	32.99	9.79	194
Halligan, Patrick	R-R	6-6	230	10-4-99	5	1	2.58	37	0	4	45	30	14	13	1	17	62	.184	.264	.227	33.88	9.29	183
Harper, Landon	R-R	6-1	176	4-8-01	2	1	1.41	22	5	1	51	33	9	8	5	9	40	.182	.220	.287	20.73	4.66	193
Harris, Hayden	L-L	6-0	186	3-2-99	2	1	1.74	19	0	1	21	17	4	4	0	9	34	.218	.299	.256	39.08	10.34	87
Hughes, Jonathan	R-R	6-2	196	1-8-97	2	1	3.58	34	0	0	50	38	21	20	1	23	44	.212	.306	.291	21.15	11.06	208
Joseph, Elison	R-R	6-0	170	1-24-01	1	0	1.33	20	0	5	20	12	3	3	1	15	30	.169	.322	.239	34.48	17.24	87
Juan, Jorge	R-R	6-8	200	3-6-99	2	4	5.11	34	0	4	37	31	24	21	3	28	53	.225	.386	.362	29.94	15.82	177
Lara, Jhancarlos	R-R	6-3	190	1-15-03	1	2	3.92	5	5	0	21	15	11	9	1	24	22	.217	.417	.275	22.92	25.00	96
Logue, Zach	L-L	6-0	165	4-23-96	0	0	0.00	1	0	0	4	3	0	0	0	1	4	.250	.286	.333	28.57	7.14	14
McSteen, Jake	R-L	6-0	215	3-12-96	1	7	5.89	35	4	0	55	64	40	36	8	16	59	.291	.333	.464	24.38	6.61	242
Mejia, Ian	R-R	6-3	205	1-31-00	8	7	3.47	24	23	1	124	108	53	48	9	56	123	.233	.322	.353	23.12	10.53	532
Munoz, Rolddy	R-R	6-2	183	4-14-00	2	2	3.98	31	1	3	41	34	20	18	2	18	56	.224	.312	.309	32.18	10.34	174
Niekro, J.J.	R-R	6-0	185	1-28-98	1	4	4.02	8	8	0	40	38	21	18	3	14	36	.253	.317	.373	21.69	8.43	166
Parrish, Drew	L-L	5-11	200	12-8-97	7	5	3.33	27	17	0	108	101	44	40	16	19	109	.245	.278	.403	24.94	4.35	437
Riley, Trey	L-R	6-3	205	4-21-98	1	6	4.80	40	0	2	45	47	26	24	3	29	51	.276	.385	.388	24.64	14.01	207
Schwellenbach, Spencer	R-R	6-1	200	5-31-00	2	0	0.00	2	2	0	13	5	0	0	0	1	17	.122	.163	.146	38.64	2.27	44
Smith, Austin	R-R	6-4	210	6-22-99	1	2	9.19	17	0	0	16	22	19	16	2	19	15	.349	.489	.476	16.85	21.35	89
Vines, Darius	R-R	6-1	190	4-30-98	2	0	1.65	3	3	0	16	13	3	3	1	8	17	.213	.300	.295	24.29	11.43	70
Vizcaya, Anthony	R-R	6-0	220	10-24-93	3	0	4.67	22	0	3	27	29	15	14	2	6	26	.269	.319	.380	22.41	5.17	116
Waldrep, Hurston	R-R	6-2	205	3-1-02	3	4	2.92	9	9	0	49	52	18	16	2	17	48	.269	.329	.337	22.43	7.94	214
Williams, Peyton	R-R	6-1	180	5-6-98	0	0	1.08	6	0	0	8	7	2	1	0	7	7	.233	.385	.233	17.95	17.95	39
Wilson, Brooks	L-R	6-2	205	3-15-96	0	1	16.20	4	0	0	3	5	6	6	1	4	6	.333	.474	.600	31.58	21.05	19

Fielding

Catcher	PCT	G	PO	A	E	DP	PB
Baldwin	.985	33	311	21	5	1	1
Rivero	.976	40	349	22	9	1	2
Tolve	.975	50	400	33	11	2	5
Zebrowski	.993	15	142	7	1	2	3

First Base	PCT	G	PO	A	E	DP
Bunnell	.989	28	166	21	2	19
Horne	.987	103	698	49	10	61
Valdes	1.000	9	58	2	0	4

Second Base	PCT	G	PO	A	E	DP
Bunnell	.958	8	13	10	1	6
Conley	.984	33	43	77	2	15
Fletcher	.990	29	52	52	1	16
Jones	1.000	1	2	1	0	0
Milligan	1.000	6	7	13	0	4
Ogans	1.000	4	9	3	0	1
Quintero	1.000	8	10	20	0	2
Sanchez	.990	48	91	112	2	33

Third Base	PCT	G	PO	A	E	DP
Bunnell	.957	13	5	17	1	2
Fletcher	1.000	3	1	8	0	1
Ogans	.969	91	66	156	7	15
Sanchez	.908	30	22	57	8	6

Shortstop	PCT	G	PO	A	E	DP
Alvarez	.966	39	53	91	5	12
Conley	.966	92	117	198	11	36
Fletcher	1.000	5	4	17	0	5
Magee	1.000	1	0	3	0	0
Sanchez	1.000	1	0	2	0	1

Outfield	PCT	G	PO	A	E	DP
Bunnell	.973	21	36	0	1	0
Dean	.995	91	215	4	1	3
Milligan	.990	97	187	8	2	3
Parker	.991	69	113	1	1	0
Quintero	.979	81	139	3	3	1
Workinger	1.000	30	61	0	0	0
Worrell	1.000	21	39	1	0	1

ROME BRAVES — *HIGH-A*

SOUTH ATLANTIC LEAGUE

Batting	B-T	Ht.	Wt.	DOB	AVG	OBP	SLG	G	PA	AB	R	H	2B	3B	HR	RBI	BB	HBP	SH	SF	SO	SB	CS	BB%	SO%
Arroyo, Carlos	R-R	5-9	170	7-11-01	.180	.278	.251	61	210	183	19	33	7	0	2	13	17	8	0	1	61	8	4	8.10	29.05
Borden, Tim	R-R	6-1	200	9-1-99	.113	.288	.151	21	66	53	1	6	2	0	0	3	9	4	0	0	27	0	1	13.64	40.91
Ceballos, Sabin	R-R	6-3	225	8-17-02	.259	.353	.354	84	377	328	54	85	20	1	3	30	37	11	0	1	72	9	3	9.81	19.10
Celedonio, Jeremy	R-R	6-1	183	12-26-01	.125	.333	.125	6	21	16	3	2	0	0	0	0	4	1	0	0	9	0	0	19.05	42.86
Clarno, Nick	R-R	6-0	205	6-25-98	.185	.307	.259	33	127	108	14	20	2	0	2	11	17	2	0	0	34	4	0	13.39	26.77
Clohisy, Patrick	L-L	5-10	190	12-6-01	.125	.263	.125	4	19	16	2	2	0	0	0	2	3	0	0	0	9	1	0	15.79	47.37
Compton, Drew	B-R	6-2	212	3-25-01	.285	.387	.405	67	284	242	26	69	14	0	5	36	34	7	0	1	47	1	0	11.97	16.55
Dimon, Dawson	R-R	6-0	185	5-17-99	.128	.236	.149	17	55	47	5	6	1	0	0	5	6	1	0	1	23	2	0	10.91	41.82
Exposito, E.J.	R-R	5-11	190	5-4-01	.238	.311	.417	116	477	424	62	101	29	4	13	50	44	3	1	5	115	31	8	9.22	24.11
Godman, Jacob	R-R	6-2	200	5-7-00	.205	.418	.282	15	55	39	9	8	1	1	0	5	15	0	0	1	12	0	0	27.27	21.82
Grady, Jace	B-R	5-11	182	5-25-01	.185	.288	.251	55	229	195	18	36	4	0	3	21	28	2	0	4	38	5	5	12.23	16.59
Guscette, Mac	R-R	6-0	200	2-14-02	.143	.286	.200	11	42	35	3	5	2	0	0	4	5	2	0	0	2	0	0	11.90	4.76
Janas, Justin	L-R	6-2	205	9-18-00	.244	.358	.344	82	310	262	32	64	14	0	4	29	29	18	0	1	53	5	3	9.35	17.10
Jones, Colby	R-R	5-11	180	9-30-03	.103	.133	.103	7	30	29	4	3	0	0	0	2	1	0	0	0	10	1	1	3.33	33.33
Kern, Kade	R-R	6-0	200	9-18-01	.140	.178	.233	14	45	43	3	6	1	0	1	7	2	0	0	0	14	1	1	4.44	31.11
Kilpatrick, Kevin	R-R	5-10	186	11-25-00	.238	.319	.332	118	542	479	78	114	20	5	5	46	51	8	0	4	140	50	9	9.41	25.83
Olsavsky, Joe	R-R	6-1	180	3-29-02	.250	.357	.354	15	56	48	8	12	5	0	0	3	8	0	0	0	18	0	0	14.29	32.14
Paolini, Stephen	L-L	6-1	195	11-23-00	.220	.314	.323	102	404	350	51	77	17	2	5	44	47	3	0	4	131	20	2	11.63	32.43
Tavarez, Ambioris	R-R	5-11	168	11-12-03	.199	.298	.320	50	208	181	23	36	7	3	3	22	22	4	0	1	80	11	4	10.58	38.46
Wall, Cory	R-R	6-4	230	3-14-00	.000	.000	.000	26	1	1	0	0	0	0	0	0	0	0	0	0	1	0	0	0.00	100.00
Ward, Nick	L-R	5-9	180	10-19-95	.222	.343	.282	80	298	248	28	55	7	1	2	30	43	4	1	2	68	9	2	14.43	22.82
Workinger, Ethan	R-R	6-0	185	10-19-01	.268	.355	.415	98	424	366	46	98	15	3	11	52	49	3	0	4	84	8	5	11.56	19.81
Worrell, Bryson	B-R	6-2	226	11-7-98	.191	.266	.296	36	128	115	13	22	3	0	3	16	12	0	0	1	42	10	1	9.38	32.81
Zebrowski, Adam	R-R	6-0	230	9-28-00	.220	.304	.361	88	372	327	43	72	10	3	10	42	34	7	0	4	109	2	1	9.14	29.30

Pitching	B-T	Ht.	Wt.	DOB	W	L	ERA	G	GS	SV	IP	Hits	Runs	ER	HR	BB	SO	AVG	OBP	SLG	SO%	BB%	BF
Arroyo, Carlos	R-R	5-9	170	7-11-01	0	0	6.75	2	0	0	1	0	1	1	0	3	1	.000	.429	.000	14.29	42.86	7
Baumann, Garrett	L-R	6-8	245	8-15-04	1	0	0.00	1	1	0	7	4	0	0	0	0	5	.182	.217	.227	21.74	0.00	23
Borden, Tim	R-R	6-1	200	9-1-99	0	0	0.00	1	0	0	0	1	0	0	0	1	0	.500	.667	.500	0.00	33.33	3
Bourassa, Ryan	R-R	6-0	230	12-18-99	2	2	2.79	25	0	6	29	15	12	9	4	11	45	.147	.228	.294	39.47	9.65	114
Braun, Lucas	R-R	6-0	185	8-26-01	4	2	4.34	12	11	0	64	63	34	31	6	16	75	.253	.311	.394	27.68	5.90	271
Bryant, Chad	R-R	6-0	210	8-3-99	2	2	6.63	9	0	0	19	16	21	14	1	24	17	.239	.458	.358	17.71	25.00	96
Burkhalter, Blake	R-R	6-0	204	9-19-00	3	3	2.71	14	14	0	70	66	23	21	3	16	63	.253	.300	.345	22.42	5.69	281
Corona, Reibyn	R-R	5-11	175	11-13-01	0	0	16.20	1	0	0	2	3	3	3	0	3	2	.375	.545	.625	18.18	27.27	11
Diaz, Giomar	R-R	6-2	190	11-23-02	1	2	3.38	6	0	0	11	10	4	4	0	7	5	.256	.362	.333	10.64	14.89	47
Dimon, Dawson	R-R	6-0	185	5-17-99	0	0	0.00	1	0	0	0	0	0	0	0	0	0	.000	.500	.000	0.00	0.00	2
Farris, Mitch	L-L	6-2	187	2-14-01	4	4	2.95	17	16	0	82	64	30	27	5	25	93	.215	.278	.320	28.35	7.62	328
Frey, Riley	L-L	6-1	185	4-19-02	3	2	2.67	13	8	1	61	51	21	18	5	18	46	.223	.282	.336	18.55	7.26	248
Gallegos, Isaac	R-R	6-3	215	9-17-02	0	2	3.32	13	0	1	19	13	9	7	1	13	25	.191	.345	.265	29.76	15.48	84
Griswold, Rob	R-R	6-1	185	7-13-98	2	4	3.47	30	0	2	49	54	28	19	5	11	37	.276	.327	.434	16.97	5.05	218
Hackenberg, Drue	R-R	6-2	220	4-1-02	3	3	3.64	12	12	0	59	46	30	24	2	28	62	.211	.327	.271	24.03	10.85	258
Harper, Landon	R-R	6-1	176	4-8-01	3	2	4.39	10	1	0	27	26	14	13	4	5	24	.243	.277	.421	21.43	4.46	112
Hernandez, Herick	L-L	5-10	192	8-11-03	0	0	6.00	1	1	0	3	4	2	2	0	0	5	.308	.308	.462	38.46	0.00	13
Johnson, Jared	R-R	6-2	225	3-15-01	7	4	2.60	38	0	8	52	41	25	15	2	27	61	.206	.313	.281	26.41	11.69	231
Joseph, Elison	R-R	6-0	170	1-24-01	1	2	2.48	19	0	2	33	21	15	9	1	13	46	.175	.261	.242	33.82	9.56	136
Kuehler, Cade	R-R	6-0	215	5-24-02	0	1	24.00	1	1	0	3	8	8	8	1	4	4	.471	.571	.882	19.05	19.05	21
Lara, Jhancarlos	R-R	6-3	190	1-15-03	1	2	3.92	15	14	0	62	55	30	27	2	36	72	.241	.356	.311	26.18	13.09	275
Maier, Adam	R-R	6-0	203	11-26-01	1	1	3.38	6	6	0	27	27	13	10	1	13	21	.260	.347	.356	17.80	11.02	118
Martinez, Daniel	L-R	5-11	190	7-28-98	0	0	2.25	1	1	0	4	1	1	1	0	4	4	.077	.333	.154	22.22	22.22	18
McDonough, LJ	R-R	6-4	200	4-2-00	1	0	0.93	8	0	0	10	7	1	1	0	9	14	.194	.356	.222	31.11	20.00	45
Minter, A.J.	L-L	6-0	215	9-2-93	0	0	0.00	1	1	0	1	1	1	0	0	0	3	.200	.200	.200	60.00	0.00	5
Munoz, Rolddy	R-R	6-2	183	4-14-00	1	1	5.23	7	0	1	10	7	7	6	1	4	19	.189	.279	.378	44.19	9.30	43
Murphy, Owen	R-R	6-1	190	9-27-03	4	2	1.54	7	7	0	41	18	9	7	2	12	60	.129	.203	.216	38.71	7.74	155
Philip, Beau	R-R	5-11	200	10-23-98	0	1	18.00	2	1	0	2	3	4	4	2	1	1	.333	.400	1.000	10.00	10.00	10
Ritchie, JR	R-R	6-2	185	6-26-03	1	1	3.60	2	2	0	10	10	5	4	2	2	8	.256	.286	.667	19.05	4.76	42
Schanaman, Shay	R-R	6-0	195	8-12-99	7	6	4.53	43	0	2	58	51	34	29	6	16	66	.239	.311	.399	27.27	6.61	242
Schwellenbach, Spencer	R-R	6-1	200	5-31-00	2	1	2.53	6	6	0	32	26	12	9	1	9	34	.215	.275	.306	25.95	6.87	131
Silva, William	R-R	6-0	185	8-2-01	0	1	8.59	11	0	2	15	23	16	14	3	6	12	.348	.421	.606	15.79	7.89	76
Smith-Shawver, AJ	R-R	6-3	205	11-20-02	0	1	4.50	1	1	0	2	1	1	1	1	0	4	.143	.143	.571	57.14	0.00	7
Smith, Austin	R-R	6-4	210	6-22-99	0	1	4.05	6	0	1	7	7	4	3	0	4	8	.259	.344	.370	25.00	12.50	32
Strickland, Samuel	R-L	6-2	218	3-26-99	2	2	1.67	39	0	3	59	46	17	11	2	15	66	.209	.258	.282	27.97	6.36	236
Thompson, Tyree	R-R	6-4	165	6-12-97	2	1	4.79	17	1	0	36	31	22	19	5	26	41	.233	.362	.383	24.85	15.76	165
Vargas, Luis	R-R	5-11	196	5-2-02	3	3	4.08	14	13	0	64	64	37	29	8	22	65	.259	.316	.457	23.90	8.09	272
Wall, Cory	R-R	6-4	230	3-14-00	3	5	3.21	26	9	0	76	66	34	27	5	21	76	.237	.295	.360	24.92	6.89	305

Fielding

Catcher	PCT	G	PO	A	E	DP	PB
Clarno	.987	30	280	19	4	2	2
Godman	.993	15	127	14	1	1	2
Guscette	1.000	11	105	9	0	0	1
Zebrowski	.986	63	599	52	9	6	3

First Base	PCT	G	PO	A	E	DP
Compton	.992	48	358	25	3	31
Exposito	.958	6	45	1	2	3
Janas	.978	64	394	43	10	35
Ward	.947	15	86	3	5	7

Second Base	PCT	G	PO	A	E	DP
Arroyo	.959	51	87	100	8	21
Borden	.950	11	17	21	2	9
Exposito	.947	24	37	52	5	11
Jones	.958	6	9	14	1	2
Olsavsky	1.000	1	1	2	0	0
Ward	.973	39	53	90	4	15

Third Base	PCT	G	PO	A	E	DP
Arroyo	.867	6	4	9	2	1
Borden	.500	5	0	2	2	0
Ceballos	.908	71	50	118	17	13
Compton	1.000	2	0	2	0	0
Exposito	1.000	6	6	9	0	1
Olsavsky	.972	14	13	22	1	4
Ward	.887	27	26	37	8	3

Shortstop	PCT	G	PO	A	E	DP
Borden	1.000	3	1	3	0	1
Exposito	.943	76	105	160	16	28
Jones	1.000	1	1	3	0	0
Tavarez	.949	48	78	110	10	18

Outfield	PCT	G	PO	A	E	DP
Arroyo	1.000	1	1	0	0	0
Celedonio	1.000	3	1	0	0	0
Clohisy	1.000	4	10	0	0	0
Grady	.952	46	73	7	4	4
Janas	1.000	4	8	0	0	0
Kern	1.000	10	26	0	0	0
Kilpatrick	.976	117	241	8	6	3
Paolini	.982	91	156	6	3	1
Workinger	.974	89	144	4	4	2
Worrell	1.000	26	45	1	0	1

AUGUSTA GREENJACKETS — *LOW-A*

CAROLINA LEAGUE

Batting	B-T	Ht.	Wt.	DOB	AVG	OBP	SLG	G	PA	AB	R	H	2B	3B	HR	RBI	BB	HBP	SH	SF	SO	SB	CS	BB%	SO%
Benitez, Diego	R-R	6-0	180	11-19-04	.137	.231	.214	37	148	131	13	18	2	1	2	10	14	2	0	0	54	3	0	9.46	36.49
Boucher, Pier-Olivier	L-R	6-2	185	12-3-99	.174	.301	.256	39	143	121	14	21	5	1	1	6	20	2	0	0	48	12	2	13.99	33.57
Celedonio, Jeremy	R-R	6-1	183	12-26-01	.197	.286	.394	19	77	66	6	13	2	1	3	10	6	3	0	2	35	3	1	7.79	45.45
Clohisy, Patrick	L-L	5-10	190	12-6-01	.256	.330	.346	22	88	78	7	20	7	0	0	8	9	0	0	1	17	3	0	10.23	19.32
Compton, Drew	B-R	6-2	212	3-25-01	.295	.406	.430	43	180	149	17	44	11	0	3	26	26	3	0	2	33	5	1	14.44	18.33
De La Cruz, Willmer	B-R	5-8	168	4-6-03	.184	.311	.224	27	91	76	7	14	1	1	0	7	13	1	0	0	32	5	2	14.29	35.16
Dimon, Dawson	R-R	6-0	185	5-17-99	.148	.233	.148	9	30	27	2	4	0	0	0	0	3	0	0	0	16	0	0	10.00	53.33
Drake, Isaiah	L-R	5-10	185	7-15-05	.163	.259	.252	69	283	246	26	40	8	4	2	11	32	1	0	3	100	23	4	11.31	35.34
Dumitru, Titus	R-R	6-2	220	5-17-03	.217	.324	.337	27	108	92	15	20	6	1	1	11	13	2	0	1	26	4	3	12.04	24.07
Figueroa, Leiker	R-R	5-10	155	1-12-05	.169	.230	.213	53	201	183	14	31	4	2	0	14	11	4	1	2	54	13	3	5.47	26.87
Garcia, Junior	L-R	6-2	190	7-13-05	.184	.315	.191	40	162	136	7	25	1	0	0	11	25	1	0	0	59	3	4	15.43	36.42
Gil, John	R-R	6-1	175	5-14-06	.204	.297	.255	39	159	137	20	28	5	1	0	7	19	0	1	2	37	14	2	11.95	23.27
Godman, Jacob	R-R	6-2	200	5-7-00	.200	.366	.300	47	164	130	19	26	5	1	2	11	31	3	0	0	40	9	2	18.90	24.39

Gonzalez, Robert	L-R	5-10	175	12-22-04	.194	.304	.287	65	253	216	26	42	8	3	2	28	34	1	0	2	88	19	2	13.44	34.78
Grady, Jace	B-R	5-11	182	5-25-01	.288	.374	.453	45	195	170	27	49	9	2	5	26	23	1	0	1	33	9	1	11.79	16.92
Guanipa, Luis	R-R	5-11	188	12-15-05	.184	.250	.200	32	136	125	7	23	2	0	0	6	11	0	0	0	35	6	4	8.09	25.74
Guerra, Mason	R-R	6-3	195	8-28-02	.133	.253	.173	24	87	75	5	10	3	0	0	5	11	1	0	0	25	0	0	12.64	28.74
Guscette, Mac	R-R	6-0	200	2-14-02	.250	.333	.250	3	9	8	0	2	0	0	0	0	1	0	0	0	1	0	0	11.11	11.11
Jones, Colby	R-R	5-11	180	9-30-03	.281	.343	.328	20	70	64	8	18	3	0	0	4	4	2	0	0	15	1	4	5.71	21.43
Kern, Kade	R-R	6-0	200	9-18-01	.199	.274	.300	80	310	277	29	55	9	2	5	24	25	5	0	3	92	16	7	8.06	29.68
Machado, Austin	L-R	6-1	205	6-11-01	.278	.490	.278	13	51	36	5	10	0	0	0	4	9	6	0	0	3	0	0	17.65	5.88
Magee, Cam	L-R	6-1	190	6-1-02	.176	.286	.219	57	220	187	21	33	5	0	1	13	22	8	0	3	75	18	4	10.00	34.09
Marcano, Jose	R-R	6-0	160	5-6-04	.200	.333	.200	4	12	10	1	2	0	0	0	2	2	0	0	0	4	0	0	16.67	33.33
Martinez, Alexander	R-R	5-11	170	11-16-04	.121	.164	.138	15	61	58	8	7	1	0	0	5	3	0	0	0	23	0	0	4.92	37.70
Olsavsky, Joe	R-R	6-1	180	3-29-02	.176	.332	.261	63	232	188	28	33	8	1	2	19	33	11	0	0	60	6	5	14.22	25.86
Owen, Harry	R-R	6-1	225	3-7-02	.222	.285	.327	50	179	162	14	36	6	1	3	16	13	2	0	2	37	0	0	7.26	20.67
Parababire, Luis	R-R	5-10	195	4-8-06	.111	.200	.111	3	10	9	0	1	0	0	0	0	1	0	0	0	6	1	0	10.00	60.00
Pineda, Alen	R-R	5-10	180	11-4-04	.091	.167	.091	3	12	11	0	1	0	0	0	0	1	0	0	0	8	0	0	8.33	66.67
Sanchez, Luis	R-R	5-7	165	1-16-04	.226	.296	.274	86	348	314	32	71	8	2	1	28	26	6	0	2	62	14	6	7.47	17.82
Steels, Jake	R-R	6-0	185	6-17-02	.231	.340	.256	12	47	39	5	9	1	0	0	3	5	2	0	1	12	2	1	10.64	25.53
Verdung, Will	R-R	6-2	200	6-8-03	.215	.343	.276	106	437	362	37	78	16	0	2	37	64	8	0	3	90	17	5	14.65	20.59
Williams, Noah	B-R	6-1	180	4-12-04	.205	.288	.299	36	132	117	10	24	3	1	2	12	12	2	0	1	40	2	2	9.09	30.30
Worrell, Bryson	B-R	6-2	226	11-7-98	.143	.143	.286	5	21	21	3	3	1	1	0	2	0	0	0	0	6	2	0	0.00	28.57

Pitching	B-T	Ht.	Wt.	DOB	W	L	ERA	G	GS	SV	IP	Hits	Runs	ER	HR	BB	SO	AVG	OBP	SLG	SO%	BB%	BF
Anderson, Ian	R-R	6-3	170	5-2-98	0	0	0.00	2	2	0	6	1	0	0	0	2	6	.050	.136	.050	27.27	9.09	22
Antonio, Rayven	R-R	6-1	190	3-2-06	0	1	3.66	5	4	1	20	21	9	8	0	12	14	.269	.374	.359	15.38	13.19	91
Arestigueta, Luis	R-R	6-3	175	10-14-05	0	1	3.50	4	3	0	18	13	8	7	2	8	17	.197	.308	.364	21.79	10.26	78
Austin, Zack	R-R	6-2	190	7-17-01	0	0	8.31	12	0	1	17	18	19	16	0	31	20	.273	.529	.333	19.05	29.52	105
Bagwell, Ethan	R-R	6-4	230	2-24-06	0	0	6.75	1	1	0	3	4	2	2	0	1	3	.400	.455	.600	25.00	8.33	12
Baumann, Garrett	L-R	6-8	245	8-15-04	6	5	3.42	19	18	0	92	85	43	35	3	23	84	.241	.295	.324	21.88	5.99	384
Boucher, Pier-Olivier	L-R	6-2	185	12-3-99	0	0	4.50	1	0	0	2	2	1	1	1	0	0	.222	.222	.556	0.00	0.00	9
Caminiti, Cameron	L-L	6-2	200	8-8-06	0	1	3.00	1	1	0	3	3	1	1	0	0	4	.250	.250	.333	33.33	0.00	12
Corona, Reibyn	R-R	5-11	175	11-13-01	4	5	6.12	28	0	4	43	51	37	29	6	22	45	.288	.385	.463	21.63	10.58	208
Diaz, Giomar	R-R	6-2	190	11-23-02	1	4	5.12	26	0	4	46	48	32	26	2	26	55	.267	.363	.389	25.70	12.15	214
Dilone, Adel	R-R	6-3	207	10-7-00	5	1	3.08	20	2	0	53	37	20	18	5	22	62	.193	.289	.313	28.44	10.09	218
Farris, Mitch	L-L	6-2	187	2-14-01	0	1	2.38	7	2	1	23	17	6	6	0	14	37	.207	.323	.244	38.54	14.58	96
Frey, Riley	L-L	6-1	185	4-19-02	3	0	1.54	5	4	0	23	15	7	4	0	4	28	.172	.209	.241	30.77	4.40	91
Fuentes, Didier	R-R	6-0	170	6-17-05	3	6	2.74	18	17	0	76	56	28	23	8	21	98	.200	.262	.350	32.13	6.89	305
Gallegos, Isaac	R-R	6-3	215	9-17-02	0	0	3.18	3	0	1	6	5	2	2	0	2	9	.217	.280	.304	36.00	8.00	25
Garcia, Anthony	R-R	6-2	200	3-28-02	1	2	5.34	12	2	0	30	36	18	18	4	14	26	.293	.369	.431	18.44	9.93	141
Gomez, Jacob	R-L	5-10	190	10-27-01	1	0	0.66	7	0	0	14	6	1	1	0	3	22	.133	.220	.156	44.00	6.00	50
Gutierrez, Rolando	L-L	6-2	190	4-6-02	0	2	8.15	8	1	0	18	21	19	16	0	12	19	.300	.402	.371	21.84	13.79	87
Hackman, Owen	R-R	6-1	185	11-2-01	2	2	1.31	5	3	0	21	11	6	3	0	7	24	.157	.244	.214	30.77	8.97	78
Hernandez, Herick	L-L	5-10	192	8-11-03	0	0	0.00	1	1	0	4	0	0	0	0	0	7	.000	.000	.000	63.64	0.00	11
Holton, Carter	L-L	5-11	201	9-4-02	0	0	13.50	1	1	0	2	1	3	3	0	4	3	.167	.500	.167	30.00	40.00	10
Keller, Seth	R-R	5-10	180	5-26-04	0	0	2.25	2	0	0	4	2	1	1	0	6	2	.143	.429	.286	9.52	28.57	21
Kern, Kade	R-R	6-0	200	9-18-01	0	0	0.00	1	0	0	1	0	0	0	0	0	0	.000	.000	.000	0.00	0.00	2
Kroeger, Jacob	L-L	6-1	190	5-18-00	0	1	2.13	7	1	1	13	9	3	3	0	17	16	.220	.441	.244	27.12	28.81	59
Kuehler, Cade	R-R	6-0	215	5-24-02	3	5	2.52	11	11	0	50	41	17	14	3	20	44	.220	.305	.371	20.95	9.52	210
Maier, Adam	R-R	6-0	203	11-26-01	2	4	4.45	13	13	0	57	58	34	28	3	12	57	.259	.308	.371	23.75	5.00	240
Marcano, Jose	R-R	6-0	160	5-6-04	0	0	0.00	1	0	0	1	0	0	0	0	1	0	.000	.333	.000	0.00	33.33	3
McDonough, LJ	R-R	6-4	200	4-2-00	2	3	5.06	25	0	4	37	38	26	21	3	24	52	.260	.365	.349	30.59	14.12	170
Morton, Kadon	R-R	6-1	195	11-19-00	2	5	6.88	17	5	0	35	41	33	27	6	17	30	.287	.361	.531	17.96	10.18	167
Olsavsky, Joe	R-R	6-1	180	3-29-02	0	0	5.40	1	0	0	2	2	1	1	1	2	0	.333	.444	.833	0.00	22.22	9
Ortiz, Hayder	R-R	6-0	160	11-14-01	1	1	7.36	7	0	0	7	10	8	6	0	7	11	.345	.500	.448	26.83	17.07	41
Philip, Beau	R-R	5-11	200	10-23-98	0	3	4.68	17	0	1	33	35	22	17	0	15	29	.285	.371	.333	20.00	10.34	145
Polo, Davis	R-R	6-1	150	10-27-04	1	9	5.16	15	12	0	59	65	37	34	5	14	53	.270	.306	.419	20.46	5.41	259
Reyes, Jeremy	R-R	6-1	170	1-11-06	1	2	3.00	4	4	0	15	13	7	5	0	12	9	.241	.379	.296	13.64	18.18	66
Ritchie, JR	R-R	6-2	185	6-26-03	1	3	1.95	7	6	0	32	23	11	7	3	10	40	.197	.277	.316	30.77	7.69	130
Rivas, Albert	R-R	6-0	155	2-18-03	2	2	4.64	14	0	3	21	20	12	11	1	6	21	.241	.300	.386	23.33	6.67	90
Rodriguez, David	L-R	6-2	196	12-31-01	2	3	4.97	7	2	0	25	28	15	14	2	9	19	.286	.343	.439	17.59	8.33	108
Samuels, Logan	R-R	6-4	170	2-18-02	0	0	0.00	1	1	0	1	1	0	0	0	0	1	.200	.200	.200	20.00	0.00	5
Sanchez, Juan	R-R	6-2	180	5-21-03	0	1	3.58	19	0	2	38	26	15	15	2	29	42	.195	.370	.286	24.28	16.76	173
Shafer, Jacob	R-R	6-8	240	4-30-02	1	1	1.35	5	5	0	20	15	6	3	0	7	24	.211	.282	.225	30.77	8.97	78
Shoemaker, Adam	L-L	6-6	205	8-24-02	2	4	6.20	24	3	2	70	61	53	48	3	61	91	.235	.390	.350	27.49	18.43	331
Silva, William	R-R	6-0	185	8-2-01	1	1	2.51	17	0	2	29	25	12	8	0	9	37	.229	.306	.294	29.84	7.26	124
Thompson, Tyree	R-R	6-4	165	6-12-97	0	0	0.00	1	0	0	5	1	0	0	0	3	7	.077	.278	.077	38.89	16.67	18
Vargas, Luis	R-R	5-11	196	5-2-02	2	0	3.45	9	3	2	31	23	14	12	2	17	39	.204	.305	.327	29.77	12.98	131
Waldrep, Hurston	R-R	6-2	205	3-1-02	0	1	18.00	1	1	0	2	5	4	4	0	2	4	.417	.500	.583	28.57	14.29	14
Wall, Cory	R-R	6-4	230	3-14-00	0	0	3.00	1	0	0	3	4	1	1	0	2	4	.364	.462	.545	30.77	15.38	13

Fielding

Catcher	PCT	G	PO	A	E	DP	PB
Dimon	.988	9	83	1	1	0	4
Godman	.978	46	410	32	10	2	3
Gonzalez	1.000	1	1	0	0	0	0
Guscette	1.000	3	19	5	0	1	0
Machado	.991	10	98	9	1	0	0
Martinez	.946	15	159	17	10	4	0
Owen	.996	47	441	25	2	7	6
Pineda	1.000	3	26	1	0	0	1

First Base	PCT	G	PO	A	E	DP
Celedonio	1.000	3	24	2	0	3
Compton	.987	35	277	21	4	20
Guerra	.977	6	41	1	1	4
Olsavsky	.982	8	51	5	1	2

Parababire	1.000	1	3	1	0	0
Verdung	.986	78	528	52	8	36

Second Base	PCT	G	PO	A	E	DP
De La Cruz	.941	14	19	29	3	2
Figueroa	.925	13	16	33	4	5
Jones	.984	17	29	34	1	5
Magee	.986	18	31	39	1	12
Olsavsky	.967	9	5	24	1	2
Sanchez	.959	49	73	112	8	19
Verdung	.978	11	12	32	1	4

Third Base	PCT	G	PO	A	E	DP
De La Cruz	.893	11	9	16	3	4
Figueroa	.816	13	10	21	7	3
Guerra	.919	18	13	21	3	2
Magee	.949	22	10	27	2	3
Olsavsky	.929	31	25	54	6	7
Sanchez	.898	35	23	56	9	5
Verdung	.895	7	7	10	2	3

Shortstop	PCT	G	PO	A	E	DP
De La Cruz	.893	11	9	16	3	4
Figueroa	.816	13	10	21	7	3
Guerra	.919	18	13	21	3	2
Magee	.949	22	10	27	2	3
Olsavsky	.929	31	25	54	6	7
Sanchez	.898	35	23	56	9	5
Verdung	.895	7	7	10	2	3

Outfield	PCT	G	PO	A	E	DP
De La Cruz	.000	1	0	0	1	0
Guanipa	.907	24	38	1	4	0
Garcia	.950	31	56	1	3	1
Gonzalez	.960	65	113	7	5	1
Steels	.963	11	21	5	1	2
Drake	.963	61	104	1	4	0
Clohisy	.968	16	26	4	1	1
Dumitru	.973	20	35	1	1	1
Kern	.991	63	101	4	1	0
Boucher	1.000	30	45	2	0	0
Celedonio	1.000	1	1	0	0	0
Grady	1.000	39	47	3	0	2
Williams	1.000	29	54	1	0	0
Worrell	1.000	5	12	0	0	0

FCL BRAVES — ROOKIE

FLORIDA COMPLEX LEAGUE

Batting	B-T	Ht.	Wt.	DOB	AVG	OBP	SLG	G	PA	AB	R	H	2B	3B	HR	RBI	BB	HBP	SH	SF	SO	SB	CS	BB%	SO%
Baez, Mario	R-R	5-9	175	8-25-06	.202	.272	.243	51	193	173	20	35	5	1	0	20	15	2	1	1	36	16	2	7.77	18.65
Benitez, Diego	R-R	6-0	180	11-19-04	.165	.276	.247	27	98	85	12	14	1	0	2	11	13	0	0	0	24	1	0	13.27	24.49
Bolt, Skye	B-R	6-2	194	1-15-94	.000	.429	.000	2	7	4	2	0	0	0	0	0	3	0	0	0	0	0	0	42.86	0.00
Casanova, Jair	R-R	5-11	170	11-14-03	.040	.111	.040	9	27	25	1	1	0	0	0	2	2	0	0	0	12	0	0	7.41	44.44
Celedonio, Jeremy	R-R	6-1	183	12-26-01	.158	.333	.211	6	24	19	4	3	1	0	0	3	5	0	0	0	9	0	0	20.83	37.50
Cordero, Carlos	B-R	6-0	170	9-11-05	.170	.235	.213	18	51	47	3	8	0	1	0	5	3	1	0	0	13	1	1	5.88	25.49
De La Cruz, Willmer	B-R	5-8	168	4-6-03	.281	.410	.344	13	39	32	3	9	2	0	0	5	7	0	0	0	6	4	1	17.95	15.38
Drake, Isaiah	L-R	5-10	185	7-15-05	.083	.421	.083	5	19	12	3	1	0	0	0	0	7	0	0	0	7	0	1	36.84	36.84
Estevez, John	L-R	6-3	190	5-17-06	.200	.367	.313	52	196	150	24	30	8	3	1	21	38	4	0	4	49	7	3	19.39	25.00
Figueroa, Leiker	R-R	5-10	155	1-12-05	.176	.222	.235	5	18	17	0	3	1	0	0	2	1	0	0	0	3	0	0	5.56	16.67
Garcia, Elian	L-L	5-10	175	10-31-04	.081	.286	.189	24	52	37	4	3	1	0	1	6	8	3	3	1	12	2	0	15.38	23.08
Garcia, Junior	L-R	6-2	190	7-13-05	.317	.432	.446	42	169	139	26	44	5	2	3	22	22	7	0	1	41	12	4	13.02	24.26
Gil, John	R-R	6-1	175	5-14-06	.286	.403	.389	51	211	175	42	50	9	0	3	20	28	7	0	1	34	26	6	13.27	16.11
Glod, Douglas	R-R	5-9	185	1-20-05	.193	.357	.296	46	171	135	17	26	4	2	2	16	34	1	0	1	62	0	3	19.88	36.26
Godman, Jacob	R-R	6-2	200	5-7-00	.500	.500	.500	1	2	2	0	1	0	0	0	1	0	0	0	0	0	0	0	0.00	0.00
Gonzalez, Robert	L-R	5-10	175	12-22-04	.091	.333	.091	5	15	11	1	1	0	0	0	0	3	1	0	0	3	0	0	20.00	20.00
Guanipa, Luis	R-R	5-11	188	12-15-05	.282	.346	.451	20	81	71	14	20	2	2	2	9	7	1	0	2	10	4	0	8.64	12.35
Liberato, Luis	L-L	5-11	175	12-18-95	.231	.412	.308	4	17	13	1	3	1	0	0	0	4	0	0	0	3	0	0	23.53	17.65
Magee, Cam	L-R	6-1	190	6-1-02	.400	.500	.400	2	6	5	0	2	0	0	0	1	1	0	0	0	2	0	0	16.67	33.33
Martinez, Alexander	R-R	5-11	170	11-16-04	.147	.200	.173	22	81	75	7	11	2	0	0	1	5	0	1	0	17	1	0	6.17	20.99
Monteverde, Carlos	L-L	6-1	177	12-10-05	.400	.514	.533	10	37	30	3	12	4	0	0	4	7	0	0	0	4	0	0	18.92	10.81
Niazoa, Roiber	R-R	6-0	175	12-23-04	.233	.385	.301	30	91	73	10	17	3	1	0	7	13	5	0	0	23	1	0	14.29	25.27
Nieblas, Angel	R-R	5-8	170	9-4-05	.208	.305	.277	36	119	101	11	21	7	0	0	10	12	3	1	2	28	5	2	10.08	23.53
Orellana, Josnaider	R-R	5-11	175	9-26-04	.155	.246	.155	22	65	58	3	9	0	0	0	5	7	0	0	0	17	1	0	10.77	26.15
Owen, Harry	R-R	6-1	225	3-7-02	.120	.154	.120	7	26	25	1	3	0	0	0	3	1	0	0	0	6	0	0	3.85	23.08
Parababire, Luis	R-R	5-10	195	4-8-06	.262	.458	.443	24	83	61	14	16	11	0	0	7	18	4	0	0	15	0	0	21.69	18.07
Pineda, Alen	R-R	5-10	180	11-4-04	.067	.208	.178	17	53	45	4	3	0	1	1	2	5	3	0	0	18	0	0	9.43	33.96
White, Eli	R-R	6-2	195	6-26-94	.000	.000	.000	1	4	4	0	0	0	0	0	0	0	0	0	0	0	0	0	0.00	0.00
Williams, Noah	B-R	6-1	190	4-12-04	.190	.346	.429	8	26	21	3	4	0	1	1	5	4	1	0	0	6	0	0	15.38	23.08

Pitching	B-T	Ht.	Wt.	DOB	W	L	ERA	G	GS	SV	IP	Hits	Runs	ER	HR	BB	SO	AVG	OBP	SLG	SO%	BB%	BF
Abreu, Cristobal	R-R	6-1	165	2-2-06	0	1	11.88	3	1	0	8	14	15	11	2	6	3	.350	.435	.575	6.52	13.04	46
Almonte, Genderson	R-R	6-2	170	12-13-03	1	0	5.06	5	0	0	5	7	3	3	1	4	5	.350	.440	.500	20.00	16.00	25
Anderson, Ian	R-R	6-3	170	5-2-98	0	0	1.80	2	2	0	5	3	1	1	0	0	7	.188	.235	.188	41.18	0.00	17
Antonio, Rayven	R-R	6-1	190	3-2-06	1	1	4.33	11	2	1	27	28	15	13	0	7	17	.269	.333	.298	14.91	6.14	114
Arestigueta, Luis	R-R	6-3	175	10-14-05	2	3	5.10	12	8	0	42	46	26	24	2	22	42	.271	.367	.382	21.32	11.17	197
Austin, Zack	R-R	6-2	190	7-17-01	1	3	7.11	9	0	2	13	13	17	10	0	13	11	.265	.439	.306	16.42	19.40	67
Bourassa, Ryan	R-R	6-0	230	12-18-99	0	0	0.00	1	0	0	1	0	0	0	0	2	1	.000	.600	.000	20.00	40.00	5
Burkhalter, Blake	R-R	6-0	204	9-19-00	0	1	11.57	2	2	0	2	3	3	3	0	2	6	.333	.455	.333	54.55	18.18	11
Doyle, Tommy	R-R	6-6	244	5-1-96	0	0	0.00	1	1	0	1	0	1	0	0	1	2	.000	.200	.000	40.00	20.00	5
Gallegos, Isaac	R-R	6-3	215	9-17-02	0	0	0.00	2	0	0	2	0	0	0	0	0	6	.000	.000	.000	66.67	0.00	9
Garcia, Anthony	R-R	6-2	200	3-28-02	0	1	4.50	9	0	0	14	11	13	7	0	8	12	.204	.333	.278	17.91	11.94	67
Guerra, Whilmer	R-R	6-2	160	10-14-05	3	4	3.38	11	6	0	37	38	21	14	3	23	23	.262	.377	.407	13.14	13.14	175
Gutierrez, Rolando	L-L	6-2	190	4-6-02	0	1	2.84	3	0	0	6	5	3	2	0	4	8	.227	.393	.455	28.57	14.29	28
Herget, Jimmy	R-R	6-3	170	9-9-93	0	0	0.00	1	0	0	1	0	0	0	0	0	1	.000	.000	.000	33.33	0.00	3
Hernandez, Miguel	R-R	6-0	174	10-1-02	0	0	3.18	4	0	0	6	4	3	2	0	3	4	.182	.280	.182	16.00	12.00	25
Militello, Justin	R-R	6-1	190	12-3-03	2	5	10.23	12	5	0	32	46	39	36	2	27	24	.348	.476	.538	14.12	15.88	170
Morton, Kadon	R-R	6-1	195	11-19-00	0	2	4.50	3	3	0	12	11	9	6	0	8	14	.239	.357	.304	25.00	14.29	56
Niazoa, Roiber	R-R	6-0	175	12-23-04	0	0	9.00	1	0	0	1	2	1	1	0	0	1	.400	.400	.600	20.00	0.00	5
Ojeda, Jose	R-R	5-10	170	5-15-05	1	1	7.45	17	0	0	19	20	21	16	0	17	18	.278	.430	.319	17.65	16.67	102
Ortiz, Hayder	R-R	6-0	160	11-14-01	1	0	19.73	10	0	2	9	9	19	19	1	16	16	.257	.527	.429	29.09	29.09	55
Patino, Marco	R-R	6-0	175	11-17-04	3	2	6.18	14	2	2	28	29	20	19	1	23	20	.279	.427	.404	15.27	17.56	131
Pirela, Yorvi	R-R	6-0	160	1-3-05	0	1	4.78	17	0	0	26	33	15	14	5	14	21	.306	.382	.519	17.07	11.38	123
Rees, Carter	R-R	6-3	205	7-22-03	1	1	6.91	11	0	0	14	14	15	11	0	15	19	.259	.431	.352	26.39	20.83	72
Reyes, Jeremy	R-R	6-1	170	1-11-06	0	1	1.25	5	4	0	22	13	5	3	0	13	23	.173	.295	.200	25.84	14.61	89

Pitching	B-T	Ht.	Wt.	DOB	W	L	ERA	G	GS	SV	IP	Hits	Runs	ER	HR	BB	SO	AVG	OBP	SLG	SO%	BB%	BF
Ritchie, JR	R-R	6-2	185	6-26-03	0	1	6.14	3	3	0	7	6	5	5	1	5	8	.231	.375	.462	24.24	15.15	33
Rivas, Albert	R-R	6-0	155	2-18-03	1	0	2.40	11	0	4	15	17	6	4	0	5	13	.304	.371	.375	20.97	8.06	62
Rodriguez, David	L-R	6-2	196	12-31-01	0	2	5.35	9	6	0	34	31	21	20	2	15	29	.250	.324	.347	20.42	10.56	142
Sanchez, Juan	R-R	6-2	180	5-21-03	1	1	2.45	4	0	0	7	8	5	2	0	4	8	.267	.389	.300	21.62	10.81	37
Smith, Austin	R-R	6-4	210	6-22-99	0	0	2.45	3	1	0	4	3	1	1	0	1	3	.250	.357	.417	21.43	7.14	14
Taveras, Jhonly	R-R	6-1	180	12-16-04	1	6	7.84	12	10	0	31	31	33	27	3	34	30	.267	.446	.414	19.11	21.66	157
Waldrep, Hurston	R-R	6-2	205	3-1-02	0	0	4.50	1	1	0	2	2	1	1	0	2	2	.250	.400	.375	20.00	20.00	10
Ynoa, Huascar	R-R	6-2	220	5-28-98	0	1	8.10	2	2	0	3	4	3	3	1	0	1	.286	.286	.571	7.14	0.00	14

Fielding

C: Martinez 22, Parababire 14, Orellana 13, Owen 7, Pineda 5, Godman 1. 1B: Niazoa 27, Pineda 13, Parababire 8, Orellana 6, Monteverde 5, Garcia 2, Celedonio 1. 2B: Baez 26, Nieblas 20, Cordero 10, De La Cruz 5, Figueroa 1. 3B: Benitez 23, Nieblas 15, Cordero 7, Gil 7, De La Cruz 6, Figueroa 3, Magee 2, Niazoa 1. SS: Gil 36, Baez 20, De La Cruz 3, Figueroa 1. LF: Estevez 20, Garcia 13, Glod 9, Garcia 9, Casanova 4, Williams 4, Monteverde 3, Liberato 1, Celedonio 1. CF: Glod 19, Guanipa 18, Garcia 9, Estevez 7, Drake 5, Gonzalez 5, Liberato 1, White 1, Bolt 1. RF: Estevez 16, Garcia 13, Garcia 12, Glod 9, Casanova 5, Celedonio 4, Williams 4, Liberato 2, Monteverde 1, Bolt 1.

DSL BRAVES — ROOKIE

DOMINICAN SUMMER LEAGUE

Batting	B-T	Ht.	Wt.	DOB	AVG	OBP	SLG	G	PA	AB	R	H	2B	3B	HR	RBI	BB	HBP	SH	SF	SO	SB	CS	BB%	SO%
Acevedo, Joan	L-R	5-11	155	9-17-06	.234	.287	.274	42	137	124	11	29	1	2	0	18	9	1	1	2	29	5	1	6.57	21.17
Baez, Michael	R-R	5-11	195	10-3-04	.204	.333	.269	38	129	108	15	22	7	0	0	13	15	6	0	0	35	0	0	11.63	27.13
Campos, Elio	R-R	5-9	157	1-2-04	.247	.339	.286	47	178	154	27	38	3	0	1	13	20	2	1	1	27	14	7	11.24	15.17
Cesa, Gabriel	R-R	5-10	166	9-5-06	.164	.289	.188	43	152	128	14	21	3	0	0	18	20	3	0	1	45	12	5	13.16	29.61
Cueche, Nixson	R-R	5-11	156	3-6-06	.198	.353	.236	42	136	106	18	21	4	0	0	17	25	2	0	3	23	5	6	18.38	16.91
De La Rosa, Samil	R-R	5-8	175	9-24-03	.273	.467	.273	5	15	11	4	3	0	0	0	1	3	1	0	0	2	1	0	20.00	13.33
Dos Passos, Manuel	R-R	5-10	165	1-8-07	.140	.354	.172	35	128	93	18	13	3	0	0	10	24	8	1	2	36	5	5	18.75	28.13
Espinal, Juan	R-R	6-2	185	9-26-06	.169	.341	.246	44	167	130	22	22	4	0	2	18	26	9	0	2	63	14	5	15.57	37.72
Ferreira, Johan	R-R	5-11	190	10-5-02	.091	.389	.091	6	18	11	3	1	0	0	0	1	5	1	0	1	2	1	0	27.78	11.11
Hernandez, Hojans	R-R	5-11	175	3-7-06	.154	.333	.167	31	99	78	11	12	1	0	0	5	19	2	0	0	23	10	4	19.19	23.23
Martinez, Michael	R-R	6-2	175	1-24-07	.222	.349	.316	48	189	158	20	35	8	2	1	14	13	18	0	0	52	5	5	6.88	27.51
Mateo, Juan	B-R	6-0	165	5-22-07	.250	.345	.333	44	165	144	20	36	7	1	1	14	21	0	0	0	16	9	6	12.73	9.70
Monteverde, Carlos	L-L	6-1	177	12-10-05	.264	.415	.347	24	94	72	14	19	6	0	0	9	19	1	0	2	23	0	2	20.21	24.47
Nunez, Joan	L-R	5-11	155	9-17-06	234	.287	.274	42	137	124	11	29	1	2	0	18	9	1	1	2	29	5	1	6.57	21.17
Osorio, Isaac	R-R	6-1	180	3-12-07	.167	.343	.167	31	99	78	9	13	0	0	0	7	17	4	0	0	33	3	0	17.17	33.33
Perdomo, Jose	R-R	5-11	180	9-20-06	.250	.318	.250	8	22	20	3	5	0	0	0	0	2	0	0	0	4	2	1	9.09	18.18
Sanchez, Alexander	B-R	5-10	170	11-30-05	.194	.278	.226	12	36	31	1	6	1	0	0	2	3	1	0	1	8	2	2	8.33	22.22

Pitching	B-T	Ht.	Wt.	DOB	W	L	ERA	G	GS	SV	IP	Hits	Runs	ER	HR	BB	SO	AVG	OBP	SLG	SO%	BB%	BF
Beltran, Jeiki	R-R	5-11	170	10-11-03	1	3	6.53	12	1	0	21	16	18	15	1	21	26	.216	.416	.324	25.74	20.79	101
Carmona, Kelvin	R-R	6-1	170	8-20-06	2	2	6.11	14	0	0	18	10	13	12	0	20	18	.189	.416	.283	22.78	25.32	79
Cedano, Edward	R-R	6-1	165	11-14-05	1	3	4.88	9	7	0	28	15	17	15	0	30	30	.161	.376	.194	24.00	24.00	125
Duarte, Fernando	R-R	6-6	180	3-12-07	0	1	9.00	9	2	0	15	10	17	15	1	22	12	.196	.469	.294	14.81	27.16	81
Estiven, Sebastian	R-R	6-4	220	12-18-01	0	5	10.38	10	8	0	22	21	26	25	0	18	26	.256	.431	.341	23.85	16.51	109
Francique, Kendy	R-R	6-2	195	9-8-04	2	3	3.48	13	0	2	21	16	9	8	2	8	16	.222	.298	.319	19.05	9.52	84
Frias, Yonathan	L-L	6-0	175	9-22-05	0	0	4.26	6	0	0	6	8	3	3	0	11	2	.320	.526	.320	5.26	28.95	38
Gonzalez, Anferni	R-R	6-4	195	1-25-06	2	2	6.17	12	1	0	23	24	22	16	2	20	16	.258	.412	.441	13.45	16.81	119
Gonzalez, Euder	R-R	6-3	180	1-15-05	0	0	27.00	1	0	0	0	1	1	1	0	3	0	.500	.800	.500	0.00	60.00	5
Gutierrez, Jean F.	R-R	6-1	170	10-25-05	0	1	3.20	12	0	1	20	17	10	7	0	16	15	.254	.441	.299	16.13	17.20	93
Hidalgo, Edwarlys	L-L	6-0	170	6-24-06	0	0	2.35	6	1	0	8	8	2	2	0	7	7	.286	.459	.357	18.92	18.92	37
Lasorsa, Rafael	R-L	6-1	163	5-27-07	1	1	3.12	13	0	0	26	22	15	9	2	12	18	.232	.318	.326	16.22	10.81	111
Marcano, Jose	R-R	6-3	170	1-4-05	0	0	0.00	3	0	0	3	2	1	0	0	2	4	.154	.267	.231	26.67	13.33	15
Marine, Yansel	L-L	6-2	160	6-11-05	0	1	6.75	14	0	0	21	29	21	16	0	17	15	.341	.444	.412	13.89	15.74	108
Marquez, Noslen	R-R	6-0	165	6-27-05	1	1	8.39	11	1	0	25	22	27	23	0	24	23	.247	.431	.315	18.55	19.35	124
Nunez, Jorge	R-R	6-2	174	8-30-07	0	0	4.02	10	0	0	16	4	9	7	0	20	13	.089	.392	.156	17.57	27.03	74
Pina, Rudit	R-R	6-3	170	3-20-06	0	3	3.93	12	10	0	37	24	18	16	1	27	43	.194	.346	.290	27.04	16.98	159
Pineda, Jose	R-R	5-11	150	1-7-05	0	4	7.85	10	8	0	18	20	20	16	1	17	13	.290	.479	.377	13.54	17.71	96
Pinero, Yander	R-R	6-3	165	6-8-07	0	1	6.75	9	3	1	24	29	20	18	0	21	27	.299	.433	.371	22.50	17.50	120
Sifontes, Lewis	L-L	5-9	155	2-7-06	1	4	7.79	11	10	0	32	37	29	28	1	22	29	.287	.399	.395	18.35	13.92	158
Vicioso, Francisco	R-R	6-0	175	11-28-04	0	1	23.63	7	0	0	3	2	7	7	0	17	5	.200	.704	.400	18.52	62.96	27
Zapata, Daury	R-R	6-1	170	11-8-02	4	1	3.57	12	0	0	18	14	9	7	0	8	14	.219	.315	.234	19.18	10.96	73

Fielding

C: Dos Passos 26, Hernandez 19, Baez 7. 1B: Cueche 20, Baez 18, Hernandez 10, Monteverde 7, Ferreira 3, Campos 3. 2B: Campos 32, Mateo 8, Sanchez 7, Acevedo 5, De La Rosa 3, Hernandez 1, Cueche 1. 3B: Acevedo 28, Cueche 20, Sanchez 5, Campos 4, De La Rosa 1, Hernandez 1, Mateo 1. SS: Mateo 33, Acevedo 13, Campos 7, Perdomo 7. LF: Martinez 28, Cesa 13, Monteverde 6, Osorio 6, Cueche 5. CF: Espinal 33, Cesa 16, Martinez 4. RF: Osorio 18, Cesa 14, Martinez 10, Monteverde 8, Espinal 5, Ferreira 3, Cueche 1.

Baltimore Orioles

SEASON SYNOPSIS: Baltimore was the hot young team in 2023 and for most of 2024, but the Orioles' vibes changed in a .500 second half with some key injuries and a team-wide offensive slump dropping them to a wild-card spot. A stunning home two-game postseason sweep at the hands of the Royals sent fans into the offseason unhappy.

HIGH POINT: The Orioles rode their offense to a strong start, winning seven out of 10 games in late June through July 7, when they won back-to-back road series at Seattle and Oakland to take a three-game lead ahead of the Yankees in the American League East. Anthony Santander homered in the 6-3 win in Oakland on July 7, the 23rd of his 44 homers on the season–a record for an Orioles switch-hitter.

LOW POINT: Baltimore's bats cooled significantly in the second half and worsened in September, when three of the club's eight shutouts occurred during a stretch of five consecutive lost series in the month. (They lost two series to Detroit and one each to Tampa Bay, Boston and San Francisco.) By the end of the slide, the Orioles trailed the Yankees by six games,

NOTABLE ROOKIES: Jackson Holliday, the 2022 No. 1 overall pick in the draft, sped to the majors but slumped and was sent back to Triple-A to tweak his swing. He hit just .189 with 69 strikeouts in 190 at-bats. Lefty Cade Povich was needed in the second half to fill a rotation slot and had some flashes but also had a 5.20 ERA and erratic control (9.7% BB).

KEY TRANSACTIONS: The Orioles acquired a frontline ace in the offseason, trading Joey Ortiz and D.L. Hall to Milwaukee for Corbin Burnes, who was a workhorse with a 15-9, 2.92 season over 194 innings. He carried a heavy burden as Kyle Bradish (Tommy John surgery) missed most of the season, while Grayson Rodriguez (shoulder) missed most of the final two months. Free agent Craig Kimbrel, signed to replace injured closer Felix Bautista (Tommy John surgery), didn't work out and was released Sept. 25. Deadline moves for lefties Gregory Soto (5.09 ERA) and Tyler Rogers (7.71 ERA in four starts) backfired, while Seranthony Dominguez (10 saves) replaced Kimbrel down the stretch as closer.

OPENING DAY PAYROLL: $94,520,400 (27th)

PLAYERS OF THE YEAR

MAJOR LEAGUE

Gunnar Henderson
SS

.281/.364/.529
37 HR, 21 SB,
92 RBIs, 118 R, 78 BB

MINOR LEAGUE

Coby Mayo
3B

(A+,AAA)
.293/.372/.592
25 HR, 73 RBIs

ORGANIZATION LEADERS

Batting		* Qualifiers
MAJORS		
* AVG	Gunnar Henderson	.281
* OPS	Gunnar Henderson	.893
HR	Anthony Santander	44
RBI	Anthony Santander	102
MINORS		
* AVG	Coby Mayo, Aberdeen/Norfolk	.293
* OBP	Douglas Hodo, Delmarva/Aberdeen/Bowie	.382
* SLG	Coby Mayo, Aberdeen/Norfolk	.592
* OPS	Coby Mayo, Aberdeen/Norfolk	.964
R	Enrique Bradfield, Bowie/Aberdeen	88
H	Samuel Basallo, Bowie/Norfolk	133
* TB	Samuel Basallo, Bowie/Norfolk	215
2B	Coby Mayo, Aberdeen/Norfolk	26
3B	Matthew Etzel, Bowie/Montgomery/Aberdeen	7
HR	Coby Mayo, Aberdeen/Norfolk	25
RBI	Daniel Johnson, Norfolk	76
BB	Jackson Holliday, Norfolk	75
SO	Jud Fabian, Bowie/Norfolk	177
SB	Enrique Bradfield, Bowie/Aberdeen	74

PITCHING		# Qualifiers
MAJORS		
W	Corbin Burnes	15
# ERA	Corbin Burnes	2.92
SO	Corbin Burnes	181
SV	Craig Kimbrel	23
MINORS		
W	Nolan Hoffman, Norfolk	8
L	3 tied	11
# ERA	Zach Fruit, Aberdeen	3.03
G	Kade Strowd, Bowie/Norfolk	46
GS	Trace Bright, Bowie	27
GS	Alex Pham, Bowie	27
SV	Keagan Gillies, Bowie	7
IP	Justin Armbruester, Norfolk	119
BB	Justin Armbruester, Norfolk	69
SO	Chayce McDermott, Norfolk	144
# AVG	Zach Fruit, Aberdeen	.201

2024 PERFORMANCE

General Manager: Mike Elias. **Farm Director:** Anthony Villa. **Scouting Director:** Matt Blood.

Class	Team	League	W	L	PCT	Finish	Manager
Majors	Baltimore Orioles	American	91	71	.562	3 (15)	Brandon Hyde
Triple-A	Norfolk Tides	International	69	81	.460	17 (20)	Buck Britton
Double-A	Bowie Baysox	Eastern	62	75	.453	9 (12)	Roberto Mercado
High-A	Aberdeen IronBirds	South Atlantic	67	65	.508	5 (12)	Felipe Alou
Low-A	Delmarva Shorebirds	Carolina	53	78	.405	11 (12)	Collin Woody
Rookie	FCL Orioles	Florida Complex	23	36	.390	12 (15)	Christian Frias
Rookie	DSL Orioles Black	Dominican	26	29	.473	29 (51)	Elvis Morel
Rookie	DSL Orioles Orange	Dominican	38	18	.679	5 (51)	Chris Madera
Overall 2024 Minor League Record			**338**	**382**	**.469**	**23rd (30)**	

ORGANIZATION STATISTICS

BALTIMORE ORIOLES

AMERICAN LEAGUE

Batting	B-T	Ht.	Wt.	DOB	AVG	OBP	SLG	G	PA	AB	R	H	2B	3B	HR	RBI	BB	HBP	SH	SF	SO	SB	CS	BB%	SO%
Banuelos, David	R-R	6-0	205	10-1-96	.000	.000	.000	1	1	1	0	0	0	0	0	0	0	0	0	0	0	0	0	0.00	0.00
Cowser, Colton	L-R	6-2	220	3-20-00	.242	.321	.447	153	561	499	77	121	24	3	24	69	52	7	0	3	172	9	4	9.27	30.66
Hays, Austin	R-R	5-11	200	7-5-95	.255	.316	.395	63	175	157	18	40	13	0	3	14	9	6	1	2	40	0	1	5.14	22.86
Henderson, Gunnar	L-R	6-3	220	6-29-01	.281	.364	.529	159	719	630	118	177	31	7	37	92	78	7	0	4	159	21	4	10.85	22.11
Holliday, Jackson	L-R	6-0	185	12-4-03	.189	.255	.311	60	208	190	28	36	4	2	5	23	15	2	0	1	69	4	0	7.21	33.17
Jimenez, Eloy	R-R	6-4	240	11-27-96	.232	.270	.316	33	100	95	7	22	5	0	1	7	4	1	0	0	23	0	0	4.00	23.00
Johnson, Daniel	L-L	5-9	200	7-11-95	.000	.000	.000	1	1	1	1	0	0	0	0	0	0	0	0	0	0	0	0	0.00	0.00
Kemp, Tony	L-R	5-6	160	10-31-91	.000	.100	.000	5	10	9	1	0	0	0	0	0	1	0	0	0	1	0	0	10.00	10.00
Kjerstad, Heston	L-R	6-3	205	2-12-99	.253	.351	.394	39	114	99	8	25	2	0	4	14	10	5	0	0	33	1	0	8.77	28.95
Mateo, Jorge	R-R	6-1	200	6-23-95	.229	.267	.401	68	208	192	30	44	14	2	5	18	10	1	2	3	48	13	2	4.81	23.08
Maton, Nick	L-R	6-2	178	2-18-97	.000	.000	.000	5	5	5	0	0	0	0	0	0	0	0	0	0	2	0	0	0.00	40.00
Mayo, Coby	R-R	6-5	230	12-10-01	.098	.196	.098	17	46	41	4	4	0	0	0	0	4	1	0	0	22	0	0	8.70	47.83
McCann, James	R-R	6-3	235	6-13-90	.234	.279	.388	66	233	214	27	50	9	0	8	31	13	2	0	4	56	1	0	5.58	24.03
McKenna, Ryan	R-R	5-11	195	2-14-97	.375	.444	1.125	9	9	8	3	3	0	0	2	2	1	0	0	0	1	0	1	11.11	11.11
Mountcastle, Ryan	R-R	6-4	220	2-18-97	.271	.308	.425	124	507	473	54	128	30	2	13	63	27	1	0	6	114	3	0	5.33	22.49
Mullins, Cedric	L-L	5-9	175	10-1-94	.234	.305	.405	147	499	444	69	104	16	3	18	54	41	5	2	2	98	32	6	8.22	19.64
Norby, Connor	R-R	5-9	180	6-8-00	.188	.188	.406	9	32	32	3	6	1	0	2	3	0	0	0	0	12	0	0	0.00	37.50
O'Hearn, Ryan	L-L	6-3	220	7-26-93	.264	.334	.427	142	494	443	60	117	21	3	15	59	46	2	0	3	69	3	1	9.31	13.97
Pache, Cristian	R-R	6-2	215	11-19-98	1.000	1.000	1.000	3	1	1	0	1	0	0	0	0	0	0	0	0	0	0	0	0.00	0.00
Rivera, Emmanuel	R-R	6-2	225	6-29-96	.313	.370	.578	27	73	64	9	20	3	1	4	14	6	1	0	2	18	0	0	8.22	24.66
Rutschman, Adley	B-R	6-2	230	2-6-98	.250	.318	.391	148	638	571	68	143	21	1	19	79	58	2	0	7	103	1	0	9.09	16.14
Santander, Anthony	B-R	6-2	230	10-19-94	.235	.308	.506	155	665	595	91	140	25	2	44	102	58	7	0	5	129	2	0	8.72	19.40
Slater, Austin	R-R	6-1	204	12-13-92	.246	.342	.333	33	79	69	10	17	3	0	1	6	8	2	0	0	23	1	1	10.13	29.11
Soto, Livan	L-R	5-10	160	6-22-00	.300	.462	.400	12	13	10	1	3	1	0	0	0	3	0	0	0	2	0	0	23.08	15.38
Stowers, Kyle	L-L	6-3	215	1-2-98	.306	.297	.500	19	37	36	3	11	4	0	1	9	0	0	0	1	13	0	1	0.00	35.14
Urias, Ramon	R-R	5-10	185	6-3-94	.254	.322	.423	100	301	272	39	69	9	2	11	37	23	5	0	1	55	1	1	7.64	18.27
Westburg, Jordan	R-R	6-2	210	2-18-99	.264	.312	.481	107	447	416	57	110	26	5	18	63	22	7	1	1	97	6	3	4.92	21.70

Pitching	B-T	Ht.	Wt.	DOB	W	L	ERA	G	GS	SV	IP	Hits	Runs	ER	HR	BB	SO	AVG	OBP	SLG	SO%	BB%	BF
Akin, Keegan	L-L	6-0	240	4-1-95	3	1	3.32	66	0	1	79	55	31	29	9	19	97	.193	.244	.347	30.99	6.07	313
Baker, Bryan	R-R	6-6	235	12-2-94	1	1	5.01	19	0	0	23	20	14	13	3	7	23	.235	.290	.435	24.73	7.53	93
Baumann, Mike	R-R	6-4	240	9-10-95	1	0	3.44	17	0	0	18	18	9	7	2	9	16	.250	.341	.389	19.51	10.98	82
Bowman, Matt	R-R	6-0	185	5-31-91	1	0	3.45	15	1	0	16	15	6	6	2	6	14	.250	.318	.383	21.21	9.09	66
Bradish, Kyle	R-R	6-3	215	9-12-96	2	0	2.75	8	8	0	39	27	12	12	2	15	53	.188	.278	.299	32.52	9.20	163
Burnes, Corbin	R-R	6-3	246	10-22-94	15	9	2.92	32	32	0	194	165	76	63	22	48	181	.226	.274	.347	23.09	6.12	784
Cano, Yennier	R-R	6-4	245	3-9-94	4	3	3.15	70	0	5	60	54	24	21	6	24	65	.242	.317	.372	26.10	9.64	249
Coulombe, Danny	L-L	5-10	190	10-26-89	1	0	2.12	33	0	1	30	15	7	7	3	5	32	.147	.187	.265	29.91	4.67	107
Davidson, Tucker	L-L	6-2	215	3-25-96	1	0	0.00	1	0	0	5	4	0	0	0	2	1	.235	.316	.235	5.26	10.53	19
Dominguez, Seranthony	R-R	6-1	225	11-25-94	0	2	3.97	25	0	10	23	20	10	10	6	9	28	.227	.296	.455	28.57	9.18	98
Eflin, Zach	R-R	6-6	220	4-8-94	5	2	2.60	9	9	0	55	51	16	16	8	11	47	.239	.277	.366	20.98	4.91	224
Heasley, Jonathan	R-R	6-3	225	1-27-97	0	1	16.88	4	0	0	5	10	11	10	2	3	4	.400	.483	.640	13.79	10.34	29
Irvin, Cole	L-L	6-4	225	1-31-94	6	5	4.86	25	16	1	107	126	66	58	17	25	76	.290	.333	.493	16.17	5.32	470
Kimbrel, Craig	R-R	6-0	215	5-28-88	7	5	5.33	57	0	23	52	40	35	31	7	31	73	.208	.329	.365	31.47	13.36	232
Kremer, Dean	R-R	6-2	210	1-7-96	8	10	4.10	24	24	0	130	110	72	59	18	51	123	.223	.297	.371	22.24	9.22	553
Krook, Matt	L-L	6-4	225	10-21-94	0	0	18.00	1	0	0	1	1	3	2	1	1	2	.200	.333	.800	33.33	16.67	6
McCann, James	R-R	6-3	235	6-13-90	0	0	18.00	1	0	0	1	2	2	2	1	0	0	.400	.400	1.000	0.00	0.00	5
McDermott, Chayce	L-R	6-3	197	8-22-98	0	0	6.75	1	1	0	4	5	3	3	1	2	3	.333	.389	.533	16.67	11.11	18
Means, John	L-L	6-4	230	4-24-93	2	0	2.61	4	4	0	21	16	6	6	2	2	16	.211	.238	.368	20.00	2.50	80
Nittoli, Vinny	R-R	6-1	210	11-11-90	0	0	0.00	2	0	0	4	2	0	0	0	0	3	.143	.143	.214	21.43	0.00	14
Perez, Cionel	R-L	6-0	175	4-21-96	2	0	4.53	62	0	2	54	47	29	27	0	28	46	.232	.338	.310	19.33	11.76	238
Povich, Cade	L-L	6-3	185	4-12-00	3	9	5.20	16	16	0	80	80	49	46	12	34	69	.256	.332	.454	19.60	9.66	352
Ramirez, Yohan	R-R	6-4	212	5-6-95	0	0	6.00	5	0	0	6	3	4	4	0	2	6	.158	.333	.158	25.00	8.33	24
Rodriguez, Grayson	L-R	6-5	230	11-16-99	13	4	3.86	20	20	0	117	109	52	50	15	36	130	.243	.305	.405	26.48	7.33	491

Rogers, Trevor	L-L	6-5	217	11-13-97	0	2	7.11	4	4	0	19	25	16	15	2	10	12	.338	.404	.514	13.33	11.11	90
Selby, Colin	R-R	6-2	220	10-24-97	0	0	0.00	3	0	0	4	1	0	0	0	2	5	.083	.267	.083	33.33	13.33	15
Smith, Burch	R-R	6-4	225	4-12-90	2	1	5.74	25	0	0	27	25	19	17	5	3	23	.248	.276	.465	21.70	2.83	106
Soto, Gregory	L-L	6-1	234	2-11-95	1	1	5.09	23	0	0	18	20	11	10	2	7	21	.286	.367	.443	26.58	8.86	79
Suarez, Albert	R-R	6-3	235	10-8-89	9	7	3.70	32	24	0	134	130	56	55	17	43	108	.255	.314	.425	19.12	7.61	565
Tate, Dillon	R-R	6-2	190	5-1-94	2	1	4.59	29	0	1	33	38	19	17	2	9	23	.284	.345	.381	15.54	6.08	148
Vespi, Nick	L-L	6-3	235	10-10-95	0	0	2.92	11	0	0	12	10	4	4	1	3	9	.222	.265	.378	18.37	6.12	49
Vieira, Thyago	R-R	6-3	265	7-1-93	0	0	0.00	1	0	0	0	1	3	3	0	4	0	1.000	1.000	3.000	0.00	80.00	5
Webb, Jacob	R-R	6-2	210	8-15-93	2	5	3.02	60	0	2	57	40	23	19	4	27	58	.192	.287	.303	24.47	11.39	237
Wells, Tyler	R-R	6-8	260	8-26-94	0	2	5.87	3	3	0	15	18	11	10	3	3	13	.281	.313	.516	19.40	4.48	67

Fielding

Catcher	PCT	G	PO	A	E	DP	PB
McCann	.986	65	528	28	8	2	0
Rutschman	.996	103	874	37	4	4	3

First Base	PCT	G	PO	A	E	DP
Mayo	1.000	4	12	1	0	2
Mountcastle	.997	114	860	74	3	57
O'Hearn	.985	55	304	19	5	28
Rivera	1.000	8	30	2	0	1
Santander	.000	1	0	0	0	0
Urias	1.000	2	9	0	0	2

Second Base	PCT	G	PO	A	E	DP
Holliday	.985	56	76	127	3	29
Kemp	1.000	5	3	5	0	0
Mateo	.981	56	79	130	4	24
Maton	.000	1	0	0	0	0
Norby	1.000	9	5	13	0	3
Soto	1.000	6	6	11	0	5
Urias	1.000	3	2	7	0	2
Westburg	.977	53	49	81	3	9

Third Base	PCT	G	PO	A	E	DP
Maton	1.000	2	0	2	0	1
Mayo	.909	12	3	7	1	0
Rivera	.966	20	11	17	1	2
Soto	.000	4	0	0	0	0
Urias	.965	93	47	119	6	8
Westburg	.986	67	39	98	2	7

Shortstop	PCT	G	PO	A	E	DP
Henderson	.961	157	232	378	25	71
Holliday	1.000	3	4	1	0	1
Mateo	1.000	6	3	7	0	1
Soto	.000	2	0	0	0	0
Westburg	.714	2	3	2	2	0

Outfield	PCT	G	PO	A	E	DP
Cowser	.997	174	308	3	1	0
Hays	.988	56	80	2	1	0
Johnson	1.000	1	1	0	0	0
Kemp	.000	1	0	0	0	0
Kjerstad	1.000	19	34	0	0	0
Mateo	1.000	4	5	0	0	0
McKenna	1.000	8	11	0	0	0
Mullins	.996	140	271	2	1	0
O'Hearn	1.000	27	33	0	0	0
Pache	.000	2	0	0	0	0
Santander	.993	130	262	7	2	2
Slater	1.000	30	36	1	0	0
Stowers	1.000	15	16	0	0	0

NORFOLK TIDES — *TRIPLE-A*

INTERNATIONAL LEAGUE

Batting	B-T	Ht.	Wt.	DOB	AVG	OBP	SLG	G	PA	AB	R	H	2B	3B	HR	RBI	BB	HBP	SH	SF	SO	SB	CS	BB%	SO%
Bellony, Isaac	B-R	6-2	220	12-15-01	-20-	1.000	-20-	1	1	0	0	0	0	0	0	0	1	0	0	0	0	0	0	100.0	0.0
Banuelos, David	R-R	6-0	205	10-1-96	.225	.360	.352	22	86	71	11	16	3	0	2	11	13	2	0	0	25	1	0	15.12	29.07
Basallo, Samuel	L-R	6-3	180	8-13-04	.222	.267	.370	21	86	81	11	18	3	0	3	10	5	0	0	0	27	1	0	5.81	31.40
Beavers, Dylan	L-R	6-4	206	8-11-01	.250	.318	.300	6	22	20	3	5	1	0	0	4	1	1	0	0	10	0	0	4.55	45.45
Bowens, TT	R-R	6-4	235	5-27-98	.155	.234	.321	24	94	84	8	13	5	0	3	14	9	0	0	1	22	0	0	9.57	23.40
Burdick, Peyton	R-R	6-0	205	2-26-97	.182	.333	.455	16	69	55	11	10	3	0	4	9	11	2	0	1	28	1	0	15.94	40.58
Castillo, Diego	R-R	5-10	185	10-28-97	.308	.438	.385	3	16	13	2	4	1	0	0	0	3	0	0	0	4	0	0	18.75	25.00
Cook, Billy	R-R	6-1	200	1-7-99	.279	.372	.485	70	304	262	42	73	15	3	11	43	34	6	0	2	69	12	5	11.18	22.70
Cooper, Garrett	R-R	6-5	235	12-25-90	.310	.393	.521	20	84	71	9	22	3	0	4	24	9	2	0	2	20	0	0	10.71	23.81
Davis, J.D.	R-R	6-3	218	4-27-93	.147	.218	.248	31	119	109	8	16	2	0	3	9	9	1	0	0	53	0	0	7.56	44.54
Fabian, Jud	R-L	6-1	195	9-27-00	.159	.232	.257	30	125	113	11	18	5	0	2	7	11	0	0	1	51	3	1	8.80	40.80
Fontana, Shayne	L-L	6-1	195	6-21-97	.225	.313	.315	73	245	213	33	48	5	1	4	17	23	5	1	2	57	11	3	9.39	23.27
Goodrum, Niko	B-R	6-3	215	2-28-92	.291	.369	.466	43	168	148	14	43	6	4	4	28	18	1	0	1	47	6	1	10.71	27.98
Handley, Maverick	R-R	5-10	210	3-10-98	.202	.325	.287	84	330	272	34	55	12	1	3	26	44	8	1	5	74	5	3	13.33	22.42
Haskin, Hudson	R-R	6-0	200	12-31-98	.213	.343	.300	90	335	277	45	59	10	1	4	24	43	13	0	2	91	22	6	12.84	27.16
Higgins, Ryan	R-R	6-1	200	1-25-00	.000	.000	.000	2	2	2	0	0	0	0	0	0	0	0	0	0	1	0	0	0.00	50.00
Holliday, Jackson	L-R	6-0	185	12-4-03	.271	.431	.477	73	346	266	75	72	25	0	10	38	75	2	0	3	77	8	1	21.68	22.25
Hunt, Blake	R-R	6-3	215	11-10-98	.179	.219	.278	42	160	151	11	27	4	1	3	7	7	1	0	1	50	1	0	4.38	31.25
Johnson, Daniel	L-L	5-9	200	7-11-95	.259	.320	.448	118	500	451	69	117	20	1	21	76	37	6	0	6	129	17	10	7.40	25.80
Kjerstad, Heston	L-R	6-3	205	2-12-99	.300	.397	.601	56	258	213	49	64	14	1	16	58	32	6	0	6	67	2	0	12.40	25.97
Krook, Matt	L-L	6-4	225	10-21-94	.000	.000	.000	42	1	1	0	0	0	0	0	0	0	0	0	0	1	0	0	0.00	100.00
Maton, Nick	L-R	6-2	178	2-18-97	.258	.363	.471	87	344	291	44	75	12	1	16	56	45	5	0	3	70	1	1	13.08	20.35
Mayo, Coby	R-R	6-5	230	12-10-01	.287	.364	.562	89	390	345	61	99	23	3	22	67	40	3	0	2	97	4	4	10.26	24.87
McKenna, Ryan	R-R	5-11	195	2-14-97	.244	.333	.444	12	52	45	8	11	3	0	2	5	6	0	1	0	10	3	0	11.54	19.23
Mountcastle, Ryan	R-R	6-4	220	2-18-97	.091	.091	.091	3	11	11	0	1	0	0	0	0	0	0	0	0	6	0	0	0.00	54.55
Norby, Connor	R-R	5-9	180	6-8-00	.297	.389	.519	80	375	320	71	95	21	1	16	57	47	4	0	4	104	13	3	12.53	27.73
Pavolony, Connor	R-R	6-1	195	10-25-99	.297	.409	.459	13	45	37	5	11	6	0	0	4	7	0	1	0	11	0	0	15.56	24.44
Peguero, Fernando	B-R	5-9	145	12-27-04	.267	.267	.267	5	15	15	0	4	0	0	0	0	0	0	0	0	7	0	0	0.00	46.67
Perez, Michael	L-R	5-10	195	8-7-92	.215	.287	.316	22	87	79	4	17	2	0	2	13	5	3	0	0	27	0	0	5.75	31.03
Robinson, Errol	R-R	5-10	170	10-1-94	.208	.300	.275	46	171	149	19	31	7	0	1	11	20	0	1	1	48	12	3	11.70	28.07
Romero, Noelberth	R-R	6-0	183	12-5-01	.228	.305	.272	39	131	114	10	26	2	0	1	10	12	2	0	3	33	0	3	9.16	25.19
Segura, Jean	R-R	5-10	220	3-17-90	.137	.250	.196	14	60	51	4	7	3	0	0	3	6	2	0	1	13	1	1	10.00	21.67
Servideo, Anthony	L-R	5-10	175	3-11-99	.183	.282	.287	34	133	115	20	21	1	1	3	10	16	0	2	0	44	4	0	12.03	33.08
Soto, Livan	L-R	5-10	160	6-22-00	.325	.378	.525	12	45	40	3	13	3	1	1	5	3	1	0	1	4	0	0	6.67	8.89
Stowers, Kyle	L-L	6-3	215	1-2-98	.240	.322	.555	58	264	229	41	55	16	1	18	55	26	4	0	5	66	0	0	9.85	25.00
Urias, Ramon	R-R	5-10	185	6-3-94	.333	.333	.667	3	9	9	1	3	0	0	1	3	0	0	0	0	4	0	0	0.00	44.44
Vavra, Terrin	L-R	6-0	185	5-12-97	.236	.342	.356	55	224	191	29	45	5	3	4	28	28	3	2	0	56	2	3	12.50	25.00
Wall, Forrest	L-R	6-0	195	11-20-95	.261	.382	.370	14	56	46	7	12	2	0	1	6	8	1	1	0	19	4	0	14.29	33.93
Westburg, Jordan	R-R	6-2	210	2-18-99	.400	.500	.800	3	12	10	4	4	1	0	1	2	1	1	0	0	1	0	0	8.33	8.33
Williams, Donta'	L-L	5-10	185	6-30-99	.211	.286	.211	6	21	19	3	4	0	0	0	1	2	0	0	0	4	0	0	9.52	19.05

Pitching	B-T	Ht.	Wt.	DOB	W	L	ERA	G	GS	SV	IP	H	R	ER	HR	BB	SO	AVG	OBP	SLG	SO%	BB%	BF
Anderson, Nick	R-R	6-4	205	7-5-90	0	0	0.00	2	0	0	2	1	0	0	0	0	2	.143	.143	.143	28.57	0.00	7
Armbruester, Justin	R-R	6-4	235	10-21-98	5	11	7.54	29	26	1	119	123	107	100	27	69	131	.261	.371	.503	23.43	12.34	559
Avila, Nick	R-R	6-4	195	7-25-97	0	1	67.50	3	0	0	1	9	10	10	0	3	2	.692	.750	1.077	12.50	18.75	16
Baker, Bryan	R-R	6-6	235	12-2-94	2	1	5.17	32	0	6	31	24	18	18	5	16	43	.205	.301	.393	32.09	11.94	134
Bowman, Matt	R-R	6-0	185	5-31-91	0	0	0.00	2	0	0	3	0	0	0	0	1	6	.000	.100	.000	60.00	10.00	10
Bradish, Kyle	R-R	6-3	215	9-12-96	1	0	5.40	2	2	0	8	11	5	5	1	4	10	.324	.410	.441	25.64	10.26	39
Charles, Wandisson	R-R	6-4	250	9-7-96	1	5	8.42	25	0	0	26	25	29	24	3	28	27	.266	.433	.447	21.09	21.88	128
Coulombe, Danny	L-L	5-10	190	10-26-89	0	0	0.00	3	0	0	3	2	0	0	0	0	2	.200	.200	.300	20.00	0.00	10
Davidson, Tucker	L-L	6-2	215	3-25-96	5	11	3.89	32	17	0	116	109	67	50	17	46	104	.242	.312	.404	20.68	9.15	503
Gonzalez, Luis	L-L	6-2	170	1-17-92	5	3	4.50	44	0	2	60	54	32	30	8	12	71	.236	.282	.432	28.86	4.88	246
Heasley, Jonathan	R-R	6-3	225	1-27-97	0	1	2.64	10	3	0	31	29	9	9	3	8	27	.252	.306	.374	21.77	6.45	124
Hennen, Ryan	R-L	6-0	180	9-30-97	0	0	1.93	2	0	0	4.2	3	1	1	1	2	4	.188	.278	.375	21.05	10.52	19
Higgins, Ryan	R-R	6-1	200	1-25-00	0	0	20.25	1	0	0	1	3	3	3	1	1	1	.429	.556	.857	11.11	11.11	9
Hoffman, Nolan	R-R	6-4	190	8-9-97	8	3	3.88	44	0	2	58	64	30	25	2	37	77	.278	.380	.352	28.21	13.55	273
Houser, Adrian	R-R	6-3	242	2-2-93	0	2	9.18	3	3	0	17	24	17	17	3	7	13	.333	.392	.528	16.46	8.86	79
Irvin, Cole	L-L	6-4	225	1-31-94	0	1	4.05	2	2	0	7	5	4	3	0	6	5	.200	.364	.240	15.15	18.18	33
Kremer, Dean	R-R	6-2	210	1-7-96	0	1	11.42	3	3	0	9	15	14	11	4	4	9	.366	.413	.707	19.57	8.70	46
Kriske, Brooks	R-R	6-3	190	2-3-94	0	0	5.00	8	0	0	9	8	5	5	2	6	9	.242	.366	.455	21.95	14.63	41
Krook, Matt	L-L	6-4	225	10-21-94	3	2	3.92	41	0	1	44	30	20	19	4	31	54	.197	.335	.316	29.03	16.67	186
Long, Ryan	R-R	6-6	240	10-19-99	0	1	11.57	1	0	0	5	8	7	6	3	0	4	.381	.381	.952	19.05	0.00	21
Martin, Corbin	R-R	6-2	225	12-28-95	1	2	4.05	29	0	0	33	41	22	15	1	21	31	.304	.406	.430	19.25	13.04	161
Maton, Nick	L-R	6-2	178	2-18-97	0	0	5.40	4	0	0	3	3	3	2	0	3	0	.231	.412	.308	0.00	17.65	17
McDermott, Chayce	L-R	6-3	197	8-22-98	4	5	3.78	22	21	0	100	81	48	42	11	60	144	.219	.332	.365	32.88	13.70	438
McGough, Trey	L-L	6-3	195	3-29-98	2	0	2.08	16	0	0	35	23	8	8	2	15	31	.185	.271	.274	22.14	10.71	140
McSweeney, Morgan	R-R	6-4	210	9-21-97	0	0	0.00	6	0	0	6.2	6	0	0	0	3	3	.240	.321	.320	10.71	10.71	28
Means, John	L-L	6-4	230	4-24-93	1	2	8.68	6	6	0	19	22	18	18	5	7	22	.293	.357	.547	25.88	8.24	85
Nittoli, Vinny	R-R	6-1	210	11-11-90	0	1	3.00	3	0	0	3	3	1	1	1	0	4	.300	.364	.600	36.36	0.00	11
Ort, Kaleb	R-R	6-4	240	2-5-92	0	1	12.08	14	0	2	13	21	19	17	2	10	16	.356	.449	.542	23.19	14.49	69
Perez, Cionel	R-L	6-0	175	4-21-96	0	1	3.86	2	0	0	2	3	1	1	0	1	1	.333	.400	.556	10.00	10.00	10
Povich, Cade	L-L	6-3	185	4-12-00	6	1	3.48	15	14	0	78	59	32	30	7	27	89	.207	.275	.347	28.16	8.54	316
Rinehart, Logan	R-R	6-3	185	9-21-97	0	0	3.68	3	0	0	7	7	3	3	1	8	6	.259	.417	.407	16.67	22.22	36
Rogers, Trevor	L-L	6-5	217	11-13-97	1	2	5.65	5	5	0	29	26	18	18	3	9	30	.236	.292	.391	25.00	7.50	120
Romero, Noelberth	R-R	6-0	183	12-5-01	0	0	18.00	1	0	0	1	2	2	2	1	0	0	.400	.400	1.000	0.00	0.00	5
Selby, Colin	R-R	6-2	220	10-24-97	0	1	4.24	18	0	4	17	15	9	8	1	8	26	.234	.315	.328	35.62	10.96	73
Smith, Burch	R-R	6-4	225	4-12-90	0	0	0.00	2	0	0	2	1	0	0	0	0	2	.143	.143	.143	28.57	0.00	7
Stallings, Garrett	R-R	6-2	200	8-8-97	0	1	5.67	11	4	0	27	31	20	17	3	13	25	.282	.360	.427	20.00	10.40	125
Stoudt, Levi	R-R	6-1	195	12-4-97	3	1	5.54	8	0	1	13	12	10	8	5	6	15	.245	.327	.592	26.79	10.71	56
Strowd, Kade	R-R	6-2	200	9-17-97	4	2	6.80	37	0	0	41	49	34	31	7	27	60	.297	.400	.479	30.77	13.85	195
Suarez, Albert	R-R	6-3	235	10-8-89	1	1	5.87	3	1	0	15	19	11	10	2	1	17	.297	.308	.500	26.15	1.54	65
Suarez, Andrew	L-L	6-0	202	9-11-92	2	1	5.93	10	0	0	14	19	11	9	2	5	12	.339	.403	.518	19.35	8.06	62
Tate, Dillon	R-R	6-2	190	5-1-94	0	0	2.16	16	0	0	17	14	4	4	1	3	15	.219	.275	.313	21.74	4.35	69
Tavera, Carlos	R-R	6-1	195	10-6-98	2	4	7.47	14	6	0	47	60	46	39	11	36	42	.314	.422	.597	18.18	15.58	231
Teheran, Julio	R-R	6-2	205	1-27-91	1	1	9.18	4	4	0	17	23	17	17	3	11	12	.333	.432	.507	14.81	13.58	81
Vespi, Nick	L-L	6-3	235	10-10-95	2	2	7.23	29	0	2	42	55	36	34	2	31	51	.313	.420	.443	24.06	14.62	212
Watson, Ryan	R-R	6-5	225	11-15-97	1	1	1.42	6	0	1	6	6	1	1	0	1	7	.231	.259	.346	25.93	3.70	27
Webb, Jacob	R-R	6-2	210	8-15-93	0	0	0.00	3	0	0	3	3	0	0	0	1	2	.273	.333	.273	16.67	8.33	12
Young, Brandon	R-R	6-6	210	8-19-98	5	4	3.44	20	18	0	89	81	39	34	7	33	96	.241	.310	.351	25.60	8.80	375
Zimmermann, Bruce	L-L	6-1	220	2-9-95	3	4	4.34	23	15	1	77	80	45	37	8	26	75	.265	.327	.404	22.46	7.78	334

Fielding

Catcher	PCT	G	PO	A	E	DP	PB
Banuelos	1.000	18	167	8	0	3	1
Basallo	.990	11	98	4	1	0	2
Handley	.990	73	721	34	8	6	1
Hunt	.997	30	269	17	1	5	0
Pavolony	.967	10	79	9	3	0	0
Perez	.993	14	136	9	1	3	2

First Base	PCT	G	PO	A	E	DP
Basallo	1.000	4	22	1	0	5
Bowens	1.000	19	122	7	0	11
Castillo	1.000	1	7	0	0	0
Cook	.994	42	294	14	2	31
Cooper	.981	14	92	11	2	10
Davis	1.000	5	28	5	0	2
Fontana	.983	32	218	12	4	15
Goodrum	1.000	3	16	2	0	1
Kjerstad	.980	8	47	3	1	10
Maton	.960	4	24	0	1	1
Mayo	.959	23	135	7	6	15
Mountcastle	1.000	2	15	0	0	0

Second Base	PCT	G	PO	A	E	DP
Castillo	1.000	1	2	2	0	0
Cook	1.000	1	1	0	0	0
Goodrum	1.000	4	7	6	0	1
Holliday	.947	43	73	106	10	29
Maton	.900	9	10	17	3	5
Norby	.943	32	41	74	7	12
Peguero	1.000	3	6	5	0	2
Robinson	1.000	3	8	2	0	1
Romero	1.000	19	35	40	0	6
Segura	.958	12	17	29	2	4
Servideo	.923	3	3	9	1	1
Soto	1.000	2	0	8	0	0
Vavra	.975	26	23	56	2	10
Westburg	.800	2	3	1	1	0

Third Base	PCT	G	PO	A	E	DP
Castillo	.500	1	0	1	1	0
Cook	.750	1	1	2	1	0
Cooper	1.000	1	0	1	0	0
Davis	.956	25	17	26	2	4
Goodrum	.920	10	9	14	2	1
Higgins	.750	1	2	1	1	0
Maton	.980	25	14	35	1	4
Mayo	.940	66	58	113	11	19
Robinson	.952	8	9	11	1	2
Romero	.857	12	3	21	4	0
Servideo	.500	2	2	0	2	0
Urias	1.000	2	0	4	0	0
Vavra	1.000	6	2	6	0	0
Westburg	1.000	1	0	1	0	0

Shortstop	PCT	G	PO	A	E	DP
Goodrum	.938	19	17	44	4	8
Holliday	.911	15	15	26	4	3
Maton	.941	36	35	61	6	14
Robinson	.953	33	49	53	5	18
Romero	.900	4	1	8	1	1
Servideo	.958	30	32	59	4	11
Soto	.958	10	13	10	1	6
Vavra	.923	12	5	19	2	1

Outfield	PCT	G	PO	A	E	DP
Beavers	1.000	5	15	0	0	0
Bowens	1.000	3	3	0	0	0
Burdick	1.000	11	23	1	0	0
Cook	.982	25	52	4	1	1
Fabian	1.000	28	66	1	0	1
Fontana	1.000	29	48	1	0	0
Haskin	.973	84	173	6	5	4

Johnson	.956	101	191	5	9	1
Kjerstad	.984	39	61	1	1	0
Krook	.000	1	0	0	0	0
Maton	1.000	12	22	1	0	0
McKenna	1.000	10	20	0	0	0
Norby	.970	45	60	4	2	1
Peguero	1.000	2	2	1	0	0
Stowers	.989	50	91	3	1	0
Vavra	1.000	6	8	1	0	0
Wall	1.000	12	31	0	0	0
Williams	1.000	6	18	0	0	0

BOWIE BAYSOX — *DOUBLE-A*

EASTERN LEAGUE

Batting	B-T	Ht.	Wt.	DOB	AVG	OBP	SLG	G	PA	AB	R	H	2B	3B	HR	RBI	BB	HBP	SH	SF	SO	SB	CS	BB%	SO%
Ardoin, Silas	R-R	6-0	215	9-19-00	.200	.299	.275	104	417	360	26	72	13	1	4	34	47	5	2	3	116	3	2	11.27	27.82
Basallo, Samuel	L-R	6-3	180	8-13-04	.289	.355	.465	106	446	398	57	115	22	0	16	55	41	2	1	4	85	9	5	9.19	19.06
Beavers, Dylan	L-R	6-4	206	8-11-01	.241	.343	.413	119	509	431	67	104	19	5	15	50	67	3	2	6	115	31	3	13.16	22.59
Bencosme, Frederick	L-R	6-0	160	12-25-02	.240	.318	.348	125	504	445	64	107	18	3	8	45	49	3	4	3	82	28	5	9.72	16.27
Bowens, TT	R-R	6-4	235	5-27-98	.246	.298	.430	81	336	309	38	76	19	1	12	52	20	4	0	3	94	7	1	5.95	27.98
Bradfield, Enrique	L-L	6-1	170	12-2-01	.287	.395	.396	27	120	101	25	29	4	2	1	9	15	3	1	0	14	15	4	12.50	11.67
Burns, Collin	L-R	5-11	187	5-20-00	.218	.293	.318	101	371	330	34	72	12	3	5	37	29	7	3	2	81	15	5	7.82	21.83
Cook, Billy	R-R	6-1	200	1-7-99	.255	.365	.392	15	63	51	10	13	2	1	1	10	8	2	0	2	11	4	0	12.70	17.46
Etzel, Matthew	L-R	6-2	211	4-30-02	.261	.338	.391	32	130	115	12	30	3	3	2	10	14	0	0	1	23	10	5	10.77	17.69
Fabian, Jud	R-L	6-1	195	9-27-00	.233	.326	.432	98	422	361	53	84	16	1	18	58	46	7	2	6	126	13	5	10.90	29.86
Florentino, Randy	L-R	5-11	182	7-5-00	.250	.250	.500	1	4	4	0	1	1	0	0	1	0	0	0	0	1	0	0	0.00	25.00
Hays, Austin	R-R	5-11	200	7-5-95	.357	.471	.857	5	17	14	5	5	1	0	2	3	3	0	0	0	4	0	0	17.65	23.53
Higgins, Ryan	R-R	6-1	200	1-25-00	.194	.283	.320	76	257	222	23	43	7	0	7	20	20	8	6	1	88	6	2	7.78	34.24
Hodo, Douglas	R-R	6-0	185	9-25-00	.267	.313	.467	14	49	45	7	12	6	0	1	4	2	1	1	0	13	5	1	4.08	26.53
Josenberger, Tavian	B-R	6-0	185	10-23-01	.300	.364	.300	7	23	20	7	6	0	0	0	1	2	0	1	0	4	5	0	8.70	17.39
Kjerstad, Heston	L-R	6-3	205	2-12-99	.308	.438	.385	4	16	13	1	4	1	0	0	3	2	1	0	0	1	0	0	12.50	6.25
Pavolony, Connor	R-R	6-1	195	10-25-99	.147	.249	.217	58	210	184	13	27	4	0	3	11	22	3	1	0	68	1	0	10.48	32.38
Retzbach, Adam	R-R	6-4	220	11-13-00	.118	.167	.118	5	18	17	0	2	0	0	0	0	0	1	0	0	9	0	0	0.00	50.00
Rhodes, John	R-R	6-0	200	8-15-00	.202	.271	.309	104	413	376	27	76	16	0	8	47	31	5	0	1	98	4	1	7.51	23.73
Romero, Noelberth	R-R	6-0	183	12-5-01	.237	.275	.342	12	41	38	5	9	1	0	1	5	1	1	1	0	14	0	1	2.44	34.15
Servideo, Anthony	L-R	5-10	175	3-11-99	.158	.283	.255	83	304	259	41	41	10	0	5	21	42	3	0	0	96	9	3	13.82	31.58
Trimble, Reed	B-R	6-0	180	6-6-00	.348	.400	.609	6	25	23	6	8	3	0	1	6	1	1	0	0	5	2	0	4.00	20.00
Valdez, Luis	B-R	5-11	165	1-22-00	.250	.368	.250	6	19	16	3	4	0	0	0	0	3	0	0	0	4	4	2	15.79	21.05
Velasquez, Alfredo	R-R	5-11	153	9-30-04	.194	.194	.226	10	31	31	2	6	1	0	0	0	0	0	0	0	5	1	0	0.00	16.13
Wagner, Max	R-R	6-0	215	8-19-01	.109	.208	.156	19	72	64	4	7	0	0	1	3	7	1	0	0	29	2	0	9.72	40.28
Willems, Creed	L-R	6-0	225	6-4-03	.262	.275	.492	16	69	65	5	17	3	0	4	14	2	0	0	2	13	1	0	2.90	18.84
Williams, Donta'	L-L	5-10	185	6-30-99	.218	.350	.286	50	177	147	18	32	8	1	0	9	29	1	0	0	42	10	7	16.38	23.73
Young, Carter	B-R	6-0	180	1-24-01	.263	.333	.368	12	42	38	0	10	4	0	0	3	4	0	0	0	8	2	0	9.52	19.05

Pitching	B-T	Ht.	Wt.	DOB	W	L	ERA	G	GS	SV	IP	Hits	Runs	ER	HR	BB	SO	AVG	OBP	SLG	SO%	BB%	BF
Bradish, Kyle	R-R	6-3	215	9-12-96	0	0	0.00	1	1	0	3	1	0	0	0	0	4	.100	.100	.100	40.00	0.00	10
Brehmer, Bradley	R-R	6-6	205	2-12-00	4	6	5.58	16	0	0	31	40	25	19	2	7	32	.310	.362	.411	22.70	4.96	141
Bright, Trace	R-R	6-4	199	10-26-00	0	11	4.18	27	27	0	112	106	58	52	13	60	120	.253	.354	.401	24.54	12.27	489
Brnovich, Kyle	L-R	6-2	190	10-20-97	6	2	3.96	19	11	0	75	56	36	33	16	28	77	.202	.288	.412	24.68	8.97	312
Burch, Tyler	R-R	6-2	190	9-2-97	0	0	21.60	2	0	0	2	5	4	4	0	1	0	.625	.600	.875	0.00	10.00	10
Charles, Wandisson	R-R	6-4	250	9-7-96	0	2	9.64	6	0	1	5	8	6	5	0	5	5	.400	.500	.450	18.52	18.52	27
Gillies, Keagan	R-R	6-8	255	1-27-98	1	3	4.94	42	0	7	47	42	30	26	4	25	54	.235	.335	.363	26.09	12.08	207
Hammer, Dan	R-R	6-2	210	9-10-97	3	1	4.46	30	0	3	42	34	21	21	5	25	49	.221	.330	.364	26.92	13.74	182
Heid, Dylan	R-R	6-1	180	5-18-98	5	3	1.69	41	0	5	64	40	23	12	2	34	60	.178	.282	.231	22.90	12.98	262
Hennen, Ryan	R-L	6-0	180	9-30-97	4	2	5.03	26	0	1	34	42	23	19	3	11	37	.309	.353	.441	24.03	7.14	154
Henzman, Lincoln	R-R	6-2	205	7-4-95	4	2	3.81	16	0	1	26	25	14	11	4	6	25	.250	.306	.410	22.94	5.50	109
Hernandez, Jakob	L-L	6-4	260	5-19-96	1	0	0.77	9	0	0	12	4	1	1	0	5	15	.108	.214	.135	35.71	11.90	42
Higgins, Ryan	R-R	6-1	200	1-25-00	0	0	0.00	2	0	0	2	2	0	0	0	0	1	.250	.250	.250	12.50	0.00	8
Johnson, Seth	R-R	6-1	205	9-19-98	0	6	2.63	18	18	0	65	51	24	19	5	35	61	.219	.320	.300	22.59	12.96	270
Lloyd, Daniel	R-R	6-3	232	8-8-00	0	1	2.25	1	0	0	4	2	1	1	1	2	5	.143	.250	.357	31.25	12.50	16
Long, Ryan	R-R	6-6	240	10-19-99	0	6	5.03	24	14	0	93	83	60	52	18	34	79	.231	.303	.456	19.60	8.44	403
McGough, Trey	L-L	6-3	195	3-29-98	0	0	1.83	12	0	2	20	10	6	4	0	6	24	.152	.227	.182	31.58	7.89	76
McSweeney, Morgan	R-R	6-4	210	9-21-97	0	0	4.22	6	0	0	11	8	6	5	0	3	11	.211	.279	.289	25.00	6.82	44
Pavolony, Connor	R-R	6-1	195	10-25-99	0	1	9.00	1	0	0	1	1	2	1	1	0	0	.250	.250	1.000	0.00	0.00	4
Peek, Zach	R-R	6-3	190	5-6-98	0	0	4.91	3	0	0	7	6	4	4	0	4	11	.222	.323	.259	35.48	12.90	31
Pham, Alex	R-R	5-11	165	10-10-99	7	4	4.24	27	27	0	119	97	59	56	14	50	138	.221	.300	.369	27.94	10.12	494
Reilly, Patrick	R-R	6-3	208	10-7-01	1	1	3.73	8	6	0	31	21	16	13	3	18	38	.194	.331	.333	28.57	13.53	133
Richmond, Nick	R-R	6-4	195	4-2-98	5	2	4.50	38	0	4	46	49	32	23	5	24	43	.274	.380	.419	20.00	11.16	215
Rinehart, Logan	R-R	6-3	185	9-21-97	1	1	2.57	19	0	1	28	17	9	8	2	12	33	.167	.259	.275	28.45	10.34	116
Roth, Houston	R-R	6-3	220	3-9-98	2	4	3.35	33	0	3	48	40	22	18	5	23	65	.231	.322	.387	32.02	11.33	203
Scroggins, Cody	R-R	6-0	195	8-17-96	0	0	2.70	4	0	0	7	6	4	2	0	1	6	.240	.286	.240	20.00	3.33	30
Stoudt, Levi	R-R	6-1	195	12-4-97	0	2	2.70	14	0	0	20	16	9	6	1	8	22	.208	.282	.325	25.88	9.41	85
Strowd, Kade	R-R	6-2	200	9-17-97	2	1	0.00	9	0	0	10	4	3	0	0	1	11	.114	.139	.114	30.56	2.78	36
Tavera, Carlos	R-R	6-1	195	10-6-98	3	0	3.08	11	2	0	38	22	15	13	1	17	42	.165	.257	.203	27.63	11.18	152
Van Loon, Peter	R-R	6-5	210	2-18-99	1	1	2.66	12	11	0	47	36	17	14	3	21	61	.217	.325	.307	31.44	10.82	194
Virbitsky, Kyle	R-R	6-7	235	10-8-98	4	1	4.44	20	0	1	26	25	13	13	3	9	30	.250	.315	.410	26.79	8.04	112
Watson, Ryan	R-R	6-5	225	11-15-97	2	0	2.76	11	0	1	16	9	5	5	1	6	16	.170	.254	.283	26.23	9.84	61
Webb, Jacob	R-R	6-2	210	8-15-93	0	0	108.00	1	0	0	0	2	4	4	0	1	0	.500	.600	.500	0.00	20.00	5
Weston, Cameron	R-R	6-2	215	8-27-00	6	10	3.41	23	14	1	92	71	43	35	11	25	108	.206	.275	.366	28.42	6.58	380
Young, Brandon	R-R	6-6	210	8-19-98	0	2	4.09	7	6	0	22	21	10	10	1	4	36	.250	.284	.369	40.91	4.55	88

Fielding

Catcher	PCT	G	PO	A	E	DP	PB
Ardoin	.985	63	601	53	10	8	5
Basallo	.983	45	429	41	8	4	6
Florentino	1.000	1	13	0	0	0	0
Pavolony	.992	25	225	23	2	1	1
Willems	.974	8	70	4	2	1	1

First Base	PCT	G	PO	A	E	DP
Ardoin	.959	10	65	5	3	6
Basallo	.995	28	174	7	1	12
Beavers	1.000	13	85	3	0	9
Bowens	.977	50	329	18	8	25
Cook	1.000	2	12	2	0	0
Higgins	.978	9	41	3	1	5
Retzbach	1.000	4	23	2	0	4
Rhodes	.976	27	153	10	4	13
Romero	1.000	2	8	1	0	0
Willems	.958	3	21	2	1	4

Second Base	PCT	G	PO	A	E	DP
Bencosme	.958	44	66	95	7	21
Burns	.980	43	54	90	3	19
Cook	.900	8	5	13	2	2
Josenberger	1.000	3	3	6	0	0
Romero	1.000	6	6	14	0	2
Servideo	.973	21	25	48	2	7
Valdez	1.000	4	3	11	0	2
Velasquez	1.000	4	3	5	0	1
Wagner	.964	9	11	16	1	5
Young	1.000	6	4	12	0	4

Third Base	PCT	G	PO	A	E	DP
Burns	.983	32	16	42	1	3
Higgins	.866	58	26	71	15	5
Romero	.714	4	3	2	2	1
Servideo	.938	39	27	48	5	6
Valdez	1.000	2	0	1	0	0
Velasquez	1.000	2	3	3	0	0
Wagner	.850	8	6	11	3	2
Young	1.000	1	0	1	0	0

Shortstop	PCT	G	PO	A	E	DP
Bencosme	.945	79	115	178	17	32
Burns	.964	27	31	49	3	12
Servideo	.924	25	22	39	5	8
Velasquez	.857	4	1	5	1	1
Young	1.000	5	7	13	0	4

Outfield	PCT	G	PO	A	E	DP
Beavers	.932	100	186	7	14	0
Bowens	1.000	13	27	1	0	0
Bradfield	.986	27	73	0	1	0
Cook	1.000	5	10	0	0	0
Etzel	.985	30	61	3	1	0
Fabian	.992	94	235	13	2	5
Hays	1.000	4	7	1	0	1
Higgins	1.000	9	13	1	0	0
Hodo	.895	13	16	1	2	0
Josenberger	.857	3	6	0	1	0
Kjerstad	1.000	3	2	0	0	0
Rhodes	1.000	75	140	4	0	2
Servideo	1.000	1	3	0	0	0
Trimble	.889	5	8	0	1	0
Valdez	1.000	1	2	0	0	0
Williams	.954	50	100	4	5	1

ABERDEEN IRONBIRDS — HIGH CLASS A

SOUTH ATLANTIC LEAGUE

Batting	B-T	Ht.	Wt.	DOB	AVG	OBP	SLG	G	PA	AB	R	H	2B	3B	HR	RBI	BB	HBP	SH	SF	SO	SB	CS	BB%	SO%
Anderson, Ethan	B-R	6-2	205	9-21-03	.353	.450	.412	5	20	17	1	6	1	0	0	1	3	0	0	0	6	3	2	15.00	30.00
Arias, Leandro	B-R	6-1	155	2-5-05	.247	.341	.301	20	85	73	3	18	4	0	0	9	9	2	0	1	18	0	1	10.59	21.18
Benavides, Cristian	R-R	6-0	155	5-11-05	.105	.150	.105	7	20	19	2	2	0	0	0	0	1	0	0	0	8	0	0	5.00	40.00
Bradfield, Enrique	L-L	6-1	170	12-2-01	.267	.345	.363	81	349	303	63	81	14	3	3	26	35	3	4	4	58	59	9	10.03	16.62
Costes, Maxwell	R-R	6-1	215	7-30-99	.192	.313	.275	40	144	120	13	23	4	0	2	15	16	6	0	2	24	0	2	11.11	16.67
Cunningham, Jake	R-R	6-4	205	7-3-02	.268	.321	.310	20	78	71	7	19	3	0	0	12	5	1	0	1	20	9	3	6.41	25.64
De Leon, Isaac	R-R	6-3	209	11-7-01	.200	.294	.250	21	68	60	9	12	3	0	0	2	7	1	0	0	26	4	2	10.29	38.24
De Los Santos, Anderson	R-R	5-11	185	1-11-04	.159	.326	.246	23	86	69	6	11	3	0	1	2	16	1	0	0	27	2	3	18.60	31.40
Estrada, Aron	B-R	5-8	142	1-13-05	.247	.337	.341	26	98	85	8	21	1	2	1	9	11	1	0	1	13	8	5	11.22	13.27
Etzel, Matthew	L-R	6-2	211	4-30-02	.306	.379	.478	51	214	186	34	57	12	4	4	37	22	2	0	4	42	31	6	10.28	19.63
Florentino, Randy	L-R	5-11	182	7-5-00	.263	.294	.365	45	143	137	12	36	9	1	1	18	5	1	0	0	30	1	2	3.50	20.98
Haskin, Hudson	R-R	6-0	200	12-31-98	.205	.404	.308	11	52	39	8	8	1	0	1	6	11	2	0	0	18	0	0	21.15	34.62
Higgins, Ryan	R-R	6-1	200	1-25-00	.265	.321	.408	15	56	49	6	13	2	1	1	10	4	1	0	2	18	0	1	7.14	32.14
Hodo, Douglas	R-R	6-0	185	9-25-00	.248	.397	.378	82	310	246	50	61	12	1	6	29	58	4	0	2	83	42	5	18.71	26.77
Honeycutt, Vance	R-R	6-3	190	5-17-03	.100	.100	.100	5	20	20	1	2	0	0	0	2	0	0	0	0	11	0	0	0.00	55.00
Horvath, Mac	R-R	6-1	195	7-22-01	.232	.328	.417	71	317	271	40	63	19	2	9	41	37	4	0	5	71	26	1	11.67	22.40
Hunt, Blake	R-R	6-3	215	11-10-98	.231	.286	.385	4	14	13	2	3	2	0	0	1	1	0	0	0	4	0	0	7.14	28.57
Josenberger, Tavian	B-R	6-0	185	10-23-01	.230	.344	.405	79	349	291	57	67	14	5	9	38	49	2	6	1	57	45	6	14.04	16.33
Kjerstad, Heston	L-R	6-3	205	2-12-99	.400	.500	.400	2	6	5	1	2	0	0	0	0	1	0	0	0	0	0	0	16.67	0.00
Maton, Nick	L-R	6-2	178	2-18-97	.273	.429	.455	4	14	11	0	3	0	1	0	1	3	0	0	0	4	0	0	21.43	28.57
Mayo, Coby	R-R	6-5	230	12-10-01	.462	.563	1.385	4	16	13	4	6	3	0	3	6	2	1	0	0	5	0	0	12.50	31.25
Mordan, Aneudis	R-R	6-1	175	6-10-04	.210	.246	.306	17	65	62	4	13	4	1	0	5	3	0	0	0	23	0	0	4.62	35.38
O'Ferrall, Griff	R-R	6-1	185	2-2-03	.300	.333	.300	5	21	20	2	6	0	0	0	0	1	0	0	0	3	1	1	4.76	14.29
Overn, Austin	L-R	6-0	175	5-10-03	.250	.375	.500	6	24	20	2	5	1	2	0	1	3	1	0	0	8	4	0	12.50	33.33
Prado, Elio	R-R	6-0	160	11-29-01	.223	.332	.327	76	305	260	32	58	11	2	4	31	40	3	0	1	65	19	9	13.11	21.31
Retzbach, Adam	R-R	6-4	220	11-13-00	.183	.317	.340	82	295	241	37	44	9	4	7	38	45	4	2	3	110	2	1	15.25	37.29
Rodriguez, Carlos	R-R	5-11	195	10-14-03	.111	.100	.222	3	10	9	0	1	1	0	0	1	0	0	0	1	1	0	0	0.00	10.00
Romero, Noelberth	R-R	6-0	183	12-5-01	.173	.236	.222	23	89	81	5	14	1	0	1	8	5	2	0	1	21	5	2	5.62	23.60
Sosa, Thomas	L-L	6-1	160	1-18-05	.181	.298	.194	19	84	72	8	13	1	0	0	3	11	1	0	0	28	8	1	13.10	33.33
Stafford, Ryan	R-R	5-10	180	1-15-03	.118	.158	.118	5	19	17	0	2	0	0	0	3	1	0	0	1	8	1	0	5.26	42.11
Tejada, Angel	R-R	5-10	160	1-30-04	.198	.220	.271	28	100	96	10	19	4	0	1	6	2	1	0	1	27	3	3	2.00	27.00
Trimble, Reed	B-R	6-0	180	6-6-00	.255	.363	.466	49	194	161	36	41	13	3	5	25	29	0	0	3	35	23	0	14.95	18.04
Urman, Cole	R-R	6-1	195	7-28-01	.273	.333	.273	3	12	11	1	3	0	0	0	0	1	0	0	0	3	0	0	8.33	25.00
Valdez, Luis	B-R	5-11	165	1-22-00	.164	.219	.209	24	73	67	9	11	1	1	0	2	5	0	0	1	24	13	2	6.85	32.88
Vasquez, Jalen	L-R	6-0	175	1-18-02	.216	.341	.334	96	356	296	43	64	15	4	4	30	54	3	0	2	99	35	8	15.17	27.81
Vavra, Terrin	L-R	6-0	185	5-12-97	.292	.320	.375	6	25	24	5	7	2	0	0	2	1	0	0	0	6	0	0	4.00	24.00
Wagner, Max	R-R	6-0	215	8-19-01	.278	.381	.611	5	21	18	3	5	1	1	1	2	3	0	0	0	6	1	0	14.29	28.57
Willems, Creed	L-R	6-0	225	6-4-03	.238	.332	.456	82	326	281	40	67	18	2	13	51	35	6	1	3	68	1	1	10.74	20.86
Young, Carter	B-R	6-0	180	1-24-01	.208	.276	.322	100	398	360	31	75	15	4	6	38	33	2	0	3	107	17	7	8.29	26.88

Pitching	B-T	Ht.	Wt.	DOB	W	L	ERA	G	GS	SV	IP	Hits	Runs	ER	HR	BB	SO	AVG	OBP	SLG	SO%	BB%	BF
Avila, Nick	R-R	6-4	195	7-25-97	0	1	2.45	6	2	0	7	6	4	2	1	3	5	.222	.323	.370	16.13	9.68	31
Barnhart, Zane	R-R	5-10	190	5-30-02	3	1	2.47	30	0	1	44	27	15	12	3	27	44	.176	.308	.261	23.66	14.52	186
Baumeister, Jackson	R-R	6-4	226	7-10-02	1	3	3.06	18	18	0	71	53	31	24	3	43	91	.210	.337	.317	29.55	13.96	308
Baumler, Carter	R-R	6-2	195	1-31-02	3	1	4.00	7	1	0	18	15	9	8	2	6	15	.227	.301	.364	20.55	8.22	73
Beck, Jared	L-L	7-0	225	7-1-00	1	1	4.00	7	0	0	9	7	4	4	1	8	12	.212	.395	.303	27.91	18.60	43
Brehmer, Bradley	R-R	6-6	205	2-12-00	2	3	2.80	19	0	1	35	29	14	11	1	15	47	.221	.304	.351	31.33	10.00	150

Name	B-T	HT	WT	DOB	W	L	ERA	G	GS	SV	IP	H	R	ER	HR	BB	SO	AVG	OBP	SLG	SO%	BB%	BF
Burch, Tyler	R-R	6-2	190	9-2-97	1	0	1.17	6	1	1	8	8	1	1	0	0	9	.258	.258	.290	29.03	0.00	31
Chace, Moises	R-R	6-1	213	6-9-03	2	2	3.46	17	9	1	52	37	22	20	5	30	76	.201	.329	.342	34.23	13.51	222
Chandler, Cooper	R-R	6-2	200	8-12-98	0	1	3.00	12	0	4	18	14	8	6	2	4	22	.209	.250	.328	30.56	5.56	72
Costes, Maxwell	R-R	6-1	215	7-30-99	0	0	1.93	4	0	0	5	3	1	1	0	0	0	.188	.188	.313	0.00	0.00	16
Cruz, Deivy	L-L	5-11	154	2-13-04	3	1	5.76	29	0	3	30	21	20	19	1	29	42	.206	.415	.265	29.58	20.42	142
De Leon, Luis	L-L	6-3	168	4-14-03	2	3	5.73	19	11	0	60	70	43	38	4	42	65	.289	.397	.384	22.65	14.63	287
De Los Santos, Juan	R-R	6-3	250	5-25-02	0	0	4.85	12	0	2	13	12	8	7	1	11	19	.235	.371	.392	30.16	17.46	63
Dorsey, Carson	L-L	6-2	165	2-25-03	0	0	108.00	1	0	0	0	2	4	4	1	3	0	1.000	1.000	2.500	0.00	60.00	5
Firoved, Graham	R-R	6-1	185	9-26-99	1	8	5.83	35	0	3	42	33	31	27	4	42	47	.219	.389	.371	23.62	21.11	199
Florentino, Randy	L-R	5-11	182	7-5-00	0	0	3.60	2	0	0	5	7	2	2	0	1	2	.333	.391	.381	8.70	4.35	23
Forret, Michael	L-R	6-3	190	4-6-04	4	4	4.35	16	9	0	60	55	37	29	8	29	75	.244	.345	.396	28.09	10.86	267
Freeberger, Dominic	R-R	6-0	205	4-5-00	2	1	11.70	11	0	0	10	15	13	13	2	6	10	.366	.449	.610	20.41	12.24	49
Fruit, Zach	R-R	6-4	203	4-12-00	3	4	3.03	25	21	1	107	78	41	36	7	55	113	.201	.302	.320	25.11	12.22	450
German, Nestor	R-R	6-3	225	2-26-02	2	0	1.78	7	0	0	25	21	5	5	2	3	33	.223	.247	.319	34.02	3.09	97
Gibson, Trey	R-R	6-5	230	5-18-02	2	4	4.21	9	7	0	36	33	19	17	1	15	37	.244	.331	.326	24.03	9.74	154
Gongora, Sebastian	L-L	6-5	215	9-1-01	0	0	5.40	1	0	0	2	2	1	1	0	0	2	.286	.286	.571	28.57	0.00	7
Guzman, Ronald	L-L	6-5	235	10-20-94	0	0	30.00	4	0	0	3	5	11	10	0	9	4	.417	.680	.500	16.00	36.00	25
Hammer, Dan	R-R	6-2	210	9-10-97	0	1	9.00	2	0	0	2	5	2	2	0	1	2	.500	.545	.600	18.18	9.09	11
Hernandez, Jakob	L-L	6-4	260	5-19-96	0	0	2.45	3	0	0	4	4	1	1	0	1	5	.267	.313	.467	31.25	6.25	16
Johnson, Preston	R-R	6-4	250	3-11-00	3	3	4.72	25	4	1	55	45	33	29	2	39	76	.222	.351	.325	30.77	15.79	247
Lloyd, Daniel	R-R	6-3	232	8-8-00	3	3	5.90	11	3	1	40	43	27	26	5	22	36	.277	.365	.439	19.89	12.15	181
McKeehan, Cooper	L-L	6-1	195	3-28-01	2	0	6.28	10	0	0	14	14	11	10	0	10	24	.246	.377	.368	34.78	14.49	69
Nierman, Hayden	S-R	6-2	170	1-27-00	0	0	3.75	11	0	0	12	13	8	5	0	11	10	.277	.426	.319	16.13	17.74	62
Nunez, Juan	R-R	5-11	190	12-7-00	2	1	2.45	7	4	0	29	22	8	8	3	10	38	.212	.282	.385	32.20	8.47	118
Portes, Edgar	R-R	6-2	165	10-2-02	5	4	3.34	25	13	2	94	77	39	35	5	49	119	.215	.316	.313	28.95	11.92	411
Rinehart, Logan	R-R	6-3	185	9-21-97	1	0	0.00	5	0	0	5	0	0	0	0	3	6	.000	.211	.000	31.58	15.79	19
Rivera, Yaqui	R-R	6-2	150	7-19-03	7	1	1.99	37	0	6	54	31	21	12	2	27	59	.161	.289	.229	25.88	11.84	228
Roth, Houston	R-R	6-3	220	3-9-98	0	1	5.79	3	0	0	5	3	3	3	1	1	8	.200	.278	.533	44.44	5.56	18
Salazar, Grabiel	R-R	6-0	165	2-19-01	0	0	3.38	4	0	0	5	4	2	2	1	0	3	.222	.211	.500	15.79	0.00	19
Sanchez, Luis	R-R	6-0	167	3-4-03	4	2	6.85	24	0	1	24	19	19	18	2	33	27	.216	.445	.307	20.93	25.58	129
Scroggins, Cody	R-R	6-0	195	8-17-96	2	0	0.00	6	0	1	8	6	1	0	0	7	4	.222	.417	.259	11.11	19.44	36
Sharkey, Teddy	R-R	5-11	215	8-1-01	2	0	5.63	5	0	0	8	3	5	5	0	11	10	.125	.378	.167	27.03	29.73	37
Van Loon, Peter	R-R	6-5	210	2-18-99	0	1	6.30	3	3	0	10	13	7	7	1	3	13	.302	.388	.442	26.53	6.12	49
Vasquez, Jalen	L-R	6-0	175	1-18-02	0	0	0.00	1	0	0	1	0	0	0	0	0	0	.000	.250	.000	0.00	0.00	4
Virbitsky, Kyle	R-R	6-7	235	10-8-98	3	1	2.59	21	0	3	31.1	29	12	9	2	6	39	.246	.279	.356	30.23	4.65	129
Wells, Levi	R-R	6-2	216	9-21-01	0	9	6.71	21	21	0	60	69	56	45	6	30	74	.280	.363	.427	25.96	10.53	285
Weston, Cameron	R-R	6-2	215	8-27-00	1	0	0.54	4	4	0	17	7	1	1	0	7	19	.137	.250	.176	31.67	11.67	60
Yates, Evan	R-R	6-1	180	9-17-02	0	0	5.79	3	0	0	5	5	3	3	0	3	9	.263	.364	.368	40.91	13.64	22
Zimmermann, Bruce	L-L	6-1	220	2-9-95	0	0	0.00	1	1	0	3	1	0	0	0	1	6	.100	.182	.100	54.55	9.09	11

Fielding

Catcher	PCT	G	PO	A	E	DP	PB
Anderson	1.000	3	28	1	0	0	0
Florentino	.975	23	186	13	5	0	1
Hunt	1.000	3	29	4	0	0	0
Mordan	.989	8	88	3	1	0	0
Retzbach	.982	55	531	24	10	4	8
Rodriguez	1.000	1	7	0	0	0	0
Stafford	.947	2	17	1	1	0	0
Urman	1.000	1	14	0	0	0	0
Willems	.986	45	468	25	7	5	5

First Base	PCT	G	PO	A	E	DP
Anderson	1.000	1	6	1	0	2
Costes	.981	25	146	7	3	10
De Leon	.952	10	54	5	3	5
De Los Santos	.985	9	58	6	1	6
Etzel	.950	11	55	2	3	10
Florentino	1.000	10	37	3	0	5
Higgins	.960	5	24	0	1	1
Mordan	1.000	7	46	3	0	2
Retzbach	1.000	22	110	9	0	8
Rodriguez	1.000	2	13	1	0	0
Romero	.985	8	65	1	1	4
Stafford	1.000	1	8	0	0	1
Tejada	.977	7	41	1	1	1
Urman	1.000	2	12	3	0	2
Willems	.994	27	163	6	1	17

Second Base	PCT	G	PO	A	E	DP
Arias	.889	4	9	7	2	1
Benavides	.960	6	11	13	1	3
Estrada	.965	14	18	37	2	6
Horvath	.971	11	13	20	1	3
Josenberger	.988	44	70	93	2	24
Maton	1.000	1	0	2	0	0
O'Ferrall	1.000	1	3	4	0	1
Romero	1.000	5	6	8	0	2
Stafford	1.000	2	8	3	0	2
Tejada	.958	10	11	12	1	2
Valdez	.897	9	9	17	3	4
Vasquez	.975	21	30	48	2	13
Vavra	1.000	2	2	9	0	4
Wagner	1.000	1	1	0	0	1
Young	.944	10	17	17	2	4

Third Base	PCT	G	PO	A	E	DP
Arias	1.000	1	0	2	0	0
Benavides	.000	1	0	0	0	0
Costes	.813	8	6	7	3	2
De Leon	.778	10	3	11	4	0
De Los Santos	1.000	12	7	16	0	2
Estrada	1.000	2	1	3	0	0
Higgins	.909	5	2	8	1	1
Horvath	.928	35	28	49	6	6
Josenberger	.000	1	0	0	0	0
Mayo	1.000	2	3	4	0	0
Romero	.571	5	2	2	3	0
Tejada	.950	7	6	13	1	2
Vasquez	.948	26	17	38	3	5
Wagner	.857	3	2	4	1	0
Young	.933	24	18	38	4	7

Shortstop	PCT	G	PO	A	E	DP
Arias	.976	11	18	23	1	6
Estrada	1.000	3	5	8	0	0
Josenberger	.000	1	0	0	0	0
Maton	1.000	3	2	5	0	1
O'Ferrall	.875	4	3	11	2	3
Romero	1.000	2	1	2	0	0
Vasquez	.931	46	56	93	11	11
Vavra	1.000	2	2	7	0	1
Young	.964	67	79	133	8	33

Outfield	PCT	G	PO	A	E	DP
Anderson	1.000	1	3	1	0	1
Bradfield	.995	79	189	9	1	5
Cunningham	1.000	16	28	1	0	1
Estrada	1.000	7	6	0	0	0
Etzel	.986	38	71	1	1	0
Florentino	.500	1	1	0	1	0
Haskin	1.000	8	13	1	0	0
Higgins	1.000	6	11	1	0	0
Hodo	.982	71	101	6	2	0
Honeycutt	.900	5	9	0	1	0
Horvath	1.000	11	17	0	0	0
Josenberger	.970	34	61	3	2	1
Kjerstad	1.000	1	1	0	0	0
Overn	.917	5	9	2	1	0
Prado	.979	59	91	4	2	0
Sosa	.935	17	28	1	2	0
Tejada	1.000	3	5	0	0	0
Trimble	.958	43	65	4	3	1
Valdez	1.000	11	10	0	0	0

BALTIMORE ORIOLES

DELMARVA SHOREBIRDS

LOW CLASS A

CAROLINA LEAGUE

BALTIMORE ORIOLES

Batting	B-T	Ht.	Wt.	DOB	AVG	OBP	SLG	G	PA	AB	R	H	2B	3B	HR	RBI	BB	HBP	SH	SF	SO	SB	CS	BB%	SO%
Acevedo, Stiven	R-R	6-4	185	8-2-02	.219	.280	.336	80	311	283	29	62	10	1	7	35	23	2	0	3	84	22	5	7.40	27.01
Amparo, Edwin	B-R	6-0	165	10-14-04	.284	.398	.395	27	98	81	14	23	3	0	2	8	15	1	0	1	22	13	6	15.31	22.45
Anderson, Ethan	B-R	6-2	205	9-21-03	.268	.333	.446	14	63	56	8	15	3	2	1	11	6	0	0	1	9	3	0	9.52	14.29
Arias, Leandro	B-R	6-1	155	2-5-05	.213	.313	.291	67	274	230	27	49	9	0	3	30	31	5	2	6	51	6	7	11.31	18.61
Benavides, Cristian	R-R	6-0	155	5-11-05	.167	.286	.167	2	7	6	1	1	0	0	0	0	1	0	0	0	3	2	0	14.29	42.86
Campos, Edrei	L-R	6-1	165	5-8-05	.250	.250	.250	5	20	20	0	5	0	0	0	1	0	0	0	0	5	1	2	0.00	25.00
Costes, Maxwell	R-R	6-1	215	7-30-99	.261	.320	.283	14	50	46	1	12	1	0	0	4	4	0	0	0	5	2	0	8.00	10.00
Cuevas, Elis	B-R	5-11	150	11-8-04	.234	.383	.359	20	81	64	10	15	2	0	2	7	14	2	0	1	18	14	5	17.28	22.22
Cunningham, Jake	R-R	6-4	205	7-3-02	.208	.311	.312	71	268	231	30	48	8	2	4	23	31	4	1	1	85	20	2	11.57	31.72
De Los Santos, Anderson	R-R	5-11	185	1-11-04	.205	.308	.339	82	339	292	36	60	7	4	8	42	40	4	1	2	106	13	9	11.80	31.27
Estrada, Aron	B-R	5-8	142	1-13-05	.296	.361	.434	91	388	348	53	103	18	3	8	43	29	8	0	3	65	31	8	7.47	16.75
Guerrero, Kevin	R-R	6-3	165	4-17-04	.205	.258	.295	76	264	244	24	50	10	3	2	20	17	1	0	2	85	7	6	6.44	32.20
Hernandez, Brayan	L-R	6-1	225	11-11-01	.114	.184	.143	29	77	70	1	8	2	0	0	5	5	1	1	0	27	1	0	6.49	35.06
Hernandez, Maikol	R-R	6-3	175	10-4-03	.179	.282	.244	62	235	201	26	36	5	1	2	19	27	3	1	3	60	10	1	11.49	25.53
Hodo, Douglas	R-R	6-0	185	9-25-00	.204	.361	.367	16	61	49	7	10	2	0	2	4	10	2	0	0	23	4	1	16.39	37.70
Honeycutt, Vance	R-R	6-3	190	5-17-03	.226	.333	.258	8	36	31	2	7	1	0	0	3	4	1	0	0	13	4	2	11.11	36.11
Mordan, Aneudis	R-R	6-1	175	6-10-04	.220	.324	.390	86	341	295	31	65	11	0	13	37	43	2	1	0	91	5	8	12.61	26.69
O'Ferrall, Griff	R-R	6-1	185	2-2-03	.232	.348	.268	15	69	56	6	13	2	0	0	8	9	2	0	2	10	1	3	13.04	14.49
Ondina, Steven	R-R	5-8	156	3-30-02	.200	.235	.200	4	17	15	2	3	0	0	0	1	0	1	0	1	3	0	1	0.00	17.65
Overn, Austin	L-R	6-0	175	5-10-03	.291	.406	.455	15	69	55	14	16	4	1	1	6	12	0	0	2	17	12	6	17.39	24.64
Peguero, Fernando	B-R	5-9	145	12-27-04	.444	.545	.722	6	22	18	5	8	1	2	0	5	4	0	0	0	7	5	0	18.18	31.82
Rodriguez, Carlos	R-R	5-11	195	10-14-03	.333	.333	.667	1	3	3	1	1	1	0	0	1	0	0	0	0	0	0	0	0.00	0.00
Rodriguez, Miguel	R-R	5-11	160	12-29-05	.203	.321	.297	19	78	64	7	13	3	0	1	9	10	2	0	2	9	2	0	12.82	11.54
Romero, Noelberth	R-R	6-0	183	12-5-01	.136	.180	.243	31	111	103	11	14	3	1	2	8	5	1	0	2	26	5	0	4.50	23.42
Sosa, Thomas	L-L	6-1	160	1-18-05	.244	.328	.369	74	308	271	45	66	18	2	4	17	33	2	0	2	86	22	9	10.71	27.92
Stafford, Ryan	R-R	5-10	180	1-15-03	.327	.444	.388	15	63	49	9	16	3	0	0	7	9	3	0	2	12	9	1	14.29	19.05
Tavera, Braylin	R-R	6-2	175	2-19-05	.173	.296	.213	84	355	300	26	52	5	2	1	26	49	4	0	2	90	27	13	13.80	25.35
Tejada, Angel	R-R	5-10	160	1-30-04	.253	.286	.376	55	200	186	18	47	10	2	3	27	7	3	1	3	35	27	4	3.50	17.50
Trimble, Reed	B-R	6-0	180	6-6-00	.278	.300	.333	5	20	18	3	5	1	0	0	2	1	0	0	1	5	3	0	5.00	25.00
Tuft, Colin	R-R	6-2	195	1-24-03	.177	.354	.274	20	79	62	12	11	3	0	1	8	10	7	0	0	27	7	3	12.66	34.18
Urman, Cole	R-R	6-1	195	7-28-01	.205	.313	.317	80	293	249	32	51	13	0	5	20	36	4	2	2	90	10	1	12.29	30.72
Valdez, Luis	B-R	5-11	165	1-22-00	.308	.438	.423	10	32	26	6	8	1	1	0	3	6	0	0	0	6	8	1	18.75	18.75
Velasquez, Alfredo	R-R	5-11	153	9-30-04	.245	.286	.301	43	155	143	16	35	6	1	0	11	9	0	1	2	27	11	3	5.81	17.42

Pitching	B-T	Ht.	Wt.	DOB	W	L	ERA	G	GS	SV	IP	Hits	Runs	ER	HR	BB	SO	AVG	OBP	SLG	SO%	BB%	BF
Alberto, Eddy	R-R	6-2	190	3-10-02	1	2	4.34	21	0	1	29	27	20	14	2	20	41	.231	.366	.368	28.87	14.08	142
Barnhart, Zane	R-R	5-10	190	5-30-02	0	0	3.12	6	0	0	9	6	5	3	0	4	12	.214	.324	.357	35.29	11.76	34
Baumler, Carter	R-R	6-2	195	1-31-02	1	0	19.29	3	0	0	2	6	5	5	1	0	2	.500	.500	.750	16.67	0.00	12
Beck, Jared	L-L	7-0	225	7-1-00	4	5	5.06	26	0	1	37	29	25	21	2	36	52	.215	.379	.281	29.71	20.57	175
Beriguete, Randy	R-R	6-4	221	11-2-02	5	1	3.46	34	0	3	42	31	20	16	1	31	35	.205	.342	.311	18.72	16.58	187
Bragg, Braxton	R-R	6-2	207	10-28-00	5	6	3.36	24	20	0	96	91	40	36	9	22	122	.242	.294	.375	30.12	5.43	405
Cartaya, Yeiber	R-R	6-5	165	1-20-03	2	0	1.11	6	3	0	24	16	5	3	0	11	31	.178	.283	.189	29.25	10.38	106
Casimiri, Jiorgeny	R-R	6-1	160	7-12-01	3	2	6.34	28	0	0	38	43	34	27	1	27	45	.279	.397	.409	23.81	14.29	189
Chandler, Cooper	R-R	6-2	200	8-12-98	0	0	2.70	4	0	0	7	7	2	2	1	1	8	.259	.286	.444	28.57	3.57	28
Cooper, Riley	L-L	6-2	264	10-19-01	5	4	3.07	24	9	1	88	76	37	30	5	38	84	.231	.314	.340	22.46	10.16	374
Correa, Eccel	R-R	6-0	170	2-1-03	2	4	4.94	18	11	1	62	66	42	34	2	29	54	.265	.347	.329	18.95	10.18	285
Cravey, Jacob	R-R	6-6	215	9-28-01	0	9	5.27	24	13	0	84	86	53	49	5	58	74	.273	.389	.410	19.47	15.26	380
Cruz, Deivy	L-L	5-11	154	2-13-04	1	0	0.00	3	0	1	4	0	0	0	0	3	4	.000	.188	.000	25.00	18.75	16
De Leon, Luis	L-L	6-3	168	4-14-03	1	2	2.25	7	7	0	28	20	13	7	1	7	41	.190	.252	.257	35.34	6.03	116
De Los Santos, Juan	R-R	6-3	250	5-25-02	0	0	15.00	3	0	0	3	6	7	5	1	1	1	.400	.438	.667	6.25	6.25	16
Forret, Michael	L-R	6-3	190	4-6-04	2	4	3.18	10	8	0	40	30	19	14	0	15	49	.211	.293	.268	29.88	9.15	164
Freeberger, Dominic	R-R	6-0	205	4-5-00	0	1	2.70	3	0	0	3	2	2	1	0	3	6	.182	.357	.182	42.86	21.43	14
Frias, Harif	R-R	6-4	163	5-19-01	3	3	6.00	27	0	2	36	37	25	24	2	26	34	.268	.387	.406	20.00	15.29	170
German, Nestor	R-R	6-3	225	2-26-02	1	3	1.49	14	12	0	48	31	13	8	0	14	57	.179	.238	.202	30.00	7.37	190
Gibson, Trey	R-R	6-5	230	5-18-02	1	5	3.40	16	9	0	56	41	26	21	2	24	81	.200	.302	.263	34.47	10.21	235
Glassey, Joe	R-R	6-3	215	7-17-01	1	0	1.17	7	0	3	8	3	2	1	1	0	7	.115	.115	.231	26.92	0.00	26
Hernandez, Brayan	L-R	6-1	225	11-11-01	0	0	12.00	2	0	0	3	5	4	4	2	3	2	.357	.471	.786	11.76	17.65	17
Leandro, Alberto	R-R	6-3	171	4-24-02	0	0	2.70	6	0	0	7	3	2	2	0	5	8	.143	.310	.190	27.59	17.24	29
Leiner, Kenny	S-R	6-3	225	7-7-01	1	0	3.24	6	0	0	8	5	7	3	0	10	11	.167	.375	.233	26.83	24.39	41
Lloyd, Daniel	R-R	6-3	232	8-8-00	0	1	5.40	4	4	0	12	16	8	7	0	4	6	.320	.393	.360	10.71	7.14	56
McKeehan, Cooper	L-L	6-1	195	3-28-01	1	0	4.26	5	0	0	6	2	4	3	0	4	11	.095	.240	.095	44.00	16.00	25
Mendez, Alejandro	R-R	6-5	254	2-28-01	0	0	4.24	13	0	2	17	18	14	8	1	8	10	.261	.365	.333	11.76	9.41	85
Money, Blake	R-R	6-7	240	11-14-01	4	7	3.15	25	14	0	103	84	48	36	7	25	119	.214	.259	.316	28.00	5.88	425
Morfe, Keeler	R-R	5-8	161	6-9-06	0	1	6.75	4	4	0	11	8	10	8	0	9	11	.205	.377	.231	20.37	16.67	54
Nierman, Hayden	S-R	6-2	170	1-27-00	1	1	5.00	7	0	1	9	10	5	5	0	4	16	.278	.350	.361	39.02	9.76	41
Peek, Zach	R-R	6-3	190	5-6-98	0	0	3.24	5	0	1	8	3	3	3	0	4	9	.107	.242	.107	27.27	12.12	33
Rodriguez, Eris	R-R	6-3	188	9-10-01	0	1	10.38	8	0	0	9	9	14	10	1	12	7	.257	.469	.457	14.29	24.49	49
Rojas, Juan	L-L	6-0	165	1-31-04	4	5	4.53	17	6	1	54	39	31	27	1	30	64	.193	.300	.238	27.47	12.88	233
Salazar, Grabiel	R-R	6-0	165	2-19-01	0	2	3.86	29	1	3	33	31	19	14	1	22	35	.250	.377	.363	23.03	14.47	152
Sanchez, Brayner	R-R	6-4	189	6-2-01	0	1	9.75	11	0	0	12	15	16	13	1	11	15	.294	.439	.471	22.73	16.67	66
Showalter, Justin	R-R	6-2	190	2-2-99	1	1	2.88	7	0	1	25	23	11	8	1	10	26	.237	.351	.299	22.81	8.77	114

Pitching	B-T	Ht.	Wt.	DOB	W	L	ERA	G	GS	SV	IP	Hits	Runs	ER	HR	BB	SO	AVG	OBP	SLG	SO%	BB%	BF
Solano, Issac	R-R	6-6	195	10-23-01	1	2	3.49	19	0	4	28	21	14	11	0	20	36	.212	.347	.273	29.51	16.39	122
Turzenski, Trent	R-R	6-6	240	5-11-01	0	1	1.23	6	0	0	7	7	3	1	1	2	10	.259	.300	.370	33.33	6.67	30
Urman, Cole	R-R	6-1	195	7-28-01	0	0	15.00	2	0	0	6	15	12	10	2	3	2	.455	.486	.727	5.41	8.11	37
Weatherly, Ty	L-R	6-6	200	9-19-00	2	4	2.02	13	10	0	36	22	13	8	1	17	48	.185	.293	.252	34.29	12.14	140

Fielding

Catcher	PCT	G	PO	A	E	DP	PB
Anderson	.962	6	50	1	2	1	2
Hernandez	1.000	2	5	1	0	1	0
Mordan	.978	50	488	37	12	3	9
Rodriguez	1.000	7	59	5	0	0	2
Stafford	.984	5	54	6	1	0	1
Tuft	.985	5	63	4	1	0	1
Urman	.984	57	585	45	10	4	7

First Base	PCT	G	PO	A	E	DP
Acevedo	.973	24	172	10	5	20
Anderson	1.000	4	34	7	0	1
Costes	.978	7	41	3	1	5
Cuevas	.951	7	38	1	2	2
De Los Santos	.962	18	99	3	4	10
Hernandez	.948	20	119	9	7	9
Mordan	.979	21	127	11	3	14
Rodriguez	.985	9	64	2	1	4
Rodriguez	1.000	1	2	1	0	0
Romero	1.000	5	23	3	0	2
Tuft	.958	4	22	1	1	0
Urman	.983	19	104	13	2	6

Second Base	PCT	G	PO	A	E	DP
Amparo	.913	11	12	30	4	2
Arias	.911	14	20	21	4	3
Estrada	.967	39	66	108	6	20
Hernandez	.939	7	11	20	2	4
O'Ferrall	1.000	3	8	11	0	1
Ondina	.857	2	5	1	1	0
Peguero	1.000	2	3	7	0	0
Romero	.935	7	7	22	2	4
Stafford	.920	5	8	15	2	1
Tejada	.973	26	52	55	3	14
Valdez	.667	1	1	1	1	1
Velasquez	.949	15	19	37	3	4

Third Base	PCT	G	PO	A	E	DP
Amparo	.643	8	1	8	5	0
Benavides	.000	1	0	0	0	0
Campos	.667	2	0	2	1	0
Costes	.000	1	0	0	1	0
Cuevas	.857	2	5	1	1	0
De Los Santos	.874	60	43	68	16	9
Estrada	.500	2	0	2	2	0
Hernandez	.905	35	24	33	6	3
Tejada	.870	23	19	21	6	4
Velasquez	.889	5	4	4	1	1

Shortstop	PCT	G	PO	A	E	DP
Amparo	.857	5	2	10	2	1
Arias	.894	42	42	68	13	17
Campos	.778	2	2	5	2	0
Estrada	.922	29	35	71	9	16
Hernandez	.902	15	12	34	5	6
O'Ferrall	.975	12	15	24	1	3
Romero	.900	13	19	17	4	5
Velasquez	.974	16	28	47	2	9

Outfield	PCT	G	PO	A	E	DP
Acevedo	.951	48	73	4	4	1
Amparo	1.000	1	1	0	0	0
Anderson	1.000	2	2	0	0	0
Campos	.000	1	0	0	0	0
Cuevas	.880	10	21	1	3	0
Cunningham	1.000	70	133	7	0	0
Estrada	1.000	20	36	0	0	0
Guerrero	1.000	59	103	10	0	6
Hodo	1.000	13	19	0	0	0
Honeycutt	1.000	6	17	0	0	0
Overn	1.000	16	40	2	0	0
Peguero	.917	4	11	0	1	0
Romero	1.000	2	3	0	0	0
Sosa	.912	60	112	2	11	1
Stafford	.800	3	4	0	1	0
Tavera	.981	77	150	2	3	0
Tejada	.000	2	0	0	0	0
Trimble	1.000	4	5	0	0	0
Tuft	1.000	8	9	1	0	0
Valdez	1.000	6	3	1	0	0
Velasquez	.875	4	7	0	1	0

FCL ORIOLES — *ROOKIE*

FLORIDA COMPLEX LEAGUE

Batting	B-T	Ht.	Wt.	DOB	AVG	OBP	SLG	G	PA	AB	R	H	2B	3B	HR	RBI	BB	HBP	SH	SF	SO	SB	CS	BB%	SO%
Almeyda, Luis	R-R	6-2	180	4-17-06	.200	.337	.316	53	190	155	20	31	1	1	5	23	31	2	0	2	49	12	5	16.32	25.79
Amparo, Edwin	B-R	6-0	165	10-14-04	.245	.400	.384	52	195	151	29	37	9	0	4	23	39	2	0	3	37	25	9	20.00	18.97
Arias, Leandro	B-R	6-1	155	2-5-05	.368	.500	.947	7	26	19	5	7	3	1	2	10	4	2	0	1	3	1	0	15.38	11.54
Benavides, Cristian	R-R	6-0	155	5-11-05	.225	.309	.338	32	81	71	13	16	2	0	2	10	8	1	0	1	24	2	1	9.88	29.63
Bucce, Yasmil	B-R	5-11	168	8-13-04	.185	.415	.262	33	94	65	7	12	2	0	1	11	23	4	0	2	21	1	0	24.47	22.34
Campos, Edrei	L-R	6-1	165	5-8-05	.262	.330	.429	33	94	84	10	22	4	2	2	14	7	2	0	1	11	5	1	7.45	11.70
Cuevas, Elis	B-R	5-11	150	11-8-04	.270	.382	.428	56	195	159	37	43	5	1	6	23	21	9	1	2	25	33	7	10.77	12.82
Cunningham, Jake	R-R	6-4	205	7-3-02	.000	.250	.000	1	4	3	1	0	0	0	0	0	1	0	0	0	1	0	0	25.00	25.00
Hernandez, Maikol	R-R	6-3	175	10-4-03	.146	.250	.244	14	48	41	5	6	2	1	0	3	3	3	0	1	11	0	0	6.25	22.92
Liranzo, Joshua	R-R	6-3	180	8-25-06	.220	.349	.264	31	109	91	12	20	4	0	0	5	18	0	0	0	30	4	1	16.51	27.52
Nolaya, Andres	R-R	6-1	185	3-27-05	.220	.342	.286	39	114	91	19	20	2	2	0	16	17	2	0	4	24	9	3	14.91	21.05
Peguero, Fernando	B-R	5-9	145	12-27-04	.239	.322	.289	56	184	159	27	38	5	0	1	21	20	1	1	3	24	32	7	10.87	13.04
Ramos, Raylin	R-R	6-1	180	12-1-04	.218	.271	.273	17	59	55	7	12	3	0	0	4	4	0	0	0	11	0	1	6.78	18.64
Robinson, Errol	R-R	5-10	170	10-1-94	.429	.500	.429	2	8	7	2	3	0	0	0	2	1	0	0	0	1	0	0	12.50	12.50
Rodriguez, Carlos	R-R	5-11	195	10-14-03	.338	.405	.415	26	74	65	9	22	5	0	0	14	8	0	0	1	19	1	1	10.81	25.68
Rodriguez, Miguel	R-R	5-11	160	12-29-05	.308	.419	.421	49	162	133	26	41	6	0	3	15	20	6	1	1	18	3	4	12.35	11.11
Ruiz, Yirber	B-R	6-1	160	10-8-04	.195	.313	.195	24	49	41	4	8	0	0	0	2	6	1	1	0	16	2	4	12.24	32.65
Tavera, Braylin	R-R	6-2	175	2-19-05	.143	.333	.143	3	9	7	1	1	0	0	0	0	1	1	0	0	3	0	1	11.11	33.33
Trimble, Reed	B-R	6-0	180	6-6-00	.143	.563	.143	5	16	7	2	1	0	0	0	1	8	0	0	1	2	1	0	50.00	12.50
Valdez, Luis	B-R	5-11	165	1-22-00	.267	.353	.300	9	34	30	9	8	1	0	0	3	4	0	0	0	6	7	1	11.76	17.65
Vavra, Terrin	L-R	6-0	185	5-12-97	.000	.250	.000	1	4	3	0	0	0	0	0	1	0	1	0	0	1	0	0	0.00	25.00
Velasquez, Alfredo	R-R	5-11	153	9-30-04	.290	.333	.387	13	33	31	10	9	1	1	0	3	1	1	0	0	5	4	0	3.03	15.15
Vicioso, Luis	R-R	5-10	188	5-7-03	.219	.313	.260	33	83	73	9	16	1	1	0	5	9	1	0	0	22	2	2	10.84	26.51
Wagner, Max	R-R	6-0	215	8-19-01	.250	.250	.250	1	4	4	0	1	0	0	0	0	0	0	0	0	0	0	0	0.00	0.00

Pitching	B-T	Ht.	Wt.	DOB	W	L	ERA	G	GS	SV	IP	Hits	Runs	ER	HR	BB	SO	AVG	OBP	SLG	SO%	BB%	BF
Alberto, Eddy	R-R	6-2	190	3-10-02	0	0	4.22	6	0	0	11	10	5	5	1	6	17	.250	.362	.425	36.17	12.77	47
Arias, Harol	R-R	6-2	180	11-7-02	4	2	6.12	18	0	1	25	27	18	17	3	19	22	.284	.410	.411	18.80	16.24	117
Bautista, Bryan	R-R	6-3	175	2-8-04	2	2	4.74	12	7	1	38	34	23	20	1	15	41	.241	.325	.340	25.47	9.32	161
Benavides, Cristian	R-R	6-0	155	5-11-05	0	1	4.50	2	0	0	2	2	2	1	0	1	3	.250	.333	.250	33.33	11.11	9
Brito, Carlos	R-R	5-11	160	8-22-02	1	3	8.49	17	0	0	23	36	23	22	3	17	19	.343	.431	.495	15.45	13.82	123
Bucce, Yasmil	S-R	5-11	168	8-13-04	1	0	0.00	2	0	0	2	3	0	0	0	0	0	.333	.333	.444	0.00	0.00	9
Campos, Edrei	L-R	6-1	165	5-8-05	0	0	27.00	2	0	0	1	4	4	4	1	0	0	.500	.556	1.000	0.00	0.00	9
Cartaya, Yeiber	R-R	6-5	165	1-20-03	0	4	4.02	11	9	0	40	32	25	18	4	29	58	.211	.337	.329	31.35	15.68	185
Chandler, Cooper	R-R	6-2	200	8-12-98	1	0	0.00	3	1	0	3	2	0	0	0	1	5	.167	.231	.167	38.46	7.69	13
Correa, Eccel	R-R	6-0	170	2-1-03	1	0	0.00	1	1	0	5.0	4	0	0	0	0	3	.200	.273	.200	13.64	0.00	22
Guzman, Ronald	L-L	6-5	235	10-20-94	0	1	2.08	4	0	1	4	2	3	1	0	6	7	.133	.381	.133	33.33	28.57	21
LaRoche, Kelvin	R-R	5-11	170	7-31-99	2	1	5.23	9	0	0	10	12	8	6	0	7	9	.308	.426	.410	19.15	14.89	47

Pitching	B-T	Ht.	Wt.	DOB	W	L	ERA	G	GS	SV	IP	Hits	Runs	ER	HR	BB	SO	AVG	OBP	SLG	SO%	BB%	BF
Leandro, Alberto	R-R	6-3	171	4-24-02	2	1	5.86	10	5	0	35	34	25	23	0	22	30	.258	.380	.333	18.18	13.33	165
Leandro, Jose	L-L	6-3	187	4-24-02	3	1	6.75	13	2	0	23	24	19	17	3	19	22	.279	.431	.453	20.18	17.43	109
Lloyd, Daniel	R-R	6-3	232	8-8-00	0	0	0.00	1	1	0	2	2	0	0	0	1	1	.250	.333	.250	11.11	11.11	9
Loeprich, Conner	R-R	6-3	215	9-13-97	0	0	0.00	1	1	0	1	1	0	0	0	0	1	.250	.250	.250	25.00	0.00	4
Maruskin, Jack	R-R	6-2	200	12-15-99	1	3	10.54	13	0	0	14	12	20	16	0	27	15	.240	.531	.320	18.52	33.33	81
Mesa, Miguel	R-R	6-2	188	2-5-03	1	4	6.27	9	6	0	19	20	15	13	0	20	24	.270	.438	.351	25.00	20.83	96
Morao, Francisco	L-L	6-2	178	11-15-05	0	2	7.40	10	8	1	24	23	21	20	0	18	26	.237	.364	.289	22.03	15.25	118
Nierman, Hayden	S-R	6-2	170	1-27-00	0	0	0.00	1	0	0	2	1	0	0	0	0	1	.143	.143	.143	14.29	0.00	7
Nolaya, Andres	R-R	6-1	185	3-27-05	0	0	0.00	1	0	0	1	2	0	0	0	0	1	.500	.500	.500	25.00	0.00	4
Ochoa, Nelvis	R-R	5-10	158	1-18-03	0	3	4.71	9	7	0	21	19	11	11	3	5	24	.253	.306	.413	27.91	5.81	86
Palacios, Jesus	R-R	6-2	167	3-7-05	2	3	5.08	10	5	0	28	21	19	16	2	21	37	.198	.336	.311	28.91	16.41	128
Parra, Andres	L-L	5-11	160	3-19-05	0	1	3.20	12	1	1	25	22	12	9	0	11	25	.234	.311	.298	23.58	10.38	106
Peguero, Fernando	S-R	5-9	145	12-27-04	0	0	0.00	1	0	0	0	0	0	0	0	0	0	.000	.000	.000	0.00	0.00	1
Rinehart, Logan	R-R	6-3	185	9-21-97	0	1	27.00	1	0	0	1	3	3	3	1	1	0	.600	.667	1.200	0.00	16.67	6
Rodriguez, Aneuris	R-R	6-3	185	6-14-04	0	3	7.97	7	3	0	20	21	23	18	2	17	18	.253	.379	.386	17.14	16.19	105
Rodriguez, Carlos	R-R	5-11	195	10-14-03	0	0	0.00	1	0	0	1	0	0	0	0	0	1	.000	.000	.000	25.00	0.00	4
Rodriguez, Eris	R-R	6-3	188	9-10-01	1	0	4.41	10	0	1	16	17	12	8	0	10	15	.270	.377	.349	18.99	12.66	79
Rojas, Juan	L-L	6-0	165	1-31-04	0	0	0.00	1	1	0	1	0	0	0	0	1	1	.000	.333	.000	33.33	33.33	3
Ruiz, Yirber	S-R	6-1	160	10-8-04	0	0	7.20	3	0	0	5	6	4	4	1	3	1	.286	.423	.571	3.85	11.54	26
Showalter, Justin	R-R	6-2	190	2-2-99	0	0	0.00	1	0	0	2	2	2	0	0	1	1	.250	.333	.250	10.00	10.00	10
Solano, Issac	R-R	6-6	195	10-23-01	1	0	0.00	2	0	0	3	3	2	0	0	2	3	.231	.333	.231	20.00	13.33	15
Van Loon, Peter	R-R	6-5	210	2-18-99	0	0	0.00	1	1	0	2	2	0	0	0	0	2	.250	.250	.250	25.00	0.00	8
Vicioso, Luis	R-R	5-10	188	5-7-03	0	0	0.00	3	0	0	3	0	0	0	0	5	5	.000	.412	.000	29.41	29.41	17

Fielding

C: Mordan 19, Bucce 18, Rodriguez 13, Baez 10, Pavolony 3, Hernandez 2, Viloria 2, Urman 1, Mantecon 1. **1B:** Mordan 16, Gonzalez 11, Castillo 10, C: Rodriguez 26, Nolaya 22, Bucce 14, Rodriguez 5. 1B: Rodriguez 16, Bucce 14, Rodriguez 13, Nolaya 11, Vicioso 5, Cuevas 5, Vavra 1. 2B: Amparo 32, Campos 15, Peguero 5, Benavides 3, Valdez 2, Velasquez 2, Robinson 1, Arias 1. 3B: Almeyda 18, Liranzo 17, Campos 8, Benavides 6, Hernandez 5, Amparo 5, Velasquez 2, Wagner 1, Cuevas 1. SS: Almeyda 24, Amparo 11, Hernandez 7, Liranzo 6, Campos 5, Arias 4, Velasquez 3. LF: Ruiz 17, Vicioso 17, Peguero 14, Benavides 14, Velasquez 3, Campos 2, Mesa 1. CF: Peguero 35, Cuevas 17, Valdez 4, Trimble 2, Cunningham 1, Tavera 1, Benavides 1. RF: Cuevas 36, Ramos 10, Vicioso 7, Velasquez 3, Benavides 3, Peguero 2, Ruiz 2, Tavera 1, Trimble 1.

DSL ORIOLES BLACK

DOMINICAN SUMMER LEAGUE

Batting	B-T	Ht.	Wt.	DOB	AVG	OBP	SLG	G	PA	AB	R	H	2B	3B	HR	RBI	BB	HBP	SH	SF	SO	SB	CS	BB%	SO%
Amparo, Felix	R-R	5-10	180	2-27-06	.321	.399	.496	41	159	131	27	42	4	2	5	36	12	9	1	6	10	19	2	7.55	6.29
Chirinos, Frainner	R-R	6-3	164	2-1-07	.171	.408	.300	32	98	70	15	12	3	0	2	8	25	3	0	0	32	3	0	25.51	32.65
Cohen, Abraham	L-L	6-1	175	6-15-06	.198	.408	.278	48	174	126	21	25	6	2	0	15	38	8	0	2	36	13	2	21.84	20.69
Corniel, Enmanuel	L-R	6-1	160	2-16-07	.147	.290	.227	29	93	75	11	11	1	1	1	11	15	1	0	2	28	2	2	16.13	30.11
Frias, Wander	B-L	5-10	155	9-5-05	.087	.283	.130	24	62	46	16	4	0	1	0	5	10	3	1	1	15	7	2	16.13	24.19
Garcia, Elvin	B-R	6-2	165	1-18-07	.294	.439	.505	36	139	109	22	32	10	5	1	20	27	2	0	1	25	12	1	19.42	17.99
Garcia, Juan	R-R	5-11	165	9-2-06	.083	.115	.125	8	27	24	1	2	1	0	0	2	1	0	1	1	15	0	0	3.70	55.56
Leonte, Raul	L-L	6-1	170	5-7-06	.270	.341	.270	14	41	37	6	10	0	0	0	3	4	0	0	0	9	2	0	9.76	21.95
Martinez, Juan	R-R	6-4	175	9-19-04	.089	.281	.156	19	57	45	5	4	3	0	0	4	11	1	0	0	10	2	0	19.30	17.54
Mejia, Jose	R-R	5-11	175	9-29-05	.300	.410	.413	44	178	150	40	45	9	1	2	19	24	4	0	0	16	28	6	13.48	8.99
Nuel, Jemone	B-R	6-0	150	1-3-07	.208	.371	.357	50	198	154	29	32	8	3	3	24	38	3	1	2	60	20	4	19.19	30.30
Ortega, Juan	R-R	5-8	177	4-10-06	.253	.423	.380	32	105	79	14	20	4	0	2	9	11	13	1	1	16	9	4	10.48	15.24
Rincon, Alexander	L-L	6-2	175	9-16-06	.284	.338	.381	45	146	134	22	38	5	4	0	9	10	1	1	0	30	12	3	6.85	20.55
Robain, Jhonanderson	R-R	6-0	176	1-14-06	.213	.403	.298	20	62	47	7	10	2	1	0	6	12	3	0	0	15	4	3	19.35	24.19
Urbina, Omar	R-R	6-1	175	9-1-05	.242	.353	.288	45	156	132	16	32	3	0	1	24	17	6	0	1	24	2	0	10.90	15.38
Valdez, Argenis	R-R	6-3	160	1-15-07	.163	.277	.221	30	101	86	9	14	5	0	0	6	12	2	0	1	25	4	3	11.88	24.75
Valenzuela, Cleudis	L-R	5-10	160	11-9-06	.213	.398	.263	31	108	80	13	17	4	0	0	8	25	1	0	2	16	7	7	23.15	14.81

Pitching	B-T	Ht.	Wt.	DOB	W	L	ERA	G	GS	SV	IP	Hits	Runs	ER	HR	BB	SO	AVG	OBP	SLG	SO%	BB%	BF
Amparo, Felix	R-R	5-10	180	2-27-06	0	0	0.00	1	0	0	2	0	0	0	0	1	1	.000	.333	.000	11.11	11.11	9
Bolivar, Angel	R-R	6-1	175	10-1-05	0	3	4.87	6	6	0	20	22	13	11	0	11	17	.286	.402	.416	18.28	11.83	93
Bonilla, Ezequiel	R-R	6-1	160	8-12-05	0	0	0.00	1	0	0	1	0	0	0	0	2	0	.000	.286	.000	0.00	28.57	7
Casado, Salvador	R-R	6-3	198	3-16-06	2	2	6.07	15	6	0	30	25	25	20	0	24	32	.231	.391	.250	23.02	17.27	139
De Los Santos, David	R-R	6-1	179	10-6-05	0	0	0.00	3	0	0	5	3	0	0	0	0	3	.176	.176	.176	17.65	0.00	17
Delgado, Adrian	R-R	6-3	182	5-12-05	3	2	6.86	16	0	2	19.2	13	21	15	0	28	23	.188	.423	.217	23.71	28.87	97
Duran, Juan	R-R	6-0	160	11-25-03	3	3	2.92	17	0	1	25	15	10	8	0	15	25	.176	.324	.247	23.58	14.15	106
Fabian, Andy	L-L	6-4	210	1-1-03	0	3	3.15	9	9	0	34	31	18	12	2	13	45	.231	.309	.313	30.20	8.72	149
Frias, Wander	S-L	5-10	155	9-5-05	0	1	40.50	2	0	0	2	6	10	9	0	4	0	.600	.733	.700	0.00	25.00	16
Gonzalez, Javier	R-R	6-0	150	9-22-05	0	2	3.93	10	8	0	34	35	19	15	0	11	38	.261	.333	.328	25.33	7.33	150
Gonzalez, Ledwin	L-L	5-11	160	6-22-06	0	1	11.88	8	0	0	8	8	11	11	0	10	8	.235	.435	.265	17.39	21.74	46
Herrera, Ronal	R-R	6-2	180	3-10-03	2	2	3.38	13	0	1	21	15	12	8	0	14	28	.200	.348	.267	30.43	15.22	92
Javier, Robinson	R-R	6-2	170	10-8-05	0	1	7.20	3	1	0	5	5	5	4	1	4	6	.263	.417	.421	25.00	16.67	24
Jules, Guachi	R-R	6-2	180	11-14-03	0	0	12.27	4	0	0	4	6	9	5	0	4	4	.333	.520	.500	16.00	16.00	25
Leonte, Raul	L-L	6-1	170	5-7-06	0	0	27.00	2	0	0	1	2	4	4	1	4	0	.400	.667	1.200	0.00	44.44	9
Luna, Esteban	R-R	5-11	168	9-28-06	1	1	1.49	9	9	0	36	21	7	6	0	16	35	.169	.273	.202	24.48	11.19	143
Magallanes, Fermin	R-R	6-7	170	2-17-02	5	1	3.95	19	0	1	27	9	16	12	0	27	42	.102	.333	.125	34.71	22.31	121
Mejia, Esteban	R-R	6-3	175	3-7-07	0	2	3.32	8	8	0	22	14	9	8	0	11	35	.187	.319	.227	38.04	11.96	92
Moscoso, Elias	R-R	5-11	162	3-27-05	1	0	13.50	12	0	1	9	9	17	13	2	20	7	.281	.579	.563	12.07	34.48	58
Naut, Harlin	R-R	6-2	161	4-26-05	0	0	0.00	1	0	0	1	0	0	0	0	0	0	.000	.000	.000	0.00	0.00	3
Robain, Jhonanderson	R-R	6-0	176	1-14-06	0	0	0.00	2	0	2	1	0	0	0	0	1	0	.000	.250	.000	0.00	25.00	4

Pitching	B-T	Ht.	Wt.	DOB	W	L	ERA	G	GS	SV	IP	Hits	Runs	ER	HR	BB	SO	AVG	OBP	SLG	SO%	BB%	BF
Rondon, Wilton	R-R	6-2	185	9-10-02	3	1	4.12	12	0	1	20	13	12	9	2	7	19	.186	.275	.300	23.46	8.64	81
Rubi, Reykelly	L-L	6-0	180	10-5-05	1	1	5.06	9	4	0	21.1	24	14	12	3	4	27	.276	.312	.425	29.03	4.30	93
Santos, Victor	L-L	6-0	153	4-19-07	1	0	6.08	9	2	0	13	10	12	9	1	8	14	.204	.328	.286	24.14	13.79	58
Sosa, Raymond	R-R	6-4	185	5-3-06	1	0	4.85	11	0	0	13	12	8	7	0	9	11	.235	.391	.255	17.19	14.06	64
Suero, Rafael	R-R	6-2	180	5-7-06	2	3	7.71	16	0	1	21	25	24	18	0	19	21	.294	.440	.388	18.92	17.12	111
Tena, Andy	L-L	6-1	172	2-22-04	0	0	9.58	8	0	0	10	13	14	11	1	15	8	.310	.500	.500	13.79	25.86	58
Torres, Eduardo	R-R	6-2	155	12-23-03	1	0	7.71	3	0	0	2	3	2	2	0	4	1	.333	.538	.889	7.69	30.77	13
Velasco, Kevin	R-R	6-11	155	1-11-06	0	0	0.00	2	2	0	8	2	0	0	0	2	9	.077	.143	.115	32.14	7.14	28

Fielding

C: Ortega 24, Urbina 21, Robain 14, Garcia 3, Frias 1. 1B: Urbina 13, Mejia 11, Amparo 10, Valenzuela 10, Chirinos 8, Martinez 5, Garcia 3, Ortega 3. 2B: Mejia 28, Valenzuela 17, Amparo 9, Frias 5. 3B: Chirinos 24, Amparo 13, Garcia 13, Nuel 9, Frias 3. SS: Nuel 37, Garcia 20. LF: Valdez 15, Corniel 12, Leonte 12, Martinez 7, Robain 5, Frias 4, Rincon 3, Cohen 3. CF: Rincon 42, Corniel 12, Cohen 9. RF: Cohen 35, Valdez 15, Martinez 7, Corniel 4.

DSL ORIOLES ORANGE

DOMINICAN SUMMER LEAGUE

Batting	B-T	Ht.	Wt.	DOB	AVG	OBP	SLG	G	PA	AB	R	H	2B	3B	HR	RBI	BB	HBP	SH	SF	SO	SB	CS	BB%	SO%
Amparo, Felix	R-R	5-10	180	2-27-06	.281	.314	.531	9	35	32	4	9	3	1	1	3	1	1	0	1	6	5	2	2.86	17.14
Astudillo, Christian	R-R	6-0	188	6-13-07	.295	.421	.359	27	96	78	8	23	5	0	0	17	12	5	1	0	16	1	1	12.50	16.67
Aybar, Junior	L-R	6-0	145	7-14-06	.247	.363	.365	38	102	85	21	21	3	2	1	20	16	0	0	1	23	18	0	15.69	22.55
Campusano, Hector	B-R	5-10	160	4-24-07	.240	.398	.341	45	166	129	29	31	7	0	2	22	29	6	0	2	28	12	8	17.47	16.87
De Los Santos, Sebastian	B-R	5-10	145	6-16-06	.215	.426	.253	33	109	79	21	17	3	0	0	11	26	3	1	0	28	12	2	23.85	25.69
Feliciano, Wilmer	L-R	6-3	190	4-6-04	.000	.000	.000	1	4	4	0	0	0	0	0	0	0	0	0	0	1	0	0	0.00	25.00
Frias, Wander	B-L	5-10	155	9-5-05	.000	.250	.000	4	8	6	2	0	0	0	0	0	1	1	0	0	3	1	0	12.50	37.50
Garcia, Angel	R-R	6-2	195	11-13-06	.219	.371	.333	38	143	114	22	25	5	1	2	25	19	9	0	1	37	3	3	13.29	25.87
Garcia, Juan	R-R	5-11	165	9-2-06	.083	.320	.111	15	50	36	5	3	1	0	0	3	9	4	0	1	15	2	0	18.00	30.00
Gomez, Saul	R-R	6-0	178	7-27-07	.294	.403	.361	44	144	119	27	35	5	0	1	21	18	5	0	2	28	5	0	12.50	19.44
Guevara, Luis	B-R	5-8	167	2-6-06	.273	.424	.318	40	144	110	33	30	5	0	0	17	28	3	0	3	21	20	1	19.44	14.58
Martinez, Stiven	R-R	6-4	198	8-8-07	.278	.417	.466	41	168	133	27	37	5	4	4	33	28	5	0	2	51	2	4	16.67	30.36
Mejia, Adriander	R-R	6-0	165	8-29-06	.291	.419	.392	50	198	158	38	46	6	2	2	34	33	4	0	3	15	6	0	16.67	7.58
Ortega, Juan	R-R	5-8	177	4-10-06	.143	.538	.286	10	26	14	7	2	2	0	0	3	7	5	0	0	8	3	0	26.92	30.77
Perez, Jose	L-R	5-10	150	5-15-05	.259	.363	.295	37	135	112	21	29	2	1	0	12	17	3	0	3	39	16	4	12.59	28.89
Ramirez, Breiny	L-L	6-4	180	5-19-06	.215	.303	.380	33	89	79	15	17	5	1	2	15	8	2	0	0	29	2	4	8.99	32.58
Rojas, Elvis	L-L	6-3	175	9-25-05	.132	.327	.237	17	49	38	6	5	2	1	0	2	11	0	0	0	16	3	1	22.45	32.65
Sanchez, Emilio	L-R	6-1	160	4-13-07	.212	.416	.281	48	203	146	37	31	2	4	0	14	48	5	1	3	35	29	2	23.65	17.24
Sanchez, Jordan	L-L	6-1	176	10-9-05	.333	.432	.605	38	155	129	33	43	13	2	6	37	23	1	0	2	31	5	2	14.84	20.00

Pitching	B-T	Ht.	Wt.	DOB	W	L	ERA	G	GS	SV	IP	Hits	Runs	ER	HR	BB	SO	AVG	OBP	SLG	SO%	BB%	BF
Beltran, Luis	R-R	6-4	175	4-6-04	3	0	4.38	18	0	1	25	10	14	12	2	28	42	.123	.360	.222	37.84	25.23	111
Bonilla, Ezequiel	R-R	6-1	160	8-12-05	5	2	3.68	16	3	1	29	22	14	12	0	23	29	.218	.362	.327	22.66	17.97	128
De Los Santos, David	R-R	6-1	179	10-6-05	0	0	1.35	6	0	0	7	6	1	1	0	4	7	.240	.345	.280	24.14	13.79	29
Espinoza, Luis	R-R	6-2	194	12-11-06	0	0	3.77	11	10	0	43	38	23	18	2	13	34	.236	.302	.360	18.89	7.22	180
Fabian, Andy	L-L	6-4	210	1-1-03	0	0	0.00	1	0	0	3	1	0	0	0	2	0	.125	.300	.125	0.00	20.00	10
Gonzalez, Ledwin	L-L	5-11	160	6-22-06	0	0	15.75	4	0	0	4	7	7	7	0	14	5	.368	.636	.368	15.15	42.42	33
Heredia, Adrian	R-R	6-1	185	11-16-04	2	0	1.83	11	11	0	44	32	10	9	2	18	56	.205	.290	.276	31.82	10.23	176
Herrera, Ronal	R-R	6-2	180	3-10-03	2	0	0.00	5	0	0	7	1	0	0	0	3	7	.050	.259	.050	25.00	10.71	28
Javier, Robinson	R-R	6-2	170	10-8-05	5	0	4.24	12	0	1	17	14	10	8	1	11	20	.219	.338	.328	25.64	14.10	78
Jules, Guachi	R-R	6-2	180	11-14-03	3	2	4.50	12	0	0	14	9	9	7	1	19	12	.184	.431	.265	16.67	26.39	72
Luna, Esteban	R-R	5-11	168	9-28-06	0	0	3.00	2	2	0	6	3	2	2	0	6	6	.143	.357	.143	21.43	21.43	28
Mejia, Esteban	R-R	6-3	175	3-7-07	0	1	3.00	2	2	0	6	4	6	2	0	4	9	.167	.276	.208	31.03	13.79	29
Mora, Jeyderson	R-R	6-0	145	3-13-05	1	2	3.72	10	8	0	29	20	15	12	0	18	28	.183	.321	.248	21.37	13.74	131
Moreta, Oscar	R-R	6-2	180	10-12-03	4	1	3.68	12	0	0	22	16	13	9	0	19	29	.203	.373	.253	28.43	18.63	102
Morfe, Keeler	R-R	5-8	161	6-9-06	0	1	0.82	7	7	0	22	11	4	2	0	8	38	.141	.221	.167	44.19	9.30	86
Naut, Harlin	R-R	6-2	161	4-26-05	0	0	1.93	6	0	1	9	7	4	2	0	4	7	.226	.324	.355	18.42	10.53	38
Rasquin, Juan	S-R	6-3	165	12-24-05	1	1	3.48	10	7	0	34	18	20	13	0	24	37	.153	.303	.203	25.34	16.44	146
Rondon, Wilton	R-R	6-2	185	9-10-02	1	1	3.38	4	0	0	5	6	3	2	0	1	6	.273	.304	.318	25.00	4.17	24
Tejada, Henry	R-R	6-0	160	9-15-04	3	1	2.00	9	1	2	18	12	9	4	0	8	16	.185	.303	.277	20.78	10.39	77
Valenzuela, Esmerlyn	S-R	6-0	170	1-2-03	3	2	8.31	16	0	3	22	22	22	20	3	18	25	.262	.410	.488	23.58	16.98	106
Velasco, Kevin	R-R	6-11	155	1-11-06	1	0	1.41	9	5	0	32	23	8	5	0	8	43	.200	.258	.235	34.68	6.45	124
Vizcaino, Santhony	R-R	6-5	160	10-18-03	4	3	6.29	15	0	2	24	26	19	17	0	13	15	.271	.357	.354	13.27	11.50	113
Yan, Jose	R-R	6-2	200	10-15-00	0	1	8.38	10	0	0	10	9	15	9	0	12	12	.225	.426	.325	22.22	22.22	54

Fielding

C: Mejia 25, Astudillo 17, Garcia 12, Ortega 8. 1B: Gomez 19, Mejia 13, De Los Santos 9, Astudillo 5, Perez 5, Aybar 4, Ortega 2, Amparo 2, Campusano 1, Feliciano 1, Garcia 1. 2B: Campusano 26, De Los Santos 20, Perez 9, Guevara 6, Amparo 4, Frias 3, Aybar 1. 3B: Perez 16, Gomez 13, Guevara 13, Aybar 8, Sanchez 8, De Los Santos 6, Amparo 2. SS: Sanchez 34, Guevara 20, Perez 9, Aybar 1. LF: Ramirez 26, Garcia 16, Campusano 14, Martinez 5, Sanchez 4, Aybar 3, Rojas 1. CF: Martinez 29, Aybar 22, Sanchez 12, Ramirez 2, Campusano 1, Garcia 1. RF: Garcia 22, Sanchez 19, Rojas 12, Campusano 6, Martinez 4, Ramirez 1.

Boston Red Sox

SEASON SYNOPSIS: The Red Sox missed the playoffs for the third straight season, their longest such streak since Bobby Valentine's disastrous one-year managerial stint. The Sox lost momentum in the second half but rallied late to avoid a third straight losing season, finishing 81-81

HIGH POINT: A strong first half left Boston 10 games above .500 by the all-star break. Four straight series wins to open July included taking two out of three in the Bronx against the Yankees and winning two of three at Fenway Park against Kansas City just before the break. Righthanders Brayan Bello, Kutter Crawford and Tanner Houck—three homegrown starters who combined for 93 starts—helped lead the way. Crawford tossed seven shutout innings in each of those series, while Houck tossed six scoreless against the Athletics, and Bello set a career-high with 11 strikeouts against them.

LOW POINT: The Sox quickly dispelled notions that they were contenders by losing their first three series (going 2-7) out of the break, the low point being a four-error, 20-7 boat race in Colorado. The Rockies hit four home runs and tied their franchise record for runs. Boston went just 4-11 against National League West teams on the season.

NOTABLE ROOKIES: Right fielder Wilyer Abreu looked like a keeper, at least against righthanded pitchers, hitting .253/.322/.459 with 33 doubles and 15 home runs to establish himself as a starter. A broken left hand ended his season in August, but not before David Hamilton, who stole 33 bases and was a capable defender at shortstop, made himself a factor for the future. Lefty Cam Booser provided one of the season's best stories; originally signed by the Twins in 2013 as a nondrafted free agent, he quit in 2017 due to a host of injuries but returned to baseball with an independent team in 2021 and reached the majors in 2024, making 43 relief appearances.

KEY TRANSACTIONS: Craig Breslow, in his first offseason as chief baseball officer, had a mixed bag, trading away Chris Sale to Atlanta for salary relief and Vaughn Grissom, who was injured most of the season. His trade for outfielder Tyler O'Neill, who led the team with 31 homers, paid short-term dividends in the last year of O'Neill's team control.

OPENING DAY PAYROLL: $176,458,748 (12th)

PLAYERS OF THE YEAR

MAJOR LEAGUE

Jarren Duran
OF
.285/.342/.492
21 HR, 34 SB
AL-best 48 2B, 14 3B

MINOR LEAGUE

Kristian Campbell
2B/OF
(A+/AA/AAA)
.330/.439/.558
20 HR, 24 SB

ORGANIZATION LEADERS

Batting		*Qualifiers
MAJORS		
* AVG	Jarren Duran	.285
* OPS	Rafael Devers	.870
HR	Rafael Devers	83
RBI	Rafael Devers	100
MINORS		
* AVG	Kristian Campbell, Greenville/Portland/Worcester	.330
* OBP	Kristian Campbell, Greenville/Portland/Worcester	.439
* SLG	Kristian Campbell, Greenville/Portland/Worcester	.558
* OPS	Kristian Campbell, Greenville/Portland/Worcester	.997
R	Kristian Campbell, Greenville/Portland/Worcester	94
H	Kristian Campbell, Greenville/Portland/Worcester	142
TB	Kristian Campbell, Greenville/Portland/Worcester	240
2B	Kristian Campbell, Greenville/Portland/Worcester	32
2B	Roman Anthony, Portland/Worcester	32
3B	Natanael Yuten, Salem	7
HR	Jhostynxon Garcia, Salem/Greenville/Portland	23
RBI	Kyle Teel, Worcester/Portland	78
BB	Chase Meidroth, Worcester	105
SO	Ahbram Liendo, Greenville/Portland	162
SB	Miguel Bleis, Salem/Greenville	38

Pitching		#Qualifiers
MAJORS		
W	Brayan Bello	14
# ERA	Tanner Houck	3.12
SO	Kutter Crawford	175
SV	Kenley Jansen	27
MINORS		
W	Robert Kwiatkowski, Worcester/Portland	13
L	Connelly Early, Greenville/Portland	9
# ERA	Hunter Dobbins, Portland/Worcester	3.08
G	Wyatt Olds, Worcester/Portland	43
GS	Jason Alexander, Worcester	27
SV	Felix Cepeda, Portland	14
IP	Jason Alexander, Worcester	138
BB	Wyatt Olds, Worcester/Portland	55
SO	Isaac Coffey, Portland	148
# AVG	Isaac Coffey, Portland	.215

2024 PERFORMANCE

General Manager: Craig Breslow. **Farm Director:** Brian Abraham. **Scouting Director:** Devin Pearson.

Class	Team	League	W	L	PCT	Finish	Manager
Majors	Boston Red Sox	American	81	81	.500	9 (15)	Alex Cora
Triple-A	Worcester Red Sox	International	79	71	.527	5 (20)	Chad Tracy
Double-A	Portland Sea Dogs	Eastern	78	60	.565	3 (12)	Chad Epperson
High-A	Greenville Drive	South Atlantic	63	69	.477	8 (12)	Iggy Suarez
Low-A	Salem Red Sox	Carolina	70	62	.530	5 (12)	Liam Carroll
Rookie	FCL Red Sox	Florida Complex	35	24	.593	6 (15)	Jimmy Gonzalez
Rookie	DSL Red Sox Blue	Dominican	27	26	.509	24 (51)	Amaury Garcia
Rookie	DSL Red Sox Red	Dominican	42	14	.750	2 (51)	Sandy Madera
Overall 2024 Minor League Record			**394**	**326**	**.547**	**4th (30)**	

ORGANIZATION STATISTICS

BOSTON RED SOX

AMERICAN LEAGUE

Batting	B-T	Ht.	Wt.	DOB	AVG	OBP	SLG	G	PA	AB	R	H	2B	3B	HR	RBI	BB	HBP	SH	SF	SO	SB	CS	BB%	SO%
Abreu, Wilyer	L-L	5-10	217	6-24-99	.253	.322	.459	132	447	399	59	101	33	2	15	58	40	3	0	5	125	8	3	8.95	27.96
Casas, Triston	L-R	6-4	252	1-15-00	.241	.337	.462	63	243	212	28	51	8	0	13	32	30	1	0	0	77	0	1	12.35	31.69
Cooper, Garrett	R-R	6-5	235	12-25-90	.171	.227	.229	24	75	70	3	12	4	0	0	5	3	2	0	0	22	0	0	4.00	29.33
Dalbec, Bobby	R-R	6-4	227	6-29-95	.133	.217	.193	37	93	83	6	11	2	0	1	8	8	1	1	0	43	3	0	8.60	46.24
Devers, Rafael	L-R	6-0	240	10-24-96	.272	.354	.516	138	601	525	87	143	34	5	28	83	67	3	0	6	147	3	0	11.15	24.46
Duran, Jarren	L-R	6-2	212	9-5-96	.285	.342	.492	160	735	671	111	191	48	14	21	75	54	6	1	3	160	34	7	7.35	21.77
Gasper, Mickey	B-R	5-9	205	10-11-95	.000	.217	.000	13	23	18	1	0	0	0	0	0	4	1	0	0	8	0	0	17.39	34.78
Gonzalez, Romy	R-R	6-1	215	9-6-96	.266	.306	.417	89	216	199	25	53	10	1	6	29	12	1	0	4	58	11	3	5.56	26.85
Grissom, Vaughn	R-R	6-2	210	1-5-01	.190	.246	.219	31	114	105	10	20	3	0	0	6	7	1	0	1	24	2	0	6.14	21.05
Hamilton, David	L-R	5-10	175	9-29-97	.248	.303	.395	98	317	294	47	73	17	1	8	28	22	1	0	0	80	33	4	6.94	25.24
Heineman, Tyler	B-R	5-10	190	6-19-91	.000	.333	.000	2	3	2	0	0	0	0	0	0	0	1	0	0	1	0	0	0.00	33.33
Jansen, Danny	R-R	6-2	215	4-15-95	.188	.323	.300	30	96	80	8	15	0	0	3	6	15	1	0	0	19	0	0	15.63	19.79
McGuire, Reese	L-R	6-0	218	3-2-95	.209	.280	.295	53	158	139	10	29	3	0	3	18	13	2	1	3	39	3	0	8.23	24.68
O'Neill, Tyler	R-R	5-11	200	6-22-95	.241	.336	.511	113	473	411	74	99	18	0	31	61	53	7	0	2	159	4	0	11.21	33.62
Rafaela, Ceddanne	R-R	5-9	152	9-18-00	.246	.274	.390	152	571	544	70	134	23	5	15	75	15	7	2	3	151	19	10	2.63	26.44
Refsnyder, Rob	R-R	6-0	205	3-26-91	.283	.359	.471	93	307	272	32	77	16	1	11	40	28	5	0	1	78	2	2	9.12	25.41
Reyes, Pablo	R-R	5-8	175	9-5-93	.183	.234	.217	21	64	60	4	11	2	0	0	5	3	1	0	0	19	1	2	4.69	29.69
Short, Zack	R-R	5-10	180	5-29-95	.000	.000	.000	2	7	7	0	0	0	0	0	0	0	0	0	0	4	0	0	0.00	57.14
Smith, Dominic	L-L	6-0	224	6-15-95	.237	.317	.390	84	278	249	29	59	20	0	6	34	25	4	0	0	65	1	1	8.99	23.38
Sogard, Nick	B-R	6-1	180	9-9-97	.273	.326	.325	31	86	77	13	21	4	0	0	8	7	0	0	2	25	3	0	8.14	29.07
Story, Trevor	R-R	6-2	213	11-15-92	.255	.340	.394	26	106	94	8	24	7	0	2	10	11	1	0	0	33	6	3	10.38	31.13
Valdez, Enmanuel	L-R	5-8	191	12-28-98	.214	.270	.363	76	223	201	23	43	12	0	6	28	17	0	1	4	53	1	1	7.62	23.77
Westbrook, Jamie	R-R	5-7	193	6-18-95	.150	.234	.350	21	48	40	4	6	2	0	2	7	4	1	0	2	14	0	0	8.33	29.17
Wong, Connor	R-R	6-1	181	5-19-96	.280	.333	.425	126	487	447	54	125	24	1	13	52	28	9	1	2	114	8	7	5.75	23.41
Yoshida, Masataka	L-R	5-8	176	7-15-93	.280	.349	.415	108	421	378	45	106	21	0	10	56	27	14	0	2	52	2	0	6.41	12.35

Pitching	B-T	Ht.	Wt.	DOB	W	L	ERA	G	GS	SV	IP	Hits	Runs	ER	HR	BB	SO	AVG	OBP	SLG	SO%	BB%	BF
Anderson, Chase	R-R	6-1	210	11-30-87	0	2	4.85	27	1	3	52	46	34	28	10	19	35	.231	.305	.417	15.63	8.48	224
Bello, Brayan	R-R	6-1	170	5-17-99	14	8	4.49	30	30	0	162	157	84	81	19	64	153	.252	.330	.394	21.79	9.12	702
Bernardino, Brennan	L-L	6-4	180	1-15-92	4	3	4.06	57	3	0	51	50	25	23	6	22	56	.256	.347	.405	24.78	9.73	226
Booser, Cam	L-L	6-3	225	5-4-92	2	3	3.38	43	0	1	43	41	17	16	5	16	43	.250	.311	.390	23.50	8.74	183
Campbell, Isaiah	R-R	6-4	230	8-15-97	0	1	16.20	8	0	0	7	14	13	12	3	2	6	.400	.432	.743	16.22	5.41	37
Crawford, Kutter	R-R	6-1	209	4-1-96	9	16	4.36	33	33	0	184	155	97	89	34	51	175	.223	.284	.419	23.06	6.72	759
Criswell, Cooper	R-R	6-6	200	7-24-96	6	5	4.08	26	18	0	99	103	52	45	10	31	73	.273	.333	.422	17.22	7.31	424
Fitts, Richard	R-R	6-3	215	12-17-99	0	1	1.74	4	4	0	21	19	6	4	0	7	9	.250	.313	.289	10.59	8.24	85
Garcia, Luis	R-R	6-2	240	1-30-87	0	0	8.22	15	0	0	15	24	15	14	4	1	13	.338	.347	.620	18.06	1.39	72
Guerrero, Luis	R-R	6-0	215	8-5-00	0	0	0.00	9	0	0	10	6	1	0	0	2	9	.182	.222	.212	25.00	5.56	36
Hill, Rich	L-L	6-5	221	3-11-80	0	1	4.91	4	0	0	4	1	2	2	1	3	5	.100	.333	.400	33.33	20.00	15
Horn, Bailey	L-L	6-2	210	1-15-98	1	1	6.50	18	0	0	18	22	14	13	5	10	13	.293	.368	.547	14.77	11.36	88
Houck, Tanner	R-R	6-5	230	6-29-96	9	10	3.12	30	30	0	179	156	75	62	11	48	154	.231	.296	.320	20.73	6.46	743
Jacques, Joe	L-L	6-4	210	3-11-95	0	0	5.40	1	0	0	2	3	1	1	0	0	2	.375	.444	.500	22.22	0.00	9
Jansen, Kenley	S-R	6-5	265	9-30-87	4	2	3.29	54	0	27	55	38	20	20	4	20	62	.196	.271	.304	28.44	9.17	218
Keller, Brad	R-R	6-5	255	7-27-95	0	2	5.84	11	0	1	25	31	18	16	4	9	19	.295	.362	.467	16.38	7.76	116
Kelly, Zack	R-R	6-3	205	3-3-95	6	3	3.97	49	3	0	57	44	31	25	10	27	61	.208	.303	.387	25.31	11.20	241
Martin, Chris	R-R	6-8	225	6-2-86	3	1	3.45	45	0	2	44	47	22	17	5	3	50	.276	.298	.382	27.78	1.67	180
Paxton, James	L-L	6-4	227	11-6-88	1	1	4.09	3	3	0	11	13	8	5	1	2	9	.289	.319	.422	19.15	4.26	47
Penrod, Zach	L-L	6-2	210	6-16-97	0	0	2.25	7	0	0	4	3	2	1	0	4	3	.200	.400	.267	15.00	20.00	20
Pivetta, Nick	R-R	6-5	214	2-14-93	6	12	4.14	27	26	0	146	128	70	67	28	36	172	.231	.277	.439	28.91	6.05	595
Priester, Quinn	R-R	6-3	210	9-15-00	1	0	1.80	1	1	0	5	4	1	1	0	1	2	.222	.300	.222	10.00	5.00	20
Ramirez, Yohan	R-R	6-4	212	5-6-95	0	0	13.50	1	0	0	1	3	3	2	0	0	1	.429	.556	.571	11.11	0.00	9
Reyes, Pablo	R-R	5-8	175	9-5-93	0	0	0.00	1	0	0	1	1	0	0	0	1	0	.250	.400	.250	0.00	20.00	5
Rodriguez, Joely	L-L	6-1	200	11-14-91	0	1	5.93	14	0	0	14	19	13	9	3	2	12	.317	.344	.533	18.75	3.13	64
Shugart, Chase	L-R	5-10	198	10-24-96	0	0	4.15	6	0	1	9	8	4	4	1	3	8	.242	.306	.364	22.22	8.33	36
Sims, Lucas	R-R	6-2	213	5-10-94	0	2	6.43	15	0	0	14	11	10	10	2	10	9	.224	.361	.429	14.75	16.39	61

Pitching	B-T	Ht.	Wt.	DOB	W	L	ERA	G	GS	SV	IP	Hits	Runs	ER	HR	BB	SO	AVG	OBP	SLG	SO%	BB%	BF
Slaten, Justin	R-R	6-4	222	9-15-97	6	2	2.93	44	0	2	55	47	21	18	4	9	58	.223	.259	.318	25.89	4.02	224
Smith, Dominic	L-L	6-0	224	6-15-95	0	0	0.00	3	0	0	3	2	0	0	0	1	0	.200	.273	.300	0.00	9.09	11
Uwasawa, Naoyuki	R-R	6-1	196	2-6-94	0	0	2.25	2	0	0	4	2	1	1	0	2	3	.143	.250	.214	18.75	12.50	16
Weissert, Greg	R-R	6-2	235	2-4-95	4	2	3.13	62	0	1	63	65	32	22	7	20	58	.274	.324	.401	22.05	7.60	263
Whitlock, Garrett	R-R	6-5	225	6-11-96	1	0	1.96	4	4	0	18	14	4	4	1	7	17	.212	.297	.318	22.67	9.33	75
Winckowski, Josh	R-R	6-4	202	6-28-98	4	2	4.14	40	6	2	76	81	44	35	10	26	60	.272	.334	.423	17.86	7.74	336
Wingenter, Trey	R-R	6-7	237	4-15-94	0	0	27.00	2	0	0	2	5	7	7	1	2	3	.417	.500	.750	21.43	14.29	14

Fielding

Catcher	PCT	G	PO	A	E	DP	PB
Heineman	1.000	1	2	1	0	0	0
Jansen	.985	28	195	2	3	1	2
McGuire	.985	48	381	10	6	2	3
Wong	.995	106	817	41	4	3	3

First Base	PCT	G	PO	A	E	DP
Casas	.990	61	450	50	5	36
Cooper	.984	12	55	8	1	6
Dalbec	1.000	21	95	14	0	9
Gasper	1.000	2	1	0	0	0
Gonzalez	1.000	20	75	14	0	7
Reyes	1.000	2	8	2	0	1
Smith	.987	77	443	76	7	45
Wong	.967	14	53	5	2	5

Second Base	PCT	G	PO	A	E	DP
Gasper	1.000	6	4	11	0	0
Gonzalez	.964	31	22	32	2	9
Grissom	.976	30	35	85	3	16
Hamilton	.978	39	51	84	3	16
Rafaela	1.000	10	4	16	0	3
Reyes	1.000	9	5	17	0	2
Short	1.000	1	1	4	0	1
Sogard	1.000	18	19	26	0	6
Valdez	.972	65	69	140	6	23
Westbrook	.982	19	21	35	1	6
Wong	1.000	6	3	3	0	0

Third Base	PCT	G	PO	A	E	DP
Dalbec	1.000	13	4	12	0	0
Devers	.960	130	102	185	12	19
Gonzalez	.880	14	8	14	3	0
Rafaela	1.000	4	0	1	0	0
Reyes	.852	11	6	17	4	1
Short	1.000	1	0	1	0	0
Sogard	1.000	7	5	15	0	3
Valdez	1.000	3	2	0	0	0
Westbrook	1.000	1	0	1	0	0

Shortstop	PCT	G	PO	A	E	DP
Gonzalez	1.000	23	21	18	0	2
Hamilton	.964	62	64	121	7	24
Rafaela	.968	82	114	158	9	36
Reyes	1.000	2	1	2	0	0
Sogard	.962	9	8	17	1	1
Story	.989	26	32	61	1	13

Outfield	PCT	G	PO	A	E	DP
Abreu	.971	131	222	9	7	2
Dalbec	1.000	2	2	0	0	0
Duran	.984	188	356	12	6	2
Gonzalez	1.000	9	7	0	0	0
O'Neill	.957	120	151	4	7	0
Rafaela	.984	88	179	5	3	2
Refsnyder	.967	83	116	2	4	0
Valdez	.000	1	0	0	0	0
Westbrook	.000	1	0	0	0	0
Wong	.000	1	0	0	0	0
Yoshida	.000	1	0	0	0	0

WORCESTER RED SOX — *TRIPLE-A*

INTERNATIONAL LEAGUE

Batting	B-T	Ht.	Wt.	DOB	AVG	OBP	SLG	G	PA	AB	R	H	2B	3B	HR	RBI	BB	HBP	SH	SF	SO	SB	CS	BB%	SO%
Abreu, Wilyer	L-L	5-10	217	6-24-99	.250	.308	.750	3	13	12	3	3	0	0	2	2	1	0	0	0	3	0	0	7.69	23.08
Alvarez, Eddy	L-R	5-8	178	1-30-90	.247	.349	.462	115	454	381	74	94	26	1	18	77	49	13	7	4	109	18	7	10.79	24.01
Anthony, Roman	L-R	6-2	200	5-13-04	.344	.463	.519	35	164	131	33	45	12	1	3	20	31	0	0	2	31	5	2	18.90	18.90
Binelas, Alex	L-R	6-1	225	5-26-00	.250	.308	.500	3	13	12	1	3	0	0	1	3	1	0	0	0	5	1	1	7.69	38.46
Campbell, Kristian	R-R	6-3	191	6-28-02	.286	.412	.486	19	85	70	17	20	2	0	4	17	13	2	0	0	18	4	2	15.29	21.18
Casas, Triston	L-R	6-4	252	1-15-00	.286	.388	.524	12	49	42	5	12	7	0	1	7	6	1	0	0	14	0	0	12.24	28.57
Contreras, Mark	L-R	6-0	195	1-24-95	.199	.312	.311	104	378	322	51	64	15	3	5	35	45	9	0	2	104	25	5	11.90	27.51
Dalbec, Bobby	R-R	6-4	227	6-29-95	.252	.337	.479	97	410	361	68	91	20	1	20	68	46	1	0	2	148	11	1	11.22	36.10
Ferguson, Max	L-R	6-0	180	8-23-99	.100	.250	.100	3	12	10	1	1	0	0	0	1	2	0	0	0	3	0	0	16.67	25.00
Gasper, Mickey	B-R	5-9	205	10-11-95	.367	.471	.592	48	204	169	38	62	14	0	8	36	30	4	0	1	20	1	1	14.71	9.80
Gonzalez, Romy	R-R	6-1	215	9-6-96	.373	.421	.667	13	57	51	8	19	2	2	3	17	4	1	0	1	10	3	2	7.02	17.54
Grissom, Vaughn	R-R	6-2	210	1-5-01	.259	.385	.373	55	234	193	27	50	4	0	6	34	36	4	0	1	45	10	1	15.38	19.23
Guthrie, Dalton	R-R	5-11	160	12-23-95	.254	.321	.303	51	156	142	19	36	4	0	1	12	13	1	0	0	32	11	3	8.33	20.51
Hamilton, David	L-R	5-10	175	9-29-97	.167	.250	.500	5	20	18	3	3	0	0	2	2	2	0	0	0	6	0	1	10.00	30.00
Heineman, Tyler	B-R	5-10	190	6-19-91	.252	.379	.403	51	199	159	26	40	4	1	6	26	28	6	4	2	32	8	1	14.07	16.08
Hickey, Nathan	L-R	5-11	210	11-23-99	.210	.340	.397	86	365	300	53	63	15	1	13	54	58	3	0	4	114	4	0	15.89	31.23
Kavadas, Niko	L-R	5-11	235	10-27-98	.281	.424	.551	83	335	263	57	74	20	0	17	63	58	10	0	4	112	0	1	17.31	33.43
Kolozsvary, Mark	R-R	5-7	185	9-4-95	.185	.349	.354	27	83	65	12	12	2	0	3	10	11	6	0	1	26	2	0	13.25	31.33
Lugo, Matthew	R-R	6-1	187	5-9-01	.250	.340	.452	35	141	124	21	31	10	0	5	19	12	5	0	0	38	7	0	8.51	26.95
Marrero, Elih	B-R	5-7	185	6-21-97	.154	.267	.462	4	15	13	3	2	1	0	1	2	1	1	0	0	8	0	0	6.67	53.33
McDonough, Tyler	B-R	5-8	180	4-2-99	.219	.315	.307	35	130	114	16	25	5	1	1	17	15	1	0	0	39	3	1	11.54	30.00
McGuire, Reese	L-R	6-0	218	3-2-95	.114	.220	.136	13	51	44	6	5	1	0	0	3	6	0	0	0	15	0	0	11.76	29.41
Meidroth, Chase	R-R	5-9	170	7-23-01	.293	.437	.400	122	558	437	87	128	20	3	7	57	105	11	0	5	71	13	6	18.82	12.72
Miller, Tyler	L-R	6-2	193	12-17-99	.000	.111	.000	4	9	8	1	0	0	0	0	0	1	0	0	0	5	0	0	11.11	55.56
O'Neill, Tyler	R-R	5-11	200	6-22-95	.000	.000	.000	1	3	3	0	0	0	0	0	0	0	0	0	0	1	0	0	0.00	33.33
Refsnyder, Rob	R-R	6-0	205	3-26-91	.333	.385	.667	4	13	12	3	4	1	0	1	1	1	0	0	0	5	0	0	7.69	38.46
Reyes, Pablo	R-R	5-8	175	9-5-93	.462	.588	.692	5	17	13	4	6	0	0	1	4	4	0	0	0	3	3	0	23.53	17.65
Rosier, Corey	L-R	5-10	180	9-7-99	.177	.267	.262	54	187	164	18	29	4	2	2	16	20	1	0	2	45	11	3	10.70	24.06
Sikes, Phillip	R-R	6-2	190	4-27-99	.100	.182	.100	3	11	10	0	1	0	0	0	1	1	0	0	0	3	1	0	9.09	27.27
Simas, Karson	R-R	5-11	175	6-2-01	.268	.311	.341	11	45	41	7	11	0	0	1	5	2	1	0	1	13	2	0	4.44	28.89
Sogard, Nick	B-R	6-1	180	9-9-97	.283	.390	.446	96	440	368	69	104	19	1	13	59	64	3	1	4	90	10	6	14.55	20.45
Story, Trevor	R-R	6-2	213	11-15-92	.375	.375	.438	4	16	16	3	6	1	0	0	2	0	0	0	0	2	1	0	0.00	12.50
Teel, Kyle	L-R	6-1	190	2-15-02	.255	.374	.343	28	123	102	23	26	3	0	2	18	20	0	0	1	29	3	0	16.26	23.58
Valdez, Enmanuel	L-R	5-8	191	12-28-98	.233	.330	.446	50	225	193	26	45	8	0	11	30	27	2	1	2	53	3	0	12.00	23.56
Westbrook, Jamie	R-R	5-7	193	6-18-95	.277	.369	.450	102	425	358	52	99	24	1	12	71	48	8	0	6	72	2	2	11.29	16.94
Yorke, Nick	R-R	5-11	200	4-2-02	.310	.408	.490	38	169	145	32	45	8	0	6	19	24	0	0	0	32	6	1	14.20	18.93
Yoshida, Masataka	L-R	5-8	176	7-15-93	.143	.250	.143	2	8	7	2	1	0	0	0	0	1	0	0	0	2	0	0	12.50	25.00

Pitching	B-T	Ht.	Wt.	DOB	W	L	ERA	G	GS	SV	IP	Hits	Runs	ER	HR	BB	SO	AVG	OBP	SLG	SO%	BB%	BF
Adames, Jose	R-R	6-2	165	1-17-93	0	1	0.00	5	0	1	4	4	6	0	1	4	6	.222	.364	.389	27.27	18.18	22
Adon, Melvin	L-R	6-3	246	6-9-94	0	1	11.88	7	0	0	8	9	11	11	2	10	12	.273	.455	.515	27.27	22.73	44

Alexander, Jason	R-R	6-2	227	3-1-93	7	6	4.42	29	27	0	138	143	76	68	12	39	129	.264	.320	.407	21.94	6.63	588
Alvarez, Eddy	L-R	5-8	178	1-30-90	0	0	0.00	1	0	0	0	0	0	0	0	0	0	.000	.000	.000	0.00	0.00	1
Benitez, Jorge	L-L	6-2	155	6-2-99	2	3	8.07	26	0	0	36	37	32	32	5	35	43	.270	.432	.438	24.02	19.55	179
Bernardino, Brennan	L-L	6-4	180	1-15-92	0	0	16.20	2	0	0	2	3	3	3	1	1	2	.375	.500	.875	20.00	10.00	10
Booser, Cam	L-L	6-3	225	5-4-92	2	2	5.91	8	0	0	11	13	8	7	0	4	21	.289	.360	.356	42.00	8.00	50
Campbell, Isaiah	R-R	6-4	230	8-15-97	0	1	2.20	14	0	0	16	14	5	4	3	5	19	.222	.286	.381	27.14	7.14	70
Cellucci, Brendan	L-L	6-4	211	6-30-98	0	0	15.00	5	0	0	6	5	10	10	0	10	7	.250	.529	.300	20.59	29.41	34
Criswell, Cooper	R-R	6-6	200	7-24-96	2	2	1.40	5	5	0	26	21	7	4	0	8	23	.223	.318	.234	21.30	7.41	108
Dobbins, Hunter	R-R	6-2	185	8-30-99	1	2	2.61	4	4	0	21	20	6	6	1	9	22	.263	.356	.342	25.00	10.23	88
Drohan, Shane	L-L	6-3	195	1-7-99	0	0	6.43	2	2	0	7	9	5	5	0	8	8	.300	.447	.400	21.05	21.05	38
Fitts, Richard	R-R	6-3	215	12-17-99	9	5	4.17	24	23	0	117	112	59	54	19	37	111	.253	.314	.438	22.56	7.52	492
Gambrell, Grant	L-R	6-4	225	11-21-97	4	6	4.09	18	16	0	84	85	40	38	6	34	65	.262	.341	.372	17.62	9.21	369
Garcia, Luis	R-R	6-2	240	1-30-87	0	0	0.00	1	0	0	1	1	0	0	0	0	0	.250	.250	.250	0.00	0.00	4
Guerrero, Luis	R-R	6-0	215	8-5-00	5	3	3.31	42	0	2	54	39	22	20	6	32	79	.198	.335	.315	33.05	13.39	239
Gutierrez, Vladimir	R-R	6-1	205	9-18-95	0	0	9.00	5	1	1	8	10	10	8	1	12	8	.294	.478	.500	17.39	26.09	46
Hagenman, Justin	R-R	6-3	205	10-7-96	4	6	4.91	28	15	0	92	90	55	50	21	31	98	.249	.318	.485	24.50	7.75	400
Hendriks, Liam	R-R	6-0	235	2-10-89	0	0	0.00	4	0	0	4	2	0	0	0	1	1	.154	.214	.154	7.14	7.14	14
Hill, Rich	L-L	6-5	221	3-11-80	0	0	0.00	1	1	0	2	0	0	0	0	1	2	.000	.286	.000	28.57	14.29	7
Horn, Bailey	L-L	6-2	210	1-15-98	3	2	2.15	21	1	3	29	17	9	7	2	14	35	.165	.258	.262	29.17	11.67	120
Jacques, Joe	L-L	6-4	210	3-11-95	0	1	15.75	4	0	0	4	8	7	7	0	6	7	.421	.560	.474	28.00	24.00	25
Keller, Brad	R-R	6-5	255	7-27-95	3	3	2.91	13	10	0	53	44	21	17	2	17	46	.224	.288	.311	21.30	7.87	216
Kelly, Zack	R-R	6-3	205	3-3-95	0	0	0.00	9	0	1	13	1	0	0	0	8	13	.026	.196	.053	28.26	17.39	46
Kwiatkowski, Robert	R-R	6-1	190	6-8-97	2	0	2.35	4	0	0	8	6	2	2	1	1	5	.222	.276	.407	17.24	3.45	29
Luetge, Lucas	L-L	6-4	205	3-24-87	4	2	3.02	31	0	6	42	36	17	14	3	13	47	.229	.287	.338	26.70	7.39	176
Martin, Chris	R-R	6-8	225	6-2-86	0	0	0.00	1	0	0	1	0	0	0	0	1	0	.000	.250	.000	0.00	25.00	4
Mata, Bryan	R-R	6-3	238	5-3-99	0	0	4.22	6	2	0	11	7	6	5	1	7	12	.194	.375	.278	25.00	14.58	48
Miller, Tyler	L-R	6-2	193	12-17-99	0	0	18.00	2	0	0	2	6	4	4	0	0	0	.600	.500	.600	0.00	0.00	12
Olds, Wyatt	R-R	6-0	183	8-5-99	3	2	8.39	17	0	1	25	26	24	23	4	25	35	.280	.452	.452	28.23	20.16	124
Penrod, Zach	L-L	6-2	210	6-16-97	4	2	5.93	15	5	0	27	26	18	18	2	20	40	.252	.379	.388	32.26	16.13	124
Pivetta, Nick	R-R	6-5	214	2-14-93	0	1	12.00	1	1	0	3	3	4	4	0	4	5	.250	.438	.250	31.25	25.00	16
Politi, Andrew	R-R	6-0	195	6-4-96	0	1	12.19	11	0	0	10	16	14	14	5	6	12	.364	.442	.795	23.08	11.54	52
Priester, Quinn	R-R	6-3	210	9-15-00	1	1	5.40	9	9	0	38	36	25	23	4	12	42	.245	.304	.367	25.93	7.41	162
Ramirez, Yohan	R-R	6-4	212	5-6-95	1	1	2.18	15	0	6	21	14	8	5	2	11	24	.189	.326	.284	26.67	12.22	90
Rodriguez, Joely	L-L	6-1	223	9-11-16	0	2	1.88	13	0	1	14.1	8	6	3	1	8	13	.157	.270	.275	20.63	12.70	63
Romano, Sal	L-R	6-5	255	10-12-93	0	1	9.24	15	0	1	25	31	26	26	5	13	15	.304	.388	.529	12.82	11.11	117
Scroggins, Cody	R-R	6-0	195	8-17-96	0	0	37.80	2	0	0	2	6	7	7	1	3	2	.545	.667	.818	13.33	20.00	15
Shugart, Chase	L-R	5-10	198	10-24-96	6	2	4.46	36	5	1	71	65	45	35	7	32	80	.242	.331	.364	25.56	10.22	313
Sims, Lucas	R-R	6-2	213	5-10-94	0	0	0.00	2	0	0	1	0	0	0	0	2	3	.000	.333	.000	50.00	33.33	6
Speas, Alex	R-R	6-3	225	3-4-98	0	1	16.88	11	0	0	8	8	15	15	0	21	14	.267	.558	.367	26.92	40.38	52
Uwasawa, Naoyuki	R-R	6-1	196	2-6-94	5	4	7.63	20	6	0	59	69	51	50	8	36	47	.296	.401	.464	16.85	12.90	279
Van Belle, Brian	R-R	6-3	185	9-3-96	8	2	4.42	30	9	2	94	109	49	46	10	30	87	.289	.343	.424	21.17	7.30	411
Webb, Jacob	L-R	6-5	246	3-23-99	0	0	19.64	4	0	0	4	9	8	8	0	3	4	.474	.542	.684	16.67	12.50	24
Weisert, Greg	R-R	6-2	235	8-25-22	0	0	1.50	4	0	0	6.0	4	1	1	1	2	7	.200	.273	.400	31.82	9.09	22
Whitlock, Garrett	R-R	6-5	225	6-11-96	0	0	0.00	1	1	0	5	2	0	0	0	1	5	.125	.176	.188	29.41	5.88	17
Winckowski, Josh	R-R	6-4	202	6-28-98	3	2	2.87	7	6	0	31	33	16	10	1	6	29	.254	.290	.315	21.01	4.35	138
Wingenter, Trey	R-R	6-7	237	4-15-94	0	0	1.50	4	0	0	6	4	1	1	0	2	11	.190	.292	.190	44.00	8.00	25
Zeferjahn, Ryan	R-R	6-5	209	2-28-98	0	3	5.47	18	1	4	25	20	18	15	3	17	31	.220	.374	.352	26.96	14.78	115

Fielding

Catcher	PCT	G	PO	A	E	DP	PB
Gasper	.994	20	159	9	1	2	2
Heineman	.988	41	371	24	5	5	3
Hickey	.982	37	317	14	6	0	2
Kolozsvary	.983	21	169	7	3	1	1
Marrero	1.000	4	40	0	0	0	0
McGuire	1.000	12	115	5	0	0	1
Teel	.980	18	193	8	4	0	5

First Base	PCT	G	PO	A	E	DP
Binelas	1.000	3	21	2	0	1
Casas	1.000	8	48	6	0	7
Dalbec	.996	37	252	16	1	27
Gasper	1.000	17	130	13	0	17
Gonzalez	.889	4	21	3	3	5
Heineman	.000	1	0	0	0	0
Hickey	.982	17	106	4	2	9
Kavadas	.988	54	396	26	5	30
Miller	1.000	1	8	0	0	1
Refsnyder	1.000	1	3	0	0	1
Sogard	.966	3	26	2	1	1
Valdez	.933	3	13	1	1	2
Westbrook	1.000	9	34	2	0	3

Second Base	PCT	G	PO	A	E	DP
Alvarez	.963	20	29	50	3	12
Campbell	1.000	2	2	4	0	1
Ferguson	1.000	1	0	3	0	1
Gasper	1.000	4	6	5	0	4
Gonzalez	.929	4	5	8	1	1
Grissom	.971	46	57	110	5	24
Hamilton	1.000	1	1	5	0	0
McDonough	1.000	1	1	3	0	0
Meidroth	1.000	19	25	42	0	11
Sogard	.960	6	12	12	1	2
Valdez	.976	28	25	57	2	10
Westbrook	.952	10	8	12	1	1
Yorke	.989	22	37	54	1	12

Third Base	PCT	G	PO	A	E	DP
Alvarez	.885	10	2	21	3	1
Campbell	1.000	3	2	2	0	0
Dalbec	.953	15	12	29	2	1
Ferguson	.750	2	1	2	1	0
Gasper	1.000	1	1	0	0	0
Guthrie	1.000	3	2	5	0	1
Kolozsvary	.000	1	0	0	0	0
Meidroth	.967	35	23	65	3	8
Miller	1.000	1	0	1	0	0
Simas	1.000	5	3	6	0	1
Sogard	1.000	23	15	36	0	4
Valdez	.909	10	5	15	2	3
Westbrook	.961	53	25	73	4	3

Shortstop	PCT	G	PO	A	E	DP
Alvarez	.925	19	18	44	5	13
Campbell	.950	14	14	24	2	5
Dalbec	.950	9	16	22	2	4
Gonzalez	.875	4	7	7	2	2
Hamilton	1.000	3	5	5	0	2
McDonough	.833	3	2	3	1	1
Meidroth	.962	51	65	110	7	30
Reyes	1.000	3	7	7	0	2
Sogard	.954	50	59	108	8	18
Story	1.000	3	4	7	0	2

Outfield	PCT	G	PO	A	E	DP
Abreu	.000	1	0	0	0	0
Alvarez	.984	71	120	3	2	0
Anthony	1.000	37	71	0	0	0
Campbell	1.000	2	7	0	0	0
Contreras	.995	104	199	2	1	0
Dalbec	.971	40	60	6	2	1
Guthrie	1.000	45	81	1	0	1
Lugo	.980	32	49	1	1	0
McDonough	.984	34	63	0	1	0
Miller	.000	1	0	0	0	0
Refsnyder	1.000	2	5	0	0	0
Reyes	1.000	1	2	1	0	0

	PCT	G	PO	A	E	DP
Rosier	.987	53	75	1	1	0
Sikes	1.000	3	13	0	0	0
Simas	1.000	6	10	0	0	0
Sogard	.909	15	10	0	1	0
Valdez	1.000	5	8	1	0	0
Westbrook	.938	26	44	1	3	0
Yorke	1.000	15	21	1	0	0

PORTLAND SEA DOGS

DOUBLE-A

EASTERN LEAGUE

Batting	B-T	Ht.	Wt.	DOB	AVG	OBP	SLG	G	PA	AB	R	H	2B	3B	HR	RBI	BB	HBP	SH	SF	SO	SB	CS	BB%	SO%
Anthony, Roman	L-R	6-2	200	5-13-04	.269	.367	.489	84	376	323	60	87	20	3	15	45	48	3	0	2	96	16	5	12.77	25.53
Binelas, Alex	L-R	6-1	225	5-26-00	.252	.354	.409	88	350	298	45	75	13	5	8	57	46	3	0	3	87	13	0	13.14	24.86
Campbell, Kristian	R-R	6-3	191	6-28-02	.362	.463	.582	56	255	213	48	77	17	3	8	35	35	6	0	1	38	17	5	13.73	14.90
Castro, Allan	B-R	6-0	170	5-24-03	.180	.274	.230	28	117	100	15	18	2	0	1	9	13	1	0	3	30	6	3	11.11	25.64
De Leon, Fraymi	B-R	5-10	155	9-28-04	.000	.250	.000	2	4	3	1	0	0	0	0	0	1	0	0	0	0	0	0	25.00	0.00
Decker, Nick	L-L	6-0	207	10-2-99	.178	.266	.344	56	203	180	28	32	12	0	6	24	21	1	0	1	89	7	1	10.34	43.84
Donlan, Matt	R-R	6-3	213	11-9-99	.146	.294	.220	16	51	41	3	6	3	0	0	4	4	5	0	1	13	0	0	7.84	25.49
Ehrhard, Drew	R-R	5-11	185	1-16-99	.265	.359	.456	21	78	68	11	18	5	1	2	8	7	3	0	0	18	0	1	8.97	23.08
Ferguson, Max	L-R	6-0	180	8-23-99	.159	.255	.293	25	94	82	13	13	2	0	3	10	11	0	0	1	27	6	2	11.70	28.72
Garcia, Jhostynxon	R-R	5-11	163	12-11-02	.263	.320	.386	30	126	114	14	30	4	2	2	10	6	4	0	1	24	2	4	4.76	19.05
Gasper, Mickey	B-R	5-9	205	10-11-95	.282	.403	.458	44	176	142	28	40	13	0	4	22	26	5	0	3	22	3	0	14.77	12.50
Gonzalez, Bryan	R-R	6-0	220	9-18-01	.000	.000	.000	2	2	2	0	0	0	0	0	0	0	0	0	0	1	0	0	0.00	50.00
Heineman, Tyler	B-R	5-10	190	6-19-91	.333	.333	.333	1	3	3	1	1	0	0	0	1	0	0	0	0	1	0	0	0.00	33.33
Hickey, Nathan	L-R	5-11	210	11-23-99	.207	.387	.329	26	106	82	14	17	10	0	0	9	23	1	0	0	28	1	1	21.70	26.42
Jordan, Blaze	R-R	6-2	220	12-19-02	.261	.305	.388	89	380	353	35	92	22	1	7	61	18	6	0	3	46	2	1	4.74	12.11
Liendo, Ahbram	B-R	5-8	170	2-1-04	.197	.274	.224	26	84	76	7	15	2	0	0	7	8	0	0	0	29	7	1	9.52	34.52
Lugo, Matthew	R-R	6-1	187	5-9-01	.315	.405	.664	43	171	146	27	46	10	4	11	35	20	2	0	0	36	9	1	11.70	21.05
Marrero, Elih	B-R	5-7	185	6-21-97	.268	.335	.451	50	183	164	25	44	12	0	6	22	16	1	1	1	39	11	3	8.74	21.31
Mayer, Marcelo	L-R	6-2	188	12-12-02	.307	.370	.480	77	335	300	60	92	28	0	8	38	30	2	0	3	66	13	2	8.96	19.70
McDonough, Tyler	B-R	5-8	180	4-2-99	.250	.312	.375	85	325	296	39	74	18	2	5	36	27	0	1	1	92	15	5	8.31	28.31
Miller, Tyler	L-R	6-2	193	12-17-99	.228	.288	.312	58	226	202	22	46	14	0	1	25	16	3	0	5	38	2	2	7.08	16.81
Paulino, Eddinson	L-R	5-10	155	7-2-02	.263	.349	.391	69	278	243	33	64	16	3	3	35	29	4	0	2	60	10	8	10.43	21.58
Ravelo, Luis	B-R	6-1	187	11-5-03	.205	.327	.205	14	52	44	7	9	0	0	0	5	7	1	0	0	9	0	0	13.46	17.31
Romero, Mikey	L-R	5-11	175	1-12-04	.243	.257	.543	16	74	70	11	17	3	0	6	12	2	0	0	2	25	0	0	2.70	33.78
Rosier, Corey	L-R	5-10	180	9-7-99	.225	.302	.304	34	116	102	9	23	5	0	1	9	11	1	0	2	23	8	0	9.48	19.83
Sikes, Phillip	R-R	6-2	190	4-27-99	.239	.329	.408	106	432	377	64	90	23	1	13	48	42	10	0	3	126	24	9	9.72	29.17
Simas, Karson	R-R	5-11	175	6-2-01	.152	.250	.217	16	53	46	5	7	3	0	0	4	1	5	1	0	15	5	2	1.89	28.30
Teel, Kyle	L-R	6-1	190	2-15-02	.298	.390	.462	84	382	325	65	97	20	0	11	60	48	4	0	5	87	9	5	12.57	22.77
Yorke, Nick	R-R	5-11	200	4-2-02	.251	.325	.366	45	197	175	21	44	8	0	4	27	18	2	0	2	36	8	2	9.14	18.27

Pitching	B-T	Ht.	Wt.	DOB	W	L	ERA	G	GS	SV	IP	Hits	Runs	ER	HR	BB	SO	AVG	OBP	SLG	SO%	BB%	BF
Bastardo, Angel	R-R	6-1	175	6-18-02	0	5	5.36	10	10	0	45	39	33	27	6	21	53	.225	.315	.370	26.63	10.55	199
Bello, Brayan	R-R	6-1	170	5-17-99	0	1	6.75	1	1	0	3	4	3	2	1	2	5	.333	.429	.750	33.33	13.33	15
Bolden, Caleb	R-R	6-2	190	12-19-98	1	2	3.88	21	10	1	58	53	28	25	2	27	58	.250	.349	.321	23.20	10.80	250
Bonnin, Bryce	R-R	6-2	190	10-11-98	0	0	5.68	3	1	0	6	7	4	4	2	4	8	.259	.355	.481	25.81	12.90	31
Booser, Cam	L-L	6-3	225	5-4-92	0	0	0.00	1	0	0	1	1	0	0	0	0	1	.250	.250	.250	25.00	0.00	4
Brand, Jonathan	R-R	5-9	200	2-20-00	2	3	4.67	28	0	0	44	44	25	23	4	19	33	.256	.340	.355	16.75	9.64	197
Bryant, Zach	R-R	6-1	210	6-5-98	4	1	4.82	19	0	3	28	30	17	15	4	11	28	.270	.344	.486	22.22	8.73	126
Cellucci, Brendan	L-L	6-4	211	6-30-98	7	3	3.07	30	0	4	59	42	25	20	4	39	84	.199	.326	.289	32.43	15.06	259
Cepeda, Felix	R-R	6-3	170	7-15-00	0	2	5.57	30	0	14	42	46	29	26	6	20	37	.271	.359	.476	18.97	10.26	195
Coffey, Isaac	R-R	6-1	205	6-21-00	11	4	3.17	24	21	0	114	89	47	40	9	51	148	.215	.335	.334	29.96	10.32	494
Denlinger, Theo	R-R	6-3	240	7-10-96	3	3	5.53	23	0	0	41	49	29	25	5	9	35	.292	.337	.458	18.92	4.86	185
Dobbins, Hunter	R-R	6-2	185	8-30-99	7	3	3.17	21	21	0	105	90	40	37	1	39	98	.232	.310	.284	22.48	8.94	436
Donlan, Matt	R-R	6-3	213	11-9-99	0	0	0.00	2	0	0	2	1	0	0	0	3	0	.167	.444	.333	0.00	33.33	9
Early, Connelly	L-L	6-3	195	4-3-02	2	3	4.50	8	8	0	36	31	24	18	1	15	48	.225	.318	.290	30.57	9.55	157
Encarnacion, Juan D.l	R-R	6-2	173	3-30-01	1	5	9.10	10	7	0	31	45	32	31	4	11	23	.352	.417	.516	15.86	7.59	145
Gonzalez, Wikelman	R-R	6-0	167	3-25-02	4	3	4.73	24	19	0	84	59	48	44	6	46	92	.198	.320	.299	25.56	12.78	360
Hendriks, Liam	R-R	6-0	235	2-10-89	0	0	0.00	2	0	0	1	2	1	0	0	1	2	.333	.429	.333	28.57	14.29	7
Hoppe, Alex	R-R	6-1	200	12-17-98	4	5	5.43	36	0	4	66	81	49	40	7	37	66	.298	.385	.426	21.02	11.78	314
Jackson, Gabriel	R-R	6-2	180	9-7-01	0	0	3.86	3	0	1	5	4	3	2	1	1	7	.211	.286	.421	33.33	4.76	21
Kwiatkowski, Robert	R-R	6-1	190	6-8-97	11	2	2.92	32	2	4	71	56	26	23	6	24	66	.214	.288	.328	22.60	8.22	292
Liu, Chih-Jung	S-R	6-0	185	4-7-99	1	1	4.00	6	4	0	18	14	8	8	4	9	29	.222	.329	.444	39.19	12.16	74
Mata, Bryan	R-R	6-3	238	5-3-99	0	1	3.38	3	3	0	8	9	3	3	0	1	6	.321	.387	.357	19.35	3.23	31
Olds, Wyatt	R-R	6-0	183	8-5-99	1	2	5.03	26	1	1	54	38	34	30	5	30	74	.193	.331	.315	30.45	12.35	243
Olivarez, Helcris	L-L	6-2	192	8-8-00	1	1	3.50	14	5	0	36	14	21	14	1	50	47	.121	.415	.155	26.70	28.41	176
Penrod, Zach	L-L	6-2	210	6-16-97	4	0	2.80	7	7	0	35	23	12	11	3	13	53	.183	.273	.286	37.06	9.09	143
Perales, Luis	R-R	6-1	160	4-14-03	1	0	1.23	2	2	0	7	4	3	1	0	2	10	.167	.250	.167	35.71	7.14	28
Sandlin, David	R-R	6-4	215	2-21-01	0	2	5.61	8	8	0	26	30	19	16	7	7	32	.286	.336	.552	28.32	6.19	113
Scroggins, Cody	R-R	6-0	195	8-17-96	0	1	6.35	6	0	0	11	13	8	8	1	6	8	.302	.400	.395	16.00	12.00	50
Sena, Reidis	R-R	5-10	160	4-7-01	0	1	7.94	7	0	2	11	13	10	10	2	8	17	.289	.396	.467	32.08	15.09	53
Slaten, Justin	R-R	6-4	222	9-15-97	0	0	27.00	1	0	0	0	1	1	1	0	1	1	.500	.667	.500	33.33	33.33	3
Troye, Christopher	R-R	6-4	225	2-8-99	2	2	4.60	28	0	2	45	36	25	23	7	31	60	.220	.338	.390	29.85	15.42	201
Webb, Jacob	L-R	6-5	246	3-23-99	10	3	4.28	37	7	1	80	82	48	38	11	27	77	.259	.324	.405	22.00	7.71	350
Wehunt, Blake	R-R	6-6	240	11-9-00	0	1	9.00	1	1	0	5	8	5	5	1	0	1	.381	.381	.619	4.76	0.00	21
Zeferjahn, Ryan	R-R	6-5	209	2-28-98	1	0	0.00	7	0	3	14	9	2	0	0	3	22	.176	.222	.176	40.74	5.56	54

Fielding

Catcher	PCT	G	PO	A	E	DP	PB
Donlan	.962	8	70	5	3	1	0
Ehrhard	1.000	1	4	0	0	0	0

Gasper	.985	16	181	14	3	0	1
Hickey	1.000	10	91	3	0	2	1
Marrero	.982	48	451	34	9	4	7
Teel	.986	57	542	38	8	3	6

First Base	PCT	G	PO	A	E	DP
Binelas	.990	42	285	27	3	24
Donlan	1.000	4	21	2	0	0
Ehrhard	1.000	13	89	10	0	6
Gasper	.987	21	135	15	2	16
Hickey	.833	1	5	0	1	1
Jordan	.989	27	169	16	2	12
Miller	.989	35	243	22	3	20

Second Base	PCT	G	PO	A	E	DP
Campbell	.957	15	24	43	3	5
De Leon	1.000	1	1	4	0	2
Ehrhard	1.000	3	3	7	0	1
Ferguson	1.000	7	11	11	0	1
Liendo	.960	12	17	31	2	6
McDonough	.982	39	67	95	3	20
Paulino	1.000	20	30	50	0	9
Ravelo	.971	10	15	19	1	4
Romero	1.000	1	2	5	0	2
Simas	1.000	4	5	13	0	0
Yorke	.984	33	54	72	2	16

Third Base	PCT	G	PO	A	E	DP
Binelas	.826	15	7	12	4	0
Campbell	1.000	1	0	2	0	1
Ferguson	1.000	7	7	12	0	2
Jordan	.910	57	26	85	11	9
Liendo	.923	9	6	18	2	2
Mayer	.750	1	0	3	1	0
Miller	.893	13	7	18	3	1
Paulino	.920	37	21	48	6	4
Simas	1.000	6	6	6	0	1

Shortstop	PCT	G	PO	A	E	DP
Campbell	.984	22	23	39	1	7
De Leon	.000	1	0	0	0	0
Ferguson	.963	8	6	20	1	4
Liendo	.842	6	2	14	3	5
Mayer	.953	66	80	122	10	16
McDonough	.909	7	4	6	1	2
Paulino	.865	11	12	20	5	9
Ravelo	.947	5	8	10	1	2
Romero	.956	14	13	30	2	4
Simas	1.000	5	5	10	0	4

Outfield	PCT	G	PO	A	E	DP
Anthony	.979	68	141	2	3	1
Campbell	1.000	11	21	0	0	0
Castro	1.000	27	49	2	0	0
Decker	.978	52	82	5	2	0
Ferguson	1.000	2	2	0	0	0
Garcia	.967	27	58	1	2	0
Lugo	.971	39	66	2	2	0
McDonough	.975	41	75	3	2	2
Miller	1.000	11	11	2	0	0
Rosier	.983	33	59	0	1	0
Sikes	.977	106	166	6	4	2
Simas	1.000	2	6	0	0	0
Yorke	1.000	12	14	1	0	0

BOSTON RED SOX

GREENVILLE DRIVE

HIGH-A

SOUTH ATLANTIC LEAGUE

Batting	B-T	Ht.	Wt.	DOB	AVG	OBP	SLG	G	PA	AB	R	H	2B	3B	HR	RBI	BB	HBP	SH	SF	SO	SB	CS	BB%	SO%
Bleis, Miguel	R-R	6-0	170	3-1-04	.190	.265	.319	52	234	210	32	40	6	0	7	25	18	4	0	2	54	22	3	7.69	23.08
Campbell, Kristian	R-R	6-3	191	6-28-02	.306	.418	.558	40	177	147	29	45	13	0	8	25	26	3	0	1	47	3	1	14.69	26.55
Castro, Allan	B-R	6-0	170	5-24-03	.243	.363	.449	95	413	345	65	84	21	4	14	48	61	5	0	2	94	11	2	14.77	22.76
Chacon, Juan	R-R	6-1	171	12-4-02	.203	.269	.302	84	334	305	37	62	18	3	2	17	25	3	0	1	109	9	3	7.49	32.63
Coffey, Cutter	R-R	6-1	190	5-21-04	.238	.321	.463	61	271	240	39	57	12	0	14	46	28	2	0	1	65	8	3	10.33	23.99
De Leon, Fraymi	B-R	5-10	155	9-28-04	.234	.347	.359	21	75	64	12	15	5	0	1	4	7	4	0	0	21	5	2	9.33	28.00
Ehrhard, Drew	R-R	5-11	185	1-16-99	.333	.400	1.111	6	10	9	3	3	1	0	2	3	1	0	0	0	2	0	0	10.00	20.00
Ehrhard, Zach	R-R	5-11	190	1-21-03	.156	.264	.195	22	91	77	9	12	3	0	0	5	11	1	0	2	25	4	1	12.09	27.47
Garcia, Jhostynxon	R-R	5-11	163	12-11-02	.311	.371	.627	53	229	209	44	65	14	2	16	37	12	8	0	0	50	1	3	5.24	21.83
Gonzalez, Bryan	R-R	6-0	220	9-18-01	.272	.337	.508	91	362	327	58	89	13	2	20	59	29	4	0	2	115	15	10	8.01	31.77
Liendo, Ahbram	B-R	5-8	170	2-1-04	.196	.294	.262	83	347	301	33	59	5	3	3	25	41	2	0	3	133	24	6	11.82	38.33
Lira, Enderso	R-R	6-1	185	10-11-03	.142	.191	.173	37	136	127	12	18	1	0	1	9	8	0	0	1	40	0	0	5.88	29.41
Lopez, Eduardo	B-R	5-11	187	5-8-02	.232	.343	.425	56	213	181	29	42	11	3	6	23	30	1	0	1	49	4	0	14.08	23.00
Lugo, Andy	R-R	5-11	160	3-15-04	.225	.295	.282	21	79	71	4	16	4	0	0	6	5	2	0	0	20	3	1	6.33	25.32
Miller, Tyler	L-R	6-2	193	12-17-99	.275	.321	.450	36	140	131	16	36	9	1	4	17	9	0	0	0	28	0	0	6.43	20.00
Montero, Juan	R-R	5-11	180	6-10-02	.188	.305	.292	16	59	48	7	9	3	1	0	5	8	1	0	2	17	0	0	13.56	28.81
Ravelo, Luis	B-R	6-1	187	11-5-03	.225	.305	.322	85	347	307	30	69	14	2	4	33	32	5	0	3	81	1	1	9.22	23.34
Riemer, Justin	B-R	6-0	170	2-6-02	.240	.397	.280	28	126	100	21	24	4	0	0	3	19	7	0	0	24	8	0	15.08	19.05
Romero, Mikey	L-R	5-11	175	1-12-04	.271	.319	.498	59	276	255	40	69	20	4	10	40	16	3	0	2	58	1	0	5.80	21.01
Rosario, Ronald	R-R	6-0	175	1-1-03	.244	.302	.359	99	427	390	43	95	19	1	8	63	32	2	0	3	82	2	1	7.49	19.20
Rose, Caden	R-R	5-11	175	10-7-01	.187	.267	.352	25	101	91	15	17	1	1	4	16	7	3	0	0	33	0	0	6.93	32.67
Simas, Karson	R-R	5-11	175	6-2-01	.188	.288	.290	21	80	69	11	13	4	0	1	6	9	1	0	1	21	2	0	11.25	26.25
Taylor, Nelson	L-L	6-1	180	1-22-03	.289	.341	.553	10	41	38	5	11	2	1	2	8	3	0	0	0	13	2	1	7.32	31.71
Turner, Will	L-L	6-1	190	9-18-02	.081	.250	.122	23	92	74	9	6	1	1	0	7	14	3	0	1	16	3	1	15.22	17.39
Ugueto, Miguel	R-R	5-11	185	9-3-02	.242	.273	.377	63	249	231	28	56	13	3	4	28	10	2	0	6	50	7	4	4.02	20.08
White, Hudson	R-R	6-1	200	8-9-02	.167	.324	.167	18	69	54	2	9	0	0	0	3	11	2	1	1	21	1	0	15.94	30.43

Pitching	B-T	Ht.	Wt.	DOB	W	L	ERA	G	GS	SV	IP	Hits	Runs	ER	HR	BB	SO	AVG	OBP	SLG	SO%	BB%	BF
Adams, Cooper	L-R	6-3	205	6-14-00	2	5	5.08	26	6	1	80	77	52	45	10	37	59	.262	.355	.442	16.86	10.57	350
Bolden, Caleb	R-R	6-2	190	12-19-98	3	0	4.96	12	0	5	16	14	11	9	2	11	25	.230	.360	.361	33.33	14.67	75
Bonnin, Bryce	R-R	6-2	190	10-11-98	3	3	4.04	19	0	0	36	20	16	16	3	16	40	.164	.266	.270	27.97	11.19	143
Brand, Jonathan	R-R	5-9	200	2-20-00	0	0	0.00	6	0	1	12	8	1	0	0	3	18	.186	.239	.209	38.30	6.38	47
Carlson, Max	R-R	6-1	190	9-13-01	1	1	2.31	5	0	1	12	8	3	3	0	5	9	.200	.304	.275	19.15	10.64	47
Dean, Noah	L-L	6-2	185	3-10-01	0	1	6.38	7	2	1	18	13	15	13	0	23	30	.194	.423	.194	30.93	23.71	97
Early, Connelly	L-L	6-3	195	4-3-02	1	6	3.72	15	15	0	68	53	33	28	6	24	90	.208	.300	.345	30.93	8.25	291
Ehrhard, Drew	R-R	5-11	185	1-16-99	0	2	2.45	3	0	0	4	4	3	1	1	0	0	.333	.385	.583	0.00	0.00	13
Encarnacion, Juan D.	R-R	6-2	173	3-30-01	2	1	4.50	9	9	0	40	39	20	20	4	13	52	.250	.318	.385	29.89	7.47	174
Feeney, Cade	R-R	6-0	195	7-31-01	0	1	3.66	20	0	3	32	27	16	13	2	2	32	.220	.228	.350	25.00	1.56	128
Fogell, Zach	L-L	5-11	190	7-23-00	5	2	3.32	33	0	1	57	45	25	21	6	32	67	.212	.328	.330	26.80	12.80	250
Jackson, Gabriel	R-R	6-2	180	9-7-01	8	2	4.89	27	2	3	74	67	46	40	9	35	59	.229	.321	.375	17.56	10.42	336
Landry, Nathan	R-L	6-2	200	5-4-99	2	1	5.24	24	0	0	46	42	30	27	2	27	48	.244	.367	.331	22.86	12.86	210
Mata, Bryan	R-R	6-3	238	5-3-99	0	0	9.00	1	1	0	2	4	2	2	0	1	0	.444	.500	.778	0.00	10.00	10
Monegro, Yordanny	R-R	6-4	180	10-14-02	6	2	2.73	15	14	0	66	42	28	20	7	26	82	.176	.263	.328	30.83	9.77	266
Mullins, Hayden	L-L	6-0	194	9-14-00	4	5	3.94	22	17	0	89	73	47	39	10	42	118	.223	.324	.351	30.33	10.80	389
Paez, Jedixson	R-R	6-1	170	1-17-04	4	3	3.48	15	7	0	65	60	27	25	10	8	78	.245	.275	.404	30.23	3.10	258
Perales, Luis	R-R	6-1	160	4-14-03	1	2	3.42	7	7	0	26	28	14	10	1	10	46	.269	.345	.337	39.66	8.62	116
Rodriguez-Cruz, Elmer	L-R	6-3	160	8-18-03	2	1	3.77	7	7	0	29	18	13	12	4	18	29	.180	.311	.330	24.37	15.13	119
Rogers, Dalton	R-L	5-11	172	1-18-01	2	7	5.12	21	19	0	83	83	63	47	4	50	89	.252	.352	.345	23.00	12.92	387

Pitching	B-T	Ht.	Wt.	DOB	W	L	ERA	G	GS	SV	IP	Hits	Runs	ER	HR	BB	SO	AVG	OBP	SLG	SO%	BB%	BF
Sandlin, David	R-R	6-4	215	2-21-01	0	2	5.12	10	10	0	32	31	20	18	7	11	50	.254	.313	.475	37.31	8.21	134
Sena, Reidis	R-R	5-10	160	4-7-01	6	4	3.56	28	0	3	48	36	24	19	7	24	67	.201	.301	.352	32.37	11.59	207
Smith, Adam	R-R	6-2	180	5-9-00	5	7	5.83	29	0	1	59	65	48	38	6	24	49	.284	.367	.432	18.42	9.02	266
Stebens, Isaac	L-R	6-0	194	12-5-01	3	3	3.68	29	0	5	51	45	23	21	4	31	73	.228	.343	.340	31.33	13.30	233
Steinbaugh, Conor	R-R	6-0	205	5-22-99	0	0	8.44	5	0	0	11	17	10	10	4	5	9	.362	.436	.660	16.36	9.09	55
Uberstine, Tyler	R-R	6-1	200	6-1-99	0	1	1.93	3	3	0	5	5	1	1	0	1	6	.278	.350	.444	30.00	5.00	20
Wehunt, Blake	R-R	6-6	240	11-9-00	1	6	4.42	13	13	0	59	46	32	29	5	19	65	.213	.280	.338	26.75	7.82	243
Wu-Yelland, Jeremy	L-L	6-2	210	6-24-99	2	1	5.67	23	0	1	33	31	28	21	1	23	42	.238	.363	.300	26.42	14.47	159

Fielding

Catcher	PCT	G	PO	A	E	DP	PB
Lira	.987	35	365	18	5	0	6
Montero	1.000	4	42	2	0	0	0
Rosario	.985	80	793	64	13	8	13
White	.986	13	136	6	2	1	0

First Base	PCT	G	PO	A	E	DP
Gonzalez	.974	74	498	25	14	33
Lopez	.993	39	264	13	2	21
Miller	.975	18	152	6	4	13
Montero	.889	1	7	1	1	0

Second Base	PCT	G	PO	A	E	DP
Campbell	1.000	19	23	51	0	9
Coffey	.667	2	4	2	3	1
De Leon	.957	11	17	28	2	7
Liendo	.955	28	40	65	5	11
Lugo	.857	7	6	12	3	1
Ravelo	.950	35	50	64	6	16
Riemer	1.000	11	15	18	0	2
Romero	.962	15	22	28	2	6
Simas	1.000	6	6	8	0	1

Third Base	PCT	G	PO	A	E	DP
Campbell	1.000	1	1	4	0	1
Coffey	.862	31	22	53	12	7
De Leon	.917	5	5	6	1	1
Gonzalez	1.000	1	2	1	0	0
Liendo	.917	44	32	78	10	10
Lugo	.913	13	6	15	2	1
Miller	.959	17	13	34	2	3
Montero	.870	11	6	14	3	0
Simas	.929	11	10	16	2	2

Shortstop	PCT	G	PO	A	E	DP
Coffey	.889	21	22	34	7	7
De Leon	.923	5	9	15	2	4
Liendo	.889	10	14	18	4	2
Ravelo	.940	46	48	93	9	14
Riemer	.940	17	17	30	3	6
Romero	.945	36	42	78	7	7

Outfield	PCT	G	PO	A	E	DP
Bleis	.945	43	83	3	5	0
Campbell	1.000	12	25	0	0	0
Castro	.993	79	145	5	1	1
Chacon	.971	74	127	8	4	3
Ehrhard	1.000	18	42	1	0	0
Garcia	.975	43	76	2	2	0
Gonzalez	1.000	13	22	2	0	0
Lopez	1.000	9	14	4	0	0
Lugo	1.000	2	1	0	0	0
Rose	1.000	25	57	1	0	0
Simas	1.000	4	13	0	0	0
Taylor	1.000	8	13	0	0	0
Turner	.971	21	31	2	1	1
Ugueto	.956	53	79	7	4	1

SALEM RED SOX — *LOW-A*

CAROLINA LEAGUE

Batting	B-T	Ht.	Wt.	DOB	AVG	OBP	SLG	G	PA	AB	R	H	2B	3B	HR	RBI	BB	HBP	SH	SF	SO	SB	CS	BB%	SO%
Alcantara, Marvin	R-R	5-10	157	11-2-04	.248	.300	.307	108	456	423	60	105	10	3	3	47	28	4	0	1	103	13	3	6.14	22.59
Anderson, Antonio	B-R	6-3	205	6-28-05	.186	.311	.270	108	482	404	53	75	17	1	5	34	69	6	0	3	122	3	4	14.32	25.31
Arias, Franklin	R-R	5-11	170	11-19-05	.257	.331	.378	36	166	148	18	38	9	0	3	26	16	1	0	1	29	5	2	9.64	17.47
Ayubi, Karim	R-R	6-2	165	12-8-03	.224	.367	.265	14	60	49	5	11	2	0	0	5	8	3	0	0	21	2	1	13.33	35.00
Bleis, Miguel	R-R	6-0	170	3-1-04	.257	.349	.398	43	195	171	24	44	10	1	4	22	21	3	0	0	38	16	7	10.77	19.49
Brannon, Brooks	R-R	5-11	210	5-4-04	.251	.326	.396	54	230	207	22	52	8	2	6	24	23	0	0	0	67	5	1	10.00	29.13
De Leon, Fraymi	B-R	5-10	155	9-28-04	.195	.307	.243	54	199	169	26	33	3	1	1	17	25	3	0	2	52	19	4	12.56	26.13
Diaz, Kelvin	R-R	5-11	148	3-17-03	.214	.257	.340	29	109	103	16	22	8	1	1	7	6	0	0	0	41	8	2	5.50	37.61
Encarnacion, Freili	R-R	6-1	181	1-26-05	.244	.290	.329	80	331	307	39	75	14	3	2	32	12	9	0	3	90	15	9	3.63	27.19
Feliz, Albert	R-R	6-2	200	4-13-02	.165	.253	.318	76	292	255	25	42	6	0	11	41	29	3	0	5	118	1	0	9.93	40.41
Garcia, Jhostynxon	R-R	5-11	163	12-11-02	.258	.365	.517	24	104	89	20	23	6	1	5	19	15	0	0	0	25	14	0	14.42	24.04
Garcia, Johanfran	R-R	5-10	196	12-8-04	.385	.467	.596	14	60	52	5	20	5	0	2	5	6	2	0	0	15	0	0	10.00	25.00
Lugo, Andy	R-R	5-11	160	3-15-04	.271	.346	.392	87	341	306	43	83	26	1	3	39	26	9	0	0	68	25	3	7.62	19.94
McElveny, Daniel	R-R	5-10	190	4-21-03	.179	.336	.231	55	214	173	23	31	4	1	1	12	35	6	0	0	56	3	2	16.36	26.17
Montero, Juan	R-R	5-11	180	6-10-02	.207	.362	.304	34	117	92	12	19	4	1	1	8	16	7	0	1	30	2	1	13.68	25.64
Musett, Andruw	R-R	5-10	198	11-21-05	.200	.319	.233	17	72	60	5	12	2	0	0	7	9	2	0	1	19	0	0	12.50	26.39
Pierre, Angel	R-R	6-0	170	9-19-03	.000	.500	.000	1	2	1	1	0	0	0	0	0	0	1	0	0	1	0	0	0.00	50.00
Rodriguez, Gerardo	R-R	5-10	177	12-8-05	.381	.409	.381	7	22	21	2	8	0	0	0	1	1	0	0	0	0	0	0	4.55	0.00
Rose, Caden	R-R	5-11	175	10-7-01	.353	.476	.529	10	42	34	9	12	6	0	0	7	5	3	0	0	10	3	1	11.90	23.81
Taylor, Nelson	L-L	6-1	180	1-22-03	.228	.336	.358	101	434	369	69	84	24	3	6	46	60	2	0	3	106	31	9	13.82	24.42
Tucker, Stanley	R-R	5-9	165	4-22-02	.195	.314	.267	69	261	221	23	43	6	2	2	25	39	0	0	1	61	23	7	14.94	23.37
Viloria, Diego	R-R	5-10	165	2-23-03	.152	.200	.152	11	36	33	3	5	0	0	0	3	1	1	0	0	4	0	0	2.78	11.11
Yuten, Natanael	L-L	6-2	143	10-9-04	.243	.304	.380	101	418	379	39	92	20	7	6	50	30	5	0	4	105	12	11	7.18	25.12
Zanetello, Nazzan	R-R	6-2	190	5-25-05	.156	.279	.279	78	345	294	38	46	11	2	7	21	42	8	0	0	151	4	1	12.17	43.77

Pitching	B-T	Ht.	Wt.	DOB	W	L	ERA	G	GS	SV	IP	Hits	Runs	ER	HR	BB	SO	AVG	OBP	SLG	SO%	BB%	BF
Bickerstaff, Calvin	R-R	6-5	205	1-22-02	0	0	2.84	4	0	0	6	3	2	2	1	0	7	.143	.143	.286	33.33	0.00	21
Blanco, Royman	R-R	6-1	170	4-17-01	10	4	3.75	33	1	6	70	76	36	29	5	19	44	.276	.326	.436	14.72	6.35	299
Carlson, Max	R-R	6-1	190	9-13-01	5	1	2.81	28	0	6	58	57	29	18	1	18	77	.254	.307	.357	30.68	7.17	251
Cohen, Luis	R-R	6-0	172	5-26-03	6	5	3.40	23	22	0	98	76	43	37	7	34	77	.213	.288	.336	19.30	8.52	399
Cruz, Nathanael	R-R	6-2	175	2-4-03	6	4	4.71	38	0	4	57	53	45	30	5	33	60	.240	.354	.398	22.81	12.55	263
De Leon, Fraymi	S-R	5-10	155	9-28-04	0	1	27.00	1	0	0	1	2	2	2	0	1	0	.500	.600	.750	0.00	20.00	5
Dean, Noah	L-L	6-2	185	3-10-01	2	3	3.96	15	13	0	61	28	29	27	5	31	86	.139	.287	.238	35.10	12.65	245
Duffy, Matthew	L-R	6-1	185	10-4-01	4	5	2.83	22	21	0	99	81	35	31	8	27	100	.223	.283	.360	24.94	6.73	401
Ehrlicher, Austin	L-R	6-5	185	6-2-03	0	0	0.00	2	0	0	6	5	2	0	0	1	10	.208	.240	.250	40.00	4.00	25
Feliz, Albert	R-R	6-2	200	4-13-02	0	0	5.06	4	0	0	5	4	3	3	0	6	5	.211	.423	.263	19.23	23.08	26
Fogell, Zach	L-L	5-11	190	7-23-00	1	0	0.00	2	0	0	5	2	0	0	0	1	7	.111	.200	.167	35.00	5.00	20
Hernandez, Francis	R-R	6-2	170	9-4-01	5	8	7.20	32	1	2	65	62	63	52	8	39	57	.252	.364	.427	19.13	13.09	298
Ingrassia, Joseph	L-L	6-1	170	7-24-02	3	1	1.85	21	12	1	58	38	15	12	2	20	93	.179	.255	.274	39.57	8.51	235
Judice, Nicholas	R-R	6-8	212	4-8-01	0	1	5.79	3	1	0	5	3	4	3	1	3	5	.200	.350	.467	25.00	15.00	20
Kilander, Griffin	R-R	6-5	205	6-30-03	0	0	1.23	4	0	0	7	1	1	1	0	3	6	.043	.154	.043	23.08	11.54	26
Kirwin, Danny	R-R	6-2	205	10-12-99	4	3	3.63	20	5	0	69	54	34	28	5	24	69	.211	.281	.320	24.21	8.42	285

Pitching	B-T	Ht.	Wt.	DOB	W	L	ERA	G	GS	SV	IP	Hits	Runs	ER	HR	BB	SO	AVG	OBP	SLG	SO%	BB%	BF
Lugo, Andy	R-R	5-11	160	3-15-04	0	0	0.00	1	0	0	0	0	0	0	0	0	1	.000	.000	.000	100.00	0.00	1
O'Donnell, Trennor	R-R	6-7	240	6-6-01	3	7	4.00	20	6	1	63	66	46	28	3	21	71	.257	.322	.346	24.65	7.29	288
Paez, Jedixson	R-R	6-1	170	1-17-04	1	1	2.53	7	5	0	32	36	13	9	1	4	35	.283	.305	.362	26.52	3.03	132
Portes, Ovis	R-R	6-4	167	12-3-04	0	1	3.43	7	5	0	21	17	11	8	0	15	25	.213	.347	.300	25.51	15.31	98
Reguillo, Dennis	R-R	5-11	165	9-9-03	2	0	8.10	17	0	1	27	37	31	24	1	29	20	.330	.479	.464	13.70	19.86	146
Rivera, Eduardo	L-L	6-7	237	6-13-03	0	1	1.99	6	4	0	23	14	10	5	1	7	30	.175	.244	.213	33.33	7.78	90
Rodriguez-Cruz, Elmer	L-R	6-3	160	8-18-03	3	4	2.51	14	13	0	61	47	26	17	1	25	73	.206	.289	.263	28.52	9.77	256
Sansone, Michael	R-L	5-9	195	11-10-99	7	4	3.11	20	3	3	72	64	32	25	4	9	68	.243	.294	.365	23.61	3.13	288
Stebens, Isaac	L-R	6-0	194	12-5-01	0	0	0.82	6	0	3	11	7	3	1	0	4	14	.179	.289	.256	31.11	8.89	45
Steinbaugh, Conor	R-R	6-0	205	5-22-99	6	2	2.86	20	1	1	57	44	22	18	3	19	52	.216	.293	.338	22.71	8.30	229
Talavera, Luis	R-R	6-3	175	2-6-02	0	2	6.60	21	0	2	30	42	25	22	1	19	20	.328	.427	.391	13.25	12.58	151
Tolbert, Cole	R-R	6-4	200	12-2-02	0	1	5.56	5	3	0	11	11	7	7	0	6	14	.268	.380	.366	28.00	12.00	50
Valera, Juan	R-R	6-3	205	5-18-06	0	1	2.35	7	7	0	23	9	6	6	1	14	28	.120	.256	.173	31.11	15.56	90
Vargas, Yeferson	R-R	6-0	177	8-4-04	0	0	2.25	1	1	0	4	2	2	1	0	2	5	.154	.267	.154	33.33	13.33	15
Wehunt, Blake	R-R	6-6	240	11-9-00	2	0	2.16	8	8	0	33	20	9	8	1	15	44	.167	.265	.225	32.35	11.03	136
Weins, CJ	R-R	6-3	223	8-15-00	0	2	4.81	19	0	3	24	19	17	13	2	16	29	.211	.327	.367	26.61	14.68	109

Fielding

Catcher	PCT	G	PO	A	E	DP	PB
Brannon	.982	21	201	21	4	0	1
Garcia	.982	10	102	9	2	1	2
McElveny	.980	49	421	22	9	1	5
Montero	.993	25	258	21	2	1	2
Musett	.966	14	125	19	5	3	3
Rodriguez	.984	7	52	10	1	0	1
Viloria	.980	11	92	6	2	0	1

First Base	PCT	G	PO	A	E	DP
Brannon	.981	14	93	10	2	6
Encarnacion	.970	35	273	15	9	20
Feliz	.983	62	443	32	8	43
Lugo	.993	19	139	10	1	6
Montero	1.000	8	36	3	0	0

Second Base	PCT	G	PO	A	E	DP
Alcantara	.976	65	84	155	6	30
Arias	.950	10	15	23	2	6
De Leon	.970	33	38	60	3	10
Lugo	1.000	7	3	10	0	0
Pierre	1.000	1	0	2	0	0
Tucker	.968	16	23	38	2	6
Zanetello	.895	5	6	11	2	0

Third Base	PCT	G	PO	A	E	DP
Alcantara	1.000	6	3	15	0	0
Anderson	.914	67	55	104	15	14
De Leon	.875	8	4	10	2	2
Encarnacion	.880	40	26	77	14	5
Lugo	.923	11	12	12	2	2
Tucker	.750	2	4	2	2	1

Shortstop	PCT	G	PO	A	E	DP
Alcantara	.949	38	50	81	7	14
Anderson	.910	23	24	37	6	7
Arias	.946	21	36	51	5	12
De Leon	1.000	6	5	10	0	3
Encarnacion	1.000	1	2	7	0	2
Zanetello	.849	48	53	82	24	14

Outfield	PCT	G	PO	A	E	DP
Ayubi	1.000	13	20	0	0	0
Bleis	.979	37	89	3	2	1
De Leon	1.000	6	11	0	0	0
Diaz	.952	29	57	3	3	0
Garcia	.976	21	40	1	1	0
Lugo	.951	50	72	6	4	1
Rose	1.000	10	22	2	0	1
Taylor	.981	94	201	3	4	1
Tucker	.979	49	85	7	2	1
Yuten	.970	95	154	5	5	1

FCL RED SOX — *ROOKIE*

FLORIDA COMPLEX LEAGUE

Batting	B-T	Ht.	Wt.	DOB	AVG	OBP	SLG	G	PA	AB	R	H	2B	3B	HR	RBI	BB	HBP	SH	SF	SO	SB	CS	BB%	SO%
Arias, Franklin	R-R	5-11	170	11-19-05	.355	.471	.584	51	206	166	41	59	16	2	6	28	34	4	0	2	36	30	4	16.50	17.48
Asencio, Yosander	B-R	5-11	160	11-14-04	.271	.393	.441	43	145	118	23	32	7	2	3	27	25	0	0	2	48	6	1	17.24	33.10
Ayubi, Karim	R-R	6-2	165	12-8-03	.198	.398	.344	38	128	96	17	19	3	1	3	14	28	4	0	0	42	3	1	21.88	32.81
Brannon, Brooks	R-R	5-11	210	5-4-04	.174	.296	.174	8	27	23	3	4	0	0	0	1	4	0	0	0	10	1	0	14.81	37.04
Cespedes, Yoeilin	R-R	5-9	181	9-8-05	.319	.400	.615	25	105	91	20	29	10	1	5	24	12	1	0	1	19	3	1	11.43	18.10
De Los Santos, Raimundo	B-R	5-10	147	2-27-05	.232	.363	.278	46	182	151	27	35	7	0	0	8	30	1	0	0	49	28	8	16.48	26.92
Diaz, Kelvin	R-R	5-11	148	3-17-03	.298	.378	.439	47	135	114	26	34	10	0	2	17	13	4	0	4	39	20	2	9.63	28.89
Jimenez, Frederik	B-R	6-0	178	11-15-04	.308	.404	.500	29	94	78	18	24	5	2	2	17	12	2	0	2	22	6	1	12.77	23.40
Linarez, Yohander	B-R	5-11	160	3-19-05	.206	.267	.262	35	116	107	9	22	3	0	1	12	8	1	0	0	32	2	0	6.90	27.59
Musett, Andruw	R-R	5-10	198	11-21-05	.255	.395	.358	46	172	137	25	35	8	0	2	20	30	3	0	2	23	1	1	17.44	13.37
Noria, Franyer	R-R	5-10	135	9-24-04	.277	.455	.313	42	112	83	20	23	1	1	0	13	21	7	0	1	22	11	3	18.75	19.64
Nunez, Starlyn	B-R	6-0	155	10-10-05	.228	.321	.412	35	134	114	20	26	8	2	3	25	15	2	0	3	24	5	1	11.19	17.91
Riemer, Justin	B-R	6-0	170	2-6-02	.296	.462	.407	10	39	27	6	8	1	1	0	4	10	0	0	2	5	1	0	25.64	12.82
Rodriguez, Gerardo	R-R	5-10	177	12-8-05	.259	.429	.333	24	70	54	15	14	1	0	1	7	16	0	0	0	12	3	1	22.86	17.14
Romero, Mikey	L-R	5-11	175	1-12-04	.455	.500	.545	3	12	11	3	5	1	0	0	1	0	1	0	0	1	0	0	0.00	8.33
Salazar, Kleyver	R-R	6-1	187	5-1-06	.226	.333	.374	49	183	155	22	35	7	2	4	31	25	1	0	2	40	2	1	13.66	21.86
Santana, Jancel	B-R	6-0	157	8-17-05	.045	.160	.045	11	25	22	3	1	0	0	0	0	3	0	0	0	15	0	0	12.00	60.00
Sierra, Armando	R-R	6-1	189	1-17-04	.269	.310	.433	34	114	104	13	28	4	2	3	15	6	1	1	2	29	0	0	5.26	25.44

Pitching	B-T	Ht.	Wt.	DOB	W	L	ERA	G	GS	SV	IP	Hits	Runs	ER	HR	BB	SO	AVG	OBP	SLG	SO%	BB%	BF
Bates, Adam	R-R	6-1	165	8-8-05	1	2	3.96	11	9	0	36	37	17	16	3	17	36	.278	.358	.414	23.84	11.26	151
Bautista, Gilberto	R-R	6-0	165	1-8-05	0	3	3.92	8	5	0	21	18	13	9	0	13	23	.220	.326	.293	24.21	13.68	95
Bryant, Zach	R-R	6-1	210	6-5-98	0	0	4.50	4	3	0	6	7	3	3	1	3	6	.318	.423	.455	23.08	11.54	26
Colmenares, Willian	R-R	6-0	183	2-3-05	2	3	13.86	12	0	1	12	19	21	19	1	23	8	.352	.538	.519	10.26	29.49	78
De La Cruz, Nicolas	L-L	6-4	252	11-18-05	0	1	1.93	6	3	0	9	5	5	2	0	12	11	.167	.405	.200	26.19	28.57	42
Diaz, Kelvin	R-R	5-11	148	3-17-03	0	0	0.00	1	0	0	1	0	0	0	0	1	1	.000	.250	.000	25.00	25.00	4
Garcia, Jesus	R-R	6-1	191	11-6-05	2	1	3.34	15	1	1	32	33	18	12	2	25	27	.266	.401	.395	17.76	16.45	152
Hernandez, Diego	R-R	6-0	154	8-12-04	2	0	6.10	10	0	1	10	9	8	7	0	17	15	.237	.482	.316	26.32	29.82	57
Jerez, Luis	R-R	6-1	217	8-26-03	0	1	5.09	10	1	0	18	19	10	10	2	9	18	.279	.380	.456	22.78	11.39	79
Judice, Nicholas	R-R	6-8	212	4-8-01	1	0	4.50	2	1	0	4	3	2	2	1	2	4	.200	.294	.467	23.53	11.76	17
Lee, Chansol	R-R	6-1	195	7-24-05	0	0	10.80	2	2	0	2	4	2	2	0	1	2	.444	.500	.667	20.00	10.00	10
Liu, Chih-Jung	B-R	6-0	185	4-7-99	1	0	0.00	1	0	0	3.0	3	0	0	0	0	5	.250	.250	.333	41.67	0.00	12
Mata, Bryan	R-R	6-3	238	5-3-99	0	0	4.50	1	1	0	2	3	1	1	0	0	2	.375	.375	.750	25.00	0.00	8
Monegro, Yordanny	R-R	6-4	180	10-14-02	0	0	3.60	3	3	0	10	8	4	4	0	3	12	.222	.300	.333	30.00	7.50	40
Portes, Ovis	R-R	6-4	167	12-3-04	2	0	0.00	4	0	2	13	5	0	0	0	4	16	.119	.196	.143	34.78	8.70	46

BOSTON RED SOX

Reguillo, Dennis	R-R	5-11	165	9-9-03	3	2	6.75	13	0	2	25	31	21	19	1	13	20	.298	.392	.394	16.67	10.83	120
Rivera, Eduardo	L-L	6-7	237	6-13-03	1	1	4.70	4	1	1	8	10	6	4	0	2	8	.303	.343	.424	22.22	5.56	36
Rodriguez, Wuilliams	R-R	6-2	199	11-3-05	2	0	3.82	12	4	0	31	24	16	13	1	11	30	.216	.298	.315	24.00	8.80	125
Rodriguez, Yonfi	R-R	5-10	160	7-30-02	5	5	4.85	16	1	1	30	37	22	16	0	21	20	.314	.420	.415	13.89	14.58	144
Salcedo, Deybi	R-R	6-1	197	7-5-04	2	1	5.18	11	7	1	33	34	21	19	2	21	33	.262	.359	.369	21.57	13.73	153
Soriano, Cristofer	R-R	6-1	160	11-23-02	2	0	7.36	16	0	1	26	24	26	21	1	29	26	.264	.438	.341	21.31	23.77	122
Talavera, Luis	R-R	6-3	175	2-6-02	0	0	0.00	1	0	0	2	0	1	0	0	1	2	.000	.125	.000	25.00	12.50	8
Valera, Juan	R-R	6-3	205	5-18-06	1	2	1.79	11	9	0	40	17	9	8	0	14	40	.128	.235	.165	25.97	9.09	154
Van Der Schaaf, Stijn	R-R	6-4	185	4-8-04	3	0	3.76	10	5	0	26	21	11	11	1	15	23	.236	.382	.348	20.91	13.64	110
Vargas, Yeferson	R-R	6-0	177	8-4-04	4	2	3.13	10	3	1	32	30	15	11	3	13	29	.256	.333	.436	21.97	9.85	132

Fielding

C: Salazar 25, Musett 22, Rodriguez 14, Brannon 5, Jimenez 1. **1B:** Jimenez 21, Musett 16, Salazar 16, Sierra 8, Rodriguez 2, Brannon 1. **2B:** Noria 13, De Los Santos 12, Arias 11, Linarez 8, Cespedes 7, Santana 6, Riemer 3, Nunez 2, Romero 1. **3B:** Nunez 27, Linarez 22, Noria 10, Rodriguez 1, De Los Santos 1. **SS:** Arias 36, Cespedes 10, Nunez 4, Riemer 4, Santana 4, Romero 2, Linarez 2, De Los Santos 1. **LF:** Asencio 18, Noria 15, Sierra 15, Ayubi 11, Rodriguez 5, Diaz 4. **CF:** De Los Santos 34, Diaz 21, Asencio 5, Ayubi 1. **RF:** Ayubi 26, Diaz 17, Asencio 13, Sierra 3, Noria 1.

DSL RED SOX BLUE — *ROOKIE*

DOMINICAN SUMMER LEAGUE

Batting	B-T	Ht.	Wt.	DOB	AVG	OBP	SLG	G	PA	AB	R	H	2B	3B	HR	RBI	BB	HBP	SH	SF	SO	SB	CS	BB%	SO%
Arroyo, Samuel	R-R	5-11	159	5-23-07	.100	.294	.175	16	51	40	1	4	3	0	0	2	10	1	0	0	16	1	0	19.61	31.37
Asencio, Vladimir	R-R	5-10	165	12-13-06	.165	.317	.195	43	164	133	21	22	2	1	0	13	21	9	0	1	39	14	5	12.80	23.78
Baker, Tavano	L-L	5-11	160	10-13-06	.243	.308	.340	40	159	144	23	35	5	3	1	18	11	3	0	1	25	6	0	6.92	15.72
Bolivar, Moises	R-R	6-0	175	7-8-07	.274	.362	.436	33	138	117	19	32	6	2	3	21	17	1	0	3	23	1	0	12.32	16.67
Brito, Josue	R-R	6-0	175	4-12-07	.212	.379	.346	37	132	104	15	22	5	0	3	14	27	1	0	0	31	7	5	20.45	23.48
Darville, Edwin	L-R	5-9	163	10-12-06	.177	.416	.302	38	137	96	18	17	3	3	1	8	36	4	0	1	50	7	2	26.28	36.50
Diaz, Jhiancarlos	L-R	6-1	174	1-12-07	.240	.363	.253	28	91	75	13	18	1	0	0	8	11	4	0	1	25	3	2	12.09	27.47
Fernandez, Ilan	R-R	6-0	160	10-30-06	.279	.385	.367	43	179	147	25	41	4	3	1	16	18	10	0	4	23	10	1	10.06	12.85
Gonzales, Justin	R-R	6-4	210	12-31-06	.327	.395	.516	43	177	159	27	52	10	4	4	26	17	1	0	0	16	7	3	9.60	9.04
Lugo, Jesus	R-R	6-0	170	10-25-06	.183	.281	.278	36	135	115	11	21	5	0	2	16	14	3	0	3	45	2	3	10.37	33.33
Marin, Liosward	L-R	5-10	158	5-15-06	.277	.406	.349	31	106	83	15	23	6	0	0	14	17	3	0	3	17	1	0	16.04	16.04
Reyna, Emanuel	R-R	6-3	196	7-5-07	.224	.323	.247	29	99	85	6	19	2	0	0	13	10	3	0	1	36	1	0	10.10	36.36
Ruiz, Yoiber	R-R	5-7	171	11-11-05	.278	.391	.315	34	128	108	22	30	4	0	0	7	14	6	0	0	16	9	1	10.94	12.50
Santana, Jancel	B-R	6-0	157	8-17-05	.250	.550	.250	6	20	12	4	3	0	0	0	0	6	2	0	0	5	2	0	30.00	25.00
Semerite, Moises	R-R	6-0	151	5-31-06	.176	.300	.441	20	40	34	6	6	2	2	1	5	5	1	0	0	18	1	0	12.50	45.00
Sirvania, Givian	R-R	5-8	150	8-2-07	.222	.385	.274	36	148	117	19	26	6	0	0	5	22	9	0	0	26	19	7	14.86	17.57
Sojo, Justim	L-R	5-11	163	5-17-07	.136	.296	.212	25	81	66	5	9	1	2	0	4	9	6	0	0	29	4	1	11.11	35.80

Pitching	B-T	Ht.	Wt.	DOB	W	L	ERA	G	GS	SV	IP	Hits	Runs	ER	HR	BB	SO	AVG	OBP	SLG	SO%	BB%	BF
Belisario, Felix	R-R	5-11	155	9-11-06	3	3	5.51	16	1	2	33	42	25	20	2	25	32	.311	.422	.444	19.75	15.43	162
Beltre, Yodrian	R-R	6-2	238	10-20-05	0	3	7.71	5	3	0	14	17	13	12	0	8	14	.279	.371	.344	20.00	11.43	70
Cabrera, Luis	R-R	6-2	180	5-13-06	3	1	7.01	12	1	0	35	35	31	27	4	22	23	.263	.366	.466	14.29	13.66	161
Carta, Enrique	R-R	5-10	180	12-23-03	3	0	1.71	12	0	1	26	11	7	5	0	11	29	.129	.240	.153	29.00	11.00	100
Chirino, Yoelvin	R-R	6-0	161	5-13-05	2	1	3.16	12	7	0	37	28	15	13	3	23	40	.212	.335	.356	25.16	14.47	159
Felix, Anthony	R-R	5-11	170	5-31-04	0	0	5.17	9	0	1	16	18	9	9	1	10	17	.277	.397	.431	21.79	12.82	78
Galvan, Gilbel	R-R	5-10	167	9-20-06	5	1	1.62	17	0	1	33	24	9	6	1	13	21	.203	.293	.271	15.67	9.70	134
Golindano, Jose	L-L	5-11	170	3-16-06	1	4	6.55	11	4	1	22	22	26	16	0	29	32	.250	.450	.341	26.67	24.17	120
Gonzalez, Yohandry	R-R	5-11	165	3-25-06	0	1	2.08	8	5	0	22	12	6	5	0	15	19	.167	.348	.194	20.65	16.30	92
Medina, Juan	R-R	5-11	190	10-28-06	2	1	7.11	6	1	0	13	14	12	10	1	13	8	.275	.448	.353	11.94	19.40	67
Pena, Jeremy	R-R	6-2	180	10-15-04	0	1	10.91	10	0	1	16	18	21	19	0	20	12	.286	.472	.333	13.48	22.47	89
Prado, Abis	L-L	6-3	190	10-17-06	0	5	5.40	12	11	0	32	30	33	19	0	35	31	.252	.428	.286	19.50	22.01	159
Reyes, Dalvinson	R-R	6-5	200	11-19-06	0	0	0.00	4	4	0	16	8	0	0	0	2	17	.148	.193	.167	29.82	3.51	57
Reynoso, William	R-R	6-0	175	8-16-05	4	0	4.94	16	0	1	27	22	17	15	0	23	12	.227	.398	.247	9.38	17.97	128
Rijo, Brahian	R-R	5-11	180	8-22-06	2	0	4.63	14	0	0	23	12	12	12	0	30	20	.154	.407	.218	17.70	26.55	113
Sanchez, Denison	R-R	6-1	164	8-30-05	1	0	4.45	16	0	1	32	26	19	16	1	27	38	.217	.409	.283	23.90	16.98	159
Semerite, Moises	R-R	6-0	151	5-31-06	0	0	0.00	1	0	0	1	0	0	0	0	1	0	.000	.333	.000	0.00	33.33	3
Travieso, Jesus	R-R	5-11	140	3-22-07	0	3	3.80	11	11	0	21	19	11	9	0	10	27	.238	.333	.288	29.03	10.75	93
Wilson, Tejahari	R-R	6-1	186	12-6-06	1	2	3.32	8	5	0	19	8	10	7	1	14	17	.133	.321	.217	21.79	17.95	78

Fielding

C: Rodriguez 31, Rivera 28, Mambel 6. **1B:** Mambel 26, Carrasquel 18, Simmons 11, Gonzales 4, Barry 3, Brito 3, Montesino 1. **2B:** Alvarado 26, Barry 23, Simmons 8, Teran 6. **3B:** Alvarado 18, Carrasquel 15, Teran 14, Simmons 11, Barry 7. **SS:** Pinto 42, Teran 18, Alvarado 1. **LF:** Azocar 27, Peguero 16, Montesino 9, Delancey 6, Fermin 1, Barry 1, Brito 1. **CF:** Fermin 39, Peguero 10, Teran 5, Montesino 3. **RF:** Brito 33, Peguero 16, Montesino 12, Azocar 3.

DSL RED SOX RED — *ROOKIE*

DOMINICAN SUMMER LEAGUE

Batting	B-T	Ht.	Wt.	DOB	AVG	OBP	SLG	G	PA	AB	R	H	2B	3B	HR	RBI	BB	HBP	SH	SF	SO	SB	CS	BB%	SO%
Alvarado, Christopher	R-R	5-10	162	6-14-07	.260	.375	.295	44	176	146	29	38	5	0	0	16	24	4	0	2	27	16	8	13.64	15.34
Azocar, Enddy	R-R	6-2	168	2-24-07	.266	.397	.309	31	116	94	17	25	2	1	0	11	18	3	0	1	15	2	7	15.52	12.93
Barry, Justin	R-R	5-11	159	8-9-06	.207	.311	.356	41	161	135	25	28	7	2	3	20	18	4	0	4	37	8	0	11.18	22.98
Brito, Edwin	R-R	5-11	195	11-23-06	.251	.361	.450	51	205	171	27	43	6	2	8	32	21	10	0	3	46	2	1	10.24	22.44
Carrasquel, Carlos	R-R	6-4	195	1-13-07	.319	.394	.372	34	127	113	15	36	4	1	0	23	9	5	0	0	26	0	0	7.09	20.47
Delancey, Chad	R-R	5-11	175	7-12-06	.305	.442	.390	23	77	59	12	18	3	1	0	12	11	5	0	2	16	4	3	14.29	20.78

Fermin, Anderson	B-R	5-11	174	9-2-06	.293	.408	.337	49	224	181	33	53	6	1	0	23	35	3	1	4	22	12	6	15.63	9.82
Gonzales, Justin	R-R	6-4	210	12-31-06	.231	.333	.538	4	15	13	2	3	1	0	1	3	2	0	0	0	4	1	0	13.33	26.67
Mambel, Alexander	R-R	6-0	191	8-4-06	.277	.302	.406	33	106	101	13	28	7	0	2	20	1	3	0	1	13	0	0	0.94	12.26
Montesino, Rafi	R-R	5-10	170	5-31-07	.175	.293	.206	28	76	63	11	11	0	1	0	3	11	0	1	1	18	2	1	14.47	23.68
Peguero, Jhoan	R-R	6-2	166	9-5-05	.251	.358	.347	49	201	167	35	42	9	2	1	22	27	3	0	4	43	15	1	13.43	21.39
Pinto, Avinson	B-R	5-11	150	5-29-07	.320	.407	.393	44	172	150	30	48	4	2	1	16	17	5	0	0	15	12	6	9.88	8.72
Rivera, Miguel	R-R	5-11	170	2-2-07	.180	.280	.191	29	107	89	9	16	1	0	0	12	13	1	0	4	21	0	0	12.15	19.63
Rodriguez, Jorge	R-R	5-10	147	2-24-06	.258	.333	.280	31	105	93	18	24	2	0	0	7	7	4	0	1	25	8	1	6.67	23.81
Simmons, Kenyon	R-R	6-1	150	4-13-07	.165	.302	.203	30	96	79	11	13	3	0	0	8	14	2	0	1	29	3	0	14.58	30.21
Teran, Efren	B-R	5-10	163	11-4-06	.205	.300	.246	40	140	122	15	25	5	0	0	16	17	0	0	1	10	3	3	12.14	7.14

Pitching	**B-T**	**Ht.**	**Wt.**	**DOB**	**W**	**L**	**ERA**	**G**	**GS**	**SV**	**IP**	**Hits**	**Runs**	**ER**	**HR**	**BB**	**SO**	**AVG**	**OBP**	**SLG**	**SO%**	**BB%**	**BF**
Alcantara, Jhon	R-R	61-4	175	9-13-05	0	1	20.25	4	0	0	3	3	9	6	0	10	1	.250	.625	.333	4.00	40.00	25
Arredondo, Breilin	R-R	5-11	151	7-10-05	4	2	3.58	18	0	0	28	23	17	11	2	17	14	.228	.366	.307	11.38	13.82	123
Beltre, Yodrian	R-R	6-2	238	10-20-05	1	0	0.82	5	5	0	22	12	3	2	0	4	20	.160	.222	.187	24.39	4.88	82
Bido, Merlin	R-R	6-0	174	2-27-06	2	3	4.17	12	6	0	41	34	21	19	1	18	33	.233	.329	.342	19.64	10.71	168
Bonaci, Yander	L-L	5-11	162	10-25-06	5	0	4.26	15	0	1	25	14	13	12	2	15	33	.163	.321	.267	30.84	14.02	107
Carta, Enrique	R-R	5-10	180	12-23-03	0	0	5.79	3	0	1	5	9	3	3	0	3	4	.409	.480	.455	16.00	12.00	25
Colina, Greider	R-R	6-2	180	4-24-05	3	0	2.12	16	0	4	30	18	11	7	0	13	29	.173	.289	.202	23.97	10.74	121
Delancey, Chad	R-R	5-11	175	7-12-06	0	0	0.00	1	0	0	0	0	0	0	0	0	0	.000	.000	.000	0.00	0.00	1
Felix, Anthony	R-R	5-11	170	5-31-04	2	0	0.93	5	0	1	10	7	3	1	0	4	9	.194	.326	.194	20.93	9.30	43
Frias, Madinson	R-R	6-2	205	4-1-05	2	1	2.23	11	11	0	40	31	12	10	0	19	24	.221	.325	.264	14.72	11.66	163
Gil, Raphy	R-R	6-1	165	11-15-05	0	0	0.90	8	0	3	10	8	7	1	0	6	8	.211	.340	.263	17.02	12.77	47
Henriquez, Juan	R-R	6-0	172	6-29-06	5	0	2.14	17	0	4	34	28	9	8	1	15	25	.233	.324	.283	17.99	10.79	139
Martinez, Jose	R-R	6-1	204	1-7-05	4	1	3.48	14	4	0	41	36	17	16	4	9	45	.240	.284	.380	27.61	5.52	163
Morillo, Dariel	R-R	5-11	204	8-4-06	1	2	3.00	8	6	0	18	13	14	6	2	12	13	.188	.333	.290	15.48	14.29	84
Muzziotti, Cesar	R-R	6-1	182	10-23-06	1	1	0.00	6	0	1	9	3	2	0	0	6	5	.115	.333	.115	13.51	16.22	37
Payano, Jeison	R-R	6-0	187	11-5-05	1	1	2.61	9	6	1	31	22	9	9	2	9	25	.195	.260	.310	20.33	7.32	123
Reyes, Dalvinson	R-R	6-5	200	11-19-06	0	0	0.00	1	1	0	1	0	0	0	0	0	2	.000	.000	.000	66.67	0.00	3
Rojas, Shnaider	R-R	6-0	170	12-5-06	3	0	6.26	11	0	0	23	30	18	16	2	19	22	.306	.434	.449	18.03	15.57	122
Ruiz, Yermain	R-R	5-11	160	11-27-05	3	1	1.77	11	11	0	46	27	13	9	3	15	37	.172	.257	.248	21.02	8.52	176
Sanchez, Oscar	L-L	6-0	180	6-26-03	2	0	1.04	10	0	0	17	6	2	2	0	7	13	.105	.227	.158	19.40	10.45	67
Veraza, Yoandys	R-R	5-11	174	9-2-06	3	1	3.03	11	1	1	36	29	14	12	2	25	25	.236	.387	.341	15.82	15.82	158
Zink, Charlie	R-R	6-4	180	1-5-06	0	0	7.71	5	5	0	7	5	6	6	0	8	5	.238	.500	.381	14.71	23.53	34

Fielding

C: Marin 30, Arroyo 15, Ruiz 14. **1B:** Gonzales 28, Reyna 20, Diaz 8, Bolivar 3. **2B:** Darville 29, Sirvania 15, Sojo 10, Ruiz 5, Diaz 2, Santana 1. **3B:** Bolivar 25, Diaz 19, Ruiz 7, Darville 7, Santana 1. **SS:** Fernandez 42, Ruiz 9, Santana 3, Diaz 2, Sirvania 1. **LF:** Lugo 20, Brito 11, Sirvania 10, Baker 10, Asencio 6, Semerite 2. **CF:** Asencio 30, Baker 11, Semerite 8, Sirvania 6, Brito 5, Gonzales 2. **RF:** Brito 15, Gonzales 14, Baker 12, Semerite 8, Asencio 6, Sirvania 5.

Chicago Cubs

SEASON SYNOPSIS: The Cubs splurged on an industry-high $8 million annual contract to lure manager Craig Counsell from the rival Brewers. But in his first season, Counsell led the Cubs to the same 83-79 record David Ross managed them to in 2023.

HIGH POINT: Japanese lefthander Shota Imanaga was one of the better starters in the National League in a 15-3, 2.91 season, ranking third in the NL in ERA and first with a 6.2 strikeout/walk ratio. He didn't give up a run in five of his first nine starts, helping the Cubs reach first place as late as May 8, and was 5-0, 0.84 before the league caught up a bit. But on Sept. 4, he threw seven innings, with Nate Pearson and Porter Hodge getting an inning apiece in the first no-hitter by the Cubs at Wrigley Field since 1972, a 12-0 win against the Pirates.

LOW POINT: For a single game, it's hard to beat April 8, as the Padres spotted the Cubs an 8-0 lead, then rallied for a 9-8 victory, the Cubs' largest blown lead in a game since 2002. The Cubs were 24-17 when they lost six consecutive series—two to the Braves and one apiece to every NL Central division foe. Only a two-game sweep of the lowly crosstown White Sox ended the streak.

NOTABLE ROOKIES: Imanaga, signed for four years and $53 million, counts as a rookie in his first year coming over from Japan. Righthander Ben Brown, armed with a fastball which averaged 96 mph, showed promise and tossed seven scoreless, hitless innings with 10 strikeouts in a May 28 start against the Brewers. He missed the last three months of the season with a neck strain. Hodge, 23, emerged as a relief option and potential future closer, saving nine games to rank second on the team.

KEY TRANSACTIONS: The Cubs acquired their starting first baseman, Michael Busch, from the Dodgers in a trade that cost them prospects Zyhir Hope, a toolsy outfielder, and lefthander Jackson Ferris. They mixed buying and selling at the trade deadline, shipping righty reliever Mark Leiter Jr. to the Yankees, while spinning Christopher Morel and two minor league pitchers, Hunter Bigge and Ty Johnson, to the Rays for third baseman Isaac Paredes. The Cubs originally signed Paredes out of Mexico in 2015 and traded him to the Tigers in a 2017 deadline deal.

OPENING DAY PAYROLL: $213,020,500 (9th)

PLAYERS OF THE YEAR

MAJOR LEAGUE

Ian Happ
OF

.243/.341/.441
25 HR, 86 RBIs, 80 BB
Third Gold Glove

MINOR LEAGUE

Matt Shaw
3B

(AA/AAA)
.284/.379/.488
21 HR, 31 SB

ORGANIZATION LEADERS

Batting		***Qualifiers**
MAJORS		
* AVG	Seiya Suzuki	.283
* OPS	Seiya Suzuki	.848
HR	Ian Happ	24
RBI	Ian Happ	86
MINORS		
* AVG	James Triantos, Tennessee/Iowa	.300
* OBP	Christian Franklin, Tennessee	.398
* SLG	Matt Shaw, Iowa/Tennessee	.488
* OPS	Matt Shaw, Iowa/Tennessee	.867
R	Jonathon Long, South Bend/Tennessee	86
H	James Triantos, Tennessee/Iowa	133
TB	Owen Caissie, Iowa	223
2B	Andy Garriola, Myrtle Beach/South Bend	29
2B	Owen Caissie, Iowa	29
3B	Alexey Lumpuy, DSL Cubs Blue	12
3B	Jacob Wetzel, Myrtle Beach/South Bend	12
HR	Matt Shaw, Iowa/Tennessee	21
HR	Andy Garriola, Myrtle Beach/South Bend	21
RBI	Andy Garriola, Myrtle Beach/South Bend	83
BB	Cristian Hernandez, Myrtle Beach/South Bend	75
SO	Felix Stevens, South Bend/Tennessee	164
SB	James Triantos, Tennessee/Iowa	47
Pitching		**#Qualifiers**
MAJORS		
W	Shota Imanaga	15
# ERA	Shota Imanaga	2.91
SO	Shota Imanaga	174
SV	Hector Neris	17
MINORS		
W	Connor Noland, Iowa/Tennessee	12
L	Brandon Birdsell, Iowa/Tennessee	9
# ERA	Sam Armstrong, South Bend/Tennessee	2.87
G	Michael Arias, Iowa/Tennessee	49
G	Cam Sanders, Iowa/Tennessee	49
GS	Brandon Birdsell, Iowa/Tennessee	26
SV	Frankie Scalzo, Iowa/Tennessee	9
IP	Brandon Birdsell, Iowa/Tennessee	136
BB	Drew Gray, South Bend	73
SO	Brandon Birdsell, Iowa/Tennessee	134
# AVG	Sam Armstrong, South Bend/Tennessee	.213

2024 PERFORMANCE

President: Jed Hoyer. **Farm Director:** Jason Kanzler. **Scouting Director:** Dan Kantrovitz.

Class	Team	League	W	L	PCT	Finish	Manager
Majors	Chicago Cubs	National	83	79	.512	8 (15)	Craig Counsell
Triple-A	Iowa Cubs	International	68	82	.453	19 (20)	Marty Pevey
Double-A	Tennessee Smokies	Southern	87	50	.635	1 (8)	Lance Rymel
High-A	South Bend Cubs	Midwest	54	78	.409	11 (12)	Nick Lovullo
Low-A	Myrtle Beach Pelicans	Carolina	62	67	.481	9 (12)	Buddy Bailey
Rookie	ACL Cubs	Arizona Complex	30	30	.500	7 (15)	Corey Ray
Rookie	DSL Cubs Blue	Dominican	28	26	.519	22 (51)	Enrique Wilson
Rookie	DSL Cubs Red	Dominican	19	35	.352	44 (51)	Carlos Ramirez
Overall 2024 Minor League Record			**348**	**368**	**.486**	**18th (30)**	

ORGANIZATION STATISTICS

CHICAGO CUBS

CHICAGO CUBS

NATIONAL LEAGUE

Batting	B-T	Ht.	Wt.	DOB	AVG	OBP	SLG	G	PA	AB	R	H	2B	3B	HR	RBI	BB	HBP	SH	SF	SO	SB	CS	BB%	SO%
Alcantara, Kevin	R-R	6-6	188	7-12-02	.100	.100	.100	3	10	10	1	1	0	0	0	0	0	0	0	0	1	0	0	0.00	10.00
Amaya, Miguel	R-R	6-0	230	3-9-99	.232	.288	.357	117	363	328	32	76	13	2	8	47	23	4	5	3	62	0	0	6.34	17.08
Bellinger, Cody	L-L	6-4	203	7-13-95	.266	.325	.426	130	569	516	72	137	23	3	18	78	45	3	0	5	89	9	2	7.91	15.64
Bethancourt, Christian	R-R	6-3	205	9-2-91	.281	.305	.509	24	59	57	9	16	4	0	3	15	2	0	0	0	14	3	0	3.39	23.73
Bote, David	R-R	6-1	205	4-7-93	.304	.333	.391	37	48	46	4	14	4	0	0	6	2	0	0	0	13	0	0	4.17	27.08
Busch, Michael	L-R	6-1	210	11-9-97	.248	.335	.440	152	567	496	73	123	28	2	21	65	63	4	0	4	162	2	1	11.11	28.57
Canario, Alexander	R-R	5-11	165	5-7-00	.280	.357	.440	15	28	25	4	7	1	0	1	2	2	1	0	0	11	1	0	7.14	39.29
Cooper, Garrett	R-R	6-5	235	12-25-90	.270	.341	.432	12	41	37	3	10	1	1	1	6	4	0	0	0	13	0	0	9.76	31.71
Crow-Armstrong, Pete	L-L	5-11	184	3-25-02	.237	.286	.384	123	410	372	46	88	13	6	10	47	21	6	8	3	98	27	3	5.12	23.90
Gomes, Yan	R-R	6-2	212	7-19-87	.154	.179	.242	34	96	91	7	14	2	0	2	7	2	1	1	1	36	0	0	2.08	37.50
Happ, Ian	B-R	6-0	205	8-12-94	.243	.341	.441	153	657	569	89	138	34	2	25	86	80	6	0	2	168	13	2	12.18	25.57
Hoerner, Nico	R-R	6-1	200	5-13-97	.273	.335	.373	151	641	582	86	159	35	1	7	48	44	12	0	3	66	31	6	6.86	10.30
Madrigal, Nick	R-R	5-8	175	3-5-97	.221	.280	.256	51	94	86	5	19	3	0	0	10	4	3	1	0	10	1	0	4.26	10.64
Mastrobuoni, Miles	L-R	5-11	185	10-31-95	.194	.245	.224	50	106	98	9	19	3	0	0	4	7	0	0	1	17	2	0	6.60	16.04
Mervis, Matt	L-R	6-2	225	4-16-98	.115	.148	.154	9	28	26	1	3	1	0	0	3	1	0	0	0	8	0	0	3.57	28.57
Morel, Christopher	R-R	5-11	145	6-24-99	.199	.302	.373	103	421	362	43	72	7	1	18	51	47	8	0	4	103	7	5	11.16	24.47
Nido, Tomas	R-R	6-0	211	4-12-94	.128	.143	.234	17	50	47	5	6	2	0	1	4	1	0	1	1	15	0	0	2.00	30.00
Paredes, Isaac	R-R	5-11	213	2-18-99	.223	.325	.307	52	212	179	23	40	6	0	3	25	24	5	0	4	37	1	0	11.32	17.45
Suzuki, Seiya	R-R	5-11	182	8-18-94	.283	.366	.482	132	585	512	74	145	27	6	21	73	63	6	0	4	160	16	6	10.77	27.35
Swanson, Dansby	R-R	6-1	190	2-11-94	.242	.312	.390	149	593	534	82	129	27	2	16	66	54	2	0	3	144	19	3	9.11	24.28
Tauchman, Mike	L-L	6-2	220	12-3-90	.248	.357	.366	109	350	298	50	74	12	1	7	29	47	4	0	1	70	6	2	13.43	20.00
Vazquez, Luis	R-R	6-0	165	10-10-99	.083	.143	.083	11	14	12	2	1	0	0	0	1	0	1	0	1	6	0	0	0.00	42.86
Wisdom, Patrick	R-R	6-2	220	8-27-91	.171	.237	.392	75	174	158	16	27	7	2	8	23	10	4	1	1	59	5	0	5.75	33.91

Pitching	B-T	Ht.	Wt.	DOB	W	L	ERA	G	GS	SV	IP	Hits	Runs	ER	HR	BB	SO	AVG	OBP	SLG	SO%	BB%	BF
Almonte, Yency	R-R	6-5	223	6-4-94	1	0	3.45	17	0	1	16	9	7	6	1	8	20	.161	.204	.268	29.85	11.94	67
Alzolay, Adbert	R-R	6-1	208	3-1-95	1	4	4.67	18	0	4	17	19	13	9	6	6	13	.279	.347	.559	17.33	8.00	75
Armstrong, Shawn	R-R	6-2	225	9-11-90	0	1	4.91	8	0	0	7	10	4	4	0	4	4	.370	.452	.444	12.50	12.50	32
Assad, Javier	R-R	6-1	200	7-30-97	7	6	3.73	29	29	0	147	143	64	61	20	63	124	.254	.333	.422	19.44	9.87	638
Bigge, Hunter	R-R	6-1	205	6-12-98	0	0	2.70	4	0	0	3	3	1	1	0	2	5	.231	.333	.231	33.33	13.33	15
Bote, David	R-R	6-1	205	4-7-93	0	0	0.00	1	0	0	1	1	0	0	0	1	0	.250	.400	.500	0.00	20.00	5
Brewer, Colten	R-R	6-4	222	10-29-92	0	0	5.66	16	0	1	21	24	16	13	1	9	22	.293	.358	.427	23.16	9.47	95
Brown, Ben	R-R	6-6	210	9-9-99	1	3	3.58	15	8	0	55	41	22	22	5	19	64	.208	.276	.330	28.83	8.56	222
Cuas, Jose	R-R	6-3	195	6-28-94	0	0	7.43	9	0	0	13	16	12	11	3	6	14	.291	.385	.509	21.54	9.23	65
Hendricks, Kyle	R-R	6-3	190	12-7-89	4	12	5.92	29	24	0	131	147	88	86	21	43	87	.286	.340	.442	15.34	7.58	567
Hodge, Porter	R-R	6-4	230	2-21-01	3	1	1.88	39	0	9	43	19	10	9	2	19	52	.132	.238	.215	31.71	11.59	164
Hollowell, Gavin	R-R	6-7	215	11-4-97	0	0	0.00	1	0	0	1	2	0	0	0	0	1	.400	.400	.400	16.67	0.00	6
Imanaga, Shota	L-L	5-8	176	9-1-93	15	3	2.91	29	29	0	173	149	66	56	27	28	174	.225	.259	.385	25.07	4.03	694
Kilian, Caleb	R-R	6-4	180	6-2-97	0	1	4.22	2	1	0	11	11	6	5	2	6	7	.268	.362	.463	14.58	12.50	48
Leiter, Mark	R-R	6-0	210	3-13-91	2	4	4.21	39	0	0	36	27	20	17	2	13	53	.196	.270	.261	34.87	8.55	152
Little, Luke	L-L	6-8	220	8-30-00	3	1	3.46	30	1	0	26	15	11	10	1	18	28	.174	.339	.256	25.69	16.51	109
Lopez, Jorge	R-R	6-3	200	2-10-93	1	1	2.03	24	0	2	27	21	6	6	3	8	31	.214	.274	.327	29.25	7.55	106
Lovelady, Richard	L-L	6-0	185	7-7-95	0	1	7.94	7	0	0	6	9	5	5	1	2	6	.346	.393	.577	21.43	7.14	28
Merryweather, Julian	R-R	6-4	215	10-14-91	1	1	6.60	15	0	0	15	18	11	11	0	9	14	.295	.405	.459	18.92	12.16	74
Mervis, Matt	L-R	6-2	225	4-16-98	0	0	81.00	1	0	0	1	7	6	6	0	0	0	.778	.778	1.111	0.00	0.00	9
Miller, Tyson	R-R	6-5	220	7-29-95	5	1	2.15	49	0	1	50	31	13	12	5	10	42	.178	.238	.293	22.11	5.26	190
Neely, Jack	R-R	6-8	225	6-5-00	0	0	9.00	6	0	0	6	8	6	6	2	2	7	.308	.357	.538	25.00	7.14	28
Neris, Hector	R-R	6-2	227	6-14-89	8	4	3.89	46	0	17	44	41	20	19	4	26	46	.247	.351	.398	23.47	13.27	196
Palencia, Daniel	R-R	5-11	160	2-5-00	0	1	6.14	10	0	1	15	14	11	10	0	12	16	.250	.391	.339	23.19	17.39	69
Paredes, Enoli	R-R	5-11	171	9-28-95	0	0	0.00	1	0	0	1	0	0	0	0	0	2	.000	.000	.000	66.67	0.00	3
Pearson, Nate	R-R	6-6	255	8-20-96	2	1	2.73	19	1	0	26	22	8	8	4	4	23	.227	.262	.402	22.33	3.88	103
Roberts, Ethan	R-R	5-10	180	7-4-97	1	1	3.71	21	0	0	27	31	11	11	3	10	26	.290	.356	.421	22.03	8.47	118

Pitching	B-T	Ht.	Wt.	DOB	W	L	ERA	G	GS	SV	IP	Hits	Runs	ER	HR	BB	SO	AVG	OBP	SLG	SO%	BB%	BF
Smyly, Drew	L-L	6-2	188	6-13-89	4	8	3.84	50	0	0	59	57	29	25	10	25	56	.252	.333	.416	21.79	9.73	257
Steele, Justin	L-L	6-2	205	7-11-95	5	5	3.07	24	24	0	135	111	54	46	12	37	135	.219	.276	.336	24.32	6.67	555
Taillon, Jameson	R-R	6-5	230	11-18-91	12	8	3.27	28	28	0	165	154	67	60	21	33	125	.243	.280	.387	18.52	4.89	675
Thompson, Keegan	R-R	6-1	210	3-13-95	2	1	2.67	24	0	2	30	19	12	9	3	18	36	.178	.294	.318	28.35	14.17	127
Tinoco, Jesus	R-R	6-4	258	4-30-95	0	0	0.00	2	0	0	4	3	0	0	0	0	3	.214	.214	.214	21.43	0.00	14
Wesneski, Hayden	R-R	6-3	210	12-5-97	3	6	3.86	28	7	0	68	56	37	29	12	21	67	.215	.279	.392	23.67	7.42	283
Wicks, Jordan	L-L	6-3	220	9-1-99	2	4	5.48	11	10	0	46	55	31	28	9	20	42	.291	.365	.497	19.81	9.43	212
Wingenter, Trey	R-R	6-7	237	4-15-94	0	0	3.00	5	0	0	6	8	2	2	1	2	3	.320	.370	.440	10.71	7.14	28
Wisdom, Patrick	R-R	6-2	220	8-27-91	0	0	0.00	1	0	0	0	1	0	0	0	1	0	.500	.667	.500	0.00	33.33	3

Fielding

Catcher	PCT	G	PO	A	E	DP	PB
Amaya	.993	116	856	31	6	3	6
Bethancourt	.993	24	135	10	1	0	0
Gomes	1.000	34	245	6	0	0	0
Nido	.993	16	135	5	1	1	1

First Base	PCT	G	PO	A	E	DP
Bellinger	1.000	22	110	7	0	4
Bote	1.000	3	3	1	0	0
Busch	.996	142	940	77	4	68
Cooper	1.000	3	22	1	0	3
Mervis	1.000	1	1	0	0	0
Wisdom	.992	27	120	7	1	8

Second Base	PCT	G	PO	A	E	DP
Bote	1.000	6	7	3	0	1
Busch	1.000	3	0	1	0	0
Hoerner	.986	144	229	337	8	61
Madrigal	1.000	15	11	19	0	4
Mastrobuoni	1.000	10	12	17	0	3
Vazquez	.000	1	0	0	0	0
Wisdom	1.000	3	0	1	0	0

Third Base	PCT	G	PO	A	E	DP
Bote	1.000	26	7	12	0	1
Busch	.000	1	0	0	0	0
Madrigal	.947	36	10	26	2	4
Mastrobuoni	.946	17	6	29	2	3
Morel	.946	74	47	112	9	8
Paredes	.930	50	24	95	9	5
Vazquez	1.000	3	1	3	0	0
Wisdom	.871	17	9	18	4	1

Shortstop	PCT	G	PO	A	E	DP
Hoerner	.972	10	9	26	1	3
Mastrobuoni	.971	10	12	22	1	4
Swanson	.990	148	166	335	5	56
Vazquez	.929	6	5	8	1	1

Outfield	PCT	G	PO	A	E	DP
Alcantara	1.000	3	2	0	0	0
Bellinger	.990	98	191	3	2	1
Canario	1.000	15	24	0	0	0
Cooper	1.000	2	1	0	0	0
Crow-Armstrong	.991	117	306	8	3	0
Happ	.997	144	307	11	1	2
Mastrobuoni	1.000	3	1	0	0	0
Suzuki	.981	73	150	5	3	3
Tauchman	.991	82	113	1	1	1
Wisdom	1.000	8	3	0	0	0

IOWA CUBS — *TRIPLE-A*

INTERNATIONAL LEAGUE

Batting	B-T	Ht.	Wt.	DOB	AVG	OBP	SLG	G	PA	AB	R	H	2B	3B	HR	RBI	BB	HBP	SH	SF	SO	SB	CS	BB%	SO%
Alcantara, Kevin	R-R	6-6	188	7-12-02	.292	.378	.469	35	148	130	23	38	8	0	5	22	17	1	0	0	43	7	1	11.49	29.05
Ballesteros, Moises	L-R	5-7	195	11-8-03	.281	.340	.454	68	285	260	30	73	15	0	10	35	23	1	0	1	60	0	1	8.07	21.05
Beesley, Bradlee	R-R	5-9	180	2-21-98	.133	.278	.133	11	18	15	0	2	0	0	0	0	3	0	0	0	6	1	0	16.67	33.33
Bethancourt, Christian	R-R	6-3	205	9-2-91	.192	.222	.192	7	27	26	0	5	0	0	0	2	1	0	0	0	7	0	0	3.70	25.93
Bote, David	R-R	6-1	205	4-7-93	.259	.341	.546	28	123	108	17	28	8	1	7	15	12	2	0	1	18	0	1	9.76	14.63
Caissie, Owen	L-R	6-3	190	7-8-02	.278	.375	.472	127	549	472	69	131	29	3	19	75	71	4	0	2	156	11	2	12.93	28.42
Canario, Alexander	R-R	5-11	165	5-7-00	.243	.336	.514	64	283	247	46	60	13	0	18	47	32	3	0	1	86	5	2	11.31	30.39
Cantrelle, Hayden	B-R	5-11	175	11-25-98	.273	.396	.424	41	160	132	21	36	7	2	3	18	23	4	1	0	48	9	0	14.38	30.00
Casali, Curt	R-R	6-2	220	11-9-88	.362	.489	.551	23	88	69	13	25	7	0	2	11	15	3	0	1	16	0	0	17.05	18.18
Celestino, Gilberto	R-L	6-0	170	2-13-99	.316	.350	.421	5	20	19	1	6	2	0	0	1	0	1	0	0	4	0	0	0.00	20.00
Crow-Armstrong, Pete	L-L	5-11	184	3-25-02	.255	.299	.509	26	117	110	22	28	9	2	5	14	6	1	0	0	32	10	0	5.13	27.35
Davis, Brennen	R-R	6-0	210	11-2-99	.214	.359	.469	47	181	145	30	31	4	0	11	28	23	11	0	2	42	1	1	12.71	23.20
Garcia, Reivaj	B-R	5-9	175	8-12-01	.346	.393	.500	7	28	26	1	9	1	0	1	4	2	0	0	0	10	0	0	7.14	35.71
Hager, Jake	R-R	6-1	170	3-4-93	.221	.269	.328	39	131	122	12	27	7	0	2	9	7	1	1	0	43	0	0	5.34	32.82
Hill, Darius	L-L	5-11	190	8-17-97	.267	.323	.355	98	392	352	49	94	23	1	2	41	31	1	1	6	70	3	6	7.91	17.86
Howard, Ed	R-R	6-1	185	1-28-02	.139	.205	.167	10	41	36	4	5	1	0	0	3	2	1	2	0	11	0	0	4.88	26.83
Hudson, Joe	R-R	5-11	210	5-21-91	.000	.143	.000	2	8	6	0	0	0	0	0	0	1	0	1	0	2	0	0	12.50	25.00
Knight, Caleb	R-R	5-9	220	1-2-96	.194	.242	.403	21	68	62	5	12	1	0	4	8	4	0	2	0	18	1	1	5.88	26.47
Madrigal, Nick	R-R	5-8	175	3-5-97	1.000	1.000	2.000	1	3	1	0	1	1	0	0	1	1	1	0	0	0	0	0	33.33	0.00
Mastrobuoni, Miles	L-R	5-11	185	10-31-95	.218	.305	.329	54	244	216	34	47	12	0	4	22	27	0	1	0	44	15	1	11.07	18.03
Mervis, Matt	L-R	6-2	225	4-16-98	.235	.329	.434	81	350	302	35	71	15	0	15	43	37	7	0	4	105	4	2	10.57	30.00
Murray, BJ	B-R	5-10	205	1-5-00	.204	.320	.348	88	353	299	46	61	10	0	11	39	50	2	0	2	86	10	1	14.16	24.36
Nido, Tomas	R-R	6-0	211	4-12-94	.500	.500	.500	1	2	2	1	1	0	0	0	0	0	0	0	0	0	0	0	0.00	0.00
Padlo, Kevin	R-R	5-11	210	7-15-96	.118	.250	.353	5	20	17	1	2	1	0	1	3	3	0	0	0	9	0	0	15.00	45.00
Peralta, David	L-L	6-1	210	8-14-87	.217	.341	.348	20	85	69	10	15	3	0	2	8	12	2	0	2	13	1	1	14.12	15.29
Pertuz, Fabian	R-R	5-11	156	9-1-00	.205	.262	.436	11	42	39	6	8	3	0	2	6	3	0	0	0	14	0	0	7.14	33.33
Reinheimer, Jack	R-R	6-1	185	7-19-92	.173	.202	.250	30	109	104	10	18	5	0	1	7	4	0	0	1	24	3	0	3.67	22.02
Roederer, Cole	L-L	5-9	180	9-24-99	.216	.319	.370	46	188	162	27	35	10	0	5	18	22	3	0	1	53	4	0	11.70	28.19
Sanchez, Ali	R-R	6-1	200	1-20-97	.240	.338	.388	41	148	129	16	31	10	0	3	21	18	1	0	0	28	0	0	12.16	18.92
Shaw, Matt	R-R	5-11	185	11-6-01	.298	.395	.534	35	152	131	18	39	8	1	7	21	17	4	0	0	30	6	3	11.18	19.74
Simoneit, William	R-R	6-3	235	10-14-96	.180	.218	.340	18	57	50	5	9	2	0	2	10	3	0	2	2	21	0	1	5.26	36.84
Slaughter, Jake	R-R	6-1	200	10-24-96	.297	.392	.486	32	130	111	17	33	6	0	5	17	15	3	0	1	32	10	1	11.54	24.62
Strumpf, Chase	R-R	6-0	170	3-8-98	.237	.343	.414	85	326	278	46	66	13	0	12	36	44	1	2	1	113	1	2	13.50	34.66
Suzuki, Seiya	R-R	5-11	182	8-18-94	.400	.500	.400	2	6	5	2	2	0	0	0	0	1	0	0	0	1	1	0	16.67	16.67
Thompson, Trayce	R-R	6-3	225	3-15-91	.240	.335	.429	45	179	154	22	37	6	1	7	22	22	1	0	2	55	3	1	12.29	30.73
Triantos, James	R-R	6-1	195	1-29-03	.302	.351	.384	26	94	86	12	26	5	1	0	12	7	0	0	1	16	9	2	7.45	17.02
Vazquez, Luis	R-R	6-0	165	10-10-99	.263	.347	.432	64	273	236	33	62	16	0	8	24	25	6	5	1	60	1	2	9.16	21.98
Windham, Bryce	L-R	5-10	190	9-25-96	.260	.337	.379	68	260	227	25	59	17	2	2	20	26	1	5	1	55	10	0	10.00	21.15
Wisdom, Patrick	R-R	6-2	220	8-27-91	.407	.528	.889	9	36	27	9	11	4	0	3	10	8	0	0	1	12	0	0	22.22	33.33

Pitching	B-T	Ht.	Wt.	DOB	W	L	ERA	G	GS	SV	IP	Hits	Runs	ER	HR	BB	SO	AVG	OBP	SLG	SO%	BB%	BF
Alzolay, Adbert	R-R	6-1	208	3-1-95	0	0	18.00	1	0	0	1	2	2	2	0	2	1	.500	.667	.750	16.67	33.33	6

Arias, Michael	R-R	6-0	155	11-15-01	3	2	5.45	33	0	4	36	40	24	22	3	36	46	.278	.429	.410	25.00	19.57	184
Bigge, Hunter	R-R	6-1	205	6-12-98	1	0	0.68	12	0	6	13	3	1	1	1	6	20	.073	.188	.171	41.67	12.50	48
Birdsell, Brandon	R-R	6-2	240	3-23-00	4	5	4.26	12	12	0	61	70	32	29	4	18	69	.290	.344	.423	26.24	6.84	263
Brewer, Colten	R-R	6-4	222	10-29-92	0	3	2.00	16	0	4	18	12	7	4	2	8	20	.182	.276	.273	26.32	10.53	76
Clarke, Chris	R-R	6-7	215	5-13-98	1	2	5.00	13	11	0	45	52	28	25	5	17	34	.294	.369	.441	17.17	8.59	198
Cuas, Jose	R-R	6-3	195	6-28-94	1	1	6.35	10	0	1	11	11	9	8	1	9	24	.256	.377	.395	45.28	16.98	53
Edwards, Carl	R-R	6-3	165	9-3-91	2	3	1.85	20	0	7	24	20	8	5	1	15	22	.227	.340	.295	21.36	14.56	103
Escobar, Edwin	L-L	6-2	225	4-22-92	5	2	4.86	31	0	0	46	40	25	25	7	33	47	.237	.364	.396	22.82	16.02	206
Franklin, Kohl	R-R	6-4	195	9-9-99	0	0	0.00	1	1	0	2	2	0	0	0	0	1	.250	.250	.250	12.50	0.00	8
Hendricks, Kyle	R-R	6-3	190	12-7-89	0	0	2.08	1	1	0	4	5	1	1	0	3	6	.294	.400	.294	30.00	15.00	20
Herget, Jimmy	R-R	6-3	170	9-9-93	0	0	0.00	4	0	0	4	3	0	0	0	0	5	.188	.235	.250	29.41	0.00	17
Hill, Darius	L-L	5-11	190	8-17-97	0	0	0.00	1	0	0	0	1	0	0	0	0	0	.500	.500	.500	0.00	0.00	2
Hodge, Porter	R-R	6-4	230	2-21-01	1	1	5.74	13	0	0	16	18	12	10	1	12	20	.281	.395	.359	26.32	15.79	76
Hollowell, Gavin	R-R	6-7	215	11-4-97	1	1	1.93	7	0	0	9	4	2	2	0	4	15	.125	.222	.156	41.67	11.11	36
Horton, Cade	R-R	6-1	211	8-20-01	1	1	7.50	5	5	0	18	17	15	15	4	11	22	.254	.346	.493	27.16	13.58	81
Houser, Adrian	R-R	6-3	242	2-2-93	0	2	3.86	4	4	0	19	15	8	8	0	5	12	.227	.303	.303	15.79	6.58	76
Kachmar, Chris	R-R	6-3	180	9-3-96	0	0	13.50	2	1	0	3	4	4	4	0	6	1	.333	.556	.500	5.56	33.33	18
Kilian, Caleb	R-R	6-4	180	6-2-97	2	0	3.22	13	7	0	45	37	18	16	2	14	38	.219	.290	.302	20.32	7.49	187
Knight, Caleb	R-R	5-9	220	1-2-96	0	0	0.00	1	0	0	1	0	0	0	0	0	0	.000	.000	.000	0.00	0.00	2
Leigh, Zac	R-R	6-0	170	11-14-97	0	0	8.31	13	0	0	13	21	12	12	1	18	16	.368	.538	.491	20.51	23.08	78
Little, Luke	L-L	6-8	220	8-30-00	0	0	4.05	4	0	1	7	3	3	3	0	7	7	.150	.414	.150	23.33	23.33	30
Lopez, Jorge	R-R	6-3	200	2-10-93	0	0	12.46	5	0	0	4	8	6	6	1	1	3	.400	.478	.600	13.04	4.35	23
Lovelady, Richard	L-L	6-0	185	7-7-95	1	2	5.84	10	0	0	12	22	8	8	0	1	20	.373	.383	.475	33.33	1.67	60
Luetge, Lucas	L-L	6-4	205	3-24-87	1	1	6.48	13	1	0	17	18	13	12	3	5	24	.265	.315	.485	32.88	6.85	73
Martin, Riley	L-L	6-1	215	3-19-98	4	4	4.48	43	0	2	60	52	35	30	6	45	91	.233	.367	.386	32.73	16.19	278
McGowin, Kyle	R-R	6-3	202	11-27-91	0	3	6.13	10	10	0	47	55	33	32	8	23	39	.296	.377	.484	18.22	10.75	214
McWilliams, Sam	R-R	6-7	230	9-4-95	4	4	6.60	34	4	0	61	58	46	45	13	41	88	.246	.358	.487	31.10	14.49	283
Merryweather, Julian	R-R	6-4	215	10-14-91	2	0	1.59	5	0	0	6	6	1	1	0	1	8	.250	.280	.250	32.00	4.00	25
Missaki, Daniel	R-R	6-0	170	4-9-96	0	1	11.12	3	1	0	6	6	7	7	1	5	8	.261	.393	.391	28.57	17.86	28
Neely, Jack	R-R	6-8	225	6-5-00	0	0	3.12	8	0	3	9	9	4	3	1	2	16	.281	.324	.469	44.44	5.56	36
Noland, Connor	R-R	6-2	215	7-20-99	5	2	5.29	10	9	0	48	56	32	28	10	15	49	.286	.333	.490	22.79	6.98	215
Nunez, Eduarniel	R-R	6-2	170	6-7-99	1	1	6.85	19	0	2	24	23	19	18	3	26	22	.261	.449	.375	18.64	22.03	118
Palencia, Daniel	R-R	5-11	160	2-5-00	2	1	4.85	33	1	5	39	31	22	21	3	22	68	.212	.322	.342	39.53	12.79	172
Pannone, Thomas	L-L	6-0	209	4-28-94	4	8	4.37	19	19	0	91	101	53	44	14	32	87	.283	.346	.485	21.97	8.08	396
Powell, Walker	R-R	6-8	210	6-11-96	0	0	5.40	2	2	0	5	8	6	3	0	5	5	.381	.483	.476	17.24	17.24	29
Roberts, Ethan	R-R	5-10	180	7-4-97	0	0	1.65	14	0	0	16	9	5	3	1	7	21	.164	.292	.236	31.34	10.45	67
Sanders, Cam	R-R	6-2	175	12-9-96	1	2	7.79	30	1	0	32	36	34	28	7	39	50	.275	.448	.496	28.74	22.41	174
Santana, Tyler	R-R	6-1	205	5-13-98	0	0	0.00	2	0	0	3	1	0	0	0	0	3	.111	.111	.111	33.33	0.00	9
Scalzo, Frankie	R-R	6-3	185	11-25-99	0	5	4.08	24	0	0	29	34	18	13	3	16	31	.296	.388	.443	22.96	11.85	135
Staumont, Josh	R-R	6-3	200	12-21-93	1	0	18.00	2	0	0	1	1	2	2	0	5	1	.250	.667	.250	11.11	55.56	9
Steele, Justin	L-L	6-2	205	7-11-95	0	0	8.10	1	1	0	3	6	3	3	0	1	4	.375	.412	.438	23.53	5.88	17
Straily, Dan	R-R	6-2	220	12-1-88	1	7	5.49	17	16	0	79	79	50	48	18	38	75	.258	.341	.503	21.37	10.83	351
Supak, Trey	R-R	6-5	268	5-31-96	4	2	4.90	16	9	0	64	75	36	35	10	21	55	.293	.352	.496	19.43	7.42	283
Taillon, Jameson	R-R	6-5	230	11-18-91	0	0	0.00	1	1	0	4	3	0	0	0	1	4	.200	.250	.267	25.00	6.25	16
Teheran, Julio	R-R	6-2	205	1-27-91	1	4	8.82	8	8	0	33	48	34	32	8	11	37	.336	.394	.629	23.13	6.88	160
Thompson, Keegan	R-R	6-1	210	3-13-95	2	1	2.96	20	0	1	27	15	11	9	3	10	38	.161	.257	.301	36.19	9.52	105
Thompson, Matthew	R-R	6-3	195	8-11-00	0	0	27.00	1	0	0	1	0	2	2	0	3	1	.000	.600	.000	20.00	60.00	5
Thompson, Riley	L-R	6-4	210	7-9-96	6	4	5.95	34	15	1	107	124	77	71	15	48	99	.288	.358	.472	20.50	9.94	483
Watkins, Chase	L-L	6-4	215	10-4-99	0	0	0.00	1	0	0	1	1	0	0	0	0	3	.250	.250	.250	75.00	0.00	4
Weiman, Blake	R-L	6-3	210	11-5-95	1	0	0.00	1	0	0	2	1	0	0	0	0	3	.167	.167	.167	50.00	0.00	6
Wesneski, Hayden	R-R	6-3	210	12-5-97	1	0	3.45	7	3	0	16	16	6	6	1	5	17	.262	.338	.311	25.00	7.35	68
Wicks, Jordan	L-L	6-3	220	9-1-99	0	4	5.57	7	7	0	21	18	14	13	5	8	24	.228	.295	.481	26.97	8.99	89
Wieck, Brad	L-L	6-8	257	10-14-91	3	2	4.94	21	0	0	27	25	17	15	4	10	29	.234	.308	.439	24.17	8.33	120
Wingenter, Trey	R-R	6-7	237	4-15-94	1	1	2.79	8	0	1	10	5	5	3	1	3	16	.147	.211	.235	42.11	7.89	38

Fielding

Catcher	PCT	G	PO	A	E	DP	PB
Ballesteros	.995	45	394	25	2	3	8
Bethancourt	1.000	3	23	3	0	0	2
Casali	.983	16	172	6	3	1	0
Hudson	1.000	2	20	0	0	0	1
Knight	1.000	12	97	10	0	3	0
Nido	1.000	1	7	0	0	0	0
Sanchez	.991	35	305	12	3	1	3
Simoneit	1.000	16	163	5	0	1	1
Windham	.988	31	308	12	4	1	1

First Base	PCT	G	PO	A	E	DP
Ballesteros	.857	2	11	1	2	2
Bote	1.000	3	18	2	0	4
Hager	1.000	11	69	12	0	8
Mervis	.990	73	475	40	5	59
Murray	.987	11	72	2	1	4
Padlo	1.000	3	20	0	0	3
Simoneit	1.000	2	8	0	0	1
Slaughter	1.000	5	26	1	0	4
Strumpf	.991	32	211	12	2	20
Windham	.987	12	69	5	1	6
Wisdom	.950	3	17	2	1	4

Second Base	PCT	G	PO	A	E	DP
Bote	.950	6	9	10	1	1
Cantrelle	.961	22	30	44	3	8
Garcia	1.000	3	3	5	0	1
Hager	.959	12	22	25	2	7
Mastrobuoni	.962	18	29	47	3	17
Pertuz	1.000	5	9	12	0	5
Reinheimer	1.000	3	7	7	0	3
Shaw	1.000	5	11	7	0	4
Slaughter	.958	18	30	38	3	11
Strumpf	.951	29	54	63	6	16
Triantos	.971	18	26	42	2	7
Vazquez	1.000	6	14	13	0	5
Windham	.969	8	15	16	1	8

Third Base	PCT	G	PO	A	E	DP
Bote	.909	9	3	17	2	2
Cantrelle	.875	2	3	4	1	0
Garcia	1.000	3	0	5	0	1
Hager	1.000	2	0	5	0	0
Knight	.500	1	0	1	1	0
Madrigal	1.000	1	1	3	0	1
Mastrobuoni	1.000	7	6	11	0	1
Murray	.940	69	44	114	10	12
Padlo	1.000	1	0	5	0	0
Pertuz	1.000	4	4	9	0	1
Shaw	.938	22	19	26	3	0
Slaughter	.923	8	1	11	1	2
Strumpf	.909	17	12	18	3	0
Vazquez	1.000	7	5	16	0	4
Wisdom	.600	3	1	2	2	0

Shortstop	PCT	G	PO	A	E	DP
Bote	1.000	9	6	11	0	2

Cantrelle	.908	14	18	41	6	13
Hager	.926	8	9	16	2	4
Howard	1.000	10	10	20	0	2
Mastrobuoni	.988	24	37	48	1	12
Pertuz	.900	2	2	7	1	2
Reinheimer	.979	27	30	62	2	14
Shaw	1.000	5	3	11	0	2
Slaughter	1.000	1	1	1	0	1
Strumpf	1.000	1	1	1	0	0
Vazquez	.955	51	64	104	8	19

Outfield	PCT	G	PO	A	E	DP
Alcantara	.972	33	68	1	2	0
Beesley	.917	7	11	0	1	0
Bote	1.000	1	1	0	0	0
Caissie	.981	114	195	7	4	2
Canario	.951	44	75	3	4	1
Cantrelle	1.000	2	7	0	0	0
Celestino	.833	5	5	0	1	0
Crow-Armstrong	1.000	25	48	5	0	0
Davis	.941	31	46	2	3	0
Hager	1.000	3	4	0	0	0
Hill	.986	81	144	1	2	0
Mastrobuoni	1.000	1	4	0	0	0
Peralta	.962	16	24	1	1	1
Roederer	.987	42	75	2	1	0
Suzuki	.000	1	0	0	0	0
Thompson	1.000	43	82	4	0	2
Triantos	1.000	2	1	0	0	0
Windham	1.000	15	28	1	0	0
Wisdom	1.000	1	2	0	0	0

TENNESSEE SMOKIES

DOUBLE-A

SOUTHERN LEAGUE

Batting	B-T	Ht.	Wt.	DOB	AVG	OBP	SLG	G	PA	AB	R	H	2B	3B	HR	RBI	BB	HBP	SH	SF	SO	SB	CS	BB%	SO%
Alcantara, Kevin	R-R	6-6	188	7-12-02	.271	.342	.409	76	325	291	38	79	13	0	9	39	30	2	0	2	80	7	3	9.23	24.62
Aliendo, Pablo	R-R	6-0	170	5-29-01	.249	.346	.462	58	231	197	29	49	10	1	10	33	24	7	0	3	75	2	0	10.39	32.47
Avitia, David	R-R	5-9	205	9-20-98	.000	.143	.000	2	7	6	0	0	0	0	0	0	0	1	0	0	4	0	0	0.00	57.14
Ballesteros, Moises	L-R	5-7	195	11-8-03	.299	.372	.495	56	223	194	27	58	9	1	9	43	22	3	0	4	33	1	0	9.87	14.80
Bateman, Brett	L-L	5-10	170	3-19-02	.241	.331	.250	28	128	112	16	27	1	0	0	5	15	0	1	0	29	8	4	11.72	22.66
Beesley, Bradlee	R-R	5-9	180	2-21-98	.000	.333	.000	1	3	2	0	0	0	0	0	0	0	1	0	0	0	0	0	0.00	0.00
Cantrelle, Hayden	B-R	5-11	175	11-25-98	.258	.343	.435	21	71	62	11	16	3	1	2	6	5	3	1	0	23	2	2	7.04	32.39
Chavers, Parker	L-R	5-9	185	7-25-98	.190	.306	.190	17	49	42	5	8	0	0	0	1	7	0	0	0	12	4	1	14.29	24.49
Cowles, Benjamin	R-R	6-0	180	2-15-00	.077	.294	.077	4	17	13	2	1	0	0	0	0	2	2	0	0	3	0	0	11.76	17.65
Franklin, Christian	R-R	5-8	195	11-30-99	.268	.398	.366	98	427	347	63	93	15	2	5	38	71	6	0	3	89	34	7	16.63	20.84
Garcia, Reivaj	B-R	5-9	175	8-12-01	.214	.246	.268	17	63	56	4	12	3	0	0	4	3	0	2	2	7	0	0	4.76	11.11
Knight, Caleb	R-R	5-9	220	1-2-96	.162	.262	.189	12	42	37	4	6	1	0	0	0	4	1	0	0	11	1	0	9.52	26.19
Long, Jonathan	R-R	5-11	210	1-20-02	.340	.455	.528	46	200	159	42	54	9	0	7	29	35	2	0	4	33	0	0	17.50	16.50
McGeary, Haydn	R-R	6-4	235	10-9-99	.208	.291	.354	102	407	356	38	74	14	1	12	63	39	5	0	5	126	7	0	9.58	30.96
Murray, BJ	B-R	5-10	205	1-5-00	.155	.246	.172	15	65	58	5	9	1	0	0	4	7	0	0	0	14	4	0	10.77	21.54
Nwogu, Jordan	R-R	6-1	230	3-10-99	.171	.244	.366	16	45	41	7	7	3	1	1	5	4	0	0	0	12	4	0	8.89	26.67
Opitz, Casey	B-R	5-9	200	7-30-98	.176	.303	.282	40	155	131	16	23	4	2	2	11	23	1	0	0	41	3	0	14.84	26.45
Pagan, Ezequiel	L-R	5-9	163	7-8-00	.184	.227	.304	67	233	217	27	40	6	1	6	15	8	5	0	3	49	7	0	3.43	21.03
Pertuz, Fabian	R-R	5-11	156	9-1-00	.238	.291	.340	42	158	147	14	35	6	0	3	17	8	3	0	0	53	4	1	5.06	33.54
Pinango, Yohendrick	L-L	5-11	170	5-7-02	.223	.316	.345	55	225	197	22	44	10	1	4	21	25	2	0	1	47	7	1	11.11	20.89
Reinheimer, Jack	R-R	6-1	185	7-19-92	.167	.304	.167	5	23	18	2	3	0	0	0	4	4	0	0	1	6	0	0	17.39	26.09
Rivera, Josh	R-R	6-2	215	10-10-00	.169	.277	.260	68	253	219	27	37	4	2	4	16	33	0	0	1	67	7	1	13.04	26.48
Roederer, Cole	L-L	5-9	180	9-24-99	.153	.293	.247	46	181	150	15	23	9	1	1	15	27	3	0	1	54	3	3	14.92	29.83
Shaw, Matt	R-R	5-11	185	11-6-01	.279	.373	.468	86	371	312	60	87	11	3	14	50	45	6	0	7	65	25	8	12.13	17.52
Simoneit, William	R-R	6-3	235	10-14-96	.230	.288	.377	18	66	61	5	14	6	0	1	8	3	2	0	0	28	2	0	4.55	42.42
Smith, Cam	R-R	6-3	215	2-22-03	.263	.300	.474	5	20	19	4	5	0	2	0	3	1	0	0	0	3	0	0	5.00	15.00
Soto, Wally	L-R	5-6	170	1-5-03	.250	.250	.500	2	4	4	1	1	1	0	0	1	0	0	0	0	2	0	0	0.00	50.00
Stevens, Felix	R-R	6-4	225	7-30-99	.226	.344	.394	65	247	208	29	47	10	2	7	35	34	4	0	1	85	2	0	13.77	34.41
Triantos, James	R-R	6-1	195	1-29-03	.300	.345	.437	89	391	357	63	107	18	5	7	40	20	8	0	6	38	38	7	5.12	9.72
Verdugo, Luis	R-R	6-0	160	10-12-00	.257	.313	.328	109	447	405	34	104	21	1	2	42	34	2	0	6	74	4	2	7.61	16.55

Pitching	B-T	Ht.	Wt.	DOB	W	L	ERA	G	GS	SV	IP	Hits	Runs	ER	HR	BB	SO	AVG	OBP	SLG	SO%	BB%	BF
Arias, Michael	R-R	6-0	155	11-15-01	3	0	3.75	16	0	1	24	24	10	10	2	12	26	.267	.353	.389	25.49	11.76	102
Armstrong, Sam	R-R	6-2	245	9-26-00	2	3	2.70	10	9	0	50	37	23	15	2	14	35	.202	.265	.262	17.50	7.00	200
Belge, Jeff	L-L	6-5	225	12-4-97	0	1	3.03	27	0	1	33	25	11	11	0	14	30	.212	.299	.271	22.39	10.45	134
Birdsell, Brandon	R-R	6-2	240	3-23-00	4	4	3.63	15	14	0	74	73	39	30	10	13	65	.256	.296	.393	21.10	4.22	308
Deppermann, Brad	R-R	6-0	195	6-15-96	0	0	0.00	3	0	0	5	4	0	0	0	4	5	.222	.364	.333	22.73	18.18	22
Endersby, Jimmy	R-R	6-1	194	1-16-98	1	2	4.43	12	8	0	41	33	21	20	4	12	35	.221	.293	.389	21.34	7.32	164
Espinoza, Manuel	R-R	5-11	150	11-17-00	0	1	3.86	3	1	0	7	5	3	3	0	2	6	.200	.250	.320	21.43	7.14	28
Franklin, Kohl	R-R	6-4	195	9-9-99	0	0	0.00	1	1	0	4	0	0	0	0	0	4	.000	.000	.000	33.33	0.00	12
Gallardo, Richard	R-R	6-1	180	9-6-01	0	2	6.06	4	3	0	16	23	14	11	1	4	17	.329	.368	.443	22.37	5.26	76
Hendricks, Kyle	R-R	6-3	190	12-7-89	1	0	3.60	1	1	0	5	6	2	2	0	0	7	.286	.286	.333	33.33	0.00	21
Hodge, Porter	R-R	6-4	230	2-21-01	0	0	0.00	2	0	0	4	1	0	0	0	1	8	.083	.154	.083	57.14	7.14	14
Horton, Cade	R-R	6-1	211	8-20-01	1	0	1.10	4	4	0	16	13	3	2	1	2	18	.228	.290	.351	29.03	3.23	62
Hull, Nick	R-R	6-0	205	8-21-99	0	0	1.38	6	1	0	13	10	2	2	0	5	14	.208	.278	.250	25.93	9.26	54
Kachmar, Chris	R-R	6-3	180	9-3-96	8	3	3.44	25	19	0	105	91	45	40	9	39	93	.232	.305	.365	21.14	8.86	440
Leeper, Ben	R-R	6-0	195	6-15-97	1	0	2.16	6	0	0	8	6	2	2	1	2	10	.194	.242	.290	30.30	6.06	33
Leigh, Zac	R-R	6-0	170	11-14-97	3	2	1.44	25	0	0	31	26	8	5	2	16	40	.226	.323	.304	29.85	11.94	134
McCullough, Brody	R-R	6-4	205	6-30-00	0	0	2.25	1	1	0	4	3	1	1	1	1	7	.200	.250	.400	43.75	6.25	16
McGowin, Kyle	R-R	6-3	202	11-27-91	2	1	2.22	5	5	0	28	17	7	7	1	4	33	.170	.215	.250	30.84	3.74	107
Missaki, Daniel	R-R	6-0	170	4-9-96	0	0	3.60	16	0	1	25	15	10	10	3	17	34	.176	.320	.306	33.01	16.50	103
Moats, Dalton	L-L	6-3	210	5-24-95	0	2	6.50	14	0	0	18	18	16	13	3	15	19	.265	.400	.456	22.35	17.65	85
Nahas, Joe	R-R	6-1	185	11-14-99	6	2	4.34	25	2	0	58	51	29	28	7	20	63	.235	.301	.387	26.36	8.37	239
Noland, Connor	R-R	6-2	215	7-20-99	7	3	2.50	16	16	0	86	76	29	24	4	21	67	.235	.281	.312	19.14	6.00	350
Nunez, Eduarniel	R-R	6-2	170	6-7-99	8	2	0.98	27	0	3	37	17	6	4	3	12	42	.137	.213	.226	30.88	8.82	136
Perry, Aaron	R-R	5-11	175	6-7-99	0	0	11.25	2	0	0	4	5	5	5	0	2	6	.294	.368	.471	31.58	10.53	19
Reindl, Jake	R-R	6-1	190	1-15-97	4	1	7.15	20	0	0	23	20	20	18	1	22	36	.241	.435	.349	31.03	18.97	116
Reyes, Carlo	R-R	6-0	212	7-4-98	2	1	2.05	19	1	1	26	23	10	6	2	8	37	.225	.282	.343	33.64	7.27	110
Roberts, Ethan	R-R	5-10	180	7-4-97	0	0	0.00	1	0	0	1	0	0	0	0	2	0	.000	.500	.000	0.00	50.00	4

Sanders, Cam	R-R	6-2	175	12-9-96	1	1	2.91	19	0	6	22	16	8	7	1	6	27	.211	.279	.263	31.40	6.98	86
Sanders, Will	L-R	6-6	230	3-30-02	0	1	6.75	1	1	0	4	8	3	3	2	1	4	.400	.429	.800	19.05	4.76	21
Santos, Antonio	R-R	6-3	223	10-6-96	9	4	3.99	14	13	0	70	48	31	31	9	25	80	.190	.275	.340	28.17	8.80	284
Scalzo, Frankie	R-R	6-3	185	11-25-99	3	0	0.00	21	0	9	26	11	1	0	0	6	17	.125	.189	.136	17.71	6.25	96
Supak, Trey	R-R	6-5	268	5-31-96	3	1	3.43	5	4	0	21	22	8	8	2	5	17	.265	.330	.398	18.68	5.49	91
Taillon, Jameson	R-R	6-5	230	11-18-91	0	1	10.13	1	1	0	3	6	4	3	0	1	4	.429	.467	.500	26.67	6.67	15
Thompson, Matthew	R-R	6-3	195	8-11-00	5	6	4.63	25	23	0	105	76	55	54	9	69	98	.207	.341	.323	21.83	15.37	449
Troop, Alex	L-L	6-5	210	7-19-96	1	4	4.60	13	5	0	43	41	22	22	6	11	38	.255	.305	.441	21.35	6.18	178
Tyranski, Mitchell	L-L	6-2	215	9-2-97	0	0	2.08	2	0	0	4	1	1	1	0	1	4	.067	.176	.067	23.53	5.88	17
Ueckert, Cayne	R-R	6-3	195	5-28-96	0	2	5.50	30	0	2	34	34	21	21	5	18	36	.258	.357	.432	23.08	11.54	156
Weiman, Blake	R-L	6-3	210	11-5-95	4	0	2.77	42	0	7	49	40	18	15	3	8	52	.219	.253	.328	26.80	4.12	194
Whitney, Blake	R-R	6-3	185	5-25-96	8	0	3.14	41	3	8	66	55	26	23	10	21	77	.227	.294	.426	28.52	7.78	270
Wong, Jake	R-R	6-2	218	9-3-96	0	0	0.00	1	1	0	2	3	0	0	0	0	2	.333	.333	.333	22.22	0.00	9

Fielding

Catcher	PCT	G	PO	A	E	DP	PB
Aliendo	.988	52	470	31	6	4	7
Avitia	1.000	2	22	2	0	1	0
Ballesteros	.980	27	242	9	5	2	5
Knight	1.000	4	35	2	0	0	0
Opitz	.989	39	322	31	4	2	2
Simoneit	1.000	15	143	4	0	0	1

First Base	PCT	G	PO	A	E	DP
Ballesteros	1.000	6	39	5	0	4
Knight	1.000	3	11	1	0	2
Long	1.000	30	221	7	0	19
McGeary	.994	70	446	24	3	43
Murray	.963	4	25	1	1	2
Simoneit	1.000	1	6	1	0	1
Stevens	.989	12	89	4	1	8
Verdugo	.989	14	85	4	1	8

Second Base	PCT	G	PO	A	E	DP
Cantrelle	.964	6	11	16	1	3
Garcia	1.000	17	21	37	0	11
Pertuz	.972	10	17	18	1	4
Shaw	.975	19	33	44	2	9
Triantos	.976	68	94	152	6	24
Verdugo	.986	19	16	57	1	13

Third Base	PCT	G	PO	A	E	DP
Cantrelle	1.000	2	2	6	0	1
Long	.923	7	4	8	1	1
Murray	.875	8	4	3	1	0
Pertuz	.750	2	2	1	1	0
Shaw	.947	42	39	50	5	2
Smith	1.000	4	4	4	0	0
Verdugo	.957	72	52	124	8	10

Shortstop	PCT	G	PO	A	E	DP
Cantrelle	.971	11	16	18	1	9
Cowles	1.000	3	5	9	0	1
Pertuz	.971	29	45	55	3	19
Reinheimer	1.000	5	10	13	0	6
Rivera	.971	68	71	164	7	30
Shaw	1.000	19	27	33	0	5
Verdugo	1.000	2	6	5	0	5

Outfield	PCT	G	PO	A	E	DP
Alcantara	.995	73	200	4	1	1
Bateman	.957	28	65	1	3	1
Beesley	1.000	1	1	0	0	0
Chavers	.926	14	25	0	2	0
Franklin	.995	95	209	9	1	3
Long	1.000	3	4	0	0	0
Nwogu	1.000	11	22	0	0	0
Pagan	.981	57	94	7	2	1
Pertuz	.000	1	0	0	1	0
Pinango	.988	47	81	2	1	1
Roederer	.979	44	90	2	2	2
Stevens	1.000	49	97	7	0	2
Triantos	1.000	7	26	0	0	0

CHICAGO CUBS

SOUTH BEND CUBS — HIGH-A

MIDWEST LEAGUE

Batting	B-T	Ht.	Wt.	DOB	AVG	OBP	SLG	G	PA	AB	R	H	2B	3B	HR	RBI	BB	HBP	SH	SF	SO	SB	CS	BB%	SO%
Alvarez, Edgar	L-R	6-4	225	2-19-01	.245	.355	.319	27	110	94	9	23	4	0	1	9	15	1	0	0	36	1	1	13.64	32.73
Armas, Ariel	R-R	6-0	180	11-29-02	.204	.316	.286	13	57	49	6	10	4	0	0	5	7	1	0	0	10	0	0	12.28	17.54
Avitia, David	R-R	5-9	205	9-20-98	.121	.250	.165	30	110	91	7	11	4	0	0	4	13	3	2	1	49	0	0	11.82	44.55
Bateman, Brett	L-L	5-10	170	3-19-02	.283	.401	.352	79	359	293	49	83	11	3	1	25	56	4	2	4	57	22	4	15.60	15.88
Chavers, Parker	L-R	5-9	185	7-25-98	.244	.344	.343	74	294	254	35	62	9	2	4	26	38	1	0	1	57	22	7	12.93	19.39
Davis, Drennen	R-R	6-0	210	11-2-99	.250	.417	.357	8	36	28	6	7	3	0	0	4	6	2	0	0	9	0	0	16.67	25.00
Garcia, Reivaj	B-R	5-9	175	8-12-01	.284	.295	.336	71	279	268	29	76	10	2	0	30	6	0	1	4	34	4	2	2.15	12.19
Garriola, Andy	R-R	6-3	235	12-15-99	.270	.356	.492	17	74	63	12	17	5	0	3	11	6	3	0	1	15	3	0	8.11	20.27
Granadillo, Dilan	B-R	5-7	175	5-18-01	.130	.259	.304	9	27	23	1	3	1	0	1	5	4	0	0	0	5	0	0	14.81	18.52
Hearn, Ethan	L-R	5-10	200	8-31-00	.231	.310	.431	65	255	225	38	52	13	1	10	34	18	9	0	3	76	5	3	7.06	29.80
Hernandez, Cristian	R-R	6-1	175	12-13-03	.229	.343	.277	23	99	83	11	19	2	1	0	9	15	0	0	1	19	7	3	15.15	19.19
Howard, Ed	R-R	6-1	185	1-28-02	.234	.289	.310	102	395	364	42	85	18	2	2	24	26	3	0	2	111	8	1	6.58	28.10
Kalmer, Brian	R-R	6-2	215	8-17-00	.196	.293	.385	83	335	291	41	57	18	2	11	43	37	4	0	3	129	0	0	11.04	38.51
Long, Jonathan	R-R	5-11	210	1-20-02	.247	.346	.417	68	289	247	44	61	12	0	10	41	34	5	0	3	68	2	0	11.76	23.53
Morel, Rafael	R-R	6-0	170	11-22-01	.226	.316	.341	84	328	287	44	65	7	1	8	32	29	9	2	1	93	6	5	8.84	28.35
Nwogu, Jordan	R-R	6-1	230	3-10-99	.240	.319	.364	80	323	283	31	68	15	1	6	42	31	4	0	5	72	19	7	9.60	22.29
Olivo, Christian	R-R	5-9	168	10-29-03	.085	.140	.085	13	51	47	4	4	0	0	0	1	3	0	1	0	13	0	0	5.88	25.49
Opitz, Casey	B-R	5-9	200	7-30-98	.193	.267	.376	31	120	109	12	21	3	1	5	11	10	1	0	0	41	1	0	8.33	34.17
Pagan, Ezequiel	L-R	5-9	163	7-8-00	.277	.382	.447	12	55	47	5	13	2	0	2	9	6	2	0	0	5	3	0	10.91	9.09
Pertuz, Fabian	R-R	5-11	156	9-1-00	.333	.333	.333	2	6	6	1	2	0	0	0	0	0	0	0	0	1	0	0	0.00	16.67
Pinango, Yohendrick	L-L	5-11	170	5-7-02	.340	.451	.610	29	122	100	20	34	8	2	5	19	20	1	0	1	15	3	3	16.39	12.30
Ramirez, Pedro	B-R	5-8	165	4-1-04	.284	.348	.381	116	515	464	56	132	19	7	4	48	43	4	0	4	93	14	6	8.35	18.06
Rojas, Jefferson	R-R	5-10	150	4-25-05	.245	.310	.336	96	419	372	47	91	10	3	6	47	35	4	0	8	64	21	8	8.35	15.27
Smith, Cam	R-R	6-3	215	2-22-03	.333	.421	.500	12	57	48	6	16	3	1	1	9	6	2	0	1	9	1	1	10.53	15.79
Soto, Wally	L-R	5-6	170	1-5-03	.136	.174	.136	7	23	22	0	3	0	0	0	2	0	1	0	0	12	0	0	0.00	52.17
Stevens, Felix	R-R	6-4	225	7-30-99	.249	.365	.503	50	219	185	31	46	8	0	13	38	28	6	0	0	79	2	0	12.79	36.07
Wetzel, Jacob	L-L	5-9	215	3-26-00	.235	.333	.353	10	39	34	3	8	2	1	0	4	4	1	0	0	9	2	1	10.26	23.08

Pitching	B-T	Ht.	Wt.	DOB	W	L	ERA	G	GS	SV	IP	Hits	Runs	ER	HR	BB	SO	AVG	OBP	SLG	SO%	BB%	BF
Armstrong, Sam	R-R	6-2	245	9-26-00	3	4	3.00	17	11	1	66	54	22	22	5	22	66	.221	.308	.340	23.91	7.97	276
Bigge, Hunter	R-R	6-1	205	6-12-98	0	0	9.00	1	0	0	1	3	1	1	0	0	2	.600	.600	.600	40.00	0.00	5
Cabrera, Yovanny	R-R	6-2	180	3-22-01	3	6	3.97	33	0	7	45	30	27	20	5	31	49	.184	.330	.325	23.67	14.98	207
Dean, Nick	R-R	6-3	180	12-26-00	4	4	4.10	15	14	0	64	59	32	29	6	17	50	.242	.291	.385	18.66	6.34	268
Deppermann, Brad	R-R	6-0	195	6-15-96	0	0	1.00	6	0	1	9	7	1	1	0	0	9	.212	.212	.303	27.27	0.00	33

Devers, Luis	R-R	6-3	178	4-24-00	4	3	5.33	20	5	0	49	44	31	29	2	28	43	.234	.344	.330	19.20	12.50	224
Gonzalez, Angel	R-R	6-2	175	8-26-02	3	4	7.94	33	0	0	45	40	44	40	3	42	57	.233	.407	.349	25.22	18.58	226
Gray, Drew	L-L	6-3	190	5-9-03	1	6	4.39	22	22	0	80	53	42	39	3	73	97	.196	.368	.292	27.64	20.80	351
Hernandez, Angel	L-L	6-2	180	5-6-00	2	2	10.61	11	0	0	19	23	23	22	2	20	13	.324	.469	.507	13.40	20.62	97
Hull, Nick	R-R	6-0	205	8-21-99	3	4	4.40	26	9	1	76	69	45	37	8	36	80	.241	.335	.371	24.32	10.94	329
Johnson, Ty	R-R	6-6	190	9-25-01	0	3	3.62	8	6	0	27	25	15	11	1	12	33	.250	.336	.340	28.45	10.34	116
Kilian, Caleb	R-R	6-4	180	6-2-97	0	0	9.00	3	0	0	4	4	4	4	0	3	5	.235	.350	.294	25.00	15.00	20
Kipp, Grant	R-R	6-6	220	11-11-99	1	3	5.50	10	7	0	36	28	22	22	3	19	38	.212	.316	.371	24.52	12.26	155
Leeper, Ben	R-R	6-0	195	6-15-97	1	1	4.26	5	0	0	6	5	3	3	1	3	8	.227	.357	.409	28.57	10.71	28
McCullough, Brody	R-R	6-4	205	6-30-00	0	1	1.69	3	2	0	11	7	2	2	0	4	8	.194	.275	.278	20.00	10.00	40
Moore, Grayson	S-R	6-3	215	7-9-01	0	1	2.57	11	0	2	14	10	6	4	1	13	15	.204	.375	.286	22.73	19.70	66
Moreno, Koen	R-R	6-2	170	8-1-01	2	3	6.17	12	0	0	23	21	17	16	1	24	19	.247	.431	.388	16.24	20.51	117
Nahas, Joe	R-R	6-1	185	11-14-99	0	0	2.38	6	0	2	11	8	3	3	1	6	11	.200	.304	.325	23.40	12.77	47
Patterson, Jack	L-L	6-0	210	8-3-95	0	2	5.60	13	0	0	18	15	14	11	1	15	19	.231	.381	.338	22.62	17.86	84
Perry, Aaron	R-R	5-11	175	6-7-99	1	2	3.86	9	2	0	30	26	14	13	3	10	29	.234	.293	.369	23.58	8.13	123
Pertuz, Fabian	R-R	5-11	156	9-1-00	0	0	54.00	1	0	0	1	5	6	6	1	1	1	.714	.700	1.143	10.00	10.00	10
Reyes, Carlo	R-R	6-0	212	7-4-98	1	1	0.00	9	0	1	13	9	3	0	0	2	19	.188	.231	.208	36.54	3.85	52
Rodriguez, Erian	R-R	6-3	190	11-23-01	1	2	3.52	11	11	0	46	38	18	18	2	21	35	.226	.318	.310	18.23	10.94	192
Romero, Jose	R-R	5-10	185	4-20-01	5	3	4.70	37	0	7	52	48	33	27	2	48	63	.253	.427	.353	25.40	19.35	248
Sanders, Will	L-R	6-6	230	3-30-02	2	7	4.56	23	22	1	93	88	58	47	11	43	105	.243	.333	.398	25.12	10.29	418
Santana, Tyler	R-R	6-1	205	5-13-98	5	3	5.43	30	1	1	70	86	50	42	10	32	61	.305	.374	.479	19.18	10.06	318
Santy, Marino	L-L	5-11	170	3-4-02	0	3	3.68	14	0	0	29	30	13	12	2	17	21	.280	.397	.421	15.91	12.88	132
Schlaffer, Tyler	R-R	6-1	180	5-24-01	0	2	7.86	13	9	0	45	56	41	39	6	30	33	.309	.415	.481	15.14	13.76	218
Smyly, Drew	L-L	6-2	188	6-13-89	0	0	0.00	1	1	0	3	0	0	0	0	0	5	.000	.000	.000	55.56	0.00	9
Thoresen, Sam	R-R	6-3	210	9-21-98	0	0	0.00	2	0	1	3	2	0	0	0	1	6	.182	.250	.182	50.00	8.33	12
Tyranski, Mitchell	L-L	6-2	215	9-2-97	2	5	3.52	31	0	4	46	31	19	18	5	20	51	.190	.283	.344	27.27	10.70	187
Viets, Hunter	R-R	6-4	220	9-27-98	0	1	8.44	3	0	0	5	8	5	5	0	5	4	.364	.464	.455	14.29	17.86	28
Watkins, Chase	L-L	6-4	215	10-4-99	5	1	3.52	33	0	0	54	49	25	21	5	19	52	.244	.314	.413	23.32	8.52	223
Wiggins, Jaxon	R-R	6-6	225	10-3-01	3	1	4.55	8	8	0	32	26	17	16	2	19	38	.222	.336	.316	27.74	13.87	137
Zeglin, Nico	R-R	6-4	200	1-19-00	2	0	0.33	9	2	0	28	14	1	1	1	9	33	.149	.238	.191	31.43	8.57	105

CHICAGO CUBS

Fielding

Catcher	PCT	G	PO	A	E	DP	PB
Armas	.959	9	111	6	5	0	1
Avitia	1.000	26	232	22	0	3	4
Granadillo	.976	9	75	5	2	1	2
Hearn	.967	58	488	34	18	6	8
Opitz	.990	31	273	29	3	1	7
Soto	1.000	4	28	4	0	1	0

First Base	PCT	G	PO	A	E	DP
Alvarez	.993	16	129	8	1	11
Garcia	1.000	6	32	0	0	3
Kalmer	.990	66	456	34	5	33
Long	.995	33	203	15	1	24
Soto	.818	1	9	0	2	0
Stevens	1.000	13	101	7	0	6

Second Base	PCT	G	PO	A	E	DP
Garcia	.955	28	41	66	5	23
Hernandez	1.000	6	8	9	0	1
Howard	.994	41	77	92	1	18
Morel	.900	4	2	7	1	1
Ramirez	.983	45	73	103	3	20
Rojas	.973	12	15	21	1	5

Third Base	PCT	G	PO	A	E	DP
Alvarez	1.000	2	2	4	0	0
Garcia	.950	33	21	55	4	5
Howard	.917	7	3	8	1	0
Long	1.000	8	3	8	0	0
Morel	.936	20	10	34	3	3
Pertuz	.333	2	0	1	2	0
Ramirez	.951	54	41	95	7	10
Smith	.920	10	8	15	2	1

Shortstop	PCT	G	PO	A	E	DP
Garcia	.909	3	4	6	1	2
Hernandez	.931	15	19	35	4	7
Howard	.927	42	52	87	11	17
Morel	.833	2	2	3	1	0
Rojas	.926	71	101	151	20	33

Outfield	PCT	G	PO	A	E	DP
Alvarez	1.000	5	11	1	0	1
Avitia	1.000	2	1	0	0	0
Bateman	.995	79	175	7	1	4
Chavers	.987	72	153	4	2	1
Davis	1.000	1	6	0	0	0
Garriola	1.000	15	24	1	0	0
Long	1.000	14	21	1	0	0
Morel	.990	60	98	6	1	1
Nwogu	.985	69	121	9	2	4
Olivo	1.000	12	23	3	0	0
Pagan	1.000	12	29	2	0	0
Pinango	.980	24	49	1	1	0
Ramirez	1.000	4	2	0	0	0
Stevens	.966	27	55	2	2	0
Wetzel	.957	10	22	0	1	0

MYRTLE BEACH PELICANS — *LOW-A*

CAROLINA LEAGUE

Batting	B-T	Ht.	Wt.	DOB	AVG	OBP	SLG	G	PA	AB	R	H	2B	3B	HR	RBI	BB	HBP	SH	SF	SO	SB	CS	BB%	SO%
Avitia, David	R-R	5-9	205	9-20-98	.000	.250	.000	1	4	3	0	0	0	0	0	0	1	0	0	0	2	0	0	25.00	50.00
Ayers, Owen	B-R	6-2	185	6-7-01	.190	.271	.302	18	70	63	6	12	4	0	1	5	6	1	0	0	14	1	0	8.57	20.00
Bowser, Drew	R-R	6-4	226	10-2-01	.162	.289	.283	58	228	191	27	31	9	1	4	20	31	4	0	2	95	0	1	13.60	41.67
Brethowr, Ivan	R-R	6-6	245	2-27-03	.169	.274	.253	23	95	83	12	14	1	0	2	7	8	4	0	0	26	3	0	8.42	27.37
Encarnacion, Jefferson	L-L	6-1	185	8-28-01	.250	.419	.375	10	43	32	6	8	1	0	1	8	10	0	0	1	14	0	0	23.26	32.56
Escobar, Jose	L-R	5-10	165	9-13-04	.209	.357	.478	23	84	67	9	14	2	2	4	15	11	5	0	1	20	0	0	13.10	23.81
Espinoza, Leonel	R-R	6-0	165	4-7-03	.260	.379	.428	59	257	215	38	56	11	5	5	20	30	11	1	0	60	10	4	11.67	23.35
Garriola, Andy	R-R	6-3	235	12-15-99	.241	.312	.482	90	381	332	49	80	24	1	18	72	35	4	0	10	119	9	2	9.19	31.23
Granadillo, Dilan	B-R	5-7	175	5-18-01	.167	.342	.167	11	39	30	5	5	0	0	0	2	8	0	1	0	8	0	0	20.51	20.51
Hernandez, Alexis	R-R	6-0	155	12-27-04	.144	.266	.184	52	204	174	24	25	1	0	2	12	28	1	1	0	76	10	0	13.73	37.25
Hernandez, Cristian	R-R	6-1	175	12-13-03	.269	.382	.406	95	414	350	56	94	25	4	5	50	60	4	0	0	95	37	5	14.49	22.95
Hernandez, Frank	R-R	5-9	185	12-10-01	.243	.318	.257	38	153	136	12	33	2	0	0	9	13	2	2	0	37	4	2	8.50	24.18
Mena, Ismael	L-L	6-3	185	11-30-02	.239	.361	.318	28	109	88	14	21	2	1	1	7	16	2	1	2	19	4	2	14.68	17.43
Olivo, Christian	R-R	5-9	168	10-29-03	.225	.300	.287	87	334	293	44	66	5	2	3	23	29	4	4	4	82	20	4	8.68	24.55
Pabon, Miguel	R-R	5-9	165	8-30-00	.222	.346	.301	68	260	216	23	48	8	0	3	20	38	4	0	2	63	0	0	14.62	24.23
Paciolla, Christopher	R-R	6-0	185	3-16-04	.205	.236	.285	66	275	263	23	54	15	0	2	19	11	0	0	1	77	3	1	4.00	28.00
Pertuz, Fabian	R-R	5-11	156	9-1-00	.147	.255	.253	27	110	95	9	14	4	0	2	10	13	1	0	1	37	1	0	11.82	33.64
Preciado, Reginald	B-R	6-3	185	5-16-03	.229	.284	.312	89	380	349	46	80	13	2	4	32	24	3	3	1	109	12	4	6.32	28.68

Batting	B-T	Ht.	Wt.	DOB	AVG	OBP	SLG	G	PA	AB	R	H	2B	3B	HR	RBI	BB	HBP	SH	SF	SO	SB	CS	BB%	SO%
Ramon, Eriandys	B-R	6-3	170	1-7-03	.184	.273	.306	27	110	98	13	18	8	2	0	5	10	2	0	0	25	3	2	9.09	22.73
Rosario, Alfonsin	R-R	6-2	215	6-21-04	.230	.344	.423	109	456	383	61	88	18	4	16	73	56	13	0	4	147	20	5	12.28	32.24
Sisneros, Cameron	L-L	6-2	230	6-1-01	.209	.306	.488	13	49	43	4	9	1	1	3	9	5	1	0	0	15	0	0	10.20	30.61
Smith, Cam	R-R	6-3	215	2-22-03	.313	.404	.771	15	57	48	10	15	2	1	6	12	8	0	0	1	12	1	0	14.04	21.05
Soto, Wally	L-R	5-6	170	1-5-03	.152	.316	.261	15	58	46	6	7	2	0	1	7	11	0	1	0	15	0	0	18.97	25.86
Suriel, Anderson	L-L	5-11	175	4-11-03	.245	.351	.367	17	57	49	7	12	3	0	1	6	4	4	0	0	17	0	1	7.02	29.82
Trice, Carter	R-R	6-0	200	8-23-02	.218	.320	.410	67	266	229	24	50	18	1	8	34	33	2	0	2	88	2	1	12.41	33.08
Wetzel, Jacob	L-L	5-9	215	3-26-00	.255	.377	.469	81	347	286	53	73	15	11	8	39	55	2	1	2	77	17	2	15.85	22.19

Pitching	B-T	Ht.	Wt.	DOB	W	L	ERA	G	GS	SV	IP	Hits	Runs	ER	HR	BB	SO	AVG	OBP	SLG	SO%	BB%	BF
Almonte, Lisandro	R-R	6-1	170	6-11-02	1	1	3.86	3	0	0	5	2	3	2	0	4	6	.133	.350	.133	30.00	20.00	20
Bello, Juan	R-R	6-1	173	4-6-04	4	5	3.21	22	22	0	90	73	32	32	5	28	91	.225	.294	.309	25.07	7.71	363
Brown, Garrett	L-R	6-7	218	11-6-99	1	1	10.34	12	0	0	16	25	20	18	1	14	9	.391	.512	.484	10.98	17.07	82
Dean, Nick	R-R	6-3	180	12-26-00	2	0	2.33	7	3	0	27	17	7	7	0	9	36	.179	.248	.211	34.29	8.57	105
Egbert, Kenten	R-R	6-3	205	7-9-01	7	2	3.04	23	16	0	98	72	39	33	8	32	104	.202	.270	.325	26.46	8.14	393
Frisch, Will	R-R	6-0	222	7-14-00	0	2	9.00	2	2	0	3	3	3	3	0	3	1	.273	.438	.364	6.25	18.75	16
Hambley, Dominic	R-R	6-2	230	4-24-03	0	2	7.58	12	0	0	19	23	22	16	0	20	20	.284	.468	.321	18.02	18.02	111
Hernandez, Angel	L-L	6-2	180	5-6-00	4	2	1.26	17	0	1	50	24	9	7	1	25	62	.147	.267	.215	31.96	12.89	194
Hernandez, Frank	R-R	5-9	185	12-10-01	0	0	0.00	1	0	1	1	1	1	0	0	0	0	.333	.250	.333	0.00	0.00	4
Johnson, Ty	R-R	6-6	190	9-25-01	1	1	3.48	10	4	1	34	23	14	13	1	10	48	.198	.286	.259	36.09	7.52	133
Lebron, Scarlyn	R-R	6-3	178	1-2-02	1	2	8.25	9	0	0	12	15	12	11	0	18	15	.300	.507	.420	21.13	25.35	71
Marshall, Shane	R-R	6-4	210	3-15-00	2	3	2.52	33	0	7	39	28	17	11	4	22	42	.206	.313	.353	25.00	13.10	168
Martinez-Gomez, Luis	R-R	6-2	178	5-27-03	1	0	0.00	3	0	1	6	7	0	0	0	0	7	.318	.348	.364	30.43	0.00	23
McGwire, Mason	R-R	6-4	190	1-5-04	0	4	5.71	15	8	0	41	40	29	26	4	34	30	.260	.397	.416	15.87	17.99	189
Mule, Nazier	R-R	6-1	210	10-15-04	1	1	3.95	13	13	0	43	28	21	19	2	32	31	.187	.358	.287	16.32	16.84	190
Noriega, Branden	L-L	6-2	180	7-9-01	1	0	8.31	3	0	0	4	3	4	4	0	7	4	.214	.522	.286	16.67	29.17	24
Patterson, Jack	L-L	6-0	210	8-3-95	0	0	33.75	2	0	0	1	5	5	5	0	1	2	.714	.750	.714	22.22	11.11	9
Perez, Kenyi	R-R	6-2	165	8-9-01	1	2	9.47	36	0	1	38	22	44	40	2	60	71	.164	.449	.261	34.63	29.27	205
Peters, Mathew	R-R	6-4	215	12-28-00	0	1	7.71	5	0	0	9	7	8	8	1	11	8	.206	.417	.324	16.67	22.92	48
Pichardo, Starlyn	R-R	6-0	175	1-12-04	0	1	4.76	7	0	0	11	7	7	6	2	17	14	.171	.414	.366	24.14	29.31	58
Reilly, Vince	R-R	5-10	160	6-7-01	7	4	3.88	32	0	6	53	43	28	23	2	16	52	.213	.275	.292	23.21	7.14	224
Reyes, Luis A.	R-R	6-3	220	10-23-03	1	0	10.80	1	0	0	2	4	2	2	0	1	1	.444	.500	.556	10.00	10.00	10
Reynoso, Francis	R-R	6-5	206	12-26-02	1	2	5.18	26	0	3	33	23	20	19	4	21	42	.189	.315	.361	28.19	14.09	149
Rodriguez, Erian	R-R	6-3	190	11-23-01	3	3	3.29	13	2	0	41	36	17	15	1	16	41	.234	.318	.318	23.70	9.25	173
Rojas, Yenrri	R-R	6-1	186	11-30-03	5	5	3.16	17	7	2	63	59	26	22	2	20	37	.253	.313	.313	14.12	7.63	262
Romero, Alfredo	R-R	6-3	175	6-27-03	0	7	8.10	14	10	0	40	55	43	36	2	22	34	.314	.388	.429	16.83	10.89	202
Rujano, Luis	R-R	6-4	200	4-22-03	4	3	5.40	20	7	0	53	60	36	32	4	25	55	.288	.368	.428	23.01	10.46	239
Santy, Marino	L-L	5-11	170	3-4-02	1	2	3.89	13	8	0	44	41	23	19	3	29	58	.247	.374	.349	28.57	14.29	203
Schlaffer, Tyler	R-R	6-1	180	5-24-01	3	1	1.87	8	6	0	34	21	9	7	1	10	34	.176	.252	.286	25.95	7.63	131
Schultz, Connor	R-R	6-4	225	2-12-99	1	2	1.82	9	1	0	30	23	13	6	2	4	30	.217	.248	.311	26.55	3.54	113
Soto, Wally	L-R	5-6	170	1-5-03	0	0	54.00	1	0	0	0	3	2	2	1	1	0	.750	.800	1.500	0.00	20.00	5
Thoresen, Sam	R-R	6-3	210	9-21-98	0	1	1.66	17	0	0	22	10	8	4	0	21	29	.143	.355	.171	30.85	22.34	94
Tyranski, Mitchell	L-L	6-2	215	9-2-97	0	0	0.00	1	0	0	2	0	0	0	0	2	4	.000	.222	.000	44.44	22.22	9
Vizcaino, Jeral	R-R	6-1	155	1-7-02	4	3	2.82	26	2	3	67	52	23	21	4	26	61	.216	.299	.311	22.18	9.45	275
Wheat, JP	R-R	6-5	185	8-3-02	0	2	7.91	10	10	0	19	15	24	17	0	34	16	.211	.477	.268	14.29	30.36	112
Wiggins, Jaxon	R-R	6-6	225	10-3-01	0	2	2.14	6	6	0	21	12	5	5	0	5	26	.162	.215	.230	32.91	6.33	79
Zeglin, Nico	R-R	6-4	200	1-19-00	5	0	1.41	16	2	3	38	24	9	6	1	7	57	.175	.235	.234	38.26	4.70	149

Fielding

Catcher	PCT	G	PO	A	E	DP	PB
Avitia	1.000	1	17	0	0	0	0
Ayers	.975	9	69	8	2	1	0
Granadillo	.973	9	66	7	2	0	0
Hernandez	.981	35	336	24	7	2	9
Pabon	.987	64	572	49	8	6	6
Soto	.960	7	69	3	3	0	3
Trice	.960	6	69	3	3	1	2

First Base	PCT	G	PO	A	E	
Bowser	.975	41	285	23	8	17
Pabon	1.000	2	18	1	0	0
Pertuz	.981	19	140	13	3	14
Preciado	.985	14	112	17	2	9
Sisneros	.989	11	85	4	1	4
Suriel	1.000	7	44	6	0	6
Trice	.996	36	268	12	1	17

Second Base	PCT	G	PO	A	E	DP
Escobar	.973	21	25	46	2	7
Hernandez	.911	34	52	61	11	12
Hernandez	.940	23	31	48	5	8
Olivo	.979	34	65	78	3	20
Pertuz	1.000	4	2	9	0	1
Preciado	.961	10	20	29	2	9
Ramon	.923	5	4	8	1	0

Third Base	PCT	G	PO	A	E	DP
Bowser	1.000	3	2	3	0	0
Olivo	1.000	3	2	2	0	0
Paciolla	.926	64	39	86	10	4
Pertuz	1.000	1	0	2	0	0
Preciado	.959	42	28	65	4	5
Ramon	1.000	8	3	14	0	2
Smith	.958	10	11	12	1	0
Trice	.500	2	0	1	1	0

Shortstop	PCT	G	PO	A	E	DP
Hernandez	.940	70	83	169	16	27
Hernandez	.950	17	22	35	3	8
Olivo	.941	25	31	65	6	8
Pertuz	1.000	3	5	8	0	0
Preciado	1.000	3	6	8	0	1
Ramon	.941	15	16	32	3	5

Outfield	PCT	G	PO	A	E	DP
Brethowr	.977	22	39	3	1	0
Encarnacion	1.000	8	8	0	0	0
Escobar	.000	1	0	0	0	0
Espinoza	.973	60	102	5	3	1
Garriola	.972	62	105	1	3	1
Mena	1.000	22	33	1	0	0
Olivo	1.000	25	51	6	0	2
Preciado	1.000	21	25	4	0	0
Rosario	.973	92	177	6	5	0
Suriel	.833	10	14	1	3	0
Trice	1.000	3	5	1	0	1
Wetzel	.992	72	118	7	1	0

ACL CUBS — *ROOKIE*

ARIZONA COMPLEX LEAGUE

Batting	B-T	Ht.	Wt.	DOB	AVG	OBP	SLG	G	PA	AB	R	H	2B	3B	HR	RBI	BB	HBP	SH	SF	SO	SB	CS	BB%	SO%
Alcantara, Derik	L-R	6-0	160	2-20-05	.278	.350	.278	5	20	18	3	5	0	0	0	2	1	1	0	0	3	2	0	5.00	15.00
Bowser, Drew	R-R	6-4	226	10-2-01	.278	.316	.639	11	38	36	6	10	4	0	3	4	2	0	0	0	16	0	0	5.26	42.11

Carico, Michael	L-R	6-0	190	9-4-02	.167	.375	.167	3	8	6	0	1	0	0	0	0	1	1	0	0	2	0	0	12.50	25.00
Cepeda, Angel	R-R	6-1	170	10-29-05	.298	.383	.428	56	240	208	40	62	8	5	3	25	27	3	0	2	59	21	6	11.25	24.58
Delgado, Joan	R-R	5-11	165	12-7-04	.281	.364	.538	53	187	160	45	45	7	8	6	29	19	4	0	4	65	16	2	10.16	34.76
Diaz, Jairo	L-R	5-10	180	7-14-04	.355	.417	.435	23	72	62	6	22	5	0	0	13	7	1	0	2	15	1	1	9.72	20.83
Diaz, Yidel	R-R	5-10	203	11-3-04	.213	.304	.262	23	69	61	8	13	3	0	0	9	8	0	0	0	25	1	0	11.59	36.23
Encarnacion, Jefferson	L-L	6-1	185	8-28-01	.118	.193	.224	32	88	76	9	9	3	1	1	9	8	0	0	4	31	3	0	9.09	35.23
Escobar, Jose	L-R	5-10	165	9-13-04	.303	.435	.465	47	178	142	35	43	4	5	3	19	30	4	1	1	23	10	6	16.85	12.92
Espinoza, Leonel	R-R	6-0	165	4-7-03	.273	.407	.364	6	27	22	3	6	0	1	0	5	4	1	0	0	5	0	0	14.81	18.52
Gutierrez, Albert	R-R	6-1	195	2-15-04	.236	.287	.379	47	176	161	19	38	8	3	3	21	12	0	0	1	48	0	0	6.82	27.27
Hager, Jake	R-R	6-1	170	3-4-93	.000	.000	.000	1	3	2	0	0	0	0	0	1	0	0	0	1	0	0	0	0.00	0.00
Lubo, Geuri	R-R	6-2	185	9-24-03	.288	.384	.403	46	164	139	25	40	5	1	3	22	20	3	0	2	32	13	4	12.20	19.51
Melendez, Yahil	L-R	6-2	175	9-5-05	.268	.394	.425	53	218	179	47	48	13	3	3	23	30	8	0	1	62	11	6	13.76	28.44
Mena, Ismael	L-L	6-3	185	11-30-02	.286	.267	.357	5	15	14	0	4	1	0	0	2	0	0	0	1	4	1	0	0.00	26.67
Pagan, Ezequiel	L-R	5-9	163	7-8-00	.143	.143	.143	2	7	7	0	1	0	0	0	1	0	0	0	0	2	0	0	0.00	28.57
Ramon, Eriandys	B-R	6-3	170	1-7-03	.340	.367	.566	47	166	159	31	54	12	6	4	23	7	0	0	0	33	3	3	4.22	19.88
Sanchez, Adan	R-R	6-0	205	5-24-05	.223	.316	.357	37	133	112	15	25	9	0	2	24	14	3	0	4	26	0	4	10.53	19.55
Strumpf, Chase	R-R	6-0	170	3-8-98	.143	.455	.286	3	11	7	4	1	1	0	0	1	2	2	0	0	5	0	0	18.18	45.45
Suriel, Anderson	L-L	5-11	175	4-11-03	.344	.415	.680	38	143	125	26	43	12	3	8	38	13	3	0	1	30	8	5	9.09	20.98
Tauchman, Mike	L-L	6-2	220	12-3-90	.000	.167	.000	2	6	5	1	0	0	0	0	0	1	0	0	0	1	0	0	16.67	16.67
Trice, Carter	R-R	6-0	200	8-23-02	.279	.396	.488	15	53	43	11	12	2	2	1	4	9	0	0	1	12	6	0	16.98	22.64
Valdez, Derniche	R-R	5-11	150	3-29-06	.271	.313	.508	17	64	59	14	16	4	2	2	10	4	0	0	1	19	2	1	6.25	29.69

Pitching	B-T	Ht.	Wt.	DOB	W	L	ERA	G	GS	SV	IP	Hits	Runs	ER	HR	BB	SO	AVG	OBP	SLG	SO%	BB%	BF
Almonte, Lisandro	R-R	6-1	170	6-11-02	1	1	1.84	9	0	1	15	5	5	3	1	5	18	.106	.271	.170	30.51	8.47	59
Alzolay, Adbert	R-R	6-1	208	3-1-95	0	0	4.50	2	1	0	2	2	3	1	0	0	3	.250	.222	.750	33.33	0.00	9
Bigge, Hunter	R-R	6-1	205	6-12-98	0	0	0.00	1	0	0	1	0	0	0	0	0	1	.000	.000	.000	33.33	0.00	3
Bracho, David	R-R	6-0	160	2-24-05	1	1	5.71	8	2	0	17	15	12	11	1	14	13	.250	.395	.367	16.88	18.18	77
Brown, Garrett	L-R	6-7	218	11-6-99	1	0	3.38	2	0	0	3	3	2	1	1	2	4	.300	.417	.600	30.77	15.38	13
Castillo, Eduardo	R-R	6-1	176	9-16-03	1	0	9.82	9	0	0	11	11	13	12	0	16	17	.289	.491	.316	29.82	28.07	57
Cruz, Miguel	L-L	6-4	200	8-3-03	0	3	9.96	13	9	1	28	30	37	31	1	45	30	.288	.510	.356	18.99	28.48	158
Cunningham, Wilson	L-L	6-8	185	5-19-03	0	1	3.72	8	0	1	10	7	4	4	1	7	14	.200	.364	.343	31.82	15.91	44
Deppermann, Brad	R-R	6-0	195	6-15-96	0	0	0.69	10	0	2	13	15	3	1	0	2	16	.306	.333	.347	30.77	3.85	52
Devers, Luis	R-R	6-3	178	4-24-00	2	2	5.40	8	0	0	12	14	12	7	0	6	16	.304	.393	.348	27.59	10.34	58
Dugarte, Diego	R-R	6-1	182	11-8-02	1	3	5.46	12	7	0	30	27	21	18	4	23	22	.257	.392	.390	16.67	17.42	132
Encarnacion, Jefferson	L-L	6-1	185	8-28-01	0	0	27.00	1	0	0	1	0	2	2	0	3	0	.000	.667	.000	0.00	50.00	6
Frisch, Will	R-R	6-0	222	7-14-00	0	1	13.50	2	2	0	3	2	4	4	0	4	3	.222	.500	.222	21.43	28.57	14
Gallardo, Richard	R-R	6-1	180	9-6-01	0	0	0.00	1	1	0	2	3	0	0	0	0	0	.500	.500	.500	0.00	0.00	6
Gonzalez, Yoendris	R-R	5-11	215	11-27-02	1	1	27.00	5	3	0	5	8	14	14	0	12	3	.400	.600	.750	8.57	34.29	35
Hambley, Dominic	R-R	6-2	230	4-24-03	2	1	3.43	12	0	1	21	13	12	8	0	23	28	.178	.429	.192	26.67	21.90	105
Imbriano, Zhiorman	L-L	6-0	180	1-30-03	0	2	10.57	12	9	0	23	29	27	27	1	22	26	.319	.462	.418	21.85	18.49	119
Kipp, Grant	R-R	6-6	220	11-11-99	0	1	10.80	3	3	0	5	8	8	6	0	1	9	.333	.385	.458	34.62	3.85	26
Lebron, Scarlyn	R-R	6-3	178	1-2-02	1	2	3.50	13	0	3	18	15	10	7	1	10	21	.242	.351	.387	26.58	12.66	79
Leeper, Ben	R-R	6-0	195	6-15-97	0	0	0.00	2	1	0	2	2	0	0	0	0	3	.250	.250	.375	37.50	0.00	8
Lopez, Jorge	R-R	6-3	200	2-10-93	0	0	27.00	1	0	0	1	4	3	3	0	0	2	.571	.571	1.143	28.57	0.00	7
Marte, Fraimin	R-R	6-3	170	7-21-01	2	0	5.87	16	0	5	23	16	17	15	2	15	28	.193	.343	.349	27.45	14.71	102
Martinez-Gomez, Luis	R-R	6-2	178	5-27-03	2	1	3.54	7	4	0	28	21	13	11	2	15	25	.200	.311	.314	20.49	12.30	122
Merryweather, Julian	R-R	6-4	215	10-14-91	0	0	0.00	1	0	0	1	0	0	0	0	0	0	.000	.000	.000	0.00	0.00	3
Missaki, Daniel	R-R	6-0	170	4-9-96	0	0	0.00	1	0	0	2	3	0	0	0	1	2	.375	.444	.500	22.22	11.11	9
Mora, Wilme	R-R	6-5	180	6-28-03	3	1	9.33	18	2	0	27	37	30	28	1	22	29	.327	.454	.451	20.57	15.60	141
Mule, Nazier	R-R	6-1	210	10-15-04	0	1	6.23	4	3	0	9	9	8	6	0	10	12	.273	.432	.333	27.27	22.73	44
Noriega, Branden	L-L	6-2	180	7-9-01	3	0	11.64	15	0	2	19	23	27	25	2	22	26	.307	.462	.507	25.00	21.15	104
Paredes, Eligio	R-R	6-1	190	7-10-02	1	0	9.00	5	0	0	6	6	6	6	0	3	9	.286	.370	.333	33.33	11.11	27
Patterson, Jack	L-L	6-0	210	8-3-95	2	0	1.86	5	0	0	10	5	2	2	0	7	13	.152	.293	.152	31.71	17.07	41
Pichardo, Starlyn	R-R	6-0	175	1-12-04	1	2	6.28	12	0	0	14	10	10	10	1	14	21	.192	.368	.308	30.88	20.59	68
Reyes, Luis A.	R-R	6-3	220	10-23-03	2	0	5.61	17	0	0	26	16	20	16	2	29	27	.174	.387	.283	21.77	23.39	124
Roberts, Ethan	R-R	5-10	180	7-4-97	0	0	0.00	1	0	0	1	0	0	0	0	0	0	.000	.000	.000	0.00	0.00	3
Rojas, Yenrri	R-R	6-1	186	11-30-03	1	0	4.02	4	2	0	16	15	7	7	1	9	19	.254	.353	.390	27.94	13.24	68
Romero, Alfredo	R-R	6-3	175	6-27-03	0	1	13.50	1	0	0	1	2	2	2	0	2	1	.333	.500	.500	12.50	25.00	8
Schultz, Connor	R-R	6-4	225	2-12-99	0	0	2.08	5	1	1	17	15	6	4	2	4	20	.231	.275	.415	28.99	5.80	69
Silverio, Freilyn	R-R	6-3	180	1-24-05	0	0	6.91	6	3	0	14	16	11	11	0	14	15	.291	.429	.418	21.13	19.72	71
Tetreault, Jackson	R-R	6-5	189	6-3-96	1	1	5.19	8	1	0	9	8	5	5	0	2	15	.242	.286	.364	42.86	5.71	35
Thoresen, Sam	R-R	6-3	210	9-21-98	0	0	3.00	3	0	0	3	1	2	1	1	1	5	.111	.273	.444	45.45	9.09	11
Ueckert, Cayne	R-R	6-3	195	5-28-96	0	0	0.00	1	0	0	1	1	0	0	0	0	2	.250	.250	.500	50.00	0.00	4
Viets, Hunter	R-R	6-4	220	9-27-98	1	1	4.05	4	0	0	7	6	3	3	2	1	4	.250	.280	.500	16.00	4.00	25
Wheat, JP	R-R	6-5	185	8-3-02	0	0	3.00	2	2	0	3	0	1	1	0	2	4	.000	.385	.000	30.77	15.38	13
Wiggins, Jaxon	R-R	6-6	225	10-3-01	0	3	10.29	4	4	0	7	4	9	8	2	12	7	.154	.421	.385	18.42	31.58	38

Fielding

C: Sanchez 27, Diaz 19, Diaz 14, Carico 3, Trice 2. **1B:** Gutierrez 33, Ramon 11, Trice 8, Bowser 5, Suriel 4, Diaz 1, Lubo 1, Sanchez 1. **2B:** Escobar 24, Cepeda 13, Ramon 10, Valdez 9, Melendez 7, Strumpf 1. **3B:** Ramon 22, Cepeda 20, Melendez 16, Trice 2, Valdez 1. **SS:** Melendez 30, Cepeda 21, Valdez 6, Ramon 5. **LF:** Encarnacion 19, Escobar 14, Lubo 9, Suriel 9, Bowser 6, Alcantara 4, Delgado 3, Trice 2, Mena 1. **CF:** Delgado 47, Suriel 7, Escobar 4, Espinoza 4, Mena 2, Pagan 1, Tauchman 1, Alcantara 1. **RF:** Lubo 34, Suriel 15, Encarnacion 7, Escobar 3, Espinoza 2, Mena 1, Pagan 1, Tauchman 1.

DSL CUBS BLUE — ROOKIE

DOMINICAN SUMMER LEAGUE

Batting	B-T	Ht.	Wt.	DOB	AVG	OBP	SLG	G	PA	AB	R	H	2B	3B	HR	RBI	BB	HBP	SH	SF	SO	SB	CS	BB%	SO%
Alcala, Henniel	R-R	5-11	175	6-22-06	.243	.367	.297	37	139	111	12	27	3	0	1	15	17	7	0	4	24	2	2	12.23	17.27
Alcantara, Derik	L-R	6-0	160	2-20-05	.360	.433	.507	22	90	75	14	27	5	0	2	24	12	0	0	3	6	8	1	13.33	6.67
Altuve, Carlos	R-R	5-11	192	1-6-05	.210	.355	.300	33	124	100	17	21	2	2	1	12	19	4	0	1	24	5	2	15.32	19.35
Cespedes, Ivan	R-R	5-11	190	8-1-05	.100	.280	.250	8	25	20	2	2	0	0	1	2	5	0	0	0	8	1	0	20.00	32.00
De Leon, Darlyn	L-R	5-8	150	2-11-05	.307	.428	.395	41	138	114	29	35	6	2	0	7	22	2	0	0	25	24	7	15.94	18.12
Espinoza, Ludwing	B-R	5-11	170	12-10-05	.221	.347	.343	43	170	140	29	31	6	4	1	18	23	5	0	2	44	8	3	13.53	25.88
Gonzalez, Diego	R-R	5-10	170	4-2-07	.208	.323	.273	29	93	77	4	16	2	0	1	10	12	2	0	2	20	4	0	12.90	21.51
Lugo, Cesar	L-L	6-0	165	2-6-07	.278	.426	.389	17	68	54	8	15	6	0	0	4	14	0	0	0	12	6	1	20.59	17.65
Lumpuy, Alexey	L-L	6-0	180	2-22-04	.257	.397	.534	45	185	148	40	38	5	12	4	19	26	9	1	1	42	20	8	14.05	22.70
Monso, Juan	L-R	5-11	160	11-10-06	.324	.455	.412	12	44	34	5	11	1	1	0	8	5	4	0	1	10	1	3	11.36	22.73
Moscote, Isaac	R-R	5-11	180	11-24-06	.174	.283	.186	28	99	86	8	15	1	0	0	8	12	1	0	0	30	3	0	12.12	30.30
Pascual, Brailin	R-R	6-2	160	12-2-04	.164	.239	.279	23	67	61	7	10	2	1	1	3	5	1	0	0	26	6	1	7.46	38.81
Ramirez, Josias	R-R	6-0	155	7-8-05	.184	.347	.375	44	170	136	21	25	6	4	4	21	30	4	0	0	32	10	4	17.65	18.82
Rosario, Enyel	B-R	6-0	160	4-6-07	.214	.281	.250	8	32	28	6	6	1	0	0	5	3	0	0	1	7	1	0	9.38	21.88
Sanchez, Sandy	B-R	5-10	150	7-15-05	.173	.344	.296	37	125	98	16	17	3	3	1	12	25	1	0	1	19	8	3	20.00	15.20
Valdez, Julio	R-R	6-2	212	1-14-05	.137	.258	.265	33	120	102	13	14	4	0	3	20	15	2	0	1	49	2	0	12.50	40.83
Velasquez, Grenyerbert	B-R	5-11	180	9-8-05	.210	.398	.340	36	133	100	23	21	3	2	2	10	29	3	0	1	30	12	2	21.80	22.56
Vivas, Leonel	R-R	6-2	168	1-22-07	.250	.727	.250	3	11	4	3	1	0	0	0	2	4	3	0	0	1	3	0	36.36	9.09

Pitching	B-T	Ht.	Wt.	DOB	W	L	ERA	G	GS	SV	IP	Hits	Runs	ER	HR	BB	SO	AVG	OBP	SLG	SO%	BB%	BF
Alvarez, Jorge	S-R	5-9	187	10-2-06	1	0	6.11	6	2	0	18	23	12	12	0	6	23	.315	.378	.438	28.05	7.32	82
Arroyo, Rowell	R-R	5-11	180	2-15-05	1	0	3.32	13	0	2	22	18	11	8	0	9	21	.225	.300	.313	23.33	10.00	90
Bracho, David	R-R	6-0	160	2-24-05	0	0	3.86	1	1	0	2	1	2	1	0	1	1	.111	.200	.111	10.00	10.00	10
Castillo, Eduardo	R-R	6-1	176	9-16-03	0	0	0.00	1	0	1	2	0	0	0	0	0	4	.000	.000	.000	66.67	0.00	6
Chala, Alberto	R-R	5-10	170	9-20-03	3	3	7.53	12	0	1	14	17	14	12	0	11	16	.283	.397	.367	21.92	15.07	73
De La Cruz, Gabriel	R-R	6-0	150	2-1-07	0	2	8.34	12	5	1	23	24	26	21	2	26	23	.279	.471	.465	19.01	21.49	121
Fajardo, Fred	R-R	6-3	194	1-27-05	2	1	3.09	15	0	1	23	16	9	8	2	11	36	.188	.286	.318	36.73	11.22	98
Flores, Moises	R-R	6-0	178	7-4-06	0	0	9.82	4	0	0	4	6	4	4	0	8	2	.375	.560	.375	8.00	32.00	25
Guzman, Jeremy	L-L	6-4	180	4-27-04	1	3	8.64	13	0	0	17	13	19	16	2	28	19	.224	.495	.362	20.65	30.43	92
Henriquez, Jordan	R-R	6-4	245	4-30-04	2	1	1.82	16	0	2	25	15	8	5	2	10	21	.174	.287	.279	20.59	9.80	102
Lopez, Ronny	R-R	6-1	185	11-18-02	1	1	1.78	10	4	0	25	11	8	5	0	20	34	.133	.311	.157	31.78	18.69	107
Madeira, Emannoel	R-R	6-3	225	8-20-06	1	3	3.35	13	11	0	38	38	19	14	0	14	34	.252	.329	.291	20.00	8.24	170
Maria, Yander	R-R	6-4	200	11-21-06	0	1	3.98	12	12	0	32	18	16	14	2	24	34	.167	.316	.250	25.37	17.91	134
Morey, Ismael	R-R	6-3	165	8-15-06	2	1	2.48	12	4	0	29	23	8	8	1	16	22	.225	.339	.324	18.18	13.22	121
Rivero, Darian	R-R	6-1	185	7-8-05	1	5	6.10	11	10	0	31	32	23	21	3	23	24	.274	.413	.453	16.00	15.33	150
Romero, Jordi	R-R	6-2	185	7-5-02	3	0	0.00	8	0	1	13	6	2	0	0	6	9	.140	.302	.140	16.67	11.11	54
Rosario, Jhon	R-R	5-10	180	9-21-04	3	0	2.30	8	0	1	16	13	6	4	0	9	16	.217	.319	.250	23.19	13.04	69
Siri, Saul	R-R	6-2	195	12-20-04	3	3	5.34	12	1	0	30	24	21	18	1	17	29	.214	.318	.295	21.97	12.88	132
Vasquez, Geovanny	R-R	6-3	190	12-15-03	1	1	7.54	9	4	0	23	17	23	19	0	24	31	.210	.449	.235	26.27	20.34	118
Vazquez, Irving	R-R	6-3	195	7-13-03	3	1	3.24	14	0	1	25	22	9	9	1	11	18	.232	.321	.305	16.36	10.00	110

Fielding

C: Alcala 27, Gonzalez 17, Altuve 12, Cespedes 3. **1B:** Altuve 21, Sanchez 11, Gonzalez 10, Alcala 10, Cespedes 3, Velasquez 1. **2B:** Moscote 17, Monso 12, Velasquez 8, Sanchez 7, Pascual 6, Rosario 6. **3B:** Velasquez 23, Sanchez 13, Pascual 12, Moscote 6, Vivas 1. **SS:** Espinoza 43, Sanchez 5, Velasquez 2, Vivas 2, Rosario 2, Pascual 1. **LF:** Lumpuy 14, De Leon 13, Lugo 13, Alcantara 11, Ramirez 4. **CF:** Ramirez 37, De Leon 11, Lumpuy 5, Lugo 1. **RF:** Valdez 24, De Leon 14, Lumpuy 12, Lugo 2, Alcantara 2, Ramirez 1.

DSL CUBS RED — ROOKIE

DOMINICAN SUMMER LEAGUE

Batting	B-T	Ht.	Wt.	DOB	AVG	OBP	SLG	G	PA	AB	R	H	2B	3B	HR	RBI	BB	HBP	SH	SF	SO	SB	CS	BB%	SO%
Campos, Daniel	R-R	5-11	170	12-20-05	.250	.351	.427	39	148	124	24	31	6	2	4	28	18	3	0	3	22	2	0	12.16	14.86
Cruz, Andrws	R-R	5-10	150	12-3-02	.265	.382	.301	37	103	83	15	22	3	0	0	16	16	1	1	2	16	11	1	15.53	15.53
Cruz, Fernando	R-R	5-11	155	11-13-06	.215	.326	.329	25	92	79	13	17	3	0	2	12	10	3	0	0	25	11	1	10.87	27.17
De Leon, Abel	R-R	5-11	180	8-20-04	.228	.353	.316	21	68	57	12	13	2	0	1	3	9	2	0	0	26	5	0	13.24	38.24
De Leon, Edgardo	R-R	6-0	170	2-22-07	.277	.431	.433	48	181	141	31	39	7	0	5	27	32	7	0	1	44	5	4	17.68	24.31
Escalante, Leroy	L-L	5-10	160	1-14-07	.231	.336	.355	41	140	121	12	28	4	1	3	14	15	4	0	0	44	9	6	10.71	31.43
Espinoza, Ronnyel	B-R	5-11	173	8-11-05	.215	.407	.308	28	87	65	10	14	1	1	1	7	20	1	1	0	15	6	2	22.99	17.24
Lugo, Cesar	L-L	6-0	165	2-6-07	.253	.417	.387	25	96	75	17	19	5	1	1	12	17	4	0	0	9	9	3	17.71	9.38
Mancebo, Axel	B-R	5-10	160	12-1-06	.082	.243	.131	21	74	61	5	5	3	0	0	4	11	2	0	0	34	9	3	14.86	45.95
Meneses, Jesus	R-R	6-2	175	12-4-06	.141	.303	.231	26	99	78	17	11	2	1	1	7	18	1	0	2	31	4	0	18.18	31.31
Nunez, Vicent	R-R	5-10	185	2-28-05	.191	.333	.217	39	144	115	19	22	3	0	0	13	20	6	0	3	39	6	1	13.89	27.08
Ortiz, Robin	R-R	6-4	200	9-12-06	.276	.390	.403	45	164	134	18	37	9	1	2	21	21	6	0	3	38	8	7	12.80	23.17
Pascual, Brailin	R-R	6-2	160	12-2-04	.235	.350	.588	7	20	17	4	4	2	2	0	2	3	0	0	0	9	0	0	15.00	45.00
Pena, Ezequiel	L-R	6-0	165	9-14-06	.259	.331	.328	38	130	116	14	30	6	1	0	13	12	1	0	1	31	13	2	9.23	23.85
Rodriguez, Jesus	L-L	5-9	165	9-18-06	.243	.376	.324	29	93	74	14	18	3	0	1	10	16	1	0	2	22	9	5	17.20	23.66
Rosario, Enyel	B-R	6-0	160	4-6-07	.312	.375	.366	26	104	93	10	29	3	1	0	11	9	1	0	1	23	6	3	8.65	22.12
Velasquez, Grenyerbert	B-R	5-11	180	9-8-05	.200	.273	.200	3	11	10	0	2	0	0	0	1	1	0	0	0	3	0	0	9.09	27.27
Vivas, Leonel	R-R	6-2	168	1-22-07	.179	.395	.286	10	38	28	5	5	1	1	0	1	7	3	0	0	11	6	0	18.42	28.95

Pitching	B-T	Ht.	Wt.	DOB	W	L	ERA	G	GS	SV	IP	Hits	Runs	ER	HR	BB	SO	AVG	OBP	SLG	SO%	BB%	BF
Alejo, Frailin	R-R	5-11	150	10-8-06	0	1	7.89	10	10	0	22	18	20	19	0	25	10	.234	.450	.351	8.93	22.32	112

Archbold, Juan	R-R	6-2	180	3-21-04	0	1	11.15	8	5	0	15	18	20	19	1	19	14	.300	.488	.417	17.07	23.17	82
Arroyo, Rowell	R-R	5-11	180	2-15-05	0	0	18.00	1	0	0	1	1	2	2	0	1	1	.333	.500	.667	16.67	16.67	6
Blanco, Elvis	R-R	6-0	170	10-27-04	0	2	32.68	11	0	0	6	5	28	23	1	33	11	.208	.672	.375	18.64	55.93	59
Camacho, Kevin	R-R	5-11	200	2-10-05	4	2	3.97	16	0	3	23	21	16	10	2	11	24	.231	.336	.407	22.43	10.28	107
Diaz, Brayan	R-R	6-1	190	1-5-01	2	2	5.15	16	0	0	36.2	34	26	21	1	17	41	.258	.370	.379	24.70	10.24	166
Duran, Julian	R-R	6-0	160	8-12-05	1	0	6.35	9	0	0	11	8	9	8	0	14	13	.190	.414	.190	22.41	24.14	58
Encarnacion, Gabriel	R-R	6-3	195	3-27-03	1	1	13.97	10	0	0	10	11	16	15	2	18	9	.314	.550	.629	14.75	29.51	61
Febrillet, Moises	R-R	6-2	165	11-1-04	0	0	6.00	11	0	0	15	14	12	10	0	13	15	.246	.400	.404	20.00	17.33	75
Florentino, Jostin	R-R	6-0	175	12-1-04	1	2	2.06	10	7	0	35	20	13	8	0	10	40	.167	.243	.192	29.41	7.35	136
Ghisays, Luis	R-R	5-11	188	4-18-06	0	5	6.37	11	11	0	35	34	29	25	4	19	32	.246	.335	.442	20.25	12.03	158
Mejias, Jeanfranco	R-R	6-5	183	4-2-05	1	2	7.00	7	0	0	9	8	7	7	0	11	12	.258	.478	.290	26.09	23.91	46
Melendez, Edwardo	R-R	6-0	177	2-16-04	3	2	7.71	14	3	0	30	27	27	26	0	20	33	.235	.367	.287	23.74	14.39	139
Osorio, Roque	R-R	6-2	169	10-17-06	0	1	8.31	10	0	0	9	6	9	8	0	15	8	.194	.500	.194	15.38	28.85	52
Payares, Santiago	L-L	6-0	155	9-5-05	0	1	27.00	1	1	0	1	3	4	4	0	2	1	.375	.500	.375	10.00	20.00	10
Pierret, Cesar	R-R	6-3	200	5-20-03	0	0	18.00	6	0	0	4	1	9	8	0	18	8	.091	.667	.091	26.67	60.00	30
Pirela, Nestor	R-R	6-1	170	2-26-06	2	1	5.79	13	0	1	23	18	16	15	1	18	23	.228	.376	.316	22.77	17.82	101
Ramos, Emilio	R-R	6-2	198	2-25-06	0	4	1.78	12	11	0	35	26	13	7	2	20	36	.211	.329	.285	24.66	13.70	146
Rangel, Carlos	R-R	5-11	183	9-25-05	1	3	8.69	16	2	1	29	48	31	28	2	14	29	.372	.449	.558	19.46	9.40	149
Rivero, Darian	R-R	6-1	185	7-8-05	0	1	2.25	1	1	0	4.0	5	1	1	0	1	1	.385	.471	.538	5.56	5.56	18
Romero, Jordi	R-R	6-2	185	7-5-02	1	0	2.51	9	0	1	14	11	4	4	0	11	12	.220	.381	.320	19.05	17.46	63
Sanchez, Stiven	R-R	5-11	170	2-27-06	1	4	19.09	12	3	0	19	35	45	41	3	30	16	.393	.571	.539	12.70	23.81	126
Vazquez, Irving	R-R	6-3	195	7-13-03	1	0	3.00	1	0	0	3	3	1	1	0	1	3	.250	.308	.250	23.08	7.69	13

Fielding

C: Nunez 23, Campos 21, De Leon 12. **1B:** Campos 18, Nunez 17, De Leon 12, De Leon 9. **2B:** Pena 18, Espinoza 12, Cruz 9, Meneses 6, Rosario 5, Pascual 4, Vivas 4, Velasquez 1. **3B:** De Leon 22, Meneses 12, Pena 9, Cruz 6, Espinoza 4, Campos 2, Vivas 2, Pascual 1. **SS:** Cruz 22, Espinoza 14, Rosario 14, Cruz 6, Vivas 3, Velasquez 2. **LF:** Rodriguez 22, Cruz 11, Escalante 11, Mancebo 5, Ortiz 4, Lugo 4, De Leon 2. **CF:** Ortiz 21, Lugo 18, Mancebo 17, Rodriguez 2, Escalante 1. **RF:** Escalante 27, Ortiz 15, Cruz 7, Rodriguez 5, Lugo 4, Mancebo 1.

Chicago White Sox

SEASON SYNOPSIS: No modern major league team has lost as much as the White Sox, who won five of their last six games but still surpassed the 1962 Mets' previous record with 121 losses. The Sox' .253 winning percentage is the fifth-worst in 'modern' MLB history (since 1903) and second-worst of the expansion era, just edging the '62 Mets (.250).

HIGH POINT: Lefthander Garret Crochet, the club's 2020 first-round pick, emerged as a top starter in baseball in the first half of the season amidst the doldrums of a lost season. He had six double-digit strikeout efforts, with a career-best 13 Ks against the whiff-prone Mariners in a June 13 start in Seattle. He threw 71 fastballs, 30 cutters and one changeup on the evening, using the fastball for his last 46 pitches.

LOW POINT: The Sox had three losing streaks reach double-digits and threatened history with a 21-game streak that tied the AL's worst mark and fell two shy of the modern MLB record. The streak lasted July 10-Aug. 5, as the Sox were outscored 49-136, an average loss of 6.5-2.3, They went a combined 7-44 in July and August.

NOTABLE ROOKIES: Even more frustrating, the White Sox weren't exceedingly young. Righty Jonathan Cannon, a 2022 third-round pick, beat Oakland 5-1 to end the 21-game losing streak and went 5-10, 4.49 overall, and the Sox won four of his final five starts. Righty Drew Thorpe, acquired in spring training from the Padres, made nine starts and showed some promise before surgery to remove bone spurs in his elbow ended his season at the end of July.

KEY TRANSACTIONS: The White Sox waived the white flag on March 14, trading ace Dylan Cease to the Padres for a mix of prospects headlined by Thorpe. Chris Getz, promoted from farm director to general manager in August 2023, signed free agent righty Erick Fedde after Fedde's KBO sojourn, and Fedde was the team's second-best starter behind Crochet before being traded to the Cardinals on July 29 in a three-team deal that also unloaded veteran outfielder Tommy Pham to St. Louis and righty flamethrower Michael Kopech to the Dodgers. Infielder Miguel Vargas, who hit .104 for the Sox after the trade, was the biggest piece Chicago got back in the underwhelming deal.

OPENING DAY PAYROLL: $142,995,900 (15th)

PLAYERS OF THE YEAR

MAJOR LEAGUE

Garrett Crochet
LHP

6-12, 3.58 ERA
209 SO, 33 BB, 146 IP
First season as SP

MINOR LEAGUE

Edgar Quero
C

(AA/AAA)
.280/.366/.463
16 HR, 70 RBIs

ORGANIZATION LEADERS

Batting		***Qualifiers**
MAJORS		
* AVG	Andrew Vaughn	.246
* OPS	Andrew Vaughn	.699
HR	Andrew Benintendi	20
RBI	Andrew Vaughn	70
MINORS		
* AVG	Mark Payton, Charlotte	.309
* OBP	Rikuu Nishida, Birmingham/Kannapolis/W-S	.418
* SLG	Edgar Quero, Birmingham/Charlotte	.463
* OPS	Mark Payton, Charlotte	.846
R	Rikuu Nishida, Birmingham/Kannapolis/W-S	114
H	Tim Elko, Birmingham/Charlotte	156
TB	Tim Elko, Birmingham/Charlotte	237
2B	Caden Connor, Kannapolis/Winston-Salem	33
3B	D.J. Gladney, Winston-Salem	6
HR	Colson Montgomery, Charlotte	18
HR	Tim Elko, Birmingham/Charlotte	18
RBI	Caden Connor, Kannapolis/Winston-Salem	76
BB	Rikuu Nishida, Birmingham/Kannapolis/W-S	86
SO	Tim Elko, Birmingham/Charlotte	173
SB	Rikuu Nishida, Birmingham/Kannapolis/W-S	49

Pitching		**#Qualifiers**
MAJORS		
W	Garrett Crochet	6
# ERA	No qualifier	
SO	Garrett Crochet	209
SV	Michael Kopech	9
MINORS		
W	Aldrin Batista, Kannapolis/Winston-Salem	10
L	Tanner McDougal, Kannapolis/Winston-Salem	11
L	Jacob Bockenstedt, Kannapolis/Winston-Salem	11
# ERA	Lucas Gordon, Kannapolis/Winston-Salem	2.23
G	Aaron McGarity, Charlotte	55
GS	Tyler Schweitzer, Birmingham/Winston-Salem	25
GS	Riley Gowens, Birmingham/Winston-Salem	25
SV	Adisyn Coffey, Birmingham/Charlotte	13
IP	Tyler Schweitzer, Birmingham/Winston-Salem	132
BB	Lucas Gordon, Kannapolis/Winston-Salem	61
SO	Riley Gowens, Birmingham/Winston-Salem	136
# AVG	Lucas Gordon, Kannapolis/Winston-Salem	.180

2024 PERFORMANCE

General Manager: Chris Getz. **Farm Director:** Paul Janish. **Scouting Director:** Mike Shirley

Class	Team	League	W	L	PCT	Finish	Manager
Majors	Chicago White Sox	American	41	121	.253	15 (15)	Pedro Grifol
Triple-A	Charlotte Knights	International	68	79	.463	16 (20)	Justin Jirschele
Double-A	Birmingham Barons	Southern	72	66	.522	4 (8)	Sergio Santos
High-A	Winston-Salem Dash	South Atlantic	60	72	.455	10 (12)	Guillermo Quiroz
Low-A	Kannapolis Cannon Ballers	Carolina	70	61	.534	3 (12)	Pat Leyland
Rookie	ACL White Sox	Arizona Complex	24	36	.400	15 (15)	Danny Gonzalez
Rookie	DSL White Sox	Dominican	20	35	.364	43 (51)	Anthony Nunez
Overall 2024 Minor League Record			**314**	**349**	**.474**	**22nd (30)**	

CHICAGO WHITE SOX

ORGANIZATION STATISTICS

CHICAGO WHITE SOX

AMERICAN LEAGUE

Batting	B-T	Ht.	Wt.	DOB	AVG	OBP	SLG	G	PA	AB	R	H	2B	3B	HR	RBI	BB	HBP	SH	SF	SO	SB	CS	BB%	SO%
Amaya, Jacob	R-R	6-0	180	9-3-98	.179	.225	.194	23	71	67	4	12	1	0	0	3	4	0	0	0	28	1	0	5.63	39.44
Baldwin, Brooks	B-R	6-2	175	8-15-00	.211	.250	.316	33	121	114	9	24	6	0	2	8	6	0	1	0	31	4	0	4.96	25.62
Benintendi, Andrew	L-L	5-9	180	7-6-94	.229	.289	.396	135	522	477	50	109	20	0	20	64	41	1	0	3	96	3	2	7.85	18.39
Colas, Oscar	L-L	5-11	209	9-17-98	.273	.368	.273	13	38	33	1	9	0	0	0	4	4	1	0	0	10	0	1	10.53	26.32
DeJong, Paul	R-R	6-0	205	8-2-93	.228	.275	.430	102	363	337	39	77	14	0	18	41	14	9	0	3	112	2	1	3.86	30.85
DeLoach, Zach	L-R	6-0	205	8-18-98	.209	.293	.328	22	75	67	10	14	5	0	1	5	8	0	0	0	21	0	1	10.67	28.00
Ellis, Duke	L-L	6-1	180	1-16-98	.000	.000	.000	8	4	4	1	0	0	0	0	0	0	0	0	0	2	4	0	0.00	50.00
Fletcher, Dominic	L-L	5-6	185	9-2-97	.206	.252	.256	72	241	223	14	46	8	0	1	17	11	3	2	1	58	0	0	4.56	24.07
Grossman, Robbie	B-L	6-0	209	9-16-89	.211	.329	.268	25	85	71	6	15	4	0	0	4	13	0	0	1	20	2	0	15.29	23.53
Jimenez, Eloy	R-R	6-4	240	11-27-96	.240	.297	.345	65	249	229	18	55	9	0	5	16	18	1	0	1	47	3	0	7.23	18.88
Julks, Corey	R-R	6-1	185	2-27-96	.214	.275	.306	66	189	173	17	37	7	0	3	14	15	0	0	1	50	5	2	7.94	26.46
Lee, Korey	R-R	6-2	210	7-25-98	.210	.244	.347	125	394	377	36	79	14	1	12	37	17	0	0	0	122	6	3	4.31	30.96
Lopez, Nicky	L-R	5-11	180	3-13-95	.241	.312	.294	124	445	398	40	96	12	3	1	21	37	4	6	0	67	5	7	8.31	15.06
Maldonado, Martin	R-R	6-0	230	8-16-86	.119	.174	.230	48	147	135	9	16	3	0	4	11	8	1	3	0	51	0	0	5.44	34.69
Mendick, Danny	R-R	5-10	195	9-28-93	.197	.243	.318	47	141	132	13	26	7	0	3	8	6	2	1	0	35	6	0	4.26	24.82
Moncada, Yoan	B-R	6-2	225	5-27-95	.275	.356	.400	12	45	40	4	11	3	1	0	0	5	0	0	0	11	1	0	11.11	24.44
Ortega, Rafael	L-R	5-11	180	5-15-91	.071	.176	.071	14	17	14	4	1	0	0	0	1	2	0	0	1	4	2	0	11.76	23.53
Pham, Tommy	R-R	6-1	223	3-8-88	.266	.330	.380	70	297	271	33	72	14	1	5	19	25	1	0	0	63	6	3	8.42	21.21
Pillar, Kevin	R-R	6-0	200	1-4-89	.160	.290	.360	17	32	25	1	4	2	0	1	4	4	1	1	1	8	2	0	12.50	25.00
Ramos, Bryan	R-R	6-2	190	3-12-02	.202	.252	.333	32	108	99	13	20	4	0	3	11	7	0	0	1	22	0	2	6.48	20.37
Remillard, Zach	R-R	6-0	185	2-21-94	.242	.342	.333	15	39	33	3	8	1	1	0	1	5	0	1	0	10	1	0	12.82	25.64
Robert, Luis	R-R	6-2	220	8-3-97	.224	.278	.379	100	425	393	47	88	19	0	14	35	28	2	0	1	141	23	6	6.59	33.18
Robinson, Chuckie	R-R	6-0	215	12-14-94	.129	.197	.129	26	76	70	2	9	0	0	0	0	5	1	0	0	20	0	0	6.58	26.32
Senzel, Nick	R-R	6-1	218	6-29-95	.100	.129	.133	10	32	30	0	3	1	0	0	0	1	0	1	0	8	0	0	3.13	25.00
Sheets, Gavin	L-L	6-5	230	4-23-96	.233	.303	.357	139	501	451	35	105	24	1	10	45	43	4	0	3	106	2	2	8.58	21.16
Shewmake, Braden	L-R	6-3	190	11-19-97	.125	.134	.203	29	67	64	4	8	2	0	1	4	1	0	0	2	10	5	1	1.49	14.93
Sosa, Lenyn	R-R	6-0	180	1-25-00	.254	.283	.359	100	369	351	28	89	13	0	8	35	12	3	2	1	77	3	1	3.25	20.87
Vargas, Miguel	R-R	6-3	205	11-17-99	.104	.217	.170	42	157	135	11	14	3	0	2	7	17	3	0	2	41	2	1	10.83	26.11
Vaughn, Andrew	R-R	6-0	215	4-3-98	.246	.297	.402	149	619	570	55	140	30	1	19	70	38	6	0	5	132	2	0	6.14	21.32

Pitching	B-T	Ht.	Wt.	DOB	W	L	ERA	G	GS	SV	IP	Hits	Runs	ER	HR	BB	SO	AVG	OBP	SLG	SO%	BB%	BF
Anderson, Justin	L-R	6-3	230	9-28-92	1	2	4.39	56	0	1	53	48	29	26	5	32	57	.234	.344	.351	23.55	13.22	
Banks, Tanner	R-L	6-1	210	10-24-91	2	2	4.13	41	1	2	48	47	30	22	5	15	55	.257	.314	.388	26.83	7.32	
Berroa, Prelander	R-R	5-11	170	4-18-00	1	0	3.32	17	0	0	19	15	7	7	2	13	26	.217	.349	.362	31.33	15.66	
Brebbia, John	L-R	6-1	200	5-30-90	0	6	6.29	54	0	2	49	52	34	34	9	17	58	.265	.333	.459	26.85	7.87	
Burke, Sean	R-R	6-6	230	12-18-99	2	0	1.42	4	3	0	19	12	4	3	2	7	22	.174	.250	.333	28.95	9.21	
Bush, Ky	L-L	6-6	240	11-12-99	0	3	5.60	4	4	0	18	20	11	11	2	16	11	.290	.425	.449	12.64	18.39	
Cannon, Jonathan	R-R	6-6	213	7-19-00	5	10	4.49	23	21	1	124	125	65	62	18	40	91	.263	.324	.440	17.43	7.66	
Clevinger, Mike	R-R	6-4	215	12-21-90	0	3	6.75	4	4	0	16	22	13	12	4	9	15	.319	.397	.594	19.23	11.54	
Crochet, Garrett	L-L	6-6	230	6-21-99	6	12	3.58	32	32	0	146	123	61	58	18	33	209	.222	.271	.371	35.13	5.55	
De Los Santos, Enyel	R-R	6-3	235	12-25-95	0	0	3.63	15	0	1	17	13	7	7	5	9	13	.213	.324	.475	18.31	12.68	
Eder, Jake	L-L	6-4	215	10-9-98	0	0	4.50	1	0	0	2	2	1	1	0	1	1	.286	.444	.286	11.11	11.11	
Ellard, Fraser	L-L	6-4	205	11-6-97	2	3	3.75	25	0	1	24	18	12	10	3	12	26	.212	.307	.353	25.74	11.88	
Fedde, Erick	R-R	6-4	203	2-25-93	7	4	3.11	21	21	0	122	105	43	42	14	34	108	.227	.281	.370	21.51	6.77	
Flexen, Chris	R-R	6-3	219	7-1-94	3	15	4.95	33	30	0	160	180	95	88	24	63	123	.283	.349	.476	17.40	8.91	
Foster, Matt	R-R	6-0	215	1-27-95	0	1	2.70	6	1	0	7	5	2	2	1	5	4	.200	.333	.360	13.33	16.67	
Garcia, Deivi	R-R	5-9	163	5-19-99	1	2	7.07	14	0	1	14	16	16	11	2	11	15	.286	.397	.411	22.06	16.18	
Hill, Tim	R-L	6-4	200	2-10-90	1	0	5.87	27	0	0	23	41	19	15	0	10	13	.387	.441	.425	11.02	8.47	
Iriarte, Jairo	R-R	6-2	160	12-15-01	0	1	1.50	6	0	0	6	3	3	1	0	8	6	.143	.367	.143	20.00	26.67	
Keller, Brad	R-R	6-5	255	7-27-95	0	2	4.86	5	2	0	17	17	10	9	5	6	13	.243	.303	.529	17.11	7.89	
Kopech, Michael	R-R	6-3	210	4-30-96	2	8	4.74	43	0	9	44	35	24	23	8	24	59	.222	.337	.380	30.89	12.57	
Kuhl, Chad	R-R	6-3	207	9-10-92	0	2	5.06	31	1	1	53	56	33	30	5	25	54	.273	.367	.410	22.50	10.42	
Leasure, Jordan	R-R	6-3	215	8-15-98	0	2	6.32	33	0	2	31	32	22	22	6	18	26	.267	.362	.492	18.31	12.68	
Leone, Dominic	R-R	5-10	215	10-26-91	0	2	6.63	23	0	0	19	20	17	14	4	14	17	.274	.382	.521	19.10	15.73	
Martin, Davis	L-R	6-2	200	1-4-97	0	5	4.32	11	10	0	50	50	25	24	5	23	47	.260	.355	.365	21.36	10.45	

Mendick, Danny	R-R	5-10	195	9-28-93	0	0	0.00	1	0	0	1	2	0	0	0	0	0	.500	.500	.500	0.00	0.00
Nastrini, Nick	R-R	6-3	215	2-18-00	0	7	7.07	9	8	0	36	32	33	28	7	36	26	.234	.397	.445	14.94	20.69
Peralta, Sammy	L-L	6-2	205	5-10-98	0	0	4.80	9	0	0	15	21	9	8	2	7	11	.323	.389	.508	15.28	9.72
Shaw, Bryan	S-R	6-1	226	11-8-87	0	1	9.00	5	0	0	4	8	5	4	1	4	4	.400	.500	.700	16.67	16.67
Shuster, Jared	L-L	6-3	210	8-3-98	2	5	4.42	39	4	0	73	74	38	36	9	33	56	.261	.333	.410	17.45	10.28
Soroka, Michael	R-R	6-5	225	8-4-97	0	10	4.74	25	9	0	80	66	49	42	13	44	84	.224	.328	.415	24.21	12.68
Thorpe, Drew	L-R	6-4	190	10-1-00	3	3	5.48	9	9	0	44	35	29	27	8	21	25	.212	.302	.424	13.16	11.05
Toussaint, Touki	R-R	6-3	215	6-20-96	1	2	7.43	11	0	0	23	35	19	19	3	18	26	.361	.462	.557	22.22	15.38
Varland, Gus	L-R	6-1	213	11-6-96	1	0	3.54	19	0	0	20	23	9	8	1	4	24	.284	.318	.383	28.24	4.71
Wilson, Steven	R-R	6-3	221	8-24-94	1	6	5.71	40	0	0	35	29	29	22	8	26	34	.227	.363	.469	20.86	15.95
Woodford, Jake	R-R	6-4	215	10-28-96	0	2	10.80	2	2	0	8	15	10	10	2	5	7	.375	.457	.650	15.22	10.87

Fielding

Catcher	PCT	G	PO	A	E	DP	PB
Lee	.995	113	824	33	4	4	8
Maldonado	.995	48	378	11	2	0	3
Robinson	.990	26	196	10	2	1	0

First Base	PCT	G	PO	A	E	DP
Sheets	.997	43	279	26	1	28
Sosa	1.000	2	5	0	0	0
Vaughn	.996	122	816	76	4	75

Second Base	PCT	G	PO	A	E	DP
Shewmake	.952	6	4	16	1	3
Baldwin	.978	24	38	50	2	7
Sosa	.988	47	72	89	2	31
Lopez	.989	83	100	180	3	33
Mendick	1.000	14	24	29	0	8
Remillard	1.000	7	4	17	0	2

Third Base	PCT	G	PO	A	E	DP
DeJong	.923	11	9	15	2	0
Mendick	.943	26	15	35	3	2
Moncada	.935	11	8	21	2	4
Ramos	.982	21	16	38	1	4
Remillard	1.000	3	2	4	0	0
Senzel	.929	6	6	7	1	0
Shewmake	1.000	8	3	13	0	0
Sosa	.967	52	38	78	4	11
Vargas	.956	36	26	60	4	9

Shortstop	PCT	G	PO	A	E	DP
Amaya	.985	23	32	32	1	9
Baldwin	1.000	9	8	19	0	9
DeJong	.958	89	110	163	12	29
Lopez	.994	45	61	92	1	24
Remillard	.857	3	1	5	1	0
Shewmake	.926	11	6	19	2	4

Outfield	PCT	G	PO	A	E	DP
Benintendi	.988	125	244	3	3	0
Colas	1.000	12	16	0	0	0
DeLoach	1.000	17	37	1	0	0
Ellis	.750	6	6	0	2	0
Fletcher	.966	73	165	8	6	1
Grossman	.976	19	40	1	1	0
Jimenez	1.000	1	1	0	0	0
Julks	.988	57	80	1	1	1
Ortega	1.000	12	18	0	0	0
Pham	.993	78	142	1	1	0
Pillar	1.000	14	17	0	0	0
Remillard	1.000	3	2	0	0	0
Robert	.992	97	254	1	2	0
Senzel	1.000	1	1	0	0	0
Sheets	.986	45	67	2	1	1
Vargas	1.000	1	2	0	0	0

CHARLOTTE KNIGHTS

TRIPLE-A

INTERNATIONAL LEAGUE

Batting	B-T	Ht.	Wt.	DOB	AVG	OBP	SLG	G	PA	AB	R	H	2B	3B	HR	RBI	BB	HBP	SH	SF	SO	SB	CS	BB%	SO%
Baldwin, Brooks	B-R	6-2	175	8-15-00	.345	.441	.655	8	35	29	6	10	3	0	2	4	5	0	1	0	2	1	1	14.29	5.71
Bernard, Wynton	R-R	6-2	195	9-24-90	.306	.328	.446	41	125	121	20	37	6	1	3	14	4	0	0	0	21	11	1	3.20	16.80
Castellano, Angelo	R-R	5-10	165	1-13-95	.241	.280	.375	33	119	112	18	27	3	0	4	11	6	0	1	0	30	3	1	5.04	25.21
Chavis, Michael	R-R	5-10	190	8-11-95	.234	.308	.414	67	266	239	40	56	16	0	9	27	20	6	0	1	63	9	1	7.52	23.68
Colas, Oscar	L-L	5-11	209	9-17-98	.246	.332	.400	109	464	402	57	99	21	4	11	51	51	4	0	7	107	12	8	10.99	23.06
DeLoach, Zach	L-R	6-0	205	8-18-98	.287	.375	.410	97	411	356	65	102	22	2	6	54	48	4	0	3	107	20	2	11.68	26.03
Difo, Wilmer	B-R	5-10	200	4-2-92	.276	.370	.405	94	362	304	45	84	14	2	7	44	44	4	5	5	79	11	2	12.15	21.82
Eberly, Weston	R-R	6-0	195	1-7-01	.200	.273	.200	4	11	10	1	2	0	0	0	1	1	0	0	0	3	0	0	9.09	27.27
Elko, Tim	R-R	6-4	240	12-27-98	.289	.361	.472	48	219	197	31	57	7	1	9	33	21	1	0	0	64	1	1	9.59	29.22
Ellis, Duke	L-L	6-1	180	1-16-98	.125	.125	.125	2	8	8	0	1	0	0	0	0	0	0	0	0	2	0	1	0.00	25.00
Fletcher, Dominic	L-L	5-6	185	9-2-97	.263	.333	.389	24	106	95	13	25	6	0	2	7	10	0	1	0	15	0	1	9.43	14.15
Grossman, Robbie	B-L	6-0	209	9-16-89	.400	.500	1.100	3	12	10	3	4	1	0	2	5	2	0	0	0	2	0	0	16.67	16.67
Hackenberg, Adam	R-R	6-1	225	9-8-99	.188	.315	.234	49	185	154	17	29	4	0	1	7	25	4	1	1	77	3	1	13.51	41.62
Julks, Corey	R-R	6-1	185	2-27-96	.333	.438	.593	7	32	27	6	9	2	1	1	2	5	0	0	0	7	1	0	15.63	21.88
Mendick, Danny	R-R	5-10	195	9-28-93	.263	.330	.514	52	197	179	29	47	12	0	11	35	17	1	0	0	43	3	5	8.63	21.83
Moncada, Yoan	B-R	6-2	225	5-27-95	.341	.413	.537	12	46	41	8	14	5	0	1	6	5	0	0	0	12	1	0	10.87	26.09
Montgomery, Colson	L-R	6-3	205	2-27-02	.214	.329	.381	130	573	485	66	104	21	3	18	63	69	15	0	3	164	8	2	12.04	28.62
Nakawake, Taishi	R-R	5-11	185	6-20-98	.125	.263	.125	7	19	16	2	2	0	0	0	0	2	1	0	0	6	0	1	10.53	31.58
Ortega, Rafael	L-R	5-11	180	5-15-91	.289	.413	.498	84	313	249	45	72	15	2	11	53	56	1	1	6	62	17	8	17.89	19.81
Payton, Mark	L-L	5-8	180	12-7-91	.309	.383	.463	112	479	417	70	129	30	2	10	53	53	0	4	5	81	5	7	11.06	16.91
Perez, Carlos	R-R	5-11	205	9-10-96	.273	.312	.430	100	398	370	47	101	20	1	12	56	20	3	1	4	42	1	1	5.03	10.55
Pham, Tommy	R-R	6-1	223	3-8-88	.294	.333	.353	4	18	17	3	5	1	0	0	1	1	0	0	0	3	2	0	5.56	16.67
Phillips, Brett	L-R	6-0	195	5-30-94	.120	.228	.280	17	57	50	5	6	3	1	1	7	7	0	0	0	27	3	0	12.28	47.37
Quero, Edgar	B-R	5-11	170	4-6-03	.295	.382	.463	26	110	95	13	28	4	0	4	17	13	1	0	1	21	0	0	11.82	19.09
Ramos, Bryan	R-R	6-2	190	3-12-02	.263	.339	.416	64	279	243	34	64	13	0	8	33	24	5	0	2	58	6	3	8.60	20.79
Remillard, Zach	R-R	6-0	185	2-21-94	.146	.213	.234	47	176	158	19	23	3	1	3	15	11	3	2	2	43	2	2	6.25	24.43
Robert, Luis	R-R	6-2	220	8-3-97	.100	.182	.250	5	22	20	3	2	0	0	1	3	0	2	0	0	6	0	0	0.00	27.27
Robinson, Chuckie	R-R	6-0	215	12-14-94	.246	.292	.382	55	216	199	22	49	4	1	7	32	13	1	0	3	56	0	2	6.02	25.93
Shewmake, Braden	L-R	6-3	190	11-19-97	.152	.152	.182	10	33	33	2	5	1	0	0	2	0	0	0	0	7	0	1	0.00	21.21
Smith-Njigba, Canaan	L-R	6-0	230	4-30-99	.261	.370	.304	8	27	23	3	6	1	0	0	2	4	0	0	0	6	3	0	14.81	22.22
Sosa, Lenyn	R-R	6-0	180	1-25-00	.275	.330	.529	24	113	102	18	28	8	0	6	18	9	0	1	1	20	2	1	7.96	17.70
Stassi, Max	R-R	5-10	200	3-15-91	.091	.375	.091	5	16	11	3	1	0	0	0	1	2	3	0	0	4	0	0	12.50	25.00
Walsh, Jared	L-L	6-0	210	7-30-93	.185	.289	.415	41	149	130	15	24	4	1	8	17	18	1	0	0	55	1	0	12.08	36.91

Pitching	B-T	Ht.	Wt.	DOB	W	L	ERA	G	GS	SV	IP	Hits	Runs	ER	HR	BB	SO	AVG	OBP	SLG	SO%	BB%	BF
Abbott, Cory	R-R	6-2	217	9-20-95	5	5	5.80	30	9	0	71	66	48	46	15	29	78	.243	.318	.449	25.57	9.51	305
Adams, Mason	R-R	6-0	200	2-23-00	0	0	5.82	5	5	0	17	20	13	11	1	9	9	.278	.366	.361	10.98	10.98	82
Anderson, Justin	L-R	6-3	230	9-28-92	1	2	2.50	16	0	6	18	14	8	5	1	4	25	.206	.247	.294	34.25	5.48	73
Barlow, Joe	R-R	6-2	210	9-28-95	0	0	10.03	12	0	0	12	18	14	13	5	8	14	.367	.448	.837	23.33	13.33	60

Bernard, Wynton	R-R	6-2	195	9-24-90	0	0	0.00	1	0	0	1	1	0	0	0	1	0	.333	.500	.333	0.00	25.00	4
Berroa, Prelander	R-R	5-11	170	4-18-00	3	5	6.41	43	0	0	46	50	38	33	7	35	49	.286	.400	.480	22.48	16.06	218
Brebbia, John	L-R	6-1	200	5-30-90	0	0	0.00	1	1	0	1	1	0	0	0	0	2	.250	.250	.250	50.00	0.00	4
Burke, Sean	R-R	6-6	230	12-18-99	2	6	4.62	16	16	0	64	47	35	33	12	36	86	.199	.310	.403	31.05	13.00	277
Bush, Ky	L-L	6-6	240	11-12-99	2	1	7.01	6	4	0	26	27	21	20	3	14	22	.270	.371	.460	18.97	12.07	116
Cannon, Jonathan	R-R	6-6	213	7-19-00	2	3	5.50	8	8	0	38	39	26	23	3	18	35	.271	.369	.424	20.83	10.71	168
Clevinger, Mike	R-R	6-4	215	12-21-90	0	0	5.40	6	6	0	22	27	13	13	4	7	20	.303	.374	.483	20.20	7.07	99
Coffey, Adisyn	R-R	6-2	185	1-22-99	1	1	2.04	35	0	10	35	26	8	8	1	17	40	.200	.293	.269	27.21	11.56	147
Cousin, Josimar	R-R	6-3	185	2-18-98	0	1	3.55	22	0	1	25	19	10	10	4	12	19	.204	.295	.344	17.92	11.32	106
Davis, Tyler	R-R	6-3	210	10-3-98	1	0	9.00	4	0	0	5	3	5	5	2	3	4	.167	.286	.500	19.05	14.29	21
Dominguez, Johan	R-R	6-4	190	1-18-96	7	5	4.43	27	22	0	112	110	60	55	17	53	90	.256	.346	.436	18.22	10.73	494
Drohan, Shane	L-L	6-3	195	1-7-99	2	0	9.00	5	0	0	4	4	4	4	0	4	5	.250	.400	.313	25.00	20.00	20
Eder, Jake	L-L	6-4	215	10-9-98	1	4	9.87	9	9	0	35	42	40	38	7	27	36	.304	.423	.551	21.43	16.07	168
Ellard, Fraser	L-L	6-4	205	11-6-97	2	3	3.76	38	0	3	41	34	19	17	4	20	59	.227	.335	.380	33.52	11.36	176
Foster, Matt	R-R	6-0	215	1-27-95	0	0	2.40	14	0	0	15	16	5	4	1	5	19	.262	.318	.361	28.79	7.58	66
Garcia, Deivi	R-R	5-9	163	5-19-99	3	6	6.18	40	5	1	51	50	38	35	5	27	62	.262	.363	.408	27.43	11.95	226
Hoopii-Tuionetoa, Anthony	R-R	6-2	190	8-11-00	0	1	13.50	9	0	0	9	11	13	13	1	5	8	.306	.372	.417	18.60	11.63	43
Horn, Bailey	L-L	6-2	210	1-15-98	1	1	11.32	9	0	0	10	14	13	13	4	10	15	.333	.462	.762	28.85	19.23	52
Keller, Brad	R-R	6-5	255	7-27-95	1	1	4.50	3	3	0	16	16	8	8	1	6	14	.262	.324	.410	20.59	8.82	68
Knebel, Corey	R-R	6-3	224	11-26-91	1	0	0.00	6	0	0	5	0	0	0	0	2	8	.000	.111	.000	44.44	11.11	18
Kuhl, Chad	R-R	6-3	207	9-10-92	1	3	4.34	13	11	0	56	51	30	27	5	33	42	.250	.362	.397	17.28	13.58	243
Lakins, Travis	R-R	6-1	220	6-29-94	0	1	6.00	14	0	1	15	17	10	10	2	7	16	.266	.347	.469	22.22	9.72	72
Leasure, Jordan	R-R	6-3	215	8-15-98	3	0	5.59	11	0	0	10	7	6	6	1	6	12	.212	.350	.394	30.00	15.00	40
Leone, Dominic	R-R	5-10	215	10-26-91	0	0	4.50	4	0	0	4	4	2	2	0	0	7	.250	.294	.250	41.18	0.00	17
Martin, Davis	L-R	6-2	200	1-4-97	0	0	0.00	2	2	0	8	5	0	0	0	3	7	.179	.258	.250	22.58	9.68	31
McGarity, Aaron	R-R	6-3	185	1-31-95	8	5	2.77	55	0	6	65	47	26	20	5	21	60	.203	.295	.306	22.30	7.81	269
McGough, Trey	L-L	6-3	195	3-29-98	4	2	1.98	14	1	0	27	21	6	6	1	8	33	.216	.274	.268	30.84	7.48	107
Mendick, Danny	R-R	5-10	195	9-28-93	0	1	10.29	5	0	0	7	15	9	8	3	3	1	.455	.500	.818	2.78	8.33	36
Mikel, Jordan	R-R	6-5	190	3-24-99	0	0	162.00	1	0	0	0	2	6	6	0	3	0	.667	.857	.667	0.00	42.86	7
Murphy, Shane	L-L	6-5	210	1-19-01	0	1	7.20	3	2	0	10	7	8	8	2	7	8	.189	.318	.405	18.18	15.91	44
Nastrini, Nick	R-R	6-3	215	2-18-00	3	9	5.29	21	18	0	85	83	62	50	17	52	98	.250	.354	.464	25.00	13.27	392
Padilla, Nicholas	R-R	6-2	220	12-24-96	0	3	3.23	25	0	0	31	21	12	11	5	16	37	.194	.302	.361	29.37	12.70	126
Peralta, Sammy	L-L	6-2	205	5-10-98	2	0	2.84	26	0	1	38	24	12	12	3	17	41	.186	.296	.302	26.97	11.18	152
Perez, Carlos	R-R	5-11	205	9-10-96	0	0	0.00	1	0	0	2	1	0	0	0	1	0	.143	.250	.286	0.00	12.50	8
Plymell, Chase	R-R	6-4	205	5-29-98	2	0	3.08	23	0	0	38	30	15	13	4	17	25	.214	.304	.357	15.72	10.69	159
Ramirez, Jose	R-R	6-0	142	3-28-01	0	1	15.43	1	1	0	2	3	4	4	1	3	2	.375	.615	.875	15.38	23.08	13
Ramsey, Lane	R-R	6-9	245	7-16-96	1	1	5.17	14	0	1	16	11	9	9	5	13	18	.193	.352	.474	25.35	18.31	71
Roach, Dalton	R-R	6-2	210	4-8-96	2	0	3.65	21	0	0	25	18	12	10	3	11	26	.200	.301	.400	25.24	10.68	103
Roberts, Max	R-L	6-6	190	7-23-97	0	0	0.00	1	0	0	2	1	0	0	0	2	2	.167	.375	.167	25.00	25.00	8
Schoenle, Garrett	L-L	6-5	185	6-21-98	0	0	0.00	1	1	0	3	0	0	0	0	1	4	.000	.100	.000	40.00	10.00	10
Sedlock, Cody	R-R	6-4	220	6-19-95	0	0	18.00	6	0	0	5	3	10	10	1	13	2	.200	.567	.533	6.67	43.33	30
Shuster, Jared	L-L	6-3	210	8-3-98	0	1	6.39	3	3	0	13	14	9	9	4	3	9	.275	.315	.608	16.36	5.45	55
Soroka, Michael	R-R	6-5	225	8-4-97	3	0	3.38	6	0	0	8	5	3	3	1	2	12	.179	.281	.321	37.50	6.25	32
Speas, Alex	R-R	6-3	225	3-4-98	0	0	15.43	2	0	0	2	2	4	4	1	2	2	.222	.364	.556	18.18	18.18	11
Then, Juan	R-R	6-1	200	2-7-00	0	0	15.88	7	0	0	6	8	10	10	4	7	5	.333	.500	.833	15.63	21.88	32
Toussaint, Touki	R-R	6-3	215	6-20-96	3	3	6.02	19	10	0	55	59	39	37	5	43	58	.276	.407	.397	21.97	16.29	264
Varland, Gus	L-R	6-1	213	11-6-96	0	0	3.86	4	0	0	5	5	2	2	1	0	5	.263	.263	.474	26.32	0.00	19
Veloz, Manuel	R-R	6-2	185	1-28-01	0	0	13.50	1	0	0	2	6	3	3	0	3	3	.545	.643	.545	21.43	21.43	14
Wilson, Steven	R-R	6-3	221	8-24-94	0	0	5.25	12	0	0	12	13	7	7	2	7	14	.277	.364	.532	25.45	12.73	55
Woodford, Jake	R-R	6-4	215	10-28-96	1	3	5.26	10	10	0	50	52	31	29	9	17	42	.269	.341	.492	19.63	7.94	214

Fielding

Catcher	PCT	G	PO	A	E	DP	PB
Eberly	1.000	4	27	1	0	0	0
Hackenberg	.990	46	386	30	4	4	2
Perez	.996	30	266	10	1	0	1
Quero	.986	24	210	7	3	1	0
Robinson	.995	47	408	28	2	5	2
Stassi	.968	4	29	1	1	0	0

First Base	PCT	G	PO	A	E	DP
Castellano	.000	1	0	0	0	0
Chavis	.988	11	72	8	1	7
Colas	.955	2	20	1	1	0
Elko	.985	46	313	24	5	30
Mendick	1.000	1	2	0	0	0
Perez	.994	49	335	22	2	46
Remillard	.982	9	50	6	1	5
Walsh	1.000	36	224	32	0	23

Second Base	PCT	G	PO	A	E	DP
Baldwin	1.000	4	5	10	0	1
Castellano	.962	10	17	33	2	8
Chavis	.966	47	71	126	7	28
Difo	.971	40	49	83	4	19
Mendick	.982	16	21	35	1	9
Nakawake	1.000	2	2	4	0	2
Ramos	1.000	1	3	4	0	2
Remillard	1.000	16	18	43	0	8
Shewmake	1.000	4	7	10	0	2
Sosa	.955	13	14	28	2	8

Third Base	PCT	G	PO	A	E	DP
Baldwin	1.000	1	0	1	0	0
Castellano	.971	18	12	22	1	3
Chavis	.900	7	2	7	1	2
Difo	.947	30	20	51	4	3
Mendick	.974	19	8	29	1	4
Moncada	.824	8	4	10	3	1
Nakawake	.833	4	2	3	1	0
Perez	1.000	1	0	1	0	0
Ramos	.930	47	27	66	7	3
Remillard	1.000	9	8	12	0	0
Shewmake	1.000	3	4	2	0	0
Sosa	.833	10	4	11	3	1

Shortstop	PCT	G	PO	A	E	DP
Baldwin	1.000	3	6	9	0	3
Castellano	.929	3	4	9	1	2
Chavis	1.000	1	1	1	0	1
Mendick	1.000	2	4	2	0	1
Montgomery	.963	125	213	275	19	79
Remillard	.974	9	16	22	1	3
Sosa	1.000	1	2	2	0	1

Outfield	PCT	G	PO	A	E	DP
Bernard	.978	33	42	2	1	1
Colas	.994	93	169	11	1	2
DeLoach	1.000	88	178	4	0	0
Ellis	1.000	2	6	0	0	0
Fletcher	.986	24	69	1	1	0
Grossman	.667	2	2	0	1	0
Julks	1.000	4	13	0	0	0
Mendick	1.000	6	7	1	0	0
Ortega	.988	76	160	5	2	0
Payton	.983	92	166	6	3	0

Pham	1.000	4	7	0	0	0
Phillips	1.000	13	23	1	0	0
Ramos	1.000	1	1	0	0	0
Remillard	1.000	5	12	0	0	0
Robert	1.000	4	8	0	0	0
Smith-Njigba	1.000	6	4	0	0	0
Walsh	1.000	5	9	0	0	0

BIRMINGHAM BARONS

DOUBLE-A

SOUTHERN LEAGUE

Batting	B-T	Ht.	Wt.	DOB	AVG	OBP	SLG	G	PA	AB	R	H	2B	3B	HR	RBI	BB	HBP	SH	SF	SO	SB	CS	BB%	SO%
Baldwin, Brooks	B-R	6-2	175	8-15-00	.322	.386	.441	74	319	286	34	92	16	0	6	37	28	3	0	2	56	16	4	8.78	17.55
Betancourt, Jhoneiker	R-R	6-1	174	5-7-00	.333	.333	.333	1	3	3	1	1	0	0	0	0	0	0	0	0	1	0	0	0.00	33.33
Burke, Jacob	R-R	6-1	208	2-26-01	.193	.290	.229	71	256	223	26	43	6	1	0	17	26	5	1	1	67	24	2	10.16	26.17
Camilletti, Mario	L-R	5-9	195	4-19-99	.239	.412	.323	47	204	155	22	37	7	0	2	14	45	2	0	2	38	3	2	22.06	18.63
Claunch, Troy	R-R	6-0	210	9-1-98	.179	.289	.179	13	45	39	3	7	0	0	0	0	4	2	0	0	13	0	0	8.89	28.89
DeGuzman, Cristopher	B-R	5-11	185	12-1-99	.152	.176	.182	13	35	33	1	5	1	0	0	3	1	0	1	0	13	1	1	2.86	37.14
Eberly, Weston	R-R	6-0	195	1-7-01	.130	.286	.130	6	28	23	2	3	0	0	0	2	5	0	0	0	8	0	0	17.86	28.57
Elko, Tim	R-R	6-4	240	12-27-98	.289	.338	.420	91	371	343	36	99	16	1	9	40	21	5	0	1	109	2	0	5.66	29.38
Ellis, Duke	L-L	6-1	180	1-16-98	.258	.341	.308	39	141	120	24	31	3	0	1	12	13	3	3	2	31	34	1	9.22	21.99
Gladney, DJ	R-R	6-3	195	7-14-01	.278	.314	.505	24	105	97	12	27	4	0	6	18	4	2	0	2	23	1	0	3.81	21.90
Gonzalez, Jacob	L-R	6-2	200	5-30-02	.225	.284	.321	94	407	365	40	82	20	0	5	42	28	5	2	7	57	10	5	6.88	14.00
Gonzalez, Juan	R-R	5-9	195	2-20-01	.000	.143	.000	3	7	6	0	0	0	0	0	0	1	0	0	0	3	0	0	14.29	42.86
Goosenberg, Shawn	R-R	6-1	195	12-5-99	.200	.268	.313	33	128	115	15	23	7	0	2	11	9	2	1	1	27	8	2	7.03	21.09
Hackenberg, Adam	R-R	6-1	225	9-8-99	.233	.305	.267	26	95	86	8	20	3	0	0	7	9	0	0	0	31	0	1	9.47	32.63
Hogan, Matt	L-R	6-0	195	1-24-00	.173	.293	.263	53	185	156	17	27	9	1	1	18	23	4	0	1	71	12	3	12.43	38.38
Matthews, Jason	R-R	6-0	187	4-9-97	.194	.289	.267	117	418	360	41	70	8	3	4	31	43	6	6	3	117	8	2	10.29	27.99
Nakawake, Taishi	R-R	5-11	185	6-20-98	.200	.200	.200	4	15	15	0	3	0	0	0	1	0	0	0	0	1	0	0	0.00	6.67
Neslony, Tyler	L-R	5-11	190	2-13-94	.226	.264	.286	43	144	133	11	30	8	0	0	13	7	1	0	3	28	5	3	4.86	19.44
Nishida, Rikuu	L-R	5-6	150	5-6-01	.333	.400	.333	11	50	45	10	15	0	0	0	2	4	1	0	0	0	4	1	8.00	0.00
Podkul, Nick	R-R	6-1	200	4-11-97	.256	.358	.402	22	95	82	12	21	4	1	2	7	12	1	0	0	26	0	0	12.63	27.37
Quero, Edgar	B-R	5-11	170	4-6-03	.275	.360	.463	72	292	255	28	70	12	0	12	53	26	9	0	2	49	1	1	8.90	16.78
Ramos, Bryan	R-R	6-2	190	3-12-02	.182	.265	.307	24	98	88	9	16	5	0	2	11	7	3	0	0	28	2	0	7.14	28.57
Smith-Njigba, Canaan	L-R	6-0	230	4-30-99	.182	.258	.273	16	62	55	3	10	2	0	1	6	5	1	0	1	15	1	0	8.06	24.19
Tatum, Terrell	L-L	5-9	167	7-27-99	.219	.317	.302	116	495	430	59	94	15	3	5	43	59	3	3	0	130	30	8	11.92	26.26
Turner, Michael	L-R	6-2	205	8-18-98	.218	.325	.282	96	385	330	38	72	13	1	2	33	50	3	0	2	77	6	0	12.99	20.00
Veras, Wilfred	R-R	6-2	180	11-15-02	.267	.319	.424	128	536	491	62	131	27	1	16	60	34	6	0	5	140	25	9	6.34	26.12
Womack, Alsander	R-R	5-9	205	3-16-99	.214	.279	.260	44	147	131	20	28	3	0	1	12	11	2	0	3	30	4	1	7.48	20.41

Pitching	B-T	Ht.	Wt.	DOB	W	L	ERA	G	GS	SV	IP	Hits	Runs	ER	HR	BB	SO	AVG	OBP	SLG	SO%	BB%	BF
Adams, Mason	R-R	6-0	200	2-23-00	7	5	2.44	18	17	0	103	90	31	28	9	19	101	.236	.292	.339	24.57	4.62	411
Adler, Eric	R-R	6-2	190	10-12-00	2	2	4.06	32	0	8	31	20	19	14	1	20	38	.189	.318	.245	29.46	15.50	129
Bush, Ky	L-L	6-6	240	11-12-99	5	3	2.12	14	14	0	81	51	23	19	6	32	78	.180	.265	.264	24.61	10.09	317
Carela, Juan	R-R	6-3	186	12-15-01	3	3	3.58	7	7	0	33	25	13	13	4	13	36	.221	.328	.389	27.27	9.85	132
Coffey, Adisyn	R-R	6-2	185	1-22-99	4	1	0.53	15	0	3	17	11	2	1	0	5	15	.177	.239	.194	22.39	7.46	67
Cousin, Josimar	R-R	6-3	185	2-18-98	0	0	0.90	8	0	0	10	6	1	1	1	2	15	.171	.216	.257	40.54	5.41	37
Dalquist, Andrew	R-R	6-1	175	11-13-00	2	3	3.06	38	0	1	47	36	18	16	2	27	52	.217	.323	.301	26.00	13.50	200
Dominguez, Johan	R-R	6-4	190	1-18-96	0	1	1.29	1	1	0	7	4	1	1	0	0	9	.160	.160	.160	36.00	0.00	25
Eder, Jake	L-L	6-4	215	10-9-98	2	5	5.09	15	15	0	74	83	43	42	8	31	86	.284	.355	.421	25.90	9.34	332
Franklin, Zach	R-R	6-1	198	10-27-98	2	0	0.90	8	0	0	10	4	1	1	0	3	17	.121	.194	.182	47.22	8.33	36
Freeman, Caleb	R-R	6-1	195	2-23-98	2	5	3.92	39	0	4	44	33	21	19	5	26	56	.208	.332	.358	29.32	13.61	191
Gowens, Riley	R-R	6-3	220	10-18-99	2	3	3.14	12	12	0	52	50	22	18	4	20	60	.251	.326	.352	26.79	8.93	224
Hoopii-Tuionetoa, Anthony	R-R	6-2	190	8-11-00	0	2	3.24	23	0	4	25	19	9	9	2	8	23	.216	.286	.330	23.23	8.08	99
Iriarte, Jairo	R-R	6-2	160	12-15-01	5	7	3.71	23	22	0	126	104	57	52	7	57	122	.228	.333	.314	22.85	10.67	534
Kelley, Jared	R-R	6-3	230	10-3-01	1	1	5.63	5	0	0	8	9	6	5	0	6	5	.281	.395	.344	13.16	15.79	38
Luna, Gil	L-L	5-10	173	7-29-99	4	3	2.80	42	0	3	45	29	20	14	0	46	48	.191	.386	.224	23.65	22.66	203
McCullough, Connor	R-R	6-1	185	10-5-99	3	1	3.38	4	1	0	13	11	5	5	3	4	13	.224	.283	.449	24.53	7.55	53
Mikel, Jordan	R-R	6-5	190	3-24-99	4	2	4.24	27	0	1	51	44	24	24	2	17	57	.233	.308	.376	26.64	7.94	214
Palisch, Jake	L-L	6-4	215	8-19-98	4	3	3.75	38	0	0	50	51	24	21	7	15	35	.270	.322	.413	16.75	7.18	209
Pallette, Peyton	R-R	6-1	180	5-9-01	1	1	1.80	8	0	0	15	7	4	3	0	5	16	.137	.241	.176	27.59	8.62	58
Plymell, Chase	R-R	6-4	205	5-29-98	3	2	3.76	15	0	0	38	35	17	16	4	8	28	.243	.287	.396	17.83	5.10	157
Ramirez, Jose	R-R	6-0	142	3-28-01	0	0	6.75	1	1	0	4	4	3	3	0	2	1	.250	.429	.438	4.76	9.52	21
Roach, Dalton	R-R	6-2	210	4-8-96	1	0	0.00	5	0	0	6	7	0	0	0	0	7	.292	.292	.458	29.17	0.00	24
Roberts, Max	R-L	6-6	190	7-23-97	0	1	5.40	10	0	1	12	9	7	7	2	13	14	.220	.400	.390	25.45	23.64	55
Schoenle, Garrett	L-L	6-5	185	6-21-98	3	2	1.64	25	5	2	55	36	11	10	1	16	68	.179	.247	.239	31.05	7.31	219
Schultz, Noah	L-L	6-9	220	8-5-03	0	3	1.48	16	16	0	61	45	15	10	2	17	73	.202	.282	.265	29.44	6.85	248
Schweitzer, Tyler	L-L	6-0	185	9-19-00	4	6	4.17	16	16	0	86	77	45	40	8	27	89	.237	.299	.375	24.65	7.48	361
Stivors, Tristan	R-R	6-4	220	9-22-98	0	0	4.24	18	0	0	23	18	13	11	1	19	24	.217	.371	.301	22.86	18.10	105
Then, Juan	R-R	6-1	200	2-7-00	1	0	7.04	7	0	0	8	8	8	6	1	5	3	.242	.359	.515	7.50	12.50	40
Thorpe, Drew	L-R	6-4	190	10-1-00	7	1	1.35	11	11	0	60	35	9	9	3	17	56	.170	.233	.228	25.00	7.59	224

Fielding

Catcher	PCT	G	PO	A	E	DP	PB
Claunch	.982	12	101	6	2	1	1
Eberly	1.000	6	60	3	0	0	0
Gonzalez	1.000	2	24	1	0	0	0
Hackenberg	1.000	24	208	19	0	1	4
Quero	.983	51	444	24	8	1	4
Turner	.985	46	427	37	7	6	7

First Base	PCT	G	PO	A	E	DP
Betancourt	1.000	1	7	0	0	2
Elko	.997	85	614	26	2	57
Gladney	1.000	1	8	0	0	2
Goosenberg	.980	25	191	6	4	18
Neslony	1.000	2	17	1	0	2
Podkul	1.000	1	13	0	0	2
Turner	.994	23	163	8	1	17
Womack	1.000	2	4	0	0	0

Second Base	PCT	G	PO	A	E	DP
Baldwin	.980	11	16	34	1	12
Camilletti	.992	38	50	74	1	20
DeGuzman	1.000	10	10	15	0	6
Gonzalez	.987	18	25	51	1	14
Goosenberg	1.000	1	1	2	0	1
Matthews	.974	20	28	48	2	5
Nakawake	1.000	2	2	3	0	2
Nishida	1.000	8	15	17	0	7
Womack	.974	36	51	63	3	17

Third Base	PCT	G	PO	A	E	DP
Baldwin	1.000	5	7	8	0	1
DeGuzman	1.000	2	0	5	0	0
Goosenberg	1.000	1	1	1	0	1
Matthews	.950	82	61	150	11	13
Nakawake	1.000	2	1	1	0	0
Podkul	.964	19	8	45	2	7
Ramos	1.000	24	13	34	0	3
Womack	1.000	5	0	6	0	0

Shortstop	PCT	G	PO	A	E	DP
Baldwin	.974	54	66	121	5	22
Gonzalez	.980	69	75	174	5	44
Matthews	.913	15	27	36	6	8

Outfield	PCT	G	PO	A	E	DP
Baldwin	1.000	3	2	0	0	0
Burke	.988	69	165	2	2	2
Camilletti	1.000	6	8	0	0	0
Ellis	1.000	35	74	1	0	0
Gladney	.967	17	29	0	1	0
Goosenberg	1.000	5	7	0	0	0
Hogan	.980	52	97	3	2	1
Neslony	.960	24	48	0	2	0
Nishida	.800	3	4	0	1	0
Smith-Njigba	.929	12	12	1	1	0
Tatum	.985	103	199	3	3	1
Veras	.967	94	173	5	6	1

WINSTON-SALEM DASH — HIGH-A

SOUTH ATLANTIC LEAGUE

Batting	B-T	Ht.	Wt.	DOB	AVG	OBP	SLG	G	PA	AB	R	H	2B	3B	HR	RBI	BB	HBP	SH	SF	SO	SB	CS	BB%	SO%
Bergolla, William	L-R	5-11	165	10-20-04	.316	.386	.368	22	90	76	9	24	0	2	0	11	7	3	2	2	8	9	2	7.78	8.89
Burke, Jacob	R-R	6-1	208	2-26-01	.118	.167	.118	5	18	17	1	2	0	0	0	1	1	0	0	0	5	0	1	5.56	27.78
Camilletti, Mario	L-R	5-9	195	4-19-99	.260	.362	.390	41	175	146	23	38	8	1	3	27	24	1	1	3	37	2	1	13.71	21.14
Chapelli, Loidel	L-R	5-8	187	12-20-01	.233	.318	.316	80	328	288	35	67	12	3	2	20	33	4	1	2	86	17	6	10.06	26.22
Connor, Caden	L-L	6-1	200	8-2-00	.269	.335	.394	43	176	160	14	43	9	1	3	21	16	0	0	0	31	1	0	9.09	17.61
Eberly, Weston	R-R	6-0	195	1-7-01	.173	.274	.284	28	96	81	9	14	3	0	2	10	8	4	1	2	29	0	0	8.33	30.21
Galanie, Ryan	R-R	6-2	215	6-20-00	.213	.338	.378	68	281	230	28	49	6	1	10	34	37	9	0	5	59	3	1	13.17	21.00
Gladney, DJ	R-R	6-3	195	7-14-01	.234	.299	.430	67	281	256	35	60	16	2	10	32	23	1	0	1	87	7	0	8.19	30.96
Gonzalez, Jacob	L-R	6-2	200	5-30-02	.273	.364	.399	36	165	143	18	39	7	1	3	15	19	2	0	1	17	7	1	11.52	10.30
Goosenberg, Shawn	R-R	6-1	195	12-5-99	.272	.348	.460	71	305	272	41	74	20	2	9	51	29	3	0	1	91	11	6	9.51	29.84
Harris, Calvin	L-R	6-0	205	11-15-01	.220	.302	.303	68	288	254	31	56	11	2	2	23	28	3	0	3	66	0	0	9.72	22.92
Kath, Wes	L-R	6-3	200	8-3-02	.226	.319	.409	116	459	399	58	90	21	2	16	58	43	13	2	2	155	6	3	9.37	33.77
Lanzilli, Chris	R-R	6-2	225	6-18-98	.245	.342	.382	33	121	102	16	25	3	1	3	17	12	4	0	2	32	3	5	9.92	26.45
Nakawake, Taishi	R-R	5-11	185	6-20-98	.173	.193	.192	32	109	104	7	18	2	0	0	8	2	1	0	2	34	0	0	1.83	31.19
Nishida, Rikuu	L-R	5-6	150	5-6-01	.337	.436	.357	26	119	98	20	33	0	1	0	6	16	2	2	1	13	10	3	13.45	10.92
Park, Eddie	L-L	6-1	187	8-22-01	.242	.325	.271	74	308	273	32	66	5	0	1	22	33	1	0	1	50	11	3	10.71	16.23
Sanchez, Wilber	R-R	5-10	160	2-21-02	.189	.318	.243	13	44	37	2	7	2	0	0	3	7	0	0	0	18	5	0	15.91	40.91
Santos, Miguel	R-R	5-11	174	3-12-01	.333	.364	.476	5	22	21	3	7	0	0	1	3	1	0	0	0	6	0	0	4.55	27.27
Saucke, Casey	R-R	6-3	198	7-24-03	.290	.333	.398	24	99	93	8	27	4	0	2	9	6	0	0	0	26	2	2	6.06	26.26
Smelley, Colby	R-R	6-2	195	3-15-00	.241	.323	.341	63	248	220	24	53	12	2	2	23	22	5	0	1	64	0	0	8.87	25.81
Sprinkle, Jordan	R-R	5-11	180	3-6-01	.207	.296	.279	92	384	333	44	69	16	1	2	29	37	6	6	2	81	27	5	9.64	21.09
Willits, Bryce	L-R	6-2	200	8-25-99	.248	.328	.336	94	379	327	40	81	12	4	3	35	40	3	1	8	81	6	3	10.55	21.37
Zavala, Samuel	L-L	6-1	175	7-15-04	.187	.340	.301	111	467	375	59	70	15	2	8	39	83	5	2	2	104	14	5	17.77	22.27

Pitching	B-T	Ht.	Wt.	DOB	W	L	ERA	G	GS	SV	IP	Hits	Runs	ER	HR	BB	SO	AVG	OBP	SLG	SO%	BB%	BF
Adler, Eric	R-R	6-2	190	10-12-00	1	0	0.00	8	0	5	9	3	0	0	0	4	14	.107	.219	.179	43.75	12.50	32
Altermatt, Nick	R-R	6-0	225	9-28-99	1	0	2.77	8	0	1	13	8	4	4	0	5	19	.178	.260	.222	38.00	10.00	50
Barlow, Joe	R-R	6-2	210	9-28-95	0	0	9.00	2	0	0	2	2	2	2	0	1	3	.250	.333	.500	33.33	11.11	9
Batista, Aldrin	R-R	6-2	185	5-4-03	2	1	1.04	5	5	0	26	16	3	3	0	6	29	.176	.242	.209	29.29	6.06	99
Bell, Luke	R-R	6-4	200	8-9-00	1	1	14.40	5	0	0	5	9	8	8	0	3	6	.391	.462	.478	23.08	11.54	26
Beutel, Ben	L-L	6-0	165	9-2-99	2	1	5.06	20	0	0	27	21	15	15	5	14	31	.219	.345	.417	26.72	12.07	116
Bockenstedt, Jacob	R-R	6-1	190	11-15-99	1	3	8.88	7	7	0	24	32	26	24	5	15	28	.311	.408	.534	23.33	12.50	120
Carela, Juan	R-R	6-3	186	12-15-01	4	4	3.77	16	16	0	74	62	35	31	5	32	78	.226	.325	.343	24.30	9.97	321
Castro, Yon	R-R	6-0	203	5-23-99	0	0	6.00	7	0	0	12	12	8	8	1	5	11	.255	.327	.340	21.15	9.62	52
Collins, Bryce	R-R	6-0	180	6-28-00	1	0	2.03	23	0	5	31	21	9	7	2	16	41	.189	.295	.279	31.78	12.40	129
Davis, Tyler	R-R	6-3	210	10-3-98	1	1	1.86	6	0	1	10	7	4	2	1	3	10	.200	.282	.314	25.00	7.50	40
Drohan, Shane	L-L	6-3	195	1-7-99	0	0	10.80	2	0	0	2	2	3	2	0	2	1	.333	.556	.500	11.11	22.22	9
Duensing, Cole	L-R	6-4	195	6-16-98	0	1	36.00	5	0	0	3	14	13	12	0	3	5	.583	.630	.958	18.52	11.11	27
Franklin, Zach	R-R	6-1	198	10-27-98	4	6	3.76	29	0	6	41	30	25	17	2	16	58	.205	.299	.288	34.32	9.47	169
Goosenberg, Shawn	R-R	6-1	195	12-5-99	0	0	0.00	1	0	0	1	2	0	0	0	0	0	.400	.400	.600	0.00	0.00	5
Gordon, Lucas	L-L	6-1	193	2-13-02	2	3	2.81	9	9	0	42	27	13	13	5	27	32	.191	.320	.355	18.93	15.98	169
Gowens, Riley	R-R	6-3	220	10-18-99	5	3	4.35	13	13	0	70	47	38	34	9	26	85	.188	.267	.360	30.25	9.25	281
Hazelwood, Everhett	R-R	6-2	210	5-12-99	0	2	10.29	9	0	0	14	21	19	16	5	11	17	.339	.453	.694	22.67	14.67	75
Housley, Connor	L-R	6-4	205	8-18-01	0	0	2.84	9	0	1	13	12	4	4	1	9	14	.245	.393	.469	22.95	14.75	61
Jacobs, Carson	R-R	6-9	215	8-17-01	0	0	1.69	5	0	0	5	3	1	1	0	6	9	.158	.385	.211	34.62	23.08	26
Jaquez, Ernesto	R-R	6-2	190	6-11-99	3	1	8.72	15	0	0	22	27	23	21	3	21	27	.300	.430	.467	23.68	18.42	114
Keener, Seth	R-R	6-1	195	10-4-01	0	1	12.60	2	2	0	5	8	7	7	0	4	7	.381	.500	.524	26.92	15.38	26
Kelley, Jared	R-R	6-3	230	10-3-01	2	1	4.26	25	0	5	44	46	25	21	3	30	38	.269	.377	.368	18.63	14.71	204
Knebel, Corey	R-R	6-3	224	11-26-91	0	0	31.50	3	0	0	2	6	7	7	1	4	2	.500	.647	1.000	11.76	23.53	17
Martin, Davis	L-R	6-2	200	1-4-97	0	0	7.11	2	2	0	6	7	5	5	1	1	7	.269	.296	.500	25.93	3.70	27
Maybach, Patrick	R-L	6-3	190	1-9-98	0	0	1.80	2	0	0	5	3	2	1	0	3	3	.176	.333	.176	14.29	14.29	21
McDaniel, Drew	R-R	6-2	185	8-26-00	2	3	8.44	5	5	0	21	30	20	20	2	6	16	.333	.388	.511	16.16	6.06	99
McDougal, Tanner	R-R	6-5	185	4-9-03	0	8	6.85	16	16	0	66	66	54	50	13	44	80	.260	.377	.488	26.23	14.43	305
Mikel, Jordan	R-R	6-5	190	3-24-99	0	0	7.36	3	0	0	7	9	6	6	3	2	6	.310	.382	.690	17.65	5.88	34
Murphy, Shane	L-L	6-5	210	1-19-01	1	3	4.14	20	14	0	91	82	47	42	14	15	78	.236	.266	.418	21.25	4.09	367
Nakawake, Taishi	R-R	5-11	185	6-20-98	0	0	0.00	1	0	0	1	2	0	0	0	0	0	.400	.400	.400	0.00	0.00	5

Pitching	B-T	Ht.	Wt.	DOB	W	L	ERA	G	GS	SV	IP	Hits	Runs	ER	HR	BB	SO	AVG	OBP	SLG	SO%	BB%	BF
Padilla, Nicholas	R-R	6-2	220	12-24-96	1	0	2.45	2	0	0	4	2	1	1	0	4	4	.167	.375	.167	25.00	25.00	16
Pallette, Peyton	R-R	6-1	180	5-9-01	3	7	4.95	24	12	2	67	68	40	37	7	29	79	.263	.343	.390	26.51	9.73	298
Ramirez, Jose	R-R	6-0	142	3-28-01	6	6	6.11	29	3	0	74	63	52	50	5	38	49	.229	.347	.364	14.89	11.55	329
Ray, Johnny	R-R	6-2	220	10-10-98	0	0	8.78	24	0	1	27	29	28	26	5	28	42	.274	.431	.509	30.66	20.44	137
Roberts, Max	R-L	6-6	190	7-23-97	3	2	3.89	27	0	3	35	33	17	15	2	20	47	.252	.355	.359	30.92	13.16	152
Rosado, Jarold	R-R	6-3	215	7-13-02	1	1	2.76	10	0	0	16	12	5	5	1	4	23	.203	.262	.373	35.38	6.15	65
Schoenle, Garrett	L-L	6-5	185	6-21-98	1	1	2.25	7	0	0	12	7	4	3	0	6	16	.167	.271	.286	33.33	12.50	48
Schultz, Noah	L-L	6-9	220	8-5-03	0	1	3.95	7	7	0	27	18	13	12	1	7	42	.182	.264	.293	38.18	6.36	110
Schweitzer, Tyler	L-L	6-0	185	9-19-00	3	3	3.74	9	9	0	46	46	21	19	4	14	47	.263	.319	.406	24.61	7.33	191
Scolaro, Jonah	L-L	5-10	193	8-3-98	0	0	23.40	4	0	0	5	9	14	13	2	8	11	.360	.543	.760	31.43	22.86	35
Seidl, Billy	R-R	6-0	220	11-9-99	2	2	5.92	15	0	0	24	23	16	16	3	18	19	.258	.395	.449	16.67	15.79	114
Smith, Hagen	L-L	6-3	215	8-19-03	0	1	3.52	3	3	0	8	7	3	3	0	2	7	.250	.364	.321	21.21	6.06	33
Vail, Tommy	R-L	6-0	195	5-18-99	2	3	1.49	12	7	0	36	21	8	6	2	20	44	.165	.279	.228	29.93	13.61	147
Veloz, Manuel	R-R	6-2	185	1-28-01	5	0	6.44	13	1	0	29	36	21	21	4	12	16	.305	.381	.517	11.94	8.96	134
Veras, Frander	L-R	6-5	185	10-8-98	0	0	7.31	22	0	0	28	29	24	23	5	27	30	.261	.411	.468	21.28	19.15	141
Willits, Bryce	L-R	6-2	200	8-25-99	0	1	0.00	1	0	0	0	1	1	0	0	0	0	1.000	.500	1.000	0.00	0.00	2

Fielding

Catcher	PCT	G	PO	A	E	DP	PB
Eberly	.985	27	235	26	4	2	0
Harris	.992	63	596	42	5	1	2
Smelley	.987	43	438	26	6	6	8

First Base	PCT	G	PO	A	E	DP
Connor	.994	23	152	9	1	17
Galanie	1.000	31	231	8	0	20
Goosenberg	.989	11	88	2	1	8
Smelley	1.000	1	7	1	0	0
Willits	.996	66	474	19	2	42

Second Base	PCT	G	PO	A	E	DP
Bergolla	1.000	2	5	8	0	2
Camilletti	.971	19	24	43	2	10
Chapelli	.969	66	91	160	8	38
Goosenberg	1.000	1	1	6	0	1
Nakawake	.900	3	4	5	1	2
Nishida	1.000	21	41	46	0	13
Santos	1.000	4	10	7	0	1
Sprinkle	.983	16	22	36	1	8

Third Base	PCT	G	PO	A	E	DP
Kath	.936	110	79	171	17	11
Nakawake	1.000	9	6	10	0	3
Sanchez	.750	6	3	0	1	0
Smelley	.000	1	0	0	0	0
Sprinkle	1.000	9	3	9	0	1
Willits	.600	1	1	2	2	0

Shortstop	PCT	G	PO	A	E	DP
Bergolla	.967	17	19	40	2	10
Gonzalez	.965	34	27	82	4	19
Nakawake	.979	19	16	30	1	7
Sanchez	1.000	7	10	13	0	5
Santos	1.000	1	1	1	0	0
Sprinkle	.945	57	57	116	10	23

Outfield	PCT	G	PO	A	E	DP
Burke	1.000	5	13	1	0	0
Camilletti	1.000	14	17	1	0	0
Connor	1.000	14	20	1	0	0
Galanie	1.000	1	2	0	0	0
Gladney	1.000	66	109	0	0	0
Goosenberg	.985	42	65	1	1	1
Lanzilli	.974	31	35	2	1	2
Nishida	1.000	5	3	0	0	0
Park	.975	74	155	3	4	0
Saucke	.952	23	38	2	2	1
Sprinkle	.500	1	1	0	1	0
Willits	.974	18	36	2	1	0
Zavala	.992	112	244	4	2	1

KANNAPOLIS CANNON BALLERS — *LOW-A*

CAROLINA LEAGUE

Batting	B-T	Ht.	Wt.	DOB	AVG	OBP	SLG	G	PA	AB	R	H	2B	3B	HR	RBI	BB	HBP	SH	SF	SO	SB	CS	BB%	SO%
Aguero, Alvaro	R-R	6-0	160	3-19-03	.326	.354	.457	14	48	46	9	15	3	0	1	7	2	0	0	0	15	4	0	4.17	31.25
Antonacci, Sam	L-R	6-0	185	2-6-03	.333	.471	.432	23	102	81	22	27	6	1	0	14	17	4	0	0	13	7	2	16.67	12.75
Appel, Jackson	B-R	6-0	195	8-31-01	.268	.400	.390	12	50	41	9	11	2	0	1	6	7	2	0	0	7	0	0	14.00	14.00
Archer, Nathan	L-R	6-0	175	3-14-03	.208	.291	.247	22	86	77	12	16	3	0	0	3	7	2	0	0	23	8	0	8.14	26.74
Arias, Frankeli	L-L	6-0	170	4-5-03	.000	.000	.000	29	1	1	0	0	0	0	0	0	0	0	0	0	1	0	0	0.00	100.00
Asigen, Albertson	R-R	5-10	175	8-27-01	.230	.344	.332	69	288	244	44	56	8	1	5	35	35	8	0	1	74	22	5	12.15	25.69
Betancourt, Jhoneiker	R-R	6-1	174	5-2-00	.200	.294	.267	4	17	15	3	3	1	0	0	3	1	1	0	0	0	0	0	5.88	0.00
Burrowes, Ryan	R-R	6-2	170	8-17-04	.204	.292	.246	77	322	280	37	57	7	1	1	33	32	5	0	5	107	22	4	9.94	33.23
Connor, Caden	L-L	6-1	200	8-2-00	.307	.390	.440	78	356	300	51	92	24	2	4	55	42	5	0	9	61	6	1	11.80	17.13
Dinesen, Mason	R-R	6-4	180	7-24-98	.286	.327	.408	23	52	49	13	14	0	0	2	7	3	0	0	0	21	2	0	5.77	40.38
Felix, Edrick	R-R	6-0	198	1-14-02	.141	.287	.155	22	87	71	7	10	1	0	0	4	10	5	0	1	24	0	0	11.49	27.59
Galanie, Ryan	R-R	6-2	215	6-20-00	.346	.432	.582	38	176	153	27	53	7	4	7	39	18	5	0	0	37	1	0	10.23	21.02
Gonzalez, Juan	R-R	5-9	195	2-20-01	.188	.305	.213	25	95	80	6	15	2	0	0	8	11	3	0	1	29	1	2	11.58	30.53
Hernandez, Arxy	R-R	6-2	170	7-29-03	.238	.313	.350	108	457	403	58	96	19	7	4	51	37	10	0	7	115	4	0	8.10	25.16
Hernandez, Ronny	R-R	6-1	200	11-9-04	.272	.387	.328	96	413	345	47	94	16	0	1	46	62	3	0	1	59	0	0	15.01	14.29
Hogan, Matt	L-R	6-0	195	1-24-00	.209	.357	.409	38	140	110	21	23	2	1	6	20	25	2	0	3	43	8	1	17.86	30.71
Kane, Mikey	R-R	6-3	195	7-11-01	.273	.374	.413	48	203	172	29	47	9	0	5	13	24	5	0	2	42	2	0	11.82	20.69
Logan, Drake	R-R	6-4	205	9-5-00	.266	.328	.430	80	323	293	37	78	20	2	8	47	21	7	0	2	120	15	2	6.50	37.15
Makarewicz, Alec	B-R	6-2	217	9-12-00	.301	.360	.442	28	125	113	16	34	10	0	2	28	11	0	0	1	28	0	2	8.80	22.40
McCants, T.J.	L-R	6-3	190	6-6-01	.230	.356	.443	16	73	61	9	14	1	3	2	6	11	1	0	0	25	4	2	15.07	34.25
Miller-Green, Lyle	R-R	6-6	229	9-4-00	.219	.351	.375	19	77	64	8	14	4	0	2	6	11	2	0	0	26	0	0	14.29	33.77
Mora, Javier	R-R	5-11	170	3-23-03	.128	.281	.179	27	96	78	14	10	4	0	0	4	15	2	0	1	30	1	0	15.63	31.25
Nishida, Rikuu	L-R	5-6	150	5-6-01	.290	.414	.367	90	418	341	84	99	13	5	1	36	66	7	3	1	51	35	8	15.79	12.20
Park, Eddie	L-L	6-1	187	8-22-01	.283	.457	.358	15	70	53	7	15	2	1	0	8	17	0	0	0	4	3	1	24.29	5.71
Perez, Jeral	R-R	6-0	179	11-6-04	.259	.344	.431	30	131	116	19	30	10	2	2	10	14	1	0	0	33	0	1	10.69	25.19
Pineda, Luis	R-R	6-1	209	3-19-02	.238	.307	.356	75	315	281	33	67	16	1	5	34	28	1	0	3	93	2	1	8.89	29.52
Sanchez, Wilber	R-R	5-10	160	2-21-02	.221	.290	.317	61	231	208	31	46	6	1	4	28	21	0	0	2	57	14	3	9.09	24.68
Wolkow, George	L-R	6-7	225	1-11-06	.241	.342	.428	76	325	278	39	67	11	4	11	52	39	5	0	3	132	6	1	12.00	40.62

Pitching	B-T	Ht.	Wt.	DOB	W	L	ERA	G	GS	SV	IP	Hits	Runs	ER	HR	BB	SO	AVG	OBP	SLG	SO%	BB%	BF
Altermatt, Nick	R-R	6-0	225	9-28-99	3	3	2.75	30	0	2	36	29	13	11	2	12	37	.220	.293	.311	25.00	8.11	148
Arias, Frankeli	L-L	6-0	170	4-5-03	3	4	4.92	28	8	1	71	70	43	39	9	34	78	.255	.345	.425	24.38	10.63	320
Asigen, Albertson	R-R	5-10	175	8-27-01	0	0	27.00	1	0	0	1	1	3	3	0	2	1	.333	.625	.333	12.50	25.00	8
Batista, Aldrin	R-R	6-2	185	5-4-03	8	4	3.51	17	17	0	85	73	39	33	8	33	87	.233	.321	.351	24.44	9.27	356
Bell, Luke	R-R	6-4	200	8-9-00	2	3	2.44	28	0	0	44	35	14	12	2	15	49	.222	.288	.291	27.53	8.43	178

Bockenstedt, Jacob	R-R	6-1	190	11-15-99	3	8	4.54	15	14	0	67	64	44	34	8	31	65	.257	.332	.418	22.41	10.69	290
Brizuela, Ricardo	R-R	6-3	198	6-30-03	3	2	4.33	10	10	0	44	43	22	21	2	10	35	.254	.304	.379	19.02	5.43	184
Collins, Bryce	R-R	6-0	180	6-28-00	0	0	3.21	11	0	0	14	14	5	5	1	6	24	.255	.328	.345	39.34	9.84	61
Combs, Aaron	R-R	6-3	190	12-28-01	2	0	0.00	6	0	0	8	5	2	0	0	4	13	.179	.303	.179	39.39	12.12	33
Davis, Tyler	R-R	6-3	210	10-3-98	0	0	3.16	15	1	0	26	22	10	9	3	18	32	.234	.363	.362	28.32	15.93	113
Dinesen, Mason	R-R	6-4	180	7-24-98	0	0	0.00	2	0	0	4	0	0	0	0	1	5	.000	.143	.000	35.71	7.14	14
Edwards, Christian	R-R	6-3	205	3-4-99	2	1	4.02	17	0	0	16	11	9	7	0	18	17	.200	.390	.255	21.79	23.08	78
George, Pierce	R-R	6-6	215	6-10-03	0	0	6.00	6	0	0	6	4	6	4	0	3	5	.182	.321	.318	17.86	10.71	28
Gonzalez, Daniel	L-L	6-3	160	11-27-01	1	0	13.50	9	0	0	9	11	18	14	0	12	17	.268	.474	.341	29.82	21.05	57
Gordon, Lucas	L-L	6-1	193	2-13-02	7	2	1.89	14	14	0	71	43	19	15	5	34	66	.173	.273	.282	23.32	12.01	283
Hartzog, Clete	L-R	6-1	183	6-12-01	2	0	1.13	6	0	1	8	3	1	1	0	3	10	.115	.207	.115	34.48	10.34	29
Hazelwood, Everhett	R-R	6-2	210	5-12-99	1	0	9.00	1	0	0	2	2	2	2	1	1	2	.250	.333	.625	22.22	11.11	9
Housley, Connor	L-R	6-4	205	8-18-01	1	0	0.66	7	0	1	14	4	1	1	0	7	21	.091	.216	.159	41.18	13.73	51
Jacobs, Carson	R-R	6-9	215	8-17-01	0	1	0.87	8	0	2	10.1	6	3	1	0	6	19	.167	.286	.167	44.19	13.95	43
Keener, Seth	R-R	6-1	195	10-4-01	4	3	3.36	14	14	0	64	46	24	24	1	32	75	.202	.317	.268	27.99	11.94	268
Maybach, Patrick	R-L	6-3	190	1-9-98	1	2	4.22	10	0	0	21	19	15	10	1	8	20	.241	.330	.367	21.74	8.70	92
McDaniel, Drew	R-R	6-2	185	8-26-00	4	1	1.82	7	7	0	40	25	9	8	3	12	49	.182	.263	.314	32.24	7.89	152
McDougal, Tanner	R-R	6-5	185	4-9-03	0	3	4.05	6	6	0	27	23	14	12	0	14	36	.230	.353	.270	30.00	11.67	120
McLaughlin, Mark	R-R	6-3	205	2-14-01	2	4	3.79	31	0	0	62	46	27	26	4	29	55	.207	.306	.302	21.32	11.24	258
Mendez, Jesus	R-R	5-11	180	7-30-04	4	6	5.93	41	0	9	58	62	43	38	2	25	55	.277	.356	.366	21.07	9.58	261
Moore, Mason	R-R	6-4	215	9-29-01	0	0	19.29	1	1	0	2	6	5	5	0	2	2	.462	.533	.692	13.33	13.33	15
Peppers, Jake	R-R	6-3	160	12-26-01	7	6	4.27	22	22	0	97	90	53	46	8	43	86	.247	.336	.364	20.62	10.31	417
Perkins, Carlton	R-R	6-3	180	11-9-02	1	3	5.57	7	4	0	21	28	15	13	2	14	29	.322	.417	.425	28.16	13.59	103
Peters, Connery	R-R	6-6	240	2-3-00	2	1	4.75	30	0	1	42	38	23	22	2	25	44	.247	.364	.364	23.40	13.30	188
Pinto, Nick	L-L	6-0	175	6-22-00	0	0	0.00	1	1	0	3	1	0	0	0	1	3	.111	.200	.222	30.00	10.00	10
Roach, Dalton	R-R	6-2	210	4-8-96	0	0	0.00	2	0	0	2	0	0	0	0	2	3	.000	.286	.000	42.86	28.57	7
Seidl, Billy	R-R	6-0	220	11-9-99	1	1	2.63	20	0	1	24	13	7	7	0	10	33	.163	.306	.175	33.33	10.10	99
Sims, Hale	R-R	6-4	290	8-30-99	0	1	10.32	9	0	2	11	20	14	13	1	5	15	.377	.443	.547	24.59	8.20	61
Sinibaldi, Justin	L-L	6-5	220	3-3-02	0	0	5.00	3	3	0	9	9	6	5	0	3	7	.257	.308	.371	17.95	7.69	39
Talavera, Emerson	R-R	5-10	160	10-1-02	1	0	12.27	6	0	0	7	12	10	10	3	3	6	.353	.395	.706	15.79	7.89	38
Taylor, Grant	R-R	6-3	220	5-20-02	0	0	1.13	4	4	0	16	9	2	2	1	1	25	.158	.172	.228	43.10	1.72	58
Vail, Tommy	R-L	6-0	195	5-18-99	3	1	1.91	14	3	0	33	14	7	7	1	16	56	.128	.240	.202	44.09	12.60	127
Veloz, Manuel	R-R	6-2	185	1-28-01	2	1	2.95	16	2	1	43	43	16	14	0	13	37	.259	.324	.349	20.33	7.14	182
Wright, Garrett	R-R	6-2	220	2-11-02	0	0	0.96	7	0	3	9	7	1	1	0	0	12	.206	.200	.235	34.29	0.00	35

Fielding

Catcher	PCT	G	PO	A	E	DP	PB
Appel	1.000	10	111	10	0	0	2
Gonzalez	.989	17	169	10	2	3	2
Hernandez	.998	54	456	29	1	3	3
Pineda	.991	52	503	27	5	3	9

First Base	PCT	G	PO	A	E	DP
Betancourt	1.000	4	26	2	0	4
Connor	1.000	39	277	19	0	21
Dinesen	.986	14	67	2	1	11
Galanie	.996	29	216	21	1	11
Gonzalez	1.000	2	11	0	0	0
Kane	.993	19	128	9	1	9
Makarewicz	.994	20	160	10	1	14
Miller-Green	.957	9	64	2	3	4

Second Base	PCT	G	PO	A	E	DP
Antonacci	1.000	12	17	29	0	2
Burrowes	.944	18	25	43	4	12
Dinesen	1.000	2	1	6	0	1
Kane	1.000	16	27	28	0	6
Mora	.966	22	26	31	2	9
Nishida	.994	40	54	110	1	15
Perez	.980	11	19	30	1	7
Sanchez	.985	18	29	35	1	7

Third Base	PCT	G	PO	A	E	DP
Antonacci	1.000	9	3	12	0	2
Dinesen	1.000	1	1	2	0	1
Felix	.868	22	17	16	5	1
Hernandez	.935	76	44	115	11	10
Kane	.967	11	7	22	1	1
Makarewicz	1.000	4	2	3	0	0
Mora	.800	2	1	3	1	1
Sanchez	.900	11	7	20	3	0

Shortstop	PCT	G	PO	A	E	DP
Burrowes	.934	55	71	114	13	23
Dinesen	.857	2	3	3	1	1
Hernandez	.890	28	32	57	11	10
Perez	.947	18	28	43	4	7
Sanchez	.960	31	42	77	5	13

Outfield	PCT	G	PO	A	E	DP
Aguero	.938	12	29	1	2	1
Archer	.976	22	40	1	1	0
Arias	.000	1	0	0	0	0
Asigen	.992	68	120	3	1	0
Connor	.980	30	44	5	1	1
Dinesen	.500	1	1	0	1	0
Galanie	.750	2	3	0	1	0
Hogan	1.000	37	82	4	0	2
Logan	.976	74	119	3	3	1
McCants	1.000	16	23	0	0	0
Miller-Green	1.000	5	3	0	0	0
Nishida	1.000	49	75	4	0	2
Park	.974	16	37	0	1	0
Wolkow	.927	74	111	4	9	1

ACL WHITE SOX — ROOKIE

ARIZONA COMPLEX LEAGUE

Batting	B-T	Ht.	Wt.	DOB	AVG	OBP	SLG	G	PA	AB	R	H	2B	3B	HR	RBI	BB	HBP	SH	SF	SO	SB	CS	BB%	SO%
Aguero, Alvaro	R-R	6-0	160	3-19-03	.105	.186	.184	20	43	38	3	4	0	0	1	4	3	1	0	1	15	1	0	6.98	34.88
Alsinois, Leandro	R-R	5-10	175	9-6-04	.245	.295	.387	50	176	163	23	40	7	2	4	21	10	2	0	1	45	6	2	5.68	25.57
Benintendi, Andrew	L-L	5-9	180	7-6-94	.600	.714	1.600	2	7	5	3	3	2	0	1	1	2	0	0	0	1	0	0	28.57	14.29
Betancourt, Jhoneiker	R-R	6-1	174	5-2-00	.286	.313	.571	8	16	14	1	4	1	0	1	3	1	0	0	1	3	0	0	6.25	18.75
Borrero, Dario	L-L	6-5	190	11-13-03	.257	.317	.376	35	121	109	16	28	7	0	2	13	7	3	1	1	20	0	0	5.79	16.53
Burrowes, Ryan	R-R	6-2	170	8-17-04	.417	.483	.417	6	29	24	5	10	0	0	0	2	3	1	0	1	8	2	1	10.34	27.59
Dinesen, Mason	R-R	6-4	180	7-24-98	.167	.231	.250	4	14	12	2	2	1	0	0	0	1	0	1	0	5	0	0	7.14	35.71
Felix, Edrick	R-R	6-0	198	1-14-02	.250	.381	.444	46	176	144	31	36	9	2	5	27	24	7	0	1	48	8	3	13.64	27.27
Fletcher, Dominic	L-L	5-6	185	9-2-97	.083	.214	.083	4	14	12	1	1	0	0	0	0	1	1	0	0	4	0	0	7.14	28.57
Flores, Stiven	R-R	5-11	180	12-26-05	.287	.338	.329	43	157	143	15	41	1	1	1	24	11	1	0	2	32	6	0	7.01	20.38
Gil, Adrian	R-R	6-0	193	11-17-05	.225	.392	.391	56	217	169	40	38	8	4	4	30	37	10	0	1	58	10	4	17.05	26.73
Gonzalez, Ivan	R-R	5-6	190	10-28-96	.000	.250	.000	5	8	6	1	0	0	0	0	0	2	0	0	0	3	0	0	25.00	37.50
Guariman, Manuel	R-R	6-0	196	2-9-04	.256	.302	.333	15	43	39	4	10	0	0	1	7	3	0	0	1	10	1	0	6.98	23.26
Hackenberg, Adam	R-R	6-1	225	9-8-99	.294	.368	.353	5	19	17	5	5	1	0	0	0	2	0	0	0	3	2	0	10.53	15.79

Hernandez, Angelo	R-R	6-1	200	9-11-05	.248	.325	.416	36	126	113	13	28	5	1	4	21	8	5	0	0	38	1	2	6.35	30.16
Hernandez, Erick	L-L	6-0	170	1-15-05	.209	.286	.349	19	49	43	4	9	1	1	1	6	3	2	0	1	15	0	1	6.12	30.61
Jimenez, Eloy	R-R	6-4	240	11-27-96	.444	.474	.667	6	19	18	1	8	1	0	1	5	1	0	0	0	2	0	0	5.26	10.53
Mogollon, Javier	R-R	5-8	160	11-1-05	.259	.406	.524	46	180	143	31	37	14	0	8	29	33	3	0	1	69	16	0	18.33	38.33
Moncada, Yoan	B-R	6-2	225	5-27-95	.533	.563	.600	5	16	15	4	8	1	0	0	2	1	0	0	0	4	0	0	6.25	25.00
Nunez, Abraham	L-R	6-2	175	2-17-06	.292	.382	.371	53	207	178	28	52	4	5	0	18	21	6	0	2	44	20	9	10.14	21.26
Pham, Tommy	R-R	6-1	223	3-8-88	.273	.273	.545	3	11	11	3	3	0	0	1	1	0	0	0	0	4	0	0	0.00	36.36
Prado, Arnold	R-R	6-3	194	11-20-04	.242	.307	.356	50	163	149	22	36	4	2	3	18	9	5	0	0	66	8	2	5.52	40.49
Robert, Luis	R-R	6-2	220	8-3-97	.143	.250	.571	3	8	7	1	1	0	0	1	1	1	0	0	0	4	0	0	12.50	50.00
Rodriguez, Guillermo	R-R	5-9	156	9-3-04	.262	.351	.354	25	74	65	9	17	6	0	0	6	9	0	0	0	19	1	4	12.16	25.68
Tejada, D'Angelo	R-R	6-0	160	11-12-05	.169	.255	.301	29	94	83	7	14	5	0	2	7	10	0	0	1	41	1	2	10.64	43.62
Wolkow, George	L-R	6-7	225	1-11-06	.333	.433	.561	15	67	57	13	19	7	0	2	4	8	2	0	0	26	3	1	11.94	38.81

Pitching	B-T	Ht.	Wt.	DOB	W	L	ERA	G	GS	SV	IP	Hits	Runs	ER	HR	BB	SO	AVG	OBP	SLG	SO%	BB%	BF
Aguero, Alvaro	R-R	6-0	160	3-19-03	0	0	0.00	1	0	0	2	3	0	0	0	2	0	.375	.500	.500	0.00	20.00	10
Barlow, Joe	R-R	6-2	210	9-28-95	0	0	0.00	1	0	0	1	1	0	0	0	0	1	.250	.250	.250	25.00	0.00	4
Betancourt, Jhoneiker	R-R	6-1	174	5-2-00	0	0	0.00	1	0	0	0	1	0	0	0	2	0	.500	.750	1.000	0.00	50.00	4
Beutel, Ben	L-L	6-0	165	9-2-99	0	0	0.00	1	0	0	1	0	0	0	0	0	2	.000	.000	.000	66.67	0.00	3
Brizuela, Ricardo	R-R	6-3	198	6-30-03	1	2	2.33	10	2	0	27	20	9	7	1	3	34	.211	.255	.305	33.33	2.94	102
Burke, Sean	R-R	6-6	230	12-18-99	0	1	6.14	3	3	0	7	8	7	5	1	5	17	.267	.371	.567	48.57	14.29	35
Chirinos, Jordany	R-R	6-3	196	5-4-06	2	2	5.27	13	9	2	41	36	25	24	2	27	43	.237	.350	.355	23.76	14.92	181
Davis, Tyler	R-R	6-3	210	10-3-98	0	0	0.00	1	0	1	1	1	0	0	0	0	1	.200	.200	.400	20.00	0.00	5
Drohan, Shane	L-L	6-3	195	1-7-99	0	0	7.36	3	0	0	4	3	3	3	1	2	9	.214	.353	.643	52.94	11.76	17
Foster, Matt	R-R	6-0	215	1-27-95	0	0	3.00	3	1	0	3	4	1	1	0	0	3	.333	.333	.417	25.00	0.00	12
Gonzalez, Daniel	L-L	6-3	160	11-27-01	3	3	1.04	20	0	2	26	16	11	3	1	19	38	.174	.321	.228	33.33	16.67	114
Gonzalez, Jeremy	L-L	6-0	168	4-1-05	0	4	11.37	7	6	0	19	26	26	24	3	17	22	.351	.464	.581	22.45	17.35	98
Hinestroza, Carlos	R-R	6-1	190	2-4-03	0	2	12.54	18	1	0	28	42	40	39	3	23	24	.333	.439	.508	15.48	14.84	155
Housley, Connor	L-R	6-4	205	8-18-01	0	0	3.38	2	0	1	3	4	4	1	0	0	2	.308	.308	.385	15.38	0.00	13
Imhoff, Anthony	L-L	6-7	195	10-3-01	0	0	2.79	6	0	1	10	9	3	3	0	9	14	.250	.408	.417	28.57	18.37	49
Jacobs, Carson	R-R	6-9	215	8-17-01	1	1	3.22	18	0	1	22	15	10	8	0	14	30	.188	.316	.225	31.58	14.74	95
Knebel, Corey	R-R	6-3	224	11-26-91	0	0	0.00	3	0	0	3	0	0	0	0	1	2	.000	.091	.000	18.18	9.09	11
Lakins, Travis	R-R	6-1	220	6-29-94	1	1	5.40	10	0	1	13	12	8	8	1	2	24	.240	.264	.400	44.44	3.70	54
Lambert, Jimmy	R-R	6-2	190	11-18-94	0	0	0.00	2	2	0	2	2	0	0	0	0	4	.250	.250	.250	50.00	0.00	8
Lima, Denny	R-R	6-0	170	8-30-04	0	1	8.10	12	3	0	20	23	18	18	3	10	21	.295	.387	.500	22.58	10.75	93
Martin, Davis	L-R	6-2	200	1-4-97	0	1	3.86	3	3	0	7	6	3	3	0	1	11	.222	.250	.296	39.29	3.57	28
Martinez, Maximo	R-R	6-2	185	6-21-04	0	2	16.62	4	3	1	9	16	17	16	5	11	10	.410	.540	.846	20.00	22.00	50
McLaughlin, Mark	R-R	6-3	205	2-14-01	0	0	27.00	1	0	0	0	0	1	1	0	2	0	.000	.667	.000	0.00	66.67	3
Mendoza, Jose	R-R	6-2	175	3-15-04	2	1	8.44	7	0	0	11	12	11	10	1	6	17	.286	.380	.381	34.00	12.00	50
Oppor, Christian	L-L	6-2	175	7-23-04	2	4	5.21	12	9	0	38	38	26	22	1	28	46	.277	.400	.380	27.06	16.47	170
Padilla, Nicholas	R-R	6-2	220	12-24-96	0	0	0.00	2	0	0	3	1	0	0	0	1	5	.125	.300	.125	50.00	10.00	10
Perkins, Carlton	R-R	6-3	180	11-9-02	2	3	3.89	15	5	3	37	32	24	16	0	21	43	.225	.331	.261	25.44	12.43	169
Redman, Pedro	R-R	6-2	190	4-19-04	0	0	10.80	2	0	0	2	2	2	2	0	4	5	.286	.545	.286	45.45	36.36	11
Reyes, Luis	R-R	6-2	190	10-13-05	0	4	5.74	12	10	0	42	51	33	27	2	21	51	.295	.379	.376	25.76	10.61	198
Rodriguez, Luis	R-R	6-2	181	12-29-03	0	1	7.36	2	0	0	4	4	5	3	0	3	4	.286	.389	.500	21.05	15.79	19
Sims, Hale	R-R	6-4	290	8-30-99	1	0	2.25	6	0	0	8	5	2	2	0	3	8	.192	.267	.231	26.67	10.00	30
Stivors, Tristan	R-R	6-4	220	9-22-98	2	0	2.35	6	0	0	8	6	2	2	0	2	14	.207	.258	.241	45.16	6.45	31
Talavera, Emerson	R-R	5-10	160	10-1-02	5	3	4.59	14	0	0	33	34	18	17	3	11	35	.266	.342	.438	23.81	7.48	147
Taylor, Grant	R-R	6-3	220	5-20-02	0	0	8.10	1	1	0	3	3	3	3	1	1	7	.231	.286	.538	50.00	7.14	14
Valladares, Marcelo	R-R	6-4	187	8-28-04	0	0	10.45	12	1	0	10	10	17	12	3	20	14	.238	.492	.452	22.22	31.75	63
Vera, Norge	R-R	6-4	185	6-1-00	0	0	0.00	1	1	0	1	0	0	0	0	1	2	.000	.250	.000	50.00	25.00	4
Veras, Frander	L-R	6-5	185	10-8-98	2	0	0.00	5	0	0	6	4	1	0	0	0	4	.182	.182	.273	18.18	0.00	22

Fielding

C: Hernandez 28, Benavides 10, Guariman 8, Eberly 7, Pineda 6, Harris 3, Claunch 3, Tamez 2. **1B:** Borrero 28, Jimenez 26, Galanie 2, Guariman 1, Connor **C:** Flores 30, Hernandez 18, Guariman 11, Gonzalez 4, Hackenberg 3, Betancourt 2. **1B:** Borrero 32, Gil 22, Flores 7, Gonzalez 1, Guariman 1, Betancourt 1. **2B:** Felix 16, Tejada 15, Gil 13, Rodriguez 11, Mogollon 5, Burrowes 1. **3B:** Felix 28, Gil 20, Tejada 9, Moncada 4, Rodriguez 4, Dinesen 1. **SS:** Mogollon 40, Rodriguez 10, Burrowes 5, Dinesen 3, Tejada 3. **LF:** Prado 34, Hernandez 15, Nunez 10, Aguero 5, Alsinois 4, Benintendi 1. **CF:** Nunez 30, Alsinois 17, Aguero 7, Wolkow 4, Robert 3, Prado 2, Fletcher 2, Pham 1. **RF:** Alsinois 27, Prado 13, Nunez 10, Wolkow 8, Aguero 2, Pham 1, Hernandez 1.

DSL WHITE SOX — *ROOKIE*

DOMINICAN SUMMER LEAGUE

Batting	B-T	Ht.	Wt.	DOB	AVG	OBP	SLG	G	PA	AB	R	H	2B	3B	HR	RBI	BB	HBP	SH	SF	SO	SB	CS	BB%	SO%
Alberto, Albert	R-R	6-3	190	3-3-06	.224	.384	.327	37	125	98	23	22	5	1	1	13	21	5	0	1	35	2	1	16.80	28.00
Alcala, Marcelo	R-R	6-0	183	3-23-06	.272	.369	.441	44	161	136	34	37	4	5	3	19	12	10	0	2	54	13	4	7.45	33.54
Alvarez, Rafael	R-R	6-2	190	2-13-05	.182	.308	.394	12	39	33	7	6	1	0	2	9	2	4	0	0	13	1	0	5.13	33.33
Castillo, Ryan	L-R	6-1	170	1-28-05	.284	.370	.358	36	128	109	21	31	2	0	2	20	14	2	1	2	28	5	1	10.94	21.88
Gil, Elier	R-R	5-11	187	9-28-05	.220	.317	.300	17	60	50	7	11	1	0	1	8	5	3	0	2	20	0	0	8.33	33.33
Gonzalez, Christian	L-L	5-11	185	9-4-06	.265	.395	.303	48	191	155	25	41	4	1	0	15	31	3	1	1	17	11	11	16.23	8.90
Herrera, Eduardo	R-R	6-3	212	10-23-06	.197	.323	.250	40	159	132	19	26	3	2	0	16	22	3	0	1	44	1	1	13.84	27.67
Mendez, Jehancarlos	R-R	6-2	180	8-9-07	.239	.309	.290	41	152	138	19	33	4	0	1	16	10	4	0	0	34	4	3	6.58	22.37
Premoli, Jesus	L-R	6-4	225	1-19-07	.219	.285	.298	44	165	151	18	33	6	0	2	20	10	4	0	0	43	1	0	6.06	26.06
Profar, Jurdrick	R-R	5-11	170	4-24-07	.264	.397	.390	48	194	159	33	42	11	0	3	16	31	4	0	0	43	8	8	15.98	22.16
Riera, Elias	R-R	6-2	180	4-18-06	.143	.357	.190	8	29	21	3	3	1	0	0	2	2	5	1	0	5	0	1	6.90	17.24
Rios, Alvaro	R-R	6-1	170	9-25-06	.241	.326	.241	30	92	79	8	19	0	0	0	9	8	3	0	2	22	0	0	8.70	23.91
Severo, Noel	R-R	6-5	200	4-26-06	.122	.317	.204	22	63	49	3	6	1	0	1	8	11	3	0	0	31	0	0	17.46	49.21

SIllet, Renny	R-R	6-2	176	4-28-07	.194	.275	.226	21	70	62	8	12	2	0	0	6	5	2	1	0	19	2	0	7.14	27.14
Suarez, Jhoangel	R-R	5-11	164	10-16-06	.190	.386	.207	31	83	58	10	11	1	0	0	8	15	6	0	4	17	6	2	18.07	20.48
Ugueto, Eyke	R-R	5-11	175	3-19-06	.244	.398	.305	40	106	82	18	20	3	1	0	15	16	5	3	0	17	3	4	15.09	16.04
Uribe, Juan	R-R	5-10	160	6-7-06	.143	.373	.163	20	67	49	4	7	1	0	0	4	18	0	0	0	27	1	0	26.87	40.30

Pitching	**B-T**	**Ht.**	**Wt.**	**DOB**	**W**	**L**	**ERA**	**G**	**GS**	**SV**	**IP**	**Hits**	**Runs**	**ER**	**HR**	**BB**	**SO**	**AVG**	**OBP**	**SLG**	**SO%**	**BB%**	**BF**
Alvarez, Rafael	R-R	6-2	190	2-13-05	0	0	0.00	1	0	0	1	0	0	0	0	0	0	.000	.250	.000	0.00	0.00	4
Barrios, Marco	R-R	6-3	195	5-25-06	2	2	7.00	17	0	0	27	19	26	21	1	36	33	.209	.434	.341	25.38	27.69	130
Bello, Angel	R-R	6-3	170	7-22-06	1	4	5.71	14	11	0	41	48	30	26	2	10	41	.287	.343	.383	22.65	5.52	181
Bernal, Carlos	R-R	6-1	188	2-18-06	1	1	3.00	13	0	2	12	11	6	4	0	6	15	.239	.352	.304	27.78	11.11	54
Boekhoudt, Jeziel	R-R	5-10	170	1-29-07	0	0	6.35	6	0	0	11	14	9	8	0	10	11	.311	.466	.511	18.97	17.24	58
Ciofani, Yerardo	L-L	5-11	185	3-9-06	5	1	7.56	14	0	0	25	36	30	21	3	18	25	.336	.436	.495	18.66	13.43	134
Cruz, Wascur	R-R	6-4	180	1-10-04	0	0	10.95	9	0	0	12	16	16	15	1	15	8	.327	.500	.469	12.12	22.73	66
Diaz, Reudis	R-R	6-1	180	2-16-06	2	1	2.04	9	7	0	35	28	13	8	2	6	34	.212	.278	.273	23.61	4.17	144
Fajardo, Yhoiker	R-R	6-3	181	10-3-06	1	4	3.91	13	13	0	51	52	29	22	2	8	64	.260	.288	.355	30.19	3.77	212
Gomez, Ricardo	R-R	6-3	158	11-9-04	2	0	10.57	16	0	2	23	36	30	27	3	15	30	.364	.454	.556	25.21	12.61	119
Hernandez, Jommy	R-R	6-3	185	4-18-06	2	3	4.05	15	0	1	27	29	17	12	1	25	21	.287	.425	.366	16.54	19.69	127
Hernandez, Oscar	R-R	6-4	190	1-18-06	0	1	3.86	6	0	0	12	13	8	5	0	6	8	.277	.352	.447	14.81	11.11	54
Malave, Jose	R-R	6-2	198	4-10-06	0	1	24.75	3	0	0	4	12	11	11	0	1	5	.522	.556	.652	18.52	3.70	27
Mateo, Alexander	R-R	6-5	205	10-28-05	0	0	9.00	2	0	0	2	3	3	2	0	1	1	.333	.455	.444	8.33	8.33	12
Rosario, Emilio	R-R	6-4	190	10-19-04	0	0	27.00	2	0	0	2	2	6	6	0	6	1	.250	.571	.500	7.14	42.86	14
Ruiz, Juan	R-R	6-2	180	12-13-05	3	1	10.89	15	0	0	21	24	27	25	1	14	11	.286	.413	.440	10.58	13.46	104
Rumbos, Manuel	R-R	6-4	170	4-17-03	0	5	3.05	8	7	0	21	14	18	7	0	19	25	.197	.387	.296	26.60	20.21	94
Suarez, Orlando	R-R	6-4	217	12-7-06	0	6	6.41	14	14	0	39	50	33	28	1	23	48	.316	.416	.386	25.67	12.30	187
Ugueto, Eyke	R-R	5-11	175	3-19-06	0	0	0.00	1	0	0	1	0	0	0	0	1	1	.000	.333	.000	33.33	33.33	3
Valdiviezo, Alexandre	R-R	6-0	203	6-4-07	0	1	7.43	10	0	1	13	20	14	11	3	9	7	.351	.456	.649	10.14	13.04	69
Ysalla, Fabian	R-R	6-0	161	12-14-04	1	4	3.79	15	3	2	36	41	22	15	2	14	24	.285	.364	.382	14.72	8.59	163

Fielding

C: Rios 30, SIllet 21, Riera 8. **1B:** Premoli 34, Castillo 18, Alvarez 6. **2B:** Uribe 14, Mendez 13, Suarez 11, Profar 10, Ugueto 8. **3B:** Herrera 32, Suarez 13, Profar 5, Alvarez 5, Ugueto 3. **SS:** Mendez 29, Profar 28, Suarez 1. **LF:** Castillo 17, Ugueto 14, Alberto 13, Alcala 13, Severo 5. **CF:** Gonzalez 44, Alcala 8, Ugueto 7. **RF:** Alberto 23, Alcala 23, Severo 12, Ugueto 2.

Cincinnati Reds

SEASON SYNOPSIS: The Reds finished ninth in the National League in runs and ninth in ERA, an apt description of their mediocrity. They went 77-85, five games worse than 2023 despite an offseason spending spree of nearly $100 million in guaranteed free-agent contracts. The slide cost manager David Bell his job in late September.

HIGH POINT: Shortstop Elly De La Cruz avoided the sophomore slump in his first full season, though his 218 strikeouts led the majors and was the fourth-highest single-season total ever. Still, De La Cruz led the majors with 67 steals, helping the Reds reach 200 stolen bases for the first time since 1988 (they had 207, tying the '88 team). He hit his 25th homer in a 7-1 win against Pittsburgh on Sept. 21, becoming the first primary shortstop in MLB history to have a season with 25 home runs and 65 steals.

LOW POINT: The Reds followed a 14-10 start by losing 20 of 26, including an eight-game losing streak to start the month of May. Six of those losses were in a homestand against Baltimore and Arizona in which Cincinnati scored just 11 runs in six games, with 18 of their 31 hits coming in the final two games. The offense suffered from the season-long absence of middle infielder Matt McLain, lost in the spring to shoulder surgery.

NOTABLE ROOKIES: Righthander Carson Spiers, son of ex-big leaguer Bill Spiers, was a versatile arm who made 10 starts and 12 relief appearances in a 5-7, 5.46 season. He was a bit too homer-prone (20 HR in 91 IP). Fellow righties Julian Aguiar, who had postseason Tommy John surgery, and 2023 first-rounder Rhett Lowder debuted but retained rookie eligibility for 2025, as did West Point grad outfielder Jacob Hurtubise.

KEY TRANSACTIONS: The offseason free-agent splurge added corner infielder Jeimer Candelario (3 years/$45 million) and righties Nick Martinez (2/$26M), Emilio Pagan (2/$16M) and Jakob Junis (1/$7M), and Martinez had a strong season. Bell lost his job in late September, replaced for the final five games by Freddy Benavides, but in October, Cincinnati hired future Hall of Famer Terry Francona—who played for the Reds in 1987— to manage the club in 2025.

OPENING DAY PAYROLL: $106,441,547 (22nd)

PLAYERS OF THE YEAR

MAJOR LEAGUE

Elly De La Cruz
SS
.259/.339/.471
25 HR, 67 SB
105 R, 69 BB

MINOR LEAGUE

Cam Collier
3B
(A+)
.248/.355/.443
20 HR, 74 RBIs

ORGANIZATION LEADERS

Batting		*Qualifiers
MAJORS		
* AVG	Elly De La Cruz	.259
* OPS	Elly De La Cruz	.810
HR	Elly De La Cruz	25
RBI	Spencer Steer	92
MINORS		
* AVG	Edwin Rios, Louisville	.286
* OBP	Edwin Rios, Louisville	.385
* SLG	Edwin Rios, Louisville	.547
* OPS	Edwin Rios, Louisville	.932
R	Cam Collier, Dayton	72
H	Hector Rodriguez, Dayton	139
TB	Hector Rodriguez, Dayton	213
2B	P.J. Higgins, Louisville	32
3B	Hector Rodriguez, Dayton	7
HR	Nicholas Northcut, Chattanooga	26
RBI	Cam Collier, Dayton	74
BB	Ariel Almonte, Daytona	67
SO	Austin Hendrick, Chattanooga	173
SB	Dominic Pitelli, Daytona/Chattanooga	43

Pitching		#Qualifiers
MAJORS		
W	Andrew Abbott	10
W	Nick Martinez	10
# ERA	No qualifier	
SO	Hunter Greene	169
SV	Alexis Diaz	28
MINORS		
W	Ryan Cardona, Dayton	9
L	Thomas Farr, Chattanooga	17
# ERA	Julian Aguiar, Dayton/Chattanooga	3.79
G	Zach Maxwell, Louisville/Chattanooga	53
GS	Thomas Farr, Chattanooga	26
SV	Tony Santillan, Louisville	16
IP	Thomas Farr, Chattanooga	126
BB	Kevin Abel, Dayton/Chattanooga	65
SO	Brian Edgington, Daytona/Dayton	121
# AVG	Kevin Abel, Dayton/Chattanooga	.232

2024 PERFORMANCE

General Manager: Nick Krall. **Farm Director:** Jeremy Farrell. **Scouting Director:** Joe Katuska.

Class	Team	League	W	L	PCT	Finish	Manager
Majors	Cincinnati Reds	National	77	85	.475	11 (15)	Terry Francona
Triple-A	Louisville Bats	International	67	82	.450	20 (20)	Pat Kelly
Double-A	Chattanooga Lookouts	Southern	45	90	.333	8 (8)	Jose Moreno
High-A	Dayton Dragons	Midwest	74	58	.561	3 (12)	Vince Harrison
Low-A	Daytona Tortugas	Florida State	64	64	.500	7 (10)	Julio Morillo
Rookie	DSL Reds	Dominican	37	18	.673	7 (51)	Jose Montilla
Rookie	ACL Reds	Arizona Complex	31	29	.517	6 (15)	Gustavo Molina
Overall 2024 Minor League Record			**343**	**371**	**.480**	**21st (30)**	

ORGANIZATION STATISTICS

CINCINNATI REDS

NATIONAL LEAGUE

Batting	B-T	Ht.	Wt.	DOB	AVG	OBP	SLG	G	PA	AB	R	H	2B	3B	HR	RBI	BB	HBP	SH	SF	SO	SB	CS	BB%	SO%
Benson, Will	L-L	6-5	230	6-16-98	.187	.274	.376	128	388	343	41	64	19	2	14	43	40	2	1	2	154	16	7	10.31	39.69
Candelario, Jeimer	B-R	6-2	222	11-24-93	.225	.279	.429	112	463	427	47	96	23	2	20	56	27	6	0	3	114	4	3	5.83	24.62
Capel, Conner	L-L	6-1	185	5-19-97	.250	.250	.250	5	8	8	1	2	0	0	0	0	0	0	0	0	2	1	0	0.00	25.00
De La Cruz, Elly	B-R	6-5	200	1-11-02	.259	.339	.471	160	696	618	105	160	36	10	25	76	69	6	2	1	218	67	16	9.91	31.32
Dunn, Blake	R-R	6-0	210	9-5-98	.154	.241	.308	19	29	26	8	4	1	0	1	1	2	1	0	0	11	2	0	6.90	37.93
Encarnacion-Strand, C.	R-R	6-0	224	12-1-99	.190	.220	.293	29	123	116	13	22	6	0	2	16	4	1	0	2	35	0	0	3.25	28.46
Espinal, Santiago	R-R	5-10	185	11-13-94	.246	.295	.356	118	391	357	32	88	12	0	9	45	24	2	4	4	54	11	1	6.14	13.81
Fairchild, Stuart	R-R	6-0	205	3-17-96	.215	.286	.368	94	233	209	33	45	8	0	8	30	17	4	2	1	60	13	1	7.30	25.75
Ford, Mike	L-R	6-0	225	7-4-92	.150	.177	.233	17	62	60	2	9	0	1	1	4	2	0	0	0	15	0	0	3.23	24.19
Fraley, Jake	L-L	6-0	206	5-25-95	.277	.330	.386	116	382	350	44	97	19	2	5	26	26	3	0	3	70	20	5	6.81	18.32
France, Ty	R-R	5-11	215	7-13-94	.251	.292	.391	52	195	179	18	45	10	0	5	20	10	2	0	4	31	1	0	5.13	15.90
Friedl, TJ	L-L	5-10	180	8-14-95	.226	.310	.380	85	341	297	35	67	5	1	13	55	26	12	2	4	52	9	1	7.62	15.25
Hinds, Rece	R-R	6-4	215	9-5-00	.261	.333	.717	24	51	46	9	12	4	1	5	11	4	1	0	0	16	2	0	7.84	31.37
Hurtubise, Jacob	L-R	6-0	180	12-11-97	.185	.297	.241	29	68	54	7	10	1	1	0	4	6	3	4	1	18	2	0	8.82	26.47
India, Jonathan	R-R	6-0	200	12-15-96	.248	.357	.392	151	637	533	84	132	28	2	15	58	80	15	2	7	125	13	2	12.56	19.62
Jordan, Levi	R-R	5-8	170	9-24-95	.100	.091	.200	7	11	10	1	1	1	0	0	1	0	0	0	1	3	0	0	0.00	27.27
Maile, Luke	R-R	6-3	225	2-6-91	.178	.268	.252	55	154	135	8	24	4	0	2	8	13	4	1	1	52	2	0	8.44	33.77
Marte, Noelvi	R-R	6-0	216	10-16-01	.210	.248	.301	66	242	229	24	48	9	0	4	18	9	3	0	1	75	9	3	3.72	30.99
Martini, Nick	L-L	5-11	205	6-27-90	.212	.272	.370	52	163	146	23	31	4	2	5	24	9	4	0	3	38	1	3	5.52	23.31
Rios, Edwin	L-R	6-3	220	4-21-94	.111	.200	.111	5	10	9	1	1	0	0	0	0	1	0	0	0	4	0	0	10.00	40.00
Rosario, Amed	R-R	6-2	190	11-20-95	.158	.186	.211	22	59	57	6	9	0	0	1	4	1	1	0	0	23	3	0	1.69	38.98
Slater, Austin	R-R	6-1	204	12-13-92	.111	.190	.111	8	21	18	2	2	0	0	0	3	2	0	0	1	6	0	0	9.52	28.57
Smith, Dominic	L-L	6-0	224	6-15-95	.192	.276	.269	9	29	26	4	5	2	0	0	0	3	0	0	0	11	0	0	10.34	37.93
Soto, Livan	L-R	5-10	160	6-22-00	.000	.000	.000	1	3	3	0	0	0	0	0	0	0	0	0	0	1	0	0	0.00	33.33
Steer, Spencer	R-R	5-11	185	12-7-97	.225	.319	.402	158	656	574	74	129	34	4	20	92	72	8	0	2	137	25	3	10.98	20.88
Stephenson, Tyler	R-R	6-4	225	8-16-96	.258	.338	.444	138	515	457	69	118	26	1	19	66	48	8	0	2	117	1	0	9.32	22.72
Thompson, Bubba	R-R	6-2	197	6-9-98	.111	.111	.167	17	18	18	5	2	1	0	0	0	0	0	0	0	11	5	0	0.00	61.11
Wiemer, Joey	R-R	6-4	220	2-11-99	.000	1.000	.000	2	1	0	0	0	0	0	0	0	1	0	0	0	0	0	0	100.00	0.00
Wynns, Austin	R-R	6-0	190	12-10-90	.368	.400	.579	7	20	19	3	7	4	0	0	2	0	1	0	0	5	0	0	0.00	25.00
Yang, Eric	R-R	5-11	185	3-26-98	.000	.000	.000	1	1	1	0	0	0	0	0	0	0	0	0	0	1	0	0	0.00	100.00

Pitching	B-T	Ht.	Wt.	DOB	W	L	ERA	G	GS	SV	IP	Hits	Runs	ER	HR	BB	SO	AVG	OBP	SLG	SO%	BB%	BF
Abbott, Andrew	L-L	6-0	192	6-1-99	10	10	3.72	25	25	0	138	127	60	57	25	52	114	.240	.309	.439	19.45	8.87	586
Aguiar, Julian	L-R	6-3	180	6-4-01	2	1	6.25	7	7	0	32	30	22	22	8	12	19	.244	.336	.488	13.57	8.57	140
Antone, Tejay	R-R	6-4	230	12-5-93	0	0	4.50	4	0	0	2	2	2	1	0	4	2	.286	.545	.429	18.18	36.36	11
Ashcraft, Graham	L-R	6-2	248	2-11-98	5	5	5.24	15	15	0	77	89	50	45	11	27	57	.282	.349	.434	16.29	7.71	350
Buchanan, David	R-R	6-3	200	5-11-89	0	0	2.70	1	0	0	3	2	1	1	0	2	1	.167	.286	.250	7.14	14.29	14
Busenitz, Alan	R-R	6-1	180	8-22-90	0	0	13.50	3	0	0	4	9	7	6	1	0	3	.429	.429	.619	14.29	0.00	21
Cruz, Fernando	R-R	6-2	237	3-28-90	3	8	4.86	69	3	0	67	54	36	36	9	35	109	.216	.314	.388	37.85	12.15	288
Diaz, Alexis	R-R	6-2	224	9-28-96	2	5	3.99	60	0	28	56	42	31	25	6	31	55	.206	.326	.338	22.73	12.81	242
Farmer, Buck	L-R	6-4	243	2-20-91	3	2	3.04	61	1	1	71	56	25	24	7	29	70	.215	.309	.369	23.41	9.70	299
Gibaut, Ian	R-R	6-3	250	11-19-93	0	0	4.50	2	0	0	2	3	1	1	0	1	1	.333	.400	.444	10.00	10.00	10
Greene, Hunter	R-R	6-5	242	8-6-99	9	5	2.75	26	26	0	150	96	47	46	12	57	169	.183	.283	.298	27.66	9.33	611
Junis, Jakob	R-R	6-3	220	9-16-92	0	0	2.85	14	5	0	41	29	13	13	4	3	32	.197	.224	.347	21.05	1.97	152
Kelly, Casey	R-R	6-3	215	10-4-89	0	0	5.06	2	0	1	5	5	3	3	1	1	4	.263	.286	.474	19.05	4.76	21
Kravetz, Evan	L-L	6-8	240	12-19-96	0	0	0.00	1	0	0	1	0	0	0	0	0	0	.000	.000	.000	0.00	0.00	2
Legumina, Casey	R-R	6-2	195	6-19-97	0	0	8.68	6	0	0	9	15	11	9	2	2	7	.341	.383	.568	14.89	4.26	47
Leibrandt, Brandon	L-L	6-4	190	12-13-92	0	0	9.95	2	0	0	6	11	7	7	3	2	5	.367	.406	.667	15.63	6.25	32
Lodolo, Nick	L-L	6-6	216	2-5-98	9	6	4.76	21	21	0	115	101	62	61	13	37	122	.231	.316	.380	24.75	7.51	493
Lowder, Rhett	R-R	6-2	200	3-8-02	2	2	1.17	6	6	0	31	25	4	4	0	14	22	.219	.305	.237	17.19	10.94	128
Maile, Luke	R-R	6-3	225	2-6-91	0	0	14.73	3	0	0	4	6	6	6	1	0	0	.353	.333	.824	0.00	0.00	18
Martinez, Nick	L-R	6-1	200	8-5-90	10	7	3.10	42	16	0	142	128	56	49	13	18	116	.237	.267	.377	20.35	3.16	570
Moll, Sam	L-L	5-9	190	1-3-92	3	2	3.35	48	0	0	38	27	16	14	3	14	38	.201	.283	.313	25.00	9.21	152

Pitching	B-T	Ht.	Wt.	DOB	W	L	ERA	G	GS	SV	IP	Hits	Runs	ER	HR	BB	SO	AVG	OBP	SLG	SO%	BB%	BF
Montas, Frankie	R-R	6-2	255	3-21-93	4	8	5.01	19	19	0	93	93	56	52	14	41	78	.256	.338	.433	18.98	9.98	411
Pagan, Emilio	L-R	6-2	208	5-7-91	4	5	4.50	38	1	1	38	40	20	19	6	11	44	.278	.323	.444	27.85	6.96	158
Richardson, Lyon	S-R	6-2	207	1-18-00	0	0	27.00	1	0	0	1	2	2	2	1	1	1	.500	.600	1.250	20.00	20.00	5
Santillan, Tony	R-R	6-3	285	4-15-97	3	3	3.00	29	1	0	30	21	11	10	4	9	46	.186	.246	.319	37.70	7.38	122
Sims, Lucas	R-R	6-2	213	5-10-94	1	4	3.57	43	0	1	35	30	14	14	6	20	40	.231	.333	.408	25.97	12.99	154
Spiers, Carson	R-R	6-3	205	11-11-97	5	7	5.46	22	10	0	91	112	59	55	20	27	80	.297	.351	.536	19.51	6.59	410
Suter, Brent	L-L	6-4	213	8-29-89	1	0	3.15	47	3	2	66	63	25	23	10	12	50	.249	.289	.419	18.52	4.44	270
Williamson, Brandon	R-L	6-6	210	4-2-98	0	0	3.77	4	3	0	14	10	7	6	4	5	12	.196	.288	.451	20.34	8.47	59
Wilson, Justin	L-L	6-2	205	8-18-87	1	5	5.59	60	0	2	47	55	30	29	10	13	51	.286	.335	.495	24.40	6.22	209
Young, Alex	L-L	6-3	220	9-9-93	0	0	0.00	3	0	0	2	4	0	0	0	0	2	.400	.400	.400	20.00	0.00	10
Zulueta, Yosver	R-R	6-1	190	1-23-98	0	0	4.96	12	0	0	16	15	10	9	2	7	20	.246	.333	.393	28.99	10.14	69

Fielding

Catcher	PCT	G	PO	A	E	DP	PB
Maile	.998	49	402	18	1	0	3
Stephenson	.996	127	945	32	4	4	4
Wynns	1.000	6	44	6	0	0	0

First Base	PCT	G	PO	A	E	DP
Candelario	.990	32	180	16	2	20
Encarnacion-Strand	1.000	29	196	19	0	13
Ford	1.000	2	15	2	0	1
France	.997	46	262	30	1	28
Rios	1.000	3	12	0	0	2
Smith	1.000	5	29	1	0	4
Steer	.998	63	372	37	1	27

Second Base	PCT	G	PO	A	E	DP
Espinal	.980	33	41	56	2	13
India	.991	133	217	239	4	53
Jordan	1.000	1	1	1	0	1
Marte	.000	1	0	0	0	0
Rosario	1.000	4	1	1	0	0
Steer	1.000	7	4	6	0	2

Third Base	PCT	G	PO	A	E	DP
Candelario	.930	54	40	80	9	6
Espinal	.968	67	26	96	4	6
Marte	.908	55	45	73	12	6

Shortstop	PCT	G	PO	A	E	DP
De La Cruz	.954	160	247	360	29	70
Espinal	1.000	6	6	10	0	1
Steer	1.000	1	0	3	0	1

Outfield	PCT	G	PO	A	E	DP
Benson	.991	143	226	5	2	0
Capel	1.000	1	2	0	0	0
Dunn	1.000	17	18	0	0	0
Espinal	1.000	8	12	0	0	0
Fairchild	1.000	91	170	1	0	1
Fraley	.990	104	193	4	2	0
Friedl	.985	82	192	3	3	1
Hinds	1.000	22	33	0	0	0
Hurtubise	1.000	21	32	3	0	0
Jordan	1.000	5	2	0	0	0
Martini	1.000	18	24	1	0	0
Rosario	1.000	6	7	0	0	0
Slater	.938	7	15	0	1	0
Steer	.972	105	172	1	5	0
Thompson	1.000	11	15	0	0	0
Wiemer	1.000	3	1	0	0	0

LOUISVILLE BATS — TRIPLE-A

INTERNATIONAL LEAGUE

Batting	B-T	Ht.	Wt.	DOB	AVG	OBP	SLG	G	PA	AB	R	H	2B	3B	HR	RBI	BB	HBP	SH	SF	SO	SB	CS	BB%	SO%
Barnhart, Tucker	L-R	5-11	192	1-7-91	.187	.247	.253	21	82	75	5	14	5	0	0	6	6	0	1	0	11	0	0	7.32	13.41
Burdick, Peyton	R-R	6-0	205	2-26-97	.189	.291	.341	47	189	164	25	31	4	0	7	16	21	3	0	1	80	4	0	11.11	42.33
Callihan, Tyler	L-R	6-1	205	6-22-00	.357	.550	.714	4	20	14	5	5	2	0	1	2	6	0	0	0	4	1	0	30.00	20.00
Capel, Conner	L-L	6-1	185	5-19-97	.218	.343	.432	74	287	234	34	51	12	1	12	33	45	2	0	5	63	9	4	15.68	21.95
Dunn, Blake	R-R	6-0	210	9-5-98	.240	.337	.354	99	421	359	62	86	16	2	7	34	45	8	8	1	113	21	2	10.69	26.84
Faltine, Trey	R-R	6-2	198	1-8-01	.250	.250	.250	1	4	4	0	1	0	0	0	0	0	0	0	0	2	0	0	0.00	50.00
Ford, Mike	L-R	6-0	225	7-4-92	.297	.381	.538	24	105	91	15	27	4	0	6	15	12	1	0	1	20	2	0	11.43	19.05
Friedl, TJ	L-L	5-10	180	8-14-95	.185	.313	.333	7	32	27	5	5	4	0	0	2	4	1	0	0	4	0	0	12.50	12.50
Gonzalez, Erik	R-R	6-3	205	8-31-91	.246	.287	.347	127	464	435	62	107	24	1	6	55	24	2	0	3	95	6	1	5.17	20.47
Higgins, P.J.	R-R	5-10	195	5-10-93	.259	.320	.385	134	568	514	50	133	32	0	11	68	45	4	0	5	140	0	1	7.92	24.65
Hinds, Rece	R-R	6-4	215	9-5-00	.208	.282	.376	99	422	380	48	79	18	2	14	47	37	3	0	2	160	20	3	8.77	37.91
Hurtubise, Jacob	L-R	6-0	180	12-11-97	.271	.389	.349	51	234	192	37	52	5	2	2	12	31	6	3	0	43	15	1	13.25	18.38
Johnson, Ivan	B-R	6-0	190	10-11-98	.289	.359	.537	46	167	149	24	43	11	4	6	22	15	2	0	1	47	3	2	8.98	28.14
Jordan, Levi	R-R	5-8	170	9-24-95	.307	.382	.489	95	401	352	59	100	23	1	13	52	30	15	0	4	78	10	4	7.48	19.45
Kemp, Tony	L-R	5-6	160	10-31-91	.237	.338	.364	35	139	118	13	28	6	0	3	17	17	2	0	2	12	4	1	12.23	8.63
Maile, Luke	R-R	6-3	225	2-6-91	.167	.286	.167	2	7	6	0	1	0	0	0	0	1	0	0	0	1	0	0	14.29	14.29
Marte, Noelvi	R-R	6-0	216	10-16-01	.151	.151	.170	12	53	53	3	8	1	0	0	2	0	0	0	0	15	1	0	0.00	28.30
Martini, Nick	L-L	5-11	205	6-27-90	.305	.420	.646	23	100	82	20	25	7	0	7	17	16	1	0	1	22	0	0	16.00	22.00
McAfee, Quincy	R-R	5-11	185	9-16-97	.250	.357	.417	9	29	24	4	6	4	0	0	0	3	1	1	0	5	1	0	10.34	17.24
McGarry, Alex	L-L	6-1	213	5-11-98	.125	.250	.125	11	28	24	5	3	0	0	0	2	4	0	0	0	14	0	0	14.29	50.00
Mount, Drew	L-R	5-11	205	3-24-96	.083	.154	.083	6	13	12	1	1	0	0	0	0	1	0	0	0	3	0	0	7.69	23.08
Perez, Hernan	R-R	6-1	213	3-26-91	.212	.275	.390	82	300	269	41	57	11	2	11	44	23	2	2	4	66	5	1	7.67	22.00
Rios, Edwin	L-R	6-3	220	4-21-94	.286	.385	.547	99	421	360	65	103	28	0	22	70	56	3	0	2	117	2	0	13.30	27.79
Soto, Livan	L-R	5-10	160	6-22-00	.283	.383	.368	67	290	247	24	70	12	0	3	34	38	3	0	2	53	3	1	13.10	18.28
Thompson, Bubba	R-R	6-2	197	6-9-98	.160	.222	.200	9	27	25	3	4	1	0	0	3	2	0	0	0	8	2	0	7.41	29.63
Trautwein, Michael	L-R	6-1	205	9-13-99	.192	.270	.365	77	290	260	35	50	15	3	8	30	25	3	1	1	100	4	1	8.62	34.48
Urbaez, Francisco	R-R	5-11	195	10-13-97	.306	.388	.459	27	100	85	18	26	7	0	2	16	12	0	2	1	19	4	0	12.00	19.00
Wendzel, Davis	R-R	5-10	206	5-23-97	.247	.331	.340	42	172	150	10	37	8	0	2	20	17	3	0	2	33	1	0	9.88	19.19
Wiemer, Joey	R-R	6-4	220	2-11-99	.190	.280	.229	30	118	105	12	20	2	1	0	3	12	1	0	0	37	4	0	10.17	31.36
Wynns, Austin	R-R	6-0	190	12-10-90	.250	.307	.404	31	114	104	10	26	4	0	4	17	9	0	0	1	29	0	0	7.89	25.44
Yang, Eric	R-R	5-11	185	3-26-98	.250	.333	.359	24	72	64	6	16	4	0	1	10	7	1	0	0	20	1	0	9.72	27.78

Pitching	B-T	Ht.	Wt.	DOB	W	L	ERA	G	GS	SV	IP	Hits	Runs	ER	HR	BB	SO	AVG	OBP	SLG	SO%	BB%	BF
Acuna, Jose	R-R	6-2	175	10-20-02	0	1	9.95	4	4	0	13	23	14	14	2	4	10	.397	.431	.672	15.38	6.15	65
Aguiar, Julian	L-R	6-3	180	6-4-01	3	1	4.40	9	9	0	47	43	25	23	6	16	41	.243	.317	.435	20.60	8.04	199
Ashcraft, Graham	L-R	6-2	248	2-11-98	1	1	3.00	2	2	0	12	10	4	4	1	2	12	.222	.250	.333	25.00	4.17	48
Benschoter, Sam	R-R	6-3	215	3-17-98	2	0	5.95	6	1	0	20	25	13	13	2	9	17	.309	.380	.531	18.48	9.78	92
Branche, Stevie	R-R	6-4	205	5-18-97	2	1	5.20	24	0	0	28	29	17	16	5	27	31	.271	.431	.495	22.46	19.57	138
Bruihl, Justin	L-L	6-2	215	6-26-97	4	0	2.31	19	0	0	23	16	8	6	0	10	24	.200	.320	.263	24.74	10.31	97
Buchanan, David	R-R	6-3	200	5-11-89	1	0	7.53	3	2	0	14	22	12	12	2	4	10	.367	.418	.533	14.71	5.88	68
Busenitz, Alan	R-R	6-1	180	8-22-90	5	4	4.07	49	2	3	66	64	35	30	6	22	60	.258	.319	.383	21.58	7.91	278

Byrne, Michael	R-R	6-3	205	4-16-97	0	0	4.05	7	0	2	7	7	3	3	0	2	11	.280	.357	.320	39.29	7.14	28
Crawford, Brooks	R-R	6-4	215	8-19-96	0	1	6.38	14	1	0	18	21	15	13	4	13	14	.304	.417	.536	16.67	15.48	84
Fransen, Arij	R-R	6-3	190	5-20-01	0	0	54.00	1	0	0	0	1	3	2	0	1	1	.333	.500	.333	25.00	25.00	4
Garcia, Pedro	R-R	5-11	220	3-21-95	0	0	27.00	1	0	0	1	2	3	3	1	3	1	.500	.625	1.250	12.50	37.50	8
Gavin, Grant	R-R	6-2	185	7-10-95	0	4	6.48	9	4	1	25	27	19	18	2	18	19	.278	.388	.412	16.24	15.38	117
Gibaut, Ian	R-R	6-3	250	11-19-93	0	1	11.74	9	1	0	8	13	10	10	3	6	6	.371	.488	.657	13.95	13.95	43
Gilbert, Tyler	L-L	6-3	223	12-22-93	0	1	13.11	7	3	0	12	24	17	17	0	6	13	.436	.484	.673	20.63	9.52	63
Kelly, Casey	R-R	6-3	215	10-4-89	0	2	7.09	6	6	0	27	35	23	21	6	14	18	.310	.383	.513	14.06	10.94	128
Kennedy, Brett	R-R	6-0	200	8-4-94	1	6	7.74	10	10	0	43	50	37	37	12	9	34	.296	.332	.574	18.48	4.89	184
Kravetz, Evan	L-L	6-8	240	12-19-96	6	4	3.67	48	0	2	49	51	24	20	9	27	53	.268	.357	.474	23.87	12.16	222
Kriske, Brooks	R-R	6-3	190	2-3-94	5	0	3.10	42	0	1	49	24	17	17	6	29	72	.148	.277	.315	36.73	14.80	196
Legumina, Casey	R-R	6-2	195	6-19-97	6	2	3.24	39	0	0	58	46	23	21	8	18	57	.218	.285	.393	24.15	7.63	236
Leibrandt, Brandon	L-L	6-4	190	12-13-92	3	4	4.41	17	17	0	84	81	43	41	15	21	80	.251	.295	.458	22.73	5.97	352
Lodolo, Nick	L-L	6-6	216	2-5-98	0	2	5.87	2	2	0	8	7	5	5	1	3	10	.259	.394	.481	30.30	9.09	33
Lowder, Rhett	R-R	6-2	200	3-8-02	0	0	0.00	1	1	0	6	3	0	0	0	0	7	.150	.190	.150	33.33	0.00	21
Maxwell, Zach	R-R	6-6	275	1-26-01	5	2	3.89	39	0	5	39	34	21	17	1	29	58	.231	.362	.313	32.40	16.20	179
Moll, Sam	L-L	5-9	190	1-3-92	1	2	6.48	9	0	1	8	11	6	6	1	3	9	.324	.410	.529	22.50	7.50	40
Murphy, John	R-R	6-4	245	12-11-96	0	0	9.00	2	0	0	2	2	2	2	1	2	1	.286	.444	.714	11.11	22.22	9
Overton, Connor	L-R	6-0	205	7-24-93	0	1	9.12	9	2	0	25	36	27	25	10	6	13	.340	.391	.689	11.21	5.17	116
Pagan, Emilio	L-R	6-2	208	5-7-91	0	0	6.00	3	0	1	3	2	2	2	0	0	3	.200	.182	.300	27.27	0.00	11
Perez, Hernan	R-R	6-1	213	3-26-91	0	0	21.00	3	0	0	3	10	7	7	0	2	0	.526	.591	.579	0.00	9.09	22
Petty, Chase	R-R	6-1	190	4-4-03	1	0	1.80	2	2	0	10	8	2	2	0	3	7	.222	.282	.389	17.50	7.50	40
Phillips, Connor	R-R	6-2	209	5-4-01	3	9	8.01	19	19	0	79	99	73	70	16	60	77	.310	.425	.542	19.69	15.35	391
Richardson, Lyon	S-R	6-2	207	1-18-00	1	7	4.67	25	19	0	98	90	60	51	8	59	93	.243	.352	.377	21.09	13.38	441
Roa, Christian	R-R	6-4	220	4-2-99	4	5	5.55	23	4	0	49	55	37	30	9	30	47	.293	.396	.484	21.17	13.51	222
Sanmartin, Reiver	L-L	6-2	160	4-15-96	0	2	7.36	18	0	0	18	25	17	15	2	7	18	.309	.378	.420	20.00	7.78	90
Santillan, Tony	R-R	6-3	285	4-15-97	2	4	3.49	38	0	16	39	32	20	15	3	23	53	.222	.341	.340	30.46	13.22	174
Sheffield, Justus	L-L	5-10	224	5-13-96	0	7	7.27	17	8	0	43	56	39	35	6	27	40	.308	.405	.489	18.52	12.50	216
Spiers, Carson	R-R	6-3	205	11-11-97	3	1	2.51	9	8	0	47	34	19	13	2	15	49	.197	.276	.283	25.39	7.77	193
Stockton, Spencer	S-R	6-3	210	4-24-96	0	0	7.65	12	0	0	20	25	20	17	5	14	16	.316	.421	.570	16.84	14.74	95
Suter, Brent	L-L	6-4	213	8-29-89	0	0	1.93	3	0	0	5	6	1	1	0	0	4	.333	.333	.500	22.22	0.00	18
Weigel, Patrick	R-R	6-6	240	7-8-94	0	2	18.00	2	0	0	2	5	5	4	0	3	1	.455	.571	.545	7.14	21.43	14
Williamson, Brandon	R-L	6-6	210	4-2-98	0	0	0.68	4	4	0	13	7	1	1	0	4	11	.163	.265	.186	22.45	8.16	49
Wynne, Randy	R-R	6-1	180	3-9-93	2	3	4.16	27	18	0	93	102	44	43	22	26	62	.282	.329	.522	15.78	6.62	393
Wynns, Austin	R-R	6-0	190	12-10-90	0	0	18.00	1	0	0	1	1	2	2	0	3	0	.500	.571	.500	0.00	42.86	7
Yang, Eric	R-R	5-11	185	3-26-98	0	0	0.00	5	0	0	4	2	0	0	0	3	1	.133	.316	.133	5.26	15.79	19
Young, Alex	L-L	6-3	220	9-9-93	2	0	1.19	23	0	0	23	12	5	3	1	7	22	.156	.244	.208	25.29	8.05	87
Zulueta, Yosver	R-R	6-1	190	1-23-98	4	2	3.83	40	0	1	54	52	29	23	3	32	65	.252	.360	.325	26.75	13.17	243

Fielding

Catcher	PCT	G	PO	A	E	DP	PB
Barnhart	.987	20	149	7	2	2	0
Higgins	.996	28	232	9	1	0	1
Maile	1.000	1	3	0	0	0	0
Trautwein	.986	60	524	35	8	4	3
Wynns	.984	28	225	17	4	4	0
Yang	.988	18	148	12	2	1	1

First Base	PCT	G	PO	A	E	DP
Ford	1.000	6	37	4	0	4
Higgins	.991	75	495	64	5	70
Martini	1.000	2	15	0	0	1
McGarry	1.000	9	42	0	0	5
Mount	.000	1	0	0	0	0
Perez	.992	16	108	14	1	13
Rios	.982	50	343	39	7	36
Urbaez	1.000	1	1	0	0	0

Second Base	PCT	G	PO	A	E	DP
Callihan	1.000	3	10	6	0	2
Johnson	.961	19	27	47	3	10
Jordan	.993	61	104	183	2	53
Kemp	.981	13	21	31	1	7
Marte	1.000	3	0	2	0	0
McAfee	.957	6	7	15	1	3
Perez	.977	25	38	47	2	11
Soto	.951	9	17	22	2	7
Urbaez	.953	19	35	26	3	7

Third Base	PCT	G	PO	A	E	DP
Gonzalez	.934	56	35	64	7	7
Higgins	.930	22	12	28	3	2
Jordan	1.000	9	6	15	0	5
Marte	.909	8	7	13	2	1
Perez	.929	30	29	49	6	8
Rios	.833	8	2	8	2	2
Urbaez	1.000	1	1	1	0	0
Wendzel	.954	26	22	40	3	4

Shortstop	PCT	G	PO	A	E	DP
Faltine	1.000	1	0	3	0	0
Gonzalez	.960	71	91	175	11	49
Marte	.800	1	2	2	1	1
Perez	.944	7	4	13	1	0
Soto	.965	58	74	120	7	41
Wendzel	.984	17	15	46	1	10

Outfield	PCT	G	PO	A	E	DP
Burdick	.983	47	113	1	2	0
Callihan	1.000	1	4	0	0	0
Capel	.991	60	108	6	1	2
Dunn	.995	95	177	4	1	2
Friedl	.933	6	14	0	1	0
Hinds	.965	90	157	8	6	2
Hurtubise	.968	52	90	2	3	0
Johnson	1.000	18	31	1	0	0
Jordan	1.000	21	45	0	0	0
Kemp	1.000	20	32	1	0	0
Martini	.960	12	24	0	1	0
McAfee	1.000	4	2	1	0	1
Mount	.000	2	0	0	0	0
Thompson	1.000	8	15	1	0	0
Trautwein	1.000	7	11	0	0	0
Wiemer	.976	29	80	3	2	0

CHATTANOOGA LOOKOUTS — *DOUBLE-A*

SOUTHERN LEAGUE

Batting	B-T	Ht.	Wt.	DOB	AVG	OBP	SLG	G	PA	AB	R	H	2B	3B	HR	RBI	BB	HBP	SH	SF	SO	SB	CS	BB%	SO%
Alford, Anthony	R-R	6-1	215	7-20-94	.222	.317	.361	12	41	36	3	8	2	0	1	5	5	0	0	0	18	0	0	12.20	43.90
Callahan, Austin	L-R	6-3	215	6-6-01	.209	.298	.326	53	216	187	21	39	11	1	3	17	24	1	1	3	65	3	1	11.11	30.09
Callihan, Tyler	L-R	6-1	205	6-22-00	.271	.345	.413	69	282	247	27	67	9	1	8	25	27	2	4	2	78	21	5	9.57	27.66
Cerda, Allan	R-R	6-3	203	11-24-99	.181	.289	.361	23	83	72	10	13	2	1	3	8	11	0	0	0	24	1	0	13.25	28.92
Chevalier, Luis	B-R	5-11	160	1-18-02	.250	.250	.250	1	4	4	1	1	0	0	0	0	0	0	0	0	2	0	0	0.00	50.00
Free, James	B-R	6-2	205	4-14-98	.225	.289	.325	11	45	40	1	9	1	0	1	4	3	1	0	1	10	0	0	6.67	22.22
Hendrick, Austin	L-L	6-0	195	6-15-01	.188	.243	.288	121	474	437	42	82	11	0	11	30	25	8	1	3	173	14	7	5.27	36.50
Hernandez, Miguel	R-R	6-0	194	4-13-99	.195	.219	.243	56	193	185	13	36	6	0	1	16	5	1	1	1	29	2	0	2.59	15.03
Ibarra, Ruben	R-R	6-5	290	4-26-99	.233	.314	.417	82	326	288	35	67	17	0	12	44	29	6	0	2	82	0	1	8.90	25.15

Johnson, Ivan	B-R	6-0	190	10-11-98	.235	.352	.417	75	273	230	34	54	17	2	7	25	36	6	0	1	85	12	3	13.19	31.14
McAfee, Quincy	R-R	5-11	185	9-16-97	.205	.282	.367	59	234	210	24	43	7	0	9	26	16	7	0	1	42	5	3	6.84	17.95
McGarry, Alex	L-L	6-1	213	5-11-98	.214	.281	.286	8	32	28	1	6	2	0	0	2	3	0	0	1	7	3	0	9.38	21.88
Nelson, Matheu	R-R	5-11	209	1-14-99	.198	.328	.287	76	300	247	26	49	10	0	4	21	30	19	1	3	68	0	0	10.00	22.67
Northcut, Nicholas	R-R	6-1	206	6-13-99	.192	.256	.440	107	425	391	45	75	15	2	26	65	28	6	0	0	128	0	0	6.59	30.12
Pitelli, Dominic	L-R	5-11	175	1-18-02	.237	.315	.290	79	319	279	35	66	8	2	1	20	32	1	5	2	82	33	5	10.03	25.71
Rogers, Jack	L-L	6-2	205	4-5-99	.186	.236	.265	65	242	226	28	42	4	1	4	19	13	2	0	1	76	2	0	5.37	31.40
Thompson, Bubba	R-R	6-2	197	6-9-98	.232	.264	.289	57	221	211	23	49	7	1	1	14	8	1	1	0	63	13	4	3.62	28.51
Thompson, Justice	R-R	6-4	205	7-8-00	.202	.278	.307	69	252	228	25	46	7	1	5	18	22	2	0	0	80	2	1	8.73	31.75
Torres, Jose	R-R	6-0	171	9-28-99	.217	.274	.319	79	279	254	35	55	11	0	5	21	17	4	1	2	82	9	3	6.09	29.39
Trautwein, Michael	L-R	6-1	205	9-13-99	.216	.356	.216	11	45	37	2	8	0	0	0	1	7	1	0	0	10	0	0	15.56	22.22
Urbaez, Francisco	R-R	5-11	195	10-13-97	.263	.347	.400	74	315	270	29	71	12	2	7	41	31	7	0	6	42	4	6	9.84	13.33
Vellojin, Daniel	L-R	5-11	160	3-15-00	.170	.293	.242	64	215	182	13	31	5	1	2	18	31	1	0	1	51	1	0	14.42	23.72
Yang, Eric	R-R	5-11	185	3-26-98	.146	.328	.188	19	61	48	4	7	2	0	0	2	11	2	0	0	15	0	0	18.03	24.59

Pitching	B-T	Ht.	Wt.	DOB	W	L	ERA	G	GS	SV	IP	Hits	Runs	ER	HR	BB	SO	AVG	OBP	SLG	SO%	BB%	BF
Abel, Kevin	R-R	6-1	195	2-19-99	6	8	5.09	18	18	0	87	76	56	49	6	57	82	.238	.356	.375	21.24	14.77	386
Acuna, Jose	R-R	6-2	175	10-20-02	0	2	0.81	9	7	0	22	21	7	2	1	6	26	.241	.302	.322	26.80	6.19	97
Aguiar, Julian	L-R	6-3	180	6-4-01	2	3	3.38	13	13	0	69	69	29	26	7	13	54	.265	.309	.396	19.08	4.59	283
Benoit, Donovan	R-R	6-3	203	1-22-99	3	2	4.97	31	0	0	58	62	44	32	5	30	48	.279	.371	.410	18.11	11.32	265
Benschoter, Sam	R-R	6-3	215	3-17-98	2	5	3.95	27	10	0	84	77	45	37	4	34	84	.245	.327	.347	23.27	9.42	361
Braithwaite, Trey	R-R	6-3	220	9-23-97	0	0	14.73	4	0	0	4	6	6	6	1	7	6	.375	.565	.625	26.09	30.43	23
Branche, Stevie	R-R	6-4	205	5-18-97	0	0	0.00	2	0	1	3	1	0	0	0	1	3	.111	.273	.222	27.27	9.09	11
Crawford, Brooks	R-R	6-4	215	8-19-96	1	3	3.17	23	0	1	54	38	22	19	4	23	59	.199	.287	.346	27.31	10.65	216
Demurias, Eddy	R-R	6-0	184	8-1-97	1	1	4.50	10	0	0	16	21	11	8	0	7	18	.313	.378	.433	24.32	9.46	74
Farr, Thomas	R-R	6-0	203	4-29-99	1	17	5.56	26	26	0	126	139	84	78	20	47	87	.283	.360	.487	15.59	8.42	558
Gavin, Grant	R-R	6-2	185	7-10-95	0	1	0.00	3	2	0	11	7	1	0	0	1	12	.184	.200	.263	30.00	2.50	40
Gozzo, Jake	R-R	6-5	221	1-5-97	0	3	8.53	24	0	4	32	37	34	30	1	24	30	.298	.397	.403	19.23	15.38	156
Heatherly, Jacob	L-L	6-1	215	5-20-98	4	3	8.06	37	0	0	41	33	39	37	1	52	57	.221	.429	.289	27.67	25.24	206
Holt, Owen	R-R	6-3	225	4-22-99	1	8	5.03	37	0	3	48	49	35	27	4	24	39	.266	.354	.418	18.66	11.48	209
Hubbart, Bryce	L-L	6-1	181	6-28-01	0	1	2.00	3	1	0	9	6	2	2	0	3	8	.194	.257	.258	22.86	8.57	35
Lowder, Rhett	R-R	6-2	200	3-8-02	4	4	4.31	16	16	0	77	80	37	37	7	18	77	.266	.312	.412	23.77	5.56	324
Maxwell, Zach	R-R	6-6	275	1-26-01	2	0	1.23	14	0	0	15	7	3	2	0	9	27	.143	.276	.184	46.55	15.52	58
Mey, Luis	R-R	6-2	160	6-24-01	0	3	4.15	19	0	1	26	23	16	12	0	19	27	.253	.400	.286	23.28	16.38	116
Moore, Andrew	L-R	6-5	205	8-11-99	2	4	4.47	27	0	0	46	39	23	23	2	37	69	.225	.374	.312	32.24	17.29	214
Parks, Hunter	R-R	6-4	187	4-28-01	0	4	6.83	8	8	0	28	27	21	21	1	28	27	.257	.424	.362	19.42	20.14	139
Petty, Chase	R-R	6-1	190	4-4-03	10	5	4.39	26	26	0	127	116	68	62	11	56	123	.244	.326	.385	22.78	10.37	540
Roxby, Braxton	R-R	6-3	215	3-12-99	0	4	5.21	39	0	3	48	49	34	28	2	24	65	.254	.360	.373	28.76	10.62	226
Rudd, Carson	R-R	6-5	190	9-17-98	1	3	3.04	33	5	4	77	56	27	26	4	57	85	.207	.355	.292	25.22	16.91	337
Sikkema, T.J.	L-L	6-0	221	7-25-98	3	0	2.65	3	3	0	17	14	5	5	2	3	20	.219	.254	.359	29.85	4.48	67
Timpanelli, Vin	R-R	6-2	210	10-2-98	1	3	7.90	10	0	0	14	19	15	12	4	10	10	.339	.435	.643	14.49	14.49	69
Urbaez, Francisco	R-R	5-11	195	10-13-97	0	0	0.00	1	0	0	0	0	4	4	0	5	0	.000	1.000	.000	0.00	83.33	6
Weigel, Patrick	R-R	6-6	240	7-8-94	1	3	0.90	19	0	10	20	15	6	2	0	9	24	.208	.321	.250	28.24	10.59	85

Fielding

Catcher	PCT	G	PO	A	E	DP	PB
Nelson	.993	65	525	37	4	5	6
Trautwein	1.000	10	92	11	0	0	0
Vellojin	.989	50	410	26	5	1	8
Yang	.994	19	165	4	1	2	3

First Base	PCT	G	PO	A	E	DP
Callahan	.977	6	36	6	1	3
Callihan	.969	4	27	4	1	5
Free	1.000	7	52	11	0	5
Ibarra	.987	69	481	37	7	65
McGarry	1.000	6	39	3	0	5
Northcut	1.000	32	198	14	0	21
Rogers	.988	13	78	5	1	14
Vellojin	1.000	5	32	1	0	3

Second Base	PCT	G	PO	A	E	DP
Callihan	.978	43	70	104	4	27
Chevalier	1.000	1	2	2	0	0
Hernandez	1.000	7	9	12	0	5
Johnson	.963	9	13	13	1	5
McAfee	.959	9	19	28	2	8
Torres	.986	19	23	45	1	9
Urbaez	.990	49	81	108	2	28

Third Base	PCT	G	PO	A	E	DP
Callahan	.975	39	22	55	2	4
Callihan	.500	1	0	1	1	0
Hernandez	.957	24	14	30	2	5
McAfee	.750	2	1	2	1	0
Northcut	.936	63	45	87	9	12
Torres	.889	12	10	6	2	4
Urbaez	1.000	2	0	3	0	0

Shortstop	PCT	G	PO	A	E	DP
Hernandez	.966	21	26	59	3	11
McAfee	.667	1	2	0	1	0
Pitelli	.971	71	94	174	8	41
Torres	.957	46	69	108	8	37

Outfield	PCT	G	PO	A	E	DP
Alford	1.000	10	20	0	0	0
Callihan	1.000	16	29	2	0	0
Cerda	.973	20	35	1	1	1
Hendrick	.971	116	192	10	6	2
Hernandez	1.000	3	6	0	0	0
Johnson	.982	57	104	6	2	4
McAfee	.973	34	68	5	2	1
Rogers	.989	47	86	0	1	0
Thompson	.990	55	98	2	1	0
Thompson	1.000	56	130	4	0	1
Urbaez	1.000	5	13	0	0	0

DAYTON DRAGONS — *HIGH-A*

MIDWEST LEAGUE

Batting	B-T	Ht.	Wt.	DOB	AVG	OBP	SLG	G	PA	AB	R	H	2B	3B	HR	RBI	BB	HBP	SH	SF	SO	SB	CS	BB%	SO%
Acosta, Victor	B-R	5-11	170	6-10-04	.186	.299	.287	107	404	345	41	64	13	5	4	36	44	12	2	1	105	14	6	10.89	25.99
Allen, Jay	R-R	6-2	190	11-22-02	.224	.372	.345	109	456	362	65	81	10	2	10	40	65	23	2	4	98	35	10	14.25	21.49
Ascanio, Johnny	B-R	5-10	150	7-4-03	.218	.348	.273	18	68	55	11	12	0	0	1	4	10	1	2	0	12	4	0	14.71	17.65
Balcazar, Leonardo	R-R	5-10	190	6-17-04	.264	.295	.354	102	410	390	33	103	13	2	6	47	14	4	0	2	100	9	4	3.41	24.39
Burns, Connor	R-R	6-1	185	12-25-01	.143	.236	.222	22	73	63	8	9	2	0	1	8	8	0	1	1	26	0	1	10.96	35.62
Collier, Cam	L-R	6-2	210	11-20-04	.248	.355	.443	119	507	427	72	106	21	1	20	74	66	8	0	6	127	2	1	13.02	25.05
Contreras, Yan	R-R	6-2	185	1-30-01	.120	.244	.213	43	129	108	18	13	2	1	2	10	14	4	2	1	48	8	2	10.85	37.21
Faile, John Michael	R-R	6-0	218	5-11-00	.231	.265	.477	16	68	65	9	15	2	1	4	10	2	1	0	0	24	0	0	2.94	35.29
Faltine, Trey	R-R	6-2	198	1-8-01	.100	.182	.100	8	25	20	1	2	0	0	0	2	2	0	3	0	11	3	0	8.00	44.00

Batting	B-T	Ht.	Wt.	DOB	AVG	OBP	SLG	G	PA	AB	R	H	2B	3B	HR	RBI	BB	HBP	SH	SF	SO	SB	CS	BB%	SO%
Graham, Carter	R-R	6-2	232	9-17-01	.188	.267	.359	34	131	117	15	22	5	0	5	15	10	3	0	1	45	3	1	7.63	34.35
Hunter, Cade	L-R	6-2	200	11-29-00	.196	.304	.296	107	429	368	50	72	14	1	7	42	48	10	0	1	136	14	0	11.19	31.70
Hurtubise, Jacob	L-R	6-0	180	12-11-97	.286	.333	.643	5	15	14	4	4	2	0	1	1	0	1	0	0	2	1	0	0.00	13.33
Ibarra, Ruben	R-R	6-5	290	4-26-99	.255	.368	.340	30	115	94	11	24	2	0	2	12	17	1	0	2	30	1	0	14.78	26.09
Jorge, Carlos	L-R	5-10	160	9-22-03	.220	.291	.394	95	402	355	50	78	20	3	12	43	31	7	0	5	125	28	4	7.71	31.09
Mount, Drew	L-R	5-11	205	3-24-96	.045	.214	.045	7	28	22	0	1	0	0	0	2	3	2	0	1	8	0	0	10.71	28.57
O'Donnell, Ethan	L-R	6-1	190	3-27-02	.269	.358	.416	104	415	361	61	97	11	6	10	40	40	11	2	1	108	31	5	9.64	26.02
Rodriguez, Hector	L-R	5-8	186	3-11-04	.274	.309	.420	125	541	507	65	139	24	7	12	61	26	2	1	5	72	12	6	4.81	13.31
Serrano, Jose	R-R	6-0	180	10-14-03	.143	.217	.214	30	92	84	5	12	0	0	2	4	8	0	0	0	45	0	0	8.70	48.91
Stewart, Sal	R-R	6-3	215	12-7-03	.279	.391	.454	80	338	280	54	78	23	1	8	46	50	4	0	4	57	10	2	14.79	16.86
Tanner, Logan	R-R	6-0	215	11-10-00	.185	.298	.342	69	259	222	28	41	12	1	7	26	35	1	0	0	86	0	1	13.51	33.20

Pitching	B-T	Ht.	Wt.	DOB	W	L	ERA	G	GS	SV	IP	Hits	Runs	ER	HR	BB	SO	AVG	OBP	SLG	SO%	BB%	BF
Abel, Kevin	R-R	6-1	195	2-19-99	1	0	2.79	6	6	0	29	23	10	9	4	8	31	.215	.280	.364	26.27	6.78	118
Adcock, Cody	R-R	6-4	210	6-21-02	2	0	4.60	9	0	0	16	13	8	8	0	7	18	.217	.314	.283	25.71	10.00	70
Aguilera, Gabriel	R-R	6-0	165	8-19-00	4	4	4.25	13	13	0	55	44	28	26	3	28	37	.217	.314	.350	15.42	11.67	240
Alfonseca, Pedro	R-R	6-0	178	9-4-97	0	2	8.04	20	0	0	28	35	31	25	1	35	30	.307	.494	.465	18.99	22.15	158
Bell, Brock	R-R	6-4	227	3-18-98	3	3	4.82	35	0	7	52	66	36	28	9	11	44	.297	.335	.500	18.57	4.64	237
Braithwaite, Trey	R-R	6-3	220	9-23-97	0	0	7.50	9	0	0	12	13	10	10	0	9	9	.271	.379	.271	15.52	15.52	58
Cardona, Ryan	R-R	6-1	200	5-7-00	9	5	3.29	22	19	1	104	74	42	38	7	43	120	.198	.283	.324	28.17	10.09	426
Contreras, Yan	R-R	6-2	185	1-30-01	0	0	33.75	1	0	0	1	7	5	5	0	3	1	.778	.769	1.000	7.69	23.08	13
Cooper, Tanner	R-R	6-3	215	9-8-99	0	0	9.82	2	0	0	4	8	4	4	2	0	1	.444	.444	.944	5.56	0.00	18
Edgington, Brian	R-R	6-0	200	9-2-98	2	2	5.40	8	8	0	42	36	27	25	5	9	41	.226	.276	.377	24.12	5.29	170
Franco, Jose	R-R	6-2	175	11-25-00	1	3	3.45	14	14	0	47	35	18	18	3	17	49	.203	.277	.320	25.65	8.90	191
Fransen, Arij	R-R	6-3	190	5-20-01	3	3	3.86	30	0	3	68	69	31	29	1	37	55	.260	.362	.351	17.80	11.97	309
Gayman, Myles	R-R	6-4	200	2-19-98	2	4	8.10	15	0	0	37	49	34	33	3	10	28	.320	.365	.464	16.37	5.85	171
Gibaut, Ian	R-R	6-3	250	11-19-93	0	0	0.00	2	0	0	2	1	0	0	0	1	4	.143	.250	.143	50.00	12.50	8
Harmon, Johnathan	R-R	6-5	195	9-4-00	3	3	4.30	10	10	0	46	41	24	22	5	13	41	.233	.295	.369	21.13	6.70	194
Hubbart, Bryce	L-L	6-1	181	6-28-01	4	5	5.88	20	10	2	67	73	44	44	11	37	62	.279	.376	.492	20.13	12.01	308
Jessee, Brody	R-R	6-4	217	12-1-00	8	3	6.11	32	0	2	63	68	47	43	5	24	66	.272	.353	.392	23.08	8.39	286
Lorant, Nestor	R-R	6-2	175	5-4-02	0	0	4.15	3	1	0	9	8	4	4	0	4	10	.242	.359	.333	25.64	10.26	39
Lowder, Rhett	R-R	6-2	200	3-8-02	2	0	2.49	5	5	0	25	18	8	7	2	6	29	.191	.255	.351	28.43	5.88	102
Lyons, Jared	R-R	6-1	190	9-27-00	3	1	2.82	8	8	0	38	28	13	12	5	20	46	.200	.300	.343	28.75	12.50	160
Menefee, Joseph	L-L	6-2	220	10-6-99	2	2	3.68	20	0	1	37	25	19	15	1	24	59	.189	.321	.242	37.11	15.09	159
Mey, Luis	R-R	6-2	160	6-24-01	2	2	2.79	21	0	8	29	15	15	9	0	24	36	.147	.315	.176	28.13	18.75	128
Miller, Simon	R-R	6-2	210	9-8-00	3	2	1.47	18	0	8	31	17	8	5	1	10	37	.156	.233	.220	30.83	8.33	120
Moore, Andrew	L-R	6-5	205	8-11-99	1	0	1.38	7	0	3	13	4	2	2	1	5	24	.095	.191	.167	51.06	10.64	47
Murphy, John	R-R	6-4	245	12-11-96	4	1	1.79	32	0	8	40	29	15	8	2	10	42	.200	.265	.297	25.77	6.13	163
Osman, Graham	L-L	6-3	183	1-29-01	1	1	7.56	9	2	0	17	20	15	14	2	14	16	.313	.432	.453	19.75	17.28	81
Overton, Connor	L-R	6-0	205	7-24-93	0	0	7.20	2	1	0	5	4	4	4	2	0	8	.211	.250	.526	40.00	0.00	20
Pelio, Mason	R-R	6-3	230	7-15-00	0	4	8.65	9	8	0	26	31	29	25	2	26	16	.295	.434	.419	11.68	18.98	137
Rivera, Javier	R-R	6-1	195	11-27-99	5	2	4.09	12	12	0	51	43	24	23	2	16	62	.219	.292	.306	28.18	7.27	220
Sanmartin, Reiver	L-L	6-2	160	4-15-96	0	0	0.00	1	0	0	1	0	0	0	0	0	0	.000	.000	.000	0.00	0.00	3
Sikkema, T.J.	L-L	6-0	221	7-25-98	3	3	3.90	17	11	0	55	52	31	24	5	13	52	.241	.301	.370	21.94	5.49	237
Sikorski, Easton	R-R	6-0	210	1-12-00	4	2	3.90	26	1	2	67	58	33	29	4	34	57	.233	.329	.365	19.86	11.85	287
Simmons, Dylan	R-R	6-3	245	10-5-00	1	1	4.09	9	0	0	22	17	11	10	2	6	23	.205	.267	.361	25.56	6.67	90
Timpanelli, Vin	R-R	6-2	210	10-2-98	0	0	3.86	4	0	1	5	4	2	2	1	3	10	.222	.364	.389	45.45	13.64	22
Vargas, Victor	R-R	6-1	175	9-3-00	1	0	1.00	2	2	0	9	7	1	1	0	1	8	.200	.243	.257	21.62	2.70	37
Williamson, Brandon	R-L	6-6	210	4-2-98	0	0	0.00	1	1	0	3	1	0	0	0	0	4	.100	.100	.200	40.00	0.00	10

Fielding

Catcher	PCT	G	PO	A	E	DP	PB
Burns	.990	22	185	12	2	0	3
Faile	1.000	1	5	1	0	0	0
Hunter	.988	47	386	28	5	3	2
Serrano	1.000	2	1	0	0	0	0
Tanner	.986	69	612	34	9	4	4

First Base	PCT	G	PO	A	E	DP
Contreras	.993	19	130	7	1	7
Faile	1.000	2	15	0	0	1
Graham	.995	27	180	12	1	12
Hunter	.984	44	284	18	5	23
Ibarra	.976	27	189	11	5	10
Mount	.964	4	26	1	1	1
Serrano	.991	15	97	10	1	7

Second Base	PCT	G	PO	A	E	DP
Acosta	.980	68	97	150	5	20
Ascanio	.960	11	17	31	2	7
Balcazar	1.000	3	4	4	0	0
Contreras	1.000	10	16	18	0	4
Jorge	1.000	3	5	6	0	2
Serrano	1.000	2	2	6	0	0
Stewart	.986	36	63	78	2	17

Third Base	PCT	G	PO	A	E	DP
Ascanio	.889	5	4	4	1	0
Collier	.908	86	49	128	18	6
Contreras	1.000	2	0	2	0	0
Faltine	1.000	2	2	4	0	0
Graham	.857	4	2	4	1	0
Serrano	1.000	3	0	1	0	0
Stewart	.936	33	24	64	6	3

Shortstop	PCT	G	PO	A	E	DP
Acosta	.936	34	36	67	7	9
Ascanio	1.000	1	1	0	0	0
Balcazar	.943	97	132	182	19	31
Contreras	.667	1	1	1	1	1

Outfield	PCT	G	PO	A	E	DP
Allen	.968	106	238	3	8	1
Contreras	.882	10	14	1	2	0
Faltine	1.000	6	6	0	0	0
Hunter	.966	22	28	0	1	0
Hurtubise	1.000	4	13	0	0	0
Jorge	.996	84	213	9	1	2
O'Donnell	.971	83	169	1	5	1
Rodriguez	.988	99	166	4	2	0

DAYTONA TORTUGAS — *LOW-A*

FLORIDA STATE LEAGUE

Batting	B-T	Ht.	Wt.	DOB	AVG	OBP	SLG	G	PA	AB	R	H	2B	3B	HR	RBI	BB	HBP	SH	SF	SO	SB	CS	BB%	SO%
Almonte, Ariel	L-L	6-1	170	12-1-03	.199	.306	.391	118	506	432	62	86	21	1	20	66	67	2	0	5	163	3	1	13.24	32.21
Ascanio, Johnny	B-R	5-10	150	7-4-03	.220	.296	.300	79	289	250	29	55	11	0	3	28	24	5	5	5	45	8	3	8.30	15.57
Burns, Connor	R-R	6-1	185	12-25-01	.195	.292	.357	68	278	241	30	47	11	2	8	36	34	0	1	2	94	0	1	12.23	33.81

Cabrera, Ricardo	R-R	5-11	178	10-31-04	.252	.331	.399	105	456	404	59	102	22	2	11	55	31	18	0	3	101	19	8	6.80	22.15
Confidan, Yerlin	L-L	6-3	170	12-16-02	.249	.343	.419	91	400	346	52	86	28	2	9	41	49	2	0	3	97	16	7	12.25	24.25
Duno, Alfredo	R-R	6-2	210	1-7-06	.267	.367	.422	32	139	116	18	31	7	1	3	16	18	2	0	3	40	2	0	12.95	28.78
Faltine, Trey	R-R	6-2	198	1-8-01	.216	.340	.351	78	251	208	38	45	10	0	6	28	33	7	1	2	96	26	2	13.15	38.25
Graham, Carter	R-R	6-2	232	9-17-01	.235	.326	.364	49	187	162	20	38	10	1	3	25	15	8	0	2	38	5	2	8.02	20.32
Henley, Kyle	R-R	6-3	180	12-15-04	.111	.200	.111	4	10	9	0	1	0	0	0	2	1	0	0	0	5	1	0	10.00	50.00
Isturiz, Eddy	R-R	5-10	182	1-16-04	.208	.323	.358	22	62	53	16	11	0	1	2	6	9	0	0	0	20	10	1	14.52	32.26
Leones, Luis	L-L	5-10	155	6-12-03	.050	.050	.050	6	20	20	0	1	0	0	0	1	0	0	0	0	12	0	0	0.00	60.00
McCrystal, Ryan	L-R	6-2	206	10-4-02	.256	.310	.333	13	42	39	2	10	3	0	0	2	3	0	0	0	9	0	0	7.14	21.43
Moon, Bernard	R-R	6-0	185	4-15-05	.000	.000	.000	1	3	3	0	0	0	0	0	0	0	0	0	0	2	0	0	0.00	66.67
Moss, Jack	L-R	6-5	215	10-30-01	.262	.343	.306	82	289	252	27	66	9	1	0	23	33	0	0	4	51	2	0	11.42	17.65
Omana, Diego	R-R	5-11	165	1-10-03	.206	.296	.262	35	125	107	9	22	3	0	1	8	14	1	0	3	32	1	1	11.20	25.60
Pineda, Esmith	R-R	5-10	183	11-13-04	.213	.316	.346	103	427	367	55	78	22	0	9	38	53	4	0	3	115	9	1	12.41	26.93
Pino, Yassel	R-R	6-2	200	10-4-01	.265	.327	.426	54	171	155	19	41	7	0	6	18	13	2	0	1	34	5	2	7.60	19.88
Pitelli, Dominic	L-R	5-11	175	1-18-02	.290	.376	.492	34	141	124	15	36	10	3	3	15	15	2	0	0	38	10	6	10.64	26.95
Reyes, Luis	R-R	5-11	193	11-15-03	.267	.325	.333	23	83	75	14	20	2	0	1	9	7	0	0	1	16	1	1	8.43	19.28
Salcedo, Andruw	B-R	5-11	175	9-29-02	.188	.350	.188	7	20	16	1	3	0	0	0	0	4	0	0	0	7	0	0	20.00	35.00
Sanchez, Carlos	L-R	6-0	177	1-12-05	.210	.356	.233	53	220	176	24	37	4	0	0	16	39	1	4	0	73	8	6	17.73	33.18
Stafura, Sammy	R-R	6-0	188	11-15-04	.255	.374	.379	77	352	290	52	74	10	4	6	37	52	5	0	3	84	27	5	14.77	23.86
Stovall, Peyton	L-R	5-11	195	2-14-03	.235	.355	.333	16	62	51	4	12	1	2	0	6	9	1	0	1	7	4	0	14.52	11.29
Valdez, Malvin	R-R	6-2	178	10-14-03	.192	.295	.242	83	307	265	27	51	9	2	0	24	32	7	2	1	90	20	6	10.42	29.32

Pitching	B-T	Ht.	Wt.	DOB	W	L	ERA	G	GS	SV	IP	Hits	Runs	ER	HR	BB	SO	AVG	OBP	SLG	SO%	BB%	BF
Adcock, Cody	R-R	6-4	210	6-21-02	1	3	3.60	19	0	5	35	25	18	14	1	20	42	.205	.338	.311	27.63	13.16	152
Aguilera, Gabriel	R-R	6-0	165	8-19-00	2	0	2.66	12	6	0	44	31	16	13	0	20	33	.199	.304	.256	18.13	10.99	182
Blandino, Alex	R-R	6-0	190	11-6-92	0	0	8.59	5	0	0	7	11	7	7	0	6	7	.393	.500	.536	19.44	16.67	36
Brutti, Ben	R-R	6-3	200	5-16-03	2	4	3.38	23	14	2	80	70	35	30	5	43	77	.233	.350	.323	21.75	12.15	354
Byrne, Michael	R-R	6-3	205	4-16-97	0	0	9.00	3	1	0	3	4	3	3	0	3	3	.364	.500	.455	21.43	21.43	14
Campbell, Logan	R-R	6-2	205	7-22-99	0	1	9.00	3	0	1	3	4	4	3	2	3	4	.308	.471	.769	23.53	17.65	17
Edgington, Brian	R-R	6-0	200	9-2-98	2	6	3.52	15	15	0	72	75	32	28	8	17	80	.272	.315	.438	27.12	5.76	295
Franco, Jose	R-R	6-2	175	11-25-00	1	0	3.64	8	8	0	30	27	12	12	4	9	41	.237	.293	.421	33.33	7.32	123
Gutierrez, Dualvert	R-R	6-0	185	1-25-01	5	0	3.14	14	8	0	49	46	17	17	3	17	43	.250	.310	.359	21.08	8.33	204
Hayden, Luke	R-R	6-1	210	12-5-02	1	0	3.60	4	0	1	5	4	3	2	0	2	6	.222	.286	.222	28.57	9.52	21
Herrera, Adrian	R-R	6-1	190	8-10-04	2	2	6.65	7	1	0	22	26	17	16	4	9	20	.302	.384	.581	20.00	9.00	100
Hodgdon, Trent	R-R	6-3	205	7-9-03	0	0	6.75	3	0	1	5	4	4	4	0	5	5	.222	.391	.389	20.83	20.83	24
Hollan, Hunter	L-L	6-5	200	3-5-02	0	0	7.30	4	2	0	12	12	12	10	0	7	9	.255	.368	.319	15.79	12.28	57
Huggins, Kenya	R-R	6-3	215	12-12-02	1	0	1.13	4	0	0	8	1	1	1	0	3	7	.167	.250	.208	25.00	10.71	28
Hurney, Jonah	L-L	5-8	180	3-3-00	4	1	3.40	28	0	7	56	43	23	21	2	13	62	.213	.265	.347	28.05	5.88	221
Isturiz, Eddy	R-R	5-10	182	1-16-04	0	0	0.00	1	0	0	1	1	0	0	0	0	0	.250	.250	.250	0.00	0.00	4
Johnson, Alexander	R-R	6-6	220	7-2-00	3	2	6.59	23	0	0	29	23	28	21	1	34	26	.228	.428	.337	18.84	24.64	138
Laureano, Anyer	R-R	6-2	188	12-29-02	4	6	3.00	29	0	2	54	30	20	18	5	37	81	.163	.313	.304	35.53	16.23	228
Lorant, Nestor	R-R	6-2	175	5-4-02	8	3	1.44	22	7	3	88	54	16	14	3	22	99	.180	.245	.267	30.18	6.71	328
Lorduy, David	R-R	6-0	198	10-15-03	1	0	0.60	5	2	0	15	8	2	1	0	3	17	.145	.190	.200	29.31	5.17	58
Martinez, Juan	R-R	6-1	160	12-30-02	1	5	3.89	11	6	0	39	31	24	17	3	16	35	.212	.293	.342	20.96	9.58	167
Miller, Simon	R-R	6-2	210	9-8-00	2	2	2.66	15	0	5	20	13	10	6	1	12	27	.183	.314	.282	30.68	13.64	88
Montero, Jose	R-R	6-2	180	7-14-03	4	6	3.47	25	16	0	96	88	44	37	4	44	87	.251	.337	.345	21.70	10.97	401
Ortiz, JeanPierre	R-R	6-0	185	2-18-04	0	0	4.70	6	0	0	8	7	4	4	0	9	9	.269	.486	.462	24.32	24.32	37
Osman, Graham	L-L	6-3	183	1-29-01	4	3	3.47	16	2	0	49	37	21	19	0	36	56	.208	.355	.292	25.34	16.29	221
Payero, Nick	R-R	6-2	200	6-21-00	1	1	3.53	12	7	0	43	42	19	17	5	9	38	.247	.291	.418	20.88	4.95	182
Pestka, Drew	R-R	6-5	225	5-18-04	1	3	3.06	11	0	1	18	15	12	6	1	10	20	.231	.325	.323	25.64	12.82	78
Portes, Ovis	R-R	6-4	167	12-3-04	0	1	14.40	4	2	0	5	5	8	8	0	10	9	.250	.531	.350	28.13	31.25	32
Quigley, Stephen	S-R	6-0	175	5-3-00	0	1	6.75	2	1	0	5	7	4	4	2	2	5	.280	.333	.520	18.52	7.41	27
Romano, Jimmy	R-R	6-1	200	6-11-03	1	0	3.52	4	0	0	8	5	3	3	2	4	3	.192	.323	.423	9.68	12.90	31
Salcedo, Andruw	S-R	5-11	175	9-29-02	0	0	0.00	1	0	0	0	1	0	0	0	1	0	.500	.667	1.000	0.00	33.33	3
Sando, Nick	L-L	6-2	203	5-11-01	6	2	3.24	22	3	3	67	47	29	24	1	32	77	.198	.313	.266	27.70	11.51	278
Schoenwetter, Cole	R-R	6-3	190	10-1-04	0	2	8.04	6	2	0	16	17	17	14	2	17	23	.274	.430	.452	29.11	21.52	79
Serwinowski, Adam	L-L	6-5	190	6-7-04	1	3	3.57	25	25	0	86	64	36	34	4	45	106	.205	.315	.301	29.04	12.33	365
Simmons, Dylan	R-R	6-3	245	10-5-00	5	4	4.34	18	0	2	29	31	15	14	2	15	30	.272	.364	.395	22.39	11.19	134
Starks, Gabe	R-R	6-1	230	12-26-01	1	3	9.00	10	0	1	14	21	21	14	0	14	13	.356	.461	.525	17.11	18.42	76

Fielding

Catcher	PCT	G	PO	A	E	DP	PB
Burns	.987	65	613	53	9	5	5
Duno	.978	21	202	17	5	1	3
McCrystal	.979	11	84	10	2	2	2
Omana	.981	33	285	29	6	4	3
Salcedo	1.000	2	21	2	0	1	2

First Base	PCT	G	PO	A	E	DP
Graham	.992	30	224	14	2	18
Moss	.996	64	426	25	2	32
Pino	.996	40	245	15	1	31
Reyes	1.000	12	70	4	0	7

Second Base	PCT	G	PO	A	E	DP
Ascanio	.997	77	113	182	1	48
Cabrera	.920	16	20	26	4	3
Faltine	1.000	22	36	49	0	10
Moon	1.000	1	2	0	0	0
Pitelli	.978	9	15	29	1	6
Stovall	.977	11	21	22	1	4

Third Base	PCT	G	PO	A	E	DP
Cabrera	.910	55	36	85	12	11
Faltine	.950	16	14	24	2	1
Graham	.927	16	11	27	3	5
Pino	.870	14	9	11	3	0
Pitelli	1.000	5	9	8	0	0
Reyes	.857	3	2	4	1	0
Sanchez	.946	25	12	41	3	2
Stovall	1.000	1	1	2	0	0

Shortstop	PCT	G	PO	A	E	DP
Cabrera	.879	17	24	27	7	10
Faltine	.833	4	2	8	2	1
Pitelli	.978	19	28	59	2	13
Sanchez	.910	24	30	51	8	10
Stafura	.961	67	95	177	11	32

Outfield	PCT	G	PO	A	E	DP
Almonte	.964	90	126	9	5	4
Confidan	.987	82	149	3	2	0
Faltine	.953	31	56	5	3	0
Henley	1.000	3	5	0	0	0
Isturiz	.933	10	12	2	1	0
Leones	.889	6	8	0	1	0
Moss	.000	1	0	0	0	0
Pineda	.978	102	165	9	4	3
Valdez	.973	84	140	5	4	0

ACL REDS — ROOKIE

ARIZONA COMPLEX LEAGUE

Batting	B-T	Ht.	Wt.	DOB	AVG	OBP	SLG	G	PA	AB	R	H	2B	3B	HR	RBI	BB	HBP	SH	SF	SO	SB	CS	BB%	SO%
Alcantara, Alfredo	R-R	5-9	165	10-25-05	.189	.322	.302	51	205	169	25	32	4	0	5	19	29	5	0	2	74	4	2	14.15	36.10
Callahan, Austin	L-R	6-3	215	6-6-01	.250	.310	.542	7	29	24	2	6	2	1	1	5	2	1	0	2	10	0	0	6.90	34.48
Chevalier, Luis	B-R	5-11	160	1-18-02	.245	.403	.439	35	126	98	23	24	6	2	3	18	23	3	2	0	24	2	1	18.25	19.05
Davies, Drew	L-R	6-2	171	12-4-05	.214	.386	.316	36	127	98	12	21	4	0	2	17	26	2	0	1	35	1	0	20.47	27.56
Espinoza, Iverson	R-R	5-10	155	1-6-03	.294	.392	.412	27	79	68	16	20	2	3	0	8	9	2	0	0	16	5	0	11.39	20.25
Faile, John Michael	R-R	6-0	218	5-11-00	.333	.457	.561	25	81	66	10	22	6	0	3	11	12	3	0	0	26	1	0	14.81	32.10
Garcia, Juan	R-R	5-11	185	5-3-03	.217	.304	.283	36	138	120	20	26	8	0	0	12	13	3	0	2	37	0	1	9.42	26.81
Henley, Kyle	R-R	6-3	180	12-15-04	.280	.372	.406	53	241	207	47	58	10	5	2	20	22	9	2	1	79	35	3	9.13	32.78
Hurtubise, Jacob	L-R	6-0	180	12-11-97	.200	.273	.300	3	11	10	1	2	1	0	0	2	0	1	0	0	4	1	0	0.00	36.36
Isturiz, Eddy	R-R	5-10	182	1-16-04	.259	.449	.362	21	78	58	12	15	4	1	0	7	19	1	0	0	19	4	1	24.36	24.36
Leones, Luis	L-L	5-10	155	6-12-03	.196	.268	.259	32	125	112	16	22	2	1	1	8	10	1	2	0	49	8	3	8.00	39.20
Lin, Sheng-En	L-R	5-11	185	9-1-05	.308	.418	.419	49	215	172	29	53	4	6	1	34	36	0	2	5	68	12	3	16.74	31.63
McAfee, Quincy	R-R	5-11	185	9-16-97	.200	.400	.267	6	20	15	3	3	1	0	0	0	4	1	0	0	3	2	0	20.00	15.00
Moon, Bernard	R-R	6-0	185	4-15-05	.304	.423	.410	47	197	161	24	49	9	1	2	30	18	16	1	1	50	6	6	9.14	25.38
Mount, Drew	L-R	5-11	205	3-24-96	.182	.400	.455	4	15	11	4	2	1	1	0	0	2	2	0	0	3	1	0	13.33	20.00
Omana, Diego	R-R	5-11	165	1-10-03	.280	.441	.320	9	35	25	6	7	1	0	0	3	7	1	1	1	10	0	0	20.00	28.57
Puerta, Jorge	R-R	5-11	178	12-5-01	.259	.328	.328	21	68	58	9	15	1	0	1	13	6	1	1	2	10	0	0	8.82	14.71
Reyes, Luis	R-R	5-11	193	11-15-03	.330	.413	.447	27	110	94	16	31	5	0	2	14	11	3	1	1	20	3	0	10.00	18.18
Rijo, Brayan	R-R	5-11	160	11-24-03	.215	.305	.290	34	107	93	11	20	5	1	0	7	11	1	2	0	31	5	1	10.28	28.97
Rogers, Jack	L-L	6-2	205	4-5-99	.125	.333	.125	3	12	8	2	1	0	0	0	2	3	0	0	1	3	0	0	25.00	25.00
Sanchez, Carlos	L-R	6-0	177	1-12-05	.214	.356	.300	21	88	70	10	15	3	0	1	11	16	0	1	1	24	2	1	18.18	27.27
Stafura, Sammy	R-R	6-0	188	11-15-04	.345	.449	.582	15	69	55	18	19	3	2	2	17	12	0	0	2	20	4	0	17.39	28.99
Torres, Jesus	R-R	6-0	160	10-2-02	.182	.280	.273	23	75	66	14	12	1	1	1	4	8	1	0	0	27	2	1	10.67	36.00

Pitching	B-T	Ht.	Wt.	DOB	W	L	ERA	G	GS	SV	IP	Hits	Runs	ER	HR	BB	SO	AVG	OBP	SLG	SO%	BB%	BF
Acuna, Jose	R-R	6-2	175	10-20-02	0	0	0.00	2	1	0	4	1	0	0	0	3	4	.077	.250	.077	25.00	18.75	16
Arellano, Joneiker	R-R	5-11	155	2-20-05	3	1	3.77	5	1	0	14	14	6	6	0	5	16	.275	.339	.373	26.67	8.33	60
Batista, Jonathan	R-R	6-3	195	2-28-02	3	4	7.30	12	4	0	37	50	36	30	5	18	46	.314	.394	.478	25.56	10.00	180
Blandino, Alex	R-R	6-0	190	11-6-92	1	0	3.86	2	0	0	2	1	1	1	0	5	1	.143	.500	.143	8.33	41.67	12
Braithwaite, Trey	R-R	6-3	220	9-23-97	0	0	1.80	5	1	1	5	4	1	1	0	1	5	.211	.250	.316	25.00	5.00	20
Byrne, Michael	R-R	6-3	205	4-16-97	0	0	0.00	1	0	0	1	0	0	0	0	0	2	.000	.000	.000	66.67	0.00	3
Campbell, Logan	R-R	6-2	205	7-22-99	1	1	1.29	4	0	1	7	7	5	1	0	3	8	.250	.389	.286	22.22	8.33	36
Cervantes, Edwin	L-L	6-3	159	9-6-04	2	1	9.89	15	1	0	24	37	27	26	2	15	31	.352	.426	.467	25.20	12.20	123
Davila, Vladimir	R-R	5-11	158	9-10-02	0	0	0.00	1	0	0	1	1	0	0	0	1	1	.250	.400	.750	20.00	20.00	5
Faile, John Michael	R-R	6-0	218	5-11-00	0	0	0.00	1	0	0	2	3	0	0	0	0	1	.333	.333	.333	11.11	0.00	9
Gaitan, Abraham	R-R	6-2	180	2-6-04	0	0	4.70	13	3	0	23	26	16	12	0	11	14	.280	.358	.387	12.96	10.19	108
Guevara, Khristian	L-L	6-3	150	8-24-04	2	1	4.85	12	2	1	30	37	18	16	7	14	17	.306	.393	.521	12.14	10.00	140
Gutierrez, Dualvert	R-R	6-0	185	1-25-01	0	1	11.57	3	3	0	5	8	6	6	1	1	6	.400	.409	.550	27.27	4.55	22
Herrera, Adrian	R-R	6-1	190	8-10-04	3	3	4.89	12	5	0	39	34	27	21	6	17	52	.241	.343	.468	31.14	10.18	167
Hollan, Hunter	L-L	6-5	200	3-5-02	0	1	6.00	1	1	0	3	4	3	2	0	4	0	.364	.533	.545	0.00	26.67	15
Lantigua, Lisnerkin	R-R	6-0	181	9-1-04	0	1	3.00	9	0	0	9	6	3	3	1	9	11	.214	.410	.393	28.21	23.08	39
Longstaff, Darcy	R-R	6-0	200	1-22-04	0	1	6.59	9	5	1	27	39	23	20	2	13	23	.345	.415	.496	17.69	10.00	130
Lopez, Jefferson	R-R	6-1	185	2-18-01	0	0	10.80	3	0	0	3	6	4	4	3	0	2	.400	.400	1.000	13.33	0.00	15
Lorduy, David	R-R	6-0	198	10-15-03	4	2	2.76	13	5	0	42	30	15	13	3	9	41	.197	.248	.309	24.85	5.45	165
Morellis, Luis	R-R	6-2	165	2-7-04	2	1	3.35	12	4	1	38	26	21	14	4	18	58	.190	.311	.314	36.02	11.18	161
Ortiz, JeanPierre	R-R	6-0	185	2-18-04	1	1	3.12	6	0	0	9	7	4	3	0	5	10	.219	.342	.313	26.32	13.16	38
Overton, Connor	L-R	6-0	205	7-24-93	1	1	3.86	6	4	0	7	4	4	3	1	2	7	.174	.296	.348	25.93	7.41	27
Payano, Nelfri	R-R	5-10	179	11-9-04	1	0	9.22	12	0	2	14	13	15	14	0	16	18	.245	.444	.264	25.00	22.22	72
Payero, Nick	R-R	6-2	200	6-21-00	0	0	3.38	2	0	0	8	6	3	3	1	2	10	.222	.267	.407	33.33	6.67	30
Pelio, Mason	R-R	6-3	230	7-15-00	0	0	0.00	2	2	0	5	1	0	0	0	3	4	.067	.263	.067	21.05	15.79	19
Pestka, Drew	R-R	6-5	225	5-18-04	1	1	2.25	3	0	0	4	4	1	1	0	0	6	.267	.313	.333	37.50	0.00	16
Polo, Juan	R-R	6-1	182	5-18-01	0	0	30.86	3	0	0	2	8	8	8	1	4	4	.571	.632	.857	21.05	21.05	19
Quintana, Ricardo	R-R	5-11	160	11-1-02	0	1	1.98	13	0	3	27	29	10	6	1	6	22	.261	.311	.324	18.49	5.04	119
Rijo, Brayan	R-R	5-11	160	11-24-03	0	1	5.40	1	0	0	2	3	2	1	0	0	0	.500	.429	.500	0.00	0.00	7
Sando, Nick	L-L	6-2	203	5-11-01	2	0	2.35	2	0	0	8	8	3	2	0	3	13	.276	.344	.310	39.39	9.09	33
Sanmartin, Reiver	L-L	6-2	160	4-15-96	0	0	0.00	2	2	0	2	1	0	0	0	0	1	.167	.286	.167	14.29	0.00	7
Scheffler, Dominic	L-L	6-4	196	7-27-04	1	2	7.62	12	6	0	28	25	25	24	1	33	42	.231	.428	.324	28.97	22.76	145
Schoenwetter, Cole	R-R	6-3	190	10-1-04	1	4	5.89	12	10	0	37	41	26	24	0	23	43	.289	.392	.394	25.15	13.45	171
Sheffield, Justus	L-L	5-10	224	5-13-96	1	0	0.00	2	0	0	3	2	0	0	0	1	6	.167	.231	.167	46.15	7.69	13
Starks, Gabe	R-R	6-1	230	12-26-01	1	0	2.30	8	0	0	16	13	4	4	2	3	21	.228	.267	.404	35.00	5.00	60

Fielding

C: Garcia 33, Puerta 20, Omana 9, Faile 3. **1B:** Chevalier 22, Reyes 22, Faile 15, Mount 4, Callahan 3. **2B:** Moon 40, Alcantara 12, Espinoza 11, McAfee 1. **3B:** Lin 32, Espinoza 15, Chevalier 8, Alcantara 7, Callahan 3, McAfee 2, Rijo 1. **SS:** Alcantara 24, Sanchez 19, Stafura 12, Lin 10. **LF:** Rijo 18, Isturiz 17, Leones 10, Davies 9, Torres 5, Chevalier 3, Hurtubise 2, Rogers 2, McAfee 1. **CF:** Henley 53, Leones 7, Rijo 1. **RF:** Davies 19, Torres 17, Leones 13, Rijo 11, Isturiz 2, Rogers 1, Espinoza 1, Hurtubise 1, Chevalier 1.

DSL REDS

ROOKIE

DOMINICAN SUMMER LEAGUE

Batting	B-T	Ht.	Wt.	DOB	AVG	OBP	SLG	G	PA	AB	R	H	2B	3B	HR	RBI	BB	HBP	SH	SF	SO	SB	CS	BB%	SO%
Abad, Pablo	R-R	6-2	165	11-5-05	.111	.273	.222	13	44	36	4	4	1	0	1	3	8	0	0	0	15	2	1	18.18	34.09
Buten, Anielson	R-R	5-9	155	9-22-05	.301	.384	.441	46	166	143	27	43	12	1	2	23	16	4	2	1	33	12	3	9.64	19.88
Cano, Ichiro	B-R	5-11	175	2-7-05	.241	.453	.315	21	75	54	9	13	2	1	0	7	20	1	0	0	16	6	1	26.67	21.33
Correa, Jesus	B-R	5-8	167	9-8-04	.232	.391	.261	28	88	69	12	16	2	0	0	7	17	1	1	0	18	10	2	19.32	20.45
Diaz, Brauli	B-R	6-0	149	1-23-06	.147	.326	.265	13	43	34	12	5	2	1	0	1	8	1	0	0	18	6	1	18.60	41.86
Gomes, Gabriel	R-R	5-9	170	3-31-04	.280	.429	.402	29	105	82	21	23	4	0	2	14	17	5	0	1	15	3	0	16.19	14.29
Jimenez, Hansel	R-R	6-1	179	12-5-06	.429	.529	.500	5	17	14	6	6	1	0	0	2	3	0	0	0	4	1	0	17.65	23.53
Joseph, Brayan	B-R	5-10	145	9-22-05	.183	.286	.254	23	84	71	6	13	5	0	0	9	11	0	0	2	21	6	1	13.10	25.00
Legito, Qyshawn	R-R	5-10	181	11-13-05	.258	.465	.452	12	43	31	11	8	0	0	2	7	10	2	0	0	11	2	0	23.26	25.58
Mora, Angelo	R-R	5-11	150	6-10-05	.313	.385	.453	37	143	128	25	40	9	0	3	21	9	6	0	0	24	3	0	6.29	16.78
Morillo, Jirvin	B-R	5-11	177	1-10-07	.152	.370	.212	12	46	33	5	5	2	0	0	2	12	0	0	1	4	1	2	26.09	8.70
Reyes, Adrian	B-R	6-1	215	11-26-04	.174	.330	.304	34	115	92	15	16	3	0	3	10	21	1	0	1	39	0	1	18.26	33.91
Romero, Yael	L-R	5-11	175	10-15-05	.292	.482	.433	45	170	120	29	35	12	1	1	16	37	10	0	3	24	2	1	21.76	14.12
Sabino, Jose	L-R	6-0	150	6-18-07	.171	.302	.200	13	43	35	4	6	1	0	0	5	7	0	0	1	10	0	1	16.28	23.26
Sanchez, Adolfo	L-L	6-1	185	9-19-06	.207	.338	.310	21	71	58	6	12	2	2	0	4	11	1	0	1	24	3	1	15.49	33.80
Soriano, Yeycol	L-L	6-0	150	9-3-05	.261	.363	.350	51	215	180	28	47	9	2	1	24	27	4	0	4	40	16	5	12.56	18.60
Torres, Rafhlmil	B-R	5-11	150	9-5-05	.204	.333	.306	47	177	147	26	30	7	1	2	19	25	4	0	1	16	13	6	14.12	9.04
Valencia, Anthuan	R-R	5-8	177	10-14-04	.255	.333	.376	47	189	165	26	42	6	1	4	30	17	4	0	3	29	19	6	8.99	15.34
Zambrano, Diorland	R-R	5-10	168	11-2-06	.217	.321	.348	16	54	46	9	10	0	0	2	3	6	1	1	0	5	2	1	11.11	9.26

Pitching	B-T	Ht.	Wt.	DOB	W	L	ERA	G	GS	SV	IP	Hits	Runs	ER	HR	BB	SO	AVG	OBP	SLG	SO%	BB%	BF
Aguero, Erlin	R-R	5-10	154	9-12-04	1	1	0.82	6	1	1	11	9	3	1	0	6	4	.243	.370	.297	8.33	12.50	48
Almeida, Jhan	R-R	6-3	185	4-29-05	4	0	1.13	8	0	1	16	11	5	2	0	8	12	.183	.290	.183	17.39	11.59	69
Cabeza, Johan	R-R	6-0	155	7-25-06	0	0	4.38	6	3	0	12	14	6	6	0	6	8	.292	.382	.375	14.29	10.71	56
Colina, Jesus	R-R	5-11	170	3-21-05	3	1	3.72	14	9	0	46	41	25	19	3	12	31	.229	.289	.318	15.98	6.19	194
Colmenares, Mauricio	R-R	6-0	170	11-4-03	4	0	1.40	11	7	1	39	25	10	6	0	10	25	.188	.262	.218	16.79	7.14	149
De La Cruz, Ariel	L-L	6-2	165	4-25-06	5	1	4.91	15	0	2	18	14	10	10	2	12	21	.206	.333	.338	25.61	14.63	82
Diaz, Oneil	R-R	6-3	198	9-10-05	3	0	1.24	14	2	2	29	13	6	4	1	22	27	.138	.331	.223	22.31	18.18	121
Lopez, Christian	L-L	6-2	207	7-6-06	0	0	2.13	3	3	0	13	6	3	3	0	1	16	.136	.156	.227	35.56	2.22	45
Lopez, Josue	R-R	6-2	175	2-6-02	0	0	0.00	2	0	1	2	0	0	0	0	5	2	.000	.500	.000	20.00	50.00	10
Mendez, Franyer	R-R	6-1	193	12-15-06	0	0	5.87	4	4	0	8	9	5	5	1	7	9	.310	.447	.483	23.68	18.42	38
Merite, Ryjeteri	L-L	6-3	150	12-16-05	0	0	2.45	3	3	0	4	3	1	1	0	2	4	.214	.313	.214	25.00	12.50	16
Pena, Ayendy	R-R	6-1	172	3-16-04	3	2	1.54	14	0	1	23	19	7	4	0	9	23	.221	.309	.233	23.47	9.18	98
Perez, Samuel	R-R	6-1	178	8-3-04	3	2	2.60	12	9	0	45	32	13	13	2	12	36	.198	.264	.284	20.22	6.74	178
Prodanovic, Nicola	R-R	6-0	190	4-5-04	2	3	10.20	12	0	0	15	11	19	17	0	24	13	.216	.506	.275	15.66	28.92	83
Salazar, Sebastian	R-R	5-11	168	12-27-05	0	2	14.21	5	4	0	6	9	10	10	1	4	9	.321	.457	.536	25.71	11.43	35
Salgado, Bryan	R-R	5-10	170	1-16-07	0	1	1.27	15	0	7	21	15	4	3	0	10	24	.203	.294	.257	28.24	11.76	85
Solano, Mendry	R-R	6-3	182	10-22-03	1	0	5.59	6	0	0	10	8	6	6	0	8	7	.250	.405	.313	16.67	19.05	42
Torres, Stharlin	R-R	6-0	182	6-19-06	2	1	1.49	13	10	0	54	32	11	9	0	13	49	.178	.234	.239	24.75	6.57	198
Villa, Sergio	R-R	6-2	155	10-20-05	0	2	6.23	14	0	0	22	23	16	15	0	10	14	.284	.366	.395	14.74	10.53	95
Villafana, Deivi	R-R	6-4	175	5-25-03	1	0	1.93	3	0	0	5	7	1	1	0	0	5	.368	.368	.474	26.32	0.00	19
Zambrano, Carlos	R-R	6-3	170	6-9-05	5	2	3.65	12	0	0	25	22	20	10	1	16	18	.237	.368	.376	15.65	13.91	115

Fielding

C: Mora 31, Gomes 12, Morillo 8, Legito 6. **1B:** Romero 39, Gomes 10, Zambrano 5, Diaz 3, Reyes 1. **2B:** Valencia 34, Buten 15, Torres 4, Zambrano 2, Diaz 1. **3B:** Cano 20, Joseph 15, Valencia 9, Diaz 5, Zambrano 3, Jimenez 2, Buten 2. **SS:** Torres 43, Joseph 8, Jimenez 3, Zambrano 2. **LF:** Buten 26, Correa 16, Abad 5, Sabino 5, Reyes 4, Sanchez 1, Soriano 1. **CF:** Soriano 43, Sanchez 9, Correa 3. **RF:** Reyes 20, Sanchez 10, Abad 8, Soriano 7, Sabino 6, Correa 6, Buten 1.

DSL ROJOS

ROOKIE

DOMINICAN SUMMER LEAGUE

Batting	B-T	Ht.	Wt.	DOB	AVG	OBP	SLG	G	PA	AB	R	H	2B	3B	HR	RBI	BB	HBP	SH	SF	SO	SB	CS	BB%	SO%
Brown, Juan	R-R	6-3	185	7-5-07	.364	.462	.455	11	39	33	4	12	1	1	0	3	4	2	0	0	12	4	0	10.26	30.77
Calzado, Yojanser	B-R	5-11	158	4-17-07	.226	.374	.285	45	172	137	30	31	2	3	0	13	31	2	1	1	44	27	5	18.02	25.58
Cano, Ichiro	B-R	5-11	175	2-7-05	.313	.408	.425	25	98	80	10	25	6	0	1	24	14	1	0	3	14	5	3	14.29	14.29
Diaz, Brauli	B-R	6-0	149	1-23-06	.138	.286	.138	15	36	29	6	4	0	0	0	1	5	1	1	0	17	4	0	13.89	47.22
Jaime, Brandon	R-R	5-9	184	11-12-04	.259	.349	.352	24	65	54	10	14	2	0	1	7	6	2	2	1	8	0	0	9.23	12.31
Joseph, Brayan	B-R	5-10	145	9-22-05	.157	.232	.157	18	56	51	4	8	0	0	0	5	5	0	0	0	15	3	1	8.93	26.79
Mariano, Naibel	R-R	6-3	182	9-6-06	.188	.328	.242	49	201	165	28	31	4	1	1	22	27	8	0	1	54	3	5	13.43	26.87
Martinez, Jaset	L-L	5-10	170	12-15-06	.261	.405	.428	45	173	138	31	36	11	3	2	24	30	4	0	1	25	2	0	17.34	14.45
Martinus, Shendrion	R-R	5-10	161	12-23-06	.260	.345	.290	30	113	100	14	26	3	0	0	13	9	4	0	0	27	3	1	7.96	23.89
Morillo, Jirvin	B-R	5-11	177	1-10-07	.296	.473	.543	27	110	81	26	24	12	1	2	21	28	0	0	1	17	2	0	25.45	15.45
Nunez, Pablo	L-L	5-10	145	10-23-06	.257	.371	.343	46	171	140	28	36	6	3	0	16	24	3	1	3	16	11	2	14.04	9.36
Revierre, Peson	B-R	6-0	159	12-18-06	.270	.411	.391	40	146	115	24	31	7	2	1	27	24	5	0	2	21	7	1	16.44	14.38
Richardson, Riangelo	R-R	5-9	159	7-1-07	.125	.276	.240	39	127	104	17	13	6	0	2	13	19	3	0	1	41	11	2	14.96	32.28
Rojas, Gilberto	R-R	6-1	165	1-19-05	.231	.412	.231	6	17	13	4	3	0	0	0	2	4	0	0	0	3	0	0	23.53	17.65
Rosillo, Emdys	L-R	6-0	170	8-4-06	.283	.443	.304	18	61	46	11	13	1	0	0	9	13	1	0	1	6	0	0	21.31	9.84
Sabino, Jose	L-R	6-0	150	6-18-07	.235	.355	.255	18	62	51	7	12	1	0	0	6	9	1	0	1	14	2	1	14.52	22.58
Sanchez, Adolfo	L-L	6-1	185	9-19-06	.222	.368	.370	24	106	81	17	18	4	1	2	14	19	2	0	4	36	8	1	17.92	33.96
Waterfort, Nayerich	R-R	5-10	154	3-30-06	.125	.333	.188	23	63	48	7	6	3	0	0	2	9	6	0	0	16	3	2	14.29	25.40
Zambrano, Diorland	R-R	5-10	168	11-2-06	.347	.452	.449	16	63	49	11	17	2	0	1	14	10	1	1	2	5	0	2	15.87	7.94

Pitching	B-T	Ht.	Wt.	DOB	W	L	ERA	G	GS	SV	IP	Hits	Runs	ER	HR	BB	SO	AVG	OBP	SLG	SO%	BB%	BF
Aguero, Erlin	R-R	5-10	154	9-12-04	0	2	6.75	7	0	1	11	12	9	8	1	10	6	.293	.473	.463	10.91	18.18	55
Aguilera, Dony	R-R	5-11	154	9-18-06	1	1	2.56	13	11	0	46	32	16	13	0	12	31	.196	.263	.245	17.22	6.67	180
Aquino, Anthony	R-R	6-2	180	4-25-06	1	0	15.00	6	0	0	6	10	11	10	0	7	11	.357	.486	.500	29.73	18.92	37
Burgos, Deivid	R-R	6-2	190	4-19-05	1	2	7.71	16	0	0	21	26	25	18	0	21	20	.295	.447	.375	17.54	18.42	114
Castillo, Anderson	R-R	6-2	180	10-12-04	0	0	9.00	2	0	0	2	1	2	2	0	4	0	.200	.545	.400	0.00	36.36	11
Castillo, Moises	R-R	5-10	172	5-23-05	0	3	3.22	11	9	0	36	28	14	13	3	14	40	.217	.327	.349	26.67	9.33	150
Colmenares, Mauricio	R-R	6-0	170	11-4-03	0	0	7.20	3	0	0	5	7	4	4	0	2	0	.350	.375	.400	0.00	8.33	24
Diaz, Jorge	L-L	6-4	187	7-14-07	0	1	19.29	9	0	0	7	5	16	15	0	17	6	.238	.545	.286	13.33	37.78	45
Gil, Michael	R-R	6-2	170	3-14-05	1	1	12.00	8	0	0	9	13	15	12	0	14	8	.342	.519	.395	15.09	26.42	53
Gonzalez, Irvin	R-R	5-10	150	6-9-06	1	4	6.07	14	12	0	43	54	30	29	2	19	27	.314	.379	.465	13.85	9.74	195
Jaime, Brandon	R-R	5-9	184	11-12-04	0	0	0.00	1	0	0	2	1	0	0	0	0	0	.143	.143	.429	0.00	0.00	7
Lopez, Christian	L-L	6-2	207	7-6-06	2	1	2.08	10	7	1	35	24	9	8	0	13	48	.186	.276	.202	33.10	8.97	145
Lopez, Josue	R-R	6-2	175	2-6-02	1	2	7.43	8	0	0	13	9	13	11	0	20	9	.191	.486	.234	12.16	27.03	74
Marchan, Manuel	R-R	6-3	165	3-28-07	3	3	8.63	14	1	1	24	34	27	23	4	19	19	.347	.450	.541	15.83	15.83	120
Meza, Carlos	R-R	6-4	209	3-2-04	2	1	10.93	13	0	0	14	17	21	17	1	24	14	.298	.535	.404	16.28	27.91	86
Nino, Dulger	R-R	6-1	185	12-29-04	4	2	5.46	16	0	3	28	35	22	17	1	17	22	.310	.409	.416	16.42	12.69	134
Palacio, Jesus	R-R	6-6	190	8-25-04	1	3	7.54	13	2	0	23	31	29	19	0	14	10	.333	.434	.409	8.77	12.28	114
Pimentel, Luis	R-R	6-2	175	8-11-03	2	0	0.00	9	0	0	14	8	3	0	0	4	15	.154	.241	.173	25.86	6.90	58
Prodanovic, Nicola	R-R	6-0	190	4-5-04	0	0	0.00	1	0	0	1	0	0	0	0	2	0	.000	.400	.000	0.00	40.00	5
Richardson, Riangelo	R-R	5-9	159	7-1-07	0	0	0.00	1	0	0	0	0	0	0	0	0	0	.000	.000	.000	0.00	0.00	1
Salazar, Sebastian	R-R	5-11	168	12-27-05	0	0	0.00	1	0	0	2	2	0	0	0	0	3	.250	.333	.375	33.33	0.00	9
Solano, Mendry	R-R	6-3	182	10-22-03	1	4	13.06	9	1	1	10	13	18	15	0	13	10	.310	.508	.476	15.38	20.00	65
Talavera, Enmanuel	R-R	6-2	170	10-7-05	3	0	2.47	13	10	0	47	34	13	13	3	9	44	.201	.240	.290	24.31	4.97	181
Torres, Stharlin	R-R	6-0	182	6-19-06	0	0	9.00	1	0	0	2	3	2	2	0	0	2	.375	.333	.750	22.22	0.00	9
Villafana, Deivi	R-R	6-4	175	5-25-03	1	0	6.75	2	0	0	4	7	4	3	0	1	4	.412	.444	.471	22.22	5.56	18
Waterfort, Nayerich	R-R	5-10	154	3-30-06	0	0	0.00	1	0	1	1	0	0	0	0	1	0	.000	.250	.000	0.00	25.00	4
Yepes, Luis	R-R	6-4	180	3-24-06	0	0	0.00	2	2	0	2	4	0	0	0	0	0	.500	.500	.625	0.00	0.00	8

Fielding

C: Jaime 20, Morillo 20, Rosillo 18, Rojas 3. **1B:** Martinez 40, Cano 8, Diaz 8, Zambrano 2, Waterfort 1. **2B:** Martinus 27, Waterfort 15, Richardson 12, Diaz 1, Joseph 1, Zambrano 1. **3B:** Cano 17, Richardson 13, Joseph 9, Zambrano 8, Brown 8, Diaz 6, Mariano 1. **SS:** Mariano 42, Joseph 8, Richardson 4, Waterfort 1. **LF:** Revierre 29, Nunez 21, Calzado 4, Sabino 2. **CF:** Calzado 29, Sanchez 22, Nunez 5. **RF:** Nunez 18, Sabino 15, Calzado 12, Revierre 10, Martinez 1.

Cleveland Guardians

SEASON SYNOPSIS: First-year manager Stephen Vogt brought the energy and helped tweak the offense, and the Guardians produced one of the greatest bullpen seasons ever to return to the top of the American League Central for the second time in three seasons. "Guards Ball" won one playoff series but lost to the Yankees in a dramatic but short five-game League Championship Series.

HIGH POINT: Cleveland won nine in a row in May, its best month of the year. But the high point was the Game 3 LCS win against the Yankees, when Jhonkensy Noel tied the game with a two-run, pinch-hit homer, followed by David Fry's walk-off 10th-inning homer in the 7-5 victory. Fry, who earned his first all-star nod with a big first half, also had a game-winning homer in Game Four of the Division Series against the Tigers.

LOW POINT: Emmanuel Clase led MLB in win probability added during a 4-2, 0.61 season, leading the American League for the third straight season in saves (47). But the Tigers and Yankees got to him, as he gave up eight runs in eight postseason innings, while other consistent options such as Hunter Gaddis (1.57 ERA in 78 games) and Cade Smith (1.91 in 74 games) was hit by the Yankees as well. Gaddis gave up the series-ending 10th-inning homer to Juan Soto, while Giancarlo Stanton tagged Smith for a three-run homer in a Game 4 loss.

NOTABLE ROOKIES: Smith, 25, went 6-1, 1.91 with 103 strikeouts, 17 walks and only one home run allowed in 75.1 innings. Former top prospect Brayan Rocchio was the team's main shortstop and hit well in the postseason after a middling .614 regular-season OPS. Noel hit just .218 but added 13 homers while shifting to right field, while DH/1B Kyle Manzardo, versatile utilityman Daniel Schneemann and Angel Martinez—shifted from shortstop to outfield to fill a hole—all contributed. Lefties Joey Cantillo (eight starts) and Erik Sabrowski (eight relief outings) both earned postseason innings.

KEY TRANSACTIONS: The Guardians made a key midseason trade, packaging prospect lefty Alex Clemmey to the Nationals for Lane Thomas. A crucial bat against lefthanded pitchers, Thomas settled in as the regular center fielder and hit just .209 but had two homers and nine RBIs in the ALDS against Detroit. Another trade brought in Alex Cobb from the Giants, but free agent lefty Matt Boyd, returning from Tommy John surgery, was a bigger late-season rotation boost.

OPENING DAY PAYROLL: $93,333,629 (28th)

PLAYERS OF THE YEAR

MAJOR LEAGUE

Jose Ramirez
3B
.279/.335/.537
39 HR, 41 SB
114 R, 118 RBIs

MINOR LEAGUE

Jaison Chourio
OF
(A)
.270/.414/.398
44 SB, 86 BB

ORGANIZATION LEADERS

Batting		*Qualifiers
MAJORS		
* AVG	Steven Kwan	.292
* OPS	Jose Ramirez	.872
HR	Jose Ramirez	39
RBI	Jose Ramirez	118
MINORS		
* AVG	Angel Genao, Lynchburg/Lake County	.330
* OBP	Cooper Ingle, Lake County/Akron	.397
* SLG	Johnathan Rodriguez, Columbus	.540
* OPS	Johnathan Rodriguez, Columbus	.930
R	Juan Brito, Columbus	92
H	Angel Genao, Lake County/Lynchburg	148
TB	Juan Brito, Columbus	244
2B	Juan Brito, Columbus	40
3B	Wuilfredo Antunez, Lynchburg	9
HR	Johnathan Rodriguez, Columbus	29
RBI	Johnathan Rodriguez, Columbus	94
BB	Juan Brito, Columbus	88
SO	Johnathan Rodriguez, Columbus	128
SB	Jaison Chourio, Lynchburg	44

Pitching		#Qualifiers
MAJORS		
W	Ben Lively	13
# ERA	Tanner Bibee	3.47
SO	Tanner Bibee	187
SV	Emmanuel Clase	47
MINORS		
W	Austin Peterson, Akron/Lake County	14
L	Alonzo Richardson, Lake County/Lynchburg	8
# ERA	Matthew Wilkinson, Lake County/Lynchburg	1.90
G	Tanner Burns, Columbus	51
GS	3-tied	27
SV	Magnus Ellerts, Akron/Lake County	13
IP	Austin Peterson, Akron/Lake County	160
BB	Will Dion, Columbus	54
SO	Matthew Wilkinson, Lake County/Lynchburg	174
# AVG	Matthew Wilkinson, Lake County/Lynchburg	.169

CLEVELAND GUARDIANS

2024 PERFORMANCE

General Manager: Mike Chernoff. **Farm Director:** James Harris. **Scouting Director:** Scott Barnsby.

Class	Team	League	W	L	PCT	Finish	Manager
Majors	Cleveland Guardians	American	92	69	.571	2 (15)	Stephen Vogt
Triple-A	Columbus Clippers	International	80	68	.541	3 (20)	Andy Tracy
Double-A	Akron RubberDucks	Eastern	80	58	.580	1 (12)	Greg DiCenzo
High-A	Lake County Captains	Midwest	77	53	.592	1 (12)	Omir Santos
Low-A	Lynchburg Hillcats	Carolina	67	62	.519	6 (12)	Jordan Smith
Rookie	ACL Guardians	Arizona Complex	27	33	.450	11 (15)	Yan Rivera
Rookie	DSL Guardians Blue	Dominican	26	24	.520	21 (51)	Jonathan Lopez
Rookie	DSL Guardians Red	Dominican	35	19	.648	9 (51)	Juan De La Cruz
Overall 2024 Minor League Record			**392**	**317**	**.553**	**2nd (30)**	

ORGANIZATION STATISTICS

CLEVELAND GUARDIANS

AMERICAN LEAGUE

Batting	B-T	Ht.	Wt.	DOB	AVG	OBP	SLG	G	PA	AB	R	H	2B	3B	HR	RBI	BB	HBP	SH	SF	SO	SB	CS	BB%	SO%
Arias, Gabriel	R-R	6-1	217	4-20-22	.222	.255	.353	53	161	153	15	34	9	1	3	15	6	1	0	1	53	5	2	3.72	32.92
Brennan, Will	L-L	6-0	200	2-2-98	.264	.309	.388	114	353	330	37	87	13	2	8	30	19	3	0	1	48	4	2	5.38	13.60
Florial, Estevan	L-R	6-1	195	11-25-97	.173	.264	.367	36	111	98	11	17	6	2	3	11	11	1	1	0	41	2	1	9.91	36.94
Freeman, Tyler	R-R	6-0	190	5-21-99	.209	.305	.321	118	383	330	48	69	14	1	7	32	28	19	3	3	53	11	6	7.31	13.84
Fry, David	R-R	6-0	215	11-20-95	.263	.356	.448	122	392	335	44	88	18	1	14	51	42	9	0	4	84	4	1	10.71	21.43
Gimenez, Andres	L-R	5-11	161	9-4-98	.252	.298	.340	152	633	583	64	147	22	1	9	63	26	15	3	6	97	30	5	4.11	15.32
Hedges, Austin	R-R	6-1	223	8-18-92	.152	.203	.220	66	146	132	12	20	3	0	2	15	6	3	3	2	50	2	0	4.11	34.25
Kwan, Steven	L-L	5-9	170	9-5-97	.292	.368	.425	122	540	480	83	140	16	3	14	44	53	5	2	0	51	12	5	9.81	9.44
Laureano, Ramon	R-R	5-11	203	7-15-94	.143	.265	.229	31	83	70	7	10	3	0	1	4	7	5	0	1	32	3	1	8.43	38.55
Manzardo, Kyle	L-R	6-0	205	7-18-00	.234	.282	.421	53	156	145	11	34	12	0	5	15	9	1	0	1	41	0	0	5.77	26.28
Martinez, Angel	B-R	6-0	200	1-27-02	.232	.298	.338	43	169	151	16	35	7	0	3	11	15	0	1	2	33	3	1	8.88	19.53
Naylor, Bo	L-R	6-0	205	2-21-00	.201	.264	.350	123	389	354	39	71	10	2	13	39	29	2	2	2	122	6	3	7.46	31.36
Naylor, Josh	L-L	5-11	250	6-22-97	.243	.320	.456	152	633	563	84	137	27	0	31	108	58	7	0	4	105	6	2	9.16	16.59
Noel, Jhonkensy	R-R	6-3	250	7-15-01	.218	.288	.486	67	198	179	25	39	7	1	13	28	13	5	0	1	63	0	0	6.57	31.82
Ramirez, Jose	B-R	5-9	190	9-17-92	.279	.335	.537	158	682	620	114	173	39	2	39	118	54	1	0	6	82	41	7	7.92	12.02
Rocchio, Brayan	B-R	5-10	170	1-13-01	.206	.298	.316	143	442	383	50	79	18	0	8	36	44	8	2	5	90	10	6	9.95	20.36
Rodriguez, Johnathan	R-R	6-3	224	11-4-99	.129	.325	.161	13	40	31	6	4	1	0	0	5	9	0	0	0	14	0	0	22.50	35.00
Schneemann, Daniel	L-R	6-0	185	1-23-97	.218	.303	.368	73	221	193	17	42	10	2	5	22	25	0	0	3	70	3	2	11.31	31.67
Straw, Myles	R-R	5-10	178	10-17-94	.250	.250	.250	7	4	4	2	1	0	0	0	0	0	0	0	0	0	2	0	0.00	0.00
Tena, Jose	L-R	5-11	195	3-20-01	.000	.000	.000	3	4	4	0	0	0	0	0	0	0	0	0	0	2	0	0	0.00	50.00
Thomas, Lane	R-R	6-0	198	8-23-95	.209	.267	.390	53	187	172	23	36	10	0	7	23	12	2	0	1	65	4	2	6.42	34.76

Pitching	B-T	Ht.	Wt.	DOB	W	L	ERA	G	GS	SV	IP	Hits	Runs	ER	HR	BB	SO	AVG	OBP	SLG	SO%	BB%	BF
Allen, Logan	R-L	6-0	190	9-5-98	8	5	5.73	20	20	0	97	113	63	62	22	41	79	.295	.367	.551	18.29	9.49	432
Avila, Pedro	R-R	5-11	210	1-14-97	5	1	3.25	50	0	1	75	68	30	27	7	30	73	.243	.318	.361	22.96	9.43	318
Barlow, Scott	R-R	6-3	210	12-18-92	3	3	4.25	63	0	2	55	44	27	26	6	31	68	.216	.328	.358	28.22	12.86	241
Beede, Tyler	R-R	6-2	216	5-23-93	1	0	8.36	13	0	0	14	16	14	13	2	9	18	.296	.418	.500	26.47	13.24	68
Bibee, Tanner	R-R	6-2	205	3-5-99	12	8	3.47	31	31	0	174	150	70	67	22	44	187	.230	.285	.406	26.34	6.20	710
Bieber, Shane	R-R	6-3	200	5-31-95	2	0	0.00	2	2	0	12	10	0	0	0	1	20	.227	.244	.318	44.44	2.22	45
Boyd, Matthew	L-L	6-3	223	2-2-91	2	2	2.72	8	8	0	40	32	16	12	4	13	46	.213	.283	.347	27.71	7.83	166
Cantillo, Joey	L-L	6-4	225	12-18-99	2	4	4.89	9	8	0	39	35	22	21	6	15	44	.238	.307	.435	26.99	9.20	163
Carrasco, Carlos	R-R	6-4	224	3-21-87	3	10	5.64	21	21	0	104	112	68	65	19	33	89	.276	.336	.505	19.91	7.38	447
Clase, Emmanuel	R-R	6-2	206	3-18-98	4	2	0.61	74	0	47	74	39	10	5	2	10	66	.154	.190	.202	24.44	3.70	270
Cobb, Alex	R-R	6-3	205	10-7-87	2	1	2.76	3	3	0	16	14	7	5	1	3	10	.241	.274	.345	16.13	4.84	62
Curry, Xzavion	R-R	6-0	195	7-27-98	0	2	5.84	7	4	0	25	29	17	16	5	5	15	.282	.315	.544	13.89	4.63	108
Gaddis, Hunter	R-R	6-6	260	4-9-98	6	3	1.57	78	0	0	75	43	16	13	4	14	66	.166	.219	.282	23.74	5.04	278
Gillispie, Connor	R-R	5-11	185	11-10-97	0	0	2.25	3	0	0	8	4	2	2	0	5	8	.154	.281	.231	25.00	15.63	32
Gose, Anthony	L-L	6-0	200	8-10-90	0	0	10.38	3	0	0	4	9	5	5	2	1	4	.429	.455	.905	18.18	4.55	22
Hedges, Austin	R-R	6-1	223	8-18-92	0	0	0.00	1	0	0	2	0	0	0	0	1	0	.000	.167	.000	0.00	16.67	6
Hentges, Sam	L-L	6-6	245	7-18-96	0	0	3.04	25	0	0	24	18	8	8	3	5	27	.212	.256	.388	29.67	5.49	91
Herrin, Tim	L-L	6-6	230	10-8-96	5	1	1.92	75	0	0	66	39	17	14	2	25	68	.173	.270	.240	26.46	9.73	257
Howard, Spencer	R-R	6-3	210	7-28-96	0	1	9.00	2	1	0	5	11	8	5	3	3	6	.407	.467	.741	20.00	10.00	30
Lively, Ben	R-R	6-4	235	3-5-92	13	10	3.81	29	29	0	151	139	67	64	23	49	118	.241	.305	.419	18.67	7.75	632
McCaughan, Darren	R-R	6-1	200	3-18-96	0	0	9.00	2	0	0	6	9	6	6	2	6	1	.391	.500	.696	3.33	20.00	30
McKenzie, Triston	R-R	6-5	165	8-2-97	3	5	5.11	16	16	0	76	69	46	43	19	49	74	.240	.351	.479	21.76	14.41	340
Morgan, Eli	R-R	5-10	190	5-13-96	3	0	1.93	32	0	0	42	30	11	9	4	11	34	.197	.255	.336	20.36	6.59	167
Parsons, Wes	R-R	6-5	206	9-6-92	0	0	0.00	2	0	0	4	4	0	0	0	0	5	.267	.267	.267	33.33	0.00	15
Sabrowski, Erik	R-L	6-4	235	10-31-97	0	0	0.00	8	0	1	13	6	0	0	0	4	19	.140	.213	.163	40.43	8.51	47
Sandlin, Nick	R-R	5-11	175	1-10-97	8	0	3.75	68	1	1	58	46	29	24	12	27	68	.222	.325	.435	27.64	10.98	246
Smith, Cade	R-R	6-5	230	5-9-99	6	1	1.91	74	0	1	75	51	16	16	1	17	103	.190	.246	.280	35.64	5.88	289
Strzelecki, Peter	R-R	6-2	216	10-24-94	0	0	2.31	10	0	0	12	11	3	3	1	3	9	.256	.319	.395	19.15	6.38	47
Walters, Andrew	R-R	6-4	220	12-8-00	1	0	0.00	9	1	0	9	1	1	0	0	5	6	.038	.188	.077	18.75	15.63	32
Williams, Gavin	L-R	6-6	250	7-26-99	3	10	4.86	16	16	0	76	72	42	41	7	32	79	.246	.323	.396	23.80	9.64	332

Fielding

Catcher	PCT	G	PO	A	E	DP	PB
Fry	1.000	23	129	2	0	0	0
Hedges	.993	65	423	15	3	2	0
Naylor	.994	115	894	36	6	4	7

First Base	PCT	G	PO	A	E	DP
Arias	1.000	4	11	4	0	2
Fry	.983	20	106	9	2	7
Manzardo	1.000	6	13	2	0	1
Naylor	.992	137	1008	69	9	110
Noel	1.000	9	33	5	0	1

Second Base	PCT	G	PO	A	E	DP
Arias	.885	6	7	16	3	1
Freeman	1.000	6	4	9	0	2
Gimenez	.986	152	233	396	9	93
Martinez	.500	1	0	1	1	0
Schneemann	1.000	6	2	9	0	2

Third Base	PCT	G	PO	A	E	DP
Arias	.960	20	16	32	2	2
Freeman	1.000	8	1	7	0	0
Fry	1.000	4	0	1	0	0
Martinez	.875	3	2	5	1	0
Ramirez	.971	126	99	207	9	23
Schneemann	.963	17	8	18	1	1
Tena	.667	2	2	0	1	0

Shortstop	PCT	G	PO	A	E	DP
Arias	.980	15	17	31	1	7
Freeman	.882	10	7	8	2	2
Rocchio	.974	142	166	284	12	75
Schneemann	.918	32	17	39	5	8

Outfield	PCT	G	PO	A	E	DP
Thomas	.970	61	94	2	3	0
Florial	.973	26	35	1	1	0
Martinez	.985	43	64	1	1	0
Brennan	.988	106	157	2	2	0
Freeman	.995	97	193	8	1	2
Kwan	.995	114	205	9	1	3
Arias	1.000	8	6	0	0	0
Fry	1.000	20	30	2	0	1
Laureano	1.000	35	52	5	0	0
Noel	1.000	55	94	2	0	1
Rodriguez	1.000	11	12	1	0	0
Schneemann	1.000	36	62	2	0	1
Straw	1.000	5	4	0	0	0

COLUMBUS CLIPPERS — *TRIPLE-A*

INTERNATIONAL LEAGUE

Batting	B-T	Ht.	Wt.	DOB	AVG	OBP	SLG	G	PA	AB	R	H	2B	3B	HR	RBI	BB	HBP	SH	SF	SO	SB	CS	BB%	SO%
Arias, Gabriel	R-R	6-1	217	2-27-00	.317	.360	.545	43	178	167	24	53	10	5	6	20	8	3	0	0	40	11	0	4.49	22.47
Brennan, Will	L-L	6-0	200	2-2-98	.371	.421	.571	9	39	35	7	13	4	0	1	6	2	1	0	0	8	4	0	5.13	20.51
Brito, Juan	B-R	5-11	162	9-24-01	.256	.365	.443	144	652	551	92	141	40	0	21	84	88	8	2	3	105	13	5	13.50	16.10
Cairo, Christian	R-R	5-8	170	6-11-01	.233	.355	.314	69	257	210	34	49	5	3	2	30	40	2	1	4	58	12	4	15.56	22.57
Cedrola, Lorenzo	R-R	5-8	152	1-12-98	.275	.350	.396	30	103	91	13	25	6	1	1	10	8	3	0	1	16	9	1	7.77	15.53
DeLauter, Chase	L-L	6-4	235	10-8-01	.304	.407	.739	6	27	23	4	7	4	0	2	7	4	0	0	0	2	0	0	14.81	7.41
Delgado, Raynel	L-R	6-1	200	4-4-00	.275	.365	.426	93	345	298	41	82	14	2	9	44	38	4	5	0	85	22	8	11.01	24.64
Donovan, Joe	R-R	5-9	180	1-20-99	.000	.000	.000	1	1	1	0	0	0	0	0	0	0	0	0	0	0	0	0	0.00	0.00
Fascia, Zac	L-R	6-0	225	9-15-98	.250	.250	.625	2	8	8	1	2	0	0	1	2	0	0	0	0	1	0	0	0.00	12.50
Florial, Estevan	L-R	6-1	195	11-25-97	.213	.320	.371	64	231	197	34	42	4	0	9	30	30	2	0	2	72	22	4	12.99	31.17
Freeman, Tyler	R-R	6-0	190	5-21-99	.417	.500	.667	6	28	24	3	10	3	0	1	4	2	2	0	0	3	3	0	7.14	10.71
Kwan, Steven	L-L	5-9	170	9-5-97	.200	.429	.200	2	7	5	3	1	0	0	0	1	2	0	0	0	0	1	0	28.57	0.00
Lavastida, Bryan	R-R	6-0	200	11-27-98	.232	.334	.387	87	345	297	46	69	18	2	8	42	37	9	1	1	79	27	5	10.72	22.90
Manzardo, Kyle	L-R	6-0	205	7-18-00	.267	.398	.548	83	364	292	65	70	20	1	20	49	61	6	0	5	67	3	1	16.76	18.41
Martinez, Angel	B-R	6-0	200	1-27-02	.274	.356	.456	55	249	215	36	59	16	1	7	27	25	4	2	3	40	5	4	10.04	16.06
Noel, Jhonkensy	R-R	6-3	250	7-15-01	.295	.359	.578	65	284	258	41	76	15	2	18	59	19	7	0	0	60	1	0	6.69	21.13
Nunez, Dom	L-R	5-8	212	1-17-95	.202	.330	.339	68	263	218	33	44	11	2	5	19	42	0	2	1	79	1	0	15.97	30.04
Pries, Micah	L-R	6-3	210	2-27-98	.227	.299	.366	68	264	238	34	54	7	1	8	34	21	4	0	1	63	4	3	7.95	23.86
Ramirez, Micael	R-R	5-9	170	6-8-99	.200	.188	.200	4	16	15	4	3	0	0	0	1	0	0	0	1	6	0	0	0.00	37.50
Rodriguez, Johnathan	R-R	6-3	224	11-4-99	.301	.390	.540	118	508	439	84	132	18	0	29	94	64	2	0	3	128	8	2	12.60	25.20
Schneemann, Daniel	L-R	6-0	185	1-23-97	.294	.428	.556	53	223	180	39	53	15	1	10	39	41	1	1	0	52	4	3	18.39	23.32
Straw, Myles	R-R	5-10	178	10-17-94	.240	.321	.329	123	495	434	62	104	18	6	3	47	53	1	3	4	95	30	1	10.71	19.19
Tena, Jose	L-R	5-11	195	3-20-01	.298	.353	.493	90	405	369	54	110	17	2	17	63	30	2	3	1	102	14	8	7.41	25.19
Valera, George	L-L	6-0	195	11-13-00	.248	.337	.452	90	374	323	51	80	15	0	17	50	45	1	0	5	101	6	2	12.03	27.01

Pitching	B-T	Ht.	Wt.	DOB	W	L	ERA	G	GS	SV	IP	Hits	Runs	ER	HR	BB	SO	AVG	OBP	SLG	SO%	BB%	BF
Aleman, Franco	R-R	6-6	235	6-26-00	1	2	1.99	24	0	2	23	14	8	5	1	10	34	.184	.311	.237	36.56	10.75	93
Allen, Logan	R-L	6-0	190	9-5-98	5	3	5.36	10	8	0	49	49	31	29	12	23	48	.265	.354	.546	22.64	10.85	212
Arias, Jaime	R-L	6-0	210	1-21-99	0	2	8.31	7	1	0	22	35	20	20	7	13	13	.380	.462	.685	12.26	12.26	106
Banda, Anthony	L-L	6-2	221	8-10-93	0	0	2.12	12	0	1	17	10	5	4	1	6	25	.172	.258	.241	37.88	9.09	66
Barria, Jaime	R-R	6-1	210	7-18-96	1	0	4.81	13	1	0	24	19	15	13	2	6	27	.213	.263	.337	28.13	6.25	96
Beede, Tyler	R-R	6-2	216	5-23-93	0	4	11.28	12	5	0	22	33	28	28	5	16	24	.351	.447	.628	20.87	13.91	115
Boyd, Matthew	L-L	6-3	223	2-2-91	0	0	0.93	2	2	0	10	3	2	1	0	0	12	.094	.094	.156	37.50	0.00	32
Burns, Tanner	R-R	6-0	210	12-28-98	5	3	4.59	51	0	3	69	57	41	35	11	47	70	.225	.346	.399	22.73	15.26	308
Cantillo, Joey	L-L	6-4	225	12-18-99	2	1	3.29	10	9	0	38	34	15	14	4	25	51	.236	.351	.382	29.82	14.62	171
Carrasco, Carlos	R-R	6-4	224	3-21-87	0	0	2.45	1	1	0	4	4	1	1	1	1	3	.286	.333	.500	20.00	6.67	15
Cedrola, Lorenzo	R-R	5-8	152	1-12-98	0	1	27.00	1	0	0	0	0	1	1	0	3	0	.000	.800	.000	0.00	60.00	5
Cobb, Alex	R-R	6-3	205	10-7-87	0	0	1.93	1	1	0	5	3	1	1	0	2	5	.188	.278	.188	27.78	11.11	18
Curry, Xzavion	R-R	6-0	195	7-27-98	2	6	6.58	12	11	0	53	57	40	39	15	21	47	.273	.342	.584	19.83	8.86	237
Dion, Will	L-L	5-10	180	4-17-00	4	4	5.48	29	27	0	117	122	83	71	21	54	116	.267	.344	.486	22.39	10.42	518
Doxakis, John	R-L	6-4	215	8-20-98	1	3	7.26	20	0	0	31	33	29	25	4	29	30	.287	.447	.461	19.35	18.71	155
Enright, Nic	R-R	6-3	205	1-8-97	2	1	1.06	16	1	3	17	9	2	2	0	5	31	.155	.222	.190	49.21	7.94	63
Gillispie, Connor	R-R	5-11	185	11-10-97	5	7	4.05	27	15	0	113	92	59	51	22	48	119	.221	.308	.441	25.00	10.08	476
Gose, Anthony	L-L	6-0	200	8-10-90	5	4	3.22	41	0	10	45	34	21	16	5	27	59	.207	.323	.335	30.73	14.06	192
Hanner, Bradley	R-R	6-4	210	2-10-99	0	0	27.00	1	0	0	0	1	1	1	1	0	0	.500	.500	2.000	0.00	0.00	2
Hentges, Sam	L-L	6-6	245	7-18-96	1	1	4.32	9	2	0	8	6	4	4	0	5	7	.200	.351	.233	18.92	13.51	37
Hickman, Mason	R-R	6-6	228	12-23-98	1	4	6.75	25	0	2	32	32	26	24	11	21	43	.252	.364	.551	28.48	13.91	151
Karinchak, James	R-R	6-3	215	9-22-95	0	0	2.70	7	0	1	7	3	2	2	0	6	12	.130	.310	.174	41.38	20.69	29
Kent, Zak	R-R	6-3	208	2-24-98	2	1	7.23	14	3	0	24	26	20	19	2	19	29	.274	.405	.411	25.00	16.38	116
Labaut, Randy	L-L	6-2	205	10-1-96	3	6	4.57	36	3	0	61	57	38	31	7	43	52	.244	.358	.397	18.57	15.36	280
Lively, Ben	R-R	6-4	235	3-5-92	1	0	3.24	2	2	0	8	5	3	3	1	0	4	.172	.172	.310	13.79	0.00	29
McCaughan, Darren	R-R	6-1	200	3-18-96	3	0	5.06	6	6	0	32	29	20	18	6	12	33	.232	.299	.472	24.09	8.76	137
McKenzie, Triston	R-R	6-5	165	8-2-97	4	4	5.23	13	10	0	53	54	34	31	10	33	56	.269	.370	.488	23.53	13.87	238

Mikolajchak, Nick	R-R	6-2	215	11-21-97	3	1	3.50	32	0	0	36	36	16	14	4	23	26	.261	.364	.413	15.95	14.11	163
Misiaszek, Andrew	R-L	6-2	215	8-24-97	4	1	4.50	16	0	0	18	12	9	9	2	10	21	.188	.316	.375	27.63	13.16	76
Morgan, Eli	R-R	5-10	190	5-13-96	0	0	2.70	14	0	0	17	13	5	5	1	8	16	.213	.304	.344	22.86	11.43	70
Nikhazy, Doug	L-L	6-0	210	8-11-99	7	3	2.87	14	13	0	75	51	24	24	8	34	75	.195	.294	.322	25.00	11.33	300
Oller, Adam	R-R	6-4	225	10-17-94	1	1	7.48	12	6	0	28	26	24	23	6	18	33	.252	.363	.505	26.40	14.40	125
Parsons, Wes	R-R	6-5	206	9-6-92	0	1	4.21	12	5	0	26	22	13	12	5	21	36	.224	.374	.449	29.27	17.07	123
Sabrowski, Erik	R-L	6-4	235	10-31-97	8	2	4.38	27	0	0	37	33	21	18	2	30	53	.244	.381	.378	31.18	17.65	170
Sandlin, Nick	R-R	5-11	175	1-10-97	0	0	0.00	1	0	0	1	0	0	0	0	1	0	.000	.250	.000	0.00	25.00	4
Stanley, Hunter	R-R	5-11	203	11-25-97	2	1	5.97	13	4	1	29	38	23	19	7	13	31	.314	.375	.620	22.79	9.56	136
Strzelecki, Peter	R-R	6-2	216	10-24-94	3	1	5.01	44	0	9	47	48	30	26	4	16	55	.264	.332	.407	27.09	7.88	203
Walters, Andrew	R-R	6-4	220	12-8-00	1	0	2.97	33	0	6	30	20	10	10	4	17	41	.180	.295	.324	31.78	13.18	129
Webb, Ryan	L-L	6-1	202	4-19-99	2	0	2.60	7	7	0	35	31	10	10	3	13	33	.235	.313	.386	22.45	8.84	147
Williams, Gavin	L-R	6-6	250	7-26-99	0	0	6.00	5	5	0	12	14	10	8	2	7	20	.286	.379	.469	34.48	12.07	58
Zapata, Juan	R-R	6-1	198	11-19-98	1	0	1.80	2	0	0	5	3	1	1	1	4	2	.167	.318	.333	9.09	18.18	22

Fielding

Catcher	PCT	G	PO	A	E	DP	PB
Fascia	1.000	2	14	0	0	0	0
Lavastida	.993	80	789	35	6	5	7
Nunez	.992	64	594	21	5	4	4
Ramirez	.958	2	22	1	1	0	0

First Base	PCT	G	PO	A	E	DP
Brito	.988	26	155	10	2	26
Manzardo	.998	63	407	32	1	46
Noel	.988	26	159	7	2	11
Nunez	1.000	1	2	0	0	0
Pries	.988	34	228	9	3	25

Second Base	PCT	G	PO	A	E	DP
Brito	.967	71	82	125	7	33
Cairo	.984	16	26	36	1	13
Delgado	.967	30	60	59	4	15
Freeman	1.000	1	1	2	0	0
Martinez	.951	21	33	45	4	17
Schneemann	1.000	4	9	7	0	4
Tena	.986	16	24	45	1	11

Third Base	PCT	G	PO	A	E	DP
Arias	.933	4	2	12	1	2
Brito	.967	20	11	18	1	1
Cairo	.919	23	22	35	5	1
Delgado	.927	63	36	91	10	7
Martinez	.900	11	7	11	2	1
Schneemann	1.000	17	9	25	0	1
Tena	.903	15	11	17	3	0

Shortstop	PCT	G	PO	A	E	DP
Arias	.974	31	28	86	3	24
Brito	.935	9	10	19	2	8
Cairo	1.000	31	41	62	0	16
Martinez	1.000	4	2	5	0	0
Schneemann	.985	18	23	43	1	10
Tena	.935	58	73	128	14	29

Outfield	PCT	G	PO	A	E	DP
Arias	.917	3	11	0	1	0
Brennan	.950	9	19	0	1	0
Brito	.939	19	30	1	2	0
Cedrola	.977	23	41	1	1	0
DeLauter	1.000	5	11	2	0	0
Florial	.971	57	99	1	3	0
Freeman	1.000	5	11	0	0	0
Kwan	1.000	2	3	0	0	0
Martinez	1.000	20	46	0	0	0
Noel	1.000	25	53	2	0	0
Pries	.964	21	26	1	1	0
Rodriguez	.980	95	187	9	4	3
Schneemann	1.000	14	28	1	0	1
Straw	.982	105	215	4	4	4
Valera	.977	69	125	5	3	1

AKRON RUBBERDUCKS — DOUBLE-A

EASTERN LEAGUE

Batting	B-T	Ht.	Wt.	DOB	AVG	OBP	SLG	G	PA	AB	R	H	2B	3B	HR	RBI	BB	HBP	SH	SF	SO	SB	CS	BB%	SO%
Bracho, Aaron	B-R	5-9	193	4-24-01	.221	.296	.338	97	405	358	41	79	14	2	8	49	36	5	0	6	80	3	1	8.89	19.75
Burgos, Jorge	L-L	5-10	165	12-26-01	.127	.200	.309	15	60	55	5	7	1	0	3	9	5	0	0	0	23	0	0	8.33	38.33
Cairo, Christian	R-R	5-8	170	6-11-01	.252	.353	.344	39	156	131	14	33	4	1	2	9	19	3	0	3	38	14	0	12.18	24.36
DeLauter, Chase	L-L	6-4	235	10-8-01	.252	.328	.441	30	128	111	18	28	6	0	5	16	14	0	0	3	19	1	1	10.94	14.84
Donovan, Joe	R-R	5-9	180	1-20-99	.115	.148	.154	9	27	26	3	3	1	0	0	0	1	0	0	0	13	0	0	3.70	48.15
Frias, Dayan	B-R	5-9	140	6-25-02	.203	.301	.303	114	429	370	42	75	16	3	5	46	49	5	1	4	104	6	6	11.42	24.24
Furman, Nate	L-R	5-8	180	7-23-01	.125	.300	.200	13	51	40	6	5	1	1	0	4	8	2	1	0	8	2	0	15.69	15.69
Halpin, Petey	L-R	6-0	200	5-26-02	.233	.314	.399	90	405	356	54	83	15	4	12	45	43	1	1	4	95	12	7	10.62	23.46
Huff, Kody	R-R	5-10	198	12-11-00	.245	.340	.364	98	389	335	45	82	17	1	7	28	44	6	1	3	87	7	0	11.31	22.37
Ingle, Cooper	L-R	5-10	185	2-23-02	.281	.379	.416	25	103	89	9	25	6	0	2	12	14	0	0	0	16	4	0	13.59	15.53
Kayfus, C.J.	L-L	6-0	188	10-28-01	.263	.366	.470	67	298	251	38	66	14	4	10	55	36	7	0	4	84	1	2	12.08	28.19
Kokx, Connor	R-R	6-1	195	2-24-00	.232	.330	.263	35	109	95	13	22	3	0	0	7	8	6	0	0	26	9	3	7.34	23.85
Lampe, Joe	L-R	5-11	185	12-5-00	.249	.323	.360	105	406	361	49	90	18	5	4	38	36	4	2	2	78	20	4	8.87	19.21
Lipscomb, Guy	L-R	6-2	195	3-11-01	.273	.380	.409	26	79	66	9	18	6	0	1	3	12	0	0	1	13	8	1	15.19	16.46
Naranjo, Joe	L-L	5-10	205	5-11-01	.211	.305	.266	34	128	109	12	23	3	0	1	13	16	0	0	3	34	2	0	12.50	26.56
Planez, Alexfri	R-R	6-2	180	8-17-01	.219	.254	.383	104	425	402	46	88	14	2	16	48	16	4	0	3	123	3	1	3.76	28.94
Ramirez, Micael	R-R	5-9	170	6-8-99	.270	.342	.348	45	160	141	11	38	2	0	3	17	15	1	2	1	27	0	2	9.38	16.88
Rodriguez, Gabriel	R-R	6-3	215	2-22-02	.139	.162	.194	11	37	36	2	5	2	0	0	3	0	1	0	0	16	0	0	0.00	43.24
Tolentino, Milan	L-R	6-1	185	11-17-01	.241	.313	.370	111	441	395	53	95	20	2	9	43	41	2	0	3	112	17	6	9.30	25.40
Turner, Tyresse	B-R	5-10	170	1-5-00	.314	.342	.514	14	39	35	6	11	2	1	1	5	2	0	1	1	10	5	0	5.13	25.64
Valdes, Yordys	B-R	5-10	170	8-16-01	.231	.317	.339	109	411	360	50	83	9	3	8	41	44	2	4	1	123	19	2	10.71	29.93
Watson, Kahlil	L-R	5-10	178	4-16-03	.220	.305	.407	96	407	359	56	79	15	2	16	41	42	3	0	3	125	15	9	10.32	30.71

Pitching	B-T	Ht.	Wt.	DOB	W	L	ERA	G	GS	SV	IP	Hits	Runs	ER	HR	BB	SO	AVG	OBP	SLG	SO%	BB%	BF
Abney, Alaska	R-R	6-1	205	5-5-00	4	0	2.33	26	0	1	39	22	11	10	0	15	34	.168	.286	.206	21.79	9.62	156
Arias, Jaime	R-L	6-0	210	1-21-99	2	2	2.25	8	6	0	32	25	10	8	2	10	30	.216	.281	.353	23.26	7.75	129
Benton, Trey	R-R	6-4	215	6-18-98	4	1	3.45	23	0	1	31	30	15	12	0	14	30	.254	.328	.314	22.39	10.45	134
Boone, Rodney	L-L	6-1	195	4-9-00	2	1	3.26	9	7	0	39	27	14	14	4	14	35	.197	.295	.321	22.29	8.92	157
Boyd, Matthew	L-L	6-3	223	2-2-91	1	0	1.00	2	2	0	9	6	1	1	0	1	8	.194	.219	.226	25.00	3.13	32
Carrasco, Carlos	R-R	6-4	224	3-21-87	0	1	6.00	1	1	0	3	3	2	2	0	0	3	.273	.273	.455	27.27	0.00	11
Carver, Ross	R-R	6-2	205	8-27-99	2	4	4.34	35	2	0	56	42	29	27	4	22	59	.206	.288	.328	25.32	9.44	233
Davenport, Aaron	R-R	6-0	185	7-25-00	7	4	2.85	27	26	0	142	116	49	45	11	52	135	.221	.299	.338	23.00	8.86	587
Denholm, Trenton	R-R	5-11	180	11-29-99	4	2	2.59	7	7	0	42	33	13	12	4	11	32	.224	.277	.374	19.88	6.83	161
Ellerts, Magnus	R-R	6-5	225	3-15-01	5	0	3.92	16	0	2	21	18	10	9	2	9	24	.240	.329	.360	27.59	10.34	87
Hankins, Ethan	R-R	6-6	200	5-23-00	0	0	0.00	1	1	0	2	2	0	0	0	2	3	.286	.444	.286	33.33	22.22	9
Hanner, Bradley	R-R	6-4	210	2-10-99	8	4	2.77	43	0	6	55	49	26	17	3	24	66	.233	.319	.333	27.73	10.08	238

Hentges, Sam	L-L	6-6	245	7-18-96	0	0	0.00	1	1	0	1	1	0	0	0	0	1	.333	.333	.333	33.33	0.00	3
Hickman, Mason	R-R	6-6	228	12-23-98	2	0	2.86	16	0	1	22	14	8	7	2	7	15	.187	.265	.307	17.86	8.33	84
Jones, Jordan	R-R	6-1	210	10-2-97	1	4	5.46	20	1	0	31	30	23	19	3	20	33	.254	.362	.441	23.24	14.08	142
Kokx, Connor	R-R	6-1	195	2-24-00	0	0	0.00	1	0	0	1	1	0	0	0	0	0	.250	.250	.250	0.00	0.00	4
Leftwich, Jack	R-R	6-4	220	9-26-98	4	7	4.25	42	1	10	59	51	28	28	10	23	68	.227	.304	.404	26.98	9.13	252
Mace, Tommy	R-R	6-6	230	11-11-98	8	7	3.71	28	27	0	146	131	72	60	17	46	104	.236	.308	.379	16.83	7.44	618
Messick, Parker	L-L	6-0	225	10-26-00	4	1	2.06	14	13	1	66	45	18	15	4	21	85	.191	.272	.285	32.32	7.98	263
Morehouse, Zane	R-R	6-4	200	11-16-99	1	1	1.76	12	0	2	15	11	4	3	0	5	20	.193	.292	.246	30.77	7.69	65
Nikhazy, Doug	L-L	6-0	210	8-11-99	0	1	3.17	11	11	0	48	31	17	17	4	19	49	.186	.270	.317	25.93	10.05	189
Peterson, Austin	R-R	6-6	234	9-19-99	7	2	2.88	13	13	0	75	57	24	24	5	15	72	.210	.254	.332	25.09	5.23	287
Sabrowski, Erik	R-L	6-4	235	10-31-97	0	1	0.77	9	0	0	12	11	7	1	0	2	26	.244	.277	.289	54.17	4.17	48
Sharpe, Davis	R-R	6-4	215	1-30-00	3	2	5.17	38	0	2	56	62	39	32	9	21	52	.282	.350	.477	21.05	8.50	247
Stanley, Hunter	R-R	5-11	203	11-25-97	0	0	9.00	2	0	0	2	3	2	2	1	0	3	.333	.333	.667	33.33	0.00	9
Thornton, Tyler	L-R	6-3	200	7-8-00	1	0	4.73	24	0	1	27	21	16	14	1	20	37	.214	.381	.286	29.37	15.87	126
Torres, Lenny	R-R	6-1	190	10-15-00	2	6	2.26	41	0	7	52	39	18	13	4	24	63	.218	.314	.307	30.29	11.54	208
Walters, Andrew	R-R	6-4	220	12-8-00	3	0	1.35	17	0	2	20	13	3	3	1	8	38	.181	.280	.264	46.34	9.76	82
Webb, Ryan	L-L	6-1	202	4-19-99	4	7	2.87	20	18	0	107	95	36	34	4	39	118	.244	.323	.326	26.76	8.84	441
Williams, Gavin	L-R	6-6	250	7-26-99	1	0	1.80	1	1	0	5	4	1	1	0	0	4	.222	.222	.333	22.22	0.00	18

Fielding

Catcher	PCT	G	PO	A	E	DP	PB
Donovan	1.000	8	68	3	0	0	0
Huff	.985	80	745	45	12	4	2
Ingle	.988	18	151	11	2	0	0
Ramirez	.994	36	304	18	2	2	6

First Base	PCT	G	PO	A	E	DP
Naranjo	.978	29	199	21	5	18
Bracho	.982	39	257	15	5	23
Frias	.992	16	110	8	1	10
Kayfus	.993	53	380	19	3	34
Huff	1.000	4	24	4	0	5

Second Base	PCT	G	PO	A	E	DP
Bracho	.909	22	31	39	7	11
Cairo	.973	18	29	43	2	10
Frias	1.000	12	11	34	0	3
Furman	1.000	7	11	16	0	3
Tolentino	1.000	17	19	37	0	6
Turner	.875	2	2	5	1	0
Valdes	.955	28	38	69	5	15
Watson	.934	38	52	76	9	17

Third Base	PCT	G	PO	A	E	DP
Cairo	1.000	3	3	6	0	2
Frias	.945	70	56	100	9	17
Furman	1.000	2	2	1	0	0
Rodriguez	.913	11	11	10	2	0
Tolentino	.953	37	34	47	4	5
Valdes	.968	18	10	20	1	3
Watson	1.000	2	1	6	0	1

Shortstop	PCT	G	PO	A	E	DP
Frias	.965	14	20	35	2	9
Tolentino	.985	57	72	124	3	24
Valdes	.980	62	97	145	5	32
Watson	.944	6	8	9	1	1

Outfield	PCT	G	PO	A	E	DP
Burgos	1.000	11	22	1	0	0
Cairo	.972	16	34	1	1	1
DeLauter	1.000	25	41	1	0	0
Halpin	.978	88	213	5	5	3
Kayfus	1.000	12	21	0	0	0
Kokx	1.000	31	61	2	0	0
Lampe	.983	98	168	2	3	2
Lipscomb	1.000	23	43	0	0	0
Planez	.974	84	135	12	4	2
Turner	.952	10	19	1	1	0
Watson	.969	45	91	4	3	2

LAKE COUNTY CAPTAINS — *HIGH-A*

MIDWEST LEAGUE

Batting	B-T	Ht.	Wt.	DOB	AVG	OBP	SLG	G	PA	AB	R	H	2B	3B	HR	RBI	BB	HBP	SH	SF	SO	SB	CS	BB%	SO%
Advincula, Jonah	L-R	6-1	197	1-6-01	.248	.374	.350	99	373	306	45	76	10	3	5	42	54	9	1	3	75	32	4	14.48	20.11
Antunez, Wuilfredo	L-R	6-0	150	5-16-02	.306	.328	.452	16	64	62	8	19	3	0	2	8	2	0	0	0	11	4	0	3.13	17.19
Bazzana, Travis	L-R	5-9	170	8-28-02	.238	.369	.396	27	122	101	20	24	7	0	3	12	17	4	0	0	31	5	0	13.93	25.41
Boyd, Justin	R-R	6-0	201	3-30-01	.165	.269	.244	40	146	127	18	21	7	0	1	8	18	0	1	0	48	4	0	12.33	32.88
Burgos, Jorge	L-L	5-10	165	12-26-01	.233	.305	.452	71	305	270	35	63	14	0	15	48	25	5	0	5	84	5	0	8.20	27.54
Collado, Maick	B-R	5-11	160	12-24-02	.218	.343	.318	94	388	321	37	70	11	0	7	45	56	7	0	4	61	2	0	14.43	15.72
Cozart, Jacob	L-R	6-3	205	1-9-03	.119	.245	.143	13	49	42	2	5	1	0	0	0	7	0	0	0	18	0	0	14.29	36.73
Devers, Jose	R-R	6-0	140	5-17-03	.216	.289	.320	102	426	384	55	83	19	0	7	37	37	3	0	2	107	14	3	8.69	25.12
Fascia, Zac	L-R	6-0	225	9-15-98	.209	.321	.358	26	79	67	9	14	1	0	3	11	10	1	1	0	19	0	0	12.66	24.05
Fox, Jake	L-R	5-11	185	2-12-03	.218	.314	.333	94	408	354	44	77	16	2	7	47	48	3	0	3	86	9	1	11.76	21.08
Furman, Nate	L-R	5-8	180	7-23-01	.338	.417	.500	37	176	154	35	52	2	1	7	28	18	3	0	0	31	8	2	10.23	17.61
Genao, Angel	B-R	5-9	150	5-19-04	.322	.377	.463	66	300	270	41	87	24	1	4	32	24	2	0	4	49	13	2	8.00	16.33
Gonzalez, Esteban	L-R	5-8	150	3-19-03	.231	.304	.308	28	115	104	8	24	5	0	1	13	11	0	0	0	36	4	4	9.57	31.30
Greene, Isaiah	L-L	6-0	180	8-29-01	.202	.311	.348	28	103	89	10	18	4	3	1	5	14	0	0	0	28	4	1	13.59	27.18
Ingle, Cooper	L-R	5-10	185	2-23-02	.313	.433	.500	68	305	252	45	79	18	1	9	55	51	2	0	0	40	3	1	16.72	13.11
Kayfus, C.J.	L-L	6-0	188	10-28-01	.338	.437	.578	40	183	154	32	52	12	2	7	37	23	5	0	1	33	4	0	12.57	18.03
Kwan, Steven	L-L	5-9	170	9-5-97	.200	.333	.800	2	6	5	2	1	0	0	1	3	1	0	0	0	0	0	0	16.67	0.00
Lipscomb, Guy	L-R	6-2	195	3-11-01	.278	.360	.379	67	283	248	43	69	10	3	3	34	29	4	0	2	43	26	5	10.25	15.19
Mooney, Alex	R-R	6-1	195	7-6-02	.235	.336	.393	105	473	405	73	95	22	3	12	55	50	14	0	4	100	43	6	10.57	21.14
Rivas, Kevin	B-R	5-7	128	4-7-03	.138	.265	.138	10	34	29	3	4	0	0	0	4	5	0	0	0	18	0	0	14.71	52.94
Tincher, Johnny	R-R	5-8	170	8-25-01	.176	.319	.256	55	216	176	16	31	5	0	3	18	33	5	0	2	56	0	1	15.28	25.93
Turner, Tyresse	B-R	5-10	170	1-5-00	.249	.353	.319	58	216	185	32	46	4	0	3	21	27	3	1	0	59	17	0	12.50	27.31
Velazquez, Ralphy	L-R	6-2	220	5-28-05	.176	.275	.250	19	80	68	5	12	2	0	1	9	10	0	0	2	20	0	0	12.50	25.00
Zarate, Angel	L-L	5-11	190	7-16-99	.183	.300	.243	39	141	115	14	21	4	0	1	12	18	3	1	4	20	7	1	12.77	14.18

Pitching	B-T	Ht.	Wt.	DOB	W	L	ERA	G	GS	SV	IP	Hits	Runs	ER	HR	BB	SO	AVG	OBP	SLG	SO%	BB%	BF
Abney, Alaska	R-R	6-1	205	5-5-00	2	0	1.08	14	0	0	17	12	2	2	2	6	18	.200	.294	.333	26.47	8.82	68
DeLucia, Dylan	R-R	6-1	205	8-1-00	0	1	2.52	8	8	0	36	25	10	10	4	9	39	.195	.254	.305	28.06	6.47	139
Denholm, Trenton	R-R	5-11	180	11-29-99	9	2	3.29	19	19	0	107	89	45	39	13	25	95	.218	.271	.367	21.49	5.66	442
Driver, Jay	R-R	6-3	195	2-25-02	1	2	1.53	40	0	2	47	42	12	8	2	24	53	.243	.343	.324	25.98	11.76	204
Ellerts, Magnus	R-R	6-5	225	3-15-01	3	3	2.31	29	0	11	35	19	9	9	2	20	59	.160	.296	.227	40.97	13.89	144
Gomez, Yorman	R-R	5-11	167	11-10-02	1	2	5.00	4	3	0	18	18	12	10	4	7	17	.247	.313	.452	21.25	8.75	80
Hajjar, Steve	R-L	6-5	240	8-7-00	2	1	7.26	30	2	0	40	20	32	32	6	40	35	.148	.350	.326	19.44	22.22	180
Harlow, Josh	R-R	6-3	215	4-18-01	1	1	2.93	9	0	1	15	10	5	5	1	10	15	.189	.338	.377	22.39	14.93	67

Hernandez, Allan	R-R	6-5	225	1-19-01	1	3	2.83	37	0	6	48	32	22	15	2	30	51	.183	.305	.263	24.17	14.22	211
Jachec, Matt	R-R	6-0	205	7-25-01	1	2	4.91	19	0	1	37	36	24	20	5	12	56	.247	.308	.390	35.22	7.55	159
Jacobs, Zach	R-R	6-1	170	9-9-01	7	3	2.36	34	5	0	80	44	23	21	5	26	80	.161	.243	.249	26.32	8.55	304
Maltrud, Rorik	R-R	6-4	223	3-21-00	4	4	4.53	12	12	0	52	53	27	26	7	22	56	.264	.338	.408	24.56	9.65	228
Messick, Parker	L-L	6-0	225	10-26-00	5	5	3.57	13	13	0	68	64	30	27	6	23	80	.249	.317	.401	28.17	8.10	284
Miller, Jake	R-R	6-2	210	7-14-00	5	3	5.83	21	4	0	42	47	27	27	6	16	37	.280	.346	.446	20.00	8.65	185
Morehouse, Zane	R-R	6-4	200	11-16-99	1	4	3.47	32	0	7	36	35	16	14	1	16	43	.248	.333	.312	26.71	9.94	161
Perez, Steven	L-L	6-0	155	4-21-01	3	0	3.68	14	0	2	15	10	6	6	1	8	12	.200	.317	.260	20.00	13.33	60
Peterson, Austin	R-R	6-6	234	9-19-99	7	2	2.44	14	14	0	85	65	26	23	3	6	87	.208	.231	.317	27.10	1.87	321
Rapp, Shawn	R-L	6-2	200	7-3-00	2	0	3.18	13	0	4	17	13	9	6	0	8	17	.213	.310	.279	23.61	11.11	72
Richardson, Alonzo	R-R	5-11	165	10-7-02	1	3	5.79	5	5	0	23	30	16	15	3	11	14	.326	.394	.587	13.33	10.48	105
Spivey, Carter	R-R	6-1	193	10-13-99	8	1	3.32	24	24	0	125	104	53	46	7	48	96	.227	.308	.320	18.50	9.25	519
Tulloch, Adam	L-L	6-2	200	7-1-00	6	0	3.60	31	0	1	60	49	27	24	4	32	61	.223	.350	.332	23.19	12.17	263
Wilkinson, Matthew	R-L	5-11	260	12-10-02	5	5	2.30	16	16	0	78	49	25	20	8	28	103	.174	.255	.302	32.70	8.89	315
Wolf, Josh	R-R	6-3	170	9-1-00	0	1	5.11	10	0	0	12	12	8	7	2	10	13	.250	.390	.375	22.03	16.95	59
Zapata, Juan	R-R	6-1	198	11-19-98	2	5	8.03	20	5	0	37	49	41	33	8	26	33	.306	.401	.550	17.55	13.83	188

Fielding

Catcher	PCT	G	PO	A	E	DP	PB
Cozart	.974	13	105	6	3	0	0
Fascia	.977	16	126	4	3	2	0
Ingle	.987	56	496	25	7	2	1
Rivas	.977	5	39	4	1	0	2
Tincher	.989	46	430	13	5	1	6

First Base	PCT	G	PO	A	E	DP
Collado	.988	76	558	24	7	36
Fascia	.974	6	33	4	1	3
Kayfus	.991	30	218	11	2	22
Rivas	.952	3	19	1	1	1
Turner	1.000	8	42	1	0	1
Velazquez	1.000	11	76	5	0	5

Second Base	PCT	G	PO	A	E	DP
Bazzana	.981	27	38	66	2	6
Devers	.974	10	17	21	1	3
Fox	.947	18	22	49	4	7
Furman	.981	25	38	64	2	16
Genao	.946	16	18	35	3	8
Mooney	.975	19	33	45	2	8
Turner	.984	18	20	40	1	5

Third Base	PCT	G	PO	A	E	DP
Collado	1.000	10	11	19	0	2
Devers	.974	18	12	26	1	1
Furman	.917	9	1	10	1	1
Genao	1.000	11	5	15	0	1
Mooney	.903	54	40	72	12	10
Turner	.925	28	23	39	5	2

Shortstop	PCT	G	PO	A	E	DP
Devers	.952	68	114	163	14	34
Genao	.908	36	29	50	8	7
Mooney	.989	26	32	59	1	7

Outfield	PCT	G	PO	A	E	DP
Advincula	.988	85	164	2	2	2
Antunez	.969	16	31	0	1	0
Boyd	1.000	36	52	1	0	1
Burgos	.974	48	69	7	2	1
Fox	.975	65	151	4	4	0
Gonzalez	.986	28	67	1	1	0
Greene	.923	20	36	0	3	0
Kayfus	.947	10	18	0	1	0
Kwan	1.000	1	2	0	0	0
Lipscomb	.983	59	112	2	2	1
Velazquez	1.000	4	8	0	0	0
Zarate	1.000	31	40	4	0	0

LYNCHBURG HILLCATS — *LOW-A*

CAROLINA LEAGUE

Batting	B-T	Ht.	Wt.	DOB	AVG	OBP	SLG	G	PA	AB	R	H	2B	3B	HR	RBI	BB	HBP	SH	SF	SO	SB	CS	BB%	SO%
Alduey, Fran	B-R	5-7	140	1-7-04	.196	.259	.268	47	168	153	20	30	5	3	0	13	11	2	1	0	54	12	5	6.55	32.14
Antunez, Wuilfredo	L-R	6-0	150	5-16-02	.255	.325	.459	80	331	294	41	75	18	9	8	54	29	3	0	3	72	15	9	8.76	21.75
Benjamin, Juan	B-R	5-8	150	4-25-03	.251	.314	.329	96	383	346	40	87	17	2	2	52	29	4	1	3	85	24	3	7.57	22.19
Cesarini, Ryan	L-R	5-10	205	12-16-02	.283	.370	.543	13	54	46	6	13	4	4	0	11	7	0	0	1	10	3	1	12.96	18.52
Chourio, Jaison	B-R	6-1	162	5-19-05	.269	.414	.398	98	432	334	69	90	24	2	5	58	86	3	0	9	69	44	11	19.91	15.97
Clark, Logun	R-R	6-2	195	6-4-03	.294	.388	.426	20	80	68	6	20	3	0	2	11	8	3	0	1	22	1	1	10.00	27.50
Durango, Luis	L-L	5-10	135	4-8-03	.250	.344	.311	41	153	132	25	33	6	1	0	14	9	10	2	0	30	21	1	5.88	19.61
Francisca, Welbyn	B-R	5-8	148	5-17-06	.325	.402	.402	29	132	117	20	38	6	0	1	15	14	1	0	0	27	8	2	10.61	20.45
Genao, Angel	B-R	5-9	150	5-19-04	.341	.383	.553	44	196	179	31	61	14	3	6	39	14	0	0	3	28	12	3	7.14	14.29
Gonzalez, Esteban	L-R	5-8	150	3-19-03	.287	.348	.464	69	299	265	54	76	17	6	6	39	18	10	0	6	61	37	9	6.02	20.40
Hawke, Tommy	L-R	5-6	160	7-7-02	.263	.379	.347	88	391	323	59	85	12	6	1	22	59	4	1	4	78	37	11	15.09	19.95
Howe, Garrett	L-R	5-11	185	7-12-02	.240	.367	.240	15	60	50	9	12	0	0	0	4	9	1	0	0	19	6	3	15.00	31.67
Knapczyk, Christian	L-R	5-9	165	12-16-01	.250	.382	.350	92	399	320	56	80	12	7	2	41	56	16	1	6	70	18	8	14.04	17.54
Lopez, Robert	L-R	5-10	150	1-2-04	.246	.354	.335	53	209	179	23	44	7	0	3	24	29	1	0	0	53	3	0	13.88	25.36
Mejias, Manuel	B-R	5-7	166	6-13-04	.214	.309	.274	77	307	266	23	57	13	0	1	23	36	2	0	3	63	3	0	11.73	20.52
Merejo, Luis	R-R	6-2	185	6-28-06	.282	.372	.466	30	121	103	20	29	8	1	3	16	11	5	0	2	30	3	0	9.09	24.79
Pastrano, Jose	B-R	5-9	145	9-12-02	.189	.348	.229	61	227	175	26	33	4	0	1	20	45	1	0	6	51	9	5	19.82	22.47
Paz, Richard	L-R	5-7	150	6-12-01	.250	.500	.250	2	6	4	1	1	0	0	0	0	1	1	0	0	3	0	0	16.67	50.00
Ramirez, Rafael	L-R	6-0	159	7-22-05	.187	.301	.319	54	216	182	23	34	10	1	4	23	30	1	0	3	71	7	4	13.89	32.87
Riebock, Barrett	L-L	6-2	190	7-30-02	.189	.276	.284	25	87	74	12	14	2	1	1	9	9	1	0	3	13	2	2	10.34	14.94
Rivas, Kevin	B-R	5-7	128	4-7-03	.145	.270	.211	24	89	76	10	11	3	1	0	5	13	0	0	0	42	1	2	14.61	47.19
Saduy, Lexer	L-L	5-10	148	10-14-02	.221	.313	.292	39	131	113	16	25	2	0	2	13	12	4	0	2	22	7	5	9.16	16.79
Thompson, Bennett	R-R	5-10	196	12-16-02	.061	.115	.143	13	52	49	2	3	1	0	1	2	2	1	0	0	19	0	0	3.85	36.54
Velazquez, Ralphy	L-R	6-2	220	5-28-05	.243	.362	.414	82	373	309	56	75	21	1	10	52	56	4	0	4	75	8	2	15.01	20.11

Pitching	B-T	Ht.	Wt.	DOB	W	L	ERA	G	GS	SV	IP	Hits	Runs	ER	HR	BB	SO	AVG	OBP	SLG	SO%	BB%	BF
Alfaro, Jervis	R-R	5-11	170	10-24-03	2	0	3.42	6	4	0	24	24	12	9	2	9	20	.258	.337	.398	19.23	8.65	104
Artiles, Reny	R-R	6-0	160	1-17-02	4	3	3.63	32	0	5	52	42	33	21	3	35	62	.220	.354	.346	25.83	14.58	240
Berry, Jake	R-L	6-10	245	5-29-01	0	1	16.20	3	0	0	3	6	8	6	1	4	5	.375	.476	.750	23.81	19.05	21
Bresnahan, Jacob	L-L	6-3	175	6-27-05	0	0	4.50	1	1	0	4	4	2	2	1	2	3	.250	.333	.563	16.67	11.11	18
Brito, Abel	R-R	6-1	175	3-4-01	3	1	6.63	25	0	0	38	37	36	28	3	38	36	.261	.426	.415	18.95	20.00	190
Clemmey, Alexander	L-L	6-6	205	7-18-05	1	4	4.67	19	19	0	69	53	39	36	4	47	97	.214	.339	.323	32.55	15.77	298
DeLucia, Dylan	R-R	6-1	205	8-1-00	0	2	4.15	3	3	0	9	7	4	4	0	3	10	.212	.297	.303	27.03	8.11	37
Favors, Caden	R-L	6-3	205	8-29-01	0	3	3.09	4	1	0	12	14	9	4	1	2	13	.275	.302	.431	24.53	3.77	53
Garcia, Jogly	R-R	6-1	170	9-8-03	0	2	8.14	7	5	0	24	36	26	22	3	14	31	.330	.430	.495	24.22	10.94	128
Gomez, Yorman	R-R	5-11	167	11-10-02	7	4	3.81	21	20	0	104	92	53	44	6	38	96	.231	.306	.347	21.52	8.52	446

Pitching	B-T	Ht.	Wt.	DOB	W	L	ERA	G	GS	SV	IP	Hits	Runs	ER	HR	BB	SO	AVG	OBP	SLG	SO%	BB%	BF
Harlow, Josh	R-R	6-3	215	4-18-01	4	3	3.51	28	0	5	41	37	24	16	5	20	47	.236	.328	.401	25.54	10.87	184
Heppner, Sean	R-R	6-2	175	9-14-02	0	0	6.94	6	0	0	12	12	10	9	1	11	15	.273	.404	.432	26.32	19.30	57
Hernandez, Melkis	L-L	6-0	186	1-18-05	1	2	4.43	6	5	0	22	25	16	11	2	16	20	.284	.400	.409	19.05	15.24	105
Humphries, Jackson	R-L	6-1	200	7-20-04	3	6	4.56	23	23	0	79	69	42	40	12	41	97	.240	.339	.417	29.13	12.31	333
Jachec, Matt	R-R	6-0	205	7-25-01	2	2	3.82	17	0	2	35	32	18	15	2	6	48	.232	.267	.333	32.88	4.11	146
Jasiak, Jack	R-R	6-1	198	3-6-01	7	5	4.57	32	2	1	67	76	39	34	6	22	62	.281	.352	.407	20.60	7.31	301
Maltrud, Rorik	R-R	6-4	223	3-21-00	4	1	2.38	12	7	0	53	38	17	14	2	14	62	.199	.250	.314	29.81	6.73	208
Martinez, Izaak	L-L	5-10	180	9-12-01	1	0	2.77	7	0	0	13	11	4	4	2	7	16	.239	.327	.478	29.09	12.73	55
Parra, Deretd	R-R	6-3	160	6-18-00	4	2	3.93	19	0	3	34	31	19	15	0	17	29	.238	.327	.315	18.95	11.11	153
Perez, Steven	L-L	6-0	155	4-21-01	1	1	2.20	23	0	4	41	27	11	10	6	19	58	.188	.285	.347	35.15	11.52	165
Richardson, Alonzo	R-R	5-11	165	10-7-02	4	5	3.57	18	15	0	91	83	44	36	5	32	59	.241	.310	.371	15.45	8.38	382
Schlesinger, Rafe	L-L	6-3	199	1-22-03	0	2	4.91	3	3	0	7	6	4	4	1	3	11	.231	.300	.346	36.67	10.00	30
Schuelke, Cam	R-R	6-0	190	1-14-02	1	0	0.00	8	0	2	9	4	2	0	0	6	11	.133	.297	.167	29.73	16.22	37
Scott, Kyle	R-R	6-1	220	4-16-02	6	5	3.00	24	13	1	96	80	48	32	7	28	96	.219	.284	.334	23.88	6.97	402
Vasquez, Wardquelin	R-R	6-3	194	7-25-01	4	2	2.75	30	0	1	69	56	34	21	1	36	76	.215	.317	.277	25.00	11.84	304
Virguez, Kendeglys	R-R	6-2	160	5-6-04	1	0	3.32	12	0	1	19	15	8	7	1	8	23	.224	.333	.313	29.49	10.26	78
Wegielnik, Robert	R-R	6-0	185	9-6-01	3	4	5.82	31	0	2	34	45	40	22	4	22	37	.306	.428	.456	20.44	12.15	181
Wilkinson, Matthew	R-L	5-11	260	12-10-02	3	1	1.12	8	8	0	40	22	7	5	2	9	71	.159	.216	.225	47.97	6.08	148
Zsak, Donovan	L-L	6-3	185	7-12-03	1	0	1.86	7	0	0	10	2	3	2	0	10	13	.069	.349	.103	30.23	23.26	43

Fielding

Catcher	PCT	G	PO	A	E	DP	PB
Clark	1.000	15	148	16	0	1	0
Lopez	.987	43	409	32	6	4	10
Mejias	.983	57	527	35	10	8	10
Paz	.875	1	6	1	1	0	1
Rivas	.982	6	52	4	1	0	0
Thompson	.991	10	101	6	1	0	5

First Base	PCT	G	PO	A	E	DP
Benjamin	.978	25	151	27	4	13
Mejias	1.000	2	5	1	0	1
Merejo	.963	20	145	13	6	18
Rivas	1.000	8	45	3	0	4
Saduy	.986	9	67	5	1	3
Velazquez	.985	67	429	30	7	26

Second Base	PCT	G	PO	A	E	DP
Alduey	.949	15	19	18	2	3
Benjamin	.943	20	37	45	5	10
Francisca	.933	3	6	8	1	3
Genao	1.000	3	6	9	0	2
Howe	1.000	5	8	10	0	2
Knapczyk	.977	48	75	92	4	20
Pastrano	.955	21	27	37	3	7
Ramirez	.939	10	15	16	2	4
Rivas	.842	7	5	11	3	1

Third Base	PCT	G	PO	A	E	DP
Alduey	.869	24	21	32	8	3
Benjamin	.884	37	34	50	11	8
Genao	1.000	2	0	8	0	0
Howe	1.000	4	1	2	0	0
Knapczyk	.875	16	11	17	4	1
Pastrano	.953	36	35	47	4	9
Ramirez	.792	12	6	13	5	1

Shortstop	PCT	G	PO	A	E	DP
Alduey	.857	6	6	12	3	0
Benjamin	.800	6	5	11	4	0
Francisca	.901	26	30	61	10	16
Genao	.938	37	44	76	8	10
Howe	.842	5	6	10	3	1
Knapczyk	.896	22	24	45	8	6
Ramirez	.838	28	20	47	13	9

Outfield	PCT	G	PO	A	E	DP
Antunez	.967	70	133	12	5	4
Cesarini	.955	13	21	0	1	0
Chourio	.990	92	201	7	2	4
Durango	.982	30	55	0	1	0
Gonzalez	.973	58	106	4	3	0
Hawke	.989	81	175	6	2	0
Merejo	.909	8	9	1	1	0
Riebock	.955	21	20	1	1	0
Saduy	.914	22	31	1	3	0
Velazquez	1.000	3	3	1	0	0

ACL GUARDIANS — *ROOKIE*

ARIZONA COMPLEX LEAGUE

Batting	B-T	Ht.	Wt.	DOB	AVG	OBP	SLG	G	PA	AB	R	H	2B	3B	HR	RBI	BB	HBP	SH	SF	SO	SB	CS	BB%	SO%
Alduey, Fran	B-R	5-7	140	1-7-04	.429	.500	.643	5	16	14	4	6	1	1	0	1	2	0	0	0	5	1	0	12.50	31.25
Baptiste, Yanki	B-R	5-11	185	11-18-04	.300	.364	.767	9	33	30	7	9	1	2	3	7	3	0	0	0	14	0	0	9.09	42.42
Bolivar, Mason	L-R	5-10	162	8-18-06	.176	.176	.353	6	17	17	2	3	1	1	0	2	0	0	0	0	7	0	1	0.00	41.18
Cedeno, Jose	L-R	5-7	140	3-1-05	.226	.353	.321	27	102	84	12	19	2	0	2	10	12	5	0	1	24	0	0	11.76	23.53
Clark, Logun	R-R	6-2	195	6-4-03	.220	.347	.463	12	49	41	8	9	1	0	3	13	5	3	0	0	18	0	1	10.20	36.73
DeLauter, Chase	L-L	6-4	235	10-8-01	.250	.333	.625	3	9	8	3	2	0	0	1	1	1	0	0	0	1	0	0	11.11	11.11
Espinola, Christopher	L-L	5-7	165	9-19-03	.216	.333	.330	30	114	97	11	21	3	1	2	14	16	1	0	0	31	2	2	14.04	27.19
Francisca, Welbyn	B-R	5-8	148	5-17-06	.328	.418	.523	45	201	174	47	57	12	2	6	28	25	2	0	0	25	11	1	12.44	12.44
Gutierrez, Carlos	L-L	5-6	135	6-18-04	.259	.328	.333	36	125	108	16	28	5	0	1	19	11	2	0	4	30	11	1	8.80	24.00
Izturis, Victor	L-R	5-9	165	3-22-05	.169	.373	.221	29	102	77	9	13	1	0	1	5	24	1	0	0	32	2	0	23.53	31.37
Leon, David	L-R	5-11	156	2-2-04	.283	.449	.350	27	78	60	15	17	1	0	1	11	17	1	0	0	14	0	1	21.79	17.95
Luis, Yerlin	B-R	5-9	155	9-9-05	.169	.289	.220	36	142	118	16	20	4	1	0	19	19	2	0	3	52	4	4	13.38	36.62
Martinez, Angel	B-R	6-0	200	1-27-02	.000	.222	.000	3	9	7	2	0	0	0	0	0	2	0	0	0	2	0	0	22.22	22.22
Martinez, Jonathan	B-R	5-9	131	8-16-06	.246	.413	.333	18	75	57	12	14	5	0	0	9	15	2	0	1	17	7	2	20.00	22.67
Mendez, Alberto	L-R	5-9	146	11-29-04	.182	.299	.350	42	167	143	16	26	9	0	5	18	21	3	0	0	47	2	1	12.57	28.14
Mercedes, Jeffrey	B-R	5-8	146	10-2-04	.282	.364	.411	35	143	124	12	35	8	1	2	20	16	1	0	2	23	1	2	11.19	16.08
Merejo, Luis	R-R	6-2	185	6-28-06	.250	.417	.421	47	200	152	41	38	12	1	4	16	35	10	0	2	48	8	3	17.50	24.00
Mijares, Yaikel	B-R	5-9	145	12-13-05	.229	.358	.338	46	191	157	28	36	8	0	3	29	28	4	1	1	59	15	0	14.66	30.89
Paz, Richard	L-R	5-7	150	6-12-01	.167	.167	.250	4	12	12	2	2	1	0	0	1	0	0	0	0	2	0	0	0.00	16.67
Pirela, Jose	L-R	6-3	181	4-9-06	.186	.293	.385	45	188	161	25	30	7	2	7	25	17	8	0	2	61	3	5	9.04	32.45
Riebock, Barrett	L-L	6-2	190	7-30-02	.234	.381	.266	31	118	94	13	22	3	0	0	9	16	7	0	1	28	9	3	13.56	23.73
Rivas, Kevin	B-R	5-7	128	4-7-03	.174	.441	.217	11	34	23	5	4	1	0	0	0	10	1	0	0	11	3	1	29.41	32.35
Silva, Heribert	L-L	5-9	152	3-31-06	.237	.344	.421	24	90	76	15	18	7	2	1	12	9	4	0	1	22	7	0	10.00	24.44

Pitching	B-T	Ht.	Wt.	DOB	W	L	ERA	G	GS	SV	IP	Hits	Runs	ER	HR	BB	SO	AVG	OBP	SLG	SO%	BB%	BF
Alcantara, Eudry	R-R	5-11	150	12-27-04	1	1	12.19	8	3	0	10	13	14	14	2	17	15	.325	.516	.600	24.19	27.42	62
Aldeano, Austin	R-R	6-1	180	6-6-04	2	1	5.18	13	7	0	49	45	30	28	7	19	39	.250	.332	.483	18.75	9.13	208
Alfaro, Jervis	R-R	5-11	170	10-24-03	2	1	3.38	11	8	0	43	37	18	16	0	8	48	.231	.291	.313	27.27	4.55	176
Boyd, Matthew	L-L	6-3	223	2-2-91	0	0	0.00	1	1	0	3	3	1	0	0	1	7	.250	.308	.250	53.85	7.69	13
Bresnahan, Jacob	L-L	6-3	175	6-27-05	1	3	2.54	11	11	0	46	32	18	13	2	16	63	.190	.259	.321	34.05	8.65	185
Cantillo, Joey	L-L	6-4	225	12-18-99	0	1	33.75	1	1	0	1	3	5	5	0	2	2	.429	.556	.571	22.22	22.22	9

Cordones, Miguel	R-R	6-6	180	9-16-99	2	4	10.80	10	0	0	20	28	26	24	4	17	26	.329	.438	.576	24.53	16.04	106
DeLucia, Dylan	R-R	6-1	205	8-1-00	0	0	0.00	2	2	0	5	3	0	0	0	0	3	.176	.176	.176	17.65	0.00	17
Flores, Luis	L-L	6-1	160	10-5-03	3	2	5.87	17	0	0	23	20	15	15	3	24	44	.227	.398	.375	38.60	21.05	114
Garcia, Jogly	R-R	6-1	170	9-8-03	1	2	4.22	12	9	1	49	54	26	23	5	11	59	.277	.324	.451	28.10	5.24	210
Hernandez, Evelio	R-R	5-11	167	9-3-03	0	0	2.16	3	1	0	8	7	2	2	0	7	10	.226	.385	.323	25.64	17.95	39
Hernandez, Melkis	L-L	6-0	186	1-18-05	4	0	4.03	12	3	1	38	35	19	17	0	11	48	.240	.304	.308	29.81	6.83	161
Jimenez, Ezequiel	R-R	6-1	182	6-10-03	0	3	7.63	7	4	0	15	19	14	13	1	8	11	.311	.403	.459	15.28	11.11	72
Kent, Zak	R-R	6-3	208	2-24-98	0	0	0.00	1	1	0	2	0	0	0	0	0	2	.000	.000	.000	33.33	0.00	6
Leon, David	L-R	5-11	156	2-2-04	0	0	20.25	1	0	0	1	6	3	3	0	1	0	.667	.636	.778	0.00	9.09	11
Misiaszek, Andrew	R-L	6-2	215	8-24-97	0	0	1.59	5	1	0	6	3	1	1	0	2	8	.150	.227	.300	36.36	9.09	22
Parra, Deretd	R-R	6-3	160	6-18-00	2	0	2.45	8	0	1	11	8	8	3	0	3	20	.186	.271	.209	40.82	6.12	49
Ramirez, Jose	R-R	5-11	155	9-3-04	1	2	6.04	21	0	2	25	27	22	17	3	31	31	.273	.449	.404	22.79	22.79	136
Rapp, Shawn	R-L	6-2	200	7-3-00	0	0	0.00	2	0	0	2	0	0	0	0	1	2	.000	.125	.000	25.00	12.50	8
Rivas, Kevin	S-R	5-7	128	4-7-03	0	0	13.50	1	0	0	1	3	2	2	0	0	1	.429	.429	.714	14.29	0.00	7
Rivera, Raudy	R-R	5-10	195	5-3-05	1	2	8.31	11	0	0	17	21	19	16	2	20	26	.309	.495	.441	27.08	20.83	96
Santos, Javier	L-R	6-0	190	6-2-03	1	2	17.74	17	0	0	12	14	29	23	2	33	15	.264	.547	.415	17.44	38.37	86
Ventimiglia, Tommy	R-R	6-4	205	10-1-03	4	2	7.03	22	0	0	24	16	21	19	0	29	23	.188	.419	.259	18.40	23.20	125
Virguez, Kendeglys	R-R	6-2	160	5-6-04	1	3	3.80	13	0	1	21	14	13	9	3	7	31	.187	.289	.413	34.07	7.69	91
Zapata, Julio	R-R	6-1	184	11-22-02	0	0	5.17	10	1	2	16	18	10	9	2	8	19	.286	.395	.508	25.00	10.53	76
Zinn, Keegan	R-R	6-3	165	3-30-05	1	4	9.82	13	7	0	33	32	39	36	5	25	45	.260	.411	.431	28.13	15.63	160

Fielding

C: Izturis 19, Cedeno 19, Leon 15, Clark 10, Paz 4, Rivas 3, Silva 1. **1B:** Merejo 36, Leon 8, Rivas 7, Baptiste 7, Izturis 3, Mercedes 3. **2B:** Mendez 26, Francisca 18, Martinez 6, Mijares 6, Mercedes 3, Rivas 1, Martinez 1. **3B:** Mercedes 27, Mijares 17, Mendez 14, Alduey 2, Baptiste 1. **SS:** Francisca 27, Mijares 22, Martinez 10, Alduey 2, Espinola 1. **LF:** Gutierrez 16, Riebock 15, Silva 9, Espinola 8, Pirela 5, Luis 4, Merejo 4, Bolivar 3. **CF:** Pirela 37, Luis 19, Riebock 3, Silva 1, Martinez 1, DeLauter 1, Gutierrez 1. **RF:** Riebock 12, Espinola 11, Silva 9, Gutierrez 8, Luis 8, Merejo 8, Pirela 3, DeLauter 2, Bolivar 1, Cedeno 1.

DSL CLEVELAND MENDOZA — ROOKIE

DOMINICAN SUMMER LEAGUE

Batting	B-T	Ht.	Wt.	DOB	AVG	OBP	SLG	G	PA	AB	R	H	2B	3B	HR	RBI	BB	HBP	SH	SF	SO	SB	CS	BB%	SO%
Arias, Dariel	L-R	6-0	152	10-7-06	.204	.307	.255	32	114	98	18	20	3	1	0	8	12	3	0	1	17	2	1	10.53	14.91
Arias, Robert	L-L	6-1	168	9-13-06	.247	.367	.347	41	180	150	37	37	7	4	0	9	25	4	0	1	15	29	4	13.89	8.33
Ayala, Yelserth	B-R	5-8	140	6-5-06	.245	.385	.302	21	66	53	10	13	1	1	0	5	10	2	1	0	12	8	1	15.15	18.18
Caceres, Juneiker	L-L	5-10	168	8-15-07	.340	.425	.504	40	167	141	28	48	11	6	0	33	19	4	0	3	18	9	0	11.38	10.78
Cadiz, Sebastian	L-R	5-11	180	2-1-06	.225	.349	.310	27	86	71	11	16	2	2	0	10	13	1	0	1	20	0	1	15.12	23.26
Caripa, Carlos	L-L	5-10	155	6-29-07	.148	.262	.216	27	103	88	10	13	4	1	0	8	13	1	0	1	18	3	0	12.62	17.48
Dalmagro, Pedro	L-R	5-11	170	12-17-05	.279	.359	.423	35	131	111	15	31	11	1	1	17	12	4	0	4	25	2	1	9.16	19.08
Frances, Juan	B-R	5-9	145	9-7-05	.235	.312	.309	30	93	81	15	19	4	1	0	10	8	2	0	2	8	2	3	8.60	8.60
Garces, Carlos	B-R	5-7	143	9-30-06	.226	.346	.321	34	130	106	16	24	6	2	0	13	18	3	0	3	15	4	6	13.85	11.54
John, Yorfran	B-R	5-10	163	9-14-04	.114	.304	.114	17	46	35	4	4	0	0	0	2	10	0	0	1	8	3	1	21.74	17.39
Marcano, Jose	L-R	5-10	155	10-3-05	.293	.336	.364	28	107	99	17	29	5	1	0	7	7	0	0	1	8	2	3	6.54	7.48
Martinez, Randy	B-R	5-9	163	4-17-07	.165	.277	.268	37	150	127	17	21	7	3	0	9	18	2	1	1	44	2	1	12.00	29.33
Rodriguez, Gabriel	L-R	6-0	161	5-3-07	.276	.510	.398	33	145	98	23	27	4	1	2	20	34	13	0	0	23	9	2	23.45	15.86
Torrealba, Osmar	L-L	5-9	161	4-2-07	.190	.373	.207	21	75	58	4	11	1	0	0	4	16	1	0	0	10	2	2	21.33	13.33
Torres, Wuinder	R-R	5-10	130	1-28-07	.293	.326	.366	22	89	82	9	24	6	0	0	16	5	0	0	2	17	2	0	5.62	19.10
Ustariz, Santiago	L-R	5-10	165	11-8-06	.115	.200	.115	8	30	26	2	3	0	0	0	3	2	1	0	1	7	0	0	6.67	23.33
Velasquez, Nomar	L-R	5-9	158	5-21-05	.268	.346	.296	27	81	71	12	19	2	0	0	12	8	1	0	1	10	5	4	9.88	12.35

Pitching	B-T	Ht.	Wt.	DOB	W	L	ERA	G	GS	SV	IP	Hits	Runs	ER	HR	BB	SO	AVG	OBP	SLG	SO%	BB%	BF
Abreu, Javier	R-R	5-11	150	5-24-06	1	0	1.98	6	0	0	14	9	6	3	0	10	11	.200	.351	.267	19.30	17.54	57
Ardiles, Wilinyer	R-R	5-11	140	8-14-07	0	4	8.88	11	9	0	25	27	28	25	2	23	10	.281	.449	.500	7.87	18.11	127
Castillo, Hector	R-R	6-0	180	5-2-07	1	1	5.50	11	0	1	18	15	11	11	4	11	14	.217	.337	.478	16.87	13.25	83
Crisostomo, Yatner	R-R	5-11	155	6-21-03	0	2	3.32	7	6	0	19	20	12	7	0	6	26	.256	.318	.333	30.59	7.06	85
Feliz, Rey	L-R	6-4	186	2-9-07	1	1	9.00	9	0	0	11	7	13	11	2	17	9	.189	.500	.351	15.00	28.33	60
Garcia, Alexander	R-R	6-0	161	7-27-06	2	0	4.64	11	2	0	21	23	12	11	1	10	30	.277	.371	.373	30.93	10.31	97
Henriquez, Jodainy	L-L	6-2	193	10-3-05	0	0	6.06	11	0	0	16	14	14	11	1	17	18	.241	.447	.379	21.18	20.00	85
Hernandez, Daiher	L-L	5-11	141	3-2-06	1	2	6.59	11	0	2	14	13	12	10	0	12	20	.245	.403	.321	29.85	17.91	67
Mariano, Diovel	R-R	6-1	175	2-23-04	2	0	2.75	9	0	0	20	20	6	6	1	5	17	.260	.321	.403	20.24	5.95	84
Mejia, Algeni	L-L	6-4	183	9-13-04	2	1	1.29	12	0	0	14	10	4	2	1	11	22	.196	.339	.353	35.48	17.74	62
Melgarejo, Oscar	R-R	5-10	169	11-29-05	1	0	8.38	5	0	0	10	16	13	9	2	9	6	.356	.464	.489	10.71	16.07	56
Meza, Jonaikel	R-R	5-11	154	3-23-07	2	0	1.62	12	0	2	17	18	9	3	1	11	15	.277	.413	.385	18.75	13.75	80
Navarro, Diego	R-R	5-11	176	12-29-02	4	2	7.59	12	1	1	21	28	19	18	3	7	18	.304	.360	.457	18.00	7.00	100
Osorio, Manuel	L-L	5-10	170	3-24-06	2	2	1.71	11	10	0	47	24	13	9	0	25	43	.156	.297	.195	23.24	13.51	185
Perez, Angel	R-R	6-2	176	5-22-04	1	2	5.40	10	9	0	33	33	21	20	1	18	36	.262	.359	.317	24.83	12.41	145
Perez, Edelvis	R-R	6-3	190	5-2-05	2	2	3.92	11	10	0	41	35	19	18	3	19	30	.235	.331	.362	17.44	11.05	172
Ruiz, Harrison	R-R	6-1	192	10-2-03	0	1	1.42	3	3	0	6	5	1	1	1	5	7	.208	.345	.333	24.14	17.24	29
Salvador, Rodarni	R-R	6-3	158	4-1-05	2	2	5.40	11	0	2	17	16	10	10	1	9	11	.246	.364	.400	14.29	11.69	77
Tejada, Abrahan	R-R	5-10	151	12-11-04	2	0	5.28	12	0	0	15	11	10	9	1	8	18	.200	.308	.345	27.69	12.31	65
Tovar, Erich	R-R	5-11	160	11-11-06	0	2	9.00	11	0	1	15	19	16	15	0	11	10	.333	.467	.491	13.33	14.67	75

Fielding

C: Arosemena 28, Cadiz 24, Herrera 20, Dalmagro 18, Leon 14, Taveras 14. **1B**: Pena 26, Merejo 22, Taveras 18, Baptiste 12, Leon 11, Borrome 9, Hidalgo **C:** Dalmagro 19, Torres 17, Cadiz 15, Ustariz 6. **1B:** Dalmagro 15, Cadiz 13, Ayala 11, Velasquez 11, John 3, Torres 3, Ustariz 2. **2B:** Marcano 12, Martinez 10, Rodriguez 8, Arias 7, Garces 6, Velasquez 5, Ayala 4, John 4. **3B:** Garces 18, Martinez 11, Arias 9, Marcano 6, Velasquez 4, Ayala 4, John 1. **SS:** Rodriguez 22, Martinez 15, Arias 10, Marcano 8. **LF:** Frances 21, Caceres 13, Torrealba 9, Arias 5, Garces 4, John 3, Velasquez 1, Ayala 1, Caripa 1. **CF:** Arias 34, Caceres 8,

Caripa 4, Torrealba 4. **RF:** Caripa 21, Caceres 14, Frances 10, Torrealba 6, Arias 3.

DSL CLEVELAND GORYL — ROOKIE

DOMINICAN SUMMER LEAGUE

Batting	B-T	Ht.	Wt.	DOB	AVG	OBP	SLG	G	PA	AB	R	H	2B	3B	HR	RBI	BB	HBP	SH	SF	SO	SB	CS	BB%	SO%
Abreus, Jhorvic	B-R	5-7	144	10-27-05	.252	.358	.348	47	187	155	24	39	8	2	1	23	25	3	0	4	32	9	7	13.37	17.11
Arosemena, Pablo	R-R	5-8	154	2-17-06	.228	.408	.354	30	103	79	19	18	5	1	1	8	19	5	0	0	22	3	2	18.45	21.36
Blasco, Alejandro	B-R	5-7	154	3-29-07	.188	.289	.342	36	135	117	19	22	6	0	4	23	16	1	0	1	29	3	2	11.85	21.48
Castillo, Yeiferth	L-L	5-8	155	11-18-06	.301	.389	.366	44	180	153	23	46	8	1	0	28	21	3	0	3	14	0	1	11.67	7.78
De La Cruz, Luis	B-R	5-11	166	9-24-06	.261	.344	.381	36	151	134	23	35	8	1	2	13	17	0	0	0	36	9	2	11.26	23.84
Fernandez, Dauri	B-R	5-9	155	3-7-07	.287	.370	.407	45	192	167	34	48	9	4	1	30	17	6	0	2	19	8	0	8.85	9.90
Guedez, Brayan	L-R	5-8	135	12-7-04	.269	.414	.321	31	99	78	21	21	2	1	0	17	18	2	0	1	16	17	2	18.18	16.16
Herrera, Reiner	L-R	5-11	170	10-20-05	.274	.397	.381	37	141	113	15	31	6	0	2	22	22	3	0	3	22	1	0	15.60	15.60
John, Yorfran	B-R	5-10	163	9-14-04	.300	.300	.300	5	10	10	1	3	0	0	0	3	0	0	0	0	4	0	1	0.00	40.00
Molero, Moises	L-L	5-9	145	2-19-05	.220	.320	.268	29	98	82	7	18	4	0	0	8	8	5	1	2	19	1	0	8.16	19.39
Morillo, Estivel	R-R	6-0	155	7-21-07	.232	.394	.333	39	175	138	26	32	6	4	0	8	34	3	0	0	37	12	6	19.43	21.14
Rodriguez, Gabriel	L-R	6-0	161	5-3-07	.200	.471	.400	4	18	10	4	2	2	0	0	4	5	1	0	1	4	0	1	27.78	22.22
Rodriguez, Johan	R-R	5-11	165	7-28-07	.255	.358	.383	40	173	141	26	36	10	1	2	26	23	3	0	6	26	7	1	13.29	15.03
Taveras, Emilio	R-R	5-10	175	9-18-02	.211	.374	.382	28	99	76	13	16	4	0	3	12	19	2	0	2	27	1	0	19.19	27.27
Taveras, Jonathan	B-R	5-8	146	9-1-05	.187	.287	.227	31	88	75	15	14	1	1	0	10	11	0	1	1	24	9	6	12.50	27.27
Taveras, Romer	L-L	5-7	145	9-11-06	.185	.436	.277	27	94	65	20	12	2	2	0	2	28	1	0	0	20	9	2	29.79	21.28
Torres, Wuinder	R-R	5-10	130	1-28-07	.182	.300	.182	7	30	22	1	4	0	0	0	5	2	3	0	3	5	1	0	6.67	16.67
Ustariz, Santiago	L-R	5-10	165	11-8-06	.232	.357	.317	25	98	82	9	19	2	1	1	8	13	3	0	0	15	2	0	13.27	15.31

Pitching	B-T	Ht.	Wt.	DOB	W	L	ERA	G	GS	SV	IP	Hits	Runs	ER	HR	BB	SO	AVG	OBP	SLG	SO%	BB%	BF
Abreu, Javier	R-R	5-11	150	5-24-06	0	0	54.00	1	1	0	1	2	4	4	0	2	1	.400	.571	.800	14.29	28.57	7
Acosta, Neiver	R-R	6-1	184	7-23-03	0	1	0.00	2	0	0	0	1	9	6	0	8	0	1.000	1.000	2.000	0.00	88.89	9
Betancourt, Joswal	R-R	6-0	170	9-14-05	2	1	5.57	13	0	1	21	22	13	13	3	11	14	.275	.368	.488	14.58	11.46	96
Cabrera, Luilli	R-R	6-3	187	10-30-05	2	1	3.74	13	0	1	22	16	13	9	1	11	26	.205	.298	.295	27.66	11.70	94
Castillo, Wagner	R-R	6-0	180	9-23-03	2	2	5.87	12	0	1	23	12	16	15	2	16	15	.162	.344	.311	15.46	16.49	97
Cruz, Estarlin	L-L	6-7	177	10-5-04	2	1	8.16	12	0	0	14	12	14	13	1	24	20	.231	.474	.308	26.32	31.58	76
Flores, Miguel	L-L	6-2	185	10-15-04	2	1	2.93	11	11	0	46	33	15	15	3	25	59	.208	.324	.333	31.22	13.23	189
Garcia, Luis	R-R	6-1	175	8-15-02	2	0	6.23	7	0	1	9	12	8	6	1	5	7	.353	.415	.529	17.07	12.20	41
Lopez, Carlos	L-L	6-0	148	6-12-06	2	1	8.84	12	0	0	18	15	20	18	1	25	25	.224	.448	.403	26.04	26.04	96
Mariano, Diovel	R-R	6-1	175	2-23-04	0	0	13.50	4	0	0	5	6	8	7	0	9	5	.286	.516	.286	16.13	29.03	31
Melgarejo, Oscar	R-R	5-10	169	11-29-05	3	0	0.00	8	1	1	14	8	0	0	0	8	6	.167	.298	.167	10.53	14.04	57
Milan, Abrahan	R-R	5-11	219	1-22-06	0	1	5.63	12	0	1	16	12	10	10	0	10	10	.211	.352	.263	13.89	13.89	72
Padilla, Erick	R-R	5-10	145	11-26-03	1	1	2.70	13	0	3	17	11	10	5	1	15	19	.190	.397	.241	24.36	19.23	78
Peraza, Santiago	R-R	5-11	135	5-17-05	1	0	0.86	10	10	0	42	21	4	4	0	19	37	.147	.268	.168	22.02	11.31	168
Perez, Erigaldi	R-R	6-2	185	1-25-06	2	0	3.63	10	10	0	40	33	17	16	1	8	26	.219	.263	.311	16.25	5.00	160
Perez, Joelvis	R-R	6-3	180	12-8-04	0	3	3.47	11	9	1	47	42	20	18	1	19	34	.244	.325	.355	17.26	9.64	197
Ramos, Renil	R-R	6-2	143	12-1-05	1	0	3.06	10	10	0	35	26	13	12	0	23	42	.206	.358	.238	26.42	14.47	159
Rivera, Alejandro	R-R	5-10	154	12-27-06	3	2	2.48	13	2	3	29	17	9	8	1	10	25	.172	.252	.253	22.32	8.93	112
Trujillo, Raul	R-R	5-11	205	5-20-07	4	1	3.32	14	0	1	19	15	10	7	1	11	19	.221	.338	.353	23.46	13.58	81
Uribe, Delni	R-R	5-10	155	3-1-07	5	3	4.29	13	0	1	21	22	23	10	0	11	22	.256	.350	.314	22.00	11.00	100
Vasquez, Eriberto	R-R	5-11	175	3-8-04	1	0	1.50	12	0	1	24	15	4	4	0	14	15	.181	.313	.217	15.15	14.14	99

Fielding

C: Arosemena 26, Herrera 22, Ustariz 15, Torres 7, Taveras 2. **1B:** Herrera 20, Taveras 20, Guedez 7, Ustariz 7, Abreus 6, Arosemena 2, Torres 2, Taveras 1. **2B:** Blasco 17, Taveras 15, Fernandez 14, Guedez 8, Abreus 6, Rodriguez 3. **3B:** Abreus 19, Blasco 19, Rodriguez 7, De La Cruz 6, Fernandez 5, Guedez 5. **SS:** Rodriguez 26, Fernandez 19, Abreus 9, Rodriguez 4, Guedez 2. **LF:** Guedez 12, Molero 11, Morillo 9, Castillo 9, De La Cruz 8, Abreus 8, Taveras 6, John 4. **CF:** Morillo 24, Taveras 14, Castillo 9, Molero 8. **RF:** Castillo 28, De La Cruz 16, Molero 7, Morillo 6, Taveras 6, Abreus 1.

Colorado Rockies

SEASON SYNOPSIS: The Rockies continued to plumb new depths, losing 100 games for the second straight season–and the second time in franchise history. They ranked last in the NL in pitching for the third straight season and on offense led the league in strikeouts for the second straight season.

HIGH POINT: The Rockies saw real improvement from their young core, mainly shortstop Ezequiel Tovar and center fielder Brenton Doyle. Doyle trimmed his strikeout rate to 25 percent (from 35%), improved his OBP by 67 points (to .317), slugged 23 homers and stole a team-high 30 bags. Tovar led the National League with 45 doubles and Colorado with 26 home runs, while ranking second in extra-base hits (75).

LOW POINT: Colorado had plenty of low points, but the bullpen provided more than its fair share as veteran closer Daniel Bard missed the season with forearm and knee issues. According to MLB.com, the Rox set a major league record by losing six games where they led by five or more runs in the ninth inning, the first coming April 30 against Miami. The worst was likely an 11-9 loss to the Dodgers on June 19 in which Colorado gave up seven in the ninth.

NOTABLE ROOKIES: Amidst the bullpen problems, righty Victor Vodnik emerged as a reliable power arm, with nine saves and a 4.28 ERA that led the club's relievers. Rule 5 pick Anthony Molina logged 60 innings, with several blowups driving his ERA near 7.00. Outfielder Jordan Beck and C/OF Hunter Goodman both hit below .200 but showed some flashes, with Goodman hitting 13 homers.

KEY TRANSACTIONS: The Rockies needed starting pitching and added Cal Quantrill as a free agent after he was non-tendered by the Guardians; he led the team in wins during a solid 8-11, 4.98 campaign, faring much better than fellow free-agent signee Dakota Hudson (2-12, 6.17), who didn't last the full season. Two of the club's better relievers, lefty Jalen Beeks and righty Nick Mears, were traded at the deadline to the Pirates and Brewers, respectively. The team's longest-tenured player, outfielder/DH Charlie Blackmon, retired at the end of the season, finishing career second in franchise history to Todd Helton in hits (1,805), runs (996) and total bases (2,956).

OPENING DAY PAYROLL: $142,571,000 (16th)

PLAYERS OF THE YEAR

MAJOR LEAGUE

Brenton Doyle
OF
.260/.317/.446
23 HR, 30 SB
Gold Glove in CF

MINOR LEAGUE

Chase Dollander
RHP
(A+/AA)
6-2, 2.59 ERA
169 SO, 47 BB, 118 IP

ORGANIZATION LEADERS

Batting		*Qualifiers
MAJORS		
* AVG	Ezequiel Tovar	.269
* OPS	Ezequiel Tovar	.734
HR	Ezequiel Tovar	26
RBI	Ezequiel Tovar	78
MINORS		
* AVG	Kyle Karros, Spokane	.311
* OBP	Jake Snider, Fresno/Spokane/ACL Rockies	.423
* SLG	Kyle Karros, Spokane	.485
* OPS	Kyle Karros, Spokane	.875
R	Braylen Wimmer, Fresno	94
H	Kyle Karros, Spokane	147
TB	Kyle Karros, Spokane	229
2B	Kyle Karros, Spokane	33
3B	Cole Carrigg, Spokane/ACL Rockies	14
HR	Zach Kokoska, Hartford	20
HR	Glenallen Hill, Fresno/Spokane	20
RBI	Kyle Karros, Spokane	78
BB	Jake Snider, Fresno/Spokane/ACL Rockies	77
SO	Greg Jones, Albuquerque/ACL Rockies	148
SB	Cole Carrigg, Spokane/ACL Rockies	53

Pitching		#Qualifiers
MAJORS		
W	Cal Quantrill	8
# ERA	Ryan Feltner	4.49
SO	Ryan Feltner	138
SV	Tyler Kinley	12
MINORS		
W	Welinton Herrera, Fresno/Spokane	11
L	Karl Kauffmann, Albuquerque	13
# ERA	Michael Prosecky, Fresno	2.72
G	Matt Koch, Albuquerque	49
G	Carson Skipper, Spokane/Hartford	49
GS	Karl Kauffmann, Albuquerque	29
SV	Zach Agnos, Spokane/Hartford	17
IP	Karl Kauffmann, Albuquerque	130
BB	Karl Kauffmann, Albuquerque	76
SO	Chase Dollander, Spokane/Hartford	169
# AVG	Michael Prosecky, Fresno	.215

2024 PERFORMANCE

General Manager: Bill Schmidt. **Farm Director:** Chris Forbes. **Scouting Director:** Danny Montgomery.

Class	Team	League	W	L	PCT	Finish	Manager
Majors	Colorado Rockies	National	61	101	.377	15 (15)	Bud Black
Triple-A	Albuquerque Isotopes	Pacific Coast	58	92	.387	10 (10)	Pedro Lopez
Double-A	Hartford Yard Goats	Eastern	76	60	.559	4 (12)	Bobby Meacham
High-A	Spokane Indians	Northwest	79	51	.608	1 (6)	Robinson Cancel
Low-A	Fresno Grizzlies	California	67	64	.511	4 (8)	Steve Soliz
Rookie	ACL Rockies	Arizona Complex	29	31	.483	8 (15)	Fred Ocasio
Rookie	DSL Rockies	Dominican	37	18	.673	8 (51)	Mauricio Gonzalez
Rookie	DSL Colorado	Dominican	28	27	.509	25 (51)	Eugenio Jose
Overall 2024 Minor League Record			**374**	**343**	**.522**	**9th (30)**	

ORGANIZATION STATISTICS

COLORADO ROCKIES

NATIONAL LEAGUE

Batting	B-T	Ht.	Wt.	DOB	AVG	OBP	SLG	G	PA	AB	R	H	2B	3B	HR	RBI	BB	HBP	SH	SF	SO	SB	CS	BB%	SO%
Amador, Adael	B-R	6-0	160	4-11-03	.171	.194	.200	10	36	35	1	6	1	0	0	0	1	0	0	0	6	1	0	2.78	16.67
Beck, Jordan	R-R	6-3	225	4-19-01	.188	.245	.276	55	184	170	14	32	6	0	3	13	12	1	0	1	65	7	1	6.52	35.33
Blackmon, Charlie	L-L	6-3	221	7-1-86	.256	.329	.412	124	499	449	59	115	24	5	12	52	43	6	0	1	86	6	2	8.62	17.23
Bouchard, Sean	R-R	6-3	215	5-16-96	.187	.290	.297	31	108	91	14	17	7	0	1	8	12	2	1	2	33	4	0	11.11	30.56
Bryant, Kris	R-R	6-5	230	1-4-92	.218	.323	.301	37	155	133	9	29	5	0	2	15	13	8	0	1	48	0	0	8.39	30.97
Cave, Jake	L-L	6-0	200	12-4-92	.251	.290	.396	123	346	323	42	81	16	5	7	37	18	1	1	3	98	5	2	5.20	28.32
Diaz, Elias	R-R	6-1	223	11-17-90	.270	.315	.378	84	327	304	26	82	18	0	5	36	17	4	0	2	64	0	0	5.20	19.57
Doyle, Brenton	R-R	6-2	200	5-14-98	.260	.317	.446	149	603	542	82	141	24	4	23	72	46	3	4	8	153	30	5	7.63	25.37
Goodman, Hunter	R-R	5-11	210	10-8-99	.190	.228	.417	70	224	211	24	40	9	0	13	36	8	3	0	2	64	1	1	3.57	28.57
Hilliard, Sam	L-L	6-5	236	2-21-94	.239	.305	.507	58	158	138	26	33	5	1	10	27	14	0	4	2	56	5	2	8.86	35.44
Jones, Greg	B-R	6-2	175	3-7-98	.200	.333	.800	6	6	5	1	1	0	0	1	1	1	0	0	0	4	0	0	16.67	66.67
Jones, Nolan	L-R	6-4	195	5-7-98	.227	.321	.320	79	297	256	28	58	13	1	3	28	36	1	1	3	91	5	4	12.12	30.64
McMahon, Ryan	L-R	6-2	219	12-14-94	.242	.325	.397	153	645	567	68	137	28	0	20	65	69	3	0	4	185	4	6	10.70	28.68
Montero, Elehuris	R-R	6-3	235	8-17-98	.205	.267	.304	67	247	224	23	46	10	0	4	28	20	0	0	3	56	0	0	8.10	22.67
Rodgers, Brendan	R-R	6-0	204	8-9-96	.267	.314	.407	135	539	501	67	134	29	1	13	54	31	4	1	2	132	1	0	5.75	24.49
Romo, Drew	B-R	5-11	205	8-29-01	.176	.208	.235	16	53	51	4	9	3	0	0	6	2	0	0	0	18	0	1	3.77	33.96
Schunk, Aaron	R-R	6-1	205	7-24-97	.234	.265	.330	39	98	94	14	22	3	0	2	7	4	0	0	0	31	0	1	4.08	31.63
Stallings, Jacob	R-R	6-5	225	12-22-89	.263	.357	.453	82	281	243	31	64	17	1	9	36	27	9	1	1	65	0	0	9.61	23.13
Toglia, Michael	B-L	6-5	226	8-16-98	.218	.311	.456	116	458	399	62	87	14	3	25	55	54	1	0	3	147	10	1	11.79	32.10
Tovar, Ezequiel	R-R	6-0	162	8-1-01	.269	.295	.469	157	695	655	83	176	45	4	26	78	23	4	5	7	200	6	5	3.31	28.78
Trejo, Alan	R-R	6-2	205	5-30-96	.143	.182	.143	28	67	63	4	9	0	0	0	1	2	1	1	0	15	0	0	2.99	22.39

Pitching	B-T	Ht.	Wt.	DOB	W	L	ERA	G	GS	SV	IP	Hits	Runs	ER	HR	BB	SO	AVG	OBP	SLG	SO%	BB%	BF
Beeks, Jalen	L-L	5-11	215	7-10-93	6	4	4.74	45	0	9	49	49	29	26	6	18	38	.261	.325	.388	18.01	8.53	211
Bird, Jake	R-R	6-3	200	12-4-95	2	2	4.50	35	0	1	40	43	21	20	5	25	31	.279	.391	.448	16.76	13.51	185
Blach, Ty	R-L	6-1	215	10-20-90	3	8	6.94	20	12	0	71	103	55	55	17	18	36	.342	.387	.585	10.91	5.45	330
Blalock, Bradley	R-R	6-2	200	12-25-00	1	3	6.07	6	6	0	30	35	22	20	4	19	20	.285	.385	.480	13.99	13.29	143
Carasiti, Matt	R-R	6-2	205	7-23-91	0	1	10.38	7	0	0	9	16	10	10	2	3	7	.410	.465	.641	16.28	6.98	43
Chivilli, Angel	R-R	6-2	162	7-28-02	2	3	4.55	30	0	1	32	31	17	16	7	10	28	.254	.316	.475	21.05	7.52	133
Criswell, Jeff	R-R	6-4	225	3-10-99	1	0	2.75	13	0	0	20	20	6	6	4	9	27	.263	.345	.474	31.03	10.34	87
Curtiss, John	R-R	6-5	220	4-5-93	0	0	15.43	3	0	0	2	6	4	4	2	0	1	.500	.500	1.167	8.33	0.00	12
Davis, Noah	R-R	6-2	195	4-22-97	0	0	5.75	9	0	0	20	31	15	13	3	7	15	.352	.400	.523	15.63	7.29	96
Feltner, Ryan	R-R	6-4	190	9-2-96	3	10	4.49	30	30	0	162	165	94	81	20	52	138	.263	.324	.408	19.94	7.51	692
Freeland, Kyle	L-L	6-4	204	5-14-93	5	8	5.24	21	21	0	113	134	73	66	22	26	85	.291	.329	.507	17.35	5.31	490
Gilbreath, Lucas	L-L	6-1	185	3-5-96	0	0	54.00	3	0	0	1	7	6	6	1	1	0	.700	.750	1.200	0.00	8.33	12
Gomber, Austin	L-L	6-5	220	11-23-93	5	12	4.75	30	30	0	165	178	89	87	30	38	116	.273	.312	.482	16.67	5.46	696
Gordon, Tanner	L-R	6-5	215	10-26-97	0	6	8.65	8	8	0	34	53	34	33	10	6	26	.356	.386	.658	16.25	3.75	160
Halvorsen, Seth	R-R	6-2	225	2-18-00	2	1	1.46	12	0	2	12	8	3	2	2	2	13	.186	.239	.326	28.26	4.35	46
Hartlieb, Geoff	R-R	6-5	240	12-9-93	0	0	9.00	5	0	0	9	13	10	9	1	4	7	.333	.386	.564	15.91	9.09	44
Hill, Jaden	R-R	6-4	234	12-22-99	0	0	5.06	9	0	0	11	8	7	6	2	4	6	.216	.311	.378	13.33	8.89	45
Hudson, Dakota	R-R	6-5	215	9-15-94	2	12	6.17	18	18	0	89	99	66	61	11	50	49	.286	.382	.436	12.13	12.38	404
Justice, Evan	L-L	6-4	205	7-7-98	0	0	0.00	1	0	0	0	0	0	0	0	1	1	.000	.500	.000	50.00	50.00	2
Kinley, Tyler	R-R	6-4	220	1-31-91	6	1	6.19	67	0	12	64	61	44	44	11	33	72	.248	.338	.455	25.26	11.58	285
Koch, Matt	L-R	6-3	215	11-2-90	0	0	81.00	2	0	1	0	3	4	3	1	1	0	.750	.800	1.750	0.00	20.00	5
Lambert, Peter	R-R	6-2	208	4-18-97	2	5	5.72	28	3	0	61	73	42	39	7	29	50	.302	.374	.471	17.86	10.36	280
Lawrence, Justin	R-R	6-3	213	11-25-94	4	4	6.49	56	0	2	60	73	52	43	9	33	45	.313	.408	.485	16.13	11.83	279
Marquez, German	R-R	6-1	230	2-22-95	0	0	6.75	1	1	0	4	5	3	3	1	4	3	.313	.450	.500	15.00	20.00	20
Mears, Nick	R-R	6-2	200	10-7-96	1	4	5.56	41	0	0	45	47	30	28	2	21	57	.264	.335	.360	28.08	10.34	203
Molina, Anthony	R-R	6-1	170	1-12-02	1	1	6.79	35	1	0	60	72	46	45	5	22	41	.305	.364	.445	15.53	8.33	264
Peralta, Luis	L-L	5-11	170	1-6-01	0	0	0.73	15	0	0	12	7	1	1	0	5	14	.175	.292	.200	28.57	10.20	49
Pint, Riley	R-R	6-5	225	11-6-97	0	0	21.60	4	0	0	3	5	8	8	2	5	7	.333	.545	.733	31.82	22.73	22
Quantrill, Cal	L-R	6-3	195	2-10-95	8	11	4.98	29	29	0	148	156	83	82	23	69	110	.273	.361	.461	16.77	10.52	656
Rogers, Josh	L-L	6-3	211	7-10-94	2	0	6.55	6	0	0	11	15	8	8	1	3	3	.349	.400	.512	6.00	6.00	50

Pitching	B-T	Ht.	Wt.	DOB	W	L	ERA	G	GS	SV	IP	Hits	Runs	ER	HR	BB	SO	AVG	OBP	SLG	SO%	BB%	BF
Senzatela, Antonio	R-R	6-1	236	1-21-95	0	1	6.57	3	3	0	12	15	10	9	3	8	7	.326	.426	.587	12.96	14.81	54
Shreve, Chasen	L-L	6-4	180	7-12-90	0	0	0.00	1	0	0	1	1	0	0	0	0	0	.250	.250	.250	0.00	0.00	4
Vodnik, Victor	R-R	6-0	200	10-9-99	5	4	4.28	64	0	9	74	72	37	35	7	37	65	.257	.345	.382	20.31	11.56	320

Fielding

Catcher	PCT	G	PO	A	E	DP	PB
Diaz	.991	67	403	27	4	1	0
Goodman	1.000	23	125	4	0	0	3
Romo	.990	15	93	10	1	1	2
Stallings	.987	76	506	24	7	1	1

First Base	PCT	G	PO	A	E	DP
Bryant	.988	10	82	3	1	10
Goodman	1.000	4	27	3	0	5
Montero	.994	54	453	21	3	47
Toglia	.991	107	847	69	8	96

Second Base	PCT	G	PO	A	E	DP
Amador	.974	10	14	24	1	8
Rodgers	.985	132	181	342	8	89
Schunk	.984	16	24	39	1	13
Trejo	.984	16	20	41	1	10

Third Base	PCT	G	PO	A	E	DP
McMahon	.966	152	98	323	15	33
Schunk	1.000	13	7	18	0	1
Trejo	1.000	7	4	5	0	1

Shortstop	PCT	G	PO	A	E	DP
Schunk	1.000	4	8	12	0	1
Tovar	.988	157	233	435	8	113
Trejo	1.000	2	0	3	0	0

Outfield	PCT	G	PO	A	E	DP
Beck	.990	54	96	3	1	1
Blackmon	1.000	27	38	2	0	0
Bouchard	.945	31	50	2	3	0
Bryant	1.000	12	19	0	0	0
Cave	.995	129	184	5	1	1
Doyle	.991	146	426	8	4	3
Goodman	.964	34	53	1	2	0
Hilliard	.963	56	78	1	3	0
Jones	.955	69	103	4	5	0
Jones	1.000	4	2	0	0	0
Toglia	1.000	16	23	1	0	0

ALBUQUERQUE ISOTOPES — *TRIPLE-A*

PACIFIC COAST LEAGUE

Batting	B-T	Ht.	Wt.	DOB	AVG	OBP	SLG	G	PA	AB	R	H	2B	3B	HR	RBI	BB	HBP	SH	SF	SO	SB	CS	BB%	SO%
Beck, Jordan	R-R	6-3	225	4-19-01	.319	.402	.558	39	189	163	36	52	11	2	8	35	23	1	0	2	44	6	1	12.17	23.28
Boone, Trevor	R-R	6-2	210	9-9-97	.235	.305	.471	48	189	170	30	40	8	1	10	23	17	0	2	0	74	10	1	8.99	39.15
Bouchard, Sean	R-R	6-3	215	5-16-96	.324	.418	.642	46	208	179	38	58	12	6	11	41	25	4	0	0	47	5	2	12.02	22.60
Bryant, Kris	R-R	6-5	230	1-4-92	.290	.333	.516	8	33	31	6	9	1	0	2	3	2	0	0	0	8	0	0	6.06	24.24
Carreras, Julio	R-R	6-1	190	1-12-00	.237	.290	.344	84	339	308	47	73	17	5	2	26	22	2	5	2	102	25	3	6.49	30.09
Clifford, Nolan	L-R	5-10	175	2-4-02	.200	.200	.200	1	5	5	1	1	0	0	0	2	0	0	0	0	1	0	0	0.00	20.00
Cope, Daniel	R-R	6-0	195	6-15-97	.143	.224	.221	21	85	77	12	11	0	0	2	4	8	0	0	0	36	0	0	9.41	42.35
Fernandez, Yanquiel	L-L	6-2	198	1-1-03	.211	.268	.313	33	138	128	10	27	7	0	2	18	9	1	0	0	28	0	0	6.52	20.29
Goodman, Hunter	R-R	5-11	210	10-8-99	.281	.367	.603	31	139	121	21	34	13	1	8	26	15	2	0	1	32	1	0	10.79	23.02
Hannah, Jameson	L-L	5-10	185	8-10-97	.291	.348	.394	38	141	127	19	37	7	0	2	20	12	0	0	2	30	1	0	8.51	21.28
Herron, Jimmy	R-L	6-0	195	7-27-96	.280	.357	.453	95	413	364	60	102	15	3	14	68	40	5	1	3	58	16	5	9.69	14.04
Hilliard, Sam	L-L	6-5	236	2-21-94	.288	.374	.542	65	305	264	57	76	15	5	14	44	38	0	0	3	77	13	2	12.46	25.25
Jones, Greg	B-R	6-2	175	3-7-98	.269	.346	.460	86	406	361	78	97	17	2	16	42	37	6	1	1	143	46	3	9.11	35.22
Jones, Nolan	L-R	6-4	195	5-7-98	.268	.381	.521	20	84	71	15	19	7	1	3	15	10	3	0	0	27	0	0	11.90	32.14
Kaiser, Connor	R-R	6-3	195	11-20-96	.221	.343	.339	90	347	289	39	64	12	2	6	28	49	5	3	1	110	5	1	14.12	31.70
Lavigne, Grant	L-R	6-2	220	8-27-99	.243	.359	.426	130	530	441	68	107	15	6	18	53	73	10	1	5	143	9	8	13.77	26.98
Lewis, AJ	R-R	5-10	195	5-31-98	.314	.432	.486	10	44	35	5	11	6	0	0	9	7	1	0	1	5	1	0	15.91	11.36
MacIver, Willie	R-R	6-1	205	10-28-96	.297	.381	.530	89	369	317	49	94	19	5	15	56	37	9	2	4	90	9	3	10.03	24.39
Montero, Elehuris	R-R	6-3	235	8-17-98	.309	.397	.582	65	297	256	44	79	16	3	16	52	36	3	0	2	78	1	0	12.12	26.26
Montes, Coco	R-R	6-1	200	10-7-96	.335	.414	.551	64	297	254	43	85	16	6	9	47	37	1	0	5	54	5	2	12.46	18.18
Navarro, Cristopher	R-R	6-0	170	6-14-99	.204	.262	.259	18	61	54	3	11	3	0	0	3	4	1	0	2	12	0	0	6.56	19.67
Perez, Jean	R-R	5-10	178	7-20-02	.222	.222	.222	3	10	9	0	2	0	0	0	1	0	0	1	0	4	0	0	0.00	40.00
Rodgers, Brendan	R-R	6-0	204	8-9-96	.250	.250	.500	1	4	4	0	1	1	0	0	3	0	0	0	0	0	0	0	0.00	0.00
Romo, Drew	B-R	5-11	205	8-29-01	.297	.339	.499	85	370	343	51	102	19	4	14	60	16	7	1	3	66	3	1	4.32	17.84
Schunk, Aaron	R-R	6-1	205	7-24-97	.291	.339	.469	69	299	275	36	80	24	2	7	43	19	2	1	2	53	11	5	6.35	17.73
Stovall, Hunter	R-R	5-6	170	9-5-96	.271	.319	.373	102	431	399	65	108	18	1	7	41	29	0	1	2	50	12	4	6.73	11.60
Toglia, Michael	B-L	6-5	226	8-16-98	.277	.363	.571	30	135	119	20	33	4	2	9	27	15	1	0	0	35	1	2	11.11	25.93
Veen, Zac	L-R	6-3	190	12-12-01	.220	.281	.476	21	92	82	12	18	3	0	6	15	7	0	3	0	24	6	1	7.61	26.09

Pitching	B-T	Ht.	Wt.	DOB	W	L	ERA	G	GS	SV	IP	Hits	Runs	ER	HR	BB	SO	AVG	OBP	SLG	SO%	BB%	BF
Adams, Chance	R-R	6-1	215	8-10-94	4	4	6.44	46	3	0	57	72	44	41	4	28	43	.309	.386	.459	16.04	10.45	268
Battenfield, Peyton	R-R	6-4	224	8-10-97	5	8	7.45	26	24	0	118	152	101	98	29	47	80	.318	.377	.590	14.81	8.70	540
Bird, Jake	R-R	6-3	200	12-4-95	1	0	5.27	14	0	0	14	20	11	8	3	7	19	.333	.429	.517	27.14	10.00	70
Blach, Ty	R-L	6-1	215	10-20-90	1	2	4.17	12	9	0	41	40	21	19	7	6	24	.253	.289	.430	14.46	3.61	166
Blalock, Bradley	R-R	6-2	200	12-25-00	0	0	0.00	2	0	0	3	1	0	0	0	0	4	.100	.100	.100	40.00	0.00	10
Carasiti, Matt	R-R	6-2	205	7-23-91	2	1	5.91	20	0	6	21	22	14	14	2	11	26	.262	.351	.452	26.80	11.34	97
Chivilli, Angel	R-R	6-2	162	7-28-02	0	0	0.00	3	0	0	3	0	0	0	0	0	5	.000	.000	.000	45.45	0.00	11
Criswell, Jeff	R-R	6-4	225	3-10-99	1	1	6.24	35	0	0	58	75	43	40	14	28	83	.311	.377	.564	29.96	10.11	277
Curtiss, John	R-R	6-5	220	4-5-93	2	5	3.96	43	0	6	50	51	27	22	4	15	41	.268	.315	.468	19.07	6.98	215
Danish, Tyler	R-R	6-0	200	9-12-94	1	6	7.71	11	10	0	40	61	43	34	4	31	26	.359	.456	.541	12.62	15.05	206
Darnell, Dugan	L-R	6-2	205	6-26-97	0	1	5.58	40	1	0	40	47	32	25	4	21	50	.290	.371	.494	26.60	11.17	188
Davis, Noah	R-R	6-2	195	4-22-97	2	3	5.77	19	8	0	69	82	55	44	7	31	72	.298	.379	.455	22.57	9.72	319
Feltner, Ryan	R-R	6-4	190	9-2-96	0	1	10.13	1	1	0	3	4	5	3	0	2	3	.364	.400	.455	20.00	13.33	15
Freeland, Kyle	L-L	6-4	204	5-14-93	0	0	3.38	2	2	0	8	5	3	3	1	5	8	.192	.323	.308	25.81	16.13	31
Gilbreath, Lucas	L-L	6-1	185	3-5-96	0	0	7.11	7	0	0	6	6	5	5	0	5	6	.250	.438	.292	18.75	15.63	32
Goldsberry, Blake	R-R	6-4	220	5-21-97	0	1	9.31	10	1	0	10	14	12	10	1	12	6	.326	.464	.535	10.71	21.43	56
Gonsalves, Stephen	L-L	6-5	218	7-8-94	2	2	7.41	17	0	0	17	18	14	14	1	22	23	.273	.462	.348	25.27	24.18	91
Gordon, Tanner	L-R	6-5	215	10-26-97	4	4	4.45	11	11	0	55	62	31	27	11	13	44	.292	.332	.538	19.13	5.65	230
Halvorsen, Seth	R-R	6-2	225	2-18-00	1	0	3.00	8	0	1	9	8	3	3	1	4	15	.235	.316	.324	39.47	10.53	38
Hartlieb, Geoff	R-R	6-5	240	12-9-93	5	1	5.47	41	0	2	54	59	35	33	8	24	56	.272	.348	.479	22.86	9.80	245
Hill, Jaden	R-R	6-4	234	12-22-99	1	0	10.29	7	0	1	7	9	8	8	1	6	13	.300	.447	.500	34.21	15.79	38
Hillman, Juan	L-L	6-1	195	5-15-97	2	5	5.46	19	9	0	56	72	43	34	9	26	33	.317	.391	.542	12.79	10.08	258

Pitching	B-T	Ht.	Wt.	DOB	W	L	ERA	G	GS	SV	IP	Hits	Runs	ER	HR	BB	SO	AVG	OBP	SLG	SO%	BB%	BF
Hollowell, Gavin	R-R	6-7	215	11-4-97	0	0	16.62	6	0	0	4	6	10	8	1	4	6	.300	.423	.600	23.08	15.38	26
Hudson, Dakota	R-R	6-5	215	9-15-94	1	2	9.53	3	3	0	11	18	14	12	2	4	10	.367	.418	.592	18.18	7.27	55
Jones, Stephen	R-R	6-4	195	7-30-97	3	1	13.08	20	0	0	21	43	41	31	5	24	26	.413	.515	.673	19.26	17.78	135
Justice, Evan	L-L	6-4	205	7-7-98	0	3	8.76	32	0	0	25	27	32	24	2	34	26	.281	.478	.385	18.98	24.82	137
Kauffmann, Karl	R-R	6-2	200	8-15-97	5	13	8.95	29	29	0	130	194	141	129	34	76	74	.356	.433	.640	11.60	11.91	638
Kelly, Antoine	L-L	6-5	205	12-5-99	0	0	9.35	9	0	0	9	6	10	9	2	10	10	.182	.372	.364	23.26	23.26	43
Kitchen, Austin	L-L	6-0	200	2-11-97	3	0	3.65	18	0	0	25	25	11	10	1	6	18	.260	.301	.333	17.48	5.83	103
Koch, Matt	L-R	6-3	215	11-2-90	6	5	4.83	49	0	5	54	73	37	29	10	8	38	.327	.351	.561	15.77	3.32	241
Lambert, Peter	R-R	6-2	208	4-18-97	0	1	5.28	10	4	0	29	24	21	17	3	13	38	.222	.303	.370	30.89	10.57	123
Lawrence, Justin	R-R	6-3	213	11-25-94	0	1	54.00	1	0	0	0	3	2	2	0	1	0	.750	.800	.750	0.00	20.00	5
Marquez, German	R-R	6-1	230	2-22-95	0	0	54.00	1	1	0	1	4	4	4	1	1	1	.667	.714	1.667	14.29	14.29	7
Palmquist, Carson	L-L	6-3	185	10-17-00	1	4	5.86	9	9	0	35	38	24	23	8	27	31	.277	.400	.504	18.67	16.27	166
Peralta, Luis	L-L	5-11	170	1-6-01	0	0	0.00	1	0	0	1	0	0	0	0	1	1	.000	.250	.000	25.00	25.00	4
Pint, Riley	R-R	6-5	225	11-6-97	2	1	4.12	35	0	1	39	26	19	18	0	38	66	.190	.389	.226	35.68	20.54	185
Ponticelli, Thomas	R-R	6-1	205	4-15-97	0	6	14.96	10	8	0	28	52	52	46	11	29	12	.400	.503	.808	7.41	17.90	162
Quezada, Andrew	L-R	6-1	185	6-28-97	0	0	4.32	4	0	0	8	8	6	4	0	10	3	.258	.439	.323	7.32	24.39	41
Rogers, Josh	L-L	6-3	211	7-10-94	2	7	6.26	19	16	0	83	112	62	58	22	16	51	.318	.349	.614	13.56	4.26	376
Rolison, Ryan	R-L	6-2	213	7-11-97	1	2	5.19	22	1	0	35	35	20	20	7	9	25	.261	.308	.478	17.48	6.29	143
Shreve, Chasen	L-L	6-4	180	7-12-90	0	0	27.00	1	0	0	1	3	3	3	3	0	0	.500	.500	2.000	0.00	0.00	6
Sommers, Jake	R-R	6-2	190	5-5-97	0	0	7.36	3	0	0	4	5	3	3	0	4	5	.333	.474	.333	26.32	21.05	19
Spain, Dylan	R-R	6-6	205	6-21-98	0	0	18.00	1	0	0	2	3	4	4	1	1	1	.333	.400	.667	10.00	10.00	10
Todd, Reagan	L-L	6-3	218	8-30-95	0	0	13.50	2	0	0	1	1	2	2	0	2	1	.167	.375	.167	12.50	25.00	8
Wilcox, Kyle	R-R	6-3	195	6-14-94	0	1	9.12	16	0	0	26	29	28	26	5	25	30	.282	.432	.505	22.56	18.80	133

Fielding

Catcher	PCT	G	PO	A	E	DP	PB
Cope	.991	13	101	4	1	0	2
Goodman	.981	12	96	6	2	0	1
Lewis	1.000	2	12	0	0	0	0
MacIver	.991	64	506	37	5	8	3
Romo	.996	60	474	45	2	6	11

First Base	PCT	G	PO	A	E	DP
Bouchard	.957	3	18	4	1	1
Bryant	1.000	3	15	2	0	1
Goodman	.947	5	33	3	2	1
Kaiser	1.000	7	54	6	0	7
Lavigne	.978	114	869	57	21	98
MacIver	1.000	1	6	1	0	1
Montero	.981	15	99	6	2	13
Toglia	.980	7	46	4	1	3

Second Base	PCT	G	PO	A	E	DP
Carreras	.975	18	35	43	2	14
Jones	.972	8	17	18	1	3
Lewis	1.000	4	7	9	0	2
Montes	.975	35	59	96	4	20
Navarro	1.000	1	1	0	0	0
Perez	1.000	2	5	8	0	3
Rodgers	.750	1	2	1	1	0
Schunk	1.000	13	23	27	0	3
Stovall	.987	71	109	184	4	62

Third Base	PCT	G	PO	A	E	DP
Carreras	.878	21	11	25	5	2
Clifford	1.000	1	0	4	0	0
Kaiser	.949	11	10	27	2	1
Montero	.872	49	25	84	16	11
Montes	1.000	11	6	27	0	1
Navarro	.833	9	6	14	4	3
Perez	.000	1	0	0	0	0
Schunk	.965	41	37	72	4	11
Stovall	1.000	9	8	11	0	2

Shortstop	PCT	G	PO	A	E	DP
Carreras	.931	43	47	88	10	18
Jones	.939	14	25	37	4	8
Kaiser	.993	66	80	193	2	45
Montes	.972	8	12	23	1	6
Navarro	.923	8	11	25	3	9
Schunk	.978	13	12	32	1	7
Stovall	1.000	1	1	3	0	1

Outfield	PCT	G	PO	A	E	DP
Beck	.987	36	72	2	1	1
Boone	.962	49	96	5	4	0
Bouchard	.986	33	71	2	1	1
Bryant	1.000	2	2	0	0	0
Fernandez	.935	31	55	3	4	1
Goodman	.929	5	13	0	1	0
Hannah	.987	34	71	3	1	2
Herron	.993	79	142	3	1	0
Hilliard	.974	64	149	0	4	0
Jones	.960	63	161	7	7	1
Jones	.962	11	22	3	1	1
Stovall	1.000	20	28	1	0	0
Toglia	1.000	23	62	0	0	0
Veen	.980	20	47	1	1	1

HARTFORD YARD GOATS — DOUBLE-A

EASTERN LEAGUE

Batting	B-T	Ht.	Wt.	DOB	AVG	OBP	SLG	G	PA	AB	R	H	2B	3B	HR	RBI	BB	HBP	SH	SF	SO	SB	CS	BB%	SO%
Amador, Adael	B-R	6-0	160	4-11-03	.230	.343	.376	100	455	383	61	88	12	1	14	52	62	5	1	2	88	35	11	13.63	19.34
Bernabel, Warming	R-R	6-1	180	6-6-02	.263	.296	.359	120	506	479	51	126	17	1	9	64	18	6	0	3	72	12	4	3.56	14.23
Boone, Trevor	R-R	6-2	210	9-9-97	.059	.086	.176	10	35	34	2	2	1	0	1	3	1	0	0	0	22	0	0	2.86	62.86
Datres, Kyle	R-R	6-0	205	1-5-96	.226	.343	.394	69	268	226	30	51	11	0	9	32	37	4	0	1	71	13	2	13.81	26.49
Fernandez, Yanquiel	L-L	6-2	198	1-1-03	.283	.339	.439	89	346	314	40	89	17	1	10	46	26	2	0	3	66	1	0	7.51	19.08
Fulford, Braxton	R-R	5-10	190	12-9-98	.241	.341	.412	92	379	323	47	78	21	2	10	46	38	13	0	4	95	10	2	10.03	25.07
Guerrero, Juan	R-R	6-1	160	9-10-01	.313	.350	.383	29	124	115	17	36	2	0	2	17	7	0	1	1	15	4	3	5.65	12.10
Kent, Nic	R-R	6-2	185	4-10-00	.248	.311	.307	101	364	326	36	81	13	0	2	35	23	7	7	1	83	10	0	6.32	22.80
Kokoska, Zach	L-L	6-1	200	10-20-98	.216	.310	.461	104	398	343	57	74	22	1	20	67	35	14	1	5	122	15	4	8.79	30.65
Lewis, AJ	R-R	5-10	195	5-31-98	.197	.291	.237	24	86	76	8	15	3	0	0	10	8	2	0	0	27	1	1	9.30	31.40
Montgomery, Benny	R-R	6-4	200	9-9-02	.283	.313	.500	11	48	46	8	13	4	0	2	10	2	0	0	0	20	3	0	4.17	41.67
Navarro, Cristopher	R-R	6-0	170	6-14-99	.121	.237	.152	13	38	33	4	4	1	0	0	1	4	1	0	0	10	0	0	10.53	26.32
Palma, Ronaiker	R-R	5-8	180	1-2-00	.242	.348	.281	55	209	178	21	43	4	0	1	18	25	4	2	0	34	7	0	11.96	16.27
Restituyo, Bladimir	R-R	5-10	151	7-2-01	.270	.312	.350	111	444	408	50	110	18	0	5	47	25	3	0	6	73	25	9	5.63	16.44
Ritter, Ryan	R-R	6-2	200	11-10-00	.270	.370	.403	91	373	318	57	86	17	2	7	32	35	16	3	1	88	17	0	9.38	23.59
Thompson, Sterlin	L-R	6-4	200	6-26-01	.245	.319	.385	119	518	462	62	113	18	4	13	57	43	9	0	4	122	12	4	8.30	23.55
Tucker, Tevin	R-R	6-0	190	2-10-00	.250	.200	.250	2	6	4	0	1	0	0	0	1	0	0	1	1	3	0	0	0.00	50.00
Veen, Zac	L-R	6-3	190	12-12-01	.268	.359	.457	36	145	127	24	34	5	2	5	14	16	2	0	0	38	10	1	11.03	26.21
Ward, Braiden	L-R	5-10	160	1-18-99	.243	.353	.358	85	323	268	50	65	8	4	5	19	24	23	6	2	81	32	5	7.43	25.08

Pitching	B-T	Ht.	Wt.	DOB	W	L	ERA	G	GS	SV	IP	Hits	Runs	ER	HR	BB	SO	AVG	OBP	SLG	SO%	BB%	BF
Adams, Blake	R-R	6-2	215	9-11-00	2	2	3.46	5	5	0	26	27	15	10	2	3	29	.265	.280	.382	26.85	2.78	108
Agnos, Zach	R-R	6-0	210	8-15-00	4	2	1.95	24	0	7	28	15	7	6	2	9	33	.158	.238	.263	30.84	8.41	107
Albright, Mason	L-L	6-0	190	11-26-02	4	8	4.59	24	23	0	116	115	64	59	13	40	80	.258	.323	.415	16.19	8.10	494
Barger, Alec	R-R	6-2	201	3-24-98	4	1	3.52	39	0	0	46	42	24	18	3	18	46	.236	.318	.343	22.77	8.91	202

Baumgartner, Collin	L-R	6-6	250	9-26-98	4	2	2.17	31	0	0	37	30	11	9	2	17	45	.221	.314	.316	28.66	10.83	157
Bido, Anderson	R-R	6-3	205	5-7-99	0	0	2.82	13	1	0	22	15	8	7	1	4	28	.181	.236	.313	31.46	4.49	89
Blalock, Bradley	R-R	6-2	200	12-25-00	0	1	6.17	2	2	0	12	16	9	8	3	2	12	.340	.380	.617	24.00	4.00	50
Cande, Jarrod	R-R	6-2	215	8-16-99	6	6	4.15	23	21	0	106	93	53	49	15	46	95	.232	.320	.409	20.61	9.98	461
Castillo, Brayan	R-R	6-0	145	9-11-00	0	0	2.38	9	0	1	11	9	3	3	1	5	13	.214	.292	.310	27.08	10.42	48
Chivilli, Angel	R-R	6-2	162	7-28-02	1	0	2.49	22	0	1	25	21	9	7	2	12	37	.226	.318	.366	34.58	11.21	107
Darnell, Dugan	L-R	6-2	205	6-26-97	0	0	0.00	3	0	1	4	2	0	0	0	1	6	.154	.214	.154	42.86	7.14	14
Dollander, Chase	R-R	6-2	200	10-26-01	2	1	2.25	9	9	0	48	34	14	12	1	19	58	.195	.291	.282	29.15	9.55	199
Goldsberry, Blake	R-R	6-4	220	5-21-97	1	0	3.38	9	0	0	11	6	5	4	1	2	10	.158	.238	.289	23.81	4.76	42
Green, Mason	L-L	6-1	195	2-5-99	1	1	7.71	4	2	0	12	18	10	10	3	5	13	.346	.414	.596	22.41	8.62	58
Halvorsen, Seth	R-R	6-2	225	2-18-00	4	2	4.84	33	0	8	35	34	21	19	2	19	41	.256	.363	.353	25.95	12.03	158
Hardy, Brendan	R-R	6-4	170	12-15-99	1	3	4.08	34	0	0	40	32	18	18	3	20	43	.224	.339	.336	25.15	11.70	171
Hill, Jaden	R-R	6-4	234	12-22-99	5	2	3.52	34	0	6	38	39	17	15	3	11	56	.255	.325	.379	32.94	6.47	170
Kitchen, Austin	L-L	6-0	200	2-11-97	2	0	1.08	5	0	0	8	9	1	1	0	2	6	.290	.333	.290	18.18	6.06	33
Kostyshock, Jacob	R-R	6-4	175	1-2-98	0	0	11.57	7	0	0	9	13	13	12	3	10	8	.333	.500	.744	14.81	18.52	54
Marquez, German	R-R	6-1	230	2-22-95	0	2	4.15	2	2	0	9	9	5	4	1	1	10	.250	.270	.417	27.03	2.70	37
McGowan, Bryce	R-R	6-1	205	3-20-00	2	0	4.12	41	0	2	44	40	23	20	5	25	47	.241	.339	.380	24.48	13.02	192
McKillican, Adam	R-R	6-5	225	1-9-98	0	0	20.25	1	0	0	1	2	3	3	1	2	1	.400	.500	1.000	12.50	25.00	8
Mejia, Juan	R-R	6-3	200	7-4-00	4	4	5.00	47	0	6	54	57	32	30	3	30	65	.275	.372	.391	26.75	12.35	243
Palmquist, Carson	L-L	6-3	185	10-17-00	6	4	3.17	18	18	0	82	59	35	29	7	33	113	.203	.297	.328	34.24	10.00	330
Peralta, Luis	L-L	5-11	170	1-6-01	3	0	1.29	5	0	0	7	4	1	1	1	2	10	.167	.259	.333	37.04	7.41	27
Quezada, Andrew	L-R	6-1	185	6-28-97	5	2	3.18	15	15	0	82	81	33	29	9	20	60	.266	.321	.408	17.96	5.99	334
Senzatela, Antonio	R-R	6-1	236	1-21-95	0	1	6.17	3	3	0	12	12	8	8	2	2	13	.261	.286	.435	26.53	4.08	49
Shawver, Evan	R-L	6-0	175	9-11-99	3	3	2.90	36	6	0	50	35	21	16	2	29	50	.199	.321	.313	23.92	13.88	209
Skipper, Carson	L-L	6-2	211	8-12-99	2	2	4.50	15	0	0	20	21	11	10	2	10	23	.259	.337	.407	25.00	10.87	92
Sommers, Jake	R-R	6-2	190	5-5-97	1	2	11.74	7	0	0	8	11	11	10	0	5	10	.306	.390	.444	24.39	12.20	41
Spain, Dylan	R-R	6-6	205	6-21-98	0	1	6.97	8	0	1	10	16	9	8	4	5	6	.348	.412	.696	11.76	9.80	51
Sullivan, Sean	R-L	6-4	190	7-22-02	2	0	1.97	7	7	0	32	28	7	7	2	7	24	.243	.293	.357	19.51	5.69	123
Todd, Reagan	L-L	6-3	218	8-30-95	0	1	4.66	8	0	0	10	13	8	5	0	2	14	.310	.348	.405	30.43	4.35	46
Van Scoyoc, Connor	R-R	6-6	234	11-26-99	7	7	4.46	23	22	0	115	110	61	57	12	43	73	.253	.326	.395	14.93	8.79	489
Vodnik, Victor	R-R	6-0	200	10-9-99	0	0	0.00	1	0	0	1	0	0	0	0	0	2	.000	.000	.000	66.67	0.00	3

Fielding

Catcher	PCT	G	PO	A	E	DP	PB
Betancourt	.984	65	611	58	11	3	9
Cordova	1.000	20	138	7	0	3	1
Messina	.988	17	148	10	2	2	2
Ordonez	.989	39	315	34	4	3	3

First Base	PCT	G	PO	A	E	DP
Betancourt	.992	35	221	18	2	21
Boone	1.000	9	58	3	0	2
Cordova	1.000	63	420	27	0	37
Kelly	.980	17	91	9	2	6
Martin	.960	5	22	2	1	2
Messinger	1.000	11	72	2	0	9

Second Base	PCT	G	PO	A	E	DP
Blomgren	.976	14	16	24	1	5
Hill	.975	12	16	23	1	4
Jorge	.975	26	53	62	3	13
Perez	.957	54	74	105	8	24
Perez	1.000	5	14	9	0	5
Ward	.956	26	40	46	4	10

Third Base	PCT	G	PO	A	E	DP
Condon	.909	5	4	6	1	0
Karros	.970	116	116	211	10	29
Messinger	1.000	2	1	1	0	0
Perez	.000	2	0	0	0	0
Perez	1.000	6	0	6	0	0

Shortstop	PCT	G	PO	A	E	DP
Blomgren	.962	16	12	39	2	6
Carrigg	.955	14	21	21	2	4
Jorge	.944	91	112	176	17	31
Ordonez	.000	1	0	0	0	0
Perez	.972	10	10	25	1	5
Perez	1.000	2	2	2	0	0

Outfield	PCT	G	PO	A	E	DP
Andrews	.985	32	61	3	1	2
Blomgren	1.000	1	1	0	0	0
Boone	1.000	4	14	0	0	0
Bugarin	.980	48	92	4	2	0
Carrigg	.991	92	213	5	2	3
Condon	1.000	14	25	0	0	0
Cordova	1.000	1	1	0	0	0
Guerrero	.969	71	120	3	4	1
Hill	.971	35	65	2	2	1
Kelly	.909	4	10	0	1	0
Martin	.993	55	130	7	1	1
Snider	.986	42	68	1	1	0
Veen	1.000	4	5	0	0	0
Ward	1.000	5	11	0	0	0

SPOKANE INDIANS — HIGH-A

NORTHWEST LEAGUE

Batting	B-T	Ht.	Wt.	DOB	AVG	OBP	SLG	G	PA	AB	R	H	2B	3B	HR	RBI	BB	HBP	SH	SF	SO	SB	CS	BB%	SO%
Andrews, EJ	R-R	6-1	210	9-28-00	.250	.322	.435	39	124	108	18	27	5	0	5	19	11	1	3	1	35	8	0	8.87	28.23
Betancourt, Bryant	L-R	5-11	170	10-12-03	.238	.316	.376	110	433	378	48	90	12	2	12	47	41	4	6	4	93	15	5	9.47	21.48
Blomgren, Jack	R-R	5-10	180	9-27-98	.252	.373	.398	31	128	103	15	26	5	2	2	8	17	4	2	2	25	10	1	13.28	19.53
Boone, Trevor	R-R	6-2	210	9-9-97	.196	.281	.373	16	57	51	8	10	0	0	3	7	3	3	0	0	18	1	1	5.26	31.58
Bugarin, Jesus	R-R	5-10	180	12-2-01	.248	.266	.363	72	279	270	30	67	10	0	7	37	5	2	1	1	73	6	1	1.79	26.16
Carrigg, Cole	B-R	6-3	190	5-8-02	.280	.358	.475	111	510	440	80	123	16	11	16	60	50	8	5	7	97	51	11	9.80	19.02
Condon, Charlie	R-R	6-6	211	4-14-03	.180	.248	.270	25	109	100	6	18	4	1	1	11	4	5	0	0	34	4	0	3.67	31.19
Cordova, Jose	R-R	6-0	180	1-11-00	.286	.358	.400	84	321	280	38	80	19	2	3	38	30	3	4	3	65	11	11	9.35	20.25
Guerrero, Juan	R-R	6-1	160	9-10-01	.302	.341	.399	92	385	358	56	108	21	1	4	49	19	4	1	3	54	23	2	4.94	14.03
Hill, Glenallen	B-R	5-9	170	9-30-00	.282	.364	.589	47	187	163	34	46	6	1	14	26	17	4	3	0	50	10	0	9.09	26.74
Jorge, Dyan	R-R	6-3	170	3-18-03	.267	.336	.319	121	541	483	82	129	13	3	2	49	48	4	2	4	122	36	10	8.87	22.55
Karros, Kyle	R-R	6-5	220	7-26-02	.311	.390	.485	123	539	472	64	147	33	2	15	78	54	9	0	4	123	12	5	10.02	22.82
Kelly, Parker	R-R	6-3	220	3-18-99	.183	.265	.233	23	69	60	8	11	1	1	0	3	6	1	1	1	24	4	1	8.70	34.78
Martin, Robby	L-R	6-3	190	8-17-99	.248	.306	.348	63	254	230	27	57	5	0	6	36	19	1	2	2	52	5	6	7.48	20.47
Messina, Cole	R-R	6-0	230	5-14-03	.140	.232	.220	17	56	50	1	7	1	0	1	6	5	1	0	0	11	0	0	8.93	19.64
Messinger, Skyler	R-R	6-3	220	11-1-98	.239	.266	.364	25	94	88	14	21	5	0	2	12	4	0	0	2	25	3	0	4.26	26.60
Ordonez, Jesus	R-R	5-8	180	12-26-99	.270	.353	.372	44	169	148	22	40	6	0	3	14	12	7	2	0	26	4	2	7.10	15.38
Perez, Andy	L-R	6-3	165	6-3-04	.226	.250	.323	16	66	62	7	14	3	0	1	10	1	1	2	0	14	5	0	1.52	21.21
Perez, Jean	R-R	5-10	178	7-20-02	.260	.288	.353	64	223	204	36	53	7	3	2	27	7	2	8	2	63	8	0	3.14	28.25

Snider, Jake	L-R	6-1	190	5-19-98	.237	.383	.353	70	272	215	45	51	6	2	5	23	42	10	3	2	54	21	2	15.44	19.85
Veen, Zac	L-R	6-3	190	12-12-01	.235	.435	.294	5	23	17	4	4	1	0	0	3	6	0	0	0	3	3	2	26.09	13.04
Ward, Braiden	L-R	5-10	160	1-18-99	.340	.426	.550	32	115	100	23	34	7	4	2	17	4	11	0	0	24	18	4	3.48	20.87

Pitching	B-T	Ht.	Wt.	DOB	W	L	ERA	G	GS	SV	IP	Hits	Runs	ER	HR	BB	SO	AVG	OBP	SLG	SO%	BB%	BF
Adams, Blake	R-R	6-2	215	9-11-00	7	3	2.76	18	17	0	101	101	36	31	7	23	96	.259	.302	.377	22.75	5.45	422
Agnos, Zach	R-R	6-0	210	8-15-00	4	1	0.73	21	0	10	25	15	5	2	1	2	30	.167	.191	.233	31.91	2.13	94
Ahearn, Tyler	R-R	6-2	202	8-25-98	1	1	12.21	14	0	1	14	19	19	19	2	9	10	.322	.432	.525	13.33	12.00	75
Amoroso, Luis	R-R	6-1	192	12-12-99	1	3	4.80	39	0	3	45	49	31	24	3	17	31	.271	.347	.381	15.20	8.33	204
Bido, Anderson	R-R	6-3	205	5-7-99	1	0	3.94	12	0	0	16	20	7	7	1	2	9	.333	.369	.450	13.85	3.08	65
Bush, Nick	L-L	6-0	195	8-23-96	0	1	6.43	2	2	0	7	12	5	5	1	4	8	.387	.457	.548	22.86	11.43	35
Carmichael, Braden	R-L	5-10	186	5-23-00	0	0	10.29	6	0	0	7	10	11	8	2	4	6	.323	.389	.613	16.67	11.11	36
Castillo, Brayan	R-R	6-0	145	9-11-00	2	3	3.66	28	0	5	32	16	14	13	4	18	39	.143	.260	.277	29.77	13.74	131
Denton, Cade	R-R	6-3	180	12-28-01	0	1	7.36	5	0	0	7	8	6	6	1	1	3	.286	.355	.500	9.68	3.23	31
Dollander, Chase	R-R	6-2	200	10-26-01	4	1	2.83	14	14	0	70	60	26	22	6	28	111	.228	.323	.327	37.00	9.33	300
Eaton, Konner	R-L	6-3	210	10-30-02	0	0	0.00	1	0	0	2	1	0	0	0	2	4	.143	.333	.143	44.44	22.22	9
Franzen, Caleb	L-L	6-3	200	6-10-01	1	0	4.74	14	0	0	25	18	13	13	3	18	11	.198	.342	.330	9.91	16.22	111
Gilbreath, Lucas	L-L	6-1	185	3-5-96	0	0	10.80	2	1	0	2	1	2	2	1	2	4	.167	.375	.667	50.00	25.00	8
Green, Mason	L-L	6-1	195	2-5-99	9	5	2.79	20	15	0	97	83	38	30	9	46	99	.233	.324	.365	24.32	11.30	407
Hammer, Bryson	L-L	6-1	186	10-8-01	3	1	2.57	11	0	0	14	14	6	4	0	6	10	.269	.367	.308	16.67	10.00	60
Herrera, Welinton	L-L	6-0	166	4-3-04	3	2	4.76	23	0	0	28	26	16	15	1	14	30	.245	.339	.368	24.79	11.57	121
Herrera, Yujanyer	R-R	6-3	175	8-17-03	1	0	3.31	6	6	0	33	26	13	12	1	11	33	.220	.290	.297	25.00	8.33	132
Hyde, Braxton	R-R	6-3	195	6-6-01	3	2	3.44	33	2	0	65	60	28	25	3	33	53	.254	.353	.343	19.13	11.91	277
Juarez, Victor	R-R	6-0	173	6-19-03	4	7	4.30	22	21	0	111	112	64	53	19	34	113	.262	.323	.471	24.04	7.23	470
Mahoney, Jack	R-R	6-3	205	8-13-01	1	1	5.33	6	5	0	25	28	15	15	4	8	24	.289	.355	.515	22.43	7.48	107
Marquez, German	R-R	6-1	230	2-22-95	0	0	0.00	1	1	0	4	1	0	0	0	2	3	.083	.214	.083	20.00	13.33	15
Pacheco, Alberto	L-L	6-1	176	11-29-02	1	1	3.43	4	3	0	21	23	8	8	0	10	13	.288	.363	.325	14.29	10.99	91
Palermo, Davison	R-R	6-4	200	12-16-99	2	5	4.95	34	0	1	40	36	25	22	6	18	37	.238	.337	.437	21.14	10.29	175
Prosecky, Michael	L-L	6-3	200	2-28-01	2	2	5.90	8	7	0	29	34	24	19	2	17	44	.293	.406	.440	31.65	12.23	139
Ramires, Felix	L-L	6-4	175	9-26-99	2	1	6.98	33	0	1	39	47	33	30	3	25	45	.297	.411	.468	23.68	13.16	190
Rolison, Ryan	R-L	6-2	213	7-11-97	0	0	5.79	3	1	0	5	7	3	3	1	3	3	.350	.435	.600	13.04	13.04	23
Sanchez, Sergio	R-R	6-0	180	1-13-01	2	1	6.41	28	0	0	39	37	29	28	8	31	50	.245	.392	.503	26.46	16.40	189
Senzatela, Antonio	R-R	6-1	236	1-21-95	0	0	3.38	2	2	0	5	4	2	2	1	2	5	.200	.273	.350	22.73	9.09	22
Skipper, Carson	L-L	6-2	211	8-12-99	7	1	1.40	34	0	9	39	30	8	6	2	8	56	.207	.252	.262	36.13	5.16	155
Staine, Connor	R-R	6-4	200	1-12-01	4	6	4.48	20	19	0	90	72	48	45	11	42	101	.220	.317	.381	26.37	10.97	383
Sullivan, Sean	R-L	6-4	190	7-22-02	7	2	2.16	14	14	0	83	62	25	20	7	8	101	.200	.227	.326	31.46	2.49	321
Torres, Carlos	R-R	6-4	240	5-3-01	5	0	3.32	15	0	0	22	21	10	8	2	4	20	.247	.289	.376	22.22	4.44	90
Weatherly, Sam	L-L	6-4	205	5-28-99	2	0	0.00	10	0	5	12	4	0	0	0	4	18	.111	.200	.139	42.86	9.52	42

Fielding

Catcher	PCT	G	PO	A	E	DP	PB
Fulford	.986	87	809	51	12	5	7
Lewis	.957	3	22	0	1	0	0
Palma	.988	47	378	31	5	0	2

First Base	PCT	G	PO	A	E	DP
Bernabel	.992	17	117	7	1	8
Boone	1.000	1	5	0	0	0
Datres	.997	43	300	30	1	23
Kent	1.000	8	58	6	0	7
Kokoska	.993	61	388	38	3	40
Thompson	.982	11	51	4	1	9

Second Base	PCT	G	PO	A	E	DP
Amador	.960	94	152	230	16	44
Datres	1.000	4	6	5	0	2
Kent	.978	25	37	52	2	10
Lewis	.962	5	10	15	1	1
Navarro	1.000	7	13	13	0	5
Thompson	.800	1	4	4	2	2
Tucker	1.000	2	2	4	0	1
Ward	.895	4	6	11	2	3

Third Base	PCT	G	PO	A	E	DP
Bernabel	.939	97	58	142	13	13
Datres	.889	12	13	19	4	2
Kent	.900	23	19	17	4	1
Navarro	.917	5	3	8	1	1
Thompson	1.000	1	0	1	0	0

Shortstop	PCT	G	PO	A	E	DP
Amador	1.000	4	6	4	0	1
Kent	.951	49	64	90	8	17
Ritter	.953	88	159	187	17	54

Outfield	PCT	G	PO	A	E	DP
Boone	1.000	6	7	1	0	0
Datres	1.000	1	2	0	0	0
Fernandez	.977	78	124	4	3	0
Guerrero	1.000	26	33	2	0	0
Kokoska	1.000	22	30	0	0	0
Montgomery	1.000	10	18	1	0	0
Restituyo	.980	102	182	13	4	3
Thompson	.967	80	141	6	5	1
Veen	1.000	25	49	2	0	0
Ward	.984	73	176	6	3	2

FRESNO GRIZZLIES — LOW-A

CALIFORNIA LEAGUE

Batting	B-T	Ht.	Wt.	DOB	AVG	OBP	SLG	G	PA	AB	R	H	2B	3B	HR	RBI	BB	HBP	SH	SF	SO	SB	CS	BB%	SO%
Andrews, EJ	R-R	6-1	210	9-28-00	.184	.294	.316	49	180	152	16	28	5	3	3	18	25	0	0	3	47	5	1	13.89	26.11
Calaz, Robert	R-R	6-2	202	11-22-05	.327	.386	.571	13	57	49	10	16	2	2	2	11	5	1	0	2	16	3	0	8.77	28.07
Castillo, Juan	R-R	6-1	170	1-16-03	.195	.267	.244	13	45	41	4	8	2	0	0	3	3	1	0	0	18	1	0	6.67	40.00
Cruz, Fadriel	L-R	5-10	170	11-12-00	.193	.312	.241	64	221	187	23	36	3	0	2	15	31	2	0	1	64	11	3	14.03	28.96
Cumbest, Brad	R-R	6-6	235	7-13-00	.140	.195	.246	49	185	171	15	24	8	2	2	19	10	2	0	2	72	0	0	5.41	38.92
Gile, Nick	R-R	5-11	210	1-12-99	.200	.308	.259	40	160	135	19	27	5	0	1	10	19	3	1	2	39	1	0	11.88	24.38
Hidalgo, Kelvin	R-R	6-2	166	3-1-05	.281	.333	.406	8	36	32	4	9	2	1	0	3	2	1	0	1	9	3	0	5.56	25.00
Hill, Glenallen	B-R	5-9	170	9-30-00	.248	.351	.448	34	149	125	31	31	7	0	6	21	17	4	1	2	35	6	0	11.41	23.49
Hinchman, Jason	R-R	6-3	220	7-19-99	.225	.336	.334	101	396	329	48	74	18	3	4	49	53	6	0	8	122	10	2	13.38	30.81
Hobson, Caleb	R-R	6-1	183	1-24-02	.249	.371	.358	111	463	377	79	94	12	4	7	37	69	7	5	5	129	46	6	14.90	27.86
Hopfe, Tommy	B-R	6-1	195	10-11-02	.250	.357	.361	10	42	36	3	9	1	0	1	2	4	2	0	0	7	2	1	9.52	16.67
Jones, Nolan	L-R	6-4	195	5-7-98	.313	.476	.688	5	21	16	6	5	0	0	2	5	5	0	0	0	4	0	0	23.81	19.05
Longwell, Aidan	L-L	6-1	205	10-17-01	.313	.403	.425	63	283	240	39	75	11	2	4	34	32	7	0	4	38	3	3	11.31	13.43
McCabe, Ben	R-R	6-0	185	2-4-00	.190	.298	.270	66	247	211	19	40	9	1	2	17	18	15	2	1	78	1	2	7.29	31.58
Mendez, Luis	L-R	5-11	157	10-30-02	.232	.315	.343	91	342	297	37	69	10	4	5	32	34	3	5	3	67	14	5	9.94	19.59

Batting	B-T	Ht.	Wt.	DOB	AVG	OBP	SLG	G	PA	AB	R	H	2B	3B	HR	RBI	BB	HBP	SH	SF	SO	SB	CS	BB%	SO%
Perez, Andy	L-R	6-3	165	6-3-04	.292	.326	.434	109	478	442	61	129	22	7	9	64	24	2	2	7	64	15	6	5.02	13.39
Perry, Darius	R-R	6-2	200	5-3-01	.174	.287	.272	66	252	213	19	37	9	0	4	24	29	6	1	3	91	0	0	11.51	36.11
Snider, Jake	L-R	6-1	190	5-19-98	.311	.497	.495	34	145	103	25	32	9	2	2	20	33	7	0	2	21	8	2	22.76	14.48
Tena, Felix	R-R	6-0	196	9-27-03	.249	.311	.371	107	458	418	38	104	21	6	6	64	23	15	1	1	101	13	6	5.02	22.05
Thomas, Jared	L-L	6-2	175	7-1-03	.333	.389	.545	8	36	33	5	11	1	0	2	4	3	0	0	0	7	1	0	8.33	19.44
Tucker, Tevin	R-R	6-0	190	2-10-00	.184	.364	.272	78	300	228	37	42	7	2	3	22	52	14	3	3	92	14	4	17.33	30.67
Wimmer, Braylen	R-R	6-4	200	12-27-00	.285	.362	.435	118	529	460	94	131	21	3	14	64	48	12	2	7	107	34	5	9.07	20.23
Wright, Blake	R-R	5-11	195	2-12-02	.270	.342	.460	16	73	63	10	17	6	0	2	13	6	2	0	2	9	1	0	8.22	12.33

Pitching	B-T	Ht.	Wt.	DOB	W	L	ERA	G	GS	SV	IP	Hits	Runs	ER	HR	BB	SO	AVG	OBP	SLG	SO%	BB%	BF
Baumgartner, Collin	L-R	6-6	250	9-26-98	2	2	1.42	14	0	1	19	7	3	3	0	6	30	.119	.209	.136	44.12	8.82	68
Becker, Austin	R-R	6-5	215	9-2-99	1	1	4.30	17	0	0	23	19	12	11	0	12	22	.218	.310	.264	21.78	11.88	101
Blasick, Nathan	L-R	6-3	210	6-26-01	1	0	1.69	5	0	0	5	3	1	1	0	5	8	.167	.348	.167	34.78	21.74	23
Brown, McCade	R-R	6-6	225	8-15-00	0	2	7.36	6	6	0	15	14	13	12	5	8	20	.233	.352	.517	28.17	11.27	71
Carmichael, Braden	R-L	5-10	186	5-23-00	0	0	4.09	12	0	0	11	13	6	5	1	1	9	.302	.333	.488	20.00	2.22	45
Correa, Yanzel	S-R	6-4	210	12-17-04	0	0	4.00	6	0	0	9	9	8	4	2	7	7	.257	.409	.543	15.91	15.91	44
Coupet, Isaiah	L-L	6-1	190	9-27-02	6	5	5.34	19	15	0	86	88	53	51	7	27	119	.260	.330	.410	31.65	7.18	376
Denton, Cade	R-R	6-3	180	12-28-01	1	1	2.86	26	0	1	28	26	12	9	1	7	23	.234	.301	.324	18.70	5.69	123
Eaton, Konner	R-L	6-3	210	10-30-02	0	0	1.00	8	0	1	9	5	1	1	0	1	12	.156	.229	.219	34.29	2.86	35
Emener, Austin	L-L	6-4	210	6-1-02	1	4	4.20	12	12	0	60	57	29	28	8	20	67	.248	.310	.430	26.27	7.84	255
Fernandez, Wuardo	R-R	6-1	168	12-14-00	0	0	11.25	9	0	0	8	12	15	10	1	12	5	.364	.571	.515	10.20	24.49	49
Flesland, Stu	R-L	6-5	207	10-1-00	3	3	3.91	32	7	0	71	69	34	31	2	27	70	.245	.324	.326	22.22	8.57	315
Franzen, Caleb	L-L	6-3	200	6-10-01	1	0	8.22	3	0	0	8	14	7	7	1	2	3	.389	.421	.583	7.89	5.26	38
Hammer, Bryson	L-L	6-1	186	10-8-01	5	3	1.25	33	0	5	50	35	17	7	1	24	52	.190	.294	.223	24.53	11.32	212
Handy, Kannon	L-L	6-3	220	6-1-00	2	4	5.82	24	2	0	39	42	30	25	6	20	46	.269	.361	.494	25.56	11.11	180
Herrera, Welinton	L-L	6-0	166	4-3-04	8	2	2.38	23	0	0	34	25	9	9	1	9	62	.202	.283	.290	44.60	6.47	139
Hill, Brady	L-R	6-0	180	11-10-00	2	5	4.71	38	0	5	42	40	25	22	5	20	49	.244	.332	.390	26.20	10.70	187
Hoffman, Tyler	R-R	6-0	182	9-1-99	2	0	7.23	35	0	0	37	31	30	30	5	35	35	.238	.412	.377	19.66	19.66	178
Justice, Evan	L-L	6-4	205	7-7-98	0	0	9.00	1	0	0	1	2	1	1	0	0	2	.400	.400	.600	40.00	0.00	5
Kaminska, Jace	R-R	6-2	235	12-9-01	5	5	2.78	17	16	0	87	80	30	27	6	12	104	.238	.272	.351	29.46	3.40	353
Loer, Justin	R-L	6-5	214	2-25-03	0	0	7.71	9	0	0	9	9	8	8	1	7	9	.250	.364	.444	20.45	15.91	44
Luciano, Ismael	R-R	6-0	170	3-4-03	4	1	6.32	8	6	0	31	32	22	22	6	17	30	.269	.367	.555	21.58	12.23	139
Madden, Jake	R-R	6-6	185	12-26-01	1	1	3.89	28	0	0	44	37	22	19	2	25	37	.224	.335	.309	19.07	12.89	194
Mahoney, Jack	R-R	6-3	205	8-13-01	5	6	3.52	17	17	0	95	87	40	37	6	22	91	.241	.288	.357	23.33	5.64	390
Mann, Hunter	R-R	6-7	225	8-15-01	1	0	4.57	18	0	0	22	20	11	11	0	7	26	.247	.323	.284	27.66	7.45	94
Marquez, German	R-R	6-1	230	2-22-95	0	1	15.43	1	1	0	2	6	4	4	2	0	5	.462	.462	1.077	38.46	0.00	13
Mena, Bryan	R-R	6-2	185	6-14-04	1	3	5.13	7	7	0	33	33	19	19	6	18	25	.273	.369	.479	17.61	12.68	142
Omlid, Hunter	R-R	6-2	200	5-31-00	0	1	3.00	3	0	0	6	3	4	2	1	3	9	.143	.250	.286	37.50	12.50	24
Pacheco, Alberto	L-L	6-1	176	11-29-02	5	4	3.79	19	18	0	100	85	47	42	11	43	100	.231	.322	.367	23.58	10.14	424
Perez, Bryan	R-R	6-2	167	9-8-03	5	8	4.26	22	22	0	112	105	62	53	8	54	124	.245	.352	.357	24.46	10.65	507
Prosecky, Michael	L-L	6-3	200	2-28-01	1	0	0.82	2	2	0	11	5	1	1	1	3	17	.132	.195	.237	41.46	7.32	41
Ulloa, Fidel	R-R	6-1	196	1-3-03	1	1	4.50	11	0	1	12	8	8	6	3	8	15	.186	.314	.419	29.41	15.69	51
Weatherly, Sam	L-L	6-4	205	5-28-99	3	1	2.85	30	0	8	41	31	18	13	3	19	51	.211	.316	.299	29.65	11.05	172

Fielding

Catcher	PCT	G	PO	A	E	DP	PB
Castillo	1.000	10	61	5	0	2	2
McCabe	.995	64	617	25	3	4	6
Perry	.989	65	597	48	7	4	3

First Base	PCT	G	PO	A	E	DP
Castillo	1.000	3	23	1	0	1
Gile	1.000	24	126	14	0	12
Hinchman	.993	56	390	29	3	38
Longwell	.989	59	431	39	5	44
Mendez	1.000	1	6	0	0	1

Second Base	PCT	G	PO	A	E	DP
Gile	.957	16	13	31	2	3
Hill	1.000	7	9	10	0	2
Mendez	.984	49	66	118	3	17
Tucker	.982	72	116	163	5	46
Wright	.500	1	1	0	1	0

Third Base	PCT	G	PO	A	E	DP
Gile	1.000	1	0	2	0	0
Hidalgo	.667	1	0	2	1	0
Mendez	.927	35	19	57	6	7
Perez	.936	32	11	62	5	7
Wimmer	.900	58	36	90	14	8
Wright	1.000	11	5	24	0	0

Shortstop	PCT	G	PO	A	E	DP
Hidalgo	.870	5	9	11	3	4
Mendez	.000	1	0	0	0	0
Perez	.951	74	96	177	14	36
Tucker	1.000	4	4	2	0	1
Wimmer	.956	54	67	129	9	31

Outfield	PCT	G	PO	A	E	DP
Andrews	.971	43	64	2	2	0
Calaz	.931	11	27	0	2	0
Cruz	1.000	49	75	0	0	0
Cumbest	.980	30	48	2	1	1
Hill	.982	26	54	0	1	0
Hinchman	1.000	46	70	2	0	1
Hobson	.996	103	239	7	1	2
Hopfe	.923	10	12	0	1	0
Jones	1.000	3	4	0	0	0
Snider	.938	18	14	1	1	0
Tena	.876	80	96	3	14	1
Thomas	1.000	5	8	0	0	0
Wimmer	.000	1	0	0	0	0

ACL ROCKIES — ROOKIE

ARIZONA COMPLEX LEAGUE

Batting	B-T	Ht.	Wt.	DOB	AVG	OBP	SLG	G	PA	AB	R	H	2B	3B	HR	RBI	BB	HBP	SH	SF	SO	SB	CS	BB%	SO%
Bautista, Erick	R-R	6-2	197	2-18-05	.157	.321	.250	41	134	108	13	17	3	2	1	12	23	3	0	0	55	2	1	17.16	41.04
Beck, Jordan	R-R	6-3	225	4-19-01	.273	.273	.273	3	11	11	2	3	0	0	0	0	0	0	0	0	1	0	0	0.00	9.09
Bernard, Derek	L-R	6-0	190	8-9-05	.296	.360	.440	48	175	159	25	47	10	5	1	25	15	1	0	0	56	9	5	8.57	32.00
Blomgren, Jack	R-R	5-10	180	9-27-98	.625	.750	.750	3	12	8	4	5	1	0	0	1	4	0	0	0	0	1	0	33.33	0.00
Calaz, Robert	R-R	6-2	202	11-22-05	.349	.462	.651	49	210	172	46	60	12	5	10	45	32	5	0	1	47	12	1	15.24	22.38
Carrigg, Cole	B-R	6-3	190	5-8-02	.375	.389	.938	4	18	16	7	6	0	3	1	5	1	0	0	1	3	2	1	5.56	16.67
Castillo, Juan	R-R	6-1	170	1-16-03	.266	.296	.367	38	135	128	18	34	8	1	1	16	5	1	0	1	29	1	0	3.70	21.48
Cumbest, Brad	R-R	6-6	235	7-13-00	.295	.413	.508	21	75	61	12	18	4	3	1	13	8	5	0	1	25	0	0	10.67	33.33
Datres, Kyle	R-R	6-0	205	1-5-96	.000	.000	.000	2	7	7	0	0	0	0	0	0	0	0	0	0	1	0	0	0.00	14.29
Decolati, Niko	R-R	6-0	215	8-12-97	.143	.333	.143	10	27	21	2	3	0	0	0	3	4	2	0	0	9	1	0	14.81	33.33

Freitez, Jesus	R-R	5-11	176	12-19-05	.125	.239	.250	20	47	40	5	5	1	2	0	4	5	1	0	0	7	1	0	10.64	14.89
Garcia, Francisco	R-R	6-0	190	11-10-02	.266	.359	.399	52	206	173	30	46	14	0	3	33	19	9	0	5	50	1	0	9.22	24.27
Gile, Nick	R-R	5-11	210	1-12-99	.227	.292	.409	15	48	44	7	10	1	2	1	8	3	1	0	0	16	0	0	6.25	33.33
Hannah, Jameson	L-L	5-10	185	8-10-97	.286	.400	.429	4	10	7	2	2	1	0	0	1	2	0	0	1	1	0	0	20.00	10.00
Hernandez, Roynier	L-R	5-11	180	12-6-04	.305	.417	.360	60	243	200	38	61	9	1	0	35	39	1	1	2	36	11	2	16.05	14.81
Herron, Jimmy	R-L	6-0	195	7-27-96	.364	.500	.636	3	14	11	4	4	0	0	1	4	2	1	0	0	1	0	0	14.29	7.14
HIdalgo, Kelvin	R-R	6-2	166	3-1-05	.288	.347	.365	58	247	222	40	64	8	3	1	33	19	2	2	2	58	18	4	7.69	23.48
Jones, Greg	B-R	6-2	175	3-7-98	.200	.273	.200	3	11	10	2	2	0	0	0	1	1	0	0	0	5	0	0	9.09	45.45
Lantigua, Andriel	R-R	6-0	190	11-29-03	.000	.100	.000	5	10	9	0	0	0	0	0	0	1	0	0	0	4	0	0	10.00	40.00
Ledesma, Bairon	R-R	5-9	180	5-3-05	.307	.389	.360	38	133	114	24	35	2	2	0	13	16	0	2	1	24	4	3	12.03	18.05
Lopez, Franklin	R-R	5-9	170	11-19-04	.184	.244	.211	11	41	38	3	7	1	0	0	4	3	0	0	0	8	0	0	7.32	19.51
Mendez, Jorge	R-R	5-10	160	8-1-03	.222	.300	.333	6	20	18	3	4	2	0	0	3	2	0	0	0	3	0	0	10.00	15.00
Messinger, Skyler	R-R	6-3	220	11-1-98	.226	.330	.344	28	109	93	15	21	6	1	1	13	11	4	0	1	29	4	1	10.09	26.61
Navarro, Cristopher	R-R	6-0	170	6-14-99	.500	.606	.769	9	33	26	10	13	1	0	2	10	6	1	0	0	5	2	1	18.18	15.15
Reyes, Yeiker	L-R	6-0	175	10-17-05	.266	.392	.328	56	233	192	40	51	8	2	0	17	36	4	1	0	57	23	10	15.45	24.46
Snider, Jake	L-R	6-1	190	5-19-98	.333	.600	.333	1	5	3	0	1	0	0	0	0	2	0	0	0	2	1	0	40.00	40.00
Veen, Zac	L-R	6-3	190	12-12-01	.571	.556	.714	3	10	7	3	4	1	0	0	3	1	0	1	1	2	2	0	10.00	20.00

Pitching	B-T	Ht.	Wt.	DOB	W	L	ERA	G	GS	SV	IP	Hits	Runs	ER	HR	BB	SO	AVG	OBP	SLG	SO%	BB%	BF
Becker, Austin	R-R	6-5	215	9-2-99	0	0	0.00	3	0	0	4	2	0	0	0	0	4	.154	.154	.154	30.77	0.00	13
Bird, Jake	R-R	6-3	200	12-4-95	0	0	9.00	1	1	0	1	1	1	1	1	0	2	.250	.250	1.000	50.00	0.00	4
Brown, McCade	R-R	6-6	225	8-15-00	1	1	6.00	6	4	0	9	6	6	6	0	9	15	.194	.422	.226	33.33	20.00	45
Bush, Nick	L-L	6-0	195	8-23-96	0	0	0.00	1	1	0	3	4	0	0	0	1	4	.364	.417	.364	33.33	8.33	12
Butler, Troy	R-R	6-2	195	3-22-03	0	0	22.09	8	0	0	7	14	18	18	2	13	10	.400	.571	.571	20.41	26.53	49
Casilla, Luichi	L-L	6-2	180	12-26-04	3	2	7.00	12	7	0	36	34	33	28	2	28	57	.236	.364	.333	32.95	16.18	173
Correa, Yanzel	S-R	6-4	210	12-17-04	1	4	7.89	16	0	2	30	38	28	26	2	17	27	.317	.427	.492	18.75	11.81	144
Davis, Noah	R-R	6-2	195	4-22-97	0	0	3.60	2	2	0	5	6	2	2	0	0	5	.286	.286	.381	23.81	0.00	21
Denton, Cade	R-R	6-3	180	12-28-01	0	0	2.25	3	0	0	4	2	1	1	0	3	7	.143	.294	.143	41.18	17.65	17
Fernandez, Wuardo	R-R	6-1	168	12-14-00	1	2	5.19	8	0	4	9	10	6	5	0	3	12	.294	.368	.412	30.77	7.69	39
Freeland, Kyle	L-L	6-4	204	5-14-93	0	0	0.00	1	1	0	2	1	0	0	0	0	1	.125	.125	.250	12.50	0.00	8
Gilbreath, Lucas	L-L	6-1	185	3-5-96	0	0	9.00	1	1	0	1	1	2	1	0	1	2	.250	.400	.500	40.00	20.00	5
Gomez, Redinson	R-R	6-2	170	7-26-04	1	0	3.81	19	0	2	26	18	12	11	1	16	26	.194	.321	.269	23.21	14.29	112
Gordon, Tanner	L-R	6-5	215	10-26-97	0	0	2.70	2	2	0	7	7	2	2	1	2	9	.259	.310	.481	31.03	6.90	29
Handy, Kannon	L-L	6-3	220	6-1-00	0	1	2.65	4	4	0	17	16	7	5	0	4	20	.242	.286	.379	28.57	5.71	70
Herrera, Marcos	R-R	6-2	182	10-11-04	2	2	5.77	12	6	0	44	50	30	28	2	28	39	.294	.404	.441	19.21	13.79	203
Hollowell, Gavin	R-R	6-7	215	11-4-97	0	0	0.00	2	0	0	2	0	0	0	0	1	3	.000	.143	.000	42.86	14.29	7
Justice, Evan	L-L	6-4	205	7-7-98	0	1	27.00	2	0	0	2	3	5	5	0	1	1	.375	.500	.375	10.00	10.00	10
Kostyshock, Jacob	R-R	6-4	175	1-2-98	0	0	13.50	1	0	0	1	1	2	1	0	1	1	.333	.600	.333	16.67	16.67	6
Lantigua, Andriel	R-R	6-0	190	11-29-03	0	0	9.00	1	0	0	1	3	1	1	0	0	2	.500	.500	.500	33.33	0.00	6
Luciano, Ismael	R-R	6-0	170	3-4-03	6	3	6.00	13	3	0	51	63	36	34	4	28	53	.309	.408	.471	22.08	11.67	240
Madden, Jake	R-R	6-6	185	12-26-01	1	0	2.57	5	0	0	7	8	3	2	0	1	6	.286	.300	.321	20.00	3.33	30
Mann, Hunter	R-R	6-7	225	8-15-01	2	0	2.87	13	0	1	16	11	5	5	1	7	24	.204	.323	.278	36.92	10.77	65
Marquez, German	R-R	6-1	230	2-22-95	0	1	8.10	2	2	0	3	6	4	3	0	1	5	.353	.389	.471	27.78	5.56	18
McKillican, Adam	R-R	6-5	225	1-9-98	0	0	0.00	3	0	0	3	0	0	0	0	1	4	.000	.100	.000	40.00	10.00	10
Mena, Bryan	R-R	6-2	185	6-14-04	2	4	4.89	13	6	2	46	47	40	25	3	24	58	.266	.357	.384	27.49	11.37	211
Ozunz, Sandy	R-R	6-3	177	5-25-06	3	0	4.14	10	5	1	37	35	18	17	1	11	45	.252	.314	.388	29.41	7.19	153
Pint, Riley	R-R	6-5	225	11-6-97	0	0	0.00	2	0	0	2	0	0	0	0	2	4	.000	.250	.000	50.00	25.00	8
Prosecky, Michael	L-L	6-3	200	2-28-01	0	1	4.15	4	4	0	9	9	4	4	0	1	17	.265	.306	.324	47.22	2.78	36
Rivera, Francis	R-R	6-4	160	9-14-00	0	0	8.22	8	2	0	0	12	7	7	0	5	9	.400	.500	.500	23.08	12.82	39
Rogers, Josh	L-L	6-3	211	7-10-94	0	0	18.00	1	1	0	1	2	2	2	1	0	1	.400	.400	1.000	20.00	0.00	5
Rolison, Ryan	R-L	6-2	213	7-11-97	1	1	0.00	4	3	0	7	3	2	0	0	3	7	.130	.231	.174	25.93	11.11	27
Silvestre, Engel	R-R	6-2	230	9-27-05	1	4	7.59	14	0	0	21	29	24	18	1	18	23	.312	.421	.419	20.18	15.79	114
Spain, Dylan	R-R	6-6	205	6-21-98	0	0	5.40	5	0	0	5	5	3	3	1	0	4	.250	.250	.600	20.00	0.00	20
Taggart, Luke	R-R	6-3	228	10-10-97	0	0	2.45	4	2	0	4	2	1	1	0	2	2	.182	.357	.182	14.29	14.29	14
Tejeda, Luis	R-R	6-2	170	12-13-04	2	3	5.92	15	1	1	24	29	22	16	2	13	19	.299	.395	.464	16.67	11.40	114
Todd, Reagan	L-L	6-3	218	8-30-95	1	0	0.00	1	0	0	1	0	0	0	0	1	1	.000	.333	.000	33.33	33.33	3
Torres, Carlos	R-R	6-4	240	5-3-01	0	0	4.50	3	2	0	4	4	2	2	0	0	6	.250	.250	.313	37.50	0.00	16
Wills, Cory	L-L	6-0	195	7-19-97	1	1	5.91	22	0	1	21	39	17	14	4	11	26	.394	.470	.667	22.61	9.57	115

Fielding

C: Castillo 34, Freitez 11, Lopez 11, Mendez 5, Lantigua 3. **1B:** Garcia 49, Navarro 7, Messinger 6, Datres 1, Freitez 1. **2B:** Hernandez 28, Ledesma 26, Gile 5, Freitez 3, Blomgren 2, Castillo 2, Datres 1, Navarro 1. **3B:** Hernandez 33, Ledesma 14, Gile 10, HIdalgo 4, Navarro 3, Messinger 2. **SS:** HIdalgo 54, Carrigg 3, Hernandez 2, Jones 2, Navarro 1, Blomgren 1. **LF:** Bernard 21, Bautista 15, Reyes 14, Cumbest 12, Freitez 2, Veen 2, Herron 2, Hannah 1, Beck 1. **CF:** Reyes 39, Calaz 21, Bautista 3, Carrigg 2, Jones 1. **RF:** Calaz 24, Bernard 16, Bautista 14, Decolati 8, Cumbest 3, Beck 1, Hannah 1, Snider 1.

DSL COLORADO — ROOKIE

DOMINICAN SUMMER LEAGUE

Batting	B-T	Ht.	Wt.	DOB	AVG	OBP	SLG	G	PA	AB	R	H	2B	3B	HR	RBI	BB	HBP	SH	SF	SO	SB	CS	BB%	SO%
Alvarez, Jjam	R-R	5-11	160	6-3-06	.340	.448	.383	13	58	47	7	16	2	0	0	5	8	2	0	1	5	3	0	13.79	8.62
Andujar, Ashly	B-R	6-1	163	7-29-07	.291	.376	.352	51	229	199	36	58	8	2	0	24	22	6	0	2	31	17	8	9.61	13.54
Arguelles, Cristian	L-L	6-0	177	6-30-07	.227	.320	.258	38	155	132	20	30	4	0	0	18	15	4	2	2	11	10	2	9.68	7.10
Brito, Roldy	B-R	5-11	183	4-8-07	.254	.360	.314	54	222	185	27	47	9	1	0	26	27	6	0	4	41	24	3	12.16	18.47
Cancro, Danny	R-R	5-10	148	4-24-07	.324	.478	.471	12	46	34	5	11	3	1	0	8	10	1	0	1	3	3	3	21.74	6.52
Chacon, Adan	L-R	6-1	191	6-24-06	.212	.307	.254	39	137	118	18	25	2	0	1	13	15	2	0	2	34	2	1	10.95	24.82

Batting	B-T	Ht.	Wt.	DOB	AVG	OBP	SLG	G	PA	AB	R	H	2B	3B	HR	RBI	BB	HBP	SH	SF	SO	SB	CS	BB%	SO%
De La Cruz, Jose	R-R	5-11	190	3-19-07	.152	.300	.227	22	81	66	8	10	3	1	0	2	13	1	1	0	24	0	0	16.05	29.63
Dihigo, Eriel	R-R	6-2	180	11-10-06	.333	.443	.435	42	168	138	31	46	9	1	1	19	21	7	1	1	18	20	2	12.50	10.71
Felix, Diego	R-R	6-0	160	7-22-06	.213	.339	.255	16	57	47	10	10	0	1	0	2	9	0	1	0	25	4	2	15.79	43.86
Feliz, Angel	L-R	6-1	157	3-2-04	.282	.380	.368	39	137	117	24	33	7	0	1	11	18	1	0	1	36	6	1	13.14	26.28
Garcia, Dariel	B-R	5-10	155	11-28-06	.241	.354	.327	51	200	162	23	39	9	1	1	21	25	5	5	3	47	11	7	12.50	23.50
Guerra, Jose	B-R	5-11	180	12-18-05	.059	.150	.059	5	20	17	2	1	0	0	0	1	2	0	0	1	4	1	0	10.00	20.00
Herrera, Herlinton	L-R	5-11	150	1-22-07	.236	.400	.291	41	167	127	18	30	3	2	0	19	33	3	2	2	27	7	1	19.76	16.17
Lopez, Gabriel	R-R	5-8	169	3-23-06	.133	.261	.147	30	90	75	14	10	1	0	0	7	9	4	2	0	24	2	2	10.00	26.67
Ortiz, Nicolas	R-R	6-0	173	12-31-06	.125	.300	.146	17	61	48	8	6	1	0	0	6	10	2	1	0	23	2	1	16.39	37.70
Tovar, Anderson	R-R	6-1	205	12-7-06	.269	.302	.320	53	212	197	26	53	10	0	0	26	7	4	0	4	34	10	11	3.30	16.04

Pitching	B-T	Ht.	Wt.	DOB	W	L	ERA	G	GS	SV	IP	Hits	Runs	ER	HR	BB	SO	AVG	OBP	SLG	SO%	BB%	BF
Almonte, Leonardi	R-R	6-2	190	3-25-05	2	2	5.51	12	0	1	16.1	22	18	10	5	7	15	.324	.403	.544	19.48	9.09	77
Barboza, Julian	R-R	6-2	196	10-16-06	1	1	6.75	9	3	1	16	10	12	12	1	7	13	.189	.338	.340	20.00	10.77	65
Compres, Brailyn	R-R	6-1	200	7-16-05	0	1	6.91	13	0	0	14	12	12	11	1	17	14	.226	.431	.321	19.18	23.29	73
Cruz, Odarlin	R-R	6-7	188	2-18-05	6	2	1.80	20	0	5	25	24	18	5	0	7	34	.238	.313	.297	29.82	6.14	114
Cruz, Rony	R-R	6-1	196	3-3-04	0	0	0.00	1	0	0	1	0	0	0	0	0	1	.000	.000	.000	33.33	0.00	3
Fernandez, Brian	R-R	6-2	176	3-20-07	0	1	11.05	7	0	0	7	9	9	9	1	8	5	.333	.526	.519	13.16	21.05	38
Ferrari, Gian	L-L	6-3	163	4-12-06	0	0	7.20	4	0	0	5	9	7	4	0	3	2	.409	.533	.545	6.67	10.00	30
Florencio, Ronaldo	R-R	6-0	165	8-13-07	2	1	3.60	17	0	4	30	34	16	12	1	5	29	.276	.305	.431	22.14	3.82	131
Garcia, Manuel	R-R	6-2	205	4-22-07	0	0	0.00	3	0	0	4	2	0	0	0	0	3	.154	.214	.231	21.43	0.00	14
Gonzalez, Maximo	R-R	5-11	175	5-5-07	0	2	3.47	12	12	0	47	33	24	18	5	25	44	.201	.320	.354	22.68	12.89	194
Henrique, Josue	R-R	6-4	193	10-3-06	2	1	4.29	15	1	1	21	24	12	10	2	14	24	.304	.430	.443	23.53	13.73	102
Hernandez, Freddy	R-R	6-1	156	8-7-06	0	0	6.00	3	0	0	3	2	2	2	0	4	1	.222	.467	.444	6.67	26.67	15
Herrera, Andres	R-R	6-4	180	6-10-06	1	2	9.64	12	1	1	14	14	18	15	2	10	9	.269	.412	.442	13.24	14.71	68
Liscano, Jhondre	R-R	6-4	183	9-30-06	0	0	1.23	6	0	0	7	10	7	1	0	5	7	.333	.429	.367	20.00	14.29	35
Martorella, Carlos	R-R	6-2	179	8-2-06	1	0	1.93	4	0	0	9	7	3	2	0	3	5	.200	.282	.286	12.82	7.69	39
Meza, Moises	R-R	6-0	188	8-19-05	2	4	4.67	9	9	0	35	28	23	18	3	17	37	.228	.336	.333	25.17	11.56	147
Paulino, Wilmis	R-R	6-0	181	1-16-06	2	1	2.42	8	0	1	26	22	13	7	3	4	18	.239	.283	.413	18.18	4.04	99
Pena, Alvey	R-R	6-1	168	10-10-06	1	0	9.00	7	0	1	8	9	12	8	1	6	2	.290	.415	.516	4.88	14.63	41
Pena, Eliezer	R-R	6-0	167	10-8-05	1	1	3.77	13	3	1	31	39	23	13	1	8	31	.315	.372	.468	22.46	5.80	138
Perez, Doilin	R-R	6-4	200	5-10-05	1	0	0.00	4	0	0	5	2	2	0	0	3	5	.125	.263	.125	26.32	15.79	19
Pujols, Oscar	R-R	6-2	165	11-15-06	2	1	2.36	7	5	0	26.2	23	11	7	3	6	29	.237	.286	.423	27.10	5.61	107
Sanchez, Enger	R-R	6-5	170	5-23-03	0	0	18.00	1	0	0	1	1	2	2	0	1	1	.200	.333	.600	16.67	16.67	6
Sanchez, Gregory	R-R	6-4	189	1-12-07	0	3	5.40	13	13	0	33	37	22	20	0	19	42	.278	.417	.353	25.00	11.31	168
Suarez, Junior	L-L	6-1	195	6-24-05	0	2	8.44	9	0	0	11	10	10	10	1	9	15	.227	.382	.341	27.27	16.36	55
Tejada, Kevin	R-R	6-5	187	5-8-05	2	1	5.79	13	0	2	23	24	16	15	4	7	19	.270	.353	.494	18.63	6.86	102
Veras, Eric	L-L	6-0	182	12-18-06	2	1	2.68	8	8	0	37	31	15	11	2	9	25	.228	.277	.338	16.89	6.08	148

Fielding

C: Lopez 23, De La Cruz 20, Ortiz 15, Guerra 4. 1B: Chacon 38, Garcia 9, Alvarez 7, Lopez 6, Guerra 1, De La Cruz 1. 2B: Brito 35, Herrera 11, Garcia 9, Alvarez 2. 3B: Dihigo 41, Cancro 11, Alvarez 3, Garcia 2, Herrera 1. SS: Andujar 45, Brito 10, Herrera 1. LF: Feliz 30, Garcia 25, Arguelles 4, Ortiz 1. CF: Arguelles 34, Felix 15, Garcia 7. RF: Tovar 52, Feliz 3, Garcia 1.

DSL ROCKIES — *ROOKIE*

DOMINICAN SUMMER LEAGUE

Batting	B-T	Ht.	Wt.	DOB	AVG	OBP	SLG	G	PA	AB	R	H	2B	3B	HR	RBI	BB	HBP	SH	SF	SO	SB	CS	BB%	SO%
Alvarez, Jjam	R-R	5-11	160	6-3-06	.281	.361	.360	42	160	139	19	39	6	1	1	15	14	4	2	1	28	4	2	8.75	17.50
Arguelles, Cristian	L-L	6-0	177	6-30-07	.400	.457	.450	12	47	40	9	16	2	0	0	7	3	2	1	1	1	1	1	6.38	2.13
Arias, Cruzmel	R-R	5-11	176	2-20-04	.258	.325	.318	44	169	151	19	39	7	1	0	20	8	7	3	0	29	0	0	4.73	17.16
Cancro, Danny	R-R	5-10	148	4-24-07	.218	.321	.323	38	158	133	34	29	8	3	0	19	16	5	2	2	27	16	0	10.13	17.09
Capellan, Jarol	L-R	5-11	176	5-23-06	.279	.417	.333	36	140	111	18	31	6	0	0	17	15	12	1	1	22	2	1	10.71	15.71
Ciriaco, Jeremy	R-R	5-10	163	8-15-06	.339	.420	.413	47	224	189	52	64	9	1	1	32	26	2	5	2	29	21	6	11.61	12.95
Dalis, Wilder	B-R	6-0	172	7-30-06	.327	.445	.450	56	256	202	44	66	12	2	3	49	42	5	2	5	34	21	7	16.41	13.28
De La Cruz, Alessander	R-R	6-1	208	1-2-06	.318	.406	.542	48	212	179	42	57	15	2	7	42	25	4	0	4	40	13	0	11.79	18.87
Dihigo, Eriel	R-R	6-2	180	11-10-06	.214	.314	.262	12	51	42	4	9	0	1	0	9	7	0	0	2	15	1	0	13.73	29.41
Felix, Diego	R-R	6-0	160	7-22-06	.190	.319	.310	21	70	58	22	11	5	1	0	6	8	3	1	0	27	10	2	11.43	38.57
Guerra, Jose	B-R	5-11	180	12-18-05	.211	.254	.263	18	64	57	7	12	3	0	0	6	3	1	1	2	11	3	0	4.69	17.19
Isea, David	R-R	5-11	165	3-25-06	.273	.273	.455	3	11	11	2	3	0	1	0	3	0	0	0	0	1	0	0	0.00	9.09
Kolokie, Aldalay	R-R	6-0	187	8-29-04	.321	.438	.425	41	170	134	25	43	8	0	2	39	21	10	1	4	16	11	3	12.35	9.41
Lopez, Gabriel	R-R	5-8	169	3-23-06	.296	.406	.333	9	32	27	6	8	1	0	0	3	5	0	0	0	7	0	0	15.63	21.88
Ortiz, Nicolas	R-R	6-0	173	12-31-06	.000	.000	.000	1	1	1	0	0	0	0	0	0	0	0	0	0	0	0	1	0.00	0.00
Renzullo, Carlos	B-R	5-8	150	9-30-06	.360	.455	.447	50	235	197	57	71	8	3	1	21	33	2	2	1	14	18	6	14.04	5.96
Reyes, Yensi	R-R	6-1	189	9-14-03	.302	.394	.509	48	189	159	36	48	11	2	6	36	20	6	1	3	47	8	4	10.58	24.87

Pitching	B-T	Ht.	Wt.	DOB	W	L	ERA	G	GS	SV	IP	Hits	Runs	ER	HR	BB	SO	AVG	OBP	SLG	SO%	BB%	BF
Cabeza, Yeremmy	R-R	6-0	165	12-21-05	3	1	5.14	7	3	0	21	24	14	12	0	4	22	.282	.319	.329	24.18	4.40	91
Camacho, Reiver	R-R	6-2	170	4-1-07	5	1	2.33	11	10	0	54	45	19	14	1	6	46	.223	.251	.287	21.70	2.83	212
Cedeno, Keywill	R-R	6-4	204	1-31-05	1	0	2.00	15	0	5	27	26	8	6	2	3	35	.250	.291	.356	31.82	2.73	110
Cubilla, Efrain	R-R	6-1	190	2-18-05	2	2	4.33	9	7	1	35	36	19	17	2	7	18	.261	.304	.355	12.16	4.73	148
Ferrari, Gian	L-L	6-3	163	4-12-06	1	0	7.71	5	0	0	5	5	5	4	1	3	3	.250	.375	.400	12.50	12.50	24
Flores, Ruver	R-R	6-1	171	3-3-05	5	2	6.47	12	0	1	32	32	26	23	4	16	32	.264	.368	.438	22.22	11.11	144
George, Aneudis	R-R	6-1	172	9-27-03	2	1	4.13	13	0	0	24	27	12	11	1	4	17	.297	.330	.429	17.00	4.00	100
Hernandez, Freddy	R-R	6-1	156	8-7-06	1	0	0.00	5	0	0	6	2	0	0	0	5	5	.111	.333	.111	20.83	20.83	24

Martorella, Carlos	R-R	6-2	179	8-2-06	1	0	5.73	10	0	2	11	13	8	7	2	4	12	.302	.360	.535	24.00	8.00	50
Medina, Jhon	L-L	6-0	195	1-9-06	4	2	2.36	10	8	0	42	35	16	11	1	12	38	.230	.306	.309	22.35	7.06	170
Meza, Moises	R-R	6-0	188	8-19-05	0	1	5.63	4	1	0	8	8	5	5	2	4	12	.258	.343	.516	34.29	11.43	35
Nascimiento, Fabian	L-L	6-2	176	12-18-06	0	0	27.00	2	0	0	2	3	6	5	0	3	3	.375	.643	.625	21.43	21.43	14
Paulino, Wilmis	R-R	6-0	181	1-16-06	1	0	3.75	4	0	1	12	16	5	5	1	5	10	.320	.375	.500	17.86	8.93	56
Perez, Doilin	R-R	6-4	200	5-10-05	0	0	11.12	4	0	0	6	7	7	7	0	3	6	.333	.462	.333	22.22	11.11	27
Pimentel, Marcos	R-R	6-1	172	9-30-06	4	4	5.33	12	12	0	51	52	35	30	6	16	39	.268	.332	.448	18.22	7.48	214
Pineda, Euri	R-R	6-2	200	8-13-05	3	0	3.06	10	0	1	18	17	7	6	1	6	26	.266	.342	.328	35.62	8.22	73
Ramirez, Anthony	R-R	6-2	175	8-17-05	1	0	9.45	4	0	0	7	13	7	7	0	2	5	.394	.429	.485	14.29	5.71	35
Ramon, Yadiel	R-R	6-2	180	8-17-07	0	2	6.94	7	4	0	12	16	11	9	2	11	8	.333	.467	.542	13.33	18.33	60
Reyes, Ulises	R-R	6-0	205	10-5-05	1	0	7.00	15	0	0	18	27	16	14	1	5	13	.338	.378	.463	14.44	5.56	90
Sanchez, Enger	R-R	6-5	170	5-23-03	0	0	12.15	5	0	1	7	12	9	9	0	8	4	.414	.538	.552	10.26	20.51	39
Tejada, Kevin	R-R	6-5	187	5-8-05	0	0	4.15	3	0	2	9	6	4	4	1	2	9	.188	.257	.406	25.71	5.71	35
Valdez, Yoan	R-R	6-1	187	8-19-05	1	1	6.75	9	0	0	16	18	13	12	0	8	14	.300	.380	.417	19.44	11.11	72
Veras, Eric	L-L	6-0	182	12-18-06	1	0	9.00	2	2	0	8	12	9	8	0	4	3	.387	.500	.452	7.50	10.00	40
Zacarias, Alison	R-R	6-3	200	11-10-05	0	1	3.96	10	9	0	39	38	20	17	1	24	39	.266	.375	.378	23.08	14.20	169

Fielding

C: Arias 32, Guerra 17, Lopez 8, Isea 3, Ortiz 1. **1B:** Capellan 28, Alvarez 21, Arias 12, Lopez 2, Ciriaco 1, Felix 1, Guerra 1, Kolokie 1. **2B:** Renzullo 33, Ciriaco 15, Cancro 9, Dalis 1, Alvarez 1. **3B:** Cancro 23, Dalis 17, Dihigo 12, Capellan 5, Alvarez 4, Ciriaco 1. **SS:** Dalis 35, Ciriaco 24. **LF:** Reyes 41, Kolokie 14, Arguelles 1, Felix 1. **CF:** Renzullo 17, Felix 16, Kolokie 14, Arguelles 10. **RF:** De La Cruz 43, Kolokie 11, Felix 2, Renzullo 1, Reyes 1.

Detroit Tigers

SEASON SYNOPSIS: The Tigers sold at the trade deadline, even as the team started playing better. The changes helped the club unleash Pitching Chaos, a bullpen-centric pitching approach surrounding Cy Young Award winner Tarik Skubal that powered the Tigers to a 31-13 stretch run and wild-card berth, their first playoff spot in a decade.

HIGH POINT: The Astros had reached at least the ALCS every year since 2017, but they ran into the white-hot Tigers, who held Houston to three runs in a road two-game sweep. Skubal tossed six scoreless innings in a 3-1 victory, and the Tigers rallied off Houston's high-priced bullpen in Game 2, loading the bases against Ryan Pressly. Andy Ibañez then cleared the bases with a double off Josh Hader en route to a 5-2 victory.

LOW POINT: Detroit went 10-17 in June, leading them to sell at the deadline, but the Tigers obviously rallied and won four of their first five playoff games before dropping the last two ALDS games to the Guardians. Detroit led Game 4 by a run before Cleveland rallied on the road for a 5-4 victory, keyed by a David Fry homer off Beau Brieske. Then Skubal cracked in Game 5, giving up a five-spot, including a grand slam to Lane Thomas, in a 7-3 defeat.

NOTABLE ROOKIES: Second baseman Colt Keith, who signed a six-year, $28.6 million extension before the season, led the team with 148 games and ranked second with 61 RBIs in a .260/.309/.380 season. Center fielder Parker Meadows thrived at the plate after returning from the minor leagues in early August, hitting well in the postseason (.806 OPS). Wenceel Perez and Justyn-Henry Malloy had their moments, and lefty-hitting Trey Sweeney replaced injured Javier Baez at shortstop in late August and provided a boost. Rookies provided plenty of key innings as bulk relievers and starters in the second half; Keider Montero tossed 98 innings, while Brant Hurter (6-1, 2.58) logged 45.1 innings over 10 outings. Relievers Sean Guenther and Brenan Hanifee pitched their way onto the postseason roster.

KEY TRANSACTIONS: Detroit signed free agent righties Jack Flaherty and Kenta Maeda in the offseason, but Maeda was banished to the bullpen after a poor start, while Flaherty was traded at the July deadline to the Dodgers for a package that included Sweeney. Other veterans who'd been signed in the offseason but were traded off in-season included outfielder Mark Canha, lefty reliever Andrew Chafin and third baseman Gio Urshela.

OPENING DAY PAYROLL: $103,834,833 (24th)

PLAYERS OF THE YEAR

MAJOR LEAGUE

Tarik Skubal
LHP
18-4, 2.39 ERA
228 SO in 192 IP
pitching triple crown

MINOR LEAGUE

Max Clark
OF
(A/A+)
.279/.372/.421
9 HR, 29 SB

ORGANIZATION LEADERS

Batting — *Qualifiers

MAJORS

* AVG	Riley Greene	.262
* OPS	Riley Greene	.827
HR	Riley Greene	24
RBI	Riley Greene	74

MINORS

* AVG	Hao-Yu Lee, Erie	.298
* OBP	Carlos Mendoza, Erie/Toledo/West Michigan	.388
* SLG	Andrew Navigato, Erie/Toledo	.491
* OPS	Hao-Yu Lee, Erie	.851
R	Carlos Mendoza, Erie/Toledo/West Michigan	87
H	Max Anderson, Erie/West Michigan	135
H	Gage Workman, Erie	135
TB	Gage Workman, Erie	230
2B	Andrew Navigato, Erie/Toledo	29
2B	Gage Workman, Erie	29
3B	3 tied	6
HR	Andrew Navigato, Erie/Toledo	21
RBI	Gage Workman, Erie	89
BB	David Smith, Lakeland	83
SO	Gage Workman, Erie	153
SB	Seth Stephenson, West Michigan	60

Pitching — #Qualifiers

MAJORS

W	Tarik Skubal	18
# ERA	Tarik Skubal	2.39
SO	Tarik Skubal	228
SV	Jason Foley	28

MINORS

W	Devin Sweet, Toledo	9
W	Tim Naughton, Erie	9
W	Jake Miller, Lakeland/W-Michigan/Erie	9
L	Carlos Marcano, West Michigan	11
# ERA	Carlos Pena, West Michigan/Erie	3.46
G	Devin Sweet, Toledo	52
GS	Wilkel Hernandez, Erie	27
SV	Eiker Huizi, Lakeland/West Michigan	10
IP	Garrett Burhenn, Erie/West Michigan	122
BB	Lael Lockhart, Erie/Toledo	59
SO	Lael Lockhart, Erie/Toledo	145
# AVG	Lael Lockhart, Erie/Toledo	.230

2024 PERFORMANCE

General Manager: Scott Harris. **Farm Director:** Ryan Garko. **Scouting Director:** Scott Bream.

Class	Team	League	W	L	PCT	Finish	Manager
Majors	Detroit Tigers	American	86	76	.531	5 (15)	A.J. Hinch
Triple-A	Toledo Mud Hens	International	69	80	.463	15 (20)	Tim Federowicz
Double-A	Erie SeaWolves	Eastern	77	58	.570	2 (12)	Gabe Alvarez
High-A	West Michigan Whitecaps	Midwest	68	63	.519	6 (12)	Tony Cappucilli
Low-A	Lakeland Flying Tigers	Florida State	80	50	.615	2 (10)	Andrew Graham
Rookie	FCL Tigers	Florida Complex	34	23	.596	4 (15)	Salvador Paniagua
Rookie	DSL Tigers 1	Dominican	30	26	.536	19 (51)	Marcos Yepez
Rookie	DSL Tigers 2	Dominican	38	18	.679	6 (51)	Sandy Acevedo
Overall 2024 Minor League Record			**396**	**318**	**.555**	**1st (30)**	

ORGANIZATION STATISTICS

DETROIT TIGERS

AMERICAN LEAGUE

Batting	B-T	Ht.	Wt.	DOB	AVG	OBP	SLG	G	PA	AB	R	H	2B	3B	HR	RBI	BB	HBP	SH	SF	SO	SB	CS	BB%	SO%
Baddoo, Akil	L-L	6-1	214	8-16-98	.137	.220	.301	31	82	73	7	10	2	2	2	5	8	0	0	1	27	1	0	9.76	32.93
Baez, Javier	R-R	6-0	190	12-1-92	.184	.221	.294	80	289	272	25	50	12	0	6	37	12	2	0	3	69	8	1	4.15	23.88
Canha, Mark	R-R	6-2	209	2-15-89	.231	.337	.350	93	377	320	42	74	17	0	7	38	42	11	0	4	79	4	0	11.14	20.95
Carpenter, Kerry	L-R	6-2	220	9-2-97	.284	.345	.587	87	296	264	37	75	16	5	18	57	22	4	0	3	75	0	2	7.43	25.34
Dingler, Dillon	R-R	6-3	210	9-17-98	.167	.195	.310	27	87	84	2	14	5	2	1	11	3	0	0	0	30	0	0	3.45	34.48
Greene, Riley	L-L	6-3	200	9-28-00	.262	.348	.479	137	584	512	82	134	27	6	24	74	64	5	0	2	156	4	2	10.96	26.71
Ibanez, Andy	R-R	5-10	205	4-3-93	.241	.295	.357	99	244	224	30	54	9	1	5	32	15	3	0	2	63	2	3	6.15	25.82
Jung, Jace	L-R	6-0	205	10-4-00	.241	.362	.304	34	94	79	14	19	5	0	0	3	15	0	0	0	29	0	1	15.96	30.85
Keith, Colt	L-R	6-2	211	8-14-01	.260	.309	.380	148	556	516	54	134	15	4	13	61	36	2	0	2	110	7	1	6.47	19.78
Kelly, Carson	R-R	6-2	212	7-14-94	.240	.325	.391	60	203	179	21	43	4	1	7	29	17	6	0	1	40	0	0	8.37	19.70
Kennedy, Buddy	R-R	5-9	190	10-5-98	.200	.308	.500	6	13	10	2	2	0	0	1	4	2	0	0	1	4	1	0	15.38	30.77
Kreidler, Ryan	R-R	6-4	208	11-12-97	.119	.200	.169	35	65	59	9	7	0	0	1	2	6	0	0	0	19	5	3	9.23	29.23
Madris, Bligh	L-R	6-0	208	2-29-96	.269	.324	.358	21	75	67	8	18	3	0	1	5	6	0	0	1	20	0	0	8.00	26.67
Malloy, Justyn-Henry	R-R	6-1	212	2-19-00	.203	.291	.366	71	230	202	18	41	7	1	8	21	23	3	0	2	85	1	1	10.00	36.96
McKinstry, Zach	L-R	6-0	180	4-29-95	.215	.277	.337	118	325	297	32	64	14	5	4	23	24	2	0	2	69	16	0	7.38	21.23
Meadows, Parker	L-R	6-5	205	11-2-99	.244	.310	.433	82	298	270	39	66	12	6	9	28	25	1	1	1	76	9	4	8.39	25.50
Perez, Wenceel	B-R	5-11	203	10-30-99	.242	.300	.383	112	425	389	51	94	16	6	9	37	32	1	2	1	92	9	5	7.53	21.65
Rogers, Jake	R-R	6-1	201	4-18-95	.197	.255	.352	102	337	310	43	61	16	1	10	36	22	3	0	2	99	1	0	6.53	29.38
Sweeney, Trey	L-R	6-2	200	4-24-00	.218	.269	.373	36	119	110	11	24	5	0	4	17	7	1	0	1	32	2	0	5.88	26.89
Torkelson, Spencer	R-R	6-1	220	8-26-99	.219	.295	.374	92	381	342	45	75	21	1	10	37	33	4	0	1	105	0	0	8.66	27.56
Urshela, Gio	R-R	6-0	215	10-11-91	.243	.286	.333	92	325	300	25	73	10	1	5	37	19	1	0	5	49	0	0	5.85	15.08
Vierling, Matt	R-R	6-3	205	9-16-96	.257	.312	.423	144	567	518	80	133	28	5	16	57	41	3	0	5	121	6	1	7.23	21.34
Vilade, Ryan	R-R	6-2	226	2-18-99	.178	.208	.244	17	49	45	5	8	0	0	1	5	2	0	1	1	12	0	0	4.08	24.49

Pitching	B-T	Ht.	Wt.	DOB	W	L	ERA	G	GS	SV	IP	Hits	Runs	ER	HR	BB	SO	AVG	OBP	SLG	SO%	BB%	BF
Brieske, Beau	R-R	6-3	200	4-4-98	4	5	3.59	46	12	1	68	55	31	27	5	30	69	.224	.310	.354	24.47	10.64	282
Chafin, Andrew	R-L	6-2	235	6-17-90	3	2	3.16	41	0	1	37	35	16	13	2	16	50	.245	.321	.315	30.86	9.88	162
Englert, Mason	S-R	6-4	206	11-1-99	1	0	5.40	12	1	0	22	23	15	13	4	5	16	.264	.312	.529	17.20	5.38	93
Faedo, Alex	R-R	6-5	225	11-12-95	5	3	3.61	37	6	0	57	49	24	23	9	28	55	.233	.328	.405	22.36	11.38	246
Flaherty, Jack	R-R	6-4	225	10-15-95	7	5	2.95	18	18	0	107	83	38	35	15	19	133	.211	.253	.372	32.05	4.58	415
Foley, Jason	R-R	6-4	215	11-1-95	3	6	3.15	69	0	28	60	51	28	21	5	20	46	.228	.293	.339	18.40	8.00	250
Guenther, Sean	L-L	5-11	194	12-29-95	3	0	0.86	17	0	0	21	9	2	2	0	2	12	.130	.178	.188	16.44	2.74	73
Hanifee, Brenan	R-R	6-5	215	5-29-98	1	1	1.84	21	3	0	29	27	7	6	2	6	23	.237	.275	.360	19.17	5.00	120
Holton, Tyler	L-L	6-2	200	6-13-96	7	2	2.19	66	9	8	94	57	25	23	7	17	77	.173	.222	.279	21.75	4.80	354
Hurter, Brant	L-L	6-6	250	9-6-98	6	1	2.58	10	1	0	45	34	13	13	4	6	38	.204	.230	.323	21.71	3.43	175
Jobe, Jackson	R-R	6-2	190	7-30-02	0	0	0.00	2	0	0	4	1	0	0	0	1	2	.071	.133	.071	12.50	6.25	16
Lange, Alex	R-R	6-3	202	10-2-95	0	3	4.34	21	0	2	19	16	16	9	0	17	21	.232	.398	.290	23.33	18.89	90
Lucas, Easton	L-L	6-4	180	9-23-96	1	0	5.40	3	0	0	3	3	2	2	0	2	2	.250	.375	.250	12.50	12.50	16
Madden, Ty	R-R	6-3	215	2-21-00	1	1	4.30	6	1	0	23	25	12	11	2	8	17	.275	.337	.396	16.83	7.92	101
Maeda, Kenta	R-R	6-1	185	4-11-88	3	7	6.09	29	17	0	112	124	80	76	22	31	96	.281	.331	.491	19.79	6.39	485
Manning, Matt	R-R	6-6	195	1-28-98	0	1	4.88	5	5	0	28	31	15	15	3	12	23	.287	.350	.426	18.70	9.76	123
McKinstry, Zach	L-R	6-0	180	4-29-95	0	0	9.00	3	0	0	2	1	2	2	1	1	0	.143	.250	.571	0.00	12.50	8
Miller, Shelby	R-R	6-3	225	10-10-90	6	8	4.53	51	0	2	56	41	31	28	9	13	49	.202	.262	.384	21.78	5.78	225
Mize, Casey	R-R	6-3	212	5-1-97	2	6	4.49	22	20	0	102	121	57	51	11	29	78	.290	.336	.436	17.26	6.42	452
Montero, Keider	R-R	6-1	145	7-6-00	6	6	4.76	19	16	0	98	100	54	52	19	31	77	.265	.325	.463	18.69	7.52	412
Olson, Reese	R-R	6-1	160	7-31-99	4	8	3.53	22	22	0	112	100	51	44	7	33	101	.238	.295	.347	21.72	7.10	465
Sammons, Bryan	L-L	6-4	235	4-27-95	1	1	3.62	6	0	0	27	16	11	11	6	9	18	.170	.250	.383	17.31	8.65	104
Skubal, Tarik	R-L	6-3	240	11-20-96	18	4	2.39	31	31	0	192	142	54	51	15	35	228	.201	.247	.311	30.28	4.65	753
Vanasco, Ricky	R-R	6-3	180	10-13-98	1	0	0.00	2	0	0	2	0	0	0	0	0	0	.000	.000	.000	0.00	0.00	6
Vest, Will	R-R	6-0	180	6-6-95	3	4	2.82	69	0	2	70	61	23	22	3	18	63	.234	.285	.310	21.80	6.23	289
Wentz, Joey	L-L	6-5	220	10-6-97	0	2	5.37	38	0	1	55	60	35	33	8	27	60	.273	.356	.418	23.62	10.63	254

Fielding

Catcher	PCT	G	PO	A	E	DP	PB
Dingler	.994	27	168	7	1	0	4
Kelly	.996	60	461	27	2	7	2
Rogers	.996	92	744	29	3	4	1

First Base	PCT	G	PO	A	E	DP
Canha	.991	31	206	13	2	22
Ibanez	.989	18	85	7	1	10
Madris	1.000	20	139	5	0	12
Torkelson	.995	90	701	58	4	59
Urshela	1.000	18	122	7	0	12
Vierling	1.000	1	2	0	0	0
Vilade	1.000	1	2	0	0	0

Second Base	PCT	G	PO	A	E	DP
Ibanez	.992	44	47	79	1	19
Jung	.000	1	0	0	0	0
Keith	.977	133	194	309	12	68
Kennedy	1.000	4	5	7	0	2
McKinstry	1.000	18	16	23	0	3

Third Base	PCT	G	PO	A	E	DP
Ibanez	1.000	19	7	15	0	2
Jung	.917	27	10	34	4	2
Kennedy	1.000	1	0	2	0	0
Kreidler	1.000	8	2	6	0	0
McKinstry	.897	38	8	27	4	2
Urshela	.966	74	37	107	5	7
Vierling	.982	51	34	74	2	6

Shortstop	PCT	G	PO	A	E	DP
Baez	.972	80	122	189	9	39
Ibanez	1.000	5	0	5	0	1
Kreidler	.975	26	20	58	2	13
McKinstry	.961	48	33	91	5	19
Sweeney	.972	36	37	104	4	20

Outfield	PCT	G	PO	A	E	DP
Baddoo	1.000	30	42	0	0	0
Canha	.983	34	59	0	1	0
Carpenter	.989	48	88	5	1	0
Greene	.986	115	203	4	3	1
Ibanez	1.000	6	8	0	0	0
Kreidler	.000	2	0	0	0	0
Madris	1.000	1	1	0	0	0
Malloy	1.000	23	24	0	0	0
McKinstry	1.000	30	27	0	0	0
Meadows	.995	82	193	0	1	0
Perez	.990	116	189	1	2	0
Vierling	.990	106	202	3	2	1
Vilade	1.000	20	30	0	0	0

TOLEDO MUD HENS — TRIPLE-A

INTERNATIONAL LEAGUE

Batting	B-T	Ht.	Wt.	DOB	AVG	OBP	SLG	G	PA	AB	R	H	2B	3B	HR	RBI	BB	HBP	SH	SF	SO	SB	CS	BB%	SO%
Baddoo, Akil	L-L	6-1	214	8-16-98	.238	.340	.418	82	377	323	57	77	21	5	9	35	48	3	0	2	100	29	8	12.73	26.53
Baez, Javier	R-R	6-0	190	12-1-92	.333	.385	.667	4	13	12	3	4	1	0	1	1	1	0	0	0	3	0	0	7.69	23.08
Bastidas, Abel	B-R	6-1	165	11-24-03	.000	.000	.000	1	1	1	0	0	0	0	0	0	0	0	0	0	1	0	0	0.00	100.00
Bemboom, Anthony	L-R	6-2	195	1-18-90	.227	.345	.341	58	224	185	25	42	15	0	2	26	33	2	1	3	52	0	0	14.73	23.21
Bigbie, Justice	R-R	6-2	200	1-24-99	.248	.333	.334	136	558	488	62	121	26	2	4	50	60	5	0	5	104	8	5	10.75	18.64
Carpenter, Kerry	L-R	6-2	220	9-2-97	.214	.267	.286	4	15	14	2	3	1	0	0	2	1	0	0	0	5	0	0	6.67	33.33
Dingler, Dillon	R-R	6-3	210	9-17-98	.308	.379	.559	71	301	263	44	81	15	0	17	52	30	3	0	5	61	5	1	9.97	20.27
Gonzalez, Alvaro	B-R	6-0	165	9-16-00	.250	.382	.393	10	34	28	4	7	2	1	0	4	5	1	0	0	12	0	0	14.71	35.29
Greene, Riley	L-L	6-3	200	9-28-00	.167	.167	.333	2	6	6	0	1	1	0	0	2	0	0	0	0	1	0	0	0.00	16.67
Hiura, Keston	R-R	5-11	208	8-2-96	.232	.312	.401	49	199	177	27	41	10	1	6	24	21	0	0	1	56	0	0	10.55	28.14
Ibanez, Andy	R-R	5-10	205	4-3-93	.333	.400	.556	3	10	9	1	3	2	0	0	1	0	1	0	0	1	0	0	0.00	10.00
Joyce, Corey	R-R	6-0	190	8-19-98	.227	.393	.318	9	28	22	5	5	2	0	0	3	6	0	0	0	7	2	0	21.43	25.00
Jung, Jace	L-R	6-0	205	10-4-00	.257	.377	.454	91	415	339	50	87	23	1	14	60	67	2	0	6	93	2	2	16.14	22.41
Kennedy, Buddy	R-R	5-9	190	10-5-98	.234	.331	.383	39	163	141	25	33	12	0	3	14	19	2	0	1	39	2	1	11.66	23.93
Kreidler, Ryan	R-R	6-4	208	11-12-97	.200	.320	.335	48	201	170	20	34	4	2	5	14	25	5	1	0	59	7	0	12.44	29.35
Leonard, Eddys	R-R	5-11	195	11-10-00	.263	.326	.455	67	282	255	35	67	15	2	10	26	17	8	0	2	74	7	3	6.03	26.24
Madris, Bligh	L-R	6-0	208	2-29-96	.222	.323	.444	108	429	365	57	81	20	2	19	60	53	3	0	3	111	21	5	12.35	25.87
Maggi, Drew	R-R	6-0	192	5-16-89	.225	.287	.405	40	123	111	18	25	5	0	5	12	9	1	1	1	35	1	0	7.32	28.46
Malloy, Justyn-Henry	R-R	6-1	212	2-19-00	.258	.403	.457	55	236	186	27	48	16	0	7	31	43	4	0	3	66	3	3	18.22	27.97
Meadows, Parker	L-R	6-5	205	11-2-99	.292	.388	.495	51	237	202	39	59	11	3	8	25	30	3	0	2	45	19	5	12.66	18.99
Mendoza, Carlos	L-R	5-7	165	12-14-99	.000	.000	.000	1	1	1	0	0	0	0	0	0	0	0	0	0	0	0	0	0.00	0.00
Mercado, Oscar	R-R	6-2	197	12-16-94	.200	.315	.289	15	54	45	4	9	1	0	1	8	8	0	0	1	11	4	0	14.81	20.37
Navigato, Andrew	R-R	5-11	188	5-28-98	.271	.363	.500	128	512	446	82	121	29	5	21	83	55	10	0	1	126	22	10	10.74	24.61
Nido, Tomas	R-R	6-0	211	4-12-94	.222	.222	.333	3	9	9	1	2	1	0	0	2	0	0	0	0	2	0	0	0.00	22.22
Perez, Wenceel	B-R	5-11	203	10-30-99	.164	.270	.382	15	63	55	10	9	2	2	2	8	8	0	0	0	15	4	0	12.70	23.81
Santana, Luis	R-R	5-6	196	7-20-99	.125	.222	.125	3	9	8	1	1	0	0	0	1	1	0	0	0	3	0	0	11.11	33.33
Scott, Stephen	L-R	5-11	207	5-23-97	.292	.337	.466	46	175	161	22	47	14	1	4	23	11	1	0	2	41	3	2	6.29	23.43
Sweeney, Trey	L-R	6-2	200	4-24-00	.381	.447	.667	11	47	42	9	16	6	0	2	9	5	0	0	0	12	4	1	10.64	25.53
Tapia, Sergio	R-R	5-10	160	8-24-02	.000	.000	.000	1	1	1	0	0	0	0	0	0	0	0	0	0	0	0	0	0.00	0.00
Torkelson, Spencer	R-R	6-1	220	8-26-99	.239	.356	.442	58	275	226	41	54	13	0	11	43	42	2	0	5	85	1	0	15.27	30.91
Unroe, Riley	B-R	5-11	180	8-3-95	.272	.378	.412	86	294	243	40	66	16	0	6	24	41	1	8	1	77	18	4	13.95	26.19
Urshela, Gio	R-R	6-0	215	10-11-91	.625	.667	.625	3	9	8	2	5	0	0	0	1	1	0	0	0	1	0	0	11.11	11.11
Vilade, Ryan	R-R	6-2	226	2-18-99	.278	.346	.449	108	442	392	47	109	24	2	13	64	39	5	0	6	108	20	7	8.82	24.43

Pitching	B-T	Ht.	Wt.	DOB	W	L	ERA	G	GS	SV	IP	Hits	Runs	ER	HR	BB	SO	AVG	OBP	SLG	SO%	BB%	BF
Adcock, Ty	R-R	6-0	213	2-7-97	1	1	9.00	6	0	0	6	9	6	6	2	3	9	.321	.406	.571	28.13	9.38	32
Anderson, Drew	R-R	6-3	205	3-22-94	2	1	3.86	9	0	1	14	16	6	6	0	9	16	.286	.385	.375	24.62	13.85	65
Anderson, Jack	R-R	6-3	197	11-23-99	2	0	5.82	8	1	0	17	19	14	11	2	6	10	.288	.338	.500	13.16	7.89	76
Bergner, Austin	R-R	6-5	210	5-1-97	0	1	9.68	10	9	0	31	45	34	33	5	26	33	.333	.442	.563	20.25	15.95	163
Bienlien, Michael	R-R	6-3	246	3-19-98	0	1	13.50	4	0	1	6	11	9	9	2	5	10	.407	.500	.667	29.41	14.71	34
Brieske, Beau	R-R	6-3	200	4-4-98	1	0	2.95	13	0	3	21	19	7	7	0	11	22	.244	.352	.333	24.18	12.09	91
Diaz, Miguel	R-R	6-0	224	11-28-94	1	0	1.97	24	1	4	32	25	7	7	0	12	44	.208	.284	.275	32.84	8.96	134
Englert, Mason	S-R	6-4	206	11-1-99	3	1	3.24	28	2	0	42	33	15	15	5	14	60	.216	.294	.353	35.29	8.24	170
Faedo, Alex	R-R	6-5	225	11-12-95	0	0	3.00	3	1	0	3	4	1	1	0	4	4	.308	.471	.385	23.53	23.53	17
Flores, Wilmer	R-R	6-4	225	2-20-01	2	3	8.53	16	0	0	25	29	27	24	3	24	23	.293	.422	.495	17.97	18.75	128
Guenther, Sean	L-L	5-11	194	12-29-95	4	4	3.31	39	2	3	52	51	28	19	4	15	52	.252	.305	.381	23.42	6.76	222
Hanifee, Brenan	R-R	6-5	215	5-29-98	1	2	5.17	34	0	1	47	47	29	27	6	14	53	.251	.305	.455	25.98	6.86	204
Hill, Garrett	R-R	6-0	185	1-16-96	0	1	4.76	16	1	0	28	23	15	15	4	25	28	.221	.372	.394	21.71	19.38	129
Hurter, Brant	L-L	6-6	250	9-6-98	2	4	5.80	19	18	0	71	82	49	46	8	23	70	.285	.356	.441	21.67	7.12	323
Jobe, Jackson	R-R	6-2	190	7-30-02	1	0	6.00	2	2	0	9	12	6	6	2	5	7	.316	.395	.579	16.28	11.63	43
Lange, Alex	R-R	6-3	202	10-2-95	1	1	3.12	9	0	0	9	7	3	3	1	1	12	.212	.235	.364	35.29	2.94	34
Lee, Chase	R-R	6-0	170	8-13-98	1	3	3.27	17	0	0	22	23	12	8	2	4	31	.261	.309	.386	32.29	4.17	96

Lockhart, Lael	S-L	6-3	225	12-31-97	4	8	5.32	20	18	0	93	85	56	55	16	50	109	.239	.347	.451	26.27	12.05	415
Lucas, Easton	L-L	6-4	180	9-23-96	1	1	3.51	21	0	1	33	29	14	13	2	15	39	.240	.324	.347	28.06	10.79	139
Madden, Ty	R-R	6-3	215	2-21-00	3	5	7.97	18	18	0	79	100	73	70	17	40	102	.304	.381	.559	27.57	10.81	370
Madris, Bligh	L-R	6-0	208	2-29-96	0	0	0.00	1	0	0	0	0	0	0	0	0	0	.000	.000	.000	0.00	0.00	1
Maeda, Kenta	R-R	6-1	185	4-11-88	0	0	3.00	1	1	0	3	3	1	1	0	0	6	.231	.231	.385	46.15	0.00	13
Maggi, Drew	R-R	6-0	192	5-16-89	0	0	0.00	1	0	0	0	0	0	0	0	0	0	.000	.000	.000	0.00	0.00	1
Magno, Andrew	R-L	5-11	190	4-30-98	4	9	6.62	35	0	0	50	60	42	37	4	32	55	.305	.410	.447	22.82	13.28	241
Manning, Matt	R-R	6-6	195	1-28-98	2	5	4.28	15	14	0	69	64	34	33	10	25	72	.244	.308	.420	24.91	8.65	289
Miller, Shelby	R-R	6-3	225	10-10-90	0	0	0.00	2	1	0	2	2	0	0	0	1	3	.222	.300	.556	30.00	10.00	10
Mize, Casey	R-R	6-3	212	5-1-97	0	0	2.63	4	4	0	14	10	4	4	0	4	17	.204	.278	.265	31.48	7.41	54
Montero, Keider	R-R	6-1	145	7-6-00	1	4	5.03	13	13	0	48	52	28	27	5	30	54	.272	.377	.455	24.11	13.39	224
Olson, Reese	R-R	6-1	160	7-31-99	0	0	0.00	2	2	0	5	2	0	0	0	2	6	.125	.222	.188	33.33	11.11	18
Poulin, PJ	R-L	6-1	195	7-25-96	1	0	3.81	20	0	0	26	23	13	11	1	11	32	.237	.315	.330	28.83	9.91	111
Reyes, Angel	R-R	6-2	205	10-17-97	0	0	7.91	10	1	0	19	22	18	17	3	18	11	.289	.449	.539	11.22	18.37	98
Sammons, Bryan	L-L	6-4	235	4-27-95	6	7	4.15	22	20	0	102	89	53	47	14	44	102	.226	.308	.407	23.08	9.95	442
Schulfer, Austin	R-R	6-2	175	12-22-95	3	1	5.14	23	1	1	35	34	21	20	5	15	45	.248	.340	.438	28.85	9.62	156
Sequeira, Gabriel	L-L	6-0	200	8-18-97	0	1	45.00	1	0	0	1	3	5	5	0	2	2	.500	.727	.833	18.18	18.18	11
Sweet, Devin	S-R	5-11	183	9-6-96	9	6	3.91	52	4	4	76	62	38	33	11	38	111	.221	.320	.416	33.94	11.62	327
Tassin, Bryce	R-R	6-2	209	1-11-97	0	0	3.74	21	3	2	34	30	15	14	8	17	35	.236	.345	.472	23.65	11.49	148
Unroe, Riley	S-R	5-11	180	8-3-95	0	0	29.45	2	0	0	4	12	12	12	3	2	0	.545	.600	1.091	0.00	8.00	25
Vanasco, Ricky	R-R	6-3	180	10-13-98	1	0	1.06	11	0	0	17	12	3	2	0	9	21	.197	.310	.213	29.58	12.68	71
Vasquez, Andrew	L-L	6-6	235	9-14-93	7	3	5.11	48	3	2	69	77	45	39	8	31	63	.278	.370	.419	19.44	9.57	324
Villalobos, Eli	R-R	6-4	195	6-26-97	0	0	31.50	3	0	0	2	6	8	7	0	6	2	.545	.706	.818	11.76	35.29	17
Watson, Troy	R-R	6-2	180	6-11-97	0	3	5.83	10	8	0	29	35	19	19	5	19	33	.302	.403	.569	23.57	13.57	140
White, Brendan	R-R	5-11	185	11-18-98	0	0	21.60	3	0	0	2	1	4	4	0	6	1	.200	.615	.200	7.69	46.15	13
Wingenter, Trey	R-R	6-7	237	4-15-94	4	4	3.31	26	0	2	33	31	16	12	4	17	48	.248	.352	.424	32.88	11.64	146
Wolf, Adam	L-L	6-6	215	12-26-96	1	0	3.24	5	1	0	8	6	3	3	0	8	8	.207	.410	.276	20.51	20.51	39

Fielding

Catcher	PCT	G	PO	A	E	DP	PB
Bemboom	.985	55	519	21	8	2	6
Dingler	.997	66	640	38	2	1	4
Nido	1.000	3	28	1	0	0	0
Scott	.988	28	305	16	4	2	4

First Base	PCT	G	PO	A	E	DP
Hiura	.986	42	271	18	4	31
Kennedy	1.000	1	6	0	0	1
Madris	.993	44	279	14	2	25
Scott	.923	2	12	0	1	2
Torkelson	1.000	51	346	40	0	34
Vilade	.991	14	102	5	1	6

Second Base	PCT	G	PO	A	E	DP
Gonzalez	1.000	6	8	7	0	0
Ibanez	1.000	1	1	6	0	1
Joyce	1.000	4	3	8	0	3
Jung	.987	18	23	51	1	9
Kennedy	.974	22	25	49	2	11
Kreidler	1.000	2	0	3	0	0
Leonard	.987	23	30	48	1	8
Maggi	.952	10	6	14	1	4
Mendoza	1.000	1	1	0	0	0
Navigato	.952	30	43	77	6	10
Santana	1.000	3	9	5	0	3
Unroe	.966	31	39	76	4	17
Vilade	.979	15	19	27	1	12

Third Base	PCT	G	PO	A	E	DP
Bastidas	.000	1	0	0	0	0
Gonzalez	.889	5	1	7	1	0
Ibanez	1.000	1	0	2	0	0
Joyce	1.000	2	0	2	0	0
Jung	.891	65	28	103	16	12
Kennedy	.951	18	9	30	2	6
Kreidler	.875	4	5	9	2	1
Leonard	.952	15	7	13	1	0
Maggi	.966	18	6	22	1	3
Navigato	.933	22	11	31	3	3
Sweeney	1.000	1	0	3	0	0
Unroe	1.000	3	2	1	0	0
Urshela	1.000	2	1	1	0	1
Vilade	.933	6	8	6	1	2

Shortstop	PCT	G	PO	A	E	DP
Baez	1.000	3	2	4	0	2
Joyce	1.000	3	2	12	0	1
Kennedy	1.000	1	1	0	0	0
Kreidler	.978	33	58	76	3	15
Leonard	.987	22	25	51	1	8
Maggi	.857	2	0	6	1	1
Navigato	.948	61	76	125	11	28
Sweeney	1.000	9	10	24	0	6
Unroe	.923	22	27	45	6	7

Outfield	PCT	G	PO	A	E	DP
Baddoo	.993	72	142	1	1	0
Bigbie	.990	120	196	2	2	0
Carpenter	1.000	2	3	0	0	0
Greene	1.000	2	2	1	0	0
Kreidler	1.000	7	22	0	0	0
Leonard	1.000	4	3	0	0	0
Madris	.922	36	52	7	5	2
Malloy	.983	43	56	1	1	1
Meadows	1.000	42	102	2	0	0
Mercado	1.000	15	21	0	0	0
Navigato	.958	13	21	2	1	1
Perez	1.000	9	8	0	0	0
Scott	.947	11	18	0	1	0
Unroe	.966	29	52	4	2	1
Vilade	.992	66	119	5	1	0

ERIE SEAWOLVES — *DOUBLE-A*

EASTERN LEAGUE

Batting	B-T	Ht.	Wt.	DOB	AVG	OBP	SLG	G	PA	AB	R	H	2B	3B	HR	RBI	BB	HBP	SH	SF	SO	SB	CS	BB%	SO%
Alfonzo, Eliezer	B-R	5-10	155	9-23-99	.255	.304	.368	97	396	364	41	93	14	0	9	52	23	4	0	4	31	2	2	5.81	7.83
Allen, Brady	R-L	6-1	218	9-3-99	.205	.278	.342	108	410	366	40	75	17	3	9	47	33	6	0	5	139	6	7	8.05	33.90
Anderson, Max	R-R	6-0	195	2-28-02	.182	.182	.273	5	22	22	0	4	2	0	0	3	0	0	0	0	3	0	0	0.00	13.64
Cabrera, Daniel	L-L	5-11	200	9-5-98	.200	.222	.360	7	27	25	5	5	1	0	1	6	1	0	0	1	5	0	0	3.70	18.52
Crouch, Josh	R-R	6-0	200	12-7-98	.250	.250	.250	1	4	4	1	1	0	0	0	0	0	0	0	0	0	0	0	0.00	0.00
Cruz, Trei	B-R	6-1	204	7-5-98	.260	.342	.396	102	440	384	57	100	23	1	9	48	49	1	2	4	112	9	8	11.14	25.45
Graham, Peyton	R-R	6-3	185	1-26-01	.667	.750	.667	1	4	3	1	2	0	0	0	0	0	1	0	0	1	0	0	0.00	25.00
Hicks, Liam	L-R	5-11	185	6-2-99	.272	.414	.368	33	145	114	20	31	5	0	2	14	23	6	0	2	14	2	0	15.86	9.66
Holton, Jake	R-R	6-0	210	3-2-98	.279	.373	.459	96	410	351	62	98	21	0	14	71	44	11	0	4	91	6	2	10.73	22.20
Hopkins, TJ	R-R	6-1	195	1-16-97	.190	.326	.329	22	95	79	10	15	5	0	2	4	16	0	0	0	24	2	1	16.84	25.26
Joyce, Corey	R-R	6-0	190	8-19-98	.345	.472	.448	8	36	29	5	10	0	0	1	5	4	3	0	0	9	2	0	11.11	25.00
Lee, Hao-Yu	R-R	5-9	190	2-3-03	.298	.363	.488	87	386	342	55	102	19	5	12	56	33	5	0	6	69	16	1	8.55	17.88
Lee, Patrick	R-R	5-10	180	10-19-99	.156	.289	.281	12	38	32	5	5	2	1	0	2	4	2	0	0	14	3	0	10.53	36.84
Malgeri, Ben	R-R	6-1	215	1-12-00	.252	.323	.409	117	470	421	67	106	22	4	12	57	43	3	0	3	148	20	4	9.15	31.49
Mendoza, Carlos	L-R	5-7	165	12-14-99	.269	.394	.374	114	515	420	86	113	17	6	5	46	70	18	5	2	89	32	5	13.59	17.28
Meyers, Chris	L-R	6-3	210	4-27-99	.256	.342	.430	122	503	442	67	113	23	0	18	58	46	13	0	2	130	4	2	9.15	25.84
Molfetta, Christian	R-R	5-10	195	10-17-96	.176	.256	.294	13	39	34	4	6	1	0	1	7	3	1	0	1	16	0	0	7.69	41.03

Batting	B-T	Ht.	Wt.	DOB	AVG	OBP	SLG	G	PA	AB	R	H	2B	3B	HR	RBI	BB	HBP	SH	SF	SO	SB	CS	BB%	SO%
Murr, Austin	L-L	6-1	218	1-26-99	.239	.333	.427	71	273	234	40	56	14	3	8	37	28	7	0	4	55	7	3	10.26	20.15
Navigato, Andrew	R-R	5-11	188	5-28-98	.000	.000	.000	2	8	8	0	0	0	0	0	0	0	0	0	0	2	0	0	0.00	25.00
Rodriguez, Julio E.	R-R	5-11	245	6-11-97	.186	.240	.278	30	104	97	10	18	6	0	1	7	5	2	0	0	22	0	0	4.81	21.15
Santana, Luis	R-R	5-6	196	7-20-99	.165	.270	.216	29	115	97	8	16	5	0	0	6	11	4	0	3	22	2	1	9.57	19.13
Scott, Stephen	L-R	5-11	207	5-23-97	.287	.378	.521	29	111	94	18	27	5	1	5	19	12	3	0	2	24	6	0	10.81	21.62
Serretti, Danny	B-R	6-0	195	5-7-00	.206	.372	.206	12	43	34	5	7	0	0	0	0	6	3	0	0	11	1	1	13.95	25.58
Workman, Gage	B-R	6-4	202	10-24-99	.280	.366	.476	126	556	483	85	135	29	6	18	89	65	3	0	3	153	30	13	11.69	27.52

Pitching	B-T	Ht.	Wt.	DOB	W	L	ERA	G	GS	SV	IP	Hits	Runs	ER	HR	BB	SO	AVG	OBP	SLG	SO%	BB%	BF
Bergner, Austin	R-R	6-5	210	5-1-97	3	2	2.34	10	10	0	50	33	17	13	5	20	64	.189	.278	.326	32.16	10.05	199
Bienlien, Michael	R-R	6-3	246	3-19-98	1	1	6.00	15	1	0	24	24	16	16	2	8	30	.255	.317	.362	28.85	7.69	104
Burhenn, Garrett	R-R	6-3	215	9-12-99	6	1	3.91	20	19	0	94	92	42	41	11	38	91	.259	.333	.420	22.41	9.36	406
Calvo, Blair	R-R	6-3	195	2-27-96	0	0	9.00	3	0	0	2	4	3	2	0	2	3	.364	.500	.364	21.43	14.29	14
Coker, Calvin	R-R	6-3	174	3-6-96	3	4	3.20	41	0	2	56	51	22	20	3	24	48	.244	.329	.349	19.92	9.96	241
Hernandez, Wilkel	R-R	6-3	195	4-13-99	5	7	4.34	28	27	0	120	119	67	58	16	55	108	.259	.344	.434	20.61	10.50	524
Higginbotham, Jake	L-L	6-0	190	1-11-96	2	5	4.33	41	2	3	62	63	33	30	10	12	78	.254	.295	.435	29.43	4.53	265
Hill, Garrett	R-R	6-0	185	1-16-96	2	3	4.15	16	1	1	22	20	14	10	1	14	33	.247	.357	.333	33.00	14.00	100
Holton, Jake	R-R	6-0	210	3-2-98	0	0	9.00	1	0	0	1	2	1	1	1	0	1	.400	.400	1.200	20.00	0.00	5
Jobe, Jackson	R-R	6-2	190	7-30-02	4	2	1.95	16	16	0	74	42	19	16	2	38	81	.163	.275	.218	27.09	12.71	299
Lockhart, Lael	S-L	6-3	225	12-31-97	2	2	1.93	7	6	0	28	20	7	6	2	9	36	.196	.259	.284	32.14	8.04	112
Madden, Ty	R-R	6-3	215	2-21-00	0	0	2.55	4	4	0	18	11	6	5	1	3	22	.172	.221	.250	32.35	4.41	68
Magno, Andrew	R-L	5-11	190	4-30-98	3	0	2.25	10	0	3	16	9	4	4	3	3	22	.164	.203	.364	37.29	5.08	59
Melton, Troy	R-R	6-4	210	12-3-00	7	8	5.10	23	23	0	101	108	61	57	19	30	119	.274	.326	.487	27.67	6.98	430
Michael, Trevin	R-R	6-2	200	9-15-97	3	2	3.35	36	1	0	54	41	21	20	7	15	61	.208	.269	.391	28.24	6.94	216
Miller, Jake	L-L	6-2	185	6-27-01	0	0	0.00	1	1	0	5	3	0	0	0	0	3	.176	.176	.176	17.65	0.00	17
Murr, Austin	L-L	6-1	218	1-26-99	1	0	9.00	1	0	0	1	1	1	1	0	1	0	.333	.500	.333	0.00	25.00	4
Naughton, Tim	R-R	6-3	195	11-14-95	9	0	3.00	43	0	0	60	48	28	20	4	33	73	.219	.324	.315	28.52	12.89	256
Owens, Tyler	R-R	5-10	185	1-9-01	1	3	3.31	13	0	2	16	13	8	6	1	7	20	.213	.294	.328	28.17	9.86	71
Peguero, Joel	R-R	5-11	160	5-5-97	3	0	3.14	43	0	2	52	46	25	18	4	17	56	.232	.301	.348	25.45	7.73	220
Pena, Carlos	L-L	5-11	160	9-7-98	8	6	3.49	25	19	0	113	100	47	44	6	44	99	.235	.312	.336	20.84	9.26	475
Petit, RJ	R-R	6-8	300	9-23-99	6	7	3.68	43	1	3	59	42	29	24	2	27	76	.199	.303	.270	31.15	11.07	244
Poulin, PJ	R-L	6-1	195	7-25-96	1	1	0.79	25	0	4	34	19	4	3	0	13	41	.162	.258	.197	30.60	9.70	134
Reyes, Angel	R-R	6-2	205	10-17-97	3	1	4.40	22	3	0	43	43	23	21	4	15	35	.257	.328	.377	18.52	7.94	189
Seelinger, Matt	R-R	6-3	190	4-19-95	1	1	1.65	20	0	2	27	17	8	5	3	10	46	.173	.248	.306	42.20	9.17	109
Silva, Eric	R-R	6-1	185	10-3-02	0	2	5.60	13	0	0	18	16	12	11	3	6	18	.242	.324	.409	24.32	8.11	74
Tassin, Bryce	R-R	6-2	209	1-11-97	1	0	1.00	5	0	0	9	3	1	1	0	3	8	.100	.182	.200	24.24	9.09	33
Weins, CJ	R-R	6-3	223	8-15-00	0	0	3.00	2	0	0	3	1	1	1	0	1	6	.111	.200	.222	54.55	9.09	11
White, Brendan	R-R	5-11	185	11-18-98	0	0	13.50	1	0	0	1	0	1	1	0	4	0	.000	.667	.000	0.00	66.67	6
Wolf, Adam	L-L	6-6	215	12-26-96	2	0	3.04	11	1	0	24	20	8	8	3	8	19	.233	.347	.395	18.81	7.92	101

Fielding

Catcher	PCT	G	PO	A	E	DP	PB
Alfonzo	.987	75	752	37	10	6	2
Crouch	1.000	1	9	1	0	0	1
Hicks	.978	18	166	12	4	0	2
Molfetta	.929	9	48	5	5	0	0
Rodriguez	.995	22	179	7	1	1	1
Scott	.987	16	147	8	2	0	0

First Base	PCT	G	PO	A	E	DP
Holton	.994	73	519	20	3	54
Meyers	1.000	45	296	13	0	22
Murr	1.000	22	151	8	0	5

Second Base	PCT	G	PO	A	E	DP
Anderson	.917	5	5	17	2	1
Joyce	1.000	1	1	0	2	0
Lee	.980	77	116	174	6	39
Mendoza	.984	48	64	123	3	25
Serretti	1.000	6	8	18	0	2
Workman	.895	5	5	12	2	3

Third Base	PCT	G	PO	A	E	DP
Cruz	1.000	1	0	2	0	0
Joyce	.909	6	6	4	1	0
Lee	.897	9	7	19	3	3
Mendoza	.932	19	11	30	3	6
Molfetta	1.000	2	0	2	0	0
Santana	.982	25	18	37	1	4
Serretti	1.000	3	4	2	0	0
Workman	.967	74	45	111	5	5

Shortstop	PCT	G	PO	A	E	DP
Cruz	.982	82	101	177	5	38
Graham	1.000	1	2	4	0	0
Joyce	1.000	1	2	0	0	0
Navigato	.857	2	2	4	1	0
Serretti	.875	2	4	3	1	
Worknan	.922	47	49	92	12	13

Outfield	PCT	G	PO	A	E	DP
Allen	.996	108	232	8	1	2
Cabrera	1.000	7	11	0	0	0
Cruz	1.000	19	38	3	0	0
Hopkins	.941	19	34	0	2	0
Lee	.950	10	20	2	1	0
Malgeri	.983	120	237	4	4	1
Mendoza	.989	50	89	1	1	0
Meyers	1.000	52	83	2	0	0
Murr	.983	33	59	0	1	0

WEST MICHIGAN WHITECAPS — HIGH CLASS A

MIDWEST LEAGUE

Batting	B-T	Ht.	Wt.	DOB	AVG	OBP	SLG	G	PA	AB	R	H	2B	3B	HR	RBI	BB	HBP	SH	SF	SO	SB	CS	BB%	SO%
Anderson, Max	R-R	6-0	195	2-28-02	.270	.321	.392	121	527	485	64	131	20	3	11	73	35	3	0	4	74	1	0	6.64	14.04
Brookman, Archer	R-R	5-11	200	1-8-99	.095	.240	.143	9	25	21	0	2	1	0	0	0	2	2	0	0	8	0	0	8.00	32.00
Callahan, Brett	L-R	6-0	195	11-2-01	.056	.190	.056	5	21	18	0	1	0	0	0	0	2	1	0	0	4	0	0	9.52	19.05
Campos, Roberto	R-R	6-3	200	6-14-03	.272	.342	.425	118	484	426	56	116	25	5	10	66	41	8	0	7	112	11	2	8.47	23.14
Clark, Max	L-L	6-1	190	12-21-04	.264	.344	.421	34	157	140	20	37	10	3	2	17	13	4	0	0	36	3	2	8.28	22.93
Crouch, Josh	R-R	6-0	200	12-7-98	.210	.286	.341	62	238	214	28	45	10	0	6	26	16	7	0	1	60	1	0	6.72	25.21
Gold, Luke	R-R	6-0	220	10-10-00	.226	.302	.385	121	497	442	68	100	24	2	14	57	36	14	0	5	128	7	3	7.24	25.75
Graham, Peyton	R-R	6-3	185	1-26-01	.185	.342	.247	53	202	162	17	30	7	0	1	15	31	8	0	1	46	8	2	15.35	22.77
Hurtado, Ricardo	R-R	5-10	100	5-23-03	.000	.333	.000	1	3	2	0	0	0	0	0	0	1	0	0	0	1	0	0	33.33	33.33
Jarvis, Jim	L-R	5-10	185	11-6-00	.216	.308	.308	71	289	250	35	54	9	1	4	23	32	3	0	4	40	11	5	11.07	13.84
Jenkins, Andrew	R-R	5-11	217	11-3-00	.286	.364	.408	14	55	49	7	14	3	0	1	6	6	0	0	0	14	0	0	10.91	25.45
Johnson, Dom	R-R	5-9	185	3-7-01	.193	.249	.270	69	265	244	23	47	8	1	3	20	11	8	0	2	71	14	3	4.15	26.79
Lee, Bennett	R-R	6-0	208	4-26-02	.166	.292	.242	49	185	157	15	26	9	0	1	13	25	3	0	0	51	0	0	13.51	27.57

DETROIT TIGERS

Batting	B-T	Ht.	Wt.	DOB	AVG	OBP	SLG	G	PA	AB	R	H	2B	3B	HR	RBI	BB	HBP	SH	SF	SO	SB	CS	BB%	SO%
Lee, Patrick	R-R	5-10	180	10-19-99	.250	.317	.407	35	120	108	18	27	8	0	3	22	10	1	0	1	31	19	3	8.33	25.83
Leonard, Eddys	R-R	5-11	195	11-10-00	.167	.250	.389	5	20	18	3	3	1	0	1	2	2	0	0	0	4	0	0	10.00	20.00
Liranzo, Thayron	B-R	6-3	195	7-5-03	.315	.470	.562	26	115	89	17	28	7	0	5	20	26	0	0	0	20	0	0	22.61	17.39
McGonigle, Kevin	L-R	5-11	185	8-18-04	.214	.368	.357	14	57	42	9	9	1	1	1	7	11	1	0	3	4	2	0	19.30	7.02
Mendoza, Carlos	L-R	5-7	165	12-14-99	.174	.296	.174	7	27	23	1	4	0	0	0	0	2	2	0	0	7	1	0	7.41	25.93
Murr, Austin	L-L	6-1	218	1-26-99	.239	.381	.433	18	84	67	12	16	5	1	2	9	13	3	0	1	15	3	2	15.48	17.86
Pacheco, Izaac	L-R	6-3	225	11-18-02	.220	.286	.354	68	280	254	24	56	11	1	7	35	22	2	0	2	96	4	1	7.86	34.29
Peck, John	R-R	6-0	185	7-18-02	.286	.333	.400	18	75	70	10	20	3	1	1	8	4	1	0	0	23	6	1	5.33	30.67
Santana, Luis	R-R	5-6	196	7-20-99	.201	.283	.311	47	184	164	23	33	3	0	5	13	13	6	0	1	30	2	0	7.07	16.30
Scott, Stephen	L-R	5-11	207	5-23-97	.143	.294	.214	5	17	14	1	2	1	0	0	0	1	2	0	0	4	0	0	5.88	23.53
Serretti, Danny	B-R	6-0	195	5-7-00	.190	.287	.293	87	320	273	28	52	13	0	5	30	36	3	2	5	91	4	3	11.25	28.44
Sibrian, Jose	R-R	5-10	175	10-24-98	.152	.250	.196	17	52	46	4	7	2	0	0	3	4	2	0	0	17	0	0	7.69	32.69
Stephenson, Seth	R-R	5-8	165	1-10-01	.263	.349	.342	111	477	415	69	109	12	3	5	36	37	19	4	2	85	60	9	7.76	17.82
Turney, Cole	L-L	6-1	215	1-16-99	.318	.430	.530	19	79	66	13	21	8	0	2	10	12	1	0	0	23	1	0	15.19	29.11

Pitching	B-T	Ht.	Wt.	DOB	W	L	ERA	G	GS	SV	IP	Hits	Runs	ER	HR	BB	SO	AVG	OBP	SLG	SO%	BB%	BF
Adametz, Joe	L-L	6-5	190	12-23-99	4	2	3.26	10	9	0	47	48	22	17	2	16	36	.268	.333	.358	18.18	8.08	198
Alba, Max	R-R	6-5	215	7-15-99	3	4	3.61	39	3	4	57	46	26	23	8	8	63	.208	.236	.380	27.51	3.49	229
Anderson, Jack	R-R	6-3	197	11-23-99	3	1	2.92	27	0	1	49	40	18	16	3	7	50	.215	.255	.339	25.51	3.57	196
Bergner, Austin	R-R	6-5	210	5-1-97	0	1	1.00	3	3	0	9	4	1	1	1	2	11	.133	.188	.300	34.38	6.25	32
Bienlien, Michael	R-R	6-3	246	3-19-98	1	0	0.94	16	0	5	29	16	3	3	0	8	24	.167	.243	.177	22.22	7.41	108
Burhenn, Garrett	R-R	6-3	215	9-12-99	0	3	2.89	7	7	0	28	24	10	9	2	4	32	.224	.259	.336	28.57	3.57	112
De Los Santos, Carlos	R-R	6-2	170	11-18-00	1	0	7.20	5	0	0	5	2	6	4	0	14	3	.133	.548	.133	9.68	45.16	31
Englert, Mason	S-R	6-4	206	11-1-99	1	0	1.69	2	1	0	5	3	1	1	0	2	5	.158	.238	.211	23.81	9.52	21
Fields, Colin	R-R	6-2	200	3-18-00	2	5	3.22	26	21	0	103	82	42	37	9	35	104	.223	.304	.342	24.88	8.37	418
Flores, Wilmer	R-R	6-4	225	2-20-01	0	0	3.38	2	0	0	3	3	1	1	0	1	4	.300	.364	.300	36.36	9.09	11
Hamm, Jaden	R-R	6-1	190	9-5-02	5	4	2.64	24	23	0	99	73	30	29	8	31	122	.202	.271	.315	30.58	7.77	399
Hess, Zack	R-R	6-6	219	2-25-97	1	0	6.30	25	0	0	30	32	22	21	3	26	34	.274	.407	.427	23.13	17.69	147
Holden, Connor	R-R	6-5	240	6-25-98	3	1	5.26	19	0	0	26	25	15	15	4	10	19	.253	.339	.444	16.67	8.77	114
Huizi, Eiker	R-R	6-0	155	9-24-00	0	1	20.25	3	0	1	3	5	7	6	1	4	1	.357	.500	.643	5.56	22.22	18
Jimenez, Marco	R-R	5-11	239	12-6-99	6	1	2.05	38	0	4	57	28	15	13	1	28	52	.149	.262	.207	23.32	12.56	223
Jobe, Jackson	R-R	6-2	190	7-30-02	0	1	2.00	3	3	0	9	4	4	2	0	2	8	.133	.188	.233	24.24	6.06	33
Kohlhepp, Tanner	L-R	6-4	210	5-27-99	7	5	4.55	46	1	5	61	52	43	31	2	30	78	.225	.333	.286	28.57	10.99	273
Marcano, Carlos	R-R	6-2	150	7-8-03	3	11	3.86	26	23	0	112	122	60	48	5	36	97	.276	.335	.387	19.88	7.38	488
Mauloni, Christopher	L-R	6-2	200	6-16-98	3	2	3.68	24	0	0	37	28	17	15	5	12	32	.212	.305	.379	21.05	7.89	152
Merrill, Matt	R-R	6-4	202	6-11-98	4	1	1.79	36	0	3	50	24	11	10	1	38	70	.146	.311	.195	33.49	18.18	209
Michael, Trevin	R-R	6-2	200	9-15-97	0	0	0.00	3	0	1	4	0	0	0	0	1	7	.000	.077	.000	53.85	7.69	13
Miller, Jake	L-L	6-2	185	6-27-01	1	2	4.50	5	0	0	20	22	11	10	2	3	20	.286	.306	.455	23.26	3.49	86
Miller, Joe	L-L	5-10	195	3-13-00	3	4	4.42	19	18	0	77	81	39	38	9	20	50	.267	.324	.442	15.11	6.04	331
Montalvo, Joseph	S-R	6-2	185	5-4-02	1	1	4.74	5	5	0	19	17	10	10	1	7	15	.239	.313	.408	18.75	8.75	80
Pena, Carlos	L-L	5-11	160	9-7-98	0	2	2.84	2	0	0	6	5	6	2	1	4	13	.200	.300	.440	41.94	12.90	31
Perez, Cleiverth	L-L	6-0	211	2-5-00	7	1	3.90	23	0	0	32	28	17	14	5	11	25	.224	.283	.424	18.12	7.97	138
Pinales, Erick	R-R	6-2	185	1-27-99	2	2	6.23	34	0	2	39	34	34	27	3	33	48	.225	.376	.344	25.26	17.37	190
Reyes, Angel	R-R	6-2	205	10-17-97	0	0	4.15	3	0	0	4	5	2	2	0	1	5	.294	.368	.471	26.32	5.26	19
Sanchez, Yosber	R-R	6-1	170	5-22-01	4	2	1.59	23	0	3	40	28	11	7	1	19	47	.194	.301	.264	28.31	11.45	166
Sequeira, Gabriel	L-L	6-0	200	8-18-97	0	0	7.07	15	0	1	14	10	12	11	1	12	20	.192	.373	.288	29.85	17.91	67
Smith, Dylan	R-R	6-2	180	5-28-00	0	5	4.40	14	13	0	57	58	28	28	7	31	59	.259	.349	.433	23.14	12.16	255
Tassin, Bryce	R-R	6-2	209	1-11-97	2	0	5.40	3	1	0	3	6	2	2	0	1	2	.375	.444	.438	11.11	5.56	18
Weins, CJ	R-R	6-3	223	8-15-00	1	1	1.69	4	0	0	5	3	2	1	1	2	0	.158	.273	.316	36.36	9.09	22

Fielding

Catcher	PCT	G	PO	A	E	DP	PB
Brookman	.955	9	62	2	3	0	2
Crouch	.993	55	539	28	4	1	5
Hurtado	1.000	1	9	1	0	1	0
Lee	.982	44	358	17	7	2	7
Liranzo	.990	13	92	5	1	1	2
Scott	.950	3	17	2	1	0	1
Sibrian	1.000	14	93	9	0	0	3

First Base	PCT	G	PO	A	E	DP
Crouch	.922	6	47	0	4	5
Gold	.991	90	651	38	6	54
Jenkins	.962	9	49	2	2	4
Murr	1.000	7	54	6	0	3
Pacheco	.971	5	29	5	1	5
Santana	1.000	18	134	10	0	11

Second Base	PCT	G	PO	A	E	DP
Anderson	.975	101	169	256	11	53
Graham	1.000	2	3	4	0	0
Jarvis	.974	9	16	22	1	4
McGonigle	1.000	2	0	5	0	1
Mendoza	1.000	1	1	3	0	1
Serretti	.983	17	18	40	1	7

Third Base	PCT	G	PO	A	E	DP
Gold	.813	8	7	6	3	0
Graham	1.000	2	0	3	0	0
Jarvis	.950	10	4	15	1	2
Leonard	1.000	2	1	4	0	0
Pacheco	.935	51	58	72	9	8
Peck	1.000	5	2	8	0	1
Santana	.941	18	11	21	2	3
Serretti	.944	40	29	55	5	8

Shortstop	PCT	G	PO	A	E	DP
Graham	.909	37	48	82	13	15
Jarvis	.958	52	69	134	9	24
McGonigle	.923	11	10	38	4	7
Peck	.981	13	19	34	1	5
Serretti	.951	20	29	49	4	8

Outfield	PCT	G	PO	A	E	DP
Callahan	.900	5	9	0	1	0
Campos	.986	107	208	3	3	0
Clark	.987	28	75	0	1	0
Gold	.931	18	25	2	2	0
Graham	1.000	4	2	0	0	0
Jenkins	1.000	1	2	0	0	0
Johnson	1.000	69	140	6	0	1
Lee	.979	27	42	4	1	0
Mendoza	1.000	6	10	0	0	0
Murr	.938	10	15	0	1	0
Stephenson	.980	109	190	6	4	1
Turney	.964	14	27	0	1	0

LAKELAND FLYING TIGERS — *LOW CLASS A*

FLORIDA STATE LEAGUE

Batting	B-T	Ht.	Wt.	DOB	AVG	OBP	SLG	G	PA	AB	R	H	2B	3B	HR	RBI	BB	HBP	SH	SF	SO	SB	CS	BB%	SO%
Bastidas, Abel	B-R	6-1	165	11-24-03	.161	.206	.226	11	34	31	4	5	2	0	0	5	1	1	0	1	10	0	0	2.94	29.41

DETROIT TIGERS

Briceno, Josue	L-R	6-4	200	9-23-04	.278	.381	.377	40	176	151	21	42	5	2	2	22	22	3	0	0	26	1	2	12.50	14.77
Brookman, Archer	R-R	5-11	200	1-8-99	.234	.349	.373	51	193	158	20	37	10	0	4	26	26	4	1	4	37	1	0	13.47	19.17
Callahan, Brett	L-R	6-0	195	11-2-01	.276	.359	.439	62	260	228	35	63	12	2	7	35	23	7	1	1	55	20	4	8.85	21.15
Campbell, Clayton	R-R	6-1	209	9-11-03	.197	.298	.286	86	343	290	28	57	14	0	4	39	38	7	0	7	79	3	1	11.08	23.03
Clark, Max	L-L	6-1	190	12-21-04	.286	.386	.421	73	333	280	55	80	11	3	7	58	48	0	1	4	58	26	2	14.41	17.42
De La Cruz, Daneurys	R-R	5-10	160	4-27-01	.212	.342	.318	41	158	132	24	28	6	1	2	12	24	2	0	0	43	3	3	15.19	27.22
De La Cruz, Jose	R-R	6-1	216	1-3-02	.236	.316	.399	117	471	419	62	99	16	2	16	75	38	12	0	2	164	9	3	8.07	34.82
De Los Santos, Raudy	R-R	5-10	155	3-18-03	.000	.667	.000	1	3	1	0	0	0	0	0	0	2	0	0	0	1	0	0	66.67	33.33
Fana, Nomar	B-R	5-11	175	9-28-02	.205	.286	.452	21	84	73	12	15	7	1	3	10	9	0	0	2	25	2	0	10.71	29.76
Gil, Samuel	R-R	5-9	165	11-1-04	.229	.327	.288	94	370	319	41	73	8	4	1	43	44	4	0	3	78	7	3	11.89	21.08
Gonzalez, Alvaro	B-R	6-0	165	9-16-00	.125	.239	.175	34	92	80	12	10	1	0	1	4	10	2	0	0	23	2	0	10.87	25.00
Graham, Peyton	R-R	6-3	185	1-26-01	.250	.382	.393	10	34	28	5	7	1	0	1	3	6	0	0	0	5	2	0	17.65	14.71
Hadeen, Woody	B-R	6-2	185	7-16-02	.111	.333	.111	4	12	9	1	1	0	0	0	0	2	1	0	0	1	2	0	16.67	8.33
Hurtado, Ricardo	R-R	5-10	180	5-23-03	.250	.409	.313	6	22	16	3	4	1	0	0	2	4	1	0	1	5	0	0	18.18	22.73
Jarvis, Jim	L-R	5-10	185	11-6-00	.270	.366	.368	45	191	163	31	44	9	2	1	18	23	3	0	2	24	14	2	12.04	12.57
Jenkins, Andrew	R-R	5-11	217	11-3-00	.239	.288	.367	29	118	109	15	26	8	0	2	16	6	2	0	1	32	0	0	5.08	27.12
Johnson, Dom	R-R	5-9	185	3-7-01	.298	.393	.442	31	122	104	23	31	6	0	3	12	14	3	0	1	25	18	1	11.48	20.49
Joyce, Corey	R-R	6-0	190	8-19-98	.077	.314	.077	8	35	26	5	2	0	0	0	1	9	0	0	0	9	2	0	25.71	25.71
Jung, Jace	L-R	6-0	205	10-4-00	.300	.467	.700	4	15	10	3	3	1	0	1	3	4	0	0	1	2	1	0	26.67	13.33
Kreidler, Ryan	R-R	6-4	208	11-12-97	.100	.182	.100	7	22	20	0	2	0	0	0	0	1	1	0	0	11	0	0	4.55	50.00
Lee, Bennett	R-R	6-0	208	4-26-02	.250	.294	.688	4	17	16	2	4	1	0	2	7	0	1	0	0	4	0	0	0.00	23.53
Lee, Patrick	R-R	5-10	180	10-19-99	.308	.471	.431	21	85	65	16	20	2	0	2	7	17	3	0	0	17	13	1	20.00	20.00
Leonard, Eddys	R-R	5-11	195	11-10-00	.214	.313	.286	10	32	28	4	6	2	0	0	2	2	2	0	0	8	2	0	6.25	25.00
MacDonald, Zach	R-R	6-1	195	8-3-03	.161	.235	.290	8	34	31	5	5	2	1	0	4	3	0	0	0	18	1	0	8.82	52.94
McGonigle, Kevin	L-R	5-11	185	8-18-04	.326	.407	.470	60	271	230	40	75	15	3	4	37	35	0	1	5	24	20	2	12.92	8.86
Montilla, Franyerber	B-R	6-0	160	4-15-05	.095	.278	.127	20	79	63	12	6	2	0	0	1	12	4	0	0	25	6	1	15.19	31.65
Pacheco, Izaac	L-R	6-3	225	11-18-02	.244	.380	.317	12	50	41	7	10	3	0	0	2	9	0	0	0	15	0	1	18.00	30.00
Peck, John	R-R	6-0	185	7-18-02	.249	.348	.373	49	207	177	25	44	8	4	2	12	24	4	0	2	48	25	4	11.59	23.19
Penney, Jack	L-R	6-0	185	8-19-02	.255	.367	.392	14	60	51	7	13	3	2	0	9	9	0	0	0	18	2	1	15.00	30.00
Pennington, Garrett	R-R	6-0	215	10-15-00	.250	.270	.444	9	37	36	3	9	1	0	2	6	1	0	0	0	5	0	0	2.70	13.51
Rubalcaba, Alonzo	R-R	5-10	210	2-22-00	.000	.172	.000	9	30	24	1	0	0	0	0	0	4	1	1	0	12	0	0	13.33	40.00
Santana, Cristian	R-R	5-11	165	11-25-03	.150	.364	.313	55	207	147	26	22	3	0	7	22	49	4	1	6	69	1	2	23.67	33.33
Santana, Luis	R-R	5-6	196	7-20-99	.385	.529	.692	4	17	13	4	5	1	0	1	2	4	0	0	0	2	0	0	23.53	11.76
Smith, David	B-R	5-11	195	2-20-01	.198	.380	.291	106	414	313	69	62	14	3	3	40	83	12	1	5	94	29	7	20.05	22.71
Strong, Jackson	L-L	6-1	185	8-26-03	.313	.361	.406	9	36	32	2	10	3	0	0	5	2	1	0	1	8	3	0	5.56	22.22
Valencia, Eduardo	R-R	6-1	180	1-25-00	.249	.326	.366	57	231	205	30	51	12	0	4	24	21	3	1	1	43	0	0	9.09	18.61

Pitching	B-T	Ht.	Wt.	DOB	W	L	ERA	G	GS	SV	IP	Hits	Runs	ER	HR	BB	SO	AVG	OBP	SLG	SO%	BB%	BF
Adametz, Joe	L-L	6-5	190	12-23-99	4	0	1.79	12	10	0	50	35	12	10	2	15	46	.200	.289	.251	23.23	7.58	198
Apker, Garrett	R-R	6-5	195	9-18-99	4	1	4.07	23	0	1	42	33	19	19	3	16	45	.223	.299	.365	26.79	9.52	168
Ashman, Micah	L-L	6-7	200	8-22-02	1	0	4.26	5	0	0	6	3	3	3	1	2	9	.136	.240	.318	36.00	8.00	25
Brookman, Archer	R-R	5-11	200	1-8-99	0	0	9.00	1	0	0	1	3	1	1	0	0	1	.500	.500	.667	16.67	0.00	6
Brown, Cameron	L-R	6-2	165	5-12-98	6	1	3.51	40	0	6	56	51	24	22	2	24	56	.243	.339	.333	22.86	9.80	245
Bruss, Thomas	R-R	6-8	280	5-18-99	2	2	4.97	34	0	1	42	43	26	23	3	27	54	.262	.388	.366	26.87	13.43	201
Castillo, Rayner	R-R	6-3	180	6-30-04	4	1	2.52	13	13	0	61	43	21	17	3	19	41	.204	.280	.275	17.30	8.02	237
Chalas, Ronny	R-R	5-10	162	8-19-02	1	2	0.93	7	0	1	10	7	3	1	0	2	10	.200	.243	.257	27.03	5.41	37
De Los Santos, Carlos	R-R	6-2	170	11-18-00	0	2	54.00	4	0	0	2	7	14	12	3	6	4	.500	.667	1.143	19.05	28.57	21
Englert, Mason	S-R	6-4	206	11-1-99	0	1	3.38	2	2	0	3	3	2	1	1	2	2	.300	.417	.600	16.67	16.67	12
Evans, Donye	R-R	6-6	220	2-15-02	2	0	1.40	17	0	4	19	11	4	3	0	8	21	.167	.282	.242	26.92	10.26	78
Flores, Wilmer	R-R	6-4	225	2-20-01	0	0	6.00	2	2	0	3	4	2	2	1	0	2	.308	.357	.615	14.29	0.00	14
Garcia, Pedro	R-R	6-1	190	2-27-02	1	2	10.67	7	3	1	14	14	17	17	0	17	14	.241	.443	.328	17.72	21.52	79
Gipson-Long, Sawyer	R-R	6-4	225	12-12-97	0	0	3.00	1	1	0	3	3	1	1	1	0	4	.250	.250	.583	33.33	0.00	12
Gonzalez, Alvaro	S-R	6-0	165	9-16-00	0	0	0.00	2	0	0	2	3	0	0	0	0	2	.300	.300	.300	20.00	0.00	10
Gudaitis, Quinn	R-R	6-7	225	4-10-99	2	0	6.23	21	0	0	22	17	19	15	1	19	23	.213	.427	.325	20.91	17.27	110
Hebbert, Duque	R-R	5-10	170	10-29-01	5	2	5.16	21	7	0	61	55	36	35	7	17	46	.240	.304	.397	18.11	6.69	254
Hill, Garrett	R-R	6-0	185	1-16-96	2	2	5.60	13	3	1	18	17	12	11	1	12	19	.246	.369	.319	22.62	14.29	84
Holden, Connor	R-R	6-5	240	6-25-98	0	2	4.03	15	0	1	22	23	16	10	3	3	23	.253	.313	.407	23.23	3.03	99
Howey, Preston	R-R	5-10	173	6-20-02	0	1	5.40	1	0	0	2	2	1	1	0	2	1	.333	.556	.667	11.11	22.22	9
Huizi, Eiker	R-R	6-0	155	9-24-00	5	2	2.36	36	0	9	46	25	15	12	1	21	48	.166	.312	.219	25.81	11.29	186
Lee, Zack	L-R	6-4	200	12-5-00	3	4	3.16	21	17	0	83	72	36	29	6	20	88	.231	.283	.356	25.96	5.90	339
Lequerica, Carlos	R-R	6-2	195	9-6-00	3	1	4.36	22	0	1	33	31	19	16	2	12	31	.250	.319	.347	21.99	8.51	141
Mauloni, Christopher	L-R	6-2	200	6-16-98	0	0	2.70	2	0	0	3	0	1	1	0	3	5	.000	.231	.000	38.46	23.08	13
Miller, Jake	L-L	6-2	185	6-27-01	8	1	1.16	18	2	1	62	40	12	8	3	14	81	.179	.227	.274	33.89	5.86	239
Miller, Joe	L-L	5-10	195	3-13-00	2	0	1.23	6	4	0	22	13	4	3	1	3	29	.171	.210	.211	35.80	3.70	81
Minton, Hayden	L-R	6-4	220	3-14-01	4	5	4.65	23	21	0	93	102	51	48	7	45	115	.276	.372	.369	26.56	10.39	433
Patten, Cole	R-R	6-4	194	8-5-99	0	1	5.06	9	5	0	27	24	16	15	3	10	21	.240	.313	.340	18.26	8.70	115
Perez, Cleiverth	L-L	6-0	211	2-5-00	0	0	4.76	5	1	1	6	7	3	3	1	0	6	.292	.292	.500	25.00	0.00	24
Pivaroff, Blake	L-R	6-0	200	6-1-01	2	0	2.95	13	2	0	18	21	8	6	1	3	18	.284	.304	.432	22.78	3.80	79
Pridgen, Patrick	R-R	6-4	220	3-26-99	3	3	5.40	17	1	0	20	21	12	12	0	13	21	.266	.383	.430	22.34	13.83	94
Randall, Josh	R-R	6-4	242	10-15-02	0	0	4.50	2	2	0	4	5	2	2	0	0	2	.278	.350	.389	10.00	0.00	20
Reyes, Gabriel	L-L	6-1	170	7-1-03	4	2	3.97	12	11	0	48	34	24	21	5	14	64	.199	.270	.345	33.86	7.41	189
Rodriguez, Erick	R-R	5-10	185	3-21-02	0	0	13.50	1	1	0	1	2	1	1	0	2	1	.500	.667	.500	16.67	33.33	6
Rodriguez, Moises	R-R	6-2	170	3-3-02	0	0	9.00	1	0	0	2	4	2	2	0	1	3	.444	.500	.444	30.00	10.00	10
Sanchez, Yosber	R-R	6-1	170	5-22-01	2	1	2.53	17	0	6	21	20	7	6	1	11	35	.247	.340	.321	37.23	11.70	94
Schulfer, Austin	R-R	6-2	175	12-22-95	0	0	0.00	2	0	0	2	0	0	0	0	0	1	.000	.000	.000	16.67	0.00	6

Sears, Andrew	L-L	6-3	200	10-30-02	6	4	2.51	22	19	0	90	61	35	25	5	50	101	.196	.330	.301	26.44	13.09	382
Sequeira, Gabriel	L-L	6-0	200	8-18-97	0	0	4.05	4	0	0	7	3	4	3	0	4	8	.136	.269	.273	30.77	15.38	26
Sloan, Ethan	L-L	5-11	190	8-4-02	0	0	10.80	2	0	0	2	2	2	2	0	4	3	.286	.583	.429	25.00	33.33	12
Stofel, Luke	R-R	6-5	235	11-25-01	1	4	5.01	30	0	0	41	41	26	23	3	19	43	.258	.348	.365	23.76	10.50	181
Stupp, Cole	R-R	6-4	205	11-10-00	0	2	6.59	5	2	0	14	12	12	10	4	12	15	.245	.424	.571	22.73	18.18	66
Villalobos, Eli	R-R	6-4	195	6-26-97	1	0	3.00	2	0	0	3	2	1	1	0	1	1	.182	.250	.364	8.33	8.33	12
Weins, CJ	R-R	6-3	223	8-15-00	1	0	2.20	10	0	0	16	9	4	4	2	7	28	.164	.258	.273	45.16	11.29	62
White, Brendan	R-R	5-11	185	11-18-98	1	0	2.25	3	1	0	4	2	1	1	1	0	4	.143	.143	.357	28.57	0.00	14
Williams, Chris	L-L	6-2	205	3-3-00	0	1	27.00	1	0	0	1	1	4	4	0	5	0	.250	.667	.250	0.00	55.56	9

Fielding

Catcher	PCT	G	PO	A	E	DP	PB
Briceno	.983	16	161	17	3	0	2
Brookman	.995	47	400	24	2	1	1
Campbell	.984	20	174	6	3	2	2
De La Cruz	1.000	1	2	0	0	0	0
Hurtado	1.000	1	6	1	0	0	0
Lee	1.000	2	23	0	0	0	0
Rubalcaba	1.000	8	69	4	0	1	1
Valencia	.987	42	364	23	5	4	2

First Base	PCT	G	PO	A	E	DP
Briceno	1.000	16	121	8	0	13
Brookman	1.000	1	6	0	0	1
Campbell	.997	39	285	14	1	25
De La Cruz	.992	35	236	15	2	23
Gonzalez	.979	5	42	4	1	4
Hurtado	1.000	2	14	0	0	0
Jenkins	.976	20	152	8	4	16
Pennington	1.000	6	36	3	0	4
Valencia	1.000	9	62	7	0	5

Second Base	PCT	G	PO	A	E	DP
Bastidas	1.000	4	5	12	0	2
De Los Santos	.833	1	3	2	1	0
Gil	.986	52	75	135	3	33
Gonzalez	.957	14	15	30	2	8
Graham	1.000	1	0	1	0	0
Hadeen	1.000	1	2	3	0	0
Jarvis	1.000	12	14	27	0	6
Joyce	.875	1	2	5	1	1
McGonigle	.987	19	36	42	1	10
Montilla	1.000	8	17	18	0	5
Peck	1.000	4	4	12	0	2
Penney	1.000	1	3	2	0	0
Santana	.928	15	35	29	5	4
Smith	1.000	4	5	8	0	4

Third Base	PCT	G	PO	A	E	DP
Bastidas	.900	7	5	4	1	0
Campbell	.913	24	17	25	4	1
Gil	.769	6	3	7	3	1
Gonzalez	.917	7	1	10	1	0
Graham	.857	3	2	4	1	0
Jarvis	.969	19	25	37	2	6
Joyce	1.000	3	1	2	0	0
Jung	.929	3	3	10	1	1
Kreidler	1.000	2	3	2	0	0
Leonard	.667	1	0	2	1	0
Pacheco	.900	10	2	16	2	1
Peck	.975	14	9	30	1	3
Penney	.955	9	2	19	1	2
Santana	.800	2	0	4	1	0
Santana	.933	31	19	51	5	5

Shortstop	PCT	G	PO	A	E	DP
Gil	.970	34	29	67	3	16
Graham	.957	5	7	15	1	3
Hadeen	1.000	3	1	1	0	1
Jarvis	.981	13	18	33	1	9
Joyce	1.000	2	2	3	0	1
Kreidler	1.000	1	1	1	0	1
Leonard	.833	3	1	4	1	0
McGonigle	.978	32	47	85	3	18
Montilla	.976	11	14	26	1	3
Peck	.961	29	39	59	4	11
Penney	.889	4	6	10	2	1

Outfield	PCT	G	PO	A	E	DP
Callahan	.955	57	101	4	5	1
Clark	.993	66	146	4	1	2
De La Cruz	.000	1	0	0	0	0
De La Cruz	.943	84	126	7	8	0
Fana	.941	21	30	2	2	0
Johnson	.962	30	48	2	2	1
Lee	.969	20	30	1	1	0
MacDonald	1.000	8	13	1	0	1
Smith	.993	98	137	5	1	1
Strong	1.000	9	15	0	0	0

FCL TIGERS — *ROOKIE*

FLORIDA COMPLEX LEAGUE

Batting	B-T	Ht.	Wt.	DOB	AVG	OBP	SLG	G	PA	AB	R	H	2B	3B	HR	RBI	BB	HBP	SH	SF	SO	SB	CS	BB%	SO%
Bastidas, Abel	B-R	6-1	165	11-24-03	.185	.277	.272	23	94	81	8	15	4	0	1	8	11	0	0	2	25	1	0	11.70	26.60
Callahan, Brett	L-R	6-0	195	11-2-01	.545	.600	.636	4	15	11	3	6	1	0	0	3	1	2	0	1	0	1	0	6.67	0.00
Cruz, Angel	R-R	5-11	165	9-27-01	.258	.309	.419	21	68	62	14	16	2	1	2	8	3	2	0	1	17	5	1	4.41	25.00
De La Cruz, Daneurys	R-R	5-10	160	4-27-01	.533	.632	.667	4	19	15	3	8	2	0	0	4	3	1	0	0	3	1	1	15.79	15.79
De Los Santos, Raudy	R-R	5-10	155	3-18-03	.244	.321	.303	42	136	119	18	29	5	1	0	17	11	3	2	1	16	9	4	8.09	11.76
Diaz, Yimmy	B-R	5-10	155	2-19-04	.168	.319	.242	35	119	95	19	16	4	0	1	10	13	9	0	2	27	0	1	10.92	22.69
Fana, Nomar	B-R	5-11	175	9-28-02	.291	.432	.511	53	228	182	44	53	8	1	10	37	44	1	0	0	57	15	1	19.30	25.00
Hernandez, Juan	L-R	6-0	160	3-27-06	.242	.341	.346	48	176	153	26	37	5	1	3	22	17	6	0	0	41	3	1	9.66	23.30
Hurtado, Ricardo	R-R	5-10	180	5-23-03	.233	.431	.388	42	161	116	25	27	9	0	3	20	33	9	0	2	40	2	1	20.50	24.84
Jenkins, Andrew	R-R	5-11	217	11-3-00	.182	.308	.182	4	13	11	2	2	0	0	0	1	2	0	0	0	3	0	0	15.38	23.08
Jimenez, Enrique	B-R	5-10	170	11-3-05	.242	.366	.376	43	183	149	23	36	9	1	3	22	28	3	0	3	44	5	2	15.30	24.04
Machado, Jesus	R-R	5-10	152	3-24-03	.175	.358	.272	44	148	114	25	20	2	0	3	18	29	4	0	1	50	9	3	19.59	33.78
Montilla, Franyerber	B-R	6-0	160	4-15-05	.273	.409	.448	48	216	172	37	47	12	0	6	29	38	3	0	2	40	24	7	17.59	18.52
Pacheco, Izaac	L-R	6-3	225	11-18-02	.250	.250	.250	1	4	4	0	1	0	0	0	0	0	0	0	0	2	0	0	0.00	50.00
Peck, John	R-R	6-0	185	7-18-02	.588	.611	.706	6	18	17	3	10	2	0	0	3	1	0	0	0	3	2	1	5.56	16.67
Perez, Reylin	B-R	6-2	160	10-5-04	.216	.328	.331	48	178	148	27	32	6	1	3	20	25	1	1	3	54	15	2	14.04	30.34
Rojas, Samuel	R-R	5-10	190	11-6-02	.143	.355	.214	22	76	56	8	8	1	0	1	7	17	2	0	1	13	1	1	22.37	17.11
Rucker, Carson	R-R	6-2	195	8-18-04	.385	.467	.692	4	16	13	1	5	4	0	0	2	0	2	0	0	5	1	1	0.00	31.25
Salas, Anibal	B-R	5-11	180	9-30-05	.195	.331	.323	39	160	133	23	26	3	1	4	18	23	4	0	0	48	3	0	14.38	30.00
Santana, Cristian	R-R	5-11	165	11-25-03	.200	.409	.400	6	22	15	4	3	0	0	1	6	3	3	0	1	5	0	0	13.64	22.73
Santana, Luis	R-R	5-6	196	7-20-99	.200	.200	.800	2	5	5	1	1	0	0	1	2	0	0	0	0	0	0	0	0.00	0.00
Sequera, Manuel	R-R	6-1	170	9-28-02	.269	.321	.423	7	28	26	3	7	1	0	1	4	2	0	0	0	6	0	0	7.14	21.43
Tapia, Sergio	R-R	5-10	160	8-24-02	.236	.327	.404	31	102	89	14	21	4	1	3	13	11	1	1	0	14	0	0	10.78	13.73
Valencia, Eduardo	R-R	6-1	180	1-25-00	.133	.125	.267	5	16	15	1	2	2	0	0	2	0	0	0	1	5	0	0	0.00	31.25

Pitching	B-T	Ht.	Wt.	DOB	W	L	ERA	G	GS	SV	IP	Hits	Runs	ER	HR	BB	SO	AVG	OBP	SLG	SO%	BB%	BF
Apker, Garrett	R-R	6-5	195	9-18-99	3	1	3.18	8	1	0	11	9	6	4	0	5	10	.220	.333	.268	20.83	10.42	48
Briceno, Ignacio	L-L	5-11	155	6-4-01	2	1	4.10	17	1	0	26	31	14	12	0	9	25	.301	.374	.369	21.74	7.83	115
Bushell, Jack	R-R	6-0	165	9-30-05	1	0	2.84	4	1	0	13	6	4	4	0	8	11	.143	.308	.214	21.15	15.38	52
Campos, Ulices	R-R	5-10	170	12-14-01	3	1	3.86	12	0	1	16	24	10	7	2	6	11	.353	.405	.471	14.86	8.11	74
Castillo, Rayner	R-R	6-3	180	6-30-04	0	1	2.79	3	3	0	10	6	3	3	1	4	15	.167	.250	.306	37.50	10.00	40
Chalas, Ronny	R-R	5-10	162	8-19-02	1	3	4.74	16	1	0	25	25	17	13	3	14	22	.269	.373	.462	19.82	12.61	111
Cruz, Angel	R-R	5-11	165	9-27-01	0	1	0.00	1	0	0	0	0	1	0	0	3	1	.000	.750	.000	25.00	75.00	4

Pitching	B-T	Ht.	Wt.	DOB	W	L	ERA	G	GS	SV	IP	Hits	Runs	ER	HR	BB	SO	AVG	OBP	SLG	SO%	BB%	BF
Diaz, Jatnk	R-R	6-4	215	8-19-04	0	4	10.67	7	4	0	14	16	19	17	2	14	13	.291	.452	.455	17.81	19.18	73
Diaz, Jose	R-R	6-5	200	5-12-00	3	0	1.37	17	0	4	26	26	10	4	1	9	23	.260	.336	.350	20.35	7.96	113
Dickerson, Blake	L-L	6-6	210	1-7-05	0	0	3.33	10	5	1	24	15	9	9	1	16	20	.181	.330	.277	19.42	15.53	103
Dunford, Andrew	R-R	6-7	235	1-5-05	0	0	108.00	1	0	0	0	0	4	4	0	4	0	.000	.800	.000	0.00	80.00	5
Evans, Donye	R-R	6-6	220	2-15-02	1	0	4.76	4	1	0	6	5	3	3	0	4	9	.238	.385	.286	34.62	15.38	26
Garcia, Pedro	R-R	6-1	190	2-27-02	1	1	3.63	11	7	0	45	46	20	18	4	21	50	.267	.355	.459	25.38	10.66	197
Hebbert, Duque	R-R	5-10	170	10-29-01	1	0	3.00	1	0	0	3	1	1	1	0	2	4	.100	.308	.100	30.77	15.38	13
Lequerica, Carlos	R-R	6-2	195	9-6-00	2	0	0.00	6	0	1	9	4	0	0	0	1	13	.143	.172	.143	44.83	3.45	29
McCall, Dylan	R-R	6-8	200	3-19-04	1	0	9.15	16	0	0	21	24	23	21	3	18	17	.300	.448	.488	16.04	16.98	106
Moreno, Frank	R-R	6-2	185	10-16-02	4	1	3.73	9	4	0	31	29	14	13	1	28	24	.246	.396	.314	16.11	18.79	149
Mota, Eliseo	R-R	6-2	185	11-7-02	1	0	3.38	11	5	0	32	32	13	12	1	20	23	.271	.389	.398	15.97	13.89	144
Pacheco, Freddy	R-R	5-11	203	4-17-98	0	0	13.50	2	2	0	2	3	3	3	0	1	0	.333	.400	.444	0.00	10.00	10
Patten, Cole	R-R	6-4	194	8-5-99	1	0	0.00	3	0	1	6	7	0	0	0	0	12	.269	.296	.269	44.44	0.00	27
Pridgen, Patrick	R-R	6-4	220	3-26-99	0	0	0.00	5	0	0	6	1	0	0	0	5	5	.063	.318	.125	22.73	22.73	22
Reyes, Gabriel	L-L	6-1	170	7-1-03	0	1	4.00	5	2	1	18	18	8	8	1	5	18	.257	.307	.386	24.00	6.67	75
Rodriguez, Moises	R-R	6-2	170	3-3-02	3	2	8.61	17	0	0	23	26	25	22	3	16	23	.295	.409	.466	20.91	14.55	110
Rogers, Johnathan	R-R	6-3	215	9-5-04	0	2	3.52	11	9	0	38	29	17	15	3	18	31	.209	.304	.295	19.25	11.18	161
Sequeira, Gabriel	L-L	6-0	200	8-18-97	0	0	9.00	1	0	0	1	1	1	1	0	1	2	.250	.500	.250	33.33	16.67	6
Stofel, Luke	R-R	6-5	235	11-25-01	0	0	0.00	1	0	0	1	1	0	0	0	0	1	.250	.250	.250	25.00	0.00	4
Stupp, Cole	R-R	6-4	205	11-10-00	2	0	0.61	12	0	3	15	6	2	1	0	5	19	.115	.246	.173	31.15	8.20	61
Valentine, Riley	R-R	6-7	195	8-20-05	2	2	7.82	6	3	0	13	12	11	11	0	10	5	.261	.393	.326	8.93	17.86	56
Villalobos, Eli	R-R	6-4	195	6-26-97	0	0	0.00	1	0	0	1	0	0	0	0	1	2	.000	.250	.000	50.00	25.00	4
White, Brendan	R-R	5-11	185	11-18-98	0	0	0.00	1	0	0	1	0	0	0	0	1	1	.000	.250	.000	25.00	25.00	4
Williams, Chris	L-L	6-2	205	3-3-00	1	0	5.40	5	1	0	7	4	4	4	0	4	6	.182	.296	.227	22.22	14.81	27
Wilson, Paul	R-L	6-3	197	12-11-04	1	2	6.62	11	8	0	35	44	35	26	4	36	34	.310	.459	.479	18.78	19.89	181

Fielding

C: Jimenez 23, Hurtado 18, Tapia 17, Rojas 9, Valencia 2. **1B:** Hurtado 20, Jimenez 15, Cruz 13, Rojas 8, De La Cruz 2, Jenkins 2. **2B:** Perez 24, Montilla 12, Bastidas 10, Hernandez 8, De Los Santos 4, Diaz 2, Santana 2, Sequera 2. **3B:** Hernandez 17, Diaz 14, Montilla 12, Bastidas 8, Perez 7, Santana 3, Peck 2, Rucker 1, Santana 1, De Los Santos 1. **SS:** Montilla 22, Hernandez 17, Perez 15, Bastidas 4, Peck 3, Rucker 1. **LF:** Diaz 16, Machado 14, Fana 11, Salas 6, De Los Santos 4, Cruz 4, De La Cruz 1, Callahan 1, Sequera 1. **CF:** De Los Santos 23, Fana 18, Machado 10, Salas 9. **RF:** Fana 21, Salas 20, Machado 13, De Los Santos 6, Callahan 2.

DSL TIGERS 1 — *ROOKIE*

DOMINICAN SUMMER LEAGUE

Batting	B-T	Ht.	Wt.	DOB	AVG	OBP	SLG	G	PA	AB	R	H	2B	3B	HR	RBI	BB	HBP	SH	SF	SO	SB	CS	BB%	SO%
Batista, Guillermo	B-R	6-1	195	11-23-06	.230	.385	.328	42	156	122	23	28	7	1	1	19	28	4	0	2	38	5	4	17.95	24.36
Caraballo, Brandy	R-R	5-9	150	9-26-05	.333	.400	.889	4	10	9	2	3	0	1	1	3	1	0	0	0	3	0	0	10.00	30.00
De Leon, Jensy	R-R	6-0	175	5-14-04	.204	.316	.224	23	57	49	5	10	1	0	0	5	6	2	0	0	12	4	3	10.53	21.05
Dickson, Jose	R-R	6-2	158	11-8-06	.273	.407	.374	44	172	139	38	38	8	3	0	16	26	6	0	1	27	18	4	15.12	15.70
Estrada, Johan	R-R	5-11	170	10-27-05	.211	.391	.408	30	92	71	17	15	6	1	2	12	21	0	0	0	20	8	2	22.83	21.74
Gudino, Jeiker	R-R	5-9	171	11-15-06	.096	.304	.115	23	69	52	4	5	1	0	0	7	11	5	0	1	10	3	1	15.94	14.49
Hoyte, Adrian	L-L	5-7	145	1-9-06	.262	.410	.393	26	78	61	16	16	6	1	0	8	12	4	0	1	15	5	0	15.38	19.23
Lao, Armando	R-R	5-10	170	11-25-06	.140	.319	.158	24	73	57	5	8	1	0	0	1	8	7	1	0	23	3	1	10.96	31.51
Luna, Wagnel	R-R	6-0	155	12-14-05	.139	.298	.188	44	124	101	14	14	0	1	1	7	20	3	0	0	36	5	1	16.13	29.03
Matos, Delvis	R-R	5-11	165	11-9-04	.250	.250	.375	3	8	8	2	2	1	0	0	0	0	0	0	0	1	0	0	0.00	12.50
Medrano, Abelardo	L-R	6-2	180	1-27-06	.178	.286	.322	36	105	90	9	16	7	0	2	9	10	4	0	1	28	2	1	9.52	26.67
Miranda, Nestor	R-R	6-3	225	2-23-06	.177	.407	.306	22	86	62	11	11	2	0	2	6	23	1	0	0	29	2	0	26.74	33.72
Ochoa, Jose	R-R	5-9	162	7-25-03	.203	.311	.281	41	152	128	25	26	4	3	0	10	19	2	1	2	28	4	3	12.50	18.42
Orozco, Maikol	R-R	5-11	175	9-9-05	.301	.449	.411	45	187	146	30	44	8	1	2	26	31	9	0	1	32	13	8	16.58	17.11
Perea, Randy	R-R	5-11	150	1-21-04	.291	.418	.473	28	67	55	11	16	2	1	2	11	11	1	0	0	19	11	3	16.42	28.36
Perez, Cristian	R-R	5-11	190	8-15-06	.285	.401	.391	46	182	151	29	43	5	1	3	32	27	3	0	1	46	6	1	14.84	25.27
Pinto, Santiago	L-L	5-11	170	2-5-06	.271	.365	.407	44	137	118	19	32	3	2	3	19	15	3	0	1	35	15	6	10.95	25.55
Rodriguez, Justin	R-R	5-10	155	3-11-04	.190	.347	.215	38	98	79	14	15	0	1	0	7	14	5	0	0	29	5	2	14.29	29.59
Tamara, Martin	R-R	6-0	185	2-5-04	.191	.319	.309	45	165	136	21	26	4	3	2	20	16	10	0	1	39	5	0	9.70	23.64

Pitching	B-T	Ht.	Wt.	DOB	W	L	ERA	G	GS	SV	IP	Hits	Runs	ER	HR	BB	SO	AVG	OBP	SLG	SO%	BB%	BF
Amarante, Gregory	L-L	5-11	186	3-18-07	1	0	6.38	12	3	0	24	16	19	17	0	21	31	.180	.342	.202	26.96	18.26	115
Anderson, Branell	R-R	6-4	180	5-23-07	0	1	8.31	9	0	0	13	12	13	12	1	12	17	.245	.406	.449	26.56	18.75	64
Castillo, Luis	R-R	6-0	180	3-19-02	1	1	7.06	17	1	3	22	24	17	17	0	16	18	.282	.402	.388	17.48	15.53	103
Coba, Jhonan	R-R	6-0	150	7-20-06	1	2	10.22	10	0	0	12	12	16	14	1	11	14	.255	.393	.404	22.95	18.03	61
De Leon, Jensy	R-R	6-0	175	5-14-04	0	0	0.00	2	0	0	4	4	0	0	0	0	1	.286	.313	.286	6.25	0.00	16
De Los Santos, Ericksson	L-L	6-6	200	3-24-06	1	1	11.37	5	1	0	6	7	9	8	0	7	3	.259	.429	.407	8.57	20.00	35
Felix, Eddy	R-R	6-2	180	8-23-03	1	3	3.27	10	10	0	44	34	20	16	2	17	64	.213	.298	.313	35.36	9.39	181
Florian, Jose	R-R	5-11	155	2-3-04	0	0	1.08	5	0	1	8	4	3	1	0	5	10	.138	.278	.138	27.78	13.89	36
Florido, Antonio	R-R	6-1	175	2-15-05	1	0	2.93	12	12	0	46	40	19	15	1	35	42	.250	.410	.338	20.39	16.99	206
Landaeta, Bryant	R-R	6-2	175	11-27-03	4	1	8.44	15	0	1	21	32	22	20	1	22	20	.356	.487	.500	17.09	18.80	117
Leon, Leonardo	R-R	6-4	180	9-21-05	0	0	5.79	4	0	1	5	5	3	3	0	6	3	.313	.478	.313	13.04	26.09	23
Melendez, Anderson	R-R	6-1	170	10-12-02	1	0	3.86	18	0	3	23	22	18	10	0	14	30	.250	.368	.318	28.04	13.08	107
Montas, Donal	R-R	6-3	190	5-5-02	4	1	5.10	21	0	3	30	26	20	17	2	16	24	.234	.344	.351	18.18	12.12	132
Palmero, Diego	R-R	6-1	190	8-1-03	0	3	12.03	6	3	0	13	17	23	19	0	14	9	.315	.494	.333	11.69	18.18	77
Perea, Randy	R-R	5-11	150	1-21-04	0	0	67.50	1	0	0	1	3	5	5	0	4	0	.600	.778	.800	0.00	44.44	9
Petri, Jorger	L-L	5-10	155	11-3-04	2	3	2.93	11	10	0	43	33	19	14	1	17	46	.217	.312	.283	26.59	9.83	173
Ramos, Albert	R-R	6-3	185	4-7-06	0	1	1.80	2	1	0	5	4	1	1	0	4	6	.222	.364	.222	27.27	18.18	22
Riera, Miguel	R-R	6-3	175	4-7-05	1	1	10.13	12	0	0	13	16	16	15	1	18	17	.327	.541	.490	22.97	24.32	74

Pitching	B-T	Ht.	Wt.	DOB	W	L	ERA	G	GS	SV	IP	Hits	Runs	ER	HR	BB	SO	AVG	OBP	SLG	SO%	BB%	BF
Rodriguez, Carlos	L-L	6-0	170	4-29-06	4	3	4.96	9	9	0	33	42	23	18	0	8	21	.313	.350	.366	14.69	5.59	143
Rodriguez, Justin	R-R	5-10	155	3-11-04	0	0	0.00	1	0	0	1	0	0	0	0	0	0	.000	.000	.000	0.00	0.00	4
Rossel, Leonardo	R-R	6-0	170	12-17-04	2	4	4.82	18	2	1	28	23	21	15	1	16	22	.228	.349	.307	17.46	12.70	126
Sanchez, Angel	R-R	6-1	164	12-20-02	4	0	1.83	14	0	3	20	16	5	4	0	5	15	.219	.275	.288	18.75	6.25	80
Vasquez, Luis	R-R	6-4	180	12-11-04	2	1	4.41	6	2	0	16	23	11	8	0	7	6	.333	.395	.406	7.89	9.21	76
Veloz, Gerard	L-L	6-1	157	11-7-04	0	0	6.35	11	0	1	11	12	9	8	0	14	9	.267	.443	.289	14.75	22.95	61

Fielding

C: Tamara 32, Gudino 17, Lao 14, Estrada 1. **1B:** Estrada 20, Rodriguez 17, Tamara 12, De Leon 10, Medrano 8, Lao 1, Batista 1. **2B:** Batista 24, Orozco 24, Luna 15, Gudino 2, De Leon 1, Rodriquez 1. **3B:** Orozco 21, Rodriguez 18, Miranda 11, Luna 7, Batista 6, De Leon 5. **SS:** Dickson 40, Luna 24. **LF:** Pinto 25, Hoyte 21, Medrano 7, Perea 5, Caraballo 3, Estrada 1, Matos 1, Perez 1, Ochoa 1. **CF:** Perez 33, Ochoa 15, Pinto 8, Perea 7. **RF:** Ochoa 22, Medrano 15, Pinto 11, Perea 9, Perez 8, Hoyte 2, Lao 1.

DSL TIGERS 2 — *ROOKIE*

DOMINICAN SUMMER LEAGUE

Batting	B-T	Ht.	Wt.	DOB	AVG	OBP	SLG	G	PA	AB	R	H	2B	3B	HR	RBI	BB	HBP	SH	SF	SO	SB	CS	BB%	SO%
Aguilera, Luis	L-R	5-11	145	1-5-07	.292	.417	.348	38	108	89	23	26	0	1	1	8	18	1	0	0	15	5	3	16.67	13.89
Berti, Willian	L-L	6-0	160	11-5-05	.236	.349	.371	33	106	89	11	21	6	0	2	21	14	2	0	1	27	1	0	13.21	25.47
Caraballo, Brandy	R-R	5-9	150	9-26-05	.387	.412	.387	12	34	31	4	12	0	0	0	3	2	0	0	1	8	5	0	5.88	23.53
Estevez, Geury	B-R	6-0	180	2-20-02	.307	.435	.438	49	193	153	34	47	9	1	3	41	24	13	0	3	27	6	2	12.44	13.99
Hernandez, Kendrick	R-R	6-2	194	9-4-06	.151	.322	.183	34	118	93	14	14	3	0	0	10	23	1	0	1	48	2	0	19.49	40.68
Lugo, Edgar	B-R	5-11	160	8-19-04	.273	.376	.455	38	142	121	19	33	11	1	3	22	18	2	1	0	25	5	2	12.68	17.61
Madero, Steven	L-R	6-2	175	9-24-06	.283	.372	.400	40	146	120	23	34	5	0	3	35	18	2	1	5	30	1	2	12.33	20.55
Marin, Nelson	R-R	5-11	165	9-29-05	.225	.371	.296	29	89	71	8	16	2	0	1	10	12	5	0	1	24	0	0	13.48	26.97
Matos, Delvis	R-R	5-11	165	11-9-04	.241	.290	.448	12	31	29	2	7	1	1	1	4	1	1	0	0	11	0	0	3.23	35.48
Moya, Jonathan	R-R	5-11	203	9-27-06	.268	.349	.420	34	126	112	20	30	6	1	3	13	8	6	0	0	42	2	0	6.35	33.33
Osorio, Javier	R-R	6-0	165	3-29-05	.304	.434	.503	50	198	161	46	49	15	4	3	22	30	7	0	0	44	19	6	15.15	22.22
Perea, Randy	R-R	5-11	150	1-21-04	.000	.500	.000	5	2	1	1	0	0	0	0	0	1	0	0	0	1	0	0	50.00	50.00
Perez, Cristian	R-R	5-11	190	8-15-06	.214	.409	.214	6	22	14	4	3	0	0	0	4	5	1	0	2	6	1	0	22.73	27.27
Pinto, Jesus	R-R	5-11	180	3-30-07	.275	.403	.438	53	196	160	46	44	12	1	4	16	30	5	0	1	41	16	9	15.31	20.92
Quezada, Junior	R-R	6-0	165	2-3-05	.179	.281	.179	27	65	56	6	10	0	0	0	0	7	1	1	0	15	3	1	10.77	23.08
Ramirez, Ronald	R-R	5-10	170	10-12-06	.343	.451	.429	42	175	140	37	48	9	0	1	18	24	7	0	4	29	6	7	13.71	16.57
Rodriguez, Angel	L-R	5-10	185	9-10-06	.222	.370	.250	31	46	36	5	8	1	0	0	3	8	1	0	1	15	0	0	17.39	32.61
Rondon, Newremberg	R-R	5-11	170	7-10-03	.313	.358	.429	46	177	163	25	51	11	1	2	27	11	1	1	1	28	1	0	6.21	15.82
Sanchez, Heison	L-R	6-0	170	9-6-04	.230	.345	.311	30	89	74	15	17	1	1	1	6	11	2	1	0	24	3	0	12.36	26.97

Pitching	B-T	Ht.	Wt.	DOB	W	L	ERA	G	GS	SV	IP	Hits	Runs	ER	HR	BB	SO	AVG	OBP	SLG	SO%	BB%	BF
Castillo, Luis	R-R	6-0	180	3-19-02	0	0	1.50	2	1	0	6	4	1	1	0	0	6	.182	.182	.273	27.27	0.00	22
De Los Santos, Ericksson	L-L	6-6	200	3-24-06	0	0	4.91	9	0	0	7	4	4	4	0	9	13	.160	.463	.160	31.71	21.95	41
Evangelista, Snarlyn	R-R	6-0	175	2-20-05	1	4	1.96	20	0	2	23	13	9	5	0	6	26	.173	.232	.227	31.71	7.32	82
Felix, Eddy	R-R	6-2	180	8-23-03	1	0	1.80	1	1	0	5	3	1	1	0	0	4	.176	.176	.235	22.22	0.00	18
Florian, Jose	R-R	5-11	155	2-3-04	0	0	0.00	2	0	0	2	2	0	0	0	0	0	.250	.250	.250	0.00	0.00	8
Grant, Frenny	L-L	6-1	170	10-14-03	5	1	4.65	19	1	0	31	27	17	16	1	15	36	.243	.351	.297	27.48	11.45	131
Guacache, Xiomer	R-R	6-3	195	2-11-04	3	2	6.28	11	10	0	39	45	27	27	4	8	34	.294	.335	.451	20.73	4.88	164
Mateo, Andy	R-R	6-4	180	10-19-05	0	1	8.18	12	0	2	11	14	13	10	0	8	7	.311	.411	.444	12.50	14.29	56
Mendez, Wuilberth	R-R	6-3	150	5-29-04	3	0	2.65	12	12	0	54	57	24	16	3	9	38	.282	.336	.366	17.12	4.05	222
Palmero, Victor	R-R	6-7	180	5-9-06	2	1	6.60	10	0	2	15	14	14	11	4	8	17	.226	.351	.516	22.97	10.81	74
Ramirez, Wanmer	R-R	6-1	190	1-6-04	7	2	2.17	19	0	3	29	23	9	7	0	12	36	.213	.317	.269	28.57	9.52	126
Ramos, Albert	R-R	6-3	185	4-7-06	2	1	4.63	14	0	0	23	18	14	12	1	13	21	.220	.377	.305	19.63	12.15	107
Reyes, Erinson	R-R	6-1	187	11-18-01	3	1	2.79	18	0	7	19.1	16	9	6	0	6	20	.225	.278	.239	25.32	7.59	79
Reyes, Franyerson	R-R	6-1	185	9-18-06	2	1	2.70	11	10	0	46.2	38	16	14	2	7	35	.235	.294	.364	19.44	3.89	180
Rodriguez, Carlos	L-L	6-0	170	4-29-06	0	0	3.00	3	0	1	6	4	2	2	0	1	2	.200	.217	.200	8.70	4.35	23
Rodriguez, Deibi	R-R	6-0	175	12-9-05	3	2	2.31	11	10	0	47	40	17	12	1	15	42	.234	.314	.275	21.54	7.69	195
Salas, Henderson	R-R	6-2	165	12-31-05	4	0	3.04	15	0	0	24	23	11	8	0	7	13	.267	.327	.314	12.87	6.93	101
Salcedo, Kelvis	R-R	6-0	180	1-23-06	2	2	3.93	12	11	0	50	47	31	22	3	18	61	.249	.324	.354	28.91	8.53	211
Sanchez, Angel	R-R	6-1	164	12-20-02	0	0	0.00	2	0	1	3	0	0	0	0	0	3	.000	.100	.000	27.27	0.00	11
Vasquez, Luis	R-R	6-4	180	12-11-04	0	0	12.27	2	0	0	4	5	5	5	0	0	5	.294	.294	.471	29.41	0.00	17

Fielding

C: Jimenez 29, Marin 25, Tamara 25, Rojas 18, Santana 13, Rondon 8, Martinez 7, Estrada 1. **1B:** Estevez 47, Cruz 35, Jimenez 12, Estrada 9, De Leon **C:** Rodriguez 31, Marin 24, Madero 19, Rondon 15, Aguilera 1. **1B:** Estevez 46, Madero 10, Marin 2, Rondon 2. **2B:** Aguilera 24, Sanchez 16, Ramirez 12, Lugo 9, Osorio 2, Estevez 1. **3B:** Hernandez 34, Osorio 23, Sanchez 11. **SS:** Ramirez 31, Osorio 27, Aguilera 5. **LF:** Berti 29, Quezada 14, Lugo 14, Matos 4, Caraballo 4, Moya 3, Perea 1, Estevez 1. **CF:** Pinto 51, Lugo 12, Caraballo 3, Perea 2, Perez 1. **RF:** Moya 31, Quezada 10, Matos 8, Lugo 7, Caraballo 6, Perez 6, Estevez 1, Berti 1.

Houston Astros

SEASON SYNOPSIS: First-year manager Joe Espada rallied Houston back from a 6-14 start to win the American League West for the seventh time in eight seasons. But a home sweep in the wild-card round against Detroit marked the Astros' first absence from the AL Championship Series since 2016.

HIGH POINT: Houston's first win after an 0-4 start came April 1, with righty Ronel Blanco finishing a no-hitter against the Blue Jays in a 10-0 victory. Blanco, who originally signed with the Astros in 2016, became the organization's latest Latin American pitching breakthrough, stepping in for injured starters such as Cristian Javier and Jose Urquidy to lead Houston's starters in ERA during a 13-6, 2.80 season with 166 strikeouts in 167 innings, and was stingier than any AL pitcher in allowing hits (6.1 per 9 IP).

LOW POINT: Jose Abreu struggled in 2023 in his first year as an Astro but bottomed out in '24, first accepting a May minor league assignment to work on his swing, then being released in mid June. The Astros still owe the 37-year-old $19.5 million for 2025, but they still ranked third in batting average (.262) despite Abreu hitting .124 in 113 at-bats.

NOTABLE ROOKIES: With all the pitching injuries, righty Spencer Arrighetti came through well, making 28 starts, striking out 171 in 145 innings and posting three double-digit strikeout outings in five August starts. Righty Shawn Dubin, a 13th-round pick in 2018, contributed out of the bullpen for 45 innings.

KEY TRANSACTIONS: Houston signed closer Josh Hader to a five-year, $95 million contract, pushing Ryan Pressly to a setup role, but Hader posted his worst career ERA (3.80) while allowing 12 home runs, even with a WHIP below 1.00. South African-born righty Tayler Scott, signed in December 2023 as a minor league free agent, had a fine 7-3, 2.23 season in relief before tiring late, allowing nine runs in his last 16 innings. The Astros were aggressive at the trade deadline, trading three players–outfielder Joey Loperfido, infielder Will Wagner and righthander Jake Bloss–to Toronto for lefty Yusei Kikuchi. The Astros didn't get to him in the postseason, but he helped them get there, pitching at least 5.1 innings in each of his 10 starts. Houston won the first nine to pull away from Seattle and Texas in the AL West.

OPENING DAY PAYROLL: $236,524,482 (5th)

PLAYERS OF THE YEAR

MAJOR LEAGUE

Yordan Alvarez
DH
.308/.392/.567
35 HR, 86 RBIs
34 2B, 69 BB

MINOR LEAGUE

Shay Whitcomb
SS/3B
(AAA)
.293/.378/.530
25 HR, 26 SB

ORGANIZATION LEADERS

Batting		*Qualifiers
MAJORS		
* AVG	Yordan Alvarez	.308
* OPS	Yordan Alvarez	.959
HR	Yordan Alvarez	35
RBI	Yordan Alvarez	86
MINORS		
* AVG	Pedro Leon, Sugar Land	.299
* OBP	Cooper Hummel, Sugar Land	.419
* SLG	Shay Whitcomb, Sugar Land	.530
* OPS	Shay Whitcomb, Sugar Land	.908
R	Jesus Bastidas, Sugar Land	92
H	Pedro Leon, Sugar Land	140
TB	Pedro Leon, Sugar Land	241
2B	Jesus Bastidas, Sugar Land	31
3B	Pascanel Ferreras, Corpus Christi/Asheville	6
HR	Shay Whitcomb, Sugar Land	25
HR	Jesus Bastidas, Sugar Land	25
RBI	Shay Whitcomb, Sugar Land	91
BB	Cooper Hummel, Sugar Land	79
SO	Ryan Johnson, Asheville	170
SB	Yamal Encarnacion, Asheville/Fayetteville	36

Pitching		#Qualifiers
MAJORS		
W	Framber Valdez	15
# ERA	Framber Valdez	198
SO	Hunter Brown	179
SV	Josh Hader	34
MINORS		
W	A.J. Blubaugh, Corpus Christi/Sugar Land	12
L	Tyler Guilfoil, Corpus Christi	11
L	Trey Dombrowski, Asheville/Corpus Christi	11
# ERA	Ryan Gusto, Sugar Land	3.70
G	Wander Suero, Sugar Land	67
GS	Ryan Gusto, Sugar Land	26
GS	Colton Gordon, C. Christi/S.Land	24
SV	Wander Suero, Sugar Land	37
IP	Ryan Gusto, Sugar Land	148
BB	Miguel Ullola, Corpus Christi/Sugar Land	77
SO	Miguel Ullola, Corpus Christi/Sugar Land	171
# AVG	Miguel Ullola, Corpus Christi/Sugar Land	.163

2024 PERFORMANCE

General Manager: Dana Brown. **Farm Director:** Jacob Buffa. **Scouting Director:** Deric Ladnier.

Class	Team	League	W	L	PCT	Finish	Manager
Majors	Houston Astros	American	88	73	.547	4 (15)	Joe Espada
Triple-A	S.L. Space Cowboys	Pacific Coast	93	56	.624	1 (10)	Mickey Storey
Double-A	Corpus Christi Hooks	Texas	52	84	.382	10 (10)	Dickie Joe Thon
High-A	Asheville Tourists	South Atlantic	51	79	.392	12 (12)	Nate Shaver
Low-A	Fayetteville Woodpeckers	Carolina	55	75	.423	10 (12)	Ricky Rivera
Rookie	FCL Astros	Florida Complex	25	27	.481	8 (15)	Carlos Lugo
Rookie	DSL Astros Blue	Dominican	25	29	.463	33 (51)	Johe Acosta
Rookie	DSL Astros Orange	Dominican	23	32	.418	39 (51)	Manny Martinez
Overall 2024 Minor League Record			**324**	**382**	**.459**	**27th (30)**	

HOUSTON ASTROS

ORGANIZATION STATISTICS

HOUSTON ASTROS

AMERICAN LEAGUE

Batting	B-T	Ht.	Wt.	DOB	AVG	OBP	SLG	G	PA	AB	R	H	2B	3B	HR	RBI	BB	HBP	SH	SF	SO	SB	CS	BB%	SO%
Abreu, Jose	R-R	6-3	235	1-29-87	.124	.167	.195	35	120	113	10	14	2	0	2	7	4	2	0	1	28	0	0	3.33	23.33
Altuve, Jose	R-R	5-6	166	5-6-90	.295	.350	.439	153	682	628	94	185	31	0	20	65	47	7	0	0	119	22	7	6.89	17.45
Alvarez, Yordan	L-R	6-5	225	6-27-97	.308	.392	.567	147	635	552	88	170	34	2	35	86	69	10	0	4	95	6	0	10.87	14.96
Amaya, Jacob	R-R	6-0	180	9-3-98	.000	.000	.000	1	1	1	0	0	0	0	0	0	0	0	0	0	0	0	0	0.00	0.00
Bregman, Alex	R-R	6-0	192	3-30-94	.260	.315	.453	145	634	581	79	151	30	2	26	75	44	5	0	4	86	3	1	6.94	13.56
Cabbage, Trey	L-R	6-2	204	5-3-97	.209	.253	.337	45	91	86	12	18	8	0	1	8	4	1	0	0	34	1	1	4.40	37.36
Caratini, Victor	B-R	5-11	225	8-17-93	.269	.336	.408	87	274	245	30	66	8	1	8	30	23	3	0	3	53	0	1	8.39	19.34
Dezenzo, Zach	R-R	6-4	220	5-11-00	.242	.277	.371	19	65	62	5	15	2	0	2	8	3	0	0	0	22	0	0	4.62	33.85
Diaz, Aledmys	R-R	6-1	195	8-1-90	.000	.000	.000	2	4	4	0	0	0	0	0	0	0	0	0	0	2	0	0	0.00	50.00
Diaz, Yainer	R-R	6-0	195	9-21-98	.299	.325	.441	148	619	585	70	175	29	3	16	84	24	2	0	8	107	2	0	3.88	17.29
Dubon, Mauricio	R-R	6-0	173	7-19-94	.269	.296	.361	137	428	402	45	108	25	0	4	47	16	2	3	5	55	3	2	3.74	12.85
Gamel, Ben	L-L	5-10	180	5-17-92	.259	.377	.362	20	69	58	13	15	3	0	1	4	11	0	0	0	17	0	0	15.94	24.64
Heyward, Jason	L-L	6-5	240	8-9-89	.218	.283	.473	24	61	55	8	12	2	0	4	9	5	0	0	0	17	1	0	8.20	27.87
Hummel, Cooper	B-R	5-10	198	11-28-94	.000	.000	.000	6	8	8	0	0	0	0	0	0	0	0	0	0	2	1	0	0.00	25.00
Kessinger, Grae	R-R	6-1	204	8-25-97	.000	.160	.000	23	25	21	4	0	0	0	0	0	3	1	0	0	7	0	0	12.00	28.00
Leon, Pedro	R-R	5-8	170	5-28-98	.100	.143	.100	7	21	20	2	2	0	0	0	0	1	0	0	0	10	2	0	4.76	47.62
Loperfido, Joey	L-R	6-3	220	5-11-99	.236	.299	.358	38	118	106	11	25	5	1	2	16	7	3	1	1	43	2	1	5.93	36.44
McCormick, Chas	R-L	6-0	208	4-19-95	.211	.271	.306	94	267	242	32	51	6	1	5	27	17	4	1	3	72	8	2	6.37	26.97
Meyers, Jake	R-L	6-0	200	6-18-96	.219	.286	.360	148	513	461	51	101	20	3	13	61	35	10	3	4	117	11	3	6.82	22.81
Pena, Jeremy	R-R	6-0	202	9-22-97	.266	.308	.394	157	650	602	78	160	28	2	15	70	25	14	3	6	111	20	6	3.85	17.08
Salazar, Cesar	L-R	5-9	185	3-15-96	.320	.387	.400	12	32	25	5	8	2	0	0	8	2	2	1	2	6	0	0	6.25	18.75
Singleton, Jon	L-L	6-0	256	9-18-91	.234	.321	.386	119	405	355	46	83	13	1	13	42	47	0	0	3	111	0	0	11.60	27.41
Tucker, Kyle	L-R	6-4	199	1-17-97	.289	.408	.585	78	339	277	56	80	13	0	23	49	56	1	0	2	54	11	0	16.52	15.93
Whitcomb, Shay	R-R	6-1	202	9-28-98	.220	.304	.293	20	46	41	1	9	3	0	0	5	5	0	0	0	8	0	0	10.87	17.39

Pitching	B-T	Ht.	Wt.	DOB	W	L	ERA	G	GS	SV	IP	Hits	Runs	ER	HR	BB	SO	AVG	OBP	SLG	SO%	BB%	BF
Abreu, Bryan	R-R	6-1	225	4-22-97	3	3	3.10	78	0	1	78	59	27	27	9	32	103	.207	.299	.344	31.69	9.85	325
Arrighetti, Spencer	R-R	6-2	186	1-2-00	7	13	4.53	29	28	0	145	139	80	73	21	65	171	.250	.334	.424	27.06	10.28	632
Bielak, Brandon	L-R	6-2	208	4-2-96	0	0	5.71	10	0	0	17	22	11	11	3	7	9	.297	.373	.486	10.84	8.43	83
Blanco, Ronel	R-R	6-0	180	8-31-93	13	6	2.80	30	29	0	167	114	56	52	22	68	166	.190	.273	.354	24.56	10.06	676
Bloss, Jake	R-R	6-3	205	6-23-01	0	1	6.94	3	3	0	12	16	9	9	5	3	11	.314	.352	.667	20.00	5.45	55
Brown, Hunter	R-R	6-2	212	8-29-98	11	9	3.49	31	30	0	170	156	71	66	18	60	179	.242	.310	.357	25.14	8.43	712
Coleman, Dylan	R-R	6-5	230	9-16-96	0	0	0.00	1	0	0	1	0	0	0	0	1	1	.000	.250	.000	25.00	25.00	4
Contreras, Luis	R-R	6-1	175	4-29-96	0	0	9.00	5	0	0	6	7	6	6	0	2	6	.292	.346	.375	23.08	7.69	26
Diaz, Miguel	R-R	6-0	224	11-28-94	0	0	0.00	1	0	0	1	0	0	0	0	0	0	.000	.000	.000	0.00	0.00	3
Dubin, Shawn	R-R	6-1	171	9-6-95	1	1	4.17	31	2	2	45	45	25	21	3	26	49	.256	.353	.375	23.67	12.56	207
Ferguson, Caleb	R-L	6-3	226	7-2-96	0	1	3.86	20	0	0	21	22	10	9	1	9	26	.265	.351	.325	27.66	9.57	94
France, J.P.	R-R	6-0	216	4-4-95	0	3	7.46	5	5	0	25	31	21	21	5	12	22	.290	.364	.505	18.18	9.92	121
Hader, Josh	L-L	5-11	180	4-7-94	8	8	3.80	71	0	34	71	43	33	30	12	25	105	.171	.248	.343	37.77	8.99	278
Henley, Blair	R-R	6-3	190	5-14-97	0	0	135.00	1	1	0	0	4	5	5	0	3	0	.800	.889	.800	0.00	33.33	9
Hernandez, Nick	R-R	6-1	212	12-30-94	0	0	7.88	5	0	0	8	10	7	7	4	1	10	.303	.324	.667	29.41	2.94	34
Javier, Cristian	R-R	6-1	213	3-26-97	3	1	3.89	7	7	0	35	30	16	15	4	19	27	.233	.329	.411	18.00	12.67	150
Kessinger, Grae	R-R	6-1	204	8-25-97	0	0	0.00	1	0	0	1	0	0	0	0	0	0	.000	.000	.000	0.00	0.00	3
Kikuchi, Yusei	L-L	6-0	210	6-17-91	5	1	2.70	10	10	0	60	42	22	18	8	14	76	.188	.234	.308	31.80	5.86	239
King, Bryan	R-L	6-1	184	11-5-96	1	0	2.39	28	0	0	26	20	7	7	1	10	32	.211	.303	.295	29.36	9.17	109
Kuhnel, Joel	R-R	6-5	290	2-19-95	0	0	18.00	1	0	0	2	4	4	4	0	0	1	.400	.455	.500	9.09	0.00	11
Martinez, Seth	R-R	6-2	200	8-29-94	3	2	3.59	44	0	1	53	49	24	21	7	18	36	.246	.321	.422	16.22	8.11	222
Montero, Rafael	R-R	6-0	190	10-17-90	1	2	4.70	41	0	0	38	35	21	20	8	19	23	.248	.348	.461	14.02	11.59	164
Mushinski, Parker	L-L	6-0	218	11-22-95	0	0	6.55	10	0	0	11	11	10	8	1	5	3	.256	.340	.395	6.00	10.00	50
Neris, Hector	R-R	6-2	227	6-14-89	2	1	4.70	16	0	1	15	14	11	8	4	2	18	.237	.270	.475	28.13	3.13	64
Ort, Kaleb	R-R	6-4	240	2-5-92	1	1	2.55	22	0	0	25	16	7	7	7	4	26	.180	.215	.438	27.96	4.30	93
Pressly, Ryan	R-R	6-2	206	12-15-88	2	3	3.49	59	0	4	57	58	25	22	4	18	58	.264	.322	.395	23.77	7.38	244
Scott, Tayler	R-R	6-3	185	6-1-92	7	3	2.23	62	1	0	69	45	21	17	7	35	71	.188	.299	.310	25.18	12.41	282

Name	B-T	Ht.	Wt.	DOB	W	L	ERA	G	GS	SV	IP	Hits	Runs	ER	HR	BB	SO	AVG	OBP	SLG	SO%	BB%	BF
Speas, Alex	R-R	6-3	225	3-4-98	0	0	4.50	1	0	0	2	2	1	1	1	1	2	.286	.375	.714	25.00	12.50	8
Suero, Wander	R-R	6-4	216	9-15-91	0	1	0.00	1	0	0	0	1	1	0	0	0	0	1.000	1.000	1.000	0.00	0.00	1
Valdez, Framber	R-L	5-11	239	11-19-93	15	7	2.91	28	28	0	176	140	60	57	13	55	169	.221	.287	.323	24.04	7.82	703
Verlander, Justin	R-R	6-5	235	2-20-83	5	6	5.48	17	17	0	90	98	56	55	15	27	74	.274	.331	.450	18.69	6.82	396
Whitley, Forrest	R-R	6-7	238	9-15-97	0	0	0.00	3	0	0	3	5	2	0	0	3	5	.313	.450	.375	25.00	15.00	20

Fielding

Catcher	PCT	G	PO	A	E	DP	PB
Caratini	.994	58	489	23	3	1	0
Diaz	.996	102	919	36	4	5	1
Salazar	.978	10	83	4	2	0	1

First Base	PCT	G	PO	A	E	DP
Abreu	.989	35	254	19	3	24
Caratini	1.000	11	68	4	0	9
Dezenzo	.988	14	81	2	1	9
Diaz	.987	11	72	5	1	8
Diaz	1.000	1	5	1	0	1
Dubon	1.000	20	79	11	0	9
Kessinger	1.000	1	8	0	0	1
Loperfido	1.000	1	6	0	0	0
Singleton	.988	94	568	64	8	60

Second Base	PCT	G	PO	A	E	DP
Altuve	.989	147	158	312	5	85
Amaya	1.000	1	2	2	0	1
Diaz	1.000	1	1	1	0	1
Dubon	1.000	22	17	43	0	7
Kessinger	1.000	6	1	4	0	1
Whitcomb	1.000	4	2	3	0	2

Third Base	PCT	G	PO	A	E	DP
Bregman	.972	142	103	242	10	23
Dezenzo	1.000	3	1	1	0	0
Dubon	.968	10	10	20	1	1
Kessinger	.917	7	5	6	1	0
Whitcomb	.833	14	12	13	5	1

Shortstop	PCT	G	PO	A	E	DP
Dubon	.941	5	7	9	1	2
Kessinger	1.000	3	2	2	0	2
Pena	.969	157	221	380	19	86

Outfield	PCT	G	PO	A	E	DP
Alvarez	.987	53	71	3	1	0
Cabbage	1.000	39	31	1	0	0
Dubon	.964	102	157	2	6	0
Gamel	1.000	26	32	0	0	0
Heyward	.971	26	32	1	1	0
Hummel	1.000	4	3	0	0	0
Leon	1.000	6	7	0	0	0
Loperfido	1.000	42	57	1	0	0
McCormick	.994	108	160	1	1	0
Meyers	.997	145	349	2	1	0
Tucker	1.000	70	124	4	0	2

SUGAR LAND SPACE COWBOYS

TRIPLE-A

PACIFIC COAST LEAGUE

Batting	B-T	Ht.	Wt.	DOB	AVG	OBP	SLG	G	PA	AB	R	H	2B	3B	HR	RBI	BB	HBP	SH	SF	SO	SB	CS	BB%	SO%
Abreu, Jose	R-R	6-3	235	1-29-87	.000	.125	.000	2	8	7	0	0	0	0	0	0	1	0	0	0	3	0	0	12.50	37.50
Amaya, Jacob	R-R	6-0	180	9-3-98	.223	.313	.336	73	291	256	36	57	10	2	5	32	32	2	0	1	70	6	0	11.00	24.05
Bastidas, Jesus	R-R	5-8	145	9-14-98	.242	.337	.448	132	606	525	92	127	31	1	25	89	54	23	0	4	140	15	3	8.91	23.10
Berryhill, Luke	R-R	6-0	227	5-28-98	.234	.332	.370	57	221	192	28	45	8	0	6	30	26	2	1	0	69	5	0	11.76	31.22
Cabbage, Trey	L-R	6-2	204	5-3-97	.243	.351	.474	66	291	247	50	60	12	3	13	43	41	1	0	2	100	22	5	14.09	34.36
Corona, Kenedy	R-R	5-10	184	3-21-00	.190	.257	.254	20	71	63	5	12	1	0	1	6	5	1	1	1	19	3	1	7.04	26.76
Dezenzo, Zach	R-R	6-4	220	5-11-00	.333	.425	.573	25	113	96	22	32	8	0	5	20	15	1	0	1	25	3	2	13.27	22.12
Gittens, Chris	R-R	6-4	250	2-4-94	.313	.421	.313	5	19	16	1	5	0	0	0	1	3	0	0	0	9	0	0	15.79	47.37
Hamilton, Quincy	L-L	5-10	190	6-12-98	.246	.350	.464	99	410	349	62	86	21	5	15	56	54	3	1	3	94	8	4	13.17	22.93
Hensley, David	R-R	6-6	190	3-28-96	.234	.352	.376	81	358	303	63	71	20	1	7	35	54	1	0	0	89	17	2	15.08	24.86
Hummel, Cooper	B-R	5-10	198	11-28-94	.277	.419	.454	101	442	350	55	97	26	3	10	59	79	9	0	4	89	15	4	17.87	20.14
Julks, Corey	R-R	6-1	185	2-27-96	.266	.358	.444	31	148	124	26	33	7	0	5	15	19	1	0	4	27	6	0	12.84	18.24
Kessinger, Grae	R-R	6-1	204	8-25-97	.262	.337	.388	67	294	263	46	69	13	1	6	22	30	0	0	1	68	7	2	10.20	23.13
Leon, Pedro	R-R	5-8	170	5-28-98	.299	.372	.514	118	533	469	78	140	25	2	24	90	43	14	3	4	144	29	11	8.07	27.02
Loftin, Jackson	R-R	6-2	195	5-14-00	.286	.444	.286	5	9	7	1	2	0	0	0	1	1	1	0	0	0	0	0	11.11	0.00
Loperfido, Joey	L-R	6-3	220	5-11-99	.272	.365	.568	39	189	162	41	44	7	1	13	33	21	4	0	2	53	9	1	11.11	28.04
Machado, Dixon	R-R	6-1	190	2-22-92	.222	.317	.301	45	182	153	12	34	3	0	3	22	23	0	2	4	25	1	0	12.64	13.74
Matthews, Brice	R-R	6-0	175	3-16-02	.143	.250	.190	12	48	42	3	6	2	0	0	5	3	3	0	0	19	3	0	6.25	39.58
McCormick, Chas	R-L	6-0	208	4-19-95	.308	.400	.385	3	15	13	1	4	1	0	0	1	1	1	0	0	5	1	0	6.67	33.33
Melton, Jacob	L-L	6-3	208	9-7-00	.260	.314	.405	47	192	173	27	45	10	0	5	20	13	1	1	1	48	11	0	6.77	25.00
Narvaez, Omar	L-R	5-11	220	2-10-92	.196	.325	.304	42	169	138	16	27	4	1	3	20	26	2	0	3	31	0	0	15.38	18.34
Palma, Miguel	R-R	5-8	170	1-4-02	.412	.474	.471	5	19	17	2	7	1	0	0	1	1	1	0	0	4	0	1	5.26	21.05
Sacco, Tommy	B-R	5-10	195	5-21-99	.275	.393	.391	22	84	69	9	19	5	0	1	8	14	0	0	1	22	3	0	16.67	26.19
Salazar, Cesar	L-R	5-9	185	3-15-96	.253	.378	.410	78	321	261	37	66	13	2	8	50	45	10	1	4	45	1	2	14.02	14.02
Stubbs, C.J.	R-R	6-3	207	11-12-96	.091	.333	.091	4	15	11	1	1	0	0	0	2	3	1	0	0	5	0	0	20.00	33.33
Wagner, Will	L-R	5-11	210	7-29-98	.307	.424	.429	70	324	261	51	80	13	2	5	41	54	3	1	5	33	3	1	16.67	10.19
Whitcomb, Shay	R-R	6-1	202	9-28-98	.293	.378	.530	108	481	413	73	121	19	2	25	91	53	8	0	7	95	26	8	11.02	19.75
Wrobleski, Ryan	R-R	6-1	196	2-2-00	.207	.303	.379	8	33	29	6	6	2	0	1	6	4	0	0	0	8	0	0	12.12	24.24

Pitching	B-T	Ht.	Wt.	DOB	W	L	ERA	G	GS	SV	IP	Hits	Runs	ER	HR	BB	SO	AVG	OBP	SLG	SO%	BB%	BF
Arrighetti, Spencer	R-R	6-2	186	1-2-00	0	0	2.16	2	2	0	8	7	2	2	0	7	10	.233	.378	.267	27.03	18.92	37
Berryhill, Luke	R-R	6-0	227	5-28-98	0	0	13.50	1	0	0	1	1	2	2	0	3	0	.250	.571	.250	0.00	42.86	7
Bloss, Jake	R-R	6-3	205	6-23-01	0	0	0.00	1	1	0	4	1	0	0	0	0	3	.077	.077	.077	23.08	0.00	13
Blubaugh, A.J.	R-R	6-2	190	7-4-00	12	4	3.83	27	25	0	125	117	58	53	14	51	128	.250	.330	.391	24.24	9.66	528
Brown, Aaron	R-R	6-4	220	3-19-99	0	3	5.32	5	5	0	22	21	14	13	5	8	15	.250	.312	.476	16.13	8.60	93
Carrasco, Deury	L-R	6-0	182	9-20-99	0	0	10.13	1	0	0	3	5	3	3	0	3	1	.455	.600	.545	6.67	20.00	15
Coleman, Dylan	R-R	6-5	230	9-16-96	2	0	6.50	36	0	1	36	28	28	26	2	42	42	.220	.429	.323	23.86	23.86	176
Contreras, Luis	R-R	6-1	175	4-29-96	4	1	1.74	47	0	2	47	22	10	9	3	20	50	.144	.247	.235	27.78	11.11	180
Diaz, Miguel	R-R	6-0	224	11-28-94	2	2	9.64	13	0	0	14	20	15	15	0	5	10	.333	.379	.483	15.15	7.58	66
Dubin, Shawn	R-R	6-1	171	9-6-95	2	0	3.60	10	0	0	10	8	4	4	0	5	13	.222	.310	.333	30.95	11.90	42
France, J.P.	R-R	6-0	216	4-4-95	0	0	7.36	1	1	0	4	4	3	3	0	4	3	.267	.421	.400	15.79	21.05	19
Gaither, Ray	R-R	6-4	224	3-4-98	2	0	3.13	51	3	1	63	57	25	22	4	35	62	.242	.339	.360	22.55	12.73	275
Gomez, Cesar	L-R	6-3	195	7-9-98	0	1	11.91	8	2	0	11	24	15	15	1	13	8	.462	.561	.596	11.94	19.40	67
Gordon, Colton	L-L	6-4	225	12-20-98	8	2	3.94	25	24	0	123	112	68	54	13	39	124	.238	.305	.391	23.75	7.47	522
Greene, Conner	R-R	6-4	195	4-4-95	6	3	4.68	34	5	0	58	55	35	30	7	32	59	.255	.349	.412	23.05	12.50	256
Gusto, Ryan	R-R	6-4	232	3-11-99	8	6	3.70	29	26	0	148	135	68	61	14	53	141	.242	.313	.367	22.63	8.51	623
Henley, Blair	R-R	6-3	190	5-14-97	3	4	5.51	15	14	0	64	71	46	39	10	42	61	.284	.408	.484	20.00	13.77	305

Hernandez, Nick	R-R	6-1	212	12-30-94	5	4	2.83	26	0	0	29	18	10	9	2	14	36	.184	.287	.265	31.30	12.17	115
Hummel, Cooper	S-R	5-10	198	11-28-94	0	0	48.60	2	0	0	2	8	9	9	2	3	0	.667	.688	1.500	0.00	18.75	16
Junk, Janson	R-R	6-2	202	1-15-96	0	2	6.14	4	4	0	15	13	10	10	2	6	10	.236	.302	.400	15.87	9.52	63
King, Bryan	R-L	6-1	184	11-5-96	1	0	2.21	34	0	3	37	28	10	9	1	14	44	.209	.298	.261	29.14	9.27	151
Kouba, Rhett	R-R	6-0	180	9-3-99	2	4	5.95	11	10	0	42.1	46	32	28	5	32	30	.277	.401	.446	14.78	15.76	203
Kuhnel, Joel	R-R	6-5	290	2-19-95	4	1	3.18	9	0	0	11	12	4	4	0	1	6	.273	.304	.364	13.04	2.17	46
Lauer, Eric	R-L	6-3	209	6-3-95	2	3	5.09	11	10	0	46	56	31	26	5	20	49	.295	.371	.426	23.00	9.39	213
Martinez, Seth	R-R	6-2	200	8-29-94	0	0	1.46	13	0	0	12	6	2	2	1	7	12	.143	.280	.238	24.00	14.00	50
McDonald, Cole	L-R	6-1	218	3-11-97	1	0	10.02	20	0	0	21	25	23	23	6	14	18	.301	.408	.566	18.37	14.29	98
Montero, Rafael	R-R	6-0	190	10-17-90	1	1	2.20	17	0	0	16	13	4	4	2	9	24	.217	.319	.350	34.29	12.86	70
Mushinski, Parker	L-L	6-0	218	11-22-95	2	1	5.44	44	0	0	45	45	29	27	4	25	55	.257	.370	.366	26.44	12.02	208
Ort, Kaleb	R-R	6-4	240	2-5-92	0	0	1.13	16	0	1	16	9	2	2	0	8	22	.161	.266	.250	34.38	12.50	64
Otto, Glenn	R-R	6-3	240	3-11-96	0	0	9.00	2	0	0	1	2	1	1	0	0	2	.400	.400	.600	40.00	0.00	5
Robaina, Julio	L-L	5-11	170	3-23-01	0	0	3.86	1	1	0	5	6	2	2	0	2	5	.316	.381	.421	23.81	9.52	21
Speas, Alex	R-R	6-3	225	3-4-98	1	3	8.00	10	0	0	9	9	8	8	1	13	14	.257	.469	.343	28.57	26.53	49
Strotman, Drew	R-R	6-3	195	9-3-96	0	1	6.59	14	0	1	14	18	10	10	3	8	17	.321	.426	.607	24.64	11.59	69
Suero, Wander	R-R	6-4	216	9-15-91	7	1	2.66	67	0	37	68	48	22	20	8	33	71	.197	.306	.340	24.83	11.54	286
Tamarez, Misael	R-R	6-1	206	1-16-00	5	5	6.46	31	11	0	71	74	58	51	17	44	69	.266	.370	.514	21.10	13.46	327
Ullola, Miguel	R-R	6-1	205	6-19-02	0	0	6.00	1	1	0	3	2	2	2	0	4	5	.182	.438	.182	31.25	25.00	16
Urquidy, Jose	R-R	6-0	217	5-1-95	0	1	5.68	2	2	0	6	7	4	4	1	1	6	.269	.296	.423	22.22	3.70	27
VanWey, Logan	R-R	6-2	205	2-14-99	9	1	3.22	60	0	4	73	59	28	26	7	40	98	.225	.339	.344	31.51	12.86	311
Verlander, Justin	R-R	6-5	235	2-20-83	0	1	10.50	2	2	0	6	9	8	7	1	3	9	.333	.400	.778	30.00	10.00	30
Washington, Mark	R-R	6-7	205	3-22-96	0	0	21.60	3	0	0	3	5	8	8	1	6	2	.333	.545	.667	9.09	27.27	22
Whitley, Forrest	R-R	6-7	238	9-15-97	4	1	1.89	32	0	0	33	25	12	7	4	15	45	.203	.293	.325	31.91	10.64	141

Fielding

Catcher	PCT	G	PO	A	E	DP	PB
Berryhill	.982	36	326	10	6	1	6
Narvaez	.988	33	314	13	4	0	1
Palma	.959	5	45	2	2	0	1
Salazar	.995	68	626	32	3	5	2
Stubbs	.970	3	31	1	1	0	1
Wrobleski	1.000	8	62	3	0	0	1

First Base	PCT	G	PO	A	E	DP
Abreu	1.000	1	11	0	0	0
Berryhill	1.000	6	35	4	0	0
Cabbage	.995	28	170	17	1	20
Dezenzo	.986	10	65	7	1	6
Gittens	1.000	3	16	1	0	2
Hensley	.988	22	153	14	2	24
Hummel	.976	21	149	12	4	15
Kessinger	.988	12	69	12	1	15
Loperfido	.990	11	87	8	1	11
Wagner	.992	33	240	16	2	26
Whitcomb	.979	6	44	3	1	8

Second Base	PCT	G	PO	A	E	DP
Amaya	.986	35	49	87	2	30
Bastidas	.973	49	72	111	5	33
Kessinger	1.000	4	6	9	0	3
Loftin	1.000	3	4	2	0	1
Machado	1.000	8	14	8	0	5
Sacco	1.000	16	18	24	0	7
Wagner	1.000	21	36	54	0	18
Whitcomb	.967	18	27	32	2	10

Third Base	PCT	G	PO	A	E	DP
Amaya	.818	7	7	11	4	1
Bastidas	.944	28	17	50	4	7
Dezenzo	.970	12	13	19	1	3
Hensley	.891	25	18	31	6	6
Kessinger	.957	16	10	34	2	2
Loftin	1.000	2	0	1	0	1
Machado	1.000	16	12	22	0	3
Matthews	1.000	4	3	7	0	0
Sacco	1.000	4	5	7	0	0
Wagner	.968	8	8	22	1	2
Whitcomb	.965	31	21	62	3	10

Shortstop	PCT	G	PO	A	E	DP
Amaya	.939	25	36	57	6	20
Bastidas	.962	42	45	105	6	25
Kessinger	.967	27	24	64	3	10
Machado	.955	18	18	45	3	13
Matthews	1.000	8	6	13	0	1
Sacco	1.000	2	5	5	0	3
Whitcomb	.974	30	44	67	3	13

Outfield	PCT	G	PO	A	E	DP
Cabbage	.966	29	55	2	2	0
Corona	1.000	20	53	1	0	0
Dezenzo	.917	3	11	0	1	0
Hamilton	.973	92	175	3	5	0
Hensley	.979	27	46	1	1	0
Hummel	.981	59	104	2	2	0
Julks	1.000	28	32	2	0	0
Leon	.991	110	219	3	2	0
Loperfido	.985	29	64	1	1	0
McCormick	1.000	2	5	0	0	0
Melton	.985	45	126	2	2	0
Whitcomb	1.000	11	23	1	0	0

CORPUS CHRISTI HOOKS — DOUBLE-A

TEXAS LEAGUE

Batting	B-T	Ht.	Wt.	DOB	AVG	OBP	SLG	G	PA	AB	R	H	2B	3B	HR	RBI	BB	HBP	SH	SF	SO	SB	CS	BB%	SO%
Arocho, Jeremy	B-R	5-10	165	10-6-98	.214	.334	.259	109	443	370	42	79	8	3	1	34	66	2	3	2	79	34	5	14.90	17.83
Baez, Luis	R-R	6-1	205	1-11-04	.216	.311	.333	14	61	51	4	11	3	0	1	9	8	0	0	2	11	2	0	13.11	18.03
Barber, Colin	L-L	5-11	200	12-4-00	.222	.287	.353	70	282	252	27	56	9	0	8	27	21	4	0	5	85	4	2	7.45	30.14
Brewer, Jordan	R-L	6-0	204	8-1-97	.224	.305	.363	84	334	295	33	66	18	1	7	31	26	10	0	3	66	10	0	7.78	19.76
Caratini, Victor	B-R	5-11	225	8-17-93	.400	.500	1.000	2	6	5	2	2	0	0	1	2	1	0	0	0	0	0	0	16.67	0.00
Cerny, Logan	R-R	6-1	185	9-28-99	.180	.231	.287	33	130	122	18	22	5	1	2	9	8	0	0	0	37	6	1	6.15	28.46
Cole, Zach	L-R	6-2	190	8-4-00	.214	.302	.408	70	295	262	29	56	17	2	10	36	24	9	0	0	113	14	2	8.14	38.31
Corona, Kenedy	R-R	5-10	184	3-21-00	.219	.326	.297	78	325	279	34	61	12	2	2	23	34	11	0	1	77	24	5	10.46	23.69
Correa, J.C.	R-R	5-9	200	9-15-98	.239	.279	.327	42	172	159	16	38	8	0	2	16	10	0	0	3	22	3	0	5.81	12.79
Cruz, Narbe	R-R	6-3	181	10-1-00	.353	.450	.412	5	20	17	1	6	1	0	0	4	3	0	0	0	3	0	0	15.00	15.00
Daniels, Zach	R-R	6-1	220	1-23-99	.148	.207	.222	16	58	54	5	8	1	0	1	4	4	0	0	0	24	4	0	6.90	41.38
Deming, Austin	R-R	6-0	200	12-21-99	.255	.357	.500	30	112	94	11	24	2	0	7	18	13	3	0	2	26	5	1	11.61	23.21
Dezenzo, Zach	R-R	6-4	220	5-11-00	.222	.308	.370	22	91	81	8	18	6	0	2	7	9	1	0	0	23	2	1	9.89	25.27
Encarnacion, Luis	R-R	5-8	170	9-25-02	.233	.267	.512	11	45	43	5	10	0	0	4	6	2	0	0	0	10	0	0	4.44	22.22
Encarnacion, Yamal	B-R	5-8	150	9-8-03	.238	.292	.333	15	49	42	7	10	4	0	0	4	4	0	1	2	7	3	3	8.16	14.29
Espinosa, Rolando	R-R	6-0	177	1-5-01	.223	.297	.385	84	300	265	36	59	11	1	10	39	29	1	0	5	101	13	2	9.67	33.67
Ferreras, Pascanel	R-R	5-10	185	11-25-01	.201	.295	.331	88	359	314	31	63	11	6	6	30	37	6	0	2	98	8	3	10.31	27.30
Hamilton, Quincy	L-L	5-10	190	6-12-98	.131	.312	.197	18	77	61	5	8	1	0	1	5	13	3	0	0	15	3	1	16.88	19.48
Huezo, Anthony	L-R	6-2	170	11-2-05	.000	.000	.000	1	3	3	0	0	0	0	0	0	0	0	0	0	2	0	0	0.00	66.67
Kato, Kobe	L-R	6-1	170	3-19-99	.000	.500	.000	1	2	1	0	0	0	0	0	0	0	1	0	0	1	0	0	0.00	50.00
Matthews, Brice	R-R	6-0	175	3-16-02	.252	.376	.497	42	181	151	28	38	8	1	9	21	24	6	0	0	61	16	4	13.26	33.70
McCormick, Chas	R-L	6-0	208	4-19-95	.167	.158	.222	5	19	18	0	3	1	0	0	1	0	0	0	1	5	1	1	0.00	26.32
Melton, Jacob	L-L	6-3	208	9-7-00	.248	.306	.442	58	251	226	32	56	10	2	10	34	18	2	0	2	56	19	4	7.17	22.31

Palma, Miguel	R-R	5-8	170	1-4-02	.201	.301	.284	53	193	169	16	34	3	1	3	14	22	2	0	0	48	1	0	11.40	24.87
Price, Collin	R-R	6-6	225	11-15-99	.222	.316	.375	83	320	275	34	61	12	0	10	30	36	4	0	5	78	5	1	11.25	24.38
Sacco, Tommy	B-R	5-10	195	5-21-99	.243	.335	.376	102	448	391	49	95	16	3	10	33	52	3	0	2	83	16	6	11.61	18.53
Stevens, Chad	R-R	6-3	215	2-3-99	.153	.242	.235	24	95	85	3	13	4	0	1	5	9	1	0	0	35	2	1	9.47	36.84
Stubbs, C.J.	R-R	6-3	207	11-12-96	.127	.222	.236	17	63	55	8	7	0	0	2	5	7	0	0	1	21	1	0	11.11	33.33
Williams, Jeron	R-R	6-1	180	9-29-00	.204	.266	.352	40	154	142	16	29	6	3	3	13	10	2	0	0	27	14	3	6.49	17.53
Wrobleski, Ryan	R-R	6-1	196	2-2-00	.207	.299	.264	35	137	121	10	25	4	0	1	8	9	7	0	0	36	6	0	6.57	26.28

Pitching	B-T	Ht.	Wt.	DOB	W	L	ERA	G	GS	SV	IP	Hits	Runs	ER	HR	BB	SO	AVG	OBP	SLG	SO%	BB%	BF
Betancourt, Carlos	R-R	6-1	160	3-27-01	1	1	5.59	11	0	0	19	21	12	12	2	10	16	.280	.364	.387	18.18	11.36	88
Bloss, Jake	R-R	6-3	205	6-23-01	3	1	1.61	8	8	0	45	19	11	8	2	13	35	.127	.195	.207	21.21	7.88	165
Blubaugh, A.J.	R-R	6-2	190	7-4-00	0	0	0.00	1	0	0	4	2	0	0	0	0	5	.143	.143	.143	35.71	0.00	14
Brockhouse, Walker	R-R	6-4	197	2-22-99	0	2	6.23	22	0	3	26	29	20	18	4	12	25	.282	.364	.437	21.01	10.08	119
Brown, Aaron	R-R	6-4	220	3-19-99	3	7	4.50	22	13	1	92	103	51	46	12	26	111	.283	.334	.462	27.75	6.50	400
Carrasco, Deury	L-R	6-0	182	9-20-99	0	0	0.00	1	0	0	1	0	0	0	0	0	1	.000	.000	.000	50.00	0.00	2
De Paula, Brayan	L-L	6-3	225	6-25-99	2	1	5.23	25	0	0	33	22	21	19	4	35	33	.191	.400	.313	21.29	22.58	155
DeLabio, Jacob	R-R	6-5	235	9-18-97	1	1	4.57	17	0	2	22	17	12	11	2	14	26	.221	.368	.377	27.37	14.74	95
Dombroski, Trey	R-L	6-5	235	3-13-01	2	3	6.41	7	5	0	27	33	19	19	10	11	29	.297	.366	.595	23.39	8.87	124
Fleury, Jose	R-R	6-0	185	3-8-02	1	4	3.82	17	9	1	68	55	34	29	9	26	74	.216	.290	.384	25.52	8.97	290
Ford, Kasey	L-R	6-6	275	1-10-98	3	2	3.93	30	0	2	37	22	21	16	2	27	34	.182	.335	.248	21.12	16.77	161
Garcia, Luis	R-R	5-11	244	12-13-96	0	1	27.00	1	1	0	1	3	4	4	2	1	2	.429	.500	1.286	25.00	12.50	8
Gomez, Cesar	L-R	6-3	195	7-9-98	2	1	1.67	26	0	2	38	31	9	7	4	7	33	.225	.265	.348	22.45	4.76	147
Guilfoil, Tyler	R-R	6-4	215	1-19-00	5	11	4.81	27	18	1	118	106	68	63	20	54	107	.242	.345	.438	20.82	10.51	514
Henderson, Layne	R-R	6-4	200	6-8-96	0	0	2.45	9	0	0	11	10	3	3	1	6	13	.238	.327	.405	26.53	12.24	49
Henley, Blair	R-R	6-3	190	5-14-97	0	0	3.00	3	0	0	3	2	1	1	0	0	6	.182	.250	.182	50.00	0.00	12
Hicks, James	R-R	6-2	190	5-9-01	2	2	5.21	12	5	0	48	61	29	28	7	13	52	.305	.361	.470	23.74	5.94	219
Javier, Cristian	R-R	6-1	213	3-26-97	0	1	8.10	1	1	0	3	3	3	3	0	2	3	.214	.313	.214	18.75	12.50	16
Knorr, Michael	R-R	6-5	245	5-12-00	0	6	5.90	11	7	0	40	39	33	26	7	20	47	.257	.339	.447	26.70	11.36	176
Mancini, Joey	L-R	6-1	195	10-4-00	5	4	1.88	18	9	1	77	54	21	16	4	30	68	.197	.292	.288	21.45	9.46	317
McDonald, Cole	L-R	6-1	218	3-11-97	2	0	1.50	20	0	1	24	13	4	4	0	11	31	.159	.271	.232	32.29	11.46	96
Melendez, Jaime	L-R	5-8	190	9-26-01	1	2	10.34	8	2	0	16	15	20	18	1	17	8	.254	.464	.339	9.41	20.00	85
Molero, Jeremy	R-R	6-2	170	11-8-99	0	0	4.50	3	0	0	2	3	1	1	0	0	2	.375	.375	.625	25.00	0.00	8
Pecko, Ethan	R-R	6-2	195	8-25-02	2	2	2.36	7	3	0	27	17	8	7	3	9	28	.187	.267	.319	27.45	8.82	102
Perez, Railin	R-R	6-3	185	9-2-01	0	0	16.20	2	0	0	2	1	3	3	0	4	1	.167	.545	.167	9.09	36.36	11
Robaina, Julio	L-L	5-11	170	3-23-01	1	5	5.08	14	10	1	62	72	46	35	10	18	57	.295	.342	.480	21.03	6.64	271
Rodning, Brody	R-L	6-1	185	1-14-96	2	1	2.70	13	0	0	13	8	5	4	0	4	17	.182	.265	.227	34.00	8.00	50
Rodriguez, Luis Angel	L-L	6-1	190	9-10-99	6	6	5.31	21	11	1	80	75	50	47	11	39	92	.247	.342	.421	26.14	11.08	352
Santa, Alimber	R-R	5-10	163	5-3-03	0	1	9.14	11	2	0	22	27	30	22	6	20	18	.297	.423	.516	16.07	17.86	112
Santos, Alex	R-R	6-4	208	2-10-02	0	5	7.83	6	5	0	23	27	25	20	5	14	24	.290	.382	.527	21.62	12.61	111
Strotman, Drew	R-R	6-3	195	9-3-96	3	1	1.88	15	0	1	24	17	7	5	0	12	26	.193	.327	.227	24.30	11.21	107
Swanson, Nic	R-R	6-2	180	7-8-99	0	0	4.15	1	1	0	4	3	2	2	1	1	3	.200	.250	.400	18.75	6.25	16
Torres, Alejandro	R-R	6-1	238	4-26-01	0	2	3.29	31	0	4	41	26	17	15	3	23	44	.179	.310	.248	25.29	13.22	174
Ullola, Miguel	R-R	6-1	205	6-19-02	5	9	4.24	27	23	1	127	72	61	60	12	73	166	.162	.293	.304	31.14	13.70	533
Urquidy, Jose	R-R	6-0	217	5-1-95	0	1	9.00	1	1	0	4	7	5	4	1	0	2	.368	.368	.632	10.53	0.00	19
Verlander, Justin	R-R	6-5	235	2-20-83	0	1	6.75	2	2	0	8	11	8	6	0	1	8	.306	.316	.389	21.05	2.63	38

Fielding

Catcher	PCT	G	PO	A	E	DP	PB
Caratini	.909	2	10	0	1	0	0
Correa	1.000	5	48	3	0	1	0
Palma	.998	46	405	38	1	4	5
Price	.987	58	517	25	7	2	6
Stubbs	.978	10	87	4	2	0	2
Wrobleski	.963	22	194	12	8	1	2

First Base	PCT	G	PO	A	E	DP
Brewer	.987	59	417	25	6	37
Correa	1.000	12	75	5	0	6
Daniels	1.000	1	3	0	0	0
Deming	.976	8	39	2	1	3
Dezenzo	1.000	4	36	1	0	6
Encarnacion	.984	10	57	3	1	6
Espinosa	1.000	6	35	6	0	5
Palma	1.000	2	10	0	0	0
Price	.995	24	173	11	1	11
Stubbs	1.000	3	24	1	0	2
Wrobleski	1.000	10	78	4	0	5

Second Base	PCT	G	PO	A	E	DP
Arocho	.981	53	94	117	4	28
Correa	.979	11	23	23	1	7
Cruz	1.000	2	3	4	0	0
Deming	1.000	1	1	1	0	0
Encarnacion	.857	3	2	4	1	2
Encarnacion	1.000	1	1	3	0	0
Espinosa	.958	7	12	11	1	3
Ferreras	.947	33	65	78	8	24
Kato	.000	1	0	0	0	0
Matthews	1.000	2	4	3	0	0
Sacco	.984	16	26	36	1	5
Stevens	1.000	4	8	6	0	4
Williams	1.000	8	11	11	0	2

Third Base	PCT	G	PO	A	E	DP
Arocho	.917	9	3	19	2	2
Correa	1.000	1	1	2	0	0
Deming	.977	19	11	32	1	2
Dezenzo	.932	16	18	23	3	1
Espinosa	.833	6	3	7	2	0
Ferreras	.968	23	20	40	2	5
Matthews	.919	13	13	21	3	3
Sacco	.895	23	13	38	6	3
Stevens	1.000	12	11	15	0	1
Williams	.870	14	10	30	6	2

Shortstop	PCT	G	PO	A	E	DP
Arocho	1.000	5	11	10	0	4
Cruz	1.000	3	3	11	0	2
Espinosa	1.000	2	0	4	0	0
Ferreras	.917	25	30	47	7	4
Matthews	.911	25	31	61	9	12
Sacco	.958	55	74	129	9	30
Stevens	.846	8	10	12	4	4
Williams	.974	14	10	27	1	2

Outfield	PCT	G	PO	A	E	DP
Arocho	1.000	36	57	1	0	1
Baez	.917	13	10	1	1	0
Barber	.967	55	85	3	3	0
Brewer	1.000	17	31	2	0	2
Cerny	.968	32	90	0	3	0
Cole	1.000	39	70	5	0	2
Corona	.995	72	175	6	1	1
Daniels	.968	14	29	1	1	0
Encarnacion	1.000	12	20	0	0	0
Espinosa	.970	58	94	4	3	0
Hamilton	1.000	17	37	1	0	0
Huezo	1.000	1	1	0	0	0
McCormick	1.000	3	6	0	0	0
Melton	.979	52	92	1	2	0

ASHEVILLE TOURISTS **HIGH-A**

SOUTH ATLANTIC LEAGUE

Batting	B-T	Ht.	Wt.	DOB	AVG	OBP	SLG	G	PA	AB	R	H	2B	3B	HR	RBI	BB	HBP	SH	SF	SO	SB	CS	BB%	SO%
Backstrom, Mahki	L-L	6-5	220	10-10-01	.088	.114	.118	11	35	34	1	3	1	0	0	0	1	0	0	0	21	1	0	2.86	60.00
Baez, Luis	R-R	6-1	205	1-11-04	.263	.300	.479	92	407	380	53	100	22	0	20	67	22	0	0	5	111	9	1	5.41	27.27
Bush, Will	L-R	6-4	230	3-4-04	.200	.200	.200	3	10	10	1	2	0	0	0	0	0	0	0	0	2	0	0	0.00	20.00
Caldera, Fernando	R-R	5-11	170	10-10-02	.123	.240	.231	23	75	65	7	8	4	0	1	6	10	0	0	0	36	0	0	13.33	48.00
Carrillo, Oliver	R-R	5-11	210	1-19-02	.223	.288	.419	62	236	215	27	48	12	0	10	28	20	0	0	1	82	0	0	8.47	34.75
Cerny, Logan	R-R	6-1	185	9-28-99	.225	.330	.443	73	318	271	57	61	17	0	14	36	39	5	0	3	109	26	1	12.26	34.28
Cruz, Narbe	R-R	6-3	181	10-1-00	.270	.347	.423	77	314	281	35	76	15	2	8	36	24	9	0	0	87	7	3	7.64	27.71
Deming, Austin	R-R	6-0	200	12-21-99	.264	.345	.453	83	346	307	44	81	22	0	12	45	29	9	0	0	98	8	2	8.38	28.32
Encarnacion, Luis	R-R	5-8	170	9-25-02	.263	.300	.419	76	287	270	35	71	12	0	10	52	13	2	0	2	57	3	1	4.53	19.86
Encarnacion, Yamal	B-R	5-8	150	9-8-03	.200	.319	.225	13	47	40	4	8	1	0	0	6	7	0	0	0	12	7	1	14.89	25.53
Ferreras, Pascanel	R-R	5-10	185	11-25-01	.309	.411	.457	21	95	81	16	25	3	0	3	12	10	4	0	0	24	2	1	10.53	25.26
Fisher, Cameron	L-R	6-2	210	6-12-01	.157	.310	.384	58	226	185	33	29	6	0	12	28	35	6	0	0	102	10	0	15.49	45.13
Garcia, John	R-R	6-0	190	9-25-00	.293	.372	.480	77	333	294	47	86	21	2	10	39	27	11	0	1	86	9	2	8.11	25.83
Gomez, Kenni	L-R	5-11	185	5-14-05	.272	.314	.358	20	86	81	12	22	2	1	1	7	3	2	0	0	31	7	2	3.49	36.05
Guillemette, Garret	R-R	6-1	210	9-4-01	.212	.298	.345	98	383	339	43	72	15	0	10	47	36	6	0	2	105	4	0	9.40	27.42
Huezo, Anthony	L-R	6-2	170	11-2-05	.200	.310	.400	7	29	25	3	5	2	0	1	2	4	0	0	0	11	2	0	13.79	37.93
Janek, Walker	R-R	6-0	190	9-24-02	.175	.214	.289	25	103	97	10	17	6	1	1	11	4	1	0	1	30	0	0	3.88	29.13
Johnson, Ryan	R-R	6-0	175	12-27-00	.202	.294	.345	105	412	362	56	73	10	0	14	33	41	7	0	2	170	9	2	9.95	41.26
Loftin, Jackson	R-R	6-2	195	5-14-00	.183	.278	.307	65	231	202	33	37	11	1	4	16	22	5	0	1	65	20	2	9.52	28.14
Matthews, Brice	R-R	6-0	175	3-16-02	.321	.423	.580	21	97	81	17	26	3	0	6	17	14	1	0	1	26	10	3	14.43	26.80
Morton, Korey	R-R	6-1	177	8-9-02	.210	.247	.210	23	86	81	7	17	0	0	0	3	3	1	0	0	25	4	3	3.49	29.07
Nunez, Alejandro	L-R	5-10	179	9-8-04	.184	.262	.263	12	42	38	2	7	1	1	0	0	4	0	0	0	15	0	0	9.52	35.71
Price, Collin	R-R	6-6	225	11-15-99	.250	.375	.467	17	72	60	10	15	4	0	3	10	12	0	0	0	20	2	0	16.67	27.78
Sherwin, Anthony	L-R	5-11	190	6-20-02	.206	.349	.361	66	238	194	25	40	9	0	7	26	39	4	0	1	90	1	5	16.39	37.82
Teter, Jacob	L-L	6-6	225	2-26-99	.667	.750	1.000	1	4	3	1	2	1	0	0	0	1	0	0	0	0	0	0	25.00	0.00
Trimble, Justin	L-R	6-4	215	6-21-03	.182	.217	.227	6	23	22	4	4	1	0	0	2	1	0	0	0	13	1	0	4.35	56.52
Whitaker, Tyler	R-R	6-4	190	8-2-02	.205	.316	.311	37	155	132	14	27	8	0	2	12	18	4	0	1	56	6	0	11.61	36.13
Williams, Jeron	R-R	6-1	180	9-29-00	.310	.366	.552	31	131	116	16	36	9	2	5	24	11	1	0	3	25	12	2	8.40	19.08

Pitching	B-T	Ht.	Wt.	DOB	W	L	ERA	G	GS	SV	IP	Hits	Runs	ER	HR	BB	SO	AVG	OBP	SLG	SO%	BB%	BF
Almonte, Davil	R-R	5-9	187	10-19-01	0	0	7.20	2	0	0	5.0	6	4	4	2	0	3	.316	.316	.737	15.79	0.00	19
Austin, Kelly	R-R	6-0	195	12-17-00	2	0	2.70	18	0	3	27	23	11	8	5	6	32	.225	.282	.402	29.09	5.45	110
Batista, Edinson	R-R	6-2	210	5-19-02	6	6	5.01	26	16	1	115	93	76	64	18	54	103	.221	.331	.413	20.60	10.80	500
Bloss, Jake	R-R	6-3	205	6-23-01	1	1	2.08	4	4	0	17	11	5	4	1	8	25	.186	.279	.288	36.76	11.76	68
Brockhouse, Walker	R-R	6-4	197	2-22-99	0	0	5.17	5	1	0	16	13	10	9	1	13	20	.232	.375	.357	27.78	18.06	72
Calderon, Carlos	R-R	6-0	210	10-4-01	0	4	9.58	14	6	1	52	83	64	55	12	30	52	.361	.442	.635	19.48	11.24	267
Carrasco, Deury	L-R	6-0	182	9-20-99	0	5	4.61	22	0	0	27	29	17	14	2	17	21	.282	.400	.398	16.67	13.49	126
Cobos, Franny	R-R	5-9	195	2-1-01	6	2	5.84	31	0	0	57	60	46	37	9	29	63	.263	.350	.469	23.60	10.86	267
Dombroski, Trey	R-L	6-5	235	3-13-01	5	8	5.70	18	13	0	71	88	52	45	11	21	83	.290	.336	.482	25.00	6.33	332
Foggo, Ian	R-R	6-1	200	6-1-98	3	2	6.17	24	0	1	23	20	18	16	4	22	33	.225	.395	.449	28.95	19.30	114
Guedez, Jose	R-R	6-0	169	9-27-01	3	4	3.24	16	12	0	67	51	30	24	4	37	77	.213	.336	.313	26.92	12.94	286
Henderson, Layne	R-R	6-4	200	6-8-96	0	1	5.25	21	0	2	24	26	17	14	3	12	33	.268	.351	.412	29.20	10.62	113
Hicks, James	R-R	6-2	190	5-9-01	3	2	3.63	9	5	0	40	45	23	16	5	9	38	.281	.324	.425	22.35	5.29	170
Langford, Colby	L-L	6-3	195	4-30-02	0	5	10.59	6	3	0	17	15	25	20	1	23	22	.246	.473	.393	23.66	24.73	93
Leach, Hudson	R-R	6-3	220	6-16-02	0	1	0.00	3	0	1	5	1	1	0	0	5	8	.067	.300	.067	40.00	25.00	20
Mancini, Joey	L-R	6-1	195	10-4-00	3	1	2.73	9	0	1	30	19	12	9	1	14	39	.184	.298	.262	32.23	11.57	121
Melendez, Jaime	L-R	5-8	190	9-26-01	1	1	5.23	7	1	0	10	5	9	6	2	15	5	.143	.404	.343	9.62	28.85	52
Molero, Jeremy	R-R	6-2	170	11-8-99	1	1	3.15	32	0	3	34	20	21	12	4	29	53	.165	.354	.314	33.54	18.35	158
Nezuh, Jackson	R-R	6-1	180	2-11-02	1	2	2.79	9	5	0	39	33	12	12	2	16	46	.231	.319	.336	28.22	9.82	163
Pecko, Ethan	R-R	6-2	195	8-25-02	0	2	7.15	6	5	0	23	31	24	18	5	8	34	.304	.345	.520	30.09	7.08	113
Pena, Alain	R-R	5-11	155	4-10-03	1	3	6.11	5	4	0	18	22	20	12	3	7	22	.293	.376	.507	25.88	8.24	85
Perez, Railin	R-R	6-3	185	9-2-01	4	2	3.42	37	0	3	53	44	23	20	4	32	62	.227	.352	.345	26.50	13.68	234
Robaina, Julio	L-L	5-11	170	3-23-01	0	0	9.00	1	1	0	2	2	2	2	0	3	2	.250	.455	.250	18.18	27.27	11
Rodning, Brody	R-L	6-1	185	1-14-96	1	0	5.87	7	0	1	8	9	7	5	0	4	9	.273	.342	.394	23.68	10.53	38
Sanchez, Wilmy	R-R	5-9	193	12-17-03	1	0	2.76	10	0	0	16	16	9	5	1	8	26	.250	.333	.391	35.62	10.96	73
Sherwin, Anthony	L-R	5-11	190	6-20-02	0	0	4.50	2	0	0	2	3	1	1	1	0	0	.375	.375	.875	0.00	0.00	8
Swanson, Nic	R-R	6-2	180	7-8-99	3	9	4.88	25	24	0	107	95	65	58	14	47	115	.234	.316	.387	25.05	10.24	459
Taylor, Andrew	R-R	6-5	190	9-23-01	1	1	5.27	5	3	1	14	16	11	8	3	5	17	.286	.339	.518	27.42	8.06	62
Torres, Alejandro	R-R	6-1	238	4-26-01	1	0	1.54	8	0	0	12	5	2	2	1	1	17	.125	.167	.225	40.48	2.38	42
True, Derek	R-R	6-2	180	4-25-01	2	6	6.90	20	15	1	76	89	64	58	13	34	80	.290	.364	.515	22.66	9.63	353
Urias, Manuel	R-R	6-6	200	3-8-01	2	10	6.19	25	12	1	105	120	81	72	25	33	107	.284	.336	.539	22.96	7.08	466

Fielding

Catcher	PCT	G	PO	A	E	DP	PB
Bush	1.000	3	23	1	0	0	0
Caldera	.923	9	51	9	5	0	2
Encarnacion	1.000	8	46	1	0	0	3
Garcia	.979	49	476	35	11	0	9
Guillemette	.980	47	452	31	10	1	7
Janek	.959	13	126	15	6	0	2
Price	1.000	7	72	1	0	0	2

First Base	PCT	G	PO	A	E	DP
Backstrom	1.000	5	32	0	0	3
Caldera	.979	6	44	2	1	3
Carrillo	.971	10	66	2	2	5
Deming	1.000	8	34	3	0	2
Encarnacion	.968	29	172	10	6	16
Fisher	.944	21	123	13	8	12
Garcia	.967	12	85	4	3	5
Guillemette	.990	38	284	20	3	24
Loftin	.000	1	0	0	0	0
Price	.963	7	50	2	2	6
Teter	1.000	1	7	0	0	2
Trimble	1.000	3	20	0	0	2

Second Base	PCT	G	PO	A	E	DP
Carrasco	1.000	1	0	1	0	1
Cruz	.943	34	51	81	8	14
Deming	1.000	10	13	20	0	5
Encarnacion	1.000	3	5	8	0	3
Encarnacion	1.000	1	3	0	0	0
Ferreras	.972	10	17	18	1	7
Johnson	.972	19	26	43	2	12
Loftin	.917	4	7	4	1	0
Nunez	.970	10	10	22	1	3
Sherwin	.975	39	42	74	3	17
Williams	1.000	11	15	23	0	7

Third Base	PCT	G	PO	A	E	DP
Cruz	.937	25	19	40	4	5
Deming	.906	61	35	90	13	8
Ferreras	.750	2	1	2	1	0
Johnson	.889	13	13	19	4	2
Matthews	.929	4	4	9	1	3
Sherwin	.857	19	9	15	4	0
Trimble	1.000	4	2	9	0	2
Williams	1.000	7	3	9	0	1

Shortstop	PCT	G	PO	A	E	DP
Cruz	.980	11	19	30	1	5
Ferreras	1.000	9	7	24	0	3
Johnson	.945	72	94	166	15	34
Loftin	.947	7	10	8	1	1
Matthews	.930	12	18	22	3	2
Nunez	1.000	1	2	1	0	0
Sherwin	.893	8	14	11	3	3
Williams	.889	13	22	26	6	8

Outfield	PCT	G	PO	A	E	DP
Backstrom	1.000	3	2	0	0	0
Baez	.959	84	114	3	5	1
Carrillo	.958	51	67	2	3	0
Cerny	1.000	67	120	5	0	2
Encarnacion	.971	22	33	1	1	1
Encarnacion	1.000	12	16	2	0	2
Fisher	.959	31	46	1	2	0
Gomez	.973	20	35	1	1	0
Huezo	1.000	7	10	1	0	0
Loftin	.973	52	103	4	3	0
Morton	.976	24	39	1	1	0
Nunez	1.000	3	3	0	0	0
Whitaker	.986	37	68	2	1	0

HOUSTON ASTROS

FAYETTEVILLE WOODPECKERS — *LOW-A*

CAROLINA LEAGUE

Batting	B-T	Ht.	Wt.	DOB	AVG	OBP	SLG	G	PA	AB	R	H	2B	3B	HR	RBI	BB	HBP	SH	SF	SO	SB	CS	BB%	SO%
Austin, Trevor	R-R	5-10	188	10-3-01	.293	.376	.347	20	85	75	3	22	4	0	0	11	6	4	0	0	15	3	0	7.06	17.65
Bush, Will	L-R	6-4	230	3-4-04	.221	.336	.360	88	325	272	32	60	12	1	8	45	41	8	0	3	89	5	0	12.62	27.38
Caldera, Fernando	R-R	5-11	170	10-10-02	.136	.278	.136	24	79	66	5	9	0	0	0	6	11	2	0	0	26	0	1	13.92	32.91
Carrillo, Oliver	R-R	5-11	210	1-19-02	.232	.382	.420	39	173	138	26	32	6	1	6	27	29	5	0	1	57	0	2	16.76	32.95
Casserilla, Xavier	R-R	6-0	210	5-16-03	.227	.317	.300	60	230	203	17	46	15	0	0	27	15	12	0	0	63	6	2	6.52	27.39
Colon, Rabel	L-R	6-0	175	8-29-03	.135	.195	.324	13	41	37	4	5	1	0	2	4	3	0	0	1	18	0	1	7.32	43.90
Daniels, Zach	R-R	6-1	220	1-23-99	.235	.316	.471	4	19	17	4	4	1	0	1	3	2	0	0	0	5	0	0	10.53	26.32
Diaz, Camilo	R-R	6-3	208	9-5-05	.125	.125	.125	3	8	8	0	1	0	0	0	0	0	0	0	0	2	0	0	0.00	25.00
Diaz, Victor	R-R	5-10	175	11-25-01	.134	.190	.247	28	105	97	8	13	2	0	3	8	6	1	0	1	39	0	0	5.71	37.14
Encarnacion, Luis	R-R	5-8	170	9-25-02	.462	.462	.769	4	13	13	2	6	1	0	1	4	0	0	0	0	1	1	0	0.00	7.69
Encarnacion, Yamal	B-R	5-8	150	9-8-03	.262	.350	.343	61	268	233	46	61	8	1	3	21	31	1	2	1	40	29	5	11.57	14.93
Gomez, Kenni	L-R	5-11	185	5-14-05	.265	.338	.415	87	367	328	44	87	23	4	6	35	34	3	0	2	83	13	8	9.26	22.62
Hernandez, Alberto	R-R	6-0	169	2-4-04	.197	.288	.251	74	271	239	35	47	7	0	2	23	29	2	0	1	61	4	2	10.70	22.51
Hernandez, Cesar	L-L	6-0	197	4-22-03	.230	.312	.304	94	382	335	52	77	15	2	2	34	30	12	0	5	85	34	7	7.85	22.25
Holy, Max	R-R	6-0	185	7-11-02	.167	.337	.182	22	83	66	7	11	1	0	0	5	16	1	0	0	26	17	1	19.28	31.33
Jaworsky, Chase	L-R	6-1	170	7-31-04	.233	.335	.346	78	328	283	45	66	20	0	4	32	29	15	0	1	68	28	6	8.84	20.73
Luciano, Waner	R-R	6-1	170	1-13-05	.187	.299	.270	72	298	252	29	47	12	0	3	22	36	6	0	4	62	1	3	12.08	20.81
Nunez, Alejandro	L-R	5-10	179	9-8-04	.256	.341	.367	92	338	297	52	76	17	2	4	32	36	3	0	1	92	18	3	10.65	27.22
Ochoa, Nehomar	R-R	6-4	210	7-31-05	.222	.317	.359	103	394	343	44	76	15	1	10	44	38	11	0	2	116	17	5	9.64	29.44
Perez, Luis	R-R	5-10	193	10-24-02	.154	.313	.154	5	16	13	2	2	0	0	0	1	2	1	0	0	5	0	3	12.50	31.25
Powell, Caden	R-R	6-2	208	10-24-03	.241	.287	.379	24	94	87	13	21	4	1	2	13	4	2	0	1	34	6	1	4.26	36.17
Ramirez, German	R-R	6-0	179	7-28-06	.000	.000	.000	3	9	9	0	0	0	0	0	0	0	0	0	0	1	0	0	0.00	11.11
Santander, Juan	R-R	6-2	180	12-9-02	.220	.302	.336	65	252	223	23	49	6	1	6	28	27	0	0	2	60	8	2	10.71	23.81
Schiavone, Jason	R-R	6-3	200	3-19-03	.156	.280	.297	20	75	64	8	10	3	0	2	7	10	1	0	0	33	3	0	13.33	44.00
Sherwin, Anthony	L-R	5-11	190	6-20-02	.211	.329	.254	21	85	71	8	15	0	0	1	9	12	1	0	1	25	0	1	14.12	29.41
Spence, Lucas	L-L	6-1	190	1-27-03	.200	.347	.288	24	98	80	10	16	0	2	1	4	15	3	0	0	22	4	2	15.31	22.45
Sullivan, Joseph	L-L	6-0	200	7-1-02	.250	.416	.324	20	89	68	13	17	5	0	0	9	13	7	0	1	11	8	4	14.61	12.36
Villarroel, Jancel	R-R	5-8	176	1-17-05	.233	.339	.321	54	227	193	30	45	9	1	2	28	20	12	0	2	57	7	2	8.81	25.11
Vogel, Drew	R-R	6-1	195	5-28-02	.085	.261	.085	22	88	71	8	6	0	0	0	4	13	4	0	0	17	10	1	14.77	19.32

Pitching	B-T	Ht.	Wt.	DOB	W	L	ERA	G	GS	SV	IP	Hits	Runs	ER	HR	BB	SO	AVG	OBP	SLG	SO%	BB%	BF
Almonte, Dawill	R-R	5-9	168	10-19-01	1	1	3.69	27	0	1	39	33	18	16	5	15	40	.228	.309	.379	24.24	9.09	165
Austin, Kelly	R-R	6-0	195	12-17-00	1	0	0.90	8	0	0	10	7	1	1	0	1	14	.189	.211	.270	36.84	2.63	38
Brito, Anderson	R-R	5-10	155	7-7-04	1	2	2.63	7	5	0	27	19	8	8	4	15	38	.204	.333	.430	34.23	13.51	111
Bush, Will	L-R	6-4	230	3-4-04	0	0	0.00	1	0	0	2	2	0	0	0	0	0	.286	.250	.286	0.00	0.00	8
Caldera, Fernando	R-R	5-11	170	10-10-02	0	0	27.00	1	0	0	1	5	3	3	1	2	0	.714	.700	1.143	0.00	20.00	10
Chirinos, Amilcar	R-R	6-3	200	11-7-01	5	3	4.15	24	0	4	35	31	25	16	1	10	39	.233	.291	.301	26.17	6.71	149
David, Ramsey	R-R	6-3	190	2-8-01	0	0	3.68	4	2	0	7	5	3	3	0	10	10	.192	.447	.192	26.32	26.32	38
Encarnacion, Yamal	S-R	5-8	150	9-8-03	0	0	36.00	1	0	0	1	4	4	4	2	1	0	.571	.667	1.429	0.00	11.11	9
Gonzalez, Rafael	R-R	5-11	195	7-18-04	0	2	6.75	6	1	1	19	16	15	14	2	13	25	.229	.360	.371	29.07	15.12	86
Hertzler, Cole	R-R	6-4	235	6-21-03	0	0	1.80	2	0	0	5	5	1	1	1	3	6	.278	.381	.444	28.57	14.29	21
Hicks, James	R-R	6-2	190	5-9-01	1	0	0.50	4	2	1	18	9	1	1	1	7	25	.143	.229	.206	35.71	10.00	70
Langford, Colby	L-L	6-3	195	4-30-02	4	2	3.32	15	5	0	41	26	16	15	4	28	54	.186	.327	.279	31.58	16.37	171
Leach, Hudson	R-R	6-3	220	6-16-02	1	3	3.60	21	0	1	30	21	17	12	3	22	36	.202	.344	.356	27.69	16.92	130
Marquez, Pedro	R-R	5-11	172	12-7-01	1	1	8.35	5	2	0	18	15	17	17	2	19	15	.227	.416	.364	16.67	21.11	90
Marte, Julio	R-R	6-5	180	4-27-03	2	7	6.84	21	11	1	75	84	69	57	6	40	90	.278	.369	.407	25.50	11.33	353
Mathiesen, Ryan	R-R	6-1	200	6-10-03	0	0	0.00	1	0	0	1	0	0	0	0	1	0	.000	.333	.000	0.00	33.33	3
Mayer, Bryce	R-R	6-3	210	2-11-02	0	0	2.84	3	2	0	6	5	3	2	0	4	10	.208	.367	.208	33.33	13.33	30
Mejia, Sandy	R-R	6-0	160	1-3-04	4	8	5.50	20	13	0	70	63	45	43	8	50	93	.237	.358	.395	28.97	15.58	321
Mercedes, Abel	R-R	6-1	185	6-29-02	2	3	5.16	40	0	6	45	21	30	26	0	55	74	.139	.384	.172	34.26	25.46	216
Murfee, Penn	R-R	6-2	195	5-2-94	0	1	108.00	1	1	0	0	3	4	4	0	1	1	.750	.800	1.000	20.00	20.00	5
Nezuh, Jackson	R-R	6-1	180	2-11-02	7	4	4.41	18	11	0	82	62	44	40	8	32	105	.207	.283	.340	30.97	9.44	339
Nunez, Juan	R-R	6-0	155	10-13-03	2	0	3.21	5	2	0	14	6	7	5	1	9	18	.125	.283	.208	30.00	15.00	60
Ogando, Joan	R-R	6-1	179	5-23-04	1	0	5.27	9	0	0	14	12	10	8	1	13	21	.240	.394	.440	31.82	19.70	66
Palmer, Twine	R-R	6-5	200	8-31-04	0	0	11.57	2	0	0	2	3	5	3	1	5	4	.273	.500	.636	25.00	31.25	16
Pecko, Ethan	R-R	6-2	195	8-25-02	2	2	2.31	13	7	2	47	31	14	12	2	20	63	.186	.275	.269	33.33	10.58	189

Pena, Alain	R-R	5-11	155	4-10-03	3	2	3.42	19	12	1	79	70	33	30	7	28	83	.233	.304	.362	25.00	8.43	332
Peralta, Engel Daniel	R-R	6-4	190	6-3-04	1	2	9.37	6	3	0	16	22	17	17	4	16	20	.328	.471	.672	23.53	18.82	85
Petschke, Ben	R-R	5-11	191	11-9-01	2	1	6.62	21	0	1	35	45	37	26	1	26	23	.308	.417	.397	13.14	14.86	175
Rodriguez, Luis	R-R	6-2	181	12-29-03	2	2	2.86	7	5	0	28	25	9	9	2	15	24	.243	.358	.369	19.51	12.20	123
Rodriguez, Raimy	R-R	6-1	185	7-16-05	3	7	6.53	25	10	1	83	74	67	60	2	76	90	.241	.422	.339	21.48	18.14	419
Sanchez, Wilmy	R-R	5-9	193	12-17-03	0	2	3.82	22	0	0	38	33	19	16	0	26	56	.236	.355	.307	33.14	15.38	169
Sanchez, Yanquiel	L-L	6-3	200	1-28-01	0	4	8.36	6	4	0	14	15	18	13	1	15	23	.273	.437	.345	31.94	20.83	72
Santa, Alimber	R-R	5-10	163	5-3-03	1	1	2.30	6	0	1	16	10	4	4	0	2	26	.185	.211	.259	44.83	3.45	58
Santander, Juan	R-R	6-2	180	12-9-02	0	0	0.00	2	0	1	3	1	0	0	0	1	3	.100	.250	.100	25.00	8.33	12
Santos, Yeriel	R-R	6-0	165	11-20-03	5	5	4.11	25	14	2	101	75	53	46	7	54	104	.204	.313	.316	24.07	12.50	432
Soto, Juan	R-R	6-2	209	4-30-03	0	1	9.53	2	1	0	6	13	6	6	1	3	7	.448	.500	.586	21.88	9.38	32
Tredwell, Alonzo	L-R	6-8	230	5-8-02	1	6	5.37	17	14	0	57	53	37	34	3	38	67	.244	.362	.346	26.07	14.79	257
Trehey, Danny	R-R	6-4	205	6-14-01	1	2	2.53	7	0	0	11	10	4	3	0	7	15	.250	.375	.300	31.25	14.58	48
True, Derek	R-R	6-2	180	4-25-01	1	1	2.49	5	3	0	22	18	8	6	1	6	27	.225	.287	.300	31.03	6.90	87

Fielding

Catcher	PCT	G	PO	A	E	DP	PB
Bush	.986	65	666	58	10	4	12
Caldera	.983	21	209	27	4	4	6
Diaz	1.000	9	101	5	0	1	2
Encarnacion	.909	1	9	1	1	0	1
Santander	.867	3	12	1	2	0	2
Schiavone	.973	13	98	9	3	0	4
Villarroel	.985	25	251	19	4	2	5

First Base	PCT	G	PO	A	E	DP
Austin	1.000	5	28	2	0	3
Bush	.969	10	60	3	2	5
Caldera	1.000	2	1	0	0	1
Carrillo	.976	21	149	13	4	10
Casserilla	.995	34	179	15	1	15
Diaz	.989	13	82	5	1	3
Encarnacion	1.000	2	16	2	0	1
Luciano	1.000	3	1	0	0	0
Nunez	1.000	3	10	0	0	1
Santander	.987	38	220	14	3	14
Schiavone	.982	7	51	3	1	6
Villarroel	.981	9	51	2	1	6

Second Base	PCT	G	PO	A	E	DP
Austin	.947	4	3	15	1	2
Encarnacion	.857	5	7	5	2	3
Hernandez	.923	18	23	25	4	2
Holy	.968	12	20	40	2	9
Jaworsky	.972	22	37	33	2	4
Luciano	.984	18	22	38	1	4
Nunez	.974	45	61	88	4	20
Sherwin	1.000	1	0	2	0	0
Villarroel	1.000	3	9	3	0	1
Vogel	.912	9	13	18	3	6

Third Base	PCT	G	PO	A	E	DP
Austin	.909	8	4	6	1	0
Casserilla	.913	29	21	42	6	3
Diaz	1.000	1	0	1	0	0
Encarnacion	1.000	3	2	0	0	0
Hernandez	.850	10	4	13	3	1
Jaworsky	1.000	8	3	9	0	1
Luciano	.965	48	38	72	4	6
Nunez	1.000	3	0	3	0	1
Powell	.842	11	7	9	3	3
Sherwin	.893	12	11	14	3	1
Vogel	.818	8	5	4	2	1

Shortstop	PCT	G	PO	A	E	DP
Hernandez	.946	48	44	97	8	7
Holy	.973	10	21	15	1	4
Jaworsky	.966	50	63	108	6	12
Luciano	.857	3	3	3	1	1
Nunez	.769	4	0	10	3	1
Powell	.929	10	18	21	3	7
Ramirez	.923	3	4	8	1	2
Vogel	.960	5	10	14	1	3

Outfield	PCT	G	PO	A	E	DP
Austin	1.000	1	1	0	0	0
Carrillo	1.000	14	21	1	0	1
Colon	1.000	10	11	0	0	0
Daniels	1.000	3	4	0	0	0
Encarnacion	.971	53	94	7	3	2
Gomez	.950	72	111	3	6	2
Hernandez	.970	80	130	1	4	0
Luciano	1.000	2	2	0	0	0
Nunez	.981	33	46	5	1	0
Ochoa	.971	100	154	12	5	4
Perez	1.000	5	6	0	0	0
Spence	1.000	23	49	3	0	0
Sullivan	1.000	13	30	1	0	0
Villarroel	1.000	5	4	0	0	0

FCL ASTROS — *ROOKIE*

FLORIDA COMPLEX LEAGUE

Batting	B-T	Ht.	Wt.	DOB	AVG	OBP	SLG	G	PA	AB	R	H	2B	3B	HR	RBI	BB	HBP	SH	SF	SO	SB	CS	BB%	SO%
Abreu, Jose	R-R	6-3	235	1-29-87	.318	.375	.545	5	24	22	5	7	2	0	1	3	1	1	0	0	2	0	0	4.17	8.33
Arias, Bryan	R-R	5-10	205	6-6-97	.115	.148	.115	6	27	26	1	3	0	0	0	1	1	0	0	0	9	0	0	3.70	33.33
Caratini, Victor	B-R	5-11	225	8-17-93	.400	.400	.400	2	5	5	0	2	0	0	0	0	0	0	0	0	1	0	0	0.00	20.00
Cauro, Carlos	R-R	6-2	184	6-14-05	.255	.336	.400	40	125	110	9	28	4	0	4	17	12	2	0	1	30	2	2	9.60	24.00
Cole, Zach	L-R	6-2	190	8-4-00	.273	.385	.545	6	26	22	4	6	1	1	1	2	3	1	0	0	8	1	0	11.54	30.77
Colon, Luis	B-R	5-8	160	12-2-03	.138	.200	.185	24	71	65	12	9	1	1	0	1	5	0	1	0	26	5	0	7.04	36.62
Colon, Rabel	L-R	6-0	175	8-29-03	.253	.426	.422	34	108	83	23	21	3	1	3	8	23	2	0	0	36	11	3	21.30	33.33
De Leon, Darwin	R-R	5-9	156	10-31-03	.429	.429	.714	2	7	7	2	3	2	0	0	1	0	0	0	0	1	0	0	0.00	14.29
Dezenzo, Zach	R-R	6-4	220	5-11-00	.450	.500	.600	5	22	20	3	9	3	0	0	4	2	0	0	0	3	0	0	9.09	13.64
Diaz, Aledmys	R-R	6-1	195	8-1-90	.333	.313	.400	4	16	15	1	5	1	0	0	2	0	0	0	1	1	0	0	0.00	6.25
Diaz, Camilo	R-R	6-3	208	9-5-05	.188	.333	.304	43	168	138	22	26	2	4	2	9	28	2	0	0	69	16	3	16.67	41.07
Diaz, Victor	R-R	5-10	175	11-25-01	.371	.378	.600	13	37	35	9	13	2	0	2	6	1	0	0	1	7	0	0	2.70	18.92
Fisher, Cameron	L-R	6-2	210	6-12-01	.194	.370	.417	11	46	36	6	7	2	0	2	3	8	2	0	0	18	2	1	17.39	39.13
Gittens, Chris	R-R	6-4	250	2-4-94	.214	.389	.214	5	18	14	0	3	0	0	0	1	4	0	0	0	4	0	0	22.22	22.22
Gonzalez, Cristian	R-R	6-3	210	10-22-01	.333	.333	.667	3	9	9	1	3	0	0	1	1	0	0	0	0	1	0	1	0.00	11.11
Huezo, Anthony	L-R	6-2	170	11-2-05	.151	.275	.303	40	142	119	15	18	4	1	4	12	16	5	0	2	57	6	2	11.27	40.14
Machado, Dixon	R-R	6-1	190	2-22-92	.286	.500	.357	4	20	14	3	4	1	0	0	1	3	3	0	0	4	0	0	15.00	20.00
Matthews, Brice	R-R	6-0	175	3-16-02	.462	.611	.615	4	18	13	4	6	2	0	0	1	5	0	0	0	2	3	2	27.78	11.11
Nieves, Hector	L-R	6-3	185	7-8-03	.157	.368	.286	29	95	70	11	11	4	1	1	8	23	1	0	1	41	7	4	24.21	43.16
Palma, Miguel	R-R	5-8	170	1-4-02	.333	.417	.381	6	24	21	1	7	1	0	0	5	2	1	0	0	6	1	1	8.33	25.00
Pratt, Karniel	R-R	5-10	170	1-3-05	.271	.417	.417	24	61	48	10	13	2	1	1	5	11	1	1	0	22	10	3	18.03	36.07
Ramirez, German	R-R	6-0	179	7-28-06	.226	.310	.280	48	187	164	21	37	4	1	1	18	19	2	0	2	53	10	10	10.16	28.34
Ramirez, Rafael	R-R	6-1	185	11-9-04	.186	.326	.300	30	86	70	10	13	2	0	2	8	12	3	0	1	33	5	2	13.95	38.37
Rives, Luis	B-L	6-2	216	10-14-04	.231	.290	.314	40	132	121	19	28	4	0	2	15	10	0	1	0	27	12	3	7.58	20.45
Sosa, Andrews	R-R	5-10	160	1-7-05	.162	.238	.189	16	42	37	2	6	1	0	0	4	2	2	0	1	9	0	0	4.76	21.43
Trujillo, Kedaur	R-R	5-11	188	3-2-04	.272	.362	.395	34	94	81	10	22	7	0	1	9	10	2	0	1	14	0	0	10.64	14.89
Valencia, Esmil	R-R	5-10	182	10-9-05	.289	.331	.376	41	160	149	21	43	3	2	2	18	5	5	0	1	28	16	5	3.13	17.50
Villarroel, Jancel	R-R	5-8	176	1-17-05	.284	.415	.478	22	82	67	11	19	3	2	2	13	11	4	0	0	14	4	3	13.41	17.07

Pitching	B-T	Ht.	Wt.	DOB	W	L	ERA	G	GS	SV	IP	Hits	Runs	ER	HR	BB	SO	AVG	OBP	SLG	SO%	BB%	BF
Aparicio, Antony	R-R	6-2	183	10-18-02	0	0	0.00	3	1	0	9	5	1	0	0	2	13	.156	.206	.156	38.24	5.88	34
Brito, Anderson	R-R	5-10	155	7-7-04	0	0	0.00	1	1	0	4	2	0	0	0	0	4	.143	.143	.214	28.57	0.00	14
Brockhouse, Walker	R-R	6-4	197	2-22-99	0	0	0.00	2	2	0	3	2	0	0	0	0	2	.182	.182	.182	18.18	0.00	11
Carrera, Jesus	R-R	5-11	160	11-27-04	1	2	3.76	10	3	0	26	21	12	11	1	7	30	.219	.276	.323	28.30	6.60	106
Colon, Luis	S-R	5-8	160	12-2-03	0	1	0.00	1	0	0	1	1	1	0	0	0	0	.250	.250	.250	0.00	0.00	4
Coronel, Enrique	R-R	6-0	175	8-25-00	0	2	7.17	13	1	2	21	23	20	17	3	13	26	.274	.371	.417	26.53	13.27	98
Cruz, Anthony	R-R	5-11	179	8-19-02	3	0	2.18	12	3	3	33	17	10	8	2	10	38	.147	.219	.250	29.69	7.81	128
Diaz, Victor	R-R	5-10	175	11-25-01	0	1	36.00	2	0	0	1	4	5	4	1	3	3	.500	.636	.875	27.27	27.27	11
Fleury, Jose	R-R	6-0	185	3-8-02	0	0	0.00	2	2	0	3	0	0	0	0	0	3	.000	.000	.000	33.33	0.00	9
Frias, Francisco	R-R	5-11	190	10-15-04	4	2	7.44	13	0	0	33	25	28	27	1	19	42	.214	.336	.333	29.37	13.29	143
Garcia, Luis	R-R	5-11	244	12-13-96	0	0	0.00	1	1	0	1	0	0	0	0	0	2	.000	.000	.000	66.67	0.00	3
Geraldo, Jorge	R-R	6-6	197	12-7-01	0	1	13.50	4	1	0	7	9	11	11	2	10	10	.290	.476	.548	23.81	23.81	42
Gil, Franklin	R-R	5-11	155	1-6-03	3	2	4.29	11	6	0	36	31	21	17	4	10	43	.221	.278	.379	28.48	6.62	151
Gonzalez, Rafael	R-R	5-11	195	7-18-04	1	1	3.44	7	3	1	18	13	8	7	0	9	25	.194	.286	.239	32.47	11.69	77
Kouba, Rhett	R-R	6-0	180	9-3-99	0	1	9.45	3	3	0	7	10	8	7	1	4	11	.345	.424	.586	33.33	12.12	33
Landeta, David	R-R	6-2	244	3-28-03	0	1	4.38	5	0	0	12	13	8	6	0	9	15	.265	.383	.327	25.00	15.00	60
Leach, Hudson	R-R	6-3	220	6-16-02	0	0	4.91	3	1	0	4	2	3	2	0	4	5	.154	.353	.154	29.41	23.53	17
Marquez, Pedro	R-R	5-11	172	12-7-01	0	0	4.32	5	1	2	8	6	6	4	0	7	17	.188	.333	.313	43.59	17.95	39
Melendez, Jaime	L-R	5-8	190	9-26-01	1	2	5.25	5	2	0	12	14	9	7	1	10	15	.286	.400	.347	25.00	16.67	60
Murray, Jayden	R-R	6-1	190	4-11-97	0	0	3.00	2	2	0	3	3	1	1	1	0	5	.231	.231	.538	38.46	0.00	13
Nunez, Juan	R-R	6-0	155	10-13-03	4	2	2.84	10	2	0	25	16	13	8	1	11	30	.176	.287	.242	27.78	10.19	108
Ogando, Joan	R-R	6-1	179	5-23-04	2	2	6.08	11	2	1	27	26	20	18	1	10	33	.252	.350	.388	27.27	8.26	121
Peralta, Engel Daniel	R-R	6-4	190	6-3-04	2	1	1.48	7	1	0	24	16	9	4	1	7	26	.180	.255	.281	26.26	7.07	99
Rodriguez, Luis	R-R	6-2	181	12-29-03	2	0	1.82	10	2	1	30	23	8	6	1	5	36	.207	.254	.270	30.51	4.24	118
Sanchez, Yanquiel	L-L	6-3	200	1-28-01	1	2	4.05	4	0	0	7	5	4	3	0	3	12	.200	.276	.200	41.38	10.34	29
Santa, Alimber	R-R	5-10	163	5-3-03	0	0	9.00	2	2	0	3	4	3	3	0	1	5	.286	.333	.357	33.33	6.67	15
Trujillo, Kedaur	R-R	5-11	188	3-2-04	0	0	0.00	3	0	0	2	3	1	0	0	3	4	.333	.500	.444	33.33	25.00	12
Varela, Jose	R-R	6-1	183	10-29-04	0	1	3.06	6	4	1	18	10	7	6	2	12	18	.164	.320	.311	24.00	16.00	75
Victorino, Luis	R-R	6-0	167	8-18-02	1	3	3.32	14	5	2	41	30	26	15	2	31	41	.199	.337	.311	22.16	16.76	185
Whitley, Forrest	R-R	6-7	238	9-15-97	0	0	13.50	1	1	0	1	2	2	1	1	2	1	.667	.800	2.000	20.00	40.00	5

Fielding

C: Cauro 17, Trujillo 15, Sosa 12, Villarroel 10, Diaz 6, Palma 6, Caratini 1. **1B:** Cauro 19, Trujillo 12, Diaz 6, Fisher 5, Gittens 5, Villarroel 5, Nieves 5, Ramirez 2, Huezo 2, Abreu 2, Diaz 1, Sosa 1, Palma 1. **2B:** Nieves 21, Colon 18, Ramirez 13, Ramirez 6, Arias 2, Villarroel 1. **3B:** Diaz 23, Ramirez 10, Ramirez 7, Dezenzo 5, Colon 4, Arias 2, Nieves 2, De Leon 1, Diaz 1, Machado 1. **SS:** Ramirez 32, Diaz 11, Gonzalez 3, Machado 3, Matthews 3, Colon 3, Ramirez 2, De Leon 1, Diaz 1. **LF:** Pratt 18, Colon 14, Rives 12, Fisher 4, Huezo 2, Nieves 2, Ramirez 1, Villarroel 1, Diaz 1, Arias 1. **CF:** Valencia 20, Huezo 20, Colon 10, Cole 5, Rives 2. RF: Valencia 19, Rives 18, Huezo 15, Colon 3, Pratt 1.

DSL ASTROS BLUE — *ROOKIE*

DOMINICAN SUMMER LEAGUE

Batting	B-T	Ht.	Wt.	DOB	AVG	OBP	SLG	G	PA	AB	R	H	2B	3B	HR	RBI	BB	HBP	SH	SF	SO	SB	CS	BB%	SO%
Brito, Samuel	R-R	5-11	170	2-1-07	.240	.325	.288	43	120	104	17	25	2	0	1	10	13	1	0	2	35	6	6	10.83	29.17
Castellano, Alejandro	R-R	5-8	159	9-24-06	.217	.373	.217	24	75	60	11	13	0	0	0	2	14	1	0	0	16	1	1	18.67	21.33
De Paula, Axell	R-R	5-10	178	10-18-04	.000	.250	.000	1	4	3	0	0	0	0	0	0	1	0	0	0	0	0	0	25.00	0.00
Diaz, Jhon	R-R	6-0	162	3-26-05	.257	.362	.321	39	130	109	23	28	4	0	1	11	12	7	0	2	23	3	2	9.23	17.69
Flores, Miguel	R-R	6-0	177	6-18-05	.000	.067	.000	6	15	14	1	0	0	0	0	1	1	0	0	0	1	0	0	6.67	6.67
Gonzalez, Cristopfer	R-R	6-5	167	7-20-05	.159	.273	.227	42	154	132	15	21	4	1	1	19	18	3	0	1	34	7	4	11.69	22.08
Lara, Wilton	R-R	5-11	175	1-21-04	.268	.364	.394	41	152	127	25	34	5	1	3	25	14	7	1	3	20	14	3	9.21	13.16
Marcelino, Marco	R-R	5-9	190	10-30-04	.203	.337	.311	27	89	74	12	15	3	1	1	8	13	2	0	0	17	5	0	14.61	19.10
Marte, Angel	R-R	5-11	185	12-28-05	.107	.314	.120	35	102	75	16	8	1	0	0	6	23	1	0	3	34	3	1	22.55	33.33
Ramirez, Amauri	L-L	6-2	203	1-24-07	.211	.315	.303	48	165	142	19	30	8	1	1	13	21	1	0	1	31	5	3	12.73	18.79
Romero, Esteban	L-R	6-2	180	12-1-06	.260	.351	.313	48	172	150	26	39	8	0	0	13	17	4	1	0	25	12	1	9.88	14.53
Salas, Hector	L-R	5-11	145	3-19-04	.271	.406	.386	49	175	140	23	38	7	3	1	20	30	3	0	2	29	18	5	17.14	16.57
Sanchez, Brayan	R-R	6-0	195	12-19-04	.232	.389	.304	28	72	56	13	13	1	0	1	6	15	0	0	1	13	2	1	20.83	18.06
Sierra, Juan	R-R	6-1	208	12-8-05	.270	.374	.497	51	195	163	33	44	10	0	9	33	22	7	0	3	40	10	3	11.28	20.51
Silverio, Franchely	R-R	6-2	201	11-19-06	.211	.291	.286	49	179	161	17	34	7	1	1	15	15	3	0	0	37	2	5	8.38	20.67
Sosa, Andrews	R-R	5-10	160	1-7-05	.333	.385	.417	4	13	12	3	4	1	0	0	2	1	0	0	0	0	0	0	7.69	0.00

Pitching	B-T	Ht.	Wt.	DOB	W	L	ERA	G	GS	SV	IP	Hits	Runs	ER	HR	BB	SO	AVG	OBP	SLG	SO%	BB%	BF
Aguilar, Luis	R-R	5-11	176	4-4-04	2	4	2.44	13	5	1	48	41	23	13	1	17	46	.227	.296	.320	22.55	8.33	204
Aranda, Angel	R-R	6-0	187	3-31-04	0	3	10.67	12	6	0	29	27	36	34	2	38	32	.260	.459	.394	21.92	26.03	146
Aybar, Angel	R-R	6-3	162	4-28-04	0	0	3.00	3	0	0	3	1	1	1	0	6	4	.125	.533	.125	26.67	40.00	15
Balza, Miguel	R-R	6-0	195	5-21-04	1	0	4.91	3	0	0	4	3	2	2	0	2	3	.231	.313	.308	18.75	12.50	16
Borquez, Nick	R-R	6-1	186	7-27-06	0	0	5.30	9	2	1	19	17	14	11	4	7	14	.236	.313	.472	16.87	8.43	83
Brito, Anderson	R-R	5-10	155	7-7-04	3	0	0.40	7	3	0	22	7	2	1	0	6	40	.091	.186	.117	46.51	6.98	86
Gantes, Anthony	R-R	6-1	165	11-25-05	2	3	2.52	13	6	0	39	33	17	11	0	13	34	.234	.293	.270	21.66	8.28	157
Gomez, Miguel	R-R	5-11	152	6-12-06	3	1	4.94	11	1	0	24	22	18	13	2	20	20	.256	.404	.395	18.35	18.35	109
Gonzalez, Edwin	R-R	6-2	153	7-19-04	1	3	4.86	13	5	0	33	22	25	18	0	33	39	.183	.388	.233	23.49	19.88	166
Landeta, David	R-R	6-2	244	3-28-03	1	1	6.48	3	2	0	8	11	7	6	0	8	10	.324	.452	.471	23.81	19.05	42
Maican, Mauricio	R-R	5-10	150	12-28-03	1	0	7.88	12	2	0	24	18	24	21	1	25	27	.212	.417	.318	22.50	20.83	120
Marte, Angel	R-R	5-11	185	12-28-05	0	0	0.00	1	0	0	1	0	0	0	0	0	2	.000	.250	.000	50.00	0.00	4
Mieses, Juan	R-R	6-0	200	3-31-06	2	1	6.55	13	2	0	22	16	18	16	1	16	19	.205	.388	.308	18.45	15.53	103
Movilio, Miguel	R-R	5-11	185	8-24-06	0	3	3.78	10	0	2	17	12	11	7	1	15	18	.197	.375	.279	21.95	18.29	82
Nunez, Miguel	L-L	6-2	180	7-7-05	0	0	8.22	6	2	1	8	7	8	7	0	11	4	.259	.500	.296	10.00	27.50	40

Pitching	B-T	Ht.	Wt.	DOB	W	L	ERA	G	GS	SV	IP	Hits	Runs	ER	HR	BB	SO	AVG	OBP	SLG	SO%	BB%	BF
Peralta, Jean	R-R	6-4	185	7-5-03	1	2	5.52	11	6	0	15	12	10	9	0	12	15	.231	.369	.346	23.08	18.46	65
Perez, Javier	R-R	6-1	220	12-22-03	0	1	1.31	9	8	0	21	10	6	3	0	4	23	.141	.187	.239	30.26	5.26	76
Presinal, Cristopher	R-R	6-2	156	11-28-04	1	6	9.00	13	3	0	28	27	38	28	0	39	29	.255	.464	.302	19.21	25.83	151
Ramos, Porfirio	R-R	5-10	163	12-3-03	4	0	1.21	13	0	2	30	20	5	4	1	9	29	.189	.271	.283	24.58	7.63	118
Rodriguez, Luis	R-R	6-2	183	6-12-03	0	0	9.00	1	1	0	1	0	1	1	0	1	2	.000	.250	.000	50.00	25.00	4
Santana, Kevin	R-R	6-4	175	1-18-07	1	0	9.82	3	0	0	4	2	5	4	0	7	6	.200	.524	.200	28.57	33.33	21
Valencia, Josue	R-R	6-2	165	8-11-05	2	1	9.45	11	0	0	13	9	14	14	2	14	8	.200	.403	.400	12.90	22.58	62

Fielding

C: Marte 25, Sanchez 23, Castellano 17, Flores 4, Sosa 1. **1B:** Salas 13, Gonzalez 12, Castellano 8, Diaz 7, Sanchez 7, Marte 7, Lara 4, Sierra 2, Sosa 2. **2B:** Brito 22, Salas 18, Diaz 15, Lara 5, Sosa 1. **3B:** Diaz 16, Lara 16, Silverio 16, Brito 10, Salas 8. **SS:** Silverio 30, Lara 14, Salas 10, Brito 4. **LF:** Romero 18, Sierra 18, Ramirez 8, Gonzalez 6, Marcelino 5, Lara 1. **CF:** Ramirez 28, Romero 14, Gonzalez 9, Sierra 5. **RF:** Marcelino 17, Sierra 17, Romero 10, Gonzalez 9, Ramirez 5.

DSL ASTROS ORANGE — ROOKIE

DOMINICAN SUMMER LEAGUE

Batting	B-T	Ht.	Wt.	DOB	AVG	OBP	SLG	G	PA	AB	R	H	2B	3B	HR	RBI	BB	HBP	SH	SF	SO	SB	CS	BB%	SO%
Almanzar, Yariell	R-R	6-2	185	5-17-06	.165	.270	.211	40	128	109	11	18	3	1	0	4	13	3	2	1	40	5	0	10.16	31.25
Caldera, Francisco	R-R	6-1	193	3-9-06	.228	.338	.307	49	151	127	13	29	4	0	2	23	16	6	0	2	26	9	1	10.60	17.22
Campos, Diego	R-R	6-1	192	10-30-06	.133	.278	.178	22	54	45	3	6	2	0	0	1	9	0	0	0	13	0	0	16.67	24.07
Capellan, Samuel	R-R	5-11	155	1-5-05	.150	.313	.313	30	99	80	14	12	3	2	2	7	15	4	0	0	30	8	2	15.15	30.30
Flores, Miguel	R-R	6-0	177	6-18-05	.278	.409	.389	10	22	18	3	5	2	0	0	2	2	2	0	0	8	0	0	9.09	36.36
Gonzalez, Cristopfer	R-R	6-5	167	7-20-05	.333	.429	.750	4	14	12	3	4	3	1	0	2	2	0	0	0	1	1	0	14.29	7.14
Liriano, Eudy	R-R	5-10	160	5-27-04	.286	.375	.286	15	8	7	1	2	0	0	0	1	1	0	0	0	2	0	0	12.50	25.00
Morgado, Leandro	R-R	5-10	155	2-16-07	.218	.271	.324	54	188	170	28	37	12	0	2	20	9	5	0	4	30	12	5	4.79	15.96
Mujica, Jesus	R-R	5-11	179	9-2-05	.215	.321	.380	41	140	121	17	26	8	0	4	12	15	4	0	0	34	3	1	10.71	24.29
Peralta, Angel	R-R	6-1	160	10-23-06	.000	.000	.000	14	3	3	0	0	0	0	0	0	0	0	0	0	3	0	0	0.00	100.00
Pereira, Sandro	B-R	5-7	147	9-30-05	.331	.464	.400	44	167	130	27	43	7	1	0	18	28	6	1	2	30	8	3	16.77	17.96
Perez, Eduardo	R-R	6-4	214	7-24-06	.214	.333	.429	19	66	56	10	12	6	0	2	7	4	6	0	0	33	2	1	6.06	50.00
Quesada, Luis	R-R	6-2	193	1-18-05	.202	.379	.415	35	124	94	16	19	3	1	5	19	18	10	0	2	26	4	1	14.52	20.97
Quintana, Roiner	R-R	5-11	157	6-20-05	.144	.304	.212	42	148	118	20	17	3	1	1	8	25	3	0	2	23	15	1	16.89	15.54
Quiroz, Alexi	R-R	6-0	205	10-26-06	.165	.398	.253	36	113	79	11	13	5	1	0	9	28	4	0	2	24	2	0	24.78	21.24
Robledo, Jose	B-R	5-7	188	9-14-03	.236	.318	.331	54	203	178	28	42	12	1	1	20	17	5	2	1	47	13	4	8.37	23.15
Sanchez, Julio	R-R	6-1	201	7-29-05	.000	.250	.000	13	4	3	1	0	0	0	0	1	1	0	0	0	3	0	0	25.00	75.00
Tejeda, Jose	R-R	6-3	205	5-14-04	.000	.000	.000	13	5	5	0	0	0	0	0	0	0	0	0	0	4	0	0	0.00	80.00
Vasquez, Yosweld	R-R	5-9	176	11-8-04	.267	.382	.407	29	103	86	15	23	9	0	1	9	13	3	1	0	15	3	1	12.62	14.56
Villalobos, Dionel	R-R	6-2	205	9-27-05	.000	.333	.000	12	3	2	0	0	0	0	0	0	1	0	0	0	1	0	0	33.33	33.33
Yan, Frailin	R-R	6-2	185	5-10-04	.176	.369	.222	47	142	108	20	19	2	0	1	12	29	4	1	0	48	9	11	20.42	33.80

Pitching	B-T	Ht.	Wt.	DOB	W	L	ERA	G	GS	SV	IP	Hits	Runs	ER	HR	BB	SO	AVG	OBP	SLG	SO%	BB%	BF
Ardines, Adrian	R-R	6-0	186	10-16-06	0	4	8.27	13	2	0	21	30	24	19	2	20	21	.333	.459	.544	18.92	18.02	111
Baez, Jhoster	R-R	6-3	205	12-11-04	1	2	3.89	12	6	0	37	30	17	16	2	19	41	.216	.319	.345	24.47	11.80	161
Caldera, Francisco	R-R	6-1	193	3-9-06	0	0	0.00	1	0	0	1	1	0	0	0	0	0	.333	.333	1.000	0.00	0.00	3
De La Cruz, Cristian	R-R	5-11	194	1-16-03	0	0	13.50	2	1	0	3	2	4	4	0	4	1	.200	.429	.200	7.14	28.57	14
Diaz, Norbis	R-R	6-0	165	8-10-04	0	1	2.93	10	9	0	28	23	10	9	1	12	23	.228	.310	.297	20.18	10.53	114
Henriquez, Marcos	R-R	6-4	190	7-3-04	1	1	15.85	13	0	0	15	19	31	27	1	28	13	.322	.547	.475	13.68	29.47	95
Liriano, Eudy	R-R	5-10	160	5-27-04	3	2	5.57	13	2	1	32	31	24	20	3	15	28	.250	.331	.435	19.72	10.56	142
Marquez, Pedro	R-R	5-11	172	12-7-01	0	0	2.79	3	2	0	10	6	4	3	0	9	11	.176	.364	.294	25.00	20.45	44
Martinez, Jeremy	R-R	6-2	200	6-7-04	3	4	5.30	16	6	1	36	30	28	21	6	21	35	.221	.331	.419	21.47	12.88	163
Mota, Eddy	R-R	6-3	210	2-13-04	0	0	0.00	5	0	0	7.2	4	0	0	0	3	4	.154	.241	.154	13.79	10.34	29
Nunez, Jesus	R-R	6-4	220	9-28-05	1	1	5.09	8	3	0	18	10	12	10	0	16	10	.169	.354	.220	12.66	20.25	79
Peralta, Angel	R-R	6-1	160	10-23-06	0	2	7.83	13	3	1	23	13	23	20	2	28	33	.155	.393	.262	27.97	23.73	118
Pichardo, Jank	R-R	6-1	170	8-4-04	4	4	6.95	15	4	2	34	34	34	26	0	27	40	.262	.405	.331	24.54	16.56	163
Rivero, Gabriel	R-R	6-0	186	11-10-04	1	1	1.40	11	2	2	26	14	7	4	0	16	34	.169	.307	.217	33.33	15.69	102
Rodriguez, Mauricio	R-R	6-6	175	7-30-04	2	0	7.32	15	0	1	20	22	20	16	1	19	21	.286	.455	.481	20.79	18.81	101
Salazar, Mario	R-R	6-2	195	1-11-05	2	3	8.53	13	0	1	19	12	23	18	1	20	16	.182	.393	.318	17.98	22.47	89
Sanchez, Julio	R-R	6-1	201	7-29-05	1	1	8.10	12	0	1	17	17	16	15	2	17	10	.298	.447	.421	13.16	22.37	76
Serrano, Jose	R-R	6-2	212	2-14-04	2	2	2.63	13	12	0	48	42	18	14	1	22	46	.236	.330	.315	22.66	10.84	203
Tejeda, Jose	R-R	6-3	205	5-14-04	1	1	24.65	11	0	0	8	12	21	21	2	24	7	.364	.650	.636	11.67	40.00	60
Villalobos, Dionel	R-R	6-2	205	9-27-05	1	3	4.56	11	3	0	26	21	16	13	2	14	15	.219	.330	.365	13.39	12.50	112

Fielding

C: Caldera 28, Quiroz 23, Vasquez 10, Campos 8, Flores 4. **1B:** Caldera 24, Quesada 14, Quiroz 14, Vasquez 9, Mujica 7, Campos 3, Flores 1, Almanzar 1. **2B:** Pereira 32, Almanzar 10, Capellan 8, Vasquez 8, Robledo 7. **3B:** Mujica 21, Robledo 20, Almanzar 12, Pereira 6, Vasquez 2. **SS:** Robledo 26, Almanzar 16, Mujica 15. **LF:** Yan 19, Morgado 17, Capellan 12, Quesada 8, Quintana 6, Pereira 1, Gonzalez 1. **CF:** Quintana 23, Morgado 20, Yan 13, Perez 2, Capellan 1, Gonzalez 1. **RF:** Morgado 15, Quesada 12, Yan 11, Perez 10, Quintana 9, Capellan 3, Gonzalez 2, Liriano 1, Almanzar 1, Campos 1, Sanchez 1, Tejeda 1.

Kansas City Royals

SEASON SYNOPSIS: After tying a franchise record with 106 losses in 2023, Kansas City overhauled its rotation and roster with a series of free-agent signings, then rode its pitching and an elite season by homegrown star Bobby Witt Jr. to improve by 30 wins. It was good enough for the franchise's first playoff appearance in a decade, a run that ended in a division-series loss to the Yankees.

HIGH POINT: Kansas City had several in the regular season, but the Wild Card Series win in Baltimore summed up the Royals' season because they gave up only one run in two games, powered by strong pitching. Lefty Cole Ragans struck out eight and walked none in six shutout innings in the playoff opener, while Seth Lugo pitched into the fifth and yielded only one run. Witt drove in the winning run in the sixth inning in each game, leading to 1–0 and 2-1 victories, both saved by new closer Lucas Erceg.

LOW POINT: Kansas City had two seven-game losing streaks, both in September, the second one ending Sept. 22 with a second straight shutout loss at home to the Giants. First baseman Vinnie Pasquantino's broken thumb and absence from the lineup was felt acutely when the club scored just 74 runs in 25 September games (11-14).

NOTABLE ROOKIES: The Royals relied more on young veterans and imports, with 2020 first-rounder Nick Loftin (.519 OPS) providing some value as a multi-position utility player early in the season before the league caught up to him.

KEY TRANSACTIONS: GM J.J. Picollo and his front office were active in the offseason, signing Lugo and righty Michael Wacha to join Ragans and Brady Singer in the rotation; the veterans combined for 62 starts and 29 wins, with Lugo earning his first all-star recognition. Fellow free-agent acquisitions Adam Frazier, Garrett Hampson, Hunter Renfroe, Will Smith and Chris Stratton weren't nearly as productive but did help change the organization's vibes and raise the floor entering the season. The hard-throwing Erceg, acquired from Oakland, was the most important in-season pickup, picking up 11 saves with a 31-3 strikeout-walk ratio in 25 innings as a Royal. Kansas City also added veterans Tommy Pham (St. Louis), Paul DeJong (White Sox) and even Yuli Gurriel (Braves) in trades in July and August, all of whom made playoff starts.

OPENING DAY PAYROLL: $115,257,261 (21st)

PLAYERS OF THE YEAR

MAJOR LEAGUE

Bobby Witt Jr.
SS
.332/.389/.588
32 HR, 31 SB
211 hits led MLB

MINOR LEAGUE

Blake Mitchell
C
(A/A+)
.232/.368/.424
18 HR, 26 SB

ORGANIZATION LEADERS

Batting		***Qualifiers**
MAJORS		
* AVG	Bobby Witt Jr.	.332
* OPS	Bobby Witt Jr.	.977
HR	Bobby Witt Jr.	32
RBI	Bobby Witt Jr.	109
MINORS		
* AVG	Drew Waters, Omaha	.290
* OBP	Drew Waters, Omaha	.379
* SLG	Drew Waters, Omaha	.494
* OPS	Drew Waters, Omaha	.873
R	John Rave, Omaha	93
H	John Rave, Omaha	129
TB	John Rave, Omaha	234
2B	Drew Waters, Omaha	33
3B	Carter Jensen, Surprise/Quad Cities/NW Arkansas	6
3B	Yandel Ricardo, DSL Royals Blue	6
HR	John Rave, Omaha	21
HR	Spencer Nivens, ACL Royals/Quad Cities	21
RBI	Cam Devanney, Omaha	77
BB	Blake Mitchell, Quad Cities/Columbia	80
SO	Trevor Werner, Quad Cities	178
SB	Tyler Tolbert, Omaha/NW Arkansas	48

Pitching		**#Qualifiers**
MAJORS		
W	Seth Lugo	16
# ERA	Seth Lugo	3.00
SO	Cole Ragans	223
SV	James McArthur	18
MINORS		
W	Ethan Bosacker, Quad Cities/Columbia	13
L	Chandler Champlain, Omaha/NW Arkansas	10
# ERA	Ethan Bosacker, Quad Cities/Columbia	2.45
G	Evan Sisk, Omaha	58
GS	Chandler Champlain, Omaha/NW Arkansas	27
SV	Evan Sisk, Omaha	15
IP	Chandler Champlain, Omaha/NW Arkansas	140
BB	Tyson Guerrero, Omaha/NW Arkansas	57
SO	Noah Cameron, Omaha/NW Arkansas	149
# AVG	Felix Arronde, Columbia	.205

2024 PERFORMANCE

General Manager: J.J. Picollo. **Farm Director:** Mitch Maier. **Scouting Director:** Danny Ontiveros.

Class	Team	League	W	L	PCT	Finish	Manager
Majors	Kansas City Royals	American	86	76	.531	6 (15)	Matt Quatraro
Triple-A	Omaha Storm Chasers	International	89	59	.601	1 (20)	Mike Jirschele
Double-A	NW Arkansas Naturals	Texas	66	71	.482	5 (10)	Tommy Shields
High-A	Quad Cities River Bandits	Midwest	68	63	.519	5 (12)	Brooks Conrad
Low-A	Columbia Fireflies	Carolina	68	63	.519	7 (12)	Jesus Azuaje
Rookie	ACL Royals	Arizona Complex	25	35	.417	12 (15)	Larry Sutton
Rookie	DSL Royals Blue	Dominican	32	22	.593	12 (51)	Sergio De Luna
Overall 2024 Minor League Record			**365**	**347**	**.513**	**14th (30)**	

ORGANIZATION STATISTICS

KANSAS CITY ROYALS

AMERICAN LEAGUE

Batting	B-T	Ht.	Wt.	DOB	AVG	OBP	SLG	G	PA	AB	R	H	2B	3B	HR	RBI	BB	HBP	SH	SF	SO	SB	CS	BB%	SO%
Alexander, CJ	L-R	6-3	215	7-17-96	.125	.125	.125	4	8	8	0	1	0	0	0	0	0	0	0	0	3	0	0	0.00	37.50
Blanco, Dairon	R-R	5-11	170	4-26-93	.258	.308	.392	88	132	120	37	31	4	0	4	13	8	1	1	1	32	31	7	6.06	24.24
DeJong, Paul	R-R	6-0	205	8-2-93	.222	.277	.417	37	119	108	15	24	3	0	6	15	9	0	0	2	44	0	1	7.56	36.97
Fermin, Freddy	R-R	5-9	200	5-16-95	.271	.319	.366	111	368	339	40	92	14	0	6	36	23	2	1	3	66	2	0	6.25	17.93
Frazier, Adam	L-R	5-10	180	12-14-91	.202	.282	.294	104	294	262	35	53	10	1	4	22	22	7	3	0	59	3	0	7.48	20.07
Garcia, Maikel	R-R	6-0	145	3-3-00	.231	.281	.332	157	626	575	84	133	27	5	7	58	42	0	4	5	103	37	2	6.71	16.45
Gentry, Tyler	R-R	6-0	210	2-1-99	.000	.000	.000	3	5	5	0	0	0	0	0	0	0	0	0	0	2	0	0	0.00	40.00
Grossman, Robbie	B-L	6-0	209	9-16-89	.125	.263	.125	16	38	32	2	4	0	0	0	2	5	1	0	0	13	0	0	13.16	34.21
Gurriel, Yuli	R-R	6-0	215	6-9-84	.241	.338	.296	18	65	54	7	13	3	0	0	6	9	0	0	2	15	1	0	13.85	23.08
Hampson, Garrett	R-R	5-11	196	10-10-94	.230	.275	.300	113	231	213	16	49	13	1	0	16	14	0	2	2	59	7	2	6.06	25.54
Isbel, Kyle	L-R	5-11	190	3-3-97	.229	.287	.367	136	426	384	62	88	13	8	8	42	27	5	8	2	88	11	2	6.34	20.66
Loftin, Nick	R-R	5-11	180	9-25-98	.189	.282	.236	57	171	148	15	28	4	0	1	14	19	1	1	2	24	1	0	11.11	14.04
Massey, Michael	L-R	6-0	190	3-22-98	.259	.294	.449	100	356	332	45	86	17	2	14	45	15	3	2	4	56	1	0	4.21	15.73
Melendez, MJ	L-R	6-1	190	11-29-98	.206	.273	.400	135	451	412	44	85	23	3	17	44	35	3	0	0	113	4	4	7.76	25.06
Pasquantino, Vinnie	L-L	6-4	245	10-10-97	.262	.315	.446	131	554	496	64	130	30	2	19	97	40	4	1	13	71	1	0	7.22	12.82
Perez, Salvador	R-R	6-3	255	5-10-90	.271	.330	.456	158	652	590	58	160	28	0	27	104	44	11	0	6	129	0	0	6.75	19.79
Pham, Tommy	R-R	6-1	223	3-8-88	.228	.250	.337	23	104	101	9	23	3	1	2	8	3	0	0	0	27	1	0	2.88	25.96
Renfroe, Hunter	R-R	6-1	230	1-28-92	.229	.297	.392	120	424	385	44	88	18	0	15	52	36	2	0	1	84	1	1	8.49	19.81
Velazquez, Nelson	R-R	6-0	190	12-26-98	.200	.274	.366	64	230	205	31	41	8	1	8	27	19	3	0	3	61	2	0	8.26	26.52
Waters, Drew	B-R	6-0	185	12-30-98	.188	.316	.250	7	19	16	2	3	1	0	0	1	2	1	0	0	6	0	0	10.53	31.58
Witt, Bobby	R-R	6-1	200	6-14-00	.332	.389	.588	161	709	636	125	211	45	11	32	109	57	8	0	8	106	31	12	8.04	14.95

Pitching	B-T	Ht.	Wt.	DOB	W	L	ERA	G	GS	SV	IP	Hits	Runs	ER	HR	BB	SO	AVG	OBP	SLG	SO%	BB%	BF
Altavilla, Dan	R-R	5-11	226	9-8-92	0	1	14.73	5	1	0	4	5	6	6	1	3	5	.313	.450	.563	23.81	14.29	21
Anderson, Nick	R-R	6-4	205	7-5-90	3	1	4.04	37	0	1	36	35	17	16	6	15	29	.259	.333	.474	18.95	9.80	153
Bowlan, Jonathan	R-R	6-6	240	12-1-96	0	1	13.50	1	1	0	3	6	4	4	3	3	3	.429	.529	1.071	17.65	17.65	17
Bubic, Kris	L-L	6-3	225	8-19-97	1	1	2.67	27	0	1	30	26	12	9	2	5	39	.232	.261	.348	32.23	4.13	121
Cruz, Steven	R-R	6-7	225	6-15-99	0	0	0.00	5	0	0	6	1	0	0	0	0	4	.056	.056	.056	22.22	0.00	18
Duffey, Tyler	R-R	6-3	220	12-27-90	1	0	5.00	9	0	0	9	7	5	5	0	8	10	.219	.381	.313	23.81	19.05	42
Erceg, Lucas	L-R	6-2	214	5-1-95	0	3	2.88	23	0	11	25	18	9	8	0	3	31	.194	.227	.237	31.96	3.09	97
Harvey, Hunter	R-R	6-3	239	12-9-94	0	0	6.35	6	0	1	6	8	4	4	1	4	5	.333	.448	.625	17.24	13.79	29
Hernandez, Carlos	R-R	6-4	245	3-11-97	0	1	3.30	27	0	0	30	24	14	11	1	16	27	.220	.318	.321	20.93	12.40	129
Klein, Will	R-R	6-5	230	11-28-99	1	0	6.35	5	0	0	6	10	4	4	0	2	6	.400	.444	.520	22.22	7.41	27
Long, Sam	L-L	6-1	185	7-8-95	3	3	3.16	43	0	1	43	34	17	15	5	17	44	.218	.297	.353	25.00	9.66	176
Lorenzen, Michael	R-R	6-3	217	1-4-92	2	0	1.57	7	6	0	29	19	6	5	2	12	22	.183	.274	.298	18.80	10.26	117
Lugo, Seth	R-R	6-4	225	11-17-89	16	9	3.00	33	33	0	207	177	75	69	16	48	181	.229	.281	.353	21.65	5.74	836
Lyles, Jordan	R-R	6-5	230	10-19-90	0	0	0.00	5	0	0	5	2	0	0	0	2	3	.118	.211	.235	15.79	10.53	19
Lynch, Daniel	L-L	6-6	200	11-17-96	2	0	3.32	16	3	1	43	29	17	16	6	14	39	.188	.270	.344	22.41	8.05	174
Marsh, Alec	R-R	6-2	220	5-14-98	9	9	4.53	26	25	0	129	123	70	65	19	39	123	.249	.316	.434	22.45	7.12	548
McArthur, James	R-R	6-7	230	12-11-96	5	7	4.92	57	0	18	57	68	36	31	8	14	49	.298	.346	.456	19.84	5.67	247
Pennington, Walter	L-L	6-2	205	4-14-98	0	0	0.00	1	0	0	1	0	0	0	0	0	1	.000	.000	.000	50.00	0.00	2
Ragans, Cole	L-L	6-4	190	12-12-97	11	9	3.14	32	32	0	186	146	71	65	15	67	223	.213	.289	.334	29.27	8.79	762
Sauer, Matt	R-R	6-4	195	1-21-99	0	0	7.71	14	0	0	16	23	14	14	3	11	9	.324	.417	.535	10.71	13.10	84
Schreiber, John	R-R	6-2	210	3-5-94	4	3	3.66	59	0	2	52	48	23	21	1	20	46	.242	.321	.318	20.54	8.93	224
Selby, Colin	R-R	6-2	220	10-24-97	0	0	6.00	2	0	0	3	2	3	2	0	2	0	.182	.308	.182	0.00	15.38	13
Singer, Brady	R-R	6-5	215	8-4-96	9	13	3.71	32	32	0	180	175	77	74	22	54	170	.253	.315	.405	22.31	7.09	762
Smith, Will	R-L	6-5	255	7-10-89	0	4	6.53	45	0	1	41	45	31	30	7	15	29	.273	.342	.467	15.59	8.06	186
Stratton, Chris	R-R	6-2	205	8-22-90	4	3	5.55	57	0	4	58	53	38	36	5	33	44	.248	.348	.397	17.12	12.84	257
Veneziano, Anthony	L-L	6-5	205	9-1-97	0	0	4.50	2	0	0	2	4	2	1	0	1	2	.400	.455	.500	18.18	9.09	11
Wacha, Michael	R-R	6-6	215	7-1-91	13	8	3.35	29	29	0	167	154	65	62	17	45	145	.246	.300	.387	21.17	6.57	685
Zerpa, Angel	L-L	6-0	220	9-27-99	2	0	3.86	60	0	0	54	59	24	23	6	19	49	.273	.336	.403	20.50	7.95	239

Fielding

Catcher	PCT	G	PO	A	E	DP	PB
Fermin	.993	91	634	35	5	2	4
Perez	.993	91	730	25	5	7	3

First Base	PCT	G	PO	A	E	DP
Frazier	.000	1	0	0	0	0
Gurriel	1.000	12	76	6	0	4
Hampson	1.000	8	16	2	0	2
Loftin	.947	7	17	1	1	1
Melendez	1.000	1	3	0	0	0
Pasquantino	.998	103	805	71	2	76
Perez	1.000	49	334	25	0	31
Renfroe	1.000	1	1	0	0	1

Second Base	PCT	G	PO	A	E	DP
Frazier	.985	43	46	83	2	12
Garcia	.973	37	44	65	3	15
Hampson	.980	24	16	33	1	8
Loftin	.980	28	35	65	2	15
Massey	.990	82	122	177	3	39

Third Base	PCT	G	PO	A	E	DP
Alexander	1.000	3	1	3	0	0
DeJong	.986	30	24	49	1	6
Frazier	.857	9	2	4	1	1
Garcia	.961	124	66	203	11	13
Hampson	1.000	2	0	1	0	0
Loftin	.974	17	15	23	1	5

Shortstop	PCT	G	PO	A	E	DP
DeJong	.000	1	0	0	0	0
Garcia	1.000	4	1	4	0	1
Hampson	1.000	8	3	2	0	0
Witt	.974	160	207	361	15	78

Outfield	PCT	G	PO	A	E	DP
Blanco	.964	72	79	1	3	0
Frazier	1.000	36	47	3	0	1
Garcia	1.000	1	1	0	0	0
Gentry	1.000	3	1	0	0	0
Grossman	1.000	2	3	0	0	0
Hampson	.983	87	113	2	2	1
Isbel	.987	136	293	1	4	1
Loftin	.000	4	0	0	0	0
Melendez	.990	124	190	2	2	1
Pham	1.000	20	34	2	0	0
Renfroe	.991	116	200	9	2	2
Velazquez	.970	21	32	0	1	0
Waters	.909	7	9	1	1	0

OMAHA STORM CHASERS — *TRIPLE-A*

INTERNATIONAL LEAGUE

Batting	B-T	Ht.	Wt.	DOB	AVG	OBP	SLG	G	PA	AB	R	H	2B	3B	HR	RBI	BB	HBP	SH	SF	SO	SB	CS	BB%	SO%
Alexander, CJ	L-R	6-3	215	7-17-96	.303	.352	.554	82	350	323	56	98	23	5	16	54	23	2	0	1	77	2	3	6.57	22.00
Brito, Chris	R-R	6-2	215	9-28-99	.500	.500	.500	1	2	2	1	1	0	0	0	2	0	0	0	0	0	0	0	0.00	0.00
Brosseau, Mike	R-R	5-11	203	3-15-94	.107	.212	.143	9	33	28	3	3	1	0	0	3	3	1	0	1	8	0	0	9.09	24.24
Devanney, Cam	R-R	6-1	195	4-13-97	.254	.336	.445	136	524	461	69	117	27	2	19	77	47	11	3	2	136	8	4	8.97	25.95
Duran, Rodolfo	R-R	5-8	181	2-19-98	.265	.299	.363	27	108	102	10	27	4	0	2	15	4	1	1	0	18	1	0	3.70	16.67
Eaton, Nate	R-R	5-11	185	12-22-96	.252	.298	.439	116	464	428	65	108	30	1	16	60	27	2	5	2	108	27	4	5.82	23.28
Fitzgerald, Ryan	L-R	6-0	185	6-17-94	.244	.336	.418	108	431	373	54	91	17	3	14	54	43	10	3	2	99	3	3	9.98	22.97
Gentry, Tyler	R-R	6-0	210	2-1-99	.251	.338	.422	121	489	431	68	108	24	1	16	59	53	4	1	0	149	8	1	10.84	30.47
Lester, Josh	L-R	6-3	180	7-17-94	.100	.250	.100	3	12	10	1	1	0	0	0	1	2	0	0	0	2	0	0	16.67	16.67
Loftin, Nick	R-R	5-11	180	9-25-98	.302	.409	.462	58	254	212	34	64	13	0	7	35	37	3	0	2	37	4	2	14.57	14.57
Mann, Devin	R-R	6-2	180	2-11-97	.257	.358	.420	101	403	343	58	88	17	0	13	52	48	7	3	2	90	4	2	11.91	22.33
Massey, Michael	L-R	6-0	190	3-22-98	.333	.370	.588	12	54	51	11	17	7	0	2	10	3	0	0	0	7	1	0	5.56	12.96
Nola, Austin	R-R	6-0	197	12-28-89	.174	.260	.298	55	191	161	19	28	5	0	5	24	17	2	10	1	45	0	0	8.90	23.56
O'Keefe, Brian	R-R	6-1	210	7-15-93	.281	.364	.554	72	280	242	36	68	12	0	18	58	34	0	0	4	55	0	1	12.14	19.64
Padlo, Kevin	R-R	5-11	210	7-15-96	.103	.213	.282	12	47	39	5	4	1	0	2	5	6	0	0	2	15	0	0	12.77	31.91
Porter, Logan	R-R	6-0	200	7-12-95	.319	.428	.575	32	138	113	22	36	9	1	6	22	22	1	0	2	34	1	0	15.94	24.64
Pratto, Nick	L-L	6-1	215	10-6-98	.242	.324	.410	115	490	429	70	104	20	2	16	61	53	1	3	4	149	15	1	10.82	30.41
Rave, John	L-L	5-9	185	12-30-97	.259	.346	.470	131	578	498	93	129	32	5	21	60	65	3	8	4	125	17	5	11.25	21.63
Russell, Stone	R-R	6-1	195	6-17-04	.167	.167	.167	3	6	6	1	1	0	0	0	0	0	0	0	0	2	0	0	0.00	33.33
Tolbert, Tyler	R-R	6-0	160	1-27-98	.141	.247	.167	27	90	78	10	11	2	0	0	3	9	2	1	0	25	8	1	10.00	27.78
Velazquez, Nelson	R-R	6-0	190	12-26-98	.239	.356	.415	56	225	188	22	45	10	1	7	33	34	1	0	2	47	6	3	15.11	20.89
Waters, Drew	B-R	6-0	185	12-30-98	.290	.379	.494	109	457	393	84	114	33	4	13	61	53	6	0	5	121	20	7	11.60	26.48

Pitching	B-T	Ht.	Wt.	DOB	W	L	ERA	G	GS	SV	IP	Hits	Runs	ER	HR	BB	SO	AVG	OBP	SLG	SO%	BB%	BF
Altavilla, Dan	R-R	5-11	226	9-8-92	1	2	3.51	37	0	3	41	33	16	16	5	22	38	.223	.322	.372	22.22	12.87	171
Avila, Luinder	R-R	6-3	195	8-21-01	0	0	10.38	1	1	0	4	5	5	5	0	4	3	.294	.409	.412	13.64	18.18	22
Bowlan, Jonathan	R-R	6-6	240	12-1-96	12	4	4.67	35	16	0	104	106	61	54	14	34	98	.262	.327	.421	21.83	7.57	449
Brentz, Jake	L-L	6-1	205	9-14-94	0	1	13.50	8	0	0	6	5	9	9	1	17	6	.227	.585	.455	14.63	41.46	41
Bubic, Kris	L-L	6-3	225	8-19-97	1	1	2.63	9	5	0	27	23	8	8	1	10	29	.223	.298	.301	25.44	8.77	114
Cameron, Noah	L-L	6-3	220	7-17-99	3	2	2.32	9	9	0	54	44	14	14	6	11	62	.220	.262	.350	28.97	5.14	214
Cerantola, Eric	R-R	6-5	225	5-2-00	1	1	3.77	13	0	0	14	13	6	6	3	8	20	.245	.349	.472	31.25	12.50	64
Cessa, Luis	R-R	6-0	222	4-25-92	2	2	3.89	11	10	0	39	44	25	17	6	16	29	.282	.347	.468	16.76	9.25	173
Champlain, Chandler	R-R	6-5	220	7-23-99	4	9	5.61	21	20	0	104	117	68	65	17	46	72	.283	.360	.465	15.48	9.89	465
Cox, Austin	L-L	6-4	235	3-28-97	2	1	4.25	38	5	0	55	53	30	26	8	38	60	.259	.373	.420	24.00	15.20	250
Cruz, Steven	R-R	6-7	225	6-15-99	6	1	3.33	47	0	3	51	43	20	19	4	24	56	.228	.324	.328	25.69	11.01	218
Davies, Zach	R-R	6-0	180	2-7-93	1	1	4.29	5	5	0	21	20	11	10	2	9	12	.247	.315	.383	12.90	9.68	93
Dipoto, Jonah	R-R	6-1	225	9-3-96	1	0	4.40	10	2	0	14	11	10	7	3	8	13	.200	.318	.473	19.70	12.12	66
Duffey, Tyler	R-R	6-3	220	12-27-90	3	3	2.35	23	0	0	31	24	9	8	2	11	34	.207	.276	.328	26.77	8.66	127
Fleming, William	R-R	6-6	220	3-6-99	0	0	5.14	5	5	0	21	24	12	12	3	7	16	.282	.358	.459	16.84	7.37	95
Guerrero, Tyson	L-L	6-1	188	2-16-99	1	3	8.71	5	5	0	21	24	21	20	5	14	14	.293	.392	.585	14.43	14.43	97
Hernandez, Carlos	R-R	6-4	245	3-11-97	3	0	5.40	25	0	5	27	22	16	16	5	12	36	.222	.310	.434	31.86	10.62	113
Hoffmann, Andrew	R-R	6-5	210	2-2-00	3	5	6.82	25	11	0	66	84	54	50	9	32	66	.310	.392	.465	20.89	10.13	316
Klein, Will	R-R	6-5	230	11-28-99	2	1	3.58	34	0	9	38	25	18	15	4	27	38	.184	.317	.287	22.89	16.27	166
Lamet, Dinelson	R-R	6-3	228	7-18-92	5	3	4.81	10	10	0	49	41	27	26	5	29	35	.234	.338	.377	16.91	14.01	207
Long, Sam	L-L	6-1	185	7-8-95	1	2	1.31	16	0	2	21	17	6	3	0	5	23	.218	.262	.282	27.38	5.95	84
Lorenzen, Michael	R-R	6-3	217	1-4-92	0	0	2.70	1	1	0	3	2	1	1	1	2	4	.167	.286	.417	28.57	14.29	14
Lynch, Daniel	L-L	6-6	200	11-17-96	8	1	3.54	21	21	0	119	117	51	47	15	32	95	.257	.306	.425	19.23	6.48	494
Marsh, Alec	R-R	6-2	220	5-14-98	1	1	1.42	5	5	0	19	8	3	3	1	6	25	.129	.229	.177	35.71	8.57	70
McMillon, John	L-R	6-3	230	1-27-98	5	2	6.53	28	0	0	30	31	22	22	7	26	35	.261	.397	.479	23.81	17.69	147
Murdock, Noah	R-R	6-8	205	8-20-98	1	0	3.76	30	0	1	38	27	18	16	0	26	46	.203	.348	.218	27.88	15.76	165
Pennington, Walter	L-L	6-2	205	4-14-98	6	3	2.26	37	2	2	60	39	18	15	6	20	79	.182	.257	.285	32.92	8.33	240
Selby, Colin	R-R	6-2	220	10-24-97	2	2	5.85	18	0	0	20	16	14	13	3	8	26	.216	.310	.405	30.59	9.41	85

Pitching	B-T	Ht.	Wt.	DOB	W	L	ERA	G	GS	SV	IP	Hits	Runs	ER	HR	BB	SO	AVG	OBP	SLG	SO%	BB%	BF
Simonelli, Anthony	R-R	6-2	200	12-23-98	1	1	4.96	10	1	0	16	10	9	9	3	8	13	.175	.294	.439	19.12	11.76	68
Sisk, Evan	L-L	6-2	209	4-23-97	6	2	1.57	58	0	15	57	33	13	10	0	26	81	.166	.271	.201	35.37	11.35	229
Taylor, Josh	L-L	6-5	245	3-2-93	0	0	16.88	3	0	0	3	7	5	5	1	2	2	.467	.529	.933	11.76	11.76	17
Tinoco, Jesus	R-R	6-4	258	4-30-95	0	0	4.05	6	0	1	7	6	3	3	0	1	10	.231	.259	.269	37.04	3.70	27
Veneziano, Anthony	L-L	6-5	205	9-1-97	4	5	4.80	31	14	0	90	90	53	48	12	42	76	.262	.344	.419	19.34	10.69	393
Wallace, Jacob	R-R	6-1	190	8-13-98	2	0	6.75	3	0	0	3	2	2	2	0	0	3	.182	.182	.364	27.27	0.00	11
Way, Beck	R-R	6-4	200	8-6-99	0	0	18.00	1	0	0	1	2	2	2	0	2	2	.400	.571	.600	28.57	28.57	7
Zerpa, Angel	L-L	6-0	220	9-27-99	1	0	0.79	8	0	0	11	9	2	1	0	2	9	.231	.268	.231	21.95	4.88	41

Fielding

Catcher	PCT	G	PO	A	E	DP	PB
Duran	.990	24	196	12	2	1	2
Nola	.994	55	461	23	3	6	0
O'Keefe	.982	54	426	17	8	1	4
Porter	1.000	23	209	11	0	0	0

First Base	PCT	G	PO	A	E	DP
Alexander	1.000	5	40	1	0	4
Lester	1.000	3	18	0	0	4
Loftin	1.000	5	36	5	0	6
Mann	.993	39	279	19	2	31
Porter	.970	4	29	3	1	2
Pratto	.995	96	738	68	4	73

Second Base	PCT	G	PO	A	E	DP
Brosseau	1.000	1	2	4	0	1
Devanney	.974	7	13	25	1	7
Eaton	.857	2	2	4	1	0
Fitzgerald	.988	41	55	107	2	22
Loftin	.988	37	67	95	2	26
Mann	.975	36	56	100	4	27
Massey	1.000	6	9	17	0	1
Padlo	1.000	8	11	19	0	4
Russell	1.000	1	1	4	0	1
Tolbert	1.000	17	24	50	0	13

Third Base	PCT	G	PO	A	E	DP
Alexander	.923	48	25	83	9	9
Brosseau	1.000	6	1	10	0	1
Devanney	.941	6	6	10	1	0
Eaton	.973	42	30	77	3	9
Fitzgerald	.963	40	24	80	4	9
Loftin	.968	12	8	22	1	2
Russell	1.000	1	0	1	0	1

Shortstop	PCT	G	PO	A	E	DP
Devanney	.968	123	145	277	14	72
Fitzgerald	.969	27	32	61	3	17
Tolbert	.800	1	2	2	1	1

Outfield	PCT	G	PO	A	E	DP
Alexander	.971	14	33	1	1	0
Eaton	.990	59	95	4	1	0
Gentry	.978	114	215	6	5	2
Loftin	1.000	6	9	1	0	0
Pratto	.938	9	15	0	1	0
Rave	.996	121	216	6	1	1
Tolbert	1.000	4	8	0	0	0
Velazquez	1.000	28	39	2	0	0
Waters	.986	101	202	7	3	3

KANSAS CITY ROYALS

NORTHWEST ARKANSAS NATURALS — *DOUBLE-A*

TEXAS LEAGUE

Batting	B-T	Ht.	Wt.	DOB	AVG	OBP	SLG	G	PA	AB	R	H	2B	3B	HR	RBI	BB	HBP	SH	SF	SO	SB	CS	BB%	SO%
Alexander, Jack	R-R	5-10	212	5-30-00	.000	.250	.000	2	8	6	2	0	0	0	0	0	2	0	0	0	2	0	0	25.00	25.00
Brito, Chris	R-R	6-2	215	9-28-99	.100	.308	.100	5	13	10	0	1	0	0	0	1	2	1	0	0	3	0	0	15.38	23.08
Cross, Gavin	L-L	6-1	210	2-13-01	.261	.342	.428	101	436	383	54	100	19	0	15	59	45	4	0	4	105	30	2	10.32	24.08
Duran, Rodolfo	R-R	5-8	181	2-19-98	.290	.333	.516	56	243	221	39	64	19	2	9	45	13	4	0	5	50	1	0	5.35	20.58
Emshoff, Kale	R-R	6-2	228	5-2-98	.218	.269	.391	23	93	87	7	19	6	0	3	10	5	1	0	0	38	0	0	5.38	40.86
Frazier, Adam	L-R	5-10	180	12-14-91	.000	.000	.000	1	4	4	0	0	0	0	0	0	0	0	0	0	1	0	0	0.00	25.00
Gonzalez, Asbel	R-R	6-2	170	1-2-06	.167	.375	.167	4	8	6	1	1	0	0	0	0	2	0	0	0	1	1	0	25.00	12.50
Gray Jr., Joe	R-R	6-0	214	3-12-00	.136	.253	.185	30	96	81	4	11	2	1	0	1	12	1	1	1	27	4	0	12.50	28.13
Hernandez, Diego	L-L	6-0	150	11-21-00	.240	.271	.352	104	395	366	39	88	15	1	8	43	16	1	8	4	97	5	7	4.05	24.56
Jensen, Carter	L-R	6-1	210	7-3-03	.233	.300	.480	41	170	150	20	35	7	3	8	28	15	1	0	4	45	1	1	8.82	26.47
Lester, Josh	L-R	6-3	180	7-17-94	.263	.329	.459	112	454	403	57	106	21	2	18	70	40	3	0	7	90	2	0	8.81	19.82
Massey, Michael	L-R	6-0	190	3-22-98	.000	.000	.000	1	4	4	0	0	0	0	0	0	0	0	0	0	4	0	0	0.00	100.00
Melendez, MJ	L-R	6-1	190	11-29-98	.111	.182	.444	3	11	9	3	1	0	0	1	2	1	0	0	1	2	0	0	9.09	18.18
Newton, Shervyen	B-R	6-3	209	4-24-99	.148	.246	.241	16	62	54	4	8	2	0	1	5	7	0	1	0	26	1	0	11.29	41.94
Padlo, Kevin	R-R	5-11	210	7-15-96	.143	.200	.250	7	30	28	4	4	0	0	1	5	2	0	0	0	10	0	0	6.67	33.33
Pineda, Jack	L-R	5-7	170	8-10-99	.234	.315	.359	39	155	128	21	30	7	0	3	23	13	3	9	2	37	4	1	8.39	23.87
Renfroe, Hunter	R-R	6-1	230	1-28-92	.000	.000	.000	1	5	4	0	0	0	0	0	1	0	0	0	1	1	0	0	0.00	20.00
Russell, Stone	R-R	6-1	195	6-17-04	.286	.375	.286	2	8	7	1	2	0	0	0	0	0	1	0	0	3	0	0	0.00	37.50
Shrum, Dillan	R-L	5-11	200	3-4-98	.234	.328	.418	111	457	397	60	93	19	3	16	57	45	12	0	3	144	0	0	9.85	31.51
Tolbert, Tyler	R-R	6-0	160	1-27-98	.260	.339	.354	101	462	393	58	102	21	2	4	38	38	10	19	2	103	40	4	8.23	22.29
Town, River	L-R	5-9	181	7-8-99	.235	.386	.306	67	249	196	33	46	7	2	1	17	41	9	0	3	33	3	5	16.47	13.25
Tresh, Luca	R-R	5-11	193	1-11-00	.250	.323	.429	97	400	352	47	88	19	1	14	58	37	4	1	6	98	0	0	9.25	24.50
Valera, Leonel	R-R	6-3	206	7-9-99	.242	.280	.330	83	290	273	42	66	11	5	1	25	13	2	1	1	70	14	1	4.48	24.14
Vaz, Javier	L-R	5-9	151	9-22-00	.263	.375	.379	115	523	433	80	114	22	2	8	42	73	6	9	2	60	16	3	13.96	11.47
Wallace, Cayden	R-R	5-10	205	8-7-01	.282	.350	.427	34	140	124	17	35	9	0	3	16	9	5	0	2	26	2	3	6.43	18.57
Wilson, Peyton	B-R	5-8	180	11-1-99	.228	.338	.380	120	517	439	69	100	19	3	14	58	68	7	0	3	115	22	3	13.15	22.24

Pitching	B-T	Ht.	Wt.	DOB	W	L	ERA	G	GS	SV	IP	Hits	Runs	ER	HR	BB	SO	AVG	OBP	SLG	SO%	BB%	BF
Avila, Luinder	R-R	6-3	195	8-21-01	6	5	3.81	19	19	0	83	71	36	35	4	43	82	.229	.330	.329	22.91	12.01	358
Barnett, Mason	R-R	6-0	218	11-7-00	5	6	4.91	19	18	0	92	89	55	50	9	36	109	.252	.329	.408	27.39	9.05	398
Block, A.J.	L-L	6-5	218	4-16-98	0	0	16.20	4	1	0	3	9	6	6	0	2	2	.500	.571	.500	9.52	9.52	21
Brady, Ryan	R-R	6-1	185	3-23-99	5	4	4.28	42	2	1	67	77	35	32	2	23	60	.288	.347	.386	20.07	7.69	299
Brentz, Jake	L-L	6-1	205	9-14-94	0	0	10.88	26	0	0	24	20	30	29	3	35	26	.230	.496	.391	18.98	25.55	137
Bubic, Kris	L-L	6-3	225	8-19-97	0	1	9.00	2	2	0	5	6	5	5	1	1	5	.300	.333	.600	23.81	4.76	21
Cameron, Noah	L-L	6-3	220	7-17-99	4	4	3.63	16	16	0	74	76	37	30	6	25	87	.259	.320	.381	27.02	7.76	322
Cerantola, Eric	R-R	6-5	225	5-2-00	2	3	2.78	24	7	1	58	35	26	18	5	42	81	.169	.319	.271	31.40	16.28	258
Champlain, Chandler	R-R	6-5	220	7-23-99	2	1	3.50	7	7	0	36	26	15	14	4	7	48	.203	.255	.344	34.53	5.04	139
Cox, Austin	L-L	6-4	235	3-28-97	1	0	0.00	4	0	0	6	1	0	0	0	2	5	.059	.158	.059	26.32	10.53	19
Fleming, William	R-R	6-6	220	3-6-99	4	6	7.75	22	15	0	84	114	75	72	10	39	44	.334	.406	.545	11.14	9.87	395
Guerrero, Tyson	L-L	6-1	188	2-16-99	3	6	3.69	22	20	0	102	80	46	42	8	43	109	.213	.308	.330	25.00	9.86	436
Harm, Parker	L-L	6-2	208	2-2-97	0	0	4.32	9	0	0	8	8	4	4	0	9	13	.242	.468	.333	27.66	19.15	47

Hoffmann, Andrew	R-R	6-5	210	2-2-00	0	1	3.60	1	1	0	5	4	2	2	0	2	3	.222	.300	.222	15.00	10.00	20
Johnson, Brandon	R-R	6-0	195	6-12-99	0	1	4.31	27	0	1	31	35	17	15	2	13	42	.276	.336	.402	29.37	9.09	143
Karcher, Ricky	R-R	6-4	230	9-18-97	0	1	5.56	12	0	0	11	10	7	7	0	8	11	.233	.365	.279	21.15	15.38	52
Kaufman, Rylan	L-L	6-4	225	6-23-99	0	0	2.70	1	0	0	3	3	2	1	1	0	5	.214	.214	.429	35.71	0.00	14
Killgore, Keylan	L-L	6-3	185	9-30-96	5	5	5.60	39	0	2	53	46	34	33	3	30	71	.236	.352	.349	30.34	12.82	234
Kudrna, Ben	R-R	6-3	175	1-30-03	2	3	5.32	9	8	0	46	50	29	27	8	21	48	.284	.371	.472	23.30	10.19	206
Lester, Josh	L-R	6-3	180	7-17-94	0	0	0.00	2	0	0	1	0	0	0	0	0	0	.000	.000	.000	0.00	0.00	4
Lorenzen, Michael	R-R	6-3	217	1-4-92	0	0	16.20	1	1	0	2	5	3	3	0	1	2	.500	.545	.500	18.18	9.09	11
Murdock, Noah	R-R	6-8	205	8-20-98	0	0	2.22	16	0	0	24	16	8	6	0	15	26	.193	.333	.253	25.49	14.71	102
Noriega, Cruz	R-R	6-1	175	10-1-97	7	4	6.01	32	9	0	76	79	52	51	9	21	73	.262	.310	.417	22.19	6.38	329
Paulino, Anderson	R-R	6-2	200	9-12-98	1	6	5.57	48	0	10	53	64	37	33	7	25	53	.292	.376	.429	21.03	9.92	252
Regalado, Nicholas	R-R	6-2	215	5-15-02	0	1	6.75	3	0	0	4	3	3	3	0	2	3	.214	.368	.214	15.79	10.53	19
Schreiber, John	R-R	6-2	224	3-5-94	0	0	13.50	2	1	0	2	4	3	3	1	0	3	.400	.400	.900	30.00	0.00	10
Simonelli, Anthony	R-R	6-2	200	12-23-98	4	2	2.35	33	0	3	57	35	17	15	3	22	74	.173	.257	.272	32.74	9.73	226
Taylor, Josh	L-L	6-5	245	3-2-93	0	0	0.00	3	0	0	3	1	1	0	0	1	1	.111	.273	.222	9.09	9.09	11
Wallace, Chase	R-R	6-2	195	11-13-98	0	1	4.97	11	0	0	13	10	7	7	1	9	8	.222	.357	.333	14.29	16.07	56
Wallace, Jacob	R-R	6-1	190	8-13-98	3	4	3.98	42	0	0	61	42	29	27	8	30	83	.192	.296	.352	32.68	11.81	254
Way, Beck	R-R	6-4	200	8-6-99	6	3	3.88	47	0	12	58	47	33	25	4	40	63	.222	.364	.344	24.14	15.33	261
Zobac, Steven	L-R	6-3	185	10-14-00	6	3	3.25	11	10	0	55	46	25	20	4	14	65	.222	.274	.377	28.63	6.17	227

Fielding

Catcher	PCT	G	PO	A	E	DP	PB
Hayes	.993	15	130	11	1	2	0
Hernandez	.987	68	550	49	8	5	4
Jensen	.988	47	372	31	5	2	4
Mitchell	1.000	1	8	0	0	0	0

First Base	PCT	G	PO	A	E	DP
Brito	1.000	12	91	1	0	3
Caglianone	.989	23	164	10	2	19
Emshoff	.943	4	32	1	2	1
Kulasingam	1.000	1	4	0	0	1
Newton	.990	14	87	9	1	8
Squires	.998	61	464	33	1	47
Werner	1.000	22	151	11	0	13

Second Base	PCT	G	PO	A	E	DP
Johnson	.985	94	190	217	6	53
Kulasingam	1.000	1	1	3	0	1
Nadal	1.000	1	2	6	0	3
Pineda	.985	30	51	82	2	23
Rodriguez	1.000	7	14	15	0	6

Third Base	PCT	G	PO	A	E	DP
Kulasingam	1.000	1	1	2	0	0
Nadal	.960	13	8	16	1	4
Newton	1.000	3	1	5	0	1
Pineda	.954	28	18	44	3	10
Werner	.955	91	65	167	11	17

Shortstop	PCT	G	PO	A	E	DP
Dickerson	.972	103	167	254	12	49
Newton	1.000	7	5	14	0	2
Nivens	.956	96	152	0	7	0
Pineda	.934	23	35	50	6	7

Outfield	PCT	G	PO	A	E	DP
Dickey	.968	75	114	6	4	1
Kulasingam	1.000	18	43	2	0	0
Nadal	.969	39	57	6	2	1
Ramirez	1.000	51	92	4	0	2
Roccaforte	.997	120	294	4	1	1
Squires	1.000	1	1	1	0	0

QUAD CITIES RIVER BANDITS — *HIGH-A*

MIDWEST LEAGUE

Batting	B-T	Ht.	Wt.	DOB	AVG	OBP	SLG	G	PA	AB	R	H	2B	3B	HR	RBI	BB	HBP	SH	SF	SO	SB	CS	BB%	SO%
Brito, Chris	R-R	6-2	215	9-28-99	.185	.350	.198	26	104	81	6	15	1	0	0	4	20	1	1	1	22	2	2	19.23	21.15
Caglianone, Jac	L-L	6-5	217	2-9-03	.241	.302	.388	29	126	116	13	28	9	1	2	14	7	3	0	0	26	2	0	5.56	20.63
Dickerson, Dustin	R-R	6-1	180	3-28-01	.224	.357	.267	105	434	352	58	79	9	0	2	38	69	5	4	3	100	9	5	15.90	23.04
Dickey, Jared	L-R	6-1	204	3-1-02	.269	.360	.424	81	331	290	39	78	12	3	9	40	32	9	0	0	64	8	4	9.67	19.34
Emshoff, Kale	R-R	6-2	228	5-2-98	.276	.343	.496	34	143	127	15	35	7	0	7	32	11	3	0	2	41	2	0	7.69	28.67
Hayes, Kyle	R-R	6-2	190	10-8-97	.146	.293	.208	15	58	48	3	7	3	0	0	5	7	3	0	0	20	0	1	12.07	34.48
Hernandez, Omar	R-R	5-11	170	12-10-01	.227	.284	.291	70	277	251	27	57	10	0	2	20	19	1	5	0	57	14	3	6.86	20.58
Jensen, Carter	L-R	6-1	210	7-3-03	.271	.386	.435	84	376	310	47	84	15	3	10	39	57	4	0	5	83	16	2	15.16	22.07
Johnson, Justin	R-R	5-11	185	4-3-00	.237	.349	.341	101	400	334	54	79	24	1	3	35	51	9	1	4	76	16	5	12.75	19.00
Kulasingam, Sam	B-R	6-2	190	7-10-01	.257	.325	.329	20	80	70	7	18	3	1	0	6	5	3	0	2	14	3	0	6.25	17.50
Mitchell, Blake	L-R	6-1	192	8-3-04	.111	.200	.111	5	20	18	2	2	0	0	0	1	1	1	0	0	7	1	0	5.00	35.00
Nadal, Deivis	L-R	6-0	150	2-8-02	.147	.235	.276	52	187	163	17	24	6	3	3	15	17	2	4	1	85	5	2	9.09	45.45
Newton, Shervyen	B-R	6-3	209	4-24-99	.224	.295	.379	31	129	116	17	26	3	0	5	16	9	3	0	1	42	0	0	6.98	32.56
Nivens, Spencer	L-R	5-11	185	11-16-01	.243	.333	.475	99	412	358	53	87	17	3	20	58	48	2	0	4	111	7	4	11.65	26.94
Pineda, Jack	L-R	5-7	170	8-10-99	.257	.362	.378	79	347	288	45	74	16	2	5	36	43	7	4	5	72	15	5	12.39	20.75
Ramirez, Jean	L-L	5-10	190	10-25-00	.192	.287	.231	50	184	156	21	30	6	0	0	9	21	0	6	1	36	9	2	11.41	19.57
Roccaforte, Carson	L-L	6-1	195	3-29-02	.208	.293	.342	122	535	471	59	98	23	5	10	62	56	3	0	5	139	34	13	10.47	25.98
Rodriguez, Lizandro	B-R	5-11	180	11-16-02	.217	.308	.304	7	26	23	4	5	2	0	0	1	3	0	0	0	6	2	0	11.54	23.08
Squires, Brett	L-R	6-2	210	2-26-00	.309	.390	.481	62	270	233	36	72	13	0	9	42	32	1	0	3	70	16	4	11.85	25.93
Werner, Trevor	R-R	6-3	225	9-3-00	.200	.292	.339	119	503	436	54	87	18	5	11	53	55	5	0	7	178	20	4	10.93	35.39

Pitching	B-T	Ht.	Wt.	DOB	W	L	ERA	G	GS	SV	IP	Hits	Runs	ER	HR	BB	SO	AVG	OBP	SLG	SO%	BB%	BF
Ackenhausen, Nate	L-L	6-2	230	9-23-01	0	0	0.00	5	0	0	9	2	0	0	0	2	9	.074	.138	.074	31.03	6.90	29
Block, A.J.	L-L	6-5	218	4-16-98	4	1	4.59	30	0	0	51	46	27	26	9	24	59	.240	.345	.443	26.11	10.62	226
Bosacker, Ethan	R-R	6-2	210	2-20-01	7	1	1.97	9	9	0	50	36	12	11	1	11	37	.202	.255	.253	19.27	5.73	192
Fenlong, Connor	R-R	6-4	225	9-22-99	1	1	3.28	15	0	1	25	24	10	9	2	9	15	.255	.340	.372	14.15	8.49	106
Garabitos, Natanael	R-R	6-0	185	8-4-00	2	1	4.46	34	0	2	42	34	25	21	5	28	33	.219	.339	.348	17.74	15.05	186
Harm, Parker	L-L	6-2	208	2-2-97	1	0	1.80	5	0	0	5	3	1	1	0	7	10	.167	.423	.278	38.46	26.92	26
Hernandez, Ben	R-R	6-2	205	7-1-01	1	1	4.79	10	0	0	21	24	11	11	1	7	14	.300	.352	.425	15.91	7.95	88
Isbell, Chase	R-R	6-2	198	9-12-00	1	2	4.50	20	0	0	28	27	16	14	4	9	31	.257	.319	.419	26.72	7.76	116
Johnson, Brandon	R-R	6-0	195	6-12-99	3	3	4.13	18	0	2	24	23	12	11	2	10	36	.250	.327	.402	34.62	9.62	104
Kudrna, Ben	R-R	6-3	175	1-30-03	4	5	3.49	14	14	0	70	56	31	27	6	32	71	.226	.317	.355	24.91	11.23	285
Martinez, Chazz	L-L	6-3	210	1-6-00	0	2	4.09	35	0	2	51	38	27	23	1	35	61	.209	.353	.280	27.23	15.63	224

McKeehan, Cooper	L-L	6-1	195	3-28-01	1	2	9.56	14	0	0	16	26	18	17	2	13	14	.377	.477	.580	16.28	15.12	86
Molsky, Tommy	R-R	6-1	160	2-6-03	0	1	9.00	2	0	0	3	4	4	3	1	1	2	.333	.357	.667	14.29	7.14	14
Morones, Andrew	R-R	6-0	200	12-19-00	1	0	0.90	8	0	0	10	5	1	1	1	5	7	.152	.263	.273	18.42	13.16	38
Mozzicato, Frank	L-L	6-3	175	6-19-03	5	10	3.45	22	22	0	102	72	46	39	9	62	91	.203	.322	.332	21.31	14.52	427
Owen, Hunter	R-L	6-6	261	1-30-02	6	7	4.24	23	22	0	102	90	54	48	8	32	80	.241	.317	.351	18.87	7.55	424
Panzini, Shane	R-R	6-3	220	10-30-01	3	3	5.29	16	7	1	51	52	31	30	8	26	48	.278	.374	.460	21.92	11.87	219
Patteson, Hunter	L-L	6-4	190	4-4-00	3	4	5.75	13	5	0	36	42	23	23	7	11	35	.292	.340	.486	22.44	7.05	156
Ramsey, Ryan	R-L	6-0	195	1-18-01	6	4	2.43	22	11	3	89	59	27	24	4	30	97	.188	.278	.262	27.40	8.47	354
Rayo, Oscar	L-L	6-1	180	1-13-02	6	0	2.13	25	7	2	85	70	20	20	2	19	78	.226	.283	.290	23.15	5.64	337
Sears, Ben	R-R	6-5	208	6-15-00	2	3	3.28	44	0	15	58	54	26	21	5	16	50	.244	.306	.339	20.33	6.50	246
Wallace, Chase	R-R	6-2	195	11-13-98	1	3	2.82	27	0	2	38	23	16	12	3	9	38	.168	.228	.277	25.33	6.00	150
Williams, Henry	R-R	6-5	200	9-18-01	5	4	3.68	22	21	1	103	86	46	42	8	39	92	.231	.313	.366	21.80	9.24	422
Zobac, Steven	L-R	6-3	185	10-14-00	5	5	3.95	14	13	0	71	66	34	31	3	15	58	.246	.293	.347	20.00	5.17	290

Fielding

Catcher	PCT	G	PO	A	E	DP	PB
Alexander	1.000	2	18	0	0	0	0
Brito	1.000	1	9	1	0	0	0
Duran	.989	37	341	23	4	5	4
Emshoff	1.000	6	60	2	0	0	0
Jensen	.980	26	228	11	5	2	6
Tresh	.996	67	665	39	3	6	13

First Base	PCT	G	PO	A	E	DP
Brito	1.000	1	5	0	0	0
Emshoff	1.000	1	6	1	0	0
Lester	.996	33	235	21	1	18
Padlo	1.000	1	10	1	0	1
Shrum	.996	104	769	37	3	57
Valera	.000	1	0	0	0	0

Second Base	PCT	G	PO	A	E	DP
Frazier	1.000	1	3	0	0	0
Massey	.833	1	4	1	1	0
Russell	1.000	2	1	2	0	1
Tolbert	1.000	6	4	15	0	3
Vaz	.997	89	160	206	1	47
Wilson	.964	40	51	84	5	14

Third Base	PCT	G	PO	A	E	DP
Lester	.987	58	31	122	2	5
Newton	.833	7	5	10	3	2
Padlo	1.000	3	1	9	0	0
Pineda	1.000	5	4	9	0	0
Valera	.945	37	22	81	6	8
Wallace	.930	33	13	53	5	6

Shortstop	PCT	G	PO	A	E	DP
Newton	.944	9	13	21	2	5
Pineda	.959	34	45	97	6	17
Tolbert	.965	52	55	111	6	15
Valera	.956	40	30	78	5	10
Vaz	.929	7	1	12	1	1

Outfield	PCT	G	PO	A	E	DP
Cross	.987	90	153	2	2	1
Gonzalez	1.000	3	3	0	0	0
Gray Jr.	.985	27	64	1	1	0
Hernandez	.972	99	195	12	6	4
Lester	1.000	9	11	0	0	0
Melendez	1.000	2	2	0	0	0
Tolbert	1.000	42	112	1	0	1
Town	1.000	60	90	5	0	2
Valera	1.000	3	3	0	0	0
Vaz	1.000	16	23	2	0	0
Wilson	.964	75	101	6	4	1

COLUMBIA FIREFLIES — LOW-A

CAROLINA LEAGUE

Batting	B-T	Ht.	Wt.	DOB	AVG	OBP	SLG	G	PA	AB	R	H	2B	3B	HR	RBI	BB	HBP	SH	SF	SO	SB	CS	BB%	SO%
Becker, Colton	R-R	6-2	200	4-26-01	.220	.304	.260	16	57	50	3	11	2	0	0	8	6	0	1	0	10	6	3	10.53	17.54
Brito, Chris	R-R	6-2	215	9-28-99	.306	.447	.438	40	160	121	26	37	10	0	2	18	31	3	1	4	18	4	1	19.38	11.25
Brown, Canyon	R-R	6-2	190	8-7-03	.000	.100	.000	3	10	9	0	0	0	0	0	0	1	0	0	0	5	0	0	10.00	50.00
Cepero, Ryan	R-R	5-10	180	2-11-03	.121	.216	.121	12	38	33	2	4	0	0	0	0	3	1	1	0	15	2	0	7.89	39.47
Charles, Austin	R-R	6-4	215	11-13-03	.257	.353	.386	117	481	409	62	105	15	4	10	64	50	14	2	6	124	36	7	10.40	25.78
Figueroa, Derlin	L-R	6-0	163	9-7-03	.223	.303	.364	118	492	431	54	96	16	3	13	56	49	3	2	5	108	15	7	9.96	21.95
Frederick, Carter	R-R	6-4	235	7-2-02	.266	.373	.344	19	75	64	13	17	5	0	0	8	11	0	0	0	21	5	0	14.67	28.00
Guzman, Diego	R-R	5-11	200	9-12-03	.124	.165	.223	36	128	121	8	15	4	1	2	4	6	0	1	0	42	3	0	4.69	32.81
Kulasingam, Sam	B-R	6-2	190	7-10-01	.154	.200	.154	4	15	13	1	2	0	0	0	3	1	0	0	1	3	1	0	6.67	20.00
Lucas, Aldrin	R-R	5-10	165	2-7-03	.143	.333	.161	21	72	56	6	8	1	0	0	7	10	6	0	0	22	2	1	13.89	30.56
McNair, Brennon	R-R	5-10	185	9-15-02	.193	.307	.353	87	320	269	39	52	15	2	8	31	39	6	4	2	107	9	6	12.19	33.44
Mitchell, Blake	L-R	6-1	192	8-3-04	.238	.376	.439	106	466	378	61	90	16	3	18	50	79	6	0	3	142	25	7	16.95	30.47
Moss, Michael Callan	R-R	6-3	230	8-31-03	.339	.488	.452	22	80	62	9	21	1	0	2	7	18	0	0	0	12	3	2	22.50	15.00
Pena, Erick	L-R	6-1	205	2-20-03	.176	.282	.319	108	427	364	40	64	16	3	10	43	51	4	5	3	171	13	3	11.94	40.05
Perdomo, Jhonny	R-R	5-10	168	6-9-02	.199	.271	.273	83	321	286	36	57	10	4	1	33	24	5	4	2	64	32	5	7.48	19.94
Rodriguez, Lizandro	B-R	5-11	180	11-16-02	.235	.322	.348	61	238	204	28	48	8	3	3	22	24	3	5	2	46	18	5	10.08	19.33
Rushford, Milo	L-L	6-0	185	2-12-04	.116	.267	.209	28	105	86	10	10	4	2	0	8	16	2	0	1	28	4	1	15.24	26.67
Salon, Dionmy	R-R	5-11	215	11-18-01	.220	.319	.268	52	194	164	18	36	8	0	0	16	20	5	3	2	25	4	0	10.31	12.89
Silva, Gabriel	R-R	5-9	218	12-10-03	.184	.258	.322	27	98	87	13	16	4	1	2	7	9	0	1	1	45	0	1	9.18	45.92
Torres, Erick	R-R	5-10	160	12-20-04	.237	.336	.298	115	514	439	70	104	13	1	4	32	57	10	5	3	72	25	11	11.09	14.01
Um, Hyungchan	R-R	6-1	190	4-24-04	.205	.333	.307	50	198	166	21	34	5	0	4	22	25	7	0	0	56	1	1	12.63	28.28
Vazquez, Daniel	R-R	6-1	150	12-15-03	.253	.353	.289	74	325	277	33	70	10	0	0	20	43	1	2	2	72	12	5	13.23	22.15

Pitching	B-T	Ht.	Wt.	DOB	W	L	ERA	G	GS	SV	IP	Hits	Runs	ER	HR	BB	SO	AVG	OBP	SLG	SO%	BB%	BF
Arronde, Felix	R-R	6-3	185	4-25-03	4	8	2.94	23	21	1	110	81	44	36	9	32	103	.205	.278	.336	23.46	7.29	439
Bernal, Jonatan	R-R	6-1	194	6-29-02	1	4	3.49	12	11	0	57	50	25	22	6	12	43	.238	.281	.348	18.86	5.26	228
Bosacker, Ethan	R-R	6-2	210	2-20-01	6	2	2.78	15	9	1	74	66	27	23	4	17	59	.235	.282	.331	19.60	5.65	301
Cawyer, Zachary	R-R	6-3	210	12-2-02	3	1	4.22	8	0	1	11	11	5	5	0	4	13	.268	.333	.366	28.26	8.70	46
Fenlong, Connor	R-R	6-4	225	9-22-99	0	2	3.47	17	0	3	23	24	12	9	0	12	22	.270	.356	.303	21.78	11.88	101
Hansell, Josh	R-R	6-6	215	2-7-02	4	2	2.52	21	6	1	64	49	24	18	0	39	71	.209	.329	.252	25.54	14.03	278
Hernandez, Ben	R-R	6-2	205	7-1-01	2	1	3.19	15	0	1	31	33	18	11	1	12	21	.275	.338	.333	15.67	8.96	134
Herrera, Eduardo	S-R	5-9	179	1-5-00	2	1	3.86	8	0	1	14	14	10	6	2	11	14	.250	.368	.429	20.59	16.18	68
Isbell, Chase	R-R	6-2	198	9-12-00	3	1	0.79	13	0	2	23	9	5	2	0	5	33	.120	.175	.120	41.25	6.25	80
Kirkland, Doug	R-R	5-11	212	12-3-00	3	4	2.16	31	0	1	42	23	16	10	2	34	58	.167	.326	.246	33.14	19.43	175
Leal, Henson	R-R	6-1	176	9-19-03	1	0	4.87	12	0	0	20	19	11	11	4	11	22	.253	.341	.493	24.44	12.22	90
Marte, Yunior	R-R	6-5	210	9-8-03	0	1	6.48	2	2	0	8	13	6	6	0	2	7	.361	.395	.528	18.42	5.26	38
Martin, Logan	R-R	6-1	180	7-17-01	4	3	3.62	25	17	3	102	87	45	41	7	32	97	.223	.285	.323	22.88	7.55	424
Martinez, Juan	R-R	5-11	195	4-6-01	1	1	4.76	10	0	0	17	17	9	9	0	10	16	.262	.377	.338	20.51	12.82	78
Michel, Ismael	R-R	6-3	175	2-14-02	4	0	1.42	19	0	2	32	18	7	5	2	17	32	.167	.297	.259	25.00	13.28	128

Pitching	B-T	Ht.	Wt.	DOB	W	L	ERA	G	GS	SV	IP	Hits	Runs	ER	HR	BB	SO	AVG	OBP	SLG	SO%	BB%	BF
Miller, Mason	L-L	6-2	200	3-30-02	1	1	7.71	3	0	0	7	11	6	6	3	4	9	.367	.429	.733	25.71	11.43	35
Novas, Elvis	R-R	6-0	205	9-2-02	0	4	2.77	19	0	9	26	19	9	8	0	6	20	.202	.245	.245	19.61	5.88	102
Patteson, Hunter	L-L	6-4	190	4-4-00	3	4	3.27	11	10	1	55	44	22	20	4	8	56	.220	.250	.335	26.29	3.76	213
Polanco, Luis	R-R	6-3	225	8-10-00	4	1	3.89	18	0	3	37	30	18	16	4	13	31	.224	.298	.358	20.39	8.55	152
Presinal, Yimi	R-R	5-11	175	9-18-04	3	0	7.20	14	0	0	20	26	22	16	1	14	23	.306	.429	.447	21.70	13.21	106
Regalado, Nicholas	R-R	6-2	215	5-15-02	5	4	3.74	27	1	0	46	46	26	19	2	23	64	.250	.340	.332	30.62	11.00	209
Reyes, Emmanuel	R-R	6-0	180	5-16-04	5	5	3.62	23	21	0	107	91	50	43	8	32	85	.228	.289	.360	19.32	7.27	440
Rios, Jesus	R-R	6-1	190	12-27-01	1	4	5.54	17	0	1	26	32	18	16	2	10	23	.296	.355	.426	18.85	8.20	122
Rosado, Jarold	R-R	6-3	215	7-13-02	0	1	1.85	27	0	4	39	30	11	8	1	11	45	.219	.275	.285	29.41	7.19	153
Rosario, Julio	R-R	6-1	205	7-12-02	2	0	2.40	7	0	0	15	14	6	4	0	4	16	.246	.306	.298	25.81	6.45	62
Veliz, Mauricio	R-R	6-2	220	7-17-02	1	4	7.54	13	13	0	45	55	42	38	4	31	37	.293	.409	.452	16.09	13.48	230
Widener, Jacob	R-L	6-7	235	6-15-01	1	0	0.00	5	0	0	8	3	0	0	0	3	15	.115	.233	.154	50.00	10.00	30
Wolters, Blake	R-R	6-4	215	10-25-04	2	3	4.20	14	14	0	56	57	32	26	4	25	46	.261	.343	.385	18.62	10.12	247
Wyatt, Hiro	R-R	6-1	185	8-25-04	2	1	2.67	6	6	0	27	17	9	8	1	9	26	.189	.282	.311	25.24	8.74	103

Fielding

Catcher	PCT	G	PO	A	E	DP	PB
Brown	1.000	3	15	4	0	0	0
Mitchell	.973	62	548	32	16	3	9
Salon	.991	37	302	26	3	5	2
Silva	.989	12	86	4	1	0	2
Um	.995	22	170	15	1	0	2

First Base	PCT	G	PO	A	E	DP
Brito	1.000	39	287	22	0	25
Figueroa	.990	50	365	19	4	36
Kulasingam	1.000	1	5	0	0	1
Lucas	.986	21	137	8	2	6
Moss	.984	22	168	12	3	10
Silva	1.000	4	38	0	0	3

Second Base	PCT	G	PO	A	E	DP
Becker	.968	15	28	32	2	4
Perdomo	.971	61	83	150	7	27
Rodriguez	.968	57	97	147	8	33

Third Base	PCT	G	PO	A	E	DP
Charles	.939	64	52	116	11	12
Figueroa	.951	43	24	74	5	6
Guzman	.970	14	11	21	1	2
Kulasingam	1.000	1	2	2	0	0
McNair	1.000	2	1	1	0	0
Perdomo	.923	10	8	16	2	1

Shortstop	PCT	G	PO	A	E	DP
Becker	1.000	1	4	0	0	0
Cepero	.974	12	15	22	1	4
Charles	.953	48	58	125	9	22
Guzman	1.000	1	1	2	0	0
Vazquez	.936	72	86	179	18	32

Outfield	PCT	G	PO	A	E	DP
Figueroa	.977	22	39	3	1	1
Frederick	.972	19	35	0	1	0
Guzman	.964	20	27	0	1	0
Kulasingam	1.000	2	3	0	0	0
McNair	.980	84	144	3	3	0
Pena	.995	109	211	5	1	1
Rushford	1.000	28	49	2	0	2
Torres	.986	112	273	10	4	2

ACL ROYALS — *ROOKIE*

ARIZONA COMPLEX LEAGUE

Batting	B-T	Ht.	Wt.	DOB	AVG	OBP	SLG	G	PA	AB	R	H	2B	3B	HR	RBI	BB	HBP	SH	SF	SO	SB	CS	BB%	SO%
Acosta, Angel	L-R	5-9	160	3-2-03	.300	.353	.333	10	34	30	5	9	1	0	0	5	3	0	0	1	6	1	1	8.82	17.65
Allende, Giullianno	L-L	6-0	165	9-4-03	.250	.360	.315	35	112	92	17	23	4	1	0	10	15	2	1	2	36	8	1	13.39	32.14
Barber, Noah	R-R	6-3	180	5-3-05	.167	.274	.241	27	63	54	11	9	1	0	1	8	8	0	1	0	30	6	1	12.70	47.62
Cabrera, Roni	R-R	6-1	175	7-31-05	.232	.327	.421	28	111	95	22	22	6	0	4	22	12	2	1	1	31	5	2	10.81	27.93
Cepero, Ryan	R-R	5-10	180	2-11-03	.318	.500	.364	9	31	22	8	7	1	0	0	2	8	0	1	0	7	3	1	25.81	22.58
Gonzalez, Asbel	R-R	6-2	170	1-2-06	.285	.398	.384	41	182	151	39	43	11	2	0	20	20	9	1	1	37	22	4	10.99	20.33
Guzman, Diego	R-R	5-11	200	9-12-03	.343	.389	.657	17	72	67	15	23	8	2	3	14	3	2	0	0	19	3	2	4.17	26.39
Hayes, Kyle	R-R	6-2	190	10-8-97	.333	.500	.333	6	20	15	4	5	0	0	0	2	5	0	0	0	2	0	0	25.00	10.00
Hernandez, Jorge	L-R	6-0	180	12-20-05	.291	.337	.399	41	173	158	20	46	8	0	3	31	10	2	1	2	35	2	1	5.78	20.23
Lucas, Aldrin	R-R	5-10	165	2-7-03	.318	.432	.439	21	82	66	11	21	3	1	1	6	12	2	1	1	12	1	2	14.63	14.63
Mendez, Jairo	L-L	6-0	155	10-6-02	.156	.204	.289	13	49	45	9	7	1	1	1	5	3	0	0	1	24	2	0	6.12	48.98
Newton, Shervyen	B-R	6-3	209	4-24-99	.158	.238	.368	6	21	19	1	3	1	0	1	2	2	0	0	0	9	0	0	9.52	42.86
Nivens, Spencer	L-R	5-11	185	11-16-01	.625	.700	1.125	2	10	8	6	5	1	0	1	3	2	0	0	0	2	0	0	20.00	20.00
Nola, Austin	R-R	6-0	197	12-28-89	.250	.250	.250	1	4	4	1	1	0	0	0	0	0	0	0	0	1	0	0	0.00	25.00
Novas, Josi	R-R	6-4	180	2-12-05	.190	.254	.348	42	173	158	20	30	8	1	5	16	9	5	0	1	80	4	1	5.20	46.24
Nuel, Omar	R-R	5-11	210	5-12-03	.200	.238	.325	12	42	40	6	8	2	0	1	6	0	2	0	0	18	3	0	0.00	42.86
Pire, Enmanuel	R-R	5-10	180	5-18-01	.288	.409	.329	28	88	73	9	21	0	0	1	9	13	2	0	0	14	0	1	14.77	15.91
Ramirez, Ramon	R-R	6-0	180	6-15-05	.265	.379	.459	49	203	170	28	45	10	1	7	33	26	6	0	1	42	1	0	12.81	20.69
Ramos, Henry	L-L	6-1	175	9-20-04	.260	.331	.309	37	140	123	23	32	3	0	1	19	12	2	1	2	37	9	3	8.57	26.43
Rushford, Milo	L-L	6-0	185	2-12-04	.192	.354	.327	16	65	52	10	10	0	2	1	4	12	1	0	0	22	6	0	18.46	33.85
Russell, Stone	R-R	6-1	195	6-17-04	.260	.352	.357	45	181	154	28	40	7	1	2	21	21	2	2	2	34	6	1	11.60	18.78
Silva, Gabriel	R-R	5-9	218	12-10-03	.182	.321	.295	14	54	44	0	8	5	0	0	5	8	1	1	0	15	0	2	14.81	27.78
Sosa, Ivan	R-R	6-2	180	9-9-04	.243	.309	.365	25	81	74	15	18	3	0	2	10	6	1	0	0	28	2	3	7.41	34.57
Um, Hyungchan	R-R	6-1	190	4-24-04	.310	.400	.500	27	116	100	13	31	7	0	4	16	12	3	0	0	25	3	0	10.34	21.55
Wallace, Cayden	R-R	5-10	205	8-7-01	.263	.333	.263	7	21	19	2	5	0	0	0	2	1	1	0	0	4	1	1	4.76	19.05
Zue, Jhosmmel	R-R	5-11	146	2-5-04	.216	.330	.375	31	106	88	18	19	5	0	3	12	14	2	0	2	35	1	1	13.21	33.02

Pitching	B-T	Ht.	Wt.	DOB	W	L	ERA	G	GS	SV	IP	Hits	Runs	ER	HR	BB	SO	AVG	OBP	SLG	SO%	BB%	BF
Baez, Dioni	R-R	6-2	185	1-24-03	1	1	3.54	15	0	0	20	15	13	8	0	14	25	.192	.330	.282	26.60	14.89	94
Bernal, Jonatan	R-R	6-1	194	6-29-02	0	1	7.50	4	4	0	6	3	5	5	0	3	8	.136	.269	.273	30.77	11.54	26
Bubic, Kris	L-L	6-3	225	8-19-97	0	1	2.70	3	3	0	3	4	1	1	0	2	8	.308	.400	.385	50.00	12.50	16
Espinoza, Weskendry	R-R	6-1	185	3-18-02	2	3	3.96	16	0	1	25	19	14	11	0	9	27	.207	.279	.304	25.71	8.57	105
Herbold, Brandon	R-R	6-6	180	8-10-04	1	2	5.68	12	8	0	38	34	25	24	5	24	43	.248	.365	.416	25.29	14.12	170
Hoffmann, Andrew	R-R	6-5	210	2-2-00	0	0	0.00	3	3	0	6	4	1	0	0	1	8	.182	.217	.318	34.78	4.35	23
Leal, Henson	R-R	6-1	176	9-19-03	0	0	5.63	5	0	0	8	7	5	5	1	3	7	.219	.286	.438	20.00	8.57	35
Marte, Yunior	R-R	6-5	210	9-8-03	0	2	9.92	7	6	0	16	28	19	18	3	8	15	.384	.446	.589	18.07	9.64	83
Martinez, Juan	R-R	5-11	195	4-6-01	2	1	5.93	10	1	0	14	11	9	9	3	8	14	.220	.328	.440	22.95	13.11	61
Martinez, Luis	L-L	6-1	180	9-17-03	0	3	14.90	16	1	0	19	33	35	32	2	20	19	.371	.482	.607	16.96	17.86	112
Mendieta, Augusto	R-R	5-11	190	8-19-04	1	0	3.68	12	0	0	15	21	7	6	0	6	12	.362	.431	.431	18.18	9.09	66
Michel, Ismael	R-R	6-3	175	2-14-02	0	0	0.87	8	0	2	10	6	1	1	1	4	20	.162	.244	.270	48.78	9.76	41

Miller, Mason	L-L	6-2	200	3-30-02	3	2	7.77	11	0	0	22	30	20	19	1	14	20	.330	.445	.429	18.18	12.73	110
Nova, Fraynel	R-R	6-0	190	5-22-02	1	2	6.38	10	1	0	24	35	22	17	2	8	25	.333	.377	.524	21.93	7.02	114
Novas, Elvis	R-R	6-0	205	9-2-02	1	0	8.44	9	0	0	11	16	11	10	2	5	14	.333	.418	.604	25.45	9.09	55
Oduber, Shawndrick	R-R	6-0	170	12-16-04	2	2	5.18	14	0	0	24	25	18	14	2	11	21	.258	.348	.392	18.75	9.82	112
Perez, Yeri	R-R	6-3	180	10-16-04	1	0	6.67	12	5	0	30	31	25	22	1	23	35	.287	.418	.444	25.93	17.04	135
Picard, Coleman	R-R	6-2	185	10-27-01	0	0	3.86	3	0	0	5	3	2	2	1	3	10	.188	.316	.438	52.63	15.79	19
Presinal, Yimi	R-R	5-11	175	9-18-04	0	0	1.59	4	0	1	6	4	3	1	0	2	4	.182	.280	.182	16.00	8.00	25
Rios, Jesus	R-R	6-1	190	12-27-01	0	2	3.65	7	0	0	12	15	8	5	0	4	10	.306	.382	.408	17.54	7.02	57
Rosario, Julio	R-R	6-1	205	7-12-02	4	2	2.45	17	0	3	29	25	15	8	1	14	40	.225	.307	.360	31.01	10.85	129
Sosa, Yenfri	L-L	6-0	170	12-29-03	2	2	4.88	12	0	0	28	24	19	15	3	22	36	.233	.380	.398	27.91	17.05	129
Valdez, Luis	R-R	6-0	170	10-25-04	1	0	5.96	9	2	0	23	27	16	15	4	6	29	.290	.337	.538	28.71	5.94	101
Valdez, Richy	R-R	6-1	180	7-29-05	0	0	21.60	4	0	0	3	4	10	8	1	6	4	.267	.560	.467	16.00	24.00	25
Van Den Brink, Gils	L-L	6-6	200	7-7-05	1	1	4.03	10	4	0	22	22	14	10	1	18	20	.268	.398	.390	19.42	17.48	103
Veliz, Mauricio	R-R	6-2	220	7-17-02	1	3	10.24	5	4	0	10	15	11	11	1	6	9	.357	.449	.500	18.37	12.24	49
Wacha, Michael	R-R	6-6	215	7-1-91	0	0	0.00	1	1	0	4	2	0	0	0	0	6	.154	.154	.154	46.15	0.00	13
Woods, Jordan	L-L	6-3	183	11-13-03	1	2	4.65	10	9	0	31	29	18	16	3	11	40	.244	.316	.395	30.08	8.27	133
Wyatt, Hiro	R-R	6-1	185	8-25-04	0	3	4.81	12	8	0	34	41	22	18	0	16	36	.304	.381	.378	22.50	10.00	160

Fielding

C: Ramirez 24, Pire 22, Um 14, Hayes 5, Silva 3, Zue 1, Nola 1. **1B:** Zue 30, Lucas 20, Silva 10, Russell 5, Newton 1, Barber 1, Hernandez 1. **2B:** Russell 33, Guzman 12, Acosta 10, Cepero 8. **3B:** Hernandez 40, Sosa 8, Russell 7, Wallace 6, Guzman 3, Newton 2. **SS:** Novas 42, Sosa 17, Newton 2, Cepero 1. **LF:** Barber 17, Rushford 14, Mendez 13, Allende 10, Ramos 8, Nivens 2, Guzman 2. **CF:** Gonzalez 39, Allende 16, Ramos 5. **RF:** Cabrera 28, Ramos 23, Nuel 10, Barber 3, Allende 2.

DSL ROYALS VENTURA — ROOKIE

DOMINICAN SUMMER LEAGUE

Batting	B-T	Ht.	Wt.	DOB	AVG	OBP	SLG	G	PA	AB	R	H	2B	3B	HR	RBI	BB	HBP	SH	SF	SO	SB	CS	BB%	SO%
Acosta, Angel	L-R	5-9	160	3-2-03	.194	.275	.278	10	40	36	3	7	3	0	0	8	3	1	0	0	5	0	1	7.50	12.50
Cerice, Jose	R-R	6-2	192	5-12-05	.314	.380	.421	47	179	159	35	50	8	3	1	25	10	8	0	2	20	4	2	5.59	11.17
Chacon, Robinson	L-R	5-11	165	4-21-07	.241	.281	.259	20	67	58	8	14	1	0	0	6	4	0	3	2	18	1	2	5.97	26.87
Cruz, Darvin	L-L	5-11	165	11-10-05	.000	.333	.000	1	3	2	1	0	0	0	0	0	1	0	0	0	1	1	0	33.33	33.33
Garcia, Anderson	R-R	6-0	195	9-14-06	.250	.250	.500	1	4	4	1	1	1	0	0	1	0	0	0	0	3	0	0	0.00	75.00
Garcia, Darison	B-R	5-11	165	5-14-07	.241	.357	.328	35	144	116	20	28	6	2	0	15	20	3	0	4	24	11	2	13.89	16.67
German, Manuel	R-R	6-1	220	4-29-05	.280	.419	.320	8	31	25	3	7	1	0	0	1	4	2	0	0	3	0	0	12.90	9.68
Gonzalez, Ricson	R-R	6-0	170	6-16-05	.274	.350	.333	37	138	117	12	32	5	1	0	20	11	5	1	4	21	0	2	7.97	15.22
Lopez, Daniel	L-L	6-2	165	9-14-05	.268	.362	.403	46	175	149	26	40	10	2	2	21	20	3	1	2	31	11	5	11.43	17.71
Luciano, Sandy	B-R	6-0	193	1-9-07	.207	.314	.276	28	102	87	11	18	6	0	0	14	14	0	0	1	7	2	1	13.73	6.86
Medina, Jose	B-R	5-10	185	4-16-05	.158	.366	.171	31	102	76	11	12	1	0	0	6	24	1	1	0	16	0	0	23.53	15.69
Medina, Raimel	R-R	5-11	165	11-15-04	.269	.403	.463	34	135	108	25	29	6	3	3	23	17	8	1	1	21	8	2	12.59	15.56
Morales, Jesus	R-R	6-0	165	8-2-07	.133	.316	.167	13	38	30	4	4	1	0	0	1	8	0	0	0	6	0	1	21.05	15.79
Mota, Edgar	R-R	6-1	170	12-14-05	.182	.286	.182	8	28	22	3	4	0	0	0	5	4	0	0	2	8	0	0	14.29	28.57
Nova, Charles	R-R	5-10	155	1-15-05	.167	.231	.167	4	13	12	0	2	0	0	0	3	1	0	0	0	1	0	0	7.69	7.69
Orasma, Alexander	B-R	6-0	165	11-19-04	.080	.207	.120	9	30	25	5	2	1	0	0	1	3	1	1	0	7	1	1	10.00	23.33
Paulino, Jose	L-L	5-11	165	10-23-05	.252	.396	.378	41	140	111	24	28	7	2	1	12	25	2	1	1	27	11	4	17.86	19.29
Ramirez, Angel	R-R	6-2	190	3-28-05	.217	.357	.261	17	56	46	9	10	2	0	0	5	9	1	0	0	7	5	0	16.07	12.50
Reyes, Omar	L-R	5-11	170	3-3-05	.095	.208	.095	8	24	21	1	2	0	0	0	2	3	0	0	0	7	1	0	12.50	29.17
Ricardo, Yandel	B-R	6-1	180	10-6-06	.213	.330	.366	45	196	164	27	35	7	6	2	23	25	4	2	1	34	14	5	12.76	17.35
Rivero, Marwin	R-R	5-11	160	10-21-06	.500	.667	.500	1	4	2	0	1	0	0	0	1	0	1	1	0	0	1	0	0.00	0.00
Roque, Pedro	R-R	5-10	160	12-21-05	.111	.400	.111	14	40	27	9	3	0	0	0	1	13	0	0	0	9	4	1	32.50	22.50
Ruiz, Sandy	R-R	5-10	160	1-24-06	.286	.545	.429	4	11	7	4	2	1	0	0	1	3	1	0	0	0	1	0	27.27	0.00
Ugarte, Jhonayker	R-R	6-2	180	3-12-07	.299	.423	.395	46	183	147	30	44	9	1	1	20	30	3	1	2	36	11	6	16.39	19.67

Pitching	B-T	Ht.	Wt.	DOB	W	L	ERA	G	GS	SV	IP	Hits	Runs	ER	HR	BB	SO	AVG	OBP	SLG	SO%	BB%	BF
Amezquita, Moises	L-L	5-10	160	7-27-04	1	0	4.76	3	0	1	6	6	3	3	0	7	7	.273	.448	.409	24.14	24.14	29
Basora, Andy	R-R	6-3	155	4-13-05	2	1	3.44	11	8	0	34	26	13	13	1	12	33	.213	.294	.311	24.26	8.82	136
Baules, Jezler	R-R	6-0	186	8-24-05	2	1	2.52	12	3	1	25	15	8	7	2	16	38	.179	.314	.262	37.25	15.69	102
Belen, Adrian	R-R	6-1	180	12-30-04	1	0	3.54	10	0	0	20	17	8	8	1	5	16	.233	.291	.370	20.25	6.33	79
Beras, Carlos	R-R	5-11	180	1-5-05	1	0	3.86	3	0	0	7	6	3	3	0	3	8	.231	.310	.385	27.59	10.34	29
Cabrera, Marwys	R-R	6-4	175	2-15-06	0	1	1.93	7	7	0	23	17	8	5	0	15	27	.207	.343	.244	27.27	15.15	99
Carmona, Samuel	R-R	6-0	160	12-23-04	2	3	7.24	11	3	1	27	30	22	22	1	8	26	.288	.353	.413	21.85	6.72	119
Colon, Manuel	R-R	5-11	148	12-24-06	0	0	12.46	3	0	0	4	7	6	6	1	3	4	.438	.455	.750	18.18	13.64	22
Cruz, Jose	R-R	6-4	200	4-29-05	3	1	1.57	10	3	0	29	17	10	5	1	16	30	.172	.287	.242	26.09	13.91	115
Del Rosario, Oliver	R-L	6-1	170	12-11-04	0	1	18.00	1	0	0	1	1	3	2	0	3	2	.250	.625	.250	25.00	37.50	8
Espinal, Cesar	R-R	6-2	165	8-25-05	1	1	1.42	8	2	1	13	11	6	2	0	8	13	.239	.364	.239	23.21	14.29	56
Gutierrez, Julio	R-R	6-1	175	3-5-05	3	1	3.97	10	0	0	23	18	13	10	1	8	16	.237	.326	.355	17.98	8.99	89
Herrera, Jorge	R-R	6-0	160	5-15-03	2	3	1.04	9	8	0	35	25	7	4	1	6	30	.207	.273	.281	22.73	4.55	132
Jhonni, Jordin	R-R	6-1	160	6-19-05	1	0	6.28	9	1	1	14	23	13	10	0	6	10	.365	.423	.429	14.08	8.45	71
Jimenez, Damian	R-R	6-5	190	9-21-04	0	2	5.27	6	5	0	14	6	11	8	0	16	7	.130	.354	.174	10.77	24.62	65
Leal, Jemir	R-R	6-2	155	4-7-03	2	0	1.89	9	1	1	19	12	5	4	0	5	16	.176	.230	.191	21.62	6.76	74
Lorenzo, Jhoan	R-R	5-11	165	1-12-05	0	1	81.00	1	0	0	0	0	3	3	0	5	1	.000	.833	.000	16.67	83.33	6
Oliveira, Jesus	R-R	6-0	160	12-31-04	2	3	5.59	10	0	0	19	16	14	12	2	18	16	.239	.420	.403	18.18	20.45	88
Pineda, Alvaro	R-R	6-2	170	6-30-04	0	1	21.60	1	1	0	2	5	5	4	0	1	3	.455	.500	.727	25.00	8.33	12
Reyes, Jhon	R-R	6-1	165	5-30-04	1	0	5.51	8	0	0	16	14	10	10	2	9	13	.233	.343	.367	18.57	12.86	70
Rivera, Juan	R-R	6-1	162	3-4-07	1	1	22.50	3	0	0	2	4	5	5	1	3	1	.364	.500	.818	7.14	21.43	14

Pitching	B-T	Ht.	Wt.	DOB	W	L	ERA	G	GS	SV	IP	Hits	Runs	ER	HR	BB	SO	AVG	OBP	SLG	SO%	BB%	BF
Rodriguez, Darwin	L-L	6-1	175	7-24-03	3	0	2.03	11	4	2	31	18	10	7	0	10	29	.168	.258	.196	24.17	8.33	120
Rodriguez, David	L-L	5-11	152	9-27-03	0	0	2.53	6	5	0	21	18	10	6	0	9	18	.240	.322	.280	20.45	10.23	88
Rodriguez, Frandy	R-R	5-9	155	1-28-06	1	0	0.84	8	0	1	11	4	1	1	0	1	7	.111	.135	.139	18.92	2.70	37
Rodriguez, Oswal	R-R	6-1	175	4-17-05	0	0	9.00	3	0	0	4	5	4	4	0	4	3	.333	.524	.400	14.29	19.05	21
Salgado, Edinson	L-L	6-0	150	1-6-05	0	0	4.50	3	3	0	8	5	4	4	1	7	13	.185	.353	.407	38.24	20.59	34
Taveras, Neftali	R-R	6-1	175	7-18-04	3	0	5.73	8	0	0	11	13	8	7	1	9	10	.302	.426	.488	18.52	16.67	54
Tovar, Geremy	L-L	6-2	176	4-25-06	0	1	12.00	3	0	0	6	5	9	8	0	7	9	.238	.484	.333	29.03	22.58	31

Fielding

C: Gonzalez 32, Medina 12, Morales 12, Mota 2. **1B:** Cerice 31, Medina 16, Reyes 5, Gonzalez 4, Ruiz 2. **2B:** Garcia 31, Acosta 6, Roque 6, Orasma 5, Reyes 3, Ricardo 3, Nova 3. **3B:** Ugarte 38, Cerice 17, Garcia 1, Orasma 1, Ruiz 1, Acosta 1. **SS:** Ricardo 41, Ugarte 5, Roque 4, Garcia 3, Orasma 3. **LF:** Medina 24, Chacon 13, Luciano 11, Ramirez 4, Rivero 1, Paulino 1, Lopez 1. **CF:** Paulino 38, Ramirez 8, Lopez 7, Medina 2, Cruz 1. **RF:** Lopez 36, Luciano 9, Medina 4, Ramirez 4, Chacon 3, Paulino 1.

DSL ROYALS FORTUNA — ROOKIE

DOMINICAN SUMMER LEAGUE

Batting	B-T	Ht.	Wt.	DOB	AVG	OBP	SLG	G	PA	AB	R	H	2B	3B	HR	RBI	BB	HBP	SH	SF	SO	SB	CS	BB%	SO%
Acosta, Angel	L-R	5-9	160	3-2-03	.381	.481	.524	6	27	21	4	8	0	0	1	7	4	1	0	1	2	2	0	14.81	7.41
Castro, Jose	R-R	6-3	160	4-21-06	.000	.200	.000	4	11	8	2	0	0	0	0	1	1	1	1	0	6	0	0	9.09	54.55
Chacon, Robinson	L-R	5-11	165	4-21-07	.255	.379	.291	17	67	55	9	14	2	0	0	5	10	1	0	0	13	3	0	14.93	19.40
Cruz, Darvin	L-L	5-11	165	11-10-05	.200	.307	.221	41	168	140	18	28	3	0	0	11	21	2	2	3	31	13	4	12.50	18.45
Garcia, Anderson	R-R	6-0	195	9-14-06	.244	.391	.337	31	110	86	17	21	3	1	1	8	19	3	0	2	38	2	0	17.27	34.55
Garcia, Darison	B-R	5-11	165	5-14-07	.200	.351	.300	9	37	30	7	6	3	0	0	5	7	0	0	0	4	4	1	18.92	10.81
German, Manuel	R-R	6-1	220	4-29-05	.333	.420	.550	21	69	60	14	20	7	0	2	13	6	3	0	0	18	3	0	8.70	26.09
Longo, Anthony	R-R	6-0	158	2-9-07	.143	.338	.179	23	74	56	9	8	2	0	0	7	14	3	0	1	10	0	2	18.92	13.51
Luciano, Sandy	B-R	6-0	193	1-9-07	.289	.429	.400	14	56	45	7	13	2	0	1	6	11	0	0	0	12	5	0	19.64	21.43
Medina, Raimel	R-R	5-11	165	11-15-04	.394	.523	.667	12	44	33	11	13	2	2	1	6	9	1	0	1	5	4	1	20.45	11.36
Mejia, Omar	R-R	6-2	160	9-20-06	.220	.353	.268	41	158	127	16	28	3	0	1	12	27	0	2	2	43	10	3	17.09	27.22
Morales, Jesus	R-R	6-0	165	8-2-07	.136	.208	.182	13	48	44	3	6	0	1	0	8	4	0	0	0	10	2	0	8.33	20.83
Mota, Edgar	R-R	6-1	170	12-14-05	.057	.214	.086	13	42	35	2	2	1	0	0	0	7	0	0	0	17	0	0	16.67	40.48
Nova, Charles	R-R	5-10	155	1-15-05	.217	.382	.301	28	110	83	15	18	4	0	1	11	22	2	0	3	20	8	1	20.00	18.18
Olmos, Juan	R-R	6-2	175	11-22-04	.203	.382	.305	23	76	59	9	12	3	0	1	7	13	4	0	0	18	4	0	17.11	23.68
Orasma, Alexander	B-R	6-0	165	11-19-04	.264	.459	.321	21	77	53	11	14	1	1	0	6	19	1	1	1	11	3	2	24.68	14.29
Ramirez, Angel	R-R	6-2	190	3-28-05	.359	.390	.462	11	41	39	7	14	2	1	0	8	2	0	0	0	4	5	1	4.88	9.76
Reyes, Omar	L-R	5-11	170	3-3-05	.205	.400	.295	15	60	44	9	9	1	0	1	7	12	3	0	1	12	5	0	20.00	20.00
Rivero, Marwin	R-R	5-11	160	10-21-06	.185	.359	.207	33	117	92	19	17	2	0	0	5	22	3	0	0	29	12	4	18.80	24.79
Roque, Pedro	R-R	5-10	160	12-21-05	.219	.321	.370	21	85	73	16	16	1	2	2	6	11	0	1	0	20	7	1	12.94	23.53
Ruiz, Sandy	R-R	5-10	160	1-24-06	.145	.269	.145	19	67	55	7	8	0	0	0	5	9	1	0	2	6	4	2	13.43	8.96
Ruiz, Tony	R-R	6-3	170	12-8-05	.202	.301	.349	39	153	129	15	26	8	1	3	22	14	6	0	4	45	0	0	9.15	29.41
Santos, Enmanuel	R-R	6-0	185	12-20-05	.151	.287	.301	25	87	73	11	11	2	0	3	8	10	4	0	0	24	5	2	11.49	27.59

Pitching	B-T	Ht.	Wt.	DOB	W	L	ERA	G	GS	SV	IP	Hits	Runs	ER	HR	BB	SO	AVG	OBP	SLG	SO%	BB%	BF
Amezquita, Moises	L-L	5-10	160	7-27-04	0	1	4.50	8	0	1	14	14	10	7	0	4	13	.264	.333	.377	21.67	6.67	60
Belen, Adrian	R-R	6-1	180	12-30-04	0	0	0.00	2	0	0	2	1	0	0	0	1	2	.143	.250	.143	25.00	12.50	8
Benitez, Sthiven	R-R	6-3	180	2-10-05	2	2	8.14	11	3	0	21	19	22	19	3	25	20	.241	.439	.418	18.69	23.36	107
Beras, Carlos	R-R	5-11	180	1-5-05	3	2	1.93	7	2	1	19	10	4	4	0	14	19	.161	.342	.177	23.75	17.50	80
Betemit, Wilson	R-R	6-1	170	7-27-03	0	1	4.26	4	4	0	6	7	3	3	0	2	6	.269	.345	.385	20.69	6.90	29
Cabrera, Marwys	R-R	6-4	175	2-15-06	1	2	3.94	4	4	0	16	17	7	7	0	6	14	.279	.343	.361	20.90	8.96	67
Colon, Manuel	R-R	5-11	148	12-24-06	1	0	6.14	5	0	1	7	9	5	5	0	4	10	.310	.412	.414	29.41	11.76	34
Cruz, Alan	R-R	6-1	160	3-3-07	0	4	20.25	10	0	0	8	14	28	18	3	13	8	.368	.569	.763	13.56	22.03	59
Del Rosario, Oliver	R-L	6-1	170	12-11-04	0	1	6.87	9	3	1	18	18	16	14	2	15	25	.269	.412	.433	29.41	17.65	85
Downs, Lloyd	R-R	6-1	170	4-13-06	0	0	10.66	8	0	1	13	12	17	15	2	15	11	.255	.448	.426	16.18	22.06	68
Espinal, Cesar	R-R	6-2	165	8-25-05	0	2	8.10	3	3	0	7	5	7	6	1	11	10	.208	.432	.375	27.03	29.73	37
Garcia, John	R-R	6-1	220	5-3-05	0	3	7.27	9	2	0	17	14	22	14	3	19	14	.222	.412	.413	16.47	22.35	85
Gonzalez, Carlos	R-R	6-1	150	2-14-06	2	0	3.13	12	2	2	23	21	13	8	1	8	18	.228	.290	.402	18.00	8.00	100
Herrera, Jorge	R-R	6-0	160	5-15-03	0	1	16.88	1	1	0	3	5	5	5	0	2	0	.455	.533	.545	0.00	13.33	15
Jhonni, Jordin	R-R	6-1	160	6-19-05	0	0	3.38	3	3	0	8	6	4	3	0	3	7	.207	.324	.310	20.59	8.82	34
Jimenez, Damian	R-R	6-5	190	9-21-04	0	0	6.00	4	1	0	9	8	6	6	0	4	10	.216	.293	.270	24.39	9.76	41
Jimenez, Nomar	L-L	6-2	172	1-3-07	1	0	0.00	2	0	0	2	2	0	0	0	5	1	.286	.583	.571	8.33	41.67	12
Lara, Diego	L-L	6-2	180	12-21-06	1	3	5.55	10	0	0	24	16	16	15	2	13	29	.186	.314	.372	27.36	12.26	106
Lorenzo, Jhoan	R-R	5-11	165	1-12-05	0	1	11.57	9	0	0	14	18	19	18	0	20	13	.316	.519	.474	16.05	24.69	81
Mejia, Jose	L-L	6-1	170	12-9-06	1	1	12.34	11	0	0	12	9	21	16	1	22	12	.214	.500	.310	17.65	32.35	68
Oliveira, Jesus	R-R	6-0	160	12-31-04	1	0	0.00	1	0	0	3	2	0	0	0	0	1	.250	.250	.500	12.50	0.00	8
Pineda, Alvaro	R-R	6-2	170	6-30-04	0	2	3.58	11	8	0	38	33	17	15	1	16	25	.239	.331	.348	15.92	10.19	157
Reyes, Jhon	R-R	6-1	165	5-30-04	0	0	4.50	3	0	1	4	1	2	2	0	2	2	.071	.188	.071	12.50	12.50	16
Rivera, Juan	R-R	6-1	162	3-4-07	1	3	4.07	7	5	0	24	18	13	11	1	13	24	.202	.324	.281	22.86	12.38	105
Rodriguez, David	L-L	5-11	152	9-27-03	0	0	1.93	4	4	0	19	10	4	4	0	3	17	.156	.206	.219	25.00	4.41	68
Rodriguez, Frandy	R-R	5-9	155	1-28-06	0	0	4.50	2	0	0	2	3	1	1	0	0	1	.333	.333	.444	11.11	0.00	9
Rodriguez, Oswal	R-R	6-1	175	4-17-05	0	2	8.78	8	0	1	13	14	16	13	0	12	12	.269	.431	.308	16.67	16.67	72
Salgado, Edinson	L-L	6-0	150	1-6-05	1	1	3.50	8	5	0	18	19	10	7	2	12	20	.264	.376	.389	23.53	14.12	85
Taveras, Neftali	R-R	6-1	175	7-18-04	1	1	11.57	4	0	0	7	8	9	9	0	5	6	.286	.429	.429	17.14	14.29	35
Toribio, Alberto	R-R	5-11	165	7-24-06	0	0	3.12	3	0	0	9	7	4	3	0	1	7	.226	.306	.387	19.44	2.78	36

Fielding

C: Olmos 20, Longo 16, Morales 9, Mota 9. **1B:** Ruiz 19, German 18, Reyes 9, Ruiz 9. **2B:** Nova 23, Roque 12, Orasma 7, Reyes 6, Acosta 3, Garcia 2, Ruiz 2. **3B:** Garcia 26, Mejia 20, Orasma 4, Ruiz 1, Acosta 1, Castro 1. **SS:** Mejia 20, Orasma 12, Roque 9, Garcia 7, Nova 3, Castro 3. **LF:** Rivero 20, Luciano 13, Medina 8, Chacon 8, Santos 3, Cruz 2. **CF:** Cruz 38, Rivero 11, Luciano 2, Medina 1, Ramirez 1. **RF:** Santos 21, Ruiz 10, Ramirez 10, Chacon 9, Medina 4, Rivero 1.

Los Angeles Angels

SEASON SYNOPSIS: The arrival of new manager Ron Washington brought positive vibes early to Anaheim, but another season-ending injury to Mike Trout, the free-agent departure of Shohei Ohtani to the Dodgers and the disintegration of a once-promising rotation turned 2024 into a slog, with a franchise-record 99 losses.

HIGH POINT: The Angels still drew nearly 2.6 million fans to The Big A, dropping less than 100,000 fans even after Ohtani's defection to that team farther west. The best on-field developments of the season were the fine full year by second-year shortstop Zach Neto (.761 OPS) and the conversion of righthander Jose Soriano to the rotation. Featuring a fastball that averaged 98 mph (97th percentile in MLB per Statcast), Soriano went 6-7, 3.42 before an August shoulder strain ended his season.

LOW POINT: A quick hit list would include Trout's left meniscus (knee) injury which sidelined him at the end of April, limiting him to 29 games, the third time in four seasons he's played fewer than 100; Anthony Rendon's injury-riddled season in which he played 57 games and failed to homer in 206 at-bats; and losing 15 of their final 18. Two of their three wins in that span came against the hapless 121-loss White Sox—who then swept the Angels in the penultimate series of the season.

NOTABLE ROOKIES: First baseman Nolan Schanuel, the club's 2023 first-round pick, grinded his way through a full season to post a credible .251/.343/.362 line with 13 homers and a team best 68 walks. With the rotation in tatters, 2019 third-round pick Jack Kochanowicz jumped from Double-A and made 11 big league starts, throwing strikes and posting a 3.99 ERA despite a 9.4% strikeout rate. Fireballing reliever Ben Joyce, whose fastball touched 105 mph, had more strikeouts (and more walks) than Kochanowicz in 30 fewer innings and picked up four saves while looking like the team's future closer.

KEY TRANSACTIONS: Free-agent signing Robert Stephenson faced one batter all season due to shoulder issues. A poor start to the season prompted the Angels to demote lefty Reid Detmers to Triple-A in June; he went 4-9, 6.70 in 17 big league starts, while elbow issues limited fellow lefty Patrick Sandoval to 16 starts before he had UCL surgery in June, likely costing him most of 2025. Closer Carlos Estevez was sent to the Phillies at the trade deadline.

OPENING DAY PAYROLL: $172,993,096 (13th)

PLAYERS OF THE YEAR

MAJOR LEAGUE

Zach Neto
SS
.249/.318/.443
23 HR, 30 SB
70 R, 77 RBIs

MINOR LEAGUE

Caden Dana
RHP
(AA)
9-7, 2.52 ERA
147 SO, 39 BB, 136 IP

ORGANIZATION LEADERS

Batting		*Qualifiers
MAJORS		
* AVG	Nolan Schanuel	.250
* OPS	Zach Neto	.761
HR	Taylor Ward	25
RBI	Zach Neto	77
MINORS		
* AVG	Gustavo Campero, Rocket City/Salt Lake	.279
* OBP	Gustavo Campero, Rocket City/Salt Lake	.392
* SLG	Gustavo Campero, Rocket City/Salt Lake	.472
* OPS	Gustavo Campero, Rocket City/Salt Lake	.864
R	Jordyn Adams, Salt Lake	78
H	Eric Wagaman, Rocket City/Salt Lake	122
TB	Eric Wagaman, Rocket City/Salt Lake	209
2B	Chad Stevens, 4-teams	30
3B	Joe Redfield, Inland Empire/Tri-City	6
3B	Caleb Bartolero, Inland Empire	6
HR	Keston Hiura, Toledo/Salt Lake	20
RBI	Imanol Vargas, Inland Empire	72
BB	Tucker Flint, Rocket City/Salt Lake	80
SO	Adrian Placencia, Inland Empire/Tri-City	149
SB	Caleb Ketchup, Tri-City/Salt Lake	64

Pitching		#Qualifiers
MAJORS		
W	Tyler Anderson	10
# ERA	Tyler Anderson	3.81
SO	Tyler Anderson	142
SV	Carlos Estevez	20
MINORS		
W	5 tied	9
L	Barrett Kent, Inland Empire	14
# ERA	Caden Dana, Rocket City	2.52
G	Alex Martinez, Inland Empire	48
GS	Joel Hurtado, Tri-City	26
GS	Barrett Kent, Inland Empire	26
SV	Camden Minacci, Tri-City/Rocket City	18
IP	Brett Kerry, Rocket City/Salt Lake	151
BB	Joel Hurtado, Tri-City	82
SO	Brett Kerry, Rocket City/Salt Lake	149
# AVG	Caden Dana, Rocket City	.184

LOS ANGELES ANGELS

2024 PERFORMANCE

General Manager: Perry Minasian. **Farm Director:** Joey Prebynski. **Scouting Director:** Tim McIlvaine.

Class	Team	League	W	L	PCT	Finish	Manager
Majors	Los Angeles Angels	American	63	99	.389	14 (15)	Ron Washington
Triple-A	Salt Lake Bees	Pacific Coast	67	82	.450	8 (10)	Keith Johnson
Double-A	Rocket City Trash Pandas	Southern	61	75	.449	7 (8)	Andy Schatzley
High-A	Tri-City Dust Devils	Northwest	53	78	.405	6 (6)	Willie Romero
Low-A	Inland Empire 66ers	California	58	72	.446	7 (8)	Dave Stapleton
Rookie	ACL Angels	Arizona Complex	32	28	.533	5 (15)	Hainley Statia
Rookie	DSL Angels	Dominican	38	18	.679	4 (51)	Hector De La Cruz
Overall 2024 Minor League Record			**309**	**353**	**.467**	**24th (30)**	

ORGANIZATION STATISTICS

LOS ANGELES ANGELS

AMERICAN LEAGUE

Batting	B-T	Ht.	Wt.	DOB	AVG	OBP	SLG	G	PA	AB	R	H	2B	3B	HR	RBI	BB	HBP	SH	SF	SO	SB	CS	BB%	SO%
Adams, Jordyn	R-R	6-2	181	10-18-99	.229	.289	.314	11	38	35	4	8	0	0	1	4	3	0	0	0	12	2	0	7.89	31.58
Adell, Jo	R-R	6-3	215	4-8-99	.207	.280	.402	130	451	405	54	84	15	2	20	62	35	7	0	3	126	15	10	7.76	27.94
Adrianza, Ehire	B-R	6-1	198	8-21-89	.192	.250	.346	8	28	26	4	5	1	0	1	2	2	0	0	0	11	0	0	7.14	39.29
Calhoun, Willie	L-R	5-8	205	11-4-94	.245	.315	.380	68	254	229	26	56	16	0	5	20	23	1	0	1	31	0	1	9.06	12.20
Campero, Gustavo	B-R	5-8	183	9-20-97	.239	.271	.348	13	48	46	6	11	0	1	1	6	0	2	0	0	8	3	0	0.00	16.67
Drury, Brandon	R-R	6-2	230	8-21-92	.169	.242	.228	97	360	325	28	55	7	0	4	15	27	5	0	3	81	1	0	7.50	22.50
Goodrum, Niko	B-R	6-3	215	2-28-92	.000	.133	.000	4	15	13	1	0	0	0	0	0	2	0	0	0	4	1	0	13.33	26.67
Guillorme, Luis	L-R	5-10	190	9-27-94	.231	.302	.298	51	117	104	6	24	5	1	0	3	11	0	1	1	23	1	2	9.40	19.66
Hicks, Aaron	B-R	6-1	205	10-2-89	.140	.222	.193	18	63	57	6	8	0	0	1	5	6	0	0	0	23	0	0	9.52	36.51
Hiura, Keston	R-R	5-11	208	8-2-96	.148	.148	.148	10	27	27	1	4	0	0	0	1	0	0	0	0	10	0	1	0.00	37.04
Kavadas, Niko	L-R	5-11	235	10-27-98	.183	.283	.333	30	106	93	11	17	2	0	4	8	11	2	0	0	41	1	0	10.38	38.68
Leblanc, Charles	R-R	6-3	195	6-3-96	.190	.393	.476	11	28	21	6	4	0	0	2	6	7	0	0	0	9	0	0	25.00	32.14
Lopez, Jack	R-R	5-10	160	12-16-92	.254	.286	.343	27	71	67	4	17	3	0	1	6	2	1	1	0	25	0	1	2.82	35.21
Moniak, Mickey	L-R	6-2	195	5-13-98	.219	.266	.380	124	418	392	48	86	17	2	14	49	21	4	0	1	114	8	4	5.02	27.27
Neto, Zach	R-R	6-0	185	1-31-01	.249	.318	.443	155	602	542	70	135	34	1	23	77	39	16	4	1	140	30	10	6.48	23.26
O'Hoppe, Logan	R-R	6-2	185	2-9-00	.244	.303	.409	136	522	479	64	117	17	1	20	56	33	8	1	1	155	2	3	6.32	29.69
Paris, Kyren	R-R	6-0	180	11-11-01	.118	.224	.216	21	59	51	4	6	2	0	1	5	7	0	0	0	17	1	0	11.86	28.81
Pillar, Kevin	R-R	6-0	200	1-4-89	.236	.291	.378	83	282	259	37	61	14	1	7	41	12	9	0	2	61	10	3	4.26	21.63
Rendon, Anthony	R-R	6-1	200	6-6-90	.218	.307	.267	57	238	206	21	45	10	0	0	14	23	5	0	4	35	6	1	9.66	14.71
Rengifo, Luis	B-R	5-10	195	2-26-97	.300	.347	.417	78	304	283	41	85	13	1	6	30	16	4	1	0	44	24	7	5.26	14.47
Sano, Miguel	R-R	6-4	272	5-11-93	.205	.295	.313	28	95	83	9	17	3	0	2	6	9	2	0	1	36	0	0	9.47	37.89
Schanuel, Nolan	L-R	6-3	195	2-14-02	.250	.343	.362	147	607	519	62	130	19	0	13	54	68	9	3	7	103	10	1	11.20	16.97
Stefanic, Michael	R-R	5-8	180	2-24-96	.218	.301	.255	40	124	110	8	24	4	0	0	8	10	3	1	0	20	0	0	8.06	16.13
Teodosio, Bryce	R-L	6-3	220	6-18-99	.083	.083	.083	5	12	12	1	1	0	0	0	0	0	0	0	0	5	0	0	0.00	41.67
Thaiss, Matt	L-R	6-0	215	5-6-95	.204	.323	.299	57	186	157	14	32	9	0	2	16	28	0	0	1	58	3	0	15.05	31.18
Trout, Mike	R-R	6-2	235	8-7-91	.220	.325	.541	29	126	109	17	24	1	2	10	14	16	1	0	0	27	6	1	12.70	21.43
Tucker, Cole	B-R	6-3	200	7-3-96	.180	.263	.300	25	57	50	3	9	4	1	0	3	6	0	0	1	17	3	1	10.53	29.82
Wagaman, Eric	R-R	6-4	210	8-14-97	.250	.270	.403	18	74	72	6	18	5	0	2	10	2	0	0	0	17	0	0	2.70	22.97
Ward, Taylor	R-R	6-1	200	12-14-93	.246	.323	.426	156	663	585	73	144	26	2	25	75	63	7	0	8	163	6	4	9.50	24.59

Pitching	B-T	Ht.	Wt.	DOB	W	L	ERA	G	GS	SV	IP	Hits	Runs	ER	HR	BB	SO	AVG	OBP	SLG	SO%	BB%	BF
Aldegheri, Samuel	L-L	6-1	180	9-19-01	1	2	4.85	3	3	0	13	15	12	7	2	10	10	.283	.403	.453	14.93	14.93	67
Anderson, Tyler	L-L	6-2	220	12-30-89	10	15	3.81	31	31	0	179	158	83	76	24	73	142	.232	.311	.394	18.56	9.54	765
Baumann, Mike	R-R	6-4	240	9-10-95	0	0	6.75	10	0	0	9	14	8	7	2	4	7	.341	.413	.585	15.22	8.70	46
Burke, Brock	L-L	6-4	210	8-4-96	2	1	3.54	21	1	0	20	16	8	8	1	7	25	.213	.280	.360	30.49	8.54	82
Canning, Griffin	R-R	6-2	180	5-11-96	6	13	5.19	32	31	0	172	174	105	99	31	66	130	.265	.334	.459	17.59	8.93	739
Cimber, Adam	R-R	6-3	195	8-15-90	3	0	7.03	28	0	0	24	20	19	19	1	14	19	.235	.377	.306	17.76	13.08	107
Cisnero, Jose	R-R	6-3	258	4-11-89	0	0	6.89	15	0	0	16	18	15	12	4	8	17	.290	.384	.516	22.97	10.81	74
Contreras, Roansy	R-R	6-0	175	11-7-99	1	4	4.33	37	3	2	52	44	28	25	8	23	40	.227	.317	.407	17.86	10.27	224
Crouse, Hans	L-R	6-4	180	9-15-98	4	3	2.84	25	0	0	25	14	10	8	2	17	34	.161	.311	.276	31.78	15.89	107
Cueto, Johnny	R-R	5-11	229	2-15-86	0	2	7.15	2	2	0	11	14	9	9	4	3	6	.298	.340	.681	12.00	6.00	50
Dana, Caden	L-R	6-4	215	12-17-03	1	2	9.58	3	3	0	10	14	12	11	5	7	8	.326	.423	.744	15.38	13.46	52
Daniel, Davis	R-R	6-1	190	6-11-97	1	4	6.23	6	6	0	30	39	22	21	5	6	28	.307	.343	.512	20.90	4.48	134
Detmers, Reid	L-L	6-2	210	7-8-99	4	9	6.70	17	17	0	87	98	67	65	18	38	109	.282	.353	.511	27.88	9.72	391
Estevez, Carlos	R-R	6-6	277	12-28-92	1	3	2.38	34	0	20	34	20	10	9	3	5	32	.169	.202	.288	25.81	4.03	124
Fulmer, Carson	R-R	6-0	210	12-13-93	0	5	4.15	37	8	0	87	81	45	40	11	40	81	.246	.334	.419	21.37	10.55	379
Garcia, Luis	R-R	6-2	240	1-30-87	5	1	3.71	45	0	4	44	37	21	18	4	14	40	.226	.297	.329	21.98	7.69	182
Garrett, Amir	R-L	6-5	239	5-3-92	0	0	5.06	6	0	0	5	4	3	3	1	5	11	.211	.375	.421	45.83	20.83	24
Guillorme, Luis	L-R	5-10	190	9-27-94	0	0	0.00	2	0	0	2	1	0	0	0	1	0	.143	.250	.286	0.00	12.50	8
Hicks, Aaron	S-R	6-1	205	10-2-89	0	0	18.00	1	0	0	1	2	2	2	1	1	0	.400	.500	1.000	0.00	16.67	6
Joyce, Ben	R-R	6-5	225	9-17-00	2	0	2.08	31	1	4	35	26	8	8	1	14	33	.210	.310	.250	23.24	9.86	142
Kochanowicz, Jack	L-R	6-7	228	12-22-00	2	6	3.99	11	11	0	65	68	30	29	7	10	25	.275	.325	.417	9.40	3.76	266
Kristofak, Zac	R-R	5-9	189	12-8-97	0	0	0.00	1	0	0	2	3	2	0	0	2	2	.375	.455	.625	18.18	18.18	11
Marte, Jose	R-R	6-3	180	6-14-96	0	0	2.33	14	0	0	19	14	6	5	1	10	14	.206	.313	.309	17.50	12.50	80

Mederos, Victor	R-R	6-2	227	6-8-01	0	1	11.81	4	0	0	5	7	7	7	1	6	5	.333	.481	.571	18.52	22.22	27
Miller, Ryan	R-R	6-0	180	3-28-96	0	1	4.15	13	0	0	13	13	7	6	2	8	11	.260	.362	.440	18.97	13.79	58
Moore, Matt	L-L	6-3	210	6-18-89	5	3	5.03	51	0	1	48	39	31	27	11	26	41	.218	.324	.436	19.52	12.38	210
Plesac, Zach	R-R	6-3	220	1-21-95	1	1	8.25	3	3	0	12	12	11	11	4	7	5	.255	.352	.574	9.26	12.96	54
Quijada, Jose	L-L	5-11	215	11-9-95	2	2	3.26	22	0	0	19	12	9	7	1	17	24	.190	.373	.254	28.57	20.24	84
Rosenberg, Kenny	L-L	6-1	195	7-9-95	0	1	6.00	7	1	0	24	28	17	16	5	8	17	.292	.346	.510	16.35	7.69	104
Sandoval, Patrick	L-L	6-3	190	10-18-96	2	8	5.08	16	16	0	80	85	49	45	8	35	81	.272	.349	.401	22.95	9.92	353
Sano, Miguel	R-R	6-4	272	5-11-93	0	0	0.00	1	0	0	0	0	0	0	0	0	0	.000	.000	.000	0.00	0.00	1
Silseth, Chase	R-R	6-0	217	5-18-00	0	1	6.75	2	2	0	8	8	7	6	3	4	12	.242	.324	.545	31.58	10.53	38
Soriano, Jose	R-R	6-3	220	10-20-98	6	7	3.42	22	20	0	113	91	50	43	8	45	97	.224	.311	.329	20.73	9.62	468
Stefanic, Michael	R-R	5-8	180	2-24-96	0	0	0.00	1	0	0	1	1	0	0	0	0	0	.250	.400	.250	0.00	0.00	5
Strickland, Hunter	R-R	6-3	225	9-24-88	3	2	3.31	72	0	1	73	56	31	27	10	24	57	.211	.280	.376	19.39	8.16	294
Suarez, Jose	L-L	5-10	225	1-3-98	1	2	6.02	22	3	1	52	57	38	35	7	27	56	.274	.367	.495	23.33	11.25	240
Tucker, Cole	S-R	6-3	200	7-3-96	0	0	0.00	1	0	0	1	1	0	0	0	1	0	.333	.500	.333	0.00	25.00	4
Wantz, Andrew	R-R	6-4	235	10-13-95	0	0	6.75	1	0	0	1	1	1	1	1	1	3	.200	.333	.800	50.00	16.67	6
Zeferjahn, Ryan	R-R	6-5	209	2-28-98	0	0	2.12	12	0	0	17	7	4	4	0	6	18	.127	.234	.145	28.13	9.38	64
Zuniga, Guillermo	R-R	6-5	230	10-10-98	0	0	5.09	15	0	2	18	16	10	10	5	8	12	.242	.329	.515	15.79	10.53	76

Fielding

Catcher	PCT	G	PO	A	E	DP	PB
O'Hoppe	.994	127	962	41	6	0	5
Thaiss	.988	46	313	10	4	1	1

First Base	PCT	G	PO	A	E	DP
Calhoun	1.000	4	30	4	0	3
Drury	1.000	14	92	9	0	11
Goodrum	1.000	1	5	0	0	1
Kavadas	1.000	5	47	1	0	2
Leblanc	.923	2	11	1	1	1
Sano	1.000	5	22	2	0	1
Schanuel	.994	144	1018	76	7	127

Second Base	PCT	G	PO	A	E	DP
Adrianza	1.000	2	1	5	0	1
Drury	.976	56	77	127	5	31
Guillorme	.987	32	32	46	1	13
Hiura	.909	5	3	7	1	1
Leblanc	1.000	4	2	5	0	1
Lopez	.986	21	32	39	1	19
Paris	.983	17	20	39	1	8
Rengifo	.975	31	57	59	3	20
Stefanic	1.000	35	50	76	0	24

Third Base	PCT	G	PO	A	E	DP
Adrianza	1.000	6	1	7	0	1
Drury	1.000	16	5	31	0	6
Goodrum	.667	3	3	1	2	0
Guillorme	.966	14	9	19	1	3
Leblanc	1.000	5	4	6	0	1
Rendon	.961	50	35	87	5	9
Rengifo	.975	48	30	89	3	8
Sano	1.000	14	6	22	0	1
Stefanic	1.000	1	0	1	0	1
Tucker	.833	9	3	17	4	1
Wagaman	.925	17	10	39	4	4

Shortstop	PCT	G	PO	A	E	DP
Guillorme	1.000	4	5	6	0	3
Lopez	.903	7	8	20	3	5
Neto	.972	155	231	405	18	103
Paris	1.000	2	2	6	0	0
Rengifo	1.000	1	0	2	0	1

Outfield	PCT	G	PO	A	E	DP
Adams	.958	11	23	0	1	0
Adell	.983	123	234	3	4	0
Calhoun	.000	1	0	0	0	0
Campero	.964	13	26	1	1	0
Hicks	1.000	13	19	0	0	0
Lopez	.000	1	0	0	0	0
Moniak	.986	118	270	3	4	0
Pillar	.993	77	133	2	1	0
Rengifo	.000	1	0	0	0	0
Teodosio	1.000	4	7	1	0	1
Trout	1.000	24	65	2	0	1
Tucker	1.000	8	13	0	0	0
Wagaman	1.000	1	1	0	0	0
Ward	.984	141	302	8	5	0

SALT LAKE BEES — *TRIPLE-A*

PACIFIC COAST LEAGUE

Batting	B-T	Ht.	Wt.	DOB	AVG	OBP	SLG	G	PA	AB	R	H	2B	3B	HR	RBI	BB	HBP	SH	SF	SO	SB	CS	BB%	SO%
Adams, Jordyn	R-R	6-2	181	10-18-99	.261	.333	.386	123	549	482	78	126	22	4	10	58	51	4	4	6	148	28	11	9.29	26.96
Adrianza, Ehire	B-R	6-1	198	8-21-89	.349	.434	.558	14	53	43	11	15	2	2	1	4	8	0	0	2	9	2	0	15.09	16.98
Blake, Andy	R-R	6-4	195	8-15-00	.200	.280	.333	13	50	45	8	9	0	0	2	7	4	1	0	0	12	2	1	8.00	24.00
Calhoun, Willie	L-R	5-8	205	11-4-94	.276	.369	.402	48	203	174	23	48	10	0	4	28	24	3	0	2	29	1	3	11.82	14.29
Campero, Gustavo	B-R	5-8	183	9-20-97	.280	.379	.340	14	59	50	8	14	3	0	0	5	5	3	1	0	9	4	0	8.47	15.25
DiChiara, Sonny	R-R	6-1	263	7-29-99	.115	.217	.154	16	61	52	5	6	2	0	0	3	6	1	1	1	27	1	0	9.84	44.26
Dozier, Hunter	R-R	6-4	220	8-22-91	.222	.268	.394	48	214	198	22	44	11	1	7	38	12	1	1	2	64	3	0	5.61	29.91
Drury, Brandon	R-R	6-2	230	8-21-92	.263	.440	.263	6	25	19	2	5	0	0	0	1	5	1	0	0	5	0	0	20.00	20.00
Ellis, Drew	R-R	6-3	205	12-1-95	.243	.373	.414	32	134	111	21	27	2	1	5	13	21	2	0	0	25	2	0	15.67	18.66
Flint, Tucker	L-L	6-2	215	4-5-01	.217	.357	.391	13	56	46	5	10	5	0	1	9	9	1	0	0	13	0	0	16.07	23.21
Goodrum, Niko	B-R	6-3	215	2-28-92	.200	.333	.200	8	30	25	3	5	0	0	0	4	5	0	0	0	9	0	0	16.67	30.00
Hiura, Keston	R-R	5-11	208	8-2-96	.354	.424	.796	37	165	147	35	52	5	0	20	42	14	4	0	0	51	1	0	8.48	30.91
Humphreys, Zach	R-R	5-10	195	10-9-97	.219	.323	.293	82	299	256	47	56	10	0	3	25	39	1	2	1	61	9	4	13.04	20.40
Kavadas, Niko	L-R	5-11	235	10-27-98	.159	.229	.341	11	48	44	4	7	2	0	2	4	4	0	0	0	18	0	0	8.33	37.50
Ketchup, Caleb	R-R	5-10	160	1-4-02	.241	.290	.345	7	31	29	5	7	1	1	0	3	2	0	0	0	11	2	1	6.45	35.48
Knowles, D'Shawn	B-R	6-0	181	1-16-01	.202	.313	.262	35	100	84	14	17	2	0	1	14	14	0	1	1	23	3	1	14.00	23.00
Leblanc, Charles	R-R	6-3	195	6-3-96	.254	.379	.437	98	414	339	56	86	20	3	12	52	68	3	0	4	103	4	3	16.43	24.88
Lopez, Jack	R-R	5-10	160	12-16-92	.274	.333	.421	104	432	387	58	106	15	3	12	57	31	5	5	4	111	15	7	7.18	25.69
Lugo, Matthew	R-R	6-1	187	5-9-01	.400	.400	1.200	1	5	5	2	2	1	0	1	3	0	0	0	0	0	0	0	0.00	0.00
Marisnick, Jake	R-R	6-4	220	3-30-91	.283	.368	.551	54	231	198	43	56	15	1	12	31	26	2	2	2	62	6	3	11.26	26.84
Martin, Jason	L-R	5-9	185	9-5-95	.286	.364	.517	70	306	269	54	77	17	3	13	45	31	3	1	2	66	5	5	10.13	21.57
Martinez, Orlando	L-L	6-0	185	2-17-98	.182	.250	.273	3	12	11	2	2	1	0	0	0	1	0	0	0	2	1	0	8.33	16.67
Matheny, Shane	L-R	6-1	205	6-5-96	.310	.412	.483	18	69	58	6	18	5	1	1	11	10	0	1	0	20	1	0	14.49	28.99
Mulrine, Anthony	R-R	6-0	205	3-30-98	.239	.338	.328	22	80	67	9	16	3	0	1	8	8	2	3	0	18	0	0	10.00	22.50
Paris, Kyren	R-R	6-0	180	11-11-01	.209	.287	.360	37	159	139	20	29	5	2	4	19	16	0	2	2	52	8	1	10.06	32.70
Sano, Miguel	R-R	6-4	272	5-11-93	.270	.325	.459	9	40	37	7	10	1	0	2	12	2	1	0	0	13	0	0	5.00	32.50
Soto, Elliot	R-R	5-9	160	8-21-89	.224	.323	.307	114	468	398	67	89	15	3	4	44	58	2	6	4	112	21	5	12.39	23.93
Soto, Livan	L-R	5-10	160	6-22-00	.214	.324	.286	9	35	28	2	6	2	0	0	3	5	0	1	1	5	1	2	14.29	14.29
Stefanic, Michael	R-R	5-8	180	2-24-96	.389	.456	.510	40	183	157	27	61	13	0	2	33	19	3	1	3	16	4	0	10.38	8.74
Stevens, Chad	R-R	6-3	215	2-3-99	.238	.289	.345	22	91	84	12	20	9	0	0	5	3	3	1	0	25	2	1	3.30	27.47
Teodosio, Bryce	R-L	6-3	220	6-18-99	.276	.339	.418	114	462	409	63	113	19	12	5	51	35	7	5	6	120	40	4	7.58	25.97

Trout, Mike	R-R	6-2	235	8-7-91	.000	.000	.000	1	1	1	0	0	0	0	0	0	0	0	0	0	1	0	0	0.00	100.00
Tucker, Cole	B-R	6-3	200	7-3-96	.251	.351	.344	54	231	195	27	49	9	0	3	26	31	0	3	2	56	1	2	13.42	24.24
Wagaman, Eric	R-R	6-4	210	8-14-97	.320	.355	.500	27	107	100	15	32	5	2	3	14	6	0	0	1	14	1	1	5.61	13.08
Wallace, Landon	B-R	6-2	170	2-27-02	.229	.315	.375	14	55	48	7	11	3	2	0	6	6	0	1	0	19	1	0	10.91	34.55
Wallach, Chad	R-R	6-2	246	11-4-91	.247	.337	.430	87	335	291	31	72	15	1	12	46	35	6	0	3	96	2	2	10.45	28.66

Pitching	B-T	Ht.	Wt.	DOB	W	L	ERA	G	GS	SV	IP	Hits	Runs	ER	HR	BB	SO	AVG	OBP	SLG	SO%	BB%	BF
Armstrong, Ivan	R-R	6-5	247	7-27-00	0	2	6.75	4	1	0	11	17	9	8	1	6	5	.362	.455	.511	9.09	10.91	55
Bachman, Sam	R-R	6-1	235	9-30-99	1	2	5.17	3	3	0	16	15	10	9	3	4	7	.246	.303	.443	10.61	6.06	66
Calhoun, Willie	L-R	5-8	205	11-4-94	0	0	18.00	1	0	0	2	7	4	4	0	0	0	.636	.583	.727	0.00	0.00	12
Cimber, Adam	R-R	6-3	195	8-15-90	0	1	7.04	11	0	0	15	26	16	12	4	5	20	.356	.434	.616	24.10	6.02	83
Cisnero, Jose	R-R	6-3	258	4-11-89	0	0	1.93	4	0	0	5	7	1	1	0	2	8	.333	.391	.381	34.78	8.70	23
Crouse, Hans	L-R	6-4	180	9-15-98	3	0	2.27	29	0	2	32	22	9	8	4	13	59	.190	.271	.345	45.74	10.08	129
Cueto, Johnny	R-R	5-11	229	2-15-86	3	0	3.09	4	4	0	23	27	9	8	4	5	15	.284	.327	.453	14.85	4.95	101
Daniel, Davis	R-R	6-1	190	6-11-97	9	7	5.42	22	21	0	118	139	74	71	15	34	122	.289	.341	.457	23.33	6.50	523
Darrell-Hicks, Michael	R-R	6-5	220	11-13-97	0	0	4.35	10	0	0	21	21	12	10	0	5	23	.269	.356	.295	25.27	5.49	91
Detmers, Reid	L-L	6-2	210	7-8-99	6	6	5.54	14	14	0	78	82	50	48	18	27	101	.262	.326	.495	29.36	7.85	344
Fulmer, Carson	R-R	6-0	210	12-13-93	0	1	3.00	1	1	0	3	3	3	1	0	2	2	.231	.333	.308	13.33	13.33	15
Garrett, Amir	R-L	6-5	239	5-3-92	3	2	5.08	26	2	0	34	34	22	19	5	16	43	.262	.351	.508	28.48	10.60	151
Guerrero, Tayron	R-R	6-8	225	1-9-91	1	3	5.73	30	0	1	33	47	22	21	1	11	32	.338	.390	.446	20.65	7.10	155
Harding, Houston	L-L	6-1	230	5-22-98	0	2	9.19	6	5	0	16	24	22	16	4	10	10	.343	.425	.629	12.35	12.35	81
Herget, Jimmy	R-R	6-3	170	9-9-93	1	2	3.97	10	0	0	11	10	7	5	4	1	7	.238	.267	.524	15.56	2.22	45
Hernandez, Aaron	R-R	6-1	170	12-2-96	1	0	9.00	2	0	0	2	2	2	2	0	3	2	.286	.455	.286	18.18	27.27	11
Humphreys, Zach	R-R	5-10	195	10-9-97	0	0	0.00	1	0	0	1	1	3	0	1	1	0	.200	.429	.800	0.00	14.29	7
Kerry, Brett	R-R	6-0	213	4-12-99	3	3	5.95	15	14	0	85	102	57	56	17	22	65	.300	.344	.506	17.47	5.91	372
Knebel, Corey	R-R	6-3	224	11-26-91	0	0	25.07	6	1	0	5	17	14	13	2	5	6	.567	.611	.933	16.22	13.51	37
Kolarek, Adam	L-L	6-3	215	1-14-89	1	1	6.97	31	0	1	31	43	29	24	4	18	33	.331	.416	.492	22.00	12.00	150
Kristofak, Zac	R-R	5-9	189	12-8-97	1	0	3.38	6	3	0	19	19	7	7	2	5	10	.264	.312	.417	12.99	6.49	77
Langford, Ryan	R-R	6-0	160	8-31-99	0	1	2.08	4	3	0	9	6	2	2	0	5	3	.207	.324	.276	8.82	14.71	34
Ledo, Luis	R-R	6-4	240	5-28-95	2	3	8.17	25	3	0	40	47	41	36	5	25	39	.297	.400	.449	20.21	12.95	193
MacGregor, Travis	R-R	6-4	215	10-15-97	1	7	3.61	41	3	0	82	77	37	33	8	29	73	.248	.325	.367	20.74	8.24	352
Marte, Jose	R-R	6-3	180	6-14-96	4	2	2.22	25	0	8	28	19	12	7	1	13	33	.190	.289	.260	28.45	11.21	116
Matheny, Shane	L-R	6-1	205	6-5-96	0	0	0.00	1	0	0	0	1	0	0	0	0	0	.500	.500	.500	0.00	0.00	2
Mederos, Victor	R-R	6-2	227	6-8-01	0	0	3.86	3	3	0	9	7	4	4	1	2	6	.212	.257	.394	17.14	5.71	35
Miller, Ryan	R-R	6-0	180	3-28-96	5	1	2.45	34	1	0	62	48	21	17	7	14	61	.212	.271	.336	24.60	5.65	248
O'Reilly, John	R-R	6-5	225	10-4-95	0	1	14.09	3	2	0	8	19	13	12	6	3	7	.442	.478	.953	15.22	6.52	46
Plesac, Zach	R-R	6-3	220	1-21-95	5	7	5.69	18	17	1	100	113	65	63	19	33	65	.286	.337	.499	15.01	7.62	433
Quijada, Jose	L-L	5-11	215	11-9-95	0	0	0.00	4	0	0	3	1	0	0	0	4	2	.125	.417	.125	16.67	33.33	12
Robertson, Nick	R-R	6-6	265	7-16-98	0	0	6.92	10	0	0	13	18	12	10	1	8	17	.321	.415	.464	25.76	12.12	66
Rosenberg, Kenny	L-L	6-1	195	7-9-95	9	7	4.21	21	21	0	115	112	57	54	25	38	105	.253	.316	.472	21.52	7.79	488
Seig, Hayden	R-R	6-5	227	9-10-98	0	2	6.75	4	1	0	12	17	10	9	1	3	7	.333	.375	.510	12.50	5.36	56
Shaw, Bryan	S-R	6-1	226	11-8-87	1	4	4.14	39	0	7	41	34	22	19	1	28	34	.227	.346	.320	18.38	15.14	185
Silseth, Chase	R-R	6-0	217	5-18-00	0	3	6.35	7	7	0	28	33	21	20	6	18	16	.300	.397	.527	12.21	13.74	131
Stephenson, Robert	R-R	6-3	205	2-24-93	0	0	0.00	1	0	0	0	0	0	0	0	1	0	.000	1.000	.000	0.00	100.0	1
Strickland, Hunter	R-R	6-3	225	9-24-88	0	0	13.50	2	0	0	2	4	3	3	0	1	2	.400	.455	.400	18.18	9.09	11
Suarez, Jose	L-L	5-10	225	1-3-98	2	3	6.54	11	11	0	52	67	42	38	10	17	62	.306	.357	.507	25.31	6.94	245
Thomas, Tyler	R-L	6-1	175	12-22-95	1	2	5.44	31	2	0	45	45	32	27	4	30	45	.265	.389	.365	21.53	14.35	209
Torres, Eric	L-L	6-0	195	9-22-99	0	1	8.59	6	0	0	7	7	7	7	0	11	8	.259	.487	.296	20.51	28.21	39
Wantz, Andrew	R-R	6-4	235	10-13-95	1	2	6.17	7	6	0	23	23	17	16	4	15	34	.256	.364	.456	31.78	14.02	107
Yovan, Kenyon	R-R	6-2	221	12-28-97	2	0	5.23	25	0	0	33	39	21	19	3	15	25	.310	.381	.444	16.89	10.14	148
Zeferjahn, Ryan	R-R	6-5	209	2-28-98	0	0	2.35	5	0	0	8	5	2	2	1	1	8	.185	.214	.407	28.57	3.57	28
Zuniga, Guillermo	R-R	6-5	230	10-10-98	1	4	5.19	25	0	2	26	25	17	15	4	8	16	.253	.312	.434	14.55	7.27	110

Fielding

Catcher	PCT	G	PO	A	E	DP	PB
Humphreys	.998	60	470	24	1	4	3
Mulrine	.994	22	165	12	1	2	2
Wallach	.991	75	626	37	6	4	11

First Base	PCT	G	PO	A	E	DP
Blake	1.000	2	14	1	0	0
Calhoun	.986	18	131	6	2	15
DiChiara	1.000	16	106	6	0	7
Dozier	.994	21	149	16	1	17
Flint	1.000	5	36	2	0	5
Goodrum	1.000	1	6	0	0	1
Hiura	.985	15	128	6	2	13
Humphreys	1.000	6	37	6	0	3
Kavadas	1.000	10	77	5	0	4
Leblanc	.997	40	275	18	1	29
Matheny	1.000	2	5	1	0	1
Sano	1.000	2	17	0	0	3
Tucker	1.000	8	54	3	0	7
Wagaman	.986	10	68	5	1	6
Wallach	.778	2	6	1	2	0

Second Base	PCT	G	PO	A	E	DP
Adrianza	1.000	4	11	12	0	7
Blake	.929	7	15	11	2	2
Drury	1.000	2	4	7	0	3
Ellis	.969	9	8	23	1	6
Goodrum	.000	1	0	0	0	0
Hiura	.922	15	18	29	4	5
Humphreys	.000	1	0	0	0	0
Leblanc	.990	25	42	54	1	16
Lopez	.966	18	20	36	2	8
Matheny	1.000	7	11	17	0	7
Paris	.909	12	12	28	4	6
Soto	.988	26	28	57	1	12
Soto	1.000	4	6	6	0	0
Stefanic	.962	18	24	52	3	17
Stevens	1.000	5	4	11	0	1
Tucker	1.000	7	16	16	0	6

Third Base	PCT	G	PO	A	E	DP
Blake	1.000	4	1	9	0	0
Dozier	.979	25	14	32	1	2
Ellis	.907	17	16	23	4	3
Goodrum	.625	4	1	4	3	0
Leblanc	.962	27	17	59	3	3
Lopez	.972	17	9	26	1	3
Matheny	.667	1	1	1	1	1

Sano	1.000	3	1	2	0	0
Soto	1.000	17	7	27	0	4
Stefanic	.882	12	6	24	4	2
Stevens	.949	17	12	25	2	3
Tucker	.909	5	4	16	2	0
Wagaman	.750	9	4	11	5	1

Shortstop	PCT	G	PO	A	E	DP
Adrianza	.968	9	10	20	1	3
Ellis	.800	4	4	4	2	1
Goodrum	1.000	1	1	2	0	1
Lopez	.956	33	45	86	6	21
Paris	.925	23	38	61	8	20
Soto	.944	5	6	11	1	2
Soto	.976	69	76	166	6	31
Stevens	1.000	1	1	3	0	0
Tucker	.917	7	9	13	2	5

Outfield	PCT	G	PO	A	E	DP
Adams	.984	119	242	8	4	2
Calhoun	1.000	2	2	0	0	0
Campero	.971	14	33	1	1	0
Dozier	1.000	5	8	0	0	0
Flint	1.000	8	21	0	0	0
Hiura	.000	1	0	0	0	0
Humphreys	1.000	2	4	0	0	0
Ketchup	1.000	7	19	1	0	0
Knowles	.933	26	40	2	3	1
Lopez	.988	40	75	5	1	0
Lugo	1.000	1	2	0	0	0
Marisnick	.989	41	86	2	1	0
Martin	.980	43	97	0	2	0
Martinez	1.000	3	12	0	0	0
Matheny	1.000	8	12	0	0	0
Soto	1.000	3	4	1	0	0
Teodosio	.983	115	281	3	5	1
Trout	1.000	1	3	0	0	0
Tucker	1.000	7	22	0	0	0
Wagaman	.800	7	4	0	1	0
Wallace	.913	14	20	1	2	0

ROCKET CITY TRASH PANDAS — DOUBLE-A

SOUTHERN LEAGUE

Batting	B-T	Ht.	Wt.	DOB	AVG	OBP	SLG	G	PA	AB	R	H	2B	3B	HR	RBI	BB	HBP	SH	SF	SO	SB	CS	BB%	SO%
Brown, Sam	L-L	6-2	218	9-12-01	.214	.298	.302	126	505	440	44	94	23	2	4	53	44	12	2	7	105	5	0	8.71	20.79
Calabrese, David	L-R	5-11	160	9-26-02	.209	.346	.345	38	136	110	14	23	3	0	4	11	23	0	3	0	41	4	2	16.91	30.15
Campero, Gustavo	B-R	5-8	183	9-20-97	.279	.394	.494	93	373	312	56	87	17	4	14	45	39	20	2	0	60	29	7	10.46	16.09
Coutney, Matt	L-R	6-1	230	7-8-99	.194	.265	.252	28	114	103	6	20	3	0	1	8	10	0	1	0	42	0	0	8.77	36.84
Emmerson, Myles	R-R	5-11	185	5-15-98	.242	.356	.313	35	119	99	14	24	4	0	1	9	17	1	1	1	28	0	1	14.29	23.53
Flint, Tucker	L-L	6-2	215	4-5-01	.246	.364	.419	121	506	422	61	104	19	3	16	58	71	9	1	3	150	15	8	14.03	29.64
Flores, Ronaldo	R-R	6-0	175	5-17-02	.250	.250	.250	1	4	4	0	1	0	0	0	0	0	0	0	0	2	0	0	0.00	50.00
Fontenelle, Cole	B-R	6-3	205	3-11-02	.278	.404	.417	22	89	72	16	20	4	0	2	9	11	5	0	1	23	12	1	12.36	25.84
Gobbel, Ben	R-R	6-1	190	11-2-99	.228	.268	.357	68	255	241	29	55	7	0	8	33	10	3	1	0	59	10	3	3.92	23.14
Guzman, Denzer	R-R	6-1	180	2-8-04	.206	.297	.304	83	342	296	26	61	9	1	6	30	36	3	4	2	90	7	6	10.53	26.32
Hamilton, Caleb	R-R	6-0	185	2-5-95	.124	.248	.230	39	134	113	11	14	0	0	4	11	17	2	1	1	47	3	0	12.69	35.07
Ketchup, Caleb	R-R	5-10	160	1-4-02	.125	.222	.500	3	9	8	2	1	0	0	1	3	1	0	0	0	4	1	0	11.11	44.44
Martinez, Orlando	L-L	6-0	185	2-17-98	.263	.353	.380	77	324	274	34	72	15	1	5	36	41	1	0	7	51	4	0	12.65	15.74
McCroskey, Mac	R-R	6-1	180	12-31-99	.216	.306	.263	71	246	213	25	46	7	0	1	16	26	2	4	1	77	11	1	10.57	31.30
Mershon, David	B-R	5-8	160	5-24-03	.254	.326	.298	29	130	114	13	29	5	0	0	8	12	1	1	2	31	5	1	9.23	23.85
Moore, Christian	R-R	6-1	210	10-21-02	.322	.378	.533	23	98	90	18	29	4	0	5	14	8	0	0	0	29	2	0	8.16	29.59
Nicholson, Ryan	L-L	6-4	220	8-29-00	.167	.214	.167	3	14	12	0	2	0	0	0	2	1	0	0	1	4	0	0	7.14	28.57
Paris, Kyren	R-R	6-0	180	11-11-01	.091	.198	.130	23	92	77	8	7	1	1	0	7	9	2	0	3	36	8	1	9.78	39.13
Payne, Tyler	R-R	5-11	210	10-25-92	.233	.280	.319	73	290	270	27	63	11	0	4	26	14	4	1	1	53	3	0	4.83	18.28
Rada, Nelson	L-L	5-10	160	8-24-05	.234	.331	.269	123	502	428	53	100	12	0	1	31	57	8	4	5	117	35	11	11.35	23.31
Stevens, Chad	R-R	6-3	215	2-3-99	.316	.359	.491	17	64	57	6	18	4	0	2	10	3	2	0	2	11	2	1	4.69	17.19
Vera, Arol	B-R	6-2	213	9-12-02	.171	.234	.223	76	277	251	19	43	10	0	1	21	19	2	3	2	84	1	5	6.86	30.32
Wagaman, Eric	R-R	6-4	210	8-14-97	.260	.335	.460	94	388	346	56	90	23	2	14	46	38	2	0	2	69	9	3	9.79	17.78
Wallace, Landon	B-R	6-2	170	2-27-02	.143	.143	.286	3	7	7	0	1	1	0	0	1	0	0	0	0	4	0	0	0.00	57.14

Pitching	B-T	Ht.	Wt.	DOB	W	L	ERA	G	GS	SV	IP	Hits	Runs	ER	HR	BB	SO	AVG	OBP	SLG	SO%	BB%	BF
Aldegheri, Samuel	L-L	6-1	180	9-19-01	0	2	5.19	4	4	0	17	16	11	10	0	9	25	.232	.316	.290	31.65	11.39	79
Armstrong, Ivan	R-R	6-5	247	7-27-00	7	2	2.79	28	1	0	58	48	21	18	6	24	60	.231	.305	.365	25.10	10.04	239
Bachman, Sam	R-R	6-1	235	9-30-99	0	4	5.26	9	9	0	39	38	29	23	6	17	34	.253	.337	.413	20.00	10.00	170
Chaney, Chase	R-R	6-1	199	12-16-99	7	11	4.30	26	25	0	138	149	73	66	19	44	103	.271	.331	.428	17.08	7.30	603
Choban, Brady	R-R	6-5	240	9-16-00	2	3	5.55	21	0	1	24	23	19	15	3	11	21	.242	.339	.358	18.75	9.82	112
Dana, Caden	L-R	6-4	215	12-17-03	9	7	2.52	23	23	0	136	89	46	38	10	39	147	.184	.256	.283	27.37	7.26	537
Darrell-Hicks, Michael	R-R	6-5	220	11-13-97	6	4	1.73	30	0	8	42	34	11	8	0	8	46	.224	.284	.263	27.06	4.71	170
Dashwood, Jack	L-L	6-6	240	11-17-97	0	0	2.70	8	0	0	10	6	3	3	1	1	15	.162	.184	.243	39.47	2.63	38
Erla, Mason	R-R	6-4	200	8-19-97	1	4	2.21	34	4	5	53	53	18	13	2	13	46	.262	.307	.322	21.00	5.94	219
Espinosa, Carlos	R-R	6-2	188	8-8-01	0	0	3.29	10	0	1	14	7	5	5	0	7	13	.149	.259	.213	24.07	12.96	54
Fermin, Jose	R-R	6-3	248	11-28-01	0	1	0.00	2	0	0	2	1	1	0	0	1	2	.143	.250	.286	22.22	11.11	9
Harding, Houston	L-L	6-1	230	5-22-98	1	0	3.38	5	1	0	19	10	7	7	2	10	18	.159	.274	.317	24.32	13.51	74
Hernandez, Aaron	R-R	6-1	170	12-2-96	0	1	4.50	5	0	0	6	4	3	3	1	1	2	.190	.261	.381	8.70	4.35	23
Jones, Nick	L-L	6-6	224	1-22-99	2	2	3.00	20	0	1	24	23	8	8	0	3	29	.258	.292	.348	30.21	3.13	96
Joyce, Ben	R-R	6-5	225	9-17-00	1	0	4.26	18	0	1	19	11	9	9	2	11	34	.164	.291	.313	43.04	13.92	79
Kerry, Brett	R-R	6-0	213	4-12-99	2	3	2.73	12	8	0	66	40	20	20	10	15	84	.170	.226	.328	33.33	5.95	252
Key, Keythel	R-R	6-3	180	10-10-03	0	0	40.50	1	1	0	1	3	3	3	0	3	0	.600	.750	.800	0.00	37.50	8
Klassen, George	R-R	6-2	170	1-26-02	2	3	5.65	7	7	0	29	24	18	18	2	22	36	.240	.365	.320	28.35	17.32	127
Kochanowicz, Jack	L-R	6-7	228	12-22-00	5	8	4.50	18	18	0	102	103	56	51	8	27	86	.259	.318	.372	19.50	6.12	441
Langford, Ryan	R-R	6-0	160	8-31-99	0	0	0.00	1	0	0	2	0	0	0	0	2	2	.000	.250	.000	25.00	25.00	8
Mederos, Victor	R-R	6-2	227	6-8-01	4	8	6.39	20	20	0	89	105	69	63	12	48	69	.301	.398	.456	16.51	11.48	418
Minacci, Camden	R-R	6-3	210	1-14-02	2	2	3.28	22	0	7	25	27	12	9	3	11	35	.276	.360	.429	31.53	9.91	111
Murphy, Luke	R-R	6-5	190	11-5-99	0	1	5.29	27	0	2	32	38	23	19	5	10	37	.288	.362	.477	24.67	6.67	150
O'Reilly, John	R-R	6-5	225	10-4-95	0	1	3.64	24	10	0	72	65	30	29	3	18	62	.244	.310	.312	20.95	6.08	296
Owen, Noah	L-R	6-4	200																				
Pelham, CD	R-L	6-6	238	2-21-95	0	0	2.00	9	0	0	9	6	4	2	0	7	11	.182	.317	.273	26.83	17.07	41
Rangel, Alan	R-R	6-2	170	8-21-97	2	0	2.61	4	4	0	21	15	7	6	2	5	25	.200	.256	.333	30.49	6.10	82
Seig, Hayden	R-R	6-5	227	9-10-98	3	5	3.68	40	1	4	59	57	27	24	5	21	59	.249	.310	.358	23.14	8.24	255
Smith, Jake	R-R	6-4	189	10-4-99	0	0	22.50	2	0	0	2	6	5	5	0	2	3	.600	.571	.700	21.43	14.29	14
Southard, Jared	R-R	6-2	220	10-4-00	0	1	5.32	18	0	0	24	20	16	14	4	17	20	.225	.373	.393	18.18	15.45	110
Torres, Eric	L-L	6-0	195	9-22-99	4	1	2.31	27	0	0	35	22	11	9	2	19	55	.176	.307	.248	36.42	12.58	151

Pitching	B-T	Ht.	Wt.	DOB	W	L	ERA	G	GS	SV	IP	Hits	Runs	ER	HR	BB	SO	AVG	OBP	SLG	SO%	BB%	BF
Yovan, Kenyon	R-R	6-2	221	12-28-97	1	0	0.84	8	0	1	11	4	3	1	0	3	12	.114	.205	.143	30.00	7.50	40

Fielding

Catcher	PCT	G	PO	A	E	DP	PB
Emmerson	.983	33	261	20	5	2	0
Hamilton	.971	38	323	17	10	4	7
Payne	.995	71	628	33	3	5	5

First Base	PCT	G	PO	A	E	DP
Brown	.991	110	782	68	8	67
Coutney	1.000	12	76	0	0	4
Flint	.978	13	78	9	2	9
Nicholson	1.000	1	3	1	0	0
Wagaman	1.000	7	54	4	0	3

Second Base	PCT	G	PO	A	E	DP
Gobbel	.958	6	5	18	1	1
Ketchup	.833	2	3	2	1	0
McCroskey	.979	46	77	109	4	25
Mershon	.983	16	20	39	1	4
Moore	1.000	19	33	32	0	7
Paris	1.000	3	6	8	0	2
Stevens	1.000	4	1	5	0	1
Vera	.984	46	77	106	3	31

Third Base	PCT	G	PO	A	E	DP
Coutney	.800	3	0	4	1	0
Fontenelle	.964	22	7	46	2	3
Gobbel	.920	58	30	85	10	11
Mershon	.857	6	5	7	2	0
Stevens	1.000	8	9	11	0	0
Vera	.926	28	8	42	4	3
Wagaman	.891	20	15	26	5	1

Shortstop	PCT	G	PO	A	E	DP
Guzman	.974	82	120	218	9	29
McCroskey	.959	24	34	83	5	13
Mershon	.857	4	6	12	3	5
Paris	.964	19	12	42	2	8
Stevens	.833	1	2	3	1	0
Vera	.913	7	10	11	2	3

Outfield	PCT	G	PO	A	E	DP
Calabrese	1.000	38	69	1	0	1
Campero	.992	62	119	1	1	1
Emmerson	.000	1	0	0	0	0
Flint	1.000	108	169	8	0	2
Hamilton	1.000	1	2	0	0	0
Martinez	.983	61	107	7	2	2
Mershon	.929	3	13	0	1	0
Rada	.992	117	252	5	2	0
Wagaman	.984	35	55	5	1	0
Wallace	1.000	2	2	0	0	0

TRI-CITY DUST DEVILS — *HIGH-A*

NORTHWEST LEAGUE

Batting	B-T	Ht.	Wt.	DOB	AVG	OBP	SLG	G	PA	AB	R	H	2B	3B	HR	RBI	BB	HBP	SH	SF	SO	SB	CS	BB%	SO%
Blake, Andy	R-R	6-4	195	8-15-00	.133	.225	.206	53	189	165	18	22	1	1	3	15	19	1	2	2	44	9	0	10.05	23.28
Blakely, Werner	L-R	6-3	185	2-21-02	.206	.314	.304	98	382	326	38	67	18	4	2	33	50	2	3	1	111	15	2	13.09	29.06
Bruggeman, Kevin	R-R	5-9	186	7-25-01	.242	.337	.329	73	282	240	31	58	10	1	3	27	28	7	6	1	67	15	3	9.93	23.76
Burns, Peter	L-R	5-10	195	10-14-99	.143	.286	.171	13	42	35	5	5	1	0	0	4	6	1	0	0	5	0	2	14.29	11.90
Coutney, Matt	L-R	6-1	230	7-8-99	.270	.353	.418	91	387	337	57	91	22	2	8	42	38	7	1	3	98	2	1	9.82	25.32
DiChiara, Sonny	R-R	6-1	263	7-29-99	.333	.426	.510	29	115	96	13	32	5	0	4	19	15	2	0	2	22	0	0	13.04	19.13
Flores, Juan	R-R	5-10	180	2-13-06	.229	.280	.319	53	210	188	17	43	11	0	2	27	12	3	3	4	58	1	2	5.71	27.62
Flores, Ronaldo	R-R	6-0	175	5-17-02	.186	.213	.291	27	91	86	5	16	6	0	1	14	2	1	2	0	25	1	0	2.20	27.47
Gobbel, Ben	R-R	6-1	190	11-2-99	.292	.374	.469	34	147	130	21	38	8	0	5	20	11	6	0	0	22	4	1	7.48	14.97
Guzman, Denzer	R-R	6-1	180	2-8-04	.291	.325	.354	19	84	79	12	23	3	1	0	5	4	0	1	0	28	3	1	4.76	33.33
Ketchup, Caleb	R-R	5-10	160	1-4-02	.207	.312	.313	120	500	425	68	88	21	3	6	37	62	5	2	5	133	62	10	12.40	26.60
Martin, Mason	L-R	6-0	220	6-2-99	.191	.313	.415	30	112	94	12	18	4	1	5	14	13	4	0	1	49	2	0	11.61	43.75
Matheny, Shane	L-R	6-1	205	6-5-96	.181	.326	.319	21	90	72	11	13	3	2	1	7	12	4	1	1	22	0	1	13.33	24.44
McCroskey, Mac	R-R	6-1	180	12-31-99	.226	.277	.387	30	102	93	10	21	4	1	3	10	7	0	1	1	30	2	1	6.86	29.41
McGillis, Will	R-R	6-3	200	1-16-99	.096	.200	.205	24	95	83	9	8	0	0	3	8	9	2	0	1	31	0	0	9.47	32.63
Pendleton, Caleb	R-R	6-2	185	4-5-02	.234	.246	.328	19	65	64	4	15	6	0	0	5	1	0	0	0	23	3	0	1.54	35.38
Placencia, Adrian	B-R	5-11	173	6-2-03	.208	.336	.268	51	224	183	23	38	4	2	1	14	31	5	3	1	75	4	5	13.84	33.48
Redfield, Joe	L-R	6-2	200	10-18-01	.237	.291	.302	56	256	232	25	55	8	2	1	23	14	4	5	1	48	15	4	5.47	18.75
Rios, Alberto	R-R	6-0	203	3-19-02	.252	.330	.301	31	115	103	8	26	5	0	0	10	10	2	0	0	32	2	2	8.70	27.83
Ruiz, Jorge	L-L	5-10	164	6-30-04	.150	.203	.191	62	241	220	21	33	4	1	1	19	12	3	4	2	50	8	4	4.98	20.75
Sanchez, Jadiel	B-R	6-2	185	5-10-01	.215	.278	.356	85	346	312	33	67	14	3	8	36	24	5	1	4	66	2	1	6.94	19.08
Stevens, Chad	R-R	6-3	215	2-3-99	.324	.374	.549	44	187	173	28	56	16	1	7	28	12	2	0	0	57	2	3	6.42	30.48
Stewart, Joe	R-R	6-5	212	5-6-98	.219	.315	.263	38	131	114	8	25	2	0	1	9	13	3	1	0	33	11	1	9.92	25.19
Vera, Arol	B-R	6-2	213	9-12-02	.202	.287	.257	31	122	109	9	22	3	0	1	4	12	1	0	0	31	2	0	9.84	25.41
Wallace, Landon	B-R	6-2	170	2-27-02	.195	.321	.339	41	141	118	18	23	8	3	1	20	15	7	1	0	42	3	1	10.64	29.79
Williams, Cam	B-R	5-10	195	2-7-98	.186	.316	.452	54	212	177	27	33	12	1	11	32	31	3	0	1	89	2	0	14.62	41.98

Pitching	B-T	Ht.	Wt.	DOB	W	L	ERA	G	GS	SV	IP	Hits	Runs	ER	HR	BB	SO	AVG	OBP	SLG	SO%	BB%	BF
Albanese, Glenn	R-R	6-7	223	10-22-98	1	0	2.35	11	0	0	15	13	4	4	2	6	20	.228	.313	.368	31.25	9.38	64
Blake, Andy	R-R	6-4	195	8-15-00	0	0	0.00	1	0	0	0	0	0	0	0	0	0	.000	.000	.000	0.00	0.00	1
Choban, Brady	R-R	6-5	240	9-16-00	2	0	2.39	21	0	0	26	21	9	7	2	6	23	.219	.272	.313	22.33	5.83	103
Clark, Chris	R-R	6-4	195	8-14-01	3	12	6.09	22	22	0	105	103	76	71	12	58	102	.258	.367	.430	21.56	12.26	473
Costeiu, Ryan	R-R	6-0	200	11-28-00	1	5	2.84	18	18	0	73	42	24	23	5	35	79	.162	.266	.297	26.60	11.78	297
Espinosa, Carlos	R-R	6-2	188	8-8-01	4	3	4.08	32	0	1	46	47	24	21	5	23	63	.264	.346	.393	30.73	11.22	205
Fermin, Jose	R-R	6-3	248	11-28-01	5	2	3.74	19	0	3	34	27	17	14	2	13	56	.220	.295	.317	40.00	9.29	140
Garcia, Leonard	L-L	6-2	165	8-11-03	5	2	3.71	28	1	0	53	47	27	22	4	28	54	.240	.341	.332	23.38	12.12	231
Gieg, Max	R-R	6-5	230	6-8-01	0	1	3.52	7	0	1	8	6	6	3	2	8	11	.200	.385	.400	28.21	20.51	39
Gonzalez, Jenrry	L-L	5-10	185	6-7-01	0	1	7.94	4	0	0	6	6	5	5	0	0	7	.286	.292	.381	29.17	0.00	24
Harding, Houston	L-L	6-1	230	5-22-98	4	2	0.98	10	8	0	46	34	9	5	1	16	43	.201	.274	.249	22.99	8.56	187
Hewlett, Stone	L-L	6-1	190	10-3-01	0	0	0.00	4	0	0	6	6	0	0	0	1	4	.261	.292	.348	16.67	4.17	24
Hurtado, Joel	R-R	6-2	180	2-6-01	9	8	4.61	26	26	0	139	137	85	71	8	82	134	.258	.371	.357	21.30	13.04	629
Key, Keythel	R-R	6-3	180	10-10-03	1	2	3.41	6	6	0	29	20	12	11	1	19	36	.200	.328	.260	29.75	15.70	121
Langford, Ryan	R-R	6-0	160	8-31-99	0	3	7.02	23	3	0	33	49	33	26	4	21	36	.327	.412	.507	20.34	11.86	177
Lindsay-Young, Christian	R-R	6-5	210	5-19-96	0	0	0.00	2	0	0	1	2	0	0	0	1	2	.333	.429	.500	28.57	14.29	7
Marcheco, Jorge	R-R	6-1	185	8-6-02	2	7	5.07	20	19	0	82	87	53	46	9	31	70	.274	.350	.416	19.23	8.52	364
Martinez, Quinton	L-L	6-4	190	1-23-99	1	1	4.56	17	1	0	24	24	12	12	0	21	19	.258	.417	.366	15.83	17.50	120
Mederos, Victor	R-R	6-2	227	6-8-01	0	1	9.00	1	1	0	6	5	6	6	1	2	5	.217	.280	.348	20.00	8.00	25
Minacci, Camden	R-R	6-3	210	1-14-02	1	4	3.33	23	0	11	24	23	10	9	1	11	33	.242	.321	.316	31.13	10.38	106
Mondak, Nick	L-L	6-4	203	6-2-98	1	2	1.95	16	0	1	28	18	9	6	2	6	43	.178	.224	.287	40.19	5.61	107
Murphy, Luke	R-R	6-5	190	11-5-99	0	0	0.86	16	0	8	21	12	2	2	0	5	30	.167	.215	.222	37.97	6.33	79

Pitching	B-T	Ht.	Wt.	DOB	W	L	ERA	G	GS	SV	IP	Hits	Runs	ER	HR	BB	SO	AVG	OBP	SLG	SO%	BB%	BF
Natera, Sammy	L-L	6-4	225	11-6-99	2	0	0.60	5	2	0	15	10	1	1	0	6	24	.196	.305	.216	40.68	10.17	59
Phansalkar, Roman	R-R	6-1	195	6-2-98	1	3	6.34	33	0	1	44	49	36	31	6	30	46	.285	.401	.488	21.60	14.08	213
Phillips, Dylan	L-L	6-0	220	6-16-99	3	3	3.31	41	0	1	54	45	24	20	1	21	64	.224	.313	.299	27.59	9.05	232
Rivera, Erik	L-L	6-2	200	4-2-01	0	1	3.31	10	8	0	35	29	17	13	5	20	39	.213	.316	.360	24.68	12.66	158
Smith, Jake	R-R	6-4	189	10-4-99	1	4	6.04	36	0	0	51	49	41	34	4	42	59	.251	.407	.390	23.98	17.07	246
Southard, Jared	R-R	6-2	220	10-4-00	2	2	3.41	20	0	0	29	23	12	11	1	10	26	.225	.302	.333	21.85	8.40	119
Suarez, Willian	R-R	6-3	209	3-21-98	2	2	6.46	24	0	1	31	31	23	22	5	15	47	.261	.362	.445	34.06	10.87	138
Urena, Walbert	R-R	6-0	170	1-25-04	2	7	4.19	16	16	0	77	66	45	36	3	54	64	.236	.371	.311	18.50	15.61	346

Fielding

Catcher	PCT	G	PO	A	E	DP	PB
Bruggeman	.990	38	289	21	3	0	10
Burns	.980	12	92	8	2	0	0
Flores	.984	39	410	34	7	4	5
Flores	.986	24	204	10	3	1	4
Pendleton	.969	17	115	11	4	1	1
Rios	.993	16	131	7	1	2	4

First Base	PCT	G	PO	A	E	DP
Blake	.955	4	20	1	1	4
Coutney	.997	78	558	39	2	55
DiChiara	.994	26	153	13	1	17
Flores	.833	1	5	0	1	2
Martin	.988	10	75	4	1	10
Matheny	.986	11	65	6	1	6
McGillis	1.000	1	13	3	0	1
Pendleton	1.000	1	1	1	0	0
Vera	1.000	2	18	1	0	1
Williams	1.000	4	22	0	0	1

Second Base	PCT	G	PO	A	E	DP
Blake	.976	9	21	20	1	5
Bruggeman	.914	10	12	20	3	3
Gobbel	.950	9	15	23	2	7
Ketchup	.987	73	127	175	4	38
Matheny	1.000	4	7	14	0	4
McCroskey	.956	18	28	37	3	9
McGillis	.961	12	19	30	2	12
Placencia	1.000	1	3	4	0	2

Third Base	PCT	G	PO	A	E	DP
Blake	.981	25	17	35	1	2
Coutney	.933	7	3	11	1	1
Gobbel	.917	25	16	39	5	3
Ketchup	1.000	1	1	2	0	0
Matheny	.923	4	2	10	1	3
McCroskey	.867	6	4	9	2	1
McGillis	.500	2	0	1	1	0
Stevens	.935	21	15	28	3	4
Vera	.909	27	13	37	5	1
Williams	.818	18	8	19	6	2

Shortstop	PCT	G	PO	A	E	DP
Blake	.952	12	15	25	2	11
Guzman	.975	18	23	56	2	13
Ketchup	.886	16	18	44	8	10
Matheny	1.000	4	7	8	0	0
McCroskey	.938	6	7	8	1	1
Placencia	.946	50	71	105	10	22
Stevens	.956	24	27	59	4	13
Vera	1.000	2	3	1	0	1

Outfield	PCT	G	PO	A	E	DP
Blakely	.964	95	180	5	7	3
Bruggeman	1.000	3	3	0	0	0
Ketchup	.950	32	54	3	3	0
Redfield	1.000	57	116	2	0	2
Ruiz	.959	62	113	3	5	1
Sanchez	.993	81	135	3	1	0
Stewart	.966	36	53	4	2	0
Wallace	.938	38	57	3	4	0
Williams	1.000	1	3	0	0	0

INLAND EMPIRE 66ERS

LOW-A

CALIFORNIA LEAGUE

Batting	B-T	Ht.	Wt.	DOB	AVG	OBP	SLG	G	PA	AB	R	H	2B	3B	HR	RBI	BB	HBP	SH	SF	SO	SB	CS	BB%	SO%
Bartolero, Caleb	R-R	5-11	175	11-4-99	.259	.330	.451	72	302	266	37	69	15	6	8	38	21	9	2	4	63	3	1	6.95	20.86
Burns, Peter	L-R	5-10	195	10-14-99	.333	.409	.436	14	44	39	5	13	2	1	0	3	2	3	0	0	10	1	0	4.55	22.73
Castillo, Kevyn	L-L	5-10	170	6-12-05	.292	.374	.415	46	196	171	21	50	7	1	4	25	20	3	1	1	53	8	4	10.20	27.04
Daly, Mitchell	R-R	6-1	185	5-16-01	.181	.306	.257	29	124	105	14	19	2	0	2	12	18	1	0	0	25	1	0	14.52	20.16
De Jesus, Randy	R-R	6-4	210	2-13-05	.277	.352	.459	100	427	379	62	105	25	4	12	60	34	11	0	2	125	3	5	7.96	29.27
DiChiara, Sonny	R-R	6-1	263	7-29-99	.222	.354	.418	53	237	194	33	43	14	0	8	38	36	5	0	2	79	1	0	15.19	33.33
Flores, Juan	R-R	5-10	180	2-13-06	.280	.345	.425	48	208	186	32	52	16	1	3	25	12	7	2	1	40	3	1	5.77	19.23
Flores, Randy	L-R	5-9	180	9-18-00	.203	.286	.329	23	92	79	16	16	4	0	2	16	8	2	1	2	12	4	1	8.70	13.04
Foster, Rio	R-R	6-3	205	6-18-03	.377	.442	.545	19	86	77	10	29	7	0	2	12	8	1	0	0	18	3	0	9.30	20.93
Garcia, Cristian	B-R	6-1	168	7-26-04	.177	.310	.280	46	200	164	22	29	11	0	2	22	29	4	0	3	62	1	1	14.50	31.00
Gill, Starlin	R-R	5-10	150	3-16-00	.194	.270	.269	24	75	67	9	13	3	1	0	8	5	2	1	0	14	3	0	6.67	18.67
Laverde, Dario	L-R	5-10	160	2-26-05	.277	.366	.390	57	246	213	28	59	10	4	2	21	27	4	0	2	56	0	0	10.98	22.76
Macias, Johan	B-R	5-9	150	1-6-03	.257	.310	.380	55	205	187	31	48	7	5	2	24	11	4	2	1	43	5	1	5.37	20.98
Moore, Christian	R-R	6-1	210	10-21-02	.545	.583	1.000	2	12	11	5	6	2	0	1	6	1	0	0	0	0	0	1	8.33	0.00
Nicholson, Ryan	L-L	6-4	220	8-29-00	.292	.403	.504	30	134	113	22	33	12	0	4	25	17	4	0	0	23	1	0	12.69	17.16
Ortiz, Capri	R-R	6-0	150	4-1-05	.265	.360	.368	113	462	400	57	106	15	7	4	46	50	10	1	1	127	22	8	10.82	27.49
Pendleton, Caleb	R-R	6-2	185	4-5-02	.213	.314	.377	20	70	61	9	13	2	1	2	12	8	1	0	0	21	0	0	11.43	30.00
Placencia, Adrian	B-R	5-11	173	6-2-03	.258	.411	.521	57	242	190	38	49	13	2	11	34	44	6	1	1	74	4	2	18.18	30.58
Ramirez, Alexander	R-R	6-2	229	8-29-02	.274	.386	.521	43	176	146	36	40	5	2	9	28	25	3	0	2	60	5	1	14.20	34.09
Redfield, Joe	L-R	6-2	200	10-18-01	.288	.380	.411	57	260	219	50	63	7	4	4	30	33	1	5	2	47	15	3	12.69	18.08
Rodriguez, Luis	R-R	6-1	176	12-22-04	.163	.294	.233	15	52	43	8	7	1	1	0	4	7	1	1	0	14	0	0	13.46	26.92
Ruiz, Jorge	L-L	5-10	164	6-30-04	.281	.353	.396	50	224	192	34	54	8	4	2	22	20	3	6	3	36	10	2	8.93	16.07
Scull, Anthony	L-L	6-0	165	1-26-04	.263	.345	.378	117	543	471	72	124	23	5	7	56	39	23	1	6	108	24	7	7.18	19.89
Torres, Luis	R-R	6-3	210	1-12-04	.100	.143	.100	7	21	20	0	2	0	0	0	0	1	0	0	0	9	0	0	4.76	42.86
Vargas, Imanol	L-R	6-3	215	6-29-98	.275	.364	.463	101	472	408	75	112	31	2	14	72	58	2	0	4	123	1	1	12.29	26.06
Villahermosa, Yeremi	B-R	5-9	150	10-16-02	.250	.371	.250	18	62	48	15	12	0	0	0	8	9	2	0	3	16	2	1	14.52	25.81
Wallace, Landon	B-R	6-2	170	2-27-02	.250	.308	.375	8	27	24	5	6	1	1	0	1	2	0	1	0	8	0	0	7.41	29.63

Pitching	B-T	Ht.	Wt.	DOB	W	L	ERA	G	GS	SV	IP	Hits	Runs	ER	HR	BB	SO	AVG	OBP	SLG	SO%	BB%	BF
Avila, Cesar	R-R	6-3	190	8-13-01	2	1	4.12	7	3	0	20	14	9	9	0	10	16	.197	.329	.239	18.82	11.76	85
Baro, Sadiel	L-L	6-2	177	11-10-04	0	0	3.00	2	0	0	3	2	1	1	0	1	2	.182	.250	.273	16.67	8.33	12
Barraza, Chris	R-R	6-0	196	12-3-99	2	2	3.32	30	0	1	41	33	17	15	1	28	43	.220	.351	.333	23.24	15.14	185
Bauman, Riley	R-R	6-0	181	8-30-02	1	7	7.64	20	19	0	84	100	79	71	4	53	83	.295	.414	.416	19.81	12.65	419
Britt, Logan	R-R	6-5	222	7-16-00	1	0	5.03	4	3	0	20	17	13	11	1	12	12	.233	.364	.329	13.64	13.64	88
Castillo, Ruben	R-R	6-1	160	6-18-01	2	2	7.19	20	5	0	51	62	43	41	5	33	51	.295	.405	.486	20.24	13.10	252
Christopherson, Will	R-R	6-4	210	8-8-99	1	0	5.09	20	0	0	41	30	26	23	2	22	54	.200	.337	.280	29.35	11.96	184
Clark, Derek	L-L	5-9	190	12-25-01	0	0	0.00	4	4	0	8	6	1	0	0	0	10	.207	.207	.345	34.48	0.00	29
Fermin, Jose	R-R	6-3	248	11-28-01	1	3	2.70	18	0	4	30	16	11	9	2	16	33	.154	.270	.250	26.83	13.01	123
Franco, Sadrac	R-R	6-0	155	6-4-00	0	1	1.08	4	0	0	8	4	6	1	2	3	16	.125	.243	.344	43.24	8.11	37
Garcia, Victor	R-R	6-1	194	3-28-04	2	0	3.68	11	0	1	22	22	9	9	0	13	22	.256	.366	.302	21.78	12.87	101

Gill, Starlin	R-R	5-10	150	3-16-00	0	0	18.00	1	0	0	1	1	2	2	0	1	0	.250	.400	.500	0.00	20.00	5
Gockel, Chase	R-R	6-1	195	1-1-00	0	0	5.40	2	0	0	2	2	4	1	0	3	1	.286	.545	.571	9.09	27.27	11
Gomez, Yendy	R-R	6-2	170	12-19-03	1	2	4.57	14	0	0	22	13	12	11	1	16	16	.173	.316	.320	16.84	16.84	95
Gonzalez, Jenrry	L-L	5-10	185	6-7-01	9	1	1.88	24	0	0	48	25	15	10	3	24	47	.157	.277	.239	24.23	12.37	194
Guanare, Fernando	R-R	6-1	140	6-21-03	0	1	8.29	21	0	0	42	67	42	39	7	20	39	.358	.433	.556	18.06	9.26	216
Hanley, Mo	L-L	6-2	195	7-19-99	0	0	13.50	3	0	0	3	10	7	5	0	1	5	.476	.522	.714	21.74	4.35	23
Holmes, Bridger	R-R	6-4	218	8-27-02	1	1	5.09	12	0	0	18	13	10	10	1	13	19	.213	.380	.311	24.05	16.46	79
Kent, Barrett	R-R	6-4	200	9-29-04	2	14	6.21	26	26	0	113	112	90	78	13	61	125	.256	.357	.427	24.27	11.84	515
Key, Keythel	R-R	6-3	180	10-10-03	1	5	6.59	9	8	0	29	39	31	21	5	23	28	.315	.441	.581	18.42	15.13	152
Klassen, George	R-R	6-2	170	1-26-02	1	0	1.80	1	1	0	5	3	1	1	0	3	10	.167	.286	.278	47.62	14.29	21
Lindsay-Young, Christian	R-R	6-5	210	5-19-96	5	3	5.66	20	7	1	68	75	50	43	7	14	71	.278	.317	.426	24.48	4.83	290
Lockhart, Fulton	R-R	6-4	183	12-30-03	0	0	2.77	9	0	1	13	7	6	4	1	9	13	.159	.286	.273	23.21	16.07	56
Martinez, Alex	R-R	5-10	170	9-15-02	5	6	2.60	48	0	12	69	55	27	20	1	31	77	.219	.306	.299	26.64	10.73	289
Martinez, Erik	R-R	5-11	193	3-21-96	0	0	18.00	1	0	0	1	2	2	2	1	0	2	.400	.400	1.000	40.00	0.00	5
Martinez, Quinton	L-L	6-4	190	1-23-99	0	0	6.60	8	0	1	15	20	11	11	3	7	11	.323	.375	.548	15.28	9.72	72
Olejnik, Peyton	R-R	6-9	174	12-4-02	0	0	2.84	4	4	0	6	2	2	2	0	3	11	.095	.240	.095	44.00	12.00	25
Phansalkar, Roman	R-R	6-1	195	6-2-98	2	2	1.84	9	0	1	15	10	6	3	1	5	10	.204	.281	.367	17.24	8.62	58
Sanchez, Andre	R-R	5-10	140	2-5-03	3	8	6.88	24	19	0	86	95	66	66	7	65	69	.285	.408	.420	16.75	15.78	412
Segura, Dawry	R-R	6-2	140	8-5-03	3	2	5.25	14	0	0	24	25	15	14	2	12	25	.263	.349	.432	22.94	11.01	109
Sifontes, Enderjer	R-R	6-0	135	11-19-02	2	0	9.69	9	0	0	13	16	14	14	0	10	14	.291	.409	.382	21.21	15.15	66
Texido, Francis	L-L	6-2	180	4-1-05	4	7	6.77	25	24	0	98	108	81	74	7	79	104	.285	.409	.443	21.85	16.60	476
Thompson, Ben	R-R	6-0	215	1-17-02	1	0	5.28	10	0	0	15	16	11	9	1	9	25	.267	.366	.400	35.21	12.68	71
Tullar, Cameron	R-L	6-2	215	6-30-00	2	2	5.84	25	1	0	49	59	37	32	4	31	51	.292	.395	.431	21.34	12.97	239
Vargas, Yeferson	R-R	6-0	177	8-4-04	1	1	2.35	7	6	0	31	18	10	8	0	16	33	.170	.290	.236	26.40	12.80	125
Victor, Najer	R-R	6-2	180	11-28-01	2	0	7.04	7	0	0	8	9	7	6	0	2	11	.281	.343	.469	30.56	5.56	36
Viloria, Luis	L-L	5-10	150	9-24-03	0	0	5.28	10	0	1	15	19	9	9	1	12	23	.306	.423	.419	29.49	15.38	78
Warwick, Jaren	R-R	6-2	175	10-10-01	1	1	4.24	12	0	0	17	15	9	8	0	10	18	.231	.338	.308	23.38	12.99	77
Zabala, Mario	R-R	6-2	195	5-8-02	0	0	54.00	2	0	0	1	0	4	4	0	5	0	.000	.750	.000	0.00	62.50	8

Fielding

Catcher	PCT	G	PO	A	E	DP	PB
Bartolero	1.000	1	8	1	0	0	0
Burns	.982	13	97	13	2	1	2
Flores	.987	46	407	33	6	2	8
Laverde	.993	43	404	24	3	2	8
Ortiz	.000	1	0	0	0	0	0
Pendleton	.994	19	163	10	1	1	5
Villahermosa	.968	14	113	9	4	0	2

First Base	PCT	G	PO	A	E	DP
Bartolero	1.000	6	17	0	0	3
DiChiara	.988	23	154	13	2	25
Garcia	.978	14	84	5	2	13
Nicholson	.990	14	97	6	1	9
Torres	1.000	7	38	2	0	3
Vargas	.992	73	490	38	4	39

Second Base	PCT	G	PO	A	E	DP
Daly	1.000	6	5	9	0	0
Flores	.946	23	34	53	5	7
Gill	1.000	17	37	28	0	12
Macias	.985	37	57	78	2	27
Moore	1.000	2	0	11	0	0
Ortiz	1.000	4	1	10	0	1
Placencia	.921	34	61	68	11	20
Rodriguez	.914	12	17	15	3	3
Villahermosa	1.000	3	2	0	0	0

Third Base	PCT	G	PO	A	E	DP
Bartolero	.912	65	46	68	11	11
Daly	.929	19	17	22	3	3
Garcia	.909	30	18	42	6	8
Gill	1.000	3	1	2	0	0
Macias	.925	20	11	26	3	2
Rodriguez	1.000	1	1	2	0	00

Shortstop	PCT	G	PO	A	E	DP
Daly	1.000	4	4	9	0	2
Gill	.000	1	0	0	0	0
Ortiz	.968	106	141	247	13	47
Placencia	.962	21	33	42	3	12
Rodriguez	1.000	2	4	5	0	2

Outfield	PCT	G	PO	A	E	DP
Bartolero	.000	2	0	0	0	0
Castillo	.987	44	76	0	1	0
De Jesus	.953	82	139	2	7	0
Foster	.957	13	22	0	1	0
Ramirez	.989	36	87	1	1	0
Redfield	.992	55	129	1	1	0
Ruiz	.976	49	116	6	3	1
Scull	.986	112	269	4	4	1
Wallace	.923	7	12	0	1	0

ACL ANGELS

ROOKIE

ARIZONA COMPLEX LEAGUE

Batting	B-T	Ht.	Wt.	DOB	AVG	OBP	SLG	G	PA	AB	R	H	2B	3B	HR	RBI	BB	HBP	SH	SF	SO	SB	CS	BB%	SO%
Alfonso, Edgar	B-R	5-9	175	3-27-04	.217	.297	.278	42	129	115	19	25	5	1	0	11	13	0	1	0	34	2	2	10.08	26.36
Duarte, Athanael	R-R	5-10	165	11-11-04	.247	.387	.376	55	213	170	31	42	7	3	3	27	32	8	1	2	45	6	4	15.02	21.13
Espinal, Edwardo	R-R	6-1	182	11-19-05	.217	.387	.306	52	206	157	40	34	9	1	1	20	43	2	2	2	58	9	3	20.87	28.16
Flores, Ronaldo	R-R	6-0	175	5-17-02	.077	.250	.308	4	16	13	2	1	0	0	1	4	3	0	0	0	4	0	0	18.75	25.00
Foster, Rio	R-R	6-3	205	6-18-03	.270	.397	.450	57	232	189	32	51	14	4	4	35	32	9	0	2	64	13	4	13.79	27.59
Garcia, Cristian	B-R	6-1	168	7-26-04	.275	.433	.449	21	90	69	11	19	6	0	2	15	19	1	0	1	19	1	0	21.11	21.11
Knowles, D'Shawn	B-R	6-0	181	1-16-01	.316	.409	.421	7	22	19	2	6	2	0	0	3	3	0	0	0	9	3	2	13.64	40.91
Laverde, Dario	L-R	5-10	160	2-26-05	.349	.391	.460	18	70	63	5	22	5	1	0	10	4	1	1	1	11	1	1	5.71	15.71
Linares, Jonathan	B-R	6-0	200	4-2-05	.200	.423	.271	35	99	70	10	14	2	0	1	8	25	2	2	0	23	3	2	25.25	23.23
Marisnick, Jake	R-R	6-4	220	3-30-91	.333	.412	.533	5	17	15	6	5	3	0	0	2	1	1	0	0	4	2	0	5.88	23.53
Martinez, Orlando	L-L	6-0	185	2-17-98	.333	.474	.400	11	39	30	8	10	0	1	0	1	8	0	0	0	3	2	0	20.51	7.69
Matheny, Shane	L-R	6-1	205	6-5-96	.241	.267	.517	8	30	29	7	7	1	2	1	6	1	0	0	0	8	1	1	3.33	26.67
McGillis, Will	R-R	6-3	200	1-16-99	.294	.455	.412	6	22	17	3	5	2	0	0	4	5	0	0	0	3	0	0	22.73	13.64
Morrobel, Felix	B-R	6-0	175	9-24-05	.308	.400	.327	15	62	52	10	16	1	0	0	4	8	0	2	0	8	5	2	12.90	12.90
Parra, Jeffry	R-R	5-11	195	1-24-98	.000	.000	.000	1	1	1	0	0	0	0	0	0	0	0	0	0	0	0	0	0.00	0.00
Pendleton, Caleb	R-R	6-2	185	4-5-02	.000	.000	.000	2	3	2	1	0	0	0	0	1	0	0	0	1	1	0	0	0.00	33.33
Ramirez, Alexander	R-R	6-2	229	8-29-02	.191	.269	.340	20	52	47	7	9	0	2	1	5	3	2	0	0	20	1	1	5.77	38.46
Ramirez, Ramon	L-L	6-2	195	1-30-05	.042	.148	.042	15	27	24	3	1	0	0	0	1	3	0	0	0	14	0	0	11.11	51.85
Rios, Alberto	R-R	6-0	203	3-19-02	.143	.333	.143	5	9	7	2	1	0	0	0	1	2	0	0	0	2	0	0	22.22	22.22
Rivero, Eliezer	R-R	6-0	180	3-29-05	.243	.396	.270	17	50	37	8	9	1	0	0	4	8	2	2	1	11	3	1	16.00	22.00
Rodriguez, Alejandro	R-R	5-11	200	12-27-99	.000	.125	.000	4	9	6	0	0	0	0	0	1	1	0	1	1	1	0	0	11.11	11.11
Rodriguez, Luis	R-R	6-1	176	12-22-04	.256	.388	.308	20	52	39	9	10	2	0	0	6	6	3	3	1	9	2	1	11.54	17.31
Rodriguez, Raudi	R-R	6-0	190	7-7-03	.233	.340	.314	29	103	86	14	20	2	1	1	9	12	3	0	2	26	4	2	11.65	25.24

Batting	B-T	Ht.	Wt.	DOB	AVG	OBP	SLG	G	PA	AB	R	H	2B	3B	HR	RBI	BB	HBP	SH	SF	SO	SB	CS	BB%	SO%
Rodriguez, Victor	R-R	5-10	185	1-24-06	.221	.299	.359	47	167	145	19	32	7	5	1	26	15	3	0	4	51	0	4	8.98	30.54
Sano, Miguel	R-R	6-4	272	5-11-93	.313	.450	.375	7	20	16	7	5	1	0	0	3	3	1	0	0	5	0	0	15.00	25.00
Santana, Natanael	R-R	6-3	190	7-27-01	.204	.314	.408	38	119	98	21	20	6	1	4	12	13	4	1	3	39	14	1	10.92	32.77
Scheffler, Matt	R-R	6-1	190	2-6-98	.000	.000	.000	1	1	1	0	0	0	0	0	0	0	0	0	0	1	0	0	0.00	100.00
Stefanic, Michael	R-R	5-8	180	2-24-96	.286	.400	.286	4	10	7	0	2	0	0	0	2	2	0	0	1	0	0	0	20.00	0.00
Stevens, Chad	R-R	6-3	215	2-3-99	.357	.438	.571	4	16	14	2	5	1	1	0	2	1	1	0	0	3	0	0	6.25	18.75
Torres, Luis	R-R	6-3	210	1-12-04	.238	.388	.317	29	80	63	6	15	3	1	0	12	11	5	0	1	22	0	0	13.75	27.50
Wallace, Landon	B-R	6-2	170	2-27-02	.091	.286	.091	4	14	11	2	1	0	0	0	0	1	2	0	0	4	1	1	7.14	28.57
White, Evan	R-L	6-1	219	4-26-96	.000	.333	.000	2	3	2	0	0	0	0	0	0	1	0	0	0	0	0	0	33.33	0.00
Williams, Cam	R-R	5-10	195	2-7-98	.333	.625	.333	2	8	3	1	1	0	0	0	1	3	1	0	1	2	1	0	37.50	25.00
Wimmer, John	R-R	6-1	170	3-21-05	.197	.356	.282	49	177	142	19	28	5	2	1	13	30	5	0	0	60	5	0	16.95	33.90

Pitching	B-T	Ht.	Wt.	DOB	W	L	ERA	G	GS	SV	IP	Hits	Runs	ER	HR	BB	SO	AVG	OBP	SLG	SO%	BB%	BF
Acosta, Adrian	R-R	6-1	170	5-20-05	0	4	6.26	13	8	0	42	42	30	29	2	36	24	.263	.425	.400	11.59	17.39	207
Albanese, Glenn	R-R	6-7	223	10-22-98	0	0	0.00	2	2	0	2	0	0	0	0	2	4	.000	.250	.000	50.00	25.00	8
Bachman, Sam	R-R	6-1	235	9-30-99	0	0	1.35	4	4	0	7	5	1	1	1	0	9	.200	.259	.320	33.33	0.00	27
Baro, Sadiel	L-L	6-2	177	11-10-04	3	4	4.98	13	7	0	56	70	39	31	2	15	55	.307	.354	.390	22.18	6.05	248
Cabrera, Anel	R-R	6-4	200	2-12-03	0	0	13.50	2	0	0	2	5	3	3	0	1	1	.556	.571	.667	7.14	7.14	14
Costeiu, Ryan	R-R	6-0	200	11-28-00	0	0	13.50	1	1	0	1	4	2	2	2	0	1	.500	.500	1.500	12.50	0.00	8
Encarnacion, Nixon	R-R	6-2	178	12-30-04	1	5	9.09	11	9	0	33	29	37	33	1	43	27	.246	.461	.331	16.17	25.75	167
Franco, Sadrac	R-R	6-0	155	6-4-00	2	0	2.61	6	2	0	10	8	3	3	2	6	9	.216	.326	.432	20.93	13.95	43
Garcia, Victor	R-R	6-1	194	3-28-04	3	3	5.12	20	3	2	46	45	30	26	3	14	48	.257	.327	.371	24.49	7.14	196
Gomez, Yendy	R-R	6-2	170	12-19-03	6	2	2.84	22	0	4	32	32	17	10	3	7	36	.262	.300	.426	27.69	5.38	130
Guerrero, Tayron	R-R	6-8	225	1-9-91	2	0	5.40	3	1	0	3	5	3	2	0	0	6	.357	.357	.429	42.86	0.00	14
Hechavarria, Jan	R-R	6-2	190	1-10-04	1	1	6.66	10	3	0	26	34	25	19	1	15	23	.321	.407	.443	18.70	12.20	123
Hernandez, Aaron	R-R	6-1	170	12-2-96	0	0	0.00	3	0	2	4	1	0	0	0	2	3	.091	.286	.091	21.43	14.29	14
Key, Keythel	R-R	6-3	180	10-10-03	3	1	5.30	11	2	0	36	40	24	21	2	16	48	.276	.358	.421	29.09	9.70	165
Ledo, Luis	R-R	6-4	240	5-28-95	0	0	8.10	3	0	0	3	6	3	3	2	1	2	.400	.438	1.000	12.50	6.25	16
Martinez, Erik	R-R	5-11	193	3-21-96	0	0	3.86	2	1	0	2	1	1	1	0	0	4	.125	.125	.250	50.00	0.00	8
Mendez, Haminton	R-R	6-1	177	6-5-04	2	3	8.48	12	5	1	40	47	44	38	7	29	35	.288	.403	.491	17.77	14.72	197
Mondak, Nick	L-L	6-4	203	6-2-98	1	0	0.00	4	0	0	5	2	1	0	0	0	6	.118	.118	.118	35.29	0.00	17
Owen, Noah	L-R	6-4	200	10-1-00	3	1	2.95	10	0	0	18	20	8	6	0	5	19	.267	.321	.333	22.62	5.95	84
Pelham, CD	R-L	6-6	238	2-21-95	0	0	0.00	1	0	0	1	0	0	0	0	2	1	.000	.500	.000	25.00	50.00	4
Quijada, Jose	L-L	5-11	215	11-9-95	0	0	3.86	5	2	0	5	4	2	2	1	0	11	.222	.263	.556	57.89	0.00	19
Quintero, Santiago	L-L	6-3	180	4-16-05	0	0	6.75	2	0	0	1	3	1	1	0	2	2	.429	.556	.571	22.22	22.22	9
Rangel, Alan	R-R	6-2	170	8-21-97	0	0	6.75	3	3	0	5	5	4	4	0	1	8	.238	.273	.333	36.36	4.55	22
Segura, Dawry	R-R	6-2	140	8-5-03	1	0	2.53	8	0	2	11	9	3	3	0	4	8	.225	.311	.300	17.78	8.89	45
Sifontes, Enderjer	R-R	6-0	135	11-19-02	3	2	3.15	14	3	1	34	32	18	12	2	26	30	.246	.371	.331	18.75	16.25	160
Silseth, Chase	R-R	6-0	217	5-18-00	0	0	0.00	2	2	0	7	4	0	0	0	0	10	.148	.207	.148	34.48	0.00	29
Thompson, Ben	R-R	6-0	215	1-17-02	0	1	3.60	5	0	1	5	2	2	2	1	7	5	.118	.375	.294	20.83	29.17	24
Viloria, Luis	L-L	5-10	150	9-24-03	1	1	7.23	20	0	1	24	25	20	19	2	17	39	.263	.377	.411	33.91	14.78	115
Zabala, Mario	R-R	6-2	195	5-8-02	0	0	8.04	12	0	0	16	17	15	14	1	16	16	.283	.443	.383	20.25	20.25	79
Zuniga, Guillermo	R-R	6-5	230	10-10-98	0	0	3.86	3	2	1	2	4	1	1	0	1	3	.364	.462	.364	23.08	7.69	13

Fielding

C: Linares 34, Rivero 16, Laverde 14, Rodriguez 3, Flores 3, Pendleton 2, Rios 1. **1B:** Duarte 42, Torres 13, Garcia 10, White 2, Williams 2, Rodriguez 1, Sano 1. **2B:** Alfonso 28, Duarte 17, Rodriguez 12, Wimmer 8, Morrobel 3, Stefanic 2, McGillis 2, Stevens 1. **3B:** Rodriguez 47, Alfonso 12, Rodriguez 5, Sano 3, McGillis 3, Stefanic 2, Matheny 2. **SS:** Wimmer 43, Morrobel 12, Matheny 4, Rodriguez 3, Stevens 3, Alfonso 2. **LF:** Foster 22, Rodriguez 18, Santana 17, Martinez 6, Marisnick 2, Wallace 1, Ramirez 1, Ramirez 1, Knowles 1. **CF:** Espinal 52, Rodriguez 7, Knowles 5, Foster 2, Martinez 1. **RF:** Foster 28, Santana 14, Ramirez 11, Rodriguez 4, Wallace 3, Martinez 3, Matheny 2, Marisnick 2, Ramirez 1, Torres 1.

DSL ANGELS — ROOKIE

DOMINICAN SUMMER LEAGUE

Batting	B-T	Ht.	Wt.	DOB	AVG	OBP	SLG	G	PA	AB	R	H	2B	3B	HR	RBI	BB	HBP	SH	SF	SO	SB	CS	BB%	SO%
Alvarez, Hayden	R-R	6-3	190	3-19-07	.250	.363	.358	50	217	176	43	44	10	3	1	29	31	2	5	3	35	32	6	14.29	16.13
Camacho, Jose	R-R	6-0	187	1-24-07	.290	.450	.366	47	171	131	24	38	5	1	1	21	25	14	0	1	25	9	6	14.62	14.62
Castillo, Byron	R-R	6-0	197	10-7-05	.211	.303	.305	32	110	95	15	20	6	0	1	12	9	4	1	1	36	7	4	8.18	32.73
Colina, Optiel	R-R	6-2	180	11-8-05	.171	.396	.171	16	49	35	5	6	0	0	0	3	8	5	1	0	16	4	1	16.33	32.65
De La Paz, Greylin	R-R	6-1	170	5-10-07	.220	.368	.260	45	152	123	22	27	2	0	1	17	23	6	0	0	40	13	3	15.13	26.32
De Pena, Wilberson	R-R	6-2	185	11-10-06	.226	.377	.274	26	77	62	11	14	1	1	0	9	10	5	0	0	14	4	0	12.99	18.18
Dishmey, Samil	L-R	6-2	175	12-22-05	.246	.385	.312	47	169	138	28	34	5	2	0	16	30	1	0	0	26	10	3	17.75	15.38
Lugo, Joswa	R-R	6-3	187	1-24-07	.301	.370	.466	53	219	193	31	58	11	3	5	37	17	6	0	3	51	18	5	7.76	23.29
Marquez, Anyelo	L-R	6-0	166	12-12-05	.294	.420	.395	53	229	177	31	52	6	3	2	38	39	3	5	5	31	20	11	17.03	13.54
Martinez, Bryan	L-R	6-2	170	12-26-05	.275	.391	.394	45	176	142	35	39	6	4	1	23	24	5	2	3	40	23	8	13.64	22.73
Medina, Rafael	R-R	6-2	210	12-7-05	.185	.346	.308	29	81	65	10	12	2	0	2	10	12	4	0	0	24	1	2	14.81	29.63
Patino, Oswaldo	L-R	5-10	160	7-3-06	.318	.407	.336	40	123	107	12	34	2	0	0	13	15	1	0	0	16	7	4	12.20	13.01
Quintero, Marlon	R-R	5-9	175	11-27-06	.240	.367	.340	16	61	50	13	12	1	2	0	4	10	0	1	0	4	3	0	16.39	6.56
Silva, Manuel	L-L	5-10	157	2-22-07	.167	.333	.167	10	15	12	4	2	0	0	0	1	3	0	0	0	6	2	0	20.00	40.00
Tiberi, Humberto	R-R	6-2	200	12-22-06	.254	.338	.325	37	131	114	16	29	8	0	0	15	11	4	1	1	33	4	3	8.40	25.19
Villaman, Axel	L-R	6-0	200	1-4-05	.196	.303	.250	26	66	56	15	11	1	1	0	7	9	0	0	1	20	3	1	13.64	30.30

Pitching	B-T	Ht.	Wt.	DOB	W	L	ERA	G	GS	SV	IP	Hits	Runs	ER	HR	BB	SO	AVG	OBP	SLG	SO%	BB%	BF
Anzola, Rolando	R-R	6-2	170	5-31-05	3	0	3.97	10	0	0	11	10	5	5	0	8	14	.233	.389	.302	25.93	14.81	54
Betances, Jhostin	R-R	6-3	147	3-1-07	0	0	13.50	6	0	0	6	6	9	9	0	7	2	.240	.441	.280	5.88	20.59	34

Colina, Daniel	R-R	6-1	194	11-16-06	3	1	1.40	12	0	1	19	7	4	3	0	16	20	.119	.299	.186	25.64	20.51	78
Cova, Andres	L-L	6-2	165	10-21-04	2	2	3.08	11	10	0	38	33	14	13	1	28	53	.236	.371	.300	30.99	16.37	171
De La Rosa, Dioris	R-R	6-4	200	10-26-06	5	1	2.79	11	10	0	52	41	17	16	1	20	57	.211	.290	.309	26.15	9.17	218
Gallardo, Fabian	R-R	6-3	180	1-24-06	2	5	5.50	12	6	0	38	42	26	23	1	16	33	.284	.374	.372	19.30	9.36	171
Gonzalez, Junior	R-R	6-4	210	9-16-05	0	1	7.56	8	0	0	8	4	7	7	1	7	7	.148	.351	.259	18.92	18.92	37
Lara, Davidxon	R-R	5-10	165	7-31-06	2	2	0.55	22	0	11	33	26	11	2	0	6	33	.211	.260	.236	25.19	4.58	131
Monte De Oca, Bryan	R-R	6-3	190	3-22-06	1	0	6.14	9	2	0	22	21	17	15	2	15	21	.266	.412	.392	20.39	14.56	103
Montilla, Christopher	R-R	6-2	170	2-8-07	0	1	16.50	6	0	0	6	9	11	11	2	11	6	.346	.585	.654	14.63	26.83	41
Poline, Jesus	R-R	6-3	170	10-22-04	1	0	3.94	11	0	0	16	15	7	7	0	11	10	.250	.387	.350	13.33	14.67	75
Reyes, Yokelvin	L-L	6-1	195	3-29-04	2	1	4.06	15	0	2	31	40	16	14	2	13	33	.320	.394	.416	23.24	9.15	142
Soto, Fabian	R-R	6-2	170	9-21-05	1	2	3.24	11	11	0	42	29	16	15	1	37	43	.197	.383	.245	22.16	19.07	194
Soto, Ubaldo	R-R	6-2	185	7-12-06	8	0	1.29	12	12	0	56	41	11	8	0	20	56	.214	.311	.234	25.34	9.05	221
Tirado, Leudy	L-L	5-10	160	9-27-05	2	0	2.30	11	5	0	27	27	12	7	2	15	27	.267	.364	.376	22.88	12.71	118
Vega, Marco	R-R	6-2	165	10-25-04	2	1	2.37	12	0	1	19	17	7	5	1	7	25	.230	.293	.324	30.49	8.54	82
Vergaa, Brayan																							

Fielding

C: Tiberi 32, Medina 15, Quintero 15, Villaman 1. **1B:** Camacho 42, Martinez 14, Colina 4. **2B:** Marquez 45, Patino 14. **3B:** De La Paz 45, Patino 18, Colina 1. **SS:** Lugo 49, Marquez 10. **LF:** Dishmey 38, Martinez 10, De Pena 8, Colina 7, Villaman 3, Tiberi 1. **CF:** Alvarez 46, Castillo 4, De Pena 4, Dishmey 3. **RF:** Castillo 26, Villaman 15, De Pena 11, Martinez 6, Colina 5, Alvarez 4, Dishmey 1.

Los Angeles Dodgers

SEASON SYNOPSIS: The Dodgers won the offseason with a bevy of free agent and trade additions highlighted by signing Shohei Ohtani, then overcame a flood of pitcher injuries to win the franchise's eighth World Series and second in the last five seasons.

HIGH POINT: The Dodgers rallied from a 2-1 Division Series deficit with 24 consecutive scoreless innings against the Padres to win that series. They navigated a six-game NLCS against the Mets by scoring 37 runs in their four victories. They took control of the World Series in Game One on Freddie Freeman's 10th-inning, walk-off grand slam to beat the Yankees. Walker Buehler started and won Game Three, then closed out Game Five with a scoreless ninth in a 7-6 comeback clincher.

LOW POINT: Veteran Clayton Kershaw, in his 17th season, made just seven starts thanks first to shoulder surgery, then a bone spur on his big toe that sidelined him in late August. He was one of 12 Dodgers starters on the IL by season's end, from homegrown starters such as Dustin May, Emmet Sheehan and Michael Grove to trade acquisitions such as Tyler Glasnow and River Ryan. The Dodgers entered the postseason with just three starters: trade deadline pickup Jack Flaherty and fellow righties Yoshinobu Yamamoto—who missed two months—and Buehler, who was coming off his second Tommy John surgery.

NOTABLE ROOKIES: Yamamoto went 7-2, 3.00 in his first MLB season after signing a 12-year, $325 million contract as a 25-year-old in the offseason, making him the world's highest-paid pitcher. Andy Pages was the lone homegrown rookie of note, starting 101 games in center field, batting .248/.305/.407 with 13 home runs. He hit two in one LCS game but didn't play in the World Series.

KEY TRANSACTIONS: Ohtani, coming off his own elbow surgery, left the Angels for the Dodgers on a record 10-year, $700 million contract, deferring all but $2 million annually to help the Dodgers augment the roster around him. The plan worked. L.A. signed left fielder Teoscar Hernandez for $23 million and traded for Glasnow after agreeing to sign him to a four-year, $115 million extension. Nevertheless, the Dodgers needed deadline reinforcements and acquired Flaherty from the Tigers, and made a three-team trade that netted versatile Tommy Edman. He started in center field, then shortstop throughout the postseason.

OPENING DAY PAYROLL: $249,823,654 (3rd)

PLAYERS OF THE YEAR

MAJOR LEAGUE

Shohei Ohtani
DH

.310/.390/.646
54 HR, 59 SB
134 R, 130 RBIs

MINOR LEAGUE

Dalton Rushing
C/OF

(AA/AAA)
.271/.385/.512
26 HR, 85 RBIs, 64 BB

ORGANIZATION LEADERS

Batting		*Qualifiers
MAJORS		
* AVG	Shohei Ohtani	.310
* OPS	Shohei Ohtani	1.036
HR	Shohei Ohtani	54
RBI	Shohei Ohtani	130
MINORS		
* AVG	Kody Hoese, Oklahoma City	.287
* OBP	Josue De Paula, Rancho Cucamonga/Great Lakes	.404
* SLG	Ryan Ward, Oklahoma City	.543
* OPS	Dalton Rushing, Tulsa/Oklahoma City	.896
R	Drew Avans, Okla. City	105
H	Andre Lipcius, Okla. City	152
TB	Ryan Ward, Okla. City/ACL Dodgers	268
2B	Kody Hoese, Okla. City	32
2B	Alex Freeland, Okla. City/Tulsa/Great Lakes	32
3B	Drew Avans, Okla. City	8
HR	Ryan Ward, Okla. City/ACL Dodgers	34
RBI	Ryan Ward, Okla. City/ACL Dodgers	104
BB	Alex Freeland, Okla. City/Tulsa/Great Lakes	91
SO	Chris Newell, Tulsa/Great Lakes	177
SB	Taylor Young, Tulsa	46

Pitching		#Qualifiers
MAJORS		
W	Gavin Stone	11
# ERA	No qualifier	
SO	Tyler Glasnow	168
SV	Evan Phillips	18
MINORS		
W	Sean Linan, Rancho Cuca./ACL Dodgers	9
L	Hyun-il Choi, Okla. City/Tulsa	11
# ERA	Jackson Ferris, Rancho Cucamonga/Great Lakes	3.20
G	John Rooney, Tulsa/Okla. City	53
GS	Jackson Ferris, Tulsa/Great Lakes	27
SV	Lucas Wepf, Tulsa/Great Lakes	13
IP	Orlando Ortiz-Mayr, Tulsa	136
BB	Jerming Rosario, Okla. City/Tulsa/Great Lakes	73
SO	Jackson Ferris, Tulsa/Great Lakes	145
# AVG	Jackson Ferris, Rancho Cucamonga/Great Lakes	.202

2024 PERFORMANCE

General Manager: Andrew Friedman. **Farm Director:** Will Rhymes. **Scouting Director:** Zach Fitzpatrick.

Class	Team	League	W	L	PCT	Finish	Manager
Majors	Los Angeles Dodgers	National	98	64	.605	1 (15)	Dave Roberts
Triple-A	Oklahoma City Baseball Club	Pacific Coast	79	71	.527	5 (10)	Travis Barbary
Double-A	Tulsa Drillers	Texas	63	74	.460	6 (10)	Scott Hennessey
High-A	Great Lakes Loons	Midwest	69	61	.531	4 (12)	Jair Fernandez
Low-A	Rancho Cucamonga Quakes	California	65	65	.500	6 (8)	John Shoemaker
Rookie	ACL Dodgers	Arizona Complex	40	20	.667	1 (15)	Juan Apodaca
Rookie	DSL LAD Bautista	Dominican	29	26	.527	20 (51)	Dunior Zerpa
Rookie	DSL LAD Mega	Dominican	25	29	.463	34 (51)	Leury Bonilla
Overall 2024 Minor League Record			**370**	**346**	**.517**	**11th (30)**	

ORGANIZATION STATISTICS

LOS ANGELES DODGERS

NATIONAL LEAGUE

Batting	B-T	Ht.	Wt.	DOB	AVG	OBP	SLG	G	PA	AB	R	H	2B	3B	HR	RBI	BB	HBP	SH	SF	SO	SB	CS	BB%	SO%
Ahmed, Nick	R-R	6-2	201	3-15-90	.229	.245	.292	17	49	48	6	11	0	0	1	2	1	0	0	0	14	1	0	2.04	28.57
Barnes, Austin	R-R	5-10	187	12-28-89	.264	.331	.307	54	156	140	12	37	3	0	1	11	14	0	2	0	36	3	0	8.97	23.08
Betts, Mookie	R-R	5-9	180	10-7-92	.289	.372	.491	116	516	450	75	130	24	5	19	75	61	1	0	4	57	16	2	11.82	11.05
Biggio, Cavan	L-R	6-2	200	4-11-95	.192	.306	.329	30	88	73	11	14	1	0	3	10	10	2	2	0	28	0	0	11.36	31.82
Edman, Tommy	B-R	5-10	180	5-9-95	.237	.294	.417	37	153	139	20	33	5	1	6	20	11	1	0	2	30	6	0	7.19	19.61
Feduccia, Hunter	L-R	6-0	215	6-5-97	.333	.429	.333	5	14	12	2	4	0	0	0	1	2	0	0	0	2	0	0	14.29	14.29
Freeman, Freddie	L-R	6-5	220	9-12-89	.282	.378	.476	147	638	542	81	153	35	2	22	89	78	10	0	8	100	9	2	12.23	15.67
Hernandez, Enrique	R-R	5-11	190	8-24-91	.229	.281	.373	126	393	362	44	83	16	0	12	42	27	0	1	3	77	0	0	6.87	19.59
Hernandez, Teoscar	R-R	6-2	215	10-15-92	.272	.339	.501	154	652	589	84	160	32	2	33	99	53	8	0	1	188	12	3	8.13	28.83
Heyward, Jason	L-L	6-5	240	8-9-89	.208	.289	.393	63	197	173	25	36	10	2	6	28	17	4	0	3	36	4	0	8.63	18.27
Kiermaier, Kevin	L-R	6-1	210	4-22-90	.203	.242	.322	34	64	59	7	12	2	1	1	8	2	1	2	0	20	1	2	3.13	31.25
Lux, Gavin	L-R	6-2	190	11-23-97	.251	.320	.383	139	487	439	59	110	24	2	10	50	44	2	0	2	110	5	2	9.03	22.59
Muncy, Max	L-R	6-0	215	8-25-90	.232	.358	.494	73	293	237	47	55	17	0	15	48	45	5	0	6	77	1	0	15.36	26.28
Ohtani, Shohei	L-R	6-4	210	7-5-94	.310	.390	.646	159	731	636	134	197	38	7	54	130	81	6	0	5	162	59	4	11.08	22.16
Outman, James	L-R	6-3	215	5-14-97	.147	.256	.265	53	156	136	12	20	4	0	4	11	16	4	0	0	55	2	1	10.26	35.26
Pages, Andy	R-R	6-1	212	12-8-00	.248	.305	.407	116	443	403	65	100	23	1	13	46	29	6	0	4	108	1	2	6.55	24.38
Rojas, Miguel	R-R	6-0	188	2-24-89	.283	.337	.410	103	337	307	41	87	21	0	6	36	23	3	2	2	34	8	2	6.82	10.09
Rosario, Amed	R-R	6-2	190	11-20-95	.273	.333	.364	5	12	11	1	3	1	0	0	2	1	0	0	0	2	1	1	8.33	16.67
Smith, Will	R-R	5-10	195	3-28-95	.248	.327	.433	128	544	476	77	118	24	2	20	75	51	9	0	8	105	1	1	9.38	19.30
Taylor, Chris	R-R	6-1	196	8-29-90	.202	.298	.300	87	246	213	28	43	7	1	4	23	28	2	1	2	76	5	1	11.38	30.89
Trammell, Taylor	L-L	6-2	220	9-13-97	.000	.000	.000	5	6	6	0	0	0	0	0	0	0	0	0	0	3	0	0	0.00	50.00
Vargas, Miguel	R-R	6-3	205	11-17-99	.239	.313	.423	30	80	71	11	17	4	0	3	9	8	0	0	1	16	1	0	10.00	20.00

Pitching	B-T	Ht.	Wt.	DOB	W	L	ERA	G	GS	SV	IP	Hits	Runs	ER	HR	BB	SO	AVG	OBP	SLG	SO%	BB%	BF
Banda, Anthony	L-L	6-2	221	8-10-93	3	2	3.08	48	2	2	50	44	19	17	5	18	50	.238	.309	.351	23.92	8.61	209
Brasier, Ryan	R-R	6-0	227	8-26-87	1	0	3.54	29	4	0	28	22	12	11	3	5	25	.218	.248	.376	22.73	4.55	110
Brogdon, Connor	R-R	6-6	205	1-29-95	0	0	18.00	1	0	0	1	2	2	2	2	0	0	.400	.400	1.600	0.00	0.00	5
Buehler, Walker	R-R	6-2	185	7-28-94	1	6	5.38	16	16	0	75	89	52	45	16	28	64	.289	.356	.506	18.60	8.14	344
Casparius, Ben	R-R	6-2	215	2-11-99	2	0	2.16	3	0	0	8	9	3	2	0	4	12	.273	.351	.333	32.43	10.81	37
Crismatt, Nabil	R-R	6-1	220	12-25-94	1	1	2.57	5	0	0	7	7	3	2	1	0	6	.269	.269	.423	23.08	0.00	26
Feyereisen, J.P.	R-R	6-2	215	2-7-93	0	1	8.18	10	0	1	11	11	10	10	3	5	9	.262	.354	.548	18.75	10.42	48
Flaherty, Jack	R-R	6-4	225	10-15-95	6	2	3.58	10	10	0	55	52	23	22	9	19	61	.245	.309	.420	26.07	8.12	234
Glasnow, Tyler	L-R	6-8	225	8-23-93	9	6	3.49	22	22	0	134	92	53	52	15	35	168	.190	.244	.347	32.18	6.70	522
Graterol, Brusdar	R-R	6-1	265	8-26-98	0	0	2.45	7	0	0	7	3	2	2	0	2	7	.120	.185	.120	25.93	7.41	27
Grove, Michael	R-R	6-3	200	12-18-96	4	4	5.12	39	2	0	51	46	31	29	6	16	54	.241	.316	.382	25.00	7.41	216
Henriquez, Edgardo	R-R	6-4	200	6-24-02	0	0	2.70	3	0	1	3	2	1	1	0	2	5	.167	.286	.167	35.71	14.29	14
Hernandez, Elieser	R-R	6-1	214	5-3-95	0	1	8.38	5	1	0	10	9	9	9	5	3	6	.231	.286	.641	14.29	7.14	42
Hernandez, Enrique	R-R	5-11	190	8-24-91	0	0	4.15	4	0	0	4	5	2	2	0	0	0	.278	.278	.389	0.00	0.00	18
Honeywell, Brent	R-R	6-2	195	3-31-95	1	1	2.62	18	1	1	34	29	11	10	3	9	17	.244	.303	.378	12.69	6.72	134
Hudson, Daniel	R-R	6-3	215	3-9-87	6	2	3.00	65	0	10	63	46	25	21	10	19	63	.198	.261	.371	24.90	7.51	253
Hurt, Kyle	R-R	6-3	240	5-30-98	0	1	1.35	3	1	0	7	8	2	1	0	1	3	.308	.333	.385	11.11	3.70	27
Kelly, Joe	R-R	6-1	174	6-9-88	1	1	4.78	35	0	0	32	31	19	17	4	16	35	.261	.369	.412	24.48	11.19	143
Kershaw, Clayton	L-L	6-4	225	3-19-88	2	2	4.50	7	7	0	30	36	19	15	2	9	24	.303	.353	.429	18.05	6.77	133
Knack, Landon	L-R	6-2	220	7-15-97	3	5	3.65	15	12	1	69	58	28	28	14	18	69	.220	.276	.428	24.13	6.29	286
Kopech, Michael	R-R	6-3	210	4-30-96	4	0	1.13	24	0	6	24	9	3	3	1	10	29	.118	.216	.197	32.95	11.36	88
Lamet, Dinelson	R-R	6-3	228	7-18-92	0	0	2.08	3	0	1	4	2	2	1	1	2	3	.133	.222	.333	16.67	11.11	18
Logue, Zach	L-L	6-0	165	4-23-96	0	0	18.00	2	0	0	2	6	4	4	1	0	4	.500	.500	.833	33.33	0.00	12
Miller, Bobby	L-R	6-5	220	4-5-99	2	4	8.52	13	13	0	56	69	53	53	17	30	52	.305	.391	.571	20.16	11.63	258
Paxton, James	L-L	6-4	227	11-6-88	8	2	4.43	18	18	0	89	82	45	44	11	48	64	.246	.338	.401	16.41	12.31	390
Petersen, Michael	R-R	6-7	195	5-16-94	3	0	6.43	11	0	0	14	14	10	10	3	8	11	.259	.359	.519	17.19	12.50	64
Phillips, Evan	R-R	6-2	215	9-11-94	5	1	3.62	61	0	18	55	48	30	22	6	17	63	.232	.291	.372	27.63	7.46	228
Ramirez, Nick	L-L	6-4	232	8-1-89	0	0	6.08	8	0	0	13	18	11	9	0	7	5	.333	.397	.426	7.94	11.11	63

Ramirez, Yohan	R-R	6-4	212	5-6-95	0	4	5.52	27	0	1	29	32	21	18	3	11	27	.283	.379	.442	20.15	8.21	134
Rojas, Miguel	R-R	6-0	188	2-24-89	0	0	0.00	1	0	0	1	1	0	0	0	0	0	.250	.250	.250	0.00	0.00	4
Ryan, River	R-R	6-2	195	8-17-98	1	0	1.33	4	4	0	20	15	4	3	1	9	18	.208	.296	.278	22.22	11.11	81
Salazar, Eduardo	R-R	6-2	177	5-5-98	0	0	0.00	1	0	0	2	3	1	0	0	2	3	.375	.500	.375	30.00	20.00	10
Stone, Gavin	R-R	6-1	175	10-15-98	11	5	3.53	25	25	0	140	133	55	55	18	37	116	.248	.297	.402	20.00	6.38	580
Treinen, Blake	R-R	6-5	225	6-30-88	7	3	1.93	50	0	1	47	33	11	10	5	11	56	.194	.250	.335	30.43	5.98	184
Vanasco, Ricky	R-R	6-3	180	10-13-98	0	0	13.50	2	0	0	2	3	3	3	0	0	1	.333	.333	.444	11.11	0.00	9
Varland, Gus	L-R	6-1	213	11-6-96	0	0	3.00	7	0	0	6	7	3	2	1	4	3	.280	.400	.480	10.00	13.33	30
Vesia, Alex	L-L	6-1	209	4-11-96	5	4	1.76	67	0	5	66	33	19	13	7	33	87	.148	.260	.291	33.08	12.55	263
Wrobleski, Justin	L-L	6-1	194	7-14-00	1	2	5.70	8	6	1	36	34	24	23	9	16	26	.248	.331	.511	16.88	10.39	154
Yamamoto, Yoshinobu	R-R	5-10	176	8-17-98	7	2	3.00	18	18	0	90	78	32	30	7	22	105	.229	.275	.365	28.53	5.98	368
Yarbrough, Ryan	R-L	6-5	205	12-31-91	4	2	3.74	32	0	1	67	52	29	28	9	25	39	.213	.303	.352	13.88	8.90	281

Fielding

Catcher	PCT	G	PO	A	E	DP	PB
Barnes	.987	45	368	10	5	2	1
Feduccia	1.000	4	32	2	0	0	0
Smith	.992	121	1000	58	8	3	5

First Base	PCT	G	PO	A	E	DP
Biggio	.971	12	61	5	2	7
Freeman	.996	147	1022	115	4	93
Hernandez	1.000	18	70	7	0	8
Rojas	.000	1	0	0	0	0

Second Base	PCT	G	PO	A	E	DP
Barnes	.000	2	0	0	0	0
Betts	1.000	18	13	20	0	3
Edman	.000	1	0	0	0	0
Hernandez	.895	10	4	13	2	0
Lux	.980	138	179	265	9	68
Rojas	1.000	13	16	27	0	6
Rosario	1.000	2	1	5	0	2
Taylor	.984	21	24	36	1	9

Third Base	PCT	G	PO	A	E	DP
Biggio	.903	14	11	17	3	2
Hernandez	.953	71	38	103	7	14
Muncy	.964	72	44	115	6	16
Rojas	.947	11	7	11	1	1
Rosario	1.000	1	1	0	0	0
Taylor	1.000	24	11	15	0	1

Shortstop	PCT	G	PO	A	E	DP
Ahmed	1.000	16	13	33	0	7
Betts	.963	65	86	150	9	30
Edman	.954	18	27	35	3	6
Hernandez	.958	9	8	15	1	3
Lux	.000	1	0	0	0	0
Rojas	.993	82	109	160	2	20
Rosario	1.000	2	2	3	0	0

Outfield	PCT	G	PO	A	E	DP
Betts	.963	43	77	1	3	0
Biggio	.000	4	0	0	0	0
Edman	.982	24	55	1	1	0
Hernandez	.989	180	253	7	3	3
Hernandez	1.000	26	33	0	0	0
Heyward	.991	61	113	1	1	0
Kiermaier	1.000	32	63	1	0	1
Outman	.990	51	94	2	1	0
Pages	.990	133	294	5	3	2
Taylor	.984	56	63	0	1	0
Trammell	1.000	3	5	0	0	0
Vargas	.971	27	30	3	1	1

OKLAHOMA CITY BASEBALL CLUB — *TRIPLE-A*

PACIFIC COAST LEAGUE

Batting	B-T	Ht.	Wt.	DOB	AVG	OBP	SLG	G	PA	AB	R	H	2B	3B	HR	RBI	BB	HBP	SH	SF	SO	SB	CS	BB%	SO%
Arauz, Jonathan	B-R	6-0	195	8-3-98	.227	.286	.324	60	245	225	25	51	11	1	3	21	19	0	0	1	56	2	0	7.76	22.86
Avans, Drew	L-L	5-9	195	6-13-96	.272	.366	.396	133	625	541	105	147	27	8	8	52	80	2	0	2	157	35	6	12.80	25.12
Cartaya, Diego	R-R	6-3	219	9-7-01	.208	.293	.350	49	208	183	24	38	8	0	6	25	20	3	0	2	57	1	0	9.62	27.40
Davis, Brendon	R-R	6-4	185	7-28-97	.296	.345	.556	8	29	27	5	8	4	0	1	6	2	0	0	0	6	0	0	6.90	20.69
Edman, Tommy	B-R	5-10	180	5-9-95	.294	.478	.471	6	23	17	5	5	0	0	1	4	6	0	0	0	2	1	0	26.09	8.70
Feduccia, Hunter	L-R	6-0	215	6-5-97	.284	.409	.428	82	350	285	41	81	17	3	6	50	59	3	0	3	72	2	1	16.86	20.57
Freeland, Alex	B-R	6-2	200	8-24-01	.243	.335	.396	39	164	144	23	35	7	0	5	18	19	1	0	0	44	2	0	11.59	26.83
Gauthier, Austin	R-R	6-0	188	5-7-99	.247	.355	.330	106	425	364	47	90	16	4	2	31	56	5	0	0	87	11	0	13.18	20.47
Guerrero, Eduardo	B-R	6-2	165	5-9-05	.000	.000	.000	1	4	4	0	0	0	0	0	0	0	0	0	0	2	0	0	0.00	50.00
Heyward, Jason	L-L	6-5	240	8-9-89	.000	.143	.000	2	7	6	0	0	0	0	0	0	1	0	0	0	2	0	0	14.29	28.57
Hoese, Kody	R-R	6-4	200	7-13-97	.287	.361	.474	127	525	464	76	133	32	2	17	79	52	4	0	4	104	1	1	9.90	19.81
Lipcius, Andre	R-R	6-0	190	5-22-98	.271	.351	.458	140	636	561	86	152	26	2	25	89	68	3	0	4	145	10	3	10.69	22.80
Muncy, Max	L-R	6-0	215	8-25-90	.286	.375	.476	6	24	21	3	6	1	0	1	4	3	0	0	0	6	0	0	12.50	25.00
Okey, Chris	R-R	5-11	200	12-29-94	.236	.282	.327	45	178	165	19	39	5	2	2	13	10	1	1	1	33	4	0	5.62	18.54
Outman, James	L-R	6-3	215	5-14-97	.279	.390	.543	69	319	265	62	74	15	2	17	46	44	6	0	3	81	11	1	13.79	25.39
Owings, Chris	R-R	5-10	185	8-12-91	.262	.381	.414	80	307	256	41	67	8	2	9	32	44	6	0	1	79	11	4	14.33	25.73
Padlo, Kevin	R-R	5-11	210	7-15-96	.216	.340	.380	47	209	171	21	37	10	0	6	29	32	2	0	4	55	9	1	15.31	26.32
Pages, Andy	R-R	6-1	212	12-8-00	.356	.421	.663	24	114	101	25	36	5	1	8	22	10	2	0	1	21	3	1	8.77	18.42
Rodriguez, Frank	R-R	5-11	197	9-28-01	.250	.250	.250	1	4	4	0	1	0	0	0	0	0	0	0	0	1	0	0	0.00	25.00
Rushing, Dalton	L-R	6-1	220	2-21-01	.273	.396	.511	37	169	139	25	38	6	0	9	26	26	3	0	1	34	2	1	15.38	20.12
Sweeney, Trey	L-R	6-2	200	4-24-00	.254	.334	.427	96	440	389	65	99	22	3	13	62	44	4	0	3	118	16	3	10.00	26.82
Taylor, Chris	R-R	6-1	196	8-29-90	.364	.462	.545	3	13	11	2	4	2	0	0	1	2	0	0	0	3	0	0	15.38	23.08
Trejo, Alan	R-R	6-2	205	5-30-96	.265	.346	.408	59	241	211	27	56	10	1	6	24	26	1	1	2	54	5	3	10.79	22.41
Vargas, Miguel	R-R	6-3	205	11-17-99	.290	.440	.566	41	191	145	35	42	14	1	8	38	38	4	0	4	33	8	6	19.90	17.28
Ward, Ryan	L-R	5-9	200	2-23-98	.258	.317	.543	120	520	473	78	122	22	7	33	101	41	2	0	4	141	11	3	7.88	27.12

Pitching	B-T	Ht.	Wt.	DOB	W	L	ERA	G	GS	SV	IP	Hits	Runs	ER	HR	BB	SO	AVG	OBP	SLG	SO%	BB%	BF
Anderson, Nick	R-R	6-4	205	7-5-90	2	0	2.08	3	0	0	4	3	3	1	1	3	5	.200	.333	.400	27.78	16.67	18
Brasier, Ryan	R-R	6-0	227	8-26-87	2	0	0.00	8	0	0	8	4	0	0	0	1	12	.143	.172	.143	41.38	3.45	29
Brogdon, Connor	R-R	6-6	205	1-29-95	0	0	3.46	13	0	1	13	13	5	5	2	5	19	.255	.321	.392	33.93	8.93	56
Buehler, Walker	R-R	6-2	185	7-28-94	0	4	5.01	8	8	0	32	39	21	18	4	16	35	.295	.369	.432	23.49	10.74	149
Casparius, Ben	R-R	6-2	215	2-11-99	4	3	3.36	16	14	0	67	47	26	25	4	35	72	.193	.300	.283	25.44	12.37	283
Choi, Hyun-il	R-R	6-2	215	5-27-00	4	6	4.28	15	14	0	74	66	40	35	7	32	56	.240	.331	.393	17.55	10.03	319
Crismatt, Nabil	R-R	6-1	220	12-25-94	1	0	5.68	4	3	0	13	15	9	8	3	0	15	.288	.288	.500	28.85	0.00	52
Dodson, Tanner	S-R	6-1	160	5-9-97	3	3	3.32	41	1	1	62	56	30	23	3	43	58	.239	.370	.355	20.42	15.14	284
Dreyer, Jack	R-L	6-2	205	2-27-99	5	2	2.95	37	0	4	43	39	22	14	4	9	52	.236	.276	.382	29.89	5.17	174
Duplantier, Jon	L-R	6-4	229	7-11-94	3	2	3.56	6	6	0	30	21	12	12	1	17	41	.204	.315	.291	33.06	13.71	124
Duran, Carlos	R-R	6-7	230	7-30-01	0	0	13.50	1	1	0	1	0	2	2	0	3	3	.000	.429	.000	42.86	42.86	7
Feyereisen, J.P.	R-R	6-2	215	2-7-93	2	6	5.48	33	6	0	43	46	30	26	7	13	33	.274	.322	.458	17.93	7.07	184
Fisher, Braydon	R-R	6-4	180	7-26-00	2	0	6.94	8	0	0	12	11	9	9	0	10	16	.256	.382	.326	29.09	18.18	55

Flynn, Michael	R-R	6-4	185	8-7-96	2	1	4.95	28	0	3	36	29	22	20	7	15	50	.220	.312	.417	32.05	9.62	156
Gage, Matt	L-L	6-3	265	2-11-93	1	3	4.29	20	0	1	21	17	10	10	2	12	27	.215	.315	.354	29.35	13.04	92
Gamboa, Alec	S-L	6-1	205	1-17-97	3	6	3.30	22	12	0	74	70	37	27	3	31	51	.251	.326	.348	16.14	9.81	316
Gonsalves, Stephen	L-L	6-5	218	7-8-94	2	0	6.00	15	0	0	18	14	12	12	3	20	23	.219	.407	.438	26.74	23.26	86
Gonsolin, Tony	R-R	6-3	205	5-14-94	0	0	2.35	3	3	0	8	7	2	2	0	2	12	.233	.303	.400	36.36	6.06	33
Gowdy, Kevin	R-R	6-4	205	11-16-97	2	2	4.38	42	1	4	51	57	28	25	1	23	45	.285	.378	.360	19.48	9.96	231
Graterol, Brusdar	R-R	6-1	265	8-26-98	0	0	5.87	8	0	0	8	13	6	5	0	2	7	.351	.375	.378	17.50	5.00	40
Grove, Michael	R-R	6-3	200	12-18-96	2	0	1.59	10	0	0	11	5	2	2	1	3	11	.128	.209	.256	25.58	6.98	43
Hahn, Jesse	R-R	6-5	205	7-30-89	4	1	4.54	35	2	1	42	30	22	21	2	33	44	.211	.374	.310	24.18	18.13	182
Harris, Ben	L-L	6-1	195	2-22-00	0	1	15.43	2	0	0	2	0	4	4	0	6	4	.000	.462	.000	30.77	46.15	13
Henriquez, Edgardo	R-R	6-4	200	6-24-02	1	0	2.84	14	0	0	13	14	6	4	0	10	18	.275	.393	.353	29.51	16.39	61
Hernandez, Elieser	R-R	6-1	214	5-3-95	4	1	2.83	6	5	0	29	22	10	9	2	8	34	.208	.263	.340	29.82	7.02	114
Hernandez, Jose	L-L	5-10	205	12-31-97	1	1	4.50	16	1	0	18	17	9	9	1	10	14	.246	.342	.362	17.72	12.66	79
Honeywell, Brent	R-R	6-2	195	3-31-95	0	0	0.00	2	0	0	4	3	0	0	0	1	2	.214	.267	.357	13.33	6.67	15
Hurt, Kyle	R-R	6-3	240	5-30-98	0	0	3.07	13	2	1	15	9	5	5	0	12	22	.170	.323	.226	33.85	18.46	65
Kelly, Joe	R-R	6-1	174	6-9-88	2	1	9.82	5	0	0	4	1	4	4	0	6	5	.091	.412	.091	29.41	35.29	17
Kershaw, Clayton	L-L	6-4	225	3-19-88	0	0	3.86	2	2	0	7	6	3	3	1	1	7	.231	.259	.346	25.93	3.70	27
Knack, Landon	L-R	6-2	220	7-15-97	4	3	3.71	14	12	0	68	55	30	28	7	31	79	.223	.311	.372	28.11	11.03	281
Lamet, Dinelson	R-R	6-3	228	7-18-92	3	1	4.82	9	8	0	37	42	20	20	5	23	40	.284	.390	.473	22.47	12.92	178
Lao, Sauryn	R-R	6-2	182	8-14-99	2	1	5.22	20	0	0	29	30	20	17	1	13	25	.268	.352	.375	19.38	10.08	129
Little, Jack	L-R	6-4	190	1-10-98	1	1	4.71	29	0	1	36	37	20	19	6	11	40	.261	.314	.514	25.97	7.14	154
Logue, Zach	L-L	6-0	165	4-23-96	0	0	3.00	1	1	0	3	5	1	1	0	0	1	.385	.385	.462	7.69	0.00	13
Lyles, Jordan	R-R	6-5	230	10-19-90	0	1	6.46	5	4	0	15	20	11	11	3	5	12	.313	.371	.594	17.14	7.14	70
Miller, Bobby	L-R	6-5	220	4-5-99	0	1	5.06	6	6	0	27	24	17	15	1	17	23	.240	.355	.330	19.01	14.05	121
Petersen, Michael	R-R	6-7	195	5-16-94	2	0	1.64	35	0	10	33	17	7	6	1	8	44	.145	.200	.222	35.20	6.40	125
Pomeranz, Drew	R-L	6-5	246	11-22-88	1	0	6.00	8	1	0	9	9	6	6	1	1	14	.257	.270	.457	37.84	2.70	37
Ramirez, Nick	L-L	6-4	232	8-1-89	3	1	4.37	28	2	0	35	38	18	17	3	7	28	.281	.317	.400	19.18	4.79	146
Romero, Christian	R-R	6-3	195	12-11-02	1	2	9.17	4	4	0	18	22	22	18	5	5	8	.306	.386	.569	9.30	5.81	86
Rooney, John	R-L	6-5	215	1-28-97	5	2	4.33	53	0	1	60	58	33	29	7	32	71	.257	.373	.403	26.10	11.76	272
Rosario, Jerming	R-R	6-1	175	5-8-02	0	1	7.20	1	1	0	5	3	4	4	0	6	5	.188	.391	.250	21.74	26.09	23
Ryan, River	R-R	6-2	195	8-17-98	0	0	2.76	5	5	0	16	13	5	5	1	6	19	.224	.303	.293	28.79	9.09	66
Salazar, Eduardo	R-R	6-2	177	5-5-98	1	2	5.61	7	7	0	34	47	22	21	3	12	21	.343	.412	.482	13.73	7.84	153
Sublette, Ryan	R-R	6-2	190	10-1-98	0	0	2.70	2	0	0	3	3	1	1	0	4	2	.231	.412	.385	11.76	23.53	17
Treinen, Blake	R-R	6-5	225	6-30-88	0	0	10.38	5	1	0	4	8	5	5	0	0	6	.400	.400	.550	30.00	0.00	20
Vallimont, Chris	R-R	6-5	240	3-18-97	1	5	8.57	10	9	0	42	53	41	40	11	27	33	.312	.410	.576	16.50	13.50	200
Vanasco, Ricky	R-R	6-3	180	10-13-98	0	2	3.47	24	0	5	23	19	11	9	2	21	27	.218	.369	.310	24.32	18.92	111
Varland, Gus	L-R	6-1	213	11-6-96	2	2	7.99	28	1	0	33	40	30	29	5	13	36	.299	.373	.470	23.84	8.61	151
Wrobleski, Justin	L-L	6-1	194	7-14-00	1	2	5.46	7	5	0	28	34	17	17	4	18	42	.306	.400	.514	31.82	13.64	132
Yamamoto, Yoshinobu	R-R	5-10	176	8-17-98	0	1	6.75	2	2	0	4	3	3	3	1	2	5	.214	.294	.500	29.41	11.76	17

Fielding

Catcher	PCT	G	PO	A	E	DP	PB
Cartaya	.980	35	330	14	7	2	2
Feduccia	.996	70	628	37	3	6	4
Okey	.993	39	364	34	3	5	6
Rodriguez	1.000	1	12	0	0	0	0
Rushing	1.000	6	53	4	0	0	1

First Base	PCT	G	PO	A	E	DP
Arauz	1.000	1	1	0	0	0
Lipcius	.995	93	702	58	4	75
Padlo	.989	33	258	13	3	29
Ward	.994	26	164	11	1	18

Second Base	PCT	G	PO	A	E	DP
Arauz	.981	42	66	90	3	26
Davis	1.000	3	4	7	0	0
Gauthier	.985	45	64	128	3	28
Guerrero	1.000	1	0	1	0	0
Hoese	.857	2	1	5	1	0
Lipcius	.939	11	21	25	3	6
Owings	.975	19	29	48	2	14
Taylor	1.000	1	2	1	0	1
Trejo	.986	33	61	78	2	22

Third Base	PCT	G	PO	A	E	DP
Arauz	.957	9	3	19	1	2
Gauthier	.923	4	5	7	1	0
Hoese	.960	96	62	156	9	21
Lipcius	.938	19	8	37	3	1
Muncy	.900	5	4	5	1	2
Owings	1.000	5	5	8	0	0
Sweeney	.833	2	1	4	1	1
Trejo	.978	18	8	36	1	2

Shortstop	PCT	G	PO	A	E	DP
Arauz	1.000	2	0	4	0	1
Davis	.900	2	3	6	1	2
Edman	.833	2	2	3	1	0
Freeland	.949	38	52	77	7	18
Owings	1.000	7	7	17	0	3
Sweeney	.959	92	100	228	14	55
Trejo	.958	9	9	14	1	3

Outfield	PCT	G	PO	A	E	DP
Avans	.996	131	273	10	1	4
Davis	1.000	1	3	0	0	0
Edman	1.000	5	6	0	0	0
Gauthier	.978	53	84	5	2	2
Heyward	1.000	2	5	0	0	0
Lipcius	.000	1	0	0	0	0
Okey	1.000	1	4	0	0	0
Outman	.972	61	139	2	4	1
Owings	.991	46	104	1	1	0
Padlo	1.000	4	6	1	0	0
Pages	.981	24	47	4	1	2
Rushing	.977	27	42	1	1	0
Taylor	1.000	1	2	0	0	0
Vargas	.966	37	56	1	2	0
Ward	1.000	72	110	4	0	1

TULSA DRILLERS

DOUBLE-A

TEXAS LEAGUE

Batting	B-T	Ht.	Wt.	DOB	AVG	OBP	SLG	G	PA	AB	R	H	2B	3B	HR	RBI	BB	HBP	SH	SF	SO	SB	CS	BB%	SO%
Alleyne, Chris	B-R	5-10	190	11-13-98	.252	.335	.378	97	325	286	37	72	14	2	6	35	33	4	0	2	87	15	9	10.15	26.77
Avila, Carlos	R-R	5-11	180	12-4-03	.111	.200	.111	6	20	18	1	2	0	0	0	2	2	0	0	0	8	0	0	10.00	40.00
Beck, Austin	R-R	6-1	200	11-21-98	.214	.294	.432	65	262	229	31	49	9	1	13	45	25	3	0	5	92	1	0	9.54	35.11
Cartaya, Diego	R-R	6-3	219	9-7-01	.236	.354	.379	46	192	161	27	38	8	0	5	27	27	3	0	1	56	1	0	14.06	29.17
Casey, Donovan	R-R	6-2	223	2-23-96	.161	.255	.184	30	98	87	10	14	2	0	0	10	7	4	0	0	31	9	2	7.14	31.63
Davis, Brendon	R-R	6-4	185	7-28-97	.224	.346	.353	115	468	388	74	87	21	1	9	43	62	13	0	5	109	24	0	13.25	23.29
Fernandez, Yeiner	R-R	5-9	170	9-19-02	.245	.337	.335	105	419	364	54	89	24	0	3	40	39	13	0	3	56	8	2	9.31	13.37
Freeland, Alex	B-R	6-2	200	8-24-01	.245	.370	.422	74	341	282	59	69	15	1	11	35	45	12	0	2	73	24	2	13.20	21.41
Gauthier, Austin	R-R	6-0	188	5-7-99	.280	.445	.488	24	110	82	20	23	3	1	4	17	22	4	0	2	16	2	2	20.00	14.55

Izarra, Jose	R-R	6-0	175	3-7-02	.164	.292	.262	28	73	61	6	10	3	0	1	4	11	0	1	0	30	3	1	15.07	41.10
Keith, Damon	R-R	6-3	195	5-28-00	.259	.340	.496	75	318	282	45	73	15	2	16	38	32	3	0	1	94	13	6	10.06	29.56
Lewis, Brandon	R-R	6-2	222	10-23-98	.208	.287	.360	73	269	236	33	49	7	1	9	39	26	2	1	4	94	0	0	9.67	34.94
Lockwood-Powell, Griffin	R-R	6-2	195	2-23-98	.231	.303	.369	111	469	420	49	97	16	0	14	55	40	5	0	4	108	2	1	8.53	23.03
Miller, Noah	B-R	5-11	190	11-12-02	.225	.257	.264	33	136	129	7	29	5	0	0	8	6	0	0	1	28	2	2	4.41	20.59
Newell, Chris	L-L	6-3	200	4-23-01	.162	.248	.253	27	113	99	9	16	3	0	2	9	11	1	0	2	37	7	0	9.73	32.74
Ramos, Jose	R-R	6-1	200	1-1-01	.221	.308	.388	123	506	443	57	98	19	2	17	64	57	1	0	5	172	7	5	11.26	33.99
Rushing, Dalton	L-R	6-1	220	2-21-01	.270	.378	.512	77	334	281	44	76	15	1	17	59	38	12	0	2	69	0	2	11.38	20.66
Sanchez, Lolo	R-R	5-11	186	4-23-99	.194	.291	.233	34	119	103	10	20	0	2	0	8	12	2	1	0	18	1	2	10.08	15.13
Santana, Cristian	R-R	6-2	175	2-24-97	.220	.281	.322	16	64	59	5	13	1	1	1	5	5	0	0	0	18	0	1	7.81	28.13
Young, Taylor	R-R	5-9	170	8-6-98	.236	.333	.329	128	547	474	66	112	28	2	4	43	59	11	0	2	138	46	10	10.79	25.23

Pitching	B-T	Ht.	Wt.	DOB	W	L	ERA	G	GS	SV	IP	Hits	Runs	ER	HR	BB	SO	AVG	OBP	SLG	SO%	BB%	BF
Alleyne, Chris	S-R	5-10	190	11-13-98	0	0	6.00	3	0	0	3	1	2	2	0	4	1	.111	.385	.111	7.69	30.77	13
Bautista, Kelvin	L-L	5-11	155	7-7-99	0	0	9.00	8	0	0	10	19	10	10	1	7	16	.422	.519	.644	29.63	12.96	54
Benitez, Jorge	L-L	6-2	155	6-2-99	0	0	10.80	8	0	0	10	9	13	12	2	15	13	.265	.510	.618	25.49	29.41	51
Boyer, Logan	R-R	6-3	215	1-24-98	0	1	1.67	22	0	5	27	18	7	5	2	12	33	.191	.290	.277	30.84	11.21	107
Cabrera, Jeisson	R-R	6-2	170	9-5-98	1	0	3.52	6	0	0	8	6	4	3	0	10	8	.222	.432	.296	21.62	27.03	37
Campos, Chris	R-R	5-10	170	8-13-00	2	4	3.62	13	10	0	65	60	30	26	10	20	68	.244	.305	.415	25.09	7.38	271
Casparius, Ben	R-R	6-2	215	2-11-99	2	1	3.32	5	5	0	22	18	12	8	2	11	34	.217	.316	.325	35.79	11.58	95
Castro, Yon	R-R	6-0	203	5-23-99	1	2	8.10	7	6	0	20	26	18	18	2	15	18	.325	.439	.450	18.18	15.15	99
Choi, Hyun-il	R-R	6-2	215	5-27-00	1	5	6.05	9	7	0	42	48	30	28	6	8	46	.284	.341	.462	24.73	4.30	186
Dreyer, Jack	R-L	6-2	205	2-27-99	0	0	0.00	9	0	0	15	6	1	0	0	3	20	.122	.173	.143	37.74	5.66	53
Duplantier, Jon	L-R	6-4	229	7-11-94	0	0	3.60	1	1	0	5	6	2	2	0	1	5	.286	.318	.381	22.73	4.55	22
Duran, Carlos	R-R	6-7	230	7-30-01	0	4	3.05	11	11	0	38	43	14	13	3	18	48	.281	.375	.392	27.27	10.23	176
Ferris, Jackson	L-L	6-4	195	1-15-04	1	3	2.54	7	7	0	28	22	8	8	2	14	26	.216	.328	.324	21.31	11.48	122
Fisher, Braydon	R-R	6-4	180	7-26-00	0	1	3.68	7	0	0	7	8	4	3	0	5	14	.276	.371	.517	40.00	14.29	35
Flynn, Michael	R-R	6-4	185	8-7-96	0	0	0.00	3	1	1	6	4	0	0	0	1	9	.200	.273	.250	40.91	4.55	22
Harris, Ben	L-L	6-1	195	2-22-00	4	4	4.93	40	0	0	46	37	27	25	7	38	61	.224	.369	.406	29.33	18.27	208
Henriquez, Edgardo	R-R	6-4	200	6-24-02	0	1	3.06	16	0	0	18	11	6	6	2	8	24	.183	.300	.333	33.80	11.27	71
Hobbs, Michael	R-R	6-3	215	7-10-99	2	1	2.97	42	0	1	58	44	21	19	3	30	52	.216	.325	.289	21.85	12.61	238
Karros, Jared	R-R	6-7	195	11-16-00	2	1	4.01	8	8	0	34	30	15	15	3	15	38	.248	.324	.364	27.34	10.79	139
Knowles, Antonio	R-R	6-1	190	1-15-00	3	5	3.62	42	2	0	55	39	23	22	5	33	60	.202	.332	.311	25.75	14.16	233
Kopp, Ronan	L-L	6-7	250	7-29-02	2	1	4.17	35	0	1	50	39	26	23	4	41	70	.220	.371	.322	30.84	18.06	227
Lao, Sauryn	R-R	6-2	182	8-14-99	0	0	1.90	20	0	2	24	22	5	5	1	8	29	.242	.303	.330	29.29	8.08	99
Little, Jack	L-R	6-4	190	1-10-98	2	1	2.18	18	0	4	21	13	7	5	0	5	23	.173	.253	.200	27.71	6.02	83
Martinez, Michael	R-R	6-1	185	7-11-99	0	0	0.00	2	0	0	2	0	0	0	0	1	2	.000	.250	.000	25.00	12.50	8
McDaniels, Garrett	L-L	6-2	180	12-15-99	0	0	0.00	2	0	0	3	2	1	0	0	1	6	.167	.231	.167	46.15	7.69	13
Meador, Jacob	R-R	6-0	183	10-26-00	0	1	3.18	3	3	0	11	6	5	4	2	9	13	.167	.375	.389	27.08	18.75	48
Morillo, Juan	R-R	6-1	150	3-19-99	5	2	4.76	41	0	1	51	45	30	27	6	29	50	.239	.347	.383	22.52	13.06	222
Ortiz-Mayr, Orlando	R-R	6-3	195	12-6-97	7	8	4.71	27	25	0	136	132	75	71	18	60	108	.253	.340	.414	18.21	10.12	593
Pilarski, Jake	R-R	6-2	215	5-12-98	1	0	3.21	13	0	0	14	16	7	5	1	7	10	.314	.400	.451	16.13	11.29	62
Romero, Christian	R-R	6-3	195	12-11-02	2	0	6.38	6	2	0	18	23	14	13	3	10	14	.303	.424	.513	15.05	10.75	93
Rosario, Jerming	R-R	6-1	175	5-8-02	3	5	4.70	16	16	0	67	47	41	35	3	56	77	.200	.370	.315	25.16	18.30	306
Suarez, Christian	L-L	5-11	160	11-25-00	4	4	4.54	32	0	0	42	35	30	21	1	24	38	.224	.332	.308	20.54	12.97	185
Sublette, Ryan	R-R	6-2	190	10-1-98	5	3	4.84	36	0	1	48	32	28	26	7	33	51	.193	.338	.373	24.52	15.87	208
Treinen, Blake	R-R	6-5	225	6-3-99	0	0	0.00	1	0	0	1	0	0	0	0	0	3	.000	.000	.000	100.0	0.00	3
Wepf, Lucas	L-R	6-5	192	12-23-99	4	4	5.67	21	0	5	27	32	19	17	3	15	38	.308	.403	.423	30.40	12.00	125
Williams, Kendall	R-R	6-6	205	8-24-00	4	10	6.70	20	20	0	93	111	77	69	13	50	50	.299	.395	.472	11.39	11.39	439
Wrobleski, Justin	L-L	6-1	194	7-14-00	5	2	3.06	13	13	0	68	57	24	23	3	13	62	.231	.277	.332	23.05	4.83	269

Fielding

Catcher	PCT	G	PO	A	E	DP	PB
Avila	1.000	6	57	2	0	0	1
Cartaya	.991	34	320	18	3	5	4
Davis	1.000	1	1	0	0	0	0
Fernandez	.970	20	181	10	6	1	4
Lockwood-Powell	.986	44	389	30	6	4	2
Rushing	.994	39	314	25	2	2	3

First Base	PCT	G	PO	A	E	DP
Davis	.985	22	129	5	2	17
Izarra	1.000	2	5	0	0	1
Lewis	.982	59	395	30	8	36
Lockwood-Powell	.997	49	337	29	1	41
Rushing	1.000	1	4	0	0	0
Santana	.989	14	88	2	1	3

Second Base	PCT	G	PO	A	E	DP
Alleyne	1.000	1	4	0	0	0
Davis	.944	4	9	8	1	1
Fernandez	.963	85	145	192	13	56
Izarra	.981	17	20	31	1	8
Young	.985	39	57	71	2	20

Third Base	PCT	G	PO	A	E	DP
Davis	.949	45	34	77	6	5
Fernandez	1.000	2	2	0	0	1
Izarra	1.000	4	0	1	0	0
Lewis	.929	10	8	18	2	1
Santana	.000	2	0	0	0	0
Young	.981	84	68	137	4	27

Shortstop	PCT	G	PO	A	E	DP
Freeland	.968	73	109	167	9	38
Gauthier	.947	21	22	50	4	11
Izarra	.944	5	8	9	1	1
Miller	.982	33	35	74	2	12
Young	.950	6	6	13	1	2

Outfield	PCT	G	PO	A	E	DP
Alleyne	.981	83	146	8	3	1
Beck	.986	45	68	1	1	0
Casey	1.000	20	36	2	0	1
Davis	.985	42	62	4	1	1
Gauthier	1.000	1	1	0	0	0
Keith	.977	58	80	5	2	1
Newell	1.000	26	51	0	0	0
Ramos	.966	123	273	13	10	4
Rushing	1.000	4	2	0	0	0
Sanchez	.980	31	44	4	1	1

GREAT LAKES LOONS

HIGH-A

MIDWEST LEAGUE

Batting	B-T	Ht.	Wt.	DOB	AVG	OBP	SLG	G	PA	AB	R	H	2B	3B	HR	RBI	BB	HBP	SH	SF	SO	SB	CS	BB%	SO%
Alonso, Juan	R-R	6-0	180	11-3-03	.231	.310	.269	19	58	52	6	12	2	0	0	5	4	2	0	0	26	1	0	6.90	44.83
Biddison, Nick	R-R	5-10	190	7-30-00	.220	.353	.358	83	306	254	30	56	10	2	7	31	40	12	0	0	81	21	2	13.07	26.47
Campbell, Dylan	R-R	5-11	205	7-2-02	.251	.331	.372	115	493	435	64	109	21	1	10	53	50	4	0	4	110	42	7	10.14	22.31
De Paula, Josue	L-L	6-3	185	5-24-05	.254	.422	.356	52	230	177	32	45	6	0	4	21	50	2	0	1	38	13	3	21.74	16.52
Freeland, Alex	B-R	6-2	200	8-24-01	.346	.518	.593	23	110	81	18	28	10	2	2	21	27	2	0	0	16	5	0	24.55	14.55
Galiz, Jesus	R-R	6-0	183	12-19-03	.042	.130	.063	14	54	48	3	2	1	0	0	2	5	0	0	1	19	0	0	9.26	35.19
Garcia, Yunior	R-R	6-0	198	7-29-01	.160	.189	.330	30	113	106	15	17	3	0	5	17	3	1	0	1	30	0	0	2.65	26.55
Gelof, Jake	R-R	6-1	195	2-25-02	.186	.277	.321	85	346	296	38	55	16	0	8	41	39	2	0	9	72	17	4	11.27	20.81
Liranzo, Thayron	B-R	6-3	195	7-5-03	.220	.344	.356	74	314	264	35	58	15	0	7	30	49	1	0	0	82	1	0	15.61	26.11
McLain, Sean	R-R	5-11	170	3-22-01	.211	.318	.326	28	110	95	10	20	4	2	1	8	12	3	0	0	36	2	2	10.91	32.73
Miller, Noah	B-R	5-11	190	11-12-02	.251	.336	.332	101	454	395	60	99	14	0	6	38	49	4	1	4	66	5	1	10.79	14.54
Mongelli, Sam	R-R	6-1	185	3-6-01	.232	.307	.334	87	348	302	49	70	11	1	6	45	33	2	4	5	97	23	3	9.48	27.87
Nevin, Kyle	R-R	6-4	200	8-22-01	.236	.320	.344	119	519	457	56	108	15	5	8	55	54	4	0	4	163	18	6	10.40	31.41
Newell, Chris	L-L	6-3	200	4-23-01	.212	.338	.465	97	413	340	61	72	15	1	23	65	60	7	2	4	140	24	6	14.53	33.90
Quiroz, Nelson	B-R	5-8	194	11-5-01	.255	.322	.299	54	202	184	24	47	5	0	1	17	16	2	0	0	16	0	0	7.92	7.92
Rodriguez, Frank	R-R	5-11	197	9-28-01	.181	.243	.210	32	115	105	11	19	3	0	0	10	7	2	0	1	28	1	0	6.09	24.35
Rodriguez, Luis	R-R	6-2	175	9-16-02	.207	.294	.260	44	171	150	21	31	5	0	1	16	18	1	0	1	60	2	0	10.53	35.09
Thompson, Jordan	R-R	6-0	175	1-9-02	.218	.304	.360	60	226	197	27	43	13	0	5	28	19	6	2	2	61	10	4	8.41	26.99
Vogel, Jake	R-R	5-11	165	10-12-01	.177	.298	.244	89	321	271	32	48	5	2	3	24	38	9	2	1	94	18	5	11.84	29.28

Pitching	B-T	Ht.	Wt.	DOB	W	L	ERA	G	GS	SV	IP	Hits	Runs	ER	HR	BB	SO	AVG	OBP	SLG	SO%	BB%	BF
Alonso, Juan	R-R	6-0	180	11-3-03	0	0	20.25	2	0	0	1	3	3	3	1	3	0	.600	.700	1.200	0.00	30.00	10
Bautista, Kelvin	L-L	5-11	155	7-7-99	6	4	4.47	32	0	1	44	41	29	22	2	21	55	.246	.332	.305	28.95	11.05	190
Biddison, Nick	R-R	5-10	190	7-30-00	0	0	0.00	1	0	0	0	2	0	0	0	0	1	.667	.667	1.000	33.33	0.00	3
Bruns, Maddux	L-L	6-2	205	6-20-02	0	1	2.22	10	10	0	28	20	10	7	0	20	37	.200	.362	.240	28.91	15.63	128
Cabrera, Jeisson	R-R	6-2	170	9-5-98	2	0	2.86	20	1	2	28	15	12	9	2	19	33	.158	.314	.232	27.97	16.10	118
Campos, Chris	R-R	5-10	170	8-13-00	3	2	3.15	12	5	0	46	36	16	16	6	10	50	.213	.260	.361	27.62	5.52	181
Copen, Patrick	R-R	6-6	220	2-15-02	3	2	4.23	9	9	0	38	36	18	18	2	29	38	.254	.390	.324	21.35	16.29	178
Crowell, Wyatt	L-L	6-0	170	10-13-01	0	1	3.54	6	6	0	20	18	8	8	1	9	24	.240	.367	.360	26.67	10.00	90
Cruz, Nicolas	R-R	5-11	160	4-23-04	0	0	0.00	3	0	0	5	2	0	0	0	0	7	.105	.105	.105	36.84	0.00	19
De La Paz, Franklin	L-L	6-2	190	3-29-99	1	1	6.59	26	0	0	29	23	24	21	2	25	37	.228	.410	.327	27.61	18.66	134
Edwards, Jonathan	R-R	6-6	185	1-26-00	1	1	15.23	17	0	1	13	25	23	22	1	23	17	.403	.570	.597	19.10	25.84	89
Ferris, Jackson	L-L	6-4	195	1-15-04	4	4	3.39	20	20	0	98	71	44	37	4	43	119	.198	.290	.279	29.17	10.54	408
Henriquez, Edgardo	R-R	6-4	200	6-24-02	0	1	2.92	8	0	0	12	7	5	4	0	5	25	.156	.269	.244	48.08	9.62	52
Heubeck, Peter	R-R	6-3	170	7-22-02	2	5	3.05	24	24	0	91	58	33	31	3	65	117	.184	.331	.241	29.92	16.62	391
Hobbs, Carson	R-R	6-1	197	2-27-02	1	0	5.92	18	0	1	24	24	17	16	4	13	27	.258	.364	.419	24.55	11.82	110
Ibarra, Joel	R-R	6-0	176	7-10-02	1	0	54.00	4	0	0	2	8	15	14	2	8	1	.615	.783	1.154	4.35	34.78	23
Jeffrey, Madison	L-R	6-0	190	3-14-00	1	0	5.58	26	0	0	31	23	22	19	0	32	29	.221	.417	.269	20.14	22.22	144
Karros, Jared	R-R	6-7	195	11-16-00	5	0	1.59	7	7	0	34	21	6	6	1	7	36	.174	.219	.273	28.13	5.47	128
Luna, Jesus	R-R	6-6	165	11-6-00	0	0	5.93	15	0	0	14	13	10	9	0	13	15	.241	.397	.278	22.06	19.12	68
Martin, Payton	R-R	6-0	170	5-19-04	3	4	3.38	13	13	0	53	48	24	20	7	18	32	.241	.308	.402	14.48	8.14	221
Martinez, Michael	R-R	6-1	185	7-11-99	3	5	2.01	36	0	1	40	26	14	9	1	24	46	.183	.304	.225	26.74	13.95	172
McDaniels, Garrett	L-L	6-2	180	12-15-99	5	1	2.49	19	0	1	25	19	9	7	0	5	34	.196	.257	.258	32.38	4.76	105
Meador, Jacob	R-R	6-0	183	10-26-00	3	4	5.44	22	15	1	89	91	56	54	11	50	83	.265	.380	.427	20.24	12.20	410
Neeck, Brandon	R-L	6-1	190	10-19-99	4	3	2.85	38	0	2	60	34	20	19	4	23	67	.163	.271	.249	27.80	9.54	241
Ramirez, Kelvin	R-R	6-4	187	6-10-01	3	8	4.78	44	1	12	53	49	32	28	6	26	61	.249	.336	.371	26.52	11.30	230
Reinoso, Livan	R-R	6-1	185	8-27-98	7	4	3.98	41	0	1	54	38	31	24	3	37	47	.202	.361	.287	19.58	15.42	240
Rodriguez, Jose	S-R	6-6	200	7-18-01	3	4	2.25	16	5	3	56	38	15	14	2	19	67	.187	.258	.261	29.78	8.44	225
Romero, Christian	R-R	6-3	195	12-11-02	3	4	2.26	15	8	2	64	51	18	16	4	23	53	.224	.303	.316	20.87	9.06	254
Rosario, Jerming	R-R	6-1	175	5-8-02	2	0	3.68	10	6	1	37	26	15	15	3	11	38	.198	.286	.298	25.68	7.43	148
Ruebeck, Christian	R-R	6-0	185	9-3-00	1	0	0.00	5	0	1	7	2	0	0	0	3	6	.091	.231	.091	23.08	11.54	26
Suarez, Christian	L-L	5-11	160	11-25-00	1	0	0.68	9	0	1	13	4	1	1	0	11	17	.093	.278	.140	31.48	20.37	54
Wepf, Lucas	L-R	6-5	192	12-23-99	1	2	1.84	22	0	8	29	12	8	6	3	10	44	.122	.216	.245	39.64	9.01	111

Fielding

Catcher	PCT	G	PO	A	E	DP	PB
Galiz	1.000	13	110	8	0	0	3
Liranzo	.991	44	410	30	4	2	9
Quiroz	.990	51	472	34	5	1	4
Rodriguez	.987	28	279	21	4	1	0

First Base	PCT	G	PO	A	E	DP
Biddison	.986	40	251	21	4	23
Garcia	.973	6	35	1	1	4
Gelof	1.000	1	2	0	0	1
Liranzo	.995	24	166	16	1	13
Nevin	.993	58	434	23	3	42
Rodriguez	.958	4	20	3	1	1

Second Base	PCT	G	PO	A	E	DP
Biddison	1.000	15	16	41	0	6
Campbell	1.000	3	4	9	0	1
Freeland	1.000	6	11	13	0	3
McLain	.941	3	9	7	1	3
Miller	.976	11	17	23	1	8
Mongelli	.954	59	98	109	10	34
Thompson	.964	41	58	77	5	16

Third Base	PCT	G	PO	A	E	DP
Biddison	.938	18	16	29	3	3
Freeland	.947	6	6	12	1	1
Gelof	.965	82	71	120	7	16
Mongelli	.918	15	16	29	4	3
Nevin	1.000	1	1	1	0	0
Thompson	.920	12	6	17	2	2

Shortstop	PCT	G	PO	A	E	DP
Freeland	.974	11	16	22	1	4
McLain	.971	25	22	45	2	7
Miller	.987	90	116	188	4	39
Mongelli	.000	1	0	0	0	0
Thompson	.923	5	5	7	1	3

Outfield	PCT	G	PO	A	E	DP
Alonso	.971	17	31	2	1	0
Biddison	1.000	10	11	0	0	0
Campbell	.981	111	242	11	5	2
De Paula	.970	39	63	2	2	1
Garcia	.909	17	18	2	2	0
Mongelli	.818	11	8	1	2	0
Newell	.980	82	145	3	3	2
Rodriguez	.977	38	40	3	1	0
Vogel	.994	89	154	4	1	0

RANCHO CUCAMONGA QUAKES — LOW-A

CALIFORNIA LEAGUE

Batting	B-T	Ht.	Wt.	DOB	AVG	OBP	SLG	G	PA	AB	R	H	2B	3B	HR	RBI	BB	HBP	SH	SF	SO	SB	CS	BB%	SO%
Albertus, Alexander	R-R	6-1	176	10-27-04	.229	.317	.329	19	82	70	8	16	4	0	1	16	10	0	0	2	15	1	0	12.20	18.29
Alonso, Juan	R-R	6-0	180	11-3-03	.229	.360	.371	86	347	280	49	64	14	4	6	45	48	13	0	6	114	3	4	13.83	32.85
De Paula, Josue	L-L	6-3	185	5-24-05	.279	.388	.447	55	251	208	37	58	11	3	6	41	34	5	0	3	57	14	0	13.55	22.71
Decker, Cameron	B-R	6-1	205	9-22-03	.250	.363	.522	62	270	228	49	57	20	3	12	53	36	5	0	1	91	0	1	13.33	33.70
Diaz, Wilman	R-R	6-2	182	11-15-03	.249	.316	.367	109	440	398	58	99	19	8	4	54	35	5	0	2	133	17	6	7.95	30.23
Galiz, Jesus	R-R	6-0	183	12-19-03	.268	.366	.426	52	216	183	32	49	16	2	3	23	19	11	0	3	61	0	0	8.80	28.24
Gelof, Jake	R-R	6-1	195	2-25-02	.310	.462	.494	24	117	87	20	27	4	3	2	26	27	0	0	3	31	3	0	23.08	26.50
George, Kendall	L-L	5-10	170	10-29-04	.279	.384	.328	86	404	341	75	95	6	4	1	31	57	3	0	3	83	36	12	14.11	20.54
Guerrero, Eduardo	B-R	6-2	165	5-9-05	.195	.300	.208	25	90	77	3	15	1	0	0	7	12	0	0	1	22	3	1	13.33	24.44
Hainline, Elijah	R-R	5-10	185	12-20-02	.118	.333	.200	30	114	85	21	10	1	0	2	5	26	2	0	1	30	8	1	22.81	26.32
Hope, Zyhir	L-L	6-0	193	1-19-05	.287	.415	.490	54	248	202	42	58	14	0	9	31	37	7	0	0	60	8	2	14.92	24.19
McLain, Sean	R-R	5-11	170	3-22-01	.217	.329	.341	67	295	249	45	54	10	3	5	31	28	15	0	3	78	6	2	9.49	26.44
Meza, Jose	R-R	6-1	160	4-22-03	.218	.324	.389	58	256	216	38	47	10	3	7	31	27	9	0	4	63	2	2	10.55	24.61
Munoz, Samuel	L-R	6-3	190	9-22-04	.229	.306	.342	90	385	336	41	77	15	4	5	50	39	2	0	8	79	6	3	10.13	20.52
Osorio, Oswaldo	L-R	6-1	171	4-12-05	.194	.316	.279	70	291	247	28	48	13	1	2	30	34	10	0	0	85	1	3	11.68	29.21
Perez, Jeral	R-R	6-0	179	11-6-04	.264	.380	.420	75	350	288	49	76	15	0	10	42	48	9	0	5	77	4	2	13.71	22.00
Quintero, Eduardo	R-R	6-0	175	9-16-05	.196	.333	.283	27	112	92	15	18	4	2	0	6	18	1	1	0	22	3	3	16.07	19.64
Rodrigues, Victor	R-R	6-3	203	9-23-04	.235	.278	.314	14	54	51	6	12	1	0	1	4	2	1	0	0	11	0	0	3.70	20.37
Rojas, Carlos	R-R	6-0	165	7-25-02	.290	.368	.357	75	310	269	37	78	13	1	1	47	29	7	0	5	48	0	0	9.35	15.48
Rojas, Miguel	R-R	6-0	188	2-24-89	.000	.250	.000	1	4	3	0	0	0	0	0	0	1	0	0	0	1	0	0	25.00	25.00
Taylor, Chris	R-R	6-1	196	8-29-90	.286	.375	.286	2	8	7	0	2	0	0	0	3	1	0	0	0	2	0	0	12.50	25.00
Thompson, Jordan	R-R	6-0	175	1-9-02	.264	.376	.491	43	189	159	30	42	12	0	8	30	25	4	0	1	49	8	2	13.23	25.93
Valladares, Jefferson	R-R	6-0	190	5-30-02	.271	.357	.396	15	56	48	7	13	4	1	0	5	5	2	0	1	11	0	0	8.93	19.64
Vetrano, Joe	L-L	6-3	220	5-10-02	.243	.362	.318	28	127	107	12	26	3	1	1	20	18	2	0	0	40	1	1	14.17	31.50
Wagner, Logan	B-R	6-1	200	3-9-04	.246	.405	.484	38	164	126	27	31	8	2	6	23	27	8	0	2	41	4	0	16.46	25.00

Pitching	B-T	Ht.	Wt.	DOB	W	L	ERA	G	GS	SV	IP	Hits	Runs	ER	HR	BB	SO	AVG	OBP	SLG	SO%	BB%	BF
Barrett, Seamus	R-R	6-7	220	12-26-00	0	1	5.59	7	0	1	10	7	7	6	1	8	14	.194	.341	.333	31.82	18.18	44
Brito, Moises	L-L	6-5	215	7-9-02	1	0	9.64	6	0	1	9	13	11	10	3	8	9	.317	.420	.610	18.00	16.00	50
Buehler, Walker	R-R	6-2	185	7-28-94	0	0	4.50	1	1	0	2	3	1	1	0	1	0	.333	.400	.333	0.00	10.00	10
Cabrera, Felix	L-L	6-3	170	4-8-02	6	4	5.44	35	0	2	43	48	29	26	5	34	44	.279	.406	.413	20.66	15.96	213
Copen, Patrick	R-R	6-6	220	2-15-02	5	2	3.15	13	11	0	54	40	20	19	1	25	60	.211	.315	.274	26.91	11.21	223
Corcho, Marco	R-R	6-2	200	5-2-05	0	1	6.10	7	0	0	10	11	7	7	1	11	12	.260	.455	.390	21.82	20.00	55
Crowell, Wyatt	L-L	6-0	170	10-13-01	0	0	1.56	7	7	0	17	6	3	3	0	11	26	.103	.297	.138	35.14	14.86	74
Day, Cam	S-R	6-2	195	7-25-02	5	6	4.68	24	15	0	102	109	60	53	5	52	94	.276	.369	.390	20.48	11.33	459
Duran, Carlos	R-R	6-7	230	7-30-01	0	2	4.61	7	7	0	14	9	12	7	1	11	22	.176	.354	.294	33.85	16.92	65
Emmett, Gabe	R-R	6-5	175	5-22-01	2	0	8.60	17	3	0	45	61	46	43	4	36	46	.323	.435	.481	19.74	15.45	233
Figueredo, Dilan	R-R	6-0	174	3-28-03	1	0	8.59	7	0	0	7	8	7	7	1	6	4	.296	.400	.704	11.43	17.14	35
Foeller, Aidan	R-R	6-3	220	3-26-02	0	0	0.00	2	0	0	3	0	0	0	0	2	4	.000	.182	.000	36.36	18.18	11
Fox, Luke	L-L	6-2	200	1-4-02	0	0	3.52	12	12	0	31	22	13	12	3	21	38	.206	.341	.318	29.46	16.28	129
Gonzalez, Jorge	R-R	6-5	203	8-30-02	4	2	6.98	14	0	0	19	15	16	15	0	15	27	.217	.371	.261	30.34	16.85	89
Gonzalez, Joseilyn	R-R	5-11	160	4-8-02	5	1	5.66	39	0	1	62	64	47	39	7	35	55	.269	.382	.416	19.16	12.20	287
Gutierrez, Roque	R-R	5-9	177	9-7-02	5	3	5.38	28	4	0	99	103	68	59	13	35	118	.263	.326	.467	27.00	8.01	437
Henriquez, Edgardo	R-R	6-4	200	6-24-02	0	0	1.74	5	5	0	10	4	2	2	0	6	21	.114	.262	.171	50.00	14.29	42
Hobbs, Carson	R-R	6-1	197	2-27-02	0	1	3.00	0	0	0	12	6	4	4	1	5	16	.143	.234	.238	34.04	10.64	47
Jang, Hyun-Seok	R-R	6-2	185	3-14-04	0	1	2.19	5	5	0	12	4	3	3	0	8	19	.100	.250	.125	39.58	16.67	48
Kelly, Joe	R-R	6-1	174	6-9-88	0	0	0.00	2	1	0	2	2	0	0	0	1	1	.333	.429	.333	14.29	14.29	7
Kershaw, Clayton	L-L	6-4	225	3-19-88	0	0	3.00	1	1	0	3	2	1	1	0	1	5	.222	.273	.444	45.45	9.09	11
Linan, Sean	R-R	6-0	185	11-7-04	6	2	4.89	13	4	0	57	58	32	31	5	24	72	.270	.355	.400	29.03	9.68	248
Luna, Jesus	R-R	6-6	165	11-6-00	0	1	2.70	6	0	0	10	5	4	3	0	6	17	.143	.268	.200	41.46	14.63	41
Makarewich, Alex	R-R	6-0	185	1-17-02	2	4	9.67	14	7	0	27	34	31	29	3	34	40	.315	.500	.500	26.67	22.67	150
Martin, Payton	R-R	6-0	170	5-19-04	0	2	4.82	6	6	0	19	18	11	10	2	17	22	.247	.409	.397	23.40	18.09	94
Martinez, Carlos	R-R	6-3	190	11-9-01	0	0	6.00	4	0	0	6	7	4	4	0	8	6	.318	.484	.364	19.35	25.81	31
McDaniels, Garrett	L-L	6-2	180	12-15-99	0	4	3.80	11	7	0	45	43	25	19	3	23	44	.251	.342	.368	22.34	11.68	197
Miller, Bobby	L-R	6-5	220	4-5-99	0	1	9.95	2	2	0	6	9	7	7	0	3	4	.321	.406	.429	12.50	9.38	32
Ortiz, Robinson	L-L	6-0	180	1-4-00	2	0	0.82	6	0	0	11	9	2	1	0	6	3	.237	.383	.316	6.38	12.77	47
Patick, Sterling	L-L	6-1	155	6-9-05	0	1	3.50	6	6	0	18	18	9	7	1	4	17	.250	.291	.347	21.52	5.06	79
Phillips, Evan	R-R	6-2	215	9-11-94	0	0	0.00	2	0	0	2	0	0	0	0	0	3	.000	.000	.000	60.00	0.00	5
Rodriguez, Jose	S-R	6-6	200	7-18-01	5	2	5.19	9	3	1	35	35	23	20	1	13	59	.250	.325	.364	37.34	8.23	158
Ruebeck, Christian	R-R	6-0	185	9-3-00	2	3	7.60	29	0	5	34	26	34	29	4	36	47	.217	.419	.408	27.81	21.30	169
Ruen, Noah	R-R	6-4	190	3-21-03	3	2	4.45	42	0	7	55	62	32	27	4	22	53	.284	.364	.385	20.95	8.70	253
Ryan, River	R-R	6-2	195	8-17-98	0	0	0.00	1	1	0	2	0	0	0	0	0	3	.000	.000	.000	50.00	0.00	6
Sanchez, Samuel	R-R	5-11	150	10-21-05	0	0	3.00	2	2	0	6	8	2	2	1	0	5	.296	.296	.444	18.52	0.00	27
Santana, Waylin	R-R	6-1	155	3-13-03	1	3	7.11	21	1	0	32	47	30	25	6	20	26	.343	.439	.569	15.85	12.20	164
Santillan, Pedro	R-R	6-4	200	7-7-01	1	2	5.81	20	0	1	26	28	22	17	2	21	16	.295	.430	.421	13.11	17.21	122
Serunkuma, Ben	R-R	5-10	170	9-19-01	0	0	0.00	1	0	0	2	1	0	0	0	0	3	.167	.167	.333	50.00	0.00	6
Shaw, Evan	L-L	6-4	205	2-2-01	2	0	2.57	5	0	1	7	6	2	2	0	2	3	.231	.276	.308	10.34	6.90	29
Swan, Eriq	R-R	6-6	240	10-31-01	0	1	5.16	10	7	0	23	25	17	13	2	16	29	.275	.385	.385	26.61	14.68	109
Tiburcio, David	R-R	6-2	195	12-29-01	2	2	6.35	28	1	0	45	53	42	32	8	26	38	.286	.375	.454	17.51	11.98	217
Wallace, Callum	R-R	6-3	190	4-6-04	2	4	7.83	27	0	3	33	35	31	29	1	31	28	.276	.437	.370	16.47	18.24	170
Yean, Reynaldo	R-R	6-4	190	1-4-04	2	2	6.08	28	0	5	24	10	16	16	1	25	44	.123	.351	.198	39.64	22.52	111
Zazueta, Christian	R-R	6-3	163	10-7-04	1	5	6.36	14	11	0	52	54	40	37	7	20	63	.265	.342	.417	27.16	8.62	232

Fielding

Catcher	PCT	G	PO	A	E	DP	PB
Galiz	.986	50	450	34	7	2	14
Rodrigues	.993	14	139	3	1	0	2
Rojas	.992	70	673	41	6	3	10
Valladares	1.000	2	19	3	0	0	0

First Base	PCT	G	PO	A	E	DP
Decker	.989	46	325	24	4	36
Galiz	1.000	1	3	0	0	0
McLain	.983	27	214	15	4	20
Rojas	1.000	4	22	3	0	2
Valladares	.907	8	43	6	5	1
Vetrano	.984	25	177	8	3	24
Wagner	.994	24	163	14	1	10

Second Base	PCT	G	PO	A	E	DP
Diaz	.965	23	33	49	3	10
Guerrero	1.000	2	1	2	0	0
Hainline	.987	17	32	44	1	15
McLain	.987	16	30	46	1	3
Osorio	.927	16	23	28	4	8
Perez	.952	56	93	126	11	32
Taylor	1.000	1	0	4	0	0
Thompson	1.000	3	4	6	0	0

Third Base	PCT	G	PO	A	E	DP
Albertus	.935	13	6	23	2	0
Diaz	.921	32	22	48	6	4
Gelof	.887	21	13	34	6	4
Guerrero	.946	12	6	29	2	6
McLain	.000	1	0	0	0	0
Osorio	.878	34	18	61	11	4
Perez	1.000	3	1	3	0	0
Thompson	.941	4	6	10	1	3
Wagner	1.000	11	5	14	0	3

Shortstop	PCT	G	PO	A	E	DP
Albertus	.947	5	5	13	1	2
Diaz	.956	42	62	112	8	25
Guerrero	.977	10	14	29	1	9
Hainline	.980	13	18	32	1	5
McLain	.959	19	26	45	3	10
Osorio	.815	8	9	13	5	3
Perez	.917	6	13	9	2	4
Thompson	.953	28	36	45	4	11

Outfield	PCT	G	PO	A	E	DP
Alonso	.954	75	118	7	6	2
De Paula	.914	43	52	1	5	0
Decker	1.000	11	23	1	0	1
Diaz	1.000	12	13	2	0	0
George	.954	65	142	3	7	1
Hope	.968	46	85	5	3	1
McLain	.000	1	0	0	0	0
Meza	.961	49	72	2	3	1
Munoz	.962	77	123	5	5	0
Quintero	.952	21	39	1	2	0
Taylor	1.000	1	3	0	0	0
Thompson	1.000	4	2	0	0	0
Valladares	1.000	5	5	0	0	0

ACL DODGERS — *ROOKIE*

ARIZONA COMPLEX LEAGUE

Batting	B-T	Ht.	Wt.	DOB	AVG	OBP	SLG	G	PA	AB	R	H	2B	3B	HR	RBI	BB	HBP	SH	SF	SO	SB	CS	BB%	SO%
Albertus, Alexander	R-R	6-1	176	10-27-04	.342	.479	.459	32	143	111	24	38	7	0	2	26	27	3	0	1	20	5	2	18.88	13.99
Avila, Carlos	R-R	5-11	180	12-4-03	.115	.273	.148	30	77	61	10	7	2	0	0	10	13	1	0	2	16	0	1	16.88	20.78
Decker, Cameron	B-R	6-1	205	9-22-03	.262	.400	.541	19	80	61	14	16	3	1	4	14	14	2	0	3	20	1	1	17.50	25.00
Diaz, Angel	R-R	5-11	180	2-4-04	.284	.400	.337	31	116	95	12	27	5	0	0	15	7	12	1	1	25	0	1	6.03	21.55
Elkins, Jaron	R-R	6-1	193	11-4-04	.285	.412	.457	57	228	186	43	53	11	3	5	30	33	8	0	1	80	20	7	14.47	35.09
Gonzalez, Bryan	R-R	5-10	160	7-15-05	.130	.310	.174	9	29	23	4	3	1	0	0	0	6	0	0	0	6	2	0	20.69	20.69
Guerrero, Eduardo	B-R	6-2	165	5-9-05	.258	.408	.328	48	169	128	23	33	3	3	0	18	30	6	0	5	29	6	0	17.75	17.16
Hernandez, Jose	R-R	6-1	145	4-30-03	.302	.394	.512	26	99	86	19	26	6	0	4	21	8	5	0	0	21	5	2	8.08	21.21
Hope, Zyhir	L-L	6-0	193	1-19-05	.316	.458	.421	7	24	19	4	6	2	0	0	5	4	1	0	0	2	1	0	16.67	8.33
Izarra, Jose	R-R	6-0	175	3-7-02	.250	.449	.417	12	49	36	8	9	1	1	1	6	10	3	0	0	12	0	1	20.41	24.49
Keith, Damon	R-R	6-3	195	5-28-00	.400	.526	.667	4	19	15	7	6	1	0	1	6	4	0	0	0	4	0	0	21.05	21.05
Lasso, Roger	B-R	6-0	180	2-27-04	.250	.318	.367	18	66	60	7	15	5	1	0	9	5	1	0	0	13	0	0	7.58	19.70
Martinus, Mairoshendrick	R-R	6-3	161	2-3-05	.211	.274	.373	50	190	166	28	35	5	2	6	31	14	3	0	7	69	9	1	7.37	36.32
Meza, Jose	R-R	6-1	160	4-22-03	.368	.486	.575	26	109	87	23	32	7	1	3	25	19	2	0	1	27	1	1	17.43	24.77
Ortega, Raynerd	R-R	6-1	154	7-8-05	.129	.282	.161	12	39	31	4	4	1	0	0	6	4	3	0	1	12	2	0	10.26	30.77
Osorio, Oswaldo	L-R	6-1	171	4-12-05	.250	.400	.250	1	5	4	0	1	0	0	0	0	1	0	0	0	1	1	0	20.00	20.00
Perez, Nicolas	R-R	6-0	175	9-20-04	.264	.381	.387	33	126	106	20	28	4	0	3	9	17	3	0	0	36	14	1	13.49	28.57
Quintero, Eduardo	R-R	6-0	175	9-16-05	.330	.459	.449	56	233	185	49	61	7	3	3	37	41	5	0	2	45	29	3	17.60	19.31
Rodrigues, Victor	R-R	6-3	203	9-23-04	.265	.345	.333	30	116	102	17	27	1	0	2	12	13	0	0	1	14	2	1	11.21	12.07
Shelton, Easton	R-R	6-5	225	9-17-05	.260	.357	.397	26	84	73	12	19	1	3	1	5	10	1	0	0	30	0	0	11.90	35.71
Valladares, Jefferson	R-R	6-0	190	5-30-02	.250	.400	.250	7	20	16	3	4	0	0	0	2	3	1	0	0	4	0	0	15.00	20.00
Vargas, Joendry	R-R	6-4	175	11-8-05	.303	.406	.493	38	171	142	40	43	9	3	4	24	21	5	0	2	39	11	5	12.28	22.81
Ward, Ryan	L-R	5-9	200	2-23-98	.714	.778	1.571	2	9	7	5	5	3	0	1	3	2	0	0	0	1	0	0	22.22	11.11

Pitching	B-T	Ht.	Wt.	DOB	W	L	ERA	G	GS	SV	IP	Hits	Runs	ER	HR	BB	SO	AVG	OBP	SLG	SO%	BB%	BF
Abad, Dailoui	R-R	6-0	168	5-2-02	0	0	27.00	1	0	0	1	2	2	2	0	0	1	.667	.750	.667	25.00	0.00	4
Benua, Alvaro	R-R	6-4	198	1-11-03	2	2	7.47	17	0	1	16	4	16	13	0	25	27	.085	.430	.085	34.18	31.65	79
Brito, Moises	L-L	6-5	215	7-9-02	0	0	6.35	8	2	1	11	9	8	8	2	9	17	.214	.353	.429	33.33	17.65	51
Cabrera, Felix	L-L	6-3	170	4-8-02	0	0	2.79	6	0	3	10	5	3	3	0	5	8	.161	.325	.226	20.00	12.50	40
Cabrera, Jeisson	R-R	6-2	170	9-5-98	0	0	0.00	2	0	0	3	0	1	0	0	0	4	.000	.000	.000	36.36	0.00	11
Chambers, Justin	L-L	6-2	212	8-14-05	0	1	17.18	4	3	0	4	4	7	7	0	5	3	.308	.500	.462	15.00	25.00	20
Corcho, Marco	R-R	6-2	200	5-2-05	2	0	2.70	14	0	2	17	9	6	5	0	8	21	.158	.294	.193	30.88	11.76	68
Cressend, Cole	R-R	6-3	185	8-16-02	2	0	3.38	10	0	0	16	17	6	6	2	7	23	.274	.357	.419	32.86	10.00	70
Crowell, Wyatt	L-L	6-0	170	10-13-01	0	0	6.00	4	4	0	6	2	4	4	0	4	9	.105	.320	.105	36.00	16.00	25
Cruz, Nicolas	R-R	5-11	160	4-23-04	5	1	6.08	12	2	0	27	33	20	18	2	16	35	.311	.411	.472	28.23	12.90	124
Figueredo, Dilan	R-R	6-0	174	3-28-03	1	0	1.84	13	0	2	15	10	4	3	0	6	14	.189	.306	.264	21.88	9.38	64
Fox, Luke	L-L	6-2	200	1-4-02	0	0	0.00	4	2	0	7	6	1	0	0	1	7	.222	.250	.296	25.00	3.57	28
Geronimo, Domingo	R-R	5-11	150	10-7-04	2	1	6.88	15	0	2	17	24	13	13	3	6	21	.343	.397	.543	26.92	7.69	78
Gonsalves, Stephen	L-L	6-5	218	7-8-94	0	0	9.00	1	0	0	1	2	1	1	1	1	2	.400	.500	1.200	33.33	16.67	6
Graterol, Brusdar	R-R	6-1	265	8-26-98	1	0	4.50	2	0	0	2	3	1	1	0	0	1	.375	.375	.500	11.11	0.00	9
Herder, Jholbran	R-R	6-2	170	11-2-04	4	1	2.57	12	3	0	35	26	11	10	0	16	24	.215	.326	.281	17.02	11.35	141
Hernandez, Jose	L-L	5-10	205	12-31-97	1	0	0.00	3	1	0	3	0	0	0	0	2	6	.000	.182	.000	54.55	18.18	11
Hobbs, Carson	R-R	6-1	197	2-27-02	1	0	0.00	5	1	0	6	2	0	0	0	2	11	.105	.227	.105	47.83	8.70	23
Ibarra, Joel	R-R	6-0	176	7-10-02	0	0	4.26	8	0	0	6	3	3	3	1	8	12	.130	.355	.261	38.71	25.81	31
Jang, Hyun-Seok	R-R	6-2	185	3-14-04	1	2	8.14	13	10	0	24	18	23	22	4	19	49	.189	.347	.347	41.53	16.10	118
Jimenez, Jhonny	R-R	6-5	180	11-9-03	0	0	9.39	6	0	0	8	13	12	8	1	9	6	.361	.478	.500	13.04	19.57	46
Linan, Sean	R-R	6-0	185	11-7-04	3	0	2.08	6	1	0	13	9	3	3	2	2	21	.196	.245	.326	42.86	4.08	49
Luna, Jesus	R-R	6-6	165	11-6-00	0	0	0.00	4	0	1	5	0	0	0	0	3	9	.000	.211	.000	47.37	15.79	19
Makarewich, Alex	R-R	6-0	185	1-17-02	0	1	7.20	3	3	0	5	5	4	4	1	3	5	.263	.417	.579	20.83	12.50	24

Maynard, William	L-R	6-3	190	6-19-03	0	0	0.00	3	1	0	3	0	1	0	0	4	0	.000	.417	.000	0.00	33.33	12
Montero, Ricardo	R-R	6-6	237	2-17-04	2	1	12.36	18	0	1	20	17	27	27	0	36	21	.250	.563	.294	17.65	30.25	119
Morales, Accimias	R-R	6-5	190	9-13-04	1	1	4.67	9	5	0	17	18	10	9	1	8	21	.269	.364	.358	27.27	10.39	77
Omosako, Kinn	R-R	6-4	210	6-24-04	2	0	2.88	16	0	0	25	18	10	8	0	13	30	.196	.312	.283	27.52	11.93	109
Patick, Sterling	L-L	6-1	155	6-9-05	0	1	5.93	6	5	1	14	11	9	9	0	7	14	.224	.339	.306	23.73	11.86	59
Ryan, River	R-R	6-2	195	8-17-98	0	0	1.50	2	2	0	6	4	1	1	0	2	10	.190	.261	.238	43.48	8.70	23
Sanchez, Samuel	R-R	5-11	150	10-21-05	2	2	4.98	11	8	0	34	35	19	19	3	7	41	.265	.302	.402	29.50	5.04	139
Santana, Waylin	R-R	6-1	155	3-13-03	0	0	2.25	1	0	0	4	4	1	1	0	0	4	.286	.333	.357	26.67	0.00	15
Santillan, Pedro	R-R	6-4	200	7-7-01	0	1	2.25	4	0	0	4	2	1	1	0	1	3	.154	.214	.154	21.43	7.14	14
Serunkuma, Ben	R-R	5-10	170	9-19-01	2	1	5.49	16	0	0	20	25	14	12	1	12	17	.333	.422	.413	18.68	13.19	91
Swan, Eriq	R-R	6-6	240	10-31-01	0	0	7.94	3	2	0	6	7	5	5	2	1	5	.318	.375	.682	20.83	4.17	24
Tillero, Jesus	R-R	6-0	190	5-2-06	0	2	5.23	9	5	0	21	19	17	12	2	14	19	.244	.375	.372	19.59	14.43	97
Vilchez, Michael	R-R	6-3	180	6-3-04	3	2	4.05	20	0	1	27	23	17	12	0	16	37	.240	.356	.323	31.36	13.56	118
Zazueta, Christian	R-R	6-3	163	10-7-04	3	0	1.93	5	0	0	19	14	4	4	2	3	23	.209	.243	.388	32.86	4.29	70

Fielding

C: Diaz 29, Rodrigues 28, Avila 8. **1B:** Shelton 18, Hernandez 10, Avila 10, Decker 10, Lasso 7, Valladares 4, Izarra 3, Diaz 2, Rodrigues 2, Ward 1. **2B:** Guerrero 22, Perez 19, Ortega 9, Gonzalez 7, Martinus 6, Izarra 2, Hernandez 1, Albertus 1. **3B:** Albertus 27, Guerrero 10, Martinus 9, Hernandez 6, Shelton 4, Vargas 4, Ortega 2, Izarra 2, Valladares 1. **SS:** Vargas 30, Guerrero 14, Perez 6, Izarra 5, Martinus 3, Gonzalez 2, Albertus 1, Ortega 1, Osorio 1. **LF:** Elkins 25, Meza 16, Decker 6, Quintero 5, Perez 3, Avila 3, Hope 2, Martinus 2, Shelton 1, Ward 1, Hernandez 1. **CF:** Quintero 38, Elkins 20, Martinus 6. **RF:** Quintero 11, Elkins 10, Meza 9, Avila 9, Martinus 7, Hernandez 6, Hope 4, Keith 4, Shelton 4, Decker 3, Valladares 1, Perez 1.

DSL DODGERS BAUTISTA — *ROOKIE*

DOMINICAN SUMMER LEAGUE

Batting	B-T	Ht.	Wt.	DOB	AVG	OBP	SLG	G	PA	AB	R	H	2B	3B	HR	RBI	BB	HBP	SH	SF	SO	SB	CS	BB%	SO%
Gonzalez, Harold	R-R	5-10	175	8-29-06	.235	.415	.316	33	131	98	34	23	5	0	1	16	25	6	1	1	23	8	4	19.08	17.56
Gonzalez, Jose	L-R	6-2	180	1-29-05	.266	.456	.422	41	149	109	27	29	5	3	2	19	34	5	0	1	27	8	5	22.82	18.12
Guaylupo, Vicente	R-R	6-1	180	5-6-06	.254	.500	.284	31	101	67	24	17	2	0	0	9	20	13	1	0	23	1	0	19.80	22.77
Herrera, Javier	B-R	5-10	160	2-9-05	.288	.470	.486	47	200	146	41	42	7	5	4	33	50	2	0	2	30	20	4	25.00	15.00
Johnson, Paris	R-R	6-2	205	3-9-05	.000	.000	.000	1	1	1	0	0	0	0	0	0	0	0	0	0	1	0	0	0.00	100.00
Ko, Ching-Hsien	L-R	6-3	215	8-11-06	.241	.450	.448	9	40	29	8	7	3	0	1	10	11	0	0	0	7	1	1	27.50	17.50
Lasso, Roger	B-R	6-0	180	2-27-04	.311	.457	.410	18	81	61	18	19	3	0	1	18	16	2	0	2	9	4	2	19.75	11.11
Laya, Yojackson	R-R	5-9	154	11-12-06	.254	.441	.313	43	181	134	33	34	6	1	0	24	36	9	2	0	30	9	3	19.89	16.57
Lorenzo, Abel	L-R	6-0	160	8-14-05	.198	.368	.282	54	231	177	34	35	5	2	2	26	39	11	0	4	48	28	9	16.88	20.78
Orellana, Erny	R-R	6-0	183	3-3-07	.167	.312	.256	34	109	90	16	15	5	0	1	16	13	6	0	0	21	3	1	11.93	19.27
Ortega, Raynerd	R-R	6-1	154	7-8-05	.233	.403	.400	18	78	60	12	14	5	1	1	11	12	5	0	0	14	5	0	15.38	17.95
Pacheco, Orlando	R-R	5-11	175	12-25-04	.196	.479	.261	23	72	46	14	9	3	0	0	6	18	7	1	0	18	1	0	25.00	25.00
Peguero, Rafy	R-R	6-0	190	9-26-06	.226	.374	.269	27	115	93	11	21	2	1	0	10	19	3	0	0	37	0	0	16.52	32.17
Quezada, Yunior	L-R	6-1	160	10-31-05	.208	.331	.416	32	121	101	16	21	6	0	5	24	14	5	0	1	30	2	0	11.57	24.79
Rojas, Eduardo	B-R	5-11	163	2-14-07	.227	.409	.297	40	172	128	22	29	5	2	0	17	36	5	1	2	34	7	4	20.93	19.77
Romero, David	B-R	5-5	135	1-6-07	.188	.409	.188	16	47	32	10	6	0	0	0	1	12	0	3	0	8	1	1	25.53	17.02
Sanchez, Edwin	R-R	6-3	180	8-2-04	.301	.487	.481	47	187	133	40	40	12	0	4	30	37	14	0	3	36	4	2	19.79	19.25
Torrez, Jose	R-R	6-1	195	10-5-04	.233	.380	.438	30	92	73	17	17	6	0	3	17	13	5	0	1	15	2	0	14.13	16.30

Pitching	B-T	Ht.	Wt.	DOB	W	L	ERA	G	GS	SV	IP	Hits	Runs	ER	HR	BB	SO	AVG	OBP	SLG	SO%	BB%	BF
Bartolozzi, Javier	R-R	6-4	193	4-14-05	3	5	4.47	13	12	0	50	56	29	25	3	11	48	.283	.319	.379	22.75	5.21	211
Batista, Erick	R-R	6-0	186	3-3-04	1	0	4.70	10	0	0	15	16	10	8	1	11	14	.271	.442	.475	18.18	14.29	77
Bonilla, Peter	L-L	6-3	195	12-16-04	1	0	4.34	11	0	0	19	11	9	9	1	11	23	.180	.307	.279	30.67	14.67	75
Cabrera, Jose	R-R	6-4	195	11-14-04	6	0	5.26	20	0	1	26	13	16	15	2	24	30	.143	.363	.253	24.19	19.35	124
Camacho, Roman	R-R	6-0	194	11-23-04	0	2	7.39	13	7	1	32	32	31	26	1	31	26	.269	.443	.336	16.46	19.62	158
Carias, Luis	R-R	6-4	170	9-30-04	0	3	3.89	12	12	0	35	33	18	15	0	20	29	.252	.355	.336	18.71	12.90	155
Castro, Jeremy	R-R	6-2	180	1-27-05	1	0	8.38	9	0	0	10	11	12	9	0	15	8	.282	.482	.359	14.29	26.79	56
De Los Santos, Joldelanio	R-R	6-0	175	9-21-03	2	0	4.08	15	0	1	18	7	9	8	0	20	34	.119	.391	.153	39.08	22.99	87
De Los Santos, Weslin	R-R	6-0	155	4-27-06	0	0	9.64	5	0	0	5	2	6	5	0	9	7	.133	.440	.200	28.00	36.00	25
Hernandez, Juan	R-R	6-2	187	11-19-02	0	1	5.79	10	0	0	14	11	10	9	0	19	23	.224	.449	.265	32.86	27.14	70
Herrera, Wuillians	R-R	6-4	183	3-12-04	2	2	4.67	14	0	1	17	12	12	9	0	16	18	.211	.407	.246	21.95	19.51	82
Lopez, Jose	R-R	6-0	185	11-13-05	3	1	8.74	10	0	0	11	10	11	11	1	19	16	.233	.460	.326	25.40	30.16	63
Marte, Josehp	R-R	6-2	190	3-13-05	1	3	10.33	18	7	0	27	32	35	31	0	29	26	.296	.455	.370	18.18	20.28	143
Morel, Franderly	L-L	6-2	160	9-12-03	1	1	2.59	16	0	4	24	18	8	7	1	18	41	.205	.346	.250	38.32	16.82	107
Muniz, Christian	R-R	6-0	168	8-16-06	0	0	4.50	4	0	0	4	3	2	2	1	3	4	.214	.353	.500	23.53	17.65	17
Nieves, Marlon	R-R	6-3	170	6-10-05	0	3	4.78	11	11	0	32	27	18	17	3	23	38	.237	.396	.360	26.39	15.97	144
Pacheco, Orlando	R-R	5-11	175	12-25-04	0	0	18.00	1	0	0	1	5	7	2	0	2	1	.625	.636	.750	9.09	18.18	11
Rada, Luis	R-R	6-3	190	9-8-05	3	0	7.17	16	0	0	21	19	18	17	0	21	26	.241	.400	.316	26.00	21.00	100
Ramirez, Michael	L-L	6-0	160	4-21-05	1	2	7.82	12	5	0	13	12	19	11	0	16	12	.235	.437	.392	16.90	22.54	71
Reyes, Yobany	R-R	6-2	195	10-18-04	0	0	1.93	2	0	0	5	3	1	1	0	1	5	.176	.222	.353	27.78	5.56	18
Rivero, Alexander	R-R	6-0	165	1-11-06	1	2	7.85	14	1	0	18	23	19	16	0	23	20	.299	.471	.442	19.42	22.33	103
Sanchez, Edwin	R-R	6-3	180	8-2-04	0	0	54.00	1	0	0	0	3	2	2	1	0	0	.600	.600	1.200	0.00	0.00	5
Tello, Angel	R-R	6-4	165	1-26-04	3	1	5.18	18	0	3	24	27	15	14	2	5	24	.276	.317	.429	23.08	4.81	104
Ventura, Robinson	R-R	6-1	169	6-28-06	0	0	27.00	11	0	0	8	10	26	23	0	20	11	.303	.593	.364	18.64	33.90	59

Fielding

C: Rojas 24, Torrez 22, Pacheco 15. **1B:** Sanchez 20, Lasso 16, Quezada 14, Pacheco 9, Torrez 3, Johnson 1. **2B:** Herrera 19, Romero 14, Laya 12, Gonzalez 8, Lorenzo 3, Ortega 3. **3B:** Gonzalez 16, Lorenzo 14, Quezada 13, Herrera 8, Laya 5, Ortega 5. **SS:** Laya 26, Herrera 14, Gonzalez 10, Ortega 9. **LF:** Peguero 19, Guaylupo 17, Gonzalez 12, Lorenzo 6, Orellana 5, Quezada 2, Herrera 2. **CF:** Orellana 22, Sanchez 18, Gonzalez 13, Guaylupo 6, Herrera 3, Lorenzo 1, Peguero 1, Quezada 1. **RF:** Lorenzo 19, Gonzalez 10, Guaylupo 8, Orellana 8, Sanchez 8, Peguero 3, Quezada 2, Herrera 2, Lasso 1.

DSL DODGERS MEGA

ROOKIE

DOMINICAN SUMMER LEAGUE

Batting	B-T	Ht.	Wt.	DOB	AVG	OBP	SLG	G	PA	AB	R	H	2B	3B	HR	RBI	BB	HBP	SH	SF	SO	SB	CS	BB%	SO%
Acosta, Agustin	L-R	6-2	173	9-7-04	.246	.391	.405	43	158	126	23	31	5	3	3	21	26	4	2	0	48	14	1	16.46	30.38
Ajoti, Allen	R-R	6-1	205	11-8-05	.200	.333	.267	8	18	15	2	3	1	0	0	0	3	0	0	0	3	0	0	16.67	16.67
Bolivar, Moises	R-R	6-0	175	7-8-07	.205	.311	.256	13	45	39	4	8	2	0	0	6	6	0	0	0	8	5	0	13.33	17.78
Espinoza, Francisco	R-R	6-1	206	3-16-07	.232	.429	.268	23	77	56	10	13	2	0	0	7	15	5	0	1	11	0	0	19.48	14.29
Familia, Railin	R-R	6-0	186	9-15-04	.284	.415	.407	36	107	81	20	23	4	0	2	14	17	4	1	4	19	4	1	15.89	17.76
Johnson, Paris	R-R	6-2	205	3-9-05	.200	.319	.325	25	94	80	16	16	6	2	0	6	12	2	0	0	32	5	1	12.77	34.04
Lantigua, Arnaldo	R-R	6-2	200	12-19-05	.301	.430	.575	49	193	153	42	46	7	1	11	42	33	4	0	3	34	6	1	17.10	17.62
Mariano, Reyli	B-R	5-7	140	11-7-06	.243	.433	.333	45	152	111	36	27	5	1	1	16	36	2	2	1	32	15	4	23.68	21.05
Medina, Elias	R-R	5-10	171	11-9-05	.321	.449	.375	19	69	56	12	18	3	0	0	11	12	1	0	0	15	11	3	17.39	21.74
Medina, Yorfran	R-R	6-4	195	1-25-05	.209	.409	.383	43	159	115	24	24	5	0	5	29	28	13	0	3	53	2	1	17.61	33.33
Mielcarek, Daniel	B-R	6-3	185	12-19-05	.190	.357	.330	35	126	100	21	19	2	0	4	24	22	4	0	0	49	11	1	17.46	38.89
Morales, Emil	R-R	6-3	191	9-22-06	.342	.478	.691	46	201	152	48	52	11	0	14	46	40	4	0	5	45	12	2	19.90	22.39
Padilla, Leider	R-R	6-0	176	11-25-06	.233	.330	.267	32	103	90	12	21	3	0	0	9	9	4	0	0	24	6	4	8.74	23.30
Paredes, Angel	R-R	6-3	170	11-11-06	.060	.192	.090	27	78	67	10	4	2	0	0	3	9	2	0	0	34	3	0	11.54	43.59
Pena, Heudy	L-R	6-0	156	3-9-07	.243	.391	.291	31	129	103	27	25	5	0	0	8	25	0	1	0	30	6	1	19.38	23.26
Quezada, Yunior	L-R	6-1	160	10-31-05	.281	.395	.469	11	38	32	8	9	3	0	1	4	4	2	0	0	8	3	1	10.53	21.05
Ramirez, Raynier	R-R	5-10	185	12-13-04	.200	.366	.393	47	191	150	28	30	4	2	7	32	33	7	0	1	54	9	1	17.28	28.27
Rosa, Euri	R-R	5-10	165	7-4-07	.171	.315	.276	26	92	76	15	13	3	1	1	6	12	4	0	0	29	6	0	13.04	31.52

Pitching	B-T	Ht.	Wt.	DOB	W	L	ERA	G	GS	SV	IP	Hits	Runs	ER	HR	BB	SO	AVG	OBP	SLG	SO%	BB%	BF
Batista, Erick	R-R	6-0	186	3-3-04	0	1	10.38	4	0	0	4	8	7	5	0	4	3	.400	.520	.450	12.00	16.00	25
Burgos, David	L-L	5-11	178	2-7-06	2	0	3.86	12	1	0	26	27	12	11	3	12	14	.293	.377	.457	13.21	11.32	106
Colon, Ilmerson	L-L	6-2	167	3-10-05	0	0	10.80	7	0	0	7	3	9	8	0	10	14	.125	.475	.167	35.00	25.00	40
Cruz, Angel	R-R	6-1	210	10-12-04	3	2	4.05	18	0	0	33	15	18	15	2	36	43	.138	.371	.202	28.48	23.84	151
Cruz, Joel	R-R	6-3	182	6-16-04	0	2	6.21	16	12	0	29	29	27	20	0	39	32	.266	.477	.349	20.38	24.84	157
De La Cruz, Yuliangel	R-R	6-3	158	1-24-05	0	3	9.42	13	10	0	29	34	35	30	2	36	27	.304	.477	.411	17.20	22.93	157
De Los Santos, Weslin	R-R	6-0	155	4-27-06	0	0	13.50	3	0	0	3	2	4	4	0	4	4	.200	.429	.200	28.57	28.57	14
Dominguez, Alexis	R-R	6-5	183	11-3-05	2	2	8.56	10	0	0	14	14	14	13	1	10	11	.269	.426	.404	16.18	14.71	68
Ferrera, Gregg	R-R	6-5	175	3-21-06	0	0	1.65	10	6	0	16	7	3	3	0	9	6	.137	.297	.137	9.38	14.06	64
Fischer, Tim	R-R	6-3	195	9-8-04	0	0	9.64	3	3	0	5	5	6	5	0	7	8	.250	.444	.300	29.63	25.93	27
Florian, Jeremy	R-R	6-4	185	5-4-05	0	0	37.80	4	0	0	2	2	7	7	0	9	2	.333	.733	.500	13.33	60.00	15
Gonzalez, Oliver	R-R	6-4	200	10-26-06	0	0	1.50	2	2	0	6	5	1	1	1	1	4	.217	.250	.391	16.67	4.17	24
Jerez, Anderson	R-R	5-10	185	7-19-04	1	4	12.71	16	2	1	23	31	37	32	2	29	19	.316	.504	.459	13.97	21.32	136
Jimenez, Jhonny	R-R	6-5	180	11-9-03	1	0	1.50	7	0	2	12	13	3	2	0	3	17	.255	.296	.314	31.48	5.56	54
Leon, Edgar	R-R	6-3	170	12-29-04	0	2	3.38	11	10	0	40	30	18	15	1	21	39	.205	.316	.301	22.41	12.07	174
Liborius, Jecsua	R-R	6-1	190	5-28-05	3	2	3.75	17	0	1	24	22	16	10	1	18	20	.239	.369	.315	17.86	16.07	112
Meneses, Gustavo	R-R	6-2	200	8-24-05	2	3	6.10	15	0	0	21	20	18	14	2	18	20	.250	.392	.375	19.61	17.65	102
Muniz, Christian	R-R	6-0	168	8-16-06	1	1	8.59	8	0	0	7	10	7	7	0	6	3	.345	.474	.483	7.89	15.79	38
Reyes, Yobany	R-R	6-2	195	10-18-04	4	3	6.00	14	0	1	21	25	17	14	0	7	20	.294	.340	.376	21.28	7.45	94
Romero, Luciano	R-R	6-2	190	1-8-05	1	0	4.70	15	0	1	23	13	14	12	0	22	19	.165	.346	.203	17.76	20.56	107
Salazar, Williams	L-L	6-2	175	2-15-05	0	3	3.77	12	7	0	31	19	15	13	2	24	36	.179	.360	.283	26.47	17.65	136
Sardina, Carlos	R-R	6-5	195	3-10-07	1	1	4.95	12	1	0	20	15	14	11	1	18	8	.203	.381	.351	8.25	18.56	97
Simarra, Yoryi	R-R	6-1	174	11-18-04	4	0	3.45	15	0	0	31	31	16	12	1	23	31	.263	.375	.331	21.38	15.86	145

Fielding

C: Rosa 22, Espinoza 20, Familia 18, Ajoti 4. **1B:** Medina 39, Familia 11, Johnson 10, Bolivar 3, Espinoza 2, Rosa 1. **2B:** Pena 23, Mielcarek 14, Mariano 11, Ramirez 7, Medina 2, Acosta 1. **3B:** Ramirez 33, Bolivar 9, Mariano 4, Quezada 4, Medina 3, Mielcarek 2, Morales 2, Familia 2. **SS:** Morales 33, Mariano 17, Medina 4, Mielcarek 4, Pena 1. **LF:** Padilla 21, Paredes 13, Mariano 11, Quezada 5, Familia 5, Johnson 4, Mielcarek 4, Lantigua 2, Acosta 2, Ajoti 1, Medina 1. **CF:** Lantigua 30, Acosta 18, Medina 7, Padilla 4, Paredes 2, Quezada 2. **RF:** Acosta 21, Johnson 14, Paredes 11, Lantigua 7, Padilla 6, Mariano 2, Familia 2.

Miami Marlins

SEASON SYNOPSIS: After making the playoffs for just the third time in a full season in 2023, the Marlins went back to being the Marlins in 2024, going into a full rebuild with a new general manager and plenty of trades that emptied the roster of veterans, impending free agents or any players who made a lot of money. The Marlins were 22 games worse than in 2023, losing 100 games for the fourth time in franchise history.

HIGH POINT: The Marlins finished on their highest note, winning five out of six to end the season. The stretch included a spoiler series win at Minnesota when the Twins were still in the playoff hunt, and a sweep of Toronto in the final three games. That was Miami's lone sweep of the year.

LOW POINT: There are almost too many to count thanks to a spate of injuries which forced Miami to use 41 pitchers on the year. That list doesn't include 2022 Cy Young Award winner Sandy Alcantara or 2023 phenom Eury Perez, both of whom missed the entire season with UCL elbow reconstruction surgeries. Starters such as Jesus Luzardo, Braxton Garrett, Edward Cabrera and Ryan Weathers all had IL stints, The team leader in innings pitched, Trevor Rogers, was traded to the Orioles in July.

NOTABLE ROOKIES: First-year GM Peter Bendix had an open casting call, especially in the rotation, thanks to injuries, with righties Vicente Bellozo (3.67 in 68 innings) and Roddery Muñoz (6.53 ERA but 95.2 mph average fastball velocity) showing some promise. The young infield of shortstop Xavier Edwards and second baseman Otto Lopez, a waiver claim, showed athleticism and promise, combining for 51 stolen bases but just seven home runs. So did 2B/3B Connor Norby (.247/.315/.445, seven HR).

KEY TRANSACTIONS: Bendix replaced Kim Ng, MLB's first female GM, after Ng resigned when ownership told her it intended to hire a president of baseball operations above her. Bendix didn't wait for the trade deadline to start selling. In May, he dealt batting champ Luis Arraez to the Padres for prospects. Norby and outfielder Kyle Stowers arrived from the Orioles for Rogers. Lefty reliever A.J. Puk and first baseman Josh Bell were shipped to the D-backs, and the team's biggest star, Jazz Chisholm Jr., was shipped to the Yankees, who turned him into a third baseman. Outfielder Bryan De La Cruz went to Pittsburgh as the Marlins began yet another rebuild.

OPENING DAY PAYROLL: $97,227,400 (26th)

PLAYERS OF THE YEAR

MAJOR LEAGUE

Xavier Edwards
SS

.328/.397/.423
31-for-33 SB
33 BB, 52 SO in 70 G

MINOR LEAGUE

Joe Mack
C

(A+/AA)
.252/.338/.468
24 HR, 78 RBIs

ORGANIZATION LEADERS

Batting		*Qualifiers
MAJORS		
* AVG	Jesus Sanchez	.252
* OPS	Jake Burger	.761
HR	Jake Burger	29
RBI	Jake Burger	76
MINORS		
* AVG	Ryan Ignoffo, Jupiter/Beloit	.324
* OBP	Ryan Ignoffo, Jupiter/Beloit	.376
* SLG	Griffin Conine, Jacksonville	.475
* OPS	Ryan Ignoffo, Jupiter/Beloit	.845
R	Colby Shade, Jupiter/Beloit	80
H	Troy Johnston, Jacksonville	132
TB	Joe Mack, Beloit/Pensacola	221
2B	Ryan Ignoffo, Jupiter/Beloit	34
3B	Mark Coley, Jupiter/Beloit	11
HR	Joe Mack, Beloit/Pensacola	24
RBI	Joe Mack, Beloit/Pensacola	78
BB	Brock Vradenburg, Jupiter/Beloit	79
SO	Mark Coley, Jupiter/Beloit	146
SB	Colby Shade, Jupiter/Beloit	45

Pitching		#Qualifiers
MAJORS		
W	Tanner Scott	6
# ERA	No qualifier	
SO	Edward Cabrera	107
SV	Tanner Scott	18
MINORS		
W	Yonny Chirinos, Jacksonville	10
W	Luis Palacios, Pensacola	10
L	3-tied	8
# ERA	Jake Brooks, Jupiter/Beloit	2.18
G	Austin Roberts, Jacksonville/Pensacola	50
GS	Evan Fitterer, Jacksonville/Pensacola	25
SV	Austin Roberts, Jacksonville/Pensacola	17
IP	Luis Palacios, Pensacola	125
BB	Evan Fitterer, Jacksonville/Pensacola	68
SO	Thomas White, Jupiter/Beloit	120
# AVG	Jake Brooks, Jupiter/Beloit	.216

2024 PERFORMANCE

General Manager: Peter Bendix. **Farm Director:** Rachel Balkovec. **Scouting Director:** Frankie Piliere.

Class	Team	League	W	L	PCT	Finish	Manager
Majors	Miami Marlins	National	62	100	.383	14 (15)	Skip Schumaker
Triple-A	Jacksonville Jumbo Shrimp	International	73	76	.490	10 (20)	Daren Brown
Double-A	Pensacola Blue Wahoos	Southern	71	65	.522	3 (8)	Kevin Randel
High-A	Beloit Sky Carp	Midwest	60	69	.465	8 (12)	Billy Gardner
Low-A	Jupiter Hammerheads	Florida State	65	65	.500	6 (10)	Nelson Prada
Rookie	FCL Marlins	Florida Complex	39	15	.722	1 (15)	Luis Dorante
Rookie	DSL Marlins	Dominican	33	23	.589	13 (51)	Carlos Mota
Rookie	DSL Miami	Dominican	26	30	.464	32 (51)	Oscar Escobar
Overall 2024 Minor League Record			**367**	**343**	**.517**	**12th (30)**	

ORGANIZATION STATISTICS

MIAMI MARLINS

NATIONAL LEAGUE

Batting	B-T	Ht.	Wt.	DOB	AVG	OBP	SLG	G	PA	AB	R	H	2B	3B	HR	RBI	BB	HBP	SH	SF	SO	SB	CS	BB%	SO%
Anderson, Tim	R-R	6-1	185	6-23-93	.214	.237	.226	65	241	234	16	50	3	0	0	9	7	0	0	0	68	4	4	2.90	28.22
Arraez, Luis	L-R	5-10	175	4-9-97	.299	.347	.372	33	148	137	22	41	8	1	0	5	8	2	1	0	11	0	0	5.41	7.43
Bell, Josh	B-R	6-4	261	8-14-92	.239	.305	.394	104	441	398	38	95	18	1	14	49	34	5	0	3	88	0	0	7.71	19.95
Bethancourt, Christian	R-R	6-3	205	9-2-91	.159	.198	.268	38	88	82	9	13	3	0	2	7	3	1	2	0	22	0	0	3.41	25.00
Bride, Jonah	R-R	5-10	200	12-27-95	.276	.357	.461	71	272	232	30	64	10	0	11	39	30	3	0	7	55	0	1	11.03	20.22
Brujan, Vidal	B-R	5-10	180	2-9-98	.222	.303	.319	102	278	248	32	55	14	2	2	16	25	4	1	0	54	5	6	8.99	19.42
Burger, Jake	R-R	6-2	230	4-10-96	.250	.301	.460	137	579	535	68	134	23	1	29	76	31	9	0	4	150	1	1	5.35	25.91
Chisholm, Jazz	L-R	5-11	184	2-1-98	.249	.323	.407	101	430	386	46	96	14	4	13	50	39	4	0	1	107	22	8	9.07	24.88
Conine, Griffin	L-R	6-1	210	7-11-97	.268	.326	.451	30	89	82	14	22	4	1	3	12	6	1	0	0	28	0	0	6.74	31.46
De La Cruz, Bryan	R-R	6-2	175	12-16-96	.245	.289	.417	105	454	424	44	104	19	0	18	51	25	2	0	2	118	3	1	5.51	25.99
Devers, Jose	L-R	6-0	174	12-7-99	.250	.250	.250	3	4	4	1	1	0	0	0	0	0	0	0	0	1	0	0	0.00	25.00
Edwards, Xavier	B-R	5-10	175	8-9-99	.328	.397	.423	70	303	265	39	87	12	5	1	26	33	0	1	4	52	31	4	10.89	17.16
Fortes, Nick	R-R	5-11	198	11-11-96	.227	.259	.318	110	335	308	28	70	16	0	4	29	11	4	7	5	41	0	1	3.28	12.24
Garcia, Avisail	R-R	6-4	250	6-12-91	.240	.255	.380	18	51	50	4	12	1	0	2	2	1	0	0	0	13	0	0	1.96	25.49
Gordon, Nick	L-R	6-0	160	10-24-95	.227	.258	.369	95	275	260	29	59	11	1	8	32	11	1	0	3	67	5	5	4.00	24.36
Gray, Tristan	L-R	6-1	215	3-22-96	.000	.000	.000	7	7	7	0	0	0	0	0	0	0	0	0	0	3	0	0	0.00	42.86
Hensley, David	R-R	6-6	190	3-28-96	.212	.293	.288	23	58	52	9	11	1	0	1	4	6	0	0	0	17	1	0	10.34	29.31
Hill, Derek	R-R	6-2	206	12-30-95	.234	.259	.402	32	114	107	11	25	4	1	4	18	2	2	2	1	39	4	1	1.75	34.21
Lopez, Otto	R-R	5-10	185	10-1-98	.270	.313	.377	117	434	403	49	109	23	1	6	39	25	1	2	2	75	20	4	5.76	17.28
Myers, Dane	R-R	6-0	205	3-8-96	.263	.333	.442	44	108	95	17	25	6	1	3	19	8	3	0	2	36	4	1	7.41	33.33
Norby, Connor	R-R	5-9	180	6-8-00	.247	.315	.445	36	162	146	29	36	8	0	7	17	15	0	0	1	52	3	3	9.26	32.10
Pache, Cristian	R-R	6-2	215	11-19-98	.183	.234	.283	35	64	60	4	11	3	0	1	7	4	0	0	0	21	1	0	6.25	32.81
Pereda, Jhonny	R-R	6-1	202	4-18-96	.231	.250	.231	20	40	39	2	9	0	0	0	4	0	1	0	0	10	0	0	0.00	25.00
Rivera, Emmanuel	R-R	6-2	225	6-29-96	.214	.294	.269	97	229	201	15	43	6	1	1	15	20	4	1	3	51	2	0	8.73	22.27
Sanchez, Ali	R-R	6-1	200	1-20-97	.167	.211	.190	31	96	84	5	14	2	0	0	4	4	1	6	1	24	2	1	4.17	25.00
Sanchez, Jesus	L-R	6-3	222	10-7-97	.252	.313	.417	149	537	489	60	123	25	1	18	64	41	4	1	2	140	16	2	7.64	26.07
Sanoja, Javier	R-R	5-7	150	9-3-02	.229	.250	.286	15	36	35	3	8	2	0	0	2	1	0	0	0	4	0	0	2.78	11.11
Stowers, Kyle	L-L	6-3	215	1-2-98	.186	.262	.295	50	172	156	12	29	7	2	2	15	13	3	0	0	61	0	0	7.56	35.47
Wall, Forrest	L-R	6-0	195	11-20-95	.333	.333	.333	3	3	3	1	1	0	0	0	0	0	0	0	0	2	1	0	0.00	66.67

Pitching	B-T	Ht.	Wt.	DOB	W	L	ERA	G	GS	SV	IP	Hits	Runs	ER	HR	BB	SO	AVG	OBP	SLG	SO%	BB%	BF
Anderson, Shaun	R-R	6-6	228	10-29-94	0	2	9.00	4	2	0	13	28	17	13	3	0	7	.424	.426	.697	10.29	0.00	68
Andriese, Matt	R-R	6-2	215	8-28-89	0	1	6.00	4	0	0	6	7	5	4	2	1	7	.280	.308	.640	26.92	3.85	26
Bachar, Lake	R-R	6-2	219	6-3-95	0	1	3.86	10	0	0	9	10	5	4	2	4	11	.278	.350	.472	27.50	10.00	40
Baumann, Mike	R-R	6-4	240	9-10-95	0	1	6.59	11	0	0	14	11	10	10	1	7	18	.224	.322	.367	30.51	11.86	59
Bellozo, Valente	R-R	5-10	170	1-4-00	3	4	3.67	13	13	0	69	69	31	28	15	21	44	.256	.312	.481	14.92	7.12	295
Bender, Anthony	R-R	6-4	205	2-3-95	5	2	4.08	59	0	1	53	50	25	24	3	18	59	.245	.317	.353	25.88	7.89	228
Bermudez, Jonathan	L-L	6-2	237	10-16-95	0	1	8.10	3	1	0	7	11	6	6	2	2	4	.393	.455	.714	12.12	6.06	33
Brazoban, Huascar	R-R	6-3	155	10-15-89	1	2	2.93	20	0	0	31	20	14	10	1	11	34	.179	.264	.259	27.20	8.80	125
Brujan, Vidal	S-R	5-10	180	2-9-98	0	0	43.20	2	0	0	2	7	8	8	2	3	1	.583	.688	1.083	6.25	18.75	16
Cabrera, Edward	R-R	6-5	217	4-13-98	4	8	4.95	20	20	0	96	82	60	53	15	50	107	.227	.328	.391	25.60	11.96	418
Chargois, JT	S-R	6-3	200	12-3-90	1	0	1.62	15	0	0	17	15	3	3	3	7	12	.234	.310	.391	16.90	9.86	71
Chirinos, Yonny	R-R	6-2	225	12-26-93	0	2	6.30	6	6	0	30	43	21	21	7	13	25	.339	.410	.591	17.36	9.03	144
Cronin, Declan	R-R	6-4	225	9-24-97	3	4	4.35	56	0	0	70	75	41	34	1	25	72	.274	.344	.350	23.53	8.17	306
Curry, Xzavion	R-R	6-0	195	7-27-98	2	0	3.00	9	1	0	18	9	6	6	3	2	13	.148	.172	.361	20.31	3.13	64
de Geus, Brett	R-R	6-2	190	11-4-97	0	2	6.35	7	0	0	6	7	5	4	0	2	4	.304	.385	.391	14.81	7.41	27
Emanuel, Kent	L-L	6-4	225	6-4-92	0	0	6.62	12	0	0	18	20	14	13	4	7	12	.282	.366	.521	14.63	8.54	82
Faucher, Calvin	R-R	6-1	190	9-22-95	2	3	3.19	53	0	6	54	49	25	19	0	26	63	.246	.339	.342	26.81	11.06	235
Garrett, Braxton	R-L	6-2	202	8-5-97	2	2	5.35	7	7	0	37	40	24	22	5	4	34	.263	.304	.414	21.12	2.48	161
Gutierrez, Vladimir	R-R	6-1	205	9-18-95	0	0	6.75	1	0	0	4	3	3	3	1	2	4	.200	.294	.400	23.53	11.76	17
Hensley, David	R-R	6-6	190	3-28-96	0	0	9.00	1	0	0	2	2	2	2	0	1	0	.333	.400	.500	0.00	10.00	10
Hoeing, Bryan	R-R	6-6	210	10-19-96	1	2	2.70	16	2	0	30	29	10	9	2	9	25	.252	.306	.348	20.16	7.26	124
Kitchen, Austin	L-L	6-0	200	2-11-97	0	1	14.14	4	1	0	7	16	12	11	1	3	4	.421	.463	.605	9.52	7.14	42

Luzardo, Jesus	L-L	6-0	218	9-30-97	3	6	5.00	12	12	0	67	61	37	37	9	22	58	.246	.311	.411	21.17	8.03	274
Maldonado, Anthony	R-R	6-4	220	2-6-98	1	1	5.68	16	1	1	19	21	12	12	1	7	11	.280	.341	.427	13.41	8.54	82
McCaughan, Darren	R-R	6-1	200	3-18-96	0	0	5.75	10	5	2	36	44	26	23	7	9	27	.297	.358	.507	16.36	5.45	165
McMillon, John	L-R	6-3	230	1-27-98	2	1	1.50	10	0	0	12	7	4	2	1	5	13	.171	.261	.244	27.66	10.64	47
Meyer, Max	L-R	6-0	196	3-12-99	3	5	5.68	11	11	0	57	62	38	36	14	19	46	.276	.339	.560	18.55	7.66	248
Munoz, Roddery	R-R	6-2	210	4-14-00	2	7	6.53	18	17	0	83	89	66	60	26	42	70	.272	.359	.575	18.47	11.08	379
Nardi, Andrew	L-L	6-3	215	8-18-98	3	2	5.07	59	0	0	50	44	29	28	7	18	70	.234	.301	.426	33.33	8.57	210
Oller, Adam	R-R	6-4	225	10-17-94	2	4	5.31	8	8	0	42	43	25	25	7	22	36	.261	.354	.436	19.05	11.64	189
Pereda, Jhonny	R-R	6-1	202	4-18-96	0	0	0.00	1	0	0	0	0	0	0	0	0	0	.000	.000	.000	0.00	0.00	1
Petersen, Michael	R-R	6-7	195	5-16-94	0	1	4.76	5	0	0	6	7	4	3	0	3	3	.318	.385	.364	11.54	11.54	26
Puk, A.J.	L-L	6-7	248	4-25-95	4	8	4.30	32	4	1	44	36	27	21	3	23	45	.218	.316	.352	23.56	12.04	191
Ramirez, Emmanuel	R-R	6-2	190	7-15-94	0	1	6.97	15	0	0	21	21	17	16	3	8	21	.263	.348	.500	22.83	8.70	92
Rivera, Emmanuel	R-R	6-2	225	6-29-96	0	0	9.00	4	0	0	4	7	4	4	1	0	0	.368	.400	.526	0.00	0.00	20
Rogers, Trevor	L-L	6-5	217	11-13-97	2	9	4.53	21	21	0	105	115	58	53	12	46	85	.276	.347	.448	18.01	9.75	472
Sanchez, Sixto	R-R	6-0	234	7-29-98	0	3	6.06	14	7	0	36	43	29	24	3	14	17	.303	.375	.430	10.49	8.64	162
Scott, Tanner	R-L	6-0	235	7-22-94	6	5	1.18	44	0	18	46	19	10	6	2	27	53	.127	.264	.180	29.12	14.84	182
Smith, Burch	R-R	6-4	225	4-12-90	2	0	4.25	25	0	0	30	39	15	14	1	9	23	.322	.368	.397	17.04	6.67	135
Soriano, George	R-R	6-2	210	3-24-99	1	1	6.75	22	0	1	29	27	23	22	7	13	29	.241	.336	.509	22.14	9.92	131
Tinoco, Jesus	R-R	6-4	258	4-30-95	1	0	2.03	21	0	3	27	13	6	6	1	5	30	.141	.194	.217	30.61	5.10	98
Tyler, Kyle	R-R	6-0	185	12-27-96	0	2	5.40	8	7	0	32	37	19	19	4	18	25	.301	.394	.423	17.61	12.68	142
Veneziano, Anthony	L-L	6-5	205	9-1-97	1	0	3.18	10	0	0	11	12	5	4	1	2	12	.286	.319	.476	25.53	4.26	47
Villalobos, Eli	R-R	6-4	195	6-26-97	0	0	2.08	3	0	0	4	3	1	1	1	2	3	.188	.278	.438	16.67	11.11	18
Weathers, Ryan	R-L	6-1	230	12-17-99	5	6	3.63	16	16	0	87	78	39	35	11	24	80	.236	.303	.390	21.80	6.54	3670

Fielding

Catcher	PCT	G	PO	A	E	DP	PB
Bethancourt	.982	36	206	10	4	2	1
Fortes	.990	109	831	38	9	3	4
Pereda	.989	18	86	7	1	1	0
Sanchez	.992	30	239	12	2	2	0

First Base	PCT	G	PO	A	E	DP
Arraez	1.000	8	6	0	0	1
Bell	.986	67	472	32	7	39
Bride	.992	38	236	20	2	29
Brujan	.000	1	0	0	0	0
Burger	.995	69	380	34	2	32
Devers	.000	1	0	0	0	0
Hensley	1.000	4	21	1	0	2
Pereda	1.000	1	0	1	0	0
Rivera	1.000	13	62	2	0	5

Second Base	PCT	G	PO	A	E	DP
Arraez	.971	33	55	77	4	21
Bride	1.000	3	2	3	0	0
Brujan	.989	31	40	50	1	16
Chisholm	1.000	3	3	3	0	1
Devers	1.000	1	0	3	0	0
Edwards	1.000	1	3	1	0	0
Gordon	1.000	6	5	6	0	1
Lopez	.989	103	172	260	5	54
Norby	.889	3	2	6	1	1
Sanoja	1.000	3	3	7	0	1

Third Base	PCT	G	PO	A	E	DP
Bride	.950	13	4	15	1	4
Brujan	.789	14	4	11	4	0
Burger	.925	59	36	99	11	8
Gray	1.000	5	1	9	0	0
Hensley	1.000	1	1	0	0	0
Lopez	.875	6	1	6	1	0
Norby	.924	30	38	47	7	4
Rivera	.979	77	33	110	3	12

Shortstop	PCT	G	PO	A	E	DP
Anderson	.963	63	66	170	9	34
Brujan	.975	28	38	77	3	12
Edwards	.971	69	88	148	7	32
Lopez	.920	8	8	15	2	1
Sanoja	1.000	4	2	1	0	1

Outfield	PCT	G	PO	A	E	DP
Brujan	.972	23	34	1	1	1
Chisholm	.991	95	223	3	2	0
Conine	.978	25	41	4	1	2
De La Cruz	.990	58	96	6	1	1
Garcia	1.000	16	38	1	0	0
Gordon	.978	78	131	3	3	0
Hensley	1.000	14	12	2	0	0
Hill	1.000	36	75	1	0	1
Lopez	.000	3	0	0	0	0
Myers	.970	43	59	6	2	1
Pache	.980	31	48	1	1	0
Sanchez	.983	125	226	3	4	2
Sanoja	1.000	7	8	1	0	0
Stowers	1.000	56	98	3	0	0
Wall	.000	1	0	0	0	0

JACKSONVILLE JUMBO SHRIMP — *TRIPLE-A*

INTERNATIONAL LEAGUE

Batting	B-T	Ht.	Wt.	DOB	AVG	OBP	SLG	G	PA	AB	R	H	2B	3B	HR	RBI	BB	HBP	SH	SF	SO	SB	CS	BB%	SO%
Amaya, Jacob	R-R	6-0	180	9-3-98	.182	.182	.182	3	11	11	0	2	0	0	0	2	0	0	0	0	2	0	0	0.00	18.18
Anderson, Tim	R-R	6-1	185	6-23-93	.444	.500	.778	2	10	9	5	4	0	0	1	2	1	0	0	0	1	0	0	10.00	10.00
Banfield, Will	R-R	6-0	215	11-18-99	.247	.296	.379	93	371	340	40	84	14	2	9	41	24	2	0	5	105	0	0	6.47	28.30
Berry, Jacob	B-R	6-0	212	5-5-01	.242	.311	.374	25	103	91	16	22	4	1	2	9	10	0	0	2	18	2	0	9.71	17.48
Bethancourt, Christian	R-R	6-3	205	9-2-91	.231	.231	.308	3	13	13	0	3	1	0	0	0	0	0	0	0	6	1	0	0.00	46.15
Bradshaw, Davis	L-R	6-2	175	4-25-98	.000	.000	.000	1	1	1	0	0	0	0	0	0	0	0	0	0	0	0	0	0.00	0.00
Bride, Jonah	R-R	5-10	200	12-27-95	.267	.409	.454	75	330	262	40	70	14	1	11	39	60	5	0	3	56	2	0	18.18	16.97
Brujan, Vidal	B-R	5-10	180	2-9-98	.143	.333	.571	2	9	7	1	1	0	0	1	3	2	0	0	0	1	0	0	22.22	11.11
Burger, Jake	R-R	6-2	230	4-10-96	.273	.385	.273	3	13	11	2	3	0	0	0	1	2	0	0	0	2	0	0	15.38	15.38
Conine, Griffin	L-R	6-1	210	7-11-97	.268	.350	.475	112	437	385	59	103	21	1	19	68	47	3	0	2	129	0	0	10.76	29.52
Costes, Marty	R-R	5-9	200	12-18-95	.234	.310	.305	71	271	239	31	56	5	0	4	26	21	7	0	4	44	3	2	7.75	16.24
Davis, Jonathan	R-R	5-8	190	5-12-92	.227	.342	.335	73	285	242	26	55	12	1	4	19	33	9	0	0	80	8	2	11.58	28.07
De Los Santos, Deyvison	R-R	5-11	185	6-21-03	.240	.284	.459	50	211	196	28	47	7	0	12	36	11	2	0	2	60	0	0	5.21	28.44
Devers, Jose	L-R	6-0	174	12-7-99	.239	.304	.362	54	208	188	28	45	8	3	3	17	15	3	1	1	35	3	1	7.21	16.83
Edwards, Xavier	B-R	5-10	175	8-9-99	.330	.376	.450	26	119	109	11	36	8	1	1	6	8	0	2	0	11	5	1	6.72	9.24
Garcia, Avisail	R-R	6-4	250	6-12-91	.105	.190	.211	5	21	19	2	2	0	1	0	0	2	0	0	0	7	0	0	9.52	33.33
Gordon, Nick	L-R	6-0	160	10-24-95	.264	.313	.347	23	80	72	8	19	1	1	1	9	3	3	0	2	16	2	2	3.75	20.00
Gray, Tristan	L-R	6-1	215	3-22-96	.245	.318	.459	100	409	364	48	89	21	3	17	58	37	4	0	4	110	0	1	9.05	26.89
Guzman, Jonathan	R-R	5-11	156	8-17-99	.179	.248	.232	47	169	151	11	27	5	0	1	7	14	0	4	0	48	1	1	8.28	28.40
Hill, Derek	R-R	6-2	206	12-30-95	.286	.444	.429	2	9	7	1	2	1	0	0	0	2	0	0	0	2	0	0	22.22	22.22
Hostetler, Bennett	R-R	6-0	195	9-23-97	.266	.301	.392	24	83	79	8	21	5	1	1	12	4	0	0	0	29	0	1	4.82	34.94
Infante, Diego	R-R	6-2	178	10-22-99	.205	.326	.231	25	92	78	5	16	2	0	0	4	14	0	0	0	39	1	0	15.22	42.39
Johnston, Troy	L-L	6-0	205	6-22-97	.276	.339	.424	125	528	479	65	132	30	4	11	63	37	10	0	2	100	17	3	7.01	18.94
Lopez, Otto	R-R	5-10	185	10-1-98	.436	.488	.718	10	43	39	6	17	5	0	2	6	3	1	0	0	6	0	1	6.98	13.95

Marsee, Jakob	L-L	6-0	180	6-28-01	.275	.370	.363	22	93	80	14	22	4	0	1	5	12	0	1	0	20	7	0	12.90	21.51
Mesa, Victor	L-L	6-0	195	9-8-01	.259	.319	.430	80	355	321	47	83	14	1	13	51	28	2	1	3	77	5	2	7.89	21.69
Myers, Dane	R-R	6-0	205	3-8-96	.248	.347	.381	29	121	105	20	26	5	0	3	10	14	2	0	0	34	4	0	11.57	28.10
Norby, Connor	R-R	5-9	180	6-8-00	.271	.338	.373	14	65	59	7	16	3	0	1	3	6	0	0	0	19	0	0	9.23	29.23
Pauley, Graham	L-R	6-1	200	9-24-00	.167	.250	.500	5	20	18	3	3	0	0	2	4	0	2	0	0	10	1	0	0.00	50.00
Pereda, Jhonny	R-R	6-1	202	4-18-96	.297	.405	.424	49	195	165	24	49	9	0	4	14	28	2	0	0	40	0	0	14.36	20.51
Ramirez, Agustin	R-R	6-0	210	9-10-01	.262	.358	.447	39	162	141	20	37	9	1	5	24	19	2	0	0	36	4	0	11.73	22.22
Roby, Sean	R-R	6-1	215	7-8-98	.125	.125	.125	2	8	8	0	1	0	0	0	0	0	0	0	0	5	0	0	0.00	62.50
Rodriguez, Cristhian	L-R	6-3	160	12-23-01	.130	.259	.174	7	27	23	4	3	1	0	0	3	4	0	0	0	9	0	0	14.81	33.33
Rosario, Dalvy	R-R	6-0	185	7-22-00	.226	.250	.306	20	64	62	7	14	5	0	0	2	2	0	0	0	22	1	0	3.13	34.38
Sanchez, Ali	R-R	6-1	200	1-20-97	.154	.154	.231	7	26	26	2	4	2	0	0	1	0	0	0	0	7	0	0	0.00	26.92
Sanoja, Javier	R-R	5-7	150	9-3-02	.291	.354	.431	111	492	436	51	127	31	6	6	58	44	2	3	7	30	14	6	8.94	6.10
Serna, Jared	R-R	5-6	168	6-1-02	.100	.217	.100	6	23	20	2	2	0	0	0	1	2	1	0	0	8	1	0	8.70	34.78
Spohn, Harrison	R-R	6-1	185	12-3-98	.216	.286	.275	16	56	51	4	11	3	0	0	3	5	0	0	0	18	0	0	8.93	32.14
Wall, Forrest	L-R	6-0	195	11-20-95	.292	.382	.333	13	55	48	6	14	2	0	0	0	6	1	0	0	11	4	0	10.91	20.00

Pitching	B-T	Ht.	Wt.	DOB	W	L	ERA	G	GS	SV	IP	Hits	Runs	ER	HR	BB	SO	AVG	OBP	SLG	SO%	BB%	BF
Alvarado, Elvis	R-R	6-4	183	2-23-99	3	4	2.79	39	0	11	48	33	18	15	2	38	71	.195	.355	.278	33.18	17.76	214
Anderson, Shaun	R-R	6-6	228	10-29-94	3	1	3.24	15	5	0	42	43	16	15	3	11	38	.270	.314	.403	22.09	6.40	172
Andriese, Matt	R-R	6-2	215	8-28-89	2	4	4.93	18	1	0	42	54	25	23	3	15	32	.314	.370	.477	16.93	7.94	189
Arias, Luarbert	R-R	6-2	176	12-12-00	8	6	3.04	44	1	4	68	54	28	23	8	27	75	.212	.303	.373	25.77	9.28	291
Bachar, Lake	R-R	6-2	219	6-3-95	0	0	9.00	1	0	0	1	3	1	1	0	0	0	.600	.600	.600	0.00	0.00	5
Bellozo, Valente	R-R	5-10	170	1-4-00	2	3	4.67	8	7	0	35	33	20	18	7	17	33	.246	.333	.478	21.15	10.90	156
Bender, Anthony	R-R	6-4	205	2-3-95	0	0	3.00	3	1	0	3	3	1	1	1	1	3	.300	.364	.600	27.27	9.09	11
Bermudez, Jonathan	L-L	6-2	237	10-16-95	1	2	5.74	7	4	0	27	27	18	17	3	15	29	.262	.355	.427	23.97	12.40	121
Brazoban, Huascar	R-R	6-3	155	10-15-89	1	1	5.91	6	0	0	11	13	9	7	2	3	10	.295	.333	.500	20.83	6.25	48
Cabrera, Edward	R-R	6-5	217	4-13-98	0	1	2.38	6	6	0	23	18	8	6	0	12	27	.220	.326	.305	28.13	12.50	96
Chargois, JT	S-R	6-3	200	12-3-90	0	0	0.71	11	2	0	13	4	1	1	0	4	14	.095	.174	.095	30.43	8.70	46
Chirinos, Yonny	R-R	6-2	225	12-26-93	10	6	3.66	21	21	0	111	108	51	45	11	37	92	.251	.316	.412	19.45	7.82	473
Cronin, Declan	R-R	6-4	225	9-24-97	0	0	4.15	3	0	0	4	5	2	2	1	4	4	.294	.429	.529	19.05	19.05	21
Curry, Xzavion	R-R	6-0	195	7-27-98	0	2	9.82	2	2	0	7	8	8	8	2	5	3	.286	.382	.607	8.82	14.71	34
de Geus, Brett	R-R	6-2	190	11-4-97	0	0	1.50	4	0	0	6	1	1	1	0	3	3	.059	.238	.059	14.29	14.29	21
Emanuel, Kent	L-L	6-4	225	6-4-92	0	5	6.33	15	7	0	48	71	37	34	6	15	41	.351	.407	.530	18.55	6.79	221
Faucher, Calvin	R-R	6-1	190	9-22-95	0	0	4.26	4	0	0	6	7	3	3	1	1	4	.280	.308	.400	15.38	3.85	26
Fitterer, Evan	R-R	6-3	192	6-26-00	1	2	7.71	6	6	0	26	29	22	22	4	19	29	.290	.429	.510	23.02	15.08	126
Garrett, Braxton	R-L	6-2	202	8-5-97	1	0	2.77	6	6	0	26	20	8	8	3	7	26	.211	.265	.337	25.49	6.86	102
Givens, Mychal	R-R	6-0	250	5-13-90	0	0	7.94	9	0	0	11	13	10	10	2	5	13	.277	.352	.468	24.07	9.26	54
Go, Woo Suk	R-R	5-11	198	8-6-98	2	0	4.29	16	0	0	21	23	10	10	4	7	14	.280	.352	.488	15.38	7.69	91
Henzman, Lincoln	R-R	6-2	205	7-4-95	0	0	0.00	1	0	0	1	1	1	0	0	2	1	.200	.429	.200	14.29	28.57	7
Hoeing, Bryan	R-R	6-6	210	10-19-96	2	1	4.82	5	1	0	9	11	6	5	0	5	10	.282	.364	.282	22.73	11.36	44
Kitchen, Austin	L-L	6-0	200	2-11-97	2	0	2.87	10	0	0	16	9	5	5	1	5	7	.167	.237	.278	11.86	8.47	59
Lindgren, Jeff	R-R	6-1	200	9-17-96	0	1	7.90	10	3	0	27	38	24	24	10	16	27	.342	.427	.649	20.45	12.12	132
Lowe, Collin	R-R	6-4	210	9-11-98	0	2	15.88	2	1	0	6	14	11	10	1	4	1	.483	.559	.621	2.94	11.76	34
Macuare, Angel	R-R	6-2	250	3-3-00	2	1	5.91	24	2	0	43	44	30	28	7	18	41	.272	.348	.475	21.93	9.63	187
Maldonado, Anthony	R-R	6-4	220	2-6-98	4	4	4.66	33	0	5	46	46	25	24	8	22	53	.258	.345	.444	26.11	10.84	203
Mazur, Adam	R-R	6-2	180	4-20-01	2	3	5.21	8	8	0	38	42	23	22	7	7	38	.271	.311	.471	23.17	4.27	164
McCaughan, Darren	R-R	6-1	200	3-18-96	2	4	4.53	11	11	0	54	49	33	27	7	18	59	.237	.303	.411	25.88	7.89	228
McMillon, John	L-R	6-3	230	1-27-98	0	0	0.00	1	0	0	1	0	0	0	0	1	2	.000	.250	.000	50.00	25.00	4
Meyer, Max	L-R	6-0	196	3-12-99	1	3	4.34	15	15	0	58	62	32	28	9	24	69	.272	.343	.452	27.06	9.41	255
Monteverde, Patrick	R-L	6-2	200	9-24-97	4	4	5.66	14	13	0	70	78	46	44	16	28	58	.278	.348	.509	18.53	8.95	313
Munoz, Roddery	R-R	6-2	210	4-14-00	4	4	4.96	12	8	0	49	38	29	27	7	24	43	.209	.316	.396	20.19	11.27	213
Oller, Adam	R-R	6-4	225	10-17-94	3	0	2.88	6	3	0	25	18	8	8	2	7	24	.200	.258	.367	24.49	7.14	98
Pilar, Anderson	R-R	6-2	210	3-2-98	0	0	3.00	8	2	0	15	11	5	5	2	7	22	.200	.302	.345	34.92	11.11	63
Puk, A.J.	L-L	6-7	248	4-25-95	0	0	0.00	1	0	0	1	0	0	0	0	0	3	.000	.000	.000	100.00	0.00	3
Pushard, Matt	R-R	6-4	245	10-27-97	0	0	0.00	1	0	0	2	1	0	0	0	0	2	.167	.167	.167	33.33	0.00	6
Ramirez, Emmanuel	R-R	6-2	190	7-15-94	4	2	3.76	25	0	10	41	31	20	17	5	16	51	.208	.283	.369	30.54	9.58	167
Roberts, Austin	R-R	6-0	205	7-27-98	1	1	3.10	12	0	2	20	14	7	7	2	11	25	.203	.309	.304	30.12	13.25	83
Sanchez, Sixto	R-R	6-0	234	7-29-98	0	0	0.00	1	0	0	1	0	0	0	0	0	1	.000	.000	.000	25.00	0.00	4
Simpson, Josh	L-L	6-2	190	8-19-97	0	1	6.52	9	0	0	10	12	10	7	3	4	15	.286	.367	.548	30.00	8.00	50
Smeltzer, Devin	R-L	6-3	195	9-7-95	1	2	3.69	24	0	1	32	28	17	13	6	13	32	.235	.338	.412	22.86	9.29	140
Snelling, Robby	R-L	6-3	210	12-19-03	0	0	1.50	1	1	0	6	7	2	1	1	1	7	.292	.320	.500	28.00	4.00	25
Soriano, George	R-R	6-2	210	3-24-99	0	3	4.38	24	0	2	39	30	19	19	8	17	44	.221	.310	.426	27.85	10.76	158
Stanavich, Dale	L-L	5-11	175	6-23-99	1	0	0.00	1	0	0	2	1	0	0	0	0	3	.143	.250	.143	37.50	0.00	8
Stevens, Tristan	R-R	6-2	200	12-8-97	0	0	0.00	1	1	0	4	3	0	0	0	2	2	.214	.353	.357	11.76	11.76	17
Tyler, Kyle	R-R	6-0	185	12-27-96	4	2	3.06	11	9	0	50	39	18	17	3	21	44	.220	.315	.305	21.57	10.29	204
Villalobos, Eli	R-R	6-4	195	6-26-97	1	1	4.50	13	0	1	18	17	10	9	3	11	22	.243	.361	.429	26.51	13.25	83
Vizcaino, Raffi	R-R	6-0	237	12-2-95	0	0	6.75	14	0	0	21	19	17	16	2	22	29	.238	.410	.363	27.62	20.95	105
Weathers, Ryan	R-L	6-1	230	12-17-99	1	0	2.35	2	2	0	8	8	4	2	0	5	13	.258	.361	.355	36.11	13.89	36

Fielding

Catcher	PCT	G	PO	A	E	DP	PB
Banfield	.989	81	719	29	8	5	2
Bethancourt	.947	2	17	1	1	1	0
Hostetler	1.000	2	11	1	0	0	0
Pereda	.992	40	360	21	3	1	1
Ramirez	.991	22	205	12	2	1	5
Sanchez	.969	3	28	3	1	1	0

First Base	PCT	G	PO	A	E	DP
Bride	.985	10	61	6	1	6
Burger	1.000	1	8	0	0	1
De Los Santos	.989	38	258	19	3	30
Gray	.989	13	81	7	1	8
Hostetler	1.000	2	19	1	0	0
Johnston	.996	87	603	66	3	65

Second Base	PCT	G	PO	A	E	DP
Amaya	1.000	1	0	5	0	0
Berry	1.000	1	1	3	0	1
Bride	1.000	9	10	20	0	10
Brujan	1.000	1	1	2	0	1
Devers	.981	29	38	65	2	19
Edwards	.933	6	4	10	1	3
Gordon	.981	14	22	31	1	8
Gray	.867	4	5	8	2	1
Guzman	.966	24	34	50	3	6
Lopez	.800	3	3	9	3	1
Norby	.960	7	5	19	1	0
Rodriguez	.967	7	11	18	1	5
Rosario	1.000	9	14	17	0	8
Sanoja	.980	38	50	96	3	24
Serna	1.000	2	4	4	0	0
Spohn	1.000	2	4	5	0	1

Third Base	PCT	G	PO	A	E	DP
Bride	.957	45	29	81	5	8
Burger	1.000	2	1	3	0	0
De Los Santos	.947	10	3	15	1	0
Devers	.955	6	9	12	1	1
Gray	.948	35	31	42	4	3
Guzman	.964	15	6	21	1	1
Hostetler	.848	20	15	24	7	3
Lopez	1.000	1	0	1	0	0
Myers	1.000	1	0	2	0	0
Norby	1.000	7	1	21	0	2
Pauley	.923	5	2	10	1	0
Roby	1.000	2	2	4	0	0
Rosario	.900	4	1	8	1	2

Shortstop	PCT	G	PO	A	E	DP
Amaya	.900	2	4	5	1	1
Anderson	1.000	2	4	5	0	3
Brujan	1.000	1	0	2	0	0
Devers	.943	18	18	32	3	5
Edwards	1.000	19	35	42	0	13
Gray	.961	39	60	89	6	17
Guzman	1.000	8	6	14	0	5
Lopez	1.000	6	11	15	0	3
Sanoja	.971	44	52	84	4	18
Serna	1.000	4	3	8	0	4
Spohn	.949	14	25	31	3	11

Outfield	PCT	G	PO	A	E	DP
Berry	.981	25	50	3	1	0
Brujan	.000	1	0	0	0	0
Conine	.978	91	172	6	4	2
Costes	1.000	37	59	2	0	0
Davis	.993	71	145	5	1	0
Garcia	.889	4	8	0	1	0
Gordon	1.000	7	14	1	0	0
Hill	1.000	3	1	0	0	0
Infante	.969	22	29	2	1	0
Johnston	.962	19	24	1	1	0
Marsee	1.000	21	39	0	0	0
Mesa	.995	81	180	5	1	1
Myers	.970	26	59	5	2	1
Rosario	1.000	6	9	0	0	0
Sanoja	.988	37	81	3	1	0
Wall	1.000	13	24	1	0	0

PENSACOLA BLUE WAHOOS — DOUBLE-A

SOUTHERN LEAGUE

Batting	B-T	Ht.	Wt.	DOB	AVG	OBP	SLG	G	PA	AB	R	H	2B	3B	HR	RBI	BB	HBP	SH	SF	SO	SB	CS	BB%	SO%
Alderman, Kemp	R-R	6-3	265	8-20-02	.174	.174	.348	6	23	23	1	4	1	0	1	3	0	0	0	0	9	0	0	0.00	39.13
Allen, Tanner	L-R	5-11	190	6-5-98	.225	.315	.349	44	148	129	17	29	10	0	2	12	14	3	2	0	34	4	3	9.46	22.97
Berry, Jacob	B-R	6-0	212	5-5-01	.238	.306	.360	104	425	386	40	92	18	1	9	45	31	7	0	1	87	12	2	7.29	20.47
Beshears, Jay	R-R	6-4	215	5-6-02	.000	.000	.000	2	6	6	0	0	0	0	0	1	0	0	0	0	1	0	0	0.00	16.67
Bramwell, Spencer	R-R	5-11	220	1-10-99	.143	.250	.286	2	8	7	0	1	1	0	0	1	1	0	0	0	3	0	0	12.50	37.50
Caballero, Jorge	R-R	6-0	170	1-10-00	.150	.320	.150	7	25	20	2	3	0	0	0	0	2	3	0	0	10	1	1	8.00	40.00
Guzman, Jonathan	R-R	5-11	156	8-17-99	.250	.250	.750	3	8	8	1	2	1	0	1	3	0	0	0	0	2	1	0	0.00	25.00
Hostetler, Bennett	R-R	6-0	195	9-23-97	.221	.262	.312	44	164	154	14	34	11	0	1	7	7	2	0	1	55	5	0	4.27	33.54
Infante, Diego	R-R	6-2	178	10-22-99	.290	.333	.333	27	99	93	11	27	1	0	1	7	6	0	0	0	30	4	0	6.06	30.30
Mack, Joe	L-R	6-1	210	12-27-02	.241	.322	.456	112	475	423	63	102	25	0	22	65	46	5	0	1	122	2	0	9.68	25.68
Marsee, Jakob	L-L	6-0	180	6-28-01	.188	.342	.303	91	401	320	61	60	8	4	7	37	61	15	3	2	91	32	6	15.21	22.69
Martorella, Nathan	L-L	6-1	224	2-18-01	.214	.283	.376	102	420	378	46	81	11	1	16	41	33	5	0	4	79	5	0	7.86	18.81
McIntosh, Paul	R-R	6-1	220	11-20-97	.246	.340	.385	117	480	418	50	103	18	2	12	55	50	10	0	2	95	8	3	10.42	19.79
Mercado, Jan	R-R	6-0	200	8-28-99	.000	.000	.000	2	6	6	0	0	0	0	0	0	0	0	0	0	5	0	0	0.00	83.33
Morissette, Cody	L-R	6-0	175	1-16-00	.200	.266	.334	112	418	380	40	76	17	2	10	46	30	5	0	3	108	16	3	7.18	25.84
Olmstead, Johnny	R-R	6-2	185	7-10-00	.287	.344	.460	26	96	87	13	25	4	1	3	15	7	1	0	1	16	3	2	7.29	16.67
Pauley, Graham	L-R	6-1	200	9-24-00	.239	.325	.384	38	160	138	19	33	8	0	4	17	18	1	0	3	35	4	0	11.25	21.88
Pintar, Andrew	R-R	6-2	190	3-23-01	.192	.287	.240	33	145	125	15	24	4	1	0	8	14	3	2	1	35	5	0	9.66	24.14
Roby, Sean	R-R	6-1	215	7-8-98	.196	.267	.314	44	172	153	17	30	1	1	5	16	16	0	0	3	52	0	0	9.30	30.23
Rosario, Dalvy	R-R	6-0	185	7-22-00	.205	.234	.262	41	131	122	17	25	2	1	1	9	5	0	3	1	36	6	2	3.82	27.48
Sanoja, Javier	R-R	5-7	150	9-3-02	.246	.279	.316	15	61	57	4	14	1	0	1	7	3	0	0	1	6	3	1	4.92	9.84
Sasaki, Shane	R-R	5-11	165	7-1-00	.240	.337	.300	66	250	217	28	52	10	0	1	8	29	3	1	0	69	21	4	11.60	27.60
Serna, Jared	R-R	5-6	168	6-1-02	.266	.343	.390	39	175	154	19	41	13	0	2	23	14	5	0	2	33	3	3	8.00	10.06
Spohn, Harrison	R-R	6-1	185	12-3-98	.183	.263	.308	89	313	279	25	51	10	2	7	29	30	1	1	2	117	6	4	9.58	37.38
Thompson, Jake	L-R	6-0	207	3-3-98	.324	.375	.432	10	40	37	4	12	2	1	0	3	1	2	0	0	12	0	0	2.50	30.00
Zamora, Joshua	R-R	5-10	190	5-18-99	.222	.276	.407	8	29	27	3	6	2	0	1	3	2	0	0	0	8	0	0	6.90	27.59
Zubia, Zach	R-R	6-4	230	11-4-97	.190	.310	.353	68	274	232	31	44	6	1	10	26	38	3	0	1	87	2	0	13.87	31.75

Pitching	B-T	Ht.	Wt.	DOB	W	L	ERA	G	GS	SV	IP	Hits	Runs	ER	HR	BB	SO	AVG	OBP	SLG	SO%	BB%	BF
Belgrave, Nigel	R-R	6-4	195	5-12-02	2	2	6.75	13	0	0	13	10	10	10	0	9	18	.196	.359	.294	28.13	14.06	64
Bellozo, Valente	R-R	5-10	170	1-4-00	2	2	4.60	6	6	0	31	31	16	16	3	7	39	.252	.295	.398	29.55	5.30	132
Bermudez, Jonathan	L-L	6-2	237	10-16-95	3	4	2.53	14	14	0	75	49	23	21	9	35	70	.187	.298	.344	22.95	11.48	305
Campbell, Paul	L-R	6-0	210	7-26-95	5	1	3.50	10	10	0	46	39	19	18	3	15	39	.238	.317	.329	20.97	8.06	186
Crigger, Kyle	R-R	6-2	180	6-4-99	0	0	2.25	3	0	0	4	2	1	1	0	3	4	.167	.333	.250	26.67	20.00	15
Eckberg, Tyler	R-R	6-4	220	9-4-97	2	0	3.13	21	0	1	32	25	13	11	3	11	28	.214	.295	.333	21.05	8.27	133
Ekness, Josh	R-R	6-4	225	2-7-02	0	0	9.00	4	0	0	4	6	4	4	2	1	7	.333	.368	.722	36.84	5.26	19
Fitterer, Evan	R-R	6-3	192	6-26-00	6	6	4.17	19	19	0	95	97	47	44	5	49	85	.265	.358	.366	20.09	11.58	423
Gibson, Cade	L-L	6-2	195	2-18-98	0	1	1.69	7	3	0	21	16	4	4	0	12	23	.219	.337	.301	26.74	13.95	86
Go, Woo Suk	R-R	5-11	198	8-6-98	2	1	10.42	18	0	2	19	31	28	22	4	11	23	.344	.422	.556	22.33	10.68	103
Henzman, Lincoln	R-R	6-2	205	7-4-95	1	1	6.08	12	0	1	13	17	12	9	1	1	10	.298	.322	.474	16.95	1.69	59
Johnson, M.D.	R-R	6-5	200	7-7-97	3	5	3.74	14	14	0	67	75	38	28	2	28	56	.275	.354	.392	18.01	9.00	311
Jozwiak, Chandler	L-L	6-0	185	2-15-99	3	4	3.66	40	2	1	52	41	25	21	6	30	45	.227	.335	.398	20.83	13.89	216
King, Justin	L-L	6-1	215	12-19-97	2	2	2.55	17	0	1	18	10	5	5	2	6	32	.164	.261	.262	46.38	8.70	69
Laskey, Adam	R-L	6-3	205	3-9-98	6	2	3.10	31	6	0	81	63	28	28	4	20	76	.217	.279	.314	23.75	6.25	320
Lindgren, Jeff	R-R	6-1	200	9-17-96	2	4	5.21	14	8	0	48	48	29	28	8	27	43	.258	.349	.457	19.91	12.50	216
Macuare, Angel	R-R	6-2	250	3-3-00	1	0	1.29	14	1	0	28	20	5	4	0	9	28	.202	.261	.273	25.23	8.11	111
McCambley, Zach	L-R	6-2	220	5-4-99	0	1	3.97	18	0	0	23	13	10	10	2	18	28	.171	.340	.250	28.57	18.37	98
Mendez, Josan	R-R	6-2	180	7-10-00	0	0	17.18	3	0	0	4	8	7	7	0	0	0	.444	.444	.500	0.00	0.00	19
Miller, Jacob	R-R	6-2	180	8-10-03	1	2	3.44	7	7	0	34	27	15	13	2	9	28	.209	.261	.279	20.29	6.52	138

Monteverde, Patrick	R-L	6-2	200	9-24-97	3	3	5.06	7	7	0	37	32	23	21	7	7	38	.229	.264	.400	25.68	4.73	148
Murphy, Patrick	L-L	6-1	205	3-7-97	1	2	6.00	11	0	0	15	16	12	10	1	9	17	.271	.368	.373	25.00	13.24	68
Palacios, Luis	L-L	6-2	160	7-1-00	10	7	4.91	24	24	0	125	145	80	68	15	29	94	.285	.326	.456	17.31	5.34	543
Pilar, Anderson	R-R	6-2	210	3-2-98	0	1	3.34	23	0	1	32	32	12	12	3	5	31	.256	.293	.384	23.31	3.76	133
Pushard, Matt	R-R	6-4	245	10-27-97	3	4	2.36	40	0	1	53	38	17	14	6	18	66	.191	.267	.337	29.73	8.11	222
Roberts, Austin	R-R	6-0	205	7-27-98	3	1	1.93	38	0	15	47	20	14	10	2	18	60	.130	.225	.201	33.52	10.06	179
Simpson, Josh	L-L	6-2	190	8-19-97	0	1	10.80	2	0	0	3	4	4	4	1	3	4	.308	.438	.538	25.00	18.75	16
Snelling, Robby	R-L	6-3	210	12-19-03	2	2	4.00	7	7	0	36	33	17	16	2	11	41	.236	.296	.329	26.97	7.24	152
Stanavich, Dale	L-L	5-11	175	6-23-99	2	0	2.25	29	0	5	40	22	12	10	5	22	59	.156	.277	.291	35.33	13.17	167
Stevens, Tristan	R-R	6-2	200	12-8-97	2	3	3.83	11	8	0	45	42	25	19	3	10	34	.247	.290	.371	18.28	5.38	186
Storm, Justin	L-L	6-7	232	9-12-01	0	0	13.50	1	0	0	1	1	1	1	0	2	0	.333	.600	.333	0.00	40.00	5
Vizcaino, Raffi	R-R	6-0	237	12-2-95	4	3	2.43	31	0	8	37	31	13	10	0	15	47	.226	.303	.299	30.92	9.87	152
White, Josh	R-R	6-1	205	11-24-00	0	0	5.40	2	0	0	2	3	1	1	1	1	3	.375	.444	1.000	33.33	11.11	9
Williams, Alex	L-R	6-3	220	10-22-99	0	0	15.75	2	0	0	4	9	7	7	0	3	7	.429	.500	.524	29.17	12.50	24

Fielding

Catcher	PCT	G	PO	A	E	DP	PB
Bramwell	1.000	2	21	4	0	0	0
Hostetler	1.000	16	134	13	0	0	2
Mack	.999	72	638	41	1	5	6
McIntosh	.993	47	370	30	3	2	2
Mercado	1.000	2	17	3	0	0	2

First Base	PCT	G	PO	A	E	DP
Berry	.975	5	39	0	1	2
Hostetler	.988	8	73	9	1	8
Martorella	.988	63	474	38	6	40
Roby	.982	7	52	4	1	4
Spohn	.000	1	0	0	0	0
Zamora	1.000	4	34	1	0	2
Zubia	.990	50	383	25	4	26

Second Base	PCT	G	PO	A	E	DP
Berry	1.000	2	1	6	0	1
Morissette	.973	103	147	253	11	55
Olmstead	.978	21	37	54	2	8
Rosario	.960	5	7	17	1	4
Sanoja	1.000	1	1	1	0	0
Serna	1.000	1	1	2	0	0
Spohn	.778	3	2	5	2	1
Zamora	1.000	1	0	3	0	0

Third Base	PCT	G	PO	A	E	DP
Berry	.877	45	31	62	13	3
Beshears	.857	2	3	3	1	0
Hostetler	.927	16	13	25	3	5
Morissette	.000	1	0	0	0	0
Pauley	.979	35	29	64	2	5
Roby	.969	37	27	66	3	4
Rosario	.800	1	2	2	1	0
Spohn	1.000	2	1	7	0	1
Zamora	1.000	1	1	0	0	0

Shortstop	PCT	G	PO	A	E	DP
Guzman	1.000	3	3	5	0	1
Olmstead	.952	4	10	10	1	1
Rosario	.944	6	13	21	2	5
Sanoja	1.000	8	9	27	0	5
Serna	.925	33	28	71	8	14
Spohn	.972	83	132	181	9	36

Outfield	PCT	G	PO	A	E	DP
Alderman	1.000	6	14	0	0	0
Allen	1.000	43	80	1	0	1
Berry	.948	50	89	3	5	1
Caballero	1.000	7	19	0	0	0
Infante	.972	25	32	3	1	0
Marsee	.990	91	201	3	2	1
Martorella	1.000	27	35	1	0	0
McIntosh	.958	34	44	2	2	1
Pintar	1.000	31	68	2	0	1
Rosario	.977	28	42	0	1	0
Sanoja	1.000	7	19	0	0	0
Sasaki	.984	67	120	3	2	0
Spohn	1.000	1	1	0	0	0
Thompson	1.000	6	6	0	0	0
Zamora	.750	2	3	0	1	0

BELOIT SKY CARP — HIGH-A

MIDWEST LEAGUE

Batting	B-T	Ht.	Wt.	DOB	AVG	OBP	SLG	G	PA	AB	R	H	2B	3B	HR	RBI	BB	HBP	SH	SF	SO	SB	CS	BB%	SO%
Alderman, Kemp	R-R	6-3	265	8-20-02	.240	.312	.344	33	138	125	12	30	5	1	2	11	13	0	0	0	32	2	0	9.42	23.19
Barstad, Cameron	L-R	6-1	195	11-29-00	.221	.322	.356	65	258	222	23	49	12	0	6	29	29	5	0	2	96	0	1	11.24	37.21
Beshears, Jay	R-R	6-4	215	5-6-02	.179	.233	.232	28	103	95	7	17	5	0	0	5	5	2	0	1	21	1	0	4.85	20.39
Bullard, Tony	R-R	6-4	212	2-17-00	.301	.383	.392	47	175	153	12	46	11	0	1	22	16	5	0	1	35	4	1	9.14	20.00
Caballero, Jorge	R-R	6-0	170	1-10-00	.268	.397	.356	49	184	149	20	40	7	0	2	8	32	1	0	2	50	2	2	17.39	27.17
Cappe, Yiddi	R-R	6-3	175	9-17-02	.225	.303	.288	60	267	240	28	54	7	1	2	19	26	1	0	0	66	7	5	9.74	24.72
Coley, Mark	R-R	6-2	193	11-22-00	.213	.328	.382	105	445	380	68	81	14	7	12	38	46	19	0	0	135	30	2	10.34	30.34
DeLeo, Jake	R-R	6-2	194	5-30-01	.236	.302	.330	59	233	212	25	50	10	2	2	20	19	1	1	0	74	1	2	8.15	31.76
Fernandez, Andrew	R-R	6-3	196	10-19-98	.129	.250	.258	11	36	31	6	4	1	0	1	3	5	0	0	0	19	0	0	13.89	52.78
Ignoffo, Ryan	R-R	5-10	215	7-21-00	.307	.327	.426	24	104	101	6	31	9	0	1	13	3	0	0	0	14	0	1	2.88	13.46
Johnson, Osiris	R-R	6-0	198	10-18-00	.189	.243	.254	55	203	185	17	35	7	1	1	21	12	2	1	3	37	16	2	5.91	18.23
Lane, Carmine	R-R	6-0	200	3-28-01	.000	.200	.000	2	5	4	0	0	0	0	0	0	1	0	0	0	2	0	0	20.00	40.00
Lara, Wilfredo	R-R	5-10	180	4-28-04	.278	.305	.456	23	95	90	12	25	5	1	3	15	4	0	0	1	19	2	0	4.21	20.00
Luttrell, Chase	L-L	6-0	200	6-1-00	.204	.272	.372	50	152	137	17	28	9	1	4	10	11	2	1	1	51	2	1	7.24	33.55
Mabry, JT	R-R	6-0	170	4-25-00	.143	.143	.143	2	7	7	0	1	0	0	0	0	0	0	0	0	3	0	0	0.00	42.86
Mack, Joe	L-R	6-1	210	12-27-02	.347	.467	.571	13	60	49	7	17	5	0	2	13	11	0	0	0	11	1	0	18.33	18.33
Marinez, Ynmanol	R-R	5-11	190	4-12-01	.050	.367	.050	8	30	20	4	1	0	0	0	0	10	0	0	0	10	1	0	33.33	33.33
Mercado, Jan	R-R	6-0	200	8-28-99	.188	.235	.313	6	17	16	1	3	2	0	0	0	1	0	0	0	8	0	0	5.88	47.06
Miller, Gage	R-R	6-0	200	3-1-03	.200	.235	.250	19	85	80	6	16	2	1	0	8	1	3	0	1	18	1	0	1.18	21.18
Montgomery, Torin	R-R	6-3	230	5-2-01	.237	.340	.341	72	291	249	28	59	8	0	6	38	34	6	0	2	95	0	0	11.68	32.65
Olmstead, Johnny	R-R	6-2	185	7-10-00	.239	.315	.393	95	397	351	55	84	17	2	11	43	32	9	0	5	72	8	1	8.06	18.14
Praytor, Sam	R-R	5-9	205	4-4-99	.234	.353	.414	38	153	128	17	30	8	0	5	25	21	3	0	1	34	0	1	13.73	22.22
Roberts, Brett	R-R	6-0	182	3-12-01	.208	.276	.342	40	164	149	18	31	4	2	4	13	13	1	1	0	48	4	1	7.93	29.27
Rosario, Dalvy	R-R	6-0	185	7-22-00	.139	.244	.278	13	42	36	8	5	2	0	1	6	5	0	1	0	15	4	1	11.90	35.71
Santiago, Carlos	B-R	5-11	145	7-24-01	.171	.233	.358	54	202	187	19	32	8	0	9	27	13	2	0	0	64	4	1	6.44	31.68
Shade, Colby	R-R	6-1	205	8-18-01	.231	.321	.364	33	137	121	18	28	5	1	3	14	13	3	0	0	38	7	3	9.49	27.74
Spohn, Harrison	R-R	6-1	185	12-3-98	.133	.188	.133	4	16	15	0	2	0	0	0	1	1	0	0	0	4	0	1	6.25	25.00
Thompson, Jake	L-R	6-0	207	3-3-98	.265	.355	.382	36	155	136	17	36	8	1	2	12	14	5	0	0	37	2	2	9.03	23.87
Vradenburg, Brock	L-R	6-7	230	3-20-02	.214	.307	.353	52	215	187	22	40	6	1	6	26	25	1	0	2	67	8	3	11.63	31.16
Zamora, Joshua	R-R	5-10	190	5-18-99	.250	.331	.427	100	424	372	56	93	15	0	17	56	42	5	1	4	84	0	0	9.91	19.81

Pitching	B-T	Ht.	Wt.	DOB	W	L	ERA	G	GS	SV	IP	Hits	Runs	ER	HR	BB	SO	AVG	OBP	SLG	SO%	BB%	BF
Belgrave, Nigel	R-R	6-4	195	5-12-02	3	1	2.29	21	0	5	35	18	9	9	2	12	39	.151	.239	.235	28.89	8.89	135

Bergin, Jesse	R-R	6-4	205	10-8-99	0	0	0.00	2	0	0	3	1	0	0	0	2	2	.111	.273	.111	18.18	18.18	11
Bierman, Gabe	R-R	6-2	200	9-3-99	0	0	3.00	2	0	0	3	3	1	1	1	0	4	.250	.250	.500	33.33	0.00	12
Brooks, Jake	R-R	6-4	202	7-8-01	0	0	0.00	1	1	0	5	2	0	0	0	0	6	.118	.118	.118	35.29	0.00	17
Buxton, Ike	R-R	6-3	208	7-18-00	2	8	5.35	19	19	0	77	90	60	46	5	42	74	.286	.378	.403	20.00	11.35	370
Crigger, Kyle	R-R	6-2	180	6-4-99	6	0	4.53	28	1	0	44	36	24	22	5	16	41	.231	.313	.378	23.30	9.09	176
Eckberg, Tyler	R-R	6-4	220	9-4-97	0	2	2.21	15	0	0	20	14	7	5	0	7	23	.197	.269	.254	28.75	8.75	80
Ekness, Josh	R-R	6-4	225	2-7-02	3	3	1.65	34	0	1	49	27	12	9	1	22	55	.159	.276	.206	27.64	11.06	199
Feliz, Ignacio	R-R	6-1	180	10-23-99	4	1	4.88	22	0	0	31	22	18	17	1	21	47	.204	.362	.269	33.81	15.11	139
Gibson, Cade	L-L	6-2	195	2-18-98	3	2	2.43	14	9	0	59	49	18	16	2	24	48	.226	.323	.304	19.12	9.56	251
Jimenez, Yeuris	R-R	6-3	218	3-23-01	1	1	4.46	23	0	0	40	39	25	20	1	16	41	.244	.328	.313	22.78	8.89	180
Jones, Holt	R-R	6-8	235	5-8-99	2	2	6.45	18	0	1	22	23	17	16	2	18	22	.261	.409	.386	20.00	16.36	110
Meachem, Xavier	R-R	5-11	210	9-6-02	1	5	2.84	31	0	8	44	41	23	14	0	29	56	.248	.367	.309	28.00	14.50	200
Meyer, Noble	R-R	6-5	185	1-10-05	0	5	5.18	11	10	0	40	25	25	23	6	32	42	.179	.354	.329	23.46	17.88	179
Milbrandt, Karson	R-R	6-2	190	4-21-04	1	8	4.33	22	22	0	98	90	56	47	5	57	91	.244	.350	.360	20.73	12.98	439
Miller, Jacob	R-R	6-2	180	8-10-03	5	4	4.02	16	16	0	81	81	40	36	7	25	65	.263	.326	.399	18.95	7.29	343
Olson, Emmett	L-L	6-4	230	5-15-02	6	6	3.74	18	18	0	87	85	42	36	6	31	76	.251	.318	.364	20.16	8.22	377
Pilar, Anderson	R-R	6-2	210	3-2-98	1	0	0.00	6	0	0	11	3	0	0	0	1	18	.086	.111	.086	50.00	2.78	36
Poland, Jared	R-R	6-0	215	1-12-00	1	0	5.40	6	1	0	7	5	4	4	1	5	3	.208	.367	.375	10.00	16.67	30
Sanchez, Edgar	R-R	6-1	190	8-2-00	4	1	1.90	36	0	0	52	27	14	11	1	26	44	.149	.265	.199	20.75	12.26	212
Schomberg, Will	R-R	5-10	170	1-30-01	1	3	7.13	6	6	0	24	22	21	19	5	23	32	.234	.405	.479	26.45	19.01	121
Sellinger, Jack	R-L	6-2	200	11-20-99	1	0	1.93	7	0	1	9	4	2	2	0	7	11	.125	.300	.156	27.50	17.50	40
Stanavich, Dale	L-L	5-11	175	6-23-99	2	3	4.15	14	0	1	17	18	14	8	1	6	24	.261	.338	.391	31.17	7.79	77
Storm, Justin	L-L	6-7	232	9-12-01	0	1	2.55	11	0	0	18	11	7	5	0	8	29	.180	.292	.213	39.73	10.96	73
Taylor, Evan	L-L	6-4	250	12-26-99	4	4	2.84	31	0	3	44	34	17	14	1	20	52	.217	.319	.280	27.81	10.70	187
White, Josh	R-R	6-1	205	11-24-00	2	1	2.95	38	3	6	58	47	20	19	3	24	77	.225	.318	.330	31.82	9.92	242
White, Thomas	L-L	6-5	210	9-29-04	5	3	2.61	13	13	0	62	51	19	18	6	21	76	.222	.295	.335	29.92	8.27	254
Williams, Alex	L-R	6-3	220	10-22-99	2	4	4.39	23	9	1	66	63	40	32	7	20	75	.252	.313	.448	27.17	7.25	276
Wurster, Caleb	L-L	5-11	182	9-21-98	0	1	15.19	8	1	0	11	16	19	18	5	10	11	.348	.475	.761	18.03	16.39	61

Fielding

Catcher	PCT	G	PO	A	E	DP	PB
Barstad	.989	54	482	60	6	6	10
Fernandez	.983	7	59	0	1	0	1
Ignoffo	.996	24	232	18	1	2	2
Lane	1.000	1	14	2	0	1	0
Mack	1.000	7	66	7	0	0	1
Mercado	1.000	5	35	6	0	0	0
Praytor	.987	33	288	19	4	1	2

First Base	PCT	G	PO	A	E	DP
Beshears	.750	1	3	0	1	0
Lane	1.000	1	2	3	0	0
Luttrell	1.000	1	11	1	0	1
Mercado	1.000	1	1	0	0	0
Montgomery	.990	65	457	32	5	36
Santiago	1.000	13	86	4	0	8
Thompson	1.000	2	21	1	0	2
Vradenburg	.982	46	361	19	7	23
Zamora	1.000	3	19	0	0	0

Second Base	PCT	G	PO	A	E	DP
Cappe	.895	10	12	22	4	3
Lara	1.000	16	25	39	0	6
Mabry	1.000	2	2	5	0	1
Miller	.980	11	21	29	1	4
Rosario	.000	1	0	0	0	0
Santiago	.968	30	48	74	4	12
Zamora	.988	63	98	156	3	30

Third Base	PCT	G	PO	A	E	DP
Beshears	.875	3	3	4	1	0
Bullard	.948	40	25	66	5	7
Cappe	.882	46	24	58	11	8
Lara	1.000	1	0	1	0	0
Marinez	.957	8	8	14	1	3
Miller	1.000	6	5	8	0	1
Rosario	.000	1	0	0	0	0
Zamora	.967	27	18	41	2	3

Shortstop	PCT	G	PO	A	E	DP
Beshears	.923	23	26	46	6	8
Lara	1.000	5	5	9	0	0
Olmstead	.944	92	125	230	21	39
Rosario	1.000	1	4	1	0	0
Spohn	1.000	4	4	7	0	2
Zamora	.938	5	7	8	1	2

Outfield	PCT	G	PO	A	E	DP
Alderman	.975	27	38	1	1	0
Caballero	1.000	32	44	0	0	0
Coley	.971	102	192	7	6	1
DeLeo	.990	55	97	3	1	0
Johnson	.990	56	95	3	1	0
Luttrell	1.000	51	64	0	0	0
Roberts	.985	33	63	4	1	0
Rosario	1.000	9	16	1	0	0
Santiago	1.000	9	9	1	0	0
Shade	.978	33	86	4	2	1
Thompson	1.000	2	5	0	0	0

JUPITER HAMMERHEADS — *LOW-A*

FLORIDA STATE LEAGUE

Batting	B-T	Ht.	Wt.	DOB	AVG	OBP	SLG	G	PA	AB	R	H	2B	3B	HR	RBI	BB	HBP	SH	SF	SO	SB	CS	BB%	SO%
Alderman, Kemp	R-R	6-3	265	8-20-02	.270	.321	.468	33	140	126	18	34	8	1	5	30	10	1	0	3	32	2	3	7.14	22.86
Allen, Tanner	L-R	5-11	190	6-5-98	.227	.346	.273	6	26	22	2	5	1	0	0	2	3	1	0	0	3	1	0	11.54	11.54
Bradshaw, Davis	L-R	6-2	175	4-25-98	.323	.382	.339	16	69	62	11	20	1	0	0	11	5	1	1	0	11	4	2	7.25	15.94
Bramwell, Spencer	R-R	5-11	220	1-10-99	.147	.237	.206	22	76	68	4	10	4	0	0	2	7	1	0	0	26	0	1	9.21	34.21
Bullard, Tony	R-R	6-4	212	2-17-00	.244	.333	.329	25	96	82	7	20	4	0	1	13	8	4	0	2	18	7	3	8.33	18.75
Cappe, Yiddi	R-R	6-3	175	9-17-02	.217	.217	.217	6	23	23	0	5	0	0	0	0	0	0	0	0	8	0	1	0.00	34.78
Caskenette, Connor	R-R	6-0	215	6-14-02	.206	.289	.250	20	76	68	8	14	3	0	0	5	8	0	0	0	17	3	1	10.53	22.37
Clayton, Cam	R-R	6-1	185	7-6-02	.154	.154	.154	3	13	13	2	2	0	0	0	1	0	0	0	0	5	0	0	0.00	38.46
Coley, Mark	R-R	6-2	193	11-22-00	.375	.459	.688	8	37	32	8	12	2	4	0	5	3	2	0	0	11	3	1	8.11	29.73
Cruz, John	L-L	6-3	171	8-29-05	.168	.259	.212	81	314	273	32	46	9	0	1	30	31	4	0	5	88	8	4	9.87	28.03
DeLeo, Jake	R-R	6-2	194	5-30-01	.204	.289	.272	39	166	147	20	30	7	0	1	14	16	2	0	1	40	15	2	9.64	24.10
Devers, Jose	L-R	6-0	174	12-7-99	.375	.375	.688	4	16	16	2	6	3	1	0	1	0	0	0	0	2	0	0	0.00	12.50
DiSpigna, Angelo	L-R	6-6	229	11-2-99	.203	.333	.348	59	225	187	24	38	8	2	5	28	32	5	0	1	71	3	4	14.22	31.56
Forrester, Garret	R-R	6-1	208	11-11-01	.232	.366	.293	25	101	82	4	19	5	0	0	11	15	3	0	1	30	1	0	14.85	29.70
Green, Payton	R-R	6-3	190	1-17-03	.184	.359	.224	18	65	49	8	9	2	0	0	3	13	1	1	1	14	4	1	20.00	21.54
Head, Dillon	L-L	5-11	180	10-11-04	.333	.333	.500	3	12	12	3	4	0	1	0	1	0	0	0	0	3	2	0	0.00	25.00
Hernandez, Jesus	R-R	5-9	150	2-20-04	.218	.323	.302	76	323	275	34	60	13	2	2	20	43	1	1	3	74	17	4	13.31	22.91
Hidalgo, Renny	R-R	5-9	165	9-5-02	.174	.283	.217	19	53	46	4	8	2	0	0	1	6	1	0	0	16	5	3	11.32	30.19
Ignoffo, Ryan	R-R	5-10	215	7-21-00	.330	.393	.484	79	321	285	42	94	25	2	5	45	32	0	0	4	35	21	5	9.97	10.90
Infante, Diego	R-R	6-2	178	10-22-99	.444	.615	.667	3	13	9	4	4	2	0	0	2	4	0	0	0	4	0	1	30.77	30.77

Jenkins-Cowart, Jacob	L-R	6-6	216	12-24-02	.190	.259	.276	28	116	105	14	20	6	0	1	7	9	1	0	1	35	3	2	7.76	30.17
Johnson, Carter	L-R	6-2	180	2-22-06	.221	.273	.292	28	121	113	9	25	3	1	1	16	7	1	0	0	40	2	1	5.79	33.06
Lane, Carmine	R-R	6-0	200	3-28-01	.161	.246	.210	21	69	62	8	10	1	1	0	0	7	0	0	0	19	2	0	10.14	27.54
Mabry, JT	R-R	6-0	170	4-25-00	.202	.272	.247	70	275	247	20	50	7	2	0	19	18	6	3	1	59	7	6	6.55	21.45
Martinez, Yeral	L-R	6-3	220	10-30-02	.163	.230	.307	63	236	215	23	35	8	4	5	19	16	3	0	1	94	8	3	6.78	39.83
McCants, Jordan	L-R	6-0	165	5-21-02	.211	.284	.303	104	431	383	49	81	14	6	3	24	36	5	2	5	120	31	10	8.35	27.84
McDowell, Micah	L-R	6-2	175	1-27-01	.250	.438	.333	4	16	12	1	3	1	0	0	3	3	1	0	0	5	0	0	18.75	31.25
Mesa, Victor	L-L	6-0	195	9-8-01	.167	.286	.250	3	14	12	1	2	1	0	0	0	2	0	0	0	4	0	1	14.29	28.57
Miller, Gage	R-R	6-0	200	3-1-03	.375	.485	.458	7	33	24	6	9	2	0	0	4	6	1	0	2	2	1	1	18.18	6.06
Morlando, P.J.	L-R	6-3	190	5-16-05	.000	.000	.000	1	1	1	0	0	0	0	0	0	0	0	0	0	0	0	0	0.00	0.00
Olmstead, Johnny	R-R	6-2	185	7-10-00	.294	.368	.471	5	21	17	2	5	1	1	0	3	1	1	2	0	7	2	1	4.76	33.33
Ortega, Victor	R-R	6-1	200	1-19-04	.233	.400	.279	13	55	43	5	10	2	0	0	2	12	0	0	0	9	0	0	21.82	16.36
Praytor, Sam	R-R	5-9	205	4-4-99	.280	.357	.420	15	57	50	4	14	4	0	1	8	6	0	1	0	12	0	0	10.53	21.05
Rataczak, Eric	L-R	6-3	215	1-19-01	.284	.377	.328	20	77	67	8	19	3	0	0	6	7	3	0	0	19	7	3	9.09	24.68
Rios, Nestor	R-R	5-9	175	1-4-05	.333	.500	.333	1	4	3	0	1	0	0	0	0	1	0	0	0	0	0	0	25.00	0.00
Roberts, Brett	R-R	6-0	182	3-12-01	.263	.300	.316	5	20	19	1	5	1	0	0	0	0	1	0	0	3	0	0	0.00	15.00
Rodriguez, Cristhian	L-R	6-3	160	12-23-01	.198	.312	.233	37	139	116	17	23	2	1	0	11	19	1	1	2	46	7	1	13.67	33.09
Sanchez, Junior	L-R	5-10	177	12-18-02	.213	.283	.278	31	120	108	17	23	5	1	0	10	10	1	0	1	28	2	1	8.33	23.33
Sasaki, Shane	R-R	5-11	165	7-1-00	.316	.458	.368	5	24	19	4	6	1	0	0	4	4	1	0	0	4	1	0	16.67	16.67
Shade, Colby	R-R	6-1	205	8-18-01	.274	.375	.397	81	346	292	62	80	19	1	5	30	31	18	2	3	97	38	5	8.96	28.03
Snyder, Michael	R-R	6-4	205	9-16-00	.150	.261	.167	19	69	60	8	9	1	0	0	6	7	2	0	0	23	4	0	10.14	33.33
Trimble, Fenwick	R-R	6-3	200	8-29-02	.258	.294	.325	29	127	120	10	31	4	2	0	12	5	1	1	0	21	11	6	3.94	16.54
Vradenburg, Brock	L-R	6-7	230	3-20-02	.201	.341	.311	73	302	244	24	49	13	1	4	38	54	0	0	4	77	12	7	17.88	25.50

Pitching	B-T	Ht.	Wt.	DOB	W	L	ERA	G	GS	SV	IP	Hits	Runs	ER	HR	BB	SO	AVG	OBP	SLG	SO%	BB%	BF
Alegre, Delvis	R-R	6-2	180	2-2-01	2	5	4.75	22	0	0	36	39	22	19	1	13	32	.273	.329	.329	20.25	8.23	158
Alvarado, Elvis	R-R	6-4	183	2-23-99	0	0	0.00	2	0	0	2	0	1	0	0	2	3	.000	.300	.000	30.00	20.00	10
Belgrave, Nigel	R-R	6-4	195	5-12-02	1	0	0.66	10	0	5	14	6	2	1	0	7	17	.136	.269	.159	32.69	13.46	52
Benitez, Keyner	L-L	6-1	165	5-23-06	0	5	3.12	13	11	1	58	43	25	20	5	26	58	.206	.303	.321	24.37	10.92	238
Bergin, Jesse	R-R	6-4	205	10-8-99	1	1	1.64	16	0	4	22	16	6	4	0	2	34	.195	.212	.220	40.00	2.35	85
Bierman, Gabe	R-R	6-2	200	9-3-99	1	0	2.57	5	0	1	7	5	2	2	1	4	5	.200	.300	.360	16.67	13.33	30
Brink, Nick	R-R	6-2	210	9-27-01	0	1	7.71	1	1	0	2	6	2	2	0	1	0	.545	.583	.636	0.00	8.33	12
Brooks, Jake	R-R	6-4	202	7-8-01	9	3	2.28	22	20	1	115	94	36	29	7	23	85	.220	.266	.329	18.40	4.98	462
Campbell, Paul	L-R	6-0	215	7-26-95	0	0	7.36	1	1	0	4	4	3	3	2	0	3	.267	.313	.667	18.75	0.00	16
Castillo, Walin	R-R	6-3	175	1-2-05	2	3	4.94	12	11	0	51	51	34	28	3	21	30	.259	.332	.391	13.57	9.50	221
Centala, Chase	R-R	6-1	175	3-18-02	0	1	3.72	6	0	0	10	8	7	4	1	4	6	.242	.316	.394	15.38	10.26	39
De La Cruz, Juan	R-R	6-3	180	3-4-05	0	1	5.63	6	4	0	16	13	11	10	2	13	14	.213	.380	.311	17.72	16.46	79
Dilone, Julio	L-R	6-1	196	3-23-00	0	0	22.09	5	0	0	4	4	13	9	0	12	6	.250	.594	.313	18.75	37.50	32
Dishmey, Eliazar	R-R	6-1	175	10-25-04	4	6	5.63	16	15	0	64	61	44	40	6	26	66	.244	.325	.396	23.57	9.29	280
Ekness, Josh	R-R	6-4	225	2-7-02	1	0	0.69	10	0	4	13	5	1	1	0	3	21	.114	.220	.159	42.00	6.00	50
Encarnacion, Breidy	R-R	6-3	185	11-9-00	0	0	0.00	3	0	0	3	1	0	0	0	3	3	.100	.308	.100	23.08	23.08	13
Evans, Justin	R-R	6-0	185	9-9-96	0	0	2.51	12	0	1	14	9	5	4	0	13	14	.184	.365	.245	22.22	20.63	63
Faherty, Jake	R-R	6-3	190	6-11-03	1	0	8.64	8	0	1	8	10	9	8	0	10	14	.294	.447	.353	29.79	21.28	47
Fernandez, Jose	R-R	6-1	155	10-16-03	0	0	5.59	8	0	0	10	8	6	6	1	11	6	.229	.413	.343	13.04	23.91	46
Garrett, Braxton	R-L	6-2	202	8-5-97	0	0	0.00	1	1	0	3	2	0	0	0	2	5	.200	.333	.200	41.67	16.67	12
Hoeing, Bryan	R-R	6-6	210	10-19-96	0	0	0.00	1	0	0	2	1	0	0	0	0	2	.143	.143	.143	28.57	0.00	7
Jimenez, Yeuris	R-R	6-3	218	3-23-01	0	2	3.97	10	0	3	11	9	6	5	0	4	8	.209	.320	.279	15.69	7.84	51
Johnson, M.D.	R-R	6-5	200	7-7-97	0	0	2.57	2	2	0	7	7	3	2	0	2	6	.269	.345	.346	20.69	6.90	29
Jones, Holt	R-R	6-8	235	5-8-99	3	3	3.25	21	0	4	28	26	15	10	1	12	37	.245	.336	.330	30.08	9.76	123
Lashutka, Luke	R-R	6-2	195	5-24-02	0	0	4.50	1	0	0	2	2	1	1	0	1	3	.250	.333	.250	33.33	11.11	9
Lawrence, Colson	R-R	6-5	210	3-3-02	0	1	18.00	4	0	0	4	8	8	8	0	4	3	.421	.522	.632	13.04	17.39	23
Lowe, Collin	R-R	6-4	210	9-11-98	8	3	3.50	26	3	1	75	70	32	29	3	10	62	.241	.274	.324	20.39	3.29	304
Luzardo, Jesus	L-L	6-0	218	9-30-97	1	0	0.00	1	1	0	6	1	0	0	0	1	6	.059	.111	.118	33.33	5.56	18
Maldonado, Nick	R-R	6-1	207	6-12-00	0	0	1.13	3	0	0	8	5	2	1	0	0	7	.172	.200	.207	23.33	0.00	30
Martinez, Liomar	R-R	6-2	165	6-25-05	0	2	6.88	6	5	0	17	17	16	13	3	19	14	.266	.443	.469	15.91	21.59	88
Meachem, Xavier	R-R	5-11	210	9-6-02	0	1	3.09	9	1	1	12	8	7	4	0	7	16	.178	.288	.267	30.77	13.46	52
Medina, Manuel	L-L	5-10	140	3-25-02	0	0	4.50	3	0	0	4	4	3	2	0	0	5	.235	.278	.294	26.32	0.00	19
Mendez, Julio	L-L	5-11	180	1-7-05	4	5	3.86	17	9	0	63	64	36	27	6	33	54	.258	.349	.403	18.95	11.58	285
Meyer, Noble	R-R	6-5	185	1-10-05	2	2	2.65	8	8	0	34	17	12	10	2	23	43	.149	.305	.246	30.50	16.31	141
Mokma, Chris	R-R	6-4	210	2-11-01	2	0	3.07	13	0	0	15	15	7	5	2	9	11	.259	.358	.431	16.42	13.43	67
Montero, Euri	R-R	6-4	170	3-28-02	0	0	6.26	21	0	1	27	30	23	19	2	18	12	.286	.415	.400	9.23	13.85	130
Monteverde, Patrick	R-L	6-2	200	9-24-97	0	0	6.35	2	2	0	6	4	4	4	3	5	6	.200	.360	.650	24.00	20.00	25
Murphy, Patrick	L-L	6-1	205	3-7-97	2	0	2.57	10	1	0	14	10	5	4	0	6	19	.196	.293	.275	32.76	10.34	58
Olson, Emmett	L-L	6-4	230	5-15-02	1	0	0.00	3	3	0	16	8	0	0	0	4	19	.145	.203	.164	32.20	6.78	59
Puk, A.J.	L-L	6-7	248	4-25-95	0	0	10.80	2	0	0	2	3	2	2	0	0	2	.375	.444	.375	22.22	0.00	9
Reynoso, Juan	R-R	6-0	165	4-4-04	3	3	4.29	37	0	2	63	55	35	30	3	48	65	.235	.379	.325	22.18	16.38	293
Sellinger, Jack	R-L	6-2	200	11-20-99	1	4	2.91	25	0	3	34	24	14	11	1	13	52	.198	.308	.248	35.62	8.90	146
Serrano, Jhoniel	R-R	6-2	178	10-17-03	0	0	46.29	3	1	0	2	6	12	12	0	10	3	.545	.750	.545	12.50	41.67	24
Simpson, Josh	L-L	6-2	190	8-19-97	0	0	0.00	3	0	0	3	1	0	0	0	3	4	.125	.364	.125	36.36	27.27	11
Stevens, Tristan	R-R	6-2	200	12-8-97	5	3	3.30	12	6	0	46	41	22	17	2	14	39	.233	.289	.318	20.53	7.37	190
Storm, Justin	L-L	6-7	232	9-12-01	4	2	1.41	20	0	2	32	18	8	5	1	19	43	.162	.290	.225	32.82	14.50	131
Tineo, Riskiel	R-R	6-3	190	2-27-03	0	1	6.10	15	0	2	21	27	15	14	3	13	18	.310	.396	.506	17.82	12.87	101
Vizcaino, Luis	R-R	6-4	199	7-9-01	0	1	6.39	8	0	0	13	13	10	9	2	12	15	.260	.406	.520	23.44	18.75	64
Weathers, Ryan	R-L	6-1	230	12-17-99	0	0	0.00	1	1	0	3	2	0	0	0	0	3	.222	.222	.222	33.33	0.00	9
White, Brandon	R-R	6-8	230	11-26-99	6	5	4.98	19	15	0	81	85	49	45	6	23	72	.266	.320	.392	20.40	6.52	353

Pitching	B-T	Ht.	Wt.	DOB	W	L	ERA	G	GS	SV	IP	Hits	Runs	ER	HR	BB	SO	AVG	OBP	SLG	SO%	BB%	BF
White, Thomas	L-L	6-5	210	9-29-04	1	1	3.18	8	8	0	34	37	15	12	0	17	44	.274	.376	.319	28.03	10.83	157
Wurster, Caleb	L-L	5-11	182	9-21-98	0	0	7.71	6	0	0	5	6	4	4	0	4	3	.316	.458	.474	12.50	16.67	24

Fielding

Catcher	PCT	G	PO	A	E	DP	PB
Bramwell	.994	19	156	13	1	0	2
Caskenette	.993	17	126	10	1	3	1
Forrester	1.000	2	16	0	0	0	1
Ignoffo	.993	59	515	38	4	3	15
Lane	.967	11	79	9	3	0	6
Ortega	.989	10	81	8	1	0	2
Praytor	.994	15	148	9	1	2	1

First Base	PCT	G	PO	A	E	DP
DiSpigna	1.000	24	180	14	0	12
Forrester	.969	15	123	4	4	7
Martinez	1.000	20	163	12	0	16
Rataczak	.977	5	38	5	1	3
Snyder	.988	11	76	7	1	7
Vradenburg	.975	55	400	24	11	33

Second Base	PCT	G	PO	A	E	DP
Cappe	.955	4	6	15	1	4
Devers	1.000	1	4	1	0	0
Green	.979	11	14	33	1	4
Hernandez	.889	4	6	10	2	1
Mabry	.979	10	19	27	1	6
McCants	.964	98	162	212	14	46
Miller	.938	4	7	8	1	1
Olmstead	.000	1	0	0	0	0
Sanchez	1.000	1	1	1	0	0

Third Base	PCT	G	PO	A	E	DP
Bullard	.939	21	19	43	4	8
Cappe	1.000	2	1	3	0	0
Clayton	1.000	1	2	7	0	0
Devers	1.000	1	0	1	0	0
Forrester	.933	5	1	13	1	1
Green	.800	4	4	4	2	0
Hernandez	.875	7	2	5	1	0
Lane	1.000	2	1	0	0	0
Mabry	.913	52	47	89	13	7
Miller	1.000	2	1	3	0	0
Olmstead	1.000	1	0	4	0	0
Rodriguez	.949	20	16	40	3	7
Sanchez	1.000	10	9	10	0	0
Snyder	1.000	6	4	9	0	0

Shortstop	PCT	G	PO	A	E	DP
Clayton	.867	2	5	8	2	2
Devers	1.000	2	3	4	0	0
Green	1.000	1	1	2	0	0
Hernandez	.935	63	63	154	15	24
Johnson	.917	24	38	62	9	13
Olmstead	.933	4	8	6	1	1
Rodriguez	.879	17	17	34	7	4
Sanchez	1.000	19	22	45	0	8

Outfield	PCT	G	PO	A	E	DP
Alderman	.909	29	48	2	5	1
Allen	1.000	5	9	0	0	0
Bradshaw	1.000	10	18	0	0	0
Coley	1.000	7	12	0	0	0
Cruz	.935	75	122	7	9	2
DeLeo	.974	32	71	3	2	0
DiSpigna	.960	27	47	1	2	0
Head	1.000	2	7	1	0	1
Hidalgo	.962	18	24	1	1	0
Infante	1.000	3	2	0	0	0
Jenkins-Cowart	1.000	27	61	3	0	1
Mabry	1.000	2	1	0	0	0
Martinez	.949	37	52	4	3	0
McDowell	1.000	3	9	1	0	0
Mesa	1.000	3	3	0	0	0
Morlando	.000	1	0	0	0	0
Rataczak	1.000	13	27	1	0	0
Roberts	.857	3	6	0	1	0
Sasaki	1.000	4	10	0	0	0
Shade	.985	77	193	5	3	0
Trimble	1.000	30	64	0	0	0

FCL MARLINS — *ROOKIE*

FLORIDA COMPLEX LEAGUE

Batting	B-T	Ht.	Wt.	DOB	AVG	OBP	SLG	G	PA	AB	R	H	2B	3B	HR	RBI	BB	HBP	SH	SF	SO	SB	CS	BB%	SO%
Alderman, Kemp	R-R	6-3	265	8-20-02	.133	.316	.200	5	19	15	2	2	1	0	0	2	4	0	0	0	5	1	0	21.05	26.32
Altamirano, Greyber	L-R	6-2	145	10-15-04	.118	.226	.204	36	106	93	9	11	2	3	0	15	11	2	0	0	27	2	0	10.38	25.47
Batista, Remington	B-R	5-10	175	1-28-05	.182	.229	.303	20	35	33	9	6	1	0	1	3	2	0	0	0	6	3	0	5.71	17.14
Bradshaw, Davis	L-R	6-2	175	4-25-98	.286	.375	.429	4	16	14	3	4	0	1	0	3	2	0	0	0	2	1	0	12.50	12.50
Chirinos, Nixon	R-R	6-0	190	10-25-05	.143	.308	.143	11	26	21	2	3	0	0	0	1	5	0	0	0	10	0	0	19.23	38.46
Colina, Oscar	R-R	6-0	150	1-28-04	.143	.400	.143	5	11	7	1	1	0	0	0	0	2	1	0	0	2	0	0	18.18	18.18
Devers, Jose	L-R	6-0	174	12-7-99	.176	.250	.176	6	20	17	1	3	0	0	0	2	1	1	0	1	7	1	0	5.00	35.00
Gerardo, Jose	R-R	6-0	179	6-12-05	.165	.278	.284	34	126	109	19	18	10	0	1	12	13	4	0	0	60	21	3	10.32	47.62
Gonzalez, Danny	R-R	6-0	160	11-26-04	.223	.336	.384	35	131	112	23	25	6	0	4	19	14	5	0	0	41	11	3	10.69	31.30
Head, Dillon	L-L	5-11	180	10-11-04	.167	.286	.667	2	7	6	1	1	0	0	1	1	1	0	0	0	2	0	0	14.29	28.57
Henriquez, Julio	R-R	5-11	190	11-4-04	.301	.437	.431	48	190	153	33	46	9	1	3	32	28	9	0	0	29	28	8	14.74	15.26
Infante, Diego	R-R	6-2	178	10-22-99	.400	.438	.533	4	16	15	2	6	2	0	0	3	1	0	0	0	3	0	0	6.25	18.75
Lopez, Fabian	B-R	6-0	165	9-18-05	.204	.266	.306	50	214	196	32	40	8	3	2	19	16	1	0	1	56	20	3	7.48	26.17
Monserrate, Jose	R-R	6-0	176	9-20-04	.368	.481	.437	38	106	87	16	32	4	1	0	8	17	2	0	0	20	18	5	16.04	10.07
Mota, Gregory	R-R	6-3	172	12-20-04	.158	.200	.158	10	20	19	3	3	0	0	0	1	0	1	0	0	12	1	0	0.00	60.00
Neymour, Cherif	B-R	5-11	150	3-4-05	.284	.339	.382	32	113	102	24	29	4	3	0	12	8	1	0	1	29	20	5	7.08	25.66
Ortega, Victor	R-R	6-1	200	1-19-04	.284	.417	.349	37	141	109	12	31	7	0	0	24	27	0	2	3	16	4	0	19.15	11.35
Peguero, Antony	R-R	6-0	175	6-14-05	.161	.270	.290	11	37	31	9	5	1	0	1	8	5	0	0	1	8	2	0	13.51	21.62
Rios, Nestor	R-R	5-9	175	1-4-05	.000	.214	.000	8	14	11	1	0	0	0	0	0	2	1	0	0	5	0	0	14.29	35.71
Roberts, Brett	R-R	6-0	182	3-12-01	.214	.267	.214	4	15	14	3	3	0	0	0	0	1	0	0	0	4	2	0	6.67	26.67
Sanchez, Carlos	B-R	5-9	175	9-20-04	.193	.315	.284	35	130	109	16	21	7	0	1	16	15	5	0	1	30	1	0	11.54	23.08
Sanchez, Junior	L-R	5-10	177	12-18-02	.276	.364	.345	19	66	58	10	16	4	0	0	8	6	2	0	0	11	9	1	9.09	16.67
Sasaki, Shane	R-R	5-11	165	7-1-00	.400	.625	.500	4	16	10	2	4	1	0	0	1	6	0	0	0	5	2	0	37.50	31.25
Simmons, Toby	B-L	5-10	175	12-2-04	.233	.377	.326	19	53	43	9	10	2	1	0	6	10	0	0	0	19	14	2	18.87	35.85
Solano, Yoffry	B-R	5-10	155	11-4-04	.268	.327	.376	40	165	149	22	40	10	3	0	19	12	2	0	2	17	12	4	7.27	10.30
Valor, Andres	R-R	6-3	180	11-8-05	.289	.374	.421	54	227	197	42	57	10	5	2	28	20	8	0	2	57	35	4	8.81	25.11

Pitching	B-T	Ht.	Wt.	DOB	W	L	ERA	G	GS	SV	IP	Hits	Runs	ER	HR	BB	SO	AVG	OBP	SLG	SO%	BB%	BF
Alegre, Delvis	R-R	6-2	180	2-2-01	0	0	0.00	1	0	0	1	0	0	0	0	0	1	.000	.000	.000	33.33	0.00	3
Arias, Josue	L-L	6-2	165	5-5-05	0	5	8.92	12	10	1	36	29	36	36	3	42	38	.221	.449	.321	20.32	22.46	187
Benitez, Keyner	L-L	6-1	165	5-23-06	0	0	0.75	3	2	1	12	7	1	1	0	2	19	.175	.227	.200	43.18	4.55	44
Bergin, Jesse	R-R	6-4	205	10-8-99	0	1	5.79	7	0	0	9	10	7	6	1	1	16	.270	.289	.432	42.11	2.63	38
Cabral, Jhon	R-R	6-1	172	8-9-05	3	0	4.40	11	0	0	14	10	8	7	1	15	21	.196	.386	.294	30.00	21.43	70
Carpio, Samuel	R-R	6-2	200	5-6-03	3	0	2.49	16	0	0	22	16	9	6	1	11	28	.211	.333	.329	31.11	12.22	90
Castillo, Walin	R-R	6-3	175	1-2-05	2	0	0.39	6	3	0	23	9	6	1	0	3	23	.111	.153	.136	27.06	3.53	85
Cesar, Luis	L-L	6-3	183	2-24-04	5	1	2.30	12	10	0	47	24	19	12	4	31	38	.150	.303	.275	19.39	15.82	196
De La Cruz, Juan	R-R	6-3	180	3-4-05	5	0	1.57	11	11	0	46	24	10	8	1	21	44	.154	.286	.205	23.78	11.35	185
De La Cruz, Rodolfo	R-R	6-2	193	2-19-04	1	0	3.60	4	0	0	5	2	2	2	1	6	3	.133	.364	.333	13.64	27.27	22
Dishmey, Eliazar	R-R	6-1	175	10-25-04	0	0	0.00	1	1	0	4	0	0	0	0	1	8	.000	.000	.000	57.14	7.14	14
Fernandez, Jose	R-R	6-1	155	10-16-03	1	0	1.74	16	0	6	21	17	4	4	0	7	25	.224	.306	.289	29.07	8.14	86
Garcia, Hamlet	R-R	6-2	175	11-23-05	3	1	1.95	8	6	0	32	19	8	7	2	17	26	.174	.287	.257	20.16	13.18	129

Garrett, Braxton	R-L	6-2	202	8-5-97	1	0	0.00	1	1	0	6	1	0	0	0	1	13	.056	.105	.056	68.42	5.26	19
Lawrence, Colson	R-R	6-5	210	3-3-02	2	1	3.76	18	0	0	26	22	14	11	2	14	35	.222	.336	.343	30.17	12.07	116
Maldonado, Nick	R-R	6-1	207	6-12-00	0	0	0.00	2	0	0	3	2	0	0	0	0	2	.222	.222	.333	22.22	0.00	9
Martinez, Liomar	R-R	6-2	165	6-25-05	1	2	3.89	11	10	0	35	21	18	15	4	20	38	.171	.293	.293	25.85	13.61	147
Medina, Manuel	L-L	5-10	140	3-25-02	3	0	0.89	18	0	5	20	9	5	2	0	5	36	.132	.211	.162	46.15	6.41	78
Mendez, Julio	L-L	5-11	180	1-7-05	0	0	0.00	1	0	1	2	2	0	0	0	1	3	.286	.375	.286	37.50	12.50	8
Perez, Michael	R-R	6-3	160	9-5-02	1	1	3.80	16	1	0	21	18	9	9	2	12	25	.228	.344	.329	26.88	12.90	93
Polanco, Natanael	R-R	6-1	170	4-24-03	3	0	1.35	17	0	1	20	7	6	3	1	12	16	.100	.241	.171	19.28	14.46	83
Puk, A.J.	L-L	6-7	248	4-25-95	0	0	0.00	1	0	0	1	0	0	0	0	0	2	.000	.000	.000	66.67	0.00	3
Ramirez, Luis	R-R	6-3	175	2-19-02	2	1	4.02	14	0	0	16	16	9	7	0	11	16	.262	.408	.377	21.05	14.47	76
Rodriguez, Darwin	R-R	6-1	180	11-10-04	0	1	12.38	8	0	0	8	16	13	11	2	8	10	.381	.480	.548	20.00	16.00	50
Serrano, Jhoniel	R-R	6-2	178	10-17-03	0	1	6.10	7	0	0	10	11	8	7	1	11	16	.268	.455	.366	29.09	20.00	55
Tineo, Riskiel	R-R	6-3	190	2-27-03	2	0	0.63	8	0	0	14	8	1	1	0	2	10	.174	.204	.217	20.41	4.08	49
Vizcaino, Luis	R-R	6-4	199	7-9-01	1	0	0.00	7	0	4	8	6	0	0	0	0	16	.194	.194	.194	51.61	0.00	31

Fielding

C: Sanchez 26, Ortega 24, Chirinos 6, Rios 5. **1B:** Henriquez 44, Gonzalez 14, Rios 2. **2B:** Solano 38, Neymour 10, Altamirano 8, Devers 2, Sanchez 1. **3B:** Neymour 19, Sanchez 18, Altamirano 18, Mota 3, Rios 1, Henriquez 1. **SS:** Lopez 46, Altamirano 10, Devers 3, Neymour 1. **LF:** Monserrate 26, Gonzalez 10, Peguero 9, Batista 4, Bradshaw 3, Roberts 3, Sasaki 3, Simmons 3, Colina 2, Gerardo 1, Infante 1, Mota 1, Alderman 1. **CF:** Valor 47, Simmons 4, Gerardo 3, Head 2, Peguero 2, Roberts 1, Colina 1. **RF:** Gerardo 31, Batista 11, Simmons 9, Gonzalez 8, Alderman 3, Infante 2, Monserrate 2, Colina 2, Valor 1.

DSL MARLINS — *ROOKIE*

DOMINICAN SUMMER LEAGUE

Batting	B-T	Ht.	Wt.	DOB	AVG	OBP	SLG	G	PA	AB	R	H	2B	3B	HR	RBI	BB	HBP	SH	SF	SO	SB	CS	BB%	SO%
Abreu, Jesus	R-R	6-1	190	9-15-05	.173	.337	.222	27	104	81	9	14	4	0	0	7	15	6	0	2	34	0	0	14.42	32.69
Almonte, Jeremy	R-R	6-0	170	10-12-05	.336	.440	.436	34	134	110	24	37	6	1	1	21	13	9	0	2	14	1	0	9.70	10.45
Almonte, Khris	R-R	6-1	160	9-6-05	.129	.206	.129	9	34	31	3	4	0	0	0	1	2	1	0	0	11	5	0	5.88	32.35
Bello, Adrian	B-R	5-11	165	5-19-06	.182	.231	.182	3	13	11	0	2	0	0	0	1	1	0	0	1	4	0	0	7.69	30.77
Castillo, Rafael	B-R	5-11	160	4-7-06	.217	.404	.264	37	141	106	18	23	3	1	0	10	31	3	0	1	42	9	2	21.99	29.79
Cova, Luis	R-R	6-1	160	2-1-07	.233	.425	.333	10	40	30	8	7	0	0	1	4	8	2	0	0	3	8	4	20.00	7.50
Cueto, Derek	R-R	5-10	167	10-26-05	.164	.329	.282	40	140	110	24	18	8	1	1	14	26	2	0	2	42	20	3	18.57	30.00
Encarnacion, Diwarys	R-R	6-2	170	10-16-05	.227	.317	.301	52	202	176	25	40	10	0	1	25	19	5	0	2	34	3	3	9.41	16.83
Felicia, Jayden	B-R	6-0	150	3-14-06	.185	.254	.231	20	71	65	7	12	3	0	0	8	6	0	0	0	13	5	0	8.45	18.31
Gaitor, Daniel	B-R	5-10	170	11-22-05	.191	.321	.292	30	106	89	15	17	2	2	1	12	13	4	0	0	35	15	3	12.26	33.02
Ibarra, Adrian	R-R	6-2	175	4-8-06	.170	.270	.227	30	100	88	16	15	2	0	1	10	9	3	0	0	26	1	2	9.00	26.00
Miller, Janero	B-L	6-2	195	1-10-06	.218	.349	.352	44	172	142	28	31	10	3	1	23	22	7	0	1	67	12	4	12.79	38.95
Mosquera, Deivis	R-R	6-2	178	11-5-04	.262	.405	.349	41	158	126	18	33	7	2	0	21	20	11	0	1	28	7	5	12.66	17.72
Perez, Robert	R-R	6-2	165	4-27-04	.239	.357	.402	35	140	117	22	28	8	1	3	18	17	5	0	1	39	13	4	12.14	27.86
Rivera, Jose	B-R	6-0	145	11-17-04	.276	.432	.310	10	37	29	5	8	1	0	0	4	8	0	0	0	11	10	1	21.62	29.73
Robledo, Kevin	R-R	5-11	176	9-15-06	.221	.420	.441	47	205	145	32	32	11	0	7	29	48	6	0	6	48	3	1	23.41	23.41
Tailor, Joseph	L-R	5-11	175	6-14-06	.280	.419	.531	49	217	175	50	49	9	7	7	19	19	23	0	0	52	13	6	8.76	23.96
Tolentino, Almen	L-R	6-1	160	1-12-07	.105	.333	.158	15	51	38	7	4	2	0	0	2	13	0	0	0	14	12	2	25.49	27.45

Pitching	B-T	Ht.	Wt.	DOB	W	L	ERA	G	GS	SV	IP	Hits	Runs	ER	HR	BB	SO	AVG	OBP	SLG	SO%	BB%	BF
Aponte, Oswaldo	R-R	6-2	185	5-2-06	0	3	5.71	11	10	0	35	26	25	22	2	24	34	.215	.353	.273	22.67	16.00	150
De La Cruz, Alejandro	R-R	6-0	190	2-5-07	2	0	4.32	11	0	0	25	17	17	12	1	33	26	.198	.448	.291	20.63	26.19	126
De La Cruz, Luis	R-R	6-0	182	8-4-02	0	0	0.00	2	0	0	4	4	0	0	0	1	7	.267	.313	.400	43.75	6.25	16
Espinoza, Eiver	R-R	6-6	168	1-11-04	2	0	0.34	11	2	0	26	7	1	1	0	7	33	.083	.181	.107	35.11	7.45	94
Espinoza, Luis	R-R	5-11	150	3-23-05	3	0	2.19	10	1	0	25	15	7	6	2	12	31	.181	.292	.301	32.29	12.50	96
Francisco, Estarlin	R-R	6-3	155	10-15-06	1	2	3.83	12	12	0	40	34	22	17	1	26	28	.236	.371	.313	15.56	14.44	180
Gutierrez, Eric	L-L	6-5	170	11-23-05	0	4	4.60	10	10	0	29	25	19	15	1	21	43	.231	.364	.306	32.58	15.91	132
Henriquez, Wilfredo	R-R	6-2	180	2-11-03	4	2	1.71	10	0	0	26	25	17	5	0	10	25	.245	.336	.353	21.55	8.62	116
Hernandez, Abraham	L-L	6-2	170	3-22-07	0	1	5.89	7	7	0	18	15	12	12	1	19	18	.227	.407	.348	20.93	22.09	86
Hernandez, Angel	R-R	6-2	194	1-24-04	1	2	7.80	9	0	1	15	14	13	13	1	10	20	.250	.353	.446	29.41	14.71	68
Jimenez, Elvin	R-R	6-2	210	3-19-05	2	2	1.76	9	0	0	15	8	6	3	1	12	22	.160	.354	.240	33.85	18.46	65
Mendez, Gerinton	R-R	6-0	180	9-4-06	1	1	5.06	9	0	0	16	12	12	9	2	19	21	.218	.442	.418	27.27	24.68	77
Ochoa, Carlos	R-R	6-2	185	9-23-06	5	0	4.15	10	2	0	30	19	16	14	0	22	39	.183	.341	.260	30.23	17.05	129
Ortega, Juan	R-R	6-2	170	6-3-05	0	0	10.80	7	0	0	7	6	9	8	1	9	7	.231	.500	.423	17.50	22.50	40
Paulino, Jose	R-R	6-3	175	10-15-06	0	1	3.86	7	7	0	21	9	12	9	0	13	23	.129	.282	.200	27.06	15.29	85
Reyes, Bryan	R-R	6-0	150	10-11-05	0	2	4.76	11	0	0	11	13	6	6	0	6	10	.289	.389	.356	18.52	11.11	54
Rodriguez, Victor	R-R	6-1	185	10-24-06	1	0	6.00	7	0	1	9	7	6	6	0	10	5	.212	.422	.242	11.11	22.22	45
Romero, Luifer	L-L	6-2	160	12-9-04	0	0	0.00	1	1	0	4	3	2	0	0	1	4	.188	.235	.188	23.53	5.88	17
Rosario, Angel	L-L	6-3	190	3-21-03	2	0	4.02	10	0	2	16	8	7	7	0	12	20	.151	.319	.189	28.99	17.39	69
Rosario, Jonathan	L-L	6-2	165	1-3-07	0	1	54.00	9	0	0	4	17	28	26	0	21	2	.567	.750	.600	3.85	40.38	52
Salas, Braulio	R-R	6-2	175	11-5-04	3	0	3.06	10	4	0	32	26	13	11	0	9	35	.226	.282	.322	26.72	6.87	131
Serrata, Elian	R-R	6-0	160	1-27-02	5	1	2.05	14	0	6	22	18	7	5	0	19	31	.214	.389	.250	28.70	17.59	108
Torrealba, Jonfreider	R-R	6-0	175	5-15-07	1	0	4.70	3	0	0	8	3	5	4	1	8	4	.115	.314	.308	11.43	22.86	35
Villegas, Mado	R-R	5-11	165	7-6-03	0	1	3.71	11	0	1	17	23	14	7	3	3	16	.315	.342	.452	20.78	3.90	77

Fielding

C: Almonte 26, Abreu 19, Robledo 10, Tolentino 6, Bello 1. **1B:** Robledo 26, Ibarra 21, Cueto 10, Abreu 5, Bello 1. **2B:** Tailor 31, Castillo 17, Rivera 7, Felicia 4, Gaitor 1. **3B:** Tailor 15, Cueto 13, Felicia 11, Encarnacion 9, Robledo 8, Ibarra 6, Castillo 3. **SS:** Encarnacion 34, Castillo 18, Felicia 3, Rivera 3. **LF:** Mosquera

29, Perez 11, Cueto 11, Almonte 6, Encarnacion 2, Cova 1. **CF:** Miller 38, Perez 9, Encarnacion 5, Almonte 3, Cova 3, Gaitor 2, Mosquera 1. **RF:** Gaitor 25, Perez 16, Mosquera 10, Cova 5, Cueto 2, Encarnacion 1, Almonte 1.

DSL MIAMI — *ROOKIE*

DOMINICAN SUMMER LEAGUE

Batting	B-T	Ht.	Wt.	DOB	AVG	OBP	SLG	G	PA	AB	R	H	2B	3B	HR	RBI	BB	HBP	SH	SF	SO	SB	CS	BB%	SO%
Almonte, Khris	R-R	6-1	160	9-6-05	.175	.243	.270	22	70	63	7	11	3	0	1	10	2	4	0	1	18	6	1	2.86	25.71
Arias, Gregori	B-R	6-0	160	10-19-06	.227	.414	.343	53	229	172	39	39	8	3	2	16	47	8	2	0	69	23	7	20.52	30.13
Bello, Adrian	B-R	5-11	165	5-19-06	.181	.296	.224	35	135	116	15	21	5	0	0	6	17	2	0	0	49	5	2	12.59	36.30
Bonifacio, Lisandro	B-R	6-0	155	8-12-05	.250	.346	.321	45	180	156	22	39	9	1	0	14	22	1	1	0	36	11	7	12.22	20.00
Castro, Jose	R-R	6-3	180	10-31-06	.148	.333	.254	52	219	169	34	25	3	0	5	22	44	4	0	2	73	8	6	20.09	33.33
Cova, Luis	R-R	6-1	160	2-1-07	.240	.365	.351	45	189	154	36	37	9	1	2	22	27	5	0	3	20	28	4	14.29	10.58
De La Cruz, Jancory	L-L	6-2	180	2-17-06	.205	.357	.336	43	182	146	24	30	6	2	3	22	30	5	0	1	49	11	4	16.48	26.92
Dean, Breyias	R-R	6-2	175	9-1-05	.258	.414	.348	43	170	132	21	34	6	0	2	22	24	12	0	1	49	9	1	14.12	28.82
Felicia, Jayden	B-R	6-0	150	3-14-06	.176	.462	.176	7	26	17	2	3	0	0	0	0	7	2	0	0	5	3	1	26.92	19.23
Gaitor, Daniel	B-R	5-10	170	11-22-05	.258	.378	.419	9	38	31	5	8	3	1	0	3	4	2	1	0	7	2	1	10.53	18.42
Made, Jose	R-R	6-2	175	4-19-06	.106	.213	.167	24	76	66	4	7	1	0	1	2	8	1	1	0	43	2	1	10.53	56.58
Martinez, Yordani	R-R	5-7	170	1-15-07	.169	.325	.266	36	155	124	15	21	4	4	0	13	20	9	1	1	28	21	2	12.90	18.06
Novoa, Kevin	R-R	5-11	175	8-27-04	.250	.425	.310	35	134	100	12	25	6	0	0	18	24	8	0	2	22	6	2	17.91	16.42
Perez, Robert	R-R	6-2	165	4-27-04	.333	.478	.389	6	23	18	2	6	1	0	0	2	3	2	0	0	4	2	3	13.04	17.39
Requena, Alexander	R-R	6-0	175	10-5-05	.272	.369	.340	35	130	103	18	28	5	1	0	13	16	4	0	7	28	0	0	12.31	21.54
Rivera, Jose	B-R	6-0	145	11-17-04	.284	.383	.343	35	120	102	23	29	4	1	0	8	16	1	0	1	32	18	4	13.33	26.67
Tolentino, Almen	L-R	6-1	160	1-12-07	.000	.333	.000	5	18	12	1	0	0	0	0	1	6	0	0	0	7	1	0	33.33	38.89

Pitching	B-T	Ht.	Wt.	DOB	W	L	ERA	G	GS	SV	IP	Hits	Runs	ER	HR	BB	SO	AVG	OBP	SLG	SO%	BB%	BF
Cuevas, Melvin	R-R	6-1	160	10-1-04	3	2	3.22	20	0	7	22	10	10	8	1	21	37	.133	.340	.213	37.00	21.00	100
De La Cruz, Luis	R-R	6-0	182	8-4-02	1	2	5.06	15	0	2	21	17	14	12	0	16	31	.221	.365	.299	31.63	16.33	98
Encarnacion, Kifraidy	L-L	6-4	187	10-26-05	0	0	2.35	2	2	0	8	2	2	2	0	5	10	.080	.258	.080	32.26	16.13	31
Fuente, Johandry	R-R	6-0	185	12-29-02	1	1	9.69	14	0	0	13	7	15	14	0	29	23	.156	.506	.244	29.87	37.66	77
Genao, Manuel	R-R	6-1	150	11-11-05	0	1	4.66	11	11	0	29	28	17	15	1	9	34	.241	.305	.319	26.36	6.98	129
Hernandez, Jeckferxon	R-R	6-3	185	9-18-02	1	2	3.38	19	0	0	19	15	8	7	0	17	27	.211	.378	.225	30.00	18.89	90
Medina, Ian	L-L	6-0	195	7-7-04	5	2	2.54	12	1	0	28	27	13	8	1	18	34	.262	.371	.359	27.42	14.52	124
Mejia, Jeyson	R-R	6-1	170	12-22-05	0	0	11.81	14	0	0	16	29	24	21	1	12	18	.387	.484	.520	19.78	13.19	91
Melo, Bayant	R-R	6-3	165	12-31-04	0	6	8.00	12	12	0	36	36	39	32	1	44	44	.255	.450	.326	23.04	23.04	191
Moreta, Franklyn	R-R	6-0	160	1-11-04	2	1	6.92	20	0	0	26	30	21	20	1	12	31	.280	.379	.393	25.00	9.68	124
Nakamura, Raisei	L-R	6-3	172	5-6-03	1	1	14.21	11	0	1	13	18	21	20	1	14	9	.360	.547	.520	12.00	18.67	75
Ortega, Juan	R-R	6-2	170	6-3-05	0	0	0.00	2	0	0	2	2	2	0	0	2	1	.250	.364	.250	9.09	18.18	11
Ortiz, Albert	R-R	5-11	146	8-7-06	0	2	9.00	8	1	0	15	14	20	15	1	15	20	.237	.438	.305	25.00	18.75	80
Palacios, Johan	R-R	6-9	175	12-26-04	1	0	4.26	16	0	1	19	9	11	9	2	18	21	.141	.345	.281	23.86	20.45	88
Polanco, Albert	R-R	6-2	174	6-30-05	1	1	2.68	11	10	0	40	26	21	12	1	29	45	.186	.335	.264	25.57	16.48	176
Puente, Robert	L-L	5-9	141	2-5-07	0	0	0.00	3	0	0	2	0	0	0	0	0	2	.000	.167	.000	33.33	0.00	6
Rodriguez, Darwin	R-R	6-1	180	11-10-04	0	0	0.00	4	0	4	4	5	1	0	0	2	6	.294	.368	.294	31.58	10.53	19
Rodriguez, Maikel	R-R	6-1	180	8-25-06	3	1	4.08	11	8	0	40	36	20	18	3	17	31	.242	.327	.369	18.45	10.12	168
Romero, Luifer	L-L	6-2	160	12-9-04	1	0	2.76	12	7	0	29	27	11	9	0	13	35	.237	.315	.307	27.56	10.24	127
Rueda, Cristian	R-R	6-1	180	1-5-05	1	2	8.00	3	1	0	9	10	8	8	2	5	10	.270	.349	.486	23.26	11.63	43
Santana, Yohanfer	R-R	6-7	200	10-13-05	0	0	9.00	3	3	0	7	5	7	7	2	4	12	.200	.355	.480	38.71	12.90	31
Smith, Brandon	R-R	6-0	165	11-9-05	1	0	5.89	18	0	0	18	14	13	12	1	13	13	.209	.341	.343	15.85	15.85	82
Suriel, Fraylin	R-R	6-1	170	5-21-04	2	2	2.95	19	0	0	18	8	11	6	2	18	22	.136	.373	.271	26.51	21.69	83
Takahashi, Hiroshi	R-R	6-1	170	6-15-06	0	0	10.80	3	0	0	3	3	4	4	0	5	3	.250	.471	.250	17.65	29.41	17
Torrealba, Jonfreider	R-R	6-0	175	5-15-07	1	2	10.00	6	0	0	9	10	10	10	3	13	7	.333	.583	.733	14.58	27.08	48
Uzcategui, Jonas	L-L	6-0	155	10-30-04	1	2	5.49	18	0	0	20	10	13	12	1	16	30	.159	.384	.222	34.88	18.60	86

Fielding

C: Requena 24, Bello 20, Novoa 10, Tolentino 5. **1B:** Dean 22, Novoa 22, Bello 10, Requena 7. **2B:** Martinez 22, Rivera 17, Arias 13, Bonifacio 5, Felicia 4. **3B:** Dean 20, Bonifacio 15, Arias 10, Martinez 9, Rivera 6, Felicia 1. **SS: Arias 26, Bonifacio 21, Rivera 7, Martinez 3. LF:** Castro 14, Almonte 12, Cova 11, De La Cruz 10, Gaitor 5, Made 5, Perez 5, Bello 1. **CF:** Cova 30, De La Cruz 25, Gaitor 2, Castro 2, Perez 1, Almonte 1. **RF:** Castro 33, Made 13, De La Cruz 8, Gaitor 1, Cova 1, Almonte 1.

Milwaukee Brewers

SEASON SYNOPSIS: First-year manager Pat Murphy mixed a rebuilt rotation, breakout rookie Jackson Chourio, an athletic defense and running game, and a bullpen built around castoffs for a magical regular season in Milwaukee. The Brewers won the NL Central for the third time in four seasons but lost a heartbreaking Wild Card Series to the visiting Mets on a ninth-inning, Game 3 home run by Pete Alonso off closer Devin Williams.

HIGH POINT: Milwaukee pulled away in August, going 19-9 after the team lost left fielder Christian Yelich to a season-ending back injury in July. The stretch included a series sweep in Atlanta by a cumulative 34-12 score, as veteran Colin Rea tossed seven scoreless innings in the opener, then finished a three-game sweep of Cleveland with seven more shutout frames in a 2-0 win 12 days later. Rea led the team with a career-best 12 wins.

LOW POINT: The Brewers had the WCS set up just the way they wanted it when Alonso took a Williams changeup to the opposite field to turn a 2-0 deficit into a 3-2 Mets lead and eventual 4-2 victory. It was the first home run Williams had yielded on his "airbender" changeup in 2024.

NOTABLE ROOKIES: Righty Tobias Myers, traded in the past for 2008 No. 1 overall pick Tim Beckham and by Tampa to Cleveland for Junior Caminero, answered the call for the Brewers in his second year in the organization. He went 9-6, 3.00 with 127 strikeouts and just 36 walks in 138 innings. Chourio, whom the Brewers signed to a guaranteed $82 million contract before the season, was their best player in the second half and looked like a future star with 21 homers, 22 steals and a .791 OPS as a 20-year-old. Third baseman Joey Ortiz provided excellent defense and hit a respectable .239/.329/.398 with 11 homers.

KEY TRANSACTIONS: Craig Counsell left Milwaukee, signing on with the Cubs as the majors' highest-paid manager, but the Brew Crew didn't miss a beat. Ortiz and lefty DL Hall arrived from Baltimore in the offseason Corbin Burnes trade. Their former No. 2 starter, Brandon Woodruff, had offseason shoulder surgery and was non-tendered. While Rea and Myers filled those rotation holes, the Brewers also traded during the season for righties Aaron Civale (from the Rays) and Frankie Montas (from the Reds). Free agent pickup Rhys Hoskins, who had missed 2023 with a knee injury, hit just .214/.303/.419 but finished second on the club with 26 homers.

OPENING DAY PAYROLL: $105,833,094 (23rd)

PLAYERS OF THE YEAR

MAJOR LEAGUE

William Contreras
C

.281/.365/.466
23 HR, 92 RBIs
37 2B, 99 R, 78 BB

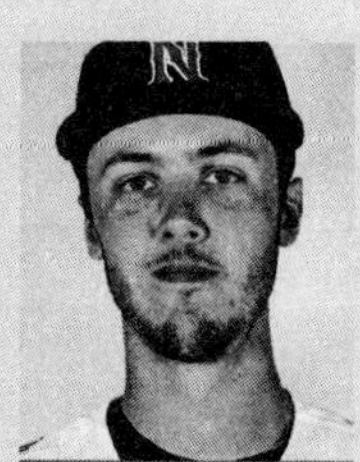

MINOR LEAGUE

Jacob Misiorowski
RHP

(AA/AAA)
3.33 ERA, 1.20 WHIP
127 SO, 60 BB, 97 IP

ORGANIZATION LEADERS

Batting		***Qualifiers**
MAJORS		
* AVG	William Contreras	.281
* OPS	William Contreras	.831
HR	Willy Adames	32
RBI	Willy Adames	112
MINORS		
* AVG	Jadher Areinamo, Wisconsin	.301
* OBP	Luke Adams, Wisconsin	.443
* SLG	Eric Bitonti, ACL Brewers/Carolina	.544
* OPS	Eric Bitonti, ACL Brewers/Carolina	.946
R	Dylan O'Rae, Wisconsin/Biloxi	80
H	Jadher Areinamo, Wisconsin	128
TB	Isaac Collins, Nashville	198
2B	Jadher Areinamo, Wisconsin	30
2B	Ernesto Martinez, Biloxi	30
3B	Isaac Collins, Nashville	7
HR	Brewer Hicklen, Nashville	22
RBI	Isaac Collins, Nashville	76
BB	Dylan O'Rae, Wisconsin/Biloxi	87
SO	Chris Roller, ACL Brewers/Nashville	151
SB	Yhoswar Garcia, Carolina	65

Pitching		**#Qualifiers**
MAJORS		
W	Collin Rea	12
# ERA	Freddy Peralta	3.68
SO	Freddy Peralta	200
SV	Trevor Megill	21
MINORS		
W	Chad Patrick, Nashville	14
L	Nate Peterson, Biloxi	9
L	Carlos F. Rodriguez, Nashville	9
# ERA	Chad Patrick, Nashville	2.90
G	Ryan Middendorf, Nashville	52
GS	Chad Patrick, Nashville	24
SV	Justin Yeager, Biloxi	20
IP	Chad Patrick, Nashville	136
BB	Aaron Ashby, Nashville	73
SO	Chad Patrick, Nashville	145
# AVG	Carlos F. Rodriguez, Nashville	.209

2024 PERFORMANCE

General Manager: Matt Arnold. **Farm Director:** Cam Castro. **Scouting Director:** Tod Johnson.

Class	Team	League	W	L	PCT	Finish	Manager
Majors	Milwaukee Brewers	National	93	69	.574	3 (15)	Pat Murphy
Triple-A	Nashville Sounds	International	78	68	.534	4 (20)	Rick Sweet
Double-A	Biloxi Shuckers	Southern	66	69	.489	5 (8)	Joe Ayrault
High-A	Wisconsin Timber Rattlers	Midwest	77	54	.588	2 (12)	Victor Estevez
Low-A	Carolina Mudcats	Carolina	78	51	.605	1 (12)	Nick Stanley
Rookie	ACL Brewers	Arizona Complex	28	32	.467	9 (15)	Rafael Neda
Rookie	DSL Brewers 1	Dominican	32	23	.582	14 (51)	Victor Rey
Rookie	DSL Brewers 2	Dominican	30	23	.566	15 (51)	Natanael Mejia
Overall 2024 Minor League Record			**389**	**320**	**.549**	**3rd (30)**	

ORGANIZATION STATISTICS

MILWAUKEE BREWERS

NATIONAL LEAGUE

Batting	B-T	Ht.	Wt.	DOB	AVG	OBP	SLG	G	PA	AB	R	H	2B	3B	HR	RBI	BB	HBP	SH	SF	SO	SB	CS	BB%	SO%
Adames, Willy	R-R	6-1	214	9-2-95	.251	.331	.462	161	688	610	93	153	33	0	32	112	74	1	0	3	173	21	4	10.76	25.15
Bauers, Jake	L-L	5-11	195	10-6-95	.199	.301	.361	117	346	302	45	60	9	2	12	43	39	5	0	0	118	13	1	11.27	34.10
Black, Tyler	L-R	5-10	190	7-26-00	.204	.316	.245	18	57	49	4	10	2	0	0	2	7	1	0	0	17	3	0	12.28	29.82
Capra, Vinny	R-R	5-8	180	7-7-96	.111	.111	.222	3	9	9	1	1	1	0	0	0	0	0	0	0	3	0	0	0.00	33.33
Chourio, Jackson	R-R	5-11	165	3-11-04	.275	.327	.464	148	573	528	80	145	29	4	21	79	39	3	1	2	121	22	7	6.81	21.12
Collins, Isaac	B-R	5-7	185	7-22-97	.118	.211	.118	11	19	17	0	2	0	0	0	0	2	0	0	0	10	1	0	10.53	52.63
Contreras, William	R-R	5-11	216	12-24-97	.281	.365	.466	155	679	595	99	167	37	2	23	92	78	3	0	3	139	9	2	11.49	20.47
Dunn, Oliver	L-R	5-10	185	9-2-97	.221	.282	.316	41	104	95	11	21	2	2	1	7	6	2	1	0	40	3	0	5.77	38.46
Frelick, Sal	L-R	5-10	182	4-19-00	.259	.320	.335	145	524	475	66	123	22	4	2	32	39	4	2	1	78	18	3	7.44	14.89
Haase, Eric	R-R	5-10	210	12-18-92	.273	.304	.515	30	69	66	10	18	1	0	5	14	3	0	0	0	28	0	0	4.35	40.58
Hicklen, Brewer	R-R	6-1	220	2-9-96	.000	.000	.000	3	5	5	0	0	0	0	0	0	0	0	0	0	4	1	0	0.00	80.00
Hoskins, Rhys	R-R	6-4	245	3-17-93	.214	.303	.419	131	517	449	59	96	14	0	26	82	53	7	0	6	149	3	0	10.25	28.82
Miller, Owen	R-R	5-11	195	11-15-96	.185	.185	.222	14	27	27	2	5	1	0	0	3	0	0	0	0	8	0	0	0.00	29.63
Mitchell, Garrett	L-R	6-3	224	9-4-98	.255	.342	.469	69	224	196	33	50	12	3	8	21	25	1	2	0	71	11	4	11.16	31.70
Monasterio, Andruw	R-R	5-11	186	5-30-97	.208	.303	.272	59	142	125	14	26	5	0	1	16	16	1	0	0	40	6	2	11.27	28.17
Ortiz, Joey	R-R	5-9	190	7-14-98	.239	.329	.398	142	511	440	58	105	25	6	11	60	56	6	3	6	103	11	6	10.96	20.16
Perkins, Blake	B-R	5-11	197	9-10-96	.240	.316	.332	121	434	383	54	92	13	2	6	43	42	3	0	6	108	23	5	9.68	24.88
Roller, Chris	R-R	5-11	190	10-8-96	.000	.000	.000	1	1	1	0	0	0	0	0	0	0	0	0	0	1	0	0	0.00	100.00
Sanchez, Gary	R-R	6-2	230	12-2-92	.220	.307	.392	89	280	245	30	54	7	1	11	37	27	5	0	3	76	0	0	9.64	27.14
Turang, Brice	L-R	6-0	176	11-21-99	.254	.316	.349	155	619	559	72	142	24	4	7	57	50	2	5	3	105	50	6	8.08	16.96
Wiemer, Joey	R-R	6-4	220	2-11-99	.154	.185	.154	19	27	26	2	4	0	0	0	0	1	0	0	0	9	1	1	3.70	33.33
Yelich, Christian	L-R	6-3	207	12-5-91	.315	.406	.504	73	315	270	44	85	12	3	11	42	40	2	1	1	58	21	1	12.70	18.41

Pitching	B-T	Ht.	Wt.	DOB	W	L	ERA	G	GS	SV	IP	Hits	Runs	ER	HR	BB	SO	AVG	OBP	SLG	SO%	BB%	BF
Ashby, Aaron	R-L	6-1	188	5-24-98	1	2	2.86	14	2	0	28	20	13	9	2	10	33	.187	.254	.299	27.73	8.40	119
Bauers, Jake	L-L	5-11	195	10-6-95	0	0	4.50	4	0	0	4	5	2	2	0	4	1	.313	.450	.500	5.00	20.00	20
Blalock, Bradley	R-R	6-2	200	12-25-00	0	0	0.00	1	0	0	1	0	0	0	0	1	0	.000	.250	.000	0.00	25.00	4
Bukauskas, J.B.	R-R	6-0	208	10-11-96	0	0	1.50	6	0	0	6	3	1	1	1	1	6	.143	.182	.286	27.27	4.55	22
Civale, Aaron	R-R	6-2	215	6-12-95	6	3	3.53	14	14	0	74	65	31	29	13	25	65	.230	.297	.422	20.90	8.04	311
Gasser, Robert	L-L	6-0	192	5-31-99	2	0	2.57	5	5	0	28	28	9	8	2	1	16	.264	.283	.330	14.04	0.88	114
Hall, DL	L-L	6-2	210	9-19-98	1	2	5.02	13	7	0	43	48	26	24	6	21	44	.282	.372	.418	22.34	10.66	197
Herget, Kevin	L-R	5-10	185	4-3-91	0	0	1.59	7	0	1	11	6	2	2	1	3	9	.150	.209	.275	20.93	6.98	43
Hernandez, Elieser	R-R	6-1	214	5-3-95	0	0	3.00	4	0	0	6	5	2	2	0	2	2	.250	.318	.350	9.09	9.09	22
Hudson, Bryan	L-L	6-8	220	5-8-97	6	1	1.73	43	0	0	62	28	12	12	7	17	62	.135	.209	.279	26.84	7.36	231
Jay, Tyler	L-L	6-1	185	4-19-94	0	0	0.00	2	0	0	3	2	0	0	0	3	3	.222	.417	.222	25.00	25.00	12
Junis, Jakob	R-R	6-3	220	9-16-92	4	0	2.42	10	1	1	26	20	9	7	4	5	19	.213	.257	.383	18.81	4.95	101
Junk, Janson	R-R	6-2	202	1-15-96	0	0	6.75	5	0	0	8	16	6	6	2	2	8	.432	.450	.649	20.00	5.00	40
Keuchel, Dallas	L-L	6-2	205	1-1-88	0	0	5.40	4	4	0	17	23	10	10	3	8	11	.329	.392	.543	13.92	10.13	79
Koenig, Jared	R-L	6-5	235	1-24-94	9	4	2.47	55	6	1	62	54	22	17	4	23	63	.229	.308	.309	23.77	8.68	265
Mears, Nick	R-R	6-2	200	10-7-96	0	1	7.30	13	0	0	12	14	10	10	5	3	18	.280	.321	.620	33.96	5.66	53
Meeker, James	R-R	6-4	222	3-22-95	0	0	0.00	1	0	0	1	1	0	0	0	1	0	.333	.500	.333	0.00	25.00	4
Megill, Trevor	L-R	6-8	250	12-5-93	1	3	2.72	48	0	21	46	33	16	14	4	14	50	.200	.264	.291	27.32	7.65	183
Miley, Wade	L-L	6-1	220	11-13-86	0	1	6.43	2	2	0	7	6	5	5	1	4	2	.250	.379	.375	6.67	13.33	30
Miller, Owen	R-R	5-11	195	11-15-96	0	0	18.00	1	0	0	2	5	4	4	1	1	0	.500	.500	.900	0.00	8.33	12
Milner, Hoby	L-L	6-3	184	1-13-91	5	1	4.73	61	1	1	65	63	38	34	6	14	64	.258	.299	.393	23.88	5.22	268
Montas, Frankie	R-R	6-2	255	3-21-93	3	3	4.55	11	11	0	57	47	33	29	10	25	70	.221	.302	.399	28.69	10.25	244
Myers, Tobias	R-R	6-1	217	8-5-98	9	6	3.00	27	25	0	138	126	52	46	18	36	127	.242	.295	.387	22.32	6.33	569
Paredes, Enoli	R-R	5-11	171	9-28-95	1	0	1.74	17	0	1	21	13	4	4	0	10	14	.181	.298	.236	16.67	11.90	84
Payamps, Joel	R-R	6-2	217	4-7-94	3	7	3.05	68	0	6	59	39	23	20	7	18	59	.184	.253	.340	25.11	7.66	235
Peguero, Elvis	R-R	6-5	237	3-20-97	7	4	2.98	52	0	2	51	52	22	17	4	27	47	.264	.357	.360	20.70	11.89	227
Peralta, Freddy	R-R	6-0	196	6-4-96	11	9	3.68	32	32	0	174	143	74	71	26	68	200	.224	.307	.387	27.59	9.38	725
Rea, Colin	R-R	6-5	218	7-1-90	12	6	4.29	32	27	1	168	169	83	80	29	43	135	.258	.311	.447	18.91	6.02	714

Rodriguez, Carlos F.	R-R	6-0	206	11-27-01	0	3	7.30	3	3	0	12	19	11	10	3	3	9	.365	.393	.596	15.79	5.26	57
Ross, Joe	R-R	6-4	232	5-21-93	3	6	3.77	25	10	0	74	72	35	31	7	29	66	.251	.319	.359	20.56	9.03	321
Uribe, Abner	R-R	6-3	225	6-20-00	2	2	6.91	14	0	3	14	15	11	11	1	12	14	.278	.409	.389	21.21	18.18	66
Vieira, Thyago	R-R	6-3	265	7-1-93	0	0	5.64	16	0	1	22	25	14	14	6	13	25	.278	.377	.500	23.58	12.26	106
White, Mitch	R-R	6-3	210	12-28-94	0	1	6.48	6	0	0	8	8	8	6	2	4	6	.258	.351	.484	15.38	10.26	39
Williams, Devin	R-R	6-2	192	9-21-94	1	0	1.25	22	0	14	22	10	3	3	1	11	38	.133	.261	.227	43.18	12.50	88
Wilson, Bryse	R-R	6-2	267	12-20-97	5	4	4.04	34	9	0	105	102	49	47	20	31	82	.252	.311	.432	18.55	7.01	442
Zastryzny, Rob	R-L	6-3	205	3-26-92	1	0	1.17	9	3	0	8	4	1	1	0	1	5	.154	.214	.192	17.24	3.45	29

Fielding

Catcher	PCT	G	PO	A	E	DP	PB
Contreras	.993	120	1054	37	8	2	6
Haase	.987	23	144	3	2	0	0
Sanchez	.977	28	205	10	5	2	3

First Base	PCT	G	PO	A	E	DP
Bauers	.989	76	424	38	5	42
Black	1.000	6	42	2	0	5
Dunn	1.000	1	1	0	0	0
Hoskins	.995	94	602	55	3	52
Miller	1.000	9	49	4	0	5
Monasterio	1.000	5	14	0	0	2
Sanchez	1.000	4	7	1	0	0

Second Base	PCT	G	PO	A	E	DP
Collins	.667	2	0	2	1	0
Dunn	1.000	1	0	1	0	0
Miller	1.000	2	0	2	0	1
Monasterio	.984	21	23	37	1	13
Ortiz	1.000	6	7	4	0	2
Turang	.989	152	240	379	7	78

Third Base	PCT	G	PO	A	E	DP
Capra	1.000	2	0	5	0	0
Dunn	1.000	27	10	36	0	4
Frelick	1.000	2	2	0	0	0
Miller	1.000	1	2	0	0	0
Monasterio	.906	26	13	35	5	4
Ortiz	.971	134	102	227	10	24

Shortstop	PCT	G	PO	A	E	DP
Adames	.963	161	204	323	20	66
Capra	1.000	1	1	2	0	0
Ortiz	1.000	10	5	10	0	4

Outfield	PCT	G	PO	A	E	DP
Bauers	1.000	18	16	0	0	0
Chourio	1.000	154	286	4	0	0
Collins	1.000	5	7	0	0	0
Frelick	.989	155	269	6	3	1
Hicklen	1.000	2	2	0	0	0
Mitchell	1.000	64	119	3	0	0
Monasterio	1.000	1	1	0	0	0
Perkins	.997	119	300	7	1	2
Roller	1.000	1	1	0	0	0
Wiemer	.917	17	11	0	1	0
Yelich	.987	48	75	3	1	1

NASHVILLE SOUNDS — TRIPLE-A

INTERNATIONALLEAGUE

Batting	B-T	Ht.	Wt.	DOB	AVG	OBP	SLG	G	PA	AB	R	H	2B	3B	HR	RBI	BB	HBP	SH	SF	SO	SB	CS	BB%	SO%
Arroyo, Christian	R-R	6-1	210	5-30-95	.237	.305	.360	30	128	114	19	27	8	0	2	13	9	3	0	2	32	1	1	7.03	25.00
Black, Tyler	L-R	5-10	190	7-26-00	.258	.374	.429	102	462	387	61	100	14	5	14	67	61	12	0	2	87	20	3	13.20	18.83
Campbell, Noah	B-R	5-11	200	6-6-99	.196	.348	.304	37	138	112	18	22	3	3	1	11	23	3	0	0	49	0	3	16.67	35.51
Capra, Vinny	R-R	5-8	180	7-7-96	.261	.348	.382	110	489	429	61	112	26	1	8	53	52	6	0	2	91	10	2	10.63	18.61
Clarke, Wes	R-R	6-0	228	10-13-99	.243	.340	.458	87	373	321	45	78	13	1	18	62	45	4	0	3	131	2	0	12.06	35.12
Collins, Isaac	B-R	5-7	185	7-22-97	.273	.386	.475	113	500	417	75	114	28	7	14	76	71	8	0	4	96	24	5	14.20	19.20
Dorrian, Patrick	L-R	6-2	188	6-26-96	.172	.275	.251	75	276	239	41	41	6	2	3	20	33	2	0	2	79	2	0	11.96	28.62
Dunn, Oliver	L-R	5-10	185	9-2-97	.310	.394	.517	8	33	29	6	9	3	0	1	3	4	0	0	0	9	2	1	12.12	27.27
Haase, Eric	R-R	5-10	210	12-18-92	.279	.367	.503	41	170	147	28	41	6	0	9	31	19	2	1	1	56	1	1	11.18	32.94
Hernandez, Yonny	B-R	5-9	140	5-4-98	.241	.333	.309	81	322	278	35	67	7	3	2	32	35	4	4	1	57	13	8	10.87	17.70
Hicklen, Brewer	R-R	6-1	220	2-9-96	.246	.363	.470	115	499	415	78	102	17	5	22	72	61	18	0	5	139	44	5	12.22	27.86
Kahle, Nick	R-R	5-8	210	2-28-98	.256	.333	.372	14	48	43	4	11	2	0	1	10	3	2	0	0	7	0	0	6.25	14.58
Mejia, Francisco	B-R	5-8	188	10-27-95	.274	.348	.428	90	376	332	46	91	14	2	11	55	38	2	0	4	65	1	0	10.11	17.29
Metzinger, Ben	R-R	5-11	195	6-26-99	.000	.000	.000	1	1	1	0	0	0	0	0	0	0	0	0	0	1	0	0	0.00	100.00
Miller, Owen	R-R	5-11	195	11-15-96	.276	.354	.392	91	381	337	56	93	18	3	5	37	37	5	0	2	70	9	5	9.71	18.37
Mitchell, Garrett	L-R	6-3	224	9-4-98	.318	.404	.636	12	52	44	7	14	2	0	4	10	6	1	0	1	10	4	1	11.54	19.23
Monasterio, Andruw	R-R	5-11	186	5-30-97	.243	.362	.297	10	47	37	7	9	2	0	0	4	7	1	0	2	10	6	0	14.89	21.28
Navarreto, Brian	R-R	6-2	233	12-29-94	.224	.272	.293	40	159	147	16	33	5	1	1	19	10	0	0	1	32	0	0	6.29	20.13
Quero, Jeferson	R-R	5-11	215	10-8-02	.000	1.000	.000	1	1	0	0	0	0	0	0	0	1	0	0	0	0	0	0	100.00	0.00
Rodriguez, Carlos D.	L-L	5-8	186	12-7-00	.245	.344	.309	31	128	110	12	27	3	2	0	10	17	0	0	1	11	2	2	13.28	8.59
Roller, Chris	R-R	5-11	190	10-8-96	.201	.275	.353	94	372	334	47	67	15	3	10	41	33	2	1	2	151	9	1	8.87	40.59
Sanchez, Gary	R-R	6-2	230	12-2-92	.167	.375	.167	2	8	6	1	1	0	0	0	0	1	1	0	0	2	0	0	12.50	25.00
Wiemer, Joey	R-R	6-4	220	2-11-99	.242	.387	.358	53	235	190	29	46	13	0	3	21	43	2	0	0	61	6	4	18.30	25.96
Yerzy, Andy	L-R	6-3	215	7-5-98	.400	.400	.400	1	5	5	0	2	0	0	0	0	0	0	0	0	1	0	0	0.00	20.00
Young, Chavez	B-R	5-10	200	7-8-97	.209	.302	.324	47	171	148	25	31	7	2	2	18	14	6	2	1	46	7	4	8.19	26.90
Zamora, Freddy	R-R	5-10	190	11-1-98	.195	.294	.250	67	255	220	27	43	6	0	2	23	28	4	0	3	55	7	2	10.98	21.57

Pitching	B-T	Ht.	Wt.	DOB	W	L	ERA	G	GS	SV	IP	Hits	Runs	ER	HR	BB	SO	AVG	OBP	SLG	SO%	BB%	BF
Ashby, Aaron	R-L	6-1	188	5-24-98	4	7	8.04	25	14	0	84	95	77	75	5	73	92	.283	.419	.396	21.96	17.42	419
Bennett, Nick	L-L	6-4	210	9-1-97	1	5	5.09	16	4	1	35	38	22	20	5	14	23	.264	.333	.465	14.38	8.75	160
Blackwood, Nolan	R-R	6-5	185	3-16-95	2	1	2.22	22	0	2	24	21	11	6	1	11	19	.231	.317	.308	18.27	10.58	104
Bukauskas, J.B.	R-R	6-0	208	10-11-96	0	0	1.80	6	0	0	5	4	1	1	0	0	3	.222	.263	.278	15.79	0.00	19
Chirino, Harold	R-R	6-2	173	1-12-98	2	4	4.67	30	0	0	35	44	28	18	4	30	32	.321	.442	.474	18.50	17.34	173
Clarke, Taylor	R-R	6-4	217	5-13-93	2	4	4.90	22	15	1	68	73	41	37	11	17	56	.274	.320	.477	19.11	5.80	293
Dorrian, Patrick	L-R	6-2	188	6-26-96	0	0	9.00	1	0	0	1	4	1	1	0	0	0	.571	.571	.571	0.00	0.00	7
Gasser, Robert	L-L	6-0	192	5-31-99	0	1	5.25	3	3	0	12	12	7	7	4	6	17	.273	.373	.636	33.33	11.76	51
Gutierrez, Vladimir	R-R	6-1	205	9-18-95	0	0	13.50	2	1	0	5	7	7	7	1	3	2	.368	.478	.684	8.70	13.04	23
Hall, DL	L-L	6-2	210	9-19-98	1	2	3.83	14	14	0	40	36	20	17	4	25	35	.247	.363	.377	19.55	13.97	179
Henderson, Logan	R-R	5-11	194	3-2-02	1	3	4.56	6	6	0	24	19	13	12	5	6	26	.211	.276	.433	26.53	6.12	98
Herget, Kevin	L-R	5-10	185	4-3-91	5	1	2.27	38	0	4	48	34	13	12	2	11	59	.204	.260	.257	32.42	6.04	182
Hernandez, Yonny	S-R	5-9	140	5-4-98	0	0	0.00	1	0	0	1	2	0	0	0	0	1	.400	.400	.400	20.00	0.00	5
Holub, Blake	R-R	6-6	230	10-23-98	1	2	8.49	25	0	1	23	26	25	22	2	22	30	.292	.421	.382	26.32	19.30	114
Hudson, Bryan	L-L	6-8	220	5-8-97	0	0	2.08	8	0	0	9	10	2	2	0	2	13	.294	.324	.353	35.14	5.41	37
Jay, Tyler	L-L	6-1	185	4-19-94	0	0	4.70	13	0	2	15	17	10	8	1	8	19	.279	.384	.410	25.68	10.81	74

Junis, Jakob	R-R	6-3	220	9-16-92	0	0	2.08	2	2	0	4	1	1	1	0	2	4	.071	.188	.071	25.00	12.50	16
Junk, Janson	R-R	6-2	202	1-15-96	3	3	2.55	18	3	2	35	30	12	10	3	15	35	.231	.324	.354	23.65	10.14	148
Kahle, Nick	R-R	5-8	210	2-28-98	0	0	0.00	2	0	0	2	0	0	0	0	0	0	.000	.000	.000	0.00	0.00	6
Koenig, Jared	R-L	6-5	235	1-24-94	0	0	1.35	6	0	0	7	3	1	1	0	2	11	.143	.217	.238	47.83	8.70	23
Kuhnel, Joel	R-R	6-5	290	2-19-95	0	0	2.45	7	0	0	7	6	2	2	0	3	10	.222	.300	.296	33.33	10.00	30
Martin, Corbin	R-R	6-2	225	12-28-95	0	1	6.43	7	0	1	7	8	5	5	1	10	7	.308	.500	.538	19.44	27.78	36
McGee, Easton	R-R	6-6	205	12-26-97	2	2	7.03	11	2	0	24	32	21	19	2	3	20	.314	.342	.451	18.02	2.70	111
McKendry, Evan	R-R	6-3	200	2-6-98	4	6	5.30	24	10	2	87	77	52	51	12	33	69	.237	.313	.415	18.65	8.92	370
McWilliams, Sam	R-R	6-7	230	9-4-95	0	0	27.00	1	0	0	1	5	3	3	1	0	0	.625	.625	1.125	0.00	0.00	8
Meeker, James	R-R	6-4	222	3-22-95	2	0	3.82	28	0	1	38	28	26	16	5	19	33	.211	.316	.383	20.63	11.88	160
Megill, Irevor	L-R	6-8	250	12-5-93	0	0	0.00	2	0	0	2	1	0	0	0	2	3	.143	.333	.143	33.33	22.22	9
Middendorf, Ryan	L-R	6-6	220	12-22-97	3	0	4.68	52	0	7	60	60	32	31	9	28	60	.261	.359	.443	22.22	10.37	270
Miley, Wade	L-L	6-1	220	11-13-86	0	0	3.00	1	1	0	3	2	1	1	0	2	3	.182	.308	.273	23.08	15.38	13
Misiorowski, Jacob	R-R	6-7	190	4-3-02	0	1	2.55	14	2	1	18	5	7	5	1	10	22	.088	.257	.158	31.43	14.29	70
Myers, Tobias	R-R	6-1	217	8-5-98	1	1	1.45	5	3	0	19	13	3	3	2	7	24	.191	.267	.279	32.00	9.33	75
Paredes, Enoli	R-R	5-11	171	9-28-95	2	0	1.73	23	0	5	26	14	6	5	0	11	41	.152	.250	.152	39.42	10.58	104
Patrick, Chad	R-R	6-1	205	8-14-98	14	1	2.90	26	24	0	136	109	50	44	16	39	145	.215	.279	.377	26.13	7.03	555
Peguero, Elvis	R-R	6-5	237	3-20-97	0	1	8.44	6	0	1	5	7	5	5	0	3	4	.318	.423	.318	15.38	11.54	26
Rodriguez, Carlos F.	R-R	6-0	206	11-27-01	9	9	4.51	25	22	1	130	100	69	65	15	61	129	.209	.308	.355	23.50	11.11	549
Ross, Joe	R-R	6-4	232	5-21-93	0	0	8.25	3	3	0	12	16	11	11	2	6	9	.356	.426	.556	16.36	10.91	55
Smith, Shane	R-R	6-4	235	4-4-00	1	0	2.70	5	0	0	7	4	2	2	0	3	7	.167	.286	.250	25.00	10.71	28
Stallings, Garrett	R-R	6-2	200	8-8-97	1	2	4.27	17	5	1	53	50	27	25	9	24	42	.258	.339	.464	19.00	10.86	221
Thompson, Darrell	L-L	6-4	185	4-27-94	2	1	2.57	15	0	1	14	8	7	4	3	12	17	.160	.338	.380	26.15	18.46	65
Uribe, Abner	R-R	6-3	225	6-20-00	1	0	1.04	7	0	1	9	3	1	1	0	7	7	.103	.316	.138	18.42	18.42	38
White, Mitch	R-R	6-3	210	12-28-94	6	4	4.06	18	7	1	58	59	28	26	2	22	68	.265	.344	.341	27.20	8.80	250
Williams, Devin	R-R	6-2	192	9-21-94	0	0	0.00	3	0	0	3	1	0	0	0	2	3	.100	.250	.100	25.00	16.67	12
Woessner, Tyler	R-R	6-4	230	10-26-99	3	5	7.22	15	5	0	39	44	35	31	9	34	29	.282	.418	.494	14.95	17.53	194
Yoho, Craig	R-R	6-3	205	10-23-99	1	1	1.26	14	0	1	14	9	4	2	0	9	18	.176	.311	.255	29.03	14.52	62
Zastryzny, Rob	R-L	6-3	205	3-26-92	4	0	3.03	30	0	2	30	20	10	10	3	11	39	.185	.258	.306	32.50	9.17	120

Fielding

Catcher	PCT	G	PO	A	E	DP	PB
Haase	.992	30	252	9	2	1	3
Kahle	1.000	9	90	4	0	0	0
Mejia	.989	69	601	31	7	1	7
Navarreto	.995	39	348	15	2	0	1
Sanchez	1.000	1	7	2	0	1	0
Yerzy	1.000	1	10	0	0	0	0

First Base	PCT	G	PO	A	E	DP
Black	.983	70	463	50	9	63
Campbell	1.000	7	51	2	0	4
Clarke	.996	34	228	14	1	18
Dorrian	.974	12	66	8	2	8
Miller	.990	29	183	21	2	20

Second Base	PCT	G	PO	A	E	DP
Arroyo	.976	24	36	46	2	12
Capra	.983	35	39	80	2	19
Collins	.989	20	28	59	1	12
Dorrian	.957	7	7	15	1	2
Hernandez	.975	42	58	100	4	20
Miller	.989	20	33	59	1	16
Monasterio	1.000	1	0	4	0	1

Third Base	PCT	G	PO	A	E	DP
Arroyo	.923	4	7	5	1	0
Black	.864	9	5	14	3	2
Capra	.960	27	18	30	2	4
Collins	.897	10	8	18	3	4
Dorrian	.975	54	42	76	3	7
Dunn	1.000	8	6	14	0	0
Hernandez	1.000	1	3	1	0	0
Miller	.987	32	31	46	1	2
Monasterio	1.000	5	4	10	0	2

Shortstop	PCT	G	PO	A	E	DP
Capra	.989	48	77	106	2	30
Hernandez	.974	30	42	72	3	20
Monasterio	1.000	3	5	6	0	3
Zamora	.967	67	108	158	9	40

Outfield	PCT	G	PO	A	E	DP
Black	.947	12	18	0	1	0
Campbell	1.000	24	38	2	0	1
Collins	.980	82	144	6	3	0
Hernandez	1.000	5	6	1	0	0
Hicklen	.986	102	201	4	3	0
Mitchell	1.000	8	16	2	0	0
Rodriguez	.984	30	60	1	1	0
Roller	.991	94	204	6	2	1
Wiemer	.958	49	113	1	5	0
Young	.971	43	97	4	3	0

BILOXI SHUCKERS — *DOUBLE-A*

SOUTHERN LEAGUE

Batting	B-T	Ht.	Wt.	DOB	AVG	OBP	SLG	G	PA	AB	R	H	2B	3B	HR	RBI	BB	HBP	SH	SF	SO	SB	CS	BB%	SO%
Acosta, Jose	B-R	5-10	170	3-20-00	.143	.250	.143	14	33	28	5	4	0	0	0	1	3	1	1	0	11	1	0	9.09	33.33
Boeve, Mike	L-R	6-3	200	5-5-02	.306	.374	.447	66	289	255	34	78	12	3	6	28	27	3	0	4	49	1	0	9.34	16.96
Brown, Eric	R-R	5-10	190	12-19-00	.185	.270	.262	105	441	390	47	72	16	1	4	38	41	6	0	4	83	20	8	9.30	18.82
Campbell, Noah	B-R	5-11	200	6-6-99	.273	.402	.410	46	169	139	17	38	7	3	2	22	28	2	0	0	50	3	0	16.57	29.59
Clarke, Wes	R-R	6-0	228	10-13-99	.250	.365	.545	13	52	44	6	11	4	0	3	10	8	0	0	0	13	1	0	15.38	25.00
Dirden, Justin	L-R	6-3	209	7-16-97	.177	.239	.241	24	88	79	7	14	1	2	0	4	7	0	0	2	32	3	0	7.95	36.36
Garcia, Eduardo	R-R	6-1	160	7-10-02	.241	.389	.448	10	36	29	5	7	1	1	1	3	3	4	0	0	12	1	1	8.33	33.33
Hall, Adam	R-R	5-11	165	5-22-99	.262	.377	.279	53	208	172	24	45	3	0	0	16	23	10	0	2	51	10	2	11.06	24.52
Kahle, Nick	R-R	5-8	210	2-28-98	.172	.271	.226	30	107	93	10	16	2	0	1	13	11	2	0	1	24	0	0	10.28	22.43
Martin, Casey	R-R	5-9	175	4-7-99	.147	.231	.254	54	199	177	23	26	2	1	5	22	17	3	0	2	62	3	1	8.54	31.16
Martinez, Ernesto	L-L	6-5	250	6-20-99	.284	.365	.466	110	457	401	52	114	30	2	13	62	40	13	0	3	77	20	5	8.75	16.85
Metzinger, Ben	R-R	5-11	195	6-26-99	.000	.333	.000	6	6	4	1	0	0	0	0	0	2	0	0	0	3	0	0	33.33	50.00
Miller, Darrien	L-R	5-10	186	3-10-01	.212	.392	.291	93	403	306	51	65	16	1	2	29	64	28	2	3	82	2	0	15.88	20.35
Murray, Ethan	R-R	5-10	201	5-13-00	.177	.273	.253	82	317	277	27	49	13	1	2	22	33	4	2	1	78	6	2	10.41	24.61
O'Rae, Dylan	L-R	5-7	160	2-14-04	.171	.310	.211	64	298	246	28	42	7	0	1	13	45	5	1	1	71	29	7	15.10	23.83
Rodriguez, Carlos D.	L-L	5-8	186	12-7-00	.298	.376	.396	84	372	326	53	97	12	4	4	42	42	1	0	3	41	15	4	11.29	11.02
Scott, Connor	L-L	6-3	208	10-8-99	.243	.305	.421	41	154	140	22	34	13	0	4	24	11	2	0	1	37	0	2	7.14	24.03
Sparks, Lamar	R-R	6-1	170	9-26-98	.277	.337	.420	103	392	357	45	99	19	1	10	43	33	0	0	2	117	12	8	8.42	29.85
Valerio, Felix	R-R	5-5	165	12-26-00	.333	.333	1.333	1	3	3	1	1	0	0	1	2	0	0	0	0	2	0	0	0.00	66.67
Warren, Zavier	B-R	5-10	215	1-8-99	.206	.308	.342	99	370	316	36	65	8	1	11	52	43	6	0	5	98	4	3	11.62	26.49
Wilken, Brock	R-R	6-4	225	6-17-02	.199	.312	.363	108	471	402	58	80	15	0	17	51	63	4	0	2	133	1	0	13.38	28.24

Batting	B-T	Ht.	Wt.	DOB	AVG	OBP	SLG	G	PA	AB	R	H	2B	3B	HR	RBI	BB	HBP	SH	SF	SO	SB	CS	BB%	SO%
Yerzy, Andy	L-R	6-3	215	7-5-98	.194	.267	.299	22	75	67	3	13	1	0	2	14	7	0	0	1	15	1	0	9.33	20.00
Zamora, Freddy	R-R	5-10	190	11-1-98	.186	.336	.291	27	107	86	11	16	3	0	2	7	13	7	0	1	20	2	1	12.15	18.69

Pitching	B-T	Ht.	Wt.	DOB	W	L	ERA	G	GS	SV	IP	Hits	Runs	ER	HR	BB	SO	AVG	OBP	SLG	SO%	BB%	BF
Blalock, Bradley	R-R	6-2	200	12-25-00	5	2	4.08	16	16	0	75	69	34	34	9	27	64	.240	.303	.373	20.19	8.52	317
Bowman, Kaleb	R-R	6-1	195	5-22-97	6	3	3.07	39	1	0	70	57	28	24	7	22	67	.229	.304	.345	23.93	7.86	280
Carlson, Sam	R-R	6-4	195	12-3-98	4	2	4.25	44	0	0	49	51	30	23	2	19	51	.267	.347	.366	23.50	8.76	217
Childers, Will	L-R	6-4	210	11-14-00	3	3	4.28	28	0	0	34	38	17	16	3	15	39	.288	.362	.409	26.00	10.00	150
Chirino, Harold	R-R	6-2	173	1-12-98	1	1	5.06	7	0	0	11	9	7	6	3	3	16	.225	.311	.500	35.56	6.67	45
Costello, Chase	R-R	6-4	215	4-13-00	1	0	0.00	3	0	0	6	1	0	0	0	4	6	.053	.217	.053	26.09	17.39	23
Gardner, Sam	R-R	6-1	205	1-4-97	2	2	2.34	22	0	0	35	18	12	9	1	12	48	.158	.234	.237	37.21	9.30	129
Henderson, Logan	R-R	5-11	194	3-2-02	6	2	3.30	9	9	0	46	34	18	17	8	7	58	.202	.236	.393	32.58	3.93	178
Holub, Blake	R-R	6-6	230	10-23-98	2	2	0.34	20	0	8	26	22	5	1	0	5	29	.220	.257	.230	27.62	4.76	105
Hunt, K.C.	L-R	6-3	200	7-14-00	1	2	2.20	6	6	0	33	24	8	8	2	9	39	.200	.262	.275	29.77	6.87	131
Kahle, Nick	R-R	5-8	210	2-28-98	0	0	0.00	1	0	0	1	0	0	0	0	0	0	.000	.000	.000	0.00	0.00	2
King, Justin	L-L	6-1	215	12-19-97	0	0	9.31	19	0	0	19	21	21	20	1	11	26	.280	.367	.413	28.89	12.22	90
Kuehner, Tate	L-L	6-1	195	2-7-01	3	1	4.04	7	6	0	36	27	18	16	5	21	33	.208	.327	.385	21.57	13.73	153
McWilliams, Sam	R-R	6-7	230	9-4-95	0	0	0.00	1	0	0	1	0	0	0	0	0	0	.000	.000	.000	0.00	0.00	3
Meeker, James	R-R	6-4	222	3-22-95	0	0	0.00	10	0	1	13	11	3	0	0	5	13	.220	.286	.240	22.81	8.77	57
Merkel, Nick	R-R	6-7	255	7-3-98	6	5	3.43	40	3	0	79	59	35	30	3	33	87	.206	.304	.275	26.28	9.97	331
Metzinger, Ben	R-R	5-11	195	6-26-99	0	0	0.00	2	0	0	2	2	0	0	0	1	0	.250	.333	.250	0.00	11.11	9
Misiorowski, Jacob	R-R	6-7	190	4-3-02	3	4	3.50	19	19	0	80	52	34	31	7	50	105	.182	.324	.291	30.26	14.41	347
Peterson, Nate	L-L	5-10	180	2-15-00	3	9	4.08	27	15	1	93	92	47	42	19	42	96	.257	.333	.478	23.76	10.40	404
Seminaris, Adam	R-L	6-0	191	10-19-98	1	8	6.15	25	10	1	75	99	54	51	5	23	73	.319	.365	.439	21.79	6.87	335
Shook, TJ	R-R	6-4	217	5-29-98	5	7	4.90	17	11	0	64	62	38	35	7	25	77	.249	.325	.414	27.40	8.90	281
Smith, Russell	L-L	6-7	255	9-10-98	2	1	2.73	29	1	0	53	40	17	16	3	28	52	.212	.318	.328	23.42	12.61	222
Smith, Shane	R-R	6-4	235	4-4-00	5	3	3.08	27	16	1	88	66	33	30	6	26	106	.207	.278	.304	29.94	7.34	354
Warren, Zavier	S-R	5-10	215	1-8-99	0	0	0.00	1	0	0	0	1	0	0	0	0	0	.500	.500	.500	0.00	0.00	2
Wichrowski, Brett	L-R	6-2	177	8-15-02	2	3	4.12	17	17	0	74	63	34	34	6	36	61	.229	.336	.342	18.83	11.11	324
Woessner, Tyler	R-R	6-4	230	10-26-99	0	2	6.81	17	5	0	37	43	30	28	2	17	49	.293	.375	.415	28.99	10.06	169
Yeager, Justin	L-R	6-4	215	1-20-98	3	6	3.88	47	0	20	51	45	27	22	3	19	56	.236	.312	.356	25.93	8.80	216
Yoho, Craig	R-R	6-3	205	10-23-99	2	1	1.17	18	0	2	23	14	7	3	0	8	46	.161	.245	.195	46.46	8.08	99

Fielding

Catcher	PCT	G	PO	A	E	DP	PB
Clarke	.985	6	59	5	1	0	2
Kahle	.996	26	244	18	1	0	1
Miller	.984	85	826	43	14	5	10
Yerzy	.984	21	178	7	3	0	0

First Base	PCT	G	PO	A	E	DP
Boeve	.984	26	171	9	3	19
Clarke	1.000	2	14	2	0	1
Martinez	.992	87	601	35	5	45
Metzinger	1.000	1	1	0	0	0
Warren	.994	27	150	24	1	11
Yerzy	1.000	1	7	0	0	1

Second Base	PCT	G	PO	A	E	DP
Acosta	.960	6	10	14	1	2
Brown	.950	5	9	10	1	2
Campbell	.667	1	1	1	1	1
Hall	1.000	4	12	2	0	1
Martin	.982	13	15	39	1	9
Murray	.981	47	70	83	3	18
O'Rae	.988	41	52	110	2	19
Warren	1.000	4	3	4	0	1
Zamora	.959	18	25	45	3	9

Third Base	PCT	G	PO	A	E	DP
Boeve	.930	23	10	30	3	3
Garcia	1.000	3	1	1	0	0
Martin	1.000	6	6	9	0	0
Murray	1.000	12	6	12	0	1
Warren	.931	13	9	18	2	3
Wilken	.936	82	53	109	11	9

Shortstop	PCT	G	PO	A	E	DP
Brown	.974	96	139	203	9	44
Hall	.900	2	2	7	1	0
Martin	.930	14	17	36	4	6
Murray	.953	21	23	38	3	8
Zamora	.864	7	3	16	3	2

Outfield	PCT	G	PO	A	E	DP
Acosta	1.000	4	10	0	0	0
Campbell	.984	40	62	1	1	0
Dirden	.976	22	39	2	1	1
Garcia	1.000	9	22	0	0	0
Hall	1.000	48	74	4	0	0
Kahle	1.000	1	2	0	0	0
Martin	1.000	19	32	0	0	0
Martinez	1.000	6	12	0	0	0
Metzinger	1.000	3	1	0	0	0
O'Rae	1.000	15	41	0	0	0
Rodriguez	.989	85	172	3	2	1
Scott	1.000	34	44	2	0	0
Sparks	.982	96	161	2	3	1
Valerio	1.000	1	2	0	0	0
Warren	.973	47	72	1	2	0

WISCONSIN TIMBER RATTLERS — HIGH-A

MIDWEST LEAGUE

Batting	B-T	Ht.	Wt.	DOB	AVG	OBP	SLG	G	PA	AB	R	H	2B	3B	HR	RBI	BB	HBP	SH	SF	SO	SB	CS	BB%	SO%
Acosta, Jose	B-R	5-10	170	3-20-00	.217	.308	.435	13	27	23	3	5	2	0	1	3	3	0	1	0	2	2	0	11.11	7.41
Adams, Luke	R-R	6-4	210	4-24-04	.227	.443	.397	101	418	295	56	67	15	1	11	56	78	40	0	5	89	28	10	18.66	21.29
Areinamo, Jadher	R-R	5-8	160	11-28-03	.301	.349	.442	110	467	425	63	128	30	0	10	68	33	2	0	7	52	32	8	7.07	11.13
Boeve, Mike	L-R	6-3	200	5-5-02	.553	.642	.632	13	53	38	10	21	3	0	0	8	13	0	0	2	5	1	1	24.53	9.43
Burke, Blake	L-L	6-3	240	6-11-03	.250	.333	.250	5	18	16	0	4	0	0	0	0	2	0	0	0	4	0	0	11.11	22.22
Chirinos, Jesus	R-R	6-0	165	7-27-01	.222	.318	.335	85	327	284	35	63	14	0	6	40	41	0	0	2	106	1	0	12.54	32.42
Doston, Terence	L-R	5-10	160	9-22-00	.231	.311	.277	45	148	130	22	30	3	0	1	10	15	1	0	2	23	9	3	10.14	15.54
Fernandez, Eduarqui	R-R	6-2	176	11-20-01	.190	.281	.316	113	430	373	51	71	19	2	8	43	48	2	0	7	147	20	9	11.16	34.19
Garcia, Eduardo	R-R	6-1	160	7-10-02	.249	.297	.387	59	246	225	29	56	15	2	4	31	5	12	0	4	76	8	3	2.03	30.89
Hall, Tayden	L-R	6-4	215	1-12-03	.221	.342	.289	76	304	249	32	55	9	1	2	25	42	7	0	6	51	5	2	13.82	16.78
Lara, Luis	B-R	5-7	155	11-17-04	.245	.332	.327	110	489	425	65	104	19	2	4	41	41	17	0	5	77	45	14	8.38	15.75
Metzinger, Ben	R-R	5-11	195	6-26-99	.000	.267	.000	5	15	11	2	0	0	0	0	0	3	1	0	0	7	0	0	20.00	46.67
O'Rae, Dylan	L-R	5-7	160	2-14-04	.266	.405	.323	62	284	229	52	61	7	3	0	18	42	12	0	1	51	33	5	14.79	17.96
Ortiz, Joey	R-R	5-9	190	7-14-98	.000	.333	.000	1	3	2	0	0	0	0	0	0	1	0	0	0	0	0	0	33.33	0.00
Perez, Hedbert	L-L	5-10	160	4-4-03	.219	.278	.397	19	79	73	7	16	5	1	2	9	6	0	0	0	23	0	1	7.59	29.11

Pratt, Cooper	R-R	6-4	195	8-18-04	.221	.258	.442	23	95	86	13	19	4	0	5	9	4	1	1	2	24	2	1	4.21	25.26
Rodriguez, Alejandro	R-R	5-11	200	12-27-99	.000	.333	.000	3	3	2	0	0	0	0	0	0	0	1	0	0	0	0	0	0.00	0.00
Rodriguez, Ramon	R-R	6-0	210	10-30-98	.252	.340	.427	74	303	262	33	66	16	0	10	38	32	5	0	4	32	5	2	10.56	10.56
Torres, Victor	R-R	6-0	180	7-29-00	.182	.182	.273	7	11	11	2	2	1	0	0	1	0	0	0	0	1	1	0	0.00	9.09
Valerio, Felix	R-R	5-5	165	12-26-00	.213	.318	.299	55	201	174	20	37	4	1	3	20	23	4	0	0	46	9	2	11.44	22.89
Vargas, Jheremy	R-R	5-10	160	5-10-03	.210	.303	.301	100	353	309	37	65	11	1	5	34	38	4	0	2	54	23	8	10.76	15.30
Wood, Matthew	L-R	5-10	190	3-2-01	.235	.346	.332	91	379	319	32	75	15	2	4	41	47	9	0	4	52	2	1	12.40	13.72

Pitching	B-T	Ht.	Wt.	DOB	W	L	ERA	G	GS	SV	IP	Hits	Runs	ER	HR	BB	SO	AVG	OBP	SLG	SO%	BB%	BF
Acosta, Jose	S-R	5-10	170	3-20-00	0	0	36.00	1	0	0	1	2	4	4	1	2	0	.400	.625	1.000	0.00	25.00	8
Aquino, Patricio	R-R	6-0	175	5-1-03	3	4	3.65	20	10	2	79	74	33	32	6	23	57	.248	.318	.393	17.27	6.97	330
Birchard, Ryan	L-R	6-0	207	7-12-03	0	3	8.71	5	5	0	10	16	11	10	2	14	13	.390	.545	.634	23.64	25.45	55
Bryant, Tyler	R-R	6-4	203	1-23-99	0	0	1.29	11	0	3	14	8	2	2	1	8	15	.163	.281	.265	26.32	14.04	57
Childers, Will	L-R	6-4	210	11-14-00	2	2	3.93	15	0	3	18	17	8	8	1	3	17	.250	.278	.353	23.61	4.17	72
Cornielle, Alexander	R-R	6-2	180	8-22-01	6	5	4.31	22	20	0	104	89	52	50	10	39	98	.233	.313	.372	22.53	8.97	435
Costello, Chase	R-R	6-4	215	4-13-00	6	3	3.83	34	0	4	42	40	20	18	3	15	57	.248	.318	.366	31.84	8.38	179
Cruz, Stiven	R-R	6-2	165	11-14-01	2	3	3.43	33	6	1	63	58	25	24	6	30	49	.256	.341	.383	18.42	11.28	266
Durow, Harrison	R-R	6-3	210	10-29-01	1	0	0.00	1	0	0	2	1	0	0	0	0	3	.143	.143	.143	42.86	0.00	7
Figueroa, Jeferson	R-R	6-0	180	8-22-00	3	1	3.16	10	0	1	26	15	10	9	1	14	28	.172	.294	.264	27.18	13.59	103
Fitzpatrick, Brian	S-L	6-7	230	6-1-00	5	2	2.69	20	7	1	70	56	25	21	4	23	76	.214	.285	.305	26.21	7.93	290
Guerrero, Miguel	R-R	6-5	216	7-15-00	1	0	13.50	2	0	0	2	0	3	3	0	4	0	.000	.400	.000	0.00	40.00	10
Hall, DL	L-L	6-2	210	9-19-98	0	0	0.00	1	1	0	1	0	0	0	0	0	1	.000	.000	.000	33.33	0.00	3
Henderson, Logan	R-R	5-11	194	3-2-02	0	1	1.35	2	2	0	7	4	1	1	0	2	10	.174	.240	.217	40.00	8.00	25
Hernandez, Joseph	R-R	5-11	150	6-15-00	1	0	7.36	5	0	0	7	9	6	6	1	2	4	.290	.333	.484	12.12	6.06	33
Herrera, Yujanyer	R-R	6-3	175	8-17-03	6	1	3.18	12	9	1	51	49	20	18	1	17	50	.254	.332	.311	22.83	7.76	219
Hunt, K.C.	L-R	6-3	200	7-14-00	4	1	2.15	11	8	0	50	37	13	12	3	12	68	.200	.247	.303	34.34	6.06	198
Jimenez, Edwin	R-R	6-3	175	12-12-01	7	0	5.02	8	6	0	43	44	26	24	5	10	36	.263	.304	.419	19.46	5.41	185
Kuehner, Tate	L-L	6-1	195	2-7-01	5	2	2.75	16	13	0	69	52	23	21	2	33	82	.211	.316	.275	28.77	11.58	285
Maldonado, Aidan	R-R	6-0	170	5-27-00	0	2	4.50	9	0	0	14	10	7	7	0	11	14	.200	.354	.280	21.54	16.92	65
Manfredi, Mark	L-L	6-4	210	1-28-00	6	4	3.91	28	12	0	76	61	41	33	7	43	95	.222	.345	.367	28.61	12.95	332
Megill, Trevor	L-R	6-8	250	12-5-93	0	0	0.00	2	1	0	2	1	0	0	0	0	2	.143	.143	.143	28.57	0.00	7
Milner, Hoby	L-L	6-3	184	1-13-91	0	0	0.00	2	0	0	2	1	0	0	0	0	1	.143	.143	.286	14.29	0.00	7
Paredes, Enoli	R-R	5-11	171	9-28-95	0	0	3.18	4	1	0	6	4	2	2	1	1	7	.190	.227	.476	31.82	4.55	22
Polancic, Jake	R-R	6-3	205	6-8-98	0	1	9.24	14	0	0	13	11	15	13	4	14	12	.234	.446	.574	18.46	21.54	65
Rodriguez, Brailin	R-R	6-2	185	8-10-02	0	0	4.91	3	0	0	7	9	5	4	3	3	6	.290	.371	.645	17.14	8.57	35
Rodriguez, Yerlin	R-R	6-2	172	3-22-02	3	1	5.94	41	0	6	50	37	38	33	4	51	71	.202	.394	.317	28.74	20.65	247
Root, Bayden	R-R	6-3	235	10-27-98	3	3	4.54	26	0	2	34	39	23	17	0	20	33	.289	.401	.333	20.37	12.35	162
Ross, Joe	R-R	6-4	232	5-21-93	0	0	0.00	1	1	0	3	3	1	0	0	0	1	.300	.300	.300	10.00	0.00	10
Rudy, Will	R-R	6-1	170	5-7-01	6	8	4.61	23	22	0	113	101	59	58	17	36	106	.241	.305	.439	22.55	7.66	470
Rund, Aaron	R-R	6-5	225	6-16-99	4	2	3.00	39	0	8	57	45	22	19	0	24	56	.214	.301	.290	23.43	10.04	239
Sanchez, Dikember	R-R	5-11	160	2-20-04	0	1	4.05	4	0	0	7	7	4	3	1	1	7	.280	.357	.480	25.00	3.57	28
Timmerman, Josh	R-R	6-4	195	8-4-02	0	0	7.71	1	1	0	5	4	4	4	1	3	3	.250	.429	.500	14.29	14.29	21
Torres, Victor	R-R	6-0	180	7-29-00	0	0	4.50	3	0	0	2	3	3	1	1	0	0	.375	.364	.875	0.00	0.00	11
Wehrle, Tyler	R-R	6-3	220	5-18-00	2	3	4.07	28	2	1	60	62	31	27	8	27	52	.268	.354	.424	19.62	10.19	265
Wichrowski, Brett	L-R	6-2	177	8-15-02	0	1	2.45	4	4	0	15	13	6	4	1	3	21	.224	.258	.379	33.87	4.84	62
Williams, Devin	R-R	6-2	192	9-21-94	0	0	0.00	1	0	0	1	0	0	0	0	0	3	.000	.000	.000	100.00	0.00	3
Yoho, Craig	R-R	6-3	205	10-23-99	1	0	0.44	16	0	7	20	8	3	1	0	6	37	.119	.221	.134	48.05	7.79	77

Fielding

Catcher	PCT	G	PO	A	E	DP	PB
Rodriguez	.993	59	557	38	4	3	3
Torres	1.000	2	29	0	0	0	0
Wood	.994	71	633	38	4	3	4

First Base	PCT	G	PO	A	E	DP
Adams	.994	20	151	12	1	14
Boeve	1.000	4	14	2	0	0
Burke	.963	3	25	1	1	5
Chirinos	.983	35	215	10	4	17
Hall	.990	71	465	24	5	59
Metzinger	1.000	3	17	1	0	2

Second Base	PCT	G	PO	A	E	DP
Acosta	1.000	2	2	5	0	0
Areinamo	.974	53	97	127	6	35
Garcia	.989	19	40	53	1	18
O'Rae	.987	41	63	93	2	20
Valerio	.968	10	12	18	1	4
Vargas	.974	12	17	20	1	8

Third Base	PCT	G	PO	A	E	DP
Acosta	1.000	1	1	1	0	0
Adams	.943	76	54	129	11	15
Areinamo	.964	19	21	33	2	2
Boeve	1.000	9	7	15	0	3
Chirinos	1.000	1	0	1	0	0
Garcia	.857	11	3	15	3	3
Ortiz	1.000	1	0	2	0	0
Vargas	.941	22	10	22	2	1

Shortstop	PCT	G	PO	A	E	DP
Areinamo	.977	30	64	64	3	12
Garcia	.952	26	40	60	5	18
Pratt	.988	22	31	50	1	15
Vargas	.500	1	1	1	2	0

Outfield	PCT	G	PO	A	E	DP
Acosta	1.000	4	4	0	0	0
Doston	.962	40	76	0	3	0
Fernandez	.985	112	192	11	3	0
Garcia	1.000	4	9	0	0	0
Lara	.992	107	245	6	2	1
O'Rae	1.000	16	33	0	0	0
Perez	.919	19	30	4	3	1
Valerio	.956	37	65	0	3	0
Vargas	.966	65	110	5	4	1

CAROLINA MUDCATS — *LOW-A*

CAROLINA LEAGUE

Batting	B-T	Ht.	Wt.	DOB	AVG	OBP	SLG	G	PA	AB	R	H	2B	3B	HR	RBI	BB	HBP	SH	SF	SO	SB	CS	BB%	SO%
Acosta, Jose	B-R	5-10	170	3-20-00	.258	.310	.273	22	71	66	8	17	1	0	0	7	5	0	0	0	14	11	2	7.04	19.72
Adamczewski, Josh	L-R	6-0	190	5-10-05	.273	.415	.515	9	41	33	7	9	5	0	1	9	7	1	0	0	10	0	0	17.07	24.39
Baez, Juan	R-R	5-9	175	6-27-05	.272	.331	.361	81	356	324	47	88	18	4	1	40	25	5	0	2	32	11	10	7.02	8.99
Bitonti, Eric	L-R	6-4	205	11-17-05	.221	.318	.487	28	132	113	20	25	6	0	8	24	16	1	0	2	39	3	0	12.12	29.55
Briceno, Miguel	R-R	5-9	155	7-6-03	.277	.320	.365	94	337	310	42	86	16	1	3	45	21	1	0	5	43	16	7	6.23	12.76
Castillo, Luis	L-L	6-0	175	10-11-03	.207	.310	.389	115	462	396	65	82	16	1	18	75	58	3	0	5	118	4	1	12.55	25.54

Di Turi, Filippo	B-R	5-11	165	11-9-05	.192	.312	.233	66	285	240	30	46	10	0	0	17	41	2	0	2	68	5	2	14.39	23.86
Diaz, Blayberg	R-R	5-11	190	1-31-03	.249	.326	.319	74	258	229	28	57	13	0	1	21	19	8	0	2	52	3	1	7.36	20.16
Dinges, Marco	R-R	6-0	190	9-5-03	.271	.364	.354	13	55	48	4	13	4	0	0	3	6	1	0	0	13	0	0	10.91	23.64
Garcia, David	B-R	5-10	201	2-6-00	.233	.393	.286	84	336	262	41	61	14	0	0	33	60	11	0	3	67	2	0	17.86	19.94
Garcia, Yhoswar	R-R	5-9	150	9-13-01	.291	.351	.346	104	394	350	59	102	12	2	1	43	31	4	4	5	68	65	13	7.87	17.26
Guilarte, Daniel	R-R	5-11	160	10-29-03	.245	.348	.328	110	468	400	72	98	18	3	3	35	63	2	0	3	115	40	12	13.46	24.57
Hall, Tayden	L-R	6-4	215	1-12-03	.378	.480	.524	26	100	82	16	31	6	3	0	14	17	0	0	1	16	0	0	17.00	16.00
Mercado, Reidy	B-R	5-11	153	1-6-01	.205	.284	.260	63	164	146	25	30	3	1	1	5	15	1	2	0	46	20	3	9.15	28.05
Nicasia, Kaylan	B-R	5-11	176	4-10-02	.227	.313	.433	29	112	97	15	22	6	1	4	12	12	1	0	2	31	10	1	10.71	27.68
Norman, Satchell	R-R	5-8	200	7-22-02	.210	.272	.286	31	114	105	5	22	6	1	0	6	9	0	0	0	30	7	1	7.89	26.32
Payne, Braylon	L-L	6-2	186	8-14-06	.438	.526	.625	4	19	16	3	7	1	1	0	5	3	0	0	0	3	4	1	15.79	15.79
Pratt, Cooper	R-R	6-4	195	8-18-04	.295	.394	.395	73	311	261	43	77	11	3	3	36	38	7	0	4	57	25	2	12.22	18.33
Rodriguez, Yophery	L-L	6-1	185	12-5-05	.250	.343	.383	110	484	420	59	105	23	6	7	60	59	2	0	3	115	7	5	12.19	23.76
Torres, Victor	R-R	6-0	180	7-29-00	.250	.227	.350	7	22	20	2	5	2	0	0	3	0	0	0	2	6	0	1	0.00	27.27
Walling, Reece	L-R	6-5	202	9-22-03	.206	.333	.323	79	312	257	37	53	15	0	5	32	47	4	0	4	90	1	0	15.06	28.85

Pitching	B-T	Ht.	Wt.	DOB	W	L	ERA	G	GS	SV	IP	Hits	Runs	ER	HR	BB	SO	AVG	OBP	SLG	SO%	BB%	BF
Austin, Morris	R-R	6-2	215	3-27-00	9	5	4.26	36	1	3	70	54	41	33	2	46	79	.218	.359	.290	25.48	14.84	310
Birchard, Ryan	L-R	6-0	207	7-12-03	1	0	3.38	3	2	0	8	6	4	3	0	5	12	.207	.333	.345	33.33	13.89	36
Briceno, Miguel	R-R	5-9	155	7-6-03	0	0	6.75	6	0	0	5	8	4	4	1	2	1	.364	.462	.545	3.85	7.69	26
Broca, Jesus	L-L	5-8	174	10-16-03	2	0	5.52	7	0	1	15	18	9	9	0	5	17	.300	.364	.367	25.76	7.58	66
Bryant, Tyler	R-R	6-4	203	1-23-99	1	0	2.53	9	0	2	11	8	3	3	1	6	18	.205	.311	.282	40.00	13.33	45
Calzadilla, Gerson	R-R	5-11	155	4-5-03	0	0	2.84	5	0	0	6	5	3	2	1	4	3	.208	.321	.333	10.71	14.29	28
Carrasco, Cristofher	R-R	5-10	175	12-24-02	2	0	3.97	9	1	2	11	6	6	5	1	8	12	.143	.308	.238	23.08	15.38	52
Corniel, Daniel	R-R	6-0	177	7-7-04	4	5	4.29	21	21	0	99	86	49	47	6	46	95	.238	.336	.360	22.95	11.11	414
Cortez, Enniel	R-R	6-0	180	5-1-06	0	2	5.32	6	6	0	24	28	14	14	3	10	24	.301	.362	.495	22.86	9.52	105
Durow, Harrison	R-R	6-3	210	10-29-01	3	4	4.97	31	0	6	58	60	37	32	3	23	58	.273	.362	.377	22.48	8.91	258
Figueroa, Jeferson	R-R	6-0	180	8-22-00	5	2	2.90	22	2	2	40	31	16	13	6	20	52	.214	.325	.386	30.77	11.83	169
Flores, Anthony	L-L	5-11	165	10-21-04	2	1	3.42	7	3	0	26	18	11	10	2	9	28	.191	.283	.298	26.42	8.49	106
Flores, Jesus	S-R	6-2	180	3-16-05	1	0	5.28	6	0	1	15	14	10	9	0	13	15	.255	.417	.291	20.83	18.06	72
Galindez, Yorman	R-R	6-1	160	2-3-03	0	0	2.45	11	11	0	40	24	11	11	2	24	64	.171	.305	.243	38.32	14.37	167
Hardin, Tyson	R-R	6-2	185	11-19-01	1	0	4.91	2	1	0	4	4	2	2	0	2	2	.286	.412	.429	11.76	11.76	17
Hernandez, Melvin	R-R	5-11	139	7-3-06	0	1	3.00	2	0	0	6	7	2	2	0	1	7	.292	.346	.375	26.92	3.85	26
Herrera, Yujanyer	R-R	6-3	175	8-17-03	3	0	2.12	4	0	0	17	10	4	4	0	6	27	.175	.250	.246	42.19	9.38	64
Hunt, K.C.	L-R	6-3	200	7-14-00	3	0	1.42	8	0	1	19	9	3	3	1	4	32	.136	.208	.197	44.44	5.56	72
Knoth, Josh	R-R	6-1	190	8-10-05	4	6	4.48	21	21	0	84	78	43	42	7	40	96	.248	.338	.378	26.59	11.08	361
Letson, Bishop	R-R	6-4	170	9-15-04	1	4	3.13	16	14	0	63	43	26	22	6	27	57	.195	.300	.335	22.18	10.51	257
Maldonado, Aidan	R-R	6-0	170	5-27-00	3	0	3.29	22	0	4	38	27	15	14	5	10	49	.201	.264	.343	32.89	6.71	149
Mogollon, Osbriel	L-L	5-10	160	4-1-04	1	1	7.71	6	0	0	14	12	14	12	0	15	10	.240	.452	.400	13.70	20.55	73
Molina, Mason	R-L	6-2	215	7-8-03	0	0	0.00	2	2	0	5	4	0	0	0	1	6	.235	.278	.235	33.33	5.56	18
Nova, Jose	R-R	6-5	185	4-2-02	1	0	6.00	7	0	0	9	8	7	6	1	12	10	.235	.469	.412	20.00	24.00	50
Pena, Jeison	R-R	6-1	165	9-14-02	3	1	5.02	30	0	2	43	39	24	24	1	26	35	.253	.366	.383	18.72	13.90	187
Prado, Eric	R-R	6-0	174	11-11-05	0	1	12.00	1	0	0	3	4	4	4	2	2	1	.364	.429	.909	7.14	14.29	14
Reyes, Anfernny	L-L	6-3	170	2-23-04	4	1	3.60	15	0	0	20	9	12	8	1	20	23	.141	.371	.203	25.56	22.22	90
Rivera, Bryan	R-R	6-1	170	6-17-05	1	2	4.39	6	4	0	27	23	15	13	0	16	26	.230	.336	.300	22.41	13.79	116
Rivero, Jesus	R-R	6-1	175	5-14-03	4	2	5.59	18	6	1	48	33	31	30	2	35	63	.201	.391	.299	29.17	16.20	216
Rodriguez, Brailin	R-R	6-2	185	8-10-02	3	2	3.23	22	0	1	47	35	21	17	2	25	47	.210	.332	.323	23.50	12.50	200
Rodriguez, Manuel	R-R	6-2	175	8-8-05	4	6	3.23	18	18	0	95	82	37	34	11	10	77	.232	.265	.388	20.64	2.68	373
Root, Bayden	R-R	6-3	235	10-27-98	2	0	2.29	15	0	6	20	15	7	5	0	16	28	.238	.378	.254	33.33	19.05	84
Sanchez, Dikember	R-R	5-11	160	2-20-04	3	2	1.38	19	0	3	33	21	7	5	2	11	29	.181	.264	.267	22.48	8.53	129
Seppings, Jack	R-R	6-1	190	7-3-02	1	0	9.00	3	0	0	4	5	6	4	0	3	2	.357	.476	.571	9.52	14.29	21
Timmerman, Josh	R-R	6-4	195	8-4-02	4	2	3.99	17	12	0	56	48	32	25	0	32	62	.227	.341	.284	24.90	12.85	249
Welch, Chandler	R-R	6-0	170	3-5-03	0	0	0.00	1	1	0	2	2	0	0	0	0	3	.333	.333	.333	50.00	0.00	6
Whiting, Blake	R-R	6-2	180	4-21-99	2	1	4.66	16	0	4	19	18	11	10	2	16	20	.254	.418	.408	21.98	17.58	91
Woodward, Jason	R-R	6-1	180	7-2-02	0	0	2.84	3	3	0	6	4	2	2	0	5	13	.174	.321	.174	46.43	17.86	28

Fielding

Catcher	PCT	G	PO	A	E	DP	PB
Diaz	.979	44	368	43	9	5	7
Dinges	1.000	2	20	2	0	0	0
Garcia	.989	75	693	59	8	9	4
Norman	.960	11	84	11	4	0	2
Torres	1.000	4	50	2	0	0	0

First Base	PCT	G	PO	A	E	DP
Bitonti	.982	14	101	11	2	4
Briceno	.993	23	138	14	1	18
Diaz	.988	27	148	11	2	17
Hall	.994	24	148	10	1	8
Nicasia	1.000	1	5	0	0	0
Norman	.978	13	79	8	2	8
Walling	.974	39	241	24	7	25

Second Base	PCT	G	PO	A	E	DP
Acosta	1.000	13	26	39	0	8
Adamczewski	.923	8	14	22	3	4
Baez	.986	18	26	44	1	7
Briceno	.958	25	29	40	3	8
Di Turi	.992	34	44	81	1	15
Guilarte	.965	41	64	73	5	22
Nicasia	.500	1	1	0	1	0

Third Base	PCT	G	PO	A	E	DP
Acosta	.727	2	5	3	3	0
Baez	.957	60	50	82	6	7
Bitonti	.875	11	6	15	3	0
Briceno	.970	33	34	31	2	10
Diaz	1.000	1	1	2	0	0
Guilarte	.941	26	21	27	3	5

Shortstop	PCT	G	PO	A	E	DP
Briceno	1.000	1	1	0	0	1
Di Turi	.964	29	39	67	4	18
Guilarte	.964	37	59	73	5	11
Pratt	.973	65	96	153	7	36

Outfield	PCT	G	PO	A	E	DP
Acosta	.000	1	0	0	0	0
Briceno	1.000	11	20	0	0	0
Castillo	.950	85	124	8	7	2
Garcia	.958	98	152	6	7	0
Mercado	.943	51	75	8	5	1
Nicasia	1.000	22	24	2	0	1
Payne	1.000	3	2	0	0	0
Rodriguez	.991	99	198	15	2	3
Walling	.988	40	76	6	1	2

ACL BREWERS

ROOKIE

ARIZONA COMPLEX LEAGUE

Batting	B-T	Ht.	Wt.	DOB	AVG	OBP	SLG	G	PA	AB	R	H	2B	3B	HR	RBI	BB	HBP	SH	SF	SO	SB	CS	BB%	SO%
Adamczewski, Josh	L-R	6-0	190	5-10-05	.336	.472	.478	32	142	113	35	38	10	0	2	18	26	3	0	0	26	8	3	18.31	18.31
Alastre, Luiyin	B-R	5-10	160	9-27-05	.260	.341	.344	50	220	192	34	50	6	2	2	27	23	2	0	3	26	11	2	10.45	11.82
Arroyo, Christian	R-R	6-1	210	5-30-95	.143	.280	.143	7	25	21	3	3	0	0	0	1	2	2	0	0	7	0	0	8.00	28.00
Baez, Juan	R-R	5-9	175	6-27-05	.333	.500	.467	5	22	15	5	5	0	1	0	2	4	2	0	1	1	0	1	18.18	4.55
Barrios, Johan	R-R	6-1	180	1-8-05	.282	.399	.394	48	173	142	34	40	3	2	3	26	26	3	0	2	41	7	3	15.03	23.70
Bitonti, Eric	I-R	6-4	205	11-17-05	.320	.451	.580	51	226	181	42	58	17	3	8	42	43	1	0	1	61	9	3	19.03	26.99
Di Turi, Filippo	B-R	5-11	165	11-9-05	.325	.481	.475	23	106	80	18	26	5	2	1	14	23	2	0	1	16	5	1	21.70	15.09
Garcia, Eduardo	R-R	6-1	160	7-10-02	.200	.250	.400	4	16	15	2	3	1	1	0	2	1	0	0	0	4	1	0	6.25	25.00
Gomez, Antony	L-L	6-1	175	4-5-06	.191	.365	.284	47	181	141	24	27	7	0	2	24	36	3	0	1	50	9	7	19.89	27.62
Hall, Adam	R-R	5-11	165	5-22-99	.333	.250	.333	1	4	3	1	1	0	0	0	1	0	0	0	1	1	0	0	0.00	25.00
Holguin, Gery	R-R	6-0	160	8-3-05	.220	.308	.384	49	201	177	31	39	13	2	4	35	22	1	0	1	57	3	1	10.95	28.36
Ibarguen, Pedro	R-R	5-10	180	7-2-06	.158	.310	.184	38	145	114	19	18	1	1	0	8	26	1	0	4	43	9	2	17.93	29.66
Lameda, Luis	B-R	5-10	160	1-17-06	.193	.387	.228	42	155	114	17	22	1	0	1	14	36	2	0	3	34	3	4	23.23	21.94
Martinez, Eric	R-R	6-0	175	4-6-04	.208	.311	.283	33	122	106	18	22	2	0	2	9	12	4	0	0	28	2	0	9.84	22.95
Mitchell, Garrett	L-R	6-3	224	9-4-98	.286	.444	.286	2	9	7	2	2	0	0	0	3	2	0	0	0	2	0	0	22.22	22.22
Moreno, Ramon	R-R	5-9	165	10-27-04	.253	.349	.352	33	106	91	15	23	5	2	0	10	14	0	0	1	40	12	2	13.21	37.74
Navarreto, Brian	R-R	6-2	233	12-29-94	.200	.250	.333	4	16	15	1	3	2	0	0	4	1	0	0	0	5	0	0	6.25	31.25
Norman, Satchell	R-R	5-8	200	7-22-02	.000	.273	.000	3	11	8	0	0	0	0	0	0	3	0	0	0	5	0	0	27.27	45.45
Ordonez, Edgardo	L-R	5-11	155	9-24-03	.272	.392	.495	30	125	103	18	28	2	0	7	26	21	0	0	1	35	0	1	16.80	28.00
Pereira, Angel	R-R	5-10	176	3-30-05	.175	.306	.325	16	49	40	7	7	1	1	1	7	6	2	0	1	16	3	0	12.24	32.65
Rodriguez, Tyler	R-R	5-10	165	2-8-06	.277	.455	.361	31	112	83	22	23	4	0	1	8	17	11	0	1	14	9	1	15.18	12.50
Roller, Chris	R-R	5-11	190	10-8-96	.000	.400	.000	1	5	3	0	0	0	0	0	0	0	2	0	0	0	1	0	0.00	0.00
Valerio, Felix	R-R	5-5	165	12-26-00	.517	.588	.690	8	34	29	9	15	3	1	0	10	4	1	0	0	5	1	0	11.76	14.71
Walther, Yannic	R-R	6-0	185	4-12-04	.182	.275	.250	16	51	44	2	8	3	0	0	2	6	0	0	1	12	0	1	11.76	23.53
Wilken, Brock	R-R	6-4	225	6-17-02	.333	.500	.667	1	4	3	0	1	1	0	0	0	0	1	0	0	0	0	0	0.00	0.00

Pitching	B-T	Ht.	Wt.	DOB	W	L	ERA	G	GS	SV	IP	Hits	Runs	ER	HR	BB	SO	AVG	OBP	SLG	SO%	BB%	BF
Barrios, Johan	R-R	6-1	180	1-8-05	0	0	18.00	1	0	0	1	3	2	2	1	0	1	.600	.667	1.200	16.67	0.00	6
Birchard, Ryan	L-R	6-0	207	7-12-03	0	0	6.00	2	2	0	3	5	2	2	0	1	5	.385	.429	.615	35.71	7.14	14
Broca, Jesus	L-L	5-8	174	10-16-03	3	0	1.80	6	0	3	10	6	4	2	0	3	12	.167	.225	.278	30.00	7.50	40
Bukauskas, J.B.	R-R	6-0	208	10-11-96	0	0	0.00	1	0	0	1	1	0	0	0	0	1	.200	.200	.200	20.00	0.00	5
Calzadilla, Gerson	R-R	5-11	155	4-5-03	1	1	11.57	4	0	0	5	10	8	6	0	3	0	.435	.519	.522	0.00	11.11	27
Carrasco, Cristofher	R-R	5-10	175	12-24-02	1	0	10.13	2	0	0	3	4	4	3	1	3	6	.364	.500	.909	37.50	18.75	16
Cortez, Enniel	R-R	6-0	180	5-1-06	2	2	5.55	7	5	0	24	30	16	15	3	3	27	.300	.346	.490	25.23	2.80	107
De Los Santos, Felipe	R-R	6-0	180	11-29-02	2	3	11.77	17	1	1	26	36	36	34	1	28	27	.321	.469	.429	18.62	19.31	145
Flores, Anthony	L-L	5-11	165	10-21-04	3	3	6.23	12	4	0	43	53	35	30	2	18	57	.291	.366	.429	27.80	8.78	205
Flores, Jesus	S-R	6-2	180	3-16-05	0	1	1.74	5	0	2	10	10	3	2	0	3	9	.233	.283	.256	19.15	6.38	47
Garcia, Rafael	R-R	6-1	158	4-28-01	1	0	6.23	5	0	0	4	5	3	3	0	5	4	.313	.476	.313	19.05	23.81	21
Gardner, Sam	R-R	6-1	205	1-4-97	0	0	0.00	2	0	0	2	1	0	0	0	0	5	.125	.125	.125	62.50	0.00	8
Geraldo, Dencer	R-R	6-1	160	3-5-03	0	2	11.81	8	0	0	5	7	12	7	0	7	7	.292	.528	.292	19.44	19.44	36
Henderson, Logan	R-R	5-11	194	3-2-02	0	0	0.00	2	2	0	5	2	0	0	0	0	10	.125	.125	.125	62.50	0.00	16
Hernandez, Melvin	R-R	5-11	139	7-3-06	2	2	5.09	12	8	0	46	59	30	26	0	14	49	.312	.371	.429	23.22	6.64	211
Jackson, Isaiah	R-R	6-5	185	9-1-01	0	0	7.62	12	0	0	13	11	16	11	3	17	19	.216	.431	.451	26.03	23.29	73
Johnson, Bjorn	L-L	6-2	185	1-11-05	0	2	8.38	8	6	0	19	26	21	18	1	18	16	.329	.444	.443	16.16	18.18	99
Knarr, Brandon	R-L	5-10	217	6-2-90	0	1	10.80	3	1	0	3	3	5	4	0	3	4	.214	.353	.429	23.53	17.65	17
McGee, Easton	R-R	6-6	205	12-26-97	0	0	4.00	5	4	0	9	11	4	4	0	1	12	.297	.316	.514	31.58	2.63	38
Meneses, Jose	L-L	6-1	150	3-9-05	2	3	10.89	7	1	0	19	27	30	23	2	24	13	.346	.509	.538	12.26	22.64	106
Nova, Jose	R-R	6-5	185	4-2-02	1	1	4.11	11	0	1	15	14	9	7	0	9	17	.233	.343	.283	24.29	12.86	70
Mogollon, Osbriel	L-L	5-10	160	4-1-04	2	0	8.20	13	0	0	19	20	17	17	1	29	15	.294	.519	.412	14.42	27.88	104
Prado, Eric	R-R	6-0	174	11-11-05	1	2	7.02	12	6	0	41	52	33	32	8	15	37	.311	.373	.551	20.00	8.11	185
Reyes, Anfernny	L-L	6-3	170	2-23-04	2	0	0.00	8	0	2	12	7	3	0	0	6	18	.149	.273	.191	32.73	10.91	55
Rivera, Bryan	R-R	6-1	170	6-17-05	0	2	5.79	12	8	0	47	45	32	30	4	24	54	.247	.352	.412	25.35	11.27	213
Robinson, Hayden	R-R	6-0	180	7-12-05	0	0	2.41	6	3	0	19	14	5	5	0	7	28	.209	.303	.284	36.84	9.21	76
Rodriguez, Aneuris	R-R	6-3	185	6-14-04	0	0	3.68	3	1	0	7	7	6	3	0	4	15	.233	.343	.367	42.86	11.43	35
Rodriguez, Brailin	R-R	6-2	185	8-10-02	0	0	13.50	2	0	1	2	5	3	3	0	0	5	.455	.455	.545	45.45	0.00	11
Sanchez, Dikember	R-R	5-11	160	2-20-04	1	1	4.02	11	0	3	16	13	10	7	1	6	28	.213	.290	.344	40.58	8.70	69
Valerio, Samuel	R-R	6-4	230	10-8-01	2	2	7.85	18	0	2	18	15	17	16	2	21	28	.227	.435	.348	30.43	22.83	92
Vire, Caden	L-L	6-6	170	9-9-03	0	0	12.19	7	0	0	10	13	16	14	3	11	12	.317	.464	.585	21.43	19.64	56
Woodward, Jason	R-R	6-1	180	7-2-02	0	1	7.94	4	4	0	6	8	7	5	1	5	6	.364	.481	.591	21.43	17.86	28
Yanez, Ismael	R-R	6-0	180	11-9-05	2	3	11.48	8	4	0	13	15	17	17	3	16	16	.300	.500	.560	22.22	22.22	72

Fielding

C: Ordonez 26, Martinez 22, Walther 13, Navarreto 2, Norman 2. **1B:** Barrios 32, Holguin 19, Lameda 14. **2B:** Adamczewski 27, Lameda 19, Rodriguez 7, Alastre 7, Baez 3, Di Turi 1, Valerio 1. **3B:** Bitonti 39, Barrios 11, Arroyo 7, Holguin 4, Baez 2, Rodriguez 1, Wilken 1. **SS:** Alastre 28, Di Turi 19, Rodriguez 15, Garcia 2. **LF:** Moreno 16, Gomez 13, Alastre 11, Pereira 7, Rodriguez 7, Valerio 5, Lameda 4, Ibarguen 2, Martinez 1. **CF:** Gomez 29, Ibarguen 22, Moreno 9, Garcia 2, Hall 1, Roller 1, Mitchell 1. **RF:** Holguin 24, Ibarguen 12, Moreno 8, Pereira 6, Lameda 6, Gomez 5.

DSL BREWERS 1 — ROOKIE

DOMINICAN SUMMER LEAGUE

Batting	B-T	Ht.	Wt.	DOB	AVG	OBP	SLG	G	PA	AB	R	H	2B	3B	HR	RBI	BB	HBP	SH	SF	SO	SB	CS	BB%	SO%
Anderson, Jose	R-R	6-0	183	11-28-06	.333	.500	.333	1	4	3	2	1	0	0	0	0	0	1	0	0	1	1	0	0.00	25.00
Corobo, Luis	R-R	5-11	183	5-2-07	.250	.368	.250	5	19	16	3	4	0	0	0	1	2	1	0	0	4	1	0	10.53	21.05
Cruz, Yohandy	R-R	6-0	157	5-26-07	.196	.293	.275	18	58	51	5	10	1	0	1	5	4	3	0	0	15	2	3	6.90	25.86
Encarnacion, Handelfry	L-L	5-11	172	6-8-07	.210	.378	.330	31	127	100	18	21	6	0	2	19	23	4	0	0	21	4	3	18.11	16.54
Garcia, Kevin	R-R	6-0	177	7-20-07	.187	.284	.347	25	88	75	13	14	1	1	3	10	10	1	0	2	28	3	0	11.36	31.82
George, Jeremy	R-R	6-0	165	10-11-06	.105	.277	.184	17	47	38	5	4	0	0	1	1	6	3	0	0	20	3	3	12.77	42.55
Gutierrez, Joan	L-R	5-11	165	10-7-05	.153	.284	.216	38	134	111	14	17	3	2	0	10	17	4	0	2	30	8	2	12.69	22.39
Made, Jesus	B-R	6-1	187	5-8-07	.331	.458	.554	51	216	175	63	58	9	6	6	28	39	2	0	0	28	28	4	18.06	12.96
Martinez, Juan	B-R	5-11	170	4-18-07	.256	.349	.351	50	195	168	24	43	6	5	0	30	20	5	0	2	23	15	1	10.26	11.79
Ortuno, Juan	R-R	5-8	165	4-26-07	.344	.464	.481	49	192	154	29	53	6	3	3	34	29	7	0	2	27	22	7	15.10	14.06
Paulino, Engel	R-R	5-9	162	12-2-06	.240	.350	.390	49	183	154	18	37	8	6	1	33	23	4	0	2	43	13	3	12.57	23.50
Pena, Joandrew	R-R	6-3	172	12-14-06	.200	.293	.313	38	133	115	15	23	4	0	3	14	10	6	0	2	50	5	0	7.52	37.59
Pena, Luis	R-R	5-11	185	11-13-06	.393	.457	.583	44	184	163	43	64	16	6	1	36	15	5	0	1	15	39	4	8.15	8.15
Puerta, Danny	L-L	5-8	150	4-1-06	.195	.320	.256	30	97	82	13	16	3	1	0	7	13	2	0	0	18	2	3	13.40	18.56
Rojas, Freider	B-R	5-8	155	10-23-05	.190	.427	.238	25	89	63	15	12	1	1	0	6	26	0	0	0	17	5	1	29.21	19.10
Saez, Jhoanjel	R-R	5-9	150	4-13-07	.250	.340	.364	15	50	44	3	11	1	2	0	3	5	1	0	0	6	4	2	10.00	12.00
Santiesteban, Idalberto	L-L	6-2	175	6-12-04	.185	.297	.204	27	64	54	15	10	1	0	0	5	7	2	0	1	15	3	1	10.94	23.44
Seijas, Kegnnalex	R-R	5-8	150	11-5-05	.143	.250	.143	2	8	7	1	1	0	0	0	0	1	0	0	0	0	0	0	12.50	0.00
Tejada, Ludwin	L-R	5-10	175	5-12-05	.194	.381	.226	18	42	31	4	6	1	0	0	3	8	2	0	1	6	1	1	19.05	14.29

Pitching	B-T	Ht.	Wt.	DOB	W	L	ERA	G	GS	SV	IP	Hits	Runs	ER	HR	BB	SO	AVG	OBP	SLG	SO%	BB%	BF
Bravo, Ayendy	R-R	5-10	180	1-24-07	4	3	2.38	12	4	1	45	31	17	12	2	16	34	.195	.272	.289	18.89	8.89	180
Camilo, Oliver	R-R	6-0	153	2-8-06	0	0	0.00	2	0	0	3	1	1	0	0	1	2	.111	.182	.111	18.18	9.09	11
Canales, Carlos	R-R	6-1	160	1-10-06	2	3	7.85	11	3	1	39	37	38	34	5	18	25	.255	.370	.448	14.45	10.40	173
Carra, Carlos	R-R	5-11	181	11-19-06	0	0	1.66	8	6	0	22	12	5	4	0	16	27	.158	.347	.184	27.55	16.33	98
Colmenarez, Gabriel	R-R	6-1	155	3-28-06	1	1	3.33	9	7	0	24	20	11	9	1	16	19	.220	.355	.341	17.27	14.55	110
Garcia, Victor	L-L	6-2	225	9-28-06	0	3	9.95	6	2	0	13	11	19	14	0	19	14	.229	.472	.292	19.44	26.39	72
Gonzalez, Lukas	R-R	6-0	140	11-23-06	1	1	4.50	10	4	0	26	24	13	13	0	17	26	.250	.390	.354	22.03	14.41	118
Guevara, Francisco	R-R	5-10	150	8-3-06	0	0	72.00	3	0	0	1	2	8	8	0	7	1	.500	.846	.500	7.69	53.85	13
Guevara, Luis	R-R	6-1	180	6-3-06	3	0	2.93	10	0	0	15	14	5	5	1	9	15	.255	.373	.418	22.39	13.43	67
Jaquez, Dariel	R-R	6-1	170	12-15-06	2	0	1.74	9	6	1	31	13	8	6	1	16	29	.129	.285	.188	23.58	13.01	123
Jimenez, Linbel	R-R	6-5	198	10-26-04	0	1	14.21	6	0	0	6	4	11	10	0	9	6	.182	.441	.182	17.65	26.47	34
King, Wenderlyn	R-R	5-9	165	8-24-05	2	3	3.35	10	6	0	38	42	15	14	1	6	43	.280	.331	.360	25.90	3.61	166
Moreno, Manuel	R-R	6-1	170	10-23-06	4	0	4.00	10	5	1	36	33	18	16	3	6	31	.236	.287	.393	20.67	4.00	150
Ospino, Jhosep	R-R	6-0	142	9-6-04	1	2	5.51	12	0	1	16	14	13	10	0	12	17	.237	.392	.322	22.97	16.22	74
Puerta, Danny	L-L	5-8	150	4-1-06	0	0	0.00	1	0	0	1	1	0	0	0	0	0	.250	.250	.250	0.00	0.00	4
Quezada, Joshua	R-R	6-2	185	5-4-04	2	2	3.44	9	5	1	34	30	14	13	3	14	40	.233	.322	.380	26.85	9.40	149
Reyes, Fabian	R-R	6-4	175	10-5-04	1	0	0.00	4	0	0	3	1	0	0	0	3	2	.100	.308	.100	15.38	23.08	13
Saldana, Ruben	R-R	5-10	153	2-1-06	0	0	5.40	9	0	1	8	8	5	5	0	5	8	.286	.371	.357	22.22	13.89	36
Sanchez, Saul	R-R	5-11	175	8-8-06	3	2	1.74	15	0	1	21	13	8	4	0	9	17	.176	.284	.216	19.32	10.23	88
Santiesteban, Idalberto	L-L	6-2	175	6-12-04	2	1	2.89	10	0	0	9	10	4	3	0	4	6	.278	.386	.306	13.64	9.09	44
Smith, Ranwell	R-R	5-11	140	8-23-05	3	0	2.25	13	0	2	20	13	5	5	0	21	13	.200	.398	.246	14.61	23.60	89
Torres, Wande	L-L	6-3	190	1-31-05	1	0	1.72	8	7	0	16	7	3	3	0	6	33	.132	.258	.132	53.23	9.68	62
Zapata, Johan	R-R	5-11	160	11-10-05	0	1	33.75	2	0	0	3	6	11	10	2	5	2	.400	.609	.800	8.70	21.74	23

Fielding

C: Rojas 23, Garcia 22, Tejada 10, Corobo 5, Seijas 2. **1B:** Pena 30, Ortuno 12, Cruz 9, Tejada 7, Rojas 2. **2B:** Martinez 17, Saez 9, Made 9, Pena 8, Ortuno 6, Gutierrez 5, Cruz 1. **3B:** Made 12, Martinez 11, Gutierrez 11, Pena 10, Ortuno 8, Pena 5, Saez 1. **SS:** Made 27, Pena 24, Ortuno 4, Martinez 2, Saez 1. **LF:** Gutierrez 19, Ortuno 13, Martinez 10, Paulino 5, Puerta 5, Cruz 4, George 2, Tejada 1. **CF:** Paulino 39, Encarnacion 14, George 2, Gutierrez 1, Anderson 1. **RF:** Puerta 24, Encarnacion 15, George 13, Paulino 4, Gutierrez 1, Rojas 1.

DSL BREWERS 2 — ROOKIE

DOMINICAN SUMMER LEAGUE

Batting	B-T	Ht.	Wt.	DOB	AVG	OBP	SLG	G	PA	AB	R	H	2B	3B	HR	RBI	BB	HBP	SH	SF	SO	SB	CS	BB%	SO%
Anderson, Jose	R-R	6-0	183	11-28-06	.282	.401	.515	45	197	163	36	46	10	2	8	34	29	4	0	1	37	14	4	14.72	18.78
Charles, Eduardo	R-R	5-10	160	4-22-06	.203	.342	.322	23	73	59	9	12	5	1	0	8	9	4	0	1	22	10	3	12.33	30.14
Corobo, Luis	R-R	5-11	183	5-2-07	.240	.324	.406	28	108	96	21	23	4	0	4	16	10	2	0	0	14	10	2	9.26	12.96
Ereu, Kevin	R-R	5-10	165	5-24-06	.250	.416	.300	38	154	120	22	30	6	0	0	6	28	6	0	0	25	7	4	18.18	16.23
Flores, Roderick	R-R	5-9	167	8-24-06	.245	.441	.349	38	145	106	27	26	6	1	1	15	33	5	0	1	33	13	3	22.76	22.76
Garcia, Luis	R-R	5-11	180	1-19-05	.368	.480	.579	12	25	19	4	7	4	0	0	3	5	0	0	1	6	1	1	20.00	24.00
George, Jeremy	R-R	6-0	165	10-11-06	.000	.167	.000	2	6	5	0	0	0	0	0	0	1	0	0	0	4	0	0	16.67	66.67
Gonzalez, Angel	L-R	5-10	171	1-18-07	.179	.368	.242	36	125	95	18	17	1	1	1	10	22	7	0	1	23	9	2	17.60	18.40
Lafond, Frandy	R-R	6-1	180	1-27-07	.267	.417	.419	35	133	105	21	28	5	1	3	17	17	10	0	0	28	15	4	12.78	21.05
Lugo, Yoneiker	R-R	5-8	155	4-27-07	.291	.412	.367	25	97	79	12	23	3	0	1	17	16	1	0	1	11	5	2	16.49	11.34
Montero, Frederi	L-R	6-2	188	1-12-07	.245	.356	.304	51	216	184	25	45	9	1	0	28	25	7	0	0	32	12	2	11.57	14.81
Polanco, Moises	R-R	5-10	150	5-30-07	.260	.420	.359	40	169	131	32	34	11	1	0	9	31	6	0	1	24	23	5	18.34	14.20
Quintana, Jorge	B-R	6-2	183	4-5-07	.250	.361	.380	53	238	200	37	50	14	3	2	31	33	3	0	2	51	22	11	13.87	21.43
Rangel, Jonathan	L-R	5-9	176	2-23-07	.272	.385	.315	30	109	92	12	25	4	0	0	16	13	4	0	0	15	10	2	11.93	13.76
Seijas, Kegnnalex	R-R	5-8	150	11-5-05	.200	.357	.250	13	28	20	3	4	1	0	0	3	6	0	0	2	2	1	0	21.43	7.14
Tovar, Pedro	L-L	6-1	160	6-23-06	.301	.357	.420	38	157	143	24	43	11	3	0	16	13	0	0	1	43	7	2	8.28	27.39

Pitching	B-T	Ht.	Wt.	DOB	W	L	ERA	G	GS	SV	IP	Hits	Runs	ER	HR	BB	SO	AVG	OBP	SLG	SO%	BB%	BF
Aparicio, Argenis	S-R	6-0	180	9-23-05	4	1	2.81	11	5	0	48	41	21	15	5	11	41	.225	.273	.379	21.03	5.64	195
Bodre, Dalvin	R-R	5-9	158	11-27-06	1	1	14.21	5	4	0	6	11	11	10	0	4	8	.379	.472	.483	21.62	10.81	37
Broca, Jesus	L-L	5-8	174	10-16-03	1	1	6.35	4	0	0	6	12	5	4	0	1	12	.444	.464	.667	42.86	3.57	28
Cabrera, Wandy	R-R	6-2	170	6-6-06	4	2	2.05	11	3	0	31	21	16	7	1	18	25	.193	.321	.275	18.94	13.64	132
Camilo, Oliver	R-R	6-0	153	2-8-06	1	0	2.08	14	0	2	17	15	8	4	2	6	12	.238	.338	.429	16.22	8.11	74
Downs, Lonell	R-R	5-9	184	4-7-07	3	1	3.86	11	3	0	37	27	19	16	0	19	35	.216	.338	.328	23.03	12.50	152
Flores, Jesus	S-R	6-2	180	3-16-05	1	0	3.00	2	2	0	9	7	3	3	0	3	13	.212	.297	.333	35.14	8.11	37
Garcia, Victor	L-L	6-2	225	9-28-06	0	0	0.00	2	0	0	2	1	0	0	0	1	1	.125	.222	.125	11.11	11.11	9
Gonzalez, Aldrin	R-R	6-1	180	4-6-06	0	1	4.63	6	5	0	12	10	6	6	1	7	10	.227	.358	.364	18.87	13.21	53
Guevara, Francisco	R-R	5-10	150	8-3-06	0	1	6.75	9	0	0	9	4	9	7	1	13	5	.129	.438	.290	10.42	27.08	48
Hoff, Paul	R-R	6-5	180	9-4-06	2	2	3.64	8	5	1	30	20	13	12	2	18	21	.190	.320	.267	16.80	14.40	125
Jimenez, Linbel	R-R	6-5	198	10-26-04	0	0	6.75	2	0	0	1	4	1	1	0	1	2	.571	.625	.571	25.00	12.50	8
Lugo, Justin	R-R	6-3	200	11-26-05	1	1	6.00	9	2	1	15	5	11	10	0	15	22	.104	.348	.188	33.33	22.73	66
Mendez, Lenin	R-R	6-3	193	9-22-04	1	1	2.95	17	0	1	21	24	10	7	1	11	10	.289	.385	.446	10.42	11.46	96
Mercado, Enderson	L-L	5-11	177	3-23-07	3	6	5.95	11	8	0	42	49	33	28	1	19	51	.292	.371	.405	26.29	9.79	194
Mercedes, Miqueas	R-R	6-3	200	7-7-06	0	0	10.13	3	1	0	5	5	6	6	1	2	6	.238	.360	.524	24.00	8.00	25
Parra, Alejandro	R-R	6-3	195	11-28-05	1	0	6.75	3	2	0	8	7	6	6	0	9	9	.259	.447	.333	23.68	23.68	38
Reyes, Fabian	R-R	6-4	175	10-5-04	1	0	1.98	9	0	0	14	10	3	3	1	7	19	.200	.305	.300	32.20	11.86	59
Rodriguez, Jean	R-R	6-2	170	6-1-07	0	3	8.20	8	3	0	19	20	20	17	1	14	14	.286	.430	.457	14.89	14.89	94
Tales, Yeferson	R-R	6-1	165	12-6-03	1	0	6.75	7	0	0	8	8	9	6	0	9	12	.250	.467	.281	26.67	20.00	45
Toledo, Josue	R-R	5-11	182	5-19-06	2	1	6.88	10	5	0	34	38	31	26	5	17	25	.279	.369	.500	15.82	10.76	158
Urena, Ever	R-R	6-0	165	1-14-05	0	0	0.00	6	0	1	5	0	0	0	0	1	3	.000	.111	.000	16.67	5.56	18
Zapata, Johan	R-R	5-11	160	11-10-05	1	0	3.12	10	0	2	17	12	6	6	3	5	9	.194	.250	.371	13.24	7.35	68

Fielding

C: Corobo 28, Lugo 23, Seijas 7, Garcia 3. **1B:** Montero 37, Charles 8, Garcia 6, Rangel 5, Seijas 2, Flores 1. **2B:** Polanco 19, Ereu 16, Rangel 10, Flores 7, Charles 2. **3B:** Flores 14, Montero 14, Quintana 13, Rangel 10, Ereu 2, Polanco 1. **SS:** Quintana 30, Polanco 12, Ereu 11. **LF:** Tovar 24, Gonzalez 21, Charles 9, Lafond 5, Flores 1. **CF:** Anderson 41, Lafond 11, Tovar 1. **RF:** Lafond 15, Gonzalez 14, Tovar 11, Flores 10, George 2, Rangel 2, Anderson 1.

Minnesota Twins

SEASON SYNOPSIS: After climbing out of a 7-13 starting hole to get within two games of first place and 17 games above .500 in early August, the Twins completely collapsed. A 9-18 September swoon dropped them out of the playoffs for the second time in three seasons.

HIGH POINT: Despite injuries to Byron Buxton and Carlos Correa sapping vitality from their lineup, the Twins won five of six against Kansas City and host Texas, with a four-run rally Aug. 17 against the Rangers propelling them to a 70-53 mark. Versatile Willi Castro had a key two-RBI single in an eighth-inning, go-ahead rally.

LOW POINT: The next day, Texas blitzed reliever Jorge Alcala for five runs en route to a 6-5 walkoff victory, and the wheels started falling off. The Twins went 12-27 the rest of the season, capped by a brutal 2-5 road trip Sept. 16-22 which included two walk-off losses in Cleveland and a Sept. 22 doubleheader sweep in Boston by a combined score of 17-4 that dropped the Twins out of the wild-card lead for good.

NOTABLE ROOKIES: By August, Minnesota was relying on three rookie righties in its five-man rotation. Simeon Woods Richardson joined the rotation in late April and made 28 starts, running out of gas in September but posting a useful 5-5, 4.17 line in 133 innings. David Festa (10.8 K/9 in 64 IP) and Zebby Matthews (6.69 ERA in nine starts), who started the year in high Class A, pitched like rookies, showing talent but vulnerabilities and inconsistency. OF/2B Austin Martin hit only one homer in 233 at-bats, while 2022 first-round pick Brooks Lee (.585 OPS) wasn't quite ready when needed after plantar fasciitis sidelined Correa for most of the second half.

KEY TRANSACTIONS: Owner Joe Pohlad's self-described "business decision" to cut roughly $30 million in payroll from the 2023 AL Central winners proved costly. While Carlos Santana (team-best 23 HR) came through as a free agent signing, offseason acquisitions such as RHPs Anthony Desclafani (injured), Jay Jackson (DFA'd in June) and Josh Staumont (released in August) definitely did not. That lack of depth was exposed after starters Chris Paddack and Joe Ryan (7-7, 3.60) went on the IL in July and August. The Twins' lone trade deadline pickup, reliever Trevor Richards, lasted less than a month before being DFA'd. At season's end, the Pohlad family, which has owned the Twins since 1984, announced it would seek a buyer for the club.

OPENING DAY PAYROLL: $124,077,590 (20th)

PLAYERS OF THE YEAR

MAJOR LEAGUE

Bailey Ober
RHP
12-9, 3.98 ERA
191 SO, 43 BB
Career-high 179 IP

MINOR LEAGUE

Zebby Matthews
RHP
(A+/AA/AAA)
6-3, 2.60 ERA
114 SO, 7 BB, 97 IP

ORGANIZATION LEADERS

Batting *Qualifiers

MAJORS

* AVG	Willi Castro	.247
* OPS	Matt Wallner	.877
HR	Carlos Santana	23
RBI	Carlos Santana	71

MINORS

* AVG	Payton Eeles, Cedar Rapids/Fort Myers/St. Paul	.306
* OBP	Payton Eeles, Cedar Rapids/Fort Myers/St. Paul	.435
* SLG	Payton Eeles, Cedar Rapids/Fort Myers/St. Paul	.497
* OPS	Payton Eeles, Cedar Rapids/Fort Myers/St. Paul	.932
R	Payton Eeles, Cedar Rapids/Fort Myers/St. Paul	87
H	DaShawn Keirsey, St. Paul	133
TB	Carson McCusker, St. Paul/Wichita	225
2B	Carson McCusker, St. Paul/Wichita	30
3B	Payton Eeles, Cedar Rapids/Fort Myers/St. Paul	8
HR	Yunior Severino, St. Paul	21
RBI	DaShawn Keirsey, St. Paul	81
BB	3 tied	67
SO	Yunior Severino, St. Paul	154
SB	Payton Eeles, Cedar Rapids/Fort Myers/St. Paul	41

Pitching #Qualifiers

MAJORS

W	Pablo Lopez	15
# ERA	Bailey Ober	3.98
SO	Pablo Lopez	198
SV	Jhoan Duran	23

MINORS

W	Randy Dobnak, St. Paul	12
L	Aaron Rozek, St. Paul/Wichita	10
L	Darren Bowen, Cedar Rapids	10
# ERA	Andrew Morris, Cedar Rapids/Wichita/St. Paul	2.37
G	Kyle Bischoff, Cedar Rapids/St. Paul/Wichita	45
GS	Caleb Boushley, St. Paul	26
SV	Nolan Santos, Cedar Rapids/Fort Myers	11
IP	Caleb Boushley, St. Paul	134
BB	Randy Dobnak, St. Paul	63
SO	Randy Dobnak, St. Paul	134
# AVG	Andrew Morris, Cedar Rapids/Wichita/St. Paul	.221

2024 PERFORMANCE

General Manager: Derek Falvey. **Farm Director:** Drew MacPhail. **Scouting Director:** Sean Johnson.

Class	Team	League	W	L	PCT	Finish	Manager
Majors	Minnesota Twins	American	82	80	.506	8 (15)	Rocco Baldelli
Triple-A	St. Paul Saints	International	70	79	.470	13 (20)	Toby Gardenhire
Double-A	Wichita Wind Surge	Texas	58	80	.420	9 (10)	Ramon Borrego
High-A	Cedar Rapids Kernels	Midwest	67	63	.515	7 (12)	Brian Dinkelman
Low-A	Fort Myers Mighty Mussels	Florida State	66	59	.528	4 (10)	Brian Meyer
Rookie	FCL Twins	Florida Complex	28	31	.475	9 (15)	Seth Feldman
Rookie	DSL Twins	Dominican	30	25	.545	18 (51)	Rafael Martinez
Overall 2024 Minor League Record			**319**	**337**	**.486**	**19th (30)**	

MINNESOTA TWINS

ORGANIZATION STATISTICS

MINNESOTA TWINS

AMERICAN LEAGUE

Batting	B-T	Ht.	Wt.	DOB	AVG	OBP	SLG	G	PA	AB	R	H	2B	3B	HR	RBI	BB	HBP	SH	SF	SO	SB	CS	BB%	SO%
Buxton, Byron	R-R	6-2	190	12-18-93	.279	.335	.524	102	388	355	62	99	27	3	18	56	20	11	0	2	99	7	2	5.15	25.52
Camargo, Jair	R-R	5-10	230	7-1-99	.000	.143	.000	5	7	6	1	0	0	0	0	0	1	0	0	0	3	0	0	14.29	42.86
Castillo, Diego	R-R	5-10	185	10-28-97	.333	.500	.500	4	8	6	3	2	1	0	0	2	2	0	0	0	1	0	0	25.00	12.50
Castro, Willi	B-R	6-1	206	4-24-97	.247	.331	.385	158	635	558	89	138	31	5	12	60	51	21	1	4	150	14	9	8.03	23.62
Correa, Carlos	R-R	6-4	220	9-22-94	.310	.388	.517	86	367	319	55	99	20	2	14	54	40	3	0	4	61	0	0	10.90	16.62
Farmer, Kyle	R-R	6-0	205	8-17-90	.214	.293	.353	107	242	215	26	46	13	1	5	25	19	6	0	2	49	3	5	7.85	20.25
Helman, Michael	R-R	5-11	195	5-23-96	.300	.300	.500	9	10	10	2	3	2	0	0	0	0	0	0	0	3	0	0	0.00	30.00
Jeffers, Ryan	R-R	6-4	235	6-3-97	.226	.300	.432	122	465	412	56	93	22	0	21	64	32	14	1	6	94	3	0	6.88	20.22
Julien, Edouard	L-R	6-0	195	4-30-99	.199	.292	.323	94	301	266	36	53	9	0	8	21	33	2	0	0	102	6	0	10.96	33.89
Keirsey, DaShawn	L-L	6-0	195	5-13-97	.154	.214	.385	6	14	13	1	2	0	0	1	1	0	1	0	0	1	0	0	0.00	7.14
Kepler, Max	L-L	6-4	225	2-10-93	.253	.302	.380	105	399	368	43	93	21	1	8	42	22	5	0	3	80	1	0	5.51	20.05
Kirilloff, Alex	L-L	6-2	195	11-9-97	.201	.270	.384	57	178	159	20	32	8	3	5	20	15	1	0	3	47	0	0	8.43	26.40
Larnach, Trevor	L-R	6-4	223	2-26-97	.259	.338	.434	112	400	355	59	92	17	0	15	52	40	3	0	2	89	4	1	10.00	22.25
Lee, Brooks	B-R	5-11	205	2-14-01	.221	.265	.320	50	185	172	9	38	6	1	3	27	11	0	0	2	27	3	0	5.95	14.59
Lewis, Royce	R-R	6-2	200	6-5-99	.233	.295	.452	82	325	292	40	68	16	0	16	47	28	0	0	5	74	0	0	8.62	22.77
Margot, Manuel	R-R	5-11	180	9-28-94	.238	.289	.337	129	343	315	37	75	17	1	4	31	21	3	1	3	54	5	0	6.12	15.74
Martin, Austin	R-R	6-0	185	3-23-99	.253	.318	.352	93	257	233	41	59	18	1	1	16	20	2	2	0	47	7	3	7.78	18.29
Miranda, Jose	R-R	6-2	210	6-29-98	.284	.322	.441	121	429	401	44	114	28	4	9	49	18	6	0	4	66	2	2	4.20	15.38
Santana, Carlos	B-R	5-11	215	4-8-86	.238	.328	.420	150	594	521	63	124	26	0	23	71	65	6	0	2	99	4	0	10.94	16.67
Vazquez, Christian	R-R	5-9	205	8-21-90	.221	.248	.327	93	315	294	29	65	10	0	7	27	11	1	5	4	65	3	1	3.49	20.63
Wallner, Matt	L-R	6-4	220	12-12-97	.259	.372	.523	75	261	220	26	57	17	1	13	37	24	16	0	1	95	3	0	9.20	36.40

Pitching	B-T	Ht.	Wt.	DOB	W	L	ERA	G	GS	SV	IP	Hits	Runs	ER	HR	BB	SO	AVG	OBP	SLG	SO%	BB%	BF
Alcala, Jorge	R-R	6-3	205	7-28-95	4	3	3.24	54	0	0	58	40	23	21	8	20	58	.190	.269	.352	24.68	8.51	235
Blewett, Scott	R-R	6-6	245	4-10-96	1	1	1.77	12	0	0	20	17	5	4	2	8	18	.224	.306	.368	21.18	9.41	85
Boushley, Caleb	R-R	6-3	190	10-1-93	0	0	4.50	2	0	0	4	6	2	2	0	2	1	.333	.400	.444	5.00	10.00	20
Bowman, Matt	R-R	6-0	185	5-31-91	0	0	2.35	5	0	0	8	2	2	2	1	4	6	.080	.258	.200	19.35	12.90	31
Castillo, Diego	R-R	6-3	268	1-18-94	0	0	2.70	7	0	0	10	8	3	3	0	8	6	.235	.372	.294	13.95	18.60	43
Castro, Willi	S-R	6-1	206	4-24-97	0	0	0.00	2	0	0	1	0	0	0	0	0	0	.000	.000	.000	0.00	0.00	4
Dobnak, Randy	R-R	6-1	230	1-17-95	0	0	5.59	5	0	0	10	11	6	6	1	5	7	.275	.356	.450	15.56	11.11	45
Duarte, Daniel	R-R	6-0	235	12-4-96	1	0	2.25	2	0	0	4	2	1	1	1	1	3	.143	.200	.429	20.00	6.67	15
Duran, Jhoan	R-R	6-5	230	1-8-98	6	9	3.64	58	0	23	54	48	30	22	4	15	66	.235	.305	.363	28.95	6.58	228
Farmer, Kyle	R-R	6-0	205	8-17-90	0	0	6.75	3	0	0	4	7	3	3	0	1	0	.389	.421	.556	0.00	5.26	19
Festa, David	R-R	6-6	185	3-8-00	2	6	4.90	14	13	0	64	62	36	35	9	23	77	.247	.314	.434	27.80	8.30	277
Funderburk, Kody	L-L	6-4	230	11-27-96	1	0	6.49	27	0	1	35	41	26	25	4	15	32	.301	.381	.478	19.88	9.32	161
Headrick, Brent	L-L	6-6	235	12-17-97	0	0	3.00	1	0	0	3	2	1	1	1	2	5	.182	.308	.545	38.46	15.38	13
Henriquez, Ronny	R-R	5-10	155	6-20-00	1	1	3.26	16	1	0	19	20	8	7	2	5	15	.267	.329	.387	18.29	6.10	82
Irvin, Cole	L-L	6-4	225	1-31-94	0	1	12.27	4	0	0	4	6	5	5	1	4	2	.375	.500	.625	9.09	18.18	22
Jackson, Jay	R-R	6-1	195	10-27-87	1	2	7.52	20	0	0	26	28	24	22	7	9	29	.267	.325	.524	25.44	7.89	114
Jax, Griffin	R-R	6-2	195	11-22-94	5	5	2.03	72	0	10	71	47	19	16	4	15	95	.184	.234	.281	34.42	5.43	276
Lopez, Pablo	L-R	6-4	225	3-7-96	15	10	4.08	32	32	0	185	180	90	84	26	41	198	.252	.298	.407	25.65	5.31	772
Matthews, Zebby	R-R	6-5	225	5-22-00	1	4	6.69	9	9	0	38	51	31	28	11	11	43	.311	.362	.567	24.29	6.21	177
Ober, Bailey	R-R	6-9	260	7-12-95	12	9	3.98	31	31	0	179	136	81	79	27	43	191	.208	.261	.391	26.94	6.06	709
Okert, Steven	L-L	6-2	202	7-9-91	3	2	5.09	44	1	1	35	37	22	20	6	16	33	.266	.352	.460	20.63	10.00	160
Paddack, Chris	R-R	6-5	217	1-8-96	5	3	4.99	17	17	0	88	102	50	49	14	21	79	.283	.323	.444	20.57	5.47	384
Richards, Trevor	R-R	6-2	205	5-15-93	0	1	4.15	10	0	1	13	8	6	6	0	11	13	.182	.356	.205	22.03	18.64	59
Ryan, Joe	R-R	6-2	205	6-5-96	7	7	3.60	23	23	0	135	110	59	54	19	23	147	.217	.257	.400	27.32	4.28	538
Sands, Cole	R-R	6-3	215	7-17-97	9	1	3.28	62	0	4	71	59	30	26	6	12	85	.221	.265	.326	29.11	4.11	292
Staumont, Josh	R-R	6-3	200	12-21-93	1	0	3.70	25	0	0	24	17	12	10	0	14	18	.200	.314	.212	17.65	13.73	102
Stewart, Brock	L-R	6-3	220	10-3-91	0	0	5.17	16	0	0	16	15	9	9	2	8	20	.254	.343	.407	29.85	11.94	67
Thielbar, Caleb	R-L	6-0	205	1-31-87	2	4	5.32	59	0	3	47	50	33	28	6	24	53	.266	.344	.410	24.54	11.11	216
Tonkin, Michael	R-R	6-7	220	11-19-89	0	0	3.86	13	0	0	16	18	7	7	0	7	22	.286	.370	.317	30.14	9.59	73
Topa, Justin	R-R	6-4	200	3-7-91	0	0	0.00	3	0	0	2	1	0	0	0	0	2	.125	.125	.125	25.00	0.00	8
Varland, Louie	L-R	6-1	205	12-9-97	0	6	7.61	16	7	0	50	68	44	42	12	16	49	.318	.371	.523	20.59	6.72	238

Pitching	B-T	Ht.	Wt.	DOB	W	L	ERA	G	GS	SV	IP	Hits	Runs	ER	HR	BB	SO	AVG	OBP	SLG	SO%	BB%	BF
Wallner, Matt	L-R	6-4	220	12-12-97	0	0	0.00	1	0	0	1	2	0	0	0	0	0	.333	.333	.500	0.00	0.00	6
Winder, Josh	R-R	6-5	210	10-11-96	0	0	3.00	4	0	0	9	7	4	3	0	1	10	.212	.263	.242	26.32	2.63	38
Woods Richardson, Simeon	R-R	6-3	210	9-27-00	5	5	4.17	28	28	0	134	125	63	62	16	48	117	.246	.310	.385	20.56	8.44	569

Fielding

Catcher	PCT	G	PO	A	E	DP	PB
Camargo	.000	2	0	0	0	0	0
Jeffers	.992	86	749	31	6	0	3
Vazquez	.995	86	772	29	4	2	1

First Base	PCT	G	PO	A	E	DP
Santana	.996	146	998	92	4	67
Farmer	1.000	1	2	0	0	0
Julien	1.000	1	1	0	0	0
Kirilloff	1.000	12	57	3	0	2
Miranda	1.000	13	86	7	0	5
Vazquez	1.000	1	1	0	0	0

Second Base	PCT	G	PO	A	E	DP
Lewis	.875	2	0	7	1	0
Lee	.920	11	7	16	2	1
Julien	.981	90	86	166	5	25
Castro	.981	40	46	60	2	13
Farmer	.985	71	38	92	2	13
Martin	1.000	14	15	19	0	3

Third Base	PCT	G	PO	A	E	DP
Castillo	1.000	3	1	3	0	0
Castro	.971	27	12	22	1	0
Farmer	1.000	29	12	27	0	3
Helman	.000	1	0	0	0	0
Lee	1.000	13	7	20	0	0
Lewis	.952	51	42	76	6	7
Miranda	.959	78	42	97	6	9
Vazquez	.000	3	0	0	0	0

Shortstop	PCT	G	PO	A	E	DP
Castro	.982	56	68	93	3	11
Correa	.983	84	119	169	5	26
Farmer	1.000	13	5	9	0	1
Lee	.974	27	34	42	2	8
Miranda	1.000	1	0	2	0	1

Outfield	PCT	G	PO	A	E	DP
Buxton	1.000	94	204	2	0	0
Castro	.984	64	121	3	2	0
Helman	.667	7	2	0	1	0
Keirsey	1.000	6	5	1	0	0
Kepler	1.000	103	172	4	0	1
Kirilloff	1.000	31	37	1	0	0
Larnach	1.000	62	91	0	0	0
Margot	.982	130	163	0	3	0
Martin	.992	80	124	1	1	0
Wallner	1.000	58	109	4	0	1

ST. PAUL SAINTS — TRIPLE-A

INTERNATIONAL LEAGUE

Batting	B-T	Ht.	Wt.	DOB	AVG	OBP	SLG	G	PA	AB	R	H	2B	3B	HR	RBI	BB	HBP	SH	SF	SO	SB	CS	BB%	SO%
Bannon, Rylan	R-R	5-8	180	4-22-96	.165	.330	.285	49	197	158	20	26	8	1	3	20	36	3	0	0	57	4	0	18.27	28.93
Bernard, Wynton	R-R	6-2	195	9-24-90	.248	.300	.357	32	140	129	12	32	6	1	2	15	8	2	0	1	23	12	1	5.71	16.43
Brigham, Jeff	R-R	6-0	195	2-16-92	.000	.000	.000	33	1	1	0	0	0	0	0	0	0	0	0	0	1	0	0	0.00	100.00
Buxton, Byron	R-R	6-2	190	12-18-93	.091	.167	.091	4	12	11	1	1	0	0	0	1	1	0	0	0	6	0	0	8.33	50.00
Camargo, Jair	R-R	5-10	230	7-1-99	.212	.290	.403	74	317	283	36	60	16	1	12	51	25	7	0	2	94	2	1	7.89	29.65
Castillo, Diego	R-R	5-10	185	10-28-97	.260	.361	.397	110	454	385	58	100	22	2	9	54	60	4	0	5	66	13	4	13.22	14.54
Eeles, Payton	L-R	5-7	180	11-16-99	.299	.419	.500	64	260	214	43	64	11	4	8	30	33	12	0	1	38	20	3	12.69	14.62
Fajardo, Yoyner	L-R	6-0	179	4-6-99	.229	.274	.362	33	114	105	16	24	2	0	4	17	6	1	0	1	34	3	3	5.26	29.82
Farmer, Kyle	R-R	6-0	205	8-17-90	.273	.333	.455	3	12	11	0	3	2	0	0	1	1	0	0	0	4	0	0	8.33	33.33
Helman, Michael	R-R	5-11	195	5-23-96	.271	.350	.487	72	314	277	49	75	18	0	14	47	29	6	0	2	76	12	1	9.24	24.20
Holland, Will	R-R	5-9	181	4-18-98	.299	.428	.556	41	145	117	32	35	10	1	6	20	17	10	0	1	31	13	2	11.72	21.38
Houghton, Maddux	R-R	5-11	190	2-23-99	.231	.231	.231	5	13	13	2	3	0	0	0	0	0	0	0	0	5	0	0	0.00	38.46
Isola, Alex	R-R	5-11	215	7-22-98	.215	.303	.333	70	274	237	28	51	13	0	5	29	31	1	0	5	53	4	1	11.31	19.34
Julien, Edouard	L-R	6-0	195	4-30-99	.242	.395	.409	49	233	186	33	45	8	1	7	20	46	1	0	0	73	6	0	19.74	31.33
Keirsey, DaShawn	L-L	6-0	195	5-13-97	.300	.368	.476	111	505	443	71	133	22	7	14	81	48	5	0	9	116	36	7	9.50	22.97
Kemp, Tony	L-R	5-6	160	10-31-91	.279	.358	.436	46	187	165	24	46	6	1	6	26	18	3	0	1	24	4	1	9.63	12.83
Kepler, Max	L-L	6-4	225	2-10-93	.400	.538	.400	3	13	10	3	4	0	0	0	0	3	0	0	0	2	0	0	23.08	15.38
Kirilloff, Alex	L-L	6-2	195	11-9-97	.200	.200	.400	1	5	5	1	1	1	0	0	0	0	0	0	0	3	0	0	0.00	60.00
Lee, Brooks	B-R	5-11	205	2-14-01	.308	.368	.606	25	114	104	22	32	7	0	8	25	10	0	0	0	16	1	0	8.77	14.04
Lewis, Royce	R-R	6-2	200	6-5-99	.172	.226	.241	8	31	29	4	5	2	0	0	0	2	0	0	0	11	1	0	6.45	35.48
Lucky, Nick	L-R	6-0	190	12-25-99	.000	.000	.000	1	1	1	0	0	0	0	0	0	0	0	0	0	1	0	0	0.00	100.00
Martin, Austin	R-R	6-0	185	3-23-99	.305	.469	.379	28	130	95	19	29	4	0	1	10	28	4	0	3	15	8	1	21.54	11.54
McCusker, Carson	R-R	6-8	250	5-22-98	.286	.337	.484	24	98	91	13	26	4	1	4	11	7	0	0	0	33	0	0	7.14	33.67
Miranda, Jose	R-R	6-2	210	6-29-98	.294	.375	.471	9	40	34	5	10	3	0	1	4	5	0	0	1	5	1	0	12.50	12.50
Morales, Jeferson	R-R	5-8	170	5-13-99	.358	.433	.585	17	60	53	12	19	7	1	1	7	6	1	0	0	11	2	0	10.00	18.33
Morris, Tanner	L-R	6-0	190	9-13-97	.133	.245	.200	14	53	45	6	6	3	0	0	2	7	0	0	1	13	0	0	13.21	24.53
Prato, Anthony	R-R	5-9	186	5-11-98	.228	.370	.350	106	413	334	60	76	20	6	3	30	67	9	2	1	85	10	1	16.22	20.58
Rodriguez, Emmanuel	L-L	5-10	210	2-28-03	.217	.400	.348	7	30	23	6	5	0	0	1	5	7	0	0	0	12	0	0	23.33	40.00
Severino, Yunior	B-R	6-0	189	10-3-99	.254	.342	.434	128	565	489	66	124	21	2	21	79	67	2	0	7	154	4	0	11.86	27.26
Shuffield, Dalton	R-R	5-10	170	3-31-99	.216	.284	.338	25	82	74	12	16	4	1	1	15	6	1	1	0	22	3	1	7.32	26.83
Varland, Louie	L-R	6-1	205	12-9-97	.000	.000	.000	17	1	1	0	0	0	0	0	0	0	0	0	0	1	0	0	0.00	100.00
Wallner, Matt	L-R	6-4	220	12-12-97	.259	.343	.544	67	297	259	45	67	15	1	19	53	32	3	0	3	91	5	0	10.77	30.64
Williams, Chris	R-R	5-11	225	11-23-96	.221	.339	.461	88	334	280	49	62	16	0	17	41	48	3	1	2	106	5	0	14.37	31.74
Winkel, Pat	L-R	6-0	200	1-27-00	.228	.279	.362	78	297	276	23	63	16	0	7	38	19	1	0	1	90	0	0	6.40	30.30

Pitching	B-T	Ht.	Wt.	DOB	W	L	ERA	G	GS	SV	IP	Hits	Runs	ER	HR	BB	SO	AVG	OBP	SLG	SO%	BB%	BF
Adams, Travis	R-R	6-1	197	1-19-00	0	2	5.21	4	3	0	19	17	11	11	4	7	9	.239	.308	.493	11.39	8.86	79
Alcala, Jorge	R-R	6-3	205	7-28-95	0	0	1.69	9	0	2	11	7	2	2	1	7	16	.194	.326	.306	37.21	16.28	43
Balazovic, Jordan	R-R	6-5	215	9-17-98	5	4	5.60	24	1	0	35	38	25	22	3	15	49	.266	.340	.406	30.06	9.20	163
Baragar, Caleb	R-L	6-3	215	4-9-94	2	3	5.96	16	4	0	26	29	21	17	5	11	26	.287	.365	.505	22.41	9.48	116
Bischoff, Kyle	R-R	6-2	210	7-29-99	0	0	4.50	3	0	0	2	0	1	1	0	1	1	.000	.125	.000	12.50	12.50	8
Blewett, Scott	R-R	6-6	245	4-10-96	5	2	3.79	38	3	1	55	58	28	23	3	17	54	.266	.324	.399	22.69	7.14	238
Boushley, Caleb	R-R	6-3	190	10-1-93	9	6	5.23	26	26	0	134	156	81	78	22	28	108	.288	.322	.494	18.75	4.86	576
Bowman, Matt	R-R	6-0	185	5-31-91	1	0	1.31	17	0	1	21	14	5	3	2	7	24	.194	.266	.306	30.00	8.75	80
Boyle, Michael	R-L	6-3	200	4-12-94	0	0	7.71	10	0	1	9	15	11	8	2	7	4	.357	.449	.571	8.00	14.00	50
Brice, Austin	R-R	6-4	238	6-19-92	0	0	35.31	8	0	0	4	8	17	17	0	15	8	.381	.658	.476	21.05	39.47	38
Brigham, Jeff	R-R	6-0	195	2-16-92	1	3	4.64	33	1	1	43	38	22	22	8	26	59	.247	.359	.442	31.89	14.05	185
Castillo, Diego	R-R	5-10	185	10-28-97	0	0	36.00	1	0	0	1	2	4	4	1	2	0	.400	.571	1.000	0.00	28.57	7
Castillo, Diego	R-R	6-3	268	1-18-94	0	5	5.59	40	0	8	37	40	25	23	4	25	42	.268	.377	.396	23.86	14.20	176
Dobnak, Randy	R-R	6-1	230	1-17-95	12	7	4.25	28	24	0	133	130	75	63	14	63	134	.253	.343	.391	22.67	10.66	591

Duran, Jhoan	R-R	6-5	230	1-8-98	0	0	9.00	2	0	0	2	4	2	2	0	0	5	.400	.400	.600	50.00	0.00	10
Festa, David	R-R	6-6	185	3-8-00	3	3	4.03	15	15	0	60	56	27	27	9	26	89	.249	.333	.431	34.90	10.20	255
Funderburk, Kody	L-L	6-4	230	11-27-96	1	0	6.08	11	0	3	13	12	9	9	1	6	22	.231	.333	.327	36.67	10.00	60
Gallegos, Giovanny	R-R	6-2	215	8-14-91	0	1	4.26	13	0	0	13	13	7	6	0	10	8	.265	.400	.306	13.33	16.67	60
Gunkel, Joe	R-R	6-5	225	12-30-91	0	5	10.54	9	7	0	27	52	33	32	7	6	11	.406	.430	.672	8.09	4.41	136
Harris, Hobie	R-R	6-3	212	6-23-93	4	6	6.79	44	0	5	54	69	46	41	11	31	62	.307	.386	.498	23.75	11.88	261
Headrick, Brent	L-L	6-6	235	12-17-97	1	0	2.00	6	4	0	18	14	7	4	3	6	23	.206	.270	.368	31.08	8.11	74
Henriquez, Ronny	R-R	5-10	155	6-20-00	1	2	3.44	34	3	3	55	59	27	21	9	17	59	.272	.326	.461	24.89	7.17	237
Jackson, Jay	R-R	6-1	195	10-27-87	0	0	3.00	3	0	0	3	2	1	1	0	0	2	.200	.200	.300	20.00	0.00	10
Jensen, Ryan	R-R	6-0	190	11-23-97	4	5	4.76	44	3	0	57	46	35	30	4	50	81	.221	.378	.346	30.92	19.08	262
Lewis, Cory	R-R	6-5	220	10-9-00	1	0	3.60	1	1	0	5	7	2	2	0	3	2	.368	.435	.421	8.70	13.04	23
MacLeod, Christian	L-L	6-4	227	4-12-00	0	1	7.20	1	1	0	5	6	5	4	1	1	5	.300	.333	.500	23.81	4.76	21
Matthews, Zebby	R-R	6-5	225	5-22-00	1	2	5.68	4	4	0	19	24	12	12	4	1	23	.304	.321	.544	28.40	1.23	81
Morris, Andrew	R-R	6-0	195	9-1-01	1	1	3.48	7	7	0	34	27	14	13	3	11	27	.218	.292	.347	19.57	7.97	138
Nowlin, Jaylen	L-L	6-1	180	1-29-01	0	0	13.50	3	0	0	2	3	4	3	1	0	2	.333	.455	.667	16.67	0.00	12
Okert, Steven	L-L	6-2	202	7-9-91	0	0	6.75	7	0	1	5	9	4	4	0	4	10	.360	.484	.400	32.26	12.90	31
Plutko, Adam	R-R	6-3	215	10-3-91	6	2	4.35	13	12	0	60	52	29	29	8	14	49	.227	.270	.389	20.08	5.74	244
Prato, Anthony	R-R	5-9	186	5-11-98	0	0	0.00	1	0	0	2	5	1	0	0	0	1	.417	.417	.417	8.33	0.00	12
Raya, Marco	R-R	6-1	170	8-7-02	0	0	0.00	1	1	0	5	5	0	0	0	0	4	.263	.263	.316	21.05	0.00	19
Richards, Trevor	R-R	6-2	205	5-15-93	0	0	18.00	1	0	0	1	1	2	2	1	1	1	.250	.400	1.000	20.00	20.00	5
Rozek, Aaron	L-L	6-2	225	8-20-95	1	6	6.23	12	10	0	52	67	38	36	4	17	41	.318	.376	.455	17.23	7.14	238
Schulfer, Austin	R-R	6-2	175	12-22-95	0	0	5.09	11	0	0	18	18	11	10	2	10	14	.269	.372	.403	17.95	12.82	78
Stankiewicz, John	R-R	6-4	230	9-8-98	0	0	0.00	1	0	0	1	0	0	0	0	0	1	.000	.000	.000	33.33	0.00	3
Staumont, Josh	R-R	6-3	200	12-21-93	0	1	4.22	8	0	0	11	9	5	5	1	3	16	.231	.279	.436	37.21	6.98	43
Stewart, Brock	L-R	6-3	220	10-3-91	0	0	2.25	4	0	0	4	2	1	1	1	2	8	.154	.267	.385	53.33	13.33	15
Thielbar, Caleb	R-L	6-0	205	1-31-87	1	0	3.00	2	0	0	3	2	1	1	1	1	5	.200	.273	.500	45.45	9.09	11
Topa, Justin	R-R	6-4	200	3-7-91	0	0	4.09	11	0	0	11	9	6	5	1	4	16	.237	.341	.395	36.36	9.09	44
Varland, Louie	L-R	6-1	205	12-9-97	5	8	4.75	17	16	0	83	84	49	44	12	32	96	.256	.323	.421	26.16	8.72	367
Weiss, Zack	R-R	6-3	210	6-16-92	2	1	5.40	18	0	0	25	36	16	15	3	11	32	.353	.424	.490	26.67	9.17	120
Whorff, Jarret	R-R	6-3	195	10-2-98	0	0	0.00	1	0	0	1	0	0	0	0	0	3	.000	.000	.000	75.00	0.00	4
Williams, Chris	R-R	5-11	225	11-23-96	0	0	54.00	1	0	0	0	1	2	2	0	1	0	.500	.667	.500	0.00	33.33	3
Winder, Josh	R-R	6-5	210	10-11-96	2	0	6.15	27	0	4	41	55	29	28	5	13	47	.320	.374	.471	24.48	6.77	192
Wittgren, Nick	R-R	6-2	216	5-29-91	1	2	5.88	35	0	2	52	60	37	34	14	12	48	.282	.326	.535	21.05	5.26	228
Woods Richardson, Simeon	R-R	6-3	210	9-27-00	0	1	6.08	3	3	0	13	16	9	9	0	5	12	.302	.373	.396	20.34	8.47	59

Fielding

Catcher	PCT	G	PO	A	E	DP	PB
Camargo	.988	45	392	24	5	2	4
Isola	1.000	2	21	1	0	0	0
Williams	.982	43	354	19	7	1	2
Winkel	.986	68	609	30	9	4	5

First Base	PCT	G	PO	A	E	DP
Camargo	.984	8	56	4	1	3
Castillo	.966	3	27	1	1	3
Isola	1.000	22	153	12	0	13
Julien	.964	7	52	2	2	4
Miranda	1.000	6	47	3	0	4
Severino	.900	91	623	55	8	65
Williams	1.000	19	106	15	0	7
Winkel	.000	1	0	0	0	0

Second Base	PCT	G	PO	A	E	DP
Bannon	1.000	2	3	10	0	1
Castillo	.980	12	16	34	1	9
Eeles	.991	30	49	62	1	9
Farmer	1.000	1	2	0	0	0
Helman	1.000	3	2	11	0	2
Holland	1.000	1	5	3	0	1
Julien	.944	39	45	90	8	18
Kemp	.988	25	31	53	1	14
Lee	1.000	2	2	4	0	1
Martin	.955	6	7	14	1	3
Morris	1.000	5	4	15	0	2
Prato	1.000	29	41	64	0	9
Shuffield	1.000	1	1	3	0	0

Third Base	PCT	G	PO	A	E	DP
Bannon	.871	12	9	18	4	2
Castillo	.951	58	38	98	7	7
Eeles	.800	3	3	1	1	0
Helman	1.000	12	8	20	0	1
Lee	1.000	3	1	5	0	0
Lewis	1.000	4	5	4	0	0
Miranda	1.000	2	0	4	0	0
Morris	.789	8	5	10	4	0
Prato	.910	42	23	58	8	7
Severino	.938	8	7	8	1	1
Shuffield	.800	2	0	4	1	0
Williams	.000	1	0	0	0	0

Shortstop	PCT	G	PO	A	E	DP
Bannon	.970	33	29	69	3	8
Castillo	.944	23	28	57	5	13
Eeles	.989	23	35	52	1	11
Farmer	1.000	1	1	3	0	0
Helman	.964	31	43	65	4	13
Holland	.957	20	34	54	4	17
Lee	.965	18	15	40	2	12
Prato	1.000	3	5	3	0	1
Shuffield	1.000	3	3	9	0	1

Outfield	PCT	G	PO	A	E	DP
Bernard	.971	32	63	3	2	0
Buxton	1.000	3	3	0	0	0
Castillo	1.000	2	2	0	0	0
Eeles	.913	11	20	1	2	1
Fajardo	.975	29	38	1	1	0
Helman	1.000	24	44	0	0	0
Holland	1.000	18	30	0	0	0
Houghton	1.000	5	9	0	0	0
Isola	.977	29	38	4	1	2
Keirsey	.984	106	246	7	4	1
Kemp	1.000	21	35	0	0	0
Kepler	1.000	2	3	0	0	0
Lucky	1.000	1	2	0	0	0
Martin	.982	21	55	0	1	0
McCusker	1.000	21	36	1	0	0
Morales	.950	13	19	0	1	0
Prato	.980	30	49	1	1	0
Rodriguez	1.000	5	7	0	0	0
Severino	.929	10	12	1	1	0
Shuffield	.926	17	22	3	2	1
Varland	.000	1	0	0	0	0
Wallner	.965	57	79	3	3	0
Williams	.973	18	32	4	1	2

WICHITA WIND SURGE

DOUBLE-A

TEXAS LEAGUE

Batting	B-T	Ht.	Wt.	DOB	AVG	OBP	SLG	G	PA	AB	R	H	2B	3B	HR	RBI	BB	HBP	SH	SF	SO	SB	CS	BB%	SO%
Cardenas, Noah	R-R	5-11	195	9-10-99	.173	.311	.276	75	305	254	32	44	11	0	5	32	43	8	0	0	71	4	4	14.10	23.28
Cossetti, Andrew	R-R	5-10	215	1-31-00	.192	.299	.344	86	368	317	34	61	18	3	8	43	41	8	0	2	115	5	1	11.14	31.25
Dearden, Tyler	L-R	6-2	185	7-6-98	.221	.276	.316	27	105	95	9	21	9	0	0	6	7	1	0	2	27	0	0	6.67	25.71
Fedko, Kyler	R-R	6-1	195	9-21-99	.227	.327	.319	76	294	251	24	57	14	0	3	21	37	2	0	4	59	7	4	12.59	20.07
Isola, Alex	R-R	5-11	215	7-22-98	.214	.295	.329	19	78	70	7	15	2	0	2	8	7	1	0	0	15	0	1	8.97	19.23
Jenkins, Walker	L-R	6-3	205	2-19-05	.160	.250	.200	6	28	25	3	4	1	0	0	1	3	0	0	0	4	2	0	10.71	14.29
Keaschall, Luke	R-R	6-1	190	8-15-02	.281	.393	.439	58	267	221	43	62	9	1	8	27	32	11	0	3	51	9	5	11.99	19.10
McCusker, Carson	R-R	6-8	250	5-22-98	.281	.357	.489	98	420	370	56	104	26	3	15	64	38	8	0	4	117	7	7	9.05	27.86

Batting	B-T	Ht.	Wt.	DOB	AVG	OBP	SLG	G	PA	AB	R	H	2B	3B	HR	RBI	BB	HBP	SH	SF	SO	SB	CS	BB%	SO%
Morales, Jeferson	R-R	5-8	170	5-13-99	.278	.356	.431	88	371	327	39	91	21	1	9	52	30	11	0	3	57	4	4	8.09	15.36
Olivar, Ricardo	R-R	5-10	176	8-10-01	.224	.325	.299	19	77	67	7	15	2	0	1	7	9	1	0	0	18	3	0	11.69	23.38
Ortega, Jorel	R-R	6-0	194	1-22-01	.214	.308	.349	121	417	364	49	78	13	3	10	44	44	6	1	2	102	11	6	10.55	24.46
Rodriguez, Emmanuel	L-L	5-10	210	2-28-03	.298	.479	.621	37	167	124	40	37	12	2	8	20	42	1	0	0	46	9	3	25.15	27.54
Rosario, Kala'i	R-R	6-0	205	7-2-02	.235	.321	.405	67	299	264	36	62	19	1	8	34	32	2	0	1	91	3	0	10.70	30.43
Ross, Ben	R-R	6-0	180	6-6-01	.212	.284	.341	123	458	410	48	87	18	1	11	38	40	3	1	4	136	20	7	8.73	29.69
Rucker, Jake	R-R	6-0	195	9-14-99	.261	.321	.372	121	515	468	55	122	23	1	9	68	35	8	1	3	77	5	4	6.80	14.95
Sabato, Aaron	R-R	6-2	230	6-4-99	.206	.303	.350	85	350	306	35	63	14	0	10	33	38	5	0	1	104	8	2	10.86	29.71
Schobel, Tanner	R-R	5-9	170	6-4-01	.211	.301	.338	122	520	455	67	96	20	4	10	53	59	1	1	4	124	13	6	11.35	23.85
Shuffield, Dalton	R-R	5-10	170	3-31-99	.228	.309	.374	38	139	123	20	28	6	0	4	19	13	2	0	1	38	7	1	9.35	27.34
Soularie, Alerick	R-R	5-11	175	7-5-99	.164	.314	.284	33	88	67	19	11	2	0	2	10	12	4	2	3	24	12	4	13.64	27.27

Pitching	B-T	Ht.	Wt.	DOB	W	L	ERA	G	GS	SV	IP	Hits	Runs	ER	HR	BB	SO	AVG	OBP	SLG	SO%	BB%	BF
Adams, Travis	R-R	6-1	197	1-19-00	5	7	3.67	22	19	0	108	95	51	44	9	28	109	.233	.284	.344	24.55	6.31	444
Alexy, A.J.	R-R	6-4	195	4-21-98	1	2	6.87	7	3	0	18	11	16	14	0	26	16	.177	.440	.258	17.58	28.57	91
Bischoff, Kyle	R-R	6-2	210	7-29-99	0	0	1.40	14	0	2	19	11	6	3	1	8	25	.164	.260	.254	32.05	10.26	78
Brice, Austin	R-R	6-4	238	6-19-92	0	0	1.08	7	0	1	8	7	3	1	0	4	19	.219	.359	.219	48.72	10.26	39
Culpepper, C.J.	R-R	6-3	193	11-2-01	1	1	4.71	6	6	0	21	19	11	11	2	7	21	.238	.322	.375	23.33	7.78	90
Engler, Scott	R-R	6-4	220	12-12-96	4	1	6.88	27	0	0	34	28	27	26	2	30	37	.226	.388	.339	23.13	18.75	160
Floyd, Taylor	R-R	6-1	185	12-8-97	4	4	4.04	44	1	2	65	54	33	29	3	27	59	.222	.315	.300	21.07	9.64	280
Fox, Mason	R-R	6-2	170	1-7-97	0	0	2.63	11	0	0	14	11	5	4	1	12	13	.239	.390	.391	22.03	20.34	59
Grace, Regi	L-R	6-2	215	12-10-99	1	4	4.19	31	0	0	43	39	24	20	4	21	34	.242	.344	.385	17.80	10.99	191
Jones, Kyle	L-R	6-1	200	2-7-00	0	0	3.60	3	2	0	10	7	4	4	1	4	7	.189	.268	.351	17.07	9.76	41
Laweryson, Cody	L-R	6-4	205	5-10-98	2	2	6.82	27	0	3	33	41	28	25	1	12	33	.301	.351	.404	21.71	7.89	152
Lewis, Cory	R-R	6-5	220	10-9-00	2	6	2.59	15	13	1	66	54	21	19	7	34	80	.227	.324	.378	28.78	12.23	278
MacLeod, Christian	L-L	6-4	227	4-12-00	1	2	3.72	8	7	1	39	27	17	16	4	20	44	.191	.296	.340	27.16	12.35	162
Marcano, Rafael	L-L	6-1	170	4-20-00	0	2	16.71	5	1	0	7	7	13	13	3	14	9	.259	.523	.630	19.57	30.43	46
Matthews, Zebby	R-R	6-5	225	5-22-00	2	1	1.95	10	9	0	55	36	17	12	2	6	63	.180	.208	.245	30.14	2.87	209
McMahon, Hunter	R-R	6-3	185	4-9-98	1	0	5.65	8	0	0	14	16	9	9	2	2	4	.302	.321	.472	7.02	3.51	57
Morris, Andrew	R-R	6-0	195	9-1-01	6	3	1.90	12	10	1	62	49	18	13	1	14	63	.210	.261	.253	25.20	5.60	250
Noble, Jack	R-R	6-2	200	4-2-00	0	0	3.00	1	0	0	3	1	1	1	0	0	1	.111	.200	.111	10.00	0.00	10
Nowlin, Jaylen	L-L	6-1	180	1-29-01	5	7	4.67	21	15	0	96	90	59	50	11	48	97	.251	.341	.399	23.10	11.43	420
Ohl, Pierson	R-R	6-1	180	9-10-99	4	7	4.68	21	15	1	102	113	63	53	14	16	70	.278	.304	.453	16.32	3.73	429
Ortega, Jorel	R-R	6-0	194	1-22-01	0	0	0.00	2	0	0	2	0	0	0	0	0	0	.000	.000	.000	0.00	0.00	5
Paredes, Mike	R-R	5-11	185	7-27-00	0	0	5.79	13	0	0	19	21	12	12	1	8	13	.280	.349	.400	15.66	9.64	83
Raya, Marco	R-R	6-1	170	8-7-02	3	4	4.27	24	24	0	93	84	44	44	8	44	99	.242	.333	.366	24.81	11.03	399
Reed, Sheldon	L-R	6-2	205	7-30-97	1	0	6.75	4	0	0	7	8	6	5	0	7	8	.276	.417	.276	22.22	19.44	36
Rodriguez, Miguel	R-R	6-0	180	2-25-99	1	7	4.96	37	0	5	45	41	35	25	1	22	42	.246	.333	.341	20.79	10.89	202
Rozek, Aaron	L-L	6-2	225	8-20-95	5	4	2.19	14	5	0	70	56	20	17	5	13	59	.215	.254	.315	21.38	4.71	276
Rucker, Jake	R-R	6-0	195	9-14-99	0	0	0.00	1	0	0	0	0	0	0	0	0	0	.000	.000	.000	0.00	0.00	1
Solomon, Jared	R-R	6-2	219	6-10-97	2	4	7.76	30	0	4	31	38	31	27	2	25	33	.295	.435	.395	20.50	15.53	161
Stankiewicz, John	R-R	6-4	230	9-8-98	2	5	4.45	41	0	2	59	65	32	29	6	15	49	.280	.327	.392	19.52	5.98	251
Velez, Ricardo	R-R	6-1	180	8-21-98	1	3	6.27	16	0	0	19	24	15	13	3	7	17	.316	.381	.447	20.00	8.24	85
Whorff, Jarret	R-R	6-3	195	10-2-98	3	3	2.93	22	5	2	46	39	17	15	4	23	45	.228	.332	.368	22.50	11.50	200
Wittgren, Nick	R-R	6-2	216	5-29-91	1	1	3.52	5	3	0	8	10	4	3	1	2	4	.313	.353	.438	11.76	5.88	34
Wosinski, Jacob	R-R	6-8	220	3-9-99	0	0	0.00	2	0	0	4	1	0	0	0	1	3	.077	.143	.077	21.43	7.14	14

Fielding

Catcher	PCT	G	PO	A	E	DP	PB
Cardenas	.984	71	624	43	11	4	8
Cossetti	.985	51	427	28	7	6	15
Isola	.974	4	33	5	1	2	0
Morales	.973	5	32	4	1	0	0
Olivar	.948	9	69	4	4	0	1

First Base	PCT	G	PO	A	E	DP
Cossetti	.994	23	152	4	1	11
Fedko	1.000	13	101	10	0	13
Isola	1.000	4	32	1	0	1
Keaschall	1.000	13	107	8	0	4
Morales	1.000	1	3	0	0	1
Ortega	.985	15	61	5	1	4
Rucker	.954	10	60	2	3	4
Sabato	.982	66	465	24	9	36
Shuffield	1.000	1	1	0	0	0

Second Base	PCT	G	PO	A	E	DP
Keaschall	1.000	10	10	29	0	4
Morales	.965	22	31	51	3	9
Ortega	1.000	30	58	64	0	16
Rucker	.990	69	114	181	3	34
Schobel	.967	9	7	22	1	3
Shuffield	1.000	1	4	4	0	1
Soularie	.000	1	0	0	0	0

Third Base	PCT	G	PO	A	E	DP
Ortega	.900	16	17	19	4	6
Ross	.957	8	8	14	1	3
Rucker	.990	40	29	69	1	6
Schobel	.939	77	49	106	10	8
Shuffield	1.000	1	2	1	0	1

Shortstop	PCT	G	PO	A	E	DP
Ortega	.992	35	48	71	1	13
Ross	.969	83	95	151	8	22
Schobel	.966	29	49	63	4	16

Outfield	PCT	G	PO	A	E	DP
Dearden	.980	26	50	0	1	0
Fedko	.990	55	100	2	1	1
Isola	1.000	10	25	0	0	0
Jenkins	1.000	3	11	0	0	0
Keaschall	1.000	11	30	1	0	0
McCusker	.977	70	124	5	3	1
Morales	.966	38	79	5	3	2
Olivar	1.000	5	11	0	0	0
Ortega	1.000	22	55	0	0	0
Rodriguez	.960	35	94	2	4	0
Rosario	.955	61	107	0	5	0
Ross	.989	32	85	4	1	3
Schobel	.923	4	12	0	1	0
Shuffield	.990	34	99	2	1	0
Soularie	.925	27	47	2	4	1

CEDAR RAPIDS KERNELS — HIGH-A

MIDWEST LEAGUE

Batting	B-T	Ht.	Wt.	DOB	AVG	OBP	SLG	G	PA	AB	R	H	2B	3B	HR	RBI	BB	HBP	SH	SF	SO	SB	CS	BB%	SO%
Baez, Nate	R-R	5-11	191	5-17-01	.239	.331	.420	82	317	276	38	66	10	2	12	32	31	8	0	2	89	0	0	9.78	28.08
Cavaco, Keoni	R-R	6-0	195	6-2-01	.144	.202	.327	34	114	104	14	15	5	1	4	13	7	1	0	2	50	0	0	6.14	43.86
Cespedes, Rubel	L-R	6-0	210	8-29-00	.282	.346	.431	110	463	418	48	118	22	2	12	72	39	3	0	2	93	5	3	8.42	20.09
Clayton, Matthew	R-R	5-11	185	5-15-99	.200	.250	.400	7	16	15	1	3	0	0	1	4	1	0	0	0	6	0	1	6.25	37.50

Culpepper, Kaelen	R-R	6-0	185	12-29-02	.210	.310	.306	17	71	62	11	13	1	1	1	3	8	1	0	0	13	2	0	11.27	18.31
De Andrade, Danny	R-R	5-11	173	4-10-04	.243	.333	.359	29	117	103	13	25	6	0	2	19	8	6	0	0	20	5	2	6.84	17.09
Dearden, Tyler	L-R	6-2	185	7-6-98	.364	.400	.455	9	35	33	3	12	3	0	0	4	0	2	0	0	8	0	0	0.00	22.86
Doncon, Rayne	R-R	6-2	176	9-22-03	.235	.320	.410	56	244	217	32	51	11	3	7	34	24	3	0	0	51	3	3	9.84	20.90
Eeles, Payton	L-R	5-7	180	11-16-99	.275	.473	.425	13	55	40	12	11	1	1	1	4	11	4	0	0	3	8	3	20.00	5.45
Garry, Willie Joe	L-L	6-0	187	5-29-00	.132	.224	.235	24	77	68	9	9	1	0	2	7	7	1	1	0	18	4	0	9.09	23.38
Gonzalez, Gabriel	R-R	5-10	165	1-4-04	.255	.327	.379	76	315	282	28	72	19	2	4	35	22	9	0	2	49	5	3	6.98	15.56
Harry, Jay	L-R	6-0	195	7-18-02	.214	.306	.349	82	340	295	36	63	14	1	8	39	30	11	0	4	65	5	4	8.82	19.12
Hess, Kyle	L-R	6-0	210	5-20-99	.195	.266	.314	53	178	159	16	31	9	2	2	15	13	3	0	2	41	5	3	7.30	23.03
Jenkins, Walker	L-R	6-3	205	2-19-05	.290	.382	.481	34	152	131	21	38	12	2	3	17	17	3	0	1	24	8	2	11.18	15.79
Keaschall, Luke	R-R	6-1	190	8-15-02	.335	.457	.544	44	197	158	37	53	12	0	7	21	30	7	0	2	29	14	1	15.23	14.72
Lucky, Nick	L-R	6-0	190	12-25-99	.152	.291	.197	22	79	66	6	10	0	0	1	4	10	3	0	0	26	2	1	12.66	32.91
Maitan, Kevin	B-R	6-2	190	2-12-00	.246	.296	.389	75	311	285	32	70	13	2	8	35	19	3	0	4	103	2	1	6.11	33.12
Olivar, Ricardo	R-R	5-10	176	8-10-01	.287	.393	.473	81	356	300	59	86	17	3	11	44	53	1	0	2	70	3	0	14.89	19.66
Ruiz, Agustin	L-R	6-2	215	9-23-99	.220	.319	.367	83	307	264	41	58	17	2	6	36	30	10	0	3	68	2	4	9.77	22.15
Ruiz, Poncho	R-R	6-2	210	2-23-02	.182	.286	.227	21	77	66	3	12	3	0	0	5	10	0	0	1	19	0	0	12.99	24.68
Salas, Jose	B-R	6-0	191	4-26-03	.227	.286	.330	102	374	339	43	77	17	3	4	33	23	5	7	0	104	16	5	6.15	27.81
Shuffield, Dalton	R-R	5-10	170	3-31-99	.227	.292	.455	13	48	44	5	10	2	1	2	9	4	0	0	0	16	2	1	8.33	33.33
Tatum, Dillon	R-R	5-11	220	5-24-00	.197	.288	.324	24	80	71	8	14	3	0	2	5	7	2	0	0	33	0	1	8.75	41.25
Urbina, Misael	R-R	5-10	190	4-26-02	.218	.335	.324	101	392	330	48	72	16	2	5	30	56	3	1	2	97	14	6	14.29	24.74
Wingrove, Rixon	L-R	6-4	260	5-23-00	.224	.298	.447	21	84	76	8	17	2	0	5	11	7	1	0	0	17	0	0	8.33	20.24

Pitching	B-T	Ht.	Wt.	DOB	W	L	ERA	G	GS	SV	IP	Hits	Runs	ER	HR	BB	SO	AVG	OBP	SLG	SO%	BB%	BF
Bengard, Spencer	R-R	6-4	220	4-19-02	1	0	1.17	6	1	1	23	18	4	3	1	3	14	.212	.247	.271	15.73	3.37	89
Bischoff, Kyle	R-R	6-2	210	7-29-99	5	2	4.05	28	0	4	40	32	18	18	2	17	52	.212	.310	.272	29.71	9.71	175
Boadas, Miguelangel	R-R	6-1	181	12-7-02	1	4	6.23	11	8	0	30	31	29	21	2	14	39	.256	.368	.364	26.71	9.59	146
Bowen, Darren	R-R	6-3	180	2-3-01	2	10	6.07	18	17	0	73	77	53	49	7	26	71	.266	.332	.422	21.65	7.93	328
Carr, Jordan	S-L	6-2	210	7-17-97	6	3	4.47	31	7	0	91	94	49	45	9	30	67	.267	.340	.389	17.01	7.61	394
Castro, Ricky	R-R	6-1	200	8-5-99	2	4	4.05	7	5	0	33	33	19	15	3	9	31	.252	.300	.412	21.99	6.38	141
Cavaco, Keoni	R-R	6-0	195	6-2-01	0	0	0.00	3	0	0	2	2	0	0	0	0	2	.222	.222	.333	22.22	0.00	9
Clayton, Matthew	R-R	5-11	185	5-15-99	0	0	21.00	2	0	0	3	9	7	7	2	1	0	.529	.550	1.000	0.00	5.00	20
Culpepper, C.J.	R-R	6-3	193	11-2-01	2	2	2.89	10	9	0	37	29	17	12	1	11	43	.215	.282	.304	28.86	7.38	149
Hall, Tanner	R-R	6-1	186	3-18-02	0	3	7.85	4	4	0	18	18	16	16	5	9	15	.247	.349	.493	17.44	10.47	86
Hamilton, Xander	L-R	6-3	216	7-7-01	0	0	6.75	7	0	0	7	9	8	5	0	2	9	.290	.343	.323	25.71	5.71	35
Klein, John	R-R	6-5	225	4-22-02	8	3	4.57	22	20	0	100	102	51	51	9	38	90	.261	.333	.399	20.41	8.62	441
Labas, A.J.	R-R	6-3	223	12-8-98	5	3	5.49	26	0	0	41	42	28	25	11	13	36	.264	.328	.516	20.34	7.34	177
Langenberg, Ty	R-R	6-2	190	12-8-01	5	2	3.90	12	11	0	60	60	31	26	7	18	60	.259	.316	.397	23.62	7.09	254
Lee, Jeremy	R-R	5-11	203	9-7-01	1	5	5.27	15	13	0	56	64	37	33	5	26	49	.283	.367	.403	18.85	10.00	260
MacLeod, Christian	L-L	6-4	227	4-12-00	3	1	2.77	12	12	0	49	41	20	15	6	25	58	.224	.322	.377	27.49	11.85	211
Marcano, Rafael	L-L	6-1	170	4-20-00	1	0	2.70	25	0	1	43	34	14	13	1	24	41	.224	.330	.342	22.78	13.33	180
Matthews, Zebby	R-R	6-5	225	5-22-00	3	0	1.59	4	4	0	23	17	4	4	1	0	28	.202	.202	.262	33.33	0.00	84
Mendez, Juan	R-R	6-4	240	10-18-98	1	1	4.79	33	0	0	36	44	25	19	3	15	45	.291	.363	.411	26.79	8.93	168
Mercedes, Juan	R-R	5-10	181	1-7-02	1	3	7.31	20	0	0	28	38	29	23	6	10	31	.309	.358	.545	22.63	7.30	137
Morris, Andrew	R-R	6-0	195	9-1-01	3	1	2.15	7	7	0	38	35	10	9	2	7	43	.240	.273	.301	27.92	4.55	154
Noble, Jack	R-R	6-2	200	4-2-00	0	0	16.20	2	0	0	3	5	6	6	1	3	4	.333	.444	.533	22.22	16.67	18
Paredes, Mike	R-R	5-11	185	7-27-00	2	2	1.80	17	3	2	45	37	10	9	1	5	45	.228	.247	.290	26.47	2.94	170
Perez, Samuel	L-L	5-11	205	11-29-99	0	0	1.80	3	0	1	5	4	1	1	1	2	5	.222	.300	.500	25.00	10.00	20
Prielipp, Connor	L-L	6-2	210	1-10-01	0	1	3.26	7	7	0	19	12	10	7	0	7	32	.176	.263	.191	41.56	9.09	77
Reed, Sheldon	L-R	6-2	205	7-30-97	0	0	8.68	14	0	0	19	24	20	18	6	13	19	.320	.409	.613	20.21	13.83	94
Santos, Nolan	R-R	6-1	205	12-7-00	1	3	4.34	14	0	3	19	16	10	9	1	6	18	.225	.278	.352	22.50	7.50	80
Stankiewicz, John	R-R	6-4	230	9-8-98	0	0	0.00	1	0	0	2	0	0	0	0	0	3	.000	.000	.000	50.00	0.00	6
Velez, Ricardo	R-R	6-1	180	8-21-98	7	1	2.72	27	0	7	36	26	16	11	2	13	51	.191	.267	.287	34.00	8.67	150
Whorff, Jarret	R-R	6-3	195	10-2-98	1	2	2.28	10	0	1	24	18	8	6	1	4	25	.207	.255	.310	26.60	4.26	94
Wosinski, Jacob	R-R	6-8	220	3-9-99	2	3	4.48	34	2	5	60	49	33	30	9	32	63	.217	.327	.394	23.95	12.17	263
Yanez, Gabriel	L-L	6-3	168	7-22-99	4	4	2.26	38	0	10	56	49	20	14	1	17	49	.240	.303	.304	21.49	7.46	228

Fielding

Catcher	PCT	G	PO	A	E	DP	PB
Baez	.986	39	352	12	5	1	3
Clayton	.970	5	29	3	1	0	2
Olivar	.984	50	467	20	8	1	5
Ruiz	1.000	16	110	12	0	1	1
Tatum	.980	23	188	11	4	1	3

First Base	PCT	G	PO	A	E	DP
Baez	.984	26	179	7	3	11
Cavaco	.992	33	235	18	2	20
Cespedes	1.000	13	77	5	0	5
Maitan	.987	38	305	10	4	28
Ruiz	.972	4	33	2	1	1
Ruiz	1.000	2	16	0	0	1
Wingrove	1.000	20	152	10	0	11

Second Base	PCT	G	PO	A	E	DP
Cespedes	.973	22	25	48	2	9
Culpepper	1.000	1	3	6	0	0
De Andrade	.944	5	5	12	1	1
Doncon	1.000	4	6	11	0	2
Eeles	.926	10	11	14	2	4
Harry	.968	39	55	96	5	14
Keaschall	.961	10	23	26	2	7
Lucky	.975	11	17	22	1	7
Salas	.983	32	42	75	2	13
Shuffield	1.000	4	5	10	0	2

Third Base	PCT	G	PO	A	E	DP
Cespedes	.941	72	34	110	9	11
Culpepper	1.000	1	2	0	0	0
Doncon	.929	11	4	22	2	3
Eeles	1.000	1	2	0	0	0
Harry	1.000	9	6	27	0	1
Lucky	1.000	1	0	2	0	0
Maitan	.969	31	22	40	2	5
Salas	.842	10	0	16	3	1
Shuffield	1.000	1	2	1	0	0

Shortstop	PCT	G	PO	A	E	DP
Culpepper	.938	15	21	39	4	8
De Andrade	.942	22	27	54	5	6
Doncon	.931	40	50	72	9	7
Eeles	.875	2	1	6	1	2
Harry	.976	21	28	55	2	10
Lucky	.943	9	13	20	2	3
Salas	.935	23	35	51	6	8
Shuffield	1.000	1	2	5	0	1

Outfield	PCT	G	PO	A	E	DP
Dearden	1.000	6	14	0	0	0
Garry	.966	22	56	0	2	0
Gonzalez	.935	67	95	5	7	0
Harry	1.000	12	17	0	0	0
Hess	1.000	51	94	1	0	0
Jenkins	1.000	17	37	1	0	0
Keaschall	1.000	5	8	0	0	0
Lucky	1.000	2	2	0	0	0

Maitan	.000	1	0	0	0	0	Ruiz	.992	68	126	2	1	0	Shuffield	.938	7	14	1	1	0
Olivar	1.000	13	23	1	0	1	Salas	.980	36	94	2	2	1	Urbina	.982	98	156	4	3	0

FORT MYERS MIGHTY MUSSELS — LOW-A

FLORIDA STATE LEAGUE

Batting	B-T	Ht.	Wt.	DOB	AVG	OBP	SLG	G	PA	AB	R	H	2B	3B	HR	RBI	BB	HBP	SH	SF	SO	SB	CS	BB%	SO%
Aguiar, Carlos	L-L	6-2	175	8-28-01	.230	.303	.446	42	155	139	18	32	11	2	5	21	15	0	0	1	45	3	0	9.68	29.03
Amick, Billy	R-R	6-0	210	11-4-02	.222	.351	.413	18	77	63	9	14	3	0	3	9	12	1	0	1	15	2	0	15.58	19.48
Bender, Derek	R-R	6-1	210	1-9-03	.200	.273	.333	19	67	60	6	12	2	0	2	8	5	1	0	0	20	1	1	7.46	29.85
Camargo, Jair	R-R	5-10	230	7-1-99	.304	.360	.478	6	25	23	2	7	1	0	1	4	2	0	0	0	7	1	0	8.00	28.00
Castro, Wilfri	R-R	5-11	165	3-21-01	.226	.385	.306	22	78	62	7	14	2	0	1	5	14	2	0	0	23	0	0	17.95	29.49
Chourio, Byron	B-R	6-2	171	5-20-05	.207	.271	.277	84	366	328	38	68	7	5	2	31	29	2	1	6	104	23	5	7.92	28.42
Clayton, Matthew	R-R	5-11	185	5-15-99	.280	.429	.398	35	119	93	19	26	5	0	2	15	12	13	0	1	24	0	1	10.08	20.17
Cruz, Rafael	R-R	6-1	166	11-13-03	.194	.225	.276	27	102	98	14	19	6	1	0	10	3	1	0	0	32	3	0	2.94	31.37
Culpepper, Kaelen	R-R	6-0	185	12-29-02	.297	.366	.541	9	41	37	6	11	3	0	2	9	3	1	0	0	2	2	1	7.32	4.88
Daniel, Omari	R-R	6-0	185	5-4-04	.154	.185	.250	17	54	52	5	8	3	1	0	1	2	0	0	0	25	1	0	3.70	46.30
DeBarge, Kyle	R-R	5-9	170	7-15-03	.235	.322	.343	26	115	102	14	24	2	3	1	21	12	1	0	0	28	15	3	10.43	24.35
Del Rosario, Angel	R-R	6-0	160	1-11-03	.238	.351	.299	56	175	147	27	35	5	2	0	13	23	3	1	1	41	25	2	13.14	23.43
Diaw, Khadim	R-R	6-1	215	8-23-03	.271	.374	.341	24	99	85	15	23	3	0	1	6	11	3	0	0	14	4	0	11.11	14.14
Doncon, Rayne	R-R	6-2	176	9-22-03	.283	.374	.464	38	163	138	21	39	13	0	4	19	21	1	0	3	38	3	1	12.88	23.31
Duran, Gregory	L-R	6-2	201	10-8-02	.235	.296	.388	30	108	98	18	23	2	2	3	15	7	2	0	1	42	0	0	6.48	38.89
Eeles, Payton	L-R	5-7	180	11-16-99	.331	.448	.517	34	154	118	32	39	7	3	3	26	23	7	0	6	27	13	4	14.94	17.53
Elvis, Cole	R-R	6-1	215	8-4-99	.113	.230	.132	21	61	53	2	6	1	0	0	2	8	0	0	0	29	2	1	13.11	47.54
Ferrer, Jaime	R-R	6-1	222	12-27-02	.269	.376	.372	24	93	78	15	21	8	0	0	9	6	8	0	1	10	6	1	6.45	10.75
Hess, Kyle	L-R	6-0	210	5-20-99	.381	.447	.738	12	47	42	9	16	5	2	2	11	3	2	0	0	7	4	1	6.38	14.89
Houghton, Maddux	R-R	5-11	190	2-23-99	.254	.346	.363	84	298	256	50	65	12	2	4	35	29	9	0	4	89	18	3	9.73	29.87
Jenkins, Walker	L-R	6-3	205	2-19-05	.273	.404	.413	33	151	121	20	33	6	1	3	33	28	0	0	2	17	4	1	18.54	11.26
Kendle, Caden	R-R	5-11	195	3-13-02	.284	.368	.373	22	76	67	10	19	6	0	0	11	8	1	0	0	8	2	2	10.53	10.53
Larnach, Trevor	L-R	6-4	223	2-26-97	.182	.286	.273	3	14	11	2	2	1	0	0	3	2	0	0	1	2	0	0	14.29	14.29
Lee, Brooks	B-R	5-11	205	2-14-01	.333	.429	.389	5	21	18	2	6	1	0	0	3	3	0	0	0	3	1	0	14.29	14.29
Lucky, Nick	L-R	6-0	190	12-25-99	.236	.368	.455	37	136	110	22	26	5	2	5	15	18	5	1	0	47	14	1	13.24	34.56
Martinez, Yohander	R-R	5-10	175	1-8-02	.185	.370	.228	55	212	162	33	30	4	0	1	19	35	13	1	1	45	5	0	16.51	21.23
McCarthy, Ryan	L-R	6-3	235	1-13-99	.233	.359	.302	29	103	86	16	20	6	0	0	7	15	2	0	0	28	4	2	14.56	27.18
Mercedes, Yasser	R-R	6-2	175	11-16-04	.125	.271	.150	10	48	40	7	5	1	0	0	3	6	2	0	0	18	3	0	12.50	37.50
Pena, Daniel	R-R	5-11	205	3-9-05	.195	.301	.293	36	143	123	16	24	3	0	3	14	16	3	0	1	32	0	0	11.19	22.38
Pena, Isaac	B-R	5-10	160	12-27-03	.185	.330	.243	64	233	189	26	35	6	1	1	18	38	4	0	2	55	8	2	16.31	23.61
Rodriguez, Emmanuel	L-L	5-10	210	2-28-03	.000	.250	.000	1	4	3	0	0	0	0	0	0	1	0	0	0	1	0	0	25.00	25.00
Rodriguez, Jose	R-R	6-2	196	6-10-05	.178	.235	.319	43	179	163	15	29	8	0	5	23	12	1	0	3	65	1	0	6.70	36.31
Rosario, Kala'i	R-R	6-0	205	7-2-02	.400	.625	1.600	2	8	5	2	2	0	0	2	3	3	0	0	0	0	0	0	37.50	0.00
Ruiz, Poncho	R-R	6-2	210	2-23-02	.265	.367	.395	71	300	253	35	67	21	0	4	36	38	5	0	4	50	3	1	12.67	16.67
Sabato, Aaron	R-R	6-2	230	6-4-99	.067	.391	.067	5	23	15	1	1	0	0	0	0	8	0	0	0	9	0	0	34.78	39.13
Thomason, Jay	L-R	6-1	200	4-11-02	.213	.306	.320	23	85	75	13	16	2	0	2	7	10	0	0	0	16	1	1	11.76	18.82
Wingrove, Rixon	L-R	6-4	260	5-23-00	.264	.369	.497	45	187	159	25	42	11	1	8	34	24	3	0	1	40	0	1	12.83	21.39
Winokur, Brandon	R-R	6-5	210	12-16-04	.249	.327	.434	94	411	362	60	90	19	3	14	54	34	10	0	4	115	23	6	8.27	27.98

Pitching	B-T	Ht.	Wt.	DOB	W	L	ERA	G	GS	SV	IP	Hits	Runs	ER	HR	BB	SO	AVG	OBP	SLG	SO%	BB%	BF
Becerra, Christian	S-R	6-1	170	6-2-03	0	0	0.00	2	0	0	4	3	1	0	0	3	4	.231	.375	.231	25.00	18.75	16
Bengard, Spencer	R-R	6-4	220	4-19-02	7	2	1.64	13	7	0	60	50	15	11	3	11	58	.222	.259	.316	24.27	4.60	239
Bloor, Kyle	R-R	6-1	190	9-4-99	1	1	1.29	4	0	0	7	4	1	1	0	2	3	.174	.259	.174	11.11	7.41	27
Bohorquez, Adrian	R-R	6-1	190	3-3-05	0	0	2.20	6	5	0	16	8	4	4	0	10	21	.143	.279	.214	30.88	14.71	68
Bonilla, Julio	R-R	6-3	180	11-15-00	1	1	7.83	19	0	3	23	23	22	20	3	18	27	.253	.393	.473	24.11	16.07	112
Bragg, Kade	R-L	6-1	190	7-2-01	0	0	1.08	6	0	1	8	5	2	1	0	5	9	.185	.353	.259	26.47	14.71	34
Castro, Ricky	R-R	6-1	200	8-5-99	4	2	3.72	8	5	1	29	20	14	12	3	10	39	.196	.267	.333	33.05	8.47	118
Clayton, Matthew	R-R	5-11	185	5-15-99	0	0	0.00	2	0	0	2	0	0	0	0	1	1	.000	.286	.000	14.29	14.29	7
Cleto, Tomas	R-R	6-2	206	10-9-00	1	1	4.96	13	1	1	16	10	11	9	1	10	16	.169	.301	.271	21.92	13.70	73
Dunn, Ross	R-L	6-3	225	2-20-02	1	5	6.46	19	16	0	61	68	50	44	8	30	60	.273	.351	.478	21.20	10.60	283
Ethridge, Ben	R-R	6-2	190	7-3-01	3	1	3.84	34	0	1	66	57	41	28	10	26	49	.230	.305	.375	17.50	9.29	280
Hall, Tanner	R-R	6-1	186	3-18-02	4	0	4.44	15	9	0	47	44	31	23	3	19	59	.243	.338	.359	28.50	9.18	207
Hamilton, Xander	L-R	6-3	216	7-7-01	6	7	4.65	35	0	9	50	39	29	26	4	24	61	.212	.324	.304	27.98	11.01	218
Headrick, Brent	L-L	6-6	235	12-17-97	0	0	0.00	1	1	0	1	2	0	0	0	1	0	.333	.500	.333	0.00	12.50	8
Holiday, Aaron	R-R	6-3	205	5-28-00	1	1	7.63	14	1	0	15	13	15	13	0	26	21	.220	.453	.237	24.42	30.23	86
Houghton, Maddux	R-R	5-11	190	2-23-99	0	0	0.00	1	0	0	0	0	0	0	0	1	0	.000	.500	.000	0.00	50.00	2
Jones, Kyle	L-R	6-1	200	2-7-00	0	0	0.00	1	1	0	3	0	0	0	0	0	4	.000	.000	.000	44.44	0.00	9
Kirby, Devin	R-R	5-10	220	8-10-99	1	0	5.40	6	0	0	13	9	8	8	0	10	20	.200	.362	.267	34.48	17.24	58
Langenberg, Ty	R-R	6-2	190	12-8-01	3	3	3.38	9	9	0	48	46	23	18	1	12	56	.251	.303	.350	27.72	5.94	202
Lares, Cesar	L-L	6-0	155	7-3-03	3	4	4.56	19	19	0	81	88	56	41	8	28	77	.272	.365	.401	20.53	7.47	375
Lee, Jeremy	R-R	5-11	203	9-7-01	2	1	2.35	6	4	0	23	16	7	6	1	9	29	.198	.283	.284	31.52	9.78	92
Lewis, Cory	R-R	6-5	220	10-9-00	0	0	0.00	1	1	0	3	1	0	0	0	1	3	.100	.182	.100	27.27	9.09	11
Maldonado, Cleiber	L-L	6-1	200	11-20-03	1	1	2.70	10	0	0	13	10	6	4	0	6	15	.213	.298	.277	26.32	10.53	57
Mercedes, Juan	R-R	5-10	181	1-7-02	1	1	2.89	13	0	0	19	14	8	6	0	11	22	.209	.333	.224	27.16	13.58	81
Moreno, Danny	R-R	6-1	180	10-10-99	1	1	3.65	17	0	0	25	23	15	10	0	18	24	.242	.379	.347	20.51	15.38	117
Narvaez, Anthony	R-R	6-1	175	7-30-03	0	0	5.63	4	4	0	8	7	5	5	3	4	10	.233	.324	.600	29.41	11.76	34
Noble, Jack	R-R	6-2	200	4-2-00	8	2	4.78	32	1	3	58	55	38	31	11	30	72	.248	.347	.446	27.38	11.41	263
Olivares, Jose	R-R	6-1	199	1-18-03	2	3	3.33	13	10	0	46	42	20	17	0	19	47	.240	.315	.309	23.86	9.64	197
Paredes, Mike	R-R	5-11	185	7-27-00	0	1	4.50	1	0	0	2	4	2	1	0	0	3	.400	.400	.600	30.00	0.00	10

Pitching	B-T	Ht.	Wt.	DOB	W	L	ERA	G	GS	SV	IP	Hits	Runs	ER	HR	BB	SO	AVG	OBP	SLG	SO%	BB%	BF
Pasqualotto, Paulshawn	R-R	6-2	200	6-14-01	3	8	6.66	26	8	2	76	96	64	56	9	29	76	.300	.365	.459	21.11	8.06	360
Perez, Samuel	L-L	5-11	205	11-29-99	2	1	2.54	35	1	2	67	52	24	19	3	22	77	.208	.276	.300	28.00	8.00	275
Prielipp, Connor	L-L	6-2	210	1-10-01	0	0	0.00	1	1	0	2	1	0	0	0	0	3	.167	.167	.167	50.00	0.00	6
Reyes, Wilker	L-L	6-0	170	2-25-02	6	2	3.67	25	0	2	42	33	25	17	2	20	49	.210	.302	.287	27.07	11.05	181
Santos, Nolan	R-R	6-1	205	12-7-00	3	2	2.39	29	0	8	49	35	17	13	1	20	62	.191	.282	.284	30.10	9.71	206
Soto, Charlee	S-R	6-5	210	8-31-05	1	7	5.23	21	20	0	74	78	52	43	6	33	87	.271	.358	.389	26.36	10.00	330
Stasiowski, Tyler	R-R	6-0	185	8-13-01	0	0	4.50	3	0	0	4	1	2	2	1	3	4	.077	.250	.308	25.00	18.75	16
Topa, Justin	R-R	6-4	200	3-7-91	0	0	0.00	1	0	0	1	0	0	0	0	1	1	.000	.333	.000	33.33	33.33	3
Weiss, Zack	R-R	6-3	210	6-16-92	0	0	0.00	2	0	0	3	1	0	0	0	1	0	.111	.200	.111	0.00	10.00	10
Whitaker, Logan	R-R	6-6	225	5-25-00	0	0	2.25	2	0	0	4	4	3	1	1	0	5	.222	.222	.444	27.78	0.00	18
Winder, Josh	R-R	6-5	210	10-11-96	0	1	9.82	2	1	0	4	7	4	4	0	0	8	.389	.389	.611	44.44	0.00	18

Fielding

Catcher	PCT	G	PO	A	E	DP	PB
Bender	1.000	8	71	8	0	1	0
Camargo	1.000	3	23	1	0	1	1
Castro	.973	16	130	16	4	1	2
Clayton	.981	23	193	9	4	1	2
Diaw	.982	13	108	4	2	0	1
Elvis	.983	8	52	5	1	0	0
Ferrer	1.000	1	1	0	0	0	0
Pena	.976	13	114	6	3	1	6
Ruiz	.985	50	495	36	8	2	6

First Base	PCT	G	PO	A	E	DP
Amick	1.000	5	20	0	0	2
Bender	1.000	11	57	2	0	5
Castro	.947	4	18	0	1	1
Clayton	1.000	2	10	0	0	0
Cruz	.958	17	129	7	6	8
Duran	.981	16	99	5	2	9
Elvis	.950	5	35	3	2	2
Martinez	1.000	2	10	0	0	0
Pena	.981	8	52	0	1	6
Ruiz	.974	12	66	10	2	6
Sabato	.966	3	26	2	1	2
Thomason	1.000	7	49	2	0	2
Wingrove	.987	43	293	20	4	22

Second Base	PCT	G	PO	A	E	DP
Cruz	1.000	3	0	4	0	0
Daniel	.962	5	11	14	1	4
DeBarge	.941	13	19	29	3	8
Del Rosario	.931	26	32	49	6	11
Eeles	.990	23	47	48	1	12
Lee	1.000	1	1	3	0	0
Lucky	.952	8	6	14	1	1
Martinez	.930	25	36	57	7	10
Pena	.941	20	33	31	4	8
Thomason	.963	7	14	12	1	3

Third Base	PCT	G	PO	A	E	DP
Amick	.941	12	10	22	2	1
Cruz	.500	2	0	1	1	0
Culpepper	1.000	1	1	4	0	1
Daniel	1.000	7	6	13	0	0
Del Rosario	1.000	1	0	1	0	0
Doncon	.914	19	7	25	3	1
Eeles	.923	5	7	5	1	0
Elvis	.900	7	2	7	1	0
Lucky	.846	7	2	9	2	1
Martinez	.947	25	15	39	3	2
Pena	.855	28	20	39	10	2
Thomason	.857	8	0	12	2	1
Winokur	.913	10	7	14	2	4

Shortstop	PCT	G	PO	A	E	DP
Culpepper	.920	6	8	15	2	6
Daniel	1.000	1	2	0	0	0
DeBarge	.848	10	10	18	5	2
Del Rosario	.833	2	3	2	1	0
Doncon	.946	15	20	33	3	6
Eeles	1.000	2	5	1	0	0
Lee	1.000	2	2	4	0	0
Lucky	.938	18	28	33	4	6
Pena	.878	12	17	26	6	5
Winokur	.934	61	67	131	14	17

Outfield	PCT	G	PO	A	E	DP
Aguiar	.975	39	75	4	2	0
Chourio	.985	80	125	4	2	0
Clayton	.500	1	1	0	1	0
Daniel	1.000	5	3	0	0	0
DeBarge	1.000	1	1	0	0	0
Del Rosario	1.000	13	14	3	0	1
Diaw	1.000	9	15	1	0	0
Duran	.941	13	14	2	1	1
Eeles	1.000	2	8	0	0	0
Ferrer	1.000	22	45	1	0	0
Hess	1.000	11	10	0	0	0
Houghton	.977	79	170	3	4	1
Jenkins	.972	12	35	0	1	0
Kendle	1.000	20	39	0	0	0
Larnach	1.000	2	4	0	0	0
Lucky	.857	3	6	0	1	0
McCarthy	.977	27	43	0	1	0
Mercedes	.909	8	9	1	1	0
Rodriguez	.750	1	3	0	1	0
Rodriguez	.893	31	25	0	3	0
Rosario	1.000	1	1	0	0	0
Winokur	.957	22	41	4	2	0

FCL TWINS — *ROOKIE*

FLORIDA COMPLEX LEAGUE

Batting	B-T	Ht.	Wt.	DOB	AVG	OBP	SLG	G	PA	AB	R	H	2B	3B	HR	RBI	BB	HBP	SH	SF	SO	SB	CS	BB%	SO%
Acuna, Bryan	R-R	6-0	176	8-11-05	.255	.423	.311	37	137	106	14	27	6	0	0	9	27	4	0	0	36	5	3	19.71	26.28
Bass, Jayson	L-R	5-11	165	4-29-06	.276	.345	.365	51	174	156	25	43	7	2	1	26	17	0	0	1	36	8	5	9.77	20.69
Camargo, Jair	R-R	5-10	230	7-1-99	.667	.800	1.000	1	5	3	1	2	1	0	0	1	1	1	0	0	1	0	0	20.00	20.00
Castro, Ariel	L-L	6-2	178	2-17-06	.204	.321	.345	36	134	113	16	23	4	0	4	25	16	4	0	1	41	5	3	11.94	30.60
Chivilli, Hendry	R-R	6-3	165	9-14-05	.207	.314	.281	46	159	135	23	28	10	0	0	11	17	5	0	2	48	15	6	10.69	30.19
Daniel, Omari	R-R	6-0	185	5-4-04	.194	.301	.290	27	73	62	18	12	3	0	1	6	9	1	0	1	24	7	1	12.33	32.88
Del Rosario, Angel	R-R	6-0	160	1-11-03	.118	.250	.176	5	20	17	2	2	1	0	0	0	3	0	0	0	6	3	1	15.00	30.00
Duran, Gregory	L-R	6-2	201	10-8-02	.030	.209	.030	14	43	33	2	1	0	0	0	4	7	1	0	2	13	0	0	16.28	30.23
Elvis, Cole	R-R	6-1	215	8-4-99	.174	.231	.217	8	26	23	3	4	1	0	0	2	2	0	0	1	8	0	0	7.69	30.77
Gonzalez, Gabriel	R-R	5-10	165	1-4-04	.250	.318	.400	5	22	20	2	5	0	0	1	2	1	1	0	0	0	0	1	4.55	0.00
Grant, Harold	R-R	5-11	160	10-29-04	.149	.269	.179	25	78	67	9	10	2	0	0	8	11	0	0	0	23	2	1	14.10	29.49
Herrera, Yilber	B-R	5-11	145	1-15-05	.226	.407	.330	45	140	106	16	24	3	1	2	14	31	2	0	1	35	7	6	22.14	25.00
Jenkins, Walker	L-R	6-3	205	2-19-05	.393	.514	.571	9	37	28	7	11	3	1	0	7	8	0	0	1	2	3	0	21.62	5.41
Lee, Brooks	B-R	5-11	205	2-14-01	.450	.476	.550	5	21	20	5	9	2	0	0	2	1	0	0	0	2	0	0	4.76	9.52
Lopez, Moises	L-R	6-1	170	5-7-06	.115	.324	.231	26	68	52	9	6	0	0	2	9	15	1	0	0	26	0	2	22.06	38.24
Mercedes, Yasser	R-R	6-2	175	11-16-04	.331	.421	.568	51	195	169	34	56	18	2	6	24	24	2	0	0	39	18	5	12.31	20.00
Nova, Anderson	L-L	6-0	165	2-14-05	.211	.300	.338	29	80	71	8	15	2	2	1	7	8	1	0	0	15	0	1	10.00	18.75
Pena, Dameury	R-R	5-10	150	9-1-05	.282	.386	.410	36	140	117	25	33	4	1	3	18	19	2	0	2	9	4	2	13.57	6.43
Pena, Daniel	R-R	5-11	205	3-9-05	.308	.438	.500	9	32	26	5	8	2	0	1	5	6	0	0	0	6	0	0	18.75	18.75
Pena, Ricardo	R-R	6-0	180	5-30-05	.360	.481	.488	33	106	86	10	31	8	0	1	12	18	2	0	0	21	1	0	16.98	19.81
Rivero, Giovanny	B-R	5-10	173	10-19-03	.148	.303	.222	15	33	27	3	4	2	0	0	0	4	2	0	0	9	0	0	12.12	27.27
Rodriguez, Emmanuel	L-L	5-10	210	2-28-03	.286	.375	.571	2	8	7	1	2	2	0	0	2	1	0	0	0	3	0	0	12.50	37.50
Roman, Javier	R-R	6-0	155	3-26-03	.302	.362	.385	31	105	96	9	29	6	1	0	11	7	2	0	0	21	0	0	6.67	20.00
Vasquez, Amilcar	B-R	5-8	170	12-26-01	.317	.379	.367	22	67	60	8	19	3	0	0	10	4	2	1	0	8	1	0	5.97	11.94

Pitching	B-T	Ht.	Wt.	DOB	W	L	ERA	G	GS	SV	IP	Hits	Runs	ER	HR	BB	SO	AVG	OBP	SLG	SO%	BB%	BF
Bloor, Kyle	R-R	6-1	190	9-4-99	0	1	10.80	6	1	0	7	12	8	8	0	2	5	.387	.424	.516	15.15	6.06	33
Bohorquez, Adrian	R-R	6-1	190	3-3-05	2	3	3.68	10	7	0	37	23	18	15	2	17	41	.174	.272	.258	27.15	11.26	151

Cleto, Tomas	R-R	6-2	206	10-9-00	1	1	3.72	4	2	0	10	7	4	4	1	6	9	.212	.333	.303	23.08	15.38	39
Cordero, Miguel	R-R	6-1	170	8-15-06	1	2	6.97	12	1	1	31	37	31	24	2	13	26	.303	.373	.484	18.18	9.09	143
Cota, Juan	R-R	6-1	170	6-2-05	1	2	7.04	7	6	0	15	15	12	12	0	10	9	.268	.400	.357	12.86	14.29	70
Crisostomo, Alejandro	R-R	6-5	184	9-11-00	1	0	7.13	14	0	0	18	14	15	14	0	22	26	.222	.422	.270	28.89	24.44	90
De Jesus, Yency	R-R	5-11	170	6-20-02	1	1	1.08	11	1	0	25	17	10	3	0	16	21	.177	.292	.260	18.58	14.16	113
Garcia, Joel	R-R	5-10	165	7-3-04	2	1	1.50	6	5	0	18	13	5	3	1	0	16	.194	.191	.299	23.53	0.00	68
Helwig, Matthew	R-R	5-11	2010	4-10-00	2	0	0.00	6	0	1	12	4	1	0	0	3	4	.108	.175	.108	10.00	7.50	40
Huffman, Andrew	R-R	6-2	225	8-20-99	0	1	2.70	2	0	0	3	4	3	1	0	2	3	.267	.353	.333	17.65	11.76	17
Jones, Kyle	L-R	6-1	200	2-7-00	0	0	0.00	2	2	0	5	1	0	0	0	1	7	.063	.118	.063	41.18	5.88	17
King, Jacob	R-R	6-4	215	10-2-01	0	0	13.50	1	1	0	1	1	1	1	0	3	1	.333	.667	.333	16.67	50.00	6
Kirby, Devin	R-R	5-10	220	8-10-99	2	1	2.55	11	0	3	25	25	10	7	0	8	31	.260	.327	.354	28.97	7.48	107
Lewis, Cory	R-R	6-5	220	10-9-00	0	0	1.80	2	2	0	5	2	1	1	0	2	7	.125	.222	.125	38.89	11.11	18
Machuca, Eider	R-R	6-2	190	8-11-04	2	2	3.00	8	2	0	18	14	8	6	1	10	17	.212	.338	.288	21.25	12.50	80
Maldonado, Cleiber	L-L	6-1	200	11-20-03	2	0	2.04	14	1	5	18	14	8	4	0	5	18	.203	.269	.246	23.08	6.41	78
Narvaez, Anthony	R-R	6-1	175	7-30-03	2	3	5.72	10	6	0	39	47	35	25	1	12	41	.288	.333	.374	22.65	6.63	181
Olivares, Jose	R-R	6-1	199	1-18-03	0	0	9.64	2	2	0	5	5	6	5	1	3	4	.250	.348	.450	17.39	13.04	23
Plutko, Adam	R-R	6-3	215	10-3-91	0	0	0.00	1	1	0	1	1	1	0	0	0	1	.200	.200	.200	20.00	0.00	5
Prielipp, Connor	L-L	6-2	210	1-10-01	0	0	0.00	1	1	0	2	1	0	0	0	0	6	.143	.250	.143	75.00	0.00	8
Questad, Dylan	R-R	6-1	200	11-2-04	2	4	10.48	12	9	0	28	35	37	33	4	29	39	.289	.424	.463	25.83	19.21	151
Reyes, Wilker	L-L	6-0	170	2-25-02	0	0	0.00	7	0	3	8	4	0	0	0	1	12	.143	.200	.214	40.00	3.33	30
Rocha, Liam	R-R	6-3	200	5-8-02	2	1	4.30	10	5	0	29	34	18	14	3	16	31	.281	.362	.430	22.46	11.59	138
Soriano, Eduardo	R-R	6-1	190	10-4-02	2	5	7.45	13	3	0	29	35	26	24	0	22	31	.313	.432	.375	22.14	15.71	140
Stone, Mitch	R-R	6-3	205	12-13-00	1	0	3.00	3	0	0	3	3	2	1	0	2	6	.250	.357	.250	42.86	14.29	14
Ventura, Ezequiel	R-R	6-1	151	6-20-02	2	2	6.47	14	0	1	32	44	27	23	3	10	31	.328	.372	.478	20.81	6.71	149
Weiss, Zack	R-R	6-3	210	6-16-92	0	0	0.00	1	1	0	1	0	0	0	0	1	2	.000	.250	.000	50.00	25.00	4

Fielding

C: Pena 24, Roman 14, Vasquez 12, Rivero 9, Pena 7, Elvis 4. **1B:** Roman 15, Duran 13, Daniel 9, Lopez 8, Pena 5, Rivero 5, Elvis 3, Bass 3, Grant 2. **2B:** Grant 18, Herrera 16, Pena 12, Lopez 9, Daniel 3, Del Rosario 2, Acuna 2, Chivilli 1, Rivero 1. **3B:** Chivilli 18, Herrera 16, Acuna 10, Daniel 6, Pena 5, Lopez 4, Lee 1, Del Rosario 1, Grant 1. **SS:** Chivilli 25, Acuna 20, Herrera 13, Lee 2. **LF:** Nova 18, Bass 13, Castro 8, Vasquez 7, Mercedes 6, Grant 4, Pena 4, Acuna 2. **CF:** Mercedes 25, Castro 15, Bass 14, Jenkins 5, Daniel 3, Rodriguez 2, Del Rosario 1, Chivilli 1. **RF:** Bass 24, Castro 12, Mercedes 12, Nova 8, Gonzalez 4, Daniel 3, Duran 1.

DSL TWINS — *ROOKIE*

DOMINICAN SUMMER LEAGUE

Batting	B-T	Ht.	Wt.	DOB	AVG	OBP	SLG	G	PA	AB	R	H	2B	3B	HR	RBI	BB	HBP	SH	SF	SO	SB	CS	BB%	SO%
Beltre, Eduardo	R-R	5-11	175	10-10-06	.326	.453	.618	43	181	144	33	47	9	0	11	36	28	7	0	2	43	10	4	15.47	23.76
De Los Santos, Daiber	R-R	6-1	160	10-6-06	.301	.384	.460	47	203	176	37	53	11	1	5	38	18	7	0	2	63	17	7	8.87	31.03
Dominguez, Ramiro	R-R	5-9	163	3-26-07	.272	.336	.376	37	143	125	23	34	7	0	2	17	12	2	0	4	21	2	1	8.39	14.69
Fragoza, Luis	R-R	6-1	160	10-26-06	.259	.439	.345	41	157	116	36	30	5	1	1	19	22	16	0	1	35	21	3	14.01	22.29
Fuenmayor, Davirik	R-R	6-0	187	5-1-07	.212	.381	.273	12	42	33	4	7	2	0	0	2	5	4	0	0	9	2	1	11.90	21.43
Hernandez, Merphy	L-L	5-11	150	12-12-06	.276	.389	.417	48	190	156	40	43	4	6	2	30	28	3	0	3	30	36	2	14.74	15.79
Hernandez, Yandro	R-R	5-11	175	5-13-05	.293	.365	.440	23	85	75	12	22	4	2	1	14	5	4	0	1	23	8	5	5.88	27.06
Leal, Victor	R-R	5-11	174	9-29-06	.230	.364	.333	42	154	126	20	29	4	0	3	15	21	6	0	1	15	4	4	13.64	9.74
Medina, Alver	R-R	5-11	160	2-11-07	.228	.345	.272	32	110	92	19	21	2	1	0	11	13	4	0	1	34	7	2	11.82	30.91
Nunez, Irvin	R-R	5-10	160	2-21-06	.299	.453	.507	27	86	67	15	20	6	1	2	18	15	4	0	0	10	6	1	17.44	11.63
Paez, Ricardo	L-L	5-10	165	4-14-07	.263	.388	.424	36	121	99	26	26	4	3	2	14	20	1	0	1	26	4	4	16.53	21.49
Rodriguez, Luis	B-R	5-9	161	3-6-07	.141	.326	.169	31	92	71	12	10	2	0	0	4	20	0	0	1	20	11	2	21.74	21.74
Silva, Carlos	R-R	5-10	168	3-1-06	.216	.357	.319	38	143	116	22	25	9	0	1	21	24	2	0	1	24	2	2	16.78	16.78
Sosa, Guillermo	L-R	6-1	155	1-29-07	.222	.451	.250	18	51	36	10	8	1	0	0	2	8	7	0	0	14	7	1	15.69	27.45
Urbina, Nestor	B-R	5-10	168	6-13-07	.243	.364	.351	37	132	111	30	27	5	2	1	11	19	2	0	0	29	9	3	14.39	21.97
Velazquez, Ruben	R-R	6-1	175	7-24-07	.242	.296	.290	22	71	62	12	15	3	0	0	11	5	1	0	3	12	3	1	7.04	16.90

Pitching	B-T	Ht.	Wt.	DOB	W	L	ERA	G	GS	SV	IP	Hits	Runs	ER	HR	BB	SO	AVG	OBP	SLG	SO%	BB%	BF
Cafe, Nestor	R-R	6-4	185	11-6-05	0	0	8.79	11	0	0	14	12	17	14	1	26	19	.226	.506	.302	22.89	31.33	83
Carranza, Aaron	R-R	6-2	165	7-11-05	1	1	7.53	10	2	0	14	13	15	12	1	13	13	.241	.432	.333	17.57	17.57	74
Castillo, Raymi	R-R	6-4	187	1-10-06	1	1	19.06	6	0	0	6	7	12	12	0	12	8	.318	.595	.409	21.62	32.43	37
Cepeda, Enyer	R-R	5-9	148	10-27-06	0	0	27.00	3	2	0	2	7	8	7	1	1	2	.500	.588	.857	11.76	5.88	17
Chacon, Anderson	R-R	5-11	160	9-5-05	0	4	5.72	10	9	0	28	39	25	18	2	13	19	.315	.385	.476	13.29	9.09	143
Compres, Manuel	R-R	6-4	226	7-9-05	2	2	14.25	13	0	1	12	6	24	19	1	24	14	.150	.507	.275	19.72	33.80	71
Garcia, Eudy	R-R	6-6	217	3-14-05	2	0	7.14	13	2	0	29	30	30	23	2	23	21	.268	.415	.402	14.19	15.54	148
Hernandez, Cristian	R-R	6-1	185	1-8-05	0	3	4.01	7	6	0	25	15	14	11	1	17	37	.170	.318	.216	34.58	15.89	107
Herrera, Fabian	R-R	6-4	205	6-5-05	2	0	3.20	15	0	3	20	25	14	7	1	9	18	.313	.385	.438	19.78	9.89	91
Manzueta, Daniel	R-R	6-1	185	2-22-06	1	1	8.68	12	0	0	9	13	11	9	0	17	11	.325	.585	.400	16.92	26.15	65
Montano, Omar	R-R	6-0	160	2-10-06	0	0	9.00	1	1	0	1	2	1	1	0	1	0	.500	.600	.500	0.00	20.00	5
Nunez, Irvin	R-R	5-10	160	2-21-06	0	0	0.00	1	0	0	1	0	0	0	0	1	2	.000	.200	.000	40.00	20.00	5
Pulido, Sebastian	R-R	6-2	203	3-9-06	4	0	5.03	13	0	1	20	19	11	11	1	4	14	.260	.345	.315	16.67	4.76	84
Ramos, Anderson	R-R	6-1	182	4-24-06	5	3	5.58	12	0	0	31	28	21	19	1	16	33	.235	.324	.311	23.74	11.51	139
Rodriguez, Melvin	R-R	6-2	195	2-27-06	3	3	2.72	11	8	0	46	39	15	14	2	12	48	.225	.291	.312	25.40	6.35	189
Rodriguez, Neftali	R-R	5-10	144	3-22-06	0	1	4.97	10	0	0	13	12	12	7	1	12	13	.261	.446	.435	19.70	18.18	66
Rojas, Santiago	R-R	6-0	165	4-8-07	0	1	4.02	11	10	0	40	35	22	18	3	27	41	.238	.363	.361	22.91	15.08	179
Rondon, Leonardo	R-R	5-10	176	5-17-07	1	1	5.40	9	7	0	32	31	21	19	1	12	28	.256	.357	.388	19.58	8.39	143
Roque, Yoel	R-R	6-2	175	1-21-07	0	2	6.93	10	3	0	25	31	26	19	1	29	33	.295	.456	.457	24.26	21.32	136
Vasquez, Jose	R-R	6-4	200	12-12-04	4	0	4.99	11	3	0	31	30	19	17	2	15	45	.250	.350	.333	32.14	10.71	140
Velazquez, Ruben	R-R	6-1	175	7-24-07	0	0	5.40	1	0	0	2	1	1	1	1	1	0	.200	.333	.800	0.00	16.67	6

Ventura, Aiberson	R-R	6-4	176	11-23-05	3	1	1.10	10	0	1	16	11	3	2	0	2	13	.193	.226	.281	20.97	3.23	62
Villanueva, Ramiro	R-R	6-0	170	5-14-06	1	1	15.00	3	2	0	3	7	5	5	0	0	2	.538	.500	.769	13.33	0.00	15

Fielding

C: Leal 25, Silva 25, Nunez 12. **1B:** Leal 19, Nunez 14, Silva 12, Fuenmayor 7, Velazquez 5, Hernandez 1, Rodriguez 1, Fragoza 1. **2B:** Dominguez 23, Rodriguez 10, Urbina 10, Sosa 9, Medina 6, De Los Santos 3, Velazquez 3. **3B:** Urbina 18, Rodriguez 15, Medina 11, Velazquez 7, Dominguez 5, Sosa 3, De Los Santos 3. **SS:** De Los Santos 40, Velazquez 6, Medina 5, Sosa 3, Dominguez 3, Fragoza 1, Urbina 1, Rodriguez 1. **LF:** Paez 19, Hernandez 13, Fragoza 9, Beltre 6, Hernandez 4, Medina 4, Sosa 2, Dominguez 2. **CF:** Hernandez 37, Beltre 10, Fragoza 7, De Los Santos 3, Paez 3. **RF:** Fragoza 22, Beltre 17, Paez 8, Hernandez 7, Fuenmayor 2, Velazquez 1.

New York Mets

SEASON SYNOPSIS: The Mets overcame a 22-33 start to be one of baseball's best teams in the second half thanks to pitching depth, some unlikely contributors and a monster finish by shortstop Francisco Lindor. They earned a wild-card spot and beat the Brewers and Phillies in the postseason before a six-game loss to the Dodgers in the National League Championship Series.

HIGH POINT: The Mets won their two postseason series on dramatic home runs. Impending free agent Pete Alonso hit a three-run homer off Devin Williams in the ninth to give the Mets a 3-2 lead in an eventual 4-2 win in the wild-card series. Then, seeking a clincher in Game Four of the Division Series, New York trailed Philadelphia 1-0 in the sixth inning before loading the bases for Lindor, who hit a grand slam of Carlos Estevez to provide the final margin in a 4-1 win.

LOW POINT: The Mets had a miserable May, going 9-19 overall and losing 15 out of 19 in one stretch. Closer Edwin Diaz, coming back from a knee injury that cost him the 2023 season, blew a save against the Phillies, then another against the Marlins in the first two series of the skid. The Mets had a three-game streak of hitting three home runs in a row and still losing, and when they gave up a six spot in the eighth inning of a 10-3 loss to the Dodgers, they were 16 games back at 22-33.

NOTABLE ROOKIES: Righty Jose Butto (7-3, 2.55, three saves) succeeded in a hybrid starter/relief role and made the postseason roster, as did lefty specialist and 30-year-old rookie Danny young. (4-1, 4.54). Tommy John surgery alumni Dedniel Nuñez, a 28-year-old org veteran, and Christian Scott had some success before each got hurt again and couldn't finish the season. Scott suffered a late July elbow strain and Nunez went on the IL for good in August.

KEY TRANSACTIONS: President of baseball operations David Stearns had a successful first offseason. Free agents Luis Severino and Sean Manaea combined for 63 starts, and the Mets won Manaea's first three playoff starts. Veteran free agents DH J.D. Martinez and center fielder Harrison Bader had their moments while journeyman infielder Jose Iglesias had one of his best offensive seasons after starting the year in Triple-A. The Mets were active at the trade deadline on the margins, trading for relievers Phil Maton and Ryne Stanek, outfielder/DH Jesse Winker and starter Paul Blackburn, who was hurt after five starts.

OPENING DAY PAYROLL: $305,624,274 (1st)

PLAYERS OF THE YEAR

MAJOR LEAGUE

Francisco Lindor
SS

.273/.344/.500
33 HR, 29 SB
107 R, 91 RBIs

MINOR LEAGUE

Brandon Sproat
RHP

(A+/AA/AAA)
7-4, 3.40 ERA
131 SO, 42 BB, 116 IP

ORGANIZATION LEADERS

Batting		*Qualifiers
MAJORS		
* AVG	Francisco Lindor	.273
* OPS	Francisco Lindor	.844
HR	Pete Alonso	34
RBI	Francisco Lindor	91
MINORS		
* AVG	Nick Morabito, Brooklyn/St. Lucie	.312
* OBP	Nick Morabito, Brooklyn/St. Lucie	.403
* SLG	Luke Ritter, Syracuse	.480
* OPS	Luke Ritter, Syracuse	.849
R	Luisangel Acuna, Syracuse	90
H	Nick Morabito, Brooklyn/St. Lucie	142
TB	Luke Ritter, Syracuse	230
2B	Matt Rudick, Binghamton	27
2B	Ryan Clifford, Brooklyn/Binghamton	27
2B	Yohairo Cuevas, St. Lucie	27
3B	Luisangel Acuna, NY Mets/Syracuse/Lara	6
HR	Luke Ritter, Binghamton/Syracuse	26
RBI	Luke Ritter, Syracuse	93
BB	Ryan Clifford, Brooklyn/Binghamton	95
SO	Luke Ritter, Syracuse	174
SB	Nick Morabito, Brooklyn/St. Lucie	59

Pitching		#Qualifiers
MAJORS		
W	Sean Manaea	12
# ERA	Sean Manaea	3.47
SO	Sean Manaea	184
SV	Edwin Diaz	20
MINORS		
W	Joander Suarez, Binghamton	10
L	Blade Tidwell, Binghamton/Syracuse	13
# ERA	Jonah Tong, Brooklyn/Binghamton/St. Lucie	3.03
G	Max Kranick, Binghamton/St. Lucie/Syracuse	45
GS	Mike Vasil, Syracuse	27
GS	Dominic Hamel, Syracuse	27
SV	Wilkin Ramos, Binghamton/Syracuse	11
IP	Mike Vasil, Syracuse	134
BB	Dominic Hamel, Syracuse	77
SO	Jonah Tong, Brooklyn/Binghamton/St. Lucie	160
# AVG	Jonah Tong, Brooklyn/Binghamton/St. Lucie	.204

2024 PERFORMANCE

General Manager: David Stearns. **Farm Director:** Andy Green. **Scouting Director:** Kris Gross.

Class	Team	League	W	L	PCT	Finish	Manager
Majors	New York Mets	National	89	73	.549	7 (15)	Carlos Mendoza
Triple-A	Syracuse Mets	International	78	71	.523	7 (20)	Dick Scott
Double-A	Binghamton R. Ponies	Eastern	69	67	.507	6 (12)	Reid Brignac
High-A	Brooklyn Cyclones	South Atlantic	65	67	.492	7 (12)	Gilbert Gomez
Low-A	St. Lucie Mets	Florida State	45	84	.349	10 (10)	Yucary De La Cruz
Rookie	FCL Mets	Florida Complex	23	28	.451	11 (15)	Danny Ortega
Rookie	DSL Mets Blue	Dominican	21	33	.389	41 (51)	Gilberto Mejia
Rookie	DSL Mets Orange	Dominican	27	27	.500	26 (51)	Felix Fermin
Overall 2024 Minor League Record			**328**	**377**	**.465**	**26th (30)**	

ORGANIZATION STATISTICS

NEW YORK METS

NATIONAL LEAGUE

Batting	B-T	Ht.	Wt.	DOB	AVG	OBP	SLG	G	PA	AB	R	H	2B	3B	HR	RBI	BB	HBP	SH	SF	SO	SB	CS	BB%	SO%
Acuna, Luisangel	R-R	5-8	181	3-12-02	.308	.325	.641	14	40	39	6	12	2	1	3	6	1	0	0	0	6	0	1	2.50	15.00
Alonso, Pete	R-R	6-3	245	12-7-94	.240	.329	.459	162	695	608	91	146	31	0	34	88	70	13	0	4	172	3	0	10.07	24.75
Alvarez, Eddy	L-R	5-8	178	1-30-90	.000	.182	.000	13	11	9	2	0	0	0	0	0	1	1	0	0	2	0	0	9.09	18.18
Alvarez, Francisco	R-R	5-10	233	11-19-01	.237	.307	.403	100	342	308	39	73	14	2	11	47	30	2	0	2	86	1	1	8.77	25.15
Bader, Harrison	R-R	6-0	210	6-3-94	.236	.284	.373	143	437	402	57	95	19	0	12	51	21	8	0	6	95	17	8	4.81	21.74
Baty, Brett	L-R	6-3	210	11-13-99	.229	.306	.327	50	171	153	15	35	3	0	4	16	16	1	1	0	42	0	0	9.36	24.56
Gamel, Ben	L-L	5-10	180	5-17-92	.217	.400	.261	18	30	23	9	5	1	0	0	0	7	0	0	0	7	1	0	23.33	23.33
Iglesias, Jose	R-R	5-11	195	1-5-90	.337	.381	.448	85	291	270	39	91	16	1	4	26	12	8	0	1	39	6	2	4.12	13.40
Lindor, Francisco	B-R	5-11	190	11-14-93	.273	.344	.500	152	689	618	107	169	39	1	33	91	56	12	0	3	127	29	4	8.13	18.43
Marte, Starling	R-R	6-1	195	10-9-88	.269	.327	.388	94	370	335	46	90	13	3	7	40	27	3	3	2	81	16	1	7.30	21.89
Martinez, J.D.	R-R	6-3	230	8-21-87	.235	.320	.406	120	495	434	46	102	24	1	16	69	49	6	0	2	141	0	0	9.90	28.48
McNeil, Jeff	L-R	6-1	195	4-8-92	.238	.308	.384	129	472	424	57	101	26	0	12	44	35	9	1	3	68	5	1	7.42	14.41
Narvaez, Omar	L-R	5-11	220	2-10-92	.154	.191	.185	28	69	65	4	10	2	0	0	5	3	0	1	0	12	0	0	4.35	17.39
Nido, Tomas	R-R	6-0	211	4-12-94	.229	.261	.361	32	90	83	9	19	2	0	3	8	4	0	2	1	20	0	0	4.44	22.22
Nimmo, Brandon	L-R	6-3	206	3-27-93	.224	.327	.399	151	663	571	88	128	25	3	23	90	77	12	0	3	158	15	0	11.61	23.83
Reyes, Pablo	R-R	5-8	175	9-5-93	.000	.000	.000	1	0	0	1	0	0	0	0	0	0	0	0	0	0	0	0	—	—
Short, Zack	R-R	5-10	180	5-29-95	.111	.273	.111	10	12	9	2	1	0	0	0	0	2	0	1	0	4	0	1	16.67	33.33
Stewart, DJ	L-R	6-0	210	11-30-93	.177	.325	.297	74	194	158	16	28	4	0	5	19	31	4	0	1	48	1	0	15.98	24.74
Taylor, Tyrone	R-R	6-1	218	1-22-94	.248	.299	.401	130	345	319	47	79	22	3	7	35	19	5	1	1	80	11	2	5.51	23.19
Torrens, Luis	R-R	6-0	217	5-2-96	.229	.292	.373	48	130	118	14	27	8	0	3	15	9	2	0	1	28	0	1	6.92	21.54
Vientos, Mark	R-R	6-4	185	12-11-99	.266	.322	.516	111	454	413	58	110	22	0	27	71	33	3	0	5	135	0	0	7.27	29.74
Wendle, Joey	L-R	6-1	195	4-26-90	.222	.243	.250	18	37	36	3	8	1	0	0	1	1	0	0	0	9	1	0	2.70	24.32
Winker, Jesse	L-L	6-2	230	8-17-93	.243	.318	.365	44	129	115	12	28	5	0	3	13	10	3	0	1	22	0	0	7.75	17.05

Pitching	B-T	Ht.	Wt.	DOB	W	L	ERA	G	GS	SV	IP	Hits	Runs	ER	HR	BB	SO	AVG	OBP	SLG	SO%	BB%	BF
Adcock, Ty	R-R	6-0	213	2-7-97	0	0	14.54	3	0	0	4	7	7	7	4	2	3	.368	.429	1.000	14.29	9.52	21
Alvarez, Eddy	L-R	5-8	178	1-30-90	0	0	0.00	1	0	0	1	1	0	0	0	0	1	.250	.400	.500	20.00	0.00	5
Blackburn, Paul	R-R	6-1	196	12-4-93	1	2	5.18	5	5	0	24	31	16	14	4	7	21	.320	.374	.495	19.44	6.48	108
Brazoban, Huascar	R-R	6-3	155	10-15-89	0	1	5.14	19	0	0	21	18	12	12	1	14	17	.234	.359	.312	18.48	15.22	92
Butto, Jose	R-R	6-1	202	3-19-98	7	3	2.55	30	7	3	74	41	21	21	6	38	79	.167	.287	.276	26.87	12.93	294
Diaz, Edwin	R-R	6-3	165	3-22-94	6	4	3.52	54	0	20	54	36	23	21	7	20	84	.188	.273	.328	38.89	9.26	216
Diekman, Jake	R-L	6-4	195	1-21-87	2	3	5.63	43	0	4	32	23	24	20	7	24	40	.202	.354	.447	27.59	16.55	145
Festa, Matt	R-R	6-1	195	3-11-93	0	1	36.00	1	0	0	1	4	5	4	0	1	1	.571	.625	.714	12.50	12.50	8
Garrett, Reed	R-R	6-2	195	1-2-93	8	5	3.77	53	0	4	57	50	28	24	6	30	83	.236	.333	.363	33.60	12.15	247
Hartwig, Grant	R-R	6-5	235	12-18-97	0	0	6.75	4	0	0	7	6	6	5	1	4	4	.240	.387	.360	12.90	12.90	31
Houser, Adrian	R-R	6-3	242	2-2-93	1	5	5.84	23	7	1	69	74	48	45	8	32	45	.272	.356	.445	14.56	10.36	309
Jay, Tyler	L-L	6-1	185	4-19-94	0	0	7.71	3	0	0	5	7	5	4	0	3	3	.333	.417	.476	12.50	12.50	24
Lopez, Jorge	R-R	6-3	200	2-10-93	1	2	3.76	28	0	2	26	25	13	11	3	11	19	.255	.342	.418	17.12	9.91	111
Lucchesi, Joey	L-L	6-5	225	6-6-93	0	2	5.23	2	2	0	10	8	6	6	1	8	7	.216	.356	.378	15.22	17.39	46
Manaea, Sean	R-L	6-5	245	2-1-92	12	6	3.47	32	32	0	182	134	75	70	21	63	184	.202	.280	.338	24.93	8.54	738
Maton, Phil	R-R	6-2	206	3-25-93	2	1	2.51	31	0	1	29	18	8	8	1	6	30	.176	.250	.235	26.55	5.31	113
Megill, Tylor	R-R	6-7	230	7-28-95	4	5	4.04	16	15	0	78	70	39	35	8	32	91	.235	.315	.372	27.00	9.50	337
Nunez, Dedniel	R-R	6-2	180	6-5-96	2	0	2.31	25	0	1	35	24	11	9	3	8	48	.189	.237	.299	35.56	5.93	135
Orze, Eric	R-R	6-4	195	8-21-97	0	1	21.60	2	0	0	2	3	4	4	1	2	1	.375	.545	.750	9.09	18.18	11
Ottavino, Adam	S-R	6-5	246	11-22-85	2	2	4.34	60	0	1	56	49	29	27	6	23	70	.230	.324	.362	28.57	9.39	245
Peterson, David	L-L	6-6	240	9-3-95	10	3	2.90	21	21	0	121	110	44	39	8	46	101	.243	.320	.349	19.80	9.02	510
Quintana, Jose	R-L	6-1	220	1-24-89	10	10	3.75	31	31	0	170	150	73	71	22	63	135	.237	.314	.396	18.83	8.79	717
Raley, Brooks	L-L	6-3	200	6-29-88	1	0	0.00	8	0	0	7	2	0	0	0	3	9	.095	.200	.143	36.00	12.00	25
Ramirez, Yohan	R-R	6-4	212	5-6-95	0	1	7.56	5	0	0	8	11	7	7	1	4	11	.306	.366	.472	26.83	9.76	41
Reid-Foley, Sean	R-R	6-3	230	8-30-95	1	2	1.66	23	0	0	22	13	10	4	0	14	25	.173	.300	.200	27.78	15.56	90
Scott, Christian	R-R	6-4	215	6-15-99	0	3	4.56	9	9	0	47	45	24	24	8	12	39	.250	.303	.433	19.80	6.09	197
Senga, Kodai	L-R	6-1	202	1-30-93	1	0	3.38	1	1	0	5	2	2	2	1	1	9	.111	.200	.278	45.00	5.00	20
Severino, Luis	R-R	6-2	218	2-20-94	11	7	3.91	31	31	0	182	166	86	79	23	60	161	.243	.313	.383	21.16	7.88	761
Smith, Drew	R-R	6-2	190	9-24-93	1	1	3.06	19	0	2	18	18	7	6	2	9	23	.265	.342	.441	29.11	11.39	79

Pitching	B-T	Ht.	Wt.	DOB	W	L	ERA	G	GS	SV	IP	Hits	Runs	ER	HR	BB	SO	AVG	OBP	SLG	SO%	BB%	BF
Stanek, Ryne	R-R	6-4	226	7-26-91	1	0	6.06	17	0	0	16	13	11	11	3	8	23	.217	.319	.417	33.33	11.59	69
Sulser, Cole	R-R	6-1	190	3-12-90	0	0	9.64	4	0	0	5	6	5	5	1	3	7	.316	.391	.632	30.43	13.04	23
Teheran, Julio	R-R	6-2	205	1-27-91	0	0	13.50	1	1	0	3	6	4	4	1	2	3	.429	.500	.714	18.75	12.50	16
Tonkin, Michael	R-R	6-7	220	11-19-89	1	2	5.14	5	0	0	7	8	10	4	1	2	6	.286	.371	.429	17.14	5.71	35
Torrens, Luis	R-R	6-0	217	5-2-96	0	0	0.00	1	0	0	0	0	0	0	0	0	0	.000	.000	.000	0.00	0.00	1
Walker, Josh	L-L	6-6	225	12-1-94	0	0	5.11	10	0	0	12	13	7	7	1	6	11	.277	.345	.426	20.00	10.91	55
Young, Alex	L-L	6-3	220	9-9-93	0	0	3.29	14	0	0	14	11	5	5	2	7	13	.216	.310	.431	22.41	12.07	58
Young, Danny	L-L	6-3	200	5-27-94	4	1	4.54	42	0	0	38	29	22	19	3	18	48	.210	.331	.319	29.09	10.91	165

Fielding

Catcher	PCT	G	PO	A	E	DP	PB
Alvarez	.993	96	775	25	6	1	11
Hudson	1.000	1	2	0	0	0	0
Narvaez	.974	28	184	4	5	3	0
Nido	.979	32	222	10	5	1	0
Torrens	.997	44	295	20	1	2	3

First Base	PCT	G	PO	A	E	DP
Alonso	.995	161	1179	99	7	117
Stewart	1.000	1	4	0	0	0
Vientos	1.000	4	18	1	0	1

Second Base	PCT	G	PO	A	E	DP
Acuna	1.000	1	0	2	0	0
Alvarez	1.000	11	7	8	0	1
Iglesias	.990	61	79	116	2	33
McNeil	.983	110	181	231	7	66
Short	.000	1	0	0	0	0
Wendle	.958	8	10	13	1	3

Third Base	PCT	G	PO	A	E	DP
Baty	.984	47	33	87	2	10
Iglesias	.980	36	11	38	1	5
Short	.875	5	1	6	1	2
Vientos	.980	108	61	179	5	15
Wendle	.714	7	1	4	2	0

Shortstop	PCT	G	PO	A	E	DP
Acuna	.977	12	9	33	1	3
Alvarez	1.000	1	2	1	0	0
Iglesias	1.000	6	1	2	0	0
Lindor	.979	151	194	358	12	74
Short	1.000	1	2	0	0	0
Wendle	1.000	3	2	7	0	0

Outfield	PCT	G	PO	A	E	DP
Bader	.986	140	278	1	4	0
Gamel	1.000	17	13	0	0	0
Marte	.986	85	138	6	2	2
McNeil	.947	32	35	1	2	0
Nimmo	.992	170	239	4	2	0
Stewart	1.000	37	45	2	0	1
Taylor	.985	135	193	3	3	0
Winker	1.000	27	31	2	0	0

SYRACUSE METS — *TRIPLE-A*

INTERNATIONAL LEAGUE

Batting	B-T	Ht.	Wt.	DOB	AVG	OBP	SLG	G	PA	AB	R	H	2B	3B	HR	RBI	BB	HBP	SH	SF	SO	SB	CS	BB%	SO%
Acuna, Luisangel	R-R	5-8	181	3-12-02	.258	.299	.355	131	587	547	90	141	20	6	7	50	32	2	2	4	96	40	14	5.45	16.35
Allen, Austin	L-R	6-2	219	1-16-94	.261	.290	.438	46	162	153	21	40	3	0	8	27	6	1	0	2	46	1	0	3.70	28.40
Azocar, Jose	R-R	5-11	181	5-11-96	.353	.382	.529	13	55	51	14	18	3	0	2	12	2	1	0	1	7	6	1	3.64	12.73
Bannon, Rylan	R-R	5-8	180	4-22-96	.254	.392	.475	79	342	276	50	70	14	1	15	57	60	4	0	2	79	7	4	17.54	23.10
Baty, Brett	L-R	6-3	210	11-13-99	.252	.349	.504	62	269	230	37	58	10	0	16	45	33	3	0	3	57	1	0	12.27	21.19
Bradley, Jackie	L-R	5-10	196	4-19-90	.209	.266	.360	25	94	86	9	18	5	1	2	9	7	0	0	1	23	5	1	7.45	24.47
Brosseau, Mike	R-R	5-11	203	3-15-94	.276	.368	.441	93	372	322	59	89	8	0	15	41	37	11	0	2	76	2	1	9.95	20.43
Choi, Ji Man	L-R	6-1	260	5-19-91	.190	.317	.357	26	104	84	7	16	2	0	4	12	17	0	0	3	29	0	0	16.35	27.88
Cortes, Carlos	L-S	5-7	197	6-30-97	.246	.330	.456	83	321	281	52	69	11	0	16	52	37	0	0	3	60	3	1	11.53	18.69
Gamel, Ben	L-L	5-10	180	5-17-92	.314	.423	.538	45	190	156	35	49	12	1	7	24	31	0	1	2	46	0	0	16.32	24.21
Gilbert, Drew	L-L	5-9	195	9-27-00	.215	.313	.393	56	247	214	24	46	8	0	10	32	25	6	0	1	51	3	1	10.12	20.65
Hudson, Joe	R-R	5-11	210	5-21-91	.216	.367	.412	34	120	97	15	21	4	0	5	16	19	4	0	0	40	4	1	15.83	33.33
Iglesias, Jose	R-R	5-11	195	1-5-90	.273	.309	.442	42	175	165	26	45	7	0	7	29	9	0	0	1	29	1	0	5.14	16.57
Kohlwey, Taylor	L-L	6-1	200	7-20-94	.088	.162	.118	11	37	34	3	3	1	0	0	2	3	0	0	0	13	0	0	8.11	35.14
Marte, Starling	R-R	6-1	195	10-9-88	.182	.167	.273	3	12	11	1	2	1	0	0	1	0	0	0	1	0	0	0	0.00	0.00
Martinez, J.D.	R-R	6-3	230	8-21-87	.375	.375	.500	2	8	8	1	3	1	0	0	3	0	0	0	0	1	0	0	0.00	12.50
Nido, Tomas	R-R	6-0	211	4-12-94	.345	.345	.517	9	30	29	3	10	2	0	1	2	0	0	1	0	6	0	0	0.00	20.00
O'Neill, Matt	R-R	5-10	205	8-20-97	.160	.259	.280	21	59	50	10	8	3	0	1	5	7	0	1	1	22	0	0	11.86	37.29
Porter, Logan	R-R	6-0	200	7-12-95	.186	.304	.305	20	69	59	5	11	1	0	2	11	8	2	0	0	24	1	0	11.59	34.78
Reyes, Pablo	R-R	5-8	175	9-5-93	.290	.371	.493	63	250	217	43	63	7	2	11	38	29	0	2	2	36	12	2	11.60	14.40
Ritter, Luke	R-R	5-11	187	2-15-97	.257	.369	.480	134	567	479	80	123	25	2	26	93	73	13	0	2	174	4	2	12.87	30.69
Rosario, Eddie	L-R	6-1	180	9-28-91	.103	.133	.310	7	30	29	1	3	1	1	1	2	1	0	0	0	8	0	0	3.33	26.67
Sanchez, Yolmer	B-R	5-8	210	6-29-92	.226	.346	.393	111	399	336	60	76	23	3	9	52	55	7	0	1	84	9	0	13.78	21.05
Schwartz, JT	L-R	6-4	215	12-17-99	.219	.287	.381	48	178	160	21	35	11	0	5	22	10	6	0	2	29	2	0	5.62	16.29
Senger, Hayden	R-R	6-1	210	4-3-97	.252	.323	.401	48	166	147	20	37	11	1	3	27	12	4	2	1	39	0	0	7.23	23.49
Stewart, DJ	L-R	6-0	210	11-30-93	.280	.434	.451	26	106	82	15	23	5	0	3	9	19	4	0	1	33	5	0	17.92	31.13
Thomas, Rhylan	L-L	5-10	170	4-15-00	.235	.286	.377	49	196	183	35	43	11	0	5	18	13	0	0	0	24	5	2	6.63	12.24
Thompson, Trayce	R-R	6-3	225	3-15-91	.228	.300	.500	62	253	224	36	51	13	0	16	44	24	1	0	4	65	6	1	9.49	25.69
Vientos, Mark	R-R	6-4	185	12-11-99	.284	.376	.500	31	133	116	21	33	5	1	6	30	16	1	0	0	38	0	0	12.03	28.57
Williams, Jett	R-R	5-6	175	11-3-03	.364	.533	.545	6	30	22	10	8	4	0	0	1	8	0	0	0	7	1	0	26.67	23.33
Young, Wyatt	L-R	5-6	160	12-5-99	.283	.346	.326	16	52	46	6	13	2	0	0	8	3	2	0	1	13	1	1	5.77	25.00

Pitching	B-T	Ht.	Wt.	DOB	W	L	ERA	G	GS	SV	IP	Hits	Runs	ER	HR	BB	SO	AVG	OBP	SLG	SO%	BB%	BF
Adcock, Ty	R-R	6-0	213	2-7-97	2	0	3.93	17	0	3	18	26	10	8	1	8	21	.329	.386	.405	23.86	9.09	88
Blackburn, Paul	R-R	6-1	196	12-4-93	0	0	1.35	1	1	0	7	4	1	1	0	1	4	.174	.208	.217	16.67	4.17	24
Butto, Jose	R-R	6-1	202	3-19-98	5	2	3.05	8	8	0	44	36	16	15	4	18	38	.218	.303	.345	20.54	9.73	185
Castaneda, Victor	R-R	6-1	185	8-27-98	0	0	33.75	1	0	0	1	5	5	5	0	4	0	.556	.692	.889	0.00	30.77	13
Colon, Jeffrey	R-R	6-1	170	11-9-99	0	0	22.50	2	0	0	2	4	5	5	0	6	2	.444	.647	.444	11.76	35.29	17
Crick, Kyle	L-R	6-4	225	11-30-92	0	1	2.25	4	0	0	4	2	1	1	0	4	7	.143	.333	.143	38.89	22.22	18
Duplantier, Jon	L-R	6-4	229	7-11-94	3	1	5.31	16	0	0	20	22	12	12	2	22	22	.293	.451	.440	21.57	21.57	102
Festa, Matt	R-R	6-1	195	3-11-93	1	0	1.76	11	0	0	15	11	3	3	1	3	19	.204	.259	.315	32.20	5.08	59
Fujinami, Shintaro	R-R	6-6	180	4-12-94	1	2	6.68	29	0	1	32	16	28	24	2	33	38	.144	.351	.216	25.68	22.30	148
Gage, Matt	L-L	6-3	265	2-11-93	0	0	3.92	20	0	6	21	17	9	9	2	10	24	.218	.307	.333	27.27	11.36	88
Garrett, Reed	R-R	6-2	195	1-2-93	0	0	0.00	2	0	0	3	2	0	0	0	1	7	.182	.250	.273	58.33	8.33	12
Geber, Jordan	R-R	6-3	205	7-31-99	0	2	4.26	4	2	0	13	12	6	6	2	8	9	.261	.370	.457	16.67	14.81	54
Griffin, David	R-R	6-0	205	7-16-96	1	2	17.36	3	0	0	5	12	10	9	0	4	5	.480	.533	.520	16.67	13.33	30

Guzman, Carlos	R-R	6-1	210	5-16-98	0	1	4.50	7	0	0	10	4	7	5	1	12	9	.118	.347	.235	18.37	24.49	49
Hamel, Dominic	R-R	6-2	206	3-2-99	5	9	6.79	27	27	0	125	141	95	94	23	77	124	.285	.384	.494	21.31	13.23	582
Hartwig, Grant	R-R	6-5	235	12-18-97	4	1	4.34	33	0	3	37	33	20	18	2	20	37	.231	.343	.336	21.76	11.76	170
Hejka, Josh	R-R	6-1	175	3-20-97	0	0	16.20	2	0	0	2	5	7	3	0	0	0	.500	.571	.600	0.00	0.00	14
Ingram, Kolton	L-L	5-9	170	10-21-96	1	0	7.20	4	0	0	5	5	4	4	1	6	3	.278	.481	.444	11.11	22.22	27
Jarvis, Justin	R-R	6-2	183	2-20-00	1	3	5.98	18	5	0	47	59	33	31	7	23	39	.304	.379	.510	17.41	10.27	224
Jay, Tyler	L-L	6-1	185	4-19-94	5	1	2.40	23	1	1	41	38	14	11	3	4	30	.248	.275	.353	18.63	2.48	161
Kranick, Max	R-R	6-3	220	7-21-97	2	1	3.57	41	4	2	63	57	28	25	12	20	53	.241	.304	.460	20.38	7.69	260
Lavender, Nathan	L-L	6-2	210	1-20-00	0	0	3.86	5	1	0	7	6	3	3	2	7	9	.222	.382	.444	26.47	20.59	34
Lucchesi, Joey	L-L	6-5	225	6-6-93	5	7	4.70	27	17	0	115	114	66	60	14	56	86	.261	.346	.398	17.30	11.27	497
McLoughlin, Trey	R-R	6-2	210	6-11-99	0	0	4.00	9	0	0	9	7	4	4	2	4	11	.219	.297	.531	29.73	10.81	37
Megill, Tylor	R-R	6-7	230	7-28-95	3	0	3.68	9	9	0	44	34	19	18	4	20	57	.214	.298	.333	31.49	11.05	181
Miller, Troy	R-R	6-4	210	2-13-97	0	0	27.00	1	1	0	2	7	7	7	3	4	3	.500	.611	1.357	16.67	22.22	18
Montes de Oca, Bryce	R-R	6-7	265	4-23-96	0	0	7.71	6	0	0	5	3	4	4	2	9	7	.188	.519	.563	25.93	33.33	27
Moreno, Luis	R-R	5-8	170	5-29-99	0	2	13.50	3	2	0	6	7	11	9	0	7	7	.304	.455	.391	21.21	21.21	33
Nittoli, Vinny	R-R	6-1	210	11-11-90	1	1	9.82	3	0	0	4	4	5	4	1	1	3	.286	.313	.643	18.75	6.25	16
Nunez, Dedniel	R-R	6-2	180	6-5-96	3	0	1.29	14	0	2	14	8	2	2	0	6	21	.163	.255	.265	38.18	10.91	55
O'Neill, Matt	R-R	5-10	205	8-20-97	0	0	0.00	1	0	0	0	0	0	0	0	0	0	.000	.000	.000	0.00	0.00	1
Orze, Eric	R-R	6-4	195	8-21-97	6	1	2.92	43	0	3	62	43	22	20	8	31	84	.194	.297	.333	32.68	12.06	257
Parsons, Hunter	R-R	6-2	215	6-24-97	0	0	6.75	5	1	0	7	5	5	5	1	8	10	.208	.394	.333	30.30	24.24	33
Peterson, David	L-L	6-6	240	9-3-95	1	1	2.79	2	2	0	10	12	4	3	0	2	11	.300	.349	.350	25.58	4.65	43
Pintaro, Jonathan	R-R	6-2	235	11-7-97	0	0	0.00	1	1	0	4	4	0	0	0	4	6	.267	.421	.333	31.58	21.05	19
Ramirez, Jawilme	R-R	6-2	170	11-28-01	0	0	0.00	1	0	0	1	1	0	0	0	1	2	.250	.400	.500	40.00	20.00	5
Ramos, Wilkin	R-R	6-5	165	10-31-00	4	2	5.40	18	0	2	18	16	14	11	1	15	16	.232	.391	.391	18.18	17.05	88
Reid-Foley, Sean	R-R	6-3	230	8-30-95	0	0	4.15	4	0	0	4	6	3	2	1	2	3	.333	.400	.500	15.00	10.00	20
Rios, Yacksel	R-R	6-3	215	6-27-93	3	1	3.30	27	0	3	30	25	13	11	2	22	30	.229	.370	.358	22.22	16.30	135
Sanchez, Yolmer	S-R	5-8	210	6-29-92	0	0	10.38	6	0	0	4	9	5	5	2	1	0	.391	.417	.739	0.00	4.17	24
Scott, Christian	R-R	6-4	215	6-15-99	3	0	2.76	9	9	0	42	29	13	13	10	12	55	.191	.250	.401	33.54	7.32	164
Scrubb, Andre	R-R	6-4	270	1-13-95	0	0	9.00	1	0	0	2	2	2	2	0	3	0	.400	.625	.600	0.00	37.50	8
Senga, Kodai	L-R	6-1	202	1-30-93	0	0	4.76	4	4	0	11	12	6	6	1	8	9	.279	.385	.465	17.31	15.38	52
Smith, Drew	R-R	6-2	190	9-24-93	1	0	9.00	4	0	0	4	5	4	4	1	1	1	.313	.353	.625	5.88	5.88	17
Sproat, Brandon	R-R	6-3	210	9-17-00	1	2	7.53	7	7	0	29	36	25	24	7	11	21	.313	.383	.574	16.28	8.53	129
Suarez, Joander	R-R	6-3	223	2-27-00	1	1	12.00	2	2	0	9	16	12	12	5	1	6	.390	.395	.780	13.95	2.33	43
Sulser, Cole	R-R	6-1	190	3-12-90	2	2	1.48	24	1	2	30	16	10	5	4	16	34	.157	.275	.294	28.10	13.22	121
Tidwell, Blade	R-R	6-4	207	6-8-01	1	9	5.93	19	17	0	85	80	65	56	17	53	77	.245	.358	.422	19.85	13.66	388
Vasil, Mike	L-R	6-5	225	3-19-00	8	10	6.04	29	27	0	134	155	98	90	24	52	109	.291	.365	.492	17.96	8.57	607
Walker, Josh	L-L	6-6	225	12-1-94	2	2	2.83	25	0	5	29	16	12	9	2	21	39	.157	.310	.225	30.95	16.67	126
Young, Alex	L-L	6-3	220	9-9-93	1	0	4.91	6	0	0	7	5	4	4	0	3	5	.192	.300	.231	16.67	10.00	30
Young, Danny	L-L	6-3	200	5-27-94	1	1	1.26	15	0	3	14	8	2	2	0	12	22	.160	.364	.200	33.33	18.18	66
Zuber, Tyler	R-R	5-11	195	6-16-95	0	3	12.38	17	0	0	16	28	23	22	2	15	18	.406	.494	.565	20.69	17.24	87

Fielding

Catcher	PCT	G	PO	A	E	DP	PB
Allen	.984	35	292	12	5	1	2
Hudson	.996	33	253	13	1	1	2
Nido	.987	9	73	5	1	1	0
O'Neill	.978	17	124	8	3	0	2
Porter	1.000	20	149	8	0	1	0
Senger	.995	46	391	25	2	3	3

First Base	PCT	G	PO	A	E	DP
Brosseau	.992	47	338	25	3	30
Choi	1.000	17	118	14	0	9
Ritter	1.000	42	294	22	0	31
Schwartz	.994	44	300	39	2	32
Senger	.000	1	0	0	0	0
Vientos	1.000	6	41	0	0	4

Second Base	PCT	G	PO	A	E	DP
Acuna	.977	30	49	81	3	20
Bannon	1.000	12	18	22	0	3
Baty	.991	27	45	69	1	19
Iglesias	.988	20	35	47	1	16
Reyes	1.000	14	25	33	0	9
Ritter	1.000	20	19	45	0	8
Sanchez	1.000	23	30	65	0	12
Young	1.000	11	19	37	0	6

Third Base	PCT	G	PO	A	E	DP
Bannon	.964	24	17	37	2	4
Baty	.937	34	26	63	6	7
Brosseau	.938	9	4	11	1	2
Iglesias	.889	2	2	6	1	0
Reyes	.946	22	21	32	3	4
Ritter	.944	32	18	49	4	3
Sanchez	1.000	13	8	15	0	1
Vientos	.944	19	12	22	2	0
Young	.750	3	2	1	1	1

Shortstop	PCT	G	PO	A	E	DP
Acuna	.962	70	81	173	10	31
Bannon	1.000	21	23	36	0	10
Iglesias	.987	19	29	49	1	12
Reyes	.941	14	17	31	3	10
Sanchez	1.000	21	29	42	0	7
Williams	.917	6	8	14	2	4
Young	.000	2	0	0	0	0

Outfield	PCT	G	PO	A	E	DP
Acuna	.975	31	73	4	2	0
Azocar	.964	13	25	2	1	0
Bannon	.917	9	11	0	1	0
Bradley	1.000	24	48	2	0	1
Brosseau	1.000	4	9	0	0	0
Cortes	.964	72	97	9	4	1
Gamel	1.000	41	68	4	0	0
Gilbert	.982	49	101	7	2	3
Kohlwey	1.000	11	15	0	0	0
Marte	1.000	3	6	1	0	0
Ritter	.961	28	47	2	2	0
Rosario	1.000	5	6	0	0	0
Sanchez	1.000	46	87	8	0	0
Stewart	.960	17	23	1	1	0
Thomas	.983	50	113	2	2	0
Thompson	.981	58	101	3	2	1

BINGHAMTON RUMBLE PONIES — DOUBLE-A

EASTERN LEAGUE

Batting	B-T	Ht.	Wt.	DOB	AVG	OBP	SLG	G	PA	AB	R	H	2B	3B	HR	RBI	BB	HBP	SH	SF	SO	SB	CS	BB%	SO%
Alvarez, Francisco	R-R	5-10	233	11-19-01	.250	.333	.625	3	9	8	2	2	0	0	1	3	1	0	0	0	2	0	0	11.11	22.22
Clifford, Ryan	L-L	6-3	200	7-20-03	.231	.359	.456	98	405	333	53	77	21	0	18	58	63	5	0	3	117	3	2	15.56	28.89
Consuegra, Stanley	R-R	6-2	167	9-24-00	.201	.262	.304	58	221	204	24	41	10	1	3	22	12	5	0	0	63	4	2	5.43	28.51
De Los Santos, Omar	R-R	6-1	172	8-8-99	.136	.167	.409	13	24	22	7	3	0	0	2	3	1	0	0	1	11	2	1	4.17	45.83
Ellis, Duke	L-L	6-1	180	1-16-98	.333	.429	.333	2	7	6	0	2	0	0	0	0	0	1	0	0	1	0	1	0.00	14.29
Gil, Mateo	R-R	6-0	180	7-24-00	.163	.198	.233	25	92	86	8	14	3	0	1	6	4	0	1	1	31	1	0	4.35	33.70
Jackson, Jeremiah	R-R	6-0	165	3-26-00	.205	.245	.373	121	482	453	49	93	19	0	19	61	23	2	0	4	123	11	2	4.77	25.52
Jordan, Rowdey	B-R	5-10	190	1-27-99	.218	.297	.329	116	466	413	53	90	19	0	9	53	42	6	1	3	123	25	7	9.01	26.39

Lantigua, Andriel	R-R	6-0	190	11-29-03	.000	.000	.000	1	4	4	0	0	0	0	0	0	0	0	0	0	3	0	0	0.00	75.00
Lorusso, Nick	R-R	6-2	212	9-11-00	.208	.387	.375	8	31	24	3	5	1	0	1	2	6	1	0	0	7	1	2	19.35	22.58
Marte, Starling	R-R	6-1	195	10-9-88	.000	.333	.000	1	3	2	0	0	0	0	0	0	1	0	0	0	1	0	0	33.33	33.33
McIlwain, Brandon	R-R	6-0	205	5-31-98	.224	.306	.342	44	171	152	16	34	7	1	3	9	14	4	1	0	44	6	3	8.19	25.73
McLean, Nolan	R-R	6-4	214	7-24-01	.159	.232	.333	35	69	63	6	10	2	0	3	8	6	0	0	0	36	0	0	8.70	52.17
O'Neill, Matt	R-R	5-10	205	8-20-97	.184	.295	.211	12	44	38	6	7	1	0	0	3	6	0	0	0	12	0	0	13.64	27.27
Osborn, Drake	R-R	5-9	190	7-22-98	.235	.287	.320	62	217	200	17	47	11	0	2	24	12	3	1	1	50	1	0	5.53	23.04
Palmer, Jaylen	R-R	6-3	208	7-31-00	.223	.316	.436	83	310	273	35	61	22	0	12	33	33	4	0	0	119	10	4	10.65	38.39
Parada, Kevin	R-R	5-11	197	8-3-01	.214	.304	.359	114	454	398	41	85	17	1	13	43	45	8	0	3	153	0	1	9.91	33.70
Peroza, Jose	R-R	6-1	221	6-15-00	.243	.341	.371	23	82	70	13	17	3	0	2	7	10	1	0	1	27	0	0	12.20	32.93
Ramirez, Alex	R-R	6-3	170	1-13-03	.210	.291	.299	123	542	481	62	101	22	3	5	46	55	1	0	3	123	40	8	10.15	22.69
Rudick, Matt	L-L	5-6	170	7-2-98	.239	.352	.366	114	491	415	54	99	27	1	8	41	64	10	0	2	106	12	7	13.03	21.59
Schwartz, JT	L-R	6-4	215	12-17-99	.295	.408	.424	64	262	217	25	64	11	1	5	27	39	4	0	2	41	7	1	14.89	15.65
Senger, Hayden	R-R	6-1	210	4-3-97	.059	.111	.059	5	18	17	1	1	0	0	0	0	1	0	0	0	6	0	0	5.56	33.33
Suozzi, Joe	R-R	6-2	215	2-28-98	.000	.188	.000	6	16	13	1	0	0	0	0	0	2	1	0	0	9	0	0	12.50	56.25
Thomas, Rhylan	L-L	5-10	170	4-15-00	.323	.377	.406	25	109	96	11	31	8	0	0	13	8	1	3	1	13	6	3	7.34	11.93
Williams, Jett	R-R	5-6	175	11-3-03	.172	.287	.241	22	101	87	12	15	4	1	0	3	10	4	0	0	25	2	2	9.90	24.75
Young, Wyatt	L-R	5-6	160	12-5-99	.288	.393	.363	102	380	320	49	92	10	1	4	31	49	7	3	1	79	16	7	12.89	20.79

Pitching	B-T	Ht.	Wt.	DOB	W	L	ERA	G	GS	SV	IP	Hits	Runs	ER	HR	BB	SO	AVG	OBP	SLG	SO%	BB%	BF
Clenney, Nolan	L-R	6-2	200	6-16-96	5	1	5.37	33	0	1	54	65	40	32	6	15	60	.301	.354	.440	24.79	6.20	242
Colon, Jeffrey	R-R	6-1	170	11-9-99	1	0	2.45	6	1	0	15	14	4	4	2	7	10	.269	.367	.385	16.67	11.67	60
Cornielly, Joshua	R-R	6-2	175	1-15-01	0	0	1.13	10	0	0	16	9	2	2	1	4	21	.158	.226	.263	33.87	6.45	62
Foster, Cameron	R-R	6-5	230	3-17-99	4	2	3.64	27	9	1	72	74	35	29	7	33	68	.266	.347	.392	21.45	10.41	317
Fujinami, Shintaro	R-R	6-6	180	4-12-94	0	0	0.00	2	0	0	2	0	0	0	0	0	5	.000	.000	.000	83.33	0.00	6
Garrett, Reed	R-R	6-2	195	1-2-93	0	1	81.00	1	0	0	0	4	3	3	0	1	1	.800	.833	1.200	16.67	16.67	6
Geber, Jordan	R-R	6-3	205	7-31-99	4	6	4.15	17	8	0	61	65	29	28	6	20	42	.274	.340	.401	15.85	7.55	265
Gervase, Paul	R-R	6-10	230	5-23-00	3	2	3.25	22	0	5	28	16	16	10	3	17	46	.157	.283	.265	38.02	14.05	121
Griffin, David	R-R	6-0	205	7-16-96	0	1	9.00	2	1	0	5	8	5	5	1	1	4	.348	.375	.696	16.67	4.17	24
Guzman, Carlos	R-R	6-1	210	5-16-98	2	1	3.72	28	0	3	39	28	19	16	6	14	42	.199	.285	.362	26.58	8.86	158
Hartwig, Grant	R-R	6-5	235	12-18-97	0	0	12.00	3	0	0	3	6	4	4	2	1	4	.462	.500	.923	28.57	7.14	14
Hawkins, Dakota	R-R	6-0	208	3-20-00	0	2	6.00	3	2	0	9	10	7	6	0	4	7	.303	.366	.455	17.07	9.76	41
Hejka, Josh	R-R	6-1	175	3-20-97	0	1	6.30	14	0	0	20	27	15	14	3	5	17	.310	.368	.471	17.89	5.26	95
Herrera, Eduardo	S-R	5-9	179	1-5-00	0	0	6.00	2	0	0	3	3	2	2	0	3	3	.273	.429	.273	21.43	21.43	14
Jarvis, Justin	R-R	6-2	183	2-20-00	5	2	2.90	10	5	1	40	29	14	13	4	7	45	.195	.241	.309	28.30	4.40	159
Juarez, Daniel	L-L	5-11	155	9-28-00	2	3	5.09	34	0	0	35	34	24	20	3	21	33	.254	.356	.381	20.63	13.13	160
Kranick, Max	R-R	6-3	220	7-21-97	0	0	1.50	2	2	0	6	3	2	1	0	2	8	.136	.208	.182	32.00	8.00	25
Lawson, Justin	R-R	6-3	198	12-1-00	1	0	0.00	1	0	0	2	0	0	0	0	0	3	.000	.167	.000	50.00	0.00	6
McLean, Nolan	R-R	6-4	214	7-24-01	2	8	4.19	18	18	0	82	76	43	38	10	32	80	.248	.335	.399	22.79	9.12	351
McLoughlin, Trey	R-R	6-2	210	6-11-99	1	0	1.89	28	0	5	33	20	8	7	2	17	39	.171	.274	.282	28.89	12.59	135
Megill, Tylor	R-R	6-7	230	7-28-95	0	0	3.38	1	1	0	3	2	1	1	1	0	4	.200	.273	.500	36.36	0.00	11
Miller, Troy	R-R	6-4	210	2-13-97	0	0	5.75	7	5	0	20	22	14	13	3	9	17	.278	.344	.456	18.89	10.00	90
Montes de Oca, Bryce	R-R	6-7	265	4-23-96	1	0	5.40	4	0	0	3	3	2	2	1	1	5	.231	.286	.538	35.71	7.14	14
Moreno, Luis	R-R	5-8	170	5-29-99	3	7	4.27	25	19	1	103	103	59	49	12	41	107	.252	.326	.396	23.31	8.93	459
Parsons, Hunter	R-R	6-2	215	6-24-97	1	1	10.13	5	0	0	5	4	7	6	2	4	9	.222	.400	.611	36.00	16.00	25
Peterson, David	L-L	6-6	240	9-3-95	1	0	0.00	1	1	0	5	5	0	0	0	0	8	.250	.250	.300	40.00	0.00	20
Pintaro, Jonathan	R-R	6-2	235	11-7-97	3	3	3.18	7	7	0	34	26	15	12	2	10	34	.215	.294	.339	25.00	7.35	136
Ramos, Wilkin	R-R	6-5	165	10-31-00	2	1	1.65	23	0	9	33	25	6	6	0	13	31	.216	.306	.241	22.96	9.63	135
Reid-Foley, Sean	R-R	6-3	230	8-30-95	0	1	16.20	3	0	0	2	1	3	3	0	5	4	.167	.545	.333	36.36	45.45	11
Robinson, Cam	R-R	6-0	205	9-6-99	3	1	3.20	28	0	1	39	35	19	14	5	23	40	.230	.337	.401	22.47	12.92	178
Santos, Junior	R-R	6-7	244	8-16-01	4	1	4.99	31	1	1	52	49	29	29	6	26	45	.244	.343	.383	19.15	11.06	235
Scrubb, Andre	R-R	6-4	270	1-13-95	0	1	3.27	6	0	0	11	6	4	4	1	6	7	.158	.289	.289	15.56	13.33	45
Shook, TJ	R-R	6-4	217	5-29-98	3	4	3.92	13	0	4	21	17	12	9	2	4	30	.218	.282	.359	35.29	4.71	85
Sproat, Brandon	R-R	6-3	210	9-17-00	4	1	2.45	11	11	0	62	39	17	17	6	15	77	.181	.234	.302	33.19	6.47	232
Stuart, Tyler	R-R	6-9	250	10-8-99	3	7	3.96	17	17	0	84	85	39	37	8	20	90	.259	.302	.399	25.35	5.63	355
Suarez, Joander	R-R	6-3	223	2-27-00	9	5	3.92	23	21	1	119	107	55	52	12	29	118	.240	.286	.372	24.48	6.02	482
Tidwell, Blade	R-R	6-4	207	6-8-01	2	4	2.41	7	5	0	37	29	13	10	1	11	44	.218	.272	.308	29.93	7.48	147
Tong, Jonah	R-R	6-1	180	6-19-03	0	0	2.89	2	2	0	9	4	3	3	1	4	14	.121	.216	.242	37.84	10.81	37
Ventura, Jordany	R-R	6-0	162	7-6-00	0	0	0.00	5	0	0	9	3	0	0	0	4	11	.097	.200	.194	31.43	11.43	35

Fielding

Catcher	PCT	G	PO	A	E	DP	PB
Alvarez	1.000	3	25	2	0	0	0
Lantigua	1.000	1	8	1	0	0	0
O'Neill	.991	11	100	5	1	0	1
Osborn	.980	53	466	25	10	2	2
Parada	.983	73	613	37	11	9	15
Senger	1.000	4	38	1	0	0	0

First Base	PCT	G	PO	A	E	DP
Clifford	.989	51	325	25	4	28
De Los Santos	1.000	1	1	0	0	0
Gil	1.000	17	108	13	0	7
Lorusso	.979	5	42	5	1	5
Palmer	1.000	8	48	4	0	2
Peroza	1.000	7	42	4	0	2
Schwartz	.997	51	350	40	1	28
Suozzi	1.000	1	12	0	0	1

Second Base	PCT	G	PO	A	E	DP
Gil	1.000	2	2	12	0	3
Jackson	.983	15	26	32	1	6
Jordan	.987	79	99	199	4	39
Palmer	.944	7	2	15	1	3
Williams	.889	5	3	5	1	1
Young	.991	30	39	71	1	12

Third Base	PCT	G	PO	A	E	DP
Gil	.846	7	8	3	2	0
Jackson	.912	29	18	34	5	6
Jordan	.909	35	24	56	8	3
Lorusso	.750	2	1	2	1	0
Palmer	.973	35	26	45	2	5
Peroza	.960	14	7	17	1	2

NEW YORK METS

	PCT	G	PO	A	E	DP
Schwartz	.842	7	6	10	3	1
Young	.867	11	9	4	2	0

Shortstop	PCT	G	PO	A	E	DP
Jackson	.957	64	83	139	10	24
Williams	.929	14	12	27	3	2
Young	.991	59	84	131	2	33

Outfield	PCT	G	PO	A	E	DP
Clifford	.956	42	83	3	4	1
Consuegra	.992	53	114	3	1	1
De Los Santos	.957	8	20	2	1	0
Ellis	1.000	2	5	0	0	0
Jackson	.923	7	11	1	1	0
Marte	.000	1	0	0	0	0
McIlwain	1.000	38	69	1	0	0
Palmer	1.000	29	57	0	0	0
Ramirez	.958	118	221	7	10	0
Rudick	.985	95	196	7	3	1
Suozzi	.857	5	5	1	1	1
Thomas	1.000	21	46	2	0	2
Williams	1.000	1	2	0	0	0

BROOKLYN CYCLONES — HIGH-A

SOUTH ATLANTIC LEAGUE

Batting	B-T	Ht.	Wt.	DOB	AVG	OBP	SLG	G	PA	AB	R	H	2B	3B	HR	RBI	BB	HBP	SH	SF	SO	SB	CS	BB%	SO%
Allen, Austin	L-R	6-2	219	1-16-94	.182	.357	.182	3	14	11	2	2	0	0	0	0	2	1	0	0	5	0	0	14.29	35.71
Alvarez, Francisco	R-R	5-10	233	11-19-01	.091	.231	.091	3	13	11	0	1	0	0	0	0	2	0	0	0	1	0	0	15.38	7.69
Antonia, Donovan	R-R	5-10	182	8-13-03	.212	.257	.212	9	35	33	5	7	0	0	0	4	2	0	0	0	11	1	1	5.71	31.43
Baez, Jesus	R-R	5-9	180	2-26-05	.267	.313	.467	8	32	30	3	8	3	0	1	4	2	0	0	0	5	1	1	6.25	15.63
Baro, Boston	L-R	6-1	175	8-23-04	.205	.286	.318	11	49	44	7	9	3	1	0	5	5	0	0	0	10	1	0	10.20	20.41
Castro, Sebastian	L-R	6-3	185	8-27-04	.154	.353	.154	5	18	13	2	2	0	0	0	1	4	0	1	0	6	0	0	22.22	33.33
Clark, Kellum	L-R	6-4	205	4-21-01	.203	.345	.235	60	229	187	19	38	4	1	0	13	36	5	0	1	80	3	1	15.72	34.93
Clifford, Ryan	L-L	6-3	200	7-20-03	.216	.412	.304	31	136	102	13	22	6	0	1	10	32	2	0	0	43	1	0	23.53	31.62
Consuegra, Stanley	R-R	6-2	167	9-24-00	.228	.337	.381	60	252	215	26	49	12	0	7	31	30	6	0	1	84	6	3	11.90	33.33
De Los Santos, Jefrey	L-R	5-11	154	5-30-03	.194	.282	.331	93	358	314	32	61	19	3	6	39	34	6	0	4	98	3	2	9.50	27.37
De Los Santos, Omar	R-R	6-1	172	8-8-99	.196	.286	.343	85	303	265	44	52	7	4	8	32	30	4	1	2	86	43	7	9.90	28.38
Gil, Mateo	R-R	6-0	180	7-24-00	.232	.272	.409	57	217	203	19	47	11	2	7	28	11	1	0	2	54	1	2	5.07	24.88
Hernandez, Jose	R-R	5-10	190	5-13-02	.104	.173	.146	14	52	48	0	5	2	0	0	5	4	0	0	0	26	2	0	7.69	50.00
Hernandez, Ronald	B-R	5-11	155	10-23-03	.167	.286	.222	10	42	36	4	6	2	0	0	4	5	1	0	0	16	1	0	11.90	38.10
Lantigua, Andriel	R-R	6-0	190	11-29-03	.000	.000	.000	1	3	3	0	0	0	0	0	0	0	0	0	0	2	0	0	0.00	66.67
Lara, Wilfredo	R-R	5-10	180	4-28-04	.244	.349	.343	78	332	283	49	69	8	4	4	29	40	7	0	2	75	13	4	12.05	22.59
Lorusso, Nick	R-R	6-2	212	9-11-00	.267	.365	.469	70	310	262	36	70	14	3	11	42	40	3	0	5	61	8	1	12.90	19.68
Lugo, William	R-R	6-2	215	1-2-02	.186	.332	.339	84	346	280	41	52	15	2	8	34	57	6	0	3	95	5	1	16.47	27.46
McLean, Nolan	R-R	6-4	214	7-24-01	.224	.297	.552	25	74	67	10	15	7	0	5	13	6	1	0	0	38	1	0	8.11	51.35
Mercado, Estarling	L-R	6-0	195	3-6-03	.182	.280	.273	13	50	44	7	8	1	0	1	6	5	1	0	0	17	0	0	10.00	34.00
Morabito, Nick	R-R	5-11	185	5-7-03	.294	.373	.374	95	427	377	60	111	15	3	3	22	42	6	0	1	80	48	11	9.84	18.74
Osborn, Drake	R-R	5-9	190	7-22-98	.347	.458	.490	16	59	49	10	17	4	0	1	4	9	1	0	0	16	1	1	15.25	27.12
Oviedo, Carlos	R-R	6-1	210	8-20-04	.000	.053	.000	6	19	18	1	0	0	0	0	1	1	0	0	0	10	0	0	5.26	52.63
Palmer, Jaylen	R-R	6-3	208	7-31-00	.071	.133	.071	4	15	14	0	1	0	0	0	0	1	0	0	0	10	2	0	6.67	66.67
Paz, Karell	B-R	6-0	215	8-11-99	.215	.298	.368	47	163	144	18	31	7	3	3	12	13	4	2	0	44	10	4	7.98	26.99
Pregent, Christian	R-R	6-3	215	12-26-00	.166	.281	.204	53	185	157	16	26	3	0	1	15	23	3	0	2	62	0	0	12.43	33.51
Reimer, Jacob	R-R	6-2	205	2-22-04	.196	.327	.261	14	55	46	3	9	3	0	0	4	8	1	0	0	7	0	1	14.55	12.73
Rodriguez, Orangel	L-R	6-0	180	4-1-05	.250	.250	.250	2	8	8	1	2	0	0	0	0	0	0	0	0	4	0	0	0.00	50.00
Smith, D'Andre	R-R	5-8	180	5-10-01	.246	.288	.338	37	139	130	11	32	6	0	2	14	5	3	0	1	24	6	2	3.60	17.27
Suero, Christopher	R-R	5-10	205	1-27-04	.228	.353	.350	87	357	294	42	67	11	2	7	45	52	7	0	4	82	15	6	14.57	22.97
Suozzi, Joe	R-R	6-2	215	2-28-98	.211	.375	.263	6	24	19	5	4	1	0	0	1	5	0	0	0	8	0	0	20.83	33.33
Tilien, Junior	R-R	6-1	168	9-9-02	.232	.302	.331	109	440	393	37	91	17	2	6	42	40	2	0	5	85	4	1	9.09	19.32
Villavicencio, Kevin	R-R	5-9	172	11-24-03	.170	.198	.226	39	112	106	11	18	4	1	0	7	3	1	1	1	27	5	2	2.68	24.11

Pitching	B-T	Ht.	Wt.	DOB	W	L	ERA	G	GS	SV	IP	Hits	Runs	ER	HR	BB	SO	AVG	OBP	SLG	SO%	BB%	BF
Adcock, Ty	R-R	6-0	213	2-7-97	1	0	0.00	2	0	0	2	0	0	0	0	1	0	.000	.143	.000	0.00	14.29	7
Ammons, Ryan	L-L	6-0	200	4-17-01	3	0	1.33	14	0	0	20	6	3	3	0	13	25	.092	.253	.123	31.65	16.46	79
Banks, Brett	L-R	6-3	210	10-3-01	2	0	3.18	11	0	1	11	6	4	4	2	6	10	.154	.267	.359	22.22	13.33	45
Castaneda, Victor	R-R	6-1	185	8-27-98	4	2	6.47	18	0	0	32	35	24	23	2	12	36	.287	.362	.451	25.35	8.45	142
Colon, Jeffrey	R-R	6-1	170	11-9-99	1	0	5.59	18	0	0	37	43	25	23	1	15	24	.289	.371	.376	14.04	8.77	171
Cornielly, Joshua	R-R	6-2	175	1-15-01	2	5	4.35	25	0	8	39	26	24	19	4	15	50	.182	.283	.322	30.12	9.04	166
Crick, Kyle	L-R	6-4	225	11-30-92	0	0	0.00	2	0	0	2	0	0	0	0	1	4	.000	.143	.000	57.14	14.29	7
De La Cruz, Felipe	L-L	6-0	160	5-26-01	3	9	4.25	25	24	0	106	103	58	50	2	45	116	.255	.335	.342	24.84	9.64	467
Diaz, Edwin	R-R	6-3	165	3-22-94	1	0	0.00	2	0	0	2	1	0	0	0	1	3	.167	.286	.500	42.86	14.29	7
Garcia, Saul	R-R	6-0	180	6-11-03	1	0	0.00	1	1	0	5	3	0	0	0	1	7	.167	.211	.278	36.84	5.26	19
Geber, Jordan	R-R	6-3	205	7-31-99	1	0	2.25	4	3	0	16	13	4	4	0	2	15	.228	.279	.263	24.19	3.23	62
Hall, Noah	R-R	6-0	195	3-30-01	0	2	10.50	4	4	0	12	20	14	14	2	9	12	.392	.475	.647	19.67	14.75	61
Hawkins, Dakota	R-R	6-0	208	3-20-00	4	4	4.30	27	9	1	84	76	43	40	10	27	74	.238	.300	.395	21.20	7.74	349
Hejka, Josh	R-R	6-1	175	3-20-97	1	2	1.77	22	0	5	36	25	9	7	0	9	31	.195	.266	.266	21.53	6.25	144
Henry, Henry	R-R	6-4	215	12-17-98	0	3	10.38	14	0	0	17	24	22	20	1	13	18	.320	.429	.520	19.78	14.29	91
Herrera, Eduardo	S-R	5-9	179	1-5-00	2	0	3.32	13	0	4	19	12	7	7	1	12	30	.176	.296	.250	37.04	14.81	81
Lambert, Ryan	R-R	6-3	222	9-2-02	0	0	0.00	2	0	1	3	2	0	0	0	1	4	.182	.250	.182	33.33	8.33	12
Lancellotti, Joey	R-R	5-11	205	1-15-98	0	0	6.14	14	0	1	15	17	13	10	1	11	11	.293	.423	.414	15.49	15.49	71
Lawson, Justin	R-R	6-3	198	12-1-00	2	4	2.49	34	1	8	61	40	23	17	3	29	52	.187	.290	.290	20.88	11.65	249
Loper, Jimmy	R-R	6-4	215	11-8-99	0	2	6.95	14	0	0	22	26	18	17	1	12	18	.295	.394	.466	17.31	11.54	104
Louis, Gregori	L-L	6-3	161	10-28-02	0	0	1.08	6	0	0	8	5	3	1	0	5	8	.167	.324	.267	21.62	13.51	37
McLean, Nolan	R-R	6-4	214	7-24-01	2	2	2.57	7	7	0	28	20	9	8	0	10	36	.206	.313	.237	32.14	8.93	112
Megill, Tylor	R-R	6-7	230	7-28-95	0	0	0.00	1	1	0	2	0	0	0	0	0	6	.000	.000	.000	100.00	0.00	6
Moreno, Luis	R-R	6-2	174	8-3-98	5	1	5.33	12	0	0	27	27	17	16	2	16	25	.260	.371	.356	20.16	12.90	124
Morris, Kade	R-R	6-3	170	6-21-02	4	3	3.43	11	10	0	58	48	26	22	4	19	57	.221	.298	.350	23.27	7.76	245
Orellana, Douglas	R-R	6-1	196	5-1-02	0	1	1.86	13	9	0	39	32	11	8	1	18	49	.222	.309	.319	30.06	11.04	163
Ovalles, Layonel	R-R	6-3	216	6-16-03	1	0	0.00	3	0	0	4	1	0	0	0	0	6	.071	.071	.071	42.86	0.00	14

Perdomo, Alan	R-R	6-4	150	8-24-01	1	1	3.86	10	0	2	9	7	4	4	1	5	4	.200	.333	.371	9.52	11.90	42
Pintaro, Jonathan	R-R	6-2	235	11-7-97	0	3	2.50	9	7	1	36	28	14	10	1	14	35	.211	.303	.301	22.88	9.15	153
Ramirez, Jawilme	R-R	6-2	170	11-28-01	4	4	3.86	21	6	0	56	51	24	24	3	26	43	.248	.335	.350	17.99	10.88	239
Reid-Foley, Sean	R-R	6-3	230	8-30-95	0	0	10.80	2	0	0	2	2	2	2	0	1	3	.286	.375	.286	37.50	12.50	8
Senga, Kodai	L-R	6-1	202	1-30-93	0	0	0.00	1	1	0	3	0	0	0	0	0	6	.000	.000	.000	66.67	0.00	9
Simon, Ben	R-R	5-11	197	3-22-02	2	3	4.04	22	1	0	36	34	17	16	2	11	35	.252	.325	.385	23.03	7.24	152
Smith, Drew	R-R	6-2	190	9-24-93	0	0	0.00	1	0	0	1	0	0	0	0	0	2	.000	.000	.000	66.67	0.00	3
Smith, Julian	R-L	6-4	210	6-3-97	1	1	15.00	8	0	0	6	7	11	10	0	10	4	.304	.515	.391	12.12	30.30	33
Sproat, Brandon	R-R	6-3	210	9-17-00	2	1	1.07	6	5	0	25	12	4	3	1	16	33	.141	.284	.200	32.35	15.69	102
Stevenson, Jake	R-R	6-4	225	3-24-97	3	1	6.37	29	0	1	30	32	23	21	2	17	39	.262	.359	.385	27.46	11.97	142
Taveras, Diosmerky	R-R	6-5	256	9-23-99	0	1	8.68	9	0	0	9	13	10	9	1	7	10	.325	.417	.500	20.83	14.58	48
Thornton, Zach	L-L	6-3	170	1-17-02	2	2	3.67	7	6	0	27	30	11	11	1	2	22	.283	.315	.415	19.82	1.80	111
Tong, Jonah	R-R	6-1	180	6-19-03	5	4	3.71	19	19	0	85	74	39	35	2	38	110	.229	.310	.328	30.30	10.47	363
Troesser, Austin	R-R	6-3	189	3-29-02	0	2	4.50	4	4	0	12	13	7	6	1	6	9	.271	.352	.417	16.67	11.11	54
Vega, Alfred	R-R	6-1	169	1-19-01	0	0	5.87	7	0	1	8	8	5	5	1	3	10	.258	.343	.419	28.57	8.57	35
Ventura, Jordany	R-R	6-0	162	7-6-00	4	2	3.89	15	3	0	37	33	19	16	5	16	42	.234	.321	.383	26.42	10.06	159
Wenninger, Jack	L-R	6-4	210	3-14-02	1	2	3.12	10	9	0	43	40	22	15	1	17	51	.237	.316	.302	26.56	8.85	192
Ziegler, Calvin	R-R	6-0	205	10-3-02	0	0	0.00	2	2	0	6	0	1	0	0	2	13	.000	.100	.000	65.00	10.00	20

Fielding

Catcher	PCT	G	PO	A	E	DP	PB
Allen	1.000	3	27	4	0	0	1
Alvarez	1.000	2	14	0	0	0	0
Hernandez	.971	4	32	1	1	0	2
Hernandez	1.000	6	64	4	0	1	1
Osborn	.987	14	144	7	2	1	1
Oviedo	.982	6	50	5	1	0	2
Pregent	.985	49	429	17	7	1	3
Rodriguez	.938	2	15	0	1	0	1
Suero	.983	52	434	33	8	1	7

First Base	PCT	G	PO	A	E	DP
Clark	1.000	27	207	9	0	18
Clifford	.989	14	83	5	1	12
Gil	1.000	26	186	21	0	13
Hernandez	1.000	2	11	2	0	0
Hernandez	1.000	3	18	2	0	2
Lorusso	.990	37	280	15	3	17
Lugo	1.000	2	9	2	0	1
Mercado	.976	5	34	6	1	6
Palmer	.909	1	9	1	1	0
Paz	1.000	1	5	2	0	0
Suero	.992	12	108	10	1	6
Tilien	.972	7	32	3	1	1

Second Base	PCT	G	PO	A	E	DP
Antonia	.846	2	4	7	2	1
Baez	1.000	1	1	4	0	1
Baro	.750	1	2	1	1	1
De Los Santos	.959	30	45	71	5	14
Gil	.970	8	12	20	1	3
Lara	.947	16	25	47	4	4
Smith	.963	18	29	50	3	9
Tilien	.989	45	65	110	2	19
Villavicencio	1.000	15	27	46	0	9

Third Base	PCT	G	PO	A	E	DP
Baez	1.000	2	2	3	0	1
Baro	1.000	3	0	4	0	0
De Los Santos	.946	23	10	25	2	1
Gil	.895	11	3	14	2	0
Lara	.833	11	10	15	5	2
Lorusso	.933	22	13	29	3	2
Lugo	.971	18	8	25	1	0
Palmer	1.000	1	0	1	0	0
Reimer	.875	10	12	9	3	2
Smith	.667	2	0	2	1	0
Tilien	.978	32	23	64	2	8
Villavicencio	1.000	3	1	1	0	1

Shortstop	PCT	G	PO	A	E	DP
Baez	.938	5	4	11	1	1
Baro	.969	7	14	17	1	4
Gil	1.000	5	5	11	0	0
Lara	.959	32	41	76	5	16
Lugo	.980	59	65	133	4	20
Tilien	.955	14	13	29	2	3
Villavicencio	.982	16	20	36	1	7

Outfield	PCT	G	PO	A	E	DP
Antonia	1.000	5	3	0	0	0
Castro	1.000	3	12	0	0	0
Clark	.976	24	39	1	1	1
Clifford	.923	18	24	0	2	0
Consuegra	.980	58	92	5	2	0
De Los Santos	.962	34	47	3	2	1
De Los Santos	.976	83	156	9	4	2
Hernandez	1.000	4	3	0	0	0
Lara	1.000	12	20	2	0	0
Mercado	1.000	1	3	1	0	0
Morabito	.978	88	177	5	4	0
Palmer	1.000	1	2	0	0	0
Paz	.971	42	65	2	2	0
Smith	1.000	10	17	0	0	0
Suero	1.000	23	27	1	0	0
Suozzi	1.000	7	7	0	0	0
Villavicencio	1.000	4	4	2	0	0

ST. LUCIE METS — *LOW-A*

FLORIDA STATE LEAGUE

Batting	B-T	Ht.	Wt.	DOB	AVG	OBP	SLG	G	PA	AB	R	H	2B	3B	HR	RBI	BB	HBP	SH	SF	SO	SB	CS	BB%	SO%
Allen, Austin	L-R	6-2	219	1-16-94	1.000	1.000	2.000	1	1	1	0	1	1	0	0	0	0	0	0	0	0	0	0	0.00	0.00
Antonia, Donovan	R-R	5-10	182	8-13-03	.143	.273	.161	20	66	56	8	8	1	0	0	3	9	1	0	0	23	2	1	13.64	34.85
Baez, Jesus	R-R	5-9	180	2-26-05	.262	.338	.444	64	284	252	40	66	14	1	10	39	25	5	0	2	46	8	0	8.80	16.20
Baro, Boston	L-R	6-1	175	8-23-04	.288	.368	.399	84	370	323	46	93	16	4	4	42	41	2	0	4	66	8	1	11.08	17.84
Benge, Carson	L-R	6-1	184	1-20-03	.273	.420	.436	15	69	55	10	15	3	0	2	8	11	3	0	0	14	3	0	15.94	20.29
Castro, Sebastian	L-R	6-3	185	8-27-04	.267	.313	.333	4	16	15	2	4	1	0	0	0	0	1	0	0	6	2	0	0.00	37.50
Clark, Kellum	L-R	6-4	205	4-21-01	.150	.346	.250	8	26	20	2	3	0	1	0	3	6	0	0	0	8	0	0	23.08	30.77
Collins, Corey	L-R	6-3	220	10-10-01	.217	.457	.348	9	35	23	3	5	0	0	1	3	9	2	0	1	8	1	0	25.71	22.86
Cuevas, Yohairo	L-L	6-3	172	9-16-03	.213	.333	.296	113	457	385	43	82	27	1	1	46	65	5	0	2	119	20	5	14.22	26.04
De Los Santos, Jefrey	L-R	5-11	154	5-30-03	.167	.167	.222	4	18	18	0	3	1	0	0	1	0	0	0	0	5	1	0	0.00	27.78
Ewing, A.J.	L-R	6-0	160	8-10-04	.228	.344	.344	71	299	250	39	57	10	2	5	35	44	2	0	3	87	8	5	14.72	29.10
Fanas, Willy	B-R	6-1	190	1-23-04	.200	.267	.268	58	225	205	21	41	5	3	1	17	16	3	0	1	61	2	4	7.11	27.11
Gilbert, Drew	L-L	5-9	195	9-27-00	.125	.273	.125	3	11	8	0	1	0	0	0	1	1	1	0	1	1	0	0	9.09	9.09
Gutierrez, Daiverson	R-R	5-11	206	9-11-05	.111	.111	.222	8	27	27	0	3	3	0	0	0	0	0	0	0	9	0	0	0.00	33.33
Henriquez, Yonatan	B-R	5-10	185	10-12-04	.169	.245	.202	26	98	89	5	15	3	0	0	7	7	2	0	0	26	0	3	7.14	26.53
Hernandez, Jose	R-R	5-10	190	5-13-02	.147	.319	.221	35	119	95	13	14	2	1	1	5	19	5	0	0	42	5	4	15.97	35.29
Hernandez, Ronald	B-R	5-11	155	10-23-03	.271	.362	.359	98	403	351	41	95	12	2	5	41	47	4	0	1	96	7	2	11.66	23.82
Houck, Colin	R-R	6-2	190	9-30-04	.206	.304	.306	112	471	408	40	84	16	5	5	51	49	10	0	4	171	8	4	10.40	36.31
Lantigua, Andriel	R-R	6-0	190	11-29-03	.000	.100	.000	2	10	9	1	0	0	0	0	0	1	0	0	0	7	0	0	10.00	70.00
Long, Jacoby	B-R	6-1	183	6-26-02	.203	.271	.234	18	70	64	5	13	0	1	0	6	5	1	0	0	15	0	1	7.14	21.43
Machado, Fabian	R-R	5-11	180	4-25-03	.125	.222	.167	7	27	24	2	3	1	0	0	1	1	2	0	0	16	1	0	3.70	59.26
Marte, Starling	R-R	6-1	195	10-9-88	.400	.400	1.000	2	5	5	1	2	0	0	1	1	0	0	0	0	2	1	0	0.00	40.00
Martinez, J.D.	R-R	6-3	230	8-21-87	.273	.385	.364	3	13	11	3	3	1	0	0	1	2	0	0	0	1	0	0	15.38	7.69
Mercado, Estarling	L-R	6-0	195	3-6-03	.177	.320	.371	60	225	186	23	33	8	2	8	27	31	8	0	0	74	3	1	13.78	32.89

Morabito, Nick	R-R	5-11	185	5-7-03	.397	.530	.513	24	101	78	14	31	2	2	1	10	18	4	0	0	18	11	4	17.82	17.82
Mosquera, Diego	R-R	5-9	156	3-14-04	.218	.294	.241	67	246	220	18	48	1	2	0	19	19	5	1	1	36	4	3	7.72	14.63
Oviedo, Carlos	R-R	6-1	210	8-20-04	.375	.444	.500	3	9	8	1	3	1	0	0	0	1	0	0	0	2	0	0	11.11	22.22
Perozo, Vincent	L-R	6-0	170	3-6-03	.173	.280	.229	73	271	231	27	40	10	0	1	21	27	9	0	4	81	4	1	9.96	29.89
Reimer, Jacob	R-R	6-2	205	2-22-04	.333	.448	.417	7	29	24	4	8	2	0	0	2	4	1	0	0	5	0	0	13.79	17.24
Rosa, Jeffry	R-R	6-1	190	9-11-04	.149	.284	.234	42	169	141	16	21	3	0	3	16	16	11	0	1	59	2	1	9.47	34.91
Roselli, Nick	L-R	5-10	200	3-31-03	.309	.433	.436	18	68	55	9	17	2	1	1	7	10	2	0	0	18	3	0	14.71	26.47
Senger, Hayden	R-R	6-1	210	4-3-97	.286	.286	.286	2	7	7	0	2	0	0	0	2	0	0	0	0	3	0	0	0.00	42.86
Serrano, Eli	L-L	6-5	193	5-1-03	.238	.333	.444	17	72	63	8	15	3	2	2	6	7	2	0	0	16	1	0	9.72	22.22
Smith, D'Andre	R-R	5-8	180	5-10-01	.176	.222	.235	5	18	17	1	3	1	0	0	1	0	1	0	0	4	0	0	0.00	22.22
Snyder, Trey	R-R	6-1	197	9-21-05	.182	.308	.182	6	26	22	5	4	0	0	0	3	4	0	0	0	6	1	1	15.38	23.08
Suero, Christopher	R-R	5-10	205	1-27-04	.265	.390	.434	25	100	83	18	22	6	1	2	15	10	7	0	0	19	5	5	10.00	19.00
Vargas, Marco	L-R	6-0	170	5-14-05	.208	.369	.238	37	168	130	31	27	4	0	0	7	34	1	0	3	38	13	2	20.24	22.62
Villavicencio, Kevin	R-R	5-9	172	11-24-03	.215	.283	.287	64	230	209	33	45	6	3	1	17	17	3	0	1	48	14	3	7.39	20.87
Williams, Jett	R-R	5-6	175	11-3-03	.250	.471	.250	5	17	12	0	3	0	0	0	0	4	1	0	0	3	2	1	23.53	17.65

Pitching	**B-T**	**Ht.**	**Wt.**	**DOB**	**W**	**L**	**ERA**	**G**	**GS**	**SV**	**IP**	**Hits**	**Runs**	**ER**	**HR**	**BB**	**SO**	**AVG**	**OBP**	**SLG**	**SO%**	**BB%**	**BF**
Alfonseca, Miguel	R-R	6-0	190	2-13-00	1	2	5.79	22	0	0	28	33	21	18	4	22	18	.295	.423	.464	13.04	15.94	138
Ammons, Ryan	L-L	6-0	200	4-17-01	1	4	2.88	18	0	3	25	18	13	8	1	19	35	.198	.348	.341	31.25	16.96	112
Aracena, Wellington	R-R	6-3	180	12-27-04	1	2	9.45	6	2	0	13	13	16	14	1	16	20	.245	.414	.321	28.57	22.86	70
Arnaud, Juan	R-R	6-2	164	6-22-03	3	1	4.02	32	0	4	40	29	23	18	1	31	49	.203	.370	.245	26.49	16.76	185
Austin, Channing	R-R	6-3	200	12-21-01	0	0	0.00	1	0	0	1	1	0	0	0	1	1	.333	.500	.667	25.00	25.00	4
Banks, Brett	L-R	6-3	210	10-3-01	0	0	4.91	4	0	1	4	5	2	2	1	2	6	.313	.389	.500	33.33	11.11	18
Barreto, Brayhans	L-L	6-4	185	5-5-01	0	4	6.53	8	1	0	21	23	17	15	3	11	21	.284	.366	.444	22.58	11.83	93
Bautista, Nick	R-R	6-3	200	2-22-02	2	1	7.77	16	0	0	22	25	19	19	3	18	23	.291	.435	.465	20.00	15.65	115
Brewer, Hoss	L-R	6-4	205	2-20-01	0	0	0.00	1	0	0	2	0	0	0	0	0	1	.000	.000	.000	16.67	0.00	6
Chirinos, Jose	R-R	6-3	170	10-16-04	0	0	9.00	1	0	0	1	1	1	1	0	2	1	.250	.500	.250	16.67	33.33	6
Cota, Irving	R-R	5-9	165	2-14-04	1	1	2.08	7	0	0	17	14	6	4	2	7	11	.209	.293	.343	14.67	9.33	75
Crick, Kyle	L-R	6-4	225	11-30-92	0	0	2.08	4	1	0	4	3	1	1	0	2	5	.200	.400	.200	25.00	10.00	20
Cuevas, Candido	R-R	6-1	202	4-24-04	0	1	4.91	3	1	0	7	6	6	4	0	10	8	.200	.405	.300	19.05	23.81	42
De Leon, Jorge	R-R	6-5	180	11-24-02	0	3	8.84	11	6	1	18	18	20	18	1	21	29	.261	.448	.406	30.21	21.88	96
Diaz, Joel	R-R	6-2	208	2-26-04	2	6	4.92	17	14	0	68	69	46	37	12	28	62	.258	.333	.446	20.53	9.27	302
Elissalt, Frank	S-R	6-2	210	3-25-02	0	0	0.00	1	0	1	0	0	0	0	0	0	1	.000	.000	.000	50.00	0.00	2
Escalante, Estarlin	R-R	6-4	235	8-22-03	0	1	3.00	5	0	0	9	7	3	3	0	3	6	.212	.278	.212	16.22	8.11	37
Ferrer, Andinson	R-R	6-3	180	5-5-04	0	0	0.00	1	0	0	3	1	0	0	0	1	5	.111	.200	.222	50.00	10.00	10
Fujinami, Shintaro	R-R	6-6	180	4-12-94	0	0	0.00	1	0	0	1	0	0	0	0	0	0	.000	.000	.000	0.00	0.00	3
Garcia, Saul	R-R	6-0	180	6-11-03	3	8	5.43	23	12	0	66	69	48	40	3	41	79	.263	.378	.370	25.08	13.02	315
Girton, Brendan	R-R	6-2	220	11-10-01	0	0	12.00	3	1	0	3	5	4	4	0	4	5	.417	.563	.417	31.25	25.00	16
Gomez, Cristofer	R-R	6-4	222	5-13-03	1	0	4.38	24	0	2	39	27	23	19	0	25	44	.191	.320	.255	26.04	14.79	169
Gomez, Franklin	L-L	6-0	145	7-6-05	3	9	4.28	23	16	0	82	82	49	39	5	41	83	.255	.351	.364	22.43	11.08	370
Gordillo, Lucas	R-R	6-0	180	7-2-02	0	1	7.71	1	0	0	2	3	4	2	0	3	3	.300	.462	.400	23.08	23.08	13
Hall, Noah	R-R	6-0	195	3-30-01	0	0	0.00	1	1	0	1	0	0	0	0	1	0	.000	.250	.000	0.00	25.00	4
Hartwig, Grant	R-R	6-5	235	12-18-97	0	0	0.00	2	2	0	2	1	0	0	0	1	2	.167	.375	.167	25.00	12.50	8
Henry, Henry	R-R	6-4	215	12-17-98	0	0	0.00	1	0	0	1	0	0	0	0	0	1	.000	.000	.000	33.33	0.00	3
Herrera, Eduardo	S-R	5-9	179	1-5-00	0	0	0.84	8	0	0	11	4	1	1	0	3	19	.118	.189	.118	51.35	8.11	37
Hodges, Hunter	R-R	6-3	225	10-3-02	0	1	54.00	1	0	0	1	1	4	4	0	4	1	.333	.714	.333	14.29	57.14	7
Hudepohl, Wyatt	R-R	6-4	220	9-25-01	1	3	4.03	8	7	0	29	31	15	13	2	18	31	.279	.377	.414	23.85	13.85	130
Kranick, Max	R-R	6-3	220	7-21-97	0	1	21.60	2	2	0	2	7	4	4	0	2	3	.583	.643	.750	21.43	14.29	14
Lanthier, Ethan	R-R	6-5	230	6-10-03	0	0	0.00	2	0	0	3	1	0	0	0	1	5	.111	.200	.111	50.00	10.00	10
Loper, Jimmy	R-R	6-4	215	11-8-99	0	1	2.57	7	0	0	14	12	4	4	0	2	19	.231	.259	.365	35.19	3.70	54
Lopez, Wilson	R-R	6-1	216	7-15-02	2	0	7.15	22	0	0	23	23	28	18	0	27	19	.247	.445	.323	14.84	21.09	128
Louis, Gregori	L-L	6-3	161	10-28-02	4	0	1.49	20	0	2	42	24	12	7	0	24	44	.166	.286	.214	25.14	13.71	175
Marsh, Chandler	R-R	6-4	235	9-6-02	0	0	0.00	1	1	0	1	2	0	0	0	2	1	.667	.800	1.000	20.00	40.00	5
Mercedes, Ernesto	R-R	6-2	180	10-14-03	0	11	5.54	18	13	0	65	51	50	40	1	60	89	.223	.395	.297	29.18	19.67	305
Montes de Oca, Bryce	R-R	6-7	265	4-23-96	0	0	22.50	3	2	0	2	4	5	5	0	5	2	.444	.643	.556	14.29	35.71	14
Moreta, Edgar	R-R	6-4	192	9-5-03	1	4	5.04	13	11	0	50	53	33	28	6	20	54	.273	.366	.433	23.68	8.77	228
Morris, Kade	R-R	6-3	170	6-21-02	0	3	3.63	7	6	0	35	34	17	14	6	11	38	.252	.311	.444	25.50	7.38	149
Nunez, Anthony	S-R	6-1	190	7-10-01	0	0	3.38	7	0	0	8	5	3	3	0	5	10	.172	.333	.241	27.78	13.89	36
Ovalles, Layonel	R-R	6-3	216	6-16-03	2	1	5.92	21	0	1	38	37	25	25	1	28	42	.257	.390	.326	23.60	15.73	178
Peguero, Jeremy	L-L	6-2	175	5-3-02	2	1	3.12	22	0	0	35	23	17	12	1	32	50	.184	.374	.272	30.67	19.63	163
Perdomo, Alan	R-R	6-4	150	8-24-01	2	1	3.74	24	1	3	43	42	22	18	2	17	33	.251	.326	.359	17.46	8.99	189
Peterson, David	L-L	6-6	240	9-3-95	0	0	0.00	3	3	0	9	2	0	0	0	1	16	.069	.100	.069	53.33	3.33	30
Ramirez, Jawilme	R-R	6-2	170	11-28-01	1	1	2.81	8	0	0	16	10	6	5	0	10	16	.182	.318	.255	23.88	14.93	67
Rodriguez, Christian	R-R	6-0	160	10-12-04	1	0	1.69	4	1	1	16	7	3	3	0	10	11	.127	.284	.145	16.18	14.71	68
Ross, Dylan	R-R	6-5	251	9-1-00	1	0	0.00	1	0	0	1	0	0	0	0	0	3	.000	.000	.000	100.00	0.00	3
Thornton, Zach	L-L	6-3	170	1-17-02	3	2	4.39	13	6	1	41	47	26	20	3	16	32	.294	.374	.425	17.49	8.74	183
Tong, Jonah	R-R	6-1	180	6-19-03	1	0	0.00	4	2	0	19	7	1	0	0	5	36	.115	.194	.180	52.94	7.35	68
Troesser, Austin	R-R	6-3	189	3-29-02	1	4	4.25	12	6	0	36	33	17	17	2	16	52	.244	.325	.326	34.44	10.60	151
Vega, Alfred	R-R	6-1	169	1-19-01	0	1	20.25	3	0	0	3	6	6	6	0	0	5	.429	.429	.643	35.71	0.00	14
Ventura, Jordany	R-R	6-0	162	7-6-00	0	0	0.00	2	1	0	2	2	1	0	0	0	2	.222	.300	.222	20.00	0.00	10
Watson, William	R-R	6-1	170	11-7-02	1	0	3.38	2	0	0	3	2	1	1	1	0	3	.200	.200	.500	30.00	0.00	10
Wenninger, Jack	L-R	6-4	210	3-14-02	3	4	5.02	15	10	0	72	67	47	40	10	23	89	.238	.300	.406	28.71	7.42	310
Witt, Tanner	R-R	6-5	215	7-11-02	0	0	0.00	1	0	0	2	0	0	0	0	0	2	.000	.000	.000	40.00	0.00	5
Yabbour, Joseph	R-R	6-0	175	7-9-03	1	1	8.24	14	0	0	20	26	21	18	2	19	28	.313	.442	.542	26.92	18.27	104

Fielding

Catcher	PCT	G	PO	A	E	DP	PB
Allen	1.000	1	1	0	0	0	0
Gutierrez	.979	6	43	3	1	0	2
Hernandez	.979	23	179	11	4	0	17
Hernandez	.988	50	474	23	6	2	15
Lantigua	1.000	1	13	1	0	0	1
Oviedo	1.000	1	7	1	0	0	0
Perozo	.975	51	466	42	13	1	22
Senger	1.000	2	21	2	0	0	0
Suero	.989	8	75	12	1	0	2

First Base	PCT	G	PO	A	E	DP
Collins	.980	7	45	4	1	2
Cuevas	.981	48	281	22	6	32
Hernandez	.969	10	56	6	2	2
Hernandez	.981	24	146	10	3	17
Lantigua	1.000	1	6	0	0	0
Mercado	.993	23	148	2	1	12
Oviedo	1.000	2	9	0	0	1
Perozo	.985	18	120	8	2	7
Suero	.961	11	69	4	3	5

Second Base	PCT	G	PO	A	E	DP
Ewing	.932	18	32	36	5	5
Roselli	.947	16	18	36	3	2
Villavicencio	.966	20	35	49	3	9
Mosquera	.968	32	46	76	4	16
Vargas	.984	15	27	33	1	7
Baro	.984	17	26	35	1	10
Antonia	1.000	3	5	8	0	1
Baez	1.000	8	18	25	0	4
De Los Santos	1.000	2	4	5	0	1
Henriquez	1.000	1	4	1	0	1
Houck	1.000	1	0	5	0	1
Smith	1.000	3	3	7	0	3

Third Base	PCT	G	PO	A	E	DP
Baez	.904	19	13	34	5	2
Baro	.943	32	32	50	5	3
Henriquez	1.000	8	2	15	0	0
Houck	.849	40	23	50	13	4
Mosquera	.857	8	3	9	2	0
Reimer	.833	5	3	7	2	0
Snyder	1.000	2	2	6	0	0
Vargas	.944	6	4	13	1	3
Villavicencio	1.000	14	6	25	0	3

Shortstop	PCT	G	PO	A	E	DP
Baez	.919	17	29	39	6	7
Baro	.919	19	25	43	6	7
Henriquez	1.000	8	7	13	0	7
Houck	.918	62	65	115	16	22
Mosquera	1.000	3	2	3	0	0
Snyder	.900	4	8	10	2	2
Vargas	.966	14	20	36	2	5
Villavicencio	1.000	5	8	8	0	2
Williams	1.000	4	5	8	0	1

Outfield	PCT	G	PO	A	E	DP
Antonia	1.000	14	19	2	0	1
Benge	.933	8	12	2	1	0
Castro	1.000	4	4	0	0	0
Clark	1.000	8	8	0	0	0
Cuevas	.959	69	104	13	5	1
De Los Santos	1.000	2	3	0	0	0
Ewing	.972	50	101	2	3	1
Fanas	.972	56	103	3	3	0
Gilbert	1.000	2	2	1	0	0
Henriquez	1.000	8	12	0	0	0
Hernandez	.800	1	4	0	1	0
Long	1.000	18	31	3	0	1
Machado	.800	6	4	0	1	0
Marte	1.000	1	1	0	0	0
Mercado	1.000	26	33	1	0	0
Morabito	.964	23	48	5	2	1
Mosquera	1.000	24	31	3	0	1
Rosa	.985	39	58	6	1	0
Serrano	1.000	16	17	3	0	0
Smith	1.000	1	3	0	0	0
Suero	1.000	5	9	0	0	0
Villavicencio	.983	22	58	0	1	0

FCL METS — ROOKIE

FLORIDA COMPLEX LEAGUE

Batting	B-T	Ht.	Wt.	DOB	AVG	OBP	SLG	G	PA	AB	R	H	2B	3B	HR	RBI	BB	HBP	SH	SF	SO	SB	CS	BB%	SO%
Allen, Austin	L-R	6-2	219	1-16-94	.100	.182	.100	3	11	10	1	1	0	0	0	0	1	0	0	0	3	1	0	9.09	27.27
Antonia, Donovan	R-R	5-10	182	8-13-03	.169	.234	.268	22	77	71	8	12	4	0	1	8	6	0	0	0	21	3	4	7.79	27.27
Castro, Sebastian	L-R	6-3	185	8-27-04	.107	.211	.179	30	95	84	9	9	1	1	1	4	8	3	0	0	30	3	2	8.42	31.58
De Oleo, Branny	R-R	6-1	156	5-15-05	.209	.284	.302	42	155	139	16	29	3	2	2	14	11	4	0	1	35	4	4	7.10	22.58
Ewing, A.J.	L-R	6-0	160	8-10-04	.254	.422	.571	19	83	63	20	16	3	1	5	14	19	0	0	1	22	5	1	22.89	26.51
Fanas, Willy	B-R	6-1	190	1-23-04	.282	.404	.538	11	47	39	8	11	5	1	1	6	7	1	0	0	8	0	0	14.89	17.02
Gilbert, Drew	L-L	5-9	195	9-27-00	.000	.364	.000	3	11	7	2	0	0	0	0	0	4	0	0	0	2	0	0	36.36	18.18
Gutierrez, Daiverson	R-R	5-11	206	9-11-05	.317	.463	.537	15	54	41	7	13	3	0	2	6	9	3	0	1	4	0	0	16.67	7.41
Henriquez, Yonatan	B-R	5-10	185	10-12-04	.289	.464	.377	40	151	114	27	33	6	2	0	10	34	3	0	0	23	15	4	22.52	15.23
Juan, Simon	R-R	5-11	195	7-13-05	.273	.337	.459	50	202	183	30	50	11	1	7	29	17	1	0	1	48	4	1	8.42	23.76
Machado, Fabian	R-R	5-11	180	4-25-03	.223	.309	.266	30	110	94	11	21	4	0	0	13	10	3	0	3	29	2	0	9.09	26.36
Mosquera, Diego	R-R	5-9	156	3-14-04	.154	.353	.154	5	17	13	1	2	0	0	0	1	4	0	0	0	3	0	2	23.53	17.65
Oviedo, Carlos	R-R	6-1	210	8-20-04	.154	.290	.192	11	32	26	1	4	1	0	0	2	4	1	1	0	13	0	0	12.50	40.63
Peroza, Jose	R-R	6-1	221	6-15-00	.500	.500	1.250	1	4	4	1	2	0	0	1	3	0	0	0	0	1	0	0	0.00	25.00
Reimer, Jacob	R-R	6-2	205	2-22-04	.000	.273	.000	4	11	8	0	0	0	0	0	1	3	0	0	0	2	0	0	27.27	18.18
Rodriguez, Jeremy	L-R	6-0	170	7-4-06	.282	.355	.400	50	217	195	25	55	10	2	3	20	21	1	0	0	37	17	8	9.68	17.05
Rodriguez, Orangel	L-R	6-0	180	4-1-05	.282	.300	.385	14	40	39	6	11	4	0	0	6	1	0	0	0	5	0	0	2.50	12.50
Rosa, Jeffry	R-R	6-1	190	9-11-04	.178	.351	.244	15	57	45	6	8	0	0	1	1	11	1	0	0	20	2	0	19.30	35.09
Sarmiento, Dangelo	R-R	6-0	160	1-4-05	.200	.385	.500	4	13	10	3	2	0	0	1	2	3	0	0	0	6	1	0	23.08	46.15
Smith, D'Andre	R-R	5-8	180	5-10-01	.235	.278	.294	5	18	17	3	4	1	0	0	3	1	0	0	0	3	3	0	5.56	16.67
Subero, Jose	R-R	6-0	160	3-8-05	.417	.417	.417	5	12	12	2	5	0	0	0	3	0	0	0	0	3	0	0	0.00	25.00
Toledo, Francisco	R-R	5-9	160	4-23-05	.225	.337	.236	30	104	89	10	20	1	0	0	8	14	1	0	0	22	1	0	13.46	21.15
Zayas, Julio	R-R	5-11	190	2-16-06	.239	.354	.367	35	131	109	16	26	3	1	3	17	18	2	0	1	22	0	0	13.74	16.79
Zitella, Jacob	R-R	5-11	195	2-24-05	.252	.355	.367	45	172	147	22	37	9	1	2	16	17	7	0	1	41	1	1	9.88	23.84

Pitching	B-T	Ht.	Wt.	DOB	W	L	ERA	G	GS	SV	IP	Hits	Runs	ER	HR	BB	SO	AVG	OBP	SLG	SO%	BB%	BF
Alvarez, Luis	R-R	6-5	185	5-5-03	1	0	4.22	7	2	1	11	9	9	5	0	12	18	.220	.429	.293	32.14	21.43	56
Anton, Jesus	R-R	6-3	175	2-17-06	0	2	9.95	5	2	0	6	7	8	7	0	14	8	.292	.564	.333	20.51	35.90	39
Aracena, Wellington	R-R	6-3	180	12-27-04	1	6	6.26	11	9	0	27	26	27	19	1	26	36	.239	.399	.339	26.09	18.84	138
Barreto, Brayhans	L-L	6-4	185	5-5-01	2	0	2.76	15	0	2	33	25	11	10	1	14	42	.208	.289	.242	30.88	10.29	136
Bihm, Gage	L-L	6-4	215	8-15-01	0	0	0.00	2	0	0	1	1	2	0	0	4	2	.200	.500	.200	20.00	40.00	10
Chirinos, Jhosep	R-R	6-4	175	4-17-04	1	0	4.50	1	0	0	2	1	1	1	0	1	2	.125	.222	.125	22.22	11.11	9
Chirinos, Jose	R-R	6-3	170	10-16-04	1	3	6.14	12	7	0	37	35	31	25	0	24	43	.245	.359	.294	25.00	13.95	172
Cota, Irving	R-R	5-9	165	2-14-04	4	0	3.49	10	1	0	28	26	16	11	4	6	42	.232	.277	.402	35.29	5.04	119
De Leon, Jorge	R-R	6-5	180	11-24-02	0	0	1.13	3	3	0	8	3	2	1	0	3	16	.107	.194	.143	51.61	9.68	31
Diaz, Joel	R-R	6-2	208	2-26-04	0	0	0.00	3	3	0	7	6	1	0	0	0	9	.222	.222	.296	33.33	0.00	27
Escalante, Estarlin	R-R	6-4	235	8-22-03	1	1	4.00	14	0	1	18	18	11	8	0	5	24	.250	.316	.306	30.38	6.33	79
Esterlin, Wilson	R-R	6-3	160	8-17-04	1	2	9.90	15	0	0	20	25	23	22	5	14	30	.301	.454	.518	27.78	12.96	108
Ferrer, Andinson	R-R	6-3	180	5-5-04	2	0	4.58	12	0	1	18	12	13	9	1	11	25	.182	.325	.288	31.25	13.75	80
Fujinami, Shintaro	R-R	6-6	180	4-12-94	0	0	0.00	1	1	0	1	0	0	0	0	0	1	.000	.000	.000	33.33	0.00	3
Gomez, Cristofer	R-R	6-4	222	5-13-03	0	0	0.00	3	0	2	5	4	0	0	0	0	3	.235	.235	.235	17.65	0.00	17
Gordillo, Lucas	R-R	6-0	180	7-2-02	2	0	3.94	15	0	0	30	32	16	13	1	13	28	.296	.370	.380	21.71	10.08	129

Pitching	B-T	Ht.	Wt.	DOB	W	L	ERA	G	GS	SV	IP	Hits	Runs	ER	HR	BB	SO	AVG	OBP	SLG	SO%	BB%	BF
Hurtado, Daviel	L-L	6-1	166	1-26-05	0	5	6.32	8	8	0	16	15	13	11	0	10	23	.259	.368	.293	33.82	14.71	68
Louis, Gregori	L-L	6-3	161	10-28-02	1	0	0.00	2	0	0	4	4	0	0	0	1	6	.286	.333	.357	40.00	6.67	15
Mercado, Franciso	R-R	6-2	150	12-7-03	0	1	4.70	5	3	0	8	6	6	4	0	5	6	.200	.333	.300	16.67	13.89	36
Moreta, Edgar	R-R	6-4	192	9-5-03	2	2	3.86	6	2	0	19	16	10	8	3	4	19	.225	.291	.380	24.05	5.06	79
Nunez, Anthony	S-R	6-1	190	7-10-01	0	0	0.00	2	1	0	2	0	0	0	0	0	2	.000	.000	.000	33.33	0.00	6
Ovalles, Layonel	R-R	6-3	216	6-16-03	0	0	0.00	3	0	0	8	1	0	0	0	3	7	.043	.148	.130	25.93	11.11	27
Peguero, Jeremy	L-L	6-2	175	5-3-02	2	0	0.87	4	0	0	10	2	1	1	0	7	16	.061	.244	.091	39.02	17.07	41
Rodriguez, Christian	R-R	6-0	160	10-12-04	1	3	3.82	13	2	0	35	34	24	15	5	27	48	.252	.384	.407	28.92	16.27	166
Victorino, Omar	R-R	6-2	170	6-9-05	0	2	5.46	10	8	0	28	20	19	17	1	33	39	.208	.422	.313	28.68	24.26	136
Yabbour, Joseph	R-R	6-0	175	7-9-03	1	1	3.24	10	0	0	25	17	11	9	2	12	35	.202	.304	.310	34.31	11.76	102

Fielding

C: Toledo 22, Zayas 16, Gutierrez 11, Rodriguez 4, Allen 3. **1B:** Zitella 18, Oviedo 10, Rodriguez 9, Castro 8, Zayas 7, Toledo 3. **2B:** De Oleo 18, Rodriguez 10, Ewing 8, Henriquez 5, Subero 4, Smith 3, Antonia 3, Mosquera 2, Sarmiento 2. **3B:** Zitella 25, Henriquez 11, De Oleo 10, Reimer 3, Rodriguez 3, Subero 1, Mosquera 1, Peroza 1, Castro 1. **SS:** Rodriguez 37, De Oleo 15, Sarmiento 1. **LF:** Castro 12, Henriquez 9, Antonia 8, Rosa 7, Machado 6, Juan 5, Fanas 4, Smith 2. **CF:** Juan 23, Ewing 11, Henriquez 9, Machado 6, Gilbert 3, Antonia 3, Castro 2. **RF:** Juan 18, Machado 13, Rosa 6, Castro 5, Antonia 4, Fanas 3, Henriquez 3, Sarmiento 1, Toledo 1.

DSL METS BLUE — *ROOKIE*

DOMINICAN SUMMER LEAGUE

Batting	B-T	Ht.	Wt.	DOB	AVG	OBP	SLG	G	PA	AB	R	H	2B	3B	HR	RBI	BB	HBP	SH	SF	SO	SB	CS	BB%	SO%
Acosta, Alex	R-R	6-1	187	11-24-05	.246	.353	.373	42	167	142	26	35	7	1	3	23	20	4	0	1	33	6	3	11.98	19.76
Aular, Jose	R-R	5-11	175	1-2-04	.278	.519	.389	20	54	36	8	10	2	1	0	9	15	3	0	0	6	1	0	27.78	11.11
Cordero, Daris	R-R	5-11	185	9-2-05	.254	.268	.299	23	71	67	5	17	3	0	0	8	1	1	0	2	23	3	1	1.41	32.39
De Aza, Diover	B-R	6-1	160	8-15-07	.228	.338	.316	16	68	57	11	13	2	0	1	7	8	2	0	1	22	2	3	11.76	32.35
Diaz, Reniel	R-R	6-0	160	4-3-06	.171	.412	.286	15	51	35	9	6	1	0	1	5	9	6	0	1	19	2	0	17.65	37.25
Fernandez, Starling	R-R	6-0	178	10-27-06	.167	.167	.167	2	6	6	0	1	0	0	0	0	0	0	0	0	2	0	0	0.00	33.33
Garcia, Keiver	B-R	5-10	145	8-6-06	.375	.444	.458	8	27	24	4	9	2	0	0	0	2	1	0	0	5	2	2	7.41	18.52
German, Haniel	R-R	6-2	185	12-5-05	.269	.337	.414	40	163	145	23	39	9	0	4	20	13	3	0	2	37	5	2	7.98	22.70
Gomez, Vladi	L-R	5-11	150	9-12-05	.216	.345	.330	26	116	97	24	21	4	2	1	15	15	4	0	0	19	17	1	12.93	16.38
Guerrero, Vladi	L-L	6-2	220	9-21-06	.195	.327	.250	41	153	128	20	25	5	1	0	12	22	3	0	0	54	3	0	14.38	35.29
Gutierrez, Daiverson	R-R	5-11	206	9-11-05	.300	.472	.475	14	53	40	7	12	7	0	0	7	7	6	0	0	5	1	0	13.21	9.43
Guzman, Randy	R-R	6-4	215	4-19-05	.275	.370	.500	12	46	40	5	11	4	1	1	7	6	0	0	0	12	1	1	13.04	26.09
Hernandez, Julian	R-R	6-0	180	9-24-05	.200	.385	.350	11	26	20	6	4	0	0	1	3	6	0	0	0	9	2	0	23.08	34.62
Herrera, Roybert	L-R	6-2	175	6-30-07	.329	.407	.443	24	91	79	16	26	4	1	1	9	6	5	0	1	23	8	1	6.59	25.27
Lantigua, Edward	R-R	6-3	174	11-13-06	.290	.443	.462	28	122	93	20	27	7	3	1	17	17	10	0	2	26	8	2	13.93	21.31
Matos, Alvaro	L-R	5-11	180	6-20-06	.250	.423	.300	7	26	20	6	5	1	0	0	1	3	3	0	0	10	7	0	11.54	38.46
Mella, Leandy	L-R	5-10	170	2-4-07	.000	.300	.000	3	10	7	1	0	0	0	0	0	3	0	0	0	3	0	0	30.00	30.00
Miranda, Adolfo	R-R	6-2	190	10-4-06	.150	.190	.150	7	21	20	0	3	0	0	0	0	1	0	0	0	12	0	0	4.76	57.14
Montano, Arnaldo	R-R	6-0	175	2-3-06	.200	.375	.280	9	32	25	3	5	2	0	0	3	6	1	0	0	8	1	1	18.75	25.00
Peralta, Waldy	R-R	6-0	150	3-3-06	.143	.265	.214	17	49	42	6	6	3	0	0	1	4	3	0	0	16	0	1	8.16	32.65
Ramirez, Justin	L-L	6-3	190	2-9-05	.157	.290	.294	14	62	51	8	8	1	0	2	6	8	2	0	1	15	0	0	12.90	24.19
Reyes, Rainer	R-R	5-11	190	5-19-03	.295	.412	.526	30	119	95	21	28	7	0	5	22	13	8	0	3	24	3	1	10.92	20.17
Rivas, Yensi	B-R	6-0	170	10-14-06	.245	.351	.329	45	185	155	26	38	5	4	0	25	20	7	0	3	50	16	7	10.81	27.03
Sanchez, Jonnhan	L-L	6-0	160	5-8-07	.053	.136	.158	7	22	19	2	1	0	1	0	1	2	0	0	1	5	1	0	9.09	22.73
Silva, Daniel	B-R	6-2	200	1-12-05	.261	.404	.283	16	57	46	6	12	1	0	0	3	10	1	0	0	15	0	1	17.54	26.32
Subero, Jose	R-R	6-0	160	3-8-05	.232	.341	.348	23	82	69	16	16	6	1	0	8	10	2	0	1	23	6	4	12.20	28.05
Terrero, Marcos	L-R	5-11	155	11-11-05	.268	.364	.393	19	66	56	10	15	3	2	0	7	9	0	0	1	8	4	1	13.64	12.12

Pitching	B-T	Ht.	Wt.	DOB	W	L	ERA	G	GS	SV	IP	Hits	Runs	ER	HR	BB	SO	AVG	OBP	SLG	SO%	BB%	BF
Arciniegas, Franklin	L-L	6-2	182	1-12-05	0	0	6.23	3	0	1	4	6	3	3	0	2	6	.316	.381	.421	28.57	9.52	21
Brito, Carlos	R-R	6-5	192	2-24-02	1	0	3.18	9	0	1	11	10	7	4	1	12	16	.227	.393	.386	28.57	21.43	56
Brito, Jean	R-R	6-3	180	3-28-06	1	0	0.00	3	0	0	3	2	0	0	0	2	5	.167	.286	.167	35.71	14.29	14
Cabrera, Luis	R-R	6-3	212	11-22-04	0	0	4.91	4	0	0	7	4	4	4	1	3	10	.160	.267	.280	33.33	10.00	30
Cornelia, Jamdrick	L-L	6-0	140	11-17-05	0	0	1.46	8	0	1	12	6	3	2	0	5	15	.146	.239	.195	31.25	10.42	48
Crespo, Anthony	R-R	6-0	197	5-4-04	2	6	3.38	11	11	0	48	35	22	18	2	22	51	.202	.294	.266	25.89	11.17	197
De La Rosa, Angel	L-L	6-2	180	11-20-05	0	0	3.86	1	0	0	2	2	1	1	0	0	2	.222	.300	.444	20.00	0.00	10
Felix, Darling	L-L	6-2	173	10-6-05	0	0	8.82	14	0	0	16	20	24	16	1	27	27	.299	.515	.388	27.27	27.27	99
Gomez, Jose	L-L	6-1	160	9-9-06	0	0	17.36	5	0	0	5	6	11	9	0	8	6	.300	.517	.300	20.69	27.59	29
Guevara, Jose	R-R	6-1	178	4-20-05	2	2	1.72	7	7	0	31	16	9	6	0	9	37	.143	.211	.188	30.08	7.32	123
Lara, Joel	R-R	6-2	210	1-11-07	2	1	2.45	9	2	1	18	18	10	5	0	5	26	.254	.308	.296	33.33	6.41	78
Lopez, Luisner	R-R	6-3	180	1-28-04	2	1	4.81	17	0	1	34	30	24	18	1	22	26	.234	.361	.336	16.56	14.01	157
Lopez, Misael	L-L	6-2	180	4-8-03	1	2	9.00	7	0	0	8	4	9	8	0	9	14	.143	.390	.214	34.15	21.95	41
Lora, Darlin	R-R	6-3	200	6-25-07	0	0	13.50	3	0	0	2	1	6	3	0	7	4	.125	.588	.125	23.53	41.18	17
Lugo, Wilmer	L-L	6-0	190	3-5-06	1	6	3.94	11	7	0	32	37	30	14	0	28	37	.287	.437	.357	22.02	16.67	168
Meza, Nomar	R-R	6-2	200	10-3-06	1	2	5.79	6	0	0	9	13	7	6	0	6	8	.342	.435	.368	17.39	13.04	46
Mijares, Elwis	R-R	6-0	180	12-29-05	1	0	0.43	4	4	0	21	14	3	1	0	1	28	.189	.211	.203	36.84	1.32	76
Moreno, Johan	R-R	6-2	200	9-10-04	0	4	4.18	8	8	0	28	21	21	13	1	16	41	.193	.318	.312	31.54	12.31	130
Portel, Danny	L-L	6-4	224	8-5-04	1	0	4.00	6	0	1	9	6	6	4	0	6	12	.194	.333	.194	30.00	15.00	40
Ramirez, Alejandro	R-R	6-2	190	4-21-04	0	0	13.50	5	0	0	9	8	13	13	0	16	9	.242	.510	.242	17.65	31.37	51
Ramos, Lenerd	R-R	6-2	190	9-23-03	0	0	6.75	3	0	0	3	3	3	2	0	2	4	.273	.429	.273	28.57	14.29	14
Rivas, Yancarlos	L-L	6-1	155	1-1-07	1	0	6.94	9	0	1	12	16	16	9	0	18	8	.348	.530	.413	12.12	27.27	66
Rochin, Christopher	R-R	6-2	200	9-18-06	0	0	0.00	1	0	0	1	0	0	0	0	0	0	.000	.000	.000	0.00	0.00	4
Rodriguez, Leyvi	R-R	6-2	195	5-17-06	0	2	6.52	10	7	0	29	19	26	21	0	30	35	.188	.401	.257	25.55	21.90	137
Valdez, Krisspy	R-R	6-9	215	11-23-03	2	0	10.20	10	0	1	15	17	18	17	0	15	20	.283	.469	.383	24.69	18.52	81

Pitching	B-T	Ht.	Wt.	DOB	W	L	ERA	G	GS	SV	IP	Hits	Runs	ER	HR	BB	SO	AVG	OBP	SLG	SO%	BB%	BF
Verdu, Jermayne	R-R	6-0	150	7-27-06	3	3	5.93	14	2	1	30	36	23	20	1	14	38	.298	.388	.430	26.95	9.93	141
Victora, Deivy	R-R	6-4	209	8-15-05	0	4	8.06	11	6	0	22	28	27	20	1	18	26	.304	.454	.424	21.85	15.13	119

Fielding

C: Aular 17, Gutierrez 11, Terrero 11, Silva 10, Montano 9, Hernandez 6. **1B:** Guerrero 22, Cordero 11, Reyes 8, Herrera 7, Guzman 6, Aular 2, Peralta 1, Silva 1. **2B:** Gomez 10, Peralta 9, Rivas 7, Matos 7, Herrera 6, Subero 5, Terrero 5, Hernandez 3, De Aza 3, Fernandez 2, Garcia 1. **3B:** Rivas 15, Cordero 14, Herrera 11, Subero 8, Gomez 5, De Aza 3, Garcia 3, Peralta 2, Guzman 1, Hernandez 1. **SS:** Rivas 23, Subero 12, De Aza 10, Peralta 5, Garcia 4, Gomez 4. **LF:** Acosta 19, Reyes 10, Guerrero 9, German 7, Diaz 4, Lantigua 2, Miranda 1, Ramirez 1, Sanchez 1. **CF:** Lantigua 19, German 9, Gomez 8, Ramirez 8, Acosta 7, Diaz 5, Mella 2. RF: German 19, Acosta 9, Lantigua 5, Reyes 5, Sanchez 5, Ramirez 4, Guzman 3, Diaz 3, Guerrero 2, Miranda 1.

DSL METS ORANGE — ROOKIE

DOMINICAN SUMMER LEAGUE

Batting	B-T	Ht.	Wt.	DOB	AVG	OBP	SLG	G	PA	AB	R	H	2B	3B	HR	RBI	BB	HBP	SH	SF	SO	SB	CS	BB%	SO%
Adderley, Bohan	R-R	6-3	180	11-10-06	.229	.356	.320	47	188	153	30	35	7	2	1	27	28	4	0	3	49	27	1	14.89	26.06
Asencio, Enderson	R-R	6-4	195	3-17-06	.275	.405	.341	32	111	91	17	25	6	0	0	12	17	3	0	0	31	8	2	15.32	27.93
Aular, Jose	R-R	5-11	175	1-2-04	.000	1.000	.000	1	1	0	0	0	0	0	0	0	0	1	0	0	0	0	0	0.00	0.00
De Aza, Diover	B-R	6-1	160	8-15-07	.216	.328	.258	31	119	97	17	21	2	1	0	16	17	1	0	4	43	3	2	14.29	36.13
Delgado, Anthony	L-R	6-0	190	1-27-07	.194	.386	.254	27	88	67	15	13	2	1	0	0	19	2	0	0	15	5	0	21.59	17.05
Diaz, Reniel	R-R	6-0	160	4-3-06	.169	.300	.271	22	70	59	12	10	2	2	0	6	10	1	0	0	24	5	0	14.29	34.29
Fernandez, Starling	R-R	6-0	178	10-27-06	.200	.333	.333	7	18	15	3	3	0	1	0	2	3	0	0	0	2	2	0	16.67	11.11
Garcia, Keiver	B-R	5-10	145	8-6-06	.237	.369	.275	43	160	131	24	31	3	1	0	10	26	2	0	1	36	16	3	16.25	22.50
Gomez, Vladi	L-R	5-11	150	9-12-05	.362	.500	.447	17	62	47	16	17	2	1	0	4	14	0	0	1	13	11	3	22.58	20.97
Guzman, Randy	R-R	6-4	215	4-19-05	.111	.200	.222	9	30	27	1	3	0	0	1	2	3	0	0	0	13	0	1	10.00	43.33
Hernandez, Julian	R-R	6-0	180	9-24-05	.278	.423	.444	9	26	18	3	5	0	0	1	7	5	1	0	2	1	0	0	19.23	3.85
Lantigua, Edward	R-R	6-3	174	11-13-06	.220	.313	.288	17	67	59	8	13	2	1	0	5	4	4	0	0	11	1	2	5.97	16.42
Mella, Leandy	L-R	5-10	170	2-4-07	.145	.293	.250	25	92	76	10	11	6	1	0	3	13	3	0	0	35	5	2	14.13	38.04
Montano, Arnaldo	R-R	6-0	175	2-3-06	.295	.404	.386	16	52	44	4	13	1	0	1	7	7	1	0	0	14	0	0	13.46	26.92
Pinango, Fidel	R-R	6-1	176	7-13-07	.203	.289	.243	30	84	74	13	15	1	1	0	2	7	2	1	0	14	8	1	8.33	16.67
Ramirez, Justin	L-L	6-3	190	2-9-05	.207	.377	.305	30	106	82	15	17	3	1	1	8	22	1	0	1	29	4	5	20.75	27.36
Reyes, Josmir	L-R	6-0	180	9-21-06	.667	.750	.667	2	4	3	1	2	0	0	0	0	1	0	0	0	0	0	0	25.00	0.00
Reyes, Rainer	R-R	5-11	190	5-19-03	.179	.333	.250	18	69	56	7	10	1	0	1	8	11	2	0	0	18	3	1	15.94	26.09
Rincon, Heriberto	R-R	6-1	160	2-16-06	.207	.303	.279	45	167	140	16	29	3	2	1	25	19	2	0	4	26	13	6	11.38	15.57
Rodriguez, Derek	R-R	6-1	187	5-5-06	.000	.154	.000	9	13	11	1	0	0	0	0	1	2	0	0	0	6	0	1	15.38	46.15
Rodriguez, Yovanny	R-R	6-0	175	11-7-06	.219	.359	.356	44	181	146	28	32	8	3	2	25	30	3	0	2	34	4	2	16.57	18.78
Solano, Rocky	B-R	6-2	170	12-28-06	.205	.289	.259	34	128	112	18	23	2	2	0	16	10	4	0	2	27	9	2	7.81	21.09
Terrero, Marcos	L-R	5-11	155	11-11-05	.200	.447	.360	11	38	25	7	5	1	0	1	3	10	2	0	1	6	1	1	26.32	15.79

Pitching	B-T	Ht.	Wt.	DOB	W	L	ERA	G	GS	SV	IP	Hits	Runs	ER	HR	BB	SO	AVG	OBP	SLG	SO%	BB%	BF
Anton, Jesus	R-R	6-3	175	2-17-06	0	0	2.70	1	1	0	3	0	1	1	0	0	4	.000	.182	.000	36.36	0.00	11
Cabrera, Luis	R-R	6-3	212	11-22-04	0	0	16.20	3	0	0	5	8	9	9	1	5	6	.348	.467	.565	20.00	16.67	30
Cadiz, Yoralbert	R-R	6-1	171	10-24-04	5	0	4.78	16	0	2	26	28	17	14	1	17	20	.269	.397	.327	15.27	12.98	131
Carreno, Nicolas	L-L	5-10	155	6-9-06	0	1	3.48	3	3	0	10	8	4	4	0	7	9	.222	.341	.250	20.45	15.91	44
Carrillo, Alvaro	R-R	6-4	175	4-5-05	1	0	2.08	7	0	1	9	4	3	2	0	9	8	.133	.381	.133	19.05	21.43	42
Cornelia, Jamdrick	L-L	6-0	140	11-17-05	1	1	3.60	9	0	2	15	16	12	6	2	7	15	.250	.333	.359	20.83	9.72	72
Crespo, Anthony	R-R	6-0	197	5-4-04	0	0	0.00	1	1	0	2	1	0	0	0	0	2	.143	.143	.143	28.57	0.00	7
De La Cruz, Jose	R-R	6-3	186	2-4-02	1	1	5.14	14	0	0	21	22	16	12	2	14	18	.259	.385	.412	17.31	13.46	104
De La Rosa, Angel	L-L	6-2	180	11-20-05	0	0	8.71	10	0	0	10	13	10	10	1	8	10	.302	.415	.372	18.87	15.09	53
Figuera, Fredayan	R-R	6-0	175	10-5-05	5	0	2.16	14	0	2	25	24	9	6	2	7	20	.261	.340	.380	19.23	6.73	104
Gomez, Jose	L-L	6-1	160	9-9-06	0	0	27.00	2	0	0	2	5	5	5	0	2	2	.500	.583	.800	16.67	16.67	12
Guevara, Jose	R-R	6-1	178	4-20-05	1	0	1.42	3	3	0	13	9	3	2	0	3	15	.191	.255	.234	29.41	5.88	51
Harvey, Maxgregori	R-R	6-2	180	11-12-06	0	1	6.75	6	0	2	9	8	9	7	0	14	9	.229	.451	.257	17.31	26.92	52
Jimenez, Jonathan	R-R	6-2	182	3-21-04	3	3	3.99	10	10	0	47	48	24	21	0	19	38	.265	.349	.304	18.01	9.00	211
Lara, Joel	R-R	6-2	210	1-11-07	2	1	5.40	6	0	0	10	13	7	6	0	3	7	.310	.356	.429	15.22	6.52	46
Lopez, Jose	R-R	6-1	180	5-22-04	0	0	2.65	9	1	1	17	12	9	5	1	7	16	.203	.294	.305	23.53	10.29	68
Lopez, Misael	L-L	6-2	180	4-8-03	0	0	15.26	5	0	0	8	12	13	13	2	13	11	.353	.531	.588	22.45	26.53	49
Mijares, Elwis	R-R	6-0	180	12-29-05	0	6	9.25	10	7	2	24	34	27	25	1	16	31	.327	.431	.442	25.20	13.01	123
Montero, Luis	L-L	6-3	172	9-9-06	0	1	3.86	2	2	0	7	9	5	3	1	1	5	.310	.333	.448	16.67	3.33	30
Morillo, Josue	R-R	6-4	212	1-13-05	2	1	4.68	10	7	0	33	20	22	17	0	23	38	.174	.338	.226	25.68	15.54	148
Obispo, Emilio	R-R	5-11	150	8-14-06	0	5	3.47	9	9	0	36	38	21	14	1	12	41	.271	.344	.364	25.95	7.59	158
Paulino, Deivy	R-R	6-2	205	6-15-05	2	4	4.31	10	9	0	40	35	26	19	1	14	39	.233	.322	.307	21.91	7.87	178
Ramirez, Alejandro	R-R	6-2	190	4-21-04	2	0	0.98	12	0	1	18	6	7	2	0	11	24	.100	.280	.100	32.00	14.67	75
Reynoso, Anthony	L-L	5-9	160	1-20-07	0	0	16.20	1	0	0	2	6	4	3	0	0	3	.545	.643	.636	21.43	0.00	14
Turmero, Nehomar	R-R	6-2	180	9-3-05	2	2	8.78	9	0	1	13	14	14	13	1	12	18	.280	.419	.480	28.13	18.75	64
Verdu, Jermayne	R-R	6-0	150	7-27-06	0	0	2.79	3	1	0	10	8	4	3	1	2	12	.222	.263	.333	31.58	5.26	38
Villegas, Johan	L-L	6-2	160	3-7-05	0	0	18.56	5	0	0	5	5	12	11	0	9	5	.238	.515	.286	15.15	27.27	33

Fielding

C: Rodriguez 33, Montano 9, Terrero 8, Hernandez 6, Aular 1, Reyes 1. **1B:** Delgado 26, Asencio 17, Montano 5, Pinango 4, Guzman 3, Reyes 3, Reyes 1. **2B:** Mella 15, Garcia 13, De Aza 11, Gomez 9, Pinango 9, Fernandez 3. **3B:** Adderley 21, Pinango 16, Garcia 13, Guzman 3, Hernandez 3, Montano 2, Fernandez 2, Gomez 1. **SS:** Adderley 22, De Aza 15, Garcia 15, Gomez 2, Pinango 2, Fernandez 1. **LF:** Solano 17, Rincon 10, Ramirez 10, Reyes 6, Diaz 5, Rodriguez 4, Lantigua 3, Asencio 3, Mella 2. **CF:** Rincon 23, Ramirez 12, Diaz 7, Lantigua 6, Gomez 5, Mella 4, Solano 3. **RF:** Rincon 12, Ramirez 10, Solano 10, Lantigua 8, Diaz 7, Asencio 6, Reyes 5, Rodriguez 1.

New York Yankees

SEASON SYNOPSIS: The Yankees ended a 15-year pennant drought, posting the best record in the American League and beating Kansas City and Cleveland to reach the World Series for the 41st time. But a misfiring offense and sloppy defense doomed them against the Dodgers, sending New York to a five-game Series defeat.

HIGH POINT: The Yankees led the American League in runs scored (third in the majors) and led MLB with 237 home runs, led by Aaron Judge, who had his second 10 WAR season in the last three. He led MLB with 58 homers, 144 RBIs, 133 walks and a 1.159 OPS. He hit seven homers in a six-game span Aug. 20-25 against Cleveland and Colorado as the Yankees won four and overtook Baltimore for first place in the AL East.

LOW POINT: Defense cost the Yankees in the World Series. A fielding miscue by Juan Soto, who double-clutched, then one-hopped a throw that allowed Shohei Ohtani to advance to third after a double, led to the tying run in an eventual 6-3, 10-inning gut-punch Game One loss. In Game Five, the Yankees made three errors in the top of the fifth to blow a five-run lead. Judge dropped a line drive to center, shortstop Anthony Volpe flubbed a throw to third base trying for a force out, and ace Gerrit Cole failed to cover first base and Mookie Betts beat Anthony Rizzo to the bag to prolong the inning, with the Dodgers scoring five unearned runs to tie the game.

NOTABLE ROOKIES: Austin Wells, a 2020 first-round pick, seized the everyday catcher job, grading out well defensively for framing and blocking while hitting 13 home runs and posting a solid .718 OPS. Righthander Luis Gil debuted in 2021 but was an official rookie in '24, got off to a great start and went 15-7, 3.50 overall, ranking second on the club in wins and strikeouts (171). Ben Rice filled in for Rizzo at first base for more than a month and had his moments, hitting seven homers, but eventually was overwhelmed, batting .171.

KEY TRANSACTIONS: The Yankees used their pitching depth to meet the Padres' demands and traded for Juan Soto in the offseason; he led the league with 128 runs scored and hit a career-high 41 homers. Soto, 26, became a free agent after the 2024 season. At the trade deadline, they acquired Jazz Chisholm Jr. from the Marlins and shifted the former shortstop and center fielder to third base, where he played well. He hit 11 homers and stole 18 bases in just 46 games for the Yankees.

OPENING DAY PAYROLL: $303,322,047 (2nd)

PLAYERS OF THE YEAR

MAJOR LEAGUE

Aaron Judge
OF

.322/.458/.701
MLB-best 58 HR,
144 RBIs, 133 BB

MINOR LEAGUE

Rafael Flores
C/1B

(A+/AA)
.279/.379/.495
21 HR, 31 2B, 66 BB

ORGANIZATION LEADERS

Batting		*Qualifiers
MAJORS		
* AVG	Aaron Judge	.322
* OPS	Aaron Judge	1.159
HR	Aaron Judge	58
RBI	Aaron Judge	144
MINORS		
* AVG	Benjamin Cowles, Somerset	.294
* OBP	Caleb Durbin, Tampa, Somerset, Scranton/WB	.396
* SLG	Rafael Flores, Hudson Valley, Somerset	.495
* OPS	Rafael Flores, Hudson Valley, Somerset	.878
R	Roderick Arias, Tampa	78
H	T.J. Rumfield, Scranton/WB/Somerset	137
TB	Spencer Jones, Somerset	218
2B	J.C. Escarra, Scranton/WB/Somerset	32
3B	Roderick Arias, Tampa/Estrellas	8
HR	Ben Rice, Scranton/WB/Somerset	24
RBI	Spencer Jones, Somerset	70
BB	Omar Martinez, Hudson Valley	73
SO	Spencer Jones, Somerset	200
SB	George Lombard, Hudson Valley/Tampa	39

Pitching		#Qualifiers
MAJORS		
W	Carlos Rodon	16
# ERA	Nestor Cortes	3.77
SO	Carlos Rodon	195
SV	Clay Holmes	30
MINORS		
W	Trystan Vrieling, Somerset	13
L	Edgar Barclay, Scranton/WB	9
# ERA	Zach Messinger, Somerset	3.06
G	Oddanier Mosqueda, Scranton/WB	55
GS	Edgar Barclay, Scranton/WB	29
SV	Anthony Misiewicz, Scranton/WB	8
IP	Trystan Vrieling, Somerset	147
BB	Edgar Barclay, Scranton/WB	70
SO	Cam Schlittler, Scranton/WB/H. Valley/Somerset	154
# AVG	Zach Messinger, Somerset	.207

2024 PERFORMANCE

General Manager: Brian Cashman. **Farm Director:** Kevin Reese. **Scouting Director:** Damon Oppenheimer.

Class	Team	League	W	L	PCT	Finish	Manager
Majors	New York Yankees	American	94	68	.580	1 (15)	Aaron Boone
Triple-A	Scranton/W-B RailRiders	International	89	60	.597	2 (20)	Shelley Duncan
Double-A	Somerset Patriots	Eastern	75	62	.547	5 (12)	Raul Dominguez
High-A	Hudson Valley Renegades	South Atlantic	73	58	.557	4 (12)	Nick Ortiz
Low-A	Tampa Tarpons	Florida State	54	74	.422	8 (10)	James Cooper
Rookie	FCL Yankees	Florida Complex	35	22	.614	2 (15)	Ryan Chipka
Rookie	DSL NYY Bombers	Dominican	30	25	.545	17 (51)	Carlos Vidal
Rookie	DSL NYY Yankees	Dominican	17	37	.315	47 (51)	Parker Guinn
Overall 2024 Minor League Record			**373**	**338**	**.525**	**8th (30)**	

ORGANIZATION STATISTICS

NEW YORK YANKEES

AMERICAN LEAGUE

Batting	B-T	Ht.	Wt.	DOB	AVG	OBP	SLG	G	PA	AB	R	H	2B	3B	HR	RBI	BB	HBP	SH	SF	SO	SB	CS	BB%	SO%
Berti, Jon	R-R	5-10	190	1-22-90	.273	.342	.318	25	74	66	10	18	0	0	1	6	6	1	1	0	14	5	1	8.11	18.92
Cabrera, Oswaldo	B-R	5-11	200	3-1-99	.247	.296	.365	109	326	299	47	74	11	0	8	36	21	1	2	3	63	4	2	6.44	19.33
Chisholm, Jazz	L-R	5-11	184	2-1-98	.273	.325	.500	46	191	176	28	48	7	0	11	23	14	0	0	1	45	18	2	7.33	23.56
Davis, J.D.	R-R	6-3	218	4-27-93	.105	.227	.158	7	22	19	1	2	1	0	0	1	3	0	0	0	9	0	0	13.64	40.91
Dominguez, Jasson	B-R	5-9	190	2-7-03	.179	.313	.304	18	67	56	8	10	1	0	2	4	11	0	0	0	19	5	0	16.42	28.36
Ellis, Duke	L-L	6-1	180	1-16-98	1.000	1.000	1.000	3	1	1	0	1	0	0	0	0	0	0	0	0	0	1	0	0.00	0.00
Grisham, Trent	L-L	5-11	224	11-1-96	.190	.290	.385	76	209	179	21	34	8	0	9	31	22	4	1	2	57	1	1	10.53	27.27
Jones, Jahmai	R-R	6-0	210	8-4-97	.238	.304	.381	33	47	42	8	10	1	1	1	4	2	2	1	0	16	1	1	4.26	34.04
Judge, Aaron	R-R	6-7	282	4-26-92	.322	.458	.701	158	704	559	122	180	36	1	58	144	133	9	0	2	171	10	0	18.89	24.29
LeMahieu, DJ	R-R	6-4	220	7-13-88	.204	.269	.259	67	228	201	19	41	5	0	2	26	19	1	1	6	35	0	1	8.33	15.35
Narvaez, Carlos	R-R	5-11	190	11-26-98	.231	.333	.231	6	15	13	0	3	0	0	0	0	2	0	0	0	6	0	0	13.33	40.00
Peraza, Oswald	R-R	6-0	200	6-15-00	.200	.273	.500	4	11	10	2	2	0	0	1	1	1	0	0	0	3	0	0	9.09	27.27
Rice, Ben	L-R	6-1	205	2-22-99	.171	.264	.349	50	178	152	20	26	6	0	7	23	20	1	0	5	48	0	1	11.24	26.97
Rizzo, Anthony	L-L	6-3	240	8-8-89	.228	.301	.335	92	375	337	38	77	12	0	8	35	27	9	0	2	65	0	0	7.20	17.33
Soto, Juan	L-L	6-2	224	10-25-98	.288	.419	.569	157	713	576	128	166	31	4	41	109	129	4	0	4	119	7	4	18.09	16.69
Stanton, Giancarlo	R-R	6-6	245	11-8-89	.233	.298	.475	114	459	417	49	97	20	0	27	72	38	2	0	2	143	0	0	8.28	31.15
Torres, Gleyber	R-R	6-1	205	12-13-96	.257	.330	.378	154	665	587	80	151	26	0	15	63	65	3	2	8	136	4	3	9.77	20.45
Trammell, Taylor	L-L	6-2	220	9-13-97	1.000	1.000	1.000	5	2	1	2	1	0	0	0	0	1	0	0	0	0	0	0	50.00	0.00
Trevino, Jose	R-R	5-10	215	11-28-92	.215	.288	.354	74	234	209	26	45	5	0	8	28	20	2	1	2	41	1	0	8.55	17.52
Verdugo, Alex	L-L	6-0	192	5-15-96	.233	.291	.356	149	621	559	74	130	28	1	13	61	49	1	2	10	93	2	1	7.89	14.98
Volpe, Anthony	R-R	5-9	180	4-28-01	.243	.293	.364	160	689	637	90	155	27	7	12	60	42	4	2	3	156	28	7	6.10	22.64
Wells, Austin	L-R	6-0	220	7-12-99	.229	.322	.395	115	414	354	42	81	18	1	13	55	47	5	1	7	87	1	2	11.35	21.01

Pitching	B-T	Ht.	Wt.	DOB	W	L	ERA	G	GS	SV	IP	Hits	Runs	ER	HR	BB	SO	AVG	OBP	SLG	SO%	BB%	BF
Andrews, Clayton	L-L	5-6	160	1-4-97	0	0	27.00	1	0	0	0	1	1	1	1	0	1	.500	.667	2.000	33.33	0.00	3
Beeter, Clayton	R-R	6-2	220	10-9-98	0	0	4.91	3	0	0	4	4	2	2	0	1	5	.286	.333	.429	33.33	6.67	15
Bickford, Phil	R-R	6-4	200	7-10-95	0	0	8.64	8	0	0	8	10	9	8	1	1	6	.278	.316	.417	15.38	2.56	39
Burdi, Nick	R-R	6-3	225	1-19-93	1	0	1.86	12	0	0	10	5	2	2	1	9	12	.147	.356	.235	26.67	20.00	45
Cabrera, Oswaldo	S-R	5-11	200	3-1-99	0	0	0.00	1	0	0	0	0	0	0	0	2	0	.000	.667	.000	0.00	66.67	3
Cole, Gerrit	R-R	6-4	220	9-8-90	8	5	3.41	17	17	0	95	78	38	36	11	29	99	.220	.290	.358	25.38	7.44	390
Cortes, Nestor	R-L	5-11	210	12-10-94	9	10	3.77	31	30	0	174	162	74	73	24	39	162	.245	.290	.421	22.82	5.49	710
Cousins, Jake	R-R	6-4	193	7-14-94	2	1	2.37	37	0	1	38	20	14	10	5	20	53	.154	.290	.292	34.19	12.90	155
De Los Santos, Enyel	R-R	6-3	235	12-25-95	0	0	14.21	5	0	0	6	13	10	10	1	3	5	.419	.514	.710	13.51	8.11	37
Effross, Scott	R-R	6-2	202	12-28-93	0	0	5.40	3	0	0	3	3	2	2	1	2	2	.250	.357	.500	14.29	14.29	14
Ferguson, Caleb	R-L	6-3	226	7-2-96	1	3	5.13	42	0	1	33	34	24	19	5	16	41	.250	.335	.426	26.45	10.32	155
Gil, Luis	R-R	6-2	185	6-3-98	15	7	3.50	29	29	0	152	104	60	59	18	77	171	.189	.297	.345	26.84	12.09	637
Gomez, Yoendrys	R-R	6-3	175	10-15-99	0	0	3.97	5	0	0	11	11	5	5	2	7	10	.250	.352	.455	18.52	12.96	54
Gonzalez, Victor	L-L	6-0	180	11-16-95	2	1	3.86	27	0	2	23	13	12	10	3	13	11	.160	.299	.296	11.34	13.40	97
Hamilton, Ian	R-R	6-1	200	6-16-95	0	1	3.82	35	0	1	38	37	17	16	2	14	41	.261	.331	.373	25.15	8.59	163
Hill, Tim	R-L	6-4	200	2-10-90	3	0	2.05	35	0	0	44	36	13	10	2	9	18	.225	.267	.281	10.40	5.20	173
Holmes, Clay	R-R	6-5	245	3-27-93	3	5	3.14	67	0	30	63	60	29	22	4	22	68	.248	.315	.347	25.09	8.12	271
Kahnle, Tommy	R-R	6-1	230	8-7-89	0	2	2.11	50	0	1	43	30	16	10	5	19	46	.190	.285	.342	25.70	10.61	179
Leiter, Mark	R-R	6-0	210	3-13-91	2	1	4.98	21	0	0	22	28	14	12	6	9	33	.301	.375	.581	31.73	8.65	104
Loaisiga, Jonathan	R-R	5-11	165	11-2-94	1	0	0.00	3	0	0	4	7	0	0	0	1	3	.368	.400	.368	15.00	5.00	20
Maciejewski, Josh	R-L	6-3	175	8-14-95	0	0	2.57	4	0	0	7	4	2	2	1	2	7	.160	.222	.320	25.93	7.41	27
Marinaccio, Ron	R-R	6-2	205	7-1-95	1	0	3.86	16	0	0	23	18	11	10	4	10	25	.217	.316	.410	25.25	10.10	99
Mayza, Tim	L-L	6-3	215	1-15-92	0	1	4.00	15	0	0	18	18	10	8	2	3	12	.261	.297	.420	16.22	4.05	74
Misiewicz, Anthony	R-L	6-1	196	11-1-94	0	0	0.00	1	0	0	1	2	0	0	0	1	1	.400	.500	.400	16.67	16.67	6
Poteet, Cody	R-R	6-1	190	7-30-94	3	0	2.22	5	4	0	24	18	7	6	2	8	16	.207	.281	.310	16.67	8.33	96
Rodon, Carlos	L-L	6-2	255	12-10-92	16	9	3.96	32	32	0	175	157	81	77	31	57	195	.235	.304	.435	26.49	7.74	736
Santana, Dennis	R-R	6-2	190	4-12-96	2	0	6.26	23	0	2	27	27	19	19	2	10	19	.262	.333	.408	16.52	8.70	115
Schmidt, Clarke	R-R	6-1	200	2-20-96	5	5	2.85	16	16	0	85	71	31	27	8	30	93	.230	.312	.356	26.35	8.50	353

Stroman, Marcus	R-R	5-7	180	5-1-91	10	9	4.31	30	29	1	155	167	81	74	19	60	113	.277	.349	.431	16.74	8.89	675
Tonkin, Michael	R-R	6-7	220	11-19-89	3	2	3.38	39	0	2	56	44	26	21	5	21	57	.214	.293	.350	24.57	9.05	232
Trevino, Jose	R-R	5-10	215	11-28-92	0	0	13.50	2	0	0	2	5	3	3	0	2	0	.455	.538	.727	0.00	15.38	13
Warren, Will	R-R	6-2	175	6-16-99	0	3	10.32	6	5	0	23	33	27	26	5	10	29	.340	.404	.608	26.36	9.09	110
Weaver, Luke	R-R	6-2	183	8-21-93	7	3	2.89	62	0	4	84	52	28	27	10	26	103	.176	.248	.334	31.12	7.85	331

Fielding

Catcher	PCT	G	PO	A	E	DP	PB
Narvaez	1.000	6	41	1	0	0	0
Rice	.000	1	0	0	0	0	0
Trevino	.990	71	552	22	6	2	5
Wells	.988	110	892	33	11	5	5

First Base	PCT	G	PO	A	E	DP
Cabrera	1.000	13	51	2	0	4
Davis	1.000	4	12	1	0	1
LeMahieu	.990	38	185	15	2	16
Rice	.993	49	273	14	2	21
Rizzo	.996	92	602	74	3	58

Second Base	PCT	G	PO	A	E	DP
Berti	1.000	2	2	1	0	0
Cabrera	.971	13	18	15	1	2
Jones	1.000	3	4	7	0	1
Torres	.969	153	234	330	18	74

Third Base	PCT	G	PO	A	E	DP
Berti	.929	18	6	33	3	4
Cabrera	.970	74	61	136	6	13
Chisholm	.940	45	35	74	7	6
Jones	1.000	3	1	1	0	0
LeMahieu	.989	36	27	67	1	4
Peraza	1.000	4	2	3	0	0

Shortstop	PCT	G	PO	A	E	DP
Cabrera	1.000	6	4	5	0	0
Volpe	.972	160	210	344	16	68

Outfield	PCT	G	PO	A	E	DP
Berti	.000	1	0	0	0	0
Cabrera	1.000	6	2	0	0	0
Chisholm	1.000	2	7	0	0	0
Dominguez	.968	17	28	2	1	0
Ellis	1.000	1	2	0	0	0
Grisham	.986	69	141	3	2	2
Jones	.917	13	11	0	1	0
Judge	1.000	118	279	4	0	2
Soto	.994	151	302	10	2	1
Trammell	1.000	4	1	0	0	0
Verdugo	.997	158	285	7	1	1

SCRANTON/WILKES-BARRE RAILRIDERS — TRIPLE-A

INTERNATIONAL LEAGUE

Batting	B-T	Ht.	Wt.	DOB	AVG	OBP	SLG	G	PA	AB	R	H	2B	3B	HR	RBI	BB	HBP	SH	SF	SO	SB	CS	BB%	SO%
Allen, Greg	B-R	6-0	185	3-15-93	.225	.338	.360	58	218	178	29	40	9	3	3	22	23	9	5	3	47	13	2	10.55	21.56
Berti, Jon	R-R	5-10	190	1-22-90	.529	.550	.765	4	20	17	6	9	1	0	1	2	2	0	0	1	2	0	0	10.00	10.00
Breaux, Josh	R-R	6-1	220	10-7-97	.143	.189	.314	11	37	35	4	5	0	0	2	5	2	0	0	0	15	0	0	5.41	40.54
Dominguez, Jasson	B-R	5-9	190	2-7-03	.309	.368	.480	44	193	175	33	54	7	1	7	25	16	1	0	1	36	15	1	8.29	18.65
Downs, Jeter	R-R	5-11	197	7-27-98	.264	.360	.498	69	274	227	43	60	17	3	10	38	30	8	2	7	68	15	6	10.95	24.82
Dunham, Elijah	L-L	5-11	213	5-29-98	.100	.308	.100	4	13	10	2	1	0	0	0	1	2	1	0	0	3	0	0	15.38	23.08
Durbin, Caleb	R-R	5-6	175	2-22-00	.287	.396	.471	82	375	310	57	89	23	2	10	60	47	11	4	3	37	29	3	12.53	9.87
Eden, Cam	R-R	6-1	205	3-31-98	.231	.286	.385	23	43	39	8	9	1	1	1	3	3	0	1	0	5	7	1	6.98	11.63
Ellis, Duke	L-L	6-1	180	1-16-98	.000	.000	.000	8	6	6	3	0	0	0	0	0	0	0	0	0	3	6	0	0.00	50.00
Escarra, J.C.	L R	6 3	205	4 24 95	.302	.403	.527	52	201	169	36	51	14	0	8	34	27	3	0	2	30	2	0	13.43	14.93
Gonzalez, Luis	L-L	6-1	185	9-10-95	.282	.374	.397	22	91	78	12	22	5	2	0	5	10	2	0	1	24	3	0	10.99	26.37
Gonzalez, Oscar	R-R	6-4	240	1-10-98	.294	.333	.469	78	306	286	51	84	22	2	8	45	15	3	0	2	62	7	0	4.90	20.26
Groshans, Jordan	R-R	6-3	200	11-10-99	.228	.302	.316	17	63	57	8	13	2	0	1	7	6	0	0	0	11	0	1	9.52	17.46
Jones, Jahmai	R-R	6-0	210	8-4-97	.304	.390	.490	34	119	102	22	31	5	1	4	16	11	4	1	1	25	10	1	9.24	21.01
LeMahieu, DJ	R-R	6-4	220	7-13-88	.000	.286	.000	2	7	5	1	0	0	0	0	0	2	0	0	0	1	0	0	28.57	14.29
Lockridge, Brandon	R-R	5-11	185	3-14-97	.295	.405	.382	72	259	217	37	64	15	2	0	32	39	1	2	0	62	34	4	15.06	23.94
Maciejewski, Josh	R-L	6-3	175	8-14-95	.000	.000	.000	20	1	1	0	0	0	0	0	0	0	0	0	0	1	0	0	0.00	100.00
Narvaez, Carlos	R-R	5-11	190	11-26-98	.254	.370	.412	96	403	335	54	85	20	0	11	58	56	8	0	4	105	9	1	13.90	26.05
Palensky, Aaron	R-R	5-10	190	9-22-98	.000	.000	.000	5	16	15	0	0	0	0	0	0	0	0	1	0	8	0	0	0.00	50.00
Peraza, Oswald	R-R	6-0	200	6-15-00	.246	.341	.394	92	406	350	62	86	13	0	13	60	43	9	1	3	85	24	7	10.59	20.94
Pereira, Everson	R-R	5-11	191	4-10-01	.265	.346	.512	40	182	162	33	43	8	1	10	27	16	4	0	0	59	5	2	8.79	32.42
Ramirez, Agustin	R-R	6-0	210	9-10-01	.224	.328	.364	29	125	107	14	24	3	0	4	20	14	3	0	1	23	5	1	11.20	18.40
Rice, Ben	L-R	6-1	205	2-22-99	.294	.428	.661	30	138	109	29	32	4	0	12	33	25	2	0	2	26	2	1	18.12	18.84
Rojas, Jose	L-R	6-0	200	2-24-93	.254	.359	.561	67	273	228	44	58	14	1	18	57	38	2	0	5	60	4	1	13.92	21.98
Rumfield, T.J.	L-R	6-4	225	5-17-00	.292	.365	.461	114	474	421	72	123	26	0	15	71	43	7	0	3	78	3	3	9.07	16.46
Serruto, Peter	R-R	6-2	195	3-17-00	.400	.400	.400	3	6	5	0	2	0	0	0	0	0	0	1	0	2	0	0	0.00	33.33
Smith, Kevin	R-R	6-0	190	7-4-96	.244	.295	.340	73	264	238	31	58	14	0	3	33	17	3	0	6	88	12	2	6.44	33.33
Torrens, Luis	R-R	6-0	217	5-2-96	.279	.339	.468	30	124	111	17	31	6	0	5	19	10	1	0	2	29	1	1	8.06	23.39
Trammell, Taylor	L-L	6-2	220	9-13-97	.256	.381	.488	106	407	336	65	86	20	2	18	63	63	6	0	2	109	20	5	15.48	26.78
VanMeter, Josh	L-R	5-9	198	3-10-95	.177	.335	.293	59	207	164	24	29	10	0	3	27	37	3	1	2	53	5	1	17.87	25.60
Vivas, Jorbit	L-R	5-10	171	3-9-01	.225	.347	.366	93	422	347	57	78	18	2	9	45	58	9	0	4	70	20	5	13.74	16.59

Pitching	B-T	Ht.	Wt.	DOB	W	L	ERA	G	GS	SV	IP	Hits	Runs	ER	HR	BB	SO	AVG	OBP	SLG	SO%	BB%	BF
Andrews, Clayton	L-L	5-6	160	1-4-97	1	3	5.84	20	0	0	25	15	16	16	3	22	28	.181	.361	.349	25.93	20.37	108
Barclay, Edgar	L-L	5-10	200	5-25-98	7	9	5.98	29	29	0	143	150	104	95	30	70	118	.265	.351	.489	18.21	10.80	648
Beeter, Clayton	R-R	6-2	220	10-9-98	3	1	2.25	10	7	0	36	18	9	9	1	21	51	.145	.267	.210	34.69	14.29	147
Bickford, Phil	R-R	6-4	200	7-10-95	4	4	3.40	39	1	5	50	41	20	19	4	16	62	.225	.296	.341	29.95	7.73	207
Brubaker, JT	R-R	6-3	185	11-17-93	0	0	4.05	5	2	0	7	4	3	3	1	6	4	.174	.345	.304	13.79	20.69	29
Burdi, Nick	R-R	6-3	225	1-19-93	1	0	2.65	18	0	1	17	9	6	5	1	11	24	.153	.296	.237	33.33	15.28	72
Calderon, Yorlin	R-R	6-3	155	8-17-01	1	0	1.17	3	0	0	8	4	2	1	1	3	5	.148	.258	.296	16.13	9.68	31
Cole, Gerrit	R-R	6-4	220	9-8-90	0	0	0.00	1	1	0	4	2	1	0	0	0	10	.125	.125	.188	62.50	0.00	16
Cousins, Jake	R-R	6-4	193	7-14-94	1	0	3.00	7	0	2	6	4	3	2	0	4	8	.200	.385	.300	30.77	15.38	26
De Los Santos, Yerry	R-R	6-2	215	12-12-97	2	2	4.12	51	1	4	59	66	35	27	9	19	55	.282	.335	.466	21.32	7.36	258
Effross, Scott	R-R	6-2	202	12-28-93	7	1	2.78	27	0	1	32	25	12	10	2	9	28	.212	.268	.305	22.05	7.09	127
Gerber, Joey	R-R	6-4	212	5-3-97	1	1	3.86	12	0	0	14	16	10	6	2	8	15	.291	.381	.527	23.08	12.31	65
Givin, Matt	R-R	6-3	180	6-17-99	0	0	0.00	1	0	0	3	2	0	0	0	2	3	.167	.286	.167	21.43	14.29	14
Gomez, Yoendrys	R-R	6-3	175	10-15-99	3	5	3.67	23	21	0	83	58	36	34	12	39	93	.197	.307	.381	27.03	11.34	344

Gonzalez, Oscar	R-R	6-4	240	1-10-98	0	1	0.00	1	0	0	0	1	2	1	1	0	0	1.000	1.000	4.000	0.00	0.00	1
Gonzalez, Victor	L-L	6-0	180	11-16-95	4	0	4.50	21	0	2	22	29	13	11	1	9	21	.315	.382	.402	20.59	8.82	102
Hamilton, Ian	R-R	6-1	200	6-16-95	0	0	0.00	1	0	0	2	0	0	0	0	0	0	.000	.000	.000	0.00	0.00	5
Liranzo, Jesus	R-R	6-2	225	3-7-95	1	1	6.35	5	0	0	6	5	4	4	2	2	8	.227	.292	.500	33.33	8.33	24
Maciejewski, Josh	R-L	6-3	175	8-14-95	2	3	5.37	19	12	0	60	63	40	36	7	26	57	.265	.341	.395	21.35	9.74	267
Marinaccio, Ron	R-R	6-2	205	7-1-95	1	3	2.04	35	0	8	40	25	9	9	2	14	41	.179	.270	.293	25.79	8.81	159
Mauricio, Alex	R-R	6-0	180	9-24-96	4	2	2.39	37	0	1	49	37	15	13	4	27	53	.207	.309	.330	25.48	12.98	208
Mayza, Tim	L-L	6-3	215	1-15-92	1	0	2.16	9	0	1	8	7	2	2	0	3	8	.219	.286	.219	22.86	8.57	35
Misiewicz, Anthony	R-L	6-1	196	11-1-94	3	2	3.90	47	0	8	55	53	27	24	8	18	69	.249	.305	.423	28.99	7.56	238
Moore, McKinley	R-R	6-6	225	8-24-98	0	0	27.00	2	0	0	1	0	2	2	0	6	1	.000	.778	.000	11.11	66.67	9
Morris, Cody	R-R	6-4	205	11-4-96	6	0	4.03	26	2	0	38	28	18	17	3	26	46	.199	.329	.291	27.06	15.29	170
Mosqueda, Oddanier	L-L	5-10	155	5-6-99	7	1	4.39	55	0	5	68	50	38	33	8	37	88	.202	.322	.335	29.73	12.50	296
Myatt, Tanner	R-R	6-7	220	5-21-98	0	0	13.50	1	0	0	2	4	3	3	0	1	0	.571	.556	.571	0.00	10.00	10
Neely, Jack	R-R	6-8	225	6-5-00	1	1	3.38	9	0	0	11	10	4	4	1	4	12	.256	.333	.410	26.67	8.89	45
Pannone, Thomas	L-L	6-0	209	4-28-94	6	1	2.34	11	11	0	62	57	18	16	6	6	49	.242	.268	.373	19.92	2.44	246
Poteet, Cody	R-R	6-1	190	7-30-94	3	0	3.92	10	10	0	44	39	20	19	5	15	49	.238	.306	.366	27.22	8.33	180
Ramirez, Nick	L-L	6-4	232	8-1-89	0	0	4.50	1	0	0	2	3	1	1	0	0	2	.375	.375	.375	25.00	0.00	8
Rojas, Jose	L-R	6-0	200	2-24-93	0	0	13.50	2	0	0	2	4	3	3	1	2	0	.400	.500	.700	0.00	16.67	12
Santana, Dennis	R-R	6-2	190	4-12-96	0	0	6.75	2	0	0	1	3	1	1	0	3	2	.429	.600	.429	20.00	30.00	10
Sauer, Matt	R-R	6-4	195	1-21-99	1	2	16.20	10	1	1	8	18	15	15	4	8	9	.409	.500	.750	16.98	15.09	53
Schlittler, Cam	R-R	6-6	210	2-5-01	0	0	21.60	1	1	0	2	1	5	4	0	4	3	.167	.615	.167	23.08	30.77	13
Schmidt, Clarke	R-R	6-1	200	2-20-96	0	0	3.00	1	1	0	3	3	1	1	0	1	5	.250	.308	.250	38.46	7.69	13
Sellers, Trent	R-R	6-1	200	10-30-99	1	0	10.80	1	0	0	2	1	2	2	0	3	2	.167	.444	.167	22.22	33.33	9
Serruto, Peter	R-R	6-2	195	3-17-00	0	0	0.00	2	0	0	2	2	0	0	0	0	0	.286	.286	.286	0.00	0.00	7
Shields, Ben	R-L	6-4	210	1-23-99	0	1	37.80	1	1	0	2	8	9	7	1	2	1	.615	.706	1.000	5.88	11.76	17
Shreve, Chasen	L-L	6-4	180	7-12-90	2	1	2.45	10	0	0	11	6	6	3	2	3	11	.154	.227	.308	25.00	6.82	44
Smith, Kevin	R-R	6-0	190	7-4-96	0	0	4.91	2	0	0	4	7	2	2	0	0	0	.412	.412	.412	0.00	0.00	17
Stuart, Baron	R-R	6-4	209	7-24-99	1	0	1.29	1	1	0	7	3	2	1	0	4	2	.143	.280	.190	8.00	16.00	25
Torrens, Luis	R-R	6-0	217	5-2-96	0	0	0.00	1	0	0	1	0	0	0	0	3	0	.000	.500	.000	0.00	50.00	6
Trivino, Lou	R-R	6-5	235	10-1-91	1	0	7.50	6	0	0	6	7	5	5	1	4	6	.292	.393	.500	20.69	13.79	29
Tully, Tanner	L-L	6-2	205	11-30-94	3	7	6.41	25	22	1	100	117	75	71	20	28	57	.285	.334	.482	12.87	6.32	443
Underwood, Duane	R-R	6-2	225	7-20-94	3	1	3.26	32	2	3	39	32	16	14	6	24	40	.227	.349	.390	23.39	14.04	171
VanMeter, Josh	L-R	5-9	198	3-10-95	0	1	15.00	3	0	0	3	6	7	5	1	1	3	.400	.444	.600	15.79	5.26	19
Warren, Art	R-R	6-3	230	3-23-93	1	1	8.78	24	0	0	27	36	26	26	8	22	29	.319	.431	.584	21.17	16.06	137
Warren, Will	R-R	6-2	175	6-16-99	6	5	5.91	23	23	0	110	114	79	72	19	39	136	.262	.333	.432	27.98	8.02	486

Fielding

Catcher	PCT	G	PO	A	E	DP	PB
Breaux	1.000	7	48	1	0	0	0
Escarra	.990	36	294	18	3	0	2
Narvaez	.984	59	527	22	9	2	4
Ramirez	.988	19	159	4	2	0	2
Rice	1.000	9	82	1	0	0	1
Serruto	1.000	1	11	0	0	0	0
Torrens	.991	22	203	11	2	1	0

First Base	PCT	G	PO	A	E	DP
Escarra	1.000	6	39	3	0	3
Groshans	1.000	5	33	3	0	3
Jones	1.000	4	13	0	0	4
LeMahieu	1.000	1	3	2	0	1
Narvaez	.982	14	104	5	2	9
Ramirez	.977	7	40	2	1	3
Rice	.991	16	111	5	1	10
Rojas	.963	12	72	7	3	3
Rumfield	.988	88	607	45	8	60
Torrens	1.000	3	19	1	0	1

Second Base	PCT	G	PO	A	E	DP
Downs	.882	4	6	9	2	1
Durbin	.994	37	72	93	1	23
Jones	.842	5	9	7	3	5
Lockridge	1.000	4	8	4	0	1
Peraza	.937	14	25	34	4	8
Smith	.939	9	16	15	2	5
Torrens	.714	2	3	2	2	0
VanMeter	.978	30	35	52	2	15
Vivas	.986	54	78	132	3	27

Third Base	PCT	G	PO	A	E	DP
Berti	.889	2	0	8	1	0
Downs	.908	28	16	53	7	3
Durbin	.939	21	15	31	3	3
Escarra	1.000	1	2	1	0	1
Groshans	.917	10	2	9	1	3
Jones	.750	9	2	13	5	0
LeMahieu	1.000	1	1	1	0	0
Narvaez	1.000	1	0	1	0	0
Peraza	1.000	15	7	33	0	3
Rojas	1.000	1	0	1	0	0
Smith	1.000	22	15	35	0	3
Torrens	.500	3	0	2	2	0
VanMeter	.955	9	5	16	1	3
Vivas	.979	35	17	78	2	8

Shortstop	PCT	G	PO	A	E	DP
Downs	.983	36	45	70	2	11
Durbin	.929	14	18	34	4	10
Peraza	.966	62	67	129	7	29
Smith	.968	41	38	83	4	15

Outfield	PCT	G	PO	A	E	DP
Allen	.970	59	92	4	3	1
Berti	1.000	3	4	0	0	0
Dominguez	.943	40	95	4	6	1
Dunham	.875	4	7	0	1	0
Durbin	1.000	9	11	0	0	0
Eden	1.000	18	27	1	0	1
Ellis	.750	4	3	0	1	0
Escarra	1.000	3	3	0	0	0
Gonzalez	.930	68	105	2	8	0
Gonzalez	.978	22	44	1	1	0
Jones	1.000	17	31	1	0	0
Lockridge	1.000	68	136	1	0	1
Palensky	1.000	6	4	0	0	0
Pereira	1.000	31	69	1	0	0
Rojas	.985	33	63	2	1	0
Trammell	1.000	104	208	2	0	1
VanMeter	1.000	10	23	1	0	0

SOMERSET PATRIOTS — DOUBLE-A

EASTERN LEAGUE

Batting	B-T	Ht.	Wt.	DOB	AVG	OBP	SLG	G	PA	AB	R	H	2B	3B	HR	RBI	BB	HBP	SH	SF	SO	SB	CS	BB%	SO%
Allen, Greg	B-R	6-0	185	3-15-93	.200	.273	.200	3	11	10	0	2	0	0	0	0	1	0	0	0	3	0	0	9.09	27.27
Anderson, Ryan	L-L	6-6	205	9-9-98	.000	.000	.000	25	1	1	0	0	0	0	0	0	0	0	0	0	1	0	0	0.00	100.00
Berti, Jon	R-R	5-10	190	1-22-90	.179	.324	.286	10	34	28	6	5	0	0	1	3	5	1	0	0	11	1	0	14.71	32.35
Burt, Max	R-R	6-1	185	8-28-96	.146	.219	.239	72	237	213	35	31	5	0	5	20	17	4	0	3	80	14	2	7.17	33.76
Cowles, Benjamin	R-R	6-0	180	2-15-00	.294	.376	.472	88	378	326	52	96	25	3	9	51	39	7	0	6	67	14	2	10.32	17.72
Crisp, Juan	R-R	6-0	170	5-23-00	.056	.150	.056	7	20	18	3	1	0	0	0	1	2	0	0	0	9	0	0	10.00	45.00
Dominguez, Jasson	B-R	5-9	190	2-7-03	.316	.350	.632	10	40	38	8	12	0	0	4	8	2	0	0	0	11	1	0	5.00	27.50
Dunham, Elijah	L-L	5-11	213	5-29-98	.248	.332	.455	99	394	347	49	86	19	4	15	56	42	3	0	2	107	19	4	10.66	27.16
Durbin, Caleb	R-R	5-6	175	2-22-00	.125	.300	.208	7	30	24	4	3	2	0	0	0	6	0	0	0	3	2	1	20.00	10.00

Escarra, J.C.	L-R	6-3	205	4-24-95	.233	.322	.374	72	292	257	41	60	18	3	4	30	28	6	0	1	38	1	2	9.59	13.01
Flores, Rafael	R-R	6-4	220	11-7-00	.274	.359	.519	65	273	241	40	66	14	0	15	33	28	4	0	0	73	6	0	10.26	26.74
Gabrielson, Cole	R-R	6-0	185	7-5-00	.256	.385	.349	16	52	43	6	11	2	1	0	6	8	1	0	0	15	3	1	15.38	28.85
Groshans, Jordan	R-R	6-3	200	11-10-99	.234	.314	.262	33	121	107	10	25	3	0	0	8	12	1	0	1	20	0	1	9.92	16.53
Hardman, Tyler	R-R	6-2	204	1-27-99	.175	.266	.294	74	309	269	36	47	6	1	8	32	33	2	0	4	120	12	2	10.68	38.83
Henson, Spencer	R-R	6-0	235	11-3-97	.063	.063	.063	5	16	16	0	1	0	0	0	0	0	0	0	0	6	0	0	0.00	37.50
Jones, Spencer	L-L	6-6	225	5-14-01	.259	.336	.452	122	544	482	73	125	30	6	17	78	54	4	0	4	200	25	9	9.93	36.76
LeMahieu, DJ	R-R	6-4	220	7-13-88	.500	.714	.500	3	7	4	2	2	0	0	0	1	3	0	0	0	1	0	0	42.86	14.29
Palensky, Aaron	R-R	5-10	190	9-22-98	.217	.349	.293	53	193	157	23	34	9	0	1	22	29	4	1	2	39	13	4	15.03	20.21
Peraza, Oswald	R-R	6-0	200	6-15-00	.125	.300	.500	5	20	16	4	2	0	0	2	2	4	0	0	0	7	1	0	20.00	35.00
Ramirez, Agustin	R-R	6-0	210	9-10-01	.289	.372	.570	58	261	228	46	66	14	1	16	49	28	3	0	2	43	13	1	10.73	16.48
Rice, Ben	L-R	6-1	205	2-22-99	.261	.382	.511	49	218	180	36	47	9	0	12	26	32	4	0	1	46	8	0	14.68	21.10
Richardson, Grant	L-L	6-0	210	7-13-99	.257	.319	.401	108	431	389	53	100	25	2	9	47	32	5	1	4	121	16	6	7.42	28.07
Rizzo, Anthony	L-L	6-3	240	8-8-89	.182	.308	.455	5	13	11	2	2	0	0	1	1	2	0	0	0	4	0	0	15.38	30.77
Rodriguez, Jesus	R-R	5-9	182	4-23-02	.226	.278	.417	23	90	84	9	19	1	0	5	14	4	2	0	0	19	2	1	4.44	21.11
Romero, Kiko	L-R	5-11	185	9-18-00	.200	.333	.500	3	12	10	1	2	0	0	1	4	2	0	0	0	3	0	0	16.67	25.00
Rumfield, T.J.	L-R	6-4	225	5-17-00	.321	.441	.357	8	34	28	5	9	1	0	0	2	6	0	0	0	4	1	0	17.65	11.76
Seigler, Anthony	B-S	5-9	200	6-20-99	.234	.350	.398	118	433	364	61	85	24	0	12	49	64	2	1	2	77	29	3	14.78	17.78
Trevino, Jose	R-R	5-10	215	11-28-92	.250	.333	.250	3	9	8	1	2	0	0	0	0	1	0	0	0	0	0	0	11.11	0.00
Vargas, Alexander	B-R	5-10	148	10-29-01	.254	.293	.375	73	256	240	23	61	7	5	4	30	11	3	0	2	65	14	9	4.30	25.39
Wegner, Jared	R-R	6-0	220	7-25-99	.211	.316	.342	93	358	304	38	64	15	2	7	39	42	7	0	5	105	9	5	11.73	29.33

Pitching	B-T	Ht.	Wt.	DOB	W	L	ERA	G	GS	SV	IP	Hits	Runs	ER	HR	BB	SO	AVG	OBP	SLG	SO%	BB%	BF
Abeyta, Blane	R-R	6-3	185	9-4-98	3	6	6.75	13	13	0	67	82	61	50	16	17	53	.294	.338	.523	17.61	5.65	301
Aguilar, Clay	L-L	6-1	210	3-26-99	0	0	27.00	2	0	0	3	10	10	10	3	2	2	.500	.565	1.050	8.70	8.70	23
Anderson, Ryan	L-L	6-6	205	9-9-98	1	3	3.00	25	1	0	30	20	13	10	1	10	34	.189	.269	.245	28.33	8.33	120
Ayers, Cole	R-R	6-3	185	8-17-99	0	2	5.00	8	0	0	9	4	5	5	1	6	11	.138	.286	.276	31.43	17.14	35
Beeter, Clayton	R-R	6-2	220	10-9-98	0	0	0.00	2	0	0	3	1	0	0	0	0	5	.100	.100	.200	50.00	0.00	10
Boyle, Sean	R-R	6-1	205	10-29-96	3	1	3.27	10	0	1	11	4	4	4	1	3	12	.111	.175	.250	30.00	7.50	40
Brubaker, JT	R-R	6-3	185	11-17-93	0	0	0.00	1	1	0	3	1	0	0	0	1	3	.100	.182	.200	27.27	9.09	11
Calderon, Yorlin	R-R	6-3	155	8-17-01	1	1	2.28	16	1	0	28	20	12	7	1	13	22	.200	.311	.280	18.49	10.92	119
Cole, Gerrit	R-R	6-4	220	9-8-90	0	0	1.13	2	2	0	8	4	1	1	1	0	9	.143	.143	.250	32.14	0.00	28
Dees, Bailey	R-R	6-8	250	2-5-99	7	7	4.25	27	26	0	138	118	71	65	19	54	145	.226	.305	.392	24.87	9.26	583
Gerber, Joey	R-R	6-4	212	5-3-97	1	0	1.76	12	0	1	15	11	3	3	1	8	18	.204	.302	.296	28.57	12.70	63
Gil, Luis	R-R	6-2	185	6-3-98	0	0	7.36	1	1	0	4	4	3	3	0	2	6	.286	.412	.500	35.29	11.76	17
Givin, Matt	R-R	6-3	180	6-17-99	0	0	3.00	1	0	0	3	2	1	1	0	1	5	.182	.250	.364	41.67	8.33	12
Gomez, Carlos	R-R	6-1	175	6-14-98	4	1	3.63	27	0	2	40	29	16	16	3	10	36	.200	.318	.303	21.05	10.53	171
Grosz, Josh	R-R	6-4	199	9-5-02	0	1	11.25	1	1	0	4	6	6	5	1	3	5	.353	.500	.647	22.73	13.64	22
Hamilton, Ian	R-R	6-1	200	6-16-95	1	0	0.00	2	0	0	2	0	0	0	0	0	6	.000	.000	.000	85.71	0.00	7
Hampton, Chase	R-R	6-2	225	8-7-01	0	0	0.00	2	2	0	6	4	0	0	0	3	4	.190	.292	.238	16.67	12.50	24
Kahnle, Tommy	R-R	6-1	230	8-7-89	0	0	0.00	3	0	0	3	0	0	0	0	0	8	.000	.000	.000	88.89	0.00	9
Liranzo, Jesus	R-R	6-2	225	3-7-95	5	1	2.67	23	0	3	30	25	10	9	2	11	39	.217	.297	.322	30.47	8.59	128
Maciejewski, Josh	R-L	6-3	175	8-14-95	0	2	7.11	7	1	0	13	16	12	10	3	3	17	.286	.322	.482	28.81	5.08	59
Mauricio, Alex	R-R	6-0	180	9-24-96	0	0	0.00	1	0	0	1	0	0	0	0	0	0	.000	.000	.000	0.00	0.00	3
Messinger, Zach	R-R	6-6	225	10-4-99	7	8	3.06	27	25	1	150	114	68	51	9	52	136	.207	.282	.322	21.97	8.40	619
Moore, McKinley	R-R	6-6	225	8-24-98	3	1	6.43	16	0	0	14	17	11	10	1	9	12	.283	.397	.450	16.44	12.33	73
Myatt, Tanner	R-R	6-7	220	5-21-98	0	0	2.35	5	0	0	8	6	2	2	0	2	13	.207	.258	.345	41.94	6.45	31
Neely, Jack	R-R	6-8	225	6-5-00	0	0	2.61	22	0	6	31	23	10	9	2	12	51	.204	.273	.345	39.23	9.23	130
Pacheco, Luis	R-R	6-2	185	4-22-99	0	0	0.00	3	0	0	4	1	0	0	0	2	3	.083	.267	.083	20.00	13.33	15
Palensky, Aaron	R-R	5-10	190	9-22-98	0	0	27.00	2	0	0	2	4	5	5	0	1	0	.500	.545	.750	0.00	9.09	11
Pestana, Leonardo	R-R	6-4	198	7-30-98	1	0	3.18	21	0	2	23	19	8	8	2	9	28	.232	.323	.341	30.11	9.68	93
Poteet, Cody	R-R	6-1	190	7-30-94	0	0	0.96	3	3	0	9	5	1	1	0	1	11	.152	.176	.182	32.35	2.94	34
Reyzelman, Eric	R-R	6-2	188	6-27-01	1	1	1.93	21	0	5	23	14	6	5	2	14	37	.167	.283	.250	37.37	14.14	99
Sauer, Matt	R-R	6-4	195	1-21-99	2	0	2.63	17	0	0	24	17	8	7	2	3	21	.191	.213	.292	22.34	3.19	94
Schlittler, Cam	R-R	6-6	210	2-5-01	2	4	4.45	7	5	0	32	37	19	16	3	13	43	.287	.356	.395	29.25	8.84	147
Schmidt, Clarke	R-R	6-1	200	2-20-96	0	0	3.24	2	2	0	8	4	3	3	2	1	13	.138	.167	.379	43.33	3.33	30
Selvidge, Brock	R-L	6-3	205	8-28-02	7	6	4.25	16	16	0	85	78	50	40	6	40	83	.245	.340	.352	22.43	10.81	370
Serruto, Peter	R-R	6-2	195	3-17-00	0	0	0.00	1	0	0	1	0	0	0	0	3	1	.000	.600	.000	20.00	60.00	5
Shields, Ben	R-L	6-4	210	1-23-99	2	2	3.12	11	9	0	52	41	21	18	3	21	65	.212	.305	.311	29.55	9.55	220
Stevens, Kevin	R-R	6-2	225	1-26-98	4	0	2.54	31	0	7	39	29	11	11	2	16	56	.204	.286	.289	34.78	9.94	161
Trivino, Lou	R-R	6-5	235	10-1-91	0	0	1.80	5	0	0	5	3	1	1	0	2	5	.176	.263	.235	26.32	10.53	19
Velasquez, Luis	R-R	5-10	155	7-1-01	3	3	4.57	30	2	1	41	33	29	21	6	31	56	.206	.345	.369	28.72	15.90	195
Vrieling, Trystan	R-R	6-4	200	10-2-00	13	7	4.58	27	25	0	147	140	79	75	13	46	132	.248	.306	.374	21.32	7.43	619
Watson, Danny	R-R	6-7	235	10-6-00	2	5	5.06	32	0	4	37	35	25	21	5	13	26	.245	.314	.399	16.25	8.13	160
White, Colby	R-R	6-0	190	7-4-98	2	0	3.34	29	1	0	32	23	15	12	3	22	40	.202	.326	.351	28.99	15.94	138

Fielding

Catcher	PCT	G	PO	A	E	DP	PB
Crisp	.964	7	46	7	2	0	1
Escarra	.976	23	221	18	6	1	4
Flores	.993	46	412	34	3	3	2
Ramirez	.981	31	284	21	6	1	4
Rice	.995	22	201	9	1	2	3
Rodriguez	.965	11	72	11	3	0	0
Serruto	.000	1	0	0	0	0	0
Trevino	1.000	3	15	1	0	0	0

First Base	PCT	G	PO	A	E	DP
Burt	1.000	9	45	3	0	0
Dunham	1.000	3	7	0	0	1
Escarra	1.000	21	161	9	0	15
Flores	.990	14	96	2	1	9
Hardman	.991	45	295	29	3	18
Henson	1.000	4	25	3	0	1
Ramirez	.972	15	95	9	3	7
Rice	.971	17	120	15	4	10
Rizzo	1.000	3	12	2	0	1
Rodriguez	.968	5	28	2	1	2
Romero	1.000	1	3	0	0	1
Rumfield	.986	8	67	2	1	6

Second Base	PCT	G	PO	A	E	DP
Burt	1.000	4	6	9	0	2
Cowles	1.000	10	18	17	0	4
Durbin	1.000	2	3	3	0	0
Groshans	.955	7	7	14	1	0
Palensky	.955	4	8	13	1	2
Seigler	.964	118	143	259	15	46
Vargas	1.000	3	3	0	0	0

Third Base	PCT	G	PO	A	E	DP
Berti	1.000	8	6	8	0	0
Burt	.961	49	38	61	4	3
Cowles	.905	20	14	24	4	1
Durbin	1.000	2	1	2	0	0

	PCT	G	PO	A	E	DP
Escarra	.966	18	6	22	1	1
Groshans	.930	27	17	36	4	5
Hardman	.892	16	15	18	4	4
LeMahieu	.000	3	0	0	0	0
Rodriguez	1.000	6	2	11	0	0
Romero	.750	3	0	3	1	0
Vargas	1.000	6	1	3	0	1

Shortstop	PCT	G	PO	A	E	DP
Burt	.965	13	22	33	2	10
Cowles	.960	64	89	128	9	22
Groshans	1.000	3	1	3	0	1
Peraza	1.000	3	0	7	0	2
Vargas	.927	64	77	113	15	16

Outfield	PCT	G	PO	A	E	DP
Allen	1.000	3	5	0	0	0
Dominguez	1.000	3	4	0	0	0
Dunham	.986	79	137	3	2	0
Escarra	1.000	3	3	1	0	0
Gabrielson	1.000	15	29	0	0	0
Jones	.978	99	218	3	5	0
Palensky	1.000	46	83	1	0	0
Richardson	.964	98	203	9	8	3
Rodriguez	1.000	1	2	0	0	0
Wegner	.993	77	137	4	1	2

HUDSON VALLEY RENEGADES — HIGH-A

SOUTH ATLANTIC LEAGUE

Batting	B-T	Ht.	Wt.	DOB	AVG	OBP	SLG	G	PA	AB	R	H	2B	3B	HR	RBI	BB	HBP	SH	SF	SO	SB	CS	BB%	SO%
Avina, Jace	R-R	5-11	180	6-6-03	.245	.317	.399	92	397	351	44	86	24	0	10	49	32	8	0	6	108	4	1	8.06	27.20
Battle, Kyle	R-R	6-0	190	12-4-97	.174	.316	.304	21	57	46	14	8	1	1	1	5	9	1	0	1	23	5	0	15.79	40.35
Brewer, Beau	R-R	6-1	215	10-28-01	.228	.290	.293	33	102	92	8	21	6	0	0	10	8	0	0	0	19	0	0	7.84	18.63
Castillo, Jackson	L-L	6-0	195	5-2-03	.314	.383	.514	21	81	70	11	22	4	2	2	20	8	1	0	2	15	5	1	9.88	18.52
Cobb, Owen	R-R	6-2	193	6-24-01	.000	.182	.000	3	12	9	2	0	0	0	0	0	1	1	0	0	4	2	0	8.33	33.33
Escanio, Brenny	B-R	5-9	145	12-16-02	.203	.291	.271	45	135	118	8	24	8	0	0	12	14	1	1	1	39	8	3	10.37	28.89
Familia, Christopher	L-L	5-11	170	6-10-00	.183	.264	.304	34	129	115	15	21	5	0	3	17	10	3	0	1	40	0	0	7.75	31.01
Flores, Rafael	R-R	6-4	220	11-7-00	.285	.403	.466	57	233	193	27	55	17	0	6	35	38	1	0	1	55	2	1	16.31	23.61
Gabrielson, Cole	R-R	6-0	185	7-5-00	.204	.343	.277	66	233	191	28	39	12	1	0	18	29	12	0	1	56	12	3	12.45	24.03
Gomez, Antonio	R-R	6-2	210	11-13-01	.238	.315	.431	47	184	160	29	38	14	1	5	20	17	2	0	2	51	2	0	9.24	27.72
Hall, Anthony	L-L	6-1	200	2-9-01	.181	.286	.241	37	133	116	11	21	5	1	0	10	17	0	0	0	45	4	0	12.78	33.83
Hardman, Tyler	R-R	6-2	204	1-27-99	.237	.292	.339	16	65	59	8	14	3	0	1	7	5	0	0	1	26	1	0	7.69	40.00
Jasso, Dylan	R-R	6-3	196	11-30-02	.258	.321	.423	27	109	97	14	25	8	1	2	13	10	0	0	2	25	0	0	9.17	22.94
Jones, Brendan	L-L	5-10	175	4-24-02	.234	.429	.404	15	63	47	9	11	2	0	2	10	16	0	0	0	13	13	0	25.40	20.63
LeMahieu, DJ	R-R	6-4	220	7-13-88	.286	.286	.429	2	7	7	1	2	1	0	0	1	0	0	0	0	1	0	0	0.00	14.29
Lombard, George	R-R	6-3	190	6-2-05	.226	.321	.296	29	131	115	10	26	8	0	0	8	14	2	0	0	26	9	4	10.69	19.85
Martin, Garrett	R-R	6-4	216	6-28-00	.216	.326	.422	87	346	287	50	62	17	3	12	43	34	14	0	2	97	17	2	9.83	28.03
Martinez, Omar	L-R	5-10	192	7-5-01	.238	.374	.404	104	430	349	53	83	15	2	13	41	73	5	0	3	101	3	0	16.98	23.49
Medina, Nelson	R-R	6-2	175	9-14-00	.115	.197	.147	50	173	156	13	18	3	1	0	14	14	2	0	1	74	8	0	8.09	42.77
Morales, Coby	L-R	6-3	225	12-5-01	.286	.417	.327	15	60	49	9	14	2	0	0	8	10	1	0	0	16	3	1	16.67	26.67
Moylan, Josh	L-R	6-4	216	7-3-02	.246	.357	.381	101	406	341	52	84	18	2	8	42	55	6	0	4	102	3	3	13.55	25.12
Riggio, Roc	L-R	5-9	180	6-11-02	.221	.349	.397	106	480	398	70	88	27	5	11	47	71	8	1	2	97	27	6	14.79	20.21
Rodriguez, Jesus	R-R	5-9	182	4-23-02	.332	.412	.507	56	243	211	39	70	14	4	5	33	29	1	0	2	30	7	3	11.93	12.35
Romero, Kiko	L-R	5-11	185	9-18-00	.208	.349	.362	72	252	207	27	43	12	1	6	21	40	5	0	0	79	9	1	15.87	31.35
Serna, Jared	R-R	5-6	168	6-1-02	.253	.341	.444	88	393	340	51	86	26	0	13	58	40	8	0	5	60	11	8	10.18	15.27
Silverio, Oscar	L-R	5-9	170	10-25-01	.000	.000	.000	1	1	1	0	0	0	0	0	0	0	0	0	0	1	0	0	0.00	100.00
Vargas, Alexander	B-R	5-10	148	10-29-01	.200	.316	.400	5	19	15	1	3	1	1	0	5	3	0	0	1	1	1	1	15.79	5.26
Vivas, Edison	R-R	6-0	184	6-3-06	.400	.400	.400	2	5	5	0	2	0	0	0	3	0	0	0	0	2	0	0	0.00	40.00
Vivas, Jorbit	L-R	5-10	171	3-9-01	.313	.389	.375	4	18	16	4	5	1	0	0	5	2	0	0	0	3	0	0	11.11	16.67

Pitching	B-T	Ht.	Wt.	DOB	W	L	ERA	G	GS	SV	IP	Hits	Runs	ER	HR	BB	SO	AVG	OBP	SLG	SO%	BB%	BF
Abeyta, Blane	R-R	6-3	185	9-4-98	3	2	2.23	14	7	0	44	38	18	11	3	5	32	.228	.267	.341	17.58	2.75	182
Arejula, Luis	R-R	6-1	170	2-20-02	3	4	2.90	23	0	1	40	33	18	13	2	21	38	.223	.326	.358	22.09	12.21	172
Austin, Kelly	R-R	6-0	195	12-17-00	3	0	1.29	10	0	0	14	10	2	2	1	2	19	.196	.241	.314	35.19	3.70	54
Ayers, Cole	R-R	6-3	185	8-17-99	3	4	3.09	36	0	3	55	47	23	19	5	20	67	.225	.300	.335	28.76	8.58	233
Balboni, Thomas	L-R	6-4	185	7-6-00	0	1	7.20	11	0	0	10	8	8	8	0	9	19	.216	.400	.297	38.00	18.00	50
Boyle, Sean	R-R	6-1	205	10-29-96	1	0	1.29	4	0	0	7	6	1	1	1	2	7	.231	.333	.385	23.33	6.67	30
Calderon, Yorlin	R-R	6-3	155	8-17-01	2	0	2.31	16	0	3	23	20	7	6	2	9	31	.220	.304	.297	30.10	8.74	103
Carr, Kyle	L-L	6-1	175	5-6-02	1	8	4.76	24	24	0	104	97	70	55	5	55	95	.250	.344	.376	21.02	12.17	452
Cohen, Harrison	R-R	6-0	190	5-28-99	3	0	0.93	12	0	0	19	10	3	2	1	1	23	.149	.171	.209	32.86	1.43	70
Crisp, Juan	R-R	6-0	170	5-23-00	1	0	12.00	2	0	0	3	2	4	4	2	4	4	.182	.400	.727	26.67	26.67	15
Diaz, Indigo	R-R	6-5	250	10-14-98	0	0	2.38	11	1	0	11	5	4	3	1	2	15	.135	.175	.243	37.50	5.00	40
Fristoe, Jackson	R-R	6-4	210	3-6-01	1	3	3.79	12	12	0	38	27	18	16	2	28	40	.201	.341	.299	24.39	17.07	164
Fulgencio, Steven	R-R	6-2	175	10-5-00	1	1	4.15	8	0	0	9	7	7	4	0	6	7	.219	.366	.281	17.07	14.63	41
Gabonia, Ocean	R-R	6-1	175	7-31-01	0	0	2.89	7	0	1	9	8	3	3	1	5	7	.235	.325	.324	17.50	12.50	40
Gilbert, Geoffrey	L-L	6-0	215	5-3-01	0	0	0.00	5	0	2	7	1	0	0	0	2	10	.043	.120	.043	40.00	8.00	25
Grosz, Josh	R-R	6-4	199	9-5-02	4	2	2.77	7	7	0	39	22	14	12	4	20	31	.169	.280	.315	20.53	13.25	151
Hendry, Brian	R-R	6-4	225	10-11-99	1	0	0.48	7	7	0	19	8	3	1	0	9	23	.125	.230	.188	31.08	12.16	74
Keane, Sebastian	R-R	6-3	187	11-2-00	6	7	4.61	26	15	1	82	73	45	42	7	41	84	.243	.350	.387	23.33	11.39	360
Keating, Matt	R-R	6-1	215	12-8-00	5	4	3.89	40	0	4	69	45	33	30	10	32	83	.181	.278	.355	29.54	11.39	281
Moore, McKinley	R-R	6-6	225	8-24-98	0	0	7.36	4	0	1	4	2	3	3	0	2	6	.154	.294	.231	35.29	11.76	17
Morrill, Hueston	R-R	6-0	168	11-27-99	3	3	3.59	36	0	3	48	44	26	19	6	15	51	.251	.320	.423	25.76	7.58	198
Pestana, Leonardo	R-R	6-4	198	7-30-98	1	0	1.86	6	0	0	10	1	2	2	0	5	15	.036	.182	.036	44.12	14.71	34
Reyzelman, Eric	R-R	6-2	188	6-27-01	0	0	0.00	6	0	0	10	2	0	0	0	4	17	.065	.194	.065	47.22	11.11	36
Schlittler, Cam	R-R	6-6	210	2-5-01	6	4	2.60	17	17	0	87	60	34	25	7	38	108	.191	.284	.306	30.25	10.64	357
Sellers, Trent	R-R	6-1	200	10-30-99	6	3	2.09	31	9	1	82	42	27	19	3	37	98	.149	.255	.227	30.34	11.46	323
Shields, Ben	R-L	6-4	210	1-23-99	3	2	2.75	14	7	0	52	35	19	16	5	10	71	.185	.241	.312	34.80	4.90	204

Pitching	B-T	Ht.	Wt.	DOB	W	L	ERA	G	GS	SV	IP	Hits	Runs	ER	HR	BB	SO	AVG	OBP	SLG	SO%	BB%	BF
Smith, Cade	L-R	6-1	190	4-9-02	0	1	5.63	2	2	0	8	4	5	5	1	3	7	.143	.250	.357	21.88	9.38	32
Stuart, Baron	R-R	6-4	209	7-24-99	8	5	3.63	22	22	0	109	98	49	44	4	42	102	.241	.318	.330	22.17	9.13	460
Valdez, Joel	L-L	6-4	171	4-28-00	2	2	3.41	36	0	4	58	42	26	22	3	29	72	.199	.315	.275	28.57	11.51	252
Vinyard, Mason	R-R	6-2	210	6-22-99	6	2	3.26	33	0	2	47	35	23	17	2	25	61	.200	.303	.297	30.35	12.44	201
Warrecker, Bryce	L-R	6-8	225	9-13-01	0	0	3.86	1	1	0	2	3	1	1	0	2	2	.333	.455	.333	18.18	18.18	11

Fielding

Catcher	PCT	G	PO	A	E	DP	PB
Camargo	.000	2	0	0	0	0	0
Jeffers	.992	86	749	31	6	0	3
Vazquez	.995	86	772	29	4	2	1

First Base	PCT	G	PO	A	E	DP
Farmer	1.000	1	2	0	0	0
Julien	1.000	1	1	0	0	0
Kirilloff	1.000	12	57	3	0	2
Miranda	1.000	13	86	7	0	5
Santana	.996	146	998	92	4	67
Vazquez	1.000	1	1	0	0	0

Second Base	PCT	G	PO	A	E	DP
Castro	.981	40	46	60	2	13
Farmer	.985	71	38	92	2	13
Julien	.981	90	86	166	5	25
Lee	.920	11	7	16	2	1
Lewis	.875	2	0	7	1	0
Martin	1.000	14	15	19	0	3

Third Base	PCT	G	PO	A	E	DP
Castillo	1.000	3	1	3	0	0
Castro	.971	27	12	22	1	0
Farmer	1.000	29	12	27	0	3
Helman	.000	1	0	0	0	0
Lee	1.000	13	7	20	0	0
Lewis	.952	51	42	76	6	7
Miranda	.959	78	42	97	6	9
Vazquez	.000	3	0	0	0	0

Shortstop	PCT	G	PO	A	E	DP
Castro	.982	56	68	93	3	11
Correa	.983	84	119	169	5	26
Farmer	1.000	13	5	9	0	1
Lee	.974	27	34	42	2	8
Miranda	1.000	1	0	2	0	1

Outfield	PCT	G	PO	A	E	DP
Buxton	1.000	94	204	2	0	0
Castro	.984	64	121	3	2	0
Helman	.667	7	2	0	1	0
Keirsey	1.000	6	5	1	0	0
Kepler	1.000	103	172	4	0	1
Kirilloff	1.000	31	37	1	0	0
Larnach	1.000	62	91	0	0	0
Margot	.982	130	163	0	3	0
Martin	.992	80	124	1	1	0
Wallner	1.000	58	109	4	0	1

NEW YORK YANKEES

TAMPA TARPONS — LOW-A

FLORIDA STATE LEAGUE

Batting	B-T	Ht.	Wt.	DOB	AVG	OBP	SLG	G	PA	AB	R	H	2B	3B	HR	RBI	BB	HBP	SH	SF	SO	SB	CS	BB%	SO%
Aguilar, Tayler	L-L	5-10	205	8-15-00	.109	.338	.182	19	74	55	8	6	1	0	1	3	17	2	0	0	26	3	0	22.97	35.14
Arias, Daury	L-L	5-11	172	8-7-01	.171	.266	.246	55	199	175	22	30	7	0	2	20	20	3	0	1	54	6	2	10.05	27.14
Arias, Roderick	B-R	6-0	178	9-9-04	.233	.335	.393	124	552	473	78	110	21	8	13	74	68	7	0	4	171	37	13	12.32	30.98
Burt, Max	R-R	6-1	185	8-28-96	.214	.267	.429	4	15	14	1	3	3	0	0	2	1	0	0	0	2	2	0	6.67	13.33
Castillo, Jackson	L-L	6-0	195	5-2-03	.256	.386	.404	82	334	270	51	69	17	1	7	32	58	2	0	4	65	16	5	17.37	19.46
Cobb, Owen	R-R	6-2	193	6-24-01	.278	.365	.352	15	63	54	13	15	4	0	0	10	7	1	0	1	15	7	0	11.11	23.81
De Los Santos, Joe	R-R	5-10	195	6-26-01	.286	.419	.371	21	86	70	13	20	6	0	0	8	14	2	0	0	26	10	3	16.28	30.23
Dominguez, Jasson	B-R	5-9	190	2-7-03	.385	.529	.462	4	17	13	2	5	1	0	0	2	4	0	0	0	3	0	0	23.53	17.65
Duran, Edinson	R-R	5-6	180	7-22-02	.218	.307	.346	24	88	78	7	17	4	3	0	2	6	4	0	0	20	1	0	6.82	22.73
Durbin, Caleb	R-R	5-6	175	2-22-00	.000	.000	.000	1	1	1	0	0	0	0	0	0	0	0	0	0	0	0	0	0.00	0.00
Escanio, Brenny	B-R	5-9	145	12-16-02	.276	.333	.368	31	96	87	11	24	4	2	0	6	8	0	0	1	21	6	1	8.33	21.88
Familia, Christopher	L-L	5-11	170	6-10-00	.318	.348	.727	5	23	22	3	7	1	1	2	5	1	0	0	0	5	0	0	4.35	21.74
Frick, Tomas	R-R	6-0	200	10-11-00	.250	.370	.368	47	173	144	23	36	11	0	2	18	23	5	0	1	28	1	0	13.29	16.18
Gomez, Antonio	R-R	6-2	210	11-13-01	.273	.385	.364	4	13	11	1	3	1	0	0	3	2	0	0	0	2	1	0	15.38	15.38
Gonzalez, Josue	R-R	5-9	170	10-30-03	.235	.299	.348	41	137	115	16	27	4	0	3	20	10	4	0	8	26	1	3	7.30	18.98
Gonzalez, Oscar	R-R	6-4	240	1-10-98	.300	.391	.700	5	23	20	4	6	0	1	2	6	3	0	0	0	4	0	0	13.04	17.39
Green, Austin	B-R	6-0	195	5-20-02	.115	.143	.115	7	28	26	0	3	0	0	0	5	0	1	0	1	11	1	0	0.00	39.29
Hall, Anthony	L-L	6-1	200	2-9-01	.167	.231	.167	3	13	12	0	2	0	0	0	1	1	0	0	0	5	0	0	7.69	38.46
Harber, Parks	R-R	6-3	225	9-25-01	.269	.389	.449	23	95	78	19	21	7	2	1	19	15	1	0	1	24	4	0	15.79	25.26
Hardman, Tyler	R-R	6-2	204	1-27-99	.235	.235	.471	4	17	17	2	4	1	0	1	5	0	0	0	0	7	0	1	0.00	41.18
Hernandez, Diomedes	R-R	5-11	165	2-6-05	.300	.383	.425	14	47	40	8	12	2	0	1	9	6	0	0	1	7	0	1	12.77	14.89
Jackson, JoJo	B-L	6-2	215	10-6-02	.190	.292	.190	6	24	21	4	4	0	0	0	2	3	0	0	0	7	0	0	12.50	29.17
Jasso, Dylan	R-R	6-3	196	11-30-02	.238	.331	.392	93	399	344	49	82	22	2	9	54	40	10	0	5	99	2	0	10.03	24.81
Jones, Brendan	L-L	5-10	175	4-24-02	.321	.537	.536	9	41	28	7	9	3	0	1	9	13	0	0	0	8	5	0	31.71	19.51
Lewis, Dillon	R-R	6-3	205	6-12-03	.250	.304	.385	14	56	52	10	13	4	0	1	6	4	0	0	0	9	3	0	7.14	16.07
Lombard, George	R-R	6-3	190	6-2-05	.232	.344	.348	81	366	310	46	72	17	2	5	37	47	7	0	2	88	30	4	12.84	24.04
Matheus, Juan	B-R	5-10	155	4-29-04	.077	.333	.154	5	18	13	2	1	1	0	0	0	5	0	0	0	6	2	0	27.78	33.33
Montero, Hans	R-R	5-9	160	12-25-03	.206	.305	.333	99	391	339	49	70	9	5	8	38	44	5	1	2	113	13	4	11.25	28.90
Montero, Willy	R-R	6-4	202	8-4-04	.244	.311	.355	120	486	434	64	106	23	2	7	58	40	5	0	7	103	15	1	8.23	21.19
Morales, Coby	L-R	6-3	225	12-5-01	.248	.356	.319	98	382	326	51	81	9	1	4	47	48	7	0	1	113	31	7	12.57	29.58
Palencia, Manuel	R-R	5-11	175	9-5-02	.281	.314	.344	29	102	96	8	27	6	0	0	12	5	0	0	1	12	1	0	4.90	11.76
Pastore, Duncan	R-R	6-3	175	5-27-00	.370	.455	.370	10	33	27	5	10	0	0	0	4	3	2	0	1	4	4	0	9.09	12.12
Peraza, Oswald	R-R	6-0	200	6-15-00	.400	.571	1.000	2	7	5	3	2	0	0	1	1	2	0	0	0	1	0	0	28.57	14.29
Perez, Dayro	R-R	5-11	180	1-31-02	.077	.172	.154	13	29	26	2	2	0	1	0	0	3	0	0	0	15	5	0	10.34	51.72
Silverio, Oscar	L-R	5-9	170	10-25-01	.182	.250	.273	7	12	11	0	2	1	0	0	2	1	0	0	0	6	0	0	8.33	50.00
Tejeda, Enmanuel	R-R	5-11	158	12-25-04	.310	.353	.369	43	185	168	26	52	7	0	1	18	11	2	0	3	36	24	4	5.95	19.46
Toole, Marshall	L-R	5-11	185	3-17-03	.255	.449	.353	17	69	51	6	13	2	0	1	9	15	3	0	0	18	8	2	21.74	26.09
Vivas, Jorbit	L-R	5-10	171	3-9-01	.091	.333	.091	4	15	11	2	1	0	0	0	0	3	1	0	0	3	1	0	20.00	20.00
Wilson, Tyler	B-R	6-2	210	7-10-02	.197	.326	.303	21	92	76	10	15	5	0	1	12	14	1	0	1	14	2	1	15.22	15.22

Pitching	B-T	Ht.	Wt.	DOB	W	L	ERA	G	GS	SV	IP	Hits	Runs	ER	HR	BB	SO	AVG	OBP	SLG	SO%	BB%	BF
Arejula, Luis	R-R	6-1	170	2-20-02	1	0	3.14	10	0	1	14	11	8	5	1	7	11	.200	.302	.345	17.46	11.11	63
Austin, Cade	R-R	6-3	230	9-28-01	2	4	3.69	26	1	1	46	34	23	19	7	14	50	.201	.277	.349	26.46	7.41	189
Barbosa, Gabriel	R-R	6-0	183	1-22-02	5	9	5.09	24	20	1	120	118	73	68	13	38	128	.252	.315	.400	24.71	7.34	518
Bow, Kris	R-R	6-4	225	11-26-00	3	2	5.45	29	0	2	40	27	30	24	5	28	43	.197	.365	.358	24.02	15.64	179

Brian, Will	L-L	5-11	220	4-25-99	0	0	0.00	1	0	0	2	2	0	0	0	0	4	.250	.250	.375	50.00	0.00	8
Brubaker, JT	R-R	6-3	185	11-17-93	0	0	0.00	1	1	0	3	2	0	0	0	0	2	.200	.200	.300	20.00	0.00	10
Cohen, Harrison	R-R	6-0	190	5-28-99	2	0	2.84	5	0	0	6	5	2	2	0	8	5	.227	.433	.273	16.67	26.67	30
Diaz, Yoljeldriz	R-R	5-11	165	7-14-01	2	1	5.34	22	0	0	30	24	18	18	1	27	35	.214	.371	.277	25.00	19.29	140
Effross, Scott	R-R	6-2	202	12-28-93	1	0	0.00	2	0	0	3	1	0	0	0	0	4	.100	.100	.200	40.00	0.00	10
Escanio, Brenny	S-R	5-9	145	12-16-02	0	0	0.00	1	0	0	0	0	0	0	0	1	1	.000	.500	.000	50.00	50.00	2
Facundo, Allen	L-L	6-0	171	9-3-02	1	1	2.40	8	7	0	30	18	10	8	1	14	38	.165	.278	.248	30.16	11.11	126
Flatt, Danny	R-R	6-4	190	6-6-04	0	2	9.31	4	4	0	10	18	14	10	4	8	9	.360	.448	.640	15.52	13.79	58
Fulgencio, Steven	R-R	6-2	175	10-5-00	0	0	4.80	19	2	1	30	26	20	16	0	21	27	.226	.355	.296	19.57	15.22	138
Gabonia, Ocean	R-R	6-1	175	7-31-01	3	3	4.01	32	0	2	49	47	26	22	4	13	55	.254	.296	.405	26.57	6.28	207
Gerber, Joey	R-R	6-4	212	5-3-97	0	0	0.00	1	0	0	2	0	0	0	0	1	4	.000	.143	.000	57.14	14.29	7
Givin, Matt	R-R	6-3	180	6-17-99	0	1	7.36	11	0	0	15	19	13	12	2	5	12	.297	.343	.484	17.14	7.14	70
Gomez, Alejandro	R-R	6-4	180	8-3-02	2	0	3.75	7	0	0	12	10	5	5	2	7	10	.217	.345	.413	18.18	12.73	55
Grosz, Josh	R-R	6-4	199	9-5-02	3	5	4.00	16	15	0	79	73	50	35	9	29	95	.245	.327	.409	27.94	8.53	340
Hampton, Chase	R-R	6-2	225	8-7-01	0	1	3.72	3	3	0	10	4	5	4	1	2	8	.129	.222	.258	22.22	5.56	36
Harvey, Ryan	R-R	6-3	195	2-8-01	2	4	6.03	11	10	0	31	26	23	21	1	19	35	.230	.355	.372	24.82	13.48	141
Hernandez, Diomedes	R-R	5-11	165	2-6-05	0	0	0.00	2	0	0	1	0	0	0	0	0	0	.000	.000	.000	0.00	0.00	2
Kahnle, Tommy	R-R	6-1	230	8-7-89	0	0	0.00	2	2	0	2	0	0	0	0	0	3	.000	.000	.000	50.00	0.00	6
Kean, Chris	R-R	6-5	210	6-12-02	1	0	0.71	11	0	2	13	9	2	1	1	2	17	.184	.231	.286	32.69	3.85	52
Lagrange, Carlos	R-R	6-7	195	5-25-03	0	1	6.91	5	5	0	14	10	13	11	0	13	19	.200	.391	.280	27.54	18.84	69
Lalane, Henry	L-L	6-7	211	5-18-04	0	1	9.00	3	3	0	6	6	6	6	1	5	7	.286	.429	.476	25.00	17.86	28
Landry, Andrew	R-R	6-1	175	2-20-02	0	2	6.98	7	7	0	19	19	18	15	1	16	12	.253	.385	.387	13.19	17.58	91
Luciano, Jordy	R-R	5-10	160	7-22-01	2	6	5.07	34	0	1	55	51	41	31	4	46	64	.248	.399	.364	24.33	17.49	263
Morrill, Hueston	R-R	6-0	168	11-27-99	2	0	2.00	5	0	1	9	6	3	2	0	4	7	.182	.289	.242	17.95	10.26	39
Myatt, Tanner	R-R	6-7	220	5-21-98	0	0	4.50	2	0	0	2	3	1	1	1	1	4	.333	.400	.667	40.00	10.00	10
Nivar, Rafelin	L-L	5-10	160	10-21-01	0	1	6.58	17	0	0	26	21	21	19	3	38	34	.223	.456	.362	24.82	27.74	137
Nixon, Aaron	R-R	6-1	205	7-19-01	4	3	5.40	39	0	5	62	46	41	37	3	48	63	.204	.353	.311	22.18	16.90	284
Pacheco, Luis	R-R	6-2	185	4-22-99	2	1	2.08	11	0	1	17	16	5	4	2	4	23	.254	.299	.365	34.33	5.97	67
Perez, Dayro	R-R	5-11	180	1-31-02	0	0	27.00	1	0	0	1	3	2	2	0	1	1	.600	.667	.600	16.67	16.67	6
Phillips, Brett	L-R	6-0	195	5-30-94	0	0	0.00	1	0	0	0	2	5	5	0	2	0	1.000	1.000	1.000	0.00	40.00	5
Rodriguez, Osiel	R-R	6-2	210	11-22-01	1	2	2.56	30	0	1	56	32	17	16	8	28	68	.164	.279	.344	29.69	12.23	229
Rose, Brady	L-L	6-5	220	10-26-00	1	1	9.26	4	1	0	12	14	13	12	1	7	8	.311	.400	.533	14.55	12.73	55
Sanchez, Juan	L-R	5-11	190	3-21-03	0	1	0.00	1	0	0	0	1	1	0	0	0	0	.500	.500	1.000	0.00	0.00	2
Semmel, Montana	R-R	6-4	225	1-1-02	4	4	6.33	28	0	6	43	42	38	30	5	29	40	.256	.372	.402	20.30	14.72	197
Serna, Luis	R-R	5-11	162	7-20-04	2	6	6.07	18	17	0	70	67	48	47	6	24	82	.250	.337	.410	27.06	7.92	303
Silverio, Oscar	L-R	5-9	170	10-25-01	0	0	0.00	1	0	0	1	0	0	0	0	1	0	.000	.250	.000	0.00	25.00	4
Smith, Cade	L-R	6-1	190	4-9-02	6	6	3.47	19	17	0	86	59	39	33	5	40	111	.191	.288	.294	31.36	11.30	354
Warrecker, Bryce	L-R	6-8	225	9-13-01	2	5	6.34	13	13	0	50	49	36	35	6	27	31	.261	.371	.436	13.84	12.05	224
Warren, Art	R-R	6-3	230	3-23-93	0	1	6.75	4	0	0	4	8	6	3	0	2	6	.364	.440	.500	24.00	8.00	25

NEW YORK YANKEES

Fielding

Catcher	PCT	G	PO	A	E	DP	PB
Duran	.980	21	188	12	4	1	5
Frick	.984	37	336	22	6	2	3
Gomez	1.000	3	21	1	0	1	0
Gonzalez	.988	40	313	27	4	2	14
Hernandez	.974	14	104	8	3	0	1
Palencia	.969	20	173	12	6	0	1
Silverio	1.000	6	33	2	0	1	0

First Base	PCT	G	PO	A	E	DP
Gonzalez	1.000	2	21	1	0	2
Harber	.987	21	143	12	2	15
Jasso	.992	68	479	34	4	53
Morales	.996	37	238	25	1	21
Pastore	1.000	3	18	0	0	1

Second Base	PCT	G	PO	A	E	DP
Arias	.947	32	54	71	7	16
Burt	1.000	1	1	2	0	0
Cobb	.938	11	14	31	3	8
Durbin	1.000	1	0	1	0	0
Escanio	.933	15	17	39	4	8
Green	1.000	6	7	19	0	3
Lombard	.974	19	27	47	2	7
Matheus	.944	4	5	12	1	2
Montero	.965	32	44	65	4	15
Perez	.846	5	5	6	2	1
Tejeda	.944	10	12	22	2	3
Vivas	.909	4	4	6	1	1

Third Base	PCT	G	PO	A	E	DP
Arias	1.000	2	1	5	0	0
Burt	1.000	1	0	2	0	1
Cobb	.909	5	5	5	1	1
Escanio	.919	12	8	26	3	3
Jasso	1.000	25	10	30	0	1
Lombard	.750	9	3	12	5	2
Montero	.898	55	33	64	11	11
Pastore	.833	7	4	6	2	1
Tejeda	.793	19	7	16	6	0

Shortstop	PCT	G	PO	A	E	DP
Arias	.926	84	92	184	22	40
Lombard	.951	44	71	124	10	25
Matheus	1.000	1	2	1	0	0
Montero	1.000	3	3	5	0	1
Peraza	1.000	1	1	1	0	0

Outfield	PCT	G	PO	A	E	DP
Aguilar	.973	19	36	0	1	0
Arias	.966	55	84	1	3	0
Castillo	.985	78	130	2	2	1
De Los Santos	1.000	14	25	1	0	0
Familia	1.000	4	4	0	0	0
Gonzalez	1.000	2	5	1	0	1
Hall	1.000	2	4	0	0	0
Jackson	1.000	3	4	0	0	0
Jones	1.000	9	19	2	0	0
Lewis	.963	11	26	0	1	0
Montero	.960	111	211	7	9	3
Montero	1.000	1	1	0	0	0
Morales	1.000	50	75	5	0	4
Perez	.857	4	12	0	2	0
Tejeda	1.000	1	1	0	0	0
Toole	1.000	16	24	0	0	0
Wilson	1.000	13	21	0	0	0

FCL YANKEES — *ROOKIE*

FLORIDA COMPLEX LEAGUE

Batting	B-T	Ht.	Wt.	DOB	AVG	OBP	SLG	G	PA	AB	R	H	2B	3B	HR	RBI	BB	HBP	SH	SF	SO	SB	CS	BB%	SO%
Altagracia, Ramiro	R-R	5-11	180	1-18-04	.333	.370	.429	24	46	42	4	14	1	0	1	10	2	1	0	1	9	0	1	4.35	19.57
Burt, Max	R-R	6-1	185	8-28-96	.000	.000	.000	1	5	5	0	0	0	0	0	0	0	0	0	0	2	0	0	0.00	40.00
Familia, Christopher	L-L	5-11	170	6-10-00	.550	.609	.850	6	23	20	3	11	3	0	1	3	3	0	0	0	3	0	0	13.04	13.04
Gomez, Antonio	R-R	6-2	210	11-13-01	.250	.400	.350	6	25	20	3	5	2	0	0	1	5	0	0	0	4	0	0	20.00	16.00
Gomez, Santiago	R-R	5-11	160	4-5-04	.321	.421	.420	36	95	81	16	26	2	0	2	16	7	7	0	0	22	9	7	7.37	23.16
Gonzalez, Josue	R-R	5-9	170	10-30-03	.240	.396	.446	36	154	121	20	29	7	0	6	22	22	10	0	1	30	4	0	14.29	19.48
Hall, Anthony	L-L	6-1	200	2-9-01	.400	.486	.667	8	35	30	7	12	2	0	2	8	5	0	0	0	9	2	0	14.29	25.71

Batting	B-T	Ht.	Wt.	DOB	AVG	OBP	SLG	G	PA	AB	R	H	2B	3B	HR	RBI	BB	HBP	SH	SF	SO	SB	CS	BB%	SO%
Hardman, Tyler	R-R	6-2	204	1-27-99	.000	.250	.000	2	8	6	2	0	0	0	0	0	1	1	0	0	2	0	0	12.50	25.00
Hernandez, Diomedes	R-R	5-11	165	2-6-05	.244	.295	.244	14	44	41	6	10	0	0	0	5	2	1	0	0	9	1	0	4.55	20.45
Matheus, Juan	B-R	5-10	155	4-29-04	.321	.429	.488	49	196	162	30	52	10	1	5	40	29	3	0	2	28	10	7	14.80	14.29
Mayea, Brando	R-R	5-11	175	9-12-05	.281	.370	.326	35	154	135	23	38	2	2	0	9	16	3	0	0	43	19	3	10.39	27.92
Mendez, Joel	R-R	6-1	180	1-28-03	.292	.405	.569	46	158	130	28	38	10	4	6	30	26	0	0	2	42	2	1	16.46	26.58
Montero, Fidel	R-R	6-0	178	12-19-03	.218	.333	.400	20	66	55	8	12	4	0	2	5	10	0	0	1	27	6	3	15.15	40.91
Ogando, Luis	R-R	5-10	175	10-11-03	.250	.361	.400	31	97	80	16	20	1	1	3	18	9	6	0	2	17	10	1	9.28	17.53
Perez, Edgleen	R-R	5-10	155	5-25-06	.283	.444	.380	51	216	166	35	47	8	1	2	24	45	4	0	1	35	4	1	20.83	16.20
Ramirez, Abrahan	L-R	5-9	150	10-8-04	.348	.447	.513	49	189	158	32	55	14	3	2	24	29	0	0	1	30	6	1	15.34	15.87
Rodriguez, Wilson	L-L	6-1	186	9-10-04	.152	.300	.152	11	40	33	6	5	0	0	0	4	7	0	0	0	15	1	2	17.50	37.50
Sanchez, Brian	L-R	6-3	170	7-4-04	.306	.394	.514	49	198	173	40	53	16	4	4	32	23	2	0	0	41	16	3	11.62	20.71
Sanchez, Juan	L-R	5-11	190	3-21-03	.000	1.000	.000	5	1	0	0	0	0	0	0	0	1	0	0	0	0	0	0	100.00	0.00
Tejeda, Enmanuel	R-R	5-11	158	12-25-04	.500	.556	.813	5	18	16	2	8	2	0	1	3	2	0	0	0	2	2	0	11.11	11.11
Terrero, Gabriel	B-R	5-6	169	9-26-05	.256	.392	.360	46	158	125	29	32	5	1	2	20	28	2	0	3	27	14	0	17.72	17.09
Tiedemann, Josh	R-R	6-2	190	6-9-04	.500	.667	.500	3	9	6	1	3	0	0	0	0	2	1	0	0	2	0	0	22.22	22.22
Urena, Engelth	R-R	5-11	196	8-17-04	.301	.420	.564	40	162	133	34	40	11	0	8	31	24	4	0	1	19	5	2	14.81	11.73

Pitching	B-T	Ht.	Wt.	DOB	W	L	ERA	G	GS	SV	IP	Hits	Runs	ER	HR	BB	SO	AVG	OBP	SLG	SO%	BB%	BF
Altagracia, Ramiro	R-R	5-11	180	1-18-04	1	0	15.43	4	0	0	2	5	5	4	1	3	1	.500	.625	.900	6.25	18.75	16
Arias, Brian	R-R	6-0	177	11-18-03	0	0	6.75	4	1	0	4	5	3	3	0	3	3	.333	.421	.400	15.79	15.79	19
Arias, Chalniel	R-R	6-3	165	9-11-03	0	1	1.59	3	1	0	6	3	1	1	0	0	5	.143	.143	.286	23.81	0.00	21
Benitez, Angel	R-R	6-7	204	9-10-03	1	1	1.74	5	3	0	10	5	6	2	0	12	12	.143	.354	.171	25.00	25.00	48
Boyle, Sean	R-R	6-1	205	10-29-96	0	0	12.00	2	2	0	3	8	4	4	0	0	3	.471	.471	.529	17.65	0.00	17
Brian, Will	L-L	5-11	220	4-25-99	0	1	16.20	1	0	0	2	3	3	3	0	1	1	.500	.571	.833	12.50	12.50	8
Brubaker, JT	R-R	6-3	185	11-17-93	0	0	4.50	1	1	0	4	1	2	2	1	1	0	.077	.143	.308	0.00	7.14	14
Castellanos, Jesus	R-R	5-11	175	1-28-02	3	3	3.63	12	0	2	17	15	9	7	1	11	16	.234	.359	.391	20.51	14.10	78
Cohen, Harrison	R-R	6-0	190	5-28-99	0	0	0.00	1	1	0	1	0	0	0	0	0	1	.000	.000	.000	33.33	0.00	3
Diaz, Indigo	R-R	6-5	250	10-14-98	0	0	0.00	3	2	0	4	2	0	0	0	0	4	.154	.154	.154	30.77	0.00	13
Diaz, Yoljeldriz	R-R	5-11	165	7-14-01	5	0	2.49	15	0	1	25	17	11	7	0	11	28	.181	.294	.191	25.69	10.09	109
Fernandez, Orvis	R-R	5-11	185	7-14-03	2	0	6.23	3	0	0	9	8	6	6	0	8	7	.242	.419	.273	16.28	18.60	43
Flatt, Danny	R-R	6-4	190	6-6-04	3	1	3.19	10	6	0	37	31	16	13	3	20	37	.228	.323	.346	22.98	12.42	161
Gerber, Joey	R-R	6-4	212	5-3-97	0	0	0.00	1	1	0	2	1	0	0	0	0	3	.143	.143	.143	42.86	0.00	7
Gomez, Alejandro	R-R	6-4	180	8-3-02	1	3	8.10	17	0	1	27	35	27	24	4	14	29	.321	.408	.523	22.31	10.77	130
Gomez, Santiago	R-R	5-11	160	4-5-04	0	1	21.60	7	0	1	5	17	14	12	3	7	1	.567	.658	.967	2.63	18.42	38
Gonzalez, Omar	R-R	6-4	175	7-25-05	0	0	6.94	10	4	0	23	12	19	18	2	19	21	.150	.320	.250	20.39	18.45	103
Guzman, Jose	R-R	5-11	185	12-26-01	4	0	6.88	13	0	1	17	20	15	13	4	14	16	.303	.440	.500	19.05	16.67	84
Hampton, Chase	R-R	6-2	225	8-7-01	0	0	2.70	2	2	0	3	3	1	1	0	4	4	.250	.438	.333	25.00	25.00	16
Hernandez, Diomedes	R-R	5-11	165	2-6-05	0	0	18.00	1	0	0	1	3	2	2	0	2	0	.500	.625	.833	0.00	25.00	8
Kean, Chris	R-R	6-5	210	6-12-02	1	1	1.31	14	1	1	21	6	5	3	0	3	27	.092	.141	.123	38.03	4.23	71
Lagrange, Carlos	R-R	6-7	195	5-25-03	0	0	6.75	4	3	0	7	4	5	5	1	7	8	.174	.355	.348	25.81	22.58	31
Lalane, Henry	L-L	6-7	211	5-18-04	1	1	4.26	3	1	0	6	3	3	3	1	4	6	.150	.280	.400	24.00	16.00	25
Landry, Andrew	R-R	6-1	175	2-20-02	1	0	1.93	4	0	0	9	9	2	2	1	3	14	.257	.316	.400	36.84	7.89	38
Liranzo, Jesus	R-R	6-2	225	3-7-95	0	1	8.10	3	3	0	3	4	3	3	1	2	4	.333	.429	.667	28.57	14.29	14
Luciano, Jordy	R-R	5-10	160	7-22-01	0	0	4.15	4	0	1	9	5	5	4	0	2	9	.172	.250	.207	28.13	6.25	32
Marte, Sabier	R-R	6-5	167	2-10-04	4	0	2.76	12	5	0	49	38	21	15	4	16	44	.204	.271	.296	21.36	7.77	206
Martina, Sunayro	R-R	6-3	165	10-9-03	2	1	8.53	11	3	0	19	19	22	18	1	13	23	.253	.406	.347	23.96	13.54	96
Mendoza, Jordarlin	R-R	6-0	175	11-14-03	0	0	3.14	5	2	0	14	15	11	5	1	11	24	.254	.397	.339	32.43	14.86	74
Moore, McKinley	R-R	6-6	225	8-24-98	0	0	3.00	3	3	0	3	1	1	1	0	2	6	.100	.308	.100	46.15	15.38	13
Nivar, Rafelin	L-L	5-10	160	10-21-01	2	0	4.05	7	0	0	13	15	14	6	4	8	14	.283	.381	.585	22.22	12.70	63
Ogando, Luis	R-R	5-10	175	10-11-03	0	0	0.00	1	0	0	1	0	1	0	0	0	0	.000	.000	.000	0.00	0.00	3
Pacheco, Luis	R-R	6-2	185	4-22-99	0	2	9.64	6	0	0	5	9	8	5	0	2	3	.375	.444	.417	11.11	7.41	27
Peres, Michael	L-L	6-0	180	9-18-03	1	0	7.71	13	0	1	14	12	18	12	1	27	20	.226	.500	.377	23.81	32.14	84
Reyzelman, Eric	R-R	6-2	188	6-27-01	0	0	0.00	4	1	0	6	2	0	0	0	1	9	.118	.211	.118	47.37	5.26	19
Rosario, Hansel	R-R	6-4	174	8-5-02	2	0	6.42	13	3	0	34	29	28	24	3	29	46	.228	.393	.370	28.22	17.79	163
Rose, Brady	L-L	6-5	220	10-26-00	0	1	8.10	2	0	1	7	7	7	6	1	3	4	.259	.344	.407	12.50	9.38	32
Ruiz, Yarison	R-R	6-4	216	3-26-00	0	2	11.57	8	2	0	7	4	13	9	0	9	11	.160	.436	.240	28.21	23.08	39
Sanchez, Juan	L-R	5-11	190	3-21-03	1	0	9.82	4	0	1	4	2	4	4	1	4	1	.167	.389	.417	5.56	22.22	18
Silverio, Oscar	L-R	5-9	170	10-25-01	0	0	47.25	2	0	0	1	5	7	7	3	3	0	.556	.667	1.556	0.00	25.00	12
Tiedemann, Josh	R-R	6-2	190	6-9-04	0	0	13.50	1	1	0	2	2	3	3	0	2	3	.222	.364	.222	27.27	18.18	11
Vinyard, Mason	R-R	6-2	210	6-22-99	0	0	0.00	1	0	0	1	0	0	0	0	0	4	.000	.000	.000	100.00	0.00	4
Vivas, Edison	R-R	6-0	184	6-3-06	0	0	13.50	1	0	0	1	1	2	1	0	2	0	.250	.500	.500	0.00	33.33	6
Warrecker, Bryce	L-R	6-8	225	9-13-01	0	2	4.05	5	5	0	13	13	7	6	1	1	13	.241	.268	.370	22.41	1.72	58

Fielding

C: Perez 34, Gonzalez 14, Urena 12, Silverio 1, Hernandez 1. **1B:** Gonzalez 22, Urena 18, Ogando 13, Hernandez 10. **2B:** Terrero 39, Ramirez 13, Gomez 10, Tejeda 3, Matheus 1. 3B: Ramirez 37, Ogando 17, Gomez 10. SS: Matheus 48, Gomez 8, Tejeda 2, Ramirez 1. LF: Sanchez 33, Mendez 23, Altagracia 4, Familia 4, Rodriguez 2, Gomez 1, Montero 1. **CF:** Mayea 34, Sanchez 20, Montero 7, Rodriguez 2, Mendez 1. **RF:** Mendez 25, Altagracia 15, Montero 12, Rodriguez 7, Hall 6, Sanchez 2, Vivas 1, Gomez 1.

DSL NYY BOMBERS — *ROOKIE*

DOMINICAN SUMMER LEAGUE

Batting	B-T	Ht.	Wt.	DOB	AVG	OBP	SLG	G	PA	AB	R	H	2B	3B	HR	RBI	BB	HBP	SH	SF	SO	SB	CS	BB%	SO%
Araujo, Juan	R-R	5-11	158	12-15-06	.200	.455	.267	11	22	15	3	3	1	0	0	2	6	1	0	0	5	2	1	27.27	22.73
Beckles, David	R-R	6-3	215	4-23-04	.000	.250	.000	3	4	3	0	0	0	0	0	0	1	0	0	0	0	0	0	25.00	0.00

Capellan, Justin	R-R	5-10	180	7-18-06	.282	.326	.436	11	43	39	9	11	3	0	1	10	2	1	0	1	8	4	0	4.65	18.60
Carrera, David	R-R	6-3	180	9-7-06	.276	.402	.418	35	122	98	19	27	10	2	0	25	15	7	0	2	32	11	2	12.30	26.23
Escudero, Luis	B-R	5-8	165	2-9-06	.287	.450	.418	44	160	122	34	35	5	4	1	19	34	3	0	1	12	26	5	21.25	7.50
Gonzalez, Adrian	R-R	6-2	170	3-31-05	.000	.400	.000	4	5	3	2	0	0	0	0	0	2	0	0	0	0	0	0	40.00	0.00
Javier, Andry	B-R	5-10	160	2-13-04	.200	.429	.200	3	7	5	1	1	0	0	0	2	1	1	0	0	0	0	1	14.29	0.00
Lacruz, Andres	B-R	5-10	158	1-25-05	.000	1.000	.000	1	1	0	0	0	0	0	0	0	1	0	0	0	0	0	0	100.00	0.00
Marquez, Jesus	R-R	6-0	183	9-2-06	.191	.284	.250	27	81	68	5	13	4	0	0	7	10	0	0	3	18	1	1	12.35	22.22
Martinez, Browm	R-R	5-10	161	11-26-06	.278	.386	.313	38	140	115	21	32	4	0	0	19	15	7	0	3	25	21	6	10.71	17.86
Martinez, Rafael	R-R	5-10	160	10-23-05	.269	.361	.308	23	61	52	8	14	2	0	0	6	8	0	0	1	11	3	2	13.11	18.03
Meran, Richard	R-R	6-0	165	6-25-06	.231	.344	.298	32	122	104	19	24	5	1	0	14	12	6	0	0	41	7	2	9.84	33.61
Pena, Anthony	R-R	5-10	157	12-27-05	.136	.269	.136	14	26	22	3	3	0	0	0	2	3	1	0	0	9	1	0	11.54	34.62
Pineda, Queni	R-R	5-10	190	5-29-07	.254	.434	.438	44	173	130	32	33	9	0	5	15	41	1	0	1	39	5	3	23.70	22.54
Reyes, Cristofer	R-R	5-10	154	8-23-07	.250	.346	.314	44	179	156	31	39	5	1	1	22	18	5	0	0	41	21	9	10.06	22.91
Rondon, Carlos	R-R	6-0	190	2-16-06	.130	.355	.130	21	62	46	10	6	0	0	0	4	13	3	0	0	19	2	1	20.97	30.65
Suarez, Luis	R-R	5-9	143	10-5-04	.300	.352	.360	25	54	50	6	15	3	0	0	7	4	0	0	0	10	3	2	7.41	18.52
Veldhuisen, Remy	L-R	6-2	190	2-11-05	.254	.407	.302	26	81	63	14	16	3	0	0	8	10	7	0	1	16	3	1	12.35	19.75
Ventura, Angel	R-R	6-1	165	3-10-06	.245	.336	.276	33	113	98	21	24	1	1	0	13	8	6	0	1	30	18	2	7.08	26.55
Verde, Kevin	R-R	5-9	160	12-12-05	.235	.282	.328	36	131	119	20	28	7	2	0	19	9	0	0	3	19	9	2	6.87	14.50
Villarroel, Carlos	R-R	6-1	188	6-4-07	.299	.390	.410	36	136	117	19	35	7	0	2	15	17	1	0	1	31	2	4	12.50	22.79
Vilorio, Francisco	R-R	6-4	212	10-31-06	.196	.294	.345	42	170	148	22	29	8	1	4	19	16	5	0	1	56	8	4	9.41	32.94
Vivas, Edison	R-R	6-0	184	6-3-06	.200	.429	.300	5	14	10	2	2	1	0	0	1	3	1	0	0	5	4	1	21.43	35.71

Pitching	B-T	Ht.	Wt.	DOB	W	L	ERA	G	GS	SV	IP	Hits	Runs	ER	HR	BB	SO	AVG	OBP	SLG	SO%	BB%	BF
Alejandro, Jerson	R-R	6-6	255	2-23-06	1	5	5.02	12	11	0	38	23	24	21	0	34	57	.178	.406	.248	31.67	18.89	180
Almonte, Carlos	R-R	6-5	220	8-18-03	2	1	2.86	10	4	0	28	23	15	9	0	11	22	.213	.307	.315	17.32	8.66	127
Araujo, Juan	R-R	5-11	158	12-15-06	0	0	0.00	1	0	0	1	1	0	0	0	0	1	.333	.333	.333	33.33	0.00	3
Arias, Rafael	R-R	6-2	190	11-5-03	1	0	1.23	4	0	0	7	4	1	1	0	2	11	.154	.214	.154	39.29	7.14	28
Brinez, Saul	R-R	6-3	170	11-10-04	2	1	4.41	8	1	0	16	15	12	8	0	11	18	.238	.364	.286	23.38	14.29	77
Burgos, Luis	R-R	6-2	186	9-6-05	0	0	3.86	2	0	0	2	2	1	1	0	1	2	.250	.333	.375	22.22	11.11	9
Delgadillo, Ismael	R-R	6-0	184	5-26-05	0	0	2.84	4	0	1	6	5	6	2	0	6	6	.227	.367	.409	20.00	20.00	30
Gomez, Chaury	R-R	6-1	166	11-6-06	1	2	9.31	9	0	0	10	5	11	10	0	16	6	.156	.453	.188	11.32	30.19	53
Herrera, Franyer	L-L	6-0	165	5-3-05	5	1	2.01	12	11	0	49	43	17	11	1	17	64	.235	.305	.301	31.53	8.37	203
Javier, Andry	S-R	5-10	160	2-13-04	0	0	0.00	1	0	0	1	2	0	0	0	0	2	.400	.400	.400	40.00	0.00	5
Jimenez, Richard	R-R	6-0	150	5-16-05	1	0	4.35	10	0	2	10	10	6	5	0	9	8	.256	.412	.385	15.69	17.65	51
Lampson, Joshawn	R-R	6-1	185	6-23-05	3	0	4.32	11	6	0	33	31	17	16	0	19	31	.250	.382	.371	20.39	12.50	152
Ledesma, Jose	L-L	6-0	170	4-10-03	2	0	1.25	18	0	8	22	10	6	3	0	14	28	.139	.279	.194	32.56	16.28	86
Leito, Joshua	R-R	5-10	170	3-20-05	1	1	6.75	11	0	0	17	26	17	13	3	5	15	.347	.378	.613	18.29	6.10	82
Manzano, Marco	L-L	6-3	176	8-24-03	0	0	0.00	1	0	0	2	2	1	0	0	1	4	.250	.300	.250	40.00	10.00	10
Martinez, Rafael	R-R	5-10	160	10-23-05	0	1	0.00	1	0	0	1	1	1	0	0	1	0	.250	.400	.250	0.00	20.00	5
Mena, Anthony	R-R	6-2	173	10-12-04	1	3	5.68	11	0	0	19	31	17	12	2	4	18	.352	.376	.443	19.35	4.30	93
Paulino, Alexis	R-R	6-0	175	5-5-03	1	1	7.86	12	1	1	26	17	26	23	1	19	35	.181	.353	.234	29.41	15.97	119
Pena, Anthony	R-R	5-10	157	12-27-05	0	0	27.00	2	0	0	1	5	3	3	0	0	0	.625	.667	.875	0.00	0.00	9
Rosario, Jose	R-R	6-2	194	8-2-05	1	0	9.00	15	0	1	15	17	19	15	1	12	17	.288	.405	.441	22.67	16.00	75
Salomon, Mariano	R-R	6-3	185	8-5-02	4	2	2.80	10	8	0	45	36	16	14	5	10	56	.214	.260	.369	30.94	5.52	181
Sanchez, Enixon	R-R	6-0	150	7-7-07	3	1	2.79	10	7	0	29	14	13	9	0	16	29	.143	.292	.204	24.17	13.33	120
Suarez, Luis	R-R	5-9	143	10-5-04	0	0	0.00	3	0	0	4	4	1	0	0	0	4	.235	.235	.235	23.53	0.00	17
Tavera, Junior	L-L	6-0	184	5-23-07	0	3	8.82	8	6	0	16	16	18	16	1	21	22	.262	.446	.459	26.51	25.30	83
Vargas, Mauricio	R-R	6-0	160	2-6-07	1	0	4.50	8	0	0	8	6	5	4	0	12	8	.214	.452	.286	19.05	28.57	42
Villarreal, Varis	R-R	5-11	157	7-1-05	0	0	3.46	10	0	0	13	6	6	5	2	7	9	.150	.280	.325	18.00	14.00	50

Fielding

C: Pineda 32, Rondon 13, Villarroel 11, Capellan 5, Marquez 3, Vivas 1. **1B:** Villarroel 20, Marquez 19, Veldhuisen 8, Rondon 5, Vivas 4, Beckles 3, Gonzalez 1, Javier 1. **2B:** Escudero 39, Martinez 9, Araujo 7, Reyes 3, Suarez 2, Verde 1, Pena 1. **3B:** Verde 24, Suarez 12, Martinez 11, Pena 7, Escudero 4, Gonzalez 1, Javier 1, Araujo 1. **SS:** Reyes 41, Verde 12, Suarez 5. **LF:** Martinez 18, Veldhuisen 17, Meran 9, Ventura 8, Carrera 7, Gonzalez 1, Lacruz 1. **CF:** Vilorio 35, Martinez 11, Ventura 8, Carrera 7, Meran 1. RF: Meran 19, Carrera 18, Ventura 15, Martinez 6, Martinez 1.

DSL NYY YANKEES — *ROOKIE*

DOMINICAN SUMMER LEAGUE

Batting	B-T	Ht.	Wt.	DOB	AVG	OBP	SLG	G	PA	AB	R	H	2B	3B	HR	RBI	BB	HBP	SH	SF	SO	SB	CS	BB%	SO%
Arias, Isael	R-R	6-0	178	8-11-05	.246	.379	.325	38	140	114	23	28	2	2	1	12	19	6	0	1	21	10	1	13.57	15.00
Asigen, Niurby	L-L	6-3	180	11-6-04	.279	.408	.311	23	76	61	11	17	2	0	0	9	13	1	0	1	15	8	1	17.11	19.74
Blanco, Geyber	R-R	5-9	155	6-11-06	.202	.267	.311	35	131	119	15	24	10	0	1	17	8	3	0	1	31	2	1	6.11	23.66
Capellan, Justin	R-R	5-10	180	7-18-06	.225	.381	.326	30	113	89	7	20	9	0	0	15	15	8	0	1	25	7	2	13.27	22.12
Coca, Jeison	R-R	5-11	158	11-10-05	.127	.258	.215	27	93	79	11	10	3	2	0	7	14	0	0	0	26	3	1	15.05	27.96
Contreras, Johan	R-R	6-1	218	3-10-05	.167	.255	.238	18	47	42	3	7	0	0	1	7	5	0	0	0	18	0	0	10.64	38.30
Flores, Diego	R-R	5-11	160	3-10-07	.162	.279	.162	15	43	37	4	6	0	0	0	4	4	2	0	0	9	2	1	9.30	20.93
Frias, Ovandy	R-R	6-0	176	1-12-04	.243	.391	.486	15	46	37	6	9	0	0	3	5	9	0	0	0	9	0	2	19.57	19.57
Gonzalez, Adrian	R-R	6-2	170	3-31-05	.111	.194	.111	11	31	27	1	3	0	0	0	2	2	1	0	1	6	0	0	6.45	19.35
Gonzalez, Diego	L-R	5-11	155	3-30-07	.050	.208	.050	6	24	20	1	1	0	0	0	3	4	0	0	0	6	0	0	16.67	25.00
Imbert, Jhon	R-R	6-1	172	9-1-03	.000	.625	.000	2	8	3	3	0	0	0	0	1	5	0	0	0	3	1	0	62.50	37.50
Jimenez, Edgar	R-R	5-10	165	11-3-06	.176	.200	.275	18	55	51	4	9	2	0	1	6	2	0	0	2	18	2	0	3.64	32.73
Lara, Gabriel	L-L	5-9	165	11-27-05	.202	.322	.250	38	146	124	19	25	1	1	1	6	18	4	0	0	19	14	4	12.33	13.01
Matic, Richard	R-R	6-0	200	7-26-07	.196	.333	.248	46	186	153	22	30	8	0	0	14	23	9	0	1	43	6	2	12.37	23.12
Medina, Dilan	R-R	6-2	190	9-29-05	.277	.370	.319	17	54	47	6	13	2	0	0	5	4	3	0	0	13	1	1	7.41	24.07
Montero, Estivenzon	R-R	6-1	189	10-9-06	.242	.361	.364	31	119	99	11	24	5	2	1	22	17	2	0	1	33	4	1	14.29	27.73

Peralta, Dexters	B-R	6-1	170	7-11-07	.219	.320	.325	46	194	169	33	37	7	1	3	13	21	4	0	0	57	26	4	10.82	29.38
Pierre, Louis	L-L	6-2	160	9-12-04	.180	.341	.252	39	138	111	17	20	4	2	0	6	25	2	0	0	44	13	3	18.12	31.88
Puello, Luis	R-R	5-11	162	1-22-06	.361	.439	.516	37	139	122	22	44	5	1	4	17	11	6	0	0	27	3	0	7.91	19.42
Rondon, Carlos	R-R	6-0	190	2-16-06	.133	.350	.133	7	20	15	2	2	0	0	0	1	5	0	0	0	5	1	0	25.00	25.00
Zapata, Yael	R-R	6-0	183	2-26-06	.037	.278	.037	11	36	27	2	1	0	0	0	3	5	4	0	0	21	3	0	13.89	58.33

Pitching	B-T	Ht.	Wt.	DOB	W	L	ERA	G	GS	SV	IP	Hits	Runs	ER	HR	BB	SO	AVG	OBP	SLG	SO%	BB%	BF
Alcantara, Stanly	R-R	6-6	187	4-12-04	0	5	17.84	12	0	0	19	28	40	37	2	34	16	.364	.598	.532	13.11	27.87	122
Almonte, Alexander	R-R	6-4	205	9-14-06	0	3	3.51	9	9	0	26	20	14	10	3	12	26	.220	.318	.363	23.85	11.01	109
Arias, Rafael	R-R	6-2	190	11-5-03	0	2	2.35	9	0	0	8	6	4	2	1	4	10	.214	.353	.357	29.41	11.76	34
Burgos, Luis	R-R	6-2	186	9-6-05	1	0	5.26	12	2	0	26	24	21	15	1	18	21	.250	.373	.302	17.80	15.25	118
Chirinos, Michell	R-R	6-2	187	12-9-03	0	6	5.52	10	8	0	31	29	25	19	2	24	46	.250	.409	.405	30.87	16.11	149
Contreras, Johan	R-R	6-1	218	3-10-05	1	0	0.00	2	0	0	1	2	0	0	0	0	2	.333	.333	.333	33.33	0.00	6
Delgadillo, Ismael	R-R	6-0	184	5-26-05	1	1	4.15	6	0	0	13	10	8	6	0	10	7	.213	.393	.298	11.29	16.13	62
Diaz, Keninson	R-R	6-2	180	3-30-04	3	2	3.00	17	0	1	27	13	12	9	0	19	34	.138	.302	.213	29.31	16.38	116
Frias, Ovandy	R-R	6-0	170	1-12-04	0	0	0.00	2	0	0	1	1	0	0	0	0	1	.167	.167	.167	16.67	0.00	6
Gomez, Chaury	R-R	6-1	166	11-6-06	0	0	3.38	4	0	0	5	6	3	2	0	2	10	.273	.320	.273	40.00	8.00	25
Gonzalez, Adrian	R-R	6-2	170	3-31-05	0	0	0.00	1	0	0	1	0	2	0	0	1	0	.000	.167	.000	0.00	16.67	6
Imbert, Jhon	R-R	6-1	172	9-1-03	0	0	9.00	1	0	0	1	1	1	1	1	1	1	.250	.571	1.000	14.29	14.29	7
Jimenez, Richard	R-R	6-0	150	5-16-05	0	0	0.00	2	0	1	4	2	0	0	0	6	4	.167	.444	.167	22.22	33.33	18
Lampson, Joshawn	R-R	6-1	185	6-23-05	0	1	18.00	1	1	0	2	3	4	4	0	5	1	.375	.571	.625	7.14	35.71	14
Luna, Jorge	R-R	6-0	165	11-4-04	1	4	3.64	12	10	0	42	34	26	17	3	18	51	.218	.311	.340	28.18	9.94	181
Manzano, Marco	L-L	6-3	176	8-24-03	1	3	4.91	9	4	0	26	20	24	14	0	22	27	.208	.376	.260	21.43	17.46	126
Marquez, Edinzo	R-R	6-2	208	12-16-04	1	1	3.45	12	12	0	44	38	21	17	0	20	50	.232	.319	.293	26.88	10.75	186
Mejia, Jesus	R-R	6-1	170	8-8-05	1	1	3.60	10	0	2	15	14	7	6	1	11	13	.246	.419	.439	17.57	14.86	74
Paulino, Alexis	R-R	6-0	175	5-5-03	0	0	1.80	3	0	0	5	3	6	1	0	6	9	.167	.393	.167	32.14	21.43	28
Rodriguez, Miguelangel	R-R	6-4	195	6-2-03	0	1	3.21	7	0	0	14	13	7	5	0	9	12	.265	.406	.347	18.75	14.06	64
Silvestre, Josue	R-R	6-7	198	7-13-04	0	1	5.40	10	0	0	10	7	10	6	1	12	11	.194	.420	.306	21.57	23.53	51
Tejada, Ronald	L-L	6-3	160	1-11-07	3	0	1.75	17	0	1	26	15	8	5	0	12	24	.163	.262	.228	22.43	11.21	107
Vargas, Emanuel	R-R	6-1	178	10-10-05	0	3	5.00	8	8	0	18	14	13	10	3	12	19	.203	.337	.362	22.62	14.29	84
Vasquez, Christopher	R-R	5-11	168	9-12-06	2	0	7.80	12	0	0	15	15	13	13	2	13	9	.273	.408	.418	12.68	18.31	71
Vasquez, Oscar	R-R	6-1	170	12-11-04	2	2	7.20	10	0	0	20	17	18	16	2	13	23	.224	.362	.395	24.47	13.83	94
Villarreal, Varis	R-R	5-11	157	7-1-05	0	1	5.79	7	0	0	9	8	6	6	1	4	11	.235	.308	.382	28.21	10.26	39

Fielding

C: Puello 24, Capellan 23, Rondon 7, Contreras 3, Flores 2, Jimenez 1. **1B:** Asigen 18, Contreras 13, Gonzalez 9, Puello 6, Jimenez 5, Flores 5, Imbert 2, Gonzalez 1. **2B:** Blanco 24, Coca 15, Jimenez 10, Frias 6, Araujo 1. **3B:** Matic 40, Blanco 10, Frias 3, Gonzalez 2, Coca 2, Jimenez 1. **SS:** Peralta 40, Coca 10, Frias 5. **LF:** Lara 23, Medina 8, Montero 8, Arias 8, Asigen 4, Zapata 3, Puello 2, Pierre 1. **CF:** Arias 22, Pierre 19, Lara 14. **RF:** Montero 24, Pierre 14, Medina 8, Zapata 4, Arias 4, Asigen 1.

Oakland Athletics

SEASON SYNOPSIS: The final season of the franchise in Oakland—the plan is to play in Sacramento for the next three seasons en route to an eventual move to Las Vegas—was bittersweet for Athletics fans, as a power-packed offense avoided a third straight last-place finish by posting a .500 record in the second half. The 69-93 A's said goodbye by ranking third in the league in home runs and last in the AL, again, in attendance.

HIGH POINT: Picked to be the majors' worst team, Oakland lost seven of its first eight but rallied to get to .500 at 17-17 following a six-game winning streak, capped May 4 with a 20-4 thrashing of Miami. The A's hit six homers, two by Brent Rooker, who went on to hit 39 homers in an all-star .293/.365/.562 campaign.

LOW POINT: Oakland and Texas played a four-game series in early May with a doubleheader, with total attendance of 15,090. But the A's last home game at the Coliseum came before a sellout crowd of 46,889 and included Barry Zito singing the national anthem and first pitches from Rickey Henderson and Dave Stewart. Rookie Mason Miller closed out the 3-2 victory against Texas, converting his 16th consecutive save chance. As Rangers second baseman (and Bay Area native, Cal grad and former Athletic) Marcus Semien put it, "It's pretty sad, because there are a lot of people who love this team in Oakland, and I don't know how the support is going to be anywhere else. So, pretty tough."

NOTABLE ROOKIES: Miller was baseball's hardest thrower, averaging 100.9 mph on his fastball, and led MLB with a 41.8% strikeout rate. Max Schuemann, a 20th-round pick in 2018, surprisingly emerged as Oakland's regular shortstop, batting .220/.311/.308 with 14 stolen bases. Rookies started 68 games for the A's on the mound, led by Rule 5 pick Mitch Spence (8-10, 4.58) and lefty Joey Estes (7-9, 5.01), who made 24 apiece, and hard-throwing righty Joey Boyle (3-6, 6.42), whose fastball averaged 97.7 mph.

KEY TRANSACTIONS: Spence was the No. 1 pick in the 2023 Rule 5 draft and was a big win. He ranked second on the team with 151 innings pitched, especially crucial as free-agent stopgaps Ross Stripling and Alex Wood both struggled with performance and health in the rotation. Oakland traded righthander Paul Blackburn, a member of its rotation (when healthy) since 2017, to the Mets in late July.

OPENING DAY PAYROLL: $60,503,298 (30th)

PLAYERS OF THE YEAR

MAJOR LEAGUE

Brent Rooker
DH
.293/.365/.562
39 HR, 112 RBIs
82 R, 59 BB

MINOR LEAGUE

Colby Thomas
OF
(AA/AAA)
.277/.342/.563
31 HR, 44 2B, 15 SB

ORGANIZATION LEADERS

Batting		***Qualifiers**
MAJORS		
* AVG	Brent Rooker	.293
* OPS	Brent Rooker	.927
HR	Brent Rooker	39
RBI	Brent Rooker	112
MINORS		
* AVG	Nate Nankil, Stockton, Lansing	.303
* OBP	Nate Nankil, Stockton, Lansing	.404
* SLG	Colby Thomas, Midland/Las Vegas	.563
* OPS	Colby Thomas, Midland/Las Vegas	.905
R	Henry Bolte, Midland/Lansing	92
H	Colby Thomas, Midland/Las Vegas	142
TB	Colby Thomas, Midland/Las Vegas	289
2B	Colby Thomas, Midland/Las Vegas	44
3B	Denzel Clarke, Midland/Mesa	8
3B	Henry Bolte, Midland/Lansing	8
HR	Colby Thomas, Midland/Las Vegas	31
RBI	Colby Thomas, Midland/Las Vegas	92
BB	Ryan Noda, Las Vegas	89
SO	Henry Bolte, Midland/Lansing	189
SB	Henry Bolte, Midland/Lansing	46

Pitching		**#Qualifiers**
MAJORS		
W	JP Sears	11
# ERA	Paul Blackburn	4.38
SO	JP Sears	137
SV	Mason Miller	28
MINORS		
W	Blake Beers, Midland/Las Vegas	11
L	Blaze Pontes, Lansing	9
L	Aaron Brooks, Las Vegas	9
# ERA	James Gonzalez, Lansing/Midland/Las Vegas	3.41
G	Pedro Santos, Midland/Las Vegas	48
GS	Blake Beers, Midland/Las Vegas	24
SV	Seth Elledge, Midland	11
IP	Blake Beers, Midland/Las Vegas	150
BB	Drew Conover, 4 teams	64
SO	Blake Beers, Midland/Las Vegas	139
# AVG	Gunnar Hoglund, Midland/Las Vegas	.197

2024 PERFORMANCE

General Manager: David Forst. **Farm Director:** Ed Sprague. **Scouting Director:** Eric Kubota.

Class	Team	League	W	L	PCT	Finish	Manager
Majors	Oakland Athletics	American	69	93	.426	13 (15)	Mark Kotsay
Triple-A	Las Vegas Aviators	Pacific Coast	74	75	.497	6 (10)	Fran Riordan
Double-A	Midland RockHounds	Texas	84	54	.609	2 (10)	Gregorio Petit
High-A	Lansing Lugnuts	Midwest	59	72	.450	9 (12)	Craig Conklin
Low-A	Stockton Ports	California	46	84	.354	8 (8)	Javier Godard
Rookie	ACL Athletics	Arizona Complex	24	36	.400	13 (15)	Tim Esmay
Rookie	DSL Athletics	Dominican	22	33	.400	40 (51)	Cooper Goldby
Overall 2024 Minor League Record			**309**	**354**	**.466**	**25th (30)**	

ORGANIZATION STATISTICS

OAKLAND ATHLETICS

AMERICAN LEAGUE

Batting	B-T	Ht.	Wt.	DOB	AVG	OBP	SLG	G	PA	AB	R	H	2B	3B	HR	RBI	BB	HBP	SH	SF	SO	SB	CS	BB%	SO%
Allen, Nick	R-R	5-8	166	10-8-98	.175	.216	.247	41	105	97	6	17	4	0	1	4	5	0	3	0	20	0	0	4.76	19.05
Alvarez, Armando	R-R	6-0	195	7-14-94	.243	.282	.270	16	39	37	7	9	1	0	0	2	2	0	0	0	8	1	0	5.13	20.51
Andujar, Miguel	R-R	6-0	211	3-2-95	.285	.320	.377	75	319	302	31	86	14	1	4	30	13	3	0	1	42	3	2	4.08	13.17
Bleday, JJ	L-L	6-2	205	11-10-97	.243	.324	.437	159	642	572	74	139	43	4	20	60	67	2	1	0	125	2	3	10.44	19.47
Brown, Seth	L-L	6-1	223	7-13-92	.231	.283	.379	124	400	372	32	86	11	1	14	44	25	2	0	1	112	4	2	6.25	28.00
Butler, Lawrence	L-R	6-3	210	7-10-00	.262	.317	.490	125	451	412	63	108	24	2	22	57	35	0	0	4	108	18	0	7.76	23.95
Cameron, Daz	R-R	6-2	185	1-15-97	.200	.258	.329	66	186	170	22	34	5	1	5	15	13	1	0	2	51	5	0	6.99	27.42
Davis, J.D.	R-R	6-3	218	4-27-93	.236	.304	.366	39	135	123	12	29	4	0	4	5	9	3	0	0	30	0	0	6.67	22.22
Diaz, Aledmys	R-R	6-1	195	8-1-90	.103	.133	.103	12	30	29	2	3	0	0	0	1	1	0	0	0	7	0	0	3.33	23.33
Gelof, Zack	R-R	6-2	205	10-19-99	.211	.270	.362	138	547	497	60	105	20	2	17	49	38	4	3	5	188	25	3	6.95	34.37
Gray, Tristan	L-R	6-1	215	3-22-96	.143	.250	.190	8	24	21	0	3	1	0	0	0	3	0	0	0	13	0	0	12.50	54.17
Harris, Brett	R-R	6-1	208	6-24-98	.146	.276	.262	36	123	103	15	15	3	0	3	12	17	2	0	1	25	0	3	13.82	20.33
Hernaiz, Darell	R-R	5-11	190	8-3-01	.192	.261	.242	48	135	120	8	23	3	0	1	12	11	1	1	2	27	1	1	8.15	20.00
Langeliers, Shea	R-R	6-0	205	11-18-97	.224	.288	.450	137	534	482	58	108	18	2	29	80	41	5	0	6	145	4	2	7.68	27.15
McCann, Kyle	L-R	6-2	217	12-2-97	.236	.318	.371	54	157	140	13	33	4	0	5	15	16	1	0	0	59	0	0	10.19	37.58
Nevin, Tyler	R-R	6-4	225	5-29-97	.204	.288	.331	87	278	245	22	50	10	0	7	20	25	5	0	3	64	1	0	8.99	23.02
Noda, Ryan	L-L	6-3	217	3-30-96	.137	.255	.211	36	111	95	8	13	4	0	1	4	14	1	1	0	37	0	0	12.61	33.33
Rooker, Brent	R-R	6-4	225	11-1-94	.293	.365	.562	145	614	546	82	160	26	2	39	112	59	5	0	4	177	11	3	9.61	28.83
Ruiz, Esteury	R-R	6-0	169	2-15-99	.200	.270	.382	29	65	55	10	11	2	1	2	8	4	2	2	2	20	5	4	6.15	30.77
Schuemann, Max	R-R	5-11	186	6-11-97	.220	.311	.308	133	459	396	55	87	14	0	7	34	47	7	5	4	119	14	1	10.24	25.93
Soderstrom, Tyler	L-R	6-1	200	11-24-01	.233	.315	.429	61	213	189	18	44	10	0	9	26	20	3	0	1	53	0	0	9.39	24.88
Toro, Abraham	B-R	6-0	223	12-20-96	.240	.293	.350	94	364	337	34	81	17	1	6	26	20	5	2	0	62	4	2	5.49	17.03
Wilson, Jacob	R-R	6-3	190	3-30-02	.250	.314	.315	28	103	92	11	23	2	2	0	3	8	1	1	1	10	0	0	7.77	9.71

Pitching	B-T	Ht.	Wt.	DOB	W	L	ERA	G	GS	SV	IP	Hits	Runs	ER	HR	BB	SO	AVG	OBP	SLG	SO%	BB%	BF
Adams, Austin	R-R	6-3	220	5-5-91	1	2	3.92	56	0	0	41	38	20	18	4	23	53	.250	.389	.408	27.75	12.04	191
Alexander, Scott	L-L	6-2	195	7-10-89	1	3	2.56	45	0	0	39	31	14	11	3	15	31	.223	.304	.338	19.38	9.38	160
Basso, Brady	R-L	6-2	213	10-8-97	1	1	4.03	7	4	0	22	23	10	10	3	5	19	.264	.301	.379	20.43	5.38	93
Bido, Osvaldo	R-R	6-3	175	10-18-95	5	3	3.41	16	9	0	63	43	25	24	3	26	63	.192	.295	.286	24.32	10.04	259
Bielak, Brandon	L-R	6-2	208	4-2-96	1	0	4.38	6	0	0	12	17	6	6	2	6	5	.333	.404	.569	8.77	10.53	57
Blackburn, Paul	R-R	6-1	196	12-4-93	4	2	4.41	9	9	0	51	45	25	25	8	14	38	.233	.288	.415	18.27	6.73	208
Boyle, Joe	R-R	6-7	240	8-14-99	3	6	6.42	13	10	0	48	42	35	34	4	40	56	.235	.382	.346	24.78	17.70	226
Brooks, Aaron	R-R	6-4	230	4-27-90	0	2	5.06	5	4	0	27	33	19	15	4	8	12	.308	.353	.486	10.08	6.72	119
Erceg, Lucas	L-R	6-2	214	5-1-95	2	3	3.68	38	0	3	37	31	17	15	3	13	41	.225	.314	.348	26.28	8.33	156
Estes, Joey	R-R	6-2	190	10-8-01	7	9	5.01	25	24	0	128	130	73	71	23	27	92	.259	.308	.473	16.94	4.97	543
Ferguson, Tyler	R-R	6-4	225	10-5-93	4	2	3.68	48	0	2	51	32	23	21	4	24	62	.178	.282	.306	29.95	11.59	207
Ginn, J.T.	R-R	6-2	200	5-20-99	1	1	4.24	8	6	0	34	36	16	16	4	9	29	.275	.331	.405	20.42	6.34	142
Harris, Hogan	R-L	6-3	230	12-26-96	4	4	2.86	21	9	0	72	65	29	23	7	33	61	.244	.333	.391	20.00	10.82	305
Holman, Grant	R-R	6-6	250	5-31-00	1	1	4.02	18	0	0	16	17	8	7	1	9	16	.270	.370	.365	21.92	12.33	73
Jimenez, Dany	R-R	6-1	182	12-23-93	1	3	4.91	25	0	1	26	21	18	14	6	19	25	.223	.350	.500	21.37	16.24	117
Junk, Janson	R-R	6-2	202	1-15-96	0	0	0.00	1	0	0	0	6	7	7	1	2	0	1.000	1.000	1.833	0.00	25.00	8
Kelly, Michael	R-R	6-4	185	9-6-92	3	2	2.59	28	0	0	31	27	11	9	2	10	22	.241	.315	.357	17.19	7.81	128
Klein, Will	R-R	6-5	230	11-28-99	0	0	27.00	3	0	0	2	2	5	5	0	4	1	.333	.545	.500	9.09	36.36	11
Lucas, Easton	L-L	6-4	180	9-23-96	0	0	14.73	3	0	0	4	8	7	6	0	3	6	.400	.478	.500	26.09	13.04	23
McFarland, T.J.	L-L	6-3	200	6-8-89	2	4	3.81	79	0	0	57	53	28	24	4	17	39	.252	.316	.367	16.60	7.23	235
Medina, Luis	R-R	6-1	175	5-3-99	2	4	5.18	8	8	0	40	43	24	23	4	20	32	.276	.356	.417	17.78	11.11	180
Miller, Mason	R-R	6-5	200	8-24-98	2	2	2.49	55	0	28	65	36	23	18	6	21	104	.160	.233	.262	41.77	8.43	249
Muller, Kyle	R-L	6-7	250	10-7-97	0	1	4.01	21	0	0	49	48	25	22	6	10	36	.255	.292	.404	17.82	4.95	202
Newcomb, Sean	L-L	6-5	255	6-12-93	1	0	6.30	7	0	0	10	9	7	7	2	8	7	.257	.409	.457	15.56	17.78	45
Nittoli, Vinny	R-R	6-1	210	11-11-90	0	1	2.25	7	0	0	8	8	2	2	1	2	5	.267	.313	.400	15.63	6.25	32
O'Loughlin, Jack	L-L	6-5	223	3-14-00	0	0	4.66	4	0	0	10	13	5	5	1	5	6	.310	.383	.429	12.77	10.64	47
Otanez, Michel	R-R	6-4	218	7-3-97	1	0	3.44	36	0	1	34	27	15	13	2	20	55	.214	.331	.302	36.42	13.25	151
Reyes, Gerardo	R-R	5-11	195	5-13-93	0	0	4.50	3	0	0	4	4	3	2	0	3	2	.267	.389	.400	11.11	16.67	18

Pitching	B-T	Ht.	Wt.	DOB	W	L	ERA	G	GS	SV	IP	Hits	Runs	ER	HR	BB	SO	AVG	OBP	SLG	SO%	BB%	BF
Sears, JP	R-L	5-11	180	2-19-96	11	13	4.38	32	32	0	181	172	93	88	28	49	137	.251	.311	.439	18.07	6.46	758
Spence, Mitch	R-R	6-1	185	5-6-98	8	10	4.58	35	24	0	151	165	79	77	20	44	126	.276	.331	.455	19.35	6.76	651
Stripling, Ross	R-R	6-1	215	11-23-89	2	11	6.01	22	14	0	85	109	65	57	7	22	49	.309	.347	.453	12.86	5.77	381
Wood, Alex	R-L	6-4	215	1-12-91	1	3	5.26	9	9	0	39	51	27	23	6	19	33	.323	.408	.519	17.74	10.22	186

Fielding

Catcher	PCT	G	PO	A	E	DP	PB
Langeliers	.995	131	1007	51	5	5	7
McCann	.987	44	288	12	4	2	5
Soderstrom	1.000	1	4	1	0	0	0

First Base	PCT	G	PO	A	E	DP
Alvarez	1.000	5	22	0	0	4
Brown	.992	45	227	25	2	17
Davis	.993	24	122	13	1	14
Diaz	1.000	4	16	3	0	1
Gray	1.000	7	25	2	0	4
Nevin	.991	38	201	13	2	18
Noda	.990	30	177	18	2	24
Soderstrom	.992	59	373	23	3	47
Toro	1.000	5	21	2	0	3

Second Base	PCT	G	PO	A	E	DP
Allen	1.000	2	0	2	0	1
Alvarez	1.000	1	1	0	0	0
Diaz	1.000	1	0	3	0	1
Gelof	.988	138	264	332	7	92
Hernaiz	1.000	3	3	1	0	0
Schuemann	1.000	9	7	15	0	5
Toro	1.000	19	25	39	0	10

Third Base	PCT	G	PO	A	E	DP
Allen	1.000	5	4	6	0	1
Alvarez	1.000	6	3	9	0	0
Davis	1.000	14	7	13	0	3
Diaz	1.000	1	1	0	0	0
Gray	1.000	2	3	5	0	0
Harris	.963	35	20	59	3	9
Hernaiz	.964	32	17	37	2	6
Nevin	.951	25	14	25	2	7
Schuemann	.941	27	15	33	3	2
Toro	.961	56	36	87	5	5

Shortstop	PCT	G	PO	A	E	DP
Allen	.949	34	45	66	6	22
Diaz	1.000	6	5	13	0	2
Hernaiz	.986	19	32	37	1	7
Schuemann	.964	93	113	213	12	41
Wilson	1.000	27	32	69	0	16

Outfield	PCT	G	PO	A	E	DP
Alvarez	1.000	2	4	0	0	0
Andujar	.986	72	129	10	2	1
Bleday	.988	157	392	8	5	1
Brown	.986	87	140	2	2	0
Butler	.985	125	253	2	4	1
Cameron	1.000	65	83	3	0	0
Nevin	1.000	31	46	0	0	0
Noda	1.000	2	1	0	0	0
Rooker	1.000	14	16	0	0	0
Ruiz	.972	28	35	0	1	0
Schuemann	1.000	10	4	0	0	0
Toro	1.000	1	2	0	0	0

LAS VEGAS AVIATORS — *TRIPLE-A*

PACIFIC COAST LEAGUE

Batting	B-T	Ht.	Wt.	DOB	AVG	OBP	SLG	G	PA	AB	R	H	2B	3B	HR	RBI	BB	HBP	SH	SF	SO	SB	CS	BB%	SO%
Alexander, CJ	L-R	6-3	215	7-17-96	.294	.410	.588	12	61	51	7	15	4	1	3	14	8	2	0	0	8	0	0	13.11	13.11
Allen, Nick	R-R	5-8	166	10-8-98	.345	.431	.497	81	379	322	64	111	26	1	7	51	49	3	1	4	41	16	8	12.93	10.82
Alvarez, Armando	R-R	6-0	195	7-14-94	.315	.407	.560	75	317	273	46	86	20	1	15	54	41	2	0	1	61	5	2	12.93	19.24
Andujar, Miguel	R-R	6-0	211	3-2-95	.389	.421	.611	5	19	18	3	7	4	0	0	6	1	0	0	0	2	0	0	5.26	10.53
Armenteros, Lazaro	R-R	5-11	182	5-22-99	.191	.321	.309	42	112	94	17	18	3	1	2	10	15	3	0	0	44	10	2	13.39	39.29
Bowman, Cooper	R-R	6-0	205	1-25-00	.218	.284	.308	38	152	133	21	29	8	2	0	17	12	1	4	2	37	8	1	7.89	24.34
Brown, Seth	L-L	6-1	223	7-13-92	.403	.416	.736	16	77	72	16	29	3	0	7	24	3	0	0	2	15	2	0	3.90	19.48
Butler, Lawrence	L-R	6-3	210	7-10-00	.255	.349	.418	27	126	110	25	28	6	0	4	9	16	0	0	0	25	7	1	12.70	19.84
Cameron, Daz	R-R	6-2	185	1-15-97	.307	.424	.577	41	165	137	32	42	15	2	6	27	27	1	0	0	35	8	2	16.36	21.21
Davidson, Logan	B-R	6-3	185	12-26-97	.300	.366	.535	87	347	310	59	93	23	4	14	51	27	7	0	3	108	7	2	7.78	31.12
Davis, J.D.	R-R	6-3	218	4-27-93	.200	.294	.267	4	17	15	2	3	1	0	0	0	2	0	0	0	6	0	0	11.76	35.29
Diaz, Aledmys	R-R	6-1	195	8-1-90	.154	.313	.308	10	32	26	3	4	1	0	1	5	6	0	0	0	5	0	0	18.75	15.63
Diaz, Jordan	R-R	5-10	175	8-13-00	.301	.362	.529	102	436	395	60	119	22	1	22	85	34	5	0	2	78	0	0	7.80	17.89
Gelof, Zack	R-R	6-2	205	10-19-99	.125	.200	.500	2	10	8	1	1	0	0	1	2	1	0	0	1	3	0	0	10.00	30.00
Gray, Tristan	L-R	6-1	215	3-22-96	.296	.350	.519	12	60	54	11	16	4	1	2	6	4	1	0	1	11	0	0	6.67	18.33
Harris, Brett	R-R	6-1	208	6-24-98	.281	.385	.419	74	317	270	52	76	9	2	8	45	41	5	0	1	62	6	3	12.93	19.56
Hernaiz, Darell	R-R	5-11	190	8-3-01	.331	.376	.493	35	157	142	23	47	8	0	5	19	12	0	0	3	22	6	1	7.64	14.01
Kuroda-Grauer, Josh	R-R	6-0	185	1-31-03	.167	.231	.167	4	13	12	1	2	0	0	0	1	0	1	0	0	1	0	0	0.00	7.69
Lugbauer, Drew	L-R	6-3	220	8-23-96	.206	.283	.408	94	322	287	41	59	13	0	15	46	31	1	0	3	131	0	0	9.63	40.68
Muncy, Max	R-R	6-1	180	8-25-02	.277	.374	.491	50	203	173	28	48	11	1	8	33	18	10	0	2	50	4	2	8.87	24.63
Nevin, Tyler	R-R	6-4	225	5-29-97	.296	.365	.667	14	63	54	11	16	6	1	4	17	6	1	0	2	11	0	0	9.52	17.46
Nieporte, Quincy	R-R	6-0	225	7-29-94	.278	.381	.333	12	43	36	5	10	2	0	0	7	6	0	0	0	10	1	0	13.95	23.26
Noda, Ryan	L-L	6-3	217	3-30-96	.224	.391	.486	101	447	348	81	78	21	2	22	54	89	8	0	2	134	5	1	19.91	29.98
Park, Hoy	L-R	6-0	200	4-7-96	.254	.374	.397	115	434	358	71	91	18	3	9	55	67	3	2	3	98	15	6	15.44	22.58
Perez, Carlos	R-R	5-10	210	10-27-90	.260	.344	.544	112	468	408	79	106	27	4	27	77	49	6	0	5	80	0	0	10.47	17.09
Piscotty, Stephen	R-R	6-4	211	1-14-91	.176	.246	.241	31	118	108	9	19	4	0	1	9	9	1	0	0	34	0	0	7.63	28.81
Pozo, Yohel	R-R	5-10	201	6-14-97	.324	.335	.538	90	361	346	49	112	27	1	15	54	7	2	0	6	30	0	1	1.94	8.31
Ruiz, Esteury	R-R	6-0	169	2-15-99	.326	.423	.581	11	52	43	6	14	2	0	3	8	6	2	0	1	10	7	1	11.54	19.23
Schuemann, Max	R-R	5-11	186	6-11-97	.174	.310	.174	6	29	23	2	4	0	0	0	1	5	0	0	1	8	1	0	17.24	27.59
Soderstrom, Tyler	L-R	6-1	200	11-24-01	.279	.385	.607	33	143	122	22	34	8	1	10	27	16	5	0	0	35	0	1	11.19	24.48
Thomas, Colby	R-R	6-0	190	1-26-01	.272	.344	.559	73	314	279	47	76	25	2	17	45	23	9	0	3	95	3	3	7.32	30.25
Toro, Abraham	B-R	6-0	223	12-20-96	.188	.235	.188	4	17	16	1	3	0	0	0	0	1	0	0	0	3	0	0	5.88	17.65
Wilson, Jacob	R-R	6-3	190	3-30-02	.396	.448	.613	26	116	106	26	42	11	0	4	17	9	1	0	0	5	0	0	7.76	4.31

Pitching	B-T	Ht.	Wt.	DOB	W	L	ERA	G	GS	SV	IP	Hits	Runs	ER	HR	BB	SO	AVG	OBP	SLG	SO%	BB%	BF
Alexander, Scott	L-L	6-2	195	7-10-89	1	0	13.50	4	0	0	3	4	5	4	0	1	5	.308	.438	.385	31.25	6.25	16
Avant, Corey	R-R	6-4	225	11-6-01	1	0	7.90	10	0	0	14	13	12	12	0	9	12	.255	.381	.294	19.05	14.29	63
Barrera, Diego	L-L	6-0	165	5-5-00	0	0	16.20	1	1	0	2	3	3	3	0	1	1	.375	.444	.375	11.11	11.11	9
Basso, Brady	R-L	6-2	213	10-8-97	4	3	5.19	16	12	2	68	69	41	39	15	22	77	.257	.313	.520	26.37	7.53	292
Baum, Tyler	R-R	6-2	195	1-14-98	0	1	9.28	9	0	0	11	13	11	11	3	11	7	.302	.455	.605	12.73	20.00	55
Beers, Blake	R-R	6-4	215	7-15-98	0	1	7.65	4	3	0	20	31	18	17	5	10	17	.365	.434	.671	17.17	10.10	99
Bido, Osvaldo	R-R	6-3	175	10-18-95	4	3	4.50	10	9	0	48	48	24	24	10	16	55	.259	.324	.454	26.96	7.84	204
Bielak, Brandon	L-R	6-2	208	4-2-96	3	3	6.08	16	13	0	67	75	48	45	10	31	49	.285	.366	.475	16.39	10.37	299
Blackburn, Paul	R-R	6-1	196	12-4-93	1	1	13.50	2	1	0	3	9	7	5	1	3	2	.563	.591	1.000	8.70	13.04	23

Boyle, Joe	R-R	6-7	240	8-14-99	1	3	5.12	15	13	1	46	26	27	26	4	39	71	.169	.345	.312	36.04	19.80	197
Briggs, Austin	R-L	6-1	205	10-11-95	0	2	13.86	10	2	0	12	15	24	19	1	20	5	.319	.514	.468	7.14	28.57	70
Brooks, Aaron	R-R	6-4	230	4-27-90	2	9	4.92	15	9	0	68	83	46	37	4	16	50	.303	.343	.442	16.72	5.35	299
Brown, Ryan	R-R	6-2	214	11-2-00	0	0	9.00	3	0	0	4	5	4	4	1	3	4	.294	.455	.706	18.18	13.64	22
Conover, Drew	R-R	6-5	185	7-27-01	0	0	54.00	1	0	0	1	5	6	6	0	5	1	.714	.833	.857	8.33	41.67	12
Correa, Danis	R-R	5-11	150	8-26-99	0	0	7.71	11	0	0	12	13	10	10	1	15	14	.289	.500	.422	21.88	23.44	64
Cushing, Jack	R-R	6-3	195	12-3-96	2	0	5.01	22	0	2	32	34	19	18	3	17	37	.260	.345	.412	25.00	11.49	148
Cusick, Ryan	R-R	6-6	235	11-12-99	0	1	10.38	2	0	0	4	8	8	5	0	4	2	.381	.519	.524	7.14	14.29	28
Dugger, Robert	R-R	6-0	198	7-3-95	5	2	4.79	20	16	0	94	83	52	50	16	56	87	.236	.337	.435	20.86	13.43	417
Emanuels, Stevie	R-R	6-5	210	1-30-99	0	0	8.40	14	0	0	15	19	15	14	5	14	19	.322	.446	.678	25.33	18.67	75
Estes, Joey	R-R	6-2	190	10-8-01	2	3	6.04	6	6	0	28	31	20	19	7	10	26	.272	.336	.596	20.80	8.00	125
Ferguson, Tyler	R-R	6-4	225	10-5-93	2	2	3.49	26	0	5	28	27	15	11	0	11	43	.245	.346	.300	33.08	8.46	130
Garland, Jake	R-R	6-5	236	9-26-00	0	0	6.75	1	1	0	4	5	3	3	2	2	7	.357	.438	.857	41.18	11.76	17
Ginn, J.T.	R-R	6-2	200	5-20-99	4	3	5.72	15	14	0	72	80	50	46	10	30	69	.278	.358	.420	21.23	9.23	325
Gonzalez, James	L-L	6-2	257	9-15-00	0	0	15.00	1	1	0	3	8	5	5	1	1	1	.471	.500	.824	5.56	5.56	18
Guante, Wander	R-R	6-1	180	6-15-00	1	1	5.79	6	1	0	19	21	15	12	3	9	14	.296	.375	.507	17.50	11.25	80
Harris, Hogan	R-L	6-3	230	12-26-96	3	4	6.35	13	13	0	57	63	42	40	8	39	65	.280	.392	.444	24.07	14.44	270
Hoglund, Gunnar	L-R	6-4	220	12-17-99	0	3	5.88	5	5	0	26	25	17	17	5	10	22	.250	.324	.460	19.82	9.01	111
Holman, Grant	R-R	6-6	250	5-31-00	4	0	0.92	23	0	3	29	13	5	3	1	13	30	.131	.237	.212	26.32	11.40	114
Jackson, Zach	R-R	6-4	230	12-25-94	5	6	7.08	35	0	0	34	30	31	27	4	43	43	.238	.429	.389	25.29	25.29	170
Jimenez, Dany	R-R	6-1	182	12-23-93	1	3	4.13	21	0	3	24	17	14	11	4	13	30	.207	.337	.378	29.41	12.75	102
Junk, Janson	R-R	6-2	202	1-15-96	0	0	3.48	2	2	0	10	13	4	4	2	0	9	.302	.302	.465	20.93	0.00	43
Klein, Will	R-R	6-5	230	11-28-99	0	1	5.06	4	0	0	5	6	3	3	1	5	5	.300	.462	.450	19.23	19.23	26
Lucas, Easton	L-L	6-4	180	9-23-96	2	0	2.87	11	1	0	16	12	6	5	2	8	13	.211	.313	.386	19.40	11.94	67
Martinez, Adrian	R-R	6-2	215	12-10-96	1	1	11.05	18	0	0	22	37	30	27	7	15	19	.370	.452	.650	16.38	12.93	116
Medina, Luis	R-R	6-1	175	5-3-99	0	0	10.50	2	2	0	6	8	7	7	1	3	7	.296	.424	.444	21.21	9.09	33
Moreno, Gerson	R-R	6-0	218	9-10-95	0	0	6.00	37	1	2	42	28	29	28	7	29	43	.194	.331	.396	23.76	16.02	181
Morris, Kade	R-R	6-3	170	6-21-02	0	1	11.12	2	1	1	6	9	7	7	2	4	2	.360	.448	.640	6.90	13.79	29
Muller, Kyle	R-L	6-7	250	10-7-97	1	1	4.62	7	4	0	25	23	13	13	6	8	19	.240	.292	.479	17.76	7.48	107
Myers, Mitch	R-R	6-2	200	1-8-99	0	0	5.40	2	0	0	3	3	2	2	1	2	1	.231	.333	.462	6.67	13.33	15
Newcomb, Sean	L-L	6-5	255	6-12-93	0	0	3.60	3	0	0	5	6	2	2	0	4	4	.316	.435	.316	17.39	17.39	23
Nittoli, Vinny	R-R	6-1	210	11-11-90	3	1	2.70	20	0	3	23	20	9	7	3	11	36	.230	.320	.391	36.00	11.00	100
O'Loughlin, Jack	L-L	6-5	223	3-14-00	3	5	6.04	32	10	0	73	96	49	49	17	34	80	.320	.386	.563	23.53	10.00	340
Otanez, Michel	R-R	6-4	218	7-3-97	7	1	5.35	29	0	1	37	30	23	22	2	25	55	.217	.363	.355	32.16	14.62	171
Peluse, Colin	R-R	6-3	230	6-11-98	0	0	8.53	5	1	0	6	8	8	6	1	6	2	.333	.452	.625	6.45	19.35	31
Perez, Carlos	R-R	5-10	210	10-27-90	0	0	4.50	2	0	0	2	3	1	1	1	1	1	.333	.400	.667	10.00	10.00	10
Perez, Francisco	S-L	6-2	227	7-20-97	1	2	7.82	34	0	0	36	47	32	31	9	20	49	.311	.392	.556	28.65	11.70	171
Pfennigs, Jake	R-R	6-7	215	9-9-99	0	0	9.00	1	0	0	2	3	2	2	0	0	0	.375	.364	.625	0.00	0.00	11
Pozo, Yohel	R-R	5-10	201	6-14-97	0	0	16.88	3	0	0	3	5	5	5	1	3	1	.455	.500	.818	6.25	18.75	16
Pruitt, Austin	R-R	5-10	185	8-31-89	1	2	8.40	9	2	1	15	17	16	14	3	7	14	.279	.371	.459	20.00	10.00	70
Reyes, Gerardo	R-R	5-11	195	5-13-93	4	1	4.87	43	0	1	44	27	27	24	10	28	60	.176	.301	.425	31.91	14.89	188
Salinas, Royber	R-R	6-3	205	4-10-01	0	0	9.95	2	2	0	6	6	7	7	1	8	8	.240	.424	.480	24.24	24.24	33
Santos, Pedro	R-R	6-4	205	1-7-00	2	3	5.89	33	0	2	37	36	24	24	5	31	43	.255	.400	.390	24.57	17.71	175
Speas, Alex	R-R	6-3	225	3-4-98	2	0	11.32	9	0	0	10	16	14	13	3	7	15	.356	.434	.622	28.30	13.21	53
Stripling, Ross	R-R	6-1	215	11-23-89	0	0	5.63	2	2	0	8	13	5	5	0	1	1	.382	.389	.412	2.78	2.78	36
Sullivan, Billy	R-R	6-2	195	4-16-99	0	0	11.81	6	0	1	5	6	13	7	0	10	4	.273	.528	.318	11.11	27.78	36
Tarnok, Freddy	R-R	6-3	185	11-24-98	0	2	13.50	6	1	0	7	9	11	11	2	4	6	.310	.412	.621	17.14	11.43	35
Watters, Jacob	R-R	6-4	230	3-3-01	1	0	9.00	1	0	0	3	3	3	3	0	5	0	.300	.533	.400	0.00	33.33	15

Fielding

Catcher	PCT	G	PO	A	E	DP	PB
Perez	.991	80	744	59	7	9	3
Pozo	.987	53	427	26	6	2	1
Soderstrom	.991	21	207	9	2	1	5

First Base	PCT	G	PO	A	E	DP
Alexander	1.000	1	6	0	0	2
Alvarez	1.000	4	30	4	0	5
Davidson	1.000	4	32	2	0	1
Diaz	.980	5	46	3	1	6
Gray	1.000	10	75	6	0	6
Harris	.000	1	0	0	0	0
Lugbauer	1.000	51	320	20	0	40
Nieporte	1.000	1	9	0	0	1
Noda	.992	52	330	23	3	29
Perez	.982	13	54	1	1	8
Pozo	1.000	19	119	6	0	10
Soderstrom	1.000	8	47	4	0	6

Second Base	PCT	G	PO	A	E	DP
Allen	.981	25	33	70	2	18
Alvarez	.982	34	49	59	2	18
Bowman	1.000	4	7	8	0	4
Davidson	.930	13	17	23	3	6
Diaz	1.000	1	0	2	0	0
Diaz	1.000	23	20	46	0	11
Gelof	1.000	2	4	6	0	2
Harris	.982	12	19	37	1	6
Hernaiz	1.000	1	0	2	0	1
Kuroda-Grauer	1.000	2	2	4	0	0
Muncy	.983	15	33	26	1	13
Park	.989	28	34	55	1	11
Schuemann	1.000	1	3	4	0	3
Toro	1.000	3	3	9	0	1

Third Base	PCT	G	PO	A	E	DP
Alexander	.875	6	7	7	2	0
Allen	1.000	5	2	6	0	1
Alvarez	.925	26	13	49	5	6
Davidson	.982	23	20	36	1	4
Davis	1.000	2	1	3	0	0
Diaz	.700	3	1	6	3	1
Diaz	1.000	4	0	6	0	0
Gray	1.000	2	1	6	0	0
Harris	.992	56	25	92	1	9
Hernaiz	1.000	3	1	9	0	1
Lugbauer	.922	28	11	48	5	5
Muncy	.700	3	3	4	3	0
Nevin	.750	4	1	2	1	0
Park	1.000	1	0	3	0	0
Toro	1.000	1	0	2	0	1

Shortstop	PCT	G	PO	A	E	DP
Allen	.984	55	75	111	3	24
Alvarez	1.000	4	3	5	0	1
Davidson	.979	15	14	32	1	4
Diaz	1.000	1	1	1	0	0
Harris	1.000	2	1	3	0	0
Hernaiz	.982	29	43	68	2	21
Kuroda-Grauer	1.000	2	5	8	0	1
Muncy	.913	31	35	80	11	19
Park	1.000	2	1	1	0	0
Schuemann	.667	1	1	1	1	0
Wilson	.942	22	24	41	4	12

Outfield	PCT	G	PO	A	E	DP
Alexander	1.000	6	8	0	0	0
Allen	.667	2	2	0	1	0
Alvarez	1.000	14	20	1	0	1
Andujar	1.000	2	3	0	0	0
Armenteros	1.000	35	49	2	0	0
Bowman	.953	33	82	0	4	0
Brown	1.000	16	32	0	0	0
Butler	.967	28	59	0	2	0
Cameron	.968	41	88	3	3	1
Davidson	.952	37	58	1	3	1
Nevin	.913	12	21	0	2	0
Noda	.978	54	88	0	2	0
Park	.994	87	155	4	1	3
Perez	1.000	1	2	0	0	0
Piscotty	.958	33	45	1	2	1

	PCT	G	PO	A	E	DP
Ruiz	.955	10	21	0	1	0
Schuemann	1.000	4	6	0	0	0
Thomas	.994	74	161	9	1	0

MIDLAND ROCKHOUNDS — *DOUBLE-A*

TEXAS LEAGUE

Batting	B-T	Ht.	Wt.	DOB	AVG	OBP	SLG	G	PA	AB	R	H	2B	3B	HR	RBI	BB	HBP	SH	SF	SO	SB	CS	BB%	SO%
Angeles, Euribiel	R-R	5-11	175	5-11-02	.222	.278	.323	33	108	99	11	22	5	1	1	10	6	2	0	1	13	4	0	5.56	12.04
Armenteros, Lazaro	R-R	5-11	182	5-22-99	.269	.406	.365	16	64	52	10	14	2	0	1	5	10	2	0	0	24	4	2	15.63	37.50
Bolte, Henry	R-R	6-3	195	8-4-03	.252	.332	.396	54	227	202	32	51	13	2	4	21	20	4	0	0	88	18	6	8.81	38.77
Bowman, Cooper	R-R	6-0	205	1-25-00	.281	.378	.466	80	371	313	62	88	18	2	12	53	46	5	3	4	75	35	5	12.40	20.22
Buelvas, Brayan	R-R	5-11	155	6-8-02	.256	.305	.364	33	131	121	11	31	8	1	1	11	8	1	0	1	34	5	1	6.11	25.95
Clarke, Denzel	R-R	6-5	220	5-1-00	.269	.339	.445	116	478	431	74	116	21	8	13	53	39	7	0	1	143	36	9	8.16	29.92
Eierman, Jeremy	R-R	5-11	205	9-10-96	.221	.282	.400	72	260	235	26	52	6	0	12	36	15	6	1	3	83	2	0	5.77	31.92
Gomez, Mario	L-R	5-10	185	12-30-02	.400	.400	.400	2	5	5	0	2	0	0	0	0	0	0	0	0	3	0	0	0.00	60.00
Groshans, Jordan	R-R	6-3	200	11-10-99	.239	.312	.352	51	199	176	28	42	9	1	3	19	20	0	0	3	36	0	1	10.05	18.09
Kurtz, Nick	L-L	6-6	230	3-11-03	.308	.400	.385	5	15	13	3	4	1	0	0	1	2	0	0	0	3	1	0	13.33	20.00
McGuire, Shane	L-R	5-10	195	4-12-99	.238	.358	.343	74	297	248	42	59	14	0	4	35	45	2	1	1	52	6	1	15.15	17.51
Milone, Brennan	R-R	6-1	198	5-6-01	.278	.361	.441	127	548	478	75	133	29	2	15	70	59	6	0	5	117	8	5	10.77	21.35
Mujica, Jose	R-R	6-0	164	3-28-01	.262	.279	.357	14	43	42	5	11	4	0	0	1	0	1	0	0	8	0	0	0.00	18.60
Nieporte, Quincy	R-R	6-0	225	7-29-94	.243	.349	.297	13	44	37	7	9	2	0	0	3	6	0	1	0	9	0	0	13.64	20.45
Perez, Junior	R-R	6-1	165	7-4-01	.220	.304	.372	97	390	341	50	75	24	2	8	52	42	1	2	4	138	28	5	10.77	35.38
Rosado, Jamaliel	R-R	6-3	195	8-15-03	.000	.286	.000	2	7	5	1	0	0	0	0	0	2	0	0	0	2	0	0	28.57	28.57
Rosario, Jeisson	L-L	5-11	191	10-22-99	.258	.355	.349	74	292	252	34	65	6	4	3	38	37	1	2	0	75	8	6	12.67	25.68
Simpson, Will	R-R	6-4	225	8-28-01	.348	.408	.493	18	76	69	10	24	4	0	2	9	7	0	0	0	18	1	0	9.21	23.68
Susac, Daniel	R-R	6-4	218	5-14-01	.257	.300	.434	88	370	343	39	88	19	3	12	50	16	7	0	4	96	7	2	4.32	25.95
Thomas, Colby	R-R	6-0	190	1-26-01	.282	.340	.568	59	261	234	32	66	19	3	14	47	17	5	0	3	47	12	1	6.51	18.01
Trenkle, Caeden	L-L	5-10	179	6-29-01	.195	.269	.301	74	267	236	29	46	11	1	4	23	25	0	1	3	82	3	0	9.36	30.71
Valenzuela, Sahid	B-R	5-7	165	9-16-97	.183	.231	.211	35	118	109	9	20	3	0	0	5	7	0	1	1	22	1	1	5.93	18.64
Wilson, Jacob	R-R	6-3	190	3-30-02	.455	.473	.705	22	93	88	18	40	13	0	3	19	2	2	0	1	10	2	1	2.15	10.75
Winkler, Jack	R-R	6-2	185	11-4-98	.223	.310	.345	127	536	470	66	105	31	1	8	57	48	13	1	4	117	28	5	8.96	21.83

Pitching	B-T	Ht.	Wt.	DOB	W	L	ERA	G	GS	SV	IP	Hits	Runs	ER	HR	BB	SO	AVG	OBP	SLG	SO%	BB%	BF
Barnett, Mason	R-R	6-0	218	11-7-00	4	2	2.61	7	7	0	41	32	14	12	4	13	52	.212	.283	.331	31.14	7.78	167
Basso, Brady	R-L	6-2	213	10-8-97	1	1	2.84	6	6	0	25	22	11	8	3	3	32	.222	.267	.374	30.48	2.86	105
Baum, Tyler	R-R	6-2	195	1-14-98	3	5	4.01	36	0	2	49	42	27	22	5	23	65	.233	.332	.367	30.81	10.90	211
Beers, Blake	R-R	6-4	215	7-15-98	11	6	3.33	24	21	0	130	108	52	48	16	39	122	.229	.298	.362	23.11	7.39	528
Briggs, Austin	R-L	6-1	205	10-11-95	2	0	4.95	16	0	1	20	22	12	11	1	12	19	.297	.387	.392	20.43	12.90	93
Cohen, Chase	L-R	6-1	183	4-26-97	2	1	2.61	17	0	0	21	14	9	6	2	11	22	.184	.295	.289	25.00	12.50	88
Correa, Danis	R-R	5-11	150	8-26-99	0	1	1.47	15	0	7	18	9	4	3	2	6	17	.141	.247	.250	23.29	8.22	73
Cushing, Jack	R-R	6-3	195	12-3-96	3	3	2.86	15	5	0	44	38	15	14	3	10	37	.228	.275	.347	20.67	5.59	179
Cusick, Ryan	R-R	6-6	235	11-12-99	3	3	4.47	27	8	4	56	49	30	28	4	33	63	.236	.353	.341	25.30	13.25	249
Dallas, Micah	R-R	6-2	215	4-14-00	0	0	0.00	2	0	0	2	1	0	0	0	0	2	.167	.167	.167	33.33	0.00	6
Elledge, Seth	R-R	6-3	240	5-20-96	3	3	2.22	34	0	11	45	27	15	11	3	9	34	.175	.228	.292	20.00	5.29	170
Emanuels, Stevie	R-R	6-5	210	1-30-99	0	0	0.00	3	0	1	3	0	0	0	0	0	3	.000	.000	.000	33.33	0.00	9
Garland, Jake	R-R	6-5	236	9-26-00	1	0	3.00	1	1	0	6	4	2	2	1	3	1	.200	.304	.350	4.35	13.04	23
Ginn, J.T.	R-R	6-2	200	5-20-99	4	1	4.15	6	6	0	30	31	18	14	3	10	28	.263	.333	.398	21.21	7.58	132
Gonzalez, James	L-L	6-2	257	9-15-00	6	4	3.14	20	14	0	97	82	42	34	5	35	86	.229	.306	.330	21.39	8.71	402
Guante, Wander	R-R	6-1	180	6-15-00	3	1	4.96	13	0	0	33	35	21	18	4	14	29	.280	.370	.448	19.59	9.46	148
Henzman, Lincoln	R-R	6-2	205	7-4-95	0	1	5.40	6	0	0	7	12	7	4	2	2	3	.387	.412	.645	8.82	5.88	34
Hoglund, Gunnar	L-R	6-4	220	12-17-99	9	4	2.84	19	18	0	105	78	35	33	12	27	97	.207	.271	.363	23.43	6.52	414
Holman, Grant	R-R	6-6	250	5-31-00	0	0	0.00	17	0	6	19	12	0	0	0	9	24	.190	.292	.238	33.33	12.50	72
Irvin, Garrett	L-L	6-0	185	2-18-99	0	0	4.50	3	0	0	4	1	2	2	1	3	3	.077	.250	.308	18.75	18.75	16
Jackson, Zach	R-R	6-4	230	12-25-94	0	1	11.57	3	0	0	2	5	3	3	1	2	4	.455	.538	.727	30.77	15.38	13
Johnson, Colton	L-L	6-4	222	7-28-98	2	2	2.25	12	0	0	20	11	7	5	3	11	23	.164	.291	.328	28.75	13.75	80
Johnston, Will	L-L	6-3	215	12-12-00	0	0	4.50	2	2	0	8	8	4	4	1	2	14	.242	.286	.364	40.00	5.71	35
Leal, David	L-L	6-5	250	4-22-97	5	3	3.57	28	2	2	63	57	32	25	4	15	52	.241	.307	.354	19.62	5.66	265
Peluse, Colin	R-R	6-3	230	6-11-98	4	3	2.05	28	1	2	53	39	13	12	3	15	42	.213	.274	.301	20.90	7.46	201
Perkins, Jack	R-R	6-1	220	12-26-99	4	1	2.96	17	15	0	76	52	28	25	2	35	100	.193	.296	.241	31.75	11.11	315
Robles, Domingo	L-L	6-2	170	4-29-98	7	2	2.98	21	13	1	85	64	29	28	7	24	87	.210	.270	.328	26.05	7.19	334
Salinas, Royber	R-R	6-3	205	4-10-01	3	1	3.68	8	8	0	37	30	18	15	5	26	42	.227	.366	.371	25.45	15.76	165
Santos, Pedro	R-R	6-4	205	1-7-00	0	0	1.80	15	0	5	15	9	3	3	0	11	26	.176	.344	.196	40.63	17.19	64
Tomioka, Shohei	R-R	6-0	190	2-29-96	2	4	4.14	39	0	1	50	38	27	23	2	26	47	.208	.310	.284	21.66	11.98	217
Walkinshaw, Jake	R-R	6-3	200	7-7-96	1	1	2.15	8	7	0	29	22	7	7	2	9	23	.208	.276	.311	19.83	7.76	116
Weisenburger, Jack	R-R	6-3	220	10-8-97	0	0	1.35	8	0	0	7	4	1	1	0	9	10	.167	.412	.250	29.41	26.47	34
Zhuang, Chen Zhong-Ao	R-R	6-1	190	8-25-00	1	0	2.05	5	4	1	22	15	6	5	2	5	18	.190	.244	.316	20.93	5.81	86

Fielding

Catcher	PCT	G	PO	A	E	DP	PB
Gomez	1.000	2	6	1	0	0	0
McGuire	.989	51	426	36	5	2	4
Mujica	.989	10	81	6	1	0	0
Susac	.990	81	727	55	8	2	7

First Base	PCT	G	PO	A	E	DP
Groshans	1.000	3	23	0	0	1
Kurtz	.964	5	27	0	1	3
McGuire	1.000	16	90	8	0	12
Milone	.996	93	711	37	3	58
Mujica	.833	1	5	0	1	0
Nieporte	.977	8	40	3	1	2
Simpson	.984	17	116	8	2	11
Susac	1.000	1	8	0	0	0
Winkler	.944	3	16	1	1	0

Second Base	PCT	G	PO	A	E	DP
Angeles	1.000	21	24	40	0	8
Bowman	.984	70	144	170	5	43
Groshans	1.000	1	2	2	0	1
Milone	.940	17	12	35	3	5
Valenzuela	1.000	15	19	23	0	4
Winkler	1.000	24	51	48	0	9

Third Base	PCT	G	PO	A	E	DP
Angeles	1.000	7	3	5	0	1
Bowman	.929	5	5	8	1	0
Eierman	1.000	19	13	33	0	3
Groshans	.981	47	18	85	2	9
Milone	.846	9	7	15	4	0
Rosado	1.000	2	1	1	0	0
Valenzuela	.956	19	16	27	2	4
Winkler	.935	41	23	78	7	5

Shortstop	PCT	G	PO	A	E	DP
Angeles	1.000	6	7	17	0	1
Bowman	.800	1	5	3	2	2
Eierman	.964	52	47	113	6	16
Wilson	.974	22	25	49	2	9
Winkler	.979	60	83	146	5	32

Outfield	PCT	G	PO	A	E	DP
Armenteros	1.000	11	24	1	0	1
Bolte	.975	47	78	0	2	0
Buelvas	.948	27	54	1	3	1
Clarke	.993	105	263	6	2	0
Perez	.987	81	152	5	2	1
Rosario	.966	47	77	7	3	1
Thomas	1.000	51	86	6	0	1
Trenkle	.979	55	91	1	2	0

LANSING LUGNUTS

HIGH-A

MIDWEST LEAGUE

Batting	B-T	Ht.	Wt.	DOB	AVG	OBP	SLG	G	PA	AB	R	H	2B	3B	HR	RBI	BB	HBP	SH	SF	SO	SB	CS	BB%	SO%
Amaya, Carlos	R-R	5-10	165	12-28-01	.222	.216	.278	10	38	36	5	8	2	0	0	5	0	0	1	1	7	0	0	0.00	18.42
Angeles, Euribiel	R-R	5-11	175	5-11-02	.279	.310	.398	85	364	344	41	96	15	4	6	54	16	1	0	3	41	15	4	4.40	11.26
Arevalo, Angel	R-R	5-11	160	10-2-03	.250	.400	.250	3	6	4	1	1	0	0	0	0	1	0	1	0	1	1	0	16.67	16.67
Bautista, Danny	R-R	6-2	185	9-20-00	.265	.343	.381	95	388	339	47	90	17	5	4	47	33	9	1	4	51	14	5	8.51	13.14
Bolte, Henry	R-R	6-3	195	8-4-03	.278	.393	.519	69	318	266	60	74	19	6	11	52	41	10	0	1	101	28	6	12.89	31.76
Buelvas, Brayan	R-R	5-11	155	6-8-02	.272	.368	.443	80	361	309	54	84	20	6	7	51	46	3	0	3	80	22	6	12.74	22.16
Butler, Jonny	L-R	6-1	200	2-12-99	.224	.328	.357	113	522	451	72	101	26	5	8	50	64	6	0	1	111	18	4	12.26	21.26
Conn, Cole	B-R	6-0	175	7-11-01	.208	.296	.301	54	199	173	21	36	7	0	3	19	21	2	0	3	42	5	1	10.55	21.11
Dickey, Jared	L-R	6-1	204	3-1-02	.237	.299	.298	34	147	131	12	31	3	1	1	15	10	3	0	3	23	2	2	6.80	15.65
Escorche, Jose	R-R	5-8	145	4-29-02	.190	.267	.219	31	118	105	12	20	3	0	0	8	8	3	2	0	36	3	2	6.78	30.51
Halter, Colby	L-R	6-1	200	8-24-01	.258	.368	.365	66	277	233	35	60	14	1	3	24	38	4	0	2	81	12	8	13.72	29.24
Kuroda-Grauer, Josh	R-R	6-0	185	1-31-03	.286	.400	.333	12	50	42	4	12	2	0	0	3	5	3	0	0	3	1	1	10.00	6.00
Lasko, Ryan	R-R	6-0	190	6-24-02	.245	.341	.342	41	179	155	22	38	7	1	2	18	20	3	0	1	35	13	1	11.17	19.55
Mann, Luke	L-R	6-2	218	4-13-00	.217	.300	.346	78	324	286	28	62	9	2	8	32	27	8	0	2	82	2	0	8.33	25.31
Masterman, Cameron	R-R	6-2	225	5-5-99	.221	.317	.401	75	301	262	37	58	14	3	9	40	34	3	0	1	110	4	2	11.30	36.54
Mujica, Jose	R-R	6-0	164	3-28-01	.174	.208	.174	6	24	23	2	4	0	0	0	0	1	0	0	0	10	0	0	4.17	41.67
Nankil, Nate	R-R	6-3	185	10-16-02	.356	.414	.452	28	116	104	14	37	7	0	1	14	8	3	0	1	25	0	1	6.90	21.55
Rijo, Elvis	R-R	5-11	165	11-27-03	.333	.500	.333	1	4	3	2	1	0	0	0	0	0	1	0	0	0	0	0	0.00	0.00
Rodriguez, CJ	R-R	5-7	200	7-7-00	.201	.320	.236	70	272	229	21	46	6	1	0	18	38	3	0	2	48	0	0	13.97	17.65
Salom, Dereck	R-R	5-10	135	2-22-01	.239	.346	.313	21	78	67	12	16	2	0	1	7	11	0	0	0	17	1	0	14.10	21.79
Schofield-Sam, T.J.	L-R	6-1	185	6-20-01	.231	.331	.343	32	124	108	12	25	6	0	2	10	9	7	0	0	19	0	1	7.26	15.32
Simpson, Will	R-R	6-4	225	8-20-01	.270	.373	.480	109	474	396	68	107	27	4	16	81	69	1	0	8	117	4	3	14.56	24.68
Valenzuela, Sahid	B-R	5-7	165	9-16-97	.173	.246	.192	30	115	104	12	18	0	1	0	7	10	0	1	0	23	2	0	8.70	20.00
Wright, Joshwan	R-R	5-8	170	11-9-00	.429	.429	.500	4	14	14	2	6	1	0	0	0	0	0	0	0	3	0	0	0.00	21.43
Yamauchi, Casey	R-R	5-9	155	8-8-00	.236	.306	.258	52	197	178	24	42	4	0	0	13	11	7	1	0	14	13	2	5.58	7.11

Pitching	B-T	Ht.	Wt.	DOB	W	L	ERA	G	GS	SV	IP	Hits	Runs	ER	HR	BB	SO	AVG	OBP	SLG	SO%	BB%	BF
Barrera, Diego	L-L	6-0	165	5-5-00	3	0	2.28	17	0	5	28	25	9	7	1	10	19	.240	.304	.327	16.38	8.62	116
Breault, Hunter	R-R	6-2	228	6-12-99	4	3	6.08	36	0	6	40	43	31	27	5	30	42	.277	.399	.452	22.22	15.87	189
Carrasco, Luis	R-R	6-1	180	12-19-01	2	5	5.14	19	7	1	63	57	40	36	8	31	43	.238	.325	.381	15.52	11.19	277
Conover, Drew	R-R	6-5	185	7-27-01	0	1	0.00	1	0	0	0	2	4	4	0	5	0	1.000	1.000	1.000	0.00	71.43	7
Dallas, Micah	R-R	6-2	215	4-14-00	2	1	3.46	10	0	1	13	11	7	5	1	4	10	.239	.294	.370	18.87	7.55	53
Dicochea, Jose	R-R	6-3	180	3-21-01	0	1	9.82	4	2	0	11	11	13	12	3	9	16	.250	.400	.477	29.09	16.36	55
Garland, Jake	R-R	6-5	236	9-26-00	6	6	3.75	25	14	1	98	94	47	41	8	33	62	.248	.322	.364	14.69	7.82	422
Gonzalez, James	L-L	6-2	257	9-15-00	1	0	3.00	6	3	0	21	22	8	7	3	2	23	.268	.294	.451	27.06	2.35	85
Guante, Wander	R-R	6-1	180	6-15-00	1	3	5.22	14	7	0	50	51	31	29	8	22	35	.268	.355	.447	16.13	10.14	217
Hall, Dylan	R-R	6-5	210	9-7-97	3	3	6.36	35	0	0	58	74	45	41	13	30	53	.316	.396	.547	19.56	11.07	271
Irvin, Garrett	L-L	6-0	185	2-18-99	3	2	5.95	35	0	1	39	45	30	26	2	25	43	.290	.396	.413	22.99	13.37	187
Johnson, Colton	L-L	6-4	222	7-28-98	1	1	3.08	29	0	9	38	40	15	13	1	13	42	.267	.333	.333	25.45	7.88	165
Johnston, Will	L-L	6-3	215	12-12-00	5	4	4.17	21	11	0	78	63	38	36	7	30	97	.218	.293	.356	29.94	9.26	324
Judkins, Grant	L-R	6-3	200	8-6-97	4	5	3.56	25	12	0	83	71	36	33	10	27	75	.228	.295	.367	21.87	7.87	343
Morales, Luis	R-R	6-3	190	9-24-02	2	4	4.22	22	22	0	81	71	39	38	8	36	84	.237	.322	.378	24.85	10.65	338
Morris, Kade	R-R	6-3	170	6-21-02	0	6	5.92	7	7	0	38	41	26	25	3	11	24	.277	.355	.439	14.20	6.51	169
Myers, Mitch	R-R	6-2	200	1-8-99	6	7	4.54	26	18	0	111	127	62	56	11	24	100	.284	.325	.400	20.92	5.02	478
Owen, Jack	L-L	6-2	204	5-26-98	3	1	7.41	35	0	0	51	75	43	42	7	17	33	.339	.393	.516	13.64	7.02	242
Pontes, Blaze	R-R	6-0	185	1-6-00	3	9	7.36	26	10	0	88	113	76	72	11	40	44	.323	.400	.491	10.84	9.85	406
Rivera, Eduardo	L-L	6-7	237	6-13-03	0	1	11.88	4	2	0	8	11	13	11	0	10	8	.314	.467	.371	17.78	22.22	45
Sanchez, Yehizon	R-R	6-2	170	11-16-00	2	6	6.18	37	0	1	51	63	43	35	3	31	44	.307	.404	.385	17.96	12.65	245
Watters, Jacob	R-R	6-4	230	3-3-01	6	3	5.04	17	10	0	61	63	36	34	2	28	56	.269	.358	.385	20.82	10.41	269
Zhuang, Chen Zhong-Ao	R-R	6-1	190	8-25-00	2	0	2.56	9	6	0	32	23	9	9	2	3	29	.195	.215	.288	23.97	2.48	121

Fielding

Catcher	PCT	G	PO	A	E	DP	PB
Amaya	.985	9	60	6	1	0	1
Conn	.977	49	388	31	10	1	1
Mujica	1.000	5	51	1	0	0	0
Rodriguez	.993	70	519	37	4	4	10

First Base	PCT	G	PO	A	E	DP
Bautista	.991	38	306	33	3	24
Conn	.967	4	28	1	1	6
Simpson	.989	93	717	31	8	69

Second Base	PCT	G	PO	A	E	DP
Arevalo	1.000	2	3	4	0	3
Escorche	.918	13	20	36	5	7
Halter	.967	52	72	130	7	23
Rijo	.800	1	3	1	1	1
Schofield-Sam	.964	25	42	64	4	17
Valenzuela	1.000	6	10	18	0	2
Wright	1.000	2	4	8	0	2
Yamauchi	.981	36	69	86	3	21

Third Base	PCT	G	PO	A	E	DP
Amaya	.000	1	0	0	1	0
Escorche	.838	16	10	21	6	0
Halter	1.000	2	1	0	0	0
Mann	.963	78	44	140	7	14

OAKLAND ATHLETICS

Salom	.924	20	20	41	5	10
Schofield-Sam	.000	1	0	0	0	0
Simpson	.947	12	10	26	2	1
Valenzuela	1.000	1	0	2	0	0
Wright	1.000	2	2	1	0	0

Shortstop	PCT	G	PO	A	E	DP
Angeles	.965	83	130	205	12	46
Escorche	1.000	3	5	2	0	0
Halter	.942	12	17	32	3	5
Kuroda-Grauer	.935	12	10	33	3	5
Valenzuela	.962	13	19	31	2	6
Yamauchi	.962	11	19	31	2	9

Outfield	PCT	G	PO	A	E	DP
Bautista	.957	38	65	1	3	1
Bolte	.960	63	115	4	5	0
Buelvas	.983	78	172	3	3	1
Butler	.973	80	174	9	5	2
Dickey	1.000	26	44	1	0	0
Lasko	1.000	41	105	9	0	2
Masterman	.966	39	80	5	3	1
Nankil	.944	22	32	2	2	0
Valenzuela	.938	9	15	0	1	0

OAKLAND ATHLETICS

STOCKTON PORTS

LOW-A

CALIFORNIA LEAGUE

Batting	B-T	Ht.	Wt.	DOB	AVG	OBP	SLG	G	PA	AB	R	H	2B	3B	HR	RBI	BB	HBP	SH	SF	SO	SB	CS	BB%	SO%
Amaya, Carlos	R-R	5-10	165	12-28-01	.209	.298	.306	37	152	134	15	28	7	0	2	4	15	2	1	0	36	1	1	9.87	23.68
Arevalo, Angel	R-R	5-11	160	10-2-03	.176	.333	.176	6	21	17	2	3	0	0	0	2	4	0	0	0	8	1	0	19.05	38.10
Beltran, Nelson	R-R	5-10	160	12-28-01	.206	.328	.276	82	342	286	37	59	7	2	3	26	42	11	1	2	107	11	3	12.28	31.29
Conn, Cole	B-R	6-0	175	7-11-01	.273	.431	.417	40	185	139	24	38	6	1	4	28	33	7	4	2	38	5	1	17.84	20.54
Cooke, Bjay	R-R	6-2	187	3-14-03	.185	.279	.281	38	165	146	20	27	3	1	3	13	16	3	0	0	54	4	0	9.70	32.73
Diaz, Davis	R-R	5-11	186	3-2-03	.226	.397	.283	14	68	53	12	12	3	0	0	6	8	7	0	0	9	0	0	11.76	13.24
Elliott, Clark	L-R	6-0	183	9-29-00	.291	.436	.473	54	236	182	44	53	9	3	6	34	36	13	2	3	51	6	2	15.25	21.61
Escorche, Jose	R-R	5-8	145	4-29-02	.128	.212	.128	14	52	47	4	6	0	0	0	3	4	1	0	0	12	1	0	7.69	23.08
Franco, Carlos	R-R	5-10	150	2-17-03	.202	.250	.220	29	116	109	8	22	2	0	0	5	6	1	0	0	22	0	0	5.17	18.97
Gomez, Mario	L-R	5-10	185	12-30-02	.238	.330	.388	24	94	80	9	19	1	1	3	11	11	1	0	2	18	0	0	11.70	19.15
Green, Rodney	L-L	6-3	190	4-12-03	.289	.368	.464	24	114	97	19	28	8	0	3	21	13	1	0	3	30	9	1	11.40	26.32
Kuroda-Grauer, Josh	R-R	6-0	185	1-31-03	.389	.476	.389	12	63	54	13	21	0	0	0	4	7	2	0	0	5	4	1	11.11	7.94
Kurtz, Nick	L-L	6-6	230	3-11-03	.400	.571	.960	7	35	25	11	10	2	0	4	12	10	0	0	0	7	0	0	28.57	20.00
Laboy, Yeniel	L-R	6-3	196	5-11-04	.138	.243	.154	21	74	65	4	9	1	0	0	6	8	1	0	0	18	1	0	10.81	24.32
Lasko, Ryan	R-R	6-0	190	6-24-02	.225	.359	.322	82	390	320	48	72	19	0	4	29	59	9	0	2	103	20	6	15.13	26.41
Leary, Cameron	L-L	6-0	180	11-13-01	.222	.309	.395	20	96	81	14	18	5	0	3	16	10	1	2	2	19	4	0	10.42	19.79
Mann, Luke	L-R	6-2	218	4-13-00	.296	.383	.516	40	183	159	26	47	9	1	8	25	20	3	0	1	42	1	0	10.93	22.95
Montero, Darlyn	B-R	6-2	170	5-11-02	.256	.318	.353	95	401	363	43	93	15	1	6	29	24	10	1	2	104	9	0	5.99	25.94
Nankil, Nate	R-R	6-3	185	10-16-02	.285	.401	.460	83	359	298	39	85	20	1	10	56	44	15	0	2	64	3	2	12.26	17.83
Naylor, Myles	R-R	6-2	195	4-15-05	.192	.321	.322	115	499	416	48	80	17	2	11	58	79	1	1	2	173	6	0	15.83	34.67
Pineda, Pedro	R-R	6-1	170	9-6-03	.122	.182	.183	22	88	82	6	10	3	1	0	5	6	0	0	0	31	2	2	6.82	35.23
Puason, Robert	R-R	6-3	165	9-11-02	.183	.260	.209	32	127	115	15	21	3	0	0	10	9	3	0	0	43	4	2	7.09	33.86
Rijo, Elvis	R-R	5-11	165	11-27-03	.215	.324	.268	43	174	149	14	32	8	0	0	20	8	16	1	0	32	2	1	4.60	18.39
Rodriguez, Joseph	R-R	6-1	165	1-4-03	.193	.323	.303	33	133	109	12	21	6	0	2	9	21	1	0	2	44	4	1	15.79	33.08
Ruiz, Esteury	R-R	6-0	169	2-15-99	.545	.563	.727	4	16	11	3	6	2	0	0	5	3	0	0	2	3	1	2	18.75	18.75
Salom, Dereck	R-R	5-10	135	2-22-01	.220	.354	.276	69	305	246	34	54	8	0	2	29	49	5	0	5	46	7	1	16.07	15.08
Schofield-Sam, T.J.	L-R	6-1	185	6-20-01	.280	.325	.386	59	277	254	30	71	11	2	4	38	7	12	0	4	47	5	1	2.53	16.97
Schwartz, Nick	R-R	5-11	190	3-7-01	.207	.323	.266	46	202	169	28	35	4	0	2	19	28	2	0	2	60	2	0	13.86	29.70
White, Tommy	R-R	6-0	242	3-2-03	.224	.303	.299	25	119	107	15	24	2	0	2	14	9	3	0	0	21	0	0	7.56	17.65
Yamauchi, Casey	R-R	5-9	155	8-8-00	.316	.389	.404	35	132	114	18	36	6	2	0	12	10	5	1	2	13	7	3	7.58	9.85

Pitching	B-T	Ht.	Wt.	DOB	W	L	ERA	G	GS	SV	IP	Hits	Runs	ER	HR	BB	SO	AVG	OBP	SLG	SO%	BB%	BF
Adamiak, Mark	R-R	6-4	230	12-15-00	5	5	4.90	45	0	2	61	62	41	33	7	28	75	.267	.353	.422	27.47	10.26	273
Alexander, Scott	L-L	6-2	195	7-10-89	0	0	4.50	2	1	0	2	2	1	1	0	0	3	.250	.250	.250	37.50	0.00	8
Alvarado, Wilfred	R-R	6-3	190	11-20-05	0	1	24.92	2	0	0	4	11	12	12	3	3	4	.458	.536	1.083	14.29	10.71	28
Anderson, Luke	R-R	6-2	205	8-5-98	2	2	5.28	18	0	1	15	14	14	9	0	20	21	.233	.446	.283	25.30	24.10	83
Avant, Corey	R-R	6-4	225	11-6-01	2	6	7.26	24	6	2	57	81	54	46	7	39	68	.329	.421	.520	23.29	13.36	292
Barrera, Diego	L-L	6-0	165	5-5-00	6	2	2.77	26	0	2	39	37	16	12	3	13	48	.248	.313	.362	29.27	7.93	164
Blackburn, Paul	R-R	6-1	196	12-4-93	0	0	40.50	1	0	0	1	2	3	3	0	2	1	.500	.667	.500	16.67	33.33	6
Brown, Ryan	R-R	6-2	214	11-2-00	2	3	4.67	21	7	4	69	57	38	36	3	21	79	.217	.274	.346	27.43	7.29	288
Castro, Felix	R-R	6-3	180	2-16-04	0	0	29.70	3	0	0	3	7	11	11	1	6	4	.438	.577	.875	15.38	23.08	26
Conover, Drew	R-R	6-5	185	7-27-01	0	3	15.80	7	2	0	14	12	27	24	1	31	15	.235	.549	.373	16.48	34.07	91
Corro, Derek	L-L	5-11	145	11-19-04	4	2	5.80	25	1	1	54	56	44	35	5	41	52	.269	.407	.433	19.70	15.53	264
Czyz, T.J.	R-R	6-2	175	9-12-00	2	0	5.44	33	0	0	41	37	26	25	6	42	35	.242	.409	.412	17.68	21.21	198
Dallas, Micah	R-R	6-2	215	4-14-00	1	2	2.83	28	0	4	35	30	17	11	4	9	40	.227	.276	.371	27.40	6.16	146
De La Rosa, Franck	R-R	6-8	200	6-9-00	1	1	5.88	9	1	0	26	26	17	17	2	19	39	.255	.387	.441	31.45	15.32	124
Dettmer, Nathan	R-R	6-4	230	4-26-02	0	2	10.24	4	3	0	10	16	11	11	2	4	11	.364	.417	.727	22.92	8.33	48
Dicochea, Jose	R-R	6-3	180	3-21-01	2	6	4.54	22	14	1	79	75	50	40	6	42	84	.250	.354	.377	23.53	11.76	357
Echavarria, Steven	R-R	6-1	180	8-6-05	0	5	6.55	19	19	0	58	74	50	42	4	36	59	.311	.408	.429	20.92	12.77	282
Finley, Jackson	R-R	6-4	222	9-15-00	2	7	5.62	25	15	0	83	94	57	52	6	42	94	.288	.385	.408	24.35	10.88	386
Franco, Carlos	R-R	5-10	150	2-17-03	0	0	18.00	1	0	0	1	3	2	2	0	0	0	.500	.500	.833	0.00	0.00	6
Hernandez, Camilo	R-R	6-1	190	9-30-03	2	0	3.26	12	0	1	19	19	9	7	1	9	13	.253	.352	.347	14.77	10.23	88
Jean, Jefferson	R-R	6-3	170	1-29-05	0	6	9.33	9	7	1	27	32	29	28	5	26	25	.288	.433	.505	17.73	18.44	141
Johnston, Will	L-L	6-3	215	12-12-00	0	1	1.93	4	2	0	14	5	3	3	0	8	26	.109	.241	.130	48.15	14.81	54
Laboy, Yeniel	L-R	6-3	196	5-11-04	0	0	0.00	1	0	0	1	1	0	0	0	0	0	.250	.250	.250	0.00	0.00	4
Manzano, Alejandro	R-R	6-2	165	2-28-02	4	3	6.16	21	8	0	76	84	60	52	11	33	82	.272	.349	.479	23.30	9.38	352
Muller, Kyle	R-L	6-7	250	10-7-97	0	1	6.00	1	1	0	3	3	2	2	0	2	3	.273	.385	.273	23.08	15.38	13
Nova, Alvin	R-R	6-4	170	5-5-05	1	1	4.50	3	2	0	8	7	5	4	0	3	7	.241	.333	.310	21.21	9.09	33
Pfennigs, Jake	R-R	6-7	215	9-9-99	1	2	4.87	8	2	0	20	21	13	11	1	7	26	.259	.315	.321	29.21	7.87	89
Reisinger, Tom	R-R	6-3	215	3-17-01	1	5	9.05	21	5	1	63	93	67	63	8	41	53	.343	.435	.528	16.36	12.65	324
Restituyo, Brayan	L-L	5-11	160	1-17-02	0	1	6.49	16	0	2	26	28	20	19	2	14	33	.277	.373	.366	26.19	11.11	126

Rivera, Eduardo	L-L	6-7	237	6-13-03	0	0	0.00	4	0	2	3	1	0	0	0	0	3	.111	.111	.111	33.33	0.00	9
Robinson, Kyle	R-R	6-6	210	7-17-03	0	0	7.71	3	2	0	7	9	7	6	1	3	9	.310	.382	.483	26.47	8.82	34
Salom, Dereck	R-R	5-10	135	2-22-01	0	0	22.50	1	0	0	2	6	5	5	3	1	0	.462	.500	1.154	0.00	7.14	14
Sha, Tzu-Chen	R-R	6-2	165	10-15-03	2	6	6.33	24	12	0	85	104	74	60	20	27	64	.298	.353	.562	16.41	6.92	390
Stripling, Ross	R-R	6-1	215	11-23-89	0	1	13.50	1	1	0	1	2	2	1	1	1	1	.400	.500	1.000	16.67	16.67	6
Tur, Yunior	R-R	6-6	200	8-9-99	2	6	4.88	27	10	1	90	95	54	49	10	35	92	.271	.348	.444	23.12	8.79	398
Vera, Norge	R-R	6-4	185	6-1-00	1	2	6.89	9	4	0	16	13	12	12	1	18	24	.224	.438	.362	30.00	22.50	80
Zhuang, Chen Zhong-Ao	R-R	6-1	190	8-25-00	3	2	1.67	9	5	0	32	26	6	6	1	4	37	.215	.246	.331	29.37	3.17	126

Fielding

Catcher	PCT	G	PO	A	E	DP	PB
Amaya	.976	32	296	26	8	3	7
Conn	.990	31	287	24	3	3	2
Diaz	1.000	9	72	6	0	1	5
Franco	.982	22	214	6	4	0	1
Gomez	.983	13	107	6	2	0	3
Schwartz	.989	27	258	20	3	0	1

First Base	PCT	G	PO	A	E	DP
Conn	1.000	2	15	1	0	3
Gomez	1.000	4	29	0	0	2
Kurtz	.982	7	48	6	1	8
Laboy	1.000	2	23	0	0	3
Montero	.988	77	534	28	7	50
Salom	1.000	2	13	2	0	0
Schofield-Sam	.986	30	187	18	3	15
Schwartz	1.000	8	61	5	0	5

Second Base	PCT	G	PO	A	E	DP
Arevalo	.947	6	3	15	1	1
Cooke	.979	27	40	52	2	13
Diaz	1.000	2	2	1	0	0
Escorche	.925	9	14	23	3	6
Laboy	.867	5	4	9	2	2
Naylor	.934	14	23	34	4	5
Puason	1.000	2	1	0	0	0
Rijo	.923	21	26	34	5	10
Salom	1.000	6	13	12	0	3
Schofield-Sam	.951	16	19	39	3	9
Yamauchi	.931	30	47	88	10	21

Third Base	PCT	G	PO	A	E	DP
Amaya	1.000	1	0	2	0	0
Diaz	1.000	2	3	2	0	0
Escorche	.600	3	1	2	2	0
Laboy	.909	10	10	10	2	1
Mann	.964	31	30	51	3	6
Rijo	.943	20	10	23	2	3
Salom	.895	38	35	50	10	8
Schofield-Sam	1.000	4	2	3	0	0
White	.973	22	11	25	1	2
Yamauchi	1.000	2	2	2	0	0

Shortstop	PCT	G	PO	A	E	DP
Cooke	1.000	1	1	3	0	1
Escorche	.667	2	3	1	2	0
Kuroda-Grauer	1.000	10	11	24	0	6
Mann	.960	7	11	13	1	2
Naylor	.915	89	115	175	27	38
Salom	.948	23	40	69	6	14
Yamauchi	1.000	1	0	1	0	0

Outfield	PCT	G	PO	A	E	DP
Beltran	.975	63	112	3	3	1
Cooke	1.000	4	1	0	0	0
Elliott	.946	41	84	4	5	1
Green	.981	22	51	0	1	0
Lasko	.990	76	189	7	2	2
Leary	1.000	19	27	0	0	0
Montero	.923	8	11	1	1	0
Nankil	.986	77	133	3	2	1
Pineda	.975	21	39	0	1	0
Puason	.972	30	32	3	1	0
Rijo	1.000	2	6	0	0	0
Rodriguez	.985	31	64	3	1	0
Ruiz	1.000	3	3	0	0	0
Schofield-Sam	1.000	3	3	0	0	0

OAKLAND ATHLETICS

ACL ATHLETICS — *ROOKIE*

ARIZONA COMPLEX LEAGUE

Batting	B-T	Ht.	Wt.	DOB	AVG	OBP	SLG	G	PA	AB	R	H	2B	3B	HR	RBI	BB	HBP	SH	SF	SO	SB	CS	BB%	SO%
Andrade, Bryan	R-R	6-1	145	2-3-05	.262	.262	.310	16	42	42	4	11	0	1	0	8	0	0	0	0	12	0	1	0.00	28.57
Arevalo, Angel	R-R	5-11	160	10-2-03	.213	.355	.426	45	169	136	24	29	7	5	4	23	26	5	0	2	59	11	0	15.38	34.91
Cooke, Bjay	R-R	6-2	187	3-14-03	.278	.480	.333	6	25	18	5	5	1	0	0	3	6	1	0	0	4	3	0	24.00	16.00
Davidson, Logan	B-R	6-3	185	12-26-97	.429	.600	.857	3	10	7	4	3	0	0	1	3	3	0	0	0	1	0	0	30.00	10.00
De La Paz, Reynaldo	R-R	6-3	190	9-11-05	.179	.318	.260	37	148	123	19	22	3	2	1	15	20	5	0	0	45	0	0	13.51	30.41
Eierman, Jeremy	R-R	5-11	205	9-10-96	.455	.571	.818	4	14	11	2	5	1	0	1	3	3	0	0	0	4	0	0	21.43	28.57
Elliott, Clark	L-R	6-0	183	9-29-00	.389	.450	.500	5	20	18	3	7	2	0	0	3	2	0	0	0	8	1	0	10.00	40.00
Fernandez, Jesus	R-R	5-11	145	2-14-06	.253	.297	.277	27	91	83	13	21	2	0	0	8	6	0	0	2	4	4	1	6.59	4.40
Freitez, Luis	R-R	6-0	180	5-17-03	.244	.380	.378	44	151	119	21	29	4	6	0	22	23	5	1	3	44	0	2	15.23	29.14
Fuentes, Erubiel	R-R	5-8	170	1-15-03	.221	.393	.253	33	125	95	11	21	3	0	0	14	21	6	3	0	27	0	0	16.80	21.60
Garrett, Ray	R-R	5-10	155	3-23-04	.260	.318	.325	27	86	77	7	20	0	1	1	13	7	0	1	1	24	4	0	8.14	27.91
Gomez, Mario	L-R	5-10	185	12-30-02	.286	.440	.329	23	92	70	17	20	3	0	0	9	19	1	1	1	18	0	0	20.65	19.57
Gonzalez, Cesar	R-R	6-2	165	1-13-05	.244	.326	.366	12	46	41	7	10	3	1	0	8	4	1	0	0	14	0	0	8.70	30.43
Halter, Colby	L-R	6-1	200	8-24-01	.000	.000	.000	1	1	1	0	0	0	0	0	0	0	0	0	0	1	0	0	0.00	100.00
Harris, Brett	R-R	6-1	208	6-24-98	.333	.500	1.333	1	4	3	2	1	0	0	1	2	1	0	0	0	0	0	0	25.00	0.00
Laboy, Yeniel	L-R	6-3	196	5-11-04	.255	.376	.284	34	125	102	17	26	1	1	0	15	20	1	0	2	22	1	2	16.00	17.60
Machado, Anderson	R-R	6-1	170	10-10-03	.556	.600	.556	3	10	9	1	5	0	0	0	1	1	0	0	0	1	0	0	10.00	10.00
Marinez, Luis	R-R	6-1	155	10-11-01	.180	.345	.295	46	177	139	25	25	7	0	3	25	30	6	0	2	58	1	1	16.95	32.77
Muncy, Max	R-R	6-1	180	8-25-02	.379	.400	.724	8	30	29	5	11	4	0	2	5	0	1	0	0	13	1	0	0.00	43.33
Ortiz, German	B-R	6-2	195	8-2-04	.292	.417	.399	46	205	168	44	49	10	1	2	17	32	4	0	0	37	3	0	15.61	18.05
Pacheco, Carlos	R-R	5-10	150	11-1-04	.257	.398	.403	48	184	144	39	37	10	1	3	13	22	13	2	2	45	11	3	11.96	24.46
Pariguan, Javier	R-R	5-10	160	2-5-04	.115	.289	.131	22	76	61	5	7	1	0	0	2	14	1	0	0	32	0	1	18.42	42.11
Pineda, Pedro	R-R	6-1	170	9-6-03	.239	.349	.380	22	87	71	5	17	5	1	1	17	12	1	1	2	27	2	1	13.79	31.03
Rijo, Elvis	R-R	5-11	165	11-27-03	.120	.281	.120	8	32	25	2	3	0	0	0	1	5	1	0	1	7	2	1	15.63	21.88
Rivera, Angel	R-R	5-9	175	2-2-03	.417	.632	.583	5	19	12	1	5	2	0	0	5	7	0	0	0	2	0	0	36.84	10.53
Rodriguez, Joseph	R-R	6-1	165	1-4-03	.274	.416	.597	20	77	62	17	17	4	2	4	10	14	1	0	0	29	1	1	18.18	37.66
Rosado, Jamaliel	R-R	6-3	195	8-15-03	.189	.373	.256	36	119	90	15	17	4	1	0	14	24	3	1	1	36	2	1	20.17	30.25
Ruiz, Esteury	R-R	6-0	169	2-15-99	.000	.000	.000	1	5	4	0	0	0	0	0	1	0	0	0	1	3	0	0	0.00	60.00
Schofield-Sam, T.J.	L-R	6-1	185	6-20-01	.429	.484	.607	7	31	28	11	12	3	1	0	2	3	0	0	0	3	1	0	9.68	9.68
Schwartz, Nick	R-R	5-11	190	3-7-01	.244	.340	.268	13	48	41	4	10	1	0	0	3	6	0	0	0	14	0	0	12.50	29.17
Toro, Abraham	B-R	6-0	223	12-20-96	.375	.500	.750	3	10	8	1	3	0	0	1	4	2	0	0	0	1	0	0	20.00	10.00
Valenzuela, Sahid	B-R	5-7	165	9-16-97	.143	.143	.143	2	7	7	1	1	0	0	0	0	0	0	0	0	2	0	0	0.00	28.57
Wilson, Jacob	R-R	6-3	190	3-30-02	.571	.647	.857	5	17	14	4	8	4	0	0	3	3	0	0	0	0	0	0	17.65	0.00
Wright, Joshwan	R-R	5-8	170	11-9-00	.273	.273	.273	3	11	11	1	3	0	0	0	0	0	0	0	0	2	1	0	0.00	18.18

Pitching	B-T	Ht.	Wt.	DOB	W	L	ERA	G	GS	SV	IP	Hits	Runs	ER	HR	BB	SO	AVG	OBP	SLG	SO%	BB%	BF
Alvarado, Wilfred	R-R	6-3	190	11-20-05	2	0	3.12	12	0	1	17	18	11	6	0	12	13	.269	.373	.343	15.48	14.29	84
Anderson, Luke	R-R	6-2	205	8-5-98	0	0	9.00	1	0	0	1	1	1	1	0	1	0	.333	.500	1.000	0.00	25.00	4

Castro, Felix	R-R	6-3	180	2-16-04	1	1	6.80	12	8	0	44	51	39	33	3	28	35	.295	.399	.439	16.83	13.46	208
Conover, Drew	R-R	6-5	185	7-27-01	0	4	5.96	8	5	0	26	21	21	17	1	23	34	.216	.398	.320	26.56	17.97	128
Correa, Danis	R-R	5-11	150	8-26-99	0	0	0.00	4	1	0	5	0	0	0	0	1	9	.000	.067	.000	60.00	6.67	15
Corro, Derek	L-L	5-11	145	11-19-04	0	1	1.13	3	1	0	8	10	8	1	0	4	3	.294	.366	.382	7.32	9.76	41
Cusick, Ryan	R-R	6-6	235	11-12-99	0	0	0.00	1	1	0	3	1	0	0	0	3	1	.125	.364	.125	9.09	27.27	11
De Jesus, Dairon	R-R	6-3	180	3-27-04	2	3	4.56	20	0	1	24	25	18	12	1	12	23	.278	.357	.500	20.54	10.71	112
Del Rosario, Joelvis	R-R	5-11	170	4-16-01	0	0	0.00	2	2	0	4	2	0	0	0	0	5	.143	.143	.143	35.71	0.00	14
Fernandez, Richard	R-R	6-1	190	9-22-02	0	0	0.00	1	1	0	1	1	0	0	0	0	1	.333	.333	.333	33.33	0.00	3
Garrett, Ray	R-R	5-10	155	3-23-04	0	0	0.00	1	0	0	1	0	0	0	0	0	0	.000	.000	.000	0.00	0.00	2
Gonzalez, Jose	R-R	6-0	160	1-5-02	2	1	7.88	19	0	0	24	35	25	21	0	6	24	.327	.365	.430	20.69	5.17	116
Hernandez, Camilo	R-R	6-1	190	9-30-03	3	1	3.18	22	0	5	28	21	15	10	0	13	33	.196	.281	.262	27.27	10.74	121
Jackson, Zach	R-R	6-4	230	12-25-94	1	1	10.13	2	0	0	3	2	3	3	1	3	6	.200	.385	.600	46.15	23.08	13
Jean, Jefferson	R-R	6-3	170	1-29-05	0	0	2.95	5	3	0	18	12	8	6	2	14	33	.179	.325	.299	39.76	16.87	83
Manzano, Alejandro	R-R	6-2	165	2-28-02	0	0	0.00	1	1	0	2	1	0	0	0	0	2	.143	.143	.143	28.57	0.00	7
Marte, Francis	R-R	6-3	180	10-31-05	0	0	3.89	11	5	1	35	33	19	15	2	18	28	.244	.331	.385	17.83	11.46	157
Martinez, Adrian	R-R	6-2	215	12-10-96	1	0	1.69	4	1	0	5	2	1	1	1	0	8	.095	.095	.238	38.10	0.00	21
Medina, Luis	R-R	6-1	175	5-3-99	0	1	27.00	1	1	0	2	6	6	6	0	0	3	.500	.538	.750	23.08	0.00	13
Newcomb, Sean	L-L	6-5	255	6-12-93	0	0	0.00	1	1	0	1	0	0	0	0	0	2	.000	.000	.000	66.67	0.00	3
Nova, Alvin	R-R	6-4	170	5-5-05	1	4	9.24	10	5	0	25	35	28	26	0	23	30	.340	.451	.485	22.56	17.29	133
Parra, Josnier	R-R	6-1	170	10-15-01	1	2	5.48	18	0	1	23	33	24	14	3	7	20	.327	.389	.604	17.70	6.19	113
Perez, Francisco	S-L	6-2	227	7-20-97	1	0	0.00	2	0	0	3	1	0	0	0	2	8	.100	.250	.200	66.67	16.67	12
Perez, Manuel	R-R	6-2	180	8-29-05	1	4	6.64	13	6	0	39	40	35	29	2	30	38	.258	.386	.355	20.11	15.87	189
Perkins, Jack	R-R	6-1	220	12-26-99	0	0	0.00	1	1	0	2	0	0	0	0	0	3	.000	.000	.000	50.00	0.00	6
Pfennigs, Jake	R-R	6-7	215	9-9-99	0	0	21.60	3	0	0	2	6	5	4	0	2	2	.545	.643	.727	14.29	14.29	14
Restituyo, Brayan	L-L	5-11	160	1-17-02	2	1	5.93	20	0	0	30	33	22	20	2	11	32	.277	.333	.420	23.53	8.09	136
Robles, Domingo	L-L	6-2	170	4-29-98	0	0	0.00	1	1	0	2	0	0	0	0	0	4	.000	.000	.000	66.67	0.00	6
Rodriguez, Franyelson	R-R	6-1	160	5-20-02	2	4	6.83	20	0	1	29	44	31	22	3	9	30	.346	.381	.591	21.28	6.38	141
Silverio, Jesus	R-R	6-2	180	7-15-02	3	3	8.28	17	0	0	25	30	24	23	2	16	31	.306	.402	.510	25.20	13.01	123
Troconis, Donny	R-R	6-4	180	10-12-05	1	4	6.80	12	8	0	42	57	48	32	5	19	45	.308	.382	.568	21.23	8.96	212
Vera, Norge	R-R	6-4	185	6-1-00	0	0	0.00	3	2	0	3	1	0	0	0	2	2	.111	.273	.111	18.18	18.18	11
Walkinshaw, Jake	R-R	6-3	200	7-7-96	0	1	5.91	6	6	0	11	13	7	7	0	3	8	.310	.370	.357	17.39	6.52	46

Fielding

C: Pariguan 22, Gomez 14, Schwartz 13, Marinez 8, Rivera 5, Gonzalez 5. **1B:** Marinez 28, Ortiz 17, Laboy 10, Gonzalez 3, Andrade 3, Gomez 2, Machado 1. **2B:** Fuentes 32, Garrett 22, Arevalo 4, Schofield-Sam 2, Wright 2, Toro 1, Halter 1, Rosado 1, Cooke 1, Freitez 1. **3B:** Rosado 29, Laboy 12, Andrade 11, Rijo 6, Schofield-Sam 4, Machado 2, Valenzuela 2, Muncy 1, Toro 1, Davidson 1, Harris 1. **SS:** Fernandez 26, Arevalo 24, Rosado 7, Muncy 4, Wilson 3, Cooke 3, Eierman 3, Garrett 2. **LF:** Pacheco 22, Ortiz 16, Freitez 13, Pineda 6, Rodriguez 6, Schofield-Sam 1, Davidson 1, Elliott 1. **CF:** Pacheco 22, Rodriguez 13, Arevalo 13, Pineda 10, Freitez 6, Elliott 3, Ruiz 1. RF: De La Paz 37, Freitez 21, Pineda 5, Fuentes 1, Elliott 1.

DSL ATHLETICS — *ROOKIE*

DOMINICAN SUMMER LEAGUE

Batting	B-T	Ht.	Wt.	DOB	AVG	OBP	SLG	G	PA	AB	R	H	2B	3B	HR	RBI	BB	HBP	SH	SF	SO	SB	CS	BB%	SO%
Baldallo, Dayker	L-R	5-10	135	11-29-03	.225	.338	.225	45	155	129	17	29	0	0	0	10	21	1	4	0	29	3	0	13.55	18.71
Cota, Brayan	L-R	6-1	170	5-14-07	.159	.361	.171	33	109	82	10	13	1	0	0	15	22	4	1	0	22	2	1	20.18	20.18
De La Cruz, Reinaldo	R-R	6-2	170	1-12-06	.271	.456	.390	20	80	59	12	16	3	2	0	9	16	4	1	0	16	7	2	20.00	20.00
Dume, Kevin	L-R	6-5	220	9-19-04	.275	.399	.377	51	203	167	21	46	5	0	4	34	33	2	0	1	56	1	1	16.26	27.59
Duran, Frandy	L-R	6-2	175	9-29-05	.286	.394	.321	10	33	28	4	8	1	0	0	2	5	0	0	0	5	0	0	15.15	15.15
Fernandez, Darling	R-R	6-2	190	12-10-05	.264	.383	.385	50	214	174	39	46	15	0	2	24	33	3	0	4	24	14	1	15.42	11.21
Gonzalez, Samuel	R-R	5-11	170	11-20-06	.126	.378	.168	42	136	95	21	12	4	0	0	14	36	3	1	1	26	3	2	26.47	19.12
Landaeta, Ramon	R-R	6-2	180	4-19-06	.247	.371	.330	33	116	97	13	24	5	0	1	12	18	1	0	0	35	2	0	15.52	30.17
Lopez, Jeison	R-R	6-1	170	4-6-06	.200	.310	.320	10	29	25	3	5	3	0	0	3	2	2	0	0	10	1	1	6.90	34.48
Montero, Edgar	R-R	6-2	190	11-21-06	.239	.398	.375	54	227	176	35	42	9	3	3	24	48	0	1	2	50	11	2	21.15	22.03
Natera, Jesus	R-R	5-10	165	7-22-06	.105	.382	.132	19	55	38	8	4	1	0	0	3	14	3	0	0	17	0	0	25.45	30.91
Pacheco, Azaeel	R-R	6-0	170	12-13-06	.158	.333	.211	13	24	19	2	3	1	0	0	1	4	1	0	0	7	0	0	16.67	29.17
Pereira, Alejandro	R-R	5-11	170	6-12-07	.192	.270	.231	28	89	78	10	15	3	0	0	10	7	2	0	2	23	0	0	7.87	25.84
Ramos, Jose	L-R	6-1	160	10-1-06	.141	.310	.195	49	188	149	24	21	2	3	0	12	35	2	1	1	62	16	4	18.62	32.98
Rojas, Sebastian	R-R	6-0	175	3-13-07	.224	.357	.313	23	85	67	15	15	3	0	1	12	8	7	1	2	11	0	0	9.41	12.94
Superlano, Jesus	R-R	5-11	165	9-20-05	.248	.317	.376	39	139	125	21	31	7	0	3	15	7	6	0	1	29	3	3	5.04	20.86
Yan, Jonatan	R-R	6-0	150	11-1-04	.190	.314	.260	35	121	100	16	19	3	2	0	9	18	1	0	2	32	6	3	14.88	26.45

Pitching	B-T	Ht.	Wt.	DOB	W	L	ERA	G	GS	SV	IP	Hits	Runs	ER	HR	BB	SO	AVG	OBP	SLG	SO%	BB%	BF
Arends, Nathan	R-R	6-2	180	9-23-06	1	1	7.71	13	0	1	14	12	13	12	0	10	9	.255	.397	.277	14.29	15.87	63
Baldallo, Dayker	L-R	5-10	135	11-29-03	0	0	16.20	2	0	0	2	6	3	3	0	0	0	.600	.545	.900	0.00	0.00	11
Chacon, Paul	R-R	6-0	180	9-8-05	0	2	7.17	12	6	1	38	45	33	30	2	23	32	.306	.418	.456	18.08	12.99	177
Contreras, Yohandri	R-R	6-3	200	10-30-06	2	3	7.80	11	5	0	30	31	26	26	1	27	20	.277	.450	.375	13.42	18.12	149
Cortes, Jonathan	R-R	6-2	200	7-31-04	0	0	4.67	14	0	2	17	11	9	9	3	10	11	.175	.307	.365	14.67	13.33	75
De Los Santos, Eliazar	R-R	6-4	220	8-15-02	0	5	5.16	11	7	0	30	31	28	17	1	20	36	.263	.380	.339	25.35	14.08	142
Gonzalez, Diomar	R-R	6-1	190	10-11-04	0	2	7.80	7	3	1	15	23	16	13	1	8	12	.354	.440	.477	15.79	10.53	76
Guzman, Freilyn	R-R	6-3	160	11-5-05	1	4	4.28	12	8	0	40	50	23	19	0	25	21	.318	.411	.350	11.35	13.51	185
Lopez, Celso	R-R	6-0	185	7-16-04	0	0	3.38	8	2	0	13	10	7	5	0	10	12	.222	.357	.311	21.43	17.86	56
Matos, Erick	R-R	6-4	195	1-20-07	4	2	3.15	10	5	0	34	25	18	12	0	28	28	.207	.362	.240	18.30	18.30	153
Medina, Amilcar	R-R	6-2	154	9-2-04	1	0	7.27	13	1	0	17	13	19	14	0	30	13	.210	.484	.274	13.68	31.58	95
Meraz, Hugo	R-R	6-4	195	6-21-05	0	0	11.70	9	0	1	10	13	18	13	0	10	14	.295	.446	.341	24.56	17.54	57
Parra, Jose	L-L	5-11	175	12-30-05	1	0	10.13	7	1	0	11	10	15	12	0	18	12	.250	.483	.300	20.00	30.00	60

Pinto, Jose	R-R	6-1	180	8-4-02	2	1	2.79	11	6	0	42	37	16	13	0	22	37	.239	.344	.355	20.11	11.96	184
Plicet, Luis	R-R	6-4	160	4-2-07	0	2	8.10	6	0	0	7	5	6	6	0	13	14	.200	.500	.280	35.00	32.50	40
Polanco, Brayan	R-R	6-6	180	2-28-05	2	3	3.24	14	0	1	17	17	9	6	0	6	15	.279	.333	.295	21.74	8.70	69
Ribeiro, Sulivan	L-L	6-4	218	12-16-03	1	0	15.26	9	0	0	8	4	15	13	0	22	4	.182	.633	.227	8.16	44.90	49
Silva, Yeferson	R-R	6-0	175	6-28-05	3	1	3.72	11	6	1	39	38	17	16	3	15	31	.255	.327	.349	18.79	9.09	165
Sirotti, Oliver	R-R	6-3	180	9-26-06	0	2	5.11	12	0	1	12	14	10	7	1	7	18	.269	.371	.346	29.03	11.29	62
Urdaneta, Roberto	R-R	6-2	170	9-22-05	0	0	1.69	8	0	1	11	2	2	2	0	8	7	.067	.293	.067	16.67	19.05	42
Zabaleta, Franco	L-L	6-2	165	10-12-06	4	5	5.18	11	5	0	33	41	28	19	0	20	39	.299	.400	.343	24.22	12.42	161

Fielding

C: Pereira 26, Natera 17, Landaeta 16, Pacheco 9. **1B:** Dume 38, Baldallo 14, Cota 8, Duran 1, Montero 1, Natera 1. **2B:** Gonzalez 39, De La Cruz 18, Superlano 4, Baldallo 3, Cota 1. **3B:** Superlano 29, Cota 24, Baldallo 6, Gonzalez 1, Montero 1. **SS:** Montero 53, De La Cruz 2, Gonzalez 2. **LF:** Fernandez 40, Baldallo 9, Ramos 3, Rojas 2, Superlano 1, Duran 1, Lopez 1. **CF:** Yan 33, Ramos 22, Lopez 8. **RF:** Ramos 25, Baldallo 16, Rojas 11, Duran 9, Yan 2, Lopez 1, De La Cruz 1.

Philadelphia Phillies

SEASON SYNOPSIS: For the first time since 2011, the Phillies won the National League East, cruising into the all-star break with an MLB-best 62-34 record. But after the break, the Phillies gave up nearly a run more per game, and after reaching the World Series in 2022, the Phillies have lost a round earlier in successive seasons, dropping a Division Series to the upstart Mets.

HIGH POINT: Philadelphia ripped off a 22-4 spurt, starting with ace Zack Wheeler's six scoreless frames against the Reds on April 25, wrapping up when Wheeler beat the Rangers 5-2 on May 23. Wheeler led the team in WAR and led National League pitchers in WHIP (0.955) during a 16-7, 2.57 campaign with 224 strikeouts in 200 innings. He was one of a franchise-record eight Phillies named to the NL All-Star Game roster.

LOW POINT: The Phillies lost three of their last four regular-season series; catcher J.T. Realmuto told MLB.com that the team knew it wasn't at its best but hoped it could "flip a switch" in the post-season. But the Mets flustered the Phils' offense, which scored just five runs in three Division Series losses. That included a Game One 6-2 loss despite seven scoreless innings from Wheeler.

NOTABLE ROOKIES: Orion Kerkering, who made the postseason roster last year after jumping from Class A, was one of four relievers manager Rob Thomson used for 60 games or more. He posted a 2.29 ERA and 74 strikeouts with just 17 walks in 63 innings. Righty Tyler Phillips went 4-1 in seven starts but allowed nine homers in 37 innings. Versatile Weston Wilson, a minor league free agent signed prior to the 2023 season, started games in the outfield corners, second and third base and earned a spot on the playoff roster.

KEY TRANSACTIONS: The Phillies mostly ran it back from 2023 in the offseason but club president Dave Dombrowski was active during the season. He traded away relievers Gregory Soto and Seranthony Dominguez to the Orioles in separate deals, receiving prospects and outfielder Austin Hays in return, but the righthanded hitter had hamstring and kidney issues that limited his availability and production. They traded for Angels closer Carlos Estevez as well, but it was Estevez, relieving Jeff Hoffman, who gave up a Game Four, series-clinching grand slam to Francisco Lindor in the Division Series.

OPENING DAY PAYROLL: $243,476,617 (4th)

PLAYERS OF THE YEAR

MAJOR LEAGUE

Zack Wheeler
RHP

16-7, 2.57 ERA
224 SO, 52 BB, 200 IP
NL-best 0.96 WHIP

MINOR LEAGUE

Aidan Miller
SS

(A/A+/AA)
.261/.366/.446
11 HR, 23 SB

ORGANIZATION LEADERS

Batting		*Qualifiers
MAJORS		
* AVG	Trea Turner	.295
* OPS	Bryce Harper	.898
HR	Kyle Schwarber	38
RBI	Kyle Schwarber	104
MINORS		
* AVG	Keaton Anthony, Clearwater, J. Shore, Reading	.327
* OBP	Keaton Anthony, Clearwater, J. Shore, Reading	.414
* SLG	Otto Kemp, 4-teams	.489
* OPS	Otto Kemp, 4-teams	.881
R	Otto Kemp, 4-teams	82
H	Justin Crawford, Jersey Shore/Reading	143
TB	Scott Kingery, Lehigh Valley	226
2B	Aidan Miller, Jersey Shore/Reading/Clearwater	28
3B	Otto Kemp, 4-teams	9
HR	Scott Kingery, Lehigh Valley	25
RBI	Carson Taylor, Reading/Lehigh Valley	77
BB	Carson Taylor, Reading/Lehigh Valley	73
SO	Carlos De La Cruz, Reading/Lehigh Valley	148
SB	Starlyn Caba, FCL Phillies, Clearwater	50

Pitching		#Qualifiers
MAJORS		
W	Zack Wheeler	16
# ERA	Zack Wheeler	2.57
SO	Zack Wheeler	224
SV	Jose Alvarado	13
MINORS		
W	Robinson Pina, Reading/Lehigh Valley	13
L	Mick Abel, Lehigh Valley	12
# ERA	Brandon Tucker, Clearwater/Jersey Shore	2.97
G	Andrew Bellatti, Lehigh Valley	46
GS	Robinson Pina, Reading/Lehigh Valley	25
GS	Tyler Phillips, Reading/L. Valley	25
SV	Max Lazar, Reading/Lehigh Valley	13
IP	Robinson Pina, Reading/Lehigh Valley	129
BB	Mick Abel, Lehigh Valley	78
SO	Eiberson Castellano, Jersey Shore/Reading	132
# AVG	Brandon Tucker, Clearwater/Jersey Shore	.233

2024 PERFORMANCE

General Manager: Dave Dombrowski. **Farm Director:** Preston Mattingly. **Scouting Director:** Brian Barber.

Class	Team	League	W	L	PCT	Finish	Manager
Majors	Philadelphia Phillies	National	95	67	.586	2 (15)	Rob Thomson
Triple-A	Lehigh Valley IronPigs	International	68	78	.466	14 (20)	Anthony Contreras
Double-A	Reading Fightin Phils	Eastern	59	78	.431	11 (12)	Al Pedrique
High-A	Jersey Shore BlueClaws	South Atlantic	74	58	.561	3 (12)	Greg Brodzinski
Low-A	Clearwater Threshers	Florida State	64	63	.504	5 (10)	Marty Malloy
Rookie	FCL Phillies	Florida Complex	33	25	.569	7 (15)	Shawn Williams
Rookie	DSL Phillies Red	Dominican	21	34	.382	42 (51)	Nerluis Martinez
Rookie	DSL Phillies White	Dominican	26	29	.473	31 (51)	Waner Santanaz
Overall 2024 Minor League Record			**345**	**365**	**.486**	**20th (30)**	

ORGANIZATION STATISTICS

PHILADELPHIA PHILLIES

NATIONAL LEAGUE

Batting	B-T	Ht.	Wt.	DOB	AVG	OBP	SLG	G	PA	AB	R	H	2B	3B	HR	RBI	BB	HBP	SH	SF	SO	SB	CS	BB%	SO%
Bohm, Alec	R-R	6-5	218	8-3-96	.280	.332	.448	143	606	554	62	155	44	2	15	97	40	6	0	6	86	5	2	6.60	14.19
Castellanos, Nick	R-R	6-4	203	3-4-92	.254	.311	.431	162	659	606	80	154	30	4	23	86	41	10	0	2	139	6	2	6.22	21.09
Clemens, Kody	L-R	6-1	200	5-15-96	.219	.258	.447	44	120	114	17	25	9	1	5	18	5	1	0	0	29	0	0	4.17	24.17
Dahl, David	L-R	6-1	197	4-1-94	.207	.242	.397	19	62	58	6	12	2	0	3	8	3	0	0	1	21	0	0	4.84	33.87
Garcia, Aramis	R-R	6-1	228	1-12-93	.000	.000	.000	3	7	7	0	0	0	0	0	0	0	0	0	0	3	0	0	0.00	42.86
Harper, Bryce	L-R	6-3	210	10-16-92	.285	.373	.525	145	631	550	85	157	42	0	30	87	76	2	1	2	138	7	4	12.04	21.87
Hays, Austin	R-R	5-11	200	7-5-95	.256	.275	.397	22	80	78	8	20	5	0	2	6	0	2	0	0	19	2	1	0.00	23.75
Kennedy, Buddy	R-R	5-9	190	10-5-98	.182	.308	.273	8	13	11	1	2	1	0	0	2	2	0	0	0	3	0	0	15.38	23.08
Marchan, Rafael	B-R	5-9	170	2-25-99	.294	.345	.549	17	56	51	8	15	4	0	3	6	3	1	1	0	8	0	0	5.36	14.29
Marsh, Brandon	L-R	6-4	215	12-18-97	.249	.328	.419	135	476	418	55	104	17	3	16	60	50	2	1	5	154	19	3	10.50	32.35
Merrifield, Whit	R-R	6-1	195	1-24-89	.199	.277	.295	53	174	156	21	31	4	1	3	11	15	2	1	0	19	11	1	8.62	10.92
Pache, Cristian	R-R	6-2	215	11-19-98	.202	.288	.269	50	118	104	9	21	5	1	0	9	13	0	0	1	43	0	0	11.02	36.44
Realmuto, J.T.	R-R	6-1	212	3-18-91	.266	.322	.429	99	413	380	50	101	18	1	14	47	27	5	0	1	102	2	2	6.54	24.70
Rojas, Johan	R-R	5-11	165	8-14-00	.243	.279	.322	120	363	338	47	82	12	3	3	32	13	4	8	0	69	25	4	3.58	19.01
Schwarber, Kyle	L-R	6-0	229	3-5-93	.248	.366	.485	150	692	573	110	142	22	0	38	104	106	5	0	8	197	5	3	15.32	28.47
Sosa, Edmundo	R-R	6-0	210	3-6-96	.257	.313	.422	90	274	249	39	64	12	4	7	31	13	8	1	2	66	7	1	4.74	24.09
Stevenson, Cal	L-L	5-9	175	9-12-96	.250	.333	.375	18	27	24	2	6	3	0	0	6	3	0	0	0	4	0	0	11.11	14.81
Stott, Bryson	L-R	6-3	200	10-6-97	.245	.315	.356	148	571	506	65	124	19	2	11	57	53	3	0	9	93	32	3	9.28	16.29
Stubbs, Garrett	L-R	5-10	170	5-26-93	.207	.296	.262	56	187	164	18	34	4	1	1	11	17	4	0	1	50	5	0	9.09	26.74
Turner, Trea	R-R	6-2	185	6-30-93	.295	.338	.469	121	539	505	88	149	25	0	21	62	27	6	0	1	98	19	4	5.01	18.18
Wilson, Weston	R-R	6-3	215	9-11-94	.284	.347	.489	41	98	88	13	25	7	1	3	10	8	1	0	1	29	3	0	8.16	29.59

Pitching	B-T	Ht.	Wt.	DOB	W	L	ERA	G	GS	SV	IP	Hits	Runs	ER	HR	BB	SO	AVG	OBP	SLG	SO%	BB%	BF
Allard, Kolby	L-L	6-1	195	8-13-97	2	0	5.00	7	4	0	27	34	15	15	5	8	23	.312	.359	.523	19.66	6.84	117
Alvarado, Jose	L-L	6-2	245	5-21-95	2	5	4.09	66	0	13	62	49	30	28	6	28	63	.215	.302	.346	24.42	10.85	258
Banks, Tanner	R-L	6-1	210	10-24-91	0	1	3.70	22	1	0	24	22	11	10	1	10	23	.234	.311	.309	21.70	9.43	106
Brogdon, Connor	R-R	6-6	205	1-29-95	0	1	27.00	3	0	0	2	3	7	6	2	6	3	.375	.643	1.250	21.43	42.86	14
Clemens, Kody	L-R	6-1	200	5-15-96	0	0	9.00	1	0	0	1	2	1	1	1	1	0	.400	.500	1.000	0.00	16.67	6
Dominguez, Seranthony	R-R	6-1	225	11-25-94	3	2	4.75	38	0	1	36	32	22	19	6	12	40	.224	.293	.406	25.48	7.64	157
Estevez, Carlos	R-R	6-6	277	12-28-92	3	2	2.57	20	0	6	21	18	8	6	2	7	18	.225	.295	.350	20.45	7.95	88
Gilbert, Tyler	L-L	6-3	223	12-22-93	0	0	3.24	6	0	0	8	10	3	3	1	2	4	.286	.342	.400	10.53	5.26	38
Hoffman, Jeff	R-R	6-5	235	1-8-93	3	3	2.17	68	0	10	66	48	20	16	6	16	89	.197	.253	.324	33.58	6.04	265
Johnson, Seth	R-R	6-1	205	9-19-98	0	1	34.71	1	1	0	2	8	9	9	1	3	0	.571	.611	.929	0.00	16.67	18
Kerkering, Orion	R-R	6-2	204	4-4-01	5	3	2.29	64	2	0	63	51	20	16	2	17	74	.223	.297	.301	28.79	6.61	257
Lazar, Max	R-R	6-1	200	6-3-99	0	0	4.61	11	0	0	14	13	7	7	2	2	9	.250	.278	.442	16.67	3.70	54
Marte, Yunior	R-R	6-2	180	2-2-95	0	0	6.92	23	0	0	26	34	22	20	5	15	23	.306	.386	.495	18.11	11.81	127
Mercado, Michael	R-R	6-4	160	4-15-99	1	2	11.08	5	2	0	13	16	16	16	9	9	10	.296	.406	.833	15.63	14.06	64
Nelson, Nick	R-R	6-1	205	12-5-95	0	0	5.06	4	0	0	5	8	3	3	0	2	8	.348	.423	.435	30.77	7.69	26
Nola, Aaron	R-R	6-2	200	6-4-93	14	8	3.57	33	33	0	199	189	84	79	30	50	197	.247	.295	.421	24.02	6.10	820
Ortiz, Luis	R-R	6-3	230	9-22-95	0	0	27.00	1	0	0	1	3	2	2	0	0	0	.750	.750	.750	0.00	0.00	4
Phillips, Tyler	R-R	6-5	225	10-27-97	4	1	6.87	8	7	0	37	45	28	28	9	7	28	.300	.338	.527	17.50	4.38	160
Pinto, Ricardo	R-R	6-0	195	1-20-94	0	0	10.97	6	0	1	11	19	14	13	2	5	8	.373	.441	.608	13.56	8.47	59
Ruiz, Jose	R-R	6-1	245	10-21-94	5	1	3.71	52	0	1	51	51	23	21	8	17	52	.260	.318	.423	23.96	7.83	217
Sanchez, Cristopher	L-L	6-1	165	12-12-96	11	9	3.32	31	31	0	182	182	76	67	11	44	153	.258	.301	.358	20.29	5.84	754
Soto, Gregory	L-L	6-1	234	2-11-95	2	4	4.08	43	0	2	35	36	19	16	2	20	44	.265	.378	.375	26.67	12.12	165
Strahm, Matt	R-L	6-2	190	11-12-91	6	2	1.87	66	0	3	63	36	14	13	4	11	79	.166	.224	.276	33.33	4.64	237
Stubbs, Garrett	L-R	5-10	170	5-26-93	0	0	15.75	4	0	0	4	6	7	7	2	2	0	.353	.421	.765	0.00	10.53	19
Suarez, Ranger	L-L	6-1	217	8-26-95	12	8	3.46	27	27	0	151	140	63	58	14	41	145	.243	.299	.379	23.16	6.55	626
Turnbull, Spencer	R-R	6-3	210	9-18-92	3	0	2.65	17	7	0	54	37	17	16	6	20	58	.188	.279	.325	26.13	9.01	222
Walker, Taijuan	R-R	6-4	235	8-13-92	3	7	7.10	19	15	0	84	107	68	66	24	37	58	.317	.386	.589	15.22	9.71	381
Wheeler, Zack	L-R	6-4	195	5-30-90	16	7	2.57	32	32	0	200	139	62	57	20	52	224	.192	.253	.328	28.46	6.61	787
Wilson, Weston	R-R	6-3	215	9-11-94	0	0	0.00	1	0	0	1	1	0	0	0	0	0	.250	.250	.250	0.00	0.00	4

Fielding

Catcher	PCT	G	PO	A	E	DP	PB
Garcia	1.000	3	15	2	0	0	0
Marchan	.985	17	126	6	2	3	0
Realmuto	.995	99	899	34	5	5	4
Stubbs	.995	52	417	16	2	2	3

First Base	PCT	G	PO	A	E	DP
Bohm	.991	15	96	10	1	5
Clemens	1.000	15	89	5	0	7
Harper	.996	141	1050	95	5	99
Wilson	1.000	3	3	0	0	0

Second Base	PCT	G	PO	A	E	DP
Clemens	1.000	8	7	12	0	2
Kennedy	1.000	2	3	4	0	1
Merrifield	.956	14	25	18	2	6
Sosa	.977	20	41	44	2	13
Stott	.993	137	221	314	4	71
Wilson	1.000	4	3	4	0	1

Third Base	PCT	G	PO	A	E	DP
Bohm	.960	128	84	253	14	15
Clemens	.889	11	4	20	3	1
Kennedy	1.000	3	1	2	0	0
Merrifield	.967	12	10	19	1	4
Sosa	.977	23	9	33	1	0
Wilson	.867	5	4	9	2	1

Shortstop	PCT	G	PO	A	E	DP
Sosa	.981	48	51	107	3	23
Stott	.935	14	11	18	2	3
Turner	.962	118	136	291	17	51

Outfield	PCT	G	PO	A	E	DP
Castellanos	.989	157	263	3	3	0
Clemens	1.000	7	5	0	0	0
Dahl	1.000	15	18	1	0	0
Hays	1.000	21	35	0	0	0
Marsh	.979	158	228	6	5	1
Merrifield	1.000	25	32	2	0	0
Pache	.973	48	69	2	2	0
Rojas	.991	116	219	6	2	1
Schwarber	1.000	5	10	0	0	0
Stevenson	1.000	16	23	1	0	0
Wilson	1.000	26	20	1	0	1

LEHIGH VALLEY IRONPIGS — *TRIPLE-A*

INTERNATIONAL LEAGUE

Batting	B-T	Ht.	Wt.	DOB	AVG	OBP	SLG	G	PA	AB	R	H	2B	3B	HR	RBI	BB	HBP	SH	SF	SO	SB	CS	BB%	SO%
Bohm, Alec	R-R	6-5	218	8-3-96	.500	.500	.750	1	4	4	0	2	1	0	0	0	0	0	0	0	1	0	0	0.00	25.00
Breaux, Josh	R-R	6-1	220	10-7-97	.154	.214	.231	4	14	13	0	2	1	0	0	0	1	0	0	0	3	0	0	7.14	21.43
Cardenas, Ruben	R-R	6-0	185	10-10-97	.269	.342	.587	26	117	104	21	28	6	0	9	28	10	2	0	1	13	5	0	8.55	11.11
Castro, Rodolfo	B-R	6-0	205	5-21-99	.209	.274	.313	19	73	67	9	14	1	0	2	7	5	1	0	0	18	0	2	6.85	24.66
Clemens, Kody	L-R	6-1	200	5-15-96	.266	.322	.489	68	301	274	43	73	13	3	14	50	20	4	0	3	63	6	1	6.64	20.93
Dahl, David	L-R	6-1	197	4-1-94	.285	.353	.502	76	295	267	36	76	12	2	14	40	28	0	0	0	71	5	4	9.49	24.07
De La Cruz, Carlos	R-R	6-8	210	10-6-99	.190	.240	.276	48	175	163	11	31	5	0	3	18	8	3	0	1	63	1	0	4.57	36.00
Fergus, Cade	R-R	6-2	195	8-22-00	.000	.000	.000	1	3	2	0	0	0	0	0	0	0	0	1	0	2	0	0	0.00	66.67
Garcia, Aramis	R-R	6-1	228	1-12-93	.159	.216	.279	76	278	258	29	41	7	0	8	25	13	6	0	1	99	6	1	4.68	35.61
Godoy, Jose	L-R	5-11	200	10-13-94	.143	.226	.161	20	63	56	6	8	1	0	0	1	4	2	1	0	12	0	0	6.35	19.05
Gonzalez, Diego	R-R	5-11	160	6-7-03	.167	.286	.167	4	7	6	0	1	0	0	0	0	1	0	0	0	2	1	0	14.29	28.57
Haley, Jim	R-R	6-1	195	2-23-95	.249	.313	.400	88	313	285	39	71	17	1	8	41	20	7	0	1	75	17	1	6.39	23.96
Hall, Darick	L-R	6-4	232	7-25-95	.236	.320	.387	114	488	432	50	102	17	0	16	72	50	4	0	2	111	2	1	10.25	22.75
Hays, Austin	R-R	5-11	200	7-5-95	.214	.353	.214	4	17	14	4	3	0	0	0	0	2	1	0	0	6	0	0	11.76	35.29
Kemp, Otto	R-R	5-11	185	9-9-99	.200	.333	.244	13	54	45	5	9	2	0	0	2	5	4	0	0	18	1	1	9.26	33.33
Kennedy, Buddy	R-R	5-9	190	10-5-98	.294	.400	.500	67	300	248	44	73	19	1	10	35	41	6	0	5	45	2	1	13.67	15.00
Kingery, Scott	R-R	5-10	180	4-29-94	.268	.316	.488	125	505	463	73	124	17	5	25	67	34	0	5	3	138	25	2	6.73	27.33
Kroon, Matt	R-R	6-0	195	12-5-96	.251	.325	.441	80	280	247	36	62	14	0	11	38	22	6	2	2	70	15	1	7.86	25.00
Lee Sang, Marcus	L-L	5-11	200	1-2-01	.333	.400	.333	2	10	9	3	3	0	0	0	0	1	0	0	0	3	0	0	10.00	30.00
Luplow, Jordan	R-R	5-11	195	9-26-93	.255	.343	.450	62	254	220	41	56	13	0	10	32	28	3	0	3	52	12	2	11.02	20.47
Marchan, Rafael	B-R	5-9	170	2-25-99	.229	.340	.297	34	141	118	16	27	2	0	2	11	19	2	0	2	28	0	0	13.48	19.86
McKenna, Ryan	R-R	5-11	195	2-14-97	.190	.296	.345	25	98	84	7	16	5	1	2	13	11	2	0	1	22	6	1	11.22	22.45
Muzziotti, Simon	L-L	6-0	175	12-27-98	.235	.297	.373	61	240	217	28	51	9	3	5	24	19	1	1	2	47	5	1	7.92	19.58
Podkul, Nick	R-R	6-1	200	4-11-97	.231	.364	.418	60	220	182	35	42	7	0	9	34	34	4	0	0	70	1	1	15.45	31.82
Quiroz, Esteban	L-R	5-4	199	2-17-92	.158	.289	.259	54	190	158	17	25	4	0	4	22	27	3	0	2	52	1	0	14.21	27.37
Roberts, Cody	R-R	6-1	195	6-16-96	.290	.373	.406	43	160	138	21	40	13	0	1	14	17	2	2	1	51	2	0	10.63	31.88
Rojas, Johan	R-R	5-11	165	8-14-00	.382	.417	.500	8	38	34	7	13	1	0	1	3	2	0	2	0	6	6	0	5.26	15.79
Schwecke, Trevor	R-R	6-1	185	12-18-97	.214	.302	.232	18	65	56	9	12	1	0	0	1	7	0	0	0	22	0	0	10.77	33.85
Shaver, A.J.	R-R	6-2	213	10-8-01	.222	.300	.222	4	10	9	1	2	0	0	0	1	1	0	0	0	5	1	0	10.00	50.00
Simoneit, William	R-R	6-3	235	10-14-96	.000	.000	.000	1	3	3	0	0	0	0	0	0	0	0	0	0	2	0	0	0.00	66.67
Sosa, Edmundo	R-R	6-0	210	3-6-96	.111	.111	.111	2	9	9	0	1	0	0	0	0	0	0	0	0	1	0	0	0.00	11.11
Stevenson, Cal	L-L	5-9	175	9-12-96	.302	.421	.486	101	397	321	68	97	25	5	8	44	68	0	5	3	66	29	5	17.13	16.62
Taylor, Carson	B-R	6-2	205	6-2-99	.316	.519	.316	6	27	19	4	6	0	0	0	2	6	2	0	0	2	0	0	22.22	7.41
Thomas, Jared	L-R	6-0	185	12-3-00	.286	.375	.286	4	8	7	2	2	0	0	0	0	1	0	0	0	5	0	0	12.50	62.50
Wilson, Ethan	L-L	6-0	210	11-7-99	.150	.150	.300	5	21	20	3	3	0	0	1	2	0	0	1	0	5	1	0	0.00	23.81
Wilson, Weston	R-R	6-3	215	9-11-94	.240	.340	.487	71	313	263	49	63	11	0	18	55	42	1	1	6	76	14	4	13.42	24.28

Pitching	B-T	Ht.	Wt.	DOB	W	L	ERA	G	GS	SV	IP	Hits	Runs	ER	HR	BB	SO	AVG	OBP	SLG	SO%	BB%	BF
Abel, Mick	R-R	6-5	190	8-18-01	3	12	6.46	24	24	0	109	119	88	78	15	78	117	.279	.390	.479	22.72	15.15	515
Allard, Kolby	L-L	6-1	195	8-13-97	3	8	5.38	20	14	0	82	98	62	49	15	34	74	.293	.357	.522	19.79	9.09	374
Alvarez, Nelson L.	R-R	6-4	220	6-11-98	0	0	0.00	1	0	0	1	0	0	0	0	0	3	.000	.000	.000	100.00	0.00	3
Bellatti, Andrew	R-R	6-1	190	8-5-91	4	2	5.48	46	0	2	43	35	28	26	4	33	42	.220	.370	.421	20.79	16.34	202
Brice, Austin	R-R	6-4	238	6-19-92	0	1	7.71	2	0	0	2	3	3	2	0	3	2	.375	.545	.500	18.18	27.27	11
Buchanan, David	R-R	6-3	200	5-11-89	9	3	4.82	22	16	0	103	119	57	55	13	33	78	.292	.345	.484	17.49	7.40	446
Burr, Ryan	R-R	6-4	220	5-28-94	2	1	2.16	15	0	1	17	14	4	4	1	5	29	.226	.284	.323	43.28	7.46	67
Burrows, Beau	R-R	6-2	210	9-18-96	0	0	8.10	9	0	0	13	15	12	12	1	18	11	.294	.478	.471	15.94	26.09	69
Castillo, Max	R-R	6-2	280	5-4-99	0	5	8.37	11	10	0	43	59	46	40	11	24	37	.330	.404	.626	17.70	11.48	209
Covey, Dylan	R-R	6-1	215	8-14-91	0	0	1.20	15	0	3	15	9	2	2	1	7	16	.176	.276	.255	27.59	12.07	58
Cuas, Jose	R-R	6-3	195	6-28-94	0	1	4.91	4	0	0	4	4	2	2	0	2	5	.286	.412	.357	29.41	11.76	17
Dipoto, Jonah	R-R	6-1	225	9-3-96	0	1	4.37	19	0	0	23	22	12	11	4	12	18	.256	.379	.407	17.14	11.43	105
Garnett, Tristan	L-L	6-6	240	3-29-98	0	0	0.00	1	0	0	1	0	0	0	0	0	2	.000	.000	.000	66.67	0.00	3
Gilbert, Tyler	L-L	6-3	223	12-22-93	4	0	2.25	31	0	7	40	33	15	10	3	8	52	.214	.267	.305	31.52	4.85	165
Godoy, Jose	L-R	5-11	200	10-13-94	0	0	0.00	1	0	0	1	1	0	0	0	0	0	.250	.250	.500	0.00	0.00	4
Gonzalez, Diego	R-R	5-11	160	6-7-03	0	0	0.00	1	0	0	1	0	0	0	0	0	0	.000	.333	.000	0.00	0.00	3

Haake, Zach	R-R	6-7	220	10-8-96	0	1	4.22	16	1	2	21	16	10	10	1	11	28	.208	.330	.325	30.43	11.96	92
Houston, Zac	R-R	6-5	260	11-30-94	2	1	10.29	14	0	0	14	15	17	16	4	14	19	.278	.458	.537	26.39	19.44	72
Johnson, Seth	R-R	6-1	205	9-19-98	2	1	2.74	5	5	0	23	15	7	7	2	14	19	.185	.313	.284	19.59	14.43	97
Kerkering, Orion	R-R	6-2	204	4-4-01	0	0	0.00	2	0	0	2	2	0	0	0	0	3	.250	.333	.250	33.33	0.00	9
Knight, Blaine	R-R	6-3	165	6-28-96	0	0	9.31	7	0	0	10	13	10	10	3	7	11	.333	.438	.641	22.92	14.58	48
Lazar, Max	R-R	6-1	200	6-3-99	4	3	2.45	29	0	10	33	24	13	9	1	10	38	.202	.273	.244	28.36	7.46	134
Lehman, Taylor	L-L	6-8	240	12-30-95	4	3	5.73	38	0	0	33	30	23	21	6	29	37	.256	.404	.496	24.50	19.21	151
Marte, Yunior	R-R	6-2	180	2-2-95	1	0	6.88	16	0	0	17	25	17	13	1	10	14	.373	.463	.463	17.50	12.50	80
McGarry, Griff	R-R	6-2	190	6-8-99	2	1	4.70	29	0	1	31	23	17	16	3	36	40	.217	.408	.358	27.21	24.49	147
McKay, Tyler	R-R	6-6	180	8-18-97	3	3	3.21	29	0	0	34	27	18	12	2	21	32	.218	.340	.290	21.33	14.00	150
Mercado, Michael	R-R	6-4	160	4-15-99	3	1	2.07	32	10	1	70	51	19	16	4	35	64	.210	.312	.309	22.30	12.20	287
Nelson, Nick	R-R	6-1	205	12-5-95	2	5	6.13	34	5	2	54	54	41	37	8	27	44	.260	.360	.438	17.96	11.02	245
Ortiz, Luis	R-R	6-3	230	9-22-95	0	0	10.80	1	0	0	2	1	2	2	1	1	0	.167	.375	.667	0.00	12.50	8
Parkinson, David	R-L	6-2	210	12-14-95	2	4	5.45	19	11	0	69	75	45	42	10	27	49	.279	.358	.454	15.96	8.79	307
Phillips, Tyler	R-R	6-5	225	10-27-97	8	5	5.08	20	20	0	119	117	71	67	14	49	100	.258	.331	.414	19.72	9.66	507
Pina, Robinson	R-R	6-5	225	11-26-98	1	4	4.97	6	6	0	29	29	16	16	4	14	25	.257	.349	.469	19.38	10.85	129
Pinto, Ricardo	R-R	6-0	195	1-20-94	4	1	5.27	16	6	0	56	67	36	33	8	28	40	.295	.376	.467	15.50	10.85	258
Quiroz, Esteban	L-R	5-4	199	2-17-92	0	0	243.00	1	0	0	0	8	9	9	2	1	0	.889	.900	1.889	0.00	10.00	10
Ramos, Eury	R-R	6-3	152	10-10-97	0	0	10.80	6	0	0	7	10	10	8	3	10	5	.357	.526	.821	13.16	26.32	38
Rangel, Alan	R-R	6-2	170	8-21-97	1	2	4.30	10	5	0	29	23	16	14	4	8	25	.217	.267	.396	21.55	6.90	116
Roberts, Cody	R-R	6-1	195	6-16-96	0	0	0.00	1	0	0	1	0	0	0	0	0	0	.000	.000	.000	0.00	0.00	3
Rucker, Michael	R-R	6-1	195	4-27-94	2	2	7.04	19	0	0	23	37	19	18	3	10	31	.356	.417	.538	26.72	8.62	116
Ruiz, Jose	R-R	6-1	245	10-21-94	0	1	1.64	10	0	3	11	7	2	2	1	3	13	.179	.238	.256	30.95	7.14	42
Schultz, Andrew	R-R	6-4	195	7-31-97	0	1	27.00	1	0	0	1	1	2	2	1	4	1	.333	.714	1.333	14.29	57.14	7
Stevenson, Cal	L-L	5-9	175	9-12-96	0	0	27.00	1	0	0	1	2	2	2	1	0	0	.500	.500	1.500	0.00	0.00	4
Tarnok, Freddy	R-R	6-3	185	11-24-98	0	3	6.33	15	4	0	21	23	15	15	5	16	28	.280	.406	.537	27.72	15.84	101
Turnbull, Spencer	R-R	6-3	210	9-18-92	0	0	9.00	1	0	0	2	2	2	2	1	1	2	.250	.333	.750	22.22	11.11	9
Tyler, Kyle	R-R	6-0	185	12-27-96	1	2	5.82	7	7	0	34	36	23	22	4	13	36	.269	.333	.440	24.32	8.78	148
Walker, Taijuan	R-R	6-4	235	8-13-92	1	0	4.09	2	2	0	11	10	5	5	0	6	2	.244	.347	.390	4.08	12.24	49

Fielding

Catcher	PCT	G	PO	A	E	DP	PB
Breaux	1.000	4	24	1	0	0	0
Garcia	.987	68	588	33	8	11	4
Godoy	.991	17	99	15	1	1	1
Marchan	.975	29	214	21	6	1	0
Roberts	.977	30	276	20	7	2	1
Thomas	1.000	2	9	0	0	0	0

First Base	PCT	G	PO	A	E	DP
Clemens	1.000	7	47	10	0	7
De La Cruz	1.000	1	8	1	0	0
Garcia	.667	3	2	0	1	0
Haley	1.000	8	51	4	0	4
Hall	.995	108	831	82	5	88
Luplow	.917	2	9	2	1	0
Podkul	.988	23	156	13	2	17
Taylor	1.000	2	20	0	0	3

Second Base	PCT	G	PO	A	E	DP
Castro	.962	8	11	14	1	4
Clemens	.989	20	35	54	1	13
Gonzalez	1.000	1	1	1	0	0
Haley	.940	58	77	143	14	39
Kennedy	1.000	4	4	16	0	1
Kingery	.950	16	21	36	3	7
Podkul	1.000	3	5	8	0	4
Quiroz	.993	33	45	90	1	21
Schwecke	1.000	8	6	17	0	5
Sosa	.000	1	0	0	0	0
Wilson	1.000	2	2	2	0	0

Third Base	PCT	G	PO	A	E	DP
Bohm	.000	1	0	0	0	0
Castro	.933	6	3	11	1	2
Clemens	.909	4	3	7	1	1
Gonzalez	.000	1	0	0	0	0
Haley	.800	4	1	7	2	0
Kemp	1.000	12	10	15	0	3
Kennedy	.925	55	40	71	9	4
Podkul	.934	22	15	42	4	5
Quiroz	.951	17	9	30	2	5
Schwecke	.889	4	2	6	1	1
Wilson	.972	24	20	50	2	8

Shortstop	PCT	G	PO	A	E	DP
Castro	1.000	1	0	1	0	0
Haley	.975	11	12	27	1	4
Kennedy	1.000	1	1	2	0	0
Kingery	.963	106	171	293	18	77
Schwecke	1.000	1	1	0	0	0
Sosa	.000	1	0	0	0	0
Wilson	.949	31	36	58	5	15

Outfield	PCT	G	PO	A	E	DP
Cardenas	.957	22	38	6	2	2
Clemens	.970	19	31	1	1	0
Dahl	.978	33	44	1	1	1
De La Cruz	.984	41	60	0	1	0
Fergus	1.000	1	2	0	0	0
Haley	1.000	2	2	0	0	0
Hays	1.000	3	1	0	0	0
Kennedy	1.000	1	2	0	0	0
Kingery	1.000	1	1	0	0	0
Kroon	.953	74	118	5	6	1
Lee Sang	1.000	2	2	0	0	0
Luplow	1.000	42	75	5	0	1
McKenna	1.000	25	42	0	0	0
Muzziotti	.983	56	105	12	2	2
Roberts	1.000	2	4	0	0	0
Rojas	1.000	8	16	1	0	0
Schwecke	1.000	3	6	0	0	0
Shaver	1.000	3	5	0	0	0
Stevenson	.996	97	222	3	1	0
Thomas	.000	1	0	0	0	0
Wilson	.964	16	27	0	1	0
Wilson	1.000	5	7	1	0	0

READING FIGHTIN PHILS — *DOUBLE-A*

EASTERN LEAGUE

Batting	B-T	Ht.	Wt.	DOB	AVG	OBP	SLG	G	PA	AB	R	H	2B	3B	HR	RBI	BB	HBP	SH	SF	SO	SB	CS	BB%	SO%
Anthony, Keaton	R-R	6-4	211	6-24-01	.120	.154	.120	6	26	25	0	3	0	0	0	1	1	0	0	0	6	0	0	3.85	23.08
Arnold, Zach	R-R	6-2	205	6-13-01	.149	.208	.179	19	72	67	6	10	2	0	0	1	2	3	0	0	24	2	1	2.78	33.33
Ball, Bryce	L-R	6-4	240	7-8-98	.193	.301	.324	54	206	176	25	34	12	1	3	19	26	2	0	2	67	0	0	12.62	32.52
Breaux, Josh	R-R	6-1	220	10-7-97	.230	.289	.414	25	97	87	8	20	4	0	4	20	8	0	0	2	27	0	0	8.25	27.84
Brito, Erick	R-R	5-8	134	5-25-02	.211	.264	.272	41	161	147	16	31	7	1	0	10	7	4	2	1	25	7	3	4.35	15.53
Crawford, Justin	L-R	6-1	175	1-13-04	.333	.380	.455	40	180	165	25	55	11	0	3	26	11	2	1	1	29	15	1	6.11	16.11
De Freitas, Arturo	R-R	5-10	170	5-28-01	.222	.378	.389	13	45	36	6	8	0	0	2	4	8	1	0	0	13	0	0	17.78	28.89
De La Cruz, Carlos	R-R	6-8	210	10-6-99	.262	.341	.427	65	279	248	36	65	13	2	8	35	24	6	0	1	85	5	1	8.60	30.47
Dissin, Jordan	R-R	6-3	185	5-29-02	.188	.435	.188	6	23	16	4	3	0	0	0	0	5	2	0	0	4	0	0	21.74	17.39
Farquhar, Trent	L-R	5-8	180	3-12-01	.389	.450	.444	5	20	18	2	7	1	0	0	0	2	0	0	0	1	0	2	10.00	5.00
Fergus, Cade	R-R	6-2	195	8-22-00	.202	.307	.336	37	137	119	14	24	4	0	4	13	14	4	0	0	54	7	2	10.22	39.42
Haley, Jim	R-R	6-1	195	2-23-95	.220	.324	.322	17	68	59	6	13	1	1	1	6	7	2	0	0	21	2	0	10.29	30.88
Kemp, Otto	R-R	5-11	185	9-9-99	.258	.353	.476	64	273	233	38	60	12	3	11	39	23	13	0	3	62	9	5	8.42	22.71

Lee Sang, Marcus	L-L	5-11	200	1-2-01	.239	.297	.397	103	425	385	61	92	12	5	13	47	30	4	1	5	100	12	6	7.06	23.53
Marsh, Brandon	L-R	6-4	215	12-18-97	.500	.556	.500	2	9	8	2	4	0	0	0	0	1	0	0	0	3	0	1	11.11	33.33
Martin, Casey	R-R	5-9	175	4-7-99	.167	.216	.297	43	153	138	21	23	4	1	4	11	7	3	0	5	46	6	0	4.58	30.07
Miller, Aidan	R-R	6-2	210	6-9-04	.190	.227	.190	5	22	21	1	4	0	0	0	2	0	1	0	0	4	1	0	0.00	18.18
Moore, Robert	B-R	5-9	170	3-31-02	.240	.323	.364	107	435	379	48	91	20	0	9	41	39	9	5	3	73	19	11	8.97	16.78
Nava, Andrick	B-R	5-10	175	10-6-01	.210	.338	.226	22	74	62	3	13	1	0	0	3	11	1	0	0	9	0	1	14.86	12.16
Pineda, Leandro	L-L	6-1	165	6-4-02	.262	.354	.548	12	48	42	6	11	3	0	3	7	5	1	0	0	5	0	0	10.42	10.42
Radcliff, Baron	L-R	6-4	228	2-9-99	.158	.232	.283	45	168	152	14	24	4	0	5	8	15	0	0	1	79	0	0	8.93	47.02
Ricketts, Caleb	L-R	6-3	225	5-10-00	.219	.331	.338	75	308	260	40	57	8	1	7	31	32	13	0	3	61	1	0	10.39	19.81
Rincones, Gabriel	L-R	6-3	225	3-3-01	.263	.357	.487	59	258	224	35	59	15	1	11	29	30	3	0	1	66	20	7	11.63	25.58
Rodriguez, Jose	R-R	5-11	175	5-13-01	.265	.329	.422	38	164	147	30	39	9	1	4	18	13	2	0	2	21	12	2	7.93	12.80
Schwecke, Trevor	R-R	6-1	185	12-18-97	.257	.326	.408	76	282	245	31	63	18	2	5	35	25	2	0	4	69	14	0	8.87	24.47
Simmons, Kendall	R-R	6-0	180	4-11-00	.252	.333	.455	64	228	202	31	51	12	1	9	27	17	8	0	1	65	6	0	7.46	28.51
Simoneit, William	R-R	6-3	235	10-14-96	.153	.297	.322	19	74	59	10	9	2	1	2	8	7	6	0	2	28	0	0	9.46	37.84
Taylor, Carson	B-R	6-2	205	6-2-99	.277	.389	.465	109	450	372	53	103	16	3	16	75	67	5	0	6	96	5	1	14.89	21.33
Wilson, Ethan	L-L	6-0	210	11-7-99	.211	.271	.347	91	352	317	31	67	14	1	9	36	25	3	1	6	75	9	5	7.10	21.31

Pitching	B-T	Ht.	Wt.	DOB	W	L	ERA	G	GS	SV	IP	Hits	Runs	ER	HR	BB	SO	AVG	OBP	SLG	SO%	BB%	BF
Aldegheri, Samuel	L-L	6-1	180	9-19-01	0	2	3.60	2	2	0	10	9	7	4	0	4	14	.214	.283	.310	30.43	8.70	46
Allard, Kolby	L-L	6-1	195	8-13-97	0	1	8.31	3	3	0	9	12	8	8	3	2	10	.316	.350	.658	25.00	5.00	40
Alvarez, Nelson L.	R-R	6-4	220	6-11-98	0	2	1.76	11	0	0	15	14	6	3	1	7	21	.230	.304	.295	30.43	10.14	69
Ash, Konnor	R-R	5-11	191	3-17-99	1	5	3.53	35	10	0	64	50	25	25	4	35	66	.215	.315	.343	24.35	12.92	271
Baker, Andrew	R-R	6-1	190	3-24-00	4	2	6.21	27	0	0	33	38	27	23	2	24	43	.284	.391	.418	26.71	14.91	161
Burrows, Beau	R-R	6-2	210	9-18-96	1	1	4.00	7	0	0	9	8	4	4	3	4	10	.250	.368	.563	26.32	10.53	38
Cabrera, Jean	R-R	6-0	145	10-20-01	1	1	4.85	6	5	0	30	37	17	16	0	8	19	.311	.379	.387	14.39	6.06	132
Castellano, Eiberson	R-R	6-3	160	5-9-01	2	3	3.79	8	8	0	40	31	19	17	5	9	50	.211	.278	.347	30.86	5.56	162
Castillo, Max	R-R	6-2	280	5-4-99	0	1	4.00	3	3	0	9	8	4	4	1	1	3	.235	.257	.382	8.57	2.86	35
Chace, Moises	R-R	6-1	213	6-9-03	2	1	3.66	4	4	0	20	14	10	8	3	7	35	.200	.273	.371	45.45	9.09	77
Contreras, Efrain	R-R	5-10	225	1-2-00	1	5	9.67	14	8	0	45	57	49	48	10	24	51	.308	.395	.589	23.72	11.16	215
Covey, Dylan	R-R	6-1	215	8-14-91	0	1	1.80	2	0	0	5	5	2	1	0	0	2	.250	.286	.300	9.52	0.00	21
Dallas, Jack	R-R	5-11	200	12-18-98	0	0	0.00	2	0	0	3	1	0	0	0	0	4	.100	.100	.100	40.00	0.00	10
Fausnaught, Braeden	L-L	6-3	235	7-29-99	1	3	3.29	5	5	0	27	30	14	10	1	8	32	.273	.325	.382	26.67	6.67	120
Francisco, Carlos A	R-R	6-4	220	7-2-99	3	4	5.17	41	1	0	54	45	34	31	7	32	52	.223	.339	.391	21.49	13.22	242
Garnett, Tristan	L-L	6-6	240	3-29-98	1	3	2.87	31	0	1	38	27	15	12	2	26	50	.197	.327	.285	30.12	15.66	166
Haake, Zach	R-R	6-7	220	10-8-96	1	2	5.79	19	3	0	28	34	19	18	5	20	28	.298	.400	.482	20.74	14.81	135
Harper, Daniel	R-R	6-4	225	6-1-99	3	1	3.60	21	0	2	25	24	11	10	2	10	23	.270	.340	.382	22.12	9.62	104
Hernandez, Cristian	R-R	6-3	180	9-23-00	1	3	3.19	31	1	2	42	40	16	15	4	9	44	.247	.293	.364	25.29	5.17	174
Johnson, Seth	R-R	6-1	205	9-19-98	0	1	3.52	2	2	0	8	8	3	3	2	1	9	.258	.303	.452	27.27	3.03	33
King, Charles	R-R	6-5	215	1-6-98	0	0	0.00	1	0	0	1	2	0	0	0	1	1	.333	.429	.500	14.29	14.29	7
Lazar, Max	R-R	6-1	200	6-3-99	0	0	0.00	8	0	3	10	3	0	0	0	0	18	.088	.088	.088	52.94	0.00	34
Martinez, Jordi	L-L	6-2	185	7-18-00	1	0	6.00	4	0	0	6	7	5	4	0	0	10	.280	.296	.480	37.04	0.00	27
Mayer, Gunner	R-R	6-6	190	7-27-00	0	1	4.50	2	0	0	2	4	4	1	0	0	4	.400	.400	.500	40.00	0.00	10
McCollum, Tommy	R-R	6-5	260	6-8-99	1	4	5.09	42	0	10	46	49	29	26	4	26	50	.271	.371	.403	23.81	12.38	210
McGowan, Christian	R-R	6-0	205	3-7-00	0	4	6.29	11	9	0	34	38	27	24	6	21	39	.271	.383	.479	23.35	12.57	167
McKay, Tyler	R-R	6-6	180	8-18-97	2	1	0.00	14	0	1	14	6	1	0	0	1	16	.128	.160	.170	32.00	2.00	50
Moore, Wesley	L-L	6-2	200	9-5-99	0	0	5.65	16	0	0	14	14	9	9	2	7	15	.250	.354	.411	23.08	10.77	65
Nava, Andrick	S-R	5-10	175	10-6-01	0	0	9.00	1	0	0	1	3	1	1	0	0	0	.500	.500	.667	0.00	0.00	6
Neunborn, Mitch	R-R	6-0	190	6-27-97	2	1	5.32	15	1	0	24	28	22	14	2	18	26	.283	.398	.465	22.03	15.25	118
Ortiz, Luis	R-R	6-3	230	9-22-95	0	0	15.43	2	0	0	2	4	4	4	1	1	3	.364	.417	.636	25.00	8.33	12
Osterberg, Matt	L-L	6-2	200	4-21-99	3	6	5.24	18	18	0	88	121	59	51	7	24	73	.325	.368	.476	18.25	6.00	400
Pina, Robinson	R-R	6-5	225	11-26-98	12	4	3.95	19	19	0	100	107	45	44	14	13	107	.268	.300	.464	25.30	3.07	423
Pipkin, Dominic	R-R	6-4	160	11-5-99	0	0	0.00	4	0	0	4	3	0	0	0	1	2	.200	.250	.333	12.50	6.25	16
Ramos, Eury	R-R	6-3	152	10-10-97	2	0	3.05	14	0	0	21	12	8	7	1	7	20	.162	.232	.243	24.39	8.54	82
Rucker, Michael	R-R	6-1	195	4-27-94	0	0	4.50	2	0	0	2	2	2	1	0	1	3	.286	.375	.286	37.50	12.50	8
Russell, Matt	R-R	6-2	190	3-28-99	0	2	4.45	25	0	0	32	34	19	16	4	19	33	.272	.385	.392	22.15	12.75	149
Schultz, Andrew	R-R	6-4	195	7-31-97	1	3	4.87	40	0	6	41	36	24	22	2	25	52	.237	.366	.362	27.96	13.44	186
Skirrow, Noah	R-R	6-3	215	7-21-98	6	5	4.66	25	17	0	95	110	64	49	9	47	64	.288	.377	.429	14.48	10.63	442
Walker, Taijuan	R-R	6-4	235	8-13-92	0	0	3.52	2	2	0	8	6	4	3	0	1	6	.214	.258	.321	19.35	3.23	31
Walling, Andrew	L-L	6-2	220	10-29-99	1	0	3.18	14	0	1	17	20	7	6	1	3	24	.290	.338	.391	32.43	4.05	74
Wells, Lachlan	L-L	6-1	185	2-27-97	6	5	3.55	16	16	0	91	83	37	36	16	11	77	.239	.270	.438	21.15	3.02	364

Fielding

Catcher	PCT	G	PO	A	E	DP	PB
Breaux	1.000	13	116	5	0	0	0
De Freitas	.989	12	84	10	1	0	1
Dissin	.962	6	48	2	2	0	2
Nava	.990	19	179	17	2	1	2
Ricketts	.994	71	623	41	4	5	13
Simoneit	.989	18	166	13	2	2	1

First Base	PCT	G	PO	A	E	DP
Anthony	1.000	4	26	2	0	4
Arnold	1.000	4	11	0	0	1
Ball	.992	37	231	18	2	17
Breaux	1.000	6	39	2	0	4
Haley	1.000	1	5	1	0	0
Nava	1.000	1	6	1	0	0
Pineda	1.000	7	48	3	0	9
Schwecke	1.000	8	39	4	0	5
Simoneit	1.000	1	6	0	0	0
Taylor	.989	74	531	32	6	44

Second Base	PCT	G	PO	A	E	DP
Arnold	1.000	3	3	10	0	1
Brito	1.000	12	22	30	0	10
Farquhar	1.000	3	6	6	0	0
Kemp	1.000	5	4	9	0	0
Martin	1.000	7	11	18	0	2
Moore	.994	45	70	107	1	27
Rodriguez	.989	28	42	52	1	9
Schwecke	1.000	10	7	25	0	8
Simmons	.948	26	32	60	5	11

Third Base	PCT	G	PO	A	E	DP
Arnold	.897	10	8	18	3	1
Brito	.875	3	3	4	1	0
Haley	.680	10	5	12	8	1
Kemp	.959	56	26	90	5	8
Martin	.786	7	2	9	3	0
Schwecke	.872	22	23	18	6	1
Simmons	.885	30	14	40	7	3
Taylor	1.000	2	1	3	0	1

Shortstop	PCT	G	PO	A	E	DP
Arnold	.889	3	1	7	1	0
Brito	.991	26	30	75	1	16
Farquhar	1.000	1	3	4	0	1
Martin	.960	21	26	46	3	6
Miller	.944	5	11	6	1	3
Moore	.950	61	69	138	11	21
Rodriguez	.867	9	12	14	4	5
Schwecke	.984	13	25	37	1	11

Outfield	PCT	G	PO	A	E	DP
Crawford	1.000	35	84	2	0	1
De La Cruz	.992	60	125	1	1	0
Fergus	.944	37	63	5	4	0
Haley	.875	4	6	1	1	0
Lee Sang	.978	94	215	3	5	0
Marsh	1.000	1	2	0	0	0
Martin	1.000	8	16	0	0	0
Pineda	1.000	4	7	0	0	0
Radcliff	.975	28	37	2	1	1
Rincones	.964	53	102	4	4	0
Schwecke	1.000	18	32	1	0	1
Wilson	.979	78	136	4	3	1

JERSEY SHORE BLUECLAWS — HIGH-A

SOUTH ATLANTIC LEAGUE

Batting	B-T	Ht.	Wt.	DOB	AVG	OBP	SLG	G	PA	AB	R	H	2B	3B	HR	RBI	BB	HBP	SH	SF	SO	SB	CS	BB%	SO%
Anthony, Keaton	R-R	6-4	211	6-24-01	.356	.418	.483	53	232	205	26	73	10	2	4	45	21	3	0	3	34	0	0	9.05	14.66
Arnold, Zach	R-R	6-2	205	6-13-01	.256	.335	.325	75	282	246	32	63	5	3	2	36	27	4	1	4	64	3	1	9.57	22.70
Bennett, Pierce	R-R	6-1	195	6-28-01	.263	.346	.368	28	107	95	13	25	4	3	0	11	12	0	0	0	15	3	1	11.21	14.02
Bergolla, William	L-R	5-11	165	10-20-04	.295	.350	.385	67	267	234	36	69	12	3	1	29	22	0	7	4	30	18	4	8.24	11.24
Boyd, Emaarion	R-R	5-11	177	8-22-03	.239	.316	.330	96	400	351	52	84	13	5	3	40	27	14	5	3	78	27	12	6.75	19.50
Brito, Erick	R-R	5-8	134	5-25-02	.263	.352	.358	70	276	240	41	63	15	1	2	20	30	3	3	0	39	14	5	10.87	14.13
Caicuto, Luis	R-R	5-10	160	3-5-03	.186	.295	.186	31	113	97	7	18	0	0	0	5	10	5	0	0	21	0	1	8.85	18.58
Castillo, Chad	L-R	6-2	225	4-19-00	.154	.267	.192	8	30	26	2	4	1	0	0	2	3	1	0	0	14	0	0	10.00	46.67
Castro, Rodolfo	B-R	6-0	205	5-21-99	.000	.000	.000	1	1	1	0	0	0	0	0	0	0	0	0	0	0	0	0	0.00	0.00
Crawford, Justin	L-R	6-1	175	1-13-04	.301	.349	.438	70	317	292	54	88	14	4	6	35	21	1	2	1	64	27	8	6.62	20.19
Dissin, Jordan	R-R	6-3	185	5-29-02	.214	.334	.349	78	302	252	43	54	7	0	9	41	39	8	0	3	77	3	1	12.91	25.50
Farquhar, Trent	L-R	5-8	180	3-12-01	.257	.386	.336	38	172	140	27	36	7	2	0	10	22	8	1	1	34	19	4	12.79	19.77
Fergus, Cade	R-R	6-2	195	8-22-00	.237	.383	.419	34	115	93	20	22	1	2	4	16	16	6	0	0	40	9	1	13.91	34.78
Gonzalez, Diego	R-R	5-11	160	6-7-03	.120	.290	.120	9	31	25	1	3	0	0	0	2	6	0	0	0	7	0	1	19.35	22.58
Kemp, Otto	R-R	5-11	185	9-9-99	.333	.440	.533	41	182	150	35	50	8	5	4	22	21	9	0	2	29	8	2	11.54	15.93
Kroon, Matt	R-R	6-0	195	12-5-96	.143	.222	.143	2	9	7	1	1	0	0	0	2	1	0	0	1	3	1	0	11.11	33.33
Leitch, Ryan	R-R	6-0	195	8-26-01	.128	.171	.231	16	41	39	3	5	1	0	1	4	2	0	0	0	15	0	0	4.88	36.59
Mendez, Hendry	L-L	6-2	175	11-7-03	.284	.386	.391	90	373	317	49	90	19	3	3	41	52	2	0	2	52	3	0	13.94	13.94
Miller, Aidan	R-R	6-2	210	6-9-04	.258	.353	.444	58	258	225	35	58	12	6	6	32	30	3	0	0	57	12	4	11.63	22.09
Muzziotti, Simon	L-L	6-0	175	12-27-98	.067	.125	.200	4	16	15	1	1	0	1	0	1	1	0	0	0	5	0	0	6.25	31.25
Nava, Andrick	B-R	5-10	175	10-6-01	.281	.353	.430	39	156	135	16	38	9	1	3	25	16	1	0	4	31	0	0	10.26	19.87
Pineda, Leandro	L-L	6-1	165	6-4-02	.260	.327	.394	78	327	292	39	76	11	2	8	45	23	8	0	4	70	3	2	7.03	21.41
Reyes, Felix	R-R	6-3	195	3-26-01	.243	.280	.375	85	353	325	42	79	19	0	8	50	19	1	0	8	61	3	0	5.38	17.28
Rincon, Bryan	B-R	5-10	185	2-8-04	.202	.336	.333	33	140	114	25	23	9	0	2	15	23	1	0	2	44	8	0	16.43	31.43
Rondon, Leonardo	B-R	5-7	160	3-10-04	.143	.143	.143	3	7	7	0	1	0	0	0	0	0	0	0	0	2	0	0	0.00	28.57
Schreffler, Troy	R-R	5-11	190	10-27-00	.227	.296	.396	82	285	255	45	58	11	4	8	39	20	6	1	3	80	23	1	7.02	28.07
Thomas, Jared	L-R	6-0	185	12-3-00	.273	.333	.273	7	24	22	2	6	0	0	0	1	2	0	0	0	6	1	0	8.33	25.00
Viars, Jordan	L-L	6-2	215	7-18-03	.180	.276	.247	27	105	89	11	16	0	0	2	10	11	2	0	3	41	0	0	10.48	39.05
Ware, Bryson	R-R	6-2	193	12-28-00	.293	.340	.465	27	106	99	13	29	6	4	1	11	6	1	0	0	31	3	0	5.66	29.25

Pitching	B-T	Ht.	Wt.	DOB	W	L	ERA	G	GS	SV	IP	Hits	Runs	ER	HR	BB	SO	AVG	OBP	SLG	SO%	BB%	BF
Aldegheri, Samuel	L-L	6-1	180	9-19-01	6	5	3.18	13	13	0	68	44	27	24	3	28	95	.182	.274	.285	34.55	10.18	275
Baker, Andrew	R-R	6-1	190	3-24-00	1	0	1.59	16	0	0	17	7	4	3	0	8	30	.125	.231	.196	46.15	12.31	65
Beckel, Brandon	R-R	6-4	225	10-20-01	0	0	3.68	5	0	0	7	9	3	3	0	5	14	.290	.378	.387	37.84	13.51	37
Buchanan, David	R-R	6-3	200	5-11-89	1	0	0.00	1	1	0	7	4	0	0	0	0	4	.167	.167	.167	16.67	0.00	24
Cabrera, Jean	R-R	6-0	145	10-20-01	5	4	3.39	14	14	0	77	59	33	29	6	25	91	.210	.283	.313	28.98	7.96	314
Castellano, Eiberson	R-R	6-3	160	5-9-01	4	2	4.12	14	12	0	63	58	34	29	6	20	86	.240	.312	.347	31.62	7.35	272
Castillo, Starlyn	R-R	6-0	210	2-24-02	2	3	3.34	8	7	0	30	20	11	11	0	20	20	.196	.352	.294	15.63	15.63	128
Chace, Moises	R-R	6-1	213	6-9-03	1	1	4.15	2	2	0	9	6	4	4	0	3	13	.194	.265	.226	37.14	8.57	35
Chenault, Ethan	R-R	6-5	200	3-28-01	0	0	3.00	6	0	0	6	3	2	2	1	3	8	.150	.261	.300	34.78	13.04	23
Dallas, Jack	R-R	5-11	200	12-18-98	5	2	3.50	39	3	0	54	47	27	21	3	18	55	.230	.307	.343	24.12	7.89	228
Dillard, Trey	R-R	6-0	195	11-15-98	1	0	5.15	30	1	1	37	28	22	21	3	30	44	.206	.357	.331	26.19	17.86	168
Eddington, Jacob	R-R	6-2	185	4-26-01	0	0	0.00	5	0	0	5	3	2	0	0	4	6	.158	.304	.263	26.09	17.39	23
Estanista, Jaydenn	R-R	6-3	180	10-3-01	1	0	3.18	15	0	3	23	18	11	8	1	10	27	.214	.320	.321	27.84	10.31	97
Fausnaught, Braeden	L-L	6-3	235	7-29-99	8	3	3.65	19	18	0	99	89	45	40	12	32	90	.241	.302	.398	22.00	7.82	409
Fowler, Jordan	L-L	6-3	180	3-9-99	0	0	1.93	3	1	0	9	8	2	2	1	2	8	.235	.278	.441	22.22	5.56	36
Garbrick, Alex	R-R	6-1	210	6-4-98	0	0	2.70	7	0	0	7	8	4	2	0	3	3	.286	.355	.321	9.68	9.68	31
Harper, Daniel	R-R	6-4	225	6-1-99	0	3	2.08	23	0	7	26	15	9	6	1	10	38	.163	.252	.217	36.54	9.62	104
Hernandez, Cristian	R-R	6-3	180	9-23-00	0	0	0.00	6	0	0	8	5	0	0	0	1	10	.179	.207	.250	34.48	3.45	29
Jimenez, Estibenzon	R-R	6-1	172	1-25-02	4	11	7.02	27	14	0	82	104	76	64	11	32	85	.301	.373	.470	21.85	8.23	389
Karaffa, Nathan	R-R	6-1	200	1-4-01	1	0	0.00	4	0	0	5	1	0	0	0	0	4	.059	.059	.059	23.53	0.00	17
King, Charles	R-R	6-5	215	1-6-98	2	2	4.26	31	0	2	38	34	19	18	1	15	41	.238	.319	.322	25.15	9.20	163
Klassen, George	R-R	6-2	170	1-26-02	1	2	4.22	5	5	0	21	16	11	10	2	9	32	.200	.297	.363	35.16	9.89	91
Leitch, Ryan	R-R	6-0	195	8-26-01	0	0	9.00	1	0	0	1	2	1	1	1	0	0	.400	.400	1.000	0.00	0.00	5
Martinez, Jordi	L-L	6-2	185	7-18-00	0	1	3.86	3	0	0	2	2	1	1	1	1	3	.222	.300	.556	30.00	10.00	10
Mayer, Gunner	R-R	6-6	190	7-27-00	3	3	4.10	41	0	4	53	38	28	24	3	36	68	.207	.341	.332	30.09	15.93	226
McGarry, Griff	R-R	6-2	190	6-8-99	0	0	0.00	1	0	0	1	0	0	0	0	0	2	.000	.000	.000	66.67	0.00	3
Moore, Wesley	L-L	6-2	200	9-5-99	0	0	2.70	12	0	1	13	10	4	4	1	3	18	.204	.264	.306	33.96	5.66	53
Neunborn, Mitch	R-R	6-0	190	6-27-97	5	5	2.39	14	14	0	68	50	26	18	5	24	70	.203	.281	.337	25.36	8.70	276
Pan, Wen Hui	R-R	6-3	220	9-19-02	0	1	1.29	14	1	1	21	13	5	3	0	7	22	.183	.268	.268	26.83	8.54	82
Petit, Jonathan	R-R	6-2	174	4-19-01	0	0	19.06	7	0	0	6	10	12	12	1	7	9	.370	.528	.630	25.00	19.44	36
Pipkin, Dominic	R-R	6-4	160	11-5-99	0	0	0.00	3	0	0	3	0	0	0	0	1	4	.000	.083	.000	33.33	8.33	12

Rao, Alex	R-R	6-4	230	10-25-99	0	1	11.12	12	0	0	11	13	16	14	0	18	14	.310	.500	.405	21.88	28.13	64
Robles, Benony	L-L	6-4	185	10-1-00	0	0	5.70	20	0	0	24	25	21	15	4	18	23	.269	.395	.484	20.00	15.65	115
Ronan, Mason	L-L	6-3	222	3-3-00	2	1	7.89	26	0	0	30	27	27	26	2	25	39	.243	.399	.369	27.27	17.48	143
Russo, Luke	L-R	6-4	199	2-21-01	4	2	2.86	7	6	0	35	24	13	11	1	15	37	.203	.307	.314	26.81	10.87	138
Steward, Casey	R-R	6-5	260	8-2-01	4	3	3.46	10	10	0	52	39	22	20	1	31	49	.206	.327	.270	21.68	13.72	226
Tarnok, Freddy	R-R	6-3	185	11-24-98	0	0	0.00	2	2	0	3	2	0	0	0	0	2	.200	.200	.200	18.18	0.00	11
Thompson, Paxton	R-R	6-1	205	10-5-99	2	0	1.64	16	0	2	22	15	5	4	2	6	23	.195	.250	.312	27.38	7.14	84
Tucker, Braydon	L-R	6-3	205	7-19-99	4	2	3.02	8	8	0	42	37	14	14	2	13	42	.243	.304	.322	24.56	7.60	171
Walling, Andrew	L-L	6-2	220	10-29-99	7	0	1.73	30	0	6	36	20	8	7	3	24	43	.161	.305	.242	28.48	15.89	151
Wilkinson, Danny	L-L	6-0	206	10-19-00	0	1	4.83	30	0	0	32	28	25	17	1	28	50	.237	.388	.373	33.56	18.79	149

Fielding

Catcher	PCT	G	PO	A	E	DP	PB
Caicuto	.987	30	290	21	4	2	4
Dissin	.992	74	732	52	6	5	18
Leitch	.984	9	57	3	1	0	1
Nava	.989	24	245	13	3	2	5
Thomas	1.000	2	17	0	0	0	0

First Base	PCT	G	PO	A	E	DP
Anthony	.997	47	292	26	1	31
Arnold	1.000	4	13	0	0	1
Bennett	.000	1	0	0	0	0
Castillo	1.000	8	40	3	0	4
Kemp	1.000	6	44	5	0	5
Nava	1.000	2	7	0	0	0
Pineda	.966	23	124	16	5	6
Reyes	.991	45	299	21	3	27
Ware	.944	2	16	1	1	1

Second Base	PCT	G	PO	A	E	DP
Arnold	.927	11	14	24	3	2
Bergolla	.984	55	84	100	3	26
Brito	.943	19	21	29	3	6
Farquhar	.967	31	43	73	4	20
Gonzalez	1.000	2	3	5	0	0
Kemp	.966	16	21	36	2	5
Rondon	.875	3	3	4	1	1
Ware	1.000	4	8	10	0	1

Third Base	PCT	G	PO	A	E	DP
Arnold	.933	62	48	78	9	7
Brito	.938	9	4	11	1	1
Farquhar	1.000	6	5	9	0	1
Gonzalez	.929	5	6	7	1	0
Kemp	.969	19	10	21	1	2
Reyes	.907	27	16	33	5	4
Ware	.900	12	9	18	3	3

Shortstop	PCT	G	PO	A	E	DP
Bergolla	1.000	11	12	19	0	2
Brito	.954	42	50	95	7	13
Castro	.500	1	0	1	1	0
Farquhar	1.000	1	0	1	0	0
Gonzalez	1.000	2	0	1	0	0
Miller	.922	48	69	97	14	24
Rincon	.914	26	31	33	6	10
Ware	1.000	7	11	17	0	3

Outfield	PCT	G	PO	A	E	DP
Arnold	.000	1	0	0	0	0
Bennett	1.000	28	58	2	0	0
Boyd	.980	96	190	3	4	1
Crawford	.991	58	106	0	1	0
Fergus	.984	33	60	3	1	1
Kemp	1.000	2	1	0	0	0
Kroon	1.000	2	2	0	0	0
Mendez	.967	47	84	5	3	1
Muzziotti	1.000	3	5	0	0	0
Pineda	.988	48	80	3	1	1
Schreffler	.984	76	121	5	2	2
Viars	.960	27	47	1	2	1
Ware	1.000	1	1	0	0	0

CLEARWATER THRESHERS — *LOW-A*

FLORIDA STATE LEAGUE

Batting	B-T	Ht.	Wt.	DOB	AVG	OBP	SLG	G	PA	AB	R	H	2B	3B	HR	RBI	BB	HBP	SH	SF	SO	SB	CS	BB%	SO%
Albrecht, Lou	R-R	6-0	210	11-7-01	.163	.250	.256	13	48	43	2	7	1	0	1	3	3	2	0	0	17	0	0	6.25	35.42
Anthony, Keaton	R-R	6-4	211	6-24-01	.322	.446	.470	44	186	149	26	48	10	0	4	21	28	6	0	1	28	3	1	15.05	15.05
Bennett, Pierce	R-R	6-1	195	6-28-01	.249	.385	.303	54	231	185	34	46	5	1	1	23	35	8	0	3	34	8	3	15.15	14.72
Burkholder, Griffin	R-R	6-2	195	8-30-05	.500	.500	1.500	1	2	2	1	1	0	1	0	0	0	0	0	0	0	0	0	0.00	0.00
Caba, Starlyn	B-R	5-10	160	12-6-05	.179	.304	.189	26	115	95	13	17	1	0	0	9	16	2	0	2	15	13	4	13.91	13.04
Caicuto, Luis	R-R	5-10	160	3-5-03	.244	.338	.325	34	143	123	14	30	10	0	0	19	12	6	0	1	22	2	0	8.39	15.38
Castro, Rodolfo	B-R	6-0	205	5-21-99	.333	.429	.833	2	7	6	2	2	0	0	1	1	1	0	0	0	1	0	0	14.29	14.29
Day, Brady	L-R	5-11	185	3-6-02	.195	.276	.208	22	87	77	8	15	1	0	0	7	8	1	0	1	16	1	1	9.20	18.39
DeMartini, Carson	L-R	6-0	185	12-27-02	.315	.385	.478	24	104	92	18	29	5	2	2	9	9	2	0	1	14	8	1	8.65	13.46
Dragoo, Joel	R-R	6-1	210	1-8-03	.319	.508	.447	15	65	47	7	15	6	0	0	12	15	3	0	0	14	3	2	23.08	21.54
Farmer, Ezra	L-L	6-0	165	6-10-03	.143	.333	.143	3	9	7	2	1	0	0	0	0	2	0	0	0	5	0	0	22.22	55.56
Farquhar, Trent	L-R	5-8	180	3-12-01	.314	.493	.429	32	144	105	19	33	7	1	1	12	35	3	0	1	26	9	1	24.31	18.06
Flores, Yemal	R-R	5-9	206	11-22-03	.190	.292	.262	14	48	42	4	8	0	0	1	4	3	3	0	0	20	0	0	6.25	41.67
Gonzalez, Diego	R-R	5-11	160	6-7-03	.265	.362	.394	44	152	132	16	35	6	1	3	21	17	3	0	0	33	2	3	11.18	21.71
Heredia, Raylin	R-R	6-0	174	11-10-03	.245	.309	.428	70	289	257	43	63	11	6	8	42	21	5	1	5	97	9	4	7.27	33.56
Hettiger, Kehden	B-R	6-2	195	5-25-04	.195	.361	.310	68	288	226	37	44	9	1	5	30	57	3	0	2	68	4	1	19.79	23.61
Kemp, Otto	R-R	5-11	185	9-9-99	.500	.650	1.000	5	20	14	4	7	2	1	1	3	3	3	0	0	3	2	1	15.00	15.00
Kotowski, Dakota	R-R	6-4	245	3-26-00	.221	.312	.363	56	218	190	30	42	7	1	6	31	19	7	0	2	81	7	3	8.72	37.16
Marchan, Rafael	B-R	5-9	170	2-25-99	.273	.467	.545	4	15	11	2	3	0	0	1	3	3	1	0	0	1	1	0	20.00	6.67
Mathison, Carter	L-L	6-1	190	1-26-03	.207	.477	.241	11	44	29	6	6	1	0	0	0	11	4	0	0	11	6	0	25.00	25.00
Miller, Aidan	R-R	6-2	210	6-9-04	.275	.401	.483	39	182	149	28	41	16	0	5	26	26	6	0	1	39	10	1	14.29	21.43
Nori, Dante	L-L	5-10	190	10-7-04	.240	.424	.280	14	66	50	10	12	0	1	0	9	16	0	0	0	14	4	2	24.24	21.21
Owusu-Asiedu, Avery	R-R	6-4	230	6-16-03	.192	.287	.327	98	357	312	46	60	11	2	9	27	37	5	1	2	129	17	3	10.36	36.13
Pouaka-Grego, Nikau	L-R	5-9	175	9-13-04	.198	.314	.302	54	205	172	23	34	10	1	2	19	24	6	1	2	43	1	1	11.71	20.98
Rincon, Bryan	B-R	5-10	185	2-8-04	.143	.250	.143	2	8	7	1	1	0	0	0	0	1	0	0	0	2	0	0	12.50	25.00
Rosario, Guillermo	R-R	6-2	190	4-22-05	.194	.231	.278	12	39	36	3	7	0	0	1	4	1	1	0	1	12	0	0	2.56	30.77
Rosario, Ricardo	R-R	5-11	160	2-8-03	.213	.273	.279	17	66	61	5	13	4	0	0	6	3	2	0	0	19	4	1	4.55	28.79
Saltiban, Devin	R-R	5-10	180	2-14-05	.237	.346	.428	97	411	346	68	82	13	1	17	53	50	10	0	4	102	22	2	12.17	24.82
Shaver, A.J.	R-R	6-2	213	10-8-01	.086	.172	.190	19	65	58	5	5	0	0	2	7	4	2	1	0	27	0	2	6.15	41.54
Shojinaga, Kodey	R-R	5-10	195	2-22-03	.143	.379	.143	15	58	42	6	6	0	0	0	4	15	1	0	0	4	0	2	25.86	6.90
Spikerman, John	B-R	6-0	177	4-2-03	.226	.360	.323	17	75	62	13	14	4	1	0	5	9	4	0	0	20	7	1	12.00	26.67
Tait, Eduardo	L-R	6-0	175	8-27-06	.269	.316	.462	28	114	104	13	28	5	0	5	24	8	0	0	2	33	0	0	7.02	28.95
Tello, Raider	R-R	6-0	205	2-25-01	.255	.345	.294	14	58	51	9	13	2	0	0	7	6	1	0	0	13	0	1	10.34	22.41
Thomas, Jared	L-R	6-0	185	12-3-00	.188	.309	.265	39	140	117	8	22	3	0	2	13	18	3	1	1	23	3	2	12.86	16.43
Viars, Jordan	L-L	6-2	215	7-18-03	.252	.355	.491	64	265	226	39	57	14	2	12	39	30	7	0	2	81	2	3	11.32	30.57
Villavicencio, Juan	L-R	5-10	155	11-24-04	.000	.111	.000	2	9	8	0	0	0	0	0	0	0	1	0	0	2	1	0	0.00	22.22
Walton, TayShaun	R-R	6-3	225	1-29-05	.200	.331	.333	36	145	120	16	24	7	0	3	16	19	5	0	1	46	7	5	13.10	31.72
Ware, Bryson	R-R	6-2	193	12-28-00	.201	.305	.345	75	308	264	34	53	11	0	9	41	33	8	0	3	74	11	5	10.71	24.03

Pitching	B-T	Ht.	Wt.	DOB	W	L	ERA	G	GS	SV	IP	Hits	Runs	ER	HR	BB	SO	AVG	OBP	SLG	SO%	BB%	BF
Amarante, Juan	L-L	5-10	177	4-14-04	2	4	6.51	7	5	0	28	38	22	20	5	13	28	.328	.392	.586	21.54	10.00	130
Andrade, Kleyderve	L-L	5-11	180	12-19-02	0	1	9.00	4	0	2	5	4	5	5	1	3	7	.211	.348	.526	30.43	13.04	23
Avila, Luis	R-R	6-1	170	5-26-03	2	3	0.68	19	0	3	26	9	5	2	0	13	30	.107	.240	.155	29.70	12.87	101
Beckel, Brandon	R-R	6-4	225	10-20-01	4	1	3.28	25	3	1	47	34	22	17	3	17	51	.199	.287	.310	26.15	8.72	195
Bortka, Josh	R-R	6-5	225	7-12-99	4	2	5.90	22	0	0	29	29	27	19	2	14	42	.261	.393	.351	31.11	10.37	135
Cain, Tegan	L-R	6-0	200	12-2-02	0	0	0.00	2	0	0	2	0	0	0	0	0	2	.000	.000	.000	33.33	0.00	6
Carmack, Kyler	R-R	6-2	180	1-6-03	0	0	9.82	3	0	0	4	5	4	4	1	4	5	.357	.526	.571	26.32	21.05	19
Chenault, Ethan	R-R	6-5	200	3-28-01	1	3	4.91	25	0	4	37	26	24	20	4	26	53	.210	.376	.363	33.76	16.56	157
Covey, Dylan	R-R	6-1	215	8-14-91	0	1	81.00	1	0	0	0	2	3	3	0	2	1	.667	.800	1.000	20.00	40.00	5
Dillard, Trey	R-R	6-0	195	11-15-98	1	0	3.38	5	0	1	8	6	4	3	1	5	11	.207	.333	.310	30.56	13.89	36
Dutton, Reese	R-R	6-2	195	5-15-01	1	0	0.00	2	0	0	6	2	0	0	0	1	6	.105	.150	.105	30.00	5.00	20
Eddington, Jacob	R-R	6-2	185	4-26-01	2	1	4.55	15	3	0	30	25	17	15	1	29	36	.231	.411	.296	25.35	20.42	142
Estanista, Jaydenn	R-R	6-3	180	10-3-01	1	0	3.77	16	0	0	31	16	15	13	4	21	44	.147	.290	.312	33.59	16.03	131
Fowler, Jordan	L-L	6-3	180	3-9-99	0	0	1.80	4	4	0	10	6	2	2	1	1	8	.167	.189	.278	21.62	2.70	37
Garbrick, Alex	R-R	6-1	210	6-4-98	0	0	6.00	5	0	0	6	4	4	4	1	5	8	.200	.357	.450	28.57	17.86	28
Garcia, Josbel	R-R	6-0	165	3-30-04	0	0	9.00	1	0	0	2	2	3	2	0	2	3	.222	.364	.333	27.27	18.18	11
Garnett, Tristan	L-L	6-6	240	3-29-98	0	0	0.00	2	0	0	2	2	0	0	0	2	4	.222	.364	.222	36.36	18.18	11
Garrett, Drew	R-R	6-6	205	6-20-00	1	2	3.54	29	0	5	41	21	18	16	1	47	56	.157	.384	.261	30.27	25.41	185
Gonzalez, Orlando	R-R	6-1	220	11-22-02	0	1	2.63	6	3	0	14	8	7	4	3	6	11	.167	.298	.417	19.30	10.53	57
Graves, Mavis	L-L	6-6	205	11-20-03	7	6	3.64	18	16	0	84	77	41	34	3	36	117	.238	.324	.319	31.79	9.78	368
Hayes, Titan	R-R	6-2	220	11-12-01	0	1	3.86	6	0	1	7	4	4	3	1	5	5	.190	.370	.333	18.52	18.52	27
Henriquez, Jonh	R-R	6-0	187	10-30-99	3	1	3.45	20	0	0	31	28	17	12	2	19	34	.237	.345	.364	24.29	13.57	140
Hernandez, Cristian	R-R	6-3	180	9-23-00	0	0	14.73	3	0	1	4	5	6	6	0	3	3	.333	.450	.667	15.00	15.00	20
Highfill, Sam	R-R	6-3	203	11-30-00	0	1	6.43	3	1	0	7	9	6	5	0	5	10	.290	.389	.323	27.78	13.89	36
Hopewell, Chase	R-R	6-4	197	1-23-01	0	3	7.20	23	0	2	30	38	25	24	5	15	28	.314	.387	.562	20.44	10.95	137
Kerkering, Orion	R-R	6-2	204	4-4-01	1	0	0.00	2	0	0	2	0	0	0	0	0	7	.000	.125	.000	87.50	0.00	8
King, Charles	R-R	6-5	215	1-6-98	0	0	0.00	1	0	0	1	0	0	0	0	0	1	.000	.000	.000	33.33	0.00	3
Klassen, George	R-R	6-2	170	1-26-02	2	0	0.71	9	9	0	38	21	4	3	1	12	57	.160	.236	.198	39.58	8.33	144
Knight, Blaine	R-R	6-3	165	6-28-96	0	0	0.00	1	0	0	1	0	0	0	0	0	1	.000	.000	.000	33.33	0.00	3
Liranzo, Angel	L-L	6-1	172	8-5-06	1	0	3.86	1	0	0	2	1	1	1	0	3	2	.125	.364	.125	18.18	27.27	11
Loyd, Hunter	R-R	6-2	205	5-7-00	1	1	30.86	3	0	0	2	11	8	8	1	3	2	.611	.667	1.000	9.52	14.29	21
McGowan, Christian	R-R	6-0	205	3-7-00	0	0	0.00	1	1	0	3	1	0	0	0	1	4	.091	.167	.091	33.33	8.33	12
Ortiz, Luis	R-R	6-3	230	9-22-95	0	0	4.50	2	0	0	2	0	1	1	0	1	3	.000	.143	.000	42.86	14.29	7
Osterberg, Matt	L-L	6-2	200	4-21-99	0	0	4.15	2	2	0	4	2	2	2	0	1	4	.133	.278	.133	22.22	5.56	18
Ottenbreit, Micah	R-R	6-4	190	5-7-03	3	9	4.88	19	19	0	94	88	53	51	8	41	99	.246	.337	.375	24.15	10.00	410
Pan, Wen Hui	R-R	6-3	220	9-19-02	0	1	3.68	3	3	0	7	6	3	3	0	2	12	.222	.300	.407	38.71	6.45	31
Pena, Jose	R-R	6-3	200	7-8-03	4	3	5.47	32	0	0	51	48	32	31	4	31	71	.241	.353	.362	30.21	13.19	235
Petit, Jonathan	R-R	6-2	174	4-19-01	2	1	7.71	19	2	1	33	31	30	28	2	25	32	.254	.404	.385	20.38	15.92	157
Pulido, Danyony	R-R	6-1	165	10-19-02	2	1	2.94	10	8	0	34	20	16	11	1	23	38	.168	.306	.261	26.39	15.97	144
Rangel, Alan	R-R	6-2	170	8-21-97	0	0	0.00	1	1	0	2	1	0	0	0	0	4	.143	.143	.143	57.14	0.00	7
Reyes, Pedro	R-R	6-3	175	11-26-02	0	0	3.00	5	3	0	18	19	12	6	1	9	16	.260	.349	.356	19.28	10.84	83
Rucker, Michael	R-R	6-1	195	4-27-94	0	0	0.00	1	0	0	1	1	0	0	0	0	2	.250	.250	.500	50.00	0.00	4
Russo, Luke	L-R	6-4	199	2-21-01	4	3	5.13	15	14	0	67	67	39	38	6	26	88	.260	.334	.442	30.03	8.87	293
Schultz, Andrew	R-R	6-4	195	7-31-97	0	0	0.00	1	0	0	1	0	0	0	0	0	3	.000	.000	.000	100.00	0.00	3
Segura, Enrique	R-R	6-3	175	12-19-04	2	4	7.17	10	9	0	43	41	35	34	7	26	42	.258	.383	.472	21.65	13.40	194
Steward, Casey	R-R	6-5	260	8-2-01	4	2	3.38	12	10	0	51	42	23	19	4	19	52	.226	.318	.366	24.53	8.96	212
Teran, Saul	R-R	6-1	165	3-20-02	3	1	3.96	22	0	7	25	20	13	11	3	19	36	.206	.345	.361	30.25	15.97	119
Thompson, Paxton	R-R	6-1	205	10-5-99	1	2	3.62	19	0	1	27	26	11	11	2	9	30	.257	.321	.406	26.79	8.04	112
Trop, Eli	R-R	6-4	225	5-4-02	0	1	5.79	4	0	0	5	4	3	3	0	1	5	.235	.364	.235	22.73	4.55	22
Tucker, Braydon	L-R	6-3	205	7-19-99	5	2	2.94	15	9	0	64	53	21	21	3	13	62	.226	.285	.338	24.22	5.08	256
Walker, Taijuan	R-R	6-4	235	8-13-92	0	0	4.50	1	1	0	4	2	2	2	0	0	4	.143	.200	.214	26.67	0.00	15
Wells, Lachlan	L-L	6-1	185	2-27-97	0	0	0.00	1	1	0	2	2	0	0	0	1	2	.250	.333	.375	22.22	11.11	9
Wilson, A.J.	L-L	6-2	210	12-17-00	0	1	3.86	5	0	0	7	4	3	3	0	7	11	.160	.344	.240	34.38	21.88	32

Fielding

Catcher	PCT	G	PO	A	E	DP	PB
Albrecht	.965	12	120	19	5	0	3
Caicuto	.988	31	303	34	4	3	3
Hettiger	.986	30	326	16	5	2	8
Marchan	1.000	3	24	3	0	0	0
Rosario	.969	4	30	1	1	0	0
Shojinaga	1.000	7	57	3	0	1	4
Tait	.994	17	158	15	1	2	2
Thomas	.997	32	276	13	1	4	0

First Base	PCT	G	PO	A	E	DP
Anthony	.996	36	231	14	1	25
Hettiger	.985	29	184	12	3	17
Kotowski	.984	38	229	16	4	17
Rosario	.983	8	57	2	1	7
Shojinaga	1.000	6	35	2	0	4
Tello	1.000	6	32	4	0	5
Ware	.957	7	41	3	2	1

Second Base	PCT	G	PO	A	E	DP
Castro	1.000	1	0	1	0	0
Day	.980	14	23	25	1	6
DeMartini	.917	3	4	7	1	2
Farquhar	1.000	4	7	5	0	1
Kemp	1.000	1	1	3	0	0
Pouaka-Grego	.952	15	22	18	2	6
Saltiban	.956	88	91	190	13	45
Ware	.973	8	13	23	1	6

Third Base	PCT	G	PO	A	E	DP
Castro	1.000	1	0	1	0	0
Day	.692	5	3	6	4	1
DeMartini	.914	12	13	19	3	3
Farquhar	1.000	8	5	12	0	1
Gonzalez	.956	34	22	43	3	3
Hettiger	.000	1	0	0	0	0
Kemp	1.000	3	0	6	0	0
Pouaka-Grego	.922	38	23	48	6	6
Tello	1.000	10	5	13	0	1

Ware	.863	25	18	26	7	4

Shortstop	PCT	G	PO	A	E	DP
Caba	.952	26	34	65	5	16
DeMartini	.913	7	7	14	2	1
Farquhar	.983	19	23	34	1	12
Gonzalez	1.000	11	8	16	0	3
Miller	.964	37	57	75	5	20
Rincon	.857	2	2	4	1	1
Villavicencio	.667	2	2	4	3	2
Ware	.942	26	23	42	4	8

Outfield	PCT	G	PO	A	E	DP
Bennett	.986	49	70	2	1	1
Burkholder	1.000	1	2	0	0	0
Dragoo	1.000	14	23	1	0	0
Farmer	1.000	3	7	0	0	0
Flores	1.000	11	17	1	0	0
Heredia	.976	67	114	9	3	4

Kotowski	1.000	2	3	0	0	0
Mathison	.857	10	10	2	2	0
Nori	1.000	13	18	1	0	0
Owusu-Asiedu	.990	97	187	5	2	4
Rosario	1.000	15	22	2	0	2
Shaver	1.000	19	39	1	0	0
Spikerman	1.000	16	35	4	0	1
Viars	.953	36	57	4	3	1
Walton	1.000	31	60	0	0	0
Ware	1.000	10	19	0	0	0

FCL PHILLIES — *ROOKIE*

FLORIDA COMPLEX LEAGUE

Batting	B-T	Ht.	Wt.	DOB	AVG	OBP	SLG	G	PA	AB	R	H	2B	3B	HR	RBI	BB	HBP	SH	SF	SO	SB	CS	BB%	SO%
Beltran, Nolan	L-R	6-0	160	1-24-05	.234	.363	.372	34	113	94	16	22	4	0	3	14	17	2	0	0	22	2	2	15.04	19.47
Caba, Starlyn	B-R	5-10	160	12-6-05	.254	.427	.335	52	225	173	44	44	6	1	2	17	51	1	0	0	34	37	8	22.67	15.11
Castro, Rodolfo	B-R	6-0	205	5-21-99	.333	.333	.333	1	3	3	1	1	0	0	0	1	0	0	0	0	0	0	0	0.00	0.00
Escobar, Aroon	R-R	5-11	180	1-1-05	.338	.495	.481	24	104	77	24	26	2	0	3	17	21	4	1	1	10	9	0	20.19	9.62
Farmer, Ezra	L-L	6-0	165	6-10-03	.286	.403	.317	26	77	63	6	18	2	0	0	9	13	0	0	1	24	3	2	16.88	31.17
Farquhar, Trent	L-R	5-8	180	3-12-01	.143	.333	.143	3	9	7	1	1	0	0	0	1	0	2	0	0	2	0	0	0.00	22.22
Ferrebus, Alirio	R-R	6-2	174	9-12-05	.324	.366	.378	10	41	37	5	12	2	0	0	6	0	3	0	1	6	1	2	0.00	14.63
Flores, Yemal	R-R	5-9	206	11-22-03	.265	.370	.515	23	81	68	10	18	3	1	4	18	10	2	0	1	31	0	1	12.35	38.27
Garcia, Jorge	L-R	5-11	145	2-6-04	.000	.195	.000	14	41	32	3	0	0	0	0	1	7	1	0	1	16	0	0	17.07	39.02
Gonzalez, Diego	R-R	5-11	160	6-7-03	.176	.273	.294	9	22	17	4	3	2	0	0	3	2	1	0	2	4	0	0	9.09	18.18
Jimenez, Manolfi	L-L	6-0	190	11-14-04	.261	.317	.380	31	101	92	17	24	2	0	3	13	6	2	0	1	22	3	3	5.94	21.78
Marin, Junior	R-R	6-2	240	3-15-04	.289	.336	.464	30	107	97	18	28	6	1	3	18	6	2	0	2	19	5	3	5.61	17.76
Mendez, Jorge	R-R	5-10	160	8-1-03	.214	.290	.321	11	31	28	3	6	0	0	1	2	1	2	0	0	5	0	0	3.23	16.13
Pena, Jerffson	L-R	6-2	185	12-16-03	.267	.364	.427	41	151	131	29	35	10	1	3	10	16	4	0	0	48	12	3	10.60	31.79
Perez, Rickardo	L-R	5-10	172	12-4-03	.297	.368	.486	32	125	111	17	33	3	0	6	26	11	2	0	1	18	0	1	8.80	14.40
Rincones, Gabriel	L-R	6-3	225	3-3-01	.167	.278	.200	9	36	30	6	5	1	0	0	3	4	1	0	1	8	3	0	11.11	22.22
Rondon, Leonardo	B-R	5-7	160	3-10-04	.179	.273	.286	14	33	28	5	5	0	0	1	9	4	0	0	1	7	1	1	12.12	21.21
Rosario, Guillermo	R-R	6-2	190	4-22-05	.237	.338	.385	51	201	169	29	40	9	2	4	27	24	4	0	4	55	2	1	11.94	27.36
Rosario, Ricardo	R-R	5-11	160	2-8-03	.091	.091	.091	4	11	11	0	1	0	0	0	0	0	0	0	0	5	1	0	0.00	45.45
Rosario, Yemil	R-R	6-2	150	4-12-04	.143	.284	.156	34	95	77	12	11	1	0	0	10	12	4	0	2	26	4	1	12.63	27.37
Shaver, A.J.	R-R	6-2	213	10-8-01	.192	.417	.308	11	36	26	7	5	3	0	0	4	8	2	0	0	12	6	0	22.22	33.33
Silva, Brahian	R-R	5-11	170	12-30-02	.500	.615	.500	6	13	10	2	5	0	0	0	2	3	0	0	0	2	1	0	23.08	15.38
Simmons, Kendall	R-R	6-0	180	4-11-00	.167	.167	.167	2	6	6	0	1	0	0	0	0	0	0	0	0	1	0	0	0.00	16.67
Tait, Eduardo	L-R	6-0	175	8-27-06	.321	.377	.500	51	212	184	29	59	13	1	6	49	13	8	0	7	31	5	0	6.13	14.62
Villavicencio, Juan	L-R	5-10	155	11-24-04	.264	.364	.365	47	187	159	29	42	7	3	1	18	22	4	0	2	44	5	3	11.76	23.53
Walton, TayShaun	R-R	6-3	225	1-29-05	.154	.214	.154	4	14	13	0	2	0	0	0	0	0	1	0	0	5	0	0	0.00	35.71

Pitching	B-T	Ht.	Wt.	DOB	W	L	ERA	G	GS	SV	IP	Hits	Runs	ER	HR	BB	SO	AVG	OBP	SLG	SO%	BB%	BF
Amarante, Juan	L-L	5-10	177	4-14-04	3	1	3.38	15	6	1	45	37	20	17	3	24	58	.228	.335	.364	30.85	12.77	188
Andrade, Kleyderve	L-L	5-11	180	12-19-02	2	2	3.38	14	0	0	21	18	14	8	1	10	31	.225	.323	.313	33.33	10.75	93
Avila, Luis	R-R	6-1	170	5-26-03	0	0	5.73	9	0	4	11	14	8	7	2	8	12	.304	.429	.457	21.43	14.29	56
Bata, Eliecer	R-R	6-3	190	3-20-04	1	1	9.00	5	0	0	7	12	7	7	1	4	3	.414	.457	.586	8.57	11.43	35
Blanco, Wilmer	R-R	6-3	170	2-21-04	2	4	6.70	12	10	0	47	56	41	35	5	29	49	.301	.413	.457	21.97	13.00	223
Bortka, Josh	R-R	6-5	225	7-12-99	0	0	0.00	1	0	0	1	1	0	0	0	1	2	.250	.500	.500	33.33	16.67	6
De La Cruz, Alexis	R-R	6-6	205	9-20-04	2	1	8.84	12	1	1	18	19	18	18	3	19	10	.275	.441	.522	10.75	20.43	93
Eddington, Jacob	R-R	6-2	185	4-26-01	0	0	1.50	5	0	0	6	5	1	1	1	5	8	.227	.393	.409	28.57	17.86	28
Fowler, Jordan	L-L	6-3	180	3-9-99	0	0	0.00	1	1	0	2	1	0	0	0	2	0	.143	.333	.143	0.00	22.22	9
Garbrick, Alex	R-R	6-1	210	6-4-98	0	0	0.00	3	0	1	4	1	0	0	0	3	5	.071	.235	.071	29.41	17.65	17
Garcia, Josbel	R-R	6-0	165	3-30-04	2	2	4.33	14	5	3	35	33	20	17	1	24	27	.254	.372	.315	17.31	15.38	156
Gatier, Claudio	L-L	6-3	180	5-25-02	1	1	9.00	7	0	2	10	13	10	10	0	10	14	.325	.472	.425	26.42	18.87	53
Gonzalez, Luis	R-R	6-0	170	7-15-05	4	1	4.13	10	2	0	33	32	15	15	2	9	34	.260	.321	.350	25.37	6.72	134
Gonzalez, Orlando	R-R	6-1	220	11-22-02	3	0	1.32	6	3	1	27	13	6	4	2	20	23	.148	.330	.250	20.54	17.86	112
Henriquez, Jonh	R-R	6-0	187	10-30-99	0	0	3.38	3	0	0	3	2	3	1	0	4	2	.222	.500	.222	14.29	28.57	14
Hernandez, Maxwel	R-R	6-2	190	5-14-03	3	3	4.95	12	8	0	40	43	23	22	0	25	30	.289	.400	.369	16.57	13.81	181
King, Charles	R-R	6-5	215	1-6-98	0	0	0.00	1	1	0	1	0	0	0	0	0	2	.000	.000	.000	66.67	0.00	3
Martinez, Jordi	L-L	6-2	185	7-18-00	0	1	9.00	1	0	0	1	2	3	1	0	1	3	.333	.429	.500	42.86	14.29	7
McGowan, Christian	R-R	6-0	205	3-7-00	0	0	0.00	2	1	0	3	2	0	0	0	1	4	.222	.300	.222	40.00	10.00	10
Pan, Wen Hui	R-R	6-3	220	9-19-02	0	0	9.00	1	1	0	1	3	1	1	0	0	1	.429	.429	.429	14.29	0.00	7
Peralta, Adilson	R-R	6-4	175	6-17-03	4	3	4.26	16	0	3	32	28	18	15	3	20	44	.235	.350	.395	30.56	13.89	144
Pipkin, Dominic	R-R	6-4	160	11-5-99	0	0	0.00	2	0	0	2	3	4	0	0	3	4	.375	.545	.625	36.36	27.27	11
Pulido, Danyony	R-R	6-1	165	10-19-02	1	2	4.55	8	7	0	32	32	19	16	2	18	39	.267	.373	.383	27.46	12.68	142
Reyes, Pedro	R-R	6-3	175	11-26-02	3	1	2.89	11	6	0	47	42	18	15	5	12	29	.239	.301	.392	15.03	6.22	193
Robles, Benony	L-L	6-4	185	10-1-00	0	0	21.60	1	0	0	2	5	5	4	1	1	3	.500	.545	1.100	27.27	9.09	11
Segura, Enrique	R-R	6-3	175	12-19-04	2	2	3.90	6	6	0	32	30	14	14	2	12	31	.248	.326	.397	22.46	8.70	138
Silva, Brahian	R-R	5-11	170	12-30-02	0	0	0.00	1	0	0	0	0	0	0	0	0	0	.000	.000	.000	0.00	0.00	1

Fielding

C: Tait 27, Rosario 22, Mendez 6, Ferrebus 4, Silva 1. **1B:** Perez 25, Rosario 20, Rosario 13, Ferrebus 4. **2B:** Villavicencio 32, Escobar 15, Rosario 9, Rondon 4, Farquhar 2, Gonzalez 1. **3B:** Beltran 26, Rosario 10, Villavicencio 7, Escobar 7, Gonzalez 7, Rondon 7, Simmons 2, Farquhar 1, Castro 1. SS: Caba 52, Villavicencio 10. **LF:** Farmer 23, Marin 17, Garcia 13, Beltran 7, Jimenez 5, Walton 3, Shaver 1. **CF:** Pena 34, Jimenez 19, Shaver 6, Rosario 4, Garcia 1. **RF:** Flores 23, Marin 13, Pena 8, Jimenez 8, Rincones 7, Shaver 4, Farmer 3.

DSL PHILLIES RED — ROOKIE

DOMINICAN SUMMER LEAGUE

Batting	B-T	Ht.	Wt.	DOB	AVG	OBP	SLG	G	PA	AB	R	H	2B	3B	HR	RBI	BB	HBP	SH	SF	SO	SB	CS	BB%	SO%
Arias, Jalvin	R-R	6-2	230	10-1-06	.233	.411	.372	14	56	43	8	10	0	0	2	9	12	1	0	0	20	1	2	21.43	35.71
Cardoza, Victor	R-R	5-11	181	1-19-06	.417	.456	.738	21	91	84	19	35	8	2	5	14	5	1	1	0	19	9	3	5.49	20.88
Carela, Leny	R-R	6-0	170	10-9-04	.198	.340	.272	36	104	81	17	16	4	1	0	13	17	2	1	3	12	14	1	16.35	11.54
Casanova, Maylerson	B-R	5-11	165	11-13-06	.173	.307	.252	42	166	139	22	24	3	1	2	16	20	7	0	0	59	15	2	12.05	35.54
Castillo, Winifer	R-R	6-3	182	11-15-06	.067	.222	.067	7	18	15	2	1	0	0	0	1	1	2	0	0	5	1	0	5.56	27.78
De Leon, Meylin	R-R	5-11	170	4-21-07	.252	.350	.318	48	177	151	26	38	8	1	0	14	20	4	0	2	36	4	2	11.30	20.34
Diaz, Joseph	R-R	6-3	185	12-8-05	.202	.290	.303	32	101	89	13	18	4	1	1	8	7	4	1	0	26	1	0	6.93	25.74
Estevez, Samuel	R-R	6-0	184	3-26-07	.217	.342	.250	47	185	152	26	33	5	0	0	16	25	5	1	2	65	18	6	13.51	35.14
Ferrebus, Alirio	R-R	6-2	174	9-12-05	.375	.471	.725	14	51	40	10	15	5	0	3	13	8	1	0	2	3	2	1	15.69	5.88
Freitas, David	R-R	6-2	190	6-30-07	.153	.250	.184	35	113	98	11	15	3	0	0	11	11	2	1	1	42	4	2	9.73	37.17
Fuentes, Yadimir	R-R	6-2	202	1-10-07	.133	.262	.162	36	126	105	13	14	3	0	0	11	16	3	0	2	23	1	2	12.70	18.25
Garcia, Adrian	B-R	6-2	170	11-27-06	.238	.324	.356	46	182	160	32	38	7	3	2	17	16	5	0	1	23	12	2	8.79	12.64
Hernandez, Fernando	R-R	5-11	165	3-30-03	.000	.000	.000	1	1	1	0	0	0	0	0	0	0	0	0	0	0	0	0	0.00	0.00
Manrique, Renair	B-R	6-0	172	2-8-06	.187	.292	.275	32	107	91	13	17	8	0	0	13	8	6	0	1	25	1	0	7.48	23.36
Mujica, Cesar	R-R	6-2	198	3-30-07	.185	.306	.215	43	160	135	13	25	4	0	0	9	15	9	0	1	47	9	2	9.38	29.38
Polanco, Yonkelvin	L-R	5-11	175	7-13-06	.164	.284	.213	22	74	61	7	10	1	1	0	7	10	1	0	2	22	8	2	13.51	29.73
Rodriguez, Esterling	L-R	5-11	140	9-8-05	.265	.420	.382	23	88	68	12	18	5	0	1	14	19	0	0	1	23	9	2	21.59	26.14
Ruiz, Ibrahim	R-R	5-11	170	11-6-06	.197	.275	.213	22	69	61	9	12	1	0	0	5	3	4	0	1	15	4	3	4.35	21.74
Silva, Brahian	R-R	5-11	170	12-30-02	.059	.333	.059	7	24	17	3	1	0	0	0	1	6	1	0	0	8	0	0	25.00	33.33
Speirs, Declan	R-R	5-11	176	6-16-05	.258	.410	.290	13	39	31	3	8	1	0	0	2	7	1	0	0	12	0	2	17.95	30.77

Pitching	B-T	Ht.	Wt.	DOB	W	L	ERA	G	GS	SV	IP	Hits	Runs	ER	HR	BB	SO	AVG	OBP	SLG	SO%	BB%	BF
Arias, Eligio	R-R	6-7	230	3-26-03	1	4	7.44	13	5	0	33	31	29	27	3	18	45	.252	.372	.439	29.80	11.92	151
Arias, Yael	R-R	6-5	176	8-16-04	2	5	6.62	14	7	0	34	34	31	25	4	16	34	.246	.348	.391	21.12	9.94	161
De La Cruz, Joshue	R-R	6-2	193	10-17-05	1	1	4.24	6	5	0	23	19	11	11	0	9	22	.224	.327	.306	22.45	9.18	98
De Los Santos, Alexander	R-R	6-1	160	8-23-06	1	3	2.13	11	9	0	38	18	12	9	0	19	38	.141	.282	.164	24.36	12.18	156
Delpino, Geremi	R-R	6-2	185	2-12-04	0	0	0.00	3	1	0	6	1	0	0	0	5	6	.053	.308	.158	23.08	19.23	26
Fernandez, Eduardo	L-L	6-0	170	9-4-04	1	0	0.00	1	0	0	3	3	2	0	0	1	4	.273	.308	.273	30.77	7.69	13
Gatier, Claudio	L-L	6-3	180	5-25-02	0	0	0.00	1	0	1	1	0	0	0	0	1	0	.000	.200	.000	0.00	20.00	5
Gonzalez, Orlando	R-R	6-1	220	11-22-02	0	0	0.00	1	1	0	2	1	0	0	0	1	1	.143	.250	.143	12.50	12.50	8
Lebron, Gregory	L-L	6-4	220	7-9-04	0	1	28.50	7	0	0	6	6	21	19	0	26	9	.273	.680	.318	18.00	52.00	50
Lopez, Gerardo	R-R	5-11	183	7-30-05	2	2	4.75	13	2	0	30	28	16	16	1	10	30	.246	.344	.325	22.90	7.63	131
Mejia, Naoel	R-R	6-5	220	7-5-02	1	1	2.65	17	0	7	17	13	7	5	0	11	18	.220	.356	.220	24.66	15.07	73
Pacheco, Brad	R-R	6-0	175	6-9-05	1	0	1.59	5	5	0	17	11	6	3	0	3	23	.190	.238	.241	36.51	4.76	63
Peralta, Pedro	R-R	5-11	185	7-27-06	0	4	6.31	9	7	0	26	29	32	18	1	24	32	.279	.423	.413	23.19	17.39	138
Ramirez, Henry	R-R	6-1	160	8-20-05	1	0	2.93	9	0	0	15	9	8	5	0	20	19	.173	.427	.212	25.33	26.67	75
Ramos, Fernando	R-R	6-0	164	1-25-03	2	0	2.79	13	0	3	29	21	11	9	0	9	26	.208	.281	.228	22.41	7.76	116
Reyes, Darling	R-R	6-1	175	10-29-04	1	2	3.96	14	0	0	25	23	20	11	0	21	28	.235	.390	.276	22.76	17.07	123
Rosario, Raymon	L-L	6-2	198	6-6-05	0	5	5.44	12	12	0	46	46	31	28	2	23	52	.256	.367	.372	24.19	10.70	215
Velazquez, Naiker	R-R	6-5	195	3-23-05	1	1	8.00	14	1	0	27	31	31	24	0	22	31	.301	.435	.398	23.48	16.67	132
Yousuf, Zuher	L-L	5-10	174	5-24-06	5	3	3.62	15	0	1	37	26	16	15	0	17	49	.190	.291	.234	30.82	10.69	159
Yrish, Rene	R-R	6-1	165	11-20-06	1	2	10.64	15	0	0	22	26	27	26	0	27	15	.325	.538	.375	12.50	22.50	120

Fielding

C: Mujica 27, Fuentes 21, Ferrebus 8, Speirs 4, Silva 2. **1B:** Diaz 25, Fuentes 12, Speirs 8, Manrique 6, Ferrebus 5, Freitas 5, Mujica 2, Silva 1. **2B:** Manrique 19, Garcia 18, Carela 16, De Leon 10, Speirs 1. **3B:** De Leon 36, Garcia 12, Carela 11, Manrique 3. **SS:** Casanova 37, Garcia 13, Carela 9. **LF:** Polanco 18, Freitas 16, Ruiz 14, Estevez 6, Diaz 4, Carela 3, Rodriguez 2, Castillo 1. **CF:** Estevez 25, Rodriguez 14, Cardoza 10, Arias 6, Ruiz 2, Polanco 2, Carela 1, Castillo 1. **RF:** Estevez 13, Freitas 11, Cardoza 10, Arias 8, Rodriguez 7, Castillo 3, Diaz 3, Polanco 2, Ruiz 1, Carela 1.

DSL PHILLIES WHITE — ROOKIE

DOMINICAN SUMMER LEAGUE

Batting	B-T	Ht.	Wt.	DOB	AVG	OBP	SLG	G	PA	AB	R	H	2B	3B	HR	RBI	BB	HBP	SH	SF	SO	SB	CS	BB%	SO%
Aguila, Denilson	B-R	5-11	165	2-28-06	.212	.352	.212	34	106	85	13	18	0	0	0	6	9	10	1	1	31	12	4	8.49	29.25
Aguilera, Freiderman	R-R	6-0	163	5-3-07	.189	.300	.242	35	111	95	15	18	5	0	0	8	13	2	1	0	46	10	2	11.71	41.44
Andrade, Dervin	R-R	6-0	200	11-1-03	.100	.182	.100	7	22	20	1	2	0	0	0	0	2	0	0	0	1	0	0	9.09	4.55
Bena, Cristobal	L-R	5-10	133	9-17-06	.146	.290	.225	30	108	89	10	13	1	3	0	4	13	5	1	0	48	6	4	12.04	44.44
Calderon, Jaeden	R-R	6-1	208	9-17-05	.282	.429	.444	46	184	142	29	40	7	2	4	24	26	13	0	3	40	7	4	14.13	21.74
Cardoza, Victor	R-R	5-11	181	1-19-06	.244	.322	.372	24	87	78	15	19	4	0	2	11	7	2	0	0	25	7	1	8.05	28.74
Cijntje, Nathanael	R-R	5-9	166	1-16-07	.333	.455	.333	4	11	9	3	3	0	0	0	0	2	0	0	0	3	1	0	18.18	27.27
Escalona, Yhoan	R-R	6-2	185	11-4-05	.148	.316	.159	31	114	88	14	13	1	0	0	10	19	4	0	3	23	4	0	16.67	20.18
Familia, Jose	L-R	6-2	163	8-16-07	.187	.344	.271	47	195	155	22	29	5	1	2	13	36	2	0	2	62	9	1	18.46	31.79
Hernandez, Andres	R-R	6-2	180	3-10-05	.212	.339	.250	22	62	52	6	11	2	0	0	2	9	1	0	0	18	2	1	14.52	29.03
Julio, Jorge	R-R	6-1	182	8-4-06	.276	.392	.398	42	148	123	22	34	7	4	0	17	21	3	0	1	19	4	2	14.19	12.84
Loreto, Francisco	R-R	6-0	178	6-21-07	.230	.358	.322	30	106	87	16	20	3	1	1	11	12	6	0	1	24	7	4	11.32	22.64
Marchan, Jose	R-R	6-1	187	12-20-05	.139	.279	.208	25	86	72	8	10	2	0	1	10	13	1	0	0	21	7	0	15.12	24.42
Navas, Anderson	R-R	6-2	175	2-16-07	.181	.246	.295	47	184	166	17	30	6	2	3	17	10	5	1	2	65	8	2	5.43	35.33
Prado, Santiago	L-R	6-0	160	10-18-06	.199	.309	.235	44	163	136	14	27	3	1	0	15	19	4	1	3	30	6	3	11.66	18.40
Quinonez, Josueth	R-R	6-1	172	2-22-07	.311	.397	.385	46	179	148	26	46	9	1	0	22	16	9	0	6	15	8	8	8.94	8.38
Ramirez, Isaac	B-R	5-10	170	10-7-05	.156	.291	.222	13	55	45	9	7	1	1	0	2	7	2	0	1	23	11	2	12.73	41.82

Pitching	B-T	Ht.	Wt.	DOB	W	L	ERA	G	GS	SV	IP	Hits	Runs	ER	HR	BB	SO	AVG	OBP	SLG	SO%	BB%	BF
Bata, Eliecer	R-R	6-3	190	3-20-04	1	0	2.03	5	1	0	13	12	3	3	0	3	12	.240	.296	.300	22.22	5.56	54

PHILADELPHIA PHILLIES

Carpio, Gelson	R-R	6-1	165	4-6-06	0	4	5.73	15	0	2	22	19	18	14	0	22	20	.250	.414	.276	19.61	21.57	102
Castillo, Edwin	R-R	6-3	190	11-22-04	0	0	17.28	10	0	0	8	9	17	16	0	23	7	.310	.625	.448	12.07	39.66	58
De La Cruz, Gustavo	R-R	6-3	190	6-6-06	0	0	4.15	4	0	0	4	1	2	2	0	9	5	.071	.458	.071	20.83	37.50	24
Diaz, Cristian	R-R	6-2	180	6-12-05	3	0	5.59	15	0	2	29	27	21	18	0	19	33	.250	.374	.315	25.19	14.50	131
Duarte, Juan	R-R	6-1	185	9-28-04	1	0	2.45	8	0	0	11	8	5	3	0	9	7	.211	.362	.237	14.58	18.75	48
Fernandez, Eduardo	L-L	6-0	170	9-4-04	2	3	5.56	12	0	0	23	19	18	14	0	17	23	.226	.371	.250	21.70	16.04	106
German, Jeffrey	R-R	6-3	175	10-26-04	0	5	4.38	13	7	2	39	42	31	19	1	23	37	.276	.397	.375	20.00	12.43	185
Guzman, Jorge	L-L	6-1	170	3-17-07	1	2	7.20	13	0	0	25	30	20	20	3	14	31	.300	.387	.500	26.05	11.76	119
Heredia, Joel	R-R	6-6	190	1-15-04	3	3	3.97	12	11	0	48	49	30	21	0	16	35	.268	.337	.339	16.83	7.69	208
Jean, Enderson	R-R	6-3	175	9-21-04	2	2	1.96	15	0	3	23	12	12	5	1	22	29	.148	.349	.210	27.10	20.56	107
Montiel, Jesus	R-R	6-4	195	9-24-06	1	0	0.00	1	0	0	1	2	0	0	0	1	0	.400	.500	.600	0.00	16.67	6
Nunez, Emmanuel	R-R	6-3	154	12-25-04	1	0	6.00	6	0	0	6	4	4	4	0	5	4	.190	.346	.286	15.38	19.23	26
Polanco, Julio	R-R	6-3	195	9-11-06	1	3	4.97	11	10	0	38	36	30	21	0	21	31	.243	.369	.270	17.32	11.73	179
Reyes, Richard	R-R	6-6	220	10-14-03	2	1	4.50	13	6	1	36	30	18	18	0	14	34	.227	.312	.295	22.08	9.09	154
Robles, Eduardo	R-R	5-9	176	6-27-05	3	3	2.61	11	9	0	48	45	25	14	1	16	41	.245	.312	.321	20.00	7.80	205
Sosa, John	L-L	6-3	200	2-14-03	1	1	12.38	12	0	1	16	20	26	22	1	31	18	.308	.540	.415	18.00	31.00	100
Vargas, Hanfermin	R-R	6-3	158	8-12-04	4	2	2.82	11	11	0	45	33	19	14	1	25	30	.206	.332	.281	15.54	12.95	193

Fielding

C: Navas 34, Escalona 11, Loreto 11, Prado 1, Andrade 1. **1B:** Calderon 19, Escalona 15, Julio 11, Navas 9, Andrade 5, Hernandez 3. **2B:** Bena 20, Prado 16, Aguila 14, Hernandez 4, Ramirez 2, Loreto 1. **3B:** Prado 27, Hernandez 11, Aguila 11, Bena 9. **SS:** Familia 47, Aguila 9, Hernandez 2. **LF:** Calderon 22, Julio 16, Marchan 9, Quinonez 7, Aguilera 4, Ramirez 3, Hernandez 2. **CF:** Quinonez 26, Cardoza 16, Aguilera 12, Cijntje 3, Ramirez 3, Hernandez 1. **RF:** Marchan 13, Aguilera 12, Julio 12, Quinonez 8, Cardoza 8, Ramirez 4, Calderon 3, Hernandez 1.

Pittsburgh Pirates

SEASON SYNOPSIS: After improving by 14 wins from 2022 to 2023, the Pirates flatlined with another 76-86 record–even though they debuted Paul Skenes, the 2023 No. 1 overall pick and 2024 Rookie of the Year. The punchless Bucs finished last in the National League in slugging and 13th in runs.

HIGH POINT: Nearly every Skenes start was an event, evoking memories of 1998 Kerry Wood and 2010 Stephen Strasburg starts. He debuted at home May 11 against the Cubs, lasting four innings, then no-hit the Cubs for six innings–striking out 11–in Wrigley Field six days later. On July 11, he threw another no-hit outing, tossing seven hitless frames against Milwaukee and striking out 11.

LOW POINT: Pittsburgh entered August on the fringe of the playoff race and above .500, but the bottom fell out in an 8-19 August, including a 10-game losing streak Aug. 4-14. Five of the losses were by one run thanks in part to a porous bullpen. They blew a 4-0 lead in a 6-5 loss to Arizona to start the streak. Closer David Bednar blew back-to-back leads in losses to the Padres and lost a tenth-inning lead to the Dodgers.

NOTABLE ROOKIES: Skenes posted a 1.96 ERA, 33% strikeout rate and 11-3 record, establishing himself as one of the best pitchers in baseball, not just among rookies. Righty Jared Jones beat him to the majors, making the Opening Day roster, throwing a firmer fastball (97.3 mph) than Skenes (96.8 mph) but struggling with home runs (18) in an encouraging 6-8, 4.14 debut. A shoulder strain limited to one start apiece in July and August. Righty Hunter Stratton, 27, got a long look in the bullpen and had his moments.

KEY TRANSACTIONS: Moves around the margins of the roster mostly failed, both preseason and in-season. Free agent Michael A. Taylor (.543 OPS, 105 SO in 269 AB) proved a bust in center field; reliever Aroldis Chapman was competent (3.79 ERA) but not good enough to flip for a prospect, as the Royals did in 2023. And trade deadline additions such as outfielder Bryan de la Cruz (.514 OPS) and shortstop Isiah Kiner-Falefa (.587 OPS, 3/41 BB/SO ratio) didn't hit, though Kiner-Falefa was steady at shortstop, pushing Oneil Cruz to center field. While 2021 No. 1 overall pick Henry Davis struggled behind the plate, trade pickup Joey Bart, whom the Giants picked No. 2 overall in 2018, hit well (.265/.337/.462, 13 HR).

OPENING DAY PAYROLL: $85,760,000 (29th)

PLAYERS OF THE YEAR

MAJOR LEAGUE

Paul Skenes
RHP
11-3, 1.96 ERA
170 SO, 32 BB, 133 IP
Started All-Star Game

MINOR LEAGUE

Bubba Chandler
RHP
(AA/AAA)
10-7, 3.08 ERA
148 SO, 41 BB, 120 IP

ORGANIZATION LEADERS

Batting		* Qualifiers
MAJORS		
* AVG	Bryan Reynolds	.275
* OPS	Bryan Reynolds	.791
HR	Bryan Reynolds	24
RBI	Bryan Reynolds	88
MINORS		
* AVG	Charles McAdoo, Greensboro, Altoona	.315
* OBP	Charles McAdoo, Greensboro, Altoona	.394
* SLG	Charles McAdoo, Greensboro, Altoona	.538
* OPS	Charles McAdoo, Greensboro, Altoona	.932
R	Termarr Johnson, Greensboro, Altoona	82
H	Liover Peguero, Indianapolis	127
TB	Liover Peguero, Indianapolis	203
TB	Matt Gorski, Indianapolis	203
2B	Liover Peguero, Indianapolis	29
3B	Mitch Jebb, Greensboro	7
HR	Matt Gorski, Indianapolis	23
HR	Shawn Ross, Greensboro	23
RBI	Liover Peguero, Indianapolis	79
BB	Termarr Johnson, Greensboro	78
SO	Josiah Sightler	142
SB	Mitch Jebb, Greensboro	43

Pitching		#Qualifiers
MAJORS		
W	Mitch Keller	11
W	Paul Skenes	11
# ERA	Mitch Keller	4.25
SO	Paul Skenes	170
SV	David Bednar	23
MINORS		
W	Bubba Chandler, Altoona/Indianapolis	10
L	Michael Plassmeyer, Indianapolis	10
L	Po-Yu Chen, Altoona	10
# ERA	Carlson Reed, Bradenton/Greensboro	1.99
G	Connor Sadzeck, Indianapolis	49
GS	Wilber Dotel, Greensboro	25
SV	Connor Sadzeck, Indianapolis	9
IP	Po-Yu Chen, Altoona	134
BB	Carlos Jimenez, Greensboro/Bradenton	69
SO	Bubba Chandler, Altoona/Indianapolis	148
# AVG	Carlson Reed, Bradenton/Greensboro	.173

2024 PERFORMANCE

General Manager: Ben Cherington. **Farm Director:** John Baker. **Scouting Director:** Justin Horowitz.

Class	Team	League	W	L	PCT	Finish	Manager
Majors	Pittsburgh Pirates	National	76	86	.469	12 (15)	Derek Shelton
Triple-A	Indianapolis Indians	International	77	70	.524	6 (20)	Miguel Perez
Double-A	Altoona Curve	Eastern	62	76	.449	10 (12)	Robby Hammock
High-A	Greensboro Grasshoppers	South Atlantic	75	55	.577	2 (12)	Blake Butler
Low-A	Bradenton Marauders	Florida State	54	77	.412	9 (10)	Jim Horner
Rookie	FCL Pirates	Florida Complex	36	23	.610	3 (15)	Kieran Mattison
Rookie	DSL Pirates Black	Dominican	19	36	.345	45 (51)	Joel Fuentes
Rookie	DSL Pirates Gold	Dominican	32	22	.593	11 (51)	Jose Mosquera
Overall 2024 Minor League Record			**355**	**359**	**.497**	**16th (30)**	

ORGANIZATION STATISTICS

PITTSBURGH PIRATES

NATIONAL LEAGUE

Batting	B-T	Ht.	Wt.	DOB	AVG	OBP	SLG	G	PA	AB	R	H	2B	3B	HR	RBI	BB	HBP	SH	SF	SO	SB	CS	BB%	SO%
Bae, Ji Hwan	L-R	6-1	185	7-26-99	.189	.247	.216	29	81	74	11	14	2	0	0	6	6	0	0	1	24	6	2	7.41	29.63
Bart, Joey	R-R	6-2	238	12-15-96	.265	.337	.462	80	282	253	38	67	11	0	13	45	22	6	0	1	73	0	0	7.80	25.89
Cook, Billy	R-R	6-1	200	1-7-99	.224	.224	.449	16	49	49	5	11	2	0	3	8	0	0	0	0	19	1	0	0.00	38.78
Cruz, Oneil	L-R	6-7	220	10-4-98	.259	.324	.449	146	599	541	72	140	34	3	21	76	51	3	0	4	181	22	1	8.51	30.22
Davis, Henry	R-R	6-0	220	9-21-99	.144	.242	.212	37	122	104	9	15	4	0	1	5	13	1	1	2	45	0	0	10.66	36.89
De La Cruz, Bryan	R-R	6-2	175	12-16-96	.200	.220	.294	44	168	160	17	32	6	0	3	17	4	1	0	3	52	2	1	2.38	30.95
Delay, Jason	R-R	5-11	200	3-7-95	.200	.333	.400	7	19	15	1	3	3	0	0	6	3	0	1	0	0	0	0	15.79	0.00
Gonzales, Nick	R-R	5-9	195	5-27-99	.270	.311	.398	94	387	359	42	97	19	3	7	49	18	5	1	4	74	5	3	4.65	19.12
Grandal, Yasmani	B-R	6-2	225	11-8-88	.228	.304	.400	72	243	215	26	49	10	0	9	27	24	0	3	1	46	1	0	9.88	18.93
Hayes, Ke'Bryan	R-R	5-10	205	1-28-97	.233	.283	.290	96	396	365	38	85	9	0	4	25	23	4	0	4	75	11	2	5.81	18.94
Joe, Connor	R-R	6-0	205	8-16-92	.228	.320	.368	123	416	364	49	83	22	1	9	36	44	6	0	2	91	2	2	10.58	21.88
Kiner-Falefa, Isiah	R-R	5-11	190	3-23-95	.240	.265	.322	50	215	208	21	50	10	2	1	10	3	4	0	0	41	8	1	1.40	19.07
Koch, Grant	R-R	5-10	195	2-5-97	.000	.125	.000	3	8	7	1	0	0	0	0	0	1	0	0	0	6	0	0	12.50	75.00
McCutchen, Andrew	R-R	5-11	195	10-10-86	.232	.328	.411	120	515	448	66	104	18	1	20	50	58	7	0	2	133	3	2	11.26	25.83
McKinney, Billy	L-L	5-11	205	8-23-94	.200	.286	.240	10	28	25	4	5	1	0	0	2	2	1	0	0	13	0	0	7.14	46.43
Olivares, Edward	R-R	6-2	190	3-6-96	.224	.291	.333	55	196	174	22	39	4	0	5	23	16	2	0	4	37	1	0	8.16	18.88
Palacios, Josh	L-R	6-1	200	7-30-95	.224	.333	.343	23	78	67	10	15	2	0	2	9	10	1	0	0	12	1	0	12.82	15.38
Peguero, Liover	R-R	6-0	210	12-31-00	.200	.200	.300	3	10	10	0	2	1	0	0	2	0	0	0	0	3	0	0	0.00	30.00
Reynolds, Bryan	B-R	6-3	205	1-27-95	.275	.344	.447	156	692	622	73	171	29	3	24	88	57	10	0	3	156	10	2	8.24	22.54
Suwinski, Jack	L-L	6-2	215	7-29-98	.182	.264	.324	88	277	247	29	45	8	0	9	26	27	1	1	1	79	9	1	9.75	28.52
Taylor, Michael A.	R-R	6-4	215	3-26-91	.193	.253	.290	113	300	269	35	52	9	1	5	21	23	0	4	4	105	12	1	7.67	35.00
Tellez, Rowdy	L-L	6-4	270	3-16-95	.243	.299	.392	132	421	383	38	93	18	0	13	56	31	2	0	5	89	1	0	7.36	21.14
Triolo, Jared	R-R	6-3	212	2-8-98	.216	.296	.315	125	446	394	41	85	10	1	9	46	42	5	0	5	118	8	1	9.42	26.46
Williams, Alika	R-R	6-1	180	3-12-99	.207	.242	.299	37	96	87	13	18	4	2	0	5	3	1	5	0	22	1	0	3.13	22.92
Yorke, Nick	R-R	5-11	200	4-2-02	.216	.286	.378	11	42	37	4	8	0	0	2	5	4	0	0	1	12	2	0	9.52	28.57

Pitching	B-T	Ht.	Wt.	DOB	W	L	ERA	G	GS	SV	IP	Hits	Runs	ER	HR	BB	SO	AVG	OBP	SLG	SO%	BB%	BF
Bednar, David	L-R	6-1	250	10-10-94	3	8	5.77	62	0	23	58	54	40	37	9	28	58	.238	.327	.410	22.14	10.69	262
Beeks, Jalen	L-L	5-11	215	7-10-93	1	0	3.92	26	0	1	21	28	13	9	0	9	17	.318	.390	.386	16.83	8.91	101
Borucki, Ryan	L-L	6-4	210	3-31-94	0	0	7.36	14	0	0	11	14	10	9	2	4	13	.311	.380	.511	25.49	7.84	51
Bruihl, Justin	L-L	6-2	215	6-26-97	0	0	9.53	7	0	0	6	9	6	6	1	1	5	.375	.407	.625	18.52	3.70	27
Burrows, Mike	R-R	6-2	195	11-8-99	1	0	2.70	1	0	0	3	2	2	1	1	3	2	.182	.357	.455	14.29	21.43	14
Chapman, Aroldis	L-L	6-4	218	2-28-88	5	5	3.79	68	0	14	62	44	31	26	5	39	98	.198	.321	.315	36.98	14.72	265
Contreras, Roansy	R-R	6-0	175	11-7-99	1	0	4.41	12	0	0	16	19	8	8	3	8	16	.292	.370	.477	21.62	10.81	74
Falter, Bailey	R-L	6-4	175	4-24-97	8	9	4.43	28	28	0	142	138	72	70	17	45	97	.260	.315	.424	16.47	7.64	589
Feigl, Brady	R-L	6-4	195	12-27-90	0	0	32.40	1	0	0	2	7	6	6	1	0	0	.636	.636	1.091	0.00	0.00	11
Fleming, Josh	L-L	6-2	220	5-18-96	1	1	4.02	25	3	1	31	34	18	14	3	14	17	.276	.355	.398	12.32	10.14	138
German, Domingo	R-R	6-2	181	8-4-92	0	1	7.84	7	2	0	21	25	19	18	4	13	18	.298	.404	.464	18.00	13.00	100
Gonzales, Marco	L-L	6-1	205	2-16-92	1	1	4.54	7	7	0	34	43	17	17	5	11	23	.312	.360	.478	15.23	7.28	151
Heller, Ben	R-R	6-3	210	8-5-91	0	1	11.25	8	0	0	12	19	16	15	1	6	15	.352	.470	.500	22.73	9.09	66
Hernandez, Jose	L-L	5-10	205	12-31-97	1	1	3.38	7	0	1	5	5	2	2	1	4	4	.238	.360	.476	16.00	16.00	25
Holderman, Colin	R-R	6-7	240	10-8-95	3	6	3.16	55	0	0	51	42	23	18	6	25	56	.223	.324	.367	25.11	11.21	223
Honeywell, Brent	R-R	6-2	195	3-31-95	0	0	2.70	2	0	0	3	3	1	1	0	2	1	.231	.333	.308	6.67	13.33	15
Jefferies, Daulton	L-R	6-0	182	8-2-95	0	0	6.30	4	0	0	10	10	7	7	2	2	8	.256	.310	.487	19.05	4.76	42
Jones, Jared	L-R	6-1	190	8-6-01	6	8	4.14	22	22	0	122	106	60	56	18	39	132	.232	.298	.432	26.19	7.74	504
Keller, Mitch	R-R	6-2	220	4-4-96	11	12	4.25	31	31	0	178	182	90	84	23	50	166	.261	.321	.446	21.47	6.47	773
Mattson, Isaac	R-R	6-2	205	7-14-95	0	0	5.06	3	0	0	5	1	3	3	0	5	6	.059	.304	.059	26.09	21.74	23
Mlodzinski, Carmen	R-R	6-2	225	2-19-99	5	5	3.38	40	4	0	51	41	22	19	3	19	46	.223	.297	.315	22.01	9.09	209
Nicolas, Kyle	R-R	6-4	223	2-22-99	2	2	3.95	51	0	0	55	51	30	24	4	31	55	.249	.354	.341	22.63	12.76	243
Ortiz, Luis	R-R	6-2	240	1-27-99	7	6	3.32	37	15	1	136	109	56	50	16	42	107	.218	.288	.372	19.24	7.55	556
Perez, Martin	L-L	6-0	200	4-4-91	2	5	5.20	16	16	0	83	105	51	48	13	32	63	.312	.376	.499	16.89	8.58	373
Priester, Quinn	R-R	6-3	210	9-15-00	2	6	5.04	10	6	0	45	52	29	25	7	13	31	.283	.333	.440	15.42	6.47	201
Ryan, Ryder	R-R	6-2	205	5-11-95	1	0	5.66	15	0	0	21	21	14	13	2	9	17	.269	.359	.436	18.28	9.68	93

Santana, Dennis	R-R	6-2	190	4-12-96	1	1	2.44	39	0	1	44	30	14	12	2	11	50	.192	.256	.314	29.07	6.40	172
Skenes, Paul	R-R	6-6	235	5-29-02	11	3	1.96	23	23	0	133	94	31	29	10	32	170	.198	.257	.295	33.07	6.23	514
Stratton, Hunter	R-R	6-4	225	11-17-96	2	1	3.58	36	0	1	38	37	17	15	3	7	33	.255	.303	.372	20.89	4.43	158
Wentz, Joey	L-L	6-5	220	10-6-97	1	0	1.50	8	0	0	12	6	2	2	0	6	13	.143	.260	.167	26.00	12.00	50
Woodford, Jake	R-R	6-4	215	10-28-96	0	4	7.09	7	5	0	27	33	27	21	4	4	19	.292	.322	.487	15.70	3.31	121

Fielding

Catcher	PCT	G	PO	A	E	DP	PB
Bart	.992	69	498	23	4	3	4
Davis	.993	34	260	9	2	3	3
Delay	1.000	6	42	2	0	0	0
Grandal	.988	71	568	9	7	0	5
Koch	1.000	2	17	0	0	0	0

First Base	PCT	G	PO	A	E	DP
Cook	.969	5	31	0	1	3
Grandal	1.000	2	4	1	0	1
Joe	.998	79	370	36	1	45
Tellez	.998	124	740	61	2	76
Triolo	1.000	9	39	1	0	1

Second Base	PCT	G	PO	A	E	DP
Bae	.000	1	0	0	0	0
Gonzales	.987	85	147	231	5	64
Kiner-Falefa	.983	16	20	39	1	8
Triolo	.995	47	71	110	1	29
Williams	.981	20	22	31	1	5
Yorke	1.000	7	8	10	0	3

Third Base	PCT	G	PO	A	E	DP
Gonzales	1.000	2	2	0	0	0
Hayes	.981	96	75	185	5	28
Kiner-Falefa	.938	9	3	12	1	0
Triolo	.985	61	29	101	2	11
Yorke	.500	1	0	1	1	0

Shortstop	PCT	G	PO	A	E	DP
Cruz	.939	112	141	231	24	53
Gonzales	.875	8	4	10	2	0
Kiner-Falefa	1.000	28	31	60	0	14
Peguero	.909	3	4	6	1	2
Triolo	1.000	9	9	16	0	5
Williams	.978	16	16	29	1	4

Outfield	PCT	G	PO	A	E	DP
Bae	1.000	27	58	1	0	1
Cook	1.000	12	25	2	0	1
Cruz	.964	23	53	0	2	0
De La Cruz	.966	44	82	2	3	1
Joe	.968	50	87	3	3	1
McCutchen	1.000	5	6	0	0	0
McKinney	1.000	11	8	1	0	0
Olivares	.987	48	76	2	1	0
Palacios	1.000	24	27	1	0	0
Reynolds	.992	140	241	11	2	2
Suwinski	.994	100	177	0	1	0
Taylor	.987	106	229	3	3	0
Triolo	1.000	1	1	0	0	0
Yorke	1.000	3	6	0	0	0

INDIANAPOLIS INDIANS — *TRIPLE-A*

INTERNATIONAL LEAGUE

Batting	B-T	Ht.	Wt.	DOB	AVG	OBP	SLG	G	PA	AB	R	H	2B	3B	HR	RBI	BB	HBP	SH	SF	SO	SB	CS	BB%	SO%
Alcantara, Sergio	B-R	6-4	151	7-10-96	.182	.357	.212	11	42	33	5	6	1	0	0	1	9	0	0	0	9	0	1	21.43	21.43
Alvarez, Andres	R-R	5-8	175	3-29-97	.271	.360	.417	78	286	247	41	67	10	4	6	35	31	4	3	1	69	7	3	10.84	24.13
Bae, Ji Hwan	L-R	6-1	185	7-26-99	.341	.433	.504	66	293	246	49	84	11	4	7	41	41	1	1	3	63	14	3	13.99	21.50
Bart, Joey	R-R	6-2	238	12-15-96	.353	.450	.412	6	20	17	2	6	1	0	0	4	3	0	0	0	3	0	0	15.00	15.00
Beer, Seth	L-R	6-0	225	9-18-96	.272	.339	.475	44	177	158	24	43	8	0	8	33	13	4	0	2	38	0	0	7.34	21.47
Bins, Carter	R-R	5-11	215	10-7-98	.275	.383	.400	15	47	40	2	11	5	0	0	6	4	3	0	0	20	0	0	8.51	42.55
Celestino, Gilberto	R-L	6-0	170	2-13-99	.271	.348	.356	67	264	236	33	64	11	0	3	25	27	1	0	0	53	9	1	10.23	20.08
Cheng, Tsung-Che	L-R	5-7	154	7-26-01	.462	.588	.538	6	17	13	5	6	1	0	0	1	4	0	0	0	2	1	0	23.53	11.76
Cook, Billy	R-R	6-1	200	1-7-99	.276	.389	.486	30	126	105	19	29	7	0	5	21	17	3	0	1	36	9	1	13.49	28.57
Davis, Henry	R-R	6-0	220	9-21-99	.307	.401	.555	57	254	218	44	67	15	0	13	43	23	11	0	0	57	8	1	9.06	22.44
Delay, Jason	R-R	5-11	200	3-7-95	.287	.357	.360	45	171	150	20	43	8	0	1	16	14	3	1	1	27	1	1	8.19	15.79
Dixon, Brenden	R-R	5-11	205	11-20-00	.143	.200	.357	6	15	14	2	2	0	0	1	2	1	0	0	0	7	1	0	6.67	46.67
Fraizer, Matt	L-R	6-3	220	1-12-98	.261	.325	.406	45	151	138	25	36	9	1	3	23	12	1	0	0	35	6	2	7.95	23.18
Glenn, Jackson	R-R	5-10	205	10-24-97	.100	.182	.200	4	11	10	1	1	1	0	0	0	1	0	0	0	1	0	0	9.09	9.09
Gonzales, Nick	R-R	5-9	195	5-27-99	.356	.429	.600	34	154	135	37	48	14	2	5	20	15	3	0	1	25	0	3	9.74	16.23
Gorski, Matt	R-R	6-2	198	12-22-97	.257	.319	.522	113	433	389	68	100	24	5	23	67	38	0	1	5	124	15	9	8.78	28.64
Grandal, Yasmani	B-R	6-2	225	11-8-88	.257	.316	.400	9	38	35	3	9	2	0	1	11	3	0	0	0	8	0	0	7.89	21.05
Jarvis, Mike	R-R	5-10	180	5-12-98	.210	.296	.355	30	71	62	8	13	1	1	2	7	7	1	0	1	23	4	2	9.86	32.39
Koch, Grant	R-R	5-10	195	2-5-97	.191	.265	.281	30	100	89	9	17	2	0	2	8	8	1	0	0	34	0	0	8.00	34.00
Lamb, Jake	L-R	6-3	215	10-9-90	.264	.350	.393	98	414	356	48	94	23	1	7	55	43	8	0	7	84	0	1	10.39	20.29
McKinney, Billy	L-L	5-11	205	8-23-94	.299	.406	.460	43	165	137	21	41	7	0	5	19	24	2	0	2	37	0	3	14.55	22.42
Nunez, Malcom	R-R	6-0	205	3-9-01	.250	.310	.365	128	526	468	59	117	21	0	11	65	42	4	0	12	108	3	1	7.98	20.53
Olivares, Edward	R-R	6-2	190	3-6-96	.263	.343	.379	27	108	95	18	25	2	0	3	12	9	3	0	1	15	9	5	8.33	13.89
Palacios, Josh	L-R	6-1	200	7-30-95	.291	.372	.489	50	208	182	32	53	19	1	5	25	22	2	1	1	47	5	4	10.58	22.60
Peguero, Liover	R-R	6-0	210	12-31-00	.257	.319	.410	128	555	495	68	127	29	4	13	79	46	3	3	8	139	14	3	8.29	25.05
Perez, Joe	R-R	6-1	198	8-12-99	.100	.182	.100	7	22	20	2	2	0	0	0	1	2	0	0	0	10	0	0	9.09	45.45
Peterson, Dustin	R-R	6-1	210	9-10-94	.167	.229	.167	9	35	30	4	5	0	0	0	3	3	0	0	2	10	2	0	8.57	28.57
Rodriguez, Endy	B-R	5-9	170	5-26-00	.333	.375	.600	4	16	15	2	5	1	0	1	4	1	0	0	0	3	0	1	6.25	18.75
Rojas, Jose	L-R	6-0	200	2-24-93	.192	.288	.423	15	59	52	8	10	3	0	3	6	7	0	0	0	12	0	0	11.86	20.34
Shockley, Dylan	R-R	5-9	195	4-10-97	.258	.324	.409	29	74	66	12	17	4	0	2	11	4	3	0	1	18	0	0	5.41	24.32
Smith-Njigba, Canaan	L-R	6-0	230	4-30-99	.212	.344	.330	54	220	179	26	38	11	2	2	18	37	0	1	2	62	6	0	16.82	28.18
Suwinski, Jack	L-L	6-2	215	7-29-98	.239	.307	.444	48	202	180	24	43	10	3	7	27	17	2	0	3	59	3	0	8.42	29.21
Williams, Alika	R-R	6-1	180	3-12-99	.311	.384	.396	41	186	164	27	51	10	2	0	13	20	0	1	1	34	2	0	10.75	18.28
Wilson, Eli	R-R	6-0	190	7-6-98	.286	.286	.857	4	7	7	1	2	1	0	1	1	0	0	0	0	2	0	1	0.00	28.57
Yorke, Nick	R-R	5-11	200	4-2-02	.355	.431	.507	40	175	152	26	54	17	0	2	26	18	3	0	1	33	7	4	10.29	18.86

Pitching	B-T	Ht.	Wt.	DOB	W	L	ERA	G	GS	SV	IP	Hits	Runs	ER	HR	BB	SO	AVG	OBP	SLG	SO%	BB%	BF
Alldred, Cam	L-L	6-3	205	7-25-96	1	3	6.88	9	9	0	34	39	28	26	3	18	34	.289	.374	.430	21.79	11.54	156
Ashcraft, Braxton	L-R	6-5	195	10-5-99	1	0	0.47	5	4	0	19	15	2	1	0	4	14	.205	.247	.274	17.72	5.06	79
Bidois, Brandan	R-R	6-2	158	6-21-01	0	0	0.00	1	0	0	1	1	0	0	0	0	1	.250	.400	.250	20.00	0.00	5
Borucki, Ryan	L-L	6-4	210	3-31-94	1	1	4.76	12	0	0	11	8	6	6	3	6	21	.195	.313	.415	43.75	12.50	48
Bruihl, Justin	L-L	6-2	215	6-26-97	0	0	3.93	18	0	0	18	20	11	8	2	10	23	.270	.389	.419	25.56	11.11	90
Burrows, Mike	R-R	6-2	195	11-8-99	1	1	4.06	10	9	0	38	38	17	17	7	15	45	.253	.325	.467	26.63	8.88	169
Case, Brad	R-R	6-6	242	9-13-96	1	1	9.64	2	0	0	5	6	6	5	2	3	1	.316	.458	.684	4.17	12.50	24
Cessa, Luis	R-R	6-0	222	4-25-92	2	5	5.26	15	13	0	63	62	46	37	9	27	48	.256	.331	.450	17.58	9.89	273
Chandler, Bubba	S-R	6-2	200	9-14-02	4	0	1.83	7	7	0	39	26	10	8	2	15	54	.183	.270	.261	33.96	9.43	159

Del Bonta-Smith, Fineas	R-R	6-0	190	2-2-97	3	1	4.64	21	0	0	33	38	19	17	7	16	28	.299	.374	.567	19.05	10.88	147
Dombkowski, Nick	R-L	6-2	210	8-9-98	2	2	4.32	14	5	0	33	36	17	16	4	25	32	.275	.391	.412	20.51	16.03	156
Falter, Bailey	R-L	6-4	175	4-24-97	0	0	6.00	1	1	0	3	5	2	2	0	0	3	.385	.385	.385	23.08	0.00	13
Feigl, Brady	R-L	6-4	195	12-27-90	7	2	4.05	39	1	2	60	58	27	27	9	15	68	.254	.309	.439	27.53	6.07	247
Fellows, Drake	L-R	6-5	216	3-6-98	0	1	5.73	3	3	0	11	10	8	7	0	9	8	.233	.352	.326	14.81	16.67	54
Fleming, Josh	L-L	6-2	220	5-18-96	0	0	5.68	7	0	0	13	12	8	8	1	2	5	.240	.296	.420	9.09	3.64	55
Flowers, J.C.	R-R	6-3	195	5-19-98	2	1	9.00	14	2	0	20	27	24	20	4	26	16	.329	.491	.537	14.29	23.21	112
Franzua, Geronimo	L-L	6-1	170	9-25-93	5	6	4.55	48	2	5	61	55	38	31	12	39	80	.240	.357	.428	29.09	14.18	275
Gau, Chris	L-R	6-2	205	2-3-97	2	1	5.73	10	1	0	22	22	15	14	4	17	18	.262	.379	.512	17.48	16.50	103
German, Domingo	R-R	6-2	181	8-4-92	7	4	5.04	15	14	0	75	72	48	42	12	33	74	.247	.329	.454	22.49	10.03	329
Gonzales, Marco	L-L	6-1	205	2-16-92	0	1	6.14	2	2	0	7	7	6	5	1	5	6	.226	.333	.452	16.67	13.89	36
Harrington, Thomas	R-R	6-2	185	7-12-01	5	1	3.33	8	8	0	46	35	18	17	5	8	38	.212	.253	.345	21.23	4.47	179
Heller, Ben	R-R	6-3	210	8-5-91	2	3	3.55	30	0	4	33	20	14	13	6	13	55	.168	.267	.361	40.74	9.63	135
Hernandez, Jose	L-L	5-10	205	12-31-97	0	0	7.04	14	0	0	15	19	12	12	1	9	21	.292	.387	.415	28.00	12.00	75
Holderman, Colin	R-R	6-7	240	10-8-95	0	0	5.87	8	1	0	8	6	5	5	1	2	10	.222	.323	.370	32.26	6.45	31
Honeywell, Brent	R-R	6-2	195	3-31-95	1	3	4.85	31	0	7	39	36	26	21	4	17	33	.250	.339	.410	19.64	10.12	168
Jefferies, Daulton	L-R	6-0	182	8-2-95	1	1	6.23	6	5	0	22	27	15	15	3	10	12	.318	.378	.565	12.24	10.20	98
Jones, Jared	L-R	6-1	190	8-6-01	0	1	4.91	3	3	0	11	9	7	6	1	3	16	.225	.279	.425	37.21	6.98	43
Lauer, Eric	R-L	6-3	209	6-3-95	2	2	5.52	8	6	0	29	31	20	18	6	11	37	.272	.339	.535	29.13	8.66	127
Mattson, Isaac	R-R	6-2	205	7-14-95	5	1	3.15	29	3	3	60	45	25	21	6	33	76	.208	.308	.347	29.80	12.94	255
McClure, Kade	R-R	6-7	220	2-12-96	0	2	15.00	7	0	0	9	13	15	15	4	8	8	.333	.469	.718	16.00	16.00	50
Mlodzinski, Carmen	R-R	6-2	225	2-19-99	0	1	6.75	15	0	0	17	22	13	13	4	8	17	.314	.400	.571	21.25	10.00	80
Nicolas, Kyle	R-R	6-4	223	2-22-99	0	0	0.84	9	0	1	11	2	1	1	0	9	13	.061	.273	.091	29.55	20.45	44
Peralta, Wily	R-R	6-1	261	5-8-89	2	2	7.44	17	4	0	33	35	28	27	7	14	29	.278	.343	.516	20.00	9.66	145
Perez, Martin	L-L	6-0	200	4-4-91	0	0	1.80	1	1	0	5	5	2	1	0	0	4	.263	.263	.421	21.05	0.00	19
Plassmeyer, Michael	L-L	6-2	197	11-5-96	5	10	7.93	28	11	0	70	96	64	62	11	13	86	.327	.371	.575	26.71	4.04	322
Priester, Quinn	R-R	6-3	210	9-15-00	3	1	3.21	7	7	0	34	29	12	12	2	7	36	.232	.274	.360	26.67	5.19	135
Ryan, Ryder	R-R	6-2	205	5-11-95	2	2	4.61	32	0	3	41	40	24	21	8	15	34	.252	.320	.459	19.32	8.52	176
Sadzeck, Connor	R-R	6-7	235	10-1-91	4	3	4.66	49	0	9	64	67	39	33	3	42	67	.265	.386	.375	21.68	13.59	309
Selby, Colin	R-R	6-2	220	10-24-97	0	0	0.00	2	0	0	2	1	0	0	0	3	2	.167	.444	.167	20.00	30.00	10
Shockley, Dylan	R-R	5-9	195	4-10-97	0	0	21.60	3	0	0	3	8	8	8	1	2	0	.471	.500	.706	0.00	10.00	20
Shortridge, Aaron	R-R	6-3	215	5-29-97	3	4	5.18	12	6	0	49	48	32	28	7	20	40	.250	.321	.443	18.60	9.30	215
Skenes, Paul	R-R	6-6	235	5-29-02	0	0	0.99	7	7	0	27	17	4	3	1	8	45	.175	.238	.247	42.86	7.62	105
Stratton, Hunter	R-R	6-4	225	11-17-96	0	0	0.00	3	0	1	4	2	0	0	0	1	4	.143	.200	.143	26.67	6.67	15
Sulser, Beau	R-R	6-2	195	5-5-94	1	1	6.53	6	3	0	21	28	15	15	4	9	22	.311	.380	.533	22.00	9.00	100
Walker, Josh	L-L	6-6	225	12-1-94	0	0	8.00	8	0	0	9	10	8	8	2	1	11	.270	.289	.486	28.95	2.63	38
Woodford, Jake	R-R	6-4	215	10-28-96	2	2	2.44	10	9	0	44	41	12	12	3	10	49	.243	.290	.361	26.63	5.43	184
Yean, Eddy	R-R	6-1	180	6-25-01	0	0	0.00	2	0	0	2	1	0	0	0	1	4	.143	.250	.286	50.00	12.50	8

Fielding

Catcher	PCT	G	PO	A	E	DP	PB
Bart	1.000	4	20	1	0	0	0
Bins	.977	15	120	8	3	0	0
Davis	.992	35	346	10	3	0	4
Delay	.989	45	361	14	4	1	2
Grandal	.985	7	61	3	1	2	1
Koch	.986	30	274	6	4	1	1
Rodriguez	.882	2	15	0	2	0	0
Shockley	.989	26	171	17	2	1	0
Wilson	1.000	1	9	1	0	0	0

First Base	PCT	G	PO	A	E	DP
Beer	.988	22	155	5	2	11
Cook	1.000	6	41	1	0	4
Gorski	.988	14	80	5	1	4
Lamb	1.000	72	456	46	0	41
McKinney	1.000	8	47	2	0	4
Nunez	.992	40	215	24	2	27
Rodriguez	1.000	1	9	0	0	0
Rojas	1.000	1	8	1	0	0

Second Base	PCT	G	PO	A	E	DP
Alcantara	1.000	2	5	5	0	2
Alvarez	.989	26	30	58	1	10
Bae	.968	21	45	45	3	11
Cheng	1.000	1	0	2	0	0
Gonzales	.958	19	26	42	3	13
Jarvis	1.000	9	15	18	0	3
Peguero	.994	48	70	95	1	18
Williams	1.000	15	22	26	0	4
Yorke	.952	23	28	52	4	9

Third Base	PCT	G	PO	A	E	DP
Alcantara	.923	7	4	8	1	0
Alvarez	.931	29	20	34	4	5
Glenn	1.000	4	7	6	0	1
Gonzales	1.000	5	2	9	0	1
Jarvis	.806	17	11	14	6	3
Nunez	.947	87	45	133	10	15
Rojas	1.000	11	10	14	0	3
Williams	1.000	8	5	8	0	2
Yorke	1.000	2	1	2	0	0

Shortstop	PCT	G	PO	A	E	DP
Alcantara	1.000	2	1	1	0	1
Alvarez	.973	20	31	40	2	6
Bae	1.000	1	0	2	0	0
Cheng	1.000	4	1	6	0	1
Gonzales	.972	13	12	23	1	3
Jarvis	1.000	1	0	3	0	0
Peguero	.965	83	102	171	10	37
Williams	.973	23	25	47	2	11
Yorke	1.000	7	10	19	0	3

Outfield	PCT	G	PO	A	E	DP
Alvarez	1.000	5	5	1	0	0
Bae	1.000	46	77	1	0	0
Celestino	.967	67	113	5	4	1
Cook	1.000	22	45	1	0	0
Fraizer	1.000	43	58	2	0	0
Gorski	.965	103	185	9	7	3
Lamb	1.000	6	11	0	0	0
McKinney	.951	30	56	2	3	2
Olivares	.979	21	46	1	1	0
Palacios	1.000	32	50	1	0	0
Perez	1.000	3	1	1	0	0
Peterson	.875	6	7	0	1	0
Rojas	.857	3	5	1	1	0
Smith-Njigba	.986	39	64	4	1	1
Suwinski	.963	44	104	1	4	0
Yorke	1.000	11	18	0	0	0

ALTOONA CURVE — DOUBLE-A

EASTERN LEAGUE

Batting	B-T	Ht.	Wt.	DOB	AVG	OBP	SLG	G	PA	AB	R	H	2B	3B	HR	RBI	BB	HBP	SH	SF	SO	SB	CS	BB%	SO%
Acuna, Francisco	R-R	5-7	150	1-12-00	.290	.405	.387	15	39	31	2	9	3	0	0	3	6	0	2	0	6	1	0	15.38	15.38
Beer, Seth	L-R	6-0	225	9-18-96	.281	.366	.397	55	228	199	19	56	7	2	4	21	18	9	0	1	48	1	0	7.89	21.05
Bins, Carter	R-R	5-11	215	10-7-98	.193	.302	.354	66	247	212	34	41	8	1	8	18	29	4	1	0	87	6	1	11.74	35.22
Bowen, Jase	R-R	6-0	190	9-2-00	.241	.298	.366	110	450	407	57	98	17	2	10	43	29	6	3	5	106	22	8	6.44	23.56
Cheng, Tsung-Che	L-R	5-7	154	7-26-01	.218	.320	.341	126	500	422	64	92	19	0	11	54	61	4	10	3	117	16	7	12.20	23.40
Cimillo, Nick	R-R	6-2	215	2-23-00	.224	.324	.366	44	185	161	17	36	9	1	4	23	22	2	0	0	32	1	0	11.89	17.30

Davis, Henry	R-R	6-0	220	9-21-99	.000	.250	.000	2	8	6	1	0	0	0	0	0	2	0	0	0	5	0	0	25.00	62.50
Dixon, Brenden	R-R	5-11	205	11-20-00	.188	.281	.340	64	224	197	23	37	6	0	8	30	24	2	0	1	69	6	0	10.71	30.80
Fajardo, Yoyner	L-R	6-0	179	4-6-99	.300	.406	.373	63	265	220	40	66	10	3	0	20	35	5	0	1	37	17	5	13.21	13.96
Fraizer, Matt	L-R	6-3	220	1-12-98	.240	.318	.365	56	218	192	25	46	7	1	5	21	20	3	1	2	59	10	3	9.17	27.06
Glenn, Jackson	R-R	5-10	205	10-24-97	.192	.252	.286	73	249	224	28	43	9	0	4	20	19	0	3	3	75	2	2	7.63	30.12
Gonzalez, Tres	L-L	5-11	185	10-4-00	.239	.313	.273	95	363	322	34	77	9	1	0	24	28	7	5	1	75	10	8	7.71	20.66
Gutierrez, Abrahan	R-R	6-0	214	10-31-99	.251	.283	.322	44	180	171	15	43	10	1	0	20	7	1	0	1	29	2	1	3.89	16.11
Harrison, Kalae	L-R	5-11	188	6-5-02	.167	.167	.167	4	12	12	1	2	0	0	0	0	0	0	0	0	3	0	1	0.00	25.00
Hendrie, Wyatt	R-R	5-10	200	2-8-99	.254	.304	.365	20	72	63	8	16	4	0	1	13	4	1	3	1	16	4	0	5.56	22.22
Jarvis, Mike	R-R	5-10	180	5-12-98	.103	.194	.172	27	99	87	7	9	3	0	1	2	9	1	1	1	31	4	1	9.09	31.31
Johnson, Termarr	L-R	5-8	175	6-11-04	.229	.316	.396	14	57	48	9	11	2	0	2	8	7	0	0	2	11	2	1	12.28	19.30
Kiner-Falefa, Isiah	R-R	5-11	190	3-23-95	.500	.500	.750	1	4	4	1	2	1	0	0	0	0	0	0	0	0	0	0	0.00	0.00
McAdoo, Charles	R-R	6-2	210	3-6-02	.269	.347	.490	27	118	104	13	28	6	1	5	11	13	0	0	1	29	3	0	11.02	24.58
Perez, Joe	R-R	6-1	198	8-12-99	.230	.297	.374	62	259	230	20	53	11	2	6	38	22	2	0	5	78	2	0	8.49	30.12
Peterson, Dustin	R-R	6-1	210	9-10-94	.220	.300	.352	45	180	159	18	35	6	0	5	23	17	2	0	2	51	2	2	9.44	28.33
Pichardo, Kervin	R-R	6-0	180	10-15-01	.252	.306	.373	118	459	421	57	106	14	2	11	49	27	6	4	0	128	8	4	5.88	27.89
Planchart, Geovanny	R-R	6-1	176	9-17-01	.222	.417	.222	3	12	9	2	2	0	0	0	1	3	0	0	0	2	0	0	25.00	16.67
Rodriguez, Endy	B-R	5-9	170	5-26-00	.208	.240	.250	6	25	24	4	5	1	0	0	1	1	0	0	0	6	0	0	4.00	24.00
Scott, Connor	L-L	6-3	208	10-8-99	.160	.207	.185	24	87	81	8	13	2	0	0	5	5	0	0	1	25	0	1	5.75	28.74
Shackelford, Aaron	L-R	5-9	215	10-16-96	.216	.263	.409	23	95	88	9	19	3	1	4	14	3	3	0	1	34	1	1	3.16	35.79
Shockley, Dylan	R-R	5-9	195	4-10-97	.167	.200	.167	11	28	24	0	4	0	0	0	1	0	1	3	0	8	0	0	0.00	28.57
Siani, Sammy	L-L	5-10	195	12-14-00	.254	.325	.368	96	394	351	49	89	13	6	5	36	35	3	3	2	81	14	5	8.88	20.56
Wilson, Eli	R-R	6-0	190	7-6-98	.164	.240	.313	25	75	67	7	11	1	0	3	6	7	0	0	1	20	3	1	9.33	26.67

Pitching	B-T	Ht.	Wt.	DOB	W	L	ERA	G	GS	SV	IP	Hits	Runs	ER	HR	BB	SO	AVG	OBP	SLG	SO%	BB%	BF
Ashcraft, Braxton	L-R	6-5	195	10-5-99	2	2	3.69	11	10	0	54	51	24	22	6	8	63	.244	.274	.411	28.64	3.64	220
Barco, Hunter	L-L	6-4	210	12-15-00	0	1	2.25	2	2	0	4	2	1	1	0	0	6	.154	.154	.154	46.15	0.00	13
Bednar, David	L-R	6-1	250	10-10-94	0	0	0.00	1	0	0	1	0	0	0	0	0	1	.000	.000	.000	25.00	0.00	4
Borucki, Ryan	L-L	6-4	210	3-31-94	0	0	5.40	3	0	0	3	3	2	2	0	2	3	.273	.400	.273	20.00	13.33	15
Carey, Jack	R-R	6-0	205	9-20-99	6	3	3.75	30	0	8	50	52	25	21	6	23	43	.269	.360	.435	19.28	10.31	223
Case, Brad	R-R	6-6	242	9-13-96	4	1	3.19	17	1	0	37	41	15	13	2	9	21	.285	.348	.382	13.04	5.59	161
Chandler, Bubba	S-R	6-2	200	9-14-02	6	7	3.70	19	16	1	80	55	36	33	7	26	94	.192	.264	.310	29.38	8.13	320
Chapman, Emmanuel	R-R	6-6	255	9-23-98	2	2	3.57	24	7	0	63	47	27	25	3	26	57	.213	.296	.317	22.44	10.24	254
Chen, Po-Yu	L-R	6-2	187	10-2-01	4	10	4.03	27	25	0	134	130	68	60	12	43	96	.255	.325	.376	16.75	7.50	573
Deese, Jaycob	R-R	6-1	195	5-30-00	0	0	4.82	5	1	0	9	14	5	5	1	4	3	.368	.429	.474	7.14	9.52	42
Dombkowski, Nick	R-L	6-2	210	8-9-98	4	4	3.17	16	7	1	48	38	21	17	5	15	39	.210	.269	.354	19.31	7.43	202
Fellows, Drake	L-R	6-5	216	3-6-98	2	5	5.74	17	10	0	53	52	36	34	6	26	49	.254	.345	.444	20.85	11.06	235
Flowers, J.C.	R-R	6-3	195	5-19-98	1	1	3.44	27	0	0	50	30	23	19	1	30	43	.174	.309	.267	20.67	14.42	208
Ford, Grant	R-R	6-1	175	3-11-98	4	3	3.95	35	2	0	57	56	31	25	2	32	58	.251	.349	.332	22.05	12.17	263
Garcia, Darvin	R-R	6-3	170	4-25-99	0	1	9.00	1	0	0	1	1	4	1	0	3	1	.200	.500	.200	11.11	33.33	9
Gau, Chris	L-R	6-2	205	2-3-97	0	4	3.47	11	5	1	23	22	13	9	3	8	20	.244	.307	.400	19.80	7.92	101
Harrington, Thomas	R-R	6-2	185	7-12-01	2	2	2.24	13	12	0	68	58	25	17	4	10	74	.227	.264	.333	27.41	3.70	270
Junker, Cameron	R-R	6-5	220	9-3-97	0	3	13.19	15	0	2	14	19	24	21	2	21	12	.328	.488	.483	14.63	25.61	82
Linarez, Valentin	R-R	6-5	226	2-14-00	1	2	6.46	17	0	0	31	33	25	22	5	19	28	.292	.392	.451	19.44	13.19	144
Mattson, Isaac	R-R	6-2	205	7-14-95	2	1	3.27	8	0	1	11	9	4	4	1	5	13	.237	.326	.342	29.55	11.36	44
McClure, Kade	R-R	6-7	220	2-12-96	0	0	18.00	2	0	0	2	5	4	4	0	1	1	.500	.545	.600	9.09	9.09	11
Meis, Justin	R-R	6-2	160	11-23-99	3	1	6.44	37	0	2	64	70	49	46	9	36	72	.280	.370	.484	24.57	12.29	293
Melendez, Cristofer	R-R	6-3	226	9-16-97	1	0	18.00	2	0	0	2	6	4	4	0	2	4	.500	.571	.750	28.57	14.29	14
Nielson, Cy	R-L	6-3	210	2-25-01	3	1	6.55	13	0	0	22	23	17	16	2	14	28	.261	.387	.386	26.17	13.08	107
Perachi, Dominic	L-L	6-4	195	2-27-01	1	2	6.15	10	8	1	41	54	30	28	4	23	40	.321	.407	.476	20.51	11.79	195
Peralta, Luis	L-L	5-11	170	1-6-01	0	0	1.86	7	0	2	10	9	2	2	1	3	14	.250	.325	.333	35.00	7.50	40
Randall, Scott	R-R	6-0	172	8-3-98	0	0	0.00	1	1	0	4	3	0	0	0	0	3	.231	.231	.308	23.08	0.00	13
Samaniego, Tyler	R-L	6-4	205	1-30-99	0	0	3.57	13	0	1	18	17	7	7	1	7	22	.243	.308	.329	28.21	8.97	78
Solometo, Anthony	L-L	6-5	220	12-2-02	1	7	5.98	20	17	0	59	60	41	39	7	35	46	.269	.382	.430	17.10	13.01	269
Sullivan, Sean	R-R	6-1	180	10-2-00	2	5	3.84	15	13	1	73	70	34	31	6	22	57	.252	.309	.406	18.69	7.21	305
Sulser, Beau	R-R	6-2	195	5-5-94	0	0	0.00	1	0	0	4	2	0	0	0	1	3	.143	.200	.143	20.00	6.67	15
Townsend, Blake	L-L	6-4	220	4-5-01	1	0	2.00	5	0	0	9	4	2	2	0	2	6	.138	.286	.138	16.67	5.56	36
Wilson, Eli	R-R	6-0	190	7-6-98	0	0	0.00	1	0	0	1	0	0	0	0	0	1	.000	.000	.000	33.33	0.00	3
Woods, Jaden	L-L	6-2	205	2-1-02	3	3	4.93	20	1	3	35	34	21	19	3	17	43	.250	.348	.353	27.04	10.69	159
Yean, Eddy	R-R	6-1	180	6-25-01	7	5	3.45	46	0	5	73	76	35	28	6	21	65	.269	.329	.378	20.50	6.62	317

Fielding

Catcher	PCT	G	PO	A	E	DP	PB
Bins	.981	54	432	21	9	4	2
Davis	1.000	2	20	0	0	0	0
Gutierrez	.980	39	325	14	7	3	0
Hendrie	.994	20	154	8	1	2	4
Planchart	1.000	3	29	2	0	1	0
Rodriguez	1.000	3	19	0	0	0	2
Shockley	.988	11	79	2	1	0	1
Wilson	.990	18	94	8	1	0	3

First Base	PCT	G	PO	A	E	DP
Beer	.978	32	219	8	5	27
Bins	1.000	8	51	2	0	7
Bowen	1.000	5	19	4	0	2
Cimillo	.991	44	314	22	3	28
Dixon	.982	11	52	4	1	4
Glenn	1.000	12	22	1	0	4
Gutierrez	.947	3	15	3	1	2
Perez	.986	30	199	11	3	25
Shackelford	.983	15	106	7	2	8

Second Base	PCT	G	PO	A	E	DP
Acuna	1.000	12	15	37	0	8
Cheng	1.000	25	29	63	0	14
Dixon	1.000	3	4	7	0	2
Glenn	.992	32	48	74	1	22
Harrison	1.000	4	4	6	0	2
Jarvis	.979	10	16	30	1	6
Johnson	.962	12	21	30	2	10
Kiner-Falefa	1.000	1	0	1	0	0
Pichardo	.976	61	75	131	5	26

Third Base	PCT	G	PO	A	E	DP
Dixon	.897	36	18	34	6	4
Perez	.909	17	20	20	4	3
Pichardo	.926	36	26	49	6	6
Glenn	.959	33	18	29	2	3
Jarvis	.964	14	11	16	1	3
McAdoo	.979	24	13	34	1	2

Shortstop	PCT	G	PO	A	E	DP
Acuna	1.000	1	4	1	0	0
Cheng	.968	107	118	241	12	50
Jarvis	1.000	5	4	12	0	2
Johnson	1.000	3	2	11	0	2
Kiner-Falefa	1.000	1	1	1	0	0
Pichardo	.939	41	47	76	8	20

Outfield	PCT	G	PO	A	E	DP
Bowen	.975	104	222	9	6	3
Fajardo	.973	32	69	3	2	0
Fraizer	.983	52	112	2	2	1
Gonzalez	1.000	81	186	6	0	1
Jarvis	1.000	1	3	1	0	0
McAdoo	1.000	5	6	0	0	0
Perez	.952	11	19	1	1	0
Peterson	1.000	22	35	0	0	0
Scott	1.000	17	41	1	0	0
Shackelford	.929	6	13	0	1	0
Siani	.992	97	239	7	2	2

GREENSBORO GRASSHOPPERS — *HIGH-A*

SOUTH ATLANTIC LEAGUE

Batting	B-T	Ht.	Wt.	DOB	AVG	OBP	SLG	G	PA	AB	R	H	2B	3B	HR	RBI	BB	HBP	SH	SF	SO	SB	CS	BB%	SO%
Alfonzo, Omar	L-R	6-1	180	8-3-03	.247	.371	.457	24	97	81	12	20	2	0	5	12	16	0	0	0	25	1	1	16.49	25.77
Brannigan, Jack	R-R	6-0	190	3-11-01	.238	.344	.490	77	341	290	61	69	15	2	18	53	40	8	1	2	89	12	3	11.73	26.10
Brown, Luke	L-R	5-9	195	3-12-99	.175	.289	.316	72	240	206	38	36	3	1	8	22	30	3	1	0	75	10	1	12.50	31.25
Campana, Sergio	R-R	6-0	160	3-29-02	.050	.259	.050	16	28	20	5	1	0	0	0	1	5	1	0	1	12	4	1	17.86	42.86
Cimillo, Nick	R-R	6-2	215	2-23-00	.293	.419	.619	52	223	181	46	53	8	0	17	48	38	2	0	1	57	2	0	17.04	25.56
Escotto, Maikol	R-R	5-10	180	6-4-02	.215	.257	.355	68	232	214	27	46	6	0	8	31	13	0	1	3	78	8	2	5.60	33.62
Gourson, Duce	L-R	6-1	190	9-20-02	.179	.319	.205	11	47	39	5	7	1	0	0	2	5	3	0	0	11	2	1	10.64	23.40
Harrison, Kalae	L-R	5-11	188	6-5-02	.159	.259	.221	49	167	145	19	23	6	0	1	14	17	3	1	1	49	3	0	10.18	29.34
Head, Hudson	L-L	6-0	180	4-8-01	.208	.303	.383	102	416	360	58	75	12	6	13	49	45	5	2	3	133	9	4	10.82	31.97
Hendrie, Wyatt	R-R	5-10	200	2-8-99	.163	.255	.224	15	55	49	6	8	0	0	1	3	4	2	0	0	20	3	0	7.27	36.36
Hilson, P.J.	R-R	5-10	175	8-25-00	.257	.317	.443	85	326	296	60	76	14	1	13	45	23	4	1	2	82	14	3	7.06	25.15
Jebb, Mitch	L-R	6-1	185	5-13-02	.253	.341	.355	113	497	431	76	109	12	7	6	42	56	3	4	3	95	43	8	11.27	19.11
Johnson, Termarr	L-R	5-8	175	6-11-04	.238	.372	.385	110	487	395	73	94	17	1	13	46	78	9	1	4	105	20	4	16.02	21.56
McAdoo, Charles	R-R	6-2	210	3-6-02	.336	.415	.561	60	258	223	40	75	15	4	9	52	27	5	0	3	56	14	3	10.47	21.71
McKinney, Billy	L-L	5-11	205	8-23-94	.200	.455	.267	6	22	15	3	3	1	0	0	0	6	1	0	0	5	1	0	27.27	22.73
Miknis, Justin	L-R	6-0	195	9-6-00	.167	.286	.667	2	7	6	1	1	0	0	1	2	1	0	0	0	4	0	0	14.29	57.14
Nolasco, Rodolfo	R-R	5-11	175	9-23-01	.173	.264	.293	21	87	75	8	13	3	0	2	12	10	0	0	2	38	0	1	11.49	43.68
Palacios, Josh	L-R	6-1	200	7-30-95	.231	.231	.769	4	13	13	2	3	1	0	2	4	0	0	0	0	4	0	0	0.00	30.77
Planchart, Geovanny	R-R	6-1	176	9-17-01	.223	.350	.325	52	200	166	19	37	6	1	3	24	31	2	0	1	50	0	2	15.50	25.00
Rivas, Javier	R-R	6-6	165	9-1-02	.125	.176	.188	10	35	32	1	4	0	1	0	0	0	2	1	0	14	0	0	0.00	40.00
Ross, Shawn	R-R	6-0	185	9-30-99	.193	.334	.459	92	375	305	52	59	10	1	23	58	57	9	1	3	132	12	1	15.20	35.20
Siani, Sammy	L-L	5-10	195	12-14-00	.324	.402	.563	20	82	71	17	23	5	0	4	12	10	0	0	1	9	2	1	12.20	10.98
Sightler, Josiah	L-L	6-3	234	10-19-99	.192	.288	.377	82	316	276	35	53	7	1	14	41	33	5	0	2	142	3	0	10.44	44.94
White, Lonnie	R-R	6-3	212	12-31-02	.167	.275	.340	89	375	324	46	54	10	2	14	44	36	13	0	2	129	15	6	9.60	34.40

Pitching	B-T	Ht.	Wt.	DOB	W	L	ERA	G	GS	SV	IP	Hits	Runs	ER	HR	BB	SO	AVG	OBP	SLG	SO%	BB%	BF
Barco, Hunter	L-L	6-4	210	12-15-00	4	1	3.34	16	14	0	62	46	23	23	5	22	77	.207	.294	.311	30.43	8.70	253
Bidois, Brandan	R-R	6-2	158	6-21-01	0	5	4.25	26	0	4	30	19	16	14	3	17	43	.179	.294	.283	33.86	13.39	127
Birdsong, Elijah	R-R	6-2	200	10-11-99	4	2	4.83	30	0	2	41	32	24	22	4	28	31	.222	.358	.340	17.51	15.82	177
Bosnic, Julian	L-L	6-3	218	12-28-99	2	3	3.03	24	0	0	39	36	18	13	1	28	40	.254	.382	.310	23.12	16.18	173
Carey, Jack	R-R	6-0	205	9-20-99	2	0	1.64	5	0	0	11	9	3	2	1	2	11	.225	.256	.300	25.58	4.65	43
Chapman, Emmanuel	R-R	6-6	255	9-23-98	2	0	3.00	12	0	0	18	12	6	6	3	6	23	.188	.257	.359	32.86	8.57	70
Cotto, Magdiel	L-L	6-3	225	6-24-02	2	1	7.71	6	0	1	7	8	7	6	2	2	6	.276	.344	.483	18.75	6.25	32
De La Paz, Yoldin	L-L	6-0	165	5-10-02	0	2	6.75	10	1	1	21	25	17	16	3	7	18	.294	.344	.482	19.35	7.53	93
Deese, Jaycob	R-R	6-1	195	5-30-00	2	4	6.64	30	1	1	42	49	36	31	8	14	28	.283	.339	.486	14.81	7.41	189
Del Bonta-Smith, Fineas	R-R	6-0	190	2-2-97	0	0	0.00	4	0	0	6	3	0	0	0	3	5	.158	.273	.158	21.74	13.04	23
Diamond, Derek	R-R	6-2	200	1-4-01	5	6	4.80	23	19	0	96	107	57	51	16	19	83	.277	.312	.469	20.29	4.65	409
Dotel, Wilber	R-R	6-3	178	9-25-02	9	5	5.33	25	25	0	106	98	68	63	21	54	106	.242	.336	.435	22.84	11.64	464
Ercolani, Alessandro	R-R	6-2	185	4-20-04	6	2	3.29	24	9	1	77	58	31	28	8	25	93	.205	.270	.329	29.71	7.99	313
Escotto, Maikol	R-R	5-10	180	6-4-02	0	0	4.91	5	0	0	4	5	2	2	1	3	2	.313	.450	.500	10.00	15.00	20
Fellows, Drake	L-R	6-5	216	3-6-98	1	0	5.23	4	0	0	10	11	6	6	0	5	11	.268	.348	.390	23.91	10.87	46
Garcia, Darvin	R-R	6-3	170	4-25-99	2	2	4.50	31	0	2	44	42	28	22	3	27	43	.255	.357	.358	21.50	13.50	200
Harbin, Ryan	R-R	6-4	195	8-6-01	0	2	5.40	28	0	1	38	34	26	23	5	24	55	.238	.366	.385	31.61	13.79	174
Jimenez, Carlos	R-R	6-2	140	7-14-02	2	0	1.93	3	0	0	5	3	1	1	0	3	4	.200	.316	.267	21.05	15.79	19
Kennedy, Michael	L-L	6-1	205	11-30-04	0	0	0.84	2	2	0	11	6	1	1	0	3	15	.167	.244	.194	36.59	7.32	41
Linarez, Valentin	R-R	6-5	226	2-14-00	3	0	3.20	18	0	2	25	18	11	9	3	12	43	.200	.308	.333	41.35	11.54	104
Massey, J.P.	R-R	6-5	205	4-1-00	3	5	5.24	20	17	0	69	64	46	40	6	39	66	.242	.358	.377	20.89	12.34	316
McMillan, Garrett	L-R	6-4	230	2-10-01	1	0	0.43	7	3	0	21	16	3	1	0	4	28	.208	.247	.247	34.57	4.94	81
Nielson, Cy	R-L	6-3	210	2-25-01	2	2	2.39	31	1	7	38	26	15	10	0	15	50	.190	.278	.255	31.65	9.49	158
Perachi, Dominic	L-L	6-4	195	2-27-01	6	3	2.08	16	10	1	74	44	20	17	0	19	81	.171	.241	.194	28.22	6.62	287
Peralta, Luis	L-L	5-11	170	1-6-01	4	0	0.60	19	0	3	30	12	3	2	0	15	50	.121	.241	.131	43.10	12.93	116
Randall, Scott	R-R	6-0	172	8-3-98	4	3	5.63	14	3	0	38	45	25	24	3	5	38	.292	.315	.442	23.46	3.09	162
Reed, Carlson	L-R	6-4	200	11-27-02	1	0	0.87	6	6	0	31	11	7	3	1	9	34	.106	.184	.154	29.82	7.89	114
Reilly, Patrick	R-R	6-3	208	10-7-01	5	4	3.38	19	19	0	88	61	38	33	14	41	108	.194	.288	.376	30.17	11.45	358
Thibo, Yunior	R-R	6-4	185	6-24-98	1	0	2.70	4	0	0	3	4	1	1	0	1	0	.286	.375	.357	0.00	6.25	16
Tomkins, Landon	R-R	6-3	200	6-23-00	1	2	5.23	9	0	1	10	11	8	6	1	7	12	.268	.404	.366	23.08	13.46	52
Walsh, Mike	R-R	6-2	195	1-17-01	0	1	1.38	10	0	4	13	9	6	2	1	7	10	.191	.291	.255	18.18	12.73	55
Woods, Jaden	L-L	6-2	205	2-1-02	1	0	2.13	20	0	1	25	20	7	6	2	11	31	.215	.311	.355	28.97	10.28	107

Fielding

Catcher	PCT	G	PO	A	E	DP	PB
Alfonzo	.990	10	90	11	1	2	3
Miknis	1.000	2	23	1	0	0	1
Planchart	.991	41	394	27	4	1	10
Ross	.980	79	747	51	16	7	7

First Base	PCT	G	PO	A	E	DP
Alfonzo	1.000	10	54	0	0	1
Cimillo	.977	29	200	8	5	15
Escotto	.993	22	132	4	1	8
McAdoo	1.000	4	27	2	0	3
McKinney	1.000	1	8	1	0	0
Planchart	1.000	5	29	3	0	2
Sightler	.986	67	486	21	7	54

Second Base	PCT	G	PO	A	E	DP
Brannigan	1.000	10	7	14	0	2
Escotto	.950	4	6	13	1	3
Gourson	1.000	8	10	26	0	4
Harrison	1.000	4	6	9	0	1
Jebb	.957	57	83	115	9	29
Johnson	.969	53	87	129	7	28
McAdoo	.667	2	1	1	1	0

Third Base	PCT	G	PO	A	E	DP
Brannigan	.964	26	15	39	2	3
Escotto	.951	26	12	27	2	0
Gourson	1.000	1	1	3	0	0
Harrison	.897	36	14	56	8	2
McAdoo	.978	40	20	71	2	4
Rivas	1.000	1	0	2	0	1
Ross	.824	10	3	11	3	0

Shortstop	PCT	G	PO	A	E	DP
Brannigan	.944	40	50	102	9	19
Escotto	.967	12	9	20	1	1
Harrison	1.000	8	11	19	0	6
Jebb	.919	35	37	65	9	15
Johnson	.950	36	43	71	6	18
Rivas	.909	9	11	19	3	4

Outfield	PCT	G	PO	A	E	DP
Brown	1.000	62	99	10	0	2
Campana	.938	13	15	0	1	0
Escotto	1.000	3	5	1	0	0
Head	.981	92	206	2	4	0
Hendrie	1.000	13	20	2	0	0
Hilson	.966	74	136	7	5	2
Jebb	1.000	10	19	1	0	0
McAdoo	1.000	9	15	2	0	0
McKinney	1.000	3	2	0	0	0
Nolasco	.966	17	27	1	1	0
Palacios	1.000	3	1	0	0	0
Siani	.947	19	36	0	2	0
Sightler	1.000	7	14	0	0	0
White	.976	83	157	6	4	1

BRADENTON MARAUDERS — LOW-A

FLORIDA STATE LEAGUE

Batting	B-T	Ht.	Wt.	DOB	AVG	OBP	SLG	G	PA	AB	R	H	2B	3B	HR	RBI	BB	HBP	SH	SF	SO	SB	CS	BB%	SO%
Alfonzo, Omar	L-R	6-1	180	8-3-03	.253	.353	.388	86	354	304	41	77	15	1	8	34	45	3	0	2	92	1	1	12.71	25.99
Alvarez, Andres	R-R	5-8	175	3-29-97	.300	.462	.500	3	13	10	1	3	2	0	0	1	2	1	0	0	4	0	1	15.38	30.77
Bae, Ji Hwan	L-R	6-1	185	7-26-99	.667	.667	1.000	1	3	3	0	2	1	0	0	1	0	0	0	0	0	0	0	0.00	0.00
Berg, Derek	R-R	6-3	200	9-21-01	.122	.200	.184	15	55	49	3	6	0	0	1	5	5	0	0	1	20	0	0	9.09	36.36
Bishop, Braylon	L-L	6-2	193	4-23-03	.206	.313	.350	58	208	180	30	37	7	2	5	18	22	6	0	0	66	17	2	10.58	31.73
Campana, Sergio	R-R	6-0	160	3-29-02	.220	.347	.322	28	75	59	8	13	3	0	1	4	12	0	1	1	27	11	2	16.00	36.00
Caro, Carlos	R-R	5-11	160	11-4-04	.217	.333	.261	7	27	23	2	5	1	0	0	0	3	1	0	0	6	1	1	11.11	22.22
Castillo, Jesus	B-S	5-10	144	7-12-03	.141	.330	.165	25	110	85	10	12	2	0	0	3	22	2	1	0	26	10	2	20.00	23.64
Custodio, Jauri	R-R	5-9	162	9-21-01	.130	.231	.217	9	26	23	3	3	0	1	0	0	1	2	0	0	9	1	0	3.85	34.62
De Los Santos, Yordanny	R-R	6-1	170	2-17-05	.195	.300	.264	25	101	87	9	17	3	0	1	9	13	0	1	0	22	10	0	12.87	21.78
Delay, Jason	R-R	5-11	200	3-7-95	.000	.333	.000	1	3	2	0	0	0	0	0	0	1	0	0	0	1	0	0	33.33	33.33
Delgado, Keiner	B-R	5-7	145	1-5-04	.231	.318	.347	89	381	337	44	78	11	2	8	29	33	10	1	0	83	25	6	8.66	21.78
Espinal, Ewry	L-R	6-0	185	12-18-02	.000	.083	.000	4	12	11	1	0	0	0	0	0	1	0	0	0	5	0	0	8.33	41.67
Forrester, Garret	R-R	6-1	208	11-11-01	.273	.413	.382	34	138	110	11	30	9	0	1	9	22	5	0	1	37	2	0	15.94	26.81
Gourson, Duce	L-R	6-1	190	9-20-02	.229	.438	.343	11	48	35	8	8	4	0	0	6	10	3	0	0	10	2	0	20.83	20.83
Gutierrez, Abrahan	R-R	6-0	214	10-31-99	.000	.100	.000	3	10	9	0	0	0	0	0	0	1	0	0	0	2	0	0	10.00	20.00
Harrison, Kalae	L-R	5-11	188	6-5-02	.206	.304	.279	20	80	68	9	14	2	0	1	11	10	0	1	1	20	7	1	12.50	25.00
Herman, Jack	R-R	5-10	190	9-30-99	.176	.236	.216	14	55	51	5	9	2	0	0	2	4	0	0	0	26	3	0	7.27	47.27
Hilson, P.J.	R-R	5-10	175	8-25-00	.135	.182	.269	17	55	52	6	7	1	0	2	3	2	1	0	0	18	1	0	3.64	32.73
Jerez, Juan	R-R	6-1	160	11-28-01	.227	.299	.375	28	98	88	13	20	7	0	2	9	9	0	1	0	33	4	1	9.18	33.67
Lege, Ethan	R-R	6-0	210	3-12-01	.204	.259	.204	15	58	54	4	11	0	0	0	3	3	1	0	0	14	0	1	5.17	24.14
Maguire, Solomon	L-R	5-10	168	3-4-03	.175	.287	.338	56	180	154	21	27	3	2	6	18	24	0	2	0	50	6	1	13.33	27.78
Miknis, Justin	L-R	6-0	195	9-6-00	.194	.350	.258	37	117	93	11	18	3	0	1	14	23	0	0	1	28	0	0	19.66	23.93
Palacios, Josh	L-R	6-1	200	7-30-95	.294	.333	.412	5	18	17	2	5	2	0	0	2	1	0	0	0	4	1	0	5.56	22.22
Patrick, Andrew	R-R	6-4	195	1-19-03	.178	.315	.222	16	54	45	4	8	2	0	0	3	9	0	0	0	19	4	1	16.67	35.19
Plaz, Axiel	R-R	5-11	165	8-12-05	.207	.302	.438	76	281	242	34	50	11	0	15	42	32	3	0	4	82	1	0	11.39	29.18
Polanco, Shalin	L-L	6-0	168	2-6-04	.191	.280	.343	104	432	382	43	73	19	3	11	49	44	1	0	2	134	11	9	10.19	31.02
Rivas, Javier	R-R	6-6	165	9-1-02	.223	.283	.393	97	367	336	41	75	19	1	12	42	16	12	3	0	118	7	3	4.36	32.15
Rodriguez, Eddy	R-R	6-0	181	11-5-03	.209	.342	.269	53	223	182	24	38	8	0	1	17	33	5	1	2	67	11	2	14.80	30.04
Severino, Jhonny	R-R	6-1	185	11-8-04	.237	.285	.500	28	123	114	16	27	6	3	6	17	8	0	0	1	37	4	1	6.50	30.08
Sosa, Miguel	R-R	5-11	181	12-4-03	.200	.343	.327	17	68	55	8	11	4	0	1	5	12	0	1	0	23	0	0	17.65	33.82
Taylor, Will	R-R	6-0	175	1-10-03	.206	.329	.349	17	76	63	11	13	3	0	2	10	9	3	0	1	20	3	1	11.84	26.32
Terrero, Enmanuel	L-L	5-9	160	9-14-02	.161	.256	.265	45	178	155	23	25	2	1	4	15	20	0	2	1	60	3	1	11.24	33.71
Toledo, Jeral	B-R	5-10	135	1-22-03	.224	.318	.302	62	239	205	29	46	10	3	0	23	28	1	2	2	48	6	5	11.72	20.08
Valdez, Esmerlyn	R-R	6-2	181	1-27-04	.226	.352	.464	107	435	358	56	81	17	1	22	61	59	13	0	5	133	4	1	13.56	30.57
Wilson, Eli	R-R	6-0	190	7-6-98	.200	.308	.200	4	13	10	0	2	0	0	0	2	2	0	0	1	5	0	0	15.38	38.46
Zapata, Wesley	B-R	5-11	152	3-2-04	.183	.266	.248	38	125	109	10	20	5	1	0	10	13	0	1	2	30	4	1	10.40	24.00

Pitching	B-T	Ht.	Wt.	DOB	W	L	ERA	G	GS	SV	IP	Hits	Runs	ER	HR	BB	SO	AVG	OBP	SLG	SO%	BB%	BF
Bimbi, Jacob	L-L	6-0	182	6-5-02	0	0	13.50	4	0	0	4	5	6	6	0	7	6	.278	.462	.389	23.08	26.92	26
Birdsong, Elijah	R-R	6-2	200	10-11-99	0	0	2.35	6	0	0	8	7	2	2	1	2	4	.233	.303	.467	12.12	6.06	33
Burrows, Mike	R-R	6-2	195	11-8-99	0	1	5.59	4	4	0	10	10	7	6	4	5	11	.263	.349	.605	25.58	11.63	43
Carrion, Danny	R-R	6-3	205	8-12-01	1	1	4.74	21	0	1	25	18	18	13	1	20	25	.207	.360	.287	22.52	18.02	111
Case, Brad	R-R	6-6	242	9-13-96	0	1	2.70	2	1	0	3	3	3	1	0	2	4	.214	.389	.286	22.22	11.11	18
Castillo, Carlos	R-R	6-1	165	2-4-06	0	2	9.64	6	1	1	14	26	16	15	2	6	16	.388	.440	.582	21.33	8.00	75
Chang, Hung-Leng	R-R	6-3	159	10-7-01	5	7	4.64	19	14	0	78	81	45	40	6	31	71	.276	.351	.422	21.07	9.20	337
Cotto, Magdiel	L-L	6-3	225	6-24-02	5	3	2.63	31	0	5	48	28	20	14	2	25	49	.169	.300	.277	24.38	12.44	201
Curtis, Khristian	R-R	6-5	210	5-9-02	2	3	4.06	18	16	1	75	62	41	34	10	39	81	.227	.329	.392	25.39	12.23	319
De La Paz, Yoldin	L-L	6-0	165	5-10-02	5	0	1.19	12	0	0	23	10	6	3	2	5	24	.125	.186	.263	27.91	5.81	86
Del Bonta-Smith, Fineas	R-R	6-0	190	2-2-97	0	0	0.00	3	0	0	4	0	0	0	0	0	6	.000	.083	.000	50.00	0.00	12
Furtado, Hunter	R-L	6-3	160	2-18-02	3	5	5.74	33	0	0	47	39	40	30	4	51	45	.222	.401	.352	19.40	21.98	232
German, Domingo	R-R	6-2	181	8-4-92	0	0	2.25	1	1	0	4	3	1	1	1	3	4	.200	.333	.400	22.22	16.67	18
Harbin, Ryan	R-R	6-4	195	8-6-01	0	0	0.00	3	1	0	4	2	0	0	0	2	7	.154	.267	.154	46.67	13.33	15
Harrington, Thomas	R-R	6-2	185	7-12-01	0	0	0.00	1	1	0	3	1	0	0	0	1	3	.125	.222	.125	33.33	11.11	9

Hartle, Josh	L-L	6-4	210	3-24-03	0	0	16.20	1	0	0	2	5	4	3	0	1	2	.556	.600	.667	20.00	10.00	10
Heller, Ben	R-R	6-3	210	8-5-91	0	0	0.00	3	0	0	4	2	0	0	0	0	8	.143	.143	.214	57.14	0.00	14
Hernandez, Luigi	R-R	6-0	185	9-21-03	3	3	7.11	23	1	2	57	54	48	45	2	56	69	.251	.432	.340	24.21	19.65	285
Jimenez, Carlos	R-R	6-2	140	7-14-02	5	3	3.42	23	11	0	71	47	35	27	5	66	88	.184	.359	.277	26.75	20.06	329
Kelly, Antwone	R-R	5-10	183	9-1-03	1	6	4.43	16	14	0	69	64	39	34	8	34	65	.247	.336	.394	21.67	11.33	300
Kennedy, Michael	L-L	6-1	205	11-30-04	2	5	4.07	16	15	0	73	66	35	33	8	16	80	.240	.296	.396	26.58	5.32	301
Kennedy, Tyler	R-R	6-3	223	6-7-02	1	3	10.23	25	0	0	22	19	29	25	2	43	31	.241	.538	.430	23.48	32.58	132
Lono, Inmer	L-L	6-1	193	2-12-04	2	0	1.65	15	0	1	33	17	9	6	3	15	31	.156	.262	.275	24.22	11.72	128
McMillan, Garrett	L-R	6-4	230	2-10-01	3	4	2.92	29	1	1	49	47	22	16	4	16	53	.253	.312	.392	25.73	7.77	206
Mendez, Greiber	R-R	6-0	150	4-3-04	0	1	3.44	9	0	1	18	14	8	7	3	8	21	.212	.329	.364	26.25	10.00	80
Miknis, Justin	L-R	6-0	195	9-6-00	1	0	0.00	3	0	0	2	1	0	0	0	1	0	.125	.222	.125	0.00	11.11	9
Mlodzinski, Carmen	R-R	6-2	225	2-19-99	0	0	9.00	1	0	0	1	2	1	1	0	0	3	.400	.400	.400	60.00	0.00	5
Mueth, Zander	R-R	6-6	205	6-22-05	1	3	3.97	7	7	0	23	8	16	10	0	24	23	.110	.364	.137	21.50	22.43	107
Oliver, Connor	L-L	6-1	170	5-26-01	1	8	5.24	24	9	1	79	77	51	46	6	36	82	.251	.340	.401	23.43	10.29	350
Randall, Scott	R-R	6-0	172	8-3-98	0	1	3.00	2	2	0	6	4	2	2	0	1	7	.190	.217	.238	30.43	4.35	23
Reed, Carlson	L-R	6-4	200	11-27-02	5	3	2.43	17	17	0	78	55	26	21	4	42	96	.199	.310	.285	29.72	13.00	323
Shortridge, Aaron	R-R	6-3	215	5-29-97	0	1	2.61	3	3	0	10	9	4	3	0	1	18	.237	.250	.237	45.00	2.50	40
Solometo, Anthony	L-L	6-5	220	12-2-02	0	1	3.12	2	2	0	9	6	3	3	1	3	4	.200	.294	.333	11.76	8.82	34
Stratton, Hunter	R-R	6-4	225	11-17-96	0	0	0.00	1	0	0	1	0	0	0	0	0	2	.000	.000	.000	50.00	0.00	4
Stumbo, Peyton	R-R	6-1	200	6-28-02	3	4	4.92	37	3	5	68	70	43	37	10	26	76	.269	.339	.442	25.68	8.78	296
Takacs, Noah	L-R	6-3	195	4-9-02	1	4	7.53	7	0	0	14	15	13	12	2	12	11	.288	.414	.577	15.71	17.14	70
Tejada, Clevari	R-R	6-1	204	9-23-04	1	2	3.60	7	3	0	25	21	11	10	1	16	18	.226	.357	.323	15.93	14.16	113
Tejada, Joaquin	R-R	5-11	160	7-16-03	0	0	13.50	1	0	0	1	1	2	2	0	3	2	.250	.500	.250	25.00	37.50	8
Tomkins, Landon	R-R	6-3	200	6-23-00	2	1	3.86	25	0	7	33	27	16	14	2	10	34	.220	.304	.301	24.64	7.25	138
Walsh, Mike	R-R	6-2	195	1-17-01	1	1	0.98	20	0	1	28	15	5	3	0	4	28	.156	.212	.188	26.92	3.85	104
Wietgrefe, Connor	L-L	6-2	200	6-6-02	0	0	0.90	5	4	0	10	6	5	1	1	2	13	.158	.195	.316	31.71	4.88	41

Fielding

Catcher	PCT	G	PO	A	E	DP	PB
Alfonzo	.991	56	528	39	5	5	10
Berg	.968	11	82	8	3	2	2
Delay	1.000	1	9	0	0	0	0
Forrester	.985	14	123	7	2	0	2
Gutierrez	.966	3	24	4	1	0	0
Miknis	.992	15	114	7	1	0	1
Plaz	.983	41	317	29	6	3	8
Wilson	1.000	3	18	3	0	1	1

First Base	PCT	G	PO	A	E	DP
Alfonzo	.983	23	159	12	3	18
Berg	1.000	4	24	0	0	3
Espinal	.667	1	2	0	1	0
Forrester	1.000	2	5	0	0	0
Jerez	.976	13	74	7	2	6
Lege	.962	7	50	0	2	2
Miknis	1.000	9	67	8	0	6
Plaz	.985	31	185	7	3	20
Rodriguez	.973	16	102	6	3	10
Valdez	.976	39	268	17	7	17

Second Base	PCT	G	PO	A	E	DP
Alvarez	1.000	1	1	2	0	0
Caro	.971	7	14	20	1	6
Castillo	1.000	8	11	24	0	5
De Los Santos	.947	5	4	14	1	2
Delgado	.965	36	59	78	5	22
Gourson	.957	7	9	13	1	3
Harrison	.979	10	27	20	1	7
Rivas	1.000	2	5	5	0	0
Toledo	.994	47	56	114	1	17
Zapata	.943	15	28	22	3	7

Third Base	PCT	G	PO	A	E	DP
Castillo	1.000	7	3	9	0	0
De Los Santos	.875	5	2	12	2	1
Forrester	.974	17	9	29	1	3
Gourson	1.000	2	0	5	0	0
Harrison	.944	6	2	15	1	3
Jerez	.909	4	5	5	1	0
Lege	.813	7	5	8	3	0
Rivas	.961	42	32	67	4	9
Severino	.905	14	8	11	2	0
Toledo	.885	10	7	16	3	1
Zapata	.902	22	15	22	4	4

Shortstop	PCT	G	PO	A	E	DP
Alvarez	1.000	2	4	4	0	3
Castillo	.912	9	12	19	3	4
De Los Santos	.962	13	17	33	2	5
Delgado	.965	46	52	113	6	19
Harrison	1.000	4	1	10	0	1
Rivas	.962	54	81	124	8	28
Severino	1.000	6	8	7	0	1

Outfield	PCT	G	PO	A	E	DP
Bae	1.000	1	1	0	0	0
Bishop	.941	55	90	5	6	1
Campana	.953	24	40	1	2	1
Castillo	.000	3	0	0	0	0
Custodio	1.000	9	9	3	0	0
Herman	1.000	10	10	0	0	0
Hilson	.964	15	26	1	1	0
Jerez	1.000	5	10	0	0	0
Maguire	.968	46	85	5	3	2
Palacios	1.000	5	6	0	0	0
Patrick	1.000	14	25	2	0	0
Polanco	.964	95	183	7	7	3
Rodriguez	.978	30	42	2	1	0
Sosa	.938	11	13	2	1	0
Taylor	.938	14	30	0	2	0
Terrero	.954	38	81	2	4	2
Valdez	.978	54	86	4	2	0

FCL PIRATES — ROOKIE

FLORIDA COMPLEX LEAGUE

Batting	B-T	Ht.	Wt.	DOB	AVG	OBP	SLG	G	PA	AB	R	H	2B	3B	HR	RBI	BB	HBP	SH	SF	SO	SB	CS	BB%	SO%
Aguiar, Roinny	B-R	5-7	160	4-1-05	.241	.337	.287	37	104	87	12	21	2	1	0	10	13	0	3	1	27	7	3	12.50	25.96
Bishop, Braylon	L-L	6-2	193	4-23-03	.333	.636	.333	3	11	6	5	2	0	0	0	2	4	1	0	0	1	0	1	36.36	9.09
Blanco, Tony	R-R	6-6	243	5-14-05	.305	.385	.505	30	109	95	10	29	5	1	4	17	12	1	0	1	31	1	0	11.01	28.44
Caro, Carlos	R-R	5-11	160	11-4-04	.305	.410	.443	42	156	131	31	40	8	2	2	17	22	2	0	1	24	9	3	14.10	15.38
De Los Santos, Yordany	R-R	6-1	170	2-17-05	.344	.407	.505	57	216	192	36	66	8	4	5	34	17	4	2	1	39	24	6	7.87	18.06
Delgado, Keiner	B-R	5-7	145	1-5-04	.400	.400	1.000	1	5	5	2	2	0	0	1	4	0	0	0	0	0	2	0	0.00	0.00
Espinal, Ewry	L-R	6-0	185	12-18-02	.086	.284	.155	25	74	58	9	5	1	0	1	5	14	2	0	0	28	6	0	18.92	37.84
Forrester, Garret	R-R	6-1	208	11-11-01	.111	.320	.111	7	25	18	2	2	0	0	0	2	2	4	0	1	5	0	0	8.00	20.00
Gutierrez, Abrahan	R-R	6-0	214	10-31-99	.286	.286	.286	2	7	7	2	2	0	0	0	1	0	0	0	0	2	0	0	0.00	28.57
Lopez, John	R-R	5-8	165	10-6-05	.238	.333	.333	9	24	21	2	5	2	0	0	4	3	0	0	0	6	0	0	12.50	25.00
Machado, Juan	L-R	5-11	145	6-4-03	.123	.390	.123	32	83	57	17	7	0	0	0	6	23	2	1	0	23	10	0	27.71	27.71
Oviedo, Eduardo	R-R	6-1	169	9-2-04	.174	.269	.232	25	78	69	8	12	2	1	0	8	9	0	0	0	41	0	0	11.54	52.56
Pena, Jhonson	R-R	5-10	155	8-3-02	.246	.331	.344	47	146	122	23	30	7	1	1	16	12	4	7	1	28	9	6	8.22	19.18
Plaz, Axiel	R-R	5-11	165	8-12-05	.158	.320	.211	8	25	19	4	3	1	0	0	6	4	1	0	1	5	0	0	16.00	20.00
Ramirez, Richard	R-R	6-0	160	7-3-05	.288	.374	.464	50	174	153	27	44	8	2	5	25	18	3	0	0	56	2	0	10.34	32.18
Scherrer, Luke	R-R	6-2	210	12-13-04	.273	.406	.345	43	139	110	22	30	8	0	0	13	18	8	1	2	21	4	2	12.95	15.11
Severino, Jhonny	R-R	6-1	185	11-8-04	.291	.373	.545	56	220	189	39	55	12	3	10	41	26	1	0	4	35	12	3	11.82	15.91

Sosa, Miguel	R-R	5-11	181	12-4-03	.318	.426	.376	29	101	85	14	27	5	0	0	8	15	1	0	0	31	1	2	14.85	30.69
Suero, Estuar	B-R	6-5	180	8-29-05	.213	.318	.307	25	88	75	9	16	5	1	0	8	11	1	0	1	31	2	2	12.50	35.23
Terrero, Enmanuel	L-L	5-9	160	9-14-02	.417	.481	.542	7	27	24	5	10	1	1	0	2	3	0	0	0	3	5	1	11.11	11.11
Tirado, Carlos	L-R	6-1	187	3-13-05	.187	.299	.307	29	87	75	9	14	9	0	0	10	10	2	0	0	18	1	0	11.49	20.69
Zapata, Wesley	B-R	5-11	152	3-2-04	.000	.250	.000	3	4	3	2	0	0	0	0	0	1	0	0	0	1	1	0	25.00	25.00
Zorrilla, John	R-R	6-1	173	5-23-04	.154	.267	.154	12	30	26	5	4	0	0	0	1	4	0	0	0	13	2	0	13.33	43.33

Pitching	B-T	Ht.	Wt.	DOB	W	L	ERA	G	GS	SV	IP	Hits	Runs	ER	HR	BB	SO	AVG	OBP	SLG	SO%	BB%	BF
Aguiar, Roinny	S-R	5-7	160	4-1-05	0	0	0.00	1	0	0	0	1	0	0	0	1	1	.500	.667	.500	33.33	33.33	3
Burrows, Mike	R-R	6-2	195	11-8-99	0	1	15.75	2	2	0	4	7	7	7	0	4	3	.368	.478	.368	13.04	17.39	23
Cabreja, Victor	L-L	6-3	180	1-10-02	4	2	4.43	12	0	1	20	29	15	10	3	4	16	.345	.363	.524	17.58	4.40	91
Case, Brad	R-R	6-6	242	9-13-96	0	0	0.00	1	0	0	1	0	0	0	0	1	1	.000	.250	.000	25.00	25.00	4
Castillo, Carlos	R-R	6-1	165	2-4-06	1	2	2.86	12	9	0	35	29	11	11	2	18	27	.228	.327	.307	18.24	12.16	148
Garces, Jose	R-R	6-2	149	6-9-04	2	1	5.32	12	5	0	24	19	16	14	1	32	19	.241	.487	.418	16.24	27.35	117
Harbin, Ryan	R-R	6-4	195	8-6-01	0	0	6.75	2	0	0	1	1	2	1	0	2	3	.167	.444	.333	33.33	22.22	9
Hernandez, Kevison	R-R	6-5	188	7-20-02	0	0	17.36	8	1	0	5	2	9	9	0	14	5	.143	.600	.286	16.67	46.67	30
Lobo, Inmer	L-L	6-1	193	2-12-04	2	0	1.98	12	0	4	14	8	3	3	2	0	19	.170	.188	.340	39.58	0.00	48
Lopez, John	R-R	5-8	165	10-6-05	0	0	0.00	2	0	0	1	1	0	0	0	0	0	.250	.250	.250	0.00	0.00	4
Malone, Brennan	R-R	6-4	205	9-8-00	0	2	4.15	10	7	0	9	8	6	4	1	9	4	.267	.463	.433	9.76	21.95	41
Martinez, Dioris	R-R	6-2	185	6-20-06	1	0	1.26	6	5	0	14	7	5	2	0	11	9	.156	.333	.200	15.79	19.30	57
Mateo, Carlos	R-R	6-2	185	10-25-05	2	3	11.74	13	7	0	23	25	36	30	1	35	21	.298	.534	.405	16.03	26.72	131
Matoma, David	R-R	6-0	154	2-2-06	0	0	0.82	15	0	3	22	15	4	2	1	9	28	.183	.261	.256	30.43	9.78	92
Mendez, Greiber	R-R	6-0	150	4-3-04	4	2	3.52	16	0	5	31	25	15	12	3	17	32	.227	.356	.327	24.06	12.78	133
Mueth, Zander	R-R	6-6	205	6-22-05	6	1	1.58	13	12	0	51	39	20	9	2	26	56	.206	.326	.307	24.89	11.56	225
Randall, Scott	R-R	6-0	172	8-3-98	0	0	0.00	2	2	0	5	2	0	0	0	1	5	.111	.200	.111	25.00	5.00	20
Regalado, Jose	L-L	6-0	189	6-15-02	2	2	4.55	19	0	0	28	19	18	14	2	26	37	.198	.376	.313	29.60	20.80	125
Rosa, Pitterson	R-R	6-2	178	11-30-04	2	1	7.27	5	0	0	9	9	7	7	1	7	7	.281	.390	.469	17.07	17.07	41
Shortridge, Aaron	R-R	6-3	215	5-29-97	0	0	0.00	2	1	0	5	3	0	0	0	1	7	.188	.235	.188	41.18	5.88	17
Solometo, Anthony	L-L	6-5	220	12-2-02	0	0	0.00	1	1	0	3	2	0	0	0	1	3	.200	.273	.200	27.27	9.09	11
Stratton, Hunter	R-R	6-4	225	11-17-96	0	0	0.00	2	0	0	2	1	0	0	0	0	1	.143	.143	.143	14.29	0.00	7
Takacs, Noah	L-R	6-3	195	4-9-02	4	3	6.20	20	0	3	25	26	19	17	2	14	22	.265	.368	.418	19.13	12.17	115
Tejada, Clevari	R-R	6-1	204	9-23-04	2	1	4.98	13	4	2	43	40	28	24	5	18	34	.250	.335	.388	18.68	9.89	182
Tejada, Joaquin	R-R	5-11	160	7-16-03	0	0	16.20	4	0	0	3	8	6	6	0	7	0	.533	.696	.667	0.00	29.17	24
Torres, Alexis	R-R	6-0	153	3-16-03	3	1	4.72	14	1	0	34	25	22	18	6	25	38	.208	.362	.383	25.50	16.78	149
Valdez, Jonawel	R-R	6-1	185	3-19-04	1	1	3.07	5	2	0	15	15	7	5	1	9	8	.278	.381	.333	12.50	14.06	64

Fielding

C: Ramirez 37, Scherrer 22, Plaz 3, Forrester 2, Gutierrez 2. **1B:** Tirado 20, Scherrer 18, Ramirez 12, Blanco 12, Plaz 3, Espinal 1, Forrester 1. **2B:** Caro 30, Aguiar 23, De Los Santos 9, Delgado 1, Lopez 1, Machado 1. **3B:** Severino 26, De Los Santos 14, Caro 13, Zorrilla 9, Zapata 2, Aguiar 2, Forrester 1. **SS:** De Los Santos 30, Severino 29, Zorrilla 2, Aguiar 1, Caro 1. **LF:** Sosa 25, Machado 16, Espinal 9, Suero 5, Oviedo 3, Pena 3, Bishop 2, Terrero 2. **CF:** Pena 38, Suero 12, Oviedo 11, Terrero 1. **RF:** Espinal 14, Machado 14, Oviedo 10, Tirado 7, Pena 6, Sosa 5, Suero 5, Terrero 3, Scherrer 2, Bishop 1.

DSL PIRATES BLACK — ROOKIE

DOMINICAN SUMMER LEAGUE

Batting	B-T	Ht.	Wt.	DOB	AVG	OBP	SLG	G	PA	AB	R	H	2B	3B	HR	RBI	BB	HBP	SH	SF	SO	SB	CS	BB%	SO%
Acevedo, Javier	L-R	5-10	145	2-27-07	.189	.381	.203	32	97	74	10	14	1	0	0	3	22	1	0	0	23	1	2	22.68	23.71
Allen, Iverson	R-R	6-0	160	8-18-07	.233	.313	.317	22	67	60	8	14	1	2	0	3	5	2	0	0	15	2	0	7.46	22.39
Aquino, Angel	R-R	6-5	207	6-18-05	.203	.302	.270	28	86	74	8	15	5	0	0	9	10	1	0	1	31	2	0	11.63	36.05
Brazoban, Bralyn	L-L	6-1	180	9-1-06	.155	.276	.209	45	174	148	23	23	4	2	0	16	22	3	0	1	61	10	1	12.64	35.06
Brioso, Edwarli	R-R	5-11	161	9-22-04	.231	.310	.346	12	30	26	5	6	0	0	1	5	3	0	1	0	14	1	4	10.00	46.67
Gimenez, Yosmar	L-R	6-2	150	5-2-06	.250	.398	.310	45	128	100	19	25	4	1	0	15	23	3	0	2	22	8	1	17.97	17.19
Herrera, Kendrick	R-R	6-0	170	1-24-07	.255	.390	.330	31	118	94	16	24	2	1	1	19	20	2	0	2	18	5	1	16.95	15.25
Kim, Jayden	R-R	5-11	150	8-2-06	.217	.280	.217	11	26	23	4	5	0	0	0	4	2	0	1	0	9	0	0	7.69	34.62
Lizardo, Jesus	B-R	5-11	170	11-4-06	.188	.297	.224	34	101	85	7	16	3	0	0	7	14	0	0	2	24	1	0	13.86	23.76
Mesta, Frankeli	B-R	6-1	175	5-29-07	.274	.353	.379	43	139	124	18	34	1	3	2	14	15	0	0	0	33	3	0	10.79	23.74
Mola, Raymond	R-R	6-2	190	12-1-05	.217	.266	.383	20	64	60	7	13	4	0	2	5	4	0	0	0	19	2	1	6.25	29.69
Nunez, Lennyn	B-R	5-10	150	8-8-03	.326	.516	.391	25	65	46	8	15	3	0	0	10	10	8	1	0	8	2	1	15.38	12.31
Ojeda, Michell	L-R	6-0	158	1-23-07	.256	.438	.341	34	113	82	18	21	5	1	0	11	24	4	1	2	17	8	0	21.24	15.04
Orelin, Christopher	R-R	5-11	157	1-31-05	.000	.500	.000	6	8	4	2	0	0	0	0	0	4	0	0	0	4	0	0	50.00	50.00
Sosa, Anthony	R-R	6-1	165	4-14-07	.111	.200	.148	32	90	81	8	9	0	0	1	12	7	2	0	0	42	0	0	7.78	46.67
Tromp, Deshandro	R-R	6-0	170	9-20-06	.163	.355	.239	40	121	92	15	15	2	1	1	13	21	7	0	1	38	3	1	17.36	31.40
Van Der Linden, Joenelly	R-R	5-10	142	7-10-06	.185	.313	.185	15	34	27	5	5	0	0	0	2	4	1	2	0	3	1	0	11.76	8.82
Villafane, Andres	L-L	5-11	175	3-17-06	.300	.351	.470	37	112	100	13	30	8	3	1	20	8	1	1	2	21	5	2	7.14	18.75
Vittini, July	R-R	6-2	190	5-29-03	.133	.308	.200	20	39	30	8	4	2	0	0	2	8	0	0	1	11	1	0	20.51	28.21
Williams, Phillando	B-R	5-9	162	9-30-06	.165	.379	.176	37	118	85	17	14	1	0	0	6	22	8	2	1	31	8	3	18.64	26.27

Pitching	B-T	Ht.	Wt.	DOB	W	L	ERA	G	GS	SV	IP	Hits	Runs	ER	HR	BB	SO	AVG	OBP	SLG	SO%	BB%	BF
Berroa, Jeremia	R-R	6-2	185	10-30-04	0	2	18.82	11	3	0	11	17	31	23	0	20	12	.370	.554	.565	16.22	27.03	74
Castillo, Daviel	R-R	6-4	205	12-10-04	1	1	19.29	6	0	0	5	4	11	10	0	8	2	.222	.462	.333	7.41	29.63	27
De La Paz, Jarlen	L-L	6-4	180	6-4-05	1	2	7.04	14	2	0	15	19	20	12	2	18	20	.311	.517	.492	22.73	20.45	88
Florentino, Dariel	R-R	6-5	175	11-4-05	0	2	5.03	11	3	0	20	18	14	11	0	19	20	.234	.404	.286	20.20	19.19	99
Hernandez, Yoerys	L-L	6-2	185	9-1-03	1	1	6.00	4	0	0	3	2	4	2	0	3	1	.200	.357	.200	7.14	21.43	14
Herrera, Angel	R-R	6-1	168	7-18-07	0	5	4.98	9	9	0	22	25	14	12	1	11	16	.301	.392	.422	16.49	11.34	97
Jaquez, Wifrailyn	R-R	6-1	170	10-5-06	0	2	3.79	11	11	0	38	30	29	16	0	18	34	.210	.320	.266	20.12	10.65	169
Joseph, Luis	R-R	6-1	180	6-15-02	2	3	4.34	10	0	0	19	11	11	9	0	21	16	.183	.402	.250	19.51	25.61	82

Pitching	B-T	Ht.	Wt.	DOB	W	L	ERA	G	GS	SV	IP	Hits	Runs	ER	HR	BB	SO	AVG	OBP	SLG	SO%	BB%	BF
Linares, Janderson	L-L	6-2	175	10-18-05	3	3	2.90	13	5	0	31	23	12	10	0	19	33	.200	.340	.252	23.24	13.38	142
Martinez, Randol	R-R	6-1	168	5-31-07	0	1	4.76	4	1	0	6	7	4	3	0	1	7	.318	.360	.409	28.00	4.00	25
Martinez, Yeison	R-R	6-0	143	8-6-07	0	0	3.60	4	1	0	5	6	3	2	0	2	7	.316	.409	.368	31.82	9.09	22
Pichardo, Bladimir	R-R	6-3	193	10-24-05	1	1	3.18	8	6	0	23	18	9	8	0	8	22	.231	.337	.308	23.91	8.70	92
Pierre, Wali	R-R	6-3	180	4-24-03	2	2	4.67	16	0	4	27	17	15	14	0	17	14	.177	.316	.250	11.97	14.53	117
Quintana, Marlon	R-R	6-2	192	6-16-06	0	2	5.40	8	4	0	25	27	15	15	1	5	18	.270	.302	.440	16.98	4.72	106
Ramirez, Irwin	R-R	6-3	175	1-10-07	2	3	3.97	12	8	0	34	25	18	15	0	29	32	.205	.361	.238	20.65	18.71	155
Ress, Patricio	R-R	6-2	165	6-26-03	2	2	2.29	11	1	1	20	12	5	5	0	16	19	.188	.349	.188	22.89	19.28	83
Reyes, Francis	R-R	6-2	180	6-30-05	1	1	5.40	13	1	0	18	15	15	11	2	20	22	.231	.418	.354	24.18	21.98	91
Romero, Rubens	R-R	6-4	165	4-4-07	0	0	19.29	11	0	0	9	13	22	20	0	20	8	.351	.618	.459	11.76	29.41	68
Tapia, Jesus	L-R	6-1	173	4-10-07	0	2	10.29	13	0	0	14	15	16	16	2	16	9	.294	.457	.588	12.86	22.86	70
Trejo, Victor	R-R	6-0		5-11-06	3	0	9.47	15	0	1	19	23	21	20	3	16	14	.307	.448	.533	14.58	16.67	96
Van Der Linden, Joenelly	R-R	5-10	142	7-10-06	0	0	0.00	1	0	0	0	0	0	0	0	0	0	.000	.000	.000	0.00	0.00	1
Zapata, Eduardo	R-R	6-2	160	8-27-03	0	1	8.78	12	0	0	13	9	17	13	1	20	16	.191	.435	.277	23.19	28.99	69

Fielding

C: Lizardo 24, Acevedo 21, Nunez 11, Vittini 9, Mola 1. **1B:** Sosa 19, Gimenez 19, Vittini 10, Mola 10, Lizardo 4. **2B:** Gimenez 11, Mesta 11, Ojeda 11, Tromp 9, Van Der Linden 5, Kim 5, Brioso 4, Herrera 3, Nunez 3, Orelin 2. **3B:** Mesta 17, Tromp 13, Ojeda 12, Herrera 6, Gimenez 5, Van Der Linden 4, Orelin 3, Brioso 1. **SS:** Herrera 14, Tromp 14, Mesta 12, Ojeda 8, Kim 6, Van Der Linden 3, Gimenez 2. **LF:** Williams 16, Villafane 15, Aquino 8, Nunez 7, Allen 6, Mola 5, Brioso 4, Sosa 3, Tromp 1. **CF:** Brazoban 30, Villafane 11, Williams 9, Allen 5, Gimenez 1. **RF:** Aquino 16, Brazoban 9, Villafane 9, Sosa 8, Allen 6, Gimenez 6, Mola 4, Williams 2, Nunez 1.

DSL PIRATES GOLD — ROOKIE

DOMINICAN SUMMER LEAGUE

Batting	B-T	Ht.	Wt.	DOB	AVG	OBP	SLG	G	PA	AB	R	H	2B	3B	HR	RBI	BB	HBP	SH	SF	SO	SB	CS	BB%	SO%
Aquino, Angel	R-R	6-5	207	6-18-05	.231	.354	.308	16	48	39	5	9	1	1	0	4	8	0	0	1	12	1	1	16.67	25.00
Brioso, Edwarli	R-R	5-11	161	9-22-04	.231	.375	.308	8	16	13	2	3	1	0	0	1	2	1	0	0	7	1	0	12.50	43.75
Dipre, Isaias	R-R	5-11	159	6-7-03	.301	.441	.579	46	171	133	34	40	9	2	8	19	27	8	1	2	31	6	0	15.79	18.13
Escudero, Samuel	R-R	5-9	155	2-27-04	.311	.410	.479	39	145	119	23	37	9	1	3	34	20	2	1	3	15	5	1	13.79	10.34
Feliz, Adbiel	B-R	6-0	175	2-23-07	.206	.306	.230	40	151	126	18	26	3	0	0	19	19	0	4	2	35	5	2	12.58	23.18
Florentino, Edward	L-R	6-4	200	11-11-06	.260	.432	.459	49	190	146	40	38	10	2	5	28	38	6	0	0	36	8	2	20.00	18.95
Herrera, Kendrick	R-R	6-0	170	1-24-07	.267	.389	.422	14	54	45	9	12	3	2	0	10	9	0	0	0	7	4	1	16.67	12.96
Jauregui, Cristian	B-R	5-11	180	2-9-06	.274	.407	.393	44	167	135	37	37	3	2	3	23	23	8	0	1	36	17	6	13.77	21.56
Kim, Jayden	R-R	5-11	150	8-2-06	.217	.438	.261	23	65	46	9	10	0	1	0	5	16	2	1	0	16	3	1	24.62	24.62
Mola, Raymond	R-R	6-2	190	12-1-05	.375	.444	.375	3	9	8	1	3	0	0	0	1	1	0	0	0	4	0	0	11.11	44.44
Morales, Daje	R-R	5-10	155	3-3-05	.206	.372	.327	37	139	107	21	22	4	3	1	17	28	1	2	1	31	11	4	20.14	22.30
Orelin, Christopher	R-R	5-11	157	1-31-05	.149	.333	.255	26	60	47	10	7	3	1	0	4	11	2	0	0	13	5	0	18.33	21.67
Perez, Angel	R-R	5-10	160	9-12-05	.238	.337	.338	26	95	80	10	19	5	0	1	14	10	3	0	2	27	1	0	10.53	28.42
Pimentel, Antonio	L-R	5-10	161	10-2-05	.217	.331	.295	41	155	129	23	28	2	4	0	13	20	3	1	2	22	12	2	12.90	14.19
Rivero, Jonathan	L-R	6-0	191	12-15-05	.276	.357	.322	25	98	87	14	24	4	0	0	16	9	2	0	0	25	2	1	9.18	25.51
Rodriguez, Angel	R-R	6-2	175	10-25-04	.218	.355	.299	36	108	87	15	19	2	1	1	11	8	11	1	1	25	5	2	7.41	23.15
Rodriguez, Miguel	R-R	5-10	152	4-7-06	.275	.355	.338	27	94	80	9	22	1	2	0	15	10	1	1	2	10	4	4	10.64	10.64
Sequera, Joseph	R-R	6-0	185	12-12-05	.228	.351	.304	32	95	79	12	18	6	0	0	6	9	6	1	0	31	0	0	9.47	32.63
Van Der Linden, Joenelly	R-R	5-10	142	7-10-06	.231	.286	.231	7	14	13	2	3	0	0	0	2	0	1	0	0	5	0	1	0.00	35.71
Villafane, Andres	L-L	5-11	175	3-17-06	.212	.229	.212	9	35	33	5	7	0	0	0	3	1	0	0	1	5	1	0	2.86	14.29
Vittini, July	R-R	6-2	190	5-29-03	.000	.333	.000	5	6	4	0	0	0	0	0	0	2	0	0	0	2	0	1	33.33	33.33
Vizcaya, Ruben	R-R	5-9	155	9-30-03	.351	.479	.432	29	48	37	10	13	3	0	0	8	8	2	0	1	7	4	1	16.67	14.58

Pitching	B-T	Ht.	Wt.	DOB	W	L	ERA	G	GS	SV	IP	Hits	Runs	ER	HR	BB	SO	AVG	OBP	SLG	SO%	BB%	BF
Almonte, Keuri	L-L	6-2	190	10-16-05	1	2	5.28	14	12	0	29	25	26	17	0	29	41	.234	.443	.280	27.33	19.33	150
Aquino, Cesar	R-R	6-1	201	2-27-05	6	1	0.98	12	6	0	46	28	9	5	1	7	37	.177	.231	.247	21.26	4.02	174
Aray, Adrian	R-R	6-2	175	9-15-06	1	0	3.07	12	4	2	29	19	12	10	0	18	28	.184	.320	.214	22.40	14.40	125
Camacho, Angel	L-L	5-11	150	1-13-04	3	2	3.72	14	1	0	29	21	17	12	1	12	43	.193	.279	.239	35.25	9.84	122
Carreno, Nicolas	L-L	5-10	155	6-9-06	0	1	3.74	8	8	0	22	11	14	9	1	17	36	.143	.330	.182	36.00	17.00	100
Chiquillo, Diego	L-L	5-11	185	12-9-02	0	0	1.69	12	0	1	16	7	4	3	0	10	17	.135	.274	.154	27.42	16.13	62
Clode, Jesus	R-R	6-2	180	8-28-01	2	0	3.04	16	0	4	27	22	12	9	1	8	30	.232	.292	.347	28.30	7.55	106
Francia, Dariel	R-R	6-2	165	7-23-06	6	2	3.48	12	1	0	34	24	17	13	1	16	42	.202	.309	.269	30.22	11.51	139
Hernandez, Yoerys	L-L	6-2	185	9-1-03	1	3	7.94	9	0	0	17	24	17	15	2	11	21	.329	.425	.425	24.14	12.64	87
Jimenez, Ronaldys	L-L	5-11	165	11-29-05	0	1	4.91	3	3	0	7	2	4	4	0	12	11	.095	.441	.095	32.35	35.29	34
Joseph, Luis	R-R	6-1	180	6-15-02	0	0	3.00	2	0	0	3	2	1	1	0	1	3	.167	.231	.167	23.08	7.69	13
Martinez, Randol	R-R	6-1	168	5-31-07	0	1	9.22	8	1	0	14	15	15	14	1	18	16	.288	.486	.442	22.22	25.00	72
Mendez, Rafael	R-R	6-3	170	8-14-02	2	1	2.74	14	0	2	23	13	9	7	1	9	30	.169	.267	.260	32.61	9.78	92
Navarro, Reinold	L-L	6-0	178	10-21-06	0	2	3.38	10	9	0	24	13	12	9	1	21	37	.144	.336	.189	31.90	18.10	116
Ordonez, Dermis	R-R	6-1	170	9-5-04	0	2	9.00	7	0	0	7	8	7	7	0	12	7	.286	.535	.393	16.28	27.91	43
Oviedo, Adolfo	R-R	6-1	165	11-17-04	5	1	1.96	12	6	0	41	33	12	9	2	11	43	.216	.284	.288	25.29	6.47	170
Pichardo, Bladimir	R-R	6-3	193	10-24-05	0	1	7.27	3	0	0	9	10	10	7	0	8	4	.294	.429	.412	9.09	18.18	44
Polanco, Brandison	R-R	6-2	170	8-1-02	2	0	0.51	12	0	5	18	5	1	1	0	5	24	.089	.159	.143	38.10	7.94	63
Quintana, Marlon	R-R	6-2	192	6-16-06	1	0	6.00	1	0	0	3	4	3	2	0	1	4	.308	.357	.385	28.57	7.14	14
Ress, Patricio	R-R	6-2	165	6-26-03	1	0	1.93	2	0	0	5	3	1	1	0	2	7	.176	.263	.176	36.84	10.53	19
Rodriguez, Luis	R-R	5-10	185	8-23-04	1	1	4.73	8	0	0	13	8	8	7	0	9	16	.163	.317	.224	26.67	15.00	60
Valdez, Jonawel	R-R	6-1	185	3-19-04	0	1	3.00	3	3	0	12	7	4	4	0	3	20	.175	.267	.200	44.44	6.67	45

Fielding

C: Sequera 28, Escudero 21, Perez 14, Vittini 2. **1B:** Florentino 22, Escudero 18, Perez 10, Rodriguez 6, Sequera 5, Dipre 2, Vittini 1. **2B:** Pimentel 19, Morales 17, Feliz 12, Van Der Linden 7, Kim 6, Orelin 3, Herrera 2, Brioso 2. **3B:** Orelin 18, Morales 16, Pimentel 12, Kim 8, Herrera 6, Brioso 1. **SS:** Feliz 30, Kim 9, Pimentel 9, Herrera 6, Morales 5, Orelin 2. **LF:** Rodriguez 11, Rodriguez 11, Vizcaya 9, Dipre 9, Villafane 7, Florentino 6, Aquino 4, Brioso 3, Jauregui 3, Mola 2. **CF:** Jauregui 30, Florentino 13, Rodriguez 11, Vizcaya 8, Rodriguez 5, Villafane 1. **RF:** Dipre 16, Rodriguez 15, Jauregui 10, Aquino 9, Florentino 8, Vizcaya 6, Rodriguez 2, Villafane 2.

St. Louis Cardinals

SEASON SYNOPSIS: The Cardinals improved by 12 wins over their 2023 last-place performance, but it wasn't enough to return the club to the postseason. Nor was it enough for St. Louis fans, as club attendance fell below 3 million over a full season for the first time since 2003 (other than 2021 which had pandemic restrictions).

HIGH POINT: St. Louis swept a doubleheader from the rival Cubs on July 13, just before the all-star break, to get within 3.5 games of first-place Milwaukee. Nolan Arenado's two-run single in the eighth inning of the nightcap gave the Redbirds a 5-4 lead and closer Ryan Helsley made it hold up, the 32nd save in the team's 50th win. Helsley finished with an MLB-leading 49 saves.

LOW POINT: A 15-24 start certainly didn't help attendance or the team's playoff chances, and a five-game losing streak Aug. 10-16, including a three-game sweep in Cincinnati, served as a death blow. St. Louis scored four runs against the Reds while falling back below .500.

NOTABLE ROOKIES: Masyn Winn took over as shortstop on Opening Day and was the team's best all-around player, defending well, showing off one of the game's best throwing arms and hitting .267/.314/.416. Catchers Pedro Pages (.657 OPS) and Ivan Herrera (first full season) filled in as best they could when a broken forearm felled Willson Contreras. With center fielder Tommy Edman out with a wrist injury, journeyman Mike Siani (.570 OPS) became the primary center fielder but made more impact with his speed (team-best 20 stolen bases) and defense than his bat. Rule 5 pick Ryan Fernandez posted a 3.51 ERA while ranking fourth on the pitching staff in appearances (62).

KEY TRANSACTIONS: Club president John Mozeliak moved aggressively last offseason to overhaul the rotation, signing free agents Sonny Gray, Kyle Gibson and Lance Lynn. They combined for 83 starts, but the team's rotation ranked 23rd in bWAR, even after acquiring righty Erick Fedde from the White Sox in a three-team deadline deal that cost them Edman. St. Louis also gave up on 2016 first-rounder Dylan Carlson, trading him to Tampa Bay. After the season, the organization shed GM Mike Girsch (reassigned) and farm director Gary LaRoque (retired), while Mozeliak announced 2025 would be his final season and that Chaim Bloom, fired after the 2023 season as Boston's chief baseball officer, had signed a five-year contract to replace Mozeliak after the 2025 season.

OPENING DAY PAYROLL: $179,553,567 (11th)

PLAYERS OF THE YEAR

MAJOR LEAGUE

Masyn Winn
SS

.267/.314/.416
15 HR, 11 SB
85 R, 41 BB, 150 G

MINOR LEAGUE

Quinn Mathews
LHP

(A/A+/AA/AAA)
8-5, 2.76 ERA
202 SO, 49 BB, 143 IP

ORGANIZATION LEADERS

Batting		*Qualifiers
MAJORS		
* AVG	Brendan Donovan	.278
* OPS	Brendan Donovan	.759
HR	Paul Goldschmidt	22
RBI	Alec Burleson	78
MINORS		
* AVG	Bryan Torres, Springfield	.331
* OBP	Bryan Torres, Springfield	.418
* SLG	Luken Baker, Memphis	.535
* OPS	Matt Koperniak, Memphis	.882
R	Nathan Church, Springfield	81
H	Bryan Torres, Springfield	148
TB	Matt Koperniak, Memphis	237
2B	Cesar Prieto, Memphis	35
3B	3 tied	5
HR	Luken Baker, Memphis	32
RBI	Luken Baker, Memphis	79
BB	Bryan Torres, Springfield	69
SO	Won-Bin Cho, Peoria	134
SB	Miguel Villarroel, Palm Beach, Peoria	39

Pitching		#Qualifiers
MAJORS		
W	Sonny Gray	13
# ERA	Sonny Gray	3.84
SO	Sonny Gray	203
SV	Ryan Helsley	49
MINORS		
W	Gordon Graceffo, Memphis	10
W	Darlin Saladin, Palm Beach/Peoria	10
W	Chen-Wei Lin, Palm Beach	10
L	Brycen Mautz, Peoria	13
# ERA	Juan Salas, Palm Beach	2.62
G	Connor Thomas, Memphis	56
GS	Michael McGreevy, Memphis	27
SV	Matt Svanson, Springfield	27
IP	Michael McGreevy, Memphis	150
BB	Edwin Nunez, Springfield	67
SO	Michael McGreevy, Memphis	138
# AVG	Quinn Mathews, 4 teams	.179

2024 PERFORMANCE

General Manager: John Mozeliak. **Farm Director:** Gary LaRocque. **Scouting Director:** Randy Flores.

Class	Team	League	W	L	PCT	Finish	Manager
Majors	St. Louis Cardinals	National	83	79	.512	9 (15)	Oliver Marmol
Triple-A	Memphis Redbirds	International	74	74	.500	9 (20)	Ben Johnson
Double-A	Springfield Cardinals	Texas	79	59	.572	4 (10)	Jose Leger
High-A	Peoria Chiefs	Midwest	59	72	.450	10 (12)	Patrick Anderson
Low-A	Palm Beach Cardinals	Florida State	83	47	.638	1 (10)	Gary Kendall
Rookie	FCL Cardinals	Florida Complex	20	33	.377	13 (15)	Roberto Espinoza
Rookie	DSL Cardinals	Dominican	26	27	.491	27 (51)	Fray Peniche
Overall 2024 Minor League Record			**341**	**312**	**.522**	**10th (30)**	

ST. LOUIS CARDINALS

ORGANIZATION STATISTICS

ST. LOUIS CARDINALS

NATIONAL LEAGUE

Batting	B-T	Ht.	Wt.	DOB	AVG	OBP	SLG	G	PA	AB	R	H	2B	3B	HR	RBI	BB	HBP	SH	SF	SO	SB	CS	BB%	SO%
Arenado, Nolan	R-R	6-2	215	4-16-91	.272	.325	.394	152	635	578	70	157	23	0	16	71	44	5	0	7	92	2	2	6.93	14.49
Baker, Luken	R-R	6-4	280	3-10-97	.175	.286	.400	21	49	40	3	7	1	1	2	10	7	0	0	2	11	1	0	14.29	22.45
Burleson, Alec	L-L	6-2	212	11-25-98	.269	.314	.420	152	595	547	71	147	20	0	21	78	35	4	1	6	76	9	4	5.88	12.77
Carlson, Dylan	B-L	6-2	205	10-23-98	.198	.275	.240	59	138	121	12	24	5	0	0	11	12	2	0	3	37	0	1	8.70	26.81
Carpenter, Matt	L-R	6-4	210	11-26-85	.234	.314	.372	59	157	137	15	32	7	0	4	15	15	2	0	2	51	0	2	9.55	32.48
Contreras, Willson	R-R	6-1	225	5-13-92	.262	.380	.468	84	358	301	48	79	17	0	15	36	45	12	0	0	96	4	1	12.57	26.82
Crawford, Brandon	L-R	6-1	223	1-21-87	.169	.263	.282	29	80	71	5	12	5	0	1	4	8	1	0	0	26	0	0	10.00	32.50
Donovan, Brendan	L-R	6-1	195	1-16-97	.278	.342	.417	153	652	587	65	163	34	3	14	73	47	13	0	5	81	5	5	7.21	12.42
Fermin, Jose	R-R	5-9	200	3-29-99	.155	.241	.197	45	79	71	7	11	1	1	0	4	7	1	0	0	11	2	1	8.86	13.92
Goldschmidt, Paul	R-R	6-3	220	9-10-87	.245	.302	.414	154	654	599	70	147	33	1	22	65	47	2	0	2	173	11	0	7.19	26.45
Gorman, Nolan	L-R	6-1	210	5-10-00	.203	.271	.400	107	402	365	42	74	15	0	19	50	34	1	0	2	151	6	1	8.46	37.56
Herrera, Ivan	R-R	5-11	220	6-1-00	.301	.372	.428	72	259	229	37	69	12	1	5	27	25	2	0	2	53	5	0	9.65	20.46
Nootbaar, Lars	L-R	6-3	210	9-8-97	.244	.342	.417	109	405	348	39	85	18	3	12	45	52	1	1	3	79	7	3	12.84	19.51
Pages, Pedro	R-R	6-1	234	9-17-98	.238	.281	.376	68	218	202	19	48	3	2	7	27	13	0	1	2	58	2	0	5.96	26.61
Pham, Tommy	R-R	6-1	223	3-8-88	.206	.286	.368	23	77	68	7	14	3	1	2	12	7	1	0	1	16	0	0	9.09	20.78
Saggese, Thomas	R-R	5-11	175	4-10-02	.204	.250	.306	18	52	49	5	10	2	0	1	4	2	1	0	0	14	0	0	3.85	26.92
Scott, Victor	L-L	5-10	190	2-12-01	.179	.219	.283	53	155	145	14	26	9	0	2	10	6	2	0	2	42	5	1	3.87	27.10
Siani, Michael	L-L	6-1	188	7-16-99	.228	.285	.285	124	334	298	42	68	7	2	2	20	21	3	11	1	92	20	3	6.29	27.54
Walker, Jordan	R-R	6-6	245	5-22-02	.201	.253	.366	51	178	164	16	33	10	1	5	20	10	2	0	2	50	1	0	5.62	28.09
Winn, Masyn	R-R	5-11	180	3-21-02	.267	.314	.416	150	637	587	85	157	32	5	15	57	41	1	3	5	109	11	5	6.44	17.11

Pitching	B-T	Ht.	Wt.	DOB	W	L	ERA	G	GS	SV	IP	Hits	Runs	ER	HR	BB	SO	AVG	OBP	SLG	SO%	BB%	BF
Armstrong, Shawn	R-R	6-2	225	9-11-90	1	0	2.84	11	0	0	13	11	4	4	1	2	12	.234	.265	.404	24.49	4.08	49
Crawford, Brandon	L-R	6-1	223	1-21-87	0	0	27.00	1	0	0	1	3	4	4	0	2	0	.429	.600	.429	0.00	20.00	10
Fedde, Erick	R-R	6-4	203	2-25-93	2	5	3.72	10	10	0	56	49	23	23	6	18	46	.246	.313	.407	20.54	8.04	224
Fernandez, Ryan	R-R	6-0	170	6-11-98	1	6	3.51	62	0	2	67	58	30	26	4	32	71	.236	.325	.341	24.91	11.23	285
Gallegos, Giovanny	R-R	6-2	215	8-14-91	2	1	6.53	21	0	1	21	24	15	15	6	10	21	.286	.362	.607	22.34	10.64	94
Gibson, Kyle	R-R	6-6	200	10-23-87	8	8	4.24	30	30	0	170	161	91	80	23	68	151	.251	.324	.418	20.91	9.42	722
Graceffo, Gordon	R-R	6-4	210	3-17-00	0	1	4.70	2	1	0	8	7	4	4	1	2	6	.250	.290	.500	19.35	6.45	31
Gray, Sonny	R-R	5-10	195	11-7-89	13	9	3.84	28	28	0	166	142	79	71	21	39	203	.228	.275	.401	30.25	5.81	671
Helsley, Ryan	R-R	6-2	230	7-18-94	7	4	2.04	65	0	49	66	50	19	15	3	23	79	.210	.275	.273	29.70	8.65	266
King, John	L-L	6-2	215	9-14-94	3	3	2.85	56	0	0	60	58	23	19	5	14	38	.258	.296	.351	15.32	5.65	248
Kittredge, Andrew	R-R	6-1	230	3-17-90	5	5	2.80	74	0	1	71	60	26	22	10	20	67	.228	.280	.395	23.34	6.97	287
Kloffenstein, Adam	R-R	6-5	243	8-25-00	0	0	0.00	1	0	0	1	0	0	0	0	0	0	.000	.000	.000	0.00	0.00	3
Leahy, Kyle	S-R	6-5	200	6-4-97	1	1	4.07	33	0	1	49	40	23	22	4	10	33	.225	.267	.354	17.28	5.24	191
Liberatore, Matthew	L-L	6-4	200	11-6-99	3	4	4.40	60	6	0	86	81	44	42	11	28	76	.251	.312	.415	21.23	7.82	358
Loutos, Ryan	R-R	6-5	215	1-29-99	0	0	0.00	3	0	0	2	2	0	0	0	1	0	.222	.300	.333	0.00	10.00	10
Lynn, Lance	S-R	6-5	270	5-12-87	7	4	3.84	23	23	0	117	113	64	50	16	44	109	.247	.316	.402	21.33	8.61	511
Matz, Steven	R-L	6-2	201	5-29-91	1	2	5.08	12	7	0	44	49	28	25	7	15	33	.287	.349	.468	17.37	7.89	190
McGreevy, Michael	L-R	6-4	215	7-8-00	3	0	1.96	4	3	0	23	16	5	5	1	2	18	.193	.221	.289	20.93	2.33	86
Mikolas, Miles	R-R	6-4	230	8-23-88	10	11	5.35	32	32	0	172	194	106	102	26	25	122	.284	.312	.485	16.94	3.47	720
O'Brien, Riley	R-R	6-4	180	2-6-95	0	0	11.25	8	0	0	8	13	10	10	2	8	11	.361	.478	.639	23.91	17.39	46
Pallante, Andre	R-R	6-0	203	9-18-98	8	8	3.78	29	20	0	121	110	55	51	8	48	94	.240	.315	.338	18.47	9.43	509
Robertson, Nick	R-R	6-6	265	7-16-98	0	0	4.38	8	0	0	12	15	6	6	3	2	14	.306	.327	.531	26.92	3.85	52
Romero, JoJo	L-L	5-11	200	9-9-96	7	3	3.36	65	0	1	59	52	23	22	8	16	51	.236	.302	.395	20.99	6.58	243
Roycroft, Chris	R-R	6-8	230	6-21-97	1	2	4.19	27	0	0	34	31	19	16	2	17	33	.238	.338	.354	21.29	10.97	155
Thompson, Zack	L-L	6-2	215	10-28-97	0	2	9.53	5	2	0	17	24	18	18	6	8	20	.324	.398	.622	24.10	9.64	83

Fielding

Catcher	PCT	G	PO	A	E	DP	PB
Contreras	.992	51	359	21	3	1	4
Herrera	.994	56	476	17	3	2	1
Pages	.994	66	489	28	3	1	3

First Base	PCT	G	PO	A	E	DP
Baker	1.000	1	1	0	0	0
Burleson	1.000	15	95	10	0	10
Carpenter	1.000	5	10	1	0	0
Goldschmidt	.996	150	1216	102	5	137
Pages	1.000	1	1	0	0	0

Second Base	PCT	G	PO	A	E	DP
Carpenter	1.000	1	0	1	0	1
Donovan	.995	53	74	136	1	26

	PCT	G	PO	A	E	DP
Fermin	1.000	11	8	18	0	2
Gorman	.975	105	147	243	10	68
Saggese	.977	13	11	31	1	7

Third Base	PCT	G	PO	A	E	DP
Arenado	.977	146	103	280	9	26
Carpenter	1.000	1	1	0	0	0
Crawford	1.000	6	2	7	0	0
Donovan	.938	9	4	11	1	2
Fermin	1.000	13	5	6	0	0
Gorman	.000	2	0	0	0	0
Saggese	.833	2	1	4	1	0

Shortstop	PCT	G	PO	A	E	DP
Crawford	.982	18	15	41	1	10
Saggese	.929	3	5	8	1	2
Winn	.971	148	191	402	18	100

Outfield	PCT	G	PO	A	E	DP
Burleson	.992	80	126	6	1	2
Carlson	.989	65	88	1	1	1
Donovan	1.000	106	164	3	0	0
Fermin	.000	1	0	0	0	0
Nootbaar	.986	128	209	2	3	2
Pham	1.000	23	25	0	0	0
Scott	.979	53	95	0	2	0
Siani	1.000	123	242	1	0	0
Walker	.985	48	64	2	1	1

MEMPHIS REDBIRDS

TRIPLE-A

INTERNATIONAL LEAGUE

Batting	B-T	Ht.	Wt.	DOB	AVG	OBP	SLG	G	PA	AB	R	H	2B	3B	HR	RBI	BB	HBP	SH	SF	SO	SB	CS	BB%	SO%
Antico, Mike	L-R	5-10	200	2-16-98	.261	.323	.433	56	224	203	30	53	10	2	7	28	17	2	1	1	49	15	2	7.59	21.88
Baker, Luken	R-R	6-4	280	3-10-97	.231	.345	.535	108	452	376	54	87	18	0	32	79	67	2	0	7	110	0	0	14.82	24.34
Carlson, Dylan	B-L	6-2	205	10-23-98	.273	.467	.545	4	15	11	2	3	0	0	1	1	3	1	0	0	2	0	0	20.00	13.33
Carpenter, Matt	L-R	6-4	210	11-26-85	.231	.412	.692	4	17	13	3	3	0	0	2	3	4	0	0	0	6	0	0	23.53	35.29
Collins, Gavin	R-R	5-10	205	7-17-95	.264	.335	.461	61	216	193	26	51	11	0	9	35	17	4	1	1	35	0	0	7.87	16.20
Contreras, Willson	R-R	6-1	225	5-13-92	.143	.182	.143	6	22	21	2	3	0	0	0	1	1	0	0	0	5	0	0	4.55	22.73
Dunn, Nick	L-R	5-8	185	1-29-97	.316	.374	.467	98	361	323	40	102	19	3	8	42	30	3	0	5	33	1	1	8.31	9.14
Fermin, Jose	R-R	5-9	200	3-29-99	.311	.424	.500	61	240	196	40	61	13	0	8	27	34	6	2	2	22	18	2	14.17	9.17
Gamboa, Arquimedes	B-R	5-11	190	9-23-97	.215	.322	.335	52	183	158	23	34	7	0	4	20	25	0	0	0	49	2	2	13.66	26.78
Gomez, Moises	R-R	5-11	200	8-27-98	.208	.284	.299	41	162	144	17	30	4	0	3	11	16	0	0	2	55	0	0	9.88	33.95
Gorman, Nolan	L-R	6-1	210	5-10-00	.205	.276	.489	23	98	88	16	18	4	0	7	16	9	0	0	1	23	0	0	9.18	23.47
Herrera, Ivan	R-R	5-11	220	6-1-00	.280	.402	.473	27	112	93	18	26	1	1	5	16	19	0	0	0	20	3	0	16.96	17.86
Koperniak, Matt	L-R	6-0	200	2-8-98	.309	.370	.512	122	513	463	64	143	28	3	20	73	43	4	0	3	96	5	6	8.38	18.71
Mendoza, Ramon	R-R	5-11	174	8-31-00	.211	.254	.281	20	63	57	7	12	4	0	0	7	4	0	0	2	16	0	1	6.35	25.40
Nootbaar, Lars	L-R	6-3	210	9-8-97	.176	.300	.235	5	20	17	5	3	1	0	0	1	3	0	0	0	4	0	0	15.00	20.00
Pages, Pedro	R-R	6-1	234	9-17-98	.222	.417	.500	7	24	18	3	4	2	0	1	2	5	1	0	0	5	0	0	20.83	20.83
Prieto, Cesar	L-R	5-9	175	5-10-99	.279	.318	.445	129	535	501	67	140	35	3	14	56	23	6	3	2	63	5	5	4.30	11.78
Raposo, Nick	R-R	5-10	200	6-3-98	.193	.251	.349	58	208	192	21	37	9	0	7	28	15	0	1	0	45	0	0	7.21	21.63
Redmond, Chandler	L-R	6-1	231	1-9-97	.200	.297	.354	20	74	65	12	13	4	0	2	6	9	0	0	0	30	0	0	12.16	40.54
Rivas, Alfonso	L-L	5-10	190	9-13-96	.229	.354	.337	96	381	315	51	72	21	2	3	38	50	12	2	2	92	1	0	13.12	24.15
Saggese, Thomas	R-R	5-11	175	4-10-02	.253	.313	.438	125	528	479	75	121	23	3	20	67	31	13	1	4	122	9	4	5.87	23.11
Scott, Victor	L-L	5-10	190	2-12-01	.210	.294	.303	81	362	314	39	66	7	2	6	30	36	3	5	4	57	30	5	9.94	15.75
Sisco, Chance	L-R	6-3	210	2-24-95	.217	.308	.348	7	26	23	2	5	0	0	1	5	1	2	0	0	11	0	0	3.85	42.31
Stauss, Wade	L-R	6-2	225	4-4-99	.147	.310	.206	15	42	34	1	5	2	0	0	3	7	1	0	0	20	0	0	16.67	47.62
Walker, Jordan	R-R	6-6	245	5-22-02	.263	.326	.427	84	377	342	37	90	23	3	9	37	31	2	0	2	73	4	3	8.22	19.36
Young, Jared	L-R	6-0	185	7-9-95	.285	.411	.506	74	286	235	46	67	15	2	11	35	41	9	1	0	53	6	4	14.34	18.53

Pitching	B-T	Ht.	Wt.	DOB	W	L	ERA	G	GS	SV	IP	Hits	Runs	ER	HR	BB	SO	AVG	OBP	SLG	SO%	BB%	BF
Bedell, Ian	R-R	6-2	214	9-5-99	2	2	5.02	9	9	0	43	36	25	24	10	24	31	.222	.333	.463	16.40	12.70	189
Bosiokovic, Jacob	R-R	6-5	240	12-21-93	4	3	5.56	47	0	1	55	52	36	34	8	35	65	.248	.356	.419	26.00	14.00	250
Cornwell, Alex	L-L	6-0	202	5-9-99	2	0	4.70	6	0	0	15	18	8	8	2	5	12	.300	.354	.450	18.46	7.69	65
Gallegos, Giovanny	R-R	6-2	215	8-14-91	0	1	11.25	4	1	0	4	5	5	5	3	2	3	.313	.389	.875	16.67	11.11	18
Garcia, Benito	R-R	6-0	165	3-10-00	0	0	8.10	1	0	0	3	6	3	3	2	2	1	.375	.444	.938	5.56	11.11	18
Graceffo, Gordon	R-R	6-4	210	3-17-00	10	8	4.85	27	26	0	130	152	79	70	20	50	107	.290	.354	.450	18.35	8.58	583
Granillo, Andre	R-R	6-4	245	5-12-00	4	2	4.82	34	0	1	47	33	26	25	6	31	57	.192	.319	.331	27.94	15.20	204
Ingram, Kolton	L-L	5-9	170	10-21-96	2	0	3.93	14	0	3	18	15	8	8	1	12	23	.227	.346	.318	29.49	15.38	78
James, Josh	R-R	6-3	234	3-8-93	1	0	19.96	9	0	0	8	13	18	17	2	15	5	.371	.569	.714	9.80	29.41	51
King, John	L-L	6-2	215	9-14-94	1	0	3.38	6	0	2	5	6	2	2	1	0	5	.273	.273	.500	22.73	0.00	22
Kloffenstein, Adam	R-R	6-5	243	8-25-00	4	5	4.74	17	17	0	89	78	47	47	13	41	73	.241	.341	.414	19.41	10.90	376
Komar, Brandon	R-R	6-0	200	5-8-99	1	0	5.24	10	0	0	22	27	14	13	2	9	19	.303	.370	.416	18.81	8.91	101
Leahy, Kyle	S-R	6-5	200	6-4-97	0	4	3.86	16	0	0	28	30	12	12	6	8	31	.275	.325	.495	25.62	6.61	121
Loutos, Ryan	R-R	6-5	215	1-29-99	3	1	3.40	47	0	18	53	53	21	20	3	23	59	.259	.332	.376	25.76	10.04	229
Lynn, Lance	S-R	6-5	270	5-12-87	0	0	12.27	1	1	0	4	7	5	5	0	2	8	.389	.450	.556	40.00	10.00	20
Mathews, Quinn	L-L	6-4	192	10-4-00	0	2	6.48	4	4	0	17	18	12	12	1	14	22	.281	.410	.438	27.85	17.72	79
Matz, Steven	R-L	6-2	201	5-29-91	0	1	3.91	7	7	0	23	24	11	10	2	5	19	.267	.313	.411	19.79	5.21	96
McGreevy, Michael	L-R	6-4	215	7-8-00	9	8	4.02	27	27	0	150	152	70	67	14	44	138	.259	.311	.403	21.63	6.90	638
Naughton, Packy	R-L	6-2	195	4-16-96	0	1	2.53	7	2	0	11	10	4	3	0	3	12	.233	.277	.349	24.49	6.12	49
O'Brien, Riley	R-R	6-4	180	2-6-95	1	0	1.35	14	0	1	13	8	3	2	0	5	9	.170	.250	.277	17.31	9.62	52
Pallante, Andre	R-R	6-0	203	9-18-98	1	0	2.20	4	3	0	16	14	4	4	0	13	9	.241	.392	.259	12.00	17.33	75
Raquet, Nick	R-L	6-0	215	12-12-95	2	9	5.80	27	6	0	68	82	46	44	9	31	58	.298	.373	.436	18.41	9.84	315
Robberse, Sem	R-R	6-1	185	10-12-01	5	4	4.59	16	14	0	84	76	46	43	13	27	76	.241	.299	.410	21.84	7.76	348
Robertson, Nick	R-R	6-6	265	7-16-98	1	2	7.48	21	0	1	22	23	19	18	3	16	21	.277	.406	.422	20.59	15.69	102
Rodriguez, Wilking	R-R	6-1	180	3-2-90	0	0	5.73	12	0	0	11	8	7	7	1	11	15	.195	.365	.293	28.85	21.15	52
Roycroft, Chris	R-R	6-8	230	6-21-97	3	4	2.17	36	0	6	46	41	15	11	3	18	45	.234	.306	.309	22.96	9.18	196
Santos, Victor	R-R	6-1	191	7-12-00	6	7	5.61	33	8	1	77	84	55	48	9	33	60	.289	.361	.457	17.96	9.88	334
Shreve, Ryan	R-R	6-6	215	6-23-98	1	0	4.18	15	0	0	32	36	17	15	4	16	24	.281	.361	.445	16.67	11.11	144
Thomas, Connor	L-L	5-11	173	5-29-98	7	4	2.89	56	3	3	90	97	34	29	8	24	79	.276	.325	.384	20.63	6.27	383
Thompson, Zack	L-L	6-2	215	10-28-97	4	6	4.40	21	20	0	90	68	46	44	10	56	108	.207	.330	.353	27.41	14.21	394

Fielding

Catcher	PCT	G	PO	A	E	DP	PB
Collins	.995	51	406	18	2	2	5
Contreras	.950	3	17	2	1	0	0
Herrera	.983	20	155	15	3	2	3
Pages	.984	7	57	4	1	2	2
Raposo	.994	58	429	38	3	2	2
Sisco	1.000	7	47	2	0	0	0
Stauss	1.000	14	90	3	0	0	1

First Base	PCT	G	PO	A	E	DP
Baker	.995	80	602	46	3	59
Carpenter	1.000	2	12	3	0	3
Collins	1.000	1	6	1	0	0
Gamboa	.000	1	0	0	0	0
Redmond	1.000	20	148	9	0	23
Rivas	.997	41	314	29	1	45
Young	1.000	5	45	2	0	4

Second Base	PCT	G	PO	A	E	DP
Dunn	.976	21	28	55	2	15
Fermin	.989	17	28	64	1	7
Gorman	.976	10	15	26	1	11
Mendoza	1.000	6	9	8	0	2
Prieto	.974	53	80	141	6	39
Saggese	.986	42	76	129	3	31

Third Base	PCT	G	PO	A	E	DP
Dunn	.929	39	20	59	6	12
Fermin	.909	7	5	5	1	0
Mendoza	.000	2	0	0	0	0
Prieto	.953	67	41	121	8	9
Saggese	.933	13	7	21	2	0
Young	.925	27	25	37	5	5

Shortstop	PCT	G	PO	A	E	DP
Fermin	.951	28	41	57	5	15
Gamboa	.953	50	73	130	10	35
Mendoza	.923	4	4	8	1	4
Prieto	1.000	2	6	4	0	2
Saggese	.965	70	99	180	10	47

Outfield	PCT	G	PO	A	E	DP
Antico	1.000	55	110	1	0	1
Carlson	1.000	2	4	0	0	0
Fermin	1.000	9	14	0	0	0
Gomez	.971	37	62	4	2	1
Koperniak	.988	122	235	7	3	1
Mendoza	1.000	7	9	0	0	0
Nootbaar	1.000	3	4	0	0	0
Rivas	.982	37	51	3	1	1
Scott	.995	80	201	5	1	1
Walker	.972	75	131	9	4	1
Young	1.000	29	44	1	0	0

SPRINGFIELD CARDINALS — *DOUBLE-A*

TEXAS LEAGUE

Batting	B-T	Ht.	Wt.	DOB	AVG	OBP	SLG	G	PA	AB	R	H	2B	3B	HR	RBI	BB	HBP	SH	SF	SO	SB	CS	BB%	SO%
Antico, Mike	L-R	5-10	200	2-16-98	.270	.337	.418	70	276	244	47	66	5	2	9	33	22	4	2	3	54	18	3	7.97	19.57
Bernal, Leonardo	B-R	6-0	200	2-13-04	.204	.291	.286	14	55	49	2	10	1	0	1	4	6	0	0	0	9	0	2	10.91	16.36
Buchberger, Jacob	R-R	6-0	215	10-1-97	.249	.338	.366	108	426	374	66	93	15	4	7	42	48	3	0	1	100	13	7	11.27	23.47
Carpenter, Matt	L-R	6-4	210	11-26-85	.167	.333	.333	2	9	6	2	1	1	0	0	1	1	1	0	1	2	0	0	11.11	22.22
Church, Nathan	L-L	5-10	180	7-12-00	.268	.331	.373	127	541	482	81	129	22	1	9	66	43	6	3	6	60	24	4	7.95	11.09
Crooks, Jimmy	L-R	6-1	210	7-19-01	.321	.410	.498	90	371	315	42	101	19	2	11	62	43	8	0	5	78	4	0	11.59	21.02
Davis, Chase	L-L	6-1	216	12-5-01	.250	.323	.429	8	31	28	3	7	2	0	1	4	3	0	0	0	5	3	0	9.68	16.13
Edman, Tommy	B-R	5-10	180	5-9-95	.207	.294	.241	8	34	29	3	6	1	0	0	4	4	0	0	1	9	0	0	11.76	26.47
Harris, Dakota	B-R	6-0	197	2-19-02	.233	.299	.313	45	168	150	20	35	9	0	1	13	9	6	1	2	41	3	1	5.36	24.40
Linarez, Carlos	R-R	6-0	170	10-24-01	.200	.222	.200	8	27	25	1	5	0	0	0	4	1	0	0	1	10	0	0	3.70	37.04
Lloyd, Matt	L-R	6-1	205	3-17-96	.269	.358	.453	120	486	413	70	111	25	0	17	77	56	7	0	10	98	16	2	11.52	20.16
McKeithan, Aaron	R-R	6-1	220	12-13-99	.264	.356	.325	55	191	163	11	43	5	1	1	16	17	8	0	3	30	0	0	8.90	15.71
Mendlinger, Noah	L-R	5-9	180	8-9-00	.282	.356	.338	103	401	355	44	100	20	0	0	45	29	13	2	2	50	4	4	7.23	12.47
Mendoza, Ramon	R-R	5-11	174	8-31-00	.239	.355	.348	53	188	155	17	37	8	0	3	24	25	4	2	2	41	2	0	13.30	21.81
Nootbaar, Lars	L-R	6-3	210	9-8-97	.259	.412	.519	8	34	27	6	7	1	0	2	4	7	0	0	0	9	0	0	20.59	26.47
Redmond, Chandler	L-R	6-1	231	1-9-97	.231	.325	.354	83	319	268	32	62	6	0	9	50	36	3	0	4	99	5	1	11.29	31.03
Rivas, Jeremy	R-R	6-0	172	3-4-03	.263	.349	.311	123	459	395	61	104	8	1	3	34	46	8	6	4	85	27	10	10.02	18.52
Rodriguez, Luis	R-R	6-0	175	2-26-00	.216	.256	.243	12	39	37	3	8	1	0	0	4	2	0	0	0	16	1	0	5.13	41.03
Rotondo, Chris	R-R	6-0	200	6-15-99	.205	.265	.310	60	187	171	25	35	7	1	3	16	11	3	2	0	65	7	2	5.88	34.76
Siani, Michael	L-L	6-1	188	7-16-99	.100	.400	.100	4	15	10	1	1	0	0	0	0	5	0	0	0	2	1	1	33.33	13.33
Stauss, Wade	L-R	6-2	225	4-4-99	.167	.375	.233	13	41	30	5	5	2	0	0	3	6	4	1	0	13	0	0	14.63	31.71
Torres, Bryan	L-R	5-11	165	7-2-97	.331	.418	.416	120	528	447	79	148	28	2	2	56	69	1	6	5	75	33	10	13.07	14.20
Yeager, R.J.	R-R	6-2	200	10-2-98	.254	.315	.400	113	467	422	62	107	17	0	15	65	32	8	0	5	60	10	2	6.85	12.85

Pitching	B-T	Ht.	Wt.	DOB	W	L	ERA	G	GS	SV	IP	Hits	Runs	ER	HR	BB	SO	AVG	OBP	SLG	SO%	BB%	BF
Baker, Trent	R-R	6-3	243	12-28-98	4	6	4.89	22	14	0	81	75	47	44	10	43	81	.244	.340	.414	22.69	12.04	357
Bedell, Ian	R-R	6-2	214	9-5-99	1	2	4.73	12	10	1	65	52	36	34	12	19	79	.218	.292	.408	29.48	7.09	268
Berrios, Osvaldo	R-R	6-2	200	11-29-99	0	0	45.00	1	0	0	1	4	5	5	2	2	3	.571	.667	1.714	33.33	22.22	9
Cornwell, Alex	L-L	6-0	202	5-9-99	7	3	4.95	19	15	0	84	93	47	46	7	35	87	.284	.359	.394	23.51	9.46	370
Gallegos, Giovanny	R-R	6-2	215	8-14-91	0	0	11.57	2	0	0	2	4	3	3	0	2	2	.364	.462	.636	15.38	15.38	13
Garcia, Benito	R-R	6-0	165	3-10-00	4	1	4.02	25	0	0	54	46	29	24	5	10	43	.229	.277	.383	19.55	4.55	220
Granillo, Andre	R-R	6-4	245	5-12-00	4	0	1.47	14	0	4	18	8	3	3	1	10	23	.129	.250	.194	31.94	13.89	72
Hence, Tink	R-R	6-1	185	8-6-02	4	3	2.71	20	20	0	80	59	35	24	5	26	109	.204	.270	.301	34.06	8.13	320
Heredia, Nathanael	L-L	6-3	190	9-10-00	2	0	2.55	18	0	1	18	12	5	5	1	7	26	.185	.284	.246	35.14	9.46	74
Hjerpe, Cooper	L-L	6-3	200	3-16-01	2	1	3.07	4	4	0	15	6	5	5	0	8	20	.122	.246	.163	35.09	14.04	57
Komar, Brandon	R-R	6-0	200	5-8-99	7	3	2.50	19	8	0	79	82	27	22	1	19	64	.271	.319	.350	19.63	5.83	326
Marrero, Andrew	R-R	5-10	196	5-8-00	3	3	6.28	41	0	3	53	46	39	37	9	29	63	.236	.346	.395	27.04	12.45	233
Mathews, Quinn	L-L	6-4	192	10-4-00	2	1	2.41	9	9	0	52	35	16	14	3	15	70	.186	.257	.277	33.82	7.25	207
Matz, Steven	R-L	6-2	201	5-29-91	0	1	0.00	2	2	0	5	3	5	0	0	1	8	.167	.211	.222	40.00	5.00	20
Middleton, Keynan	R-R	6-3	215	9-12-93	0	0	2.25	5	0	0	4	1	1	1	1	6	2	.083	.389	.333	11.11	33.33	18
Mills, Zane	R-R	6-4	220	7-4-00	4	1	5.08	11	2	0	28	32	17	16	2	8	20	.294	.350	.459	16.67	6.67	120
Nunez, Edwin	R-R	6-3	185	11-5-01	0	9	7.68	29	17	0	80	75	73	68	9	67	81	.245	.410	.389	20.40	16.88	397
Pereira, Wilfredo	R-R	6-0	197	4-26-99	5	2	6.29	22	6	0	69	85	53	48	11	32	63	.296	.372	.505	19.50	9.91	323
Rajcic, Max	R-R	6-0	210	8-3-01	10	11	4.33	25	24	0	131	133	73	63	18	44	131	.260	.329	.426	23.06	7.75	568
Ralston, Jack	R-R	6-6	231	8-13-97	7	1	2.73	40	0	3	63	44	20	19	9	29	80	.196	.292	.351	31.13	11.28	257
Raquet, Nick	R-L	6-0	215	12-12-95	0	0	0.56	8	0	0	16	10	1	1	0	7	15	.189	.279	.245	24.59	11.48	61
Roby, Tekoah	R-R	6-1	185	9-18-01	2	2	6.75	7	7	0	33	43	27	25	10	12	33	.307	.370	.579	21.43	7.79	154
Rodriguez, Luis	R-R	6-0	175	2-26-00	0	0	0.00	1	0	0	0	0	0	0	0	0	0	.000	.000	.000	0.00	0.00	1
Shreve, Ryan	R-R	6-6	215	6-23-98	6	2	4.20	25	0	0	41	42	20	19	4	9	46	.268	.306	.401	27.06	5.29	170
Svanson, Matt	R-R	6-5	235	1-31-99	4	3	2.69	53	0	27	64	68	30	19	4	25	59	.276	.359	.370	20.85	8.83	283

Pitching	B-T	Ht.	Wt.	DOB	W	L	ERA	G	GS	SV	IP	Hits	Runs	ER	HR	BB	SO	AVG	OBP	SLG	SO%	BB%	BF
Taveras, Leonardo	R-R	6-5	190	9-7-98	1	4	4.27	47	0	1	65	59	38	31	7	45	71	.234	.360	.381	23.05	14.61	308

Fielding

Catcher	PCT	G	PO	A	E	DP	PB
Bernal	1.000	10	90	5	0	1	1
Crooks	.996	81	686	39	3	1	7
Linarez	1.000	7	54	5	0	0	0
McKeithan	.986	33	274	9	4	1	3
Rodriguez	.978	11	87	3	2	2	1
Stauss	.973	13	105	4	3	0	0

First Base	PCT	G	PO	A	E	DP
Buchberger	1.000	1	1	0	0	0
Carpenter	1.000	1	2	0	0	1
Lloyd	1.000	16	75	5	0	8
Redmond	.989	51	323	21	4	25
Yeager	.994	84	505	31	3	63

Second Base	PCT	G	PO	A	E	DP
Harris	.977	28	36	50	2	11
Mendlinger	.968	65	96	115	7	37
Mendoza	.990	34	41	57	1	15
Torres	.989	29	43	50	1	19

Third Base	PCT	G	PO	A	E	DP
Buchberger	.928	97	49	158	16	16
Harris	.944	7	4	13	1	2
Lloyd	1.000	1	3	2	0	0
Mendlinger	.900	5	0	9	1	1
Mendoza	.952	13	2	18	1	2
Redmond	1.000	1	0	2	0	0
Yeager	.964	24	17	36	2	3

Shortstop	PCT	G	PO	A	E	DP
Harris	.974	11	12	26	1	7
Mendlinger	.941	4	8	8	1	5
Mendoza	.929	5	3	10	1	2
Rivas	.966	123	124	274	14	51

Outfield	PCT	G	PO	A	E	DP
Antico	.993	75	140	3	1	0
Buchberger	.895	6	16	1	2	0
Church	.986	132	268	12	4	2
Davis	1.000	8	20	1	0	0
Lloyd	.963	53	77	0	3	0
Mendlinger	.958	42	67	1	3	1
Nootbaar	1.000	6	15	0	0	0
Rotondo	.981	60	101	3	2	1
Siani	1.000	4	7	0	0	0
Torres	.980	92	196	1	4	0

PEORIA CHIEFS

HIGH-A

MIDWEST LEAGUE

Batting	B-T	Ht.	Wt.	DOB	AVG	OBP	SLG	G	PA	AB	R	H	2B	3B	HR	RBI	BB	HBP	SH	SF	SO	SB	CS	BB%	SO%
Adkison, Chase	R-R	6-0	205	6-5-00	.219	.325	.313	11	40	32	2	7	3	0	0	4	4	2	0	2	6	0	0	10.00	15.00
Baez, Joshua	R-R	6-3	220	6-28-03	.225	.306	.388	71	260	227	27	51	7	0	10	30	24	4	1	3	97	19	5	9.23	37.31
Bernal, Leonardo	B-R	6-0	200	2-13-04	.270	.343	.419	96	382	341	46	92	17	2	10	53	37	2	0	2	87	7	5	9.69	22.77
Cho, Won-Bin	L-L	6-1	200	8-20-03	.227	.307	.305	107	428	374	48	85	15	4	2	28	36	9	5	4	134	13	8	8.41	31.31
Curialle, Michael	R-R	6-1	199	6-16-01	.220	.296	.366	77	278	246	30	54	13	1	7	36	21	7	1	3	85	3	1	7.55	30.58
Davis, Chase	L-L	6-1	216	12-5-01	.301	.388	.451	30	129	113	14	34	6	1	3	18	13	3	0	0	29	1	1	10.08	22.48
Encarnacion, Anyelo	R-R	5-11	164	1-2-04	.208	.333	.347	24	88	72	7	15	5	1	1	7	13	1	1	1	28	1	3	14.77	31.82
Harris, Dakota	B-R	6-0	197	2-19-02	.298	.340	.473	52	206	188	25	56	9	0	8	34	9	3	4	0	35	4	4	4.37	16.99
Hernandez, Sammy	R-R	5-9	185	6-1-04	.130	.375	.391	8	33	23	6	3	0	0	2	6	6	3	1	0	8	0	0	18.18	24.24
Iadisernia, Alex	L-L	5-10	180	10-11-00	.227	.311	.328	101	410	357	45	81	21	3	3	38	39	7	1	6	96	20	9	9.51	23.41
Jobert, Brayden	L-R	6-1	215	11-14-00	.243	.338	.286	21	80	70	6	17	3	0	0	7	8	2	0	0	21	2	1	10.00	26.25
Kretzschmar, Kade	L-R	6-2	205	6-9-00	.179	.256	.179	14	44	39	3	7	0	0	0	1	4	0	1	0	12	1	0	9.09	27.27
Levenson, Zach	R-R	6-2	210	3-6-02	.215	.317	.367	70	294	251	33	54	12	1	8	30	33	6	0	3	67	7	3	11.22	22.79
Linarez, Carlos	R-R	6-0	170	10-24-01	.162	.241	.230	28	83	74	5	12	2	0	1	5	8	0	0	1	20	1	0	9.64	24.10
Moore, Brody	R-R	5-11	183	7-20-00	.260	.319	.332	108	446	404	60	105	16	2	3	37	32	4	4	2	86	30	10	7.17	19.28
Moquete, Darlin	R-R	5-8	175	9-19-99	.244	.308	.437	80	311	279	57	68	9	3	13	33	25	2	2	2	77	19	4	8.04	24.76
Paige, Trey	L-R	6-0	215	11-9-00	.254	.323	.305	16	65	59	2	15	3	0	0	5	6	0	0	0	19	1	0	9.23	29.23
Richardson, Tre	R-R	5-10	165	12-2-01	.241	.333	.329	61	249	216	26	52	10	3	1	31	24	6	3	0	59	14	5	9.64	23.69
Rodriguez, Luis	R-R	6-0	175	2-26-00	.182	.182	.182	4	11	11	1	2	0	0	0	2	0	0	0	0	4	0	0	0.00	36.36
Rotondo, Chris	R-R	6-0	200	6-15-99	.285	.377	.391	41	175	151	21	43	4	0	4	22	18	5	0	1	47	7	5	10.29	26.86
Salazar, Johnfrank	R-R	6-1	159	8-5-03	.206	.257	.255	31	114	102	8	21	2	0	1	11	6	2	1	3	19	0	1	5.26	16.67
Sullivan, William	L-R	6-3	205	11-25-00	.169	.285	.277	51	172	148	17	25	4	0	4	18	16	8	0	0	61	1	1	9.30	35.47
Tarlow, Graysen	R-R	5-11	190	7-7-01	.167	.275	.179	30	91	78	5	13	1	0	0	5	12	0	0	1	23	0	0	13.19	25.27
Tovalin, Osvaldo	L-R	6-2	225	10-31-99	.194	.252	.262	60	224	206	21	40	8	0	2	18	7	9	2	0	40	5	2	3.13	17.86
Villarroel, Miguel	R-R	6-0	165	12-23-01	.254	.288	.325	51	181	169	15	43	7	1	1	13	5	3	4	0	47	14	5	2.76	25.97

Pitching	B-T	Ht.	Wt.	DOB	W	L	ERA	G	GS	SV	IP	Hits	Runs	ER	HR	BB	SO	AVG	OBP	SLG	SO%	BB%	BF
Arias, Benjamin	R-R	6-5	195	11-5-01	0	0	6.75	9	0	0	19	17	16	14	1	8	22	.239	.341	.394	26.83	9.76	82
Berrios, Osvaldo	R-R	6-2	200	11-29-99	2	3	2.34	24	0	8	35	34	16	9	3	9	44	.250	.295	.338	29.53	6.04	149
Bradt, Tyler	R-R	5-11	196	2-11-01	4	3	3.92	37	0	2	60	44	30	26	1	28	71	.212	.313	.269	29.10	11.48	244
Cuenca, Angel	R-R	6-1	160	7-10-01	0	1	10.80	2	0	0	3	8	4	4	0	3	3	.500	.579	.625	15.79	15.79	19
Garcia, Benito	R-R	6-0	165	3-10-00	0	1	3.38	8	0	1	13	15	6	5	2	1	9	.268	.281	.464	15.52	1.72	58
Garcia, Roy	R-R	6-0	190	8-28-00	4	1	4.41	31	0	1	51	48	29	25	6	25	59	.241	.341	.377	25.65	10.87	230
Hansen, Pete	R-L	6-2	205	7-28-00	5	7	3.86	24	24	0	128	138	59	55	10	41	134	.275	.341	.388	24.14	7.39	555
Hayes, Hunter	R-R	6-1	185	8-5-00	1	2	6.89	11	0	0	16	19	14	12	1	6	20	.297	.366	.422	28.17	8.45	71
Henderson, Ixan	L-L	6-2	180	1-29-02	2	2	2.90	6	6	0	31	33	11	10	3	14	26	.284	.368	.414	19.55	10.53	133
Heredia, Nathanael	L-L	6-3	190	9-10-00	2	2	2.36	21	0	4	27	17	9	7	0	23	27	.183	.361	.237	21.95	18.70	123
Hjerpe, Cooper	L-L	6-3	200	3-16-01	0	3	3.35	11	11	0	38	25	14	14	3	20	56	.189	.321	.288	35.22	12.58	159
Jacobson, Tanner	R-R	6-1	190	1-24-00	3	10	4.08	40	0	5	64	51	33	29	9	33	75	.222	.333	.365	27.17	11.96	276
King, Joseph	R-R	6-1	194	2-23-01	0	0	2.51	9	0	4	14	9	4	4	1	2	18	.176	.208	.255	33.96	3.77	53
Linarez, Carlos	R-R	6-0	170	10-24-01	0	0	0.00	1	0	0	1	1	0	0	0	0	0	.250	.250	.500	0.00	0.00	4
Mathews, Quinn	L-L	6-4	192	10-4-00	3	1	2.68	7	7	0	44	24	14	13	2	9	58	.160	.228	.253	34.73	5.39	167
Mautz, Brycen	L-L	6-3	190	7-17-01	3	13	5.18	24	24	0	122	130	75	70	20	47	128	.270	.346	.450	23.79	8.74	538
Mills, Zane	R-R	6-4	220	7-4-00	4	0	3.35	21	0	1	40	38	17	15	5	19	47	.247	.333	.377	27.01	10.92	174
Paniagua, Inohan	R-R	6-1	148	2-6-00	7	9	3.82	25	20	0	115	92	54	49	11	50	123	.220	.327	.356	25.00	10.16	492
Pereira, Wilfredo	R-R	6-0	197	4-26-99	1	0	2.29	8	2	0	20	12	5	5	0	10	21	.176	.278	.250	25.93	12.35	81
Rincon, Hancel	R-R	6-2	160	4-28-02	9	7	3.80	24	24	0	133	126	58	56	13	48	105	.252	.322	.412	18.78	8.59	559
Rodriguez, Dionys	L-R	6-0	188	9-3-00	3	1	2.32	33	0	3	50	33	18	13	4	21	52	.182	.282	.282	24.64	9.95	211
Rodriguez, Gustavo J.	R-R	6-3	160	1-8-01	0	1	4.76	16	0	1	23	28	14	12	0	10	26	.289	.358	.371	23.85	9.17	109
Saladin, Darlin	R-R	5-11	150	12-28-02	6	3	3.43	12	11	0	63	59	24	24	3	16	72	.249	.306	.346	27.91	6.20	258
Winquest, Cade	R-R	6-2	205	4-30-00	0	2	3.10	9	2	1	29	19	10	10	1	18	28	.186	.323	.235	22.58	14.52	124

Fielding

Catcher	PCT	G	PO	A	E	DP	PB
Adkison	.990	10	98	3	1	1	1
Bernal	.991	78	714	61	7	4	4
Hernandez	.988	8	79	3	1	0	0
Linarez	1.000	24	191	17	0	1	0
Tarlow	.994	20	160	16	1	1	0

First Base	PCT	G	PO	A	E	DP
Curialle	.950	6	34	4	2	4
Jobert	.977	20	126	4	3	12
Linarez	1.000	2	3	0	0	0
Rodriguez	1.000	3	18	1	0	1
Salazar	.989	31	175	9	2	19
Sullivan	.979	37	210	20	5	22
Tovalin	.993	44	282	20	2	24

Second Base	PCT	G	PO	A	E	DP
Encarnacion	.965	14	33	22	2	9
Harris	.974	29	58	55	3	9
Moore	1.000	5	10	17	0	6
Moquete	.941	18	29	35	4	8
Richardson	.980	59	100	146	5	30
Villarroel	.971	10	12	21	1	3

Third Base	PCT	G	PO	A	E	DP
Curialle	.921	66	35	70	9	5
Encarnacion	.900	10	3	6	1	0
Harris	.944	14	9	25	2	4
Paige	.955	11	11	10	1	2
Tovalin	.857	14	9	15	4	2
Villarroel	.886	24	17	22	5	3

Shortstop	PCT	G	PO	A	E	DP
Encarnacion	1.000	1	1	4	0	0
Harris	.946	11	15	20	2	3
Moore	.982	103	156	231	7	43
Richardson	1.000	1	1	2	0	1
Villarroel	.919	17	26	31	5	16

Outfield	PCT	G	PO	A	E	DP
Baez	.973	53	104	3	3	1
Cho	.995	104	206	2	1	1
Davis	.968	30	58	2	2	0
Iadisernia	.979	92	141	2	3	0
Kretzschmar	1.000	12	19	0	0	0
Levenson	.991	57	105	2	1	0
Moquete	.975	23	38	1	1	0
Rotondo	.978	40	87	3	2	0

PALM BEACH CARDINALS — *LOW-A*

FLORIDA STATE LEAGUE

Batting	B-T	Ht.	Wt.	DOB	AVG	OBP	SLG	G	PA	AB	R	H	2B	3B	HR	RBI	BB	HBP	SH	SF	SO	SB	CS	BB%	SO%
Adkison, Chase	R-R	6-0	205	6-5-00	.269	.368	.377	51	194	167	19	45	7	1	3	23	21	5	1	0	37	1	1	10.82	19.07
Baez, Joshua	R-R	6-3	220	6-28-03	.340	.459	.500	15	61	50	8	17	5	0	1	11	8	3	0	0	17	10	0	13.11	27.87
Campos, Ryan	L-R	5-9	180	10-16-02	.319	.396	.407	26	106	91	17	29	8	0	0	16	13	0	0	2	13	0	1	12.26	12.26
Caraballo, Heriberto	R-R	5-8	191	2-18-05	.045	.125	.091	7	24	22	1	1	1	0	0	1	2	0	0	0	9	0	0	8.33	37.50
Cordoba, Jose	R-R	5-11	165	1-3-03	.232	.293	.351	91	371	336	37	78	19	3	5	46	24	6	2	2	69	16	4	6.47	18.60
Davis, Chase	L-L	6-1	216	12-5-01	.232	.337	.401	74	315	267	39	62	21	0	8	48	40	4	0	4	79	5	1	12.70	25.08
Encarnacion, Anyelo	R-R	5-11	164	1-2-04	.215	.317	.282	52	209	181	34	39	6	0	2	18	24	3	1	0	54	7	3	11.48	25.84
Espinoza, Lizandro	R-R	5-7	158	11-20-02	.201	.302	.314	102	354	303	52	61	10	3	6	38	37	8	2	3	97	16	4	10.45	27.40
Friedrick, Ross	L-R	6-4	230	11-26-00	.199	.277	.292	79	307	271	19	54	8	1	5	45	26	5	0	5	80	0	0	8.47	26.06
Gazdar, Jon Jon	R-R	5-11	180	3-3-02	.262	.357	.344	19	71	61	12	16	3	1	0	8	7	2	1	0	5	2	1	9.86	7.04
Grant, Adari	R-R	5-8	163	1-2-04	.152	.250	.212	37	112	99	18	15	3	0	1	7	8	5	0	0	38	6	3	7.14	33.93
Hernandez, Maikel	B-R	6-0	163	2-20-03	.167	.221	.194	22	78	72	4	12	2	0	0	4	4	1	1	0	20	0	0	5.13	25.64
Hernandez, Sammy	R-R	5-9	185	6-1-04	.264	.372	.363	78	350	295	43	78	19	2	2	40	38	14	1	2	60	3	2	10.86	17.14
Honeyman, Travis	R-R	6-2	190	10-2-01	.321	.367	.446	14	60	56	13	18	7	0	0	1	3	1	0	0	8	1	1	5.00	13.33
Jobert, Brayden	L-R	6-1	215	11-14-00	.184	.320	.320	77	301	244	36	45	8	2	7	32	38	13	0	5	81	13	3	12.62	26.91
Kretzschmar, Kade	L-R	6-2	205	6-9-00	.273	.381	.369	74	312	260	40	71	11	4	2	34	39	9	0	4	56	6	3	12.50	17.95
Kross, Josh	B-R	6-2	200	2-2-03	.216	.383	.311	23	94	74	11	16	5	1	0	11	15	5	0	0	10	0	0	15.96	10.64
Loaiza, Alejandro	R-R	5-11	163	12-23-03	.250	.308	.250	4	13	12	1	3	0	0	0	0	1	0	0	0	5	0	0	7.69	38.46
Madron, Bryce	L-L	5-8	175	7-1-01	.233	.367	.260	22	90	73	19	17	2	0	0	8	16	0	0	1	14	0	2	17.78	15.56
Martin, Christian	L-R	5-10	170	1-16-03	.206	.432	.221	23	96	68	18	14	1	0	0	5	24	3	1	0	13	5	0	25.00	13.54
McGee, Cade	R-R	6-1	195	1-12-03	.197	.289	.258	20	77	66	8	13	1	0	1	8	9	0	1	1	19	1	1	11.69	24.68
Mendlinger, Noah	L-R	5-9	180	8-9-00	.231	.286	.231	4	14	13	0	3	0	0	0	1	1	0	0	0	2	0	0	7.14	14.29
Paige, Trey	L-R	6-0	215	11-9-00	.262	.358	.372	74	330	282	52	74	15	5	2	27	41	2	2	2	78	5	2	12.42	23.64
Petrutz, Ian	L-L	6-0	205	8-26-02	.344	.482	.433	28	115	90	21	31	6	1	0	20	17	7	1	0	10	5	1	14.78	8.70
Pino, Luis	R-R	5-10	175	2-7-04	.185	.228	.278	17	58	54	7	10	2	0	1	2	3	0	0	0	23	0	0	5.17	39.66
Richardson, Tre	R-R	5-10	165	12-2-01	.108	.263	.185	25	81	65	8	7	1	2	0	6	11	3	1	1	25	2	2	13.58	30.86
Salazar, Johnfrank	R-R	6-1	159	8-5-03	.285	.373	.375	57	229	200	25	57	15	0	1	22	24	4	1	0	29	0	1	10.48	12.66
Suarez, Jose	R-R	6-2	200	8-9-04	.252	.312	.384	41	173	159	21	40	8	2	3	24	12	2	0	0	46	5	3	6.94	26.59
Villarroel, Miguel	R-R	6-0	165	12-23-01	.333	.372	.427	66	285	267	38	89	14	4	1	35	15	2	0	1	60	25	1	5.26	21.05
Wetherholt, JJ	L-R	5-10	190	9-10-02	.295	.405	.400	29	126	105	18	31	5	0	2	20	16	4	0	1	15	2	0	12.70	11.90

Pitching	B-T	Ht.	Wt.	DOB	W	L	ERA	G	GS	SV	IP	Hits	Runs	ER	HR	BB	SO	AVG	OBP	SLG	SO%	BB%	BF
Arias, Benjamin	R-R	6-5	195	11-5-01	6	1	3.21	20	0	2	48	38	18	17	3	9	49	.216	.268	.341	25.79	4.74	190
Calderon, Augusto	R-R	6-0	190	10-6-00	1	6	4.87	33	1	1	61	49	38	33	6	25	68	.218	.314	.369	25.95	9.54	262
Clemente, Randel	R-R	6-3	173	11-17-01	4	2	9.82	19	0	0	22	14	25	24	2	30	37	.179	.407	.282	34.26	27.78	108
Cuenca, Angel	R-R	6-1	160	7-10-01	4	2	3.33	33	0	0	49	49	25	18	3	16	40	.255	.318	.349	18.96	7.58	211
Davila, Jose	R-R	6-3	177	11-9-02	6	5	3.54	22	21	0	109	98	47	43	0	46	113	.244	.334	.306	24.51	9.98	461
Gastelum, Luis	R-R	6-2	168	9-27-01	5	2	2.81	30	0	8	48	46	24	15	4	11	70	.243	.287	.386	34.48	5.42	203
Giulianelli, Ettore	R-R	6-3	190	3-30-03	0	0	3.96	20	0	0	25	17	12	11	2	31	39	.193	.413	.318	32.23	25.62	121
Gomez, Henry	R-R	6-1	163	10-17-01	6	3	3.03	39	0	12	62	61	26	21	1	26	44	.258	.353	.322	15.88	9.39	277
Hayes, Hunter	R-R	6-1	185	8-5-00	2	1	1.50	15	0	0	36	32	6	6	1	11	31	.246	.313	.308	21.53	7.64	144
Henderson, Ixan	L-L	6-2	180	1-29-02	6	2	2.10	16	11	1	73	51	23	17	2	27	79	.190	.274	.276	26.33	9.00	300
Herrera, Yordy	L-L	6-2	150	12-2-04	0	0	6.75	2	0	0	3	0	2	2	0	5	3	.000	.429	.000	21.43	35.71	14
Kublick, Hunter	R-R	6-4	200	7-1-03	6	2	4.22	15	7	0	49	56	31	23	1	26	42	.286	.369	.388	18.67	11.56	225
Lin, Chen-Wei	R-R	6-7	188	11-22-01	10	5	2.79	22	22	0	116	85	41	36	3	36	123	.204	.281	.276	26.62	7.79	462
Mathews, Quinn	L-L	6-4	192	10-4-00	3	1	1.47	6	6	0	31	14	6	5	2	11	52	.133	.222	.200	44.44	9.40	117
Naughton, Packy	R-L	6-2	195	4-16-96	0	0	0.00	4	0	0	5	3	0	0	0	0	6	.176	.176	.235	35.29	0.00	17
Ortega, Wilmer	R-R	6-1	169	4-4-01	0	0	18.00	1	0	0	1	2	2	2	1	0	3	.400	.400	1.000	60.00	0.00	5
Robberse, Sem	R-R	6-1	185	10-12-01	0	1	1.50	3	3	0	6	9	2	1	0	1	4	.375	.400	.458	16.00	4.00	25
Roby, Tekoah	R-R	6-1	185	9-18-01	0	1	5.40	3	3	0	5	4	3	3	0	3	6	.211	.318	.263	27.27	13.64	22
Rodriguez, Gustavo J.	R-R	6-3	160	1-8-01	0	1	3.38	6	0	3	11	10	4	4	1	4	9	.270	.318	.432	20.45	9.09	44
Rodriguez, Wilking	R-R	6-1	180	3-2-90	0	1	13.50	1	1	0	1	0	1	1	0	0	2	.000	.333	.000	66.67	0.00	3
Saladin, Darlin	R-R	5-11	150	12-28-02	4	0	1.95	11	10	0	60	44	14	13	1	17	62	.207	.268	.268	26.84	7.36	231
Salas, Gerado	R-R	6-0	189	2-14-03	9	5	2.62	22	22	0	113	93	43	33	9	25	119	.222	.274	.344	26.21	5.51	454

Savacool, Jason	R-R	6-1	210	5-21-02	4	4	3.62	22	17	0	97	80	44	39	7	48	81	.231	.330	.338	20.20	11.97	401
Sequera, Leonel	R-R	6-0	190	8-6-05	1	0	2.13	7	6	0	38	30	11	9	0	14	25	.217	.292	.254	16.23	9.09	154
Showalter, Zack	R-R	6-2	195	1-23-04	1	2	2.62	24	0	8	34	25	15	10	0	18	59	.203	.340	.228	38.56	11.76	153
Sparks, Nolan	R-R	5-10	195	8-12-02	3	0	2.35	10	0	1	15	9	8	4	1	7	18	.167	.262	.278	29.51	11.48	61
Watson, Michael	L-L	6-2	190	6-18-02	0	0	0.68	11	0	1	13	9	1	1	0	5	24	.200	.275	.244	47.06	9.80	51
Willis, Alec	R-R	6-5	220	3-30-03	0	0	0.00	2	0	0	3	1	0	0	0	2	4	.111	.273	.111	36.36	18.18	11
Ynfante, Nelfy	R-R	6-3	168	2-1-05	2	0	2.70	8	0	1	13	12	4	4	1	7	12	.231	.328	.327	19.67	11.48	61

Fielding

Catcher	PCT	G	PO	A	E	DP	PB
Adkison	.991	31	290	26	3	2	2
Campos	.983	20	163	9	3	1	1
Caraballo	.986	7	63	5	1	0	0
Grant	1.000	1	3	0	0	0	0
Hernandez	.984	22	170	15	3	1	2
Hernandez	.989	56	510	43	6	1	4
Loaiza	1.000	1	17	2	0	0	0

First Base	PCT	G	PO	A	E	DP
Friedrick	.991	70	495	34	5	47
Jobert	.959	7	44	3	2	4
Kross	.987	21	138	9	2	16
Loaiza	1.000	2	11	0	0	0
Salazar	.973	39	274	16	8	22

Second Base	PCT	G	PO	A	E	DP
Encarnacion	.982	24	34	73	2	17
Espinoza	1.000	4	8	8	0	0
Gazdar	1.000	3	2	7	0	1
Grant	.929	25	49	42	7	7
Martin	.990	23	36	66	1	17
Mendlinger	1.000	1	1	7	0	0
Paige	.933	5	6	8	1	1
Richardson	.963	22	34	45	3	8
Villarroel	.958	30	46	69	5	19

Third Base	PCT	G	PO	A	E	DP
Encarnacion	1.000	10	5	10	0	0
Gazdar	.968	15	10	20	1	3
McGee	.952	19	14	26	2	4
Paige	.948	67	45	118	9	7
Salazar	.955	19	11	31	2	3
Villarroel	.833	6	2	3	1	0

Shortstop	PCT	G	PO	A	E	DP
Encarnacion	1.000	20	28	48	0	8
Espinoza	.958	64	104	147	11	37
Grant	.000	1	0	0	0	0
Villarroel	.963	32	32	71	4	15
Wetherholt	.976	24	33	50	2	10

Outfield	PCT	G	PO	A	E	DP
Baez	.947	9	18	0	1	0
Cordoba	.982	83	155	8	3	2
Davis	.993	71	135	2	1	0
Espinoza	.985	33	64	2	1	0
Jobert	.970	68	119	9	4	0
Kretzschmar	.987	59	74	2	1	1
Madron	1.000	20	40	0	0	0
Mendlinger	1.000	2	2	0	0	0
Petrutz	1.000	24	35	0	0	0
Pino	1.000	17	24	1	0	1
Suarez	.980	31	46	2	1	1

FCL CARDINALS — *ROOKIE*

FLORIDA COMPLEX LEAGUE

Batting	B-T	Ht.	Wt.	DOB	AVG	OBP	SLG	G	PA	AB	R	H	2B	3B	HR	RBI	BB	HBP	SH	SF	SO	SB	CS	BB%	SO%
Batista, Arfeni	R-R	6-0	161	9-4-04	.186	.234	.310	39	137	129	14	24	4	0	4	12	5	3	0	0	60	4	1	3.65	43.80
Cabrera, Romtres	R-R	6-0	182	9-13-03	.129	.222	.129	12	36	31	4	4	0	0	0	1	4	0	0	1	16	2	1	11.11	44.44
Caraballo, Heriberto	R-R	5-8	191	2-18-05	.149	.269	.219	36	134	114	16	17	2	0	2	8	13	6	0	1	27	0	0	9.70	20.15
De La Rosa, Samil	R-R	5-8	175	9-24-03	.185	.288	.269	34	126	108	17	20	3	0	2	11	12	4	1	1	26	9	3	9.52	20.63
Encarnacion, Anyelo	R-R	5-11	164	1-2-04	.255	.386	.468	14	57	47	10	12	1	0	3	7	10	0	0	0	23	4	0	17.54	40.35
Gomez, Moises	R-R	5-11	200	8-27-98	.000	.214	.000	4	14	11	1	0	0	0	0	0	2	1	0	0	4	0	0	14.29	28.57
Guerrero, Justin	R-R	6-1	195	5-20-03	.133	.221	.183	21	68	60	2	8	0	0	1	8	5	2	0	1	19	0	0	7.35	27.94
Guerrero, Yancel	R-R	6-1	169	4-16-04	.254	.354	.455	42	158	134	26	34	3	3	6	27	11	11	0	2	56	8	0	6.96	35.44
Guzman, Raul	R-R	5-11	180	9-14-02	.164	.292	.180	25	72	61	6	10	1	0	0	4	9	2	0	0	31	1	0	12.50	43.06
Honeyman, Travis	R-R	6-2	190	10-2-01	.412	.545	.647	6	22	17	4	7	4	0	0	2	5	0	0	0	3	1	1	22.73	13.64
Loaiza, Alejandro	R-R	5-11	163	12-23-03	.103	.205	.221	26	78	68	7	7	0	1	2	9	6	3	0	1	29	1	0	7.69	37.18
Lopez, Chris	R-R	5-9	175	6-28-05	.097	.121	.129	12	33	31	2	3	1	0	0	3	1	0	0	1	12	0	0	3.03	36.36
Mejia, Jonathan	B-R	5-11	185	4-12-05	.299	.395	.425	49	205	174	35	52	9	2	3	20	25	4	0	2	52	18	4	12.20	25.37
Pena, Yordalin	R-R	6-3	177	9-17-04	.242	.356	.358	47	194	165	24	40	9	2	2	18	26	3	0	0	42	11	5	13.40	21.65
Pino, Luis	R-R	5-10	175	2-7-04	.333	.444	.556	23	90	72	13	24	7	0	3	17	12	4	0	2	22	3	1	13.33	24.44
Ramos, Yaisel	R-R	6-4	185	2-20-03	.140	.287	.150	36	123	100	12	14	1	0	0	7	17	4	1	1	47	7	1	13.82	38.21
Rodriguez, Luis	R-R	6-1	210	10-7-04	.235	.316	.294	6	19	17	5	4	1	0	0	3	2	0	0	0	5	0	0	10.53	26.32
Suarez, Jose	R-R	6-2	200	8-9-04	.271	.338	.429	37	154	140	23	38	8	1	4	18	11	3	0	0	43	3	2	7.14	27.92
Taveras, Felix	L-R	6-1	186	3-8-03	.184	.301	.320	40	147	125	17	23	2	3	3	15	21	0	0	0	46	7	1	14.29	31.29
Vargas, Miguel	L-L	6-0	176	3-14-04	.161	.270	.242	23	74	62	5	10	3	1	0	7	10	0	0	2	24	3	1	13.51	32.43

Pitching	B-T	Ht.	Wt.	DOB	W	L	ERA	G	GS	SV	IP	Hits	Runs	ER	HR	BB	SO	AVG	OBP	SLG	SO%	BB%	BF
Batista, Yadiel	L-L	6-3	170	4-17-04	0	5	3.88	11	10	0	46	46	22	20	4	16	45	.257	.320	.374	22.84	8.12	197
Beltre, Alexander	R-L	6-1	169	11-5-02	1	0	4.63	12	0	0	12	13	8	6	1	5	12	.289	.389	.378	22.22	9.26	54
Clemente, Randel	R-R	6-3	173	11-17-01	2	0	3.08	20	0	0	26	16	10	9	0	20	43	.178	.327	.222	38.05	17.70	113
Cuello, Antoni	R-R	6-5	186	11-7-02	0	1	4.97	19	0	0	29	31	18	16	3	18	24	.282	.394	.427	18.05	13.53	133
Fabian, Samuel	R-R	6-4	177	5-21-03	1	1	1.51	21	0	3	36	30	7	6	3	11	43	.226	.293	.323	29.05	7.43	148
Galvez, Jovi	R-R	6-2	223	7-5-04	0	3	9.49	11	0	1	12	9	20	13	0	22	9	.188	.506	.229	11.39	27.85	79
Gastelum, Luis	R-R	6-2	168	9-27-01	0	0	0.00	2	0	0	3	0	0	0	0	0	3	.000	.000	.000	33.33	0.00	9
Harrison, Charles	R-R	6-1	191	12-23-01	0	2	9.00	3	0	0	3	6	4	3	0	3	7	.400	.500	.533	38.89	16.67	18
Hayes, Hunter	R-R	6-1	185	8-5-00	0	0	1.35	3	0	1	7	6	2	1	0	2	7	.240	.321	.400	25.00	7.14	28
Heredia, Roblin	L-R	6-0	200	7-22-02	0	0	12.46	5	0	0	4	8	8	6	0	4	5	.364	.462	.682	19.23	15.38	26
Herrera, Yordy	L-L	6-2	150	12-2-04	6	1	2.84	16	0	0	32	23	11	10	2	18	59	.202	.316	.298	44.03	13.43	134
Kublick, Hunter	R-R	6-4	200	7-1-03	0	1	2.57	2	2	0	7	5	2	2	1	0	11	.208	.208	.333	45.83	0.00	24
Martinez, Miguel	R-R	6-0	143	1-26-03	1	0	0.00	5	0	0	5	0	1	0	0	3	1	.000	.250	.000	4.76	14.29	21
Menes, Ruben	R-R	6-3	185	4-17-02	0	1	3.72	5	4	0	19	14	9	8	2	10	19	.194	.293	.361	23.17	12.20	82
Naughton, Packy	R-L	6-2	195	4-16-96	0	0	3.86	4	4	0	5	6	3	2	0	1	9	.316	.333	.421	42.86	4.76	21
Oliver, Ronny	R-R	6-2	155	1-1-04	2	4	5.27	12	8	0	41	31	28	24	0	30	36	.204	.353	.296	19.25	16.04	187
Ortega, Wilmer	R-R	6-1	169	4-4-01	1	2	5.54	11	0	0	13	14	10	8	2	4	15	.280	.327	.520	27.27	7.27	55
Sequera, Leonel	R-R	6-0	190	8-6-05	1	5	5.27	12	12	0	41	49	34	24	4	14	43	.292	.358	.429	22.63	7.37	190
Severino, Juan	R-R	6-0	165	6-6-04	0	2	6.25	18	2	0	32	34	23	22	2	22	34	.274	.397	.427	22.52	14.57	151
Villanueva, Victor	R-R	6-1	170	3-26-01	1	3	5.59	11	0	0	10	8	10	6	0	5	9	.195	.283	.268	19.57	10.87	46
Yanez, Omar	R-R	6-2	190	12-7-02	0	0	1.93	10	0	0	9	6	2	2	0	10	14	.182	.386	.212	31.82	22.73	44
Ynfante, Nelfy	R-R	6-3	168	2-1-05	4	2	3.29	13	11	0	52	51	23	19	2	17	62	.254	.311	.388	28.31	7.76	219

Fielding

C: Caraballo 34, Loaiza 15, Lopez 11, Guerrero 3, Rodriguez 1. **1B:** Vargas 20, Guerrero 13, Guzman 11, Loaiza 11, Guerrero 7, Caraballo 4. **2B:** Mejia 35, De La Rosa 16, Guzman 5, Encarnacion 3, Guerrero 1, Batista 1, Vargas 1. **3B:** Guerrero 33, Batista 12, Guzman 10, De La Rosa 6, Encarnacion 3, Loaiza 1. **SS:** Batista 27, Mejia 16, Encarnacion 9, Guerrero 7, Guzman 1. **LF:** Taveras 33, Ramos 9, Pino 7, Pena 6, Cabrera 3. CF: Pena 36, Ramos 18, Pino **1.** RF: Suarez 32, Pino 13, Ramos 8, Gomez 3, De La Rosa 2, Pena 1.

DSL CARDINALS — ROOKIE

DOMINICAN SUMMER LEAGUE

Batting	B-T	Ht.	Wt.	DOB	AVG	OBP	SLG	G	PA	AB	R	H	2B	3B	HR	RBI	BB	HBP	SH	SF	SO	SB	CS	BB%	SO%
Amoroso, Brayan	R-R	6-2	198	7-7-07	.227	.325	.295	36	151	132	17	30	6	0	1	21	17	2	0	0	47	1	0	11.26	31.13
Arthur, Andru	L-L	6-1	176	11-1-05	.261	.423	.353	41	156	119	28	31	5	0	2	13	23	12	0	2	36	11	4	14.74	23.08
Asprilla, Paulo	R-R	5-8	177	4-28-06	.250	.368	.266	21	77	64	10	16	1	0	0	4	11	1	1	0	19	0	0	14.29	24.68
Cabrera, Juan Pablo	R-R	5-11	185	11-11-06	.234	.380	.266	21	79	64	16	15	0	1	0	8	14	1	0	0	14	0	0	17.72	17.72
Guribe, Edward	R-R	6-1	195	11-16-06	.282	.325	.465	19	77	71	11	20	5	1	2	16	4	1	0	1	23	2	0	5.19	29.87
Junco, Yoerny	B-R	5-9	165	11-8-04	.267	.351	.366	35	151	131	22	35	6	2	1	19	16	2	0	2	30	7	5	10.60	19.87
Lebron, Cristofer	R-R	6-2	170	3-20-07	.206	.286	.258	30	112	97	13	20	2	0	1	13	9	3	0	3	29	3	3	8.04	25.89
Lucena, Yaxson	L-R	6-0	190	7-23-07	.246	.338	.333	33	130	114	17	28	4	0	2	15	13	3	0	0	26	3	0	10.00	20.00
Padilla, Yairo	B-R	6-0	170	6-28-07	.287	.391	.404	35	162	136	33	39	5	4	1	17	17	7	1	1	29	22	5	10.49	17.90
Rodriguez, Rainiel	R-R	5-10	197	1-4-07	.345	.462	.683	41	184	142	35	49	12	3	10	38	30	6	0	6	25	1	1	16.30	13.59
Rojas, Daniel	R-R	5-8	151	11-16-05	.248	.292	.338	39	154	145	15	36	2	4	1	11	8	1	0	0	33	5	5	5.19	21.43
Roquez, Fernando	L-R	6-2	181	9-1-05	.148	.354	.306	36	144	108	16	16	4	2	3	12	33	2	0	1	55	1	3	22.92	38.19
Saez, Christian	L-R	6-2	185	2-20-07	.176	.317	.261	35	145	119	16	21	5	1	1	10	22	3	0	1	44	2	1	15.17	30.34
Taveras, Bracewell	B-R	6-0	182	6-5-06	.327	.351	.421	27	114	107	12	35	2	1	2	22	5	0	0	2	22	2	0	4.39	19.30
Velasquez, Facundo	B-R	6-2	179	1-16-06	.266	.393	.475	47	196	158	36	42	7	4	6	33	28	7	0	3	68	5	3	14.29	34.69

Pitching	B-T	Ht.	Wt.	DOB	W	L	ERA	G	GS	SV	IP	Hits	Runs	ER	HR	BB	SO	AVG	OBP	SLG	SO%	BB%	BF
Baez, Jarol	R-R	6-1	200	10-21-05	2	0	2.05	15	0	0	22	18	8	5	1	21	16	.243	.423	.324	16.49	21.65	97
Bolivar, Andrew	R-R	6-1	170	10-20-05	0	0	4.22	12	10	0	43	32	22	20	1	26	53	.211	.337	.250	28.65	14.05	185
Carrera, Emisael	R-R	6-0	185	2-22-06	0	0	21.60	2	0	0	2	4	4	4	1	3	2	.444	.583	1.000	16.67	25.00	12
Chinchilla, Gabriel	R-R	6-3	163	10-20-06	1	1	1.57	6	4	0	23	12	5	4	0	10	16	.150	.261	.163	17.39	10.87	92
Cruz, Xavier	R-R	6-3	153	9-4-05	3	1	4.11	10	0	0	15	19	8	7	1	4	10	.311	.364	.410	15.15	6.06	66
Franco, Branneli	R-R	6-3	187	2-5-07	0	3	6.16	12	12	0	38	38	30	26	5	24	37	.253	.378	.427	20.56	13.33	180
Garcia, Jesus	S-R	5-11	141	1-25-06	1	2	5.24	18	0	0	34	40	28	20	0	13	38	.290	.350	.348	23.90	8.18	159
Gonzalez, Oliver	R-R	6-4	200	10-26-06	2	0	3.86	8	5	0	23	23	13	10	3	8	29	.261	.327	.432	29.29	8.08	99
Hernandez, Justin	R-R	6-4	180	4-22-05	0	1	4.91	10	0	0	11	9	6	6	0	17	21	.225	.467	.275	34.43	27.87	61
Lopez, Reiner	R-R	6-8	196	4-11-06	0	0	8.49	12	1	0	12	15	14	11	0	10	10	.294	.463	.373	14.93	14.93	67
Mack, Bernard	L-L	6-3	160	10-24-05	2	1	3.13	17	0	3	23	15	10	8	0	17	21	.190	.337	.203	21.43	17.35	98
Martinez, Guanchi	R-R	6-0	185	8-17-06	2	4	5.09	15	2	3	23	27	18	13	0	9	13	.300	.398	.411	11.50	7.96	113
Moran, Jefferson	R-R	6-1	155	6-4-04	3	1	4.54	9	7	0	34	38	19	17	3	14	32	.290	.365	.397	21.62	9.46	148
Paulino, Brailyn	R-R	6-0	185	4-26-06	1	2	6.38	15	1	1	24	19	20	17	1	29	22	.221	.455	.302	17.89	23.58	123
Perez, Kener	R-R	6-2	180	10-3-04	1	4	8.31	7	0	0	13	18	16	12	1	8	12	.346	.485	.462	16.90	11.27	71
Ramirez, Keiverson	R-R	6-1	170	4-5-06	4	2	1.62	11	11	0	50	33	12	9	1	12	48	.183	.242	.217	24.62	6.15	195
Reyes, Alan	R-R	5-9	176	10-25-03	1	2	3.33	16	0	5	27	23	16	10	1	11	28	.230	.316	.350	24.56	9.65	114
Suriel, Jose	R-R	6-3	240	10-9-04	2	1	4.15	9	0	0	13	6	8	6	0	14	19	.146	.367	.171	31.67	23.33	60
Vargas, Giovanni	R-R	6-1	179	3-3-06	1	2	6.75	13	0	1	16	15	12	12	0	17	17	.246	.410	.295	21.79	21.79	78

Fielding

C: Rodriguez 26, Asprilla 16, Cabrera 12. **1B:** Saez 34, Roquez 19, Amoroso 2. **2B:** Lebron 24, Taveras 23, Junco 9. **3B:** Junco 24, Rojas 20, Guribe 8, Lebron 4. **SS:** Padilla 35, Rojas 20. **LF:** Arthur 25, Lucena 21, Roquez 9. **CF:** Velasquez 41, Arthur 15. **RF:** Amoroso 33, Lucena 11, Roquez 9.

San Diego Padres

SEASON SYNOPSIS: The Padres improved by 11 wins over 2023, unearthed some new heroes and swept the Braves in a wild-card series before falling to the rival Dodgers in the Division Series.

HIGH POINT: Game Three of the DS was the high-water mark for the Padres, as they had split the first two games in Los Angeles, then pounded Walker Buehler for six runs in the second inning, then held on for a 6-5 victory. San Diego's best month of the season had been September, they'd won eight of 13 from the Dodgers in the regular season and were a win away from reaching the NLCS for the second time in three seasons.

LOW POINT: San Diego didn't score for the last 24 innings of the DS. The Padres' offense had sagged throughout September, when they scored 100 runs in a 16-8 month, a half-run per game below their season average. But back-to-back shutouts for a lineup that led the NL in hits (but ranked just sixth in runs) was dispiriting.

NOTABLE ROOKIES: Jackson Merrill shifted from shortstop to center field—a position he'd not played as a pro—in spring training. He won the job, becoming the third player in the last half-century to start Opening Day in center before his 21st birthday (joining Ken Griffey Jr. and Andruw Jones). Then he thrived, leading the Padres in games (156), bWAR (4.4), doubles (31) and slugging in a .292/.326/.500 season with 24 homers and 16 stolen bases. He finished second to Pirates righthander Paul Skenes for the National League's Rookie of the Year award. Righty Randy Vasquez, acquired in the Soto trade from the Yankees, provided 20 starts and 98 innings, going 4-7, 4.87.

KEY TRANSACTIONS: The Soto trade also netted Michael King, who thrived in his first year as a full-time starter, going 13-9, 2.95 with 201 strikeouts in 174 innings, then won two playoff starts. A spring-training trade of prospects—including Drew Thorpe, who was acquire with King in the Soto trade—to the White Sox added Dylan Cease to front the rotation. Cease led San Diego in starts (33), innings (189) and strikeouts (224) while going 14-11, 3.47, but he was hit hard on short rest in Game Four of the Division Series. GM AJ Preller was his usual aggressive self at the deadline, reshaping the club's bullpen by acquiring lefty Tanner Scott and righty Jason Adam and adding lefty veteran Martin Perez to patch the back of the rotation.

OPENING DAY PAYROLL: $161,937,554 (14th)

PLAYERS OF THE YEAR

MAJOR LEAGUE

Michael King
RHP
13-9, 2.95 ERA
201 SO, 63 BB
Career-high 173 IP

MINOR LEAGUE

Leodalis De Vries
SS
(A)
.238/.361/.442
11 HR, 13 SB, 75 G

ORGANIZATION LEADERS

Batting		*Qualifiers
MAJORS		
* AVG	Luis Arraez	.318
* OPS	Jurickson Profar	.839
HR	Manny Machado	29
RBI	Manny Machado	105
MINORS		
* AVG	Tirso Ornelas, El Paso	.297
* OBP	Romeo Sanabria, L. Elsinore/S. Ant./F. Wayne	.462
* SLG	Eguy Rosario, El Paso	.531
* OPS	Eguy Rosario, El Paso	.892
R	Matthew Batten, El Paso	82
H	Tirso Ornelas, El Paso	144
TB	Tirso Ornelas, El Paso	241
2B	Romeo Sanabria, L. Elsinore/S. Ant./F. Wayne	30
3B	Clay Dungan, San Antonio/El Paso	8
3B	Nate Mondou, El Paso	8
HR	Tirso Ornelas, El Paso	23
RBI	Tirso Ornelas, El Paso	89
BB	Romeo Sanabria, L. Elsinore/S. Ant./F. Wayne	84
SO	Cole Cummings, San Antonio	173
SB	Homer Bush, Fort Wayne	43

Pitching		# Qualifiers
MAJORS		
W	Dylan Cease	14
# ERA	Michael King	2.95
SO	Dylan Cease	224
SV	Robert Suarez	36
MINORS		
W	Jared Kollar, San Antonio/El Paso	11
L	Austin Krob, San Antonio	11
# ERA	Henry Baez, F. Wayne/S. Antonio	2.99
G	Jayvien Sandridge, San Antonio/El Paso	52
GS	Gabe Mosser, El Paso	26
GS	Henry Baez, San Antonio/Fort Wayne	26
SV	Austin Davis, El Paso	14
IP	Gabe Mosser, El Paso	133
BB	Jagger Haynes, Fort Wayne	66
SO	Austin Krob, San Antonio	120
# AVG	Henry Baez, F. Wayne/S. Antonio	.212

2024 PERFORMANCE

General Manager: A.J. Preller. **Farm Director:** Ryley Westman. **Scouting Director:** Chris Kemp.

Class	Team	League	W	L	PCT	Finish	Manager
Majors	San Diego Padres	National	93	69	.574	4 (15)	Mike Shildt
Triple-A	El Paso Chihuahuas	Pacific Coast	64	86	.427	9 (10)	Pete Zamora
Double-A	San Antonio Missions	Texas	62	74	.456	7 (10)	Luke Montz
High-A	Fort Wayne TinCaps	Midwest	53	79	.402	12 (12)	Mike Daly
Low-A	Lake Elsinore Storm	California	71	58	.550	3 (8)	Lukas Ray
Rookie	ACL Padres	Arizona Complex	24	36	.400	14 (15)	Luis Mendez
Rookie	DSL Padres Brown	Dominican	15	41	.268	50 (51)	Diego Cedeno
Overall 2024 Minor League Record			**315**	**403**	**.439**	**29th (30)**	

ORGANIZATION STATISTICS

SAN DIEGO PADRES

NATIONAL LEAGUE

Batting	B-T	Ht.	Wt.	DOB	AVG	OBP	SLG	G	PA	AB	R	H	2B	3B	HR	RBI	BB	HBP	SH	SF	SO	SB	CS	BB%	SO%
Ahmed, Nick	R-R	6-2	201	3-15-90	.143	.143	.143	2	7	7	1	1	0	0	0	0	0	0	0	0	2	0	0	0.00	28.57
Arraez, Luis	L-R	5-10	175	4-9-97	.318	.346	.398	117	524	500	61	159	24	2	4	41	16	6	1	1	18	9	3	3.05	3.44
Azocar, Jose	R-R	5-11	181	5-11-96	.219	.269	.247	61	79	73	13	16	2	0	0	2	5	0	1	0	19	5	1	6.33	24.05
Batten, Matthew	R-R	5-11	180	6-22-95	.333	.333	1.000	1	3	3	0	1	0	1	0	0	0	0	0	0	0	0	0	0.00	0.00
Bogaerts, Xander	R-R	6-2	218	10-1-92	.264	.307	.381	111	463	428	50	113	15	1	11	44	28	1	0	6	79	13	3	6.05	17.06
Campusano, Luis	R-R	5-11	232	9-29-98	.227	.281	.361	91	299	277	37	63	13	0	8	40	20	1	0	1	41	0	0	6.69	13.71
Cronenworth, Jake	L-R	6-0	187	1-21-94	.241	.324	.390	155	656	577	72	139	29	3	17	83	61	11	1	3	118	5	2	9.30	17.99
Diaz, Elias	R-R	6-1	223	11-17-90	.190	.292	.429	12	24	21	1	4	2	0	1	3	3	0	0	0	5	0	0	12.50	20.83
Higashioka, Kyle	R-R	6-1	202	4-20-90	.220	.263	.476	84	263	246	29	54	10	1	17	45	15	0	1	1	74	2	0	5.70	28.14
Johnson, Bryce	B-R	6-1	195	10-27-95	.206	.286	.238	47	73	63	9	13	2	0	0	4	7	0	3	0	12	1	1	9.59	16.44
Kim, Ha-Seong	R-R	5-9	168	10-17-95	.233	.330	.370	121	470	403	60	94	16	3	11	47	58	2	4	3	77	22	5	12.34	16.38
Lockridge, Brandon	R-R	5-11	185	3-14-97	.167	.167	.417	12	12	12	4	2	0	0	1	1	0	0	0	0	4	2	0	0.00	33.33
Machado, Manny	R-R	6-3	218	7-6-92	.275	.325	.472	152	643	593	77	163	30	0	29	105	45	1	0	4	124	11	2	7.00	19.28
McCoy, Mason	R-R	5-11	185	3-31-95	.204	.278	.245	19	57	49	7	10	2	0	0	3	5	0	3	0	19	1	0	8.77	33.33
Merrill, Jackson	L-R	6-3	195	4-19-03	.292	.326	.500	156	593	554	77	162	31	6	24	90	29	1	4	5	101	16	3	4.89	17.03
Pauley, Graham	L-R	6-1	200	9-24-00	.125	.125	.313	13	32	32	4	4	0	0	2	5	0	0	0	0	15	0	0	0.00	46.88
Peralta, David	L-L	6-1	210	8-14-87	.267	.335	.415	91	260	236	35	63	11	0	8	28	22	2	0	0	54	2	0	8.46	20.77
Profar, Jurickson	B-R	6-0	184	2-20-93	.280	.380	.459	158	668	564	94	158	29	0	24	85	76	18	5	5	101	10	3	11.38	15.12
Rosario, Eguy	R-R	5-7	150	8-25-99	.245	.286	.528	30	57	53	5	13	6	0	3	6	2	1	1	0	20	0	0	3.51	35.09
Solano, Donovan	R-R	5-8	210	12-17-87	.286	.343	.417	96	309	283	31	81	13	0	8	35	22	3	0	1	65	2	1	7.12	21.04
Sullivan, Brett	L-R	6-1	195	2-22-94	.188	.235	.375	7	17	16	1	3	0	0	1	2	1	0	0	0	4	0	0	5.88	23.53
Tatis, Fernando	R-R	6-3	217	1-2-99	.276	.340	.492	102	438	398	64	110	21	1	21	49	32	7	0	1	96	11	3	7.31	21.92
Wade, Tyler	L-R	6-1	188	11-23-94	.217	.285	.239	90	156	138	28	30	3	0	0	8	11	2	4	0	29	8	1	7.05	18.59

Pitching	B-T	Ht.	Wt.	DOB	W	L	ERA	G	GS	SV	IP	Hits	Runs	ER	HR	BB	SO	AVG	OBP	SLG	SO%	BB%	BF
Adam, Jason	R-R	6-3	229	8-4-91	3	0	1.01	27	0	0	27	14	3	3	1	7	31	.152	.235	.228	30.39	6.86	102
Avila, Pedro	R-R	5-11	210	1-14-97	1	0	9.00	4	0	0	8	5	8	8	1	6	9	.192	.353	.462	25.71	17.14	35
Brito, Jhony	R-R	6-2	210	2-17-98	1	2	4.12	26	0	0	44	49	23	20	4	10	29	.283	.321	.387	15.68	5.41	185
Cease, Dylan	R-R	6-2	195	12-28-95	14	11	3.47	33	33	0	189	137	80	73	18	65	224	.200	.269	.332	29.40	8.53	762
Cosgrove, Tom	L-L	6-2	190	6-14-96	0	1	11.66	18	0	0	15	23	19	19	3	6	15	.354	.440	.523	19.74	7.89	76
Darvish, Yu	R-R	6-5	220	8-16-86	7	3	3.31	16	16	0	82	65	32	30	12	22	78	.217	.274	.387	23.56	6.65	331
Davis, Austin	L-L	6-4	235	2-3-93	0	0	9.00	7	0	0	7	6	8	7	0	5	6	.240	.406	.320	18.18	15.15	33
De Los Santos, Enyel	R-R	6-3	235	12-25-95	1	2	4.46	44	0	1	40	39	21	20	11	13	48	.250	.312	.538	28.24	7.65	170
Edwards, Carl	R-R	6-3	165	9-3-91	0	0	0.00	1	0	0	0	1	0	0	0	2	0	1.000	1.000	1.000	0.00	66.67	3
Estrada, Jeremiah	S-R	6-1	185	11-1-98	6	3	2.95	62	0	1	61	42	22	20	4	23	94	.188	.259	.277	37.30	9.13	252
Gillaspie, Logan	R-R	6-2	215	4-17-97	0	0	7.15	9	0	0	11	15	9	9	2	0	7	.319	.327	.511	14.29	0.00	49
Hoeing, Bryan	R-R	6-6	210	10-19-96	1	1	1.52	18	0	0	24	14	5	4	2	5	18	.173	.221	.272	20.93	5.81	86
Jacob, Alek	L-R	6-3	190	6-16-98	0	0	2.45	7	0	0	15	9	4	4	1	2	19	.173	.228	.269	33.33	3.51	57
King, Michael	R-R	6-3	210	5-25-95	13	9	2.95	31	30	0	174	144	71	57	17	63	201	.221	.296	.346	27.69	8.68	726
Kolek, Stephen	R-R	6-3	210	4-18-97	3	0	5.21	42	0	0	47	59	30	27	4	12	39	.303	.352	.410	18.48	5.69	211
Matsui, Yuki	L-L	5-8	165	10-30-95	4	2	3.73	64	0	0	63	46	27	26	8	27	69	.204	.284	.381	26.85	10.51	257
Mazur, Adam	R-R	6-2	180	4-20-01	1	3	7.49	8	8	0	34	40	28	28	6	21	22	.301	.399	.534	13.92	13.29	158
Morejon, Adrian	L-L	5-11	224	2-27-99	3	2	2.83	60	0	2	64	63	24	20	4	21	71	.256	.314	.390	26.10	7.72	272
Musgrove, Joe	R-R	6-5	230	12-4-92	6	5	3.88	19	19	0	100	94	44	43	14	23	101	.251	.310	.419	24.63	5.61	410
Peralta, Wandy	L-L	6-0	227	7-27-91	3	2	3.99	46	0	0	38	33	19	17	6	13	22	.231	.315	.378	13.58	8.02	162
Perez, Martin	L-L	6-0	200	4-4-91	3	1	3.46	10	10	0	52	46	20	20	9	17	44	.235	.301	.393	20.28	7.83	217
Reynolds, Sean	L-R	6-8	250	4-19-98	0	0	0.82	9	0	0	11	10	1	1	0	5	21	.238	.327	.310	42.86	10.20	49
Scott, Tanner	R-L	6-0	235	7-22-94	3	1	2.73	28	0	4	26	26	10	8	1	9	31	.257	.318	.337	27.68	8.04	112
Suarez, Robert	R-R	6-2	210	3-1-91	9	3	2.77	65	0	36	65	52	21	20	7	16	59	.217	.265	.333	22.87	6.20	258
Vasquez, Randy	R-R	6-0	165	11-3-98	4	7	4.87	20	20	0	98	119	56	53	13	29	62	.304	.360	.473	14.39	6.73	431
Waldron, Matt	R-R	6-2	185	9-26-96	7	11	4.91	27	26	0	147	145	84	80	21	40	133	.255	.315	.430	21.28	6.40	625

Fielding

Catcher	PCT	G	PO	A	E	DP	PB
Campusano	.996	86	697	24	3	0	6
Diaz	1.000	12	64	2	0	0	1
Higashioka	.987	83	669	20	9	1	9
Sullivan	.978	5	44	1	1	0	0

First Base	PCT	G	PO	A	E	DP
Arraez	.989	61	435	24	5	30
Batten	1.000	1	5	2	0	1
Campusano	1.000	2	4	0	0	0
Cronenworth	.994	85	594	45	4	63
Pauley	1.000	1	1	0	0	1
Profar	1.000	2	13	1	0	1
Solano	.993	26	130	11	1	14
Sullivan	1.000	2	1	0	0	0

Second Base	PCT	G	PO	A	E	DP
Ahmed	1.000	1	2	3	0	0
Arraez	1.000	9	12	26	0	7
Bogaerts	.981	85	127	187	6	42
Cronenworth	.993	70	115	163	2	36
Rosario	1.000	2	2	2	0	1
Solano	.000	1	0	0	0	0
Wade	1.000	15	9	9	0	2

Third Base	PCT	G	PO	A	E	DP
Machado	.970	100	78	147	7	11
Pauley	.909	6	5	5	1	0
Rosario	.971	26	10	24	1	3
Solano	1.000	32	18	47	0	6
Wade	.958	31	16	30	2	1

Shortstop	PCT	G	PO	A	E	DP
Ahmed	1.000	1	1	5	0	0
Bogaerts	.952	20	20	40	3	6
Kim	.974	121	145	263	11	64
McCoy	1.000	19	20	33	0	7
Wade	.960	13	10	14	1	2

Outfield	PCT	G	PO	A	E	DP
Azocar	1.000	61	58	0	0	0
Johnson	1.000	43	43	2	0	0
Lockridge	1.000	8	10	0	0	0
Merrill	.993	155	392	8	3	4
Peralta	.989	65	87	1	1	0
Profar	.996	148	230	4	1	0
Tatis	.973	96	171	6	5	1
Wade	1.000	21	13	0	0	0

EL PASO CHIHUAHUAS — *TRIPLE-A*

PACIFIC COAST LEAGUE

Batting	B-T	Ht.	Wt.	DOB	AVG	OBP	SLG	G	PA	AB	R	H	2B	3B	HR	RBI	BB	HBP	SH	SF	SO	SB	CS	BB%	SO%
Azocar, Jose	R-R	5-11	181	5-11-96	.282	.311	.416	51	226	209	29	59	10	3	4	29	7	4	1	5	35	24	5	3.10	15.49
Batten, Matthew	R-R	5-11	180	6-22-95	.251	.325	.376	121	546	479	82	120	24	3	10	78	51	6	2	8	111	22	1	9.34	20.33
Bogaerts, Xander	R-R	6-2	218	10-1-92	.182	.400	.273	4	15	11	1	2	1	0	0	0	4	0	0	0	4	0	0	26.67	26.67
Campusano, Luis	R-R	5-11	232	9-29-98	.371	.405	.514	8	37	35	8	13	2	0	1	7	2	0	0	0	5	0	0	5.41	13.51
Diaz, Elias	R-R	6-1	223	11-17-90	.250	.357	.583	4	14	12	4	3	1	0	1	6	2	0	0	0	3	0	0	14.29	21.43
Dungan, Clay	L-R	5-11	190	6-2-96	.252	.357	.439	93	388	326	49	82	24	8	7	61	50	6	1	5	90	16	4	12.89	23.20
Hollis, Connor	R-R	5-7	170	11-18-94	.273	.360	.364	7	26	22	4	6	2	0	0	5	2	1	1	0	3	0	2	7.69	11.54
Johnson, Bryce	B-R	6-1	195	10-27-95	.288	.407	.431	74	319	260	53	75	15	5	4	34	43	11	2	3	65	20	3	13.48	20.38
Kopack, Addison	R-R	6-2	215	8-6-01	.400	.400	.400	2	5	5	1	2	0	0	0	1	0	0	0	0	3	0	1	0.00	60.00
Locastro, Tim	R-R	6-1	200	7-14-92	.333	.449	.479	33	120	96	26	32	8	0	2	11	11	10	2	1	18	8	2	9.17	15.00
Lockridge, Brandon	R-R	5-11	185	3-14-97	.325	.420	.423	32	143	123	24	40	6	0	2	13	18	2	0	0	30	12	2	12.59	20.98
McCoy, Mason	R-R	5-11	185	3-31-95	.260	.329	.382	108	432	385	52	100	26	3	5	50	39	2	4	2	105	25	8	9.03	24.31
Mercado, Oscar	R-R	6-2	197	12-16-94	.226	.307	.425	78	307	266	47	60	10	5	11	42	28	6	1	6	49	12	4	9.12	15.96
Mitchell, Cal	L-L	6-0	205	3-8-99	.277	.359	.512	122	469	408	69	113	26	2	22	70	55	0	1	5	95	12	6	11.73	20.26
Mondou, Nate	L-R	5-7	205	3-24-95	.267	.367	.404	101	443	371	55	99	20	8	5	55	55	8	2	7	89	11	4	12.42	20.09
Ornelas, Tirso	L-R	6-2	200	3-11-00	.297	.367	.497	128	548	485	76	144	24	2	23	89	53	4	0	6	88	7	2	9.67	16.06
Pauley, Graham	L-R	6-1	200	9-24-00	.228	.342	.390	70	301	254	39	58	15	1	8	41	40	5	0	2	57	2	4	13.29	18.94
Peralta, David	L-L	6-1	210	8-14-87	.182	.308	.182	3	13	11	3	2	0	0	0	1	2	0	0	0	5	0	0	15.38	38.46
Plawecki, Kevin	R-R	6-2	208	2-26-91	.260	.340	.443	75	299	262	39	68	15	0	11	38	32	1	2	2	43	0	0	10.70	14.38
Rosario, Eguy	R-R	5-7	150	8-25-99	.263	.361	.531	95	413	354	67	93	24	4	21	70	51	5	0	3	88	19	5	12.35	21.31
Sanabria, Jose	R-R	5-10	150	10-30-02	.200	.257	.277	24	71	65	8	13	3	1	0	1	4	1	1	0	20	1	2	5.63	28.17
Seagle, Chandler	R-R	5-10	190	5-23-96	.180	.219	.280	38	107	100	10	18	7	0	1	5	5	0	2	0	40	0	1	4.67	37.38
Solano, Donovan	R-R	5-8	210	12-17-87	.318	.392	.455	12	51	44	7	14	3	0	1	8	5	1	0	1	8	0	0	9.80	15.69
Sullivan, Brett	L-R	6-1	195	2-22-94	.263	.347	.485	101	453	396	70	104	25	6	17	63	49	4	0	4	60	3	0	10.82	13.25
Valenzuela, Brandon	B-R	6-0	225	10-2-00	.195	.292	.234	27	90	77	6	15	3	0	0	4	11	0	1	1	21	0	1	12.22	23.33

Pitching	B-T	Ht.	Wt.	DOB	W	L	ERA	G	GS	SV	IP	Hits	Runs	ER	HR	BB	SO	AVG	OBP	SLG	SO%	BB%	BF
Bachar, Lake	R-R	6-2	219	6-3-95	6	3	3.89	46	1	0	72	72	34	31	11	32	85	.263	.339	.471	27.42	10.32	310
Brito, Jhony	R-R	6-2	210	2-17-98	0	2	9.00	6	6	0	14	22	17	14	2	9	9	.349	.438	.571	12.33	12.33	73
Camarena, Daniel	L-L	6-0	210	11-9-92	1	6	9.75	14	7	0	36	51	39	39	13	25	29	.340	.433	.713	15.93	13.74	182
Carpenter, Ryan	L-L	6-5	230	8-22-90	2	6	8.85	14	14	0	59	81	59	58	19	31	44	.331	.409	.649	15.66	11.03	281
Cienfuegos, Miguel	L-L	6-4	195	2-10-97	1	2	7.66	5	5	0	22	29	19	19	3	15	10	.326	.426	.539	9.26	13.89	108
Cosgrove, Tom	L-L	6-2	190	6-14-96	1	3	4.85	32	0	0	30	25	18	16	4	14	34	.219	.315	.404	26.15	10.77	130
Crismatt, Nabil	R-R	6-1	220	12-25-94	1	3	5.53	15	13	0	55	66	36	34	5	24	50	.293	.362	.422	19.61	9.41	255
Cruz, Omar	L-L	6-0	210	1-26-99	1	2	4.42	14	5	0	39	33	20	19	1	23	48	.231	.335	.294	28.74	13.77	167
Davis, Austin	L-L	6-4	235	2-3-93	4	4	3.40	47	0	14	48	35	19	18	0	26	61	.206	.335	.265	29.47	12.56	207
Edwards, Carl	R-R	6-3	165	9-3-91	1	3	5.31	9	9	0	41	43	26	24	7	26	44	.274	.375	.459	23.91	14.13	184
Estrada, Jeremiah	S-R	6-1	185	11-1-98	0	0	2.08	8	0	3	9	4	2	2	0	3	20	.138	.212	.241	60.61	9.09	33
Festa, Matt	R-R	6-1	195	3-11-93	0	1	4.50	16	0	1	16	18	8	8	0	7	16	.286	.351	.349	21.62	9.46	74
Fry, Paul	L-L	6-0	205	7-26-92	4	4	4.76	51	0	1	74	86	42	39	6	30	57	.298	.366	.412	17.48	9.20	326
Gillaspie, Logan	R-R	6-2	215	4-17-97	4	2	3.77	44	0	7	45	40	23	19	5	19	42	.234	.308	.368	21.54	9.74	195
Groome, Jay	L-L	6-6	262	8-23-98	0	0	3.60	3	3	0	5	1	2	2	1	5	5	.063	.318	.250	22.73	22.73	22
Hernandez, Nick	R-R	6-1	212	12-30-94	0	0	1.90	17	0	0	24	19	6	5	1	9	34	.224	.310	.329	34.00	9.00	100
Jacob, Alek	L-R	6-3	190	6-16-98	3	1	5.53	42	0	2	54	65	46	33	12	31	65	.294	.386	.552	25.49	12.16	255
Kollar, Jared	R-R	6-0	195	7-24-98	2	2	4.72	11	8	0	48	45	27	25	6	17	35	.250	.312	.406	17.16	8.33	204
Kopps, Kevin	R-R	6-0	200	3-2-97	1	3	5.86	40	0	0	51	57	38	33	5	38	33	.289	.402	.431	13.47	15.51	245
Mazur, Adam	R-R	6-2	180	4-20-01	1	3	7.83	5	5	0	23	28	20	20	4	6	22	.301	.343	.548	22.22	6.06	99
Milacki, Bobby	R-R	6-2	210	11-6-96	0	1	13.00	5	0	0	9	16	13	13	3	6	8	.390	.468	.756	16.67	12.50	48
Morejon, Adrian	L-L	5-11	224	2-27-99	0	1	2.84	6	0	0	6	4	2	2	2	1	6	.174	.208	.522	25.00	4.17	24
Mosser, Gabe	R-R	6-4	185	6-8-96	7	7	5.40	28	26	0	133	146	83	80	15	48	103	.279	.340	.438	17.61	8.21	585
Nance, Tommy	R-R	6-6	235	3-19-91	2	2	4.05	26	0	2	33	43	23	15	4	8	35	.319	.360	.489	23.33	5.33	150
Otto, Glenn	R-R	6-3	240	3-11-96	0	2	4.63	8	2	0	12	9	6	6	1	10	15	.209	.370	.279	27.78	18.52	54
Pena, Francis	R-R	6-1	170	1-25-01	3	2	5.17	15	0	0	16	15	11	9	2	6	16	.246	.324	.410	23.19	8.70	69

Pitching	B-T	Ht.	Wt.	DOB	W	L	ERA	G	GS	SV	IP	Hits	Runs	ER	HR	BB	SO	AVG	OBP	SLG	SO%	BB%	BF
Reynolds, Sean	L-R	6-8	250	4-19-98	2	0	6.17	39	3	0	54	58	41	37	4	33	67	.276	.379	.462	26.69	13.15	251
Roberson, Josh	R-R	6-3	175	5-12-96	0	0	9.58	10	0	0	10	17	14	11	1	9	10	.362	.475	.574	16.95	15.25	59
Routzahn, Ethan	R-R	6-4	225	3-19-98	5	1	2.35	14	0	0	23	20	7	6	1	3	17	.233	.275	.337	18.68	3.30	91
Sanchez, Fernando	L-L	6-0	198	9-13-00	0	0	0.00	1	0	0	2	2	0	0	0	0	0	.286	.286	.286	0.00	0.00	7
Sandridge, Jayvien	L-L	6-5	220	2-11-99	1	1	4.76	31	0	0	40	37	24	21	7	35	56	.243	.387	.434	29.32	18.32	191
Vasquez, Randy	R-R	6-0	165	11-3-98	2	6	8.21	10	10	0	42	60	40	38	10	13	44	.333	.385	.572	22.00	6.50	200
Waldron, Matt	R-R	6-2	185	9-26-96	1	0	4.58	4	4	0	20	18	11	10	3	3	17	.234	.277	.416	20.24	3.57	84
Watson, Nolan	R-R	6-2	195	1-25-97	4	2	6.81	8	8	0	36	40	30	27	11	13	38	.276	.338	.600	23.75	8.13	160
Westphal, Luke	L-L	6-3	230	6-14-89	1	2	7.27	13	3	0	26	26	21	21	3	23	23	.255	.389	.422	18.25	18.25	126
Wolf, Jackson	L-L	6-7	205	4-22-99	3	9	7.08	26	18	0	89	110	77	70	13	57	76	.302	.401	.484	17.59	13.19	432

Fielding

Catcher	PCT	G	PO	A	E	DP	PB
Campusano	.981	5	48	5	1	0	3
Diaz	1.000	2	4	1	0	0	1
Plawecki	.997	35	274	12	1	3	0
Seagle	.996	37	249	10	1	1	1
Sullivan	.997	71	622	23	2	2	8
Valenzuela	.971	13	97	5	3	2	2

First Base	PCT	G	PO	A	E	DP
Batten	1.000	14	91	4	0	8
Kopack	.900	1	8	1	1	1
Locastro	1.000	9	58	5	0	5
Mondou	.991	57	397	46	4	50
Ornelas	.988	10	78	5	1	8
Pauley	1.000	20	146	16	0	19
Plawecki	.992	31	219	21	2	21
Solano	1.000	4	31	6	0	1
Sullivan	1.000	3	22	1	0	2
Valenzuela	.988	14	74	5	1	9

Second Base	PCT	G	PO	A	E	DP
Batten	.975	37	70	87	4	29
Bogaerts	1.000	2	4	4	0	3
Dungan	.981	46	60	96	3	23
Hollis	.929	3	7	6	1	3
Locastro	1.000	2	1	3	0	0
McCoy	.889	2	4	4	1	0
Mondou	1.000	34	57	61	0	22
Pauley	1.000	21	39	59	0	14
Rosario	1.000	2	1	8	0	1
Sanabria	1.000	9	22	27	0	8
Solano	1.000	2	6	4	0	2

Third Base	PCT	G	PO	A	E	DP
Batten	.971	39	31	70	3	6
Dungan	.959	23	11	36	2	2
Mondou	.857	3	1	5	1	0
Pauley	.952	15	7	33	2	5
Rosario	.941	67	45	114	10	18
Sanabria	.963	14	9	17	1	4

Shortstop	PCT	G	PO	A	E	DP
Batten	.987	20	19	55	1	7
Dungan	.905	17	15	42	6	9
McCoy	.979	106	120	297	9	58
Rosario	1.000	10	13	27	0	9

Outfield	PCT	G	PO	A	E	DP
Azocar	.990	49	101	2	1	0
Batten	.833	3	5	0	1	0
Dungan	1.000	10	19	1	0	0
Hollis	.833	5	5	0	1	0
Johnson	1.000	70	135	3	0	1
Locastro	.962	23	25	0	1	0
Lockridge	1.000	32	70	0	0	0
Mercado	.960	63	119	2	5	0
Mitchell	.985	100	192	5	3	1
Ornelas	.989	94	181	3	2	0
Pauley	1.000	13	22	0	0	0
Peralta	1.000	3	6	0	0	0
Rosario	.938	9	14	1	1	1

SAN ANTONIO MISSIONS — *DOUBLE-A*

TEXAS LEAGUE

Batting	B-T	Ht.	Wt.	DOB	AVG	OBP	SLG	G	PA	AB	R	H	2B	3B	HR	RBI	BB	HBP	SH	SF	SO	SB	CS	BB%	SO%
Castanon, Marcos	R-R	6-0	195	3-23-99	.227	.315	.373	110	466	405	37	92	20	0	13	54	45	10	0	6	104	3	0	9.66	22.32
Cummings, Cole	L-R	6-2	205	6-20-98	.219	.306	.345	123	517	452	63	99	23	2	10	54	50	9	0	6	173	10	2	9.67	33.46
Dale, Jarryd	R-R	6-2	200	9-11-00	.141	.187	.271	33	93	85	7	12	2	0	3	6	3	2	2	1	28	1	1	3.23	30.11
De La Cruz, Michael	B-R	5-9	190	5-15-93	.209	.306	.255	71	274	235	27	49	8	0	1	24	33	1	2	2	37	6	2	12.04	13.50
Didder, Ray-Patrick	R-R	5-9	199	10-1-94	.169	.315	.294	111	441	360	42	61	16	1	9	31	57	21	0	3	116	28	5	12.93	26.30
Dungan, Clay	L-R	5-11	190	6-2-96	.218	.342	.306	34	152	124	19	27	5	0	2	10	24	1	0	3	35	9	2	15.79	23.03
Dunn, Lucas	R-R	6-0	205	4-30-99	.200	.294	.293	29	86	75	13	15	3	2	0	5	9	1	1	0	30	0	0	10.47	34.88
Hollis, Connor	R-R	5-7	170	11-18-94	.241	.318	.306	86	362	320	39	77	11	2	2	25	23	14	2	1	57	18	5	6.35	15.75
Marsee, Jakob	L-L	6-0	180	6-28-01	.176	.336	.318	24	109	85	15	15	6	0	2	5	19	2	2	1	24	12	1	17.43	22.02
Martorella, Nathan	L-L	6-1	224	2-18-01	.292	.393	.427	25	107	89	18	26	6	0	2	14	16	0	0	2	17	3	0	14.95	15.89
Mears, Joshua	R-R	6-3	230	2-21-01	.174	.230	.478	18	74	69	9	12	3	0	6	13	4	1	0	0	35	1	1	5.41	47.30
Murphy, Kai	L-L	5-8	173	8-26-00	.375	.500	.625	3	10	8	2	3	2	0	0	3	1	1	0	0	2	0	0	10.00	20.00
Perez Jr., Robert	R-R	6-0	170	6-26-00	.225	.334	.343	120	476	405	50	91	21	0	9	46	52	16	0	3	148	14	9	10.92	31.09
Reks, Zach	L-R	6-2	190	11-12-93	.127	.278	.208	64	242	197	18	25	7	0	3	19	38	4	1	2	71	1	2	15.70	29.34
Reyes, Ripken	B-R	5-7	185	4-1-97	.225	.348	.311	119	506	408	56	92	15	4	4	42	45	34	15	4	63	16	7	8.89	12.45
Sanabria, Romeo	L-R	6-2	200	5-2-02	.270	.375	.333	32	136	111	9	30	4	0	1	19	21	0	0	4	38	0	2	15.44	27.94
Tenerowicz, Robbie	R-R	5-11	228	1-6-95	.230	.356	.366	97	404	331	42	76	15	0	10	40	32	36	0	5	69	4	1	7.92	17.08
Valentine, Chase	R-R	5-11	160	4-22-02	.000	.273	.000	7	12	8	1	0	0	0	0	0	3	0	1	0	5	0	0	25.00	41.67
Valenzuela, Brandon	B-R	6-0	225	10-2-00	.241	.317	.381	84	347	307	38	74	16	0	9	43	33	3	0	4	80	0	2	9.51	23.05
Vilar, Anthony	L-R	5-10	190	4-1-99	.138	.303	.213	26	100	80	15	11	3	0	1	6	18	1	1	0	32	3	0	18.00	32.00
Zabala, Juan	R-R	5-10	190	7-3-99	.225	.287	.314	59	209	191	19	43	8	0	3	19	16	1	0	1	55	2	4	7.66	26.32

Pitching	B-T	Ht.	Wt.	DOB	W	L	ERA	G	GS	SV	IP	Hits	Runs	ER	HR	BB	SO	AVG	OBP	SLG	SO%	BB%	BF
Baez, Henry	R-R	6-3	175	10-12-02	5	1	3.06	9	9	0	50	42	17	17	6	15	31	.230	.291	.383	15.42	7.46	201
Bergert, Ryan	R-R	6-1	210	3-8-00	2	10	4.78	23	23	0	98	99	59	52	7	33	87	.268	.330	.425	20.86	7.91	417
Blanchard, Jason	R-L	6-0	185	6-25-97	1	3	3.71	41	0	1	61	60	28	25	0	23	72	.261	.323	.322	27.69	8.85	260
Brito, Raul	R-R	6-1	180	5-23-97	3	4	3.31	33	1	2	54	38	22	20	5	23	63	.204	.306	.355	29.03	10.60	217
Camarena, Daniel	L-L	6-0	210	11-9-92	0	2	2.93	12	1	0	15	16	9	5	2	5	10	.258	.324	.371	14.49	7.25	69
Castro, Manuel	R-R	5-8	180	5-11-02	0	0	0.00	2	0	0	4	4	0	0	0	2	7	.267	.353	.333	38.89	11.11	18
Cienfuegos, Miguel	L-L	6-4	195	2-10-97	5	2	5.63	13	7	0	56	64	38	35	10	14	45	.287	.335	.484	18.22	5.67	247
Cruz, Omar	L-L	6-0	210	1-26-99	5	0	3.59	20	2	2	48	36	20	19	3	13	70	.205	.283	.301	35.35	6.57	198
Cruz, Yovanny	R-R	6-0	180	8-23-99	1	2	4.55	23	0	1	30	36	17	15	2	16	35	.308	.418	.470	24.82	11.35	141
Dale, Jarryd	R-R	6-2	200	9-11-00	0	0	13.50	2	0	0	2	4	3	3	1	0	0	.400	.400	.700	0.00	0.00	10
Geraldo, Jose	R-R	6-3	200	1-30-99	0	0	2.70	9	0	0	13	11	4	4	0	3	19	.234	.308	.319	35.85	5.66	53
Go, Woo Suk	R-R	5-11	198	8-6-98	0	2	4.38	10	0	1	12	14	7	6	0	4	15	.280	.333	.380	27.78	7.41	54
Kollar, Jared	R-R	6-0	195	7-24-98	9	3	3.04	18	15	0	83	84	29	28	6	18	77	.257	.297	.388	22.13	5.17	348
Krob, Austin	L-L	6-3	205	9-20-99	4	11	4.43	26	25	0	124	129	70	61	8	44	120	.273	.342	.388	22.43	8.22	535
Lawson, Reggie	R-R	6-4	205	8-2-97	1	0	8.10	13	0	0	13	13	13	12	0	17	14	.260	.465	.380	19.44	23.61	72
Lizarraga, Victor	R-R	6-3	180	11-30-03	5	6	4.03	21	21	0	96	79	50	43	8	42	102	.226	.322	.360	25.06	10.32	407

Loewen, Carter	R-R	6-4	240	9-28-98	1	2	5.12	38	3	1	51	44	31	29	4	31	65	.232	.345	.363	28.51	13.60	228
Mazur, Adam	R-R	6-2	180	4-20-01	3	1	1.95	6	6	0	32	23	8	7	1	5	32	.202	.233	.263	26.67	4.17	120
Milacki, Bobby	R-R	6-2	210	11-6-96	1	0	3.13	26	0	0	46	49	20	16	2	7	41	.271	.304	.370	21.47	3.66	191
Miller, Mitchell	L-L	6-6	185	6-13-97	0	0	10.80	4	0	0	3	7	5	4	0	2	5	.412	.500	.471	25.00	10.00	20
Morgan, David	R-R	6-0	185	10-26-99	2	2	5.35	22	0	0	34	29	20	20	2	16	27	.244	.350	.395	18.88	11.19	143
Nett, Braden	R-R	6-3	185	6-18-02	0	0	1.93	1	1	0	5	4	1	1	1	5	3	.250	.429	.438	14.29	23.81	21
Och, Ryan	R-L	6-0	205	7-18-98	2	2	2.76	19	0	3	29	24	11	9	0	11	42	.226	.298	.368	34.71	9.09	121
Paplham, Cole	R-R	6-3	215	3-19-00	0	0	0.00	3	0	0	4	1	0	0	0	1	6	.083	.214	.083	42.86	7.14	14
Pena, Francis	R-R	6-1	170	1-25-01	0	2	2.05	19	0	1	26	18	9	6	1	5	31	.186	.248	.237	29.25	4.72	106
Peralta, Wandy	L-L	6-0	227	7-27-91	0	0	0.00	1	0	0	1	0	0	0	0	0	1	.000	.000	.000	33.33	0.00	3
Roberson, Josh	R-R	6-3	175	5-12-96	2	1	2.70	19	0	4	20	10	6	6	1	11	21	.143	.259	.229	25.93	13.58	81
Rodriguez, Bradgley	R-R	6-1	160	11-16-03	0	1	3.14	12	0	4	14	8	5	5	0	7	21	.154	.267	.192	35.00	11.67	60
Routzahn, Ethan	R-R	6-4	225	3-19-98	4	2	2.38	31	0	6	42	37	15	11	2	17	30	.233	.311	.321	16.57	9.39	181
Sandridge, Jayvien	L-L	6-5	220	2-11-99	3	3	3.38	21	0	4	21	19	9	8	0	14	39	.247	.366	.312	41.49	14.89	94
Snelling, Robby	R-L	6-3	210	12-19-03	2	8	6.01	16	16	0	73	90	52	49	14	33	67	.309	.380	.550	20.24	9.97	331
Valentine, Chase	R-R	5-11	160	4-22-02	0	0	0.00	2	0	0	3	0	0	0	0	0	0	.000	.000	.000	0.00	0.00	9
Whiting, Sam	R-R	6-3	220	12-15-00	0	3	6.48	6	6	0	17	27	15	12	0	9	10	.365	.442	.486	11.63	10.47	86
Wolf, Jackson	L-L	6-7	205	4-22-99	1	1	3.95	6	0	0	14	15	8	6	0	7	17	.278	.365	.407	26.98	11.11	63

Fielding

Catcher	PCT	G	PO	A	E	DP	PB
De La Cruz	.984	30	240	5	4	2	4
Valenzuela	.987	58	572	45	8	5	11
Vilar	.963	22	167	15	7	0	6
Zabala	.985	32	253	16	4	0	1

First Base	PCT	G	PO	A	E	DP
Cummings	.968	5	27	3	1	3
Dale	1.000	2	7	0	0	1
De La Cruz	1.000	2	1	0	0	0
Dunn	1.000	1	7	1	0	2
Martorella	1.000	23	154	14	0	15
Sanabria	.968	21	142	10	5	17
Tenerowicz	.989	81	600	34	7	52
Valenzuela	.983	8	53	5	1	6

Second Base	PCT	G	PO	A	E	DP
Castanon	.988	23	33	51	1	18
Dale	1.000	2	4	3	0	1
De La Cruz	.952	19	27	33	3	8
Didder	.966	7	12	16	1	7
Dungan	1.000	1	2	5	0	3
Hollis	.984	29	59	64	2	11
Reyes	.992	54	96	144	2	41
Tenerowicz	1.000	1	1	2	0	0
Valentine	1.000	3	2	5	0	1
Vilar	1.000	2	2	5	0	1

Third Base	PCT	G	PO	A	E	DP
Castanon	.957	77	37	141	8	20
Dale	.933	18	8	34	3	0
Didder	.889	2	1	7	1	1
Dungan	1.000	2	0	5	0	0
Dunn	.846	10	3	8	2	1
Hollis	.947	8	8	10	1	2
Reyes	.925	14	11	26	3	4
Tenerowicz	1.000	7	5	14	0	0
Valentine	1.000	2	0	7	0	0

Shortstop	PCT	G	PO	A	E	DP
Dale	1.000	1	0	2	0	0
Didder	.951	101	105	246	18	38
Dungan	.933	3	3	11	1	3
Dunn	1.000	2	2	4	0	0
Hollis	1.000	2	3	4	0	1
Reyes	.983	31	35	79	2	14
Vilar	1.000	1	1	0	0	0

Outfield	PCT	G	PO	A	E	DP
Cummings	.990	109	189	11	2	4
Dale	1.000	5	9	0	0	0
Dungan	.987	27	74	0	1	0
Dunn	1.000	10	18	1	0	0
Hollis	.992	42	124	2	1	2
Marsee	.983	24	57	2	1	1
Mears	.971	18	32	1	1	0
Murphy	1.000	3	14	1	0	0
Perez Jr.	.973	110	206	8	6	2
Reks	.988	47	85	0	1	0
Reyes	.959	21	44	3	2	1

FORT WAYNE TINCAPS — *HIGH-A*

MIDWEST LEAGUE

Batting	B-T	Ht.	Wt.	DOB	AVG	OBP	SLG	G	PA	AB	R	H	2B	3B	HR	RBI	BB	HBP	SH	SF	SO	SB	CS	BB%	SO%
Bender, Colton	R-R	5-9	195	1-13-99	.167	.235	.233	45	168	150	11	25	7	0	1	15	14	0	2	2	41	0	0	8.33	24.40
Beshears, Jay	R-R	6-4	215	5-6-02	.235	.308	.343	57	241	213	25	50	17	0	2	19	20	4	0	3	43	4	3	8.30	17.84
Bush, Homer	R-R	6-3	200	10-13-01	.272	.362	.347	86	341	294	52	80	10	0	4	16	30	12	2	1	59	43	9	8.80	17.30
Camou, Alain	L-R	5-11	150	11-1-03	.059	.105	.059	6	20	17	1	1	0	0	0	1	1	0	1	1	1	0	0	5.00	5.00
Campbell, Jacob	R-R	6-0	200	5-21-00	.174	.224	.326	13	49	46	4	8	2	1	1	5	2	1	0	0	16	1	0	4.08	32.65
Cedeno, Nerwilian	B-R	5-11	175	3-16-02	.216	.303	.347	106	406	357	51	77	14	6	7	34	39	6	3	1	107	9	6	9.61	26.35
Dale, Jarryd	R-R	6-2	200	9-11-00	.269	.345	.346	8	29	26	4	7	0	1	0	3	3	0	0	0	10	1	0	10.34	34.48
Doersching, Griffin	R-R	6-4	251	8-12-98	.209	.302	.387	72	292	253	22	53	15	0	10	32	32	3	0	3	75	3	1	10.96	25.68
Dunn, Lucas	R-R	6-0	205	4-30-99	.173	.272	.296	33	115	98	8	17	3	0	3	13	12	2	1	2	28	2	2	10.43	24.35
Fabian, Albert	L-L	6-0	215	12-21-01	.256	.362	.400	27	105	90	13	23	7	0	2	18	14	1	0	0	19	2	2	13.33	18.10
Hoffman, Wyatt	R-R	5-9	170	3-16-99	.224	.316	.358	23	76	67	11	15	6	0	1	7	8	1	0	0	24	2	1	10.53	31.58
Kopack, Addison	R-R	6-2	215	8-6-01	.105	.171	.158	11	41	38	4	4	2	0	0	3	3	0	0	0	19	1	1	7.32	46.34
Long, Ethan	R-R	6-3	215	5-10-01	.240	.296	.420	13	54	50	6	12	3	0	2	9	3	1	0	0	19	1	0	5.56	35.19
McClaughry, Nik	R-R	5-9	159	9-14-99	.149	.253	.216	83	298	255	31	38	10	2	1	18	28	8	6	1	89	5	2	9.40	29.87
Mears, Joshua	R-R	6-3	230	2-21-01	.215	.262	.408	54	206	191	27	41	5	1	10	28	11	2	0	2	69	8	3	5.34	33.50
Murphy, Kai	L-L	5-8	173	8-26-00	.235	.342	.353	117	482	408	57	96	24	3	6	43	61	6	5	2	107	10	7	12.66	22.20
Ortiz, Devin	R-R	6-2	215	2-7-99	.245	.345	.319	117	473	408	57	100	12	0	6	50	56	7	0	2	84	10	8	11.84	17.76
Robertson, Tyler	R-R	6-4	200	3-10-00	.278	.349	.389	72	266	234	26	65	11	0	5	38	24	2	4	1	66	16	5	9.02	24.81
Salas, Ethan	L-R	6-2	185	6-1-06	.206	.288	.311	111	469	412	38	85	27	2	4	53	47	3	0	7	98	10	3	10.02	20.90
Sanabria, Romeo	L-R	6-2	200	5-2-02	.262	.343	.393	34	140	122	14	32	10	0	2	19	15	1	0	2	31	0	1	10.71	22.14
Verdugo, Rosman	R-R	6-0	180	2-2-05	.186	.262	.299	25	109	97	13	18	6	1	1	10	9	1	2	0	32	1	0	8.26	29.36
Vilar, Anthony	L-R	5-10	190	4-1-99	.257	.378	.390	74	300	249	34	64	9	3	6	43	44	5	1	1	76	8	0	14.67	25.33
Vincent, Colton	R-R	6-1	182	1-25-00	.308	.438	.308	5	16	13	4	4	0	0	0	1	2	1	0	0	3	0	0	12.50	18.75
Vogt, Nick	R-R	6-1	185	8-4-00	.205	.288	.261	50	198	176	19	36	7	0	1	16	18	3	0	1	62	10	1	9.09	31.31

Pitching	B-T	Ht.	Wt.	DOB	W	L	ERA	G	GS	SV	IP	Hits	Runs	ER	HR	BB	SO	AVG	OBP	SLG	SO%	BB%	BF
Baez, Henry	R-R	6-3	175	10-12-02	2	3	2.95	17	17	0	76	56	35	25	4	25	78	.201	.279	.283	24.76	7.94	315
Camarena, Daniel	L-L	6-0	210	11-9-92	0	1	4.50	2	0	0	2	1	3	1	1	1	1	.143	.250	.571	12.50	12.50	8
Castro, Manuel	R-R	5-8	180	5-11-02	1	3	3.49	39	0	12	57	56	31	22	3	14	68	.258	.303	.373	28.69	5.91	237
Cienfuegos, Miguel	L-L	6-4	195	2-10-97	3	4	3.91	9	7	0	46	40	24	20	4	12	29	.230	.283	.345	15.51	6.42	187
Collett, Keegan	R-R	6-3	215	7-27-98	0	0	3.55	11	0	0	13	8	5	5	2	9	14	.178	.339	.333	25.00	16.07	56

SAN DIEGO PADRES

Darvish, Yu	R-R	6-5	220	8-16-86	0	1	16.20	1	1	0	3	7	6	6	1	1	3	.412	.444	.588	16.67	5.56	18
Galindo, Ruben	R-R	6-1	175	1-24-01	3	2	3.09	13	1	0	23	19	10	8	1	10	25	.221	.309	.349	25.77	10.31	97
Geerdes, Will	R-R	6-2	220	3-21-00	3	4	5.79	34	0	0	51	49	38	33	7	25	48	.257	.350	.435	21.15	11.01	227
Geraldo, Jose	R-R	6-3	200	1-30-99	3	1	5.34	26	0	0	32	32	19	19	2	19	40	.260	.361	.415	27.78	13.19	144
Gonzalez, Joan	S-R	6-3	165	5-27-98	4	2	4.13	34	0	1	52	48	30	24	6	28	52	.253	.360	.400	22.61	12.17	230
Gustin, Harry	S-L	6-0	160	5-6-02	0	1	2.16	8	0	0	8	7	2	2	1	3	8	.226	.286	.355	22.86	8.57	35
Haynes, Jagger	L-L	6-3	170	9-20-02	2	6	4.64	23	22	0	111	90	59	57	11	66	114	.225	.342	.383	24.00	13.89	475
Landinez, Yerry	S-R	6-1	170	1-20-01	0	0	0.00	1	0	0	0	1	2	1	0	2	0	1.000	1.000	1.000	0.00	66.67	3
Lesko, Dylan	R-R	6-2	195	9-7-03	1	9	6.46	16	16	0	70	55	51	50	11	52	79	.224	.379	.420	25.00	16.46	316
Lowe, Isaiah	R-R	6-1	220	5-7-03	2	3	4.05	7	7	0	33	35	18	15	2	17	22	.276	.365	.409	14.86	11.49	148
Matos, Dwayne	R-R	6-1	155	11-7-00	1	2	4.45	23	0	2	30	23	20	15	4	14	13	.211	.310	.367	10.00	10.77	130
Miller, Mitchell	L-L	6-6	185	6-13-97	1	3	7.40	17	0	3	21	22	19	17	2	20	24	.265	.435	.422	22.22	18.52	108
Morgan, David	R-R	6-0	185	10-26-99	1	1	4.67	18	0	3	27	24	15	14	3	10	36	.231	.304	.385	31.30	8.70	115
Morgan, Tyler	R-R	6-0	200	11-4-00	4	7	4.76	37	5	1	74	67	41	39	7	27	56	.247	.316	.376	18.12	8.74	309
Nett, Braden	R-R	6-3	185	6-18-02	5	2	4.03	19	18	0	60	48	33	27	3	35	70	.215	.326	.305	26.42	13.21	265
Och, Ryan	R-L	6-0	205	7-18-98	1	1	4.73	18	0	1	27	29	15	14	1	15	41	.282	.385	.398	33.06	12.10	124
Paplham, Cole	R-R	6-3	215	3-19-00	0	1	10.38	4	0	0	4	7	5	5	1	3	4	.350	.435	.550	17.39	13.04	23
Pena, Francis	R-R	6-1	170	1-25-01	3	0	0.86	11	0	2	21	13	3	2	0	7	17	.178	.250	.260	21.25	8.75	80
Pinales, Enmanuel	R-R	6-2	185	4-16-01	3	9	3.49	22	21	0	111	94	46	43	14	43	101	.230	.304	.407	21.96	9.35	460
Reyes, Jose Luis	R-R	6-3	190	8-20-02	2	2	2.74	6	2	0	23	19	7	7	1	9	14	.235	.333	.346	14.89	9.57	94
Rodriguez, Bradgley	R-R	6-1	160	11-16-03	2	0	2.59	29	0	1	42	29	16	12	2	23	45	.197	.322	.293	25.71	13.14	175
Routzahn, Ethan	R-R	6-4	225	3-19-98	0	0	0.00	3	0	1	5	1	0	0	0	2	7	.056	.150	.056	35.00	10.00	20
Sanchez, Fernando	L-L	6-0	198	9-13-00	3	4	3.97	15	5	1	48	47	27	21	1	21	55	.250	.345	.330	25.00	9.55	220
Smeltz, Jackson	L-L	6-3	210	9-14-98	2	3	4.11	11	0	0	15	17	9	7	0	3	23	.266	.319	.313	31.94	4.17	72
Varmette, Will	R-R	6-2	195	2-28-03	0	2	9.82	8	0	0	7	10	12	8	0	10	12	.303	.457	.364	26.09	21.74	46
Vilar, Anthony	L-R	5-10	190	4-1-99	0	0	0.00	3	0	0	3	1	0	0	0	1	0	.111	.200	.111	0.00	10.00	10
Whiting, Sam	R-R	6-3	220	12-15-00	0	1	2.28	10	6	0	28	18	7	7	1	17	28	.189	.328	.274	23.73	14.41	118
Yost, Eric	R-R	6-1	190	10-15-02	1	1	4.10	6	4	0	26	29	13	12	0	8	17	.287	.345	.337	15.45	7.27	110

Fielding

Catcher	PCT	G	PO	A	E	DP	PB
Bender	.990	25	193	15	2	1	1
Kopack	1.000	3	30	1	0	0	1
Salas	.986	67	595	43	9	2	7
Vilar	.980	37	353	31	8	2	9
Vincent	1.000	1	4	0	0	0	0

First Base	PCT	G	PO	A	E	DP
Doersching	.982	47	307	27	6	19
Dunn	1.000	4	23	2	0	2
Fabian	1.000	6	33	5	0	5
Kopack	1.000	2	17	0	0	2
Long	.980	6	47	2	1	9
Ortiz	.991	26	192	21	2	22
Sanabria	.982	32	207	16	4	24
Vilar	.988	14	74	8	1	12

Second Base	PCT	G	PO	A	E	DP
Camou	1.000	1	0	1	0	0
Cedeno	.982	100	183	253	8	63
Dale	1.000	3	7	6	0	2
Hoffman	.889	1	4	4	1	0
McClaughry	1.000	8	16	13	0	1
Ortiz	1.000	4	9	8	0	3
Verdugo	1.000	1	1	2	0	0
Vilar	1.000	17	30	42	0	13

Third Base	PCT	G	PO	A	E	DP
Beshears	1.000	13	7	22	0	3
Camou	.875	3	2	5	1	0
Dunn	.895	8	7	10	2	2
Hoffman	.500	3	0	1	1	0
McClaughry	1.000	3	1	6	0	1
Ortiz	.914	79	58	113	16	16
Verdugo	.921	24	17	41	5	6
Vilar	1.000	2	2	1	0	0

Shortstop	PCT	G	PO	A	E	DP
Beshears	.950	39	35	79	6	15
Dale	.929	5	7	6	1	2
Hoffman	.963	17	29	49	3	17
McClaughry	.942	70	81	146	14	32
Ortiz	1.000	2	1	4	0	0
Vilar	1.000	1	1	0	0	0

Outfield	PCT	G	PO	A	E	DP
Bender	1.000	2	3	0	0	0
Bush	.995	84	193	5	1	3
Camou	1.000	2	4	0	0	0
Campbell	1.000	9	18	1	0	0
Cedeno	1.000	1	2	0	0	0
Doersching	1.000	4	8	0	0	0
Dunn	.966	18	25	3	1	1
Fabian	1.000	8	7	0	0	0
Hoffman	1.000	1	1	0	0	0
Kopack	1.000	3	4	0	0	0
Long	.500	2	1	0	1	0
McClaughry	.000	1	0	0	0	0
Mears	.976	54	80	0	2	0
Murphy	.996	115	223	7	1	2
Ortiz	1.000	1	2	0	0	0
Robertson	.979	69	133	4	3	0
Vincent	1.000	4	3	0	0	0
Vogt	.990	50	98	3	1	1

LAKE ELSINORE STORM — LOW-A

CALIFORNIA LEAGUE

Batting	B-T	Ht.	Wt.	DOB	AVG	OBP	SLG	G	PA	AB	R	H	2B	3B	HR	RBI	BB	HBP	SH	SF	SO	SB	CS	BB%	SO%
Barnett, Sean	R-R	6-2	200	6-22-03	.280	.333	.420	12	54	50	11	14	2	1	1	2	2	2	0	0	13	1	0	3.70	24.07
Beshears, Jay	R-R	6-4	215	5-6-02	.320	.489	.454	28	133	97	30	31	7	0	2	11	31	3	0	2	27	1	2	23.31	20.30
Bogaerts, Xander	R-R	6-2	218	10-1-92	.571	.625	.571	2	8	7	3	4	0	0	0	1	1	0	0	0	1	0	0	12.50	12.50
Butterworth, Brandon	R-R	5-11	168	8-29-02	.219	.318	.281	24	110	96	16	21	6	0	0	13	11	3	0	0	20	8	3	10.00	18.18
Camou, Alain	L-R	5-11	150	11-1-03	.202	.232	.270	25	95	89	6	18	2	2	0	6	4	0	0	2	13	0	1	4.21	13.68
Campbell, Jacob	R-R	6-0	200	5-21-00	.248	.365	.401	59	266	222	37	55	9	2	7	51	31	11	0	2	58	7	4	11.65	21.80
Campusano, Luis	R-R	5-11	232	9-29-98	.133	.188	.333	4	16	15	2	2	0	0	1	4	1	0	0	0	3	0	0	6.25	18.75
Choi, B.Y.	L-R	6-3	203	4-30-02	.207	.311	.304	24	106	92	17	19	4	1	1	10	13	1	0	0	35	0	0	12.26	33.02
Coffman, Spence	R-R	6-1	170	1-7-04	.222	.290	.259	9	31	27	0	6	1	0	0	1	2	1	0	1	8	0	0	6.45	25.81
Costello, Jack	R-R	6-1	195	5-17-01	.284	.388	.529	25	121	102	22	29	5	1	6	30	14	4	0	1	8	2	1	11.57	6.61
De Vries, Leodalis	B-R	6-2	183	10-11-06	.237	.361	.441	75	360	299	63	71	22	3	11	38	50	9	0	2	84	13	2	13.89	23.33
Durfee, Brendan	L-R	6-4	221	7-31-01	.288	.413	.479	20	92	73	11	21	8	0	2	18	13	4	0	2	18	0	0	14.13	19.57
Gonzalez, JD	L-R	5-11	165	10-3-05	.205	.322	.230	48	199	161	26	33	4	0	0	31	27	4	0	7	55	0	0	13.57	27.64
Head, Dillon	L-L	5-11	180	10-11-04	.237	.317	.366	21	104	93	13	22	5	2	1	9	9	2	0	0	25	3	4	8.65	24.04
Hoffman, Wyatt	R-R	5-9	170	3-16-99	.218	.356	.319	72	270	216	35	47	11	1	3	30	34	14	3	3	91	15	6	12.59	33.70
Hollow, Kaden	L-R	6-1	210	3-17-01	.161	.235	.242	19	68	62	10	10	5	0	0	4	6	0	0	0	24	0	0	8.82	35.29
Jackson, Ryan	R-R	5-10	180	11-27-01	.261	.404	.283	13	57	46	7	12	1	0	0	7	8	3	0	0	8	3	0	14.04	14.04
Karpathios, Braedon	L-L	6-1	186	6-19-03	.252	.388	.385	119	534	429	79	108	29	2	8	57	95	4	0	6	145	5	3	17.79	27.15
King, Lamar	R-R	6-3	215	12-7-03	.266	.352	.426	25	108	94	18	25	7	1	2	15	10	3	0	1	27	0	0	9.26	25.00

Linares, Oswaldo	R-R	5-11	150	4-28-03	.203	.324	.280	57	219	182	23	37	8	0	2	20	33	1	0	3	45	0	2	15.07	20.55
Long, Ethan	R-R	6-3	215	5-10-01	.271	.406	.393	41	175	140	23	38	8	0	3	30	33	0	0	2	49	0	0	18.86	28.00
Roberts, Kai	L-R	6-4	200	3-15-01	.340	.414	.470	24	117	100	25	34	6	2	1	17	13	1	1	2	27	14	0	11.11	23.08
Rodriguez, Carlos	B-R	5-10	155	5-12-03	.174	.310	.217	7	29	23	3	4	1	0	0	4	5	0	0	1	6	0	0	17.24	20.69
Sanabria, Jose	R-R	5-10	150	10-30-02	.221	.309	.275	73	302	262	34	58	11	0	1	38	32	2	3	2	65	6	1	10.60	21.52
Sanabria, Romeo	L-R	6-2	200	5-2-02	.311	.433	.493	59	270	219	42	68	16	0	8	40	48	1	0	2	46	3	0	17.78	17.04
Valentine, Chase	R-R	5-11	160	4-22-02	.252	.356	.360	72	264	222	43	56	9	0	5	31	31	6	3	2	76	6	4	11.74	28.79
Verdugo, Rosman	R-R	6-0	180	2-2-05	.250	.363	.407	81	372	312	57	78	18	2	9	50	54	3	0	3	102	6	3	14.52	27.42
Vincent, Colton	R-R	6-1	182	1-25-00	.241	.343	.379	16	67	58	7	14	4	2	0	12	8	1	0	0	16	0	0	11.94	23.88
Vogt, Nick	R-R	6-1	185	8-4-00	.266	.341	.419	52	227	203	42	54	10	3	5	29	19	4	1	0	61	17	2	8.37	26.87
Wilson, Ryan	R-R	6-1	195	1-12-02	.214	.361	.282	99	427	341	52	73	11	3	2	43	61	20	0	5	65	5	2	14.29	15.22

Pitching	B-T	Ht.	Wt.	DOB	W	L	ERA	G	GS	SV	IP	Hits	Runs	ER	HR	BB	SO	AVG	OBP	SLG	SO%	BB%	BF
Addkison, Zac	R-R	6-4	225	6-24-02	0	0	1.23	5	0	0	7	7	1	1	1	6	9	.259	.394	.370	26.47	17.65	34
Balboni, Thomas	L-R	6-4	185	7-6-00	4	1	4.46	30	0	2	34	29	19	17	1	20	60	.221	.340	.328	38.22	12.74	157
Camarena, Daniel	L-L	6-0	210	11-9-92	0	0	5.40	3	0	0	5	5	3	3	1	3	1	.294	.400	.529	5.00	15.00	20
Campbell, Jacob	R-R	6-0	200	5-21-00	0	0	0.00	1	0	0	1	2	0	0	0	1	0	.400	.500	.400	0.00	16.67	6
Chacon, Javier	L-L	5-11	190	12-24-02	6	2	3.61	33	5	2	77	57	38	31	6	41	93	.204	.316	.341	28.27	12.46	329
Collett, Keegan	R-R	6-3	215	7-27-98	1	2	8.53	12	0	1	19	22	19	18	3	19	19	.293	.438	.547	19.79	19.79	96
Cosgrove, Tom	L-L	6-2	190	6-14-96	0	0	5.40	2	1	0	2	2	1	1	1	1	3	.286	.375	.714	37.50	12.50	8
Eichelberger, Breck	R-R	6-4	195	3-15-00	1	0	8.49	7	1	0	12	18	13	11	1	13	10	.353	.507	.451	14.29	18.57	70
German, Luis	R-R	6-2	160	10-14-01	1	3	6.26	34	0	3	42	28	34	29	0	57	47	.193	.441	.228	21.86	26.51	215
Gustin, Harry	S-L	6-0	160	5-6-02	2	3	4.01	21	2	1	43	42	29	19	3	18	54	.247	.323	.353	27.98	9.33	193
Gutierrez, Luis	L-L	6-0	175	7-31-03	3	3	4.62	14	13	0	62	76	42	32	6	17	51	.300	.345	.431	18.41	6.14	277
Hoffman, Wyatt	R-R	5-9	170	3-16-99	0	1	5.79	4	0	0	5	4	5	3	1	0	1	.235	.263	.529	5.26	0.00	19
Jose, Bernard	R-R	5-11	160	3-3-03	2	0	4.50	9	0	0	16	20	11	8	2	7	10	.294	.377	.441	12.99	9.09	77
Koenig, Ian	L-R	6-2	225	4-10-01	2	3	5.44	13	12	0	43	43	28	26	7	11	46	.254	.304	.473	25.27	6.04	182
Landinez, Yerry	S-R	6-1	170	1-20-01	2	0	6.04	22	0	1	28	24	21	19	1	20	32	.229	.367	.400	24.81	15.50	129
Lowe, Isaiah	R-R	6-1	220	5-7-03	5	3	3.00	17	13	0	72	56	27	24	2	29	89	.211	.300	.306	29.67	9.67	300
Lugo, Alejandro	R-R	6-0	165	8-20-02	6	2	3.08	25	1	0	53	48	23	18	5	26	39	.241	.330	.372	16.96	11.30	230
Mallitz, Josh	R-R	6-3	195	10-20-01	0	0	8.10	3	0	0	3	7	3	3	0	2	2	.467	.529	.467	11.76	11.76	17
Matos, Dwayne	R-R	6-1	155	11-7-00	2	3	6.09	18	0	2	34	39	25	23	1	9	41	.287	.336	.500	27.33	6.00	150
Mendez, Miguel	R-R	6-2	165	7-1-02	3	5	3.86	22	20	0	82	68	35	35	4	55	86	.227	.362	.350	23.37	14.95	368
Miralles, Maikel	R-R	5-11	160	10-22-04	1	3	5.30	16	5	0	37	45	28	22	2	20	35	.296	.382	.414	20.11	11.49	174
Montgomery, Carson	R-R	6-3	205	8-13-02	0	1	3.86	3	2	0	7	4	4	3	1	6	10	.167	.333	.333	33.33	20.00	30
Moreno, Adan	R-R	6-1	185	9-8-04	0	0	0.00	1	0	0	2	1	0	0	0	1	2	.167	.444	.167	22.22	11.11	9
Moreno, Johan	R-R	6-1	180	3-26-03	5	2	5.62	17	5	0	42	48	32	26	6	28	38	.284	.382	.456	19.00	14.00	200
Musgrove, Joe	R-R	6-5	230	12-4-92	0	0	5.40	1	1	0	3	4	2	2	0	0	2	.308	.357	.615	14.29	0.00	14
Neighbors, Tyson	R-R	6-1	220	10-9-02	0	0	3.86	4	0	0	5	5	2	2	0	4	9	.263	.391	.316	39.13	17.39	23
Olmedo, Kleiber	R-R	6-1	155	8-23-04	1	0	4.58	8	1	1	18	14	9	9	1	10	19	.215	.325	.308	24.68	12.99	77
Pascual, Yovannki	L-L	5-11	185	8-4-02	1	0	7.04	5	0	0	8	9	7	6	0	6	7	.300	.432	.333	18.92	16.22	37
Peralta, Wandy	L-L	6-0	227	7-27-91	1	0	0.00	2	1	0	2	0	0	0	0	1	2	.000	.125	.000	25.00	12.50	8
Qin, Zack	L-L	6-1	198	7-3-05	0	1	2.57	5	0	1	7	6	4	2	1	2	9	.222	.267	.370	30.00	6.67	30
Reyes, Jose Luis	R-R	6-3	190	8-20-02	4	7	6.94	18	16	0	70	88	61	54	8	22	72	.300	.364	.495	21.95	6.71	328
Robinson, Kobe	R-R	6-2	160	3-3-01	4	1	6.96	20	0	1	32	41	27	25	1	21	34	.304	.415	.407	20.73	12.80	164
Rodriguez, Bradgley	R-R	6-1	160	11-16-03	0	0	1.69	4	0	2	5	2	1	1	0	1	9	.111	.158	.111	47.37	5.26	19
Rosario, Jonney	R-R	5-10	185	7-28-04	0	0	9.00	1	0	0	1	2	1	1	0	4	1	.400	.667	.400	11.11	44.44	9
Ruiz, Xavier	R-R	6-1	180	11-19-02	3	2	2.22	36	0	8	53	43	16	13	0	18	55	.218	.288	.299	25.11	8.22	219
Salazar, Braian	L-L	6-2	165	6-12-05	0	2	3.75	8	0	1	12	7	7	5	1	11	21	.163	.400	.302	35.00	18.33	60
Sanchez, Fernando	L-L	6-0	198	9-13-00	1	1	2.70	8	6	0	27	25	10	8	1	7	33	.236	.289	.311	28.95	6.14	114
Smeltz, Jackson	L-L	6-3	210	9-14-98	0	0	3.00	2	0	0	3	2	1	1	0	1	3	.222	.333	.222	23.08	7.69	13
Valdez, Miguel	R-R	6-0	170	8-1-03	0	0	7.11	10	0	1	13	17	13	10	2	6	9	.340	.397	.540	15.52	10.34	58
Valentine, Chase	R-R	5-11	160	4-22-02	0	0	9.82	2	0	0	4	7	4	4	1	0	2	.389	.389	.667	11.11	0.00	18
Varmette, Will	R-R	6-2	195	2-28-03	4	4	6.13	28	2	1	47	36	35	32	4	34	64	.222	.370	.358	30.77	16.35	208
Whiting, Sam	R-R	6-3	220	12-15-00	2	1	3.58	8	8	0	28	30	11	11	2	9	24	.275	.339	.440	19.83	7.44	121
Yost, Eric	R-R	6-1	190	10-15-02	4	2	4.89	18	14	0	81	94	47	44	7	27	80	.293	.357	.421	22.22	7.50	360

Fielding

Catcher	PCT	G	PO	A	E	DP	PB
Campbell	.966	5	53	3	2	1	0
Campusano	1.000	2	12	0	0	0	0
Durfee	.991	12	106	6	1	0	3
Gonzalez	.979	42	407	22	9	0	8
Hollow	.958	5	45	1	2	0	0
Linares	.970	50	447	30	15	5	10
Rodriguez	.985	6	63	3	1	0	2
Vincent	.965	12	107	3	4	1	0

First Base	PCT	G	PO	A	E	DP
Costello	.981	11	94	8	2	8
Hollow	1.000	6	38	0	0	5
King	.952	16	112	7	6	13
Long	.994	24	163	6	1	11
Sanabria	.983	56	360	34	7	30
Wilson	.986	22	135	9	2	10

Second Base	PCT	G	PO	A	E	DP
Bogaerts	1.000	2	2	3	0	0
Butterworth	.978	8	14	31	1	6
Camou	.974	10	13	25	1	5
Choi	1.000	6	10	17	0	4
Hoffman	.962	7	8	17	1	7
Jackson	1.000	2	1	3	0	0
Sanabria	.984	42	70	119	3	22
Valentine	.975	44	87	111	5	19
Verdugo	.951	12	14	25	2	2

Third Base	PCT	G	PO	A	E	DP
Beshears	.865	21	13	19	5	4
Camou	1.000	8	3	18	0	2
Choi	.969	12	12	19	1	0
Costello	1.000	5	4	5	0	0
Hoffman	.917	9	10	12	2	2
Jackson	1.000	10	3	17	0	2
Long	.900	4	5	4	1	0
Sanabria	.979	19	15	31	1	1
Valentine	1.000	4	1	6	0	0
Verdugo	.884	39	24	75	13	7

Shortstop	PCT	G	PO	A	E	DP
Beshears	1.000	5	3	10	0	0
Butterworth	.987	16	31	44	1	8
Choi	.947	5	6	12	1	4
Coffman	1.000	1	2	2	0	0
De Vries	.962	58	67	133	8	26
Hoffman	.980	15	21	28	1	7
Jackson	1.000	1	0	3	0	1
Valentine	.945	17	17	35	3	9
Verdugo	.915	14	18	25	4	5

Outfield	PCT	G	PO	A	E	DP
Barnett	.920	9	23	0	2	0
Campbell	.968	48	83	7	3	2
Coffman	1.000	8	6	2	0	0
Costello	1.000	5	7	2	0	0
Head	1.000	19	35	0	0	0
Hoffman	.989	37	82	4	1	2
Hollow	1.000	3	7	1	0	0
Karpathios	.982	109	209	13	4	0
Linares	.000	1	0	0	0	0

Long	1.000	1	2	1	0	0	Valentine	1.000	2	5	0	0	0	Wilson	.984	71	123	4	2	0
Roberts	.981	20	53	0	1	0	Vincent	1.000	4	8	0	0	0							
Sanabria	.962	12	25	0	1	0	Vogt	.990	49	101	3	1	1							

ACL PADRES

ROOKIE

ARIZONA COMPLEX LEAGUE

Batting	B-T	Ht.	Wt.	DOB	AVG	OBP	SLG	G	PA	AB	R	H	2B	3B	HR	RBI	BB	HBP	SH	SF	SO	SB	CS	BB%	SO%
Camou, Alain	L-R	5-11	150	11-1-03	.500	.500	.750	1	4	4	1	2	1	0	0	3	0	0	0	0	2	0	0	0.00	50.00
Campbell, Jacob	R-R	6-0	200	5-21-00	.250	.250	.250	1	4	4	1	1	0	0	0	0	0	0	0	0	3	0	0	0.00	75.00
Castro, Jesus	R-R	5-10	158	7-7-04	.086	.217	.086	25	71	58	5	5	0	0	0	2	9	1	2	1	21	0	0	12.68	29.58
Choi, B.Y.	L-R	6-3	203	4-30-02	.262	.405	.424	55	217	172	34	45	12	2	4	18	35	7	2	1	47	12	2	16.13	21.66
Coffman, Spence	R-R	6-1	170	1-7-04	.295	.364	.341	53	200	176	32	52	8	0	0	24	19	1	2	2	29	19	2	9.50	14.50
Conliffe, Kashon	R-R	5-11	150	7-5-05	.193	.333	.264	50	174	140	21	27	4	3	0	11	28	2	3	1	51	19	5	16.09	29.31
De Leon, Luis	B-R	5-8	155	1-8-06	.071	.235	.071	19	53	42	3	3	0	0	0	1	8	1	2	0	25	2	1	15.09	47.17
Dunn, Lucas	R-R	6-0	205	4-30-99	.279	.373	.326	13	51	43	8	12	2	0	0	3	7	0	0	1	16	6	0	13.73	31.37
Grant, Donte	L-R	6-0	175	8-29-04	.300	.417	.333	11	36	30	5	9	1	0	0	3	5	1	0	0	12	7	1	13.89	33.33
Hollis, Connor	R-R	5-7	170	11-18-94	.417	.500	.500	4	14	12	3	5	1	0	0	0	2	0	0	0	2	1	0	14.29	14.29
Hollow, Kaden	L-R	6-1	210	3-17-01	.286	.472	.440	31	124	91	24	26	9	1	1	11	29	3	1	0	28	2	0	23.39	22.58
Javier, Ismael	B-R	5-8	160	8-27-05	.218	.301	.309	38	126	110	12	24	8	1	0	8	10	3	3	0	34	3	4	7.94	26.98
Jones, L.J.	R-R	6-0	225	6-27-99	.418	.470	.714	27	100	91	15	38	9	0	6	27	8	1	0	0	16	1	0	8.00	16.00
King, Lamar	R-R	6-3	215	12-7-03	.275	.400	.417	37	145	120	20	33	7	5	0	17	16	9	0	0	26	0	0	11.03	17.93
Kopack, Addison	R-R	6-2	215	8-6-01	.308	.382	.516	27	102	91	15	28	7	3	2	13	10	1	0	0	28	1	2	9.80	27.45
Long, Ethan	R-R	6-3	215	5-10-01	.750	.750	1.250	1	4	4	2	3	2	0	0	4	0	0	0	0	1	0	0	0.00	25.00
Mears, Joshua	R-R	6-3	230	2-21-01	.222	.417	.667	3	12	9	4	2	1	0	1	3	2	1	0	0	4	2	0	16.67	33.33
Montesino, Daniel	L-L	6-0	180	2-12-04	.176	.360	.294	8	25	17	4	3	2	0	0	3	5	1	0	2	4	2	0	20.00	16.00
Rodriguez, Carlos	B-R	5-10	155	5-12-03	.212	.296	.303	42	153	132	15	28	4	4	0	15	15	2	1	3	46	1	0	9.80	30.07
Rojas, Yendry	L-R	6-0	185	1-27-05	.230	.310	.303	54	189	165	18	38	8	2	0	23	19	1	2	2	37	10	2	10.05	19.58
Sanchez, Hugo	L-R	6-0	180	11-6-02	.236	.317	.375	26	82	72	14	17	4	3	0	12	9	0	0	1	33	2	0	10.98	40.24
Turbi, Emil	B-R	5-8	150	11-26-04	.143	.213	.167	14	48	42	5	6	1	0	0	2	3	1	1	1	15	2	2	6.25	31.25
Vincent, Colton	R-R	6-1	182	1-25-00	.321	.392	.435	41	154	131	16	42	13	1	0	29	12	6	1	4	29	3	0	7.79	18.83

Pitching	B-T	Ht.	Wt.	DOB	W	L	ERA	G	GS	SV	IP	Hits	Runs	ER	HR	BB	SO	AVG	OBP	SLG	SO%	BB%	BF
Addkison, Zac	R-R	6-4	225	6-24-02	2	1	5.40	15	2	0	25	26	16	15	3	8	27	.268	.333	.464	25.00	7.41	108
Balzer, Bryan	L-R	6-1	190	10-27-04	0	0	6.43	6	2	0	7	8	5	5	0	3	7	.296	.406	.407	21.88	9.38	32
Burkett, Langston	L-R	6-6	220	4-2-05	1	2	9.39	10	1	0	15	20	18	16	0	15	12	.333	.482	.483	14.46	18.07	83
Camarena, Daniel	L-L	6-0	210	11-9-92	0	0	27.00	1	1	0	1	4	3	3	1	0	1	.571	.571	1.429	14.29	0.00	7
Castro, Jesus	R-R	5-10	158	7-7-04	0	0	4.50	3	0	0	2	2	1	1	0	1	1	.250	.333	.625	11.11	11.11	9
Cecil, Adler	L-L	6-3	155	5-1-05	1	2	7.54	18	3	2	23	20	21	19	2	34	34	.238	.484	.381	26.98	26.98	126
Cruz, Humberto	R-R	6-1	190	12-18-06	0	0	0.00	2	2	0	2	1	0	0	0	1	2	.143	.250	.143	25.00	12.50	8
Edwards, Carl	R-R	6-3	165	9-3-91	0	1	5.40	2	2	0	5	6	7	3	2	2	5	.273	.333	.591	20.83	8.33	24
Gil, Igor	L-L	5-11	170	3-23-01	0	1	8.53	17	2	0	19	27	19	18	0	21	23	.338	.481	.375	21.70	19.81	106
Gonzalez, Jesus	L-L	5-10	160	6-12-01	0	0	4.50	4	2	0	4	5	2	2	0	3	7	.313	.421	.438	36.84	15.79	19
Gutierrez, Luis	L-L	6-0	175	7-31-03	1	1	4.61	3	1	0	14	15	7	7	1	2	16	.278	.304	.370	28.07	3.51	57
Jose, Bernard	R-R	5-11	160	3-3-03	2	2	4.99	21	0	3	31	27	19	17	3	27	36	.237	.389	.360	25.00	18.75	144
Koenig, Ian	L-R	6-2	225	4-10-01	0	0	0.00	3	3	0	4	1	0	0	0	3	2	.083	.267	.083	13.33	20.00	15
Landinez, Yerry	S-R	6-1	170	1-20-01	2	0	6.75	7	3	0	9	9	7	7	1	8	12	.273	.419	.485	27.91	18.60	43
Leija, Aldo	R-R	6-2	160	6-30-04	2	1	4.57	13	3	0	22	20	12	11	2	13	26	.256	.366	.397	27.96	13.98	93
Lopez, Jesus	R-R	5-11	175	3-14-06	0	3	6.68	12	5	0	34	40	30	25	3	19	38	.290	.383	.522	23.46	11.73	162
Lugo, Alejandro	R-R	6-0	165	8-20-02	0	0	0.00	1	0	0	1	1	0	0	0	1	2	.250	.400	.500	40.00	20.00	5
Martinez, Henry	R-R	6-4	190	3-2-04	1	1	7.30	8	1	0	12	14	10	10	2	11	12	.292	.433	.521	20.00	18.33	60
Miller, Mitchell	L-L	6-6	185	6-13-97	0	2	1.93	3	1	0	5	5	6	1	0	4	8	.263	.391	.316	34.78	17.39	23
Miralles, Maikel	R-R	5-11	160	10-22-04	1	2	4.20	11	0	3	15	11	9	7	1	8	21	.200	.292	.255	31.82	12.12	66
Morales, Gabe	L-L	6-3	175	4-14-99	0	0	0.00	1	1	0	1	0	0	0	0	0	1	.000	.000	.000	33.33	0.00	3
Moreno, Johan	R-R	6-1	180	3-26-03	0	1	4.50	4	0	0	10	12	9	5	1	7	7	.286	.400	.524	14.00	14.00	50
Olmedo, Kleiber	R-R	6-1	155	8-23-04	3	1	6.75	16	2	2	33	46	28	25	4	15	37	.326	.389	.511	23.42	9.49	158
Otto, Glenn	R-R	6-3	240	3-11-96	0	2	17.18	3	3	0	4	5	7	7	2	4	4	.333	.474	.867	21.05	21.05	19
Paplham, Cole	R-R	6-3	215	3-19-00	0	0	0.00	1	0	0	1	1	0	0	0	1	1	.333	.500	.333	25.00	25.00	4
Parra, Abraham	R-R	6-2	170	12-29-05	0	4	9.59	13	7	0	36	47	40	38	3	26	40	.318	.435	.459	21.62	14.05	185
Pascual, Yovannki	L-L	5-11	185	8-4-02	1	2	2.88	10	3	0	25	26	11	8	1	9	26	.274	.337	.400	25.00	8.65	104
Qin, Zack	L-L	6-1	198	7-3-05	1	0	0.82	6	2	0	11	9	1	1	0	3	14	.220	.273	.220	31.82	6.82	44
Reyes, Jimmy	R-R	5-10	170	11-15-05	0	0	8.22	6	0	1	8	4	8	7	1	11	6	.174	.474	.348	15.79	28.95	38
Salazar, Braian	L-L	6-2	165	6-12-05	0	1	5.76	12	4	0	25	26	18	16	1	18	34	.274	.397	.347	29.31	15.52	116
Salinas, Ruben	R-L	6-0	154	1-13-03	4	3	6.75	16	3	0	24	32	24	18	2	8	24	.308	.379	.423	20.69	6.90	116
Smeltz, Jackson	L-L	6-3	210	9-14-98	0	0	0.00	2	1	0	2	2	0	0	0	2	4	.250	.400	.375	40.00	20.00	10
Valdez, Miguel	R-R	6-0	170	8-1-03	2	3	5.70	18	0	0	30	32	26	19	5	15	32	.278	.368	.478	23.36	10.95	137

Fielding

C: Rodriguez 24, Castro 18, Vincent 12, Hollow 8. **1B:** Kopack 19, Rodriguez 17, Sanchez 10, Hollow 10, Jones 5, Castro 3, King 1, Vincent 1, Long 1. **2B:** Javier 35, De Leon 8, Dunn 8, Coffman 6, Rojas 4, Turbi 3, Hollis 3, Choi 3. **3B:** Rojas 44, Kopack 9, Turbi 5, Dunn 4, Choi 2, Coffman 1, Camou 1, Javier 1, Jones 1, Sanchez 1. **SS:** Choi 50, Rojas 11, Coffman 3, De Leon 1. **LF:** Coffman 21, Jones 13, De Leon 9, Vincent 8, Montesino 7, Conliffe 5, Turbi 3, Hollow 1. **CF:** Conliffe 26, Coffman 23, Grant 10, Turbi 4, De Leon 1. **RF:** Conliffe 21, Vincent 21, Hollow 11, Jones 5, Kopack 2, Mears 2, Montesino 1, Turbi 1, Campbell 1.

DSL PADRES BROWN

ROOKIE

DOMINICAN SUMMER LEAGUE

Batting	B-T	Ht.	Wt.	DOB	AVG	OBP	SLG	G	PA	AB	R	H	2B	3B	HR	RBI	BB	HBP	SH	SF	SO	SB	CS	BB%	SO%
Alcantara, Fabian	R-R	6-0	170	12-12-05	.182	.339	.321	51	171	137	21	25	7	0	4	19	29	4	0	1	57	12	1	16.96	33.33

Alfonzo, Dayquer	R-R	6-1	190	8-2-07	.311	.436	.393	26	78	61	10	19	5	0	0	9	14	1	0	2	22	2	1	17.95	28.21
Arias, Jesmaylin	L-L	5-11	175	4-20-07	.339	.452	.475	20	73	59	8	20	6	1	0	12	11	2	0	1	13	1	0	15.07	17.81
Bericoto, Jose	R-R	6-0	160	4-23-07	.111	.306	.185	12	38	27	3	3	0	1	0	3	8	0	2	1	7	1	1	21.05	18.42
Downer, Jhojan	R-R	5-10	170	6-9-07	.154	.316	.179	33	98	78	10	12	2	0	0	5	18	1	0	1	33	3	2	18.37	33.67
Garcia, Alexander	L-R	6-0	170	10-26-05	.324	.409	.595	15	44	37	7	12	4	0	2	4	5	1	0	1	11	2	0	11.36	25.00
Giron, Estiven	R-R	5-11	170	5-25-05	.186	.338	.339	20	74	59	7	11	3	0	2	7	13	1	0	1	12	0	0	17.57	16.22
Guerrero, Tom	R-R	6-0	170	1-5-06	.190	.292	.238	7	24	21	2	4	1	0	0	4	3	0	0	0	9	0	1	12.50	37.50
Guzman, Walfrent	R-R	5-11	185	3-17-05	.107	.257	.143	12	35	28	1	3	1	0	0	4	6	0	0	1	16	0	0	17.14	45.71
Hernandez, Jason	R-R	5-11	160	1-11-06	.310	.417	.451	24	84	71	13	22	3	2	1	18	10	3	0	0	15	6	4	11.90	17.86
Javier, Johendry	L-R	5-11	150	9-12-06	.140	.290	.160	24	62	50	7	7	1	0	0	10	10	1	0	1	18	0	0	16.13	29.03
Martinez, Eddson	L-L	5-5	145	8-21-07	.229	.383	.271	19	61	48	8	11	2	0	0	5	10	2	1	0	12	2	2	16.39	19.67
Martinez, Juan	R-R	6-3	175	2-1-07	.189	.379	.243	46	145	111	11	21	6	0	0	11	22	12	0	0	45	1	4	15.17	31.03
Morla, Yorvin	B-R	5-10	150	12-24-05	.227	.405	.281	49	169	128	27	29	3	2	0	8	31	8	1	1	31	20	8	18.34	18.34
Ponce, Isaac	R-R	6-2	192	11-1-06	.216	.370	.245	37	128	102	13	22	3	0	0	13	19	6	1	0	28	1	1	14.84	21.88
Rios, Endy	L-R	6-0	155	2-15-07	.194	.240	.258	37	100	93	10	18	4	1	0	5	6	0	0	1	26	3	3	6.00	26.00
Sierra, Joan	R-R	5-10	175	8-13-06	.163	.385	.288	34	110	80	18	13	5	1	1	10	27	2	1	0	26	7	1	24.55	23.64
Tamburini, Kevin	L-R	6-1	150	4-26-06	.324	.387	.368	20	75	68	13	22	1	1	0	7	7	0	0	0	15	2	0	9.33	20.00
Tejeda, Eduarlin	B-R	5-9	150	2-24-05	.204	.313	.204	18	65	54	8	11	0	0	0	3	7	2	1	1	16	2	2	10.77	24.62
Tejeda, Jefren	L-L	6-1	170	7-24-03	.000	.000	.000	1	4	4	0	0	0	0	0	0	0	0	0	0	0	0	0	0.00	0.00
Valdez, Moises	R-R	5-8	165	11-28-05	.172	.333	.241	15	38	29	3	5	2	0	0	5	7	0	2	0	12	1	0	18.42	31.58
Velazquez, Ramses	L-L	6-0	180	10-14-04	.235	.469	.324	17	50	34	7	8	3	0	0	4	15	0	1	0	19	7	0	30.00	38.00
Winklaar, Clay	R-R	6-1	185	9-13-06	.069	.257	.069	37	109	87	4	6	0	0	0	5	11	11	0	0	36	2	1	10.09	33.03

Pitching	B-T	Ht.	Wt.	DOB	W	L	ERA	G	GS	SV	IP	Hits	Runs	ER	HR	BB	SO	AVG	OBP	SLG	SO%	BB%	BF
Agramonte, Alexander	R-R	5-11	165	9-23-04	0	2	6.00	2	2	0	9	12	8	6	0	6	3	.343	.452	.486	7.14	14.29	42
Belliard, Raymel	R-R	6-1	155	12-9-05	0	0	15.00	4	0	0	3	6	6	5	0	4	4	.400	.526	.467	21.05	21.05	19
Chourio, Winyer	R-R	6-2	180	11-4-03	2	0	0.66	6	1	0	14	9	2	1	0	5	15	.176	.250	.176	26.79	8.93	56
Crespo, Christian	R-R	6-2	190	1-30-03	0	0	0.00	2	0	0	3	2	0	0	0	0	4	.182	.182	.182	36.36	0.00	11
Davila, Manuel	R-R	6-0	140	8-8-07	1	2	3.46	6	6	0	26	20	13	10	0	7	29	.217	.308	.326	27.10	6.54	107
De La Rosa, Jose	R-R	6-0	175	11-20-04	0	3	7.20	6	6	0	20	20	17	16	3	16	12	.270	.443	.432	12.37	16.49	97
Hernandez, Edinson	R-R	6-2	175	6-9-06	2	5	6.98	13	5	0	30	22	29	23	2	35	36	.208	.401	.283	25.17	24.48	143
Hernandez, Edwyn	L-L	6-0	180	7-28-07	0	2	7.90	11	0	1	14	18	14	12	1	6	10	.310	.382	.431	14.71	8.82	68
Herrera, Joseph	L-L	5-8	145	11-10-05	1	2	5.50	13	5	0	38	41	35	23	2	31	36	.272	.404	.364	19.05	16.40	189
Martinez, Pedro	L-L	5-10	175	2-2-07	0	3	5.79	8	5	1	19	14	13	12	3	16	15	.219	.404	.391	16.85	17.98	89
Mejia, Rordy	R-R	6-0	180	4-28-05	0	1	5.66	11	4	1	21	23	14	13	4	7	16	.295	.364	.500	18.18	7.95	88
Minaya, Johan	R-R	6-1	165	10-22-04	2	2	3.44	11	3	2	34	24	16	13	2	13	30	.205	.319	.291	21.58	9.35	139
Navarro, Cristian	R-R	6-2	181	5-31-07	0	3	9.13	13	3	0	23	25	25	23	1	23	14	.278	.435	.367	12.17	20.00	115
Nova, Dionicio	R-R	6-2	185	4-20-04	1	2	5.49	8	1	0	20	23	20	12	0	13	17	.319	.436	.375	18.09	13.83	94
Ortega, Jose	R-R	6-3	160	6-11-05	0	2	14.34	10	0	0	11	13	17	17	0	7	14	.283	.441	.370	23.73	11.86	59
Padilla, Samuel	R-R	6-0	180	8-22-05	0	0	9.00	3	1	0	2	1	2	2	0	5	4	.143	.538	.143	30.77	38.46	13
Pena, Adrian	L-L	6-0	170	11-23-04	1	0	0.00	2	0	0	1	0	0	0	0	0	0	.000	.000	.000	0.00	0.00	3
Reyes, Jimmy	R-R	5-10	170	11-15-05	0	2	5.40	3	3	0	12	14	9	7	0	4	5	.286	.375	.388	8.93	7.14	56
Rios, Endy	L-R	6-0	155	2-15-07	0	0	0.00	1	0	0	0	1	0	0	0	0	1	.500	.500	.500	50.00	0.00	2
Salomon, Javier	L-L	5-11	180	7-12-07	0	3	9.13	11	8	0	23	22	29	23	4	23	19	.259	.440	.447	16.24	19.66	117
Smith, Shurland	R-R	6-0	168	9-14-06	1	2	8.64	15	0	0	17	18	21	16	1	19	11	.261	.448	.377	11.46	19.79	96
Solano, Leandro	R-R	6-2	160	2-18-05	2	2	5.59	14	0	1	19	19	16	12	1	10	9	.271	.402	.386	10.23	11.36	88
Soriano, Sebastian	L-L	6-5	205	4-17-02	1	2	6.67	13	1	1	27	45	34	20	1	16	24	.366	.449	.528	16.33	10.88	147
Valenzuela, Jordan	R-R	6-2	190	5-20-05	1	1	5.09	6	2	2	18	16	11	10	0	7	22	.239	.320	.313	29.33	9.33	75

Fielding

C: Ocopio 26, Hernandez 17, Diaz 14, Contreras 7, Cruz 1. **1B:** Garcia 28, Diaz 16, Valdez 16, Ocopio 6, Chevalier 2, Cruz 1, Hernandez 1, Perez 1. **2B:** Valdez 16, **C:** Downer 30, Giron 10, Ponce 10, Alfonzo 10, Guzman 6. **1B:** Sierra 14, Martinez 11, Garcia 10, Tamburini 9, Ponce 8, Guzman 6, Alfonzo 6, Giron 2. **2B:** Morla 36, Hernandez 5, Tejeda 5, Rios 4, Sierra 3, Tamburini 3, Javier 3, Tejeda 1. **3B:** Martinez 35, Javier 9, Sierra 8, Rios 7, Valdez 3, Tejeda 2, Guerrero 1. **SS:** Hernandez 15, Rios 14, Tejeda 8, Javier 8, Morla 7, Guerrero 6, Valdez 4. **LF:** Winklaar 20, Velazquez 13, Martinez 7, Sierra 6, Valdez 6, Alcantara 5, Rios 4, Garcia 2. **CF:** Alcantara 41, Martinez 8, Bericoto 4, Valdez 3, Velazquez 2, Winklaar 1, Arias 1. **RF:** Arias 20, Winklaar 16, Bericoto 7, Rios 5, Martinez 4, Alcantara 3, Sierra 3, Tejeda 2, Velazquez 2, Garcia 2.

DSL PADRES GOLD — *ROOKIE*

DOMINICAN SUMMER LEAGUE

Batting	B-T	Ht.	Wt.	DOB	AVG	OBP	SLG	G	PA	AB	R	H	2B	3B	HR	RBI	BB	HBP	SH	SF	SO	SB	CS	BB%	SO%
Arias, Jesmaylin	L-L	5-11	175	4-20-07	.202	.255	.287	28	102	94	8	19	5	0	1	15	6	1	0	1	28	1	1	5.88	27.45
Bericoto, Jose	R-R	6-0	160	4-23-07	.100	.308	.200	11	26	20	3	2	0	1	0	3	6	0	0	0	9	0	1	23.08	34.62
Castillo, Darian	B-R	5-7	150	9-12-06	.306	.449	.365	34	108	85	23	26	3	1	0	14	20	2	1	0	15	10	0	18.52	13.89
Contreras, Santiago	L-R	6-2	155	8-16-05	.179	.444	.262	37	126	84	25	15	3	2	0	12	32	8	2	0	40	7	3	25.40	31.75
Garcia, Alexander	L-R	6-0	170	10-26-05	.175	.431	.325	19	58	40	7	7	4	1	0	8	11	7	0	0	17	0	0	18.97	29.31
Garza, Andres	L-R	5-11	165	6-12-07	.143	.288	.190	23	52	42	10	6	2	0	0	2	9	0	0	1	13	0	1	17.31	25.00
Giron, Estiven	R-R	5-11	170	5-25-05	.291	.420	.327	19	69	55	8	16	2	0	0	8	10	3	0	1	18	0	0	14.49	26.09
Guerrero, Tom	R-R	6-0	170	1-5-06	.100	.174	.100	11	23	20	0	2	0	0	0	1	2	0	0	1	9	0	0	8.70	39.13
Guzman, Walfrent	R-R	5-11	185	3-17-05	.053	.357	.211	11	28	19	6	1	0	0	1	5	8	1	0	0	10	0	0	28.57	35.71
Hacen, Kevin	R-R	6-2	160	1-30-06	.189	.315	.270	42	149	122	19	23	5	1	1	21	18	6	0	3	42	5	1	12.08	28.19
Hernandez, Alcides	L-R	5-8	160	4-27-05	.252	.431	.304	42	153	115	23	29	4	1	0	15	32	5	0	1	19	8	2	20.92	12.42
Hernandez, Jason	R-R	5-11	160	1-11-06	.146	.311	.167	16	61	48	4	7	1	0	0	7	8	4	0	1	13	2	0	13.11	21.31
Marquez, Gustavo	R-R	6-0	160	12-28-04	.252	.420	.326	49	178	135	25	34	3	2	1	21	33	7	2	1	41	17	5	18.54	23.03
Martinez, Eddson	L-L	5-5	145	8-21-07	.203	.388	.250	22	85	64	16	13	3	0	0	9	18	2	0	1	21	6	6	21.18	24.71
Ocopio, Yoiber	R-R	5-10	175	8-24-04	.261	.442	.381	49	181	134	27	35	10	3	0	12	33	12	0	2	35	12	0	18.23	19.34

Ricardo, Ibrain	B-R	5-9	165	7-25-07	.500	.571	.500	8	14	10	8	5	0	0	0	3	2	1	0	1	0	0	0	14.29	0.00
Severino, Frailyn	R-R	5-10	155	12-14-06	.253	.364	.307	34	88	75	13	19	4	0	0	8	8	5	0	0	17	3	2	9.09	19.32
Tejeda, Eduarlin	B-R	5-9	150	2-24-05	.227	.376	.280	25	93	75	12	17	2	1	0	11	16	2	0	0	24	5	3	17.20	25.81
Tovar, Yimy	R-R	6-0	160	4-7-06	.230	.405	.358	49	195	148	33	34	10	3	1	28	36	9	0	2	28	14	5	18.46	14.36
Turbi, Emil	B-R	5-8	150	11-26-04	.211	.423	.237	16	53	38	10	8	1	0	0	4	11	3	1	0	14	3	1	20.75	26.42
Valdez, Moises	R-R	5-8	165	11-28-05	.229	.368	.314	28	88	70	9	16	3	0	1	7	15	1	1	1	16	2	1	17.05	18.18
Velazquez, Ramses	L-L	6-0	180	10-14-04	.000	.364	.000	6	11	6	0	0	0	0	0	1	3	1	0	1	3	0	0	27.27	27.27

Pitching	B-T	Ht.	Wt.	DOB	W	L	ERA	G	GS	SV	IP	Hits	Runs	ER	HR	BB	SO	AVG	OBP	SLG	SO%	BB%	BF
Agramonte, Alexander	R-R	5-11	165	9-23-04	1	3	8.25	11	1	1	24	32	26	22	4	15	20	.327	.432	.500	16.81	12.61	119
Batista, Erick	R-R	6-0	155	9-7-05	0	3	14.46	6	3	0	9	8	19	15	2	14	13	.235	.491	.441	24.53	26.42	53
Beltre, Yoesmerli	R-R	6-4	180	5-31-06	1	0	5.63	6	0	0	8	8	10	5	0	9	5	.267	.450	.400	12.20	21.95	41
Burgos, Roberto	R-R	6-2	185	10-6-03	2	2	3.54	13	1	1	28	19	16	11	1	18	24	.192	.333	.293	19.51	14.63	123
Chourio, Winyer	R-R	6-2	180	11-4-03	2	3	2.88	6	6	0	25	13	12	8	1	14	19	.149	.327	.241	17.12	12.61	111
Crespo, Christian	R-R	6-2	190	1-30-03	1	1	0.00	2	0	0	2	1	2	0	0	1	3	.143	.400	.286	30.00	10.00	10
Davila, Manuel	R-R	6-0	140	8-8-07	3	0	1.37	5	4	0	26	23	5	4	0	3	23	.242	.294	.284	22.55	2.94	102
De La Rosa, Jose	R-R	6-0	175	11-20-04	0	2	6.32	5	5	0	16	17	14	11	0	15	15	.279	.425	.344	18.75	18.75	80
Diaz, Leandry	R-R	6-3	210	9-4-02	2	1	5.54	9	0	0	13	12	8	8	0	12	16	.273	.433	.318	26.23	19.67	61
Eluscat, Marco	L-L	6-1	145	7-5-06	0	0	7.94	8	0	0	11	14	10	10	1	7	9	.318	.407	.523	16.67	12.96	54
Jimenez, Ibrahyn	L-L	6-1	170	2-19-07	1	1	3.60	7	4	0	25	20	14	10	1	11	15	.222	.314	.267	14.71	10.78	102
Jimenez, Ronaldys	L-L	5-11	165	11-29-05	0	0	1.13	4	4	0	8	2	1	1	0	3	12	.077	.226	.077	38.71	9.68	31
Maracara, Luis	R-R	6-0	175	8-19-07	2	2	3.18	11	10	0	45	44	19	16	2	16	52	.263	.340	.353	27.08	8.33	192
Mendez, Darlin	R-R	6-1	210	7-19-04	1	0	6.75	17	0	4	20	21	17	15	2	16	22	.273	.402	.403	22.45	16.33	98
Minaya, Johan	R-R	6-1	165	10-22-04	1	0	13.50	2	0	0	2	3	5	3	1	3	2	.375	.538	.875	15.38	23.08	13
Nova, Dionicio	R-R	6-2	185	4-20-04	2	0	3.00	3	0	0	3	1	1	1	1	2	1	.125	.300	.500	10.00	20.00	10
Ojeda, Danny	R-R	6-1	175	10-11-04	1	1	6.23	4	0	1	4	1	3	3	0	7	5	.083	.429	.083	23.81	33.33	21
Ortiz, Anderson	R-R	6-1	200	9-13-05	1	1	5.29	10	0	0	17	27	12	10	1	8	17	.351	.414	.468	19.54	9.20	87
Peguero, Esmerlin	R-R	6-1	180	4-17-05	0	0	0.00	2	1	0	2	2	0	0	0	1	1	.286	.500	.286	10.00	10.00	10
Polanco, Dariel	R-R	5-11	150	9-28-05	2	3	3.24	11	10	0	50	48	20	18	6	8	24	.254	.292	.381	11.82	3.94	203
Reyes, Elvis	R-R	6-2	180	4-28-03	1	4	6.82	13	6	0	33	23	26	25	1	29	34	.202	.395	.263	22.22	18.95	153
Sanchez, Angel	R-R	5-9	168	4-20-06	1	1	2.57	14	0	0	21	17	12	6	1	12	17	.215	.337	.342	17.17	12.12	99
Valenzuela, Jordan	R-R	6-2	190	5-20-05	1	1	12.46	8	0	0	13	14	21	18	0	21	12	.269	.493	.288	16.00	28.00	75

Fielding

C: Hernandez 26, Ocopio 21, Garza 12, Giron 7, Guzman 3. **1B:** Hacen 16, Ocopio 16, Garcia 11, Giron 9, Guzman 7, Garza 4, Severino 1, Valdez 1. **2B:** Castillo 26, Hernandez 13, Tejeda 13, Ricardo 6, Severino 6, Tovar 3, Turbi 2, Guerrero 2, Valdez 1. **3B:** Hacen 29, Severino 21, Tovar 6, Turbi 4, Tejeda 4, Valdez 3, Guerrero 2. **SS:** Tovar 38, Turbi 8, Guerrero 7, Tejeda 7, Hernandez 1, Ricardo 1, Castillo 1. **LF:** Contreras 18, Valdez 18, Martinez 9, Marquez 7, Severino 3, Bericoto 3, Turbi 2, Velazquez 2. **CF:** Marquez 39, Martinez 13, Arias 2, Bericoto 2, Contreras 2, Severino 1. **RF:** Arias 23, Contreras 18, Bericoto 6, Garcia 5, Valdez 5, Velazquez 3, Marquez 2, Tejeda 1, Turbi 1, Garza 1, Hernandez 1.

San Francisco Giants

SEASON SYNOPSIS: For the seventh time in eight years—with a 107-win aberration in 2021—the Giants weren't a factor, finishing fourth in the National League West for the second straight year. The franchise made huge changes after the season ended, firing president of baseball operations Farhan Zaidi. Ownership chose Buster Posey, the retired catcher, to guide the Giants' new direction.

HIGH POINT: San Francisco invested in this team, including a March free-agent signing of lefthander Blake Snell. While the reigning Cy Young Award winner started slowly thanks in part to missing much of spring training, Snell hit his stride in July, striking out 15 in six scoreless innings on July 27 against Colorado. He followed with the first complete game of his career, a no-hitter with 11 strikeouts on Aug. 2 against the Reds. Seven of his last 14 starts were scoreless outings of five innings or more.

LOW POINT: The Giants' wild-card chase fell off the rails in August as they lost the first three games of a four-game set to the Braves, whom they trailed by 1.5 games entering the series for a wild-card spot. They lost the first two games in 10 innings, losing 1-0 in the opener while being four-hit; listing 4-3 the next night; then getting blown out 13-2 as the Braves chased Robbie Ray with five runs in the first inning.

NOTABLE ROOKIES: A first-round pick in 2017, Heliot Ramos had gotten cups of coffee the previous two years before getting a full shot in center field after Korean signee Jung Hoo Lee got hurt. Ramos ran with it, earning an all-star berth while batting .269/.322/.469 with 22 home runs. Tyler Fitzgerald, never regarded as a significant prospect, homered in five straight games in July and established himself as the everyday shortstop, though he hit only one home run in September. Three rookies took significant rotation turns, and while Keaton Winn (3-8, 7.16) struggled, a pair of 22-year-olds, lefty Kyle Harrison (7-7, 4.56) and righty Hayden Birdsong (5-6, 4.75, 11 K/9 IP), showed real promise.

KEY TRANSACTIONS: The Giants signed Snell (2 years/$62 million) and third baseman Matt Chapman (3/$54M), and Chapman had a big year with a team-best 27 homers, his usual stellar defense and 7.1 bWAR. He signed a six-year, $151 million extension late in the season. Lee, who signed for six years and $113 million, missed all but 37 games with a shoulder injury.

OPENING DAY PAYROLL: $211,044,828 (10th)

PLAYERS OF THE YEAR

MAJOR LEAGUE

Matt Chapman
3B
.247/.328/.463
27 HR, 78 RBIs
Fifth Gold Glove

MINOR LEAGUE

Bryce Eldridge
1B
(A/A+/AA/AAA)
.292/.374/.516
23 HR, 92 RBIs

ORGANIZATION LEADERS

Batting		*Qualifiers
MAJORS		
* AVG	Heliot Ramos	.269
* OPS	Matt Chapman	.791
HR	Matt Chapman	27
RBI	J.D. Davis	69
MINORS		
* AVG	Trenton Brooks, Sacramento	.302
* OBP	Trenton Brooks, Sacramento	.410
* SLG	Bryce Eldridge, 4-teams	.516
* OPS	Bryce Eldridge, 4-teams	.890
R	Jonah Cox, Eugene/San Jose	80
H	Bryce Eldridge, 4-teams	130
TB	Bryce Eldridge, 4-teams	230
2B	Carter Howell, Richmond	30
3B	Jonah Cox, Eugene/San Jose	8
HR	Bryce Eldridge, 4-teams	23
RBI	Bryce Eldridge, 4-teams	92
BB	Quinn McDaniel, Eugene	67
SO	Quinn McDaniel, Eugene	166
SB	Jonah Cox, Eugene/San Jose	58

Pitching		#Qualifiers
MAJORS		
W	Logan Webb	13
# ERA	Logan Webb	3.47
SO	Logan Webb	172
SV	Camilo Doval	23
MINORS		
W	Trent Harris, Eugene/San Jose/Richmond	9
W	Nick Sinacola, Eugene/Richmond	9
L	Carson Seymour, Sacramento	10
# ERA	Dylan Carmouche, San Jose/Eugene	3.38
G	Tyler Myrick, Sacramento/Richmond	47
GS	John Bertrand, Sacramento/Richmond	29
SV	Tyler Myrick, Sacramento/Richmond	13
IP	John Bertrand, Sacramento/Richmond	156
BB	Carson Seymour, Sacramento	60
SO	Carson Ragsdale, Sacramento/Richmond	147
# AVG	Jack Choate, Eugene/Richmond	.231

2024 PERFORMANCE

General Manager: Farhan Zaidi. **Farm Director:** Kyle Haines. **Scouting Director:** Michael Holmes.

Class	Team	League	W	L	PCT	Finish	Manager
Majors	Los Angeles Dodgers	National	98	64	.605	1 (15)	Dave Roberts
Triple-A	Oklahoma City Dodgers	Pacific Coast	79	71	.527	5 (10)	Travis Barbary
Double-A	Tulsa Drillers	Texas	63	74	.460	6 (10)	Scott Hennessey
High-A	Great Lakes Loons	Midwest	69	61	.531	4 (12)	Jair Fernandez
Low-A	Rancho Cucamonga Quakes	California	65	65	.500	6 (8)	John Shoemaker
Rookie	ACL Dodgers	Arizona Complex	40	20	.667	1 (15)	Juan Apodaca
Rookie	DSL LAD Bautista	Dominican	29	26	.527	20 (51)	Dunior Zerpa
Rookie	DSL LAD Mega	Dominican	25	29	.463	34 (51)	Leury Bonilla
Overall 2024 Minor League Record			**370**	**346**	**.517**	**11th (30)**	

ORGANIZATION STATISTICS

SAN FRANCISCO GIANTS

NATIONAL LEAGUE

Batting	B-T	Ht.	Wt.	DOB	AVG	OBP	SLG	G	PA	AB	R	H	2B	3B	HR	RBI	BB	HBP	SH	SF	SO	SB	CS	BB%	SO%
Ahmed, Nick	R-R	6-2	201	3-15-90	.232	.278	.303	52	172	155	13	36	6	1	1	15	10	1	3	3	35	1	1	5.81	20.35
Bailey, Patrick	B-R	6-0	210	5-29-99	.234	.298	.339	121	448	401	46	94	16	1	8	46	39	0	1	7	100	4	0	8.71	22.32
Brooks, Trenton	L-L	5-10	195	7-3-95	.120	.241	.120	12	29	25	3	3	0	0	0	1	4	0	0	0	6	1	0	13.79	20.69
Canha, Mark	R-R	6-2	209	2-15-89	.288	.376	.329	32	85	73	4	21	3	0	0	4	9	2	0	1	17	3	0	10.59	20.00
Casali, Curt	R-R	6-2	220	11-9-88	.194	.293	.250	41	125	108	12	21	3	0	1	8	13	2	2	0	22	0	0	10.40	17.60
Chapman, Matt	R-R	6-0	215	4-28-93	.247	.328	.463	154	647	575	98	142	39	2	27	78	64	6	0	2	158	15	2	9.89	24.42
Conforto, Michael	L-R	6-1	215	3-1-93	.237	.309	.450	130	488	438	56	104	27	3	20	66	42	5	0	3	118	0	1	8.61	24.18
Encarnacion, Jerar	R-R	6-4	250	10-22-97	.248	.277	.425	35	119	113	13	28	5	0	5	19	5	0	0	1	34	1	0	4.20	28.57
Estrada, Thairo	R-R	5-10	185	2-22-96	.217	.247	.343	96	381	364	43	79	15	2	9	47	10	5	0	2	76	2	2	2.62	19.95
Fitzgerald, Tyler	R-R	6-3	205	9-15-97	.280	.334	.497	96	341	314	53	88	19	2	15	34	22	4	0	1	108	17	4	6.45	31.67
Flores, Wilmer	R-R	6-2	213	8-6-91	.206	.277	.318	71	242	214	19	44	12	0	4	26	20	3	0	5	33	0	0	8.26	13.64
Hill, Derek	R-R	6-2	206	12-30-95	.250	.308	.417	5	13	12	3	3	0	1	0	2	1	0	0	0	3	0	0	7.69	23.08
Knapp, Andrew	B-R	6-1	189	11-9-91	.167	.167	.167	3	6	6	0	1	0	0	0	0	0	0	0	0	2	0	0	0.00	33.33
Lee, Jung Hoo	L-R	6-0	171	8-20-98	.262	.310	.331	37	158	145	15	38	4	0	2	8	10	1	0	2	13	2	3	6.33	8.23
Luciano, Marco	R-R	6-1	178	9-10-01	.211	.259	.303	27	81	76	10	16	5	1	0	3	5	0	0	0	28	0	1	6.17	34.57
Matos, Luis	R-R	5-11	160	1-28-02	.213	.237	.347	45	156	150	14	32	5	0	5	25	5	0	0	1	24	0	0	3.21	15.38
McCray, Grant	L-R	6-2	190	12-7-00	.202	.238	.379	37	130	124	13	25	3	2	5	10	6	0	0	0	56	5	0	4.62	43.08
McKenna, Ryan	R-R	5-11	195	2-14-97	.000	.000	.000	4	6	6	1	0	0	0	0	0	0	0	0	0	4	1	0	0.00	66.67
Murphy, Tom	R-R	6-1	206	4-3-91	.118	.211	.235	13	38	34	3	4	1	0	1	2	4	0	0	0	14	0	0	10.53	36.84
Ramos, Heliot	R-R	6-1	188	9-7-99	.269	.322	.469	121	518	475	54	128	23	3	22	72	37	2	0	4	135	6	1	7.14	26.06
Reetz, Jakson	R-R	6-0	205	1-3-96	.143	.200	.429	6	15	14	1	2	1	0	1	1	1	0	0	0	5	0	0	6.67	33.33
Sabol, Blake	L-R	6-4	225	1-7-98	.313	.421	.375	11	38	32	3	10	2	0	0	1	5	1	0	0	9	0	0	13.16	23.68
Schmitt, Casey	R-R	6-2	215	3-1-99	.252	.283	.477	40	113	107	11	27	4	1	6	16	4	1	0	1	25	0	0	3.54	22.12
Slater, Austin	R-R	6-1	204	12-13-92	.200	.330	.244	43	112	90	12	18	1	0	1	9	16	3	0	3	31	2	1	14.29	27.68
Soler, Jorge	R-R	6-4	235	2-25-92	.240	.330	.419	93	392	341	57	82	23	1	12	40	44	3	0	3	97	1	0	11.22	24.74
Villar, David	R-R	6-1	215	1-27-97	.257	.270	.457	11	37	35	3	9	4	0	1	4	1	0	0	1	13	0	0	2.70	35.14
Wade, LaMonte	L-L	6-1	205	1-1-94	.260	.380	.381	117	401	331	45	86	16	0	8	34	62	4	1	3	90	2	1	15.46	22.44
Walton, Donovan	L-R	5-9	190	5-25-94	.136	.240	.273	9	25	22	3	3	0	0	1	2	2	1	0	0	7	0	0	8.00	28.00
Wisely, Brett	L-R	5-10	180	5-8-99	.238	.278	.345	91	272	252	25	60	13	1	4	31	13	2	2	3	65	2	3	4.78	23.90
Yastrzemski, Mike	L-L	5-10	178	8-23-90	.231	.302	.437	140	474	428	60	99	16	9	18	57	38	6	1	1	124	3	2	8.02	26.16

Pitching	B-T	Ht.	Wt.	DOB	W	L	ERA	G	GS	SV	IP	Hits	Runs	ER	HR	BB	SO	AVG	OBP	SLG	SO%	BB%	BF
Avila, Nick	R-R	6-4	195	7-25-97	1	0	8.49	8	0	0	12	17	12	11	2	3	14	.340	.364	.640	25.45	5.45	55
Baumann, Mike	R-R	6-4	240	9-10-95	0	0	27.00	1	0	0	1	3	2	2	0	0	1	.600	.600	1.000	20.00	0.00	5
Beck, Tristan	R-R	6-4	165	6-24-96	0	0	1.69	7	1	0	16	14	3	3	2	4	14	.230	.284	.393	20.90	5.97	67
Birdsong, Hayden	R-R	6-4	215	8-30-01	5	6	4.75	16	16	0	72	57	39	38	11	43	88	.216	.332	.390	27.94	13.65	315
Bivens, Spencer	R-R	6-5	205	6-28-94	3	1	3.14	27	2	1	49	47	20	17	9	11	37	.250	.294	.431	18.32	5.45	202
Black, Mason	R-R	6-3	230	12-10-99	1	5	6.44	9	8	0	36	46	26	26	7	15	31	.309	.381	.517	18.34	8.88	169
Burgos, Raymond	L-L	6-5	170	11-29-98	0	0	9.00	1	0	0	1	3	1	1	0	1	1	.500	.571	.500	14.29	14.29	7
Doval, Camilo	R-R	6-2	185	7-4-97	5	3	4.88	62	0	23	59	54	35	32	5	39	78	.241	.353	.393	28.78	14.39	271
Fitzgerald, Tyler	R-R	6-3	205	9-15-97	0	0	9.00	3	0	0	3	6	3	3	0	0	0	.429	.429	.500	0.00	0.00	14
Harrison, Kyle	R-L	6-2	200	8-12-01	7	7	4.56	24	24	0	124	125	65	63	18	42	118	.263	.328	.433	22.18	7.89	532
Hicks, Jordan	R-R	6-2	220	9-6-96	4	7	4.10	29	20	1	110	112	54	50	12	47	96	.265	.349	.414	19.96	9.77	481
Hjelle, Sean	R-R	6-11	228	5-7-97	3	4	3.90	58	0	0	81	84	37	35	10	14	75	.268	.308	.398	22.26	4.15	337
Howard, Spencer	R-R	6-3	210	7-28-96	1	1	5.63	7	2	0	24	33	16	15	2	11	21	.327	.389	.495	18.42	9.65	114
Jackson, Luke	R-R	6-2	210	8-24-91	4	2	5.40	36	0	0	35	35	22	21	5	15	33	.263	.340	.421	21.85	9.93	151
Jefferies, Daulton	L-R	6-0	182	8-2-95	0	2	17.36	2	1	0	5	14	13	9	2	2	4	.483	.516	.966	12.90	6.45	31
McDonald, Trevor	R-R	6-2	200	2-26-01	0	0	0.00	1	0	0	3	0	0	0	0	1	1	.000	.100	.000	10.00	10.00	10
Miller, Erik	L-L	6-5	240	2-13-98	4	5	3.88	73	10	0	67	50	33	29	7	38	87	.205	.313	.344	30.63	13.38	284
Ray, Robbie	L-L	6-2	225	10-1-91	3	2	4.70	7	7	0	31	20	16	16	6	15	43	.189	.320	.387	33.33	11.63	129
Rodriguez, Randy	R-R	6-0	166	9-5-99	3	2	4.30	35	1	0	52	47	29	25	4	18	53	.240	.311	.372	23.98	8.14	221
Rogers, Taylor	L-L	6-3	190	12-17-90	1	4	2.40	64	0	0	60	53	22	16	7	22	64	.237	.309	.397	25.70	8.84	249

Rogers, Tyler	R-R	6-3	181	12-17-90	3	4	2.82	77	0	1	70	67	23	22	7	6	51	.245	.278	.374	17.59	2.07	290
Roupp, Landen	R-R	6-2	205	9-10-98	1	2	3.58	23	4	0	50	43	21	20	2	26	47	.226	.323	.326	21.66	11.98	217
Snell, Blake	L-L	6-4	225	12-4-92	5	3	3.12	20	20	0	104	65	38	36	6	44	145	.174	.263	.263	34.69	10.53	418
Teng, Kai-Wei	R-R	6-4	260	12-1-98	0	0	9.82	4	0	0	11	15	12	12	2	8	7	.326	.436	.500	12.73	14.55	55
Walker, Ryan	R-R	6-2	200	11-26-95	10	4	1.91	76	1	10	80	50	19	17	5	18	99	.179	.251	.265	32.14	5.84	308
Walton, Donovan	L-R	5-9	190	5-25-94	0	0	0.00	1	0	0	1	2	0	0	0	0	0	.400	.400	.400	0.00	0.00	5
Warren, Austin	R-R	6-0	170	2-5-96	0	0	1.69	6	0	0	11	9	2	2	1	5	7	.243	.333	.351	16.67	11.90	42
Webb, Logan	R-R	6-1	220	11-18-96	13	10	3.47	33	33	0	205	202	83	79	11	50	172	.258	.302	.355	20.45	5.95	841
White, Mitch	R-R	6-3	210	12-28-94	0	0	11.81	3	0	0	5	8	7	7	1	5	1	.333	.448	.583	3.45	17.24	29
Winn, Keaton	R-R	6-4	230	2-20-98	3	8	7.16	12	12	0	55	56	44	44	9	20	48	.268	.338	.493	20.17	8.40	238
Yastrzemski, Mike	L-L	5-10	178	8-23-90	0	0	18.00	1	0	0	1	2	2	2	0	3	0	.400	.625	.400	0.00	37.50	8

Fielding

Catcher	PCT	G	PO	A	E	DP	PB
Bailey	.997	115	904	55	3	7	9
Casali	.981	41	345	20	7	0	1
Knapp	1.000	3	21	0	0	0	1
Murphy	1.000	12	68	1	0	0	4
Reetz	1.000	6	39	0	0	0	0
Sabol	.957	8	66	1	3	0	0

First Base	PCT	G	PO	A	E	DP
Brooks	1.000	9	61	2	0	8
Canha	.992	19	116	7	1	10
Encarnacion	.950	2	17	2	1	2
Fitzgerald	1.000	2	7	1	0	1
Flores	.993	56	376	33	3	41
Villar	1.000	10	79	11	0	5
Wade	.999	94	650	77	1	59
Wisely	.000	1	0	0	0	0

Second Base	PCT	G	PO	A	E	DP
Estrada	.995	94	121	264	2	63
Fitzgerald	.950	6	6	13	1	2
Luciano	.963	9	10	16	1	2
Schmitt	.977	19	18	25	1	5
Walton	1.000	8	10	16	0	1
Wisely	.987	50	45	103	2	23

Third Base	PCT	G	PO	A	E	DP
Canha	.000	1	0	0	0	0
Chapman	.963	154	100	290	15	34
Flores	1.000	2	1	3	0	0
Schmitt	.941	9	0	16	1	1
Wisely	1.000	3	0	2	0	0

Shortstop	PCT	G	PO	A	E	DP
Ahmed	.985	51	61	134	3	33
Fitzgerald	.958	72	87	166	11	30
Luciano	.865	9	15	17	5	1
Schmitt	.969	10	12	19	1	6
Wisely	.993	37	39	95	1	20

Outfield	PCT	G	PO	A	E	DP
Canha	1.000	9	2	0	0	0
Conforto	.987	106	152	5	2	1
Encarnacion	1.000	18	13	0	0	0
Fitzgerald	.909	12	20	0	2	0
Hill	1.000	5	6	0	0	0
Lee	1.000	37	79	1	0	0
Matos	.986	47	69	1	1	0
McCray	.978	37	87	0	2	0
McKenna	1.000	4	3	0	0	0
Ramos	.996	118	225	4	1	0
Slater	.977	43	40	2	1	0
Wade	1.000	12	10	1	0	0
Wisely	1.000	1	1	0	0	0
Yastrzemski	.982	136	212	5	4	1

SACRAMENTO RIVER CATS — *TRIPLE-A*

PACIFIC COAST LEAGUE

Batting	B-T	Ht.	Wt.	DOB	AVG	OBP	SLG	G	PA	AB	R	H	2B	3B	HR	RBI	BB	HBP	SH	SF	SO	SB	CS	BB%	SO%
Ahmed, Nick	R-R	6-2	201	3-15-90	.200	.273	.200	3	11	10	1	2	0	0	0	2	1	0	0	0	2	0	0	9.09	18.18
Auerbach, Brett	R-R	5-9	185	8-27-98	.281	.357	.444	62	223	196	30	55	12	4	4	23	21	3	2	1	55	5	2	9.42	24.66
Bench, Justin	R-R	6-0	185	8-28-99	.375	.375	.375	3	8	8	1	3	0	0	0	0	0	0	0	0	2	0	0	0.00	25.00
Biggio, Cavan	L-R	6-2	200	4-11-95	.163	.413	.326	12	63	43	7	7	1	0	2	6	17	2	0	1	13	2	1	26.98	20.63
Bishop, Hunter	L-R	6-5	210	6-25-98	.245	.316	.386	97	413	363	61	89	18	3	9	59	34	7	1	8	113	10	4	8.23	27.36
Brooks, Trenton	L-L	5-10	195	7-3-95	.302	.410	.453	94	407	331	62	100	18	1	10	58	63	3	2	8	61	10	1	15.48	14.99
Cavanaugh, Drew	B-R	6-0	190	1-27-02	.300	.400	.300	9	35	30	6	9	0	0	0	5	4	1	0	0	7	0	0	11.43	20.00
Conforto, Michael	L-R	6-1	215	3-1-93	.200	.333	.200	2	6	5	0	1	0	0	0	0	1	0	0	0	1	0	0	16.67	16.67
Diaz, Yusniel	R-R	6-1	215	10-7-96	.176	.358	.373	20	67	51	10	9	1	0	3	5	15	0	0	1	14	4	0	22.39	20.90
Eldridge, Bryce	L-R	6-7	219	10-20-04	.258	.343	.258	8	35	31	3	8	0	0	0	2	4	0	0	0	11	0	0	11.43	31.43
Encarnacion, Jerar	R-R	6-4	250	10-22-97	.352	.438	.616	33	146	125	21	44	3	0	10	33	18	2	0	1	35	1	0	12.33	23.97
Estrada, Thairo	R-R	5-10	185	2-22-96	.333	.390	.493	19	83	75	16	25	3	0	3	8	5	2	1	0	14	1	0	6.02	16.87
Fitzgerald, Tyler	R-R	6-3	205	9-15-97	.310	.402	.718	17	87	71	17	22	5	0	8	21	9	4	0	3	24	1	2	10.34	27.59
Francisco, Javier	R-R	6-1	162	11-11-02	.294	.294	.412	6	17	17	1	5	0	1	0	4	0	0	0	0	6	0	0	0.00	35.29
Hill, Turner	L-L	5-10	180	4-4-99	.188	.211	.188	6	20	16	1	3	0	0	0	4	1	0	1	2	2	1	0	5.00	10.00
Knapp, Andrew	B-R	6-1	189	11-9-91	.227	.370	.386	13	55	44	10	10	2	1	1	3	9	1	1	0	12	0	0	16.36	21.82
Koss, Christian	R-R	6-1	182	1-27-98	.257	.332	.415	54	197	171	32	44	10	1	5	19	14	6	4	2	45	5	0	7.11	22.84
Lopez, Otto	R-R	5-10	185	10-1-98	.167	.167	.167	2	6	6	1	1	0	0	0	0	0	0	0	0	1	0	0	0.00	16.67
Luciano, Marco	R-R	6-1	178	9-10-01	.250	.380	.380	83	384	316	55	79	9	1	10	42	65	2	0	1	103	4	3	16.93	26.82
Martorano, Brandon	R-R	6-2	198	1-6-98	.200	.302	.364	18	63	55	6	11	0	0	3	10	8	0	0	0	18	0	0	12.70	28.57
Matos, Luis	R-R	5-11	160	1-28-02	.256	.328	.451	80	375	328	42	84	22	0	14	53	28	11	0	8	40	8	2	7.47	10.67
McCray, Grant	L-R	6-2	190	12-7-00	.272	.347	.471	47	213	191	35	52	12	4	6	29	21	1	0	0	54	8	3	9.86	25.35
McKenna, Ryan	R-R	5-11	195	2-14-97	.227	.308	.348	18	79	66	13	15	2	0	2	8	8	1	1	3	18	6	1	10.13	22.78
Meckler, Wade	L-R	5-10	178	4-21-00	.288	.357	.508	44	196	177	27	51	9	3	8	27	19	0	0	0	25	3	1	9.69	12.76
Munguia, Ismael	L-L	5-10	158	10-20-98	.250	.368	.368	50	178	144	32	36	9	1	2	17	22	6	4	2	23	7	4	12.36	12.92
Pinder, Chase	R-R	5-10	185	3-16-96	.250	.400	.344	20	80	64	8	16	3	0	1	5	15	1	0	0	17	1	1	18.75	21.25
Porter, Logan	R-R	6-0	200	7-12-95	.253	.329	.387	21	85	75	8	19	4	0	2	7	9	0	0	1	24	1	0	10.59	28.24
Ramos, Heliot	R-R	6-1	188	9-7-99	.296	.388	.565	30	134	115	23	34	3	2	8	21	16	2	0	1	37	2	0	11.94	27.61
Reetz, Jakson	R-R	6-0	205	1-3-96	.254	.368	.431	58	235	197	31	50	20	0	5	34	29	7	1	1	48	1	0	12.34	20.43
Sabol, Blake	L-R	6-4	225	1-7-98	.246	.340	.388	97	403	345	50	85	14	1	11	54	48	3	3	4	98	11	1	11.91	24.32
Sands, Donny	R-R	6-2	190	5-16-96	.176	.250	.196	13	56	51	5	9	1	0	0	5	5	0	0	0	16	0	0	8.93	28.57
Schmitt, Casey	R-R	6-2	215	3-1-99	.274	.343	.469	74	335	292	45	80	16	1	13	58	31	4	0	8	70	11	2	9.25	20.90
Soler, Jorge	R-R	6-4	235	2-25-92	.286	.375	.286	2	8	7	1	2	0	0	0	1	1	0	0	0	1	0	0	12.50	12.50
Villar, David	R-R	6-1	215	1-27-97	.260	.361	.441	106	482	408	70	106	26	0	16	77	60	8	0	6	124	2	1	12.45	25.73
Wade, LaMonte	L-L	6-1	205	1-1-94	.143	.455	.143	3	11	7	3	1	0	0	0	0	4	0	0	0	2	0	0	36.36	18.18
Walton, Donovan	L-R	5-9	190	5-25-94	.306	.380	.441	99	387	340	53	104	17	4	7	51	39	4	0	4	46	4	1	10.08	11.89
Whalen, Brady	L-R	6-6	180	1-15-98	.143	.267	.190	20	75	63	10	9	3	0	0	4	11	0	0	1	21	0	0	14.67	28.00
Wilson, Will	R-R	6-0	184	7-21-98	.188	.300	.224	26	100	85	6	16	3	0	0	5	10	4	0	1	26	0	0	10.00	26.00
Wisely, Brett	L-R	5-10	180	5-8-99	.301	.389	.487	41	181	156	30	47	9	1	6	21	23	0	1	1	28	5	4	12.71	15.47

Pitching	B-T	Ht.	Wt.	DOB	W	L	ERA	G	GS	SV	IP	Hits	Runs	ER	HR	BB	SO	AVG	OBP	SLG	SO%	BB%	BF
Andrews, Tanner	R-R	6-3	220	11-15-95	3	6	6.95	38	0	2	56	64	49	43	8	36	76	.281	.380	.482	28.46	13.48	267
Auerbach, Brett	R-R	5-9	185	8-27-98	0	0	0.00	1	0	0	0	0	0	0	0	0	0	.000	.000	.000	0.00	0.00	1
Avila, Nick	R-R	6-4	195	7-25-97	3	0	6.75	8	0	0	9	7	7	7	1	4	13	.206	.289	.412	34.21	10.53	38
Beck, Tristan	R-R	6-4	165	6-24-96	0	1	7.90	5	5	0	14	22	14	12	3	3	17	.355	.385	.565	26.15	4.62	65
Bertrand, John	L-L	6-3	205	2-8-98	1	0	1.80	2	2	0	10	6	4	2	0	5	6	.167	.268	.167	14.63	12.20	41
Birdsong, Hayden	R-R	6-4	215	8-30-01	1	0	5.00	2	2	0	9	8	5	5	1	6	14	.242	.366	.394	33.33	14.29	42
Bivens, Spencer	R-R	6-5	205	6-28-94	5	1	2.92	27	0	8	49	42	16	16	3	17	42	.231	.304	.363	20.49	8.29	205
Black, Mason	R-R	6-3	230	12-10-99	5	6	4.59	20	20	0	84	78	48	43	12	39	87	.245	.333	.414	23.71	10.63	367
Burgos, Raymond	L-L	6-5	170	11-29-98	2	2	1.69	14	0	0	27	21	9	5	3	5	27	.219	.279	.375	25.71	4.76	105
Cobb, Alex	R-R	6-3	205	10-7-87	1	0	0.00	1	1	0	5	2	0	0	0	1	4	.125	.176	.125	23.53	5.88	17
Cody, Kyle	R-R	6-7	225	8-9-94	0	1	9.00	3	0	0	4	6	5	4	0	6	5	.353	.520	.471	19.23	23.08	26
Cotter, Cameron	R-R	6-3	220	12-17-98	0	0	9.00	1	0	0	1	1	2	1	0	3	1	.333	.571	.333	14.29	42.86	7
Crawford, Reggie	L-L	6-4	235	12-4-00	0	0	1.04	7	0	0	9	3	1	1	0	7	11	.115	.314	.115	31.43	20.00	35
Cruz, Jose	R-R	6-1	178	5-18-00	0	0	0.00	2	0	0	2	0	0	0	0	3	4	.000	.333	.000	44.44	33.33	9
Dabovich, R.J.	R-R	6-3	208	1-11-99	0	1	10.38	4	0	0	4	6	6	5	0	6	5	.316	.500	.474	18.52	22.22	27
Doval, Camilo	R-R	6-2	185	7-4-97	1	0	3.18	5	0	0	6	2	2	2	0	1	7	.105	.150	.211	35.00	5.00	20
Dula, Hunter	L-R	6-1	205	3-8-99	0	0	11.57	3	0	0	5	10	6	6	2	2	2	.417	.481	.667	7.41	7.41	27
Enlow, Blayne	R-R	6-3	170	3-21-99	0	1	8.22	2	2	0	8	10	7	7	0	3	7	.303	.378	.455	18.92	8.11	37
Garcia, Nick	L-R	6-4	215	4-20-99	3	1	6.04	16	0	0	22	22	15	15	4	23	19	.259	.422	.482	17.43	21.10	109
Garza, Justin	R-R	5-10	170	3-20-94	5	2	3.42	37	0	4	53	51	23	20	6	18	60	.255	.327	.410	26.67	8.00	225
Gates, Evan	R-R	6-0	210	1-13-98	1	0	7.20	20	0	0	35	49	31	28	6	14	32	.327	.377	.540	19.05	8.33	168
Helvey, Clay	R-R	6-3	195	2-14-97	7	6	5.17	39	0	0	71	67	47	41	8	35	97	.246	.340	.401	30.50	11.01	318
Hjelle, Sean	R-R	6-11	228	5-7-97	0	0	0.00	3	0	0	4	2	0	0	0	0	6	.154	.214	.154	42.86	0.00	14
Howard, Spencer	R-R	6-3	210	7-28-96	3	3	6.57	22	10	0	62	69	45	45	12	27	87	.285	.358	.492	31.64	9.82	275
Ingram, Kolton	L-L	5-9	170	10-21-96	4	2	3.08	25	0	3	26	17	9	9	6	15	26	.191	.314	.404	24.53	14.15	106
Jefferies, Daulton	L-R	6-0	182	8-2-95	1	0	3.44	4	2	0	18	14	8	7	2	5	17	.212	.284	.333	22.67	6.67	75
Jensen, Wil	R-R	6-4	180	9-2-97	0	0	9.00	3	0	0	5	8	5	5	0	6	7	.364	.500	.455	25.00	21.43	28
Matzek, Tyler	L-L	6-3	230	10-20-90	0	0	5.79	5	0	0	5	4	4	3	2	3	3	.211	.318	.526	13.64	13.64	22
McDonald, Trevor	R-R	6-2	200	2-26-01	2	3	4.72	10	8	0	48	46	26	25	4	14	36	.257	.325	.419	17.82	6.93	202
Myrick, Tyler	R-R	6-0	205	6-25-98	3	2	3.18	26	0	7	34	28	15	12	2	19	37	.228	.345	.301	25.52	13.10	145
Ragsdale, Carson	R-R	6-8	225	5-25-98	2	4	5.03	13	12	0	54	60	35	30	10	26	57	.291	.369	.544	24.05	10.97	237
Ray, Robbie	L-L	6-2	225	10-1-91	1	0	2.53	3	2	0	11	4	3	3	1	4	12	.114	.205	.257	30.77	10.26	39
Rodriguez, Julio	R-R	6-3	180	2-10-00	0	0	3.00	2	0	0	3	3	1	1	1	0	3	.273	.273	.545	27.27	0.00	11
Rodriguez, Randy	R-R	6-0	166	9-5-99	1	1	1.69	10	0	1	11	7	2	2	0	4	10	.184	.262	.263	23.81	9.52	42
Romero, Tommy	R-R	6-2	222	7-8-97	4	1	3.14	19	8	1	72	56	28	25	8	37	66	.219	.321	.375	22.07	12.37	299
Roupp, Landen	R-R	6-2	205	9-10-98	0	1	3.80	8	6	0	21	14	9	9	1	14	30	.187	.315	.253	33.33	15.56	90
Sanchez, Juan	L-L	5-9	165	11-12-00	4	0	3.93	23	0	4	34	17	17	15	2	28	35	.145	.315	.231	23.49	18.79	149
Seymour, Carson	R-R	6-6	260	12-16-98	7	10	4.82	29	28	0	134	151	84	72	20	60	132	.288	.369	.461	22.11	10.05	597
Small, Ethan	L-L	6-2	200	2-14-97	0	0	6.00	10	0	0	9	10	6	6	0	2	10	.278	.316	.333	26.32	5.26	38
Snell, Blake	L-L	6-4	225	12-4-92	1	0	3.07	4	4	0	15	7	5	5	1	6	25	.143	.250	.265	44.64	10.71	56
Stashak, Cody	R-R	6-2	180	6-4-94	1	2	5.45	27	0	2	36	45	23	22	8	12	44	.304	.352	.520	27.16	7.41	162
Strotman, Drew	R-R	6-3	195	9-3-96	0	0	4.61	9	0	0	14	12	7	7	1	15	12	.250	.456	.375	17.65	22.06	68
Teng, Kai-Wei	R-R	6-4	260	12-1-98	3	6	8.60	23	13	0	75	92	75	72	14	44	61	.305	.399	.536	17.04	12.29	358
Walton, Donovan	L-R	5-9	190	5-25-94	2	1	2.25	10	0	0	12	11	5	3	2	6	2	.268	.347	.439	4.08	12.24	49
Warren, Austin	R-R	6-0	170	2-5-96	0	1	4.70	24	0	2	23	22	14	12	4	6	27	.244	.296	.411	27.55	6.12	98
Watson, Ryan	R-R	6-5	225	11-15-97	0	0	3.97	10	0	0	11	9	5	5	2	5	13	.225	.326	.425	28.26	10.87	46
Whisenhunt, Carson	L-L	6-3	209	10-20-00	3	5	5.42	25	25	0	105	116	69	63	14	53	135	.280	.367	.463	28.36	11.13	476
Young, Alex	L-L	6-3	220	9-9-93	0	0	13.50	2	0	0	2	5	3	3	1	1	1	.500	.545	1.100	9.09	9.09	11

Fielding

Catcher	PCT	G	PO	A	E	DP	PB
Auerbach	1.000	4	21	3	0	0	0
Cavanaugh	.979	9	87	6	2	1	0
Knapp	1.000	10	100	6	0	0	0
Martorano	.963	7	75	4	3	0	0
Porter	.987	9	68	6	1	0	3
Reetz	.994	48	488	23	3	6	2
Sabol	.990	62	554	29	6	5	9
Sands	.983	6	57	1	1	0	0

First Base	PCT	G	PO	A	E	DP
Brooks	.991	62	418	32	4	45
Eldridge	.983	7	54	3	1	6
Encarnacion	1.000	5	42	6	0	6
Fitzgerald	1.000	1	5	0	0	1
Knapp	1.000	3	15	0	0	1
Porter	1.000	9	59	3	0	1
Sabol	.979	21	126	12	3	13
Sands	1.000	1	4	0	0	1
Villar	.990	38	281	29	3	35
Wade	1.000	2	14	4	0	2
Whalen	.983	7	51	6	1	8

Second Base	PCT	G	PO	A	E	DP
Auerbach	1.000	24	33	49	0	16
Bench	1.000	1	1	2	0	1
Biggio	1.000	5	12	9	0	3
Estrada	.985	18	35	31	1	12
Fitzgerald	1.000	2	6	3	0	1
Koss	1.000	3	4	5	0	3
Lopez	.500	1	1	0	1	0
Luciano	.940	21	28	35	4	14
Schmitt	1.000	6	8	15	0	1
Walton	1.000	56	94	117	0	35
Wilson	.906	7	11	18	3	8
Wisely	.987	24	23	51	1	10

Third Base	PCT	G	PO	A	E	DP
Auerbach	1.000	6	4	15	0	3
Bench	1.000	1	0	2	0	0
Biggio	1.000	1	1	1	0	0
Fitzgerald	1.000	3	1	8	0	1
Francisco	.900	6	3	6	1	1
Koss	1.000	1	0	2	0	0
Schmitt	.980	56	35	114	3	17
Villar	.951	54	28	88	6	5
Walton	.971	13	7	26	1	2
Whalen	1.000	1	0	1	0	0
Wilson	.969	16	7	24	1	1

Shortstop	PCT	G	PO	A	E	DP
Ahmed	.889	3	4	4	1	3
Fitzgerald	1.000	10	13	23	0	4
Koss	.965	46	61	130	7	28
Lopez	1.000	1	1	0	0	0
Luciano	.939	58	58	111	11	31
Schmitt	.957	10	17	28	2	5
Walton	1.000	23	27	46	0	15
Wilson	1.000	1	3	1	0	0
Wisely	.955	5	9	12	1	3

Outfield	PCT	G	PO	A	E	DP
Auerbach	1.000	33	49	2	0	0
Biggio	1.000	5	8	0	0	0
Bishop	.982	89	160	6	3	1
Brooks	1.000	3	2	0	0	0
Conforto	1.000	2	4	0	0	0
Diaz	1.000	15	21	0	0	0
Encarnacion	1.000	19	40	1	0	0
Fitzgerald	1.000	1	2	0	0	0
Hill	1.000	6	3	0	0	0
Koss	.000	2	0	0	0	0

Lopez	.000	1	0	0	0	0
Martorano	1.000	7	9	1	0	0
Matos	.986	77	139	3	2	1
McCray	.965	46	105	5	4	0
McKenna	1.000	12	21	1	0	0
Meckler	1.000	42	74	1	0	0
Munguia	1.000	47	77	1	0	0
Pinder	1.000	16	34	2	0	0
Ramos	.944	25	33	1	2	0
Reetz	.000	1	0	0	0	0
Sabol	.900	10	9	0	1	0
Walton	1.000	5	7	0	0	0
Whalen	1.000	10	13	0	0	0
Wisely	.970	15	30	2	1	0

RICHMOND FLYING SQUIRRELS — DOUBLE-A

EASTERN LEAGUE

Batting	B-T	Ht.	Wt.	DOB	AVG	OBP	SLG	G	PA	AB	R	H	2B	3B	HR	RBI	BB	HBP	SH	SF	SO	SB	CS	BB%	SO%
Auerbach, Brett	R-R	5-9	185	8-27-98	.215	.311	.308	22	74	65	7	14	4	1	0	3	8	1	0	0	18	4	1	10.81	24.32
Bericoto, Victor	R-R	6-1	155	12-3-01	.261	.309	.384	115	479	445	58	116	22	0	11	60	30	2	0	2	115	6	4	6.26	24.01
Bishop, Hunter	L-R	6-5	210	6-25-98	.242	.314	.358	26	105	95	9	23	5	0	2	6	9	1	0	0	33	5	0	8.57	31.43
Brown, Vaun	R-R	6-0	215	6-23-98	.144	.188	.265	47	145	132	18	19	5	1	3	16	7	1	1	4	71	8	0	4.83	48.97
Cerda, Allan	R-R	6-3	203	11-24-99	.200	.273	.500	6	22	20	3	4	0	0	2	3	2	0	0	0	8	0	0	9.09	36.36
Dues, Damon	L-R	6-0	180	6-21-98	.185	.302	.198	30	96	81	8	15	1	0	0	3	13	1	0	1	28	4	1	13.54	29.17
Eldridge, Bryce	L-R	6-7	219	10-20-04	.270	.325	.459	9	40	37	4	10	2	1	1	4	3	0	0	0	8	1	0	7.50	20.00
Glowenke, Jimmy	R-R	5-10	200	6-5-99	.199	.300	.309	105	392	337	47	67	16	0	7	30	32	18	2	3	88	5	2	8.16	22.45
Higgins, Matt	L-R	6-1	215	7-2-99	.262	.339	.330	32	119	103	11	27	4	0	1	15	12	1	0	2	27	2	1	10.08	22.69
Hill, Turner	L-L	5-10	180	4-4-99	.266	.364	.324	57	222	188	23	50	7	2	0	20	24	6	2	2	31	14	3	10.81	13.96
Howell, Carter	R-R	6-0	200	2-7-99	.272	.347	.391	115	505	445	64	121	30	7	3	42	47	6	3	4	99	15	4	9.31	19.60
Kachel, Andrew	L-R	6-0	170	12-24-00	.228	.343	.386	18	67	57	6	13	3	0	2	11	7	3	0	0	16	1	0	10.45	23.88
Koss, Christian	R-R	6-1	182	1-27-98	.386	.453	.627	25	96	83	16	32	12	1	2	21	10	1	1	1	12	6	1	10.42	12.50
Martorano, Brandon	R-R	6-2	198	1-6-98	.215	.304	.316	24	92	79	11	17	5	0	1	9	10	1	0	2	32	0	2	10.87	34.78
Matos, Luis	R-R	5-11	160	1-28-02	.333	.500	.333	1	4	3	0	1	0	0	0	1	1	0	0	0	0	0	0	25.00	0.00
McCray, Grant	L-R	6-2	190	12-7-00	.210	.313	.420	50	208	181	27	38	14	3	6	24	24	3	0	0	67	6	0	11.54	32.21
McKenna, Ryan	R-R	5-11	195	2-14-97	.077	.143	.077	3	14	13	1	1	0	0	0	0	0	1	0	0	4	0	0	0.00	28.57
Meckler, Wade	L-R	5-10	178	4-21-00	.324	.405	.378	10	42	37	6	12	2	0	0	2	5	0	0	0	10	0	0	11.90	23.81
Morgan, Zach	R-R	6-0	180	3-30-00	.226	.293	.333	24	93	84	13	19	3	0	2	6	8	0	1	0	22	3	0	8.60	23.66
Munguia, Ismael	L-L	5-10	158	10-20-98	.317	.404	.461	43	194	167	30	53	9	0	5	21	15	10	1	1	14	11	3	7.73	7.22
Pomares, Jairo	L-R	6-0	185	8-4-00	.238	.280	.434	82	336	311	38	74	19	3	12	47	12	6	2	0	84	9	2	3.57	25.00
Rosario, Dilan	R-R	6-0	185	6-16-01	.185	.309	.272	31	97	81	10	15	2	1	1	7	15	0	0	1	29	4	1	15.46	29.90
Sabol, Blake	L-R	6-4	225	1-7-98	.200	.250	.600	3	12	10	3	2	1	0	1	4	0	1	0	1	3	0	0	0.00	25.00
Soularie, Alerick	R-R	5-11	175	7-5-99	.222	.271	.333	22	72	63	7	14	4	0	1	9	5	0	2	2	16	3	2	6.94	22.22
Sugastey, Adrian	R-R	6-1	210	10-23-02	.210	.241	.304	52	191	181	14	38	10	2	1	22	5	3	0	2	38	0	0	2.62	19.90
Thomas, Andy	L-R	6-1	210	6-17-98	.225	.313	.312	115	432	378	49	85	16	1	5	38	43	6	4	1	87	4	2	9.95	20.14
Toribio, Luis	L-R	6-1	185	9-28-00	.209	.307	.383	69	239	206	32	43	8	2	8	33	27	3	1	2	90	0	2	11.30	37.66
Velasquez, Diego	B-R	6-1	150	10-1-03	.313	.389	.374	42	170	147	14	46	4	1	1	20	16	3	3	1	29	3	4	9.41	17.06
Whalen, Brady	L-R	6-6	180	1-15-98	.169	.270	.246	17	74	65	5	11	2	0	1	7	9	0	0	0	17	0	0	12.16	22.97
Wilson, Will	R-R	6-0	184	7-21-98	.224	.299	.315	84	360	317	36	71	14	0	5	40	34	1	5	3	70	6	3	9.44	19.44
Wishkoski, Justin	R-R	6-3	195	1-20-01	.243	.331	.340	32	120	103	17	25	4	0	2	13	10	4	2	1	21	2	1	8.33	17.50
Wyatt, Logan	L-R	6-4	230	11-15-97	.156	.240	.333	14	50	45	5	7	2	0	2	5	5	0	0	0	16	1	0	10.00	32.00

Pitching	B-T	Ht.	Wt.	DOB	W	L	ERA	G	GS	SV	IP	Hits	Runs	ER	HR	BB	SO	AVG	OBP	SLG	SO%	BB%	BF
Bednar, Will	R-R	6-2	230	6-13-00	1	2	7.71	21	5	0	33	26	30	28	7	36	43	.217	.396	.450	27.04	22.64	159
Bertrand, John	L-L	6-3	205	2-8-98	7	9	4.32	28	27	0	146	153	75	70	14	40	119	.270	.320	.419	19.44	6.54	612
Birdsong, Hayden	R-R	6-4	215	8-30-01	4	2	2.05	11	11	0	48	33	16	11	5	20	61	.188	.281	.318	30.65	10.05	199
Choate, Jack	L-L	6-6	249	4-18-01	1	4	5.82	8	8	0	34	34	24	22	3	18	41	.262	.382	.369	25.79	11.32	159
Cody, Kyle	R-R	6-7	225	8-9-94	2	0	5.06	12	0	0	16	19	10	9	2	5	16	.292	.343	.415	22.86	7.14	70
Corry, Seth	L-L	6-2	195	11-3-98	2	4	6.75	25	0	0	36	33	28	27	2	22	26	.252	.377	.366	15.95	13.50	163
Cotter, Cameron	R-R	6-3	220	12-17-98	2	2	4.09	8	0	3	11	14	5	5	0	3	9	.311	.354	.378	18.75	6.25	48
Crawford, Reggie	L-L	6-4	235	12-4-00	1	1	4.66	7	1	0	10	5	7	5	2	5	19	.147	.326	.353	44.19	11.63	43
Cruz, Jose	R-R	6-1	178	5-18-00	2	1	9.31	25	0	0	29	28	30	30	4	35	42	.248	.435	.442	27.27	22.73	154
Cumming, Dylan	R-R	6-4	175	5-14-99	3	7	5.03	18	13	0	82	96	54	46	9	35	88	.288	.366	.456	23.28	9.26	378
Dula, Hunter	L-R	6-1	205	3-8-99	0	0	5.40	2	0	0	2	2	1	1	0	1	2	.333	.429	.667	28.57	14.29	7
Frisbee, Matt	R-R	6-5	215	11-18-96	1	5	5.12	10	9	0	39	44	22	22	3	23	40	.286	.379	.422	22.60	12.99	177
Garcia, Nick	L-R	6-4	215	4-20-99	0	2	1.54	26	0	5	35	25	10	6	0	14	40	.192	.271	.262	27.78	9.72	144
Gates, Evan	R-R	6-0	210	1-13-98	2	1	1.27	19	0	3	35	20	6	5	0	17	39	.164	.264	.230	27.86	12.14	140
Harris, Trent	R-R	6-2	200	1-22-99	1	0	6.00	2	0	0	3	1	2	2	0	1	1	.100	.182	.200	9.09	9.09	11
Helvey, Clay	R-R	6-3	195	2-14-97	0	0	0.00	2	0	0	3	1	0	0	0	0	5	.111	.111	.111	55.56	0.00	9
Ingram, Kolton	L-L	5-9	170	10-21-96	0	0	0.00	1	0	0	1	0	0	0	0	2	0	.000	.500	.000	0.00	50.00	4
Jensen, Wil	R-R	6-4	180	9-2-97	4	5	3.43	32	6	1	84	76	33	32	7	27	99	.235	.297	.355	28.05	7.65	353
Kiest, Tanner	R-R	6-3	200	9-16-94	7	6	2.62	42	0	5	58	43	26	17	0	31	68	.206	.324	.239	27.20	12.40	250
Lonsway, Seth	L-L	6-2	210	10-7-98	2	1	1.38	6	5	0	33	29	8	5	2	7	26	.242	.305	.325	19.70	5.30	132
Madison, Ben	R-R	6-3	205	9-15-97	1	1	6.62	23	0	0	34	32	33	25	2	31	45	.250	.401	.344	26.79	18.45	168
McDonald, Trevor	R-R	6-2	200	2-26-01	0	2	3.21	3	3	0	14	13	6	5	0	4	8	.232	.306	.321	12.90	6.45	62
Morreale, Nick	R-R	6-5	220	7-27-97	1	1	1.70	9	8	0	37	26	7	7	3	13	30	.202	.285	.302	20.83	9.03	144
Murphy, Ryan	R-R	6-1	190	10-8-99	1	4	3.35	11	11	0	43	39	19	16	4	14	46	.242	.317	.398	25.56	7.78	180
Myrick, Tyler	R-R	6-0	205	6-25-98	1	3	5.14	21	0	6	28	31	18	16	3	8	29	.274	.344	.398	22.83	6.30	127
Olivarez, Helcris	L-L	6-2	192	8-8-00	0	0	9.00	2	0	0	2	3	3	2	0	3	4	.333	.500	.333	30.77	23.08	13
Olsen, Mat	R-R	5-11	185	7-8-00	1	2	4.02	35	0	5	47	44	23	21	2	17	39	.262	.339	.351	19.90	8.67	196
Ragsdale, Carson	R-R	6-8	225	5-25-98	3	3	3.49	14	14	0	67	46	28	26	9	31	90	.197	.294	.359	33.46	11.52	269
Rodriguez, Julio	R-R	6-3	180	2-10-00	1	0	6.91	12	0	0	14	18	12	11	0	14	15	.321	.465	.393	20.55	19.18	73
Silva, Eric	R-R	6-1	185	10-3-02	4	2	4.35	28	0	2	41	30	23	20	5	18	51	.199	.291	.364	29.31	10.34	174
Sinacola, Nick	L-R	6-2	205	10-29-99	5	2	4.08	15	15	0	68	64	33	31	8	18	59	.247	.301	.405	20.92	6.38	282

Pitching	B-T	Ht.	Wt.	DOB	W	L	ERA	G	GS	SV	IP	Hits	Runs	ER	HR	BB	SO	AVG	OBP	SLG	SO%	BB%	BF
Swiney, Nick	R-L	6-3	185	2-12-99	4	2	5.25	41	2	0	72	73	46	42	11	33	79	.260	.346	.416	24.31	10.15	325
Thomas, Andy	L-R	6-1	210	6-17-98	0	0	18.00	1	0	0	1	2	2	2	1	0	0	.400	.400	1.400	0.00	0.00	5
Toribio, Luis	L-R	6-1	185	9-28-00	0	0	0.00	1	0	0	1	1	0	0	0	0	2	.200	.200	.200	40.00	0.00	5

Fielding

Catcher	PCT	G	PO	A	E	DP	PB
Auerbach	1.000	3	28	2	0	1	0
Martorano	1.000	14	118	12	0	1	1
Morgan	.983	19	165	11	3	0	4
Sabol	1.000	2	19	1	0	0	1
Sugastey	.993	40	384	21	3	3	1
Thomas	.987	67	573	33	8	1	5

First Base	PCT	G	PO	A	E	DP
Bericoto	.989	64	433	28	5	49
Eldridge	.973	8	66	5	2	8
Higgins	.981	14	93	9	2	6
Kachel	1.000	5	41	1	0	2
Thomas	.986	29	172	35	3	16
Toribio	.909	1	9	1	1	1
Whalen	.989	13	82	8	1	10
Wyatt	1.000	12	69	6	0	9

Second Base	PCT	G	PO	A	E	DP
Auerbach	.920	7	13	10	2	3
Dues	.971	17	22	45	2	6
Glowenke	.984	68	86	163	4	39
Kachel	1.000	2	2	5	0	0
Koss	.833	2	0	5	1	2
Rosario	.974	12	19	18	1	5
Soularie	.857	10	12	18	5	2
Velasquez	.922	13	17	30	4	7
Wilson	.950	4	9	10	1	3
Wishkoski	1.000	12	20	30	0	7

Third Base	PCT	G	PO	A	E	DP
Auerbach	.905	10	3	16	2	4
Dues	1.000	2	4	2	0	0
Glowenke	.957	22	11	33	2	5
Kachel	1.000	10	8	19	0	1
Morgan	1.000	1	1	3	0	0
Rosario	1.000	8	3	6	0	0
Toribio	.899	63	34	91	14	8
Whalen	1.000	1	0	1	0	0
Wilson	.938	16	6	24	2	1
Wishkoski	.875	20	14	21	5	1

Shortstop	PCT	G	PO	A	E	DP
Dues	.750	1	1	2	1	1
Glowenke	.965	14	21	34	2	11
Koss	.967	22	43	44	3	19
Rosario	.973	12	14	22	1	4
Velasquez	.945	30	36	67	6	11
Wilson	.970	61	95	133	7	31
Wishkoski	1.000	3	2	7	0	1

Outfield	PCT	G	PO	A	E	DP
Auerbach	1.000	1	1	1	0	0
Bericoto	.955	43	78	7	4	0
Bishop	.971	18	34	0	1	0
Brown	.946	34	53	0	3	0
Cerda	1.000	6	5	1	0	1
Dues	1.000	10	24	1	0	0
Higgins	1.000	12	17	2	0	1
Hill	.989	56	91	1	1	0
Howell	1.000	96	205	6	0	1
Martorano	1.000	9	17	2	0	0
Matos	1.000	1	4	0	0	0
McCray	.989	43	86	2	1	1
McKenna	1.000	1	4	0	0	0
Meckler	1.000	6	15	0	0	0
Munguia	.945	40	66	3	4	0
Pomares	.949	55	91	2	5	0
Soularie	1.000	10	19	0	0	0
Whalen	.000	1	0	0	0	0

EUGENE EMERALDS — *HIGH-A*

NORTHWEST LEAGUE

Batting	B-T	Ht.	Wt.	DOB	AVG	OBP	SLG	G	PA	AB	R	H	2B	3B	HR	RBI	BB	HBP	SH	SF	SO	SB	CS	BB%	SO%
Arteaga, Aeverson	R-R	6-1	170	3-16-03	.183	.287	.244	21	94	82	12	15	3	1	0	2	12	0	0	0	26	2	0	12.77	27.66
Bandura, Scott	L-R	6-4	190	8-2-01	.227	.332	.374	56	247	211	46	48	9	2	6	38	31	3	0	2	69	19	2	12.55	27.94
Bench, Justin	R-R	6-0	185	8-28-99	.203	.261	.250	17	71	64	5	13	3	0	0	8	2	3	2	0	15	2	0	2.82	21.13
Brown, Vaun	R-R	6-0	215	6-23-98	.167	.231	.278	10	39	36	3	6	2	1	0	4	1	2	0	0	18	3	1	2.56	46.15
Ceballos, Sabin	R-R	6-3	225	8-17-02	.295	.364	.549	32	140	122	25	36	10	0	7	30	15	0	0	3	32	0	3	10.71	22.86
Cerda, Allan	R-R	6-3	203	11-24-99	.214	.313	.714	4	16	14	3	3	1	0	2	3	1	1	0	0	7	0	0	6.25	43.75
Cox, Jonah	R-R	6-3	190	8-4-01	.225	.324	.350	43	185	160	30	36	3	4	3	15	22	2	0	1	59	20	6	11.89	31.89
Eldridge, Bryce	L-R	6-7	219	10-20-04	.335	.442	.618	48	215	173	35	58	11	1	12	41	35	2	0	5	52	3	0	16.28	24.19
Foster, Cole	B-R	6-1	193	10-8-01	.117	.160	.169	21	81	77	4	9	1	0	1	5	4	0	0	0	39	2	0	4.94	48.15
Frechette, Garrett	L-L	6-3	210	12-31-00	.261	.299	.348	22	78	69	5	18	3	0	1	13	1	4	1	3	23	0	1	1.28	29.49
Gavello, Thomas	L-R	5-10	180	6-6-01	.193	.322	.307	79	304	254	36	49	8	0	7	32	36	13	0	1	104	9	2	11.84	34.21
Higgins, Matt	L-R	6-1	215	7-2-99	.272	.382	.379	62	270	224	28	61	12	0	4	33	37	4	1	2	63	7	2	13.70	23.33
Hill, Turner	L-L	5-10	180	4-4-99	.270	.383	.414	46	207	174	28	47	12	2	3	21	28	4	1	0	21	15	4	13.53	10.14
Kachel, Andrew	L-R	6-0	170	12-24-00	.261	.383	.335	54	228	188	32	49	6	1	2	18	31	7	1	1	59	11	3	13.60	25.88
McDaniel, Quinn	R-R	5-11	180	9-27-02	.236	.345	.390	116	511	433	62	102	20	4	13	56	67	7	1	3	166	40	7	13.11	32.49
Meckler, Wade	L-R	5-10	178	4-21-00	.429	.526	.500	4	19	14	2	6	1	0	0	1	4	0	0	1	3	1	0	21.05	15.79
Morgan, Zach	R-R	6-0	180	3-30-00	.206	.328	.302	59	239	199	22	41	10	0	3	24	34	3	1	2	41	5	1	14.23	17.15
Nolasco, Rodolfo	R-R	5-11	175	9-23-01	.234	.331	.418	67	275	239	31	56	14	0	10	33	30	5	0	1	97	9	3	10.91	35.27
O'Tremba, Tanner	R-R	6-0	212	12-6-99	.194	.320	.312	57	224	186	33	36	8	1	4	25	24	11	0	1	68	10	3	10.71	30.36
Payton, Jack	R-R	5-11	200	8-7-01	.206	.292	.302	18	72	63	5	13	3	0	1	8	5	3	0	1	15	0	0	6.94	20.83
Perez, Onil	R-R	6-1	187	9-10-02	.236	.334	.303	79	350	297	32	70	15	1	1	30	39	8	0	6	58	20	4	11.14	16.57
Shliger, Luke	L-R	5-9	180	9-25-01	.279	.362	.443	18	70	61	6	17	4	0	2	11	7	1	1	0	21	1	0	10.00	30.00
Suarez, Alexander	R-R	6-2	200	12-20-01	.282	.323	.475	63	217	202	40	57	12	0	9	27	9	4	0	2	56	15	3	4.15	25.81
Szykowny, Charlie	L-R	6-4	210	6-30-00	.235	.300	.379	40	170	153	16	36	10	0	4	18	10	5	0	2	38	4	1	5.88	22.35
Tibbs, James	L-L	6-0	205	10-1-02	.134	.216	.239	17	74	67	5	9	1	0	2	4	7	0	0	0	25	0	0	9.46	33.78
Velasquez, Diego	B-R	6-1	150	10-1-03	.274	.357	.389	71	318	270	38	74	16	3	3	26	32	5	7	4	54	18	6	10.06	16.98
Wishkoski, Justin	R-R	6-3	195	1-20-01	.261	.349	.375	81	324	283	37	74	15	1	5	36	28	11	0	2	57	16	3	8.64	17.59

Pitching	B-T	Ht.	Wt.	DOB	W	L	ERA	G	GS	SV	IP	Hits	Runs	ER	HR	BB	SO	AVG	OBP	SLG	SO%	BB%	BF
Bednar, Will	R-R	6-2	230	6-13-00	0	2	3.18	6	4	0	11	5	6	4	1	8	20	.122	.308	.244	38.46	15.38	52
Blair, Daniel	R-R	6-3	205	4-8-99	2	9	5.88	35	2	1	78	90	55	51	8	28	77	.293	.360	.446	22.06	8.02	349
Carmouche, Dylan	S-L	6-6	225	8-22-01	0	2	5.34	7	7	0	30	38	20	18	6	9	39	.311	.361	.549	29.32	6.77	133
Castillo, Wilkelma	R-R	6-0	170	1-6-00	1	2	7.67	13	3	0	27	30	24	23	3	14	29	.288	.377	.481	23.58	11.38	123
Choate, Jack	L-L	6-6	249	4-18-01	1	3	2.90	19	18	0	78	64	30	25	5	19	87	.217	.279	.308	26.85	5.86	324
Cody, Kyle	R-R	6-7	225	8-9-94	0	1	15.43	3	0	0	2	3	4	4	0	2	3	.273	.385	.364	23.08	15.38	13
Corry, Seth	L-L	6-2	195	11-3-98	1	2	2.39	13	0	2	26	13	7	7	1	13	31	.149	.299	.241	28.97	12.15	107
Cotter, Cameron	R-R	6-3	220	12-17-98	6	4	2.27	35	0	5	48	35	19	12	2	9	48	.200	.243	.286	25.81	4.84	186
Cumming, Dylan	R-R	6-4	175	5-14-99	3	0	1.87	9	7	0	34	20	8	7	1	10	50	.177	.277	.239	38.46	7.69	130
Dula, Hunter	L-R	6-1	205	3-8-99	1	2	3.19	30	0	5	37	25	14	13	3	12	37	.192	.257	.346	25.69	8.33	144
Frisbee, Matt	R-R	6-5	215	11-18-96	1	0	0.00	4	0	1	5	4	0	0	0	0	5	.222	.222	.222	27.78	0.00	18
Gavello, Thomas	L-R	5-10	180	6-6-01	0	0	45.00	1	0	0	1	6	5	5	0	2	0	.750	.800	1.000	0.00	20.00	10
Harris, Trent	R-R	6-2	200	1-22-99	5	2	2.00	20	0	1	45	31	12	10	5	12	60	.196	.251	.310	34.88	6.98	172

Kane, Tom	L-L	6-1	195	10-31-01	1	2	5.40	23	1	1	32	27	22	19	4	20	33	.223	.352	.405	22.76	13.79	145
Lonsway, Seth	L-L	6-2	210	10-7-98	2	3	3.86	13	12	0	63	63	37	27	2	20	57	.256	.326	.329	20.80	7.30	274
Madison, Ben	R-R	6-3	205	9-15-97	2	1	3.38	8	0	1	16	7	8	6	0	7	28	.121	.235	.172	41.18	10.29	68
Manzano, Mikell	R-R	6-0	140	11-30-02	1	0	4.05	3	1	0	7	7	3	3	2	0	8	.259	.259	.556	29.63	0.00	27
McDonald, Trevor	R-R	6-2	200	2-26-01	0	1	4.86	5	5	0	17	17	9	9	3	10	25	.262	.407	.431	30.49	12.20	82
Mercedes, Manuel	R-R	6-4	190	9-21-02	4	9	5.28	26	25	0	116	128	75	68	13	54	89	.284	.369	.449	16.92	10.27	526
Mikulski, Matt	L-L	6-4	205	5-8-99	1	4	5.58	37	0	2	60	56	39	37	9	41	55	.248	.373	.447	19.93	14.86	276
Morreale, Nick	R-R	6-5	220	7-27-97	3	3	3.89	25	0	0	44	40	23	19	4	12	50	.240	.297	.371	26.88	6.45	186
Perdomo, Cesar	L-L	6-0	170	2-9-02	3	6	4.00	13	13	0	54	57	37	24	5	24	55	.265	.347	.400	22.73	9.92	242
Rodriquez, Julio	R-R	6-3	180	2-10-00	4	0	2.19	24	0	1	37	34	13	9	2	12	46	.245	.323	.309	29.49	7.69	156
Sinacola, Nick	L-R	6-2	205	10-29-99	4	1	2.68	10	2	0	40	28	13	12	4	7	38	.192	.234	.329	24.68	4.55	154
Strickland, Austin	R-R	6-2	210	5-31-02	2	0	5.46	18	0	0	30	32	24	18	3	18	26	.274	.377	.385	18.84	13.04	138
Tucker, Cody	R-R	6-5	210	3-1-99	3	2	6.28	23	0	0	39	40	31	27	7	17	48	.268	.347	.490	27.75	9.83	173
Vinicio, Esmerlin	L-L	6-2	141	1-31-03	1	4	7.40	6	6	0	24	23	20	20	5	19	22	.253	.400	.451	19.13	16.52	115
Vogel, Tyler	R-R	6-0	175	11-16-00	3	1	4.74	15	1	0	25	26	14	13	3	12	22	.265	.357	.388	19.64	10.71	112
Whitman, Joe	L-L	6-5	200	9-17-01	2	3	4.96	11	11	0	53	51	32	29	5	11	54	.252	.299	.416	24.43	4.98	221
Wolf, Josh	R-R	6-3	170	9-1-00	0	0	6.43	6	2	0	7	7	5	5	1	6	6	.259	.412	.407	17.65	17.65	34
Wynja, Hayden	L-L	6-9	220	10-14-98	2	3	4.95	15	11	0	56	52	35	31	7	23	59	.233	.320	.395	23.32	9.09	253

Fielding

Catcher	PCT	G	PO	A	E	DP	PB
Gavello	.962	7	73	2	3	0	3
Morgan	.993	43	400	33	3	2	10
Payton	.977	4	43	0	1	0	2
Perez	.990	60	537	38	6	4	12
Shliger	.994	18	155	14	1	0	3

First Base	PCT	G	PO	A	E	DP
Bench	1.000	1	11	1	0	2
Eldridge	.976	44	306	13	8	28
Frechette	.985	17	124	4	2	8
Higgins	.976	21	156	8	4	14
Kachel	1.000	23	165	7	0	14
Morgan	1.000	9	75	5	0	4
Payton	.968	8	58	2	2	7
Szykowny	.973	8	63	9	2	7
Wishkoski	1.000	3	23	0	0	2

Second Base	PCT	G	PO	A	E	DP
Bench	1.000	2	4	7	0	2
Foster	1.000	4	7	12	0	4
Gavello	.978	41	71	103	4	15
Kachel	.909	3	2	8	1	2
McDaniel	.971	84	116	189	9	43

Third Base	PCT	G	PO	A	E	DP
Bench	.800	2	0	4	1	0
Ceballos	.955	25	22	42	3	8
Gavello	.882	20	6	24	4	2
Kachel	.947	11	5	13	1	0
Szykowny	.957	15	9	36	2	2
Wishkoski	.921	61	46	93	12	6

Shortstop	PCT	G	PO	A	E	DP
Arteaga	.988	20	34	45	1	11
Bench	.952	4	5	15	1	5
Foster	.947	17	16	55	4	8
Gavello	.921	10	10	25	3	4
Velasquez	.960	66	71	167	10	28
Wishkoski	.926	17	16	47	5	10

Outfield	PCT	G	PO	A	E	DP
Bandura	.972	54	106	0	3	0
Bench	1.000	8	18	1	0	1
Brown	.875	10	6	1	1	0
Cerda	1.000	4	8	0	0	0
Cox	.992	42	114	9	1	3
Frechette	.000	1	0	0	0	0
Higgins	.970	27	32	0	1	0
Hill	.990	42	97	3	1	1
Kachel	1.000	6	7	2	0	0
McDaniel	.977	27	40	2	1	0
Meckler	1.000	4	2	0	0	0
Nolasco	.936	50	85	3	6	2
O'Tremba	.970	49	91	5	3	1
Perez	.667	1	2	0	1	0
Suarez	.992	58	114	3	1	1
Tibbs	.903	17	28	0	3	0

SAN JOSE GIANTS — *LOW-A*

CALIFORNIA LEAGUE

Batting	B-T	Ht.	Wt.	DOB	AVG	OBP	SLG	G	PA	AB	R	H	2B	3B	HR	RBI	BB	HBP	SH	SF	SO	SB	CS	BB%	SO%
Ahuna, Maui	L-R	6-1	170	3-11-02	.236	.355	.281	23	107	89	11	21	1	0	1	13	16	1	0	1	28	5	0	14.95	26.17
Bandura, Scott	L-R	6-4	190	8-2-01	.276	.389	.362	27	126	105	16	29	7	1	0	14	14	6	0	1	24	5	3	11.11	19.05
Bench, Justin	R-R	6-0	185	8-28-99	.230	.337	.329	42	189	161	23	37	10	0	2	14	16	10	2	0	44	3	1	8.47	23.28
Cassiani, Estanlin	L-L	5-11	155	12-30-02	.225	.289	.240	67	253	222	49	50	5	0	0	19	13	8	7	3	39	7	1	5.14	15.42
Cavanaugh, Drew	B-R	6-0	190	1-27-02	.230	.364	.333	38	154	126	17	29	7	0	2	19	23	4	0	1	45	0	0	14.94	29.22
Christian, Jakob	R-R	6-5	225	9-17-02	.267	.378	.500	9	37	30	5	8	4	0	1	5	5	1	0	1	8	0	0	13.51	21.62
Cox, Jonah	R-R	6-3	190	8-4-01	.297	.412	.384	57	275	229	50	68	6	4	2	24	36	9	1	0	62	38	3	13.09	22.55
Darby, Zander	L-R	6-3	197	11-26-00	.234	.351	.489	13	57	47	7	11	0	0	4	14	9	0	0	1	17	0	0	15.79	29.82
Davidson, Bo	L-R	6-2	205	7-5-02	.328	.438	.608	53	226	189	40	62	12	7	9	40	32	5	0	0	54	6	3	14.16	23.89
Diaz, Lisbel	R-R	6-2	201	7-20-05	.279	.333	.433	55	255	233	43	65	12	3	6	36	14	6	0	2	48	8	3	5.49	18.82
Eldridge, Bryce	L-R	6-7	219	10-20-04	.263	.323	.478	51	229	205	34	54	14	0	10	45	17	3	0	4	61	2	0	7.42	26.64
Foster, Cole	B-R	6-1	193	10-8-01	.247	.336	.370	56	254	219	33	54	16	1	3	36	19	12	1	3	50	5	2	7.48	19.69
Francisco, Javier	R-R	6-1	162	11-11-02	.186	.285	.280	36	137	118	15	22	9	1	0	14	13	4	0	2	36	2	1	9.49	26.28
Hanchey, Ty	L-R	5-11	175	12-20-99	.254	.356	.354	50	222	189	27	48	8	1	3	25	28	3	0	2	41	2	1	12.61	18.47
Hipwell, Robert	L-R	6-2	215	3-6-03	.196	.360	.402	29	136	107	19	21	5	1	5	21	21	7	0	1	40	0	0	15.44	29.41
Jenkins, Jeremiah	L-L	6-4	238	5-5-03	.295	.367	.545	11	49	44	6	13	3	1	2	7	4	1	0	0	16	0	0	8.16	32.65
Jordan, Dakota	R-R	6-0	215	5-9-03	.000	.000	.000	2	7	7	1	0	0	0	0	1	0	0	0	0	2	1	0	0.00	28.57
Lewis, Nadir	L-L	6-1	195	11-22-00	.155	.275	.241	19	69	58	6	9	2	0	1	4	10	0	0	1	24	0	1	14.49	34.78
Martin, Walker	L-R	6-2	188	2-20-04	.202	.358	.333	25	123	99	13	20	3	2	2	16	21	3	0	0	57	2	0	17.07	46.34
Meckler, Wade	L-R	5-10	178	4-21-00	.235	.339	.314	13	59	51	5	12	1	0	1	6	8	0	0	0	10	0	0	13.56	16.95
Ortiz, Jose	R-R	5-10	160	2-13-05	.000	.000	.000	1	3	3	0	0	0	0	0	0	0	0	0	0	1	0	0	0.00	33.33
Payton, Jack	R-R	5-11	200	8-7-01	.246	.408	.385	33	157	122	22	30	9	1	2	17	27	7	0	1	30	0	0	17.20	19.11
Peralta, Ramon	R-R	5-11	165	10-2-03	.163	.236	.200	23	90	80	7	13	1	1	0	7	7	1	1	1	28	0	0	7.78	31.11
Perez, Juan	R-R	6-1	182	9-22-04	.100	.250	.100	3	12	10	3	1	0	0	0	0	1	1	0	0	6	0	0	8.33	50.00
Quintas, Cesar	R-R	6-1	175	3-25-03	.228	.320	.386	101	440	381	55	87	18	3	12	57	38	16	0	5	96	3	1	8.64	21.82
Rayo, Elian	R-R	6-0	202	3-4-03	.243	.328	.356	72	305	267	35	65	15	0	5	36	32	3	0	3	99	0	0	10.49	32.46
Reckley, Ryan	B-R	5-10	160	9-6-04	.243	.308	.343	19	78	70	10	17	4	0	1	8	6	1	0	1	30	0	1	7.69	38.46
Shliger, Luke	L-R	5-9	180	9-25-01	.228	.395	.312	62	276	215	35	49	11	2	1	22	50	10	0	1	50	10	4	18.12	18.12
Sio, Jean Carlos	L-R	6-0	167	4-3-04	.240	.378	.360	72	308	250	42	60	14	2	4	36	43	13	1	1	63	11	3	13.96	20.45
Szykowny, Charlie	L-R	6-4	210	6-30-00	.340	.405	.505	54	242	206	32	70	16	6	2	38	20	8	0	8	45	0	0	8.26	18.60

Tibbs, James	L-L	6-0	205	10-1-02	.415	.429	.512	9	42	41	9	17	4	0	0	2	1	0	0	0	11	0	0	2.38	26.19
Williamson, Guillermo	L-L	6-1	200	3-16-04	.238	.335	.408	79	325	282	32	67	12	0	12	50	37	5	0	1	100	1	1	11.38	30.77

Pitching	B-T	Ht.	Wt.	DOB	W	L	ERA	G	GS	SV	IP	Hits	Runs	ER	HR	BB	SO	AVG	OBP	SLG	SO%	BB%	BF
Bednar, Will	R-R	6-2	230	6-13-00	1	0	3.60	5	4	0	10	8	4	4	1	3	13	.222	.293	.417	31.71	7.32	41
Bostick, Josh	R-R	6-4	200	10-20-01	2	9	4.78	26	23	1	107	99	62	57	11	44	121	.248	.334	.408	26.02	9.46	465
Bresnahan, Jacob	L-L	6-3	175	6-27-05	0	4	10.98	7	7	0	20	21	25	24	4	17	21	.269	.402	.526	21.65	17.53	97
Burgos, Raymond	L-L	6-5	170	11-29-98	0	0	0.00	1	0	0	2	0	0	0	0	0	1	.000	.000	.000	16.67	0.00	6
Carmouche, Dylan	S-L	6-6	225	8-22-01	8	2	2.74	20	17	0	92	78	36	28	4	41	90	.238	.324	.314	24.00	10.93	375
Cobb, Alex	R-R	6-3	205	10-7-87	0	1	6.30	4	4	0	10	12	7	7	1	4	17	.279	.347	.395	34.69	8.16	49
Flores, Junior	R-R	6-1	170	2-13-02	5	3	5.03	32	0	4	54	52	38	30	2	41	49	.252	.388	.316	18.99	15.89	258
Garza, Justin	R-R	5-10	170	3-20-94	0	0	7.71	2	0	0	2	1	3	2	0	2	3	.125	.300	.125	30.00	20.00	10
Harris, Trent	R-R	6-2	200	1-22-99	3	1	1.14	14	0	4	32	16	6	4	1	12	44	.147	.231	.211	36.36	9.92	121
Hernandez, Alix	R-R	6-2	155	7-16-04	0	1	11.42	7	0	0	9	10	14	11	1	11	9	.313	.542	.469	18.75	22.92	48
Hillier, Cole	R-R	6-2	205	12-7-00	4	4	3.70	31	0	6	58	55	33	24	4	34	62	.241	.346	.355	22.79	12.50	272
Hjelle, Sean	R-R	6-11	228	5-7-97	0	0	13.50	2	0	0	1	3	2	2	0	1	1	.429	.500	.429	12.50	12.50	8
Jackson, Luke	R-R	6-2	210	8-24-91	0	0	0.00	2	0	0	2	0	0	0	0	1	1	.000	.143	.000	14.29	14.29	7
Johnson, Marques	R-R	6-2	210	7-4-00	1	0	2.84	5	0	0	6	2	3	2	0	8	10	.095	.367	.143	33.33	26.67	30
Kane, Tom	L-L	6-1	195	10-31-01	2	2	2.31	15	0	2	23	22	13	6	1	9	27	.244	.304	.311	26.21	8.74	103
Lansville, Cale	R-R	6-1	205	1-6-03	3	4	4.36	20	14	1	74	84	51	36	5	22	69	.271	.330	.381	20.35	6.49	339
Manning, Timmy	L-L	6-2	195	9-10-01	3	2	2.74	14	0	1	23	16	13	7	0	12	20	.188	.293	.247	19.80	11.88	101
Manzano, Mikell	R-R	6-0	140	11-30-02	1	0	4.50	5	0	1	16	19	8	8	2	2	9	.306	.318	.532	13.64	3.03	66
Mejias, Ubert	R-R	6-3	230	3-24-01	4	7	4.70	26	24	0	123	143	78	64	12	25	85	.290	.323	.436	16.10	4.73	528
Pagan, Kanoa	R-R	6-2	190	9-29-98	0	1	12.71	6	0	0	6	11	9	8	0	3	6	.367	.457	.433	17.14	8.57	35
Palencia, Brayan	R-R	5-11	142	1-14-03	2	1	2.91	19	0	1	53	51	22	17	1	18	43	.254	.315	.338	19.55	8.18	220
Perdomo, Cesar	L-L	6-0	170	2-9-02	5	1	1.26	13	1	2	43	35	9	6	0	11	50	.219	.276	.250	28.57	6.29	175
Pferrer, Cameron	R-R	5-11	182	12-18-98	1	0	2.08	6	0	0	9	7	2	2	0	1	11	.219	.235	.375	32.35	2.94	34
Pleasants, Elijah	R-R	6-4	193	5-4-00	0	0	2.33	11	0	2	27	19	9	7	0	18	23	.194	.333	.245	19.17	15.00	120
Rademacher, Shane	R-R	6-3	215	1-30-01	7	2	4.89	26	7	0	85	101	55	46	14	29	102	.293	.347	.467	27.13	7.71	376
Ray, Robbie	L-L	6-2	225	10-1-91	1	0	3.09	3	3	0	12	8	4	4	2	2	18	.190	.227	.381	40.91	4.55	44
Rayo, Elian	R-R	6-0	202	3-4-03	0	0	0.00	1	0	0	1	2	0	0	0	0	0	.400	.400	.400	0.00	0.00	5
Rodriguez, Michael	L-L	6-5	250	1-8-00	1	1	6.92	10	0	0	13	16	13	10	1	11	6	.314	.448	.392	8.82	16.18	68
Small, Ethan	L-L	6-2	200	2-14-97	0	0	0.00	1	0	0	1	1	0	0	0	0	2	.250	.250	.500	50.00	0.00	4
Snell, Blake	L-L	6-4	225	12-4-92	0	0	0.00	1	1	0	4	0	0	0	0	0	7	.000	.000	.000	58.33	0.00	12
Strickland, Austin	R-R	6-2	210	5-31-02	3	0	3.20	12	0	1	20	21	8	7	0	7	24	.266	.341	.342	27.27	7.95	88
Sullivan, Billy	R-R	6-2	195	4-16-99	1	1	6.23	4	0	0	4	3	3	3	1	4	2	.200	.381	.400	9.52	19.05	21
Tucker, Cody	R-R	6-5	210	3-1-99	2	0	2.42	13	0	2	26	13	8	7	2	12	34	.137	.248	.253	31.19	11.01	109
Vanderhei, Ryan	R-R	6-6	185	6-1-01	2	3	3.58	14	7	1	38	32	18	15	1	20	37	.230	.347	.295	22.16	11.98	167
Villers, Ian	R-R	6-6	245	9-1-00	2	2	5.97	21	0	4	35	39	26	23	3	17	23	.285	.375	.438	14.38	10.63	160
Vinicio, Esmerlin	L-L	6-2	141	1-31-03	6	0	3.59	19	5	0	58	40	25	23	0	32	55	.205	.336	.241	22.92	13.33	240
Warren, Austin	R-R	6-0	170	2-5-96	1	0	9.00	2	0	0	2	4	3	2	0	0	2	.364	.364	.545	18.18	0.00	11
Watson, Ryan	R-R	6-5	225	11-15-97	0	0	0.00	1	0	0	1	1	0	0	0	1	0	.333	.500	.333	0.00	25.00	4
Whisenhunt, Carson	L-L	6-3	209	10-20-00	0	0	0.00	2	2	0	5	1	0	0	0	3	6	.063	.250	.063	30.00	15.00	20
Whitman, Joe	L-L	6-3	185	9-17-01	1	5	4.29	12	12	0	50	43	28	24	2	26	54	.229	.321	.309	24.77	11.93	218
Wolf, Josh	R-R	6-3	170	9-1-00	2	0	0.71	7	0	0	13	6	1	1	0	5	21	.140	.229	.163	43.75	10.42	48

Fielding

Catcher	PCT	G	PO	A	E	DP	PB
Cavanaugh	.985	29	238	23	4	1	3
Hanchey	.982	36	299	32	6	3	14
Payton	.980	10	91	5	2	2	2
Perez	1.000	3	34	2	0	0	0
Shliger	.993	54	507	41	4	1	8

First Base	PCT	G	PO	A	E	DP
Eldridge	.979	41	301	21	7	26
Francisco	.984	10	57	4	1	11
Jenkins	1.000	8	49	3	0	9
Payton	.987	19	146	4	2	13
Rayo	.941	2	15	1	1	1
Williamson	.973	55	367	28	11	28

Second Base	PCT	G	PO	A	E	DP
Bench	.955	26	43	63	5	11
Cox	.000	1	0	0	0	0
Darby	.982	12	23	32	1	6
Foster	.979	8	19	27	1	12
Francisco	.974	21	29	45	2	10
Rayo	1.000	2	5	5	0	0
Reckley	.973	18	30	42	2	11
Sio	.972	50	95	112	6	24

Third Base	PCT	G	PO	A	E	DP
Bench	1.000	2	3	1	0	1
Francisco	1.000	1	1	0	0	0
Hipwell	.923	24	20	28	4	1
Rayo	.932	52	38	85	9	7
Sio	.769	6	1	9	3	2
Szykowny	.912	47	30	94	12	10

Shortstop	PCT	G	PO	A	E	DP
Ahuna	.870	10	14	26	6	9
Bench	.983	15	21	37	1	8
Foster	.965	48	57	110	6	22
Martin	.877	24	43	50	13	13
Peralta	.933	23	37	47	6	9
Reckley	1.000	1	0	2	0	0
Sio	.880	15	12	32	6	4

Outfield	PCT	G	PO	A	E	DP
Bandura	.975	26	37	2	1	0
Cassiani	.953	67	118	3	6	0
Christian	.944	9	16	1	1	0
Cox	.975	57	152	1	4	1
Davidson	.982	49	103	8	2	1
Diaz	.986	55	128	10	2	1
Hanchey	1.000	2	2	0	0	0
Jordan	1.000	2	2	0	0	0
Lewis	.964	17	27	0	1	0
Meckler	1.000	12	28	1	0	1
Ortiz	1.000	1	4	1	0	0
Quintas	.985	97	195	8	3	2
Tibbs	1.000	8	18	1	0	0
Williamson	1.000	2	1	0	0	0

ACL GIANTS — *ROOKIE*

ARIZONA COMPLEX LEAGUE

Batting	B-T	Ht.	Wt.	DOB	AVG	OBP	SLG	G	PA	AB	R	H	2B	3B	HR	RBI	BB	HBP	SH	SF	SO	SB	CS	BB%	SO%
Ahuna, Maui	L-R	6-1	170	3-11-02	.342	.405	.658	11	42	38	10	13	3	0	3	10	2	2	0	0	14	3	1	4.76	33.33
Arias, Rayner	R-R	6-2	185	4-29-06	.250	.371	.364	25	105	88	16	22	8	1	0	16	12	5	0	0	27	3	3	11.43	25.71
Arteaga, Aeverson	R-R	6-1	170	3-16-03	.444	.500	1.000	3	10	9	4	4	0	1	1	3	1	0	0	0	5	1	0	10.00	50.00

Bandura, Scott	L-R	6-4	190	8-2-01	.167	.286	.167	2	7	6	0	1	0	0	0	1	1	0	0	0	3	0	0	14.29	42.86
Brown, Vaun	R-R	6-0	215	6-23-98	.286	.429	.429	6	28	21	6	6	0	0	1	4	3	3	0	1	4	0	0	10.71	14.29
Castillo, Javier	R-R	6-1	170	11-14-03	.151	.286	.161	29	112	93	10	14	1	0	0	7	17	1	0	1	27	0	0	15.18	24.11
Diaz, Lisbel	R-R	6-2	201	7-20-05	.329	.411	.539	22	90	76	15	25	4	0	4	19	8	4	0	2	15	1	1	8.89	16.67
Diaz, Nomar	R-R	6-1	180	4-15-04	.250	.406	.458	10	32	24	3	6	2	0	1	4	4	3	0	1	8	1	1	12.50	25.00
Dupere, Jared	L-R	5-11	200	1-23-99	.125	.222	.250	9	36	32	5	4	1	0	1	3	4	0	0	0	14	1	0	11.11	38.89
Gutierrez, Carlos	L-R	5-10	174	8-22-04	.333	.385	.583	3	13	12	1	4	0	0	1	3	1	0	0	0	1	0	1	7.69	7.69
Hanchey, Ty	L-R	5-11	175	12-20-99	.346	.486	.731	10	35	26	11	9	1	0	3	10	6	2	0	1	7	1	0	17.14	20.00
Koss, Christian	R-R	6-1	182	1-27-98	.292	.419	.625	9	31	24	5	7	2	0	2	7	6	0	0	1	2	2	0	19.35	6.45
Laya, Derwin	R-R	6-3	187	9-15-03	.290	.393	.384	43	168	138	19	40	5	1	2	27	22	4	0	4	33	0	0	13.10	19.64
Maduro, Jediael	L-L	6-1	188	12-26-03	.237	.329	.271	20	70	59	9	14	2	0	0	10	6	3	0	2	13	0	0	8.57	18.57
Martin, Walker	L-R	6-2	188	2-20-04	.229	.413	.382	44	189	144	32	33	4	0	6	22	40	5	0	0	71	4	1	21.16	37.57
McIntyre, Donovan	L-L	6-2	165	12-10-02	.200	.333	.356	22	55	45	8	9	2	1	1	6	8	1	1	0	23	1	2	14.55	41.82
McKenna, Ryan	R-R	5-11	195	2-14-97	.412	.524	.647	5	21	17	6	7	1	0	1	10	4	0	0	0	5	0	0	19.05	23.81
Meckler, Wade	L-R	5-10	178	4-21-00	.228	.343	.263	16	67	57	11	13	2	0	0	5	9	1	0	0	13	5	0	13.43	19.40
Morales, Lazaro	R-R	5-11	160	4-16-04	.150	.370	.200	8	27	20	3	3	1	0	0	2	6	1	0	0	10	1	0	22.22	37.04
Ortiz, Jose	R-R	5-10	160	2-13-05	.306	.455	.400	27	112	85	24	26	3	1	1	13	14	11	0	2	20	10	2	12.50	17.86
Payton, Jack	R-R	5-11	200	8-7-01	.361	.477	.500	10	44	36	9	13	5	0	0	4	6	2	0	0	10	2	0	13.64	22.73
Peralta, Ramon	R-R	5-11	165	10-2-03	.313	.452	.542	24	104	83	18	26	9	2	2	16	17	4	0	0	29	3	0	16.35	27.88
Perez, Juan	R-R	6-1	182	9-22-04	.284	.368	.330	33	125	109	15	31	5	0	0	14	11	4	0	1	38	0	0	8.80	30.40
Pierre, Mauricio	R-R	6-3	180	11-23-03	.194	.324	.269	38	111	93	18	18	4	0	1	10	17	1	0	0	26	4	1	15.32	23.42
Ramos, Jose	R-R	5-11	143	10-25-02	.283	.426	.384	47	177	138	39	39	7	2	1	18	34	2	1	2	33	13	2	19.21	18.64
Reckley, Ryan	B-R	5-10	160	9-6-04	.283	.450	.489	32	120	92	24	26	3	2	4	15	24	4	0	0	33	4	0	20.00	27.50
Reynoso, Dario	R-R	5-10	180	3-22-05	.206	.381	.323	50	202	155	36	32	7	1	3	17	41	4	0	2	75	8	3	20.30	37.13
Sandoval, Eliam	L-L	6-2	175	2-4-04	.232	.339	.358	31	112	95	9	22	7	1	1	16	14	2	0	1	46	4	0	12.50	41.07
Soularie, Alerick	R-R	5-11	175	7-5-99	.125	.125	.375	2	8	8	1	1	0	1	0	0	0	0	0	0	2	0	0	0.00	25.00

Pitching	**B-T**	**Ht.**	**Wt.**	**DOB**	**W**	**L**	**ERA**	**G**	**GS**	**SV**	**IP**	**Hits**	**Runs**	**ER**	**HR**	**BB**	**SO**	**AVG**	**OBP**	**SLG**	**SO%**	**BB%**	**BF**
Andrews, Clayton	L-L	5-6	160	1-4-97	0	0	33.75	2	1	0	1	4	5	5	1	2	2	.500	.600	.875	20.00	20.00	10
Avendano, Christian	R-R	6-0	168	9-4-03	0	3	7.16	13	0	0	16	16	14	13	0	13	21	.246	.372	.354	26.58	16.46	79
Bello, Jose	R-R	6-1	164	5-29-05	0	0	7.71	1	0	0	2	3	4	2	0	1	2	.250	.308	.250	15.38	7.69	13
Burgos, Raymond	L-L	6-5	170	11-29-98	1	0	0.00	2	0	0	4	3	0	0	0	0	6	.214	.214	.214	42.86	0.00	14
Castillo, Wilkelma	R-R	6-0	170	1-6-00	3	2	5.02	12	1	0	29	25	20	16	6	15	34	.236	.328	.443	27.20	12.00	125
Chires, Samir	R-R	6-0	160	9-17-03	0	0	3.65	3	2	0	12	9	5	5	1	10	5	.214	.368	.357	8.77	17.54	57
Cobb, Alex	R-R	6-3	205	10-7-87	0	0	2.70	1	1	0	3	3	1	1	0	2	3	.273	.385	.273	23.08	15.38	13
Cody, Kyle	R-R	6-7	225	8-9-94	4	0	0.00	6	0	1	9	3	1	0	0	2	10	.107	.219	.143	30.30	6.06	33
Estrella, Mauricio	R-R	6-2	180	4-15-04	2	2	9.53	14	2	1	23	30	28	24	4	9	25	.313	.382	.521	22.73	8.18	110
Hernandez, Alix	R-R	6-2	155	7-16-04	2	1	3.29	14	1	1	41	34	19	15	4	20	58	.228	.348	.356	31.87	10.99	182
Hillier, Cole	R-R	6-2	205	12-7-00	0	0	0.00	1	0	1	2	0	0	0	0	1	2	.000	.167	.000	33.33	16.67	6
Johnson, Marques	R-R	6-2	210	7-4-00	0	0	0.00	1	1	0	1	0	0	0	0	0	2	.000	.000	.000	66.67	0.00	3
Lansville, Cale	R-R	6-1	205	1-6-03	0	1	3.38	2	2	0	3	3	1	1	0	2	3	.273	.385	.273	23.08	15.38	13
Laya, Derwin	R-R	6-3	187	9-15-03	0	0	0.00	1	0	0	1	0	0	0	0	0	0	.000	.000	.000	0.00	0.00	3
Manning, Timmy	L-L	6-2	195	9-10-01	1	0	2.00	8	0	0	9	7	2	2	0	3	15	.219	.286	.250	42.86	8.57	35
Manzano, Mikell	R-R	6-0	140	11-30-02	3	1	3.80	10	6	0	43	45	20	18	1	14	30	.268	.326	.351	16.30	7.61	104
Martinez, Keyner	R-R	6-1	165	8-16-04	1	1	3.03	19	0	3	33	27	15	11	2	16	23	.227	.329	.353	16.31	11.35	141
McDonald, Trevor	R-R	6-2	200	2-26-01	1	1	3.52	5	4	0	8	7	3	3	1	2	9	.250	.300	.393	30.00	6.67	30
Miles, Spencer	L-R	6-3	180	7-26-00	0	0	4.91	5	3	0	7	9	4	4	0	2	10	.300	.344	.433	31.25	6.25	32
Molina, Carlos	L-L	6-0	190	2-7-05	0	1	4.26	9	0	0	13	13	13	6	1	10	11	.271	.393	.396	18.03	16.39	61
Pagan, Kanoa	R-R	6-2	190	9-29-98	1	0	3.00	5	1	1	6	2	4	2	0	3	9	.095	.240	.095	36.00	12.00	25
Palencia, Brayan	R-R	5-11	142	1-14-03	0	0	3.86	4	3	0	14	15	11	6	3	2	19	.259	.306	.552	30.16	3.17	63
Ray, Robbie	L-L	6-2	225	10-1-91	0	1	5.14	4	4	0	7	7	4	4	1	0	15	.250	.250	.500	53.57	0.00	28
Rengel, Jose	L-L	6-0	168	9-8-05	3	2	7.50	15	5	0	48	54	47	40	2	37	47	.280	.406	.425	19.67	15.48	239
Rodriguez, Johan	R-R	6-0	170	11-12-02	3	3	5.58	14	3	0	40	30	30	25	0	42	55	.201	.381	.255	28.21	21.54	195
Rodriguez, Michael	L-L	6-5	250	1-8-00	1	0	1.93	3	0	0	5	2	1	1	1	3	6	.143	.333	.357	33.33	16.67	18
Roupp, Landen	R-R	6-2	205	9-10-98	0	0	0.00	3	2	0	5	2	0	0	0	0	12	.118	.118	.118	70.59	0.00	17
Simon, Liam	R-R	6-4	220	10-16-00	1	2	12.19	11	6	0	10	9	19	14	1	19	16	.237	.525	.342	25.81	30.65	62
Small, Ethan	L-L	6-2	200	2-14-97	0	0	3.00	3	3	0	3	2	1	1	0	0	4	.200	.182	.400	36.36	0.00	11
Sullivan, Billy	R-R	6-2	195	4-16-99	0	1	18.69	5	0	0	4	8	10	9	0	4	9	.400	.536	.550	32.14	14.29	28
Szapucki, Thomas	R-L	6-2	210	6-12-96	0	0	0.00	1	1	0	1	1	0	0	0	0	2	.250	.250	.250	50.00	0.00	4
Teng, Kai-Wei	R-R	6-4	260	12-1-98	0	0	9.82	2	1	0	4	5	4	4	2	2	4	.333	.444	.733	22.22	11.11	18
Vanderhei, Ryan	R-R	6-6	185	6-1-01	0	0	6.23	6	2	0	9	9	7	6	1	3	11	.250	.308	.444	28.21	7.69	39
Villers, Ian	R-R	6-6	245	9-1-00	1	1	3.46	9	2	0	13	10	6	5	0	4	16	.227	.314	.250	31.37	7.84	51
Vogel, Tyler	R-R	6-0	175	11-16-00	1	0	0.00	4	1	0	5	1	0	0	0	3	7	.071	.222	.071	38.89	16.67	18
Warren, Austin	R-R	6-0	170	2-5-96	0	0	0.00	2	1	0	2	0	0	0	0	0	2	.000	.000	.000	33.33	0.00	6
Winn, Keaton	R-R	6-4	238	2-20-98	0	0	2.45	1	0	0	4	2	1	1	1	2	6	.154	.267	.462	40.00	13.33	15
Wolf, Josh	R-R	6-3	170	9-1-00	2	2	5.82	11	0	0	17	17	12	11	0	13	25	.266	.385	.344	31.65	16.46	79

Fielding

C: Perez 29, Castillo 16, Payton 7, Diaz 6, Hanchey 6. **1B:** Laya 32, Maduro 15, Castillo 9, Ramos 5, Diaz 1, Payton 1. **2B:** Reckley 27, Ramos 18, Peralta 10, Morales 4, Reynoso 4, Soularie 2, Koss 2. **3B:** Reynoso 27, Ramos 17, Peralta 10, Laya 9, Koss 2. **SS:** Martin 39, Reynoso 15, Peralta 4, Koss 3, Ramos 2. **LF:** Sandoval 24, McIntyre 8, Pierre 8, McKenna 5, Dupere 4, Diaz 3, Ramos 3, Gutierrez 2, Maduro 1, Bandura 1, Brown 1. **CF: Ortiz 14, Arias 14, Meckler 12, McIntyre 8, Pierre 6, Dupere 4, Reckley 3, Morales 3, Brown 2, Gutierrez 1. RF:** Pierre 21, Diaz 20, Ortiz 13, Arias 7, Sandoval 3, McIntyre 2, Dupere 1, Bandura 1, Brown 1.

DSL GIANTS BLACK — ROOKIE

DOMINICAN SUMMER LEAGUE

Batting	B-T	Ht.	Wt.	DOB	AVG	OBP	SLG	G	PA	AB	R	H	2B	3B	HR	RBI	BB	HBP	SH	SF	SO	SB	CS	BB%	SO%
Alexander, Jesus	L-R	6-2	185	9-4-05	.321	.387	.429	6	31	28	4	9	3	0	0	6	3	0	0	0	6	0	0	9.68	19.35
Astudillo, Jose	R-R	5-10	150	2-27-04	.357	.375	.357	4	16	14	4	5	0	0	0	6	0	1	0	1	0	0	0	0.00	0.00
Colorado, Juan	R-R	6-0	165	9-18-06	.248	.330	.309	45	185	165	22	41	3	2	1	23	18	2	0	0	66	5	1	9.73	35.68
Concepcion, Carlos	R-R	6-1	189	1-6-06	.244	.362	.366	47	199	164	28	40	9	1	3	28	23	9	0	3	61	7	4	11.56	30.65
Crespo, Ricardo	L-L	5-10	168	9-26-06	.268	.442	.304	21	78	56	18	15	2	0	0	6	17	2	1	2	12	0	4	21.79	15.38
Dos Santos, Vinicius	R-R	6-2	176	6-5-07	.218	.358	.273	20	67	55	7	12	3	0	0	5	7	5	0	0	21	2	0	10.45	31.34
Duran, Alessandro	B-R	5-10	170	7-2-05	.308	.444	.354	22	83	65	16	20	3	0	0	9	14	2	1	0	12	0	0	16.87	14.46
Estevez, Evan	R-R	6-3	165	8-14-07	.290	.369	.387	43	179	155	23	45	5	2	2	21	19	2	0	3	55	6	3	10.61	30.73
Gonzalez, Anyelo	L-R	5-11	165	9-24-04	.193	.308	.261	28	108	88	12	17	4	1	0	14	16	0	1	3	12	0	1	14.81	11.11
Guzman, Angel	L-L	5-11	170	11-15-05	.305	.475	.523	45	201	151	50	46	6	3	7	34	45	4	1	0	39	15	4	22.39	19.40
Level, Jhonny	B-R	5-10	154	3-29-07	.275	.393	.517	48	215	178	44	49	11	1	10	46	30	5	1	1	36	18	9	13.95	16.74
Marquez, Anthony	R-R	5-11	155	9-23-06	.279	.405	.369	38	149	122	28	34	4	2	1	17	19	7	1	0	25	10	1	12.75	16.78
Pena, Fernando	R-R	5-11	175	3-28-07	.222	.440	.222	8	25	18	4	4	0	0	0	2	6	1	0	0	5	0	0	24.00	20.00
Riera, Dennys	R-R	5-9	165	2-17-05	.244	.383	.349	30	107	86	21	21	6	0	1	12	14	6	0	1	24	2	2	13.08	22.43
Sanchez, Yohendry	R-R	6-0	207	11-9-06	.241	.489	.448	12	45	29	8	7	3	0	1	7	10	5	0	1	11	1	1	22.22	24.44
Sarduy, Boris	L-R	6-1	155	2-3-07	.152	.394	.261	20	66	46	14	7	2	0	1	7	16	3	0	1	20	1	2	24.24	30.30
Tejada, Oliver	R-R	5-11	180	12-9-06	.300	.405	.488	46	205	170	36	51	11	3	5	39	22	10	0	3	38	13	9	10.73	18.54
Villegas, Diego	L-L	5-10	170	3-23-04	.371	.500	.600	10	44	35	11	13	2	0	2	9	9	0	0	0	9	1	0	20.45	20.45

Pitching	B-T	Ht.	Wt.	DOB	W	L	ERA	G	GS	SV	IP	Hits	Runs	ER	HR	BB	SO	AVG	OBP	SLG	SO%	BB%	BF
Caraballo, Jan	R-R	6-6	181	10-20-03	5	2	2.45	18	0	4	37	27	14	10	1	16	40	.200	.288	.259	26.14	10.46	153
Castro, Kendry	R-R	6-2	160	1-11-07	3	1	9.77	15	1	0	16	16	20	17	1	29	12	.267	.516	.350	12.90	31.18	93
Cayama, Argenis	R-R	6-1	180	9-15-06	0	0	4.50	2	2	0	4	6	2	2	0	0	6	.333	.333	.389	33.33	0.00	18
De La Torre, Luis	L-L	6-0	188	9-6-03	4	0	3.14	14	1	0	29	23	15	10	0	11	39	.228	.339	.257	31.97	9.02	122
Estrada, Ricardo	L-L	6-0	170	6-25-02	5	0	1.22	13	8	0	44	25	10	6	0	14	53	.157	.234	.201	30.29	8.00	175
Feliz, Ankeily	R-R	6-1	185	6-27-03	2	0	8.37	14	1	1	24	35	24	22	0	13	20	.343	.429	.451	16.81	10.92	119
Franco, Marlon	R-R	6-2	165	9-18-02	3	1	1.65	12	9	0	49	38	19	9	2	5	46	.211	.262	.289	23.59	2.56	195
Fuentes, Alexander	R-R	6-7	242	1-13-05	2	2	4.39	12	11	1	41	45	22	20	1	11	33	.283	.364	.352	17.93	5.98	184
Gonzalez, Jose	R-R	6-1	180	6-15-02	2	3	6.94	11	8	0	35	36	30	27	0	20	40	.267	.387	.356	24.39	12.20	164
Gonzalez, Moises	R-R	6-2	175	10-25-02	0	1	9.39	7	0	0	8	12	8	8	0	5	2	.364	.447	.545	5.26	13.16	38
Jimenez, Jeison	R-R	6-6	233	9-11-03	3	0	4.35	17	0	1	21	11	14	10	0	18	25	.155	.368	.183	26.32	18.95	95
Laroche, Alberto	R-R	5-11	171	12-1-05	0	0	0.00	2	1	0	3	3	1	0	0	0	2	.273	.250	.273	16.67	0.00	12
Lopez, Jesus	R-R	6-2	170	3-3-05	4	1	5.59	16	0	0	29	43	21	18	3	10	30	.341	.401	.468	20.98	6.99	143
Meza, Jose	R-R	5-11	180	4-24-06	2	1	2.63	18	0	4	27	24	14	8	2	14	17	.229	.333	.324	13.82	11.38	123
Millan, Antonio	L-L	6-2	165	1-14-03	2	1	3.80	20	0	7	21	13	9	9	0	18	27	.181	.341	.222	29.67	19.78	91
Narvaez, Brayan	R-R	6-2	175	10-20-04	3	0	3.92	12	11	0	44	40	21	19	2	10	45	.247	.302	.352	25.14	5.59	179

Fielding

C: Duran 19, Gonzalez 18, Sanchez 11, Pena 7, Alexander 3. **1B:** Guzman 31, Estevez 9, Gonzalez 6, Villegas 6, Alexander 2, Riera 1, Sarduy 1. **2B:** Marquez 25, Sarduy 17, Riera 13, Astudillo 2. **3B:** Colorado 41, Riera 12, Sarduy 1. **SS:** Level 42, Marquez 13, Riera 1. **LF:** Estevez 21, Dos Santos 14, Crespo 12, Guzman 6, Sarduy 1. **CF:** Tejada 42, Crespo 9, Concepcion 2, Estevez 1. **RF:** Concepcion 39, Estevez 8, Guzman 5, Dos Santos 2.

DSL GIANTS ORANGE — ROOKIE

DOMINICAN SUMMER LEAGUE

Batting	B-T	Ht.	Wt.	DOB	AVG	OBP	SLG	G	PA	AB	R	H	2B	3B	HR	RBI	BB	HBP	SH	SF	SO	SB	CS	BB%	SO%
Alexander, Jesus	L-R	6-2	185	9-4-05	.392	.446	.628	41	166	148	22	58	14	3	5	34	16	0	0	2	22	1	0	9.64	13.25
Arosemena, Erick	R-R	6-0	170	4-2-05	.229	.443	.417	17	70	48	12	11	2	2	1	12	14	6	0	2	15	2	0	20.00	21.43
Benitez, Yoxander	R-R	6-2	165	11-1-06	.232	.338	.319	25	80	69	10	16	2	2	0	12	11	0	0	0	20	4	2	13.75	25.00
Blanco, Miguel	R-R	6-0	155	10-26-05	.255	.398	.336	44	171	137	27	35	4	2	1	25	30	3	0	1	35	5	2	17.54	20.47
Brito, Carlos	B-R	5-8	198	3-25-06	.122	.317	.184	18	63	49	7	6	0	0	1	8	12	2	0	0	19	2	1	19.05	30.16
Camacaro, Keiberg	R-R	5-11	158	8-24-06	.225	.398	.314	32	133	102	24	23	5	2	0	13	22	8	0	1	28	4	1	16.54	21.05
Camacho, Santiago	B-R	5-11	176	1-27-07	.363	.507	.549	31	138	102	28	37	11	1	2	22	28	5	0	3	21	3	0	20.29	15.22
De La Rosa, Moises	R-R	6-2	190	11-29-04	.205	.352	.366	36	142	112	18	23	4	4	2	16	19	8	0	3	39	3	3	13.38	27.46
Frias, Luis	R-R	5-11	155	8-7-04	.224	.327	.329	38	167	143	27	32	6	3	1	11	18	4	2	0	50	13	5	10.78	29.94
Gonzalez, Howard	R-R	6-0	165	11-6-06	.152	.278	.196	15	54	46	4	7	2	0	0	6	7	1	0	0	21	1	0	12.96	38.89
Jimenez, Albert	R-R	6-1	174	10-28-06	.264	.339	.405	45	186	163	22	43	12	1	3	26	18	2	0	3	41	0	1	9.68	22.04
Moya, Jeyson	R-R	6-1	165	10-28-06	.104	.315	.164	23	89	67	9	7	2	1	0	5	19	2	0	1	34	2	0	21.35	38.20
Pena, Fernando	R-R	5-11	175	3-28-07	.240	.406	.280	11	32	25	4	6	1	0	0	2	3	4	0	0	11	0	0	9.38	34.38
Ramirez, Jorge	R-R	5-11	155	3-7-06	.300	.424	.400	23	85	70	11	21	2	1	1	13	11	4	0	0	20	1	2	12.94	23.53
Rivas, Yosneiker	L-R	5-10	161	10-6-05	.245	.408	.345	41	181	139	29	34	9	1	1	15	36	3	2	1	42	3	4	19.89	23.20
Vasquez, Brandon	L-L	5-10	165	12-6-06	.187	.282	.253	28	103	91	14	17	4	1	0	8	11	1	0	0	17	6	2	10.68	16.50
Villegas, Diego	L-L	5-10	170	3-23-04	.250	.403	.300	19	77	60	8	15	1	1	0	9	14	2	0	1	18	1	0	18.18	23.38
Willias, Franco	R-R	6-0	184	4-6-05	.260	.359	.420	39	154	131	26	34	8	2	3	11	7	14	1	1	34	8	5	4.55	22.08

Pitching	B-T	Ht.	Wt.	DOB	W	L	ERA	G	GS	SV	IP	Hits	Runs	ER	HR	BB	SO	AVG	OBP	SLG	SO%	BB%	BF
Bello, Jose	R-R	6-1	164	5-29-05	0	2	2.49	7	7	0	25	18	7	7	1	4	36	.202	.253	.303	37.89	4.21	95
Berson, Juan	R-R	6-1	185	4-22-04	5	1	4.13	19	0	1	24	18	12	11	1	12	16	.217	.359	.325	15.53	11.65	103
Bracho, Lender	R-R	6-0	150	2-24-05	1	2	2.40	17	0	2	30	31	11	8	0	7	25	.274	.320	.345	20.49	5.74	122
Cabello, Brayan	R-R	6-0	155	12-6-03	4	2	4.80	17	0	0	30	25	17	16	3	13	31	.225	.328	.360	23.66	9.92	131
Calcurian, Omar	R-R	5-11	168	5-25-05	2	0	2.84	12	0	1	19	17	6	6	0	4	18	.233	.282	.315	23.08	5.13	78
Cayama, Argenis	R-R	6-1	180	9-15-06	0	1	2.21	8	8	0	20	15	6	5	0	9	23	.203	.322	.270	26.14	10.23	88
De Frias, Haniel	L-R	6-4	175	10-28-04	1	1	13.50	6	1	0	4	6	6	6	1	3	6	.353	.450	.706	30.00	15.00	20

De Leon, Randry	R-R	6-4	201	7-21-05	0	2	3.19	12	11	0	42	34	17	15	3	16	46	.224	.316	.316	26.44	9.20	174
Fernandez, Dilan	R-R	5-11	168	4-6-05	0	1	3.97	12	7	0	34	29	20	15	1	12	25	.225	.299	.341	17.36	8.33	144
Gonzalez, Moises	R-R	6-2	175	10-25-02	0	0	0.00	1	0	0	1	1	1	0	0	0	0	.250	.200	.250	0.00	0.00	5
Guerra, Edwin	R-R	6-1	198	11-29-04	1	1	4.25	14	3	1	30	33	18	14	1	14	28	.270	.364	.369	19.58	9.79	143
Heredia, Delvis	L-R	5-11	190	10-27-04	3	0	2.70	16	0	0	27	20	8	8	1	14	16	.222	.333	.322	14.55	12.73	110
Hernandez, Luis	R-R	6-1	211	10-4-05	1	0	5.40	2	0	0	2	2	1	1	0	2	2	.286	.500	.429	20.00	20.00	10
Leon, Jhon	R-R	6-3	180	2-4-04	0	1	7.27	15	0	0	17	20	14	14	4	18	18	.290	.462	.493	19.78	19.78	91
Mejias, Frainer	R-R	6-1	170	1-10-06	7	1	2.72	20	1	0	36	26	20	11	1	11	47	.195	.283	.323	30.72	7.19	153
Perez, Alfonso	R-R	6-2	175	8-14-05	0	3	4.42	11	8	0	39	34	21	19	2	18	29	.241	.347	.326	16.76	10.40	173
Rojas, Jose	R-R	6-1	145	1-2-04	4	6	2.56	21	0	4	39	33	17	11	2	9	31	.221	.273	.322	19.25	5.59	161
Villarreal, Elkyns	R-R	6-0	160	11-18-06	0	3	3.45	12	10	0	31	27	20	12	1	17	24	.231	.352	.291	16.90	11.97	142

Fielding

C: Camacho 25, Ramirez 20, Pena 10, Alexander 6. **1B:** Alexander 30, Villegas 17, Jimenez 11, Ramirez 1. **2B:** Benitez 22, Willias 19, Rivas 11, Camacaro 5, Moya 2. **3B:** Jimenez 31, Willias 17, Moya 7, Rivas 7. **SS:** Camacaro 23, Rivas 22, Moya 12. **LF:** Blanco 15, De La Rosa 15, Vasquez 11, Brito 9, Frias 5, Arosemena 2, Gonzalez 1. **CF:** Frias 30, Blanco 25, De La Rosa 1, Vasquez 1. **RF:** De La Rosa 16, Gonzalez 14, Vasquez 12, Arosemena 6, Brito 5, Frias 2, Blanco 2.

Seattle Mariners

SEASON SYNOPSIS: For the third time in four seasons, Seattle was good but not good enough and narrowly missed out on a playoff spot. This time, the Mariners led the American League West into early August before a strikeout-addled offense dragged them down. Winning eight of their last 10 still left them one game shy of a wild-card spot.

HIGH POINT: The Mariners won 17 of 22 during a late May to June stretch to get to 44-31 and establish a 10-game lead in the division, with a home sweep of the Rangers capping it off. Logan Gilbert tossed eight shutout frames in a 5-0 win against the Rangers to give the M's a ninth straight home series victory and told reporters, "It really feels like a playoff atmosphere in mid June, which is kind of weird to say."

LOW POINT: Barely two months later, Seattle's lead was gone as Houston heated up and Seattle went 21-33 in a 66-day stretch which cost manager Scott Servais and hitting coach Jarrett DeHart their job in late August. The stretch included a late July home sweep at the hands of the lowly Angels that included shortstop J.P. Crawford getting hit by a pitch that broke a finger on his right hand; he wound up missing more than a month.

NOTABLE ROOKIES: Despite their offensive shortcomings, the Mariners didn't turn to their talented farm system for hitting help. Their lone notable rookie was righthander Emerson Hancock, who filled in for Bryan Woo (forearm) in the first month-plus of the season as the team's fifth starter. The sixth overall pick in 2020 made 12 starts overall.

KEY TRANSACTIONS: Hall of Famer Edgar Martinez stepped in as interim hitting coach and former Seattle catcher Dan Wilson, previously working in the organization's minor league system, stepped in as first-time manager, leading the club to a 21-13 record down the stretch. The Mariners were buyers at the trade deadline, adding outfielder Randy Arozarena from Tampa Bay and reliever Yimi Garcia from Toronto after designating veteran first baseman Ty France for assignment and trading him to Cincinnati. Their biggest addition may have been outfielder Victor Robles, signed in June and given a two-year deal later in the season after a career-best .328/.393/.467 line with Seattle after being cut by the Nationals.

OPENING DAY PAYROLL: $135,738,647 (18th)

PLAYERS OF THE YEAR

MAJOR LEAGUE

Logan Gilbert
RHP
9-12, 3.23 ERA
220 SO, 37 BB, 209 IP
MLB-best 0.89 WHIP

MINOR LEAGUE

Lazaro Montes
OF
(A/A+)
.288/.397/.484
21 HR, 78 BB, 105 RBIs

ORGANIZATION LEADERS

Batting		*Qualifiers
MAJORS		
* AVG	Julio Rodriguez	.273
* OPS	Cal Raleigh	.748
HR	Cal Raleigh	34
RBI	Cal Raleigh	100
MINORS		
* AVG	Carlos Jimenez, ACL Mariners/Modesto	.318
* OBP	Carlos Jimenez, ACL Mariners/Modesto	.426
* SLG	Jason Vosler, Tacoma	.573
* OPS	Jason Vosler, Tacoma	.944
R	Michael Arroyo, Everett/Modesto	101
H	Jason Vosler, Tacoma	141
TB	Jason Vosler, Tacoma	267
2B	Ben Williamson, Everett/Arkansas	34
3B	Tai Peete, Modesto	9
HR	Jason Vosler, Tacoma	31
RBI	Jason Vosler, Tacoma	110
BB	Lazaro Montes, Everett/Modesto	78
SO	Charlie Pagliarini, Modesto	171
SB	Ryan Bliss, Tacoma	50
SB	Samad Taylor, Tacoma	50

Pitching		#Qualifiers
MAJORS		
W	George Kirby	14
# ERA	Bryce Miller	2.94
SO	Logan Gilbert	220
SV	Andres Munoz	22
MINORS		
W	Michael Morales, Everett/Arkansas	13
L	Casey Lawrence, Tacoma	11
# ERA	Brandyn Garcia, Everett/Arkansas	2.25
G	Carlos Vargas, Tacoma	55
GS	Casey Lawrence, Tacoma	29
SV	Troy Taylor, Everett/Arkansas	21
IP	Casey Lawrence, Tacoma	165
BB	Ashton Izzi, Modesto	59
SO	Michael Morales, Everett/Arkansas	147
# AVG	Elijah Dale, Modesto	.201

2024 PERFORMANCE

General Manager: Jerry Dipoto. **Farm Director:** Justin Toole. **Scouting Director:** Scott Hunter.

Class	Team	League	W	L	PCT	Finish	Manager
Majors	Seattle Mariners	American	85	77	.525	7 (15)	S. Servais/D. Wilson
Triple-A	Tacoma Rainiers	Pacific Coast	82	68	.547	2 (10)	John Russell
Double-A	Arkansas Travelers	Texas	80	57	.584	3 (10)	Christian Colon
High-A	Everett AquaSox	Northwest	64	68	.485	4 (6)	Ryan Scott
Low-A	Modesto Nuts	California	73	57	.562	2 (8)	Zach Vincej
Rookie	ACL Mariners	Arizona Complex	28	32	.467	10 (15)	Luis Caballero
Rookie	DSL Mariners	Dominican	16	39	.291	48 (51)	Jose Amancio
Overall 2024 Minor League Record			**343**	**321**	**.517**	**13th (30)**	

SEATTLE MARINERS

ORGANIZATION STATISTICS

SEATTLE MARINERS

AMERICAN LEAGUE

Batting	B-T	Ht.	Wt.	DOB	AVG	OBP	SLG	G	PA	AB	R	H	2B	3B	HR	RBI	BB	HBP	SH	SF	SO	SB	CS	BB%	SO%
Arozarena, Randy	R-R	5-11	185	2-28-95	.231	.356	.377	54	239	199	32	46	14	0	5	23	28	11	0	1	68	4	3	11.72	28.45
Bliss, Ryan	R-R	5-6	165	12-13-99	.222	.290	.397	33	71	63	10	14	3	1	2	9	5	1	2	0	22	5	3	7.04	30.99
Canzone, Dominic	L-R	5-11	190	8-16-97	.196	.271	.381	67	188	168	20	33	7	0	8	17	18	0	0	2	53	1	0	9.57	28.19
Castillo, Luis	R-R	6-2	200	12-12-92	.000	.000	.000	30	1	1	0	0	0	0	0	0	0	0	0	0	1	0	0	0.00	100.00
Clase, Jonatan	B-R	5-9	150	5-23-02	.195	.233	.220	19	43	41	4	8	1	0	0	3	2	0	0	0	14	3	0	4.65	32.56
Crawford, J.P.	L-R	6-2	202	1-11-95	.202	.304	.321	105	451	392	55	79	16	2	9	37	52	6	0	1	102	5	0	11.53	22.62
France, Ty	R-R	5-11	215	7-13-94	.223	.312	.350	88	340	300	28	67	14	0	8	31	28	11	0	1	83	0	1	8.24	24.41
Garver, Mitch	R-R	6-1	220	1-15-91	.172	.286	.341	114	430	367	37	63	17	0	15	51	53	7	0	3	133	0	0	12.33	30.93
Haggerty, Sam	B-R	5-11	175	5-26-94	.067	.125	.067	8	16	15	1	1	0	0	0	1	1	0	0	0	4	1	0	6.25	25.00
Haniger, Mitch	R-R	6-2	214	12-23-90	.208	.286	.334	121	423	380	42	79	12	0	12	44	40	2	0	1	126	0	0	9.46	29.79
Locklear, Tyler	R-R	6-1	210	11-24-00	.156	.224	.311	16	49	45	3	7	1	0	2	3	3	1	0	0	20	1	0	6.12	40.82
Marlowe, Cade	L-R	6-1	210	6-24-97	.250	.333	.250	8	9	8	1	2	0	0	0	0	1	0	0	0	1	0	0	11.11	11.11
Moore, Dylan	R-R	6-0	205	8-2-92	.201	.320	.367	135	441	368	53	74	23	4	10	42	53	14	1	5	123	32	6	12.02	27.89
Polanco, Jorge	B-R	5-11	208	7-5-93	.213	.296	.355	118	469	417	43	89	11	0	16	45	46	4	0	2	137	4	2	9.81	29.21
Raleigh, Cal	B-R	6-3	235	11-26-96	.220	.312	.436	153	628	546	73	120	16	0	34	100	70	6	0	6	176	6	1	11.15	28.03
Raley, Luke	L-R	6-4	235	9-19-94	.243	.320	.463	137	455	404	58	98	19	2	22	58	27	20	2	2	135	11	2	5.93	29.67
Rivas, Leo	B-R	5-10	150	10-10-97	.233	.333	.274	43	86	73	10	17	1	1	0	8	10	1	2	0	24	3	0	11.63	27.91
Robles, Victor	R-R	6-0	194	5-19-97	.328	.393	.467	77	262	229	41	75	20	0	4	26	16	10	5	2	44	30	1	6.11	16.79
Rodriguez, Julio	R-R	6-3	228	12-29-00	.273	.325	.409	143	613	567	76	155	17	0	20	68	38	6	0	2	156	24	5	6.20	25.45
Rojas, Josh	L-R	6-1	207	6-30-94	.225	.304	.336	143	476	422	48	95	19	2	8	31	46	3	1	2	108	10	4	9.66	22.69
Taylor, Samad	R-R	5-8	160	7-11-98	.400	.400	.400	3	5	5	2	2	0	0	0	0	0	0	0	0	1	0	0	0.00	20.00
Turner, Justin	R-R	5-11	202	11-23-84	.264	.363	.403	48	190	159	22	42	7	0	5	24	20	7	0	4	35	0	0	10.53	18.42
Urias, Luis	R-R	5-10	202	6-3-97	.191	.303	.394	41	109	94	11	18	7	0	4	16	9	6	0	0	34	0	0	8.26	31.19
Vosler, Jason	L-R	6-1	220	9-6-93	.179	.233	.286	10	30	28	2	5	1	1	0	3	2	0	0	0	9	0	0	6.67	30.00
Zavala, Seby	R-R	5-11	205	8-28-93	.154	.214	.282	18	43	39	4	6	2	0	1	2	3	0	1	0	16	0	0	6.98	37.21

Pitching	B-T	Ht.	Wt.	DOB	W	L	ERA	G	GS	SV	IP	Hits	Runs	ER	HR	BB	SO	AVG	OBP	SLG	SO%	BB%	BF
Baumann, Mike	R-R	6-4	240	9-10-95	2	0	5.51	18	0	0	16	13	11	10	4	8	16	.213	.306	.475	22.22	11.11	72
Bazardo, Eduard	R-R	6-0	190	9-1-95	2	0	4.88	23	0	0	28	20	15	15	2	9	33	.204	.271	.296	30.56	8.33	108
Bolton, Cody	R-R	6-3	230	6-19-98	0	0	4.34	17	0	0	19	18	11	9	3	9	17	.247	.325	.438	20.48	10.84	83
Bowman, Matt	R-R	6-0	185	5-31-91	0	0	13.50	1	0	0	1	1	1	1	1	1	0	.333	.500	1.333	0.00	25.00	4
Castillo, Luis	R-R	6-2	200	12-12-92	11	12	3.64	30	30	0	175	158	73	71	25	47	175	.238	.293	.412	24.34	6.54	719
Chargois, JT	S-R	6-3	200	12-3-90	2	1	2.75	21	0	0	20	9	6	6	3	6	18	.134	.227	.299	24.00	8.00	75
de Geus, Brett	R-R	6-2	190	11-4-97	0	0	2.70	4	0	0	3	4	1	1	0	0	2	.333	.429	.417	14.29	0.00	14
Diaz, Jhonathan	L-L	6-0	170	9-13-96	0	1	4.66	5	1	0	10	14	6	5	2	3	8	.318	.362	.568	17.02	6.38	47
Garcia, Yimi	R-R	6-1	230	8-18-90	0	0	6.00	10	0	0	9	7	6	6	3	4	7	.206	.289	.500	18.42	10.53	38
Gilbert, Logan	R-R	6-6	215	5-5-97	9	12	3.23	33	33	0	209	148	83	75	26	37	220	.196	.236	.353	27.40	4.61	803
Hancock, Emerson	R-R	6-4	213	5-31-99	4	4	4.75	12	12	0	61	62	37	32	12	19	39	.259	.327	.456	14.66	7.14	266
Hernandez, Jonathan	R-R	6-3	190	7-6-96	0	0	11.57	3	0	0	2	2	3	3	0	2	3	.222	.364	.222	27.27	18.18	11
Kirby, George	R-R	6-4	215	2-4-98	14	11	3.53	33	33	0	191	181	82	75	22	23	179	.245	.272	.393	23.01	2.96	778
Miller, Bryce	R-R	6-2	180	8-23-98	12	8	2.94	31	31	0	180	131	62	59	21	45	171	.200	.254	.338	24.29	6.39	704
Miller, Tyson	R-R	6-5	220	7-29-95	0	0	3.09	9	0	0	12	8	5	4	2	1	12	.186	.222	.395	26.67	2.22	45
Munoz, Andres	R-R	6-2	222	1-16-99	3	7	2.12	60	0	22	59	31	16	14	6	26	77	.153	.259	.257	33.19	11.21	232
Rivas, Leo	S-R	5-10	150	10-10-97	0	0	0.00	2	0	0	2	2	1	0	0	0	0	.222	.222	.333	0.00	0.00	9
Rojas, Josh	L-R	6-1	207	6-30-94	0	0	9.00	2	0	0	2	1	2	2	1	2	0	.167	.375	.667	0.00	25.00	8
Santos, Gregory	R-R	6-2	190	8-28-99	0	1	4.91	8	0	0	7	7	4	4	0	1	6	.241	.290	.310	19.35	3.23	31
Saucedo, Tayler	L-L	6-4	205	6-18-93	2	0	3.49	53	0	3	39	35	15	15	3	18	38	.240	.331	.356	22.89	10.84	166
Snead, Kirby	L-L	6-1	218	10-7-94	0	0	4.35	11	0	0	10	12	5	5	0	7	7	.293	.396	.439	14.58	14.58	48
Snider, Collin	R-R	6-4	195	10-10-95	3	4	1.94	42	0	0	42	36	14	9	5	13	47	.231	.290	.378	27.81	7.69	169
Speier, Gabe	L-L	5-11	200	4-12-95	0	2	5.70	29	0	0	24	19	15	15	2	14	33	.226	.340	.345	31.73	13.46	104
Stanek, Ryne	R-R	6-4	226	7-26-91	6	3	4.38	46	0	7	39	35	21	19	5	17	44	.230	.314	.375	25.58	9.88	172
Taylor, Troy	R-R	6-0	195	9-9-01	0	0	3.72	21	0	1	19	15	8	8	4	7	25	.203	.272	.419	30.86	8.64	81
Thornton, Trent	R-R	6-0	190	9-30-93	4	3	3.61	71	0	1	72	63	32	29	8	19	77	.238	.299	.396	26.19	6.46	294

Voth, Austin	R-R	6-2	215	6-26-92	2	5	3.69	68	0	0	61	46	31	25	9	18	61	.204	.271	.367	24.60	7.26	248
Woo, Bryan	R-R	6-2	205	1-30-00	9	3	2.89	22	22	0	121	96	41	39	14	13	101	.211	.237	.337	21.40	2.75	472

Fielding

Catcher	PCT	G	PO	A	E	DP	PB
Garver	1.000	25	183	9	0	2	0
Raleigh	.995	135	1138	51	6	8	5
Zavala	.989	18	91	3	1	0	0

First Base	PCT	G	PO	A	E	DP
France	.994	87	580	65	4	54
Locklear	1.000	16	91	7	0	5
Moore	1.000	11	36	1	0	0
Raley	.996	41	224	16	1	14
Rojas	1.000	1	1	0	0	0
Turner	.991	31	192	27	2	10
Vosler	1.000	5	18	3	0	3

Second Base	PCT	G	PO	A	E	DP
Bliss	.987	25	36	42	1	14
France	1.000	1	1	1	0	0
Moore	1.000	37	39	65	0	9
Polanco	.981	112	138	222	7	45
Rivas	1.000	11	2	10	0	0
Rojas	1.000	11	9	29	0	5

Third Base	PCT	G	PO	A	E	DP
Moore	1.000	45	24	47	0	4
Rivas	1.000	2	0	1	0	0
Rojas	.964	131	79	186	10	15
Turner	.000	1	0	0	0	0
Urias	.929	38	27	51	6	7

Shortstop	PCT	G	PO	A	E	DP
Crawford	.991	104	113	212	3	36
Moore	.968	49	60	89	5	15
Rivas	.968	26	17	43	2	8

Outfield	PCT	G	PO	A	E	DP
Arozarena	1.000	53	114	1	0	0
Canzone	1.000	62	100	0	0	0
Clase	1.000	17	21	0	0	0
Haggerty	.875	7	6	1	1	0
Haniger	.971	90	162	4	5	0
Marlowe	1.000	7	4	0	0	0
Moore	1.000	23	35	0	0	0
Raley	.982	105	165	2	3	0
Robles	.986	80	140	3	2	1
Rodriguez	.985	131	334	4	5	1
Rojas	1.000	6	8	0	0	0
Taylor	1.000	3	1	0	0	0
Vosler	1.000	2	3	0	0	0

TACOMA RAINIERS — TRIPLE-A

PACIFIC COAST LEAGUE

Batting	B-T	Ht.	Wt.	DOB	AVG	OBP	SLG	G	PA	AB	R	H	2B	3B	HR	RBI	BB	HBP	SH	SF	SO	SB	CS	BB%	SO%
Anderson, Brian	R-R	6-2	215	5-19-93	.270	.358	.439	42	176	148	22	40	7	0	6	28	20	3	0	5	39	0	0	11.36	22.16
Bliss, Ryan	R-R	5-6	165	12-13-99	.269	.377	.456	93	433	360	67	97	25	3	12	54	61	5	1	6	97	50	13	14.09	22.40
Canzone, Dominic	L-R	5-11	190	8-16-97	.287	.354	.513	29	130	115	19	33	5	0	7	22	12	1	0	2	24	2	0	9.23	18.46
Chavis, Michael	R-R	5-10	190	8-11-95	.290	.366	.485	46	191	169	31	49	10	1	7	29	16	5	0	1	36	1	0	8.38	18.85
Clase, Jonatan	B-R	5-9	150	5-23-02	.274	.373	.483	59	280	234	47	64	11	4	10	34	40	0	1	5	72	26	9	14.29	25.71
Crawford, J.P.	L-R	6-2	202	1-11-95	.182	.357	.182	4	14	11	1	2	0	0	0	0	2	1	0	0	4	0	0	14.29	28.57
Ellis, Duke	L-L	6-1	180	1-16-98	.212	.291	.385	32	117	104	17	22	2	2	4	20	11	1	0	1	30	17	1	9.40	25.64
Gilliam, Isiah	B-R	6-3	220	7-23-96	.222	.396	.435	38	139	108	24	24	9	1	4	15	31	0	0	0	44	6	3	22.30	31.65
Haggerty, Sam	B-R	5-11	175	5-26-94	.310	.388	.338	19	81	71	8	22	2	0	0	5	8	1	1	0	19	7	1	9.88	23.46
Hunt, Blake	R-R	6-3	215	11-10-98	.293	.372	.533	24	86	75	15	22	4	1	4	20	6	4	0	1	10	0	0	6.98	11.63
Kato, Kobe	L-R	6-1	170	3-19-99	.356	.435	.492	16	69	59	16	21	6	1	0	13	8	1	0	1	15	6	1	11.59	21.74
Locklear, Tyler	R-R	6-1	210	11-24-00	.260	.371	.430	70	318	265	53	69	15	3	8	41	39	10	0	4	76	5	0	12.26	23.90
Marlowe, Cade	L-R	6-1	210	6-24-97	.235	.341	.395	90	411	344	60	81	8	4	13	45	55	4	1	7	133	43	7	13.38	32.36
Miller, Andrew	R-R	6-2	230	9-2-97	.083	.154	.083	3	13	12	0	1	0	0	0	1	1	0	0	0	5	0	0	7.69	38.46
Packard, Spencer	L-R	5-10	210	10-12-97	.279	.358	.416	40	176	154	24	43	15	0	2	28	19	1	0	2	26	0	0	10.80	14.77
Papierski, Michael	B-R	6-2	224	2-26-96	.242	.358	.372	83	336	277	42	67	18	0	6	46	49	4	1	5	67	1	0	14.58	19.94
Perez, Michael	L-R	5-10	195	8-7-92	.176	.300	.392	16	60	51	8	9	2	0	3	8	8	1	0	0	15	0	0	13.33	25.00
Polanco, Jorge	B-R	5-11	208	7-5-93	.333	.474	1.000	4	19	15	6	5	1	0	3	6	4	0	0	0	4	0	0	21.05	21.05
Rivas, Leo	B-R	5-10	150	10-10-97	.296	.441	.424	63	266	203	50	60	12	1	4	32	55	1	3	4	51	24	6	20.68	19.17
Scheffler, Matt	R-R	6-1	190	2-6-98	.250	.400	.333	4	15	12	3	3	1	0	0	3	2	1	0	0	3	1	0	13.33	20.00
Slaughter, Jake	R-R	6-1	200	10-24-96	.276	.345	.430	85	368	330	48	91	21	0	10	60	29	7	0	2	98	11	7	7.88	26.63
Solak, Nick	R-R	5-9	185	1-11-95	.311	.406	.446	90	347	296	52	92	13	0	9	53	41	8	0	2	53	10	1	11.82	15.27
Taylor, Samad	R-R	5-8	160	7-11-98	.262	.352	.380	136	599	508	93	133	19	4	11	75	68	6	11	6	156	50	15	11.35	26.04
Thomas, Rhylan	L-L	5-10	170	4-15-00	.322	.365	.373	47	196	177	34	57	6	0	1	18	13	0	4	2	12	10	1	6.63	6.12
Urias, Luis	R-R	5-10	202	6-3-97	.260	.378	.413	77	350	288	50	75	12	1	10	56	48	9	0	4	57	8	1	13.71	16.29
Vavra, Terrin	L-R	6-0	185	5-12-97	.182	.231	.182	3	13	11	0	2	0	0	0	2	1	0	0	1	6	0	0	7.69	46.15
Vosler, Jason	L-R	6-1	220	9-6-93	.303	.371	.573	119	524	466	92	141	25	4	31	110	46	7	0	4	113	4	1	8.78	21.56
Warmoth, Logan	R-R	5-10	195	9-6-95	.200	.308	.273	20	67	55	9	11	1	0	1	7	8	1	2	1	18	3	1	11.94	26.87
Washington, Curtis	R-R	6-2	180	5-22-00	.000	.250	.000	2	4	3	1	0	0	0	0	0	1	0	0	0	1	1	0	25.00	25.00
Zavala, Seby	R-R	5-11	205	8-28-93	.188	.325	.376	33	123	101	17	19	7	0	4	16	16	5	0	1	43	0	1	13.01	34.96

Pitching	B-T	Ht.	Wt.	DOB	W	L	ERA	G	GS	SV	IP	Hits	Runs	ER	HR	BB	SO	AVG	OBP	SLG	SO%	BB%	BF
Abbott, Cory	R-R	6-2	217	9-20-95	0	0	9.00	1	1	0	3	4	3	3	2	2	2	.333	.429	.833	14.29	14.29	14
Adcock, Ty	R-R	6-0	213	2-7-97	1	0	7.71	3	0	0	2	2	2	2	0	3	2	.222	.417	.222	16.67	25.00	12
Barker, Luke	R-R	6-3	230	3-11-92	0	0	10.80	5	0	0	7	6	8	8	1	9	6	.261	.455	.391	18.18	27.27	33
Bazardo, Eduard	R-R	6-0	190	9-1-95	1	1	4.29	21	0	0	21	18	13	10	2	11	29	.220	.312	.341	31.18	11.83	93
Bolton, Cody	R-R	6-3	230	6-19-98	1	2	3.07	33	0	2	29	25	12	10	2	12	34	.225	.310	.324	26.98	9.52	126
Bowman, Matt	R-R	6-0	185	5-31-91	2	0	3.60	8	0	0	10	10	4	4	2	1	11	.250	.268	.475	26.83	2.44	41
Buttrey, Ty	L-R	6-6	240	3-31-93	0	2	9.00	29	1	0	29	39	30	29	6	14	31	.320	.379	.631	22.14	10.00	140
Castano, Blas	R-R	5-10	162	9-8-98	5	4	5.13	14	14	0	74	79	46	42	13	24	74	.277	.344	.484	23.34	7.57	317
de Geus, Brett	R-R	6-2	190	11-4-97	0	4	6.60	32	0	7	30	41	24	22	3	11	21	.320	.379	.430	15.00	7.86	140
Devenski, Chris	R-R	6-3	211	11-13-90	0	1	2.35	23	0	3	23	14	6	6	1	10	31	.169	.258	.277	33.33	10.75	93
Diaz, Jhonathan	L-L	6-0	170	9-13-96	9	3	4.36	23	22	0	118	121	62	57	9	52	120	.266	.357	.398	22.90	9.92	524
Fleming, Josh	L-L	6-2	220	5-18-96	2	2	4.50	19	0	1	16	15	10	8	2	5	13	.246	.299	.426	19.12	7.35	68
Gragg, Logan	R-R	6-5	200	8-8-98	0	0	2.08	4	1	0	9	5	2	2	1	4	7	.167	.286	.300	20.00	11.43	35
Hahn, Jesse	R-R	6-5	205	7-30-89	1	0	3.12	8	0	0	9	4	3	3	0	4	10	.138	.242	.138	30.30	12.12	33
Hancock, Emerson	R-R	6-4	213	5-31-99	7	3	3.43	17	17	0	94	85	36	36	10	37	66	.241	.316	.384	16.71	9.37	395
Hembree, Heath	R-R	6-4	220	1-13-89	0	0	3.00	3	0	0	3	1	1	1	1	0	4	.100	.100	.400	40.00	0.00	10
Hernandez, Jonathan	R-R	6-3	190	7-6-96	0	0	5.25	13	0	0	12	18	7	7	1	6	9	.360	.439	.520	15.79	10.53	57
Holloway, Jordan	R-R	6-6	230	6-13-96	2	0	10.02	35	0	0	32	37	37	36	5	48	43	.289	.475	.469	24.02	26.82	179
Jefferson, Chris	L-R	6-2	200	1-24-97	0	1	6.23	4	1	0	4	2	4	3	1	7	4	.143	.429	.357	19.05	33.33	21

Kaminsky, Rob	R-L	6-0	195	9-2-94	1	0	7.66	15	8	0	47	71	44	40	7	17	45	.338	.391	.510	19.57	7.39	230
Kelley, Trevor	R-R	6-2	210	10-20-92	3	2	3.52	54	0	1	54	52	28	21	7	33	62	.256	.358	.419	25.73	13.69	241
Keuchel, Dallas	L-L	6-2	205	1-1-88	7	4	3.93	13	13	0	71	64	36	31	10	22	45	.245	.307	.414	15.63	7.64	288
Kitchen, Austin	L-L	6-0	200	2-11-97	1	1	14.73	4	0	0	4	9	8	6	1	2	2	.429	.478	.619	8.33	8.33	24
Krehbiel, Joey	R-R	6-3	250	12-20-92	5	3	3.26	54	0	10	58	41	27	21	5	25	55	.193	.278	.335	22.82	10.37	241
Lawrence, Casey	R-R	6-0	180	10-28-87	11	11	5.95	29	29	0	165	199	111	109	34	48	108	.296	.347	.527	14.86	6.60	727
Llovera, Mauricio	R-R	5-11	224	4-17-96	2	0	4.86	14	1	0	17	13	10	9	3	8	12	.217	.310	.417	16.90	11.27	71
Mariot, Michael	R-R	6-0	190	10-20-88	9	7	5.84	28	25	0	126	136	85	82	21	33	101	.276	.330	.470	18.67	6.10	541
Martinez, Bernie	R-R	6-0	195	12-24-96	0	0	0.00	1	0	0	2	0	0	0	0	2	2	.000	.333	.000	33.33	33.33	6
Miller, Tyson	R-R	6-5	220	7-29-95	0	0	2.25	4	0	0	4	3	1	1	0	2	6	.231	.313	.308	37.50	12.50	16
Payero, Nick	R-R	6-2	200	6-21-00	0	1	5.19	2	2	0	9	11	9	5	3	4	2	.297	.366	.649	4.88	9.76	41
Peralta, Sammy	L-L	6-2	205	5-10-98	1	1	9.24	12	0	0	13	16	13	13	3	8	12	.314	.417	.588	20.00	13.33	60
Poppen, Sean	R-R	6-3	210	3-15-94	0	0	10.80	2	0	0	3	4	4	4	2	2	5	.286	.375	.714	31.25	12.50	16
Ruffcorn, Jason	R-R	6-2	215	7-27-98	1	0	0.00	3	0	0	5	2	0	0	0	3	3	.154	.294	.154	17.65	17.65	17
Salazar, Eduardo	R-R	6-2	177	5-5-98	1	0	5.40	4	0	0	3	3	3	2	0	3	1	.273	.400	.545	6.67	20.00	15
Santos, Gregory	R-R	6-2	190	8-28-99	0	0	1.42	7	0	0	6	3	1	1	0	7	7	.143	.357	.143	25.00	25.00	28
Saucedo, Tayler	L-L	6-4	205	6-18-93	0	0	0.00	1	0	0	1	0	0	0	0	0	1	.000	.000	.000	33.33	0.00	3
Snead, Kirby	L-L	6-1	218	10-7-94	4	5	7.68	40	0	1	36	45	32	31	6	17	34	.304	.385	.500	19.77	9.88	172
Snider, Collin	R-R	6-4	195	10-10-95	0	1	3.44	17	1	0	18	23	10	7	2	8	22	.299	.360	.455	25.58	9.30	86
Speier, Gabe	L-L	5-11	200	4-12-95	0	0	1.80	15	0	1	15	9	3	3	0	5	10	.167	.237	.204	16.95	8.47	59
Stoudt, Levi	R-R	6-1	195	12-4-97	3	4	6.92	12	11	0	52	60	42	40	15	30	36	.290	.386	.560	14.94	12.45	241
Tabor, Matt	R-R	6-2	180	7-14-98	0	0	6.48	7	0	0	8	11	6	6	1	8	7	.344	.463	.531	17.07	19.51	41
Vargas, Carlos	R-R	6-4	210	10-13-99	2	5	3.54	55	0	2	53	58	29	21	6	18	40	.276	.341	.400	17.09	7.69	234
Vosler, Jason	L-R	6-1	220	9-6-93	0	0	0.00	1	0	0	1	2	0	0	0	0	0	.500	.500	.750	0.00	0.00	4
Warmoth, Logan	R-R	5-10	195	9-6-95	0	0	9.00	1	0	0	1	2	1	1	0	1	0	.400	.500	.600	0.00	16.67	6
Woo, Bryan	R-R	6-2	205	1-30-00	0	0	0.00	3	3	0	11	5	0	0	0	0	17	.128	.128	.179	43.59	0.00	39

Fielding

Catcher	PCT	G	PO	A	E	DP	PB
Hunt	.987	23	143	5	2	1	2
Miller	1.000	3	28	1	0	1	0
Papierski	.992	77	615	22	5	9	7
Perez	.992	16	118	7	1	0	2
Scheffler	1.000	3	27	1	0	0	0
Zavala	.985	32	252	11	4	2	1

First Base	PCT	G	PO	A	E	DP
Anderson	1.000	10	73	7	0	11
Chavis	1.000	9	63	5	0	8
Gilliam	1.000	1	1	0	0	0
Locklear	.998	53	427	36	1	57
Packard	.977	6	41	1	1	6
Papierski	.971	3	33	1	1	3
Slaughter	.913	2	20	1	2	2
Vosler	.997	70	535	40	2	59

Second Base	PCT	G	PO	A	E	DP
Bliss	.976	33	53	68	3	16
Chavis	1.000	1	5	2	0	2
Haggerty	.967	8	14	15	1	4
Kato	.988	16	23	58	1	16
Polanco	1.000	2	3	3	0	1
Slaughter	.969	48	84	105	6	31
Taylor	.976	39	69	96	4	35
Urias	1.000	2	2	3	0	0
Vavra	1.000	3	5	8	0	1
Warmoth	.935	5	9	20	2	8

Third Base	PCT	G	PO	A	E	DP
Anderson	.919	24	15	53	6	5
Bliss	.882	9	7	23	4	2
Chavis	.964	28	14	66	3	6
Slaughter	.968	11	7	23	1	0
Taylor	1.000	2	3	4	0	3
Urias	.963	69	48	135	7	14
Vosler	.500	2	0	2	2	0
Warmoth	1.000	7	6	15	0	2

Shortstop	PCT	G	PO	A	E	DP
Bliss	.972	53	72	137	6	40
Crawford	1.000	4	6	7	0	1
Haggerty	1.000	2	8	1	0	0
Rivas	.967	63	77	183	9	39
Taylor	.945	26	48	72	7	21
Urias	1.000	3	4	5	0	1
Warmoth	.952	7	6	14	1	3

Outfield	PCT	G	PO	A	E	DP
Bliss	1.000	2	5	0	0	0
Canzone	1.000	27	56	2	0	1
Clase	.987	59	151	5	2	3
Ellis	.986	30	69	2	1	0
Gilliam	1.000	9	18	1	0	1
Haggerty	1.000	10	8	2	0	0
Marlowe	.995	90	192	3	1	1
Packard	1.000	23	36	1	0	0
Solak	1.000	79	122	3	0	1
Taylor	1.000	70	113	10	0	1
Thomas	.984	49	60	3	1	0
Vosler	.958	25	45	1	2	0
Washington	1.000	2	5	0	0	0

ARKANSAS TRAVELERS — DOUBLE-A

TEXAS LEAGUE

Batting	B-T	Ht.	Wt.	DOB	AVG	OBP	SLG	G	PA	AB	R	H	2B	3B	HR	RBI	BB	HBP	SH	SF	SO	SB	CS	BB%	SO%
Anchia, Jake	R-R	5-10	210	3-5-97	.210	.246	.358	79	290	271	33	57	13	0	9	39	9	5	1	4	85	3	1	3.10	29.31
Caguana, Jose	R-R	5-10	175	4-5-02	.333	.333	.333	1	3	3	1	1	0	0	0	0	0	0	0	0	1	0	0	0.00	33.33
Ford, Harry	R-R	5-10	200	2-21-03	.249	.377	.367	116	523	430	72	107	26	2	7	45	74	16	1	2	115	35	9	14.15	21.99
Kato, Kobe	L-R	6-1	170	3-19-99	.074	.167	.074	9	30	27	2	2	0	0	0	1	3	0	0	0	13	1	1	10.00	43.33
Labrada, Victor	L-L	5-9	165	1-16-00	.233	.315	.383	54	218	193	30	45	10	2	5	27	18	5	1	0	67	25	7	8.26	30.73
Locklear, Tyler	R-R	6-1	210	11-24-00	.291	.401	.532	41	188	158	30	46	12	1	8	26	23	6	0	0	49	4	1	12.23	26.06
McCullough, Morgan	L-R	5-6	180	12-19-97	.210	.335	.353	54	203	167	25	35	8	2	4	20	30	2	2	1	53	9	4	14.78	26.11
Miller, Andrew	R-R	6-2	230	9-2-97	.143	.222	.143	4	9	7	0	1	0	0	0	2	1	0	0	1	3	1	0	11.11	33.33
Oliva, Jared	R-R	6-1	200	11-27-95	.294	.378	.463	69	248	214	45	63	7	4	7	40	24	6	2	2	45	37	3	9.68	18.15
Packard, Spencer	L-R	5-10	210	10-12-97	.285	.405	.392	50	227	186	27	53	5	0	5	29	34	5	0	2	38	2	0	14.98	16.74
Polcovich, Kaden	B-R	5-10	185	2-21-99	.228	.339	.340	81	287	241	31	55	12	3	3	30	33	9	1	3	74	17	7	11.50	25.78
Rambusch, Blake	R-R	5-8	175	8-31-99	.264	.369	.297	60	216	182	35	48	4	1	0	12	25	6	2	1	37	20	7	11.57	17.13
Ramirez, Ben	L-R	6-1	200	12-2-98	.207	.262	.271	90	329	299	29	62	13	0	2	19	20	3	4	2	87	9	4	6.08	26.44
Rodden, Brock	B-R	5-9	170	5-25-00	.208	.261	.342	64	266	240	27	50	13	2	5	31	18	1	2	5	74	8	3	6.77	27.82
Rodriguez, Alberto	L-L	5-10	227	10-6-00	.241	.287	.329	93	384	353	33	85	18	2	3	47	22	3	1	5	103	10	4	5.73	26.82
Sanchez, Lolo	R-R	5-11	186	4-23-99	.308	.357	.538	3	14	13	2	4	1	1	0	1	1	0	0	0	5	0	1	7.14	35.71
Schreck, RJ	L-R	6-1	210	7-12-00	.143	.294	.250	8	34	28	4	4	1	1	0	1	4	2	0	0	7	1	0	11.76	20.59
Tenerowicz, Robbie	R-R	5-11	228	1-6-95	.269	.344	.404	16	62	52	6	14	1	0	2	9	3	4	1	2	17	0	0	4.84	27.42
Williamson, Ben	R-R	6-0	190	11-5-00	.272	.365	.374	95	411	356	50	97	23	2	3	43	44	9	0	2	97	15	6	10.71	23.60
Windish, Hogan	R-R	5-11	222	5-10-99	.218	.332	.383	124	518	436	66	95	25	1	15	62	65	12	0	5	167	19	2	12.55	32.24
Witherspoon, Grant	L-L	6-1	200	9-27-96	.153	.250	.255	41	157	137	13	21	3	1	3	16	17	1	1	1	53	2	2	10.83	33.76
Young, Cole	L-R	6-0	180	7-29-03	.271	.369	.390	124	552	469	67	127	25	2	9	57	67	8	3	4	87	23	11	12.14	15.76

Pitching	B-T	Ht.	Wt.	DOB	W	L	ERA	G	GS	SV	IP	Hits	Runs	ER	HR	BB	SO	AVG	OBP	SLG	SO%	BB%	BF
Alcantara, Raul	L-L	6-0	167	1-22-01	6	3	3.44	37	2	0	71	53	36	27	4	42	65	.205	.320	.317	20.97	13.55	310
Alford, Peyton	L-L	6-0	190	8-15-97	8	2	2.20	43	0	7	57	25	14	14	4	23	63	.134	.235	.242	29.30	10.70	215
Bayless, Jarod	R-R	6-4	225	12-29-96	1	1	4.76	19	0	2	23	22	15	12	3	9	16	.250	.400	.409	14.41	8.11	111
Castano, Blas	R-R	5-10	162	9-8-98	0	4	3.31	15	12	0	52	50	25	19	2	19	34	.253	.327	.308	15.25	8.52	223
Curvelo, Luis	R-R	6-1	170	10-21-00	4	0	2.57	49	0	3	67	39	20	19	5	18	78	.168	.239	.267	30.59	7.06	255
Davila, Garrett	L-L	6-2	180	1-17-97	3	1	3.63	44	0	4	62	52	25	25	3	18	70	.227	.290	.314	27.56	7.09	254
Evans, Logan	R-R	6-4	215	6-5-01	9	5	3.20	32	22	0	107	84	46	38	7	42	98	.217	.302	.323	21.92	9.40	447
Garcia, Brandyn	L-L	6-4	225	5-27-00	0	2	2.83	13	13	0	48	38	17	15	3	21	49	.221	.322	.314	23.56	10.10	208
Gragg, Logan	R-R	6-5	200	8-8-98	5	0	3.71	28	0	0	51	41	24	21	7	16	44	.215	.278	.382	21.05	7.66	209
Haberer, Jake	R-R	6-2	225	2-9-95	1	0	5.28	13	1	0	15	16	9	9	1	12	15	.267	.400	.383	20.00	16.00	75
Hill, Kyle	R-R	5-11	200	5-12-97	4	2	5.91	38	0	1	35	34	25	23	5	19	46	.248	.346	.431	28.75	11.88	160
Joyce, Jimmy	R-R	6-2	210	1-13-99	4	6	5.49	27	9	0	59	50	40	36	3	34	58	.227	.346	.318	21.97	12.88	264
Kingsbury, Jimmy	R-R	6-1	187	2-13-99	0	0	13.50	1	0	0	2	4	3	3	0	1	1	.400	.500	.400	8.33	8.33	12
Kuhn, Travis	R-R	5-10	195	5-20-98	4	6	3.33	44	0	3	54	51	27	20	1	23	64	.248	.340	.306	26.78	9.62	239
Mercedes, Juan	R-R	6-2	190	4-3-00	10	5	2.87	27	27	0	144	132	54	46	16	26	126	.239	.280	.400	21.28	4.39	592
Morales, Michael	R-R	6-2	205	8-13-02	4	1	3.88	12	12	0	65	58	31	28	11	13	67	.234	.273	.435	25.38	4.92	264
Morgan, Reid	R-R	6-0	187	3-24-97	1	3	4.66	40	0	2	46	48	30	24	6	17	43	.271	.338	.424	21.18	8.37	203
Onyshko, Ben	R-L	6-2	205	10-18-96	0	0	9.64	7	0	0	9	12	11	10	2	8	8	.333	.490	.583	16.33	16.33	49
Ruffcorn, Jason	R-R	6-2	215	7-27-98	0	0	6.75	4	0	1	4	7	3	3	1	0	5	.389	.389	.722	27.78	0.00	18
Taylor, Troy	R-R	6-0	195	9-9-01	3	3	1.17	29	0	16	31	16	6	4	0	9	31	.151	.216	.179	26.72	7.76	116
Van Scoter, Reid	L-L	6-0	190	11-25-98	5	7	4.01	22	22	0	101	93	50	45	7	29	85	.250	.307	.401	20.63	7.04	412
Wirchansky, Dan	L-L	6-1	200	7-2-97	8	6	2.84	27	17	0	111	88	43	35	10	30	89	.214	.269	.333	19.96	6.73	446

Fielding

Catcher	PCT	G	PO	A	E	DP	PB
Anchia	.984	71	617	40	11	3	4
Caguana	1.000	1	11	0	0	0	0
Ford	.989	67	537	25	6	3	5
Miller	1.000	2	11	1	0	0	1

First Base	PCT	G	PO	A	E	DP
Locklear	.988	37	307	20	4	25
Packard	.929	2	11	2	1	1
Ramirez	.991	43	297	24	3	27
Tenerowicz	1.000	4	22	3	0	3
Windish	.986	55	382	32	6	27

Second Base	PCT	G	PO	A	E	DP
Kato	1.000	1	1	0	0	1
McCullough	1.000	15	17	39	0	8
Polcovich	1.000	4	7	11	0	3
Rambusch	1.000	4	4	6	0	0
Rodden	.969	34	61	66	4	17
Williamson	1.000	5	11	6	0	0
Windish	.971	41	66	99	5	18
Young	.993	37	71	77	1	18

Third Base	PCT	G	PO	A	E	DP
McCullough	.966	9	0	28	1	1
Ramirez	.942	48	29	102	8	7
Rodden	1.000	9	4	14	0	0
Tenerowicz	1.000	2	2	3	0	1
Williamson	.963	70	57	125	7	16
Windish	.786	6	3	8	3	1

Shortstop	PCT	G	PO	A	E	DP
McCullough	.978	27	28	63	2	9
Rodden	.904	15	18	29	5	4
Williamson	1.000	13	11	30	0	4
Young	.970	84	99	188	9	36

Outfield	PCT	G	PO	A	E	DP
Ford	.833	8	15	0	3	0
Kato	1.000	7	8	1	0	1
Labrada	.984	51	118	3	2	1
McCullough	1.000	3	6	0	0	0
Miller	1.000	1	1	0	0	0
Oliva	1.000	64	132	4	0	3
Packard	1.000	41	75	1	0	0
Polcovich	1.000	68	140	1	0	0
Rambusch	.984	52	122	3	2	0
Rodriguez	.979	89	182	4	4	0
Sanchez	1.000	3	3	0	0	0
Schreck	1.000	7	9	0	0	0
Witherspoon	.965	39	83	0	3	0

EVERETT AQUASOX — *HIGH-A*

NORTHWEST LEAGUE

Batting	B-T	Ht.	Wt.	DOB	AVG	OBP	SLG	G	PA	AB	R	H	2B	3B	HR	RBI	BB	HBP	SH	SF	SO	SB	CS	BB%	SO%
Arroyo, Michael	R-R	5-8	160	11-3-04	.290	.397	.519	60	290	241	47	70	15	2	12	40	34	11	0	4	75	10	5	11.72	25.86
Batista, Freuddy	R-R	6-0	182	12-12-99	.237	.275	.381	72	287	270	30	64	12	0	9	36	13	2	0	2	73	3	0	4.53	25.44
Cali, Caleb	R-R	6-3	230	8-20-00	.232	.346	.424	91	390	328	52	76	17	2	14	59	55	4	0	3	111	7	2	14.10	28.46
Charping, Connor	R-R	6-0	210	4-12-99	.257	.385	.284	23	91	74	13	19	2	0	0	9	12	4	0	1	12	2	3	13.19	13.19
Davis, Colin	R-R	6-0	190	2-8-99	.131	.241	.219	46	159	137	11	18	3	0	3	14	13	7	1	1	43	2	1	8.18	27.04
Duvall, Ty	L-R	5-11	200	7-11-97	.143	.294	.214	5	17	14	1	2	1	0	0	1	2	1	0	0	4	0	0	11.76	23.53
Emerson, Colt	L-R	6-0	185	7-20-05	.225	.331	.317	29	139	120	19	27	5	0	2	12	15	4	0	0	30	9	1	10.79	21.58
Fitz-Gerald, Hunter	L-R	6-4	230	12-9-00	.278	.349	.426	73	301	270	33	75	20	1	6	35	28	2	0	1	78	2	2	9.30	25.91
Hood, Josh	R-R	6-2	202	7-21-00	.246	.323	.418	109	474	419	75	103	21	3	15	59	48	2	0	5	115	21	5	10.13	24.26
Knight, Bill	R-R	6-1	195	8-24-99	.210	.322	.376	113	479	404	67	85	23	4	12	64	45	24	1	5	114	29	6	9.39	23.80
Labrada, Victor	L-L	5-9	165	1-16-00	.308	.413	.532	47	185	156	33	48	12	4	5	24	25	3	0	0	34	24	4	13.51	18.38
Miller, Andrew	R-R	6-2	230	9-2-97	.259	.295	.434	40	156	143	20	37	7	0	6	28	9	0	0	4	45	0	0	5.77	28.85
Moncada, Gabe	L-L	6-2	175	12-17-01	.202	.327	.291	69	266	223	29	45	14	0	2	21	38	4	0	1	72	1	1	14.29	27.07
Montes, Lazaro	L-R	6-3	210	10-22-04	.260	.378	.427	51	233	192	36	50	8	0	8	33	35	3	0	3	69	4	3	15.02	29.61
Polanco, Jorge	B-R	5-11	208	7-5-93	.200	.429	.200	2	7	5	0	1	0	0	0	0	2	0	0	0	2	0	0	28.57	28.57
Rodden, Brock	B-R	5-9	170	5-25-00	.302	.413	.484	67	310	258	47	78	14	3	9	33	42	8	0	2	57	21	8	13.55	18.39
Sanchez, Axel	R-R	5-10	170	12-10-02	.198	.278	.273	100	393	344	46	68	7	2	5	35	35	6	1	7	111	15	9	8.91	28.24
Schreck, RJ	L-R	6-1	210	7-12-00	.261	.401	.464	78	344	276	48	72	20	0	12	44	57	9	0	2	47	7	1	16.57	13.66
Sundstrom, Jared	R-R	6-3	225	6-21-01	.263	.380	.434	112	499	415	72	109	28	2	13	63	71	9	0	3	117	26	6	14.23	23.45
Washington, Curtis	R-R	6-2	180	5-22-00	.200	.429	.200	2	7	5	0	1	0	0	0	0	1	1	0	0	2	0	1	14.29	28.57
Williamson, Ben	R-R	6-0	190	11-5-00	.315	.408	.459	29	130	111	16	35	11	1	1	21	15	3	0	1	21	4	0	11.54	16.15

Pitching	B-T	Ht.	Wt.	DOB	W	L	ERA	G	GS	SV	IP	Hits	Runs	ER	HR	BB	SO	AVG	OBP	SLG	SO%	BB%	BF
Burgos, Juan	R-R	6-0	155	12-22-99	2	5	3.38	38	3	5	61	47	27	23	5	23	70	.210	.293	.313	27.13	8.91	258
Cleveland, Tyler	L-R	6-3	185	9-9-99	2	2	3.38	36	0	0	37	31	17	14	5	23	48	.230	.348	.430	29.27	14.02	164
Cummings, Ty	R-R	6-2	205	11-1-01	4	5	4.17	25	25	0	117	118	60	54	13	46	124	.263	.339	.420	24.70	9.16	502
Davila, Nick	R-R	6-3	202	11-21-98	3	3	4.98	13	0	2	22	17	14	12	3	3	28	.210	.250	.432	31.11	3.33	90

Davis, Colin	R-R	6-0	190	2-8-99	0	0	0.00	1	0	0	1	0	0	0	0	0	0	.000	.000	.000	0.00	0.00	4
Diaz, Gleiner	R-R	6-0	170	9-20-03	0	0	6.35	5	0	0	6	4	4	4	1	7	6	.200	.429	.500	21.43	25.00	28
Garcia, Brandyn	L-L	6-4	225	5-27-00	6	0	1.84	14	12	0	68	56	15	14	1	26	85	.223	.323	.279	29.51	9.03	288
Hawks, Ryan	R-R	6-2	235	11-24-00	6	9	5.59	25	25	0	121	139	80	75	22	35	95	.285	.344	.473	17.69	6.52	537
Hembree, Heath	R-R	6-4	220	1-13-89	0	0	6.75	3	0	0	3	3	2	2	1	4	6	.273	.467	.545	40.00	26.67	15
Hernandez, Joseph	R-R	5-11	150	6-15-00	3	2	7.23	20	0	0	19	22	18	15	2	14	15	.297	.433	.419	15.46	14.43	97
Jefferson, Chris	L-R	6-2	200	1-24-97	2	1	5.32	35	1	1	46	49	30	27	8	25	45	.271	.367	.481	21.33	11.85	211
Kingsbury, Jimmy	R-R	6-1	187	2-13-99	2	4	2.40	39	2	2	60	42	24	16	4	21	57	.193	.283	.280	22.89	8.43	249
Laws, Holden	L-L	6-2	166	12-8-99	2	3	3.66	42	0	0	47	31	20	19	4	20	33	.189	.291	.293	17.28	10.47	191
Melenge, Harold	L-L	5-10	170	1-15-02	0	0	40.50	1	1	0	1	4	6	6	0	3	1	.500	.667	.750	8.33	25.00	12
Morales, Michael	R-R	6-2	205	8-13-02	9	1	2.36	15	15	0	84	78	23	22	2	25	80	.246	.303	.331	23.12	7.23	346
Ovando, Anyelo	R-R	6-5	222	12-25-00	0	0	3.60	3	0	0	5	2	3	2	0	5	7	.118	.348	.118	30.43	21.74	23
Payero, Nick	R-R	6-2	200	6-21-00	2	0	2.93	5	5	0	28	25	13	9	3	7	27	.236	.281	.377	23.68	6.14	114
Peavyhouse, Shaddon	R-R	6-3	205	8-18-98	4	9	5.75	29	13	0	83	99	58	53	8	40	82	.293	.379	.405	21.08	10.28	389
Perez, Marcelo	R-R	5-10	180	11-16-99	4	9	6.81	25	25	0	104	142	83	79	18	29	91	.323	.375	.522	18.84	6.00	483
Pope, Bryan	R-R	6-2	195	1-27-99	0	2	7.36	20	0	0	22	36	23	18	3	13	19	.360	.439	.570	16.52	11.30	115
Raeth, Stefan	L-R	6-1	180	8-31-00	3	2	3.77	42	0	7	45	43	22	19	4	20	37	.244	.332	.381	18.41	9.95	201
Ruffcorn, Jason	R-R	6-2	215	7-27-98	4	4	3.51	35	0	4	41	33	24	16	5	14	47	.212	.277	.365	26.70	7.95	176
Saathoff, Allan	R-R	6-1	230	9-18-99	1	2	4.85	26	0	0	30	25	18	16	4	23	24	.227	.370	.382	17.39	16.67	138
Sanchez, Steven	R-R	6-0	160	8-19-03	0	0	0.00	1	0	0	1	1	0	0	0	0	0	.500	.500	1.000	0.00	0.00	3
Santos, Gregory	R-R	6-2	190	8-28-99	0	0	0.00	1	0	0	1	0	0	0	0	0	1	.000	.000	.000	33.33	0.00	3
Schomberg, Will	R-R	5-10	170	1-30-01	1	1	3.27	4	4	0	22	18	9	8	3	6	19	.222	.292	.420	21.35	6.74	89
Sosa, Gabriel	R-R	6-2	182	4-17-01	1	1	9.35	8	0	0	9	11	9	9	2	5	14	.289	.370	.526	30.43	10.87	46
Tabor, Matt	R-R	6-2	180	7-14-98	0	0	0.00	1	0	0	2	1	0	0	0	0	1	.143	.250	.143	12.50	0.00	8
Taylor, Troy	R-R	6-0	195	9-9-01	0	1	1.50	11	0	5	12	6	2	2	0	5	14	.143	.234	.143	29.79	10.64	47
Tomczak, Anthony	R-R	6-2	200	10-17-00	0	0	9.45	25	0	0	27	44	35	28	5	19	29	.352	.453	.552	19.59	12.84	148
Townsend, Blake	L-L	6-4	220	4-5-01	1	1	2.45	28	0	0	29	21	13	8	1	17	30	.200	.348	.333	22.56	12.78	133
Widger, C.J.	L-L	6-6	170	5-25-99	2	1	6.30	10	0	0	10	7	7	7	1	6	15	.194	.311	.361	33.33	13.33	45
Woo, Bryan	R-R	6-2	205	1-30-00	0	0	6.75	1	1	0	3	1	2	2	1	2	2	.125	.300	.500	20.00	20.00	10

Fielding

Catcher	PCT	G	PO	A	E	DP	PB
Batista	.997	72	608	57	2	6	15
Charping	.991	23	206	14	2	0	1
Duvall	.971	5	33	1	1	1	1
Miller	.997	35	308	13	1	1	5

First Base	PCT	G	PO	A	E	DP
Cali	.981	9	47	4	1	3
Fitz-Gerald	.992	68	553	35	5	42
Moncada	.978	60	443	38	11	35

Second Base	PCT	G	PO	A	E	DP
Arroyo	.936	45	78	112	13	20
Cali	.000	1	0	0	0	0
Hood	.982	15	21	34	1	4
Polanco	.667	1	1	1	1	0
Rodden	.982	54	91	133	4	27
Sanchez	.943	20	29	54	5	11

Third Base	PCT	G	PO	A	E	DP
Cali	.920	72	43	119	14	11
Emerson	.909	9	8	12	2	2
Hood	.967	20	19	40	2	0
Rodden	.938	9	4	26	2	2
Williamson	.954	25	23	60	4	5

Shortstop	PCT	G	PO	A	E	DP
Arroyo	.882	4	5	10	2	0
Emerson	.969	19	19	43	2	9
Hood	.956	36	43	87	6	18
Sanchez	.956	73	102	179	13	29
Williamson	1.000	1	2	3	0	1

Outfield	PCT	G	PO	A	E	DP
Davis	.984	40	60	3	1	1
Hood	.983	25	56	2	1	0
Knight	.964	105	204	10	8	4
Labrada	1.000	30	36	4	0	0
Miller	1.000	2	3	1	0	0
Montes	.949	43	73	2	4	1
Schreck	.983	59	110	3	2	0
Sundstrom	.980	100	195	4	4	1
Washington	1.000	2	2	1	0	0

MODESTO NUTS — *LOW-A*

CALIFORNIA LEAGUE

Batting	B-T	Ht.	Wt.	DOB	AVG	OBP	SLG	G	PA	AB	R	H	2B	3B	HR	RBI	BB	HBP	SH	SF	SO	SB	CS	BB%	SO%
Arroyo, Michael	R-R	5-8	160	11-3-04	.279	.404	.500	60	302	244	54	68	11	5	11	49	39	15	0	4	61	8	1	12.91	20.20
Belbin, Jarrod	L-R	6-2	220	6-22-00	.177	.311	.226	18	74	62	5	11	1	1	0	8	11	1	0	0	22	1	0	14.86	29.73
Caguana, Jose	R-R	5-10	175	4-5-02	.179	.291	.269	20	79	67	11	12	3	0	1	6	11	0	0	1	18	0	0	13.92	22.78
Cali, Caleb	R-R	6-3	230	8-20-00	.337	.443	.535	26	122	101	23	34	10	2	2	22	18	2	0	1	27	2	1	14.75	22.13
Caron, Josh	R-R	6-0	215	8-3-03	.277	.352	.383	13	54	47	2	13	2	0	1	10	5	1	0	1	9	2	0	9.26	16.67
Charping, Connor	R-R	6-0	210	4-12-99	.285	.420	.404	44	193	151	32	43	11	2	1	24	28	10	0	4	31	10	1	14.51	16.06
Cova, Ricardo	R-R	5-9	145	5-24-04	.200	.283	.264	29	127	110	21	22	3	2	0	12	10	4	0	3	25	2	1	7.87	19.69
Donofrio, Anthony	L-R	6-3	195	6-28-00	.262	.380	.400	20	79	65	12	17	5	2	0	9	13	0	0	1	15	5	0	16.46	18.99
Dorighi, Carter	L-R	6-0	190	6-11-03	.196	.254	.268	16	63	56	9	11	1	0	1	10	5	0	0	2	13	1	0	7.94	20.63
Eike, Brandon	R-R	6-0	220	10-1-01	.278	.370	.430	21	92	79	19	22	6	0	2	15	8	4	0	1	13	0	0	8.70	14.13
Emerson, Colt	L-R	6-0	185	7-20-05	.293	.440	.427	40	193	150	36	44	12	1	2	25	35	6	0	2	27	6	1	18.13	13.99
Farmelo, Jonny	L-R	6-2	205	9-9-04	.264	.398	.421	46	221	178	39	47	10	3	4	25	36	5	0	2	52	18	2	16.29	23.53
Gonzalez, Junior	R-R	5-8	186	5-10-00	.229	.349	.429	11	43	35	4	8	2	1	1	6	6	1	0	1	11	0	1	13.95	25.58
Jimenez, Carlos	L-L	5-10	170	2-14-03	.295	.393	.456	53	252	217	41	64	12	7	3	26	33	2	0	0	60	14	3	13.10	23.81
Jones, Carson	L-L	6-2	190	9-29-00	.251	.326	.425	102	454	398	71	100	20	5	13	68	41	6	1	6	142	37	5	9.03	31.28
Montes, Lazaro	L-R	6-3	210	10-22-04	.309	.411	.527	65	309	256	46	79	13	2	13	72	43	5	0	5	59	1	0	13.92	19.09
Pagliarini, Charlie	L-R	6-2	210	12-12-00	.232	.378	.439	105	450	362	76	84	30	3	13	59	73	13	0	2	171	6	1	16.22	38.00
Peete, Tai	L-R	6-2	193	8-11-05	.269	.343	.408	115	528	468	72	126	26	9	7	71	55	0	0	5	162	45	5	10.42	30.68
Perez, Milkar	B-R	5-11	200	10-16-01	.281	.386	.417	93	399	338	57	95	24	2	6	41	56	3	0	2	84	2	0	14.04	21.05
Rodriguez, Edryn	R-R	5-8	150	4-23-03	.204	.292	.278	19	65	54	9	11	4	0	0	6	8	0	0	3	24	0	0	12.31	36.92
Sharp, Jacob	R-R	5-10	190	9-15-01	.255	.339	.435	44	191	161	32	41	11	0	6	29	18	5	0	5	19	3	2	9.42	9.95
Smith, Aidan	R-R	6-3	190	7-23-04	.284	.402	.470	77	358	296	63	84	26	1	9	42	52	8	0	2	87	28	5	14.53	24.30
St. Laurent, Austin	R-R	6-1	188	7-13-02	.222	.364	.556	3	11	9	3	2	1	1	0	1	2	0	0	0	2	0	0	18.18	18.18
Suisbel, Luis	B-R	6-1	190	5-23-03	.276	.351	.436	119	552	475	76	131	23	4	15	90	49	14	0	14	144	4	0	8.88	26.09
Washington, Curtis	R-R	6-2	180	5-22-00	.225	.276	.317	44	159	142	20	32	3	2	2	22	9	2	3	3	38	11	3	5.66	23.90

Pitching	B-T	Ht.	Wt.	DOB	W	L	ERA	G	GS	SV	IP	Hits	Runs	ER	HR	BB	SO	AVG	OBP	SLG	SO%	BB%	BF
Beilenson, Charlie	R-R	6-0	215	12-10-99	0	0	2.45	4	0	0	4	2	1	1	0	5	4	.154	.389	.231	22.22	27.78	18
Bello, Yensy	R-R	5-10	180	12-2-02	0	0	81.00	1	0	0	0	3	4	3	0	2	1	.750	.833	1.250	16.67	33.33	6
Boehm, Gage	R-R	6-5	255	11-21-01	1	2	13.50	8	0	0	8	13	15	12	0	8	15	.351	.478	.459	32.61	17.39	46
Brierley, Chandler	L-L	6-8	195	5-12-98	1	0	30.38	9	0	0	5	8	21	18	0	12	9	.308	.609	.308	19.57	26.09	46
Cranton, Hunter	R-R	6-3	215	10-24-00	1	1	3.24	9	0	3	8	7	4	3	0	4	14	.233	.343	.300	40.00	11.43	35
Dale, Elijah	S-R	5-11	175	1-7-01	5	8	4.46	26	24	0	109	83	66	54	7	57	111	.201	.329	.276	22.52	11.56	493
Day, Ernie	R-R	6-4	230	10-24-01	2	2	13.73	24	0	0	20	26	31	30	1	32	19	.325	.529	.450	15.70	26.45	121
Fajardo, German	R-R	5-11	165	1-29-01	3	2	5.10	35	0	0	65	61	48	37	3	41	73	.240	.378	.370	23.03	12.93	317
Ford, Walter	R-R	6-3	198	12-28-04	1	2	7.22	8	6	0	39	54	35	31	4	11	32	.327	.385	.533	17.39	5.98	184
Geraldo, Jose	R-R	5-10	185	12-3-99	0	0	0.00	2	0	1	2	0	0	0	0	1	3	.000	.143	.000	42.86	14.29	7
Gough, Tyler	S-R	6-2	205	8-12-03	7	4	4.33	23	23	0	96	88	55	46	3	47	99	.244	.337	.325	23.91	11.35	414
Hopkins, Brody	R-R	6-4	200	1-18-02	4	3	2.90	18	18	0	84	62	35	27	2	40	95	.207	.328	.273	26.54	11.17	358
Izzi, Ashton	R-R	6-3	165	11-18-03	6	5	2.85	26	26	0	111	95	43	35	4	59	95	.230	.331	.322	19.71	12.24	482
Lemos, Pedro Da Costa	R-R	6-0	179	5-22-03	5	4	4.32	31	11	0	90	93	52	43	8	40	88	.260	.349	.363	21.15	9.62	416
Limoncelli, Michael	L-R	6-2	185	5-30-00	3	1	5.54	25	0	0	26	17	23	16	1	38	28	.183	.443	.247	20.00	27.14	140
Long, Trevor	R-R	6-1	198	5-22-01	1	0	1.08	9	0	1	8	3	1	1	0	3	8	.107	.265	.179	23.53	8.82	34
Lora, Aneury	R-R	6-2	155	3-30-04	0	0	3.00	2	2	0	9	5	3	3	0	4	5	.167	.297	.267	13.51	10.81	37
McGraw, Teddy	R-R	6-2	210	10-30-01	0	0	4.15	4	4	0	9	9	4	4	0	4	8	.273	.375	.273	20.00	10.00	40
McNairy, Jacob	R-R	6-2	205	11-22-99	0	0	6.00	1	0	0	3	5	2	2	0	0	2	.385	.385	.538	15.38	0.00	13
Moore, Brock	R-R	6-6	230	5-17-00	0	0	0.00	1	0	0	1	0	0	0	0	2	2	.000	.400	.000	40.00	40.00	5
Munoz, Jean	R-R	6-1	155	9-17-02	2	2	10.18	11	1	0	20	24	25	23	1	24	19	.296	.460	.469	16.67	21.05	114
Ovando, Anyelo	R-R	6-5	222	12-25-00	3	4	4.67	31	0	0	52	42	35	27	3	33	68	.218	.358	.363	27.87	13.52	244
Perez, Brayan	L-L	6-0	170	9-5-00	3	0	3.19	39	0	5	62	48	27	22	0	18	64	.209	.284	.265	24.33	6.84	263
Perez, Milkar	S-R	5-11	200	10-16-01	0	0	0.00	2	0	0	2	1	0	0	0	2	0	.143	.333	.143	0.00	22.22	9
Quintana, Adrian	R-R	6-0	175	11-20-02	0	2	5.52	17	0	0	29	34	20	18	2	10	23	.286	.368	.387	16.91	7.35	136
Riley, Will	R-R	6-0	200	4-13-02	0	0	0.00	2	0	0	2	1	0	0	0	0	3	.125	.222	.125	33.33	0.00	9
Rodriguez, Edryn	R-R	5-8	150	4-23-03	0	0	9.00	1	0	0	1	2	1	1	0	0	0	.400	.400	.600	0.00	0.00	5
Sanchez, Steven	R-R	6-0	160	8-19-03	0	0	0.00	1	0	0	3	1	0	0	0	1	1	.100	.182	.100	9.09	9.09	11
Schomberg, Will	R-R	5-10	170	1-30-01	6	1	2.69	15	15	0	70	48	25	21	3	40	97	.190	.327	.282	31.49	12.99	308
Sosa, Gabriel	R-R	6-2	182	4-17-01	3	1	4.55	27	0	4	30	26	20	15	2	17	44	.226	.357	.322	30.56	11.81	144
Tatiz, Yeury	R-R	6-3	175	11-22-00	1	2	3.00	21	0	0	24	15	10	8	0	18	22	.172	.368	.230	19.30	15.79	114
Tomczak, Anthony	R-R	6-2	200	10-17-00	1	0	0.93	9	0	2	10	7	1	1	0	4	7	.200	.317	.229	17.07	9.76	41
Truitt, Evan	R-R	6-0	187	5-2-03	0	0	7.45	10	0	0	10	8	8	8	2	8	6	.222	.364	.417	13.64	18.18	44
Wainscott, Jesse	R-R	6-1	200	6-15-00	4	3	4.53	43	0	6	48	43	27	24	3	34	50	.236	.369	.341	22.22	15.11	225
Washington, Curtis	R-R	6-2	180	5-22-00	0	0	19.29	3	0	0	2	5	7	5	0	4	1	.417	.556	.583	5.56	22.22	18
White, Jack	L-L	6-3	210	10-4-99	7	4	4.76	38	0	3	70	61	41	37	5	47	88	.233	.362	.344	27.67	14.78	318
Widger, C.J.	L-L	6-6	170	5-25-99	3	4	4.60	27	0	3	29	18	17	15	2	17	44	.180	.325	.300	35.20	13.60	125

Fielding

Catcher	PCT	G	PO	A	E	DP	PB
Caguana	.980	20	186	15	4	3	3
Caron	.975	12	113	5	3	1	9
Charping	.992	44	454	23	4	2	7
Gonzalez	1.000	11	75	8	0	0	4
Sharp	.987	44	434	28	6	1	8

First Base	PCT	G	PO	A	E	DP
Belbin	.984	10	58	2	1	10
Cali	.979	7	43	4	1	4
Pagliarini	.981	24	188	16	4	25
Perez	.977	78	520	40	13	49
Suisbel	.992	17	124	3	1	16

Second Base	PCT	G	PO	A	E	DP
Arroyo	.964	49	100	138	9	32
Cova	.980	10	18	30	1	8
Dorighi	1.000	2	4	4	0	1
Emerson	1.000	1	1	2	0	1
Pagliarini	.967	56	96	109	7	29
Rodriguez	.930	17	33	33	5	9
St. Laurent	1.000	2	3	8	0	1

Third Base	PCT	G	PO	A	E	DP
Belbin	1.000	1	1	0	0	0
Cali	.861	13	5	26	5	3
Cova	.667	3	3	1	2	0
Eike	.938	15	9	21	2	2
Emerson	.900	4	2	7	1	1
Pagliarini	.750	6	0	3	1	0
Peete	.879	17	8	21	4	3
Suisbel	.911	81	49	135	18	12

Shortstop	PCT	G	PO	A	E	DP
Arroyo	.900	10	12	15	3	6
Dorighi	.938	14	28	33	4	8
Emerson	.918	36	63	94	14	28
Peete	.921	71	93	175	23	28
St. Laurent	1.000	1	2	2	0	1
Suisbel	1.000	7	6	18	0	2

Outfield	PCT	G	PO	A	E	DP
Cali	.750	2	3	0	1	0
Cova	.972	18	33	2	1	0
Donofrio	1.000	20	27	1	0	1
Farmelo	.968	42	92	0	3	0
Jimenez	.888	48	83	4	11	0
Jones	.968	83	148	3	5	1
Montes	.963	51	76	1	3	0
Pagliarini	.000	1	0	0	0	0
Peete	.983	24	57	2	1	0
Smith	.985	74	121	7	2	2
Washington	.984	43	61	2	1	0

ACL MARINERS — *ROOKIE*

ARIZONA COMPLEX LEAGUE

Batting	B-T	Ht.	Wt.	DOB	AVG	OBP	SLG	G	PA	AB	R	H	2B	3B	HR	RBI	BB	HBP	SH	SF	SO	SB	CS	BB%	SO%
Aguilar, Starlin	L-R	5-11	170	1-26-04	.240	.315	.340	42	168	150	17	36	8	2	1	17	14	3	0	1	33	5	0	8.33	19.64
Alcantara, Kelvin	L-L	6-0	165	9-15-05	.287	.381	.433	48	194	164	29	47	6	3	4	40	25	2	0	3	45	2	0	12.89	23.20
Belbin, Jarrod	L-R	6-2	220	6-22-00	.344	.424	.528	33	144	125	25	43	6	4	3	33	15	3	0	1	20	7	1	10.42	13.89
Caguana, Jose	R-R	5-10	175	4-5-02	.240	.380	.496	40	163	129	27	31	7	1	8	26	27	4	0	3	51	4	0	16.56	31.29
Celesten, Felnin	B-R	6-1	175	9-15-05	.352	.431	.568	32	144	125	30	44	10	4	3	27	18	0	0	1	28	5	2	12.50	19.44
Cova, Ricardo	R-R	5-9	145	5-24-04	.316	.407	.500	44	204	174	40	55	11	3	5	29	25	3	0	2	28	16	4	12.25	13.73
Crenshaw, Dustin	L-R	6-2	190	11-12-01	.214	.214	.214	3	14	14	3	3	0	0	0	0	0	0	0	0	2	0	0	0.00	14.29
Cruz, Juan	R-R	5-11	140	4-30-04	.277	.404	.404	17	58	47	13	13	0	0	2	6	9	1	1	0	17	3	0	15.52	29.31
De Andrade, Sebastian	R-R	5-9	165	5-11-06	.200	.300	.259	26	100	85	11	17	2	0	1	11	12	1	0	2	22	1	0	12.00	22.00
Dorighi, Carter	L-R	6-0	190	6-11-03	.583	.615	.917	3	13	12	5	7	2	1	0	3	1	0	0	0	1	0	0	7.69	7.69
Emerson, Colt	L-R	6-0	185	7-20-05	.250	.250	.250	1	4	4	1	1	0	0	0	0	0	0	0	0	1	0	0	0.00	25.00
Feliz, George	R-R	5-10	160	9-21-02	.227	.326	.387	48	192	163	30	37	5	0	7	26	21	4	2	2	52	8	1	10.94	27.08

Batting	B-T	Ht.	Wt.	DOB	AVG	OBP	SLG	G	PA	AB	R	H	2B	3B	HR	RBI	BB	HBP	SH	SF	SO	SB	CS	BB%	SO%
Garcia, Yunior	R-R	6-0	198	7-29-01	.300	.343	.467	8	35	30	8	9	2	0	1	7	3	0	0	2	10	0	0	8.57	28.57
Gonzalez, Carlos	R-R	5-11	175	11-20-03	.209	.349	.284	25	83	67	14	14	1	2	0	4	15	0	0	1	16	0	1	18.07	19.28
Gonzalez, Junior	R-R	5-8	186	5-10-00	.262	.371	.381	39	151	126	25	33	3	0	4	21	21	2	0	2	47	3	1	13.91	31.13
Gonzalez, Martin	R-R	5-10	165	9-28-04	.209	.301	.286	31	103	91	10	19	5	1	0	12	10	2	0	0	30	0	0	9.71	29.13
Jimenez, Carlos	L-L	5-10	170	2-14-03	.365	.489	.615	28	131	104	30	38	9	1	5	27	24	2	0	1	33	8	2	18.32	25.19
Kato, Kobe	L-R	6-1	170	3-19-99	.346	.500	.500	7	34	26	8	9	1	0	1	3	7	1	0	0	5	1	2	20.59	14.71
Mendez, Bryant	R-R	5-7	165	9-15-03	.203	.281	.301	44	153	133	15	27	9	2	0	11	10	6	0	4	43	9	3	6.54	28.10
Rambusch, Blake	R-R	5-8	175	8-31-99	.375	.583	.500	9	36	24	7	9	1	1	0	6	9	3	0	0	1	5	2	25.00	2.78
Ravelo, Rangel	R-R	6-0	235	4-24-92	.364	.364	.364	3	11	11	2	4	0	0	0	1	0	0	0	0	0	0	0	0.00	0.00
Rodriguez, Edryn	R-R	5-8	150	4-23-03	.300	.467	.500	5	15	10	4	3	2	0	0	3	3	1	0	1	4	0	0	20.00	26.67
Ventura, Dervy	B-R	5-10	165	1-20-04	.273	.430	.440	50	193	150	33	41	6	2	5	23	42	0	0	1	38	8	1	21.76	19.69
Washington, Curtis	R-R	6-2	180	5-22-00	.222	.364	.556	3	11	9	2	2	1	1	0	2	1	1	0	0	2	0	0	9.09	18.18

Pitching	B-T	Ht.	Wt.	DOB	W	L	ERA	G	GS	SV	IP	Hits	Runs	ER	HR	BB	SO	AVG	OBP	SLG	SO%	BB%	BF
Bello, Yensy	R-L	5-10	180	12-2-02	2	1	0.64	13	0	1	14	10	5	1	0	5	15	.204	.291	.265	26.32	8.77	57
Brierley, Chandler	L-L	6-8	195	5-12-98	0	0	0.00	1	0	1	1	0	0	0	0	1	1	.000	.333	.000	33.33	33.33	3
Cardozo, Kristian	R-R	6-2	175	11-10-02	2	0	3.68	12	0	0	15	14	9	6	2	10	14	.246	.371	.421	20.00	14.29	70
Cleveland, Tyler	L-R	6-3	185	9-9-99	0	0	4.50	1	0	0	2	2	1	1	0	0	4	.250	.250	.375	50.00	0.00	8
Diaz, Gleiner	R-R	6-0	170	9-20-03	1	3	3.57	16	0	2	23	22	16	9	1	9	23	.250	.355	.364	21.30	8.33	108
Ford, Walter	R-R	6-3	198	12-28-04	3	2	3.27	12	10	0	41	47	20	15	5	9	42	.285	.320	.418	23.86	5.11	176
Haberer, Jake	R-R	6-2	225	2-9-95	1	0	0.00	4	0	0	4	1	0	0	0	0	5	.071	.188	.071	31.25	0.00	16
Hembree, Heath	R-R	6-4	220	1-13-89	0	0	3.38	3	3	0	3	4	1	1	0	1	4	.333	.385	.333	30.77	7.69	13
Jackson, Jordan	R-R	6-6	204	10-14-98	0	0	27.00	3	1	0	1	5	6	4	0	2	4	.556	.636	.667	36.36	18.18	11
Joyce, Jimmy	R-R	6-2	210	1-13-99	0	1	4.50	1	1	0	2	2	1	1	0	1	3	.250	.400	.500	30.00	10.00	10
Llovera, Mauricio	R-R	5-11	224	4-17-96	0	0	3.00	3	2	0	3	5	1	1	0	0	2	.385	.385	.538	14.29	0.00	14
Lora, Aneury	R-R	6-2	155	3-30-04	1	1	5.51	12	5	0	33	41	22	20	1	12	30	.306	.360	.388	19.87	7.95	151
Martinez, Jeter	R-R	6-4	180	2-16-06	0	4	3.86	13	11	0	40	30	24	17	1	31	49	.207	.361	.283	26.63	16.85	184
Medina, Abdiel	R-R	5-11	155	1-20-02	0	0	13.91	11	0	0	11	19	17	17	3	10	10	.380	.475	.680	16.39	16.39	61
Melenge, Harold	L-L	5-10	170	1-15-02	2	0	3.29	13	1	1	38	36	18	14	3	9	34	.243	.300	.351	21.12	5.59	161
Morillo, David	R-R	6-2	168	9-26-01	1	2	11.57	8	0	0	9	15	12	12	0	4	11	.385	.479	.513	22.92	8.33	48
Munoz, Jean	R-R	6-1	155	9-17-02	0	0	7.43	9	0	0	13	12	12	11	0	7	20	.235	.328	.275	32.79	11.48	61
Pazos, Francisco	R-R	5-9	200	11-16-05	3	4	4.09	13	0	0	33	39	23	15	2	13	20	.310	.382	.405	13.61	8.84	147
Pinto, Juan	L-L	6-2	165	8-26-04	0	3	6.91	14	8	0	27	25	25	21	0	28	30	.234	.407	.364	21.43	20.00	140
Prins, Connor	R-R	6-2	160	10-4-03	1	1	3.07	8	0	0	15	11	10	5	0	12	10	.208	.373	.302	14.93	17.91	67
Quintana, Adrian	R-R	6-0	175	11-20-02	1	2	3.21	11	0	0	14	12	6	5	3	5	18	.226	.293	.434	31.03	8.62	58
Rodriguez, Wuilliams	R-R	6-4	195	2-20-04	1	0	1.84	14	0	1	15	12	3	3	1	11	20	.222	.348	.352	30.30	16.67	66
Romero, Jose	R-R	6-1	160	7-26-04	3	2	4.25	12	5	0	36	37	26	17	1	16	37	.252	.331	.306	21.76	9.41	170
Sanchez, Steven	R-R	6-0	160	8-19-03	0	0	4.02	14	0	0	16	17	9	7	1	8	12	.270	.361	.333	16.67	11.11	72
Schaeffer, Brandon	L-L	6-2	195	2-11-00	0	0	10.13	5	4	0	5	9	6	6	0	5	4	.391	.500	.478	13.79	17.24	29
Speier, Gabe	L-L	5-11	200	4-12-95	0	0	0.00	1	1	0	1	1	0	0	0	0	0	.250	.250	.250	0.00	0.00	4
Tabor, Matt	R-R	6-2	180	7-14-98	0	0	0.00	4	0	0	4	5	1	0	0	2	7	.263	.333	.263	33.33	9.52	21
Talavera, Roiber	R-R	6-0	160	3-31-04	3	2	3.99	11	2	0	29	21	16	13	1	16	35	.193	.321	.275	26.72	12.21	131
Tovar, Eduardo	R-R	5-11	165	10-10-03	1	1	11.05	10	0	0	7	10	14	9	0	13	11	.294	.510	.353	22.45	26.53	49
Wilson, Dylan	R-R	6-0	160	12-1-05	1	2	5.06	12	6	0	32	38	27	18	2	29	35	.297	.425	.461	21.74	18.01	161
Zerpa, Jose	R-R	6-2	180	10-19-04	1	1	4.22	10	0	1	11	13	7	5	1	7	9	.317	.429	.415	18.37	14.29	49

Fielding

C: Gonzalez 31, De Andrade 18, Caguana 14, Gonzalez 3. **1B:** Belbin 20, Gonzalez 20, Caguana 15, Garcia 7, Gonzalez 4, Ravelo 3, Rodriguez 2. **2B:** Ventura 37, Mendez 9, Aguilar 9, Cova 4, Rambusch 3, Kato 3, Belbin 2, Rodriguez 1, Crenshaw 1, Dorighi 1. **3B:** Gonzalez 26, Aguilar 14, Mendez 8, Ventura 5, Belbin 4, Cova 4, Rodriguez 2, Kato 2, Crenshaw 1, Dorighi 1. **SS:** Celesten 29, Mendez 28, Ventura 4, Crenshaw 1, Dorighi 1, Emerson 1. **LF:** Alcantara 18, Cova 17, Jimenez 12, Belbin 8, Cruz 4, Feliz 4, Kato 3, Ventura 3, Aguilar 3, Rambusch 2. **CF:** Feliz 23, Cova 14, Jimenez 13, Cruz 6, Alcantara 4, Washington 3. **RF:** Alcantara 29, Feliz 20, Cruz 7, Cova 4, Garcia 3, Belbin 2, Caguana 2, Rambusch 1.

DSL MARINERS — *ROOKIE*

DOMINICAN SUMMER LEAGUE

Batting	B-T	Ht.	Wt.	DOB	AVG	OBP	SLG	G	PA	AB	R	H	2B	3B	HR	RBI	BB	HBP	SH	SF	SO	SB	CS	BB%	SO%
Baez, Manuel	R-R	5-9	192	5-22-05	.083	.214	.083	19	28	24	2	2	0	0	0	0	2	2	0	0	13	0	0	7.14	46.43
Beltran, Gustavo	R-R	5-8	145	5-17-05	.165	.313	.177	39	96	79	10	13	1	0	0	9	15	2	0	0	20	0	1	15.63	20.83
Bolivar, Luis	R-R	6-1	160	2-9-04	.175	.329	.238	34	82	63	10	11	4	0	0	9	13	2	3	1	25	4	3	15.85	30.49
Castillo, Deuri	L-R	5-10	170	6-18-04	.213	.372	.287	44	156	122	21	26	3	3	0	9	27	5	0	2	46	20	2	17.31	29.49
De Cesare, Manuel	R-R	6-4	185	5-8-07	.247	.286	.304	47	168	158	12	39	7	1	0	14	7	2	0	1	40	1	1	4.17	23.81
Francis, Joshua	B-R	5-11	155	11-19-06	.170	.343	.226	33	67	53	9	9	1	1	0	5	13	1	0	0	21	2	1	19.40	31.34
Garcia, Alexander	R-R	5-10	155	10-30-05	.219	.349	.314	46	129	105	11	23	7	0	1	16	16	6	0	2	36	3	4	12.40	27.91
Guanchez, Gabriel	R-R	6-2	196	3-14-07	.214	.283	.290	43	145	131	9	28	7	0	1	24	10	3	0	1	51	0	0	6.90	35.17
Guilarte, German	R-R	5-10	167	3-6-03	.184	.345	.218	40	110	87	10	16	3	0	0	5	20	2	0	1	24	2	0	18.18	21.82
Gutierrez, Jean C.	R-R	6-1	175	10-25-05	.167	.286	.222	27	63	54	6	9	0	0	1	6	7	2	0	0	24	0	0	11.11	38.10
Joseph, Dawel	R-R	6-2	185	5-15-07	.133	.274	.173	47	179	150	16	20	6	0	0	2	27	2	0	0	52	3	2	15.08	29.05
Meyer, Danery	R-R	6-4	202	9-8-06	.000	.000	.000	12	1	1	0	0	0	0	0	0	0	0	0	0	1	0	0	0.00	100.00
Nunez, Zeus	R-R	6-1	185	11-19-06	.191	.288	.245	37	125	110	7	21	3	0	1	6	13	2	0	0	44	2	0	10.40	35.20
Ponce, Eduardo	R-R	5-9	172	9-2-06	.229	.368	.393	47	174	140	23	32	7	2	4	17	27	5	0	2	24	3	0	15.52	13.79
Robles, Kay	R-R	6-2	180	3-9-05	.120	.194	.152	39	103	92	9	11	3	0	0	3	3	6	0	2	50	6	1	2.91	48.54
Romero, Leandro	R-R	6-1	170	11-8-06	.223	.359	.304	49	181	148	23	33	8	2	0	13	30	2	0	1	46	4	4	16.57	25.41

Pitching	B-T	Ht.	Wt.	DOB	W	L	ERA	G	GS	SV	IP	Hits	Runs	ER	HR	BB	SO	AVG	OBP	SLG	SO%	BB%	BF
Aray, Cristian	R-R	5-10	155	4-5-07	0	3	4.13	11	8	0	33	28	15	15	3	13	30	.233	.312	.375	21.74	9.42	138

Arrieche, Gregori	R-R	6-2	205	12-19-01	1	1	2.76	5	5	0	16	10	5	5	0	4	21	.167	.254	.300	31.34	5.97	67
Beltran, Gustavo	R-R	5-8	145	5-17-05	0	1	27.00	1	0	0	0	2	1	1	0	0	1	.667	.667	1.000	33.33	0.00	3
Castillo, Deuri	L-R	5-10	170	6-18-04	0	0	0.00	1	0	0	1	1	0	0	0	1	2	.250	.400	.250	40.00	20.00	5
Cazarez, Juan	R-R	5-11	172	9-5-05	1	4	9.00	5	5	0	20	32	22	20	1	2	20	.368	.391	.517	21.74	2.17	92
Del Orbe, Alisson	S-R	6-3	185	9-6-01	2	0	2.95	8	0	1	18	22	8	6	0	6	24	.293	.346	.400	29.63	7.41	81
Gomez, Olivier	R-R	6-1	145	12-4-01	0	2	4.11	8	0	0	15	12	12	7	1	15	16	.214	.384	.357	21.92	20.55	73
Guevara, Anderson	R-R	5-10	170	11-4-04	1	1	1.45	13	4	0	31	15	6	5	1	18	50	.146	.305	.194	38.76	13.95	129
Guilarte, German	R-R	5-10	167	3-6-03	1	1	4.26	3	0	0	6	6	4	3	0	1	4	.240	.269	.280	15.38	3.85	26
Gutierrez, Jean C.	R-R	6-1	175	10-25-05	0	0	0.00	1	0	0	0	1	5	5	1	3	0	1.000	1.000	4.000	0.00	60.00	5
Jaspe, Carlos	R-R	6-1	155	6-5-07	0	0	18.00	8	0	0	6	7	12	12	1	15	5	.292	.585	.542	12.20	36.59	41
Jimenez, Anderson	R-R	6-0	160	8-3-07	1	3	6.41	9	7	0	20	17	16	14	0	13	26	.230	.374	.270	28.57	14.29	91
Jimenez, Federik	R-R	6-0	175	7-27-04	1	1	4.19	15	0	0	19	7	12	9	0	26	22	.111	.408	.111	22.45	26.53	98
Jimenez, Juan	R-R	6-1	225	12-9-06	0	0	0.00	1	0	0	0	1	4	4	0	3	0	1.000	1.000	2.000	0.00	75.00	4
Jimenez, Yoryi	R-R	6-1	175	10-28-03	1	0	6.85	15	0	0	24	24	23	18	1	17	31	.258	.395	.323	26.05	14.29	119
Lanza, Erick	R-R	6-2	169	9-1-06	0	0	16.20	4	0	0	5	11	9	9	0	7	3	.440	.563	.560	9.09	21.21	33
Meyer, Danery	R-R	6-4	202	9-8-06	1	0	11.93	12	0	0	14	16	24	19	1	25	13	.281	.517	.439	14.77	28.41	88
Meza, Kendal	R-R	6-0	160	12-13-05	0	5	2.25	12	11	0	36	20	13	9	0	32	48	.163	.354	.195	29.63	19.75	162
Navarro, Ruddy	R-R	6-1	155	7-21-06	0	1	0.75	3	3	0	12	9	3	1	0	2	16	.220	.298	.220	34.04	4.26	47
Orbe, Eliezer	L-L	6-0	165	11-7-05	0	1	32.40	3	1	0	2	1	6	6	0	7	2	.167	.615	.333	15.38	53.85	13
Perez, Roberto	R-R	5-9	145	1-27-04	3	3	2.84	17	3	0	38	29	18	12	1	11	46	.206	.269	.305	29.49	7.05	156
Ramirez, Jheifer	R-R	6-0	155	6-21-07	0	2	8.85	12	7	0	20	20	22	20	0	34	20	.267	.533	.320	16.67	28.33	120
Ramirez, Ruben	R-R	6-2	204	2-6-05	2	3	3.97	17	0	4	34	25	19	15	2	16	46	.192	.298	.292	30.46	10.60	151
Sato, Mathias	L-R	5-11	163	1-28-07	0	3	5.54	16	1	0	26	34	29	16	1	18	27	.304	.409	.393	20.45	13.64	132
Silvera, Fernando	L-L	5-11	190	12-8-02	1	4	8.49	9	0	1	12	12	15	11	1	13	14	.267	.460	.378	22.22	20.63	63

Fielding

C: Guanchez 23, Ponce 19, Guilarte 16, Baez 16, Robles 1. **1B:** Guilarte 23, Beltran 18, Garcia 15, Ponce 11, Baez 2, Guanchez 1, Gutierrez 1. **2B:** Romero 30, Castillo 18, Beltran 8, Francis 5, Garcia 4, Ponce 1. **3B:** Nunez 33, Romero 11, Beltran 9, Francis 8, Garcia 2. **SS:** Joseph 46, Romero 11, Garcia 2. **LF:** Garcia 24, Bolivar 21, Gutierrez 9, Castillo 8, Francis 6, De Cesare 2, Robles 2, Ponce 1, Guilarte 1. **CF:** Robles 27, Castillo 22, Bolivar 10, Francis 7, De Cesare 2, Guilarte 1. **RF:** De Cesare 40, Gutierrez 14, Robles 9, Bolivar 2, Garcia 1, Nunez 1.

Tampa Bay Rays

SEASON SYNOPSIS: After making five straight playoff appearances, the Rays defined 'mid' for MLB in 2024. A mix of injured pitchers, middling performance and a midseason sell-off kept Tampa from ever hitting its stride, never getting more than three games over .500 or more than five games below that mark.

HIGH POINT: Thanks to injuries to rotation members Shane McClanahan, Drew Rasmussen and Jeffrey Springs, the Rays had to lean on some different starters, and righty Taj Bradley for a time was up to the challenge. He posted 24 consecutive scoreless innings in July over parts of five starts, including three scoreless starts against the Guardians, Yankees and Blue Jays. Bradley, veteran Zack Littell, a healthy Shane Baz and righty Ryan Pepiot gave the Rays building blocks for a future rotation.

LOW POINT: It actually came after the season, when Hurricane Milton struck the Tampa Bay area Oct. 9 and caused millions of dollars in damages. The symbol of the damage came to be the Rays' maligned home ballpark, Tropicana Field, as the Teflon-coated fiberglass roof was ripped to shreds and many of the clubs' offices laid open to the elements. As a result, the Rays will play the 2025 season at Steinbrenner Field, the Grapefruit League home of the Yankees and Florida State League home to the Low-A Tampa Tarpons during the regular minor league season.

NOTABLE ROOKIES: Tampa finished 14th in the AL in runs and OPS, so the second-half boost from top prospect Junior Caminero (.248/.299/.424, 6 HR) provided tantalizing hope for improvement in 2025. But Australia-born third baseman Curtis Mead (.569 OPS) struggled in the big leagues.

KEY TRANSACTIONS: The Rays traded right-hander Tyler Glasnow to the Dodgers in the offseason for Pepiot and outfielder Jonny DeLuca. judged the trade market as thin and jumped in as a seller, reconfiguring its roster. They jettisoned veteran starters Aaron Civale (Milwaukee) and Zach Eflin (Baltimore), as well as 2020 playoff hero Randy Arozarena, who was traded to Seattle. Tampa also sent reliever Jason Adam to San Diego and dealt its top offensive player, third baseman Isaac Paredes, to the Cubs for a package headed by versatile but strikeout-prone Christopher Morel. They also acquired outfielder Dylan Carlson from the Cardinals for reliever Shawn Armstrong.

OPENING DAY PAYROLL: $101,023,112 (25th)

PLAYERS OF THE YEAR

MAJOR LEAGUE

Ryan Pepiot
RHP

8-8, 3.60 ERA
142 SO, 48 BB
Career-high 130 IP

MINOR LEAGUE

Carson Williams
SS

(AA)
.256/.353/.469
20 HR, 33 SB

ORGANIZATION LEADERS

Batting		*Qualifiers
MAJORS		
* AVG	Yandy Diaz	.281
* OPS	Yandy Diaz	.755
HR	Brandon Lowe	21
RBI	Yandy Diaz	65
MINORS		
* AVG	Chandler Simpson, Montgomery/Bowling Green	.355
* OBP	Chandler Simpson, Montgomery/Bowling Green	.410
* SLG	Bobby Seymour, Durham/Montgomery	.523
* OPS	Tre' Morgan, Charleston/B. Green/Montgomery	.891
R	Chandler Simpson, Montgomery/Bowling Green	90
H	Chandler Simpson, Montgomery/Bowling Green	160
TB	Bobby Seymour, Durham/Montgomery	238
2B	Cooper Kinney, Bowling Green	32
3B	Brayden Taylor, Montgomery/Bowling Green	8
HR	Bobby Seymour, Durham/Montgomery	28
RBI	Bobby Seymour, Durham/Montgomery	95
BB	Brayden Taylor, Montgomery/Bowling Green	76
SO	Bobby Seymour, Durham/Montgomery	156
SB	Chandler Simpson, Montgomery/Bowling Green	104

Pitching		#Qualifiers
MAJORS		
W	Taj Bradley	8
W	Zach Littell	8
W	Ryan Pepiot	8
L	Taj Bradley	11
# ERA	No qualifier	
SO	Taj Bradley	154
SV	Pete Fairbanks	23
MINORS		
W	Logan Workman, Durham/Montgomery	11
L	Duncan Davitt, Montgomery/Bowling Green	10
# ERA	Ian Seymour, Montgomery/Durham	2.35
G	Keyshawn Askew, Montgomery	51
GS	Cole Wilcox, Durham/Montgomery	28
SV	Austin Vernon, Montgomery	9
IP	Logan Workman, Durham/Montgomery	146
BB	Yoniel Curet, Montgomery/Bowling Green	60
SO	Ian Seymour, Durham/Montgomery	162
# AVG	Ian Seymour, Montgomery/Durham	.187

2024 PERFORMANCE

General Manager: Erik Neander. **Farm Director:** Blake Butera. **Scouting Director:** Chuck Ricci.

Class	Team	League	W	L	PCT	Finish	Manager
Majors	Tampa Bay Rays	American	80	82	.494	10 (15)	Kevin Cash
Triple-A	Durham Bulls	International	72	78	.480	11 (20)	Morgan Ensberg
Double-A	Montgomery Biscuits	Southern	80	57	.584	2 (8)	Kevin Boles
High-A	Bowling Green Hot Rods	South Atlantic	75	54	.581	1 (12)	Rafael Valenzuela
Low-A	Charleston RiverDogs	Carolina	69	61	.531	4 (12)	Sean Smedley
Rookie	FCL Rays	Florida Complex	35	24	.593	5 (15)	Hector Gimenez
Rookie	DSL Rays	Dominican	24	32	.429	37 (51)	Albert Lantigua
Rookie	DSL Tampa Bay	Dominican	24	32	.429	38 (51)	Henry Lugo
Overall 2024 Minor League Record			**379**	**338**	**.529**	**6th (30)**	

ORGANIZATION STATISTICS

TAMPA BAY RAYS

AMERICAN LEAGUE

Batting	B-T	Ht.	Wt.	DOB	AVG	OBP	SLG	G	PA	AB	R	H	2B	3B	HR	RBI	BB	HBP	SH	SF	SO	SB	CS	BB%	SO%
Aranda, Jonathan	L-R	6-0	210	5-23-98	.234	.308	.430	44	143	128	22	30	7	0	6	14	12	2	0	1	32	0	0	8.39	22.38
Arozarena, Randy	R-R	5-11	185	2-28-95	.211	.318	.394	100	409	350	45	74	19	0	15	37	45	11	0	3	101	16	7	11.00	24.69
Brantly, Rob	L-R	6-0	190	7-14-89	.111	.111	.111	3	9	9	0	1	0	0	0	0	0	0	0	0	2	0	0	0.00	22.22
Caballero, Jose	R-R	5-9	185	8-30-96	.227	.283	.347	139	483	441	53	100	24	1	9	44	27	9	3	3	133	44	16	5.59	27.54
Caminero, Junior	R-R	6-1	157	7-5-03	.248	.299	.424	43	177	165	15	41	9	1	6	18	11	1	0	0	38	2	0	6.21	21.47
Carlson, Dylan	B-L	6-2	205	10-23-98	.219	.299	.316	37	127	114	7	25	2	0	3	14	10	3	0	0	38	2	0	7.87	29.92
DeLuca, Jonny	R-R	6-0	200	7-10-98	.217	.278	.331	107	362	332	29	72	12	4	6	31	24	4	2	0	77	16	6	6.63	21.27
Diaz, Yandy	R-R	6-2	215	8-8-91	.281	.341	.414	145	621	563	55	158	31	1	14	65	50	4	0	4	95	0	0	8.05	15.30
Driscoll, Logan	L-R	5-10	195	11-3-97	.171	.189	.257	15	37	35	2	6	0	0	1	5	1	0	0	1	6	0	0	2.70	16.22
Goodrum, Niko	B-R	6-3	215	2-28-92	.188	.235	.188	9	18	16	1	3	0	0	0	0	1	0	1	0	6	0	1	5.56	33.33
Jackson, Alex	R-R	5-11	238	12-25-95	.122	.201	.237	58	155	139	17	17	7	0	3	12	12	2	1	1	53	1	0	7.74	34.19
Lowe, Brandon	L-R	5-10	185	7-6-94	.244	.311	.473	107	425	385	56	94	19	3	21	58	33	5	0	2	112	5	1	7.76	26.35
Lowe, Josh	L-R	6-4	205	2-2-98	.241	.302	.391	106	387	353	37	85	19	2	10	34	32	0	0	2	123	25	1	8.27	31.78
Mead, Curtis	R-R	6-0	171	10-26-00	.238	.282	.287	38	132	122	10	29	3	0	1	7	6	2	0	1	30	2	0	4.55	22.73
Misner, Kameron	L-L	6-4	218	1-8-98	.067	.067	.067	8	15	15	0	1	0	0	0	0	0	0	0	0	10	0	0	0.00	66.67
Morel, Christopher	R-R	5-11	145	6-24-99	.191	.258	.289	49	190	173	13	33	4	2	3	9	14	2	0	1	56	1	2	7.37	29.47
Palacios, Richie	L-R	5-10	180	5-16-97	.223	.346	.318	92	316	264	46	59	8	1	5	21	45	5	0	1	67	19	1	14.24	21.20
Paredes, Isaac	R-R	5-11	213	2-18-99	.245	.357	.435	101	429	363	41	89	19	1	16	55	52	12	0	2	68	0	1	12.12	15.85
Pinto, Rene	R-R	5-10	195	11-2-96	.214	.292	.429	19	49	42	5	9	3	0	2	6	4	1	1	1	18	0	0	8.16	36.73
Ramirez, Harold	R-R	5-10	232	9-6-94	.268	.284	.305	48	169	164	21	44	3	0	1	13	3	1	0	1	33	5	2	1.78	19.53
Rortvedt, Ben	L-R	5-9	191	9-25-97	.228	.317	.303	112	328	290	27	66	13	0	3	31	34	4	0	0	88	1	0	10.37	26.83
Rosario, Amed	R-R	6-2	190	11-19-95	.307	.331	.417	76	275	264	22	81	17	3	2	26	7	3	0	1	48	9	4	2.55	17.45
Shenton, Austin	L-R	6-0	205	1-22-98	.214	.340	.405	19	50	42	3	9	5	0	1	3	8	0	0	0	14	0	0	16.00	28.00
Siri, Jose	R-R	6-2	175	7-22-95	.187	.255	.366	130	448	402	50	75	16	1	18	47	31	7	2	4	170	14	7	6.92	37.95
Walls, Taylor	B-R	5-10	185	7-10-96	.183	.282	.248	84	252	218	27	40	5	3	1	14	31	0	0	3	67	16	4	12.30	26.59

Pitching	B-T	Ht.	Wt.	DOB	W	L	ERA	G	GS	SV	IP	Hits	Runs	ER	HR	BB	SO	AVG	OBP	SLG	SO%	BB%	BF
Adam, Jason	R-R	6-3	229	8-4-91	4	2	2.49	47	0	4	47	26	17	13	4	16	50	.164	.250	.277	27.78	8.89	180
Alexander, Tyler	R-L	6-2	203	7-14-94	6	5	5.10	23	9	0	108	110	61	61	23	24	90	.263	.307	.480	19.78	5.27	455
Armstrong, Shawn	R-R	6-2	225	9-11-90	2	2	5.40	38	7	1	47	56	30	28	5	19	50	.292	.360	.443	23.36	8.88	214
Baz, Shane	R-R	6-2	190	6-17-99	4	3	3.06	14	14	0	79	57	28	27	9	27	69	.200	.276	.319	21.63	8.46	319
Bigge, Hunter	R-R	6-1	205	6-12-98	0	0	2.57	15	1	1	14	14	4	4	2	3	19	.255	.293	.418	32.76	5.17	58
Bradley, Taj	R-R	6-2	190	3-19-01	8	11	4.11	25	25	0	138	122	68	63	22	47	154	.235	.300	.408	26.64	8.13	578
Civale, Aaron	R-R	6-2	215	6-12-95	2	6	5.07	17	17	0	87	93	51	49	16	27	84	.270	.329	.455	22.22	7.14	378
Cleavinger, Garrett	R-L	6-1	220	4-23-94	7	5	3.75	68	0	6	60	52	29	25	6	31	71	.231	.338	.342	26.69	11.65	266
Devenski, Chris	R-R	6-3	211	11-13-90	2	1	6.75	19	0	0	27	28	25	20	9	14	24	.259	.344	.583	19.67	11.48	122
Eflin, Zach	R-R	6-6	220	4-8-94	5	7	4.09	19	19	0	110	115	55	50	14	13	87	.261	.285	.423	18.91	2.83	460
Fairbanks, Pete	R-R	6-6	225	12-16-93	3	3	3.57	46	0	23	45	36	20	18	4	17	44	.217	.288	.313	23.78	9.19	185
Kelly, Kevin	R-R	6-2	200	11-28-97	5	2	2.67	68	0	1	71	59	25	21	7	9	63	.226	.264	.352	22.66	3.24	278
Kuhnel, Joel	R-R	6-5	290	2-19-95	0	0	1.13	5	0	0	8	4	1	1	1	0	4	.143	.143	.286	14.29	0.00	28
Littell, Zack	R-R	6-4	220	10-5-95	8	10	3.63	29	29	0	156	164	68	63	22	31	141	.265	.306	.426	21.49	4.73	656
Lopez, Jacob	L-L	6-4	220	3-11-98	0	0	5.23	4	1	0	10	5	7	6	2	7	8	.135	.304	.324	17.39	15.22	46
Lovelady, Richard	L-L	6-0	185	7-7-95	3	5	3.77	28	0	2	29	25	13	12	2	9	20	.236	.305	.321	16.81	7.56	119
Maton, Phil	R-R	6-2	206	3-25-93	1	2	4.58	40	0	2	35	29	19	18	6	18	30	.225	.342	.434	19.74	11.84	152
Montgomery, Mason	L-L	6-2	195	6-17-00	0	0	1.86	9	0	0	10	6	2	2	0	5	17	.188	.297	.281	45.95	13.51	37
Pepiot, Ryan	R-R	6-3	215	8-21-97	8	8	3.60	26	26	0	130	102	58	52	17	48	142	.212	.292	.364	26.35	8.91	539
Poche, Colin	L-L	6-3	225	1-17-94	1	2	3.86	43	0	2	37	30	16	16	7	13	33	.217	.281	.391	21.57	8.50	153
Ramirez, Erasmo	R-R	6-0	220	5-2-90	3	0	4.35	13	0	1	21	12	12	10	5	10	15	.164	.271	.384	17.65	11.76	85
Rasmussen, Drew	R-R	6-1	211	7-27-95	0	2	2.83	16	4	1	29	25	10	9	0	6	35	.229	.267	.275	30.17	5.17	116
Rodriguez, Manuel	R-R	5-11	210	8-6-96	3	4	2.15	40	0	2	38	29	13	9	3	11	34	.212	.292	.307	21.52	6.96	158
Rortvedt, Ben	L-R	5-9	191	9-25-97	0	0	4.50	1	0	0	2	3	1	1	1	2	1	.333	.455	.778	9.09	18.18	11
Springs, Jeffrey	L-L	6-3	218	9-19-92	2	2	3.27	7	7	0	33	34	12	12	5	11	37	.264	.324	.419	26.06	7.75	142
Sterner, Justin	R-R	6-1	215	8-29-96	0	0	2.25	2	0	0	4	5	2	1	0	1	4	.294	.316	.412	21.05	5.26	19

Pitching	B-T	Ht.	Wt.	DOB	W	L	ERA	G	GS	SV	IP	Hits	Runs	ER	HR	BB	SO	AVG	OBP	SLG	SO%	BB%	BF
Sulser, Cole	R-R	6-1	190	3-12-90	1	0	0.00	6	2	0	12	3	0	0	0	6	8	.086	.214	.086	18.60	13.95	43
Uceta, Edwin	R-R	6-0	155	1-9-98	2	0	1.51	30	0	5	42	26	8	7	2	8	57	.174	.222	.255	35.85	5.03	159
Waguespack, Jacob	R-R	6-6	235	11-5-93	0	0	5.40	4	1	0	10	13	7	6	1	10	11	.317	.451	.439	21.57	19.61	51
Zuber, Tyler	R-R	5-11	195	6-16-95	0	0	2.70	2	0	0	3	3	1	1	1	2	4	.231	.333	.462	26.67	13.33	15

Fielding

Catcher	PCT	G	PO	A	E	DP	PB
Brantly	1.000	3	17	1	0	0	0
Driscoll	.991	15	100	6	1	0	1
Jackson	.987	58	444	18	6	2	4
Pinto	.992	19	126	2	1	0	1
Rortvedt	.989	111	755	26	9	2	6

First Base	PCT	G	PO	A	E	DP
Aranda	1.000	23	133	7	0	10
Caminero	1.000	1	13	2	0	0
Diaz	.989	112	784	45	9	67
Goodrum	.667	2	2	0	1	0
Lowe	1.000	13	71	7	0	9
Mead	1.000	1	2	0	0	0
Paredes	.992	17	111	9	1	12
Shenton	1.000	10	62	3	0	3
Siri	1.000	1	1	0	0	0

Second Base	PCT	G	PO	A	E	DP
Aranda	1.000	6	4	12	0	1
Caballero	.971	30	23	43	2	9
Goodrum	1.000	1	1	3	0	0
Lowe	1.000	58	80	123	0	26
Mead	.967	21	22	36	2	8
Morel	.967	21	25	63	3	7
Palacios	.964	37	48	84	5	15
Rosario	.982	21	29	26	1	3

Third Base	PCT	G	PO	A	E	DP
Aranda	.000	1	0	0	0	0
Caballero	.986	37	17	51	1	5
Caminero	.933	39	27	56	6	5
Mead	.939	14	11	20	2	1
Palacios	.667	2	1	3	2	0
Paredes	.963	78	39	115	6	14
Rosario	.947	14	4	14	1	4

Shortstop	PCT	G	PO	A	E	DP
Caballero	.968	88	85	187	9	37
Goodrum	1.000	1	2	3	0	1
Palacios	.000	1	0	0	0	0
Rosario	1.000	12	8	17	0	3
Walls	.988	83	80	172	3	33

Outfield	PCT	G	PO	A	E	DP
Arozarena	.988	96	165	4	2	0
Carlson	1.000	31	55	0	0	0
DeLuca	.991	112	219	6	2	2
Goodrum	1.000	4	2	0	0	0
Lowe	.979	96	189	2	4	1
Misner	1.000	6	12	0	0	0
Morel	.923	11	12	0	1	0
Palacios	1.000	53	83	0	0	0
Ramirez	1.000	9	16	0	0	0
Rosario	1.000	20	40	1	0	0
Siri	.980	128	336	1	7	1

TAMPA BAY RAYS

DURHAM BULLS — *TRIPLE-A*

INTERNATIONAL LEAGUE

Batting	B-T	Ht.	Wt.	DOB	AVG	OBP	SLG	G	PA	AB	R	H	2B	3B	HR	RBI	BB	HBP	SH	SF	SO	SB	CS	BB%	SO%
Aranda, Jonathan	L-R	6-0	210	5-23-98	.237	.368	.424	32	144	118	22	28	1	0	7	19	23	2	0	1	47	0	0	15.97	32.64
Barreat, Elis	R-R	5-9	158	5-22-03	.200	.200	.400	2	5	5	0	1	1	0	0	0	0	0	0	0	1	0	0	0.00	20.00
Basabe, Osleivis	R-R	5-11	188	9-13-00	.248	.293	.336	66	283	262	26	65	8	0	5	29	14	4	0	3	51	4	3	4.95	18.02
Brantly, Rob	L-R	6-0	190	7-14-89	.250	.316	.394	52	179	160	21	40	6	1	5	19	12	4	0	1	35	0	0	6.70	19.55
Caminero, Junior	R-R	6-1	157	7-5-03	.276	.331	.498	53	236	217	33	60	9	0	13	34	16	2	0	1	50	1	1	6.78	21.19
Cardenas, Ruben	R-R	6-0	185	10-10-97	.281	.346	.530	49	205	185	31	52	11	1	11	28	12	7	0	1	43	5	4	5.85	20.98
Chang, Yu	R-R	6-1	180	8-18-95	.293	.431	.512	14	51	41	6	12	3	0	2	7	9	1	0	0	15	2	1	17.65	29.41
DeLuca, Jonny	R-R	6-0	200	7-10-98	.300	.440	.650	6	25	20	6	6	1	0	2	6	4	1	0	0	1	1	0	16.00	4.00
Driscoll, Logan	L-R	5-10	195	11-3-97	.292	.367	.473	70	294	260	40	76	24	1	7	37	28	4	0	2	61	1	0	9.52	20.75
Dyer, Matthew	R-R	6-2	185	7-14-98	.250	.400	.500	2	5	4	0	1	1	0	0	1	1	0	0	0	2	0	0	20.00	40.00
Goodrum, Niko	B-R	6-3	215	2-28-92	.316	.422	.605	9	45	38	11	12	2	0	3	12	6	1	0	0	10	1	0	13.33	22.22
Hernandez, Heriberto	R-R	5-11	195	12-16-99	.187	.322	.407	44	183	150	26	28	4	1	9	20	27	4	0	2	49	2	0	14.75	26.78
Hinojosa, C.J.	R-R	5-10	185	7-15-94	.223	.284	.329	106	387	350	39	78	14	1	7	33	25	6	3	3	70	3	2	6.46	18.09
Jackson, Alex	R-R	5-11	238	12-25-95	.238	.322	.533	28	118	105	17	25	5	1	8	20	12	1	0	0	27	0	0	10.17	22.88
Lowe, Brandon	L-R	5-10	185	7-6-94	.235	.381	.647	6	21	17	3	4	1	0	2	8	4	0	0	0	9	0	0	19.05	42.86
Lowe, Josh	L-R	6-4	205	2-2-98	.255	.309	.471	13	55	51	7	13	0	1	3	13	4	0	0	0	24	0	0	7.27	43.64
Mangum, Jake	B-L	6-1	179	3-8-96	.317	.357	.442	104	428	398	57	126	30	1	6	56	23	4	0	3	73	20	8	5.37	17.06
Mead, Curtis	R-R	6-0	171	10-26-00	.288	.359	.481	91	410	364	60	105	19	6	13	41	29	13	0	4	64	11	6	7.07	15.61
Misner, Kameron	L-L	6-4	218	1-8-98	.248	.360	.442	113	519	439	77	109	26	4	17	55	73	5	0	2	152	30	3	14.07	29.29
Palacios, Richie	L-R	5-10	180	5-16-97	.222	.333	.222	5	21	18	0	4	0	0	0	0	3	0	0	0	1	0	0	14.29	4.76
Peters, Tristan	L-R	5-11	180	2-29-00	.238	.344	.402	123	478	408	67	97	21	5	12	46	63	4	1	2	94	8	7	13.18	19.67
Pinto, Rene	R-R	5-10	195	11-2-96	.191	.257	.373	53	230	209	29	40	5	0	11	31	16	3	0	2	84	0	0	6.96	36.52
Piper, Kenny	R-R	5-9	190	7-12-98	.188	.278	.386	29	115	101	18	19	5	0	5	17	11	2	0	1	33	3	0	9.57	28.70
Schnell, Nick	L-R	6-1	180	3-27-00	.213	.263	.337	26	96	89	10	19	2	0	3	8	5	1	1	0	38	2	0	5.21	39.58
Seymour, Bobby	L-R	6-4	250	10-7-98	.269	.353	.601	57	218	193	35	52	7	0	19	44	24	1	0	0	76	3	0	11.01	34.86
Shenton, Austin	L-R	6-0	205	1-22-98	.258	.361	.497	83	363	310	49	80	12	1	20	65	48	3	0	2	110	0	0	13.22	30.30
Simon, Ronny	B-R	5-7	150	4-17-00	.283	.356	.429	130	527	466	72	132	30	4	10	56	47	7	4	3	99	20	7	8.92	18.79
Smith, Dominic	L-L	6-0	224	6-15-95	.263	.337	.375	21	89	80	10	21	3	0	2	11	8	1	0	0	26	1	0	8.99	29.21
Turner, Gionti	R-R	6-2	178	8-17-00	.147	.194	.265	15	36	34	4	5	1	0	1	2	2	0	0	0	9	1	0	5.56	25.00
Walls, Taylor	B-R	5-10	185	7-10-96	.381	.435	.714	5	23	21	6	8	5	1	0	5	2	0	0	0	6	1	0	8.70	26.09

Pitching	B-T	Ht.	Wt.	DOB	W	L	ERA	G	GS	SV	IP	Hits	Runs	ER	HR	BB	SO	AVG	OBP	SLG	SO%	BB%	BF
Alexander, Tyler	R-L	6-2	203	7-14-94	1	4	4.54	7	5	0	36	39	22	18	5	6	33	.273	.302	.469	21.85	3.97	151
Alvarez, Nelson L.	R-R	6-4	220	6-11-98	1	0	3.94	12	0	0	16	11	8	7	0	15	15	.208	.371	.245	21.43	21.43	70
Baz, Shane	R-R	6-2	190	6-17-99	3	3	4.12	10	10	0	39	39	18	18	2	23	44	.260	.365	.373	24.72	12.92	178
Bigge, Hunter	R-R	6-1	205	6-12-98	0	1	5.40	8	0	2	7	5	4	4	3	3	16	.192	.276	.577	55.17	10.34	29
Bradley, Taj	R-R	6-2	190	3-19-01	1	0	0.82	2	2	0	11	2	1	1	1	3	15	.057	.132	.143	39.47	7.89	38
Brantly, Rob	L-R	6-0	190	7-14-89	0	0	10.13	3	0	1	3	3	3	3	2	2	1	.300	.385	.900	7.69	15.38	13
Brigden, Trevor	L-R	6-3	210	9-19-95	3	1	7.64	32	0	1	35	43	31	30	8	15	45	.303	.371	.556	28.30	9.43	159
Cuevas, Jonny	R-R	6-3	200	11-19-00	1	0	18.90	2	0	0	3	3	7	7	0	7	3	.231	.500	.231	15.00	35.00	20
Devenski, Chris	R-R	6-3	211	11-13-90	0	0	6.00	3	0	0	6	7	4	4	1	0	8	.292	.292	.542	33.33	0.00	24
Fairbanks, Pete	R-R	6-6	225	12-16-93	0	0	0.00	2	0	0	2	2	0	0	0	0	2	.286	.286	.286	28.57	0.00	7
Flynn, Michael	R-R	6-4	185	8-7-96	0	1	6.35	6	0	0	6	6	4	4	0	4	9	.261	.357	.391	32.14	14.29	28
Garcia, Carlos	R-R	6-3	185	11-28-98	3	2	4.50	40	5	2	64	56	39	32	6	34	66	.237	.344	.373	23.66	12.19	279
Gomez, Michael	R-R	6-3	210	8-15-96	3	4	5.01	39	0	1	56	54	37	31	5	22	68	.250	.332	.384	27.76	8.98	245

Hinojosa, C.J.	R-R	5-10	185	7-15-94	0	0	20.25	2	0	0	1	2	3	3	0	1	1	.333	.600	.500	10.00	10.00	10
Jimenez, Antonio	L-L	5-11	145	5-6-01	1	0	4.32	16	1	0	25	23	12	12	3	7	22	.242	.294	.400	21.57	6.86	102
Kelly, Kevin	R-R	6-2	200	11-28-97	0	0	0.00	5	0	0	5	4	1	0	0	0	8	.222	.222	.222	44.44	0.00	18
Kuhnel, Joel	R-R	6-5	290	2-19-95	2	0	4.30	13	0	0	15	18	8	7	1	3	14	.305	.339	.441	22.58	4.84	62
Leverett, Adam	L-R	6-4	190	9-19-98	0	1	5.25	3	3	0	12	7	7	7	2	4	5	.171	.265	.341	10.20	8.16	49
Lopez, Jacob	L-L	6-4	220	3-11-98	4	7	4.26	21	19	0	89	71	47	42	12	45	106	.218	.320	.351	27.89	11.84	380
Lovelady, Richard	L-L	6-0	185	7-7-95	1	0	1.86	10	0	0	10	5	3	2	0	1	12	.147	.194	.147	32.43	2.70	37
Mejia, Enmanuel	R-R	5-11	185	12-22-98	7	5	7.83	42	5	1	54	56	50	47	12	36	59	.262	.379	.472	22.96	14.01	257
Montgomery, Mason	L-L	6-2	195	6-17-00	1	7	6.26	31	14	2	88	105	63	61	19	36	105	.294	.363	.515	26.05	8.93	403
Odorizzi, Jake	R-R	6-2	190	3-27-90	0	2	11.81	2	2	0	5	8	7	7	1	5	2	.364	.517	.545	6.90	17.24	29
Poche, Colin	L-L	6-3	225	1-17-94	0	0	6.75	3	0	0	3	3	2	2	0	1	1	.273	.333	.364	8.33	8.33	12
Ramirez, Erasmo	R-R	6-0	220	5-2-90	3	4	3.23	37	0	4	53	50	21	19	7	15	64	.248	.303	.406	28.83	6.76	222
Rasmussen, Drew	R-R	6-1	211	7-27-95	0	2	8.59	5	2	0	7	11	7	7	2	0	8	.344	.364	.594	24.24	0.00	33
Record, Joe	R-R	6-3	232	1-12-95	1	3	4.47	46	3	3	58	60	39	29	4	31	70	.255	.347	.374	25.83	11.44	271
Rock, Joe	L-L	6-6	200	7-29-00	7	8	4.58	27	23	0	140	160	81	71	17	35	132	.284	.330	.433	21.60	5.73	611
Rodriguez, Manuel	R-R	5-11	210	8-6-96	1	0	1.09	23	0	5	25	19	3	3	2	6	28	.218	.281	.310	29.17	6.25	96
Sanchez, Angel	R-R	6-1	190	11-28-89	4	2	2.36	6	5	0	27	28	12	7	2	6	15	.275	.312	.382	13.76	5.50	109
Seymour, Ian	L-L	6-0	210	12-13-98	4	1	2.33	10	10	0	54	43	16	14	7	19	63	.213	.296	.366	27.88	8.41	226
Springs, Jeffrey	L-L	6-3	218	9-19-92	0	3	4.50	9	9	0	30	33	18	15	3	4	31	.277	.304	.395	24.60	3.17	126
Sterner, Justin	R-R	6-1	215	8-29-96	2	4	3.28	34	1	2	47	35	19	17	7	17	60	.208	.295	.357	31.41	8.90	191
Sulser, Cole	R-R	6-1	190	3-12-90	1	0	2.08	9	0	0	13	9	3	3	1	2	11	.196	.229	.326	22.92	4.17	48
Uceta, Edwin	R-R	6-0	155	1-9-98	1	2	5.77	22	0	0	34	38	25	22	8	16	47	.277	.357	.504	29.75	10.13	158
Waguespack, Jacob	R-R	6-6	235	11-5-93	1	1	5.32	9	4	0	22	26	13	13	2	5	32	.283	.323	.391	32.32	5.05	99
White, Colby	R-R	6-0	190	7-4-98	0	2	17.61	9	1	0	8	10	17	15	3	10	10	.294	.478	.559	21.74	21.74	46
Whitten, Kyle	R-R	6-3	190	9-22-98	1	0	4.32	11	1	0	17	12	9	8	4	10	17	.194	.306	.435	23.61	13.89	72
Wicklander, Patrick	R-L	6-1	205	12-31-99	0	0	16.20	2	0	0	3	6	6	6	1	6	1	.400	.571	.733	4.76	28.57	21
Wilcox, Cole	R-R	6-5	232	7-14-99	3	3	4.62	8	8	0	39	39	23	20	4	17	28	.264	.351	.399	16.67	10.12	168
Wiles, Nathan	R-R	6-4	228	7-2-98	6	3	5.54	35	11	0	88	104	62	54	14	26	72	.294	.349	.503	18.37	6.63	392
Workman, Logan	R-R	6-4	215	12-6-98	1	1	4.30	5	5	0	23	24	11	11	2	11	26	.270	.353	.371	25.24	10.68	103
Zarraga, Alfredo	R-R	5-11	158	11-16-00	1	1	5.93	10	1	0	14	15	9	9	1	10	16	.273	.385	.400	24.62	15.38	65
Zuber, Tyler	R-R	5-11	195	6-16-95	3	0	2.49	18	0	4	22	16	7	6	3	6	29	.200	.264	.363	33.33	6.90	87

Fielding

Catcher	PCT	G	PO	A	E	DP	PB
Brantly	.986	25	209	9	3	0	3
Driscoll	.990	48	452	29	5	3	5
Jackson	.995	18	187	8	1	1	1
Pinto	.991	43	396	26	4	4	2
Piper	1.000	20	200	12	0	0	1

First Base	PCT	G	PO	A	E	DP
Aranda	.988	14	79	4	1	5
Brantly	.978	8	42	3	1	2
Cardenas	1.000	16	103	5	0	6
Goodrum	.667	1	2	0	1	0
Schnell	1.000	2	17	1	0	2
Seymour	.992	46	328	24	3	26
Shenton	.991	50	307	21	3	30
Smith	1.000	20	111	20	0	10

Second Base	PCT	G	PO	A	E	DP
Aranda	1.000	7	7	12	0	1
Barreat	.750	2	0	3	1	0
Basabe	.950	15	21	36	3	3
Caminero	.943	8	14	19	2	2
Goodrum	1.000	3	1	4	0	1
Hinojosa	.983	14	24	33	1	9
Lowe	1.000	4	9	3	0	2
Mead	.977	35	56	72	3	14
Palacios	1.000	2	1	6	0	1
Simon	.954	66	105	145	12	28
Turner	.944	8	7	10	1	5

Third Base	PCT	G	PO	A	E	DP
Basabe	1.000	4	2	7	0	3
Brantly	1.000	2	1	4	0	0
Caminero	.923	44	37	59	8	7
Cardenas	.000	1	0	0	0	0
Dyer	1.000	1	0	2	0	1
Hinojosa	.778	6	2	5	2	0
Mead	.950	61	31	84	6	8
Shenton	.883	31	11	42	7	3
Simon	.850	10	5	12	3	0

Shortstop	PCT	G	PO	A	E	DP
Basabe	.982	46	58	103	3	26
Chang	.971	13	11	23	1	5
Goodrum	1.000	3	3	5	0	0
Hinojosa	.982	87	96	170	5	28
Simon	.889	5	3	5	1	0
Turner	1.000	1	2	2	0	0
Walls	1.000	4	1	10	0	1

Outfield	PCT	G	PO	A	E	DP
Cardenas	.980	23	48	1	1	0
DeLuca	.917	4	10	1	1	1
Driscoll	1.000	1	1	0	0	0
Dyer	.000	1	0	0	0	0
Goodrum	1.000	2	6	0	0	0
Hernandez	.967	34	58	1	2	0
Lowe	.882	10	14	1	2	0
Mangum	.990	100	200	6	2	2
Misner	.993	106	272	7	2	1
Palacios	1.000	2	1	0	0	0
Peters	.996	115	219	4	1	2
Schnell	.956	23	42	1	2	0
Simon	.983	44	52	5	1	0
Turner	.889	4	8	0	1	0

MONTGOMERY BISCUITS — *DOUBLE-A*

SOUTHERN LEAGUE

Batting	B-T	Ht.	Wt.	DOB	AVG	OBP	SLG	G	PA	AB	R	H	2B	3B	HR	RBI	BB	HBP	SH	SF	SO	SB	CS	BB%	SO%
Ariza, Luis	R-R	5-11	155	5-8-04	.182	.308	.182	4	13	11	1	2	0	0	0	0	1	1	0	0	4	0	0	7.69	30.77
Auer, Mason	R-R	6-1	210	3-1-01	.190	.264	.325	86	331	295	32	56	14	4	6	30	25	6	2	3	87	23	7	7.55	26.28
Baker, Dru	R-R	5-11	205	3-22-00	.288	.344	.328	110	467	424	50	122	13	2	0	44	34	4	2	3	96	42	12	7.28	20.56
Barreat, Elis	R-R	5-9	158	5-22-03	.111	.111	.111	3	9	9	0	1	0	0	0	0	0	0	0	0	2	0	0	0.00	22.22
Battles, Jalen	R-R	6-1	210	12-19-99	.229	.295	.302	76	286	258	36	59	12	2	1	25	21	4	1	2	70	5	0	7.34	24.48
Dyer, Matthew	R-R	6-2	185	7-14-98	.212	.306	.322	39	135	118	17	25	6	2	1	9	15	1	1	0	46	5	0	11.11	34.07
Etzel, Matthew	L-R	6-2	211	4-30-02	.232	.300	.392	36	140	125	20	29	3	1	5	19	11	2	0	2	49	4	1	7.86	35.00
Genoves, Ricardo	R-R	6-2	190	5-14-99	.215	.308	.462	28	108	93	14	20	8	0	5	14	12	1	1	1	29	0	0	11.11	26.85
Hernandez, Heriberto	R-R	5-11	195	12-16-99	.268	.359	.560	60	245	209	40	56	17	1	14	40	29	3	0	4	68	3	1	11.84	27.76
Isaac, Xavier	L-L	6-3	240	12-17-03	.211	.346	.349	31	133	109	14	23	4	1	3	17	21	2	0	1	54	1	1	15.79	40.60
Keegan, Dominic	R-R	6-0	210	8-1-00	.285	.371	.435	104	442	375	58	107	23	3	9	60	50	7	0	10	90	0	0	11.31	20.36
Morgan, Tre'	L-L	6-1	191	7-16-02	.211	.322	.342	21	91	76	12	16	2	1	2	13	12	1	0	1	17	1	1	13.19	18.68

Murray, Tanner	R-R	6-1	190	9-3-99	.290	.328	.424	111	448	420	56	122	29	3	7	66	21	4	0	3	73	4	0	4.69	16.29
Piper, Kenny	R-R	5-9	190	7-12-98	.217	.317	.382	58	243	207	31	45	9	2	7	31	27	5	0	4	72	2	0	11.11	29.63
Sandoval, Joshuan	R-R	6-2	215	12-18-97	.214	.313	.357	5	16	14	0	3	2	0	0	0	2	0	0	0	7	0	0	12.50	43.75
Schnell, Nick	L-R	6-1	180	3-27-00	.262	.328	.425	81	326	294	43	77	19	1	9	41	25	5	0	2	78	9	5	7.67	23.93
Seymour, Bobby	L-R	6-4	250	10-7-98	.290	.349	.466	66	292	262	39	76	17	1	9	51	22	4	0	4	80	2	0	7.53	27.40
Simpson, Chandler	L-R	6-2	170	11-18-00	.351	.401	.407	78	358	322	56	113	13	1	1	20	29	0	4	3	27	73	12	8.10	7.54
Taylor, Brayden	L-R	6-1	180	5-22-02	.194	.290	.435	30	125	108	17	21	2	3	6	17	15	0	1	1	46	3	1	12.00	36.80
Turner, Gionti	R-R	6-2	178	8-17-00	.150	.261	.200	7	23	20	2	3	1	0	0	4	3	0	0	0	12	1	1	13.04	52.17
Vasquez, Willy	R-R	6-2	191	9-6-01	.212	.264	.320	97	371	344	29	73	18	2	5	41	24	1	0	2	118	11	6	6.47	31.81
Williams, Carson	R-R	6-1	180	6-25-03	.256	.352	.469	115	505	433	83	111	20	6	20	69	58	9	0	5	144	33	11	11.49	28.51

Pitching	B-T	Ht.	Wt.	DOB	W	L	ERA	G	GS	SV	IP	Hits	Runs	ER	HR	BB	SO	AVG	OBP	SLG	SO%	BB%	BF
Alvarez, Nelson L.	R-R	6-4	220	6-11-98	1	1	4.66	15	0	0	19	15	10	10	4	7	23	.211	.282	.423	29.49	8.97	78
Askew, Keyshawn	L-L	6-4	190	1-5-00	3	3	1.40	51	0	1	64	43	20	10	0	39	66	.193	.342	.233	23.74	14.03	278
Auer, Mason	R-R	6-1	210	3-1-01	0	1	0.00	1	0	0	0	2	1	0	0	0	0	.667	.667	.667	0.00	0.00	3
Belge, Jeff	L-L	6-5	225	12-4-97	1	1	4.20	11	0	0	15	9	7	7	3	8	17	.167	.274	.370	27.42	12.90	62
Cuevas, Jonny	R-R	6-3	200	11-19-00	1	0	1.76	6	1	0	15	13	4	3	0	6	12	.228	.313	.263	18.75	9.38	64
Curet, Yoniel	R-R	6-2	190	11-3-02	4	0	1.75	5	5	0	26	16	5	5	3	11	37	.180	.291	.315	35.92	10.68	103
Dahle, Nate	R-R	6-6	235	10-9-97	2	1	6.43	10	0	0	14	11	10	10	3	7	10	.229	.339	.438	16.95	11.86	59
Davitt, Duncan	R-R	6-3	235	9-23-99	2	4	4.76	10	10	0	51	43	29	27	7	19	56	.230	.311	.406	26.29	8.92	213
Erbe, Haden	R-R	6-3	225	8-13-98	2	5	6.75	27	2	1	35	36	30	26	4	25	38	.261	.380	.406	22.75	14.97	167
Gervase, Paul	R-R	6-10	230	5-23-00	1	0	3.57	15	0	0	18	11	7	7	2	3	31	.169	.217	.277	44.93	4.35	69
Harney, Sean	L-R	6-0	190	7-10-98	0	0	2.00	6	1	0	9	3	2	2	2	2	6	.107	.167	.321	20.00	6.67	30
Hartman, Jack	R-R	6-3	205	7-13-98	2	1	3.78	15	0	5	17	13	8	7	2	6	16	.213	.290	.344	23.19	8.70	69
Hunley, Sean	R-R	6-4	220	7-5-99	6	3	1.67	30	11	0	75	52	14	14	5	13	52	.195	.244	.273	18.06	4.51	288
Jimenez, Antonio	L-L	5-11	145	5-6-01	3	0	3.44	25	0	2	37	31	15	14	0	15	36	.221	.302	.243	22.64	9.43	159
Leverett, Adam	L-R	6-4	190	9-19-98	7	6	3.91	20	17	0	90	85	41	39	6	26	58	.249	.307	.337	15.55	6.97	373
Lunn, Connor	R-R	6-3	215	7-8-98	0	0	3.86	4	0	0	5	2	2	2	0	3	5	.133	.278	.133	27.78	16.67	18
Martin, Trevor	R-R	6-5	238	12-15-00	1	3	6.62	14	12	0	50	53	44	37	9	19	50	.260	.333	.456	21.93	8.33	228
McKay, Brendan	L-L	6-2	220	12-18-95	0	0	1.00	5	5	0	18	11	3	2	1	1	17	.169	.194	.231	25.37	1.49	67
Menendez, Antonio	R-R	6-4	215	3-11-99	6	3	3.14	39	0	0	63	48	25	22	3	35	79	.214	.337	.281	29.15	12.92	271
Peoples, Ben	L-R	6-1	175	5-1-01	3	3	3.42	12	12	0	55	41	21	21	6	23	57	.204	.297	.348	24.89	10.04	229
Pepiot, Ryan	R-R	6-3	215	8-21-97	0	0	0.00	1	1	0	3	1	0	0	0	2	7	.091	.231	.091	53.85	15.38	13
Reifert, Evan	R-R	6-4	190	5-14-99	2	0	1.96	35	0	0	41	22	10	9	3	16	65	.155	.242	.225	40.37	9.94	161
Seymour, Ian	L-L	6-0	210	12-13-98	5	3	2.36	17	17	0	91	54	24	24	4	22	99	.171	.244	.253	28.29	6.29	350
Vernon, Austin	R-R	6-8	265	2-8-99	2	3	4.21	46	0	9	51	44	33	24	2	29	66	.232	.344	.374	28.82	12.66	229
Whitten, Kyle	R-R	6-3	190	9-22-98	4	1	3.98	15	0	1	20	21	12	9	2	6	17	.269	.321	.397	19.77	6.98	86
Wicklander, Patrick	R-L	6-1	205	12-31-99	2	2	4.60	23	0	0	45	32	23	23	4	28	37	.194	.320	.315	18.69	14.14	198
Wilcox, Cole	R-R	6-5	232	7-14-99	7	4	3.18	20	20	0	105	106	40	37	4	27	82	.266	.318	.343	18.89	6.22	434
Workman, Logan	R-R	6-4	215	12-6-98	10	5	2.71	24	23	0	123	99	42	37	10	33	112	.218	.276	.337	22.67	6.68	494
Zarraga, Alfredo	R-R	5-11	158	11-16-00	3	4	2.70	36	0	8	43	27	20	13	3	22	60	.173	.292	.244	32.43	11.89	185

Fielding

Catcher	PCT	G	PO	A	E	DP	PB
Ariza	1.000	2	12	0	0	0	0
Genoves	1.000	22	200	12	0	2	1
Keegan	.994	77	679	35	4	2	6
Piper	.986	37	323	26	5	2	4

First Base	PCT	G	PO	A	E	DP
Dyer	1.000	2	6	1	0	1
Etzel	1.000	3	17	0	0	0
Genoves	1.000	2	11	1	0	4
Isaac	.987	21	140	9	2	7
Morgan	1.000	12	75	6	0	9
Murray	1.000	3	28	2	0	3
Sandoval	.960	4	22	2	1	3
Schnell	.984	34	231	13	4	21
Seymour	.996	60	450	28	2	38

Second Base	PCT	G	PO	A	E	DP
Barreat	.923	3	2	10	1	2
Battles	.995	58	79	118	1	27
Murray	.983	54	94	141	4	27
Taylor	1.000	13	19	25	0	4
Turner	1.000	1	4	1	0	1
Vasquez	.907	10	19	20	4	5

Third Base	PCT	G	PO	A	E	DP
Battles	.893	12	3	22	3	0
Dyer	1.000	7	6	11	0	0
Murray	.955	32	32	52	4	8
Taylor	.943	16	19	31	3	5
Turner	1.000	1	1	1	0	0
Vasquez	.904	69	35	78	12	3

Shortstop	PCT	G	PO	A	E	DP
Battles	1.000	3	3	7	0	1
Murray	.953	17	27	34	3	8
Vasquez	.870	5	9	11	3	2
Williams	.979	113	145	278	9	48

Outfield	PCT	G	PO	A	E	DP
Auer	.978	78	170	7	4	3
Baker	1.000	105	225	10	0	3
Dyer	1.000	27	63	1	0	0
Etzel	1.000	29	55	0	0	0
Hernandez	.986	45	67	6	1	3
Isaac	1.000	2	5	0	0	0
Morgan	1.000	5	9	0	0	0
Schnell	.988	42	83	1	1	1
Simpson	.994	76	173	3	1	1
Turner	1.000	5	10	2	0	0

BOWLING GREEN HOT RODS — *HIGH-A*

SOUTH ATLANTIC LEAGUE

Batting	B-T	Ht.	Wt.	DOB	AVG	OBP	SLG	G	PA	AB	R	H	2B	3B	HR	RBI	BB	HBP	SH	SF	SO	SB	CS	BB%	SO%
Ariza, Luis	R-R	5-11	155	5-8-04	.000	.083	.000	3	12	11	1	0	0	0	0	0	1	0	0	0	5	0	0	8.33	41.67
Barreat, Elis	R-R	5-9	158	5-22-03	.273	.360	.500	7	25	22	5	6	0	1	1	5	3	0	0	0	5	0	1	12.00	20.00
Barrios, Gregory	R-R	6-0	180	4-8-04	.240	.310	.286	43	198	175	23	42	6	1	0	11	17	2	0	3	29	18	3	8.59	14.65
Broecker, Bryan	R-R	6-2	200	1-26-02	.200	.292	.200	7	24	20	3	4	0	0	0	1	3	0	0	1	9	2	0	12.50	37.50
Bush, Homer	R-R	6-3	200	10-13-01	.272	.367	.408	28	121	103	16	28	4	2	2	14	13	3	1	1	28	14	3	10.74	23.14
Cermak, Ryan	R-R	6-0	205	6-2-01	.200	.314	.303	45	185	155	23	31	3	2	3	17	21	6	0	3	61	12	0	11.35	32.97
Diaz, Jhon	L-L	5-7	160	10-1-02	.185	.270	.267	42	163	146	17	27	1	1	3	13	15	2	0	0	50	7	0	9.20	30.67
Galarraga, Angel	L-R	6-1	178	8-1-02	.229	.333	.257	17	45	35	4	8	1	0	0	2	5	1	2	1	9	0	0	11.11	20.00
Genoves, Ricardo	R-R	6-2	190	5-14-99	.265	.370	.425	37	135	113	18	30	9	0	3	13	16	4	0	2	38	2	0	11.85	28.15

Haas, Hunter	R-R	6-0	180	4-7-02	.193	.278	.301	108	416	362	36	70	17	2	6	41	36	9	3	6	110	11	4	8.65	26.44
Herron, Tyler	R-R	6-1	190	6-19-03	.000	.000	.000	1	3	3	0	0	0	0	0	0	0	0	0	0	2	0	0	0.00	66.67
Horvath, Mac	R-R	6-1	195	7-22-01	.221	.291	.381	31	127	113	21	25	4	1	4	18	11	1	0	2	44	9	1	8.66	34.65
Isaac, Xavier	L-L	6-3	240	12-17-03	.287	.381	.535	71	302	258	51	74	17	1	15	61	37	4	0	3	91	14	2	12.25	30.13
James, Kamren	R-R	6-2	205	5-25-00	.228	.305	.349	41	168	149	18	34	6	0	4	15	8	9	1	1	47	4	2	4.76	27.98
Jones, Brock	L-L	5-11	197	3-28-01	.224	.326	.445	94	377	326	56	73	19	1	17	49	44	6	0	1	142	32	4	11.67	37.67
Kinney, Cooper	L-R	6-1	200	1-27-03	.289	.352	.494	87	361	322	46	93	32	2	10	63	32	2	0	5	80	6	3	8.86	22.16
Ledbetter, Colton	L-R	6-2	205	11-15-01	.273	.339	.484	109	446	395	60	108	23	6	16	65	36	7	0	8	126	34	7	8.07	28.25
Levins, Tatem	L-R	6-0	206	5-29-99	.219	.321	.347	74	293	251	32	55	8	0	8	29	32	7	0	3	70	1	0	10.92	23.89
Martinez, Raudelis	L-R	6-0	180	5-30-02	.070	.167	.070	13	48	43	3	3	0	0	0	2	5	0	0	0	7	0	0	10.42	14.58
Morgan, Tre'	L-L	6-1	191	7-16-02	.371	.447	.558	53	231	197	41	73	17	1	6	44	26	3	0	2	18	10	1	11.26	7.79
Myers, Noah	L-R	6-1	190	11-11-99	.241	.326	.354	23	92	79	10	19	3	0	2	10	9	1	3	0	26	9	0	9.78	28.26
Paulino, Enzo	L-R	5-11	179	5-25-04	.091	.167	.091	4	12	11	0	1	0	0	0	0	1	0	0	0	3	0	0	8.33	25.00
Robertson, Blake	L-R	6-5	200	5-19-01	.131	.221	.197	18	68	61	5	8	2	1	0	3	5	2	0	0	28	1	0	7.35	41.18
Simpson, Chandler	L-R	6-2	170	11-18-00	.364	.431	.372	32	147	129	34	47	1	0	0	9	15	0	2	0	16	31	5	10.20	10.88
Spikes, Ryan	R-R	5-8	185	3-13-03	.219	.282	.337	93	343	306	39	67	11	2	7	26	23	6	3	5	102	14	4	6.71	29.74
Taylor, Brayden	L-R	6-1	180	5-22-02	.269	.389	.513	84	383	316	71	85	25	5	14	45	61	3	0	3	95	26	6	15.93	24.80
Turner, Gionti	R-R	6-2	178	8-17-00	.203	.289	.297	25	83	74	8	15	2	1	1	6	5	4	0	0	27	5	3	6.02	32.53

Pitching	B-T	Ht.	Wt.	DOB	W	L	ERA	G	GS	SV	IP	Hits	Runs	ER	HR	BB	SO	AVG	OBP	SLG	SO%	BB%	BF
Baumeister, Jackson	R-R	6-4	226	7-10-02	2	0	1.24	7	5	1	29	12	5	4	1	5	44	.122	.173	.173	41.90	4.76	105
Boucher, Adam	R-R	6-5	235	10-29-01	2	2	6.75	12	0	0	16	20	12	12	5	5	16	.299	.347	.582	22.22	6.94	72
Chavez, Seth	R-R	6-2	200	10-4-99	0	1	5.40	3	0	0	5	5	3	3	2	1	5	.250	.286	.550	23.81	4.76	21
Christianson, Jake	R-R	6-3	190	10-22-99	4	1	3.74	31	0	2	53	41	27	22	6	19	56	.206	.284	.337	24.89	8.44	225
Cook, Alex	R-R	6-2	220	3-29-01	2	2	1.69	8	8	0	37	27	9	7	2	12	38	.197	.267	.285	25.33	8.00	150
Cortorreal, Aneudy	R-R	6-3	200	12-13-99	0	0	3.72	7	0	1	10	6	4	4	3	6	12	.176	.317	.441	29.27	14.63	41
Cuevas, Jonny	R-R	6-3	200	11-19-00	4	2	3.19	25	1	4	42	41	27	15	6	19	37	.246	.323	.401	19.79	10.16	187
Curet, Yoniel	R-R	6-2	190	11-3-02	5	7	3.28	21	21	0	93	67	40	34	6	49	122	.198	.323	.295	30.35	12.19	402
Dahle, Nate	R-R	6-6	235	10-9-97	3	0	3.16	22	0	0	37	36	15	13	2	9	48	.240	.283	.347	30.19	5.66	159
Davitt, Duncan	R-R	6-3	235	9-23-99	5	6	2.94	16	16	0	86	66	29	28	8	23	85	.212	.275	.353	24.78	6.71	343
Edington, Derrick	R-R	6-8	210	7-22-99	3	1	5.92	20	0	3	24	24	19	16	5	9	27	.255	.336	.457	25.23	8.41	107
Fondtain, T.J.	L-L	6-4	210	2-22-01	4	2	3.38	32	4	1	61	43	25	23	11	13	67	.195	.242	.386	28.39	5.51	236
Gainey, Garrett	L-L	6-1	200	6-22-00	0	0	0.00	1	0	0	2	1	0	0	0	0	1	.167	.167	.333	16.67	0.00	6
Garcia, Roel	R-R	6-4	245	11-21-98	8	5	4.30	26	18	0	103	107	53	49	15	27	97	.264	.319	.447	22.10	6.15	439
Gaston, Sandy	R-R	6-3	200	12-16-01	0	2	9.00	10	0	0	11	10	11	11	0	17	11	.244	.475	.390	18.03	27.87	61
Genoves, Ricardo	R-R	6-2	190	5-14-99	1	0	9.00	1	0	0	1	1	2	1	1	0	0	.333	.250	1.333	0.00	0.00	4
Goss, JJ	R-R	6-3	185	12-25-00	2	0	2.35	17	0	3	23	20	8	6	0	10	28	.235	.316	.341	28.57	10.20	98
Hakanson, Jeff	R-R	6-0	185	8-4-98	1	2	5.33	21	0	1	25	18	16	15	5	15	20	.196	.330	.424	17.86	13.39	112
Harney, Sean	L-R	6-0	190	7-10-98	2	0	3.91	17	0	1	25	21	11	11	4	6	21	.233	.297	.400	20.59	5.88	102
Hartman, Jack	R-R	6-3	205	7-13-98	2	1	3.08	19	0	2	26	27	10	9	3	8	32	.270	.327	.410	28.83	7.21	111
Hopkins, Brody	R-R	6-4	200	1-18-02	1	3	3.45	7	7	0	31	21	13	12	1	13	38	.186	.290	.248	29.01	9.92	131
Johnson, Marcus	R-R	6-6	200	12-11-00	0	1	3.09	4	4	0	12	13	4	4	1	1	9	.295	.304	.409	19.57	2.17	46
Johnson, Ty	R-R	6-6	190	9-25-01	2	1	0.78	6	3	1	23	10	2	2	0	4	39	.133	.195	.160	46.43	4.76	84
Lancaster, Jackson	L-L	6-1	195	3-22-99	1	4	5.59	23	0	2	29	31	22	18	4	13	42	.261	.333	.420	31.11	9.63	135
Lesko, Dylan	R-R	6-2	195	9-7-03	1	3	9.42	6	3	0	14	8	15	15	2	23	21	.163	.446	.286	28.38	31.08	74
Martin, Trevor	R-R	6-5	238	12-15-00	5	2	2.88	14	14	0	72	60	28	23	5	19	88	.221	.279	.331	29.63	6.40	297
Murphy, Chandler	L-R	6-3	203	12-18-00	3	1	2.44	11	10	0	52	37	17	14	5	10	54	.197	.249	.319	26.21	4.85	206
Rosario, Gerlin	R-R	6-3	211	2-15-02	0	0	4.61	8	0	0	14	13	9	7	2	14	19	.255	.435	.392	27.54	20.29	69
Snyder, Jack	R-R	6-2	205	8-4-98	0	1	1.50	6	0	1	6	5	1	1	0	0	2	.238	.238	.286	9.52	0.00	21
Sommers, Drew	L-L	6-3	250	8-14-00	6	3	4.00	41	0	2	54	54	28	24	2	20	65	.256	.326	.327	27.90	8.58	233
Whitten, Kyle	R-R	6-3	190	9-22-98	0	0	2.25	3	0	0	4	4	1	1	1	0	5	.250	.250	.500	31.25	0.00	16
Wild, Owen	R-R	6-2	230	7-30-02	6	1	2.72	17	15	0	86	73	27	26	8	22	113	.224	.282	.362	31.92	6.21	354

Fielding

Catcher	PCT	G	PO	A	E	DP	PB
Ariza	1.000	3	26	7	0	0	1
Galarraga	.981	14	101	2	2	0	3
Genoves	.995	22	179	4	1	0	1
Herron	1.000	1	10	1	0	0	0
James	.990	29	278	17	3	1	6
Levins	.999	64	656	30	1	4	8
Martinez	1.000	3	22	1	0	0	0

First Base	PCT	G	PO	A	E	DP
Barreat	1.000	1	2	0	0	0
Broecker	1.000	6	40	3	0	2
Genoves	1.000	10	63	5	0	1
Isaac	.995	60	405	18	2	23
James	1.000	7	36	3	0	2
Kinney	1.000	9	64	1	0	3
Martinez	.979	9	44	2	1	5
Morgan	.993	22	131	8	1	13
Paulino	1.000	3	15	2	0	1
Robertson	1.000	7	42	5	0	2
Turner	1.000	1	5	0	0	0

Second Base	PCT	G	PO	A	E	DP
Barreat	.889	5	8	8	2	1
Haas	.976	44	43	81	3	17
Horvath	.857	2	3	3	1	0
Kinney	.994	53	73	105	1	19
Martinez	1.000	1	0	1	0	0
Spikes	.942	14	19	30	3	6
Taylor	1.000	6	5	16	0	2
Turner	1.000	8	10	10	0	3

Third Base	PCT	G	PO	A	E	DP
Barreat	1.000	1	0	1	0	0
Haas	.939	19	14	32	3	4
Horvath	.980	24	18	30	1	3
Kinney	.978	17	12	32	1	0
Spikes	.914	29	22	42	6	5
Taylor	.908	32	34	45	8	6
Turner	1.000	10	5	11	0	1

Shortstop	PCT	G	PO	A	E	DP
Barrios	.957	43	48	86	6	14
Haas	.923	46	40	92	11	11
Taylor	.958	41	53	85	6	11

Outfield	PCT	G	PO	A	E	DP
Bush	1.000	27	56	1	0	0
Cermak	.990	41	96	4	1	1
Diaz	.934	34	54	3	4	0
Horvath	1.000	2	7	0	0	0
Jones	1.000	71	126	4	0	1
Ledbetter	.985	96	192	2	3	1
Morgan	1.000	5	5	0	0	0
Myers	1.000	21	34	1	0	0
Paulino	1.000	2	4	0	0	0
Robertson	.857	5	6	0	1	0
Simpson	.973	32	71	1	2	0
Spikes	1.000	50	91	2	0	0
Turner	1.000	6	8	1	0	0

CHARLESTON RIVERDOGS

LOW-A

CAROLINA LEAGUE

Batting	B-T	Ht.	Wt.	DOB	AVG	OBP	SLG	G	PA	AB	R	H	2B	3B	HR	RBI	BB	HBP	SH	SF	SO	SB	CS	BB%	SO%
Barete, Cristopher	L-L	5-7	155	12-10-01	.185	.255	.239	28	104	92	9	17	3	1	0	9	9	0	2	1	22	9	1	8.65	21.15
Barreat, Elis	R-R	5-9	158	5-22-03	.213	.250	.246	18	64	61	3	13	2	0	0	4	2	1	0	0	15	2	2	3.13	23.44
Broecker, Bryan	R-R	6-2	200	1-26-02	.176	.341	.211	47	180	142	14	25	5	0	0	11	32	4	1	1	51	9	2	17.78	28.33
Colmenarez, Carlos	L-R	5-9	170	11-15-03	.202	.337	.256	94	368	297	35	60	7	3	1	42	54	9	1	5	108	15	8	14.67	29.35
Delgado, Enderson	B-R	5-11	184	9-21-04	.255	.382	.391	56	235	192	27	49	14	0	4	21	28	12	2	1	54	1	1	11.91	22.98
Diaz, Jhon	L-L	5-7	160	10-1-02	.219	.283	.401	65	269	242	34	53	7	2	11	37	21	2	0	4	60	23	7	7.81	22.30
Gillen, Theo	L-R	6-2	195	9-12-05	.154	.353	.192	8	34	26	4	4	1	0	0	2	8	0	0	0	14	1	0	23.53	41.18
Gonzalez, JD	L-R	5-11	165	10-3-05	.074	.148	.136	24	89	81	7	6	2	0	1	2	7	0	1	0	40	1	0	7.87	44.94
Gonzalez, Ricardo	B-R	5-11	186	7-6-04	.203	.296	.247	95	364	316	24	64	11	0	1	37	39	4	2	3	75	18	3	10.71	20.60
Hujsak, Connor	R-R	6-2	200	1-25-02	.277	.326	.518	21	89	83	14	23	6	1	4	21	6	0	0	0	21	5	0	6.74	23.60
Marget, Brady	L-R	6-5	195	9-15-02	.250	.404	.333	12	47	36	6	9	0	0	1	5	9	1	0	1	6	1	0	19.15	12.77
Martinez, Raudelis	L-R	6-0	180	5-30-02	.224	.298	.323	77	303	263	36	59	11	3	3	39	27	4	1	8	43	10	1	8.91	14.19
Mateo, Angel	R-R	6-2	190	2-13-05	.224	.323	.344	101	409	352	46	79	24	0	6	40	43	10	0	4	104	26	6	10.51	25.43
Morgan, Tre'	L-L	6-1	191	7-16-02	.320	.398	.440	26	115	100	19	32	4	1	2	11	10	3	0	0	13	9	5	8.70	11.30
Myers, Noah	L-R	6-1	190	11-11-99	.279	.447	.399	62	244	183	38	51	11	1	3	22	56	2	0	3	54	24	5	22.95	22.13
Paulino, Enzo	L-R	5-11	179	5-25-04	.209	.262	.306	38	145	134	11	28	8	1	1	14	8	2	0	1	39	0	2	5.52	26.90
Peguero, Odalys	B-R	5-9	172	1-25-03	.167	.293	.196	78	294	245	25	41	7	0	0	18	41	3	4	1	67	25	0	13.95	22.79
Perez, Jose	R-R	5-9	170	3-12-04	.231	.405	.262	26	85	65	7	15	2	0	0	6	18	1	1	0	14	2	1	21.18	16.47
Pitre, Emilien	L-R	5-11	160	10-4-02	.299	.402	.403	21	92	77	14	23	6	1	0	14	12	2	0	1	11	7	2	13.04	11.96
Polanco, Narciso	L-R	5-10	161	10-28-04	.226	.324	.336	97	415	354	47	80	20	2	5	31	50	3	2	3	95	26	7	12.05	22.89
Robertson, Blake	L-R	6-5	200	5-19-01	.300	.393	.486	20	84	70	13	21	4	0	3	11	11	1	0	2	21	5	0	13.10	25.00
Sandoval, Joshuan	R-R	6-2	215	12-18-97	.143	.217	.286	10	23	21	1	3	0	0	1	3	1	1	0	0	10	0	1	4.35	43.48
Santana, Adrian	B-R	5-11	155	7-18-05	.240	.300	.305	103	455	417	55	100	21	3	0	35	34	2	1	1	72	51	9	7.47	15.82
Shin, Wooyeoul	R-R	6-0	215	12-30-01	.212	.352	.326	58	236	193	36	41	6	2	4	18	36	6	0	1	59	22	2	15.25	25.00
Smith, Aidan	R-R	6-3	190	7-23-04	.306	.395	.486	20	86	72	17	22	7	0	2	11	12	0	0	2	16	13	1	13.95	18.60

Pitching	B-T	Ht.	Wt.	DOB	W	L	ERA	G	GS	SV	IP	Hits	Runs	ER	HR	BB	SO	AVG	OBP	SLG	SO%	BB%	BF
Alberto, Alexander	R-R	6-8	190	11-2-01	1	1	1.59	16	0	5	23	13	5	4	0	10	21	.173	.292	.200	23.33	11.11	90
Barreat, Elis	R-R	5-9	158	5-22-03	0	0	0.00	1	0	0	0	0	0	0	0	1	0	.000	.500	.000	0.00	50.00	2
Boucher, Adam	R-R	6-5	235	10-29-01	5	3	3.57	24	0	3	40	33	19	16	3	17	55	.223	.307	.318	32.74	10.12	168
Canizalez, Joel	R-R	6-1	185	9-22-02	0	0	6.00	1	0	0	3	2	2	2	0	5	1	.222	.467	.222	6.67	33.33	15
Chavez, Seth	R-R	6-2	200	10-4-99	1	5	2.81	29	0	3	42	34	18	13	2	13	44	.224	.301	.329	25.43	7.51	173
De Jesus, Cesar	L-L	6-1	140	9-28-03	0	2	25.41	6	0	0	6	12	16	16	0	10	6	.414	.564	.724	15.38	25.64	39
De La Rosa, Manuel	L-L	6-0	155	4-19-03	0	0	27.00	2	0	0	2	5	7	7	0	6	2	.417	.650	.583	10.00	30.00	20
Dowd, Drew	L-L	6-1	190	1-3-02	7	6	2.85	22	19	0	111	91	41	35	6	45	99	.230	.319	.336	21.81	9.91	454
Edwards, Garrett	R-R	6-5	195	1-3-02	0	0	4.76	3	3	0	6	8	3	3	1	2	7	.333	.385	.667	26.92	7.69	26
Fowler, Dalton	L-L	6-7	200	1-7-00	2	4	4.84	34	1	1	45	35	38	24	3	33	55	.202	.337	.324	26.44	15.87	208
Garcia, Engert	R-R	5-11	190	4-30-00	3	5	3.74	19	6	1	53	47	26	22	1	33	50	.240	.358	.296	21.55	14.22	232
Gill Hill, Gary	R-R	6-2	160	9-19-04	4	4	3.15	22	21	0	109	94	39	38	9	27	105	.235	.287	.345	24.25	6.24	433
Halemanu, Cade	R-R	6-4	215	8-9-00	2	2	11.48	11	0	0	13	19	18	17	3	8	15	.311	.403	.525	20.83	11.11	72
Harrison, Trevor	R-R	6-4	225	8-8-05	2	0	3.15	9	9	0	40	32	15	14	2	18	48	.221	.311	.338	29.27	10.98	164
Hernandez, Luis	R-R	6-4	195	4-1-01	7	1	4.08	17	0	0	35	28	20	16	6	25	47	.219	.355	.383	30.13	16.03	156
Lindsey, Andrew	R-R	6-3	216	11-15-99	1	1	3.38	2	1	0	8	5	3	3	1	6	9	.179	.324	.286	25.71	17.14	35
Mejia, Samuel	R-R	6-1	160	6-17-02	4	2	5.98	33	0	5	53	57	38	35	7	20	61	.270	.340	.469	25.96	8.51	235
Murphy, Chandler	L-R	6-3	203	12-18-00	1	2	2.66	12	9	0	41	29	12	12	0	13	36	.199	.278	.226	22.09	7.98	163
Nichols, T.J.	R-R	6-5	189	6-24-02	4	6	2.90	18	14	0	71	64	24	23	3	22	66	.246	.303	.342	22.92	7.64	288
Pilon, Jeremy	L-L	6-0	185	9-11-05	1	0	3.21	4	3	0	14	7	6	5	0	14	22	.149	.339	.191	35.48	22.58	62
Rodriguez, Andy	R-R	6-1	182	7-28-02	2	0	1.06	9	0	2	17	5	2	2	0	6	15	.094	.200	.113	25.00	10.00	60
Rosario, Gerlin	R-R	6-3	211	2-15-02	3	1	2.52	26	1	8	50	32	16	14	3	15	65	.179	.244	.263	32.99	7.61	197
Rumbol, Jonalbert	R-R	5-9	170	11-11-98	1	4	3.60	24	0	2	40	38	21	16	1	20	35	.260	.366	.336	20.00	11.43	175
Sandoval, Joshuan	R-R	6-2	215	12-18-97	0	0	0.00	2	0	0	2	0	0	0	0	1	0	.000	.167	.000	0.00	16.67	6
Snelsire, Hayden	R-R	6-1	213	1-16-01	1	2	2.27	21	1	3	44	35	17	11	4	23	48	.213	.310	.341	25.53	12.23	188
Stevens, Will	R-R	6-2	210	7-18-01	2	3	6.34	29	0	3	33	32	28	23	1	38	31	.252	.441	.323	18.02	22.09	172
Stevenson, Owen	R-R	6-4	205	9-1-02	1	0	7.71	9	0	0	14	14	12	12	1	12	12	.259	.394	.426	18.18	18.18	66
Suarez, Santiago	R-R	6-2	175	1-11-05	7	6	4.11	23	23	0	112	103	55	51	12	21	115	.243	.281	.371	25.67	4.69	448
Urbina, Jose	R-R	6-3	180	11-2-05	0	0	5.29	4	4	0	17	14	10	10	4	4	12	.230	.288	.475	18.18	6.06	66
Villaman, Chris	L-L	6-2	217	3-16-01	6	1	2.03	13	8	0	49	34	11	11	2	7	57	.199	.235	.298	31.67	3.89	180
Wild, Owen	R-R	6-2	230	7-30-02	1	0	3.06	7	7	0	35	35	12	12	3	9	38	.263	.308	.444	26.57	6.29	143

Fielding

Catcher	PCT	G	PO	A	E	DP	PB
Broecker	1.000	31	274	38	0	2	2
Delgado	.988	41	380	28	5	3	5
Gonzalez	.994	18	163	14	1	0	0
Martinez	.983	36	324	25	6	2	5
Perez	1.000	1	2	0	0	0	0
Sandoval	.977	5	37	6	1	1	0

First Base	PCT	G	PO	A	E	DP
Broecker	1.000	2	8	0	0	1
Delgado	1.000	4	30	5	0	2
Marget	1.000	11	78	1	0	11
Martinez	.989	26	169	10	2	12
Morgan	.994	20	152	13	1	13
Paulino	.980	23	138	7	3	15
Perez	.980	6	49	1	1	2
Robertson	.990	12	95	8	1	6
Shin	.992	30	223	24	2	27

Second Base	PCT	G	PO	A	E	DP
Barreat	1.000	3	4	6	0	0
Colmenarez	.945	43	84	89	10	22
Gonzalez	.991	26	48	65	1	17
Peguero	.974	14	12	26	1	5
Perez	1.000	2	2	1	0	0
Pitre	.986	17	38	33	1	13
Polanco	.969	30	43	80	4	11

Third Base	PCT	G	PO	A	E	DP
Barreat	1.000	4	1	1	0	0
Colmenarez	.873	37	21	41	9	6
Gonzalez	.960	21	17	31	2	4
Peguero	.944	18	16	35	3	4
Perez	1.000	7	3	11	0	1
Polanco	1.000	45	27	75	0	5

Shortstop	PCT	G	PO	A	E	DP
Colmenarez	.857	3	2	4	1	1

	PCT	G	PO	A	E	DP
Gonzalez	.974	36	49	101	4	12
Polanco	.947	9	10	26	2	6
Santana	.968	84	104	198	10	40

Outfield	PCT	G	PO	A	E	DP
Barete	.922	29	41	6	4	0
Barreat	.938	10	15	0	1	0
Broecker	1.000	4	4	0	0	0
Diaz	.963	63	122	8	5	0
Gillen	1.000	7	24	0	0	0
Hujsak	1.000	18	30	0	0	0
Mateo	.973	94	169	9	5	0
Morgan	1.000	6	12	1	0	1
Myers	.991	59	109	3	1	1
Paulino	.964	15	25	2	1	0
Peguero	.953	46	55	6	3	0
Perez	1.000	10	18	1	0	1
Robertson	.929	8	13	0	1	0
Shin	.972	21	33	2	1	0
Smith	1.000	17	32	0	0	0

FCL RAYS — ROOKIE

FLORIDA COMPLEX LEAGUE

Batting	B-T	Ht.	Wt.	DOB	AVG	OBP	SLG	G	PA	AB	R	H	2B	3B	HR	RBI	BB	HBP	SH	SF	SO	SB	CS	BB%	SO%
Ariza, Luis	R-R	5-11	155	5-8-04	.217	.314	.367	21	70	60	7	13	4	1	1	9	9	0	0	1	15	1	0	12.86	21.43
Auer, Mason	R-R	6-1	210	3-1-01	.143	.400	.143	2	10	7	4	1	0	0	0	0	3	0	0	0	1	4	0	30.00	10.00
Aybar, Nicandro	B-R	6-1	170	9-8-04	.271	.361	.350	51	205	177	29	48	8	3	0	29	24	1	3	0	28	13	5	11.71	13.66
Basabe, Osleivis	R-R	5-11	188	9-13-00	.270	.404	.541	12	47	37	8	10	0	2	2	8	9	0	0	1	1	2	2	19.15	2.13
Caminero, Junior	R-R	6-1	157	7-5-03	.235	.409	.824	6	22	17	4	4	1	0	3	5	5	0	0	0	2	0	0	22.73	9.09
Cermak, Ryan	R-R	6-0	205	6-2-01	.300	.517	.600	7	29	20	9	6	3	0	1	3	7	2	0	0	6	3	1	24.14	20.69
Contreras, Jose	R-R	6-1	200	5-5-05	.250	.349	.388	50	187	160	29	40	10	3	2	33	18	7	1	1	40	6	4	9.63	21.39
Cotes, Felix	B-R	5-11	176	8-13-05	.269	.321	.308	7	29	26	3	7	1	0	0	2	2	0	1	0	5	2	0	6.90	17.24
Delgado, Enderson	B-R	5-11	184	9-21-04	.286	.382	.464	9	34	28	0	8	3	1	0	9	4	1	0	1	5	0	0	11.76	14.71
Driscoll, Logan	L-R	5-10	195	11-3-97	.143	.143	.286	2	7	7	1	1	1	0	0	0	0	0	0	0	1	0	0	0.00	14.29
Garcia, Yirer	R-R	5-11	165	9-18-05	.239	.368	.303	48	192	155	35	37	7	0	1	16	27	6	1	2	25	4	2	14.06	13.02
Guerrero, Brailer	L-R	6-1	215	6-25-06	.330	.452	.466	28	126	103	17	34	4	2	2	18	22	1	0	0	32	13	3	17.46	25.40
James, Kamren	R-R	6-2	205	5-25-00	.556	.692	.889	3	13	9	3	5	0	0	1	2	4	0	0	0	1	0	0	30.77	7.69
Lara, Erick	L-R	6-2	165	6-10-06	.167	.290	.222	33	132	108	14	18	4	1	0	13	20	0	1	3	30	5	2	15.15	22.73
Levins, Tatem	L-R	6-0	206	5-29-99	.222	.200	.556	2	10	9	2	2	0	0	1	3	0	0	0	1	2	0	0	0.00	20.00
Martinez, Larry	R-R	5-11	170	8-6-05	.295	.398	.369	44	176	149	25	44	7	2	0	24	16	10	0	1	10	3	1	9.09	5.68
Monzon, Jose	L-R	6-0	160	11-17-05	.253	.369	.332	54	225	190	36	48	8	2	1	18	34	1	0	0	38	11	5	15.11	16.89
Myers, Noah	L-R	6-1	190	11-11-99	.417	.462	.583	3	13	12	4	5	2	0	0	2	1	0	0	0	3	4	0	7.69	23.08
Paulino, Enzo	L-R	5-11	179	5-25-04	.358	.404	.679	13	57	53	14	19	3	1	4	15	4	0	0	0	9	2	2	7.02	15.79
Peguero, Juanfel	B-R	5-11	142	12-31-04	.225	.365	.248	46	161	129	26	29	3	0	0	23	27	2	2	1	41	7	8	16.77	25.47
Perez, Jose	R-R	5-9	170	3-12-04	.295	.464	.476	41	138	105	31	31	7	3	2	20	29	4	0	0	22	3	0	21.01	15.94
Sanabria, Jose	R-R	6-1	180	2-10-05	.167	.295	.246	37	139	114	24	19	4	1	1	14	18	4	0	3	36	9	1	12.95	25.90
Suarez, Wilson	B-R	5-11	183	6-17-05	.375	.375	.375	4	8	8	1	3	0	0	0	3	0	0	0	0	0	0	0	0.00	0.00
Tamares, Miguel	B-R	5-10	150	9-6-04	.202	.369	.250	41	157	124	21	25	2	2	0	16	28	5	0	0	42	14	3	17.83	26.75
Walls, Taylor	B-R	5-10	185	7-10-96	.118	.250	.294	5	20	17	2	2	0	0	1	1	2	1	0	0	2	1	0	10.00	10.00

Pitching	B-T	Ht.	Wt.	DOB	W	L	ERA	G	GS	SV	IP	Hits	Runs	ER	HR	BB	SO	AVG	OBP	SLG	SO%	BB%	BF
Alberto, Alexander	R-R	6-8	190	11-2-01	0	1	4.91	8	0	0	11	11	10	6	0	9	16	.262	.385	.405	30.19	16.98	53
Bitsko, Nick	R-R	6-4	225	6-16-02	0	0	38.57	4	1	0	2	5	10	10	1	8	3	.417	.650	.750	15.00	40.00	20
Canizalez, Joel	R-R	6-1	185	9-22-02	4	1	2.61	12	3	0	38	31	13	11	2	15	21	.221	.314	.314	13.21	9.43	159
De Jesus, Cesar	L-L	6-1	140	9-28-03	0	0	2.84	4	0	0	6	5	4	2	1	3	8	.200	.286	.400	28.57	10.71	28
De La Rosa, Manuel	L-L	6-0	155	4-19-03	1	1	4.61	9	0	0	14	7	9	7	0	12	12	.156	.387	.156	19.35	19.35	62
Dryer, Conor	L-R	6-3	205	8-18-98	0	0	2.70	13	1	0	17	8	5	5	0	8	18	.140	.279	.140	26.47	11.76	68
Edington, Derrick	R-R	6-8	210	7-22-99	1	0	0.00	3	0	0	4	3	0	0	0	2	5	.200	.294	.200	29.41	11.76	17
Edwards, Garrett	R-R	6-5	195	1-3-02	0	0	1.23	4	3	0	7	5	1	1	0	2	7	.185	.241	.259	24.14	6.90	29
Florian, Renaldito	R-R	5-11	161	3-26-02	1	1	6.10	13	0	0	21	22	15	14	2	13	20	.278	.368	.392	21.05	13.68	95
Halemanu, Cade	R-R	6-4	215	8-9-00	1	0	6.75	5	1	0	5	5	9	4	1	7	4	.250	.429	.400	14.29	25.00	28
Harney, Sean	L-R	6-0	190	7-10-98	0	0	4.26	4	3	0	6	8	4	3	0	5	8	.333	.433	.375	26.67	16.67	30
Harrison, Trevor	R-R	6-4	225	8-8-05	2	2	3.58	8	7	0	33	32	13	13	3	8	39	.262	.303	.402	29.55	6.06	132
Hartman, Jack	R-R	6-3	205	7-13-98	0	0	0.00	1	0	0	1	0	0	0	0	1	2	.000	.250	.000	50.00	25.00	4
Hernandez, Luis	R-R	6-4	195	4-1-01	1	0	0.00	3	0	0	7	4	3	0	1	1	5	.167	.200	.333	19.23	3.85	26
Hernandez, Maikel	R-R	6-1	184	6-8-05	4	0	1.48	17	0	3	30	19	7	5	1	8	17	.176	.244	.287	14.29	6.72	119
Johnson, Marcus	R-R	6-6	200	12-11-00	0	0	0.00	3	2	0	5	1	0	0	0	2	4	.071	.188	.071	25.00	12.50	16
Lancaster, Jackson	L-L	6-1	195	3-22-99	1	2	7.20	4	1	0	5	6	4	4	1	0	6	.333	.300	.722	30.00	0.00	20
Lovelady, Richard	L-L	6-0	185	7-7-95	0	0	54.00	1	1	0	1	3	4	4	0	1	1	.600	.667	.600	16.67	16.67	6
Mall, Dalton	R-R	6-3	225	8-27-99	0	0	0.00	1	0	0	0	1	3	3	0	2	0	1.000	1.000	1.000	0.00	50.00	4
Medina, Roberto	L-L	6-1	170	1-19-05	6	0	4.18	11	2	1	28	19	14	13	2	19	33	.192	.333	.343	27.27	15.70	121
Pilon, Jeremy	L-L	6-0	185	9-11-05	2	2	3.28	12	9	0	47	32	21	17	3	32	61	.196	.337	.325	30.65	16.08	199
Rodriguez, Andy	R-R	6-1	182	7-28-02	3	2	4.03	20	0	4	22	15	11	10	5	10	25	.183	.280	.390	26.60	10.64	94
Rumbol, Jonalbert	R-R	5-9	170	11-11-98	1	0	0.00	2	0	0	3	0	0	0	0	0	1	.000	.000	.000	11.11	0.00	9
Russell, Jonathan	R-R	6-1	180	3-14-05	0	4	6.89	12	6	0	31	37	25	24	1	19	31	.298	.408	.379	20.95	12.84	148
Sanchez, Ramon	R-R	6-3	160	11-14-01	1	1	6.23	14	0	3	13	15	11	9	0	6	11	.283	.371	.415	17.74	9.68	62
Saturria, Michael	R-R	6-4	190	9-1-02	4	2	2.76	17	0	2	29	28	13	9	0	15	36	.237	.328	.356	26.47	11.03	136
Snelsire, Hayden	R-R	6-1	213	1-16-01	0	0	0.00	2	1	0	2	1	0	0	0	2	2	.167	.375	.167	25.00	25.00	8
Snyder, Jack	R-R	6-2	205	8-4-98	0	0	0.00	1	1	0	1	1	0	0	0	1	1	.333	.500	.333	25.00	25.00	4
Springs, Jeffrey	L-L	6-3	218	9-19-92	0	0	4.50	3	3	0	2	5	1	1	0	1	5	.455	.500	.545	41.67	8.33	12
Stevenson, Owen	R-R	6-4	205	9-1-02	0	0	9.00	1	0	0	1	2	3	1	1	0	0	.400	.333	1.400	0.00	0.00	6
Urbina, Jose	R-R	6-3	180	11-2-05	1	3	4.50	13	8	0	48	37	26	24	4	25	45	.208	.314	.331	21.74	12.08	207
Valdez, Alexis	R-R	6-3	194	6-2-05	1	1	8.53	11	0	0	13	14	12	12	1	16	13	.280	.455	.400	19.70	24.24	66
Ventura, Wander	R-R	6-2	170	2-26-03	0	0	5.10	12	5	0	30	31	22	17	2	20	23	.265	.381	.410	16.55	14.39	139
Waguespack, Jacob	R-R	6-6	235	11-5-93	0	0	0.00	1	1	0	1	0	0	0	0	0	3	.000	.000	.000	75.00	0.00	4

Fielding

C: Garcia 30, Martinez 16, Delgado 6, Ariza 5, Driscoll 2, James 2, Levins 2, Suarez 1. **1B:** Martinez 20, Ariza 14, Garcia 11, Paulino 9, Perez 6, Suarez 2, Delgado 1. **2B:** Peguero 20, Perez 12, Aybar 12, Monzon 9, Cotes 4, Lara 3, Basabe 3, Caminero 1, Sanabria 1. **3B:** Monzon 19, Aybar 13, Lara 10, Perez 10, Peguero 9, Caminero 4. **SS:** Monzon 26, Peguero 14, Lara 14, Basabe 5, Walls 5, Aybar 1. **LF:** Sanabria 17, Contreras 15, Aybar 13, Perez 10, Tamares 5, Paulino 2. **CF:** Tamares 24, Guerrero 12, Aybar 11, Sanabria 8, Contreras 4, Cermak 2, Myers 2, Monzon 1, Auer 1. **RF:** Contreras 26, Guerrero 13, Sanabria 10, Tamares 9, Perez 2, Cermak 2.

DSL RAYS — ROOKIE

DOMINICAN SUMMER LEAGUE

Batting	B-T	Ht.	Wt.	DOB	AVG	OBP	SLG	G	PA	AB	R	H	2B	3B	HR	RBI	BB	HBP	SH	SF	SO	SB	CS	BB%	SO%
Acevedo, Eduardo	L-L	5-10	170	9-25-05	.234	.349	.328	35	152	128	19	30	4	4	0	10	18	5	0	1	24	9	7	11.84	15.79
Brachi, Angel	R-R	5-10	165	1-5-07	.247	.348	.276	47	206	174	27	43	3	1	0	12	12	16	2	2	31	18	8	5.83	15.05
Chauran, Kleiver	B-R	5-11	165	11-23-05	.221	.373	.343	45	177	140	23	31	8	3	1	29	31	4	0	2	43	4	1	17.51	24.29
Frias, Alan	R-R	6-2	206	10-26-05	.600	.750	1.400	3	8	5	3	3	1	0	1	1	3	0	0	0	2	0	0	37.50	25.00
Galan, Emiliano	R-R	6-1	205	11-11-06	.252	.314	.351	34	121	111	16	28	2	0	3	16	9	1	0	0	17	5	0	7.44	14.05
Gonzalez, Deinys	R-R	5-9	178	1-24-07	.203	.348	.322	46	178	143	25	29	8	0	3	18	19	14	0	2	37	6	2	10.67	20.79
Guillen, Xavier	B-R	5-10	167	9-2-04	.308	.471	.308	5	18	13	3	4	0	0	0	1	3	1	1	0	3	2	2	16.67	16.67
Lugo, Erick	R-R	6-0	165	9-15-06	.318	.423	.409	16	52	44	7	14	4	0	0	3	6	2	0	0	15	1	0	11.54	28.85
Marin, Jahir	R-R	5-10	169	1-11-07	.000	.412	.000	6	18	10	3	0	0	0	0	0	7	0	1	0	7	0	1	38.89	38.89
Martinez, Alfonzo	R-R	6-0	180	11-28-05	.273	.333	.455	3	12	11	2	3	0	1	0	1	1	0	0	0	2	1	0	8.33	16.67
Matias, Carlos	R-R	6-2	195	11-10-06	.247	.331	.370	42	166	146	17	36	7	1	3	22	15	4	0	1	37	7	0	9.04	22.29
Pinero, Aaron	R-R	5-9	180	5-15-07	.234	.335	.276	43	167	145	18	34	6	0	0	11	17	5	0	0	29	5	1	10.18	17.37
Santana, Jean	R-R	5-11	180	10-22-06	.156	.324	.202	40	138	109	11	17	3	1	0	12	24	3	2	0	33	5	3	17.39	23.91
Santana, John	L-R	6-3	176	9-24-05	.246	.296	.316	30	125	114	15	28	1	2	1	16	7	2	0	2	32	4	2	5.60	25.60
Tapia, Roosbert	R-R	6-2	177	6-23-05	.261	.341	.344	46	179	157	21	41	3	2	2	13	16	4	0	2	20	8	4	8.94	11.17
Tea, Railin	B-R	5-9	162	7-19-06	.196	.354	.290	43	176	138	34	27	6	2	1	17	23	12	1	2	31	19	3	13.07	17.61
Tovar, Jose	R-R	5-10	168	11-23-05	.288	.400	.374	42	170	139	19	40	10	1	0	20	22	6	0	3	25	3	1	12.94	14.71

Pitching	B-T	Ht.	Wt.	DOB	W	L	ERA	G	GS	SV	IP	Hits	Runs	ER	HR	BB	SO	AVG	OBP	SLG	SO%	BB%	BF
Alcala, Damian	R-R	6-1	164	6-10-05	2	1	4.42	10	0	0	18	21	13	9	0	10	11	.292	.369	.403	13.10	11.90	84
Aranguren, Jhonny	R-R	6-1	184	10-24-06	1	3	6.00	8	1	0	12	14	12	8	0	5	15	.269	.350	.308	25.00	8.33	60
Cabrera, Baldemix	R-R	6-2	191	3-28-03	0	2	2.93	4	4	0	15	12	6	5	1	5	16	.222	.311	.278	25.81	8.06	62
Campos, Alexander	R-R	6-1	190	4-14-03	2	4	3.43	14	12	0	60	59	29	23	5	9	43	.255	.280	.403	17.34	3.63	248
Castro, Cesar	R-R	6-1	205	7-14-05	1	1	5.54	8	0	0	13	13	11	8	0	6	11	.255	.328	.333	18.97	10.34	58
Chessman, Frank	R-R	5-11	170	5-8-07	1	2	5.26	16	0	1	26	25	20	15	2	19	20	.260	.392	.385	16.67	15.83	120
Clemente, Jharold	R-R	5-10	200	8-5-02	3	1	4.14	14	11	0	54	50	26	25	5	12	52	.244	.304	.376	23.11	5.33	225
Cruz, Ransel	R-R	6-2	144	9-17-05	0	1	7.71	9	6	0	19	16	19	16	2	11	16	.229	.349	.371	19.05	13.10	84
Gamez, Alvaro	L-L	6-3	175	2-19-05	1	5	5.97	14	3	0	35	29	28	23	2	26	30	.230	.368	.317	19.35	16.77	155
Hilario, Danny	R-R	6-0	185	9-17-04	2	1	3.65	15	0	3	25	26	12	10	0	14	29	.265	.351	.378	25.44	12.28	114
Infante, Jordi	R-R	6-3	193	10-10-04	2	1	7.36	15	0	2	26	33	23	21	0	19	27	.324	.425	.412	21.09	14.84	128
Jimenez, Jhomber	R-R	6-3	198	12-24-05	2	3	12.86	10	1	0	14	13	20	20	0	28	15	.255	.536	.373	17.86	33.33	84
Leal, Antawn	R-R	6-0	175	9-24-06	0	0	4.91	4	1	0	4	1	2	2	0	3	1	.111	.385	.111	7.69	23.08	13
Lugo, Yannelbinson	R-R	6-0	166	1-13-04	1	2	11.08	8	6	0	13	21	18	16	1	13	2	.382	.500	.655	2.82	18.31	71
Mesa, Yolvin	R-R	6-1	160	9-5-05	1	0	5.00	16	1	2	27	25	22	15	0	11	25	.240	.341	.288	19.84	8.73	126
Palma, Moises	R-R	6-4	195	9-1-04	2	2	3.71	17	0	4	27	24	15	11	0	12	24	.233	.333	.340	19.83	9.92	121
Pateti, Samuel	R-R	6-1	186	10-2-06	3	1	3.55	13	0	1	25	19	16	10	0	12	22	.202	.290	.266	20.56	11.21	107
Ramirez, Ricardo	R-R	6-3	204	9-30-05	0	0	9.64	4	3	0	9	8	10	10	1	11	13	.242	.444	.485	28.89	24.44	45
Savinon, Starlin	L-L	6-0	182	10-30-04	0	2	5.84	9	5	0	25	28	16	16	1	10	15	.308	.369	.396	14.56	9.71	103
Silgado, Yeison	R-R	5-11	160	10-28-04	0	0	5.93	10	2	1	14	11	9	9	0	12	11	.224	.371	.306	17.74	19.35	62
Tamayo, Jean	R-R	6-0	169	1-25-07	0	0	4.50	1	0	0	2	1	1	1	0	1	1	.200	.286	.600	14.29	14.29	7

Fielding

C: Tovar 27, Gonzalez 22, Lugo 9, Marin 3. **1B:** Tapia 40, Gonzalez 11, Tovar 4, Lugo 3. **2B:** Santana 23, Chauran 13, Pinero 13, Brachi 11. **3B:** Santana 18, Pinero 16, Chauran 14, Brachi 10, Tapia 2. **SS:** Brachi 26, Chauran 18, Pinero 14. **LF:** Tea 25, Galan 16, Matias 8, Santana 3, Acevedo 3, Guillen 1, Martinez 1. **CF:** Tea 17, Santana 15, Matias 14, Acevedo 11. **RF:** Galan 16, Matias 15, Acevedo 13, Santana 7, Guillen 4, Martinez 2, Frias 1.

DSL TAMPA BAY — ROOKIE

DOMINICAN SUMMER LEAGUE

Batting	B-T	Ht.	Wt.	DOB	AVG	OBP	SLG	G	PA	AB	R	H	2B	3B	HR	RBI	BB	HBP	SH	SF	SO	SB	CS	BB%	SO%
Batista, Domingo	L-R	6-1	170	2-8-07	.296	.434	.400	38	159	125	22	37	5	1	2	28	29	3	0	2	40	4	2	18.24	25.16
Bautista, Israfell	B-R	6-2	155	10-13-06	.277	.347	.311	40	168	148	40	41	3	1	0	14	15	2	1	2	32	39	5	8.93	19.05
Blanco, Carlos	L-R	6-0	175	1-23-04	.125	.288	.167	21	59	48	7	6	2	0	0	7	7	4	0	0	13	0	0	11.86	22.03
De Sousa, Carlos	R-R	6-1	166	2-24-06	.194	.282	.245	30	112	98	15	19	5	0	0	10	9	3	2	0	38	7	0	8.04	33.93
Del Rosario, Ismael	L-R	6-1	185	1-19-07	.147	.296	.181	36	144	116	16	17	2	1	0	14	24	1	2	1	55	8	3	16.67	38.19
Frias, Alan	R-R	6-2	206	10-26-05	.156	.333	.250	20	81	64	11	10	1	1	1	5	13	4	0	0	32	0	0	16.05	39.51
Guillen, Xavier	B-R	5-10	167	9-2-04	.273	.417	.488	36	151	121	35	33	7	5	3	21	24	6	0	0	39	15	3	15.89	25.83
Martinez, Alfonzo	R-R	6-0	180	11-28-05	.305	.401	.484	40	152	128	24	39	4	2	5	20	15	7	0	2	31	10	4	9.87	20.39
Moris, Yohangel	B-R	6-0	160	11-22-05	.180	.316	.315	35	134	111	16	20	4	1	3	11	22	0	1	0	43	3	2	16.42	32.09
Palma, Alberth	R-R	6-0	170	2-2-06	.270	.360	.310	36	153	126	23	34	5	0	0	19	16	4	3	4	15	18	4	10.46	9.80
Pineda, Leonardo	R-R	5-11	185	4-21-07	.253	.378	.364	45	196	162	26	41	10	1	2	21	31	2	0	1	43	12	4	15.82	21.94
Rodriguez, Alfredo	R-R	5-11	187	9-9-05	.238	.302	.308	41	159	143	17	34	4	3	0	20	10	4	0	2	35	4	4	6.29	22.01
Torres, Andres	L-R	5-11	145	5-1-07	.238	.349	.320	41	172	147	28	35	5	2	1	27	24	1	0	0	33	12	2	13.95	19.19
Trinidad, Wilian	L-R	5-8	165	10-6-05	.251	.372	.335	49	219	179	29	45	7	4	0	24	33	3	1	3	49	21	11	15.07	22.37
Vargas, Raul	R-R	5-9	154	9-15-06	.115	.370	.135	21	73	52	14	6	1	0	0	2	20	1	0	0	18	1	1	27.40	24.66

TAMPA BAY RAYS

Pitching	B-T	Ht.	Wt.	DOB	W	L	ERA	G	GS	SV	IP	Hits	Runs	ER	HR	BB	SO	AVG	OBP	SLG	SO%	BB%	BF
Arias, John	L-L	6-2	187	5-18-05	0	0	2.35	4	0	0	8	7	3	2	0	8	8	.250	.405	.250	21.62	21.62	37
Berbesi, Alan	R-R	5-3	189	8-19-02	1	1	2.41	10	1	1	19	14	7	5	0	9	21	.206	.313	.294	26.25	11.25	80
Bierd, Frediry	R-R	5-11	156	2-28-04	1	1	7.71	15	0	0	26	29	27	22	6	18	17	.279	.392	.510	13.60	14.40	125
Cabral, Ismael	R-R	6-1	194	12-19-03	0	3	3.21	12	11	0	42	34	27	15	1	21	28	.218	.330	.288	14.74	11.05	190
De La Cruz, Misael	R-R	6-4	195	1-29-05	0	0	10.45	14	0	0	10	8	13	12	0	19	10	.211	.531	.342	15.63	29.69	64
Eusebio, Oliver	R-R	6-0	200	1-5-05	2	2	10.08	19	0	2	25	36	40	28	1	24	19	.327	.464	.436	13.57	17.14	140
Florian, Frailin	L-L	6-6	222	8-5-04	1	5	8.38	16	0	1	19	16	21	18	1	29	34	.219	.472	.301	31.48	26.85	108
Guzman, Ricardo	R-R	6-0	185	8-19-04	0	0	12.00	2	0	0	3	4	4	4	0	2	1	.400	.571	.500	7.14	14.29	14
Javier, Jimmy	R-R	6-5	220	11-13-04	1	2	9.97	16	1	0	22	22	30	24	1	34	23	.272	.512	.407	18.70	27.64	123
Lopez, Xavier	R-R	6-2	160	5-30-05	0	1	5.75	7	7	0	20	24	15	13	1	7	20	.308	.396	.436	21.98	7.69	91
Moreno, Moises	R-R	6-2	169	11-1-05	3	1	8.55	16	0	0	20	26	23	19	3	24	27	.299	.475	.494	22.88	20.34	118
Paez, Gabriel	L-L	6-3	183	7-4-06	1	1	18.00	4	0	0	4	3	8	8	0	8	6	.214	.522	.214	26.09	34.78	23
Pena, Rubender	R-R	5-10	183	8-18-04	1	3	4.91	13	10	0	51	57	34	28	1	19	45	.279	.361	.363	19.31	8.15	233
Radney, Chariel	L-L	6-0	189	3-27-05	1	1	2.41	12	0	1	19	10	9	5	0	12	18	.152	.282	.182	23.08	15.38	78
Ramos, Efrailin	R-R	5-11	165	12-13-05	3	3	3.75	21	0	2	36	27	17	15	2	20	49	.203	.321	.316	30.82	12.58	159
Rojas, Cesar	R-R	6-3	162	5-12-02	2	2	8.36	18	0	0	28	23	33	26	2	36	37	.225	.441	.353	25.87	25.17	143
Roman, Endry	R-R	6-5	196	7-23-02	0	0	9.53	5	1	0	6	9	6	6	0	4	5	.346	.469	.577	15.63	12.50	32
Savinon, Starlin	L-L	6-0	182	10-30-04	1	1	1.10	7	2	2	16	8	3	2	0	6	14	.151	.233	.189	23.33	10.00	60
Teus, Yereny	L-L	5-10	157	8-1-03	5	2	2.50	14	12	0	54	35	15	15	3	17	71	.186	.261	.255	34.30	8.21	207
Toscano, Miguel	R-R	6-3	170	5-12-06	1	3	3.15	12	11	0	40	41	18	14	1	10	27	.261	.318	.363	15.79	5.85	171

Fielding

C: Rodriguez 22, Torres 19, De Sousa 15, Blanco 6. **1B:** Rodriguez 15, Torres 12, De Sousa 12, Blanco 11, Moris 8. **2B:** Bautista 21, Trinidad 14, Batista 10, Vargas 8, Palma 5. **3B:** Moris 21, Batista 18, Trinidad 16, Palma 6, Vargas 1. **SS:** Palma 21, Trinidad 19, Bautista 17, Vargas 3, Moris 1. **LF:** Martinez 21, Del Rosario 15, Frias 7, Guillen 7, Pineda 7, Vargas 3, Blanco 3. **CF:** Pineda 37, Del Rosario 16, Martinez 7. **RF:** Guillen 30, Martinez 7, Del Rosario 7, Frias 7, Vargas 5, Blanco 2.

Texas Rangers

SEASON SYNOPSIS: The follow-up to Texas' 2023 World Series championship never fully launched, as the Rangers spent much of their season waiting for their offense to catch fire and for their older pitchers such as Jacob deGrom and Max Scherzer to get healthy. Texas fell off the pace in May and never even climbed above .500 again, finishing at 78-84.

HIGH POINT: Texas briefly led the AL West, winning four straight series (against the Nationals and Royals at home, and at Kansas City and Oakland) to climb to 22-17. The offense seemed to be coming around with three double-digit outputs in the final five games of the run, including a 12-11 thriller in Oakland to salvage a May 8 doubleheader split. Veteran Kirby Yates continued to establish himself as the team's closer, notching his seventh save in the doubleheader en route to a 7-2, 1.17 campaign with 33 saves in 61 games.

LOW POINT: The road proved rough all season for the Rangers, who gave up 5.2 runs per game away from home (just 3.9 at home), and it was a road trip just before the trade deadline that sealed Texas' fate. After climbing to within a game of .500 by sweeping the lowly White Sox, Texas posted a 1-5 road trip, getting swept at Toronto before losing the last two in St. Louis by a combined score of 18-2. Texas' offense posted a .685 team OPS after a .789 line in 2023.

NOTABLE ROOKIES: Postseason hero Evan Carter struggled with back issues that sidelined him the last four months of the season, short-circuiting his rookie year, but 2023 first-rounder Wyatt Langford did his best to fill in. In his first full pro season, Langford played 134 games, hit 16 homers, stole 19 bases and shrugged off some growing pains to slash .253/.325/.415. Jake Latz, after two previous cups of coffee, established himself as a relatively consistent lefty reliever.

KEY TRANSACTIONS: Ballyhooed prospects and injury-plagued veterans came and went through Texas' rotation all year, such as Max Scherzer (four different injured list stints, nine starts) and Tyler Mahle (an off-season free-agent returned from Tommy John surgery in August for three starts) and star Jacob deGrom, coming back from his second UCL surgery to make three September starts. The club's Vanderbilt duo of Jack Leiter and Kumar Rocker, first-round picks in 2021 and '22, combined for eight starts in September. All five could be in the 2025 rotation.

OPENING DAY PAYROLL: $223,355,753 (6th)

PLAYERS OF THE YEAR

MAJOR LEAGUE

Corey Seager
SS

.278/.353/.512
30 HR, 74 RBIs
53 BB, 96 SO

MINOR LEAGUE

Sebastian Walcott
SS

(A+/AA)
.265/.344/.452
10 HR, 26 SB

ORGANIZATION LEADERS

Batting		*Qualifiers
MAJORS		
* AVG	Corey Seager	.278
* OPS	Corey Seager	.865
HR	Corey Seager	30
RBI	Adolis Garcia	85
MINORS		
* AVG	Josh Hatcher, Frisco/Round Rock	.294
* OBP	Jax Biggers, Round Rock	.390
* SLG	Alejandro Osuna, Hickory/Frisco	.507
* OPS	Alejandro Osuna, Hickory/Frisco	.869
R	Blaine Crim, Round Rock	87
H	Blaine Crim, Round Rock	140
TB	Blaine Crim, Round Rock	237
2B	Sebastian Walcott, Hickory/Frisco	34
3B	Sebastian Walcott, Hickory/Frisco	9
HR	Blaine Crim, Round Rock	20
HR	Gleider Figuereo, Hickory/Down East	20
RBI	Blaine Crim, Round Rock	86
BB	Jax Biggers, Round Rock	71
SO	Sam Huff, Round Rock	150
SB	Anthony Gutierrez, ACL Rangers/Hickory	43

Pitching		#Qualifiers
MAJORS		
W	Nathan Eovaldi	12
# ERA	Nathan Eovaldi	3.80
SO	Nathan Eovaldi	166
SV	Kirby Yates	33
MINORS		
W	Winston Santos, Hickory/Frisco	11
L	Adrian Sampson, Round Rock	10
# ERA	David Davalillo, Down East/Hickory	1.88
G	Grant Wolfram, Round Rock/Frisco	46
GS	Adrian Sampson, Round Rock	27
SV	Skylar Hales, Hickory/Frisco	10
IP	Adrian Sampson, Round Rock	137
BB	Ryan Garcia, Round Rock/Frisco	57
SO	Kohl Drake, Down East/Hickory/Frisco	148
# AVG	Kohl Drake, Down East/Hickory/Frisco	.196

2024 PERFORMANCE

General Manager: Chris Young. **Farm Director:** Josh Bonifay. **Scouting Director:** Kip Fagg.

Class	Team	League	W	L	PCT	Finish	Manager
Majors	Texas Rangers	American	78	84	.481	11 (15)	Bruce Bochy
Triple-A	Round Rock Express	Pacific Coast	71	77	.480	7 (10)	Doug Davis
Double-A	Frisco RoughRiders	Texas	84	54	.609	1 (10)	Carlos Cardoza
High-A	Hickory Crawdads	South Atlantic	62	70	.470	9 (12)	Chad Comer
Low-A	Down East Wood Ducks	Carolina	65	63	.508	8 (12)	Carlos Maldonado
Rookie	ACL Rangers	Arizona Complex	36	24	.600	3 (15)	Guilder Rodriguez
Rookie	DSL Rangers Blue	Dominican	26	28	.481	28 (51)	Ruben Sosa
Rookie	DSL Rangers Red	Dominican	39	17	.696	3 (51)	Nick Janssen
Overall 2024 Minor League Record			**383**	**333**	**.535**	**5th (30)**	

TEXAS RANGERS

ORGANIZATION STATISTICS

TEXAS RANGERS

AMERICAN LEAGUE

Batting	B-T	Ht.	Wt.	DOB	AVG	OBP	SLG	G	PA	AB	R	H	2B	3B	HR	RBI	BB	HBP	SH	SF	SO	SB	CS	BB%	SO%
Carter, Evan	L-R	6-2	190	8-29-02	.188	.272	.361	45	162	144	23	27	6	2	5	15	15	2	0	1	43	2	0	9.26	26.54
Duffy, Matt	R-R	6-2	190	1-15-91	.286	.500	.286	4	10	7	2	2	0	0	0	0	2	1	0	0	1	0	0	20.00	10.00
Duran, Ezequiel	R-R	5-11	185	5-22-99	.246	.288	.321	92	285	268	26	66	11	0	3	20	14	2	0	1	63	1	2	4.91	22.11
Fabian, Sandro	R-R	5-11	180	3-6-98	.000	.000	.000	3	5	5	0	0	0	0	0	0	0	0	0	0	0	0	0	0.00	0.00
Foscue, Justin	R-R	5-11	205	3-2-99	.048	.091	.071	15	44	42	3	2	1	0	0	1	2	0	0	0	18	0	0	4.55	40.91
Garcia, Adolis	R-R	6-1	205	3-2-93	.224	.284	.400	154	637	580	68	130	27	0	25	85	45	6	0	6	177	11	5	7.06	27.79
Grossman, Robbie	B-L	6-0	209	9-16-89	.238	.336	.362	45	122	105	13	25	4	0	3	10	16	0	0	1	25	1	0	13.11	20.49
Harris, Dustin	L-R	6-3	185	7-8-99	.333	.429	1.000	2	7	6	1	2	1	0	1	3	1	0	0	0	2	0	0	14.29	28.57
Heim, Jonah	B-R	6-4	220	6-27-95	.220	.267	.336	131	491	459	45	101	12	1	13	59	26	4	0	2	90	1	1	5.30	18.33
Hill, Derek	R-R	6-2	206	12-30-95	.256	.289	.465	16	45	43	5	11	0	0	3	5	2	0	0	0	14	2	1	4.44	31.11
Huff, Sam	R-R	6-4	240	1-14-98	.000	.250	.000	3	4	3	0	0	0	0	0	0	1	0	0	0	2	0	0	25.00	50.00
Jankowski, Travis	L-R	6-2	190	6-15-91	.200	.266	.242	104	207	190	19	38	5	0	1	12	12	5	0	0	44	11	1	5.80	21.26
Jung, Josh	R-R	6-2	214	2-12-98	.264	.298	.421	46	188	178	19	47	5	1	7	16	8	1	0	1	48	4	0	4.26	25.53
Kelly, Carson	R-R	6-2	212	7-14-94	.235	.291	.343	31	110	102	11	24	5	0	2	8	8	0	0	0	15	0	0	7.27	13.64
Knizner, Andrew	R-R	6-1	225	2-3-95	.167	.183	.211	37	93	90	5	15	1	0	1	9	1	1	0	1	22	0	0	1.08	23.66
Langford, Wyatt	R-R	6-1	225	11-15-01	.253	.325	.415	134	557	499	74	126	25	4	16	74	51	4	0	3	115	19	3	9.16	20.65
Lowe, Nathaniel	L-R	6-4	220	7-7-95	.265	.361	.401	140	565	486	62	129	16	1	16	69	71	4	0	4	125	2	0	12.57	22.12
Ornelas, Jonathan	R-R	6-0	196	5-26-00	.216	.256	.270	18	40	37	1	8	2	0	0	3	2	0	1	0	13	0	0	5.00	32.50
Seager, Corey	L-R	6-4	215	4-27-94	.278	.353	.512	123	533	475	68	132	21	0	30	74	53	3	0	2	96	1	1	9.94	18.01
Semien, Marcus	R-R	6-0	195	9-17-90	.237	.308	.391	159	718	650	101	154	27	2	23	74	64	3	0	1	105	8	3	8.91	14.62
Smith, Josh H.	L-R	5-10	172	8-7-97	.258	.337	.394	149	592	523	67	135	30	1	13	62	46	18	2	3	121	11	2	7.77	20.44
Taveras, Leody	B-R	6-2	195	9-8-98	.229	.289	.352	151	529	480	59	110	17	3	12	44	42	0	3	4	112	23	6	7.94	21.17
Walsh, Jared	L-L	6-0	210	7-30-93	.226	.317	.321	17	60	53	9	12	2	0	1	7	7	0	0	0	21	0	0	11.67	35.00
Wendzel, Davis	R-R	5-10	206	5-23-97	.128	.163	.234	27	49	47	2	6	2	0	1	2	1	1	0	0	12	0	0	2.04	24.49

Pitching	B-T	Ht.	Wt.	DOB	W	L	ERA	G	GS	SV	IP	Hits	Runs	ER	HR	BB	SO	AVG	OBP	SLG	SO%	BB%	BF
Anderson, Chase	R-R	6-1	210	11-30-87	0	0	9.95	2	0	0	6	9	7	7	2	2	7	.321	.387	.679	22.58	6.45	31
Anderson, Grant	R-R	6-0	180	6-21-97	0	1	8.10	23	0	1	27	33	24	24	11	10	29	.303	.367	.615	24.17	8.33	120
Anderson, Shaun	R-R	6-6	228	10-29-94	0	0	5.40	2	0	0	3	6	2	2	0	1	3	.375	.412	.500	17.65	5.88	17
Bradford, Cody	L-L	6-4	197	2-22-98	6	3	3.54	14	13	0	76	64	32	30	10	13	70	.218	.253	.379	22.73	4.22	308
Burke, Brock	L-L	6-4	210	8-4-96	0	0	9.22	13	0	0	14	21	14	14	3	9	16	.350	.444	.600	22.22	12.50	72
Chafin, Andrew	R-L	6-2	235	6-17-90	1	1	4.19	21	0	0	19	17	10	9	3	15	20	.250	.381	.397	23.81	17.86	84
Church, Marc	R-R	6-3	189	3-30-01	0	0	0.00	1	0	0	1	1	0	0	0	0	1	.250	.250	.500	25.00	0.00	4
deGrom, Jacob	L-R	6-4	180	6-19-88	0	0	1.69	3	3	0	11	11	2	2	1	1	14	.262	.295	.405	31.82	2.27	44
Dunning, Dane	R-R	6-4	225	12-19-94	5	7	5.31	26	15	0	95	97	60	56	18	40	91	.260	.340	.461	21.62	9.50	421
Eovaldi, Nathan	R-R	6-2	217	2-13-90	12	8	3.80	29	29	0	171	147	74	72	23	42	166	.229	.282	.386	23.85	6.03	696
Festa, Matt	R-R	6-1	195	3-11-93	6	0	4.37	18	0	0	23	17	13	11	2	7	23	.205	.272	.361	25.00	7.61	92
Garabito, Gerson	R-R	6-0	160	8-19-95	0	2	4.78	18	2	0	26	23	15	14	4	12	22	.240	.342	.396	19.13	10.43	115
Gray, Jon	R-R	6-4	225	11-5-91	5	6	4.47	23	19	0	103	107	54	51	11	28	86	.262	.308	.404	19.59	6.38	439
Heaney, Andrew	L-L	6-2	200	6-5-91	5	14	4.28	32	31	0	160	159	84	76	23	41	159	.251	.307	.410	22.94	5.92	693
Hernandez, Jonathan	R-R	6-3	190	7-6-96	3	1	5.05	26	1	0	41	39	25	23	6	26	36	.258	.367	.444	19.89	14.36	181
Latz, Jake	R-L	6-2	185	4-8-96	2	3	3.71	46	0	0	44	39	20	18	6	27	40	.241	.349	.377	20.83	14.06	192
Leclerc, Jose	R-R	6-0	195	12-19-93	6	5	4.32	64	0	1	67	56	33	32	7	32	89	.227	.323	.348	30.90	11.11	288
Leiter, Jack	R-R	6-1	205	4-21-00	0	3	8.83	9	6	0	36	44	39	35	7	17	31	.297	.374	.527	17.92	9.83	173
Lorenzen, Michael	R-R	6-3	217	1-4-92	5	6	3.81	19	18	0	102	82	43	43	15	48	75	.225	.322	.393	17.90	11.46	419
Mahle, Tyler	R-R	6-3	210	9-29-94	0	1	4.97	3	3	0	13	14	7	7	1	4	10	.280	.339	.420	17.86	7.14	56
Pennington, Walter	L-L	6-2	205	4-14-98	1	0	3.12	15	1	0	17	19	7	6	1	11	16	.275	.390	.391	19.51	13.41	82
Pruitt, Austin	R-R	5-10	185	8-31-89	0	0	12.46	4	0	0	4	8	6	6	3	3	1	.400	.458	.900	4.17	12.50	24
Robert, Daniel	L-R	6-4	210	8-30-94	1	0	3.18	4	0	0	6	6	2	2	1	2	6	.273	.385	.409	23.08	7.69	26
Robertson, David	R-R	5-11	195	4-9-85	3	4	3.00	68	0	2	72	53	25	24	5	27	99	.202	.288	.282	33.45	9.12	296
Rocker, Kumar	R-R	6-5	245	11-22-99	0	2	3.86	3	3	0	12	12	6	5	1	6	14	.267	.352	.333	25.45	10.91	55
Rodriguez, Yerry	R-R	6-2	198	10-15-97	1	0	6.88	12	0	0	17	16	13	13	5	11	12	.242	.359	.515	15.38	14.10	78
Sborz, Josh	R-R	6-3	215	12-17-93	2	2	3.86	17	0	0	16	16	8	7	1	4	17	.246	.290	.354	24.64	5.80	69
Scherzer, Max	R-R	6-3	208	7-27-84	2	4	3.95	9	9	0	43	40	20	19	7	10	40	.242	.288	.436	22.60	5.65	177

Pitching	B-T	Ht.	Wt.	DOB	W	L	ERA	G	GS	SV	IP	Hits	Runs	ER	HR	BB	SO	AVG	OBP	SLG	SO%	BB%	BF
Tinoco, Jesus	R-R	6-4	258	4-30-95	0	0	8.10	9	0	0	10	11	9	9	2	7	9	.268	.400	.439	18.00	14.00	50
Urena, Jose	R-R	6-2	208	9-12-91	5	8	3.80	33	9	1	109	105	51	46	13	39	70	.254	.321	.399	15.12	8.42	463
White, Owen	R-R	6-3	199	8-9-99	0	0	24.00	3	0	0	3	9	8	8	1	1	0	.529	.556	.882	0.00	5.56	18
Winn, Cole	R-R	6-2	190	11-25-99	0	1	7.79	13	0	0	17	18	15	15	2	4	14	.261	.325	.391	18.18	5.19	77
Yates, Kirby	L-R	5-10	205	3-25-87	7	2	1.17	61	0	33	62	23	10	8	3	28	85	.113	.225	.182	35.86	11.81	237

Fielding

Catcher	PCT	G	PO	A	E	DP	PB
Heim	.993	119	967	37	7	5	0
Huff	1.000	2	9	0	0	0	0
Kelly	.995	24	181	6	1	1	2
Knizner	.992	34	247	5	2	1	0

First Base	PCT	G	PO	A	E	DP
Duran	1.000	12	76	7	0	10
Foscue	1.000	1	6	0	0	1
Lowe	.995	138	983	92	5	73
Walsh	.983	16	104	10	2	11
Wendzel	.000	1	0	0	0	0

Second Base	PCT	G	PO	A	E	DP
Duran	1.000	5	4	3	0	0
Foscue	1.000	2	1	2	0	0
Ornelas	1.000	4	1	1	0	0
Semien	.989	159	214	389	7	77
Smith	.000	1	0	0	0	0
Wendzel	1.000	2	1	0	0	0

Third Base	PCT	G	PO	A	E	DP
Duffy	1.000	4	2	3	0	0
Duran	.972	28	13	56	2	3
Jung	.969	40	28	66	3	7
Ornelas	.909	7	6	14	2	0
Smith	.979	83	60	126	4	8
Wendzel	1.000	18	5	22	0	0

Shortstop	PCT	G	PO	A	E	DP
Duran	.963	9	10	16	1	4
Ornelas	1.000	6	7	9	0	1
Seager	.983	113	137	271	7	52
Smith	.951	49	50	85	7	13

Outfield	PCT	G	PO	A	E	DP
Carter	.987	44	73	3	1	1
Duran	.950	24	35	3	2	1
Fabian	1.000	3	1	0	0	0
Garcia	.985	131	253	5	4	3
Grossman	1.000	17	12	0	0	0
Hill	.944	13	16	1	1	0
Jankowski	.965	72	82	1	3	0
Langford	.991	120	208	8	2	1
Ornelas	.000	1	0	0	0	0
Smith	1.000	5	5	0	0	0
Taveras	.992	148	376	9	3	2

ROUND ROCK EXPRESS — TRIPLE-A

PACIFIC COAST LEAGUE

Batting	B-T	Ht.	Wt.	DOB	AVG	OBP	SLG	G	PA	AB	R	H	2B	3B	HR	RBI	BB	HBP	SH	SF	SO	SB	CS	BB%	SO%
Barrero, Jose	R-R	6-2	211	4-5-98	.188	.277	.345	49	188	165	25	31	6	1	6	25	13	8	0	2	63	10	1	6.91	33.51
Biggers, Jax	L-R	5-8	175	4-7-97	.275	.390	.382	119	452	364	63	100	22	4	3	55	71	2	8	7	87	12	5	15.71	19.25
Chavez, Frainyer	B-R	5-8	170	5-24-99	.256	.309	.312	35	137	125	13	32	7	0	0	12	9	1	1	1	33	5	2	6.57	24.09
Crim, Blaine	R-R	5-10	200	6-17-97	.277	.370	.469	134	586	505	87	140	33	2	20	86	70	7	0	4	101	7	1	11.95	17.24
De Goti, Alex	R-R	6-0	192	8-19-94	.266	.343	.330	30	107	94	11	25	3	0	1	9	10	1	2	0	23	3	2	9.35	21.50
Duffy, Matt	R-R	6-2	190	1-15-91	.218	.296	.280	56	216	193	29	42	6	0	2	16	22	0	0	1	45	1	2	10.19	20.83
Duran, Ezequiel	R-R	5-11	185	5-22-99	.277	.302	.554	19	86	83	18	23	4	2	5	16	3	0	0	0	19	5	1	3.49	22.09
Easley, Jayce	B-R	5-8	151	8-2-99	.200	.273	.200	6	12	10	0	2	0	0	0	0	1	0	1	0	3	1	0	8.33	25.00
Fabian, Sandro	R-R	5-11	180	3-6-98	.270	.343	.462	116	501	448	57	121	31	2	17	81	45	6	0	2	76	4	4	8.98	15.17
Foscue, Justin	R-R	5-11	205	3-2-99	.276	.420	.477	48	219	174	35	48	8	0	9	33	39	5	0	1	37	2	2	17.81	16.89
Hardy, Theo	B-R	6-1	185	11-27-01	.000	.200	.000	2	5	4	1	0	0	0	0	1	1	0	0	0	1	1	0	20.00	20.00
Harris, Dustin	L-R	6-3	185	7-8-99	.272	.358	.391	131	564	486	81	132	22	3	10	53	61	8	2	7	123	35	10	10.82	21.81
Hartl, Ben	R-R	5-11	200	1-7-03	.400	.400	.600	2	5	5	0	2	1	0	0	1	0	0	0	0	1	0	0	0.00	20.00
Hatcher, Josh	L-L	6-2	200	9-3-98	.000	.111	.000	2	9	8	0	0	0	0	0	0	1	0	0	0	4	0	0	11.11	44.44
Hauver, Trevor	L-R	5-11	205	11-19-98	.246	.360	.425	104	420	353	53	87	28	1	11	60	59	5	0	2	125	1	1	14.05	29.76
Hernandez, Elier	R-R	6-3	197	11-21-94	.289	.386	.474	20	88	76	14	22	6	1	2	10	11	1	0	0	21	1	3	12.50	23.86
Hill, Derek	R-R	6-2	206	12-30-95	.350	.415	.631	42	176	157	35	55	12	4	8	17	15	3	0	1	42	7	1	8.52	23.86
Huff, Sam	R-R	6-4	240	1-14-98	.246	.310	.416	111	477	435	49	107	33	1	13	69	39	2	0	1	150	0	0	8.18	31.45
Jung, Josh	R-R	6-2	214	2-12-98	.235	.235	.235	4	17	17	1	4	0	0	0	1	0	0	0	0	5	0	0	0.00	29.41
Knapp, Andrew	B-R	6-1	189	11-9-91	.294	.383	.457	81	345	293	44	86	19	1	9	44	43	3	0	6	83	1	4	12.46	24.06
Knizner, Andrew	R-R	6-1	225	2-3-95	.105	.150	.105	5	20	19	0	2	0	0	0	0	0	1	0	0	4	0	0	0.00	20.00
Langford, Wyatt	R-R	6-1	225	11-15-01	.200	.273	.200	3	11	10	2	2	0	0	0	0	1	0	0	0	0	0	0	9.09	0.00
Lowe, Nathaniel	L-R	6-4	220	7-7-95	.182	.250	.273	3	12	11	1	2	1	0	0	1	1	0	0	0	0	0	0	8.33	0.00
Ornelas, Jonathan	R-R	6-0	196	5-26-00	.251	.322	.326	88	368	331	42	83	10	3	3	29	30	5	1	1	87	9	2	8.15	23.64
Piotto, Konner	L-R	5-9	195	1-1-98	.226	.324	.323	12	37	31	5	7	1	1	0	3	4	1	0	1	13	0	0	10.81	35.14
Smith, Marcus	L-L	5-11	185	9-11-00	.154	.214	.179	13	42	39	3	6	1	0	0	3	2	1	0	0	21	2	2	4.76	50.00
Strahm, Kellen	R-R	6-0	215	4-25-97	.265	.380	.368	41	166	136	24	36	5	3	1	24	26	1	0	3	37	14	0	15.66	22.29
Wendzel, Davis	R-R	5-10	206	5-23-97	.289	.384	.492	34	151	128	24	37	8	0	6	22	16	5	0	2	20	4	1	10.60	13.25
Whatley, Matt	R-R	5-8	200	1-7-96	.199	.294	.319	50	164	141	14	28	2	0	5	15	20	0	1	2	38	4	1	12.20	23.17
Witte, Jantzen	R-R	6-0	195	1-4-90	.238	.331	.430	47	175	151	22	36	8	0	7	26	22	0	0	2	41	0	2	12.57	23.43

Pitching	B-T	Ht.	Wt.	DOB	W	L	ERA	G	GS	SV	IP	Hits	Runs	ER	HR	BB	SO	AVG	OBP	SLG	SO%	BB%	BF
Ahlstrom, Robby	L-L	6-3	195	6-19-99	3	0	3.98	15	1	0	20	24	9	9	2	8	15	.300	.374	.475	16.48	8.79	91
Anderson, Aidan	R-R	6-1	195	6-21-97	7	4	5.28	36	2	4	58	56	38	34	11	19	62	.246	.310	.452	24.51	7.51	253
Anderson, Ben	R-R	6-4	200	5-2-98	0	0	5.40	1	0	0	2	2	1	1	1	0	0	.286	.286	.714	0.00	0.00	7
Anderson, Chase	R-R	6-1	210	11-30-87	0	2	6.94	4	4	0	12	17	11	9	3	5	12	.327	.386	.558	21.05	8.77	57
Anderson, Grant	R-R	6-0	180	6-21-97	3	0	2.93	26	0	1	28	22	11	9	0	14	34	.216	.317	.265	28.33	11.67	120
Anderson, Shaun	R-R	6-6	228	10-29-94	3	0	2.53	4	4	0	21	18	6	6	2	4	22	.228	.262	.405	26.19	4.76	84
Barraclough, Kyle	R-R	6-3	229	5-23-90	1	4	3.74	31	4	4	55	44	25	23	3	35	67	.213	.337	.300	27.13	14.17	247
Birlingmair, Reid	L-R	5-10	210	11-13-96	0	2	9.00	14	0	0	19	28	20	19	4	22	18	.359	.495	.603	17.48	21.36	103
Brennan, Tim	R-R	6-4	212	12-18-96	1	4	6.54	17	10	0	43	51	33	31	8	28	20	.309	.421	.515	10.15	14.21	197
Burke, Brock	L-L	6-4	210	8-4-96	0	0	5.31	16	0	0	20	25	12	12	1	13	17	.313	.396	.450	17.71	13.54	96
Chi, Bryan	R-R	6-0	205	3-22-99	0	1	18.41	5	1	0	7	14	16	15	3	10	6	.424	.574	.939	12.50	20.83	48
Church, Marc	R-R	6-3	189	3-30-01	1	1	3.22	17	0	1	22	20	9	8	1	7	24	.235	.290	.318	25.81	7.53	93
Crismatt, Nabil	R-R	6-1	220	12-25-94	0	1	7.36	8	0	0	11	18	10	9	1	4	10	.360	.400	.600	18.18	7.27	55
Cueto, Johnny	R-R	5-11	229	2-15-86	2	1	5.92	8	8	0	38	39	25	25	5	8	30	.264	.306	.432	18.75	5.00	160
deGrom, Jacob	L-R	6-4	180	6-19-88	0	0	0.00	2	2	0	5	1	0	0	0	1	7	.067	.125	.067	43.75	6.25	16
Duffy, Danny	L-L	6-3	205	12-21-88	0	1	5.50	10	2	0	18	14	12	11	2	17	17	.215	.378	.415	20.73	20.73	82

Dunning, Dane	R-R	6-4	225	12-19-94	0	1	5.28	4	3	0	15	14	11	9	1	6	18	.226	.304	.339	26.09	8.70	69
Festa, Matt	R-R	6-1	195	3-11-93	1	0	1.04	6	0	1	9	6	3	1	1	3	13	.188	.257	.281	37.14	8.57	35
Garabito, Gerson	R-R	6-0	160	8-19-95	1	4	3.42	13	10	0	55	45	22	21	6	12	55	.220	.286	.351	24.23	5.29	227
Garcia, Ryan	R-R	6-0	180	1-24-98	2	3	3.43	8	8	0	42	36	16	16	5	17	50	.232	.314	.381	28.09	9.55	178
Greene, Shane	R-R	6-4	200	11-17-88	0	1	16.88	6	1	0	8	7	15	15	0	14	11	.241	.531	.414	22.45	28.57	49
Hernandez, Jonathan	R-R	6-3	190	7-6-96	1	1	2.70	8	0	1	10	11	3	3	2	4	14	.282	.349	.487	32.56	9.30	43
Ingram, Kolton	L-L	5-9	170	10-21-96	0	0	0.00	2	0	0	2	2	0	0	0	1	0	.250	.333	.250	0.00	11.11	9
Jennings, Steven	R-R	6-2	175	11-13-98	1	0	5.59	17	2	0	29	31	18	18	7	8	26	.263	.310	.500	20.63	6.35	126
Kelly, Antoine	L-L	6-5	205	12-5-99	2	0	9.37	18	0	0	16	19	17	17	1	21	22	.279	.462	.397	24.18	23.08	91
Krauth, Nick	R-R	6-3	170	9-6-99	0	0	4.50	3	0	0	8	6	4	4	3	4	5	.207	.324	.517	14.71	11.76	34
Latz, Jake	R-L	6-2	185	4-8-96	0	0	1.59	4	1	0	6	4	1	1	0	5	5	.222	.391	.222	20.83	20.83	24
Lee, Chase	R-R	6-0	170	8-13-98	0	0	1.69	8	0	0	11	12	4	2	0	7	11	.273	.373	.364	21.15	13.46	52
Leiter, Jack	R-R	6-1	205	4-21-00	6	4	3.51	17	16	0	77	62	35	30	10	35	110	.217	.310	.371	33.33	10.61	330
Lorenzen, Michael	R-R	6-3	217	1-4-92	0	0	6.35	3	3	0	11	12	8	8	1	9	13	.273	.400	.477	23.64	16.36	55
Mahle, Tyler	R-R	6-3	210	9-29-94	0	0	1.93	3	3	0	9	6	2	2	0	2	8	.194	.242	.290	24.24	6.06	33
Mendoza, Damian	L-R	6-1	175	1-25-01	0	1	0.00	1	0	0	2	3	1	0	0	2	1	.333	.455	.444	9.09	18.18	11
Oviedo, Ivan	R-R	6-2	175	10-14-02	0	1	1.80	2	0	0	5	4	2	1	0	4	4	.235	.435	.235	16.67	16.67	24
Pennington, Walter	L-L	6-2	205	4-14-98	1	0	0.00	2	0	0	4	4	1	0	0	1	3	.286	.333	.286	20.00	6.67	15
Polley, Triston	L-L	6-0	190	12-19-96	1	0	4.26	7	0	0	6	5	3	3	1	7	3	.208	.394	.333	9.09	21.21	33
Pruitt, Austin	R-R	5-10	185	8-31-89	3	1	8.10	9	0	0	10	18	9	9	2	3	5	.383	.420	.617	10.00	6.00	50
Robbins, Jimmy	L-L	6-3	190	12-22-97	0	1	6.10	9	0	0	10	10	7	7	1	8	10	.263	.383	.447	21.28	17.02	47
Robert, Daniel	L-R	6-4	210	8-30-94	4	2	2.70	35	0	7	43	22	15	13	3	13	52	.144	.220	.229	30.95	7.74	168
Rocker, Kumar	R-R	6-5	245	11-22-99	0	0	1.80	2	2	0	10	4	2	2	1	1	18	.118	.143	.265	51.43	2.86	35
Rodriguez, Yerry	R-R	6-2	198	10-15-97	1	4	6.08	11	0	1	13	14	16	9	1	10	21	.269	.381	.404	31.82	15.15	66
Sampson, Adrian	R-R	6-2	210	10-7-91	8	10	5.64	28	27	0	137	174	106	86	19	46	120	.305	.365	.500	18.84	7.22	637
Sborz, Josh	R-R	6-3	215	12-17-93	0	0	7.45	11	0	0	10	6	8	8	0	10	15	.176	.356	.294	33.33	22.22	45
Scherzer, Max	R-R	6-3	208	7-27-84	0	1	3.60	4	4	0	15	10	6	6	3	4	25	.189	.259	.415	43.10	6.90	58
Serrano, Florencio	R-R	6-1	205	2-23-00	0	0	23.14	4	1	0	5	9	12	12	3	12	3	.409	.629	.864	8.57	34.29	35
Shreve, Chasen	L-L	6-4	180	7-12-90	2	0	1.61	20	0	1	22	8	4	4	1	9	24	.113	.210	.183	29.63	11.11	81
Solomon, Peter	R-R	6-4	211	8-16-96	6	5	6.50	22	11	0	72	74	60	52	15	41	70	.266	.361	.504	21.60	12.65	324
Taylor, Blake	L-L	6-3	220	8-17-95	4	2	5.80	34	0	0	40	54	28	26	5	26	40	.323	.415	.503	20.41	13.27	196
Tinoco, Jesus	R-R	6-4	258	4-30-95	1	1	3.80	15	0	1	21	20	12	9	3	10	27	.260	.348	.429	30.34	11.24	89
Weems, Avery	R-L	6-2	205	6-6-97	0	2	8.31	4	1	0	4	5	5	4	1	2	3	.278	.350	.500	15.00	10.00	20
White, Owen	R-R	6-3	199	8-9-99	2	8	5.64	29	15	1	99	107	68	62	14	48	87	.276	.363	.425	19.46	10.74	447
Wiles, Collin	R-R	6-4	222	5-30-94	0	1	8.10	2	2	0	7	10	7	6	1	4	6	.370	.438	.593	18.75	12.50	32
Winn, Cole	R-R	6-2	190	11-25-99	0	1	3.45	10	0	2	16	14	7	6	2	4	20	.237	.303	.356	30.30	6.06	66
Wolfram, Grant	L-L	6-6	235	12-12-96	3	1	3.34	44	0	6	57	47	22	21	5	26	61	.226	.316	.370	25.63	10.92	238

Fielding

Catcher	PCT	G	PO	A	E	DP	PB
Huff	.990	79	679	35	7	6	7
Knapp	.995	40	383	20	2	4	3
Knizner	1.000	2	11	1	0	0	0
Piotto	1.000	5	22	2	0	0	0
Whatley	.980	32	273	17	6	2	4

First Base	PCT	G	PO	A	E	DP
Crim	.992	122	818	58	7	81
Duffy	1.000	1	11	0	0	1
Foscue	1.000	15	94	6	0	12
Harris	1.000	3	16	1	0	1
Hartl	1.000	1	6	0	0	0
Knapp	1.000	3	24	5	0	2
Lowe	1.000	2	12	1	0	1
Wendzel	1.000	3	26	0	0	2
Witte	1.000	2	13	1	0	1

Second Base	PCT	G	PO	A	E	DP
Biggers	.990	58	82	121	2	22
Chavez	1.000	4	7	10	0	2
De Goti	.980	15	23	27	1	5
Duffy	.984	32	52	74	2	20
Easley	1.000	4	2	6	0	1
Foscue	.979	32	44	49	2	7
Ornelas	.968	16	24	37	2	9
Wendzel	1.000	1	0	1	0	0
Witte	1.000	3	6	5	0	1

Third Base	PCT	G	PO	A	E	DP
Barrero	1.000	1	1	1	0	0
Biggers	.964	12	10	17	1	2
Chavez	.948	31	24	49	4	12
De Goti	1.000	8	10	12	0	3
Duffy	.833	12	4	11	3	0
Duran	.920	7	10	13	2	1
Harris	.952	12	8	12	1	2
Jung	1.000	3	1	5	0	1
Knapp	1.000	1	0	2	0	0
Ornelas	.895	13	2	15	2	3
Wendzel	.919	18	11	23	3	2
Witte	.976	40	20	61	2	8

Shortstop	PCT	G	PO	A	E	DP
Barrero	.935	28	37	49	6	9
Biggers	.972	44	63	113	5	23
De Goti	1.000	6	3	6	0	1
Duran	1.000	7	7	10	0	2
Hardy	.500	1	0	1	1	0
Ornelas	.942	57	62	132	12	28
Wendzel	.940	12	19	28	3	5

Outfield	PCT	G	PO	A	E	DP
Barrero	1.000	22	47	0	0	0
Biggers	1.000	4	5	0	0	0
Duran	1.000	2	1	0	0	0
Easley	.000	1	0	0	0	0
Fabian	.954	112	234	15	12	3
Harris	.984	113	246	3	4	0
Hatcher	1.000	3	4	0	0	0
Hauver	1.000	96	167	1	0	0
Hernandez	.974	18	38	0	1	0
Hill	.988	38	79	0	1	0
Langford	1.000	2	3	0	0	0
Ornelas	1.000	4	10	1	0	0
Smith	1.000	12	10	0	0	0
Strahm	.961	41	70	3	3	1

FRISCO ROUGHRIDERS — *DOUBLE-A*

TEXAS LEAGUE

Batting	B-T	Ht.	Wt.	DOB	AVG	OBP	SLG	G	PA	AB	R	H	2B	3B	HR	RBI	BB	HBP	SH	SF	SO	SB	CS	BB%	SO%
Acosta, Max	R-R	6-1	187	10-29-02	.288	.353	.425	104	434	386	57	111	23	3	8	58	34	8	0	6	58	26	9	7.83	13.36
Cepeda, Geisel	R-R	6-5	220	1-17-98	.205	.293	.286	50	183	161	25	33	10	0	1	17	17	3	2	0	23	8	0	9.29	12.57
Chavez, Frainyer	B-R	5-8	170	5-24-99	.247	.336	.347	78	297	259	36	64	8	3	4	30	34	1	2	1	61	15	2	11.45	20.54
De Goti, Alex	R-R	6-0	192	8-19-94	.195	.309	.242	45	150	128	16	25	4	1	0	3	17	4	1	0	33	8	4	11.33	22.00
Freeman, Cody	R-R	5-8	180	1-5-01	.264	.320	.432	123	518	470	68	124	33	2	14	63	37	5	0	6	94	15	1	7.14	18.15
Hardy, Theo	B-R	6-1	185	11-27-01	.154	.313	.385	5	16	13	3	2	1	1	0	1	2	1	0	0	4	0	0	12.50	25.00
Hatcher, Josh	L-L	6-2	200	9-3-98	.300	.350	.448	107	454	417	60	125	20	3	12	68	30	4	0	3	122	23	7	6.61	26.87
Hicks, Liam	L-R	5-11	185	6-2-99	.260	.364	.353	80	349	292	47	76	15	0	4	33	41	10	0	6	44	1	1	11.75	12.61
Hurdle, Devin	R-R	6-1	190	6-18-00	1.000	1.000	1.000	1	1	1	0	1	0	0	0	2	0	0	0	0	0	0	0	0.00	0.00

Johnson, Cooper	R-R	6-1	209	4-25-98	.235	.355	.474	79	300	251	40	59	18	0	14	46	44	3	1	1	78	0	0	14.67	26.00
Jung, Josh	R-R	6-2	214	2-12-98	.400	.500	.500	3	12	10	1	4	1	0	0	2	0	2	0	0	4	0	0	0.00	33.33
Kapers, Scott	R-R	5-10	198	11-27-96	.154	.244	.359	12	45	39	4	6	2	0	2	7	5	0	0	1	13	0	0	11.11	28.89
Lowe, Nathaniel	L-R	6-4	220	7-7-95	.111	.333	.444	3	12	9	4	1	0	0	1	3	2	1	0	0	0	0	0	16.67	0.00
Mateo, Daniel	R-R	6-1	165	7-3-01	.161	.221	.259	61	208	193	21	31	4	0	5	17	13	2	0	0	51	10	3	6.25	24.52
Mejia, Esteban	R-R	5-11	165	11-3-04	.000	.000	.000	1	3	3	0	0	0	0	0	0	0	0	0	0	1	0	0	0.00	33.33
Mieses, Luis	L-L	6-3	180	5-31-00	.281	.304	.461	33	136	128	12	36	5	0	6	20	4	1	0	2	31	0	0	2.94	22.79
Mitchell, Tucker	R-R	6-1	210	2-10-01	.100	.192	.143	21	78	70	7	7	1	1	0	3	7	1	0	0	16	0	0	8.97	20.51
Ortiz, Abimelec	L-L	6-0	230	2-22-02	.243	.328	.432	115	476	419	68	102	21	2	18	64	50	4	0	3	104	2	4	10.50	21.85
Osuna, Alejandro	L-L	6-0	185	10-10-02	.306	.379	.523	57	265	235	46	72	18	3	9	32	22	6	1	1	57	7	3	8.30	21.51
Rodriguez, Keyber	R-R	5-10	178	10-24-00	.234	.285	.369	94	387	355	49	83	18	3	8	52	23	4	1	4	75	7	3	5.94	19.38
Strahm, Kellen	R-R	6-0	215	4-25-97	.279	.363	.389	69	300	262	52	73	10	2	5	25	35	1	0	2	61	15	1	11.67	20.33
Walcott, Sebastian	R-R	6-4	190	3-14-06	.348	.375	.609	5	24	23	4	8	3	0	1	7	1	0	0	0	7	1	0	4.17	29.17
Zavala, Aaron	L-R	6-0	193	6-24-00	.224	.333	.305	118	498	416	53	93	17	1	5	52	63	9	2	8	139	12	5	12.65	27.91

Pitching	B-T	Ht.	Wt.	DOB	W	L	ERA	G	GS	SV	IP	Hits	Runs	ER	HR	BB	SO	AVG	OBP	SLG	SO%	BB%	BF
Acker, Dane	R-R	6-2	189	4-1-99	5	4	3.05	26	18	1	97	87	44	33	11	40	104	.236	.315	.369	25.06	9.64	415
Ahlstrom, Robby	L-L	6-3	195	6-19-99	3	1	1.85	30	0	4	44	29	11	9	3	23	57	.187	.296	.277	31.84	12.85	179
Anderson, Aidan	R-R	6-1	195	6-21-97	2	1	5.40	6	0	0	10	8	8	6	2	4	11	.222	.310	.444	25.58	9.30	43
Anderson, Ben	R-R	6-4	200	5-2-98	6	7	3.48	22	20	0	106	104	44	41	9	28	93	.261	.315	.391	21.48	6.47	433
Birlingmair, Reid	L-R	5-10	210	11-13-96	2	2	3.97	27	0	3	34	34	18	15	3	14	40	.256	.357	.376	25.81	9.03	155
Bradford, Cody	L-L	6-4	197	2-22-98	0	0	0.00	2	1	0	5	2	0	0	0	0	5	.125	.125	.188	31.25	0.00	16
Bratt, Mitch	L-L	6-1	190	7-3-03	2	2	5.45	7	6	0	33	34	25	20	4	12	33	.260	.327	.420	22.45	8.16	147
Chi, Bryan	R-R	6-0	205	3-22-99	2	0	4.66	19	1	1	46	53	26	24	6	23	38	.288	.374	.457	18.01	10.90	211
Clark, Seth	R-L	6-3	220	11-18-99	1	2	4.32	40	0	4	50	44	25	24	8	36	54	.237	.381	.398	23.38	15.58	231
Collyer, Gavin	R-R	6-1	165	5-12-01	0	1	27.00	1	0	0	1	3	3	3	0	1	1	.600	.667	1.000	16.67	16.67	6
deGrom, Jacob	L-R	6-4	180	6-19-88	0	0	1.50	2	2	0	6	3	1	1	0	0	8	.150	.150	.250	40.00	0.00	20
DeVito, Ricky	S-R	6-3	195	8-21-98	4	0	4.00	41	0	3	54	34	27	24	2	53	74	.185	.382	.245	29.96	21.46	247
Drake, Kohl	L-L	6-5	220	7-17-00	2	1	3.10	5	5	0	20	11	7	7	3	11	20	.155	.268	.310	24.39	13.41	82
Dunning, Dane	R-R	6-4	225	12-19-94	0	0	0.00	1	1	0	2	1	0	0	0	0	0	.143	.143	.143	0.00	0.00	7
Garabito, Gerson	R-R	6-0	160	8-19-95	0	0	2.08	1	1	0	4	3	2	1	0	2	7	.188	.278	.188	38.89	11.11	18
Garcia, Ryan	R-R	6-0	180	1-24-98	8	4	3.95	16	16	0	82	65	37	36	6	40	76	.217	.320	.324	21.90	11.53	347
Hales, Skylar	R-R	6-4	220	10-24-01	3	0	2.10	24	0	4	30	26	7	7	1	8	31	.241	.303	.352	26.05	6.72	119
Hoopii-Tuionetoa, Anthony	R-R	6-2	190	8-11-00	1	0	0.00	10	0	1	12	7	1	0	0	4	16	.167	.239	.214	34.04	8.51	47
Jennings, Steven	R-R	6-2	175	11-13-98	6	1	2.40	25	0	0	41	27	12	11	3	15	37	.185	.259	.281	22.70	9.20	163
Kelley, Jackson	R-R	6-0	185	4-26-00	4	1	3.38	14	0	2	19	13	7	7	0	5	25	.194	.267	.239	33.33	6.67	75
Kelly, Antoine	L-L	6-5	205	12-5-99	0	0	9.00	1	0	0	1	1	1	1	0	1	2	.250	.400	.750	40.00	20.00	5
Kindreich, Larson	L-L	6-4	210	6-21-99	1	2	4.76	11	0	0	11	11	7	6	0	14	19	.250	.424	.386	32.20	23.73	59
Krauth, Nick	R-R	6-3	170	9-6-99	8	7	5.78	23	17	0	100	112	70	64	7	51	71	.286	.385	.441	15.24	10.94	466
Latz, Jake	R-L	6-2	185	4-8-96	2	0	12.46	4	0	0	4	6	6	6	1	4	8	.316	.458	.579	33.33	16.67	24
Lobus, Ryan	R-R	6-2	180	9-8-00	1	0	3.00	4	0	2	6	6	2	2	1	0	10	.261	.261	.478	43.48	0.00	23
Magdaleno, Bryan	L-L	6-1	202	2-22-01	0	0	0.00	4	0	0	4	1	0	0	0	0	7	.077	.143	.077	50.00	0.00	14
Mahle, Tyler	R-R	6-3	210	9-29-94	0	0	4.50	2	2	0	6	4	3	3	0	1	5	.182	.217	.273	21.74	4.35	23
Maton, Jacob	R-R	6-1	195	8-22-99	0	0	0.00	1	0	0	2	0	0	0	0	0	1	.000	.000	.000	14.29	0.00	7
Mendoza, Damian	L-R	6-1	175	1-25-01	0	0	4.08	8	0	1	18	19	11	8	1	4	16	.275	.315	.348	21.33	5.33	75
Owens, Tyler	R-R	5-10	185	1-9-01	2	0	2.80	26	0	8	35	33	13	11	2	9	35	.252	.305	.330	24.48	6.29	143
Polley, Triston	L-L	6-0	190	12-19-96	2	1	3.32	16	0	0	22	14	8	8	1	15	20	.182	.323	.247	21.51	16.13	93
Rocker, Kumar	R-R	6-5	245	11-22-99	0	0	0.46	5	5	0	20	9	1	1	0	3	29	.132	.169	.191	40.85	4.23	71
Rodriguez, Andy	R-R	6-1	165	12-8-98	4	2	3.17	38	2	3	71	48	26	25	6	30	50	.196	.281	.331	17.79	10.68	281
Santos, Winston	R-R	6-0	160	4-15-02	5	3	4.89	10	10	0	46	39	26	25	8	14	57	.227	.306	.424	29.53	7.25	193
Sborz, Josh	R-R	6-3	215	12-17-93	0	0	36.00	2	0	0	1	2	4	4	0	1	2	.400	.571	.400	28.57	14.29	7
Serrano, Florencio	R-R	6-1	205	2-23-00	0	3	5.19	9	1	2	17	18	12	10	1	9	16	.269	.378	.358	19.51	10.98	82
Stephan, Josh	R-R	6-3	185	11-1-01	2	5	4.94	12	11	0	58	67	32	32	9	17	55	.289	.343	.453	21.91	6.77	251
Teodo, Emiliano	R-R	6-1	165	2-14-01	5	4	1.98	20	19	0	86	53	25	19	4	50	110	.178	.307	.248	30.73	13.97	358
Wolfram, Grant	L-L	6-6	235	12-12-96	1	0	0.00	2	0	0	4	0	0	0	0	1	8	.000	.083	.000	66.67	8.33	12
Wynyard, Kai-Noa	R-R	6-0	176	6-22-02	0	0	0.00	1	0	0	1	1	0	0	0	1	2	.333	.500	.333	50.00	25.00	4

Fielding

Catcher	PCT	G	PO	A	E	DP	PB
Hicks	.990	43	383	15	4	3	6
Johnson	.996	75	681	44	3	4	6
Kapers	1.000	9	82	1	0	0	0
Mitchell	1.000	13	121	6	0	1	3

First Base	PCT	G	PO	A	E	DP
Chavez	1.000	9	49	6	0	5
Hatcher	.993	38	262	20	2	27
Hicks	.895	3	14	3	2	2
Lowe	1.000	1	1	1	0	0
Mitchell	1.000	7	43	2	0	6
Ortiz	.990	82	573	46	6	72

Second Base	PCT	G	PO	A	E	DP
Acosta	.961	36	71	75	6	27
Chavez	.993	37	70	77	1	28
De Goti	.978	32	60	74	3	15
Freeman	1.000	8	14	21	0	7
Hardy	.958	5	14	9	1	7
Rodriguez	.980	26	45	52	2	18

Third Base	PCT	G	PO	A	E	DP
Chavez	.927	16	12	26	3	7
Freeman	.984	102	69	176	4	27
Jung	1.000	2	0	1	0	0
Mejia	.000	1	0	0	0	0
Rodriguez	.878	18	10	26	5	3
Walcott	.800	1	3	1	1	0

Shortstop	PCT	G	PO	A	E	DP
Acosta	.978	67	79	144	5	35
Chavez	.977	16	18	25	1	6
De Goti	1.000	7	11	12	0	3
Rodriguez	.981	49	63	139	4	28
Walcott	1.000	2	1	8	0	2

Outfield	PCT	G	PO	A	E	DP
Cepeda	1.000	50	99	4	0	0
Hatcher	.978	47	88	2	2	1
Mateo	.962	61	127	1	5	1
Mieses	.969	21	28	3	1	1
Ortiz	.974	18	38	0	1	0
Osuna	.978	59	135	1	3	0
Strahm	.987	68	153	3	2	1
Zavala	.988	101	157	12	2	2

TEXAS RANGERS

HICKORY CRAWDADS

HIGH-A

SOUTH ATLANTIC LEAGUE

Batting	B-T	Ht.	Wt.	DOB	AVG	OBP	SLG	G	PA	AB	R	H	2B	3B	HR	RBI	BB	HBP	SH	SF	SO	SB	CS	BB%	SO%
Basabe, Edgar	R-R	6-0	155	4-27-04	.500	.500	.500	1	4	4	0	2	0	0	0	0	0	0	0	0	1	2	0	0.00	25.00
Blackwell, Benjamin	R-R	5-11	185	4-6-99	.186	.271	.227	63	219	194	24	36	6	1	0	14	21	2	0	1	59	16	4	9.59	26.94
Cauley, Cameron	R-R	5-10	170	2-6-03	.235	.297	.411	93	404	370	60	87	17	6	12	37	33	0	0	1	118	27	2	8.17	29.21
Cueva, Danyer	L-R	6-1	160	5-27-04	.245	.317	.396	17	60	53	10	13	5	0	1	5	5	1	0	1	21	2	1	8.33	35.00
Disla, Arturo	R-R	6-2	240	10-8-00	.256	.324	.512	34	139	125	17	32	8	0	8	21	11	2	0	1	36	2	2	7.91	25.90
Dreiling, Dylan	L-L	5-11	197	4-17-03	.198	.340	.279	24	106	86	12	17	4	0	1	9	19	0	0	1	20	5	3	17.92	18.87
Easley, Jayce	B-R	5-8	151	8-2-99	.175	.310	.198	66	217	177	30	31	4	0	0	16	33	2	4	1	65	16	3	15.21	29.95
Figuereo, Gleider	L-R	6-0	165	6-27-04	.207	.263	.364	54	213	198	19	41	7	0	8	20	12	3	0	0	56	2	0	5.63	26.29
Galan, Yosy	R-R	6-4	200	4-25-01	.180	.280	.327	88	326	284	38	51	8	5	8	31	32	8	1	1	123	28	5	9.82	37.73
Gutierrez, Anthony	R-R	6-3	180	11-25-04	.241	.317	.315	71	271	241	35	58	11	2	1	19	21	7	0	2	59	37	6	7.75	21.77
Hardy, Theo	B-R	6-1	185	11-27-01	.207	.333	.345	11	36	29	6	6	1	0	1	2	6	0	0	1	9	2	0	16.67	25.00
Hurdle, Devin	R-R	6-1	190	6-18-00	.175	.278	.206	22	72	63	5	11	2	0	0	6	6	3	0	0	19	1	2	8.33	26.39
Mateo, Daniel	R-R	6-1	165	7-3-01	.262	.347	.310	14	49	42	4	11	2	0	0	5	5	1	0	1	17	3	1	10.20	34.69
Mejia, Esteban	R-R	5-11	165	11-3-04	.000	.167	.000	2	6	5	0	0	0	0	0	0	1	0	0	0	3	0	0	16.67	50.00
Mieses, Luis	L-L	6-3	180	5-31-00	.270	.299	.471	50	204	189	23	51	14	3	6	40	9	1	0	5	35	3	1	4.41	17.16
Mitchell, Tucker	R-R	6-1	210	2-10-01	.192	.282	.308	28	117	104	12	20	3	0	3	13	12	1	0	0	27	1	0	10.26	23.08
Moller, Ian	R-R	6-0	190	10-26-02	.208	.343	.287	84	321	265	31	55	13	1	2	21	54	1	0	1	82	16	0	16.82	25.55
Moore, Malcolm	L-R	6-2	210	7-31-03	.209	.298	.374	25	104	91	14	19	6	0	3	12	8	4	0	1	29	3	1	7.69	27.88
Moreno, Jesus	R-R	5-11	170	4-16-01	.303	.333	.364	11	36	33	3	10	2	0	0	6	2	0	0	1	9	0	0	5.56	25.00
Morrobel, Yeison	L-L	6-2	170	12-8-03	.211	.287	.323	115	471	421	42	89	20	0	9	52	38	8	0	4	106	7	4	8.07	22.51
Osuna, Alejandro	L-L	6-0	185	10-10-02	.272	.339	.486	45	196	173	31	47	6	2	9	29	14	4	4	1	52	10	3	7.14	26.53
Piotto, Konner	L-R	5-9	195	1-1-98	.266	.367	.371	40	148	124	18	33	3	2	2	15	17	4	1	2	31	5	1	11.49	20.95
Scott, Quincy	R-R	6-4	215	1-15-03	.219	.326	.275	103	383	324	29	71	13	1	1	41	43	11	0	5	89	10	4	11.23	23.24
Smith, Marcus	L-L	5-11	185	9-11-00	.180	.291	.270	31	103	89	12	16	2	0	2	9	13	1	0	0	40	4	1	12.62	38.83
Soto, Marco	B-R	5-11	145	3-8-04	.141	.222	.156	19	72	64	2	9	1	0	0	5	5	2	0	1	18	2	1	6.94	25.00
Stark, Cal	R-R	6-1	204	7-27-02	.200	.273	.500	4	11	10	3	2	0	0	1	3	0	1	0	0	4	0	0	0.00	36.36
Walcott, Sebastian	R-R	6-4	190	3-14-06	.261	.342	.443	116	491	433	60	113	31	9	10	49	52	3	0	3	125	26	8	10.59	25.46

Pitching	B-T	Ht.	Wt.	DOB	W	L	ERA	G	GS	SV	IP	Hits	Runs	ER	HR	BB	SO	AVG	OBP	SLG	SO%	BB%	BF
Bonzagni, Paul	R-R	6-3	195	4-1-02	2	0	3.55	5	5	0	25	25	12	10	2	6	28	.248	.303	.366	25.69	5.50	109
Bratt, Mitch	L-L	6-1	190	7-3-03	6	4	3.03	17	15	0	77	62	28	26	6	16	84	.220	.265	.358	27.81	5.30	302
Brewer, Michael	R-R	6-5	215	8-8-00	1	1	4.86	12	0	2	17	14	12	9	3	10	19	.233	.333	.450	26.03	13.70	73
Chi, Bryan	R-R	6-0	205	3-22-99	0	1	0.00	4	0	0	7	6	2	0	0	2	8	.214	.290	.214	25.81	6.45	31
Church, Marc	R-R	6-3	189	3-30-01	0	0	10.80	3	0	0	3	4	4	4	2	3	5	.267	.389	.667	27.78	16.67	18
Clark, Seth	R-L	6-3	220	11-18-99	0	0	0.00	2	0	0	2	2	1	0	0	1	4	.222	.300	.333	40.00	10.00	10
Collyer, Gavin	R-R	6-1	165	5-12-01	3	3	3.24	40	0	7	50	46	33	18	3	32	78	.237	.374	.361	32.77	13.45	238
Curry, Aidan	R-R	6-5	185	7-5-02	3	9	6.44	23	20	0	94	94	73	67	20	43	103	.255	.342	.466	24.41	10.19	422
Davalillo, David	R-R	6-1	175	9-21-02	2	1	2.10	5	5	0	30	30	7	7	1	10	34	.261	.320	.365	27.20	8.00	125
Drake, Kohl	L-L	6-5	220	7-17-00	5	3	2.53	8	8	0	43	32	13	12	4	11	57	.206	.262	.335	33.93	6.55	168
Gessner, Josh	R-R	6-1	205	6-25-00	0	1	3.00	10	0	0	12	6	4	4	0	13	4	.143	.357	.167	7.14	23.21	56
Gonzalez, Jose	R-R	6-3	200	8-5-01	0	1	6.75	1	1	0	4	2	3	3	1	2	4	.143	.250	.357	25.00	12.50	16
Hales, Skylar	R-R	6-4	220	10-24-01	1	0	4.39	20	0	6	27	22	13	13	0	9	35	.220	.282	.290	31.53	8.11	111
Hardy, Theo	S-R	6-1	185	11-27-01	0	0	0.00	1	0	0	0	0	0	0	0	0	0	.000	.000	.000	0.00	0.00	1
Kelley, Jackson	R-R	6-0	185	4-26-00	3	0	3.00	28	0	4	45	24	15	15	6	19	56	.154	.267	.308	30.94	10.50	181
Kindreich, Larson	L-L	6-4	210	6-21-99	0	0	1.62	12	0	3	17	11	3	3	1	9	20	.190	.299	.328	29.85	13.43	67
Lobus, Ryan	R-R	6-2	180	9-8-00	4	5	3.31	17	10	0	71	52	28	26	8	18	99	.203	.274	.379	35.11	6.38	282
Lopez, Leandro	R-R	6-1	200	6-17-02	1	1	9.00	5	2	0	13	13	14	13	1	11	15	.250	.391	.346	23.44	17.19	64
Magdaleno, Bryan	L-L	6-1	202	2-22-01	0	0	0.00	7	0	4	8	0	0	0	0	2	14	.000	.077	.000	53.85	7.69	26
Maton, Jacob	R-R	6-1	195	8-22-99	3	5	4.64	37	0	4	54	61	36	28	5	16	52	.277	.333	.468	21.22	6.53	245
McCarty, D.J.	R-R	6-2	145	9-9-02	2	7	4.43	21	19	0	91	90	50	45	11	34	110	.252	.342	.398	26.83	8.29	410
Mendoza, Brayan	L-L	6-0	155	1-19-04	1	0	3.48	2	2	0	10	10	6	4	2	1	13	.250	.286	.475	30.95	2.38	42
Mendoza, Damian	L-R	6-1	175	1-25-01	2	0	4.85	19	1	1	39	41	23	21	6	15	43	.265	.327	.419	24.86	8.67	173
Mollerus, Josh	R-R	6-3	215	10-6-99	2	4	5.40	20	0	0	23	23	16	14	6	15	33	.256	.358	.522	31.13	14.15	106
Montalvo, Joseph	S-R	6-2	185	5-4-02	4	2	2.44	13	13	0	59	48	21	16	8	19	73	.217	.287	.394	29.92	7.79	244
Morel, Yohanse	R-R	6-0	170	8-23-00	0	3	10.55	17	0	3	21	24	26	25	5	15	23	.289	.396	.494	22.77	14.85	101
Oviedo, Ivan	R-R	6-2	175	10-14-02	0	0	0.00	2	0	1	6	1	0	0	0	3	5	.045	.192	.045	19.23	11.54	26
Peters, DJ	R-R	6-5	225	12-12-95	1	2	5.52	23	0	1	29	29	19	18	4	21	34	.257	.376	.407	24.11	14.89	141
Porter, Brock	R-R	6-4	208	6-3-03	0	2	6.48	3	3	0	8	4	6	6	1	13	8	.143	.467	.250	17.78	28.89	45
Ramirez, Luis	R-R	6-2	200	4-6-01	1	5	8.45	24	4	0	38	49	37	36	6	28	34	.302	.418	.475	17.53	14.43	194
Rodriguez, Adrian	R-R	6-5	192	5-18-01	3	1	6.64	35	0	1	42	26	34	31	6	54	74	.171	.403	.355	34.91	25.47	212
Rosario, Alejandro	R-R	6-1	184	1-6-02	2	2	2.40	8	7	0	41	33	13	11	0	8	60	.214	.258	.273	36.81	4.91	163
Santos, Winston	R-R	6-0	160	4-15-02	6	3	2.80	12	12	0	64	53	21	20	3	20	81	.217	.282	.332	30.45	7.52	266
Savage, Luke	R-R	6-1	200	8-10-01	1	0	4.50	1	0	0	2	3	1	1	0	1	1	.375	.444	.500	11.11	11.11	9
Serrano, Florencio	R-R	6-1	205	2-23-00	2	1	3.34	14	1	0	30	23	14	11	2	16	24	.215	.315	.355	18.90	12.60	127
Simeon, Victor	R-R	6-2	160	12-4-00	0	0	81.00	1	0	0	0	1	3	3	0	4	1	.500	.833	.500	16.67	66.67	6
Stark, Cal	R-R	6-1	204	7-27-02	0	0	0.00	1	0	0	0	0	0	0	0	0	1	.000	.000	.000	100.00	0.00	1
Tiger, Izack	R-R	6-2	185	2-8-01	1	2	4.02	4	4	0	16	13	7	7	3	11	21	.213	.333	.443	29.17	15.28	72
Weems, Avery	R-L	6-2	205	6-6-97	0	1	14.73	3	0	0	4	8	6	6	0	1	4	.444	.474	.556	21.05	5.26	19
Wynyard, Kai-Noa	R-R	6-0	176	6-22-02	0	0	6.75	1	0	0	3	3	2	2	1	3	3	.300	.462	.700	23.08	23.08	13

Fielding

Catcher	PCT	G	PO	A	E	DP	PB
Mitchell	.986	13	140	4	2	0	1
Moller	.989	82	860	36	10	1	7
Moore	.982	13	152	8	3	0	3
Moreno	.988	8	79	3	1	0	2
Piotto	.993	15	146	5	1	0	1
Stark	1.000	1	13	0	0	0	0

First Base	PCT	G	PO	A	E	DP
Disla	1.000	29	199	5	0	14
Mieses	.996	45	227	18	1	17
Mitchell	.976	11	76	6	2	7
Piotto	.990	17	91	6	1	4
Scott	.987	37	208	13	3	18

Second Base	PCT	G	PO	A	E	DP
Blackwell	.976	27	30	51	2	5
Cauley	.983	40	40	79	2	13
Cueva	.894	15	15	27	5	4
Easley	.967	21	19	40	2	3
Hardy	.941	8	12	20	2	2
Hurdle	.932	16	18	23	3	2
Mejia	1.000	2	1	3	0	0
Piotto	.000	1	0	0	0	0
Soto	1.000	6	5	12	0	4

Third Base	PCT	G	PO	A	E	DP
Blackwell	.943	26	17	33	3	3
Cueva	1.000	2	2	0	0	0
Easley	.979	22	12	35	1	1
Figuereo	.913	50	37	58	9	5
Hardy	1.000	2	1	1	0	0
Hurdle	.909	6	1	9	1	0
Soto	.923	12	6	18	2	1
Walcott	.886	20	15	24	5	0

Shortstop	PCT	G	PO	A	E	DP
Blackwell	.913	7	7	14	2	3
Cauley	.941	45	39	73	7	9
Easley	.000	1	0	0	0	0
Soto	1.000	1	1	2	0	1
Walcott	.910	79	101	142	24	28

Outfield	PCT	G	PO	A	E	DP
Basabe	1.000	1	2	0	0	0
Dreiling	1.000	23	36	1	0	1
Easley	1.000	21	38	0	0	0
Galan	.987	72	144	4	2	0
Gutierrez	.985	71	191	6	3	2
Mateo	.950	14	18	1	1	0
Morrobel	.978	84	126	6	3	1
Osuna	1.000	37	67	1	0	0
Scott	.983	59	108	7	2	1
Smith	1.000	29	32	0	0	0

DOWN EAST WOOD DUCKS — *LOW-A*

CAROLINA LEAGUE

Batting	B-T	Ht.	Wt.	DOB	AVG	OBP	SLG	G	PA	AB	R	H	2B	3B	HR	RBI	BB	HBP	SH	SF	SO	SB	CS	BB%	SO%
Alvarez, Erick	R-R	5-10	150	2-1-05	.238	.272	.328	62	250	235	20	56	12	3	1	25	10	2	0	3	61	4	0	4.00	24.40
Barroso, Beycker	R-R	5-10	160	1-24-03	.229	.342	.374	39	156	131	14	30	5	1	4	17	14	9	1	1	40	6	4	8.97	25.64
Blackmon, JoJo	L-L	6-0	183	3-31-03	.166	.250	.276	43	164	145	16	24	4	0	4	15	16	1	0	2	71	6	2	9.76	43.29
Brock, Julian	R-R	6-3	220	6-3-01	.254	.318	.376	95	393	351	54	89	17	4	6	41	31	5	0	6	111	7	6	7.89	28.24
Cabrera, Yeremi	L-L	5-11	155	7-2-05	.185	.298	.247	23	94	81	10	15	3	1	0	6	8	5	0	0	28	7	0	8.51	29.79
Cook, Casey	L-R	6-0	195	10-2-02	.197	.293	.239	20	82	71	6	14	3	0	0	3	5	5	0	1	16	3	0	6.10	19.51
Cueva, Danyer	L-R	6-1	160	5-27-04	.177	.214	.223	34	140	130	14	23	3	0	1	14	7	0	0	3	42	6	0	5.00	30.00
De Jesus, Jose	B-L	6-1	170	1-8-05	.252	.310	.270	28	126	115	15	29	2	0	0	1	8	2	0	1	22	8	5	6.35	17.46
Disla, Arturo	R-R	6-2	240	10-8-00	.281	.359	.438	87	359	320	35	90	17	0	11	50	32	7	0	0	65	2	1	8.91	18.11
Figuereo, Gleider	L-R	6-0	165	6-27-04	.243	.346	.474	63	269	230	44	56	9	4	12	32	35	2	0	2	74	1	0	13.01	27.51
Guerrero, Pablo	R-R	6-2	200	7-31-06	.227	.271	.289	27	107	97	7	22	3	0	1	15	6	1	0	3	25	1	0	5.61	23.36
Hartl, Ben	R-R	5-11	200	1-7-03	.324	.481	.432	14	52	37	5	12	1	0	1	8	9	4	0	2	14	1	0	17.31	26.92
Hurdle, Devin	R-R	6-1	190	6-18-00	.154	.154	.308	3	13	13	2	2	0	1	0	1	0	0	0	0	4	0	0	0.00	30.77
Jones, Keith	L-L	6-2	210	4-29-02	.174	.174	.174	6	23	23	0	4	0	0	0	1	0	0	0	0	9	0	0	0.00	39.13
Lopez, Jesus	L-R	6-1	180	5-24-05	.242	.306	.351	55	232	211	22	51	12	1	3	21	18	2	0	1	68	1	2	7.76	29.31
Macias, Antonis	B-L	5-11	185	2-1-05	.226	.305	.302	15	59	53	3	12	4	0	0	1	5	1	0	0	19	0	1	8.47	32.20
Mejia, Esteban	R-R	5-11	165	11-3-04	.217	.301	.313	50	186	166	18	36	8	1	2	17	16	4	0	0	52	7	1	8.60	27.96
Mendez, Wady	L-L	6-0	155	10-14-04	.233	.336	.291	76	262	227	31	53	8	1	1	14	32	3	0	0	93	23	3	12.21	35.50
Moreno, Jesus	R-R	5-11	170	4-16-01	.050	.174	.200	7	23	20	1	1	0	0	1	2	3	0	0	0	9	0	0	13.04	39.13
Perich, Rafe	B-R	6-3	225	5-22-02	.120	.333	.160	9	33	25	2	3	1	0	0	2	8	0	0	0	8	0	0	24.24	24.24
Pollard, Chandler	R-R	6-2	173	5-3-04	.239	.317	.326	96	326	285	43	68	10	3	3	26	29	6	1	5	106	39	5	8.90	32.52
Smith, Marcus	L-L	5-11	185	9-11-00	.190	.305	.305	60	239	200	22	38	7	2	4	17	32	3	0	4	82	17	4	13.39	34.31
Soto, Marco	R-R	5-11	145	3-8-04	.143	.217	.143	14	46	42	4	6	0	0	0	1	4	0	0	0	17	1	0	8.70	36.96
Specht, Tommy	L-R	6-3	200	6-24-04	.177	.262	.219	65	244	215	25	38	6	0	1	22	20	6	0	3	69	7	2	8.20	28.28
Torres, Marcos	L-L	6-3	163	9-30-04	.178	.280	.300	93	343	297	28	53	8	5	6	35	38	5	0	3	118	12	9	11.08	34.40
Vargas, Echedry	R-R	5-11	170	2-27-05	.276	.321	.454	97	422	392	65	108	24	2	14	48	21	6	1	2	89	29	9	4.98	21.09

Pitching	B-T	Ht.	Wt.	DOB	W	L	ERA	G	GS	SV	IP	Hits	Runs	ER	HR	BB	SO	AVG	OBP	SLG	SO%	BB%	BF
Anazco, Angel	L-L	6-3	195	11-17-01	0	1	27.00	1	0	0	0	2	1	1	0	1	1	.667	.750	1.000	25.00	25.00	4
Bonzagni, Paul	R-R	6-3	195	4-1-02	4	1	3.68	17	11	0	64	50	29	26	4	23	67	.216	.300	.303	25.48	8.75	263
Bormie, Wilian	R-R	6-3	175	2-23-03	6	3	3.47	23	8	0	80	63	34	31	8	42	96	.220	.322	.338	28.49	12.46	337
Curtis, Kolton	S-R	6-4	170	5-5-04	4	7	2.85	23	15	0	82	58	36	26	7	42	80	.194	.301	.331	23.19	12.17	345
Danielson, Joey	R-R	6-3	235	1-11-01	3	1	3.24	7	0	1	8	6	5	3	0	3	6	.207	.303	.207	17.65	8.82	34
Davalillo, David	R-R	6-1	175	9-21-02	6	1	1.79	17	16	0	80	59	18	16	2	22	79	.199	.259	.274	24.69	6.88	320
Drake, Kohl	L-L	6-5	220	7-17-00	2	1	1.67	10	6	0	43	32	10	8	2	9	71	.205	.262	.263	42.26	5.36	168
Gonzalez, Jose	R-R	6-3	200	8-5-01	3	7	2.26	20	12	0	88	69	30	22	3	20	117	.214	.265	.285	33.33	5.70	351
Hartl, Ben	R-R	5-11	200	1-7-03	0	0	0.00	1	0	0	0	0	0	0	0	0	0	.000	.000	.000	0.00	0.00	1
Ireland, Thomas	L-L	6-1	170	6-27-02	1	1	2.16	5	4	0	25	16	6	6	1	8	22	.186	.270	.256	22.00	8.00	100
Jekielek, Jake	R-R	6-0	195	9-4-02	0	1	20.25	2	0	0	1	2	3	3	0	1	1	.250	.333	.250	11.11	11.11	9
Larsen, Kyle	R-R	6-2	240	6-14-03	3	4	5.36	15	11	0	45	41	34	27	3	36	43	.234	.381	.343	19.63	16.44	219
Lobus, Ryan	R-R	6-2	180	9-8-00	3	0	1.53	6	2	0	18	12	4	3	2	4	25	.188	.246	.313	36.23	5.80	69
Loomis, Eric	R-R	6-0	195	3-27-02	0	1	3.00	2	0	0	3	1	2	1	0	4	6	.091	.375	.091	37.50	25.00	16
Magdaleno, Bryan	L-L	6-1	202	2-22-01	6	3	1.76	25	0	5	31	18	10	6	1	19	47	.171	.310	.248	36.72	14.84	128
Matter, Case	R-R	6-2	180	1-16-02	0	2	1.42	12	0	1	13	7	6	2	0	14	18	.152	.350	.174	30.00	23.33	60
Mejia, Aneudis	R-R	5-11	165	12-13-03	0	1	4.50	2	1	0	6	3	3	3	1	6	8	.143	.333	.333	29.63	22.22	27
Mendoza, Brayan	L-L	6-0	155	1-19-04	4	4	2.18	22	17	0	91	78	34	22	6	24	96	.231	.294	.325	25.74	6.43	373
Mota, Alberto	R-R	5-11	170	2-17-03	0	3	2.25	20	0	1	32	20	12	8	0	24	46	.183	.328	.248	34.33	17.91	134
Oviedo, Ivan	R-R	6-2	175	10-14-02	2	0	2.76	14	0	1	33	20	10	10	1	19	37	.179	.316	.259	27.21	13.97	136
Perry, Kamdyn	R-R	6-4	200	8-9-05	0	1	9.00	2	1	0	5	5	5	5	1	3	4	.250	.348	.550	17.39	13.04	23
Rosario, Alejandro	R-R	6-1	184	1-6-02	2	3	2.11	10	10	0	47	36	14	11	2	5	69	.200	.230	.272	36.90	2.67	187
Sanchez, Justin	L-L	6-0	183	10-11-03	3	2	5.19	20	0	2	43	42	28	25	3	27	50	.243	.351	.353	24.75	13.37	202

Pitching	B-T	Ht.	Wt.	DOB	W	L	ERA	G	GS	SV	IP	Hits	Runs	ER	HR	BB	SO	AVG	OBP	SLG	SO%	BB%	BF
Savage, Luke	R-R	6-1	200	8-10-01	3	4	3.77	29	0	6	45	35	21	19	2	21	42	.219	.347	.313	21.21	10.61	198
Scarborough, Caden	R-R	6-5	180	4-1-05	0	0	8.31	2	1	0	4	5	4	4	1	4	5	.278	.435	.444	21.74	17.39	23
Simeon, Victor	R-R	6-2	160	12-4-00	3	2	1.98	25	0	5	36	15	14	8	1	19	54	.120	.257	.216	36.49	12.84	148
Susac, Anthony	R-R	6-3	212	7-31-02	1	0	0.00	8	0	0	9	6	1	0	0	6	12	.176	.300	.265	30.00	15.00	40
Tiger, Izack	R-R	6-2	185	2-8-01	2	0	2.41	5	4	0	19	12	5	5	1	7	22	.188	.278	.266	30.14	9.59	73
Trentadue, Josh	L-L	6-2	185	1-25-02	3	5	4.46	24	8	1	71	71	42	35	2	29	92	.250	.330	.338	28.66	9.03	321
Valdez, Luis	L-L	6-2	158	7-18-03	0	1	9.53	3	1	0	6	12	12	6	2	3	5	.400	.472	.767	13.89	8.33	36
Villavicencio, Adonis	R-R	6-2	200	12-22-00	0	2	4.56	15	0	3	24	23	13	12	1	16	30	.264	.398	.310	27.78	14.81	108
Wynyard, Kai-Noa	R-R	6-0	176	6-22-02	1	1	2.85	24	0	3	47	37	15	15	1	24	41	.222	.330	.329	20.50	12.00	200

Fielding

Catcher	PCT	G	PO	A	E	DP	PB
Barroso	1.000	3	27	4	0	0	0
Brock	.991	74	742	55	7	7	10
Hartl	1.000	6	64	6	0	0	0
Lopez	.989	42	418	30	5	4	5
Moreno	1.000	4	40	3	0	2	0

First Base	PCT	G	PO	A	E	DP
Alvarez	1.000	13	90	5	0	5
Barroso	.987	20	142	7	2	7
Disla	.989	59	399	39	5	35
Guerrero	.985	17	125	8	2	7
Hartl	.943	6	28	5	2	2
Mejia	1.000	4	22	2	0	2
Torres	.988	16	79	3	1	4

Second Base	PCT	G	PO	A	E	DP
Alvarez	.946	24	32	38	4	8
Cook	.955	17	26	37	3	8
Cueva	.925	14	18	19	3	2
Figuereo	.875	2	4	3	1	1
Hurdle	.909	2	4	6	1	2
Macias	1.000	4	11	8	0	2
Pollard	.971	53	62	103	5	19
Soto	1.000	6	5	13	0	0
Vargas	.978	10	18	26	1	4

Third Base	PCT	G	PO	A	E	DP
Alvarez	.600	2	2	1	2	0
Barroso	.889	4	1	7	1	0
Disla	.000	1	0	0	1	0
Figuereo	.904	60	39	84	13	3
Hurdle	.667	1	0	2	1	0
Mejia	.958	41	27	65	4	3
Perich	.538	9	4	3	6	0
Pollard	.829	13	8	21	6	2
Soto	1.000	3	2	3	0	0

Shortstop	PCT	G	PO	A	E	DP
Cueva	.941	21	33	47	5	14
Mejia	1.000	5	9	12	0	3
Pollard	.921	14	12	23	3	5
Soto	.947	5	5	13	1	1
Vargas	.920	86	112	200	27	28

Outfield	PCT	G	PO	A	E	DP
Alvarez	1.000	15	18	2	0	0
Blackmon	.985	39	62	3	1	1
Cabrera	.977	23	40	3	1	3
De Jesus	1.000	28	49	2	0	0
Jones	.750	5	3	0	1	0
Macias	1.000	8	12	0	0	0
Mendez	.990	61	99	4	1	0
Pollard	1.000	13	22	1	0	0
Smith	.990	58	98	3	1	0
Specht	.990	62	94	3	1	0
Torres	.993	80	133	3	1	0

ACL RANGERS — ROOKIE

ARIZONA COMPLEX LEAGUE

Batting	B-T	Ht.	Wt.	DOB	AVG	OBP	SLG	G	PA	AB	R	H	2B	3B	HR	RBI	BB	HBP	SH	SF	SO	SB	CS	BB%	SO%
Arredondo, Angel	R-R	5-8	190	10-25-06	.184	.411	.263	29	107	76	16	14	3	0	1	7	24	6	0	1	24	2	3	22.43	22.43
Barroso, Beycker	R-R	5-10	160	1-24-03	.250	.475	.393	12	40	28	6	7	4	0	0	4	11	1	0	0	4	0	1	27.50	10.00
Basabe, Edgar	R-R	6-0	155	4-27-04	.219	.275	.266	31	69	64	8	14	3	0	0	7	5	0	0	0	18	6	1	7.25	26.09
Blackmon, JoJo	L-L	6-0	183	3-31-03	.083	.389	.167	4	18	12	5	1	1	0	0	1	5	1	0	0	3	0	0	27.78	16.67
Cabrera, Yeremi	L-L	5-11	155	7-2-05	.301	.438	.571	49	210	163	52	49	11	3	9	39	40	3	0	4	42	17	4	19.05	20.00
Castillo, Yolfran	R-R	6-3	165	2-8-07	.333	.379	.350	15	66	60	10	20	1	0	0	6	5	0	0	1	7	4	2	7.58	10.61
Cauley, Cameron	R-R	5-10	170	2-6-03	.444	.545	1.444	3	11	9	4	4	0	0	3	4	2	0	0	0	3	0	1	18.18	27.27
Cueva, Danyer	L-R	6-1	160	5-27-04	.294	.294	.353	5	17	17	3	5	1	0	0	3	0	0	0	0	2	0	0	0.00	11.76
De Jesus, Jose	B-L	6-1	170	1-8-05	.335	.407	.445	50	215	182	46	61	10	5	0	28	21	5	1	6	42	21	8	9.77	19.53
Espinoza, Alfredo	R-R	6-0	160	9-23-04	.158	.304	.211	15	23	19	3	3	1	0	0	5	4	0	0	0	6	0	0	17.39	26.09
Foscue, Justin	R-R	5-11	205	3-2-99	.412	.524	.765	6	21	17	2	7	3	0	1	3	4	0	0	0	2	1	0	19.05	9.52
Guerrero, Pablo	R-R	6-2	200	7-31-06	.301	.367	.522	51	210	186	34	56	14	3	7	38	18	3	0	3	63	1	1	8.57	30.00
Gutierrez, Anthony	R-R	6-3	180	11-25-04	.267	.267	.333	5	15	15	3	4	1	0	0	0	0	0	0	0	4	6	0	0.00	26.67
Lemos, Kleimer	B-R	6-1	175	6-3-05	.260	.269	.429	18	78	77	8	20	6	2	1	15	0	1	0	0	20	1	1	0.00	25.64
Macias, Antonis	B-L	5-11	185	2-1-05	.350	.519	.463	30	108	80	16	28	7	1	0	13	25	3	0	0	14	4	5	23.15	12.96
Marquez, Luis	R-R	5-10	150	8-31-05	.254	.345	.380	48	171	142	27	36	9	0	3	25	23	0	0	6	32	4	4	13.45	18.71
Martin, Max	L-R	6-1	205	5-5-05	.230	.314	.356	37	153	135	30	31	7	2	2	26	15	2	0	1	41	6	0	9.80	26.80
Mejia, Esteban	R-R	5-11	165	11-3-04	.331	.416	.525	35	137	118	23	39	12	1	3	13	16	2	0	1	35	11	2	11.68	25.55
Mieses, Luis	L-L	6-3	180	5-31-00	.385	.619	.538	6	21	13	0	5	0	1	0	6	7	1	0	0	0	0	0	33.33	0.00
Morel, Braylin	R-R	6-2	180	1-19-06	.307	.407	.575	41	182	153	35	47	10	5	7	37	21	6	0	2	43	12	2	11.54	23.63
Narvaez, Efrenyer	R-R	5-11	155	7-25-02	.219	.289	.288	27	83	73	8	16	3	1	0	8	4	4	0	2	20	0	1	4.82	24.10
Osorio, Hector	L-L	6-0	150	4-6-05	.286	.456	.364	31	104	77	20	22	1	1	1	22	21	4	1	1	19	7	1	20.19	18.27
Piotto, Konner	L-R	5-9	195	1-1-98	.182	.250	.364	4	12	11	2	2	0	1	0	0	1	0	0	0	2	1	0	8.33	16.67
Romero, Josue	R-R	5-9	190	9-19-02	.091	.231	.182	6	13	11	2	1	1	0	0	0	2	0	0	0	3	0	0	15.38	23.08
Soto, Marco	B-R	5-11	145	3-8-04	.500	.556	.667	7	9	6	2	3	1	0	0	3	2	0	0	1	2	0	0	22.22	22.22
Sulbaran, Juan	R-R	5-11	165	10-1-05	.257	.337	.338	24	86	74	15	19	6	0	0	10	4	6	0	2	14	1	0	4.65	16.28
Vargas, Jhocsuanth	R-R	5-11	170	8-31-06	.250	.357	.500	6	14	12	4	3	0	0	1	4	2	0	0	0	1	0	0	14.29	7.14

Pitching	B-T	Ht.	Wt.	DOB	W	L	ERA	G	GS	SV	IP	Hits	Runs	ER	HR	BB	SO	AVG	OBP	SLG	SO%	BB%	BF
Agreda, Ismael	R-R	6-0	150	10-8-03	2	2	3.55	7	5	0	25	20	13	10	2	17	29	.208	.339	.333	25.22	14.78	115
Anazco, Angel	L-L	6-3	195	11-17-01	0	0	4.61	9	0	1	14	9	7	7	0	11	22	.180	.349	.320	34.92	17.46	63
Arias, Jordy	R-R	5-11	185	8-4-05	0	1	10.80	2	1	0	5	7	9	6	0	6	8	.350	.464	.650	27.59	20.69	29
Bradford, Cody	L-L	6-4	197	2-22-98	0	0	0.00	1	1	0	1	0	0	0	0	0	1	.000	.000	.000	33.33	0.00	3
Brennan, Tim	R-R	6-4	212	12-18-96	1	0	0.00	2	1	0	4	1	0	0	0	0	4	.077	.077	.077	30.77	0.00	13
Brewer, Michael	R-R	6-5	215	8-8-00	0	0	6.75	10	0	1	13	11	12	10	0	8	24	.220	.350	.300	40.00	13.33	60
Brito, Biembenido	R-R	6-3	180	2-13-03	4	1	7.76	18	1	0	31	31	29	27	6	24	48	.258	.400	.458	32.00	16.00	150
Burke, Brock	L-L	6-4	210	8-4-96	0	0	0.00	2	2	0	2	1	0	0	0	0	4	.143	.143	.143	57.14	0.00	7
Bursick-Harrington, Logan	R-R	6-4	185	1-22-01	2	2	7.00	5	0	1	18	22	19	14	2	13	22	.301	.427	.493	24.72	14.61	89
Cueto, Johnny	R-R	5-11	229	2-15-86	0	0	3.00	1	1	0	3	3	1	1	1	0	4	.250	.250	.500	33.33	0.00	12
Espinoza, Alfredo	R-R	6-0	160	9-23-04	0	0	9.00	4	0	0	2	2	2	2	0	0	1	.250	.500	.250	8.33	0.00	12

Pitching	B-T	Ht.	Wt.	DOB	W	L	ERA	G	GS	SV	IP	Hits	Runs	ER	HR	BB	SO	AVG	OBP	SLG	SO%	BB%	BF
Ireland, Thomas	L-L	6-1	170	6-27-02	2	1	5.65	13	6	0	43	51	33	27	4	15	53	.288	.364	.412	26.77	7.58	198
Keaney, Daniel	R-R	6-4	185	8-24-04	3	2	4.38	12	3	3	39	39	24	19	5	13	50	.255	.335	.412	28.74	7.47	174
Kindreich, Larson	L-L	6-4	210	6-21-99	0	0	5.40	2	0	0	2	1	1	1	0	2	3	.167	.375	.167	37.50	25.00	8
Larsen, Kyle	R-R	6-2	240	6-14-03	2	0	4.20	5	3	0	15	13	10	7	3	7	20	.220	.309	.407	29.41	10.29	68
Leath, Jackson	R-R	6-1	192	6-19-99	0	0	0.00	2	0	0	2	2	0	0	0	0	0	.286	.286	.286	0.00	0.00	7
Lee, Chase	R-R	6-0	170	8-13-98	1	0	2.70	3	1	0	3	4	1	1	0	0	7	.286	.286	.429	50.00	0.00	14
Mahle, Tyler	R-R	6-3	210	9-29-94	0	0	0.00	1	1	0	3	1	0	0	0	1	5	.111	.200	.111	50.00	10.00	10
Mejia, Aneudis	R-R	5-11	165	12-13-03	0	0	7.71	5	1	0	9	11	8	8	1	7	11	.297	.400	.514	24.44	15.56	45
Morse, Brendan	R-R	6-3	185	5-24-04	0	3	9.44	13	5	0	34	54	42	36	7	20	29	.360	.449	.573	16.48	11.36	176
Mota, Alberto	R-R	5-11	170	2-17-03	2	1	3.32	12	1	2	19	17	8	7	2	9	29	.236	.333	.361	34.52	10.71	84
Munoz, Luimy	R-R	6-2	160	7-28-02	4	3	8.42	14	5	0	26	28	28	24	1	14	36	.272	.372	.359	29.51	11.48	122
Oviedo, Ivan	R-R	6-2	175	10-14-02	0	0	0.00	1	0	0	1	1	1	0	0	0	2	.200	.200	.600	40.00	0.00	5
Perry, Kamdyn	R-R	6-4	200	8-9-05	2	1	6.58	10	4	0	26	26	23	19	2	18	22	.268	.410	.351	18.03	14.75	122
Peters, DJ	R-R	6-5	225	12-12-95	1	0	2.00	6	0	1	9	3	4	2	1	3	18	.103	.235	.207	52.94	8.82	34
Porter, Brock	R-R	6-4	208	6-3-03	0	2	7.36	5	4	0	11	6	11	9	1	11	10	.150	.393	.225	17.86	19.64	56
Pruitt, Austin	R-R	5-10	185	8-31-89	0	0	2.25	3	2	0	4	5	1	1	0	0	4	.294	.294	.471	23.53	0.00	17
Reed, Michael	S-R	6-4	218	4-27-95	2	2	3.14	20	0	1	29	17	13	10	0	29	38	.159	.353	.206	27.34	20.86	139
Rocker, Kumar	R-R	6-5	245	11-22-99	0	1	6.43	3	2	0	7	11	8	5	1	1	8	.355	.364	.484	24.24	3.03	33
Romero, Josue	R-R	5-9	190	9-19-02	0	0	27.00	1	0	0	1	4	3	3	1	0	0	.571	.571	1.000	0.00	0.00	7
Sanchez, Justin	L-L	6-0	183	10-11-03	0	0	0.00	2	1	0	3	3	0	0	0	0	2	.250	.250	.333	16.67	0.00	12
Scarborough, Caden	R-R	6-5	180	4-1-05	2	1	6.00	4	1	0	6	8	4	4	0	5	8	.320	.433	.360	26.67	16.67	30
Simeon, Victor	R-R	6-2	160	12-4-00	0	1	18.00	1	0	0	1	2	3	2	0	3	2	.500	.714	1.000	28.57	42.86	7
Soto, Marco	S-R	5-11	145	3-8-04	0	0	13.50	2	0	0	2	4	3	3	0	1	1	.500	.455	.750	9.09	9.09	11
Tiger, Izack	R-R	6-2	185	2-8-01	0	0	2.31	4	4	0	12	11	3	3	0	3	16	.256	.304	.372	34.78	6.52	46
Trausch, Michael	L-L	6-2	190	2-13-04	3	0	3.00	17	2	1	27	25	11	9	0	25	39	.255	.427	.296	29.77	19.08	131
Valverde, Michael	L-L	6-2	211	12-7-02	1	0	5.40	5	0	0	8	6	5	5	0	7	8	.207	.342	.241	21.05	18.42	38
Villavicencio, Adonis	R-R	6-2	200	12-22-00	2	0	0.98	8	0	2	18	12	4	2	0	3	21	.185	.217	.215	30.00	4.29	70
Wiles, Collin	R-R	6-4	222	5-30-94	0	0	0.00	2	2	0	2	2	0	0	0	0	1	.250	.333	.250	11.11	0.00	9

Fielding

C: Narvaez 24, Sulbaran 24, Espinoza 7, Vargas 5, Romero 3, Piotto 2, Barroso 1. **1B:** Guerrero 36, Martin 18, Foscue 4, Lemos 3, Espinoza 2, Macias 1, Mieses 1, Narvaez 1. **2B:** Macias 23, Marquez 16, Mejia 11, Arredondo 8, Lemos 3, Soto 2. **3B:** Mejia 23, Lemos 16, Marquez 13, Barroso 6, Macias 3, Soto 3, Arredondo 2, Narvaez 1. **SS:** Marquez 22, Arredondo 19, Castillo 15, Cueva 5, Cauley 3, Barroso 1, Mejia 1. **LF:** Cabrera 16, De Jesus 13, Basabe 13, Morel 10, Osorio 8, Mieses 3, Martin 2, Barroso 1, Macias 1. **CF:** De Jesus 30, Cabrera 17, Osorio 11, Gutierrez 5, Basabe 3, Morel 1. **RF:** Morel 24, Osorio 10, Martin 10, Basabe 8, Cabrera 5, De Jesus 5, Guerrero 3, Blackmon 1, Barroso 1.

DSL RANGERS BLUE — *ROOKIE*

DOMINICAN SUMMER LEAGUE

Batting	B-T	Ht.	Wt.	DOB	AVG	OBP	SLG	G	PA	AB	R	H	2B	3B	HR	RBI	BB	HBP	SH	SF	SO	SB	CS	BB%	SO%
Arias, Joaquin	L-L	6-1	160	10-4-06	.244	.300	.267	10	50	45	10	11	1	0	0	7	3	1	0	1	5	3	0	6.00	10.00
Batista, Andry	R-R	6-4	170	3-26-07	.247	.422	.390	43	192	146	32	36	3	3	4	33	42	3	0	1	56	15	2	21.88	29.17
Celesten, Yeisy	L-R	5-11	160	6-28-05	.277	.445	.386	24	110	83	14	23	7	1	0	11	23	3	0	1	20	4	2	20.91	18.18
Cuello, Adriel	R-R	6-1	175	12-15-05	.308	.357	.487	10	43	39	6	12	2	1	1	4	3	0	1	0	10	1	3	6.98	23.26
De La Cruz, Johmphy	R-R	6-0	180	4-12-07	.155	.325	.194	41	163	129	18	20	5	0	0	10	32	1	0	1	64	10	5	19.63	39.26
Flames, Daniel	B-R	5-11	160	10-27-06	.262	.490	.305	44	205	141	43	37	6	0	0	22	56	7	1	0	32	12	6	27.32	15.61
Guzman, Michael	R-R	6-1	165	1-31-06	.305	.455	.475	17	77	59	13	18	5	1	1	16	15	2	0	1	14	6	0	19.48	18.18
Herrera, Angel	L-L	5-11	160	9-16-05	.234	.379	.318	44	196	154	34	36	6	2	1	17	33	5	1	3	37	27	5	16.84	18.88
Lantigua, Claudiel	B-R	5-9	150	7-1-07	.276	.373	.322	46	178	152	33	42	5	1	0	15	22	2	1	1	38	7	5	12.36	21.35
Leen, Klendy	R-R	5-11	190	6-12-07	.139	.378	.177	30	111	79	14	11	0	0	1	7	28	3	0	1	41	3	0	25.23	36.94
Linares, Winder	L-L	5-10	155	10-13-06	.250	.387	.328	38	147	116	26	29	4	1	1	20	24	2	5	0	28	10	2	16.33	19.05
Marcano, Jose	R-R	5-10	160	10-25-06	.281	.382	.382	47	215	178	32	50	7	1	3	38	25	6	3	3	28	5	1	11.63	13.02
Montero, Neurelin	R-R	5-10	170	5-26-06	.231	.583	.231	6	24	13	4	3	0	0	0	1	9	2	0	0	3	0	0	37.50	12.50
Palacios, Nathaniel	B-R	6-1	170	9-29-06	.155	.260	.238	27	100	84	14	13	1	0	2	8	8	5	0	3	34	3	2	8.00	34.00
Ramirez, Manni	R-R	6-5	190	4-25-07	.224	.311	.348	53	229	201	33	45	10	0	5	30	21	5	0	1	65	0	4	9.17	28.38
Sanchez, Javier	R-R	5-11	160	8-17-07	.300	.452	.417	39	155	120	15	36	9	1	1	20	25	9	0	1	18	3	1	16.13	11.61

Pitching	B-T	Ht.	Wt.	DOB	W	L	ERA	G	GS	SV	IP	Hits	Runs	ER	HR	BB	SO	AVG	OBP	SLG	SO%	BB%	BF
Anazco, Angel	L-L	6-3	195	11-17-01	0	1	4.50	1	1	0	2	2	1	1	0	1	4	.250	.333	.250	44.44	11.11	9
Armas, Keiber	R-R	6-1	170	3-24-03	1	4	6.29	14	8	0	44	51	40	31	0	31	51	.291	.414	.400	23.72	14.42	215
Astudillo, Anthony	R-R	6-0	165	7-11-05	0	0	4.85	4	3	0	13	16	7	7	1	5	9	.314	.375	.412	16.07	8.93	56
Caraballo, Uilfe	R-R	5-9	160	2-16-05	0	1	4.22	6	1	0	21	21	16	10	1	12	19	.266	.392	.329	19.39	12.24	98
De Jesus, Yunier	R-R	6-1	170	11-28-05	1	1	10.95	8	0	0	12	14	19	15	0	13	14	.286	.439	.388	20.90	19.40	67
De La Cruz, Johmphy	R-R	6-0	180	4-12-07	0	0	0.00	1	0	0	0	0	0	0	0	0	0	.000	.000	.000	0.00	0.00	1
Garcia, Luis	L-L	6-4	220	2-18-04	0	0	6.66	20	0	1	24	19	19	18	0	21	31	.211	.388	.322	26.72	18.10	116
Gonzalez, Yeferson	R-R	6-0	165	1-11-07	0	0	18.00	3	0	0	7	12	14	14	1	6	9	.364	.523	.545	20.45	13.64	44
Heredia, Manuel	R-R	6-2	165	12-13-02	2	1	6.61	10	0	2	16	21	18	12	0	10	16	.304	.395	.406	19.75	12.35	81
Hernandez, Christopher	R-R	6-0	160	4-8-06	2	0	2.87	8	7	0	31	17	16	10	0	24	42	.162	.338	.210	30.88	17.65	136
Jorge, Inmanol	R-R	6-3	175	2-3-06	2	1	6.10	12	0	1	21	24	17	14	1	13	16	.300	.412	.425	16.49	13.40	97
Lafalaise, Jesus	R-R	6-1	175	2-4-05	0	2	5.84	7	5	0	25	26	19	16	1	20	21	.306	.445	.518	19.09	18.18	110
Leen, Klendy	R-R	5-11	190	6-12-07	0	0	0.00	1	0	0	1	1	0	0	0	0	0	.333	.250	.667	0.00	0.00	4
Lopez, Gilberto	R-R	6-1	175	3-30-04	2	1	4.73	10	0	2	32	39	18	17	2	20	39	.302	.400	.450	26.00	13.33	150
Lopez, Jesus	R-R	6-1	170	7-10-07	0	1	10.50	4	2	0	6	5	10	7	1	11	7	.217	.486	.391	18.92	29.73	37
Martinez, Felix	R-R	6-0	180	7-5-02	1	0	0.00	5	0	0	6	2	2	0	0	7	9	.095	.367	.095	30.00	23.33	30
Martinez, Frank	R-R	6-2	165	4-30-02	2	0	3.52	6	0	1	15	10	8	6	2	10	15	.182	.318	.327	22.73	15.15	66
Morales, Moises	R-R	6-1	175	2-15-04	1	0	1.50	2	0	0	6	2	1	1	0	4	6	.105	.292	.158	25.00	16.67	24
Nivar, Jormy	R-R	6-3	170	5-7-03	4	2	1.25	9	8	0	36	25	11	5	0	2	41	.187	.204	.239	29.71	1.45	138

Pitching	B-T	Ht.	Wt.	DOB	W	L	ERA	G	GS	SV	IP	Hits	Runs	ER	HR	BB	SO	AVG	OBP	SLG	SO%	BB%	BF
Ortiz, Walkin	R-R	6-6	200	12-7-01	2	0	10.29	7	0	0	7	9	8	8	1	11	7	.310	.535	.517	16.28	25.58	43
Paniagua, Angel	R-R	6-1	180	10-18-05	1	1	9.28	4	0	0	11	7	11	11	0	10	9	.179	.365	.282	17.31	19.23	52
Rivera, Bernardo	R-R	6-0	165	3-17-05	2	3	6.75	9	4	0	29	22	28	22	1	23	39	.196	.366	.277	26.90	15.86	145
Sanchez, Javier	R-R	5-11	160	8-17-07	0	0	0.00	1	0	0	1	1	0	0	0	0	0	.200	.200	.200	0.00	0.00	5
Silvestre, Jose	R-R	6-0	165	8-9-06	0	6	9.19	10	10	0	31	39	38	32	2	26	37	.298	.443	.473	22.16	15.57	167
Tejada, Danery	R-R	6-0	180	10-21-02	1	1	18.00	5	0	1	4	4	9	8	0	11	3	.267	.571	.333	10.71	39.29	28
Tovar, Jhemiangel	R-R	6-4	195	4-21-03	1	1	3.86	8	0	1	14	17	9	6	0	4	13	.298	.349	.351	20.31	6.25	64
Ulloa, Noel	R-R	6-3	190	6-4-03	0	0	0.00	3	0	0	4	1	0	0	0	2	9	.083	.214	.083	64.29	14.29	14
Yean, Ariel	R-R	6-2	165	9-14-05	0	0	32.40	5	0	0	5	12	19	18	4	9	3	.545	.692	1.182	7.69	23.08	39

Fielding

C: Sanchez 21, Marcano 20, Leen 10, Montero 6. **1B:** Leen 18, Palacios 16, Batista 13, De La Cruz 9, Sanchez 3, Celesten 1. **2B:** Lantigua 40, De La Cruz 13, Celesten 3, Flames 1. **3B:** Celesten 20, De La Cruz 14, Guzman 12, Cuello 5, Flames 3, Palacios 2, Lantigua 1. **SS:** Flames 40, Cuello 5, Guzman 4, Lantigua 4, De La Cruz 3. **LF:** Herrera 37, Arias 10, Batista 7, De La Cruz 2, Linares 2. **CF:** Linares 32, Batista 18, Herrera 7, Arias 1. **RF:** Ramirez 48, Batista 7, Linares 3, De La Cruz 1.

DSL RANGERS RED — ROOKIE

DOMINICAN SUMMER LEAGUE

Batting	B-T	Ht.	Wt.	DOB	AVG	OBP	SLG	G	PA	AB	R	H	2B	3B	HR	RBI	BB	HBP	SH	SF	SO	SB	CS	BB%	SO%
Arias, Joaquin	L-L	6-1	160	10-4-06	.265	.395	.338	24	87	68	14	18	3	1	0	10	16	0	1	2	18	5	1	18.39	20.69
Baquera, Sebastian	R-R	5-7	176	1-11-07	.314	.483	.488	27	116	86	24	27	6	0	3	25	21	8	0	1	18	4	1	18.10	15.52
Batista, Andry	R-R	6-4	170	3-26-07	.275	.362	.375	10	47	40	8	11	0	2	0	7	4	2	0	1	12	0	0	8.51	25.53
Bruzual, Daniel	R-R	6-0	170	2-1-05	.275	.342	.304	21	76	69	17	19	2	0	0	9	7	0	0	0	10	3	0	9.21	13.16
Castillo, Yolfran	R-R	6-3	165	2-8-07	.414	.552	.471	20	97	70	27	29	4	0	0	20	22	2	0	2	8	6	2	22.68	8.25
Cuello, Adriel	R-R	6-1	175	12-15-05	.175	.277	.228	22	65	57	10	10	3	0	0	4	5	3	0	0	21	4	2	7.69	32.31
Flames, Daniel	B-R	5-11	160	10-27-06	.655	.725	.862	10	40	29	7	19	2	2	0	11	7	3	0	1	5	2	0	17.50	12.50
Gamez, Jesus	R-R	6-0	190	3-4-03	.000	.000	.000	12	2	2	1	0	0	0	0	0	0	0	0	0	2	0	0	0.00	100.00
Guzman, Michael	R-R	6-1	165	1-31-06	.261	.386	.322	34	141	115	21	30	4	0	1	22	20	4	0	1	30	8	1	14.18	21.28
Lemos, Kleimer	B-R	6-1	175	6-3-05	.484	.535	.855	15	71	62	20	30	7	2	4	26	5	3	0	1	12	2	2	7.04	16.90
Marcano, Jose	R-R	5-10	160	10-25-06	.238	.333	.238	5	24	21	5	5	0	0	0	4	2	1	0	0	3	0	1	8.33	12.50
Martha, Curley	R-R	5-11	165	9-19-06	.282	.395	.427	54	248	206	48	58	11	2	5	42	28	12	0	2	55	19	4	11.29	22.18
Mendoza, Aniel	R-R	6-2	185	9-13-04	.266	.380	.442	44	188	154	38	41	6	3	5	31	26	4	0	3	37	5	2	13.83	19.68
Montero, Neurelin	R-R	5-10	170	5-26-06	.190	.469	.310	19	64	42	11	8	3	1	0	4	13	9	0	0	12	0	0	20.31	18.75
Pinder, Rashawn	L-L	5-8	145	6-4-07	.271	.390	.394	55	270	221	48	60	10	4	3	31	36	9	1	3	58	22	3	13.33	21.48
Rondon, Joswuill	L-L	5-11	165	12-19-05	.300	.300	.300	4	10	10	0	3	0	0	0	1	0	0	0	0	2	0	0	0.00	20.00
Sanchez, Javier	R-R	5-11	160	8-17-07	.000	.500	.000	2	8	4	0	0	0	0	0	0	4	0	0	0	1	0	0	50.00	12.50
Santana, Paulino	R-R	6-2	180	11-17-06	.292	.465	.364	53	260	195	46	57	6	4	0	30	52	12	0	1	38	20	5	20.00	14.62
Santos, Steven	R-R	5-11	200	7-6-07	.210	.418	.284	28	110	81	21	17	3	0	1	6	23	6	0	0	29	8	2	20.91	26.36
Tovar, Deward	L-L	5-11	180	4-4-06	.241	.364	.434	43	173	145	23	35	7	3	5	31	25	3	0	0	54	4	1	14.45	31.21
Vargas, Jhocsuanth	R-R	5-11	170	8-31-06	.316	.348	.474	8	23	19	2	6	0	0	1	8	2	0	0	2	2	0	1	8.70	8.70
Wong, Williams	L-R	5-10	180	10-12-05	.197	.356	.279	45	190	147	27	29	9	0	1	23	35	3	2	3	27	2	2	18.42	14.21

Pitching	B-T	Ht.	Wt.	DOB	W	L	ERA	G	GS	SV	IP	Hits	Runs	ER	HR	BB	SO	AVG	OBP	SLG	SO%	BB%	BF
Arias, Jordy	R-R	5-11	185	8-4-05	3	0	0.00	5	3	0	19	11	1	0	0	7	21	.172	.264	.188	29.17	9.72	72
Arias, Yeimison	R-R	6-1	165	1-9-05	1	1	4.64	6	3	1	21	21	11	11	3	3	23	.241	.283	.402	25.00	3.26	92
Chiquillo, Alejandro	R-R	6-1	180	12-6-02	3	0	0.67	7	6	0	27	15	5	2	0	10	30	.163	.252	.196	29.13	9.71	103
Delgado, Jesus	L-L	5-10	176	9-15-03	2	0	2.45	12	5	0	33	29	18	9	2	20	54	.227	.344	.328	35.53	13.16	152
Gamez, Jesus	R-R	6-0	190	3-4-03	2	1	3.25	10	0	2	28	19	10	10	2	12	40	.204	.308	.355	37.38	11.21	107
Garcia, Jaiker	R-R	6-4	175	12-23-04	1	3	6.41	11	10	0	39	46	34	28	4	18	43	.286	.368	.447	23.63	9.89	182
Garcia, Luis	L-L	6-4	220	2-18-04	0	1	14.40	6	0	0	5	8	10	8	0	6	3	.348	.559	.435	8.82	17.65	34
Gonzalez, Yeferson	R-R	6-0	165	1-11-07	2	2	6.61	8	0	2	16	13	12	12	1	16	21	.220	.405	.288	26.58	20.25	79
Heredia, Manuel	R-R	6-2	165	12-13-02	0	0	15.43	1	0	0	2	4	4	4	0	1	1	.444	.417	.667	7.69	7.69	13
Hernandez, Christopher	R-R	6-0	160	4-8-06	1	0	9.00	2	1	0	6	5	6	6	1	8	9	.227	.452	.364	29.03	25.81	31
Jorge, Inmanol	R-R	6-3	175	2-3-06	0	0	3.86	1	0	0	2	4	1	1	0	0	2	.400	.400	.400	20.00	0.00	10
Martinez, Emmanuel	L-L	6-1	170	8-28-03	2	2	5.40	12	2	1	28	20	18	17	1	24	49	.204	.378	.296	38.58	18.90	127
Martinez, Frank	R-R	6-2	165	4-30-02	1	0	3.32	8	0	2	22	17	14	8	3	18	33	.224	.381	.355	34.02	18.56	97
Morales, Moises	R-R	6-1	175	2-15-04	0	1	1.93	12	0	3	23	13	5	5	2	8	28	.160	.250	.272	30.43	8.70	92
Nivar, Jormy	R-R	6-3	170	5-7-03	2	0	3.60	2	2	0	10	13	6	4	0	3	9	.310	.370	.333	19.15	6.38	47
Nunez, German	R-R	6-3	155	5-24-02	6	0	2.89	12	11	0	53	38	19	17	4	11	74	.204	.266	.317	36.45	5.42	203
Ortiz, Walkin	R-R	6-6	200	12-7-01	0	1	10.38	3	0	0	4	2	5	5	1	5	1	.182	.444	.455	5.56	27.78	18
Paniagua, Angel	R-R	6-1	180	10-18-05	1	0	9.53	4	0	0	6	4	6	6	0	9	6	.190	.433	.238	20.00	30.00	30
Peralta, Eddy	R-R	6-2	165	1-27-03	2	0	5.40	14	0	1	22	7	13	13	0	21	41	.100	.351	.129	42.27	21.65	97
Rivera, Bernardo	R-R	6-0	165	3-17-05	0	1	1.80	2	1	0	10	6	3	2	0	4	13	.176	.275	.206	32.50	10.00	40
Rodriguez, Geury	L-L	6-0	155	10-19-04	1	1	2.79	7	3	1	19	13	6	6	0	6	26	.188	.263	.217	34.21	7.89	76
Rubio, Johander	R-R	6-1	185	7-6-06	2	1	6.61	11	9	0	33	27	25	24	0	39	40	.227	.419	.286	24.84	24.22	161
Silvestre, Jose	R-R	6-0	165	8-9-06	0	0	0.00	1	0	0	1	0	0	0	0	1	0	.000	.250	.000	0.00	25.00	4
Tovar, Jhemiangel	R-R	6-4	195	4-21-03	1	1	5.87	5	0	1	8	7	6	5	0	7	10	.241	.405	.310	27.03	18.92	37
Ulloa, Noel	R-R	6-3	190	6-4-03	0	1	8.64	7	0	1	8	10	8	8	0	5	9	.313	.442	.438	20.93	11.63	43
Urbaez, Rayner	R-R	6-0	175	2-13-03	4	0	0.33	17	0	2	27	14	3	1	0	10	23	.156	.243	.211	22.12	9.62	104
Valverde, Michael	L-L	6-2	211	12-7-02	2	0	3.46	8	0	1	13	9	8	5	0	7	25	.184	.322	.224	42.37	11.86	59
Wong, Williams	L-R	5-10	180	10-12-05	0	0	45.00	1	0	0	1	4	5	5	0	0	0	.571	.625	1.286	0.00	0.00	8

Fielding

C: Baquera 24, Montero 18, Bruzual 13, Vargas 8, Sanchez 2, Santos 1. **1B:** Santos 23, Mendoza 14, Lemos 13, Bruzual 5, Marcano 3, Batista 3. **2B:** Wong 37, Cuello 9, Flames 9, Martha 3, Mendoza 2, Lemos 2. **3B:** Guzman 29, Martha 16, Wong 10, Castillo 4. **SS:** Martha 36, Castillo 16, Guzman 6, Flames 1. **LF:** Pinder 37, Santana 12, Arias 6, Batista 2, Rondon 2, Cuello 1, Tovar 1. **CF:** Santana 41, Pinder 17. **RF:** Tovar 26, Arias 19, Cuello 10, Batista 7, Gamez 2, Rondon 2, Pinder 1.

Toronto Blue Jays

SEASON SYNOPSIS: After making the playoffs the previous two seasons, the Blue Jays were never really in it in 2024. They fell below .500 at the end of April and never reached the mark again, with their 74-88 final record a 15-game fall from 2023 and their worst record since 2019.

HIGH POINT: Dave Stieb, in 1990, remains the only Blue Jay ever to throw a no-hitter, inexplicably, after being known for several near-misses throughout the 1980s. Second-year righthander Bowden Francis, transitioning from the bullpen to the rotation in '24, matched Stieb by carrying two no-hitters into the ninth inning in the same season, just 18 days apart. On Aug. 24, he gave up a leadoff homer in the ninth to the Angels' Taylor Ward in a 3-1 victory. On Sept. 11, he gave up a leadoff homer in the ninth to the Mets' Francisco Lindor. New York rallied for the victory but Francis established himself as a rotation piece, going 8-5, 3.30 overall.

LOW POINT: The Jays tumbled to 11th in the American League in runs, and shortstop Bo Bichette was a barometer. After three straight seasons with at least 175 hits, Bichette started slowly, had a left calf strain when he started to heat up that sidelined him twice after June, and played one game in September before breaking a bone in his right hand to end his worst MLB season. After hitting 73 homers the previous three seasons, he hit four in 81 games in 2024.

NOTABLE ROOKIES: Late-blooming Spencer Horwitz provided some needed offensive pop while splitting time between first and second base, posting a .790 OPS in his age-26 season. Addison Barger got some run at third base and outfield but hit just .197, with some power, in 208 at-bats. Panamanian Leo Jimenez helped replace Bichette as the second-half shortstop but didn't remind anyone of peak Bichette.

KEY TRANSACTIONS: The Jays signed Cuban righthander Yariel Rodriguez to a six-year, $34 million deal in February. Rodriguez went 1-8, 4.47 in 21 big league starts. Toronto actively sold at the trade deadline, trading Isiah Kiner-Falefa (to the Pirates); veteran catcher Danny Jansen (Red Sox); free-agent signing Kevin Kiermaier (Dodgers); and relievers Yimi Garcia (Mariners) and Trevor Richards (Twins). Toronto's biggest card to play was Yusei Kikuchi, and it extracted three players–righthander Jake Bloss, infielder Will Wagner and outfielder Joey Loperfido—from the Astros for the Japanese lefthander.

OPENING DAY PAYROLL: $221,862,600 (7th)

PLAYERS OF THE YEAR

MAJOR LEAGUE

Vladimir Guerrero Jr.
1B
.323/.396/.544
30 HR, 103 RBIs
44 2B, 72 BB

MINOR LEAGUE

Alan Roden
OF
(AAA)
.293/.391/.475
16 HR, 64 BB, 75 SO

ORGANIZATION LEADERS

Batting		*Qualifiers
MAJORS		
* AVG	Vladimir Guerrero Jr.	.323
* OPS	Vladimir Guerrero Jr.	.940
HR	Vladimir Guerrero Jr.	30
RBI	Vladimir Guerrero Jr.	103
MINORS		
* AVG	Josh Kasevich, Buffalo/New Hampshire	.296
* OBP	Alan Roden, Buffalo/New Hampshire	.391
* SLG	Arjun Nimmala, Dunedin/FCL Blue Jays	.482
* OPS	Alan Roden, Buffalo/New Hampshire	.866
R	Josh Kasevich, Buffalo/New Hampshire	74
H	Josh Kasevich, Buffalo/New Hampshire	154
TB	Alan Roden, Buffalo/New Hampshire	214
2B	Josh Kasevich, Buffalo/New Hampshire	28
3B	Arjun Nimmala, Dunedin/FCL Blue Jays	70
HR	Damiano Palmegiani, Buffalo/Dunedin	21
RBI	Alan Roden, Buffalo/New Hampshire	75
BB	Riley Tirotta, Buffalo/Dunedin/New Hampshire	72
SO	Devonte Brown, New Hampshire	148
SB	Dasan Brown, Vancouver/New Hampshire	35

Pitching		#Qualifiers
MAJORS		
W	Jose Berrios	16
# ERA	Jose Berrios	3.60
SO	Chris Bassitt	168
SV	Chad Green	17
MINORS		
W	Luis Quinones, Buffalo/FCL Blue Jays	11
L	Abdiel Mendoza, New Hampshire/Buffalo	12
# ERA	Rafael Sanchez, Vancouver/New Hampshire	3.64
G	Mason Fluharty, Buffalo	56
GS	Devereaux Harrison, New Hampshire	26
GS	Trenton Wallace, New Hampshire/Buffalo	26
SV	Grayson Thurman, Vancouver	7
IP	Devereaux Harrison, New Hampshire	132
BB	Juaron Watts-Brown, Dunedin/Vancouver	60
SO	Juaron Watts-Brown, Dunedin/Vancouver	131
# AVG	Trenton Wallace, New Hampshire/Buffalo	.225

2024 PERFORMANCE

General Manager: Ross Atkins. **Farm Director:** Joe Sclafani. **Scouting Director:** Shane Farrell.

Class	Team	League	W	L	PCT	Finish	Manager
Majors	Toronto Blue Jays	American	74	88	.457	12 (15)	John Schneider
Triple-A	Buffalo Bisons	International	68	80	.459	18 (20)	Casey Candaele
Double-A	N. Hampshire Fisher Cats	Eastern	52	84	.382	12 (12)	Cesar Martin
High-A	Vancouver Canadians	Northwest	68	61	.527	2 (6)	Brent Lavallee
Low-A	Dunedin Blue Jays	Florida State	69	61	.531	3 (10)	Jose Mayorga
Rookie	FCL Blue Jays	Florida Complex	12	44	.214	15 (15)	Andy Fermin
Rookie	DSL Blue Jays	Dominican	30	24	.556	16 (51)	Daniel Canellas
Overall 2024 Minor League Record			**299**	**354**	**.458**	**28th (30)**	

TORONTO BLUE JAYS

ORGANIZATION STATISTICS

TORONTO BLUE JAYS

AMERICAN LEAGUE

Batting	B-T	Ht.	Wt.	DOB	AVG	OBP	SLG	G	PA	AB	R	H	2B	3B	HR	RBI	BB	HBP	SH	SF	SO	SB	CS	BB%	SO%
Barger, Addison	L-R	6-0	210	11-12-99	.197	.250	.351	69	225	208	20	41	11	0	7	28	14	1	0	1	60	2	0	6.22	26.67
Berroa, Steward	B-R	5-9	178	6-5-99	.189	.333	.216	28	45	37	7	7	1	0	0	1	8	0	0	0	14	6	2	17.78	31.11
Bichette, Bo	R-R	6-0	190	3-5-98	.225	.277	.322	81	336	311	29	70	16	1	4	31	20	3	0	2	64	5	1	5.95	19.05
Biggio, Cavan	L-R	6-2	200	4-11-95	.200	.323	.291	44	131	110	15	22	4	0	2	9	14	6	0	0	42	2	0	10.69	32.06
Clase, Jonatan	B-R	5-9	150	5-23-02	.350	.435	.550	7	23	20	3	7	1	0	1	2	1	2	0	0	3	0	1	4.35	13.04
Clement, Ernie	R-R	6-0	170	3-22-96	.263	.284	.408	139	452	434	48	114	21	3	12	51	11	3	2	2	41	12	3	2.43	9.07
De Los Santos, Luis	R-R	6-1	160	6-9-98	.172	.226	.241	13	31	29	2	5	2	0	0	1	2	0	0	0	10	0	0	6.45	32.26
Guerrero, Vladimir	R-R	6-2	245	3-16-99	.323	.396	.544	159	697	616	98	199	44	1	30	103	72	5	0	4	96	2	2	10.33	13.77
Heineman, Tyler	B-R	5-10	190	6-19-91	.100	.308	.100	6	13	10	2	1	0	0	0	0	3	0	0	0	5	0	0	23.08	38.46
Horwitz, Spencer	L-R	5-10	190	11-14-97	.265	.357	.433	97	381	328	46	87	19	0	12	40	42	7	0	4	70	0	0	11.02	18.37
Jansen, Danny	R-R	6-2	215	4-15-95	.212	.303	.369	61	228	198	27	42	13	0	6	18	25	2	0	3	42	0	0	10.96	18.42
Jimenez, Leo	R-R	5-10	215	5-17-01	.229	.329	.358	63	210	179	18	41	11	0	4	19	12	16	0	3	59	0	0	5.71	28.10
Kiermaier, Kevin	L-R	6-1	210	4-22-90	.195	.236	.310	82	217	200	24	39	7	2	4	18	10	1	5	1	66	5	0	4.61	30.41
Kiner-Falefa, Isiah	R-R	5-11	190	3-23-95	.292	.338	.420	82	281	257	32	75	8	2	7	33	13	6	3	2	37	3	1	4.63	13.17
Kirk, Alejandro	R-R	5-8	245	11-6-98	.253	.319	.359	103	386	340	23	86	19	1	5	54	35	2	0	9	51	0	0	9.07	13.21
Loperfido, Joey	L-R	6-3	220	5-11-99	.197	.236	.343	43	144	137	13	27	8	3	2	9	6	1	0	0	52	2	1	4.17	36.11
Lukes, Nathan	L-R	5-11	180	7-12-94	.303	.371	.447	22	91	76	13	23	4	2	1	10	10	0	2	3	9	1	0	10.99	9.89
Martinez, Orelvis	R-R	5-11	200	11-19-01	.333	.333	.333	1	3	3	0	1	0	0	0	0	0	0	0	0	1	0	0	0.00	33.33
Schneider, Davis	R-R	5-9	190	1-26-99	.191	.282	.343	135	454	397	48	76	19	1	13	46	47	5	0	5	144	6	0	10.35	31.72
Serven, Brian	R-R	6-0	207	5-5-95	.159	.243	.222	28	71	63	6	10	4	0	0	3	5	2	1	0	22	0	0	7.04	30.99
Springer, George	R-R	6-3	220	9-19-89	.220	.303	.371	145	614	545	74	120	19	3	19	56	60	6	0	2	115	16	1	9.77	18.73
Turner, Justin	R-R	5-11	202	11-23-84	.256	.350	.372	91	349	301	37	77	17	0	6	31	39	6	0	3	60	0	2	11.17	17.19
Varsho, Daulton	L-R	5-10	207	7-2-96	.214	.293	.407	136	513	459	73	98	21	7	18	58	48	4	1	1	137	10	2	9.36	26.71
Vogelbach, Daniel	L-R	6-0	270	12-17-92	.186	.278	.300	31	79	70	5	13	5	0	1	8	9	0	0	0	17	0	0	11.39	21.52
Wagner, Will	L-R	5-11	210	7-29-98	.305	.337	.451	24	86	82	8	25	6	0	2	11	4	0	0	0	16	0	0	4.65	18.60

Pitching	B-T	Ht.	Wt.	DOB	W	L	ERA	G	GS	SV	IP	Hits	Runs	ER	HR	BB	SO	AVG	OBP	SLG	SO%	BB%	BF
Bassitt, Chris	R-R	6-5	217	2-22-89	10	14	4.16	31	31	0	171	180	91	79	18	70	168	.270	.352	.397	22.16	9.23	758
Berrios, Jose	R-R	6-0	205	5-27-94	16	11	3.60	32	32	0	192	168	79	77	31	54	153	.235	.300	.406	19.47	6.87	786
Burr, Ryan	R-R	6-4	220	5-28-94	0	2	4.13	34	4	0	33	29	16	15	4	12	47	.228	.300	.402	33.57	8.57	140
Cabrera, Genesis	L-L	6-2	180	10-10-96	3	3	3.59	69	0	2	63	63	31	25	10	29	50	.268	.348	.443	18.45	10.70	271
Clement, Ernie	R-R	6-0	170	3-22-96	0	0	9.00	1	0	0	1	2	1	1	0	0	0	.400	.400	.600	0.00	0.00	5
Cuas, Jose	R-R	6-3	195	6-28-94	0	0	9.00	4	0	0	3	3	3	3	1	4	3	.250	.500	.500	16.67	22.22	18
de Geus, Brett	R-R	6-2	190	11-4-97	0	0	15.43	2	0	0	2	3	4	4	0	2	1	.333	.455	.667	9.09	18.18	11
Eisert, Brandon	L-L	6-2	205	1-19-98	0	0	4.05	3	0	0	7	5	3	3	0	4	2	.227	.346	.273	7.69	15.38	26
Espino, Paolo	R-R	5-10	212	1-10-87	0	1	8.31	3	1	0	9	14	8	8	3	5	3	.378	.455	.811	6.82	11.36	44
Francis, Bowden	R-R	6-5	220	4-22-96	8	5	3.30	27	13	0	104	74	41	38	17	22	92	.196	.253	.371	22.55	5.39	408
Frias, Luis	R-R	6-3	245	5-23-98	0	0	21.60	4	0	0	3	8	8	8	1	3	5	.421	.500	.737	22.73	13.64	22
Garcia, Yimi	R-R	6-1	230	8-18-90	3	0	2.70	29	0	5	30	16	9	9	3	8	42	.154	.228	.298	36.52	6.96	115
Gausman, Kevin	L-R	6-2	205	1-6-91	14	11	3.83	31	31	0	181	165	86	77	20	56	162	.238	.296	.392	21.43	7.41	756
Green, Chad	L-R	6-3	215	5-24-91	4	6	3.21	53	0	17	53	41	20	19	8	14	46	.216	.271	.379	21.90	6.67	210
Heineman, Tyler	S-R	5-10	190	6-19-91	0	0	0.00	1	0	0	1	1	0	0	0	0	0	.250	.250	.250	0.00	0.00	4
Kikuchi, Yusei	L-L	6-0	210	6-17-91	4	9	4.75	22	22	0	116	125	63	61	17	30	130	.272	.318	.431	26.16	6.04	497
Kiner-Falefa, Isiah	R-R	5-11	190	3-23-95	0	0	4.50	2	0	0	2	1	1	1	0	2	0	.167	.333	.167	0.00	22.22	9
Little, Brendon	L-L	6-2	195	8-11-96	1	2	3.74	49	0	1	46	41	21	19	7	19	36	.238	.318	.390	18.65	9.84	193
Lucas, Easton	L-L	6-4	180	9-23-96	0	0	11.57	2	0	0	5	6	6	6	1	4	2	.333	.455	.611	9.09	18.18	22
Manoah, Alek	R-R	6-6	285	1-9-98	1	2	3.70	5	5	0	24	17	16	10	5	8	26	.189	.282	.378	25.24	7.77	103
Mayza, Tim	L-L	6-3	215	1-15-92	0	1	8.03	35	0	0	25	36	24	22	3	12	16	.340	.397	.528	13.22	9.92	121
Nance, Tommy	R-R	6-6	235	3-19-91	0	3	4.09	20	0	0	22	18	12	10	2	9	19	.222	.304	.370	20.43	9.68	93
Parsons, Wes	R-R	6-5	206	9-6-92	0	0	10.80	2	0	0	5	6	6	6	2	2	2	.286	.348	.619	8.70	8.70	23
Pearson, Nate	R-R	6-6	255	8-19-96	0	1	5.63	41	0	2	40	45	26	25	8	17	51	.285	.352	.494	28.02	9.34	182
Pop, Zach	R-R	6-4	220	9-19-96	2	4	5.59	58	0	1	48	45	36	30	9	19	33	.243	.317	.422	15.79	9.09	209
Richards, Trevor	R-R	6-2	205	5-15-93	2	1	4.64	45	2	0	52	36	30	27	7	24	49	.189	.278	.332	22.48	11.01	218

Pitching	B-T	Ht.	Wt.	DOB	W	L	ERA	G	GS	SV	IP	Hits	Runs	ER	HR	BB	SO	AVG	OBP	SLG	SO%	BB%	BF
Robertson, Nick	R-R	6-6	265	7-16-98	0	0	0.00	1	0	0	1	0	0	0	0	0	0	.000	.000	.000	0.00	0.00	3
Rodriguez, Yariel	R-R	6-0	165	3-10-97	1	8	4.47	21	21	0	87	74	46	43	11	40	85	.229	.319	.387	23.10	10.87	368
Rodriguez, Yerry	R-R	6-2	198	10-15-97	0	0	15.43	4	0	0	5	10	9	8	2	2	5	.455	.481	.864	18.52	7.41	27
Romano, Jordan	R-R	6-5	210	4-21-93	1	2	6.59	15	0	8	14	16	10	10	4	4	13	.286	.344	.554	20.97	6.45	62
Swanson, Erik	R-R	6-3	225	9-4-93	2	2	5.03	45	0	0	39	36	22	22	11	14	37	.235	.304	.516	22.02	8.33	168
Tate, Dillon	R-R	6-2	190	5-1-94	0	0	5.40	4	0	0	3	4	2	2	0	3	4	.308	.438	.385	25.00	18.75	16
White, Mitch	R-R	6-3	210	12-28-94	1	0	5.40	4	0	0	10	10	6	6	1	4	6	.270	.333	.459	14.29	9.52	42
Yarbrough, Ryan	R-L	6-5	205	12-31-91	1	0	2.01	12	0	0	31	18	7	7	2	7	26	.173	.256	.260	22.22	5.98	117

Fielding

Catcher	PCT	G	PO	A	E	DP	PB
Heineman	1.000	5	37	2	0	1	0
Jansen	.993	53	424	16	3	0	1
Kirk	.991	93	706	46	7	6	7
Serven	.994	27	168	5	1	0	3

First Base	PCT	G	PO	A	E	DP
Biggio	1.000	5	5	0	0	0
De Los Santos	1.000	2	4	0	0	0
Guerrero	.990	121	873	70	10	90
Horwitz	.996	41	236	21	1	24
Turner	1.000	12	61	6	0	2
Wagner	1.000	1	2	0	0	0

Second Base	PCT	G	PO	A	E	DP
Biggio	.979	25	41	52	2	12
Clement	1.000	4	2	6	0	2
Horwitz	.982	39	35	75	2	16
Jimenez	.976	21	35	47	2	15
Kiner-Falefa	.993	40	49	84	1	20
Martinez	.833	1	1	4	1	0
Schneider	1.000	56	47	87	0	16
Wagner	.988	21	29	53	1	12

Third Base	PCT	G	PO	A	E	DP
Barger	.925	36	28	46	6	7
Biggio	1.000	4	2	4	0	0
Clement	.954	96	60	147	10	16
De Los Santos	.926	11	8	17	2	0
Guerrero	.941	12	12	20	2	3
Kiner-Falefa	.989	38	26	65	1	9
Turner	.714	5	0	5	2	0

Shortstop	PCT	G	PO	A	E	DP
Bichette	.971	81	76	159	7	35
Clement	.979	41	55	87	3	21
Jimenez	.983	43	43	75	2	14
Kiner-Falefa	.980	15	18	32	1	9

Outfield	PCT	G	PO	A	E	DP
Clement	.000	1	0	0	0	0
Kiner-Falefa	.000	1	0	0	0	0
Lukes	.982	23	50	4	1	0
Kiermaier	.982	81	167	1	3	0
Barger	.983	37	54	3	1	0
Schneider	.988	93	155	3	2	0
Springer	.991	124	219	3	2	0
Varsho	.994	162	320	5	2	1
Berroa	1.000	21	27	1	0	0
Biggio	1.000	10	22	0	0	0
Clase	1.000	6	12	0	0	0
Loperfido	1.000	45	93	1	0	0

BUFFALO BISONS — *TRIPLE-A*

INTERNATIONAL LEAGUE

Batting	B-T	Ht.	Wt.	DOB	AVG	OBP	SLG	G	PA	AB	R	H	2B	3B	HR	RBI	BB	HBP	SH	SF	SO	SB	CS	BB%	SO%
Arnold, Bryce	R-R	5-10	175	7-24-01	.286	.286	.571	3	14	14	3	4	1	0	1	7	0	0	0	0	1	0	0	0.00	7.14
Barger, Addison	L-R	6-0	210	11-12-99	.260	.391	.466	57	249	204	41	53	15	0	9	38	40	4	0	0	48	4	1	16.06	19.28
Barry, Braden	R-R	6-4	190	2-6-02	.273	.333	.364	3	12	11	0	3	1	0	0	2	1	0	0	0	5	0	0	8.33	41.67
Berroa, Steward	B-R	5-9	178	6-5-99	.281	.371	.454	79	300	260	54	73	9	3	10	47	35	3	1	1	71	34	8	11.67	23.67
Bichette, Bo	R-R	6-0	190	3-5-98	.286	.286	.357	4	14	14	1	4	1	0	0	2	0	0	0	0	2	0	0	0.00	14.29
Cancel, Gabriel	R-R	6-0	205	12-8-96	.228	.362	.439	33	138	114	21	26	6	0	6	15	23	1	0	0	43	3	1	16.67	31.16
Clarke, Phil	L-R	5-11	190	3-24-98	.230	.352	.323	50	193	161	21	37	6	0	3	21	27	4	0	1	28	3	0	13.99	14.51
Clase, Jonatan	B-R	5-9	150	5-23-02	.244	.288	.363	35	146	135	19	33	10	0	2	11	9	0	0	2	38	12	4	6.16	26.03
De Los Santos, Luis	R-R	6-1	160	6-9-98	.260	.375	.441	43	154	127	25	33	5	0	6	16	21	3	0	1	35	3	1	13.64	22.73
Eden, Cam	R-R	6-1	205	3-31-98	.198	.299	.322	91	332	283	34	56	10	2	7	35	39	3	3	3	91	26	7	11.75	27.41
Henry, Payton	R-R	6-0	229	6-24-97	.274	.337	.432	27	104	95	13	26	6	0	3	18	7	2	0	0	19	0	0	6.73	18.27
Hiraldo, Miguel	R-R	5-9	197	9-5-00	.205	.289	.233	22	83	73	8	15	2	0	0	8	7	2	0	1	29	3	1	8.43	34.94
Horwitz, Spencer	L-R	5-10	190	11-14-97	.335	.456	.514	57	259	212	41	71	22	2	4	38	44	3	0	0	41	3	3	16.99	15.83
Jansen, Danny	R-R	6-2	215	4-15-95	.308	.357	.615	4	14	13	2	4	1	0	1	6	1	0	0	0	4	0	0	7.14	28.57
Jimenez, Leo	R-R	5-10	215	5-17-01	.271	.416	.431	57	226	181	40	49	8	0	7	23	30	15	0	0	34	3	1	13.27	15.04
Kasevich, Josh	R-R	6-1	200	1-17-01	.325	.382	.433	41	173	157	23	51	8	0	3	23	14	1	0	1	25	3	0	8.09	14.45
Kiner-Falefa, Isiah	R-R	5-11	190	3-23-95	.333	.333	.333	2	6	6	1	2	0	0	0	0	0	0	0	0	0	0	0	0.00	0.00
Lantigua, Rafael	R-R	5-7	153	4-28-98	.265	.367	.336	130	521	446	61	118	20	0	4	33	70	3	1	1	100	16	6	13.44	19.19
Lukes, Nathan	L-R	5-11	180	7-12-94	.333	.403	.469	54	231	207	30	69	7	0	7	31	22	2	0	0	36	4	2	9.52	15.58
Martinez, Orelvis	R-R	5-11	200	11-19-01	.267	.346	.523	74	319	281	54	75	19	1	17	49	27	8	0	2	76	0	0	8.46	23.82
McDowell, Max	R-R	6-1	208	1-12-94	.172	.254	.320	55	190	169	24	29	4	0	7	23	12	7	1	1	64	1	0	6.32	33.68
Morris, Tanner	L-R	6-0	190	9-13-97	.500	.750	.500	1	4	2	1	1	0	0	0	0	2	0	0	0	1	1	0	50.00	25.00
Palmegiani, Damiano	R-R	6-0	195	1-24-00	.210	.311	.381	123	501	433	63	91	17	0	19	69	53	12	0	3	141	2	1	10.58	28.14
Raposo, Nick	R-R	5-10	200	6-3-98	.246	.361	.311	20	72	61	5	15	1	0	1	5	10	1	0	0	14	0	0	13.89	19.44
Robertson, Will	L-L	6-0	215	12-26-97	.226	.319	.429	119	464	403	64	91	23	1	19	71	50	7	0	4	145	3	2	10.78	31.25
Roden, Alan	L-R	5-11	215	12-22-99	.314	.406	.510	71	286	245	41	77	15	3	9	48	35	4	0	2	41	8	0	12.24	14.34
Serven, Brian	R-R	6-0	207	5-5-95	.265	.390	.379	40	159	132	17	35	6	0	3	15	26	1	0	0	46	0	0	16.35	28.93
Spain, Garrett	L-R	5-10	178	9-21-00	.143	.250	.286	2	8	7	0	1	1	0	0	0	1	0	0	0	3	0	0	12.50	37.50
Tirotta, Riley	R-R	6-3	195	8-21-98	.240	.360	.425	85	342	287	40	69	15	1	12	49	45	9	0	1	96	6	2	13.16	28.07
Turconi, Michael	L-R	5-10	185	6-24-99	.196	.257	.227	27	105	97	16	19	3	0	0	11	8	0	0	0	35	1	0	7.62	33.33
Votto, Joey	L-R	6-2	220	9-10-83	.143	.275	.214	15	51	42	6	6	0	0	1	4	8	0	0	1	22	0	0	15.69	43.14
Wagner, Will	L-R	5-11	210	7-29-98	.400	.516	.600	7	31	25	6	10	2	0	1	2	5	1	0	0	4	0	0	16.13	12.90

Pitching	B-T	Ht.	Wt.	DOB	W	L	ERA	G	GS	SV	IP	Hits	Runs	ER	HR	BB	SO	AVG	OBP	SLG	SO%	BB%	BF
Bash, Andrew	R-R	6-0	190	8-1-96	4	0	2.97	27	16	0	79	58	30	26	4	35	72	.204	.304	.278	21.82	10.61	330
Bechtold, Andrew	R-R	6-1	185	4-18-96	1	0	12.46	4	0	0	4	8	6	6	1	7	6	.381	.536	.524	21.43	25.00	28
Bloss, Jake	R-R	6-3	205	6-23-01	0	4	6.91	8	8	0	27	33	23	21	5	15	25	.289	.374	.482	19.08	11.45	131
Boyer, Ryan	R-R	6-2	225	5-4-97	0	1	18.00	4	0	0	4	7	9	8	2	4	4	.368	.458	.842	16.67	16.67	24
Burnette, Jimmy	L-L	6-2	205	10-19-98	0	0	7.20	8	0	1	10	12	8	8	0	7	7	.300	.431	.325	13.73	13.73	51
Burr, Ryan	R-R	6-4	220	5-28-94	0	0	11.25	5	0	0	4	6	6	5	0	4	9	.300	.417	.400	37.50	16.67	24
Cancel, Gabriel	R-R	6-0	205	12-8-96	0	0	0.00	1	0	0	0	1	0	0	0	0	0	.500	.500	.500	0.00	0.00	2

Cooke, Connor	R-R	6-1	203	11-2-99	1	2	4.55	33	0	5	32	25	18	16	3	28	30	.208	.358	.367	20.27	18.92	148
Cuas, Jose	R-R	6-3	195	6-28-94	1	1	6.89	16	0	1	16	22	12	12	3	7	16	.333	.413	.545	21.33	9.33	75
Dallas, Chad	R-R	5-11	206	6-26-00	2	4	6.34	14	14	0	61	73	44	43	10	24	50	.296	.367	.470	17.79	8.54	281
Danner, Hagen	R-R	6-1	215	9-30-98	3	0	3.15	33	0	7	34	32	15	12	4	13	34	.244	.308	.405	23.29	8.90	146
de Geus, Brett	R-R	6-2	190	11-4-97	0	0	0.00	3	0	0	3	3	0	0	0	0	3	.250	.250	.333	25.00	0.00	12
Eisert, Brandon	L-L	6-2	205	1-19-98	4	2	3.86	42	4	3	54	51	23	23	7	21	66	.252	.327	.406	29.07	9.25	227
Espino, Paolo	R-R	5-10	212	1-10-87	2	7	4.88	20	19	0	87	100	54	47	13	23	57	.291	.340	.491	15.16	6.12	376
Fisher, Braydon	R-R	6-4	180	7-26-00	2	1	6.38	17	0	0	18	24	15	13	2	14	21	.312	.413	.494	22.83	15.22	92
Fluharty, Mason	R-L	6-2	215	8-13-01	5	4	3.63	56	0	3	67	54	31	27	8	25	76	.222	.303	.391	27.44	9.03	277
Francis, Bowden	R-R	6-5	220	4-22-96	3	1	0.93	6	4	0	19	8	4	2	1	3	24	.121	.171	.167	34.29	4.29	70
Fraze, Nick	R-R	6-3	180	10-24-97	0	2	3.79	17	4	1	36	33	16	15	5	14	35	.239	.325	.399	22.29	8.92	157
Frias, Luis	R-R	6-3	245	5-23-98	0	0	0.96	9	0	0	9	8	2	1	0	5	12	.211	.302	.211	27.91	11.63	43
Garcia, Yimi	R-R	6-1	230	8-18-90	0	1	10.80	2	0	0	2	2	2	2	0	1	2	.333	.429	.333	28.57	14.29	7
Green, Chad	L-R	6-3	215	5-24-91	0	0	0.00	3	0	0	3	2	0	0	0	1	1	.182	.250	.364	8.33	8.33	12
Hernandez, Adrian	R-R	5-8	190	1-22-00	1	2	22.50	4	0	0	4	8	12	10	0	6	5	.400	.567	.450	16.67	20.00	30
Juenger, Hayden	R-R	6-0	180	8-9-00	3	4	4.19	54	0	2	69	67	35	32	6	26	64	.259	.333	.402	21.69	8.81	295
Kaprielian, James	R-R	6-3	225	3-2-94	3	4	7.11	12	12	0	49	62	42	39	13	34	40	.302	.401	.556	16.53	14.05	242
Kuhnel, Joel	R-R	6-5	290	2-19-95	1	0	1.04	6	0	0	9	9	1	1	0	4	1	.281	.351	.313	2.70	10.81	37
Little, Brendon	L-L	6-2	195	8-11-96	0	2	4.15	16	0	0	17	17	9	8	0	13	25	.262	.385	.277	31.65	16.46	79
Lucas, Easton	L-L	6-4	180	9-23-96	0	1	1.37	6	3	0	20	8	5	3	0	5	21	.123	.205	.185	28.77	6.85	73
Macko, Adam	L-L	6-0	170	12-30-00	0	0	9.00	1	1	0	3	4	3	3	2	3	3	.308	.438	.846	18.75	18.75	16
Manoah, Alek	R-R	6-6	285	1-9-98	0	2	6.50	4	4	0	18	23	13	13	4	7	26	.315	.370	.562	32.10	8.64	81
Mayers, Mike	R-R	6-2	220	12-6-91	2	5	6.10	31	3	0	41	45	32	28	4	22	46	.278	.378	.407	23.71	11.34	194
McDowell, Max	R-R	6-1	208	1-12-94	0	0	24.30	3	0	0	3	11	9	9	1	3	3	.524	.583	.810	12.50	12.50	24
Mendoza, Abdiel	R-R	5-10	160	9-19-98	1	0	5.06	3	0	0	5	3	5	3	2	5	5	.150	.346	.450	19.23	19.23	26
Pardinho, Eric	R-R	5-10	155	1-5-01	2	1	5.34	24	0	0	29	25	22	17	3	18	29	.234	.346	.355	22.48	13.95	129
Pop, Zach	R-R	6-4	220	9-19-96	0	1	1.54	11	0	4	12	9	3	2	0	5	12	.200	.280	.244	24.00	10.00	50
Quinones, Luis	R-R	6-0	205	7-2-97	11	0	5.15	35	0	0	73	69	44	42	4	51	83	.246	.368	.352	24.48	15.04	339
Ramirez, Emmanuel	R-R	6-2	190	7-15-94	0	0	8.31	5	0	0	4	6	5	4	2	1	5	.316	.350	.684	23.81	4.76	21
Robbins, Jimmy	L-L	6-3	190	12-22-97	0	0	7.71	2	0	0	2	2	2	2	1	2	3	.250	.400	.625	30.00	20.00	10
Robertson, Nick	R-R	6-6	265	7-16-98	0	0	0.00	2	0	0	2	1	0	0	0	0	0	.143	.143	.143	0.00	0.00	7
Rodriguez, Yariel	R-R	6-0	165	3-10-97	0	1	1.33	8	7	0	20	12	4	3	0	13	33	.167	.299	.167	37.93	14.94	87
Rodriguez, Yerry	R-R	6-2	198	10-15-97	0	0	1.35	6	0	0	7	3	1	1	0	9	10	.136	.375	.182	31.25	28.13	32
Romano, Jordan	R-R	6-5	210	4-21-93	0	0	0.00	2	0	0	1	1	0	0	0	4	1	.250	.625	.250	12.50	50.00	8
Sanchez, Aaron	R-R	6-4	212	7-1-92	3	6	7.92	14	14	0	61	64	60	54	13	39	41	.263	.380	.469	14.04	13.36	292
Schultz, Paxton	L-R	6-3	205	1-5-98	6	4	4.11	40	7	0	92	80	45	42	10	44	112	.237	.323	.383	28.43	11.17	394
Stadler, Fitz	R-R	6-9	230	4-2-97	0	0	15.00	3	0	0	3	1	5	5	0	9	5	.100	.550	.100	25.00	45.00	20
Sulser, Beau	R-R	6-2	195	5-5-94	3	7	5.29	17	8	0	48	55	39	28	13	13	37	.284	.336	.510	17.45	6.13	212
Swanson, Erik	R-R	6-3	225	9-4-93	1	1	11.34	18	0	0	17	28	26	21	7	13	17	.373	.467	.760	18.89	14.44	90
Tate, Dillon	R-R	6-2	190	5-1-94	0	0	1.80	5	0	2	5	1	1	1	0	1	5	.067	.167	.067	27.78	5.56	18
Tiedemann, Ricky	L-L	6-4	220	8-18-02	0	1	6.00	4	4	0	9	8	6	6	3	12	11	.242	.469	.545	22.45	24.49	49
Wallace, Trenton	L-L	6-1	200	3-31-99	0	3	6.27	9	9	0	33	37	23	23	7	27	32	.287	.414	.527	19.75	16.67	162
Watson, Troy	R-R	6-2	180	6-11-97	3	5	8.61	26	7	0	46	66	51	44	14	30	48	.332	.418	.613	20.69	12.93	232

Fielding

Catcher	PCT	G	PO	A	E	DP	PB
Clarke	.984	32	231	10	4	1	5
Henry	.985	24	181	15	3	1	2
Jansen	.957	3	22	0	1	0	1
McDowell	.995	49	399	22	2	2	4
Raposo	1.000	15	119	10	0	0	0
Serven	.997	37	332	16	1	1	2

First Base	PCT	G	PO	A	E	DP
Barger	1.000	2	11	1	0	0
Clarke	1.000	10	47	3	0	5
De Los Santos	1.000	3	18	1	0	0
Horwitz	.995	35	201	17	1	17
Palmegiani	.987	45	258	37	4	36
Tirotta	.979	55	341	30	8	30
Turconi	1.000	1	4	0	0	0
Votto	.986	10	63	9	1	7

Second Base	PCT	G	PO	A	E	DP
Arnold	1.000	3	6	5	0	3
De Los Santos	1.000	3	3	2	0	0
Hiraldo	.947	22	38	51	5	10
Horwitz	.970	11	12	20	1	3
Jimenez	1.000	9	16	22	0	5
Lantigua	.984	55	65	125	3	31
Martinez	.916	38	52	79	12	14
Morris	1.000	1	2	0	0	0
Turconi	1.000	10	18	24	0	3
Wagner	1.000	5	8	7	0	1

Third Base	PCT	G	PO	A	E	DP
Barger	.957	20	11	34	2	1
Cancel	.947	25	7	29	2	7
De Los Santos	.860	20	14	23	6	3
Kasevich	.900	7	0	9	1	0
Kiner-Falefa	.000	1	0	0	0	0
Lantigua	.885	16	3	20	3	2
Martinez	.917	23	9	24	3	3
Palmegiani	.929	44	32	46	6	6
Tirotta	.900	8	8	10	2	1
Turconi	.909	3	7	3	1	0
Wagner	1.000	1	0	1	0	0

Shortstop	PCT	G	PO	A	E	DP
Barger	.971	12	12	21	1	5
Bichette	.818	3	2	7	2	2
Cancel	.895	5	6	11	2	2
De Los Santos	1.000	12	20	29	0	4
Jimenez	.993	45	59	79	1	18
Kasevich	.957	36	62	48	5	13
Lantigua	.977	36	59	69	3	16
Turconi	.950	11	14	24	2	4

Outfield	PCT	G	PO	A	E	DP
Barger	.962	18	23	2	1	1
Barry	1.000	3	8	0	0	0
Berroa	.988	73	164	2	2	0
Cancel	.000	1	0	0	0	0
Clase	.986	32	68	1	1	0
Eden	1.000	91	200	5	0	0
Horwitz	1.000	3	6	0	0	0
Lantigua	.984	28	59	3	1	0
Lukes	1.000	47	84	5	0	0
Palmegiani	.949	19	35	2	2	0
Robertson	.983	100	168	7	3	0
Roden	1.000	64	134	8	0	3
Spain	1.000	2	5	1	0	0
Tirotta	1.000	5	1	0	0	0
Turconi	1.000	1	2	0	0	0

NEW HAMPSHIRE FISHER CATS — *DOUBLE-A*

EASTERN LEAGUE

Batting	B-T	Ht.	Wt.	DOB	AVG	OBP	SLG	G	PA	AB	R	H	2B	3B	HR	RBI	BB	HBP	SH	SF	SO	SB	CS	BB%	SO%
Britton, Zach	L-R	6-1	200	9-9-98	.205	.290	.312	55	231	205	24	42	10	0	4	28	21	4	0	1	74	5	1	9.09	32.03
Brooks, Robert	R-R	5-7	215	11-21-98	.203	.299	.339	23	67	59	4	12	2	0	2	7	7	1	0	0	25	0	0	10.45	37.31

Brown, Dasan	R-R	5-11	185	9-25-01	.217	.284	.302	32	119	106	12	23	7	1	0	2	6	4	2	0	34	13	2	5.04	28.57
Brown, Devonte	R-R	5-9	207	10-15-99	.231	.344	.363	101	413	350	53	81	12	2	10	43	54	7	0	2	148	15	2	13.08	35.84
Clarke, Phil	L-R	5-11	190	3-24-98	.307	.421	.366	29	121	101	15	31	6	0	0	8	16	4	0	0	5	2	0	13.22	4.13
De Jesus, Alex	R-R	6-1	170	3-22-02	.260	.328	.377	99	425	385	48	100	19	1	8	45	35	4	0	0	119	6	5	8.24	28.00
De La Rosa, Marcos	B-R	5-11	160	1-28-02	.000	.333	.000	1	3	2	0	0	0	0	0	0	1	0	0	0	2	0	0	33.33	66.67
Doughty, Cade	R-R	6-1	195	3-26-01	.213	.248	.287	30	114	108	6	23	3	1	1	9	5	0	1	0	31	0	2	4.39	27.19
Hiraldo, Miguel	R-R	5-9	197	9-5-00	.227	.286	.299	45	168	154	22	35	8	0	1	16	9	4	0	1	40	10	4	5.36	23.81
Jemison, Andrew	R-R	6-0	195	10-22-00	.063	.118	.125	6	17	16	0	1	1	0	0	0	1	0	0	0	6	0	0	5.88	35.29
Kasevich, Josh	R-R	6-1	200	1-17-01	.284	.333	.364	87	393	363	51	103	20	0	3	41	26	2	0	2	42	10	1	6.62	10.69
LaRue, Nate	R-R	6-3	217	7-27-01	.000	.105	.000	6	19	17	1	0	0	0	0	0	2	0	0	0	12	0	0	10.53	63.16
Martinez, Gabriel	R-R	5-9	170	7-24-02	.212	.270	.322	102	397	363	28	77	20	1	6	38	28	2	0	4	62	2	2	7.05	15.62
McAdoo, Charles	R-R	6-2	210	3-6-02	.185	.287	.323	37	143	124	15	23	6	1	3	15	14	4	0	1	43	4	1	9.79	30.07
McCarty, Ryan	R-R	5-9	182	4-22-99	.241	.304	.395	73	286	261	40	63	13	0	9	24	18	6	0	1	74	5	5	6.29	25.87
Nunez, Rainer	R-R	6-2	180	12-4-00	.275	.349	.416	105	433	385	40	106	14	2	12	54	44	1	0	3	87	2	0	10.16	20.09
Paulino, Eddinson	L-R	5-10	155	7-2-02	.294	.294	.353	4	17	17	1	5	1	0	0	1	0	0	0	0	6	1	0	0.00	35.29
Pinango, Yohendrick	L-L	5-11	170	5-7-02	.179	.244	.274	33	127	117	6	21	8	0	1	11	9	1	0	0	27	1	0	7.09	21.26
Rios, Kekai	R-R	5-10	205	6-6-97	.135	.196	.250	18	56	52	3	7	3	0	1	3	4	0	0	0	14	1	0	7.14	25.00
Rivera, Josh	R-R	6-2	215	10-10-00	.170	.226	.198	34	115	106	8	18	3	0	0	5	7	1	0	1	38	2	1	6.09	33.04
Roden, Alan	L-R	5-11	215	12-22-99	.267	.373	.432	54	244	206	31	55	11	1	7	27	29	7	0	2	34	6	1	11.89	13.93
Santiago, Glenn	R-R	5-10	165	12-14-00	.130	.238	.222	22	63	54	7	7	2	0	1	9	6	2	0	1	15	1	0	9.52	23.81
Schreck, RJ	L-R	6-1	210	7-12-00	.255	.377	.521	28	114	94	17	24	8	1	5	18	16	3	0	1	27	5	2	14.04	23.68
Sosa, Andres	R-R	5-9	210	11-7-97	.202	.333	.324	57	208	173	22	35	7	1	4	16	25	9	1	0	63	1	0	12.02	30.29
Spain, Garrett	L-R	5-10	178	9-21-00	.167	.249	.301	102	369	329	35	55	9	1	11	32	34	2	2	0	99	12	2	9.21	26.83
Tirotta, Riley	R-R	6-3	195	8-21-98	.286	.438	.464	18	73	56	11	16	2	1	2	8	16	0	0	1	19	2	2	21.92	26.03
Turconi, Michael	L-R	5-10	185	6-24-99	.246	.369	.324	76	296	244	33	60	13	0	2	29	44	5	1	2	82	9	1	14.86	27.70

Pitching	B-T	Ht.	Wt.	DOB	W	L	ERA	G	GS	SV	IP	Hits	Runs	ER	HR	BB	SO	AVG	OBP	SLG	SO%	BB%	BF
Bechtold, Andrew	R-R	6-1	185	4-18-96	1	5	5.28	29	0	0	29	31	23	17	1	13	26	.267	.336	.379	19.70	9.85	132
Boyer, Ryan	R-R	6-2	225	5-4-97	2	2	2.08	30	0	6	30	20	8	7	3	6	36	.182	.250	.282	29.75	4.96	121
Brock, T.J.	R-R	6-1	200	8-10-99	1	0	1.29	7	0	0	7	3	1	1	0	6	14	.130	.323	.174	45.16	19.35	31
Burnette, Jimmy	L-L	6-2	205	10-19-98	1	2	4.03	35	0	5	38	30	19	17	0	20	46	.210	.319	.287	27.71	12.05	166
Churchill, Ian	L-L	6-2	190	2-28-99	0	2	9.72	19	0	1	17	18	20	18	0	14	18	.269	.437	.418	20.69	16.09	87
Clifton, Trevor	R-R	6-4	170	5-11-95	1	4	5.91	15	0	0	21	25	16	14	3	13	26	.291	.388	.465	25.00	12.50	104
Dominguez, Michael	R-R	5-10	175	8-17-00	2	8	4.56	22	22	0	97	76	50	49	17	56	83	.216	.324	.426	20.10	13.56	413
Estrada, Lazaro	R-R	5-10	180	4-24-99	3	5	4.47	11	11	0	52	47	28	26	4	19	55	.240	.307	.388	25.00	8.64	220
Fisher, Braydon	R-R	6-4	180	7-26-00	0	0	2.76	14	0	0	16	12	9	5	1	7	26	.203	.314	.322	36.62	9.86	71
Fraze, Nick	R-R	6-3	180	10-24-97	1	2	4.24	17	4	1	40	32	19	19	7	12	35	.218	.289	.422	21.08	7.23	166
Garkow, Nate	R-R	5-11	190	9-4-97	0	0	0.00	3	0	0	3	1	0	0	0	1	4	.100	.182	.200	36.36	9.09	11
Gregory, Hunter	R-R	6-3	215	11-16-98	5	4	5.54	43	2	1	76	72	50	47	6	38	91	.247	.348	.387	26.69	11.14	341
Harrison, Devereaux	R-R	6-0	190	11-8-00	5	8	4.65	26	26	0	132	125	72	68	18	55	111	.248	.319	.422	19.54	9.68	568
Hernandez, Adrian	R-R	5-8	190	1-22-00	1	0	3.04	33	0	0	47	37	19	16	5	21	49	.213	.307	.339	24.14	10.34	203
Jennings, Ryan	R-R	6-0	190	6-23-99	0	2	0.90	10	1	2	10	5	3	1	0	4	12	.135	.273	.135	27.27	9.09	44
Kelly, Justin	R-R	6-1	195	12-2-98	0	0	2.30	14	0	0	16	11	4	4	0	7	10	.204	.295	.315	16.39	11.48	61
Larkin, Conor	R-R	6-1	205	3-17-99	0	1	9.82	2	0	0	4	3	5	4	1	4	4	.214	.450	.429	20.00	20.00	20
Lavallee, Johnathan	R-R	6-4	240	8-11-99	0	1	3.09	12	0	3	12	3	5	4	0	14	15	.088	.353	.118	28.30	26.42	53
Macko, Adam	L-L	6-0	170	12-30-00	5	5	4.87	16	16	0	81	69	45	44	7	30	90	.231	.317	.371	26.39	8.80	341
Melean, Alejandro	R-R	6-0	175	10-11-00	2	1	7.50	8	0	0	18	17	15	15	3	9	10	.250	.333	.441	12.82	11.54	78
Mendoza, Abdiel	R-R	5-10	160	9-19-98	8	12	3.62	32	9	1	82	72	50	33	8	27	68	.232	.308	.370	19.43	7.71	350
Miranda, Kevin	R-R	5-10	170	11-14-98	1	1	2.86	5	3	0	22	14	8	7	4	5	15	.182	.241	.403	18.07	6.02	83
Nunez, Juan	R-R	6-2	185	1-23-96	0	0	2.53	9	0	0	11	5	3	3	2	3	10	.147	.268	.353	23.81	7.14	42
Palmer, Trent	R-R	6-1	230	4-2-99	1	4	10.64	12	3	0	22	23	27	26	0	23	18	.271	.456	.329	15.79	20.18	114
Pardinho, Eric	R-R	5-10	155	1-5-01	0	0	1.01	21	0	1	27	14	6	3	1	10	37	.149	.229	.213	34.91	9.43	106
Ponce, Gabriel	R-R	6-2	205	4-29-99	0	1	6.75	1	0	0	1	3	1	1	0	1	2	.500	.571	.667	28.57	14.29	7
Sanchez, Rafael	R-R	6-1	215	8-22-99	2	1	2.28	4	4	0	24	18	7	6	3	9	15	.200	.273	.389	14.85	8.91	101
Santos, Dahian	R-R	5-11	160	2-26-03	1	1	6.00	15	2	0	27	17	20	18	3	20	31	.175	.333	.320	25.83	16.67	120
Tolhurst, Anders	R-R	6-4	190	9-13-99	2	1	4.54	23	0	1	34	37	20	17	10	9	47	.280	.322	.583	32.64	6.25	144
Van Eyk, CJ	R-R	6-1	198	9-15-98	3	8	5.68	30	16	2	95	111	63	60	10	38	78	.294	.371	.450	18.14	8.84	430
Wallace, Trenton	L-L	6-1	200	3-31-99	4	3	2.68	17	17	0	81	57	24	24	13	30	97	.197	.283	.363	29.85	9.23	325

Fielding

Catcher	PCT	G	PO	A	E	DP	PB
Britton	.994	34	302	7	2	0	5
Brooks	.994	23	155	17	1	1	1
Clarke	.989	17	182	5	2	0	3
LaRue	.981	6	45	8	1	1	1
Rios	.973	16	137	8	4	2	1
Sosa	1.000	47	387	21	0	5	3

First Base	PCT	G	PO	A	E	DP
Clarke	1.000	5	35	4	0	1
De Jesus	.857	1	5	1	1	0
McAdoo	.957	3	19	3	1	2
McCarty	.991	18	99	9	1	5
Nunez	.982	87	566	48	11	47
Santiago	.986	10	67	6	1	6
Sosa	1.000	4	26	1	0	2
Tirotta	1.000	10	54	7	0	6
Turconi	1.000	5	33	4	0	4

Second Base	PCT	G	PO	A	E	DP
Brown	1.000	9	7	18	0	0
Doughty	.986	18	30	38	1	10
Hiraldo	.955	40	55	92	7	17
Jemison	1.000	1	1	3	0	0
Kasevich	1.000	1	3	3	0	0
McCarty	.963	26	31	48	3	7
Paulino	1.000	1	1	2	0	1
Rivera	1.000	4	2	9	0	3
Turconi	.977	39	44	82	3	14

Third Base	PCT	G	PO	A	E	DP
De Jesus	.930	74	56	91	11	13
Doughty	.875	10	2	12	2	2
Jemison	.667	2	3	1	2	0
Kasevich	1.000	1	2	1	0	0
McAdoo	.926	29	13	37	4	1
McCarty	1.000	10	9	20	0	0
Santiago	1.000	2	1	2	0	0
Tirotta	.864	6	6	13	3	2
Turconi	1.000	6	3	7	0	0

Shortstop	PCT	G	PO	A	E	DP
De Jesus	.974	9	15	23	1	3
Jemison	.909	2	7	3	1	0
Kasevich	.980	84	112	181	6	41
Paulino	1.000	2	5	5	0	1
Rivera	.941	30	39	57	6	10
Turconi	.929	10	12	14	2	1

Outfield	PCT	G	PO	A	E	DP
Britton	1.000	3	4	0	0	0
Brown	.972	85	168	4	5	0
Brown	.987	30	74	0	1	0
De La Rosa	.000	1	0	0	0	0
Jemison	.500	1	1	0	1	0
Martinez	.994	81	148	8	1	1
McAdoo	1.000	2	7	0	0	0
McCarty	1.000	5	7	0	0	0
Pinango	.983	28	57	1	1	0
Roden	.979	52	93	1	2	0
Santiago	1.000	9	11	1	0	0
Schreck	.974	22	38	0	1	0
Spain	.992	97	228	8	2	0
Tirotta	1.000	2	5	0	0	0
Turconi	1.000	7	16	0	0	0

VANCOUVER CANADIANS — HIGH-A

NORTHWEST LEAGUE

Batting	B-T	Ht.	Wt.	DOB	AVG	OBP	SLG	G	PA	AB	R	H	2B	3B	HR	RBI	BB	HBP	SH	SF	SO	SB	CS	BB%	SO%
Arias, Victor	L-L	5-11	150	8-24-03	.324	.425	.353	11	40	34	5	11	1	0	0	4	6	0	0	0	5	1	3	15.00	12.50
Arnaez, Jean	R-R	5-9	160	8-22-02	.233	.280	.327	51	161	150	14	35	8	0	2	12	6	4	0	1	32	0	1	3.73	19.88
Arnold, Bryce	R-R	5-10	175	7-24-01	.297	.357	.324	13	43	37	6	11	1	0	0	3	2	2	1	1	16	1	0	4.65	37.21
Baylor, Jamari	R-R	5-10	190	8-25-00	.194	.315	.278	33	130	108	20	21	0	0	3	12	14	6	0	2	40	6	1	10.77	30.77
Bohrofen, Jace	L-R	6-2	205	10-19-01	.254	.364	.433	112	485	409	63	104	27	2	14	57	60	12	0	3	115	10	3	12.37	23.71
Brooks, Robert	R-R	5-7	215	11-21-98	.262	.340	.476	27	97	84	12	22	4	1	4	10	10	1	0	2	26	0	0	10.31	26.80
Brown, Dasan	R-R	5-11	185	9-25-01	.257	.363	.411	74	329	280	51	72	15	2	8	39	39	8	0	1	79	22	2	11.85	24.01
Coffey, Cutter	R-R	6-1	190	5-21-04	.185	.309	.272	22	97	81	10	15	4	0	1	9	13	2	0	1	25	1	0	13.40	25.77
De La Rosa, Marcos	B-R	5-11	160	1-28-02	.174	.253	.314	55	95	86	11	15	6	0	2	8	6	3	0	0	41	4	3	6.32	43.16
Deschamps, Nicolas	L-R	5-11	180	8-25-02	.200	.349	.314	12	43	35	7	7	1	0	1	1	5	3	0	0	16	0	0	11.63	37.21
Ferrer, Jose	R-R	5-11	175	3-1-99	.000	.000	.000	2	1	1	0	0	0	0	0	0	0	0	0	0	0	0	0	0.00	0.00
Goodwin, Nick	R-R	6-0	190	9-6-01	.201	.282	.318	109	451	402	37	81	16	2	9	44	33	13	0	3	116	7	4	7.32	25.72
Harry, Jay	L-R	6-0	195	7-18-02	.210	.259	.420	27	108	100	9	21	9	0	4	14	6	1	0	1	32	0	1	5.56	29.63
Hernandez, Jommer	R-R	5-11	181	10-19-00	.242	.313	.288	42	147	132	11	32	3	0	1	12	12	2	0	1	42	0	0	8.16	28.57
Hornung, Jackson	R-R	6-2	215	2-6-01	.258	.341	.373	112	463	407	43	105	25	2	6	47	45	8	0	3	114	0	0	9.72	24.62
Machado, Estiven	B-R	5-9	170	10-4-02	.191	.292	.271	67	219	188	20	36	7	1	2	17	25	3	0	3	45	1	5	11.42	20.55
McCarty, Ryan	R-R	5-9	182	4-22-99	.248	.326	.400	42	187	165	21	41	8	1	5	26	17	3	0	2	36	7	4	9.09	19.25
Orf, Brennan	L-R	6-3	225	9-6-01	.240	.358	.419	57	215	179	31	43	12	4	4	18	33	1	0	2	49	0	1	15.35	22.79
Pinto, Adrian	R-R	5-6	156	9-22-02	.300	.355	.571	17	76	70	17	21	8	1	3	14	4	2	0	0	10	2	0	5.26	13.16
Rios, Kekai	R-R	5-10	205	6-6-97	.000	.250	.000	2	4	3	0	0	0	0	0	0	1	0	0	0	2	0	0	25.00	50.00
Rock, Dylan	R-R	6-0	210	8-21-98	.184	.293	.272	71	263	228	26	42	11	0	3	18	26	9	0	0	74	3	1	9.89	28.14
Rudd, Jaden	L-L	5-10	185	8-16-02	.233	.333	.288	24	84	73	7	17	2	1	0	4	11	0	0	0	26	4	0	13.10	30.95
Santiago, Glenn	R-R	5-10	165	12-14-00	.214	.279	.291	36	130	117	15	25	3	0	2	14	11	0	1	1	33	3	2	8.46	25.38
Sharp, Jacob	R-R	5-10	190	9-15-01	.226	.316	.381	25	96	84	11	19	4	0	3	9	6	5	0	0	11	0	0	6.25	11.46
Stone, Alex	R-R	6-5	235	11-3-01	.273	.304	.318	9	23	22	3	6	1	0	0	3	0	1	0	0	5	0	0	0.00	21.74
Ward, Je'Von	L-R	6-2	190	10-25-99	.279	.393	.443	62	252	201	42	56	12	0	7	35	41	2	0	8	55	7	2	16.27	21.83
Wehler, Jeffrey	R-R	6-0	195	1-10-99	.259	.315	.364	64	248	228	23	59	6	0	6	25	16	3	0	1	51	9	3	6.45	20.56
Williams, Peyton	L-L	6-5	255	9-14-00	.289	.362	.476	77	334	294	42	85	20	1	11	50	36	0	0	4	76	0	0	10.78	22.75

Pitching	B-T	Ht.	Wt.	DOB	W	L	ERA	G	GS	SV	IP	Hits	Runs	ER	HR	BB	SO	AVG	OBP	SLG	SO%	BB%	BF
Amalfi, Alex	R-R	6-1	185	2-18-01	3	1	3.28	36	0	2	69	60	29	25	1	26	87	.240	.309	.328	30.53	9.12	285
Arnaez, Jean	R-R	5-9	160	8-22-02	0	0	0.00	1	0	0	0	0	0	0	0	0	0	.000	.500	.000	0.00	0.00	2
Bonds, Bo	R-R	5-11	200	1-10-01	4	1	4.26	10	0	1	13	8	6	6	1	5	17	.178	.275	.289	33.33	9.80	51
Carter, Irv	R-R	6-4	210	10-9-02	1	0	5.94	10	0	0	17	16	11	11	3	6	20	.254	.310	.492	28.17	8.45	71
Estrada, Lazaro	R-R	5-10	180	4-24-99	2	3	1.96	9	9	0	41	28	16	9	4	12	53	.192	.263	.329	32.72	7.41	162
Ferrer, Jose	R-R	5-11	175	3-1-99	0	0	54.00	1	0	0	1	4	4	4	0	1	0	.667	.750	.667	0.00	12.50	8
Gallagher, Pat	R-R	6-0	196	6-30-00	8	5	4.15	22	21	1	91	93	47	42	6	31	83	.271	.339	.397	21.34	7.97	389
Jennings, Ryan	R-R	6-0	190	6-23-99	0	3	2.13	11	11	0	51	41	18	12	3	19	56	.218	.300	.319	26.54	9.00	211
Kelly, Justin	R-R	6-1	195	12-2-98	2	1	2.55	15	0	3	18	17	6	5	1	4	22	.243	.284	.329	29.73	5.41	74
Larkin, Conor	R-R	6-1	205	3-17-99	2	0	2.57	26	0	3	28	17	9	8	3	17	37	.172	.299	.303	31.62	14.53	117
Lavallee, Johnathan	R-R	6-4	240	8-11-99	3	3	3.55	28	0	3	38	26	17	15	3	16	54	.195	.287	.301	35.53	10.53	152
McElvain, Chris	R-R	6-0	205	9-15-00	3	3	4.56	11	11	0	49	51	26	25	4	21	54	.263	.336	.418	24.66	9.59	219
Miranda, Kevin	R-R	5-10	178	11-14-98	2	1	3.57	6	3	0	18	15	7	7	1	5	10	.234	.300	.344	14.29	7.14	70
Mollerus, Josh	R-R	6-3	215	10-6-99	1	4	3.90	23	0	5	30	18	17	13	2	19	44	.175	.313	.262	34.11	14.73	129
Munson, Aaron	L-R	5-10	180	3-15-02	0	2	7.04	21	0	1	23	24	19	18	0	19	27	.286	.415	.345	25.23	17.76	107
O'Halloran, Connor	R-L	6-2	190	9-1-02	2	7	7.06	14	14	0	66	67	54	52	8	36	60	.262	.374	.441	19.61	11.76	306
Ohashi, Rafael	R-R	6-1	185	10-8-02	2	0	4.10	23	1	0	37	30	18	17	2	23	32	.226	.362	.331	19.63	14.11	163
Paulino, Naswell	L-L	5-11	160	4-17-00	4	0	5.20	24	0	1	28	28	18	16	3	16	27	.272	.372	.417	21.95	13.01	123
Peterson, Kai	L-L	6-1	190	8-14-02	0	1	4.42	18	0	2	18	11	11	9	0	14	28	.164	.349	.224	32.56	16.28	86
Pierce, Carson	R-R	6-3	215	9-10-01	2	3	2.72	18	9	0	46	36	17	14	2	17	51	.211	.288	.298	26.56	8.85	192
Rogers, Grant	R-R	6-7	230	5-22-01	1	1	3.11	6	6	0	38	36	13	13	1	6	36	.263	.304	.343	24.32	4.05	148
Rojas, Kendry	L-L	6-2	190	11-26-02	3	3	2.43	11	10	0	56	50	19	15	4	12	61	.238	.286	.348	26.99	5.31	226
Sanchez, J.J.	L-L	5-11	185	9-8-99	0	0	0.00	4	0	0	4	4	1	0	0	2	10	.222	.333	.278	47.62	9.52	21
Sanchez, Rafael	R-R	6-1	215	8-22-99	5	2	4.03	16	15	0	83	90	43	37	4	23	92	.277	.325	.382	26.14	6.53	352
Thurman, Grayson	R-R	6-3	205	12-27-98	6	4	3.82	48	0	7	61	55	28	26	9	18	72	.239	.294	.409	28.35	7.09	254
Tolhurst, Anders	R-R	6-4	190	9-13-99	4	1	1.73	21	0	3	26	19	7	5	0	5	28	.200	.250	.253	26.67	4.76	105
Urbaez, Geison	R-R	6-1	180	7-5-00	1	1	3.72	15	6	0	36	25	17	15	1	18	28	.191	.299	.305	18.18	11.69	154
Watson, Ryan	R-R	6-4	207	4-26-99	2	0	3.72	5	4	1	29	33	12	12	2	3	28	.284	.303	.388	23.53	2.52	119
Watts-Brown, Juaron	R-R	6-3	190	2-23-02	1	6	6.35	9	9	0	45	42	32	32	11	31	57	.244	.361	.477	27.27	14.83	209
Yeager, Chay	S-R	5-11	180	9-11-02	4	5	5.50	42	0	2	54	48	35	33	6	33	41	.239	.361	.373	17.01	13.69	241

Fielding

Catcher	PCT	G	PO	A	E	DP	PB
Brooks	.991	23	206	11	2	2	2
Deschamps	.979	11	90	5	2	1	2
Hernandez	.979	39	337	41	8	3	10
Hornung	.997	37	312	25	1	1	16
Rios	1.000	1	3	0	0	0	1
Sharp	.981	25	245	16	5	2	3
Stone	1.000	4	23	2	0	0	1

First Base	PCT	G	PO	A	E	DP
Arnaez	.988	14	80	5	1	7
Baylor	1.000	10	75	2	0	3
Hornung	.979	24	181	3	4	12
Orf	.984	27	176	8	3	16
Santiago	.980	6	43	6	1	2
Williams	.997	56	366	21	1	35

Second Base	PCT	G	PO	A	E	DP
Arnaez	.992	36	47	73	1	10
Arnold	.917	11	16	17	3	5
Baylor	.962	7	12	13	1	2
De La Rosa	1.000	6	5	12	0	1
Goodwin	1.000	1	4	4	0	3
Harry	1.000	11	5	18	0	4
Machado	1.000	17	20	37	0	4
McCarty	1.000	5	5	12	0	1
Pinto	.966	12	26	30	2	9
Santiago	.955	8	12	9	1	1
Wehler	.992	32	50	67	1	16

Third Base	PCT	G	PO	A	E	DP
Arnaez	.000	1	0	0	0	0
Arnold	1.000	1	0	3	0	1
Baylor	1.000	13	9	12	0	3
Coffey	.976	18	8	33	1	1
De La Rosa	.867	13	5	21	4	4
Goodwin	.973	39	22	50	2	2
Harry	1.000	1	1	3	0	1
Machado	1.000	2	2	3	0	0
McCarty	.932	33	23	46	5	5
Santiago	1.000	2	4	3	0	1
Wehler	.865	17	9	23	5	0

Shortstop	PCT	G	PO	A	E	DP
Coffey	1.000	4	2	9	0	0
Goodwin	.990	62	78	120	2	26
Harry	.982	15	21	34	1	4
Machado	.954	48	44	101	7	20
Santiago	.966	8	11	17	1	2
Wehler	1.000	1	3	0	0	0

Outfield	PCT	G	PO	A	E	DP
Arias	1.000	12	21	0	0	0
Baylor	1.000	4	7	1	0	0
Bohrofen	.994	111	175	3	1	1
Brown	1.000	70	152	6	0	3
De La Rosa	1.000	30	27	0	0	0
Harry	1.000	2	5	0	0	0
Hornung	1.000	11	10	0	0	0
Orf	.978	25	44	1	1	0
Pinto	1.000	1	2	0	0	0
Rock	1.000	65	97	3	0	2
Rudd	.974	24	38	0	1	0
Santiago	.968	14	29	1	1	0
Ward	.990	64	95	2	1	0
Wehler	1.000	9	16	0	0	0

DUNEDIN BLUE JAYS

LOW-A

FLORIDA STATE LEAGUE

Batting	B-T	Ht.	Wt.	DOB	AVG	OBP	SLG	G	PA	AB	R	H	2B	3B	HR	RBI	BB	HBP	SH	SF	SO	SB	CS	BB%	SO%
Aponte, Yhoangel	R-R	5-10	190	2-12-04	.189	.312	.312	83	340	285	37	54	13	2	6	38	41	11	0	3	102	14	3	12.06	30.00
Arias, Victor	L-L	5-11	150	8-24-03	.279	.386	.454	76	332	280	53	78	19	3	8	40	36	14	0	2	72	17	7	10.84	21.69
Arnold, Bryce	R-R	5-10	175	7-24-01	.195	.342	.329	76	284	231	36	45	11	1	6	30	45	7	0	1	77	7	2	15.85	27.11
Balogh, Ricardo	B-R	6-3	175	7-9-02	.205	.314	.273	14	51	44	4	9	3	0	0	2	7	0	0	0	12	0	0	13.73	23.53
Barry, Braden	R-R	6-4	190	2-6-02	.170	.308	.230	36	120	100	15	17	1	1	1	10	17	3	0	0	44	11	1	14.17	36.67
Beltre, Manuel	R-R	5-10	155	6-9-04	.236	.334	.326	107	446	386	58	91	16	2	5	46	43	15	0	2	83	23	5	9.64	18.61
Cunningham, Carter	L-R	6-4	210	11-6-00	.197	.381	.316	25	105	76	14	15	3	0	2	12	19	6	0	4	23	3	1	18.10	21.90
De La Rosa, Marcos	B-R	5-11	160	1-28-02	.237	.362	.395	15	47	38	6	9	0	0	2	5	5	3	0	1	20	1	2	10.64	42.55
De Los Santos, Luis	R-R	6-1	160	6-9-98	.500	.500	1.750	1	4	4	2	2	0	1	1	2	0	0	0	0	2	0	0	0.00	50.00
Deschamps, Nicolas	L-R	5-11	180	8-25-02	.235	.342	.422	33	120	102	16	24	4	3	3	17	15	2	0	1	43	1	4	12.50	35.83
Doughty, Cade	R-R	6-1	195	3-26-01	.304	.414	.565	8	29	23	6	7	1	1	1	3	4	1	0	1	5	0	0	13.79	17.24
Duran, Edward	R-R	5-11	170	5-29-04	.245	.346	.313	77	327	278	35	68	15	2	0	41	39	6	0	4	50	15	3	11.93	15.29
Feliz, Cristian	L-L	6-4	190	9-7-02	.189	.304	.394	76	303	259	46	49	11	0	14	37	30	13	0	1	129	2	0	9.90	42.57
Freethy, J.R.	B-R	5-11	185	12-23-02	.182	.408	.236	20	76	55	13	10	0	0	1	4	17	4	0	0	18	4	0	22.37	23.68
Gomez, Luis	R-R	#VALUE!	NULL	5-24-94	.000	.000	.000	1	1	1	0	0	0	0	0	0	0	0	0	0	0	0	0	0.00	0.00
Hernandez, Alexis	R-R	6-0	170	10-5-02	.219	.333	.331	48	177	151	25	33	5	0	4	16	21	5	0	0	42	17	1	11.86	23.73
Jemison, Andrew	R-R	6-0	195	10-22-00	.259	.333	.333	10	34	27	5	7	2	0	0	2	4	0	0	2	7	0	0	11.76	20.59
Joseph, Jean	R-R	5-11	160	2-4-05	.222	.304	.356	68	273	239	34	53	15	1	5	32	20	10	0	4	67	3	3	7.33	24.54
Keys, Sean	L-R	6-2	225	5-26-03	.293	.378	.451	22	98	82	11	24	4	3	1	20	13	0	0	3	21	2	1	13.27	21.43
LaRue, Nate	R-R	6-3	217	7-27-01	.500	.667	1.000	1	3	2	1	1	1	0	0	2	1	0	0	0	1	0	0	33.33	33.33
Lukes, Nathan	L-R	5-11	180	7-12-94	.364	.417	.364	3	12	11	3	4	0	0	0	1	1	0	0	0	4	0	0	8.33	33.33
Meza, Adrian	B-R	5-8	155	1-4-05	.171	.237	.200	13	38	35	3	6	1	0	0	2	3	0	0	0	9	0	0	7.89	23.68
Micheletti, Eddie	L-R	6-1	200	12-29-01	.292	.422	.458	20	90	72	7	21	6	0	2	12	13	4	0	1	14	0	0	14.44	15.56
Minoso, Maykel	R-R	5-8	170	7-3-05	.121	.171	.152	9	35	33	3	4	1	0	0	1	2	0	0	0	8	0	1	5.71	22.86
Mitchell, Nick	L-R	5-9	178	9-3-03	.289	.350	.467	22	103	90	18	26	2	1	4	13	7	3	0	3	20	3	0	6.80	19.42
Munoz, Yeuni	R-R	6-1	190	10-4-03	.165	.294	.286	29	109	91	13	15	3	1	2	7	14	3	0	1	42	1	1	12.84	38.53
Nimmala, Arjun	R-R	6-1	170	10-16-05	.232	.313	.476	82	361	319	59	74	18	6	16	46	30	9	0	3	113	9	1	8.31	31.30
Orf, Brennan	L-R	6-3	225	9-6-01	.083	.154	.333	4	13	12	2	1	0	0	1	1	1	0	0	0	3	0	0	7.69	23.08
Palmegiani, Damiano	R-R	6-0	195	1-24-00	.333	.417	.667	6	24	21	3	7	1	0	2	2	3	0	0	0	6	0	0	12.50	25.00
Parker, Aaron	R-R	5-9	200	1-17-03	.235	.380	.519	24	100	81	14	19	8	0	5	14	17	2	0	0	27	1	0	17.00	27.00
Paulino, Eddinson	L-R	5-10	155	7-2-02	.000	.053	.000	6	19	18	0	0	0	0	0	0	1	0	0	0	4	0	0	5.26	21.05
Perez, Daniel	L-L	6-2	195	12-9-01	.179	.242	.268	36	126	112	4	20	2	4	0	8	9	1	1	2	55	2	2	7.14	43.65
Pinto, Adrian	R-R	5-6	156	9-22-02	.313	.353	.313	4	18	16	3	5	0	0	0	2	1	0	1	0	4	0	0	5.56	22.22
Rios, Kekai	R-R	5-10	205	6-6-97	.154	.154	.308	3	13	13	0	2	2	0	0	5	0	0	0	0	2	0	0	0.00	15.38
Robertis, Robert	L-L	5-11	188	11-29-02	.214	.329	.314	25	85	70	9	15	4	0	1	12	12	1	0	2	22	4	1	14.12	25.88
Rudd, Jaden	L-L	5-10	185	8-16-02	.130	.319	.222	19	69	54	11	7	2	0	1	7	10	5	0	0	16	2	1	14.49	23.19
Salinas, Roque	L-L	5-8	180	11-8-02	.368	.429	.421	6	21	19	3	7	1	0	0	3	2	0	0	0	2	2	0	9.52	9.52
Sosa, Andres	R-R	5-9	210	11-7-97	.000	.250	.000	1	4	3	1	0	0	0	0	0	0	1	0	0	1	0	0	0.00	25.00
Tibbitts, Brock	R-R	6-4	210	10-4-02	.282	.374	.372	23	91	78	15	22	4	0	1	6	11	1	0	1	12	2	0	12.09	13.19
Tirotta, Riley	R-R	6-3	195	8-21-98	.235	.552	.471	7	29	17	7	4	1	0	1	5	11	1	0	0	6	6	0	37.93	20.69
Toman, Tucker	B-R	5-11	190	11-12-03	.221	.301	.318	80	326	289	28	64	12	2	4	29	27	7	0	3	104	5	2	8.28	31.90
Votto, Joey	L-R	6-2	220	9-10-83	.211	.348	.368	13	46	38	5	8	3	0	1	7	7	1	0	0	14	1	0	15.22	30.43
Williams, Peyton	L-L	6-5	255	9-14-00	.111	.385	.111	3	13	9	0	1	0	0	0	0	4	0	0	0	1	0	0	30.77	7.69

Pitching	B-T	Ht.	Wt.	DOB	W	L	ERA	G	GS	SV	IP	Hits	Runs	ER	HR	BB	SO	AVG	OBP	SLG	SO%	BB%	BF
Alcalde, Eliander	R-R	5-9	171	8-9-03	3	2	3.14	34	0	5	66	49	26	23	3	32	58	.207	.302	.270	21.01	11.59	276

Barriera, Brandon	L-L	6-2	180	3-4-04	0	0	13.50	1	1	0	1	2	2	2	0	1	1	.333	.500	.333	12.50	12.50	8
Bash, Andrew	R-R	6-0	190	8-1-96	0	0	0.00	1	0	0	2	0	0	0	0	0	5	.000	.000	.000	100.00	0.00	5
Bautista, Gilberto	R-R	6-0	165	1-8-05	2	0	2.70	4	3	0	17	17	8	5	2	2	16	.266	.294	.422	23.53	2.94	68
Bautista, Jorge	R-R	6-0	155	12-10-00	3	5	5.63	9	8	0	46	49	37	29	10	17	37	.274	.343	.503	18.41	8.46	201
Bello, Felipe	R-R	6-3	197	2-1-00	0	1	4.66	7	0	2	10	11	5	5	0	5	3	.314	.381	.343	7.14	11.90	42
Bonds, Bo	R-R	5-11	200	1-10-01	1	1	4.28	22	0	5	27	26	13	13	2	14	43	.260	.350	.350	36.75	11.97	117
Boyer, Ryan	R-R	6-2	225	5-4-97	0	0	4.50	2	0	0	2	1	1	1	1	0	5	.143	.143	.571	71.43	0.00	7
Brock, T.J.	R-R	6-1	200	8-10-99	0	0	0.00	3	0	0	3	0	0	0	0	0	4	.000	.000	.000	40.00	0.00	10
Carter, Irv	R-R	6-4	210	10-9-02	6	1	3.18	27	0	1	57	36	22	20	5	31	58	.185	.319	.303	24.68	13.19	235
Castro, Cristopher	L-L	6-1	150	8-17-02	1	1	3.65	5	3	0	12	15	11	5	1	9	13	.288	.387	.462	20.97	14.52	62
Colmenares, Samuel	R-R	5-10	187	11-25-04	0	1	81.00	1	1	0	1	3	6	6	1	3	1	.600	.750	1.400	12.50	37.50	8
Danner, Hagen	R-R	6-1	215	9-30-98	0	0	0.00	1	0	0	1	0	0	0	0	0	2	.000	.000	.000	66.67	0.00	3
Espino, Sebastian	R-R	6-3	176	5-29-00	1	1	6.08	12	0	0	13	15	11	9	1	8	18	.283	.381	.434	28.13	12.50	64
Estrada, Lazaro	R-R	5-10	180	4-24-99	0	1	1.93	2	2	0	5	5	2	1	0	2	5	.263	.333	.368	23.81	9.52	21
Flores, Eminen	R-R	5-11	160	2-27-03	1	1	6.11	5	1	0	18	18	13	12	4	14	16	.257	.388	.500	18.82	16.47	85
Flynn, Bennett	R-R	6-1	175	5-29-01	0	0	1.50	5	0	0	6	2	1	1	0	3	5	.105	.261	.105	21.74	13.04	23
Garkow, Nate	R-R	5-11	190	9-4-97	4	0	2.14	12	0	0	21	9	5	5	1	10	30	.127	.244	.211	36.59	12.20	82
Guerra, Daniel	R-R	6-6	230	3-13-04	1	2	4.28	6	6	0	27	17	14	13	2	14	28	.179	.282	.274	25.23	12.61	111
Holcombe, Colby	R-R	6-7	225	12-12-02	0	0	1.80	6	5	0	15	10	3	3	0	7	12	.189	.295	.226	19.67	11.48	61
Huntzinger, Jerry	R-R	6-2	180	2-15-99	0	1	4.50	7	0	0	8	7	4	4	0	5	8	.259	.444	.296	22.22	13.89	36
Kaprielian, James	R-R	6-3	225	3-2-94	0	0	0.00	1	1	0	4	2	0	0	0	4	5	.154	.353	.154	29.41	23.53	17
Leon, Keiner	R-R	5-11	190	10-29-03	2	3	6.10	26	0	2	31	35	24	21	5	21	37	.292	.392	.525	25.87	14.69	143
Macko, Adam	L-L	6-0	170	12-30-00	0	0	1.00	3	3	0	9	5	1	1	1	2	12	.161	.212	.258	36.36	6.06	33
Manoah, Alek	R-R	6-6	285	1-9-98	0	0	32.40	1	1	0	2	5	7	6	1	4	2	.500	.625	.900	12.50	25.00	16
Maroudis, Landen	R-R	6-3	195	12-16-04	1	0	0.84	3	2	0	11	3	1	1	0	4	12	.088	.184	.118	31.58	10.53	38
Martin, Colby	R-R	5-11	195	4-2-01	1	1	7.27	9	0	0	9	8	9	7	0	14	8	.242	.479	.364	16.67	29.17	48
Miranda, Kevin	R-R	5-10	178	11-14-98	1	1	4.66	5	0	1	10	8	5	5	2	6	9	.222	.349	.444	20.93	13.95	43
Mracna, Christian	R-R	6-5	220	6-9-00	0	0	1.35	6	0	0	7	3	2	1	1	10	8	.136	.441	.318	23.53	29.41	34
Munson, Aaron	L-R	5-10	180	3-15-02	0	2	3.03	21	0	2	30	25	13	10	2	14	41	.221	.321	.310	31.30	10.69	131
O'Halloran, Connor	R-L	6-2	190	9-1-02	4	2	3.13	7	7	0	37	31	18	13	5	13	45	.220	.287	.376	28.66	8.28	157
Ortiz, Julio	R-R	6-3	165	12-30-00	0	3	4.19	13	0	3	19	10	13	9	0	19	34	.152	.344	.182	37.36	20.88	91
Palmer, Trent	R-R	6-1	230	4-2-99	0	0	6.75	3	2	0	5	4	4	4	0	8	7	.200	.448	.250	24.14	27.59	29
Perez, Fernando	R-R	6-3	170	2-12-04	3	2	4.06	17	17	0	82	63	40	37	6	24	86	.211	.276	.328	25.83	7.21	333
Perry, Nolan	R-R	6-2	195	9-2-03	1	1	2.93	14	14	0	46	35	20	15	2	39	57	.212	.362	.279	27.54	18.84	207
Peterson, Kai	L-L	6-1	190	8-14-02	6	3	4.60	22	0	2	31	19	19	16	1	29	63	.173	.370	.255	42.57	19.59	148
Pierce, Carson	R-R	6-3	215	9-10-01	0	2	3.57	8	1	0	18	17	11	7	0	9	15	.258	.338	.348	18.75	11.25	80
Powell, Jordan	R-R	6-2	200	7-28-98	0	0	11.50	16	0	0	18	19	24	23	4	29	22	.271	.495	.471	20.95	27.62	105
Rogers, Grant	R-R	6-7	230	5-22-01	2	5	4.26	15	14	0	74	67	40	35	9	22	70	.238	.296	.390	22.65	7.12	309
Rojas, Kendry	L-L	6-2	190	11-26-02	0	0	6.75	1	1	0	4	4	3	3	0	1	3	.250	.294	.438	17.65	5.88	17
Rojas, Yondrei	R-R	5-10	180	11-22-02	7	2	4.36	33	0	6	43	38	26	21	5	22	57	.229	.340	.349	29.08	11.22	196
Rudd, Jaden	L-L	5-10	185	8-16-02	0	0	0.00	1	0	0	0	0	0	0	0	2	0	.000	.750	.000	0.00	50.00	4
Sanchez, J.J.	L-L	5-11	185	9-8-99	6	4	3.11	31	0	5	46	33	22	16	1	35	52	.204	.370	.253	24.88	16.75	209
Santos, Dahian	R-R	5-11	160	2-26-03	0	0	5.40	4	0	0	7	4	4	4	2	6	13	.167	.355	.500	41.94	19.35	31
Schueler, Jay	R-R	6-3	195	6-5-01	0	0	7.00	8	0	1	9	10	7	7	3	7	7	.294	.455	.647	15.91	15.91	44
Stanifer, Gage	R-R	6-3	201	11-18-03	3	5	6.34	19	17	0	60	55	42	42	5	50	64	.252	.400	.390	23.19	18.12	276
Swanson, Erik	R-R	6-3	225	9-4-93	0	0	0.00	1	0	0	1	0	0	0	0	0	2	.000	.000	.000	66.67	0.00	3
Tiedemann, Ricky	L-L	6-4	220	8-18-02	0	0	1.13	3	3	0	8	3	1	1	1	2	15	.111	.172	.296	51.72	6.90	29
Todd, Jonathan	L-R	6-6	225	8-21-01	0	0	0.00	3	0	0	3	0	1	0	0	1	6	.000	.091	.000	54.55	9.09	11
Torres, Luis	L-L	6-1	165	2-24-05	2	0	4.88	9	1	1	24	14	14	13	0	15	33	.169	.311	.205	32.04	14.56	103
Urbaez, Geison	R-R	6-1	180	7-5-00	0	0	4.50	3	0	0	6	8	3	3	0	1	4	.333	.360	.375	16.00	4.00	25
Urena, Franly	R-R	5-8	160	6-8-04	0	0	1.86	6	0	0	10	5	2	2	0	11	12	.152	.364	.182	27.27	25.00	44
Vasquez, Juanmi	L-L	5-11	140	12-1-03	4	1	4.93	16	1	0	38	37	23	21	7	30	38	.253	.389	.432	21.11	16.67	180
Watson, Ryan	R-R	6-4	207	4-26-99	0	1	3.06	3	3	0	18	12	7	6	0	4	16	.194	.254	.290	23.88	5.97	67
Watts-Brown, Juaron	R-R	6-3	190	2-23-02	3	5	3.43	12	12	0	58	45	29	22	3	29	74	.211	.305	.338	30.33	11.89	244

Fielding

Catcher	PCT	G	PO	A	E	DP	PB
Deschamps	.986	28	268	16	4	2	3
Duran	.981	67	660	58	14	8	14
LaRue	1.000	1	13	1	0	0	0
Minoso	.983	9	104	13	2	2	1
Parker	.984	12	115	8	2	0	1
Rios	1.000	2	14	1	0	0	0
Sosa	1.000	1	11	3	0	0	0
Tibbitts	.992	13	116	13	1	0	2

First Base	PCT	G	PO	A	E	DP
Balogh	.981	8	51	1	1	4
Cunningham	1.000	12	75	4	0	11
Deschamps	1.000	3	5	1	0	0
Duran	.979	9	45	2	1	2
Feliz	.980	62	411	20	9	37
Jemison	1.000	4	27	2	0	4
Keys	1.000	5	33	0	0	2
Orf	1.000	2	11	0	0	0
Perez	.972	9	68	2	2	3
Tibbitts	1.000	10	63	4	0	6
Tirotta	1.000	2	13	1	0	1
Votto	1.000	11	58	4	0	6
Williams	1.000	2	12	0	0	0

Second Base	PCT	G	PO	A	E	DP
Arnold	.960	60	71	120	8	29
Beltre	.993	39	59	81	1	22
De La Rosa	1.000	1	2	1	0	0
Doughty	1.000	2	1	4	0	1
Freethy	.976	12	19	22	1	6
Meza	1.000	3	1	4	0	1
Paulino	1.000	1	1	2	0	1
Pinto	.889	3	2	6	1	1
Toman	.983	16	24	34	1	5

Third Base	PCT	G	PO	A	E	DP
Arnold	1.000	1	1	1	0	0
Balogh	.875	4	3	4	1	1
Beltre	.965	39	18	37	2	3
De La Rosa	.909	13	5	15	2	2
De Los Santos	.667	1	0	2	1	0
Doughty	.900	5	4	5	1	0
Jemison	1.000	6	4	8	0	1
Keys	.889	15	16	16	4	2
Meza	1.000	7	1	5	0	0
Palmegiani	1.000	4	2	2	0	0
Paulino	1.000	1	1	1	0	0
Toman	.963	46	31	48	3	4

Shortstop	PCT	G	PO	A	E	DP
Arnold	1.000	4	2	7	0	3
Beltre	.969	29	40	54	3	12
Freethy	1.000	5	3	8	0	2
Meza	1.000	3	5	9	0	2
Nimmala	.949	74	108	173	15	34
Paulino	1.000	3	1	3	0	1

Toman	.980	17	18	31	1	4

Outfield	PCT	G	PO	A	E	DP
Aponte	.976	77	162	1	4	0
Arias	.992	62	116	1	1	0
Barry	.982	30	53	1	1	0
Cunningham	1.000	9	11	0	0	0
De La Rosa	.000	1	0	0	0	0
Feliz	.000	2	0	0	0	0
Freethy	.875	3	7	0	1	0
Hernandez	1.000	40	71	2	0	0
Joseph	.992	66	123	4	1	0
Lukes	1.000	3	5	1	0	1
Micheletti	.970	15	31	1	1	0
Mitchell	1.000	21	40	1	0	0
Munoz	.978	24	40	4	1	0
Orf	1.000	2	4	0	0	0
Perez	1.000	17	17	0	0	0
Pinto	1.000	1	1	0	0	0
Robertis	1.000	21	32	1	0	0
Rudd	.971	18	33	0	1	0
Salinas	1.000	5	10	0	0	0
Tirotta	1.000	3	2	0	0	0

FCL BLUE JAYS

ROOKIE

FLORIDA COMPLEX LEAGUE

Batting	B-T	Ht.	Wt.	DOB	AVG	OBP	SLG	G	PA	AB	R	H	2B	3B	HR	RBI	BB	HBP	SH	SF	SO	SB	CS	BB%	SO%
Aponte, Yhoangel	R-R	5-10	190	2-12-04	.139	.238	.250	12	42	36	3	5	1	0	1	4	2	3	0	1	15	2	1	4.76	35.71
Barry, Braden	R-R	6-4	190	2-6-02	.333	.350	.389	5	20	18	4	6	1	0	0	2	1	0	0	1	5	1	0	5.00	25.00
Bonilla, Enmanuel	R-R	6-1	180	1-22-06	.186	.257	.299	53	214	194	26	36	6	2	4	21	13	6	0	1	76	3	2	6.07	35.51
Cano, Gregori	L-R	6-0	180	7-18-04	.185	.292	.239	33	106	92	10	17	5	0	0	8	12	2	0	0	33	3	2	11.32	31.13
Chirinos, Kendry	R-R	5-11	170	10-6-04	.300	.402	.443	43	164	140	19	42	8	3	2	18	16	8	0	0	41	7	2	9.76	25.00
De La Cruz, Faruk	R-R	5-10	145	3-11-05	.167	.270	.218	28	89	78	10	13	4	0	0	9	11	0	0	0	29	2	0	12.36	32.58
De La Rosa, Marcos	B-R	5-11	160	1-28-02	.111	.273	.111	6	22	18	1	2	0	0	0	1	3	1	0	0	5	1	0	13.64	22.73
De Los Santos, Luis	R-R	6-1	160	6-9-98	.286	.333	.571	3	9	7	2	2	2	0	0	2	1	0	0	1	2	0	0	11.11	22.22
Deschamps, Nicolas	L-R	5-11	180	8-25-02	.300	.462	.400	4	13	10	2	3	1	0	0	1	3	0	0	0	5	0	0	23.08	38.46
Doughty, Cade	R-R	6-1	195	3-26-01	.500	.571	.667	2	7	6	2	3	1	0	0	1	1	0	0	0	0	0	0	14.29	0.00
Escanio, Aneudi	B-R	5-9	150	11-27-04	.118	.296	.188	35	108	85	8	10	2	2	0	4	22	0	0	1	37	3	4	20.37	34.26
Gomez, Luis	R-R	#VALUE!	NULL	5-24-94	.000	.333	.000	5	12	8	1	0	0	0	0	0	2	2	0	0	4	0	0	16.67	33.33
Guzman, David	L-L	5-7	160	2-7-06	.223	.348	.277	34	115	94	6	21	5	0	0	8	18	1	0	2	20	0	0	15.65	17.39
Jemison, Andrew	R-R	6-0	195	10-22-00	.250	.250	.250	1	4	4	0	1	0	0	0	0	0	0	0	0	0	0	0	0.00	0.00
LaRue, Nate	R-R	6-3	217	7-27-01	.273	.429	.455	5	14	11	0	3	2	0	0	0	3	0	0	0	3	1	0	21.43	21.43
Meza, Adrian	B-R	5-8	155	1-4-05	.179	.320	.198	37	128	106	15	19	2	0	0	5	15	7	0	0	20	3	2	11.72	15.63
Meza, Luis	R-R	5-8	150	9-23-04	.274	.361	.290	24	72	62	7	17	1	0	0	7	6	3	0	1	17	1	0	8.33	23.61
Minoso, Maykel	R-R	5-8	170	7-3-05	.198	.291	.277	33	117	101	14	20	3	1	1	12	13	1	0	2	15	6	0	11.11	12.82
Munoz, Yeuni	R-R	6-1	190	10-4-03	.267	.389	.333	5	18	15	1	4	1	0	0	2	1	2	0	0	6	0	0	5.56	33.33
Nimmala, Arjun	R-R	6-1	170	10-16-05	.238	.467	.571	8	30	21	4	5	2	1	1	1	9	0	0	0	7	0	0	30.00	23.33
Orf, Brennan	L-R	6-3	225	9-6-01	.200	.333	.200	6	18	15	3	3	0	0	0	0	3	0	0	0	5	0	0	16.67	27.78
Peguero, Jonathan	L-R	5-10	165	7-23-04	.180	.250	.280	19	56	50	1	9	2	0	1	8	4	1	0	1	16	0	0	7.14	28.57
Perez, Daniel	L-L	6-2	195	12-9-01	.161	.278	.290	12	36	31	4	5	1	0	1	2	5	0	0	0	14	1	2	13.89	38.89
Pinto, Adrian	R-R	5-6	156	9-22-02	.471	.500	.824	5	18	17	3	8	3	0	1	4	1	0	0	0	2	0	0	5.56	11.11
Rios, Kekai	R-R	5-10	205	6-6-97	.462	.500	.615	5	14	13	2	6	2	0	0	4	1	0	0	0	4	0	0	7.14	28.57
Robertis, Robert	L-L	5-11	188	11-29-02	.286	.412	.357	5	17	14	0	4	1	0	0	2	3	0	0	0	4	1	0	17.65	23.53
Rudd, Jaden	L-L	5-10	185	8-16-02	.250	.400	.250	5	15	12	1	3	0	0	0	1	3	0	0	0	2	2	0	20.00	13.33
Salinas, Roque	L-L	5-8	180	11-8-02	.400	.438	1.000	5	16	15	4	6	0	0	3	9	1	0	0	0	0	0	0	6.25	0.00
Shaw, Sam	L-R	5-10	175	2-26-05	.220	.361	.304	51	209	168	22	37	6	1	2	14	35	3	0	2	21	10	8	16.75	10.05
Sosa, Andres	R-R	5-9	210	11-7-97	.250	.500	.500	4	12	8	3	2	2	0	0	1	3	1	0	0	3	0	0	25.00	25.00
Tejada, Railin	R-R	5-10	160	2-10-05	.151	.330	.192	30	94	73	13	11	1	1	0	2	15	5	0	1	27	1	0	15.96	28.72
Vasquez, Carlos	L-R	5-8	150	6-4-05	.215	.327	.274	46	163	135	15	29	6	1	0	20	22	2	1	3	42	4	4	13.50	25.77
Votto, Joey	L-R	6-2	220	9-10-83	.000	.143	.000	3	7	5	1	0	0	0	0	1	1	0	0	1	0	0	0	14.29	0.00
Williams, Peyton	L-L	6-5	255	9-14-00	.400	.625	.600	5	16	10	3	4	2	0	0	4	5	1	0	0	1	0	0	31.25	6.25

Pitching	B-T	Ht.	Wt.	DOB	W	L	ERA	G	GS	SV	IP	Hits	Runs	ER	HR	BB	SO	AVG	OBP	SLG	SO%	BB%	BF
Bautista, Jorge	R-R	6-0	155	12-10-00	0	0	0.00	2	2	0	10	5	1	0	0	5	9	.147	.275	.176	22.50	12.50	40
Bello, Felipe	R-R	6-3	197	2-1-00	1	2	7.71	10	0	0	16	26	16	14	3	4	10	.394	.425	.606	13.70	5.48	73
Brock, T.J.	R-R	6-1	200	8-10-99	0	0	0.00	1	1	0	1	0	0	0	0	1	2	.000	.250	.000	50.00	25.00	4
Castro, Cristopher	L-L	6-1	150	8-17-02	2	4	4.78	12	9	0	43	29	24	23	5	31	50	.191	.332	.329	26.74	16.58	187
Chasse, Ryan	L-L	6-3	250	12-11-99	0	1	9.00	4	0	0	4	1	5	4	0	9	4	.091	.524	.091	19.05	42.86	21
Colmenares, Samuel	R-R	5-10	187	11-25-04	0	4	5.59	11	8	0	39	32	25	24	4	29	44	.227	.358	.369	25.43	16.76	173
Dallas, Chad	R-R	5-11	206	6-26-00	0	1	4.76	2	2	0	6	4	3	3	1	0	10	.200	.200	.350	50.00	0.00	20
Elliott, Evan	R-R	6-3	210	1-10-01	0	0	7.94	5	0	0	6	6	7	5	0	10	3	.300	.559	.400	8.82	29.41	34
Espino, Paolo	R-R	5-10	212	1-10-87	0	0	0.00	1	1	0	2	1	0	0	0	0	5	.143	.143	.286	71.43	0.00	7
Flores, Eminen	R-R	5-11	160	2-27-03	2	2	3.48	10	7	0	44	29	20	17	2	29	42	.188	.337	.286	22.11	15.26	190
Gomez, Luis	R-R	#VALUE!	NULL	5-24-94	0	1	36.00	1	0	0	1	4	5	4	0	0	1	.571	.625	.714	12.50	0.00	8
Gomez, Raudy	R-R	5-10	160	11-14-04	1	3	7.24	15	0	0	27	28	24	22	2	22	23	.267	.425	.362	17.16	16.42	134
Guerra, Daniel	R-R	6-6	230	3-13-04	0	6	6.42	11	9	0	41	50	31	29	0	27	41	.311	.403	.398	20.92	13.78	196
Guerra, Jorge	R-R	5-11	165	6-6-04	0	0	7.78	14	0	0	20	27	21	17	4	19	15	.314	.450	.547	13.51	17.12	111
Kaprielian, James	R-R	6-3	225	3-2-94	0	0	6.75	1	1	0	4	3	3	3	0	1	4	.200	.250	.333	25.00	6.25	16
Meza, Carlos	R-R	6-0	160	11-19-04	0	6	9.62	16	0	0	29	49	35	31	5	12	27	.377	.429	.546	18.24	8.11	148
Miranda, Kevin	R-R	5-10	178	11-14-98	0	1	7.71	1	1	0	2	3	2	2	0	0	1	.333	.333	.444	11.11	0.00	9
Nunez, Juan	R-R	6-2	185	1-23-96	0	0	3.52	5	0	0	8	7	3	3	0	9	12	.233	.452	.267	28.57	21.43	42
Ortiz, Julio	R-R	6-3	165	12-30-00	1	2	6.16	15	0	0	19	8	14	13	1	18	26	.121	.344	.182	28.89	20.00	90
Quinones, Luis	R-R	6-0	205	7-2-97	0	0	0.00	1	1	0	1	0	0	0	0	1	2	.000	.250	.000	50.00	25.00	4
Rojas, Kendry	L-L	6-2	190	11-26-02	0	0	0.00	1	1	0	3	2	0	0	0	1	5	.182	.308	.182	38.46	7.69	13
Santos, Dahian	R-R	5-11	160	2-26-03	0	0	0.00	1	1	0	2	0	0	0	0	1	4	.000	.143	.000	57.14	14.29	7
Sauer, Kelena	R-R	6-3	205	9-26-02	0	0	4.15	3	2	0	4	6	2	2	0	0	3	.300	.333	.350	14.29	0.00	21
Severino, Lluveres	R-R	6-1	180	8-9-03	2	2	8.72	17	0	1	22	39	23	21	3	15	14	.411	.496	.558	12.39	13.27	113

Simon, Johan	L-L	6-1	166	7-1-01	1	0	2.08	3	1	0	13	9	3	3	1	0	16	.184	.184	.327	32.65	0.00	49
Tiedemann, Ricky	L-L	6-4	220	8-18-02	0	0	81.00	1	1	0	0	2	3	3	0	2	1	.667	.800	.667	20.00	40.00	5
Torres, Luis	L-L	6-1	165	2-24-05	1	3	2.17	17	0	2	29	17	15	7	2	10	32	.167	.275	.235	26.67	8.33	120
Urena, Franly	R-R	5-8	160	6-8-04	1	4	4.88	13	5	0	31	31	24	17	5	20	35	.258	.381	.467	23.81	13.61	147
Vasquez, Juanmi	L-L	5-11	140	12-1-03	0	0	0.00	1	1	0	4	2	1	0	0	1	5	.154	.214	.231	35.71	7.14	14
Watson, Ryan	R-R	6-4	207	4-26-99	0	2	7.52	5	3	0	20	25	17	17	5	4	25	.313	.353	.563	29.41	4.71	85

Fielding

C: Minoso 23, Peguero 13, Meza 12, De La Cruz 6, Deschamps 4, LaRue 4, Rios 4, Sosa 2, Gomez 1. **1B:** De La Cruz 19, Cano 18, Perez 9, Minoso 7, Orf 4, Williams 4, Votto 2, Gomez 2, De Los Santos 1, Vasquez 1. **2B:** Vasquez 44, Escanio 7, Pinto 4, Chirinos 4, Meza 1. **3B:** Chirinos 39, Cano 15, Escanio 3, De Los Santos 2, Doughty 2, Minoso 1. **SS:** Meza 36, Escanio 15, Nimmala 8, Jemison 1. **LF:** Shaw 39, Tejada 10, Escanio 2, Salinas 2, Aponte 2, Barry 1, Guzman 1, Munoz 1, Robertis 1, Rudd 1. **CF:** Bonilla 47, Shaw 4, Aponte 4, Barry 3. **RF:** Guzman 25, Tejada 10, De La Rosa 6, Escanio 6, Rudd 4, Aponte 4, Salinas 3, Robertis 3, Munoz 3, Orf 2, Perez 2, Shaw 2, Bonilla 1.

DSL BLUE JAYS — ROOKIE

DOMINICAN SUMMER LEAGUE

Batting	B-T	Ht.	Wt.	DOB	AVG	OBP	SLG	G	PA	AB	R	H	2B	3B	HR	RBI	BB	HBP	SH	SF	SO	SB	CS	BB%	SO%
Archila, Pascual	L-L	5-10	172	1-23-07	.242	.415	.333	35	161	120	29	29	5	0	2	14	29	8	2	2	35	5	0	18.01	21.74
Arias, Andres	R-R	6-4	180	10-6-06	.309	.441	.418	16	69	55	15	17	6	0	0	2	11	2	0	0	15	3	1	15.94	21.74
Arrieche, Esmeiquel	R-R	5-7	152	12-21-06	.156	.393	.156	25	90	64	13	10	0	0	0	9	25	0	1	0	23	0	0	27.78	25.56
Bain, J.T.	R-R	6-1	160	7-2-07	.121	.293	.121	12	41	33	5	4	0	0	0	0	6	2	0	0	17	3	0	14.63	41.46
Beckles, David	R-R	6-3	215	4-23-04	.202	.343	.281	28	108	89	18	18	4	0	1	11	17	2	0	0	13	0	0	15.74	12.04
Flores, Rafael	R-R	5-10	172	3-28-07	.281	.409	.359	49	189	153	33	43	8	2	0	18	22	11	3	0	35	19	4	11.64	18.52
Gaxiola, Aldo	R-R	6-2	187	6-10-06	.286	.383	.464	31	133	112	18	32	8	0	4	25	13	6	0	2	20	1	0	9.77	15.04
Guzman, Angel	B-R	5-11	160	12-7-06	.263	.350	.344	40	183	160	24	42	9	2	0	19	22	0	0	1	30	2	2	12.02	16.39
Licourt, Yorman	B-R	6-2	192	2-6-04	.282	.377	.430	41	178	149	21	42	8	1	4	25	22	2	0	2	55	1	0	12.36	30.90
Montealto, Jarold	B-R	5-9	170	12-30-05	.178	.298	.188	36	124	101	7	18	1	0	0	17	18	1	0	4	33	1	1	14.52	26.61
Ramon, Dariel	R-R	5-7	160	3-17-06	.233	.404	.281	52	193	146	32	34	5	1	0	27	34	10	0	3	27	11	2	17.62	13.99
Reyes, Endry	R-R	5-10	168	12-13-06	.155	.320	.310	21	75	58	12	9	4	1	1	16	12	3	0	2	21	1	0	16.00	28.00
Rojas, Franklin	R-R	5-10	176	3-19-07	.258	.398	.348	27	114	89	7	23	3	1	1	17	17	5	0	2	16	0	0	14.91	14.04
Rosas, Juan	R-R	6-0	180	5-5-06	.125	.385	.500	3	13	8	2	1	0	0	1	5	3	1	0	1	2	0	0	23.08	15.38
Soto, Juarlin	L-R	6-0	170	12-23-06	.250	.428	.316	46	201	152	34	38	6	2	0	14	44	4	0	1	43	0	2	21.89	21.39
Soto, Randy	B-R	5-10	160	11-16-06	.269	.485	.351	47	194	134	23	36	11	0	0	16	44	14	0	2	26	1	2	22.68	13.40

Pitching	B-T	Ht.	Wt.	DOB	W	L	ERA	G	GS	SV	IP	Hits	Runs	ER	HR	BB	SO	AVG	OBP	SLG	SO%	BB%	BF
Abad, Carlos	R-R	6-1	165	10-18-03	0	0	5.40	4	0	0	3	4	8	2	1	9	6	.267	.542	.533	25.00	37.50	24
Barroso, Geremy	R-R	6-2	180	2-14-06	3	0	6.75	13	0	0	15	17	15	11	0	6	13	.298	.354	.421	20.00	9.23	65
Barvosa, Andersson	L-L	6-1	198	8-6-05	1	0	2.35	5	0	0	8	5	2	2	0	7	7	.179	.378	.250	18.92	18.92	37
Bueno, Ismauro	L-R	5-10	170	4-3-07	0	0	6.46	9	0	0	15	15	14	11	1	6	15	.250	.370	.383	20.55	8.22	73
De Jesus, Rafael	R-R	5-11	175	9-9-04	0	0	11.57	2	0	0	2	4	3	3	1	2	3	.444	.500	.778	25.00	16.67	12
De Los Santos, Antony	R-R	6-3	160	4-17-07	0	0	8.10	3	0	0	3	3	3	3	0	2	4	.231	.375	.231	25.00	12.50	16
Dominguez, Diego	R-R	6-0	178	7-2-04	2	5	5.40	15	0	4	30	35	26	18	0	18	33	.285	.375	.341	22.76	12.41	145
Espiritu, Victor	R-R	6-0	195	12-3-04	4	1	4.87	15	4	0	41	37	27	22	2	18	38	.234	.316	.323	21.47	10.17	177
Gallegos, Edgar	R-R	6-5	198	1-10-06	2	3	7.57	17	0	2	27	37	23	23	3	11	21	.325	.409	.447	15.91	8.33	132
Gonzalez, Eduar	L-L	5-11	155	5-1-06	3	2	3.78	12	11	0	48	48	22	20	2	18	51	.255	.324	.319	24.40	8.61	209
Hechavarria, Silvano	R-R	6-4	200	3-18-03	5	2	1.84	10	10	0	49	28	11	10	3	16	57	.162	.237	.266	29.38	8.25	194
Loreto, Josue	R-R	6-1	187	7-8-07	2	1	4.30	10	0	0	15	16	9	7	0	8	8	.276	.382	.379	11.76	11.76	68
Martinez, Danny	L-L	6-6	175	10-16-05	0	2	10.66	12	0	0	13	13	18	15	0	13	12	.271	.438	.313	18.75	20.31	64
Medina, Johandi	R-R	5-9	174	3-30-07	1	0	4.50	10	0	0	12	12	7	6	1	6	10	.267	.377	.356	18.87	11.32	53
Omosako, Sann	R-R	6-1	200	12-2-05	2	2	2.44	11	9	0	55	54	17	15	5	4	47	.251	.271	.349	21.17	1.80	222
Ramirez, Juan	R-R	6-0	170	4-30-06	0	0	21.60	2	0	0	2	4	5	4	0	5	1	.444	.643	.556	7.14	35.71	14
Rivero, Angel	R-R	5-11	172	11-28-06	1	3	4.93	11	10	0	35	38	22	19	0	9	38	.271	.325	.343	25.00	5.92	152
Suarez, Ramon	L-L	5-11	156	6-12-04	3	0	0.79	14	0	5	23	13	6	2	0	5	36	.167	.217	.218	42.86	5.95	84
Tucent, Pedro	R-R	6-3	190	10-18-02	1	3	5.36	10	10	0	42	45	34	25	2	21	35	.271	.366	.361	17.95	10.77	195

Fielding

C: Arrieche 25, Soto 23, Rojas 8, Rosas 3. **1B:** Soto 23, Gaxiola 20, Reyes 9, Beckles 7, Rojas 2. **2B:** Guzman 19, Soto 19, Flores 12, Montealto 7. **3B:** Montealto 26, Flores 18, Gaxiola 13, Reyes 4. **SS:** Soto 22, Guzman 20, Flores 14. **LF:** Ramon 27, Beckles 17, Flores 7, Licourt 6, Reyes 1, Bain 1. **CF:** Archila 32, Ramon 15, Bain 9. **RF:** Licourt 30, Arias 16, Ramon 10, Bain 1.

Washington Nationals

SEASON SYNOPSIS: The Nats' rebuild made progress and the major league team was frisky for half a season before losing steam in the second half, particularly on the mound as fatigue slowed a young rotation. The Nationals finished 71-91 for the second straight year, their fifth straight losing season since their 2019 World Series championship, but the roster got appreciably younger and more athletic.

HIGH POINT: D.C. area native James Wood, a key piece of the return in the Juan Soto trade, graduated to the big league club July 1, signaling a new phase in the rebuild. He homered for the first time July 6 while driving in five in a 14-6 win against the Cardinals, and by September, Washington sported an all-rookie outfield. Center fielder Jacob Young was around all season while 2023 first-round pick Dylan Crews joined the club Aug. 26.

LOW POINT: Opposing pitchers shut out the Nationals 18 times (the White Sox had 19), including three shutouts in a row in September, once against the Cubs and twice to the playoff-bound Royals. The last shutout, Sept. 25, was the same day the Nats sent down all-star shortstop C.J. Abrams after he was spotted at a local casino at 8 a.m. the morning of a day game. Abrams led the team in home runs but finished the season in Triple-A Rochester. Washington finished 14th in the 15-team NL in runs scored.

NOTABLE ROOKIES: Wood struck out a lot but showed impressive building-block tools with a .264/.354/.427 line, with nine homers and 14 steals. Young played a terrific center field, led the team with 150 games played and 33 stolen bases while hitting .256/.316/.331. Lefty Mitchell Parker, a fifth-round pick in 2018, held a rotation spot all season, with a 4.29 ERA in 151 innings. Fellow lefty DJ Herz joined him with 19 starts and had three outings of at least five innings and one or fewer hits allowed.

KEY TRANSACTIONS: The Nats sold some veterans at the deadline, trading away relievers Dylan Floro (to Arizona) and Hunter Harvey to the Royals (he got hurt soon thereafter) and outfielders Lane Thomas (Cleveland) and Jesse Winker (to the Mets) to make room for Wood and eventually Crews.

OPENING DAY PAYROLL: $126,862,600 (19th)

PLAYERS OF THE YEAR

MAJOR LEAGUE

MacKenzie Gore
LHP

10-12, 3.90
181 SO, 65 BB
Career-high 166 IP

MINOR LEAGUE

Dylan Crews
OF

(AA/AAA)
.270/.342/.451
13 HR, 25 SB

ORGANIZATION LEADERS

Batting		*Qualifiers
MAJORS		
* AVG	Luis Garcia	.282
* OPS	Luis Garcia	.762
HR	C.J. Abrams	20
RBI	Luis Garcia	70
MINORS		
* AVG	Phillip Glasser, Wilm./Fred./Harris.	.298
* OBP	Phillip Glasser, Wilm./Fred./Harris.	.398
* SLG	Travis Blankenhorn, Rochester	.499
* OPS	Travis Blankenhorn, Rochester	.821
R	Elijah Green, Fredericksburg	74
H	Andrew Pinckney, Rochester/Harrisburg	134
TB	Brady House, Rochester/Harrisburg	200
2B	Daylen Lile, Wilmington/Harrisburg	23
2B	Jeremy De La Rosa, Wilm./Fred./Harrisburg	23
2B	Phillip Glasser, Wilm./Fred./Harrisburg	23
3B	Daylen Lile, Wilmington/Harrisburg	10
HR	Travis Blankenhorn, Rochester	26
RBI	Brandon Pimentel, Fredericksburg	85
BB	Jack Dunn, Rochester	64
SO	Elijah Green, Fredericksburg	206
SB	Dashyll Tejeda, DSL Nationals	46

Pitching		#Qualifiers
MAJORS		
W	MacKenzie Gore	10
# ERA	MacKenzie Gore	3.90
SO	MacKenzie Gore	181
SV	Kyle Finnegan	38
MINORS		
W	Andry Lara, Wilmington/Harrisburg	11
L	Jose Atencio, Wilmington/Fredericksburg	12
# ERA	Brad Lord, Wilmington/Rochester/Harrisburg	2.43
G	Rico Garcia, Rochester	55
G	Amos Willingham, Rochester	55
GS	Thaddeus Ward, Rochester	28
SV	Rico Garcia, Rochester	20
IP	Kyle Luckham, Rochester/Harrisburg	144
BB	Thaddeus Ward, Rochester	94
SO	Jarlin Susana, Fredericksburg/Wilmington	157
# AVG	Brad Lord, Wilmington/Rochester/Harrisburg	.224

2024 PERFORMANCE

General Manager: Mike Rizzo. **Farm Director:** Eddie Longosz. **Scouting Director:** Brad Ciolek.

Class	Team	League	W	L	PCT	Finish	Manager
Majors	Washington Nationals	National	71	91	.438	13 (15)	Dave Martinez
Triple-A	Rochester Red Wings	International	77	71	.520	8 (20)	Matthew LeCroy
Double-A	Harrisburg Senators	Eastern	68	70	.493	7 (12)	Delino DeShields
High-A	Wilmington Blue Rocks	South Atlantic	57	75	.432	11 (12)	Mario Lisson
Low-A	Fredericksburg Nationals	Carolina	74	57	.565	2 (12)	Jake Lowery
Rookie	FCL Nationals	Florida Complex	25	29	.463	10 (15)	Luis Ordaz
Rookie	DSL Nationals	Dominican	23	30	.434	36 (51)	Sandy Martinez
Overall 2024 Minor League Record			**324**	**332**	**.494**	**17th (30)**	

WASHINGTON NATIONALS

ORGANIZATION STATISTICS

WASHINGTON NATIONALS

NATIONAL LEAGUE

Batting	B-T	Ht.	Wt.	DOB	AVG	OBP	SLG	G	PA	AB	R	H	2B	3B	HR	RBI	BB	HBP	SH	SF	SO	SB	CS	BB%	SO%
Abrams, CJ	L-R	6-2	191	10-3-00	.246	.314	.433	138	602	541	79	133	29	6	20	65	40	16	1	4	128	31	12	6.64	21.26
Adams, Riley	R-R	6-4	260	6-26-96	.224	.292	.336	41	130	116	10	26	5	1	2	8	10	2	0	2	35	1	0	7.69	26.92
Baker, Darren	L-R	5-10	180	2-11-99	.500	.500	.643	9	14	14	1	7	2	0	0	0	0	0	0	0	3	0	0	0.00	21.43
Blankenhorn, Travis	L-R	6-0	238	8-3-96	.129	.156	.161	13	32	31	2	4	1	0	0	5	1	0	0	0	9	0	0	3.13	28.13
Call, Alex	R-R	5-11	189	9-27-94	.343	.425	.525	30	113	99	15	34	9	0	3	14	12	2	0	0	19	5	1	10.62	16.81
Chaparro, Andres	R-R	6-0	200	5-4-99	.215	.280	.413	33	132	121	12	26	12	0	4	15	7	4	0	0	24	1	1	5.30	18.18
Crews, Dylan	R-R	6-0	203	2-26-02	.218	.288	.353	31	132	119	12	26	5	1	3	8	11	1	0	1	26	12	3	8.33	19.70
Gallo, Joey	L-R	6-5	250	11-19-93	.161	.277	.336	76	260	223	24	36	9	0	10	27	32	4	0	1	102	3	1	12.31	39.23
Garcia, Luis	L-R	6-2	220	5-16-00	.282	.318	.444	140	528	500	58	141	25	1	18	70	27	0	0	1	86	22	5	5.11	16.29
Garrett, Stone	R-R	6-2	224	11-22-95	.600	.667	1.400	2	6	5	2	3	1	0	1	3	1	0	0	0	0	0	0	16.67	0.00
Lipscomb, Trey	R-R	6-2	200	6-14-00	.200	.268	.232	61	211	190	20	38	3	0	1	10	16	2	1	1	40	11	2	7.58	18.96
Meneses, Joey	R-R	6-3	240	5-6-92	.231	.291	.302	76	313	281	19	65	11	0	3	42	21	5	0	6	63	2	0	6.71	20.13
Millas, Drew	B-R	6-0	198	1-15-98	.246	.306	.316	20	62	57	7	14	1	0	1	1	5	0	0	0	16	4	0	8.06	25.81
Nunez, Nasim	B-R	5-9	168	8-18-00	.246	.370	.262	51	78	61	14	15	1	0	0	1	12	0	5	0	15	8	2	15.38	19.23
Ramirez, Harold	R-R	5-10	232	9-6-94	.243	.273	.365	25	77	74	7	18	4	1	1	16	2	1	0	0	17	1	0	2.60	22.08
Robles, Victor	R-R	6-0	194	5-19-97	.120	.281	.120	14	33	25	3	3	0	0	0	2	5	1	1	1	9	4	1	15.15	27.27
Rosario, Eddie	L-R	6-1	180	9-28-91	.183	.226	.329	67	235	219	26	40	11	0	7	26	13	0	1	2	54	8	1	5.53	22.98
Ruiz, Keibert	B-R	6-0	227	7-20-98	.229	.260	.359	127	485	459	46	105	21	0	13	57	16	5	0	5	54	3	1	3.30	11.13
Senzel, Nick	R-R	6-1	218	6-29-95	.209	.303	.359	64	235	206	25	43	10	0	7	18	27	1	0	0	53	1	3	11.49	22.55
Tena, Jose	L-R	5-11	195	3-20-01	.274	.305	.363	41	164	157	14	43	5	0	3	15	7	0	0	0	39	6	1	4.27	23.78
Thomas, Lane	R-R	6-0	198	8-23-95	.253	.331	.407	77	341	300	42	76	16	3	8	40	32	5	0	4	72	28	12	9.38	21.11
Vargas, Ildemaro	B-R	6-0	195	7-16-91	.246	.295	.316	97	303	272	21	67	16	0	1	30	19	2	5	5	31	9	4	6.27	10.23
Winker, Jesse	L-L	6-2	230	8-17-93	.257	.374	.419	101	379	315	51	81	18	0	11	45	53	7	2	2	84	14	4	13.98	22.16
Wood, James	L-R	6-6	240	9-17-02	.264	.354	.427	79	336	295	43	78	13	4	9	41	39	2	0	0	97	14	8	11.61	28.87
Yepez, Juan	R-R	6-1	200	2-19-98	.283	.335	.429	62	249	226	32	64	15	0	6	26	18	1	1	3	42	2	1	7.23	16.87
Young, Jacob	R-R	5-11	180	7-27-99	.256	.316	.331	150	521	468	75	120	24	1	3	36	30	12	9	2	102	33	10	5.76	19.58

Pitching	B-T	Ht.	Wt.	DOB	W	L	ERA	G	GS	SV	IP	Hits	Runs	ER	HR	BB	SO	AVG	OBP	SLG	SO%	BB%	BF
Adon, Joan	R-R	6-2	245	8-12-98	0	0	6.75	8	1	0	11	12	8	8	2	4	6	.293	.362	.463	12.50	8.33	48
Barnes, Jacob	R-R	6-2	231	4-14-90	8	3	4.36	63	0	0	66	67	36	32	10	20	55	.266	.314	.444	19.86	7.22	277
Barnes, Matt	R-R	6-4	208	6-17-90	0	0	6.75	14	0	0	13	16	11	10	1	4	10	.291	.339	.418	16.67	6.67	60
Brzykcy, Zach	R-R	6-2	232	7-12-99	0	0	14.29	6	0	0	6	9	9	9	2	3	4	.360	.429	.640	14.29	10.71	28
Corbin, Patrick	L-L	6-4	226	7-19-89	6	13	5.62	32	32	0	175	208	114	109	25	54	139	.298	.348	.486	18.19	7.07	764
Ferrer, Jose A.	L-L	6-1	229	3-3-00	1	0	3.38	31	0	1	32	27	12	12	1	6	25	.227	.271	.277	19.38	4.65	129
Finnegan, Kyle	R-R	6-2	200	9-4-91	3	8	3.68	65	0	38	64	61	31	26	9	24	60	.249	.315	.400	22.14	8.86	271
Floro, Dylan	L-R	6-2	203	12-27-90	3	3	2.06	51	0	0	52	42	14	12	1	13	40	.222	.271	.265	19.61	6.37	204
Garcia, Robert	R-L	6-4	225	6-14-96	3	6	4.22	72	0	0	60	55	34	28	4	16	75	.237	.288	.323	29.88	6.37	251
Gore, MacKenzie	L-L	6-2	192	2-24-99	10	12	3.90	32	32	0	166	171	93	72	15	65	181	.263	.339	.398	24.76	8.89	731
Gray, Josiah	R-R	6-1	210	12-21-97	0	2	14.04	2	2	0	8	15	13	13	2	5	9	.405	.455	.703	20.45	11.36	44
Harvey, Hunter	R-R	6-3	239	12-9-94	2	4	4.20	43	0	0	45	43	24	21	4	12	50	.249	.312	.416	26.32	6.32	190
Herz, DJ	R-L	6-2	175	1-4-01	4	9	4.16	19	19	0	89	76	45	41	11	36	106	.224	.303	.359	27.75	9.42	382
Irvin, Jake	R-R	6-6	227	2-18-97	10	14	4.41	33	33	0	188	173	97	92	29	52	156	.244	.299	.428	20.29	6.76	769
LaSorsa, Joe	L-L	6-5	215	4-29-98	0	0	4.58	16	0	0	18	17	9	9	4	5	14	.258	.315	.439	18.92	6.76	74
Law, Derek	R-R	6-3	225	9-14-90	7	4	2.60	75	0	1	90	82	31	26	7	24	76	.246	.294	.348	20.82	6.58	365
Parker, Mitchell	L-L	6-4	224	9-27-99	7	10	4.29	29	29	0	151	154	82	72	18	43	133	.259	.309	.408	20.59	6.66	646
Rainey, Tanner	R-R	6-2	250	12-25-92	0	0	4.76	50	0	0	51	47	28	27	8	29	44	.239	.346	.416	19.05	12.55	231
Ribalta, Orlando	R-R	6-7	245	3-5-98	0	0	13.50	4	0	0	3	10	5	5	0	2	3	.500	.565	.600	13.04	8.70	23
Rutledge, Jackson	R-R	6-8	251	4-1-99	0	0	3.24	3	1	0	8	8	3	3	1	2	9	.258	.324	.452	26.47	5.88	34
Salazar, Eduardo	R-R	6-2	177	5-5-98	0	1	2.96	25	0	0	27	31	10	9	2	12	24	.282	.358	.391	19.51	9.76	123
Vargas, Ildemaro	S-R	6-0	195	7-16-91	0	0	4.50	2	0	0	2	3	1	1	1	0	0	.375	.444	.750	0.00	0.00	9
Weems, Jordan	L-R	6-4	212	11-7-92	1	1	6.70	41	0	0	42	49	35	31	7	24	35	.288	.383	.482	17.86	12.24	196
Williams, Trevor	R-R	6-3	231	4-25-92	6	1	2.03	13	13	0	67	51	17	15	3	18	59	.214	.265	.294	22.69	6.92	260
Willingham, Amos	R-R	6-4	217	8-21-98	0	0	18.00	1	0	0	1	2	2	2	1	0	1	.400	.400	1.000	20.00	0.00	5

Fielding

Catcher	PCT	G	PO	A	E	DP	PB
Adams	.983	40	279	10	5	2	3
Millas	.993	18	143	8	1	1	1
Ruiz	.998	116	921	39	2	8	4

First Base	PCT	G	PO	A	E	DP
Chaparro	1.000	12	80	9	0	11
Gallo	1.000	59	426	24	0	45
Lipscomb	.952	5	18	2	1	3
Meneses	1.000	50	358	29	0	39
Vargas	1.000	2	2	0	0	0
Yepez	.995	47	351	19	2	43

Second Base	PCT	G	PO	A	E	DP
Baker	1.000	4	2	3	0	1
Garcia	.981	129	221	305	10	84
Lipscomb	.875	2	3	4	1	1
Nunez	.000	2	0	0	1	0
Tena	1.000	8	12	12	0	9
Vargas	1.000	32	60	59	0	24

Third Base	PCT	G	PO	A	E	DP
Lipscomb	.950	55	28	104	7	12
Senzel	.961	47	28	95	5	8
Tena	.897	35	16	62	9	11
Vargas	.947	47	10	62	4	6

Shortstop	PCT	G	PO	A	E	DP
Abrams	.968	136	160	349	17	68
Nunez	.967	33	38	80	4	19
Vargas	.955	7	9	12	1	2

Outfield	PCT	G	PO	A	E	DP
Baker	.000	1	0	0	0	0
Blankenhorn	1.000	3	6	0	0	0
Call	.974	33	73	2	2	2
Crews	1.000	34	66	1	0	0
Gallo	.966	11	27	1	1	0
Robles	.963	14	25	1	1	0
Rosario	.979	61	91	1	2	1
Thomas	.977	77	162	5	4	3
Vargas	.947	15	18	0	1	0
Winker	.981	68	98	5	2	1
Wood	.971	79	129	4	4	1
Young	.980	149	388	5	8	2

ROCHESTER RED WINGS — *TRIPLE-A*

INTERNATIONAL LEAGUE

Batting	B-T	Ht.	Wt.	DOB	AVG	OBP	SLG	G	PA	AB	R	H	2B	3B	HR	RBI	BB	HBP	SH	SF	SO	SB	CS	BB%	SO%
Adams, Riley	R-R	6-4	260	6-26-96	.285	.385	.528	40	170	144	27	41	8	0	9	21	16	8	0	1	44	1	0	9.41	25.88
Alu, Jake	L-R	5-10	186	4-6-97	.230	.299	.332	60	221	196	24	45	11	0	3	24	21	0	0	4	30	8	1	9.50	13.57
Baker, Darren	L-R	5-10	180	2-11-99	.285	.348	.340	112	483	435	70	124	20	2	0	49	43	0	3	2	91	38	5	8.90	18.84
Blankenhorn, Travis	L-R	6-0	238	8-3-96	.238	.322	.499	106	453	399	65	95	22	2	26	72	41	9	2	2	118	2	4	9.05	26.05
Call, Alex	R-R	5-11	189	9-27-94	.222	.362	.413	75	312	252	45	56	13	1	11	50	54	3	0	3	60	13	2	17.31	19.23
Chaparro, Andres	R-R	6-0	200	5-4-99	.286	.419	.657	10	43	35	7	10	1	0	4	10	8	0	0	0	9	0	0	18.60	20.93
Cluff, Jackson	L-R	5-11	181	12-3-96	.225	.331	.388	84	307	258	44	58	11	2	9	41	37	5	5	2	92	19	0	12.05	29.97
Crews, Dylan	R-R	6-0	203	2-26-02	.265	.340	.455	49	238	211	34	56	10	3	8	30	20	5	0	2	42	10	2	8.40	17.65
Dunn, Jack	R-R	6-1	185	9-5-96	.236	.362	.352	115	443	364	56	86	11	2	9	41	64	9	4	2	72	14	4	14.45	16.25
Gallo, Joey	L-R	6-5	250	11-19-93	.177	.378	.484	19	82	62	17	11	1	0	6	15	19	1	0	0	23	0	0	23.17	28.05
Garrett, Stone	R-R	6-2	224	11-22-95	.247	.338	.336	71	274	235	30	58	12	0	3	20	29	4	0	1	83	1	1	10.58	30.29
Gonzales, Jarrett	R-R	5-9	185	3-27-98	.000	.333	.000	4	3	2	0	0	0	0	0	0	1	0	0	0	1	0	0	33.33	33.33
Hassell, Robert	L-L	6-1	195	8-15-01	.125	.188	.156	17	69	64	5	8	2	0	0	3	5	0	0	0	17	3	0	7.25	24.64
House, Brady	R-R	6-4	215	6-4-03	.250	.280	.375	54	236	224	30	56	10	0	6	32	7	3	0	2	68	1	1	2.97	28.81
Kieboom, Carter	R-R	6-2	211	9-3-97	.265	.365	.386	91	359	306	53	81	16	0	7	42	46	4	0	3	72	3	2	12.81	20.06
Lindsly, Brady	L-R	6-1	221	3-3-98	.231	.295	.330	66	243	212	20	49	12	0	3	27	19	1	8	2	65	1	0	7.82	26.75
Lipscomb, Trey	R-R	6-2	200	6-14-00	.283	.346	.392	65	264	240	31	68	14	0	4	35	22	1	0	0	50	8	5	8.33	18.94
Mejia, Erick	B-R	5-11	195	11-9-94	.192	.292	.314	66	203	172	28	33	4	1	5	25	26	0	1	4	39	13	2	12.81	19.21
Meneses, Joey	R-R	6-3	240	5-6-92	.254	.322	.471	51	211	189	29	48	14	0	9	30	18	2	0	2	38	0	0	8.53	18.01
Millas, Drew	B-R	6-0	198	1-15-98	.311	.361	.518	60	241	222	32	69	13	3	9	35	18	0	0	1	34	10	1	7.47	14.11
Pinckney, Andrew	R-R	6-3	205	12-7-00	.253	.333	.337	23	93	83	11	21	2	1	1	6	7	3	0	0	37	5	1	7.53	39.78
Ramirez, Harold	R-R	5-10	232	9-6-94	.375	.516	.417	7	31	24	1	9	1	0	0	4	6	1	0	0	7	0	1	19.35	22.58
Robles, Victor	R-R	6-0	194	5-19-97	.350	.435	.500	6	23	20	4	7	1	1	0	3	3	0	0	0	6	1	0	13.04	26.09
Stubbs, C.J.	R-R	6-3	207	11-12-96	.273	.500	.545	7	16	11	2	3	3	0	0	2	4	1	0	0	7	0	0	25.00	43.75
Tena, Jose	L-R	5-11	195	3-20-01	.179	.256	.359	10	43	39	6	7	4	0	1	5	4	0	0	0	13	1	0	9.30	30.23
Vega, Onix	R-R	5-9	200	9-7-98	.200	.429	.200	2	7	5	1	1	0	0	0	0	2	0	0	0	1	0	0	28.57	14.29
Wood, James	L-R	6-6	240	9-17-02	.353	.463	.595	52	231	190	44	67	16	0	10	37	40	0	0	1	42	10	1	17.32	18.18
Yepez, Juan	R-R	6-1	200	2-19-98	.263	.357	.438	74	319	274	38	72	15	0	11	41	40	2	0	3	45	3	2	12.54	14.11
Young, Jacob	R-R	5-11	180	7-27-99	.214	.313	.214	3	16	14	1	3	0	0	0	0	2	0	0	0	2	1	0	12.50	12.50

Pitching	B-T	Ht.	Wt.	DOB	W	L	ERA	G	GS	SV	IP	Hits	Runs	ER	HR	BB	SO	AVG	OBP	SLG	SO%	BB%	BF
Acosta, Daison	R-R	6-2	160	8-24-98	0	0	0.00	4	0	0	6	3	0	0	0	4	9	.150	.292	.150	37.50	16.67	24
Adon, Joan	R-R	6-2	245	8-12-98	4	5	5.35	23	13	0	69	71	48	41	9	42	57	.263	.380	.415	17.48	12.88	326
Alston, Garvin	R-L	6-4	175	3-12-97	0	0	6.87	9	0	0	18	15	15	14	3	11	17	.221	.325	.412	21.25	13.75	80
Alu, Jake	L-R	5-10	186	4-6-97	0	0	13.50	3	0	0	2	3	3	3	1	2	1	.333	.455	.778	9.09	18.18	11
Alvarez, Andrew	L-L	6-3	215	6-13-99	4	7	4.58	16	16	0	79	81	40	40	9	33	61	.267	.346	.406	17.73	9.59	344
Barnes, Jacob	R-R	6-2	231	4-14-90	0	0	0.00	7	0	2	8	1	0	0	0	2	10	.040	.111	.040	37.04	7.41	27
Bleier, Richard	L-L	6-3	215	4-16-87	1	1	4.32	15	0	1	17	20	8	8	2	2	10	.313	.324	.531	14.71	2.94	68
Brzykcy, Zach	R-R	6-2	232	7-12-99	1	0	1.13	7	0	0	8	3	1	1	1	1	7	.115	.148	.269	25.93	3.70	27
Cate, Tim	L-L	6-0	185	9-30-97	7	3	5.86	53	1	3	55	56	41	36	6	32	61	.264	.367	.387	24.60	12.90	248
Garcia, Rico	R-R	5-9	201	1-10-94	6	3	3.94	55	0	20	62	47	31	27	9	30	89	.208	.309	.363	34.10	11.49	261
Gonzales, Jarrett	R-R	5-9	185	3-27-98	0	0	4.50	1	0	0	2	2	1	1	0	2	0	.250	.400	.375	0.00	20.00	10
Gray, Josiah	R-R	6-1	210	12-21-97	0	0	8.00	2	2	0	9	10	8	8	2	1	5	.278	.308	.500	12.82	2.56	39
Gsellman, Robert	R-R	6-4	200	7-18-93	0	2	8.75	17	4	0	36	45	36	35	4	19	34	.310	.391	.497	20.12	11.24	169
Herz, DJ	R-L	6-2	175	1-4-01	3	3	3.89	10	10	0	39	24	21	17	3	32	44	.176	.333	.257	26.19	19.05	168
LaSorsa, Joe	L-L	6-5	215	4-29-98	2	2	2.25	42	0	0	56	45	17	14	7	11	41	.216	.265	.385	18.22	4.89	225
Lord, Brad	R-R	6-3	210	2-14-00	2	3	3.93	12	12	0	55	56	25	24	4	20	57	.262	.338	.388	23.75	8.33	240
Luckham, Kyle	R-R	6-2	205	10-1-99	1	2	10.20	4	4	0	15	22	19	17	5	10	10	.338	.429	.615	12.99	12.99	77
Medina, Adonis	R-R	6-1	187	12-18-96	8	3	3.76	49	0	0	65	63	28	27	7	26	60	.260	.339	.405	21.90	9.49	274
Mejia, Erick	S-R	5-11	195	11-9-94	0	0	0.00	1	0	0	1	1	0	0	0	1	1	.250	.400	.250	20.00	20.00	5
Nogosek, Stephen	R-R	6-2	205	1-11-95	1	2	9.77	11	0	0	16	15	18	17	5	18	15	.263	.430	.632	18.75	22.50	80
Parker, Mitchell	L-L	6-4	224	9-27-99	0	0	0.00	1	1	0	4	1	1	0	0	1	5	.077	.133	.077	33.33	6.67	15
Reyes, Luis	R-R	6-2	175	9-26-94	2	4	6.80	32	1	0	44	55	44	33	4	25	27	.304	.398	.442	12.68	11.74	213
Ribalta, Orlando	R-R	6-7	245	3-5-98	5	2	3.72	35	0	0	36	28	16	15	4	24	45	.215	.338	.338	28.66	15.29	157

Romero, Carlos	R-R	6-6	179	7-15-99	0	1	5.23	14	0	0	21	19	14	12	3	12	12	.253	.385	.493	12.77	12.77	94
Rucker, Michael	R-R	6-1	195	4-27-94	0	0	3.86	4	0	0	5	4	2	2	1	0	3	.235	.235	.412	17.65	0.00	17
Rutledge, Jackson	R-R	6-8	251	4-1-99	4	9	6.40	27	27	0	122	128	89	87	17	77	128	.271	.381	.436	22.74	13.68	563
Salazar, Eduardo	R-R	6-2	177	5-5-98	1	0	0.75	10	0	0	12	9	2	1	0	3	17	.200	.265	.244	34.69	6.12	49
Stuart, Tyler	R-R	6-9	250	10-8-99	1	1	7.56	4	4	0	17	17	14	14	1	10	13	.270	.382	.444	17.11	13.16	76
Tice, Ty	L-R	5-9	185	7-4-96	1	1	5.16	22	1	1	30	28	18	17	5	23	31	.250	.378	.464	22.96	17.04	135
Walters, Nash	R-R	6-5	210	5-18-97	0	0	6.08	10	0	0	13	16	9	9	3	7	10	.296	.377	.556	16.39	11.48	61
Ward, Thaddeus	R-R	6-3	204	1-16-97	8	6	5.64	28	28	0	120	113	78	75	13	94	107	.256	.401	.378	19.31	16.97	554
Watkins, Spenser	R-R	6-2	195	8-27-92	7	7	4.56	25	23	0	118	124	65	60	12	39	92	.270	.331	.430	18.15	7.69	507
Weems, Jordan	L-R	6-4	212	11-7-92	2	0	4.15	12	0	1	13	15	12	6	1	7	15	.278	.361	.500	24.59	11.48	61
Willingham, Amos	R-R	6-4	217	8-21-98	6	3	3.69	55	0	1	68	61	31	28	5	31	71	.237	.324	.358	24.23	10.58	293
Zeuch, T.J.	R-R	6-7	245	8-1-95	0	1	11.69	11	1	0	22	44	30	29	9	9	12	.404	.467	.716	9.84	7.38	122

Fielding

Catcher	PCT	G	PO	A	E	DP	PB
Adams	1.000	27	181	11	0	2	2
Gonzales	1.000	2	2	0	0	0	0
Lindsly	.989	64	540	20	6	3	7
Millas	.987	55	439	19	6	2	6
Stubbs	1.000	7	47	4	0	1	0
Vega	.917	2	10	1	1	0	1

First Base	PCT	G	PO	A	E	DP
Adams	1.000	3	19	1	0	2
Blankenhorn	.980	6	46	3	1	3
Chaparro	1.000	6	47	6	0	6
Dunn	1.000	2	4	0	0	0
Gallo	1.000	6	35	1	0	5
Kieboom	.984	10	57	4	1	8
Lipscomb	.992	14	110	9	1	15
Mejia	.000	1	0	0	0	0
Meneses	.987	42	274	38	4	30
Ramirez	1.000	1	8	1	0	1
Yepez	.992	64	462	41	4	63

Second Base	PCT	G	PO	A	E	DP
Alu	.979	25	34	60	2	18
Baker	.985	61	90	170	4	42
Cluff	1.000	25	35	69	0	16
Dunn	1.000	2	3	6	0	2
Lipscomb	.989	22	35	51	1	12
Mejia	.959	17	26	45	3	10
Tena	1.000	2	2	4	0	1

Third Base	PCT	G	PO	A	E	DP
Alu	.900	5	4	5	1	1
Dunn	1.000	11	5	19	0	2
House	.961	51	37	85	5	11
Kieboom	.938	40	22	68	6	5
Lipscomb	1.000	25	20	38	0	7
Mejia	.947	19	10	26	2	4
Tena	.500	2	0	1	1	0

Shortstop	PCT	G	PO	A	E	DP
Cluff	.974	54	78	147	6	40
Dunn	.986	85	125	222	5	53
Lipscomb	1.000	1	2	4	0	1
Mejia	.947	7	17	19	2	2
Tena	1.000	4	4	11	0	3

Outfield	PCT	G	PO	A	E	DP
Alu	1.000	21	34	0	0	0
Baker	1.000	51	82	1	0	0
Blankenhorn	1.000	60	83	2	0	0
Call	.982	74	165	2	3	0
Cluff	1.000	3	4	0	0	0
Crews	.992	47	127	3	1	0
Dunn	1.000	17	31	1	0	0
Gallo	1.000	4	7	0	0	0
Garrett	.983	63	108	7	2	2
Hassell	1.000	17	46	2	0	0
Lipscomb	1.000	5	4	1	0	0
Mejia	.962	16	24	1	1	1
Meneses	1.000	4	7	0	0	0
Pinckney	.977	23	42	1	1	1
Ramirez	1.000	2	1	0	0	0
Robles	1.000	4	1	0	0	0
Wood	1.000	51	98	2	0	1
Young	1.000	3	5	0	0	0

HARRISBURG SENATORS

DOUBLE-A

EASTERN LEAGUE

Batting	B-T	Ht.	Wt.	DOB	AVG	OBP	SLG	G	PA	AB	R	H	2B	3B	HR	RBI	BB	HBP	SH	SF	SO	SB	CS	BB%	SO%
Arruda, J.T.	B-R	5-10	180	10-20-97	.220	.299	.310	119	442	387	45	85	20	3	3	35	41	4	7	3	93	9	2	9.28	21.04
Barley, Jordy	R-R	5-11	175	12-3-99	.157	.289	.231	37	129	108	12	17	2	0	2	8	20	0	1	0	44	10	3	15.50	34.11
Cluff, Jackson	L-R	5-11	181	12-3-96	.294	.429	.588	7	21	17	4	5	2	0	1	2	3	1	0	0	2	2	1	14.29	9.52
Crews, Dylan	R-R	6-0	203	2-26-02	.274	.343	.446	51	211	186	26	51	11	3	5	38	16	5	0	3	50	15	3	7.58	23.70
De La Rosa, Jeremy	L-L	6-0	215	1-16-02	.161	.239	.298	44	180	161	12	26	5	1	5	18	16	1	0	2	52	4	4	8.89	28.89
Garcia, Dermis	R-R	6-1	200	1-7-98	.182	.274	.332	108	424	373	39	68	12	1	14	38	44	4	0	2	127	2	1	10.38	29.95
Garrett, Stone	R-R	6-2	224	11-22-95	.269	.424	.308	8	35	26	2	7	1	0	0	2	7	0	0	0	7	1	0	20.00	20.00
Glasser, Phillip	L-R	6-0	200	12-3-99	.172	.294	.172	18	68	58	4	10	0	0	0	5	6	4	0	0	10	1	2	8.82	14.71
Harris, Trey	R-R	5-9	220	1-15-96	.207	.257	.271	51	202	188	13	39	10	1	0	16	10	3	0	1	47	2	3	4.95	23.27
Hassell, Robert	L-L	6-1	195	8-15-01	.271	.357	.371	60	264	229	33	62	6	1	5	21	29	3	1	2	55	12	4	10.98	20.83
House, Brady	R-R	6-4	215	6-4-03	.234	.310	.423	75	306	274	38	64	11	1	13	34	24	7	0	1	75	5	2	7.84	24.51
Lawson, Cortland	R-R	6-2	200	5-12-00	.217	.284	.266	105	391	350	39	76	15	1	0	31	30	4	3	4	88	10	5	7.67	22.51
Lile, Daylen	L-R	5-11	195	11-30-02	.255	.343	.371	73	316	275	34	70	15	4	3	21	33	5	1	2	58	11	3	10.44	18.35
Made, Kevin	R-R	5-9	160	9-10-02	.158	.226	.211	21	85	76	9	12	1	0	1	5	6	1	1	1	22	2	1	7.06	25.88
Morales, Yohandy	R-R	6-4	209	10-9-01	.269	.362	.384	69	282	245	25	66	11	1	5	34	31	5	0	1	69	4	3	10.99	24.47
Pinckney, Andrew	R-R	6-3	205	12-7-00	.259	.328	.366	114	487	437	54	113	20	3	7	44	36	10	2	2	130	22	9	7.39	26.69
Pineda, Israel	R-R	5-11	217	4-3-00	.163	.206	.191	75	262	246	13	40	4	0	1	19	14	0	0	2	68	2	0	5.34	25.95
Ruiz, Keibert	B-R	6-0	227	7-20-98	.111	.111	.111	2	9	9	0	1	0	0	0	0	0	0	0	0	2	1	0	0.00	22.22
Senzel, Nick	R-R	6-1	218	6-29-95	.571	.700	.714	3	10	7	2	4	1	0	0	1	3	0	0	0	2	0	0	30.00	20.00
Stubbs, C.J.	R-R	6-3	207	11-12-96	.207	.327	.368	53	206	174	22	36	10	0	6	16	20	11	1	0	76	3	0	9.71	36.89
Suggs, Matt	R-R	5-9	195	5-31-00	.429	.500	.429	2	8	7	1	3	0	0	0	0	1	0	0	0	2	0	0	12.50	25.00
Thomas, Lane	R-R	6-0	198	8-23-95	.308	.438	.462	4	16	13	2	4	2	0	0	2	3	0	0	0	2	2	0	18.75	12.50
Vega, Onix	R-R	5-9	200	9-7-98	.190	.301	.229	34	124	105	10	20	1	0	1	8	17	0	1	1	21	2	0	13.71	16.94
Wallace, Cayden	R-R	5-10	205	8-7-01	.186	.222	.209	11	45	43	6	8	1	0	0	3	2	0	0	0	7	1	0	4.44	15.56
Wilson, Cody	R-R	6-0	200	7-4-96	.190	.284	.266	88	273	237	30	45	12	0	2	19	25	7	2	2	101	13	1	9.16	37.00
Witt, Paul	R-R	5-11	170	10-29-97	.201	.240	.396	48	181	169	16	34	9	0	8	25	8	1	2	1	44	0	0	4.42	24.31

Pitching	B-T	Ht.	Wt.	DOB	W	L	ERA	G	GS	SV	IP	Hits	Runs	ER	HR	BB	SO	AVG	OBP	SLG	SO%	BB%	BF
Acosta, Daison	R-R	6-2	160	8-24-98	4	3	2.89	43	0	2	53	39	20	17	4	24	73	.199	.299	.306	32.44	10.67	225
Alston, Garvin	R-L	6-4	175	3-12-97	1	2	3.00	35	0	0	42	37	18	14	1	23	44	.234	.339	.323	23.53	12.30	187
Alvarez, Andrew	L-L	6-3	215	6-13-99	4	2	2.89	10	10	0	53	41	19	17	4	20	53	.209	.286	.306	24.42	9.22	217
Brzykcy, Zach	R-R	6-2	232	7-12-99	0	0	3.38	12	0	0	13	7	5	5	1	7	18	.156	.269	.244	33.96	13.21	53
Cronin, Matt	L-L	6-2	210	9-20-97	0	0	2.70	16	0	2	17	17	7	5	0	8	19	.262	.342	.338	26.03	10.96	73
Cuevas, Michael	R-R	6-2	165	6-29-01	5	11	5.91	33	18	2	105	110	74	69	6	47	81	.269	.355	.372	17.09	9.92	474
Ferrer, Jose A.	L-L	6-1	229	3-3-00	0	0	1.69	5	0	0	5	1	1	1	0	3	4	.067	.222	.133	22.22	16.67	18

Gray, Josiah	R-R	6-1	210	12-21-97	0	0	3.00	2	2	0	9	7	3	3	1	3	7	.212	.278	.364	19.44	8.33	36
Grissom, Marquis	R-R	6-2	202	7-19-01	0	1	2.87	27	0	5	31	26	15	10	4	6	30	.224	.268	.379	23.44	4.69	128
Guasch, Richard	R-R	6-4	205	4-10-98	2	0	4.50	9	0	0	10	12	7	5	0	4	10	.273	.365	.295	19.23	7.69	52
Henry, Cole	R-R	6-4	215	7-15-99	0	1	3.95	5	5	0	14	11	8	6	2	9	13	.220	.344	.380	21.31	14.75	61
Knowles, Lucas	L-L	6-2	185	3-14-98	1	3	3.28	11	4	0	25	27	13	9	0	12	20	.287	.373	.340	18.02	10.81	111
Lara, Andry	R-R	6-4	180	1-6-03	9	7	3.63	19	19	0	104	89	44	42	14	35	93	.233	.299	.403	22.04	8.29	422
Lord, Brad	R-R	6-3	210	2-14-00	8	1	1.40	12	12	0	71	50	13	11	4	23	75	.201	.274	.281	27.27	8.36	275
Luckham, Kyle	R-R	6-2	205	10-1-99	5	8	4.47	23	21	0	129	135	70	64	15	25	93	.269	.313	.416	17.16	4.61	542
Peterson, Todd	R-R	6-5	230	1-22-98	1	4	4.70	31	2	0	38	41	23	20	3	17	30	.263	.331	.391	17.14	9.71	175
Powell, Holden	R-R	6-0	190	9-9-99	3	6	4.78	32	0	0	38	35	24	20	4	26	46	.241	.371	.407	26.29	14.86	175
Reyes, Samuel	R-R	5-11	180	3-13-96	5	2	3.95	42	3	1	66	58	35	29	7	24	63	.231	.300	.363	22.58	8.60	279
Ribalta, Orlando	R-R	6-7	245	3-5-98	1	0	1.00	16	0	5	18	10	2	2	1	8	32	.161	.254	.274	45.07	11.27	71
Romero, Carlos	R-R	6-6	179	7-15-99	1	0	0.47	16	0	5	19	12	5	1	0	8	27	.188	.288	.234	36.49	10.81	74
Saenz, Dustin	L-L	5-11	197	6-2-99	1	5	8.46	8	8	0	28	46	30	26	2	14	19	.374	.429	.504	13.57	10.00	140
Schoff, Tyler	R-R	6-4	220	12-6-98	4	0	3.66	25	0	3	32	22	14	13	3	10	33	.195	.268	.292	25.98	7.87	127
Shuman, Seth	R-R	6-1	195	12-1-97	1	2	3.78	4	4	0	17	20	10	7	2	6	14	.286	.346	.414	17.95	7.69	78
Sinclair, Jack	R-R	6-4	170	5-3-99	5	3	2.20	43	0	8	57	35	16	14	3	20	65	.180	.275	.263	28.63	8.81	227
Solesky, Chase	R-R	6-3	201	9-26-97	2	5	3.02	17	15	0	83	72	29	28	6	20	51	.233	.285	.343	15.04	5.90	339
Stuart, Tyler	R-R	6-9	250	10-8-99	0	0	2.08	4	4	0	22	16	6	5	1	7	32	.205	.292	.269	35.56	7.78	90
Theophile, Rodney	R-R	6-5	230	9-16-99	2	2	2.33	9	9	0	39	31	10	10	1	24	39	.225	.355	.268	23.35	14.37	167
Tice, Ty	L-R	5-9	185	7-4-96	1	2	5.20	26	0	1	28	23	17	16	4	18	33	.225	.355	.402	26.61	14.52	124
Walters, Nash	R-R	6-5	210	5-18-97	2	0	0.00	13	0	4	16	7	0	0	0	4	14	.132	.220	.170	23.33	6.67	60
Williams, Trevor	R-R	6-3	231	4-25-92	0	0	2.45	2	2	0	7	8	2	2	0	1	5	.296	.345	.296	17.24	3.45	29
Witt, Paul	R-R	5-11	170	10-29-97	0	0	9.00	1	0	0	1	2	1	1	0	0	1	.400	.400	.600	20.00	0.00	5

Fielding

Catcher	PCT	G	PO	A	E	DP	PB
Pineda	.992	73	587	54	5	5	17
Ruiz	1.000	2	14	3	0	0	0
Stubbs	.987	35	263	31	4	0	5
Suggs	1.000	2	18	0	0	0	0
Vega	.996	31	255	17	1	1	2

First Base	PCT	G	PO	A	E	DP
Cluff	1.000	1	6	1	0	0
Garcia	.989	76	546	63	7	52
Harris	.975	5	36	3	1	2
Morales	.983	39	260	28	5	23
Stubbs	1.000	9	65	3	0	3
Witt	1.000	10	84	6	0	5

Second Base	PCT	G	PO	A	E	DP
Arruda	.987	98	139	236	5	48
Barley	.941	18	28	36	4	7
Cluff	1.000	2	0	5	0	1
Glasser	1.000	11	12	32	0	2
Lawson	.979	10	18	29	1	4
Witt	.923	2	8	4	1	0

Third Base	PCT	G	PO	A	E	DP
Arruda	1.000	13	10	20	0	2
Cluff	1.000	1	1	1	0	0
House	.947	64	46	98	8	7
Lawson	1.000	2	1	2	0	0
Morales	.950	20	17	21	2	3
Senzel	.833	3	1	4	1	1
Wallace	1.000	10	10	12	0	1
Witt	.925	30	20	29	4	3

Shortstop	PCT	G	PO	A	E	DP
Arruda	.929	5	4	9	1	1
Barley	.922	18	21	26	4	5
Cluff	1.000	3	8	6	0	1
House	.800	1	2	2	1	0
Lawson	.966	91	133	208	12	48
Made	.988	21	27	57	1	6

Outfield	PCT	G	PO	A	E	DP
Cluff	1.000	2	1	0	0	0
Crews	1.000	49	117	2	0	2
De La Rosa	.968	38	58	2	2	0
Garcia	1.000	5	8	1	0	0
Garrett	1.000	6	8	0	0	0
Harris	.947	13	18	0	1	0
Hassell	.984	58	121	6	2	2
Lile	.992	70	132	0	1	0
Pinckney	.981	108	204	8	4	3
Thomas	1.000	3	3	1	0	0
Wilson	.983	76	164	5	3	0

WILMINGTON BLUE ROCKS

HIGH CLASS A

SOUTH ATLANTIC LEAGUE

Batting	B-T	Ht.	Wt.	DOB	AVG	OBP	SLG	G	PA	AB	R	H	2B	3B	HR	RBI	BB	HBP	SH	SF	SO	SB	CS	BB%	SO%
Baca, Tyler	B-L	5-9	180	5-22-00	.000	.000	.000	1	2	2	0	0	0	0	0	0	0	0	0	0	0	0	0	0.00	0.00
Boissiere, Branden	L-L	6-1	205	3-23-00	.209	.298	.294	48	189	163	19	34	5	0	3	23	18	4	0	3	48	0	0	9.52	25.40
Brown, Marcus	L-R	6-0	187	9-14-01	.155	.209	.192	55	207	193	22	30	7	0	0	19	9	4	1	0	37	1	0	4.35	17.87
Cruz, Armando	R-R	5-10	160	1-16-04	.227	.250	.318	20	70	66	6	15	1	1	1	7	2	0	2	0	14	1	0	2.86	20.00
De La Rosa, Jeremy	L-L	6-0	215	1-16-02	.167	.224	.378	42	170	156	22	26	10	1	7	29	12	0	0	2	56	7	1	7.06	32.94
Diaz, Geraldi	L-R	5-11	205	7-8-00	.086	.158	.086	13	38	35	3	3	0	0	0	0	2	1	0	0	11	0	0	5.26	28.95
Dugas, Gavin	R-R	5-10	204	5-19-00	.198	.321	.269	63	234	197	24	39	11	0	1	14	18	18	0	1	75	6	2	7.69	32.05
Frizzell, Will	L-R	6-3	225	2-21-99	.118	.238	.136	36	130	110	10	13	2	0	0	6	17	1	0	2	49	2	0	13.08	37.69
Glasser, Phillip	L-R	6-0	200	12-3-99	.305	.401	.436	75	324	275	47	84	16	1	6	31	40	5	2	2	45	14	4	12.35	13.89
Harris, Trey	R-R	5-9	220	1-15-96	.185	.237	.242	33	135	124	8	23	2	1	1	13	8	1	0	2	25	2	0	5.93	18.52
Hassell, Robert	L-L	6-1	195	8-15-01	.259	.276	.370	8	29	27	6	7	1	1	0	4	1	0	0	1	4	0	0	3.45	13.79
Infante, Sammy	R-R	6-1	185	6-22-01	.130	.259	.217	14	54	46	5	6	1	0	1	3	7	1	0	0	18	1	0	12.96	33.33
Lile, Daylen	L-R	5-11	195	11-30-02	.271	.352	.410	57	244	210	35	57	8	6	3	24	21	8	0	5	39	14	2	8.61	15.98
Made, Kevin	R-R	5-9	160	9-10-02	.239	.353	.327	72	301	251	30	60	17	1	1	27	39	7	1	3	74	11	1	12.96	24.58
McHenry, John	B-R	5-10	190	6-18-01	.129	.276	.177	26	77	62	10	8	3	0	0	4	8	5	1	1	29	3	2	10.39	37.66
McKenzie, Jared	L-L	6-0	180	5-16-01	.248	.303	.343	76	317	286	32	71	11	2	4	31	17	7	3	4	92	11	5	5.36	29.02
Murzi, Ivan	R-R	6-0	165	5-28-01	.111	.333	.111	4	13	9	1	1	0	0	0	1	3	0	1	0	7	0	0	23.08	53.85
Naranjo, Joe	L-L	5-10	205	5-11-01	.206	.303	.304	59	221	194	23	40	13	0	2	22	26	1	0	0	64	1	0	11.76	28.96
Nunez, Elijah	L-L	5-10	180	12-6-01	.136	.310	.136	33	113	88	17	12	0	0	0	6	23	0	0	2	30	12	3	20.35	26.55
Pena, Viandel	B-R	5-7	148	11-22-00	.276	.343	.346	78	316	283	36	78	12	4	0	30	28	1	4	0	71	20	2	8.86	22.47
Quintana, Roismar	R-R	6-1	175	2-6-03	.250	.388	.275	14	49	40	5	10	1	0	0	2	7	2	0	0	16	2	1	14.29	32.65
Rivero, Yoander	R-R	5-9	155	11-22-01	.000	.333	.000	4	12	8	0	0	0	0	0	0	4	0	0	0	6	1	0	33.33	50.00
Romero, Maxwell	L-R	6-1	218	4-29-01	.188	.277	.347	82	308	271	25	51	14	1	9	33	27	7	1	2	102	0	0	8.77	33.12
Stehly, Murphy	R-R	5-10	205	9-27-98	.225	.314	.330	61	242	209	26	47	12	2	2	25	17	12	0	4	62	4	2	7.02	25.62
Suggs, Matt	R-R	5-9	195	5-31-00	.166	.271	.290	49	166	145	21	24	4	1	4	16	17	4	0	0	57	4	0	10.24	34.34
Thomas, Johnathon	R-R	5-7	175	3-1-00	.191	.270	.258	85	269	236	24	45	8	4	0	17	15	11	6	1	89	23	7	5.58	33.09

Batting	B-T	Ht.	Wt.	DOB	AVG	OBP	SLG	G	PA	AB	R	H	2B	3B	HR	RBI	BB	HBP	SH	SF	SO	SB	CS	BB%	SO%
Vega, Onix	R-R	5-9	200	9-7-98	.290	.421	.323	9	38	31	3	9	1	0	0	1	7	0	0	0	7	1	0	18.42	18.42
Wallace, Cayden	R-R	5-10	205	8-7-01	.222	.462	.222	4	13	9	3	2	0	0	0	2	4	0	0	0	2	0	0	30.77	15.38
White, T.J.	B-R	6-2	210	7-23-03	.202	.294	.364	111	430	371	43	75	14	2	14	49	48	2	0	4	133	4	0	11.16	30.93
Witt, Paul	R-R	5-11	170	10-29-97	.190	.307	.317	19	75	63	8	12	5	0	1	4	9	2	0	1	17	0	0	12.00	22.67

Pitching	B-T	Ht.	Wt.	DOB	W	L	ERA	G	GS	SV	IP	Hits	Runs	ER	HR	BB	SO	AVG	OBP	SLG	SO%	BB%	BF
Amaral, Austin	R-R	6-0	200	12-4-01	1	2	6.75	4	0	0	8	11	7	6	1	7	7	.324	.439	.412	17.07	17.07	41
Arias, Wander	R-R	6-4	230	11-3-99	4	3	3.79	35	2	1	57	42	33	24	3	26	59	.202	.295	.317	24.48	10.79	241
Atencio, Jose	R-R	5-11	165	9-18-01	4	11	3.41	19	19	0	106	121	58	40	11	33	70	.288	.345	.440	15.15	7.14	462
Brzykcy, Zach	R-R	6-2	232	7-12-99	0	0	0.90	8	1	0	10	2	1	1	0	6	12	.067	.222	.100	33.33	16.67	36
Caceres, Bryan	R-R	6-1	170	2-19-00	3	9	4.83	26	23	0	110	121	65	59	6	52	81	.283	.370	.393	16.20	10.40	500
Cavalli, Cade	R-R	6-4	232	8-14-98	0	0	3.18	2	2	0	6	0	2	2	0	4	8	.000	.238	.000	38.10	19.05	21
Collins, Brendan	R-R	6-4	215	9-10-99	2	2	3.50	40	0	4	54	50	22	21	2	32	64	.249	.358	.348	26.23	13.11	244
Cornelio, Riley	R-R	6-3	195	6-6-00	9	11	5.56	26	26	0	126	128	84	78	15	65	114	.261	.348	.429	20.21	11.52	564
Cronin, Matt	L-L	6-2	210	9-20-97	2	0	0.65	24	0	8	28	11	4	2	0	3	35	.118	.143	.161	35.71	3.06	98
Davis, Marc	R-R	6-3	195	11-11-99	0	2	9.82	4	2	0	7	7	8	8	1	6	7	.250	.382	.536	20.59	17.65	34
Denaburg, Mason	R-R	6-4	195	8-8-99	0	0	7.50	5	0	0	6	7	5	5	2	5	2	.318	.429	.591	7.14	17.86	28
Diaz, Dannel	L-L	5-11	185	3-5-97	1	1	10.80	9	0	0	12	13	14	14	0	10	10	.295	.418	.432	18.18	18.18	55
Diaz, Moises	R-R	6-0	195	4-27-01	0	1	1.69	8	0	0	11	10	3	2	0	2	9	.244	.279	.341	20.93	4.65	43
Farrell, Luke	L-R	6-6	200	6-7-91	2	1	2.79	6	0	0	10	13	4	3	0	3	5	.342	.419	.474	11.63	6.98	43
Gomez, Miguel	R-R	6-3	170	9-10-01	3	2	2.89	32	1	3	47	41	16	15	2	15	41	.234	.306	.343	21.24	7.77	193
Grissom, Marquis	R-R	6-2	202	7-19-01	2	1	1.25	14	0	4	22	17	4	3	0	7	26	.210	.281	.235	29.21	7.87	89
Guasch, Richard	R-R	6-4	205	4-10-98	2	2	2.76	16	0	2	16	9	6	5	0	13	26	.161	.338	.268	36.62	18.31	71
Henry, Cole	R-R	6-4	215	7-15-99	0	0	0.00	3	0	0	3	1	0	0	0	5	4	.125	.462	.250	30.77	38.46	13
Huff, Chance	R-R	6-4	220	4-19-00	3	2	4.29	37	0	0	50	44	31	24	7	39	44	.234	.368	.415	19.05	16.88	231
Lara, Andry	R-R	6-4	180	1-6-03	2	4	2.35	6	6	0	31	23	11	8	2	9	39	.205	.264	.295	32.23	7.44	121
Lee, Evan	L-L	6-1	205	6-18-97	0	0	60.75	3	0	0	1	5	9	9	0	7	1	.556	.750	.556	6.25	43.75	16
Lord, Brad	R-R	6-3	210	2-14-00	0	0	0.00	1	1	0	4	0	2	0	0	6	3	.000	.389	.000	16.67	33.33	18
Perez, Marlon	L-L	5-10	180	3-16-00	1	1	6.15	27	0	0	34	32	26	23	4	23	43	.250	.355	.445	27.56	14.74	156
Peterson, Todd	R-R	6-5	230	1-22-98	1	0	1.46	11	0	6	12	9	5	2	1	6	12	.191	.283	.277	22.64	11.32	53
Pogue, Nick	R-R	6-5	235	9-13-99	1	0	5.60	13	0	0	18	21	11	11	2	8	17	.296	.386	.465	20.48	9.64	83
Romero, Carlos	R-R	6-6	179	7-15-99	1	0	3.60	14	0	0	20	20	8	8	1	10	26	.253	.341	.392	28.57	10.99	91
Schoff, Tyler	R-R	6-4	220	12-6-98	0	0	9.95	6	0	0	6	12	7	7	1	1	7	.400	.419	.633	22.58	3.23	31
Schultz, Thomas	R-R	6-6	243	8-3-99	0	0	5.47	23	0	0	25	26	15	15	6	9	19	.274	.333	.537	17.92	8.49	106
Shuman, Seth	R-R	6-1	195	12-1-97	1	1	4.60	8	8	0	31	29	18	16	6	9	24	.242	.311	.417	18.05	6.77	133
Simpson, Jared	L-L	6-4	205	6-28-00	0	0	0.00	2	0	0	2	2	1	0	0	0	2	.222	.222	.222	22.22	0.00	9
Susana, Jarlin	R-R	6-6	235	3-23-04	3	3	4.18	10	10	0	47	41	24	22	2	18	74	.230	.305	.320	36.82	8.96	201
Tepper, Mikey	L-R	6-0	210	6-2-02	0	1	4.50	4	4	0	14	18	10	7	0	8	13	.316	.388	.474	19.40	11.94	67
Theophile, Rodney	R-R	6-5	230	9-16-99	3	4	4.44	11	11	0	51	42	29	25	2	23	54	.225	.308	.299	25.12	10.70	215
Vasquez, Samuel	R-R	6-3	170	9-20-99	0	0	7.50	6	0	0	6	8	5	5	1	3	11	.308	.379	.538	37.93	10.34	29
Young, Luke	R-R	6-3	170	10-31-01	4	11	4.58	28	16	1	98	98	56	50	15	31	73	.266	.333	.439	17.76	7.54	411
Zinn, Jaren	R-R	6-4	205	8-5-98	2	0	4.22	26	0	3	32	20	16	15	4	33	39	.183	.386	.349	26.90	22.76	145

Fielding

Catcher	PCT	G	PO	A	E	DP	PB
Diaz	.978	13	87	2	2	0	1
Murzi	1.000	4	28	2	0	0	0
Romero	.996	73	628	46	3	2	2
Suggs	.990	40	284	26	3	0	5
Vega	.989	8	83	8	1	0	1

First Base	PCT	G	PO	A	E	DP
Boissiere	.996	36	237	7	1	25
Dugas	1.000	12	69	11	0	5
Frizzell	.979	15	88	6	2	11
Glasser	1.000	1	6	1	0	0
Harris	1.000	9	45	4	0	5
Naranjo	.984	52	327	43	6	38
Quintana	1.000	1	3	0	0	0
Stehly	1.000	2	18	2	0	2
Suggs	1.000	1	1	0	0	0
White	.977	13	84	2	2	9

Second Base	PCT	G	PO	A	E	DP
Brown	1.000	21	30	48	0	12
Cruz	1.000	4	6	7	0	1
Dugas	.961	24	29	44	3	10
Glasser	.976	23	29	53	2	9
Infante	.917	2	5	6	1	3
Made	.964	6	9	18	1	8
McHenry	1.000	8	9	17	0	5
Pena	.961	48	92	104	8	27
Rivero	1.000	3	7	7	0	2
Stehly	1.000	1	1	0	0	0

Third Base	PCT	G	PO	A	E	DP
Dugas	.933	19	14	14	2	2
Glasser	.925	21	17	32	4	7
Harris	.000	1	0	0	0	0
Infante	.893	12	2	23	3	2
McHenry	.947	10	5	13	1	3
Stehly	.910	57	47	75	12	7
Suggs	1.000	1	0	2	0	0
Wallace	1.000	3	2	3	0	0
Witt	.975	18	10	29	1	1

Shortstop	PCT	G	PO	A	E	DP
Brown	.965	34	34	76	4	15
Cruz	.899	16	24	38	7	8
Glasser	1.000	1	1	0	0	0
Infante	1.000	1	1	1	0	0
Made	.960	66	106	157	11	41
McHenry	1.000	1	1	0	0	0
Pena	.942	16	26	39	4	8
Rivero	1.000	1	1	1	0	1
Stehly	1.000	1	1	2	0	0

Outfield	PCT	G	PO	A	E	DP
Baca	1.000	1	1	0	0	0
De La Rosa	.950	36	73	3	4	1
Dugas	1.000	10	13	1	0	0
Glasser	.975	33	38	1	1	0
Harris	1.000	17	35	2	0	1
Hassell	1.000	7	10	0	0	0
Lile	.977	52	126	2	3	1
McHenry	.875	8	7	0	1	0
McKenzie	.969	76	150	4	5	1
Nunez	.985	32	63	1	1	1
Pena	.962	12	24	1	1	0
Quintana	.952	14	20	0	1	0
Suggs	1.000	2	2	0	0	0
Thomas	.983	81	166	8	3	0
White	.972	43	69	1	2	0
Witt	1.000	1	1	0	0	0

FREDERICKSBURG NATIONALS — *LOW CLASS A*

CAROLINA LEAGUE

Batting	B-T	Ht.	Wt.	DOB	AVG	OBP	SLG	G	PA	AB	R	H	2B	3B	HR	RBI	BB	HBP	SH	SF	SO	SB	CS	BB%	SO%
Baca, Tyler	B-L	5-9	180	5-22-00	.259	.375	.333	21	64	54	10	14	2	1	0	4	8	2	0	0	15	1	0	12.50	23.44
Bazzell, Kevin	R-R	6-1	205	3-29-03	.273	.433	.386	14	60	44	7	12	3	1	0	9	11	3	0	2	10	1	2	18.33	16.67
Brown, Marcus	L-R	6-0	187	9-14-01	.235	.304	.380	51	207	187	31	44	12	3	3	22	14	5	0	1	42	5	2	6.76	20.29

Colmenares, Jose	R-R	5-10	165	8-23-02	.218	.339	.267	62	248	206	23	45	4	0	2	24	29	10	0	3	41	1	0	11.69	16.53
Cooper, Everett	L-R	6-1	184	7-31-03	.225	.349	.280	71	262	218	26	49	10	1	0	20	39	3	0	1	39	13	2	14.89	14.89
Cox, Brenner	L-R	6-3	195	5-11-04	.204	.352	.349	90	353	284	52	58	11	3	8	42	56	10	1	2	126	29	6	15.86	35.69
Cruz, Armando	R-R	5-10	160	1-16-04	.224	.268	.266	77	315	286	32	64	9	0	1	18	17	2	5	5	39	18	5	5.40	12.38
De La Rosa, Jeremy	L-L	6-0	215	1-16-02	.306	.348	.597	16	67	62	10	19	8	2	2	9	3	1	0	0	16	3	4	4.48	23.88
Diaz, Kelvin	R-R	6-2	143	10-3-02	.265	.297	.412	10	38	34	8	9	2	0	1	7	2	0	1	1	14	1	1	5.26	36.84
Dugas, Gavin	R-R	5-10	204	5-19-00	.340	.438	.524	27	122	103	26	35	10	0	3	20	12	6	0	0	27	7	1	9.84	22.13
Farmer, Caleb	R-R	6-2	205	9-8-99	.182	.300	.276	61	237	203	19	37	6	2	3	15	26	8	0	0	60	3	1	10.97	25.32
Gallo, Joey	L-R	6-5	250	11-19-93	.200	.500	.800	2	8	5	1	1	0	0	1	1	3	0	0	0	1	0	0	37.50	12.50
Glasser, Phillip	L-R	6-0	200	12-3-99	.381	.444	.587	15	72	63	19	24	7	0	2	12	8	0	0	1	13	8	0	11.11	18.06
Green, Elijah	R-R	6-3	225	12-4-03	.208	.293	.355	106	468	414	74	86	14	4	13	54	46	5	0	2	206	39	3	9.83	44.02
Infante, Sammy	R-R	6-1	185	6-22-01	.267	.340	.395	24	97	86	13	23	6	1	1	13	8	2	0	1	25	7	1	8.25	25.77
King, Seaver	R-R	6-0	190	4-25-03	.295	.367	.385	20	90	78	15	23	1	3	0	10	9	1	0	2	13	10	1	10.00	14.44
Lomavita, Caleb	R-R	5-11	200	11-18-02	.213	.310	.246	17	71	61	15	13	2	0	0	10	5	4	0	1	13	3	2	7.04	18.31
McHenry, John	B-R	5-10	190	6-18-01	.128	.244	.248	37	134	109	14	14	4	0	3	10	17	1	3	4	42	7	1	12.69	31.34
McKenzie, Jared	L-L	6-0	180	5-16-01	.314	.400	.514	9	40	35	6	11	1	0	2	6	4	1	0	0	3	2	1	10.00	7.50
Morales, Yohandy	R-R	6-4	209	10-9-01	.417	.440	.750	6	25	24	5	10	2	0	2	7	1	0	0	0	1	1	0	4.00	4.00
Mota, Jorgelys	R-R	6-3	170	6-3-05	.255	.315	.333	29	111	102	11	26	4	2	0	9	5	4	0	0	39	3	2	4.50	35.14
Murzi, Ivan	R-R	6-0	165	5-28-01	.250	.400	.500	3	5	4	0	1	1	0	0	0	1	0	0	0	2	0	0	20.00	40.00
Ochoa Leyva, Nathaniel	R-R	6-4	215	10-15-03	.214	.297	.295	90	320	285	38	61	12	1	3	32	29	5	0	1	116	12	3	9.06	36.25
Peoples, Nick	B-R	6-5	205	7-24-04	.188	.321	.331	48	159	133	26	25	7	0	4	14	18	8	0	0	72	3	2	11.32	45.28
Petersen, Sam	R-R	6-0	195	1-20-03	.364	.400	.591	7	25	22	6	8	3	1	0	2	1	1	0	1	6	5	0	4.00	24.00
Pimentel, Brandon	L-L	6-3	210	6-16-00	.274	.329	.393	111	465	420	49	115	22	2	8	85	22	16	0	7	106	18	4	4.73	22.80
Quintana, Roismar	R-R	6-1	175	2-6-03	.250	.348	.364	64	256	220	30	55	9	2	4	30	31	3	0	2	52	2	2	12.11	20.31
Ramirez, Rafael	L-R	6-0	159	7-22-05	.170	.290	.264	17	62	53	4	9	3	1	0	0	9	0	0	0	24	0	3	14.52	38.71
Rombach, Nate	R-R	6-4	222	11-26-00	.261	.311	.369	30	119	111	9	29	6	0	2	14	8	0	0	0	34	0	0	6.72	28.57
Stehly, Murphy	R-R	5-10	205	9-27-98	.158	.273	.211	5	22	19	2	3	1	0	0	2	2	1	0	0	7	0	0	9.09	31.82
Vaquero, Cristhian	B-R	6-3	180	9-13-04	.190	.291	.303	103	401	347	51	66	16	4	5	32	39	11	2	2	137	29	6	9.73	34.16

Pitching	B-T	Ht.	Wt.	DOB	W	L	ERA	G	GS	SV	IP	Hits	Runs	ER	HR	BB	SO	AVG	OBP	SLG	SO%	BB%	BF
Agostini, Gabriel	L-L	6-0	160	7-24-04	0	1	34.71	1	1	0	2	7	9	9	0	4	1	.583	.647	.667	5.88	23.53	17
Amaral, Austin	R-R	6-0	200	12-4-01	4	2	3.09	9	1	0	23	20	11	8	3	12	16	.235	.327	.400	20.93	13.95	98
Arguelles, Anthony	R-R	5-10	195	8-16-00	3	0	2.87	27	0	11	31	17	11	10	1	15	39	.160	.272	.226	30.95	11.90	126
Atencio, Jose	R-R	5-11	165	9-18-01	3	1	3.14	6	4	0	29	39	10	10	0	1	31	.325	.336	.392	25.41	0.82	122
Baldo, Merrick	R-R	6-1	200	7-17-00	2	1	4.20	37	0	6	45	44	25	21	5	22	56	.249	.333	.373	27.72	10.89	202
Beeker, Merritt	R-L	6-2	187	11-12-01	1	0	11.37	5	0	0	6	6	8	8	1	6	7	.240	.387	.400	22.58	19.35	31
Bloebaum, Adam	L-L	6-6	225	5-3-01	1	0	2.57	4	0	0	7	4	2	2	0	1	15	.160	.192	.360	57.69	3.85	26
Bollenbacher, Matthew	R-R	6-1	203	11-9-99	2	2	3.39	35	0	3	58	65	26	22	2	13	65	.281	.328	.372	25.90	5.18	251
Clemmey, Alexander	L-L	6-6	205	7-18-05	0	1	4.30	6	6	0	23	14	12	11	0	16	26	.187	.326	.200	27.96	17.20	93
Cranz, Robert	R-R	6-3	200	5-28-03	1	0	0.00	4	0	0	6	2	0	0	0	1	7	.100	.143	.100	33.33	4.76	21
Davis, Marc	R-R	6-3	195	11-11-99	4	2	2.23	17	17	0	69	44	21	17	3	34	72	.184	.296	.285	25.90	12.23	278
Denaburg, Mason	R-R	6-4	195	8-8-99	6	3	4.04	35	0	1	56	47	37	25	2	34	47	.225	.344	.287	18.73	13.55	251
Diaz, Dannel	L-L	5-11	185	3-5-97	0	0	4.50	14	2	0	24	15	12	12	1	12	33	.183	.292	.280	34.38	12.50	96
Diaz, Moises	R-R	6-0	195	4-27-01	3	1	1.99	28	0	1	45	39	15	10	0	13	32	.232	.286	.292	17.58	7.14	182
Garcia, Robert	R-L	6-4	225	6-14-96	1	0	0.00	1	0	0	2	0	0	0	0	0	4	.000	.000	.000	66.67	0.00	6
Gomez, Miguel	R-R	6-3	170	9-10-01	1	0	2.25	2	0	0	4	2	1	1	0	0	2	.154	.214	.308	14.29	0.00	14
Gray, Josiah	R-R	6-1	210	12-21-97	0	1	9.00	1	1	0	3	3	3	3	1	1	2	.250	.357	.750	14.29	7.14	14
Hall, Bubba	R-R	6-1	212	4-10-00	6	2	2.78	42	0	0	68	51	25	21	4	15	72	.208	.258	.327	27.27	5.68	264
McHenry, John	S-R	5-10	190	6-18-01	0	0	27.00	1	0	0	0	1	1	1	1	0	0	.500	.500	2.000	0.00	0.00	2
Meckley, Xander	R-R	6-2	235	7-12-03	1	0	0.00	3	0	1	6	4	0	0	0	4	5	.211	.375	.263	20.83	16.67	24
Otanez, Johan	R-R	6-1	168	2-19-02	1	0	4.82	14	0	0	19	14	15	10	0	20	23	.203	.402	.261	25.00	21.74	92
Polanco, Bryan	R-R	6-2	190	9-12-01	7	4	4.06	22	17	0	93	89	44	42	11	45	74	.255	.345	.395	18.36	11.17	403
Rodriguez, Kevin	R-R	6-1	145	8-13-00	4	1	4.37	29	0	1	47	47	26	23	1	18	33	.263	.345	.352	16.26	8.87	203
Roman, Angel	L-L	5-11	162	9-24-03	0	0	2.70	7	2	0	17	18	7	5	0	5	22	.277	.342	.354	29.73	6.76	74
Romero, Brayan	R-R	6-1	180	1-6-02	0	2	5.52	7	7	0	29	32	23	18	2	9	13	.276	.331	.397	10.24	7.09	127
Saenz, Dustin	L-L	5-11	197	6-2-99	0	1	3.86	2	2	0	7	6	5	3	0	0	4	.222	.214	.259	14.29	0.00	28
Sanchez, Bryan	R-R	6-1	175	8-12-02	1	7	6.66	24	8	0	50	60	45	37	4	39	42	.299	.420	.398	16.80	15.60	250
Sanchez, Camilo	R-R	6-2	164	6-28-03	0	1	5.00	4	1	0	9	11	5	5	1	5	8	.324	.410	.588	20.51	12.82	39
Schultz, Thomas	R-R	6-6	243	8-3-99	3	1	1.82	18	0	8	25	14	5	5	2	9	32	.165	.242	.271	33.68	9.47	95
Shuman, Seth	R-R	6-1	195	12-1-97	0	2	3.27	4	4	0	11	13	7	4	0	2	12	.295	.333	.318	25.00	4.17	48
Sthele, Travis	R-R	6-0	198	9-21-01	6	8	4.81	23	21	0	101	111	59	54	8	46	79	.277	.354	.392	17.48	10.18	452
Sullivan, Liam	L-L	6-6	255	5-16-02	0	0	1.93	2	2	0	9	11	2	2	0	5	17	.297	.381	.405	40.48	11.90	42
Susana, Jarlin	R-R	6-6	235	3-23-04	1	7	4.47	14	14	0	56	47	30	28	0	30	83	.226	.333	.284	34.16	12.35	243
Sykora, Travis	R-R	6-6	220	4-28-04	5	3	2.33	20	20	0	85	50	27	22	2	27	129	.168	.241	.248	39.21	8.21	329
Tepper, Mikey	L-R	6-0	210	6-2-02	1	1	3.42	10	1	0	26	15	10	10	1	14	32	.161	.284	.269	29.36	12.84	109
Vasquez, Samuel	R-R	6-3	170	9-20-99	6	2	3.61	36	0	6	47	38	25	19	3	38	42	.222	.366	.316	19.44	17.59	216
Walters, Nash	R-R	6-5	210	5-18-97	0	0	0.00	3	0	0	4	0	0	0	0	0	6	.000	.000	.000	50.00	0.00	12

Fielding

Catcher	PCT	G	PO	A	E	DP	PB
Bazzell	.986	7	64	4	1	0	0
Colmenares	.987	59	545	50	8	6	2
Farmer	.992	51	456	46	4	2	6
Lomavita	1.000	10	90	13	0	1	1
Murzi	1.000	3	11	0	0	0	0
Rombach	.977	6	36	6	1	0	0

First Base	PCT	G	PO	A	E	DP
Farmer	1.000	5	34	3	0	3
Morales	1.000	6	35	6	0	0
Ochoa Leyva	1.000	3	16	1	0	1
Pimentel	.993	92	625	44	5	58
Quintana	.994	23	156	8	1	11
Rombach	.950	8	50	7	3	5
Stehly	1.000	1	8	0	0	1

Second Base	PCT	G	PO	A	E	DP
Brown	1.000	9	11	17	0	4
Cooper	.981	69	107	145	5	31

	PCT	G	PO	A	E	DP
Diaz	1.000	9	6	24	0	4
Dugas	.930	15	21	32	4	4
Glasser	1.000	3	2	10	0	0
Infante	.960	8	11	13	1	5
McHenry	1.000	5	8	11	0	4
Ochoa Leyva	.962	9	13	12	1	4
Ramirez	.950	14	13	25	2	2

Third Base	PCT	G	PO	A	E	DP
Brown	.959	19	13	34	2	2
Diaz	1.000	1	2	4	0	1
Dugas	1.000	4	1	2	0	0
Glasser	1.000	5	2	4	0	0
Infante	.950	7	4	15	1	2
McHenry	.917	12	9	13	2	2
Mota	.913	29	25	38	6	2
Ochoa Leyva	.891	55	53	61	14	3
Stehly	1.000	3	3	6	0	3

Shortstop	PCT	G	PO	A	E	DP
Brown	.951	18	21	57	4	10
Cruz	.950	76	136	169	16	39
Glasser	1.000	2	5	5	0	2
Infante	.000	1	0	0	0	0
King	.945	20	27	42	4	10
Ochoa Leyva	.906	20	26	32	6	8
Ramirez	1.000	1	1	3	0	1

Outfield	PCT	G	PO	A	E	DP
Baca	.966	21	28	0	1	0
Cox	.956	90	139	12	7	0
De La Rosa	1.000	12	17	1	0	0
Green	.964	100	233	8	9	4
McHenry	.952	19	18	2	1	0
McKenzie	1.000	8	13	1	0	0
Ochoa Leyva	1.000	1	1	0	0	0
Peoples	.933	47	69	1	5	0
Petersen	.909	6	9	1	1	0
Quintana	1.000	16	18	1	0	0
Vaquero	.976	103	186	14	5	1

FCL NATIONALS — *ROOKIE*

FLORIDA COMPLEX LEAGUE

Batting	B-T	Ht.	Wt.	DOB	AVG	OBP	SLG	G	PA	AB	R	H	2B	3B	HR	RBI	BB	HBP	SH	SF	SO	SB	CS	BB%	SO%
Acevedo, Andy	L-L	6-1	170	11-26-05	.171	.292	.183	29	97	82	6	14	1	0	0	4	12	2	1	0	23	11	0	12.37	23.71
Alu, Jake	L-R	5-10	186	4-6-97	.393	.452	.500	9	31	28	5	11	3	0	0	6	3	0	0	0	3	1	0	9.68	9.68
Arias, Luis	R-R	6-0	165	7-19-05	.192	.286	.253	35	113	99	12	19	6	0	0	15	13	0	1	0	27	5	3	11.50	23.89
Batista, Carlos	R-R	6-1	170	11-3-05	.140	.273	.230	37	123	100	16	14	0	0	3	11	18	1	2	2	53	12	2	14.63	43.09
Bautista, Jeremy	R-R	6-0	175	10-20-04	.167	.167	.167	4	6	6	0	1	0	0	0	0	0	0	0	0	2	0	0	0.00	33.33
Diaz, Geraldi	L-R	5-11	205	7-8-00	.143	.333	.429	5	18	14	2	2	1	0	1	2	3	1	0	0	4	0	0	16.67	22.22
Diaz, Kelvin	R-R	6-2	143	10-3-02	.149	.259	.213	35	109	94	14	14	6	0	0	7	12	2	1	0	40	7	2	11.01	36.70
Diaz, Winder	B-R	6-3	170	9-5-02	.211	.379	.303	39	141	109	18	23	4	0	2	9	24	6	1	1	43	4	1	17.02	30.50
Garcia, Juan	R-R	6-0	170	2-17-03	.262	.326	.476	13	46	42	6	11	0	0	3	6	3	1	0	0	15	0	1	6.52	32.61
Infante, Sammy	R-R	6-1	185	6-22-01	.429	.545	.429	4	11	7	2	3	0	0	0	1	3	0	0	1	2	2	0	27.27	18.18
Marcano, Agustin	R-R	6-0	160	6-28-06	.176	.440	.176	7	25	17	4	3	0	0	0	2	8	0	0	0	5	0	0	32.00	20.00
Maricuto, Jermaine	L-R	5-10	155	10-7-05	.267	.371	.300	9	35	30	4	8	1	0	0	3	5	0	0	0	7	0	0	14.29	20.00
McKenzie, Jared	L-L	6-0	180	5-16-01	.188	.235	.313	6	17	16	1	3	2	0	0	2	1	0	0	0	6	0	0	5.88	35.29
Mojica, Misael	L-R	6-0	155	12-29-04	.177	.350	.203	34	103	79	10	14	2	0	0	6	20	2	0	2	30	2	2	19.42	29.13
Mota, Jorgelys	R-R	6-3	170	6-3-05	.191	.271	.265	43	181	162	17	31	3	0	3	17	13	5	0	1	60	12	5	7.18	33.15
Nunez, Elijah	L-L	5-10	180	12-6-01	.091	.259	.182	8	27	22	3	2	2	0	0	4	5	0	0	0	3	2	0	18.52	11.11
Peoples, Nick	B-R	6-5	205	7-24-04	.176	.333	.373	18	63	51	7	9	5	1	1	8	9	3	0	0	24	1	1	14.29	38.10
Ramirez, Enmanuel	R-R	6-1	170	11-5-03	.257	.325	.326	42	160	144	18	37	6	2	0	19	15	0	0	1	30	0	1	9.38	18.75
Rivero, Yoander	R-R	5-9	155	11-22-01	.167	.294	.250	41	163	132	18	22	5	0	2	13	24	1	3	3	29	3	1	14.72	17.79
Rombach, Nate	R-R	6-4	222	11-26-00	.287	.368	.475	29	114	101	20	29	8	1	3	9	12	1	0	0	29	2	0	10.53	25.44
Rosario, Helder	R-R	6-1	165	1-26-05	.128	.328	.170	19	63	47	10	6	2	0	0	2	14	0	2	0	20	3	0	22.22	31.75
Soto, Elian	L-R	6-1	182	1-10-06	.175	.349	.228	41	146	114	17	20	4	1	0	8	27	4	0	1	51	0	0	18.49	34.93
Stehly, Murphy	R-R	5-10	205	9-27-98	.222	.300	.278	7	20	18	3	4	1	0	0	1	0	2	0	0	4	0	0	0.00	20.00
Tavares, Carlos	L-L	6-2	190	9-17-05	.276	.409	.460	30	115	87	15	24	13	0	1	18	23	0	0	5	22	0	0	20.00	19.13

Pitching	B-T	Ht.	Wt.	DOB	W	L	ERA	G	GS	SV	IP	Hits	Runs	ER	HR	BB	SO	AVG	OBP	SLG	SO%	BB%	BF
Amaral, Austin	R-R	6-0	200	12-4-01	1	1	4.05	4	2	0	7	7	3	3	0	5	11	.280	.387	.280	35.48	16.13	31
Arguelles, Anthony	R-R	5-10	195	8-16-00	0	0	0.00	4	0	0	4	2	0	0	0	0	6	.143	.143	.143	42.86	0.00	14
Bloebaum, Adam	L-L	6-6	225	5-3-01	0	3	2.00	16	0	2	18	20	7	4	2	5	22	.286	.333	.457	28.21	6.41	78
Brzykcy, Zach	R-R	6-2	232	7-12-99	1	0	2.25	3	1	0	4	3	1	1	0	0	6	.214	.214	.286	42.86	0.00	14
Cavalli, Cade	R-R	6-4	232	8-14-98	0	0	0.00	1	1	0	3	1	0	0	0	1	5	.111	.200	.222	50.00	10.00	10
Ciuffetelli, Christian	R-R	6-2	200	12-27-99	1	0	5.00	8	0	0	9	15	5	5	2	3	8	.366	.409	.634	18.18	6.82	44
Colon, Leodarlyn	R-R	6-4	190	12-1-04	0	4	3.65	14	10	0	44	48	29	18	4	24	35	.276	.376	.443	17.33	11.88	202
Diaz, Dannel	L-L	5-11	185	3-5-97	0	0	16.88	2	0	1	3	4	5	5	1	3	4	.400	.467	.800	26.67	20.00	15
Dowdell, Kevin	L-L	6-1	210	12-3-99	1	0	5.00	10	0	0	9	10	5	5	1	9	7	.294	.442	.412	16.28	20.93	43
Farias, Victor	R-R	6-2	150	7-17-02	0	1	27.00	1	1	0	2	3	5	5	0	2	2	.375	.545	.500	18.18	18.18	11
Farrell, Luke	L-R	6-6	200	6-7-91	0	1	3.18	3	3	0	6	4	3	2	0	1	6	.182	.217	.227	26.09	4.35	23
Ferrer, Jose A.	L-L	6-1	229	3-3-00	1	0	2.70	3	0	0	3	2	1	1	0	1	5	.167	.231	.167	38.46	7.69	13
Fortunato, Marcos	R-R	6-0	175	9-12-03	1	2	12.66	10	0	1	11	12	15	15	1	11	11	.286	.455	.429	20.00	20.00	55
Guasch, Richard	R-R	6-4	205	4-10-98	0	2	3.38	4	0	0	5	6	3	2	1	0	11	.286	.286	.476	52.38	0.00	21
Luis, Andy	L-R	6-0	150	1-14-03	0	1	10.57	12	0	0	15	25	23	18	0	13	14	.368	.488	.544	16.67	15.48	84
Ogando, Adrian	R-R	6-2	190	11-20-03	0	2	7.61	14	0	0	24	24	25	20	2	11	15	.258	.352	.462	13.89	10.19	108
Otanez, Johan	R-R	6-1	168	2-19-02	0	0	0.90	9	0	1	10	5	2	1	0	4	14	.147	.256	.235	35.90	10.26	39
Perez, Doimil	R-R	6-3	170	11-3-03	5	2	4.97	17	0	0	29	35	24	16	2	16	39	.297	.393	.466	27.86	11.43	140
Portorreal, Leuris	R-R	6-3	160	8-13-05	2	5	3.83	13	11	0	52	55	34	22	5	21	40	.272	.352	.421	17.39	9.13	230
Ramirez, Aldo	R-R	6-0	191	5-6-01	1	1	10.00	8	2	0	9	9	12	10	0	5	7	.243	.349	.297	16.28	11.63	43
Ramirez, Reilin	R-R	6-2	180	5-19-04	2	2	4.68	14	0	2	25	20	17	13	2	13	25	.217	.333	.315	23.15	12.04	108
Roman, Angel	L-L	5-11	162	9-24-03	3	0	2.97	16	1	1	33	28	14	11	0	11	33	.222	.308	.254	23.08	7.69	143
Romero, Brayan	R-R	6-1	180	1-6-02	0	1	2.52	12	9	0	39	31	16	11	2	9	39	.212	.263	.288	24.84	5.73	157
Saenz, Dustin	L-L	5-11	197	6-2-99	0	0	2.25	3	3	0	8	3	2	2	0	3	7	.107	.194	.107	22.58	9.68	31
Sanchez, Camilo	R-R	6-2	164	6-28-03	3	1	5.82	11	9	0	43	39	28	28	4	21	42	.241	.340	.383	22.34	11.17	188
Sandy, Will	L-L	6-4	210	9-17-99	1	0	5.54	11	0	1	13	18	9	8	0	4	15	.321	.367	.429	24.59	6.56	61
Shuman, Seth	R-R	6-1	195	12-1-97	1	0	3.86	2	1	0	5	4	2	2	0	0	9	.222	.222	.222	50.00	0.00	18
Tepper, Mikey	L-R	6-0	210	6-2-02	1	0	4.32	5	0	0	8	7	6	4	0	5	10	.226	.368	.258	26.32	13.16	38
Zapata, Genderson	R-R	6-3	170	6-26-04	0	0	54.00	1	0	0	0	2	4	2	1	2	0	.667	.800	1.667	0.00	40.00	5

Fielding

C: Rombach 24, Rosario 19, Marcano 5, Maricuto 4, Diaz 4, Bautista 2. **1B:** Tavares 22, Soto 18, Diaz 12, Garcia 12, Diaz 1. **2B:** Mojica 29, Arias 11, Diaz 10, Alu 6, Rivero 4, Infante 3, Stehly 1. **3B:** Mota 39, Arias 13, Stehly 5, Diaz 3, Infante 1. **SS:** Rivero 36, Diaz 12, Diaz 12, Mojica 1. LF: Soto 18, Acevedo 13, Peoples 13, Tavares 9, Batista 7, Ramirez 2, Alu 2. **CF:** Batista 22, Acevedo 15, Diaz 14, Nunez 8, Ramirez 3. **RF:** Ramirez 35, Batista 7, Peoples 7, McKenzie 6, Diaz 2, Acevedo 2, Soto 1.

WASHINGTON NATIONALS

DSL NATIONALS — ROOKIE

DOMINICAN SUMMER LEAGUE

Batting	B-T	Ht.	Wt.	DOB	AVG	OBP	SLG	G	PA	AB	R	H	2B	3B	HR	RBI	BB	HBP	SH	SF	SO	SB	CS	BB%	SO%
Cabrera, Manuel	R-R	5-10	155	2-16-06	.265	.421	.354	40	146	113	17	30	5	1	1	14	17	14	1	1	36	12	3	11.64	24.66
Culmer, Rohan	R-R	5-10	170	1-20-07	.174	.355	.217	16	32	23	6	4	1	0	0	4	6	1	1	1	8	1	0	18.75	25.00
Feliz, Angel	R-R	6-3	185	11-16-06	.310	.381	.468	49	194	171	42	53	9	3	4	20	21	0	0	2	36	27	8	10.82	18.56
Garcia, Rodrigo	R-R	6-0	173	4-13-07	.154	.306	.231	19	49	39	4	6	1	1	0	3	6	3	0	1	20	0	0	12.24	40.82
Hernandez, Diego	R-R	5-11	158	3-15-07	.222	.300	.247	31	91	81	14	18	2	0	0	8	7	2	1	0	12	7	1	7.69	13.19
Hurtado, Victor	L-L	6-3	175	5-24-07	.218	.310	.331	39	155	133	14	29	6	0	3	22	17	2	0	3	33	3	1	10.97	21.29
Liriano, Hector	L-R	6-2	180	5-17-06	.246	.352	.359	52	199	167	24	41	8	1	3	18	25	4	0	3	59	7	2	12.56	29.65
Marcano, Agustin	R-R	6-0	160	6-28-06	.148	.303	.148	10	33	27	5	4	0	0	0	1	6	0	0	0	9	1	0	18.18	27.27
Marmolejos, Eddy	R-R	6-0	175	2-13-07	.252	.352	.329	48	179	155	20	39	9	0	1	17	21	3	0	0	47	4	3	11.73	26.26
Obispo, Juan	R-R	6-0	180	5-9-06	.209	.294	.297	37	102	91	14	19	2	0	2	11	6	5	0	0	25	10	3	5.88	24.51
Pena, Jose	R-R	6-2	170	9-29-06	.140	.240	.140	15	50	43	6	6	0	0	0	4	5	1	0	1	11	0	0	10.00	22.00
Requena, Angel	R-R	6-1	160	6-8-07	.274	.351	.345	27	94	84	8	23	2	2	0	3	7	3	0	0	16	5	2	7.45	17.02
Rojas, Eyeksson	R-R	5-10	160	9-5-05	.321	.424	.500	10	33	28	9	9	0	1	1	3	5	0	0	0	2	3	1	15.15	6.06
Santos, Robert	R-R	6-0	175	11-25-05	.188	.255	.277	37	110	101	12	19	2	2	1	11	9	0	0	0	45	9	3	8.18	40.91
Solano, Edwin	R-R	5-11	168	3-14-06	.174	.274	.243	38	135	115	15	20	2	0	2	12	11	6	0	3	40	4	1	8.15	29.63
Tavarez, Feldi	R-R	6-0	160	12-20-06	.234	.323	.365	40	157	137	17	32	6	0	4	21	18	0	2	0	26	9	4	11.46	16.56
Tejeda, Dashyll	R-R	6-0	170	3-16-06	.304	.432	.456	38	155	125	31	38	7	3	2	19	20	9	0	1	25	46	8	12.90	16.13

Pitching	B-T	Ht.	Wt.	DOB	W	L	ERA	G	GS	SV	IP	Hits	Runs	ER	HR	BB	SO	AVG	OBP	SLG	SO%	BB%	BF
Carela, Enmanuel	R-R	5-11	160	3-10-07	1	1	3.92	12	0	1	21	18	11	9	1	9	17	.231	.330	.372	18.68	9.89	91
De La Cruz, Marlon	R-R	6-2	155	11-3-05	2	4	7.15	11	11	0	39	36	34	31	3	32	48	.243	.408	.399	25.13	16.75	191
Familia, Jeffrey	L-L	5-11	160	11-11-05	4	2	3.77	15	0	1	31	24	15	13	2	17	32	.212	.328	.354	23.70	12.59	135
Feliz, Jose	R-R	6-1	170	10-9-05	1	3	2.96	10	10	0	46	32	20	15	2	11	54	.193	.247	.271	30.00	6.11	180
Gimenez, Greyson	R-R	6-0	152	9-21-04	0	1	8.53	14	0	0	19	25	19	18	2	12	14	.325	.448	.494	14.43	12.37	97
Hernandez, Jose	R-R	6-6	200	11-1-03	2	1	8.68	11	2	0	19	13	18	18	1	32	13	.210	.480	.323	13.00	32.00	100
Lunar, Darrel	R-R	6-3	150	2-7-06	2	1	4.00	15	4	0	36	31	18	16	1	13	41	.230	.314	.304	26.80	8.50	153
Martina, Clarence	R-R	6-2	195	12-16-04	0	2	12.00	6	0	0	6	5	10	8	0	8	7	.238	.467	.286	23.33	26.67	30
Martinez, Anel	R-R	6-3	190	7-6-05	1	2	9.45	11	0	0	13	17	19	14	0	15	18	.298	.467	.404	23.68	19.74	76
Oliveros, Deiver	R-R	6-7	180	6-25-03	3	2	7.80	11	0	0	30	39	28	26	4	13	23	.320	.397	.541	16.31	9.22	141
Reyes, Juan	L-L	6-2	180	3-24-05	0	3	4.15	8	8	0	13	8	6	6	0	4	11	.182	.280	.250	22.00	8.00	50
Reynoso, Franniel	R-R	6-3	175	11-9-06	1	3	6.98	10	7	0	30	38	28	23	2	23	21	.309	.444	.447	13.73	15.03	153
Rivero, Enyerber	R-R	6-6	175	4-25-05	0	0	5.76	13	0	0	25	25	18	16	0	20	13	.266	.400	.351	10.83	16.67	120
Robles, Jean	R-R	6-1	170	10-20-06	0	1	3.95	14	0	1	27	23	15	12	1	14	30	.223	.352	.330	24.00	11.20	125
Sanchez, Jose	R-R	6-3	180	2-6-06	4	1	2.91	15	0	3	22	16	8	7	2	12	28	.208	.315	.325	30.43	13.04	92
Thomas, Jhoan	R-R	6-3	185	11-16-06	1	1	3.86	11	3	0	30	23	19	13	0	25	30	.213	.375	.259	21.74	18.12	138
Vera, Alejandro	L-L	6-1	192	12-31-05	1	2	8.88	11	8	0	25	25	26	25	1	39	22	.272	.504	.402	16.06	28.47	137

Fielding

C: Tavarez 35, Marcano 10, Pena 9, Garcia 5. **1B:** Cabrera 28, Requena 17, Solano 5, Pena 5, Culmer 2, Garcia 1, Tejeda 1, Santos 1. **2B:** Hernandez 26, Solano 20, Requena 5, Culmer 5, Cabrera 4, Rojas 4, Marmolejos 1. **3B:** Marmolejos 42, Cabrera 9, Solano 6, Culmer 3, Requena 1. **SS:** Feliz 47, Solano 7, Hernandez 4. **LF:** Hurtado 28, Santos 19, Obispo 8, Requena 2, Rojas 2, Solano 1, Liriano 1. **CF:** Tejeda 37, Obispo 9, Hurtado 5, Santos 5, Rojas 3. **RF:** Liriano 38, Santos 14, Obispo 6, Hurtado 2, Requena 1, Rojas 1.

MINOR LEAGUES

Realignment, Roster Cuts Affect Minor Leagues

BY JOSH NORRIS

It's been four seasons since the sport emerged from the pandemic with a smaller, realigned minor league environment. After a few years of adjustment, things seem more commonplace. It's true that more patience is required while prospects develop—the loss of the Appalachian and New York-Penn Leagues stripped away a buffer between the complex leagues and full-season ball—but the day-to-day operations are running as smoothly as ever.

The next wave of changes, however, might be on the way.

The final days of the 2024 season brought to a close a pair of franchises whose stadiums weren't up to the facility standards required by Major League Baseball. In the Carolina League, the Down East Wood Ducks closed up shop. The team—itself a salve after the Rangers sought a less sunny atmosphere than the California League—will play as an independent league team beginning in 2025.

Instead, the Rangers' High-A team in Hickory, N.C. will move to Low-A, and the team will open a new affiliate in Spartanburg, S.C.

The second shift came in the Southern League, where the Braves' Double-A affiliate will move from Pearl, Miss. to Columbus, Ga. The move also leaves the state of Mississippi as a whole with just one affiliated club—the Biloxi Shuckers, Milwaukee's Double-A team—after the Jackson Generals were one of the teams cut in the initial round of realignment.

Those two clubs were the beginning, but they certainly won't be the end. The list almost also included the Mariners' Low-A team in Modesto, Calif., as well.

In July, the team itself posted a story announcing that the 2024 season would be its last at John Thurman Field because negotiations between the team and city to extend its lease had failed.

"We're disappointed we were unable to agree upon an extension," Nuts general manager Veronica Hernandez said at the time. "I know we and the city worked very hard to find common ground and unfortunately were unable to accomplish our goal."

The club received a reprieve, however, when the Modesto city council agreed to authorize a one-year extension of the team's lease on their stadium.

The Carolina Mudcats will become the Wilson Warbirds in 2026.

Plenty of questions remain regarding the team's long-term future—local media estimate that John Thurman Stadium will require $32 million to get up to code—but for now baseball in Modesto lives for another season.

One certain move is on the way for the 2026 season.

The final out in 2025 will mark the closing bell for the Carolina Mudcats—the Brewers' Low-A affiliate in the Carolina League—who will stay in North Carolina but will move from Five County Stadium in Zebulon to a newly constructed stadium in Wilson. The team will change names, too, dropping the Mudcats moniker and instead becoming the Wilson Warbirds.

A little bit further in the offing, the Giants' High-A team hit a wall in an effort to stay in Eugene.

The team currently shares a stadium—PK Park—with the University of Oregon, which utilizes the park from February through May in the regular season, which leaves the stadium's two occupants with two months of overlapping schedules. The issue came to a bit of a head during the 2024 postseason. The Ducks hosted a super regional series, which meant the Emeralds had to hit the road for a series originally slated in Eugene.

Worcester and 11 other Triple-A teams are now owned by Diamond Baseball Holdings.

The stadium situation puts the Emeralds' future in baseball purgatory. Unless they reach an agreement with the UO, they have to move somewhere at some point. If the two sides reach an eleventh-hour agreement, the stadium will require significant upgrades to be in compliance with MLB's facility standards.

If not, the team has to move. Where and when is less clear. The Northwest League currently stands at just six teams, down from eight before realignment took hold. Keeping the Emeralds in the league's Pacific Northwest footprint would require finding a suitable area and getting shovels in the ground, two things—at least publicly—that have not happened yet.

Two of the teams involved in the changes coming for 2025—the Hickory Crawdads and Hub City Spartanburgers—have more in common than their affiliation with the Rangers. Both clubs are owned by Diamond Baseball Holdings, a group formed in December 2021 and led by top executives Pat Battle and Peter Freund.

DBH opened its march through the minor leagues with 10 clubs. Since then, that number has grown to 36. Its most recent acquisition was the Omaha Storm Chasers, the Royals' Triple-A affiliate in the International League.

The Royals and Storm Chasers have been partnered for the last 55 years, the longest pairing in Triple-A. As has been the case with DBH's other acquisitions, no changes were made to the front office staff.

Here's how the current breakdown of DBH-owned teams looks.

Triple-A (12): Albuquerque, Charlotte, Gwinnett, Iowa, Louisville, Memphis, Norfolk, Oklahoma City, Omaha, Scranton/Wilkes-Barre, St. Paul, Worcester

Double-A (12): Altoona, Arkansas, Binghamton, Birmingham, Columbus (formerly Mississippi), Harrisburg, Midland, New Hampshire, Portland, Springfield, Tulsa, Wichita

High-A (7): Hickory, Hudson Valley, Lansing, Rome, Salem, Vancouver, Winston-Salem

Low-A (5): Augusta, Fresno, Spartanburg, Inland Empire, San Jose

While DBH is likely to continue acquiring more minor league clubs in the coming years, MLB regulations prohibit it—or any group—from owning more than 14 teams at any MiLB classification, meaning it can only acquire two more clubs from either Double-A or Triple-A before it exhausts its quota.

Behind the scenes, the biggest on-field story in the minor leagues was the move to smaller roster limits. During the 2023 season, teams were capped at 180 players on domestic rosters. In 2024, that number was slashed to 165.

Though 15 players might not seem like a lot, the dropoff was felt acutely in front offices and by farm directors.

"You can't take fliers on guys anymore," one MLB front office official told Baseball America in February 2024.

In the past, spring training was the time where players had to battle to make a roster. Before the MLB takeover of the minors following the 2020 season, teams had much larger offseason minor league rosters. Each short-season and Rookie-level team guaranteed a club an additional 35 additional roster spots.

The Yankees, who in 2019 had five short-season affiliates between the Dominican Summer, Gulf Coast, Appalachian and New York-Penn leagues, could bring close to 250 players to camp.

Now, making the offseason roster might be tougher than surviving spring training cutdowns.

Each team is allowed to move up to 15 players onto the 60-day minor league injured list in mid March. Those 60-day IL players will not count toward the roster limit until they are activated.

In the case of most teams, there are a number of players, most notably pitchers rehabbing from Tommy John surgeries, who are guaranteed to move onto the 60-day IL as soon as they are eligible.

With a 175-player offseason limit and a 165-player in-season limit, a team with 11 or more players slated for the 60-day IL will actually find themselves with roster spots opening up in mid March. It's conceivable that a team could break camp on minor league spring training without releasing anyone.

The roster caps were also felt in another significant area of change in the minors. The 2024 season marked the first year of an earlier start date in the complex leagues in Arizona and Florida.

In previous years, the ACL and FCL began their seasons in July, after months of extended spring training. This year, those leagues moved their Opening Days up to May 4. The shorter roster caps left those clubs with fewer pitchers, which meant teams ran out of arms quickly and had to regularly cut games short.

The Dominican Summer League continued its regularly scheduled summer start dates.

In 2019, the final season before the minor leagues realigned, there were 124 seven-inning games between the ACL and FCL. In 2023, that number reached 265, more than double the pre-realignment figure. This past season, the two complex leagues played 389 seven-inning games, just 45 less than the number nine-inning games.

As is the case every season, some of those seven-inning games—especially in Florida, can be attributed to the weather—but it's clear that the impact of the smaller rosters was felt quickly and sharply in the minor leagues.

On the field, a pair of prospects rose from unheralded to elite.

The star of the season was Red Sox prospect Kristian Campbell, a Georgia Tech alum who was Boston's supplemental fourth-round pick in 2023. Campbell did not rank among his team's Top 30 after his first pro at-bats. A season later, he'd moved from High-A to Triple-A and laid claim to Baseball America's Minor League Player of the Year.

To get there, he hit .330/.439/.558 with 32 doubles, 20 home runs, 77 RBIs and 24 stolen bases. His 180 wRC+ was the best marker in the minors in 2024.

Since the Prospect Handbook launched in 2001, Campbell is the first Minor League POY who did not rank among his organization's preseason Top 30. This wasn't a misevaluation by the entire industry, but rather a testament to Campbell's work ethic and the advances in Red Sox hitting development.

He worked diligently throughout the offseason to add strength and bat speed and made alterations to his bat path to allow for more optimal contact at better angles.

"The bat speed is a big thing," Campbell said. "I worked on it a lot in the offseason with the Red Sox. My bat path had to change a little bit. We tweaked that in the offseason and I just spent time working on it every day."

A player cannot see results without putting in the work, and the Red Sox were effusive in their praise of Campbell's efforts behind the scenes.

"He's the kind of guy who bought into the programming, bought into what he felt like he needed to improve and what we provided for him in terms of training and focus," Abraham said. "He added about 15 to 20 pounds of muscle and strength. When we talk about impacting the baseball, that's a big thing."

ORGANIZATION STANDINGS

Cumulative minor league records for all 30 organizations, with annual winning percentages back to 2019. This is the combined record for all MiLB teams from Triple-A to the rookie levels.

		2024						
Rk	**MLB Org**	**W**	**L**	**PCT**	**2023**	**2022**	**2021**	**2019**
1	Tigers	396	318	.555	.522	.522	.480	.462
2	Guardians	392	317	.553	.475	.528	.521	.499
3	Brewers	389	320	.549	.525	.516	.497	.494
4	Red Sox	394	326	.547	.502	.529	.588	.464
5	Rangers	383	333	.535	.513	.522	.534	.567
6	Rays	379	338	.529	.543	.576	.623	.564
7	Giants	379	340	.527	.514	.503	.529	.509
8	Yankees	373	338	.525	.539	.548	.595	.518
9	Rockies	374	343	.522	.522	.549	.546	.482
10	Cardinals	341	312	.522	.478	.487	.398	.462
11	Dodgers	370	346	.517	.582	.545	.533	.557
12	Mariners	343	321	.517	.544	.493	.571	.487
13	Marlins	367	343	.517	.485	.501	.505	.504
14	Royals	365	347	.513	.472	.426	.509	.496
15	D-backs	360	359	.501	.490	.469	.443	.552
16	Pirates	355	359	.497	.529	.517	.537	.526
17	Nationals	324	332	.494	.438	.486	.415	.475
18	Phillies	345	365	.486	.553	.483	.484	.509
19	Twins	319	337	.486	.515	.532	.507	.525
20	Cubs	348	368	.486	.494	.499	.453	.484
21	Reds	343	371	.480	.495	.463	.505	.467
22	White Sox	314	349	.474	.434	.441	.404	.492
23	Orioles	338	382	.469	.503	.463	.463	.517
24	Angels	309	353	.467	.482	.523	.463	.409
25	Athletics	309	354	.466	.451	.426	.436	.470
26	Mets	328	377	.465	.468	.485	.457	.494
27	Astros	324	382	.459	.470	.457	.484	.529
28	Blue Jays	299	354	.458	.494	.479	.525	.496
29	Padres	315	403	.439	.487	.522	.462	.523
30	Braves	283	371	.433	.466	.502	.513	.469

POSTSEASON RESULTS

League (Level)	Champion	Runner-Up
International (AAA)	Omaha (KC)	Columbus (CLE)
Pacific Coast (AAA)	Sugar Land (HOU)	Reno (ARI)
Eastern (AA)	Erie (DET)*	Somerset (NYY)
Southern (AA)	Birmingham (CWS)	Montgomery (TB)
Texas (AA)	Arkansas (SEA)	Midland (OAK)
Midwest (A+)	Lake County (CLE)	Wisconsin (MIL)
Northwest (A+)	Spokane (COL)	Vancouver (TOR)
South Atlantic (A+)	Bowling Green (TB)	Hudson Valley (NYY)
California (A)	Modesto (SEA)*	Lake Elsinore (SD)
Carolina (A)	Fredericksburg (WSH)	Kannapolis (CWS)
Florida State (A)	Palm Beach (STL)	Lakeland (DET)
Arizona Complex (R)	Dodgers (LAD)	D-backs (ARI)
Florida Complex (R)	Tigers (DET)	Pirates (PIT)
Dominican Summer (R)	Red Sox Red (BOS)	Angels (LAA)

* Repeat champion from 2023

ANTAYA FOR THE BOSTON GLOBE VIA GETTY IMAGES

Campbell redefines his potential

PLAYER OF THE YEAR

BY GEOFF PONTES

No one saw Kristian Campbell's 2024 season coming.

When the Red Sox drafted the Georgia Tech product in the fourth round in 2023, his scouting report described a "slash-and-dash specialist." The second baseman was an under-the-radar selection in every sense. Campbell appeared on zero post-draft breakout lists and did not rank among Boston's Top 30 Prospects heading into 2024.

Kristian Campbell

Yet, less than a year later, the 22-year-old Campbell was Minor League Player of the Year.

Campbell was the obvious choice, especially in a season filled with injuries and disappointing performances among many of baseball's best prospects. He climbed from High-A Greenville to Triple-A Worcester, improving his results at each level.

Campbell's final line of .330/.439/.558 was among the best in the minor leagues. He hit 20 home runs and stole 24 bases in 115 games. His 180 wRC+ was the best in the minors.

His rise is atypical. Since the Prospect Handbook launched in 2001, Campbell is the first POY who did not rank among his organization's preseason Top 30. This wasn't a misevaluation by the industry, but rather a testament to Campbell's work ethic and the advances in Red Sox hitting development.

Campbell immersed himself in Boston's bat speed training program over the offseason. He also altered his bat path, allowing him to make greater impact at better angles to optimize ball flight. With the assistance of coaching, along with challenge-based training environments embraced by the Red Sox staff, Campbell created buzz in minor league spring training.

Over the course of a year, Campbell transformed from a hitter with below-average power potential to someone evaluators believe is capable of hitting 25 or more home runs.

"The bat speed is a big thing," Campbell said. "I worked on it a lot in the offseason with the Red Sox. My bat path had to change a little bit. We tweaked that in the offseason and I just spent time working on it every day."

Level by level, Campbell felt more comfortable with the swing changes. The results followed, even as the competition got tougher. He credited his success to the amount of pitches he saw throughout the season, whether in games or by using technology such as the Trajekt pitching machines available at the Red Sox's spring training facility in Fort Myers, Fla., and also at Boston's Fenway Park and Worcester's Polar Park.

"Seeing pitches at each level, you get better and better throughout the season," Campbell said. "The competition is tougher. It's not technically getting easier, though it can look like it does at times. It's really about trying to stay as consistent as possible."

Drafted as a shortstop, Campbell appeared most often at second base, followed by shortstop and center field. He appears most comfortable at second.

"He's the kind of guy who bought into the programming, bought into what he felt like he needed to improve and what we provided for him in terms of training and focus," Red Sox farm director Brian Abraham said. "He added about 15 to 20 pounds of muscle and strength. When we talk about impacting the baseball, that's a big thing."

Campbell stands as the poster child for the quality of Boston's improved hitting development program and the organization's ability to improve players. ■

LAST 10 WINNERS

2013: Byron Buxton, Cedar Rapids/Fort Myers (Twins)
2014: Kris Bryant, Iowa (Cubs)
2015: Blake Snell, Charlotte/Montgomery/Durham (Rays)
2016: Yoan Moncada, Salem/Portland (Red Sox)
2017: Ronald Acuña Jr., Florida/Mississippi/Gwinnett (Braves)
2018: Vladimir Guerrero Jr., New Hampshire/Buffalo (Blue Jays)
2019: Gavin Lux, SS, Tulsa/Oklahoma City (Dodgers)
2021: Bobby Witt Jr., SS, NW Arkansas/Omaha (Royals)
2022: Gunnar Henderson, SS, Bowie/Norfolk (Orioles)
2023: Jackson Holliday, SS, Del./Aber./Bowie/Norfolk (Orioles)

Full list: search "Baseball America awards"

TOM DIPACE

Campbell wasn't the only Red Sox prospect to take a starring role in 2024. Outfielder Roman Anthony, who broke out a season prior, obliterated upper-level pitching en route to a .291/.396/.498 slash line. He added 32 doubles, 18 home runs and 21 stolen bases to those totals.

On the mound, the season belonged to Quinn Mathews, a Cardinals lefty who earned Baseball America's Minor League Pitcher of the Year.

The Stanford alum made headlines for his playoff workload in 2023, particularly a 156-pitch complete game effort against Texas in the super regionals. Undeterred, St. Louis selected in the fourth round and shut him down for the year.

After an offseason to rest, Mathews quickly laid waste to all in his path. In a season that started in Low-A Palm Beach and finished in Triple-A Memphis, Mathews racked up a minor league-best 202 strikeouts over 143.1 innings.

The only resistance he encountered came at his last stop, where hitters touched him for 12 runs—all earned—over 16.2 innings. The speedbumps gave him fuel for his sophomore season.

"Going into the winter, there's going to be a bitter, sour taste—and that's my motivation," Mathews said. "I've got to give the hitters credit. I will remember September, and that's going to give me the little edge going through the offseason."

Other highlights from the season included slugging first baseman Deyvison De Los Santos—who was selected by Cleveland in the Rule 5 draft, returned to D-backs and then traded to Miami at the deadline—mashing 40 home runs and reaching the cusp of the big leagues. He was the first minor leaguer to reach the 40-homer threshold since 2021, M.J. Melendez achieved the feat in 2021. De Los Santos' 120 RBIs also led the minor leagues, as did his 307 total bases.

Rays outfielder Chandler Simpson entered pro ball with a reputation as one of college baseball's premier speed merchants. Speed, as it turns out, travels.

Simpson swiped 104 bases and was caught just 17 times in a season split between High-A and Double-A. In doing so, he became the first player to reach the century mark since 2012, when Billy Hamilton racked up 155 steals. Simpson's total outpaced Orioles prospect Enrique Bradfield's second-place finish by 30 bags.

For years, fans have clamored for some version of the automatic ball-strike system to come to the big leagues. The technology has been tested, re-tested and tested again at several levels of the minor leagues, but perhaps the biggest sign that some version of the system is destined for the leagues came during the Triple-A season.

Chandler Simpson stole 104 bases, the most in the minors since 2012.

MARY DECICCO/MLB PHOTOS VIA GETTY IMAGES

In the first half of the year, ball-strike duties in the International and Pacific Coast leagues were split between pure ABS—the technology's word is final—and human umpires with the ABS as a backstop for teams to challenge. In the second half of the season, the leagues went solely to the challenge system, which afforded teams two appeals to the technology per game. If a team was correct, it kept its challenge. If a team missed twice, it could no longer challenge any ball-strike calls.

MLB commissioner Rob Manfred announced in late November that the system would be tested in the Grapefruit and Cactus leagues during spring training 2025 with the goal of bringing it into the regular season the following year.

That is not yet a certain decision, and doing so would require an agreement between the league and the umpires union.

In the Arizona Fall League, MLB took the next steps toward addressing another issue: Checked swings. In games at Salt River Fields, teams could ask Hawk-eye to judge whether a hitter's bat crossed a 45-degree line extended forward from the front of home plate.

Much like the ABS, the checked-swing challenge system will undergo plenty of further review. Simply establishing a rule, however, is a big step in the right direction.

Abramson Keeps Reinventing

BY J.J. COOPER

EXECUTIVE OF THE YEAR

LAST 10 WINNERS

2014: Sam Bernabe, Iowa (Pacific Coast)
2015: Dave Oster, Lake Elsinore (California)
2016: Tom Kayser, president, Texas League
2017: Ryan Keur, Daytona (Florida State)
2018: Bob Murphy, Dayton (Midwest)
2019: Don Logan, Las Vegas (Pacific Coast)
2020: Adam Giardino, broadcaster
2021: K.L. Wombacher, president/GM, Hillsboro (Northwest)
2022: Kristin Call, GM, Myrtle Beach (Carolina)
2023: Rob Zerjac, president/CEO, Wisconson (Brewers)
For full list, search "Baseball America awards"

As Hartford Yard Goats general manager Mike Abramson admits, he and the Yard Goats staff have a problem.

Success is wonderful. But it's hard to ever stop and enjoy what you've done, because what has made Hartford successful is a group of like-minded individuals who aren't ever happy to rest on their success.

The stadium can always be improved. The on-field entertainment can be better. Something can be new and better every single night, even if that means jettisoning something that's already pretty good.

Probably 10 times a year I say to the guys I work most closely with in the office, I say 'Can we all just enjoy this for 10 minutes?' Because we never do. We bemoan every little thing. We're always asking 'how can we make this better?' "

That approach is working for Hartford and Abramson. He is Baseball America's 2024 MiLB Executive of the Year as he leads a team that has made the Yard Goats a consistently successful operation that figures out ways to grow each and every year.

"We have a large group of people here who have been here since we opened the ballpark, and everybody shares in sort of that relentless pursuit of something new. That's definitely why we're successful," Abramson said. "It's a bunch of people who have the same mindset. Nobody's ever irritated with somebody else when they're like, 'Hey, what if we blow up this thing?'"

Mike Abramson

It hasn't always been easy. After a painful and long gestation period that included the entire 2016 season as a road team when the team's stadium missed its completion date by months, Hartford moved into Dunkin' Donuts Park in 2017. And like most MiLB teams moving into a new stadium, they had immediate success.

"There are examples of organizations that open ballparks and went from last to first and then ended up back around the middle the pack before long and then lower in the pack after a few years," Abramson said. "It is easy to feel like you are the king of the world when you're in a new ballpark and everybody loves you, but that the attrition comes for you so quickly."

Attrition had not come for the Yard Goats. They draw more fans per game now than they did in Year 1 or 2 of the new stadium.

In 2024, that never-satisified mentality paid off in an improved on-field entertainment experience. From the on-field host introduction in the first to a sing-along in the late innings, the approach is designed so that fans share a common experience.

"I look at our games like a concert," Abramson said. "When people come out, I want them to be on a journey. I want them to feel like they went through something with the whole crowd, and then everybody left, and they were like, 'Wow, that was amazing. We all experienced it together.'"

When Abramson looked at smiling fans signing together every night, he knew they'd found something that added to the experiencee.

"The show was fine. Everybody who came out probably was like, it's great, that's amazing. I never felt like it was good. I never felt like it clicked until this year, and that was in the seventh season," Abramson said.

"Just like a concert, there's a reason why the hits come at the end of a concert. It's so the whole experience crescendos, and everybody sort of crescendos at the same time."

Vincej guides Modesto to top

MANAGER OF THE YEAR

BY SHANE LANTZ

Two seasons into his managerial career, Zach Vincej is already starting to compile an intriguing résumé.

Vincej led the Mariners' Low-A Modesto affiliate to its second consecutive California League championship in 2024. The Nuts went 73-57 and had the best run differential in the league, built by big performances from some of Seattle's most exciting young prospects.

At just 33 years old, Vincej is already being recognized around the industry as one of the best young managers out there.

His Cal League peers took note, voting him best manager prospect in annual Best Tools voting. Now, he is Baseball America Minor League Manager of the Year.

"What a great honor," Vincej said. "You know, I think of it more as an (organizational) award for me, because all the resources, all the guidance that I've gotten from the Mariners, it's been incredible.

"To have an award like this, it shows that the hard work is paying off, but it's also a testament to my staff, and how great my players are at the same time."

BRIAN WESTERHOLT/FOUR SEAM IMAGES

Zach Vincej

Since he stepped into the role as Modesto manager in 2023, Vincej has coached players the Mariners see as their brightest young stars. That list includes 2024 standouts such as right fielder Lazaro Montes—the California League MVP—shortstop Colt Emerson, second baseman Michael Arroyo, third baseman Tai Peete and center fielder Jonny Farmelo.

Having been a player just a few short years ago, including a cup of coffee with the 2018 Mariners, Vincej relates well to the current crop of ballplayers. His even-keeled personality seems like a good fit for the young players, who are often just getting their start in pro ball.

"I try to keep the guys loose, and I'm not saying that an older guy cannot do that, but I just feel like I can relate to the guys a little more just because of how close we are in age," Vincej said.

"And although the guys are 18, 19, 20 years old, I still feel like that's a good position to be in for myself, just knowing that I've worked with that group a lot in the last few years."

As Vincej puts it, the opportunity to be a coach fell into his lap. His playing career reached its end amid the Covid pandemic, and he decided to "move his life along" by going back to get his degree.

He had been drafted out of Pepperdine by the Reds in 2012 and had a brief stint in Cincinnati in 2017 before being claimed on waivers by the Mariners.

Vincej finished his playing career with one season in the Orioles' organization in 2019. After that, he went back to Pepperdine to finish his degree. While there, Vincej's old coach asked if he wanted to give coaching a try.

That experience led to the Mariners hiring him in early 2022 as a coach with Triple-A Tacoma, and he was named Modesto's manager for 2023.

Vincej has had lots of great managers over the years, but the one he most models himself after is current Triple-A Louisville manager Pat Kelly, who recently became just the seventh minor league skipper ever to reach 2,000 career wins.

Vincej watched Kelly closely while playing for him in the Reds' farm system. He saw a great motivator who brought plenty of fire but also fostered an energetic and positive clubhouse environment, which Vincej hopes he'll be able to provide his future players. ■

LAST 10 WINNERS

2013: Gary DiSarcina, Triple-A Pawtucket (Red Sox)
2014: Mark Johnson, Low-A Kane County (Cubs)
2015: Tony DeFrancesco, Triple-A Fresno (Astros)
2016: Dave Wallace, Double-A Akron (Indians)
2017: Stubby Clapp, Triple-A Memphis (Cardinals)
2018: Drew Saylor, High-A Rancho Cucamonga (Dodgers)
2019: Corey Ragsdale, High-A Down East (Rangers)
2021: Chris Widger, High-A Quad Cities (Royals)
2022: Gil Velazquez, Triple-A Reno (D-backs)
2023: Brian Dinkelman, High-A Cedar Rapids (Twins)

For full list, search "Baseball America awards"

CLASSIFICATION ALL-STARS

TRIPLE-A

Pos	Player, Team (Organization)	Age	AVG	OBP	SLG	PA	H	2B	3B	HR	RBI	BB	SO	SB
C	Adrian Del Castillo, Reno (D-backs)	24	.312	.399	.603	474	129	36	3	26	75	55	80	0
1B	Kyle Manzardo, Columbus (Guardians)	23	.267	.398	.548	364	78	20	1	20	49	61	67	3
2B	Jackson Holliday, Norfolk (Orioles)	20	.271	.431	.477	346	72	25	0	10	38	75	77	8
3B	Coby Mayo Norfolk (Orioles)	22	.287	.364	.562	390	99	23	3	22	67	40	97	4
SS	Chase Meidroth, Worcester (Red Sox)	22	.293	.437	.400	558	128	20	3	7	57	105	71	13
OF	Owen Caissie, Iowa (Cubs)	21	.278	.375	.472	549	131	29	3	19	75	71	156	11
OF	Heston Kjerstad Norfolk (Orioles)	25	.300	.397	.601	258	64	14	1	16	58	32	67	2
OF	James Wood, Rochester (Nationals)	21	.353	.463	.595	231	67	16	0	10	37	40	42	10
DH	Andres Chaparro, Reno/Rochester (ARI/WSH)	25	.328	.405	.572	457	132	27	1	23	85	49	82	3

Pos	Pitcher, Team (Organization)	Age	W	L	ERA	G	SV	IP	H	BB	SO	HR	K-BB%	WHIP
SP	Noah Cameron, Omaha (Royals)	24	3	2	2.32	9	0	54	44	11	62	6	23.8	1.01
SP	Yilber Diaz, Reno (D-backs)	23	3	4	3.22	10	0	50	47	18	63	4	21.3	1.29
SP	Michael McGreevy, Memphis (Cardinals)	23	9	8	4.02	27	0	150	152	44	138	14	14.7	1.31
SP	Cade Povich, Norfolk (Orioles)	24	6	1	3.48	15	0	78	59	27	89	7	19.6	1.11
SP	Quinn Priester, Indianapolis (Pirates)	23	4	2	4.38	16	0	72	65	19	78	6	19.9	1.17
RP	Jack Dreyer, Oklahoma City (Dodgers)	25	5	2	2.95	37	4	43	39	9	52	4	24.7	1.13

DOUBLE-A

Pos	Player, Team (Organization)	Age	AVG	OBP	SLG	PA	H	2B	3B	HR	RBI	BB	SO	SB
C	Kyle Teel, Portland (Red Sox)	22	.298	.390	.462	382	97	20	0	11	60	48	87	9
1B	Deyvison De Los Santos, Amarillo (D-backs)	21	.372	.426	.696	162	55	4	1	14	37	12	36	1
2B	Kristian Campbell, Portland (Red Sox)	22	.362	.463	.582	255	77	17	3	8	35	35	38	17
3B	Matt Shaw, Tennessee (Cubs)	22	.279	.373	.468	371	87	11	3	14	50	45	65	25
SS	Carson Williams, Montgomery (Rays)	21	.256	.352	.469	505	111	20	6	20	69	58	144	33
OF	Roman Anthony, Portland (Red Sox)	20	.269	.367	.489	376	87	20	3	15	45	48	96	16
OF	Emmanuel Rodriguez, Wichita (Twins)	21	.298	.479	.621	167	37	12	2	8	20	42	46	9
OF	Chandler Simpson, Montgomery (Rays)	23	.351	.401	.407	358	113	13	1	1	20	29	27	73
DH	Jimmy Crooks, Springfield (Cardinals)	22	.321	.410	.498	371	101	19	2	11	62	43	78	4

Pos	Pitcher, Team (Organization)	Age	W	L	ERA	G	SV	IP	H	BB	SO	HR	K-BB%	WHIP
SP	Caden Dana, Rocket City (Angels)	20	9	7	2.52	23	0	136	89	39	147	10	20.1	0.94
SP	Jackson Jobe, Erie (Tigers)	21	4	2	1.95	16	0	74	42	38	81	2	14.4	1.09
SP	Noah Schultz, Birmingham (White Sox)	20	0	3	1.48	16	0	61	45	17	73	2	22.6	1.02
SP	Emiliano Teodo, Frisco (Rangers)	23	5	4	1.98	20	0	86	53	50	110	4	16.8	1.19
SP	Drew Thorpe, Birmingham (White Sox)	23	7	1	1.35	11	0	60	35	17	56	3	17.4	0.87
RP	Troy Taylor, Arkansas (Mariners)	22	3	3	1.17	29	16	31	16	9	31	0	19.0	0.82

MIKE JANES/FOUR SEAM IMAGES

Kristian Campbell did it all as he climbed from High-A to Triple-A in the Red Sox system.

CLASSIFICATION ALL-STARS

HIGH-A

Pos	Player, Team (Organization)	Age	AVG	OBP	SLG	PA	H	2B	3B	HR	RBI	BB	SO	SB
C	Cooper Ingle, Lake County (Guardians)	22	.313	.433	.500	305	79	18	1	9	55	51	40	3
1B	Bryce Eldridge, Eugene (Giants)	19	.335	.442	.618	215	58	11	1	12	41	35	52	3
2B	Michael Arroyo, Everett (Mariners)	19	.290	.397	.519	290	70	15	2	12	40	34	75	10
3B	Kyle Karros, Spokane (Rockies)	21	.311	.390	.485	539	147	33	2	15	78	54	123	12
SS	Brayden Taylor, Bowling Green (Rays)	22	.269	.389	.513	383	85	25	5	14	45	61	95	26
OF	Henry Bolte, Lansing (Athletics)	20	.278	.393	.519	318	74	19	6	11	52	41	101	28
OF	Cole Carrigg Spokane (Rockies)	22	.280	.358	.475	510	123	16	11	16	60	50	97	51
OF	Jhostynxon Garcia, Greenville (Red Sox)	21	.311	.371	.627	229	65	14	2	16	37	12	50	1
DH	Tre' Morgan, Bowling Green (Rays)	21	.371	.447	.558	231	73	17	1	6	44	26	18	10

Pos	Pitcher, Team (Organization)	Age	W	L	ERA	G	SV	IP	H	BB	SO	HR	K-BB%	WHIP
SP	Sam Aldegheri, Jersey Shore (Phillies)	22	6	5	3.18	13	0	68	44	28	95	3	24.4	1.06
SP	Jackson Baumeister, Aberdeen/Bowling Green (BAL/TB)	21	3	3	2.53	25	1	100	65	48	135	4	21.1	1.13
SP	Jaden Hamm, West Michigan (Tigers)	21	5	4	2.64	24	0	99	73	31	122	8	22.8	1.05
SP	Sean Sullivan, Spokane (Rockies)	21	7	2	2.16	14	0	83	62	8	101	7	29.0	0.84
SP	Matt Wilkinson, Lake County (Guardians)	21	5	5	2.30	16	0	78	49	28	103	8	23.8	0.98
RP	Cameron Cotter, Eugene (Giants)	25	6	4	2.27	35	5	48	35	9	48	2	21.0	0.92

LOW-A

Pos	Player, Team (Organization)	Age	AVG	OBP	SLG	PA	H	2B	3B	HR	RBI	BB	SO	SB
C	Blake Mitchell, Columbia (Royals)	19	.238	.376	.439	466	90	16	3	18	50	79	142	25
1B	Romeo Sanabria, Lake Elsinore (Padres)	22	.311	.433	.493	270	68	16	0	8	40	48	46	3
2B	Demetrio Crisantes, Visalia (D-backs)	19	.333	.429	.478	295	83	16	1	6	40	38	47	20
3B	Gleider Figuereo, Down East (Rangers)	20	.243	.346	.474	269	56	9	4	12	32	35	74	1
SS	Kevin McGonigle, Lakeland (Tigers)	19	.326	.407	.470	271	75	15	3	4	37	35	24	20
OF	Jaison Chourio, Lynchburg (Guardians)	19	.269	.414	.398	432	90	24	2	5	58	86	69	44
OF	Lazaro Montes, Modesto (Mariners)	19	.309	.411	.527	309	79	13	2	13	72	43	59	1
OF	Aidan Smith, Modesto/Charleston (SEA/TB)	19	.288	.401	.473	444	106	33	1	11	53	64	103	41
DH	Bo Davidson, San Jose (Giants)	21	.328	.438	.608	226	62	12	7	9	40	32	54	6

Pos	Pitcher, Team (Organization)	Age	W	L	ERA	G	SV	IP	H	BB	SO	HR	K-BB%	WHIP
SP	Gary Gill Hill, Charleston (Rays)	19	4	4	3.15	22	0	109	94	27	105	9	18.0	1.11
SP	Isaiah Lowe, Lake Elsinore (Padres)	21	5	3	3.00	17	0	72	56	29	89	2	20.0	1.18
SP	Carlson Reed, Bradenton (Pirates)	21	5	3	2.43	17	0	78	55	42	96	4	16.7	1.25
SP	Elmer Rodriguez-Cruz, Salem (Red Sox)	20	3	4	2.51	14	0	61	47	25	73	1	18.8	1.18
SP	Travis Sykora, Fredericksburg (Nationals)	20	5	3	2.33	20	0	85	50	27	129	2	31.0	0.91
RP	Gerlin Rosario, Charleston (Rays)	22	3	1	2.52	26	8	50	32	15	65	3	25.4	0.94

ROOKIE COMPLEX

Pos	Player, Team (Organization)	Age	AVG	OBP	SLG	PA	H	2B	3B	HR	RBI	BB	SO	SB
C	Eduardo Tait, FCL Phillies	17	.321	.377	.500	212	59	13	1	6	49	13	31	5
1B	Engelth Urena, FCL Yankees	19	.301	.420	.564	162	40	11	0	8	31	24	19	5
2B	Jesus Made, DSL Brewers	17	.331	.458	.554	216	58	9	6	6	28	39	28	28
3B	Emil Morales, DSL Dodgers	17	.342	.478	.691	201	52	11	0	14	46	40	45	12
SS	Franklin Arias, FCL Red Sox	18	.355	.471	.584	206	59	16	2	6	28	34	36	30
OF	Yeremi Cabrera, ACL Rangers	18	.301	.438	.571	210	49	11	3	9	39	40	42	17
OF	Robert Calaz, ACL Rockies	18	.349	.462	.651	210	60	12	5	10	45	32	47	12
OF	Eduardo Quintero, ACL Dodgers	18	.330	.459	.449	233	61	7	3	3	37	41	45	29
DH	Eric Bitonti, ACL Brewers	18	.320	.451	.580	226	58	17	3	8	42	43	61	9

Pos	Pitcher, Team (Organization)	Age	W	L	ERA	G	SV	IP	H	BB	SO	HR	K-BB%	WHIP
SP	Cesar Aquino, DSL Pirates	19	6	1	0.98	12	0	46	28	7	37	1	17.2	0.76
SP	Jacob Bresnahan, ACL Guardians	19	1	3	2.54	11	0	46	32	16	63	2	25.4	1.04
SP	Juan De La Cruz, FCL Marlins	19	5	0	1.57	11	0	46	24	21	44	1	12.4	0.98
SP	Zander Mueth, FCL Pirates	19	6	1	1.58	13	0	51	39	26	56	2	13.3	1.27
SP	Ubaldo Soto, DSL Angels	17	8	0	1.29	12	0	56	41	20	56	0	16.3	1.09
RP	Manuel Medina, FCL Marlins	22	3	0	0.89	18	5	20	9	5	36	0	39.7	0.69

Red Sox outfielder Roman Anthony mashed his way to Triple-A.

Cardinals lefthander Quinn Mathews was Minor League Pitcher of the Year.

FIRST TEAM

Pos	Player, Organization (Levels)	Age	AVG	OBP	SLG	AB	H	HR	RBI	BB	SO	SB
C	Adrian Del Castillo, D-backs (AAA)	24	.312	.399	.603	413	129	26	75	55	80	0
1B	Bryce Eldridge, Giants (A,A+,AA,AAA)	19	.289	.372	.513	446	129	23	91	59	132	6
2B	Kristian Campbell, Red Sox (A+,AA,AAA)	22	.330	.439	.558	430	142	20	77	74	103	24
3B	Coby Mayo, Orioles (A+,AAA)	22	.293	.372	.592	358	105	25	73	42	102	4
SS	Carson Williams, Rays (AA)	21	.256	.352	.469	433	111	20	69	58	144	33
OF	Roman Anthony, Red Sox (AA,AAA)	20	.291	.396	.498	454	132	18	65	79	127	21
OF	Jaison Chourio, Guardians (A)	19	.269	.414	.398	334	90	5	58	86	69	44
OF	Dalton Rushing, Dodgers (AA,AAA)	23	.271	.384	.512	420	114	26	85	64	103	2
DH	Michael Arroyo, Mariners (A, A+)	19	.285	.400	.509	485	138	23	89	73	136	18

Pos	Pitcher, Organization (Levels)	Age	W	L	ERA	G	GS	IP	H	BB	SO	WHIP
SP	Bubba Chandler, Pirates (AA,AAA)	21	10	7	3.08	26	23	120	81	41	148	1.02
SP	Caden Dana, Angels (AA)	20	9	7	2.52	23	23	136	89	39	147	0.94
SP	Chase Dollander, Rockies (A+,AA)	22	6	2	2.59	23	23	118	94	47	169	1.19
SP	Quinn Mathews, Cardinals (A,A+,AA,AAA)	23	8	5	2.76	26	26	143	91	49	202	0.98
SP	Zebby Matthews, Twins (A+,AA,AAA)	24	6	3	2.60	18	17	97	77	7	114	0.87
RP	Craig Yoho, Brewers (A+,AA,AAA)	24	4	2	0.94	48	0	58	31	23	101	0.94

SECOND TEAM

Pos	Player, Organization (Levels)	Age	AVG	OBP	SLG	AB	H	HR	RBI	BB	SO	SB
C	Cooper Ingle, Guardians (A+,AA)	22	.305	.419	.478	341	104	11	67	65	56	7
1B	Tre' Morgan, Rays (A,A+,AA)	21	.324	.408	.483	373	121	10	68	48	48	20
2B	Luke Keaschall, Twins (A+,AA)	21	.303	.420	.483	379	115	15	48	62	80	23
3B	Matt Shaw, Cubs (AA, AAA)	22	.284	.379	.488	443	126	21	71	62	95	31
SS	Angel Genao, Guardians (A,A+)	20	.330	.379	.499	449	148	10	71	38	77	25
OF	Jhostynxon Garcia, Red Sox (A, A+,AA)	21	.286	.356	.536	412	118	23	66	33	99	17
OF	Chandler Simpson, Rays (A+,AA)	23	.355	.410	.397	451	160	1	29	44	43	104
OF	Colby Thomas, Athletics (AA,AAA)	23	.277	.342	.563	513	142	31	92	40	142	15
DH	Deyvison De Los Santos, D-backs/Marlins (AA,AAA)	21	.294	.343	.571	538	158	40	120	34	144	1

Pos	Pitcher, Organization (Levels)	Age	W	L	ERA	G	GS	IP	H	BB	SO	WHIP
SP	Yilber Diaz, D-backs (AA,AAA)	23	6	9	3.80	21	19	104	85	47	140	1.27
SP	Alejandro Rosario, Rangers (A,A+)	22	4	5	2.24	18	17	88	69	13	129	0.93
SP	Travis Sykora, Nationals (A)	20	5	3	2.33	20	20	85	50	27	129	0.91
SP	Jonah Tong, Mets (A,A+,AA)	21	6	4	3.03	25	23	113	85	47	160	1.17
SP	Matt Wilkinson, Guardians (A,A+)	21	8	6	1.90	24	24	119	71	37	174	0.91
RP	Andrew Walters, Guardians (AA,AAA)	23	4	0	2.32	50	0	50	33	25	79	1.15

MIKE JANES/FOUR SEAM IMAGES (ANTHONY), EDDIE KELLY (MATHEWS)

Lake County provides optimism

BY JIM INGRAHAM

TEAM OF THE YEAR

The Guardians organization is on a roll.

It started at the 2023 Winter Meetings, when Cleveland won the first overall pick in the 2024 draft lottery.

It continued when the Guardians won 92 games and the American League Central division title.

It continued when Cleveland advanced to the AL Championship Series and when Stephen Vogt was voted AL Manager of the Year.

Another accolade for the 2024 Guardians: The organization's High-A Lake County affiliate is the Baseball America Minor League Team of the Year.

That is a lot of hardware, and a lot of winning, even for a franchise on a roll.

Tugboat Wilkinson

"Winning is part of development," Guardians assistant GM James Harris said. "The goal is to play what we call 'Guards ball' and be the best version of ourselves that we can be."

Under manager Omir Santos, the Lake County Captains were all of that, and more, in 2024. The team went 77-53 (.592) then beat Wisconsin in the best-of-three championship series to win the Midwest League title.

The Captains led the MWL in runs scored and fewest runs allowed. They led in walks and on-base percentage and ranked second in stolen bases and slugging. Lake County pitchers allowed the fewest baserunners.

"When we looked at our roster at the start of the year, we were quite excited," Harris said. "Then at midseason, we moved some guys up and got even more excited."

Among those midseason additions were 21-year-old lefthander Matt "Tugboat" Wilkinson, who was summoned to Lake County from Low-A Lynchburg, where in eight starts he allowed five earned runs with 71 strikeouts in 40.1 innings.

Also promoted to Lake County at midseason was 19-year-old first baseman Ralphy Velazquez, Cleveland's first-round pick in 2023.

"Getting Tugboat and Ralphy during the middle of the season really strengthened the team," Harris said. "That's when we knew we were going to be competitive. Ralphy came in . . . the youngest on the team. You could think he would think, 'It's all about me,' but he didn't. He came in ready to work."

Even more exciting was the addition of 2024 No. 1 overall pick Travis Bazzana, the Australia-born second baseman from Oregon State. Coming off a full college season, Bazzana's numbers in 27 games for Lake County were modest—he hit .238/.369/.396 with three home runs—but his presence energized the team and, especially, the fans.

Harris said that deciding at which level Bazzana would begin his professional career was an easy call.

"Travis was an advanced player out of college, and he was in great shape," Harris said. "We figured Lake County would be an easy transition for him, so why not just let him go out and play and get the opportunity to get acclimated to pro ball?

"The team was already established, so we wanted to get Travis and Ralphy acclimated to pro ball, just like anyone else."

Counting first-round picks Bazzana and Velazquez, Lake County featured five of the Guardians' top 10 prospects at one point or another. The list includes 2023 draft breakthroughs in catcher Cooper Ingle, the Midwest League MVP, and first baseman C.J. Kayfus. ■

LAST 10 WINNERS

2013: High-A Daytona Cubs/Florida State (Cubs)
2014: Double-APortland Sea Dogs/Eastern (Red Sox)
2015: Double-A Biloxi Shuckers/Southern (Brewers)
2016: Low-A Rome Braves/South Atlantic (Braves)
2017: Double-A Midland RockHounds/Texas (Athletics)
2018: Low-A Bowling Green Hot Rods/Midwest (Rays)
2019: Double-A Amarillo/Texas (Padres)
2021: Triple-A Durham/International (Rays)
2022: Low-A Charleston/Carolina (Rays)
2023: Triple-A Norfolk/International (Orioles)

Full list: search "Baseball America awards"

MINOR LEAGUES

BRIAN WESTERHOLT/FOUR SEAM IMAGES

FULL-SEASON TEAM LEADERS

WINS

Team	
Sugar Land Space Cowboys (Pacific Coast)	93
Omaha Storm Chasers (International)	89
Scranton/W-B RailRiders (International)	89
Tennessee Smokies (Southern)	87
Frisco RoughRiders (Texas)	84

LOSSES

Albuquerque Isotopes (Pacific Coast)	92
Chattanooga Lookouts (Southern)	90
El Paso Chihuahuas (Pacific Coast)	86
Corpus Christi Hooks (Texas)	84
New Hampshire Fisher Cats (Eastern)	84
St. Lucie Mets (Florida State)	84
Stockton Ports (California)	84

BATTING AVERAGE

Reno Aces (Pacific Coast)	.286
Las Vegas Aviators (Pacific Coast)	.279
Albuquerque Isotopes (Pacific Coast)	.273
Indianapolis Indians (International)	.271
Tacoma Rainiers (Pacific Coast)	.270

RUNS

Las Vegas Aviators (Pacific Coast)	921
Reno Aces (Pacific Coast)	910
Tacoma Rainiers (Pacific Coast)	909
Worcester Red Sox (International)	869
Albuquerque Isotopes (Pacific Coast)	865

HOME RUNS

Las Vegas Aviators (Pacific Coast)	232
Durham Bulls (International)	203
Syracuse Mets (International)	203
Albuquerque Isotopes (Pacific Coast)	201
Reno Aces (Pacific Coast)	198

STOLEN BASES

Aberdeen IronBirds (South Atlantic)	363
Delmarva Shorebirds (Carolina)	307
Charleston RiverDogs (Carolina)	305
Tacoma Rainiers (Pacific Coast)	286
Lynchburg Hillcats (Carolina)	281

EARNED RUN AVERAGE

Down East Wood Ducks (Carolina)	3.02
Palm Beach Cardinals (Florida State)	3.10
Midland RockHounds (Texas)	3.13
Birmingham Barons (Southern)	3.15
Akron RubberDucks (Eastern)	3.18

STRIKEOUTS

Iowa Cubs (International)	1465
Toledo Mud Hens (International)	1461
Norfolk Tides (International)	1435
Sacramento River Cats (Pacific Coast)	1430
Durham Bulls (International)	1420

WALKS ALLOWED

Las Vegas Aviators (Pacific Coast)	753
Reno Aces (Pacific Coast)	720
Syracuse Mets (International)	692
Columbus Clippers (International)	690
Fayetteville Woodpeckers (Carolina)	689
Rancho Cucamonga Quakes (California)	689

Chandler Simpson

TOM PRIDDY/FOUR SEAM IMAGES

INDIVIDUAL BATTING

BATTING AVERAGE*

Minimum 378 PA

Chandler Simpson (Bowling Green, Montgomery)	.355
Nick Allen (Las Vegas)	.345
Demetrio Crisantes (ACL D-backs Black, Visalia)	.341
Bryson Brigman (Amarillo, Reno)	.335
Bryan Torres (Springfield)	.331

RUNS

Rikuu Nishida (Birmingham, Kannapolis, W-S)	114
Drew Avans (Okla. City)	105
Michael Arroyo (Everett, Modesto)	101
Alex Freeland (Great Lakes, Okla. City, Tulsa)	100
Braylen Wimmer (Fresno)	94
Kristian Campbell (Greenville, Portland, Worcester)	94

HITS

Chandler Simpson (Bowling Green, Montgomery)	160
Deyvison De Los Santos (Amarillo, Jacksonv., Reno)	158
Tim Elko (Birmingham, Charlotte)	156
Josh Kasevich (Buffalo, New Hampshire)	154
Tim Tawa (Amarillo, Reno)	153

TOP HITTING STREAKS

Cameron Decker (Rancho Cucamonga)	22
Aidan Smith (Modesto, Charleston)	21
William Bergolla Jr., (Jersey Shore, Winston-Salem)	21
Chandler Simspon (Mongtomery)	20
Luis Pena (DSL Brewers 1)	20

MOST HITS (ONE GAME)

Nathan Lukes (Buffalo)	6
Eli White (Gwinnett)	6
Cameron Decker (Rancho Cucamonga)	6
73 tied	5

TOTAL BASES

Deyvison De Los Santos (Amarillo, Jacksonv., Reno)	307
Colby Thomas (Las Vegas, Midland)	289
Tim Tawa (Amarillo, Reno)	285
Ryan Ward (ACL Dodgers, Okla. City)	268
Jason Vosler (Tacoma)	267

EXTRA-BASE HITS

Colby Thomas (Las Vegas, Midland)	80
Deyvison De Los Santos (Amarillo, Jacksonv., Reno)	67
Tim Tawa (Amarillo, Reno)	67
Ryan Ward (ACL Dodgers, Okla. City)	66
Adrian Del Castillo (Reno)	65

DOUBLES

Albert Almora (Reno)	45
Colby Thomas (Las Vegas, Midland)	44
Juan Brito (Columbus)	40
Jared Serna (Hudson Valley, Jacksonville, Pensacola)	39
Angel Genao (Lake County, Lynchburg)	38

TRIPLES

Cole Carrigg (ACL Rockies, Spokane)	14
Alexey Lumpuy (DSL Cubs Blue)	12
Jacob Wetzel (Myrtle Beach, South Bend)	12
Bryce Teodosio (Salt Lake)	12
Mark Coley (Beloit, Jupiter)	11

HOME RUNS

Deyvison De Los Santos (Amarillo, Jacksonv., Reno)	40
Ryan Ward (ACL Dodgers, Okla. City)	34
Luken Baker (Memphis)	32
Jason Vosler (Tacoma)	31
Tim Tawa (Amarillo, Reno)	31
Colby Thomas (Las Vegas, Midland)	31

RUNS BATTED IN

Deyvison De Los Santos (Amarillo, Jacksonv., Reno)	120
Jason Vosler (Tacoma)	110
Kyle Garlick (Reno)	105
Lazaro Montes (Everett, Modesto)	105
Ryan Ward (ACL Dodgers, Okla. City)	104

MOST RBIs(ONE GAME)

Heston Kjerstad (Norfolk)	10
Cameron Decker (Rancho Cucamonga)	10
5 tied	9

WALKS

Chase Meidroth (Worcester)	105
Rylan Bannon (St. Paul, Syracuse)	96
Ryan Clifford (Binghamton, Brooklyn)	95
Braedon Karpathios (Lake Elsinore)	95
Jakob Marsee (Jacksonville, Pensacola, San Antonio)	92

INTENTIONAL WALKS

Oscar Colas (Charlotte)	4
Ryan Ward (ACL Dodgers, Okla. City)	4
Deyvison De Los Santos (Amarillo, Jacksonville, Reno)	4
Adrian Del Castillo (Reno)	4
Dustin Harris (Round Rock)	4
Gavin Cross (NW Arkansas)	4
Lazaro Montes (Everett, Modesto)	4

STRIKEOUTS

Elijah Green (Fredericksburg)	206
Spencer Jones (Somerset)	200
Henry Bolte (Lansing, Midland)	189
Trevor Werner (Quad Cities)	178
Chris Newell (Great Lakes, Tulsa)	177
Jud Fabian (Bowie, Norfolk)	177

STOLEN BASES

Chandler Simpson (Bowling Green, Montgomery)	104
Enrique Bradfield (Aberdeen, Bowie)	74
Caleb Ketchup (Salt Lake, Tri-City)	64
Dylan O'Rae (Biloxi, Wisconsin)	62
Justin Dean (Gwinnett, Mississippi)	61

CAUGHT STEALING

Chandler Simpson (Bowling Green, Montgomery) 17
Geraldo Quintero (Mississippi) 16
Edwin Amparo (Delmarva, FCL Orioles) 15
Nick Morabito (Brooklyn, St. Lucie) 15
Samad Taylor (Tacoma) 15

ON-BASE PERCENTAGE*

Minimum 378 PA

Mickey Gasper (Portland, Worcester) .439
Kristian Campbell (Greenville, Portland, Worcester) .439
Chase Meidroth (Worcester) .437
Payton Eeles (Cedar Rapids, Fort Myers, St. Paul) .435
Nick Allen (Las Vegas) .431

SLUGGING PERCENTAGE*

Minimum 378 PA

Adrian Del Castillo (Reno) .603
Coby Mayo (Aberdeen, Norfolk) .592
Jason Vosler (Tacoma) .573
Andres Chaparro (Reno, Rochester) .572
Deyvison De Los Santos (Amarillo, Jacksonv., Reno) .571

ON-BASE PLUS SLUGGING (OPS)*

Minimum 378 PA

Adrian Del Castillo (Reno) 1.002
Kristian Campbell (Greenville, Portland, Worc.) .997
Andres Chaparro (Reno, Rochester) .977
Mickey Gasper (Portland, Worcester) .970
Coby Mayo (Aberdeen, Norfolk) .964

HIT BY PITCH

Luke Adams (Wisconsin) 40
Robbie Tenerowicz (Arkansas, San Antonio) 40
Ripken Reyes (San Antonio) 34
Braiden Ward (Hartford, Spokane) 34
Otto Kemp (4 levels) 29

SACRIFICE BUNTS

Tyler Tolbert (NW Arkansas, Omaha) 20
Ripken Reyes (San Antonio) 15
Jack Pineda (NW Arkansas, Quad Cities) 13
Samad Taylor (Tacoma) 11
Austin Nola (ACL Royals, Omaha) 10
Tsung-Che Cheng (Altoona, Indianapolis) 10
Diego Velasquez (Eugene, Richmond) 10
Joe Redfield (Inland Empire, Tri-City) 10

SACRIFICE FLIES

Luis Suisbel (Modesto) 14
Malcom Nunez (Indianapolis) 12
Jake Gelof (Great Lakes, Rancho Cuca.) 12
Andy Garriola (Myrtle Beach, South Bend) 11
Dominic Keegan (Montgomery) 10
Matt Lloyd (Springfield) 10
Charlie Szykowny (Eugene, San Jose) 10

GROUNDED INTO DOUBLE PLAY

Jordan Diaz (Las Vegas) 26
Cesar Prieto (Memphis) 21
Eric Wagaman (Rocket City, Salt Lake) 20
Robbie Tenerowicz (Arkansas, San Antonio) 20
Josh Kasevich (Buffalo, New Hampshire) 20
Rainer Nunez (New Hampshire) 20
Luke Ritter (Syracuse) 20

BATTING AVERAGE BY POSITION

CATCHERS

Ryan Ignoffo (Jupiter, Beloit) .324
Adrian Del Castillo (Reno) .312
Cooper Ingle (Lake County, Akron) .305
Moises Ballesteros (Tennessee, Iowa) .289
Kyle Teel (Portland, Worcester) .288

FIRST BASEMEN

Andres Chapparo (Reno, Rochester) .328
Keaton Anthony (Clearwater, J. Shore, Reading) .327
Tre' Morgan (Charleston, B. Green, Mont.) .324
Jason Vosler (Tacoma) .303
Trenton Brooks (Sacramento) .302

SECOND BASEMEN

Bryson Brigman (Amarillo, Reno) .335
Peyton Eeles (Ft. Myers, C. Rapids, St. Paul) .306
Rikuu Nishida (Kannap., W-S, Birmingham) .304
Nick Yorke (Worcester, Indianapolis) .303
Jadher Areinamo (Wisconsin) .301

THIRD BASEMEN

Kyle Karros (Spokane) .311
Alejo Lopez (Gwinnett) .307
Miguel Villarroel (Palm Beach, Peoria) .303
CJ Alexander (Las Vegas, Omaha) .302
Coby Mayo (Aberdeen, Norfolk) .293

SHORTSTOPS

Kristian Campbell (Greenv., Port., Worcest.) .330
Angel Genao (Lynchburg, Lake County) .330
William Bergolla (Jersey Shore, Winston-Salem) .300
Josh Kasevich (N. Hampshire, Buffalo) .296
Chase Meidroth (Worcester) .293

OUTFIELDERS

Chandler Simpson (Bowling Green, Montgomery) .355
Bryan Torres (Springfield) .331
Jake Mangum (Durham) .317
Justin Crawford (Jersey Shore, Reading) .313
Nick Morabito (St. Lucie, Brooklyn) .312

INDIVIDUAL PITCHING

EARNED RUN AVERAGE*

Minimum 110 IP

David Davalillo (Down East, Hickory) 1.88
Matt Wilkinson (Lynchburg, Lake County) 1.90
Sean Sullivan (Spokane, Hartford) 2.11
Jake Brooks (Jupiter, Beloit) 2.18
Lucas Gordon (Kannapolis, Winston-Salem) 2.23

WORST ERA*

Karl Kauffmann (Albuquerque) 8.95
Justin Armbruester (Norfolk) 7.54
Peyton Battenfield (Albuquerque) 7.45
Dom Hamel (Syracuse) 6.79
Jackson Rutledge (Rochester) 6.40

WINS

Chad Patrick (Nashville) 14
Austin Peterson (Akron, Lake County) 14
6 tied 13

LOSSES

Thomas Farr (Chattanooga) 17
Barrett Kent (Inland Empire) 14
Blade Tidwell (Binghamton, Syracuse) 13
Brycen Mautz (Peoria) 13
Karl Kauffmann (Albuquerque) 13

GAMES

Wander Suero (Sugar Land) 67
Logan VanWey (Sugar Land) 60
Evan Sisk (Omaha) 58
Connor Thomas (Memphis) 56
Mason Fluharty (Buffalo) 56

GAMES STARTED

Thomas Pannone (Iowa, Scranton/WB) 30
Casey Lawrence (Tacoma) 29
Karl Kauffmann (Albuquerque) 29
Edgar Barclay (Scranton/WB) 29
John Bertrand (Richmond, Sacramento) 29

COMPLETE GAMES

Michael McGreevy (Memphis) 3
Ian Mejia (Gwinnett, Mississippi) 3
Jack Kochanowicz (Rocket City) 2
Tyler Phillips (Lehigh Valley) 2
Gabriel Barbosa (Tampa) 2
Hurston Waldrep (Aug, FCL Braves, Gwin, Miss.) 2

SHUTOUTS

Ian Mejia (Mississippi, Gwinnett) 2
24 tied 1

GAMES FINISHED

Wander Suero (Sugar Land) 62
Rico Garcia (Rochester) 46
Matt Svanson (Springfield) 46
Justin Yeager (Biloxi) 43
Cameron Cotter (Eugene, Richmond, Sacramento) 41

HOLDS

Brooks Kriske (Louisville, Norfolk) 15
Luis Contreras (Sugar Land) 15
Alan Busenitz (Louisville) 14
Francisco Perez (ACL Athletics, Las Vegas) 14
Trevor Kelley (Tacoma) 14
Carlos Vargas (Tacoma) 14
Luis Curvelo (Arkansas) 14
Matt Pushard (Jacksonville, Pensacola) 14

SAVES

Wander Suero (Sugar Land) 37
Matt Svanson (Springfield) 27
Troy Taylor (Arkansas, Everett) 21
Rico Garcia (Rochester) 20
Justin Yeager (Biloxi) 20

INNINGS PITCHED

Casey Lawrence (Tacoma) 165
Austin Peterson (Akron, Lake County) 160
John Bertrand (Richmond, Sacramento) 156
Thomas Pannone (Iowa, Scranton/WB) 151.1
Brett Kerry (Rocket City, Salt Lake) 150.2

WALKS

Thaddeus Ward (Rochester) 94
Joel Hurtado (Tri-City) 82
Francis Texido (Inland Empire) 79
Mick Abel (Lehigh Valley) 78
Dominic Hamel (Syracuse) 77
Jackson Rutledge (Rochester) 77
Miguel Ullola (Corpus Christi, Sugar Land) 77

STRIKEOUTS

Quinn Mathews (4 levels) 202
Matthew Wilkinson (Lake County, Lynchburg) 174
Miguel Ullola (Corpus Christi, Sugar Land) 171
Chase Dollander (Hartford, Spokane) 169
Parker Messick (Akron, Lake County) 165

HITS ALLOWED

Casey Lawrence (Tacoma) 199
Karl Kauffmann (Albuquerque) 194
Adrian Sampson (Round Rock) 174
Joe Rock (Durham) 160
Jose Atencio (Fredericksburg, Wilmington) 160

HOME RUNS ALLOWED

Casey Lawrence (Tacoma) 34
Karl Kauffmann (Albuquerque) 34
Edgar Barclay (Scranton/WB) 30
Peyton Battenfield (Albuquerque) 29
Justin Armbruester (Norfolk) 27
Brett Kerry (Rocket City, Salt Lake) 27

STRIKEOUTS PER NINE (STARTERS)*

Minimum 100 IP

Jarlin Susana (Fredericksburg, Wilmington) 13.6
Matt Wilkinson (Lynchburg, Lake County) 13.2
Chayce McDermott (Norfolk) 13.0
Chase Dollander (Spokane, Hartford) 12.9
Jonah Tong (St. Lucie, Brooklyn, Binghamton) 12.7

STRIKEOUTS PER NINE (RELIEVERS)*

Minimum 50 IP

Craig Yoho (Wisconsin, Biloxi, Nashville) 15.8
Edgardo Henriquez (4-levels) 14.9
Jojo Ingrassia (Salem) 14.4
Domingo Gonzalez (Mississip., Gwinnett) 14.2
Zach Maxwell (Chattanooga, Louisville) 14.2

OPPONENT AVERAGE (STARTERS)*

Minimum 100 IP

Miguel Ullola (Corpus Christi, Sugar Land) .161
Matt Wilkinson (Lynchburg, Lake County) .168
Carlson Reed (Bradenton, Greensboro) .173
Quinn Mathews (4 levels) .178
Lucas Gordon (Kannapolis, Winston-Salem) .179

OPPONENT AVERAGE (RELIEVERS)*

Minimum 50 IP

Juan Valera (FCL Red Sox, Salem) .123
Peyton Alford (Arkansas) .132
Matt Merrill (West Michigan) .143
Marco Jimenez (West Michigan) .145
Tommy Vail (Kannapolis, Winston-Salem) .147

MOST STRIKEOUTS (ONE GAME)

Drue Hackenberg (Mississippi) 16
Matt Wilkinson (Lynchburg) 15
Brett Kerry (Rocket City) 14
Trevor Martin (Bowling Green) 14
Jean Cabrera (Jersey Shore) 14

WILD PITCHES

Julio Polanco (DSL Phillies White) 24
Elvis Blanco (DSL Cubs Red) 23
Abel Mercedes (Fayetteville) 23
Raimy Rodriguez (Fayetteville) 23
Josue Arias (FCL Marlins) 22
Gregory Lebron (DSL Phillies Red) 22

BALKS

Yorman Gomez (Lake County, Lynchburg) 11
Aaron Davenport (Akron) 10
Jayvien Sandridge (El Paso, San Antonio) 8
Esmerlin Vinicio (Eugene, San Jose) 8
Welinton Herrera (Fresno, Spokane) 8
Omar Victorino (FCL Mets) 8

HIT BATTERS

Raimy Rodriguez (Fayetteville) 27
Isaac Coffey (Portland) 25
Elijah Dale (Modesto) 22
Riley Bauman (Inland Empire) 20
Cesar Lares (Fort Myers) 20
Edwin Nunez (Springfield) 20

GROUNDBALL DOUBLE PLAYS

John Bertrand (Richmond, Sacramento) 23
Paul Fry (El Paso) 18
Karl Kauffmann (Albuquerque) 18
Brandon Komar (Memphis, Springfield) 18

MINOR LEAGUES

INTERNATIONAL LEAGUE TRIPLE-A

Awards selected by Major League Baseball

Coby Mayo

MIKE JANES/FOUR SEAM IMAGES

CHAMPION: Omaha has three league titles as a member of the Pacific Coast League and four others in the defunct American Association. In 2024, the Storm Chasers won the International League for the first time, besting Columbus two games to one in the championship series. Omaha switched leagues most recently during the minor league reconfiguration of 2021. Omaha lost the Triple-A National Championship to Sugar Land of the PCL.

MOST VALUABLE PLAYER: Columbus outfielder Johnathan Rodriguez hit .301/.390/.540 with 29 home runs and 94 RBIs. The 24-year-old made his MLB debut with the Guardians in May. Cleveland drafted him out of a Puerto Rico high school in the third round in 2017.

PITCHER OF THE YEAR: Nashville righthander Chad Patrick led the IL with 14 wins, 145 strikeouts, a 2.90 ERA and 1.09 WHIP. The 26-year-old was the Brewers' fourth-round pick out of Purdue in 2021.

TOP MLB PROSPECT: Norfolk third baseman Coby Mayo is one of the Orioles' top prospects and earned his first callup by hitting .287/.364/.562 with 22 home runs in 89 games. Baltimore drafted Mayo in the fourth round in 2020 out of South Florida prep power Stoneman Douglas.

MANAGER OF THE YEAR: Omaha manager Mike Jirschele led the Storm Chasers to a league-best 89-59 record. He is a longtime Royals minor league manager who has guided the affiliate when it was a member of three different Triple-A leagues.

INTERNATIONAL LEAGUE ALL-STARS

Pos	Player	Team	AVG	OPS	HR
C	Dillon Dingler	Toledo	.308	.938	17
1B	Kyle Manzardo	Columbus	.267	.946	20
2B	Connor Norby	Norfolk	.293	.878	17
3B	Coby Mayo	Norfolk	.287	.926	22
SS	Andrew Navigato	Toledo	.271	.863	21
OF	Ji Hwan Bae	Indianapolis	.341	.937	7
OF	Heston Kjerstad	Norfolk	.300	.998	17
OF	Johnathan Rodriguez	Columbus	.301	.930	29
DH	Matt Koperniak	Memphis	.309	.882	20
UT	Nick Yorke	Indianapolis	.333	.918	8
Pos	**Pitcher**	**Team**	**G**	**ERA**	**SO**
SP	Bryce Elder	Gwinnett	17	3.73	102
SP	Chad Patrick	Nashville	26	2.90	145
SP	Cade Povich	Norfolk	15	3.48	89
SP	Brandon Young	Norfolk	20	3.44	96
RP	Walter Pennington	Omaha	39	2.13	82

OVERALL STANDINGS

East Division	W	L	PCT	GB	Manager	Attendance	Avg	Last Penn
Scranton/Wilkes-Barre R-R (Yankees)	89	60	.597	—	Shelley Duncan	314,145	4,620	2016
Worcester Red Sox (Red Sox)	79	71	.527	10.5	Chad Tracy	479,636	6,852	Never
Syracuse Mets (Mets)	78	71	.523	11.0	Dick Scott	350,777	4,941	1976
Rochester Red Wings (Nationals)	77	71	.520	11.5	Matthew LeCroy	445,338	6,454	1997
Jacksonville Jumbo Shrimp (Marlins)	73	76	.490	16.0	Daren Brown	354,445	4,923	Never
Durham Bulls (Rays)	72	78	.480	17.5	Morgan Ensberg	496,715	6,623	2022
Lehigh Valley IronPigs (Phillies)	68	78	.466	19.5	Anthony Contreras	588,788	8,066	Never
Charlotte Knights (White Sox)	68	79	.463	20.0	Justin Jirschele/Pat Listach	439,087	6,273	1999
Norfolk Tides (Orioles)	69	81	.460	20.5	Buck Britton	423,552	6,138	2023
Buffalo Bisons (Blue Jays)	68	80	.459	20.5	Casey Candaele	472,463	6,654	2004

East Division	W	L	PCT	GB	Manager	Attendance	Avg	Last Penn
Omaha Storm Chasers (Royals)	89	59	.601	—	Mike Jirschele	285,679	4,024	2024
Columbus Clippers (Guardians)	80	68	.541	9.0	Andy Tracy	530,992	7,586	2019
Nashville Sounds (Brewers)	78	68	.534	10.0	Rick Sweet	500,241	7,046	*2005
Indianapolis Indians (Pirates)	77	70	.524	11.5	Miguel Perez	588,363	8,405	2000
Memphis Redbirds (Cardinals)	74	74	.500	15.0	Ben Johnson	199,992	2,703	*2018
Gwinnett Stripers (Braves)	72	78	.480	18.0	Kanekoa Texeira	188,669	2,620	Never
St. Paul Saints (Twins)	70	79	.470	19.5	Toby Gardenhire	457,012	6,437	Never
Toledo Mud Hens (Tigers)	69	80	.463	20.5	Tim Federowicz	458,450	6,457	2006
Iowa Cubs (Cubs)	68	82	.453	22.0	Marty Pevey	409,712	5,853	Never
Louisville Bats (Reds)	67	82	.450	22.5	Pat Kelly	361,825	5,096	2001

* Pacific Coast League title won prior to 2021 minor league realignment

International League divisions do not determine the playoff field. The team with the best first-half record plays the best second-half team in the finals.

Playoffs: Omaha defeated Columbus 2-1 in best-of-three championship series. Sugar Land defeated Omaha in Triple-A National Championship Game.

CLUB BATTING

	AVG	G	AB	R	H	2B	3B	HR	RBI	BB	SO	SB	OBP	SLG
Indianapolis Indians	.271	147	4933	775	1336	289	30	142	729	566	1307	126	.350	.428
Columbus Clippers	.263	148	4888	805	1287	260	29	195	762	660	1262	200	.356	.448
Gwinnett Stripers	.263	150	5085	740	1338	241	23	122	696	630	1263	217	.349	.392
Scranton/W-B RailRiders	.262	149	4840	854	1267	277	23	176	808	655	1227	251	.358	.438
Worcester Red Sox	.259	150	4873	869	1260	252	18	176	808	786	1358	168	.369	.426
Durham Bulls	.258	150	5113	782	1318	257	29	203	723	551	1360	120	.337	.438
Omaha Storm Chasers	.257	148	4911	792	1263	287	25	193	749	583	1349	125	.341	.444
Memphis Redbirds	.256	148	4874	701	1249	261	24	180	667	541	1096	99	.337	.430
Jacksonville Jumbo Shrimp	.256	149	4955	652	1268	252	28	135	607	520	1253	86	.332	.400
Charlotte Knights	.255	147	4902	729	1252	250	23	158	674	566	1295	126	.337	.412
Toledo Mud Hens	.255	149	4934	760	1258	308	29	170	708	679	1406	182	.349	.433
Buffalo Bisons	.254	148	4897	775	1246	244	13	162	720	672	1338	139	.354	.409
Rochester Red Wings	.254	148	4882	755	1242	247	18	154	700	622	1208	166	.344	.407
St. Paul Saints	.252	149	4938	771	1243	267	31	174	732	673	1372	169	.348	.424
Syracuse Mets	.250	149	4894	810	1225	234	19	203	774	596	1255	119	.338	.430
Iowa Cubs	.250	150	4982	718	1244	282	14	179	673	618	1443	126	.338	.420
Louisville Bats	.246	149	4978	701	1223	270	19	148	649	564	1414	123	.328	.397
Lehigh Valley IronPigs	.245	146	4815	717	1179	224	21	181	682	547	1325	164	.328	.413
Nashville Sounds	.244	146	4842	744	1181	218	40	133	688	651	1348	170	.342	.388
Norfolk Tides	.243	150	4989	780	1214	244	24	186	741	656	1527	134	.338	.414

CLUB PITCHING

	ERA	G	CG	SHO	SV	IP	H	R	ER	HR	BB	SO	AVG
Omaha Storm Chasers	4.21	148	0	9	41	1287	1177	662	602	152	587	1266	.242
Gwinnett Stripers	4.33	150	1	9	30	1306	1211	685	628	165	579	1374	.245
Nashville Sounds	4.40	146	0	8	39	1277	1157	699	624	140	608	1286	.241
Jacksonville Jumbo Shrimp	4.43	149	0	8	36	1290	1241	699	635	173	557	1309	.252
Scranton/W-B RailRiders	4.57	149	2	9	43	1284	1193	727	652	177	575	1314	.243
Memphis Redbirds	4.57	148	5	8	37	1276	1272	698	648	156	575	1194	.259
Columbus Clippers	4.70	148	1	6	38	1278	1168	746	667	198	690	1392	.243
Durham Bulls	4.77	150	1	8	28	1312	1312	783	696	177	526	1420	.258
Worcester Red Sox	4.81	150	1	11	30	1273	1231	757	680	141	602	1327	.252
Indianapolis Indians	4.83	147	0	5	35	1276	1251	760	685	173	564	1348	.255
Syracuse Mets	4.96	149	0	5	36	1274	1230	777	703	179	692	1253	.253
Louisville Bats	5.06	149	1	5	33	1295	1330	809	728	181	622	1251	.267
Iowa Cubs	5.07	150	1	6	38	1301	1330	810	733	171	674	1465	.263
Toledo Mud Hens	5.07	149	0	6	25	1289	1305	793	727	162	643	1461	.260
St. Paul Saints	5.08	149	1	6	32	1286	1377	799	726	175	529	1359	.272
Charlotte Knights	5.09	147	1	5	30	1279	1190	786	723	183	673	1310	.246
Norfolk Tides	5.10	150	1	5	23	1309	1312	836	742	170	647	1435	.258
Rochester Red Wings	5.11	148	0	1	29	1262	1245	785	717	155	661	1177	.258
Lehigh Valley IronPigs	5.12	146	3	1	32	1254	1274	798	714	165	662	1192	.264
Buffalo Bisons	5.17	148	0	12	29	1272	1287	821	730	177	670	1273	.261

CLUB FIELDING

	PCT	PO	A	E	DP
Gwinnett	.984	3917	1250	84	103
Rochester	.984	3786	1327	85	144
Memphis	.982	3827	1357	93	144
Syracuse	.982	3823	1302	92	114
Nashville	.982	3830	1191	91	118
Omaha	.982	3860	1340	95	134
Charlotte	.981	3836	1227	98	124
Jacksonville	.980	3871	1255	103	119
Durham	.979	3937	1160	107	96
Louisville	.979	3886	1276	109	146
Worcester	.979	3818	1238	109	114
Columbus	.978	3835	1121	110	119
Scranton/WB	.978	3851	1210	116	105
Indianapolis	.978	3827	1180	115	105
Toledo	.977	3868	1222	118	105
Buffalo	.977	3815	1125	117	101
Iowa	.977	3903	1173	121	122
St. Paul	.977	3859	1267	123	113
Lehigh Valley	.976	3762	1347	126	138
Norfolk	.975	3928	1131	132	115

INDIVIDUAL BATTING

Batter, Club	AVG	G	AB	R	H	2B	3B	HR	RBI	BB	SO	SB
Jake Mangum, Durham	.317	104	398	57	126	30	1	6	56	23	73	20
Mark Payton, Charlotte	.309	112	417	70	129	30	2	10	53	53	81	5
Matt Koperniak, Memphis	.309	122	463	64	143	28	3	20	73	43	96	5
Alejo Lopez, Gwinnett	.307	112	411	63	126	21	2	4	55	47	64	21
Johnathan Rodriguez, Columbus	.301	118	439	84	132	18	0	29	94	64	128	8
DaShawn Keirsey Jr., St. Paul	.300	111	443	71	133	22	7	14	81	48	116	36
Chase Meidroth, Worcester	.293	122	437	87	128	20	3	7	57	105	71	13
Connor Norby, Norfolk/Jacksonville	.293	94	379	78	111	24	1	17	60	53	123	13
T.J. Rumfield, Scranton/WB	.292	114	421	72	123	26	0	15	71	43	78	3
Javier Sanoja, Jacksonville	.291	111	436	51	127	31	6	6	58	44	30	14

INDIVIDUAL PITCHING

Pitcher, Club	W	L	ERA	G	GS	CG	SV	IP	H	R	ER	BB	SO
Chad Patrick, Nashville	14	1	2.90	26	24	0	0	136	109	50	44	39	145
Thomas Pannone, Iowa/Scranton WB	10	9	3.54	30	30	1	0	152	158	71	60	38	136
Michael McGreevy, Memphis	9	8	4.02	27	27	3	0	150	152	70	67	44	138
Randy Dobnak, St. Paul	12	7	4.25	28	24	0	0	133	130	75	63	63	134
Jason Alexander, Worcester	7	6	4.42	29	27	0	0	138	143	76	68	39	129
Carlos F. Rodriguez, Nashville	9	9	4.51	25	22	0	1	130	100	69	65	61	129
Joe Rock, Durham	7	8	4.58	27	23	1	0	140	160	81	71	35	132
Gordon Graceffo, Memphis	10	8	4.85	27	26	1	0	130	152	79	70	50	107
Caleb Boushley, St. Paul	9	6	5.23	26	26	0	0	134	156	81	78	28	108
Edgar Barclay, Scranton/WB	7	9	5.98	29	29	1	0	143	150	104	95	70	118

DEPARTMENT LEADERS

BATTING

OBP	Chase Meidroth, Worcester	.437
SLG	Edwin Rios, Louisville	.547
OPS	Edwin Rios, Louisville	.932
Runs	John Rave, Omaha	93
Hits	Matt Koperniak, Memphis	143
TB	Juan Brito, Columbus	244
XBH	Juan Brito, Columbus	61
2B	Juan Brito, Columbus	40
3B	DaShawn Keirsey, St. Paul	7
	Isaac Collins, Nashville	7
HR	Luken Baker, Memphis	32
RBI	Johnathan Rodriguez, Columbus	94
SAC	Austin Nola, Omaha	10
BB	Chase Meidroth, Worcester	105
HBP	Brewer Hicklen, Nashville	18
SO	Luke Ritter, Syracuse	174
SB	Brewer Hicklen, Nashville	44
CS	Luisangel Acuna, Syracuse	14

FIELDING

C	PCT	Bryan Lavastida, Columbus	.993
	PO	Bryan Lavastida, Columbus	789
	A	Nick Raposo, Buffalo, Memphis	48
	DP	Aramis Garcia, Lehigh Valley	11
	E	Pat Winkel, St. Paul	9
	E	Carlos Narvaez, Scranton/WB	9
	CS	Aramis Garcia, Lehigh Valley	31
	SB	Pat Winkel, St. Paul	85
	PB	Moises Ballesteros, Iowa	8
1B	PCT	Darick Hall, Lehigh Valley	.995
	PO	Darick Hall, Lehigh Valley	831
	A	Darick Hall, Lehigh Valley	82
	DP	Darick Hall, Lehigh Valley	88
	E	Tyler Black, Nashville	9
2B	PCT	No Qualifier	
	PO	Ronny Simon, Durham	105
	A	Levi Jordan, Louisville	183
	DP	Levi Jordan, Louisville	53
	E	Jim Haley, Lehigh Valley	14
3B	PCT	No Qualifier	
	PO	Coby Mayo, Norfolk	58
	PO	Alejo Lopez, Gwinnett	58
	A	Malcom Nunez, Indianapolis	133
	DP	Coby Mayo, Norfolk	19
	E	Jace Jung, Toledo	16
SS	PCT	Cam Devanney, Omaha	.968
	PO	Colson Montgomery, Charlotte	252
	A	Scott Kingery, Lehigh Valley	293
	DP	Colson Montgomery, Charlotte	79
	E	Colson Montgomery, Charlotte	195
OF	PCT	Myles Straw, Columbus	.982
	PO	Myles Straw, Columbus	212
	A	Oscar Colas, Charlotte	11
	DP	Alan Roden, Buffalo	3
	DP	Johnathan Rodriguez, Columbus	3
	E	Oscar Gonzalez, Scranton/WB	8

PITCHING

G	Evan Sisk, Omaha	58
GS	Thomas Pannone, Iowa/Scranton	30
GF	Rico Garcia, Rochester	46
SV	Rico Garcia, Rochester	20
W	Chad Patrick, Nashville	14
L	Mick Abel, Lehigh Valley	12
IP	Thomas Pannone, Iowa/Scranton	152.1
H	Joe Rock, Durham	160
R	Justin Armbruester, Norfolk	107
ER	Justin Armbruester, Norfolk	107
HBP	Thaddeus Ward, Rochester	15
BB	Thaddeus Ward, Rochester	94
SO	Chad Patrick, Nashville	145
SO/9	Chad Patrick, Nashville	9.57
BB/9	Caleb Boushley, St. Paul	1.88
WP	Aaron Ashby, Nashville	17
Balks	Brian Moran, Gwinnett	5
HR	Edgar Barclay, Scranton/WB	30
AVG	Carlos F. Rodriguez, Nashville	.209

PACIFIC COAST LEAGUE TRIPLE-A

Awards selected by Major League Baseball

CHAMPION: Sugar Land has existed as an affiliated minor league team for four seasons. The Astros' top affiliate finished as Pacific Coast League runner-up in 2021. Now, in 2024, the Space Cowboys are champions. Sugar Land swept Reno in the PCL championship series and then trounced Omaha of the International League by a score of 13-6 in the Triple-A National Championship Game.

MOST VALUABLE PLAYER: Despite spending a month in the big leagues with the D-backs, Reno catcher Adrian Del Castillo still led the PCL with 65 extra-base hits—and also a 1.002 OPS. Everything clicked for Del Castillo in 2024, three years after Arizona drafted him in the second round out of Miami. He hit .312/.399/.603 with 26 home runs in 105 games in a season in which he made his MLB debut.

PITCHER OF THE YEAR: The Rangers drafted Vanderbilt righthander Jack Leiter second overall in 2022. He had his most successful pro season at Round Rock two years later, recording a 3.51 ERA in 77 innings to go with 110 strikeouts and 35 walks. Leiter made his MLB debut in April and received two other callups to Texas.

TOP MLB PROSPECT: First baseman Deyvison De Los Santos played in both Triple-A leagues in 2024, starting with Reno of the PCL and ending with Jacksonville in the Marlins' system after he was traded for A.J. Puk. In the PCL, De Los Santos hit .289/.338/.588 with 14 of his 40 home runs on the season.

MANAGER OF THE YEAR: Sugar Land manager Mickey Storey guided the Space Cowboys to 93 wins, the most in the minor leagues and the highest win total since the minor leagues were reconfigured in 2021. Sugar Land was the only minor league team to reach 90 wins in 2024.

Adrian Del Castillo

PACIFIC COAST LEAGUE ALL-STARS

Pos	Player	Team	AVG	OPS	HR
C	Adrian Del Castillo	Reno	.312	1.002	26
1B	Jason Vosler	Tacoma	.303	.944	31
2B	Jordan Diaz	Las Vegas	.301	.891	22
3B	Andres Chaparro	Reno	.328	.977	23
SS	Nick Allen	Las Vegas	.345	.928	7
OF	Pedro Leon	Sugar Land	.299	.886	24
OF	James Outman	Oklahoma City	.279	.933	17
OF	Colby Thomas	Las Vegas	.272	.903	17
DH	Shay Whitcomb	Sugar Land	.293	.908	25
UT	Armando Alvarez	Las Vegas	.315	.967	15
Pos	**Pitcher**	**Team**	**G**	**ERA**	**SO**
SP	A.J. Blubaugh	Sugar Land	27	3.83	128
SP	Colton Gordon	Sugar Land	25	3.83	124
SP	Ryan Gusto	Sugar Land	29	3.70	141
SP	Jack Leiter	Round Rock	17	3.51	110
RP	Grant Holman	Las Vegas	23	0.92	30
RP	Wander Suero	Sugar Land	67	2.66	71

OVERALL STANDINGS

East Division	W	L	PCT	GB	Manager	Attendance	Avg	Last Penn
Sugar Land Space Cowboys (Astros)	93	56	.624	—	Mickey Storey	280,956	3,849	2024
Oklahoma City Dodgers (Dodgers)	79	71	.527	14.5	Travis Barbary	387,988	5,243	2023
Round Rock Express (Rangers)	71	77	.480	21.5	Doug Davis	366,025	5,084	Never
El Paso Chihuahuas (Padres)	64	86	.427	29.5	Pete Zamora	491,296	6,551	2016
Albuquerque Isotopes (Rockies)	58	92	.387	35.5	Pedro Lopez	503,525	6,714	1994
West Division	**W**	**L**	**PCT**	**GB**	**Manager**	**Attendance**	**Avg**	**Last Penn**
Tacoma Rainiers (Mariners)	82	68	.547	—	John Russell	401,027	5,494	2021
Sacramento River Cats (Giants)	80	70	.533	2.0	Dave Brundage	409,700	5,536	2019
Reno Aces (D-backs)	79	70	.530	2.5	Blake Lalli	355,269	4,801	2022
Las Vegas Aviators (Athletics)	74	75	.497	7.5	Fran Riordan	481,802	6,511	1988
Salt Lake Bees (Angels)	67	82	.450	14.5	Keith Johnson	469,478	6,344	1979

Pacific Coast League divisions do not determine the playoff field. The team with the best first-half record plays the best second-half team in the finals.
Playoffs: Sugar Land defeated Reno 2-0 in best-of-three championship series. Sugar Land defeated Omaha in Triple-A National Championship Game.

STEPHEN SMITH/FOUR SEAM IMAGES

MINOR LEAGUES

CLUB BATTING

	AVG	G	AB	R	H	2B	3B	HR	RBI	BB	SO	SB	OBP	SLG
Reno Aces	.286	149	5201	910	1490	310	37	198	871	589	1137	80	.364	.475
Las Vegas Aviators	.279	149	5149	921	1438	332	31	232	876	641	1298	111	.365	.491
Albuquerque Isotopes	.273	150	5246	865	1431	286	57	201	805	587	1431	186	.351	.464
Tacoma Rainiers	.270	150	5022	909	1355	257	30	170	847	718	1327	286	.366	.434
Sacramento River Cats	.265	150	5092	837	1347	255	29	170	783	689	1261	115	.357	.426
El Paso Chihuahuas	.264	150	5056	829	1335	294	51	156	782	619	1135	194	.349	.435
Oklahoma City	.263	150	5172	840	1361	268	39	186	773	702	1393	145	.355	.438
Round Rock Express	.260	148	4992	753	1298	277	29	138	712	635	1303	129	.348	.410
Salt Lake Bees	.259	149	5026	799	1303	250	42	143	724	614	1425	171	.344	.411
Sugar Land	.259	149	5009	844	1296	262	26	186	799	718	1339	194	.359	.433

CLUB PITCHING

	ERA	G	CG	SHO	SV	IP	H	R	ER	HR	BB	SO	AVG
Sugar Land	4.42	149	0	5	50	1324	1231	725	650	146	684	1379	.246
Oklahoma City	4.49	150	0	4	33	1325	1254	735	661	126	644	1374	.250
Sacramento River Cats	4.91	150	0	8	34	1326	1306	800	723	175	649	1430	.258
Round Rock Express	4.94	148	0	5	31	1298	1289	798	712	165	634	1340	.257
Tacoma Rainiers	5.08	150	2	9	28	1308	1368	813	739	188	566	1152	.268
Salt Lake Bees	5.20	149	1	2	22	1306	1432	840	755	196	517	1238	.278
Reno Aces	5.29	149	0	6	33	1314	1352	847	773	159	720	1347	.267
El Paso Chihuahuas	5.65	150	0	5	30	1313	1441	904	824	185	658	1274	.279
Las Vegas Aviators	5.97	149	0	5	28	1306	1366	949	867	211	753	1362	.269
Albuquerque Isotopes	6.59	150	1	1	22	1311	1615	1096	960	229	687	1153	.304

CLUB FIELDING

	PCT	PO	A	E	DP
Albuquerque	.983	3950	1453	94	150
El Paso	.982	3938	1370	96	132
Sacramento	.982	3978	1314	98	136
Oklahoma City	.981	3976	1334	104	132
Round Rock	.980	3895	1180	106	114
Las Vegas	.979	3919	1264	110	126
Tacoma	.979	3925	1442	117	157
Reno	.979	3943	1323	115	148
Sugar Land	.979	3972	1221	114	135
Salt Lake	.976	3918	1290	128	126

INDIVIDUAL BATTING

Batter, Club	AVG	G	AB	R	H	2B	3B	HR	RBI	BB	SO	SB
Bryson Brigman, Reno	.334	113	365	63	122	18	3	9	61	26	62	10
Andres Chaparro, Reno	.332	95	367	69	122	26	1	19	75	41	73	3
Adrian Del Castillo, Reno	.312	105	413	90	129	36	3	26	75	55	80	0
Jason Vosler, Tacoma	.303	119	466	92	141	25	4	31	110	46	113	4
Trenton Brooks, Sacramento	.302	94	331	62	100	18	1	10	58	63	61	10
Jordan Diaz, Las Vegas	.301	102	395	60	119	22	1	22	85	34	78	0
Pedro Leon, Sugar Land	.299	118	469	78	140	25	2	24	90	43	144	29
Tirso Ornelas, El Paso	.297	128	485	76	144	24	2	23	89	53	88	7
Shay Whitcomb, Sugar Land	.293	108	413	73	121	19	2	25	91	53	95	26
Albert Almora Jr., Reno	.292	127	520	79	152	45	2	9	69	42	81	20

INDIVIDUAL PITCHING

Pitcher, Club	W	L	ERA	G	GS	CG	SV	IP	H	R	ER	BB	SO
Ryan Gusto, Sugar Land	8	6	3.70	29	26	0	0	140	135	68	61	53	141
AJ Blubaugh, Sugar Land	12	4	3.83	27	25	0	0	125	117	58	53	51	128
Colton Gordon, Sugar Land	8	2	3.94	25	24	0	0	123	112	68	54	39	124
Carson Seymour, Sacramento	7	10	4.82	29	28	0	0	134	151	84	72	60	132
Gabe Mosser, El Paso	7	7	5.40	28	26	0	0	133	146	83	80	48	103
Adrian Sampson, Round Rock	8	10	5.64	28	27	0	0	137	174	106	86	46	120
Michael Mariot, Tacoma	9	7	5.84	28	25	0	0	126	136	85	82	33	101
Casey Lawrence, Tacoma	11	11	5.95	29	29	1	0	165	199	111	109	48	108
Karl Kauffmann, Albuquerque	5	13	8.95	29	29	1	0	130	194	141	129	76	74

DEPARTMENT LEADERS

BATTING

OBP	Cooper Hummel, Sugar Land	.419
SLG	Adrian Del Castillo, Reno	.603
OPS	Adrian Del Castillo, Reno	1.002
Runs	Drew Avans, Okla. City	105
Hits	Andre Lipcius, Okla. City	152
Hits	Albert Almora, Reno	152
TB	Jason Vosler, Tacoma	267
XBH	Adrian Del Castillo, Reno	65
2B	Albert Almora, Reno	45
3B	Clay Dungan, El Paso	8
3B	Nate Mondou, El Paso	8
HR	Ryan Ward, Okla. City	33
RBI	Jason Vosler, Tacoma	110
SAC	Samad Taylor, Tacoma	11
BB	Ryan Noda, Las Vegas	89
HBP	Jesus Bastidas, Sugar Land	23
SO	Kyle Garlick, Reno	171
SB	Ryan Bliss, Tacoma	50
SB	Samad Taylor, Tacoma	50
CS	Samad Taylor, Tacoma	15

FIELDING

C PO	Mike Papierski, Tacoma	.992
PO	Carlos Perez, Las Vegas	744
A	Carlos Perez, Las Vegas	59
DP	Michael Papierski, Tacoma	9
E	4 tied	7
CS	Carlos Perez, Las Vegas	31
SB	Hunter Feduccia, Okla. City	102
PB	Chad Wallach, Salt Lake	11
PB	Drew Romo, Albuquerque	11
1B PCT	Blaine Crim, Round Rock	.992
PO	Grant Lavigne, Albuquerque	869
A	Blaine Crim, Round Rock	58
DP	Grant Lavigne, Albuquerque	21
E	Grant Lavigne, Albuquerque	21
2B PCT	No qualifiers	
PO	Bryson Brigman, Reno	145
A	Bryson Brigman, Reno	161
DP	Hunter Stovall, Albuquerque	62
E	Bryson Brigman, Reno	8
3B PCT	No qualifiers	
PO	Kody Hoese, Okla. City	62
A	Kody Hoese, Okla. City	156
DP	Eguy Rosario, El Paso	18
E	Elehuris Montero, Albuquerque	16
SS PCT	Mason McCoy, El Paso	.979
PO	Luis Urias, Tacoma	48
A	Mason McCoy, El Paso	297
DP	Mason McCoy, El Paso	62
E	Trey Sweeney, Okla. City	14
OF PCT	Kyle Garlick, Reno	.977
PO	Albert Almora, Reno	180
A	Greg Jones, Albuquerque	7
DP	Jonatan Clase, Tacoma	3
E	Greg Jones, Albuquerque	7

PITCHING

G	Wander Suero, Sugar Land	67
GS	Casey Lawrence, Tacoma	29
GS	Karl Kauffmann, Albuquerque	29
GF	Wander Suero, Sugar Land	62
SV	Wander Suero, Sugar Land	37
W	A.J. Blubaugh, Sugar Land	12
L	Karl Kauffmann, Albuquerque	13
IP	Casey Lawrence, Tacoma	165
H	Casey Lawrence, Tacoma	199
R	Karl Kauffmann, Albuquerque	141
ER	Karl Kauffmann, Albuquerque	129
HBP	Jhonathan Diaz, Tacoma	13
BB	Karl Kauffmann, Albuquerque	76
SO	Ryan Gusto, Sugar Land	141
SO/9	A.J. Blubaugh, Sugar Land	9.24
BB/9	Michael Mariot	2.35
WP	Carson Seymour, Sacramento	13
Balks	Humberto Castellanos, Reno	5
HR	Karl Kauffmann, Albuquerque	34
HR	Casey Lawrence, Tacoma	34
AVG	Colton Gordon, Sugar Land	.2389

EASTERN LEAGUE DOUBLE-A

Awards selected by Major League Baseball

CHAMPION: The Erie SeaWolves went back-to-back in the Eastern League, defeating Somerset two games to none in the championship series. Erie has league titles in 2024 and 2023 after finishing as runner-up in 2022. Prior to this current run, the SeaWolves had never so much as appeared in the league finals. Erie has been the Tigers' Double-A affiliate since 1999, its first year in the EL. This year's SeaWolves club was remarkably well-balanced and ranked second in the league with 692 runs and a 3.51 ERA.

MOST VALUABLE PLAYER: Portland's Kristian Campbell locked in his Minor League Player of the Year case with his excellence in the upper minors, particularly at Double-A. The 22-year-old middle infielder hit .362/.463/.582 with eight home runs and 17 stolen bases in 56 games. The Red Sox's development of their 2023 fourth-rounder out of Georgia Tech is truly remarkable. Campbell remade himself in one offseason and went 20-20 while ranking second in the minor leagues with a .439 on-base percentage.

PITCHER OF THE YEAR: Binghamton right-hander Brandon Sproat pitched at three levels in 2024, his pro debut, after the Mets drafted him in the second round out of Florida in 2023. He saved his best work for Double-A, where he logged his only two double-digit strikeout games. Sproat made 11 starts for Binghamton, striking out 77 and walking 15 while recording a 2.45 ERA.

TOP MLB PROSPECT: Bowie's Samuel Basallo hit 16 home runs as a 19-year-old catcher at Double-A. He batted .289/.355/.465 in 106 games and is the shining beacon of the Orioles' revamped international scouting effort.

MANAGER OF THE YEAR: Hartford's Bobby Meacham guided his club to a 76-60 mark in his first year as a Rockies minor league manager.

Samuel Basallo

MIKE JANES/FOUR SEAM IMAGES

EASTERN LEAGUE ALL-STARS

Pos	Player	Team	AVG	OPS	HR
C	Agustin Ramirez	Somerset	.289	.942	16
1B	Carson Taylor	Reading	.277	.854	16
2B	Hao-Yu Lee	Erie	.298	.851	12
3B	Gage Workman	Erie	.280	.842	18
SS	Marcelo Mayer	Portland	.307	.850	8
OF	Roman Anthony	Portland	.269	.856	15
OF	Spencer Jones	Somerset	.259	.788	17
OF	Gabriel Rincones Jr.	Reading	.263	.844	11
DH	Kyle Teel	Portland	.298	.852	11
UT	Kristian Campbell	Portland	.362	1.045	8
Pos	**Pitcher**	**Team**	**G**	**ERA**	**SO**
SP	Jackson Jobe	Erie	16	1.95	81
SP	Brad Lord	Harrisburg	12	1.40	75
SP	Parker Messick	Akron	14	2.06	85
SP	Brandon Sproat	Binghamton	11	2.45	77
RP	Eric Pardinho	New Hampshire	21	1.01	37
RP	Andrew Walters	Akron	17	1.35	38

OVERALL STANDINGS

Northeast Division	W	L	PCT	GB	Manager	Attendance	Avg	Last Penn
Portland Sea Dogs (Red Sox)	78	60	.565	—	Chad Epperson	395,461	6,084	2006
Hartford Yard Goats (Rockies)	76	60	.559	1.0	Bobby Meacham	411,351	6,140	Never
Somerset Patriots (Yankees)	75	62	.547	2.5	Raul Dominguez	348,390	5,279	2022
Binghamton Rumble Ponies (Mets)	69	67	.507	8.0	Reid Brignac	146,061	2,318	2014
Reading Fightin Phils (Phillies)	59	78	.431	18.5	Al Pedrique	414,262	6,277	2001
New Hampshire Fisher Cats (Blue Jays)	52	84	.382	25.0	Cesar Martin	237,029	3,704	2018

Southwest Division	W	L	PCT	GB	Manager	Attendance	Avg	Last Penn
Akron RubberDucks (Guardians)	80	58	.580	—	Greg DiCenzo	265,008	3,897	2021
Erie SeaWolves (Tigers)	77	58	.570	1.5	Gabe Alvarez	190,780	2,891	2024
Harrisburg Senators (Nationals)	68	70	.493	12.0	Delino DeShields	275,733	4,055	1999
Richmond Flying Squirrels (Giants)	64	74	.464	16.0	Dennis Pelfrey	435,295	6,595	Never
Bowie Baysox (Orioles)	62	75	.453	17.5	Roberto Mercado	234,807	3,505	2015
Altoona Curve (Pirates)	62	76	.449	18.0	Robby Hammock	305,598	4,630	2017

Southwest: Erie defeated Akron 2-1. **Northeast:** Somerset defeated Hartford 2-0. **Championship Series:** Erie defeated Somerset 2-0

CLUB BATTING

	AVG	G	AB	R	H	2B	3B	HR	RBI	BB	SO	SB	OBP	SLG
Portland Sea Dogs	.257	138	4570	711	1174	285	25	125	658	534	1201	194	.341	.412
Erie SeaWolves	.254	135	4479	692	1138	231	30	127	634	519	1184	150	.341	.404
Hartford Yard Goats	.248	136	4463	625	1109	194	18	115	571	429	1130	207	.327	.377
Somerset Patriots	.240	137	4443	667	1066	229	28	148	612	537	1298	204	.328	.404
Richmond Flying Squirrels	.238	138	4559	592	1083	230	26	88	542	448	1203	123	.315	.357
Reading Fightin Phils	.237	137	4409	603	1043	205	25	133	552	462	1218	152	.320	.385
Akron RubberDucks	.232	138	4481	582	1038	189	31	113	532	501	1254	148	.313	.363
Altoona Curve	.231	138	4536	572	1049	181	24	97	505	453	1268	137	.308	.346
New Hampshire Fisher Cats	.230	136	4447	533	1023	208	14	93	489	477	1228	115	.313	.346
Bowie Baysox	.226	137	4477	553	1012	194	21	115	511	507	1249	187	.311	.356
Binghamton Rumble Ponies	.225	136	4395	548	991	218	10	111	496	507	1325	147	.313	.355
Harrisburg Senators	.220	138	4400	491	966	182	20	82	445	445	1254	136	.300	.326

CLUB PITCHING

	ERA	G	CG	SHO	SV	IP	H	R	ER	HR	BB	SO	AVG
Akron RubberDucks	3.18	138	1	15	36	1214	993	496	429	95	444	1247	.223
Erie SeaWolves	3.51	135	0	10	22	1186	1011	529	463	113	460	1297	.229
Harrisburg Senators	3.57	138	4	14	38	1189	1047	541	472	93	456	1137	.236
Bowie Baysox	3.79	137	0	9	31	1207	1002	605	509	124	511	1319	.224
Binghamton Rumble Ponies	3.83	136	1	12	33	1177	1056	570	501	119	429	1233	.238
Hartford Yard Goats	3.86	136	1	13	33	1171	1068	570	502	111	461	1180	.242
Somerset Patriots	3.89	137	1	10	33	1188	1004	600	513	114	468	1272	.225
Richmond Flying Squirrels	4.22	138	0	11	30	1208	1104	640	566	108	546	1281	.242
Altoona Curve	4.29	138	1	8	29	1210	1148	655	577	105	494	1129	.250
Portland Sea Dogs	4.30	138	0	7	40	1192	1067	662	570	111	568	1329	.238
New Hampshire Fisher Cats	4.41	136	3	6	24	1171	1008	640	574	130	524	1179	.230
Reading Fightin Phils	4.44	137	2	10	26	1167	1184	661	575	124	458	1209	.260

CLUB FIELDING

	PCT	PO	A	E	DP		PCT	PO	A	E	DP
Erie	.981	3558	1057	87	92	Binghamton	.975	3532	1079	119	85
Harrisburg	.981	3568	1174	93	94	Hartford	.975	3513	1118	121	98
New Hampshire	.977	3514	1042	106	83	Somerset	.974	3564	1080	124	82
Altoona	.977	3629	1167	113	119	Portland	.973	3575	1131	133	90
Akron	.976	3643	1105	115	105	Richmond	.972	3624	1195	138	111
Reading	.976	3500	1110	113	91	Bowie	.969	3622	1066	149	91

INDIVIDUAL BATTING

Batter, Club	AVG	G	AB	R	H	2B	3B	HR	RBI	BB	SO	SB
Kyle Teel, Portland	.298	84	325	65	97	20	0	11	60	48	87	9
Hao-Yu Lee, Erie	.298	87	342	55	102	19	5	12	56	33	69	16
Benjamin Cowles, Somerset	.294	88	326	52	96	25	3	9	51	39	67	14
Samuel Basallo, Bowie	.289	106	398	57	115	22	0	16	55	41	85	9
Wyatt Young, Binghamton	.288	102	320	49	92	10	1	4	31	49	79	16
Josh Kasevich, New Hampshire	.284	87	363	51	103	20	0	3	41	26	42	10
Gage Workman, Erie	.280	126	483	85	135	29	6	18	89	65	153	30
Tyler Holton, Erie	.279	96	351	62	98	21	0	14	71	44	91	6
Carson Taylor, Reading	.277	109	372	53	103	16	3	16	75	67	96	5
Rainer Nunez, New Hampshire	.275	105	385	40	106	14	2	12	54	44	87	2

INDIVIDUAL PITCHING

Pitcher, Club	W	L	ERA	G	GS	CG	SV	IP	H	R	ER	BB	SO
Aaron Davenport, Akron	7	4	2.85	27	26	0	0	142	116	49	45	52	135
Zach Messinger, Somerset	7	8	3.06	27	25	0	1	150	114	68	51	52	136
Isaac Coffey, Portland	11	4	3.17	24	21	0	0	114	89	47	40	51	148
Carlos Pena, Erie	8	6	3.49	25	19	0	0	113	100	47	44	44	99
Tommy Mace, Akron	8	7	3.71	28	27	0	0	146	131	72	60	46	104
Joander Suarez, Binghamton	9	5	3.92	23	21	0	1	119	107	55	52	29	118
Po-Yu Chen, Altoona	4	10	4.03	27	25	0	0	134	130	68	60	43	96
Trace Bright, Bowie	0	11	4.18	27	27	0	0	112	106	58	52	60	120
Alex Pham, Bowie	7	4	4.24	27	27	0	0	119	97	59	56	50	138
Bailey Dees, Somerset	7	7	4.25	27	26	0	0	138	118	71	65	54	145

DEPARTMENT LEADERS

BATTING

OBP	Carlos Mendoza, Erie	.394
SLG	Roman Anthony, Portland	.489
OPS	Roman Anthony, Portland	.856
Runs	Carlos Mendoza, Erie	86
Hits	Gage Workman, Erie	135
TB	Gage Workman, Erie	230
XBH	Spencer Jones, Somerset	53
2B	Carter Howell, Richmond	30
	Spencer Jones, Somerset	30
3B	Carter Howell, Richmond	7
HR	Zach Kokoska, Hartford	20
RBI	Gage Workman, Erie	89
SAC	Tsung-Che Cheng, Altoona	10
BB	Carlos Mendoza, Erie	70
HBP	Braiden Ward, Hartford	23
SO	Spencer Jones, Somerset	200
SB	Alex Ramirez, Binghamton	40
CS	Gage Workman, Erie	13

FIELDING

C PO	Caleb Ricketts, Reading	.994
PO	Braxton Fulford, Hartford	809
A	Israel Pineda, Harrisburg	54
DP	Kevin Parada, Binghamton	9
E	Braxton Fulford, Hartford	12
CS	Braxton Fulford, Hartford	38
SB	Eliezer Alfonzo, Erie	95
PB	Israel Pineda, Harrisburg	17
1B PCT	No Qualifier	
PO	Rainer Nunez, New Hampshire	566
A	Dermis Garcia, Harrisburg	63
DP	Jake Holton, Erie	54
E	Rainer Nunez, New Hampshire	11
2B PCT	J.T. Arruda, Harrisburg	.987
PO	Adael Amador, Hartford	230
A	Anthony Seigler, Somerset	259
DP	J.T. Arruda, Harrisburg	48
E	Adael Amador, Hartford	16
3B PCT	Warming Bernabel, Hartford	.939
PO	Warming Bernabel, Hartford	58
A	Warming Bernabel, Hartford	142
DP	Dayan Frias, Akron	17
E	Ryan Higgins, Bowie	15
SS PCT	Tsung-Che Cheng, Altoona	.968
PO	Ryan Ritter, Hartford	159
A	Tsung-Che Cheng, Altoona	241
DP	Ryan Ritter, Hartford	54
E	Frederick Bencosme, Bowie	17
OF PCT	Spencer Jones, Somerset	.978
PO	3 tied	176
A	Jud Fabian, Bowie	9
DP	Jud Fabian, Bowie	5
E	Alex Ramirez, Binghamton	6

PITCHING

G	Juan Mejia, Hartford	47
GS	5 tied	27
GF	Tommy McCollumn, Reading	28
SV	Felix Cepeda, Portland	14
W	Trystan Vrieling, Somerset	13
L	Abidel Mendoza, New Hampshire	12
IP	Zach Messinger, Somerset	150
H	John Michael Bertrand, Richmond	153
R	Trystan Vrieling, Somerset	79
ER	Trystan Vrieling, Somerset	75
HBP	Isaac Coffey, Portland	25
BB	Trace Bright, Bowie	60
SO	Isaac Coffey, Portland	148
SO/9	Isaac Coffey, Portland	11.72
BB/9	Kyle Luckham, Harrisburg	1.74
WP	Alex Hoppe, Portland	15
Balks	Helcris Olivarez, Portland, Richmond	6
HR	Bailey Dees, Somerset	19
HR	Troy Melton, Erie	19
AVG	Zach Messinger, Somerset	.207

SOUTHERN LEAGUE DOUBLE-A

Awards selected by Major League Baseball

CHAMPION: Birmingham swept Montgomery in the Southern League Championship Series, winning Game 2 in dramatic fashion. The Barons squandered a 1-0 lead in the game and made use of the automatic runner to win in the 10th inning. Shawn Goosenberg moved to third base on a wild pitch by Montgomery's Austin Vernon and then scored on a one-out single by DJ Gladney. It was Birmingham's first SL title since 2013. Birmingham's Sergio Santos was in his first year as Barons manager.

MOST VALUABLE PLAYER: Tennessee third baseman Matt Shaw hit .279/.373/.468 with 14 home runs and 25 stolen bases in 86 games before the Cubs promoted him to Triple-A Iowa. The 2023 first-rounder out of Maryland made a call to his former Terrapins hitting coach to get his swing back on track after he hit just .234 through his first 50 games.

PITCHER OF THE YEAR: Birmingham lefthander Noah Schultz thoroughly dominated SL competition in 16 starts after he joined the league on May 25. The 20-year-old recorded a 1.48 ERA in 61 innings, while striking out 73 and walking 17. The White Sox's 2022 first-rounder allowed just two home runs.

TOP MLB PROSPECT: Montgomery shortstop Carson Williams can do a little bit of everything. The Rays' 2021 first-rounder batted .256/.353/.469 with 20 home runs and 33 stolen bases in 115 games. He led the SL with 69 RBIs and 83 runs scored. League managers voted Williams the best defensive shortstop in the league as well as its most exciting player.

MANAGER OF THE YEAR: Kevin Boles' Montgomery Biscuits loaded up on Rays prospects in the second half. Carson Williams was there all season, but the club added talents such as Chandler Simpson, Xavier Isaac, Brayden Taylor and Tre' Morgan midstream. Montgomery led the SL with 650 runs scored and ranked second with a 3.31 ERA.

Carson Williams

MIKE JANES/FOUR SEAM IMAGES

SOUTHERN LEAGUE ALL-STARS

Pos	Player	Team	AVG	OPS	HR
C	Edgar Quero	Birmingham	.275	.823	12
1B	Ernesto Martinez Jr.	Biloxi	.284	.831	13
2B	James Triantos	Tennessee	.300	.782	7
3B	Matt Shaw	Tennessee	.279	.841	14
SS	Carson Williams	Montgomery	.256	.821	20
OF	Gustavo Campero	Rocket City	.279	.888	14
OF	Chandler Simpson	Montgomery	.351	.808	1
OF	Eric Wagaman	Rocket City	.260	.795	14
DH	Dominic Keegan	Montgomery	.285	.806	9
UT	Brooks Baldwin	Birmingham	.322	.827	6
Pos	**Pitcher**	**Team**	**G**	**ERA**	**SO**
SP	Caden Dana	Rocket City	23	2.52	147
SP	Noah Schultz	Birmingham	16	1.48	73
SP	Ian Seymour	Montgomery	17	2.36	99
SP	Drew Thorpe	Birmingham	11	1.35	56
RP	Blake Holub	Biloxi	20	0.34	29
RP	Evan Reifert	Montgomery	35	1.96	65

OVERALL STANDINGS

North Division	W	L	PCT	GB	Manager	Attendance	Avg	Last Penn
Tennessee Smokies (Cubs)	87	50	.635	—	Lance Rymel	292,445	4,365	2023
Birmingham Barons (White Sox)	72	66	.522	15.5	Sergio Santos	234,488	3,608	2024
Rocket City Trash Pandas (Angels)	61	75	.449	25.5	Andy Schatzley	319,417	4,563	Never
Chattanooga Lookouts (Reds)	45	90	.333	41.0	Jose Moreno	213,890	3,395	2017
South Division	**W**	**L**	**PCT**	**GB**	**Manager**	**Attendance**	**Avg**	**Last Penn**
Montgomery Biscuits (Rays)	80	57	.584	—	Kevin Boles	163,959	2,562	2007
Pensacola Blue Wahoos (Marlins)	71	65	.522	8.5	Kevin Randel	285,821	4,203	2022
Biloxi Shuckers (Brewers)	66	69	.489	13.0	Joe Ayrault	155,256	2,426	Never
Mississippi Braves (Braves)	63	73	.463	16.5	Angel Flores	118,621	2,081	2021

North: Birmingham def. Tennessee 2-1. **South:** Montgomery def. Biloxi 2-1. **Championship Series:** Birmingham defeated Montgomery 2-0.

CLUB BATTING

	AVG	G	AB	R	H	2B	3B	HR	RBI	BB	SO	SB	OBP	SLG
Montgomery Biscuits	.256	137	4526	650	1160	232	36	110	611	457	1269	222	.329	.396
Tennessee Smokies	.241	137	4418	610	1063	188	27	106	548	533	1163	176	.328	.367
Birmingham Barons	.237	138	4465	534	1057	189	12	77	493	475	1189	197	.317	.336
Rocket City Trash Pandas	.230	136	4359	538	1004	182	14	94	488	507	1217	166	.319	.343
Biloxi Shuckers	.227	135	4337	566	986	185	21	91	518	564	1161	135	.328	.343
Mississippi Braves	.226	136	4307	484	975	175	21	59	437	409	1154	226	.299	.318
Pensacola Blue Wahoos	.222	136	4379	541	971	185	18	117	487	458	1237	143	.304	.352
Chattanooga Lookouts	.213	135	4337	477	924	166	15	111	442	414	1312	125	.291	.335

CLUB PITCHING

	ERA	G	CG	SHO	SV	IP	H	R	ER	HR	BB	SO	AVG
Birmingham Barons	3.15	138	1	12	27	1195	961	472	418	83	480	1245	.221
Montgomery Biscuits	3.30	137	0	18	27	1200	944	502	440	92	453	1211	.215
Tennessee Smokies	3.43	137	0	17	39	1195	983	514	455	104	436	1213	.223
Mississippi Braves	3.72	136	7	17	32	1157	1035	529	478	85	492	1193	.239
Biloxi Shuckers	3.81	135	0	11	34	1172	1020	557	496	102	468	1297	.233
Pensacola Blue Wahoos	3.84	136	0	11	36	1185	1056	577	506	102	454	1183	.237
Rocket City Trash Pandas	3.86	136	3	5	31	1180	1054	575	506	110	430	1193	.237
Chattanooga Lookouts	4.52	135	1	9	27	1160	1087	674	583	87	604	1167	.250

CLUB FIELDING

	PCT	PO	A	E	DP
Montgomery	.983	3599	1079	83	97
Birmingham	.982	3586	1149	88	114
Tennessee	.981	3586	1055	88	102
Chattanooga	.980	3479	1131	94	134
Rocket City	.979	3539	1184	101	97
Biloxi	.979	3517	1062	100	88
Mississippi	.979	3471	1095	100	99
Pensacola	.978	3556	1215	105	95

INDIVIDUAL BATTING

Batter, Club	AVG	G	AB	R	H	2B	3B	HR	RBI	BB	SO	SB
Chandler Simpson, Montgomery	.351	78	322	56	113	13	1	1	20	29	27	73
James Triantos, Tennessee	.300	89	357	63	107	18	5	7	40	20	38	38
B.J. Murray, Montgomery	.290	111	420	56	122	29	3	7	66	21	73	4
Dru Baker, Montgomery	.288	110	424	50	122	13	2	0	44	34	96	42
Dominic Keegan, Montgomery	.285	104	375	58	107	23	3	9	60	50	90	0
Ernesto Martinez Jr., Biloxi	.284	110	401	52	114	30	2	13	62	40	77	20
Gustavo Campero, Rocket City	.279	93	312	56	87	17	4	14	45	39	60	29
Lamar Sparks, Biloxi	.277	103	357	45	99	19	1	10	43	33	117	12
Christian Franklin, Tennessee	.268	98	347	63	93	15	2	5	38	71	89	34
Wilfred Veras, Birmingham	.267	128	491	62	131	27	1	16	60	34	140	25

INDIVIDUAL PITCHING

Pitcher, Club	W	L	ERA	G	GS	CG	SV	IP	H	R	ER	BB	SO
Caden Dana, Rocket City	9	7	2.52	23	23	1	0	136	89	46	38	39	147
Logan Workman, Montgomery	10	5	2.71	24	23	0	0	123	99	42	37	33	112
Ian Mejia, Mississippi	8	7	3.47	24	23	3	1	124	108	53	48	56	123
Jairo Iriarte, Birmingham	5	7	3.71	23	22	0	0	126	104	57	52	57	122
Chase Chaney, Rocket City	7	11	4.30	26	25	0	0	138	149	73	66	44	103
Chase Petty, Chattanooga	10	5	4.39	26	26	0	0	127	116	68	62	56	123
Luis Palacios, Pensacola	10	7	4.91	24	24	0	0	125	145	80	68	29	94
Thomas Farr, Chattanooga	1	17	5.56	26	26	0	0	126	139	84	78	47	87

DEPARTMENT LEADERS

BATTING

OBP	Christian Franklin, Tennessee	.398
SLG	Gustavo Campero, Rocket City	.494
OPS	Gustavo Campero, Rocket City	.888
Runs	Carson Williams, Montgomery	83
Hits	Wilfred Veras, Birmingham	131
TB	Wilfred Veras, Birmingham	208
XBH	Joe Mack, Pensacola	47
2B	Ernesto Martinez, Biloxi	30
3B	Cody Milligan, Mississippi	6
3B	Carson Williams, Montgomery	6
HR	Nicholas Northcut, Chattanooga	26
RBI	Carson Williams, Montgomery	69
SAC	Jason Matthews, Birmingham	6
BB	Christian Franklin, Tennessee	71
HBP	Darrien Miller, Biloxi	28
SO	Austin Hendrick, Chattanooga	173
SB	Chandler Simpson, Montgomery	73
CS	Geraldo Quintero, Mississpii	16

FIELDING

C PCT	Joe Mack, Pensacola	.999
PO	Darrien Miller, Biloxi	826
A	Darrien Miller, Biloxi	43
DP	Michael Turner, Birmingham	6
E	Darrien Miller, Biloxi	14
CS	Darrien Miller, Biloxi	34
SB	Darrien Miller, Biloxi	133
PB	Darrien Miller, Biloxi	10
1B PCT	Sam Brown, Mississippi	.991
PO	Sam Brown, Rocket City	782
A	Sam Brown, Rocket City	68
DP	Sam Brown, Rocket City	67
E	Bryson Horne, Mississippi	10
2B PCT	Cody Morissette, Pensacola	.973
PO	Cody Morissette, Pensacola	147
A	Cody Morissette, Pensacola	253
DP	Cody Morissette, Pensacola	55
E	Cody Morissette, Pensacola	11
3B PCT	No qualifier	
PO	Keshawn Ogans, Mississippi	66
A	Keshawn Ogans, Mississippi	156
DP	Keshawn Ogans, Mississippi	15
E	Jacob Berry, Pensacola	13
SS PCT	Carson Williams, Montgomery	.979
PO	Carson Williams, Montgomery	145
A	Carson Williams, Montgomery	278
DP	Carson Williams, Montgomery	48
E	Cal Conley, Mississippi	11
OF PCT	Cody Milligan, Mississippi	.995
PO	Kevin Alcantara, Tennessee	195
A	Austin Hendrick, Chattanooga	9
DP	4 tied	3
E	Austin Hendrick, Chattanooga	6

PITCHING

G	Keyshawn Askew, Montgomery	51
GS	Thomas Farr, Chattanooga	26
GS	Chase Petty, Chattanooga	26
GF	Justin Yeager, Biloxi	43
SV	Justin Yeager, Biloxi	20
W	Luis Palacios, Pensacola	10
W	Logan Workman, Montgomery	10
W	Chase Petty, Chattanooga	10
L	Thomas Farr, Chattanooga	17
IP	Caden Dana, Rocket City	135.6
H	Chase Chaney, Rocket City	149
R	Thomas Farr, Chattanooga	84
ER	Thomas Farr, Chattanooga	78
HBP	Jairo Iriarte, Birmingham	17
BB	Matthew Thompson, Tennessee	69
SO	Jake Gozzo, Chattanooga	14
SO/9	Caden Dana, Rocket City	9.75
BB/9	Luis Palacios, Pensacola	2.09
WP	Jake Gozzo, Chattanooga	14
HR	Thomas Farr, Chattanooga	20
AVG	Caden Dana, Rocket City	.184

TEXAS LEAGUE DOUBLE-A

Awards selected by Major League Baseball

CHAMPION: After ending as Texas League runners-up in 2023, Arkansas finished the job in 2024 by defeating Midland two games to one in the championship series. Arkansas shortstop Cole Young scored the winning run in the bottom of the ninth in the deciding Game Three. Right fielder Alberto Rodriguez delivered the walk-off hit. Young starred all postseason, going 9-for-20 with a home run, three doubles, six walks and seven runs scored in six games. Travelers righthander and Mariners prospect Logan Evans came up huge in the deciding game by going six innings, allowing one run on five hits while striking out nine.

MOST VALUABLE PLAYER: Springfield catcher Jimmy Crooks led the TL with a .498 slugging percentage. The lefthanded hitter blasted 11 home runs in 90 games while batting .321/.410/.498 and catching 81 games. The Cardinals drafted Crooks out of Oklahoma in the fourth round in 2022.

PITCHER OF THE YEAR: Springfield righthander Tink Hence made 20 starts and recorded a 2.71 ERA in 79.2 innings. The 21-year-old struck out 109 and walked 26. The 2020 supplemental second-rounder moved one step closer to St. Louis and is poised to debut in 2025.

TOP MLB PROSPECT: Dalton Rushing continued crushing at Tulsa. The 23-year-old batted .271/.378/.513 with 17 home runs in 77 games. The Dodgers' top pick in the 2022 draft seamlessly moved to Triple-A Oklahoma City, where he focused on learning left field. Rushing hit 26 home runs in 2024 while making more and higher quality contact. Now that he can play a position not manned by Will Smith in Los Angeles, his MLB debut is on the short list.

MANAGER OF THE YEAR: Springfield's Jose Leger led the Cardinals to 79-59 record on the strength of the highest runs scored total in the league, thanks largely to a TL-best .348 on-base percentage.

Dalton Rushing

TEXAS LEAGUE ALL-STARS

Pos	Player	Team	AVG	OPS	HR
C	Jimmy Crooks	Springfield	.321	.908	11
1B	Brennan Milone	Midland	.278	.802	15
2B	Cooper Bowman	Midland	.281	.844	12
3B	Cody Freeman	Frisco	.264	.752	14
SS	Alex Freeland	Tulsa	.245	.792	11
OF	Carson McCusker	Wichita	.281	.846	15
OF	Alejandro Osuna	Frisco	.306	.902	9
OF	Colby Thomas	Midland	.282	.908	14
DH	Dalton Rushing	Tulsa	.270	.890	17
UT	Tim Tawa	Amarillo	.270	.827	21
Pos	**Pitcher**	**Team**	**G**	**ERA**	**SO**
SP	Tink Hence	Springfield	20	2.71	109
SP	Quinn Mathews	Springfield	9	2.41	70
SP	Zebby Matthews	Wichita	10	1.95	63
SP	Andrew Morris	Wichita	12	1.90	63
RP	Matt Svanson	Springfield	53	2.69	59
RP	Troy Taylor	Arkansas	29	1.17	31

MIKE JANES/FOUR SEAM IMAGES

OVERALL STANDINGS

North Division	W	L	PCT	GB	Manager	Attendance	Avg	Last Penn
Arkansas Travelers (Mariners)	80	57	.584	—	C. Colon/Michael Fransoso	327,279	4,959	2024
Springfield Cardinals (Cardinals)	79	59	.572	1.5	Jose Leger	263,648	3,877	2012
Northwest Arkansas Naturals (Royals)	66	71	.482	14.0	Tommy Shields	230,599	3,494	2021
Tulsa Drillers (Dodgers)	63	74	.460	17.0	Scott Hennessey	341,751	5,178	2018
Wichita Wind Surge (Twins)	58	80	.420	22.5	Ramon Borrego	301,886	4,375	Never
South Division	**W**	**L**	**PCT**	**GB**	**Manager**	**Attendance**	**Avg**	**Last Penn**
Frisco RoughRiders (Rangers)	84	54	.609	—	Carlos Cardoza	371,149	5,540	2022
Midland RockHounds (Athletics)	84	54	.609	—	Gregorio Petit	225,274	3,362	2017
San Antonio Missions (Padres)	62	74	.456	21.0	Luke Montz	265,011	3,897	2013
Amarillo Sod Poodles (D-backs)	58	79	.423	25.5	Tim Bogar	340,033	5,152	2023
Corpus Christi Hooks (Astros)	52	84	.382	31.0	Dickie Joe Thon	279,467	4,110	2006

North: Arkansas defeated. Springfield 2-1. **South:** Midland defeated Frisco 2-1. **Championship Series:** Arkansas defeated Midland 2-1.

CLUB BATTING

	AVG	G	AB	R	H	2B	3B	HR	RBI	BB	SO	SB	OBP	SLG
Springfield Cardinals	.266	138	4595	683	1221	203	14	94	627	521	1011	171	.348	.377
Midland RockHounds	.253	138	4599	674	1163	262	31	120	618	479	1295	209	.329	.402
Frisco RoughRiders	.250	138	4540	673	1136	232	25	117	605	481	1076	150	.329	.390
Amarillo Sod Poodles	.246	137	4551	619	1118	211	19	149	584	482	1334	90	.324	.399
NW Arkansas Naturals	.244	137	4558	662	1114	225	27	128	604	499	1191	146	.326	.390
Arkansas Travelers	.240	137	4462	628	1072	220	27	90	557	535	1277	241	.333	.362
Wichita Wind Surge	.231	138	4578	623	1058	240	20	123	580	562	1276	129	.324	.373
Tulsa Drillers	.231	137	4484	644	1036	208	17	132	586	559	1334	165	.326	.373
Corpus Christi Hooks	.218	136	4403	510	958	181	26	114	468	499	1250	216	.306	.348
San Antonio Missions	.214	136	4345	539	930	194	11	90	478	542	1219	131	.320	.326

CLUB PITCHING

	ERA	G	CG	SHO	SV	IP	H	R	ER	HR	BB	SO	AVG
Midland RockHounds	3.13	138	1	15	44	1222	973	494	425	103	452	1227	.219
Arkansas Travelers	3.50	137	1	13	39	1214	1013	554	472	101	429	1155	.225
Frisco RoughRiders	3.67	138	0	12	39	1210	1032	552	494	102	544	1253	.231
San Antonio Missions	4.01	136	0	10	30	1195	1134	601	533	86	453	1225	.252
Wichita Wind Surge	4.11	138	0	3	25	1219	1103	642	557	99	500	1176	.240
Springfield Cardinals	4.30	138	0	8	40	1200	1117	655	573	131	510	1279	.245
Tulsa Drillers	4.31	137	0	10	21	1189	1067	636	569	115	630	1238	.241
Corpus Christi Hooks	4.38	136	0	6	22	1190	1026	664	579	145	553	1247	.231
NW Arkansas Naturals	4.60	137	0	9	30	1203	1112	679	615	103	561	1305	.244
Amarillo Sod Poodles	5.15	137	0	3	27	1192	1229	778	682	172	527	1158	.266

CLUB FIELDING

	PCT	PO	A	E	DP
Northwest Arkansas	.983	3608	1171	82	92
Midland	.983	3665	1186	85	93
Frisco	.982	3631	1135	85	129
Springfield	.980	3599	1050	97	107
Arkansas	.979	3641	1154	103	91
Amarillo	.978	3577	1219	106	106
San Antonio	.978	3586	1224	108	108
Wichita	.977	3658	1118	113	95
Tulsa	.976	3568	1164	116	120
Corpus Christi	.974	3570	1084	122	94

INDIVIDUAL BATTING

Batter, Club	AVG	G	AB	R	H	2B	3B	HR	RBI	BB	SO	SB
Bryan Torres, Springfield	.331	120	447	79	148	28	2	2	56	69	75	33
Josh Hatcher, Frisco	.300	107	417	60	125	20	3	12	68	30	122	23
Max Acosta, Frisco	.288	104	386	57	111	23	3	8	58	34	58	26
Noah Mendlinger, Springfield	.282	103	355	44	100	20	0	0	45	29	50	4
Carson McCusker, Wichita	.281	98	370	56	104	26	3	15	64	38	117	7
Brennan Milone, Midland	.278	127	478	75	133	29	2	15	70	59	117	8
Ben Williamson, Arkansas	.272	95	356	50	97	23	2	3	43	44	97	15
Cole Young, Arkansas	.271	124	469	67	127	25	2	9	57	67	87	23
Tim Tawa, Amarillo	.270	105	411	62	111	22	2	21	64	40	96	11
A.J. Vukovich, Amarillo	.270	121	456	59	123	29	3	17	80	48	153	6

INDIVIDUAL PITCHING

Pitcher, Club	W	L	ERA	G	GS	CG	SV	IP	H	R	ER	BB	SO
Danny Wirchansky, Arkansas	8	6	2.84	27	17	0	0	111	88	43	35	30	89
Juan Mercedes, Arkansas	10	5	2.87	27	27	1	0	144	132	54	46	26	126
Blake Beers, Midland	11	6	3.33	24	21	0	0	130	108	52	48	39	122
Mason Barnett, Midland/NW Ark.	9	8	4.20	26	25	0	0	133	121	69	62	49	161
Miguel Ullola, Corpus Christi	5	9	4.24	27	23	0	1	127	72	61	60	73	166
Mason Rajcic, Springfield	10	11	4.33	25	24	0	0	131	133	73	63	44	131
Austin Krob, San Antonio	4	11	4.43	26	25	0	0	124	129	70	61	44	120
Orlando Ortiz-Mayr, Tulsa	7	8	4.71	27	25	0	0	136	132	75	71	60	108
Tyler Guilfoil, Corpus Christi	5	11	4.81	27	18	0	1	118	106	68	63	54	107

DEPARTMENT LEADERS

BATTING

OBP	Bryan Torres, Springfield	.418
SLG	Jimmy Crooks, Springfield	.498
OPS	Carson McCusker, Wichita	.846
Runs	Nathan Church, Springfield	81
Hits	Bryan Torres, Springfield	148
TB	Brennan Milone, Midland	211
XBH	A.J. Vukovich, Amarillo	49
XBH	Cody Freeman, Frisco	49
2B	Cody Freeman, Frisco	33
3B	Denzel Clarke, Midland	8
HR	Ivan Melendez, Amarillo	22
RBI	A.J. Vukovich, Amarillo	80
SAC	Tyler Tolbert, NW Arkansas	19
BB	Harry Ford, Arkansas	74
HBP	Robbie Tenerowicz, Ark./S. Antonio	40
SO	Cole Cummings, San Antonio	173
SB	Taylor Young, Tulsa	46
CS	Cole Young, Arkansas	11

FIELDING

C	PCT	Jimmy Crooks, Springfield	.996
	PO	Luca Tresh, NW Arkansas	728
	PO	Daniel Susac, Midland	727
	A	Daniel Susac, Midland	55
	DP	Luca Tresh, NW Arkansas	6
	DP	Andrew Cossetti, Wichita	6
	E	Jake Anchia, Arkansas	11
	E	Noah Cardenas, Wichita	11
	CS	Daniel Susac, Midland	35
	SB	Daniel Susac, Midland	99
	PB	Caleb Roberts, Amarillo	21
1B	PCT	Dillan Shrum, NW Arkansas	.996
	PO	Dillan Shrum, NW Arkansas	769
	A	Abimelec Ortiz, Frisco	46
	DP	Abimelec Ortiz, Frisco	72
	E	Aaron Sabato, Wichita	9
2B	PCT	No qualifier	
	PO	Javier Vaz, NW Arkansas	160
	A	Javier Vaz, NW Arkansas	206
	DP	Yeiner Fernandez, Tulsa	56
	E	Yeiner Fernandez, Tulsa	18
3B	PCT	Cody Freeman, Frisco	.984
	PO	Cody Freeman, Frisco	69
	A	Cody Freeman, Frisco	176
	DP	Taylor Young, Tulsa	27
	DP	Cody Freeman, Frisco	27
	E	Jacob Buchberger, Springfield	16
SS	PCT	Jorbit Vivas, Springfield	.966
	PO	Jeremy Rivas, Springfield	124
	A	Jeremy Rivas, Springfield	274
	DP	Jeremy Rivas, Springfield	51
	E	Ray-Patrick Didder, San Antonio	18
OF	PCT	Cole Cummings, San Antonio	.989
	PO	Jose Ramos, Tulsa	273
	A	Jose Ramos, Tulsa	13
	DP	Jose Ramos, Tulsa	4
	DP	Cole Cummings, San Antonio	4
	E	Jose Ramos, Tulsa	10

PITCHING

G	Matt Svanson, Springfield	53
GS	Juan Mercedes, Arkansas	27
GF	Matt Svanson, Springfield	46
SV	Matt Svanson, Springfield	27
W	Blake Beers, Midland	11
L	Tyler Guilfoil, Corpus Christi	11
L	Austin Krob, San Antonio	11
IP	Juan Mercedes, Arkansas	144.3
H	Max Rajcic, Springfield	133
R	Kendall Williams, Tulsa	77
ER	William Fleming, NW Arkansas	72
HBP	Edwin Nunez, Springfield	20
BB	Miguel Ullola, Corpus Christi	73
SO	Miguel Ullola, Corpus Christi	166
SO/9	Miguel Ullola, Corpus Christi	11.73
BB/9	Juan Mercedes, Arkansas	1.62
WP	Edwin Nunez, Springfield	18
HR	Tyler Guilfoil, Corpus Christi	20
AVG	Miguel Ullola, Corpus Christi	.162

MIDWEST LEAGUE HIGH-A

Awards selected by Major League Baseball

CHAMPION: Minor League Team of the Year Lake County dispatched Wisconsin two games to one in the Midwest League championship series—and they did it with significant prospect heft. Captains shortstop Angel Genao came up big all postseason by batting 6-for-14 with a home run, three doubles, eight walks and five RBIs. In the second half, Lake County featured both of the Guardians' last two first-round picks, first baseman Ralphy Velazquez and second baseman Travis Bazzana, drafted No. 1 overall out of Oregon State in July. Velazquez delivered a three-run home run in the Lake County's 9-4 victory in the deciding Game 3 of the MWL finals. It was a fitting conclusion for a Lake County team that led the league in both runs scored and ERA.

MOST VALUABLE PLAYER: Lake County had serious prospect cachet in 2024. Catcher Cooper Ingle helped lead the first-half charge. Drafted out of Clemson in the fourth round in 2023, Ingle is a lefthanded-hitting catcher with offensive upside. He hit .314/.433/.500 with nine home runs in 68 games to earn a promotion to Double-A Akron.

PITCHER OF THE YEAR: The Tigers found a good one in the fifth round in 2023 in the form of Middle Tennessee State righthander Jaden Hamm. He had a big year with West Michigan in 2024, striking out 122 and walking 31 in 99 innings while posting a 2.64 ERA.

TOP MLB PROSPECT: Marlins lefthander Thomas White pitched his way out of Low-A by the end of May. The 19-year-old continued to thrive at Beloit, recording a 2.61 ERA in 62 innings while notching 76 strikeouts and 21 walks. No teen pitcher was more dominant in 2024 than White.

MANAGER OF THE YEAR: Wisconsin manager Victor Estevez won the West Division and finished with the second-best record in the MWL at 77-54.

Thomas White

PAUL R. GIERHART

MIDWEST LEAGUE ALL-STARS

Pos	Player	Team	AVG	OPS	HR
C	Cooper Ingle	Lake County	.313	.933	9
1B	Will Simpson	Lansing	.270	.853	16
2B	Jadher Areinamo	Wisconsin	.301	.791	10
3B	Cam Collier	Dayton	.248	.798	20
SS	Angel Genao	Lake County	.322	.840	4
OF	Henry Bolte	Lansing	.278	.912	11
OF	Brayan Buelvas	Lansing	.272	.811	7
OF	Ethan O'Donnell	Dayton	.269	.774	10
DH	Brett Squires	Quad Cities	.309	.871	9
UT	Sal Stewart	Dayton	.279	.845	8
Pos	**Pitcher**	**Team**	**G**	**ERA**	**SO**
SP	Jaden Hamm	West Michigan	24	2.64	122
SP	Austin Peterson	Lake County	14	2.44	87
SP	Thomas White	Beloit	13	2.61	76
SP	Matt Wilkinson	Lake County	16	2.30	103
RP	Lucas Wepf	Great Lakes	22	1.84	44

OVERALL STANDINGS

East Division	W	L	PCT	GB	Manager	Attendance	Avg	Last Penn
Lake County Captains (Guardians)	77	53	.592	—	Omir Santos	207,742	3,406	2024
Dayton Dragons (Reds)	74	58	.561	4.0	Vince Harrison	528,778	8,012	Never
Great Lakes Loons (Dodgers)	69	61	.531	8.0	Jair Fernandez	200,892	3,189	2016
West Michigan Whitecaps (Tigers)	68	63	.519	9.5	Tony Cappucilli	372,943	5,827	2015
Lansing Lugnuts (Athletics)	59	72	.450	18.5	Craig Conklin	266,389	4,297	2003
Fort Wayne TinCaps (Padres)	53	79	.402	25.0	Mike Daly	341,015	5,590	2009

West Division	W	L	PCT	GB	Manager	Attendance	Avg	Last Penn
Wisconsin Timber Rattlers (Brewers)	77	54	.588	—	Victor Estevez	229,129	3,696	2012
Quad Cities River Bandits (Royals)	68	63	.519	9.0	Brooks Conrad	169,603	2,736	2021
Cedar Rapids Kernels (Twins)	67	63	.515	9.5	Brian Dinkelman	150,102	2,383	2023
Beloit Sky Carp (Marlins)	60	69	.465	16.0	Billy Gardner	99,224	1,654	1995
Peoria Chiefs (Cardinals)	59	72	.450	18.0	Patrick Anderson	164,658	2,533	2002
South Bend Cubs (Cubs)	54	78	.409	23.5	Nick Lovullo	310,023	4,770	2022

East: Lake County def. Dayton 2-0. **West:** Wisconsin def. Quad Cities 2-0. **Championship Series:** Lake County defeated Wisconsin 2-1.

CLUB BATTING

	AVG	G	AB	R	H	2B	3B	HR	RBI	BB	SO	SB	OBP	SLG
Lansing Lugnuts	.246	131	4362	620	1073	211	40	82	568	521	1080	160	.335	.369
South Bend Cubs	.244	132	4377	590	1069	191	30	93	532	496	1181	146	.328	.365
Wisconsin Timber Rattlers	.243	131	4192	600	1020	209	18	77	529	530	946	244	.341	.357
Lake County Captains	.243	130	4288	632	1043	201	19	103	584	588	1073	204	.342	.371
Cedar Rapids Kernels	.239	130	4202	572	1006	216	30	110	531	467	1112	105	.326	.384
Peoria Chiefs	.235	131	4230	530	995	177	22	84	492	406	1207	170	.313	.347
West Michigan Whitecaps	.232	131	4259	565	990	201	22	90	511	444	1095	158	.317	.353
Quad Cities River Bandits	.232	131	4241	577	985	197	27	98	526	563	1249	181	.328	.361
Beloit Sky Carp	.229	129	4227	529	968	192	22	103	496	458	1259	107	.314	.358
Dayton Dragons	.228	132	4259	601	973	176	31	114	523	493	1265	175	.320	.365
Great Lakes Loons	.223	130	4209	592	939	174	16	97	527	573	1235	203	.323	.341
Fort Wayne TinCaps	.223	132	4264	532	951	207	20	75	494	496	1178	147	.312	.334

CLUB PITCHING

	ERA	G	CG	SHO	SV	IP	H	R	ER	HR	BB	SO	AVG
Lake County Captains	3.55	130	1	9	35	1128	927	507	445	102	463	1170	.221
West Michigan Whitecaps	3.57	131	0	13	30	1141	958	528	453	86	459	1164	.226
Quad Cities River Bandits	3.68	131	0	10	31	1138	962	518	465	92	452	1066	.231
Great Lakes Loons	3.74	130	0	7	39	1142	884	538	475	75	605	1263	.213
Beloit Sky Carp	3.76	129	0	4	27	1118	947	554	467	74	525	1184	.228
Peoria Chiefs	3.81	131	0	8	31	1138	1020	534	481	99	461	1224	.239
Wisconsin Timber Rattlers	3.83	131	0	10	40	1146	990	546	488	95	494	1191	.233
Cedar Rapids Kernels	4.14	130	1	6	35	1119	1069	603	515	106	400	1138	.248
Fort Wayne TinCaps	4.19	132	1	6	28	1150	1002	621	536	96	552	1144	.235
Dayton Dragons	4.37	132	0	10	46	1155	1036	633	561	91	508	1176	.236
South Bend Cubs	4.53	132	0	6	29	1153	1021	657	581	93	645	1178	.238
Lansing Lugnuts	5.04	131	0	5	25	1141	1196	701	639	117	471	982	.270

CLUB FIELDING

	PCT	PO	A	E	DP
Quad Cities	.981	3414	1160	89	109
Wisconsin	.980	3437	1079	92	110
Great Lakes	.978	3427	1032	100	97
Peoria	.978	3413	997	100	92
Beloit	.977	3353	1104	105	83
Fort Wayne	.975	3450	1118	118	106
Cedar Rapids	.975	3358	1066	115	84
West Michigan	.974	3424	1105	120	98
Lake County	.974	3385	1009	117	78
Dayton	.974	3465	1002	120	70
Lansing	.973	3423	1196	126	110
South Bend	.971	3460	1096	136	95

INDIVIDUAL BATTING

Batter, Club	AVG	G	AB	R	H	2B	3B	HR	RBI	BB	SO	SB
Jadher Areinamo, Wisconsin	.301	110	425	63	128	30	0	10	68	33	52	32
Ricardo Olivar, Cedar Rapids	.287	81	300	59	86	17	3	11	44	53	70	3
Pedro Ramirez, South Bend	.284	116	464	56	132	19	7	4	48	43	93	14
Brett Bateman, South Bend	.283	79	293	49	83	11	3	1	25	56	57	22
Rubel Cespedes, Cedar Rapids	.282	110	418	48	118	22	2	12	72	39	93	5
Euribiel Angeles, Lansing	.279	85	344	41	96	15	4	6	54	16	41	15
Hector Rodriguez, Dayton	.274	125	507	65	139	24	7	12	61	26	72	12
Roberto Campos, West Michigan	.272	118	426	56	116	25	5	10	66	41	112	11
Brayan Buelvas, Lansing	.272	80	309	54	84	20	6	7	51	46	80	22
Carter Jensen, Quad Cities	.271	84	310	47	84	15	3	10	39	57	83	16

INDIVIDUAL PITCHING

Pitcher, Club	W	L	ERA	G	GS	CG	SV	IP	H	R	ER	BB	SO
Trenton Denholm, Lake County	9	2	3.29	19	19	1	0	107	89	45	39	25	95
Carter Spivey, Lake County	8	1	3.32	24	24	0	0	125	104	53	46	48	96
Enmanuel Pinales, Fort Wayne	3	9	3.49	22	21	0	0	111	94	46	43	43	101
Hancel Rincon, Peoria	9	7	3.80	24	24	0	0	133	126	58	56	48	105
Inohan Paniagua, Peoria	7	9	3.82	25	20	0	0	115	92	54	49	50	123
Pete Hansen, Peoria	5	7	3.86	24	24	0	0	128	138	59	55	41	134
Carlos Marcano, West Michigan	3	11	3.86	26	23	0	0	112	122	60	48	36	97
Mitch Myers, Lansing	6	7	4.54	26	18	0	0	111	127	62	56	24	100
Will Rudy, Wisconsin	6	8	4.61	23	22	0	0	113	101	59	58	36	106
Jagger Haynes, Fort Wayne	2	6	4.64	23	22	0	0	111	90	59	57	66	114

DEPARTMENT LEADERS

BATTING

OBP	Luke Adams, Wisconsin	.443
SLG	Will Simpson, Lansing	.480
OPS	Ricardo Olivar, Cedar Rapids	.866
Runs	Alex Mooney, Lake County	73
Hits	Hector Rodriguez, Dayton	139
TB	Hector Rodriguez, Dayton	213
XBH	Will Simpson, Lansing	47
2B	Jadher Areinamo, Wisconsin	30
3B	Mark Coley, Beloit	7
3B	Hector Rodriguez, Dayton	7
3B	Pedro Ramirez, South Bend	7
HR	Chris Newell, Great Lakes	23
RBI	Will Simpson, Lansing	81
SAC	Jose Salas, Cedar Rapids	7
BB	Luke Adams, Wisconsin	78
HBP	Luke Adams, Wisconsin	40
SO	Trevor Werner, Quad Cities	178
SB	Seth Stephenson, West Michigan	60
CS	Luis Lara, Wisconsin	14

FIELDING

C PCT	Matthew Wood, Wisconsin	.994
PO	Leonardo Bernal, Peoria	714
A	Leonardo Bernal, Peoria	61
DP	Cameron Barstad, Beloit	6
DP	Ethan Hearn, South Bend	6
E	Ethan Hearn, South Bend	18
CS	Leonardo Bernal, Peoria	38
SB	Ethan Hearn, South Bend	98
PB	Thayron Liranzo, G. Lakes/W. Mich.	11
1B PCT	Luke Gold, West Michigan	.991
PO	Will Simpson, Lansing	717
A	Luke Gold, West Michigan	38
DP	Will Simpson, Lansing	69
E	Will Simpson, Lansing	8
2B PCT	Justin Johnson, Quad Cities	.985
PO	Justin Johnson, Quad Cities	353
A	Max Anderson, West Michigan	256
DP	Nerwilian Cedeno, Fort Wayne	63
E	Max Anderson, West Michigan	11
3B PCT	Trevor Werner, Quad Cities	.955
PO	Jake Gelof, Great Lakes	71
A	Trevor Werner, Quad Cities	167
DP	Trevor Werner, Quad Cities	17
E	Cam Collier, Dayton	18
SS PCT	Noah Miller, Great Lakes	.987
PO	Dustin Dickerson, Quad Cities	167
A	Dustin Dickerson, Quad Cities	254
DP	Dustin Dickerson, Quad Cities	49
E	Johnny Olmstead, Beloit	21
OF PCT	Carson Roccaforte, Quad Cities	.997
PO	Carson Roccaforte, Quad Cities	294
A	Eduarqui Fernandez, Wisconsin	10
DP	Brett Bateman, South Bend	4
DP	Jordan Nwogu, South Bend	4
E	Gabriel Gonzalez, Cedar Rapids	7

PITCHING

G	Tanner Kohlhepp, West Michigan	46
GS	3 tied	24
GF	Ben Sears, Quad Cities	38
SV	Ben Sears, Quad Cities	15
W	3 tied	9
L	Brycen Mautz, Peoria	13
IP	Hancel Rincon, Peoria	132.2
H	Pete Hansen, Peoria	138
R	Blaze Pontes, Lansing	76
ER	Blaze Pontes, Lansing	72
HBP	Inohan Paniagua, Peoria	18
BB	Drew Gray, South Bend	73
SO	Pete Hansen, Peoria	134
SO/9	Inohan Paniagua, Peoria	9.60
BB/9	Mitch Myers, Lansing	1.95
WP	Yerlin Rodriguez, Wisconsin	21
HR	Brycen Mautz, Peoria	20
AVG	Trenton Denholm, Lake County	.218

NORTHWEST LEAGUE HIGH-A

Awards selected by Major League Baseball

CHAMPION: Spokane compiled the best record in the Northwest League at 79-51. The Rockies affiliate carried that success through the postseason by winning the best-of-five championship series in four games. College Player of the Year Charlie Condon, drafted third overall by the Rockies in July, helped redeem a substandard pro debut by going 2-for-3 with a walk and an RBI in Spokane's 3-2 victory in Game Four of the finals.

MOST VALUABLE PLAYER: Spokane third baseman Kyle Karros led the NWL with a .311 batting average and 78 RBIs, missing the league's triple crown by one home run. He hit 15, while Spokane teammate Cole Carrigg hit a league-leading 16. The Rockies drafted Karros, who is the son of longtime MLB first baseman Eric Karros, in the fifth round in 2023 out of UCLA.

PITCHER OF THE YEAR: Spokane lefthander Sean Sullivan spent most of his first full season in the NWL, pitching to a 2.16 ERA in 83.1 innings, while striking out 101 and walking just eight in 14 starts. Colorado drafted Sullivan out of Wake Forest in the second round in 2023. He finished his season with seven starts for Double-A Hartford.

TOP MLB PROSPECT: The 19-year-old Bryce Eldridge played at all four full-season levels in 2024, hitting 23 home runs that tied for the most by a teenager. The Eugene first baseman hit 12 home runs in 48 games in the league before being quickly ushered to Double-A for nine games and Triple-A for eight. The Giants drafted Eldridge 16th overall in 2023 and committed to using the two-way Virginia prep as a hitter only after he was highly regarded as an amateur pitcher. So far, so good.

MANAGER OF THE YEAR: Vancouver's Brent Lavallee took the top manager honors despite the Canadians finishing with the third-most wins in the six-team league. Vancouver has appeared in the NWL championship series in all three of his seasons at the helm. Lavallee is a native of British Columbia who manages Canada's only affiliated minor league team.

Bryce Eldridge

MIKE JANES/FOUR SEAM IMAGES

NORTHWEST LEAGUE ALL-STARS

Pos	Player	Team	AVG	OPS	HR
C	Jackson Hornung	Vancouver	.258	.714	6
1B	Peyton Williams	Vancouver	.289	.838	11
2B	Michael Arroyo	Everett	.290	.916	12
3B	Kyle Karros	Spokane	.311	.875	15
SS	Diego Velasquez	Eugene	.274	.746	3
OF	Cole Carrigg	Spokane	.280	.833	16
OF	Andrew Pintar	Hillsboro	.304	.919	9
OF	RJ Schreck	Everett	.261	.865	12
DH	Jared Sundstrom	Everett	.263	.814	13
UT	Brock Rodden	Everett	.302	.897	9
Pos	**Pitcher**	**Team**	**G**	**ERA**	**SO**
SP	Chase Dollander	Spokane	14	2.83	111
SP	Brandyn Garcia	Everett	14	1.84	85
SP	Spencer Giesting	Hillsboro	10	1.50	67
SP	Sean Sullivan	Spokane	14	2.16	101
RP	Zach Agnos	Spokane	21	0.73	30
RP	Carson Skipper	Spokane	34	1.40	56

OVERALL STANDINGS

Team	W	L	PCT	GB	Manager	Attendance	Avg	Last Penn
Spokane Indians (Rockies)	79	51	.608	—	Robinson Cancel	254,807	3,920	2024
Vancouver Canadians (Blue Jays)	68	61	.527	10.5	Brent Lavallee	274,892	4,659	2023
Hillsboro Hops (D-backs)	69	62	.527	10.5	Javier Colina	153,571	2,363	2019
Everett AquaSox (Mariners)	64	68	.485	16.0	Ryan Scott	135,695	2,120	2010
Eugene Emeralds (Giants)	59	72	.450	20.5	Jeremiah Knackstedt	154,442	2,413	2022
Tri-City Dust Devils (Angels)	53	78	.405	26.5	Willie Romero	121,949	1,876	Never

Championship Series: Spokane defeated Vancouver 3-1.

NORTHWEST LEAGUE | STATISTICS

CLUB BATTING

	AVG	G	AB	R	H	2B	3B	HR	RBI	BB	SO	SB	OBP	SLG
Spokane Indians	.266	130	4380	666	1163	186	35	106	580	405	1085	258	.337	.397
Everett AquaSox	.246	132	4405	695	1083	240	24	134	631	595	1232	187	.346	.402
Hillsboro Hops	.242	131	4377	557	1058	196	32	82	497	440	1138	150	.318	.357
Eugene Emeralds	.241	131	4315	621	1039	213	22	105	562	552	1286	232	.339	.373
Vancouver Canadians	.239	129	4198	557	1002	214	18	101	505	484	1172	88	.328	.370
Tri-City Dust Devils	.220	131	4254	531	936	199	29	78	482	463	1291	170	.306	.335

CLUB PITCHING

	ERA	G	CG	SHO	SV	IP	H	R	ER	HR	BB	SO	AVG
Hillsboro Hops	3.61	131	1	6	36	1154	986	573	463	80	497	1171	.231
Spokane Indians	3.88	130	1	17	35	1153	1057	570	497	112	456	1220	.243
Vancouver Canadians	4.01	129	1	14	35	1114	992	557	496	85	458	1215	.239
Tri-City Dust Devils	4.18	131	0	5	28	1142	1031	622	530	86	591	1239	.240
Eugene Emeralds	4.36	131	0	5	20	1140	1059	644	552	114	451	1207	.244
Everett AquaSox	4.46	132	0	4	26	1165	1156	661	578	129	486	1152	.256

CLUB FIELDING

	PCT	PO	A	E	DP
Vancouver	.981	3342	1034	87	87
Spokane	.979	3460	1054	98	92
Everett	.973	3496	1205	129	94
Hillsboro	.973	3461	1143	130	99
Tri-City	.969	3426	1097	143	109
Eugene	.969	3420	1151	145	98

INDIVIDUAL BATTING

Batter, Club	AVG	G	AB	R	H	2B	3B	HR	RBI	BB	SO	SB
Kyle Karros, Spokane	.311	123	472	64	147	33	2	15	78	54	123	12
Juan Guerrero, Spokane	.302	92	358	56	108	21	1	4	49	19	54	23
Gavin Conticello, Hillsboro	.282	126	489	64	138	31	7	9	65	46	115	20
Cole Carrigg, Spokane	.280	111	440	80	123	16	11	16	60	50	97	51
Manuel Pena, Hillsboro	.275	116	451	45	124	27	2	4	51	33	106	10
Matt Coutney, Tri-City	.270	91	337	57	91	22	2	8	42	38	98	2
Dylan Jorge, Spokane	.267	121	483	82	129	13	3	2	49	48	122	36
Jared Sundstrom, Everett	.263	112	415	72	109	28	2	13	63	71	117	26
Jackson Hornung, Vancouver	.258	112	407	43	105	25	2	6	47	45	114	0
Jose Fernandez, Hillsboro	.256	101	363	40	93	7	2	7	43	17	85	10

INDIVIDUAL PITCHING

Pitcher, Club	W	L	ERA	G	GS	CG	SV	IP	H	R	ER	BB	SO
Avery Short, Hillsboro	7	9	3.51	24	23	1	0	128	113	58	50	36	112
Ty Cummings, Everett	4	5	4.17	25	25	0	0	117	118	60	54	46	124
Victor Juarez, Spokane	4	7	4.30	22	21	0	0	111	112	64	53	34	113
Joel Hurtado, Tri-City	9	8	4.61	26	26	0	0	139	137	85	71	82	134
Manuel Mercedes, Eugene	4	9	5.28	26	25	0	0	116	128	75	68	54	89
Ryan Hawks, Everett	6	9	5.59	25	25	0	0	121	139	80	75	35	95

DEPARTMENT LEADERS

BATTING

OBP	Kyle Karros, Spokane	.390
SLG	Kyle Karros, Spokane	.485
OPS	Kyle Karros, Spokane	.875
Runs	Dyan Jorge, Spokane	82
Hits	Kyle Karros, Spokane	147
TB	Kyle Karros, Spokane	229
XBH	Kyle Karros, Spokane	50
2B	Kyle Karros, Spokane	33
3B	Cole Carrigg, Spokane	11
HR	Cole Carrigg, Spokane	16
RBI	Kyle Karros, Spokane	78
SAC	Jean Perez, Spokane	8
BB	Jared Sundstrom, Everett	71
HBP	Bill Knight, Everett	13
SO	Quinn McDaniel, Eugene	166
SB	Caleb Ketchup, Tri-City	62
CS	Jose Cordova, Spokane	11
CS	Cole Carrigg, Spokane	11

FIELDING

C	PO	Freuddy Batista, Everett	.997
	A	Bryant Betancourt, Spokane	58
	DP	Freuddy Batista, Everett	6
	E	Bryant Betancourt, Spokane	11
	CS	Jommer Hernandez, Vancouver	28
	CS	Freuddy Batista, Everett	28
	CS	Bryant Betancourt, Spokane	28
	SB	Onil Perez, Eugene	91
	PB	Jackson Hornung, Vancouver	16
1B	PCT	No qualifiers	
	PO	Kevin Sim, Hillsboro	563
	A	Matt Coutney, Tri-City	39
	DP	Matt Coutney, Tri-City	55
	E	Matt Coutney, Tri-City	397
2B	PCT	Manuel Pena, Hillsboro	.965
	PO	Manuel Pena, Hillsboro	162
	A	Manuel Pena, Hillsboro	221
	DP	Manuel Pena, Hillsboro	56
	E	Manuel Pena, Hillsboro	14
3B	PCT	Kyle Karros, Spokane	.970
	PO	Kyle Karros, Spokane	116
	A	Kyle Karros, Spokane	211
	DP	Kyle Karros, Spokane	29
	E	Caleb Cali, Everett	14
SS	PCT	Dylan Jorge, Spokane	.944
	PO	Dyan Jorge, Spokane	112
	A	Axel Sanchez, Everett	179
	DP	Dyan Jorge, Spokane	38
	E	Dyan Jorge, Spokane	17
OF	PCT	Cole Carrigg, Spokane	.991
	PO	Cole Carrigg, Spokane	213
	A	Gavin Conticello, Hillsboro	12
	DP	Daran Brown, Vancouver	3
	DP	Cole Carrigg, Spokane	3
	E	Bill Knight, Everett	8

PITCHING

G	Grayson Thurman, Vancouver	48
GS	Joel Hurtado, Tri-City	26
GF	Hunter Dula, Eugene	27
SV	Alfred Morillo, Hillsboro	13
W	Mason Green, Spokane	9
W	Michael Morales, Everett	9
L	Manuel Mercedes, Eugene	9
L	Ryan Hawks, Everett	9
L	Shaddon Peavyhouse, Everett	9
IP	Joel Hurtado, Tri-City	138.2
H	Marcelo Perez, Everett	142
R	Joel Hurtado, Tri-City	85
ER	Marcelo Perez, Everett	79
SO	Joel Hurtado, Tri-City	134
SO/9	Ty Cummimgs, Everett	9.57
BB/9	Avery Short, Hillsboro	2.52
WP	Mason Green, Spokane	12
Balks	Felix Ramires, Spokane	7
HR	Ryan Hawks, Everett	22
AVG	Avery Short, Hillsboro	.238

SOUTH ATLANTIC LEAGUE HIGH-A

Awards selected by Major League Baseball

CHAMPION: Bowling Green has won its league in four of the past six completed seasons. This year the Hot Rods defeated Hudson Valley two games to one in the South Atlantic League championship series. Bowling Green previously won the SAL in 2021 and 2022, and it also won a title in 2018 as a member of the Midwest League, when it was a Low-A circuit. Trade acquisition Mac Horvath played a key role for Bowling Green. The third baseman went 6-for-18 with a home run, a triple and three doubles in five postseason games. Righthander Jackson Baumeister, like Horvath part of the Zach Eflin trade with the Orioles, started and won the Game 3 finale.

MOST VALUABLE PLAYER: Greensboro third baseman Charles McAdoo hit .336/.415/.561 with nine home runs in 60 games. The Pirates drafted him in the 13th round in 2023 out of San Jose State. Pittsburgh traded McAdoo to the Blue Jays at the deadline for utility infielder Isiah Kiner-Falefa.

PITCHER OF THE YEAR: Hudson Valley righthander Cam Schlittler helped set the tone for the Renegades' SAL-leading 3.25 ERA. He went 6-4, 2.60 with 108 strikeouts and 38 walks in 86.2 innings.

TOP MLB PROSPECT: Rays 2022 first-rounder Xavier Isaac hit .287/.381/.535 with 15 home runs in 71 games for Bowling Green. The 20-year-old first baseman finished the season with Double-A Montgomery, adding three more home runs in 31 games.

MANAGER OF THE YEAR: Jersey Shore manager Greg Brodzinski led his club to the third-best record in the SAL but was not one of the league's four playoff teams.

Xavier Isaac

SOUTH ATLANTIC LEAGUE ALL-STARS

Pos	Player	Team	AVG	OPS	HR
C	John Garcia	Asheville	.293	.852	10
1B	Xavier Isaac	Bowling Green	.287	.916	15
2B	Cooper Kinney	Bowling Green	.289	.846	10
3B	Charles McAdoo	Greensboro	.336	.976	9
SS	Brayden Taylor	Bowling Green	.269	.902	14
OF	Phillip Glasser	Wilmington	.305	.837	6
OF	Colton Ledbetter	Bowling Green	.273	.823	16
OF	Nick Morabito	Brooklyn	.294	.747	3
DH	Bryan Gonzalez	Greenville	.272	.845	20
UT	Sebastian Walcott	Hickory	.261	.785	10
Pos	**Pitcher**	**Team**	**G**	**ERA**	**SO**
SP	Jackson Baumeister	Bowling Green	25	2.53	135
SP	Dominic Perachi	Greensboro	16	2.08	81
SP	Cam Schlittler	Hudson Valley	17	2.60	108
SP	Trent Sellers	Hudson Valley	31	2.09	98
RP	Matt Cronin	Wilmington	24	0.65	35
RP	Cy Nielson	Greensboro	31	2.39	50

OVERALL STANDINGS

North Division	W	L	PCT	GB	Manager	Attendance	Avg	Last Penn
Greensboro Grasshoppers (Pirates)	75	55	.577	—	Blake Butler	253,050	3,954	2011
Jersey Shore BlueClaws (Phillies)	74	58	.561	2.0	Greg Brodzinski	284,136	4,371	2010
Hudson Valley Renegades (Yankees)	73	58	.557	2.5	Nick Ortiz	195,791	3,012	Never
Aberdeen IronBirds (Orioles)	67	65	.508	9.0	Felipe Alou Jr.	125,115	1,955	Never
Brooklyn Cyclones (Mets)	65	67	.492	11.0	Gilbert Gomez	173,405	2,752	Never
Wilmington Blue Rocks (Nationals)	57	75	.432	19.0	Mario Lisson	163,031	2,630	*2019
South Division	**W**	**L**	**PCT**	**GB**	**Manager**	**Attendance**	**Avg**	**Last Penn**
Bowling Green Hot Rods (Rays)	75	54	.581	—	Rafael Valenzuela	137,683	2,295	2024
Rome Braves (Braves)	64	64	.500	10.5	Cody Gabella	78,369	1,399	2016
Greenville Drive (Red Sox)	63	69	.477	13.5	Iggy Suarez	304,653	4,687	2023
Hickory Crawdads (Rangers)	62	70	.470	14.5	Chad Comer	114,548	1,848	2015
Winston-Salem Dash (White Sox)	60	72	.455	16.5	Guillermo Quiroz	255,895	4,127	*2003
Asheville Tourists (Astros)	51	79	.392	24.5	Nate Shaver	183,987	2,920	2014

* Carolina League title won prior to 2021 minor league realignment

North: Hudson Valley def. Greensboro 2-1. **South:** Bowling Green def. Rome 2-0. **Championship Series:** Bowling Green def. Hudson Valley 2-1.

BRIAN WESTERHOLT/FOUR SEAM IMAGES

CLUB BATTING

	AVG	G	AB	R	H	2B	3B	HR	RBI	BB	SO	SB	OBP	SLG
Jersey Shore BlueClaws	.258	132	4388	671	1133	194	51	77	590	483	1044	188	.340	.378
Bowling Green Hot Rods	.246	129	4175	641	1026	211	30	122	562	480	1268	262	.332	.398
Winston-Salem Dash	.235	132	4305	557	1012	184	28	82	497	527	1180	141	.326	.348
Asheville Tourists	.234	130	4266	613	998	218	10	154	565	450	1509	160	.317	.398
Hudson Valley Renegades	.233	131	4161	608	971	254	26	100	555	599	1209	156	.339	.379
Greenville Drive	.232	132	4401	633	1021	217	32	131	561	472	1268	136	.314	.385
Aberdeen IronBirds	.229	132	4194	595	962	204	44	83	511	568	1185	363	.326	.358
Rome Emperors	.225	128	4135	545	932	181	23	72	473	517	1199	178	.322	.333
Greensboro Grasshoppers	.224	130	4213	710	942	154	28	175	617	581	1414	178	.327	.398
Hickory Crawdads	.222	132	4191	540	931	189	32	88	480	472	1253	230	.309	.346
Brooklyn Cyclones	.222	132	4206	534	932	185	31	82	467	549	1272	181	.319	.339
Wilmington Blue Rocks	.212	132	4160	514	882	179	28	60	443	454	1279	145	.303	.312

CLUB PITCHING

	ERA	G	CG	SHO	SV	IP	H	R	ER	HR	BB	SO	AVG
Hudson Valley Renegades	3.25	131	0	19	26	1120	835	496	405	78	485	1245	.206
Rome Emperors	3.47	128	1	15	29	1110	956	530	428	81	425	1192	.230
Bowling Green Hot Rods	3.49	129	1	12	25	1107	922	493	430	116	392	1262	.222
Jersey Shore BlueClaws	3.81	132	0	13	27	1151	941	574	487	79	535	1322	.222
Greensboro Grasshoppers	3.84	130	0	9	32	1133	945	560	484	115	479	1245	.225
Brooklyn Cyclones	3.94	132	0	14	34	1138	995	570	498	59	494	1198	.233
Aberdeen IronBirds	4.07	132	0	10	32	1146	966	603	518	79	656	1357	.227
Hickory Crawdads	4.27	132	0	10	37	1127	988	606	535	127	515	1365	.231
Greenville Drive	4.29	132	0	12	26	1150	1001	651	548	115	521	1332	.231
Wilmington Blue Rocks	4.30	132	0	4	32	1120	1054	620	535	97	537	1081	.249
Winston-Salem Dash	5.02	132	0	11	30	1137	1046	696	634	123	571	1234	.243
Asheville Tourists	5.11	130	1	3	20	1109	1093	762	630	157	542	1247	.254

CLUB FIELDING

	PCT	PO	A	E	DP
Bowling Green	.981	3322	908	82	62
Winston-Salem	.980	3410	1042	92	97
Brooklyn	.976	3415	1158	113	86
Jersey Shore	.975	3454	991	115	89
Hickory	.974	3382	875	112	64
Wilmington	.972	3359	1095	128	106

	PCT	PO	A	E	DP
Greensboro	.972	3399	1067	129	94
Aberdeen	.971	3437	1015	133	94
Hudson Valley	.970	3360	1102	140	82
Rome	.968	3330	1069	146	93
Greenville	.966	3451	1047	160	82
Asheville	.963	3327	1037	168	86

INDIVIDUAL BATTING

Batter, Club	AVG	G	AB	R	H	2B	3B	HR	RBI	BB	SO	SB
William Bergolla Jr., J. Shore/W-S	.300	89	310	45	93	12	5	1	40	29	38	27
Nick Morabito, Brooklyn	.294	95	377	60	111	15	3	3	22	42	80	48
Cooper Kinney, Bowling Green	.289	87	322	46	93	32	2	10	63	32	80	6
Hendry Mendez, Jersey Shore	.284	90	317	49	90	19	3	3	41	52	52	3
Colton Ledbetter, Bowling Green	.273	109	395	60	108	23	6	16	65	36	126	34
Bryan Gonzalez, Greenvillle	.272	91	327	58	89	13	2	20	59	29	115	15
Braden Taylor, Bowling Green	.269	84	316	71	85	25	5	14	45	61	95	26
Ethan Workinger, Rome	.268	98	366	46	98	15	3	11	52	49	84	8
Luis Baez, Asheville	.263	92	380	53	100	22	0	20	67	22	111	9
Sebastian Walcott, Hickory	.261	116	433	60	113	31	9	10	49	52	125	26

INDIVIDUAL PITCHING

Pitcher, Club	W	L	ERA	G	GS	CG	SV	IP	H	R	ER	BB	SO
Zach Fruit, Aberdeen	3	4	3.03	25	21	0	1	107	78	41	36	55	113
Jose Atencio, Wilmington	4	11	3.41	19	19	0	0	106	121	58	40	33	70
Baron Stuart, Hudson Valley	8	5	3.63	22	22	0	0	109	98	49	44	42	102
Felipe De La Cruz, Brooklyn	3	9	4.25	25	24	0	0	106	103	58	50	45	116
Bryan Caceres, Wilmington	3	9	4.83	26	23	0	0	110	121	65	59	52	81
Nic Swanson, Asheville	3	9	4.88	25	24	0	0	107	95	65	58	47	115
Edinson Batista, Asheville	6	6	5.01	26	16	1	1	115	93	76	64	54	103
Wilber Dotel, Greensboro	9	5	5.33	25	25	0	0	106	98	68	63	54	106
Riley Cornelio, Wilmington	9	11	5.56	26	26	0	0	126	128	84	78	65	114

DEPARTMENT LEADERS

BATTING

OBP	Brayden Taylor, Bowling Green	.389
SLG	Brayden Taylor, Bowling Green	.513
OPS	Brayden Taylor, Bowling Green	.902
Runs	Kevin Kilpatrick, Rome	78
Hits	Kevin Kilpatrick, Rome	114
TB	Sebastian Walcott, Hickory	192
XBH	Sebastian Walcott, Hickory	50
2B	Cooper Kinney, Bowling Green	32
3B	Sebastian Walcott, Hickory	9
HR	Shawn Ross, Greensboro	23
RBI	Luis Baez, Asheville	67
SAC	William Bergolla Jr., J. Shore/W-S	9
BB	Samuel Zavala, Winston-Salem	83
HBP	Justin Janas, Rome	18
HBP	Gavin Dugas, Wilmington	18
SO	Ryan Johnson, Asheville	170
SB	Enrique Bradfield, Aberdeen	59
CS	Emaarion Boyd, Jersey Shore	12

FIELDING

C	PO	Maxwell Romero Jr., Wilmington	.996
	PO	Ian Moller, Hickory	860
	A	Ronald Rosario, Greenville	64
	DP	Ronald Rosario, Greenville	8
	E	Shawn Ross, Greensboro	16
	CS	Maxwell Romero, Wilmington	35
	SB	Ronald Rosario, Greenville	146
	PB	Jordan Dissin, Jersey Shore	18
1B	PCT	No qualifiers	
	PO	Bryan Gonzalez, Greenville	498
	A	Joe Naranjo, Wilmington	43
	A	Justin Janas, Rome	43
	DP	Josiah Sightler, Greensboro	54
	E	Bryan Gonzalez, Greenville	14
2B	PCT	Roc Riggio, Hudson Valley	.958
	PO	Roc Riggio, Hudson Valley	124
	A	Roc Riggio, Hudson Valley	244
	DP	Roc Riggio, Hudson Valley	45
	E	Roc Riggio, Hudson Valley	16
3B	PCT	Wes Kath, Winston-Salem	.936
	PO	Wes Kath, Winston-Salem	79
	A	Wes Kath, Winston-Salem	171
	DP	Sabin Ceballos, Rome	13
	E	Sabin Ceballos, Rome	17
SS	PCT	No qualifiers	
	PO	Kevin Made, Wilmington	106
	A	Jared Serna, Hudson Valley	171
	DP	Kevin Made, Wilmington	41
	E	Sebastian Walcott, Hickory	24
OF	PCT	Kevin Kilpatrick, Rome	.976
	PO	Kevin Kilpatrick, Rome	241
	A	Enrique Bradfield Jr., Aberdeen	8
	A	Kevin Kilpatrick, Rome	8
	DP	Enrique Bradfield Jr., Aberdeen	5
	E	Kevin Kilpatrick, Rome	6

PITCHING

G	Shay Schanaman, Rome	43
GS	Riley Cornelio, Wilmington	26
GF	Jared Johnson, Rome	25
SV	4 tied	8
W	Wilber Dotel, Greensboro	9
W	Riley Cornelio, Wilmington	9
L	3 tied	11
IP	Bryan Caceres, Wilmington	110
H	Riley Cornelio, Wilmington	128
R	Riley Cornelio, Wilmington	84
ER	Riley Cornelio, Wilmington	78
HBP	Edinson Batista, Asheville	18
BB	Riley Cornelio, Wilmington	65
SO	Jackson Baumeister, Aber./B. Green	135
SO/9	Felipe De La Cruz, Brooklyn	9.85
BB/9	Jose Atencio, Wilmington	2.81
WP	Yoniel Curet, Bowling Green	15
HR	Manuel Urias, Asheville	25
AVG	Zach Fruit, Aberdeen	.201

CALIFORNIA LEAGUE LOW-A

Awards selected by Major League Baseball

CHAMPION: Modesto defended its California League title by defeating Lake Elsinore two games to one in the championship series. Second-year manager Zach Vincej guided both Nuts teams to glory. Modesto began the 2024 season with several of the Mariners' top young position players—including Michael Arroyo, Colt Emerson, Jonny Farmelo, Lazaro Montes and Aidan Smith—and raced to a 41-23 record. The team fell to 32-34 in the second half following a series of promotions, an injury to Farmelo and a trade of Smith. Modesto eked out a 2-1 win in the Game 3 finale.

MOST VALUABLE PLAYER: Modesto right fielder Lazaro Montes mashed 13 of his 21 home runs in the Cal League. The 19-year-old Cuban lefthanded hitter put up a .309/.411/.527 slash line in 65 games prior to a June 25 promotion to High-A Everett.

PITCHER OF THE YEAR: Fresno righthander Jace Kaminska dominated Low-A hitters with his high-ride fastball in the low 90s and big-breaking curveball in the mid 70s. The 22-year-old showed the best control in the league by walking just 12 batters in 87.1 innings while striking out 104 and posting a 2.78 ERA. The Rockies drafted Kaminska in the 10th round in 2023 out of Nebraska.

TOP MLB PROSPECT: Born in Cuba, Lazaro Montes moved to the Dominican Republic as a teenager to train with Aldo Marrero, who is best known for his work with Yordan Alvarez. The Mariners signed Montes for $2.5 million in 2022 and have watched him blossom into one of the top power sources in the lower levels of the minor leagues. He led all teenage hitters with 105 RBIs in 2024, when he focused on making more contact without sacrificing power.

MANAGER OF THE YEAR: San Jose manager Ydwin Villegas led the Giants to a league-best 74-57 record before falling to Modesto in the first round of the league playoffs.

Lazaro Montes

BILL MITCHELL

CALIFORNIA LEAGUE ALL-STARS

Pos	Player	Team	AVG	OPS	HR
C	Carlos Rojas	R. Cucamonga	.290	.725	1
1B	Romeo Sanabria	Lake Elsinore	.311	.926	8
2B	Demetrio Crisantes	Visalia	.333	.907	6
3B	Braylen Wimmer	Fresno	.285	.797	14
SS	Tai Peete	Modesto	.269	.751	7
OF	Druw Jones	Visalia	.275	.814	6
OF	Lazaro Montes	Modesto	.309	.938	13
OF	Nate Nankil	Stockton	.285	.861	10
DH	Angel Ortiz	Visalia	.300	.852	8
UT	Luis Suisbel	Modesto	.276	.787	15
Pos	**Pitcher**	**Team**	**G**	**ERA**	**SO**
SP	Jace Kaminska	Fresno	17	2.78	104
SP	Isaiah Lowe	Lake Elsinore	17	3.00	89
SP	Daniel Nunez	Visalia	20	3.21	72
SP	Will Schomberg	Modesto	15	2.69	97
RP	Welinton Herrera	Fresno	23	2.38	62
RP	Cesar Perdomo	San Jose	13	1.26	50

OVERALL STANDINGS

North Division	W	L	PCT	GB	Manager	Attendance	Avg	Last Penn
San Jose Giants (Giants)	74	57	.565	—	Ydwin Villegas	122,824	1,890	2021
Modesto Nuts (Mariners)	73	57	.562	0.5	Zach Vincej	81,310	1,291	2024
Fresno Grizzlies (Rockies)	67	64	.511	7.0	Steve Soliz	256,446	4,007	Never
Stockton Ports (Athletics)	46	84	.354	27.5	Javier Godard	105,952	1,605	2008
South Division	**W**	**L**	**PCT**	**GB**	**Manager**	**Attendance**	**Avg**	**Last Penn**
Lake Elsinore Storm (Padres)	71	58	.550	—	Lukas Ray	102,920	1,559	2022
Visalia Rawhide (D-backs)	67	64	.511	5.0	Dee Garner	123,760	1,934	2019
Rancho Cucamonga Quakes (Dodgers)	65	65	.500	6.5	John Shoemaker	152,895	2,389	2018
Inland Empire 66ers (Angels)	58	72	.446	13.5	Dave Stapleton	137,068	2,142	2013

North: Modesto def. San Jose 2-0. **South:** Lake Elsinore def. Visalia 2-0. **Championship Series:** Modesto defeated Lake Elsinore 2-1.

MINOR LEAGUES

CLUB BATTING

	AVG	G	AB	R	H	2B	3B	HR	RBI	BB	SO	SB	OBP	SLG
Modesto Nuts	.266	130	4521	833	1201	270	55	113	748	664	1316	206	.368	.425
Inland Empire 66ers	.262	130	4473	746	1172	243	52	105	648	545	1266	120	.354	.410
Visalia Rawhide	.253	131	4427	713	1118	202	44	69	611	629	1173	185	.354	.365
San Jose Giants	.249	131	4455	702	1109	229	37	93	646	581	1265	111	.352	.380
Rancho Cucamonga Quakes	.246	130	4357	729	1072	218	45	92	654	643	1304	128	.355	.380
Lake Elsinore Storm	.245	129	4332	757	1062	230	20	01	652	699	1221	115	.360	.367
Fresno Grizzlies	.240	131	4358	642	1048	191	42	83	551	545	1237	192	.336	.361
Stockton Ports	.235	130	4427	615	1040	187	18	82	549	599	1260	120	.341	.341

CLUB PITCHING

	ERA	G	CG	SHO	SV	IP	H	R	ER	HR	BB	SO	AVG
San Jose Giants	4.01	131	0	9	33	1168	1095	639	521	76	509	1178	.246
Fresno Grizzlies	4.10	131	1	8	22	1161	1052	602	529	102	481	1284	.239
Visalia Rawhide	4.36	131	0	3	29	1161	1013	662	562	95	639	1387	.234
Modesto Nuts	4.58	130	0	5	28	1161	1018	707	591	56	687	1248	.232
Lake Elsinore Storm	4.69	129	0	7	28	1145	1127	699	597	84	594	1233	.255
Rancho Cucamonga Quakes	5.28	130	0	7	28	1145	1130	773	672	97	689	1282	.257
Inland Empire 66ers	5.43	130	0	3	23	1155	1142	796	697	83	676	1200	.257
Stockton Ports	5.89	130	0	3	25	1147	1245	859	750	125	630	1230	.275

CLUB FIELDING

	PCT	PO	A	E	DP
Fresno	.976	3484	1166	116	108
Inland Empire	.974	3464	1011	118	103
Visalia	.974	3482	1156	123	121
Lake Elsinore	.971	3435	1099	136	91
San Jose	.967	3504	1142	158	100
Rancho Cucamonga	.967	3434	1128	156	105
Stockton	.967	3440	1035	155	100
Modesto	.962	3482	1134	183	115

INDIVIDUAL BATTING

Batter, Club	AVG	G	AB	R	H	2B	3B	HR	RBI	BB	SO	SB
Angel Ortiz, Visalia	.300	88	327	60	98	22	5	8	53	37	70	4
Andy Perez, Fresno	.292	109	442	61	129	22	7	9	64	24	64	15
Nate Nankil, Stockton	.285	83	298	39	85	20	1	10	56	44	64	3
Braylen Wimmer, Fresno	.285	118	460	94	131	21	3	14	64	48	107	34
Aidan Smith, Modesto	.284	77	296	63	84	26	1	9	42	52	87	28
Milkar Perez, Modesto	.281	93	338	57	95	24	2	6	41	56	84	2
Kenny Castillo, Visalia	.280	88	346	36	97	21	0	4	55	21	93	2
Kendall George, Rancho Cucamonga	.279	86	341	75	95	6	4	1	31	57	83	36
Randy De Jesus, Inland Empire	.277	100	379	62	105	25	4	12	60	34	125	3
Luis Suisbel, Modesto	.276	119	475	76	131	23	4	15	90	49	144	4

INDIVIDUAL PITCHING

Pitcher, Club	W	L	ERA	G	GS	CG	SV	IP	H	R	ER	BB	SO
Ashton Izzi, Modesto	6	5	2.85	26	26	0	0	111	95	43	35	59	95
Bryan Perez, Fresno	5	8	4.26	22	22	0	0	112	105	62	53	54	124
Elijah Dale, Modesto	5	8	4.46	26	24	0	0	109	83	66	54	57	111
Ubert Mejias, San Jose	4	7	4.70	26	24	0	0	123	143	78	64	25	85
Jos Bostick, San Jose	2	9	4.78	26	23	0	1	107	99	62	57	44	121
Barrett Kent, Inland Empire	2	14	6.21	26	26	0	0	113	112	90	78	61	125

DEPARTMENT LEADERS

BATTING

OBP	Druw Jones, Visalia	.409
SLG	Angel Ortiz, Visalia	.471
OPS	Aidan Smith, Modesto	.872
Runs	Braylen Wimmer, Fresno	94
Hits	Luis Susibel, Modesto	131
TB	Luis Susibel, Modesto	207
XBH	Jansel Luis, Visalia	46
XBH	Charlie Pagliarini, Modesto	46
2B	Imanol Vargas, Inland Empire	31
3B	Jansel Luis, Visalia	10
HR	Luis Suisbel, Modesto	15
RBI	Lazaro Montes, Modesto	80
SAC	Estanlin Cassiani, San Jose	19
BB	Druw Jones, Visalia	74
HBP	Elvis Rijo, Stockton	16
HBP	Cesar Quintas, San Jose	16
SO	Myles Naylor, Stockton	173
SB	Caleb Hobson, Fresno	46
CS	Kendall George, Rancho Cuamonga	12

FIELDING

C	PCT	Carlos Rojas, Rancho Cucamonga	.992
	PO	Kenny Castillo, Visalia	724
	A	Darius Perry, Fresno	48
	DP	Oswaldo Linares, Lake Elsinore	5
	E	Oswaldo Linares, Lake Elsinore	15
	CS	Carlos Rojas, Rancho Cucamonga	25
	SB	Carlos Rojas, Rancho Cucamonga	89
	PB	Adrian De Leon, Visalia	16
1B	PCT	No qualifier	
	PO	Darlyn Montero, Stockton	534
	A	Milkar Perez, Modesto	40
	DP	Darlyn Montero, Stockton	50
	E	Milkar Perez, Modesto	13
2B	PCT	No qualifier	
	PO	Tevin Tucker, Fresno	116
	A	Tevin Tucker, Fresno	163
	DP	Tevin Tucker, Fresno	46
	E	Jeral Perez, Rancho Cuca.	11
	E	Adrian Placencia, Inland Empire	11
3B	PCT	No qualifier	
	PO	Luis Suisbel, Modesto	49
	A	Luis Suisbel, Modesto	135
	DP	Luis Suisbel, Modesto	12
	DP	Ruben Santana, Visalia	12
	E	Luis Suisbel, Modesto	18
SS	PCT	Capri Ortiz, Inland Empire	.968
	PO	Capri Ortiz, Inland Empire	141
	A	Capri Ortiz, Inland Empire	247
	DP	Capri Ortiz, Inland Empire	47
	E	Myles Naylor, Stockton	27
OF	PCT	Caleb Hobson, Fresno	.996
	PO	Caleb Hobson, Fresno	227
	A	Jefferson Pena, Visalia	8
	A	Lisbel Diaz, San Jose	8
	DP	3 tied	2
	E	Felix Tena, Fresno	13

PITCHING

G	Alex Martinez, Inland Empire	48
GS	Barrett Kent, Inland Empire	26
GS	Ashton Izzi, Modesto	26
GF	Alex Martinez, Inland Empire	36
SV	Alex Martinez, Inland Empire	12
W	Jenrry Gonzalez, Inland Empire	9
L	Barrett Kent, Inland Empire	14
IP	Ubert Mejias, San Jose	122.2
H	Ubert Mejias, San Jose	143
R	Barrett Kent, Inland Empire	90
ER	Barrett Kent, Inland Empire	78
HBP	Elijah Dale, Modesto	22
BB	Francis Texido, Inland Empire	79
SO	Barrett Kent, Inland Empire	125
SO/9	Josh Bostick, San Jose	10.15
BB/9	Ubert Mejias, San Jose	1.83
WP	Elijah Dale, Modesto	21
HR	Tzu-Chen Sha, Stockton	20
BAA	Elijah Dale, Modesto	.201

CAROLINA LEAGUE LOW-A

Awards selected by Major League Baseball

CHAMPION: Fredericksburg won its first Carolina League title in its fourth season of existence, defeating Kannapolis two games to one in the league championship series. Nationals righthander Travis Sykora struck out nine of the 15 batters he faced in five scoreless innings of the Game 3 finale. Charleston had won the last three Carolina League titles before losing in the first round in 2024.

MOST VALUABLE PLAYER: Two years after older brother Jackson Chourio lit up the Carolina League, Jaison Chourio emerged as a top prospect in his full-season debut with Lynchburg. The 19-year-old, switch-hitting center fielder batted .270/.414/.398 with five home runs and 44 stolen bases in 98 games. He led the league with 86 walks. A fractured left wrist ended Chourio's season in late August.

PITCHER OF THE YEAR: Texas high school righthander Travis Sykora wasn't pleased that he lasted until the third round of the 2023 draft. He wasn't thrilled that the Nationals started him in extending spring training in 2024, either. Once Sykora reported to Fredericksburg in May, he dominated. The 20-year-old led all Low-A pitchers with 129 strikeouts in 85 innings while recording a 2.33 ERA and later starring for the FredNats in the Carolina League playoffs.

TOP MLB PROSPECT: Carolina League managers were so impressed with Jaison Chourio that they voted him best batting prospect, best strike-zone judgment and best defensive outfielder in the league's Best Tools voting. They also chose him as most exciting player.

MANAGER OF THE YEAR: First-year Carolina manager Nick Stanley led the Mudcats to a league-best 78-51 record with one of the youngest rosters in the league.

Jaison Chourio

MIKE JANES/FOUR SEAM IMAGES

CAROLINA LEAGUE ALL-STARS

Pos	Player	Team	AVG	OPS	HR
C	Blake Mitchell	Columbia	.238	.815	18
1B	Caden Connor	Kannapolis	.307	.830	4
2B	Aron Estrada	Delmarva	.296	.795	8
3B	Gleider Figuereo	Down East	.243	.820	12
SS	Cristian Hernandez	Myrtle Beach	.269	.788	5
OF	Jaison Chourio	Lynchburg	.269	.812	5
OF	Rikuu Nishida	Kannapolis	.290	.781	1
OF	Jacob Wetzel	Myrtle Beach	.255	.846	8
DH	Esteban Gonzalez	Lynchburg	.287	.812	6
UT	Cooper Pratt	Carolina	.295	.789	3
Pos	**Pitcher**	**Team**	**G**	**ERA**	**SO**
SP	David Davalillo	Down East	17	1.79	79
SP	Gary Gill Hill	Charleston	22	3.15	105
SP	Jojo Ingrassia	Salem	21	1.85	93
SP	Travis Sykora	Fredericksburg	20	2.33	129
RP	Gerlin Rosario	Charleston	26	2.52	65
RP	Nico Zeglin	Myrtle Beach	16	1.41	57

OVERALL STANDINGS

North Division	W	L	PCT	GB	Manager	Attendance	Avg	Last Penn
Carolina Mudcats (Brewers)	78	51	.605	—	Nick Stanley	119,954	1,904	Never
Fredericksburg Nationals (Nationals)	74	57	.565	5.0	Jake Lowery	232,690	3,693	2024
Salem Red Sox (Red Sox)	70	62	.530	9.5	Liam Carroll	185,784	2,858	2013
Lynchburg Hillcats (Guardians)	67	62	.519	11.0	Jordan Smith	97,282	1,569	2017
Down East Wood Ducks (Rangers)	65	63	.508	12.5	Carlos Maldonado	74,996	1,293	2017
Delmarva Shorebirds (Orioles)	53	78	.405	26.0	Collin Woody	172,786	2,658	*2000
South Division	**W**	**L**	**PCT**	**GB**	**Manager**	**Attendance**	**Avg**	**Last Penn**
Kannapolis Cannon Ballers (White Sox)	70	61	.534	—	Pat Leyland	195,795	3,012	*2005
Charleston RiverDogs (Rays)	69	61	.531	0.5	Sean Smedley	256,695	4,278	2023
Columbia Fireflies (Royals)	68	63	.519	2.0	Jesus Azuaje	217,809	3,457	Never
Myrtle Beach Pelicans (Cubs)	62	67	.481	7.0	Buddy Bailey	249,349	3,958	2016
Fayetteville Woodpeckers (Astros)	55	75	.423	14.5	Ricky Rivera	189,104	3,050	Never
Augusta GreenJackets (Braves)	49	80	.380	20.0	Wynston Sawyer	254,054	3,970	*2008

* South Atlantic League title won prior to 2021 minor league realignment

North: Fredericksburg def. Carolina 2-0. **South:** Kannapolis def. Charleston 2-1. **Championship Series:** Fredericksburg defeated Kannapolis 2-1

MINOR LEAGUES

CLUB BATTING

	AVG	G	AB	R	H	2B	3B	HR	RBI	BB	SO	SB	OBP	SLG
Kannapolis Cannon Ballers	.253	131	4354	692	1103	207	36	74	603	587	1270	167	.350	.368
Carolina Mudcats	.248	129	4175	628	1036	206	27	56	525	552	1033	234	.340	.351
Lynchburg Hillcats	.247	129	4157	648	1026	209	48	59	560	593	1067	281	.347	.363
Fredericksburg Nationals	.232	131	4272	632	989	198	34	73	533	483	1341	231	.323	.345
Down East Wood Ducks	.227	128	4112	506	933	167	29	76	435	407	1312	188	.306	.337
Salem Red Sox	.224	132	4360	580	975	201	30	69	498	522	1332	204	.316	.331
Charleston RiverDogs	.223	130	4114	542	918	189	21	53	464	574	1084	305	.326	.318
Delmarva Shorebirds	.223	131	4165	513	928	166	28	72	451	500	1202	307	.313	.328
Myrtle Beach Pelicans	.223	129	4162	581	927	194	38	100	516	554	1349	157	.322	.360
Fayetteville Woodpeckers	.222	130	4181	570	927	187	17	69	486	508	1213	222	.321	.324
Columbia Fireflies	.219	131	4089	556	897	163	27	79	459	573	1208	220	.324	.330
Augusta GreenJackets	.202	129	4021	433	811	140	26	37	366	522	1266	210	.303	.277

CLUB PITCHING

	ERA	G	CG	SHO	SV	IP	H	R	ER	HR	BB	SO	AVG
Down East Wood Ducks	3.02	128	0	14	29	1100	856	461	369	58	485	1292	.212
Columbia Fireflies	3.48	131	0	9	35	1142	989	535	442	71	443	1107	.232
Salem Red Sox	3.61	132	0	9	33	1164	980	603	467	67	465	1232	.226
Charleston RiverDogs	3.71	130	0	15	36	1126	957	534	464	78	484	1177	.230
Fredericksburg Nationals	3.75	131	0	10	38	1144	1000	564	477	59	516	1183	.235
Kannapolis Cannon Ballers	3.79	131	0	12	24	1127	951	545	474	70	508	1231	.229
Lynchburg Hillcats	3.82	129	2	11	27	1111	986	612	472	83	519	1224	.235
Carolina Mudcats	3.90	129	1	4	39	1111	906	543	482	71	556	1203	.225
Delmarva Shorebirds	3.94	131	0	10	26	1138	990	633	498	55	573	1286	.230
Myrtle Beach Pelicans	4.03	129	1	10	29	1109	906	585	497	58	607	1178	.223
Augusta GreenJackets	4.04	129	1	10	29	1108	997	594	497	65	530	1215	.238
Fayetteville Woodpeckers	4.68	130	2	8	24	1117	952	672	581	82	689	1349	.229

CLUB FIELDING

	PCT	PO	A	E	DP
Charleston	.976	3377	1141	112	102
Columbia Fireflies	.974	3425	1159	120	92
Kannapolis	.973	3380	1093	122	89
Carolina	.973	3334	1091	124	102
Fayetteville	.970	3352	1005	136	78
Down East	.969	3299	1036	137	76
Myrtle Beach	.968	3328	1111	149	79
Fredericksburg	.967	3432	1121	154	92
Augusta	.964	3323	1093	167	82
Salem	.962	3491	1121	184	88
Lynchburg	.957	3333	988	192	87
Delmarva	.957	3413	1040	202	92

INDIVIDUAL BATTING

Batter, Club	AVG	G	AB	R	H	2B	3B	HR	RBI	BB	SO	SB
Caden Connor, Kannapolis	.307	78	300	51	92	24	2	4	55	42	61	6
Aron Estrada, Delmarva	.296	91	348	53	103	18	3	8	43	29	65	31
Yhoswar Garcia, Carolina	.291	104	350	59	102	12	2	1	43	31	68	65
Rikuu Nishida, Kannapolis	.290	90	341	84	99	13	5	1	36	66	51	35
Arturo Disla, Down East	.281	87	320	35	90	17	0	11	50	32	65	2
Echedry Vargas, Down East	.276	97	392	65	108	24	2	14	48	21	89	29
Brandon Pimentel, Fredericksburg	.274	111	420	49	115	22	2	8	85	22	106	18
Ronny Hernandez, Kannapolis	.272	96	345	47	94	16	0	1	46	62	59	0
Juan Baez, Carolina	.272	81	324	47	88	18	4	1	40	25	32	11
Jaison Chourio, Lynchburg	.269	98	334	69	90	24	2	5	58	86	69	44

INDIVIDUAL PITCHING

Pitcher, Club	W	L	ERA	G	GS	CG	SV	IP	H	R	ER	BB	SO
Drew Dowd, Charleston	7	6	2.85	22	19	0	0	111	91	41	35	45	99
Felix Arronde, Columbia	4	8	2.94	23	21	0	1	110	81	44	36	32	103
Gary Gill Hill, Charleston	4	4	3.15	22	21	0	0	109	94	39	38	27	105
Emmanuel Reyes, Columbia	5	5	3.62	23	21	0	0	107	91	50	43	32	85
Santiago Suarez, Charleston	7	6	4.11	23	23	0	0	112	103	55	51	21	115

DEPARTMENT LEADERS

BATTING

OBP	Rikuu Nishida, Kannapolis	.414
SLG	Andy Garriola, Myrtle Beach	.482
OPS	Caden Connor, Kannapolis	.830
Runs	Rikuu Nishida, Kannapolis	84
Hits	Brandon Pimentel, Fredericksburg	115
TB	Blake Mitchell, Columbia	166
XBH	Andy Garriola, Myrtle Beach	43
2B	Andy Lugo, Salem	26
3B	Jacob Wetzel, Myrtle Beach	11
HR	Luis Castillo, Carolina	18
HR	Blake Mitchell, Columbia	18
HR	Andy Garriola, Myrtle Beach	18
RBI	Brandon Pimentel, Fredericksburg	85
SAC	4 tied	5
BB	Jaison Chourio, Lynchburg	86
HBP	Christian Knapczyk, Lynchburg	16
HBP	Brandon Pimentel, Fredericksburg	16
SO	Elijah Green, Fredericksburg	206
SB	Yhoswar Garcia, Carolina	65
CS	Braylin Tavera, Delmarva	13
CS	Yhoswar Garcia, Carolina	13

FIELDING

C PO	Julian Brock, Down East	.991
PO	Julian Brock, Down East	742
A	David Garcia, Carolina	59
DP	David Garcia, Carolina	9
E	Blake Mitchell, Columbia	16
CS	David Garcia, Carolina	42
SB	Will Bush, Fayetteville	149
PB	Will Bush, Fayetteville	12
1B PCT	Brandon Pimentel, Fredericksburg	.993
PO	Brandon Pimentel, Fredericksburg	625
A	Will Verdung, Augusta	52
DP	Brandon Pimentel, Fredericksburg	58
E	Freili Encarnacion, Salem	9
2B PCT	No qualifier	
PO	Everett Cooper, Fredericksburg	107
A	Marvin Alcantara, Salem	155
DP	Lizandro Rodriguez, Columbia	33
E	Alexis Hernandez, Myrtle Beach	11
3B PCT	No qualifier	
PO	Antonio Anderson, Salem	55
A	Austin Charles, Columbia	116
DP	Antonio Anderson, Salem	14
E	Anderson De Los Santos, Delmarva	16
SS PCT	No qualifier	
PO	Armando Cruz, Fredericksburg	136
A	Echedry Vargas, Down East	200
DP	Adrian Santana, Charleston	40
E	Echedry Vargas, Down East	27
OF PCT	Erick Pena, Columbia	.994
PO	Erick Torres, Columbia	273
A	Yophery Rodriguez, Carolina	15
DP	Elijah Green, Fredericksburg	4
E	Elijah Green, Fredericksburg	9
E	George Wolkow, Kannapolis	9

PITCHING

G	Bubba Hall, Fredericksburg	42
GS	Alexander Clemmey, Fred./Lynch.	25
GF	Jesus Mendez, Kannapolis	28
SV	Anthony Arguelles, Fredericksburg	11
W	Royman Blanco, Salem	10
L	Davis Polo, Augusta	9
L	Jacob Cravey, Delmarva	9
IP	Santiago Suarez, Charleston	111.2
H	Travis Sthele, Fredericksburg	111
R	Julio Marte, Fayetteville	69
ER	Raimy Rodriguez, Fayetteville	60
HBP	Raimy Rodriguez, Fayetteville	27
BB	Raimy Rodriguez, Fayetteville	76
SO	Travis Sykora, Fredericksburg	129
SO/9	Santiago Suarez, Charleston	9.27
BB/9	Santiago Suarez, Charleston	1.69
WP	Abel Mercedes, Fayetteville	23
HR	Bryan Polanco, Fredericksburg	11
AVG	Felix Arronde, Columbia	.205

FLORIDA STATE LEAGUE LOW-A

Awards selected by Major League Baseball

CHAMPION: Palm Beach won its second outright title as a Cardinals affiliate, defeating Lakeland two games to one in the Florida State League championship series. Shortstop JJ Wetherholt, drafted seventh overall out of West Virginia in July, shined all postseason by hitting .421/.522/.684 with a home run, a triple, six RBIs, four walks and four runs in five games.

MOST VALUABLE PLAYER: Kevin McGonigle was one of the purest high school hitters in the 2023 draft. The Tigers drafted the lefthanded-hitting Pennsylvania prep shortstop 37th overall with a competitive-balance pick. McGonigle started hot in the FSL and never stopped hitting for Lakeland. When the Tigers promoted him to High-A West Michigan in late July, he had hit .326/.407/.470 with 35 walks and 24 strikeouts in 60 FSL games, which was good for a 150 wRC+ in the run-suppressing environment.

PITCHER OF THE YEAR: Righthander Nestor Lorant began the season in the Daytona bullpen and moved into the rotation in July, making seven starts. The 22-year-old Venezuelan went 8-3, 1.44 with 99 strikeouts and 22 walks in 87.2 innings over 22 appearances.

TOP MLB PROSPECT: The Tigers drafted Indiana prep center fielder Max Clark third overall in 2023, on the heels of his High School Player of the Year season. He thrived at Lakeland in 2024, hitting .286/.386/.421 with seven home runs and 26 stolen bases in 73 games.

MANAGER OF THE YEAR: Palm Beach manager Gary Kendall led his Cardinals to an FSL-best 83-47 record. Palm Beach didn't dominate with power but led the league in a few key categories, including a .243 batting average and, on the pitching side, a 3.10 ERA, 3.6 walk rate per nine innings and just 51 home runs allowed. Playing in cavernous Roger Dean Stadium plays a role in defining Palm Beach's team attributes.

Max Clark

TOM DIPACE

FLORIDA STATE LEAGUE ALL-STARS

Pos	Player	Team	AVG	OPS	HR
C	Ryan Ignoffo	Jupiter	.333	.877	5
1B	Esmerlyn Valdez	Bradenton	.226	.816	22
2B	Devin Saltiban	Clearwater	.237	.774	17
3B	Jesus Baez	St. Lucie	.262	.782	10
SS	Kevin McGonigle	Lakeland	.326	.877	4
OF	Victor Arias	Dunedin	.279	.840	8
OF	Max Clark	Lakeland	.286	.807	7
OF	Jordan Viars	Clearwater	.252	.846	12
DH	Jackson Castillo	Tampa	.256	.790	7
UT	Miguel Villarroel	Palm Beach	.333	.799	1
Pos	**Pitcher**	**Team**	**G**	**ERA**	**SO**
SP	George Klassen	Clearwater	10	0.84	67
SP	Chen-Wei Lin	Palm Beach	22	2.79	123
SP	Nestor Lorant	Daytona	22	1.44	99
SP	Darlin Saladin	Palm Beach	11	1.95	62
RP	Jake Miller	Lakeland	18	1.16	81
RP	Zack Showalter	Palm Beach	24	2.62	59

OVERALL STANDINGS

East Division	W	L	PCT	GB	Manager	Attendance	Avg	Last Penn
Palm Beach Cardinals (Cardinals)	83	47	.638	—	Gary Kendall	45,968	754	2024
Jupiter Hammerheads (Marlins)	65	65	.500	18.0	Nelson Prada	42,543	655	2023
Daytona Tortugas (Reds)	64	64	.500	18.0	Julio Morillo	98,541	1,615	2011
St. Lucie Mets (Mets)	45	84	.349	37.5	Yucary De La Cruz	72,568	1,100	2022
West Division	**W**	**L**	**PCT**	**GB**	**Manager**	**Attendance**	**Avg**	**Last Penn**
Lakeland Flying Tigers (Tigers)	80	50	.615	—	Andrew Graham	40,392	673	2012
Dunedin Blue Jays (Blue Jays)	69	61	.531	11.0	Jose Mayorga	54,366	863	2017
Fort Myers Mighty Mussels (Twins)	66	59	.528	11.5	Brian Meyer	83,409	1,489	2018
Clearwater Threshers (Phillies)	64	63	.504	14.5	Marty Malloy	164,074	2,646	2021
Tampa Tarpons (Yankees)	54	74	.422	25.0	James Cooper	57,578	993	2010
Bradenton Marauders (Pirates)	54	77	.412	26.5	Jim Horner	68,539	1,054	2016

East: Palm Beach def. Daytona 2-0. **West:** Lakeland def. Clearwater 2-0. **Championship Series:** Palm Beach defeated Lakeland 2-1.

CLUB BATTING

	AVG	G	AB	R	H	2B	3B	HR	RBI	BB	SO	SB	OBP	SLG
Palm Beach Cardinals	.243	130	4303	639	1046	213	32	53	561	537	1072	136	.340	.344
Tampa Tarpons	.239	128	4113	626	982	204	31	74	559	565	1177	242	.338	.357
Lakeland Flying Tigers	.236	130	4119	653	971	190	30	82	564	629	1123	215	.345	.356
Fort Myers Mighty Mussels	.235	125	4034	632	949	201	31	84	553	539	1173	195	.337	.363
Clearwater Threshers	.230	127	4017	615	924	182	23	102	550	598	1189	167	.345	.363
Daytona Tortugas	.229	128	4161	573	953	200	22	91	500	555	1269	177	.326	.353
Jupiter Hammerheads	.226	130	4209	530	950	198	34	40	447	497	1232	234	.315	.317
St. Lucie Mets	.223	129	4180	533	933	166	34	55	464	560	1259	140	.328	.319
Dunedin Blue Jays	.223	130	4164	628	928	195	34	101	542	563	1307	158	.332	.359
Bradenton Marauders	.209	131	4160	541	871	184	21	111	477	554	1379	160	.312	.344

CLUB PITCHING

	ERA	G	CG	SHO	SV	IP	H	R	ER	HR	BB	SO	AVG
Palm Beach Cardinals	3.10	130	1	13	38	1147	941	476	395	51	461	1224	.224
Daytona Tortugas	3.67	128	0	11	34	1120	933	537	456	65	549	1200	.227
Lakeland Flying Tigers	3.73	130	0	12	34	1107	931	535	459	78	465	1195	.228
Jupiter Hammerheads	3.89	130	1	10	37	1143	1009	595	494	69	530	1118	.234
Fort Myers Mighty Mussels	4.13	125	0	7	33	1075	969	615	493	82	474	1182	.237
Bradenton Marauders	4.18	131	2	7	27	1136	949	633	527	95	636	1221	.226
Dunedin Blue Jays	4.19	130	2	7	36	1135	919	619	528	99	664	1297	.221
Clearwater Threshers	4.33	127	0	7	29	1081	911	593	520	82	567	1293	.227
St. Lucie Mets	4.57	129	0	7	20	1121	1016	691	569	74	671	1274	.240
Tampa Tarpons	4.81	128	2	4	25	1081	929	676	578	98	580	1176	.230

CLUB FIELDING

	PCT	PO	A	E	DP		PCT	PO	A	E	DP
Lakeland	.976	3321	1125	108	105	Jupiter	.970	3430	1151	141	89
Palm Beach	.976	3442	1154	113	96	Bradenton	.969	3407	1122	146	102
Dunedin	.975	3404	984	113	89	Tampa	.966	3242	1050	151	103
Daytona	.974	3359	1151	121	105	St. Lucie	.965	3362	1099	162	86
Clearwater	.972	3243	964	120	102	Fort Myers	.961	3224	987	170	75

INDIVIDUAL BATTING

Batter, Club	AVG	G	AB	R	H	2B	3B	HR	RBI	BB	SO	SB
Ryan Ignoffo, Jupiter	.330	79	285	42	94	25	2	5	45	32	35	21
Boston Baro, St. Lucie	.288	84	323	46	93	16	4	4	42	41	66	8
Ronald Hernandez, St. Lucie	.271	98	351	41	95	12	2	5	41	47	96	7
Ricardo Cabrera, Daytona	.252	105	404	59	102	22	2	11	55	31	101	19
Brandon Winokur, Fort Myers	.249	94	362	60	90	19	3	14	54	34	115	23
Yerlin Confidan, Daytona	.249	91	346	52	86	28	2	9	41	49	97	16
Cony Morales, Tampa	.248	98	326	51	81	9	1	4	47	48	113	31
Willy Montero, Tampa	.244	120	434	64	106	23	2	7	58	40	103	15
Dylan Jasso, Tampa	.238	93	344	49	82	22	2	9	54	40	99	2
Devin Saltiban, Clearwater	.237	97	346	68	82	13	1	17	53	50	102	22

INDIVIDUAL PITCHING

Pitcher, Club	W	L	ERA	G	GS	CG	SV	IP	H	R	ER	BB	SO
Jake Brooks, Jupiter	9	3	2.28	22	20	1	1	115	94	36	29	23	85
Juan Salas, Palm Beach	9	5	2.62	22	22	1	0	113	93	43	33	25	119
Chen-Wei Lin, Palm Beach	10	5	2.79	22	22	0	0	116	85	41	36	36	123
Jose Davila, Palm Beach	6	5	3.54	22	21	0	0	109	98	47	43	46	113
Gabriel Barbosa, Tampa	5	9	5.09	24	20	2	1	120	118	73	68	38	128

DEPARTMENT LEADERS

BATTING

OBP	Davis Smith, Lakeland	.380
SLG	Arjun Nimmala, Dunedin	.476
OPS	Esmerlyn Valdez, Bradenton	.816
Runs	Roderick Arias, Tampa	78
Hits	Roderick Arias, Tampa	110
TB	Roderick Arias, Tampa	186
XBH	Ariel Almonte, Daytona	42
XBH	Roderick Arias, Tampa	42
2B	Yerlin Confidan, Daytona	28
3B	Roderick Arias, Tampa	8
HR	Esmerlyn Valdez, Bradenton	22
RBI	Jose De La Cruz, Lakeland	75
SAC	Johnny Ascanio, Daytona	5
BB	David Smith, Lakeland	83
HBP	Colby Shade, Jupiter	18
HBP	Ricardo Cabrera, Daytona	18
SO	Roderick Arias, Tampa	171
SB	Colby Shade, Jupiter	38
CS	Roderick Arias, Tampa	13

FIELDING

C PCT	Edward Duran, Dunedin	.981
PO	Edward Duran, Dunedin	660
A	Edward Duran, Dunedin	58
DP	Edward Duran, Dunedin	8
E	Edward Duran, Dunedin	14
CS	Edward Duran, Dunedin	31
SB	Edward Duran, Dunedin	109
PB	Vincent Perozo, St. Lucie	22
1B PCT	No Qualifier	
PO	Ross Frederick, Palm Beach	495
A	Ross Frederick, Palm Beach	34
DP	Dylan Jasso, Tampa	53
E	Brock Vradenburg, Jupiter	11
2B PCT	Jordan McCants, Jupiter	.964
PO	Jordan McCants, Jupiter	162
A	Jordan McCants, Jupiter	212
DP	Johnny Ascanio, Daytona	48
E	Jordan McCants, Jupiter	14
3B PCT	No qualifier	
PO	JT Mabry, Jupiter	47
A	Trey Paige, Palm Beach	118
DP	Hans Montero, Tampa	11
DP	Ricardo Cabrera, Daytona	11
E	JT Mabry, Jupiter	13
E	Colin Houck, St. Lucie	13
SS PCT	No qualifier	
PO	Arjun Nimmala, Dunedin	108
A	Roderick Arias, Tampa	184
DP	Roderick Arias, Tampa	40
E	Roderick Arias, Tampa	22
OF PCT	No qualifier	
PO	Colby Shade, Jupiter	186
A	Yohairo Cuevas, St. Lucie	12
DP	3 tied	4
E	John Cruz, Jupiter	9

PITCHING

G	Cameron Brown, Lakeland	40
GS	Adam Serwinowski, Daytona	25
GF	Henry Gomez, Palm Beach	29
SV	Henry Gomez, Palm Beach	12
W	Chen-Wei Lin, Palm Beach	10
L	Ernesto Mercedes, St. Lucie	11
IP	Gabriel Barbosa, Tampa	120.1
H	Gabriel Barbosa, Tampa	118
R	Gabriel Barbosa, Tampa	73
ER	Gabriel Barbosa, Tampa	68
HBP	Cesar Lares, Fort Myers	20
BB	Carlos Jimenez, Bradenton	66
SO	Gabriel Barbosa, Tampa	128
SO/9	Gabriel Barbosa, Tampa	9.57
BB/9	Jake Brooks, Jupiter	1.81
WP	Ernesto Mercedes, St. Lucie	20
HR	Gabriel Barbosa, Tampa	13
AVG	Chen-Wei Lin, Palm Beach	.204

ARIZONA COMPLEX LEAGUE

Awards selected by Major League Baseball

CHAMPION: The Dodgers swept their way to an Arizona Complex League title by defeating the Giants 7-1 in the single-elimination semifinals and sweeping the D-backs in the best-of-three finals. Keyed by top-of-the-order talents Joendry Vargas and Eduardo Quintero, the Dodgers won by 8-1 and 7-6 margins in the finals. The shortstop Vargas went 5-for-15 with a home run, a double and two RBIs in three ACL postseason games, while the center fielder Quintero reached base five times in three games and scored four runs.

MOST VALUABLE PLAYER: Dominican outfielder Robert Calaz showed big power in his 2023 pro debut and continued to mash in his first year in the U.S. The 18-year-old Rockies prospect was an easy pick for MVP after winning the ACL triple crown with a .349 average, 10 home runs and 45 RBIs. Calaz batted .349/.462/.651 in 49 games and continued to hit at Low-A Fresno following an Aug. 2 promotion.

PITCHER OF THE YEAR: The Guardians went over slot to sign Washington high school lefthander Jacob Bresnahan for $375,000 in the 13th round in 2023. The 6-foot-4 southpaw dominated the ACL as a 19-year-old in 2024, leading the league with 63 strikeouts and posting a 2.54 ERA in 46 innings. Cleveland dealt Bresnahan to the Giants for veteran starter Alex Cobb at the trade deadline.

TOP MLB PROSPECT: Mariners shortstop Felnin Celesten has shined on the field, but trouble staying healthy has limited him to just 32 games in two seasons. Signed out of the Dominican Republic in 2023, Celesten did not debut in his signing year because of a hamstring injury that he suffered during a June intrasquad game. The Mariners assigned him to the ACL for May 4 Opening Day in 2024, and he hit .352/.431/.568 in 32 games before having hamate surgery.

MANAGER OF THE YEAR: Dodgers manager Juan Apodaca helped his club cruise to the top record in the league at 40-20 and ultimately an ACL title.

ARIZONA COMPLEX LEAGUE ALL-STARS

Pos	Player	Team	AVG	OPS	HR
C	Edgardo Ordonez	ACL Brewers	.272	.887	7
1B	Pablo Guerrero	ACL Rangers	.301	.889	7
2B	Demetrio Crisantes	ACL D-backs	.355	.952	1
3B	Eric Bitonti	ACL Brewers	.320	1.031	8
SS	Felnin Celesten	ACL Mariners	.352	.999	3
OF	Yeremi Cabrera	ACL Rangers	.301	1.009	9
OF	Robert Calaz	ACL Rockies	.349	1.113	10
OF	Braylin Morel	ACL Rangers	.307	.982	7
DH	Ricardo Cova	ACL Mariners	.316	.907	5
UT	Welbyn Francisca	ACL Guardians	.328	.941	6

Felnin Celesten

BILL MITCHELL

Pos	Pitcher	Team	G	ERA	SO
SP	Jervis Alfaro	ACL Guardians	11	3.38	48
SP	Jacob Bresnahan	ACL Guardians	11	2.54	63
SP	Eric Dominguez	ACL D-backs	9	2.20	53
SP	David Lorduy	ACL Reds	13	2.76	41
RP	Ricardo Brizuela	ACL White Sox	10	2.33	34
RP	Yendy Gomez	ACL Angels	22	2.84	36

OVERALL STANDINGS

Central Division	W	L	PCT	GB	Manager
ACL D-backs	39	21	.650	—	Gift Ngoepe
ACL Giants	33	27	.550	6	Jacob Heyward
ACL Cubs	30	30	.500	9	Corey Ray
ACL Rockies	29	31	.483	10	Fred Ocasio
ACL Athletics	24	36	.400	15	Tim Esmay

East Division	W	L	PCT	GB	Manager(s)
ACL Dodgers	40	20	.667	—	Juan Apodaca
ACL Angels	32	28	.533	8	Hainley Statia
ACL Reds	31	29	.517	9	Gustavo Molina
ACL Brewers	28	32	.467	12	Rafael Neda
ACL Guardians	27	33	.450	13	Yan Rivera

West Division	W	L	PCT	GB	Manager
ACL Rangers	36	24	.600	—	Guilder Rodriguez
ACL Mariners	28	32	.467	8	Luis Caballero
ACL Royals	25	35	.417	11	Larry Sutton
ACL Padres	24	36	.400	12	Luis Mendez
ACL White Sox	24	36	.400	12	Danny Gonzalez

CLUB BATTING

	AVG	G	AB	R	H	2B	3B	HR	RBI	BB	SO	SB	OBP	SLG
ACL Rangers	.285	60	1871	396	533	118	26	43	346	286	474	106	.388	.445
ACL Dodgers	.277	60	1800	376	498	85	21	40	314	306	526	109	.395	.414
ACL Cubs	.276	60	1803	348	498	101	40	42	285	219	518	98	.361	.446
ACL Rockies	.276	60	1898	355	523	93	32	24	302	260	534	95	.372	.396
ACL Mariners	.275	60	1973	389	542	97	28	50	338	312	529	85	.380	.428
ACL D-backs	.270	60	2040	393	550	104	29	26	321	274	547	115	.363	.387
ACL Giants	.258	60	1854	373	478	91	14	42	300	344	618	73	.389	.390
ACL Padres	.256	60	1756	277	449	104	25	14	232	251	509	95	.359	.367
ACL Reds	.256	60	1858	330	475	83	25	27	262	299	642	98	.372	.371
ACL Royals	.256	60	1921	341	491	96	12	42	283	237	605	89	.349	.384
ACL White Sox	.255	60	1777	286	454	85	18	43	250	211	587	86	.348	.396
ACL Brewers	.251	60	1840	359	462	87	18	34	293	354	529	93	.380	.373
ACL Athletics	.246	60	1869	337	460	85	24	25	272	336	599	49	.374	.357
ACL Angels	.236	60	1759	307	416	85	26	21	249	312	564	79	.364	.350
ACL Guardians	.234	60	1834	321	429	93	14	42	269	304	573	86	.357	.369

CLUB PITCHING

	ERA	G	CG	SHO	SV	IP	H	R	ER	HR	BB	SO	AVG
ACL D-backs	4.20	60	0	1	18	529	464	302	247	30	331	626	.237
ACL Mariners	4.59	60	0	3	7	498	515	338	254	28	276	519	.264
ACL Dodgers	4.82	60	0	2	15	475	403	285	254	30	281	581	.232
ACL Reds	4.97	60	0	3	10	487	499	317	269	41	248	546	.266
ACL Giants	5.03	60	1	1	9	476	433	325	266	36	275	554	.242
ACL Rangers	5.30	60	0	0	13	481	474	344	283	40	276	610	.254
ACL Angels	5.38	60	1	3	15	478	501	337	286	35	268	493	.268
ACL White Sox	5.46	60	0	3	13	455	450	330	276	32	272	567	.258
ACL Rockies	5.50	60	0	1	14	480	521	346	293	29	257	561	.277
ACL Royals	5.60	60	0	1	7	498	533	369	310	38	271	565	.273
ACL Athletics	5.64	60	0	1	10	488	535	399	306	28	262	516	.275
ACL Guardians	5.74	60	0	0	8	483	461	355	308	41	301	598	.249
ACL Padres	6.07	60	0	3	11	458	504	364	309	41	303	522	.281
ACL Cubs	6.23	60	0	2	17	464	427	371	321	29	380	533	.249
ACL Brewers	6.55	60	0	0	15	478	538	406	348	37	304	563	.281

CLUB FIELDING

	PCT	PO	A	E	DP
ACL Dodgers	.973	1424	437	52	45
ACL Rockies	.969	1439	518	62	46
ACL D-backs	.968	1587	545	71	59
ACL Padres	.965	1375	468	66	38
ACL Angels	.965	1435	470	69	42
ACL White Sox	.965	1366	415	65	38
ACL Cubs	.962	1392	457	74	46
ACL Reds	.961	1462	460	79	43

	PCT	PO	A	E	DP
ACL Guardians	.959	1449	419	79	28
ACL Giants	.956	1429	519	89	45
ACL Rangers	.955	1443	439	89	40
ACL Royals	.955	1494	483	94	46
ACL Brewers	.954	1434	469	91	42
ACL Athletics	.949	1464	522	106	46
ACL Mariners	.948	1495	479	108	48

INDIVIDUAL BATTING

Batter, Club	AVG	G	AB	R	H	2B	3B	HR	RBI	BB	SO	SB
Robert Calaz, Rockies	.349	49	172	46	60	12	5	10	45	32	47	12
Eriandys Ramon, Cubs	.340	47	159	31	54	12	6	4	23	7	33	3
Jose De Jesus, Rangers	.335	50	182	46	61	10	5	0	28	21	42	21
Eduardo Quintero, Dodgers	.330	56	185	49	61	7	3	3	37	41	45	29
Welbyn Francisca, Guardians	.328	45	174	47	57	12	2	6	28	25	25	11
Eric Bitonti, Brewers	.320	51	181	42	58	17	3	8	42	43	61	9
Ricardo Cova, Mariners	.316	44	174	40	55	11	3	5	29	25	28	16
Sheng-En Lin, Reds	.308	49	172	29	53	4	6	1	34	36	68	12
Braylin Morel, Rangers	.307	41	153	35	47	10	5	7	37	21	43	12
Roynier Hernandez, Rockies	.305	60	200	38	61	9	1	0	35	39	36	11

INDIVIDUAL PITCHING

Pitcher, Club	W	L	ERA	G	GS	CG	SV	IP	H	R	ER	BB	SO
Johly Garcia, Guardians	1	2	4.22	12	9	0	1	49	54	26	23	11	59
Sadiel Baro, Angels	3	4	4.98	13	7	0	0	56	70	39	31	15	55
Austin Aldeano, Guardians	2	1	5.18	13	7	0	0	49	45	30	28	19	39
Ismael Luciano, Rockies	6	3	6.00	13	3	0	0	51	63	36	34	28	53
Jose Rengel, Giants	3	2	7.50	15	5	0	0	48	54	47	40	37	47

DEPARTMENT LEADERS

BATTING

OBP	Robert Calaz, ACL Rockies	.462
SLG	Robert Calaz, ACL Rockies	.651
OPS	Robert Calaz, ACL Rockies	1.113
Runs	Yeremi Cabrera, ACL Rangers	52
Hits	Yassel Soler, ACL D-backs Black	66
TB	Robert Calaz, ACL Rockies	112
XBH	Eric Bitonti, ACL Brewers	28
2B	Eric Bitonti, ACL Brewers	17
3B	Joan Delgado, ACL Cubs	8
HR	Robert Calaz, ACL Rockies	10
RBI	Robert Calaz, ACL Rockies	45
SAC	4-tied	3
BB	Edwardo Espinal, ACL Angels	43
BB	Eric Bitonti, ACL Brewers	43
HBP	Bernard Moon, ACL Reds	16
SO	Jaron Elkins, ACL Dodgers	80
SO	Josi Novas, ACL Royals	80
SB	Kyle Henley, ACL Reds	35
CS	Yeiker Reyes, ACL Rockies	10

FIELDING

C PCT	Jonathan Linares, ACL Angels	.996
PO	Alberto Barriga, ACL D-backs Black	366
A	Alberto Barriga, ACL D-backs Black	53
DP	Alberto Barriga, ACL D-backs Black	7
E	Jose Caguana, ACL Mariners	8
CS	Alberto Barriga, ACL D-backs Black	24
SB	Edgardo Ordonez, ACL Brewers	69
PB	Stiven Flores, ACL White Sox	14
1B PCT	Athanael Duarte, ACL Angels	.989
PO	Francisco Garcia, ACL Rockies	295
A	Francisco Garcia, ACL Rockies	26
DP	Francisco Garcia, ACL Rockies	38
E	German Ortiz, ACL Athletics	7
2B PCT	Bernard Moon, ACL Reds	.939
PO	Stone Russell, ACL Royals	61
A	Stone Russell, ACL Royals	69
DP	Dervy Ventura, ACL Mariners	24
E	Bernard Moon, ACL Reds	8
E	Ryan Reckley, ACL Giants Black	8
3B PCT	Yassel Soler, ACL D-Backs	.961
PO	Victor Rodriguez, ACL Angels	31
A	Yassel Soler, ACL D-backs Black	89
DP	Yassel Soler, ACL D-backs Black	15
E	Victor Rodriguez, ACL Angels	14
SS PCT	B.Y. Choi, ACL Padres	.962
PO	B.Y. Choi, ACL Padres	76
A	Kelvin Hidalgo, ACL Rockies	120
DP	Kelvin Hidalgo, ACL Rockies	29
E	Josi Novas, ACL Royals	17
OF PCT	Kyle Henley, ACL Reds	1.000
PO	Kyle Henley, ACL Reds	118
A	Alexander Ramirez, ACL Angels	5
DP	Kyle Henley, ACL Reds	2
DP	Carlos Pacheco, ACL Athletics	2
E	Braylin Morel, ACL Rangers	5

PITCHING

G	4 tied	22
GS	Jacob Bresnahan, ACL Guardians	11
	Jeter Martinez, ACL Mariners	11
GF	Yendy Gomez, ACL Angels	18
SV	Darlin Pinales, ACL D-Backs	7
W	Ismael Luciano, ACL Rockies	6
L	Nixon Encarnacion, ACL Angels	5
IP	Sadiel Baro, ACL Angels	56
H	Sadiel Baro, ACL Angels	70
R	Donny Troconis, ACL Athletics	48
ER	Jose Rengel, ACL Giants Black	40
HBP	Ricardo Montero, ACL Dodgers	14
BB/9	Miguel Cruz, ACL Cubs	45
SO	Jacob Bresnahan, ACL Guardians	63
SO/9	Jogly Garcia, ACL Guardians	10.84
BB/9	Jogly Garcia, ACL Guardians	2.02
WP	Samuel Valerio, ACL Brewers	21
Balks	Dawel Serda, ACL D-backs Black	6
HR	Eric Prado, ACL Brewers	8
AVG	Austin Aldeano, ACL Guardians	.250

FLORIDA COMPLEX LEAGUE

Awards selected by Major League Baseball

CHAMPION: The wild card Tigers defeated the Marlins 3-1 in the single-elimination Florida Complex League semifinal game to win a date with the Pirates in the league finals. The Tigers kept rolling in the finals, defeating the Pirates by scores of 4-3 and 12-1 to win the best-of-three series. In the finale, Tigers shortstop Franyerber Montilla went 3-for-4 with two runs, four RBIs and two walks out of the leadoff spot. Tigers righthander Pedro Garcia tossed six innings, allowing one run and picked up the win.

MOST VALUABLE PLAYER: The Red Sox signed shortstop Franklin Arias out of Venezuela in 2023. He performed well in his pro debut that season but reached a new level in his 2024 follow-up. The 18-year-old Arias led the FCL with a .355 average, .471 on-base percentage and .584 slugging percentage, while hitting six home runs and stealing 30 bases in 51 games.

PITCHER OF THE YEAR: Few organizations draft and develop high school pitchers like the Pirates. Their 2023 second-round righthander Zander Mueth is a perfect example. Drafted out of high school in Illinois, he made his pro debut in 2024 and led the FCL with a 1.58 ERA in 51.1 innings while striking out 56 and walking 26. The 19-year-old spent the final month-plus of the season with Low-A Bradenton.

TOP MLB PROSPECT: League MVP Franklin Arias of the Red Sox spent the final six weeks of the season with Low-A Salem. He had one of the best overall seasons by an 18-year-old in 2024, batting .309/.409/.487 in 87 games and vaulting onto the Top 100 Prospects.

MANAGER OF THE YEAR: The Marlins hit an FCL-low 16 home runs in 55 games but finished with the league's best winning percentage on the strength of a 3.03 ERA that was more than a run lower than the next best team. Luis Dorante was rewarded as the league's manager of the year. His Marlins lost to the eventual FCL champion Tigers in the semifinal winner-take-all game.

Franklin Arias

MIKE JANES/FOUR SEAM IMAGES

FLORIDA COMPLEX LEAGUE ALL-STARS

Pos	Player	Team	AVG	OPS	HR
C	Eduardo Tait	FCL Phillies	.321	.877	6
1B	Engelth Urena	FCL Yankees	.301	.984	8
2B	Carlos Caro	FCL Pirates	.305	.853	2
3B	Abrahan Ramirez	FCL Yankees	.348	.960	2
SS	Franklin Arias	FCL Red Sox	.355	1.055	6
OF	Nomar Fana	FCL Tigers	.291	.943	10
OF	Yasser Mercedes	FCL Twins	.331	.989	6
OF	Brian Sanchez	FCL Yankees	.306	.908	4
DH	Jhonny Severino	FCL Pirates	.291	.918	10
UT	Yordany De Los Santos	FCL Pirates	.344	.912	5

Pos	Pitcher	Team	G	ERA	SO
SP	Juan De La Cruz	FCL Marlins	11	1.57	44
SP	Zander Mueth	FCL Pirates	13	1.58	56
SP	Juan Valera	FCL Red Sox	11	1.79	40
SP	Nelfy Ynfante	FCL Cardinals	13	3.29	62
RP	David Matoma	FCL Pirates	15	0.82	28
RP	Manuel Medina	FCL Marlins	18	0.89	36

OVERALL STANDINGS

East Division	W	L	PCT	GB	Manager
FCL Marlins	39	15	.722	—	Luis Dorante
FCL Astros	25	27	.481	13.0	Carlos Lugo
FCL Nationals	25	29	.463	14.0	Luis Ordaz
FCL Mets	23	28	.451	14.5	Sixto Ortega
FCL Cardinals	20	33	.377	18.5	Roberto Espinoza

North Division	W	L	PCT	GB	Manager
FCL Yankees	35	22	.614	—	Ryan Chipka
FCL Tigers	34	23	.596	1.0	Salvador Paniagua
FCL Phillies	33	25	.569	2.5	Shawn Williams
FCL Blue Jays	12	44	.214	22.5	Andy Fermin

South Division	W	L	PCT	GB	Manager(s)
FCL Pirates	36	23	.610	—	Kieran Mattison
FCL Rays	35	24	.593	1.0	Hector Gimenez
FCL Red Sox	35	24	.593	1.0	Jimmy Gonzalez
FCL Twins	28	31	.475	8.0	Seth Feldman
FCL Orioles	23	36	.390	13.0	Christian Frias
FCL Braves	20	39	.339	16.0	Nestor Perez

CLUB BATTING

	AVG	G	AB	R	H	2B	3B	HR	RBI	BB	SO	SB	OBP	SLG
FCL Yankees	.294	57	1740	347	511	101	17	47	305	299	418	111	.407	.452
FCL Red Sox	.262	59	1651	311	433	92	16	35	264	292	468	122	.379	.401
FCL Pirates	.262	59	1627	295	426	84	17	29	240	241	469	98	.367	.388
FCL Phillies	.256	58	1743	317	447	76	10	40	278	251	457	100	.362	.380
FCL Twins	.253	59	1600	255	404	90	10	23	215	257	432	79	.365	.364
FCL Rays	.252	59	1821	349	459	82	24	23	286	313	397	107	.372	.361
FCL Orioles	.242	59	1545	264	374	56	10	26	209	254	364	144	.358	.342
FCL Marlins	.241	55	1730	306	417	89	21	16	243	229	483	208	.343	.345
FCL Mets	.238	52	1559	235	371	69	12	30	187	223	403	62	.343	.355
FCL Tigers	.238	58	1801	332	428	86	8	46	276	315	518	97	.364	.371
FCL Astros	.235	52	1581	236	372	61	15	32	176	217	526	111	.340	.354
FCL Blue Jays	.213	57	1672	210	356	73	12	17	178	254	481	52	.331	.301
FCL Braves	.213	59	1645	233	350	67	14	16	188	273	460	81	.337	.300
FCL Cardinals	.211	53	1666	243	351	59	13	35	197	207	587	82	.314	.325
FCL Nationals	.202	54	1601	228	324	75	5	19	173	267	532	67	.325	.291

CLUB PITCHING

	ERA	G	CG	SHO	SV	IP	H	R	ER	HR	BB	SO	AVG
FCL Marlins	3.03	55	0	6	19	464	306	193	156	26	254	528	.186
FCL Astros	4.14	52	0	3	13	420	336	245	193	26	202	515	.213
FCL Cardinals	4.16	53	0	4	5	444	406	255	205	26	235	510	.240
FCL Rays	4.26	59	0	1	13	483	413	273	229	32	273	486	.229
FCL Pirates	4.28	59	0	5	18	427	366	256	203	33	292	406	.236
FCL Mets	4.32	52	0	4	7	406	345	255	195	24	249	530	.227
FCL Red Sox	4.35	59	0	5	12	432	401	252	209	19	270	417	.249
FCL Phillies	4.41	58	0	4	16	463	447	268	227	34	265	468	.257
FCL Tigers	4.41	58	0	5	12	479	451	277	235	30	289	450	.251
FCL Nationals	4.78	54	0	0	9	441	442	300	234	30	203	448	.258
FCL Twins	4.80	59	0	5	14	423	412	287	226	19	216	445	.251
FCL Yankees	5.23	57	0	0	11	451	399	334	262	43	284	485	.234
FCL Orioles	5.45	59	0	3	6	416	403	299	252	25	285	438	.252
FCL Blue Jays	5.60	57	0	1	3	451	445	327	281	43	281	471	.259
FCL Braves	5.68	59	0	2	11	437	451	340	276	24	294	398	.267

CLUB FIELDING

	PCT	PO	A	E	DP
FCL Tigers	.974	1438	525	52	56
FCL Phillies	.972	1390	508	55	60
FCL Red Sox	.969	1296	466	56	46
FCL Marlins	.966	1391	489	67	41
FCL Blue Jays	.964	1354	461	67	49
FCL Yankees	.962	1352	431	70	34
FCL Rays	.960	1450	516	82	30
FCL Astros	.957	1259	358	72	23

	PCT	PO	A	E	DP
FCL Orioles	.957	1249	389	74	32
FCL Pirates	.956	1280	470	80	52
FCL Nationals	.956	1323	489	84	46
FCL Twins	.954	1270	396	81	30
FCL Mets	.950	1218	383	84	27
FCL Cardinals	.949	1331	435	95	30
FCL Braves	.948	1312	470	97	39

INDIVIDUAL BATTING

Batter, Club	AVG	G	AB	R	H	2B	3B	HR	RBI	BB	SO	SB
Franklin Arias, Red Sox	.355	51	166	41	59	16	2	6	28	34	36	30
Abrahan Ramirez, Yankees	.348	49	158	32	55	14	3	2	24	29	30	6
Yordany De Los Santos, Pirates	.344	57	192	36	66	8	4	5	34	17	39	24
Yasser Mercedes, Twins	.331	51	169	34	56	18	2	6	24	24	39	18
Juan Matheus, Yankees	.321	49	162	30	52	10	1	5	40	29	28	10
Eduardo Tait, Phillies	.321	51	184	29	59	13	1	6	49	13	31	5
Junior Garcia, Braves	.317	42	139	26	44	5	2	3	22	22	41	12
Miguel Rodriguez, Orioles	.308	49	133	26	41	6	0	3	15	20	18	3
Brian Sanchez, Yankees	.306	49	173	40	53	16	4	4	32	23	41	16
Engelth Urena, Yankees	.301	40	133	34	40	11	0	8	31	24	19	5

INDIVIDUAL PITCHING

Pitcher, Club	W	L	ERA	G	GS	CG	SV	IP	H	R	ER	BB	SO
Zander Mueth, Pirates	6	1	1.58	13	12	0	0	51	39	20	9	26	56
Saiber Marte, Yankees	4	0	2.76	12	5	0	0	49	38	21	15	16	44
Neify Ynfante, Cardinals	4	2	3.29	13	11	0	0	52	51	23	19	17	62
Leuris Portorreal, Nationals	2	5	3.83	13	11	0	0	52	55	34	22	21	40
Jose Urbina, Rays	1	3	4.50	13	8	0	0	48	37	26	24	25	45

DEPARTMENT LEADERS

BATTING

OBP	Franklin Arias, FCL Red Sox	.471
SLG	Franklin Arias, FCL Red Sox	.584
OPS	Franklin Arias, FCL Red Sox	1.055
Runs	Nomar Fana, FCL Tigers	44
Runs	Starlyn Caba, FCL Phillies	44
Hits	Yordany De Los Santos, FCL Pirates	66
TB	Jhonny Severino, FCL Pirates	103
XBH	Yasser Mercedes, FCL Twins	26
2B	Yasser Mercedes, FCL Twins	18
3B	Andres Valor, FCL Marlins	5
HR	Nomar Fana, FCL Tigers	10
HR	Jhonny Severino, FCL Pirates	10
RBI	Eduardo Tait, FCL Phillies	49
SAC	Jhonson Pena, FCL Pirates	7
BB	Starlyn Caba, FCL Phillies	51
HBP	Yancel Guerrero, FCL Cardinals	11
SO	Enmanuel Bonilla, FCL Blue Jays	76
SB	Starlyn Caba, FCL Phillies	37
CS	German Ramirez, FCL Astros	10

FIELDING

C PCT	Heriberto Caraballo, FCL Cardinals	.991
A	Richard Ramirez, FCL Pirates	53
DP	Enrique Jimenez, FCL Tigers	18
E	Richard Ramirez, FCL Pirates	10
CS	Richard Ramirez, FCL Pirates	30
SB	Edgleen Perez, FCL Yankees	56
PB	Yirer Garcia, FCL Rays	12
1B PCT	Julio Henriquez, FCL Marlins	.975
PO	Julio Henriquez, FCL Marlins	327
A	Julio Henriquez, FCL Marlins	24
DP	Julio Henriquez, FCL Marlins	30
E	Roiber Niazoa, FCL Braves	10
2B PCT	Carlos Vasquez, FCL Blue Jays	.956
PO	Yoffry Solano, FCL Marlins	61
A	Carlos Vasquez, FCL Blue Jays	97
DP	Carlos Vasquez, FCL Blue Jays	30
E	Gabriel Terrero, FCL Yankees	12
3B PCT	Kendry Chirinos, FCL Blue Jays	.923
PO	Kendry Chirinos, FCL Blue Jays	31
A	Jorgelys Mota, FCL Nationals	69
DP	Kendry Chirinos, FCL Blue Jays	9
E	Yancel Guerrero, FCL Cardinals	13
SS PCT	Starlyn Caba, FCL Phillies	.974
PO	Fabian Lopez, FCL Marlins	71
A	Starlyn Caba, FCL Phillies	119
DP	Starlyn Caba, FCL Phillies	36
E	Fabian Lopez, FCL Marlins	17
OF PCT	Andres Valor, FCL Marlins	.976
PO	Enmanuel Bonilla, FCL Blue Jays	108
A	Brando Mayea, FCL Yankees	5
DP	Brando Mayea, FCL Yankees	3
E	Enmanuel Bonilla, FCL Blue Jays	6

PITCHING

G	Samuel Fabian, FCL Cardinals	21
GS	Zander Mueth, FCL Pirates	12
	Leonel Sequera, FCL Cardinals	12
GF	Andy Rodriguez, FCL Rays	17
SV	Jose Fernandez, FCL Marlins	6
W	Roberto Medina, FCL Rays	6
W	Yordy Herrera, FCL Cardinals	6
L	4 tied	6
IP	Nelfy Ynfante, FCL Cardinals	52
H	Wilmer Blanco, FCL Phillies	56
R	Wilmer Blanco, FCL Phillies	41
ER	Justin Militello, FCL Braves	36
ER	Josue Arias, FCL Marlins	36
SO	Nelfy Ynfante, FCL Cardinals	62
SO/9	Nelfy Ynfante, FCL Cardinals	10.73
BB/9	Nelfy Ynfante, FCL Cardinals	2.94
WP	Josue Arias, FCL Marlins	22
Balks	Omar Victorino, FCL Mets	8
HR	Alexis Torres, FCL Pirates	6
AVG	Saiber Marte, FCL Yankees	.204

ALL-STAR **FUTURES GAME**

BY GEOFF PONTES

We have singled out the prospects whose tools shined brightest in this year's Futures Game, which was won by the National League 6-1 thanks to home runs by Cam Collier and Drake Baldwin.

Best Player: Emiliano Teodo, RHP, Rangers

Teodo thrilled the home crowd as the American League starter. He became the first pitcher in Futures Game history to throw two perfect innings. Teodo needed 14 pitches in total, including just six pitches in the first inning, to complete the feat. Teodo is one of the Rangers' better pitching development stories in recent years, as his revamped sinker shape has put him on the road to success.

Best Hitter: Drake Baldwin, C, Braves

Baldwin hit one of the two NL homers. His solo shot in the top of the sixth was the hardest-hit ball of the game. The smash came off the bat at 107.3 mph at 21 degrees, traveling 411 feet. Baldwin also drove in a run in his first at-bat, as his sacrifice fly to center field brought in Ethan Salas.

Best Power: Cam Collier, 3B, Reds

Collier had one of the best batting practices alongside the Guardians' Ralphy Velazquez, showing consistent pull-side power in BP. Collier hit the first home run of the game to open the scoring in the third. He got hold of a 1-0 fastball down the heart of the plate and deposited it into the home bullpen in right-center field. The ball came off the bat at 105.1 mph at 32 degrees traveling 409 feet, as estimated by Statcast.

Best Fastball: Winston Santos, RHP, Rangers

Santos led all Futures Game pitchers with four swinging strikes against his four-seam fastball. Santos sat 98.1 mph on his fastball, ranging between 15 inches of induced vertical break and 19.5 inches of induced vertical break. His best fastball was a swinging strike against Druw Jones where he hit 97.2 mph and 19.5 inches of induced vertical break with 7.8 inches of horizontal run.

Best Breaking Ball: Brandon Sproat, RHP, Mets

Sproat tied with the Reds' Rhett Lowder for the most swinging strikes against his breaking ball. Sproat sat 85.6 mph on his slider with 11 to 14 inches of horizontal break and north of 2,700 rpms. He generated two whiffs on the three sliders he threw during his one inning of work at the Futures Game.

FUTURES GAME BOX SCORE

NATIONAL LEAGUE 6, AMERICAN LEAGUE 1
JULY 13 IN DALLAS

NL Futures	AB	R	H	RBI	AL Futures	AB	R	H	RBI
Crawford,LF	3	0	1	0	Clark,CF	4	0	1	0
Triantos,LF	1	0	0	0	Young,2B	3	0	1	0
Crews,RF	3	0	0	0	Keaschall,2B	1	0	0	0
Johnson,2B	2	1	1	0	Walcott,SS	2	0	0	0
Perez,2B	2	1	1	0	Mayer,SS	2	0	0	0
Eldridge,1B	2	1	1	0	Basallo,C	1	0	0	0
DeLosSantosPH-1B	2	0	0	1	Teel,C	2	0	2	0
Salas,C	2	1	1	0	Isaac,1B	4	0	0	0
Liranzo,PH-C	1	0	0	0	Montgomery,3B	0	0	0	0
Jones,CF	1	0	0	1	Lee,3B	1	0	0	0
Collier,3B	2	1	1	1	Chourio,LF	2	0	1	1
Shaw,PH-3B	2	1	0	0	Simpson,LF	1	0	0	0
Miller,SS	1	0	0	1	Ford,DH	0	0	0	0
Pratt,SS	1	0	0	0	Velazquez,PH-DH	1	0	0	0
Baldwin,DH	2	1	1	2					
Totals	**27**	**6**	**7**	**6**	**Totals**	**27**	**0**	**5**	**1**

NATIONAL LEAGUE	**001**	**301**	**1**	**6**	**7**	**3**
AMERICAN LEAGUE	**000**	**100**	**0**	**1**	**5**	**1**

NL: HR: Collier (1, 3rd inning off Dana, 0 on, 0 out); Baldwin (1, 6th inning off Perez, F, 0 on, 1 out). **TB:** Baldwin 4; Collier 4; Crawford; Eldridge; Johnson; Perez, J; Salas. **RBI:** Baldwin 2 (2); Collier (1); De Los Santos (1); Jones, D (1); Miller (1). **Runners left in scoring position, 2 out:** Crawford 2; Shaw 2. **SF:** Baldwin. **Team RISP:** 1-for-6. **Team LOB:** 7. **SB:** Crews (1, 2nd base off Morales/Teel).

AL: 2B: Teel 2 (2, Lowder, Chandler). **TB:** Chourio; Clark; Teel 4; Young. **RBI:** Chourio (1). **Runners left in scoring position, 2 out:** Isaac; Jones; Lee; Young 2; Clark. **GIDP:** Basallo. **Team RISP:** 1-for-11. **Team LOB:** 11. **SB:** Jones (1, 2nd base off White, T/Salas). **E:** Simpson (1, fielding).

NL Futures	IP	H	R	ER	BB	SO	AL Futures	IP	H	R	ER	BB	SO
Dollander	1	1	0	0	1	0	Teodo	2	0	0	0	0	1
Meyer	1	1	0	0	1	2	Dana	1	2	1	1	0	1
Sproat	1	0	0	0	0	0	Schultz	0.1	3	3	3	1	1
White	0.2	1	1	1	3	1	Blugabugh	0.2	0	0	0	0	0
Snelling	0.1	0	0	0	0	0	Morales	0.2	0	0	0	1	2
Lowder	1	0	0	0	0	1	Kudrna	0.1	0	0	0	1	0
Mathews	1	0	0	0	2	2	Perez	1	1	1	1	0	0
Chandler	1	1	0	0	1	1	Santos	1	1	1	0	1	1
Totals	7	5	1	1	5	7	Totals	7	7	6	5	4	6

WP: Blubaugh; Santos. HBP: Miller (by Schultz); Crews (by Morales). **Pitches-strikes:** Dollander 16-8; Meyer 18-10; Sproat 12-8; White, T 28-11; Snelling 4-3; Lowder 14-10; Mathews 13-9; Chandler 14-9; Teodo 14-12; Dana 14-8; Schultz 23-12; Blubaugh 3-2; Morales 22-11; Kudrna 8-1; Perez, F 11-7; Santos 24-16.. **Inherited runners-scored:** Snelling 3-0; Blubaugh 3-1; Kudrna 2-0.

Umpires: HP: Felix Neon. **1B:** Matt Blackborow. **2B:** Casey James. **3B:** Sean Sparling. **Official Scorer:** Will Rudd.

Weather: 74 degrees, roof closed. **Wind:** 0 mph. **First Pitch:** 3:12 p.m. **T:** 2:02.

Best Changeup: Bubba Chandler, RHP, Pirates

Chandler threw just four changeups, and only one was a strike, but he was the only pitcher to generate a swinging strike from his offspeed. Chandler had one of the top fastballs in the game as well.

MINOR LEAGUE BEST TOOLS

	INTERNATIONAL LEAGUE	PACIFIC COAST LEAGUE	EASTERN LEAGUE	SOUTHERN LEAGUE	TEXAS LEAGUE
Best Batting Prospect	Jackson Holliday	Adrian Del Castillo	Marcelo Mayer	Brooks Baldwin	Dalton Rushing
Best Power Prospect	James Wood	Shay Whitcomb	Roman Anthony	Joe Mack	Deyvison De Los Santos
Best Strike-Zone Judgment	Jackson Holliday	Will Wagner	Adael Amador	Chandler Simpson	Liam Hicks
Best Baserunner	Luisangel Acuña	Cade Marlowe	Adael Amador	Chandler Simpson	Cooper Bowman
Fastest Baserunner	Victor Scott II	Greg Jones	Joe Lampe	Chandler Simpson	Tyler Tolbert
Best Pitching Prospect	David Festa	AJ Blubaugh	Brandon Sproat	Noah Schultz	Emiliano Teodo
Best Fastball	Paul Skenes	Michel Otañez	Bubba Chandler	Jacob Misiorowski	Edgardo Henriquez
Best Breaking Pitch	Anthony Maldonado	Hans Crouse	Zach Messinger	Cade Horton	Emiliano Teodo
Best Changeup	Devin Sweet	Carson Whisenhunt	Ryan Webb	Drew Thorpe	Tink Hence
Best Control	Bowden Francis	Davis Daniel	Tyler Stuart	Drew Parrish	Zebby Matthews
Best Reliever	Walter Pennington	Tyler Ferguson	Seth Halvorsen	Hayden Harris	Troy Taylor
Best Defensive C	Dillon Dingler	Carlos Perez	Kyle Teel	Edgar Quero	Cooper Johnson
Best Defensive 1B	Troy Johnston	Ryan Noda	Jake Holton	Tim Elko	Dillan Shrum
Best Defensive 2B	Connor Norby	Jesus Bastidas	Jimmy Glowenke	Cody Morissette	Frainyer Chavez
Best Defensive 3B	Devin Mann	Andres Chapparo	Ben Cowles	Matt Shaw	Ben Williamson
Best Defensive SS	Cam Devanney	Mason McCoy	Tsung-Che Cheng	Carson Williams	Keyber Rodriguez
Best Infield Arm	Colson Montgomery	Casey Schmitt	Ryan Ritter	Carson Williams	Jack Winkler
Best Defensive OF	Dylan Crews	Pedro Leon	Jud Fabian	Jakob Marsee	Denzel Clarke
Best OF Arm	Matt Gorski	Sandro Fabian	Jud Fabian	Mason Auer	Jose Ramos
Most Exciting Player	James Wood	Shay Whitcomb	Roman Anthony	Carson Williams	Emmanuel Rodriguez
Best Manager Prospect	Chad Tracy	Travis Barbary	Chad Epperson	Sergio Santos	Carlos Cardoza

	MIDWEST LEAGUE	NORTHWEST LEAGUE	SOUTH ATLANTIC LEAGUE	CALIFORNIA LEAGUE	CAROLINA LEAGUE	FLORIDA STATE LEAGUE
Best Batting Prospect	Alex Freeland	Kyle Karros	Justin Crawford	Colt Emerson	Jaison Chourio	Kevin McGonigle
Best Power Prospect	Chris Newell	Lazaro Montes	Xavier Isaac	Lazaro Montes	Blake Mitchell	Cristian Feliz
Best Strike-Zone Judgment	Luke Adams	Jake Snider	Termarr Johnson	Braedon Karpathios	Jaison Chourio	Kevin McGonigle
Best Baserunner	Dylan O'Rae	Caleb Ketchup	Chandler Simpson	Jonah Cox	Adrian Santana	George Lombard Jr.
Fastest Baserunner	Homer Bush Jr.	Jonah Cox	Chandler Simpson	Kendall George	Elijah Green	Max Clark
Best Pitching Prospect	Quinn Mathews	Chase Dollander	Noah Schultz	Brody Hopkins	Gary Gill Hill	Thomas White
Best Fastball	Edgardo Henriquez	Chase Dollander	Luis Perales	Reynaldo Yean	Jarlin Susana	George Klassen
Best Breaking Pitch	Quinn Mathews	Spencer Giesting	Noah Schultz	Brody Hopkins	Alex Clemmey	Cade Smith
Best Changeup	Craig Yoho	Ryan Costeiu	Josh Cornielly	Dylan Carmouche	Alejandro Rosario	Luis Serna
Best Control	Austin Peterson	Sean Sullivan	Hunter Barco	Jace Kaminska	Manuel Rodriguez	Fernando Perez
Best Reliever	Edgardo Henriquez	Zach Agnos	Daniel Harper	Welinton Herrera	Bryan Magdaleno	Josh Ekness
Best Defensive C	Ethan Salas	Juan Flores	Shawn Ross	Darius Perry	Blake Mitchell	Connor Burns
Best Defensive 1B	Brett Squires	Matt Coutney	Keaton Anthony	Bryce Eldridge	Caden Connor	Yohairo Cuevas
Best Defensive 2B	Jadher Areinamo	Brock Rodden	William Bergolla Jr.	Michael Arroyo	Rikuu Nishida	Kevin McGonigle
Best Defensive 3B	Luke Adams	Kyle Karros	Jack Brannigan	Andy Perez	Gleider Figuereo	Javier Rivas
Best Defensive SS	Gregory Barrios	Dyan Jorge	Kevin Made	Leodalis De Vries	Cooper Pratt	George Lombard Jr.
Best Infield Arm	Jose Devers	Kyle Karros	Sebastian Walcott	Andy Perez	Austin Charles	Roderick Arias
Best Defensive OF	Luis Lara	Cole Carrigg	Enrique Bradfield Jr.	Druw Jones	Jaison Chourio	Avery Owusu-Asiedu
Best OF Arm	Luis Lara	Cole Carrigg	Cole Gabrielson	Ryan Lasko	Brenner Cox	Raylin Heredia
Most Exciting Player	Max Clark	Cole Carrigg	Sebastian Walcott	Leodalis De Vries	Jaison Chourio	Aidan Miller
Best Manager Prospect	Victor Estevez	Robinson Cancel	Greg Brodzinski	Zach Vincej	Nick Stanley	Jose Mayorga

DOMINICAN SUMMER LEAGUE

Awards selected by Major League Baseball

CHAMPION: Red Sox Red defeated the Angels two games to one. In the Game 3 finale, the Red Sox won 6-0 and allowed just two hits.

MOST VALUABLE PLAYER: Dodgers Mega shortstop Emil Morales led the league with 14 home runs and a 1.169 OPS as a 17-year-old.

PITCHER OF THE YEAR: Angels righthander Ubaldo Soto led the DSL with eight wins and ranked second with a 1.29 ERA in 56 innings.

TOP MLB PROSPECT: The Dodgers' Emil Morales hit .342/.478/.691 in 46 games and had one of the better DSL seasons of recent vintage.

MANAGER OF THE YEAR: Giants Black manager Juan Ciriaco guided his club to a league-best .755 winning percentage, going 40-13.

DOMINICAN SUMMER LEAGUE ALL-STARS

Pos	Player	Team	AVG	OPS	HR
C	Rainiel Rodriguez	DSL Cardinals	.345	1.145	10
1B	Jesus Alexander	DSL Giants Black	.381	1.034	5
2B	Carlos Renzullo	DSL Rockies	.360	.902	1
3B	Jesus Made	DSL Brewers 1	.331	1.012	6
SS	Emil Morales	DSL LAD Mega	.342	1.169	14
OF	Eduardo Beltre	DSL Twins	.326	1.071	11
OF	Arnaldo Lantigua	DSL LAD Mega	.301	1.005	11
OF	Jordan Sanchez	DSL Orioles Orange	.333	1.037	6
DH	Alessander De La Cruz	DSL Rockies	.318	.948	7
UT	Luis Peña	DSL Brewers 1	.393	1.040	1
Pos	**Pitcher**	**Team**	**G**	**ERA**	**SO**
SP	Cesar Aquino	DSL Pirates Gold	12	0.98	37
SP	Franyer Herrera	DSL NYY Bombers	12	2.01	64
SP	Christian Lopez	DSL Reds	13	2.09	64
SP	Ubaldo Soto	DSL Angels	12	1.29	56
RP	Davidxon Lara	DSL Angels	22	0.55	33
RP	Ramon Suarez	DSL Blue Jays	14	0.79	36

DSL CHAMPIONSHIP: DSL Red Sox Red defeated DSL Angels 2-1

CENTRAL

Team	W	L	PCT	GB
DSL Giants Black	40	13	.755	—
DSL Angels	38	18	.679	3.5
DSL Arizona Red	36	20	.643	5.5
DSL Blue Jays	30	24	.556	10.5
DSL Cardinals	26	27	.491	14.0
DSL Nationals	23	30	.434	17.0
DSL White Sox	20	35	.364	21.0
DSL Mariners	16	39	.291	25.0

NORTHWEST

Team	W	L	PCT	GB
DSL Orioles Orange	38	18	.679	—
DSL Brewers 1	32	23	.582	5.5
DSL LAD Bautista	29	26	.527	8.5
DSL CLE Mendoza	26	24	.520	9.0
DSL Padres Gold	26	29	.473	11.5
DSL Rojos	25	30	.455	12.5
DSL Cubs Red	19	35	.352	18.0
DSL Pirates Black	19	36	.345	18.5

EAST

Team	W	L	PCT	GB
DSL Marlins	33	23	.589	—
DSL NYY Bombers	30	25	.545	2.5
DSL Tigers 1	30	26	.536	3.0
DSL Giants Orange	29	27	.518	4.0
DSL Colorado	28	27	.509	4.5
DSL Rangers Blue	26	28	.481	6.0
DSL Mets Blue	21	33	.389	11.0
DSL Phillies Red	21	34	.382	11.5

NORTH

Team	W	L	PCT	GB
DSL CLE Goryl	35	19	.648	—
DSL Pirates Gold	32	22	.593	3.0
DSL Brewers 2	30	23	.566	4.5
DSL Cubs Blue	28	26	.519	7.0
DSL Red Sox Blue	27	26	.509	7.5
DSL LAD Mega	25	29	.463	10.0
DSL Tampa Bay	24	32	.429	12.0
DSL Astros Orange	23	32	.418	12.5
DSL Royals Fortuna	17	34	.333	16.5

WEST

Team	W	L	PCT	GB
DSL Red Sox Red	42	14	.750	—
DSL Reds	37	18	.673	4.5
DSL Royals Ventura	32	22	.593	9.0
DSL Orioles Black	26	29	.473	15.5
DSL Astros Blue	25	29	.463	16.0
DSL Rays	24	32	.429	18.0
DSL Athletics	22	33	.400	19.5
DSL Braves	15	37	.288	25.0
DSL Padres Brown	15	41	.268	27.0

SOUTH

Team	W	L	PCT	GB
DSL Rangers Red	39	17	.696	—
DSL Tigers 2	38	18	.679	1.0
DSL Rockies	37	18	.673	1.5
DSL Twins	30	25	.545	8.5
DSL Mets Orange	27	27	.500	11.0
DSL Phillies White	26	29	.473	12.5
DSL Miami	26	30	.464	13.0
DSL NYY Yankees	17	37	.315	21.0
DSL Arizona Black	12	43	.218	26.5

INDIVIDUAL BATTING LEADERS

Player, Team	AVG	G	AB	R	H	2B	3B	HR	RBI	BB	SO	SB
Luis Peña, Brewers	.393	44	163	43	64	16	6	1	36	15	15	39
Jesus Alexander, Giants	.381	47	176	26	67	17	3	5	40	19	28	1
Carlos Renzullo, Rockies	.360	50	197	57	71	8	3	1	21	33	14	18
Rainiel Rodriguez, Cardinals	.345	41	142	35	49	12	3	10	38	30	25	1
Juan Ortuno, Brewers	.344	49	154	29	53	6	3	3	34	29	27	22
Ronald Ramirez, Tigers	.343	42	140	37	48	9	0	1	18	24	29	6
Emil Morales, Dodgers	.342	46	152	48	52	11	0	14	46	40	45	12
Juneiker Caceres, Guardians	.340	40	141	28	48	11	6	0	33	19	18	9
Jeremy Ciriaco, Rockies	.339	47	189	52	64	9	1	1	32	26	29	21
Victor Cardoza, Phillies	.333	45	162	34	54	12	2	7	25	12	44	16

INDIVIDUAL PITCHING LEADERS

Player, Team	W	L	ERA	G	GS	CG	SV	IP	H	R	ER	BB	SO
Cesar Aquino, Pirates	6	1	0.98	12	6	0	0	46	28	9	5	7	37
Ubaldo Soto, Angels	8	0	1.29	12	12	0	0	56	41	11	8	20	56
Keiverson Ramirez, Cardinals	4	2	1.62	11	11	0	0	50	33	12	9	12	48
Marlon Franco, Giants	3	1	1.65	12	9	0	0	49	38	19	9	5	46
Manuel Osorio, Guardians	2	2	1.71	11	10	0	0	47	24	13	9	25	43
Stharlin Torres, Red	2	1	1.76	14	10	0	0	56	35	13	11	13	51
Jormy Nivar, Rangers	6	2	1.76	11	10	0	0	46	38	17	9	5	50
Yermain Ruiz, Red Sox	3	1	1.77	11	11	0	0	46	27	13	9	15	37
Silvano Hechavarria, Blue Jays	5	2	1.84	10	10	0	0	49	28	11	10	16	57
Franyer Herrera, Yankees	5	1	2.01	12	11	0	0	49	43	17	11	17	64

FREITAS AWARDS

Excellence That Starts Off The Field

Triple-A

SACRAMENTO (PACIFIC COAST)

Even as rumors eventually became reality, there was still nothing more important to the Sacramento River Cats than delivering on a highly-anticipated 25th anniversary season.

Did they ever.

The Triple-A affiliate of the Giants—and soon to be temporary host to the Athletics at Sutter Health Park—earned the Freitas Award this season not only for their grace and execution under difficult circumstances in 2024, but for a banner year for the organization.

On the field, the River Cats finished 80-70 on the season, good for 13 more wins than 2023.

Off the field, the team enjoyed a significant boost in attendance in multiple metrics that serve as a true hallmark of their overall success.

The River Cats saw an 8.8% increase in per-game turnstile numbers, sold their highest number of season ticket memberships since their inaugural year in 2000 and averaged 5,463 fans per game, eclipsing more than 400,000 total fans over the course of the season for the first time in the post-pandemic era.

Double-A

SOMERSET (EASTERN)

A standard of excellence that began in the independent Atlantic League is alive and well for the Somerset Patriots.

Now affiliated with the Yankees, the franchise has thrived on and off the field for 25 years.

The recognition continues a tradition as one of the top organizations in professional baseball, one that traces back to the team's beloved late founder Steve Kalafer. It is proudly carried on today by his sons, co-chairmen Jonathan and Josh Kalafer.

Since the opening of what's now called TD Bank Ballpark in 1999, those fans have been coming out in big numbers. First they supported the most successful franchise in Atlantic League history, and now they root for the successful Double-A affiliate of the Yankees. Somerset has made three straight postseason appearances.

Longtime president and GM Patrick McVerry made sure the Patriots made a smooth transition from independent to affiliated baseball, a journey that began in 2021 when MLB took over operation of the minor leagues.

The feeling appears to be mutual, with the Yankees-Somerset partnership having been an unquestionable success over its first four years.

Class A

COLUMBIA (CAROLINA)

The list of things to be proud of in looking back at the 2024 season was a lengthy one for Columbia Fireflies president Brad Shank.

Sure, there was success on the field with a franchise-best .519 winning percentage and record-tying 68 wins in the Low-A Carolina League as an affiliate of the Royals.

And yes, there's plenty of tangible evidence of off-field success as well, whether that's drawing 217,809 fans to beautiful Segra Park last year, exceptional turnouts for non-baseball events or even a record-setting turnout for the early-March Clemson-South Carolina college game that helps make up the Palmetto Series.

But what stands out the most for Shank was working hard to create a culture where his staff genuinely wants to go to work every day and can express their creativity.

That in turn creates a positive atmosphere at the ballpark for a dedicated fanbase, as well as a willingness to integrate the franchise into a community that continues to embrace it.

—MIKE ASHMORE

MINOR LEAGUES

LAST 10 WINNERS

TRIPLE-A	DOUBLE-A	CLASS A	SHORT-SEASON
2013: Indianapolis (International)	**2013:** Tulsa (Texas)	**2013:** Clearwater (Florida State)	**2010:** Idaho Falls (Pioneer)
2014: Charlotte (International)	**2014:** Montgomery (Southern)	**2014:** West Michigan (Midwest)	**2011:** Vancouver (Northwest)
2015: Salt Lake (Pacific Coast)	**2015:** Richmond (Eastern)	**2015:** Myrtle Beach (Carolina)	**2012:** Billings (Pioneer)
2016: Round Rock (Pacific Coast)	**2016:** Pensacola (Southern)	**2016:** San Bernardino (California)	**2013:** State College (NY-Penn)
2017: Fresno (Pacific Coast)	**2017:** Reading (Eastern)	**2017:** Charleston (South Atlantic)	**2014:** Brooklyn (NY-Penn)
2018: Oklahoma City (Pacific Coast)	**2018:** Tennessee (Southern)	**2018:** Winston-Salem (Carolina)	**2015:** Grand Junction (Pioneer)
2019: Nashville (Pacific Coast)	**2019:** Tulsa (Texas)	**2019:** Lexington (South Atlantic)	**2016:** Pulaski (Appalachian)
2021: Las Vegas (Pacific Coast)	**2021:** Hartford (Eastern)	**2021:** Greensboro (South Atlantic)	**2017:** Hillsboro (Northwest)
2022: St. Paul (International)	**2022:** Portland (Eastern)	**2022:** Wisconson (Midwest)	**2018:** Spokane (Northwest)
2023: Albuquerque (Pacific Coast)	**2023:** Amarillo (Texas)	**2023:** South Bend (Midwest)	**2019:** Hudson Valley (NY-Penn)

Salt River nabs AFL title

BILL MITCHELL

Salt River won the Arizona Fall League championship for the first time since 2019.

BY JOSH NORRIS

For the first time since 2019, the Salt River Rafters are champions of the Arizona Fall League.

The Rafters earned the crown by upending the Surprise Saguaros—winners of the league's last two titles—by a 3-2 score while playing as the visiting team at their home park of Salt River Fields.

Surprise opened the scoring when Rangers prospect Max Acosta reached Salt River starter Dustin Saenz for an RBI single. Salt River answered with single runs in each of the next two frames. The first on a Ben Ross sacrifice fly, which sent Robert Hassell III scampering home. An inning later, Twins outfielder Kala'i Rosario gave the Rafters the lead on a double to left field.

Rosario drove in Salt River's final run two innings later on a double play in the fifth inning, and Surprise answered on another Acosta single in the bottom of the frame.

From that point on, it was a battle of the bullpens. Royals righthander Luinder Avila and Rangers fireballer Marc Church held serve the rest of the way, but their zeroes were matched by Salt River's trio of Alfredo Morillo (Diamondbacks), Luis Pacheco (Yankees) and Evan Justice (Rockies), who held Surprise to just a hit and two walks over the duration.

Things got messy in the ninth when Justice plunked Orioles catcher Creed Willems and walked Royals prospect Jac Caglianone, but a grounder to short from Rangers outfielder Alejandro Osuna snuffed the rally, ended the game and set off Salt River's celebration.

The Fall League season was marked by new heights from some of the participants. Yankees infielder Caleb Durbin swiped 29 bags, breaking the league's all-time mark, and finished the year with a .312/.427/.548 line that included five doubles, five home runs, 17 walks and just six strikeouts.

Scottsdale's Josue Briceño also put his name in the record books. The slugging Detroit first baseman ended the fall with a .433/.509/.867 slash line, 10 home runs and 27 RBIs. Those numbers earned him the first triple crown in the history of the AFL, which began in 1992.

Briceño, who was named the league's MVP was also the first player to finish a fall with double-digit home runs since Mike Olt did so in 2011.

Phillies top prospect Andrew Painter, who has not pitched a game in the regular season since 2022, showed no signs of rust in his return to the mound.

The tall righthander overpowered hitters with the same arsenal he used to carve the competition two years ago, when he raced from Low-A to Double-A in his first full pro season and earned BA's inaugural Pitcher of the Year award. Painter finished the AFL with 18 strikeouts over 15.2 innings. He allowed just four runs on 10 hits and four walks.

Padres infielder Leodalis De Vries joined a star-studded club by hitting an AFL home run as an 18-year-old. The list also includes current Padres teammate Ethan Salas, Mariners cornerstone Julio Rodriguez and Phillies megastar Bryce Harper.

STANDINGS

Team	W	L	PCT	GB
Surprise	18	10	.643	-
Glendale	16	14	.533	3
Salt River	16	14	.533	3
Scottsdale	16	14	.533	3
Mesa	14	16	.467	5
Peoria	8	20	.286	10

INDIVIDUAL BATTING LEADERS

(Minimum 2 Plate Appearances/League Games)

Player, Team	AVG	G	AB	R	H	HR	RBI
Josue Briceño, SCO	.433	25	90	22	39	10	27
Thomas Saggese, GDD	.391	18	64	16	25	2	10
Denzel Clarke, MSS	.382	19	76	25	29	2	13
Drake Baldwin, PEJ	.377	13	53	10	20	1	9
Sammy Siani, SCO	.375	22	80	21	30	3	18
Colt Emerson, PEJ	.370	13	54	9	20	0	10
Nick Kurtz, MSS	.353	13	51	11	18	2	11
Gino Groover, SRR	.338	18	65	12	22	0	1
Max Acosta, SUR	.338	20	71	14	24	1	17
Jonathon Long, MSS	.338	18	74	17	25	6	19

INDIVIDUAL PITCHING LEADERS

(Minimum .4 Innings Pitched/League Games)

Player, Team	W	L	ERA	IP	H	BB	SO
Samy Natera Jr., MSS	1	0	0.75	12	5	4	17
Josh Stephan, SUR	1	2	2.25	20	15	5	21
Andrew Painter, GDD	2	0	2.30	16	10	4	18
Jose Acuna, GDD	0	1	2.77	13	8	11	16
Danny Kirwin, MSS	1	0	2.84	13	14	1	16
Luinder Avila, SUR	0	0	3.07	16	11	8	17
Cale Lansville, SCO	0	2	3.45	16	23	5	18
Alex Santos II, SUR	0	1	3.57	18	12	7	26
Preston Johnson, SUR	1	1	3.75	12	10	7	7
Griff McGarry, GDD	2	0	3.75	12	8	11	15

GLENDALE DESERT DOGS

Name	AVG	AB	R	H	2B	3B	HR	RBI	BB	SO	SB
Thomas Saggese	.391	64	16	25	7	0	2	10	16	15	3
C. Encarnacion-Strand	.385	26	2	10	2	0	0	7	4	9	1
Nathan Church	.364	55	10	20	1	1	0	6	3	5	3
Michael Turner	.359	39	7	14	2	0	1	12	7	5	0
Colson Montgomery	.313	32	13	10	2	0	3	11	10	6	4
Leonardo Bernal	.304	46	3	14	1	0	1	8	5	9	1
Otto Kemp	.289	45	15	13	2	0	6	22	11	15	1
Gabriel Rincones Jr.	.273	77	18	21	4	0	2	9	11	7	9
Tim Elko	.267	45	12	12	3	0	4	13	4	21	0
Tyler Callihan	.263	80	17	21	3	2	2	10	9	20	5
Matt McLain	.254	59	8	15	1	1	3	10	16	19	10
Edwin Arroyo	.253	75	18	19	4	1	0	5	6	19	7
Sean McLain	.240	50	12	12	2	0	4	12	9	21	1
Zyhir Hope	.228	92	16	21	3	1	5	21	8	25	2
DJ Gladney	.196	56	4	11	0	0	1	3	4	19	1
Bryan Rincon	.188	64	10	12	2	1	0	7	9	15	8
Jake Gelof	.172	58	9	10	2	1	2	11	11	20	1
Jordan Dissin	.161	31	2	5	1	0	0	1	5	17	0

Name	W	L	ERA	G	GS	SV	IP	H	BB	SO	AVG
Luis Mey	0	0	0.00	8	0	6	9	1	2	8	.037
Andrew Painter	2	0	2.30	6	6	0	16	10	4	18	.189
Trent Baker	1	1	2.57	3	1	0	7	2	4	2	.091
Jose Acuna	0	1	2.77	4	3	0	13	8	11	16	.186
Griff McGarry	2	0	3.75	5	4	0	12	8	11	15	.200
Carson Rudd	0	0	3.86	5	0	0	9	8	10	10	.235
Connor Phillips	2	2	4.19	6	4	0	19	17	14	26	.236
Ixan Henderson	1	1	4.50	5	2	0	12	12	8	16	.255
Jerming Rosario	1	1	4.50	6	2	1	16	13	8	24	.220
Christian McGowan	2	1	4.60	5	2	0	16	23	9	11	.343
Alex Cornwell	0	0	4.66	7	0	0	10	13	5	9	.325
Eriq Swan	0	0	5.19	4	2	0	9	7	1	14	.219
Kelvin Bautista	1	0	5.40	6	0	0	7	6	7	3	.231
Tristan Garnett	1	1	5.63	8	0	0	8	12	5	11	.353
Anthony Hoopii-Tuionetoa	0	0	5.79	8	0	0	9	10	3	9	.270
Matt Svanson	0	1	5.91	9	0	1	11	11	2	15	.256
Eric Adler	0	0	7.00	6	0	1	9	12	3	4	.364
Andrew Dalquist	0	0	7.36	9	0	0	11	13	7	10	.295
Brycen Mautz	0	0	8.10	8	0	0	10	9	7	11	.237
Grant Taylor	2	0	9.39	4	4	0	8	15	7	13	.385
Kelvin Ramirez	1	1	10.13	9	0	0	8	8	11	8	.276
Arij Fransen	0	2	10.32	8	0	0	11	15	7	11	.306
Peyton Pallette	0	1	12.71	4	0	0	6	10	2	6	.385
Alex Makarewich	0	0	13.50	6	0	0	6	9	11	8	.346
Wesley Moore	0	1	22.24	6	0	0	6	14	8	4	.467

MESA SOLAR SOX

Name	AVG	AB	R	H	2B	3B	HR	RBI	BB	SO	SB
Denzel Clarke	.382	76	25	29	2	3	2	13	13	22	9
Nick Kurtz	.353	51	11	18	3	2	2	11	9	16	0
Jonathon Long	.338	74	17	25	4	1	6	19	11	20	1
Tre' Morgan	.338	80	14	27	8	1	1	15	8	8	1
Niko Kavadas	.329	70	17	23	6	1	6	18	17	29	0
Moises Ballesteros	.316	79	14	25	4	0	5	16	10	15	0
Brooks Brannon	.309	68	8	21	4	0	2	6	4	21	0
Xavier Isaac	.286	56	12	16	6	0	3	5	11	27	0
Daniel Susac	.286	21	5	6	1	0	2	7	5	5	1
Mac Horvath	.270	37	6	10	2	0	0	8	4	12	3
David Avitia	.263	19	3	5	1	0	0	3	1	5	0
David Mershon	.263	38	12	10	1	2	0	7	14	9	4
Max Ferguson	.235	68	11	16	4	0	1	10	14	20	3
Caden Rose	.224	85	12	19	4	0	2	16	16	29	5
Henry Bolte	.222	36	9	8	1	1	1	3	5	15	2
Benjamin Cowles	.213	75	7	16	6	1	0	7	8	18	1
Drew Swift	.172	29	4	5	1	0	0	4	3	10	1
Cole Fontenelle	.169	65	11	11	0	1	1	5	13	30	2

Name	W	L	ERA	G	GS	SV	IP	H	BB	SO	AVG
Samy Natera Jr.	1	0	0.75	5	3	0	12	5	4	17	.128
Zach Fogell	0	0	0.96	8	0	1	9	2	4	10	.069
Micah Dallas	0	0	1.13	8	0	0	8	3	2	8	.120
Conor Steinbaugh	0	1	1.80	4	0	0	5	4	2	8	.200
Alexander Alberto	0	0	2.70	6	0	0	7	5	6	8	.200
Danny Kirwin	1	0	2.84	5	1	0	13	14	1	16	.264
Houston Harding	0	0	3.00	4	0	0	9	4	5	10	.129
Tyler Uberstine	0	0	3.12	7	0	0	9	13	6	7	.382
Jack Dashwood	1	0	3.60	9	0	2	10	10	2	17	.238
Vince Reilly	1	0	3.72	8	0	2	10	7	5	9	.206
T.J. Fondtain	0	3	5.28	6	5	0	15	18	5	15	.290
Grant Kipp	3	2	5.60	6	6	0	18	19	10	21	.271
Mitch Myers	1	1	6.48	6	3	0	17	17	7	9	.266
Jack Hartman	1	0	6.55	7	0	0	11	13	4	11	.271
Logan Britt	0	1	6.75	7	0	0	8	10	6	3	.313
Luis Rujano	3	0	7.00	5	2	0	9	6	9	12	.176
Jake Walkinshaw	1	2	7.36	6	5	0	18	27	6	15	.338
Sam Thoresen	0	1	7.50	6	0	0	6	12	10	7	.414
Derrick Edington	0	0	7.59	7	0	1	11	15	6	7	.385
Wander Guante	0	1	7.84	9	0	1	10	13	5	8	.310
Brandon Dufault	0	0	8.44	5	0	0	5	5	9	5	.238
Cooper Adams	1	1	9.49	6	3	0	12	16	7	9	.320
Tyler Baum	0	1	9.72	8	0	0	8	14	2	14	.368
Jackson Lancaster	0	1	12.10	6	2	0	10	17	5	14	.378
Shane Marshall	0	1	14.14	6	0	0	7	15	4	6	.429

PEORIA JAVELINAS

Name	AVG	AB	R	H	2B	3B	HR	RBI	BB	SO	SB
Drake Baldwin	.377	53	10	20	1	1	1	9	8	9	0
Colt Emerson	.370	54	9	20	9	0	0	10	6	14	8
Kemp Alderman	.306	36	8	11	1	0	6	8	4	13	1
Juan Baez	.295	78	16	23	4	2	2	15	13	18	3
Jared Sundstrom	.278	79	16	22	2	1	3	16	8	27	1
Romeo Sanabria	.276	58	14	16	4	0	0	4	8	19	0
Andrew Pintar	.271	107	21	29	2	0	3	17	14	28	9
Luis Lara	.256	86	14	22	4	1	1	9	12	17	10
Ramón Rodríguez	.250	12	1	3	0	0	0	2	3	2	0
David McCabe	.231	39	4	9	2	0	0	4	4	16	0
Ethan Salas	.228	92	14	21	6	0	4	21	13	27	4
Leodalis De Vries	.179	67	4	12	3	0	2	9	7	21	3
Brendan Durfee	.160	25	5	4	1	0	0	0	6	12	0
Brock Wilken	.155	84	12	13	1	0	4	9	12	32	0
Drew Compton	.140	57	6	8	2	0	2	10	7	16	0
Dalvy Rosario	.133	30	5	4	2	0	1	4	4	14	3
Jay Beshears	.115	52	7	6	1	0	1	4	8	22	1
Cole Young	.000	3	1	0	0	0	0	0	2	2	0

MINOR LEAGUES

Name	W	L	ERA	G	GS	SV	IP	H	BB	SO	AVG
Travis Kuhn	0	0	2.00	9	0	0	9	7	9	11	.219
Isaac Gallegos	0	0	3.38	7	0	0	11	6	11	17	.162
Harry Gustin	0	0	3.86	7	0	0	7	8	3	9	.258
Jimmy Kingsbury	1	1	3.86	7	0	0	9	11	6	11	.289
Landon Harper	0	0	4.11	6	0	0	15	17	3	14	.279
Ryan Birchard	1	1	4.20	5	5	0	15	9	19	19	.188
Will Childers	0	0	4.50	9	0	1	10	8	6	17	.211
Jordan Jackson	0	0	5.19	7	0	0	9	12	5	6	.324
David Morgan	1	1	6.23	9	0	3	9	7	10	13	.233
Jimmy Joyce	1	1	6.55	6	0	0	11	8	12	11	.222
Brandon White	1	3	6.75	6	4	0	19	20	9	15	.274
Nick Merkel	0	1	6.92	7	0	0	13	13	12	18	.241
Jason Ruffcorn	0	1	7.24	8	0	0	14	16	6	21	.286
Ryan Bergert	1	3	7.36	5	5	0	15	16	12	19	.262
Coleman Crow	0	0	8.00	4	2	0	9	14	2	6	.341
Justin King	1	0	8.10	4	0	0	7	7	7	3	.318
Gabe Mosser	0	2	10.24	4	3	0	10	17	4	7	.386
Justin Storm	0	0	10.80	8	0	0	10	14	5	9	.333
Adam Maier	0	2	11.20	5	5	0	14	25	8	13	.385
Hayden Harris	0	0	11.42	7	0	0	9	12	4	16	.324
Patrick Monteverde	0	2	12.67	6	6	0	16	31	8	12	.397
Ryan Bourassa	0	2	13.50	8	0	0	7	14	5	13	.412
Mark Manfredi	1	0	13.50	7	0	1	5	6	13	6	.286
Jun-Seok Shim	0	0	19.80	6	0	0	5	6	12	5	.333
Luis German	0	0	20.25	4	0	0	3	6	5	0	.429

SALT RIVER RAFTERS

Name	AVG	AB	R	H	2B	3B	HR	RBI	BB	SO	SB
Gino Groover	.338	65	12	22	1	0	0	11	8	13	0
Kristian Robinson	.319	69	14	22	4	1	1	9	8	22	9
Caleb Durbin	.312	93	26	29	5	1	5	21	17	6	29
Skyler Messinger	.299	67	8	20	1	0	1	12	5	22	2
Kala'i Rosario	.291	79	18	23	0	1	3	16	11	24	3
Tommy Troy	.290	93	15	27	7	1	3	12	10	27	4
Robert Hassell III	.281	89	17	25	7	1	4	19	8	22	5
Ben Ross	.280	82	18	23	5	2	1	15	15	19	3
Phillip Glasser	.270	37	7	10	2	0	0	6	5	10	0
Jose Cordova	.265	49	6	13	4	0	0	5	2	15	3
Cayden Wallace	.250	12	3	3	1	0	0	1	2	3	0
Antonio Gomez	.244	41	6	10	1	0	0	2	8	11	3
Maxwell Romero Jr.	.234	47	7	11	4	0	1	8	13	15	1
Garrett Martin	.225	71	15	16	2	1	5	16	11	22	2
Juan Guerrero	.208	72	12	15	7	0	4	18	3	20	3
Ryan Ritter	.150	40	15	6	2	0	2	4	18	19	3

Name	W	L	ERA	G	GS	SV	IP	H	BB	SO	AVG
Evan Justice	1	0	0.00	9	0	3	9	0	1	11	.000
Luis Pacheco	0	0	1.86	8	0	2	10	9	2	7	.243
Carlos Lagrange	2	0	2.08	5	4	0	9	4	15	10	.148
Carlos Torres	2	1	2.08	9	0	0	9	5	2	12	.156
Yu-Min Lin	0	0	3.00	3	3	0	9	9	3	9	.257
McCade Brown	1	0	3.18	8	0	1	11	8	11	16	.200
Harrison Cohen	0	0	3.38	3	0	0	3	2	1	4	.200
Luke Young	0	1	3.38	10	0	1	11	8	4	7	.200
Liam Rocha	1	0	4.26	7	0	0	13	12	9	12	.250
Philip Abner	2	1	4.32	8	0	0	8	13	5	10	.351
Kyle Amendt	0	0	4.76	5	0	1	6	4	4	8	.190
Chase Solesky	0	1	4.85	6	2	0	13	17	1	20	.309
Alfred Morillo	0	0	5.00	8	0	1	9	7	6	12	.206
Dustin Saenz	2	1	5.52	6	3	0	15	19	4	12	.317
Jack Noble	1	1	5.56	7	0	0	11	11	7	10	.282
Kade Bragg	1	1	7.24	8	2	0	14	9	13	13	.180
Dylan Ray	0	0	7.62	5	5	0	13	18	5	18	.327
Michael Prosecky	1	0	7.63	8	0	0	15	22	9	23	.333
Jacob King	0	1	7.71	8	0	0	9	14	6	10	.333
Matt Cronin	0	0	7.88	8	0	0	8	12	6	4	.353
Ryan Harvey	0	1	8.10	6	0	0	7	7	8	7	.304
Gabriel Hughes	1	2	8.31	6	6	0	17	20	10	14	.286
Devin Kirby	1	0	9.53	6	0	0	11	11	13	8	.262
Michael Cuevas	0	0	9.82	7	0	0	7	18	7	8	.450
Jackson Fristoe	0	3	13.50	6	5	0	11	18	14	7	.391
Ben Ross	0	0	18.00	1	0	0	1	3	2	0	.600

SCOTTSDALE SCORPIONS

Name	AVG	AB	R	H	2B	3B	HR	RBI	BB	SO	SB
Josue Briceño	.433	90	22	39	5	2	10	27	15	21	0
Thayron Liranzo	.375	48	9	18	6	1	2	7	11	9	0
Sammy Siani	.375	80	21	30	5	0	3	18	11	16	6
Kervin Pichardo	.309	55	13	17	5	2	1	12	11	10	2
Geovanny Planchart	.294	34	5	10	1	0	2	6	9	7	0
Bryce Eldridge	.293	41	7	12	3	0	2	6	3	16	0
Jett Williams	.286	84	11	24	4	1	3	12	8	23	0
Bo Davidson	.283	60	6	17	4	1	1	9	8	22	3
Charlie Szykowny	.274	62	7	17	1	1	2	8	2	12	2
Adrian Pinto	.274	84	13	23	2	1	1	8	14	13	7
Termarr Johnson	.250	40	9	10	2	2	1	4	14	11	3
Eddinson Paulino	.226	53	9	12	1	0	1	10	4	11	1
Jett Williams	.225	80	15	18	3	2	2	9	17	30	7
Jeff McNeil	.222	9	1	2	0	0	0	1	1	0	0
Drew Gilbert	.208	72	18	15	2	0	4	9	17	14	2
Jacob Reimer	.208	53	7	11	0	1	2	13	15	13	1
Drew Cavanaugh	.200	30	3	6	2	0	0	2	4	10	0
Peyton Graham	.179	28	2	5	1	1	0	3	2	11	0

Name	W	L	ERA	G	GS	SV	IP	H	BB	SO	AVG
T.J. Brock	0	0	0.00	7	0	1	7	2	3	11	.087
Ryan Jennings	1	0	0.00	9	0	2	10	5	4	14	.152
Valentin Linarez	1	0	0.87	7	0	0	10	3	8	11	.086
Johnathan Lavallee	1	1	1.74	8	0	0	10	10	0	9	.244
CJ Weins	0	0	2.35	7	0	1	8	4	5	8	.148
Derek Diamond	0	0	2.45	7	1	0	11	7	2	12	.171
Cale Lansville	0	2	3.45	6	4	1	16	23	5	18	.333
Jonathan Pintaro	1	0	3.48	4	2	0	10	9	6	10	.237
Lazaro Estrada	1	0	3.86	4	1	0	12	7	4	19	.167
Saul Garcia	0	0	4.32	8	0	0	8	6	7	9	.214
Jawilme Ramirez	2	0	4.50	8	0	0	8	9	1	10	.300
Khristian Curtis	1	1	4.67	7	3	0	17	13	8	16	.206
Noah Hall	0	1	5.40	3	2	0	7	8	7	3	.308
Tyler Vogel	1	1	5.63	9	0	0	8	5	5	6	.179
Elijah Pleasants	3	1	5.68	6	5	0	19	18	6	20	.247
Kendry Rojas	0	1	5.74	6	5	0	16	17	8	13	.274
Eric Silva	0	0	5.84	8	0	0	12	12	6	12	.261
Marques Johnson	0	0	6.00	7	0	0	6	6	6	11	.240
Eddy Yean	0	2	6.75	9	0	1	9	13	6	8	.333
Rayner Castillo	1	2	7.13	6	4	0	18	19	13	14	.275
William Kempner	0	0	7.36	4	0	0	4	2	3	7	.154
Brandan Bidois	0	0	8.22	7	0	0	8	7	9	14	.241
Jake Miller	3	1	9.18	6	3	0	17	26	3	24	.347
Dylan Ross	0	1	17.47	6	0	0	6	10	7	4	.400

SURPRISE SAGUAROS

Name	AVG	AB	R	H	2B	3B	HR	RBI	BB	SO	SB
Carter Jensen	.425	40	11	17	3	0	4	11	14	10	1
Jake Cunningham	.391	23	7	9	0	0	2	8	2	7	1
Chase DeLauter	.340	47	10	16	5	0	1	11	12	6	2
Max Acosta	.338	71	14	24	8	1	1	17	8	15	8
Creed Willems	.338	80	14	27	5	1	2	11	6	14	0
Cody Freeman	.308	65	13	20	7	0	2	8	11	14	2
Alejandro Osuna	.306	98	25	30	8	0	2	16	22	26	2
Daniel Vazquez	.298	47	9	14	3	0	0	4	7	13	2
Kody Huff	.250	44	6	11	1	0	0	8	6	11	4
Jac Caglianone	.236	89	14	21	4	0	5	21	8	19	2
Douglas Hodo	.228	57	17	13	6	1	1	6	19	21	9
Quincy Hamilton	.225	71	13	16	1	0	1	9	12	18	6
Brett Squires	.222	81	13	18	4	0	1	10	3	32	3
Collin Price	.219	73	9	16	3	0	2	15	14	21	2
Milan Tolentino	.202	84	19	17	4	1	0	10	20	30	12
Austin Deming	.194	67	5	13	2	0	3	12	6	21	2

Name	W	L	ERA	G	GS	SV	IP	H	BB	SO	AVG
Andrew Misiaszek	0	0	0.00	6	0	0	5	2	2	8	.111
Anthony Simonelli	0	0	0.00	8	0	1	8	4	3	8	.160
Avery Weems	0	0	1.29	6	0	2	7	6	1	9	.250
Zane Barnhart	1	0	1.69	7	0	0	5	5	3	7	.238
Tyler Burch	0	0	2.25	4	0	0	4	2	1	3	.143
Josh Stephan	1	2	2.25	6	3	0	20	15	5	21	.200
Luinder Avila	0	0	3.07	5	3	0	15	11	8	17	.200
Allan Hernandez	2	0	3.48	7	0	1	10	9	5	12	.231
Alex Santos II	0	1	3.57	6	3	0	18	12	7	26	.188

Preston Johnson	1	1	3.75	5	0	0	12	10	7	7	.222
Zak Kent	3	0	3.78	5	3	0	17	8	9	18	.140
Marc Church	0	0	4.05	7	0	2	7	5	1	10	.208
Alaska Abney	0	0	4.91	9	0	0	7	11	2	11	.344
Leandro Lopez	2	0	5.21	7	3	0	19	20	14	24	.267
Nic Swanson	0	1	5.59	7	0	0	10	10	5	16	.263
Shane Panzini	1	2	5.74	6	3	0	16	20	7	15	.328
Jose Fleury	2	0	6.00	5	3	0	12	14	5	10	.275
Dylan DeLucia	1	1	6.75	6	3	0	19	20	10	11	.267
Juan Rojas	2	1	7.50	6	6	0	18	22	12	11	.314
Brandon Johnson	1	0	9.35	8	0	1	9	12	4	11	.308
Chazz Martinez	0	0	10.50	7	0	0	6	5	6	6	.238
Joey Mancini	1	0	10.57	7	0	0	8	13	5	8	.382
Skylar Hales	0	0	11.12	7	0	1	6	13	2	6	.464
Houston Roth	0	0	13.50	6	0	0	5	4	4	9	.200
Alejandro Torres	0	1	14.40	7	0	0	5	7	10	6	.333

MINOR LEAGUES

INDEPENDENT LEAGUES

Partner Leagues Finding Ways To Grow

BY J.J. COOPER

It's now been over 30 years since the first modern independent leagues sprung up with the 1993 arrival of the Northern and Frontier Leagues.

Plenty has happened over those three decades. In the couple of years after the St. Paul Saints first showed the potential for indy ball, anyone with a dream and a stadium lease tried to start an indy league, whether they had the funding to do so or not.

But that gold rush ended quickly, with only the best operators and leagues hanging around to the 21st century. That first decade of the 2000s and the first half of the 2010s were equally tumultuous. The Northern League's best operators left to form the American Association. The Central League became the United League. The Northeast League turned into the Can-Am League.

So amazingly, the conversion from "independent" leagues to "partner" leagues in 2021 has actually been much less dramatic than the shuffling that happened before that. The 2024 season was the fourth in this new arrangement, but it also is a marker of lengthy stability by "indy ball" standards.

There are four partner leagues, same as there were in 2021. Those leagues have expanded as they have put the coronavirus pandemic behind them.

Between those four leagues, there were 50 teams in 2024 up from 42 in 2022. The Frontier League has added two teams. The Atlantic League has added two and the Pioneer League has added four.

This is a significant achievement, because when the pandemic arrived in 2020, the leagues seemed on shakier footing. Multiple teams shut down after the 2019 season. The Can-Am League folded and indy ball drew only 5.355 million fans. The pandemic in 2020 made those fears of instability grow.

Five years later, the leagues have returned to normalcy. For much of the past 30 years, there have been 46-48 indy ball teams around the country. The leagues have changed and some cities have come, gone and returned again.

But the water level for partner leagues/indy ball has at close to 50 teams for the entirety of the 21st century drawing around six million fans. In 2004, there were 46 indy ball teams, even if only two leagues (the Atlantic and Frontier Leagues) remain

SCOTT STRAZZANTE/SAN FRANCISCO CHRONICLE VIA GETTY IMAGES

The Pioneer League moved into Oakland with the Ballers as the A's moved out

from there. And in 2003, there were 48.

The Central, Northern and Northeast Leagues may have dissolved but their best teams ended up in the Frontier and American Association.

In 2014, there were six indy ball leagues, but there were 46 teams.

The reduction of the affiliated minors has led to a big shakeup, and the Pioneer League has become a viable partner league in the Northwest and California, an area that has struggled to sustain independent professional baseball. Talent has grown as the MLB draft has been cut to 20 rounds.

Taken as a whole, the partner leagues are still running around the same number of teams as they have for the past two decades and drawing around the same number of fans through the gates.

The four partner leagues drew 5.798 million fans in 2024 in announced attendance. In 2014, they drew 6.1 million fans. That's down, but is right in line with the dips that have been seen in affiliated baseball.

Partner leagues have matured into stable entities, which may have seemed hard to believe in 1994, but is right in line with what's been seen for the past decade.

Fogel Dominates Pioneer League

PLAYER OF THE YEAR

Adam Fogel was a solid regular for Hawaii and then Kentucky. But with the shortened 20-round draft, he never heard his name called in the draft.

And that may end up being the best thing that could have happened to him. It's been a circuitous route, but Fogel just wrapped up one of the best seasons seen in the independent/partner leagues in years.

Adam Fogel

He hit .388/.495/.773 with a Pioneer League record 35 home runs. He tossed in another 27 doubles as well. Missoula has long been considered a good place to hit, and the Pioneer League is an offense-heavy league, but Fogel hit everywhere he played. He hit 18 of his 35 home runs on the road and he hit .403 on the road.

His 2024 season made him Baseball America's Independent/Partner Leagues Player of the Year. And it was a wonderful validation of the decisions Fogel made a year ago.

Fogel almost gave up on playing baseball when he found he needed Tommy John surgery in 2023. But before long, he decided to give baseball another try.

Fogel became a Paddlehead. And as soon as the season began, he became a star. Fogel had never hit 10 home runs in a season in college. He hit 10 in his first 21 games with Missoula. He had hits in 23 of his first 24 games, including four three-hit games and two four-hit games.

"The balls off the bat. I came up playing with (Orioles slugger) Chris Davis. That was a similar sound. It's just different. He started to realize that every time he would go up there, he knew he was going to impact the game," Missoula manager Michael Schlact said.

It helped that Fogel's mindset had changed. At one point, he thought he deserved to get a shot at affiliated ball. Now, he wanted to prove he deserved to be in Missoula's lineup every day.

"Say I go and get popped (drafted) after my junior year, would I still be playing? I was no way nearly as mature as a player or a person. Even when I went to Ottawa, I went with an attitude of 'why am I here?'" Fogel said. "That was a blessing in disguise. I went to Missoula with a completely different attitude. I haven't earned sh–. I am going to work my ass off everyday. I'm going to earn my spot and prove myself every single day."

For now, Fogel is signed to return to Missoula to see what kind of encore he can produce to a season where he did everything. But Schlact, his manager, hopes the next time he sees him in a uniform, it's in affiliated ball.

"My hope as our manager is that he's not with us. Quite honestly if Adam Fogel does this and doesn't get signed, what are we doing? If that's not enough, what do I have to do?" Schlact said. "Hopefully this and the year he's had. He's improved his defense. Give him a chance."

PREVIOUS WINNERS

1996: Darryl Motley, OF, Fargo-Moorhead (Northern)
1997: Mike Meggers, OF, Winnipeg/Duluth (Northern)
1998: Morgan Burkhart, 1B, Richmond (Frontier)
1999: Carmine Cappucio, OF, New Jersey (Northeast)
2000: Anthony Lewis, 1B, Duluth-Superior (Northern)
2001: Mike Warner, OF, Somerset (Atlantic)
2002: Bobby Madritsch, LHP, Winnipeg (Northern)
2003: Jason Shelley, RHP, Rockford (Frontier)
2004: Victor Rodriguez, SS, Somerset (Atlantic)
2005: Eddie Lantigua, 3B, Quebec (Can-Am)
2006: Ian Church, OF, Kalamazoo (Frontier)
2007: Darryl Brinkley, OF, Calgary (Northern)
2008: Patrick Breen, OF, Orange County (Golden)
2009: Greg Porter, OF, Wichita (American Association)
2010: Beau Torbert, OF, Sioux Falls (American Association)
2011: Chris Collabello, 1B, Worcester (Can-Am League)
2012: Blake Gailen, OF, Lancaster (Atlantic)
2013: C.J. Ziegler, 1B, Wichita (American Association)
2014: Balbino Fuenmayor, 1B, Quebec (Can-Am League)
2015: Joe Maloney, OF, Rocland (Can-Am League)
2016: Art Charles, 1B, New Jersey (Can-Am League)
2017: Alonzo Harris, OF, York (Atlantic League)
2018: Jordany Valdespin, INF, Long Island (Atlantic League)
2019: Keon Barnum, 1B, Chicago (American Association)
2021: Adam Brett Walker, OF, Milwaukee (American Association)
2022: Courtney Hawkins, OF, Lexington (Atlantic League)
2023: Bryan Torres, OF, Milwaukee (American Association)

TAYLOR DENTON/MISSOULA PADDLEHEADS

AMERICAN ASSOCIATION

Kane County went a perfect 7-0 in the playoffs to win the team's first American Association title and its third title overall, including its time in the Midwest League. Cornelius Randolph was named the Miles Wolff Cup Final MVP as he went 6-for-12 with two RBIs, three runs and a stolen base.

East Division	W	L	PCT	GB
Cleburne Railroaders *	60	40	.600	-
Kane County Cougars †	55	45	.550	5
Chicago Dogs †	55	45	.550	5
Lake Country DockHounds †	53	47	.530	7
Milwaukee Milkmen	49	51	.490	11
Gary SouthShore RailCats	30	70	.300	30
West Division	**W**	**L**	**PCT**	**GB**
Winnipeg Goldeyes *	56	43	.566	-
Sioux Falls Canaries †	55	44	.556	1
Fargo-Moorhead RedHawks †	53	47	.530	3.5
Sioux City Explorers †	49	51	.490	7.5
Kansas City Monarchs	46	54	.460	10.5
Lincoln Saltdogs	38	62	.380	18.5

*** Division Champ. †Wild-Card**

PLAYOFFS—Quarterfinals: Kane County defeated Lake Country 2-0; Chicago defeated Cleburn 2-1; Winnipeg defeated Sioux Falls 2-1 and Fargo-Moorhead 2-1 in best-of-3 series. **Semifinals:** Winnipeg defeated Fargo-Moorhead 2-1 and Kane County defeated Chicago 2-0 in best-of-three series. **Finals:** Kane County defeated Winnipeg 3-0 in best-of-five series.

Attendance: Kane County 274,694; Chicago 220,500; Winnipeg 183,046; Lincoln 162,132; Gary SouthShore 152,985; Fargo-Moorhead 150,965; Lake Country 87,440; Sioux Falls 85,475; Cleburne 82,134; Milwaukee 80,844; Kansas City 69,814; Sioux City 60,449.

All-Star Team: C: Jaxx Groshans, Cleburne. **1B:** Jacob Teter, Chicago. **2B:** Carter Aldrete, Cleburne. **SS:** Shed Long, Cleburne. **3B:** Claudio Finor, Kane County. **OF:** Cornelius Randolph, Kane County, Ismael Alcantara, Fargo-Moorhead, Hill Alexander, Cleburne. **DH:** Ryan Hernandez, Lake Country. **UTIL:** Dayson Croes, Winnipeg. **SP:** Joey Matulovich, Winnipeg. **RP:** Joey Marciano, Chicago. **Player of the Year:** Jacob Teter, Chicago. **Manager of the Year:** Logan Watkins, Winnipeg. **Rookie Position Player of the Year:** Ryan Hernandez, Lake Country. **Rookie Pitcher of the Year:** Sebastian Rodriguez, Milwaukee.

BATTING LEADERS

Player	AVG	OBP	SLG	AB	R	H	HR	RBI	SB
Jacob Teter, Chi.	.349	.474	.673	358	72	125	28	95	10
John Nogowski, SC	.346	.461	.553	358	69	124	15	76	7
Dayson Croes, Win.	.342	.397	.452	374	54	128	5	51	10
Cornelius Randolph, KC	.342	.447	.527	292	62	100	11	58	10
Carter Aldrete, Cle	.341	.412	.557	402	89	137	21	74	20
Miles Simington, Win.	.329	.391	.503	362	61	119	7	65	28
Mike Hart, SF	.323	.420	.476	229	37	74	6	42	12
Trendon Craig, KC	.321	.406	.487	302	60	97	8	41	16
Brantley Bell, Chi.	.320	.392	.485	394	74	126	12	57	54
Frankie Tostado, KC	.318	.377	.501	343	49	109	9	57	1

PITCHING LEADERS

Player	W	L	ERA	G	IP	H	BB	SO
Joey Matulovich, Win.	11	3	2.12	20	123	80	22	145
Julian Garcia, KC	5	1	2.54	22	92	69	22	115
Greg Mahle, KC	10	2	2.94	15	83	69	18	65
Ty Culbreth, SF	12	2	2.94	19	119	109	28	73
Johnathon Tripp, Cle.	7	2	2.97	20	112	102	35	84
Foster Pace, Lin.	5	3	3.11	15	84	71	23	63
Tyler Grauer, F-M	8	4	3.26	16	86	82	20	69
Tanner Brown, SF	10	6	3.33	20	111	108	56	113
Travis Seabrooke, Win.	8	3	3.63	21	109	115	24	87
Sebastian Rodriguez, Mil.	11	4	3.71	21	114	101	38	95

CHICAGO DOGS

PLAYER	AVG	AB	R	H	2B	3B	HR	RBI	SB
Antonio Barranca	.167	60	9	10	1	7	9	20	1
Brantley Bell	.320	394	74	126	12	57	45	62	54
Marty Costes	.276	29	2	8	2	5	1	8	0
Narciso Crook	.264	386	79	102	26	73	55	114	21
Nick Dalesandro	.300	253	41	76	3	31	27	66	23
Chase Harris	.213	127	17	27	2	12	11	39	3
Jesus Lujano	.221	145	20	32	0	12	14	26	11
David Maberry	.139	101	6	14	4	6	6	26	0
Derek Maiben	.318	85	8	27	0	7	8	10	4
General McArthur	.114	35	5	4	0	2	1	16	2
Nick Novak	.215	228	35	49	1	22	31	47	9
Pavin Parks	.111	63	5	7	1	8	9	27	2
Zion Pettigrew	.259	193	35	50	3	24	25	46	3
Chad Pike	.267	30	5	8	1	4	5	13	0
Bryan Reyes	.083	24	0	2	0	0	2	10	0
Gus Sosa	.264	163	19	43	2	22	17	43	3
Dusty Stroup	.253	312	58	79	21	62	28	79	15
Jacob Teter	.349	358	72	125	28	95	84	76	10
Johnni Turbo	.271	339	36	92	7	42	32	50	6

PLAYER	W	L	ERA	G	SV	IP	H	BB	SO
John Baker	5	4	4.11	19	0	105	101	32	91
Jason Bilous	1	2	5.33	8	0	25	21	12	32
Jake Carroll	2	3	6.42	14	0	41	42	29	29
Cal Coughlin	1	2	5.96	16	0	23	24	12	28
Connor Curlis	1	0	0.77	2	0	12	4	1	13
Zach Davidson	3	1	4.40	10	0	31	23	18	39
Cal Djuraskovic	2	2	5.30	29	2	36	44	14	30
Tyler Driver	0	0	7.98	9	0	15	21	5	3
Lukas Galdoni	4	3	3.06	25	3	62	47	21	47
Brooks Gosswein	4	6	5.27	13	0	70	75	42	43
Tom King	2	1	6.14	16	0	22	19	16	21
Steven Lacey	3	3	4.40	15	0	61	56	26	49
Joey Marciano	5	3	1.78	41	26	56	30	25	74
Brady Miller	4	0	3.62	8	0	37	47	12	24
Chad Pike	1	1	3.71	9	0	17	15	8	15
Davis Pratt	1	1	8.28	16	0	25	32	12	18
Brian Schlitter	2	2	7.15	21	3	23	35	6	15
Kenny Serwa	6	6	4.22	20	1	119	116	23	103
Augie Voight	0	0	13.14	9	0	12	23	12	8
Matt Walker	4	2	4.40	14	0	45	48	18	43

CLEBURNE RAILROADERS

Name	AVG	AB	R	H	HR	RBI	BB	SO	SB
Carter Aldrete	.341	402	89	137	21	74	47	73	20
Hill Alexander	.306	395	65	121	14	70	40	72	6
Michael Berglund	.080	25	3	2	0	2	7	13	0
Bret Boswell	.251	343	60	86	13	62	52	84	8
Blaze Brothers	.194	201	40	39	1	17	40	77	24
Cam Cannon	.304	23	4	7	1	6	2	3	0
Thomas Dillard	.260	331	82	86	16	62	93	84	22
Trent Giambrone	.164	55	4	9	2	4	6	16	1
Blake Grant-Parks	.326	129	23	42	2	30	18	26	0
Jaxx Groshans	.284	282	58	80	15	66	61	53	7
Korey Holland	.311	238	47	74	8	38	27	49	10
Shed Long Jr.	.310	381	76	118	9	74	64	78	16
Jesus Lujano	.329	149	23	49	2	23	10	20	8
Brian O'Grady	.244	340	67	83	24	78	69	91	9
Gus Sosa	.255	47	8	12	1	9	5	15	1

Name	W	L	ERA	G	SV	IP	H	BB	SO
Dylan Bice	3	1	2.54	21	5	28	17	16	36
Luke Boyd	7	3	4.36	19	1	76	90	18	59
Beau Burrows	2	1	6.10	16	0	21	26	11	33
Jake Cantleberry	1	0	4.38	9	0	12	11	10	14
Joe Corbett	2	0	6.98	17	5	19	25	8	26
Jacob Gilliland	4	2	5.40	15	0	18	17	10	18
Juan Hillman	0	1	0.84	2	0	11	9	3	5
Kyle Johnston	2	3	8.67	17	0	46	67	17	43
Kasey Kalich	1	3	8.67	9	0	27	32	21	33
Justin Kleinsorge	0	4	11.28	8	0	22	40	8	11
Theo McDowell	2	2	3.46	29	0	39	25	33	56
Kade Mechals	5	2	4.80	19	0	45	58	18	48

Name	W	L	ERA	G	SV	IP	H	BB	SO
Jalen Miller	3	3	5.20	12	0	54	43	52	61
Chris Muller	0	0	3.43	33	4	42	32	19	51
Jacques Pucheu	5	3	4.33	12	0	62	56	27	44
Brady Puckett	1	2	3.95	14	0	27	28	16	20
Kristian Scott	6	3	2.66	34	8	41	29	28	33
Caleb Smith	1	1	5.40	6	0	20	22	8	20
Johnathon Tripp	7	2	2.97	20	0	112	102	35	84
Antonio Velez	5	2	4.58	15	0	75	91	17	44
Mark Washington	3	1	5.79	30	2	37	40	23	33

FARGO-MOORHEAD REDHAWKS

Name	AVG	AB	R	H	HR	RBI	BB	SO	SB
Ismael Alcantara	.306	353	72	108	9	57	32	82	70
Evan Alexander	.226	283	49	64	9	42	46	74	18
Peter Brookshaw	.237	287	43	68	9	34	38	77	9
Marcus Chiu	.284	197	33	56	4	37	25	52	6
Sam Dexter	.242	343	47	83	4	48	22	56	6
Juan Fernandez	.349	215	44	75	3	22	22	30	2
Mike Hallquist	.277	119	19	33	2	11	15	39	6
Jake Hjelle	.252	107	13	27	3	11	8	46	3
Ben Livorsi	.211	90	17	19	1	7	23	22	0
Chase McDaniel	.160	25	2	4	0	3	3	6	0
Nick Novak	.241	54	8	13	0	4	5	15	3
Alec Olund	.349	106	26	37	4	23	16	23	7
Dakota Phillips	.184	76	9	14	3	11	4	26	0
Kona Quiggle	.221	267	32	59	2	35	35	89	13
Jordan Siket	.266	79	8	21	1	4	4	15	0
Parker Stroh	.222	45	8	10	0	4	8	13	0
Dillon Thomas	.288	132	19	38	5	28	14	34	7
C.J. Valdez	.233	232	29	54	8	34	15	55	5
Drew Ward	.250	260	35	65	9	51	57	65	2

Name	W	L	ERA	G	SV	IP	H	BB	SO
Garrett Alexander	3	2	5.40	39	2	50	55	36	63
Nile Ball	5	2	3.61	12	0	57	58	27	47
Colten Davis	7	6	4.25	20	0	108	119	62	83
Alex DuBord	2	3	5.67	36	17	33	35	25	49
Jake Dykhoff	5	3	2.21	42	1	57	47	18	56
Davis Feldman	7	1	2.87	11	0	60	54	22	45
Brett Garcia	1	2	5.30	13	0	19	12	10	16
Tyler Grauer	8	4	3.26	16	0	86	82	20	69
Parker Harm	2	2	5.85	19	0	20	13	18	27
Brenden Heiss	1	4	9.11	8	1	27	27	32	20
Kolby Kiser	3	7	6.26	26	0	82	91	40	61
Nolan LaMere	0	0	6.35	10	1	17	20	15	13
Noah McBride	0	0	9.95	14	0	13	17	9	11
Braunny Muñoz	1	2	4.95	5	0	20	28	5	12
Jake Osowski	0	0	9.42	9	0	14	21	8	9
Kelvan Pilot	2	1	3.90	21	1	60	40	44	53
Orlando Rodriguez	4	4	4.29	15	0	80	71	52	74
Cade Torgerson	1	3	7.05	28	0	45	62	21	27

GARY SOUTHSHORE RAILCATS

Name	AVG	AB	R	H	HR	RBI	BB	SO	SB
Anthony Abbatine	.178	73	6	13	1	3	10	32	3
Olivier Basabe	.247	352	40	87	4	42	38	59	9
Jacob Bockelie	.162	68	6	11	2	6	9	20	0
LG Castillo	.249	365	41	91	2	40	14	87	8
Jose Contreras	.252	238	29	60	12	39	13	86	10
Francisco Del Valle	.233	219	28	51	5	24	15	40	3
Gio Díaz	.250	384	40	96	1	38	23	49	30
Cooper Edwards	.154	78	4	12	0	2	9	27	1
Brandon Fields	.191	21	1	4	0	1	1	13	0
Marcos Gonzalez	.261	257	39	67	10	38	27	53	3
Kenny Levari	.174	23	1	4	0	1	2	11	0
Yanio Pérez	.147	34	3	5	0	4	4	8	0
Guillermo Quintana	.239	284	37	68	3	23	28	43	3
Carlos Rincón	.256	274	39	70	13	39	30	56	0
Howard Rodriguez	.233	103	14	24	1	9	10	28	7
Miguelangel Sierra	.260	235	33	61	16	38	26	80	0
Jackson Valera	.269	242	30	65	3	26	17	27	1

Name	W	L	ERA	G	SV	IP	H	BB	SO
Nate Alexander	3	8	3.96	47	7	50	50	29	65
Andres Diaz	6	6	6.40	24	0	104	133	39	76
Destin Dotson	0	1	18.26	11	0	11	11	29	8
Chris Erwin	5	6	5.21	16	0	74	81	39	70
Casey Grimm	2	2	5.12	27	0	39	42	19	25
Ethan Hankins	0	2	9.82	4	0	11	13	9	17
Denson Hull	0	2	5.20	30	0	36	28	30	45
Stephen Knapp	0	0	9.22	10	1	14	25	5	8
Peyton Long	4	12	5.50	21	0	113	131	29	69
Deyni Olivero	0	1	3.57	3	0	18	17	4	11
Franklin Pérez	0	4	9.45	15	0	33	55	24	15
Julio Pinto	0	4	6.75	40	1	41	38	33	38
Carlos Sanabria	1	9	6.39	28	0	82	80	59	82
Josh Smith	0	0	3.49	47	3	49	46	15	47
Tai Tiedemann	5	10	6.19	22	0	116	146	53	70
Joan Valdez	2	2	4.19	36	0	34	25	23	32

KANE COUNTY COUGARS

Name	AVG	AB	R	H	HR	RBI	BB	SO	SB
Josh Allen	.306	304	70	93	15	55	56	75	9
Trendon Craig	.321	302	60	97	8	41	32	70	16
Galli Cribbs	.187	241	35	45	4	31	26	84	15
Jared Cushing	.250	24	3	6	1	5	1	6	0
Jonah Davis	.233	296	46	69	12	48	32	109	7
Hayden Dunhurst	.174	155	19	27	1	13	16	73	0
Claudio Finol	.309	320	58	99	11	56	38	58	10
Todd Lott	.298	363	50	108	8	67	27	60	2
Alex McGarry	.257	144	23	37	4	14	14	34	2
Ernny Ordonez	.280	218	33	61	5	30	13	43	10
Cornelius Randolph	.343	292	62	100	11	58	60	54	10
Simon Reid	.280	200	33	56	4	29	23	39	0
Harrison Smith	.256	199	27	51	4	35	16	52	10
Armond Upshaw	.280	293	54	82	9	39	47	83	32
Je'Von Ward	.292	89	13	26	1	11	13	20	8

Name	W	L	ERA	G	SV	IP	H	BB	SO
Tyler Beardsley	0	3	3.82	29	13	35	37	10	38
Nick Belzer	7	4	3.95	14	0	68	72	34	40
Mike Brewer	4	2	5.32	38	1	47	45	30	63
Antonio Carreon	0	2	8.16	3	0	14	23	4	9
C.J. Carter	3	1	3.40	36	0	45	27	27	55
Jack Fox	9	4	5.28	21	0	104	133	38	63
A.J. Jones	2	2	5.01	24	0	59	68	23	35
Greg Mahle	10	2	2.94	15	0	83	69	18	65
Jordan Martinson	1	1	5.36	44	1	49	56	31	53
Westin Muir	6	9	5.72	16	0	83	103	29	54
Logan Nissen	2	1	2.25	25	0	28	25	6	28
Ryan Nutof	1	1	2.25	17	10	16	13	10	23
Ryan Richardson	1	0	4.58	19	1	35	45	7	18
Tommy Sommer	3	4	3.92	19	0	99	100	34	79
Spencer Stockton	1	3	5.00	4	0	18	19	2	21
Vin Timpanelli	1	2	2.70	15	0	20	15	8	27
Alex Troop	2	0	1.80	2	0	10	7	0	16
Garrett Williams	1	3	6.27	31	0	37	39	32	55

KANSAS CITY T-BONES

Name	AVG	AB	R	H	HR	RBI	BB	SO	SB
Ross Adolph	.302	358	79	108	16	57	44	113	14
Bryan Aguilar	.195	77	9	15	0	5	14	16	3
Danny Amaral	.213	150	29	32	1	16	30	22	27
Abiatal Avelino	.292	72	9	21	1	11	5	12	1
Josh Bissonette	.279	340	39	95	1	33	36	67	2
Tucker Bradley	.232	99	15	23	2	7	16	13	4
Cam Cannon	.198	81	13	16	4	12	9	18	0
Lorenzo Cedrola	.275	102	17	28	0	12	2	6	2
Trent Giambrone	.298	218	35	65	7	40	22	30	1
Isiah Gilliam	.333	105	17	35	6	26	17	26	3
Moisés Gómez	.283	60	12	17	4	14	3	14	1
Herbert Iser	.252	238	27	60	5	36	23	52	0
Hayden Jones	.203	187	19	38	9	27	4	45	0
Chris Lanzilli	.167	30	5	5	0	0	7	7	0
Carson Maxwell	.235	34	7	8	0	4	4	8	1
Justin O'Conner	.308	104	15	32	6	17	6	42	0
Channy Ortiz	.195	195	22	38	1	17	20	33	1
Jhailyn Ortiz	.342	76	10	26	4	12	4	13	0
Blake Rutherford	.328	64	10	21	3	20	6	8	2
Joe Suozzi	.196	46	6	9	1	7	9	20	0

Travis Swaggerty	.269	268	51	72	7	41	46	59	20
Frankie Tostado	.318	343	49	109	9	57	30	45	1
Chavez Young	.247	73	15	18	1	9	10	11	9

Name	W	L	ERA	G	SV	IP	H	BB	SO
A.J. Alexy	2	2	6.26	20	3	23	17	20	29
Junior Cerda	2	1	3.00	8	0	12	5	8	10
Connor Curlis	1	4	5.26	15	0	53	56	18	47
Yefri Del Rosario	0	0	7.45	7	0	10	11	4	10
Julian Garcia	5	1	2.54	22	0	92	69	22	115
Grant Gavin	3	2	4.06	8	0	38	41	6	57
Jackson Goddard	3	7	5.19	19	0	87	93	38	88
Ashton Goudeau	1	0	0.90	2	0	10	7	3	6
Jeff Hakanson	1	2	2.13	10	2	13	6	6	17
Matt Hall	2	2	4.82	6	0	28	24	13	38
Damon Jones	1	0	3.46	12	0	13	11	9	13
JC Keys	4	0	2.81	22	0	32	25	22	33
Zack Leban	3	4	5.66	33	3	49	50	24	45
Will McAffer	0	2	9.00	5	0	18	32	8	18
Jackson McClelland	4	3	5.70	25	3	30	32	12	28
Hunter McMahon	3	4	4.76	22	0	68	82	15	55
Kevin Milam	1	3	6.91	11	0	42	60	16	26
Gabriel Ponce	2	3	5.97	20	2	38	39	14	45
Yefry Ramírez	1	2	6.65	5	0	22	31	11	14
Duncan Snider	1	2	4.70	7	0	38	42	13	37
Jonathan Sprinkle	1	1	7.11	10	0	13	12	10	20
Nate Tellier	3	3	2.98	35	0	54	38	22	41
Michael Watson	1	1	1.13	3	0	16	9	7	14
Collin Wiles	0	1	3.48	5	0	21	28	4	20

LAKE COUNTRY DOCKHOUNDS

Name	AVG	AB	R	H	HR	RBI	BB	SO	SB
Josh Altmann	.264	390	68	103	19	71	35	99	24
Samuel Benjamin	.200	55	14	11	2	10	8	20	0
JT Benson	.286	91	16	26	2	20	9	19	9
Marcus Chiu	.205	78	10	16	0	5	9	22	2
Marek Chlup	.252	274	41	69	7	43	39	92	23
Justin Connell	.287	167	32	48	2	18	27	29	16
Deivy Grullón	.295	234	34	69	6	43	21	69	1
Ryan Hernandez	.295	349	55	103	29	92	37	83	1
Cesar Izturis	.253	95	11	24	0	11	6	18	9
Thomas Jones	.169	83	15	14	4	9	12	31	2
Justin Lavey	.202	94	16	19	2	13	14	17	5
Carson Maxwell	.243	70	11	17	0	7	13	21	7
Josh Morgan	.241	58	7	14	2	7	11	13	0
Luke Napleton	.220	50	4	11	1	7	8	19	0
Henderson Perez	.192	26	3	5	0	3	1	4	0
Demetrius Sims	.283	300	64	85	8	38	38	88	31
Curtis Terry	.352	219	38	77	16	51	13	35	0
Blake Tiberi	.296	385	70	114	2	45	62	59	18
Chavez Young	.393	107	23	42	3	16	9	20	13
Ray Zuberer	.320	231	44	74	8	29	32	48	23

Name	W	L	ERA	G	SV	IP	H	BB	SO
Braden Boisvert	4	3	6.82	16	1	30	27	13	46
Bryan Bonnell	5	7	4.26	16	0	89	104	17	51
Jake Cantleberry	3	0	2.04	22	0	18	7	11	25
Brett Conine	7	4	4.19	19	0	105	101	46	87
Jon Duplantier	0	0	0.00	4	0	18	6	6	30
Luke Hansel	2	6	6.44	9	0	50	58	33	38
Blake Kunz	1	1	5.09	28	0	35	29	21	41
Shelby Lackey	0	1	5.12	33	1	39	29	38	55
JT Moeller	2	0	3.03	22	1	30	23	12	29
Mitch Mueller	2	0	3.68	19	0	22	14	4	32
Matt Mullenbach	2	4	3.20	37	0	65	52	33	41
Kelvan Pilot	5	1	4.29	8	0	42	36	21	37
Brady Puckett	0	3	8.67	6	0	27	29	17	21
Alexis Rivero	3	2	5.56	19	5	23	22	18	16
Brody Rodning	0	0	1.93	13	0	14	8	3	25
Sterling Sharp	1	2	3.28	8	0	36	42	10	27
Duncan Snider	2	4	6.79	11	0	50	45	43	48
John Swanda	9	3	5.93	16	0	88	108	34	86
Matt Swilley	1	1	8.31	6	0	17	23	19	17
Alan Zhang Carter	2	1	0.72	31	11	38	16	24	61

LINCOLN SALTDOGS

Name	AVG	AB	R	H	HR	RBI	BB	SO	SB
Nick Anderson	.219	155	20	34	5	21	22	30	15
Alex Baeza	.284	296	48	84	10	56	40	89	1
Kyle Battle	.244	119	19	29	7	25	14	40	3
Dakota Conners	.279	316	43	88	1	29	37	59	9
Drew Devine	.225	311	46	70	6	41	46	59	17
Jack Dragum	.262	252	22	66	3	19	22	29	3
Justin Farmer	.154	26	4	4	0	0	5	12	0
Spencer Henson	.259	201	27	52	10	35	18	50	1
Max Hewitt	.275	233	19	64	0	22	17	30	6
Gary Mattis	.218	101	15	22	1	7	9	20	13
Matt Pita	.262	168	25	44	4	22	15	38	2
Dalton Reeves	.239	71	10	17	4	17	10	17	0
Luke Roskam	.242	256	43	62	8	31	43	68	6
Aaron Takacs	.292	336	40	98	8	52	50	63	23
Logan Williams	.211	95	13	20	2	8	11	39	1

Name	W	L	ERA	G	SV	IP	H	BB	SO
Pablo Arevalo	5	5	6.13	24	0	47	50	20	27
Abdallah Aris	5	8	4.53	20	0	107	114	39	81
Dylan Beck	0	2	7.66	7	0	22	28	16	7
Walter Borkovich	1	0	6.17	9	0	12	13	8	13
Zach Keenan	6	9	4.63	20	0	113	117	31	77
Dan Kubiuk	2	2	1.05	41	16	43	26	12	39
Brandon McCabe	1	4	4.50	34	3	30	23	22	35
Ian Oxnevad	2	2	4.38	17	0	25	18	11	20
Foster Pace	5	3	3.11	15	0	84	71	23	63
Jack Parisi	1	4	6.60	11	0	45	38	36	40
Karan Patel	4	7	5.67	16	0	81	84	49	68
Bryan Perez	1	1	7.97	39	0	35	33	34	60
Tony Roca	1	0	9.24	9	0	13	19	7	15
Wyatt Sparks	2	2	4.14	39	0	50	52	16	46
Mitch Stone	0	2	8.78	9	0	13	14	13	14
Cam Wynne	1	4	6.75	13	0	41	52	16	42
David Zoz	1	4	3.19	42	1	42	51	18	50

MILWAUKEE MILKMEN

Name	AVG	AB	R	H	HR	RBI	BB	SO	SB
Jaylin Davis	.240	263	40	63	13	48	55	88	3
Griffin Doersching	.349	66	14	23	4	21	6	15	0
Brennen Dorighi	.154	26	3	4	0	2	2	8	0
Willie Escala	.301	146	22	44	4	23	11	36	5
Chase Estep	.287	359	66	103	12	56	46	80	9
Kyle Huckstorf	.227	88	13	20	2	8	8	32	12
Trey Law	.228	219	22	50	0	23	17	53	5
Abdiel Layer	.233	266	34	62	10	35	21	77	12
Wendell Marrero	.271	225	43	61	2	30	25	39	8
Roy Morales	.365	74	12	27	0	11	4	9	0
Erik Ostberg	.311	380	74	118	12	62	44	69	2
Reggie Pruitt	.201	318	54	64	6	28	43	108	34
Brett Rodriguez	.187	123	15	23	0	9	20	50	7
Oscar Santos	.223	300	33	67	11	57	29	102	2
Jose Sermo	.261	329	63	86	22	56	45	126	0
Armani Smith	.222	167	30	37	2	27	25	64	3
John Taylor	.128	39	4	5	0	2	1	17	3

Name	W	L	ERA	G	SV	IP	H	BB	SO
Shane Barringer	1	6	5.60	16	0	80	100	31	70
Rodrigo Benoit	1	4	6.39	24	0	31	36	16	35
Victor Capellan	1	3	7.13	22	7	24	30	21	19
José Chacin	0	2	7.00	6	0	18	25	8	12
Juan Echevarria	1	0	13.70	10	0	22	36	14	27
Pablo Garabitos	1	1	5.79	6	0	14	15	6	15
Ben Gerl	1	0	8.59	19	1	22	34	21	16
Nyan Hernandez	3	3	4.30	35	0	52	45	25	51
Jordan Johnson	1	2	2.25	38	13	44	26	13	50
Jhordany Mezquita	4	1	3.13	16	1	55	47	19	51
Greg Minier	2	7	6.24	12	0	62	68	27	57
Aaron Mishoulam	0	1	4.50	5	0	12	11	11	12
Alirio Negrette	2	2	10.45	12	0	10	17	7	6
Blake Purnell	0	2	6.11	10	0	18	23	9	17
Alexis Rivero	2	1	10.80	11	0	12	19	9	4
Sebastian Rodriguez	11	4	3.71	21	0	114	101	38	95

Name	W	L	ERA	G	SV	IP	H	BB	SO
Calvin Schapira	1	1	4.96	4	0	16	19	7	14
Mark Simon	5	2	2.47	42	0	47	33	21	54
Brody Sorenson	1	0	3.92	8	0	21	22	11	9
Victor Vargas	4	1	2.11	7	0	43	37	9	35
Davis Welch	0	2	5.89	10	0	37	43	18	25
Ryley Widell	5	5	5.23	23	0	86	81	62	77
Christian Young	2	1	2.70	4	0	20	15	8	24

SIOUX CITY EXPLORERS

Name	AVG	AB	R	H	HR	RBI	BB	SO	SB
Jacob Barfield	.240	25	0	6	0	1	4	8	0
Will Busch	.167	36	3	6	0	2	7	14	0
Cam Cannon	.246	179	21	44	6	33	13	47	1
Dwight Childs	.133	30	5	4	0	2	2	11	0
Justin Connell	.350	80	16	28	4	14	10	17	13
Jake Green	.286	42	14	12	0	7	13	7	1
Chase Harris	.272	147	24	40	1	19	32	38	16
D'Shawn Knowles	.261	88	17	23	1	13	16	19	5
Daniel Lingua	.245	347	70	85	1	37	60	90	49
Osvaldo Martínez	.291	302	34	88	5	42	35	48	8
Daniel Montano	.312	301	55	94	5	52	59	75	4
John Nogowski	.346	358	69	124	15	76	71	30	7
Jake Ortega	.192	219	30	42	3	26	23	53	5
Scott Ota	.274	373	61	102	13	74	37	47	23
Daniel Pérez	.288	163	28	47	4	28	27	47	2
Henderson Perez	.095	21	1	2	0	2	0	8	0
Nick Shumpert	.267	318	54	85	7	29	30	84	40
Zac Vooletich	.239	176	26	42	2	20	27	34	24
Delvin Zinn	.137	51	3	7	1	4	4	10	2

Name	W	L	ERA	G	SV	IP	H	BB	SO
Brandon Brosher	3	5	4.53	48	1	44	31	27	49
Austin Drury	4	5	5.10	16	0	90	96	36	94
Santiago Florez	0	0	4.09	10	0	11	9	6	8
Nate Gercken	1	0	5.56	40	3	44	51	18	26
Jacob Gilliland	0	0	5.25	7	0	12	11	8	9
Pedro González	1	0	6.75	10	0	16	22	6	9
Jaren Jackson	2	6	6.04	18	0	67	85	32	52
Evan Johnson	0	1	9.58	6	0	10	8	8	11
Kyle Marman	4	2	2.30	41	19	47	35	21	68
Kade Mechals	1	0	2.03	9	1	13	11	3	13
Braunny Muñoz	4	3	7.31	17	0	57	72	27	51
Joey Murray	5	8	5.94	19	0	94	88	63	86
Brendan O'Donnell	0	0	8.79	10	0	14	25	10	14
J.D. Scholten	6	2	5.40	11	0	60	71	28	29
John Sheaks	3	6	6.53	24	0	80	99	34	65
Heitor Tokar	1	0	3.95	8	0	14	16	5	15
Antonio Velez	0	1	5.23	4	0	21	26	7	18
Jared Wetherbee	6	5	4.39	16	0	84	68	55	93
Zach Willeman	5	4	3.42	41	3	50	28	30	67

SIOUX FALLS CANARIES

Name	AVG	AB	R	H	HR	RBI	BB	SO	SB
Trevor Achenbach	.257	308	54	79	19	62	54	91	6
Jordan Barth	.254	374	58	95	12	48	17	58	15
Shamoy Christopher	.146	48	5	7	3	8	1	20	0
Hunter Clanin	.289	308	42	89	12	55	31	74	12
Scott Combs	.165	133	12	22	2	11	6	37	0
Kendall Foster	.148	27	4	4	0	2	5	9	1
Mike Hart	.323	226	37	73	6	41	32	56	12
Jabari Henry	.242	256	48	62	19	52	47	81	1
Derek Maiben	.275	149	23	41	1	10	21	16	5
Tate Meiners	.222	27	3	6	0	6	1	5	0
Drew Mount	.286	105	18	30	2	8	14	17	10
Ernny Ordonez	.225	80	11	18	3	15	13	20	8
Josh Rehwaldt	.290	348	68	101	23	66	44	104	20
Spencer Sarringar	.222	234	32	52	5	33	35	56	9
Liam Spence	.239	255	38	61	5	34	49	62	9
Wyatt Ulrich	.254	288	53	73	3	21	46	48	18

Name	W	L	ERA	G	SV	IP	H	BB	SO
Tanner Brown	10	6	3.33	20	0	111	108	56	113
Dylan Chalmers	2	1	7.17	20	0	38	52	21	22
Jose Cruz	3	1	5.25	16	0	24	24	12	13
Ty Culbreth	12	2	2.94	19	0	119	109	28	73
Matt Dunaway	1	4	5.62	29	1	42	48	17	31
Chris Hardin	1	0	9.35	14	0	17	20	11	10
Charlie Hasty	1	3	2.87	38	20	38	26	8	36
Christian Johnson	1	4	6.55	33	0	55	65	30	48
Neil Lang	7	1	3.10	14	0	58	64	13	30
Seth Miller	6	4	3.84	19	0	101	107	44	45
Brady Stover	1	1	3.26	31	0	30	26	15	37
Zach Veen	3	3	2.20	39	0	41	30	21	44
Mitchell Walters	2	5	8.67	12	0	46	60	32	42
Ryan Zimmerman	5	9	6.22	22	0	103	119	49	85

WINNIPEG GOLDEYES

Name	AVG	AB	R	H	HR	RBI	BB	SO	SB
Nick Anderson	.218	133	17	29	3	14	21	37	4
Andy Armstrong	.241	274	41	66	2	39	19	73	7
Edwin Arroyo	.213	94	10	20	1	13	9	10	10
Ramon Bramasco	.286	294	58	84	4	38	50	57	11
Gio Brusa	.194	67	9	13	1	8	9	28	0
Dayson Croes	.342	374	54	128	5	51	27	41	10
Rob Emery	.293	314	54	92	11	70	21	53	7
Roby Enriquez	.296	270	47	80	3	42	24	30	6
Kevin Garcia	.188	128	11	24	1	9	13	23	1
Ryan Holgate	.191	84	10	16	2	9	6	29	1
Keshawn Lynch	.203	212	36	43	2	26	34	41	10
Jake McMurray	.274	285	45	78	2	32	41	39	2
Max Murphy	.289	374	72	108	17	73	41	107	7
Miles Simington	.329	362	61	119	7	65	29	41	28

Name	W	L	ERA	G	SV	IP	H	BB	SO
Landen Bourassa	8	7	4.01	20	0	119	121	25	96
Justin Courtney	1	0	2.04	14	5	18	10	5	30
Colton Eastman	2	9	7.34	15	0	65	81	36	46
Marshall Kasowski	1	1	2.38	2	0	11	9	2	15
Mitchell Lambson	2	0	4.74	4	0	25	23	6	15
Joey Matulovich	11	3	2.12	20	0	123	80	22	145
Ben Onyshko	1	0	1.03	30	0	44	26	12	47
Thomas Ponticelli	0	2	2.37	14	0	19	14	3	16
Zac Reininger	9	5	4.49	19	0	114	141	24	65
Travis Seabrooke	8	3	3.63	21	1	109	115	24	87
Joey Steele	1	1	2.41	17	7	19	14	5	16
Tasker Strobel	4	3	3.76	39	0	53	53	16	40
Grant Townsend	0	1	8.38	9	0	10	10	10	10
Nick Trogrlic-Iverson	6	4	3.06	41	7	62	48	13	66
Ryder Yakel	2	3	3.56	31	2	66	60	16	82

ATLANTIC LEAGUE

York picked up its fourth Atlantic League title with a sweep of Charleston in the Atlantic League championship series. Charleston actually led 1-0 heading to the bottom of the ninth in Game 3, but David Washington hit an RBI double to tie it. A swinging bunt by Alerick Soularie moved Washington to third. Jacob Rhinesmith then hit a grounder to second, but he beat the throw to first to avoid the double play, which meant Washington's run counted, giving the Revolution a dramatic title-clinching walk-off ground out.

North Division	W	L	PCT	GB
*York Revolution	80	45	.640	-
&Lancaster Stormers	71	55	.563	9.5
Long Island Ducks	64	62	.508	16.5
Staten Island FerryHawks	55	69	.444	24.5
Hagerstown Flying Boxcars	36	89	.288	44

South Division	W	L	PCT	GB
*Gastonia Baseball Club	83	43	.659	-
High Point Rockers	74	52	.587	9
&Charleston Dirty Birds	69	57	.548	14
Southern Maryland Blue Crabs	53	72	.424	29.5
Lexington Legends	42	83	.336	40.5

**First-half champion. & Second-half champion. ^Wild-Card*

Playoffs—Semifinals: York defeated Lancaster 3-1 and Charleston defeated Gastonia 3-1 in best-of-5 series. **Finals:** York defeated Charleston 3-0 in best-of-5 series.

Attendance: Long Islands 290,073; Lancaster 246,807; York 202,502; Hagerstown 175,061; Charleston 157,687; Southern Maryland 156,253;

Lexington 112,537; High Point 102,994; Staten Island 81,419; Gastonia 71,462.

All-Star Team: C-Rusber Estrada, Charleston. **1B-**Keon Barnum, Charleston. **2B-**Justin Wylie, Gastonia. **SS-**Matt McDermott, York. **3B-**Jake Gatewood, Gastonia. **DH-**Luis Castro, Staten Island. **OF-**Rudy Martin, Jr., York; Gaige Howard, Lancaster; Donovan Casey, York.

SP-Noah Bremer, Lancaster; Max Green, Lancaster; Jon Olsen, York. **Reliever-**Matt Turner, York. **Closer-**Endrys Briceno, Southern Maryland.

All-Defense Team: C-Aaron Antonini, Long Island. **1B-**David Washington, York. **2B-**D.J. Burt, High Point. **SS-**Matt McDermott, York. **3B-**Jake Gatewood, Gastonia. **OF-**Ben Aklinski, High Point; Jared Carr, Charleston; Kolby Johnson, Staten Island. **P-**Michael Horrell, York.

Player of the Year: Keon Barnum, Charleston. **Pitcher of the Year:** Jon Olsen, York. **Defensive Player of the Year:** Jared Carr, Charleston. **Manager of the Year:** Rick Forney, York.

BATTING LEADERS

Player, Team	AVG	OBP	SLG	AB	R	H	HR	RBI	SB
Luis Castro, SI	.356	.449	.636	343	77	122	24	80	22
Donovan Casey, York	.348	.398	.575	322	78	112	16	96	33
Rudy Martin Jr., York	.326	.427	.495	402	108	131	12	57	78
Gaige Howard, Lanc.	.325	.437	.452	425	94	138	5	54	24
Ryan Grotjohn, HP	.324	.424	.502	321	66	104	9	43	22
Matt Bottcher, LI	.323	.396	.504	337	67	109	10	52	23
Damon Dues, Lanc.	.322	.388	.478	314	69	101	6	42	30
Jacob Rhinesmith, York	.316	.411	.461	421	88	133	9	67	32
Kolby Johnson, SI	.308	.380	.459	429	93	132	11	62	32
Matt McDermott, York	.307	.375	.495	515	115	158	19	68	56

PITCHING LEADERS

Player, Team	W	L	ERA	G	IP	H	BB	SO
Jon Olsen, York	12	3	3.60	25	128	120	26	136
Noah Bremer, Lan.	10	7	4.06	29	135	138	42	132
Max Green, Lan.	12	5	4.35	30	120	125	55	124
David Lebron, Char.	8	7	4.52	23	123	121	47	120
Christian Capuano, SI	10	3	4.53	19	101	100	34	104
Ryan Conroy, Gast.	7	6	4.77	22	108	107	41	83
Michael Horrell, York	6	8	5.03	30	116	133	43	86
Garrett Martin, SM	6	10	5.28	25	140	142	45	122
Ian Kahaloa, SM	10	9	5.48	25	131	130	60	138
Aaron Fletcher, York	6	5	5.56	24	128	146	55	95

CHARLESTON DIRTY BIRDS

Name	AVG	AB	R	H	HR	RBI	BB	SO	SB
Keon Barnum	.301	468	90	141	41	115	82	142	0
Gabriel Cancel	.282	195	50	55	17	39	43	50	30
Jared Carr	.294	432	97	127	14	69	57	87	58
Angelo Castellano	.357	98	16	35	3	16	12	12	8
Luis Curbelo	.143	77	8	11	2	13	8	23	1
Delino DeShields	.256	262	54	67	4	33	48	49	36
Drew Ellis	.231	39	5	9	1	6	6	9	1
Phil Ervin	.271	391	76	106	19	68	55	81	27
Rusber Estrada	.279	366	72	102	22	84	59	116	0
Clint Frazier	.258	167	30	43	6	28	25	35	9
Willy García	.169	83	10	14	2	12	7	24	0
Dariel Gomez	.146	55	6	8	1	7	10	22	0
Courtney Hawkins	.219	64	9	14	5	14	4	27	0
Matt Hibbert	.167	48	6	8	2	9	7	21	4
Kevin Maitan	.333	54	13	18	3	14	7	11	0
AJ Orrico	.115	26	7	3	0	2	9	2	3
Tillman Pugh	.277	383	71	106	21	68	59	93	20
Joseph Rosa	.284	257	49	73	9	42	49	61	15
Juan Santana	.280	414	60	116	9	60	27	46	14
Jonathan Soto	.268	138	22	37	3	23	16	35	2
Jesus Tavarez	.254	126	19	32	2	15	20	30	1
Lyndon Weaver	.115	26	7	3	0	0	6	11	2

Name	W	L	ERA	G	SV	IP	H	BB	SO
Adrian Almeida	7	4	4.33	20	0	71	56	44	77
Maceo Campbell	0	0	7.65	14	0	20	26	18	18
Casey Cobb	0	4	8.82	9	0	33	42	18	27
Juan Diaz	1	0	4.76	5	0	11	11	4	11
Mason Fox	2	0	1.20	15	5	15	4	8	21
Pedro Garcia	1	0	0.60	13	7	15	9	6	11
Ricardo Gomez	0	2	6.89	18	4	16	17	12	15
Nick Horvath	4	4	6.75	21	2	27	28	12	32
David Lebron	8	7	4.52	23	0	123	121	47	120
Stevie Ledesma	4	2	4.80	18	1	75	81	31	52
Mack Lemieux	1	4	5.36	11	0	47	48	32	33
Alex Mack	0	1	6.35	13	0	23	23	18	22
Joan Martinez	0	4	4.93	46	2	49	49	16	45
Kyle McGowin	1	0	2.70	2	0	10	10	1	11
Pearson McMahan	0	2	6.10	30	1	31	30	31	26
Carlos Meza	0	0	4.22	7	0	11	6	8	13
Jalen Miller	3	2	7.47	14	1	37	40	23	40
Seth Nightingale	1	2	3.95	36	1	41	31	22	40
Cristofer Ogando	8	0	4.02	24	0	69	54	22	90
Gerald Ogando	2	3	6.50	28	0	44	54	25	58
Bryan Quillens	8	4	4.45	50	1	63	51	28	56
Gabriel Rodríguez	2	5	7.58	18	0	65	64	52	67
Keyvius Sampson	4	0	3.86	8	0	37	32	20	35
Kevin Smith	4	4	5.79	12	0	56	55	31	64
Trey Supak	1	0	2.35	4	0	23	16	2	28
Edison Suriel	4	1	3.06	36	2	47	37	31	43

GASTONIA BASEBALL CLUB

Name	AVG	AB	R	H	HR	RBI	BB	SO	SB
Alan Alonso	.239	134	21	32	4	10	15	37	7
Clint Coulter	.313	198	32	62	8	36	11	33	7
Braxton Davidson	.141	85	5	12	2	9	14	45	1
Eric De La Rosa	.225	369	59	83	14	53	41	145	36
Austin Dennis	.278	36	5	10	0	3	3	6	4
Marc Flores	.279	276	46	77	12	58	44	74	2
Jake Gatewood	.295	427	87	126	33	121	70	92	13
Hidekel Gonzalez	.225	244	33	55	10	34	10	66	7
Joe Gray	.250	32	3	8	0	2	3	4	0
Jake Hoover	.229	105	19	24	2	19	6	28	2
Alex Jackson	.180	39	6	7	1	3	6	8	5
Richie Martin	.244	156	39	38	5	15	13	19	22
Brandon Martorano	.184	49	12	9	4	6	5	18	0
Patrick Mazeika	.284	162	33	46	14	42	19	23	0
Dean Miller	.258	159	32	41	9	34	23	54	5
Zach Racusin	.280	25	1	7	0	1	1	3	0
Jack Reinheimer	.269	216	42	58	6	21	30	51	19
Jacob Robson	.277	137	28	38	8	27	33	58	18
JJ Schwarz	.197	76	7	15	2	13	7	26	0
Josh Stowers	.301	399	91	120	17	73	54	75	49
Kevin Watson	.302	368	69	111	13	66	55	60	40
Cam Williams	.184	38	6	7	2	4	2	18	1
Justin Wylie	.249	426	93	106	34	84	76	105	25

Name	W	L	ERA	G	SV	IP	H	BB	SO
Bryan Blanton	5	3	4.62	35	1	37	31	21	36
Trevor Clifton	0	1	0.92	20	7	20	11	6	23
Ryan Conroy	7	6	4.76	22	0	108	107	41	83
John Creel	1	2	9.85	20	0	28	31	19	18
Brett Daniels	3	4	7.75	16	1	74	86	31	54
Greg Duncan	0	0	6.39	11	0	13	19	5	10
Trent Fennell	6	2	3.90	38	2	62	46	56	69
Harrison Francis	2	3	6.62	9	0	35	37	27	34
Kent Hasler	0	0	4.91	11	0	11	8	5	18
Nick Horvath	7	0	3.29	28	0	38	25	14	44
Gunnar Kines	2	3	5.68	11	0	52	61	14	46
Gabe Klobosits	5	5	2.18	45	11	45	30	27	46
Zac Lowther	4	0	2.82	11	0	54	43	31	74
Brett Matthews	2	0	6.30	8	0	10	6	12	6
Ian McKinney	4	0	4.38	12	0	51	51	17	43
Morgan McSweeney	2	1	4.19	8	0	34	33	20	35
Jake Miednik	6	1	2.79	34	0	71	46	37	62
Steffon Moore	1	2	7.82	16	0	13	9	14	18
Ljay Newsome	5	1	4.15	11	0	56	51	13	54
Tyler Palm	1	0	2.77	11	0	13	11	4	7
Nate Peden	1	0	1.46	17	0	25	12	8	27
Sean Poppen	2	1	5.11	12	0	25	26	10	35
Phoenix Sanders	3	0	1.73	24	12	26	16	6	33
Julian Smith	1	2	10.24	9	0	10	15	8	14
Cory Thompson	6	0	4.22	33	0	43	39	14	48

Nick Wells	3	0	2.55	7	0	35	27	17	42
Zac Westcott	0	1	2.03	2	0	13	7	4	9
Mike Wright Jr.	2	4	7.77	10	0	49	65	20	28

HAGERSTOWN FLYING BOXCARS

Name	AVG	AB	R	H	HR	RBI	BB	SO	SB
Osvaldo Abreu	.251	418	51	105	11	46	37	94	20
Abiatal Avelino	.230	87	16	20	1	10	3	19	5
Blake Berry	.260	219	26	57	3	26	42	57	0
Joe Campagna	.251	203	22	51	7	33	23	55	0
Cito Culver	.273	418	59	114	14	57	52	103	6
Luis Yanel Diaz	.283	46	5	13	3	12	2	9	1
Nick Diaz	.194	31	3	6	0	1	5	13	0
Welington Dotel	.289	429	49	124	5	39	26	113	15
Dariel Gomez	.241	232	36	56	8	28	30	78	0
Osmy Gregorio	.264	246	24	65	4	27	23	53	12
Mike Gulino	.130	23	2	3	0	4	5	7	0
Tyler Hill	.215	219	17	47	3	21	12	78	2
Alan Marrero	.132	68	3	9	0	1	7	17	1
Demetrius Moorer	.199	211	33	42	0	15	44	70	17
Andrew Moritz	.313	268	46	84	4	24	43	44	3
Andres Noriega	.212	33	3	7	0	5	5	5	1
Eury Pérez	.292	161	19	47	1	18	9	17	19
Brandon Pugh	.105	57	1	6	0	2	1	19	0
Nellie Rodriguez	.205	151	19	31	6	21	25	66	0
Dilan Rosario	.143	35	2	5	0	5	3	14	1
Christian Sepulveda	.281	89	14	25	2	10	6	15	10
Magneuris Sierra	.333	63	10	21	1	8	7	12	7
Curtis Terry	.217	175	17	38	5	23	17	42	0
Jaylyn Williams	.347	95	13	33	3	14	5	26	0
Justin Williams	.177	96	11	17	3	11	12	25	0

Name	W	L	ERA	G	SV	IP	H	BB	SO
Malik Binns	3	5	7.79	13	0	52	63	38	40
Aneudy Cortorreal	0	2	3.00	37	6	39	21	34	52
Mike DeSanti	0	0	7.32	18	0	20	17	19	22
Yeudy García	3	9	6.36	13	0	64	76	35	40
Nick Gardewine	0	1	6.17	9	0	12	11	4	13
Carlos Gomez	2	1	6.32	12	0	16	13	9	15
Marvin Gorgas	3	10	6.62	24	0	86	103	43	72
Gunnar Groen	0	4	9.90	6	0	20	28	19	13
Domingo Jimenez	1	1	3.82	27	3	31	14	13	41
Alex Katz	0	0	6.50	14	0	18	21	8	19
Rafael Kelly	3	4	4.88	58	4	63	61	29	62
Mike Kickham	7	14	5.69	25	0	119	149	40	100
Rob Klinchock	2	3	4.75	55	0	66	65	27	59
Taylor Lepard	0	3	7.71	12	0	16	20	13	10
José Lopez	2	1	2.16	18	0	17	16	12	21
Parker Markel	2	6	6.28	18	0	76	77	53	61
Brett Matthews	1	1	7.43	26	0	23	27	18	21
Joe Palumbo	0	1	7.63	6	0	15	18	17	15
Jack Parisi	0	1	7.04	12	0	15	19	10	11
Domenic Picone	0	2	4.95	9	0	40	42	14	32
Edubray Ramos	1	1	4.67	36	0	35	39	5	43
Anthony Rodriguez	0	4	8.00	8	0	27	34	17	16
Dylan Sabia	1	1	5.53	16	0	28	42	13	14
Rodolfo Sanchez	1	3	7.08	33	2	34	36	24	34
Enrique Santana	0	2	11.25	18	3	16	17	15	12
Yoelvín Silven	1	1	5.94	33	1	36	46	11	33
Chase Solesky	3	4	5.67	9	0	33	37	9	29
Nick Trabacchi	0	2	7.36	7	0	18	23	13	17

HIGH POINT ROCKERS

Name	AVG	AB	R	H	HR	RBI	BB	SO	SB
Ben Aklinski	.247	478	94	118	29	92	66	123	29
Aidan Brewer	.235	51	11	12	2	9	6	22	0
D.J. Burt	.234	364	59	85	7	49	60	60	32
Evan Edwards	.272	368	66	100	22	70	56	88	13
Martin Figueroa	.280	347	71	97	10	36	80	76	10
Fritz Genther	.292	24	5	7	1	3	1	10	1
Ryan Grotjohn	.324	321	66	104	9	43	55	69	22
Gilberto Jimenez	.278	162	27	45	3	19	19	34	5
Gavin Johns	.303	33	5	10	0	3	1	8	0
Quincy Latimore	.250	68	11	17	3	15	9	21	0
Nick Longhi	.298	57	11	17	7	17	3	15	0
Trey Martin	.168	95	12	16	2	5	17	32	5
Michael Martínez	.279	136	15	38	2	19	7	29	0
Clayton Mehlbauer	.196	168	22	33	6	18	23	69	6
Colin Moran	.290	190	27	55	8	24	20	27	0
Quincy Nieporte	.240	96	11	23	3	13	7	21	0
Connor Owings	.276	457	70	126	19	94	79	99	5
Brian Parreira	.225	311	37	70	10	46	40	56	0
Jake Washer	.264	167	17	44	2	27	7	30	1
Nolan Watson	.077	26	2	2	0	0	2	15	0
Zander Wiel	.188	218	31	41	13	33	33	69	5

Name	W	L	ERA	G	SV	IP	H	BB	SO
Derrick Adams	3	3	3.86	8	0	42	27	13	35
Cam Bedrosian	7	3	2.81	14	0	77	58	22	87
Ben Braymer	3	2	3.55	7	0	33	25	10	34
Will Carter	1	1	2.28	27	1	28	22	14	27
Cooper Casad	2	1	3.71	6	0	27	23	3	15
Dakota Chalmers	3	3	4.00	21	6	27	13	15	52
Jacob Edwards	7	4	3.12	42	1	69	64	19	63
Nate Espelin	0	0	6.10	7	0	10	5	7	7
Taylor Guerrieri	3	3	4.37	11	0	45	39	14	37
Kyle Halbohn	2	1	1.99	19	0	23	29	4	17
Mickey Jannis	3	0	3.06	4	0	18	19	6	10
Brandon Leibrandt	2	0	0.93	4	0	19	12	7	24
Justin Lewis	1	0	4.32	12	0	17	13	5	20
Jameson McGrane	2	3	3.21	34	14	34	27	10	57
David McKay	3	1	4.63	21	0	23	20	6	20
Ryan Meisinger	1	1	1.09	23	1	25	18	2	34
Zach Muckenhirn	3	1	4.24	25	0	34	30	16	38
Braeden Ogle	1	0	2.38	20	1	23	13	16	33
Neil Ramírez	5	4	4.83	17	0	69	67	18	75
Jeremy Rhoades	5	3	4.15	13	0	69	72	24	68
Stephen Ridings	1	0	3.06	9	0	32	30	13	41
Austin Ross	2	0	2.15	27	1	29	25	12	36
Yuhi Sako	0	0	1.74	2	0	10	9	6	14
Garrett Schilling	1	1	4.09	50	3	51	46	22	51
Jonah Scolaro	5	4	4.52	19	0	94	81	46	94
Peter Solomon	0	2	5.68	3	0	13	17	3	19
Matt Solter	3	2	6.03	7	0	31	36	15	25
Zach Vennaro	0	1	2.73	31	0	30	15	12	40
Austin Warner	1	2	2.79	10	0	19	16	10	19
Ryan Weiss	3	4	4.34	9	0	46	44	20	73

LANCASTER BARNSTORMERS

Name	AVG	AB	R	H	HR	RBI	BB	SO	SB
Joseph Carpenter	.286	402	55	115	14	65	28	97	6
Jack Conley	.254	169	27	43	6	29	19	32	11
Isan Díaz	.304	296	54	90	17	64	34	76	9
Damon Dues	.322	314	69	101	6	42	35	64	30
Shawon Dunston	.264	318	71	84	14	49	55	82	49
Justin Farmer	.233	146	19	34	5	26	10	43	8
Kyle Hess	.433	30	8	13	3	10	4	1	2
Gaige Howard	.325	425	94	138	5	54	83	87	24
Jordan Howard	.227	44	7	10	3	10	6	19	5
Niko Hulsizer	.261	257	57	67	16	58	45	97	3
Kyle Kasser	.254	197	27	50	0	12	23	34	5
Trace Loehr	.261	410	64	107	10	58	31	63	14
Nick Lucky	.281	114	23	32	3	18	12	38	7
Mason Martin	.318	267	62	85	27	73	29	68	8
Chris Proctor	.258	407	72	105	12	64	42	90	46
Cristian Santana	.423	142	28	60	13	47	14	34	0
Chad Sedio	.279	172	24	48	7	28	16	40	2
Joe Stewart	.305	154	34	47	5	30	12	32	17

Name	W	L	ERA	G	SV	IP	H	BB	SO
A.J. Alexy	2	1	2.57	14	0	14	8	9	21
Nile Ball	4	2	5.74	12	0	53	53	24	52
Caleb Baragar	1	1	2.25	3	0	16	9	5	18
Noah Bremer	10	7	4.06	29	0	135	138	42	132
Oscar De La Cruz	4	3	4.11	14	0	72	70	28	52
Phillip Diehl	4	3	2.29	41	3	39	29	5	50
Scott Engler	2	0	2.66	18	1	20	13	6	25
Max Green	12	5	4.35	30	0	120	125	55	124

INDEPENDENT LEAGUES

Name	W	L	ERA	G	SV	IP	H	BB	SO
James Hoyt	2	3	6.38	26	3	24	28	11	21
Kyle Johnson	0	1	6.10	32	3	31	33	20	30
Jack Labosky	3	2	2.92	10	0	65	66	7	44
Nolan Long	1	2	8.14	15	0	24	37	17	23
Brad Markey	1	2	8.59	4	0	15	21	5	10
Steffon Moore	1	1	7.45	29	0	29	31	33	45
Stephen Nogosek	1	1	4.32	33	13	33	24	11	43
Carter Raffield	1	0	5.65	13	0	14	11	13	19
Jackson Rees	7	1	4.25	42	0	42	31	44	61
Ted Stuka	0	2	3.96	25	1	25	16	27	31
Matt Swarmer	5	4	3.80	16	0	88	85	20	99
Augie Sylk	2	2	4.39	8	0	27	25	16	23
Brady Tedesco	3	5	5.15	20	0	93	102	38	82
Carsie Walker	2	4	7.90	15	0	49	70	26	25
Adam Wibert	2	1	8.42	21	1	31	34	24	26

LEXINGTON LEGENDS

Name	AVG	AB	R	H	HR	RBI	BB	SO	SB
Jacob Barfield	.239	130	20	31	5	23	7	37	4
Austin Bates	.252	107	13	27	2	16	4	11	2
Matt Bottcher	.323	337	67	109	10	52	36	62	23
Wilmin Candelario	.162	37	5	6	0	1	4	20	1
Kole Cottam	.304	418	75	127	26	87	56	92	4
Ryan Davis	.192	26	7	5	1	2	6	11	1
Pedro Gonzalez	.274	372	71	102	29	76	54	147	18
Roberto Gonzalez	.245	102	12	25	1	9	10	17	4
Osmy Gregorio	.252	111	12	28	4	21	6	23	5
Luis Hernandez	.145	69	2	10	0	6	0	31	0
Gabe Howell	.208	106	9	22	2	10	9	36	5
Korry Howell	.276	286	58	79	14	37	37	71	31
Ryan January	.212	33	7	7	2	3	9	15	0
Drew Jemison	.271	118	20	32	6	18	14	27	3
Gavin Johns	.281	82	4	23	0	6	0	19	2
Kingston Liniak	.211	90	8	19	2	10	4	30	1
Chris Monroe	.127	63	6	8	1	9	2	27	0
Luis Navarro	.192	47	3	9	0	5	2	11	0
Keenan O'Brien	.226	257	35	58	1	25	25	106	7
Tristan Pompey	.185	92	12	17	2	8	14	29	1
Mikey Reynolds	.192	94	14	18	1	10	12	22	6
JT Riddle	.220	186	29	41	7	32	18	33	5
Nilo Rijo	.189	122	19	23	3	7	20	30	5
Will Riley	.048	21	1	1	0	4	4	4	0
Payton Robertson	.184	114	21	21	3	11	13	34	14
Jason Rooks	.200	20	2	4	0	0	2	11	1
Aldenis Sanchez	.204	98	16	20	2	10	13	29	11
Jesus Tavarez	.258	159	23	41	4	19	12	31	3
Brady Whalen	.218	285	54	62	14	50	42	45	16
Justin Williams	.216	116	19	25	5	16	16	27	4

Name	W	L	ERA	G	SV	IP	H	BB	SO
Aldry Acosta	2	5	2.05	16	0	22	13	6	15
Jose Acuna	1	4	6.21	9	0	33	34	45	27
Carson Atwood	3	0	3.66	19	0	20	28	4	14
Dustin Beggs	5	11	6.45	30	0	120	148	40	71
Parker Bugg	0	1	5.51	6	0	16	20	6	12
Victor Capellan	2	1	7.23	26	0	24	36	4	24
Neraldo Catalina	0	0	9.28	11	0	11	9	17	9
Kyle Cody	0	0	2.79	5	0	10	5	9	16
Harold Cortijo	2	1	4.18	6	0	28	23	17	21
Luis De La Rosa	1	2	6.75	14	0	44	45	32	42
Nick Galese	1	0	10.80	3	0	12	20	11	3
Nick Gardewine	0	0	0.90	21	9	20	7	8	25
Osiris German	0	2	4.30	16	2	15	7	12	20
Donald Goodson	1	1	6.11	19	2	18	17	14	16
Jean Herrera	2	0	0.00	15	0	14	5	2	9
Nic Laio	7	5	4.10	19	0	86	75	31	93
John LaRossa	0	1	9.69	14	0	13	12	15	11
Jett Lodes	1	2	4.55	28	0	28	28	16	27
Alex MacKinnon	0	0	6.45	19	0	22	26	21	20
Carlos Martinez	0	2	6.17	19	2	23	25	18	28
Justin Miller	2	9	7.43	18	0	86	100	56	70
Gerald Ogando	0	2	4.30	11	0	15	14	7	14
David Reckers	1	2	8.74	5	0	23	31	16	13
Matt Reitz	3	8	5.67	17	0	94	98	22	53

Name	W	L	ERA	G	SV	IP	H	BB	SO
Jesse Remington	0	2	15.32	7	0	12	17	10	6
Javier Reynoso	2	5	8.51	23	0	61	82	30	36
Joe Joe Rodriguez	0	3	7.49	32	0	40	44	26	54
Raymells Rosa	1	1	6.75	14	0	17	16	8	17
Wesley Scott	2	3	4.70	9	0	44	27	26	40
Elio Serrano	2	0	7.46	20	1	25	30	23	29

LONG ISLAND DUCKS

Name	AVG	AB	R	H	HR	RBI	BB	SO	SB
Aaron Antonini	.289	356	57	103	15	62	40	54	4
Jackie Bradley Jr.	.400	165	36	66	12	35	23	22	6
Leobaldo Cabrera	.319	119	27	38	4	20	22	26	12
Ivan Castillo	.297	300	52	89	11	48	23	32	16
Yoelquis Céspedes	.262	84	6	22	1	10	6	20	0
Tyler Dearden	.361	202	37	73	12	46	15	39	2
Joe DeLuca	.225	40	3	9	2	8	5	15	1
JC Encarnación	.253	297	63	75	17	56	29	90	39
Manuel Geraldo	.245	196	26	48	2	19	17	59	11
Héctor Gómez	.220	109	10	24	2	20	2	13	1
Joe Gray	.143	21	1	3	0	1	1	6	0
Nick Heath	.264	227	51	60	8	36	47	74	27
Yonny Hernández	.325	120	24	39	0	14	22	18	20
Kevin Higgins	.225	98	9	22	1	4	2	33	3
Kole Kaler	.311	190	33	59	0	20	22	34	14
Scott Kelly	.251	207	39	52	1	21	24	26	4
Taylor Kohlwey	.240	171	17	41	2	21	28	33	2
Ryan McBroom	.268	314	60	84	19	68	50	72	8
Alex McGarry	.195	82	11	16	2	8	10	23	8
Tyler Osik	.211	38	1	8	0	1	4	6	0
Alexis Pantoja	.222	108	15	24	1	11	6	22	1
Zach Racusin	.309	162	18	50	1	17	15	20	5
Frank Schwindel	.325	240	44	78	14	56	28	33	0
Chance Sisco	.261	222	42	58	16	45	31	69	0
Chad Smith	.180	39	5	7	1	3	1	15	2
Joe Suozzi	.194	31	5	6	1	3	5	12	1
Jonathan Waite	.111	27	2	3	0	0	10	9	0
Rixon Wingrove	.305	59	13	18	3	9	10	12	1

Name	W	L	ERA	G	SV	IP	H	BB	SO
Al Alburquerque	2	1	3.66	21	2	20	21	7	24
Justin Alintoff	3	2	4.46	38	1	75	76	23	60
Trevor Bettencourt	2	2	6.26	21	0	23	27	11	34
Rolando Casihis	0	0	10.80	18	0	18	26	13	15
Wei-Yin Chen	5	5	6.37	17	0	88	118	29	63
Daniel Corcino	6	9	6.07	23	0	105	136	45	74
Sam Delaplane	3	2	4.63	23	1	23	20	18	44
Chris Ellis	1	1	5.45	7	0	35	38	16	41
Jake Fishman	2	0	2.25	14	0	12	9	7	20
David Griffin	2	1	4.45	12	0	30	32	8	26
Miguel Guerrero	1	1	5.90	28	0	29	25	20	29
Josh James	0	0	8.10	23	0	20	26	20	28
John LaRossa	2	1	6.43	10	0	14	11	14	15
Emilio Marquez	1	2	2.81	8	0	26	23	7	33
Tim Melville	0	1	11.17	12	0	10	15	10	15
Mike Montgomery	6	7	5.65	22	0	100	117	40	72
Charlie Neuweiler	0	2	11.39	6	0	21	40	13	18
Wladimir Pinto	1	1	6.92	13	0	13	13	16	13
Jimmy Robbins	6	6	5.94	16	0	77	92	40	68
Sal Romano	2	1	4.72	8	1	34	35	9	25
Ramon Santos	6	1	0.58	45	14	47	25	21	76
Matt Seelinger	0	0	0.44	21	11	21	9	8	31
Mitchell Senger	0	2	4.38	2	0	12	12	1	9
Nick Tropeano	4	2	5.48	15	0	46	50	23	39
Bobby Vath	0	1	8.90	14	0	30	38	18	31
Peyton Williams	4	2	5.11	42	0	37	39	19	35
Stephen Woods	5	5	5.29	16	0	80	105	39	82

SOUTHERN MARYLAND BLUE CRABS

Name	AVG	AB	R	H	HR	RBI	BB	SO	SB
Alan Alonso	.198	116	16	23	6	17	9	39	7
Michael Baca	.225	160	23	36	1	14	18	27	10
Anthony Brocato	.246	390	73	96	29	83	65	132	2
Josh Broughton	.257	436	63	112	9	53	29	61	19
Travis Demeritte	.221	77	14	17	2	5	18	21	2

Payton Eeles	.292	24	8	7	3	4	3	2	2
Matt Hibbert	.201	169	34	34	3	16	29	71	10
Aaron Hill	.231	398	72	92	20	68	65	109	38
Juan Kelly	.252	441	76	111	17	75	64	107	24
Caleb Marquez	.211	199	23	42	5	25	20	84	2
Brandon Pugh	.226	53	10	12	0	2	7	22	6
Isaias Quiroz	.174	218	22	38	4	15	23	89	0
Anthony Ray	.238	214	31	51	2	21	23	41	4
Jomar Reyes	.274	175	22	48	8	34	11	25	2
Michael Wielansky	.304	359	77	109	10	55	59	55	10
Miles Williams	.243	276	36	67	16	50	24	108	2
Gabe Wurtz	.200	110	9	22	4	25	13	32	0
Ian Yetsko	.234	209	24	49	8	25	10	77	6

Name	W	L	ERA	G	SV	IP	H	BB	SO
Kyle Arjona	1	1	8.63	30	0	49	63	29	37
Endrys Briceno	5	4	2.06	44	20	52	39	22	84
A.J. Candelario	1	2	3.31	8	0	35	28	16	45
Derek Casey	3	4	7.20	31	1	55	66	27	67
Jason Creasy	6	2	2.80	47	0	61	54	18	72
Spencer Johnston	5	5	5.98	15	0	81	86	19	69
Ian Kahaloa	10	9	5.48	25	0	131	130	60	138
Neil Lang	1	0	8.47	4	0	17	24	11	18
Garrett Martin	6	10	5.28	25	0	140	142	45	122
Trevor McGee	0	2	5.81	24	0	48	53	45	30
Alex Merithew	2	1	2.97	12	0	30	27	12	25
Hunter Schilperoort	1	4	5.36	34	1	49	54	28	56
Shawn Semple	3	7	5.23	20	0	93	104	25	75
Cody Thompson	2	4	3.80	40	1	66	55	26	69
Daryl Thompson	6	15	6.87	26	0	152	200	44	106

STATEN ISLAND FERRYHAWKS

Name	AVG	AB	R	H	HR	RBI	BB	SO	SB
Stephen Alemais	.100	20	2	2	0	1	1	5	1
Abiatal Avelino	.194	67	7	13	2	9	7	7	3
Roldani Baldwin	.212	85	10	18	1	8	5	24	1
Robert Brooks	.354	79	23	28	6	20	24	14	3
Will Butcher	.318	44	6	14	1	8	4	10	0
Luis Castro	.356	343	77	122	24	80	58	62	22
Alejandro De Aza	.269	245	43	66	7	40	32	50	5
Kyle Dernedde	.291	148	24	43	0	10	19	54	2
Joe Dunand	.252	238	38	60	7	28	28	45	0
Calvin Estrada	.253	95	17	24	3	14	14	25	6
Wilkerman Garcia	.113	53	8	6	0	3	11	14	1
Jeison Guzmán	.225	178	21	40	5	23	14	69	3
Jordan Howard	.258	31	4	8	1	1	4	11	2
Korry Howell	.135	52	6	7	1	3	5	15	3
Kolby Johnson	.308	429	93	132	11	62	32	83	32
Jackson Loftin	.239	88	14	21	2	12	9	21	11
Drew Maggi	.235	102	8	24	3	15	8	18	4
Dave Martinez	.244	41	2	10	0	4	1	14	0
Clayton Mehlbauer	.160	25	4	4	0	0	1	10	0
David Melfi	.149	101	12	15	3	15	10	42	1
Taylor Motter	.340	106	17	36	8	24	20	25	1
Andres Noriega	.222	27	6	6	1	2	4	8	0
Ben Norman	.259	440	67	114	19	74	53	101	13
Pablo Sandoval	.248	475	58	118	10	79	46	114	0
Nate Scantlin	.273	465	77	127	5	57	36	98	30
Matt Scheffler	.250	80	13	20	2	9	11	18	2
Xavier Vargas	.229	35	2	8	0	4	6	10	0

Name	W	L	ERA	G	SV	IP	H	BB	SO
Christian Allegretti	6	3	4.64	34	0	66	59	24	70
Robbie Baker	2	3	3.04	47	11	50	44	18	65
Christian Capuano	10	3	4.53	19	0	101	100	34	104
Anthony DeFabbia	1	2	8.31	7	0	17	23	12	14
John Esposito	1	3	7.06	7	0	22	25	12	12
Mark Faello	0	2	6.14	20	0	44	52	22	45
Nate Griep	1	1	6.27	19	0	19	18	15	20
Cam Hill	0	3	6.91	6	0	27	39	9	19
Josh James	0	0	3.78	17	1	17	14	12	29
Joe Jones	0	2	5.46	28	0	31	28	21	34
William Kirwan	2	2	5.81	22	0	53	70	25	37
Aaron Leasher	7	2	2.21	12	0	73	57	23	66
Taylor Lepard	3	6	4.96	13	0	65	74	27	51
Brian McKenna	1	2	1.91	37	6	42	34	8	60
Brennen Oxford	3	1	2.63	12	0	14	13	8	11
Anthony Quattrocchi	0	1	4.76	5	0	11	12	8	4
Matt Reitz	0	3	8.14	7	0	24	32	7	17
Nate Roe	3	3	5.01	14	0	41	41	31	45
Mike Shawaryn	6	9	6.59	21	0	111	139	45	79
James Sherfy	0	1	6.91	14	1	14	13	9	16
Noe Toribio	3	4	6.70	9	0	43	52	16	37
Bryan Warzek	2	5	3.79	44	0	59	46	26	72
J.P. Woodward	0	4	3.68	45	4	51	55	22	36

YORK REVOLUTION

Name	AVG	AB	R	H	HR	RBI	BB	SO	SB
Roldani Baldwin	.333	30	5	10	4	10	0	6	0
Jordy Barley	.143	35	2	5	0	3	3	12	2
Jamari Baylor	.255	47	5	12	3	12	7	14	3
Michael Berglund	.236	140	28	33	5	32	29	44	5
Donovan Casey	.348	322	78	112	16	96	31	71	33
John Cristino	.182	22	4	4	0	1	1	11	0
Chase Dawson	.389	36	10	14	2	6	5	4	3
Ciaran Devenney	.198	162	37	32	11	31	35	70	2
Kevin Higgins	.370	27	1	10	0	1	1	5	1
Kobe Kato	.255	231	51	59	7	27	46	56	27
Rudy Martin	.326	402	108	131	12	57	68	88	78
Trey Martin	.253	253	49	64	8	44	26	82	16
Matt McDermott	.309	508	113	157	18	66	39	115	54
Paul Mondesi	.180	50	3	9	1	6	2	11	0
Alexis Pantoja	.240	75	7	18	1	14	4	8	2
Joe Perez	.277	47	9	13	2	8	1	12	2
Alfredo Reyes	.278	363	49	101	5	53	32	103	31
Jacob Rhinesmith	.316	421	88	133	9	67	63	45	32
Alejandro Rivero	.183	60	6	11	2	5	7	16	3
Christian Sepulveda	.148	27	4	4	1	3	3	9	4
Alerick Soularie	.305	105	22	32	6	30	9	24	11
Paxton Wallace	.171	41	8	7	1	3	9	11	1
David Washington	.260	408	84	106	35	96	46	198	19
Colton Welker	.347	190	39	66	11	59	32	38	1
Zander Wiel	.323	226	46	73	17	58	25	56	5

Name	W	L	ERA	G	SV	IP	H	BB	SO
Frankie Bartow	3	2	5.94	38	4	36	41	15	32
Denny Bentley	4	0	3.40	46	1	50	48	17	57
Will Carter	0	0	3.86	14	0	12	16	5	15
Nelvin Correa	3	1	3.86	22	0	21	20	4	25
Aaron Fletcher	6	5	5.55	24	0	128	146	55	95
Oliver Garcia	0	1	2.79	10	0	10	12	4	10
Aaron Holiday	2	0	1.13	16	0	16	9	5	23
Michael Horrell	6	8	5.03	30	0	116	133	43	86
Neil Lang	0	0	10.13	6	0	11	17	7	5
Ethan Lindow	11	5	5.06	21	0	101	121	37	71
Moises Lugo	3	0	1.15	16	0	16	12	7	23
Zach Neff	8	7	6.29	24	0	117	147	42	90
Jon Olsen	12	3	3.60	25	3	128	120	26	136
Brett Schulze	1	3	7.20	17	6	15	12	15	15
Will Stewart	1	4	7.90	20	0	49	61	36	53
Tom Sutera	4	2	4.13	37	1	65	61	17	44
Matt Turner	4	1	2.44	49	17	48	37	18	62
Chris Vallimont	6	2	2.13	13	0	55	36	17	68
Alex Valverde	5	0	4.39	36	1	55	47	26	63

FRONTIER LEAGUE

Quebec won its third straight Frontier League title as Anthon Quirion hit a three-run walk-off home run for a 7-6 win over Washington. This is the first time any Frontier League has won three straight titles.

West Division	W	L	PCT	GB
*Washington Wild Things	67	28	.705	-
^Gateway Grizzlies	59	36	.621	8
^Lake Erie Crushers	51	44	.537	16
Schaumburg Boomers	51	45	.531	16.5
Florence Y'alls	44	51	.463	23
Evansville Otters	41	55	.427	26.5
Windy City Thunderbolts	40	56	.417	27.5

Team	W	L	PCT	GB
Joliet Slammers	38	58	.396	29.5
East Division	**W**	**L**	**PCT**	**GB**
*Québec Capitales	64	32	.667	-
^Tri-City ValleyCats	53	41	.564	10
^Ottawa Titans	53	42	.558	10.5
New York Boulders	52	44	.542	12
Trois-Rivières Aigles	44	51	.463	19.5
New England Knockouts	38	56	.404	25
New Jersey Jackals	35	61	.365	29
Sussex County Miners	33	63	.344	31

**Division Champ. ^Wild Card*

Playoffs—Wild Card: Lake Erie defeated Gateway and Ottawa defeated Tri-City. **Semifinals:** Quebec defeated Ottawa 2-1 and Washington defeated Lake Erie 2-0 in best-of-five series. **Finals:** Quebec defeated Washington 3-1 in best-of-five series.

Attendance: Schaumburg 231,322; Québec 160,628; New York 130,615; Joliet 104,426; Florence 100,587; Evansville96,488; Lake Erie 96,084; Sussex County 88,180; Gateway 87,385; Ottawa 85,214; New Jersey 81,528; New England 51,295.

All-Star Team: C-John Cristino, New England. **1B-**Matthew Warkentin, Joliet. **2B-**Alec Craig, Schaumburg. **3B-**AJ Wright, Ottawa. **SS-**Austin Dennis, New York. **OF-**Caleb McNeely, Washington; Justin Gideon, Québec; TJ Reeves, Florence. **DH-T**yreque Reed, Washington. **SP-**James Bradwell, Québec. **RP-**Gyeongju Kim, Washington.

Most Valuable Player: Cabe McNeely, Washington. **Pitcher of the Year:** James Bradwell, Quebec. **Rookie of the Year:** TJ Reeves, Florence. Manager of the Year: Patrick Scalabrini, Quebec.

BATTING LEADERS

Player, Team	AVG	OBP	SLG	AB	R	H	HR	RBI	SB
Tyreque Reed, Wash.	.341	.418	.552	223	38	76	12	52	1
Raphael Gladu, T-R	.340	.411	.445	353	51	120	6	55	21
Brendon Dadson, T-R	.337	.442	.473	279	42	94	6	46	5
Steve Barmakian, NY	.331	.419	.436	266	52	88	2	39	17
Kyle Novak, T-C	.329	.376	.431	246	33	81	4	39	2
Austin Dennis, NY	.328	.396	.438	384	75	126	5	43	39
Gabe Holt, Gate.	.324	.384	.394	330	50	107	2	37	13
Ed Johnson, Flo.	.320	.395	.435	322	56	103	3	43	26
Peter Zimmermann, Gate.	.316	.419	.597	313	64	99	23	66	20
Cory Acton, SC	.311	.399	.403	318	47	99	6	42	31

PITCHING LEADERS

Player, Team	W	L	ERA	G	IP	H	BB	SO
Kevin Pindel, WC	9	7	2.00	19	122	123	27	95
Ryan Sandberg, Queb.	7	2	2.18	24	103	74	20	107
Zach Kirby, Wash.	10	4	2.42	17	104	86	25	100
Anthony Escobar, LE	8	4	2.43	19	111	94	36	86
James Bradwell, Queb	12	0	2.72	23	109	96	33	97
Kobe Foster, Wash.	10	1	2.91	18	118	102	23	126
Jack Eisenbarger, LE	8	4	2.91	19	111	84	47	111
Deylen Miley, Gate.	8	4	3.14	19	103	62	48	161
Tucker Smith, T-R	8	4	3.24	20	128	114	21	94
Teague Conrad, Gate.	7	4	3.29	18	101	81	49	90

EVANSVILLE OTTERS

Name	AVG	AB	R	H	HR	RBI	BB	SO	SB
Alex Adams	.273	33	6	9	0	1	6	11	0
Randy Bednar	.259	320	60	83	13	47	33	85	12
Austin Bost	.171	70	6	12	1	7	2	18	0
Logan Brown	.242	186	16	45	3	27	6	36	1
J.J. Cruz	.250	68	6	17	1	5	7	21	3
Riley Delgado	.278	90	14	25	0	8	8	9	2
Gio DiGiacomo	.281	160	30	45	0	21	21	47	11
Justin Felix	.190	121	22	23	5	13	23	59	2
Nick Gonzalez	.094	32	2	3	0	2	2	10	0
Jake Green	.230	100	9	23	1	7	8	14	0
Troy Hamilton	.130	23	3	3	0	1	2	2	0
Mason House	.136	22	5	3	1	2	8	18	0
Clayton Keyes	.167	24	4	4	0	4	5	15	1
Amani Larry	.194	31	2	6	0	2	3	4	3
Patrick Lee	.410	39	12	16	3	12	12	9	10
Gary Mattis	.303	162	36	49	2	15	21	35	21
David Mendham	.309	333	46	103	5	49	67	58	15
Blake Mozley	.226	84	10	19	0	9	6	29	1
Alec Olund	.235	204	28	48	6	42	21	48	6
Pavin Parks	.283	184	33	52	9	42	28	50	10
Mike Peabody	.187	75	9	14	2	16	5	28	0
Dakota Phillips	.265	132	23	35	12	39	17	55	2
Jomar Reyes	.231	156	21	36	2	17	10	30	4
Bryan Rosario	.095	21	5	2	0	0	7	6	4
Mason White	.255	231	29	59	5	36	19	54	17
Donivan Williams	.250	28	7	7	2	4	2	10	2
Delvin Zinn	.245	196	31	48	1	14	19	30	19

Name	W	L	ERA	G	SV	IP	H	BB	SO
Jon Beymer	4	2	3.83	38	1	56	50	29	67
Parker Brahms	6	6	4.47	18	0	95	93	39	71
Johan Castillo	1	2	6.38	6	0	24	32	9	15
Casey Delgado	2	2	2.88	10	0	41	36	14	35
Tyler Driver	1	0	4.86	12	0	17	12	14	15
Tristan Harvin	2	4	6.20	13	0	45	53	22	45
Grif Hughes	1	1	3.07	36	1	44	33	17	61
Chip Korbacher	1	1	3.82	20	0	38	23	28	38
James Krick	1	0	6.52	8	0	10	10	7	11
Terance Marin	0	7	7.90	7	0	27	44	13	14
Michael McAvene	1	7	3.00	32	8	33	32	15	38
Jakob Meyer	0	0	2.05	16	0	26	18	16	26
Pat Miner	1	0	8.69	13	0	20	26	4	19
Pavin Parks	2	1	2.51	14	7	14	12	2	18
Tyler Ras	1	0	6.86	8	0	20	26	7	20
Braden Scott	5	10	4.17	20	0	121	121	43	128
Zach Smith	7	8	3.81	20	0	113	115	50	125
Alex Valdez	2	0	1.26	12	0	14	9	5	17
Ryan Wiltse	2	2	4.50	21	0	40	39	15	34

FLORENCE FREEDOM

Name	AVG	AB	R	H	HR	RBI	BB	SO	SB
Jeremiah Burks	.167	30	7	5	1	2	6	13	1
Ashton Creal	.205	78	9	16	2	9	10	29	8
Dalton Davis	.395	86	24	34	6	14	13	10	1
Brian Fuentes	.275	371	73	102	12	74	60	95	3
Langston Ginder	.215	79	11	17	3	12	4	22	0
Sergio Gutierrez	.235	234	39	55	13	44	21	99	9
Stephen Hrustich	.290	228	44	66	14	51	22	55	4
Ed Johnson	.320	322	56	103	3	43	29	55	26
Thomas Jones	.143	35	7	5	0	4	6	16	1
Justin Lavey	.278	108	17	30	5	20	6	26	2
Craig Massey	.265	306	47	81	1	41	42	48	5
Blaze O'Saben	.299	147	29	44	2	12	10	32	20
T.J. Reeves	.293	324	60	95	18	71	29	100	1
Zade Richardson	.303	304	48	92	11	66	34	84	0
Hank Zeisler	.301	355	81	107	10	63	53	88	7

Name	W	L	ERA	G	SV	IP	H	BB	SO
Randy Abshier	2	0	5.21	5	0	19	19	13	11
Gage Bihm	0	2	9.75	6	0	12	18	11	9
Logan Campbell	3	0	2.19	12	0	25	20	10	29
Dante Chirico	1	1	7.33	6	0	23	32	8	17
Matt Fernandez	2	2	2.19	10	1	25	23	5	17
Ty Good	1	2	8.80	7	0	30	34	23	21
Gunnar Groen	1	1	13.94	6	0	10	14	10	11
Shane Gustafson	0	0	5.23	5	0	10	18	4	7
Luke Helton	0	1	9.82	2	0	11	16	7	9
Kent Klyman	0	3	4.22	36	5	43	37	24	55
Blake Loubier	1	3	12.23	6	0	18	24	27	12
Edgar Martinez	2	3	4.44	11	0	51	49	43	44
Hunter Mink	2	0	3.38	5	0	21	18	11	15
Cam Pferrer	3	0	1.50	14	3	18	13	6	23
Carter Poiry	2	4	10.94	14	0	26	30	28	22
Reed Smith	6	3	4.75	13	0	72	72	25	53
Ben Terwilliger	4	2	4.75	28	5	36	30	18	39
Ross Thompson	3	5	6.98	23	2	59	81	28	50
Jonaiker Villalobos	4	8	4.99	20	0	110	144	30	95
Alex Wagner	2	2	4.82	25	2	47	51	13	44
Ryan Watson	1	0	2.76	3	0	16	20	1	17
Evan Webster	2	1	4.50	8	0	36	47	3	20
Darrien Williams	0	1	6.15	35	2	41	38	24	37

GATEWAY GRIZZLIES

Name	AVG	AB	R	H	HR	RBI	BB	SO	SB
José Alvarez	.276	221	27	61	2	29	17	42	5
Cole Brannen	.211	247	58	52	9	29	43	74	30
Victor Castillo	.318	176	31	56	3	29	23	34	18
Abdiel Diaz	.272	320	48	87	6	50	45	46	26
Kyle Gaedele	.162	198	26	32	4	10	27	69	4
Gabe Holt	.324	330	50	107	2	37	27	23	13
Kevin Krause	.251	267	35	67	10	48	31	38	1
David Maberry	.217	69	8	15	1	4	6	21	0
Edwin Mateo	.229	319	46	73	2	17	36	61	22
Andrew Moritz	.204	93	19	19	3	13	18	20	5
Tyler Shelnut	.175	40	3	7	1	4	6	14	0
Elias Stevens	.191	21	2	4	1	3	1	10	0
D.J. Stewart	.310	332	39	103	13	66	21	46	13
Dale Thomas	.228	79	12	18	2	12	13	24	5
Mark Vierling	.264	87	10	23	1	7	10	19	1
Tate Wargo	.311	74	13	23	0	12	4	15	5
Peter Zimmermann	.316	313	64	99	23	66	42	71	20

Name	W	L	ERA	G	SV	IP	H	BB	SO
Joel Condreay	1	1	5.04	24	0	30	30	17	32
Teague Conrad	7	4	3.29	18	0	101	81	49	90
Tyler Cornett	5	2	6.49	14	0	53	63	29	52
Leoni De La Cruz	2	3	4.19	39	14	39	28	19	52
Alvery De Los Santos	3	1	3.42	23	2	68	67	27	65
Nate Garkow	3	0	1.72	17	1	16	4	8	37
Justin Goossen-Brown	3	5	4.91	35	1	44	52	18	23
Matt Hickey	4	3	2.11	41	4	43	34	17	46
Kaleb Hill	2	1	6.32	12	0	37	35	28	27
Deylen Miley	8	4	3.14	19	0	103	62	48	161
Ryne Moore	1	2	7.50	5	0	18	26	9	14
Collin Sullivan	9	5	3.62	18	0	102	78	41	106
Nathanial Tate	1	2	5.13	17	0	26	29	18	26
Gage Vailes	0	1	5.31	18	0	20	18	12	14
Lukas Veinbergs	5	4	2.30	26	6	82	64	38	72
Alec Whaley	5	1	2.47	42	0	44	38	14	38

JOLIET SLAMMERS

Name	AVG	AB	R	H	HR	RBI	BB	SO	SB
Jake Allgeyer	.250	52	4	13	1	7	4	13	0
Chris Davis	.246	220	31	54	2	20	32	68	7
Jeissy De la Cruz	.247	291	43	72	2	25	48	63	11
Braden Duhon	.242	95	11	23	0	5	12	26	7
Andrew Fernandez	.242	124	20	30	2	13	16	30	5
Giovanni Garbella	.168	113	8	19	1	11	16	43	2
Spencer Griffin	.095	21	3	2	0	2	1	11	0
Brandon Heidal	.178	146	15	26	1	11	18	38	1
Cal Hejza	.171	82	6	14	0	6	4	13	3
Liam McArthur	.281	367	51	103	3	36	53	61	13
Broc Mortensen	.000	20	2	0	0	0	3	12	1
Victor Nova	.228	303	49	69	7	36	54	59	9
Adam Pottinger	.294	34	7	10	0	6	4	10	1
Jonathan Sierra	.254	323	23	82	3	43	23	57	1
Drew Stengren	.276	134	14	37	0	23	21	16	0
Tommy Stevenson	.194	108	8	21	2	12	12	42	0
Antonio Valdez	.278	302	49	84	3	38	28	63	15
Matt Warkentin	.299	391	76	117	24	83	24	90	4

Name	W	L	ERA	G	SV	IP	H	BB	SO
Jake Armstrong	4	9	4.85	18	0	91	89	37	64
Nick Bautista	0	1	8.03	11	0	12	14	9	14
Ricky Castro	0	0	3.00	3	0	15	9	9	18
Ian Delleman	0	4	6.00	28	1	27	25	21	43
Andrew Dietz	1	2	10.35	5	0	20	28	16	8
Geno Encina	4	3	1.15	11	0	63	35	9	42
Zach Grace	1	3	5.79	26	0	42	54	22	45
David Harrison	1	1	5.28	34	1	31	31	18	28
Greyson Linderman	1	1	0.82	10	1	11	8	3	18
Dwayne Marshall	4	8	5.19	20	0	85	84	37	85
Jacob Morin	1	1	2.91	30	1	34	35	5	32
Frank Plesac	3	0	4.01	37	1	49	57	15	17
Brett Sanchez	4	6	4.42	18	0	96	98	31	79
Landon Smiddy	1	2	7.76	7	0	31	37	20	20
Cameron Smith	3	2	2.72	41	4	43	38	8	41
Matt Walker	0	0	2.45	4	0	22	15	2	15
Cole Wesneski	3	2	4.34	18	3	19	17	6	11
Zac Westcott	6	8	4.96	21	0	118	122	42	91

LAKE ERIE CRUSHERS

Name	AVG	AB	R	H	HR	RBI	BB	SO	SB
Jason Agresti	.265	223	23	59	4	20	23	37	0
Vincent Byrd	.233	245	34	57	15	47	20	101	0
Alberti Chavez	.275	367	41	101	3	24	33	53	5
Sean Cheely	.125	32	9	4	0	2	5	10	4
Burle Dixon	.228	233	36	53	4	26	38	72	9
Alex Epp	.243	37	4	9	0	3	6	11	0
Walner Espinal	.200	105	13	21	1	12	10	42	1
Sam Franco	.224	85	10	19	4	13	3	30	6
Alfredo González	.288	139	21	40	9	32	15	34	8
Jake Guenther	.272	290	45	79	4	37	33	31	12
Jack Harris	.246	317	44	78	9	37	19	92	6
Scout Knotts	.252	222	38	56	5	32	34	53	9
Ethan Skender	.246	138	16	34	4	18	12	25	17
Logan Thomason	.248	303	42	75	6	31	37	85	15
Jose Torrealba	.171	41	6	7	1	5	1	20	0
Michel Triana	.086	58	5	5	1	3	5	21	2
Johnny Tuccillo	.266	177	30	47	5	20	30	32	4
Ron Washington	.228	276	36	63	10	38	38	84	16
Jarrod Watkins	.251	350	48	88	6	38	27	65	8

Name	W	L	ERA	G	SV	IP	H	BB	SO
Cal Carver	2	2	1.66	38	0	49	42	21	53
Sam Curtis	0	0	2.38	12	0	11	7	4	6
Pedro Echemendía	3	7	5.91	11	0	56	71	17	34
Jack Eisenbarger	8	4	2.91	19	0	111	84	47	111
Anthony Escobar	8	4	2.43	19	0	111	94	36	86
Trevor Kuncl	4	4	2.47	41	21	44	42	9	59
Matt Mulhearn	5	9	5.27	18	0	94	107	40	40
Enrique Ozoa	2	0	4.50	15	0	18	24	15	9
Kenny Pierson	1	3	4.58	41	0	39	42	25	43
Darrien Ragins	7	3	3.78	16	0	86	78	36	72
Leonardo Rodríguez	2	0	3.71	29	0	53	40	32	59
Christian Scafidi	1	0	1.37	47	0	53	32	13	54
Sammy Tavarez	3	3	3.32	44	2	41	34	23	59
Matt Valin	3	2	4.81	8	0	39	23	30	47

NEW ENGLAND KNOCKOUTS

Name	AVG	AB	R	H	HR	RBI	BB	SO	SB
Luis Atiles	.203	197	31	40	2	23	34	40	7
Jake Boone	.292	366	58	107	11	53	22	59	28
Keagan Calero	.224	152	26	34	2	13	11	24	13
John Cristino	.293	345	65	101	26	72	33	114	4
J.R. DiSarcina	.233	326	54	76	4	35	29	91	9
Pat Galvin	.227	22	5	5	0	2	1	5	0
Jalen Garcia	.238	231	31	55	11	48	12	59	14
Nick Hassan	.205	39	9	8	0	5	2	6	0
Mark Herron	.217	83	8	18	3	11	7	23	1
Ramon Jimenez	.224	183	20	41	5	23	26	68	11
Tommy Kretzler	.247	186	23	46	4	20	15	56	5
Noah Lucier	.245	184	21	45	0	10	23	47	11
Zach May	.241	58	10	14	1	7	12	22	0
Brady West	.228	224	28	51	6	26	30	71	3
Austin White	.304	362	61	110	1	40	55	55	60
Jack Wold	.293	318	51	93	15	56	20	51	2

Name	W	L	ERA	G	SV	IP	H	BB	SO
Trevor Anibal	1	3	7.53	12	0	29	36	16	22
Casey Bargo	0	5	7.49	12	0	34	35	28	32
Heisell Baro	1	1	4.05	41	0	47	35	28	47
Brendan Bell	1	5	9.85	28	1	25	38	23	14
Richard Brito	3	0	3.77	7	0	43	32	15	40
Anderson Comás	0	4	6.70	13	0	43	51	36	24
Matt Cronin	4	9	8.02	21	0	89	115	54	53
Nic Daniels	1	0	4.91	18	0	22	20	25	19
Dan Goggin	1	3	3.63	39	0	45	40	28	42
Joe Kemlage	3	4	7.51	17	0	50	62	26	36
Matt Maloney	0	0	4.09	7	0	11	16	6	11
James Marinan	0	3	14.18	4	0	13	23	12	7

Name	W	L	ERA	G	SV	IP	H	BB	SO
Reeves Martin	7	2	2.47	38	9	51	43	14	52
Mike McKenna	3	0	1.76	16	0	15	10	10	16
Liam O'Sullivan	4	10	4.63	21	1	134	151	19	68
Kyle Petri	0	0	3.72	13	0	10	14	11	10
Michael Quigley	2	1	3.47	6	0	23	19	23	18
Sam Ryan	7	6	5.13	21	0	95	106	32	93
Ben Seiler	2	3	5.37	28	2	70	74	52	55
Neil Uskali	2	2	8.57	5	0	21	33	8	15
Brad VanAsdlen	1	2	16.36	13	0	11	18	12	5
Luke Williamson	1	2	7.71	19	0	14	22	18	16

NEW JERSEY JACKALS

Name	AVG	AB	R	H	HR	RBI	BB	SO	SB
Luis Acevedo	.321	112	24	36	2	18	15	19	12
Arbert Cipion	.241	237	47	57	12	47	36	72	35
John Daly	.222	117	14	26	0	7	6	37	2
Ryan Ford	.207	232	28	48	10	39	12	82	10
Fritz Genther	.294	153	15	45	3	23	17	44	11
Miguel Gómez	.303	145	16	44	3	28	7	15	0
Yovan Gonzalez	.100	20	1	2	0	0	2	4	0
Clayton Mehlbauer	.305	118	23	36	11	22	17	45	1
Frank Nigro	.239	209	19	50	3	20	24	53	1
Robb Paller	.201	144	20	29	4	18	30	52	1
Bryson Parks	.254	248	48	63	2	23	23	74	34
Nilo Rijo	.269	186	36	50	4	34	28	47	27
Kevin Rolon	.212	66	12	14	2	9	7	27	4
Hemmanuel Rosario	.290	224	33	65	9	31	19	58	6
Jordan Scott	.279	219	31	61	11	36	32	48	6
Edwin Tavarez	.186	97	11	18	1	11	19	35	3
Trent Taylor	.272	290	44	79	2	21	26	61	42
Xavier Valentin	.237	186	24	44	3	18	17	48	11
Cam Williamson	.178	90	6	16	1	10	11	22	2

Name	W	L	ERA	G	SV	IP	H	BB	SO
Alex Barker	3	5	4.94	10	0	55	66	18	39
Dazon Cole	2	2	4.60	41	6	43	36	35	36
Reinaldo De Paula	1	5	8.13	8	0	34	50	15	40
Mike DeSanti	0	1	5.74	14	1	16	18	14	17
Michael Gutierrez	0	3	9.28	3	0	11	14	15	7
Andrew Kramer	2	2	3.54	28	0	28	20	24	30
Jake Kuchmaner	2	3	5.02	8	0	43	42	24	34
Chris Mormile	0	1	2.90	42	1	40	39	19	38
Zack Morris	2	1	3.63	7	0	17	18	2	16
Austin Parsley	0	4	7.33	6	0	27	43	5	21
Edgar Rodriguez	0	3	7.86	8	0	26	27	26	18
Joe Joe Rodriguez	0	0	3.74	21	2	22	20	13	26
Dylan Sabia	3	6	4.85	14	0	72	87	25	45
Yuhi Sako	6	3	3.40	16	0	93	81	22	78
Danny Sullivan	0	1	9.19	10	0	16	20	15	14
Joe Testa	3	3	3.79	7	0	38	41	5	33
Jalon Tyson-Long	6	6	3.89	22	0	81	73	39	80
Wilfrido Valenzuela	1	3	8.40	6	0	30	33	19	18
Danny Vazquez	0	4	13.78	8	0	16	19	25	7
Ryan Velazquez	2	2	6.69	29	0	38	38	29	36
Matt Voelker	7	1	6.20	31	0	54	59	35	33

NEW YORK BOULDERS

Name	AVG	AB	R	H	HR	RBI	BB	SO	SB
Marshall Awtry	.181	94	19	17	2	12	28	41	1
Steve Barmakian	.331	266	52	88	2	39	40	30	17
Isaac Bellony	.318	220	38	70	10	42	24	58	1
Casey Dana	.277	206	41	57	6	30	18	48	8
Joe DeLuca	.266	290	50	77	15	56	59	87	8
Austin Dennis	.328	384	75	126	5	43	38	38	39
Christian Ficca	.284	67	6	19	0	11	8	15	0
Garrett Frechette	.156	32	3	5	0	1	3	5	0
Nick Gotta	.274	307	56	84	2	34	54	51	14
Chris Kwitzer	.271	388	56	105	14	62	23	91	4
Sam Linscott	.273	55	9	15	2	10	5	7	3
Assaf Lowengart	.154	52	9	8	3	11	7	29	2
Ryan McCoy	.365	52	14	19	2	6	12	17	1
Jake Reinisch	.227	66	6	15	2	12	11	22	2
David Vinsky	.253	360	51	91	12	64	53	116	4
Tom Walraven	.232	112	10	26	1	18	18	26	2

Name	W	L	ERA	G	SV	IP	H	BB	SO
Peter Allegro	2	3	3.60	38	1	45	40	13	60
Brandon Backman	8	6	4.66	18	0	95	97	33	114
Isaac Baez	0	1	6.97	2	0	10	14	3	5
Garrett Coe	2	0	3.93	16	0	34	25	15	30
Garrett Cooper	8	6	5.55	18	0	94	116	29	66
Jackson Cunningham	1	0	4.47	31	0	44	48	17	31
Aaron Dona	1	6	6.75	20	1	63	69	30	61
Colton Easterwood	2	2	6.32	41	1	47	46	20	47
Jonah Jenkins	0	2	9.53	3	0	11	15	8	11
Mitchell Senger	10	4	3.66	17	0	96	84	28	81
Jackson Sigman	0	0	4.05	14	0	13	11	7	12
Dylan Smith	7	2	1.56	34	13	40	15	34	54
Erik Stock	2	5	4.91	17	0	70	84	24	47
Blaine Traxel	7	5	3.59	19	0	120	123	29	85
Tyler Vail	3	1	3.30	27	0	44	41	9	40

OTTAWA TITANS

Name	AVG	AB	R	H	HR	RBI	BB	SO	SB
Evan Berkey	.200	35	6	7	0	1	4	5	3
Lamar Briggs	.265	234	25	62	1	30	22	45	4
Aaron Casillas	.299	194	23	58	0	23	10	29	2
Victor Cerny	.228	92	9	21	0	14	13	22	0
Jason DiCochea	.279	140	24	39	5	24	23	16	1
Michael Fuhrman	.213	225	41	48	4	31	30	83	12
Jake Hjelle	.245	49	8	12	1	4	5	14	2
Christian Ibarra	.241	266	29	64	4	37	38	46	1
Peyton Isaacson	.260	288	38	75	4	43	31	62	1
Brendan O'Donnell	.294	194	31	57	10	42	21	44	3
Laz Rivera	.231	26	3	6	1	2	1	5	1
Jake Sanford	.140	86	12	12	3	12	10	25	0
Jamey Smart	.266	342	36	91	4	59	32	63	2
Jackie Urbaez	.256	277	50	71	8	34	50	75	13
Malik Williams	.200	30	7	6	1	5	3	3	0
A.J. Wright	.304	342	75	104	13	52	59	75	4
Taylor Wright	.240	308	50	74	9	40	22	70	25

Name	W	L	ERA	G	SV	IP	H	BB	SO
CJ Blowers	0	1	0.87	5	0	31	26	11	16
Matt Dallas	4	2	3.50	40	3	46	50	23	27
Burle Dixon	2	1	2.81	9	0	16	11	7	10
Shane Gray	6	6	4.33	20	0	112	118	41	66
McLain Harris	3	2	3.59	33	2	43	34	11	40
Tyler Jandron	8	6	3.61	20	0	112	110	38	90
Jonah Jenkins	0	1	6.14	11	0	15	11	12	16
Breyln Jones	0	0	4.20	13	0	15	16	19	10
Grant Larson	7	4	3.61	17	0	105	108	21	81
Bryan Peña	7	6	3.94	21	0	80	64	54	99
Erasmo Pinales	2	4	2.84	38	23	38	29	32	41
Billy Price	2	0	5.40	5	0	15	19	6	13
Scott Prins	3	4	5.96	18	0	54	73	22	38
Brooks Walton	1	0	7.24	4	0	14	20	5	8
Kyle White	1	2	4.71	22	0	42	44	31	27

QUEBEC CAPITALES

Name	AVG	AB	R	H	HR	RBI	BB	SO	SB
Tyler Blaum	.202	114	20	23	2	13	17	32	1
Ruben Castro	.260	50	4	13	0	7	8	12	3
Kyle Crowl	.271	292	65	79	8	51	63	86	9
Guillermo García	.299	137	20	41	4	29	19	35	1
Justin Gideon	.287	335	56	96	20	65	50	78	19
David Glaude	.296	98	20	29	1	13	18	19	4
Francisco Hernandez	.222	126	24	28	5	15	25	36	10
Jonathan Lacroix	.288	292	41	84	3	44	63	73	12
Marc-Antoine Lebreux	.265	317	72	84	12	47	61	87	20
Jake MacKenzie	.223	296	58	66	5	42	48	47	46
Tyler Osik	.318	129	17	41	1	20	9	19	1
Juremi Profar	.263	57	6	15	0	6	3	9	0
Anthony Quirion	.231	273	44	63	7	52	38	71	14
Jeremy Rivera	.192	26	3	5	0	0	6	8	1
Tommy Seidl	.247	259	51	64	11	47	41	85	44
Mathieu Sirois	.259	85	14	22	5	26	6	27	3
Jesmuel Valentín	.271	258	65	70	9	49	45	47	9

Name	W	L	ERA	G	SV	IP	H	BB	SO
CJ Blowers	0	1	0.87	5	0	31	26	11	16
Matt Dallas	4	2	3.50	40	3	46	50	23	27
Burle Dixon	2	1	2.81	9	0	16	11	7	10
Shane Gray	6	6	4.33	20	0	112	118	41	66
McLain Harris	3	2	3.59	33	2	43	34	11	40
Tyler Jandron	8	6	3.61	20	0	112	110	38	90
Jonah Jenkins	0	1	6.14	11	0	15	11	12	16
Breyln Jones	0	0	4.20	13	0	15	16	19	10
Grant Larson	7	4	3.61	17	0	105	108	21	81
Bryan Peña	7	6	3.94	21	0	80	64	54	99
Erasmo Pinales	2	4	2.84	38	23	38	29	32	41
Billy Price	2	0	5.40	5	0	15	19	6	13
Scott Prins	3	4	5.96	18	0	54	73	22	38
Brooks Walton	1	0	7.24	4	0	14	20	5	8
Kyle White	1	2	4.71	22	0	42	44	31	27

SCHAUMBURG BOOMERS

Name	AVG	AB	R	H	HR	RBI	BB	SO	SB
Felix Aberouette	.229	96	15	22	4	15	11	22	0
Anthony Calarco	.298	255	30	76	9	48	21	50	0
Alec Craig	.291	299	70	87	2	43	95	63	21
Ty Crittenberger	.246	57	9	14	0	4	7	15	4
Chase Dawson	.289	377	73	109	4	63	42	44	44
Tyler Depreta-Johnson	.243	321	47	78	1	33	35	53	5
Christian Fedko	.296	308	58	91	5	50	60	29	14
Kyle Fitzgerald	.247	190	38	47	8	34	31	39	4
Willie Joe Garry	.195	41	1	8	0	5	2	12	3
Seth Gray	.225	120	20	27	4	23	12	25	4
Allante Hall	.230	87	10	20	1	7	14	29	0
Ryan McCarthy	.364	44	6	16	3	9	2	8	1
Jake Meyer	.217	106	11	23	0	10	11	24	0
Brett Milazzo	.268	183	27	49	1	23	20	25	9
Evan Orzech	.214	89	18	19	1	14	23	19	1
Will Prater	.220	173	23	38	2	15	17	44	4
Aaron Simmons	.273	271	51	74	12	54	41	59	3
Andrew Sojka	.298	104	17	31	2	21	12	19	7
Paxton Wallace	.233	146	18	34	2	17	17	32	2

Name	W	L	ERA	G	SV	IP	H	BB	SO
Cole Cook	6	5	3.76	21	0	122	126	38	135
Antonio Frias	2	2	5.82	7	0	39	37	27	42
Aaron Glickstein	6	6	5.25	23	0	96	110	30	66
Matt Helwig	2	2	3.50	16	1	18	15	7	22
Jackson Hickert	4	5	6.71	13	0	63	72	39	52
Jake Joyce	4	4	2.50	41	16	40	34	24	49
Brendan Knoll	2	5	5.43	11	0	56	62	28	40
Cristian Lopez	3	4	3.84	29	0	68	58	32	71
Hambleton Oliver	1	3	2.96	17	0	24	27	9	20
Jacob Smith	5	1	4.32	22	0	94	75	51	113
Cole Stallings	3	0	3.79	13	0	19	19	14	15
Dylan Stutsman	5	1	3.57	37	5	40	35	14	44
Mitch White	3	3	3.42	37	1	50	31	25	52
John Wilson	3	0	2.45	5	0	29	27	8	20
Dallas Woolfolk	2	2	4.15	35	2	43	45	13	39

SUSSEX COUNTY MINERS

Name	AVG	AB	R	H	HR	RBI	BB	SO	SB
Cory Acton	.311	318	47	99	6	42	47	65	31
Oraj Anu	.300	367	48	110	13	60	21	99	1
Hunter D'Amato	.274	186	28	51	1	19	18	31	11
Gehrig Ebel	.196	46	6	9	1	3	6	15	0
Willie Escala	.178	118	15	21	2	12	13	34	3
Evan Giordano	.242	298	40	72	5	35	35	61	1
Tony Gomez	.244	238	35	58	2	24	26	62	11
Sam Linscott	.164	67	9	11	0	7	7	9	5
Gabriel Maciel	.276	250	34	69	3	24	25	31	14
John Mead	.186	86	5	16	2	5	8	25	0
Kyle Richards	.174	86	10	15	1	8	12	25	0
Alec Sayre	.246	309	25	76	4	36	52	85	8
Evan Sleight	.157	89	8	14	2	14	6	23	1
Jordan Smith	.139	36	3	5	0	1	2	12	0
Gavin Stupienski	.280	229	28	64	8	37	16	45	0

Name	W	L	ERA	G	SV	IP	H	BB	SO
Jimmy Boyce	2	7	6.89	20	0	78	99	25	51
Kellen Brothers	4	8	4.30	17	0	92	112	26	85
Angel Cespedes	0	0	9.51	14	0	24	32	20	21
Bobby Curry	2	2	3.89	27	0	44	51	18	33
Robbie Hitt	1	1	2.16	26	13	25	19	10	27
Jose Ledesma	4	7	5.63	21	0	78	90	39	54
Tyler Luneke	1	1	3.58	27	0	33	27	20	41
Mark Moclair	1	1	5.17	4	0	16	14	18	15
Charlie Neuweiler	2	5	4.18	11	0	60	63	29	59
Billy Parsons	2	4	3.73	30	1	41	38	10	44
Mike Reagan	4	9	5.49	19	0	98	104	48	94
Matt Stil	2	3	5.21	31	2	38	31	28	48
Eston Stull	3	0	2.19	28	3	49	37	16	77
Tyler Thornton	5	11	5.69	19	0	98	121	50	56
Ronnie Voacolo	0	1	5.82	18	1	22	34	6	20

TRI-CITY VALLEYCATS

Name	AVG	AB	R	H	HR	RBI	BB	SO	SB
Dylan Broderick	.274	241	49	66	5	41	33	40	7
Chris Burgess	.250	176	32	44	10	29	24	60	1
Oscar Campos	.307	293	52	90	11	64	20	22	2
Ryan Cash	.250	276	44	69	1	34	37	57	8
Tyson Gingerich	.268	190	35	51	1	30	23	43	15
Jaxon Hallmark	.277	375	54	104	3	44	23	72	15
Demias Jimerson	.234	128	24	30	4	23	14	43	9
Cam Jones	.194	36	5	7	0	4	7	6	1
Robbie Merced	.253	91	21	23	5	18	17	29	12
Kyle Novak	.329	246	33	81	4	39	17	26	2
Elvis Peralta	.210	224	34	47	6	32	29	61	8
Brad Roberto	.143	28	3	4	0	4	6	4	1
Brett Rodriguez	.163	49	5	8	1	8	3	18	0
Ian Walters	.247	336	49	83	7	44	42	71	1
Javeyan Williams	.261	287	57	75	5	35	37	72	29

Name	W	L	ERA	G	SV	IP	H	BB	SO
Wes Albert	3	2	4.81	9	0	43	39	17	34
Dan Beebe	2	1	1.91	8	0	42	31	13	32
Greg Blackman	0	1	5.71	12	1	17	24	10	17
Chas Cywin	3	5	5.07	14	0	71	81	25	36
Nick DeCarlo	1	0	4.20	15	0	30	33	12	46
Austin Dill	3	1	2.82	28	5	54	47	23	53
Rolando Heredia-Bustos	1	2	4.06	10	0	31	25	10	16
Easton Klein	7	3	3.78	18	0	102	96	41	63
Arlo Marynczak	6	5	3.67	22	1	76	60	37	86
Nathan Medrano	4	4	4.97	37	4	54	68	25	50
Tom Peltier	0	0	11.45	8	0	11	22	7	8
Alfredo Ruiz	4	3	4.50	12	0	64	48	33	44
Gino Sabatine	6	1	4.56	21	1	49	53	24	18
Jhon Vargas	7	5	6.13	18	0	109	127	43	89
Connor Wilford	1	2	3.80	8	0	21	21	11	11
Zeke Wood	5	1	1.89	22	7	38	25	21	53

TROIS RIVIERES AIGLES

Name	AVG	AB	R	H	HR	RBI	BB	SO	SB
Steve Brown	.239	260	35	62	7	35	22	62	17
Jacob Carroll	.303	33	4	10	0	6	2	10	1
Dalton Combs	.289	343	52	99	10	65	38	47	13
Luis Curbelo	.220	236	38	52	9	25	13	46	3
Brendon Dadson	.337	279	42	94	6	46	52	48	5
Willie Estrada	.319	226	30	72	7	34	13	47	8
Mario Feliciano	.241	79	5	19	0	7	5	10	0
Raphael Gladu	.340	353	51	120	6	55	34	47	21
Thomas Green	.215	200	30	43	1	19	14	55	23
Brandon Hernandez	.256	82	11	21	1	8	9	17	4
Rodrigo Orozco	.280	132	14	37	1	18	13	23	1
L.P. Pelletier	.299	365	79	109	9	44	42	68	30
Yassel Pino	.197	61	4	12	1	3	5	18	1
Payton Robertson	.202	104	22	21	2	11	16	19	11
Parker Rowland	.160	25	1	4	0	3	1	8	0
Eddy Savoie	.283	46	4	13	0	6	5	10	0
James Smibert	.246	244	38	60	5	35	34	50	7
Mathieu Vallee	.341	44	8	15	0	7	2	12	2

Name	W	L	ERA	G	SV	IP	H	BB	SO
Braeden Allemann	4	4	4.41	23	0	65	67	37	70
Shaun Atamanchuk	2	0	5.93	33	0	41	46	33	36
Frankie Giuliano	0	0	4.09	22	0	22	19	13	17
Osman Gutierrez	5	7	5.77	18	0	94	94	47	84
Logan Hofmann	3	3	7.78	16	0	37	45	17	31
Alex Mack	1	1	2.60	4	0	17	8	9	20
Hernando Mejia	1	5	3.79	34	2	38	37	22	26
Michell Miliano	2	4	6.75	30	3	37	42	23	41
Kosei Naito	3	3	5.40	44	7	53	56	15	46
Sam Poliquin	0	1	8.71	8	0	10	15	4	4
Harry Rutkowski	3	1	4.09	43	1	44	40	20	41
Tucker Smith	8	4	3.24	20	0	128	114	21	94
Jesen Therrien	6	6	4.17	18	0	108	105	31	118
Yunior Thibo	2	1	4.50	26	3	32	26	23	31
Didier Vargas	2	6	6.01	16	0	70	81	26	75

WASHINGTON WILD THINGS

Name	AVG	AB	R	H	HR	RBI	BB	SO	SB
Evan Berkey	.238	147	32	35	4	16	22	48	9
Tommy Caufield	.283	354	63	100	11	59	43	100	29
Carson Clowers	.230	165	17	38	3	19	18	48	18
Andrew Czech	.264	315	53	83	18	48	68	89	2
Derek Gellos	.154	39	6	6	1	6	2	9	0
Wagner Lagrange	.297	269	39	80	12	42	13	45	3
Quincy Latimore	.192	78	14	15	4	11	8	27	3
Brandon McIlwain	.300	160	28	48	8	29	18	30	10
Caleb McNeely	.298	353	72	105	23	74	42	97	28
Jalen Miller	.271	140	25	38	5	17	16	28	13
Alexander Ovalles	.197	76	13	15	2	6	15	24	6
Baron Radcliff	.152	33	3	5	2	5	6	12	0
Tyreque Reed	.341	223	38	76	12	52	27	37	1
Cole Roberts	.222	36	1	8	0	2	4	9	2
Ricardo Sanchez	.214	154	18	33	0	14	29	27	0
J.C. Santini	.216	153	14	33	2	14	23	41	0
Ethan Wilder	.285	228	31	65	1	27	26	56	9

Name	W	L	ERA	G	SV	IP	H	BB	SO
Malik Barrington	6	4	4.54	17	0	85	59	45	100
Alex Carrillo	3	1	3.31	35	1	35	26	17	49
Jordan DiValerio	10	2	3.39	20	0	122	140	18	75
Aaron Forrest	2	0	3.27	3	0	11	8	6	8
Kobe Foster	10	1	2.91	18	0	118	102	23	126
Dariel Freglo	9	4	4.07	19	0	108	98	29	90
Christian James	3	1	2.40	36	2	45	27	15	61
Gyeongju Kim	3	3	1.59	43	28	45	28	13	52
Zach Kirby	10	4	2.42	17	0	104	86	25	100
Nick MacDonald	4	1	2.63	32	0	41	34	19	35
Ryan Munoz	4	2	1.67	20	2	32	24	8	19
Brendan Nail	1	1	2.89	18	0	19	15	8	29
Marlon Perez	0	0	5.06	4	0	11	10	2	8
Hunter Stevens	0	0	2.79	7	1	10	4	6	13

WINDY CITY THUNDERBOLTS

Name	AVG	AB	R	H	HR	RBI	BB	SO	SB
Armando Albert	.169	71	6	12	0	3	10	18	4
Ronnie Allen	.196	51	13	10	1	9	13	28	0
Garrett Broussard	.316	57	12	18	0	3	11	12	0
Robert Chayka	.242	273	43	66	3	38	35	88	13
Reed Chumley	.204	49	6	10	2	5	8	22	0
Paul Coumoulos	.200	35	1	7	0	2	1	7	1
Brennen Dorighi	.242	223	28	54	7	35	21	71	7
Joe Encarnacion	.188	69	8	13	2	10	9	22	1
JJ Figueroa	.193	140	8	27	2	16	5	46	1
Joey Grabanski	.175	40	1	7	0	1	2	12	1
Kyle Harbison	.171	70	5	12	0	1	4	29	2
J.R. Heavilin	.259	27	2	7	0	1	6	7	1
Jaylen Hubbard	.150	60	9	9	0	0	5	18	3
Joe Johnson	.230	318	41	73	6	48	37	106	6
Henry Kusiak	.277	282	43	78	3	38	19	80	5
Christian Kuzemka	.254	327	35	83	11	59	32	62	3
Kingston Liniak	.223	202	26	45	9	26	12	60	4
Ethan Lopez	.247	73	9	18	0	4	5	19	1
Cam Phelts	.256	309	51	79	0	20	30	78	53
Tommy Rodriguez	.197	152	23	30	3	9	11	61	11
Emmanuel Sanchez	.269	271	32	73	2	27	21	59	13
Tyler Sandoval	.293	41	4	12	0	6	5	18	1
Michael Seegers	.226	84	5	19	0	11	9	13	5
Wyatt Stapp	.212	33	6	7	0	1	8	7	1

Name	W	L	ERA	G	SV	IP	H	BB	SO
Will Armbruester	4	8	3.97	20	0	116	101	37	71
Michael Barker	3	8	6.37	19	0	95	102	64	83
Dan Brown	2	3	4.94	22	0	27	18	33	38
AJ Chacon	0	0	9.26	9	0	12	19	11	7
Greg Duncan	1	1	1.50	13	5	12	11	2	14
Ruddy Gomez	4	4	4.24	13	0	70	62	33	79
Bryce Hellgeth	1	1	2.02	27	0	36	30	14	27
Eric Hildebrand	0	1	11.84	17	0	19	30	17	13
Tyler LaPorte	3	1	3.03	39	13	36	25	15	52
Jack Mahoney	5	4	3.45	52	0	60	57	24	61
John Mikolaicyk	3	6	5.44	19	0	94	95	58	77
Tyler Naumann	1	3	6.23	12	1	22	29	8	29
Jacob Newman	0	3	12.04	15	0	25	37	31	25
Kevin Pindel	9	7	2.00	19	0	122	123	27	95
Caleb Riedel	3	3	3.48	18	0	34	27	21	48
Taylor Sugg	0	2	7.16	5	0	16	20	13	10

PIONEER LEAGUE

The Yolo High Wheelers beat the Glacier Range Riders to win a Pioneer League title in its first year in the league. Yolo scored three runs in the bottom of the ninth after having already rallied to tie the game earlier thanks to a Tanner Smith grand slam. Yolo second baseman Bobby Lada hit his second home run of the game for the walk-off decider.

Team	W	L	PCT	GB
*Missoula PaddleHeads	62	34	.646	-
%Oakland Ballers	58	38	.604	4
Northern Colorado Owlz	54	41	.568	7.5
^Yolo High Wheelers	53	41	.564	8
Boise Hawks	52	44	.542	10
^Glacier Range Riders	48	48	.500	14
Billings Mustangs	46	50	.479	16
Rocky Mountain Vibes	44	50	.468	17
Ogden Raptors	41	55	.427	21
Idaho Falls Chukars	40	56	.417	22
Great Falls Voyagers	38	58	.396	24
Grand Junction Jackalopes	37	58	.389	24.5

**First-half Champ. %Second-half Champ. ^Wild Card*

Playoffs Semifinals: Yolo defeated Missoula 2-0 and Glacer Range defeated Oakland 2-1 in best-of-3 series. **Finals:** Yolo defeated Glacier Range 3-1 in best-of-5 series.

Attendance: Boise 150,906; Ogden 142,918; Rocky Mountain 121,419; Billings 108,693; Glacier Range 108,501; Idaho Falls 92,551; Oakland 92,046; Missoula 82,088; Grand Junction 79,417; Great Falls 70,380.

Most Valuable Player: Adam Fogel, Missoula. **Pitcher of the Year:** Ben Ferrer, Yolo. **Rookie of the Year:** Adam Fogel, Missoula. **International Player of the Year:** Roberto Pena, Missoula. **Reliever of the Year:** Jonathan Haab, Billings. **Manager of the Year:** Billy Horton, Yolo.

BATTING LEADERS

Player, Team	AVG	OBP	SLG	AB	R	H	HR	RBI	SB
Adam Fogel, Miss.	.388	.495	.773	348	114	135	35	115	2
Mike Rosario, Miss.	.387	.469	.544	344	100	133	10	72	12
Braylin Marine, Yolo	.383	.445	.531	337	80	129	9	68	23
Patrick Chung, Miss.	.374	.477	.584	358	107	134	11	63	15
Xane Washington, GF	.372	.453	.583	374	93	139	13	86	25
Jose Gonzalez, Yolo	.370	.473	.640	322	83	119	19	84	11
Kelly Dugan, GJ	.369	.469	.711	225	56	83	22	68	1
Jackson Coutts, NC	.365	.437	.615	356	76	130	20	110	0
Ernie Yake, RM	.365	.445	.468	348	92	127	3	61	22
Connor Bagnieski, Ogden	.362	.432	.500	276	46	100	6	62	1

PITCHING LEADERS

Player, Team	W	L	ERA	G	IP	H	BB	SO
Ben Ferrer, Yolo	10	4	4.35	22	99	100	28	108
Mike Peterson, Boise	10	8	4.38	19	115	119	36	100
Cameron Repetti, Yolo	8	4	4.48	19	98	98	40	90
Alfredo Villa, Miss.	9	2	5.12	19	102	106	38	114
Luke Malone, Boise	6	8	5.20	19	97	140	23	80
Evan Massie, GJ	7	4	5.21	19	97	116	44	85
Chase Gearing, NC	8	3	5.40	21	97	119	37	81
Chase Jessee, NC	9	6	5.42	19	103	110	54	109
Carlos Lomeli, RM	9	5	5.74	20	102	118	29	58
Owen Sharts, IF	4	7	5.85	19	103	115	51	119

BILLINGS MUSTANGS

Name	AVG	AB	R	H	HR	RBI	BB	SO	SB
Evan Blum	.301	123	24	37	7	23	14	39	0
Kyle Booker	.203	74	12	15	0	9	13	23	7
Dustin Crenshaw	.306	36	12	11	1	6	7	6	1
Wyatt Crenshaw	.203	74	12	15	1	6	5	22	2
Connor Denning	.319	204	47	65	9	49	35	49	1
Blake Evans	.262	225	37	59	4	37	20	57	7
Casey Harford	.286	189	29	54	2	25	11	41	0
Travis Holt	.244	86	17	21	3	18	12	12	3
Jacob Kline	.282	262	38	74	12	50	19	65	0
Briley Knight	.268	97	18	26	3	16	16	19	3
Dylan Leach	.302	129	32	39	8	19	31	49	2
Gary Lora	.303	142	23	43	3	31	23	27	3
Isaac Lovings	.200	35	12	7	0	3	9	14	0
Pat Mills	.305	167	47	51	12	54	45	49	6
Mitch Moralez	.283	177	29	50	2	24	19	34	3
Jason Rooks	.295	95	25	28	3	24	27	35	2
Brendan Ryan	.331	332	94	110	11	64	55	58	52
Jake Sisto	.250	20	2	5	1	5	1	8	0
Abe Valdez	.268	168	33	45	4	36	34	52	0
Gabe Wurtz	.277	282	45	78	17	64	20	70	2

Name	W	L	ERA	G	SV	IP	H	BB	SO
Greg Blackman	4	3	4.17	11	0	54	49	19	57
Jacob Bradshaw	1	1	8.49	6	0	12	16	5	4
James Deloatch	2	4	11.81	9	0	32	58	24	23
Sayer Diederich	0	2	12.08	8	0	13	26	7	9
Justin Fuson	2	4	8.21	8	0	34	49	17	33
Jonathan Haab	4	1	2.21	41	12	41	35	24	61
Joey Hennessey	0	0	6.83	21	0	28	30	17	26
Earl Johnson	2	0	5.74	8	0	16	21	7	10
Dawson Lane	0	0	3.78	11	0	17	16	4	24
Logan Lee	3	2	8.71	7	0	31	47	12	18
Pat Maybach	4	1	3.68	6	0	37	38	7	35
Ethan McRae	2	5	8.23	18	0	74	101	25	38
Brendan Medoro	6	1	4.72	35	1	76	103	28	47
Austin Mora	2	1	11.96	11	1	23	42	10	9
Kyle Mosley	0	1	10.03	6	0	12	26	7	9
Luke Rettig	1	5	8.74	13	0	34	61	16	25
AJ Riddle	1	1	9.30	11	0	20	32	15	23
Ethan Ross	2	3	7.31	8	0	32	48	10	20
Shane Spencer	2	4	5.23	8	0	43	48	11	37
Grant Taylor	2	3	6.29	7	0	34	36	9	48
Luke Trueman	2	3	8.18	8	0	33	62	8	28
Cam Tullar	1	1	8.71	8	0	21	35	6	21
Daniel Willie	1	2	7.25	29	0	58	79	26	42

BOISE HAWKS

Name	AVG	AB	R	H	HR	RBI	BB	SO	SB
Tyner Hughes	.283	205	41	58	4	37	9	46	7
Tyler Jorgensen	.233	343	45	80	4	65	23	68	16
Max Jung-Goldberg	.247	178	36	44	2	25	30	53	11
Joey Kalafut	.271	166	16	45	0	19	25	35	1
Kole Kaler	.331	172	48	57	3	24	34	25	12
Nich Klemp	.294	255	46	75	5	41	32	38	3
Ben Livorsi	.286	98	24	28	5	25	13	20	0
Noah Marcelo	.278	346	69	96	6	47	47	70	23
Patrick Meriño	.257	210	49	54	10	44	30	69	8
Trevor Minder	.260	150	20	39	1	14	19	39	4
Michael O'Hara	.277	202	38	56	2	24	18	35	5
D.J. Poteet	.305	141	36	43	1	27	17	34	12
Armani Sanchez	.226	31	5	7	1	6	2	10	2
Carter Sanford	.233	43	12	10	1	6	10	12	0
Bubba Thompson	.258	31	10	8	0	4	5	12	1
Nick Ultsch	.349	361	81	126	10	86	36	66	6
Troy Viola	.343	385	78	132	28	94	38	83	2
Micah Yonamine	.338	411	97	139	24	96	40	95	2

Name	W	L	ERA	G	SV	IP	H	BB	SO
Emilio Alfonzo	1	3	6.95	27	2	45	51	28	62
Connor Butler	0	1	6.04	18	1	22	17	25	42
Cam Dayton	1	0	4.89	30	2	35	39	15	37
Robbie Dudzinski	4	3	6.86	8	0	39	44	20	28
Casey Dykstra	1	2	2.84	35	7	38	26	20	51
Andrew Edwards	6	0	4.55	34	0	63	61	24	76
Mike Esposito	0	1	5.40	11	0	10	10	11	16
Ronaldo Fernandez	0	0	7.58	13	1	19	21	14	25
Reed Garland	3	2	7.20	12	1	40	47	32	44
Evan Kowalski	2	1	5.89	37	3	63	75	25	49
Luke Malone	6	8	5.20	19	0	97	140	23	80
Blake McFadden	1	0	2.88	37	0	25	19	10	33
Isaac Mendez	6	2	3.14	11	0	63	58	15	73
Mike Peterson	10	8	4.38	19	0	115	119	36	100
Luke Schafer	0	5	8.37	9	0	43	64	20	34
Brayden Spears	6	2	3.74	10	0	53	46	20	56
Tristan Walton	0	3	11.17	3	0	10	19	8	7
Ryan Wentz	2	1	4.00	3	0	18	23	5	18
Blake Whiting	0	0	2.95	18	1	18	20	4	27

GLACIER RANGE RIDERS

Name	AVG	AB	R	H	HR	RBI	BB	SO	SB
Andy Atwood	.282	369	71	104	10	62	39	72	33
Antonio Barranca	.218	55	9	12	2	5	10	27	0
Austin Bates	.050	20	1	1	0	1	1	2	0
Nick Block	.232	112	21	26	1	22	14	32	3
Chad Castillo	.352	324	62	114	11	89	35	66	2
T.J. Clarkson	.268	56	11	15	3	10	7	8	0
John Daly	.324	71	18	23	2	15	12	22	11
Mason Dinesen	.371	140	38	52	8	33	20	38	27
Ben Fitzgerald	.295	254	60	75	17	59	38	69	3
Nick Gore	.194	36	7	7	0	4	5	9	0
Freddy Guilamo	.220	182	27	40	4	29	28	76	1
Gabe Howell	.322	273	76	88	9	47	27	64	16
Jerry Huntzinger	.284	74	15	21	2	11	14	19	4
Christian Kirtley	.289	332	73	96	20	88	68	82	9
Kingston Liniak	.347	98	22	34	8	29	10	21	3
Ryan McCarthy	.400	125	36	50	8	18	16	24	11
J.D. McLaughlin	.237	194	34	46	4	27	24	59	15
River Orsak	.340	53	7	18	0	7	6	8	1
Ty Penner	.254	205	33	52	6	29	37	68	0
Ajay Sczepkowski	.228	136	22	31	4	16	7	39	8
Drew Sims	.286	49	5	14	1	9	8	15	0
Gavin Tonkel	.170	112	16	19	5	14	15	47	5

Name	W	L	ERA	G	SV	IP	H	BB	SO
Trevor Baker	1	1	4.98	8	0	22	30	4	23
Cooper Benson	4	1	4.33	14	0	71	66	29	78
Ty Bothwell	1	1	8.31	3	0	13	10	10	16
Tyler Clayton	0	3	9.49	10	0	25	34	11	19
Justin Coleman	2	2	2.29	15	0	20	18	11	29
Luke Cooper	1	1	7.47	26	1	31	45	11	33
Cam Cowan	0	4	6.37	28	3	30	36	19	35
Jared Engman	1	2	4.45	7	0	28	30	10	17
Brady Held	3	6	7.14	16	0	52	71	32	59
Connor Housley	2	0	4.22	8	2	11	8	5	11
Jerry Huntzinger	3	4	6.41	31	0	53	62	27	64
Cullen Kafka	4	3	5.75	11	0	41	45	29	42
Jack Lynch	0	2	6.70	34	5	42	40	23	46
Aidan McEvoy	1	1	5.11	29	0	44	36	31	69
Noah Owen	0	2	5.60	9	2	18	24	2	23
Seth Pinkerton	0	1	4.50	17	0	18	12	16	18
Jonathan Pintaro	1	0	4.40	3	0	14	13	1	23
Montana Quigley	5	1	3.12	24	0	35	30	6	32
Kaleb Sophy	5	6	5.68	17	0	84	94	46	92
Rayne Supple	1	0	6.06	15	1	16	18	13	19

Name	W	L	ERA	G	SV	IP	H	BB	SO
Ricky Tibbett	1	1	4.84	17	4	22	21	4	17
Patrick Wicklander	3	0	3.34	6	0	35	33	12	47
Nick Zegna	5	3	6.34	26	0	82	88	42	74

GRAND JUNCTION JACKALOPES

Name	AVG	AB	R	H	HR	RBI	BB	SO	SB
Alec Ackerman	.250	28	4	7	0	5	1	5	0
Mike Bathauer	.200	60	4	12	0	1	4	13	0
Julian Boyd	.280	322	75	90	10	45	26	85	46
Holden Breeze	.207	29	4	6	0	3	5	6	0
Chayce Bryant	.263	38	5	10	2	7	3	9	0
Jeff Disla	.107	28	1	3	0	0	2	18	1
Kelly Dugan	.369	225	56	83	22	68	37	48	1
Lavoisier Fisher	.210	81	14	17	5	13	12	28	0
Jonathan Gonzalez	.250	104	16	26	1	11	3	22	1
Calyn Halvorson	.312	237	56	74	12	50	28	36	6
Brody Harding	.333	81	22	27	0	10	14	12	5
Damian Henderson	.288	118	23	34	10	30	21	34	1
Sam Kuchinski	.305	187	37	57	15	57	32	54	0
Sam Olsson	.208	24	3	5	0	0	0	5	0
Andres Rios	.352	341	80	120	16	82	49	61	5
David Rivera	.327	220	37	72	7	32	15	40	5
Druw Sackett	.247	275	56	68	7	41	32	81	21
Austin Shumaker	.333	78	16	26	1	11	11	17	4
Ethan Smith	.286	189	46	54	5	30	24	63	16
Matt Turner	.234	64	4	15	1	12	1	20	0
Omar Veloz	.292	171	25	50	2	30	4	33	0
Conrad Villafuerte	.286	245	42	70	2	36	24	35	1

Name	W	L	ERA	G	SV	IP	H	BB	SO
Aydan Alger	1	4	6.82	31	4	32	38	17	48
JC Ariza	2	7	7.69	22	0	55	73	23	47
Connor Barton	0	0	8.22	13	0	23	39	14	11
Ethan Brown	2	0	3.86	14	0	12	9	8	14
Hunter Bryan	4	2	6.75	30	7	56	80	26	58
Will Buraconak	1	5	7.56	12	0	58	85	32	52
Riley Egloff	1	0	6.60	10	0	15	20	5	18
Nathan Gilman	0	5	13.11	8	0	23	47	21	15
Elijah Johnson	1	3	10.17	9	0	26	34	29	28
Diego Jordan	0	1	8.49	23	0	30	42	7	22
Cole Lee	2	1	8.39	15	0	25	34	21	26
Will Levine	0	2	9.91	28	2	26	25	34	36
Drew Marrufo	0	1	10.88	22	0	22	36	19	23
Zach Martinez	2	0	6.11	10	0	18	18	14	20
Evan Massie	7	4	5.21	19	0	97	116	44	85
Frank Racioppo	0	3	6.65	5	0	22	28	14	12
Joshua Romero	0	1	10.55	20	0	21	40	5	24
Brandon Ross	5	4	6.91	15	0	57	80	34	50
Dustin Schorie	1	3	10.26	15	0	43	65	33	32
Stephen Still	5	5	7.79	18	0	84	116	32	117
Trey Valka	0	0	10.80	10	0	12	7	15	14
Josh Verdon	0	5	17.05	11	0	25	55	28	22
Bruce Yamamoto	0	1	8.88	21	0	24	32	18	11

GREAT FALLS VOYAGERS

Name	AVG	AB	R	H	HR	RBI	BB	SO	SB
Mahki Backstrom	.350	177	47	62	12	41	20	65	3
Marcos Castillo	.283	46	7	13	2	11	3	12	1
Cael Chatham	.306	49	6	15	0	2	11	19	0
Antonio Fernandez	.256	176	28	45	4	24	19	53	0
AJ Fritz	.342	41	9	14	1	8	4	9	1
Roberto Gonzalez	.273	55	7	15	0	9	9	5	3
Caden Green	.342	117	25	40	0	16	11	31	1
Hylan Hall	.321	243	53	78	8	47	19	58	8
Jordan Hamberg	.080	25	2	2	0	1	3	10	0
Ryan Holgate	.319	72	11	23	4	15	11	21	0
Devin Hurdle	.229	105	18	24	1	13	9	35	11
Jack Lynch	.292	377	58	110	11	71	35	99	10
Ryan Major	.332	340	90	113	7	44	33	62	17
Livingston Morris	.205	88	13	18	6	20	7	32	0
Jeff Nicol	.341	44	9	15	4	13	5	11	0
Frank Podkul	.279	215	29	60	10	43	27	71	1
Kody Putnam	.240	96	14	23	1	18	10	31	1
Freddy Rojas	.313	294	66	92	12	60	58	76	13
Kyle Schroedle	.238	21	7	5	0	5	2	5	0
Oscar Serratos	.325	209	40	68	4	35	20	53	32
Will Spear	.083	24	3	2	0	1	2	10	0
Xane Washington	.372	374	93	139	13	86	53	87	25
Hernan Yanez	.327	147	31	48	3	28	17	31	0

Name	W	L	ERA	G	SV	IP	H	BB	SO
Kenny Carrillo	0	6	7.90	18	0	49	66	45	47
CJ Czerwinski	3	2	6.08	8	0	40	44	13	47
Braden Forsyth	1	2	7.79	24	1	32	40	24	35
AJ Fritz	2	1	5.16	4	0	23	24	7	21
Danny Galvan	1	5	7.21	13	0	64	98	25	49
Jordan Hamberg	1	1	1.93	3	0	14	10	10	23
Shandon Herrera	0	2	12.46	7	0	13	25	11	12
Matt Hickey	0	2	13.72	7	0	20	41	12	18
Tyler Johnson	1	3	9.00	13	0	22	25	18	22
Nolan LaMere	2	1	9.69	13	0	13	25	9	5
Nate Madej	8	3	4.46	16	0	79	67	65	82
Nick Marshall	3	6	6.65	13	0	65	77	34	71
Riley Phillips	1	1	12.19	7	0	10	11	14	15
Jason Pineda	6	4	5.47	22	0	82	82	43	71
Luke Powell	0	0	8.53	23	0	25	37	19	29
Jeff Praml	0	2	13.83	3	0	14	28	4	12
Dayan Reinoso	1	2	7.29	28	2	33	41	22	41
Trae Robertson	2	3	7.71	23	0	44	60	32	48
Austin Stubber	0	1	12.27	6	0	15	24	9	14
José Torrealba	0	2	5.56	15	5	23	20	10	29
Steve Washilewski	3	2	9.20	19	0	61	79	38	43

IDAHO FALLS CHUKARS

Name	AVG	AB	R	H	HR	RBI	BB	SO	SB
Myles Austin	.219	32	10	7	0	6	3	8	4
Robert Barham	.293	58	10	17	1	12	5	16	0
Brandon Bohning	.230	270	55	62	6	34	28	75	5
Craig Corliss	.294	51	5	15	0	9	8	13	0
Noah Gent	.280	25	6	7	0	0	4	7	0
Roberto Gonzalez	.462	132	25	61	2	35	13	11	1
Chase Hanson	.275	222	35	61	6	41	30	58	3
Theo Hardy	.357	84	26	30	1	18	12	16	0
Nick Iannantone	.283	152	30	43	1	28	24	33	0
Jacob Jablonski	.292	332	59	97	17	80	57	109	12
Kyle Jenkins	.304	56	16	17	0	10	11	12	3
Kevin Johnson	.316	95	16	30	0	15	13	19	5
Anthony Mata	.307	137	31	42	3	20	16	32	9
Tom McCaffrey	.216	74	8	16	2	13	7	24	0
Ryan McCarthy	.315	181	38	57	4	29	40	41	0
Chris Monroe	.349	66	15	23	4	13	18	17	0
Grady Morgan	.349	126	29	44	2	15	12	19	0
Garret Ostrander	.216	37	7	8	0	2	7	6	0
Gabe Ramos	.182	33	5	6	0	4	6	11	0
Trevor Rogers	.311	322	79	100	14	79	65	77	0
Ben Rosengard	.337	104	22	35	0	8	13	32	4
Jacob Shanks	.294	160	35	47	4	33	17	43	16
Zaid Walker	.250	104	21	26	0	12	11	22	5
Brian Williams	.120	25	9	3	0	6	5	5	2
Tyler Wyatt	.330	373	94	123	17	78	49	74	19

Name	W	L	ERA	G	SV	IP	H	BB	SO
Bryant Bagshaw	0	2	15.80	8	0	14	34	8	13
Dusty Baird	0	1	7.53	27	0	49	68	23	44
Robbie Brown	1	0	11.86	12	0	22	47	12	13
Connor Caporale	1	2	17.72	3	0	11	19	13	11
Austyn Coleman	1	5	9.24	9	0	37	68	17	17
Garrett Crowley	3	3	5.60	40	4	53	72	34	83
Tyler Dyball	0	1	9.00	27	1	38	56	16	27
Gary Grosjean	2	2	5.49	7	0	41	51	17	29
Connor Harrison	4	3	4.28	26	0	61	73	17	49
Luke Hempel	0	0	5.20	31	2	36	44	10	49
Rob Hughes	1	0	2.87	16	2	16	19	5	14
Trevor Jackson	0	3	8.35	31	1	37	44	47	46
Casey Minchey	2	3	9.36	7	0	34	45	22	11
Tyler Naumann	3	2	5.94	8	0	36	50	18	30
Steven Ordorica	3	3	6.42	33	1	41	66	11	27
Nicolò Pinazzi	1	0	5.18	18	0	24	25	15	31
Sergio Ramirez	0	1	14.29	10	0	11	11	15	10

Name	W	L	ERA	G	SV	IP	H	BB	SO
Caleb Reyes	4	5	7.86	12	0	53	74	33	35
Owen Sharts	4	7	5.85	19	0	103	115	51	119
Garrett VanDeventer	0	3	12.75	4	0	12	25	11	7
Brian Williams	7	5	7.53	17	0	69	84	35	60

MISSOULA PADDLEHEADS

Name	AVG	AB	R	H	HR	RBI	BB	SO	SB
Patrick Chung	.374	358	107	134	11	63	62	46	15
Gio DiGiacomo	.348	23	6	8	1	5	4	5	2
Josh Elvir	.281	217	49	61	7	51	36	70	0
Adam Fogel	.388	348	114	135	35	115	61	88	2
Colin Gordon	.315	260	66	82	11	60	54	74	3
Tyler Johnson	.182	22	8	4	3	6	7	9	0
Jaylon Lee	.318	44	11	14	2	15	3	11	4
Luis Navarro	.376	93	18	35	4	25	12	13	0
Roberto Pena	.327	389	89	127	24	101	46	126	28
Carlos Perez	.330	88	23	29	4	17	7	25	2
Mike Rosario	.387	344	100	133	10	72	47	62	12
Collin Runge	.340	241	60	82	11	57	33	39	4
Alec Sanchez	.330	306	86	101	20	92	42	77	15
Taylor Smith	.245	188	34	46	6	39	35	62	0
Cameron Thompson	.255	282	70	72	9	56	52	54	17
Hayden Travinski	.224	76	10	17	2	14	5	18	0
Kamron Willman	.359	192	58	69	10	55	23	38	3
Reece Yeargain	.103	39	6	4	0	8	7	9	1

Name	W	L	ERA	G	SV	IP	H	BB	SO
Trent Anderson	2	0	7.39	19	0	28	34	12	24
Mason Bryant	0	0	8.78	8	0	13	18	10	13
Christian Ciuffetelli	0	0	4.70	13	0	15	8	11	21
Jonathan Clark	2	2	10.73	12	0	49	70	28	49
Dawson Day	5	1	4.46	12	0	40	43	12	69
Robbie Dudzinski	1	3	8.27	4	0	21	30	6	12
Garrett Eddy	0	2	10.64	16	0	22	35	17	15
Reece Fields	1	3	9.84	15	0	47	69	24	47
Andrew Garcia	1	3	9.37	43	6	40	48	42	53
Jonah Jenkins	0	2	10.38	5	0	17	27	8	20
Jestin Jones	3	3	6.24	41	0	79	91	52	91
Jimmy Loper	0	0	1.54	9	0	12	7	4	22
Noah McBride	5	1	2.10	24	0	26	20	18	34
Nick Parker	6	3	5.86	15	0	71	76	37	89
Collin Runge	2	0	5.06	3	0	16	16	3	5
Arman Sabouri	2	0	5.51	28	0	33	36	17	34
Connor Schultz	3	1	4.09	4	0	22	34	5	22
Ethan Swanson	4	1	4.29	44	8	42	33	38	66
Mark Timmins	5	2	6.31	38	1	41	51	17	40
Alfredo Villa	9	2	5.12	19	0	102	106	38	114

NORTHERN COLORADO OWLZ

Name	AVG	AB	R	H	HR	RBI	BB	SO	SB
Jonny Barditch	.280	25	5	7	0	2	7	8	1
Chris Brady	.184	49	9	9	1	7	4	19	0
Jackson Coutts	.365	356	76	130	20	110	40	68	0
Euro Diaz	.336	262	60	88	6	58	37	53	2
Henry George	.318	333	100	106	12	66	69	57	20
Dario Gomez	.345	316	105	109	30	98	46	88	30
Abdel Guadalupe	.369	65	15	24	3	26	12	11	2
Kevin Jimenez	.325	338	73	110	6	65	40	68	27
Garrett Kueber	.253	225	53	57	5	39	44	74	14
Sam Low	.048	21	7	1	1	1	7	3	2
Dave Matthews	.354	316	101	112	19	81	76	79	30
Damon Maynard	.252	143	36	36	1	22	22	42	3
Jacob McCaskey	.177	51	6	9	1	9	5	19	1
Omar Ortiz	.266	64	7	17	3	6	5	19	1
Danny Perez	.259	143	24	37	6	31	23	33	1
Kevin Santiago	.279	158	26	44	9	42	33	47	3
Evan Scavotto	.264	265	52	70	9	43	52	90	8
Reece Yeargain	.254	130	25	33	5	24	8	23	2

Name	W	L	ERA	G	SV	IP	H	BB	SO
Robb Adams	6	5	4.97	15	0	76	94	31	82
Will Buraconak	2	2	7.20	7	0	30	39	24	24
Tyler Curtis	4	5	7.03	20	0	87	128	23	72
Nathan Draves	1	2	7.34	13	0	38	58	19	43
Chase Gearing	8	3	5.40	21	0	97	119	37	81
Chase Jessee	9	6	5.42	19	0	103	110	54	109
Brandon Kaminer	0	0	8.70	23	0	30	48	20	24
Dutch Landis	4	3	4.21	45	13	47	46	19	50
Carter Linton	5	3	7.01	47	1	51	56	33	68
Kris Massey	2	0	5.96	22	0	23	20	28	22
Jacob McCaskey	2	1	5.44	35	0	45	53	23	44
Reese Miller	1	0	2.40	14	0	15	9	3	30
Starling Perez	0	0	13.14	11	0	12	19	23	8
Dalton Ross	1	2	4.67	50	0	54	62	25	54
Mark Tindall	4	6	8.84	21	0	75	115	44	55

OAKLAND BALLERS

Name	AVG	AB	R	H	HR	RBI	BB	SO	SB
Brett Barrera	.356	348	85	124	23	91	53	63	13
Tyler Best	.350	20	3	7	0	3	3	4	0
Brad Burckel	.250	252	40	63	11	55	25	98	13
Brett Carson	.317	350	90	111	13	65	59	98	18
Tripp Clark	.312	138	30	43	4	23	11	26	3
Dan Covino	.214	70	13	15	2	5	11	24	1
J.P. Gates	.333	69	12	23	3	11	6	14	0
Kyle Guerra	.253	95	20	24	1	9	16	29	5
Payton Harden	.319	310	66	99	4	31	47	80	27
Coleton Horner	.241	116	20	28	2	16	14	30	0
Dondrei Hubbard	.315	346	70	109	16	71	36	47	8
Myles Jefferson	.320	147	34	47	3	27	17	26	13
Ian Jenkins	.046	22	0	1	0	3	0	8	0
Josh Leslie	.248	145	18	36	4	25	11	28	5
Tyler Lozano	.231	160	29	37	4	27	17	32	5
Noah Martinez	.317	325	68	103	21	71	72	90	2
Jaylen Smith	.264	246	36	65	10	38	17	46	13
Daunte Stuart	.329	140	28	46	7	22	17	21	8
Stephen Wilmer	.310	290	66	90	9	57	49	85	5
Drew Woodcox	.163	49	6	8	3	10	2	15	0

Name	W	L	ERA	G	SV	IP	H	BB	SO
Reed Butz	1	1	6.59	27	0	68	73	30	75
Christian Cosby	7	3	4.59	19	0	80	74	31	124
T.J. Czyz	1	1	11.91	6	0	11	15	9	14
Jake Dahle	4	2	4.93	35	2	42	47	18	28
Chandler David	4	0	3.30	22	7	46	37	15	39
Abraham DeLeon	1	2	7.88	24	1	38	51	23	39
Aaron Eden	2	4	9.19	9	0	31	50	17	33
Brody Eglite	5	0	3.55	26	0	51	40	19	55
J.P. Gates	0	1	3.32	8	0	22	17	13	19
Justin Kleinsorge	5	4	3.94	12	0	64	63	18	67
Carson Lambert	2	4	6.89	24	7	64	75	18	65
Braydon Nelson	1	2	3.64	22	4	30	23	12	34
Kyle Pijaszek	2	0	5.26	27	1	39	40	24	21
Elijah Pleasants	2	0	4.32	5	0	17	15	4	23
Conner Richardson	6	0	4.10	32	0	42	37	22	53
Luke Short	3	0	3.10	7	0	29	23	6	37
Zach St. Pierre	7	5	5.33	24	0	83	87	39	87
Connor Sullivan	1	0	1.69	12	2	21	11	11	30
Kelsie Whitmore	0	2	12.17	13	0	24	44	14	14

OGDEN RAPTORS

Name	AVG	AB	R	H	HR	RBI	BB	SO	SB
Connor Bagnieski	.362	276	46	100	6	62	36	35	1
Landen Barns	.308	315	59	97	2	50	21	51	2
Drew Brutcher	.363	124	22	45	6	25	26	26	4
Chris Coipel	.247	73	19	18	5	17	15	19	0
Jack Cone	.344	352	97	121	12	58	42	54	17
Tru Fontenot	.264	140	24	37	1	11	7	30	6
Ray Gil	.302	215	52	65	18	53	27	83	1
Matt Golda	.183	60	8	11	0	8	4	14	0
Elliot Good	.298	151	32	45	5	25	19	38	4
Thomas Greely	.169	71	9	12	0	4	5	12	1
Anthony Herron	.156	32	3	5	1	10	3	12	0
Pearce Howard	.360	389	78	140	4	62	22	60	6
Cole Jordan	.322	258	59	83	8	51	31	43	12
Kenny Oyama	.242	120	29	29	1	16	15	20	5
Christopher Sargent	.316	358	67	113	19	95	34	75	5
Chuck Steele	.222	36	6	8	0	3	5	9	1

Name	W	L	ERA	G	SV	IP	H	BB	SO
Carson Angeroth	1	0	8.49	7	0	12	16	6	11
Brayden Bonner	2	1	4.50	27	2	30	31	10	23
Ryan Cloude	0	0	6.92	11	0	13	21	10	16
Guillermo Cuevas	0	1	13.89	4	0	12	24	14	17
Cam Edmonson	0	0	4.85	13	0	13	10	10	18
Eli Elliott	3	1	6.18	8	0	39	41	19	30
Alex Friesen	1	1	12.89	11	0	15	21	18	19
Elijah Gill	6	2	9.36	11	0	50	77	33	45
Christian Griffin	3	1	5.31	38	0	41	47	28	41
Shane Gustafson	4	3	5.70	36	0	54	68	31	67
Matt Hess	5	5	5.40	12	0	52	64	22	38
Chris Macca	4	4	6.72	15	0	74	101	35	48
Dylan Matsuoka	1	1	5.40	20	2	20	21	13	21
Gabe Pacheco	1	3	7.38	25	1	57	76	43	49
Jon Rice	1	0	5.97	24	0	29	17	34	35
Nico Saltaformaggio	2	2	7.51	19	0	62	89	20	60
Adrian Santa Cruz	2	5	7.15	8	0	34	46	24	33
Mitch Stone	3	3	7.68	8	0	34	41	19	35
Shawn Triplett	0	1	3.56	28	0	43	38	22	39
Rafi Vazquez	5	9	7.25	19	0	91	137	34	72
Quinn Waterhouse	1	5	8.06	41	6	41	46	31	40

ROCKY MOUNTAIN VIBES

Name	AVG	AB	R	H	HR	RBI	BB	SO	SB
Alex Adams	.286	28	7	8	0	3	5	11	1
Kurtis Byrne	.333	84	12	28	4	26	11	15	0
Austin Chouinard	.259	139	19	36	5	29	12	31	0
Austin Davis	.328	366	87	120	10	56	54	77	49
Tyler Davis	.241	79	6	19	1	15	2	27	0
Joshua Day	.350	363	93	127	18	82	49	71	11
Trevor Halsema	.330	339	64	112	10	70	38	62	13
Billy Hancock	.239	67	11	16	0	5	11	23	0
Devyn Lopez	.237	114	18	27	2	16	12	34	4
Eddie McCabe	.291	268	51	78	3	49	44	57	2
Glenn Miller	.354	65	8	23	3	17	3	16	2
Mason Minzey	.239	92	29	22	3	10	27	34	2
Carter Mize	.397	63	14	25	3	14	7	13	0
Steven Rivas	.342	404	91	138	31	124	30	95	13
Mason Sykes	.304	158	37	48	3	29	11	38	1
Dane Tofteland	.313	316	79	99	17	77	63	87	3
Ernie Yake	.365	348	92	127	3	61	42	48	22

Name	W	L	ERA	G	SV	IP	H	BB	SO
Derrick Cherry	2	5	7.97	25	1	50	67	38	48
Christian Day	7	5	6.49	19	0	87	121	30	59
Garrett Hill	1	0	9.75	11	0	12	20	10	14
Caden Kratz	1	2	6.59	15	0	14	15	7	17
Bryan Krolikowski	0	0	5.40	8	0	13	19	3	8
Carlos Lomeli	9	5	5.74	20	0	102	118	29	58
Nick McClanahan	0	0	4.85	15	0	13	16	13	14
Trey Morrill	3	3	5.03	37	6	39	42	21	52
Daniel Nunan	3	3	8.17	21	0	62	92	33	52
Jaxon O'Neal	4	2	4.50	36	0	40	32	15	33
Zach Ottinger	1	7	7.89	16	0	59	73	41	39
Max Pettey	2	1	8.61	20	0	23	36	10	22
Nick Powers	3	5	7.83	14	0	67	92	31	53
Bryson Spagnuolo	0	2	7.41	28	5	34	47	26	24
Wyatt Tucker	1	1	5.19	24	0	26	28	13	23
Kelsey Ward	4	4	7.88	22	0	78	77	68	87

YOLO HIGH WHEELERS

Name	AVG	AB	R	H	HR	RBI	BB	SO	SB
Kirkland Banks	.278	270	40	75	7	39	22	49	10
Braedon Blackford	.326	285	55	93	13	65	44	78	5
Edwin DeLaCruz	.256	39	4	10	1	4	2	12	0
Alex Epp	.200	25	2	5	0	3	3	10	1
Alejandro Figueredo	.308	234	40	72	7	53	43	46	1
David Glancy	.313	99	19	31	4	20	17	17	6
Jose Gonzalez	.370	322	83	119	19	84	57	75	11
Travis Holt	.143	49	7	7	0	6	4	13	1
Bobby Lada	.328	342	77	112	17	83	22	80	28
Taylor Lomack	.335	281	76	94	2	31	54	57	31
Braylin Marine	.383	337	80	129	9	68	38	65	23
Angel Mendoza	.172	192	33	33	3	21	22	76	3
Mason Minzey	.279	86	14	24	0	9	16	27	1
Ed Niemann	.338	77	8	26	2	13	2	8	0
Brayland Skinner	.298	363	82	108	8	49	44	74	41
Tanner Smith	.280	300	61	84	12	52	49	55	11

Name	W	L	ERA	G	SV	IP	H	BB	SO
Kris Anglin	2	0	3.89	31	0	35	26	21	45
Ethan Bates	0	0	3.07	10	0	15	17	8	10
Ty Buckner	1	1	3.38	31	11	32	24	14	33
Ben Ferrer	10	4	4.35	22	0	99	100	28	108
Reed Garland	2	1	3.32	12	0	22	15	25	17
Brendan Knoll	2	4	3.94	9	0	48	50	23	26
Andrew LaCour	0	1	1.84	14	0	15	10	7	20
Dawson Lane	0	3	7.23	9	0	37	58	19	44
Connor Langrell	2	1	1.97	38	4	46	35	6	46
Noah Lewis	0	1	6.00	16	0	30	36	18	12
Brandon McPherson	6	2	5.22	16	0	90	102	30	78
Brandon Mitchell	5	2	7.28	17	0	80	92	49	62
Cameron Repetti	8	4	4.48	19	1	98	98	40	90
Jack Zalasky	6	1	4.03	38	1	38	42	8	30

U.S. PRO BASEBALL LEAGUE

During the regular season, the Birmingham Bloomfield Beavers were the worst team in the four-team USPBL. But come playoff time, that just meant they had a tougher path to the title.

The Beavers beat every other team in the league, topping third-place Eastside, second-place Westside and first-place Utica in a trio of games to claim the USPBL championship. Dyson Johnson was named the championship game MVP as he allowed two runs in 6.2 innings in the deciding game. League MVP Matt Piotrowski drove in two and Ray Hilbrich went 2-for-3 with a double.

East Division	W	L	PCT	GB
Utica Unicorns	25	20	.556	-
Eastside Diamond Hoppers	23	22	.511	2
West Division	**W**	**L**	**PCT**	**GB**
Westside Woolly Mammoths	24	20	.545	—
Birmingham Bloomfield Beavers	17	27	.386	7

Playoffs—First Round: Birmingham defeated Eastside. **Semifinals:** Birmingham defeated Westside. **Finals:** Birmingham defeated Utica 3-2 in championship game.

All-Star Team: C-Ethan Krizen, Unicorns. **1B**-Noah Marcoux, Hoppers. **2B**-Matt Piotrowski, Beavers. **SS**-Colby Seltzer, Mammoths. **3B**-Austin Ochoa, Unicorns. **OF**-Chase Rodriguez, Beavers; Nick Pastore, Mammoths; Francis Florentino, Mammoths; Ray Hilbrich, Beavers. **DH**-Fox Leum, Mammoths. **UTL**-Drew Fleming, Mammoths; Jared Weber, Unicorns.

SP-Greg Loukinen, Beavers; Pierce Banks, Hoppers; John Kelly, Hoppers. **P**-Matt Colucci, Unicorns; Brett Erwin, Beavers; Nate Blain, Mammoths.

Most Valuable Player: Matt Piotrowski, Birmingham . **Pitcher of the Year:** Greg Loukinen, Birmingham.

INTERNATIONAL

Japan Strengthens Case Atop World Baseball

BY J.J. COOPER

Madonna Japan beat Team USA in the Women's World Cup final to continue their title streak

The World Baseball Softball Confederation produces world rankings, but often, those rankings have seemed baffling.

In 2018, the U.S. ranked second, well behind Japan, even though Team USA was at that time the defending World Baseball Classic champion, 18U world champion, 15U world champion and 12U world champion. Japan remained No. 1, even though it finished third at the 2017 WBC, fourth at the 18U World Cup, third at the 18U World Cup, fourth at the 12U World Cup and even third at the 18U World Cup qualifier.

Whenever the two teams played, Team USA won, but because Japan participated in more WBSC events, their appearances at Asian Games and 21U events was enough to make up for Team USA winning titles while Japan ended up with silver and bronze medal finishes.

But Japan's status at the No. 1 team in the WBSC men's baseball rankings in 2024 is well earned. And Team USA's slipping to fifth place in the rankings is partly because of events on the field, and not just because of participation points.

On the field, Japan once again has regained the upper hand. As everyone remembers, Team USA fell to Japan in the World Baseball Classic in 2023. Team USA then went on to finish fourth in the 18U World Cup later in 2023. The 18U used to be an event Team USA dominated, so a non-medal finish was truly shocking.

But it didn't get better for the United States in 2024. Team USA opted not to participate in the 15U Americas qualifier. The WBSC did not decide to offer the team an at large spot, which meant that Team USA was left out of the 15U World Cup this summer. As usual, Team USA didn't participate in the 23U World Cup this year either. So Mexico, Taiwan and Venezuela have passed Team USA in the WBSC rankings.

Japan's status as the best in the world is well earned at this point. Samurai Japan has won the 23U and 15U World Cups this year. They won the 18U World Cup in 2023 as well as the World Baseball Classic.

The only World Cup title Team USA currently holds is the 12U title from 2023.

Japan is now 4-0 in head-to-head games against Team USA's top-level national teams since 2020 with wins at Premier12, the World Baseball Classic and two wins at the Olympic Games. The last senior level Team USA win over Japan was in the 2019 Premier12 tournament.

Tawain Pulls Off Premier12 Shocker

Taiwan pulled off a stunning upset, beating Japan 4-0 to win the Premier12 tournament championship, while Team USA beat Venezuela 6-1 to claim the bronze medal.

Center fielder Chieh-Hsien Chen hit a three-run home run to lead Taiwan's offense while D-Backs pitcher Yu-Min Lin threw four scoreless, one-hit innings to start off the shutout. Relievers Yi Chang, Kuan-Yu Chen and Kai-Wei Lin combined to hold Japan to three hits over the final five

PREMIER 12

SUPER ROUND IN JAPAN

STANDINGS

Team	W	L	Team	W	L
Taiwan	6	3	Australia	2	3
Japan	8	1	Mexico	2	3
USA	5	4	Dominican Republic	1	4
Venezuela	5	4	Netherlands	2	3
South Korea	3	2	Cuba	1	4
Panama	3	2	Puerto Rico	1	4

Top six teams advanced to Super Round. Taiwan defeated Japan 4-0 in gold medal game. USA defeatedVenezuela 6-1 in bronze medal game.

BATTING LEADERS

PLAYER	TEAM	AVG	AB	R	H	HR	RBI	SB
Chieh-Hsien Chen	TPE	.625	24	5	15	2	6	2
Alen Hanson	DOM	.545	11	0	6	0	3	0
Hernán Pérez	VEN	.533	15	6	8	2	3	0
Alonso Gaitan	MEX	.526	19	5	10	1	4	0
Didi Gregorius	NED	.500	22	6	11	2	4	0
Chandler Simpson	USA	.459	37	8	17	0	6	9
Delano Selassa	NED	.455	11	4	5	0	0	0
Toshiya Sato	JPN	.455	11	3	5	0	3	0
Sharlon Schoop	NED	.450	20	3	9	2	5	0
Shogo Sakakura	JPN	.444	18	6	8	1	4	0

PITCHING LEADERS

PLAYER	TEAM	W	L	ERA	G	IP	H	BB	SO
Rich Hill	USA	0	0	0.00	3	10	5	2	14
Yi Chang	TPE	3	0	0.00	5	8	4	1	9
Shoma Fujihira	JPN	0	0	0.00	6	6	4	0	12
Antonio Menendez	USA	2	0	1.35	4	7	5	1	8
Kuo-Hao Chiang	TPE	1	0	1.42	3	6	7	4	7
Zac Grotz	USA	0	0	1.42	2	6	7	1	4
Oddanier Mosqueda	VEN	1	0	1.42	5	6	1	1	12
Tzu-Peng Huang	TPE	1	1	1.50	3	12	5	1	9
Pedro Fernández	DOM	0	1	1.50	1	6	4	1	6
Touki Toussaint	USA	0	0	1.50	2	6	4	3	9

Premier 12 All-World Team

SP: Rich Hill (USA). RP Oddaner Mosqueda (Venez.). C: Shogo Sakakura (Japan). 1B: Carlos Jesus Perez (Venezuela), 2B: Kaito Kozono (Japan) 3B: Matt Shaw (USA). SS: Didi Gregorius (Netherlands). OF: Chandler Simpson (USA), Chieh-Hsien Chen (Chinese Taipei) and Shota Morishita (Japan). DH: Ryan Ward (USA).

U15 WORLD CUP

FINAL STANDINGS

Team	W	L	Team	W	L
Japan	8	1	Dominican Republic	5	3
Puerto Rico	7	2	Venezuela	4	4
Taiwan	7	2	Italy	3	5
Nicaragua	5	4	Netherlands	3	5
Colombia	4	4	South Africa	1	7
Mexico	3	5	Guan	0	8

Top six teams advanced to Super Round, while other six teams continued in consolation round.

Gold Medal Game: Japan defeated Puerto Rico 7-6.

Bronze Medal Game: Taiwan defeated Nicaragua 7-6.

MVP: Kei Kawakami (Japan)

All-World Team: P: Gean Carlos Lopez (NCA). C: Edward Pineiro (PUR). 1B: Patrick Silva (ITA). 2B: Adniel Quiles (PUR). 3B: Yuga Arai (JPN). SS: Kei Kawakami (JPN). LF: Anthony Badillo (PUR). CF: Joel Vargas (MEX). RF: Valentin Carrasquillo (PUR). DH: Ander Elorriaga (COL).

scoreless innings.

This is arguably the biggest international win in Taiwanese baseball history (the team is called Chinese Taipei in international competitions). Taiwan has won the Asian Games before and even claimed a silver medal in the 1992 Olympics, but this is the first gold medal at a world championships for professional baseball players.

"The result went over what we anticipated. We never expected such an outcome," Chen told the World Baseball Softball Confederation after the game. "This win will give everybody in our baseball team more confidence and the awareness that we can compete with everybody."

Chen, Taiwan's captain, was named the tournament MVP. He hit .625 (15-for-24) with two home runs, five runs scored and six RBIs.

Team Japan has won seven consecutive Women's World Cup titles stretching back to 2008

WBSC MEN'S RANKINGS

Rk.	Team	Points	2024 Points
1	Japan	5756	1339
2	Mexico	4118	358
2	Taiwan	4118	755
4	Venezuela	3941	677
5	United States	3687	100
6	South Korea	3680	429
7	Netherlands	3534	562
8	Puerto Rico	3122	1083
9	Cuba	2814	119
10	Pama	2587	134
11	Colombia	2441	427
12	Dominican Republic	2302	317
13	Italy	2214	275
14	Czech Republic	2032	132
15	Australia	1865	207
16	Nicaragua	1828	927
17	Germany	1399	176
18	Great Britain	1326	184
19	Israel	1121	35
20	China	900	453

In the bronze medal game, Casey Lawrence threw six scoreless innings, holding Venezuela to four hits and no walks while striking out seven. Rays prospects Chandler Simpson and Carson Williams each had a double as part of two hits.

Madonna Japan Rolls Again

For a few moments, it seemed possible that Japan's domination of women's baseball could end.

But in the gold medal game, the champs showed that they aren't going anywhere. Madonna Japan knocked off Team USA 11-6 to win its seventh consecutive Women's World Cup. The streak, which stretches back to 2008, has gone on so long that multiple generations of players have played a role. Japan's 39-game international winning streak was halted by an eighth-inning Team USA win in round robin play. That was in a game where both teams had clinched spots in the gold medal game.

With a title on the line, Japan jumped out to an early lead and just kept adding to it. Japan got a home run from first baseman Yuki Kawabata in a four-run third against Team USA starter Jillian Alabayati.

Why is Japan so dominant in women's baseball? Because they encourage girls and women to play the sport.. High school girls baseball is popular in Japan, and multiple NPB teams have women's teams as well, which means playing pro baseball is a viable option.It shows on the field. Japan played a very polished, relentless approach.

Team USA showed it's narrowing the gap with young talent. USA's 17-year-old first baseman Naomi Ryan batted in the middle of the lineup all week. Remi Schaber is 21. Pitcher/outfielder Olivia Pichardo is 20.

23U WORLD CUP

STANDINGS

Team	W	L	Team	W	L
Japan	8	1	Netherlands	4	4
Puerto Rico	7	2	Taiwan	4	4
Nicaragua	6	3	Australia	4	4
China	5	4	Colombia	2	6
Venezuela	3	5	Great Britain	2	6
South Korea	4	4	South Africa	1	7

Format: Top six teams advanced to Super Round, while the other six teams continued in consolation round.

Gold Medal Game: Japan defeated Puerto Rico 5-0.

Bronze Medal Game: Nicaragua defeated China 3-1.

Most Valuable Player: Edgardo Villegas, Puerto Rico.

WOMENS WORLD CUP

STANDINGS

Team	W	L	Team	W	L
Japan	5	1	Mexico	2	4
United States	5	1	Venezuela	1	4
Canada	4	2	Taiwan	0	5

Gold Medal Game: Japan defeated United States 11-6.

Bronze Medal Game: Canada defeated Mexico 4-2.

Most Valuable Player: Miu Shiraishi, Japan.

ALL-WORLD TEAM: LHP: Elizabeth Gilder (Canada). RHP: Miyu Shimizu (Japan). C: Nanako Hanabusa (Japan). 1B: Naomi Ryan (USA). 2B: Alex Hugo (USA). SS: Mia Valcke (Canada). 3B: Edith De Leija (Mexico). LF: Miu Shiraishi (Japan). CF. Sena Catterall (Canada). RF: Miwa Naraoka (Japan). DH: Remi Schaber (USA).

BATTING LEADERS

PLAYER	TEAM	AVG	AB	R	H	HR	RBI	TB
Yi-Hsuan Chiu	TPE	.563	16	1	9	0	3	9
Miu Shiraishi	JPN	.563	16	8	9	0	8	13
Sena Catterall	CAN	.500	18	10	9	0	1	10
Miwa Naraoka	JPN	.474	19	7	9	0	3	12
Mia Valcke	CAN	.429	21	6	9	0	3	10
Andreanne Leblanc	CAN	.421	19	3	8	0	9	13
Iori Miura	JPN	.421	19	3	8	0	7	11
Akari Hoshikawa	JPN	.375	16	9	6	0	0	8
Haruna Tadano	JPN	.375	16	4	6	0	5	6
Edith De Leija	MEX	.368	19	0	7	0	1	8
Samaria Benitez	MEX	.350	20	3	7	0	2	7
Yuki Kawabata	JPN	.316	19	3	6	1	5	9
Naomi Ryan	USA	.294	17	5	5	0	2	5
Hsiao-Mei Chen	TPE	.267	15	2	4	0	0	4
Daniela Leal	MEX	.267	15	3	4	0	0	6
Zoe Hicks	CAN	.263	19	2	5	0	6	7
Ashton Lansdell	USA	.235	17	7	4	0	2	5
Diana Ibarra	MEX	.133	15	4	2	0	0	2

PITCHING LEADERS

PLAYER	TEAM	W	L	ERA	G	IP	H	BB	SO
Jaida Lee	CAN	1		00.00	1	5	1	3	4
Ayami Sato	JPN	0		00.00	1	5	4	0	5
Frandelis Garcia	VEN	0		00.00	2	5	3	5	7
Natsuki Kubo	JPN	1		00.00	3	5	3	1	6
Wakana Mori	JPN	1		11.00	2	7	7	3	6
Maricela Aguillera	MEX	0		11.35	3	10	9	8	7
Narda Andrade	MEX	1		01.40	2	5	3	1	0
Raine Padgham	CAN	1		01.62	2	9	9	4	4
Alexane Fournier	CAN	1		02.00	2	7	2	7	7
Akino Tanaka	JPN	1		02.33	2	6	6	1	6
Sophy Gagne	CAN	1		12.63	3	5	5	3	3
Angelia Ledezma	VEN	1		02.63	2	5	9	5	2
Jamie Baum	USA	0		02.74	2	8	7	2	4

INTERNATIONAL

Diablos Rojos Convincingly Claim Title

The class of the Mexican League in 2024, as it often is, was clearly the Mexico Diablos Rojos (Red Devils). Mexico ran away with the Southern Division title, finishing 20 games better than any of the other nine teams in the division.

The team was led by long-time MLB star Robinson Cano, who led the league with a .431 average. On the mound, long-time MLB star Trevor Bauer went 10-0, 2.48 and led the league with 120 strikeouts.

After sweeping its quarterfinal series, Los Diablos Rojos did get tested in the South Division Championship series. Oaxaca beat Bauer, Erick Leal and Jake Sanchez to take a 3-0 series lead in the best-of-7 series. After Mexico won Games 4 and 5, Oaxaca jumped out to an eight-run lead in Game 6, only to see Mexico score eight runs in the fourth to tie it and RBI singles by Diosbel Arias and Franklin Barreto gave Mexico a lead it wouldn't relinquish in the sixth. A Patrick Mazeika sac fly scored Jesus Fabela in the bottom of the ninth of Game 7 to send Los Diablos Rojos to the Series Del Rey.

After surviving such a scare, the championship series proved much easier. Mexico outscored Monterrey 37-8 in a four-game sweep.

The title was Mexico's 17th Mexican League title in the 99-year history of the league.

The caliber of play in the league has continued to pick up. With a reduced number of roster spots on MiLB affiliated teams, recognizable big league names peppered the rosters. Cano and Bauer might have been the biggest names, but Sam Travis, Lewis Diaz and Barreto also starred.

STANDINGS

Northern Division	W	L	PCT	GB
Monterrey	53	37	.589	-
Dos Laredos	54	39	.581	0.5
Laguna	52	39	.571	1.5
Tijuana	52	40	.565	2
Monclova	51	40	.560	2.5
Aguascalientes	48	43	.527	5.5
Saltillo	44	48	.478	10
Durango	37	55	.402	17
Jalisco	36	56	.391	18
Chihuahua	33	60	.355	21.5

Southern Division	W	L	PCT	GB
Mexico	71	19	.789	-
Queretaro	50	38	.568	20
Yucatan	45	40	.529	23.5
Veracruz	46	44	.511	25
Oaxaca	46	44	.511	25
Puebla	45	44	.506	25.5
Tabasco	47	46	.505	25.5
Leon	37	53	.411	34
Campeche	32	55	.368	37.5
Quintana Roo	25	64	.281	45.5

Playoffs—Quarterfinals: Mexico defeated Yucatan 4-0,Oaxaca deafeatd Queretaro 4-0, M onterrey defeated Monclova 4-3 and Dos Laredos defeated Laguna 4-1 in best-of-seven series. **Semifinals:** Monterrey defeated Dos Laredos 4-2 and Mexico defeated Oaxaca 4-3 in best-of-seven series. **Finals:** Mexico defeated Monterrey 4-0 in best-of-seven series.

BATTING LEADERS

Player, Team	AVG	OBP	SLG	AB	R	H	HR	RBI	SB
Robinson Cano, MEX	**.431**	.475	.639	327	62	141	14	77	0
Vimael Manchin, JAL	.401	.494	.579	304	64	122	7	54	10
Yurisbel Gracial, QRO	.382	.437	.670	348	95	133	24	83	2
Lewin Díaz, 2 Teams	.375	.452	.647	269	52	101	19	77	1
Wilfredo Tovar, AGS	.371	.440	.497	350	72	130	7	44	4
Jose Marmolejos, MEX	.364	.470	.559	261	64	95	10	48	3
Alexi Amarista, OAX	.361	.402	.579	368	67	133	15	57	1
Henry Urrutia, 2 Teams	.358	.426	.500	288	46	103	7	48	2
Keven Lamas, 2 Teams	.354	.426	.551	274	54	97	11	46	3
Sam Travis, 3 Teams	.350	.430	.470	334	69	117	4	47	4
Yosmany Guerra, QRO	.349	.451	.481	241	42	84	4	41	1
Balbino Fuenmayor, MVA	.346	.370	.571	240	35	83	13	54	0
Angel Reyes, AGS	.346	.412	.587	327	67	113	19	70	13
Aldrem Corredor, MVA	.343	.425	.538	329	49	113	14	69	1
Frankin Barreto, MEX	.343	.430	.576	321	77	110	16	63	8
Andretty Cordero, AGS	.342	.389	.537	363	66	124	14	78	6
Nicholas Torres, LAG	.341	.424	.550	320	65	109	15	66	10
Danry Vasquez, LAR	.339	.410	.530	330	53	112	6	57	7
Miguel Guzman, PUE	.336	.364	.475	339	60	114	8	38	5
Alen Hanson, QRO	.335	.375	.552	328	71	110	16	49	8
Kelvin Gutiérrez, QRO	.333	.408	.495	321	62	107	11	70	6
Fernando Villegas, SLT	.328	.406	.502	317	70	104	12	58	4
Manuel Boscan, DUR	.327	.409	.491	336	46	110	10	66	9
Zoilo Almonte, MTY	.326	.375	.599	307	50	100	22	63	0
Jonathan Villar, LAG	.325	.399	.417	326	48	106	3	39	24
Julian Ornelas, MEX	.320	.379	.549	306	66	98	16	84	7
Art Charles, YUC	.294	.457	.742	252	62	74	33	81	0
Billy Hamilton, 2 Teams	.257	.327	.330	230	38	59	0	16	**37**

PITCHING LEADERS

Player, Team	W	L	ERA	IP	H	HR	BB	SO
Zac Grotz, MVA	7	1	**2.35**	77	75	4	19	81
Trevor Bauer, MEX	10	0	2.48	83	66	4	21	**120**
David Reyes, VER	9	6	2.49	**123**	95	16	14	85
Erick Leal, MEX	8	1	2.91	80	69	6	24	95
Matt Dermody, TIJ	9	3	3.03	95	88	7	26	89
Emilio Vargas, LAR	6	5	3.20	112	97	12	30	99
Tyler Viza, MTY	7	2	3.30	79	82	8	20	62
Yoanner Negrin, YUC	6	3	3.35	78	65	6	24	65
Robert Stock, LAR	9	4	3.38	99	109	2	41	104
Nate Antone, LAR	6	4	3.42	95	100	8	31	98
Ronald Medrano, AGS	7	4	3.54	81	71	10	22	68
Felix Doubront, 2 Teams	3	11	3.88	114	105	8	39	85
Nick Struck, TAB	8	8	3.88	95	97	12	35	64
Cameron Gann, TIG	5	7	3.89	86	76	5	44	84
Cesar Valdez, YUC	**10**	6	4.06	106	117	14	12	73
Wilmer Rios, MVA	6	5	4.10	86	91	5	21	51
Stephen Tarpley, MTY	7	3	4.11	81	84	5	35	75
Luis I. Rodriguez, JAL	5	3	4.31	77	95	8	16	56
Zach Mort, SLT	8	4	4.34	87	110	10	19	79
Juan P. Oramas, TAB	**10**	6	4.44	93	97	16	41	71

JAPAN

BayStars Win Long Awaited Title

For the first time in 26 years, the Yokohama DeNA BayStars are Japan Series champions.

After finishing just above .500 during the regular season, Yokohama made it out of the first round, survived the one-game deficit that they began the Climax Series with to beat Yomiuri and then beat Fukuoka, clinching the title with an 11-2 win in Game 6. The BayStars' .507 winning percentage is the worst for any Japan Series champion.

Pitching was the story of the BayStars title. Katuski Azuma, Anthony Kay and Andre Jackson allowed one run combined in three starts. All three worked at least seven innings.

The win was also the first by a female owner in Japan Series history. Tomoko Namba has owned the BayStars since 2015.

The season marked the long-awaited breakout by Fukuoka righthander Carter Stewart. After opting to sign in Japan after a dispute with the Braves, Stewart has had to work his way into the Hawks rotation. But this year, he went 9-4, 1.95 and was a starter in the Japan Series.

Long-time star Norichika Aoki announced his retirement at the end of the season. Aoki, 42, played 21 pro seasons including six seasons in the U.S. with the seven different MLB teams. He had 1,949 hits in the NPB and another 774 in the U.S.

After the season, Chiba Lotte righthander Roki Sasaki announced that he would be posted to come to the U.S. Much like Shohei Ohtani did years ago, Sasaki is coming over before he has the requisite NPB service time to qualify as a "foreign professional."

Because he's coming over before being able to be treated as a free agent, Sasaki was limited to signing a MiLB contract. That means that Chiba Lotte will receive only a very modest posting fee, far from the $50 million the Orix Buffaloes received when Yoshinobu Yamamoto was posted after the 2023 season.

Yomiuri ace Tomoyuki Sugano also announced he was planning to come to the U.S. to pitch. Sugano, 35, is a two-time Sawamura Award winner as the best pitcher in Japan. He finished with the second best ERA in the Central League in 2024, going 15-3, 1.67 with just 16 walks in 167 innings.

CENTRAL LEAGUE

Team	W	L	T	PCT	GB
Yomiuri Giants	77	59	7	.566	--
Hanshin Tigers	74	63	6	.540	3.5
Yokohama DeNA BayStars	71	69	3	.507	8
Hiroshima Toyo Carp	68	70	5	.493	10
Yakult Swallows	62	77	4	.446	16.5
Chunichi Dragons	60	75	8	.444	16.5

Playoffs—First round: Yokohama defeated Hanshin 2-0 in best-of-three series. **Climax Series:** Yokohama defeated Yomirui 4-3 in best-of-seven series. **Japan Series:** Yokohama defeated Fukuoka 4-2 in best-of-7 series.

CENTRAL LEAGUE BATTING LEADERS

Player, Team	AVG	AB	R	H	HR	RBI	SB
Tyler Austin, BayStars	.316	445	396	66	2	238	69
Domingo Santana, Swallows	.315	484	419	57	0	212	70
Shugo Maki, BayStars	.294	561	517	76	0	254	74
Seiya Hosokawa, Dragons	.292	600	534	59	0	255	67
Shogo Akiyama, Carp	.289	587	547	60	1	192	30
Hideki Nagaoka, Swallows	.288	611	566	63	1	208	58
Naoki Yoshikawa, Giants	.287	602	536	65	4	202	46
Koji Chikamoto, Tigers	.285	639	562	71	5	204	45
Toshiro Miyazaki, BayStars	.283	469	410	49	0	182	56
Kazuma Okamoto, Giants	.280	611	535	70	0	268	83
Kaito Kozono, Carp	.280	588	540	52	3	178	61
Shogo Sakakura, Carp	.279	462	427	43	1	176	44
Yoshihiro Maru, Giants	.278	595	525	51	1	208	45
Shota Morishita, Tigers	.275	526	458	64	2	202	73
Keita Sano, BayStars	.273	566	524	51	0	201	62
Takayoshi Noma, Carp	.271	443	391	40	5	133	28
Teruaki Sato, Tigers	.268	496	451	58	4	198	70
Jose Osuna, Swallows	.267	585	539	54	0	223	72
Masaya Yano, Carp	.260	495	430	45	6	143	38
Yusuke Ohyama, Tigers	.259	545	483	63	0	185	68
Yuki Okabayashi, Dragons	.256	460	425	34	3	125	12
Munetaka Murakami, Swallows	.244	610	500	82	1	236	86
Ryosuke Kikuchi, Carp	.241	497	453	27	0	155	38
Takumu Nakano, Tigers	.232	634	547	63	2	154	32

OTHER NOTABLE HITTERS

Player, Team	AVG	AB	R	H	HR	RBI	SB
Elier Hernandez, Giants	.294	221	34	65	8	30	0
Coco Montes, Giants	.272	151	14	41	1	14	1
Sheldon Neuse, Tigers	.231	134	8	31	1	8	1
Mike Ford, BayStars	.200	20	1	4	1	2	0
Andre Jackson, BayStars	.098	41	1	4	0	1	0
Jeremy Beasley, Tigers	.000	21	2	0	0	0	0

CENTRAL LEAGUE PITCHING LEADERS

Pitcher, Team	W	L	ERA	IP	H	HR	BB	SO
Hiroto Takahashi, Dragons	12	4	1.38	144	107	1	34	130
Tomoyuki Sugano, Giants	15	3	1.67	167	132	6	16	111
Hiroto Saiki, Tigers	13	3	1.83	168	140	4	38	137
Daichi Ohsera, Carp	6	6	1.86	155	118	5	49	98
Shosei Togo, Giants	12	8	1.95	180	129	12	44	156
Katsuki Azuma, (DB)	13	4	2.16	183	166	11	27	140
Hiroki Tokoda, Carp	11	9	2.48	167	170	9	48	95
Masato Morishita, Carp	10	10	2.55	152	137	6	29	98
Shoki Murakami, Tigers	7	11	2.58	154	143	7	33	130
Koutaro Ohtake, Tigers	11	7	2.80	145	134	8	33	91
Iori Yamasaki, Giants	10	6	2.81	147	140	8	42	103
Andre Jackson, BayStars	8	7	2.90	143	109	8	51	121
Shinnosuke Ogasawara, Dragons	5	11	3.12	144	151	9	22	82

OTHER NOTABLE PITCHERS

Pitcher, Team	W	L	ERA	IP	H	HR	BB	SO
Taisei Ota, Giants	1	2	0.88	41	28	0	8	54
Raidel Martinez, Dragons	2	3	1.09	58	35	1	12	59
Shinya Matsuyama, Dragons	2	3	1.33	54	38	0	17	57
Hiroki Ohnishi, Swallows	9	1	1.34	60	53	3	12	31
Tatsuya Shimizu, Dragons	3	1	1.40	58	41	1	18	52
Daichi Ishii, Tigers	4	1	1.48	49	34	0	14	58
Javy Guerra, Tigers	1	4	1.55	58	47	3	11	48
Javy Guerra, Tigers	1	4	1.55	58	47	3	11	48
Takuma Kirishiki, Tigers	3	1	1.79	65	48	0	18	60
Ryoji Kuribayashi, Carp	0	6	1.96	55	33	3	16	65
Yuhei Takanashi, Giants	4	3	2.04	35	26	1	15	29
Suguru Iwazaki, Tigers	4	4	2.20	57	48	3	15	46
Hiromasa Funabasama, Giants	4	0	2.37	38	28	4	8	23
Kohei Morihara, BayStars	2	6	2.41	60	54	3	12	59
Alberto Baldonado, Giants	2	3	2.44	52	40	1	28	63
Reiji Kozawa, Swallows	6	6	2.55	78	64	6	23	66
Sotaro Shimauchi, Carp	11	6	2.77	55	43	2	27	53
Kazuto Taguchi, Swallows	1	4	2.94	34	34	2	9	22
Naofumi Kizawa, Swallows	3	3	3.06	53	50	4	20	46
Taichi Ishiyama, Swallows	1	0	4.35	41	53	2	14	39

OTHER NORTH AMERICAN PITCHERS

Pitcher, Team	W	L	ERA	IP	H	HR	BB	SO
Jeremy Beasley, Tigers	0	0	0.00	5	2	0	3	1
Javy Guerra, Tigers	0	1	1.29	35	18	1	7	26
Robert Corniel, Carp	2	2	1.53	47	24	5	19	54
Thomas Hatch, Carp	1	4	1.55	58	47	3	11	48
Taylor Hearn, Carp	1	1	1.71	26	20	1	9	25
Yofrec Diaz, BayStars	8	3	2.47	78	53	6	24	75
Anthony Kay, BayStars	0	0	2.65	17	15	1	7	14
J.B. Wendelken, BayStars	6	4	3.01	117	99	9	23	126
Foster Griffin, Giants	6	9	3.42	137	130	6	53	119
Kyle Keller, Giants	0	3	7.36	22	28	5	10	18

PACIFIC LEAGUE

Team	W	L	T	PCT	GB
Fukuoka SoftBank Hawks	91	49	3	.650	--
Hokkaido Nippon-Ham Fighters	75	60	8	.556	13.5
Chiba Lotte Marines	71	66	6	.518	18.5
Tohoku Rakuten Golden Eagles	67	72	4	.482	23.5
Orix Buffaloes	63	77	3	.450	28
Saitama Seibu Lions	49	91	3	.350	42

Playoffs: First round: Hokkaido defeated Chiba Lotte 2-1 in best-of-three series. **Climax Series:** Fukouka defeated Hokkaido 4-0 in best-of-seven series. **Japan Series:** Yokohama defeated Fukuoka 4-2 in best-of-7 series..

PACIFIC LEAGUE BATTING LEADERS

Player, Team	AVG	AB	R	H	HR	RBI	SB
Kensuke Kondoh, Hawks	.314	535	436	66	2	227	72
Ryosuke Tatsumi, Eagles	.294	597	537	68	12	225	58
Tomoya Mori, Buffaloes	.281	457	395	46	1	164	46
Toshiya Satoh, Marines	.278	452	410	41	0	149	45
Ryoya Kurihara, Hawks	.273	598	527	74	2	248	87
Neftali Soto, Marines	.269	542	491	43	2	221	88
Ukyo Shuto, Hawks	.269	477	428	63	5	146	26
Daichi Suzuki, Eagles	.266	460	406	41	5	141	41
Sosuke Genda, Lions	.264	577	522	41	7	176	21
Kenta Imamiya, Hawks	.262	538	462	60	4	172	39
Ryoma Nishikawa, Buffaloes	.258	553	519	42	0	180	46
Yuya Ogoh, Eagles	.257	642	565	64	6	202	49
Yuya Gunji, Fighters	.256	495	441	52	0	163	49
Hideto Asamura, Eagles	.253	552	471	51	0	180	60
Chusei Mannami, Fighters	.252	556	508	60	0	216	60
Kotaro Kurebayashi, Buffaloes	.247	523	465	32	0	146	38
Hotaka Yamakawa, Hawks	.247	611	550	66	1	266	99
Gregory Polanco, Marines	.243	468	416	47	0	191	60
Itsuki Murabayashi, Eagles	.241	571	518	51	3	162	50
Go Matsumoto, Fighters	.236	486	437	46	1	126	19
Ariel Martinez, Fighters	.234	459	393	42	4	159	57
Hiroto Kobukata, Eagles	.229	522	450	50	4	129	23
Shuta Tonosaki, Lions	.227	500	436	41	1	147	41

OTHER NORTH AMERICAN HITTERS

Player, Team	AVG	AB	R	H	HR	RBI	SB
Franmil Reyes, Fighters	.290	335	39	97	25	65	0
Orlando Calixte, Dragons	.261	372	30	97	7	36	2
Leandro Cedeno, Buffaloes	.260	304	29	79	15	37	0
Maikel Franco, Eagles	.218	229	20	50	8	30	0
Dayan Viciedo, Dragons	.209	43	2	9	1	2	0
Alex Dickerson, Dragons	.205	88	9	18	3	5	1
Brandon Tysinger, Lions	.188	16	0	3	0	0	0
Adam Walker, Hawks	.169	65	2	11	1	3	1
Andrew Stevenson, Fighters	.161	62	3	10	0	0	1
Marwin Gonzalez, Buffaloes	.131	61	3	8	1	2	0
Anthony Garcia, Lions	.131	61	3	8	1	4	0
Christian Rodriguez, Dragons	.130	54	3	7	0	1	0
Franchy Cordero, Lions	.129	70	5	9	1	4	0
Cody Thomas, Buffaloes	.000	18	0	0	0	0	0

PACIFIC LEAGUE PITCHING LEADERS

Pitcher, Team	W	L	ERA	IP	H	HR	BB	SO
Livan Moinelo, Hawks	11	5	1.88	163	107	11	47	155
Natsuki Takeuchi, Lions	10	6	2.17	145	120	6	22	107
Tatsuya Imai, Lions	10	8	2.34	173	132	8	70	187
Kohei Arihara, Hawks	14	7	2.36	183	142	12	37	137
Takahisa Hayakawa, Eagles	11	6	2.54	170	156	10	35	160
Hiromi Itoh, Fighters	14	5	2.65	176	150	14	39	161
Takayuki Katoh, Fighters	10	9	2.70	167	174	15	17	103
Chihiro Sumida, Lions	9	10	2.76	179	161	11	35	154
Takayuki Kishi, Eagles	6	11	2.83	143	144	13	29	73
Atsuki Taneichi, Marines	7	8	3.05	147	128	5	38	148
Sachiya Yamasaki, Fighters	10	6	3.17	148	142	17	28	74
Kazuya Ojima, Marines	12	10	3.58	163	157	15	36	132

OTHER NOTABLE PITCHERS

Pitcher, Team	W	L	ERA	IP	H	HR	BB	SO
Shota Suzuki, Marines	2	2	0.73	49	32	2	18	42
Seiryu Kotajima, Buffaloes	2	1	0.79	46	30	2	17	43
Sora Suzuki, Eagles	2	0	1.66	49	24	0	21	48
Rikuto Yokoyama, Marines	3	1	1.71	42	27	1	13	37
Kouya Fujii, Hawks	2	1	1.80	40	28	2	20	45
Andres Machado, Buffaloes	5	3	2.03	53	36	1	18	58
Ryusei Kawano, Fighters	1	4	2.13	42	33	5	11	33
Yuki Tsumori, Hawks	5	2	2.13	42	31	1	20	38
Seigi Tanaka, Fighters	4	4	2.17	50	33	4	17	47
Darwinzon Hernandez, Hawks	3	3	2.25	48	34	2	14	72
Tomohito Sakai, Eagles	2	2	2.33	46	35	0	15	29
Albert Abreu, Lions	2	5	2.39	49	38	1	20	33
Naoya Masuda, Marines	1	4	2.59	42	27	2	14	35
Yuki Matsumoto, Hawks	2	2	2.89	47	37	3	17	47
Takahiro Norimoto, Eagles	3	4	3.46	52	57	2	11	44
Roberto Osuna, Hawks	0	3	3.76	38	36	3	10	23
Taisei Yanagawa, Fighters	1	3	4.09	22	11	0	15	20
Yoshihisa Hirano, Buffaloes	1	1	4.22	11	19	1	5	11

OTHER NORTH AMERICAN PITCHERS

Pitcher, Team	W	L	ERA	IP	H	HR	BB	SO
Luis Perdomo, Buffaloes	1	0	0.64	28	20	1	3	19
Aneurys Zabala, Fighters	0	0	1.20	15	7	1	8	15
James Dykstra, Marines	1	0	1.64	11	10	2	8	11
Livan Moinelo, Hawks	11	5	1.88	163	107	11	47	155
Carter Stewart, Hawks	9	4	1.95	120	79	6	51	105
Roki Sasaki, Marines	10	5	2.35	111	83	2	32	129
Albert Abreu, Lions	2	5	2.39	49	38	1	20	33
Anderson Espinoza, Buffaloes	7	9	2.63	134	122	2	48	113
Cristopher Mercedes, Marines	4	8	2.71	126	97	12	34	91
Nik Turley, Eagles	0	1	2.93	15	15	2	12	13
Luis Castillo, Buffaloes	3	5	2.96	94	75	5	18	74
Drew VerHagen, Fighters	2	2	3.12	49	44	5	10	41
Patrick Murphy, Fighters	1	2	3.26	39	31	2	15	30
Dallas Keuchel, Marines	2	4	3.60	40	37	3	15	29
Michael Feliz, Dragons	0	1	5.19	17	15	2	8	10
Jefry Yan, Lions	0	0	5.58	31	32	3	19	35
Jimmy Cordero, Marines	0	1	7.20	5	8	1	2	1

NETHERLANDS

Neptunus Rolls

Curaçao Neptunus won its 12th Holland Series as Tom de Blok finished out the series with a complete game 5-1 win, it was his second win of the Holland Series. de Blok was 2-0, 1.06 in the Holland Series.

Neptunus made easy work of HCAW, sweeping the Holland Series after winning both of its semifinal games as well. The team was the clear class of the league, going 22-2 in the regular season. Pitching was the key to Neptunus' success. The team has three aces in de Blok, Juancarlos Sulbaran and Shairon Martis, as well as the best bullpen in the league, thanks to Ryan Huntington and Keon Postelmans.

Christian Diaz was named the MVP of the Holland Series. After being among the best hitters in the league all season, Diaz hit .625 (10-for-16) in the Holland Series with three doubles and four RBIs.

STANDINGS

Team	W	L	T	Pts
Curaçao Neptunus	22	2	0	44
Amsterdam Pirates	19	5	0	38
HCAW	16	7	1	33
DSS	12	10	2	26
RCH-Pinguins	11	12	1	23
Oosterhout Twins	11	13	0	22
UVV	10	13	1	21
Worldwide Pharma Logistics Hoofddorp Pioniers	4	19	1	9
Quick Amersfoort	0	24	0	0

Playoffs—Semifinals. Neptunus defeated DSS 2-0 and HCAW defeated Amsterdam 2-0 in best-of-three series. **Holland Series:** Neptunus defeated HCAW 4-0 in best-of-seven series.

BATTING LEADERS

Player, Team	AVG	AB	R	H	HR	RBI	SB
Luca Pastor, AMS	.429	63	10	27	0	9	1
Luuk Visser, QUI	.397	63	21	25	0	10	4
Christian Diaz, NEP	.395	195	45	77	4	45	2
Jeldwin Orman, RCH	.378	180	39	68	1	29	12
Stijn Van Der Meer, NEP	.364	151	42	55	1	19	6
Marnix Ruben, TWI	.357	182	54	65	0	35	31
Terrence Garcia, TWI	.342	158	30	54	2	26	4
Tilsaimy Melfor, RCH	.341	170	26	58	6	47	1
Dwayne Kemp, NEP	.336	220	36	74	1	51	21
Darryl Collins, NEP	.333	165	38	55	0	31	10

PITCHING LEADERS

Player, Team	W	L	ERA	IP	H	HR	BB	SO
Ryan Huntington, NEP	3	2	1.09	41	31	0	12	49
Koen Postelmans, NEP	7	1	1.25	50	35	1	18	58
Tom De Blok, NEP	10	1	1.29	105	70	1	30	95
Juancarlos Sulbaran, NEP	12	0	1.43	101	64	1	26	91
Shairon Martis, NEP	12	0	1.53	106	75	1	17	88
Lars Huijer, HCA	10	4	1.58	148	97	3	42	166
Wyatt Lankford, TWI	10	3	1.68	86	52	1	23	107
Pim Vijfvinkel, AMS	5	4	2.10	69	62	1	20	44
Nelmerson Angela, AMS	4	3	2.12	81	68	0	28	48
Kaj Timmermans, HCA	9	6	2.34	115	93	0	30	89

ITALY

ParmaClima Wins SerieA

Matteo Bocchi threw five scoreless innings, allowing just one hit as Parma shut out San Marino 6-0 in Game 5 to finish off its first Italian Baseball Series title since 2010 and its 11th overall.

Former Mariners third baseman Alex Liddi was named the Italian Series MVP. He hit a two-run home run in the seventh inning of the deciding game, and he drove in five runs in the series to lead all players. It was Liddi's first title since he came back to Italy to play.

Poviglio's Frank Garcia remains one of the aces of Italian baseball, as he went 10-4, 2.23. Collecchio's Dariel De La Torre led the league with 180 strikeouts.

STANDINGS

Group A	W	L	PCT	GB
Parma	20	10	.667	-
Foritudo Bologna	20	10	.667	-
San Marino	19	11	.633	1
Hotsand Macerata	15	15	.500	5
Grosseto 1952	10	20	.333	10
New Energy Grosseto	6	24	.200	14
Group B	**W**	**L**	**PCT**	**GB**
Collecchio	17	3	.850	-
Verona	12	8	.600	5
Poviglio	9	9	.500	7
Modena	7	11	.389	9
Settimo	5	11	.313	10
Milano 1946	6	14	.300	11
Group C	**W**	**L**	**PCT**	**GB**
Rovigo	14	6	.700	-
Crocetta	12	8	.600	2
New Rimini	11	8	.579	2.5
Cagliari	8	12	.400	6
Rocnhi	7	12	.368	6.5
Padova	7	13	.350	7
Group D	**W**	**L**	**PCT**	**GB**
Nettuno	19	1	.950	-
Godo	13	7	.650	6
Athletics	12	8	.600	7
Firentina	12	8	.600	7
Lions Nettuno	4	16	.200	15
Padule	0	20	.000	19
Group E	**W**	**L**	**PCT**	**GB**
Reggio	18	2	.900	-
Codogno	13	7	.650	5
Oltretorrente	10	10	.500	8
Catalana	9	11	.450	9
Senago	5	15	.250	13
Torino	5	15	.250	135

Playoffs—Semifinals: Parma defeated Macerata 4-3 and San Marino defeated Bologna 4-1 in best-of-7 series **Finals:** Parma defeated San Marino 4-1 in best-of-5 series.

Kia Dominates KBO Series

Hyung-Woo Choi, the oldest player to ever homer in a Korean Series game, hit a home run to start the comeback, and Socrates Brito scored on an infield single by Kim Tae Gun, as Kia knocked off Samsung 7-5 in Game 5 to finish off a 4-1 win in the best-of-7 series.

Kim Sun Bim was voted Korean Series MVP after going 10-for-17 with three doubles and a triple.

GENE WANG/GETTY IMAGES

Kim Do Yeong

The win continued a truly remarkable streak for the Tigers. This was their 12th Korean Series title in 12 Korean Series appearances. Any time Kia has made it to the championship series, it has won it all.

For the Lions, it was their 11th loss in 19 Korean Series appearances, and it extended the team's title drough to 10 years.

Samsung slugger Lewin Diaz, a former Twins and Marlins first baseman, did all he could. He hit two-run home runs in back-to-back at-bats in the deciding Game 5. He had also homered in back-to-back at-bats earlier in the postseason as well.

It was a fitting win, as Kia was the class of the league all season. The Tigers ran away from the field in the regular season, paced by starter James Naile (12-5, 2.53) as well as 20-year-old star Kim Do Yeong (.347/.420/.647) and Kim Sun Bin (.329/.380/.447).

Do Yeong is quickly establishing himself as a star. The 20-year-old flirted with a 40-40 season, finishing with 38 home runs to go with 40 stolen bases. He finished second to Matt Davidson's 46 home runs, and he finished sixth in stolen bases.

Davision continued to star for the NC Dinos, hitting .306 with the league-leading 46 homers. LG's Austin Dean hit 32 home runs, as did KT's Mel Rojas Jr.

Gullermo Heredia led the league with a .360 batting average.

While Naile led the league with a 2.53 ERA, it was Kyle Hart who topped the league with 13 wins in a 13-3, 2.69 season. Eight of the top 10 pitchers in the league were foreign imports.

STANDINGS

Team	W	L	T	PCT	GB
Kia Tigers	87	55	2	.613	-
Samsung Lions	78	64	2	.549	9
LG Twins	76	66	2	.535	11
Doosan Bears	74	68	2	.521	13
KT Wiz	72	70	2	.507	15
SSG Landers	72	70	2	.507	15
Lotte Giants	66	74	4	.471	20
Hanwha Eagles	66	76	2	.465	21
NC Dinos	61	81	2	.430	26
Kiwoom Heroes	58	86	0	.403	30

Playoffs—Wild Card: KT defeated Doosan 2-0 in best-of-3 series. **Semifinal Series:** LG defeated KT 3-1 in best-of-five series. **Playoff Final:** Samsung defeated LG 3-1 in best-of-5 series. **Korea Series:** Kia defeated Samsung 4-1 in best-of-7 series.

INDVIDUAL BATTING LEADERS

Player, Team	AVG	AB	R	H	2B	3B	HR	RBI	SB
Guillermo Heredia, SSG	.360	541	82	195	31	1	21	118	4
Victor Reyes, LOTTE	.352	574	88	202	40	3	15	111	5
Kim Do Yeong, KIA	.347	544	143	189	29	10	38	109	40
Koo Ja Wook, SAMSUNG	.343	493	92	169	39	1	33	115	13
Song Sung Mun, KIWOOM	.340	527	88	179	29	4	19	104	21
Hong Chang Ki, LG	.336	524	96	176	18	3	5	73	10
Mel Rojas Jr., KT	.329	572	108	188	39	1	32	112	2
Kim Sun Bin, KIA	.329	423	48	139	23	0	9	57	5
Park Min Woo, NC	.328	457	75	150	26	2	8	50	32
Kim Hye Seong, KIWOOM	.326	509	90	166	26	4	11	75	30
Austin Dean, LG	.319	527	99	168	32	3	32	132	12
Kim Ji Chan, SAMSUNG	.316	453	102	143	16	3	3	36	42
Yang Eui Ji, DOOSAN	.314	430	57	135	18	1	17	94	2
Na Seung Yeup, LOTTE	.312	407	59	127	35	4	7	66	1
Socrates Brito, KIA	.310	552	92	171	30	3	26	97	13
Heo Kyoung Min, DOOSAN	.309	417	69	129	28	0	7	61	5
Go Seung Min, LOTTE	.308	481	79	148	27	6	14	87	5
Park Chan Ho, KIA	.307	515	86	158	24	1	5	61	20
Matthew Davidson, NC	.306	504	90	154	25	1	46	119	0
Kang Min Ho, SAMSUNG	.303	403	48	122	19	1	19	77	3

INDIVIDUAL PITCHING LEADERS

Player	W	L	ERA	IP	H	HR	BB	SO
James Naile, KIA	12	5	2.53	149	154	11	35	138
Kyle Hart, NC	13	3	2.69	157	124	11	38	182
Charlie Barnes, LOTTE	9	6	3.35	151	140	18	46	171
Ariel Jurado, KIWOOM	10	8	3.36	190	185	19	32	169
Connor Seabold, SAMSUNG	11	6	3.43	160	135	21	40	158
Won Tae In, SAMSUNG	15	6	3.66	160	150	17	42	119
Enmanuel De Jesus, KIWOOM	13	11	3.68	171	171	22	44	178
Son Ju Young, LG	9	10	3.79	145	157	11	54	112
Denyi Reyes, SAMSUNG	11	4	3.81	144	159	15	30	114
Aaron Wilkerson, LOTTE	12	8	3.84	197	210	18	27	167
Ryu Hyun Jin, HANWHA	10	8	3.87	158	182	12	33	135
Yang Hyeon Jong, KIA	11	5	4.10	171	174	21	41	129
William Cuevas, KT	7	12	4.10	173	158	17	59	154
Dietrich Enns, LG	13	6	4.19	168	169	16	50	157
Gwak Been, DOOSAN	15	9	4.24	168	142	11	76	154
Ha Yeong Min, KIWOOM	9	8	4.37	150	168	8	58	101
Wesley Benjamin, KT	11	8	4.63	150	141	28	48	156
Park Se Woong, LOTTE	6	11	4.78	173	188	13	56	124
Um Sang Back, KT	13	10	4.88	157	164	26	42	159
Kim Kwang Hyun, SSG	12	10	4.93	162	162	24	73	154

De Paula Finds Fame In Taiwan

In the late 2000s and early 2010s, Jose De Paula was a hard-throwing promising pitching prospect in the Padres' system. It never fully clicked for him in the U.S., but he did make it to the majors with the Yankees in 2015.

That proved to be De Paula's last season playing in the U.S. He went to Mexico for four years, but he truly found his place when he came to Taiwan to join Brothers Elephant in 2020.

Jose De Paula

GENE WANG/GETTY IMAGES

De Paula quickly became the Brothers' ace. He went 16-9, 3.20 in 2020, and was even better in 2021, going 16-4, 1.77.

For the past five years, even as he's aged, he's continued to be a solid starter.

And this year, as a 36-year-old, he was at his best at the biggest moment. De Paula gave up three runs in the first inning of Game 1, of the Taiwan Series. But he then settled down to throw six scoreless innings to pick up the opening win. He was just as good in in the clinching Game 5, allowing one run, six hits and a walk over seven innings. De Paula got two of the four wins in the series.

Brothers has now won three titles in the past four years, after finishing as runners-up six times in a seven-year stretch. Since De Paula arrived, Brothers is 3-1 in Taiwan Series.

Tseng Song En was named the Taiwan Series MVP, as he went 11-for-21 with two home runs and seven RBIs.

UniLions ace Gu Lin was named the league MVP after he went 10-2, 1.66 to lead the league in ERA. Tseng Tzu Yu was named the rookie of the year. The Hawks' 21-year-old shortstop hit .270/.344/.336.

One-time Tigers outfielder Steven Moya led the league with 30 home runs. His 99 RBI also paced the CPBL. UniLions' Mario Sanchez, a pitcher in the Nationals, Phillies and Twins' systems from 2012-2022, led the league with 167 strikeouts.

STANDINGS

First Half	W	L	T	GB
Uni-Preisdent Lions	37	23	.617	-
Rakuten Monkeys	33	27	.550	4
Brothers Elephant	32	28	.533	5
Fubon Guardians	29	31	.483	8
Wei Chuan Dragons	26	34	.433	11
TSG Hawks	23	37	.383	14

Second Half	W	L	PCT	GB
Brothers Elephant	38	22	.633	-
Wei Chuan Dragons	32	28	.533	6
Uni-Preisdent Lions	29	30	.492	8.5
Rakuten Monkeys	29	30	.492	8.5
TSG Hawks	26	33	.441	11.5
Fubon Guardians	24	35	.407	13.5

Playoffs—Semifinals: Uni-President defeated Rakuten 3-1 in best-of-5 series. **Taiwan Series:** Brothers defeats UniLions 4-1 in best-of-seven series.

INDIVIDUAL BATTING LEADERS

Player, Team	AVG	AB	R	H	2B	3B	HR	RBI	SB
Lin Li, Monkeys	.353	337	65	119	13	2	5	34	19
Chen Chieh Hsien, U-Lions	.334	401	71	134	13	7	2	55	7
Chiu Chih Cheng, U-Lions	.326	445	81	145	21	6	4	63	13
Li Kai Wei, Dragons	.319	423	58	135	16	0	2	34	14
Lin Hung Yu, Monkeys	.307	335	40	103	18	0	9	61	2
Tseng Song En, Brothers	.304	392	57	119	24	0	10	52	3
Hsu Chi Hung, Brothers	.301	332	53	100	19	1	9	62	4
Chen Chen Wei, Monkeys	.295	484	77	143	15	14	10	54	30
Chu Yu Hsien, Monkeys	.295	404	50	119	16	0	12	59	1
Steven Moya, Hawks	.294	432	71	127	24	2	30	99	1
Chen Chun Hsiu, Brothers	.290	321	40	93	20	0	7	47	2
Pan Chieh Kai, U-Lions	.283	332	40	94	11	2	5	48	3
Wang Po Hsuan, Hawks	.283	375	51	106	14	5	1	38	14
Tung Tzu En, Guardians	.281	345	31	97	13	0	1	30	2
Wang Po Jung, Hawks	.280	403	53	113	25	2	6	60	13
Giljegiljaw Kungkuan, Dragons	.279	455	60	127	21	0	23	78	0
Chiang Kun Yu, Brothers	.278	324	44	90	15	1	2	50	6
Kuo Tian Shin, Dragons	.275	393	51	108	23	3	1	30	9
Tseng Tzu Yu, Hawks	.270	456	68	123	10	4	4	36	13
Lee Tsung Hsien, Guardians	.268	385	49	103	22	2	1	29	11
Liang Chia Jung, Monkeys	.266	368	35	98	16	1	3	37	0
Chen Wun Jie, Hawks	.265	404	55	107	27	3	4	42	11
Lin An Ko, U-Lions	.257	408	63	105	21	1	20	93	5
Shen Hao Wei, Guardians	.254	405	48	103	17	3	9	60	3
Chen Chung Ting, U-Lions	.246	362	37	89	9	3	2	39	9
Liu Ji Hong, Dragons	.244	434	43	106	23	1	9	56	3
Yueh Cheng Hua, Brothers	.242	434	75	105	15	4	5	31	23
Ma Chieh Sen, Monkeys	.237	367	23	87	16	1	0	34	0
Yueh Tung Hua, Brothers	.211	356	48	75	12	1	8	43	8

INDIVIDUAL PITCHING LEADERS

Player, Team	W	L	ERA	IP	H	HR	BB	SO
Ruei Yang Gu Lin, U-Lions	10	2	1.66	125	106	3	28	150
Marcelo Martinez, Monkeys	13	3	2.04	150	131	10	34	114
Nivaldo Rodriguez, Guardians	10	4	2.16	154	135	7	39	156
Mario Sanchez, U-Lions	14	5	2.49	159	130	10	37	167
Brock Dykxhoorn, U-Lions	8	4	2.58	122	107	7	34	95
Tyler Eppler, Dragons	10	11	2.75	151	124	10	40	118
Daniel Mengden, Brothers	10	3	2.86	154	132	9	43	114
Drew Gagnon, Dragons	10	8	2.98	121	119	10	49	87
José De Paula, Brothers	10	5	3.05	127	118	6	21	91
Pedro Fernandez, Monkeys	10	8	3.50	152	162	6	35	113
Shih Peng Chen, Guardians	7	7	3.68	122	138	7	35	77

INTERNATIONAL

Las Tunas Defends Title

Once an afterthought, Las Tunas has become the domiant power of Cuban baseball. Las Tunas failed to win a title from 1977-2018, but the Lenadores won their third title in six years and their second in a row by knocking off Pinar Del Rio in the National Series.

Matanzas outfielder Jose Amaury Norona was named the Serie Nacional MVP. Norona hit .351 with 19 home runs and 79 RBIs. Alfredo Despaigne returned after playing in Japan for a decade. The 37-year-old remained productive, hitting .378 with a league-best 20 home runs.

STANDINGS

Team	W	L	PCT	GB
Pinar Del Rio	50	24	.676	-
Granma	47	27	.635	3
Las Tunas	42	28	.600	6
Santiago De Cuba	42	33	.560	8.5
Ciego de Avila	41	34	.547	9.5
Industriales	41	34	.547	9.5
Matanzas	40	35	.533	10.5
Sancti Spiritus	40	35	.533	10.5
Guantanamo	40	35	.533	10.5
Villa Clara	38	37	.507	12.5
Mayabeque	36	39	.480	14.5
Artemsia	35	40	.467	15.5
Camaguey	32	43	.427	18.5
Holguin	26	49	.347	24.5
Cienfuegos	24	51	.320	26.5
Isla De La Juventud	20	50	.286	28

Playoffs: Semifinals: Pinar Del Rio defeated Industriales 4-2 and Las Tunas defeated Granma 4-1 in best-of-7 series. Finals: Las Tunas defeated Pinar Del Rio 4-1 in best-of-7 series.

BATTING LEADERS

Player, Team	AVG	AB	R	H	2B	3B	HR	RBI
William Saavedra, PRI	.411	197	37	81	9	1	14	55
Ariel Sánchez, MTZ	.397	252	54	100	20	3	4	51
Yosvani Alarcón, LTU	.396	265	65	105	22	3	12	69
Raico Santos, GRA	.394	188	44	74	13	0	7	40
Yunier Mendoza, SSP	.385	226	33	87	9	0	2	22
José Jiménez, ART	.383	261	45	100	22	0	9	50
Alfredo Despaigne, GRA	.378	172	55	65	3	0	20	59
Jorge Rojas, PRI	.372	226	41	84	17	1	9	52
Jeison Martínez, MAY	.370	265	69	98	18	1	8	52
Yordanis Samón, CMG	.369	225	27	83	14	0	6	54
Rodolexis Moreno, SSP	.368	291	56	107	11	4	1	24
Héctor Labrada, CAV	.366	183	34	67	14	1	4	49
Leonelkis Escalante, GTM	.365	285	56	104	20	3	1	50
Osvaldo Abreu, GRA	.360	267	61	96	25	0	4	34
Alexander Pozo, MAY	.359	220	39	79	14	2	2	29
Robert Delgado, GTM	.357	269	60	96	16	3	9	67
Alexei Ramírez, PRI	.357	269	59	96	18	0	14	70
Guillermo Avilés, GRA	.354	254	56	90	17	1	11	69
Yariel Duque, MTZ	.352	256	42	90	9	0	7	56
Yudier Rondón, LTU	.351	231	53	81	23	2	2	33
José Noroña, MTZ	.351	248	79	87	11	0	19	79
Yulieski Remón, GRA	.348	282	47	98	24	0	3	59
Juan Arencibia, PRI	.348	250	69	87	8	2	0	33
Edilse Silva, HOL	.347	274	37	95	20	0	6	51
Yasniel González, MAY	.347	199	46	69	10	0	12	58
Yasiel Santoya, IND	.347	239	45	83	19	0	4	44
Alexis Varona, SSP	.346	217	38	75	22	0	10	51
Roberto Baldoquín, LTU	.346	185	48	64	19	1	10	41
Yoelquis Guibert, SCU	.343	230	63	79	16	2	15	68
Leovanni Brooks, GTM	.341	170	28	58	9	1	2	37
Yordanys Alarcón, LTU	.340	265	29	90	16	0	4	48
Yordan Manduley, HOL	.340	253	34	86	17	2	5	40
Yoasán Guillén, MAY	.339	183	32	62	13	1	4	29
Denis Peña, LTU	.338	240	47	81	17	1	13	55
Dunieski Barroso, SSP	.337	199	23	67	11	0	7	52
Osmel Solano, ART	.337	193	30	65	12	0	2	24
Francisco Martínez, SCU	.337	285	62	96	14	4	3	37
Ariel Hechavarría, IND	.337	187	41	63	8	1	9	34
Carlos De La Tejera, ART	.336	247	45	83	20	0	5	39
Oscar Valdés, IND	.336	235	46	79	12	1	11	57
Rafael Viñales, LTU	.336	232	50	78	17	0	18	68
Darian Palma, GRA	.335	233	42	78	14	1	6	47
Fernando De La Paz, CAV	.335	188	39	63	8	0	4	27
Hubert Sánchez, GRA	.335	191	34	64	9	0	6	38
Jeffrey Pérez, IJV	.333	183	31	61	8	3	2	19
Luís Machado, VCL	.333	177	30	59	10	2	2	37
Frederich Cepeda, SSP	.333	201	46	67	15	0	11	44
Ronaldo Castillo, CAV	.332	211	35	70	9	0	5	31
Lázaro Ponce, MAY	.328	241	31	79	13	1	3	38
Aníbal Medina, MTZ	.328	262	72	86	12	4	0	36
Yaser González, PRI	.328	265	47	87	15	0	17	60
Dainier Gálvez, IJV	.328	204	32	67	14	2	3	27
Minardo Dieguez, IJV	.327	162	18	53	4	0	1	14
Rubén Valdés, CAV	.327	284	46	93	15	1	11	60
Elicer Arrechavaleta, VCL	.324	256	55	83	19	3	1	20
Michael Thompson, CMG	.324	259	58	84	10	3	3	23
Adrián Pérez, MTZ	.322	211	45	68	7	2	1	42

PITCHING LEADERS

Player, Team	W	L	ERA	G	IP	R	ER	BB	SO
Ediel Ponce, CAV	8	2	2.15	13	71	21	17	39	43
Danny Betancourt, SCU	6	1	2.60	15	80	29	23	14	39
Raikol Suárez, CFG	7	6	2.70	16	103	43	31	34	66
Andy Vargas, IND	7	5	2.81	15	93	37	29	25	61
Mario Valle, PRI	5	2	3.42	16	71	33	27	23	46
Rodolfo Díaz, LTU	3	5	3.55	29	71	38	28	23	60
Osdani Rodríguez, VCL	9	6	3.57	18	86	47	34	37	38
Leandro Martínez, GRA	6	2	3.65	14	81	33	33	12	49
Yunieski García, ART	6	7	3.70	14	88	48	36	30	71
Yohanny Hernández, SSP	7	3	3.81	18	76	38	32	31	31
Dachel Duquesne, CAV	9	5	3.83	18	120	55	51	35	72
Albert Valladares, MAY	9	6	3.83	17	92	47	39	37	36
José Bermudes, MAY	6	5	3.91	21	101	54	44	29	43
Enyer Fernández, GTM	8	4	3.96	17	89	45	39	52	70
Luis Marrero, CAV	5	5	3.97	16	91	55	40	24	42
Carlos Benavides, SSP	4	5	4.06	18	75	38	34	35	53
Branlis Rodríguez, PRI	5	1	4.11	16	81	44	37	28	55
Yoendris Montero, SCU	2	4	4.25	31	72	40	34	14	17
César García, GRA	7	3	4.28	14	80	43	38	26	44
Kevin Soto, CAV	6	3	4.73	18	84	54	44	31	40
Joel Tejeda, GTM	5	5	4.82	21	71	39	38	22	52
Jesús Pérez, HOL	4	6	4.91	17	88	50	48	23	59
Ramiro Rodríguez, HOL	3	6	5.12	35	70	44	40	38	51
Osvaldo Acuña, SCU	8	3	5.31	19	80	52	47	55	50
Yunier Castillo, GRA	7	5	5.40	19	77	53	46	52	54
Roilan Averohff, MTZ	4	3	5.43	21	71	54	43	50	37
Yusmel Velázquez, CMG	3	8	5.47	16	77	55	47	28	37
Alex Pérez, CFG	1	6	5.60	15	80	66	50	37	32
Jenier Alvarez, PRI	6	3	5.76	17	70	50	45	36	43
Wilson Paredes, HOL	4	9	5.94	15	73	51	48	37	26
Yusdel Tuero, MAY	7	4	6.17	16	77	62	53	45	23
Pedro Mesa, MTZ	5	3	6.43	19	70	61	50	24	23
Eric Valenzuela, IJV	3	9	6.59	19	72	60	53	49	36

Ozzie Guillen led Venezuela to a drought-ending Caribbean Series title.

LUIS GUTIERREZ/NORTE PHOTO/GETTY IMAGES

Venezuela Wins First Caribbean Series In 15 Years

In front of a sellout crowd at Miami's LoanDepot Park, Series MVP Ricardo Pinto threw 5.2 innings of a shutout as Venezuela knocked off the Dominican Republic 3-0. It was the first title for a Venezuelan club in 15 years and the nation's eighth Caribbean Series title overall.

It was a well-rounded offense that got Ozzie Guillen's club the title. After a sac fly scored a run in the fourth, Hernan Perez's fifth-inning run-scoring triple and an RBI groundout by Odubel Herrera gave Venezuela all the runs it needed.

CARIBBEAN SERIES

Team	W	L	PCT	GB
Venezuela	7	1	.875	-
Panama	6	2	.750	1.0
Dom. Rep.	4	4	.500	3.0
Puerto Rico	3	3	.500	3.0
Curacao	3	5	.375	4.0
Mexico	2	4	.333	4.0
Nicaragua	0	6	.000	6.0

Playoffs—Finals: Venezuela defeated Dominican Republic 3-0 in championship game.

AUSTRALIAN BASEBALL LEAGUE

Team	W	L	PCT	GB
Adelaide	29	11	.725	-
Perth	24	15	.615	4.5
Brisbane	22	18	.550	7.0
Melbourne	21	19	.525	8.0
Canberra	12	27	.308	16.5
Sydney	11	29	.275	18.0

Playoffs—Semifinals: Adelaide defeated Melbourne 2-1 and Perth defeated Brisbane 2-1 in best-of-three series. **Finals:** Adelaide defeated Perth 2-1 n a best-of-three series.

INDIVIDUAL BATTING LEADERS

Player, Team	AVG	AB	R	H	2B	3B	HR	RBI	BB	SO	SB
Cory Acton, CAN	.333	111	24	37	6	0	3	17	15	25	13
Alex Skepton, BRI	.330	109	25	36	6	0	8	23	12	34	4
Jarryd Dale, MEL	.327	107	15	35	4	0	1	11	8	22	3
Nick Ward, ADE	.324	145	40	47	8	0	6	26	20	17	6
Quincy Latimore, ADE	.322	146	26	47	11	0	5	35	17	32	6
Raudelis Martinez, PER	.303	122	14	37	6	0	0	15	20	19	3
Liam Spence, ADE	.301	103	22	31	6	0	2	19	24	21	3
Jake Dowey, PER	.301	123	23	37	7	1	5	24	21	23	2
Rixon Wingrove, ADE	.297	138	21	41	11	0	4	31	15	27	2
Tayden Hall, BRI	.296	135	19	40	9	0	5	25	17	20	2

INDIVIDUAL PITCHING LEADERS

Player, Team	W	L	ERA	G	SV	IP	H	BB	SO	AVG
Lachlan Wells, ADE	6	0	0.94	9	0	40	28	7	63	.165
Tyler Beardsley, PER	5	2	2.21	10	0	53	51	13	50	.255
Yuhi Sako, CAN	2	2	2.21	11	0	37	28	11	39	.200
Shunuske Nakamori, SYD	2	2	2.38	6	0	34	35	6	39	.257
Braeden Fausnaught, ADE	4	2	2.53	10	0	32	33	16	33	.262
Steven Kent, MEL	4	2	3.00	8	0	33	36	8	28	.275
Luke Wilkins, ADE	2	0	3.00	9	0	42	41	12	24	.263
Kobe Foster, PER	3	1	3.11	8	0	38	35	7	38	.241
Tim Atherton, SYD	2	3	3.47	9	0	49	53	6	52	.275
Lewis Thorpe, MEL	2	3	3.60	10	0	50	46	20	41	.241

DOMINICAN LEAGUE

Team	W	L	PCT	GB
Gigantes del Cibao	29	20	.592	-
Estrellas Orientales	29	21	.580	0.5
Leones del Escogido	26	24	.520	3.5
Tigres del Licey	25	25	.500	4.5
Aguilas Cibaenas	22	28	.440	7.5
Toros del Este	18	31	.367	11

Playoffs—Round Robin: Estrellas Orientales and Tigres Del Licey advance. **Finals:** Tigres Del Licey defeated Estrellas Orientales 4-3 in best-of-seven series.

INDIVIDUAL BATTING LEADERS

Player	AVG	OBP	SLG	AB	R	H	HR	RBI	BB	SO	SB
Simon, Ronny, TOR	.323	.432	.494	164	36	53	5	21	32	28	14
González, Erik, ESC	.321	.370	.429	168	25	54	1	28	16	24	11
Castro, Starlin, AGU	.319	.394	.429	119	15	38	2	19	15	21	0
Bonifácio, Emilio, LIC	.319	.391	.369	141	27	45	0	15	17	23	14
Rodriguez, Hector, ESC	.309	.344	.487	152	23	47	3	11	7	23	4
Hernandez, Yadiel, AGU	.302	.407	.343	169	21	51	0	20	28	21	1
Muñoz, Yairo, AGU	.301	.348	.411	163	30	49	2	13	11	18	4
Lagares, Juan, AGU	.299	.362	.386	127	24	38	2	14	10	18	7
Reyes, Franmil, ESC	.296	.353	.546	152	28	45	9	34	14	43	1
Urrutia, Henry, GIG	.288	.380	.367	139	8	40	1	20	21	22	1

INDIVIDUAL PITCHING LEADERS

Player, Team	W	L	ERA	G	IP	H	HR	BB	SO	AVG
Espino, Paolo, TOR	4	3	2.40	9	49	34	1	10	49	.193
Rogers, Esmil, TOR	3	3	3.31	10	49	50	8	24	26	.259
Valdez, Cesar, LIC	1	4	3.46	10	52	58	2	9	26	.280
Alexander, Tyler, ESC	3	4	3.83	10	47	43	5	9	44	.243
Valdes, Raul, TOR	4	6	4.99	10	49	48	9	18	35	.250

MEXICAN PACIFIC LEAGUE

Team	W	L	PCT	GB
Guasave	39	29	.574	-
Hermosillo	37	31	.544	2
Los Mochis	36	32	.529	3
Mazatlan	36	32	.529	3
Culiacan	34	32	.515	4
Jalisco	35	33	.515	4
Mexicali	34	34	.500	5
Obregon	33	35	.485	6
Monterrey	26	37	.413	11
Navojoa	25	40	.385	13

Playoffs—Semifinals: Hermosillo defeated Mexicali 4-0 and Mazatlan defeated Culiacan 4-1 in best-of-seven series. **Finals:** Hermosillo defeated Mazatlan 4-0 in best-of-seven series.

INDIVIDUAL BATTING LEADERS

Player, Team	AVG	AB	R	H	2B	3B	HR	RBI	BB	SO	SB
Taiki Sekine, OBR	.345	174	20	60	10	2	0	5	9	16	4
Norberto Obeso, MXC	.338	160	32	54	10	0	0	11	36	24	3
Roberto Valenzuela, MTY	.335	191	32	64	14	1	2	18	31	17	4
Jesus Valdez, MAZ	.320	194	17	62	10	0	3	31	10	23	2
Allen Córdoba, OBR	.318	255	49	81	8	3	2	24	29	39	15
Jose Gaitan, MAZ	.316	196	21	62	15	1	2	19	16	46	3
Jared Serna, JAL	.310	232	37	72	14	2	7	30	18	46	13
Alejandro Flores, MXC	.307	163	17	50	10	1	2	23	28	41	3
Jasson Atondo, HER	.306	183	21	56	14	0	1	23	18	20	5
Andres Alvarez, CUL	.305	187	24	57	7	0	5	16	14	42	7

INDIVIDUAL PITCHING LEADERS

Player, Team	W	L	ERA	G	SV	IP	H	BB	SO	AVG
Manny Barreda, CUL	5	3	1.96	12	0	69	45	19	51	.185
Nick Struck, MOC	7	3	2.34	13	0	69	67	24	34	.260
David Reyes, MXC	8	3	2.43	14	0	78	80	16	48	.271
Manuel Flores, MAZ	4	2	2.44	13	0	66	64	20	54	.255
Jeff Kinley, GSV	6	0	2.47	11	0	58	53	19	43	.249
Fredy Quintero, MOC	3	4	2.61	14	0	59	57	16	27	.252
Braulio Torres-Perez, MAZ	5	3	2.66	12	0	64	56	18	52	.238
Marcelo Martinez, MXC	6	2	2.77	14	0	68	54	18	68	.216
Jose Bravo, CUL	7	2	2.85	12	0	66	63	15	56	.254
Hector Villalobos, MAZ	6	5	2.94	13	0	64	55	26	54	.231

PUERTO RICAN LEAGUE

Team	W	L	PCT	GB
Santurce	25	15	.625	-
Carolina	24	16	.600	1
Caguas	21	19	.525	4
Ponce	21	19	.525	4
Mayaguez	18	22	.450	7
RA12	11	29	.275	14

Playoffs—Semifinals: Carolina defeated Ponce 4-3 and Caguas defeated Santurce 4-1 in best-of-7 series. **Finals:** Caguas defeated Carolina 5-3 in a best-of-nine series.

INDIVIDUAL BATTING LEADERS

Player, Team	AVG	AB	R	H	2B	3B	HR	RBI	BB	SO	SB
Brian Rey, MAY	.331	124	21	41	4	3	1	15	14	11	2
Bryan Torres, CAR	.299	137	23	41	4	0	1	13	23	20	13
Vimael Machín, CAG	.297	148	17	44	6	0	2	19	19	20	2
Shed Long Jr., SAN	.296	98	16	29	10	0	1	8	16	9	3
Roy Morales, SAN	.291	117	8	34	3	0	1	18	15	10	1
Nelson Velázquez, CAG	.280	82	11	23	5	0	3	12	7	16	4
Ruben Castro, RA12	.276	145	22	40	5	1	1	5	15	30	12
Johnathan Rodriguez, CAR	.269	145	20	39	4	0	3	17	22	28	1
Dwight Smith Jr., CAG	.269	108	17	29	7	1	2	10	10	22	4
Yariel Gonzalez, SAN	.267	101	7	27	0	0	1	9	8	16	1

INDIVIDUAL PITCHING LEADERS

Player, Team	W	L	ERA	G	SV	IP	H	BB	SO	AVG
Jason García, SAN	3	0	0.68	22	0	27	8	16	27	.092
Miller Hogan, CAR	2	2	1.10	8	0	33	23	2	30	.195
Adalberto Flores, SAN	3	1	1.53	9	0	35	23	10	29	.180
Orlando Rodriguez, CAR	1	1	1.84	15	1	29	28	13	25	.259
Eduardo Rivera, CAR	3	3	1.85	10	1	44	32	18	48	.200
Derrick Adams, CAG	0	1	2.08	8	0	30	25	13	21	.227
Daryl Thompson, MAY	6	1	2.09	10	0	47	41	4	34	.227
Andres Santiago, PON	1	0	2.15	12	0	29	24	8	21	.231
Luis Cruz, MAY	1	6	2.31	10	0	51	40	20	44	.223
Pedro Echemendia, PON	2	4	2.45	9	0	44	36	11	32	.220

VENEZUELAN LEAGUE

Team	W	L	PCT	GB
La Guaira	30	26	.536	-
Aragua	29	26	.527	1
Magallanes	24	33	.421	7
Caribes	21	35	.375	9

Playoffs—Round Robin: La Guaria and Lara advance. Finals: La Guaria defeated Lara 4-1 in best-of-7 series.

INDIVIDUAL BATTING LEADERS

Player, Team	AVG	AB	R	H	2B	3B	HR	RBI	BB	SO	SB
Gabriel Noriega, CAR	.376	197	29	74	14	1	3	44	9	34	2
Alexi Amarista, ARA	.363	226	37	82	14	3	1	22	14	12	0
Carlos D. Rodriguez, MAG	.354	147	26	52	9	1	1	14	22	11	6
Jose A. Martínez, ARA	.346	205	31	71	13	0	9	48	33	23	0
Wilson Garcia, LAG	.346	191	36	66	13	1	8	41	21	16	0
Leonardo Reginatto, LAG	.344	227	42	78	13	0	8	46	15	29	1
Jose Martinez, MAR	.343	175	25	60	7	2	1	28	21	18	3
David Rodríguez, MAR	.338	201	35	68	12	0	4	32	37	33	0
Jose Rondon, CAR	.338	213	44	72	17	1	14	42	28	39	1
Yorman Rodriguez, ARA	.336	152	18	51	11	1	3	30	9	18	2

INDIVIDUAL PITCHING LEADERS

Player, Team	W	L	ERA	G	SV	IP	H	BB	SO	AVG
Osmer Morales, MAR	7	0	2.26	12	0	60	53	20	51	.231
Max Castillo, LAR	5	0	2.72	11	0	50	52	12	39	.271
Jorge Tavarez, ZUL	2	4	3.28	13	0	58	53	20	35	.243
Felix Doubront, MAR	5	2	3.58	12	0	65	68	19	44	.275
Albert Suárez, CAR	4	2	3.79	11	0	55	62	12	34	.286
Ricardo Pinto, LAG	1	2	4.00	10	1	45	51	16	33	.291
Angelk Rondón, ZUL	1	3	4.11	12	0	46	50	26	21	.278
Jesus Vargas, CAR	3	2	4.66	13	0	48	61	17	32	.318
Luis Martinez, MAG	2	4	5.44	12	0	48	51	21	40	.276
Edgar Escobar, ORI	4	4	6.27	13	0	52	60	28	31	.300

COLLEGE

C. MORGAN ENGEL/NCAA PHOTOS VIA GETTY IMAGES

Tennessee avenged past postseason disappointments with a magical 60-win season

Tennessee Hangs On To Claim First Title

BY TEDDY CAHILL

Some national championships come as coronations, teams rolling through the College World Series finals to the trophy presentation. Some national championships, however, are ground out; every out, every run is fought for.

Tennessee had to fight for the 2024 national title. It won more games this season than any team in the last 22 years and collected every trophy it could have. Yet, every step of the way, it had to fight.

The Volunteers didn't win the SEC regular season title until the final day of the season. They lost their opening game of the SEC Tournament, sending them through the loser's bracket. They were forced to a Game 3 in super regionals by Evansville, the Cinderella of the NCAA Tournament. Tennessee then lost the opening game of the CWS championship series to Texas A&M, pressing its backs against the wall.

Even before this season, it was a fight for the program. Tennessee was making its third appearance in the CWS in the last four years but had gone 0-2 in 2021 and 1-2 in 2023. In between, the 2022 team was the No. 1 overall seed in the NCAA Tournament but was upset at home by Notre Dame in super regionals.

So, of course, Game 3 of the championship series on Monday didn't come easy. Tennessee never trailed on the night, thanks in part to a leadoff home run from Christian Moore. But every time it pushed ahead, A&M punched back. Even Tennessee's runs didn't come easily, especially its sixth run, which proved decisive. On that play, Hunter Ensley had to make a last-second adjustment in his dive into home plate to avoid getting tagged.

In the end, Tennessee found a way, just like it has all season long. The Volunteers held on to defeat the Aggies, 6-5, and win the first national championship in program history.

"No better team to win for the University of Tennessee than a bunch of guys who were truly the definition of a team," Vols coach Tony Vitello said. "And no better play for our program to, I think, be the winning run on that slide, a guy that's just built with a ton of grit. His teammates follow his leadership and it's a great example of how this group got things done."

This Tennessee team is arguably the greatest team in college baseball history. It finished the season 60-13, setting an SEC record for overall wins. It is the first team to win 60 games in a season since Florida State in 2002, and it won more games than any national champion since Wichita State

COACHING CAROUSEL

School	In (Previous Job)	Out (Reason/New Job)
Alcorn State	Carlton Hardy (Savannah State head coach)	Reggie Williams
Arkansas-Pine Bluff	Logan Stout (travel ball coach)	Carlos James
Arkansas State	Mike Silva (Nicholls State head coach)	Tommy Raffo
Cal State Bakersfield	Jordon Banfield (Oakland head coach)	Jeremy Beard
Campbell	Chris Marx (Purdue pitching coach)	Justin Haire (Ohio State)
Charleston Southern	Karl Kuhn (Charleston Southern pitching coach)	Marc MacMillan
The Citadel	Russell Triplett (Newberry S.C. coach)	Tony Skole
Coastal Carolina	Kevin Schnall (Coastal Carolina assistant)	Gary Gilmore (retired)
Dayton	Scott Loiseau (Penn State associated head coach)	Jayson King (Vanderbilt assistant)
Delaware State	Pedro Swann (Maryland Eastern Shore)	JP Blandin (retired)
Eastern Kentucky	Walt Jones (Eastern Kentucky assistant)	Chris Prothro
Houston Christian	Clay VanderLaan (Houston Christian assistant)	Lance Berkman
Indiana State	Tracy Archuleta (Southern Indiana)	Mitch Hannahs (South Florida)
Liberty	Bradley LeCroy (VCU)	Scott Jackson
Long Beach State	TJ Bruce (TCU associate head coach)	Bryan Peters (interim)
Longwood	Ray Noe (VMI assistant)	Chad Oxendine (Coastal Carolina assistant)
Manhattan	Steven Rosen (interim)	Dave Miller
Minnesota	Ty McDevitt (Minnesota assistant)	John Anderson (retired)
Missouri State	Joey Hawkins(Missouri State associate head coach)	Keith Guttin (retired)
Niagara	Matt Spatafora (Niagara assistant)	Rob McCoy
Nicholls State	Brent Haring (LSU director of operations)	Mike Silva (Arkansas State)
Oakland	Brian Nelson (interim)	Jordon Banfield
Ohio State	Justin Haire (Campbell)	Bill Mosiello (TCU assistant)
Pacific	Reed Peters (San Joaquin Delta Calif. JC)	Chris Rodriguez
Pepperdine	Tyler LaTorre (Westmont Calif.)	Rick Hirtensteiner
South Carolina	Paul Mainieri	Mark Kingston
S.C.-Upstate	Kane Sweeney (S.C.-Upstate assistant)	Mike McGuire (Wintrop)
South Florida	Mitch Hannahs (Indiana State)	Billy Mohl
Southern Indiana	Chris Ramirez (Lenoir-Rhyne)	Tracy Archuleta (Indiana State)
Stephen F. Austin	Matt Vanderburg (West Texas A&M)	Johnny Cardenas (retired)
Texas	Jim Schlossnagle (TCU)	David Pierce
Texas A&M	Michael Earley (Texas A&M assistant)	Jim Schlossnagle
Utah Valley	Nate Rasmussen (Utah Valley assistant)	Eddie Smith (Washington)
VCU	Sean Thompson (VCU assistant)	Bradley LeCroy (Liberty)
Washington	Eddie Smith (Utah Valley)	Jason Kelly (Texas A&M assistant)
West Virginia	Steve Sabins (West Virginia assistant)	Randy Mazey (retired)
William & Mary	Rob McCoy (Niagara)	Mike McRae
Winthrop	Mike McGuire (S.C. Upstate)	Tom Riqinos
Youngstown State	Trevor Charpie (Youngstown State assistant)	Dan Bertolini

in 1989, which went 68-16 in a very different era of the sport. The Volunteers won both the SEC regular-season and tournament titles. They had one losing weekend all year and none since the middle of March (which was also the only time they lost consecutive games all season). By the end, Tennessee was the No. 1 overall seed in the NCAA Tournament and the first No. 1 overall seed to win the national championship since Miami in 1999.

The Volunteers have star power at the heart of the team. All-American second baseman Moore was a first-round draft pick. Third baseman Billy Amick was a second-round pick. Left fielder Dylan Dreiling, the College World Series Most Outstanding Player, was also a second-round pick. Righthander Drew Beam was a third-round pick and All-American first baseman Blake Burke was a supplemental first-round pick. Each goes down as one of the best players at their positions in program history.

There will be big leaguers from this team, but that was never the story of the 2024 Volunteers. In his six years in Knoxville, Vitello has coached teams with more talent than this one. Just two years removed, the 2022 squad already has three big leaguers with more to come.

What this year's Volunteers mastered, however, was the perfect blend of talent and grit, an attitude that Vitello has tried to instill from the day he was hired. When he arrived at Tennessee in the summer of 2017, Tennessee was stuck near the bottom of the SEC standings. It had made the SEC Tournament just three times in the previous 10 years and hadn't made the NCAA Tournament since 2005.

Vitello, a first-time head coach, knew Tennessee needed to find an identity to compete in the rugged SEC. Tennessee at the time couldn't match facilities with Arkansas or Mississippi State. It didn't have LSU's tradition. It couldn't lean on in-state players like Florida or Texas A&M.

What Vitello settled on was building a gritty program that played with an edge. The notion directed his hires, from assistant coaches Frank Anderson and Josh Elander, who have been with him throughout his tenure, to support staff like Quentin Eberhardt, the program's director of sports performance. It also guided their efforts in recruiting and in practice.

The final result was an attitude on full display in the 2024 team and embodied in players like Ensley, Moore and lefthander Zander Sechrist, who started and won the final game.

"We gotta play with some attitude," Vitello said. "We gotta play with some grit. And we're going to have to get some guys that maybe don't want to say yes to a school with a better winning record than us. Guys like that, like (Moore) and some others with some attitude, have done a lot for this program."

That attitude, that grit is what led Ensley to crash into the center field fence at full speed to make a catch last Sunday. He was shaken up on the play and had to be replaced in center field the next game by Kavares Tears. He, too, barreled into the wall to make a catch.

"It's the way I grew up, (with a) blue-collar family," Ensley said. "My whole family is just tough. Growing up with them, that was kind of what was preached. You show up every day you work hard, you play hard and if it doesn't go your way, work harder and do better.

"Obviously in center field I'm willing to run through a wall for this team. I would do it a million times over."

The mindset instilled in the program isn't just limited to grit or an edge. The Volunteers were also a close-knit group who loved playing together and for their coaches. That camaraderie ran through the program, helping to get contributions from up and down the roster.

Sechrist was one such player.

A senior who makes his living on pitchability rather than pure stuff, he worked his way into the rotation and eventually became the team's best pitcher down the stretch. On Monday, he held A&M to one run in 5.1 innings. He struck out seven and worked around six hits and a walk. Tennessee won each of his last six starts, a run in which he pitched to a 1.34 ERA beginning on the final day of the regular season against South Carolina.

COLLEGE WORLD SERIES CHAMPIONS

Year	Champion	Coach	Record	Runner-Up	Most Outstanding Player
1948	Southern California	Sam Barry	40-12	Yale	None selected
1949	Texas*	Bibb Falk	23-7	Wake Forest	Charles Teague, 2B, Wake Forest
1950	Texas	Bibb Falk	27-6	Washington State	Ray VanCleef, OF, Rutgers
1951	Oklahoma*	Jack Baer	19-9	Tennessee	Sid Hatfield, 1B/P, Tennessee
1952	Holy Cross	Jack Barry	21-3	Missouri	Jim O'Neill, P, Holy Cross
1953	Michigan	Ray Fisher	21-9	Texas	J.L. Smith, P, Texas
1954	Missouri	Hi Simmons	22-4	Rollins	Tom Yewcic, C, Michigan State
1955	Wake Forest	Taylor Sanford	29-7	Western Michigan	Tom Borland, P, Oklahoma State
1956	Minnesota	Dick Siebert	33-9	Arizona	Jerry Thomas, P, Minnesota
1957	California*	George Wolfman	35-10	Penn State	Cal Emery, 1B/P, Penn State
1958	Southern California	Rod Dedeaux	35-7	Missouri	Bill Thom, P, Southern California
1959	Oklahoma State	Toby Greene	27-5	Arizona	Jim Dobson, 3B, Oklahoma State
1960	Minnesota	Dick Siebert	34-7	Southern California	John Erickson, 2B, Minnesota
1961	Southern California*	Rod Dedeaux	43-9	Oklahoma State	Littleton Fowler, P, Oklahoma State
1962	Michigan	Don Lund	31-13	Santa Clara	Bob Garibaldi, P, Santa Clara
1963	Southern California	Rod Dedeaux	37-16	Arizona	Bud Hollowell, C, Southern California
1964	Minnesota	Dick Siebert	31-12	Missouri	Joe Ferris, P, Maine
1965	Arizona State	Bobby Winkles	54-8	Ohio State	Sal Bando, 3B, Arizona State
1966	Ohio State	Marty Karow	27-6	Oklahoma State	Steve Arlin, P, Ohio State
1967	Arizona State	Bobby Winkles	53-12	Houston	Ron Davini, C, Arizona State
1968	Southern California*	Rod Dedeaux	45-14	Southern Illinois	Bill Seinsoth, 1B, Southern California
1969	Arizona State	Bobby Winkles	56-11	Tulsa	John Dolinsek, OF, Arizona State
1970	Southern California	Rod Dedeaux	51-13	Florida State	Gene Ammann, P, Florida State
1971	Southern California	Rod Dedeaux	53-13	Southern Illinois	Jerry Tabb, 1B, Tulsa
1972	Southern California	Rod Dedeaux	50-13	Arizona State	Russ McQueen, P, Southern California
1973	Southern California*	Rod Dedeaux	51-11	Arizona State	Dave Winfield, OF/P, Minnesota
1974	Southern California	Rod Dedeaux	50-20	Miami	George Milke, P, Southern California
1975	Texas	Cliff Gustafson	56-6	South Carolina	Mickey Reichenbach, 1B, Texas
1976	Arizona	Jerry Kindall	56-17	Eastern Michigan	Steve Powers, DH/P, Arizona
1977	Arizona State	Jim Brock	57-12	South Carolina	Bob Horner, 3B, Arizona State
1978	Southern California*	Rod Dedeaux	54-9	Arizona State	Rod Boxberger, P, Southern California
1979	Cal State Fullerton	Augie Garrido	60-14	Arkansas	Tony Hudson, P, Cal State Fullerton
1980	Arizona	Jerry Kindall	45-21	Hawaii	Terry Francona, OF, Arizona
1981	Arizona State	Jim Brock	55-13	Oklahoma State	Stan Holmes, OF, Arizona State
1982	Miami	Ron Fraser	57-18	Wichita State	Dan Smith, P, Miami
1983	Texas	Cliff Gustafson	66-14	Alabama	Calvin Schiraldi, P, Texas

Sechrist is one of the few players who were a part of all three CWS teams in the last four years. He said the 2024 team stood out from any he played for.

"We had unfinished business, especially this being the third time we've been here in the last four years," he said. "'21 we didn't do well. '22 you could arguably say that was the best college baseball team ever. '23 we got to experience winning at least a game here, but the job wasn't finished. And '24 just felt a little different.

"I'm just blessed today to get the job done."

The deciding win took a little bit of everything from the roster. Eight players had at least one hit. Dreiling homered again, becoming the first player to homer in every game of a CWS finals. Moore capped one of the greatest seasons in program history with a home run. Sechrist turned in another strong start and the bullpen held off a powerful, determined A&M lineup.

It ended with a raucous celebration. Vitello leapt into the stands to celebrate with Tennessee fans. Peyton Manning came onto the field to soak in the atmosphere. Players hugged each other and did snow angels in confetti.

It was the perfect ending for a team that had fought for each other for five long months. Throughout the CWS, the Volunteers talked about wanting to soak up the moments and enjoy their last couple weeks together.

The Volunteers certainly enjoyed it. They'll be forever linked together in Tennessee and college baseball history.

Texas A&M Loses Coach

Less than 24 hours after the Aggies lost to Tennessee in the College World Series finals, Texas hired away Texas A&M head coach Jim Schlossnagle.

Texas athletic director Chris Del Conte fired coach David Pierce, who led the program for eight years and guided the Longhorns to three CWS

Year	Champion	Coach	Record	Runner-Up	MOST OUTSTANDING PLAYER
1984	Cal State Fullerton	Augie Garrido	66-20	Texas	John Fishel, OF, Cal State Fullerton
1985	Miami*	Ron Fraser	64-16	Texas	Greg Ellena, DH, Miami
1986	Arizona	Jerry Kindall	49-19	Florida State	Mike Senne, OF, Arizona
1987	Stanford	Mark Marquess	53-17	Oklahoma State	Paul Carey, OF, Stanford
1988	Stanford	Mark Marquess	46-23	Arizona State	Lee Plemel, P, Stanford
1989	Wichita State	Gene Stephenson	68-16	Texas	Greg Brummett, P, Wichita State
1990	Georgia	Steve Webber	52-19	Oklahoma State	Mike Rebhan, P, Georgia
1991	Louisiana State*	Skip Bertman	55-18	Wichita State	Gary Hymel, C, Louisiana State
1992	Pepperdine*	Andy Lopez	48-11	Cal State Fullerton	Phil Nevin, 3B, Cal State Fullerton
1993	Louisiana State	Skip Bertman	53-17	Wichita State	Todd Walker, 2B, Louisiana State
1994	Oklahoma*	Larry Cochell	50-17	Georgia Tech	Chip Glass, OF, Oklahoma
1995	Cal State Fullerton*	Augie Garrido	57-9	Southern California	Mark Kotsay, OF/P, Cal State Fullerton
1996	Louisiana State*	Skip Bertman	52-15	Miami	Pat Burrell, 3B, Miami
1997	Louisiana State*	Skip Bertman	57-13	Alabama	Brandon Larson, SS, Louisiana State
1998	Southern California	Mike Gillespie	49-17	Arizona State	Wes Rachels, 2B, Southern California
1999	Miami*	Jim Morris	50-13	Florida State	Marshall McDougall, 2B, Florida State
2000	Louisiana State*	Skip Bertman	52-17	Stanford	Trey Hodges, P, Louisiana State
2001	Miami*	Jim Morris	53-12	Stanford	Charlton Jimerson, OF, Miami
2002	Texas*	Augie Garrido	57-15	South Carolina	Huston Street, P, Texas
2003	Rice	Wayne Graham	58-12	Stanford	John Hudgins, P, Stanford
2004	Cal State Fullerton	George Horton	47-22	Texas	Jason Windsor, P, Cal State Fullerton
2005	Texas*	Augie Garrido	56-16	Florida	David Maroul, 3B, Texas
2006	Oregon State	Pat Casey	50-16	North Carolina	Jonah Nickerson, P, Oregon State
2007	Oregon State*	Pat Casey	49-18	North Carolina	Jorge Reyes, P, Oregon State
2008	Fresno State	Mike Batesole	47-31	Georgia	Tommy Mendonca, 3B, Fresno State
2009	Louisiana State	Paul Mainieri	56-17	Texas	Jared Mitchell, OF, Louisiana State
2010	South Carolina	Ray Tanner	54-16	UCLA	Jackie Bradley Jr., OF, South Carolina
2011	South Carolina*	Ray Tanner	55-14	Florida	Scott Wingo, 2B, South Carolina
2012	Arizona*	Andy Lopez	48-17	South Carolina	Robert Refsnyder, OF, Arizona
2013	UCLA*	John Savage	49-17	Mississippi State	Adam Plutko, P, UCLA
2014	Vanderbilt	Tim Corbin	51-21	Virginia	Dansby Swanson, 2B, Vanderbilt
2015	Virginia	Brian O'Connor	44-24	Vanderbilt	Josh Sborz, P, Virginia
2016	Coastal Carolina	Gary Gilmore	55-18	Arizona	Andrew Beckwith, P, Coastal Carolina
2017	Florida	Kevin O'Sullivan	52-19	Louisiana State	Alex Faedo, P, Florida
2018	Oregon State	Pat Casey	55-12-1	Arkansas	Adley Rutschman, C, Oregon State
2019	Vanderbilt	Tim Corbin	59-12	Michigan	Kumar Rocker, RHP, Vanderbilt
2020	Canceled due to pandemic				
2021	Mississippi State	Chris Lemonis	50-18	Vanderbilt	Will Bednar, RHP, Mississippi State
2022	Ole Miss	Mike Bianco	42-23	Oklahoma	Dylan DeLucia, RHP, Ole Miss
2023	Louisiana State	Jay Johnson	54-17	Florida	Paul Skenes, RHP, Louisiana State
2024	Tennessee	Tony Vitello	60-13	Texas A&M	Dylan Dreiling, OF, Tennessee

appearances. A day later, Schlossnagle had accepted the job.

The move will be the most expensive in college baseball history. It will cost Texas $2.7 million just to hire Schlossnagle, the largest buyout ever paid to hire a college baseball coach by more than double. His salary is also sure to be among the highest in the sport.

Schlossnagle and Del Conte worked together for several years at TCU, and their partnership helped the Horned Frogs reach the CWS four times. Del Conte left TCU in December 2016 to become AD at Texas. Schlossnagle then left TCU after the 2021 season, but for A&M, not Texas. Now, they will be reunited in Austin with the goal of taking Texas back to the pinnacle of the sport.

Schlossnagle, the 2016 Baseball America Coach of the Year, is 946-455 in 23 seasons coaching A&M, TCU and UNLV. He has led his teams to Omaha seven times, including two of the last three seasons at A&M. He coached the Aggies to a 53-15 record this season and a runner-up finish at the CWS, the best in program history.

Schlossnagle arrives in Austin at a key inflection point for the Longhorns. Texas just moved to the SEC. While the program has still been a relatively regular Omaha participant over the last 15 years, it hasn't won a national championship since 2005. Last year, LSU won its seventh CWS title to pass Texas for the second-most national championships in college baseball history.

Schlossnagle's move adds spice to a rivalry about to be rekindled in earnest. Though Texas and A&M are athletic archrivals, their meetings on the diamond have been mostly limited to midweek games since A&M left the Big 12 for the SEC more than a decade ago. Now that they are conference mates again, they will resume annual weekend series. Next year's showdown didn't need anything extra, but the move poured gasoline on the rivalry's fire.

RPI RANKINGS

The Ratings Percentage Index is an important tool used by the NCAA in selecting at-large teams for the 64-team Division I tournament. These were the top 100 finishers for 2024. A team's rank in the final Baseball America Top 25 is indicated in parentheses, and College World Series teams are bolded.

Team	Record	Team	Record
1. Tennessee (1)	60-13	51. Auburn	27-26
2. Texas A&M (2)	53-15	52. Evansville (23)	39-26
3. Kentucky (3)	46-16	53. St. John's	38-18
4. North Carolina (4)	48-16	54. ETSU	36-20
5. Florida St. (5)	49-17	55. Indiana	33-26
6. Arkansas (15)	44-16	56. Ga. Southern	33-26
7. Georgia (10)	43-17	57. Portland	37-19
8. Clemson (11)	44-16	58. Georgetown	36-21
9. NC State (7)	38-23	59. Troy	37-22
10. Virginia (8)	46-17	60. Texas Tech	33-26
11. Florida (6)	36-30	61. Louisville	32-24
12. Indiana St.	44-15	62. Cincinnati	32-25
13. Oregon St. (9)	45-16	63. Lamar	44-15
14. Wake Forest	38-22	64. California	36-19
15. LSU	43-23	65. UNC Greensboro	33-21
16. Okla. St. (18)	42-19	66. Creighton	35-17
17. UC Santa Barb. (20)	44-14	67. Ohio St.	29-26
18. Oklahoma (19)	40-21	68. Virginia Tech	32-22
19. Miss. St. (17)	40-23	69. Nicholls	34-22
20. Duke (24)	40-20	70. South Alabama	31-25
21. San Diego	41-15	71. Kansas	31-23
22. East Carolina (16)	46-17	72. App State	33-21
23. DBU	45-15	73. VCU	38-23
24. UC Irvine (25)	45-14	74. Hawaii	33-16
25. South Carolina	37-25	75. Old Dominion	31-26
26. Vanderbilt	38-23	76. S. California	31-28
27. Southern Miss.	43-20	77. Rutgers	28-25
28. Alabama	33-24	78. Sam Houston	34-24
29. Nebraska	40-22	79. Notre Dame	27-25
30. West Virginia (13)	36-24	80. Murray St.	37-20
31. UCF	37-21	81. Miami (FL)	27-30
32. UConn (14)	35-26	82. Tulane	36-26
33. Louisiana Tech	45-19	83. Utah	33-22
34. Coastal Carolina	36-25	84. Kennesaw St.	32-24
35. Arizona (21)	36-23	85. Campbell	31-22
36. Ole Miss	27-29	86. Arizona St.	32-26
37. Kansas St. (22)	35-26	87. Michigan	32-28
38. UNCW	40-21	88. Pittsburgh	26-29
39. Northeastern	38-17	89. Boston College	22-31
40. Oregon (12)	40-20	89. UIC	34-20
41. Louisiana	42-20	91. Purdue	32-24
42. TCU	33-21	92. Samford	36-22
43. Illinois	35-21	93. Grand Canyon	36-25
44. Xavier	30-27	94. CSUN	30-24
45. Georgia Tech	33-25	95. USC Upstate	36-24
46. James Madison	36-25	96. Wichita St.	32-29
47. Col. of Charleston	41-14	97. Stetson	41-22
48. Maryland	34-22	98. Saint Louis	37-16
49. Texas	36-24	99. Penn St.	29-24
50. Wofford	42-20	100. Western Ky.	36-22

Home Runs Skyrocket, Again

The 2024 season saw more home runs than have ever been hit before in D-I college baseball. That broke the record set just last year, when the long-thought unbreakable 1998 "Gorilla Ball" record was broken.

D-I teams hit 19,038 home runs in 2024, an average of 1.17 per game. That tops the 2023 mark of 1.14 home runs per game, which blew away the 1998 record of 1.06 home runs per game.

It's not an easy time to be a pitcher. Teams scored 6.8 runs per game in 2024. That's the most since 2010, the final year before BBCOR bats were instituted into the game.

There are plenty of theories as to what is leading to the offensive explosion, but there is no one clear and overriding factor.

One suggestion is that bat manufacturers have figured out how to produce better performing bats within the BBCOR regulations.

The problem with that theory is these bats are tested every year. According to officials who do the NCAA-sanctioned bat testing at Washington State,

COLLEGE ALL-AMERICA TEAM

FIRST TEAM

Pos.	Name	Year	AVG	OBP	SLG	AB	R	H	HR	RBI	BB	SO	SB
C	Walker Janek, Sam Houston State	Jr.	.364	.476	.709	220	55	80	17	58	40	45	13
1B	Blake Burke, Tennessee	Jr.	.377	.448	.701	281	73	106	20	61	35	48	11
2B	Travis Bazzana, Oregon State	Jr.	.407	.568	.911	214	84	87	28	66	76	37	16
3B	Charlie Condon, Georgia	R-So.	.433	.556	1.009	231	84	100	37	78	57	41	3
SS	Kyle DeBarge, Louisiana	Jr.	.356	.418	.699	256	65	91	21	72	24	30	10
OF	James Tibbs III, Florida State	Jr.	.363	.488	.777	251	75	91	28	95	58	37	8
OF	Drew Burress, Georgia Tech	Fr.	.381	.512	.821	218	73	83	25	67	58	37	8
OF	Jace LaViolette, Texas A&M	So.	.307	.453	.736	254	87	78	29	78	64	78	7
DH	Christian Moore, Tennessee	Jr.	.378	.455	.797	291	82	110	33	73	38	47	5
UT	Jac Caglianone, Florida	Jr.	.419	.544	.875	248	83	104	35	72	58	26	4

Pos.	Name	Year	W	L	ERA	G	CG	SV	IP	H	BB	SO	AVG
SP	Hagen Smith, Arkansas	Jr.	9	2	2.04	16	0	0	84	41	34	161	.144
SP	Chase Burns, Wake Forest	Jr.	10	1	2.70	16	0	0	100	62	30	191	.175
SP	Ryan Johnson, Dallas Baptist	Jr.	11	3	2.21	16	2	0	106	83	14	151	.215
SP	Trey Yesavage, East Carolina	Jr.	11	1	2.03	15	1	0	93.1	49	32	145	.154
RP	Charlie Beilenson, Duke	Sr.	7	3	2.01	34	0	12	62.2	42	18	92	.181
RP	Wyatt Lunsford-Shenkman, East Carolina	Jr.	3	2	1.55	24	0	5	46.1	37	21	79	.218
UT	Jac Caglianone, Florida	Jr.	5	2	4.76	16	0	0	73.2	62	50	83	.225

SECOND TEAM

Pos.	Name	Year	AVG	OBP	SLG	AB	R	H	HR	RBI	BB	SO	SB
C	Cole Messina, South Carolina	Jr.	.326	.465	.701	224	64	73	19	1	21	71	8
1B	Corey Collins, Georgia	Sr.	.354	.574	.772	158	55	56	6	0	20	58	0
2B	Henry Godbout, Virginia	So.	.372	.472	.645	172	51	64	18	1	9	47	6
3B	Alec Makarewicz, NC State	Sr.	.378	.438	.753	259	66	98	25	0	24	84	1
SS	Josh Kuroda-Grauer, Rutgers	So.	.335	.444	.665	248	72	83	24	2	18	64	10
OF	Vance Honeycutt, North Carolina	Jr.	.318	.410	.714	255	88	81	13	2	28	70	28
OF	Braden Montgomery, Texas A&M	Jr.	.322	.454	.733	236	65	76	14	1	27	85	5
OF	Nolan Schubart, Oklahoma State	So.	.370	.513	.838	173	55	64	10	1	23	68	0
DH	Cam Smith, Florida State	So.	.387	.488	.654	269	82	104	22	1	16	57	4
UT	Carson Benge, Oklahoma State	So.	.335	.444	.665	248	72	83	24	2	18	64	10

Pos.	Name	Year	W	L	ERA	G	GS	SV	IP	H	BB	SO
SP	Jamie Arnold, Florida State	So.	11	3	2.98	19	18	1	106	90	26	159
SP	Ryan Gallagher, UC Santa Barbara	Jr.	10	1	2.22	14	14	0	89	50	25	96
SP	Brian Holiday, Oklahoma State	Jr.	7	3	2.95	16	16	0	113	82	19	128
SP	Brett Sears, Nebraska	Sr.	9	1	2.16	17	16	1	104	72	19	101
RP	Evan Aschenbeck, Texas A&M	Sr.	6	1	1.78	32	0	10	76	55	12	87
RP	Griffin Herring, LSU	So.	6	1	1.79	21	1	6	50	39	13	67
UT	Carson Benge, Oklahoma State	So.	3	2	3.16	18	4	3	37	26	11	44

THIRD TEAM

Pos.	Name	Year	AVG	OBP	SLG	AB	R	H	HR	RBI	BB	SO	SB
C	Jacob Cozart, NC State	Jr.	.305	.437	.601	223	60	68	7	1	19	54	0
1B	Roman Kuntz, Morehead State	Sr.	.366	.482	.860	235	71	86	15	1	33	100	2
2B	Daniel Dickinson, Utah Valley	So.	.367	.469	.661	245	73	90	14	2	18	53	32
3B	Tommy White, LSU	Jr.	.330	.401	.638	279	61	92	12	1	24	70	2
SS	Jalin Flores, Texas	So.	.340	.408	.626	241	52	82	22	0	18	56	2
OF	Dakota Jordan, Mississippi State	So.	.354	.459	.671	240	57	85	14	1	20	72	3
OF	Lyle Miller-Green, Austin Peay State	Gr.	.393	.533	.900	219	94	86	17	2	30	94	13
OF	Ryan Waldschmidt, Kentucky	Jr.	.333	.469	.610	213	66	71	17	0	14	46	25
DH	Jakob Christian, San Diego	Jr.	.364	.460	.828	198	59	72	14	0	26	67	9
UT	Ethan Bates, Louisiana Tech	Sr.	.337	.436	.609	258	68	87	21	2	15	74	2

Pos.	Name	Year	W	L	ERA	G	GS	SV	IP	H	BB	SO
SP	Brooks Caple, Lamar	Sr.	7	3	2.40	15	15	0	98	58	27	102
SP	Luke Holman, LSU	Jr.	9	4	2.75	16	16	0	92	57	33	127
SP	Aidan Knaak, Clemson	Fr.	5	1	3.35	15	15	0	83	67	29	108
SP	Ryan Prager, Texas A&M	Jr.	9	1	2.95	19	19	0	98	83	20	124
RP	LP Langevin, Louisiana	Jr.	6	1	3.73	23	3	7	63	40	33	106
RP	Dalton Pence, North Carolina	So.	5	1	2.45	36	0	8	59	40	27	74
UT	Ethan Bates, Louisiana Tech	Sr.	2	1	3.43	36	0	17	45	29	20	52

the bats have continued to test within similar ranges year after year. Those results haven't changed much since the BBCOR regulations arrived.

This year, the performance of the NCAA baseball became the prevailing theory. Multiple coaches describe the current NCAA baseball as being extremely "hot." It seems to carry farther than baseballs of a few years ago.

But the baseball theory also has issues. It may be a contributing factor, but there's evidence that it's not the overriding factor, because when it comes to Division I baseball, we have a near perfect control group–Division II baseball. And using the same baseball, D-II baseball has not see the home run increase that is happening across D-I.

Division I's home run rate in 2022 topped one home run per game (1.03) for the first time since the drop-five era of "gorilla ball" in the late 1990s. Division II's home run rate dipped slightly (0.88). In 2023, the D-I home run rate set an all-time record (1.14), while D-II's rate stayed relatively flat (0.84). The 2024 season broke the home run rate record again in D-I (1.17), but D-II's home run rate is almost identical to what it was in 2022 (0.87).

It's possible that the rise in D-I home run rate is being driven by older/stronger players who gained extra eligibility because of the coronavirus pandemic. That was also true for D-II, but it's possible that more D-I hitters took advantage of additional years of eligibility.

It's also possible that the reduced number of draft rounds (20 instead of the previous 40) and the rise of NIL payments have affected D-I more significantly than D-II.

There is some data that supports this point. Thanks to the combination of shorter drafts, liberalized transfer rules, extended eligibility and NIL, D-I baseball is an older sport than it was just a few years ago, and older players generally hit for more power. The share of at-bats taken by seniors has jumped from 26.5% in 2014 to 39% in 2024.

That playing time has been taken somewhat from the freshman class, which went from 16.7% of at-bats in 2014 to 12.4% in 2024, but there also have been reductions in playing time for sophomores and juniors as well.

But freshman, sophomore and juniors are also homering more than in the past.

The ever-changing strike zone may also be playing a part. College coaches say that the strike zone has become more narrow and taller as umpires are now evaluated off the "Trackman strike zone." That means pitchers have lost the ability to nibble on the edges of the plate. They are now forced to pitch more up and down, where misses are more likely to be squared up.

The walk rate in college baseball is up. At 11.34% of all plate appearances, it's continued to climb almost without exception over the past decade. While that is a long-running trend, the evidence for a smaller strike zone is that the strikeout rate actually peaked in 2021 and has declined in every year since. Batters struck out in 20.96% of plate appearances in 2021. This season, the strikeout percentage finished with a mrk of 19.63%.

And then there is the question of bat tampering. A simple Google search shows that there are plenty of "bat shaving" companies, all of whom claim that their bats will look identical externally to a full-complaint BBCOR bat, while providing massively improved performance.

COLLEGE WORLD SERIES

STANDINGS

Bracket One	W	L
Tennessee	3	0
Florida State	2	2
North Carolina	1	2
Virginia	0	2

Bracket Two	W	L
Texas A&M	3	0
Florida	2	2
Kentucky	1	2
North Carolina State	0	2

CWS FINALS (BEST OF THREE)

June 22: Texas A&M 9, Tennessee 5
June 23: Tennessee 4, Texas A&M 1
June 24: Tennessee 6, Texas A&M 5

ALL-TOURNAMENT TEAM

C: Jaxon West, Florida State. **1B:** Jac Caglianone, Florida. **2B:** Christian Moore, Tennessee. **3B:** Alec Makarewicz, NC State. **SS:** Dean Curley, Tennessee. **OF:** *Dylan Dreiling, Tennessee; Jamie Ferrer, Florida State; Vance Honeycutt, North Carolina. **DH:** Kaden Kent, Texas A&M. **P:** Evan Aschenbeck, Texas A&M; Zander Sechrist, Tennessee.

**Named Most Outstanding Player.*

BATTING

(Minimum 8 PA)

Player	AVG	R	H	2B	3B	HR	RBI	SB
Jac Caglianone, Fla.	.583	4	7	1	0	2	4	1
Dylan Dreiling, Texas	.542	6	13	1	0	3	11	1
Jacob Cozart, NC State	.500	0	3	0	0	0	1	0
Garrett Pennington, NC St.	.429	5	3	1	0	0	0	0
Henry Godbout, Virg.	.429	1	3	0	0	0	1	0
Max Williams, FSU	.421	3	8	1	0	1	3	0
Kaeden Kent, Texas A&M	.417	2	10	1	0	1	7	0
Ryan Nicholson, Kent.	.417	3	5	0	0	2	2	0
Blake Burke, Texas	.407	7	11	2	0	1	5	1
Parks Harber, UNC	.400	1	4	1	0	0	0	0

PITCHING

(Minimum 6 IP)

Pitcher	W-L	ERA	G	SV	IP	H	BB	SO
Nate Snead, Texas	1-0	1.12	5	1	8	4	5	4
Fisher Jameson, Fla.	0-0	1.17	2	0	8	4	3	8
Logan Whitaker, NC St.	0-0	1.29	1	0	7	2	3	10
Ryan Prager, Texas A&M	1-0	1.69	2	0	11	10	1	10
Drew Beam, Texas	1-0	2.00	2	0	9	7	4	14
Brandon Neely, Fla.	0-0	2.25	3	1	8	5	1	15
Zander Sechrist, Texas	2-0	2.31	2	0	12	11	2	10
Chris Cortez, Texas A&M	1-0	2.45	3	0	7	6	8	13
Evan Aschenbeck, Texas A&M	0-0	2.53	4	1	11	11	4	15
Justin Lamkin, Texas A&M	1-1	2.53	3	0	11	9	3	17

REGIONALS

MAY 31-JUNE 3

64 teams, 16 four-team, double-elimination tournaments. Winners advance to super regionals.

KNOXVILLE, TENN.

Host: Tennessee (No. 1 national seed)
Participants: No. 1 Tennessee (60-13), No. 2 Southern Mississippi (43-20), No. 3 Indiana (33-26-1), No. 4 Northern Kentucky (35-24)
Champion: Tennessee (3-0)
Runner-up: Southern Mississippi (2-2)
Outstanding player: Dylan Dreiling, OF, Tennessee

LEXINGTON, KY.

Host: Kentucky (No. 2 national seed)
Participants: No. 1 Kentucky (46-16), No. 2 Indiana State (44-15), No. 3 Illinois (35-21), No. 4 Western Michigan (32-23)
Champion: Kentucky (3-0)
Runner-up: Indiana State (2-2)
Outstanding player: Ryan Nicholson, 1B, Kentucky

COLLEGE STATION, TEXAS

Host: Texas A&M (No. 3 national seed)
Participants: No. 1 Texas A&M (53-15), No. 2 Louisiana (42-20), No. 3 Texas (36-24), No. 4 Grambling State (26-28)
Champion: Texas A&M (3-0)
Runner-up: Louisiana (2-2)
Outstanding player: Braden Montgomery, OF, Texas A&M

CHAPEL HILL, N.C.

Host: North Carolina (No. 4 national seed)
Participants: No. 1 North Carolina (48-16), No. 2 LSU (43-23), No. 3 Wofford (42-20), No. 4 Long Island (33-25)
Champion: North Carolina (3-1)
Runner-up: LSU (3-2)
Outstanding player: Gavin Gallaher, 3B, North Carolina

FAYETTEVILLE, ARK.

Host: Arkansas (No. 5 national seed)
Participants: No. 1 Arkansas (44-16), No. 2 Louisiana Tech (45-19), No. 3 Kansas State (35-26), No. 4 Southeast Missouri State (36-27)
Champion: Kansas State (3-0)
Runner-up: Southeast Missouri State (2-2)
Outstanding player: Kaelen Culpepper, SS, Kansas State

CLEMSON, S.C.

Host: Clemson (No. 6 national seed)
Participants: No. 1 Clemson (44-16), No. 2 Vanderbilt (38-23), No. 3 Coastal Carolina (36-25), No. 4 High Point (35-27)
Champion: Clemson (3-0)
Runner-up: Coastal Carolina (2-2)
Outstanding player: Jacob Hinderleider, SS, Clemson

ATHENS, GA.

Host: Georgia (No. 7 national seed)
Participants: No. 1 Georgia (43-17), No. 2 UNCW (40-21), No. 3 Georgia Tech (33-25), No. 4 Army (31-23)
Champion: Georgia (3-0)
Runner-up: Georgia Tech (2-2)
Outstanding player: Corey Collins, 1B, Georgia

TALLAHASSEE, FLA.

Host: Florida State (No. 8 national seed)
Participants: No. 1 Florida State (49-17), No. 2 Alabama (33-24), No. 3 Central Florida (37-21), No. 4 Stetson (41-22)
Champion: Florida State (3-0)
Runner-up: Central Florida (2-2)
Outstanding player: Jamie Arnold, LHP, Florida State

NORMAN, OKLA.

Host: Oklahoma (No. 9 national seed)
Participants: No. 1 Oklahoma (40-21), No. 2 Duke (40-20), No. 3 UConn (35-26), No. 4 Oral Roberts (27-32-1)
Champion: UConn (3-1)
Runner-up: Oklahoma (3-2)
Outstanding player: Korey Morton, OF, UConn

RALEIGH, N.C.

Host: NC State (No. 10 national seed)
Participants: No. 1 NC State (38-23), No. 2 South Carolina (37-25), No. 3 James Madison (36-25), No. 4 Bryant (36-21)
Champion: NC State (3-0)
Runner-up: James Madison (2-2)
Outstanding player: Alec Makarewicz, 3B, NC State

STILLWATER, OKLA.

Host: Oklahoma State (No. 11 national seed)
Participants: No. 1 Oklahoma State (42-19), No. 2 Nebraska (40-22), No. 3 Florida (36-30), No. 4 Niagara (38-17)
Champion: Florida (4-1)
Runner-up: Oklahoma State (2-2)
Outstanding player: Ashton Wilson, OF, Florida

CHARLOTTESVILLE, VA.

Host: Virginia (No. 12 national seed)
Participants: No. 1 Virginia (46-17), No. 2 Mississippi State (40-23), No. 3 St. John's (38-18-1), No. 4 Penn (24-25)
Champion: Virginia (3-0)
Runner-up: Mississippi State (2-2)
Outstanding player: Jay Woolfolk, RHP, Virginia

TUCSON, ARIZ.

Host: Arizona (No. 13 national seed)
Participants: No. 1 Arizona (36-23), No. 2 Dallas Baptist (45-15), No. 3 West Virginia (36-24), No. 4 Grand Canyon (36-25)
Champion: West Virginia (3-0)
Runner-up: Grand Canyon (2-2)
Outstanding player: Derek Clark, LHP, West Virginia

SANTA BARBARA, CALIF.

Host: UC Santa Barbara (No. 14 national seed)
Participants: No. 1 UC Santa Barbara (44-14), No. 2 San Diego (41-15), No. 3 Oregon (40-20), No. 4 Fresno State (33-29)
Champion: Oregon (3-0)
Runner-up: UC Santa Barbara (2-2)
Outstanding player: Carter Garate, 3B, Oregon

CORVALLIS, ORE.

Host: Oregon State (No. 15 national seed)
Participants: No. 1 Oregon State (45-16), No. 2 UC Irvine (45-14), No. 3 Nicholls State (38-22), No. 4 Tulane (36-26)
Champion: Oregon State (3-0)
Runner-up: UC Irvine (2-2)
Outstanding player: Travis Bazzana, 2B, Oregon State

GREENVILLE, N.C.

Host: East Carolina (No. 16 national seed)
Participants: No. 1 East Carolina (46-17), No. 2 Wake Forest (38-22), No. 3 VCU (38-23), No. 4 Evansville (39-26)
Champion: Evansville (3-1)
Runner-up: East Carolina (3-2)
Outstanding player: Kip Fougerousse, 1B, Evansville

SUPER REGIONALS

JUNE 7-10

16 teams, best-of-three series.
Winners advance to College World Series.

EVANSVILLE AT TENNESSEE

Site: Knoxville
Tennessee wins 2-1, advances to CWS.

OREGON STATE AT KENTUCKY

Site: Lexington
Kentucky wins 2-0, advances to CWS.

OREGON AT TEXAS A&M

Site: Bryan-College Station
Texas A&M wins 2-0, advances to CWS.

WEST VIRGINIA AT NORTH CAROLINA

Site: Chapel Hill
North Carolina wins 2-0, advances to CWS.

FLORIDA AT CLEMSON

Site: Clemson
Florida wins 2-0, advances to CWS.

NC STATE AT GEORGIA

Site: Athens
NC State wins 2-1, advances to CWS.

UCONN AT FLORIDA STATE

Site: Tallahassee
Florida State wins 2-0, advances to CWS.

KANSAS STATE AT VIRGINIA

Site: Charlottesville
Virginia wins 2-0, advances to CWS.

Condon Hits Way To POY

PLAYER OF THE YEAR

BY ANTHONY DASHER

A What Michelangelo was with a paintbrush, Georgia's Charlie Condon is with a bat.

Perhaps that's why the Bulldogs' career home run leader approaches each at-bat as a new work of art, an opportunity to create a fresh offensive masterpiece every time he steps to the plate.

"I just look at each individual at-bat as a blank canvas," Condon said. "It's knowing that each individual at-bat is what it is—it's its own thing. You can't start looking at stats, trends, streaks, because those things start snowballing, whether it's good or bad."

DANNY PARKER/FOUR SEAM IMAGES

Charlie Condon

Georgia head coach Wes Johnson, who has been around many special talents during his career in the Southeastern Conference, said Condon is the best college hitter he's seen.

"His plate discipline, just his mind. He gets off his A-swing a lot." Johnson said. "So it's been a lot of fun to watch."

Considering Johnson was the pitching coach for LSU last year and saw Dylan Crews—the No. 2 overall pick by the Nationals in 2023—that's quite the statement.

"I'm talking about in the batter's box too, right?" Johnson said. "I mean, obviously Dylan (Crews) is a very dynamic player. He is really a premium defender. He can run, as well. But you talk in the batter's box, I haven't had one better than Charlie Condon."

A quick glance at the numbers corroborates Johnson's point. It's also why Condon is this year's College Player of the Year.

Condon ranks first in Division I with a .433 batting average and 1.009 slugging percentage. He hit 37 home runs, which led the nation heading into the College World Series. Condon collected 100 hits, scored 84 runs and posted a .556 on-base percentage, all of which ranked top five nationally. He drove in 78 runs to rank 11th, though that standing was largely a function of him batting second for the Bulldogs.

Major league teams weren't beating down his door in 2021, when he was a high school senior at The Walker School outside Atlanta.

When home-state Georgia offered him an opportunity as a preferred walk-on, he jumped at the chance.

After redshirting his freshman year in 2022 to add more muscle and weight to his 6-foot-6 frame, Condon burst on the scene by hitting .386 with 25 homers and 67 RBIs to win BA's Freshman of the Year honors in 2023.

Even with the pressure to succeed, Condon has maintained his high level of play, both to his benefit and that of the Bulldogs, whose season ended in Athens with a loss to N.C. State in super regionals.

For one last hurrah, Condon homered in his final at-bat as a Bulldog.

PREVIOUS WINNERS

1982: Jeff Ledbetter, OF/LHP Florida St.
1983: Dave Magadan, 1B, Alabama
1984: Oddibe McDowell, OF, Arizona St.
1985: Pete Incaviglia, OF, Oklahoma State
1986: Casey Close, OF, Michigan
1987: Robin Ventura, 3B, Oklahoma State
1988: John Olerund, 1B/LHP, Washington St.
1989: Ben McDonald, RHP, Louisiana State
1990: Mike Kelly, OF, Arizona State
1991: David McCarthy, 1B, Stanford
1992: Phil Nevin, 3B, Cal State Fullerton
1993: Brooks Kieschnick, DH/RHP, Texas
1994: Jason Varitek, C, Georgia Tech
1995: Todd Helton, 1B/LHP, Tennessee
1996: Kris Benson, RHP, Clemson
1997: J.D. Drew, OF, Florida State
1998: Jeff Austin, RHP, Stanford
1999: Jason Jennings, RHP, Baylor
2000: Mark Teixeira, 3B, Georgia Tech
2001: Mark Prior, RHP, S. California
2002: Khalil Greene, SS, Clemson
2003: Rickie Weeks, 2B, Southern
2004: Jered Weaver, RHP, Long Beach St.
2005: Alex Gordon, 3B, Nebraska
2006: Andrew Miller, LHP, North Carolina
2007: David Price, LHP, Vanderbilt
2008: Buster Posey, C/RHP, Florida State
2009: Stephen Strasburg, RHP, San Diego St.
2010: Anthony Rendon, 3B, Rice
2011: Trevor Bauer, RHP, UCLA
2012: Mike Zunino, C, Florida
2013: Kris Bryant, 3B, San Diego
2014: A.J. Reed, 1B/LHP, Kentucky
2015: Andrew Benintendi, OF, Arkansas
2016: Klye Lewis, OF, Mercer
2017: Brendan McKay, LHP/1B, Louisville
2018: Brady Singer, RHP, Florida
2019: Adley Rutschman, C, Oregon State
2021: Kumar Rocker, RHP, Vanderbilt
2022: Ivan Melendez, 1B, Texas
2023: Paul Skenes, RHP, LSU

COACH OF THE YEAR

Vitello Builds Vols Into A Power

BY TEDDY CAHILL

With confetti raining down at Charles Schwab Field in Omaha, Tennessee coach Tony Vitello raised the national championship trophy aloft. His Volunteers had just won the 2024 College World Series, cementing their legacy as one of the best teams of all-time.

Tennessee won 60 games this season, more than any team in 22 years. The Volunteers collected every trophy they could, winning both the Southeastern Conference regular season crown and SEC Tournament on their way to Omaha greatness. They were the No. 1 overall seed in the NCAA Tournament, becoming the first No. top-seeded team to win the championship since Miami did it in 1999.

Tony Vitello

JAMIE SCHWABEROW_NCAA PHOTOS VIA GETTY IMAGES

It was a complete team effort. The Volunteers led the nation in home runs, ranked 11th in scoring and finished sixth in ERA. They had All-Americans, Freshman All-Americans, present first-round picks, future first-rounders and some gritty, veteran college players amid the stars.

At the heart of it all was Vitello, the program's architect and the man responsible for bringing Tennessee from the cellar of the SEC to the pinnacle of college baseball.

Vitello did it in a truly modern way, embracing the transfer portal, the rule changes around name, image and likeness rights and the offensive surge in college baseball. But he also did it through traditional recruiting, hard work and a dedication to player development.

Vitello's story—and Tennessee's, because the two are intertwined—is uniquely of the moment, but also one that followed a blueprint familiar to any program-building in college baseball over the years. Vitello took over in Knoxville in 2017 and built Tennessee into a powerhouse, reaching the greatest heights this June in Omaha.

When Vitello arrived in Knoxville in the summer of 2017, there was history and tradition on Rocky Top, but it had been a difficult 12 years since the Volunteers had last made the NCAA Tournament.

Vitello knew he needed to upgrade the talent level and find a niche for the program if it was going to make headway in the nation's premier baseball conference.

What could set Tennessee apart? After long internal consideration, Vitello settled on building the Volunteers around a gritty, competitive mentality. That influenced his coaching staff hires and how they recruited players.

"We've got to play with some attitude," Vitello said. "We've got to play with some grit. And we're going to have to get some guys who maybe don't want to say 'yes' to a school with a better winning record than us.".

PREVIOUS WINNERS

1982: Gene Stephenson, Wichita State
1983: Barry Shollenberger, Alabama
1984: Augie Garrido, Cal State Fullerton
1985: Ron Polk, Mississippi State
1986: Skip Bertman, LSU/Dave Snow, LMU
1987: Mark Marquess, Stanford
1988: Jim Brock, Arizona State
1989: Dave Snow, Long Beach State
1990: Steve Webber, Georgia
1991: Jim Hendry, Creighton
1992: Andy Lopez, Pepperdine
1993: Gene Stephenson, Wichita State
1994: Jim Morris, Miami
1995: Pat Murphy, Arizona State
1996: Skip Bertman, Louisiana State
1997: Jim Wells, Alabama
1998: Pat Murphy, Arizona State
1999: Wayne Graham, Rice
2000: Ray Tanner, South Carolina
2001: Dave Van Horn, Nebraska
2002: Augie Garrido, Texas
2003: George Horton, Cal State Fullerton
2004: David Perno, Georgia
2005: Rick Jones, Tulane
2006: Pat Casey, Oregon State
2007: Dave Serrano, UC Irvine
2008: Mike Fox, North Carolina
2009: Paul Mainieri, Louisiana State
2010: Ray Tanner, South Carolina
2011: Kevin O'Sullivan, Florida
2012: Mike Martin, Florida State
2013: John Savage, UCLA
2014: Tim Corbin, Vanderbilt
2015: Brian O'Connor, Virginia
2016: Jim Schlossnagle, Texas Christian
2017: Dan McDonnell, Louisville
2018: David Pierce, Texas
2019: Mike Martin, Florida State
2021: Chris Lemonis, Mississippi State
2022: Mike Bianco, Mississippi
2023: Jay Johnson, LSU

Burress On Path To Stardom

FRESHMAN OF THE YEAR

BY MATT EDDY

Baseball America has selected college All-American teams in each season since it launched in 1981, missing only 2020 because the pandemic truncated the season. In 42 seasons of All-American teams, a total of 24 freshmen have earned first-team honors. The list includes 10 position players, 12 pitchers and a pair of two-way players.

The list now also includes Georgia Tech freshman outfielder Drew Burress.

The 19-year-old Burress ranked second in the ACC to Wake Forest's Nick Kurtz with a .512 on-base percentage. His 25 home runs trailed only Florida State's James Tibbs III and North Carolina's Vance Honeycutt for the conference lead.

BRIAN WESTERHOLT/FOUR SEAM IMAGES

Drew Burress

Tibbs and Kurtz are fellow first-team All-Americans. Along with Honeycutt, they are 21-year-old juniors poised to be first-round picks this year. History suggests that Burress has a great chance to join them as a first-round pick when he is draft-eligible in 2026.

Burress's 25 home runs were most among first team freshman All-Americans in the more than 40 years BA has selected the freshman All-Americans. As a first-team All-American, Burress joins an illustrious group.

Of the previous nine position players who made the All-America team as freshmen, eight went on to be first round picks, including Pat Burrell, Alex Bregman, Rafael Palmeiro and Robin Ventura.

St. John's Jeremy Baltz is the only position player to make both the freshman and All-America first team who didn't get drafted in the first round.

PREVIOUS WINNERS

1993: Brett Laxton, RHP, Louisiana State
1994: R.A. Dickey, RHP, Tennessee
1995: Kyle Peterson, RHP, Stanford
1996: Pat Burrell, 3B, Miami
1997: Brian Roberts, SS, North Carolina
1998: Xavier Nady, 2B, California
1999: James Jurries, 2B, Tulane
2000: Kevin Howard, 3B, Miami
2001: Michael Aubrey, OF/LHP, Texas
2002: Stephen Drew, SS, Florida State
2003: Ryan Braun, SS, Miami
2004: Wade LeBlanc, LHP, Alabama
2005: Joe Savery, LHP, Rice
2006: Pedro Alvarez, 3B, Vanderbilt
2007: Dustin Ackley, 1B, North Carolina
2008: Chris Hernandez, LHP, Miami
2009: Anthony Rendon, 3B, Rice
2010: Matt Purke, LHP, Texas Christian
2011: Colin Moran, 3B, North Carolina
2012: Carlos Rodon, LHP, N.C. State
2013: Alex Bregman, SS, Louisiana State
2014: Zack Collins, C, Miami
2015: Brendan McKay, LHP/1B, Louisville
2016: Seth Beer, OF, Clemson
2017: Matt Wallner, OF/RHP, Southern Miss
2018: Kevin Abel, RHP, Oregon State
2019: Kumar Rocker, RHP, Vanderbilt
2021: Jack Leiter, RHP, Vanderbilt
2022: Tommy White, 3B/DH, N.C.. State
2023: Charlie Condon, 1B/OF, Georgia

FRESHMAN ALL-AMERICA TEAMS

FIRST TEAM

Pos.		AVG	OBP	SLG	AB	R	H	HR	RBI	SB
C	Luke Stevenson, North Carolina	.284	.420	.535	215	43	61	14	58	2
1B	Henry Ford, Virginia	.336	.409	.597	253	60	85	17	69	3
2B	Steven Milam, LSU	.326	.415	.516	221	51	72	8	40	7
3B	Gavin Grahovac, Texas A&M	.298	.390	.596	285	83	85	23	66	4
SS	Justin Lebron, Alabama	.338	.429	.546	216	50	73	12	37	7
OF	Caden Bogenpohl, Missouri St.	.293	.446	.639	205	62	60	20	45	7
OF	Drew Burress, Georgia Tech	.381	.512	.821	218	73	83	25	67	8
OF	Brandon Compton, Arizona St.	.354	.427	.661	189	45	67	14	51	3
DH	Daniel Cuvet, Miami	.351	.429	.736	231	52	81	24	75	2
UTL	Erik Paulsen, Stony Brook	.299	.392	.458	177	23	53	4	24	0

		W	L	ERA	G	GS	SV	IP	H	BB	SO
SP	Jason DeCaro, North Carolina	6	1	3.81	18	18	0	90	74	44	78
SP	Kenton Deverman, Evansville	9	2	4.22	18	16	0	111	112	23	83
SP	Aidan Knaak, Clemson	5	1	3.35	15	15	0	83	67	29	108
SP	Dominic Voegele, Kansas	7	2	3.89	15	15	0	81	72	29	80
RP	Gabe Gaeckle, Arkansas	3	3	2.32	22	0	7	43	26	19	57
RP	Ricky Ojeda, UC Irvine	6	1	3.46	25	0	1	52	41	25	74
UTL	Erik Paulsen, Stony Brook	2	1	3.21	15	1	6	42	44	10	24

SECOND TEAM

C: Garrett Wright, Bowling Green State. **1B:** Luke Gaffney, Purdue. **2B:** TJ Pompey, Texas Tech. **3B:** Chris Haciopan, Maryland. SS: Dean Curley, Tennessee. **OF:** AJ Gracia, Duke. **OF:** Tre Phelps, Georgia. **OF:** Zion Rose, Louisville. **DH:** Kade Lewis, Butler. **SP:** Brett Laman, Abilene Christian. **SP:** Tommy LaPour, Wichita State. **SP:** Christian Lim, Stanford. **SP:** Chase Morgan, Louisiana. **RP:** Jacob Dudan, NC State. **RP:** Ethan Norby, East Carolina. **UTL:** Kyle Johnson, Duke

NCAA DIVISION I LEADERS

HITTING (MINIMUM 140 AT-BATS)

BATTING AVERAGE

Rk.	Player, Team	Class	AVG	OBP	SLG	G	AB	2B	3B	HR	RBI	BB	SO	SB
1	Charlie Condon, Georgia	So.	.433	.556	1.009	60	231	20	1	37	78	57	41	3
2	Joshua Kuroda-Grauer, Rutgers	Jr.	.428	.492	.590	53	222	19	1	5	45	23	18	24
3	Jac Caglianone, Florida	Jr.	.419	.544	.875	66	248	8	0	35	72	58	26	4
3	Ben Watson, Virginia Tech	Sr.	.419	.466	.595	54	222	21	3	4	48	20	24	3
5	JT Marr, Penn St.	Sr.	.416	.464	.575	53	221	17	0	6	54	20	25	3
6	Kien Vu, Arizona St.	So.	.413	.497	.793	47	150	11	2	14	56	21	43	12
7	Edwin Delacruz, Ark.-Pine Bluff	Sr.	.409	.505	.578	46	154	16	2	2	35	23	32	11
8	Travis Bazzana, Oregon St.	Jr.	.407	.568	.911	60	214	16	4	28	66	76	37	16
9	Edgar Alvarez, Nicholls	Sr.	.405	.514	.678	58	227	21	1	13	67	53	32	1
9	Jon Jon Gazdar, Austin Peay	Jr.	.405	.484	.667	56	237	21	1	13	55	27	14	9
9	Sean Keys, Bucknell	Jr.	.405	.535	.798	46	163	19	3	13	57	35	26	4
12	Ben Rounds, Harvard	Sr.	.403	.506	.685	39	149	16	1	8	34	28	25	3
13	Tyler MacGregor, Northeastern	Sr.	.402	.484	.786	55	234	29	2	19	80	33	40	15
14	Myles Smith, UC Irvine	Jr.	.401	.533	.637	48	182	13	0	10	49	50	30	5
14	Joel Dragoo, Presbyterian	Jr.	.401	.508	.797	56	197	20	2	18	67	43	33	11
16	Julian Greenwell, Wright St.	Sr.	.399	.474	.699	45	183	20	1	11	53	21	16	5
17	Eric Rataczak, Niagara	Jr.	.396	.485	.698	55	222	14	1	17	71	31	25	2
18	Lyle Miller-Green, Austin Peay	Sr.	.393	.533	.900	56	219	17	2	30	94	54	38	13
19	Chase Swain, Manhattan	So.	.392	.464	.575	40	153	9	2	5	41	23	31	15
20	Khalil Walker, New Mexico	Jr.	.391	.490	.516	50	161	11	0	3	19	30	24	2
21	Kendal Ewell, UIC	Sr.	.390	.494	.795	55	210	20	1	21	69	35	54	8
22	Ethan Conrad, Marist	So.	.389	.467	.704	55	226	18	13	9	52	27	32	17
22	Treyvin Moss, Northern Ky.	Sr.	.389	.452	.675	57	244	22	7	11	66	28	20	30
24	Juan Cruz, Alabama St.	So.	.388	.430	.641	47	170	10	0	11	57	12	27	1
24	Dalton McIntyre, Southern Miss.	Jr.	.388	.447	.473	60	237	12	1	2	34	24	28	10
24	Brady Short, Central Conn. St.	Jr.	.388	.473	.511	42	178	10	3	2	31	29	27	3
27	Cade Sullivan, Western Mich.	Sr.	.387	.478	.599	55	222	15	1	10	54	39	30	6
27	Dean Ferrara, Fairfield	Jr.	.387	.442	.520	56	248	12	3	5	40	20	29	7
27	Ty Jackson, Florida A&M	Sr.	.387	.509	.643	47	168	11	4	8	41	39	25	9
27	Caden Kendle, UC Irvine	Sr.	.387	.479	.550	51	212	19	3	6	61	29	31	1
27	Cam Smith, Florida St.	So.	.387	.488	.654	66	269	22	1	16	57	44	48	4
27	Nick Iannantone, ETSU	Sr.	.387	.505	.539	56	217	14	2	5	42	51	24	0
33	Dylan Palmer, Hofstra	So.	.386	.453	.440	57	241	6	2	1	31	25	27	27
34	Josiah Ragsdale, Iona	So.	.385	.470	.646	50	192	13	8	7	37	28	41	22
34	Lucas Spence, SIUE	Jr.	.385	.473	.552	56	221	14	4	5	36	29	33	12
36	Kyle Walker, Grambling	Jr.	.384	.508	.611	54	203	11	1	11	43	34	18	12
36	Ben Patacsil, Portland	Sr.	.384	.464	.537	50	177	4	1	7	50	22	22	4
38	Jack Frank, Michigan St.	Sr.	.383	.467	.622	51	209	17	3	9	40	32	38	19
39	John Anderson, Samford	Sr.	.382	.467	.682	57	217	24	1	13	69	35	39	2
39	Rafe Perich, Lehigh	Jr.	.382	.492	.572	42	152	11	0	6	41	34	23	4
39	Evan Bouldin, Delaware St.	So.	.382	.434	.553	49	217	16	0	7	39	20	25	1
42	Jacob Steels, Cal Poly	Sr.	.381	.491	.558	54	215	12	1	8	34	34	31	0
42	Jake Holland, New Mexico	Sr.	.381	.445	.798	44	168	15	2	17	60	20	30	0
42	Drew Burress, Georgia Tech	Fr.	.381	.512	.821	58	218	15	3	25	67	58	37	8
42	Mitchell Sanford, New Orleans	Jr.	.381	.460	.708	57	226	21	4	15	68	26	46	18
42	Gage Miller, Alabama	Jr.	.381	.474	.702	55	218	12	2	18	56	27	24	0
47	Brice Martinez, Wofford	Sr.	.380	.440	.537	62	255	20	4	4	57	24	31	15
47	Patrick Clohisy, Saint Louis	Jr.	.380	.488	.663	43	163	15	5	7	44	27	19	24
47	CJ Richmond, Western Mich.	Jr.	.380	.479	.667	55	213	18	2	13	67	34	69	4
47	Clayton Gray, Austin Peay	Jr.	.380	.450	.680	55	250	24	3	15	68	31	30	13
47	Griffin Palfrey, Columbia	Jr.	.380	.471	.690	35	129	18	2	6	49	15	20	3
47	Zion Rose, Louisville	Fr.	.380	.455	.584	44	166	9	5	5	32	19	18	10
47	Garrett Wright, Bowling Green	Fr.	.380	.503	.581	40	129	8	0	6	28	13	11	5
54	Banks Tolley, App State	Sr.	.379	.484	.781	55	224	12	0	26	77	33	46	6
54	Blake Burke, Tennessee	Jr.	.379	.449	.702	72	285	30	1	20	61	35	48	11
54	Aaron Parker, UC Santa Barbara	Jr.	.379	.460	.632	48	190	12	0	12	51	27	38	0
57	Brandon Eike, VCU	Sr.	.378	.470	.661	61	251	27	1	14	62	40	45	0
57	Alec Makarewicz, NC State	Sr.	.378	.438	.753	61	259	25	0	24	84	26	50	1
57	Damian Bravo, Texas Tech	So.	.378	.438	.583	47	180	21	2	4	44	20	42	2
57	Tyler Wilson, Grand Canyon	Sr.	.378	.441	.691	58	233	18	2	17	65	24	34	1
57	Cole McConnell, Louisiana Tech	Sr.	.378	.461	.671	60	249	17	1	18	71	29	71	1
57	John Quinlan, Cornell	Jr.	.378	.439	.568	33	148	9	2	5	20	13	21	10
63	Eddie Hacopian, Maryland	Jr.	.377	.474	.573	56	220	16	0	9	51	36	25	6
63	Dalton Beck, UIW	So.	.377	.433	.716	57	236	20	3	18	67	23	42	8
63	Hunter Dorraugh, San Jose St.	Sr.	.377	.447	.714	48	199	9	2	18	49	18	41	0
63	Kade Lewis, Butler	Fr.	.377	.436	.618	53	207	12	4	10	51	18	35	3

MIKE JANES/FOUR SEAM IMAGES

Jac Caglianone hit .419. His 35 home runs trailed D-I leader Charlie Condon by only two.

EDDIE KELLY

Oregon State's Travis Bazzana hit .407. He was the No. 1 pick in the 2024 draft.

67	Nin Burns II, Texas Southern	Sr.	.376	.503	.582	45	141	11	0	6	45	34	23	8
68	Joseph Eichelberger, Jackson St.	Jr.	.375	.451	.490	53	200	10	2	3	53	25	34	16
68	Ian Farrow, FGCU	Sr.	.375	.504	.750	47	176	17	2	15	44	38	49	10
68	Alex Lane, Northeastern	Sr.	.375	.474	.685	54	216	13	0	18	80	37	49	14
68	Christian Moore, Tennessee	Jr.	.375	.451	.797	72	296	19	2	34	74	38	49	5
68	Marshall Toole, Wofford	Jr.	.375	.461	.617	62	256	15	10	9	64	38	49	43
73	Mark Shallenberger, Evansville	Sr.	.374	.514	.687	65	243	21	2	17	64	45	28	6
74	Jacob Donahue, Central Mich.	Sr.	.373	.440	.475	52	204	10	1	3	23	13	38	18
75	Henry Godbout, Virginia	So.	.372	.472	.645	51	172	18	1	9	47	29	20	6
75	Austin Kryszczuk, UNLV	Sr.	.372	.477	.779	52	199	20	2	19	75	31	33	0
75	Gino D'Alessio, Abilene Christian	Sr.	.372	.451	.546	58	218	11	0	9	63	31	31	5
78	Cade Conway, Charleston So.	Sr.	.371	.443	.474	50	194	9	1	3	33	21	43	26
78	Tatsunori Negishi, N.C. A&T	Sr.	.371	.477	.588	51	194	16	1	8	37	29	29	2
80	Carter Dorighi, Butler	Jr.	.370	.435	.547	55	243	16	3	7	48	27	32	16
80	Nolan Schubart, Oklahoma St.	So.	.370	.513	.838	49	173	10	1	23	68	49	62	0
80	Lucas Loos, Eastern Ill.	Sr.	.370	.442	.810	53	211	22	1	23	61	27	36	9
83	Cameron Sisneros, ETSU	Sr.	.369	.493	.766	56	214	16	0	23	86	49	20	1
83	Josh Tate, Ga. Southern	So.	.369	.475	.489	59	233	14	1	4	30	39	32	27
83	Zac Zyons, Bryant	Jr.	.369	.473	.601	44	168	13	1	8	33	17	32	3
83	Garrett Howe, Samford	Sr.	.369	.480	.573	58	225	18	2	8	44	44	32	23
83	Fenwick Trimble, James Madison	Jr.	.369	.452	.635	61	244	21	1	14	65	29	23	16
88	Justin Starke, VMI	Sr.	.368	.494	.647	56	204	12	3	13	51	43	30	18
88	Ryan Stafford, Cal Poly	Jr.	.368	.444	.568	57	234	23	3	6	46	26	39	10
90	Daniel Dickinson, Utah Valley	So.	.367	.367	.469	58	245	14	2	18	53	34	28	32
90	Sam Antonacci, Coastal Carolina	Jr.	.367	.523	.504	61	226	13	0	6	47	50	40	15
90	Jose Gonzalez, Bethune-Cookman	Sr.	.367	.461	.552	57	210	10	4	7	56	31	28	5
90	Carter Cunningham, East Carolina	Sr.	.367	.464	.653	63	251	17	2	17	66	38	38	6
90	Keith Jones II, New Mexico St.	Sr.	.367	.472	.710	54	221	19	3	17	67	35	47	11
90	Parker Schmidt, UNLV	Sr.	.367	.449	.473	43	150	7	3	1	28	22	27	6
96	Phil Stahl, Monmouth	Sr.	.366	.433	.497	46	161	6	0	5	36	20	22	0
96	Easton Carmichael, Oklahoma	So.	.366	.406	.563	61	254	19	5	7	64	20	43	12
96	Roman Kuntz, Morehead St.	Sr.	.366	.482	.860	61	235	15	1	33	100	50	34	2
96	Austin St. Laurent, App State	Jr.	.366	.424	.618	55	246	12	4	14	60	16	21	9
96	Jace Rinehart, USC Upstate	Jr.	.366	.412	.673	60	257	22	3	17	59	16	40	11

COLLEGE

ON-BASE PERCENTAGE

Rank	Player, Pos., Team	OBP
1.	Corey Collins, Georgia	.574
2.	Travis Bazzana, Oregon St.	.568
3.	Charlie Condon, Georgia	.556
4.	Jac Caglianone, Florida	.544
5.	Sean Keys, Bucknell	.535
6.	Myles Smith, UC Irvine	.533
7.	Lyle Miller-Green, Austin Peay	.533
8.	Nick Kurtz, Wake Forest	.531
9.	Woody Hadeen, UC Irvine	.524
10.	Sam Antonacci, Coastal Carolina	.523

SLUGGING PERCENTAGE

Rank	Player, Pos., Team	SLG
1.	Charlie Condon, Georgia	1.009
2.	Travis Bazzana, Oregon St.	.911
3.	Lyle Miller-Green, Austin Peay	.900
4.	Jac Caglianone, Florida	.875
5.	Roman Kuntz, Morehead St.	.860
6.	Cary Arbolida, Houston	.847
7.	Nolan Schubart, Oklahoma St.	.838
8.	Jakob Christian, San Diego	.828
9.	Drew Burress, Georgia Tech	.821
10.	John Bay, Austin Peay	.817

RUNS BATTED IN

Rank	Player, Pos., Team	RBI
1.	Roman Kuntz, Morehead St.	100
2.	James Tibbs III, Florida St.	95
3.	Lyle Miller-Green, Austin Peay	94
4.	Cameron Sisneros, ETSU	86
5.	Brooks Bryan, Troy	85
5.	Braden Montgomery, Texas A&M	85
7.	Alec Makarewicz, NC State	84
8.	Alex Lane, Northeastern	80
8.	Tyler MacGregor, Northeastern	80
10.	Jacob Jenkins-Cowart, East Carolina	79

HOME RUNS

Rank	Player, Pos., Team	HR
1.	Charlie Condon, Georgia	37
2.	Jac Caglianone, Florida	35
3.	Christian Moore, Tennessee	34
4.	Roman Kuntz, Morehead St.	33
5.	Lyle Miller-Green, Austin Peay	30
6.	Jace Laviolette, Texas A&M	29
7.	Travis Bazzana, Oregon St.	28
7.	Vance Honeycutt, North Caro.	28
7.	Jared Jones, LSU	28
7.	James Tibbs III, Florida St.	28

DOUBLES

Rank	Player, Pos., Team	2B
1.	Blake Burke, Tennessee	30
2.	Tyler MacGregor, Northeastern	29
3.	Brandon Eike, VCU	27
3.	Garrett Pennington, NC State	27
5.	Carlos Martinez, UMass Lowell	26
5.	Michael Snyder, Oklahoma	26
7.	Owen Ayers, Marshall	25
7.	Ryan Campos, Arizona St.	25
7.	Michael Carpentier, Cal. Baptist	25
7.	Zach Ehrhard, Oklahoma St.	25
7.	Carson Hansen, Milwaukee	25
7.	Jacob Lojewski, FGCU	25
7.	Alec Makarewicz, NC State	25
7.	Avery Neaves, Col. of Charleston	25
7.	Ben Newton, Fresno St.	25

TRIPLES

Rank	Player, Pos., Team	3B
1.	Ethan Conrad, Marist	13
2.	Alejandro Covas, Youngstown St.	10
2.	Marshall Toole, Wofford	10
4.	Janmikell Bastardo, Florida A&M	8
4.	Cameron Pittman, Radford	8
4.	Josiah Ragsdale, Iona	8
7.	Emilio Corona, Arizona	7
7.	Cooper Hext, McNeese	7
7.	Treyvin Moss, Northern Ky.	7
7.	Tyler Shaneyfelt, Northern Ky.	7

STOLEN BASES

Rank	Player, Pos., Team	SB
1.	Justin Sierra, FDU	44
2.	Marshall Toole, Wofford	43
3.	Jackson Strong, Canisius	42
4.	Trent Rice, Oakland	41
5.	Brendan Jones, Kansas St.	40
5.	Jordan McCladdie, Jackson St.	40
7.	JT Benson, Louisville	34
7.	Rodney Hibler Jr., Jackson St.	34
7.	Kole Myers, Troy	34
10.	7 tied at	33

RUNS

Rank	Player, Pos., Team	R
1.	Lyle Miller-Green, Austin Peay	94
2.	Sam Antonacci, Coastal Carolina	90
3.	Vance Honeycutt, North Carolina	88
4.	Jace Laviolette, Texas A&M	87
5.	Ryley Preece, Morehead St.	86
6.	Travis Bazzana, Oregon St.	84
6.	Charlie Condon, Georgia	84
8.	Jac Caglianone, Florida	83
8.	Gavin Grahovac, Texas A&M	83
8.	Christian Moore, Tennessee	83
8.	Marshall Toole, Wofford	83

HITS

Rank	Player, Pos., Team	H
1.	Christian Moore, Tennessee	111
2.	Blake Burke, Tennessee	108
3.	Jac Caglianone, Florida	104
3.	Cam Smith, Florida St.	104
5.	Charlie Condon, Georgia	100
6.	Alec Makarewicz, NC State	98
7.	Brice Martinez, Wofford	97
8.	Dean Ferrara, Fairfield	96
8.	Jon Jon Gazdar, Austin Peay	96
8.	Marshall Toole, Wofford	96

TOTAL BASES

Rank	Player, Pos., Team	TB
1.	Christian Moore, Tennessee	236
2.	Charlie Condon, Georgia	233
3.	Jac Caglianone, Florida	217
4.	Roman Kuntz, Morehead St.	202
5.	Blake Burke, Tennessee	200
6.	Lyle Miller-Green, Austin Peay	197
7.	Travis Bazzana, Oregon St.	195
7.	Alec Makarewicz, NC State	195
7.	James Tibbs III, Florida St.	195
10.	Jace Laviolette, Texas A&M	188

WALKS

Rank	Player, Pos., Team	BB
1.	Nick Kurtz, Wake Forest	78
2.	Travis Bazzana, Oregon St.	76
3.	Jace Laviolette, Texas A&M	64
4.	Woody Hadeen, UC Irvine	62
4.	Kole Myers, Troy	62
6.	Ryley Preece, Morehead St.	60
7.	Jared Jones, LSU	59
7.	Mike Sirota, Northeastern	59
7.	Jack Winsett, Rider	59
10.	Five tied at	58

TOUGHEST TO STRIKE OUT

Rank	Player, Pos., Team	AB/SO
1.	Jonathan Luders, Seton Hall	21.1
2.	Alejandro Garza, Cal Poly	20.5
3.	Camden Janik, Illinois	20.5
4.	Kamau Neighbors, CSUN	20.0
5.	Jon Jon Gazdar, Austin Peay	16.9
6.	Hunter Pasqualini, Cen. Conn. St.	15.9
7.	Tommy Barth, ETSU	15.2
8.	Isaiah Barkett, Stetson	14.9
9.	Alex Gouveia, UC Davis	14.3
10.	Ricky Teel, Winthrop	14.3

HIT BY PITCH

Rank	Player, Pos., Team	HBP
1.	JT Landwehr, Mount St. Mary's	39
2.	Luke Beckstein, Northeastern	36
3.	Jakob Simons, CSUN	29
4.	Corey Collins, Georgia	28
4.	Mark Shallenberger, Evansville	28
6.	Sam Antonacci, Coastal Carolina	27
6.	Matt Masciangelo, Sacramento St.	27
6.	Mac Moise, FGCU	27
9.	Josh Kross, Cincinnati	26
9.	Joichiro Oyama, UC Irvine	26
9.	Riley Silva, Nebraska	26
9.	Paul Tammaro, UConn	26

SACRIFICE BUNTS

Rank	Player, Pos., Team	SAC
1.	Riley Silva, Nebraska	18
2.	Ben Palmer, Southeast Mo. St.	17
3.	Garrison Weiss, Prairie View	16
3.	Will Worthington, San Diego	16
5.	Zayd Brannigan, Western Ky.	15
6.	Tyler Gordon, Miami (OH)	14
6.	Shamaar McDuffie, Kennesaw St.	14
6.	Sam McNulty, Boston College	14
9.	JT Landwehr, Mount St. Mary's	13
9.	Mason Le, CSUN	13
9.	Jaylin Rae, Western Ky.	13

SACRIFICE FLIES

Rank	Player, Pos., Team	SF
1.	Matt King, UTSA	11
2.	Easton Carmichael, Oklahoma	10
2.	Dallas Duarte, Hawaii	10
2.	Griff O'Ferrall, Virginia	10
5.	Cooper Benzin, VCU	9
5.	Dixon Black, Wofford	9
5.	Gino D'Alessio, Abilene Christian	9
5.	Marco Dinges, Florida St.	9
5.	Dylan Nevar, Western Mich.	9

EAST CAROLINA UNIVERSITY

Trey Yesavage went 11-1, 2.02 for East Carolina with 145 strikeouts in 93 innings

KATE WOOLSON/TEXAS RANGERS /GETTY IMAGES

Hagen Smith struck out 161 batters in just 84 innings for Arkansas

PITCHING (MINIMUM 40 INNINGS PITCHED)

Rk.	Pitcher, Team	Class	W	L	ERA	G	GS	SV	IP	H	R	ER	BB	SO
1.	Evan Aschenbeck, Texas A&M	Sr.	6	1	1.78	32	0	10	75.2	55	17	15	12	87
2.	Charlie Beilenson, Duke	Sr.	7	3	2.01	34	0	12	62.2	42	19	14	18	92
3.	Trey Yesavage, East Carolina	Jr.	11	1	2.02	15	15	0	93.1	49	21	21	32	145
4.	Hagen Smith, Arkansas	Jr.	9	2	2.04	16	16	0	84	41	22	19	34	161
5.	Brett Sears, Nebraska	Sr.	9	1	2.16	17	16	1	104	17	29	25	19	101
6.	Ryan Johnson, DBU	Jr.	11	3	2.21	16	16	0	106	83	32	26	14	151
7.	Ryan Gallagher, UC Santa Barbara	Jr.	10	1	2.22	14	14	0	89	50	26	22	25	96
8.	Brooks Caple, Lamar	Sr.	7	3	2.40	15	15	0	97.2	58	31	26	27	102
9.	Nate Knowles, William & Mary	Jr.	8	3	2.48	19	19	0	80	50	32	22	39	112
10.	Tyler Bremner, UC Santa Barbara	So.	11	1	2.54	19	9	0	88.2	57	27	25	21	104
11.	Daniel Eagen, Presbyterian	Jr.	5	2	2.67	14	14	0	77.2	49	30	23	28	121
11.	Bryson Van Sickle, Utah	Sr.	5	1	2.67	15	15	1	94.1	79	32	28	21	69
13.	Justin Lehman, Army West Point	Jr.	5	4	2.68	13	12	0	74	63	26	22	25	49
14.	Chase Burns, Wake Forest	Jr.	10	1	2.70	16	16	0	100	62	32	30	30	191
15.	Ryan Verdugo, CSU Bakersfield	Jr.	3	6	2.72	14	14	0	89.1	66	33	27	40	93
16.	Luke Holman, LSU	Jr.	9	4	2.75	16	16	0	91.2	57	36	28	33	127
17.	Luke Delongchamp, Bryant	Jr.	5	2	2.76	14	14	0	65.1	59	31	20	18	59
18.	Connor Wietgrefe, Minnesota	Jr.	8	4	2.77	15	13	0	78	81	35	24	26	74
19.	Blayze Berry, UAB	Sr.	9	3	2.82	15	15	0	92.2	84	39	29	25	99
20.	Sam Downs, UMBC	Sr.	4	1	2.83	20	6	5	70	61	28	22	34	57
20.	Dominic Castellano, UCF	Jr.	7	0	2.83	22	1	3	60.1	34	21	19	25	68
22.	Brennan Stuprich, Southeastern La.	Jr.	6	3	2.87	14	14	0	84.2	77	37	27	27	49
22.	Brian Curley, VCU	So.	6	0	2.87	19	0	3	78.1	74	28	25	35	78
22.	Caleb Granger, Florida A&M	Jr.	8	2	2.87	15	15	0	87.2	90	35	28	24	73
25.	Tristan Walton, UT Martin	Sr.	6	3	2.88	15	15	0	93.2	75	37	30	46	98
26.	Kellen O'Connor, CSU Bakersfield	Sr.	2	4	2.89	13	13	0	81	79	33	26	24	64
27.	Zach Cameron, Niagara	Sr.	8	1	2.90	24	0	11	59	44	24	19	20	59
28.	Andrew Williams, Georgetown	Jr.	4	3	2.91	16	10	0	65	62	32	21	28	49
29.	Michael Foltz, George Washington	Sr.	4	1	2.92	13	13	0	74	46	30	24	23	55
29.	Jacob Weatherley, Little Rock	Sr.	6	3	2.92	24	0	3	61.2	55	22	20	30	77
31.	Nick Wissman, Dayton	Sr.	11	1	2.93	25	0	7	67.2	66	26	22	11	64
31.	Tanner Boccabello, Bethune-Cookman	Jr.	8	3	2.93	16	15	0	98.1	114	40	32	16	73
33.	Brian Holiday, Oklahoma St.	Jr.	7	3	2.95	16	16	0	113	82	41	37	19	128
33.	Andrew Devine, Austin Peay	Sr.	6	0	2.95	10	10	0	58	36	22	19	17	60
33.	Ryan Prager, Texas A&M	Jr.	9	1	2.95	19	19	0	97.2	83	36	32	20	124
36.	Mario Pesca, St. John's (NY)	So.	6	1	2.96	15	15	0	76	70	31	25	38	53
37.	Jakob Wright, Cal Poly	So.	9	3	2.97	15	15	0	88	71	35	29	42	101
37.	Tony Roca, North Florida	Sr.	5	4	2.97	13	13	0	63.2	56	25	21	21	69
39.	Jamie Arnold, Florida St.	So.	11	3	2.98	19	18	1	105.2	90	45	35	26	159
40.	Connor Maggi, Gardner-Webb	Jr.	2	0	3.00	29	0	2	60	49	24	20	15	73
41.	Carter Gaston, Portland	So.	11	2	3.01	16	11	2	80.2	73	29	27	22	65
42.	Davian Garcia, FGCU	Fr.	5	3	3.03	16	8	1	59.1	52	24	20	20	71
43.	Aiden May, Oregon St.	Jr.	7	1	3.05	14	14	0	73.2	61	27	25	23	84
44.	Andrew Herrmann, Louisiana	Jr.	6	3	3.09	14	12	0	67	55	33	23	26	61
45.	Nate Snead, Tennessee	So.	10	2	3.11	29	1	6	75.1	71	28	26	26	61
45.	Eddie Smink, Stony Brook	So.	5	4	3.11	11	11	0	55	43	23	19	27	56
47.	Zander Sechrist, Tennessee	Sr.	6	1	3.12	20	19	0	78	76	31	27	16	76
48.	Colin Daniel, UAB	So.	7	4	3.13	14	14	0	92	95	43	32	18	76
49.	Jacob Faulkner, Princeton	Sr.	8	1	3.14	20	20	0	66	61	30	23	12	52
49.	Patrick Gardner, FDU	Jr.	8	2	3.14	16	4	0	86	55	39	30	18	28

WINS

Rank	Pitcher, Team	W
1.	Michael Ross, Samford	13
1.	AJ Causey, Tennessee	13
3.	Mason Martinez, Grambling	12
3.	Matthew Matthijs, North Carolina	12
5.	Tyler Bremner, UC Santa Barbara	11
5.	Nick Wissman, Dayton	11
5.	Trey Yesavage, East Carolina	11
5.	Carter Gaston, Portland	11
5.	Jamie Arnold, Florida St.	11
5.	Ryan Johnson, DBU	11
5.	RJ Sales, UNCW	11

SAVES

Rank	Pitcher, Team	SV
1.	Ethan Bates, Louisiana Tech	17
2.	Mason Burns, Western Ky.	15
3.	Bridger Holmes, Oregon St.	13
4.	Reece Lawler, UIC	12
4.	Charlie Beilenson, Duke	12
6.	Austin Gordon, Clemson	11
6.	Matt Ager, UC Santa Barbara	11
6.	Micah Ashman, Utah	11
6.	Zach Cameron, Niagara	11
6.	Mike McKenna, Hofstra	11
6.	Cole Stallings, Stetson	11

STRIKEOUTS

Rank	Pitcher, Team	SO
1.	Chase Burns, Wake Forest	191
2.	Hagen Smith, Arkansas	161
3.	Jamie Arnold, Florida St.	159
4.	Ryan Johnson, DBU	151
5.	Trey Yesavage, East Carolina	145
6.	Nick Brink, Portland	130
7.	Merritt Beeker, Ball St.	128
7.	Brody Brecht, Iowa	128
7.	Brian Holiday, Oklahoma St.	128
10.	Luke Holman, LSU	127

STRIKEOUTS PER NINE

Rank	Pitcher, Team	SO/9
1.	Hagen Smith, Arkansas	17.25
2.	Chase Burns, Wake Forest	17.19
3.	LP Langevin, Louisiana	15.22
4.	Riley Huge, Winthrop	14.98
5.	Brody Brecht, Iowa	14.71
6.	Merritt Beeker, Ball St.	14.22
7.	Daniel Eagen, Presbyterian	14.02
8.	Deven Sheerin, Mount St. Mary's	14.01
9.	Trey Yesavage, East Carolina	13.98
10.	Ben Hess, Alabama	13.96

FEWEST HITS PER NINE

Rank	Pitcher, Team	H/9
1.	Hagen Smith, Arkansas	4.39
2.	Trey Yesavage, East Carolina	4.72
3.	Jacob Mayers, Nicholls	4.97
4.	Ryan Gallagher, UC Santa Barbara	5.06
5.	Dominic Castellano, UCF	5.07
6.	Brody Brecht, Iowa	5.29
7.	Connor Foley, Indiana	5.29
8.	Brooks Caple, Lamar University	5.34
9.	Chase Burns, Wake Forest	5.58
10.	Andrew Devine, Austin Peay	5.59

FEWEST WALKS PER NINE

Rank	Pitcher, Team	BB/9
1.	Kyle Roche, Richmond	0.42
2.	Calvin Bickerstaff, Kent St.	0.79
3.	Peyton Calitri, Tennessee Tech	0.95
4.	Ryan Johnson, DBU	1.19
5.	Cam Walty, Arizona	1.30
6.	Carter Rustad, Missouri	1.38
7.	Armando Sierra, Mississippi Val.	1.40
8.	Evan Aschenbeck, Texas A&M	1.43
8.	Eric Steensma, UT Martin	1.43
10.	Luke Roggenburk, St. Bonaventure	1.44

TEAM LEADERS

SCORING

Rank	Team	G	R	R/G
1.	Austin Peay	56	608	10.9
2.	Wofford	62	617	10.0
3.	Columbia	44	416	9.5
4.	Morehead St.	61	571	9.4
5.	Northern Ky.	59	545	9.2
6.	Virginia	63	581	9.2
7.	Bowling Green	53	488	9.2
8.	UC Irvine	59	536	9.1
9.	Georgia	60	544	9.1
10.	Wright St.	56	505	9.0
11.	Tennessee	73	657	9.0
12.	Florida St.	66	588	8.9
13.	App State	55	484	8.8
14.	Troy	59	516	8.7
15.	Samford	58	506	8.7
16.	Campbell	53	460	8.7
17.	Coastal Carolina	61	528	8.7
18.	Northeastern	55	474	8.6
19.	Merrimack	59	504	8.5
20.	ETSU	56	478	8.5
21.	Virginia Tech	54	459	8.5
22.	Oregon St.	61	518	8.5
23.	Texas A&M	68	575	8.5
24.	North Carolina	64	541	8.5
25.	New Mexico	54	454	8.4
26.	Delaware	57	478	8.4
27.	Duke	60	501	8.4
28.	Niagara	55	458	8.3
29.	Arizona St.	58	482	8.3
30.	Col. of Charleston	55	457	8.3
31.	Nicholls	60	494	8.2
32.	Texas Tech	59	485	8.2
33.	Iowa	54	443	8.2
34.	New Mexico St.	54	443	8.2
35.	Oakland	58	475	8.2
36.	Grambling	54	441	8.2
37.	Oklahoma St.	61	498	8.2
38.	Murray St.	57	464	8.1
39.	Louisville	56	455	8.1
40.	Wake Forest	60	487	8.1
41.	Jackson St.	56	452	8.1
42.	Clemson	60	484	8.1
43.	USC Upstate	60	484	8.1
44.	Oklahoma	61	492	8.1
45.	Indiana	60	482	8.0
46.	Purdue	57	457	8.0
47.	Georgia Tech	58	461	7.9
48.	UNC Greensboro	54	427	7.9
49.	East Carolina	63	498	7.9
50.	Fairfield	58	458	7.9

BATTING AVERAGE

Rank	Team	AVG
1.	Austin Peay	.359
2.	Wofford	.334
3.	Columbia	.333
4.	Morehead St.	.324
5.	Northern Ky.	.321
6.	Virginia	.320
7.	Bowling Green	.319
8.	UC Irvine	.318
9.	Georgia	.315
10.	Wright St.	.315

HOME RUNS

Rank	Team	HR
1.	Austin Peay	184
2.	Wofford	151
3.	Columbia	146
4.	Morehead St.	136
5.	Northern Ky.	136
6.	Virginia	131
7.	Bowling Green	129
8.	UC Irvine	120
9.	Georgia	118
10.	Wright St.	118

DOUBLES

Rank	Team	2B
1.	Austin Peay	160
2.	Wofford	159
3.	Columbia	156
4.	Morehead St.	151
5.	Northern Ky.	148
6.	Virginia	143
7.	Bowling Green	142
8.	UC Irvine	141
9.	Georgia	140
10.	Wright St.	138

TRIPLES

Rank	Team	3B
1.	Austin Peay	33
2.	Wofford	33
3.	Columbia	26
4.	Morehead St.	25
5.	Northern Ky.	24
6.	Virginia	24
7.	Bowling Green	24
8.	UC Irvine	23
9.	Georgia	23
10.	Wright St.	22

SLUGGING PERCENTAGE

Rank	Team	SLG
1.	Austin Peay	.661
2.	Wofford	.607
3.	Columbia	.589
4.	Morehead St.	.568
5.	Northern Ky.	.567
6.	Virginia	.565
7.	Bowling Green	.558
8.	UC Irvine	.557
9.	Georgia	.551
10.	Wright St.	.551

STOLEN BASES

Rank	Team	SB
1.	Austin Peay	178
2.	Wofford	162
3.	Columbia	162
4.	Morehead St.	157
5.	Northern Ky.	157
6.	Virginia	151
7.	Bowling Green	147

Rank Team	
8. UC Irvine	141
9. Georgia	137
10. Wright St.	136

WALKS

Rank Team	BB
1. Austin Peay	422
2. Wofford	394
3. Columbia	382
4. Morehead St.	382
5. Northern Ky.	382
6. Virginia	378
7. Bowling Green	377
8. UC Irvine	364
9. Georgia	361
10. Wright St.	360

PITCHING

EARNED RUN AVERAGE

Rank Team	ERA
1. Hawaii	3.78
2. Lamar University	3.79
3. UC Santa Barbara	3.84
4. Texas A&M	3.86
5. Arkansas	3.87
6. Tennessee	3.89
7. DBU	4.01
8. East Carolina	4.05
9. Col. of Charleston	4.05
10. Oregon St.	4.07
11. Oklahoma St.	4.08
12. San Diego	4.15
13. Mississippi St.	4.17
14. Cal Poly	4.22
15. North Carolina	4.30
16. Army West Point	4.35
17. St. John's (NY)	4.35
18. LSU	4.36
19. Portland	4.39
20. UCF	4.43
21. Arizona	4.46
22. Louisiana	4.48
23. UNCW	4.49
24. Duke	4.50
25. Indiana St.	4.52
26. Nebraska	4.60
27. Long Beach St.	4.61
28. Clemson	4.63
29. Old Dominion	4.67
30. Georgetown	4.69
31. Grand Canyon	4.69
32. TCU	4.70
33. Bethune-Cookman	4.70
34. William & Mary	4.75
35. San Francisco	4.75
36. Sacred Heart	4.76
37. Sam Houston	4.77
38. Yale	4.80
39. UC Davis	4.81
40. Seton Hall	4.82
41. Kansas	4.82
42. California	4.84
43. VCU	4.86
44. Southern California	4.87
45. Oregon	4.88
46. UC Irvine	4.90
47. Texas	4.91
48. Stetson	4.92
49. Saint Louis	4.93
50. Florida St.	4.93

STRIKEOUTS PER NINE

Rank Team	SO/9
1. Arkansas	12.1
2. Wake Forest	11.9
3. TCU	11.5
4. LSU	11.5
5. Iowa	11.1
6. Oklahoma St.	11.0
7. Texas A&M	10.9
8. Florida	10.7
9. Florida St.	10.7
10. Georgia	10.6

FEWEST WALKS PER NINE

Rank Team	BB/9
1. Arizona	2.6
2. Nebraska	2.9
3. UT Arlington	2.9
4. Sam Houston	3.0
5. Tennessee	3.0
6. Hawaii	3.1
7. Fresno St.	3.1
8. Col. of Charleston	3.1
9. Utah	3.1
10. Sacramento St.	3.2

FIELDING

FIELDING PERCENTAGE

Rank Team	PCT
1. Notre Dame	.985
2. Cal Poly	.982
3. Florida	.982
4. DBU	.982
5. Virginia Tech	.982
6. San Diego	.981
7. Navy	.981
8. Arkansas	.981
8. CSUN	.981
10. Northwestern	.980
11. Delaware	.980
12. Mississippi St.	.980
13. Kentucky	.980
14. Duke	.980
15. Louisiana Tech	.980
16. Washington	.979
17. Illinois	.979
18. UConn	.979
19. Michigan	.979
20. Rider	.979
21. UIC	.979
22. NIU	.979
23. Florida St.	.979
24. Fresno St.	.978
25. St. John's (NY)	.978
26. Belmont	.978
27. Lamar University	.978
28. Boston College	.978
29. Texas A&M	.978
30. Rutgers	.978
31. The Citadel	.978
32. Georgia Tech	.978
33. Mercer	.978
34. Creighton	.978
35. Auburn	.978
36. LSU	.977
37. TCU	.977
38. Oral Roberts	.977
39. East Carolina	.977
40. Hawaii	.977
41. Vanderbilt	.977
42. Oregon	.977
43. Illinois St.	.977
44. App State	.977
45. Iowa	.977
46. Wofford	.977
47. Southern Miss.	.976
48. Sam Houston	.976
49. NC State	.976
50. West Virginia	.976

DOUBLE PLAYS

Rank Team	DP
1. Coastal Carolina	65
2. Michigan	62
3. Col. of Charleston	61
3. Rice	61
3. UC Davis	61
6. James Madison	59
7. UNCW	58
8. DBU	56
8. Florida A&M	56
8. Purdue	56

1. Tennessee

Coach: Tony Vitello. Overall: 60-13

Player, Pos, Yr	AVG	OBP	SLG	AB	R	H	2B	3B	HR	RBI	SB
Colby Backus, OF, Jr	.387	.500	.968	31	16	12	3	0	5	12	2
Blake Burke, 1B, Jr	.379	.449	.702	285	74	108	30	1	20	61	11
Christian Moore, INF, Jr	.375	.451	.797	296	83	111	19	2	34	74	5
Dylan Dreiling, OF, So	.341	.459	.715	246	72	84	19	2	23	75	4
Kavares Tears, OF, So	.324	.427	.643	244	73	79	16	1	20	62	4
Billy Amick, INF, Jr	.306	.387	.639	255	67	78	14	1	23	65	3
Hunter Ensley, OF, Jr	.296	.390	.532	216	45	64	15	0	12	48	4
Robin Villeneuve, UT, Jr	.288	.447	.513	80	20	23	3	0	5	22	0
Dean Curley, INF, Fr	.285	.386	.502	221	51	63	10	1	12	50	9
Dalton Bargo, UT, So	.280	.373	.551	107	27	30	5	0	8	27	2
Reese Chapman, OF, So	.274	.398	.519	106	22	29	5	0	7	31	2
Bradke Lohry, INF, Jr	.241	.452	.345	29	14	7	3	0	0	8	0
Cannon Peebles, C, So	.216	.379	.328	116	30	25	7	0	2	24	2
Cal Stark, C, Sr	.212	.353	.511	137	35	29	6	1	11	30	1

Pitcher, Year	W	L	ERA	G	GS	SV	IP	H	BB	SO
Dylan Loy, Fr	2	0	2.37	21	5	0	30	21	10	37
Nate Snead, So	10	2	3.11	29	1	6	75	71	26	61
Zander Sechrist, Sr	6	1	3.12	20	19	0	78	76	16	76
Aaron Combs, Jr	3	1	3.35	24	2	6	46	34	23	66
Andrew Behnke, So	3	1	3.54	23	0	0	28	23	9	39
Kirby Connell, Sr	4	1	3.67	36	0	4	49	49	13	49
JJ Garcia, So	3	0	3.97	11	0	0	11	8	2	18
Drew Beam, Jr	9	2	4.22	19	19	0	102	103	27	99
AJ Causey, Jr	13	3	4.43	19	6	1	91	93	22	125
Chris Stamos, Sr	3	1	4.50	22	11	0	32	24	16	35
Matthew Dallas, Fr	1	0	4.76	15	2	0	17	11	10	22
Marcus Phillips, So	0	0	4.95	19	2	3	20	15	15	22
AJ Russell, So	0	1	5.02	6	4	0	14	12	8	21

EDDIE KELLY

Braden Montgomery hit .322/.455/.733 to help lead Texas A&M to Omaha.

2. Texas A&M

Coach: Jim Schlossnagle. Overall: 53-15

Player, Pos, Yr	AVG	OBP	SLG	AB	R	H	2B	3B	HR	RBI	SB
Hayden Schott, OF, Sr	.335	.418	.498	263	45	88	15	2	8	63	1
Jackson Appel, C, Sr	.331	.422	.534	236	48	78	16	1	10	41	16
Kaeden Kent, INF, So	.327	.414	.491	110	23	36	6	0	4	28	0
Braden Montgomery, OF, Jr	.322	.454	.733	236	65	76	14	1	27	85	5
Jace Laviolette, OF, So	.305	.449	.726	259	87	79	16	3	29	78	7
Gavin Grahovac, UT, Fr	.298	.390	.596	285	83	85	16	0	23	66	4
Ali Camarillo, INF, Jr	.288	.384	.432	250	50	72	13	1	7	36	9
Ted Burton, INF, Sr	.284	.438	.479	215	46	61	13	1	9	44	11
Caden Sorrell, UT, Fr	.275	.369	.555	182	44	50	8	5	11	43	9
Travis Chestnut, INF, Sr	.262	.441	.411	107	41	28	5	1	3	13	18
Blake Binderup, P, So	.231	.367	.359	39	6	9	0	1	1	7	0
Hank Bard, C, Sr	.222	.349	.333	36	6	8	1	0	1	9	0
Ryan Targac, INF, Sr	.213	.306	.344	61	11	13	5	0	1	13	1

Pitcher, Year	W	L	ERA	G	GS	SV	IP	H	BB	SO
Evan Aschenbeck, Sr	6	1	1.78	32	0	10	76	55	12	87
Brad Rudis, Jr	6	0	2.55	24	2	0	35	35	12	35
Zane Badmaev, Sr	3	0	2.59	17	1	1	24	18	5	29
Chris Cortez, Jr	10	3	2.78	25	3	0	65	43	37	102
Isaac Morton, Fr	1	0	2.87	10	4	0	16	6	17	22
Ryan Prager, Jr	9	1	2.95	19	19	0	98	83	20	124
Shane Sdao, So	5	1	2.96	20	5	2	49	42	9	55
Brock Peery, Sr	2	1	3.54	24	0	0	20	6	17	22
Josh Stewart, Jr	2	2	4.26	25	0	0	32	31	9	39
Weston Moss, Fr	3	0	4.56	20	2	0	24	22	10	26
Justin Lamkin, So	3	3	5.21	19	16	0	66	64	22	88
Tanner Jones, Jr	3	1	6.33	15	12	0	48	61	19	47
Kaiden Wilson, Fr	0	2	9.82	10	0	0	11	17	7	15

3. Kentucky

Coach: Nick Mingione. Overall: 46-16

Player, Pos, Yr	AVG	OBP	SLG	AB	R	H	2B	3B	HR	RBI	SB
Nick Lopez, INF, Sr	.345	.400	.537	229	57	79	22	2	6	53	3
Ryan Waldschmidt, OF, Jr	.333	.469	.610	213	66	71	17	0	14	46	25
Ryan Nicholson, INF, Sr	.306	.405	.689	206	47	63	10	0	23	63	3
Émilien Pitre, INF, Jr	.301	.420	.519	239	57	72	20	1	10	58	26
Mitchell Daly, INF, Sr	.300	.431	.500	190	42	57	15	1	7	45	10
Patrick Herrera, INF, Jr	.288	.494	.390	59	15	17	4	1	0	16	1
Nolan McCarthy, OF, Jr	.288	.380	.480	198	43	57	12	1	8	41	8
Devin Burkes, C, Jr	.239	.372	.361	205	49	49	14	1	3	35	19
Grant Smith, INF, Sr	.235	.335	.343	166	34	39	3	0	5	34	6
Ty Crittenberger, OF, Sr	.222	.323	.481	27	8	6	1	0	2	3	7
James McCoy, INF, So	.218	.369	.387	142	35	31	4	1	6	25	8
Reuben Church, INF, Sr	.182	.372	.273	33	6	6	3	0	0	5	0

Pitcher, Year	W	L	ERA	G	GS	SV	IP	H	BB	SO
Ryan Hagenow, Sr	2	0	2.41	14	0	3	19	16	8	17
Robert Hogan, Jr	1	0	3.10	24	0	1	41	25	21	42
Johnny Hummel, Sr	4	0	3.48	24	0	7	31	17	11	41
Trey Pooser, Sr	7	1	3.50	19	13	2	90	70	35	82
Cameron O'Brien, Sr	3	0	4.54	36	0	0	36	29	14	50
Evan Byers, Jr	3	1	4.73	22	0	0	27	29	13	23
Mason Moore, Jr	9	4	5.05	18	18	0	93	79	54	83
Jackson Nove, Jr	1	0	6.16	28	0	2	31	25	23	42
Travis Smith, So	3	4	6.21	13	6	0	38	39	22	33
Dominic Niman, Sr	8	5	6.85	17	16	0	71	82	25	67
Drew Lafferty, Fr	1	1	6.86	8	8	0	21	23	9	17
Cooper Robinson, Jr	2	0	7.24	13	1	0	14	18	11	19
Colby Frieda, Jr	0	0	7.71	12	0	0	12	13	10	17

4. North Carolina

Coach: Scott Forbes. Overall: 48-16

Player, Pos, Yr	AVG	OBP	SLG	AB	R	H	2B	3B	HR	RBI	SB
Parks Harber, 1B, Sr	.343	.425	.648	233	57	80	9	1	20	63	4
Casey Cook, OF, So	.341	.431	.605	258	67	88	12	1	18	78	7
Anthony Donofrio, OF, Sr	.326	.435	.547	236	60	77	19	6	7	53	19
Vance Honeycutt, OF, Jr	.318	.410	.714	255	88	81	13	2	28	70	28

Player, Pos, Yr	AVG	OBP	SLG	AB	R	H	2B	3B	HR	RBI	SB
Gavin Gallaher, INF, Fr	.314	.392	.491	175	41	55	7	0	8	38	5
Alex Madera, INF, Sr	.303	.407	.386	228	53	69	9	2	2	34	9
Luke Stevenson, C, Fr	.284	.420	.535	215	43	61	8	2	14	58	2
Alberto Osuna, DH, Sr	.281	.376	.537	231	43	65	17	0	14	56	1
Colby Wilkerson, INF, Sr	.270	.370	.381	215	48	58	13	1	3	33	1
Johnny Castagnozzi, INF, Sr	.233	.333	.302	43	6	10	3	0	0	6	0
Jackson Van De Brake, INF, Sr	.213	.390	.300	80	21	17	4	0	1	11	5

Pitcher, Year	W	L	ERA	G	GS	SV	IP	H	BB	SO
Kyle Percival, So	4	0	2.42	22	0	0	22	20	11	20
Dalton Pence, So	5	1	2.45	36	0	8	59	40	27	74
Connor Bovair, Sr	1	0	3.62	23	1	1	27	28	8	27
Matthew Matthijs, So	12	4	3.72	36	0	0	58	49	18	56
Jason DeCaro, Fr	6	1	3.81	18	18	0	90	74	44	78
Shea Sprague, So	3	2	4.25	17	15	0	78	78	18	70
Ben Peterson, Sr	3	2	4.70	19	3	1	31	31	20	30
Aidan Haugh, Jr	4	3	4.83	22	8	0	54	58	27	61
Olin Johnson, Fr	1	0	4.96	7	6	0	16	20	8	10
Matt Poston, Sr	5	2	5.12	29	0	4	39	34	21	52
Cameron Padgett, So	1	0	5.22	17	2	0	29	34	10	20
Folger Boaz, Fr	3	1	5.77	9	9	0	39	48	19	38

5. Florida State

Coach: Link Jarrett. Overall: 49-17

Player, Pos, Yr	AVG	OBP	SLG	AB	R	H	2B	3B	HR	RBI	SB
Cam Smith, INF, So	.387	.488	.654	269	82	104	22	1	16	57	4
James Tibbs III, OF, Jr	.363	.488	.777	251	75	91	18	1	28	95	8
Marco Dinges, C, Jr	.323	.415	.583	235	60	76	12	2	15	69	2
Jaime Ferrer, OF, Jr	.317	.418	.665	230	54	73	8	3	22	67	3
Max Williams, OF, So	.311	.384	.582	225	57	70	11	4	14	46	5
Daniel Cantu, 1B, Sr	.308	.412	.509	234	51	72	16	2	9	43	4
Drew Faurot, INF, So	.286	.348	.465	217	45	62	19	1	6	29	10
Alex Lodise, INF, So	.281	.363	.470	217	50	61	14	0	9	44	6
Jaxson West, C, So	.274	.398	.404	146	36	40	8	1	3	29	2
Cal Fisher, INF, Fr	.273	.402	.515	66	14	18	1	0	5	13	0
McGwire Holbrook, C, Sr	.272	.352	.395	81	14	22	4	0	2	16	1
DeAmez Ross, OF, So	.253	.339	.368	95	26	24	3	1	2	19	8

Pitcher, Year	W	L	ERA	G	GS	SV	IP	H	BB	SO
Jamie Arnold, So	11	3	2.98	19	18	1	106	90	26	159
Brennen Oxford, Sr	2	1	3.43	32	0	6	58	54	28	70
Connor Hults, Jr	3	1	3.89	27	0	4	35	30	15	36
Carson Dorsey, Jr	8	4	4.60	23	11	3	76	82	37	88
Cam Leiter, So	5	1	4.63	7	7	0	35	32	22	56
John Abraham, Fr	5	2	4.72	25	3	1	34	20	31	42
Ben Barrett, So	1	0	5.27	8	0	1	14	17	4	12
Conner Whittaker, Jr	5	0	5.28	17	9	1	60	63	15	47
Joe Charles, Jr	1	0	5.94	30	0	2	33	28	19	37
Yoel Tejeda Jr., So	1	2	5.95	13	2	0	20	24	17	15
Andrew Armstrong, Sr	5	0	6.91	23	9	0	43	50	18	33
Matt Sauser, Fr	0	0	6.97	7	3	0	10	12	8	9
Brady Louck, Fr	1	1	7.06	14	4	0	22	27	15	27
Noah Short, Sr	1	1	7.71	22	0	1	21	19	21	30
Hudson Rowan, Fr	0	1	9.20	17	0	0	15	9	22	28

6. Florida

Coach: Kevin O'Sullivan. Overall: 36-30

Player, Pos, Yr	AVG	OBP	SLG	AB	R	H	2B	3B	HR	RBI	SB
Jac Caglianone, UT, Jr	.419	.544	.875	248	83	104	8	0	35	72	4
Ty Evans, OF, Jr	.316	.406	.580	193	44	61	10	1	13	43	2
Hayden Yost, OF, Fr	.284	.400	.358	67	10	19	5	0	0	4	4
Ashton Wilson, UT, So	.279	.405	.471	68	15	19	7	0	2	16	2
Tyler Shelnut, INF, Sr	.261	.360	.530	249	45	65	19	0	16	52	4
Michael Robertson, OF, So	.256	.319	.360	172	27	44	12	0	2	26	5
Colby Shelton, INF, So	.254	.374	.551	256	60	65	14	1	20	56	6
Tanner Garrison, C, Sr	.246	.348	.351	57	9	14	3	0	1	6	0
Brody Donay, C, So	.246	.323	.527	167	32	41	5	0	14	32	1
Luke Heyman, C, So	.246	.342	.481	264	46	65	14	0	16	52	1
Cade Kurland, INF, So	.245	.346	.457	245	51	60	8	1	14	44	5
Dale Thomas, INF, Sr	.225	.348	.344	151	23	34	9	0	3	21	4
Armando Albert, INF, Sr	.194	.431	.222	36	6	7	1	0	0	4	3
Jaylen Guy, OF, Sr	.143	.338	.163	49	7	7	1	0	0	2	2
Landon Russell, UT, So	.115	.172	.231	26	0	3	1	1	0	2	0

JAMES GILBERT/GETTY IMAGES

Cam Smith was the best hitter in a loaded Florida State lineup.

Pitcher, Year	W	L	ERA	G	GS	SV	IP	H	BB	SO
Fisher Jameson, Jr	5	0	3.99	34	1	3	68	60	18	79
Jac Caglianone, Jr	5	2	4.76	16	16	0	74	62	50	83
Frank Menendez, Fr	1	0	4.96	17	0	0	16	18	13	14
Brandon Neely, Jr	3	4	5.13	28	6	5	79	72	28	108
Jake Clemente, Fr	2	0	5.34	19	2	0	29	26	20	39
Liam Peterson, Fr	3	6	6.43	18	16	0	63	64	44	77
Ryan Slater, Jr	5	2	6.70	30	3	1	50	62	17	44
Alex Philpott, Fr	2	2	6.90	14	3	0	30	31	16	28
Luke McNeillie, Fr	4	6	7.07	26	2	2	36	33	21	43
Cade Fisher, So	4	3	7.13	26	9	1	59	67	29	76
Blake Purnell, Jr	0	0	7.78	21	0	0	20	28	6	21
Grayson Smith, Fr	0	1	8.66	15	0	0	18	19	11	25
Pierce Coppola, So	1	4	8.75	8	8	0	24	27	12	35

7. NC State

Coach: Elliott Avent. Overall: 38-23

Player, Pos, Yr	AVG	OBP	SLG	AB	R	H	2B	3B	HR	RBI	SB
Alec Makarewicz, INF, Sr	.378	.438	.753	259	66	98	25	0	24	84	1
Garrett Pennington, INF, Sr	.350	.435	.665	257	75	90	27	0	18	65	1
Josh Hogue, OF, So	.314	.398	.450	140	26	44	5	1	4	28	2
Jacob Cozart, C, Jr	.305	.437	.601	223	60	68	7	1	19	54	0
Eli Serrano III, OF, So	.285	.380	.431	246	56	70	9	0	9	39	7
Drew Lanphere, INF, Fr	.273	.367	.377	77	13	21	2	0	2	14	0
Chase Nixon, OF, Jr	.255	.402	.284	102	11	26	3	0	0	14	0
Matt Heavner, INF, So	.253	.357	.358	95	14	24	4	0	2	10	0
Brandon Butterworth, INF, Jr	.250	.369	.420	224	46	56	13	2	7	33	13
Luke Nixon, INF, Fr	.238	.394	.349	172	37	41	5	1	4	34	14
Alex Sosa, C, Fr	.230	.356	.398	113	16	26	1	0	6	24	1
Noah Soles, OF, Sr	.224	.388	.385	143	35	32	6	1	5	22	5
Robert Nedry, INF, Fr	.000	1.000	.000	0	0	0	0	0	0	0	0

Pitcher, Year	W	L	ERA	G	GS	SV	IP	H	BB	SO
Ryan Marohn, Fr	4	2	3.97	16	10	1	59	68	25	46
Jacob Dudan, Fr	4	2	4.50	27	0	6	48	37	34	56
Derrick Smith, So	3	2	4.55	24	0	8	30	19	11	41
Shane Van Dam, So	4	0	4.58	16	0	1	37	30	20	38

Pitcher, Year	W	L	ERA	G	GS	SV	IP	H	BB	SO
Cooper Consiglio, Fr	5	4	4.97	15	5	0	42	29	24	38
Sam Highfill, Sr	7	2	4.97	17	17	0	87	71	43	82
Logan Whitaker, Sr	3	1	5.49	13	9	0	59	59	22	69
Andrew Shaffner, So	0	0	5.56	7	0	1	11	10	5	8
Hollis Fanning, Sr	2	1	7.41	15	1	0	17	26	4	14
Dominic Fritton, So	3	7	7.64	17	17	0	73	72	47	72
Win Scott, Jr	0	1	9.00	8	0	0	10	8	8	10
Jaxon Lucas, Fr	1	0	9.43	15	1	0	21	30	12	22

8. Virginia

Coach: Brian O'Connor. Overall: 45-17

Player, Pos, Yr	AVG	OBP	SLG	AB	R	H	2B	3B	HR	RBI	SB
Henry Godbout, INF, So	.372	.472	.645	172	51	64	18	1	9	47	6
Eric Becker, INF, Fr	.362	.468	.669	127	36	46	9	3	8	46	4
Bobby Whalen, OF, Sr	.359	.446	.465	170	41	61	10	1	2	35	7
Jacob Ference, C, Sr	.350	.465	.710	200	55	70	13	4	17	43	12
Casey Saucke, INF, Jr	.344	.407	.578	256	56	88	18	0	14	65	9
Henry Ford, INF, Fr	.336	.409	.597	253	60	85	13	1	17	69	3
Ethan Anderson, C, Jr	.331	.435	.508	248	67	82	20	0	8	40	5
Griff O'Ferrall, INF, Jr	.324	.367	.454	284	64	92	20	1	5	52	17
Anthony Stephan, INF, Jr	.306	.440	.455	134	28	41	10	2	2	23	7
Harrison Didawick, OF, So	.292	.414	.642	240	78	70	13	1	23	68	14
Luke Hanson, INF, So	.286	.387	.490	147	34	42	7	1	7	37	3

Pitcher, Year	W	L	ERA	G	GS	SV	IP	H	BB	SO
Bryson Moore, Fr	2	0	1.38	7	4	0	13	16	8	10
Dean Kampschror, Jr	2	0	3.48	18	0	0	10	7	8	10
Evan Blanco, So	8	3	3.62	18	18	0	99	101	27	99
Chase Hungate, So	7	2	3.74	30	0	2	53	49	13	37
Angelo Tonas, Sr	3	0	3.76	33	0	1	38	39	10	30
Matt Augustin, Fr	2	0	4.13	22	1	0	28	29	13	25
Joe Savino, Jr	3	2	4.50	9	8	0	30	28	11	24
Matthew Buchanan, Jr	0	0	4.76	9	1	0	11	13	6	10
Ryan Osinski, Jr	4	1	4.80	27	0	0	30	34	14	13
Jay Woolfolk, Jr	4	2	5.92	24	7	0	62	65	40	67
Owen Coady, Sr	1	1	5.94	15	7	1	33	36	22	29
Blake Barker, Jr	2	1	7.31	27	0	1	28	37	18	26
Jack O'Connor, So	0	1	7.50	9	3	2	18	26	7	24
Aidan Teel, So	2	2	7.88	20	0	6	24	27	16	32
Cullen McKay, So	2	1	8.45	13	7	0	33	33	28	39
Kevin Jaxel, So	4	1	10.38	13	4	0	26	36	18	21

9. Oregon State

Coach: Mitch Canham. Overall: 45-16

Player, Pos, Yr	AVG	OBP	SLG	AB	R	H	2B	3B	HR	RBI	SB
Travis Bazzana, INF, Jr	.407	.568	.911	214	84	87	16	4	28	66	16
Micah McDowell, OF, Sr	.302	.405	.632	136	42	52	12	2	6	33	3
Trent Caraway, INF, Fr	.339	.431	.516	62	16	21	5	0	2	10	4
Easton Talt, C, So	.318	.423	.409	44	9	14	1	0	1	8	2
Dallas Macias, INF, So	.315	.389	.512	213	42	67	14	2	8	41	9
Jabin Trosky, INF, So	.287	.362	.357	115	22	33	3	1	1	20	3
Elijah Hainline, INF, Jr	.280	.402	.537	214	50	60	16	3	11	45	6
Jacob Krieg, INF, So	.278	.453	.535	144	40	40	10	0	9	40	0
Gavin Turley, OF, So	.277	.412	.589	231	53	64	13	1	19	74	6
Wilson Weber, C, Jr	.276	.380	.569	116	32	32	7	3	7	22	0
Tyce Peterson, INF, So	.275	.412	.550	40	13	11	2	0	3	9	1
Canon Reeder, OF, So	.273	.380	.379	66	14	18	5	1	0	13	5
Brady Kasper, OF, Sr	.271	.398	.496	129	28	35	6	1	7	33	2
Mason Guerra, INF, Jr	.243	.360	.467	214	44	52	13	1	11	55	0
Tanner Smith, C, Jr	.221	.359	.423	104	23	23	4	1	5	19	1

Pitcher, Year	W	L	ERA	G	GS	SV	IP	H	BB	SO
Bridger Holmes, Jr	3	4	1.93	26	0	13	33	16	15	47
Tyler Mejia, So	2	0	2.53	9	1	0	11	14	5	10
Joey Mundt, Sr	2	0	2.67	24	0	0	30	17	12	33
Aiden May, Jr	7	1	3.05	14	14	0	74	61	23	84
Jacob Kmatz, Jr	7	3	3.38	16	16	0	88	66	22	96
Nelson Keljo, So	3	0	3.98	20	3	0	43	45	14	60
Ian Lawson, Sr	2	0	4.07	12	1	1	24	24	17	23
Noah Ferguson, Jr	1	0	4.40	13	0	0	14	11	14	19
Kellan Oakes, So	3	1	4.43	18	0	0	22	18	12	17
Drew Talavs, Fr	0	0	4.63	11	0	0	12	18	3	11
Eric Segura, Fr	6	1	4.93	15	15	0	69	66	23	72
Jaren Hunter, Sr	1	2	4.96	13	8	1	45	51	18	25
AJ Hutcheson, So	4	2	5.96	22	0	0	26	16	12	21
Matthew Morrell, Fr	1	0	7.50	15	0	1	12	17	10	7

10. Georgia

Coach: Wes Johnson. Overall: 43-17

Player, Pos, Yr	AVG	OBP	SLG	AB	R	H	2B	3B	HR	RBI	SB
Charlie Condon, 1B, So	.433	.556	1.009	231	84	100	20	1	37	78	3
Corey Collins, C, Sr	.354	.574	.772	158	55	56	6	0	20	58	0
Tre Phelps, INF, Fr	.353	.441	.699	136	34	48	11	0	12	40	2
Paul Toetz, INF, Sr	.348	.448	.543	138	30	48	10	1	5	23	4
Slate Alford, INF, Jr	.300	.370	.539	267	55	80	13	0	17	69	1
Fernando Gonzalez, C, Sr	.292	.364	.532	171	39	50	10	2	9	53	0
Dylan Goldstein, OF, Sr	.273	.421	.570	165	49	45	11	1	12	43	0
Clayton Chadwick, OF, Sr	.269	.418	.444	160	39	43	16	0	4	26	4
Kolby Branch, INF, So	.267	.366	.538	225	49	60	10	0	17	58	2
Henry Hunter, C, Jr	.264	.379	.500	72	20	19	5	0	4	12	1
Sebastian Murillo, INF, Sr	.253	.396	.361	83	21	21	3	0	2	14	1
Logan Jordan, C, Sr	.241	.425	.430	79	10	19	3	0	4	19	0
Trey King, INF, Fr	.231	.310	.269	26	10	6	1	0	0	1	0
Dillon Carter, OF, Sr	.220	.439	.500	82	34	18	2	0	7	15	2

Pitcher, Year	W	L	ERA	G	GS	SV	IP	H	BB	SO
Zach DeVito, Sr	2	0	2.79	11	1	0	10	7	7	6
DJ Radtke, So	1	0	3.45	17	0	0	16	11	11	20
Charlie Goldstein, Sr	4	1	3.72	11	7	0	36	35	14	43
Leighton Finley, So	6	1	4.14	17	16	1	76	74	28	76
Christian Mracna, Sr	4	2	5.32	20	10	1	46	48	25	73
Jarvis Evans, So	3	2	5.49	16	8	0	39	38	27	47
Kolten Smith, So	9	3	5.56	20	4	0	70	73	20	105
Brian Zeldin, Sr	3	3	5.66	23	0	6	56	55	30	51
Zachary Harris, So	5	2	6.87	20	7	0	38	45	18	45
Josh Roberge, Sr	3	1	7.00	22	0	1	36	44	19	37
Max DeJong, Sr	0	0	7.20	10	0	0	10	11	4	7
Chandler Marsh, Jr	2	0	7.20	12	1	1	15	15	8	21
Daniel Padysak, Sr	1	0	7.66	15	2	0	22	23	15	21
Brandt Pancer, Sr	0	0	10.80	10	1	0	10	9	10	11

11. Clemson

Coach: Erik Bakich. Overall: 44-16

Player, Pos, Yr	AVG	OBP	SLG	AB	R	H	2B	3B	HR	RBI	SB
Blake Wright, INF, Sr	.340	.382	.652	256	68	87	10	2	22	75	0
Cam Cannarella, OF, So	.337	.417	.561	246	58	83	16	3	11	60	0
Jacob Hinderleider, INF, Sr	.336	.407	.580	238	44	80	17	1	13	60	9
Jack Crighton, UT, So	.313	.377	.391	115	16	36	7	1	0	12	3
Alden Mathes, OF, Sr	.308	.445	.504	224	64	69	12	1	10	33	5
Jimmy Obertop, UT, Sr	.303	.438	.656	218	62	66	11	0	22	56	1
Tristan Bissetta, OF, So	.298	.401	.511	141	29	42	7	1	7	34	3
Jacob Jarrell, C, So	.289	.388	.526	97	21	28	5	0	6	24	0
Andrew Ciufo, INF, Jr	.280	.378	.387	93	19	26	2	1	2	16	5
Nolan Nawrocki, INF, Fr	.264	.352	.400	125	28	33	5	0	4	24	11
Jarren Purify, INF, Fr	.248	.345	.358	165	32	41	7	1	3	28	11
Will Taylor, OF, Jr	.230	.465	.480	100	28	23	2	1	7	19	6
Cooper Blauser, INF, Fr	.103	.270	.241	29	4	3	1	0	1	3	0

Pithcer, Year	W	L	ERA	G	GS	SV	IP	H	BB	SO
Jacob McGovern, Fr	3	0	1.96	11	0	0	18	13	8	20
Drew Titsworth, Fr	4	0	3.15	19	0	0	20	10	12	26
Aidan Knaak, Fr	5	1	3.35	15	15	0	83	67	29	108
Billy Barlow, So	6	1	4.28	15	10	0	48	50	20	42
Austin Gordon, Jr	2	2	4.35	22	5	11	39	33	18	53
Tristan Smith, So	2	1	4.47	12	12	0	50	47	32	66
Matthew Marchal, Sr	5	0	4.71	16	3	1	36	38	15	35
Lucas Mahlstedt, Jr	4	1	4.73	28	0	1	53	56	15	39
Ethan Darden, So	5	5	5.13	19	11	0	67	81	15	42
Reed Garris, Jr	2	1	5.55	20	0	0	24	20	6	25
Rocco Reid, Jr	2	1	5.82	15	3	0	22	19	15	26
Joe Allen, So	1	0	6.35	12	0	0	23	16	13	25
Nick Clayton, Sr	2	0	6.64	15	0	0	20	21	13	23
Rob Hughes, Sr	1	1	9.53	13	0	3	11	14	8	12

12. Oregon

Coach: Mark Wasikowski. Overall: 40-20

Player, Pos, Yr	AVG	OBP	SLG	AB	R	H	2B	3B	HR	RBI	SB
Chase Meggers, C, So	.316	.395	.480	152	32	48	8	1	5	33	2
Maddox Molony, INF, Fr	.315	.402	.566	143	32	45	4	1	10	31	2
Drew Smith, INF, So	.314	.422	.451	204	38	64	16	0	4	29	5
Jeffery Heard, OF, Jr	.299	.386	.469	177	34	53	16	1	4	30	1
Carter Garate, INF, So	.289	.390	.402	194	41	56	13	0	3	27	2
Bennett Thompson, C, Jr	.286	.391	.423	168	35	48	8	3	3	24	8
Anson Aroz, C, So	.281	.365	.466	146	27	41	9	0	6	25	2
Bryce Boettcher, OF, Sr	.276	.372	.500	192	46	53	7	0	12	35	15
Dominic Hellman, INF, So	.271	.317	.508	59	6	16	2	0	4	9	0
Mason Neville, OF, So	.268	.369	.664	149	36	40	5	3	16	43	8
Jacob Walsh, 1B, Jr	.254	.348	.548	228	38	58	13	0	18	56	1
Justin Cassella, OF, Sr	.250	.399	.460	124	29	31	5	0	7	28	12
Ryan Cooney, INF, Fr	.203	.323	.468	79	16	16	1	1	6	12	0

Pitcher, Year	W	L	ERA	G	GS	SV	IP	H	BB	SO
Bradley Mullan, Sr	4	1	1.66	26	0	4	38	28	22	33
Logan Mercado, Sr	1	1	3.65	27	0	8	44	40	21	47
Ryan Featherston, Fr	1	2	3.76	19	0	2	41	26	20	41
Ian Umlandt, So	4	0	3.94	8	4	0	30	18	10	23
Grayson Grinsell, So	7	2	4.08	17	14	0	79	54	44	99
Kevin Seitter, Sr	8	4	4.52	15	15	0	82	72	34	80
Toby Twist, Fr	0	0	4.60	4	2	0	16	14	9	21
RJ Gordon, Jr	7	6	5.13	17	17	0	95	92	46	87
Brock Moore, Sr	4	1	5.81	17	1	1	31	28	20	52
Michael Freund, Sr	3	1	5.92	11	3	1	24	32	7	20
Collin Clarke, Fr	0	0	6.41	13	1	0	20	31	4	14
Turner Spoljaric, So	0	2	14.18	10	3	0	13	23	11	7

13. West Virginia

Coach: Randy Mazey. Overall: 36-24

Player, Pos, Yr	AVG	OBP	SLG	AB	R	H	2B	3B	HR	RBI	SB
J.J. Wetherholt, INF, Jr	.331	.472	.589	124	30	41	8	0	8	30	6
Reed Chumley, INF, Sr	.311	.404	.653	196	45	61	15	2	16	50	3
Logan Sauve, C, So	.308	.379	.484	182	42	56	8	0	8	37	2
Sam White, INF, So	.305	.406	.498	213	47	65	9	1	10	42	5
Brodie Kresser, INF, Jr	.278	.409	.424	144	27	40	7	1	4	24	13
Spencer Barnett, INF, Fr	.269	.380	.365	104	20	28	4	0	2	21	4
Kyle West, INF, Jr	.260	.344	.536	196	38	51	10	1	14	43	8
Michael Perazza, OF, Fr	.258	.313	.371	62	7	16	4	0	1	7	1
Skylar King, OF, So	.258	.335	.406	155	33	40	8	0	5	26	9
Ben Lumsden, INF, So	.251	.365	.429	175	33	44	10	0	7	25	3
Grant Hussey, 1B, Jr	.242	.339	.489	186	34	45	8	1	12	37	7
Ellis Garcia, INF, So	.241	.291	.310	116	11	28	5	0	1	16	7
Aaron Jamison, OF, Fr	.230	.329	.419	74	17	17	3	1	3	16	8
Nick Barone, 1B, So	.080	.233	.080	25	3	2	0	0	0	2	0

Pitcher, Year	W	L	ERA	G	GS	SV	IP	H	BB	SO
Jospeph Fredericks, Fr	0	0	1.13	18	0	0	16	8	12	10
Gavin Van Kempen, So	7	1	3.14	13	5	0	29	20	14	35
Carson Estridge, So	1	2	3.21	21	4	4	42	35	20	48
Derek Clark, Sr	8	3	3.23	14	13	0	98	83	23	91
Max Yehl, So	2	0	3.99	24	0	2	29	26	18	32
Hambleton Oliver, Sr	2	2	4.69	21	1	3	40	38	22	39
Tyler Switalski, Jr	5	3	5.10	18	14	0	67	67	35	58
Aidan Major, Jr	5	4	5.59	14	12	0	66	62	35	77
David Hagaman, Jr	2	3	5.91	14	1	2	35	30	19	49
Hayden Cooper, Sr	1	4	6.40	17	8	0	52	73	16	32
Chase Meyer, Fr	1	1	8.38	13	1	0	19	17	24	28
Robby Porco, So	2	1	8.71	13	1	0	10	10	17	11

14. UConn

Coach: Jim Penders. Overall: 35-26

Player, Pos, Yr	AVG	OBP	SLG	AB	R	H	2B	3B	HR	RBI	SB
Korey Morton, OF, Sr	.325	.375	.539	243	44	79	19	0	11	49	19
Paul Tammaro, INF, Sr	.306	.443	.414	232	55	71	11	1	4	37	16
Luke Broadhurst, 3B, Sr	.303	.408	.587	208	38	63	10	2	15	58	4
Matt Garbowski, C, Jr	.285	.387	.399	158	18	45	6	0	4	20	0
Bryan Padilla, INF, Sr	.278	.376	.444	198	31	55	13	1	6	39	2
Jacob Studley, OF, Sr	.271	.363	.467	214	42	58	12	0	10	27	4
Tyler Minick, INF, Fr	.266	.304	.525	139	22	37	7	1	9	28	4
Caleb Shpur, OF, Sr	.265	.372	.383	196	48	52	14	0	3	22	26
Maddix Dalena, 1B, So	.242	.358	.511	190	39	46	12	0	13	43	1
T.C. Simmons, OF, Sr	.222	.355	.349	63	12	14	4	2	0	4	1
Matt Malcom, C, Sr	.213	.352	.551	89	22	19	3	0	9	20	0
Ryan Daniels, ph, So	.183	.319	.367	60	10	11	2	0	3	13	5
Drew Kron, OF, So	.175	.250	.225	40	6	7	2	0	0	5	1
Ryan Hyde, C, Sr	.105	.227	.158	38	5	4	2	0	0	5	0

EDDIE KELLY

J.J. Wetherholt couldn't defend his 2023 D-I batting title, but he did hit .331.

Pitcher, Year	W	L	ERA	G	GS	SV	IP	H	BB	SO
Brady Afthim, Jr	2	3	2.84	22	0	8	25	17	15	27
Braden Quinn, Jr	2	3	3.63	29	0	4	45	42	22	67
Stephen Quigley, Sr	6	3	4.01	19	17	0	103	113	25	87
Jack Sullivan, Jr	2	0	4.05	16	0	1	13	12	6	15
Ben Schild, Fr	3	0	4.71	8	4	0	21	17	15	19
Ian Cooke, Jr	5	2	4.81	17	10	0	67	57	25	85
Garrett Coe, Sr	8	5	5.23	21	17	0	103	100	45	86
Kieran Finnegan, Sr	0	1	5.56	11	0	0	11	11	4	11
Gabe Van Emon, Sr	4	5	5.88	17	10	0	60	61	26	64
Joe Cinnella, Sr	3	3	6.16	23	3	0	31	38	13	27
Thomas Ellisen, Jr	0	1	6.52	17	0	0	19	16	14	12
Joe Carrea, Jr	0	0	7.84	17	0	0	10	17	8	14

15. Arkansas

Coach: Dave Van Horn. Overall: 44-16

Player, Pos, Yr	AVG	OBP	SLG	AB	R	H	2B	3B	HR	RBI	SB
Peyton Stovall, INF, Jr	.340	.409	.535	200	39	68	12	0	9	38	2
Peyton Holt, UT, Sr	.322	.412	.507	152	31	49	2	1	8	27	6
Ben McLaughlin, INF, Sr	.302	.447	.490	202	42	61	11	0	9	42	0
Hudson White, C, Jr	.297	.396	.525	158	30	47	12	0	8	33	0
Jared Sprague-Lott, INF, Sr	.290	.425	.491	169	45	49	7	0	9	28	4
Ross Lovich, OF, Sr	.286	.408	.429	84	19	24	4	1	2	16	2
Wehiwa Aloy, INF, So	.270	.355	.485	237	45	64	9	0	14	56	7
Jack Wagner, UT, Sr	.260	.344	.500	50	10	13	3	0	3	11	1
Nolan Souza, INF, Fr	.255	.366	.509	110	21	28	7	0	7	28	3
Parker Rowland, C, Sr	.241	.410	.414	29	5	7	2	0	1	4	1
Will Edmunson, OF, Jr	.241	.362	.333	87	26	21	5	0	1	10	6

Player, Pos, Yr	AVG	OBP	SLG	AB	R	H	2B	3B	HR	RBI	SB
Kendall Diggs, OF, Jr	.229	.346	.395	205	35	47	11	1	7	34	4
Ty Wilmsmeyer, OF, Sr	.214	.319	.256	117	20	25	2	0	1	13	4
Jayson Jones, UT, So	.194	.301	.403	72	11	14	3	0	4	17	3
Ryder Helfrick, C, Fr	.179	.320	.321	84	18	15	3	0	3	8	1

Pitcher, Year	W	L	ERA	G	GS	SV	IP	H	BB	SO
Christian Foutch, So	1	0	0.81	20	0	1	22	19	7	20
Jake Faherty, Jr	0	1	1.84	16	0	1	15	8	9	26
Hagen Smith, Jr	9	2	2.04	16	16	0	84	41	34	161
Gabe Gaeckle, Fr	3	3	2.32	22	0	7	43	26	19	57
Colin Fisher, Fr	6	1	2.67	10	7	0	27	24	8	27
Stone Hewlett, Sr	1	0	3.46	23	0	4	13	6	8	23
Brady Tygart, Jr	4	3	3.94	14	13	0	59	46	36	69
Gage Wood, So	3	2	4.46	22	3	2	40	42	8	56
Mason Molina, Jr	4	2	4.47	15	13	0	58	39	36	81
Will McEntire, Sr	5	0	4.83	30	1	4	54	56	18	65
Cooper Dossett, So	3	1	5.17	14	0	0	16	7	7	20
Koty Frank, Sr	2	0	5.58	20	0	4	31	30	9	30
Ben Bybee, So	2	1	5.83	11	7	0	29	30	12	36
Parker Coil, So	0	0	7.23	16	0	0	19	25	6	23
Dylan Carter, Jr	1	0	8.18	8	0	0	11	12	6	6

16. East Carolina

Coach: Cliff Godwin. Overall: 46-17

Player, Pos, Yr	AVG	OBP	SLG	AB	R	H	2B	3B	HR	RBI	SB
Carter Cunningham, UT, Sr	.367	.464	.653	251	77	92	17	2	17	66	6
Bristol Carter, OF, Fr	.346	.406	.440	159	30	55	7	1	2	31	4
Ryan McCrystal, C, Jr	.346	.402	.521	188	26	65	10	1	7	39	2
Jacob Jenkins-Cowart, OF, Jr	.340	.386	.558	265	61	90	19	0	13	79	7
Ryley Johnson, OF, Jr	.339	.461	.476	227	75	77	9	5	4	33	23
Dixon Williams, INF, So	.308	.406	.490	208	44	64	11	0	9	43	5
Cam Clonch, UT, Sr	.300	.400	.440	50	6	15	1	0	2	14	0
Justin Wilcoxen, C, Sr	.293	.369	.502	229	40	67	6	0	14	47	2
Jacob Starling, INF, Sr	.282	.404	.500	188	42	53	12	1	9	44	9
Colby Wallace, UT, Fr	.261	.363	.304	69	15	18	1	1	0	6	0
Joey Berini, INF, Sr	.225	.310	.329	213	37	48	4	3	4	36	3
Luke Nowak, OF, Jr	.222	.347	.346	81	21	18	2	1	2	16	6

Pitcher, Year	W	L	ERA	G	GS	SV	IP	H	BB	SO
Wyatt Lunsford-Shenkman, Jr	3	2	1.55	24	1	5	46	37	21	79
Trey Yesavage, Jr	11	1	2.03	15	15	0	93	49	32	145
Aaron Groller, Sr	2	1	3.34	24	4	1	32	34	10	26
Danny Beal, Sr	8	2	3.38	35	0	4	72	65	23	52
Zach Root, So	6	2	3.56	13	12	0	68	56	21	76
Ethan Norby, Fr	4	0	3.79	20	10	2	59	54	25	63
Jake Hunter, Jr	3	2	4.05	14	6	1	40	31	16	37
Jackson DiLorenzo, Fr	2	2	4.62	20	0	0	25	23	10	26
Erik Ritchie, So	1	1	6.67	28	4	0	30	22	27	33
Christopher Kahler, Sr	1	1	7.62	21	6	1	39	48	16	40
Jaden Winter, Jr	2	2	7.96	22	2	0	26	31	20	31

17. Mississippi State

Coach: Chris Lemonis. Overall: 40-23

Player, Pos, Yr	AVG	OBP	SLG	AB	R	H	2B	3B	HR	RBI	SB
Dakota Jordan, OF, So	.354	.459	.671	240	57	85	14	1	20	72	3
David Mershon, INF, So	.347	.454	.500	222	60	77	12	2	6	41	27
Connor Hujsak, INF, Sr	.325	.413	.555	200	52	65	13	3	9	49	8
Aaron Downs, INF, Jr	.305	.394	.347	95	16	29	4	0	0	9	0
Bryce Chance, OF, So	.286	.370	.429	217	36	62	11	1	6	36	8
Nolan Stevens, OF, Fr	.269	.321	.423	26	2	7	1	0	1	2	0
Joe Powell, C, Sr	.269	.343	.462	93	17	25	3	0	5	18	0
Dylan Cupp, INF, Fr	.258	.367	.318	66	13	17	4	0	0	13	4
Hunter Hines, INF, Jr	.257	.346	.486	249	41	64	9	0	16	56	0
Amani Larry, INF, Sr	.252	.394	.413	230	53	58	13	0	8	33	11
Logan Kohler, INF, Sr	.244	.351	.389	193	34	47	10	0	6	32	2
Ethan Pulliam, INF, Fr	.227	.307	.348	66	7	15	5	0	1	11	1
Nate Chester, INF, Jr	.206	.386	.265	34	7	7	2	0	0	3	0
Johnny Long, C, Sr	.188	.354	.214	117	21	22	0	0	1	12	2

Pitcher, Year	W	L	ERA	G	GS	SV	IP	H	BB	SO
Nate Dohm, Jr	4	0	1.23	8	6	0	29	23	4	37
Tyler Davis, Sr	6	1	2.80	28	0	5	35	28	14	41
Tyson Hardin, Jr	3	3	3.22	25	2	2	36	33	23	36
Khal Stephen, Jr	8	3	3.28	16	16	0	96	76	21	107
Brooks Auger, Jr	1	2	3.35	20	5	2	46	37	17	50
Pico Kohn, So	1	1	3.38	9	8	0	29	26	11	35
Jurrangelo Cijntje, So	8	2	3.67	16	16	0	91	70	30	113
Cam Schuelke, Jr	5	3	4.21	32	0	2	47	41	23	47
Karson Ligon, Jr	1	0	4.56	15	2	0	24	17	21	21
Nolan Stevens, Fr	2	3	4.73	14	1	0	27	27	8	28
Gavin Black, So	0	0	5.93	12	0	0	14	13	8	22
Evan Siary, So	0	3	7.48	10	4	0	22	28	6	22
Luke Dotson, Fr	0	0	8.25	11	0	0	12	15	5	19
Colby Holcombe, Jr	1	1	10.38	12	1	0	22	26	12	28

EDDIE KELLY

Carson Benge hit 18 home runs, and he also won three games on the mound.

18. Oklahoma State

Coach: Josh Holliday. Overall: 42-19

Player, Pos, Yr	AVG	OBP	SLG	AB	R	H	2B	3B	HR	RBI	SB
Nolan Schubart, OF, So	.370	.513	.838	173	55	64	10	1	23	68	0
Carson Benge, UT, So	.335	.444	.665	248	72	83	24	2	18	64	10
Zach Ehrhard, UT, Jr	.330	.458	.627	233	75	77	25	1	14	57	7
Aidan Meola, INF, Jr	.329	.416	.590	161	32	53	12	0	10	47	0
Lane Forsythe, INF, Sr	.287	.414	.371	202	53	58	6	1	3	29	12
Kollin Ritchie, INF, Fr	.271	.419	.457	140	25	38	3	1	7	28	4
Avery Ortiz, INF, Fr	.258	.374	.447	190	36	49	9	0	9	34	6
Ian Daugherty, C, Jr	.252	.358	.511	139	25	35	6	0	10	32	1
Colin Brueggemann, 1B, Jr	.251	.344	.507	223	44	56	13	1	14	50	0
Tyler Wulfert, INF, Sr	.229	.313	.376	157	28	36	8	0	5	23	3
Jaxson Crull, OF, Sr	.224	.366	.398	98	28	22	5	0	4	18	4
Donovan LaSalle, OF, Fr	.194	.383	.333	36	5	7	2	0	1	3	0
Charlie Carter, C, Fr	.070	.209	.088	57	6	4	1	0	0	2	0

Pitcher, Year	W	L	ERA	G	GS	SV	IP	H	BB	SO
Robert Cranz, Jr	2	1	1.63	30	0	2	50	26	12	59
Brian Holiday, Jr	7	3	2.95	16	16	0	113	82	19	128
Carson Benge, So	3	2	3.16	18	4	3	37	26	11	44
Janzen Keisel, Jr	2	1	3.38	11	8	0	35	23	22	40
Sam Garcia, Sr	7	3	3.64	16	16	0	89	77	19	115
Gabe Davis, So	2	4	4.17	18	5	3	45	36	25	55
Tommy Molsky, So	6	3	4.83	19	2	0	41	40	27	66
Brennan Phillips, So	2	0	4.91	11	2	0	15	18	5	16

Pitcher, Year	W	L	ERA	G	GS	SV	IP	H	BB	SO
Dominick Reid, So	1	0	5.28	9	4	0	15	18	8	23
Drew Blake, So	4	0	5.50	23	0	0	18	24	7	20
Evan O'Toole, Sr	2	0	5.83	17	0	1	29	36	11	34
Ryan Bogusz, Sr	1	1	7.47	19	3	0	31	38	15	34
Bryson Hudgens, Sr	1	0	8.10	7	0	0	10	20	4	14

19. Oklahoma

Coach: Skip Johnson. Overall: 40-21

Player, Pos, Yr	AVG	OBP	SLG	AB	R	H	2B	3B	HR	RBI	SB
John Spikerman, OF, Jr	.367	.429	.542	166	42	61	12	4	3	32	11
Easton Carmichael, C, So	.366	.406	.563	254	59	93	19	5	7	64	12
Michael Snyder, INF, Sr	.354	.465	.638	229	57	81	26	3	11	59	16
Carter Frederick, OF, Jr	.343	.400	.543	35	10	12	1	0	2	9	0
Isaiah Lane, INF, Fr	.321	.464	.396	53	14	17	2	1	0	6	3
Bryce Madron, OF, Sr	.318	.439	.607	211	68	67	19	3	12	53	14
Jackson Nicklaus, INF, Jr	.303	.429	.533	195	47	59	9	3	10	37	6
Anthony MacKenzie, INF, Sr	.291	.407	.453	203	50	59	10	1	7	44	6
Jason Walk, UT, Fr	.281	.376	.414	128	26	36	4	2	3	19	13
Scott Mudler, C, Jr	.279	.367	.401	147	25	41	6	0	4	31	1
Kendall Pettis, OF, Sr	.276	.398	.398	196	47	54	8	2	4	34	10
Jaxon Willits, INF, Fr	.268	.376	.484	190	37	51	11	0	10	39	1
Rocco Garza-Gongora, INF, So	.224	.338	.259	58	8	13	2	0	0	11	1

Pitcher, Year	W	L	ERA	G	GS	SV	IP	H	BB	SO
Ryan Lambert, Jr	4	0	2.57	23	0	1	21	14	12	19
Reid Hensley, Jr	0	0	3.21	17	0	0	14	9	10	22
Kyson Witherspoon, So	8	3	3.71	17	11	1	80	69	40	90
Carson Atwood, Sr	1	2	3.96	26	4	0	36	33	14	30
Dylan Crooks, Jr	1	0	4.11	25	0	0	31	31	3	20
Grant Stevens, Sr	6	1	4.28	18	9	0	55	65	20	54
Braden Davis, Jr	9	4	4.30	16	16	0	92	70	41	117
Jace Miner, Jr	1	1	4.50	13	0	0	10	11	7	12
Jett Lodes, Sr	2	1	4.80	17	1	0	30	21	17	31
Malachi Witherspoon, So	2	2	5.64	21	0	5	22	22	10	29
Carter Campbell, Sr	4	1	5.64	28	1	1	45	45	20	35
Brendan Girton, Sr	0	1	7.32	16	10	1	36	44	31	47
James Hitt, Jr	2	4	8.41	17	7	0	35	49	14	32
Will Carsten, Sr	0	1	8.66	13	2	0	18	26	12	12

20. UC Santa Barbara

Coach: Andrew Checketts. Overall: 44-14

Player, Pos, Yr	AVG	OBP	SLG	AB	R	H	2B	3B	HR	RBI	SB
Aaron Parker, C, Jr	.379	.460	.632	190	42	72	12	0	12	51	0
Jessada Brown, UT, Jr	.350	.429	.560	200	42	70	12	0	10	42	6
Brendan Durfee, C, Sr	.349	.455	.566	175	41	61	11	0	9	35	2
LeTrey McCollum, OF, Jr	.320	.400	.383	128	33	41	8	0	0	14	10
Nick Oakley, INF, Sr	.315	.401	.479	219	46	69	11	5	5	49	8
Ivan Brethowr, OF, Jr	.275	.402	.566	189	38	52	10	0	15	39	6
Zander Darby, INF, Jr	.275	.347	.420	193	37	53	6	2	6	33	5
Jonathan Mendez, INF, Fr	.272	.354	.389	180	32	49	9	0	4	30	4
Jonah Sebring, INF, Sr	.271	.337	.486	177	37	48	13	2	7	37	9
Justin Trimble, UT, Jr	.248	.380	.461	206	38	51	8	0	12	50	4
Reiss Calvin, INF, Jr	.214	.409	.330	112	27	24	7	0	2	15	9
Corey Nunez, INF, So	.194	.306	.290	31	8	6	0	0	1	10	1

Pitcher, Year	W	L	ERA	G	GS	SV	IP	H	BB	SO
Ryan Gallagher, Jr	10	1	2.22	14	14	0	89	50	25	96
Tyler Bremner, So	11	1	2.54	19	9	0	89	57	21	104
Mike Gutierrez, Sr	10	0	3.18	16	16	0	91	70	34	86
Cole Tryba, Fr	3	2	3.64	27	1	3	47	42	14	65
Jackson Flora, Fr	3	2	3.83	23	4	5	47	43	25	40
Matt Ager, Jr	3	4	4.02	24	9	11	63	59	28	59
Calvin Proskey, Fr	1	0	6.10	8	0	0	10	10	11	6
Reed Moring, So	1	3	7.12	16	3	0	30	42	20	31
Frank Camarillo, So	2	0	7.97	13	1	0	20	27	12	18

21. Arizona

Coach: Chip Hale. Overall: 36-23

Player, Pos, Yr	AVG	OBP	SLG	AB	R	H	2B	3B	HR	RBI	SB
TJ Adams, OF, Fr	.357	.413	.619	42	10	15	2	3	1	3	4
Brendan Summerhill, OF, So	.324	.399	.550	238	50	77	18	6	8	59	7
Garen Caulfield, INF, Jr	.310	.391	.469	239	38	74	19	2	5	42	0
Mason White, INF, So	.305	.392	.603	239	55	73	10	2	19	65	5
Blake McDonald, C, Sr	.297	.404	.418	91	15	27	5	0	2	18	0
Andrew Cain, INF, Fr	.290	.357	.520	100	15	29	8	0	5	23	0
Richie Morales, INF, Jr	.283	.397	.342	152	38	43	9	0	0	19	4
Adonys Guzman, C, So	.265	.384	.324	136	21	36	5	0	1	17	0
Emilio Corona, OF, Sr	.262	.322	.444	214	42	56	7	7	6	30	15
Maddox Mihalakis, INF, So	.259	.311	.386	166	24	43	10	1	3	32	1
Easton Breyfogle, OF, Fr	.252	.366	.381	139	28	35	9	3	1	14	7
Tommy Splaine, C, Jr	.230	.304	.361	183	28	42	5	2	5	23	1
Brandon Rogers, OF, So	.185	.284	.231	65	12	12	0	0	1	2	2
Xavier Esquer, INF, Fr	.129	.206	.161	31	3	4	1	0	0	1	0

Pitcher, Year	W	L	ERA	G	GS	SV	IP	H	BB	SO
Tony Pluta, So	2	1	3.07	25	0	2	29	23	2	21
Cam Walty, Sr	8	2	3.29	16	14	0	90	98	13	75
Clark Candiotti, Sr	7	4	3.39	16	16	0	96	88	23	103
Jackson Kent, So	3	4	4.08	15	15	0	86	83	27	89
Casey Hintz, So	3	1	4.13	27	0	2	33	48	12	24
Kyler Heyne, Jr	3	0	4.15	25	0	0	26	29	7	31
Dawson Netz, Sr	2	0	4.29	20	0	0	21	19	5	27
Jaeden Swanberg, Sr	2	1	4.76	19	0	0	17	17	4	16
Bradon Zastrow, Sr	1	2	4.84	17	3	0	22	27	13	26
Eric Orloff, Jr	1	3	5.11	24	0	0	25	26	8	23
Trevor Long, Sr	1	1	5.27	12	0	0	14	13	5	8
Anthony Susac, Jr	2	2	6.59	21	5	3	29	41	7	36
Matthew Martinez, Jr	0	0	7.04	15	0	0	15	20	6	17
Raul Garayzar, Jr	0	2	11.12	8	3	1	11	22	6	12

22. Kansas State

Coach: Pete Hughes. Overall: 35-26

Player, Pos, Yr	AVG	OBP	SLG	AB	R	H	2B	3B	HR	RBI	SB
Kaelen Culpepper, INF, Jr	.328	.419	.574	244	50	80	15	6	11	59	17
Brady Day, INF, Jr	.318	.426	.513	236	47	75	15	2	9	56	16
Brendan Jones, OF, Jr	.303	.442	.500	234	69	71	13	3	9	35	40
Jaden Parson, INF, Sr	.293	.400	.374	123	22	36	4	0	2	17	9
Chuck Ingram, OF, Sr	.279	.344	.484	244	49	68	11	3	11	31	9
Jayden Lobliner, C, So	.268	.355	.402	97	13	26	2	1	3	17	0
David Bishop, INF, Jr	.261	.314	.370	184	31	48	6	1	4	29	16
Nick English, C, Fr	.249	.340	.369	217	32	54	17	0	3	37	11
Kyan Lodice, OF, Jr	.238	.336	.419	105	17	25	3	2	4	12	7
Danniel Rivera, SS, Sr	.218	.378	.282	142	28	31	3	0	2	24	10
Cayden Phillips, C, Jr	.216	.268	.333	51	2	11	3	0	1	11	0
Raphael Pelletier, C, Jr	.210	.363	.398	181	31	38	7	0	9	29	0

Pitcher, Year	W	L	ERA	G	GS	SV	IP	H	BB	SO
Cole Wisenbaker, So	4	0	2.67	22	0	0	34	29	14	29
Tyson Neighbors, Jr	1	2	3.96	22	0	9	39	30	19	61
Jackson Wentworth, Jr	5	6	4.24	28	8	6	87	75	27	115
Mason Buss, So	2	0	4.26	13	1	0	19	21	6	11
J.J. Slack, Sr	2	1	4.26	15	0	0	25	24	13	28
Blake Dean, Fr	4	4	4.72	29	3	1	61	61	28	64
Owen Boerema, Sr	6	3	4.96	19	19	0	98	90	48	110
Preston Martinez, Jr	0	0	5.40	11	0	0	10	13	9	14
Adam Arther, Fr	0	1	5.68	14	0	0	19	17	7	12
Josh Wintroub, Sr	2	4	6.67	17	13	0	55	74	15	56
Tyler Ruhl, Jr	1	2	7.16	8	6	0	16	19	15	17
Jacob Frost, Jr	3	1	7.49	14	8	0	46	52	23	40
Andrew Evans, So	4	2	10.08	11	2	0	25	35	9	19

23. Evansville

Coach: Wes Carroll. Overall: 39-26

Player, Pos, Yr	AVG	OBP	SLG	AB	R	H	2B	3B	HR	RBI	SB
Mark Shallenberger, OF, Sr	.374	.514	.687	243	72	91	21	2	17	64	6
Cal McGinnis, INF, Jr	.348	.394	.530	198	38	69	14	2	6	39	1
Kip Fougerousse, INF, Sr	.348	.428	.678	270	71	94	21	1	22	71	1
Harrison Taubert, OF, Jr	.292	.400	.500	240	54	70	21	1	9	49	8
Simon Scherry, SS, Sr	.289	.376	.419	253	57	73	15	0	6	44	16
Ty Rumsey, OF, Jr	.282	.391	.441	195	45	55	8	1	7	45	16
Brent Widder, INF, Sr	.280	.384	.494	261	46	73	20	0	12	58	2
Chase Hug, UT, Sr	.278	.446	.508	126	30	35	11	0	6	31	2
Evan Waggoner, C, Jr	.271	.416	.300	70	11	19	2	0	0	9	0
Brodie Peart, INF, Fr	.270	.328	.361	122	20	33	5	0	2	17	2
Brendan Hord, C, Sr	.242	.378	.475	198	51	48	19	0	9	44	0
Kaleb Wilkey, C, Fr	.130	.259	.152	46	7	6	1	0	0	5	0

Pitcher, Year	W	L	ERA	G	GS	SV	IP	H	BB	SO
Ethan Bell, So	2	1	3.68	8	0	0	15	7	8	19
Shane Harris, Sr	8	6	3.82	27	6	4	75	70	31	72
Kenton Deverman, Fr	9	2	4.22	18	16	0	111	112	23	83
Max Hansmann, So	2	1	6.05	26	0	2	39	34	32	41
Jakob Meyer, Sr	4	4	6.07	30	0	4	46	36	24	50
Donovan Schultz, Sr	5	2	6.15	17	17	0	91	101	34	74
Jace Kressin, Sr	1	0	6.41	18	0	0	20	17	9	22
Drew Fieger, Jr	0	2	7.65	27	0	0	38	44	26	32
Kevin Reed, Fr	5	3	7.98	17	15	0	59	77	28	40
Nick Smith, Sr	2	5	13.07	18	9	0	42	69	30	42

24. Duke

Coach: Chris Pollard. Overall: 40-20

Player, Pos, Yr	AVG	OBP	SLG	AB	R	H	2B	3B	HR	RBI	SB
Ben Miller, INF, Sr	.360	.438	.645	228	56	82	18	1	15	49	2
Zac Morris, INF, Sr	.343	.439	.629	245	69	84	12	2	18	59	13
Chase Krewson, UT, Fr	.331	.417	.469	130	35	43	3	0	5	22	2
Logan Bravo, INF, Sr	.315	.432	.630	219	59	69	16	1	17	59	9
Alex Stone, C, Sr	.312	.365	.547	247	45	77	19	0	13	59	0
Andrew Yu, C, Jr	.311	.340	.556	45	11	14	2	0	3	15	0
Devin Obee, OF, Jr	.309	.399	.599	217	57	67	11	2	16	50	6
AJ Gracia, UT, Fr	.305	.440	.559	220	56	67	14	0	14	58	5
Wallace Clark, INF, Jr	.285	.451	.446	186	44	53	11	2	5	42	5
Harrison Rodgers, 2B, Sr	.259	.375	.444	27	9	7	1	2	0	5	0
Kyle Johnson, UT, Fr	.253	.398	.480	75	16	19	6	1	3	11	2
Macon Winslow, C, Fr	.250	.340	.386	132	18	33	6	0	4	17	0
Tyler Albright, OF, So	.222	.288	.315	54	11	12	2	0	1	6	1

Pitcher, Year	W	L	ERA	G	GS	SV	IP	H	BB	SO
Charlie Beilenson, Sr	7	3	2.01	34	0	12	63	42	18	92
David Boisvert, Jr	2	1	2.16	18	4	0	25	13	10	26
Gabriel Nard, So	3	2	2.60	30	1	0	45	42	20	34
Jonathan Santucci, Jr	6	1	3.41	13	13	0	58	40	36	90
Andrew Healy, So	3	1	3.76	12	12	0	41	32	17	42
Jimmy Romano, Jr	1	1	3.91	29	0	0	25	22	10	34
Kyle Johnson, Fr	4	1	4.38	15	10	0	49	44	19	53
Tim Noone, Sr	4	3	5.11	23	8	0	44	41	13	43
James Tallon, So	2	0	5.29	24	1	0	32	27	18	37
Ryan Higgins, Jr	2	2	5.96	22	7	0	48	36	27	54
Owen Proksch, So	3	0	6.10	22	0	0	21	21	16	19
Fran Oschell III, Jr	0	3	6.94	22	1	0	23	16	28	22
Edward Hart, So	1	0	8.38	14	0	0	10	11	5	9
Jackson Emus, Sr	0	1	8.66	15	1	0	18	17	12	31

25. UC Irvine

Coach: Ben Orloff. Overall: 45-14

Player, Pos, Yr	AVG	OBP	SLG	AB	R	H	2B	3B	HR	RBI	SB
Myles Smith, OF, Jr	.401	.533	.637	182	56	73	13	0	10	49	5
Caden Kendle, OF, Sr	.387	.479	.590	212	56	82	19	3	6	61	1
Woody Hadeen, INF, Sr	.358	.524	.415	229	82	82	11	1	0	34	12
Dub Gleed, INF, Jr	.351	.469	.550	131	23	46	8	0	6	35	1
Anthony Martinez, 1B, So	.316	.422	.492	256	54	81	18	0	9	74	1
Will Bermudez, INF, Jr	.301	.420	.447	206	43	62	12	3	4	48	0
Joichiro Oyama, OF, Sr	.296	.442	.511	223	64	66	13	4	9	55	9
Thomas McCaffrey, C, Sr	.281	.371	.520	171	32	48	7	2	10	46	3
Abraham Garcia-Pacheco, C, Sr	.277	.425	.394	94	18	26	8	0	1	22	1
Chase Call, UT, Jr	.261	.397	.500	188	45	49	17	2	8	47	0
Luke Spillane, OF, Sr	.247	.396	.338	77	18	19	5	1	0	7	5
James Castagnola, INF, So	.244	.407	.378	45	14	11	3	0	1	5	0
Jacob Stinson, OF, Sr	.237	.356	.342	38	11	9	1	0	1	8	0
Frankie Carney, INF, So	.208	.295	.245	53	13	11	2	0	0	7	1

Pitcher, Year	W	L	ERA	G	GS	SV	IP	H	BB	SO
Nick Rincover, Sr	1	0	2.60	19	1	0	17	17	10	16
Ricky Ojeda, Fr	6	1	3.46	25	0	1	52	41	25	74
Nick Pinto, Sr	9	2	3.91	17	16	0	94	105	23	99
Ricky Tibbett, Sr	4	1	3.93	30	0	10	50	45	24	54
Brandon Luu, Fr	5	1	4.09	14	10	0	44	44	19	25
David Butler, Jr	0	0	4.50	9	0	0	10	8	3	9
Riley Kelly, So	3	0	5.29	9	4	0	17	14	12	18
Ryder Brooks, So	2	1	5.30	22	1	0	36	45	12	32
Tim Grack, Fr	2	1	5.60	16	8	0	35	38	21	39
Trevor Hansen, Fr	6	4	5.69	16	16	0	74	91	34	74
David Utagawa, Jr	3	1	6.25	27	0	1	32	29	15	36

EDDIE KELLY

Jonathan Santucci was 6-1, 3.41 for a 40-win Duke team.

COLLEGE

NCAA regional teams in bold.

AMERICA EAST CONFERENCE

	Conference W	Conference L	Overall W	Overall L
Bryant	17	7	36	22
UMBC	14	10	27	25
NJIT	12	11	26	28
UMass Lowell	11	12	24	31
UAlbany	10	13	15	34
Binghamton	10	14	21	29
Maine	8	15	12	36

ALL-CONFERENCE TEAM: SP: Luke Delongchamp, Bryant; Gabe Driscoll, Binghamton; Luke Johnson, UMBC; Austin Wainer, Bryant. RP: Ryan Proto, UMass Lowell. 1B: Jeremiah Jenkins, Maine. 2B: Zac Zyons, Bryant. 3B: Devan Bade, Binghamton. SS: Chris Einemann, Bryant. OF: Mike Gunning, Binghamton; Gavin Noriega, Bryant; Carlos Martinez, UMass Lowell. DH: Evin Sullivan, Binghamton. UTIL: Cade Ladehoff, NJIT.

INDIVIDUAL BATTING LEADERS

(Minimum 140 at-bats)

	AVG	OBP	SLG	AB	2B	3B	HR	RBI	SB
Zac Zyons, Bryant	.369	.473	.601	168	13	1	8	33	3
AJ Soldra, NJIT	.345	.406	.483	116	8	1	2	16	5
Cole Campbell, NJIT	.341	.434	.444	135	5	0	3	26	9
Jeremiah Jenkins, Maine	.341	.451	.762	185	12	0	22	50	0
Carlos Martinez, UMass-L	.338	.414	.545	213	26	0	6	49	1
Matt Smith, Bryant	.331	.379	.496	133	9	2	3	28	0
Gavin Noriega, Bryant	.330	.468	.670	206	12	2	18	58	9
Devan Bade, Binghamton	.326	.380	.508	181	11	2	6	34	1
Cade Ladehoff, NJIT	.324	.355	.582	244	17	2	14	60	0
Myles Sargent, Maine	.324	.388	.435	108	7	1	1	14	2
Carmine Petosa, Bryant	.320	.473	.640	200	22	0	14	60	0
Justin Taylor, UMBC	.319	.425	.465	185	9	0	6	40	7
Will Binder, Albany	.318	.435	.480	173	14	1	4	30	2
Evin Sullivan, Bingh.	.316	.377	.458	155	12	2	2	22	2
Luke Filippi, Albany	.309	.406	.387	181	8	3	0	34	6
Anthony Swenda, UMBC	.308	.448	.513	195	16	0	8	49	6
Danny Wyatt, UMBC	.301	.372	.531	143	11	2	6	45	3
Kevin Putsky, NJIT	.300	.385	.547	203	12	1	12	44	4
Matt Ryan, UMBC	.295	.450	.513	193	18	0	8	38	10
Ryan Proto, UMass-L	.292	.417	.393	178	11	2	1	30	5
Alex Luccini, UMass-L	.290	.364	.484	221	16	0	9	39	16
Ryan Ferremi, Albany	.288	.427	.394	170	9	0	3	26	4
Justin Hackett, Bryant	.288	.404	.459	111	10	0	3	15	2
Albert Choi, NJIT	.287	.393	.479	188	16	1	6	31	17
Chris Einemann, Bryant	.286	.351	.401	147	9	1	2	31	7

INDIVIDUAL PITCHING LEADERS

(Minimum 40 innings pitched)

	W	L	ERA	G	SV	IP	H	BB	SO
Luke Delongchamp, Bryant	5	2	2.76	14	0	65	59	18	59
Sam Downs, UMBC	4	1	2.83	6	5	70	61	34	57
Jayden Shertel, UMBC	3	6	3.60	13	0	70	70	35	46
Gabe Driscoll, Bingh.	4	5	3.71	13	0	68	62	15	67
Joe Georgini, NJIT	6	2	4.29	2	3	57	72	20	31
Austin Wainer, Bryant	7	3	4.52	16	0	86	91	27	69
Miles Cota, UMass-L	2	2	4.61	9	0	57	60	26	38
Nelson Berkwich, Bingh.	5	5	4.77	14	0	77	77	31	71
Luke Johnson, UMBC	5	4	4.82	14	0	80	80	22	81
Dylan Banner, Ualbany	4	2	4.85	7	0	52	39	14	40
Aidan Kidd, NJIT	5	4	5.11	15	0	76	75	40	97
Michael Simes, UMass-L	2	4	5.13	9	0	60	56	18	43
Jason Krieger, Maine	1	4	5.26	13	0	65	70	43	54
Gianni Gambardella, Maine	2	4	5.68	8	1	51	52	22	45
Luc Lavigueur, Maine	4	3	6.75	9	1	59	81	32	47
Holden deJong, NJIT	3	6	6.82	12	0	62	67	39	61
Brandon Peterson, NJIT	1	4	7.83	14	0	56	79	41	49

AMERICAN ATHLETIC CONFERENCE

	Conference W	Conference L	Overall W	Overall L
East Carolina	19	8	46	17
UTSA	17	10	32	24
Tulane	15	12	36	26
Wichita State	15	12	32	29
UAB	13	14	26	29
Florida Atlantic	12	15	28	29
Charlotte	12	15	24	34
Rice	11	16	23	36
South Florida	11	16	26	29
Memphis	10	17	23	32

ALL-CONFERENCE TEAM: SP: Blayze Berry, UAB; Trey Yesavage, East Carolina; Ulises Quiroga, UTSA; Caden Favors, Wichita State. RP: Wyatt Lunsford-Shenkman, East Carolina. C: Justin Wilcoxen, East Carolina. 1B: Carter Cunningham, East Carolina. 2B: Bobby Boser, South Florida. SS: Matt King, UTSA. 3B: Gavin Schulz, Tulane. OF: Jacob Jenkins-Cowart, East Carolina; Ryley Johnson, East Carolina; Mason Lytle, UTSA. DH: Alexander Olivo, UTSA. UTL: Ben Rozenblum, South Florida. Player of the Year: Carter Cunningham, 1B, East Carolina. Pitcher of the Year: Trey Yesavage, East Carolina. Newcomer Position Player of the Year: Mason Lytle, OF, UTSA. Newcomer Pitcher of the Year: Tommy LaPour, Wichita State. Defensive Player of the Year: Ryley Johnson, OF, East Carolina. Coach of the Year: Cliff Godwin, East Carolina.

INDIVIDUAL BATTING LEADERS

(Minimum 140 at-bats)

	AVG	OBP	SLG	AB	2B	3B	HR	RBI	SB
Carter Cunningham, ECU	.367	.464	.653	251	17	2	17	65	6
Mason Lytle, UTSA	.352	.380	.590	244	19	3	11	43	17
Caleb Hill, UTSA	.347	.455	.553	219	13	1	10	40	8
Bristol Carter, ECU	.346	.406	.440	159	7	1	2	31	4
Alexander Olivo, UTSA	.346	.467	.503	159	10	0	5	33	2
Ryan McCrystal, ECU	.346	.402	.521	188	10	1	7	39	2
Christian Adams, FAU	.343	.465	.522	207	13	0	8	31	7
J. Jenkins-Cowart, ECU	.340	.386	.558	265	19	0	13	79	7
Ryley Johnson, ECU	.339	.461	.476	227	9	5	4	33	23
Matt King, UTSA	.336	.388	.464	220	14	1	4	41	4
Brady Marget, Tulane	.331	.427	.524	248	14	2	10	59	0
Pierre Seals, Mem	.327	.436	.553	199	11	2	10	33	16
Camden Johnson, WSU	.326	.389	.414	239	13	1	2	32	7
Daunte Stuart, Mem	.325	.430	.533	212	16	2	8	38	8
Derek Williams, WSU	.318	.425	.615	192	13	1	14	44	5
Logan Braunschweig, UAB	.314	.442	.402	194	9	1	2	27	21
Joaquin Monque, USF	.311	.395	.383	167	6	0	2	26	7
Lane Haworth, WSU	.311	.397	.504	135	12	1	4	27	2
Connor Rasmussen, Tulane	.310	.423	.487	226	15	2	7	51	7
John Montes, USF	.309	.391	.510	194	12	0	9	43	7
Dixon Williams, ECU	.308	.406	.490	208	11	0	9	43	5
Ben Dukes, Rice	.307	.392	.387	163	3	2	2	17	7
Rafael Betancourt, USF	.306	.374	.425	160	10	0	3	20	2
Gavin Schulz, Tulane	.303	.378	.517	234	13	2	11	51	7
Will Marcy, Mem	.303	.398	.406	155	13	0	1	19	13

INDIVIDUAL PITCHING LEADERS

(Minimum 40 innings pitched)

	W	L	ERA	G	SV	IP	H	BB	SO
Trey Yesavage, ECU	11	1	2.02	15	0	93	49	32	145
Blayze Berry, UAB	9	3	2.82	15	0	93	84	25	99
Collin Daniel, UAB	7	3	3.03	13	0	86	88	17	73
Caden Favors, WSU	9	4	3.12	17	0	107	103	20	107
Ruger Riojas, UTSA	10	3	3.25	26	7	69	68	18	75
Danny Beal,ECU	8	2	3.38	35	4	72	65	23	52
Root, Zach, ECU	6	2	3.56	13	0	68	56	21	76
C.J. Williams, FAU	5	5	4.04	15	0	82	76	35	72
Ulises Quiroga, UTSA	7	2	4.18	13	0	65	59	24	53

	W	L	ERA	G	SV	IP	H	BB	SO
Parker Smith, RICE	5	5	4.23	15	0	89	82	31	78
Tommy LaPour, WSU	6	2	4.25	16	0	78	65	37	69
Chandler Welch, TLN	7	4	4.65	17	0	89	109	24	88
Luc Fladda, TLN	5	3	4.77	18	0	83	93	21	61
Cole Reynolds, CLT	4	6	4.85	15	0	72	61	39	84
AJ Wilson, CLT	5	3	4.85	27	0	59	48	24	86
Braxton Shelton, UAB	2	7	4.99	15	0	70	73	28	38
J.D. McCracken, RICE	4	7	5.35	16	0	77	71	52	65
Seth Garner, MEM	2	1	5.40	17	0	58	65	27	46
Trey Beard, FAU	4	4	5.51	16	0	65	58	35	68
Hunter Mink, USF	3	7	5.66	14	0	76	74	27	83
Jack Cebert, USF	7	6	5.72	15	0	74	91	19	61
Daniel Garza, UTSA	4	3	5.99	18	2	68	84	14	67
David Warren, MEM	4	6	6.16	14	0	76	85	34	51
Caden Robinson, MEM	1	4	6.34	14	0	61	61	39	43

ATLANTIC COAST CONFERENCE

	Conference		Overall	
Atlantic Division	**W**	**L**	**W**	**L**
Clemson	20	10	44	16
NC State	18	11	38	23
Florida State	17	12	49	17
Louisville	16	14	32	24
Wake Forest	15	15	38	22
Notre Dame	9	21	27	25
Boston College	8	22	22	31

	Conference		Overall	
Coastal Division	**W**	**L**	**W**	**L**
North Carolina	22	8	48	16
Virginia	18	12	46	17
Duke	16	14	40	20
Georgia Tech	15	15	33	25
Virginia Tech	14	16	32	22
Miami	11	19	26	30
Pitt	10	20	26	28

ALL-CONFERENCE TEAM: SP: Aidan Knaak, SP, Clemson; Jonathan Santucci, Duke; Chase Burns, Wake Forest; Jamie Arnold, Florida State; Gage Ziehl, Miami. RP: Charlie Beilenson, RP, Duke. C: Jacob Cozart, NC State. 1B: Nick Kurtz, Wake Forest. 2B: Zac Morris, Duke. 3B: Ben Miller, Duke. SS: Griff O'Ferrall, Virginia. OF: James Tibbs III, Florida State; Drew Burress, Georgia Tech; Casey Cook, North Carolina; Vance Honeycutt, North Carolina. DH/UT: Ethan Anderson, Virginia. Player of the Year: James Tibbs III, OF, Florida State. Pitcher of the Year: Chase Burns, SP, Wake Forest. Freshman of the Year: Drew Burress, OF, Georgia Tech. Defensive Player of the Year: Vance Honeycutt, OF, North Carolina. Coach of the Year: Scott Forbes, North Carolina.

INDIVIDUAL BATTING LEADERS

(Minimum 140 at-bats)

	AVG	OBP	SLG	AB	2B	3B	HR	RBI	SB
Ben Watson, VT	.419	.466	.595	222	21	3	4	48	3
Cam Smith, Florida State	.387	.488	.654	269	22	1	16	57	4
Drew Burress, GT	.381	.512	.821	218	15	3	25	67	8
Zion Rose, Louisv.	.380	.455	.584	166	9	5	5	32	10
Alec Makarewicz, NC State	.378	.438	.753	259	25	0	24	84	1
Henry Godbout, Virginia	.370	.465	.642	173	18	1	9	48	6
James Tibbs III, FSU	.363	.488	.777	251	18	1	28	95	8
Bobby Whalen, Virginia	.361	.448	.467	169	10	1	2	35	7
Ben Miller, Duke	.360	.438	.645	228	18	1	15	49	2
Eric Becker, Virginia	.360	.468	.656	125	7	3	8	46	4
Dom Popa, Pitt	.352	.456	.448	210	13	2	1	26	6
Jacob Ference, Virginia	.352	.467	.704	199	13	3	17	41	12
Garrett Pennington, NC State	.350	.435	.665	257	27	0	18	65	1
Chris Cannizzaro, VT	.346	.413	.626	179	12	1	12	49	4
Zac Morris, Duke	.343	.439	.629	245	12	2	18	59	13
Parks Harber, UNC	.343	.425	.648	233	9	1	20	63	4
Casey Cook, UNC	.341	.431	.605	258	12	1	18	78	7
Daniel Cuvet, Miami	.341	.417	.724	232	15	1	24	73	2
Blake Wright, Clemson	.340	.382	.652	256	10	2	22	75	0
Cam Cannarella, Clemson	.337	.417	.561	246	16	3	11	60	0
Casey Saucke, Virginia	.336	.398	.559	256	18	0	13	64	9
Jacob Hinderleider, Clemson	.336	.407	.580	238	17	1	13	60	9
Clay Grady, VT	.335	.394	.410	188	3	4	1	20	7
Henry Ford, Virginia	.333	.407	.595	252	13	1	17	67	3
Trey Yunger, GT	.332	.401	.441	211	8	0	5	29	12

INDIVIDUAL PITCHING LEADERS

(Minimum 40 innings pitched)

	W	L	ERA	G	SV	IP	H	BB	SO
Charlie Beilenson, Duke	7	3	2.01	0	12	63	42	18	92
Chase Burns, WF	11	1	2.55	17	0	106	62	32	204
Jamie Arnold, FSU	11	3	2.98	18	1	106	90	26	159
Aidan Knaak, Clemson	5	1	3.35	15	0	83	67	29	108
Evan Blanco, UVA	8	3	3.62	18	0	99	101	27	99
Jason Decaro, UNC	6	1	3.81	18	0	90	74	44	78
Gage Ziehl, Miami	6	3	3.87	16	0	107	99	29	95
Evan Webster, Louisv.	5	3	4.18	15	0	71	75	20	62
Shea Sprague, UNC	3	2	4.25	15	0	78	78	18	70
Jack Radel, N. Dame	4	3	4.58	10	0	53	54	19	39
Carson Dorsey, FSU	8	4	4.60	11	3	76	82	37	88
Matt Bedford, N. Dame	3	6	4.65	15	0	62	55	28	40
Brett Renfrow, UVA Tech	6	4	4.92	15	0	75	72	32	78
Sam Highfill, NC State	7	2	4.97	17	0	87	71	43	82
Jack Sokol, Pitt	7	3	5.09	14	0	74	84	33	57
Ethan Darden, Clemson	5	5	5.13	11	0	67	81	15	42
Cam Jones, GT	4	2	5.31	8	3	59	58	20	41
John West, BC	1	4	5.42	14	0	78	91	30	66
Michael Farinelli, BC	0	6	5.76	10	2	55	64	23	42
Josh Hartle, WF	6	3	5.79	15	0	75	91	25	81

ATLANTIC SUN CONFERENCE

	Conference		Overall	
	W	**L**	**W**	**L**
Austin Peay	20	10	36	21
FGCU	20	10	30	26
Stetson	20	10	41	22
Kennesaw State	19	10	32	24
Jacksonville	18	12	27	31
Lipscomb	15	15	22	34
EKU	14	16	20	37
Central Arkansas	12	18	26	30
North Florida	11	17	21	30
North Alabama	10	19	18	35
Queens	10	20	14	41
Bellarmine	9	21	10	45

ALL-CONFERENCE TEAM: SP: Jesse Barker, Central Arkansas; Davian Garcia, FGCU; Blake Aita, Kennesaw State. RP: Bo Rhudy, Kennesaw State. C: Nick Hassan, Kennesaw State. 1B: Casey Sorg, Bellarmine. 2B: Ambren Voitik, Austin Peay. 3B: Brody Szako, Austin Peay. SS: Jon Jon Gazdar, Austin Peay. OF: Lyle Miller-Green, Austin Peay; Ron Franklin, EKU; Dillon Lewis, Queens. DH: Ian Farrow, FGCU. Player of the Year: Lyle Miller-Green, Austin Peay. Defensive Player of the Year: Jon Jon Gazdar, Austin Peay. Pitcher of the Year: Jesse Barker, Central Arkansas. Freshman of the Year: Kyle Jones, Stetson. Coach of the Year: Roland Fanning, Austin Peay.

INDIVIDUAL BATTING LEADERS

(Minimum 140 at-bats)

	AVG	OBP	SLG	AB	2B	3B	HR	RBI	SB
Jon Jon Gazdar, Austin Peay	.405	.484	.667	237	21	1	13	55	9
Lyle Miller-Green, Austin Peay	.393	.533	.900	219	17	2	30	94	13
Clayton Gray, Austin Peay	.380	.450	.680	250	24	3	15	68	13
Gus Freeman, Austin Peay	.375	.506	.617	120	14	0	5	33	5
Ian Farrow, FGCU	.375	.504	.750	176	17	2	15	44	10
Dillon Lewis, Queens	.371	.444	.729	229	14	1	22	63	20
John Bay, Austin Peay	.365	.471	.817	208	20	1	24	72	11
Jaden Brown, Austin Peay	.365	.429	.601	148	9	1	8	43	2
Conner Davis, EKU	.358	.412	.569	204	18	5	5	36	7
Kyle Jones, Stetson	.355	.459	.476	248	15	0	5	32	23
Ambren Voitik, Austin Peay	.353	.422	.593	204	14	1	11	48	13
Casey Sorg, Bellarmine	.348	.416	.638	207	12	3	14	49	9
Chandler Howard, Jacksonville	.347	.456	.568	118	9	1	5	38	0
Chris Cole, Kennesaw State	.345	.463	.427	110	7	1	0	10	17
Evan Dempsey, FGCU	.339	.432	.552	183	8	5	7	48	11
Harrison Brown, Austin Peay	.333	.427	.614	189	11	0	14	57	4

Player	AVG	OBP	SLG	AB	2B	3B	HR	RBI	SB
Brayden Eidson, Kennesaw State	.330	.374	.459	218	13	0	5	43	9
Jacob Lojewski, FGCU	.325	.407	.560	234	25	3	8	55	2
Nick Hassan, Kennesaw State	.323	.397	.481	189	15	0	5	38	11
Will Aubel, Bellarmine	.322	.381	.425	174	5	2	3	25	23
Gehrig Frei, North Alabama	.320	.420	.597	206	12	0	15	49	1
Brody Szako, Austin Peay	.319	.429	.628	188	11	1	15	59	1
Zeb Allen, Central Arkansas	.315	.432	.442	197	5	4	4	25	10
David Coppedge, Lipscomb	.313	.433	.625	128	8	1	10	24	6
Isaac Bouton, Kennesaw State	.311	.426	.566	212	16	1	12	47	0

INDIVIDUAL PITCHING LEADERS

(Minimum 40 innings pitched)

Player	W	L	ERA	G	SV	IP	H	BB	SO
Andrew Devine, Austin Peay	6	0	2.95	10	0	58	36	17	60
Tony Roca, North Florida	5	4	2.97	13	0	64	56	21	69
Davian Garcia, FGCU	5	3	3.03	8	1	59	52	20	71
Jesse Barker, Central Arkansas	3	6	3.40	15	1	109	83	28	119
Brycen Parrish, North Alabama	1	4	3.58	0	2	55	54	24	57
Richard Long, Jacksonville	8	2	3.80	15	0	83	68	28	62
Blake Aita, Kennesaw State	7	4	3.90	16	0	85	76	28	84
Aric McAtee, Stetson	3	3	4.18	9	0	67	70	27	73
Peter Holden, North Florida	4	4	4.34	14	0	66	67	44	79
Braden Osbolt, Kennesaw State	5	2	4.48	14	0	70	80	25	51
Anthony DeFabbia, Stetson	9	1	4.52	12	0	70	75	31	54
Justin Henschel, FGCU	5	2	4.91	8	2	66	69	34	55
Smith Pinson, Kennesaw State	4	8	4.92	14	1	75	67	26	57
Daniel Paret, Stetson	5	3	5.26	14	0	63	67	33	63
Mason Griffin, Central Arkansas	6	4	5.64	1	1	59	70	34	58
Lucas Hartman, FGCU	6	4	5.72	8	1	61	58	25	60
Alex Brewer, Lipscomb	5	5	5.75	15	0	83	95	30	58
Jacob James, North Alabama	5	6	5.75	14	1	77	75	57	105
Anthony Pingeton, N. Alabama	3	5	5.75	11	1	56	72	16	41
Jacob Bradshaw, N. Alabama	3	4	5.86	14	0	74	84	41	47

ATLANTIC 10 CONFERENCE

Team	Conference W	Conference L	Overall W	Overall L
Saint Louis	16	8	37	16
VCU	15	8	38	22
Dayton	14	9	33	22
Richmond	13	11	27	32
George Washington	13	11	31	26
UMass	13	11	24	29
Saint Joseph's	13	11	29	26
Rhode Island	11	13	19	28
Davidson	10	14	24	28
Fordham	10	14	19	33
St. Bonaventure	8	16	18	31
George Mason	7	17	21	32

ALL-CONFERENCE TEAM: SP: Michael Foltz, George Washington; Jackson Holmes, Saint Louis; Brian Curley, VCU. RP: Nick Wissman, Dayton. C: Connor Dykstra, George Mason. 1B: Eli Putnam Davidson. 2B: Ethan Sitzman, Saint Louis. SS: Ryan Weingartner, Saint Joseph's. 3B: Brandon Eike, VCU. OF: David Pedanou, Dayton; Adam Rankie, St. Bonaventure; Patrick Clohisy, Saint Louis. DH: Mike Gervasi, Massachusetts. Player of the Year: Brandon Eike, VCU. Pitcher of the Year: Nick Wissman, Dayton. Defensive Player of the Year: Aaron Whitley, Richmond. Rookie of the Year: David Mendez, Dayton. Coach of the Year: Darin Hendrickson, Saint Louis.

INDIVIDUAL BATTING LEADERS

(Minimum 140 at-bats)

Player	AVG	OBP	SLG	AB	2B	3B	HR	RBI	SB
Patrick Clohisy, Saint Louis	.383	.667	.493	162	15	5	7	44	24
Brandon Eike, VCU	.378	.661	.470	251	27	1	14	62	0
Aaron Whitley, Richmond	.367	.633	.474	158	12	0	10	26	18
Ellis Schwartz, G. Washington	.355	.485	.456	200	12	1	4	42	24
E Putnam, Davidson	.354	.682	.459	192	15	0	16	58	4
Brett Young, G. Washington	.352	.495	.474	182	14	3	2	41	16
Adam Rankie, St. Bonaventure	.348	.490	.399	210	15	3	3	38	5
Eddie Yamin IV, Dayton	.342	.608	.429	199	14	0	13	54	4
David Mendez, Dayton	.342	.505	.442	190	9	2	6	49	23
N Jouras, Davidson	.340	.535	.414	159	8	4	5	29	9
David Pedanou, Dayton	.338	.478	.427	201	13	3	3	25	33
Tyler Fogarty, Saint Louis	.336	.616	.415	211	18	4	11	51	15
DJ Pacheco, Richmond	.335	.530	.438	200	11	2	8	36	7
Phil Bernstein, Richmond	.330	.448	.428	221	17	0	3	45	9
Cian Sahler, Fordham	.329	.401	.401	167	7	1	1	32	6
Cole Smith, Saint Louis	.327	.400	.403	205	6	0	3	50	15
Easton Richter, Saint Louis	.327	.524	.433	147	10	2	5	34	11
McGwire Tuffy, G. Washington	.322	.420	.436	174	11	0	2	30	12
Owen Petrich, Saint Joseph's	.317	.517	.355	230	11	1	11	60	4
Jordan Jaffe, Richmond	.317	.546	.418	183	12	0	10	44	2
Ryan Weingartner, Saint Joseph's	.316	.596	.410	228	13	3	15	59	18
M. O'Shaughnessy, Davidson	.315	.569	.451	130	7	1	8	41	1
Ryan Thiesse, Fordham	.316	.379	.397	206	11	1	0	14	12
Robbie Lavey, G. Washington	.315	.429	.397	168	10	0	3	22	8
Conlan Wall, Saint Joseph's	.313	.379	.494	195	9	2	0	33	18

INDIVIDUAL PITCHING LEADERS

(Minimum 40 innings pitched)

Player	W	L	ERA	G	SV	IP	H	BB	SO
Michael Foltz, G. Washington	5	1	2.25	12	0	72	42	20	54
Brian Curley, VCU	6	0	2.87	0	3	78	74	35	78
Nick Wissman, Dayton	11	1	2.93	0	7	68	66	11	64
Christian Gordon, VCU	8	2	3.62	16	0	80	72	32	102
Ryan Desanto, Saint Joseph's	4	2	3.72	14	0	75	54	35	88
Kyle Roche, Richmond	5	8	3.74	16	0	87	105	4	72
Esteban Rodriguez, Richmond	5	2	4.50	12	0	76	76	38	90
Robbie O'Connor, UMass	3	6	4.72	14	0	74	71	20	51
Connor Fennell, Dayton	4	4	4.74	12	1	74	74	13	66
Will McCausland, Saint Joseph's	4	4	4.78	15	0	81	105	20	91
Michael Salina, St. Bonaventure	2	6	4.78	12	0	58	65	23	64
Teddy Brennan, G. Washington	2	7	4.81	14	0	73	72	43	75
Domenic Picone, Saint Joseph's	5	2	4.84	13	0	67	52	41	78
Jackson Holmes, Saint Louis	9	3	4.90	15	0	72	81	18	46
Ryan Peterson, George Mason	2	2	4.95	11	0	67	64	25	39
W Perkins, Davidson	6	4	5.31	14	0	85	103	16	76
Declan Lavelle, Fordham	6	6	5.42	15	0	91	106	27	63
Charlie Weber, Saint Louis	2	4	5.72	12	0	57	63	28	44
Konner Eaton, George Mason	3	2	5.93	12	0	55	56	31	69
I Fix, Davidson	2	4	5.96	8	1	51	59	48	55

BIG EAST CONFERENCE

Team	Conference W	Conference L	Overall W	Overall L
UConn	17	4	35	26
St. John's	14	7	38	18
Georgetown	13	7	36	20
Xavier	12	9	30	27
Villanova	8	13	17	34
Creighton	7	13	35	17
Seton Hall	7	14	24	30
Butler	5	16	20	35

ALL-CONFERENCE TEAM: SP: Ian Cooke, UConn, Everett Catlett, Georgetown; Mario Pesca, St. John's; Ryan Reich, Seton Hall. RP: Brady Afthim, UConn; Michael Gillen, Seton Hall. C: Jimmy Keenan, St. John's. 1B: Christian Ficca, Georgetown. 2B: Jared Cushing, Xavier. 3B: Luke Broadhurst, UConn. SS: Carter Dorighi, Butler. OF: Joey Urban, Butler; Korey Morton, UConn; Garrett Scavelli, St. John's. DH: Joe Hollerbach, Georgetown. Player of the Year: Christian Ficca, Georgetown, 1B. Pitcher of the Year: Ian Cooke, UConn, SP. Freshman of the Year: Kade Lewis, Butler, 1B. Coaching Staff of the Year: St. John's, Mike Hampton.

INDIVIDUAL BATTING LEADERS

(Minimum 140 at-bats)

Player	AVG	OBP	SLG	AB	2B	3B	HR	RBI	SB
Lewis, BU	.377	.436	.618	207	12	4	10	51	3
Dorighi, BU.	.370	.435	.547	243	16	3	7	48	16
N. Sailors, CU.	.355	.474	.560	200	14	3	7	55	18
N. Clifford, CU	.348	.469	.497	155	8	0	5	37	13
C Ficca, GU.	.345	.448	.570	223	15	1	11	64	1
Hack, HALL	.344	.411	.448	96	7	0	1	11	5
Keenan, SJU.	.335	.403	.615	218	21	2	12	57	1
Morton, UCONN.	.333	.382	.556	243	18	0	12	53	19

	AVG	OBP	SLG	AB	2B	3B	HR	RBI	SB
Mayberry, SJU.	.333	.429	.426	195	13	1	1	37	5
Wachsmann, XAV	.333	.438	.699	93	2	1	10	20	1
Urban, BU	.332	.412	.490	208	15	0	6	41	1
Moroknek, BU	.327	.411	.588	211	14	1	13	44	4
J Hollerbach, GU	.327	.415	.495	202	7	0	9	45	0
K Caster, GU	.322	.395	.638	174	11	4	12	48	9
T. Gillen, CU	.319	.480	.451	113	5	2	2	27	12
Scavelli, SJU.	.316	.401	.502	209	13	4	6	38	2
Sylvester, HALL.	.314	.441	.474	175	6	2	6	34	11
Tammaro, UCONN	.308	.441	.415	234	11	1	4	37	16
Lyons, HALL.	.308	.379	.356	104	3	1	0	15	7
T. Deters, CU	.305	.422	.569	197	14	4	10	48	9

INDIVIDUAL PITCHING LEADERS

(Minimum 40 innings pitched)

	W	L	ERA	G	SV	IP	H	BB	SO
A Citron, GU	4	0	2.45	25	2	44	26	30	36
Cunningham, SJU	1	0	2.66	33	1	41	38	14	41
Balzan, HALL	2	1	2.70	17	0	47	36	21	51
A Williams, GU	4	3	2.91	16	0	65	62	28	49
Pesca, SJU.	6	1	2.96	15	0	76	70	38	53
C Bowker, GU	5	1	3.00	13	0	48	40	20	59
E Catlett, GU	6	1	3.36	16	2	78	69	35	84
Marinaro, SJU	6	3	3.38	22	0	48	31	16	58
Kolhosser, SJU	9	2	3.43	15	0	76	73	26	51
Quinn, UCONN	2	3	3.77	28	4	43	42	22	64
Hansen, HALL	3	7	3.96	14	0	73	61	18	56
Mastroianni, GU	6	1	4.02	19	0	63	53	41	47
S. Quigley, UCONN	6	3	4.07	18	0	97	109	22	83
E. Nissen, CU	2	2	4.23	15	0	45	41	13	40
Reich, HALL	3	3	4.41	13	0	65	52	33	84

BIG SOUTH CONFERENCE

	Conference W	Conference L	Overall W	Overall L
Presbyterian	18	6	29	27
High Point	17	7	35	27
USC Upstate	16	8	36	24
Charleston Southern	12	12	22	32
Longwood	10	14	23	29
UNC Asheville	10	14	22	28
Gardner-Webb	9	15	22	31
Winthrop	8	15	19	29
Radford	7	16	16	34

ALL-CONFERENCE TEAM: C: Eric Grintz, High Point. INF: Cael Chatham, High Point; Grant Sherrod, USC Upstate; Brody Fahr, Presbyterian College; Alec Burns, Gardner-Webb. OF: Joel Dragoo, Presbyterian College; Robbie Burnett, UNC Asheville; Cade Conway, Charleston Southern. UTL: Noah Sullivan, USC Upstate. DH: Peyton Carr, High Point. SP: Daniel Eagen, Presbyterian College; Gus Hughes, High Point; Charlie McDaniel, Presbyterian College. RP: Connor Maggi, Gardner-Webb; Evan Truitt, Charleston Southern. Player of the Year: Joel Draggo, Presbyterian College. Pitcher of the Year: Daniel Eagen, Presbyterian College. Newcomer of the Year: Cade Conway, Charleston Southern. Freshman of the Year: Vance Sheahan, USC Upstate. Coach of the Year: Elton Pollock, Presbyterian College.

INDIVIDUAL BATTING LEADERS

(Minimum 140 at-bats)

	AVG	OBP	SLG	AB	2B	3B	HR	RBI	SB
Joel Dragoo, Presbyterian	.401	.508	.797	197	20	2	18	67	11
Cade Conway, Charleston So.	.373	.445	.477	193	9	1	3	32	27
Jace Rinehart, USC Upstate	.364	.410	.670	261	23	3	17	59	11
Cameron Pittman, Radford	.357	.437	.519	185	8	8	2	24	14
Breckin Nace, Radford	.356	.467	.525	59	5	1	1	8	1
Koby Kropf, USC Upstate	.355	.432	.701	234	21	0	20	68	5
Zack Whitacre, Radford	.346	.435	.539	191	12	2	7	31	15
Noah Campanelli, Longwood	.343	.447	.464	166	5	3	3	30	33
Chandler Tuupo, Charleston So.	.340	.445	.539	191	14	0	8	44	5
Ty Kaufman, UNC Asheville	.332	.422	.390	187	6	1	1	27	23
Vance Sheahan, USC Upstate	.330	.409	.420	188	11	0	2	29	6
Hayden Harris, Longwood	.326	.407	.468	190	18	0	3	30	7
Alec Burns, Gardner-Webb	.325	.444	.682	154	8	1	15	36	1
Robbie Burnett, UNC Asheville	.323	.454	.656	189	9	0	18	45	15
Noah Sullivan, USC Upstate	.322	.450	.606	208	8	0	17	56	6
Brody Fahr, Presbyterian	.320	.423	.463	203	12	4	3	43	4
Miggy Echazaretta, High Point	.319	.481	.429	119	7	0	2	20	19
Cael Chatham, High Point	.318	.448	.609	233	15	1	17	55	4
Eric Grintz, High Point	.313	.424	.564	179	9	0	12	33	5
Grant Sherrod, USC Upstate	.308	.369	.526	253	11	1	14	79	6
Adam Stuart, High Point	.305	.381	.528	246	15	2	12	52	5
Charlie Evans, Winthrop	.303	.386	.517	145	8	1	7	26	4
Daniel Gernon, USC Upstate	.300	.435	.448	210	8	4	5	35	15
Brayden Simpson, High Point	.300	.425	.561	223	18	2	12	46	14
Cameron Johnson, UNC Ashe.	.298	.396	.482	191	10	2	7	38	5

INDIVIDUAL PITCHING LEADERS

(Minimum 40 innings pitched)

	W	L	ERA	G	SV	IP	H	BB	SO
Daniel Eagen, Presbyterian	6	2	2.67	14	0	78	49	28	122
Connor Maggi, Gardner-Webb	2	0	3.05	0	2	59	49	15	70
Gus Hughes, High Point	6	4	3.77	16	0	103	80	41	111
Charlie Mcdaniel, Presbyterian	7	1	3.80	15	0	92	87	22	86
Evan Truitt, Charleston Southern	4	3	3.80	1	6	64	65	19	49
Colby Guy, UNC Asheville	7	4	4.35	13	0	70	64	34	68
Henry Proger, USC Upstate	6	4	4.39	15	0	80	81	29	59
Matt Little, High Point	6	2	4.39	13	0	82	95	21	55
Brett Wozniak, High Point	8	2	4.57	15	0	87	102	39	51
Noah Sullivan, USC Upstate	8	1	4.69	12	2	79	77	22	54
Owen Sarna, Winthrop	4	4	4.74	9	0	49	59	21	38
Dylan Howard, Radford	3	5	4.78	14	0	70	76	19	76
Blake Brogdon, Gardner-Webb	2	5	5.08	12	0	57	58	23	45
Reese Lumpkin, Winthrop	2	8	5.10	12	0	67	77	26	55
Riley Huge, Winthrop	5	5	5.26	13	0	67	56	29	111
Caleb Jones, Winthrop	3	1	5.26	2	0	50	56	19	49
Mathieu Curtis, USC Upstate	6	2	5.67	16	0	73	79	16	64
Fenix Digiacomo, Presbyterian	3	5	5.75	14	0	67	70	23	65
Scott Rouse, Radford	4	5	5.94	14	0	70	71	33	78
Cole Schiff, UNC Asheville	3	2	6.64	12	0	61	70	39	53

BIG 12 CONFERENCE

	Conference W	Conference L	Overall W	Overall L
Oklahoma	23	7	40	21
Oklahoma State	19	9	42	19
Texas	20	10	36	24
West Virginia	19	11	36	24
Cincinnati	17	13	32	25
Kansas State	15	15	35	26
Kansas	15	15	31	23
UCF	14	15	37	21
TCU	14	16	33	21
Texas Tech	12	17	33	26
Baylor	10	20	22	31
Houston	7	21	26	28
BYU	7	23	21	31

ALL CONFERENCE TEAM: C: Jake English, Kansas. IF: Brady Day, Kansas State; Michael Snyder, Oklahoma; Jalin Flores, Texas; Jared Thomas, Texas; JJ Wetherholt, West Virginia. OF: Carson Benge, Oklahoma State; Zach Ehrhard, Oklahoma State; Max Belyeu, Texas. DH: Easton Carmichael, Oklahoma. UT: Josh Kross, Cincinnati. SP: Braden Davis, Oklahoma; Brian Holiday, Oklahoma State; Payton Tolle, TCU; Derek Clark, West Virginia. RP: Ben Abeldt, TCU; Gage Boehm, Texas. Player of the Year: Max Belyeu, Texas. Pitcher of the Year: Payton Tolle, TCU. Freshman of the Year: Dominic Voegele, Kansas. Newcomer of the Year: Payton Tolle, TCU. Coach of the Year: Skip Johnson, Oklahoma.

INDIVIDUAL BATTING LEADERS

(Minimum 2.5 at-bats per team game)

	AVG	OBP	SLG	AB	2B	3B	HR	RBI	SB
Bravo Damian, Texas Tech	.378	.438	.583	180	21	2	4	44	2
Nolan Schubart, Oklahoma State	.370	.513	.838	173	10	1	23	68	0
Easton Carmichael, Oklahoma	.366	.406	.563	254	19	5	7	64	12
Cary Arbolida, Houston	.359	.462	.847	131	9	2	17	40	4

Player	AVG	OBP	SLG	AB	2B	3B	HR	RBI	SB
Michael Snyder, Oklahoma	.354	.465	.638	229	26	3	11	59	16
Sam Myers, TCU	.353	.405	.491	173	12	3	2	24	2
John Nett, Kansas	.352	.443	.521	219	17	1	6	37	9
Jared Thomas, Texas	.349	.434	.635	249	15	4	16	47	18
Kimble Schuessler, Texas	.343	.420	.601	178	14	1	10	30	0
Matt Prevesk, UCF	.342	.409	.474	234	10	3	5	35	2
Jalin Flores, Texas	.340	.408	.656	241	22	0	18	56	2
Carson Benge, Oklahoma State	.335	.444	.665	248	24	2	18	64	10
Logan Maxwell, TCU	.335	.447	.482	170	12	2	3	25	10
Kodey Shojinaga, Kansas	.335	.402	.485	233	20	0	5	46	0
Enzo Apodaca, Baylor	.333	.415	.514	210	14	3	6	42	2
Josh Hegemann, Cincinnati	.333	.449	.394	180	8	0	1	28	16
Wesley Jordan, Baylor	.331	.455	.632	133	11	1	9	32	4
Zach Ehrhard, Oklahoma State	.330	.458	.627	233	25	1	14	57	7
Max Belyeu, Texas	.329	.423	.667	210	15	1	18	53	3
Kaelen Culpepper, Kansas State	.327	.419	.569	248	15	6	11	60	17
Justin Murray, Houston	.325	.419	.486	212	11	1	7	40	9
Green Austin, Texas Tech	.322	.435	.546	174	13	1	8	45	6
Kerrington Cross, Cincinnati	.321	.451	.534	221	10	2	11	53	16
Woodcox Drew, Texas Tech	.321	.403	.642	165	11	0	14	48	3
Christian Mitchelle, Cincinnati	.319	.371	.417	163	4	0	4	22	9
Jack Zyska, UCF	.319	.420	.565	216	15	1	12	52	5
Bryce Madron, Oklahoma	.318	.439	.607	211	19	3	12	53	14
Peyton Powell, Texas	.318	.406	.485	239	11	1	9	44	2
Jake English, Kansas	.318	.458	.604	192	13	0	14	53	0
Braden Calise, UCF	.318	.384	.403	154	7	0	2	19	4
Josh Kross, Cincinnati	.317	.438	.638	221	14	0	19	65	1
Harold Coll, Houston	.317	.394	.601	208	20	0	13	55	13
Brady Day, Kansas State	.317	.426	.513	240	16	2	9	58	16
Ty Johnson, Baylor	.313	.393	.414	198	8	3	2	20	10
Ben Hartl, Kansas	.309	.460	.599	152	11	0	11	35	1
Reed Chumley, West Virginia	.307	.402	.643	199	15	2	16	50	3
Bazzell Kevin, Texas Tech	.306	.401	.473	186	13	0	6	32	4
Logan Sauve, West Virginia	.305	.374	.476	187	8	0	8	37	2
Jackson Nicklaus, Oklahoma	.303	.429	.533	195	9	3	10	37	6
Sam White, West Virginia	.302	.403	.493	215	9	1	10	43	5
Lauden Brooks, Cincinnati	.301	.391	.415	193	10	3	2	34	13
Brendan Jones, Kansas State	.301	.445	.496	236	13	3	9	35	40
Mike Koszewski, Kansas	.300	.408	.336	110	4	0	0	18	4
Kash Gavin, Texas Tech	.300	.365	.561	237	17	0	15	51	3
Kenneth Jimenez, Houston	.295	.476	.419	105	4	0	3	16	2
Anthony Mackenzie, Oklahoma	.291	.407	.453	203	10	1	7	44	5
Chase Brunson, TCU	.291	.390	.426	148	8	0	4	25	5
Jaden Parsons, Kansas State	.289	.393	.375	128	5	0	2	17	9
Lane Forsythe, Oklahoma State	.287	.414	.371	202	6	1	3	29	12
Rylan Galvan, Texas	.287	.392	.506	174	14	0	8	37	3

INDIVIDUAL PITCHING LEADERS

(Minimum 40 innings pitched)

	W	L	ERA	G	SV	IP	H	BB	SO
Dominic Castellano, UCF	6	0	2.83	1	3	60	34	25	68
Brian Holiday, Oklahoma State	7	3	2.95	16	0	113	82	19	128
Payton Tolle, TCU	7	4	3.21	14	0	81	57	37	125
Ethan Calder, Baylor	5	3	3.23	3	2	56	50	12	41
Derek Clark, West Virginia	8	2	3.23	13	0	98	83	23	91
Sam Garcia, Oklahoma State	7	3	3.64	16	0	89	77	19	115
Max Grubbs, Texas	6	4	3.67	12	0	74	78	18	50
Kyson Witherspoon, Oklahoma	8	3	3.71	11	1	80	69	40	90
Reese Dutton, Kansas	7	5	3.78	15	0	86	87	33	82
Dominic Voegele, Kansas	7	2	3.89	15	0	81	72	29	80
Dom Stagliano, UCF	4	4	4.10	14	0	75	54	22	66
Ace Whitehead, Texas	4	2	4.16	10	0	67	59	24	48
Jackson Wentowrth, Kansas St.	5	6	4.24	8	6	87	75	27	115
Braden Davis, Oklahoma	9	4	4.30	16	0	92	70	41	117
Ben Vespi, UCF	4	4	4.62	16	0	78	83	27	75
Owen Boerema, Kansas State	7	3	4.88	20	0	107	97	50	120
Robinson Kyle, Texas Tech	4	7	5.09	15	0	76	82	38	79
Tyler Switalski, West Virginia	5	3	5.10	14	0	67	67	35	58
Nathan Taylor, Cincinnati	8	2	5.45	16	0	73	75	33	70
Aidan Major, West Virginia	5	4	5.59	12	0	66	62	35	77
Tommy Boba, Cincinnati	5	6	5.60	15	0	71	68	30	64
Lebarron Johnson, Texas	3	4	5.60	15	0	72	79	44	84
Mason Marriott, Baylor	3	7	5.94	14	0	70	75	37	65
Antoine Jean, Houston	3	3	5.97	14	0	63	81	29	67
Bryce Robison, BYU	2	7	6.85	13	0	67	84	24	51
Seth Logue, Cincinnati	2	4	6.88	8	0	68	74	25	57
Ben Hansen, BYU	4	7	6.95	13	0	66	84	30	48

BIG TEN CONFERENCE

	Conference		Overall	
	W	L	W	L
Illinois	18	6	35	21
Nebraska	16	8	40	22
Indiana	15	9	33	26
Iowa	14	10	31	23
Michigan	14	10	32	28
Purdue	13	11	33	24
Penn State	12	12	29	24
Ohio State	12	12	29	26
Minnesota	11	13	25	23
Michigan State	11	13	24	27
Maryland	10	14	34	22
Rutgers	6	18	28	25
Northwestern	4	20	18	34

ALL-CONFERENCE TEAM: SP: Brody Brecht, Iowa; Brett Sears, Nebraska; Connor Wietgrefe, Minnesota; Jacob Denner, Michigan. C: Camden Janik, Illinois. 1B: Eddie Hacopian, Maryland. 2B: Sam Hojnar, Maryland. SS: Josh Kuroda-Grauer, Rutgers. 3B: Raider Tello, Iowa. OF: Devin Taylor, Indiana; Stephen Hrustich, Michigan; Jack Frank, Michigan State. DH: Jacob Schroeder, Illinois. UTL: Mitch Voit, Michigan. Player Of The Year: Josh Kuroda-Grauer, SS, Rutgers. Pitcher Of The Year: Brett Sears, RHP, Nebraska. Freshman Of The Year: Luke Gaffney, 1B, Purdue. Coach Of The Year: Dan Hartleb, Illinois.

INDIVIDUAL BATTING LEADERS

(Minimum 140 at-bats)

	AVG	OBP	SLG	AB	2B	3B	HR	RBI	SB
Josh Kuroda-Grauer, Rutgers	.428	.492	.590	222	19	1	5	45	24
J.T. Marr, Penn St.	.416	.464	.575	221	17	0	6	54	3
Jack Frank, Mich. St.	.383	.467	.622	209	17	3	9	40	19
Eddie Hacopian, Maryland	.377	.474	.573	220	16	0	9	51	6
Rhett Stokes, Nebraska	.360	.409	.487	150	16	0	1	18	6
Joshua Fitzgerald, Minn.	.360	.467	.632	136	10	0	9	38	11
Luke Gaffney, Purdue	.359	.449	.646	209	15	3	13	64	1
Devin Taylor, Indiana	.357	.449	.660	241	11	1	20	54	5
Raider Tello, Iowa	.357	.434	.575	221	19	4	7	60	6
Camden Janik, Illinois	.356	.440	.533	225	15	2	7	49	1
Case Sanderson, Nebraska	.338	.469	.450	151	6	1	3	26	0
Bennett Markinson, Northwest.	.337	.408	.495	202	10	2	6	34	0
Nick Mitchell, Indiana	.335	.458	.512	203	15	3	5	49	7
Davis Cop, Iowa	.335	.388	.483	209	10	0	7	59	0
Joey Brenczewski, Indiana	.333	.415	.451	162	10	0	3	42	4
Bryce Molinaro, Penn St.	.329	.409	.560	207	13	1	11	45	7
Camden Gasser, Purdue	.329	.507	.387	155	6	0	1	29	17
Chris Hacopian, Maryland	.327	.431	.586	220	10	1	15	42	2
Andy Nelson, Iowa	.325	.442	.527	169	7	0	9	44	9
Adam Cecere, Penn St.	.324	.474	.676	185	14	0	17	53	7
Logan Sutter, Purdue	.324	.453	.618	136	16	0	8	37	5
Trevor Cohen, Rutgers	.324	.400	.406	207	8	3	1	30	10
Tony Santa Maria, Rutgers	.324	.436	.586	210	11	1	14	55	13
Dillon Kark, Mich. St.	.324	.361	.466	219	17	1	4	42	2
Matt Maloney, Penn St.	.321	.398	.444	162	14	0	2	37	1
Ty Doucette, Rutgers	.321	.388	.556	162	11	0	9	49	0
Henry Kaczmar, Ohio St.	.320	.417	.476	225	10	2	7	36	5
Pete Durocher, Rutgers	.318	.387	.441	179	7	3	3	29	7
Weber Neels, Minn.	.317	.422	.528	180	14	0	8	43	0
Brody Harding, Illinois	.316	.394	.512	209	11	0	10	40	2
Tyler Cerny, Indiana	.315	.378	.525	257	24	0	10	60	6
Mitchell Okuley, Ohio St.	.314	.453	.464	194	17	0	4	43	6
Brock Tibbitts, Indiana	.312	.404	.472	176	12	2	4	43	2
Cameron Love, Rutgers	.312	.388	.447	199	12	3	3	27	6
Kyle Huckstorf, Iowa	.311	.398	.523	151	8	3	6	40	13
John Volpe, Rutgers	.311	.426	.443	167	7	0	5	35	10
Connor Milton, Illinois	.309	.433	.573	110	5	0	8	17	2
Bobby Marsh, Penn St.	.309	.381	.464	194	10	1	6	47	4

MIKE JANES/FOUR SEAM IMAGES

Brody Brecht had a breakout season as a starter for Iowa, going 4-3, 3.33

Tyler Pettorini, Ohio St.	.309	.383	.500	220	9	3	9	49	9
Nick Williams, Mich. St.	.309	.427	.459	181	15	0	4	37	3
Connor Caskenette, Purdue	.309	.429	.574	188	11	0	13	69	2
Keenan Taylor, Purdue	.309	.421	.577	97	11	0	5	28	2
Josh Caron, Nebraska	.308	.388	.579	240	15	1	16	65	3
Jo Stevens, Purdue	.307	.431	.531	179	9	2	9	43	8
Jacob Schroeder, Illinois	.306	.434	.613	160	7	0	14	41	4
Jake Perry, Minn.	.305	.398	.557	203	20	2	9	43	3
Coltin Quagliano, Illinois	.304	.354	.495	214	12	1	9	55	0
Ryan Mckay, Mich. St.	.302	.348	.381	189	7	1	2	31	4
Stephen Hrustich, Michigan	.300	.450	.606	213	16	2	15	46	5
Joseph Mershon, Ohio St.	.299	.451	.471	174	10	4	4	29	16

INDIVIDUAL PITCHING LEADERS

(Minimum 40 innings pitched)

	W	L	ERA	G	SV	IP	H	BB	SO
Brett Sears, Nebraska	9	1	2.16	17	1	104	72	19	101
Connor Wietgrefe, Minn.	8	4	2.77	15	0	78	81	26	74
Brody Brecht, Iowa	4	3	3.33	15	0	78	46	49	128
Kurt Barr, Michigan	5	3	3.41	21	0	90	72	41	60
Mason Mcconnaughey, Nebraska	9	3	3.45	17	0	73	65	24	91
Justin Sinibaldi, Rutgers	4	4	3.47	13	0	83	68	22	65
Cooper Omans, Illinois	4	1	3.73	14	0	60	47	28	56
Jacob Denner, Michigan	9	5	3.89	28	4	86	84	24	70
Cade Obermueller, Iowa	4	3	3.92	13	0	60	39	41	73
Joseph Dzierwa, Mich. St.	6	3	4.07	14	0	84	73	27	91
Landon Beidelschies, Ohio St.	6	7	4.15	15	0	85	71	31	91
Travis Luensmann, Penn St.	7	2	4.44	16	0	81	60	61	74
Jordan Morales, Purdue	7	6	4.54	15	0	85	98	23	75
Kenny Lippman, Maryland	4	4	4.55	18	2	65	60	36	64
Connor Foley, Indiana	4	2	4.71	14	0	63	37	49	82
TY Bothwell, Indiana	7	3	4.78	18	1	85	87	25	91
Jack Crowder, Illinois	8	2	4.88	16	0	90	72	38	80
Kyle Pottoff, Northwest.	3	6	5.00	18	0	72	81	20	39
Mason Horwat, Penn St.	4	1	5.34	21	2	56	56	23	28
Luke Wagner, Purdue	7	2	5.42	15	0	73	94	22	55
Mitch Voit, Michigan	5	3	5.49	10	0	62	72	16	41
Matt McClure, Northwest.	3	6	5.65	18	0	65	80	18	44
Nick Powers, Mich. St.	7	4	5.71	14	0	80	90	22	65
Jack Dyke, Northwest.	1	2	5.81	20	2	53	64	17	34
Luke Benneche, Northwest.	3	2	5.82	20	0	65	73	34	34
Logan Koester, Maryland	6	6	6.00	14	0	72	89	28	40
Jaden Henline, Penn St.	3	4	6.09	15	0	68	88	15	41
Garrett Shearer, Northwest.	3	9	6.38	21	3	55	64	29	53
Tucker Novotny, Minn.	2	5	6.75	15	0	52	62	26	62
Chase Allen, Michigan	3	3	7.27	19	0	64	81	32	33
Marcus Morgan, Iowa	2	4	7.45	16	0	54	49	53	64
Will Semb, Minn.	1	5	7.54	14	0	66	83	32	73
Nolan Morr, Northwest.	2	4	8.20	19	1	53	74	13	48

BIG WEST CONFERENCE

	Conference		Overall	
	W	L	W	L
UC Santa Barbara	26	4	44	14
UC Irvine	22	8	45	14
Hawai'i	20	10	37	16
Cal Poly	20	10	35	22
UC San Diego	17	13	30	23
CSUN	16	14	30	24
UC Davis	13	17	29	27
Long Beach State	10	20	25	29
Cal State Bakersfield	8	22	15	38
Cal State Fullerton	7	23	16	38
UC Riverside	6	24	16	36

ALL-CONFERENCE TEAM: SP: Tyler Bremner, UC Santa Barbara; Ryan Gallagher, UC Santa Barbara; Jakob Wright, Cal Poly. RP: Ricky Ojeda, UC Irvine. CP: Izaak Martinez, UC San Diego. C: Aaron Parker, UC Santa Barbara. 1B: Anthony Martinez, UC Irvine. 2B: Nick Oakley, UC Santa Barbara. 3B: Alejandro Garza, Cal Poly. SS: Woody Hadeen, UC Irvine. OF: Caden Kendle, UC Irvine; Myles Smith, UC Irvine; Jake Steels, Cal Poly. DH: Ivan Brethowr, UC Santa Barbara. UTL: Brendan Durfee, UC Santa Barbara Player of the Year: Myles Smith, UC Irvine. Pitcher of the Year: Ryan Gallagher, UC Santa Barbara. Defensive Player of the Year: Ryan Stafford, Cal Poly. Freshman Field Player of the Year: Alejandro Garza, Cal Poly. Freshman Pitcher of the Year Griffin Naess, Cal Poly. Coach of the Year: Andrew Checketts, UC Santa Barbara.

INDIVIDUAL BATTING LEADERS

(Minimum 140 at-bats)

	AVG	OBP	SLG	AB	2B	3B	HR	RBI	SB
Myles Smith, UC Irvine	.401	.533	.637	182	13	0	10	49	5
Caden Kendle, UC Irvine	.387	.479	.590	212	19	3	6	61	1
Jake Steels, Cal Poly	.381	.494	.558	215	12	1	8	34	8
Aaron Parker, UC Santa Barbara	.379	.460	.632	190	12	0	12	51	0
Ryan Stafford, Cal Poly	.368	.444	.568	234	23	3	6	46	10
Cole Koniarsky, UC Riverside	.361	.411	.471	208	13	2	2	31	0
Bubba Rocha, UC Riverside	.358	.467	.431	137	10	0	0	22	2
Woody Hadeen, UC Irvine	.358	.524	.415	229	11	1	0	34	12
Austin Machado, Hawai'i	.351	.473	.516	188	19	0	4	48	0
Jessada Brown, UC S. Barbara	.350	.429	.560	200	12	0	10	42	6
Brendan Durfee, UC S. Barbara	.349	.455	.566	175	11	0	9	35	2
Jordan Donahue, Hawai'i	.349	.458	.467	195	17	0	2	30	10
Alejandro Garza, Cal Poly	.346	.396	.400	205	11	0	0	28	1
Max Bernal, Cal State Bakers.	.343	.425	.455	99	3	1	2	19	0
Jake Tsukada, Hawai'i	.337	.439	.402	169	5	0	2	38	3
Ryan Fenn, Cal Poly	.325	.362	.461	228	18	2	3	43	10
Jakob Simons, CSUN	.321	.477	.632	193	10	1	16	56	17
Kevin Fitzer, CSUN	.321	.429	.631	168	13	3	11	42	11
Letrey Mccollum, UC . Barbara	.320	.400	.383	128	8	0	0	14	10
Anthony Potestio, UC San Diego	.318	.395	.439	107	7	0	2	20	3
Emiliano Gonzalez, UC San Diego	.317	.390	.488	164	10	0	6	46	2
Anthony Martinez, UC Irvine	.316	.422	.492	256	18	0	9	74	1
Nick Oakley, UC S. Barbara	.315	.401	.479	219	11	5	5	49	8
Connor Charpiot, Long Beach St.	.314	.402	.450	169	11	0	4	29	5
Dominic Martinez, UC Riverside	.313	.348	.408	147	8	3	0	19	0

COLLEGE

INDIVIDUAL PITCHING LEADERS

(Minimum 40 innings pitched)

	W	L	ERA	G	SV	IP	H	BB	SO
Izaak Martinez, UC San Diego	4	3	1.85	0	9	63	40	20	61
Ryan Gallagher, UC S. Barbara	10	1	2.22	14	0	89	50	25	96
Tyler Bremner, UC S. Barbara	11	1	2.54	9	0	89	57	21	104
Ryan Verdugo, Cal State Bakers.	3	6	2.72	14	0	89	66	40	93
Kellen O'Connor, Cal State Bakers.	2	4	2.89	13	0	81	78	24	64
Jakob Wright, Cal Poly	9	3	2.97	15	0	88	71	42	101
Anthony Eyanson, UC San Diego	6	2	3.07	9	1	82	55	24	85
Mike Gutierrez, UC S. Barbara	10	0	3.18	16	0	91	70	34	86
Myles Patton, Long Beach State	4	3	3.26	11	0	66	52	24	85
Alex Giroux, Hawai'i	7	3	3.43	5	1	66	63	14	66
Griffin Naess, Cal Poly	7	0	3.58	12	0	73	62	25	62
Bryan Green, UC Davis	1	3	3.86	12	0	63	59	30	62
Nick Pinto, UC Irvine	9	2	3.91	16	0	94	105	23	99
Kellan Montgomery, Long Beach St.	3	4	3.95	15	0	87	88	20	73
Randy Abshier, Hawai'i	5	4	4.00	15	0	81	72	24	90
Matt Ager, UC Santa Barbara	3	4	4.02	9	11	63	59	28	59
Noel Valdez, UC Davis	1	7	4.14	15	0	78	88	17	51
Mikiah Negrete, Cal State Fuller.	4	5	4.61	15	0	84	108	25	67
Harrison Bodendorf, Hawai'i	4	3	4.61	11	2	57	53	28	64
Matthew Dalquist, UC San Diego	6	3	4.71	13	0	73	72	17	68

COASTAL ATHLETIC ASSOCIATION

	Conference		Overall	
	W	L	W	L
Charleston	21	5	41	14
UNCW	20	7	40	21
Northeastern	18	9	38	17
Delaware	16	11	31	26
William & Mary	13	14	32	26
Hofstra	13	14	24	33
Campbell	12	15	31	22
Stony Brook	12	15	24	28
Monmouth	11	16	18	30
Elon	10	17	21	32
N.C. A&T	9	17	25	28
Towson	5	20	15	39

ALL-CONFERENCE TEAM: SP: Nate Knowles, William & Mary; Carlos Martinez, Hofstra; RJ Sales, UNCW. RP: Davis Aiken, Charleston; Luke Craig, UNCW. C: Canyon Brown, N.C. A&T. IF: Jac Croom, UNCW; Tyler MacGregor, Northeastern; Kevin Madden, Charleston; Cole Mathis, Charleston; Tanner Thach, UNCW; OF: Lawson Harrill, Campbell; Alex Lane, Northeastern; Trevor Marsh, UNCW; Avery Neaves, Charleston. UT: Grant Knipp, Campbell. DH: Cole Singsank, Charleston. Co-Players Of The Year: Tyler MacGregor, 1B, Northeastern and Tanner Thach, 1B, UNCW. Pitcher Of The Year: Nate Knowles, RHP, William & Mary. Defensive Player Of The Year: Luke Beckstein, 2B, Northeastern. Rookie Of The Year: Erik Paulsen, DH/P, Stony Brook. Coach Of The Year: Chad Holbrook, Charleston.

INDIVIDUAL BATTING LEADERS

(Minimum 140 at-bats)

	AVG	OBP	SLG	AB	2B	3B	HR	RBI	SB
Tyler MacGregor, Northeastern	.402	.484	.786	234	29	2	19	80	15
Dylan Palmer, Hofstra	.386	.453	.440	241	6	2	1	31	27
Alex Lane, Northeastern	.375	.474	.685	216	13	0	18	80	14
Tatsunori Negishi, N.C. A&T	.371	.477	.588	194	16	1	8	37	2
Phil Stahl, Monmouth	.366	.433	.497	161	6	0	5	36	0
Trevor Marsh, UNCW	.363	.431	.597	248	13	0	15	50	6
Kenny Mallory Jr., Elon	.351	.459	.521	194	12	0	7	38	6
Lawson Harrill, Campbell	.351	.492	.777	202	17	0	23	56	9
Ben Parker, William & Mary	.340	.473	.581	215	16	3	10	48	16
Elijah Dickerson, Towson	.339	.400	.484	221	21	1	3	30	7
Joe Delossantos, William & Mary	.338	.439	.597	216	14	0	14	67	17
Avery Neaves, Charleston	.338	.475	.715	207	25	4	15	44	8
Jordan Peyton, Towson	.336	.398	.481	214	9	2	6	41	8
Matt Pelcher, Hofstra	.335	.403	.406	155	8	0	1	30	1
Cole Mathis, Charleston	.335	.472	.650	200	17	2	14	57	14
Will Baumhofer, Charleston	.333	.473	.481	189	10	3	4	28	16
Charlie Granatell, Elon	.329	.414	.507	207	16	0	7	37	1
Steve Harrington, Hofstra	.327	.414	.488	205	8	2	7	32	2
Tanner Thach, UNCW	.324	.406	.700	250	11	1	27	75	4
Kevin Madden, Charleston	.320	.368	.562	219	14	0	13	48	7
Jack Goodman, Northeastern	.320	.387	.523	197	12	2	8	42	18
Dalen Thompson, Campbell	.313	.396	.554	195	13	2	10	47	20
Brown-Eiring Matt, Stony Brook	.312	.376	.485	202	15	1	6	43	10
Aaron Graeber, Delaware	.312	.413	.608	199	13	2	14	52	11
Luke Beckstein, Northeastern	.311	.515	.406	180	6	1	3	28	13

INDIVIDUAL PITCHING LEADERS

(Minimum 40 innings pitched)

	W	L	ERA	G	SV	IP	H	BB	SO
Nate Knowles, William & Mary	8	3	2.48	19	0	80	50	39	112
Smink Eddie, Stony Brook	5	4	3.11	11	0	55	43	27	56
Zack Potts, William & Mary	6	4	3.17	12	1	65	60	14	57
Connor Campbell, Charleston	8	2	3.37	16	0	83	85	19	47
RJ Sales, UNCW	11	3	3.41	16	0	95	70	48	93
Jake Brink, Charleston	8	3	3.69	15	0	93	79	38	62
Mark Hindy, William & Mary	5	3	3.75	0	1	60	56	20	73
Aidan Hunter, Charleston	7	1	3.76	14	0	77	78	28	56
Alec Couture, Monmouth	3	4	3.98	14	0	84	84	28	65
Carlos Martinez, Hofstra	6	4	4.02	15	0	78	72	32	95
Coley Kilpatrick, N.C. A&T	7	3	4.02	14	0	85	80	37	68
Rhein Colin, Stony Brook	4	3	4.50	4	1	58	51	12	40
JT Raab, Stony Brook	4	4	4.54	11	1	71	70	15	52
Drew Helmstetter, Monmouth	2	5	4.57	14	0	83	81	25	59
Kevin Opanel, Monmouth	3	5	4.84	12	0	71	65	35	48
Zach Sabers, Campbell	6	0	5.04	12	0	64	59	33	51
Justin Mitrovich, Elon	4	6	5.06	14	0	80	87	30	96
Wyatt Scotti, Northeastern	7	5	5.20	15	0	71	83	16	48
Ben Sieracki, Elon	3	5	5.30	7	3	56	58	29	42
Cole Peschl, Campbell	3	3	5.48	13	0	69	73	19	83
Doug Marose, Delaware	4	2	5.53	15	0	70	81	17	48
Rizzo Nicholas, Stony Brook	3	6	5.63	11	0	62	72	27	35
Eli Atiya, Delaware	4	2	5.64	1	3	59	62	22	52
Michael O'Hanlon, Hofstra	7	4	5.75	15	0	92	92	26	81
Jacob Shafer, UNCW	4	6	5.99	16	0	77	86	30	61
Max Simpson, Towson	2	4	6.44	10	3	59	71	21	46
Diego Barrett, N.C. A&T	1	4	8.12	10	0	54	70	28	47

CONFERENCE USA

	Conference		Overall	
	W	L	W	L
LA Tech	18	6	45	19
Dallas Baptist	17	7	45	15
WKU	15	9	36	22
Sam Houston	13	11	34	24
Liberty	11	13	24	34
FIU	11	13	27	30
NM State	10	14	25	29
MTSU	8	16	20	36
Jax State	5	19	18	34

ALL-CONFERENCE TEAM: SP: Jaron DeBerry, DBU; Ryan Johnson, DBU; Luke Nichols, LA Tech; Coltin Atkinson, Sam Houston. RP: Conner Mackay, DBU; Sam Broderson, LA Tech.C: Walker Janek, Sam Houston. INF: Chayton Krauss, DBU; Miguel Santos, DBU; Brennen Norton, Jax State; Dalton Davis, LA Tech. OF: Ethan Mann, DBU; Cole McConnell, LA Tech; Keith Jones II, NM State. DH: Ryne Guida, FIU. UTL: Ethan Bates, LA Tech. Player of the Year: Ethan Bates, LA Tech. Pitcher of the Year: Ryan Johnson, DBU. Defensive Player of the Year: Walker Janek, Sam Houston. Newcomer of the Year: Michael Dattalo, DBU. Freshman of the Year: Luke Pettitte, DBU. Keith LeClair Co-Coaches of the Year: Dan Heefner, DBU; Lane Burroughs, LA Tech. Assistant Coach of the Year: Cliff Pennington, DBU.

INDIVIDUAL BATTING LEADERS

(Minimum 140 at-bats)

	AVG	OBP	SLG	AB	2B	3B	HR	RBI	SB
Cole McConnell, LA Tech	.385	.469	.684	244	17	1	18	71	1
Keith Jones II, NM State	.367	.472	.710	221	19	3	17	67	11
Walker Janek, Sam Houston	.364	.476	.709	220	15	5	17	58	13
Chayton Krauss, Dallas Baptist	.358	.415	.626	246	16	1	16	66	7
Gabe Jennings, MTSU	.353	.417	.597	221	16	1	12	44	6
Tom Poole, Dallas Baptist	.352	.488	.704	159	13	2	13	37	9

Player	AVG	OBP	SLG	AB	2B	3B	HR	RBI	SB
Jeffrey David, Sam Houston	.351	.406	.514	222	14	2	6	44	6
Michael Dattalo, Dallas Baptist	.345	.395	.517	232	14	1	8	47	3
Titus Dumitru, NM State	.337	.435	.624	181	16	0	12	40	4
Ryne Guida, FIU	.335	.420	.536	224	18	0	9	56	0
Brylan West, FIU	.333	.454	.605	195	16	2	11	42	3
Mitch Namie, NM State	.333	.453	.508	183	13	2	5	35	1
Ethan Bates, LA Tech	.332	.427	.602	256	20	2	15	73	2
Kane Kepley, Liberty	.329	.482	.524	210	12	1	9	31	25
Bear Madliak, Jax State	.328	.400	.488	201	11	3	5	31	7
Drennen Norton, Jax State	.327	.419	.573	211	9	2	13	44	8
Alex Ulloa, FIU	.327	.406	.519	214	8	0	11	38	2
Miguel Santos, Dallas Baptist	.325	.381	.528	252	10	1	13	52	12
Ethan Mann, Dallas Baptist	.322	.412	.639	227	22	1	16	59	10
Dalton Davis, LA Tech	.321	.420	.587	218	11	1	15	53	8
Eston Snider, MTSU	.314	.380	.432	220	10	2	4	27	13
Jorge Corona, LA Tech	.314	.387	.561	239	14	0	15	48	0
Blake Cavill, WKU	.313	.443	.527	201	19	0	8	47	1
Michael Ballard, LA Tech	.313	.392	.412	243	12	0	4	37	2
Jackson Galloway, MTSU	.311	.356	.517	180	12	2	7	40	6
Romeo Ballesteros, NM State	.311	.417	.350	177	4	0	1	25	12
Ethan Lizama, WKU	.309	.373	.536	207	16	2	9	42	5
Armando Becerra, FIU	.305	.406	.532	154	9	1	8	29	1
Joey Baran, WKU	.303	.429	.402	122	6	0	2	26	2
Trace Phillips, MTSU	.303	.360	.551	198	8	1	13	46	4

INDIVIDUAL PITCHING LEADERS

(Minimum 40 innings pitched)

	W	L	ERA	G	SV	IP	H	BB	SO
Ryan Johnson, Dallas Baptist	11	3	2.21	16	0	106	83	14	151
Jerrod Jenkins, Dallas Baptist	6	0	3.43	6	1	60	45	26	57
Jaron Deberry, Dallas Baptist	7	1	3.50	15	0	90	73	38	89
Michael Watson, Sam Houston	7	1	3.50	13	0	72	52	25	91
Coltin Atkinson, Sam Houston	6	5	3.81	15	0	85	88	20	78
Cole Hertzler, Liberty	6	6	4.16	14	0	84	72	33	94
Luke Nichols, LA Tech	4	4	4.46	16	0	79	74	29	82
Nick Moran, Liberty	4	3	4.68	14	0	67	74	24	59
Chandler Alderman, MTSU	3	5	4.83	10	0	63	64	24	70
Will Baker, Jax State	3	6	5.53	11	1	67	82	19	44
Jack Bennett, WKU	6	4	5.66	12	1	70	72	17	69
Austin Cornelius, Jax State	3	4	5.75	12	2	61	83	16	25
Reed Smith, LA Tech	7	5	5.99	17	0	77	91	18	78
Gavi Coldiron, Sam Houston	3	6	6.00	13	0	60	65	16	38
Hayden Walker, NM State	6	4	6.45	11	0	67	83	33	57
James Sells, MTSU	6	6	6.50	5	0	62	69	25	46
Trey Meza, NM State	5	6	7.26	10	0	79	97	41	70
Joel Pineiro, FIU	2	4	7.80	15	0	58	66	35	53
Jackson Sleeper, Jax State	1	4	8.46	13	0	61	78	24	61

HORIZON LEAGUE

	Conference W	Conference L	Overall W	Overall L
Wright State	20	10	32	24
Northern Kentucky	19	11	35	24
Oakland	18	12	31	27
Milwaukee	13	17	19	36
Purdue Fort Wayne	11	19	19	37
Youngstown State	9	21	16	44

ALL-CONFERENCE TEAM: SP: Luke Hansel, Milwaukee; Tanner Gillis, Northern Kentucky; Brandon Decker, Oakland; Jacob Gehring, Youngstown State. RP: Kevin Fee, Purdue Fort Wayne.C: Sammy Sass, Wright State. 1B: Liam McFadden-Ackman, Northern Kentucky. 2B: John Odom, Northern Kentucky. 3B: Cleary Simpson, Northern Kentucky. SS: Trey Law, Youngstown State. OF: Carson Hansen, Milwaukee; Treyvin Moss, Northern Kentucky; Ben Vore, Wright State. DH: Julian Greenwell, Wright State. Player of the Year: Liam McFadden-Ackman, Northern Kentucky. Pitcher of the Year: Brandon Decker, Oakland. Reliever of the Year: Kevin Fee, Purdue-Fort Wayne. Freshman of the Year: Alejandro Covas, Youngstown State. Coaches of the Year: Dizzy Peyton, Northern Kentucky; Alex Sogard, Wright State.

INDIVIDUAL BATTING LEADERS

(Minimum 140 at-bats)

	AVG	OBP	SLG	AB	2B	3B	HR	RBI	SB
Julian Greenwell, Wright State	.399	.474	.699	183	20	1	11	53	5
Treyvin Moss, N. Kentucky	.389	.452	.672	244	22	7	11	66	30
Sammy Sass, Wright State	.362	.421	.638	221	20	1	13	62	6
Brandon Heidal, Oakland	.360	.483	.597	211	15	4	9	43	12
Justin Osterhouse, Purdue-FW	.355	.424	.609	138	8	0	9	38	11
L. McFadden-Ackman, N. Kentucky	.354	.483	.721	226	15	1	22	77	16
Tyler Shaneyfelt, N. Kentucky	.352	.482	.477	193	4	7	2	37	18
Trey Law, Youngstown State	.350	.421	.439	246	15	2	1	26	8
John Odom, N. Kentucky	.340	.425	.667	150	15	2	10	32	12
Drew Baker, Wright State	.339	.458	.614	127	9	1	8	23	4
Reggie Bussey, Oakland	.336	.465	.423	220	11	4	0	31	31
Cleary Simpson, N. Kentucky	.336	.493	.517	211	12	4	6	49	16
Alejandro Covas, Youngstown St.	.329	.421	.545	222	7	10	7	41	12
Jacob Walker, Purdue-FW	.329	.416	.507	219	19	1	6	31	12
Jay Luikart, Wright State	.325	.415	.619	231	12	1	18	66	2
Patrick Fultz, Wright State	.320	.424	.479	169	13	1	4	40	3
Lucas Day, Oakland	.318	.422	.559	195	17	0	10	46	7
Justin Hausser, Milwaukee	.317	.373	.445	227	18	1	3	21	5
Gus Gregory, Wright State	.315	.445	.414	111	5	0	2	16	8
Carson Hansen, Milwaukee	.315	.404	.601	203	25	0	11	63	7
Carter Hain, Oakland	.314	.384	.510	153	6	3	6	52	6
Tyler Bickers, Milwaukee	.313	.410	.421	195	16	1	1	33	5
Grant Thoroman, Purdue Ft. Wayne	.310	.404	.498	213	14	4	6	38	14
Ben Vore, Wright State	.308	.390	.664	214	11	4	19	75	15
Boston Smith, Wright State	.307	.403	.698	192	10	4	19	47	7

INDIVIDUAL PITCHING LEADERS

(Minimum 40 innings pitched)

	W	L	ERA	G	SV	IP	H	BB	SO
Luke Hansel, Milwaukee	4	5	3.41	15	0	90	74	43	84
Kevin Fee, Purdue Fort Wayne	7	3	3.48	0	5	65	75	27	46
Tanner Gillis, N. Kentucky	8	3	5.00	14	0	76	67	28	81
Adrian Montilva, Milwaukee	2	3	5.43	14	0	61	66	32	71
Brandon Decker, Oakland	7	6	5.44	13	7	103	101	34	105
Chet Lax, Wright State	4	1	6.23	9	0	56	77	18	45
Jake Shirk, Wright State	4	4	6.41	14	0	79	91	17	64
Carter Sabol, Purdue Ft. Wayne	4	6	6.47	15	0	79	91	40	74
Shane McAlinden, Oakland	3	2	6.97	8	0	61	78	15	50
Jacob Gehring, Youngstown S.	4	7	7.03	15	0	79	99	37	57
Clay Brock, Northern Kentucky	8	3	7.06	15	0	79	98	30	70
Hunter Pidek, Oakland	4	8	7.44	15	0	75	100	29	55
Ben Gerl, Northern Kentucky	5	7	7.70	16	0	83	91	45	69
Mac Ayres, Purdue Fort Wayne	2	6	7.71	15	0	77	107	37	57

IVY LEAGUE

	Conference W	Conference L	Overall W	Overall L
Columbia	17	4	26	18
Princeton	12	9	18	26
Cornell	11	10	17	21
Penn	11	10	24	25
Yale	11	10	18	23
Harvard	9	12	13	26
Dartmouth	7	14	13	26
Brown	6	15	11	28

ALL-CONFERENCE TEAM: SP: Joe Sheets, Columbia; Thomas Santana, Columbia; Callan Fang, Harvard. RP: Jacob Faulkner, Princeton. C: Mark Quatrani, Cornell. 1B: Max Jensen, Cornell. 2B: Griffin Palfrey, Columbia. 3B: Wyatt Henseler, Penn. SS: Sam Miller, Columbia. OF: Skye Selinsky, Columbia; John Quinlan, Cornell; Ben Rounds, Harvard. UTL: Nick DiPietrantonio, Princeton. DH: Cole Hage, Columbia. Player Of The Year: Wyatt Henseler, Penn. Pitcher Of The Year: Callan Fang, Harvard. Rookie Of The Year: Mark Quatrani, Cornell. Coach Of The Year: Brett Boretti, Columbia.

INDIVIDUAL BATTING LEADERS

(Minimum 140 at-bats)

	AVG	OBP	SLG	AB	2B	3B	HR	RBI	SB
Ben Rounds, Harv	.403	.506	.685	149	16	1	8	34	3
John Quinlan, Cor	.378	.439	.568	148	9	2	5	20	10
Mark Quatrani, Cor	.362	.492	.714	105	2	1	11	43	1
Wyatt Henseler, Penn	.360	.465	.755	200	9	2	22	56	0
COR Max Jensen, Cor	.358	.455	.561	148	8	2	6	37	5
Sam Miller, Col	.353	.411	.647	170	12	1	12	43	4
Nathan Cmeyla, Dart	.348	.400	.607	135	12	1	7	30	0
Jack Cooper, Col	.333	.382	.714	168	16	0	16	59	3
Cole Hage, Col	.329	.471	.658	161	10	2	13	38	6
Alec Atkinson, Yale	.326	.420	.438	144	6	2	2	22	18
Elliot Krewson, Dart	.320	.391	.386	153	7	0	1	22	5
Eric Jeon, Col	.320	.391	.523	153	12	2	5	32	2
Davis Baker, Penn	.319	.393	.521	213	14	4	7	44	14
Jake Koonin, Prin	.319	.402	.528	163	22	0	4	41	11
Nick Spaventa, Penn	.318	.408	.492	179	10	0	7	40	0
Nathan Brasher, Brown	.315	.416	.390	146	9	1	0	21	18
Jackson Hower, Dart	.311	.385	.370	119	7	0	0	19	2
Ryan Taylor, Penn	.306	.404	.470	183	15	3	3	39	13
Cole Fellows, Col	.305	.374	.508	128	8	3	4	31	2
Jake Bold, Prin	.295	.434	.442	156	7	2	4	19	2
George Cooper, Harv	.294	.335	.400	160	5	3	2	24	5
Nick DiPietrantonio, Prin	.293	.330	.485	167	10	2	6	26	4
Skye Selinsky, Col	.293	.403	.615	174	21	1	11	45	7
DJ Dillehay, Brown	.291	.362	.468	158	10	3	4	28	2
Anton Lazits, Col	.291	.416	.582	158	11	1	11	38	6

INDIVIDUAL PITCHING LEADERS

(Minimum 40 innings pitched)

	W	L	ERA	G	SV	IP	H	BB	SO
Jacob Faulkner, Prin	8	1	3.14	20	4	66	61	12	52
Sean Matson, Harv	3	3	3.25	11	0	64	53	27	77
Colton Shaw, Yale	3	7	4.26	11	0	68	62	33	70
Paxton Meyers, Brown	4	4	4.43	11	0	65	66	40	57
Reid Easterly, Yale	2	6	4.44	13	0	75	80	20	69
Callan Fang, Harv	3	3	4.64	12	0	64	56	20	83
Derek Yoo, Col	5	2	4.80	12	0	60	54	22	46
Thomas Santana, Col	4	1	4.87	13	0	44	39	18	40
Cole Zaffiro, Penn	5	5	4.94	14	0	75	65	35	90
Daniel Cohen, Yale	3	4	4.99	11	0	61	58	24	51
Ethan Hamill, Cor	3	3	5.71	12	1	58	62	25	28
Marco Dumsky, Dart	3	4	5.80	10	0	40	41	19	50
Joe Sheets, Col	4	4	5.89	13	0	55	55	29	48
Truman Pauley, Harv	1	4	6.14	15	1	44	37	41	41
Will Sword, Prin	2	4	6.52	12	0	48	52	29	43
Noah Keller, Cor	1	6	6.55	13	0	45	61	30	41
Jack Seppings, Brown	3	6	7.36	13	0	59	75	28	53
Sean Episcope, Prin	0	4	7.36	10	0	44	59	12	44
Ryan Dromboski, Penn	3	5	7.57	13	0	63	70	28	71
Huxley Holcombe, Cor	2	2	7.78	14	0	42	48	30	26
Santhosh Gottam, Brown	2	8	7.89	13	0	65	91	20	50
Jack Metzger, Dart	2	3	7.99	16	6	42	65	10	38

METRO ATLANTIC ATHLETIC CONFERENCE

	Conference		Overall	
	W	L	W	L
Fairfield	20	4	34	24
Niagara	20	4	38	17
Rider	18	6	28	23
Mount St. Mary's	13	11	22	34
Canisius	11	13	18	30
Marist	10	14	19	35
Manhattan	10	14	22	30
Quinnipiac	10	14	20	30
Siena	8	16	12	40
Iona	6	18	12	38
Saint Peter's	6	18	12	40

ALL-CONFERENCE TEAM: C: Ethan Hibbard, Fairfield. 1B: Eric Rataczak, Niagara. 2B: Zach Selinger, Fairfield; Daniel Perez, Manhattan. 3B: Dean Ferrara, Fairfield. SS: Chase Swain, Manhattan. OF: Jackson Strong, Canisius; Matt Bucciero, Fairfield; Josiah Ragsdale, Iona. P: Colin McVeigh, Fairfield; Deven Sheerin, Mount St. Mary's; PJ Craig, Rider. DH: Scott Seeker, Mount St. Mary's. UTIL: Ethan Conrad, Marist. Player of the Year: Eric Rataczak, Niagara. Pitcher of the Year: Colin McVeigh, Fairfield. Relief Pitcher of the Year: Zach Cameron, Niagara. Rookie of the Year: Deven Sheerin, Mount St. Mary's. Coach of the Year: Rob McCoy, Niagara.

INDIVIDUAL BATTING LEADERS

(Minimum 140 at-bats)

	AVG	OBP	SLG	AB	2B	3B	HR	RBI	SB
Eric Rataczak, Niagara	.396	.485	.698	222	14	1	17	71	2
Chase Swain, Manhattan	.392	.464	.575	153	9	2	5	41	15
Dean Ferrara, Fairfield	.391	.444	.522	253	12	3	5	43	7
Ethan Conrad, Marist	.385	.462	.707	239	19	14	10	56	19
Josiah Ragsdale, Iona	.385	.470	.646	192	13	8	7	37	22
Jared Zimbardo, Quinnipiac	.353	.473	.579	190	16	3	7	34	26
Jackson Strong, Canisius	.351	.483	.616	185	10	3	11	35	43
Scott Seeker, Mount St. Mary's	.348	.474	.610	210	21	2	10	61	7
Ethan Hibbard, Fairfield	.343	.459	.662	210	16	0	17	61	2
Nick Monile, Niagara	.341	.449	.447	170	5	2	3	36	9
Brian Skettini, Rider	.340	.429	.581	191	12	2	10	53	1
Daniel Perez, Manhattan	.328	.441	.414	186	7	0	3	30	14
Nick Grover, Niagara	.326	.448	.460	187	14	1	3	38	19
Keegan O'Connor, Quinnipiac	.325	.412	.557	203	10	2	11	48	7
Kyle Neri, Rider	.321	.429	.525	162	9	3	6	27	4
Brady Desjardins, Niagara	.317	.421	.477	218	12	1	7	46	6
Tyler Figueroa, Siena	.315	.392	.523	197	13	2	8	35	6
Carter Groen, Iona	.314	.393	.506	172	13	4	4	29	0
Luke Nomura, Fairfield	.313	.416	.528	233	15	1	11	38	14
Gavin Schrader, Niagara	.312	.413	.518	199	14	0	9	47	3
Rees Kozar, Niagara	.308	.411	.503	159	5	1	8	33	4
Carlin Dick, Canisius	.302	.446	.549	182	15	0	10	33	21
Matt Bucciero, Fairfield	.301	.384	.576	229	12	3	15	61	5
Nick Sturino, Fairfield	.301	.440	.449	156	7	2	4	32	5
Zach Selinger, Fairfield	.301	.451	.448	163	9	0	5	28	4

INDIVIDUAL PITCHING LEADERS

(Minimum 40 innings pitched)

	W	L	ERA	G	SV	IP	H	BB	SO
Zach Cameron, Niagara	8	1	2.90	0	11	59	44	20	59
Brendan Yagesh, Mt. St. Mary's	2	4	3.26	8	0	66	62	34	69
Jack Wren, Marist	3	2	3.70	6	5	58	48	20	54
Colin McVeigh, Fairfield	10	2	4.16	14	0	89	75	24	101
Blake Helmstetter, Fairfield	5	4	4.61	10	2	66	65	22	62
Deven Sheerin, Mt. St. Mary's	6	5	4.76	2	1	70	49	32	109
Clayton Poliey, Rider	4	3	4.78	12	1	64	67	29	51
Connor O'neill, Manhattan	3	4	4.96	6	10	53	61	31	44
Peyton Consigli, Canisius	2	7	4.98	14	0	69	66	28	69
Justin Guiliano, Canisius	3	7	5.11	13	0	69	69	32	68
PJ Craig, Rider	7	3	5.17	16	0	92	91	34	65
Felix Morin, Canisius	5	3	5.35	10	0	72	79	23	58
Bowen Baker, Fairfield	5	5	5.51	13	0	64	71	24	68
Andrelys Payamps, Iona	5	5	5.64	14	0	61	67	57	69
Justin Solimine, Manhattan	2	5	5.84	14	0	62	62	43	64
Arnad Mulamekic, Siena	2	4	6.20	10	0	54	56	39	58
Aaron Zenus, Quinnipiac	1	4	6.30	12	0	50	58	31	45
Maximilian Ramirez, Niagara	4	5	6.38	15	0	55	63	43	49
Marcus Monro, Saint Peter's	2	5	6.53	7	0	62	76	36	53
Alistair Morin, Siena	1	7	6.97	14	0	62	69	43	61
Brian Young, Rider	7	6	6.99	14	0	66	85	24	59
Mason Ulsh, Quinnipiac	3	7	7.63	14	0	74	91	31	60
Billy Rozakis, Siena	1	9	7.69	10	0	53	79	26	40
Jonny Gillig, Saint Peter's	2	8	7.69	11	1	60	66	47	48
Michael Lorenzetti, Iona	0	6	9.64	12	0	51	61	42	43

MID-AMERICAN CONFERENCE

	Conference W	Conference L	Overall W	Overall L
Bowling Green	24	6	33	20
Western Michigan	19	11	32	22
Ball State	18	12	35	23
Kent State	17	13	27	27
Miami	17	13	27	27
Toledo	16	14	27	32
Northern Illinois	14	16	21	33
Ohio	13	17	18	32
Akron	10	20	15	39
Eastern Michigan	9	21	14	38
Central Michigan	8	22	17	38

ALL-CONFERENCE TEAM: C: Garrett Wright, Bowling Green. 1B: Cade Sullivan, Western Michigan. 2B: Sam Seidel, Bowling Green. SS: Michael Hallquist, Ball State. 3B: Ryland Zaborowski, Miami. OF: Nathan Archer, Bowling Green; Zach MacDonald, Miami; Garret Pike, Toledo; Josh Johnson, Kent State. DH: CJ Richmond, Western Michigan. SP: Jared Schaeffer, Akron; Merritt Beeker, Ball State; Keegan Johnson, Ball State; Calvin Bickerstaff, Kent State. Grant Umberger, Toledo. RP: Carson Byers, Miami. Player of the Year: Nathan Archer, Bowling Green. Pitcher of the Year: Merritt Beeker, Ball State. Freshman Player of the Year: Garrett Wright, Bowling Green. Freshman Pitcher of the Year: Keegan Johnson, Ball State. Defensive Player of the Year: Michael Hallquist, Ball State. Coach of the Year: Kyle Hallock, Bowling Green.

INDIVIDUAL BATTING LEADERS

(Minimum 140 at-bats)

	AVG	OBP	SLG	AB	2B	3B	HR	RBI	SB
Cade Sullivan, W. Michigan	.387	.478	.599	222	15	1	10	54	6
Garrett Wright, Bowling Green	.380	.503	.581	129	8	0	6	28	5
CJ Richmond, W. Michigan	.380	.479	.667	213	18	2	13	67	4
Jacob Donahue, C. Michigan	.373	.440	.475	204	10	1	3	23	18
DJ Newman, Bowling Green	.371	.455	.664	143	6	3	10	37	10
Pike Garret, Toledo	.360	.435	.669	239	9	1	21	55	13
Brendan Kleiman, E. Michigan	.358	.455	.508	120	6	0	4	27	2
Dylan Nevar, W. Michigan	.353	.444	.637	215	7	3	16	71	2
Gideon Antle, Ohio	.350	.398	.599	197	17	1	10	48	4
Drew Loikits, C. Michigan	.347	.398	.463	95	3	1	2	14	4
Giano Zuccaro, E. Michigan	.341	.437	.509	167	12	2	4	30	4
Zach Macdonald, Miami	.337	.462	.683	208	6	3	20	62	15
Josh Johnson, Kent State	.336	.426	.607	211	11	2	14	62	20
Tyler Ross, Bowling Green	.331	.432	.563	160	10	3	7	37	6
Michael Hallquist, Ball State	.331	.396	.674	242	18	1	21	56	6
Eric Erato, Northern Illinois	.330	.418	.453	203	15	2	2	31	12
Lucas Johnson, E. Michigan	.327	.422	.455	165	10	1	3	26	5
Decker Scheffler, Ball State	.325	.396	.486	243	10	4	7	45	14
Blake McRae, E. Michigan	.324	.434	.453	179	9	1	4	32	7
Ty Batusich, Miami	.322	.401	.454	227	18	0	4	50	2
M. Bowman, Akron	.321	.424	.531	196	12	4	7	46	3
Nick Husovsky, Ball State	.320	.406	.448	125	7	0	3	17	0
Sam Seidel, Bowling Green	.319	.415	.481	185	12	3	4	31	9
AJ Rausch, Ohio	.318	.392	.481	154	7	0	6	27	11
Jack Krause, Bowling Green	.317	.464	.550	180	9	0	11	51	14
Cory Taylor, E. Michigan	.316	.375	.555	155	10	3	7	38	9
Kyle Schroedle, E. Michigan	.316	.398	.595	158	12	1	10	37	3
JR Nelson, Ohio	.312	.381	.377	199	10	0	1	13	12
Blake Bevis, Ball State	.310	.372	.537	229	16	0	12	55	2
Josh Swinehart, W. Michigan	.309	.378	.473	165	9	0	6	40	2

INDIVIDUAL PITCHING LEADERS

(Minimum 40 innings pitched)

	W	L	ERA	G	SV	IP	H	BB	SO
Grant Umberger, Toledo	5	5	3.81	15	0	76	70	34	80
Bergman Jackson, Toledo	4	6	3.94	7	1	59	62	18	52
Carson Byers, Miami	5	1	3.97	0	3	59	44	40	73
Merritt Beeker, Ball State	9	3	4.11	15	0	81	67	32	128
J. Schaeffer, Akron	3	8	4.32	13	0	81	94	13	61
Nolan Vlcek, Western Michigan	5	4	4.64	13	1	85	89	22	91
Nate Blain, Ball State	4	5	4.74	5	4	74	73	35	57
Peyton Olejnik, Miami	9	1	4.76	4	1	64	60	27	84
Keegan Johnson, Ball State	8	3	4.96	15	0	65	56	41	83
Calvin Bickerstaff, Kent State	4	4	5.08	11	0	57	56	5	56
Ben Vitas, Central Michigan	2	7	5.58	10	0	71	95	16	47
Drew Beckner, Eastern Michigan	2	8	5.64	9	0	69	64	48	61
Johnson Noah, Toledo	4	3	5.80	15	0	71	81	20	71
Lukas Galdoni, Miami	3	2	5.91	6	4	56	65	29	55
Adam Brouwer, Northern Illinois	7	5	6.14	14	0	73	84	25	55
Nic Good, Bowling Green	6	2	6.17	15	0	66	79	27	55
Bobby Jones, Eastern Michigan	5	5	6.28	13	0	86	89	24	79
Dillion Masters, Ohio	2	4	6.31	11	0	67	83	40	57
S. Atkins, Akron	3	8	6.34	12	0	61	72	30	45
J. Kelley, Akron	3	1	6.38	8	0	55	55	27	53
Patrick Mastrian IV, Miami	3	4	6.41	13	0	59	63	33	37
Blake Gaskey, Ohio	2	7	6.42	14	0	69	75	32	57
Eric Chalus, Kent State	5	3	6.56	14	0	73	94	24	71
Brady Miller, Western Michigan	6	6	6.75	16	0	85	114	25	75
Nick Vardavas, Miami	1	8	7.13	13	0	59	84	34	41

MISSOURI VALLEY CONFERENCE

Team	Conference W	Conference L	Overall W	Overall L
Indiana State	22	5	44	15
Murray State	17	10	37	20
Evansville	17	10	39	26
Illinois State	16	11	30	27
UIC	16	11	35	20
Southern Illinois	12	15	33	27
Belmont	12	15	26	32
Missouri State	11	16	23	34
Valparaiso	6	21	14	38
Bradley	6	21	13	37

ALL-CONFERENCE TEAM: SP: Brennyn Cutts, Indiana State; SP: Kenton Deverman, Evansville; Brandt Thompson, Missouri State. RP: Zach Davidson, Indiana State. UTIL: Reece Lawler, UIC. C: Dylan Leach, Missouri State. 1B: Luis Hernandez, Indiana State. 2B: Nick Rodriguez, Missouri State. 3B: Mason Landers, Belmont. SS: Drew Vogel, Murray State; Randal Diaz, Indiana State; Zane Zielinski, UIC. OF: Kendal Ewell, UIC; Mark Shallenberger, Evansville; Daniel Pacella, Illinois State. Joe Carter Player of the Year: Kendal Ewell, UIC. Pitcher of the Year: Brennyn Cutts, Indiana State. Defensive Player of the Year: Grant Magill, Indiana State. Newcomer of the Year: Kendal Ewell, UIC. Freshman of the Year: Kenton Deverman, Evansville. Dan Callahan Coach of the Year: Mitch Hannahs, Indiana State.

INDIVIDUAL BATTING LEADERS

(Minimum 140 at-bats)

	AVG	OBP	SLG	AB	2B	3B	HR	RBI	SB
Ewell, UIC	.390	.494	.795	210	20	1	21	69	8
Shallenberge, UE	.374	.514	.687	243	21	2	17	64	6
Zielinski, UIC	.363	.449	.583	223	17	4	8	42	20
R. Diaz, INS	.360	.437	.632	253	15	0	18	55	7
L. Hernandez, INS	.359	.421	.694	248	14	0	23	76	5
Beau Durbin, BRAD	.358	.415	.529	187	15	1	5	29	4
McGinnis, UE	.348	.394	.530	198	14	2	6	39	1
Fougerousse, UE	.348	.428	.678	270	21	1	22	71	1
M. Vallee, SIU	.341	.443	.459	229	12	0	5	41	15
L. Lawrence, ILS	.333	.396	.461	243	13	3	4	48	10
N. Rodriguez, MOST	.332	.432	.582	220	11	1	14	48	10
Vogel, MUR	.330	.441	.657	233	12	2	20	61	16
D. Pacella, ILS	.328	.429	.583	204	16	0	12	61	0
S. Loden, SIU	.328	.436	.621	177	13	0	13	50	6
T. Herron, ILS	.325	.386	.419	117	6	1	1	17	1
D. Listi, INS	.324	.464	.431	216	14	0	3	31	3
Bessette, UIC	.319	.416	.521	188	12	1	8	34	4
Tauken, MUR	.319	.385	.580	207	16	1	12	54	0
T. Gollert, MOST	.318	.394	.524	233	18	0	10	41	2
Slaughter, BEL	.317	.416	.457	208	8	0	7	33	23
Nicoloudes, UIC	.314	.427	.449	118	8	1	2	16	0
Landers, BEL	.312	.375	.602	231	11	1	18	56	6
Heaton, BEL	.310	.402	.596	213	13	0	16	62	1
Rando, BEL	.308	.417	.513	195	12	2	8	41	8
Garner, MUR	.306	.437	.551	216	8	0	15	56	16

INDIVIDUAL PITCHING LEADERS

(Minimum 40 innings pitched)

	W	L	ERA	G	SV	IP	H	BB	SO
B. Cutts, INS	7	1	3.69	18	0	83	67	40	75
B. Thompson, MOST	5	2	3.78	16	0	79	69	22	75
L. Hayden, INS	7	2	3.81	16	0	78	73	47	91
Harris, UE	8	6	3.82	27	4	75	70	31	72
Deverman, UE	9	2	4.22	18	0	111	112	23	83
A. Foeller, SIU	5	3	4.52	15	0	78	75	36	105
Ruzicka, BEL	4	5	4.52	15	0	74	62	46	56
J. Schaaf, MOST	3	4	4.58	16	0	57	55	27	39
Vernon, MUR	9	3	4.67	15	0	91	108	18	85
B. Bak, UIC	4	3	4.77	15	0	89	101	25	76
T. Perry, ILS	7	6	5.21	15	0	76	68	46	62
Pennington, MUR	4	5	5.26	15	0	77	76	23	77
C. Mabee, ILS	6	3	5.35	15	0	79	105	18	61
Schueler, UIC	5	2	5.59	14	0	76	89	22	56
Schultz, UE	6	2	6.15	17	0	91	101	34	74
Noah Edders, BRAD	5	6	6.27	15	0	79	87	34	76
Travis Lutz, BRAD	2	9	6.75	15	0	73	97	23	71
Baratta, BEL	4	4	7.16	17	0	72	84	35	52
Lyons, UIC	4	4	7.56	14	0	58	89	17	32
Jack Stellan, BRAD	0	5	8.00	20	0	54	71	29	32
T. Chadwick, ILS	3	7	8.49	15	0	58	69	34	49

MOUNTAIN WEST CONFERENCE

	Conference W	Conference L	Overall W	Overall L
Air Force	18	12	27	28
New Mexico	17	13	28	26
Fresno State	16	14	32	27
Nevada	16	14	25	26
San José State	16	14	24	32
UNLV	12	18	26	26
San Diego State	10	20	17	37

ALL-CONFERENCE TEAM: RHP: Doyle Gehring, Air Force. LHP: Seungmin Shim, Air Force. RHP: Jason Doktorczyk, Nevada. RHP: Omar Serrano, San Diego State. RHP: Austin Cates, UNLV. C: Jake Holland, New Mexico. INF: Jay Thomason, Air Force; Tommy Hopfe, Fresno State; Reed Spenrath, New Mexico; Dalton Bowling, San José State; Hunter Dorraugh, San José State; Austin Kryszczuk, UNLV. OF: Grady Morgan, Fresno State; Will Asby, New Mexico; Robert Hamchuck, San José State. Tony Gwynn Player of the Year: Jay Thomason, Air Force; Jake Holland, New Mexico. Pitcher of the Year: Seungmin Shim, Air Force. Freshman of the Year: Finley Bates, San Diego State. Coach of the Year: Mike Kazlausky, Air Force.

INDIVIDUAL BATTING LEADERS

(Minimum 140 at-bats)

	AVG	OBP	SLG	AB	2B	3B	HR	RBI	SB
K. Walker, NM	.391	161	44	63	19	11	0	3	30
J. Holland, NM	.381	168	47	64	60	15	2	17	20
Huntern Dorraugh, SJ	.377	199	45	75	49	9	2	18	18
Kryszczuk, LV	.372	199	59	74	75	20	2	19	31
Schmidt, LV	.367	150	33	55	28	7	3	1	22
Tommy Hopfe, FS	.360	247	57	89	45	19	3	7	21
Jay Thomason, AF	.358	215	71	77	55	14	5	21	30
Charlie Jones, AF	.344	154	32	53	54	9	2	13	13
R. Spenrath, NM	.340	209	54	71	51	18	4	14	41
Eddie Saldivar, FS	.335	257	58	86	33	19	4	7	18
W. Asby, NM	.333	213	59	71	59	17	2	12	30
Hefft, LV	.328	198	47	65	33	12	3	3	24
Shaun Montoya, SD	.327	220	50	72	17	9	2	3	20
Rocco Peppi, FS	.327	211	43	69	56	16	0	14	7
Spencer Chase, AF	.326	215	48	70	32	11	4	6	27
T. Wood, NM	.325	160	44	52	32	8	4	3	39
Nolan Wilson, LV	.323	201	35	65	50	20	2	7	9
Sam Kulasingam, AF	.323	229	57	74	36	16	3	6	26
Charles, LV	.320	181	46	58	32	11	2	10	14
Higgins, LV	.320	194	52	62	31	15	1	7	26

INDIVIDUAL PITCHING LEADERS

(Minimum 40 innings pitched)

	W	L	ERA	G	SV	IP	H	BB	SO
Shim Seungmin, AF	8	2	3.22	17	1	95	94	24	87
Jesse Gutierrez, SJ	4	4	3.47	21	1	57	61	19	54
Jason Doktorczyk, NV	6	4	3.95	13	0	84	79	22	91
Omar Serrano, SD	5	6	4.02	14	0	81	87	29	77
Cates, LV	6	5	4.08	14	0	90	103	15	107
Ethan Ross, SJ	6	5	4.86	18	0	83	91	48	72
Gehring Doyle, AF	1	3	4.94	24	10	58	62	18	57
Jake Riding, FS	5	6	5.06	19	0	69	68	15	67
Noah Beal, FS	4	4	5.13	16	0	79	90	23	93
Jake Dixon, FS	5	5	5.64	17	0	83	103	30	85
B. Russell, NM	4	4	5.87	16	0	61	61	17	45
Micky Thompson, SJ	5	4	6.39	16	0	82	94	35	57
Simon, LV	5	3	6.47	13	0	56	62	27	32
Ben Weber, AF	5	4	6.49	17	0	68	82	22	44
Xavier Cardenas, SD	2	6	6.58	14	0	67	62	59	58

NORTHEAST CONFERENCE

	Conference W	Conference L	Overall W	Overall L
Sacred Heart	25	8	35	23
LIU	24	9	33	25
Merrimack	22	11	33	26
Wagner	21	12	26	30
Delaware State	20	13	22	27
FDU	18	14	26	30
Central Connecticut	17	15	18	24
Le Moyne	15	17	22	27
Stonehill	13	17	18	29
Coppin State	11	21	12	33
Norfolk State	7	26	12	41
Maryland Eastern Shore	0	30	0	48

ALL-CONFERENCE TEAM: SP: Kieran Etwaru, Delaware St. SP: Patrick Gardner, FDU. SP: Garrett Yawn, LIU. RP: Alec Burnett, Wagner. C: Matthew Chatelle, Merrimack. 1B: Braydon Dolbashian, Merrimack. 2B: Evan Bouldin, Delaware St. 3B: Hunter D'Amato, FDU. SS: Jancarlos Colon, Delaware St. OF: Christian Gemelli, Merrimack; Zack Kovalchik, Sacred Heart; Jake Mastillo, LIU. DH: Frankie Ferrentino, Merrimack. Player of the Year: Evan Bouldin, Delaware St. Pitcher of the Year: Kieran Etwaru, Delaware St. Rookie fot he Year: Dawson Bryce, Merrimack. Coach of the Year: Pat Egan, Sacred Heart.

INDIVIDUAL BATTING LEADERS

(Minimum 140 at-bats)

	AVG	OBP	SLG	AB	2B	3B	HR	RBI	SB
Brady Short, C. Connecticut	.388	.473	.511	178	10	3	2	31	3
Bouldin Evan, Delaware State	.382	.434	.553	217	16	0	7	39	1
Gianno Merlonghi, C. Connecticut	.378	.417	.529	119	10	1	2	31	2
Hunter D'Amato, FDU	.364	.450	.536	220	17	3	5	51	27
Gemelli Chris, Merrimack	.362	.446	.621	232	13	1	15	54	13
Bryce Dawson, Merrimack	.357	.413	.619	252	19	1	15	59	11
Bronson Taylor, Maryland E. Shore	.355	.427	.591	110	11	0	5	24	2
Jaryn Sample, Delaware State	.339	.400	.418	177	6	1	2	28	3
Blaine Lidsky, Stonehill	.339	.385	.519	189	9	2	7	48	2
Andrew Roden, Le Moyne	.338	.440	.581	160	13	1	8	36	2
Trey Ciulla-Hall, Stonehill	.337	.443	.668	184	10	3	15	54	9
Xavier Ulrich, Wagner	.331	.384	.431	130	11	1	0	33	2
Manny Jackson, Norfolk State	.330	.360	.442	224	16	0	3	30	2
Seth Surrett, LIU	.329	.451	.468	222	12	2	5	39	14
Jancarlos Colon, Delaware State	.328	.443	.419	198	10	4	0	25	21
Tim Mcguire, Sacred Heart	.326	.418	.484	184	12	4	3	37	5
Dante D'Amore, Sacred Heart	.324	.424	.599	142	6	0	11	47	3
Benjamin Fierenzi, LIU	.324	.428	.423	213	8	2	3	41	10
Bouldin Krew, Delaware State	.320	.457	.579	178	13	0	11	55	3
Chatelle Ma, Merrimack	.319	.380	.563	160	6	0	11	46	3
Ferrentino Frankie, Merrimack	.318	.380	.611	239	13	0	19	67	0
Jalan Jones, Norfolk State	.318	.390	.490	192	15	3	4	30	11
Zack Kovalchik, Sacred Heart	.315	.401	.514	222	13	2	9	49	16
Alex Ungar, Sacred Heart	.314	.390	.471	191	14	5	2	37	17

	AVG	OBP	SLG	AB	2B	3B	HR	RBI	SB
Dolbashian Braydon, Merrimack	.309	.408	.681	188	9	2	19	53	2

INDIVIDUAL PITCHING LEADERS

(Minimum 40 innings pitched)

	W	L	ERA	G	SV	IP	H	BB	SO
Patrick Gardner, FDU	8	2	3.14	14	0	86	62	34	93
Ryan Bilka, Wagner	3	3	3.19	11	1	68	56	34	65
Kieran Etwaru, Delaware State	7	0	4.03	13	0	74	66	33	74
Joe Trombley, Sacred Heart	3	2	4.28	13	0	61	65	25	39
Jake Babuschak, Sacred Heart	9	3	4.47	15	0	93	93	28	79
Garrett Yawn, LIU	5	3	4.48	16	0	90	95	43	105
Elijah Foster, Sacred Heart	5	1	4.53	15	0	60	47	48	80
Ryan Brayde, Merrimack	6	1	4.58	14	0	73	70	27	70
Connor Hayden, Wagner	6	6	4.60	15	0	74	82	30	45
Frankie Wright, Wagner	6	6	4.62	16	0	86	105	29	53
Max Parker, Le Moyne	4	4	4.65	14	0	91	107	27	66
Jacob Crystal, Le Moyne	3	8	4.70	14	0	88	94	26	73
Jake Neuman, C. Connecticut	4	5	5.11	12	0	69	62	49	45
Braydon Gray, Stonehill	3	3	5.26	6	0	50	60	22	27
Peter Haas, Stonehill	3	6	5.33	10	0	54	67	22	49
Ryan Douglas, Stonehill	4	7	5.50	13	0	74	98	15	45
Joey Kosowsky, FDU	3	9	5.59	8	1	56	72	26	37
John Horton, Norfolk State	2	6	5.75	11	0	72	81	38	70
Zac Capps, FDU	5	6	5.83	15	0	79	81	32	100
Dalton Barham, Norfolk State	4	8	5.86	14	0	81	96	42	82

OHIO VALLEY CONFERENCE

	Conference W	Conference L	Overall W	Overall L
Little Rock	19	8	32	24
Southeast Missouri	18	9	36	27
Morehead State	17	10	37	24
Southern Indiana	14	13	27	32
Tennessee Tech	13	14	29	26
Eastern Illinois	13	14	20	33
SIUE	12	15	21	34
UT Martin	12	15	21	35
Lindenwood	9	18	16	38
Western Illinois	8	19	13	37

ALL-CONFERENCE TEAM: C: Hayden Gilliland, Tennessee Tech. 1B: Roman Kuntz, Morehead State. 2B: Nick Gooden, Morehead State. SS: Colton Becker, Morehead State. 3B: Nico Baumbach, Little Rock. OF: Ryley Preece, Morehead State; Josh Cameron, Southeast Missouri; Lucas Spence, SIUE. DH: J.R. Heavilin, Western Illinois. UT: Lucas Loos, Eastern Illinois. SP: Tristan Walton, UT Martin; Hoss Brewer, Little Rock; Peyton Calitri, Tennessee Tech. RP: Jacob Weatherley, Little Rock; Kyle Miller, Southeast Missouri. Player of the Year: Roman Kuntz, Morehead State. Pitcher of the Year: Jacob Weatherley, Little Rock. Freshman of the Year: Grant Parson, Southern Indiana. Coach of the Year: Chris Curry, Little Rock.

INDIVIDUAL BATTING LEADERS

(Minimum 140 at-bats)

	AVG	OBP	SLG	AB	2B	3B	HR	RBI	SB
Lucas Spence, SIUE	.385	.473	.552	221	14	4	5	36	12
Lucas Loos, EIU	.370	.442	.810	211	22	1	23	61	9
Roman Kuntz, MOR	.366	.482	.860	235	15	1	33	100	2
Ren Tachioka, USI	.363	.453	.421	190	6	1	1	23	17
Hayden Robbins, MOR	.349	.431	.557	212	9	1	11	57	11
Trenton Pallas, EIU	.349	.412	.480	152	8	0	4	22	3
Nick Gooden, MOR	.348	.429	.538	253	18	0	10	62	2
Colton Becker, MOR	.346	.429	.614	254	22	2	14	60	29
Dawson Hokuf, LWU	.344	.448	.533	180	16	0	6	33	0
Nico Baumbach, LR	.343	.400	.556	216	22	0	8	52	0
Ryley Preece, MOR	.340	.483	.636	247	16	0	19	62	19
Preston Ford, TTU	.335	.395	.527	188	10	1	8	40	14
Mac Danford, UTM	.333	.417	.623	204	14	0	15	55	1
Ty Stauss, SEMO	.329	.447	.545	213	17	1	9	52	2
Andrew Fernandez, UTM	.327	.412	.505	214	13	2	7	44	8
Hayden Gilliland, TTU	.325	.433	.569	209	12	0	13	56	0
Cole Gober, EIU	.323	.376	.514	220	12	0	10	38	14
Troy Baunsgard, TTU	.317	.390	.509	224	20	1	7	32	0
Will Smith, UTM	.315	.417	.514	216	12	2	9	37	4
T. Thompson-Allen, USI	.314	.387	.429	226	4	2	6	30	14
Jake Wright, LR	.313	.408	.480	198	12	0	7	36	8
JR Heavilin, WIU	.310	.390	.480	171	11	0	6	29	1
Ethan Willoughby, SIUE	.309	.368	.404	223	13	1	2	37	12
Josh Cameron, SEMO	.309	.389	.581	236	14	1	16	61	6
Brooks Kettering, SEMO	.308	.435	.474	247	12	1	9	40	8

INDIVIDUAL PITCHING LEADERS

(Minimum 40 innings pitched)

	W	L	ERA	G	SV	IP	H	BB	SO
Tristan Walton, UTM	6	4	2.88	15	0	94	75	46	98
Jacob Weatherley, LR	6	3	2.92	24	9	62	55	30	77
Peyton Calitri, TTU	7	4	3.34	15	0	94	98	10	85
Grant Parson, USI	4	3	3.90	11	0	60	46	28	60
Gavin Seebold, USI	7	2	3.93	16	0	71	70	18	58
Hoss Brewer, LR	4	5	3.95	15	0	84	79	36	101
Jaxson Pease, TTU	6	3	4.62	19	3	60	59	22	46
Eli Brown, LWU	2	6	5.01	14	0	79	73	25	65
Landon Smiddy, TTU	4	5	5.05	14	0	77	91	27	80
Haden Dow, SEMO	4	2	5.13	18	0	79	84	31	58
Josh Newell, LWU	5	4	5.21	14	0	66	83	16	41
Luke Helton, MOR	9	2	5.30	16	0	105	112	28	98
Brian Strange, SEMO	5	2	5.59	16	0	77	82	39	56
Eric Steensma, UTM	3	8	5.83	15	0	76	80	12	40
Jack Cline, LR	2	2	5.83	18	1	59	58	26	41
Zach Buschschulte, LWU	1	9	5.88	13	0	57	67	22	30
Jackson Wells, LR	5	3	5.91	15	0	64	72	38	68
Casey Parrenoud, EIU	3	4	6.45	13	0	53	61	21	42
Jeb Bartle, UTM	2	5	6.57	17	0	75	90	31	45
Tyler Kapraun, WIU	4	4	6.81	15	0	78	95	42	66
Colton Coca, EIU	3	3	6.89	19	2	63	70	38	55
Bryce Riggs, EIU	4	2	7.35	17	0	56	70	29	46
Tyler Delong, SIUE	3	6	8.28	15	0	71	87	46	58
Jason Buhl, WIU	3	9	8.29	14	0	76	95	44	48

PACIFIC-12 CONFERENCE

	Conference W	Conference L	Overall W	Overall L
Oregon State	19	10	45	16
Oregon	19	11	40	20
California	17	13	36	19
Arizona	20	10	36	23
Utah	16	14	33	22
Arizona State	17	13	32	26
USC	17	12	31	28
Stanford	11	19	22	33
Washington State	9	21	21	32
Washington	10	20	19	31
UCLA	9	21	19	33

ALL-CONFERENCE TEAM: C: Ryan Campos, Arizona State; Caleb Lomavita, California. 1B: Jacob Tobias, Arizona State; Peyton Schulze, California. INF: Mason White, Arizona; Garen Caulfield, Arizona; Jarren Advincula, California; PJ Moutzouridis, California; Maddox Moloney, Oregon; Travis Bazzana, Oregon State; Core Jackson, Utah; Aiva Arquette, Washington; Cole Cramer, Washington State. INF/OF: Owen Cobb, Stanford. OF: Brendan Summerhill, Arizona; Kien Vu, Arizona State; Nick McLain, Arizona State; Gavin Turley, Oregon State; Kai Roberts, Utah. DH: Brandon Compton, Arizona State. LHP: Jackson Kent, Arizona; Christian Lim, Stanford; Bryson Van Sickle, Utah; Micah Ashman, Utah. RHP: Clark Candiotti, Arizona; Cam Walty, Arizona; Aiden May, Oregon State; Bridger Holmes, Oregon State; Jacob Kmatz, Oregon State; Josh Blum, USC; Xavier Martinez, USC; Grant Taylor, Washington State. Player of the Year: Travis Bazzana, Oregon State. Pitcher of the Year: Bryson Van Sickle, Utah. Freshman of the Year: Brandon Compton, Arizona State. Defensive Player of the Year: Cam Clayton, Washington. Coach of the Year: Chip Hale, Arizona.

INDIVIDUAL BATTING LEADERS

(Minimum 140 at-bats)

	AVG	OBP	SLG	AB	2B	3B	HR	RBI	SB
Kien Vu, Arizona State	.413	.497	.793	150	11	2	14	56	12
Travis Bazzana, Oregon State	.404	.563	.899	218	16	4	28	67	15

Ryan Campos, Arizona State	.364	.461	.610	236	25	0	11	56	5
Core Jackson, Utah	.363	.463	.516	215	15	3	4	41	17
Kai Roberts, Utah	.356	.430	.562	233	21	3	7	58	32
Brandon Compton, Arizona St.	.354	.427	.661	189	16	0	14	51	3
Cole Cramer, Washington State	.345	.425	.487	197	15	2	3	37	7
Nick McLain, Arizona State	.342	.457	.663	187	18	3	12	54	6
Nathan Swarts, Washington St.	.329	.406	.555	155	15	4	4	22	5
Cort MacDonald, Stanford	.325	.397	.411	209	7	1	3	29	12
Aiva Arquette, Washington	.325	.384	.574	209	14	1	12	36	6
Jarren Advincula, California	.325	.404	.458	212	9	2	5	31	8
Brendan Summerhill, Arizona	.324	.399	.550	238	18	6	8	59	7
Peyton Schulze, California	.323	.375	.552	223	21	0	10	59	0
Jacob Tobias, Arizona State	.322	.418	.621	227	14	0	18	58	1
Caleb Lomavita, California	.322	.395	.586	227	13	1	15	52	12
Hunter Antillon, Utah	.321	.438	.453	137	6	0	4	25	1
Owen Cobb, Stanford	.320	.363	.500	228	16	2	7	33	6
Ryan Jackson, Southern Calif.	.318	.403	.455	233	18	1	4	39	8
Chase Meggers, Oregon	.316	.395	.480	152	8	1	5	33	2
Dallas Macias, Oregon State	.315	.390	.521	219	14	2	9	43	9
Ethan Mendoza, Arizona State	.315	.367	.443	203	11	3	3	24	0
Drew Smith, Oregon	.314	.422	.451	204	16	0	4	29	5
Seth Gwynn, California	.311	.425	.507	148	8	0	7	29	11
Garen Caulfield, Arizona	.310	.391	.469	239	19	2	5	42	0
Jimmy Nati, Stanford	.308	.372	.533	214	22	1	8	45	6
Roch Cholowsky, UCLA	.308	.399	.500	198	12	1	8	33	6
Mason White, Arizona	.305	.392	.603	239	10	2	19	65	5
AJ Guerrero, Washington	.303	.364	.572	201	9	0	15	50	0
Drake Digiorno, Utah	.301	.388	.442	206	15	1	4	32	8
AJ Salgado, UCLA	.300	.362	.422	180	5	4	3	20	6
Jeffery Heard, Oregon	.299	.386	.469	177	16	1	4	30	1
PJ Moutzouridis, California	.299	.389	.457	221	15	1	6	42	7
Temo Becerra, Stanford	.298	.357	.351	188	8	1	0	18	2
Harris Williams, Arizona State	.297	.402	.471	172	13	1	5	27	7
Joey Kramer, Washington St.	.295	.355	.483	207	6	0	11	34	1
Ethan Hott, Stanford	.294	.372	.359	153	10	0	0	13	4
Steven Ondina, Arizona St.	.291	.357	.429	189	4	2	6	29	9
Mulivai Levu, UCLA	.291	.355	.455	165	7	1	6	33	1
Carter Garate, Oregon	.289	.390	.402	194	13	0	3	27	2

INDIVIDUAL PITCHING LEADERS

(Minimum 40 innings pitched)

	W	L	ERA	G	SV	IP	H	BB	SO
Bryson Van Sickle, Utah	5	1	2.67	15	0	94	79	21	69
Aiden May, Oregon State	7	1	3.05	14	0	74	61	23	84
Cameron Walty, Arizona	8	2	3.29	16	0	90	98	13	75
Jacob Kmatz, Oregon State	7	3	3.38	16	0	88	66	22	96
Clark Candiotti, Arizona	7	4	3.39	16	0	96	88	23	103
Grayson Grinsell, Oregon	7	2	4.08	17	0	79	54	44	99
Jackson Kent, Arizona	3	4	4.08	15	0	86	83	27	89
Grant Taylor, Washington St,	5	4	4.21	15	0	83	71	28	99
Christian Lim, Stanford	4	6	4.32	14	0	77	66	36	86
Luke Jewett, UCLA	2	5	4.35	14	0	83	87	34	72
Kevin Seitter, Oregon	8	3	4.52	15	0	82	72	34	80
Connor Markl, Arizona State	6	4	4.68	14	0	65	67	35	63
Ben Jacobs, Arizona State	7	3	4.75	20	0	66	61	36	102
Luke Short, California	6	2	4.81	14	0	67	72	23	58
Connor Wilford, Washington St.	4	6	4.91	15	0	84	100	30	64
RJ Gordon, Oregon	7	6	5.13	17	0	95	92	46	87
Eric Segura, Oregon State	6	1	5.23	16	0	72	68	28	75
Duke Brotherton, Washington St.	5	8	5.43	21	1	66	79	24	44
Michael Barnett, UCLA	5	3	5.47	14	0	79	98	25	55
Tyler Stromsborg, Southern Calif.	4	9	5.50	15	0	69	88	15	53
Merit Jones, Utah	3	5	5.66	14	1	68	79	33	68
Jared Engman, Washington	0	8	5.82	14	0	60	62	28	44
Matt Scott, Stanford	4	10	5.96	16	0	80	73	36	103
Trevor Moore, Stanford	3	1	6.00	28	1	57	71	24	57
Trey Newmann, California	4	6	6.13	15	0	62	56	35	60
Nick Dugan, Stanford	2	4	6.49	18	3	69	84	29	60
Calvin Kirchoff, Washington	4	5	7.25	15	0	67	81	34	49
Spencer Jones, Washington St.	2	3	7.50	22	0	54	65	22	31

PATRIOT LEAGUE

	Conference		Overall	
	W	L	W	L
Army West Point	16	8	31	23
Navy	15	10	28	23
Holy Cross	14	11	26	27
Bucknell	12	13	22	24
Lehigh	9	16	24	23
Lafayette	8	16	14	35

ALL-CONFERENCE TEAM: SP: Justin Lehman, Army West Point; Matthew Ronnebaum, Army West Point; Tyler Grenn, Navy. RP: Andrew Berg, Army West Point. C: Derek Berg, Army West Point. 1B: Ethan Swidler, Lafayette. 2B: Billy Kender, Bucknell. SS: Tyler Young, Lehigh. 3B: Sean Keys, Bucknell. OF: William Parker, Army West Point; Jacob Corson, Bucknell; Jake Whitlinger, Lehigh. At-Large: Michael Trommer, Bucknell. Player of the Year: Sean Keys, Bucknell. Pitcher of the Year: Justin Lehman, Army West Point. Rookie of the Year: Chris Morabito, Bucknell. Defensive Player of the Year: Eduardo Diaz, Navy. Gene Depew Coach of the Year: Ed Kahovec, Holy Cross.

INDIVIDUAL BATTING LEADERS

(Minimum 140 at-bats)

	AVG	OBP	SLG	AB	2B	3B	HR	RBI	SB
Sean Keys, Bucknell	.405	.535	.798	163	19	3	13	57	4
Rafe Perich, Lehigh	.382	.492	.572	152	11	0	6	41	4
Billy Kender, Bucknell	.348	.471	.551	138	12	2	4	19	0
Brock Murtha, Navy	.345	.473	.508	177	16	2	3	35	20
Chris Barr, Army West Point	.341	.446	.471	170	8	4	2	21	16
Michael Trommer, Bucknell	.336	.440	.496	137	8	1	4	31	2
Ethan Swidler, Lafayette	.327	.460	.572	159	12	0	9	35	1
Jake Whitlinger, Lehigh	.319	.454	.375	160	7	1	0	18	21
William Parker, Army	.318	.400	.571	198	11	0	13	62	10
Tyler Young, Lehigh	.307	.371	.413	179	14	1	1	29	13
Logan Keller, Navy	.300	.357	.463	203	11	2	6	36	12
Coleson Titus, Army	.293	.434	.377	167	8	0	2	22	5
Jacob Corson, Bucknell	.291	.428	.605	172	13	1	13	47	2
Derek Berg, Army	.290	.404	.605	200	16	1	15	38	11
Andrew Manning, Navy	.285	.395	.424	172	9	3	3	33	6
Jimmy King, Holy Cross	.282	.369	.345	174	8	0	1	23	21
Colin Brown, Holy Cross	.279	.418	.382	136	11	0	1	23	2
Braden Golinski, Army	.276	.391	.490	192	10	2	9	31	12
Chris Morabito, Bucknell	.275	.365	.438	80	3	2	2	17	0
Victor Izquierdo, Navy	.275	.372	.376	178	15	0	1	42	1
Sam Ruta, Army West Point	.275	.446	.607	178	14	0	15	53	5
Connor Cooney, Holy Cross	.273	.375	.367	150	3	4	1	23	9
Ethan Ellis, Army West Point	.273	.336	.364	121	8	0	1	26	4
Blaze Fadio, Lafayette	.271	.397	.446	166	11	0	6	40	10
Gianni Royer, Holy Cross	.270	.386	.418	141	7	1	4	24	17

INDIVIDUAL PITCHING LEADERS

(Minimum 40 innings pitched)

	W	L	ERA	G	SV	IP	H	BB	SO
Justin Lehman, Army	5	4	2.68	12	0	74	63	25	49
Marcus Danchision, Lehigh	2	4	3.42	6	3	53	40	17	50
Brady Bendik, Navy	6	3	4.21	11	0	68	66	27	53
Matthew Ronnebaum, Army	6	3	4.34	12	2	77	74	29	66
Tyler Grenn, Navy	6	5	4.48	13	0	72	71	27	34
Tyler O'Neill, Bucknell	5	5	4.89	12	2	70	80	28	71
Mike Ruggieri, Army	2	6	5.26	13	0	67	64	40	70
Alex Bryant, Holy Cross	5	3	5.32	13	0	68	70	37	73
Matthew Shirah, Navy	3	5	5.53	12	0	54	38	38	60
Jaden Wywoda, Holy Cross	4	5	5.61	10	2	59	84	16	41
Mikey Myro, Bucknell	3	3	5.65	9	0	51	51	27	32
Danny Macchiarola, Holy Cross	6	5	5.74	13	0	69	75	27	67
Teddy Tolliver, Lehigh	2	4	5.87	12	0	54	64	17	22
Adam Bogosian, Lafayette	2	2	7.28	0	3	56	83	28	48

SOUTHEASTERN CONFERENCE

	Conference		Overall	
East Division	W	L	W	L
Tennessee	22	8	60	13
Kentucky	22	8	46	15
Georgia	17	13	43	17

EDDIE KELLY

Tennessee second baseman Christian Moore hit .375 with 34 home runs

Vanderbilt	13	17	38	23
South Carolina	13	17	37	25
Florida	13	17	36	30
Missouri	9	21	23	32

	Conference		Overall	
West Division	**W**	**L**	**W**	**L**
Arkansas	20	10	44	16
Texas A&M	19	11	52	15
Mississippi State	17	13	39	23
LSU	13	17	43	23
Alabama	13	17	33	24
Ole Miss	11	19	27	29
Auburn	8	22	27	26

ALL-CONFERENCE TEAM: C: Jackson Appel, Texas A&M. 1B: Jac Caglianone, Florida. 2B: Christian Moore, Tennessee. 3B: Charlie Condon, Georgia. SS: Justin Lebron, Alabama. SS: David Mershon, Mississippi State. OF: Braden Montgomery, Texas A&M; Jace LaViolette, Texas A&M; Dylan Dreiling, Tennessee. DH/UT: Ike Irish, Auburn. DH/UT: Nick Lopez, Kentucky. SP: Hagen Smith, Arkansas; Khal Stephen, Mississippi State. RP: Evan Aschenbeck, Texas A&M. Player of the Year: Charlie Condon, Georgia. Pitcher of the Year: Hagen Smith, Arkansas. Freshman of the Year: Gavin Grahovac, Texas A&M. Scholar-Athlete of the Year: Drew Beam, Tennessee. Coach of the Year: Nick Mingione, Kentucky.

INDIVIDUAL BATTING LEADERS

(Minimum 140 at-bats)

	AVG	OBP	SLG	AB	2B	3B	HR	RBI	SB
Charlie Condon, UG	.433	.556	1.009	231	20	1	37	78	3
Jac Caglianone, UF	.419	.544	.875	248	8	0	35	72	4
Gage Miller, UA	.381	.474	.702	218	12	2	18	56	0
Blake Burke, UT	.379	.449	.702	285	30	1	20	61	11
Christian Moore, UT	.375	.451	.797	296	19	2	34	74	5
Corey Collins, UG	.354	.574	.772	158	6	0	20	58	0
Dakota Jordan, MS	.354	.459	.671	240	14	1	20	72	3
David Mershon, MS	.347	.454	.500	222	12	2	6	41	27
Nick Lopez, UK	.345	.400	.537	229	22	2	6	53	3
Dylan Dreiling, UT	.341	.459	.715	246	19	2	23	75	4
Peyton Stovall, AR	.340	.409	.535	200	12	0	9	38	2
Justin Lebron, UA	.338	.429	.546	216	9	0	12	37	7
RJ Austin, VU	.335	.402	.471	242	14	2	5	54	28
Hayden Schott, AM	.335	.418	.498	263	15	2	8	63	1
Ryan Waldschmidt, UK	.333	.469	.610	213	17	0	14	46	25
Jackson Appel, AM	.331	.422	.534	236	16	1	10	41	16
Tommy White, LS	.330	.401	.638	279	12	1	24	70	3
Cole Messina, SC	.326	.465	.701	224	19	1	21	71	8
Steven Milam, LS	.326	.415	.516	221	12	3	8	40	7
Connor Hujsak, MS	.325	.413	.555	200	13	3	9	49	8
Kavares Tears, UT	.324	.427	.643	244	16	1	20	62	4
Ethan Lege, UM	.323	.424	.645	155	11	0	13	38	4
Braden Montgomery, AM	.322	.454	.733	236	14	1	27	85	5
Ian Petrutz, UA	.321	.447	.479	215	14	1	6	40	2
Mac Guscette, UA	.321	.418	.442	156	7	0	4	39	0
Ike Irish, AU	.319	.403	.627	185	11	2	14	59	5
Matthew Polk, VU	.316	.372	.492	187	16	1	5	21	8
Jayden Davis, VU	.315	.394	.435	168	12	1	2	36	2
Michael Braswell Iii, LS	.311	.411	.453	212	12	3	4	36	3
TJ McCants, UA	.306	.374	.583	235	16	2	15	50	14
Ethan Petry, SC	.306	.471	.639	219	8	1	21	53	4
Billy Amick, UT	.306	.387	.639	255	14	1	23	65	3
Ryan Nicholson, UK	.306	.405	.689	206	10	0	23	63	3
Jace Laviolette, AM	.305	.449	.726	259	16	3	29	78	7
Ben Mclaughlin, AR	.302	.447	.490	202	11	0	9	42	0
Jared Jones, LS	.301	.454	.747	229	14	2	28	59	3
Emilien Pitre, UK	.301	.420	.519	239	20	1	10	58	26
Mitchell Daly, UK	.300	.431	.500	190	15	1	7	45	10
Slate Alford, UG	.300	.370	.539	267	13	0	17	69	1
Jonathan Vastine, VU	.299	.384	.545	211	18	2	10	42	12
Gavin Grahovac, AM	.298	.390	.596	285	16	0	23	66	4
Hudson White, AR	.297	.396	.525	158	12	0	8	33	0
Trevor Austin, MO	.297	.433	.568	192	11	1	13	33	0
Hunter Ensley, UT	.296	.390	.532	216	15	0	12	48	4
Cooper Mcmurray, AU	.296	.449	.603	179	13	0	14	56	0
Mason Maners, AU	.296	.426	.549	142	9	3	7	17	7
Blake Jackson, SC	.293	.465	.483	147	9	2	5	27	16
Fernando Gonzalez, UG	.292	.364	.532	171	10	2	9	53	0
Cooper Weiss, AU	.291	.403	.487	189	11	1	8	37	27

INDIVIDUAL PITCHING LEADERS

(Minimum 40 innings pitched)

	W	L	ERA	G	SV	IP	H	BB	SO
Evan Aschenbeck, AM	6	1	1.78	32	10	76	55	12	87
Hagen Smith, AR	9	2	2.04	16	0	84	41	34	161
Luke Holman, LS	9	4	2.75	16	0	92	57	33	127
Ryan Prager, AM	9	1	2.95	19	0	98	83	20	124
Nate Snead, UT	10	2	3.11	29	6	75	71	26	61
Zander Sechrist, UT	6	1	3.12	20	0	78	76	16	76
Khal Stephen, MS	8	3	3.28	16	0	96	76	21	107
Gage Jump, LS	6	2	3.47	17	1	83	66	22	101
Trey Pooser, UK	7	1	3.50	19	2	90	70	35	82
Jurrangelo Cijntje, MS	8	2	3.67	16	0	91	70	30	113
Fisher Jameson, UF	5	0	3.99	34	2	68	60	18	79
Leighton Finley, UG	6	1	4.14	17	1	76	74	28	76
Drew Beam, UT	9	2	4.22	19	0	102	103	27	99
Bryce Cunningham, VU	7	4	4.36	16	0	85	69	34	96
Aj Causey, UT	13	3	4.43	19	1	91	93	22	125
Dylan Eskew, SC	3	5	4.60	19	0	63	58	26	40
Jac Caglianone, UF	5	2	4.76	16	0	74	62	50	83
Greg Farone, UA	4	3	5.02	17	0	72	75	24	68
Mason Moore, UK	9	4	5.05	18	0	93	79	54	83
Brandon Neely, UF	3	4	5.13	28	5	79	72	28	108
Carter Holton, VU	6	5	5.19	15	0	69	63	27	98
Eli Jones, SC	3	4	5.24	17	0	69	90	20	56
Zane Adams, UA	4	5	5.37	16	0	59	62	27	47
Riley Maddox, UM	3	7	5.48	15	0	69	79	23	53
Kolten Smith, UG	9	3	5.56	20	0	70	73	20	105
Chase Allsup, AU	4	3	5.63	13	0	62	72	16	74
Ben Hess, UA	5	5	5.80	15	0	68	60	35	106
Carter Rustad, MO	5	6	6.37	14	0	65	72	10	58
Dominic Niman, UK	8	5	6.85	17	0	71	82	25	67
Logan Lunceford, MO	2	5	6.97	14	0	61	73	26	53

SOUTHERN CONFERENCE

	Conference W	Conference L	Overall W	Overall L
UNC Greensboro	15	6	33	21
Samford	14	7	36	22
ETSU	13	8	36	20
Western Carolina	13	8	28	26
Wofford	12	8	42	20
VMI	7	14	27	29
Mercer	6	14	29	29
The Citadel	3	18	21	32

ALL-CONFERENCE TEAM: SP: Colton Cosper, Mercer; Rob Ready, UNCG; Hunter Shuey, UNCG; Michael Ross, Samford; Zac Cowan, Wofford. RP: Carson Lore, Samford; Jonathan Todd, Western Carolina. C: Justin Starke, VMI. 1B: Cameron Sisneros, ETSU. 2B: John Anderson, Samford. SS: Garrett Howe, Samford. 3B: Dixon Black, Wofford. OF: Ty Dalley, Mercer; Nate Stocum, Western Carolina; Marshall Toole, Wofford. DH: Caleb Cozart, UNCG. Player of the Year: Caleb Cozart, UNCG. Pitcher of the Year: Michael Ross, Samford. Freshman of the Year: Daniel Jackson, Wofford. Coach of the Year: Cody Ellis, UNCG

INDIVIDUAL BATTING LEADERS

(Minimum 140 at-bats)

	AVG	OBP	SLG	AB	2B	3B	HR	RBI	SB
Nick Iannantone, ETSU	.387	.505	.539	217	14	2	5	42	0
John Anderson, Samford	.382	.467	.682	217	24	1	13	69	2
Brice Martinez, Wofford	.380	.440	.537	255	20	4	4	57	15
Marshall Toole, Wofford	.375	.461	.617	256	15	10	9	64	43
Cameron Sisneros, ETSU	.369	.493	.766	214	16	0	23	86	1
Garrett Howe, Samford	.369	.480	.573	225	18	2	8	44	23
Justin Starke, VMI	.368	.494	.647	204	12	3	13	51	18
Zach Ketterman, WCU	.360	.453	.670	197	13	3	14	50	7
Daniel Jackson, Wofford	.357	.460	.599	207	10	2	12	69	4
Noah Gent, ETSU	.351	.408	.558	208	17	4	6	63	1
Andrew Bennett, Samford	.351	.457	.531	194	12	1	7	39	4
Dixon Black, Wofford	.350	.461	.617	243	16	5	13	76	13
Ty Swaim, VMI	.346	.418	.484	217	14	2	4	47	27
Lucas Manning, Wofford	.343	.493	.435	108	6	2	0	20	13
Cody Miller, ETSU	.340	.442	.426	197	9	1	2	33	19
Jack Renwick, Wofford	.336	.389	.504	232	18	3	5	57	16
Wells Sykes, Citadel	.333	.382	.492	195	10	6	3	26	7
Nate Stocum, WCU	.333	.419	.676	219	15	0	20	56	2
Caleb Cozart, UNCG	.332	.474	.742	190	10	1	22	73	1
Trey Morgan, VMI	.327	.437	.472	199	14	0	5	38	18
Tommy Barth, ETSU	.319	.412	.495	182	10	2	6	32	6
Garrett Staton, Samford	.319	.390	.633	248	19	1	19	69	7
Aidan Brewer, UNCG	.318	.373	.540	211	13	2	10	48	12
Ty Dalley, Mercer	.316	.388	.693	225	18	2	21	71	0
Jd Yakubinis, ETSU	.315	.361	.460	124	11	2	1	30	1
Tyler Hare, Wofford	.315	.418	.586	222	10	1	16	63	2

INDIVIDUAL PITCHING LEADERS

(Minimum 40 innings pitched)

	W	L	ERA	G	SV	IP	H	BB	SO
Michael Ross, Samford	13	0	3.27	15	0	96	86	21	88
Zac Cowan, Wofford	10	2	3.35	17	0	110	102	29	124
Rob Ready, UNCG	3	1	3.95	12	0	66	74	22	41
Camden Wicker, Wofford	4	3	4.28	17	2	76	70	24	57
Colton Cosper, Mercer	7	3	4.35	17	2	93	105	16	59
Ben Hutchins, Citadel	3	6	4.50	21	3	60	61	13	40
Julien Peissel, UNCG	4	2	4.70	14	0	75	74	32	64
Jace Hyde, ETSU	7	3	4.90	16	0	72	66	25	85
Carter Fink, ETSU	6	2	4.95	16	0	64	64	17	46
Michael Harpster, ETSU	8	1	5.27	14	0	67	69	23	62
Sam Swygert, Citadel	4	4	5.75	18	0	67	68	33	58
Trey Morgan, VMI	3	7	6.01	55	0	79	96	17	57
Landon Slemp, Citadel	3	6	6.23	17	0	65	77	33	44
Dante Visconti, WCU	4	1	6.33	21	0	54	51	29	45
Jess Ackerman, Mercer	5	6	6.38	23	1	66	69	28	71
George Derek Floyd, Citadel	2	5	6.44	26	0	57	72	24	56
Gavin Mortenson, WCU	4	6	6.51	20	0	65	67	36	63
Will Riley, ETSU	5	6	6.78	14	0	78	96	23	84

SOUTHLAND CONFERENCE

	Conference W	Conference L	Overall W	Overall L
Lamar	17	7	44	15
Nicholls	16	8	38	20
New Orleans	14	10	31	26
McNeese	11	13	32	27
Northwestern State	11	13	22	33
Southeastern	10	14	30	28
Incarnate Word	10	14	26	31
A&M-Corpus Christi	10	14	22	35
Heartland Christian	9	15	18	31

ALL-CONFERENCE TEAM: C: Miguel Useche, New Orleans. 1B: Edgar Alvarez, Nicholls. 2B: Isaac Webb, Texas A&M-Corpus Christi. SS: TJ Salvaggio, Southeastern. 3B: Shea Thomas, Southeastern. OF: Mitchell Sanford, New Orleans; Samuel Benjamin, HCU; Cooper Hext, McNeese. DH: Dalton Beck, UIW. UT: Bryce Calloway, New Orleans. SP: Brooks Caple, Lamar; Colton Mercer, New Orleans; Brennan Stuprich, Southeastern. RP: Nico Saltaformaggio, Nicholls. Player of the Year: Edgar Alvarez, Nicholls. Hitter of the Year: Mitchell Sanford, New Orleans. Pitcher of the Year: Brooks Caple, Lamar. Relief Pitcher of the Year: Nico Saltaformaggio, Nicholls. Freshman of the Year: Larson Fabre, Southeastern. Newcomer of the Year: Dalton Beck, UIW. Clay Gould Coach of the Year: Will Davis, Lamar.

INDIVIDUAL BATTING LEADERS

(Minimum 140 at-bats)

	AVG	OBP	SLG	AB	2B	3B	HR	RBI	SB
Edgar Alvarez, Nicholls	.405	.514	.678	227	21	1	13	67	1
Mitchell Sanford, New Orleans	.381	.460	.708	226	21	4	15	68	18
Dalton Beck, UIW	.377	.433	.716	236	20	3	18	67	8
Miguel Useche, New Orleans	.349	.461	.545	209	22	2	5	45	1
Webb Issac, A&M-Corpus	.339	.396	.456	239	10	3	4	30	19
Zak Skinner, Lamar	.339	.389	.557	221	16	1	10	53	2
River Orsak, Lamar	.338	.408	.641	231	12	2	18	65	9
Modgling Cole, A&M-Corpus	.333	.383	.407	150	6	1	1	20	6
Brayden Evans, Lamar	.326	.417	.591	215	14	2	13	43	4
Cameron Caley, UIW	.324	.473	.545	213	14	3	9	46	4
Trinidad Sebastian, A&M-Corpus	.320	.392	.409	203	14	2	0	38	5
Gerardo Villarreal, Nicholls	.317	.393	.407	167	9	0	2	35	0
Victor Castillo, New Orleans	.317	.478	.546	183	6	3	10	33	2
Cooper Hext, McNeese	.314	.407	.519	239	11	7	8	34	25
Bryce Calloway, New Orleans	.313	.390	.560	150	6	2	9	39	3
Garrett Felix, Nicholls	.312	.425	.489	221	17	2	6	46	11
Reese Lipoma, NW State	.312	.410	.380	221	13	1	0	29	14
Basiel Williams, Nicholls	.310	.396	.500	184	11	0	8	49	11
Samuel Benjamin, HCU	.309	.389	.606	188	11	0	15	39	11
Tanner Wilson, Lamar	.307	.393	.425	153	9	0	3	17	1
Diego Villescas, New Orleans	.306	.407	.494	180	9	2	7	29	10
Shea Thomas, Southeastern	.305	.373	.507	223	15	0	10	41	0
Daniel Calabrese, UIW	.304	.358	.399	148	11	0	1	22	3
Braden Duhon, McNeese	.302	.348	.365	222	10	2	0	33	14
Trevor Roper, HCU	.300	.348	.376	170	13	0	0	20	4

INDIVIDUAL PITCHING LEADERS

(Minimum 40 innings pitched)

	W	L	ERA	G	SV	IP	H	BB	SO
Brooks Caple, Lamar	7	3	2.40	15	0	98	58	27	102
Brennan Stuprich, Southeastern	6	3	2.87	14	0	85	77	27	49
Hunter Hesseltine, Lamar	7	3	3.59	14	0	78	84	14	48
Watson Matthew, A&M-Corpus	3	4	3.74	11	0	65	55	29	74
Devin Desandro, Nicholls	6	5	3.84	3	2	63	62	15	42
Colton Mercer, New Orleans	6	5	4.01	15	0	74	74	26	82
Cameron LeJeune, McNeese	7	2	4.14	7	6	74	89	26	57
Jacob Ellis, Lamar	8	1	4.22	15	0	85	68	30	72
Nico Saltaformaggio, Nicholls	7	4	4.32	0	2	73	78	22	66
Jacob Mayers, Nicholls	5	1	4.58	16	0	71	39	76	106
Michael Quevedo, Nicholls	5	1	4.75	14	0	72	70	21	68
Josh Salinas, UIW	5	3	4.89	14	0	77	66	29	76
Garcia Zach, A&M-Corpus	4	3	4.94	13	0	82	99	23	64
Parker Edwards, HCU	5	5	5.33	10	0	51	49	14	34

Dakota Lee, Southeastern	1	3	5.94	14	0	64	74	35	39
Ty Abraham, McNeese	4	3	6.22	4	0	59	63	31	58
Isaiah Zavala, UIW	4	6	6.33	13	0	87	103	29	77
Grant Edwards, New Orleans	5	5	6.41	15	0	73	94	26	67
Zach Voss, McNeese	2	6	6.60	15	0	74	83	26	45
Hunsaker Riley, A&M-Corpus	4	5	6.82	12	1	65	79	20	51
Dawson Flowers, NW State	4	5	7.26	13	0	66	75	22	34
Chase Prestwich, NW State	4	6	8.25	14	0	64	79	35	56

SOUTHWESTERN ATHLETIC CONFERENCE

	Conference		Overall	
East Division	**W**	**L**	**W**	**L**
Florida A&M	22	8	29	27
Bethune-Cookman	19	10	31	26
Alabama State	18	12	29	27
Jackson State	17	13	37	21
Alabama A&M	9	20	13	38
Mississippi Valley State	3	27	11	35

	Conference		Overall	
West Division	**W**	**L**	**W**	**L**
Texas Southern	19	6	24	24
Grambling State	18	8	26	28
Prairie View A&M	17	10	28	27
Southern	15	12	22	28
Arkansas-Pine Bluff	6	20	15	34
Alcorn State	4	25	5	43

ALL-CONFERENCE TEAM: C: Edwin DeLaCruz, Arkansas-Pine Bluff. 1B: Juan Cruz, Alabama State. 2B: Randy Flores, Alabama State. 3B: Cameron Bufford, Grambling State. SS: CJ Castillo, Texas Southern. DH: Jose Gonzalez, Bethune-Cookman. OF: Ali LaPread, Alabama State; Tiger Borom, Grambling State; Ty Jackson, Florida A&M. SP: Tanner Boccabello, Bethune-Cookman; SP: Caleb Granger, Florida A&M. RP: Pablo Torres, Bethune-Cookman. Co-Coach of the Year: Jamey Shouppe, Florida A&M; Michael Robertson, Texas Southern. Player of the Year: Ali LaPread, Alabama State. Hitter of the Year: Edwin DeLaCruz, Arkansas-Pine Bluff. Pitcher of the Year: Caleb Granger, Florida A&M. Relief Pitcher of the Year: Pablo Torres, Bethune-Cookman. Freshman of the Year: Juan Cruz, Alabama State. Newcomer of the Year: Tanner Boccabello, Bethune-Cookman.

INDIVIDUAL BATTING LEADERS

(Minimum 140 at-bats)

	AVG	OBP	SLG	AB	2B	3B	HR	RBI	SB
Edwin DeLaCruz, Ark.-Pine Bluff	.428	.520	.600	145	15	2	2	34	11
Juan Cruz, Alabama State	.388	.430	.641	170	10	0	11	57	1
Kyle Walker, Grambling State	.381	.510	.604	202	10	1	11	44	12
Ben Vanmaanen, Ark.-Pine Bluff	.375	.446	.583	72	9	0	2	27	2
Joseph Eichelberger, Jackson State	.374	.449	.500	206	10	2	4	55	18
Ty Jackson, Florida A&M	.374	.495	.621	174	11	4	8	41	9
Tyeler Hawkins, Southern	.373	.515	.660	150	10	3	9	47	23
Kj White, Southern	.364	.468	.392	143	4	0	0	22	15
Ty Washington, Miss. Valley State	.363	.463	.452	124	6	1	1	21	4
Jose Gonzalez, Bethune-Cookman	.361	.456	.554	202	10	4	7	53	5
Jordan Mccladdie, Jackson State	.361	.440	.513	230	14	6	3	46	40
Cameron Bufford, Grambling State	.360	.486	.565	200	9	1	10	58	16
Michael Burroughs, Prairie View A&M	.359	.443	.552	192	16	3	5	53	9
Myles White, Jackson State	.352	.473	.460	176	11	4	0	44	6
Gavin Terry, Arkansas-Pine Bluff	.351	.439	.433	134	5	0	2	16	10
True Fontenot, Florida A&M	.350	.422	.483	180	6	0	6	51	6
Madison Griggs, Texas Southern	.343	.471	.522	134	9	0	5	35	7
Benny Hernandez, Miss. Valley State	.343	.403	.610	105	5	1	7	36	2
Randy Flores, Alabama State	.341	.424	.558	226	14	4	9	42	31
Khyle Radcliffe, Southern	.340	.418	.537	188	15	2	6	46	19
Lenny Montesano, Jackson State	.336	.393	.583	223	15	2	12	60	3
Rodney Hibler, Jackson State	.335	.464	.509	218	13	5	5	37	35
Garrett Palladino, Alcorn State	.335	.404	.433	164	7	3	1	19	18
Michael Smith, Prairie View A&M	.333	.511	.600	165	13	2	9	50	22
Ashton Inman, Grambling State	.333	.445	.439	189	5	0	5	53	0

INDIVIDUAL PITCHING LEADERS

(Minimum 40 innings pitched)

	W	L	ERA	G	SV	IP	H	BB	SO
Caleb Granger, Florida A&M	10	2	2.97	16	0	94	98	25	77
Tanner Boccabello, B-C	7	3	2.99	14	0	90	105	16	68
Christian Womble, Jackson St.	4	3	3.67	6	8	61	45	47	59
Daniel Gaviria, B-C	6	3	4.11	13	0	72	81	16	51
Domenic Martinez, Texas So.	3	3	4.57	12	0	63	58	31	50
Carson Kelly, Florida A&M	8	3	4.71	10	1	71	73	25	48
Mason Martinez, Grambling St	12	3	4.74	17	0	114	116	41	85
Jorhan Laboy, Alabama State	6	4	4.89	13	2	88	103	30	66
Isaiah Williams, Jackson State	6	4	5.08	12	1	78	76	47	91
Luis Rodriguez, Alabama State	6	4	5.11	9	3	56	40	52	70
Marcos Gamboa, B-C	3	5	5.76	13	0	59	64	29	34
Garrett Vandeventer, Jackson St	5	6	5.81	18	0	115	138	54	79
Calvin McClendon, Ark-Pine Bluff	1	10	5.99	13	0	77	83	35	59
Jacob Ehling, Ark-Pine Bluff	4	5	6.00	11	0	72	95	20	44
Matthew Krall, Prairie View	6	1	6.08	13	0	64	69	35	42
Jose Almazan, Alabama State	4	5	6.10	10	1	59	71	30	48
Jacob Granger, Florida A&M	4	4	6.13	13	0	69	88	29	30
Michael Dews, Prairie View	4	4	6.29	14	0	73	98	21	75
Drew Lasseigne, Southern	5	6	6.37	14	0	71	107	18	63
Dalton Alford, Texas Southern	2	7	7.16	11	0	55	56	31	51
James Snipes, Miss. Valley St.	1	4	7.19	6	0	51	69	20	25
Elijah Breeden, Prairie View	3	2	7.26	1	0	66	91	23	49
Jaedon Willis, Ark-Pine Bluff	2	5	7.43	12	0	50	67	36	26
Armando Sierra, Miss Valley St	2	5	7.97	9	0	61	96	10	32
Kewan Braziel, Alcorn State	1	11	8.08	16	0	81	115	50	49
Anthony Mateo, Alabama A&M	1	7	8.17	13	0	68	110	12	36
Phillip Bryant, Grambling State	5	3	8.74	12	1	58	57	50	43
Jesus Campa, Miss. Valley St	1	6	9.13	12	0	45	59	32	25
Josiah Castro, Texas Southern	3	5	9.78	8	1	46	62	25	31

SUMMIT LEAGUE

	Conference		Overall	
	W	**L**	**W**	**L**
St. Thomas	16	10	22	24
Omaha	16	13	18	32
North Dakota State	14	12	20	30
Oral Roberts	13	15	27	32
Northern Colorado	13	16	16	38
South Dakota State	11	17	20	29

ALL-CONFERENCE TEAM: C: Max Moris, St. Thomas. 1B: Drew Stahl, Oral Roberts. 2B: Cade Stuff, SDSU. 3B: Holden Breeze, Oral Roberts. SS: Jake Schaffner, NDSU. OF: Cael Frost, SDSU; Matt Goetzmann, Omaha; Brigs Richartz, St. Thomas. DH: Dawson Parry, SDSU. UT: Jordan Sagedahl, SDSU. SP: Jakob Hall, Oral Roberts; Harrison Kreiling, Omaha; Nic McCay, SDSU. RP: Joey Danielson, NDSU. Player of the Year: Cael Frost, South Dakota State. Pitcher of the Year: Jakob Hall, Oral Roberts. Newcomer of the Year: Cael Frost, South Dakota State. Defensive Player of the Year: Matt Goetzmann, Omaha. Coach of the Year: Evan Porter, Omaha.

INDIVIDUAL BATTING LEADERS

(Minimum 140 at-bats)

	AVG	OBP	SLG	AB	2B	3B	HR	RBI	SB
Kai Wagner, Northern Colorado	.364	.435	.612	165	12	1	9	41	1
Holden Breeze, Oral Roberts	.345	.429	.515	229	10	1	9	48	2
Matthew Maulik, St. Thomas	.343	.412	.547	181	6	2	9	44	4
Cael Frost, South Dakota St.	.343	.433	.742	198	16	0	21	59	1
Brigs Richartz, St. Thomas	.337	.403	.524	187	13	2	6	34	3
Jake Schaffner, North Dakota St.	.337	.436	.421	190	9	2	1	17	16
Joe Roder, St. Thomas	.331	.448	.500	130	2	1	6	25	0
M Nyrop, St. Thomas	.326	.402	.707	92	8	0	9	32	0
Dawson Parry, South Dakota St.	.325	.404	.629	194	14	0	15	60	0
Elijah Rodriguez, Oral Roberts	.324	.413	.420	238	13	2	2	43	17
Max Moris, St. Thomas	.322	.405	.461	180	9	2	4	35	1
Cadyn Schwabe, North Dakota St.	.321	.425	.423	196	7	5	1	24	12
Garrett Fisher, Northern Colorado	.318	.440	.500	148	9	0	6	31	0
Kyle Booker, Oral Roberts	.317	.407	.461	230	12	0	7	47	12
Matt Goetzmann, Omaha	.317	.438	.485	202	12	5	4	31	17
Tyler Bishop, Omaha	.317	.395	.524	208	13	3	8	38	1
Bryce Ronken, South Dakota St.	.313	.389	.545	112	7	2	5	17	3

Player	AVG	OBP	SLG	AB	2B	3B	HR	RBI	SB
Carter Monda, Northern Colo.	.310	.410	.398	113	7	0	1	19	7
Henry Zipay, Omaha	.303	.403	.426	155	8	1	3	16	1
Reece Anderson, South Dakota St.	.302	.391	.459	159	6	2	5	21	1
Drew Lechnir, Omaha	.300	.400	.432	190	10	0	5	26	2
Ben Vujovich, St. Thomas	.299	.403	.385	187	6	2	2	24	17
Cade Stuff, South Dakota State	.298	.373	.421	178	11	1	3	31	0
Mikey Gottschalk, St. Thomas	.296	.409	.358	162	6	2	0	24	6
Alex Rodgers, Oral Roberts	.293	.403	.384	232	15	0	2	27	15

INDIVIDUAL PITCHING LEADERS

(Minimum 40 innings pitched)

Player	W	L	ERA	G	SV	IP	H	BB	SO
Nic McCay, South Dakota State	4	2	3.64	13	0	72	62	36	96
Jacob Mrosko, St. Thomas	3	3	3.91	9	0	46	25	32	57
Jakob Hall, Oral Roberts	10	3	4.12	16	0	107	100	21	110
Murphy Gienger, Northern Colo	5	3	4.52	6	0	74	72	37	61
Logan Knight, North Dakota St	5	4	5.20	14	0	73	76	38	77
Caleb, Riedel, Omaha	6	4	5.47	15	0	74	72	32	89
Brooks Fowler, Oral Roberts	5	5	5.54	16	1	80	80	32	83
Jake Storey, Northern Colorado	3	4	5.88	10	0	57	59	30	48
Kolby Gartner, St. Thomas	4	5	6.11	3	1	53	53	30	49
Charlie Bell, Omaha	2	6	6.35	14	0	68	75	25	69
Walker Retz, St. Thomas	3	3	6.40	8	1	52	62	23	44
Landon Koenig, North Dakota St	1	4	7.54	14	0	60	86	25	41
Leland Wilson, North Dakota St	1	6	8.05	8	0	54	69	33	41
Jake Goble, South Dakota State	3	8	8.62	11	0	63	99	28	57
Dylan Smith, Northern Colorado	2	10	9.93	15	0	68	125	25	54

SUN BELT CONFERENCE

East Division	Conference W	Conference L	Overall W	Overall L
Louisiana	23	7	42	20
Southern Miss	20	10	43	20
Troy	18	12	37	22
James Madison	17	13	36	25
Georgia Southern	17	13	33	26
App State	16	13	33	21
Coastal Carolina	16	14	36	25
Old Dominion	15	15	31	26
South Alabama	14	16	31	25
Texas State	13	17	27	29
Georgia State	13	17	25	32
ULM	11	19	25	30
Marshall	9	21	18	37
Arkansas State	7	20	21	32

ALL-CONFERENCE TEAM: P: Chase Morgan, Louisiana; Bryce Blevins, Marshall; Billy Oldham, Southern Miss. RP: LP Langevin, Louisiana. C: Brooks Bryan, Troy. 1B: Trey LaFleur, Louisiana. 2B: Blake Barthol, Coastal Carolina. SS: Kyle DeBarge, Louisiana. 3B: Sam Antonacci, Coastal Carolina. OF: Banks Tolley, App State; Graham Brown, Coastal Carolina; Fenwick Trimble, James Madison. DH: Slade Wilks, Southern Miss. UT: Austin St. Laurent, App State. Player of the Year: Kyle DeBarge, Louisiana. Pitcher of the Year: LP Langevin, Louisiana. Newcomer of the Year: Banks Tolley, App State. Freshman of the Year: Chase Morgan, Louisiana. Tony Robichaux Leadership Award: Sam Blancato, Georgia Southern. Ron Maestri Coach of the Year: Matt Deggs, Louisiana.

INDIVIDUAL BATTING LEADERS

(Minimum 140 at-bats)

Player	AVG	OBP	SLG	AB	2B	3B	HR	RBI	SB
Dalton McIntyre, Southern Miss	.388	.447	.473	237	12	1	2	34	10
Banks Tolley, App State	.379	.484	.781	224	12	0	26	77	6
Josh Tate, Georgia Southern	.369	.475	.489	233	14	1	4	30	27
Fenwick Trimble, James Madison	.369	.452	.635	244	21	1	14	65	16
Sam Antonacci, Coastal Carolina	.367	.523	.504	226	13	0	6	47	15
Austin St. Laurent, App State	.366	.424	.618	246	12	4	14	60	9
Trey LaFleur, Louisiana	.364	.435	.670	176	16	1	12	42	10
Ethan Kavanagh, Troy	.361	.495	.447	208	12	0	2	51	6
Kyle DeBarge, Louisiana	.355	.418	.699	256	19	3	21	72	10
Graham Brown, Coastal Carolina	.353	.456	.601	218	18	0	12	62	10
Kyle Mock, Troy	.351	.475	.569	188	14	0	9	50	2
Will Mize, Georgia State	.344	.370	.628	250	18	1	17	60	4
Ryne Farber, Texas State	.340	.466	.468	141	10	1	2	25	8
Slade Wilks, Southern Miss	.333	.414	.590	249	20	1	14	69	2
Easton Winfield, ULM	.332	.414	.546	205	8	3	10	40	18
Mike Mancini, James Madison	.329	.419	.586	237	10	3	15	49	29
Aidan Gilroy, Troy	.328	.474	.492	177	13	2	4	37	4
Caden Bodine, Coastal Carolina	.328	.411	.523	241	20	0	9	71	3
Duncan Pastore, Louisiana	.327	.404	.442	199	11	0	4	37	5
Aaron Lugo, Texas State	.326	.428	.580	193	15	2	10	49	14
Brennan Hudson, Georgia State	.326	.478	.622	135	4	0	12	32	1
Bryce Blaser, ULM	.326	.392	.442	181	13	1	2	23	3
Cam Harthan, Marshall	.325	.384	.408	169	2	3	2	15	17
Micah Morgan, South Alabama	.324	.434	.505	111	5	0	5	28	0
Kole Myers, Troy	.323	.487	.570	223	11	4	12	44	34
Michelle Artzberger, ULM	.323	.438	.547	161	12	0	8	43	4
Kent Schmidt, Georgia Southern	.321	.432	.425	212	16	0	2	42	2
Drew Holderbach, App State	.321	.465	.550	209	19	1	9	48	6
Derek Bender, Coastal Carolina	.320	.422	.519	231	9	2	11	63	10
Luke Yuhasz, Louisiana	.318	.398	.579	107	5	1	7	21	5

INDIVIDUAL PITCHING LEADERS

(Minimum 40 innings pitched)

Player	W	L	ERA	G	SV	IP	H	BB	SO
Andrew Herrmann, Louisiana	6	3	3.09	12	0	67	55	26	61
Drayton Brown, Texas State	2	3	3.14	11	0	57	52	24	47
Chase Morgan, Louisiana	5	3	3.18	13	1	74	59	20	69
Mitchell Gross, Ga. Southern	3	5	3.34	6	2	70	65	18	65
Bryce Blevins, Marshall	3	5	3.45	11	0	86	85	20	71
Colby Allen, Southern Miss	10	2	3.58	2	7	65	62	18	82
LP Langevin, Louisiana	6	1	3.73	3	7	63	40	33	106
Niko Mazza, Southern Miss	9	3	3.99	16	0	90	79	36	95
Jackson Steensma, App State	6	2	4.03	14	0	67	60	21	74
Max Kuhle, James Madison	5	4	4.13	8	1	61	54	31	67
John Holobetz, Old Dominion	4	5	4.31	4	0	63	57	20	52
Cam Hill, South Alabama	4	3	4.39	14	0	70	77	23	43
Luke Lyon, Troy	8	3	4.40	11	0	74	72	23	54
Billy Oldham, Southern Miss	7	3	4.48	16	0	94	84	28	97
Dylan Heine, Arkansas State	2	2	4.65	14	0	62	61	26	30
Donovan Burke, James Madison	7	2	4.67	14	0	94	106	26	72
Riley Eikhoff, Coastal Carolina	6	1	5.00	16	0	76	91	15	56
Ty Fisher, Georgia Southern	7	5	5.10	16	0	85	90	26	69
Austin Eaton, Texas State	4	4	5.27	10	0	56	63	22	43
Beau Blanchard, ULM	2	5	5.40	12	0	55	52	17	52
Drew Harlow, Marshall	6	7	5.61	14	0	85	81	24	80
Ben Johnson, Ga. Southern	5	3	5.80	9	2	59	69	26	57
Dante Chirico, App State	4	2	6.25	13	0	68	62	32	59
Grayson Stewart, Troy	4	2	6.67	10	0	59	57	21	66
Bradley Wilson, App State	2	4	9.00	13	0	58	68	43	49

WEST COAST CONFERENCE

Team	Conference W	Conference L	Overall W	Overall L
San Diego	20	4	41	14
Portland	19	5	39	19
Saint Mary's	17	8	35	22
Gonzaga	14	10	20	32
Santa Clara	12	12	26	26
LMU	9	15	24	30
Pepperdine	9	15	15	38
Pacific	5	19	11	44
San Francisco	4	20	21	34

ALL-CONFERENCE TEAM: C: Ariel Armas, San Diego. INF: Christian Almanza, Saint Mary's. INF: Christian Dicochea, LMU. INF: Ben Patacsil, Portland. INF/OF: Jakob Christian, San Diego. OF: Jake Holcroft, Portland. OF: Coleman Schmidt, Saint Mary's. P: Nick Brink, Portland. P: Derik Eaquinto, Saint Mary's. P: Carter Gaston, Portland. P: Blake Hammond, Santa Clara. P: Logan Reddemann, San Diego. P: Austin Smith, San Diego. Coach Of The Year: Brock Ungricht, San Diego. Player Of The Year: Jakob Christian, San Diego. Pitcher Of The Year: Carter Gaston, Portland. Freshman Of The Year: Logan Reddemann, San Diego. Defensive Player Of The Year: Ariel Armas, San Diego

INDIVIDUAL BATTING LEADERS

(Minimum 140 at-bats)

	AVG	OBP	SLG	AB	2B	3B	HR	RBI	SB
Ben Patacsil, Portland	.384	.464	.537	177	4	1	7	50	4
Jakob Christian, San Diego	.364	.460	.828	198	14	0	26	67	9
Jake Holcroft, Portland	.348	.430	.541	233	17	2	8	59	21
Christian Almanza, Saint Mary's	.343	.459	.778	207	16	1	24	69	1
Christian Dicochea, LMU	.342	.455	.518	199	15	1	6	27	10
Dalton Mashore, Saint Mary's	.338	.429	.634	216	17	4	13	41	11
Coleman Schmidt, Saint Mary's	.333	.366	.631	225	16	6	13	40	10
Tyler Howard, Portland	.331	.395	.493	136	11	1	3	20	0
Jonjon Berring, Santa Clara	.327	.448	.627	150	12	3	9	28	15
Jack Gurevitch, San Diego	.324	.450	.509	216	11	1	9	36	5
Connor Harrison, Saint Mary's	.322	.410	.541	146	8	0	8	36	0
Brady Bean, Portland	.321	.405	.503	165	10	1	6	38	2
Brendan Bobo, LMU	.317	.432	.573	199	13	1	12	58	16
Spencer Scott, Portland	.316	.447	.445	155	11	0	3	27	0
Austin Smith, San Diego	.314	.429	.471	204	11	0	7	39	3
Connor Bradshaw, Pepperdine	.309	.398	.464	207	12	1	6	39	7
Justin Decriscio, San Diego	.308	.372	.419	198	13	0	3	42	10
Will Worthington, San Diego	.304	.368	.361	191	8	0	1	38	7
Connor Walsh, Pepperdine	.303	.396	.457	188	11	0	6	38	6
Ryan Pierce, Saint Mary's	.302	.347	.559	222	12	0	15	55	2
Tommy Eisenstat, Gonzaga	.301	.337	.420	193	9	1	4	30	4
Tanner Griffith, Saint Mary's	.300	.458	.371	70	2	0	1	8	10
Ariel Armas, San Diego	.298	.399	.429	198	8	0	6	29	6
Brady Renck, Pepperdine	.298	.380	.502	215	10	5	8	34	10
Benny Casillas, LMU	.295	.386	.350	200	4	2	1	36	14
Dustin Allen, San Diego	.294	.391	.390	218	10	4	1	29	9
Evan Scavotto, Portland	.292	.388	.396	154	8	1	2	20	1
Diego Baqueiro, LMU	.291	.376	.474	196	17	2	5	45	3
Jack Costello, San Diego	.291	.369	.470	234	17	2	7	60	3
Hudson Shupe, Gonzaga	.289	.356	.428	152	10	1	3	24	3

INDIVIDUAL PITCHING LEADERS

(Minimum 40 innings pitched)

	W	L	ERA	G	SV	IP	H	BB	SO
Carter Gaston, Portland	11	2	3.01	11	2	81	73	22	65
Joe Soberon, San Francisco	4	6	3.20	14	0	79	66	31	67
Derik Eaquinto, Saint Mary's	6	2	3.46	14	0	83	67	27	75
Austin Smith, San Diego	7	0	3.49	9	5	57	47	26	49
Nick Brink, Portland	10	4	3.61	15	0	100	85	23	130
Owen Hackman, LMU	7	3	3.69	13	0	76	58	28	85
Josh Randall, San Diego	4	2	3.73	14	0	72	61	27	84
Blake Hammond, Santa Clara	3	4	3.76	5	5	69	66	28	83
Logan Reddemann, San Diego	7	4	4.01	13	0	76	81	19	66
Justin Feld, Gonzaga	4	2	4.16	10	0	63	63	36	62
Lance Santerre, San Francisco	2	4	4.57	13	0	63	62	23	63
Sam Stuhr, Portland	3	2	4.61	16	0	80	77	45	100
Brandon Gomez, Santa Clara	2	5	5.26	12	0	67	74	19	52
Jakob Guardado, Pacific	1	6	5.84	11	0	57	83	23	28
Liam Paddack, Gonzaga	3	7	6.09	12	0	65	57	56	77
Nick Bonn, Pepperdine	1	7	6.54	13	0	76	96	19	48
Matthew Boyer, Pepperdine	3	7	7.44	12	1	62	82	16	46
Connor Linchey, Saint Mary's	4	4	7.78	12	0	61	87	18	45
Ethan Shaver, Pacific	2	7	8.81	14	0	64	102	19	44

WESTERN ATHLETIC CONFERENCE

	Conference		Overall	
	W	L	W	L
Grand Canyon	23	7	36	25
Abilene Christian	18	12	33	25
Utah Valley	18	12	29	29
California Baptist	18	12	38	24
Tarleton State	17	13	32	29
UT Arlington	16	14	22	34
UTRGV	15	15	29	25
Sacramento State	14	16	26	31
Utah Tech	10	20	14	42
Seattle U	10	20	17	36
Stephen F. Austin	6	24	10	44

ALL-CONFERENCE TEAM: SP: Brett Lanman, LHP, Abilene Christian. SP: Isaac Lyon, So., RHP, Grand Canyon. RP: Grant Garza, Sr., RHP, Tarleton State. C: Burke Camper, Sr., Utah Valley. 1B: Gino D'Alessio, Grad, Abilene Christian. 2B: Daniel Dickinson, So., Utah Valley. SS: Josh Paino, Jr., California Baptist. 3B: Mitchel Simon, Sr., California Baptist. OF: Miller Ladusau, Sr., Abilene Christian. OF: Nicholas Dumesnil, So., California Baptist. OF: Tyler Wilson, Sr., Grand Canyon. DH: Beau Ankeney, Jr., Grand Canyon. Player of the Year: Tyler Wilson, Grand Canyon. Pitcher of the Year: Brett Lanman, Abilene Christian. Freshman of the Year: Brett Lanman, Abilene Christian. Defensive Player of the Year: Josh Paino, California Baptist. Coach of the Year: Gregg Wallis, Grand Canyon.

INDIVIDUAL BATTING LEADERS

(Minimum 140 at-bats)

	AVG	OBP	SLG	AB	2B	3B	HR	RBI	SB
Tyler Wilson, GCU	.378	.441	.691	233	18	2	17	65	1
Gino D'Alessio, ACU	.372	.451	.546	218	11	0	9	63	5
Daniel Dickinson, UVU	.367	.469	.661	245	14	2	18	53	32
Nick Dumesnil, CBU	.362	.440	.702	235	19	2	19	45	9
Eddy Pelc, GCU	.352	.470	.526	196	15	2	5	50	6
Miller Ladusau, ACU	.351	.462	.573	211	23	0	8	47	11
Steven Lancia, UTRGV	.344	.420	.479	192	12	1	4	32	0
Benjamin Greer, ACU	.338	.436	.477	151	15	0	2	25	16
Cole Miears, TSU	.336	.473	.488	217	12	0	7	45	13
Cole Kleckner, SU	.335	.398	.376	221	9	0	0	15	10
Dustin Crenshaw, GCU	.333	.385	.446	177	9	1	3	23	4
Cris Enriquez, TSU	.332	.407	.491	214	11	1	7	58	0
Derek Gellos, SU	.330	.430	.508	197	16	2	5	36	0
Eli Paton, GCU	.319	.399	.509	216	15	1	8	41	5
Garrett Broussard, UVU	.319	.386	.488	207	14	0	7	47	1
Gunner Gouldsmith, SAC	.318	.381	.429	245	13	1	4	38	9
Mason Hammonds, TSU	.318	.394	.467	242	19	1	5	33	12
Martin Vazquez, UTRGV	.318	.397	.602	211	9	0	17	55	0
Grant Heiser, SU	.317	.398	.565	161	13	3	7	28	0
Garret Ostrander, CBU	.316	.417	.355	155	6	0	0	26	5
CJ Valdez, UTRGV	.316	.424	.575	193	16	2	10	47	2
Emilio Barreras, GCU	.316	.388	.401	187	9	2	1	34	0
Jayden Smith, UVU	.308	.432	.459	172	13	2	3	23	11
Sam Kane, SU	.303	.355	.512	201	15	0	9	41	0

INDIVIDUAL PITCHING LEADERS

(Minimum 40 innings pitched)

	W	L	ERA	G	SV	IP	H	BB	SO
Walt Quinn, GCU	3	3	2.22	22	1	45	41	16	34
Nico Rodriguez, UTRGV	5	0	2.35	23	4	38	25	11	43
Caden Greanead, ACU	2	1	2.59	22	2	42	38	19	40
Ryan Hetzler, CBU	5	1	2.59	25	4	42	44	14	38
Reese Bassinger, TSU	5	2	3.06	27	0	68	59	17	57
Aaron Morris, UTU	1	1	3.09	25	0	32	28	21	25
Grant Garza, TSU	10	1	3.13	24	0	63	59	18	47
Nathan Hemmerling, CBU	5	4	3.22	27	3	59	53	26	47
Brett Lanman, ACU	7	2	3.48	16	0	72	56	32	79
Jacob Wilson, CBU	5	5	3.55	19	0	38	31	16	36
Kade Brown, SAC	3	3	3.72	22	8	39	27	18	54
Grant Richardson, GCU	4	1	3.73	14	0	51	45	30	70
Tyler Stewart, SAC	4	4	3.75	14	0	70	65	16	55
Caylon Dygert, UTA	6	3	3.79	14	0	90	99	16	48
Hunter Watkins, GCU	2	1	3.83	18	2	47	53	13	47
Lukas Pirko, CBU	5	3	3.84	15	1	73	76	22	76
Zach Tjelmeland, UTRGV	6	3	3.86	14	0	84	87	24	82
Nicholas Robb, UTA	2	2	3.89	19	4	42	49	10	29
Evan Gibbons, SAC	6	5	3.89	15	0	81	69	19	60
Isaac Lyon, GCU	6	1	3.97	17	1	82	94	16	79
Brett Garcia, ACU	3	5	3.98	22	3	41	32	16	67

SMALL COLLEGES

NCAA DIVISION II

Tampa won its first Division II title since 2019, knocking off defending national champion Angelo State (Texas) 8-3 in the championship game.

Tampa scored six runs in the sixth inning to blow the game open. Stephen Klein hit a two-run double and J.P. Gates followed with a two-run home run to right field. E.J. Cumbo, the all-time D-II hits leader, hit his 400th career hit in the championship game. He joined Phil Stephenson and Khalil Greene as the only NCAA players to reach 400 career hits.

In addition to his home run, he joined with Alex Canney to shut down Angelo State. Gates allowed no runs in four innings after Canney worked five innings. Gates was named the tournament's Most Outstanding Player.

Tampa now has nine national titles, including six since 2000.

DIVISION II WORLD SERIES

Site: Cary, N.C.
Participants: 1. Central Missouri. 2. Tampa. 3. Catawba (N.C.). 4. Pint Loma (Calif.). 5. Indiana (Pa.). 6. Southern New Hampshire. 7. Indianapolis. 8. Angelo State (Texas).
Champion: Tampa.
Runner-up: Angelo State (Texas).

LEADERS: BATTING AVERAGE

(Minimum 140 at bats)

Rk.	Player, Pos., Team	Class	AVG	OBP	SLG
1.	Carson Boles, Lincoln (Tenn.) Memorial	Jr.	.475	.572	.863
2.	Payton Conte, California (Pa.)	Jr.	.469	.526	.663
3.	Hayden Jatczak, Saginaw (Mich,) Valley	Sr.	.468	.551	.827
4.	Jonathan Logsdon, Albany St. (Ga.)	Sr.	.467	.582	.725
5.	Jesse Velders, MSU Denver	Jr.	.460	.562	.860
6.	Mackenzie Wainwright, Salem (W.V.)	Fr.	.449	.532	.871
7.	Alec Boucher, D'Youville (N.Y.)	Jr.	.448	.541	.612
8.	Jack Hines, Augustana (S.D.)	Sr.	.445	.485	.852
9.	Darrien McDowell, West Florida	Jr.	.442	.565	.902
10.	Taj Bates, Benedict (S.C.)	Jr.	.438	.537	.634

EARNED RUN AVERAGE

(Minimum 40 innings pitched)

Rk.	Pitcher, Team	Class	W	L	ERA
1.	Trace Hartman, Charleston (W.V.)	Fr.	5	0	1.78
2.	Alex Mykut, Millersville (Pa.)	Sr.	10	2	1.84
3.	Brent Francisco, East Stroudsburg (Pa.)	Sr.	12	1	1.91
4.	Jake Covey, Concordia University Irvine (Calif.)	Jr.	7	2	1.94
5.	Corbin Foy, Mercyhurst (Pa.)	Sr.	5	1	2.08
6.	Chase Oberle, Ouachita (Ark.) Baptist	Jr.	6	4	2.23
7.	Cole Gayman, Mo. Southern St.	Jr.	11	2	2.25
7.	Caleb Marks, Trevecca (Tenn.) Nazarene	Jr.	8	0	2.25
9.	Anson Merrick, Lander (S.C.)	Jr.	5	0	2.36
10.	Chris Morris, West Virginia St.	Jr.	7	2	2.41

CATEGORY LEADERS: BATTING

*Minimum 140 at bats

Dept.	Player, Pos., Team	Class	G	Total
OBP*	Jonathan Logsdon, Albany St. (GA)	Sr.	49	.582
SLG*	Darrien McDowell, West Florida	Jr.	58	.902
R	Carson Ogilvie, Lubbock (Texas) Christian	Sr.	61	94
H	Hayden Jatczak, Saginaw Valley	Sr.	59	108
2B	Carson Ogilvie, Lubbock (Texas) Christian	Sr.	61	30
3B	Hayden Blair, Lubbock (Texas) Christian	Sr.	43	10
HR	Darrien McDowell, West Florida	Jr.	58	27
RBI	Tripp Clark, Angelo State (Texas)	Sr.	65	92
SB	Jeff Sabater, Millersville (Pa.)	So.	54	57

CATEGORY LEADERS: PITCHING

*Minimum 40 innings

Dept.	Pitcher, Team	Class	Total
W	Skylar Gonzalez, Tampa	Sr.	16
SV	James Sashin, Point Loma (Calif.P	Sr.	18
G	EJ White, Indianapolis	Sr.	32
GS	Alex Canney, Tampa	Jr.	19
SO	Jacob Kroeger, Maryville (Mo.)	Sr.	117
SO/9*	Eric Gustofson, Mansfield (Pa.)	Sr.	13.74
BB/9*	Logan Pierce, Central Washington	Fr.	0.43
WHIP*	Brent Francisco, East Stoudsburg (Pa.)	Sr.	0.78

NCAA Division III

Misericordia (Pa.) won the first national title in school history with a 10-5 win over Wisconsin-Whitewater in the deciding Game 3 of the D-III College World Series. Wisconsin-Whitewater had forced a decisive Game 3 by winning Game 2 16-10.

But Misericordia scored seven runs in the first inning of Game 3 to quench the drama of the deciding game. Gabe Bunn went 4-for-4 with three RBI and three runs scored in the clinching game.

Garrett McIlhenney was the World Series MVP. The win was Misericordia head coach Pete Egbert's 600th.

DIVISION III WORLD SERIES

Site: Eastlake, Ohio.
Participants: 1. Endicott (Mass.). 2. Salve Regina (R.I.). 3. Wisconsin-Whitewater. 4. Ponoma-Pitzer (Calif.). 5. Misericordia (Pa.). 6. Randolph-Macon (Va,). 7. Birmingham (Ala.) Southern. 8. Lynchburg (Va.)
Champion: Misericordia (Pa.).
Runner-up: Wisconsin-Whitewater..

LEADERS: BATTING AVERAGE

(Minimum 120 at bats)

RK.	Player, Pos., Team	Class	AVG	OBP	SLG
1.	Mason Cox, Martin Luther (Ontario)	Sr.	.469	.534	.758
2.	Nick Marshall, Greensboro (N.C.)	So.	.468	.554	.862
3.	Jacob Charon, Lawrence (Wisc.)	Sr.	.468	.570	.851
4.	Tommy Kreider, SUNY New Paltz (N.Y.)	Jr.	.466	.561	.655
5.	Chris Knowles, Gustavus Adolphus (Minn.)	Sr.	.456	.522	.779
6.	Mike Ramundo, Alvernia (Pa.)	Sr.	.447	.505	.654
7.	Joe Lukancic, Aurora (Ill.)	Fr.	.447	.485	.585
8.	Sam Strazza, Union (N.Y.)	Jr.	.446	.555	.772
9.	Daniel Rogers, Loras (Iowa)	Sr.	.444	.538	.747
10.	Andrew Kell, Salisbury (Md.)	Jr.	.444	.545	.718

EARNED RUN AVERAGE

(Minimum 30 innings pitched)

Rk.	Pitcher, Team	Class	W	L	ERA
1.	Jackson Teer, Trinity (TX)	So.	8	1	1.05
2.	Sayers Collins, East Texas Baptist	Sr.	12	1	1.23
3.	Jack Haveson, Montclair (N.J.) St.	Sr.	7	1	1.24
4.	Ryan LaPierre, Westfield (Mass.) St.	Sr.	9	0	1.63
5.	Dylan Weber, Chris. Newport (Va.)	Sr.	9	2	1.66
6.	Josh Berzonski, Penn St. Harrisburg	So.	6	2	1.70
7.	Kyle Lewis, Marymount (VA)	Sr.	2	4	1.71
8.	Matt Wallingford, Husson (Maine)	Jr.	5	3	1.74
9.	Johnny Dougherty, Farmingdale (N.Y.) St.	Sr.	8	1	1.76
10.	Luc Rising, Rochester (N.Y.) Inst. of Tech.	Fr.	3	1	1.80

CATEGORY LEADERS: BATTING

*Minimum 120 at bats

Dept.	Player, Pos., Team	Class	G	Total
OBP*	Zach Haines, Valley Forge (Pa.)	So.	30	.612
SLG*	Caleb Cyr, John Hopkins (Md.)	Sr.	42	.899
R	Matt Scolan, Wisconsin-Whitewater	Jr.	56	81
H	Matt Scolan, Wisconsin-Whitewater	Jr.	56	92
2B	Alex Christie, Hanover (Ind.)	Sr.	48	28
	Eric Colaco, Denison (Ohio)	Sr.	50	28
3B	Noah Meffert, George Fox (Ore.)	Jr.	37	10
HR	CJ Colyer, Pacific (Oreg.)	Sr.	41	23
RBI	Isaac Kim, Pomona-Pitzer (Calif.)	Jr.	44	82
SB	Danny MacDougall, Endicott (Mass.)	Jr.	51	48

CATEGORY LEADERS: PITCHING

*Minimum 30 innings

Dept.	Pitcher, Team	Class	Total
W	Cord Butler, N.C. Wesleyan	Sr.	12
W	Sayers Collins, East Texas Baptist	Sr.	12
W	Joe Valenti, Misericordia (Pa.)	Sr.	12
SV	Braden Simms, Piedmont (Ga.)	Jr.	12
GS	Drew Ramos, Randolph-Macon (Ga.)	Sr.	17
SO	Dylan Weber, Chris. Newport (Va.)	Sr.	140
SO/9*	Jakob Runkel, Grinnell	So.	15.68
BB/9*	Alexander Wilkie-Viscio, Gettysburg (Pa.)	So.	0.31
WHIP*	Luc Rising, Rochester (N.Y.) Inst. of Tech.	Fr.	0.71

NAIA

Hope International (Calif.) won five straight elimination games to win its first NAIA national title the hard way. After losing their first game at the NAIA World Series, the Bulldogs never lost again. They beat Tennessee Wesleyan 14-6 in the title game. Hope International's JJ Cruz was named tournament MVP.

NAIA WORLD SERIES

Site: Lewiston, Idaho.
Participants: Arizona Christian. Cumberlands (Ky.). Georgia Gwinnett. Hope International (Calif.). Indiana Southeast. Kansas Wesleyan. Reinhardt (Ga.). Southeastern (Fla.). Tennessee Wesleyan. William Carey (Miss.).
Champion: Hope International (Calif.).
Runner-up: Tennessee Wesleyan.
All-Americans: C: Charlie Muniz, Cumberlands (Ky.). **C**: Tyler Horner, Oregon Tech. **1B**: Miguel Oropeza, Talladega (Ala.). **2B**: JJ Cruz, Hope International (Calif.). **SS**: Drew Barragan, Embry-Riddle (Ariz.). **3B**: Jaidan Quinn, Concordia (Neb.). **INF**: Drew Fleming, Concorida (Mich.). **OF**: Blaze O'Saben, Georgia Gwinnett. **OF**: Evan St. Claire, Cumberlands (Ky.). **OF**: Cayden Nicoletto, Columbia (Mo.). **OF**: Ajay Sczepkowski, Georgia Gwinnett. **SP**: Darien Smith, Southeastern (Fla.). **SP**: Cesar Avila, Cumberlands (Ky.). **SP**: Blayne Huter, Webber International (Fla.). **SP**: Isaac Rohde, LSU Shreveport (La.). **RP**: Chad Pike, Oklahoma City. **DH**: Arderrius Townsend, Blue Mountain Christian (Miss.)

LEADERS: BATTING AVERAGE

(Minimum 140 at bats)

RK. Player, Team	Class	AVG	OBP	SLG
1. Miguel Oropeza, Talladega (Ala.)	Jr.	.508	.612	.852
2. Joshua Duarte, Georgetown (Ky.)	Sr.	.491	.569	.823
3. Trey Furrey, Jessup	Sr.	.489	.566	.848
4. Patrick McGinn, Indiana Tech	Sr.	.483	.568	.552
5. Bryson Lofton, Bryan (Tenn.)	So.	.458	.529	.858

EARNED RUN AVERAGE

(Minimum 40 innings pitched)

Rk. Pitcher, Team	Class	W	L	ERA
1. Isaac Rohde, LSU Shreveport	Sr.	4	2	1.68
2. James Velasquez, Hastings	Jr.	6	3	1.71
3. Blayne Huter, Weber (Fla.) International	Jr.	8	2	1.74
4. Darien Smith, Southeastern (Fla.)	Sr.	12	0	1.87
5. Francisco Moscoso, Friends (Kan.)	Jr.	9	3	1.89

CATEGORY LEADERS: BATTING

*Minimum 140 at bats

Dept.	Player, Pos., Team	Class	G	Total
OBP*	Miguel Oropeza, Talladega (Ala.)	Jr.	57	.612
SLG*	Drew Fleming, Concordia (Mich.)	Sr.	57	.990
HR	Charlie Muniz, Cumberlands (Ky.)	Jr.	60	36
RBI	Charlie Muniz, Cumberlands (Ky.)	Jr.	60	101
SB	Victor Rivera, Talladega (Ala.)	Fr.	56	53

CATEGORY LEADERS: PITCHING

Dept.	Pitcher, Team	Class	Total
W	Cesar Avila, Cumberlands (Ky.)	Jr.	13
SV	Chad Pike, Oklahoma City	Gr.	14
IP	Luke Schafer, Indiana Southeast	Sr.	103
SO	Blake Peyton, Tennessee Wesleyan	Sr.	143

NJCAA Division I

Blinn (Texas) JC beat Northwest Florida JC 12-5 to win its first ever NJCAA D-I World Series. Lucas Davenport pitched a complete game for Blinn, earning Most Outstanding Pitcher honors. Blinn's Caden Clime went 15-for-27 (.556) with five home runs, 15 runs and 17 RBIs to be named the series Most Outstanding Hitter and MVP.

NJCAA DIVISION I WORLD SERIES

Site: Grand Junction, Colo.
Participants: Blinn (Texas), Georgia Highlands, Florence-Darlington (S.C.) Tech. Northwest Florida State. Southern Nevada. Johnson County (Kan.). Crowder (Mo.) Shelton State (Ala.) Southern Nevada. Iowa Western. McLennan (Texas).
Champion: Blinn (Texas).
Runner-up: Northwest Florida State.

LEADERS: BATTING AVERAGE

Minimum 140 at bats)

RK. Player, Pos., Team	Class	AVG	OBP	SLG
1. Elliott Peterson, Southeast (N.C.)	So.	.517	.585	.894
2. Julio Guerrero, North Central Missouri	So.	.503	.585	.820
3. Caden Powell, Seminole State (Okla.)	So.	.502	.561	1.088
4. Robby Bolin, Barton (N.C.)	So.	.464	.566	.661
5. Edwin Olmeda, USC Lancaster	Fr.	.461	.553	.688

EARNED RUN AVERAGE

(Minimum 40 innings pitched)

Rk. Pitcher, Team	Class	W	L	ERA
1. Gavin Micklinghoff, McHenry (Ill.)	Fr.	8	1	1.09
2. Brian Panneton, Wharton County (Texas)	So.	9	1	1.12
3. Dalton Boruff, Kaskaskia (Ill.)	So.	9	4	1.71
4. Garrison Sumner, Salt Lake (Utah)	So.	9	2	1.82
5. Joey Colucci, Harford (Md.)	So.	9	1	1.86

CATEGORY LEADERS: BATTING

***Minimum 140 at bats**

Dept.	Player, Pos., Team	Class	G	Total
OBP*	Aidan Kuni, McLennan (Texas)	So.	58	.624
SLG*	Caden Powell, Seminole State (Okla.)	So.	58	1.088
HR	Caden Powell, Seminole State (Okla.)	So.	55	32
RBI	Caden Powell, Seminole State (Okla.)	So.	55	104
SB	R ichard Bonomolo, Wabash Valley (Ill.)	Fr.	59	62

CATEGORY LEADERS: PITCHING

Dept.	Pitcher, Team	Class	Total
W	Brandon Stone, Johnson County (Kan.)	Fr.	14
SV	Easten Smith, Fort Scott (Kan.)	Fr.	12
IP	Brandon Stone, Johnson County (Kan.)	Fr.	104
SO	Tyler Boudreau, Midland (Texas)	Fr.	128

NJCAA Division II

For the fifth time in 12 years, LSU Eunice won the NJCAA D-II World Series. This time, LSU Eunice knocked off Brunswick (N.C.) 9-3 in the deciding game. Dawson Willis went 3-for-4 and Weston Fulk went 3-for-5 to lead LSU-Eunice to the win, while Liam Watt picked up the win.

NJCAA DIVISION II WORLD SERIES

Site: Enid, Okla.
Participants: 1. LSU Eunice; 2. Brunswick (N.C.); 3. East Central (Miss.). 4. Heartland (Ill.). 5. St. John's (Fla.) River. 6. Madison (Wisc.). 7. Southeastern (N.C.). 8. Kellogg (Mich.). 9. Des Moines (Iowa) Area. 10. South Arkansas. 11. Montgomery (Pa.). 12. Westchester (N.Y.).
Champion: LSU Eunice.
Runner-up: Brunswick (N.C.)

LEADERS: BATTING AVERAGE
(Minimum 120 at bats)

RK. Player, Pos., Team	Class	AVG	OBP	SLG
1. Brady Krzciok, Macomb (Mich.)	So.	.521	.625	.901
2. Julio Guerrero, North Central Missouri	Fr.	.503	.585	.820
3. Kyle Koehler, Cuyahoga (Ohio)	Fr.	.497	.565	.945
4. Aaron Piasecki, Kellogg (Mich.)	So.	.481	.481	.746
5. Alex Harrell, Ark. State Mountain Home	So.	.469	.469	.755

EARNED RUN AVERAGE
(Minimum 40 innings pitched)

Rk. Pitcher, Team	Class	W	L	ERA
1. Michael Carpenter, Madison	So.	10	3	1.03
2. Cesar Morales, Frederick	So.	9	0	1.41
3. Ian Koosman, Paradise Valley	Fr.	7	1	1.52
4. Mathew Murtaugh, SUNY Sullivan County	So.	8	1	1.74
5. Alec Beversdorf, LSU Eunice	Fr.	7	2	1.84

CATEGORY LEADERS: BATTING
*Minimum 120 at bats

Dept.	Player, Pos., Team	Class	G	Total
OBP*	Brady Krzciok, Macomb	So.	39	.625
SLG*	Kyle Koehler, Kellogg	Fr.	55	1.016
HR	Derek Cerda, West Oklahoma State	So.	52	21
RBI	Harrison Bowman, Iowa Central	Fr.	56	94
SB	Preston Leon, Lansing (Mich.)	Fr.	48	59

CATEGORY LEADERS: PITCHING

Dept.	Pitcher, Team	Class	Total
W	Owen Schexnaydre, LSU Eunice	So.	15
SV	Lucas Dawson, Jackson (Miss.)	Fr.	13
IP	Blake Lobell, LSU Eunice	So.	102
SO	Blake Lobell, LSU Eunice	So.	129

NJCAA Division III

Rowan Gloucester (N.J.) beat Dallas-Eastfield (Texas) 18-3 to win its ninth NJCAA World Series title. This is back-to-back titles for the Roadrunners, and three straight runners-up finishes for Dallas-Eastfield.

Caden Dulin was named tournament MVP.

NJCAA DIVISION III WORLD SERIES

Site: Greeneville, Tenn.
Participants: 1. Rowan Gloucester (N.J.); 2. Dallas-Eastfield (Texas). 3. Niagara County (N.Y.). 4. Joliet (Ill.). 5. Northern Essex (Mass.). 6. Camp (Va.). 7. Herkimer (N.Y.). 8. St. Cloud Tech (Minn.). 9.
Champion: Rowan Gloucester..
Runner-up: Dallas-Eastfield (Texas).

LEADERS: BATTING AVERAGE
(Minimum 120 at bats)

RK. Player, Pos., Team	Class	AVG	OBP	SLG
1. Rocko Brzezniak, Brookdale (N.J.)	So.	.568	.636	.925
2. Caden Dulin, Rowan Gloucester (N.J.)	So	.496	.571	.746
3. Jackson Rains, North Arkansas	So.	.489	.580	.748
4. Christopher Picarella, Nassau (N.Y.)	Fr.	.484	.571	.624
5. Nick LoVarco, Brookdale (N.J.)	So.	.473	.537	.941

EARNED RUN AVERAGE
(Minimum 40 innings pitched)

Rk. Pitcher, Team	Class	W	L	ERA
1. Andrew Johnson, SUNY Niagara	So.	8	1	1.22
2. Jayden Voelker, North Essex (Mass.)	Fr.	8	2	1.48
3. Ryan Cole, Brookdale (N.J.)	So.	9	2	1.94
4. Jose Laguna, Bunker Hill (Mass.)	Fr.	5	1	1.94
5. Sotaro Ishida, Herkimer (N.Y.)	Fr.	6	3	1.96

California Junior Colleges

Saddleback knocked off San Joaquin Delta 8-5 to win the California Community College Athletic Association title. It was Saddleback's first title since 2004.

Ben Castelli went 7-for-15 to be named tournament MVP.

CALIFORNIA CC ATHLETIC ASSOCIATION

Site: Walnut.
Participants: Saddleback, West Valley, Santa Ana, San Joaquin Delta.
Champion: Saddleback.
Runner-up: San Joaquin Delta.

LEADERS: BATTING AVERAGE
(Minimum 140 at bats)

RK. Player, Pos., Team	Class	AVG	OBP	SLG
1. Cody Turner, Antelope Valley	So.	.490	.556	.932
2. Max Debiec, Folsom Lake	So.	.449	.500	.775
3. Dominic Rodriguez, San Joaquin Delta	Fr.	.448	.533	.731
4. Matteo Mendoza, Marin	So.	.445	.546	.635
5. Connor Ross, Solano	So.	.433	.529	.793

EARNED RUN AVERAGE
(Minimum 40 innings pitched)

Rk. Pitcher, Team	Class	W	L	ERA
1. Derek Valdez, Cerritos	Fr.	13	2	1.50
2. Cameron Goffar, San Diego Mesa	So.	6	3	1.54
3. Franky Lopez, Cerritos	Fr.	12	0	1.88
4. Alex Ramos, Golden West	So.	11	2	1.88
4. Jack Wade, Saddleback	Fr.	7	3	1.94

COLLEGIATE NATIONAL TEAM STATS

INTERNATIONAL FRIENDSHIP SERIES

Year indicates 2023-24 class standing

Player, Pos.	Year	School	AVG	OBP	SLG	G	AB	R	H	2B	3B	HR	RBI	BB	SO	SB
Drew Burress, OF	Fr.	Georgia Tech	.444	.545	.611	5	18	5	8	0	0	1	3	4	3	3
Nolan Schubart, OF/INF	So.	Oklahoma State	.429	.704	1.000	6	14	6	6	2	0	2	7	13	3	0
RJ Austin Jr., UTIL	So.	Vanderbilt	.316	.350	.579	5	19	3	6	2	0	1	1	1	3	4
Max Belyeu, OF	So.	Texas	.308	.400	.308	4	13	3	4	0	0	0	4	2	6	4
Kyle Walker, INF	So.	Grambling State	.300	.364	.300	4	10	1	3	0	0	0	0	1	3	0
Dean Curley, INF	Fr.	Tennessee	.263	.364	.579	5	19	4	5	3	0	1	5	2	4	0
Brooks Bryan, C	So.	Troy	.214	.353	.5 00	4	14	3	3	1	0	1	6	3	2	0
Caden Bodine, C	So.	Coastal Carolina	.167	.333	.417	4	12	4	2	0	0	1	2	3	0	1
Marek Houston, INF	So.	Wake Forest	.143	.368	.143	5	14	4	2	0	0	0	3	4	4	2
Anthony Martinez, INF	So.	UC Irvine	.133	.278	.133	5	15	0	2	0	0	0	0	1	1	0
Danny Dickinson, INF	So.		.063	.063	.063	4	16	3	1	0	0	0	0	0	3	3

Pitcher, Pos.	Year	School	W	L	ERA	G	SV	IP	H	R	ER	BB	SO	AVG
Matt Scott, RHP	So.	Stanford	0	0	0.00	1	0	4	1	0	0	1	2	.077
Jamie Arnold, LHP	So.	Florida State	1	0	0.00	1	0	4	0	0	0	1	7	.000
Kyson Witherspoon, RHP	So.	Oklahoma	0	0	0.00	1	0	4	1	0	0	2	6	.091
Nelson Keljo, LHP	So.	Oregon State	1	0	0.00	2	0	3	4	0	0	2	4	.267
Gabriel Gaeckle, RHP	Fr.	Arkansas	0	0	0.00	2	0	3	0	1	0	3	4	.000
Gabe Davis, RHP	So.	Oklahoma State	0	0	0.00	2	0	3	0	1	0	0	4	.000
Tyler Bremmer, RHP	So.	UC Santa Barbara	0	0	0.00	1	0	3	0	0	0	2	4	.000
Tucker Biven, RHP	So.	Louisville	1	0	0.00	1	0	3	2	0	0	0	5	.250
Alton Davis II, LHP	So.	Georgia	1	0	0.00	2	0	3	0	0	0	0	3	.000
Ben Abeldt, LHP	So.	TCU	0	0	0.00	2	0	2	2	2	0	0	3	.182
Malachi Witherspoon, RHP	So.	Oklahoma	0	0	0.00	1	0	1	0	0	0	0	1	.000
Nate Snead, RHP	So.	Tennesse	0	0	0.00	1	0	1	0	0	0	0	0	.000
Ben Jacobs, LHP	So.	Arizona State	1	0	2.08	1	0	4	3	1	1	0	7	.231
Patrick Forbes, RHP	So.	Louisville	0	0	2.25	1	0	4	3	1	1	0	5	.231
Derrick Smith, RHP	So.	NC State	0	0	3.38	2	1	3	3	1	1	3	3	.375
Anthony Eyanson, RHP	So.		1	0	6.75	1	0	1	1	1	1	2	3	.200
Kolten Smith, RHP	So.	Georgia	0	0	10.80	2	0	2	3	2	2	2	1	.500

SUMMER LEAGUE TOUR

Player, Pos.	Year	School	AVG	OBP	SLG	G	AB	R	H	2B	3B	HR	RBI	BB	SO	SB
Tre Phelps, INF	Fr.	Georgia	.385	.429	.769	4	13	3	5	0	1	1	4	0	5	0
Luke Stevenson, C	Fr.	North Carolina	.333	.429	.333	3	6	1	2	0	0	0	1	0	3	0
Henry Ford, INF/OF	Fr.	Virginia	.308	.400	.308	4	13	2	4	0	0	0	1	2	3	0
AJ Gracia, OF	Fr.	Duke	.300	.533	.300	4	10	2	3	0	0	0	0	5	1	1
Jamal George, C/INF	So.	Alabama State	.222	.300	.222	3	9	0	2	0	0	0	4	1	4	0
Zion Rose, C	Fr.	Louisville	.214	.267	.214	4	14	2	3	0	0	0	1	0	4	2
Justin Lebron, INF	Fr.	Alabama	.200	.429	.300	4	10	3	2	1	0	0	1	1	2	0
Gavin Grahovac, INF	Fr.		.083	.313	.083	4	12	2	1	0	0	0	2	4	5	1
Daniel Cuvet, INF	Fr.	Miami	.071	.133	.071	4	14	0	1	0	0	0	0	1	5	0
Kyle Johnson, OF/LHP	Fr.	Duke	.000	.143	.000	2	6	1	0	0	0	0	1	1	3	0
Eric Becker, INF	Fr.	Virginia	.000	.286	.000	3	5	0	0	0	0	0	0	2	5	1
Alex Sosas, C	Fr.	NC State	.000	.500	.000	1	2	1	0	0	0	0	0	1	2	0

Pitcher, Pos.	Year	School	W	L	ERA	G	SV	IP	H	R	ER	BB	SO	AVG
Liam Peterson, RHP	Fr.	Florida	0	0	0.00	1	0	4	1	0	0	0	7	.077
Dominic Voegele, RHP	Fr.	Kansas	1	0	0.00	1	0	4	1	0	0	1	4	.083
Jacob Dudan, RHP	Fr.	NC State	0	0	0.00	2	1	2	0	0	0	2	2	.000
Brett Renfrow, RHP	Fr.	Virginia Tech	0	0	0.00	1	0	2	0	0	0	1	2	.000
Dylan Loy, LHP	Fr.	Tennessee	1	0	0.00	1	0	2	1	0	0	0	3	.143
Kyle Johnson, OF/LHP	Fr.	Duke	1	0	0.00	1	0	2	0	0	0	1	4	.000
Pablo Torres, RHP	So.	Bethune-Cookman	0	0	0.00	1	0	2	0	0	0	0	3	.000
Miller Green, LHP	Fr.	Vanderbilt	0	0	0.00	1	0	1	0	0	0	1	2	.000
Joey Volchko, RHP	Fr.	Stanford	0	0	2.25	1	0	4	1	1	1	2	7	.077
Jason DeCaro, RHP	Fr.	North Carolina	0	0	6.00	1	0	3	6	2	2	0	3	.429
Brennan Seiber, RHP	Fr.	Vanderbilt	0	0	9.00	1	0	2	2	2	2	1	0	.250
Eric Segura, RHP	Fr.	Oregon State	0	0	9.00	1	0	2	2	2	2	0	3	.250
Matthew Matthijs, RHP	So.	North Carolina	0	0	9.00	2	1	2	4	2	2	0	4	.400
Ethan McElvain, LHP	Fr.	Vanderbilt	0	0	18.00	1	0	1	2	2	2	1	1	.400
Cooper Consiglio, LHP	Fr.	NC State	0	1	27.00	1	0	1	2	2	2	1	2	.500

COLLEGE SUMMER LEAGUES

For players who played for multiple teams: 1: Stats with first team. 2: Stats with second team. 3: Stats with third team. T: combined stats.

CAPE COD LEAGUE

ECCBL East	W	L	T	PTS
#-Yarmouth-Dennis	24	12	4	52
@-Chatham	20	20	0	40
@-Harwich	16	24	0	32
@-Orleans	15	25	0	30
Brewster	13	25	2	28
CCBL West	**W**	**L**	**T**	**PTS**
#-Hyannis	24	14	2	50
@-Cotuit	22	17	1	45
@-Wareham	22	17	1	45
@-Bourne	21	16	3	45
Falmouth	16	23	1	33

PLAYOFFS: First Round: Yarmouth-Dennis defeated Orleans; Harwich defeated Chatham; Cotuit defeated Wareham; Bourne defeated Hyannis in one-game first round series. **Semifinals:** Bourne defeated Cotuit 2-1 and Harwich defeated Yarmouth-Dennis 2-0 in best-of-3 series. **Finals:** Harwich Mariners defeated Bourne Braves, 2-1, in best-of-three championship series.

All-STAR TEAM: C: Ryder Helfrick, Brewster, Arkansas. 1B: Tanner Thach, Cotuit, UNC Wilmington. 2B: Jarren Advincula, Cotuit, California. 3B: Murf Grey, Wareham, Fresno State. SS: Wehiwa Aloy, Y-D, Arkansas. OF: Ethan Petry, Y-D, South Carolina. OF: Ethan Conrad, Bourne, Wake Forest. OF: Nick Dumesnil, Brewster, Cal Baptist. DH: Ike Irish, Chatham, Auburn. RHP Braden Osbolt, Y-D, Kennesaw State. RHP Itsuki Takemoto, Orleans, Hawaii. RHP Jake Clemente, Brewster, Florida. RHP Aaron Savary, Hyannis, Iowa. RHP Sean Youngerman, Y-D, Oklahoma State. RHP Callan Fang, Orleans, Harvard. RHP Michael Ebner, Cotuit, USC. RHP Tate McGuire, Wareham, Arkansas. RHP Griffin Hugus, Bourne, Miami. RHP Blaine Wynk, Hyannis, Ohio State. RHP Gage Wood, Falmouth, Arkansas. RHP Trevor Moore, Y-D, Stanford

Reserves. C: Easton Carmichael, Y-D, Oklahoma. 1B: Eli Putnam, Wareham, Davidson. 2B: Yohan Desserault, Wareham, Stetson. 2B: Eric Snow, Hyannis, Auburn. 3B: Daniel Cuvet, Brewster, Miami. 3B: Braden Holcomb, Bourne, Vanderbilt. SS: Aiva Arquette, Chatham, Oregon State. OF/DH: Brandon Compton, Cotuit, Arizona State. OF: Ben Ziegler-Namoa, Orleans, Hawaii.

INDIVIDUAL BATTING LEADERS

Player, Team	AVG	AB	R	H	2B	3B	HR	RBI	SB
Jarren Advincula, COT	.392	130	29	51	4	0	1	17	4
Ethan Conrad, BOU	.385	109	27	42	5	0	2	19	19
Ethan Petry, Y-D	.360	100	26	36	7	0	11	25	0
Braden Holcomb, BOU	.333	123	19	41	6	0	3	25	7
Brandon Compton, COT	.331	133	26	44	3	0	6	30	2
Murf Gray, WAR	.329	140	22	46	9	0	5	27	5
Eric Snow, HYA	.326	92	15	30	3	0	2	18	5
Ike Irish, CHA	.325	120	23	39	5	1	2	12	8
Ashton Larson, CHA	.316	117	17	37	9	0	1	18	8
Daniel Cuvet, BRE	.314	102	17	32	3	0	6	20	1

INDIVIDUAL PITCHING LEADERS

Player, Team	W	L	ERA	G	SV	IP	H	BB	SO
Itsuki Takemoto, ORL	3	1	0.71	9	0	25	12	7	23
Aaron Savary, HYA	2	1	1.42	7	0	25	12	20	32
Callan Fang, ORL	3	1	2.15	7	0	29	15	9	39
Blaine Wynk, HYA	1	1	2.55	7	0	25	18	9	22
Sean Youngerman, Y-D	2	1	2.55	7	0	25	18	10	33
Jake Clemente, BRE	1	2	3.00	6	0	27	16	11	29
Michael Foltz Jr., ORL	0	3	3.03	9	0	36	23	17	24
Tyler Fay, BOU	4	1	3.16	9	0	31	28	6	22
Cody Bowker, ORL	1	4	3.28	9	0	36	26	7	36
Ryan DeSanto, HAR	1	2	3.33	6	0	24	20	4	20

BOURNE

Batting	AVG	AB	R	H	2B	3B	HR	RBI	SB
Blake Barthol	.218	55	13	12	1	0	1	9	4
Tristan Bissetta	.267	45	9	12	1	0	4	11	1
Caden Bodine	.158	19	1	3	1	0	0	3	0
Evan Conrad	.385	109	27	42	5	0	2	19	19
Davis Gillespie	.268	82	15	22	5	0	0	7	1
Clay Grady	.197	71	12	14	1	0	0	5	9
Matthew Graveline	.138	29	5	4	0	1	0	3	2
Adonys Guzman	.036	28	2	1	0	0	0	1	0
Ben Hartl	.167	24	3	4	2	0	0	4	0
Braden Holcomb	.333	123	19	41	6	0	3	25	7
Marek Houston	.306	85	17	26	2	0	0	8	7
Isaiah Jackson	.193	57	11	11	4	0	1	12	4
Camden Kozeal	.252	107	14	27	9	0	2	11	4
David Lewis	.462	13	2	6	1	0	0	2	0
Chase Meggers	.342	38	7	13	5	1	0	7	0
Garrett Michel	.207	87	14	18	4	0	3	16	3
Mason Neville	.125	32	3	4	1	0	0	2	0
Jack Penney	.271	48	11	13	0	0	0	5	2
Nick Roselli	.148	27	7	4	1	0	0	1	0
John Schroeder	.250	24	3	6	0	0	2	9	1
Chris Stanfield	.252	119	19	30	4	1	2	17	14
Landyn Vidourek	.138	29	3	4	2	0	1	4	3
Nick Wang	.111	9	1	1	1	0	0	0	0

Pitching	W	L	ERA	G	SV	IP	H	BB	SO
John Abraham	0	0	2.00	6	1	9	8	1	14
Zane Adams	2	0	4.76	5	0	17	18	2	14
Joe Ariola	2	1	5.09	8	0	23	22	15	28
Packy Bradley-Cooney	1	0	5.14	4	0	7	6	7	10
Beau Bryans	2	0	3.00	5	0	15	9	6	14
Ben Bybee	0	0	4.11	4	0	15	12	5	15
Zach Crotchfelt	0	2	6.97	8	0	10	12	6	17
Tyler Fay	4	1	3.16	9	0	31	28	6	22
Miler Green	0	0	7.04	4	0	8	6	3	12
Griffin Hugus	2	0	2.31	11	0	23	16	4	24
Kyle LaCalameto	0	0	6.00	2	0	3	3	2	3
Justin LeGuernic	0	0	9.00	5	0	5	6	6	5
Will McCausland	2	0	1.23	4	0	15	9	4	21
Ethan McElvain	0	0	0.77	3	0	12	9	5	15
Matt McShane	0	1	9.45	2	0	7	8	5	8
Chase Meyer	2	1	1.77	7	0	20	10	13	26
Jackson Mitchell	0	0	6.75	4	0	8	9	3	6
Cam Nelson	0	0	10.80	2	0	2	0	2	1
Tucker Novotny	0	0	5.14	2	0	7	9	7	5
Cameron Padgett	0	1	5.40	6	0	17	20	8	17
Wyatt Parliament	0	1	6.00	1	0	3	5	2	3
Preston Prince	1	1	11.57	3	0	5	6	7	9
Brayden Risedorph	0	1	2.70	3	0	7	8	3	6
Nolan Sparks	0	3	7.24	4	0	14	15	7	20
Jonathan Stevens	0	0	0.00	1	0	3	3	2	3
Bradley Stewart	0	0	9.00	2	0	3	1	6	7
J.D. Thompson	2	1	1.93	5	1	14	10	3	18
Jacob Vogel	0	0	0.00	1	0	1	1	3	1
Justin West	0	1	3.00	8	0	15	15	6	25
Connor Wietgrefe	1	0	0.82	2	0	11	7	1	12
Donovan Zsak	0	1	2.45	2	0	7	1	6	12

BREWSTER

Batting	AVG	AB	R	H	2B	3B	HR	RBI	SB
Blake Binderup	.167	36	5	6	0	0	0	1	0
Gio Cueto	.182	11	0	2	1	0	0	1	0
Daniel Cuvet	.314	102	17	32	3	0	6	20	1
Brody Donay	.227	97	14	22	4	0	6	13	3
Nick Dumesnil	.311	135	27	42	12	0	4	15	26
Drew Faurot	.263	99	13	26	6	0	3	16	4
Andrew Fischer	.231	65	9	15	4	1	3	14	2
Ryder Helfrick	.261	142	28	37	3	0	11	37	8
Jayden Hylton	.130	23	4	3	1	0	0	1	2
Michael Iannazzo	.500	6	1	3	1	0	1	2	0

Batting	AVG	AB	R	H	2B	3B	HR	RBI	SB
RJ Johnson Jr.	.080	25	1	2	0	0	0	1	2
Max Kaufer	.205	39	5	8	0	1	0	3	1
Kaeden Kent	.257	105	10	27	5	0	1	13	2
Dallas Macias	.279	61	13	17	0	0	0	10	1
Chase Mora	.259	27	1	7	0	0	0	5	1
Tyler Pettorini	.087	23	2	2	0	0	0	2	2
J.D. Rogers	.287	94	18	27	3	0	1	4	12
DeAmez Ross	.170	47	2	8	0	0	0	3	1
Carsten Sabathia	.154	13	0	2	0	0	0	0	0
Nolan Schubart	.300	30	11	9	2	0	3	5	1
Colby Shelton	.205	44	7	9	0	0	1	6	2
Cooper Vest	.203	64	8	13	2	0	0	2	0

Pitching	W	L	ERA	G	SV	IP	H	BB	SO
Jake Clemente	1	2	3.00	6	0	27	16	11	29
Ashton Crowther	0	2	5.73	4	0	11	12	5	10
Grant Cunningham	0	3	13.50	5	0	6	9	4	7
Gabe Davis	0	0	8.10	2	0	3	4	1	9
Parker Detmers	0	1	7.48	10	1	22	21	16	22
Sonny Fauci	0	0	6.00	2	1	3	2	4	4
Boston Flannery	0	1	6.75	7	0	12	18	13	4
Patrick Forbes	0	0	3.29	4	0	14	9	6	22
Colby Frieda	0	1	4.91	4	0	11	15	3	16
Luke Guth	1	1	6.56	8	0	23	27	11	22
Levi Huesman	2	0	7.66	9	0	22	33	11	27
Zach Johnston	1	0	7.20	8	1	15	18	9	12
Andrew Koshy	0	1	20.25	2	0	1	1	3	2
Robert Lasbury	0	0	0.00	1	0	0	0	0	1
Jacob Marlowe	1	0	2.95	8	0	18	21	2	14
Isaac Morton	0	0	2.25	1	0	4	2	0	3
Evan O'Toole	0	1	8.00	3	0	9	9	4	6
Kellan Oakes	1	0	6.94	8	0	12	11	8	15
Kyle Percival	0	1	11.25	2	0	4	5	4	4
D.J. Primeaux	2	3	4.88	12	0	24	20	12	26
Will Ray	0	2	4.91	14	2	22	24	2	23
Rocco Reid	0	2	12.79	2	0	6	9	3	6
Michael Salina	1	0	3.60	1	0	5	5	3	3
Noah Samol	0	1	6.75	1	0	3	2	5	6
Luke Schmolke	1	0	6.32	7	0	16	21	8	12
Darien Smith	1	2	6.60	5	0	15	20	10	17
Seth Tomczak	1	1	4.96	5	1	16	22	0	15
Ryan Ure	0	0	2.89	4	0	9	5	7	8
Alex Valentin	0	0	0.00	2	0	3	0	1	2

CHATHAM

Batting	AVG	AB	R	H	2B	3B	HR	RBI	SB
Alva Arquette	.291	103	15	30	4	1	3	21	2
John Bay	.254	71	16	18	6	0	4	16	2
Will Bermudez	.269	26	6	7	2	0	1	7	2
Luke Cantwell	.206	63	12	13	0	0	2	8	1
Ty Dalley	.154	13	1	2	1	0	0	0	0
Jayden Davis	.256	125	20	32	8	0	2	12	2
Cole Fellows	.167	6	2	1	0	0	0	0	0
Will Gasparino	.083	24	3	2	1	0	1	2	2
Eddie Hacopian	.400	5	2	2	1	0	0	0	0
Ike Irish	.325	120	23	39	5	1	2	12	8
Daniel Jackson	.188	16	1	3	0	0	1	2	0
Kyle Johnson	.200	15	0	3	1	0	0	1	0
Ty Johnson	.175	40	5	7	0	0	1	6	1
Jett Johnston	.000	22	1	0	0	0	0	1	0
Chayton Krauss	.259	58	8	15	3	0	4	14	1
Chase Krewson	.000	11	0	0	0	0	0	0	0
Ashton Larson	.316	117	17	37	9	0	1	18	8
Kyle Lodise	.239	109	19	26	4	0	3	12	9
Austin Overn	.314	86	14	27	6	2	3	13	9
Eli Paton	.160	25	3	4	0	0	0	1	2
Logan Poteet	.000	6	0	0	0	0	0	0	0
Bryce Roddey	.091	11	2	1	0	0	0	0	0
Campbell Smithwick	.303	76	14	23	6	0	0	12	3
Caleb Stelly	.042	24	1	1	0	0	0	1	3
Landon Stripling	.100	20	1	2	0	0	0	1	1
Robin Villenueve	.280	50	12	14	4	0	3	7	1
Cohen Wilbanks	.000	1	0	0	0	0	0	0	0
Jordan Williams	.231	13	0	3	0	0	0	2	0
Luke Yuhasz	.438	16	4	7	0	0	1	4	0

Pitching	W	L	ERA	G	SV	IP	H	BB	SO
John Armstrong	0	1	2.08	3	0	4	4	4	3
Micah Ashman	1	0	1.93	4	0	9	6	2	13
Murphy Brooks	0	0	9.00	4	0	6	10	6	3
Evan Chrest	0	2	7.94	3	0	11	15	5	13
Chance Cox	1	1	4.96	8	0	16	19	10	11
Phil Fox	1	0	0.00	2	0	4	4	0	5
Tanner Franklin	2	0	0.75	8	0	12	7	12	19
Drake George	1	1	4.22	3	0	11	13	4	11
Pierce George	0	0	5.87	4	1	8	8	4	11
Lucas Hartman	1	0	3.12	2	0	9	5	3	6
Titan Hayes	0	0	0.00	6	3	7	2	3	12
Jacob Heath	1	1	0.93	4	0	10	6	1	10
Garrett Helsel	1	1	6.17	2	0	12	10	3	17
Griffin Herring	1	0	1.69	3	0	11	3	6	10
Quinn Holt	0	1	4.32	2	0	8	11	5	4
Ryan Jenkins	0	1	7.88	2	0	8	11	4	3
Cam Johnson	0	0	16.20	4	0	3	4	11	2
Carson Johnson	0	1	18.00	1	0	3	6	3	3
Kyle Johnson	0	0	9.00	1	0	2	2	2	2
Jett Johnston	0	0	3.00	3	0	3	2	3	4
Tyler Kozera	1	0	4.19	6	0	19	22	6	15
Karson Ligon	0	0	5.40	4	1	10	10	9	10
J.D. McReynolds	0	1	16.88	3	1	3	3	3	4
Augie Mojica	0	0	6.43	3	0	7	8	2	6
Hayden Murphy	2	1	2.89	9	3	19	9	6	28
Tyler Murphy	1	1	4.63	3	0	12	11	5	9
Jackson Nedrow	0	0	3.60	2	0	5	7	0	1
Liam Paddack	0	1	6.92	4	0	13	10	7	22
Garrett Payne	1	1	4.40	6	0	14	8	5	13
Devin Pressley	0	0	3.12	4	0	9	5	2	10
Xavier Richards	1	1	8.31	5	0	4	5	4	1
Gabe Van Emon	2	0	2.65	5	1	17	8	6	22
Jacob Weaver	0	3	8.80	5	0	15	20	9	7
Andrew Williams	0	0	4.32	5	1	8	4	8	6
Kyson Witherspoon	0	0	1.00	2	0	9	8	0	10
Malachi Witherspoon	0	0	7.11	5	0	6	5	8	9
Brian Zeldin	2	1	5.91	3	0	11	10	4	14

COTUIT

Batting	AVG	AB	R	H	2B	3B	HR	RBI	SB
Jarren Advincula	.392	130	29	51	4	0	1	17	4
Chris Arroyo	.167	6	1	1	0	0	1	2	0
Christian Becerra	.273	77	8	21	3	0	0	7	3
Max Belyeu	.222	54	9	12	1	0	2	9	1
Brooks Bryan	.125	16	1	2	1	0	0	0	2
Tyler Cerny	.198	106	14	21	6	0	1	7	4
Brandon Compton	.331	133	26	44	3	0	6	30	2
Charles Davalan	.242	62	11	15	5	0	1	11	3
A.J. Gracia	.267	15	3	4	0	0	1	3	1
Nathan Hall	.333	75	17	25	1	1	1	7	7
Luke Hanson	.333	24	5	8	1	0	0	2	1
Trevor Haskins	.000	5	0	0	0	0	0	0	0
Reece Holbrook	.167	6	1	1	0	0	0	0	0
Grant Jay	.141	78	14	11	3	0	3	11	2
Sean Keys	.176	17	2	3	0	0	0	0	0
Matt Klein	.375	72	13	27	0	0	1	11	1
P.J. Moutzouridis	.222	9	1	2	0	0	0	0	2
Nolan Nawrocki	.258	97	13	25	2	0	3	15	3
Cannon Peebles	.167	6	1	1	0	0	0	1	1
Nick Rodriguez	.200	5	1	1	0	0	0	0	0
Devin Taylor	.296	98	18	29	4	1	5	16	2
Tanner Thach	.275	138	27	38	6	0	8	25	0
Kien Vu	.171	35	5	6	1	0	0	4	2
Brock Wills	.000	3	0	0	0	0	0	1	0
Easton Winfield	.216	51	7	11	4	0	1	7	0

Pitching	W	L	ERA	G	SV	IP	H	BB	SO
Christian Becerra	1	0	3.00	3	1	6	5	2	6
Merritt Beeker	3	0	0.79	3	0	11	5	5	10

	W	L	ERA	G	SV	IP	H	BB	SO
Andrew Behnke	0	0	9.95	4	0	6	11	2	10
Max Belyeu	0	0	3.00	1	0	3	2	3	2
Harrison Bodendorf	0	0	3.55	6	0	13	17	6	13
Ryan Buckler	0	0	6.00	1	0	3	5	0	1
Mason Davenport	0	0	4.76	3	0	6	6	2	8
Harry Deliyannis	0	0	0.00	1	0	1	0	1	1
Zach Dueñas	1	1	1.59	5	0	6	3	4	6
Michael Ebner	4	1	1.90	8	1	24	8	6	22
James Ellwanger	1	2	2.77	5	0	13	10	5	22
Anthony Eyanson	0	0	3.00	2	0	6	7	1	6
Cade Fisher	0	1	1.59	3	1	6	2	2	6
Max Hansmann	0	0	2.70	2	0	3	4	2	6
Luke Hanson	0	0	67.50	1	0	1	3	3	1
Colton Hartman	0	1	15.26	4	0	8	14	8	9
Camron Hill	0	2	11.57	3	0	9	13	7	9
Mark Hindy	0	0	0.00	3	1	1	0	2	1
Dylan Howanitz	0	0	7.88	7	0	8	9	5	8
Aidan Hunter	0	1	8.80	6	0	15	22	10	12
Thatcher Hurd	1	0	1.86	2	0	10	4	3	7
Ben Jacobs	0	0	0.00	2	0	5	1	4	8
Janzen Keisel	0	1	6.75	3	0	8	6	5	8
Logan Lunceford	0	0	1.80	3	0	10	3	7	12
Isaac Lyon	0	0	4.32	4	0	8	11	2	10
Max Martzolf	0	1	2.25	3	0	4	2	3	5
Ian May	1	0	1.59	2	0	6	4	2	4
Cullen McKay	0	0	7.11	3	0	6	5	4	7
Bryce McKnight	0	0	0.00	1	0	1	1	1	3
Aaron Mishoulam	0	0	4.50	1	0	2	2	0	1
Luis Misla	0	0	10.57	5	0	8	7	6	8
Gabriel Nard	2	1	3.94	8	1	16	15	6	15
Jack O'Malley	0	0	4.50	2	0	2	0	4	0
Tyler O'Neill	0	1	7.15	3	0	11	20	3	7
Brock Pare	0	0	9.00	2	0	3	3	3	2
Brycen Parrish	3	0	5.00	4	0	9	10	3	10
Owen Pierce	0	0	13.50	1	0	2	3	0	1
Lukas Pirko	0	0	5.40	5	0	10	12	4	15
Joe Sabbath	0	0	4.50	1	0	2	2	1	2
Beau Sampson	1	0	0.00	2	0	4	3	1	6
Cam Schuelke	2	1	3.52	6	2	8	10	3	9
Taylor Seay	1	2	4.15	3	0	13	15	4	11
Jacob Shafer	0	0	4.50	5	0	8	9	3	11
Tanner Thach	0	0	3.86	2	0	2	4	0	3
Mike Villani	0	0	1.93	3	1	5	4	0	6
Joey Volchko	1	1	2.37	5	0	19	20	13	29
Hunter Watkins	0	0	2.45	3	0	7	5	2	6

FALMOUTH

Batting	AVG	AB	R	H	2B	3B	HR	RBI	SB
Isaiah Barkett	.267	86	13	23	2	2	0	4	8
Jack Bell	.125	56	3	7	0	0	1	5	2
Robby Bolin	.138	29	4	4	0	0	0	1	5
Karson Bowen	.315	89	14	28	6	0	1	7	2
Joey Brenczewski	.125	8	0	1	0	0	0	2	0
Matt Bucciero	.000	12	0	0	0	0	0	0	0
Trent Caraway	.276	98	17	27	5	0	4	21	5
Dylan Carey	.304	92	16	28	5	0	1	13	6
Blake Cavill	.286	14	1	4	0	0	0	1	0
Henry Cooke	.286	14	3	4	0	0	2	4	1
Francis Ferguson	.000	1	0	0	0	0	0	0	0
Frankie Ferrentino	.000	3	0	0	0	0	0	1	0
Luke Gaffney	.276	105	17	29	3	0	1	15	2
Jayson Jones	.269	108	16	29	8	0	3	17	2
Gavin Kilen	.253	91	19	23	2	0	2	10	0
Donovan LaSalle	.202	89	15	18	3	0	4	16	2
Christian Martin	.182	22	3	4	1	0	0	3	1
Scott Mudler	.211	38	6	8	1	1	0	8	0
Jimmy Nati	.059	17	1	1	0	0	0	0	1
Kollin Ritchie	.056	18	1	1	0	0	0	0	0
Patrick Roche	.375	16	1	6	0	0	0	4	1
Zlon Rose	.295	78	14	23	3	1	3	13	4
Chase Spencer	.091	11	2	1	0	0	0	2	0
Jack Thorbahn	.000	2	1	0	0	0	0	0	0
Tab Tracy	.368	19	4	7	0	0	0	2	0
Gavin Turley	.297	74	12	22	4	0	3	17	5
Jaxon Willits	.297	91	17	27	1	0	2	15	6

Pitching	W	L	ERA	G	SV	IP	H	BB	SO
Brett Antolick	0	1	15.00	4	0	6	10	7	10
Bowen Baker	2	0	4.76	12	0	23	25	8	18
Sean Brennan	0	0	4.64	5	0	21	27	11	19
Tom Chmielewski	0	1	10.13	4	0	5	10	2	4
Valek Cisneros	0	1	7.11	4	0	6	6	8	6
Parker Coil	0	4	7.11	10	2	25	27	7	25
Matthew Dallas	1	2	5.76	6	0	25	28	18	25
Russell Derbyshire	0	0	67.50	2	0	1	4	2	1
Francis Ferguson	4	0	5.64	14	0	30	26	13	20
Hayden Frank	0	0	3.27	3	0	11	11	2	15
Santhosh Gottam	1	0	6.75	2	0	5	5	2	5
Nick Gravel	1	0	3.00	7	0	12	6	5	9
Colby Guy	0	2	8.68	3	0	9	10	8	10
Edward Hart	1	1	3.22	12	2	22	29	11	17
Mac Heuer	0	0	2.70	3	0	7	5	5	7
Justin Lessing	0	0	3.24	4	0	8	7	5	10
Ryan McCarroll	0	1	2.25	1	0	4	2	2	1
Tate McKee	0	0	4.91	3	0	7	7	6	7
Jaden Noot	3	0	7.15	6	0	11	15	5	8
Ethan Phillips	0	1	13.50	2	0	3	5	2	5
Peter Phillips	0	0	0.73	5	0	12	10	4	4
MJ Seo	0	1	5.06	3	0	5	4	7	2
Jack Seppings	1	2	2.51	5	0	14	11	6	20
Tanner Smith	0	1	2.25	3	0	8	3	8	7
Riley Stanford	0	3	5.40	13	1	22	28	8	23
Cam Tilly	0	1	12.27	3	0	4	3	4	1
Gavin Wilhelm	0	1	6.75	6	2	8	6	8	8
Gage Wood	2	0	1.42	6	0	19	11	8	29
Kade Woods	0	0	9.00	1	0	1	1	2	0

HARWICH

Batting	AVG	AB	R	H	2B	3B	HR	RBI	SB
Michael Anderson	.246	114	13	28	7	0	5	20	0
Bryan Arendt	.130	23	0	3	3	0	0	2	3
Tommy Barth	.276	76	11	21	2	1	1	10	3
Ryan Black	.286	14	0	4	0	0	0	0	0
Jack Bowery	.000	1	0	0	0	0	0	0	0
Robbie Burnett	.160	25	3	4	0	0	1	2	1
Bristol Carter	.293	58	14	17	1	0	0	5	10
Daniel Dickinson	.205	83	10	17	2	1	0	8	9
Vince Fattore	.192	26	5	5	1	0	1	3	1
Henry Godbout	.306	36	6	11	3	0	1	4	2
Luke Heyman	.186	59	5	11	0	0	2	4	0
Aden Hill	.321	28	4	9	1	1	1	8	2
Cade Kurland	.257	101	16	26	5	0	2	13	7
Chance Mako	.000	0	1	0	0	0	0	0	0
Cam Maldonado	.258	124	22	32	4	1	5	24	13
Sam McNulty	.196	46	8	9	1	0	0	2	1
Carmelo Musacchia	.125	16	0	2	0	0	0	0	0
Jake Ogden	.234	124	15	29	3	0	4	16	0
Aiden Robbins	.385	26	7	10	1	0	1	6	1
Matt Scannell	.205	122	11	25	2	1	2	14	8
Wilson Weber	.300	30	8	9	0	0	1	5	0
Ryan Weingartner	.204	93	17	19	2	0	4	15	10
Macon Winslow	.195	87	14	17	2	0	2	10	0

Pitching	W	L	ERA	G	SV	IP	H	BB	SO
Tommy Allman	1	1	6.75	3	0	7	7	2	4
Bryan Arendt	0	0	0.00	1	0	1	0	1	0
Bryson Bales	1	1	2.95	7	0	21	17	7	21
Michael Benzor	0	0	12.27	6	0	7	4	12	10
Jack Bowery	1	3	4.76	10	1	28	33	10	16
Donovan Burke	2	1	3.80	4	0	21	24	2	13
Ryan DeSanto	1	2	3.33	6	0	24	20	4	20
Andrew Evans	0	2	6.65	8	0	23	35	8	20
Jason Finkelstein	0	0	7.50	3	0	6	4	6	2
Joseph Fredericks	0	0	54.00	1	0	1	5	4	1
Jacob Frost	0	1	3.38	2	0	8	5	4	10
J.T. Gibson	0	0	3.55	6	0	13	10	13	14

Pitching	W	L	ERA	G	SV	IP	H	BB	SO
Peter Haas	0	0	5.40	5	1	8	8	2	7
Joseph Hauser	0	0	15.00	1	0	3	6	2	1
Jake Hilton	2	0	5.68	4	0	6	6	4	8
Olin Johnson	0	2	7.80	5	0	15	21	6	14
Griffin Kirn	1	0	2.18	4	0	21	17	5	13
Josh Lajoie	0	0	9.00	1	0	1	2	0	1
Haiden Leffew	1	3	5.19	5	0	17	14	10	17
Danny Macchiarola	0	2	5.68	5	0	13	13	5	10
Chance Mako	2	1	7.30	8	0	12	7	18	11
Cooper McGrath	0	0	6.23	3	0	4	5	4	9
Justin Mitrovich	1	1	5.19	7	2	17	21	11	17
Blake Morningstar	1	0	6.75	8	0	21	22	12	33
Jake Ogden	0	0	0.00	1	0	0	1	0	0
Colton Shaw	0	1	1.13	4	1	8	8	2	7
Mike Simes	0	0	0.00	2	0	7	4	3	2
Sam Tookoian	1	1	6.06	7	2	16	12	7	23
Cole Wisenbaker	1	1	1.69	3	1	5	7	1	5
Kevin Zarnoch	0	0	0.00	4	2	8	5	2	13

HYANNIS

Batting	AVG	AB	R	H	2B	3B	HR	RBI	SB
J.P. Acosta	.417	12	3	5	1	0	0	4	1
George Athanasiadis	.000	1	0	0	0	0	0	0	0
Dalton Bargo	.225	71	16	16	4	0	3	12	3
Carson Boles	.240	25	4	6	1	0	0	4	0
Parker Brosius	.250	24	9	6	1	0	1	5	4
Dawson Bryce	.250	4	0	1	1	0	0	1	0
Dawson Cash	.000	2	0	0	0	0	0	0	0
Blake Cavill	.186	43	7	8	1	0	2	5	0
Wallace Clark	.304	46	12	14	4	0	1	11	1
Michael Dattalo	.295	129	15	38	9	0	1	28	4
Manny Garza	.222	18	2	4	0	0	0	0	0
Jon Jon Gazdar	.314	70	14	22	4	0	2	17	4
Nick Groves	.364	66	18	24	2	0	0	14	10
Casey Hintz	.111	9	3	1	0	0	0	1	0
Camden Janik	.267	30	7	8	2	0	0	3	0
Kane Kepley	.244	127	31	31	6	0	3	19	21
Jake Koonin	.000	4	0	0	0	0	0	0	0
Alex Lodise	.295	61	7	18	4	0	1	4	1
Cannon Peebles	.205	44	5	9	1	0	1	6	2
Eddy Pelc	.241	29	8	7	0	0	0	5	3
Eddie Saldivar	.143	21	5	3	2	0	0	3	0
Anthony Silva	.194	72	14	14	4	1	2	11	2
Eric Snow	.326	92	15	30	3	0	2	18	5
Steve Solorzano	.000	3	0	0	0	0	0	0	0
Josh Tate	.294	68	14	20	1	0	0	10	7
Jaxson West	.281	64	9	18	1	0	0	12	3
Mason White	.177	96	19	17	6	1	2	13	1
Zach Yorke	.125	24	3	3	0	0	1	7	0

Pitching	W	L	ERA	G	SV	IP	H	BB	SO
Trey Beard	0	0	6.55	3	0	11	15	3	12
Kade Brown	2	1	4.70	10	0	15	17	3	19
Dominick Carbone	0	0	4.61	10	1	14	14	9	12
Ciaran Caughey	1	0	8.31	3	0	9	9	5	6
Pierce Coppola	0	1	6.14	2	0	7	5	5	15
Cade Crossland	1	0	5.68	5	0	6	5	4	7
Stone Cushing	0	0	4.15	5	0	9	11	8	7
Chandler Dorsey	0	0	0.00	3	0	8	3	4	13
Ryan Dromboski	0	1	1.80	3	0	10	12	7	12
Joseph Dzierwa	1	0	0.00	3	0	11	10	5	10
Jackson Emus	0	0	9.00	1	0	1	2	1	1
Sean Fitzpatrick	1	0	2.70	9	1	13	11	4	16
Andres Galan	1	0	5.27	4	0	14	12	5	14
Alizaeh Gutierrez	0	0	2.35	3	0	8	6	4	4
Casey Hintz	3	0	3.27	11	0	22	16	6	28
Maison Martinez	1	0	18.00	4	0	5	9	4	4
Nic McCay	0	1	7.71	2	0	5	8	4	6
Drake Meeks	0	0	8.68	6	0	9	12	8	11
Aaron Mishoulam	2	1	5.00	9	0	18	19	10	13
Jacob Moore	1	0	7.56	6	0	8	10	4	9
Reed Moring	3	1	3.52	7	1	15	12	8	16
Luke Nichols	0	3	9.39	5	0	15	19	7	16
Josh Och	1	0	0.00	8	3	10	1	3	17
Braxton Pearson	0	0	4.91	2	0	4	8	2	4
Jason Reitz	1	0	1.42	4	0	13	7	6	11
Aaron Savary	2	1	1.42	7	0	25	12	20	32
Paul Schmitz	1	1	4.50	3	0	6	7	6	9
Steve Solorzano	1	0	5.06	3	0	5	4	3	8
Joe Steeber	0	0	3.60	2	1	5	4	1	4
Grant Stevens	0	2	4.35	3	0	10	11	2	10
Blaine Wynk	1	1	2.55	7	0	25	18	9	22

ORLEANS

Batting	AVG	AB	R	H	2B	3B	HR	RBI	SB
Robbie Ayers	.200	35	7	7	2	0	1	3	0
Chris Barr	.259	54	10	14	2	0	0	7	3
Daniel Bucciero	.216	74	12	16	4	0	4	11	1
Roch Cholowsky	.218	55	5	12	3	0	1	5	0
Ian Daugherty	.231	39	4	9	1	0	1	7	0
Khadim Diaw	.326	46	6	15	1	0	0	3	0
Evan Griffis	.163	49	3	8	1	0	1	4	4
Jake Gurevitch	.278	90	7	25	4	1	2	16	1
Jimmy Keenan	.100	20	0	2	0	0	0	1	0
Mike Mancini	.230	100	13	23	4	4	1	10	2
Bennett Markinson	.340	50	7	17	5	0	1	11	0
Lorenzo Meola	.162	111	18	18	7	0	2	7	6
Landon Moran	.216	88	14	19	3	0	1	5	6
Hudson Shupe	.310	129	21	40	5	0	0	11	3
Austin Smith	.190	84	6	16	0	0	1	4	0
J-P Smith	.163	49	3	8	2	0	1	4	0
Colin Tuft	.143	35	3	5	0	1	0	1	4
Isaac Wachsmann	.188	32	3	6	2	0	1	5	0
Eddie Yamin IV	.045	22	0	1	0	0	0	1	0
Ben Zeigler-Namoa	.311	90	13	28	5	0	3	17	1

Pitching	W	L	ERA	G	SV	IP	H	BB	SO
Matt Ager	0	1	8.59	2	0	7	8	4	8
Joe Allen	0	1	5.12	10	0	19	20	10	18
Tucker Biven	2	2	3.97	9	2	11	12	5	16
Cody Bowker	1	4	3.28	9	0	36	26	7	36
Matthew Dalquist	0	3	11.90	8	0	20	39	10	16
Callan Fang	3	1	2.15	7	0	29	15	9	39
Michael Foltz Jr.	0	3	3.03	9	0	36	23	17	24
Caleb Freeman	0	0	5.06	4	0	5	3	5	2
Max Gitlin	1	0	4.76	6	0	6	8	4	3
Miles Gosztola	3	0	1.59	10	0	23	13	9	24
Chase Hoover	0	0	67.50	1	0	1	4	1	0
Luke Jackson	0	1	2.35	5	0	8	8	4	8
Alex Kranzler	0	1	4.15	11	1	13	16	9	14
Luc Lavigueur	0	0	9.00	1	0	1	3	1	0
Lucas Litteral	1	1	7.27	8	2	17	22	9	19
Dawson Logie	0	0	0.00	1	0	1	0	0	2
Sean Matson	0	0	0.00	7	4	7	4	4	7
Braden Quinn	0	0	12.00	2	0	3	4	3	6
Mauricio Rodriguez	0	0	0.00	3	1	4	0	1	2
Brennan Seiber	0	2	3.00	7	0	18	13	3	23
Jack Seward	0	0	0.00	2	0	2	1	0	3
Saul Soto	1	0	7.15	12	2	11	13	8	4
Itsuki Takemoto	3	1	0.71	9	0	25	12	7	23
Evan Truitt	0	2	4.91	3	0	11	10	3	4
Jayden Voelker	0	1	4.76	3	0	6	6	2	7
Brendan Walker	0	1	16.62	5	0	4	6	4	8
Matt Watson	0	0	2.08	2	0	9	6	2	8
Jarek Woodward	0	0	0.00	1	0	1	0	0	0

WAREHAM

Batting	AVG	AB	R	H	2B	3B	HR	RBI	SB
Bobby Boser	.319	72	19	23	6	0	2	8	5
Reese Chapman	.195	82	9	16	3	0	3	14	0
Gio Cueto	.056	18	1	1	0	0	0	1	0
Yohann Dessureault	.308	104	17	32	8	0	4	17	8
Hunter Dobbins	.364	11	0	4	1	0	0	3	0
Ty Dooley	.000	5	0	0	0	0	0	0	0

Batting	AVG	AB	R	H	2B	3B	HR	RBI	SB
Nate Earley	.280	75	9	21	8	0	2	3	0
Rylan Galvan	.300	10	2	3	0	0	1	3	0
Murf Gray	.329	140	22	46	9	0	5	27	5
Bayram Hot	.125	16	2	2	0	0	0	0	1
Jacob Jarrell	.215	79	17	17	4	0	2	8	0
Antonio Jimenez	.203	128	23	26	6	1	5	13	5
Michael Lippe	.172	58	9	10	2	1	0	9	1
William Parker	.333	9	4	3	0	0	1	2	0
David Pedanou	.250	8	1	2	1	0	0	1	0
Eli Putnam	.291	117	18	34	7	3	5	19	9
Jace Rinehart	.244	90	9	22	6	1	1	9	2
Aris Rivera	.077	13	1	1	0	0	0	3	0
Brendan Summerhill	.286	84	19	24	5	1	2	14	12
Colby Turner	.240	100	16	24	5	0	1	7	2
Sam White	.267	90	14	24	5	0	2	16	3
Max Williams	.273	11	1	3	0	0	1	1	0

Pitching	W	L	ERA	G	SV	IP	H	BB	SO
Heath Andrews	2	2	4.08	6	0	18	19	5	16
Gavin Black	1	0	1.80	8	0	15	10	8	17
A.J. Colarusso	0	1	10.29	3	0	7	13	4	2
Zane Coppersmith	1	0	3.18	10	0	11	14	2	14
Jake Cubbler	0	0	3.86	2	0	2	1	1	1
Ethan Darden	2	1	10.61	5	0	9	14	7	4
David Eckaus	0	0	6.23	4	0	4	6	4	4
Brok Eddy	0	1	5.14	3	1	7	9	2	8
Jake Faherty	0	0	2.25	5	3	8	3	2	14
Jacob Faulkner	3	0	1.90	13	0	24	17	5	13
Christian Foutch	0	0	0.00	2	0	1	0	2	2
Patrick Galle	3	0	5.19	12	1	17	12	15	19
Bryce Gluckman	0	0	27.00	3	0	1	4	4	1
Darin Horn	0	2	6.19	6	0	16	18	9	12
Cole Leaman	1	3	9.15	7	0	21	27	14	17
Hudson Lee	0	0	1.93	5	1	5	1	6	8
Jaxon Lucas	1	0	4.96	11	0	16	18	14	16
Lucas Mahlstedt	1	0	1.42	8	0	13	6	6	14
Matt Maloney	0	0	6.30	9	0	10	15	6	13
Tate McGuire	2	1	3.81	7	0	26	24	12	33
Sam Mettert	3	1	4.50	11	1	18	18	12	22
Griffin O'Connor	1	0	6.50	6	0	18	17	9	10
Tony Pluta	0	0	2.33	11	0	19	21	6	14
Hudson Rowan	0	1	11.25	2	0	4	3	2	2
Braeden Sloan	1	2	6.92	4	0	13	10	6	19
Jack Smith	0	0	0.00	2	0	1	0	3	0
Anthony Steele	0	0	31.50	2	0	2	6	7	2
Anthony Susac	0	1	2.92	8	3	12	11	5	20
Yoel Tejeda Jr.	0	1	4.76	3	0	11	14	4	16
Julian Tonghini	0	0	1.93	3	0	5	4	2	6
Anthony Watts	0	0	15.00	2	0	3	3	3	3

YARMOUTH-DENNIS

Batting	AVG	AB	R	H	2B	3B	HR	RBI	SB
Wehiwa Aloy	.309	81	16	25	3	0	8	24	2
RJ Austin	.321	56	10	18	6	0	2	9	6
Michael Ball	.297	37	8	11	2	0	2	4	0
Cameron Boardman	.000	0	0	0	0	0	0	0	0
Jake Brown	.320	25	2	8	0	0	1	2	1
Drew Burress	.125	64	16	8	3	0	1	3	3
Phoenix Call	.246	122	17	30	2	1	1	9	16
Easton Carmichael	.299	127	22	38	10	0	5	23	6
Jackson Chirello	.313	64	12	20	1	1	1	6	7
Gavin Gallaher	.202	84	4	17	5	0	2	15	3
Carter Garate	.241	29	2	7	0	0	0	3	0
Ryan Gerety	.250	4	0	1	0	0	0	0	2
Cameron Kim	.122	74	6	9	0	0	0	6	1
Jonathan Kim	.097	31	2	3	0	0	0	1	1
Skylar King	.294	17	3	5	0	0	1	2	0
Talmadge LeCroy	.333	42	3	14	3	0	1	2	0
Anthony Martinez	.278	90	16	25	4	0	3	17	0
Cade McGee	.185	54	9	10	0	0	1	5	0
Brady Neal	.194	31	6	6	1	0	1	4	0
Ethan Petry	.360	100	26	36	7	0	11	25	0
Charlie Saum	.113	53	6	6	1	0	3	8	1
Ryan Sprock	.276	29	3	8	0	0	0	5	0
Will Tippett	.204	54	9	11	1	0	2	3	3

Pitching	W	L	ERA	G	SV	IP	H	BB	SO
Caleb Anderson	1	0	5.00	10	0	18	17	9	26
Carson Ballard	0	1	3.63	5	0	17	21	4	17
Micah Bucknam	1	0	4.22	6	0	21	23	10	24
Aiven Cabral	5	1	2.81	9	0	16	13	4	22
Ian Cooke	0	0	14.73	2	0	4	10	1	2
Noah Czajkowski	0	0	10.38	3	0	4	7	3	5
Ramsey David	0	0	1.50	3	0	12	9	7	14
Dylan Delvecchio	1	1	3.06	11	1	18	15	10	21
Brooks Ey	0	1	9.00	1	0	2	3	0	3
Ethan Firoved	0	0	4.15	4	0	13	11	7	16
Gavin Jones	0	0	5.40	9	0	10	12	8	8
Will Jones	1	0	5.40	1	0	5	5	0	4
Justin Lee	1	1	4.74	10	0	19	18	12	25
Aiden Moffett	2	1	5.54	8	0	13	7	13	14
Kellan Montgomery	0	0	1.38	3	0	13	10	6	10
Trevor Moore	1	0	0.00	10	8	14	8	6	28
Toran O'Harran	0	0	9.53	6	0	6	6	13	6
Braeden Osbolt	2	0	2.28	5	0	24	17	8	15
Bryan Peck	0	1	4.15	5	0	13	15	6	17
Daniel Powell	0	0	0.00	1	0	3	1	0	2
Jason Reitz	0	0	6.00	1	0	3	3	5	2
Jakob Russell	0	0	7.71	2	0	2	3	3	3
Marko Sipila	1	0	2.84	3	2	6	4	2	9
Nolan Sliver	0	1	5.40	5	0	10	8	8	13
Ryan Sprock	3	0	4.50	6	0	14	8	7	22
Pablo Torres	1	0	6.35	4	0	6	7	4	7
Dylan Vigue	2	2	3.86	5	0	23	21	8	26
Caleb Williams	0	1	7.36	2	0	4	6	3	5
Sean Youngerman	2	1	2.55	7	0	25	18	10	33

ALASKA LEAGUE

	W	L	PCT	GB
Anchorage Bucs	29	12	.707	-
Mat-Su Miners	26	16	.619	3.5
Peninsula Oilers	23	19	.548	6.5
Anchorage Glacier Pilots	13	29	.310	16.5
Chugiak-Eagle River Chinooks	12	27	.308	16

CHAMPIONSHIP: Anchorage Bucs had the best record. The Championship game between Anchorage and Mat-Su was cancelled.

INDIVIDUAL BATTING LEADERS

	AVG	AB	R	H	2B	3B	HR	RBI	SB
Chase Wilcox, INF, Miners	.350	123	26	43	8	1	0	20	17
Cole Carlon, 1B/LHP, Bucs	.349	126	28	44	5	1	3	18	9
Max Roffwarg, SS, Oilers	.320	103	13	33	2	0	0	16	9
Ryan Callahan, INF, Bucs	.311	103	21	32	3	1	1	20	2
Colin Robson, OF, Oilers	.308	146	23	45	11	0	4	24	22
Tommy Eisenstat, 1B, Bucs	.288	111	12	32	4	1	1	19	5
Drake Kerr, OF, Miners	.276	134	19	37	5	2	0	17	23
Andrew Lamb, C/UT, Bucs	.276	105	20	29	14	0	0	18	3
Louie Zulaica, IF, Chinooks	.260	123	11	32	6	1	0	14	3
Brody Briggs, C, Bucs	.259	108	20	28	6	0	0	12	6

INDIVIDUAL PITCHING LEADERS

	W	L	ERA	G	SV	IP	H	BB	SO
Drew Koenen, Miners	0	1	0.00	15	9	16	5	6	17
Garvey Rumary, Bucs	4	0	0.26	9	0	35	14	12	36
Tucker Timmerman	3	1	0.27	8	0	33	23	7	29
Andrew Rudd, Bucs	2	1	0.61	14	5	29	23	6	21
Brodie Purcell, Bucs	1	0	0.63	10	4	14	4	3	16
Mose Hayes, Oilers	2	0	1.17	9	1	31	20	14	29
Ben DeTaeye, Miners	2	0	1.24	10	0	29	15	12	31
Jack Hostetler, Miners	3	2	1.41	6	0	32	16	7	37
Ashton Johnson, Miners	3	1	1.42	7	0	12.2	7	3	14
Payton Allen, Pilots	1	1	1.51	10	3	36	18	12	19

ATLANTIC COLLEGIATE LEAGUE

Wolff Division	W	L	PCT	GB
Essex Legends	22	11	.667	-
Bergen Metros	19	10	.655	1
Jersey Shore Stallions	12	19	.387	9
New Brunswick MATRIX	13	13	.500	5.5
Ocean Ospreys	11	17	.397	8.5
New York Phenoms	10	18	.362	9.5
Kaiser Division	**W**	**L**	**PCT**	**GB**
Atlantic Whitecaps	21	9	.700	-
East Coast Sandhogs	19	11	.633	2
New York Crush	18	10	.643	2
Hitters Club Hawkeyes	13	16	.448	7.5
Bayside Blue Claws	13	15	.464	7
LIB Neptunes	14	11	.560	4.5
Old Town Road Patriots	11	18	.379	9.5
New York Valor	5	23	.179	15

CHAMPIONSHIP: New York Crush defeated Essex Legends, 13-7, in championship game.

INDIVIDUAL BATTING LEADERS

	AVG	AB	R	H	2B	3B	HR	RBI	SB
Kyle Bailey, C, Crush	.458	72	16	33	8	0	0	18	2
Jace Gilligan, C, Ospreys	.389	72	12	28	7	0	0	19	6
Christopher Sais, 1B, S'hogs	.389	72	13	28	5	1	2	20	8
Luis Ramirez, INF, Metros	.385	78	18	30	6	2	5	30	11
Keldrin Rodriguez, OF, Crush	.375	64	18	24	7	2	3	19	8
Myles Seid, C, Legends	.372	94	14	35	11	0	1	24	2
Johnny Catuosco, OF, H'eyes	.361	72	17	26	5	3	0	9	1
Joey Cohen, OF, Hawkeyes	.359	92	21	33	3	0	1	14	19
Frank Scrivanic, SS, Ospreys	.357	84	17	30	6	2	0	18	5
Ian Kaiser, OF, Legends	.337	104	28	35	7	2	0	16	13

INDIVIDUAL PITCHING LEADERS

	W	L	ERA	G	SV	IP	H	BB	SO
Joey Ciancimino, Phenoms	1	1	0.98	6	0	28	15	9	34
Sammuel Urena, Crush	4	0	1.50	8	0	48	36	7	36
Michael Andrew, Whitecaps	2	0	1.88	7	0	29	21	8	26
Justin DeCastro, Blue Claws	3	0	2.08	4	0	26	19	5	28
Peter Nenadich, Hawkeyes	1	1	2.10	7	0	26	22	10	31
Matthow King, MATRIX	2	1	2.28	5	0	24	12	8	19
Daniel Goodman, Sandhogs	2	0	2.70	9	0	30	30	13	28
Alexander Burciaga, Blue Claws	2	1	2.73	8	0	30	29	14	26
Tyler Lopez, Whitecaps	3	1	2.83	7	0	29	24	9	32
Brandon Paider, Crush	3	1	2.83	6	0	35	40	7	19

CAL RIPKEN COLLEGIATE LEAGUE

North	W	L	PCT	GB
Gaithersburg Giants	23	13	.639	-
Bethesda Big Train	21	15	.583	2
Cropdusters Baseball	17	19	.472	6
SS-T Thunderbolts	12	24	.333	11
South	**W**	**L**	**PCT**	**GB**
Alexandria Aces	25	11	.694	-
Southern Maryland Senators	16	20	.444	9
Metro South County Braves	16	20	.444	9
D.C. Grays	14	22	.389	11

CHAMPIONSHIP: Bethesda Big Train defeated Gaithersburg Giants, 2-0, in championship series.

INDIVIDUAL BATTING LEADERS

	AVG	AB	R	H	2B	3B	HR	RBI	SB
Andrew Williamson, OF, BT	.462	106	38	49	16	2	9	33	8
Jeff Sabater, OF, T Bolts	.381	84	21	32	7	1	0	11	21
AJ Martin, INF, Giants	.375	88	19	33	7	1	5	26	3
Jack Pokorak, INF, Braves	.365	85	26	31	8	0	6	25	3
Ethan Plyler, INF, Aces	.354	99	17	35	6	1	1	26	7
Carter Groen, OF, Senators	.347	95	26	33	5	1	9	24	10
Tim Nicholson, C, Aces	.345	110	36	38	5	0	2	18	12
James Layman, INF, Grays	.340	103	21	35	4	0	0	7	8
Kevin Milewski, C, Aces	.339	109	10	37	7	0	6	25	1
Christopher Diaz, OF, BT	.338	77	20	26	1	2	1	7	4

INDIVIDUAL PITCHING LEADERS

	W	L	ERA	G	SV	IP	H	BB	SO
Michael Sills, Grays	2	1	2.20	6	0	29	21	5	31
Ethan Houghtaling, Aces	5	0	2.62	8	0	45	39	13	51
Matt Hoover, Senators	4	1	2.70	7	0	33	41	8	32
Zach Kwasny, Aces	4	2	3.20	7	0	39	40	10	51
Jake Roberti, Grays	3	1	3.55	8	0	38	32	8	39
Kyndall Cassidy, Braves	2	2	4.33	8	0	27	29	7	18
Jack Robinson, Big Train	4	1	4.56	12	0	26	22	20	27
Parker Edwards, Braves	1	2	4.80	8	0	30	26	15	32
Mark Loubier, Senators	0	4	5.29	8	0	34	29	19	22
Rohan Mishra, Thunderbolts	2	1	6.16	10	0	31	38	9	23

CALIFORNIA COLLEGIATE LEAGUE

South	W	L	PCT	GB
Conejo Oaks	25	12	.676	-
Santa Barbara Foresters	20	11	.645	2
Arroyo Seco Saints	21	15	.583	3.5
Orange County Riptide	20	17	.541	5
Ventura County Pirates	10	13	.435	8
Academy Barons	13	23	.361	11.5
San Diego SunRays	6	23	.207	15

North	W	L	PCT	GB
Walnut Creek Crawdads	23	14	.622	-
San Luis Obispo Blues	21	13	.618	0.5
Sonoma Stompers	21	15	.583	1.5
San Francisco Seagulls	15	18	.455	6
Alameda Merchants	13	19	.406	7.5
Menlo Park Legends	10	25	.286	12

CHAMPIONSHIP: Conejo defeated Walnut Creek, 2-0, in best-of-three championship series.

INDIVIDUAL BATTING LEADERS

	AVG	AB	R	H	2B	3B	HR	RBI	SB
Justin Rubin, SS, Oaks	.391	87	25	34	9	2	1	24	12
Jack Holman, 1B, Foresters	.381	84	16	32	8	1	2	24	1
Ryan Lordier, INF, Seagulls	.376	93	13	35	4	0	0	20	7
Ace Reese, INF, Riptide	.369	84	17	31	8	1	1	22	1
Isiaih Walker, UT, Crawdads	.360	125	31	45	6	1	2	30	11
Easton Elliot, INF, Saints	.352	105	22	37	5	1	0	21	17
Cam Calvillo, INF, Crawdads	.341	132	28	45	7	0	3	26	7
Tommy Kendlinger, OF, Oaks	.337	92	26	31	1	5	1	18	18
Robert Pitts Jr., OF, Pirates	.333	66	13	22	5	2	0	8	13
Ethan Royal, OF, Blues	.330	112	24	37	7	0	1	22	10

INDIVIDUAL PITCHING LEADERS

	W	L	ERA	G	SV	IP	H	BB	SO
Drew Aguiar, Crawdads	3	2	1.59	15	0	40	25	10	42
Jaxon Byrd, Crawdads	4	0	1.99	8	0	41	29	13	35
Dwyer Lewis, Seaguls	3	1	2.54	6	0	39	39	4	38
John Damozonio, Blues	3	0	2.79	6	0	29	20	19	48
Dante Zamudio, Barons	1	3	2.84	8	0	38	41	11	38
Trajan Lee, Saints	1	1	3.07	8	0	29	24	14	35
Cody Howard, Foresters	3	0	3.08	5	0	26	23	9	27
Logan Groff, Blues	3	0	3.15	7	0	40	27	13	42
Cody Albright, Blues	3	0	3.26	8	0	39	41	21	28
Jackson Howell, Blues	2	2	3.45	6	0	29	24	12	23

COASTAL PLAIN LEAGUE

East	W	L	PCT	GB
Peninsula Pilots	34	13	.723	-
Wilmington Sharks	26	19	.578	7
Wilson Tobs	25	19	.568	7.5
Morehead City Marlins	25	21	.543	8.5
Tri-City Chili Peppers	19	29	.396	15.5
Holly Springs Salamanders	15	31	.326	18.5
Greenville Yard Gnomes	12	34	.261	21.5
West	**W**	**L**	**PCT**	**GB**
Martinsville Mustangs	30	17	.638	-
Forest City Owls	28	18	.609	1.5
Florence Flamingos	26	18	.591	2.5

	W	L	PCT	GB
Asheboro ZooKeepers	27	20	.574	3
Lexington County Blowfish	26	22	.542	4.5
Boone Bigfoots	23	25	.479	7.5
Macon Bacon	17	31	.354	13.5
HP Thomasville HiToms	16	32	.333	14.5

CHAMPIONSHIP: Wilmington defeated Lexington , 2-0, in best-of-three championship series.

INDIVIDUAL BATTING LEADERS

	AVG	AB	R	H	2B	3B	HR	RBI	SB
Lucas Carmichael, OF, M'ngs	.410	144	34	59	8	1	1	42	6
Jaden James, 3B, Owls	.366	131	37	48	12	0	5	40	12
Jak Kail, INF, Tobs	.365	148	28	54	16	1	2	28	8
Grayson Fitzwater, 1B, Pilots	.349	149	39	52	15	0	5	36	6
Zach Evans, INF, ZopKeepers	.338	130	30	44	12	1	5	20	7
Evan Bouldin, 2B, CP	.333	138	21	46	7	0	6	24	3
Danny Stephens, INF, Sal'ers	.321	112	21	36	3	1	3	14	14
Brayden Corn, OF, Flamingos	.320	122	23	39	2	1	0	17	25
Danny Estrada, OF, CP	.316	174	38	55	10	1	1	18	6
Owen Blackledge, OF, ZK	.314	140	30	44	11	0	6	25	9

INDIVIDUAL PITCHING LEADERS

	W	L	ERA	G	SV	IP	H	BB	SO
Jack Decker, Marlins	5	1	1.15	15	1	39	18	16	53
Travis Lavendier, Sharks	4	0	1.37	9	0	46	27	18	23
Reece Miller, Tobs	5	1	1.47	8	0	43	22	14	54
Brian Ereu, Pilots	3	0	2.39	11	0	49	37	8	38
Jonah Milchuck, Tobs	2	2	2.57	10	0	42	38	6	29
Jaxon Lloyd, Mustangs	3	1	3.35	10	0	46	34	17	35
William Morris, Owls	2	1	3.55	16	2	38	34	8	39
Koen van t Klooster, Marlins	1	2	3.58	12	0	38	39	13	36
John Jones, Owls	4	1	3.61	10	0	42	48	16	35
Mason Manriquez, ZooKeepers	2	1	3.92	11	1	41	35	27	47

FLORIDA COLLEGIATE SUMMER LEAGUE

	W	L	PCT	GB
Leesburg Lightning	20	11	.645	-
Winter Garden Squeeze	21	12	.636	-
DeLand Suns	16	15	.516	4
Sanford River Rats	15	16	.484	5
Orlando Snappers	12	19	.391	8
Winter Park Diamond Dawgs	12	23	.343	10

CHAMPIONSHIP: Leesburg Lightning defeated Deland Suns, 2-0, in best-of-three championship series.

INDIVIDUAL BATTING LEADERS

	AVG	AB	R	H	2B	3B	HR	RBI	SB
Michael Furry, CF, Lightning	.406	69	27	28	7	0	3	16	5
Stewart Puckett, 3B, RR	.393	89	25	35	7	0	5	26	6
Garrett Byrd, CF, Squeeze	.376	93	26	35	11	1	1	16	10
Titan Kamaka, SS, Squeeze	.376	109	22	41	13	4	3	29	6
Jalen Hairston, 3B, RR	.367	49	11	18	5	0	1	15	13
Xavier Lopez, OF, River Rats	.356	87	19	31	5	3	0	23	11
Damion Kenealy, INF, Suns	.345	58	10	20	5	0	1	16	0
Aris Rivera, C, Suns	.338	68	7	23	2	0	1	17	0
Mathew Farner, SS, Suns	.328	64	16	21	7	0	0	9	7
Jordy Oriach, RF, Lightning	.326	86	16	28	5	0	0	13	1

INDIVIDUAL PITCHING LEADERS

	W	L	ERA	G	SV	IP	H	BB	SO
Haro Baez, Suns	1	0	0.74	7	1	24	13	6	23
Tyler Donay, Lightning	2	2	1.52	8	0	30	18	10	30
Micah Takac, Squeeze	5	0	1.55	6	0	29	23	4	25
Jace Trautner, Lightning	2	1	1.82	6	0	25	19	6	17
Lucas Hartman, Snappers	1	1	1.99	4	0	23	15	10	26
Joel Core, Suns	3	0	2.49	9	0	22	13	13	37
Tanner Walker, Lightning	2	0	2.53	12	1	22	14	8	26
Logan Wirt, Suns	1	1	2.78	6	0	23	16	16	29
Jacob Iverson, Squeeze	3	0	2.92	11	0	25	20	18	29
Tyler Mecchella, D Dawgs	0	1	3.08	7	0	26	23	12	27

FUTURES COLLEGIATE LEAGUE

	W	L	PCT	GB
Norwich Sea Unicorns	37	21	.638	-
Westfield Starfires	34	22	.625	2.000
New Britain Bees	30	25	.545	5.500
Vermont Lake Monsters	29	26	.527	6.500
Worcester Bravehearts	28	28	.509	8.000
Nashua Silver Knights	27	29	.482	9.000
Brockton Rox	18	38	.321	18.000
Futures League Road Warriors	10	24	.294	15.000

CHAMPIONSHIP: Norwich Sea Unicorns defeated Westfield Starfires, 2-0, in best-of-three championship series.

INDIVIDUAL BATTING LEADERS

	AVG	AB	R	H	2B	3B	HR	RBI	SB
Owen Pincince, OF, B'hearts	.376	173	42	65	10	1	1	23	4
Drew Loikits, INF, Silver K's	.335	164	31	55	10	1	1	33	6
Mark Quatrani, C, Lake M's	.333	144	22	48	5	1	4	34	0
Connor Campbell, OF, Rox	.328	119	25	39	4	1	1	17	12
Gianno Merlonghi, OF, S'fires	.314	175	40	55	7	2	2	33	16
Aidan Redahan, INF, S'fires	.306	160	25	49	8	1	2	29	1
Tommy Ahlers, OF, Silver K's	.303	211	46	64	14	2	0	35	26
Joe Muzio, INF, Road W's	.297	91	14	27	6	2	1	9	10
Chone James, C, Lake M's	.289	142	30	41	12	1	1	19	0
Matt Milone, OF, B'hearts	.287	136	18	39	10	0	3	28	14

INDIVIDUAL PITCHING LEADERS

	W	L	ERA	G	SV	IP	H	BB	SO
Jake Jachym, Starfites	5	1	2.70	12	0	46.2	42	13	27
Andrew Chenevert, Silver K's	5	0	4.38	11	0	49.1	56	17	36
Benjamin Oliveira, Bees	3	4	5.03	11	0	48.1	45	22	46
James Nichols, Rox	2	4	5.28	10	0	46	46	18	33
Chase Carey, Road Warriors	1	4	5.72	16	1	28.1	35	17	24

GREAT LAKES LEAGUE

	W	L	PCT	GB
Hamilton Joes	26	9	.743	-
Lima Locos	21	15	.583	5.5
Muskegon Clippers	20	16	.556	6.5
Michigan Monarchs	17	19	.472	9.5
Xenia Scouts	17	19	.472	9.5
S Ohio Copperheads	13	22	.371	13
Grand Lake Mariners	11	25	.306	15.5

CHAMPIONSHIP: Hamilton Joes defeated Muskegon Clippers, 2-0, in best-of-three championship series.

INDIVIDUAL BATTING LEADERS

	AVG	AB	R	H	2B	3B	HR	RBI	SB
Brayden Fraasman, RF, Joes	.370	92	23	34	7	1	2	16	6
Blake Bowen, 3B, Locos	.364	110	29	40	7	0	3	29	7
Tanner Mally, SS, Monarchs	.359	117	26	42	8	2	0	19	12
Sebastian Alexander, CF, Lo's	.355	110	35	39	8	2	2	30	35
Alonzo Paul, C, Monarchs	.354	82	18	29	0	0	1	9	6
Jacob Gumieny, SS, M'chs	.351	94	16	33	8	0	0	12	1
Kimo Fukofuka, OF, M'chs	.350	100	28	35	11	1	1	20	12
Noah Ruiz, INF, Scouts	.346	133	28	46	4	2	1	29	29
Justin Osterhouse, INF, Clip's	.343	105	23	36	7	1	4	30	9
Jackson Rains, OF, Mariners	.339	115	23	39	9	0	5	22	1

INDIVIDUAL PITCHING LEADERS

	W	L	ERA	G	SV	IP	H	BB	SO
Matteo Pare, Locos	3	1	1.91	7	0	33	29	6	19
Zach Vriesenga, Clippers	2	2	2.08	10	0	31	27	7	26
Joshua Hickey, Scouts	2	2	2.52	13	4	36	39	13	18
Cooper Fiehrer, Joes	2	0	2.56	8	1	32	29	6	27
Andrew Hickman, Scouts	1	1	3.13	15	1	32	34	7	11
Will DeMasse, Clippers	4	1	3.67	10	0	34	32	14	28
Jacob Pallo, Clippers	4	1	4.18	8	0	32	30	22	26
Brenden Holland, Scouts	4	1	4.53	8	0	44	40	22	39
Thomas Howard, Locos	3	4	4.66	7	0	29	31	12	27
Adam Wade, Scouts	3	3	4.67	8	0	35	31	20	41

HAMPTONS COLLEGIATE LEAGUE

	W	L	T	PTS
Sag Harbor Whalers	21	15	.583	-
North Fork Ospreys	20	15	.569	0.5
Shelter Island Bucks	20	16	.556	1
Southampton Breakers	17	17	.500	3
South Shore Clippers	16	18	.472	4
Westhampton Aviators	11	24	.319	9.5

CHAMPIONSHIP: Southampton Breakers defeated Shelter Island Bucks, 2-0, in best-of-three championship series.

INDIVIDUAL BATTING LEADERS

	AVG	AB	R	H	2B	3B	HR	RBI	SB
Jack Gold, INF, Whalers	.450	100	37	45	14	0	9	34	10
Zev Moore, INF, Aviators	.382	102	25	39	10	0	2	23	20
Nick Pratt, C, Ospreys	.376	101	27	38	6	0	5	30	3
Joseph Dwyer, INF, Ospreys	.371	105	31	39	9	0	4	28	20
Anthony Equale, INF, O's	.363	91	25	33	8	0	2	17	5
Aidan Paradine, C, Bucks	.355	76	19	27	5	0	2	19	0
Teddy Cashman, OF, Whalers	.349	83	18	29	8	0	3	20	5
Collin Quintano, INF, B'kers	.344	93	12	32	12	0	3	25	0
Kai Aoki, OF, Ospreys	.342	76	18	26	2	0	0	11	0
EJ Ettinger, INF, Clippers	.338	80	13	27	2	0	0	9	3

INDIVIDUAL PITCHING LEADERS

	W	L	ERA	G	SV	IP	H	BB	SO
Will Darrell, Whalers	4	1	2.52	6	0	25	19	17	27
Brent Herrmann, Ospreys	1	1	2.63	5	0	24	25	14	23
Aiden Urbom, Bucks	4	0	2.81	6	0	32	24	9	27
Bobby Finn, Clippers	1	1	2.88	6	0	25	15	19	37
Zach Karson, Breakers	1	2	2.90	6	0	31	30	9	25
Chris Batuyios, Clippers	4	0	3.00	6	0	24	24	15	29
Alex Ardemagni, Ospreys	4	0	3.13	10	0	23	31	6	21
Logan Detty, Bucks	2	2	3.21	8	0	28	26	11	16
Ray White, Aviators	2	3	3.66	7	0	32	37	7	17
Aden Soroca, Breakers	3	0	3.71	7	1	34	23	13	29

JAYHAWK COLLEGIATE LEAGUE

East Division	W	L	PCT	GB
Hutchinson Monarchs	27	7	.794	-
Kansas Cannons	25	11	.694	3
Derby Twins	24	11	.686	3.5
Haysville Aviators	21	13	.618	6
Great Bend BatCats	22	14	.611	6
Dirtbag Baseball	11	17	.393	13
Kingman Islanders	11	20	.355	14.5
Newton Rebels	8	26	.235	19
Diamond Kings	6	24	.200	19

INDIVIDUAL BATTING LEADERS

	AVG	AB	R	H	2B	3B	HR	RBI	SB
Riley Schrader, INF, Aviators	.528	89	34	47	8	1	1	26	8
Kyler Horsman, UT, BadCats	.437	71	29	31	3	0	3	22	8
Jaden Gustafson, OF, M'rchs	.391	115	38	45	11	2	4	32	8
Cooper Wesslund, INF, M'rchs	.361	97	32	35	4	0	0	22	19
Nolan Freund, INF, Islanders	.356	132	18	47	8	1	3	27	11
Richard Gutierrez, 2B, Twins	.353	85	24	30	5	0	4	24	3
Easton Norris, OF, Aviators	.349	83	32	29	7	3	0	17	10
Kyler Warren, 3B, Twins	.345	84	25	29	4	0	1	19	6
Jackson Bell, Aviators	.337	89	7	30	2	0	0	22	1
Brett Smajstrla, OF, M'rchs	.337	83	25	28	6	2	1	21	7

INDIVIDUAL PITCHING LEADERS

	W	L	ERA	G	SV	IP	H	BB	SO
Shane Holman, Kings	1	3	1.47	7	0	31	38	9	25
Rugar Bravo, Cannons	6	0	2.05	9	0	44	37	12	38
Gavin Oswald, Cannons	4	1	2.10	7	0	34	28	14	21
Nate Herchock, Twins	1	1	2.27	6	0	32	23	21	35
Tyler Stuhlsatz, BadCats	2	1	2.30	13	0	31	44	6	17
Ian Regal, Monarchs	2	2	2.34	7	0	35	20	14	32
Camden Cornelius, Monarchs	5	0	2.40	13	0	30	21	18	38
Jace Minor, Monarchs	3	0	2.41	8	0	37	29	16	37
Drew Iverson, Cannons	5	2	2.46	8	0	33	33	9	38
Jakob Holzer, Cannons	4	2	2.52	9	0	39	42	9	33

MINK LEAGUE

	W	L	PCT	GB
St. Joseph Mustangs	40	9	.816	-
Clarinda A's	33	16	.673	7
Jefferson City	25	18	.581	12
Sedalia Bombers	17	20	.459	17
Chillicothe Mudcats	21	24	.467	17
Carroll Merchants	19	26	.422	19
Warren Co. Crop Dusters	13	27	.325	22.5
Nevada Griffons	10	27	.270	24

CHAMPIONSHIP: St. Joseph Mustangs defeated Clarinda A's, 2-1, in best-of-three championship series.

INDIVIDUAL BATTING LEADERS

	AVG	AB	R	H	2B	3B	HR	RBI	SB
Sean Bazmore, INF, A's	.371	197	49	73	10	3	1	47	33
Khi Holiday, OF, A's	.369	168	70	62	5	3	0	30	37
Jake McClure, OF, Merchants	.364	110	27	40	2	2	0	12	8
Tyler Macon, INF, A's	.352	159	46	56	3	6	1	24	39
Bryce Humphrey, OF, G'fons	.342	76	21	26	3	0	4	22	24
Layth Holiday, OF, A's	.338	160	39	54	7	1	0	25	24
Darius Freeman, OF, M'tangs	.327	147	35	48	11	3	2	31	25
Cam Lee, OF, Renegades	.323	124	32	40	6	3	1	24	32
Sam Paule, INF, Bombers	.323	93	19	30	4	0	1	21	9
Logan Harris, OF, Merchants	.322	121	20	39	3	4	0	17	12

INDIVIDUAL PITCHING LEADERS

	W	L	ERA	G	SV	IP	H	BB	SO
Cullen McBride, Merchants	5	0	2.19	10	0	49.1	44	9	37
Byler Reither, Renegades	3	3	3.20	9	0	50.2	39	20	44
Grant Burson, Bombers	3	3	4.00	7	0	45	40	18	33
Koby Linder, Mudcats	3	4	4.57	14	0	45.1	48	26	37
Jose Calcano, A's	5	1	5.09	10	0	53	47	19	20
Caleb Tucker, Merchants	2	3	5.48	9	0	44.1	44	16	27
Billy Robertson, Merchants	2	4	7.40	11	0	45	50	25	40

NEW ENGLAND COLLEGIATE LEAGUE

Coastal Division	W	L	PCT	GB
Newport Gulls	27	16	-	.628
Mystic Schooners	23	20	4	.535
Marthas Vineyard Sharks	20	22	6.5	.476
Ocean State Waves	19	23	7.5	.452
North Shore Navigators	19	24	8	.442
North Division	**W**	**L**	**PCT**	**GB**
Vermont Mountaineers	30	11	.732	-
Sanford Mainers	26	18	.591	5.5
Keene SwampBats	26	18	.591	5.5
Upper Valley Nighthawks	18	25	.419	13
West Division	**W**	**L**	**PCT**	**GB**
Bristol Blues	24	18	.571	-
Valley Blue Sox	21	22	.488	3.5
North Adams SteepleCats	13	31	.295	12
Danbury Westerners	11	30	.268	12.5

CHAMPIONSHIP: Newport Gulls defeated Sanford Mainers, 2-0, in best-of-three championship series.

INDIVIDUAL BATTING LEADERS

	AVG	AB	R	H	2B	3B	HR	RBI	SB
Dixon Williams, 3B, Gulls	.390	100	35	39	7	0	4	33	17
Chris Hacopian, SS, Sharks	.370	135	34	50	8	0	9	32	9
Donovan Cash, 1B, Waves	.367	147	26	54	8	1	3	27	11
Devan Bade, 3B, Mainers	.358	134	28	48	8	1	6	30	8
Niko Brini, OF, Gulls	.347	147	30	51	11	0	1	18	11
Joe Jaconski, OF, SwampBats	.341	129	36	44	9	3	7	33	8
Michael Iannazzo, SS, W'ers	.338	133	31	45	6	0	1	15	16
Luke Mistone, 1B, S'Cats	.333	126	14	42	4	0	2	18	2
Reese Robinett, 1B, Sharks	.331	118	22	39	11	0	9	32	2
Easton Brenner, OF, Blues	.326	89	13	29	5	3	0	15	12

INDIVIDUAL PITCHING LEADERS

	W	L	ERA	G	SV	IP	H	BB	SO
Will Jones, Navigators	2	1	0.76	7	0	35	20	3	37
Connor Ball, Mainers	3	0	1.90	8	1	38	37	9	31
Ryan Buckler, Navigators	2	2	1.90	12	1	38	24	17	36
Aidan Coleman, Gulls	5	0	2.65	7	0	37	36	7	45
Nick Falter, Mountaineers	4	1	2.75	8	0	36	35	9	43
Benjamin Shenosky, S'Bats	3	1	2.95	11	0	37	34	7	31
Connor Harris, Schooners	4	1	3.25	8	0	36	29	8	29
Brian Young, Sharks	3	3	3.68	10	0	44	37	12	44
Tanner Duke, SteepleCats	3	2	3.82	7	0	35	37	17	40
Dan Driscoll, Schooners	3	1	4.02	8	0	40	29	11	34

NORTHWOODS LEAGUE

Great Lakes East Division	W	L	PCT	GB
Kalamazoo Growlers	24	13	.649	-
Traverse City Pit Spitters	22	15	.595	2
Rockford Rivets	21	15	.583	2.5
Royal Oak Leprechauns	16	21	.432	8
Kenosha Kingfish	15	21	.417	8.5
Battle Creek Battle Jacks	13	23	.361	10.5
Kokomo Jackrabbits	11	26	.297	13
Great Lakes West Division	**W**	**L**	**PCT**	**GB**
Madison Mallards	26	10	.722	-
Wausau Woodchucks	24	11	.686	1.5
Green Bay Rockers	19	15	.559	6
Wisconsin Rapids Rafters	20	17	.541	6.5
Fond du Lac Dock Spiders	16	20	.444	10
Lakeshore Chinooks	11	24	.314	14.5
Great Plains East Division	**W**	**L**	**PCT**	**GB**
Duluth Huskies	21	14	.600	-
Eau Claire Express	20	15	.571	1
Waterloo Bucks	18	18	.500	3.5
Rochester Honkers	17	17	.500	3.5
Thunder Bay Border Cats	17	18	.486	4
La Crosse Loggers	11	25	.306	10.5
Minnesota Mud Puppies	4	14	.222	8.5
Great Plains West Division	**W**	**L**	**PCT**	**GB**
St. Cloud Rox	25	11	.694	-
Willmar Stingers	21	15	.583	4
Mankato MoonDogs	21	16	.568	4.5
Bismarck Larks	16	18	.471	8
Minot Hot Tots	16	20	.444	9
Badlands Big Sticks	10	25	.286	14.5

CHAMPIONSHIP: Kalamazoo Growlers defeated La Crosse Logger, 8-7, championship game.

INDIVIDUAL BATTING LEADERS

	AVG	AB	R	H	2B	3B	HR	RBI	SB
Maddox Mihalakis, 1B, Riv's	.429	170	52	73	19	5	8	61	8
Andrew Sojka, OF, Stingers	.398	236	85	94	22	5	22	73	43
Max Buettenback, C, S'gers	.395	205	49	81	14	1	9	62	30
Matthew Miura, OF, Loggers	.378	217	64	82	11	2	2	41	34
Case Sanderson, 1B Loggers	.359	167	48	60	13	0	6	51	5
Ben Higdon, OF, Rox	.352	213	60	75	13	2	11	48	17
Jake Schaffner, 2B, Mallards	.351	168	51	59	5	2	2	35	18
Max Galvin, OF, Woodchucks	.344	244	59	84	18	0	13	70	19
Lucas Moore, OF, Bucks	.340	250	53	85	13	3	0	47	48
RJ Hamilton, OF, Loggers	.339	168	46	57	16	1	1	34	42

INDIVIDUAL PITCHING LEADERS

	W	L	ERA	G	SV	IP	H	BB	SO
Kai Taylor, Larks	7	1	2.48	22	1	58	57	12	58
Tyler Conklin, Big Sticks	5	0	2.85	11	0	60	52	23	48
Eamon Horwedel, Growlers	7	3	3.13	11	0	72	68	10	41
Liam Martin, Mud Puppies	1	1	3.82	7	0	33	31	15	27
Lucas Burgum, Larks	3	4	6.59	16	0	57	75	33	51

PERFECT GAME COLLEGIATE LEAGUE

East Division	W	L	PCT	GB
Amsterdam Mohawks	35	7	.833	-
Saugerties Stallions	29	12	.698	5.5
Mohawk Valley DiamondDawgs	25	15	.616	9
Utica Blue Sox	23	18	.560	11.5
Watertown Rapids	22	18	.549	12
Oneonta Outlaws	15	21	.421	17
Boonville Lumberjacks	10	28	.269	23
Albany Baseball Club	10	28	.269	23
Glens Falls Dragons	8	30	.218	25
West Division	**W**	**L**	**PCT**	**GB**
Batavia Muckdogs	34	8	.802	-
Elmira Pioneers	24	18	.571	10
Auburn Doubledays	24	18	.570	10
Jamestown Tarp Skunks	19	25	.432	16
Niagara Falls Americans	16	24	.402	17
Geneva Red Wings	14	25	.363	18.5
Newark Pilots	15	28	.349	19.5

CHAMPIONSHIP: Amsterdam Mohawks defeated Almira Pioneers, 2-0, in best-of-three championship series.

INDIVIDUAL BATTING LEADERS

	AVG	AB	R	H	2B	3B	HR	RBI	SB
Cade Ladehoff, INF, M'hawks	.408	125	31	51	16	0	5	35	6
Andy Schroeder, OF, P'neers	.388	98	26	38	5	3	0	23	16
Evan Haeger, OF, Mohawks	.371	97	35	36	11	2	2	28	8
Norris McClure, UT, Blue Sox	.367	109	18	40	10	5	1	22	18
Cristino Tufano, INF, DD	.364	143	30	52	9	1	0	18	13
Lucas Lopez, INF, Muckdogs	.356	132	35	47	10	1	0	31	18
Justin Ford, INF, Stallions	.355	110	27	39	4	4	2	31	7
Kevin Denty, OF, Blue Sox	.353	102	32	36	6	1	3	20	6
Jackson Natili, C, Mohawks	.351	94	26	33	10	0	1	15	8
Javar Williams, OF, Mohawks	.343	105	27	36	7	2	0	21	14

INDIVIDUAL PITCHING LEADERS

	W	L	ERA	G	SV	IP	H	BB	SO
Gage Rowe, Doubledays	4	0	1.34	7	0	40	26	14	36
Matt Misiti, Muckdogs	4	0	1.36	9	0	40	23	40	33
Ryan Peters, Rapids	3	1	1.66	5	0	38	33	9	36
Gage Hayes, Tarp Skunks	5	1	1.93	9	0	47	24	11	43
Marcus Sanders, DD	1	1	2.17	10	0	37	26	23	30
Lucas West, Doubledays	3	1	2.57	8	0	49	32	14	35
Connor Freeman, Pioneers	5	1	2.84	8	0	44	35	28	40
Hayden Givens-Craig, TS	1	1	3.20	12	3	39	45	10	33
Michael Benedict, Muckdogs	4	0	3.32	9	0	41	40	23	30
Mason Collins, Rapids	5	1	3.34	10	0	57	39	26	47

PROSPECT LEAGUE

Eastern Conference

Northeast	W	L	PCT	GB
Chillicothe Paints	17	10	.630	-
Johnstown Mill Rats	13	14	.481	4
Lafayette Aviators	12	17	.414	6
Champion City Kings	11	16	.407	6
Central	**W**	**L**	**PCT**	**GB**
REX Baseball	17	10	.630	-
Normal CornBelters	14	12	.538	2.5
Danville Dans	13	13	.500	3.5
Full Count Rhythm	13	14	.481	4
Dubois County Bombers	7	18	.280	9

Western Conference

Northwest	W	L	PCT	GB
Clinton LumberKings	19	10	.655	-
Illinois Valley Pistol Shrimp	18	12	.600	1.5
Springfield Lucky Horseshoes	16	13	.552	3
Burlington Bees	11	16	.407	7
South	**W**	**L**	**PCT**	**GB**
Cape Catfish	17	10	.630	-
Jackson Rockabillys	16	12	.571	1.5
O'Fallon Hoots	12	16	.429	5.5
Alton River Dragons	11	16	.407	6
Thrillville Thrillbillies	10	18	.357	7.5

CHAMPIONSHIP: Illinois Valley Pistol Shrimp defeated REX Baseball, 2-0, in best-of-three championship series.

INDIVIDUAL BATTING LEADERS

	AVG	AB	R	H	2B	3B	HR	RBI	SB
Alec Gonzalez, INF, Aviators	.400	115	30	46	8	1	2	37	10
Eric Colaco, OF, Paints	.396	164	53	65	15	1	7	46	38
Bryson Lofton, INF, Hoots	.392	130	35	51	14	1	7	42	3
Kyle Gibson, INF, P Shrimp	.385	187	60	72	17	0	1	34	25
Landen Johnson, INF, CB	.372	191	40	71	11	2	6	39	0
Jhors Gomez, INF, Paints	.370	135	31	50	8	3	7	31	20
Jalen Martinez, OF, L'Kings	.358	151	36	54	12	0	3	33	5
Merik Carter, INF, Rockabillys	.358	165	38	59	17	2	2	35	22
Baden Hackworth, OF, Hoots	.351	131	23	46	11	1	3	33	10
Cooper Donlin, OF, Bees	.350	137	31	48	6	2	1	20	4

INDIVIDUAL PITCHING LEADERS

	W	L	ERA	G	SV	IP	H	BB	SO
Ean DiPasquale, LumberKings	4	0	1.30	11	1	42	28	8	40
Breyllin Suriel, REX	2	1	1.62	18	8	39	22	13	46
Ian Korn, Mill Rats	3	1	1.63	8	0	39	24	11	52
Aaron Moss, REX	4	1	1.77	8	0	46	45	7	41
Tyler Moniz-Witten, REX	0	0	1.84	15	1	29	24	11	20
Dylan Peck, Catfish	4	0	1.91	6	0	28	16	10	28
Carter White, Paints	5	0	2.29	14	1	35	26	21	59
Jorge Romero, Catfish	5	1	2.32	11	0	50	38	18	49
Anthony Solis, Pistol Shrimp	3	3	2.54	8	0	28	24	12	35
Sam George, LumberKings	1	2	2.57	6	0	28	31	11	34

SOUTH FLORIDA COLLEGIATE LEAGUE

North Division	W	L	PCT	GB
Delray Beach Lightning	26	13	.667	-
Boca Raton Beach Boys	25	15	.625	1.5
Boynton Beach Buccaneers	21	18	.538	5
West Palm Beach Iguanas	20	19	.513	6
Palm Beach Xtreme	20	19	.512	6
Boca Raton Lions	13	18	.422	9
Delray Beach Wave	9	27	.250	15.5
South Division	**W**	**L**	**PCT**	**GB**
Boca Raton Blazers	32	9	.780	-
West Boca Snappers	25	17	.595	7.5
Miami Gardens Makos	18	15	.545	10
Coconut Creek X Team	18	17	.514	11
Florida Pokers	13	23	.365	16.5
Coconut Creek Diamond Ducks	12	24	.333	17.5
Ft. Lauderdale Hooks	6	24	.210	20.5

CHAMPIONSHIP: West Boca Snappers defeated Boca Raton Blazers, 2-1, in best-of-three championship series.

INDIVIDUAL BATTING LEADERS

	AVG	AB	R	H	2B	3B	HR	RBI	SB
Will Hampton, INF, Blazers	.394	94	37	37	8	1	1	18	12
Johnny Bruno, OF, Lions	.388	80	25	31	6	0	4	18	16
Brandon Marchese, 1B, X	.365	115	24	42	12	1	1	32	2
Danny Rogers, INF, L'ning	.356	87	25	31	5	2	4	21	10
Nathanael Coupet, C, Blazers	.345	110	23	38	10	0	4	36	6
Ryker Waite, INF, Blazers	.344	90	51	31	6	2	1	16	54
Dominic Letort, 1B, BBoys	.337	95	23	32	9	0	1	21	7
Jeo Hernandez, OF, Pokers	.329	82	15	27	6	1	1	15	9
Conner Hilton, UT, Iguanas	.326	92	20	30	2	1	2	18	11
Jesus Rodriguez, OF, X Team	.322	87	23	28	4	0	1	18	3

INDIVIDUAL PITCHING LEADERS

	W	L	ERA	G	SV	IP	H	BB	SO
Zach Redner, Pokers	3	0	0.87	6	0	31	17	4	57
Bransen Angel, Pokers	3	1	1.74	7	0	31	24	11	37
Josh Lee, Lightning	1	0	2.30	12	0	31	20	7	53
Zac Dodson, Snappers	4	1	2.43	8	0	37	24	11	49
Cameron Hillery, Iguanas	0	1	2.62	13	0	34	29	19	29
Dawson Montesa, Blazers	4	0	2.63	9	0	41	25	17	65
Cael Brannon, Snappers	3	1	3.00	9	1	36	22	24	39
Drew Dickson, Wave	1	2	3.03	6	0	30	28	12	45
Marc DeNunzio, Xtreme	5	2	3.46	9	0	39	32	17	59
Gavin Barnell, Xtreme	3	1	3.57	7	0	35	22	26	32

SUNBELT LEAGUE

	W	L	PCT	GB
Choccolocco Monsters	22	9	.710	-
Gainesville GolDiggers	18	10	.643	2.5
Atlanta Crackers	19	13	.594	3.5
Waleska Wild Things	14	13	.519	6
Cartersville Cannons	13	16	.448	8
Alpharetta Aviators	11	16	.407	9
Atlanta Blues	9	18	.333	11
Brookhaven Bucks	7	18	.280	12

CHAMPIONSHIP: Choccolocco Monsters defeated Atlanta Crackers, 2-0, in best-of-three championship series.

INDIVIDUAL BATTING LEADERS

	AVG	AB	R	H	2B	3B	HR	RBI	SB
Hutson Miles, INF, WT	.406	64	20	26	0	0	1	9	5
Logan Floyd, INF, WT	.391	69	15	27	7	1	0	16	0
Emory Guilford, OF, Aviators	.389	72	15	28	7	0	0	9	7
Noah Darden, OF, GD	.387	75	19	29	1	2	0	8	17
Jaden Anderson, OF, C'kers	.366	101	28	37	10	0	7	27	2
Cayden Sheffield, C, WT	.350	80	18	28	6	0	2	24	0
Hayes Harrison, P, Monsters	.333	81	18	27	8	0	3	22	7
Brady McDevitt, OF, Cannons	.333	102	19	34	5	0	2	6	0
Makana Peters, 3B, GD	.333	69	17	23	3	0	4	15	3
Cole Tremain, OF, Monsters	.329	76	14	25	8	1	3	11	12

INDIVIDUAL PITCHING LEADERS

	W	L	ERA	G	SV	IP	H	BB	SO
Dawson Campbell, Monsters	3	1	1.66	7	0	38	32	9	31
Howell Polk, Monsters	3	1	2.16	6	0	25	19	9	23
Sahil Patel, Gol'Diggers	2	1	2.38	8	0	34	22	20	48
Christian Donaldson, Crackers	1	1	2.58	8	0	38	32	11	40
Alex Johnson, Bucks	1	0	2.70	9	1	20	23	11	18
Gavon Wray, Blues	1	1	2.74	5	0	23	22	7	24
Cian Khajavi, Bucks	3	0	2.86	7	0	28	23	15	27
Blythe Keisler, Aviators	3	0	2.92	9	0	37	36	10	29
Brady Owens, Cannons	2	2	3.03	7	0	30	17	22	39
Wyatt Dodgens, Gol'Diggers	2	1	3.25	6	0	28	26	5	29

VALLEY LEAGUE

North Division	W	L	PCT	GB
Purcellville Cannons	26	14	.650	-
Strasburg Express	23	17	.575	3
New Market Rebels	20	20	.500	6
Winchester Royals	20	20	.500	6
Woodstock River Bandits	16	24	.400	10
Front Royal Cardinals	15	25	.375	11
South Division	**W**	**L**	**PCT**	**GB**
Charlottesville Tom Sox	26	13	.667	-
Harrisonburg Turks	22	17	.564	4
Covington Lumberjacks	20	20	.500	6.5
Culpeper Cavaliers	20	20	.500	6.5
Staunton Braves	17	23	.425	9.5
Waynesboro Generals	14	26	.350	12.5

CHAMPIONSHIP: Charlottesville TomSox defeated Purcellville Cannons, 2-1, in best-of-three championship series.

INDIVIDUAL BATTING LEADERS

	AVG	AB	R	H	2B	3B	HR	RBI	SB
Colby Wallace, UT, Tom Sox	.370	92	21	34	6	1	1	16	4
Connor Chisolm, OF, Express	.364	107	29	39	7	0	0	17	20
Mosh, 2B, Royals	.356	104	28	37	7	1	1	18	11
Ryan Wynn, INF, Tom Sox	.351	97	22	34	7	3	1	20	1
Kyle Musser, OF, Rebels	.341	91	18	31	6	1	0	13	10
Christopher Katz, OF, Turks	.340	144	33	49	12	1	2	32	1
Connor Maryniak, SS, Cavs	.337	86	20	29	5	1	2	17	7
Thomas Marsala, C, L'jacks	.336	131	24	44	9	0	1	20	8
Austin Lafferty, OF, Royals	.333	111	21	37	6	1	2	32	3

	AVG	AB	R	H	2B	3B	HR	RBI	SB
Broedy Poppell, C, Cardinals	.331	148	27	49	10	0	2	25	27

INDIVIDUAL PITCHING LEADERS

	W	L	ERA	G	SV	IP	H	BB	SO
Matthew Sheppard, Generals	4	0	2.53	13	2	32	25	10	26
Evan McDade, Braves	1	3	3.27	15	1	33	37	8	18
Dutch DeProspero, Royals	2	1	3.38	8	0	37	25	20	27
Braydon Gray, River Bandits	2	1	3.51	7	0	33	31	9	21
Vincent Dolcemaschio, Royals	2	2	3.71	8	0	34	41	10	35
Jason Cheifetz, Turks	3	0	4.08	8	0	35	41	9	21
Shawn Mannering, Rebels	2	2	4.42	10	0	39	42	18	42
Brok Eddy, Cavaliers	2	3	4.59	8	0	33	25	10	42
Garrett Wright, Rebels	1	3	4.78	14	0	38	33	27	41
Lane Duff, Turks	1	3	5.14	12	0	35	40	11	29

WEST COAST LEAGUE

North Division	W	L	PCT	GB
Wenatchee AppleSox	35	19	.648	-
Bellingham Bells	32	22	.593	3
Edmonton Riverhawks	32	22	.593	3
Victoria HarbourCats	29	25	.537	6
Nanaimo NightOwls	26	28	.481	9
Kelowna Falcons	20	34	.370	15
Port Angeles Lefties	16	38	.296	19
Kamloops NorthPaws	15	39	.278	20
South Division	**W**	**L**	**PCT**	**GB**
Corvallis Knights	41	13	.759	-
Portland Pickles	40	14	.741	1
Bend Elks	32	22	.593	9
Ridgefield Raptors	31	23	.574	10
Yakima Valley Pippins	21	33	.389	20
Cowlitz Black Bears	21	33	.389	20
Walla Walla Sweets	21	33	.389	20
Springfield Drifters	20	34	.370	21

CHAMPIONSHIP: Portland Pickles defeated Wenatchee AppleSox, 6-5, championship game.

INDIVIDUAL BATTING LEADERS

	AVG	AB	R	H	2B	3B	HR	RBI	SB
Aidan Dougherty, OF, A'Sox	.380	171	41	65	9	5	1	43	21
Hunter Katschke, INF, R'tors	.367	147	40	54	12	1	9	43	9
Justin Stransky, C, Raptors	.364	143	29	52	7	0	4	34	10
Easton Amundson, UT, Elks	.355	121	25	43	12	1	3	31	1
Jeremy Giesegh, OF, Lefties	.348	221	36	77	7	4	3	30	12
Max Hartman, OF, AppleSox	.327	196	51	64	9	1	2	28	17
Nate Kirkpatrick, INF, Bells	.327	220	31	72	17	2	4	35	10
Bryce McFeely, OF R'hawks	.325	123	18	40	10	1	0	25	3
Taylor Takata, INF, Raptors	.323	155	45	50	7	0	1	22	9
Kevin Takeuchi, INF, Knights	.323	201	43	65	16	0	5	45	10

INDIVIDUAL PITCHING LEADERS

	W	L	ERA	G	SV	IP	H	BB	SO
Freddy Rodriguez, Pickles	6	0	1.02	8	0	44	22	16	54
Murphy Gienger, Pickles	3	1	1.80	11	0	45	34	14	46
Halen Knoll, Riverhawks	4	3	2.54	12	0	60	51	22	49
Quincy Vassar, AppleSox	4	3	2.92	10	0	49	47	14	38
Zach Hangas, Sweets	4	1	3.10	10	0	61	46	18	39
Jackson Elder, Elks	3	1	3.71	8	0	44	44	10	34
Ethan Salscheider, Pippins	4	5	3.88	11	0	65	74	28	37
Aidan Boice, NightOwls	2	5	3.92	10	0	44	40	11	36
Billy Dotson, Drifters	4	5	4.25	13	1	59	63	14	22
Reid Madariaga, Elks	3	1	4.57	12	1	43	48	16	31

HIGH SCHOOL

HIGH SCHOOL

Griffin Dominates His State

EDDIE KELLY

Konnor Griffin's 85 stolen bases was the seventh-most ever in a high school season.

PREVIOUS WINNERS

1992: Preston Wilson, OF/RHP, Bamberg-Ehrhardt (S.C.) HS
1993: Trot Nixon, OF/LHP, New Hanover HS, Wilmington, N.C.
1994: Doug Million, LHP, Sarasota (Fla.) HS
1995: Ben Davis, C, Malvern (Pa.) Prep
1996: Matt White, RHP, Waynesboro Area (Pa.) HS
1997: Darnell McDonald, OF, Cherry Creek HS, Englewood, Colo.
1998: Drew Henson, 3B/RHP, Brighton (Mich.) HS
1999: Josh Hamilton, OF/LHP, Athens Drive HS, Raleigh, N.C.
2000: Matt Harrington, RHP, Palmdale (Calif.) HS
2001: Joe Mauer, C, Cretin-Derham Hall HS, St. Paul, Minn.
2002: Scott Kazmir, LHP, Cypress Falls HS, Houston
2003: Jeff Allison, RHP, Veterans Memorial HS, Peabody, Mass.
2004: Homer Bailey, RHP, LaGrange (Texas) HS
2005: Justin Upton, SS, Great Bridge HS, Chesapeake, Va.
2006: Adrian Cardenas, SS/2B, Mons. Pace HS, Opa Locka, Fla.
2007: Mike Moustakas, SS, Chatsworth (Calif.) HS
2008: Ethan Martin, RHP/3B, Stephens County HS, Toccoa, Ga.
2009: Bryce Harper, C, Las Vegas HS
2010: Kaleb Cowart, RHP/3B, Cook HS, Adel, Ga.
2011: Dylan Bundy, RHP, Owasso (Okla.) HS
2012: Byron Buxton, OF, Appling County HS, Baxley, Ga.
2013: Clint Frazier, OF, Loganville (Ga.) HS
2014: Alex Jackson, OF, Rancho Bernardo (Calif.) HS
2015: Kyle Tucker, OF, Plant HS, Tampa
2016: Mickey Moniak, OF, La Costa Canyon HS, Carlsbad, Calif.
2017: MacKenzie Gore, LHP, Whiteville (N.C.) HS
2018: Cole Winn, RHP, Orange (Calif.) Lutheran HS
2019: Bobby Witt Jr., SS, Colleyville (Texas) Heritage HS
2020: No award given in truncated season
2021: Jackson Jobe, RHP/SS, Heritage Hall HS, Oklahoma City
2022: Jackson Holliday, SS, Stillwater (Okla.) HS
2023: Max Clark, OF, Franklin (Ind.) Community HS

PLAYER OF THE YEAR

BY BRETT HUDSON

In a summer traveling around the most prestigious high school showcases and to Taiwan with USA Baseball's 18U National Team, the most valuable lesson Konnor Griffin learned is to put his headphones in.

The headphones are a metaphor. He is not physically inserting AirPods, in this case, but the results are very much real.

Griffin was in the midst of a rare slump early last summer, suffering a difficult 2-for-12 weekend while he was trying to solidify his status as a top 2024 prospect and secure a spot on Team USA.

He did not feel like himself in the batter's box. Back home with his father, he regained that feeling and did everything he could to keep it.

"I was letting too many people mess with my mind a little bit," Griffin said. "A lot of people were giving me advice, and I really just had to go back to my parents, (who told) me about having a small circle of people to trust.

"It's always just been me and my dad with hitting. Some scouts would tell me things I need to change—some coaches would—and I'm trying to listen and please everybody. But that's what I feel like was causing the most trouble because I was thinking so much.

"Once I was able to do that, I kind of put the headphones on when other people are around and try not to listen to everyone. When people try to talk to me about my swing, I'm going to listen. I'm going to be coachable (and) say, 'Yes, sir.'

"But I have to let it go through one ear and out the other."

With the headphones in place, Griffin returned to Jackson Preparatory School in Mississippi for his senior year. He led the Patriots to their seventh consecutive 6A state championship, hitting .559/.690/.966 with nine home runs. He set school records with 85 stolen bases and 47 walks.

Griffin maintained his status as the top prep prospect for the 2024 draft. And now he can add another accolade: BA High School Player of the Year.

"I felt like I was myself again," Griffin said. "Once I got some good swings off and I was rolling, I felt like, 'All right, I'm the player who can be at the top of these mock drafts and all of these rankings.'"

For a top-flight prospect interested in keeping a small circle, Griffin would be hard-pressed to find a better spot for it.

Jackson Prep is located in Flowood, a suburb of state capital Jackson. It is a hotbed for talent in Mississippi. It is located five miles from the Double-A Mississippi Braves and fewer than 200 miles away from four Southeastern Conference schools.

Griffin credits LSU assistant coach Josh Jordan for the headphones approach.

Jordan described to Griffin how well Dylan Crews did it on his way to becoming the second overall pick in 2023.

For the time being, the headphones mentality has helped Griffin remain productive on the field and largely unchanged off of it. And it should serve him well in pro ball as well.

HIGH SCHOOL TOP 50

Rank	School	Coach	Record
1	Catholic HS, Baton Rouge, La.	Brad Bass	38-2
2	Corona (Calif.) HS	Andy Wise	30-3
3	Lowndes HS, Valdosta, Ga.	Ryan Page	35-6
4	Stoneman Douglas HS, Parkland, Fla.	Todd Fitz-Gerald	26-5
5	Jackson Prep HS, Flowood, Miss.	Brent Heavener	39-4
6	Granada HS, Livermore, Calif.	Corrigan Willis	32-1
7	TomBall (Texas) HS	Doug Rush	41-3
8	Farragut HS, Knoxville, Tenn.	Matt Buckner	40-5
9	Jones HS, Madison, Ala.	Jared Smith	44-9
10	Flower Mound (Texas) HS	Danny Wallace	40-6
11	Brother Rice HS, Bloomfield Hills, Mich.	Bob Riker	42-1
12	Casteel HS, Queen Creek, Ariz.	Matt Denny	25-6
13	Richland (Wash.) HS	Grant Richardson	27-0
14	Tampa Jesuit HS	Miguel Menendez	26-6
15	Gloucester Catholic HS, Gloucester City, N.J.	Dennis Barth	27-2
16	Etowah HS, Woodstock, Ga.	Greg Robinson	35-5
17	Magnolia Heights HS, Senatobia, Miss.	Chris McMinn	35-5
18	James Island HS, Charleston, S.C.	Matt Spivey	29-3
19	Orange (Calif.) Lutheran HS	Eric Borba	28-7
20	Central HS, Phenix City, Ala.	AJ Kehoe	41-5
21	Millard West HS, Omaha, Neb.	Steve Frey	33-5
22	Grapevine (Texas) HS	Jimmy Webster	40-5
23	La Cueva HS, Albuquerque, N.M.	Gerard Pineda	27-3
24	Pleasure Ridge Park HS, Louisville	Brad Burns	41-3
25	Sunset HS, Beaverton, Ore.	John Barnes	28-2
26	Cardinal Newman HS, Santa Rosa, Calif.	Derek DeBenedetti	28-5
27	Malvern (Pa.) Prep	Freddy Hilliard	34-3
28	Trinity HS, Louisville	Rick Arnold	39-6
29	Lincoln (Neb.) East HS	Mychal Lanik	32-2
30	Olathe (Kan.) West HS	Austin Fisher	27-2
31	Harlem (Ga.) HS	Jimmie Lewis	40-1
32	Wayzata HS, Plymouth, Minn.	Bobby DeWitt	23-1
33	Nazareth Academy, Le Grange Park, Ill.	Lee Milano	37-1
34	Cherry Creek HS, Greenwood Village, Colo.	Marc Johnson	25-5
35	Mason (Ohio) HS	Curt Bly	28-6
36	Har-Ber HS, Springdale, Ark.	Dustin Helmkamp	30-5
37	Pearland (Texas) HS	David Rogers	37-9
38	Bishop Hendricken HS, Warwick, R.I.	Ed Holloway	28-1
39	Boston College HS	Steve Healy	20-5
40	West Linn (Ore.) HS	Joe Monahan	27-4
41	T.C. Roberson HS, Asheville, N.C.	Eric Filipek	28-4
42	Archbishop Moeller HS, Cincinnati	Tim Held	30-3
43	Saint Mary's HS, Stockton, Calif.	Jason Lindholm	30-6
44	Owyhee HS, Meridian, Ida.	Russ Wright	24-2
45	St. John's College HS, Washington D.C.	Mark Gibbs	27-6
46	Delbarton HS, Morristown, N.J.	Bruce Shatel	30-3
47	Lake Central HS, St. John, Ind.	Mike Swartzentruber	25-9
48	Barlow HS, Redding, Conn.	Matt Griffiths	29-2
49	Amity Regional HS, Woodbridge, Conn.	Sal Coppola	20-5
50	St. Peters HS, Staten Island, N.Y.	Bobby Glennerster	31-3

MIKE JANES/FOUR SEAM IMAGES

Griffin was drafted by the Pirates in July.

ALL-AMERICA TEAM

PJ Morlando

TOM DIPACE

Bryce Rainer

LARRY GOREN/FOUR SEAM IMAGES

Hunter Carns, C, First Coast HS, Jacksonville, FL
Carns has an atypical high school catcher profile thanks to his standout athleticism and speed that could also allow him to play outfield. He generates surprising power thanks to tremendous hand quickness and should be able to make up for the swing-and-miss in his game thanks to plenty of impact.

PJ Morlando, CI, Summerville HS, Summerville, SC
Morlando is the top first baseman in the prep class, though he has also played outfield. His calling card is a lethal hit/power combination from an unconventionally wide stance. That setup hasn't prevented him from making contact, and he uses the entire field while showing off some of the best raw power in the class.

Caleb Bonemer, CI, Okemos HS, Okemos, MI
Bonemer is a tooled-up righthanded hitter with an exciting power/speed combination who might have a chance to stick at shortstop. If he can't, he has the tools to be a great defender at third base. He has a stiff operation in the box but was one of the more impressive performers last summer on the showcase circuit.

Bryce Rainer, MI, Harvard-Westlake HS, Studio City, CA
The top prep shortstop in the class, Rainer has huge tools and turned in an excellent season in Southern California with prep powerhouse Harvard-Westlake. He projects for plus power and already has a 70-grade arm that is an asset on the left side of the infield. He has clean and reliable actions and glove work.

Tyson Lewis, MI, Millard West HS, Omaha, NE
Lewis is a standout athlete with plus speed and quick, snappy hands in the box that could make him a strong pure hitter. He added more strength and amplified his tool set this spring and has turned in double-plus run times in workouts. He has an excellent athletic foundation and up-the-middle upside.

Konnor Griffin, OF, Jackson Prep, Flowood, MS
The High School Player of the Year has unmatched tools and upside in this draft. He's a double-plus runner with plus raw power and plus arm strength who could be a plus defender at multiple positions. Scouts have praised his swing and offensive consistency this spring. Griffin also is legit as a pro pitching prospect.

Slade Caldwell, OF, Valley View HS, Jonesboro, AR
Caldwell is a short, filled-out lefthanded-hitting outfielder who is a consistent performer with a top-of-the-order tool set. He's a plus runner who covers plenty of ground in center field and pressures defenses on the bases. He might have the top bat-to-ball skills among preps, hinting at above-average hitting ability as well.

Braylon Payne, OF, Fort Bend Elkins HS, Missouri City, TX
Payne is young for the class and one of the better straight-line runners with double-plus speed that should allow him to be an above-average center fielder and potential table-setter. His bat-to-ball skills are solid, and he's done a nice job cleaning up the direction and consistency of his lower half in his swing.

Theo Gillen, DH, Westlake HS, Austin, TX
Injuries have cut into Gillen's playing time in high school, but when he's healthy he's been one of the most dangerous hitters in the class. He's a physical, lefthanded batter who should hit for average and power, while his plus run tool should make him a good outfielder if he needs to move off shortstop.

Dax Whitney

BILL MITCHELL

Kash Mayfield

EDDIE KELLY

Cam Caminiti, SP, Saguaro HS, Scottsdale, AZ
Originally a member of the 2025 class, Caminiti won't turn 18 until after the draft. He has an overpowering fastball that sits consistently in the mid 90s. The lefthander's developing secondaries are buttressed by advanced touch and feel from an athletic delivery. His uncle is 15-year big leaguer Ken Caminiti.

William Schmidt, SP, Catholic HS, Baton Rouge, LA
Schmidt's feel for spin is the envy of the 2024 class. The righthander consistently drops in a hammer breaking ball that earns double-plus projections and has helped Schmidt push to the top of the prep pitching ranks. He also has a projectable frame and a fastball tracking in the right direction and has touched 98 mph this spring.

Dax Whitney, SP, Blackfoot HS, Blackfoot, ID
Few players are drafted out of Idaho in the top 10 rounds, but Whitney forced scouts to get familiar with the state after establishing himself as the top arm in the Northwest. The righthander has an elite pitcher's frame at 6-foot-5, a fastball up to 96 mph and multiple breaking balls that could be above-average.

Kash Mayfield, SP, Elk City HS, Elk City, OK
Mayfield has a picturesque delivery and fantastic operation that has helped him develop into one of the best strike-throwers in the 2024 class. The lefthander showed more velocity and now sits in the low 90s consistently with a mid-70s breaking ball and changeup he throws with conviction to round out a solid arsenal.

Boston Bateman, SP, Camarillo HS, Camarillo, CA
Few draft prospects, high school or college, are more imposing than Bateman. For that, the 6-foot-8, 240-pound lefthander has earned the nickname "Sasquatch." He attacks hitters with a mid-90s fastball and a pair of high-spin breaking balls. He made strides this spring with his delivery and command.

Second Team

Pos.	Player	School
C	Anderson French	Red Land HS, Lewisberry, Pa.
CI	Kale Fountain	Norris HS, Firth, Neb.
CI	Chase Harlan	Central Bucks East HS, Doylestown, Pa.
MI	Kellon Lindsey	Hardee HS, Wauchula, Fla.
MI	Wyatt Sanford	Independence HS, Frisco, Texas
OF	Griffin Burkholder	Freedom HS, South Riding, Va.
OF	Derek Curiel	Orange (Calif.) Lutheran HS
OF	Garrett Shull	Enid (Okla.) HS
DH	Carter Johnson	Oxford (Ala.) HS
SP	Chase Mobley	Durant HS, Plant City, Fla.
SP	Levi Sterling	Notre Dame HS, Sherman Oaks, Calif.
SP	Dasan Hill	Grapevine (Texas) HS

AMATEUR/YOUTH CHAMPIONS 2024

ALL-AMERICAN AMATEUR BASEBALL ASSOCIATION (AAABA)

Event	Site	Champion	Runner-up
World Series (21U)	Johnstown, Pa.	Columbus TNT Knights	Buffalo East Coast Orville's

AMERICAN LEGION BASEBALL

Event	Site	Champion	Runner-up
World Series (19U)	Shelby, N.C.	Troy, Ala.	Midland, Mich.

BABE RUTH BASEBALL

Event	Site	Champion	Runner-up
Cal Ripken (9U)	Florence, Ala.	Tulare 9U	Freedom Farm 9U
Cal Ripken 11-year-old (70 feet)	Florence, Ala.	Altamonte 11U	Florence Navy 11U
13-year-old	Glen Allen, Va.	Oahu, Hawaii	Glen Allen, Va.
14-year-olds	Eagle Pass, Texas	Mexico 14U	Torrance 14U
13-to-16-year-olds	Reed Springs, Mo.	Torrance 16U	Korea 16U

LITTLE LEAGUE BASEBALL

Event	Site	Champion	Runner-up
Little League (11-12)	South Williamsport, Pa.	Florida	Taiwan
Junior League (12-14)	Taylor, Mich.	Taiwan	Michigan
Senior League (13-16)	Easley, S.C.	Venezuela	South Carolina
Intermediate (50-70)	Livermore, Calif.	Louisiana	South Korea

REVIVING BASEBALL IN INNER CITIES (RBI)

Event	Site	Champion
Junior (13-15)	Vero Beach, Fla.	Chicago White Sox RBI
Senior (16-18)	Vero Beach, Fla.	Chicago White Sox RBI

DRAFT

Guardians Pick Aussie Travis Bazzana 1-1

DRAFT

BY CARLOS COLLAZO

Coming on the heels of an excellent 2023 draft class, the 2024 class was skeptically viewed throughout the draft process thanks to an historically weak high school demographic and a college pitching contingent that included more reliever risk than is typical.

Teams picking at the top of the draft were more excited than those picking in the middle and back of the first round, thanks to excellent seasons from a top-end group that culminated in a consensus group of 10 players led by Georgia's Charlie Condon and Oregon State's Travis Bazzana.

Condon won the 2024 college player of the year award after a sensational season that fully exploited the hot-hitting offensive environment in college baseball and ranked as the No. 1 player in the class. He led the country with a .443 average, set a BBCOR-era home run record with 37, brought home a Golden Spikes award for the first-time ever for a Georgia player.

MIKE JANES/FOUR SEAM IMAGES

Travis Bazzana

In the end, it was Bazzana who heard his name called first when the Guardians—recipients of the first overall pick despite just 2% odds in the second-ever draft lottery—made him the first-ever Australian born player and first-ever second baseman selected with the first overall pick. Bazzana ranked as the No. 2 player in the class, won the Pac-12 Conference's player of the year award in the final season of the league as it's been known for years and finished his college career as a .360 hitter and the all-time program leader with 251 hits.

While Bazzana earned 1-1 status, Condon tied

FIRST-ROUND BONUS PROGRESSION

After dipping during the coronavirus pandemic and its after effects, MLB draft spending is once again growing at a relatively dramatic rate. This is to be expected, as the collective bargaining agreement mandates that as MLB revenues rise, draft bonus spending allotments rise at the same rate. But the nature of recent growth has made up for the stagnation that existed in the 2019-2022 range. These past two drafts are the first time that the draft has shown double-digit first round bonus growth in back-to-back years since 1998-1999. In every year since a massive increase in one year was followed by a dip the next year. Gerrit Cole, the No. 1 pick in the 2011 draft, held the bonus record for eight years until Adley Rutschman broke it in 2019. That was by design, as the CBA strictly limited bonuses at the start of the bonus pool allotment era. But that record has now been broken four times in the past five years, even as the spread between the top pick and the rest of the first rounds allotments have been flattened.

Year	Average	Change	Year	Average	Change	Year	Average	Change	Year	Average	Change
1965	$42,516	—	1980	$74,025	8.70%	1995	$918,019	16.10%	2010	$2,220,966	-8.80%
1966	$44,430	4.50%	1981	$78,573	6.10%	1996*	$944,404	2.90%	2011	$2,653,375	19.50%
1967	$42,898	-3.40%	1982	$82,615	5.10%	1997	$1,325,536	40.40%	2012	$2,475,167	-6.70%
1968	$43,850	2.20%	1983	$87,236	5.60%	1998	$1,637,667	23.10%	2013	$2,641,538	6.70%
1969	$43,504	-0.80%	1984	$105,391	20.80%	1999	$1,809,767	10.50%	2014	$2,612,109	-1.10%
1970	$45,230	3.90%	1985	$118,115	12.10%	2000	$1,872,586	3.50%	2015	$2,774,945	6.23%
1971	$45,197	-0.10%	1986	$116,300	-1.60%	2001	$2,154,280	15.00%	2016	$2,897,557	4.42%
1972	$44,952	-0.50%	1987	$128,480	10.50%	2002	$2,106,793	-2.20%	2017	$3,880,723	25.4%
1973	$48,832	8.60%	1988	$142,540	10.90%	2003	$1,765,667	-16.20%	2018	$3,754,123	-3.37%
1974	$53,333	9.20%	1989	$176,008	23.50%	2004	$1,958,448	10.90%	2019	$3,791,729	1.01%
1975	$49.33	-7.50%	1990	$252,577	43.50%	2005	$2,018,000	3.00%	2020	$4,080,307	7.61%
1976	$49,631	0.60%	1991	$365,396	44.70%	2006	$1,933,333	-4.20%	2021	$4,009,424	-1.74%
1977	$48,813	-1.60%	1992	$481,893	31.90%	2007	$2,098,083	8.50%	2022	$4,074,268	1.62%
1978	$67,892	39.10%	1993	$613,037	27.20%	2008	$2,458,714	17.20%	2023	$4,561,460	12.0%
1979	$68,094	0.20%	1994	$790,357	28.90%	2009	$2,434,800	-1.00%	2024	$5,036,544	10.4%

Wake Forest righthander Chase Burns (selected second overall by the Reds) for the top bonus in the class when the Rockies signed him for $9.25 million.

Eight Straight College Picks

We always expected this year's first round to be heavy on college players, and that wound up being the case on a record-setting night.

This was the first time we've ever seen eight consecutive college players lead off a draft, and it's also the most college-heavy we've seen the first 10 picks of the draft:

Guardians: 2B Travis Bazzana
Reds: RHP Chase Burns
Rockies: OF Charlie Condon
A's: 1B Nick Kurtz
White Sox: LHP Hagen Smith
Royals: TWP Jac Caglianone
Cardinals: SS JJ Wetherholt
Angels: 2B Christian Moore

Previously, the high-water mark for college players selected in the first 10 picks was six, which happened in 1985, 2018 and 2019. In the first 30 picks overall, 20 players came from the college demographic.

That tracks with the overall BA board for talent among the first 30 picks, as 21 of our top 30 players on the final board were players from a four-year university.

In fact, the first round was relatively unsurprising given the assumption that after the first 10 picks things could descend quickly into chaos. Three high school players went a bit earlier than expected, but PJ Morlando (ranked 52nd, drafted 16th), Braylon Payne (ranked 54th, drafted 17th) and Dante Nori (ranked 80th, drafted 27th) were all considered legitimate day one talents.

Cardinals Have Rare Top-10 Pick

The Cardinals' No. 7 overall pick was their only selection of the first night. Despite the lack of draft capital, they managed to land a player in West Virginia shortstop JJ Wetherholt who ranked No. 7 on the BA Draft board. Some scouts in the industry thought he had a case to be the top player in the class.

Wetherholt was a common projection to be the Guardians' pick at No. 1 overall. After Cleveland selected his pure-hitting peer Travis Bazzana, Wetherholt slid six more spots to the Cardinals, who found themselves picking inside the first 10 picks for the first time since 1998 when they selected JD Drew fifth overall.

Wetherholt's plus or better pure hitting ability, solid-average or better game power, plus speed and chance to stick at shortstop at the next level make him one of the most well-rounded players in the class.

More players will join Wetherholt in a Cardinals jersey on day two when the team makes the sixth pick of the third round at No. 80.

High School Arms Make Noise

A defining feature of this year's draft class was the relatively light top-end high school talent in

BONUS SPENDING BY TEAM

A year after the 2023 draft spending topped $350 million for the first time, the spending in the 2042 MLB Draft came close to reaching $375 million. Even with four top 10 round picks not signing, the $374,345,077 was more than $24 million above the previous 2023 bonus record.

The average team spent $12.5 million in 2024, up from $11.7 million in 2022. The Guardians $20.4 million spent was more than $3 million more than the previous record for a individual team spending. The Pirates held the record with the $17.1 million in bonus spending in 2023.

The CBA that went into effect in 2012 curtailed spending by instituting harsh penalties for teams that exceeded their bonus pools by more than five percent. It also ended the practice of awarding major league contracts to draftees. But as revenues within the game have increased, so too have the bonus pools MLB allocates to teams for the first 10 rounds. No team has yet been willing to exceed the five percent mark.

The new CBA that added the draft lottery system also included a $25,000 bump in the maximum bonus that teams could spend after the 10th round without counting toward a team's bonus allotment.

TEAM	2024	2023	2022
Angels	$13,990,500	$10,015,225	$8,352,250
Astros	$7,515,412	$8,234,500	$7,972,630
Athletics	$16,908,900	$15,882,600	$9,448,700
Blue Jays	$10,356,050	$7,856,185	$9,536,100
Braves	$9,453,100	$9,988,500	$11,886,600
Brewers	$12,504,900	$12,498,100	$7,572,500
Cardinals	$11,739,100	$7,618,500	$7,744,300
Cubs	$11,481,900	$10,695,000	$11,583,000
D-backs	$13,462,000	$12,055,000	$15,470,200
Dodgers	$7,418,800	$8,583,000	$5,559,990
Giants	$8,927,350	$11,433,525	$6,886,220
Guardians	$20,416,100	$10,221,275	$11,635,000
Mariners	$10,479,900	$13,990,500	$8,421,500
Marlins	$11,360,000	$13,692,400	$11,300,900
Mets	$11,018,000	$9,869,850	$14,716,560
Nationals	$15,925,200	$16,150,000	$12,688,200
Orioles	$12,691,800	$11,414,800	$17,735,600
Padres	$11,014,600	$7,161,600	$11,647,800
Phillies	$8,784,400	$6,761,100	$7,417,100
Pirates	$15,370,525	$17,123,300	$14,543,800
Rangers	$8,252,600	$11,442,900	$10,700,500
Rays	$9,727,600	$12,172,100	$8,511,700
Red Sox	$12,250,000	$11,851,200	$9,204,750
Reds	$17,665,800	$15,321,500	$12,225,800
Rockies	$18,206,100	$13,192,450	$14,338,300
Royals	$14,594,600	$14,002,200	$11,042,000
Tigers	$13,712,500	$17,677,450	$9,221,900
Twins	$13,136,650	$15,245,600	$10,971,500
White Sox	$16,292,500	$10,967,800	$7,557,900
Yankees	$9,688,190	$6,970,900	$7,969,500
TOTAL	$374,345,077	$350,089,060	$313,862,800
AVERAGE	$12,478,169	$11,669,635	$10,462,093

the first round. However, the pitching depth of the prep class was as deep as ever, full of intriguing, projectable arms with stuff or exciting foundations of command.

There were questions about how much the industry would tap into that depth, as high school pitchers have fallen increasingly out of favor thanks to their increased risk profiles and long player development timeline. But after just two high school pitchers came off the board in the first round—lefthanders Cam Caminiti to the Braves at 24 and Kash Mayfield to the Padres at 25—twelve high school pitchers went in the next 74 picks.

That's partially a function of draft logistics, as it's easier to slide-to-slide a prep pitcher to a second or third pick and pay that player more than college players, but also a sign that the industry was simply willing to invest in a strong area of the draft despite the elevated risk profiles.

The high school pitchers selected on day one were (BA rank in parentheses):

24. Braves: LHP Cam Caminiti (No. 21)
25. Padres: LHP Kash Mayfield (No. 25)
36. Guardians: RHP Braylon Doughty (No. 47)
37. Pirates: RHP Levi Sterling (No. 55)

ROB TRINGALI/MLB PHOTOS VIA GETTY IMAGES

Cam Caminiti

41. Royals: LHP David Shields (No. 60)
49. Tigers: RHP Owen Hall (No. 86)
57. Padres: LHP Boston Bateman (No. 77)
55. Mariners: RHP Ryan Sloan (No. 26)
57. Brewers: RHP Bryce Meccage (No. 71)
67. Brewers: RHP Chris Levonas (No. 74)
68. White Sox: LHP Blake Larson (No. 121)
69. Twins: LHP Dasan Hill (No. 48)
72. Tigers: LHP Ethan Schiefelbein (No. 91)

HIGHEST BONUSES EVER

Both Chase Burns and Charlie Condon set a new draft bonus record. Their $9.25 million bonuses topped Paul Skenes' bonus by $50,000.

Player, Pos.	Team, Year (Pick)	Bonus
Chase Burns, RHP	Reds, 2024 (No. 2)	$9,250,000
Charlie Condon, OF	Rockies, 2024 (No. 3)	$9,250,000
Paul Skenes, RHP	Pirates, 2023 (No. 1)	$9,200,000
Dylan Crews, OF	Nationals, 2023 (No. 2)	$9,000,000
Travis Bazzana, 2B	Guardians, 2024 (No. 1)	$8,950,000
Spencer Torkelson, 1B	Tigers, 2020 (No. 1)	$8,416,300
Jackson Holliday, SS	Orioles, 2022 (No. 1)	$8,190,000
Druw Jones, OF	D-backs, 2022 (No. 2)	$8,189,400
Adley Rutschman, C	Orioles, 2019 (No. 1)	$8,100,000
Gerrit Cole, RHP	Pirates, 2011 (No. 1)	$8,000,000
Wyatt Langford, OF	Rangers, 2023 (No. 4)	$8,000,000
Hagen Smith, LHP	White Sox, 2024 (No. 5)	$8,000,000
Jack Leiter, RHP	Rangers, 2021 (No. 2)	$7,922,000
Bobby Witt Jr., SS	Royals, 2019 (No. 2)	$7,787,400
Max Clark, OF	Tigers, 2023 (No. 3)	$7,767,500
Stephen Strasburg, RHP	Nationals, 2009 (No. 1)*	$7,500,000
Bubba Starling, OF	Royals, 2011 (No. 5)	$7,500,000
Casey Mize, RHP	Tigers, 2018 (No. 1)	$7,500,000
Jac Caglianone, TWP	Royals, 2024 (No. 5)	$7,497,500
Hunter Greene, RHP/SS	Reds, 2017 (No. 2)	$7,230,000
Andrew Vaughn, 1B	White Sox, 2019 (No. 3)	$7,221,200
Termarr Johnson, SS	Pirates, 2022 (No. 4)	$7,219,000
Walker Jenkins, OF	Twins, 2023 (No. 5)	$7,144,200
Joey Bart, C	Giants, 2018 (No. 2)	$7,025,000
Brendan McKay, 1B/LHP	Rays, 2017 (No. 4)	$7,005,000
Austin Martin, SS	Blue Jays, 2020 (No. 5)	$7,000,825
Kyle Wright, RHP	Braves, 2017 (No. 5)	$7,000,000
Nick Kurtz, 1B	Athletics, 2024 (No. 4)	$7,000,000
Jackson Jobe, RHP	Tigers, 2021 (No. 3)	$6,900,000
JJ Wetherholt, SS	Cardinals, 2024 (No. 7)	$6,900,000
Royce Lewis, SS	Twins, 2017 (No. 1)	$6,725,000
Jordan Lawlar, SS	D-backs, 2021 (No. 6)	$6,713,300

**Part of major league contract.*

First-Ever Second Baseman With No. 1 Overall Pick

The biggest story surrounding the first day of the draft was always who the Guardians would select 1-1, the first No. 1 overall pick in franchise history.

It was difficult to figure out who the team was honing in on in the weeks and days leading up the draft. Ultimately, they selected second baseman Travis Bazzana, putting him in the history books not just for being Cleveland's first and only No. 1 overall selection, but also for being the draft's first-ever 1-1 second baseman.

Prior to this draft, every other position on the field had at least one player taken with the first overall pick. It took nearly 50 years before it happened at second base. Turns out, it only took an Australian native with a precocious hit tool, uncanny ability to tap into his power, plus speed, standout athleticism and off-the-field makeup and work ethic that is praised throughout the entire industry to finally get it done.

Bazzana also gives the Pac-12 a 1-1 player to send off the final season of the conference, which is perhaps a fitting cherry on top.

NO. 1 OVERALL PICKS

Yr Team: Player, Pos., School	Bonus
1965 Athletics: Rick Monday, OF, Arizona State	$100,000
1966 Mets: Steve Chilcott, C, Antelope Valley HS, Lancaster, Calif.	$75,000
1967 Yankees: Ron Blomberg, 1B, Druid Hills HS, Atlanta	$65,000
1968 Mets: Tim Foli, SS, Notre Dame HS, Sherman Oaks, Calif.	$74,000
1969 Senators: Jeff Burroughs, OF, Centennial HS, Long Beach	$88,000
1970 Padres: Mike Ivie, C, Walker HS, Atlanta	$75,000
1971 White Sox: Danny Goodwin, C, Peoria (Ill.) HS	Did not sign
1972 Padres: Dave Roberts, 3B, Oregon	$70,000
1973 Rangers: David Clyde, LHP, Westchester HS, Texas	*$65,000
1974 Padres: Bill Almon, SS, Brown	*$90,000
1975 Angels: Danny Goodwin, C, Southern	*$125,000
1976 Astros: Floyd Bannister, LHP, Arizona State	$100,000
1977 White Sox: Harold Baines, OF, St. Michaels (Md.) HS	$32,000
1978 Braves: Bob Horner, 3B, Arizona State	*$162,000
1979 Mariners: Al Chambers, 1B, Harris HS, Harrisburg, Pa.	$60,000
1980 Mets: Darryl Strawberry, OF, Crenshaw HS, Los Angeles	$152,500
1981 Mariners: Mike Moore, RHP, Oral Roberts	$100,000
1982 Cubs: Shawon Dunston, SS, Jefferson HS, New York	$135,000
1983 Twins: Tim Belcher, RHP, Mount Vernon Nazarene (Ohio)	Did not sign
1984 Mets: Shawn Abner, OF, Mechanicsburg (Pa.) HS	$150,500
1985 Brewers: B.J. Surhoff, C, North Carolina	$150,000
1986 Pirates: Jeff King, 3B, Arkansas	$180,000
1987 Mariners: Ken Griffey Jr., OF, Moeller HS, Cincinnati	$160,000
1988 Padres: Andy Benes, RHP, Evansville	$235,000
1989 Orioles: Ben McDonald, RHP, Louisiana State	*$350,000
1990 Braves: Chipper Jones, SS, The Bolles School, Jacksonville	$275,000
1991 Yankees: Brien Taylor, LHP, East Carteret HS, Beaufort, N.C.	$1,550,000
1992 Astros: Phil Nevin, 3B, Cal State Fullerton	$700,000
1993 Mariners: Alex Rodriguez, SS, Westminster Christian HS, Miami	*$1,000,000
1994 Mets: Paul Wilson, RHP, Florida State	$1,550,000
1995 Angels: Darin Erstad, OF, Nebraska	$1,575,000
1996 Pirates: Kris Benson, RHP, Clemson	$2,000,000
1997 Tigers: Matt Anderson, RHP, Tigers	$2,505,000
1998 Phillies: Pat Burrell, 3B, Miami	*$3,150,000
1999 Devil Rays: Josh Hamilton, OF, Athens Drive HS, Raleigh	$3,960,000
2000 Marlins: Adrian Gonzalez, 1B, Eastlake HS, Chula Vista, Calif.	$3,000,000
2001 Twins: Joe Mauer, C, Cretin-Derham Hall, St. Paul	$5,150,000
2002 Pirates: Bryan Bullington, RHP, Ball State	$4,000,000
2003 Devil Rays: Delmon Young, OF, Camarillo (Calif.) HS	*$3,700,000
2004 Padres: Matt Bush, SS, Mission Bay HS, San Diego	$3,150,000
2005 D-backs: Justin Upton, SS, Great Bridge HS, Chesapeake, Va.	$6,100,000
2006 Royals: Luke Hochevar, RHP, Fort Worth (American Assoc.)	*$3,500,000
2007 Devil Rays: David Price, LHP, Vanderbilt	*$5,600,000
2008 Rays: Tim Beckham, SS, Griffin (Ga.) HS	$6,150,000
2009 Nationals: Stephen Strasburg, RHP, San Diego State	*$7,500,000
2010 Nationals: Bryce Harper, OF, JC of Southern Nevada	*$6,250,000
2011 Pirates: Gerrit Cole, RHP, UCLA	$8,000,000
2012 Astros: Carlos Correa, SS, Puerto Rico Baseball Acad., Gurabo, P.R.	$4,800,000
2013 Astros: Mark Appel, RHP, Stanford	$6,350,000
2014 Astros: Brady Aiken, LHP, Cathedral Catholic, San Diego	Did not sign
2015 D-backs: Dansby Swanson, SS, Vanderbilt	$6,500,000
2016 Phillies: Mickey Moniak, OF, La Costa Canyon HS, Carlsbad, Calif.	$6,100,000
2017 Twins: Royce Lewis, SS, JSerra Catholic HS, San Juan Capistrano, Calif.	$6,750,000
2018 Tigers: Casey Mize, RHP, Auburn	$7,500,000
2019 Orioles: Adley Rutschman, C, Oregon State	$8,100,000
2020 Tigers: Spencer Torkelson, 3B, Arizona State	$8,416,300
2021 Pirates: Henry Davis, C, Louisville	$6,500,000
2022 Orioles: Jackson Holliday, SS, Stillwater (Okla.) HS	$8,190,000
2023 Pirates: Paul Skenes, RHP, Louisiana State	$9,200,000
2024 Guardians: Travis Bazzana, Oregon State	$8.950,000

Four Top 10 Round Picks Don't Sign

The 2024 draft included four players selected inside the top 10 rounds who didn't agree to deals with their teams, the most since the 2018 draft which included four high school players selected inside the first 36 picks.

The players who didn't sign in 2024 included Rays supplemental second round pick SS Tyler Bell, Brewers supplemental second round pick RHP Chris Levonas, Angels third round pick LHP Ryan Prager and Mets ninth round pick RHP Jaxon Jelkin.

Teams lose the slot value of the picks they don't sign from their bonus pool allotment, though top-three round picks who don't sign come with compensation picks in future drafts—meaning the Rays, Brewers and Angels will have extra picks in the 2025 draft.

Draft Spending

When rounding to the nearest tenth there were nine teams who went to the full 5% overage, which is the max you can go over your bonus pool before incurring future draft pick penalties. In the 13 years of the bonus pool era, no team has been willing to go beyond that 5% overage.

Twenty-three teams went over their bonus pool allotment in some capacity, while one team (the D-backs) spent their exact bonus pool. Six teams did not go over, including the Rockies and Twins, who remain the only teams in the league who have never spent more than their available bonus pool.

These numbers are extremely similar to a year ago, and five of the six teams who didn't spend their entire bonus pool still spent at least 99.5% of their pool. In the 2023 draft, three teams spent less than 99.5% of their total bonus pool. This year only the Rays fell below that mark and left $250,000 on the table of their final bonus pool after not signing, though that doesn't include the bonus pool value they lost for not signing 66th overall pick Tyler Bell.

The expectation for this year's first round was that there would be plenty of underslot deals. That was, indeed, the case, as 16 of the first 30 picks signed for less than slot value. Four players signed for exactly slot value and just a third of the first rounders (10 players) signed for overslot deals.

Teams spent $151,096,325 on first round picks this year, which accounts for 40.4% of the total signing bonus dollars ($374,345,077) teams handed out to drafted players this year.

Five players signed for more than $1 million below slot value:

(1.1) Travis Bazzana, $1.6 million
(1.8) Christian Moore, $1.5 million
(1.4) Nick Kurtz, $1.4 million
(1.16) PJ Morlando, $1.3 million
(1.17) Braylon Payne, $1.1 million

Shortstop and ninth overall pick Konnor Griffin secured the most over-slot money among first rounders this year, adding $315,425 to his $6.2 million slot value at the back of the top 10. Collegians Jac Caglianone and Hagen Smith each added more than $200,000 to their slot values.

In total, teams secured $9.6 million in savings towards the bonus pool with their first overall picks, which is neck-in-neck with the $9.7 million savings total from first rounders in the 2023 draft.

The Padres and the Mariners tied for the most senior signs among the first 10 rounds with six apiece, though the tie-breaker that puts the Padres squarely on the pedestal for this category is their $1.55 million in combined underslot savings from those picks. The Mariners checked in at $1.51 million in combined savings.

The Braves and White Sox both selected four senior signs in the first 10 rounds, tied for third among all orgs, and saved $794K and $608K towards the pool, respectively, with those picks. The Brewers can be an honorable mention for this category. They selected just two seniors among the first 10 rounds but combined for $919K in savings towards the pool with those picks.

The Angels spent $2,062,500 towards the pool on day three, which narrowly beat the Brewers for the most in this category, though both teams are in a tier of their own here. The Angels primarily spent that money on 11th-rounder Trey Gregory-Alford, the No. 98 player in the class, but 18th-rounder David Mershon signed for $405,000 and is one of just three players from this draft class already in Double-A.

The Brewers spent $1,912,500 towards the pool on day three, which is seemingly a function of not signing Chris Levonas and then pushing the savings created for that pick to a number of players who signed on deadline day: 13th-rounder Joey Broughton ($385K towards the pool), 15th-rounder Travis Smith ($312K towards the pool), 16th-rounder Jayden Dubanewicz ($515K towards the pool) and 18th-rounder Tyler Renz ($700K towards the pool).

The Cubs spent $570K towards the pool on day three, while the Orioles spent $502,500, and the Blue Jays spent $500K.

There were 615 players selected in this year's draft. A full 77 percent (474) were selected from four-year colleges. Only 18.7% (115) pick were high school players, and junior colleges were 4.3% (26).

Of players who signed, 80.5% (459) were from four-year colleges, 15.3% (87) were from high schools and 4.2% (24) were from junior colleges.4YR: 80.52% (459, 96.84%)

)

THE BONUS RECORD

Rick Monday, the No. 1 overall pick in baseball's first draft in 1965, signed with the Athletics for $100,000—a figure that no draftee bettered for a decade. The record has been broken many times since, including in 2019, when Adley Rutschman signed with the Orioles as the No. 1 overall pick for $8,100,000. Spencer Torkelson broke in 2020. Paul Skenes set a new record in 2023, but it was then eclipsed by Chase Burns and Charlie Condon in 2024.

The longest bonus record stretch dates back to Todd Demeter, whose $208,000 bonus in 1979 held the mark for nine years until 1988 when Andy Benes topped him.

The list below represents only cash bonuses and doesn't include guaranteed money from major league deals, college scholarship plans or incentives. It doesn't include draft picks who signed after being granted free agency.

Year	Player, Pos., Club (Round)	Bonus
1965	Rick Monday, OF, Athletics (1)	$100,000
1975	Danny Goodwin, C, Angels (1)	$125,000
1978	Kirk Gibson, OF, Tigers (1)	$150,000
	*Bob Horner, 3B, Braves (1)	$162,000
1979	Todd Demeter, 1B, Yankees (2)	$208,000
1988	Andy Benes, RHP, Padres (1)	$235,000
1989	Tyler Houston, C, Braves (1)	$241,500
	*Ben McDonald, RHP, Orioles (1)	$350,000
	*John Olerud, 1B, Blue Jays (3)	$575,000
1991	Mike Kelly, OF, Braves (1)	$575,000
	Brien Taylor, LHP, Yankees (1)	$1,550,000
1994	Paul Wilson, RHP, Mets (1)	$1,550,000
	Josh Booty, 3B, Marlins (1)	$1,600,000
1996	Kris Benson, RHP, Pirates (1)	$2,000,000
1997	Rick Ankiel, LHP, Cardinals (2)	$2,500,000
	Matt Anderson, RHP, Tigers (1)	$2,505,000
1998	*J.D. Drew, OF, Cardinals (1)	$3,000,000
	*Pat Burrell, 3B, Phillies (1)	$3,150,000
	Mark Mulder, LHP, Athletics (1)	$3,200,000
	Corey Patterson, OF, Cubs (1)	$3,700,000
1999	Josh Hamilton, OF, Devil Rays (1)	$3,960,000
2000	Joe Borchard, OF, White Sox (1)	$5,300,000
2005	Justin Upton, SS, D-backs (1)	$6,100,000
2008	Tim Beckham, SS, Rays (1)	$6,150,000
	Buster Posey, C, Giants (1)	$6,200,000
2009	Donavan Tate, OF, Padres (1)	$6,250,000
	*Stephen Strasburg, RHP, Nationals (1)	$7,500,000
2011	Gerrit Cole, RHP, Pirates (1)	$8,000,000
2019	Adley Rutschman, C, Orioles (1)	$8,100,000
2020	Spencer Torkelson, 3B, Tigers (1)	$8,416,300
2023	Paul Skenes, RHP, Pirates (1)	$9,200,000
2024	Chase Burns, RHP, Reds (2)	$9,250,000
	Charlie Condon, OF, Rockies (3)	$9,250,000

**Part of major league contract.*

DRAFT

BONUSES VS. PICK VALUES

For the first time in MLB draft history, the slot value for a pick topped $10 million. The Cleveland Guardians won the draft lottery, which meant they were handed the No. 1 pick in the 2024 draft, which carried a slot value of $10,570,600, an 8.7% increase from the $9,721,000 slot value for the Pirates No. 1 pick in 2023. No player has yet received a $10 million bonus however, as Travis Bazzana, the No. 1 pick, signed for $8,950,000 while Chase Burns and Charlie Condon set draft bonus records by signing for $9,250,000 apiece.

The slot values for the draft are determined each year by matching the growth in revenues in baseball.

The total bonus pool value for all clubs in the 2024 draft checked in at $334,375,000, which is more than $27 million more than the total bonus pool value from the 2023 draft—$307,335,300

Player, Pos., Team (Round/Overall Pick)	Bonus	Pick Value
1. Chase Burns, RHP, Wake Forest (1st round/No. 2)	$9,250,000	$9,785,000
2. Charlie Condon, OF, Georgia (1st round/No. 3)	$9,250,000	$9,070,800
3. Travis Bazzana, 2B, Oregon State (1st round/No. 1)	$8,950,000	$10,570,600
4. Hagen Smith, LHP, Arkansas (1st round/No. 5)	$8,000,000	$7,763,700
5. Jac Caglianone, TWP, Florida (1st round/No. 6)	$7,497,500	$7,213,800
6. Nick Kurtz, 1B, Wake Forest (1st round/No. 4)	$7,000,000	$8,370,800
7. JJ Wetherholt, SS, West Virginia (1st round/No. 7)	$6,900,000	$6,823,700
8. Konnor Griffin, SS, Jackson Prep HS (1st round/No. 9)	$6,532,025	$6,216,600
9. Bryce Rainer, SS, Harvard-Westlake HS (1st round/No. 11)	$5,797,500	$5,712,100
10. Seaver King, SS, Wake Forest (1st round/No. 10)	$5,150,000	$5,953,800
11. Cam Smith, 3B, Florida State (1st round/No. 14)	$5,070,700	$5,070,700
12. Braden Montgomery, OF, Texas A&M (1st round/No. 12)	$5,000,000	$5,484,600
13. Christian Moore, 2B, Tennessee (1st round/No. 8)	$4,997,500	$6,502,800
14. Jurrangelo Cijntje, SHP, Mississippi State (1st round/No. 15)	$4,880,900	$4,880,900
15. James Tibbs, OF, Florida State (1st round/No. 13)	$4,747,500	$5,272,300
16. Theo Gillen, OF, Westlake HS (1st round/No. 18)	$4,370,400	$4,372,900
17. Trey Yesavage, RHP, ECU (1st round/No. 20)	$4,175,000	$4,073,400
18. Vance Honeycutt, OF, North Carolina (1st round/No. 22)	$4,000,000	$3,802,200
19. Carson Benge, OF, Oklahoma State (1st round/No. 19)	$3,997,500	$4,219,200
20. Kaelen Culpepper, SS, Kansas State (1st round/No. 21)	$3,934,400	$3,934,400
21. Luke Dickerson, SS, Morris Knolls HS (2nd round/No. 44)	$3,800,000	$2,122,200
22. Cam Caminiti, LHP, Saguaro HS (1st round/No. 24)	$3,553,800	$3,556,300
23. Kash Mayfield, LHP, Elk City HS (1st round/No. 25)	$3,442,100	$3,442,100
24. Braylon Payne, OF, Elkins HS (1st round/No. 17)	$3,440,000	$4,534,100
25. PJ Morlando, OF, Summerville HS (1st round/No. 16)	$3,400,000	$4,704,700
26. Kellon Lindsey, SS, Hardee HS (1st round/No. 23)	$3,297,500	$3,676,400
27. Walker Janek, C, Sam Houston State (1st round/No. 28)	$3,130,000	$3,132,500
28. Slade Caldwell, OF, Valley View HS (1st round/No. 29)	$3,087,000	$3,045,500
29. Tyson Lewis, SS, Millard West HS (2nd round/No. 51)	$3,047,500	$1,804,900
30. Malcolm Moore, C, Stanford (1st round/No. 30)	$3,000,000	$2,971,300
31. Tommy White, 3B, LSU (2nd round/No. 40)	$3,000,000	$2,332,100
32. Ryan Sloan, RHP, York Community HS (2nd round/No. 55)	$3,000,000	$1,641,800
33. Caleb Bonemer, SS, Okemos HS (2nd round/No. 43)	$2,997,500	$2,172,800
34. Ryan Waldschmidt, OF, Kentucky (1st round PPI/No. 31)	$2,904,000	$2,904,000
35. Carter Johnson, SS, Oxford HS (2nd round/No. 56)	$2,800,000	$1,603,400
36. Ben Hess, RHP, Alabama (1st round/No. 26)	$2,747,500	$3,332,900
37. Brody Brecht, RHP, Iowa (1st round supp./No. 38)	$2,700,000	$2,452,200
38. Griff O'Ferrall, SS, Virginia (1st round PPI/No. 32)	$2,697,500	$2,835,400
39. Braylon Doughty, RHP, Chaparral HS (1st round supp./No. 36)	$2,569,200	$2,569,200
40. Levi Sterling, RHP, Notre Dame HS (1st round supp./No. 37)	$2,508,900	$2,511,400
41. Boston Bateman, LHP, Adolfo Camarillo HS (2nd round/No. 52)	$2,500,000	$1,762,500
42. Bryce Meccage, RHP, The Pennington School (2nd round/No. 57)	$2,500,000	$1,562,100
43. Dante Nori, OF, Northville HS (1st round/No. 27)	$2,497,500	$3,228,300
44. Wyatt Sanford, SS, Independence HS (2nd round/No. 47)	$2,497,500	$1,984,800
45. Griffin Burkholder, OF, Freedom HS (2nd round/No. 63)	$2,497,500	$1,352,000
46. Kyle DeBarge, SS, Louisiana-Lafayette (1st round supp./No. 33)	$2,400,000	$2,766,100
47. Caleb Lomavita, C, California (1st round supp./No. 39)	$2,325,000	$2,395,000
48. David Shields, LHP, Mt. Lebanon HS (2nd round/No. 41)	$2,300,000	$2,278,000
49. Bryce Cunningham, RHP, Vanderbilt (2nd round/No. 53)	$2,297,500	$1,721,200
50. JD Dix, SS, Whitefish Bay HS (1st round supp./No. 35)	$2,150,000	$2,632,500
Total	$204,588,425	$204,122,000

The high school players did get paid the most on average. The average signing bonus for high school players was $1,364,704. For four-year college players it was $544,770 and for junior college players it was $231,931. The median signing bonus for high school players was $822,500, for four-year college players it was $150,000. It was also $150,000 for junior college players.

The total signing bonus dollars broken down into sub-categories by year is as follows: College juniors: $209,311,050; high school draftees: HS: $118,729,225; college sophomores: $24,615,200; college seniors: $14,289,262; JUCO soph. $3,063,500 and JUCO freshmen: $1,587,840.

DRAFT 2024 TOP 100 PICKS

Team, Player, Pos., School	Bonus
1. CLE, Travis Bazzana, 2B, Oregon State	$8,950,000
2. CIN, Chase Burns, RHP, Wake Forest	9,250,000
3. COL, Charlie Condon, OF, Georgia	9,250,000
4. OAK, Nick Kurtz, 1B, Wake Forest	7,000,000
5. CWS, Hagen Smith, LHP, Arkansas	8,000,000
6. KC, Jac Caglianone, TWP, Florida	7,497,500
7. STL, JJ Wetherholt, SS, West Virginia	6,900,000
8. LAA, Christian Moore, 2B, Tennessee	4,997,500
9. PIT, Konnor Griffin, SS, Jackson Prep, Flowood, Miss.	6,532,025
10. WSH, Seaver King, SS, Wake Forest	5,150,000
11. DET, Bryce Rainer, SS, Harvard-Westlake HS, Studio City, Calif.	5,797,500
12. BOS, Braden Montgomery, OF, Texas A&M	5,000,000
13. SF, James Tibbs, OF, Florida State	4,747,500
14. CHC, Cam Smith, 3B, Florida State	5,070,700
15. SEA, Jurrangelo Cijntje, SHP, Mississippi State	4,880,900
16. MIA, P.J. Morlando, OF, Summerville HS	3,400,000
17. MIL, Braylon Payne, OF, Elkins HS	3,440,000
18. TB, Theodore Gillen, OF, Westlake HS, Austin, Tex.	4,370,400
19. NYM, Carson Benge, OF, Oklahoma State	3,997,500
20. TOR, Trey Yesavage, RHP, East Carolina	4,175,000
21. MIN, Kaelen Culpepper, SS, Kansas State	3,934,400
22. BAL, Vance Honeycutt, OF, North Carolina	4,000,000
23. LAD, Kellon Lindsey, SS, Hardee HS, Wauchula, Fla.	3,297,500
24. ATL, Cam Caminiti, LHP, Saguaro HS, Scottsdale, Ariz.	3,553,800
25. SD, Kash Mayfield, LHP, Elk City (Okla.) HS	3,442,100
26. NYY, Ben Hess, RHP, Alabama	2,747,500
27. PHI, Dante Nori, OF, Northville (Mich.) HS	2,497,500
28. HOU, Walker Janek, C, Sam Houston	3,130,000
29. AZ, Slade Caldwell, OF, Valley View HS, Jonesboro, Ark.	3,087,000
30. TEX, Malcolm Moore, C, Stanford	3,000,000
31. AZ, Ryan Waldschmidt, OF, Kentucky	2,904,000
32. BAL, Griff O'Ferrall, SS, Virginia	2,697,500
33. MIN, Kyle DeBarge, SS, Louisiana Lafayette	2,400,000
34. MIL, Blake Burke, 1B, Tennessee	2,100,000
35. AZ, JD Dix, SS, Whitefish Bay (Wis.) HS	2,150,000
36. CLE, Braylon Doughty, RHP, Chaparral HS, Temecula, Calif.	2,569,200
37. PIT, Levi Sterling, RHP, Notre Dame HS, Sherman Oaks, Calif.	2,508,900
38. COL, Brody Brecht, RHP, Iowa	2,700,000
39. WSH, Caleb Lomavita, C, California	2,325,000
40. OAK, Tommy White, 3B, LSU	3,000,000
41. KC, David Shields, LHP, Mt. Lebanon HS, Pittsburgh	2,300,000
42. COL, Jared Thomas, OF, Texas	2,000,000
43. CWS, Caleb Bonemer, SS, Okemos (Mich.) HS	2,997,500
44. WSH, Luke Dickerson, SS, Morris Knolls HS, Rockaway, N.J.	3,800,000
45. LAA, Chris Cortez, RHP, Texas A&M	1,597,500
46. NYM, Jonathan Santucci, LHP, Duke	2,031,700
47. PIT, Wyatt Sanford, SS, Independence HS	2,497,500
48. CLE, Jacob Cozart, C, NC State	2,050,000
49. DET, Owen Hall, RHP, Edmond North HS	1,747,500
50. BOS, Payton Tolle, LHP, TCU	2,000,000
51. CIN, Tyson Lewis, SS, Millard West HS	3,047,500
52. SD, Boston Bateman, LHP, Adolfo Camarillo HS	2,500,000
53. NYY, Bryce Cunningham, RHP, Vanderbilt	2,297,500
54. CHC, Cole Mathis, 3B, College Of Charleston	1,681,200
55. SEA, Ryan Sloan, RHP, York Community HS	3,000,000
56. MIA, Carter Johnson, SS, Oxford HS	2,800,000
57. MIL, Bryce Meccage, RHP, The Pennington School	2,500,000
58. TB, Emilien Pitre, 2B, Kentucky	1,522,700
59. TOR, Khal Stephen, RHP, Mississippi State	1,116,750
60. MIN, Billy Amick, 3B, Tennessee	1,453,700
61. BAL, Ethan Anderson, C, Virginia	1,172,500
62. ATL, Carter Holton, LHP, Vanderbilt	1,347,500
63. PHI, Griffin Burkholder, OF, Freedom HS	2,497,500
64. AZ, Ivan Luciano, C, El Shaddai Christian Academy	990,000
65. TEX, Dylan Dreiling, OF, Tennessee	1,287,600
66. TB, Tyler Bell, SS, Lincoln Way East HS	Did Not Sign
67. MIL, Chris Levonas, RHP, Christian Brothers Academy	Did Not Sign
68. CWS, Blake Larson, LHP, IMG Academy	1,397,500
69. MIN, Dasan Hill, LHP, Grapevine HS	1,997,500
70. MIA, Aiden May, RHP, Oregon State	900,000
71. CIN, Luke Holman, RHP, LSU	997,500
72. DET, Ethan Schiefelbein, LHP, Corona Senior HS	1,797,500
73. OAK, Gage Jump, LHP, LSU	2,000,000
74. LAA, Ryan Johnson, RHP, Dallas Baptist	1,747,500
75. OAK, Josh Kuroda-Grauer, SS, Rutgers	1,043,900
76. KC, Drew Beam, RHP, Tennessee	1,097,500
77. COL, Cole Messina, C, South Carolina	1,011,900
78. CWS, Nick McLain, OF, Arizona State	800,000
79. WSH, Kevin Bazzell, C, Texas Tech	980,300
80. STL, Brian Holiday, RHP, Oklahoma State	800,000
81. LAA, Ryan Prager, LHP, Texas A&M	Did Not Sign
82. NYM, Nate Dohm, RHP, Mississippi State	797,500
83. PIT, Josh Hartle, LHP, Wake Forest	850,000
84. CLE, Joey Oakie, RHP, Ankeny Centennial HS	2,000,000
85. DET, Josh Randall, RHP, University Of San Diego	697,500
86. BOS, Brandon Neely, RHP, Florida	700,000
87. CIN, Mike Sirota, OF, Northeastern	863,300
88. SD, Cobb Hightower, SS, East Rowan HS	852,300
89. NYY, Thatcher Hurd, RHP, LSU	836,400
90. CHC, Ronny Cruz, SS, Miami Christian School	620,000
91. SEA, Hunter Cranton, RHP, Kansas	50,000
92. MIA, Gage Miller, 2B, Alabama	800,800
93. MIL, Jaron DeBerry, RHP, Dallas Baptist	25,000
94. TB, Nathan Flewelling, C, St. Joseph HS	774,000
95. TOR, Johnny King, LHP, Naples HS	1,247,500
96. MIN, Khadim Diaw, C, Loyola Marymount University	597,500
97. BAL, Austin Overn, OF, USC	847,500
98. LAD, Chase Harlan, 3B, Central Bucks East HS	1,747,500
99. ATL, Luke Sinnard, RHP, Indiana	735,300
100. PHI, John Spikerman, SS, Oklahoma	672,500

EMILEE CHINN/CINCINNATI REDS

Chase Burns

2024 CLUB-BY-CLUB SELECTIONS

Order Of Selection In Parentheses | Players Signed In Bold

ARIZONA DIAMONDBACKS (16)

1. Slade Caldwell, OF, Valley View HS, Jonesboro, Ark.
1s. Ryan Waldschmidt, OF, Kentucky
1s. JD Dix, SS, Whitefish Bay (Wis.) HS
2. Ivan Luciano, C, El Shaddai Christian Academy, Dorado, P.R.
3. Daniel Eagen, RHP, Presbyterian
4. Tytus Cissell, SS, Howell HS, St. Charles, Mo.
5. Connor Foley, RHP, Indiana
6. Mason Marriott, RHP, Baylor
7. Luke Craig, LHP, UNC Wilmington
8. Travis Garnett, LHP, William & Mary
9. Ben McLaughlin, 3B, Arkansas
10. Trent Youngblood, OF, Transylvania (Ky.)
11. Bo Walker, OF, Starr's Mill HS, Fayetteville, Ga.
12. John West, RHP, Boston College
13. Kyle Ayers, RHP, TCU
14. Braden Quinn, LHP, Connecticut
15. Rocco Reid, LHP, Clemson
16. Dawson Brown, RHP, Georgia Tech
17. Drake Frize, RHP, San Diego
18. Jackson Hotchkiss, OF, Battle Ground (Wash.) HS
19. Tyler Bayer, RHP, South Forsyth HS, Cumming, Ga.
20. Hunter Carns, C, First Coast HS, Jacksonville, Fla.

ATLANTA BRAVES (9)

1. Cam Caminiti, LHP, Saguaro HS, Scottsdale, Ariz.
2. Carter Holton, LHP, Vanderbilt
3. Luke Sinnard, RHP, Indiana
4. Herick Hernandez, LHP, Miami
5. Nicholas Montgomery, C, Cypress (Calif.) HS
6. Ethan Bagwell, RHP, Collinsville (Ill.) HS
7. Brett Sears, RHP, Nebraska
8. Logan Samuels, RHP, Montevallo (Ala.)
9. Owen Hackman, RHP, Loyola Marymount
10. Jacob Kroeger, LHP, Maryville (Mo.)
11. Patrick Clohisy, OF, Saint Louis
12. Cayman Goode, RHP, Freeman HS, Tuckahoe, Va.
13. Colby Jones, SS, Northwest Florida JC
14. Mason Guerra, 1B, Oregon State
15. Owen Carey, OF, Londonderry
16. Titus Dumitru, OF, New Mexico State
17. Jacob Shafer, RHP, UNC Wilmington
18. Jake Steels, OF, Cal Poly
19. Dalton McIntyre, OF, Southern Miss
20. Eric Hartman, OF, Holy Trinity HS, Okotoks, AB

BALTIMORE ORIOLES (1)

1. Vance Honeycutt, OF, North Carolina
1s. Griff O'Ferrall, SS, Virginia
2. Ethan Anderson, C, Virginia
3. Austin Overn, OF, Southern California
4. Chase Allsup, RHP, Auburn
5. Ryan Stafford, C, Cal Poly
6. DJ Layton, SS, Charlotte Christian HS
7. Carson Dorsey, LHP, Florida State
8. Colin Tuft, C, Tulane
9. Jack Crowder, RHP, Illinois
10. Christian Rodriguez, RHP, Cal State Fullerton
11. Sebastian Gongora, LHP, Louisville
12. Andrew Tess, C, Calvary Christian HS, Clearwater, Fla.
13. Brandon Downer, RHP, California Baptist
14. Cohen Achen, RHP, Lindsey Wilson (Ky.)
15. Carter Rustad, RHP, Missouri
16. Nate George, OF, Minooka (Ill.) Community HS
17. Iziah Salinas, LHP, Cowley County (Kan.) JC
18. Michael Caldon, RHP, Felician (N.J.)
19. Braylon Whitaker, OF, Cox Mill HS, Concord, N.C.
20. Evan Yates, RHP, Cal State Fullerton

BOSTON RED SOX (43)

1. Braden Montgomery, OF, Texas A&M
2. Payton Tolle, LHP, TCU
3. Brandon Neely, RHP, Florida
4. Zach Ehrhard, OF, Oklahoma State
5. Brandon Clarke, LHP, State JC of Florida
6. Blake Aita, RHP, Kennesaw State
7. Will Turner, OF, South Alabama
8. Conrad Cason, TWP, Greater Atlanta Christian HS, Norcross, Ga.
9. Hudson White, C, Arkansas
10. Devin Futrell, LHP, Vanderbilt
11. Steven Brooks, RHP, Cal Poly
12. Brady Tygart, RHP, Arkansas
13. Shea Sprague, LHP, North Carolina
14. Alex Bouchard, RHP, Lehigh
15. Joey Gartrell, RHP, Portland
16. Griffin Kilander, RHP, Wayne State (Mich,.)
17. Yan Cruz, OF, Academia Presbiteriana HS, Carolina, P.R.
18. Cole Tolbert, RHP, Mississippi
19. D'Angelo Ortiz, 3B, Miami Dade JC
20. Ben Hansen, RHP, BYU

CHICAGO CUBS (27)

1. Cam Smith, 3B, Florida State
2. Cole Mathis, 3B, College of Charleston
3. Ronny Cruz, SS, Miami Christian HS
4. Ty Southisene, SS, Basic HS, Henderson, Nev.
5. Ariel Armas, C, San Diego
6. Ryan Gallagher, RHP, UC Santa Barbara
7. Ivan Brethowr, OF, UC Santa Barbara
8. Edgar Alvarez, 1B, Nicholls State
9. Brooks Caple, RHP, Lamar
10. Matt Halbach, 3B, UC San Diego
11. Eli Lovich, OF, Blue Valley West HS, Stillwell, Kansas
12. Daniel Avitia, RHP, Grand Canyon
13. Evan Aschenbeck, LHP, Texas A&M
14. Cameron Sisneros, 1B, East Tennessee State
15. Hayden Frank, LHP, Lipscomb
16. Christian Gordon, LHP, Virginia Commonwealth
17. Ben Johnson, RHP, Georgia Southern
18. Thomas Mangus, RHP, Navarro (Texas) JC
19. Owen Ayers, C, Marshall
20. Brayden Risedorph, RHP, Indiana

CHICAGO WHITE SOX (3)

1. Hagen Smith, LHP, Arkansas
2. Caleb Bonemer, SS, Okemos (Mich.) HS
2s. Blake Larson, LHP, IMG Academy, Bradenton, Fla.
3. Nick McLain, OF, Arizona State
4. Casey Saucke, OF, Virginia
5. Sam Antonacci, IF, Coastal Carolina
6. Jackson Appel, C, Texas A&M
7. Phil Fox, RHP, Pittsburgh
8. Aaron Combs, RHP, Tennessee
9. Jack Young, RHP, Iowa
10. Cole McConnell, OF, Louisiana Tech
11. Blake Shepardson, RHP, San Francisco
12. Nathan Archer, OF, Bowling Green
13. Pierce George, RHP, Alabama
14. Justin Sinibaldi, LHP, Rutgers
15. Mason Moore, RHP, Kentucky
16. T.J. McCants, OF, Alabama
17. Lyle Miller-Green, TWP, Austin Peay
18. Liam Paddack, LHP, Gonzaga

DRAFT

19. Nick Pinto, LHP, UC Irvine
20. Myles Bailey, 1B, Lincoln HS, Tallahassee, Fla.

CINCINNATI REDS (7)

1. Chase Burns, RHP, Wake Forest
2. Tyson Lewis, SS, Millard West HS, Omaha, Neb.
2s. Luke Holman, RHP, LSU
3. Mike Sirota, OF, Northeastern
4. Peyton Stovall, 2B, Arkansas
5. Tristan Smith, LHP, Clemson
6. Jacob Friend, C, Davidson
7. Myles Smith, OF, UC Irvine
8. Luke Hayden, RHP, Indiana State
9. Ryan McCrystal, C, ECU
10. Yanuel Casiano, C, Albergue Olímpico Baseball Academy, Salinas, P.R.
11. Edgar Colon, RHP, Valera HS, Miami
12. Will Cannon, RHP, Auburn
13. Anthony Stephan, OF, Virginia
14. Adrian Areizaga, SS, Leadership Christian Academy, Guaynabo, P.R.
15. Jordan Little, RHP, Virginia Tech
16. Jimmy Romano, RHP, Duke
17. Trent Hodgdon, RHP, South Carolina Upstate
18. Jalen Hairston, 3B, State JC of Florida Manatee
19. Owen Pote, RHP, No School
20. Mason Russell, LHP, Casteel HS, Queen Creek, Ariz.

CLEVELAND INDIANS (24)

1. Travis Bazzana, 2B, Oregon State
1s. Braylon Doughty, RHP, Chaparral HS, Temecula, Calif.
2. Jacob Cozart, C, NC State
3. Joey Oakie, RHP, Ankeny (Iowa) Centennial HS
4. Rafe Schlesinger, LHP, Miami
5. Aidan Major, RHP, West Virginia
6. Caden Favors, LHP, Wichita State
7. Cameron Sullivan, RHP, Mt. Vernon (Va.)
8. Donovan Zsak, LHP, Rutgers
9. Sean Matson, RHP, Harvard
10. Chase Mobley, RHP, Durant HS, Plant City, Fla.
11. Garrett Howe, SS, Samford
12. Sean Heppner, RHP, British Columbia
13. Bennett Thompson, C, Oregon
14. Ryan Cesarini, OF, Saint Joseph's
15. Conner Whittaker, RHP, Florida State
16. Jacob Remily, RHP, Maryknoll HS, Honolulu
17. Logan McGuire, RHP, Georgia Tech
18. Izaak Martinez, LHP, UC San Diego
19. Cam Schuelke, RHP, Mississippi State
20. Cam Walty, RHP, Arizona

COLORADO ROCKIES (23)

1. Charlie Condon, OF, Georgia
1s. Brody Brecht, RHP, Iowa
2. Jared Thomas, OF, Texas
3. Cole Messina, C, South Carolina
4. Blake Wright, 3B, Clemson
5. Lebarron Johnson, RHP, Texas
6. Konner Eaton, LHP, George Mason
7. Fidel Ulloa, RHP, LSU
8. Luke Jewett, RHP, UCLA
9. Tommy Hopfe, 1B, Fresno State
10. Fisher Jameson, RHP, Florida
11. Alan Espinal, C, Vanderbilt
12. Everett Catlett, LHP, Georgetown
13. Justin Loer, LHP, LSU
14. Sam Gerth, RHP, Navarro (Texas) JC
15. Luke Thelen, RHP, Western Michigan
16. Kevin Fitzer, 1B, Cal State Northridge
17. Nolan Clifford, SS, Creighton
18. Tyler Hampu, RHP, Austin Peay
19. Nathan Blasick, RHP, New Orleans
20. Hunter Omlid, RHP, Arizona State

DETROIT TIGERS (5)

1. Bryce Rainer, SS, Harvard-Westlake HS, Studio City, Calif.
2. Owen Hall, RHP, Edmond North (Okla.) HS
2s. Ethan Schiefelbein, LHP, Corona (Calif.) HS
3. Josh Randall, RHP, San Diego
4. Michael Massey, RHP, Wake Forest
5. Jack Penney, SS, Notre Dame
6. Woody Hadeen, SS, UC Irvine
7. Jackson Strong, OF, Canisius
8. Ethan Sloan, LHP, Regis (Colo.)
9. Zach Swanson, RHP, Toutle Lake (Wash.) HS
10. R.J. Sales, RHP, UNC Wilmington
11. Micah Ashman, LHP, Utah
12. Jude Warwick, SS, Downers Grove (Ill.) North HS
13. Lucas Elissalt, RHP, Chipola (Fla.) JC
14. Preston Howey, RHP, St. Mary's
15. Zach MacDonald, OF, Miami
16. Anson Seibert, RHP, Blue Valley Southwest HS, Overland Park, Kan.
17. Gabriel Rosado, C, Carlos Beltran Baseball Academy, Florida, P.R.
18. Bryce Alewine, RHP, Southern Union State (Ala.) JC
19. Chase Davis, LHP, Leon HS, Tallahassee, Fla.
20. Dawson Price, RHP, Eastern Oklahoma JC

HOUSTON ASTROS (32)

1. Walker Janek, C, Sam Houston State
3. Ryan Forcucci, RHP, UC San Diego
4. Parker Smith, RHP, Rice
5. Cole Hertzler, RHP, Liberty
6. Caden Powell, SS, Seminole State (Okla.) JC
7. Joseph Sullivan, OF, South Alabama
8. Dylan Howard, RHP, Radford
9. Ryan Smith, RHP, Illinois
10. Ramsey David, RHP, Southeastern La.
11. Jason Schiavone, C, James Madison
12. Ryan Verdugo, RHP, Cal State Bakersfield
13. Bryce Boettcher, OF, Oregon
14. Ryan Mathiesen, RHP, The Master's (Calif.)
15. Drew Vogel, SS, Murray State
16. Bryce Mayer, RHP, Missouri
17. Ethan Wagner, OF, P27 Academy, Lexington, S.C.
18. Grant Burleson, RHP, Western Kentucky
19. Twine Palmer, RHP, Connors State (Okla.)
20. Ky McGary, OF, O'Connor HS, Phoenix

KANSAS CITY ROYALS (2)

1. Jac Caglianone, TWP, Florida
2. David Shields, LHP, Mt. Lebanon HS, Pittsburgh
3. Drew Beam, RHP, Tennessee
4. Louis-Philippe Langevin, RHP, Louisiana Lafayette
5. A.J. Causey, RHP, Tennessee
6. Tanner Jones, RHP, Texas A&M
7. Dennis Colleran, RHP, Northeastern
8. Nick Conte, RHP, Duke
9. Canyon Brown, C, North Carolina A&T
10. Nate Ackenhausen, LHP, LSU
11. Zachary Cawyer, RHP, TCU
12. Tommy Molsky, RHP, Oklahoma State
13. Sam Kulasingam, 3B, Air Force
14. Kyle DeGroat, RHP, Wallkill Senior
15. Tyler Davis, LHP, Mississippi State
16. Andrew Morones, RHP, CS Fullerton
17. Dane Burns, LHP, No School
18. Corey Cousin, OF, Slidell (La.) HS
19. Dash Albus, LHP, Abilene Christian
20. Carter Frederick, OF, Oklahoma

LOS ANGELES ANGELS (15)

1. Christian Moore, 2B, Tennessee

2. Chris Cortez, RHP, Texas A&M
2s. Ryan Johnson, RHP, Dallas Baptist
3. Ryan Prager, LHP, Texas A&M
4. Austin Gordon, RHP, Clemson
5. Dylan Jordan, RHP, Viera HS, Melbourne, Fla.
6. Peyton Olejnik, RHP, Miami
7. Bridger Holmes, RHP, Oregon State
8. Randy Flores, SS, Alabama State
9. Derek Clark, LHP, West Virginia
10. Ryan Nicholson, 1B, Kentucky
11. Trey Gregory-Alford, RHP, Coronado HS, Colorado Springs, Col.
12. Fran Oschell, RHP, Duke
13. Fulton Lockhart, RHP, Central Florida
14. Najer Victor, RHP, Central Florida
15. Bailan Caraballo, OF, Reborn Christian
16. Will Gervase, LHP, Wake Forest
17. Lucas Ramirez, OF, American Heritage School, Plantation, Fla.
18. David Mershon, SS, Mississippi State
19. Connor Gatwood, RHP, Baker HS, Mobile, Ala.
20. Zachary Redner, RHP, Hillsborough (Fla.) JC

LOS ANGELES DODGERS (25)

1. Kellon Lindsey, SS, Hardee HS, Wauchula, Fla.
3. Chase Harlan, 3B, Central Bucks East HS, Doylestown, Pa.
4. Jakob Wright, LHP, Cal Poly
6. Brooks Auger, RHP, Mississippi State
7. Elijah Hainline, SS, Oregon State
8. Brendan Tunink, OF, Newman Central Catholic HS
9. Kole Myers, OF, Troy
10. Seamus Barrett, RHP, Loyola Marymount
11. Aidan Foeller, RHP, Southern Illinois Carbondale
12. Cody Morse, LHP, Weatherford (Texas) JC
13. Mike Villani, RHP, Long Beach State
14. Will Gagnon, RHP, Reedley (Calf.) JC
15. Erik Parker, SS, North Gwinnett HS, Suwanee, Ga.
16. Evan Shaw, LHP, Kansas
17. Jackson Nicklaus, SS, Oklahoma
18. Isaac Ayon, RHP, Oregon
19. Chase Williams, OF, Northwest Florida State JC
20. Hunter Elliott, LHP, Ole Miss

MIAMI MARLINS (4)

1. PJ Morlando, OF, Summerville (S.C.) HS
2. Carter Johnson, SS, Oxford (Ala.) HS
2s. Aiden May, RHP, Oregon State
3. Gage Miller, 2B, Alabama
4. Fenwick Trimble, OF, James Madison
5. Grant Shepardson, RHP, Mountain Vista HS, Highlands Ranch, Colo.
6. Payton Green, SS, Georgia Tech
7. Nick Brink, RHP, Portland
8. Jacob Jenkins-Cowart, OF, ECU
9. Dub Gleed, 3B, UC Irvine
10. Michael Snyder, 3B, Oklahoma
11. Jake Faherty, RHP, Arkansas
12. Connor Caskenette, C, Purdue
13. Cody Schrier, SS, UCLA
14. Cam Clayton, SS, Washington
15. Coen Niclai, C, Service HS, Anchorage, Ala.
16. Eric Rataczak, 1B, Niagara
17. Micah McDowell, OF, Oregon State
18. Nate Payne, LHP, Central Dauphin HS, Hqarrisburg, Pa.
19. Luke Lashutka, RHP, St Leo (Fla.)
20. Chase Centala, RHP, Central Florida

MILWAUKEE BREWERS (28)

1. Braylon Payne, OF, Fort Bend Elkins HS, Missouri City, Texas
1s. Blake Burke, 1B, Tennessee
2. Bryce Meccage, RHP, The Pennington (N.J.) HS
2s. Chris Levonas, RHP, Christian Brothers Academy, Lincroft, N.J.
3. Jaron DeBerry, RHP, Dallas Baptist
4. Marco Dinges, C, Florida State
5. John Holobetz, RHP, Old Dominion
6. Chandler Welch, RHP, Tulane
7. Mason Molina, LHP, Arkansas
8. Sam Garcia, LHP, Oklahoma State
9. Griffin Tobias, RHP, Lake Central HS, St. John, Ind.
10. Ethan Dorchies, RHP, Cary-Grove HS, Cary, Ill.
11. Caedmon Parker, RHP, TCU
12. Tyson Hardin, RHP, Mississippi State
13. Joseph Broughton, LHP, Northville (Mich.) HS
14. James Nunnallee, C, Lightridge HS, Aldie, Va.
15. Travis Smith, RHP, Kentucky
16. Jayden Dubanewicz, RHP, Stoneman Douglas
17. Cooper Malamazian, SS, Nazareth HS, La Grange Park, Ill.
18. Tyler Renz, RHP, Fox Lane HS, Bedford, N.Y.
19. Noah Wech, RHP, Manitowoc (Wisc.) Lincoln HS
20. Henry Brummel, RHP, Pontiac (Ill.) HS

MINNESOTA TWINS (13)

1. Kaelen Culpepper, SS, Kansas State
1s. Kyle DeBarge, SS, Louisiana-Lafayette
2. Billy Amick, 3B, Tennessee
2s. Dasan Hill, LHP, Grapevine (Texas) HS
3. Khadim Diaw, C, Loyola Marymount
4. Jaime Ferrer, OF, Florida State
5. Caden Kendle, OF, UC Irvine
6. Derek Bender, C, Coastal Carolina
7. Eli Jones, RHP, South Carolina
8. Jakob Hall, RHP, Oral Roberts
9. Jason Doktorczyk, RHP, Nevada
10. Peyton Carr, 3B, High Point
11. Michael Carpenter, LHP, Madison (Wisc.) JC
12. Christian Becerra, RHP, California
13. Xavier Kolhosser, RHP, St Johns
14. Jacob Kisting, RHP, Bradley
15. Cole Peschl, RHP, Campbell
16. Aidan Haugh, RHP, North Carolina
17. Jay Thomason, 3B, Air Force
18. Michael Ross, RHP, Samford
19. Logan Whitaker, RHP, NC State
20. Merit Jones, RHP, Utah

NEW YORK METS (12)

1. Carson Benge, OF, Oklahoma State
2. Jonathan Santucci, LHP, Duke
3. Nate Dohm, RHP, Mississippi State
4. Eli Serrano, OF, NC State
5. Trey Snyder, SS, Liberty North (Mo.) HS
6. Corey Collins, 1B, Georgia
7. William Watson, RHP, Southern California
8. Ryan Lambert, RHP, Oklahoma
9. Jaxon Jelkin, RHP, Houston
10. Brendan Girton, RHP, Oklahoma
11. Nick Roselli, 2B, Binghamton
12. Ethan Lanthier, RHP, Kansas
13. R.J. Gordon, RHP, Oregon
14. Tanner Witt, RHP, Texas
15. Owen Woodward, RHP, Houston
16. Josh Blum, RHP, Southern California
17. Jacoby Long, OF, Miami
18. Jace Hampson, RHP, Lynnwood HS, Bothell, Wash.
19. Frank Elissalt, RHP, Nova Southeastern
20. Adam Haight, SS, Cedar Park Christian HS, Bothel, Wash.

NEW YORK YANKEES (30)

1. Ben Hess, RHP, Alabama
2. Bryce Cunningham, RHP, Vanderbilt
3. Thatcher Hurd, RHP, LSU

4. Gage Ziehl, RHP, Miami
5. Greysen Carter, RHP, Vanderbilt
6. Griffin Herring, LHP, LSU
7. Wyatt Parliament, RHP, Virginia Tech
8. Tyler Wilson, OF, Grand Canyon
9. Tanner Bauman, LHP, Auburn
10. Joe De Los Santos, OF, William & Mary
11. Mack Estrada, RHP, Northwest Florida State JC
12. Brendan Jones, OF, Kansas State
13. Dillon Lewis, OF, Queens Charlotte
14. Austin Green, 2B, Texas Tech
15. Marshall Toole, OF, Wofford
16. Xavier Rivas, LHP, Mississippi
17. JoJo Jackson, OF, Georgia State
18. Gus Hughes, RHP, High Point
19. Brandon Decker, RHP, Oakland
20. Cole Royer, RHP, Pierce County HS, Blackshear, Ga.

OAKLAND ATHLETICS (29)

1. Nick Kurtz, 1B, Wake Forest
2. Tommy White, 3B, LSU
2s. Gage Jump, LHP, LSU
3. Josh Kuroda-Grauer, SS, Rutgers
4. Rodney Green, OF, California
5. Sam Stuhr, RHP, Portland
6. Josiah Romeo, RHP, Mayfield East HS, Caledon East, Ont.
7. Dylan Fien, C, Great Oak
8. Davis Diaz, C, Vanderbilt
9. Jared Sprague-Lott, 3B, Arkansas
10. Cameron Leary, OF, Boston College
11. Kyle Robinson, RHP, Texas Tech
12. Ali Camarillo, SS, Texas A&M
13. Riley Huge, LHP, Winthrop
14. Ryan Magdic, LHP, Missouri
15. Blake Hammond, RHP, Santa Clara
16. Connor Spencer, RHP, Mississippi
17. Aidan Layton, RHP, Seton Hill
18. Tucker Novotny, LHP, Minnesota
19. Gunner Gouldsmith, SS, Sacramento State
20. Dylan Volantis, LHP, Westlake HS, Thousand Oaks, Calif.

PHILADELPHIA PHILLIES (14)

1. Dante Nori, OF, Northville (Mich.) HS
2. Griffin Burkholder, OF, Freedom HS, South Riding, Va.
3. John Spikerman, SS, Oklahoma
4. Carson DeMartini, SS, Virginia Tech
5. Carter Mathison, OF, Indiana
6. Kodey Shojinaga, C, Kansas
7. Joel Dragoo, OF, Presbyterian
8. Camron Hill, LHP, Georgia Tech
9. Marcus Morgan, RHP, Iowa
10. Brady Day, SS, Kansas State
11. Titan Hayes, RHP, Austin Peay
12. A.J. Wilson, LHP, UNC Charlotte
13. Tegan Cain, RHP, Kansas
14. Jared Spencer, LHP, Indiana State
15. Luke Gabrysh, RHP, Saint Joseph's
16. Eli Trop, RHP, Pennsylvania
17. Ryan Degges, RHP, Charlotte
18. Kevin Warunek, LHP, Longwood
19. Erik Ritchie, LHP, East Carolina
20. Kyler Carmack, RHP, Mississippi

PITTSBURGH PIRATES (18)

1. Konnor Griffin, SS, Jackson Prep, Flowood, Miss.
1s. Levi Sterling, RHP, Notre Dame HS, Sherman Oaks, Calif.
2. Wyatt Sanford, SS, Independence HS, Frisco, Texas
3. Josh Hartle, LHP, Wake Forest
4. Eddie Rynders, SS, Wisconsin Lutheran HS, Milwaukee
5. Will Taylor, OF, Clemson
6. Matt Ager, RHP, UC Santa Barbara
7. Connor Wietgrefe, LHP, Minnesota
8. Gavin Adams, RHP, Florida State
9. Duce Gourson, SS, UCLA
10. Derek Berg, C, Army
11. Jacob Bimbi, LHP, Western Kentucky
12. Camden Janik, C, Illinois
13. Matt McShane, RHP, Saint Joseph's
14. Ian Farrow, OF, Florida Gulf Coast
15. Ethan Lege, 3B, Mississipi
16. Brian Curley, RHP, VCU
17. Andrew Patrick, OF, Wright State
18. Jake Shirk, RHP, Wright State
19. Joe Vogatsky, RHP, James Madison
20. Taylor Penn, RHP, Woodford County HS, Versailles, Ky.

SAN DIEGO PADRES (6)

1. Kash Mayfield, LHP, Elk City (Okla.) HS
2. Boston Bateman, LHP, Camarillo (Calif.) HS
3. Cobb Hightower, SS, East Rowan HS, Salisbury, N.C.
4. Tyson Neighbors, RHP, Kansas State
4C. Kavares Tears, OF, Tennessee
4C. Clark Candiotti, RHP, Arizona
5. Kale Fountain, 3B, Norris HS, Firth, Neb.
6. Darrien McDowell, OF, West Florida
7. Kai Roberts, OF, Utah
8. Nick Wissman, RHP, Dayton
9. Zach Evans, SS, Lenoir-Rhyne U
10. Jack Costello, 3B, San Diego
11. Sean Barnett, TWP, Wingate
12. Brandon Butterworth, SS, NC State
13. Matthew Watson, RHP, Texas A&M - Corpus Christi
14. Brendan Durfee, C, UC Santa Barbara
15. Tanner Smith, RHP, Harvard
16. Kasen Wells, OF, Weatherford (Texas) JC
17. Ryan Jackson, SS, Southern California
18. Victor Figueroa, 1B, Florida Southwestern JC
19. Vicarte Domingo, RHP, British Columbia
20. Chase Fralick, C, McIntosh HS, Peachtree City, Ga.

SAN FRANCISCO GIANTS (10)

1. James Tibbs, OF, Florida State
4. Dakota Jordan, OF, Mississippi State
5. Jakob Christian, OF, San Diego
6. Robert Hipwell, 3B, Santa Clara
7. Greg Farone, LHP, Alabama
8. Niko Mazza, RHP, Southern Miss
9. Zane Zielinski, SS, Illinois Chicago
10. Cade Vernon, RHP, Murray State
11. Andy Polanco, OF, Central Pointe Christian HS, Kissimme, Fla.
12. Zander Darby, 3B, UC Santa Barbara
13. Drake George, RHP, Lewis-Clark (Idaho) State
14. Jeremiah Jenkins, 1B, Maine
15. Evan Gray, RHP, St. Louis
16. Tyler Switalski, LHP, West Virginia
17. Hunter Dryden, RHP, Whitworth (Wash.)
18. Ryan Slater, RHP, Florida
19. Ryan Ure, LHP, Oklahoma State
20. Fernando Gonzalez, C, Georgia

SEATTLE MARINERS (20)

1. Jurrangelo Cijntje, SHP, Mississippi State
2. Ryan Sloan, RHP, York HS, Elmhurst, Ill.
3. Hunter Cranton, RHP, Kansas
4. Josh Caron, C, Nebraska
5. Charlie Beilenson, RHP, Duke
6. Grant Knipp, TWP, Campbell
7. Brock Moore, RHP, Oregon
8. Will Riley, RHP, Virginia Military Institute
9. Aiden Butler, RHP, Polk State (Fla.) JC
10. Anthony Donofrio, OF, North Carolina

11. Christian Little, RHP, LSU
12. Evan Truitt, RHP, Charleston Southern
13. Brandon Eike, 3B, VCU
14. Austin St. Laurent, 3B, Appalachian State
15. Thomas Higgins, RHP, Georgia Southern
16. Wyatt Lunsford-Shenkman, RHP, ECU
17. Harrison Krieling, RHP, Nebraska Omaha
18. Matt Tiberia, RHP, Lynn (Mass.)
19. Brian Walters, RHP, Miami
20. Ryan Picollo, OF, Saint Joseph's

ST. LOUIS CARDINALS (19)

1. JJ Wetherholt, SS, West Virginia
3. Brian Holiday, RHP, Oklahoma State
4. Ryan Campos, C, Arizona State
5. Braden Davis, LHP, Oklahoma
6. Josh Kross, C, Cincinnati
7. Andrew Dutkanych, RHP, Vanderbilt
8. Jack Findlay, LHP, Notre Dame
9. Cade McGee, 3B, Texas Tech
10. Bryce Madron, OF, Oklahoma
11. Jon Jon Gazdar, SS, Austin Peay
12. Ian Petrutz, OF, Alabama
13. Nolan Sparks, RHP, Rochester (N.Y.)
14. Mason Burns, RHP, Western Kentucky
15. Sam Brodersen, RHP, Louisiana Tech
16. Deniel Ortiz, 3B, Walters State (Tenn.) JC
17. Brandt Thompson, RHP, Missouri State
18. Christian Martin, SS, Virginia Tech
19. Brendan Lawson, SS, P27 Academy, Lexington, S.C.
20. Owen Rice, LHP, Milwaukee

TAMPA BAY RAYS (22)

1. Theo Gillen, OF, Westlake HS, Austin, Tex.
2. Emilien Pitre, 2B, Kentucky
2s. Tyler Bell, SS, Lincoln-Way East HS, Frankfort, Ill.
3. Nathan Flewelling, C, St. Joseph Catholic HS, Red Deer, Alb.
4. Nate Knowles, RHP, William & Mary
5. Jacob Kmatz, RHP, Oregon State
6. Janzen Keisel, RHP, Oklahoma State
7. Ryan Andrade, RHP, Pittsburgh
8. Jayden Voelker, RHP, Northern Essex (Mass.) JC
9. Garrett Gainey, LHP, South Carolina
10. Trey Pooser, RHP, Kentucky
11. Cade Citelli, RHP, Houston
12. Jack Lines, SS, TNXL Academy
13. Connor Hujsak, OF, Mississippi State
14. Ryan Schiefer, RHP, Arizona State
15. Derek Datil, OF, Antonio Lucchetti HS, Arecibo, P.R.
16. Brady Marget, 1B, Tulane
17. Andres Galan, RHP, California
18. Dominic Niman, LHP, Kentucky
19. Tony Santa Maria, 3B, Rutgers
20. Kaleb Corbett, RHP, Louisville

TEXAS RANGERS (8)

1. Malcolm Moore, C, Stanford
2. Dylan Dreiling, OF, Tennessee
3. Casey Cook, OF, North Carolina
4. David Hagaman, RHP, West Virginia
5. Devin Fitz-Gerald, SS, Stoneman Douglas HS, Parkland, Fla.
6. Garrett Horn, LHP, Liberty
7. Rafe Perich, 3B, Lehigh
8. Anthony Susac, RHP, Arizona
9. Keith Jones, OF, New Mexico State
10. Jake Jekielek, RHP, Northwood (Mich.)
11. Dalton Pence, LHP, North Carolina
12. Josh Springer, C, Corona (Calif.) HS
13. Aidan Deakins, LHP, Wabash Valley (Ill.) JC
14. Ben Hartl, C, Kansas
15. Brooks Fowler, RHP, Oral Roberts
16. Eric Loomis, RHP, Missouri State
17. Joey Danielson, RHP, North Dakota State
18. Kadyn Leon, RHP, Lake Travis (Fla.) HS
19. Cade Obermueller, LHP, Iowa
20. Mac Rose, C, McLennan (Texas) JC

TORONTO BLUE JAYS (11)

1. Trey Yesavage, RHP, ECU
2. Khal Stephen, RHP, Mississippi State
3. Johnny King, LHP, Naples (Fla.) HS
4. Sean Keys, 3B, Bucknell
4s. Nick Mitchell, OF, Indiana
5. Jackson Wentworth, RHP, Kansas State
6. Aaron Parker, C, UC Santa Barbara
7. Austin Cates, RHP, UNLV
8. Eddie Micheletti, OF, Virginia Tech
9. Colby Holcombe, RHP, Mississippi State
10. Carter Cunningham, OF, East Carolina
11. Troy Guthrie, RHP, Parrish (Fla.) Community HS
12. Carson Messina, RHP, Summerville (S.C.) HS
13. Brock Tibbitts, C, Indiana
14. J.R. Freethy, 2B, Nevada
15. Jonathan Todd, RHP, Western Carolina
16. Colby Martin, RHP, Southeastern La.
17. Gavin Smith, SS, Basha HS, Chandler, Ariz.
18. Holden Wilkerson, RHP, Virginia Military Institute
19. D'Marion Terrell, 1B, Thompson HS, Alabaster, Ala.
20. Bryce Martin-Grudzielanek, SS, UC San Diego

WASHINGTON NATIONALS (17)

1. Seaver King, SS, Wake Forest
1s. Caleb Lomavita, C, California
2. Luke Dickerson, SS, Morris Knolls HS, Rockaway, N.J.
3. Kevin Bazzell, C, Texas Tech
4. Jackson Kent, LHP, Arizona
5. Randal Diaz-Morales, SS, Indiana State
6. Davian Garcia, RHP, Florida Gulf Coast
7. Robert Cranz, RHP, Oklahoma State
8. Sam Petersen, OF, Iowa
9. Jackson Ross, 3B, Mississippi
10. Luke Johnson, RHP, Maryland-Baltimore County
11. Merritt Beeker, LHP, Ball State
12. Xander Meckley, RHP, Coastal Carolina
13. Bryant Olson, LHP, Mercer
14. Yoel Tejeda, RHP, Florida State
15. Sir Jamison Jones, C, St. Rita HS, Chicago
16. Nolan Hughes, LHP, Xavier
17. Gavin Bruni, LHP, Ohio State
18. Teo Banks, OF, Tulane
19. Ryan Minckler, RHP, Niagara
20. Colby Shelton, 3B, Florida

DRAFT

APPENDIX

Billy Bean: Bean played part-time in six big league seasons but is better known for his post-playing career role as MLB's first ambassador for inclusion.

His role later expanded to senior vice president and special assistant to the commissioner.

Bean concealed his sexuality from teammates in his playing days but came out as gay in 1999, four years after his retirement.

Bean was a lefthanded-hitting outfielder who earned third-team All-America honors at Loyola Marymount in 1986. The Tigers drafted him in the fourth round that year.

Bean made his MLB debut on April 25, 1987, less than a year after being drafted. He collected four hits in his first game, tying a major league record.

Despite his quick callup, Bean spent most of his early pro career at Triple-A before signing with Kintetsu in Japan in 1992. That experience paved the way for his most successful MLB stretch, as a fourth outfielder with the Padres from 1993 to 1995.

Bean died of acute myeloid leukemia on Aug. 6 in New York. He was 60.

Sean Burroughs: Burroughs reached the pinnacle of his profession.

First-round pick. Top prospect. Olympic gold medalist. Big leaguer.

Burroughs' fall from grace was just as pronounced. Out of baseball in his mid 20s, he moved to Las Vegas and fell into a years-long pattern of substance abuse, motel-hopping and paranoia.

But Burroughs' desire to play baseball helped him get his life back on track.

Kevin Towers served as general manager when the Padres drafted Burroughs ninth overall in 1998 out of Long Beach's Wilson High, the same school where his father Jeff had been drafted first overall in 1969.

A dozen years later, Towers was instrumental in giving Burroughs a second chance, this time as GM of the D-backs. Towers signed Burroughs in November 2010.

Burroughs did not play in 2008, 2009 or 2010, but his sweet lefthanded swing never deserted him. He hit .412 in 34 games for Triple-A Reno, improbably making it back to the big leagues.

Burroughs served as primary pinch-hitter and backup third baseman for a 94-win D-backs team that won the National League West in 2011.

The remainder of Burroughs' playing career was remarkable but less magical. He bounced around the Twins and Dodgers organizations and then the independent Atlantic League, playing until he was 36 years old.

Lauded as a future MLB batting champion as a prospect, Burroughs hit .324 on his way up the minor league ladder before making the Padres' Opening Day roster as a 21-year-old in 2002.

Power never materialized for Burroughs, who hit .280/.340/.359 (91 OPS+) through his first five big league seasons before exiting baseball for awhile. His career highlights include ranking as the No. 4 overall prospect heading into 2002 and winning the only Olympic gold medal in USA Baseball history in 2000.

Burroughs died on May 9 in Long Beach after going into cardiac arrest. He had just dropped off his son before a baseball game. He was 43.

Orlando Cepeda: Cepeda won the National League Rookie of the Year award unanimously in 1958, the Giants' first year in San Francisco, and then made the NL all-star team in each of the next six seasons.

In 1959, Cepeda made history as the first Puerto Rican player to start the All-Star Game.

In 1961, he finished runner-up for NL MVP after he led the league with 46 home runs and 142 RBIs. A year later, he helped power the Giants to the World Series, which they lost in seven games.

Cepeda hit 222 home runs in his first seven MLB seasons. Just 10 players have ever hit more to begin a career. Cepeda would have kept building on that total if not for a major knee injury in 1965 that cost him almost the entire season.

Yet, because the Giants came up with Cepeda and Willie McCovey, a pair of Hall of Fame first basemen, at the same time, Cepeda's time in San Francisco did not always go smoothly.

He and McCovey took turns playing left field. Neither was a natural.

After Cepeda recovered from his knee injury, the Giants traded him to the Cardinals for lefthander Ray Sadecki in May 1966.

Cepeda announced his presence immediately. He hit a career-high .325 and led the NL with 111 RBIs in 1967, when he won his only MVP award and the Cardinals defeated the Red Sox in the World Series.

Cepeda remained a steady run-producer through his age-32 season in 1970, when he hit 34 homers for the Braves. A knee injury he suffered that season impacted his availability for the rest of his career.

HY PESKIN/GETTY IMAGES

Orlando Cepeda

Cepeda retired 50 years ago, but he still ranks fourth for home runs by a Puerto Rican player with 379. Juan Gonzalez, Carlos Beltran and Carlos Delgado later passed him.

Cepeda appeared on the Hall of Fame ballot for the full 15 seasons of eligibility but came up a few votes short in his final try, at 73.5%. The Veterans Committee elected him in 1999.

Cepeda died on June 28 in Concord, Calif. He was 86.

Mike Cubbage: Cubbage wore many hats in his nearly 50 years in the game.

Drafted out of Virginia in the second round of the secondary phase of the 1971 draft, Cubbage reached MLB with the Rangers in 1974. But he didn't earn regular playing time until he was traded to the Twins as part of the package for Bert Blyleven in June 1976.

Cubbage played regularly or semi-regularly at third base for Minnesota for five seasons from 1976 to 1980. He topped out at nine home runs in a season but was a lefthanded hitter with strong on-base skills who often walked more than he struck out.

In eight MLB seasons, Cubbage hit .258/.330/.369 with 34 home runs.

Cubbage played his final MLB season in 1981 with the Mets and embarked on a managerial career in their system. He worked his way from short-season to Triple-A before joining the big league coaching staff in 1990.

Cubbage served as Mets interim manager for seven games in 1991 but was better known as third base coach for New York and later the Red Sox. He later scouted for the Rays and served as an assistant for the Nationals.

Cubbage died Aug. 11. He was 74.

Jose De Leon: De Leon's career would likely be looked at in a different light if he pitched in the 21st century.

These days it is widely understood that a pitcher's win-loss record is often affected dramatically by the team he plays for as well as the variability of luck that is a part of the game.

That wasn't the case in the 1980s, so De Leon's career is remembered as much for his two seasons of losing a league-high 19 games as it is for his sporadic bouts of brilliance.

When he was locked in, De Leon could dominate. He led the National League in strikeouts (204) with the Cardinals in 1989. He finished sixth in the NL with a 2.71 ERA in 1991.

But luck did not shine on De Leon's career. In 1985, he went a brutal 2-19, but the Pirates were shut out in seven of his starts, and they scored a total of two runs in his first four starts.

Traded to the Cardinals in 1988, he posted the first winning record of his career and then went 16-12 in 1989, his career year. But 1990 ended in a way reminiscent of 1985 and he went 7-19.

De Leon was always hard to hit and was durable, but he also struggled with his control. For his career, he went 86-119 with a 3.76 ERA over 1,897 innings and 13 seasons.

De Leon died on Feb. 25. He was 63.

Carl Erskine: Erskine pitched for five National League-pennant winning Brooklyn Dodgers teams, including the 1955 World Series champions.

The Dodgers lost to the Yankees in the World Series five times between 1941 and 1953—and later a sixth time in 1956—before finally defeating the Yankees in 1955.

Before he died on April 16 in Anderson, Ind., at the age of 97, Erskine was the last surviving member of the "Boys of Summer" Dodgers, whose fearsome lineup featured Hall of Famers Jackie Robinson, Duke Snider, Roy Campanella, Pee Wee Reese and Gil Hodges. Sandy Koufax was a rookie on the 1955 team.

Erskine won 118 games with a 3.87 ERA for the Dodgers in between the end of World War II and the franchise's last season in Brooklyn in 1957. Only Don Newcombe won more for Brooklyn in that time.

Erskine went 20-6 with a 3.54 ERA in 1953, when he finished ninth in NL MVP voting. He made his first and only all-star team the following year.

Erskine spent two seasons in Los Angeles following the Dodgers' move out West, retiring after the 1959 season with a 122-78 record, 4.00 ERA and 981 strikeouts in 1,718.2 innings. He threw two no-hitters in his career.

He made 11 postseason appearances—all against the Yankees in the World Series—and was roughed up for a 5.83 ERA, though he did establish a since-broken World Series record with 14 strikeouts in Game 3 in 1953.

After his playing career, Erskine was heavily involved with the Special Olympics. His son Jimmy was born with Down Syndrome in 1960 and outlived his prognosis by decades, dying at age 63 in 2023.

Billy Gardner: Gardner's baseball career covered so many levels that it's hard to decide where he made his most significant impact.

A slick-fielding second baseman, Gardner played for three teams that won the World Series, but he never got into a World Series game.

After his 10-year MLB career ended, Gardner soon established himself as an excellent major league coach and manager. He had multiple stints as a coach but quickly found that managing in the minor leagues suited him even better.

Gardner took over the Double-A Pittsfield club in 1967 and served as a manager in the minors for the next 10 years, much of it with the Royals, before another stint as an MLB coach.

His return to minor league manager in 1979 paid off two years later when the Twins promoted him to the big leagues after firing Johnny Goryl.

Gardner's managerial career peaked with a 81-81 finish in 1984 that earned him a third-place finish in AL Manager of the Year voting. He managed the Twins until 1985, when he was fired after five straight losing season. But that '85 club included the nucleus of the 1987 World Series champions.

Gardner had one more return to the majors. The Royals asked him to replace John Wathan, who had to step down in 1987 because of a brain tumor. Gardner was fired in October.

Gardner died on Jan. 3. He was 96. His son Billy Gardner Jr. has had a long managerial career himself, winning more than 1,600 games. He served as High-A Beloit's manager in 2023.

Wayne Graham: Graham, the winningest coach in Rice history—and the only coach to lead the program to a national championship—died on Sept. 3. He was 88.

Graham led the Owls for 26 seasons from 1992 to 2018. In that time, he led Rice to 23 NCAA Tournament appearances, 11 super regionals, seven trips to the College World Series and the 2003 national championship.

Prior to Graham taking the reins, the Owls had made a regional just twice. He accumulated an all-time record of 1,173-528-2.

Prior to his time at Rice, Graham was responsible for turning San Jacinto Junior College, outside Houston, into a national powerhouse.

His first team in 1981 included Roger Clemens before he transferred to Texas. Later he would coach Andy Pettitte before the Yankees drafted him in 1990.

Starting in 1984, Graham led the Gators to seven straight 50-win seasons. San Jacinto won five juco national championships during that stretch, including a three-peat between 1985 and 1987.

Baseball America named Graham its Junior College Coach of the Century and its College Coach of the Year in 1999.

Graham coached many draft picks at Rice, including 19 first-rounders. Righthander Matt Anderson was drafted first overall in 1997.

In 2004, the trio of Philip Humber, Jeff Niemann and Wade Townsend made draft history when all three were selected among the top 10 picks.

Perhaps most notably, Graham coached eventual first-round pick and six-time MLB all-star Lance Berkman. In 1997, Berkman hit .431/.538/1.031 with 41 home runs, making him one of four college hitters ever to top 40 in a season.

At a time when college baseball mid-majors face long odds of making a long Omaha run, Graham's accomplishments at Rice—a small, private research university—are even more pronounced.

Jerry Grote: Jerry Koosman jumped into Jerry Grote's arms following the final out of the 1969 World Series, creating one of the most iconic baseball images of all time.

Grote was the primary catcher for the pitching-rich Mets teams of the 1960s and '70s, including the "miracle" 1969 champions and the improbable 1973 National League pennant winners.

Hall of Famer Tom Seaver loved throwing to

Grote, while NL catching rival Johnny Bench regarded Grote as the best defensive catcher in the league.

The Texas-born Grote was signed by the Astros in 1962 and traded to the Mets following the 1965 season. He instantly became a regular in New York and made his first of two all-star teams in 1968, when he hit .282/.357/.349 in 124 games.

That season, Grote helped guide the Mets pitching staff to a 2.72 ERA, the 14th-lowest of the expansion era.

Grote had a few standout seasons with the bat but was generally an on-base-oriented hitter who shined defensively. He hit 39 home runs in 16 big league seasons while batting .252/.316/.326. He threw out 38% of basestealers

Grote died April 7 in Austin, Texas. He was 81.

Don Gullet: If injuries hadn't derailed his career, Gullett seemed destined to be one of the best pitchers of the 1970s and '80s. Instead, the lefthander threw his final pitch of his pro career before he turned 28.

But Gullett's career is not one that asks what could have been. What he did was impressive enough in its own right.

As a 19-year-old, Gullett jumped to the majors and a role in the National League pennant-winning Reds' bullpen in 1970. He pitched effectively while making three appearances in the World Series. A year later, he went 16-6, 2.65 as a starter for Cincinnati. He battled hepatitis in 1972, but bounced back to become a fixture in the Reds' rotation from 1973 to '76.

Gullett was part of three consecutive World Series champions. He was the ace of the Big Red Machine's rotation in 1975 and won his only World Series start in 1976 as the Reds swept the Yankees. He then joined the Yankees as a free agent and worked out of the bullpen for New York as it won it all in 1977.

He didn't know it at that point, but Gullett's pitching career was nearly over. He made just eight starts in 1978, a season in which he tore his rotator cuff in multiple places. He spent two seasons trying to rehab, but he never got to the point where he could pitch in even a minor league game.

Gullett retired in 1980 when he was still 29 years old. He went 109-50 with a 3.11 ERA in nine MLB seasons. His .686 winning percentage ranks top 10 all time for pitchers with at least 100 decisions. Among lefthanders, only Clayton Kershaw and Whitey Ford fared better.

GETTY IMAGES

Bud Harrelson

After a decade away, he returned to the game, serving as the Reds' pitching coach from 1993 to 2005.

Gullett died on Feb. 14. He was 73.

Bud Harrelson: Harrelson, a scrappy big league shortstop, major league coach and manager and later part owner of the independent Long Island Ducks, died on Jan. 11. He was 79.

Harrelson is best known for his association with the Mets and is the only person to take part in both of the franchise's World Series championship teams. He was a slick-fielding shortstop for the 1969 Miracle Mets and third base coach for the 1986 champions who won 108 games.

The Mets signed Harrelson out of San Francisco State in 1963. In 1967 he assumed regular shortstop duties in New York as a 23-year-old. The mid-'60s Mets were rich in pitching talent—Tom Seaver, Nolan Ryan, Jerry Koosman, Tug McGraw—that would propel them to a World Series victory against the powerful Orioles in 1969.

The core of the '69 Mets also won the 1973 NL pennant, with Harrelson providing a highlight when he and the Reds' Pete Rose fought on the field after Rose slid hard into second base during Game 3 of the Championship Series.

Harrelson was a .250 hitter at his peak whose value was tied to his ability to draw walks, get on base and field his position. He won the NL Gold Glove in 1971 and is the Mets' all-time leader for defensive WAR, per Baseball-Reference. Harrelson also ranks fourth on the Mets' games played list and is third in walks.

Harrelson played briefly for the Phillies and Rangers before retiring after the 1980 season. For his career he hit .236/.327/.288 with seven home runs. He made two all-star teams and received MVP votes in three seasons.

Harrelson joined the Mets' coaching staff in 1985 and later succeeded Davey Johnson when the manager was fired in May 1990. A second-half fade in 1991 led to Harrelson's ouster after two incomplete seasons.

In 2000, Harrelson became part-owner of the new Long Island franchise in the Atlantic League. He managed the Ducks in their inaugural season and later coached home games.

Whitey Herzog: No National League team won more games or more pennants in the 1980s than Herzog's Cardinals.

The colorful Hall of Fame manager popularized "Whiteyball," a style of play that worked like a charm on the artificial turf in St. Louis—and also carpeted NL East road parks in Montreal, Philadelphia and Pittsburgh. The Cardinals played 67% of their games in those four parks.

Herzog's Cardinals won the 1982 World Series and narrowly missed adding titles in 1985 and '87, losing in seven games both times. Hall of Fame shortstop Ozzie Smith epitomized the team's style of play.

For the entire decade of the 1980s, St. Louis led the NL in fielding percentage, batting average, on-base percentage, stolen bases and lowest strikeout rate.

They ranked dead last in home runs.

Herzog assembled a roster full of fast, surehanded, contact-oriented players who converted balls in play into outs and wreaked havoc on the bases. His pitchers threw strikes and kept the ball on the ground.

Managing the Cardinals made Herzog famous, but he made his mark in baseball long before that point. He spent eight seasons in the major leagues as a part-time outfielder for four teams between 1956 and 1963.

Herzog scouted and coached for two seasons with the Kansas City Athletics after his playing career before joining the Mets as farm director. Players developed on his watch helped propel the Mets to a World Series championship in 1969 and a pennant in 1973.

Passed over as Mets manager in 1972, Herzog left the organization to embark on a managerial career. He spent one season with the Rangers and one with the Angels before finding his place with the up-and-coming Royals in 1975. Kansas City won the American League West in 1976, '77 and '78.

A clash with GM Joe Burke forced Herzog out of Kansas City after the 1979 season, but that decision preceded his historic run with the Cardinals. The rest was history.

Herzog died on April 15 in St. Louis. He was 92.

Ken Holtzman: On an Athletics pitching staff loaded with stars, it was lefthander Holtzman who started Game 1 of the World Series three years in a row.

Oakland won the American League West each season from 1971 to 1975 and were World Series champions three years in a row from 1972 to '74. Holtzman won two of his three Game 1 starts and in 70.1 career postseason innings went 6-4 with a 2.30 ERA.

Holtzman spent 15 seasons in the big leagues, winning 174 games and recording a 3.49 ERA. In his peak seasons he went 120-94, 3.25 in 1,828 innings from 1969 to 1975.

The Cubs drafted Holtzman out of Illinois in the first draft in 1965. He made his MLB debut that September and was a mainstay in Chicago through 1971, when the Cubs traded him to the A's for Rick Monday. He threw no-hitters for the Cubs in 1969 and 1971.

Holtzman made two all-star teams in Oakland and was there for the bulk of the club's '70s dynasty. He and Reggie Jackson were traded to the Orioles early in the 1976 season as A's owner Charlie Finley sold his stars rather than contend with the dawning of free agency.

Holtzman added a fourth World Series ring with the 1977 Yankees. He died April 14 in St. Louis. He was 78.

Ed Kranepool: Just three position players have appeared in a major league game as a 17-year-old in the expansion era.

Kranepool is one of the three.

In their first year of existence in 1962, the Mets signed Kranepool out of Monroe High in the Bronx. He hit .301 in 41 minor league games and made his MLB debut on Sept. 22 of that year, still more than a month shy of his 18th birthday.

Kranepool spent 18 seasons with the Mets, primarily as a first baseman, and still holds the franchise record for games played.

Kranepool made an all-star team as a 20-year-old in 1965, the only season in which he appeared

APPENDIX

in at least 150 games. He was a platoon first baseman for the 1969 World Series champions and homered in a Game 3 win against the Orioles.

Kranepool's 1,418 hits rank third in Mets franchise history. When he retired after the 1979 season, he had batted .261/.316/.377 with 118 home runs.

Kranepool died on Sept. 8 in Boca Raton, Fla. He was 79.

Mike Martin: Martin, the winningest coach in college sports history, died on Jan. 31 after a battle with Lewy body dementia. He was 79.

Martin was the head coach of Florida State, his alma mater, for 40 years before retiring in 2019. In all 40 of those seasons, he led the Seminoles to at least 40 wins and the NCAA Tournament, an unmatched record of consistency.

Martin went 2,209-736-4 as a head coach. He took 17 teams to the College World Series and finished as runner-up twice—in 1986 and 1999—though he never won a national championship.

Martin was twice named the Baseball America College Coach of the Year, an award that no man has won more than twice. He coached a record three College Players of the Year: Jeff Ledbetter (1982), J.D. Drew (1997) and Buster Posey (2008).

He coached a No. 1 pick in the MLB draft (Drew) and NFL draft (Jameis Winston). He coached fathers and sons and his own son, Mike Martin Jr.

Those records, accolades and accomplishments all tell a story of consistent success and place Martin as one of the greatest college baseball coaches of all time. And that's who he was. Between his playing and coaching career, he was a part of the program for 47 years.

The Seminoles now play on Mike Martin Field. His No. 11 is synonymous with his name in Tallahassee and beyond.

Willie Mays: Twenty-four.

Few players embody a jersey number quite like Willie Mays.

The number 24 will forever be associated with "The Catch," Mays' improbable, over-the-shoulder grab of Vic Wertz's drive during Game 1 of the 1954 World Series.

Mays' No. 24 inspired generations of ballplayers who followed. Rickey Henderson wore it. So did Barry Bonds and Ken Griffey Jr.

It will forever be a sacred baseball number, like Jackie Robinson's 42 or Roberto Clemente's 21.

BETTMANN ARCHIVE/GETTY IMAGES

Willie Mays

And with good reason. Mays has a strong case as the greatest player in MLB history. He is certainly the most well-rounded.

Mays hit .301 for his career and amassed 3,293 hits. When he retired, his 660 home runs trailed only Babe Ruth for the most ever.

He won 12 Gold Gloves, the most of any center fielder. He stole 339 bases in his career and led MLB in the category during the station-to-station '50s.

Mays won two National League MVP awards for the Giants, one in New York in 1954 and one in San Francisco in 1965. He was worthy of several more MVPs. He made 24 all-star teams.

Of course.

Mays died on June 18, the same day that MLB staged a minor league game at Rickwood Field, the 114-year-old park where Mays debuted for the Birmingham Black Barons in 1948. It was part of a celebration of Negro Leagues history, in which Mays is a key figure. Mays made his first pro appearance with Birmingham, but his roots in The Magic City run deeper. He was born in Westfield, Ala., outside Birmingham, and attended high school in Fairfield. His father, Cat, played for the local industrial league team.

Mays was 93 when he died, but his legacy—and his No. 24—will live forever.

Dave McCarty: McCarty holds a distinction held by just 42 others.

The Stanford first baseman was Baseball

America College Player of the Year in 1991.

That season he hit .420 with 24 home runs and 66 RBIs. The Cardinal lost in regionals that year but had reached Omaha a year earlier in 1990.

The Twins drafted McCarty third overall in 1991. Heading into 1993 he ranked as the No. 16 prospect in baseball. He hit .385 with eight home runs in 40 games with Triple-A Portland that year to earn a May callup to the Twins.

McCarty struggled to replicate that production outside the Pacific Coast League, batting .226/.275/.310 in three years with the Twins before bouncing around to six other clubs as a reserve player in parts of 11 MLB seasons.

The Red Sox claimed McCarty on waivers in August 2003. He hit .407 down the stretch and made his first postseason appearance. He had a part-time role on the 2004 World Series champions but did not play in October.

McCarty died of a cardiac event on April 19 in Oakland. He was 54.

Ryan Minor: For much of the 1990s, a never-ending parade of Orioles prospects were hailed as the successor to Cal Ripken Jr.

Ryan Minor is the one who actually did it. Briefly.

It was Minor's start at third base on Sept. 20, 1998, that ended Ripken's consecutive games played streak at 2,632.

That moment ensured that Minor will always be a part of baseball history, but he was also yet another player who found out how hard it is to replace a legend.

Ripken's final MLB game was Oct. 6, 2001. Minor's last game came the very next day, when he went 0-for-4 for the Expos in a win against the Mets.

While his MLB career was relatively brief, Minor's athletic career was lengthy and filled with highlights. The 6-foot-7 third baseman was also an exceptional college basketball player. He averaged more than 20 points per game in each of his final two seasons at Oklahoma and was a second-round pick of the Philadelphia 76ers in 1996.

Minor was just as impactful on the diamond. He helped lead the Sooners to the national title in 1994, teaming with his twin brother Damon. Minor ranked 35th on the Baseball America Top 100 Prospects list in 1998. He made it to the majors after just two seasons in the minors. He struggled at the plate in the big leagues but played four more seasons in the minors after his last MLB game. He then became a coach in the Orioles' and Tigers' systems.

Minor died on Dec. 22 after a battle with colon cancer. He was 49.

Reyes Moronta: Moronta died in a motorcycle crash in his native Dominican Republic on July 28. He was 31.

Moronta signed with the Giants as an international free agent in 2011 when he was already 18. He spent four years in short-season leagues before notching 12 saves for Low-A Augusta in 2015.

At High-A San Jose the following season, Moronta first earned attention as a prospect. He struck out 93 in 59 innings and saved 14 games.

Moronta ranked as the Giants' No. 12 prospect heading into 2017 and made his MLB debut as a September callup that season.

He earned a regular bullpen role for the 2018 and 2019 Giants, but tore the labrum in his shoulder in the latter season, which wiped out his 2020.

Moronta pitched in 177 MLB games, posting a 3.06 ERA in 171.1 innings.

Hector Ortiz Ortiz, a major league catcher and later an MLB and minor league coach who spent much of his career with the Rangers, died on Feb. 28. He was 54.

Ortiz was a grinder as a player. A 35th-round pick of the Dodgers in 1988, Ortiz spent 11 seasons in the minor leagues before making his big league debut in 1998. He bounced back and forth between Triple-A and the majors for much of the next few years.

When he retired, Ortiz had spent 18 seasons in the minor leagues in addition to 93 games in the majors.

Ortiz stayed around the game as a coach and minor league manager. He spent 2015 to 2020 on the Rangers' big league staff as a bullpen coach, first base coach and catching coordinator, but before and after that he worked with Texas minor leaguers.

Fritz Peterson: Peterson was the best pitcher on some of the blandest Yankees teams of the past 100 years.

From 1968 to 1972, Peterson went 81-66 with a 2.88 ERA in 1,269 innings for Yankees teams that hovered near .500. The lefthander led the American League in lowest walk rate in each of his five peak seasons and made the all-star team in 1970.

Peterson compiled nearly 17 bWAR from

1968–72, which ranked top 20 during one of the best eras ever for pitchers.

Peterson went 133-131 in 11 big league seasons. His 3.30 ERA was almost exactly league average.

Peterson made headlines in 1973 when he and Yankees teammate Mike Kekich made a "life swap," in which they switched wives and children with each other.

Peterson died on Oct. 19, 2023 in Winona, Minn. He was 81.

Pete Rose: As a ball player, Pete Rose's defiance fueled his greatness. Later, it ignited his downfall.

Growing up in Cincinnati, Rose was no scout's idea of a prospect. He had minimal power. His poor arm limited him defensively.

Rose was determined, however, and he used aggression, hustle and a family connection to secure a contract from the hometown Reds in 1960. The more people doubted him, the better he seemed to play.

After just two minor league seasons, Rose was Cincinnati's regular second baseman and the National League Rookie of the Year in 1963. He was a marvel on the field, especially during his first 16 seasons with the Reds.

Rose won NL batting titles in 1968, '69 and '73. He was MVP in 1973. Rose served as a catalyst for the famous Big Red Machine, which won World Series in 1975 and '76. He set an NL record with a 44-game hit streak in 1978.

When Rose left Cincinnati as a 37-year-old third baseman following the 1978 season, he had amassed 3,164 hits. His ticket to Cooperstown was punched.

But the Rose kept going. He signed with the Phillies, and in 1980 helped them win their first World Series. Later, he signed with the Expos. He cleared 4,000 career hits in 1984 and set his sights on Ty Cobb's record of 4,189.

To get there required Rose to write his own name in the lineup as Reds player-manager, at a time when he was a 44-year-old first baseman with zero power. He accomplished his mission, passing Cobb on Sept. 11, 1985.

Rose retired as the all-time leader with 4,256 hits, 3,215 singles, 3,562 games and 15,890 plate appearances. The 1976 Reds have a case as the best lineup ever, thanks largely to the greatness of Rose, Johnny Bench, Joe Morgan and Tony Perez.

Baseball writers voted Bench, Morgan and Perez into the Hall of Fame, but Rose never

GETTY IMAGES

Pete Rose

appeared on a ballot. Not because he didn't perform like a Hall of Famer, but because he committed baseball's cardinal sin—and then defiantly denied it for more than a decade.

Rose received a permanent ban from baseball on Aug. 24, 1989, for betting on games while active. Much later, Rose later admitted to betting on the Reds both as a player and while managing the team. He also served a five-month prison sentence for tax evasion in 1990.

For the last 35 years of Rose's life—he died on Sept. 30 in Las Vegas at age 83—he made a living off his baseball celebrity by signing autographs for fans.

But he did so far removed from the game he loved.

Luis Tiant: On a scouting trip to Cuba in 1957, Bobby Avila discovered 16-year-old right-hander Luis Tiant on the island's Juvenile League all-star team. Two years later, he recommended him to the Mexico City Tigers of the Mexican League.

Tiant spent three seasons with Mexico City before Avila, second baseman for the Indians and the first Mexico-born all-star, recommended that Cleveland sign him.

The Indians purchased Tiant's contract for $35,000 in the summer of 1961, and he reached the major leagues three years later. He excelled in six seasons in Cleveland, posting a 2.84 ERA which was 20% better than league average. He led

Luis Tiant

RICH PILLING/MLB PHOTOS VIA GETTY IMAGES

Fernando Valenzuela

JAYNE KAMIN-ONCEA/GETTY IMAGES

APPENDIX

a Cleveland pitching staff that led the American League in strikeouts five years in a row.

In 1968, the year of the pitcher, the Cardinals' Bob Gibson dominated headlines with a 1.12 ERA. In the AL, Tiant went 21-9 with a league-leading 1.60 ERA in 258.1 innings.

Tiant began to alter his pitching mechanics while in the minor leagues with Atlanta in 1971. He added a delivery quirk in which he rotated his body away from home plate, turning his back to the batter before unleashing the ball. The Red Sox took note and quickly signed him.

In Boston, Tiant earned his most acclaim. He made two all-star teams, factored in three Cy Young Award races and was the ace for the 1975 Red Sox, who pushed the dynastic Reds to seven games in a classic World Series before eventually losing.

Tiant helped make it a classic. He made three starts in the World Series, going 2-0 with a 3.60 ERA over 25 innings. He pitched two complete games, including a 173-pitch effort in Game 4.

Tiant pitched in 19 major league seasons. His 229 wins are far and away the most by a Cuban pitcher, as are his 2,416 strikeouts and 65 WAR.

Tiant has his champions for the Hall of Fame, an honor which will now have to be bestowed posthumously. He died on Oct. 8 in Wells, Maine. He was 83.

Fernando Valenezuela: Fernando-mania was magical. In 1981, any time Valenzuela and his screwball stepped onto the mound, anything seemed possible.

The 20-year-old threw a complete game for a win on Opening Day. And then he did it again. And again. And again.

In his first eight starts, he recorded eight complete games. He picked up eight wins. In mid-May, the lefthanded rookie was 8-0. 0.50. The rest of his season was excellent, as he went on to be both Rookie of the Year and the Cy Young winner.

But those first eight starts, they seemed almost impossible to believe. And they transformed Dodgers fandom. Los Angeles' Mexican-Americans had a star to love. The Dodgers drew 35,000 fans per game in 1979. By 1981, they were drawing 42,500 fans per game, largely because Valenzuela drew an average of 48,500 fans every time he pitched at home.

Valenzuela won a World Series in that rookie season. He did it all before he turned 21.

He was an All-Star for six straight seasons from 1981-1986. His durabilty was remarkable, and maybe a curse. He threw more than 250 innings in every season from 1982-1987 and led the league in complete games and batters faced three different times.

Valenzuela's last all-star appearance came as a 25-year-old. He pitched in the majors until he was 36, and he made appearances in the Mexican Pacific League until he was 46.

But those memories of him looking to the

sky mid-delivery as a 20-year-old are the indelible images, when he became the biggest star in baseball.

Valenzuela died on Oct. 22. He was 63.

Ozzie Virgil: When Ozzie Virgil made his MLB debut for the New York Giants in 1956, he was the first Dominican major leaguer.

By the end of the 1980s, the Dominican Republic produced more major league players than any country but the United States. Today, it's impossible to envision MLB without the likes of Juan Soto, Jose Ramirez or Elly De La Cruz.

It all started with Virgil, whose family emigrated to the U.S. when he was 13. He graduated from Clinton High in the Bronx and served in the Marines from 1950 to '52 prior to his baseball career.

Twenty-four years old when he made his MLB debut as a September callup, Virgil was a light-hitting third baseman—career .231 average and .594 OPS—whose versatility kept him in the big leagues for parts of nine seasons with the Giants, Tigers, Kansas City Athletics, Orioles and Pirates.

Virgil stayed in the game as a coach for 19 seasons after his playing days, most notably as third base coach for the 1984 Padres.

His son, Ozzie Virgil Jr., made two all-star teams as a catcher for the Phillies and Braves in the 1980s.

Jimy Williams: Decorated major league manager Jimy Williams died on Jan. 26 in Tarpon Springs, Fla.

Williams spent eight seasons as a player, reaching the big leagues with the Cardinals as a utility infielder for cups of coffee in 1966 and '67.

Williams' playing career was ended by a shoulder injury, but he immediately made a successful transition to managing, first in the Angels' minor league system from 1974 to '79.

The Blue Jays hired Williams as third base coach in 1980, and he took over as manager in 1986 after Bobby Cox left for the Braves. Williams' Toronto teams were successful but never reached higher than second place in the AL East.

After a 12-24 start, the Blue Jays fired Williams on May 14, 1989. The team rebounded under Cito Gaston to finally win the East. Williams teamed up again with Cox, serving as the Braves' third base coach until 1996.

The Red Sox hired Williams as manager in 1997. Once again he shepherded winning teams but could not get over the hump in the rugged AL East. The 1998 and '99 Red Sox won wild cards, the latter advancing to the AL Championship Series.

The Red Sox fired Williams in August 2001, and he latched on with the Astros in 2002. He would manage Houston for three seasons, again winning frequently but falling short of winning a division.

After Williams' Astros started 44-44 in 2004, the club fired him. Once again his successor, this time Phil Garner, managed the team to a postseason berth.

Williams went out on a high note as the Phillies' bench coach for the 2008 World Series champions.

Williams went 910-790 (.535) in 12 seasons as a big league manager. He was named 1999 AL Manager of the Year.

Williams' sons Brady and Shawn followed in his footsteps. Both are long-time minor league managers and coaches. Shawn manages the Rookie-level Florida Complex League Phillies. Brady is the Rays' big league third base coach.

Pat Zachry: Zachry won the National League Rookie of the Year award with the 1976 Reds, better known as the "Big Red Machine," and pitched for four teams in 10 big league seasons.

Cincinnati drafted Zachry in the 19th round in 1970 out of high school in Waco, Texas. After six minor league seasons, he made his MLB debut for the reigning World Series champions as a 24-year-old.

Zachry's rookie season in 1976 was his best. He quickly ascended to the rotation and went 14-7 with a 2.74 ERA in 38 appearances, including 28 starts. He struck out 143 in 204 innings. He ranked fifth in the NL in ERA and fifth with 6.3 strikeouts per nine innings.

Zachry pitched effectively in the 1976 postseason, going 2-0 in two starts and allowing four earned runs in 11.2 innings to help the Reds win their second straight World Series.

At the 1977 trade deadline, the Reds dealt Zachry and three other players to the Mets for Hall of Fame righthander Tom Seaver. Zachry spent the bulk of his career with the Mets, making an all-star team for the 96-loss 1978 team.

Zachry later pitched for the Dodger and Phillies, retiring after the 1985 season with a career record of 69-67 with a 3.52 ERA that was almost exactly league average.

Zachry died on April 4 in Austin, Texas. He was 71.

STATISTICS INDEX

APPENDIX